the Next EXIT®

USA Interstate Highway Service Guide

Restaurants • Gas Stations • Hotels • RV Camping • And Much More

the Next EXIT®
USER GUIDE

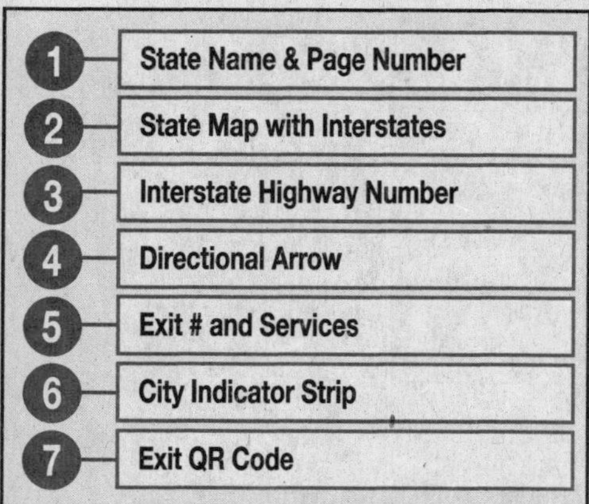

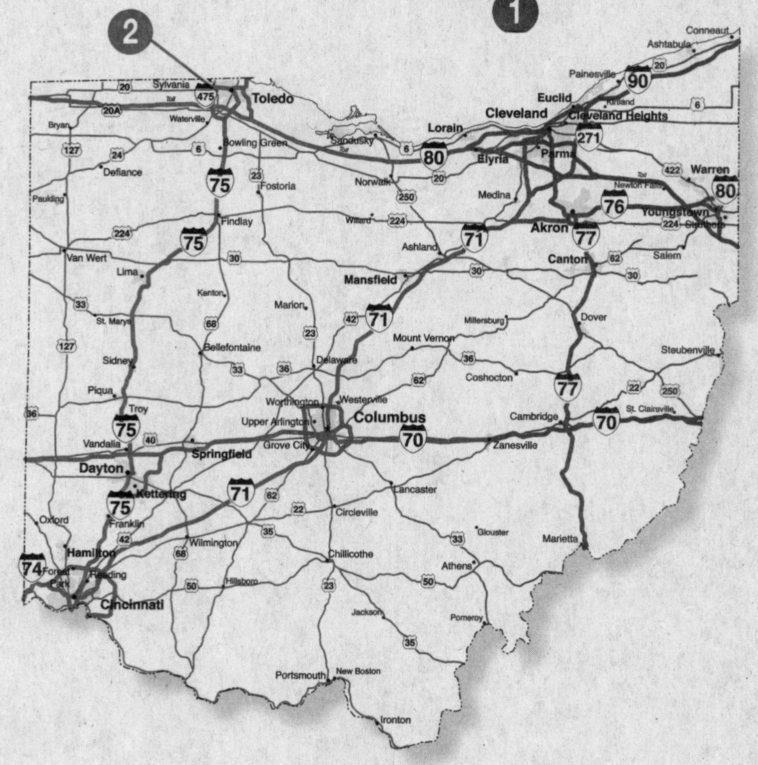

Exit

Most states number exits by the nearest mile marker(mm). A few states use consecutive numbers, in which case mile markers are given in ( ). Mile markers are the little green vertical signs beside the interstate at one mile intervals which indicate distance from the southern or western border of a state. Odd numbered interstates run north/south, even numbered run east/west.

Services

Services are listed alphabetically by category **[gas icon] = gas [food icon] = food [lodging icon] = lodging [RS] = rest stop [other icon] = other** services including camping. "[H]" indicates an exit from which a hospital may be accessed, but it may not be close to the exit. Services located away from the exit may be referred to by "access to," or "to" and a distance may be given. A directional notation is also given, such as **N**, **S**, **E** or **W**

Directional Arrows

Follow exits DOWN the page if traveling from North to South or East to West, UP the page if traveling South to North or West to East.

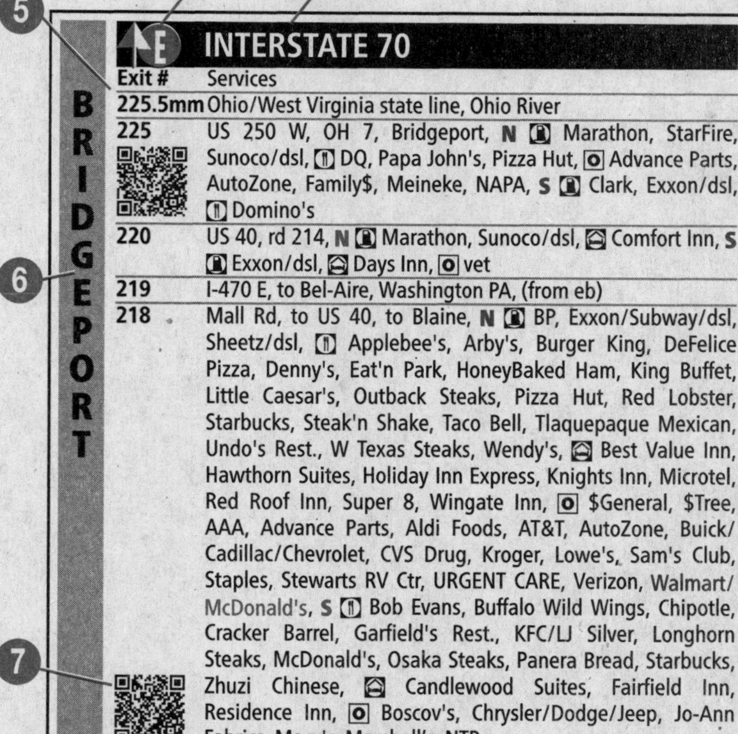

INTERSTATE 70 (E)

BRIDGEPORT

Exit #	Services
225.5mm	Ohio/West Virginia state line, Ohio River
225	US 250 W, OH 7, Bridgeport, **N** [gas] Marathon, StarFire, Sunoco/dsl, [food] DQ, Papa John's, Pizza Hut, [other] Advance Parts, AutoZone, Family$, Meineke, NAPA, **S** [gas] Clark, Exxon/dsl, [food] Domino's
220	US 40, rd 214, **N** [gas] Marathon, Sunoco/dsl, [lodging] Comfort Inn, **S** [gas] Exxon/dsl, [lodging] Days Inn, [other] vet
219	I-470 E, to Bel-Aire, Washington PA, (from eb)
218	Mall Rd, to US 40, to Blaine, **N** [gas] BP, Exxon/Subway/dsl, Sheetz/dsl, [food] Applebee's, Arby's, Burger King, DeFelice Pizza, Denny's, Eat'n Park, HoneyBaked Ham, King Buffet, Little Caesar's, Outback Steaks, Pizza Hut, Red Lobster, Starbucks, Steak'n Shake, Taco Bell, Tlaquepaque Mexican, Undo's Rest., W Texas Steaks, Wendy's, [lodging] Best Value Inn, Hawthorn Suites, Holiday Inn Express, Knights Inn, Microtel, Red Roof Inn, Super 8, Wingate Inn, [other] $General, $Tree, AAA, Advance Parts, Aldi Foods, AT&T, AutoZone, Buick/Cadillac/Chevrolet, CVS Drug, Kroger, Lowe's, Sam's Club, Staples, Stewarts RV Ctr, URGENT CARE, Verizon, Walmart/McDonald's, **S** [food] Bob Evans, Buffalo Wild Wings, Chipotle, Cracker Barrel, Garfield's Rest., KFC/LJ Silver, Longhorn Steaks, McDonald's, Osaka Steaks, Panera Bread, Starbucks, Zhuzi Chinese, [lodging] Candlewood Suites, Fairfield Inn, Residence Inn, [other] Boscov's, Chrysler/Dodge/Jeep, Jo-Ann Fabrics, Macy's, Marshall's, NTB

the Next EXIT® USER GUIDE

Abbreviations & Symbols used in the Next EXIT®

AFB ....Air Force Base
B&B ....Bed&Breakfast
Bfd...........Battlefield
CNG..........Compressed Natural Gas
Ctr ....Center
Coll ....College
Cyn ....canyon
dsl.............diesel
$................Dollar
EVC ....Electric Vehicle Charger
LNG ....Liquid Natural Gas
Mem ....Memorial
Mkt ....Market
Mtn ....Mountain
mm ....mile marker
N ....north side of exit
S ....south side of exit
E ....east side of exit
W ....west side of exit

NM............National Monument
NHS..........Nat Hist Site
NWR.........Nat Wildlife Reserve
NF.............National Forest
H ....Hospital
.............Airport
.............Picnic Area/Tables
NP.............National Park
NRA..........Nat Rec Area
pk ....park
pkwy.........parkway
rest. ....restaurant
nb ....northbound
sb ....southbound
eb ....eastbound
wb.............westbound
SP.............state park
SF.............state forest
Sprs..........springs

st ....street, state
sta ....station
TPK...........Turnpike
USPO ....Post Office
vet ....veterinarian
whse.........warehouse
@..............truckstop (full service)
red print....RV accessible
.............Handicapped accessible
.............Telephone
.............Gas
.............Food
.............Lodging
.............Other
Rs ....Rest Stop / Rest Area

More digital options are available at www.theNextExit.com

TABLE OF CONTENTS

WHAT HAVE YOU DONE WITH YOUR MOTHER?!

Will Watson

Somewhere deep in the unconscious state of sleep I felt the car abruptly maneuver to the shoulder of the interstate. Another moment later the rear doors of our van burst open, and the bright, slanted morning sun and the strong odor of sagebrush; ubiquitous along Interstate 15 in rural south-central Utah; came spilling into the back of the car painfully jolting my sleeping brother and I awake. Our weary eyes were met by the black silhouette of our father against the morning sun. His expression was quite the opposite of ours, which quickly brought us boys around. I'll never forget the next words out of his mouth: "Boys! What HAVE you done with your mother?!"

By the late 1980s it was widely accepted amongst our friends and acquaintances that our family was a tad bit eccentric. This came only in small part from our reputation of doing things other folks might find absurd such as the utilization of an 8 passenger Chevy Beauville van to accommodate 11 people (as in, two adults plus nine kids) on long road-going excursions for weeks on end. All packed up, we'd wave goodbye to our modest little house at the dead end of a gravel road buried deep in the Smoky Mountains of North Carolina. We were bound for faraway places with strange sounding names, such as Provo, Utah; Flagstaff, Arizona; or Rexburg, Idaho. There was no telling beforehand where we would end up, or what experiences we would have along the way. These excursions could easily encompass 5500 miles round trip and last for up to three weeks at a time. We would find ourselves winding through the motion-sickness-inducing canyons near Bighorn National Park, caught in ice storms outside Oklahoma City or gorging on cheese curds as Windsor, Wisconsin shrank away in our rear-view mirror. Remarkably, all persons involved in said escapades lived to tell about it. I'm one of these individuals.

By now you've probably done the math, but to help you out a bit; there are not enough seats in an 8-passenger van to accommodate 11 people. This model of vehicle, however, had a cargo area behind the back seat of the car, just long enough for a child age about age 10 or younger to make a "nest" of blankets and lay flat. That meant that about 4 of us met the minimum size requirements for laying in the nest area. And hey...this was the 80's! Bike helmets weren't really even a thing yet, and trampolines didn't have safety nets. Music in our van was played on a thing called a "tape deck". My parents figured, why not just toss the surplus pocket-sized children over in the back; the space surely intended by the manufacturer for cargo only. A space that had no seat belts, let alone, SEATS. This put the older children up front in what we from the back began sarcastically calling "First Class". I recall there being some sort of loose assigned seating system in force up front in an attempt to stave off arguments, but this usually proved too chaotic to manage the whole trip and soon deteriorated into a first-come game usually won by the older kids who were only after the window seats anyway.

Continued Next Page

Ordering fast food with our crew must have been comical to outsiders. We frequented value menus to get all of us fed in an economically friendly way. We figured that since we would be spending less in this way, we could order a few more burgers in case anyone wound up hungry later. The giggles and could-you-repeat-thats which came from the pickup windows became almost expected after placing our order for 20+ dollar menu hamburgers.

The concept of vehicle entertainment systems was new in those days, but anyway our family never had any use for such things. No, our entertainment came from whatever went whizzing by outside the car windows, with dad's commentary of course.

For extra security, my parents took to numbering each of us to keep track of who was in the car at any given time and having us sequentially "sound off" after each pit stop before the car would go into gear. This system proved effective at keeping track of the gaggle of children for many years. There was no such system in place however, for keeping track of the PARENTS. This time, puttering southbound along a rural section of central Utah's Interstate 15, my brother and I asleep in the infamous cargo area, it seemed as though the worst had happened and the flaw in the system had been found.

With less kids in the car on this particular journey, overcome by the weariness that eventually befalls all road trippers, my mother seized the opportunity to utilize the rarely vacant back seat of the old van to catch a few winks. I later came to learn that after a brief and assumingly solo out-and-back bathroom run by my father into a lonely gas station located along that corridor and kindly letting his sleeping passengers be - drove some 80+ miles before realizing anything was amiss. Soon, the rising sun began painting such a picturesque desert scene that it couldn't simply be enjoyed alone. "Debby". He called to the back seat with no response. "Debby! You should get up and see this." Still no answer from the back seat. A tad impatient now, he growled "Debby! Debby! DEBBY!" Still no answer. Upping his game, he began tossing soft objects over the seat – all while driving – in an elevated attempt to rouse her. But there was no one by that name in the car, and projectiles were simply landing on a vacant seat!

Now, finding ourselves on the shoulder of a ranch exit in rural south-central Utah with my father's looming figure demanding answers, through bleary eyes my brother and I began growing more concerned by the moment as we began piecing things together. We stared blankly at each other so as to say "What did WE do with our mother??" By then, Dad had already torn the car apart only to find the evidence of where she had been

napping - a wad of blankets in the back seat. The next hour or so was a blur. Literally. Frantically we sped as fast as legally possible back to the theorized point of "ground zero".

By the time we found her, she had been interviewed by a policeman, offered breakfast, two jobs, and room and board from the nice owners for a chance to rebuild her life after being abandoned at an isolated gas station in rural Utah by her apparently no-good husband. We joked for decades about my mother's conversation with the gas station cashier lady. "What was the last thing you said to him?" She'd wondered. Once we had mom safely back in the fold, the jokes started and just wouldn't stop. "Careful how you treat your father!" My mother said for years after. "If you start to get on his bad side, he'll leave you on the side of the road!" My poor father never did live this down, and had to wear the infamous reputation for a long time.

This incident did highlight the need for several important upgrades to our on-board attendance system. First, the person getting out of the car needed to alert the guy who is driving of their intentions no matter what, no matter when. Secondly, the driver should include everyone in the sequential head count – even the parents.

The wheels of time roll on don't they? I find myself behind the wheel mostly these days. As we plan and take our own family road trips, I relay this story to my own kids with instructive fondness. We all have a casual chuckle about it, but when we all pile out of the car and I say "Fifteen minutes everybody! Fifteen minutes!", Everyone is usually all back in their seats in ten. ◆

ALABAMA

INTERSTATE 10

LOXLEY

Exit #	Services
66.5mm	Alabama/Florida state line
66mm	**Welcome Ctr full facilities, , litter barrels, vending, petwalk,**
53	rd 64, Wilcox Rd, N Marathon/Oasis/Chester's/Stuckey's/Subway/dsl/scales/24hr/@, Riverside RV Park, Styx River Resort, S Chevron/dsl, Azalea Acres RV Park, fireworks, Hilltop RV Park(1.5 mi), Wilderness RV Park
49	Rd 68, Baldwin Beach Express, to Gulf Shores, Orange Beach, Gulf SP, S Buc-ee's/dsl
44	AL 59, Loxley, N Love's/Arby's/dsl/scales/24hr/@, Bay Inn, S Exxon/Circle K/Burger King/dsl, RaceWay/dsl, Burger King, Hardee's, McDonald's, Waffle House, Loxley Motel(3mi), WindChase Inn, to Gulf SP
38	AL 181, Malbis, N Briquettes Steakhouse, CA Dreaming, Chick-fil-A, Cracker Barrel, foosackly's Chicken, Freddy's, Half Shell Oyster House, Logan's Roadhouse, Marble Slab, Marco's Pizza, McDonald's, Moe's SW Grill, Olive Garden, Panera Bread, Pizza Hut, Poor Mexican, Popeyes, Sonic, Starbucks, Stix Asian, Taco Bell, Waffle House, Wendy's, Comfort Inn, Holiday Inn Express, Home2 Suites, La Quinta, $Tree, Advance Parts, Barnes&Noble, Belk, Best Buy, Dillard's, Goodyear/auto, Michael's, Old Navy, PetSmart, Publix, Ross, Tuesday Morning, Verizon, Walgreens, World Mkt, S CEFCO/dsl, Chevron/dsl, Shell, Burger King, Don Carlos, Dunkin', Firehouse Subs, Island Wing Co, Mellow Mushroom, Papa John's, Whataburger, Zaxby's, Malbis Motel(1mi), Woodspring Suites, AT&T, Honda, Hyundai, Lowe's, Nissan, Sam's Club/gas, Toyota, URGENT CARE, VW
35	US 90, US 98, N Marathon, Mobil, Beef O'Brady's, China Fun, Courtyard, Fairfield Inn, Bass Pro Shops, JC Penney, Kohl's, Piggly Wiggly, to Blakeley SP, Walgreens, S Exxon/dsl, Shell, Arby's, Bangkok Thai, Boudreaux's Cajun Grill, Braumhower's Grill, Burger King, Cici's Pizza, David's Catfish, Dickey's BBQ, Domino's, Dragon City Buffet, Dunkin', El Rancho Mexican, Firehouse Subs, Five Guys, foosackly's Chicken, Hooters, Longhorn Steaks, McDonald's, Mediterranean Sandwich, Nagoya Japanese, O'Charley's, Poke Bowl Sushi, Smoothie King, Starbucks, Subway, Top of the Bay, Waffle House, Waffle House(2), Zaxby's, Comfort Suites, Eastern Shore Motel, Hampton Inn, Hilton Garden, Homewood Suites, Microtel, $Tree, AT&T, Dick's, Fresh Mkt, GNC, Hobby Lobby, Home Depot, H, Office Depot, Petco, TJ Maxx
30	US 90/98, Battleship Pkwy, N BlueGill Rest., Ed's Seafood Shed, Oyster House, S same as 27
27	US 90/98, Battleship Pkwy, Gov't St, S Cafe Del Rio, Felix's Fish Camp, R&R Seafood, Ralph&Kacoo's Seafood, to USS Alabama
26b	Water St, Mobile, downtown, N Dauphin's Fine Dining, Roosters, Candlewood Suites, Hampton Inn, Holiday Inn, Quality Inn, Renaissance Hotel, to Visitors Ctr
26a	Canal St(from eb), same as 26b
25b	Virginia St, Mobile
25a	Texas St(from wb, no return)
24	Broad St, to Duval St, Mobile, N Chevron/dsl
23	Michigan Ave, N Shell/dsl
22b a	AL 163, Dauphin Island Pkwy, N OYO, $General, Family$, S Chevron, Exxon/Subway, Mobil/dsl, Checkers, Hart's Chicken, Waffle House, $General
20	I-65 N, to Montgomery

MOBILE

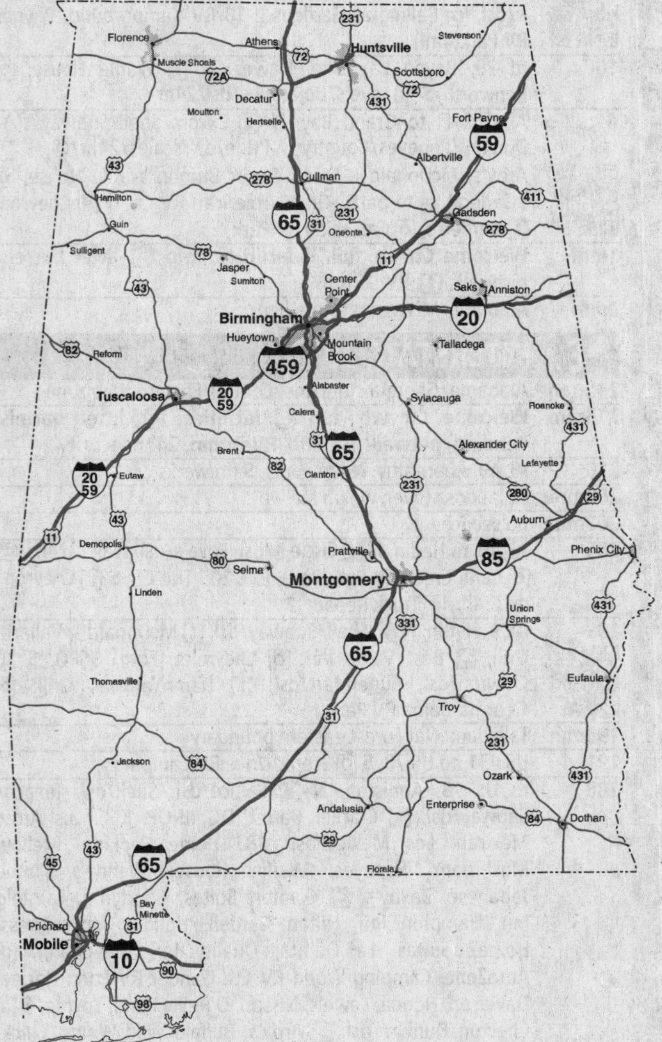

THEODORE

Exit #	Services
17	AL 193, Tillmans Corner, to Dauphin Island, N BP, Beef-O-Brady's, Firehouse Subs, Five Guys, foosackly's Chicken, IHOP, Jersey Mike's, Jimmy John's, Moe's SW, Panda Express, RockNRoll Sushi, Ruby Tuesday, Starbucks, Whataburger, Zaxby's, ALDI, AT&T, auto repair, H, Lowe's, URGENT CARE, Verizon, Walmart/Subway
15b a	US 90, Tillmans Corner, to Mobile, N Chevron, Murphy Express/dsl, RaceWay/dsl, Arby's, Aztecas Mexican, Burger King, Domino's, Godfather's, Hooters, KFC, Krystal, Little Caesar's, McDonald's, Papa John's, Popeyes, Russell's BBQ, Shrimp Basket, Subway, Taco Bell, Waffle House, Baymont Inn, Comfort Suites, Days Inn, Extend-a-Suites, Hampton Inn, Holiday Inn, Holiday Inn Express, Home2 Suites, InTown Suites, La Quinta, Motel 6, Quality Inn, Red Roof Inn, Regency Inn, Super 8, Super Inn, $General, $Tree, AutoZone, BigLots, Family$, Firestone/auto, Mike's Transmissions, O'Reilly Parts, PepBoys, vet, Walgreens, Winn-Dixie, S Exxon, RaceWay/dsl, Shell/dsl, Waffle House, Advance Parts, B&R Campers, Johnny's RV Ctr, Peterbilt, tires, transmissions, USPO, vet
13	Theodore, N Clark/dsl, Pilot/Wendy's/dsl/scales/24hr, Shell/Subway, Burger King, Church's TX Chicken,

AL

= gas = food = lodging = other = rest stop

THEODORE

INTERSTATE 10 Cont'd

13 Continued
McDonald's, Waffle House, Walmart Mkt/dsl, $Tree, Advance Parts, auto repair, Family$, Rouse's Mkt, S Circle K/dsl, Bellingraf Gardens, I-10 RV Kampground, Paynes RV Park(4mi)

10 rd 39, Bayou La Batre, Dawes, N Waffle House, Kenworth, S Love's/Bojangles/dsl/24hr

4 AL 188 E, to Grand Bay, N Exxon, Shell/Subway, TA/Dunkin'/Popeyes/Country Pride/dsl/scales/24hr/@, Arby's, McDonald's, Sam's Super Burger, Waffle House, $General, auto parts, Great American RV Ctr, S Chevron, Hardee's, Creekside RV Park

1mm **Welcome Ctr eb, full facilities, info, litter barrels, petwalk, RV Dump**

0mm Alabama/Mississippi state line

ABERNATHY

INTERSTATE 20

215mm Alabama/Georgia state line, Central/Eastern time zone

213mm **Welcome Ctr wb, full facilities, litter barrels, vending, petwalk, info, RV Dump, 24hr security**

210 AL 49, Abernathy, N fireworks, S fireworks

209mm Tallapoosa River, weigh sta wb

208mm no services

205 AL 46, to Heflin, N Circle K/dsl, Love's/dsl/scales/24hr/@, Cane Creek RV Park(2mi), Exit 205 Tire Ctr, S Chevron/dsl/24hr, Truck Repair

199 AL 9, Heflin, N Shell/Subway/dsl, McDonald's, Vallarta Grill, Best Value Inn, Chevrolet, Ford, USPO, S Chevron/dsl, SuperMart/dsl, DamnYankees Grill, Georgia-Bama RV Park

198mm Talladega Nat Forest eastern boundary

191 US 431, to US 78, S Scenic Drive RV Camping

ANNISTON

188 to US 78, Anniston, N Samco/dsl, Shell/dsl, Texaco/Subway/dsl, Cracker Barrel, DQ, IHOP, KFC, Los Arcos Mexican, Los Mexicanos, M&J Home Cooking, Mellow Mushroom, Popeyes, Waffle House, Wendy's, Yume Japanese, Zaxby's, Comfort Suites, Courtyard, Fairfield Inn, Hampton Inn, Hilton Garden, Holiday Inn Express, Home2 Suites, La Quinta, Quality Inn, Sleep Inn, AutoZone, Camping World RV Ctr, Gander RV Park, Harley-Davidson, Honda, Lowe's, Nissan, O'Reilly Parts, Toyota, S Chevron/Dunkin'/dsl, Arby's, Buffalo Wild Wings, Chick-fil-A, Chicken Salad Chick, Chipotle, Firehouse Subs, Five Guys, Jim 'N Nick's BBQ, Longhorn Steaks, Mexico Lindo Grill, Moe's SW, Olive Garden, Panda Express, Panera Bread, TX Roadhouse, AAA, AT&T, Best Buy, Dick's, GNC, Hobby Lobby, Home Depot, Kohl's, Old Navy, PetSmart, Publix, Ross, Sams Club/dsl, Target, TJ Maxx, Verizon

185 AL 21, to Ft McClellan, Anniston, N Chevron/dsl, Marathon/dsl, Shell/dsl, Texaco, Applebee's, Arby's, Baskin-Robbins, Bojangles, Burger King, Capt D's, CiCi's Pizza, Dunkin', Garfrerick's Cafe, HoneyBaked Ham, Jack's Rest., Logan's Roadhouse, McDonald's, Papa John's, Pizza Hut, Red Lobster, Sonic, Starbucks, Struts, Taco Bell, Waffle House, Western Sizzlin, Red Carpet Inn, ALDI, BooksAMillion, Cobb Auto, CVS Drug, Dillard's, Firestone/auto, Ford, JC Penney, Martin's Foods, NAPA, S 76, Circle K/dsl/scales, Murphy USA/dsl, RaceTrac, RaceWay, Jefferson's Rest, Mango's Grill, Waffle House, Wendy's, EconoLodge, Key West Inn, Motel 6, Red Roof Inn, Super 8, $Tree, Cobb Automotive, H, Walmart/EVC

179 AL 202, to US 78, to Munford, Coldwater, N Chevron/Subway/dsl, China King, El Agave Grill, Jack's Rest., Johnson's Deli, $General, Anniston Army Depot, Walgreens, S Texaco/dsl

EASTABOGA

173 AL 5, Eastaboga, S Mapco, Sunoco, to Speedway/Hall of Fame

168 AL 77, to Talladega, N Exxon/Domino's, Marathon/KFC/Taco Bell, Pilot/Arby's/dsl/scales/24hr, Jack's Rest., Waffle House, S AOC/Burger King, Chevron/Subway/dsl, TA/Popeyes/dsl/scales/24hr, McDonald's, MT Grill, Rana's Mexican, Comfort Inn, Days Inn, Hall of Fame, to Speedway

165 Embry, Lincoln, N Hi-Tech/dsl, Pilot/Subway/dsl/scales/24hr, Paradise Island RV Park, S 165 TP/Huddle House/dsl, I-20TrkStp/rest./dsl/scales/24hr, Doghouse Grill, McCaig Motel

164mm Coosa River

162 US 78, Riverside, N Safe Harbor RV Park, S Chevron/dsl, Best Value Inn/rest

158 US 231, Pell City, N Marathon/dsl, Murphy USA/dsl, Arby's, Azteca Mexican, Buffalo Wild Wings, Chick-fil-A, City Mkt Grill, Cracker Barrel, Freddy's, Golden Rule BBQ, Hwy 55 Cafe, Jade E Chinese, Krystal, Wendy's, Zaxby's, Comfort Suites, Hampton Inn, Holiday Inn Express, $Tree, AT&T, City Tire, Home Depot, H, URGENT CARE, Walgreens, Walmart/Subway, S Circle K/dsl, Texaco/dsl, Valero, Burger King, Jack's Rest., Jersey Mike's, KFC, Maya's Mexican, McDonald's, Milo's Burgers, Starbucks, Subway, Taco Bell, Waffle House, Quality Inn, AutoZone, Chrysler/Dodge/Jeep, Ford, O'Reilly Parts

156 US 78 E, to Pell City, S QT/dsl, Shell/dsl

153 US 78, Chula Vista

152 Cook Springs

147 Brompton, N Sunoco, Valero TC/Sonic/dsl/scales/24hr, S Love's/McDonald's/Subway/dsl/scales/24hr/@, Valero/dsl/deli

LEEDS

144 US 411, Leeds, N 76/dsl, RaceWay/dsl, Shell/Subway, Arby's, Cracker Barrel, Dunkin', El Patron, Logan's Roadhouse, Milo's Burgers, Popeyes, The Purple Onion, Waffle House, Wendy's, Zaxby's, Best Western+, Comfort Inn, Super 8, $Tree, Publix, Verizon, S Chevron, RaceWay/dsl, Capt D's, Chick-fil-A, El Cazador Mexican, Guadalajara Mexican, KFC, Little Caesar's, Mango's Grill, McDonald's, Taco Bell, Waffle House, Whataburger, Days Inn, $General, AT&T, AutoZone, Lowe's, Walgreens, Walmart/Subway

140 US 78, Leeds, N Distinctive Outlets/famous brands, S Buc-ee's/dsl, Chevron, Subway, America's Best Value Inn, Hampton Inn, Bass Pro Shop

139mm Cahaba River

INTERSTATE 20 Cont'd

Exit #	Services
136	I-459 S, to Montgomery, Tuscaloosa
135	US 78, Old Leeds Rd, N Shell/dsl, B'ham Race Course
133	US 78, to Kilgore Memorial Dr, (wb return at 132), N Chevron, Exxon/Circle K/dsl, Golden Rule BBQ, Hamburger Heaven, Krystal, Waffle House, Red Roof+, same as 132, $General, O'Reilly Parts, TJ Tires, S Shell, Gus' Hot Dogs, Marty's GM, McDonald's, Wings R King, Hampton Inn, Holiday Inn Express, Quality Inn, Mavis
132b a	US 78, Crestwood Blvd, N Chevron, Exxon/Circle K/dsl, Golden Rule BBQ, Hamburger Heaven, Krystal, TJ Tires, Waffle House, Red Roof+, $General, Aamco, O'Reilly Parts, same as 133, S Chevron, Circle K, Marathon/dsl, Murphy Express/dsl, Shell, Texaco/dsl, Arby's, Bojangles, Burger King, Capt D's, Chick-fil-A, Domino's, El Cazador Mexican, Honeybaked Ham, Hungry Howie's, Jack's, KFC, King Buffet, Los Arcos Mexican, McDonald's, Milo's Burgers, New China Buffet, Pancho's Mexican, Starbucks, Sushi Village, Taco Bell, The Crab Barracks, The Juicy Seafood, Zaxby's, Comfort Inn, $Tree, Advance Parts, AlLDI, Burlington Coats, Firestone/auto, Home Depot, H, Office Depot, PepBoys, Ross, TJ Maxx, Tuesday Morning, URGENT CARE, Verizon, Walgreens, Walmart
130b	US 11, 1st Ave, N Chevron, Petro, Sunoco, AutoZone, Family$, Piggly Wiggly, S Texaco/dsl, McDonald's, Pacific Seafood, Relax Inn, Sky Inn
130a	I-59 N, Gadsden
129.5mm	I-59 S and I-20 W run together from B'ham to Meridian, MS
129	Airport Blvd, N Ramada, S Amoco/dsl, BP/dsl, Mobil, Best Wings, Kabob House, Budgetel Inn, Holiday Inn
128	AL 79, Tallapoosa St, N Circle K/Subway/dsl/scales, Shell/Wings/dsl, S park
126b	31st St, N Shell/dsl, Texaco/dsl, McDonald's, Family$
126a	US 31, US 280, 26th St, Carraway Blvd, N KFC, Wings & Things, S The Pit BBQ
125b	22nd St, N Subway, Sheraton, Westin
125a	17th St, to downtown
124b a	I-65, S to Montgomery, N to Nashville
123	US 78, Arkadelphia Rd, N Chevron, Marathon, Pilot/Wendy's/dsl/scales/24hr(0.5mi), Shell/dsl, Popeyes, Days Inn, S H, to Legion Field
121	Bush Blvd(from wb, no return), Ensley, N Exxon, Marathon, WingOut
120	AL 269, 20th St, Ensley Ave, N Marathon, KFC, Honda, S Chevron, H, Toyota/Scion, Truck Repair
119b	Ave I(from wb)
119a	Lloyd Noland Pwky, N Shell/dsl, Sunoco/dsl, Fairfield Seafood, Family$, tire repair, S BP/Wings, Mobil, H
118	AL 56, Valley Rd, Fairfield, S BP/Wings, Milo's Burgers, Budgetel Inn, Home Depot, URGENT CARE
115	Allison-Bonnett Memorial Dr, tire repair, N 76/dsl, Citgo, RaceWay/dsl, Shell/dsl, Church's TX Chicken, Hardee's, Huddle House, Jack's, Los Machetes, Los Reyes Mexican, Subway, Waffle House, Zaxby's, Advance Parts, O'Reilly Parts, USPO
113	18th Ave, to Hueytown, S Chevron/dsl, Marathon, McDonald's
112	18th St, 19th St, Bessemer, N RaceWay/dsl, Shell, Jack's Rest., tire/repair, S Chevron, Sunoco/dsl, KFC, Rally's, Subway, Sykes BBQ, Advance Parts, FMS Drug, Lowe's, NAPA, O'Reilly Parts, Walgreens
110	AL Adventure Pkwy, N Splash Adventure Funpark, S H
108	US 11, AL 5 N, Academy Dr, N Circle K, Cracker Barrel,

GADSDEN ENSLEY BESSEMER

Exit #	Services
108	Continued Seafood King, The Juicy Seafood, Waffle House, Best Western+, Comfort Inn, Fairfield Inn, Holiday Inn Express, Quality Inn, Red Roof+, WoodSpring Suites, Chevrolet, Chrysler/Dodge/Jeep, Nissan, S Chevron/Church's TX Chicken/dsl, Murphy USA/dsl, Shell, Burger King, Domino's, Jack's, Little Caesar's, Los Sombreros, McDonald's, Milo's Burgers, Sonic, Wendy's, Zaxby's, Economy Inn, Hamilton Inn, Motel 6, $Tree, BigLots, Ford, H, PepBoys, to civic ctr, Verizon, Walmart/Subway
106	I-459 N, to Montgomery
104	Rock Mt Lake, S Flying J/Subway/dsl/LP/24hr
100	to Abernant, N Love's/McDonald's/Subway/dsl/scales/24hr, Speedway/dsl, Burger King, S Citgo, Marathon, Petro/Marathon/Iron Skillet/Popeyes/dsl/scales/24hr/@, $General, Tannehill SP(3mi)
97	US 11 S, AL 5 S, to W Blocton, S Chevron/KFC/dsl, Citgo/dsl, Exxon/Subway/dsl, Jack's Rest., La Tortilla Grill, Cahaba River NWR
89	Mercedes Dr, N Greystone Inn, S Mercedes Auto Plant
86	Vance, to Brookwood, N Marathon/Huddle House/Subway/dsl, Shell/dsl/rest./24hr
85mm	**both lanes, full facilities, litter barrels, vending, petwalk, RV dump**
79	US 11, University Blvd, Coaling, S Chevron/dsl, Texaco/dsl
77	Cottondale, N Chevron/McDonald's, Pilot/Wendy's/dsl/scales/24hr, TA/BP/Taco Bell/dsl/scales/24hr/@, Arby's, Holiday Inn Express, Pizza Hut, Hampton Inn, Microtel, Blue Beacon, Harley Davidson, SpeedCo, USPO, S QT, Chevrolet
76	US 11, E Tuscaloosa, Cottondale, N Chevron, Shell/dsl, Texaco, Burger King, Cracker Barrel, Waffle House, Howard Johnson, Red Roof+, SureStay Inn, Wingate Inn, Woodspring Suites, Sunset 2 RV Park, transmissions, S Pilot/Subway/dsl/scales/24hr, Texaco/dsl, Jack's, Rodeway Inn, Goodyear, Walmart Mkt/gas
73	US 82, McFarland Blvd, Tuscaloosa, N Chevron/dsl, Circle K, Shell, Applebee's, Arby's, Blaze Pizza, Buffalo Wild Wings, Burger King, Capt D's, Chick-fil-A, Chipotle, Dunkin', Five Guys, Full Moon BBQ, Jason's Deli, Krystal, Longhorn Steaks, Moe's SW Grill, Olive Garden, Panera Bread, Popeyes, Red Lobster, Shrimp Basket, Slim Chickens, T Town Seafood, TCBY, Waffle House, Yummi Crab, Avid Hotel, Best Value Inn, Best Western, Comfort Suites, Holiday Inn Express, La Quinta, Masters Inn, TownePlace, $General, Aamco, Advance Parts, AT&T, Barnes&Noble, Belk, Best Buy, CVS Drug, Firestone/auto, Goodyear/auto, Home Depot, H, JC Penney, Mavis, Michael's, Midas, Old Navy, PepBoys, Ross, SteinMart, Target, vet, S Circle K, Marathon, Buffet City, Checkers, Crimson Wings, Hardee's, KFC, Logan's Roadhouse, McDonald's, Papa John's, Sharks Fish, Sonic, Subway, Taco Bell, Taco Casa, Ambassador Inn, Candlewood Suites, Country Inn&Suites, Days Inn, EconoLodge, Motel 6, Quality Inn, Ramada Inn, Super 8, Travelodge, $General, $Tree, Chrysler/Dodge/Jeep, NAPA, Office Depot, Sam's Club/gas, TJ Maxx, U-Haul, Walmart/Subway
71b	I-359, Al 69 N, to Tuscaloosa, N H, to Stillman Coll, U of AL
71a	AL 69 S, to Moundville, S Chevron, Citgo/dsl, Mapco/dsl, Shell/dsl, Arby's, Baumhower's Rest., Chick-fil-A, Hooters, IHOP, Milo's Burgers, Outback Steaks, Pizza Hut, Red Crab, Starbucks, Waffle House, Wendy's, Whataburger, Zaxby's, Baymont Inn, Courtyard, Fairfield Inn, Hilton Garden, SpringHill Suites, Advance Parts, Goodyear/auto, Kia/Mazda/VW, Lowe's, O'Reilly Parts, PepBoys, to Mound SM, URGENT CARE

COALING TUSCALOOSA

= gas = food = lodging = other = rest stop

INTERSTATE 20 Cont'd

Exit #	Services
68	Northport-Tuscaloosa Western Bypass
64mm	Black Warrior River
62	Fosters, N Chevron/Subway/dsl, $General, Foodland, USPO, vet
52	US 11, US 43, Knoxville, N Circle K/dsl
45	AL 37, Union, S Chevron/Subway/dsl, Texaco/dsl, Se7ens Rest, Econolodge, Travel Inn, Greene Co Greyhound Park
40	AL 14, Eutaw, N to Tom Bevill Lock/Dam, S Love's/Hardees/Godfather's/dsl/scales/24hr/@, H
39mm	**wb, full facilities, litter barrels, vending, petwalk, RV Dump**
38mm	**eb, full facilities, litter barrels, vending, petwalk, RV Dump**
32	Boligee, N Marathon/rest./dsl/24hr, S Chevron/Subway/dsl
27mm	Tenn-Tom Waterway, Tombigbee River
23	rd 20, Epes, to Gainesville
17	AL 28, Livingston, S Chevron/Subway/dsl, Exxon/L&B/dsl/24hr, Shell/dsl, Burger King, Diamond Jim's/Mrs Donna's, McDonald's, Tres Hermanos, Comfort Inn, Western Inn
8	AL 17, York, S Marathon/New Orleans Grill/dsl/scales/@, Best Inn, $General, tire repair
1	to US 80 E, Cuba, S Citgo/dsl, tire repair
0.5mm	**Welcome Ctr eb, full facilities, litter barrels, pet walk, RV dump, vending**
0.3mm	I-20 E and I-59 N run together from Meridian, MS to B'ham
0mm	Alabama/Mississippi state line

INTERSTATE 22

Exit #	Services
96	I-65, N to Nashville, S to Birmingham, I-22 begins/ends
93	rd 77
91	rd 105, to Brookside
89	rd 65, to Adamsville, Graysville
87	rd 112, to Graysville
85	US 78, Birmingham, N BP
81	rd 45, W Jefferson
78	rd 81, Dora, Sumiton, N TJ's/dsl
72	rd 61, Cordova
70	rd 22, Cordova, Parish
65	Bevill Ind Pkwy, Jasper, N Hampton Inn(3mi), Holiday Inn Express(3mi), H, to Walker Co Lake, S Love's/McDonald's/Subway/dsl/scales/24hr, Burger King, Cracker Barrel, Waffle House, Zaxby's, Sleep Inn/EVC, Buick/Cadillac/Chevrolet/GMC
63	AlL 269, Jasper, Parish, N Chevron/dsl
61	AL 69, Jasper, Tuscaloosa, N RJ's, Deano's Hickory Pit
57	AL 118 E, Jasper, N Chevron, Shell/dsl, The Barn Rest.
53	to AL 118
52	AL 118, Carbon Hill
46	rd 11, Carbon Hill, Nauvoo, N Chevron, S Chevron/dsl, Shell
39	AL 13, Natural Bridge, Eldridge
34	AL 233, Glen Allen, Natural Bridge
30	AL 129, Brilliant, Winfield, S Chevron/deli/dsl, Shell/deli/dsl, Huddle House, Hampton Inn, Appalachian Foothills RV Camping/repair
26	AL 44, Brilliant, Guin, S Holiday Inn, H
22	rd 45
16	US 43, US 278, Hamilton, Guin, S Shell/dsl
14	Hamilton, N Love's/dsl/scales/24hr, Texaco/dsl, Huddle House, Days Inn(1mi), EconoLodge(1mi), Keywest Inn, Speedco, Turkey Hill RV Camping
11	AL 17, Hamilton, Sulligent, N Citgo/dsl, H
7	Hamilton, Weston, N H
3	rd 33
0mm	Alabama/Mississippi State Line

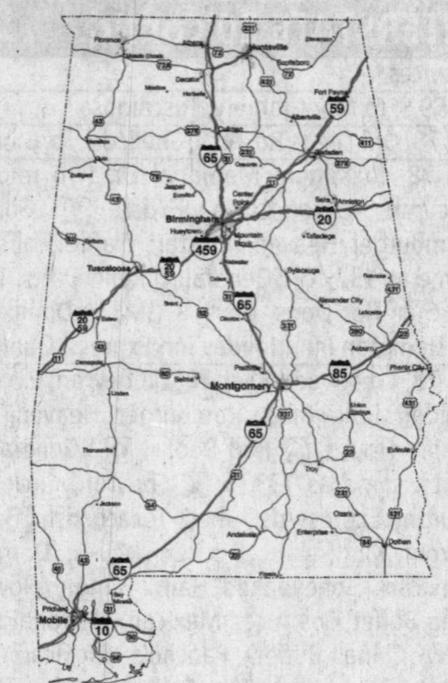

INTERSTATE 59

Exit #	Services
241.5mm	Alabama/Georgia state line, Central/Eastern time zone
241mm	**Welcome Ctr sb, full facilities, litter barrels, vending, petwalk, RV Dump**
239	to US 11, Sulphur Springs Rd
231	AL 40, AL 117, Hammondville, Valley Head, E camping(5mi), DeSoto SP, W Fuel City
224	49th St, Ft Payne, W Mapco
222	US 11, Ft Payne, E Arby's, Barone's Pizza, Domino's, Fazoli's, Jack's Rest., KFC, Krystal, Pizza Hut, Toke Japanese, Wingstop, Quality Inn, Chevrolet, Express Oil Change, Foodland/dsl, W Citgo/dsl, Marathon
218	AL 35, Ft Payne, E Capt D's, Cattle Stampede Steaks, Don Chico Mexican, DQ, Gallardo's Mexican, Jack's, Jefferson's Burgers, Little Caesar's, McDonald's, New China, Papa John's, Sonic, Taco Bell, Zaxby's, $General, Advance Parts, Alabama Museum, AutoZone, BigLots, Chrysler/Dodge/Jeep, O'Reilly Parts, URGENT CARE, W Circle K/dsl, Mapco/dsl, Murphy USA/dsl, Applebee's, Burger King, Chick-fil-A, Chow King, Cracker Barrel, Huddle House, Los Arcos, Osaka Japanese, Popeyes, Santa Fe Steaks, Waffle House, Days Inn, EconoLodge, Hampton Inn, Holiday Inn Express, $Tree, AT&T, Ford/Lincoln, GNC, H, Lowe's, Verizon, Walgreens, Walmart, Will's Creek RV Park
205	AL 68, Collinsville, E Delta, Jack's Rest., Travelers Inn, to Little River Canyon, Weiss Lake, W BP/dsl, MapCo, Burger King
188	AL 211, to US 11, Gadsden, E Marathon, H, Noccalula Falls Camping, W Marathon/dsl/e85
183	US 431, US 278, Gadsden, E Marathon/dsl, Shell, Texaco/dsl, Waffle House, Days Inn, HomeLodge, Motel 6, Rodeway Inn, st police, W Chevron, Exxon, Marathon, KFC, McDonald's, Subway, Taco Bell
182	I-759, Gadsden
181	AL 77, Rainbow City, to Gadsden, E Petro/Popeyes/dsl/scales/24hr/@, Barney's Roadhouse, Jack's, EconoLodge, W Circle K/dsl, Murphy Express/dsl, Arby's, Cracker Barrel, Domino's, El Patron, Hardee's, Hector's Kitchen, Krab Kingz, Lucky Wok, McDonald's, Old Mexico Grille, Subway, Waffle House, Wendy's, Best Western+, Comfort Suites, Fairfield Inn, Hampton Inn,

INTERSTATE 59 Cont'd

STEELE

181 Continued
Holiday Inn Express, $General, $Tree, O'Reilly Parts, Walmart

174 Steele, E Love's/Subway/Godfather's/dsl/scales/24hr/@, W Marathon/dsl, Sunoco/Hunt Bro.s Pizza/truckwash/dsl

168mm **sb, full facilities, litter barrels, vending, petwalk, RV Dump**

166 US 231, Whitney, to Ashville, E BP, Chevron/dsl, W Texaco/dsl, Dawg House Diner, Jack's Rest., Subway

165mm **nb, full facilities, litter barrels, vending, petwalk, RV Dump**

ARGO

156 AL 23, to US 11, Springville, to St Clair Springs, W Murphy USA/dsl, Shell/dsl, Burger King, China Stix, El Patron Mexican, Pizza Hut, Taco Bell, Waffle House, Zaxby's, $Tree, AT&T, Walmart

154 AL 174, Springville, to Odenville, E Exxon/dsl, W BP/Subway, Chevron, Citgo, MapCo, Shell/dsl, Choppin Block Rest., Domino's, Gulf Seafood, Jack's Rest., McDonald's, Smoke House BBQ

148 to US 11, Argo, E Shell, Jack's, Subway

143 Mt Olive Church Rd, Deerfoot Pkwy, E Shell/dsl/CNG

141 to Trussville, Pinson, E Bama/dsl, Shell/dsl, Texaco/dsl, Applebee's, Cracker Barrel, Guthrie's, McDonald's, Papa John's, Pizza Hut, Taco Bell, Waffle House, Wendy's, Comfort Inn, Holiday Inn Express, Quality Inn, Harley-Davidson, W Chevron, Marathon, Shell/dsl, Texaco, Arby's, Buffalo Wild Wings, Burger King, Chick-fil-A, Costa's Mediterranean, DQ, East Buffet, El Patron, Full Moon BBQ, Jack's, Konomi Japanese, Krystal, LongHorn Steaks, Milo's Burgers, Palace Asian, Whataburger, Zaxby's, $Tree, Ace Hardware, Advance Parts, BigLots, CVS Drug, GNC, Kohl's, Marshall's, PetSmart, Sam's Club/gas, vet, Walgreens, Walmart/Subway

137 I-459 S, to Montgomery, Tuscaloosa

134 to AL 75, Roebuck Pkwy, W Chevron, Circle K, Murphy USA/dsl, Shell/dsl, Arby's, Burger King, Chick-fil-A, Crab Barrack, Domino's, Hardee's, McDonald's, Milo's Burgers, Papa John's, Pizza Hut, Subway, Wingstop, Rodeway Inn, $Tree, AlLDI, AT&T, CVS, Family$, Honda, H, O'Reilly Parts, URGENT CARE, Vo Tires, Walgreens, Walmart/Burger King

133 4th St, to US 11(from nb), same as 134, W Papa John's, $General, USPO

132 US 11 N, 1st Ave, E same as 131, W Chevron, Shell/dsl, Krispy Kreme, city park

131 Oporto-Madrid Blvd(from nb), E BP/Circle K, Chevron, Church's TX Chicken, Little Caesar's, CVS, Family$, O'Reilly Parts, same as 132, U-Haul

130 I-20, E to Atlanta, W to Tuscaloosa

125mm I-59 S and I-20 W run together from B'ham to Mississippi. See I-20, exits 129-1.

INTERSTATE 65

ARDMORE

366mm Alabama/Tennessee state line

365 AL 53, Ardmore, E Budget Inn

364mm **Welcome Ctr sb, full facilities, litter barrels, vending, petwalk, info, RV Dump**

361 Elkmont, W BP/dsl, Momma D's Rest., repair

354 US 31 S, Athens, W Chevron/dsl, Circle K, Valero, Capt D's, Domino's, Jack's Rest., Little Caesar's, McDonald's, Rooster's Cafe, Subway, Mark Motel, $General, Advance Parts, city park, CVS, HomeTown Mkt, H, Northgate RV Park, Walgreens

351 US 72, to Athens, Huntsville, E Exxon, RaceWay/dsl, Shell/Subway, Valero/dsl, Buffalo Wild Wings, Burger King,

351 Continued
Casa Blanca, Cracker Barrel, Dunkin', Jack's, Las Trejas Mexican, Lawler's BBQ, McDonald's/RV Parking, Panda Express, Taco Bell, Waffle House, Wendy's, Econolodge, Hampton Inn, Quality Inn, Travel Inn, $General, Publix, Russell Stover, Verizon, vet, W Citgo/dsl, Marathon, Murphy USA, Applebee's, Arby's, Bojangle's, Burger King, Burrito Express, Catfish Cabin, Chick-fil-A, Chipotle, D&L Seafood, Firehouse Subs, Hardee's, IHOP, Jiang's Golden Phoenix, KFC, Krystal, Logan's Roadhouse, Papa John's, Papa Murphy's, Pizza Hut, Popeyes, Smith's Seafood, Sonic, Starbucks, Steak-Out, Subway, Taco Bell, Touchdown Wings, Zaxby's, Best Western, Days Inn, Fairfield Inn/EVC, Holiday Inn Express, Sleep Inn, Super 8, $General, $Tree, Advance Parts, ALDI, Big Lots, Chevrolet, Chrysler/Dodge/Jeep, Ford, Goodyear/auto, H, Lowe's, O'Reilly Parts, O'Reilly Parts, Pepboys, SaveALot Foods, Staples, to Joe Wheeler SP, Tuesday Morning, Walmart/EVC

347 Brownsferry Rd, Huntsville, E Buc-ee's/dsl, W Chevron, $General, Reddy RV Park, Swan Creek RV Park

340b I-565, to Alabama Space & Rocket Ctr, to Huntsville

340a AL 20, to Decatur, W Great American RV Ctr

337mm Tennessee River

HARTSELLE

334 AL 67, Priceville, to Decatur, E Marathon/dsl, RaceWay/dsl, JW's Steaks, Days Inn, Super 8, $General, Family$, Foodland, USA Tires, W Chevron/dsl, Mapco/dsl, Pilot/Subway/Wendy's/dsl/scales/24hr, Burger King, DQ, Hardee's, Krystal, McDonald's, Moe's BBQ, Pizza Hut, Taco Bell, Taste of China, Waffle House, Comfort Inn, H, Johnston RV Ctr, Publix

328 AL 36, Hartselle, E Cracker Barrel, W Chevron/dsl, Cowboys/dsl, Exxon, Mobil/dsl, Huddle House, Red Roof Inn, $General, vet

325 Thompson Rd, to Hartselle

322 AL 55, to US 31, to Falkville, Eva, E Marathon/Chester's/dsl, W Chevron, Love's/McDonald's/Subway/dsl/scales/24hr/@, $General

318 US 31, to Lacon

310 AL 157, Cullman, West Point, E Chevron/Popeyes, Circle K/dsl, Conoco/Subway/dsl, Shell/dsl, Texaco/Wendy's/dsl, Arby's, Bueno Vista Mexican, Burger King, Cracker Barrel, Denny's, KFC, Lawler's BBQ, Little Caesar's, Logan's Roadhouse, McAlister's Deli, McDonald's, Panda Express, Ruby Tuesday, Taco Bell, Waffle House, Zaxby's, Best Western, Comfort Suites, Hampton Inn, Holiday Inn Express, La Quinta, Quality Inn, Sleep Inn, Buick/GMC, Ford/Lincoln, H, Verizon, Walmart, W Exxon/dsl, Marathon/dsl, Red Roof Inn

308 US 278, Cullman, E Days Inn, Smith Farms, W Chevron, $General, Chrysler/Dodge/Jeep, flea mkt

305 to Al 69

ARKADELPHIA

304 AL 69 N, Good Hope, to Cullman, E Exxon/dsl, Jet-Pep/dsl, Pilot/Wendy's/Dunkin'/dsl/scales/24hr, Shell/dsl/scales, Hardee's, Waffle House, EconoLodge, H, Johnston RV Ctr, W Marathon, to Smith Lake Camping, $General

301mm no services

299 AL 69 S, to Jasper, E Marathon/dsl, Millican RV Ctr, repair/tires, W Chevron/dsl, Petro/Burger King/Popeyes/Papa John's/dsl/scales/24hr, Shell/McDonald's/dsl, Bubba Ritos, Jack's Rest., Pop's Place BBQ, $General

291 AL 91, Arkadelphia, E Exxon/dsl, $General, Country View RV Park(1mi), W Shell/dsl/24hr/parking/@

291mm Warrior River

289 to Blount Springs, W Citgo, to Rickwood Caverns SP

287 US 31 N, to Blount Springs, E Marathon/dsl

284 US 31 S, AL 160 E, Hayden, E Shamrock/dsl, Sunoco/dsl, Valero/Sonic/dsl, Jack's, URGENT CARE, W tires

AL

= gas = food = lodging = other = rest stop

INTERSTATE 65 Cont'd

WARRIOR

Exit #	Services
282	AL 140, Warrior, E Chevron/Subway/dsl, Exxon/McDonald's, Shell/Dunkin'/Little Caesar's/dsl, Annie Mae's Wings, Hardee's, W Marathon, Huddle House
281	US 31, Warrior
280	to US 31, Warrior, E Chevron/dsl, vet
279mm	Warrior River
275	to US 31, Morris
272	Mt Olive Rd, E Shell/dsl, LDS Temple, W Citgo/dsl, Shell/dsl, Jack's Rest., $General
271	Fieldstown Rd, E Chevron/dsl, Exxon, Murphy USA/dsl, RaceTrac/dsl, Arby's, Buffalo Wild Wings, Capt D's, Chick-fil-A, DQ, Jack's, Jim'n Nick's BBQ, Kemp's Kitchen, KFC, Krystal, Little Caesar's, Los Arcos, McDonald's, Milo's Burgers, Moe's SW, Panera Bread, Pasquales Pizza, Shrimp Basket, Starbucks, Subway, Taco Bell, Taziki's Cafe, Waffle House, Wendy's, Zaxby's, Microtel, SpringHill Suites, $General, $Tree, Advance Parts, AT&T, AutoZone, CVS, Hobby Lobby, Kia, NAPA, PepBoys, Publix, TJ Maxx, URGENT CARE, Verizon, Walgreens, Walmart/McDonald's, W Shell/dsl, Cracker Barrel, Best Western

FULTONDALE

Exit #	Services
267	Walkers Chapel Rd, to Fultondale, E BP/dsl, Exxon, Murphy Express/dsl, Shell/Subway/dsl, Applebee's, Arby's, Bojangles, Burger King, Casa Fiesta, Chick-fil-A, Chili's, Domino's, Firehouse Subs, Five Guys, Fullmoon BBQ, Hardee's, Jack's Rest., Logan's Roadhouse, McDonald's, O'Charley's, Outback Steaks, Stix Asian, Taco Bell, Waffle House, Whataburger, Zaxby's, Comfort Inn, Comfort Suites, Fairfield Inn, Holiday Inn Express, Home2 Suites, La Quinta, $General, AAA, ALDI, Books-A-Million, CVS, GNC, JC Penney, Lowe's, O'Reilly Parts, Ross, Target, URGENT CARE, USPO, Verizon, Volvo/Mack Trucks, Walgreens, Winn-Dixie, W Chevron/dsl
265b	US 31, Fultondale, E Shell/dsl, Days Inn, Econolodge
265a	I-22 W, to Memphis
264	41st Ave, W CNG, Flying J/Denny's/dsl/LP/scales/24hr
263	33rd Ave, E Shell/dsl, W Exxon
262b a	16th St, Finley Ave, E Chevron, Marathon/dsl, Sunoco/dsl, Kenworth, W Chevron, Fuel City/dsl, Capt D's, McDonald's, Popeyes
261b a	I-20/59, E to Gadsden, W to Tuscaloosa
260b a	6th Ave N, E Citgo, Marathon, Shell, Mrs Winner's, Tourway Inn, Chevrolet, Chrysler/Dodge/Jeep, Hyundai, Nissan, Subaru, W Chevron/dsl, Tire Pros, to Legion Field
259b a	University Blvd, 4th Ave, 5th Ave, E Chevron/dsl, Burger King, Capt D's, McDonald's, Ted's Cafeteria, H, W Shell/dsl
258	Green Springs Ave, E Marathon, Shell, Sunoco/dsl, Exotic Wings
256b a	Oxmoor Rd, E Marathon, Mobil/dsl, Shell, Sunoco, Acapulco Grill, Alfredo's Pizza, Burger King, Domino's, KFC, McDonald's, Paw Paw Patch, Pizza Hut, Popeyes, Purple Onion, Shrimp Basket, Taco Bell, Zaxby's, Howard Johnson, $Tree, AlLDI, AutoZone, BigLots, Firestone/auto, Midas, Office Depot, Omega Tire Pros, PepBoys, Publix, Tire & Brakes, Tuesday Morning, Walgreens, Walmart Mkt, W Chevron, Shell/dsl, Hamburger Heaven, Hardee's, Jim'n Nick's BBQ, Best Inn, Comfort Inn, Econo Lodge, Motel 6, Quality Inn, Super 8, Batteries+, vet
255	Lakeshore Dr, E Circle K, H, to Samford U, URGENT CARE, W Marathon, Shell, Chick-fil-A, Chili's, Cook Out, Costas BBQ, Dunkin', Godfather's Pizza, Hooters, La Quetzalteca, Margaronas Mexican, McAlister's Deli, McDonald's, Milo's Burger, Moe's SW Grill, Mr Wang's,

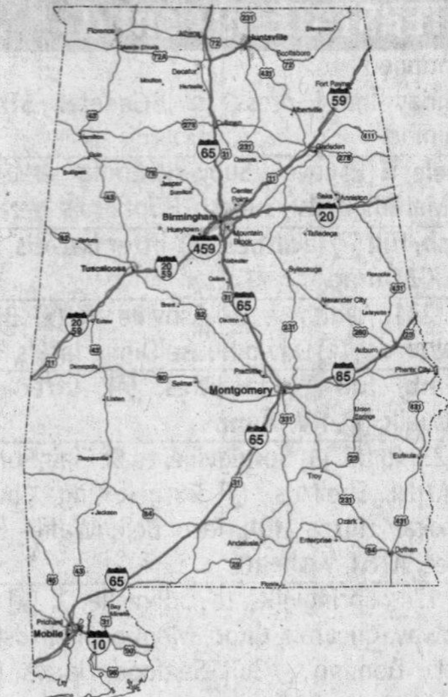

AL

PELHAM

Exit #	Services
255	Continued Okinawa Grill, Starbucks, Subway, Taco Bell, Taco Casa, Wendy's, Whataburger, Best Western, Country Inn&Suites, Drury Inn, Extended Stay, Hampton Inn, Hilton Garden, Holiday Inn, InTowne Suites, La Quinta, Sheraton, Sonesta Suites, Suburban Studios, TownePlace, $Tree, AT&T, Hobby Lobby, Lowe's, Mavis Tire & Brakes, Sam's Club/gas, Walmart/Subway
254	Alford Ave, Shades Crest Rd, E Shell, vet, W Chevron, Marathon
252	US 31, Montgomery Hwy, E Chevron, Citgo, Shell, Sunoco, Arby's, Bruster's, Capt D's, ChuckECheese's, Hardee's, Milo's Burger, Waffle House, Days Inn, Red Roof Inn, GMC, H, NAPA, PepBoys, Verizon, vet, Volvo, VW, W Chevron, Exxon/dsl, Shell/dsl, Sunoco/dsl, Archie's BBQ, Burger King, FishMkt Rest., Full Moon BBQ, Habanero's Mexican, J&C Seafood, Krispy Kreme, Krystal, Mandarin House, McDonald's, Papa John's, Pho Pho Asian, Purple Onion, Salvatore's Pizza, Starbucks, EconoLodge, $Tree, Acura, Advance Parts, AutoZone, Cadillac, Chevrolet, Chrysler/Dodge/Jeep, Firestone, Goodyear/auto, Honda, Hyundai, Nissan, Publix, TJ Maxx
250	I-459, to US 280
247	rd 17, Valleydale Rd, E Circle K, Hardee's, Jeffersons Wings, ALDI, AutoWhiz, Lowe's, W Circle K, RaceWay/dsl, Shell/dsl, Arby's, IHOP, Milo's Burgers, Papa John's, RagTime Café, Tony's Hot Dogs, Waffle House, Zapatas Mexican, Homewood Suites, InTown Suites, La Quinta, Publix, Walgreens
246	AL 119, Cahaba Valley Rd, E to Oak Mtn SP, W Chevron, Circle K/dsl/scales, Murphy USA/dsl, Racetrac, Shell/dsl, Applebee's, Arby's, Capt D's, Chick-fil-A, Cracker Barrel, Creekside BBQ, DQ, Dunkin', Hooters, Johnny Ray's BBQ, KFC, Margarita Grill, McAlister's Deli, McDonald's, Purple Onion, Sonic, Starbucks, Taco Bell, Two Pesos Mexican, TX Roadhouse, Wendy's, Whataburger, Best Western, Comfort Suites, Fairfield Inn, Hampton Inn, Holiday Inn Express, Quality Inn, Ramada, Sleep Inn, Travelodge, Woodspring Suites, $Tree, Advance Parts, AutoZone, Firestone/auto, Harley-Davidson, Kia, Mazda, Verizon, Walmart
242	rd 52, Pelham, E Chevron/dsl, Exxon/dsl, Shell/dsl, CVS Drug, Publix, W Good Sam Camping(1mi), H
238	US 31, Alabaster, E Murphy USA/dsl, Arby's, Buffalo Wild Wings, Chick-fil-A, DQ, Firehouse Subs, Full Moon BBQ, HoneyBaked Ham, Jim'n Nick's BBQ, Longhorn Steaks,

INTERSTATE 65 Cont'd

SAGINAW

238 Continued
McDonald's, Mizu Japanese, Moe's SW Grill, O'Charley's, Olive Garden, Panda House, Panera Bread, Starbucks, Taco Bell, Candlewood Suites, Holiday Inn, $Tree, AT&T, Belk, Books-A-Million, Dick's, GNC, HomeGoods, JC Penney, Lowe's, NTB, Old Navy, PetSmart, Ross, Target, TJ Maxx, URGENT CARE, Walmart/Subway, W Chevron/dsl, Shell/dsl, Whataburger, Shelby Motel, H

234 Shelby County Airport, E Exxon/Subway, W Chevron/dsl, Shell/dsl, Camping World RV Ctr

231 US 31, Saginaw, E Citgo, Murphy USA/dsl, Shell/Circle K, Bojangles, Capt D's, Cracker Barrel, McDonald's, Milo's Burgers, Pizza Hut, Subway, Taco Bell, Waffle House, Zaxby's, Hampton Inn, Quality Inn, AT&T, AutoZone, Burton RV Ctr, Publix, Rolling Hills RV Park, URGENT CARE, Walmart/Subway, W QT

228 AL 25, to Calera, E Citgo, Marathon/dsl, W BP, Shell, Little Caesar's, $General, Family$, to Brierfield Iron Works SP(15mi)

227mm Buxahatchie Creek

CLANTON

219 Union Grove, Thorsby, E Chevron/dsl, Exxon/Subway/dsl, Bone BBQ, Peach Queen Camping, W Shell/dsl, Burger King, Jack's Rest., Smokey Hollow Rest.

213mm **both lanes, full facilities, litter barrels, vending, petwalk, RV Dump**

212 AL 145, Clanton, E Chevron/dsl, Nissan, Toyota, W Citgo, Texaco/Subway, Buick/Chevrolet/GMC, Chrysler/Dodge/Jeep, H, One Big Peach

208 Clanton, E Love's/Arby's/dsl/scales/24hr, $General, Higgins Ferry RV Park(8mi), W Exxon/dsl, PITA, Shoney's, Clanton Inn, Heaton Pecans, Yellow Hammer Campground

205 US 31, AL 22, to Clanton, E Mobil, Petro, Shell/dsl, McDonald's, Waffle House, Whataburger, Best Western, Days Inn, Holiday Inn Express, Scottish Inn, Peach Park, to Confed Mem Park(9mi), W Chevron/dsl, Circle K, Murphy USA/dsl, Boomerang's Grill, Burger King, Capt D's, Jack's Rest., KFC, New China Buffet, Papa John's, Pizza Hut, San Marcos Mexican, Subway, Taco Bell, Wendy's, Zaxby's, Key West Inn, $General, $Tree, auto repair, Durbin Farms Mkt, Walmart

200 to Verbena, E Texaco/dsl, W Sunoco

195 World's Largest Confederate Flag

186 US 31, Pine Level, E Confederate Mem Park(13mi), W Chevron/dsl, Exxon/dsl, Texaco/Subway/dsl, Shann's Kitchen, H

MILLBROOK

181 AL 14, to Prattville, E Chevron/dsl, Entec/dsl, Jack's, W BP, Circle K, QV, Shell/DQ/dsl, Cracker Barrel, Los Toros, McDonald's, Ruby Tuesday, Subway, Waffle House, Wendy's, EconoLodge, Hometowne Suites, La Quinta, Quality Inn, Super 8, H

179 US 82 W, Millbrook, E Chevron/dsl, Country Inn&Suites, Key West Inn, Sleep Inn, Springhill Suites, K&K RV Ctr/Park, W Murphy Express/dsl, RaceWay/dsl, Shell/dsl, Applebee's, Arby's, Beef'O'Brady's, Bruster's, Burger King, Capt. D's, Chappy's Deli, Chick-fil-A, Chicken Salad Chick, Chipotle, CiCi's Pizza, Cook Out, El Patron, Five Guys, Hardee's, IHOP, Jack's, Jim'n Nick's BBQ, KFC, Krystal, Las Casitas Mexican, Logan's Roadhouse, Longhorn Steaks, McAlister's Deli, McDonald's, Mexico Tipico, Midtown Pizza Kitchen, Moe's SW Grill, O'Charley's, Olive Garden, Outback Steaks, Panda Express, Popeyes, Sonic, Starbucks, Steak'n Shake, Subway, Waffle House, Courtyard, Days Inn, Hampton Inn, Home2 Suites, Howard Johnson, Rodeway Inn, $General, $Tree, ALDI, AT&T, AutoZone, Bass Pro Shops,

179 Continued
Belk, BigLots, Books-A-Million, Chevrolet, CVS Drug, Firestone/auto, Ford, GNC, Hobby Lobby, Home Depot, JC Penney, Kohl's, Lowe's, Michael's, O'Reilly Parts, Office Depot, PepBoys, PetSmart, Publix, Ross, Target, TJ Maxx, U-Haul, URGENT CARE, Verizon, vet, Walmart

176 AL 143 N(from nb, no return), Millbrook, Coosada

173 AL 152, North Blvd, to US 231

172mm Alabama River

172 Clay St, Herron St, E Embassy Suites, Hampton Inn, Renaissance Hotel, W Chevron/dsl

171 I-85 N, Day St

170 Fairview Ave, E Citgo/Subway, Sunoco/dsl, Church's TX Chicken, McDonald's, Wing Master, $General, $Tree, Advance Parts, AutoZone, CVS Drug, Family$, O'Reilly Parts, Piggly Wiggly, Walgreens

HOPE HULL

169 Edgemont Ave(from sb), E Liberty

168 US 80 E, US 82, South Blvd, E Circle K/dsl, TA/Marathon/Country Pride/dsl/24hr/@, Arby's, Burger King, Capt D's, KFC, McDonald's, Popeyes, Taco Bell, Waffle House, America's Inn, Budget Inn, SureStay, H, The Woods RV Park, W Chevron/dsl, RaceWay/dsl, DQ, Hardee's, Wendy's, Candlelight Inn, Super 8

167 US 80 W, to Selma

164 US 31, Hyundai Blvd, Hope Hull, E Liberty, Saveway/dsl/scales/24hr, Shell/dsl, El Amigo Mexican, Montgomery Camping, W Chevron, Exxon/Subway, Burger King, Hardee's, McDonald's, Waffle House, Comfort Suites, Fairfield Inn, Hampton Inn, Holiday Inn, Motel 6, Quality Inn, auto repair

158 to US 31, Tyson, E Love's/Subway/Godfather's/Chester's/dsl/scales/24hr, Shell/DQ/Stuckey's, Montgomery South RV Park, W Conoco, Flying J/Denny's/dsl/scales/24hr

151 AL 97, to Letohatchee, E Marathon/dsl

142 AL 185, to Ft Deposit, E Petro+/dsl, Shell/dsl, Priester's Pecans, auto parts, W Chevron

133mm **both lanes, full facilities, litter barrels, vending, petwalk, RV Dump**

130 AL10 E, AL 185, to Greenville, E Chevron/dsl, PaceCar/dsl, Shell, Arby's, Capt D's, Hardee's, KFC, McDonald's, Old Mexico, Papa John's, Pizza Hut, Waffle House, Wendy's, Days Inn, Quality Inn, $General, Advance Parts, CVS Drug, O'Reilly Parts, Super Foods, to Sherling Lake Park, Walgreens, W Circle K, Exxon/Subway/dsl, Mobil, Murphy USA/dsl, Bates Turkey Cafe, Burger King, Cracker Barrel, Krystal, Shoney's, Sonic, Taco Bell, Wintzell's Oyster House, Best Western, Comfort Inn, Hampton Inn, Holiday Inn Express, $Tree, AT&T, Chevrolet, URGENT CARE, Walmart/Subway

128 AL 10, to Greenville, E Shell/Smokehouse, H, W Marathon

114 AL 106, to Georgiana, E Hank Williams Museum, W Chevron, Marathon, auto repair

107 rd 7, to Garland

101 to Owassa, E Marathon/dsl, W dsl repair, Owassa RV Park

96 AL 83, to Evergreen, E Chevron, Shell, Hardee's, KFC/Taco Bell, McDonald's, Shrimp Basket, Subway, Waffle House, Wendy's, Zaxby's, Sleep Inn, H, Piggly Wiggly, W Spirit/Subway/dsl, The Shack, EconoLodge, Evergreen Inn, Red Roof Inn

93 US 84, to Evergreen, E Liberty/dsl, W Love's/Arby's/dsl/scales/24hr, Shell/dsl

89mm **sb, full facilities, litter barrels, vending, petwalk, RV Dump**

85mm **nb, full facilities, litter barrels, vending, petwalk, RV Dump**

= gas = food = lodging = other = rest stop

INTERSTATE 65 Cont'd

ATMORE

CREOLA

Exit #	Services
83	AL 6, to Lenox, E Marathon/dsl, RV Park(4mi)
77	AL 41, to Range, to Range, W Shell/dsl
69	AL 113, to Flomaton, E Chevron/dsl, Shell/dsl/scales/24hr, Valero/Subway/dsl, dsl repair, Magnolia Branch Camping
57	AL 21, Atmore, E Chevron/dsl, Shell/dsl, Hardee's, McDonald's, Popeyes, Sonic, Taco Bell, Waffle House, Fairfield Inn, Hampton Inn, Holiday Inn Express, Wind Creek Indian Gaming, W Shell/dsl, to Kelley SP
54	Escambia Cty Rd 1, E Chevron/Subway/dsl, to Creek Indian Res, W Shell/diner/dsl, $General
45	to Perdido, W Chevron/dsl
37	AL 287, Gulf Shores Pkwy, to Bay Minette, E Marathon/dsl
34	to AL 59, to Bay Minette, Stockton
31	AL 225, to Stockton, E to Blakeley SP, W Shell/Subway/dsl, Landing RV Park(2mi)
29mm	Tensaw River
28mm	Middle River
25mm	Mobile River
22	Creola, E River Delta RV Park(1mi)
19	US 43, to Satsuma, E Chevron/dsl/24hr, Pilot/Arby's/dsl/scales/24hr, McDonald's, Waffle House, La Quinta, W BP/dsl, Chevron/dsl, I-65 RV Park(1.5mi)
15	AL 41, E Chevron/DQ/dsl, China Chef, Godfather's Pizza, Pizza Hut, $Tree, AT&T, CVS, Family$, O'Reilly Parts, Rouse's Mkt, Walgreens, W Shell/Circle K, Shell/Subway/dsl, $General
13	AL 158, AL 213, to Saraland, Popeyes, E Murphy USA/dsl, Shell/dsl, Chicken Salad Chick, foosackly's Chicken, Krystal, Rock N Roll Sushi, Waffle House, Whataburger, Wintzell's Oyster House, Comfort Suites, Country Inn Suites, Microtel, Motel 6, Quality Inn, Red Lion Inn, Red Roof Inn, $Tree, AT&T, URGENT CARE, Walmart/McDonald's, W Exxon/Subway, Cracker Barrel, Baymont Inn, Fairfield Inn, Hampton Inn, Holiday Inn Express, TownePlace Suites, Publix, to Chickasabogue Campground
10	W Lee St, E Shell/Circle K, M Star Hotel
9	I-165 S, to I-10 E, to Mobile
8b a	US 45, to Prichard, E Exxon/Circle K/dsl, tires/repair, W 1st Stop, Chevron/dsl, Energize/dsl, Love's/Subway/dsl/scales/24hr, Valero/dsl, Burger King, Cozy Brown's Kitchen, Domino's, Hardee's, McDonald's, $General, Advance Parts, O'Reilly Parts
5b	US 98, Moffett Rd, E Chevron/dsl, BJ's BBQ, Burger King, Church's TX Chicken, McDonald's, Sub King, AutoZone, Brakes for Less, Family$, W Super 8, auto repair
5a	Spring Hill Ave, E Burger King, Dreamland BBQ, McDonald's, Mr Transmission, PepBoys, W Shell/dsl, Hibachi Express, Starbucks, Waffle House, Zaxby's, Extended Stay America, Wingate Inn, H
4	Dauphin St, E Circle K/dsl, Checkers, Chick-fil-A, Cracker Barrel, Krystal, McDonald's, Taco Bell, Waffle House, Extenda Suites, Holiday Inn Express, Red Roof Inn, $General, Buick/GMC, Lowe's, Mercedes, same as 3 & 5a, Walmart/McDonald's, W H
3	Airport Blvd, E Shell, Burger King, Cane's, Logan's Roadhouse, McDonald's, Morrison's Cafeteria, Starbucks, Wendy's, Marriott, $Tree, Acura, BigLots, Cadillac, Dillard's, Firestone/auto, Ford, Harley-Davidson, Honda, Infiniti, Land Rover, Marshall's, Nissan, Old Navy, Sam's Club/gas, Target, Verizon, W BudgetZone/dsl, Shell/dsl, Arby's, BJ's Rest., Boiling Pot, Brick & Spoon, Burger King,

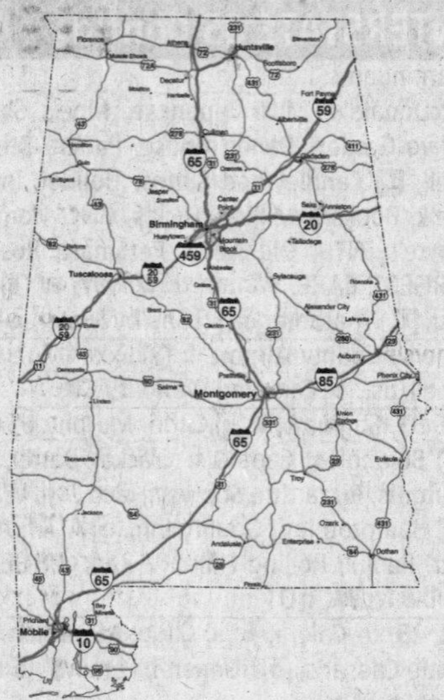

Exit #	Services
3	Continued Carrabba's, China Doll, Chipotle, ChuckECheese, Culver's, Firehouse Subs, Honeybaked Ham, Hooters, IHOP, Jason's Deli, Los Rancheros Mexican, Moe's SW Grill, O'Charley's, Olive Garden, Osaka Japanese, Outback Steaks, Panda Express, Popeyes, Red Lobster, Starbucks, Subway, Taco Bell, Waffle House, Baymont Inn, Best Value Inn, Courtyard, Days Inn, Drury Inn, Econo Lodge, Fairfield Inn, Family Inn, Hampton Inn, Hilton Garden, Holiday Inn, Homewood Suites, InTowne Suites, Motel 6, Quality Inn, Residence Inn, Travelodge, Woodspring Suites, $Tree, AT&T, BooksAMillion, Fresh Mkt Foods, Home Depot, H, Office Depot, PepBoys, PetSmart, TJ Maxx, to USAL, U-Haul, vet, Walgreens
1b a	US 90, Government Blvd, E Raceway/dsl, Dickey's BBQ, Firehouse Subs, Five Guys, McAlister's Deli, Newk's Eatery, Panda Buffet, Starbucks, Steak'n Shake, Home2 Suites, Tru Hilton, $Tree, AT&T, Audi/Porsche/VW, Best Buy, BMW, Chevrolet, Costco/gas, Dick's, Dodge, Family$, Hobby Lobby, Kia, Lexus, Lincoln/Volvo, Mazda, Old Navy, Petco, Ross, Subaru, Toyota, Verizon, W Shell/dsl, Waffle House
0mm	I-10. I-65 begins/ends on I-10, exit 20., E to Pensacola, W to New Orleans

INTERSTATE 85

Exit #	Services
80mm	Alabama/Georgia state line, Chattahoochee River
79	US 29, to Lanett, E Circle K, Murphy USA, Arby's, Burger King, Capt D's, Chuck's BBQ, DQ, Dunkin', Jack's, KFC, Krystal, Little Caesar's, McDonald's, Pizza Hut, Popeyes, San Marcos Mexican, Subway, Taco Bell, Waffle House, Wendy's, Wing Stop, $General, $Tree, Advance Parts, H, repair, Walmart, W Exxon/QV, Marathon, RaceWay/dsl, Domino's, Guthrie's, Sonic, EconoLodge, AutoZone, CVS Drug, Kroger, O'Reilly Parts, to West Point Lake, vet
78.5mm	**Welcome Ctr sb, full facilities, litter barrels, vending, petwalk,**
77	AL 208, to Huguley, E Jet Pep/Church's TX Chicken/dsl, Shell/Circle K/dsl, Waffle House, Quality Inn, Chevrolet, Chrysler/Dodge/Ford/Lincoln, Ford, W Hampton Inn, fireworks
76mm	Eastern/Central time zone
70	AL 388, to Cusseta, E BigCat/dsl, Mobil/dsl/scales/24hr/@, W fireworks
66	Andrews Rd, to US 29
64	US 29, to Opelika, E Valero/Circle K/dsl, W Exxon, Marathon

AL

INTERSTATE 85 Cont'd

Exit #	Services
62	US 280/431, to Opelika, E bp/dsl, Chevron/dsl, Marathon/dsl, Shell/Circle K/Church's TX Chicken/dsl, Burger King, McDonald's, Subway, Taco Bell, Wasabi Japanese, Wok'n Roll Rest., EconoLodge, Quality Inn, Red Carpet Inn, Red Roof Inn, $General, W GrubMart, JetPep, Capt. D's, Cracker Barrel, Sizzlin Steaks, Waffle House, Comfort Inn, OYO Hotel, Buick/Chevrolet/GMC, Chrysler/Dodge/Jeep, Ford, H&W Tire, Harley-Davidson
60	AL 51, AL 169, to Opelika, E RaceWay/dsl, Hardee's, $General, W Citgo, auto repair, H
58	US 280 W, to Opelika, E Eagle/Guthrie's/dsl, Freddy's, Wild Wing Cafe, Hampton Inn, Holiday Inn Express, Home2 Suites, La Quinta, golf, W Arby's, Brick Oven Pizza, Buffalo Wild Wings, BurgerFi, Chick-fil-A, Chicken Salad Chick, Chipotle, El Patron Mexican, Huddle House, Jersey Mike's, Longhorn Steaks, Marble Slab, McDonald's, Moe's SW Grill, New Tokyo, Newk's Eatery, Olive Garden, Panda Express, Sonic, Starbucks, Taziki's, Waffle House, Whataburger, Zaxby's, Fairfield Inn, Microtel, Motel 6, Best Buy, Books-A-Million, Dick's, Hobby Lobby, Home Depot, H, Kohl's, Kroger/dsl, Lowe's, Office Depot, Old Navy, PetCo, Ross, Target, TJ Maxx, URGENT CARE, World Mkt
57	Bent Creek Rd, W Citgo, Exxon, Baumhower's Victory Grille, Venditori's Italian, Waffle House, Wendy's, Hilton Garden, Sam's Club/gas
51	US 29, Auburn, E Chevron/dsl, Marathon, Courtyard, Hampton Inn, Tru, Cadillac/Chevrolet, Leisure Time RV Park/Camping, Nissan, to Chewacla SP, Toyota, W Chevron/Subway/dsl, Murphy USA, Arby's, Burger King, Dunkin', El Dorado Mexican, El Ranchero , Firehouse Subs, Jack's, Jim'n Nick's BBQ, Krystal, Little Caesar's, McDonald's, Philly Connection, Pizza Hut, Shrimp Basket, Sonic, Taco Bell, Waffle House, Wendy's, Zaxby's, Auburn Lodge, Clarion, Holiday Inn Express, Microtel, Pannie George's Kitchen, Quality Inn, Sleep Inn, Advance Parts, Ford/Lincoln, Kia, tires/repair, to Auburn U, URGENT CARE, Walmart, Winn-Dixie
50	Cox Rd, W Buc-ee's/dsl
44mm	**both lanes, full facilities, litter barrels, vending, petwalk, RV Dump, 24hr security**
42	US 80, AL 186 E, Wire Rd, E to Tuskegee NF, W Sunoco/Torch 85/rest./dsl/24hr
38	AL 81, to Tuskegee, E to Tuskegee NHS, Tuskegee University, Shell, Popeyes
32	AL 49 N, to Tuskegee, E Sunoco/dsl
26	AL 229 N, to Tallassee, E Chevron/Guthrie's/dsl
22	US 80, to Shorter, E Exxon, Love's/McDonald's/Subway/dsl/scales/24hr, Petro/rest./dsl/scales/24hr, Burger King, Popeyes, Days Inn, $General, Wind Drift RV Park
16	Waugh, to Cecil, E Circle K/Subway/dsl
15	AL 108 W, Pike Rd
11	US 80, AL 110, to Mitylene, to Mt Meigs, E Murphy USA/dsl, Shell/Subway/dsl, Texaco, Ztec, Anthony's Rest., Bojangles, Burger King, Cracker Barrel, Krystal, McDonald's, Milo's, Popeyes, Taco Bell, Top China, Waffle House, Candlewood Suites, Comfort Inn, Fairfield Inn, Holiday Inn Express, La Quinta, Sleep Inn, Hobby Lobby, Home Depot, O'Reilly Parts, Walmart/Subway, W Chevron/dsl, Microtel
9	AL 271, to AL 110, to Auburn U/Montgomery, E Arby's, BoneFish Grill, Buffalo Wild Wings, Chick-fil-A, Chili's, Chipotle Mexican, Firebirds Grill, Full Moon BBQ, Ixtapa Mexican, Outback Steaks, Panera Bread, Pieology,

AUBURN

Exit #	Services
9	Continued Red Robin, Smoothie King, Sonic, Starbucks, Taziki's Cafe, TX Roadhouse, Wendy's, Whataburger, Zoe's Kitchen, Hampton Inn, Homewood Suites, TownePlace Suites, $Tree, AT&T, Books-A-Million, Costco/gas, Dick's, Dillard's, Firestone/auto, Jo-Ann Fabrics, Kohl's, Michael's, Old Navy, PetSmart, Ross, Target, URGENT CARE, Verizon, vet, Whole Foods Mkt, W H
6	US 80, US 231, AL 21, East Blvd, E Citgo, Exxon/dsl, Marathon, RaceWay/dsl, Arby's, Baumhowers Rest., Burger King, Chick-fil-A, Golden Corral, Jason's Deli, KFC, Longhorn Steaks, Los Vaqueros Mexican, McDonald's, Olive Garden, Popeyes, Rock Bottom Cafe, Schlotzsky's, Taco Bell, Waffle House, Wendy's, Zaxby's, Best Value, Best Western, Comfort Inn, Courtyard, EconoLodge, Extended Stay, Holiday Inn Express, Residence Inn, Sleep Inn, Sonesta Suites, Springhill Suites, Suburban Studios, Wingate Inn, Woodspring Suites, $General, $Tree, Acura, Family$, Ford/Lincoln, Home Depot, Honda, Hyundai, Lowe's, Office Depot, PetCo, Subaru, TJ Maxx, UHaul, USPO, Walmart/McDonald's, W Chevron/Pizza Hut, Mapco/dsl, Arby's, Capt D's, Euphoria BBQ, Hardee's, Hibachi Buffet, IHOP, Jan's Rest., Krispy Kreme, Krystal, McDonald's, Red Lobster, Taco Bell, Wendy's, Clarion Inn, Comfort Suites, Drury Inn, Express Inn, Rest Inn, Travelodge, $General, Audi/VW, BMW, Buick/Cadillac/GMC, Chevrolet, Chrysler/Dodge/Jeep, Firestone/auto, Infiniti, JC Penney, Kia, Kingdom Tire, Mercedes, Nissan, Sam's Club/gas/EVC, Toyota/Lexus, Volvo
4	Perry Hill Rd, E Chappy's Deli, Fresh Mkt, W Circle K, Texaco/dsl, Subway, Hilton Garden, Homewood Suites, $General, Express Oil Change
3	Ann St, E Chevron, Arby's, Capt D's, Domino's, KFC, Krystal, McDonald's, Taco Bell, Waffle House, Zaxby's, Red Roof Inn, Pepboys, W Circle K, Murphy USA/dsl, PaceCar, Ztec, Burger King, Chick-fil-A, Hardee's, Popeyes, Wendy's, Extended Stay, $Tree, AT&T, O'Reilly Parts, Ross, Verizon, Walmart/Subway
2	Forest Ave, E CVS Drug, W H
1	Court St, Union St, downtown, E Marathon/dsl, Shell, W to Ala St U
0mm	I-85 begins/ends on I-65, exit 171 in Montgomery

INTERSTATE 459 (Birmingham)

Exit #	Services
33b a	I-59, N to Gadsden, S to Birmingham
32	US 11, Trussville, N Marathon/dsl, S Chevron/dsl, RaceWay/dsl, Arby's, Cajun Steamer, Casa Fiesta Mexican, Chili's, China Palace, Chipotle, Coldstone, El Cazador Mexican, Firehouse Subs, Habanero's Rest., Hooters, Jack's Rest., Jim'n Nick's BBQ, KFC, Logan's Roadhouse, McDonald's, Mizu Japanese, Olive Garden, Panda Express, Red Lobster, Red Robin, Starbucks, Subway, Waffle House, Zaxby's, Courtyard, Hampton Inn, Hilton Garden, AT&T, Belk, Best Buy, Books-A-Million, Buick/GMC, GNC, Home Depot, Hyundai, JC Penney, Lowe's, Michael's, Pepboys, Target, TJ Maxx, Verizon
31	Derby Parkway, N B'ham Race Course, S Ruth's Place
29	I-20, E to Atlanta, W to Birmingham
27	Grants Mill Rd, N Chevron, Taco Bell, Mercedes, S Shell/dsl, Audi/Porsche, BMW, Chrysler/Dodge/Jeep, Land Rover, Lexus, Mini
23	Liberty Parkway, S Billy's Grill, DQ, Taziki's Greek, Hilton Garden
19	US 280, Mt Brook, Childersburg, N Chevron/dsl, Cheesecake Factory, Chuy's Mexican, Flemings Rest., Lime Tex Mex, PF Chang's, Real & Rosemary, Seasons Grille, Shake Shack, Taco Mama, Urban Cookhouse, Village Tavern, AT&T, Barnes&Noble, Belk, Verizon, S Chevron, Circle K,

TRUSSVILLE

AL

INTERSTATE 459 (Birmingham) Cont'd

19 Continued
Mapco, Marathon, Shell, Shell, Arby's, Black Market Grill, Black Pearl Asian, Buffalo Wild Wings, Burger King, Carrabba's, Casa Fiesta, Chick-fil-A, Chili's, Chipotle Mexican, Chuck E. Cheese, Cracker Barrel, Dreamland BBQ, Edgar's Rest., Eli's Grill, Flying Biscuit, Full Moon BBQ, Jimmy John's, Kobe Japanese, Longhorn Steaks, McDonald's, Mellow Mushroom, Milo's Burgers, Mooyah Burgers, Pablo's, Panda Express, Papa John's, Pappadeaux, Perry's Steaks, Saltgrass Steaks, Schlotzsky's, Starbucks, Steak'n Shake, Subway, Suriname 280, Taco Bell, Taziki's Greek, Wendy's, Whataburger, Best Western, Courtyard, Days Inn, DoubleTree, Drury Inn, Extended Stay, Hampton Inn, Homewood Suites, Hyatt Place, La Quinta, Marriott, Motel 6, Quality Inn, Sonesta Suites, SpringHill Suites, ALDI, AT&T, Autozone, Best Buy, CVS Drug, Firestone/auto, Fresh Mkt Foods, Goodyear/auto, Home Depot, H, Kohl's, Mavis, NTB, Staples, Target, vet, Walgreens, Winn-Dixie, World Mkt

17 Acton Rd, **N** Shell/dsl, Dunkin', Grand Cantina Mexican, McDonald's

15b a I-65, N to Birmingham, S to Montgomery

13 US 31, Hoover, Pelham, **N** Chevron/dsl, Shell/dsl, Sunoco/dsl, Archie's BBQ, Baja CA Grill, Burger King, Chick-fil-A, Fish Mkt Rest., Habanero's, J&C Seafood, Krispy Kreme, Krystal, La Fiesta Mexican, McDonald's, Purple Onion, Salvatori's Pizza, Starbucks, Taco Bell, $Tree, Acura, AutoZone, Cadillac, Chevrolet, Firestone/auto, Goodyear/auto, Honda, Hyundai, Midas, Nissan, O'Reilly Parts, Publix, TJ Maxx, vet, **S** Chevron, Exxon, Mobil, Shell/dsl, Amigo's Mexican, Arby's, Bonefish Grill, Brixx Pizza, Cajun Steamer, Chick-fil-A, Chipotle Mexican, Dave & Buster's, Domino's, Firebird's Grill, J Alexander's Rest., Jake's Soulfood, Jason's Deli, Jim'n Nicks BBQ, McDonald's, Moe's SW Grill, Newk's Eatery, OEC Japanese, Olive Garden, Outback Steaks, Rock-N-Roll Sushi, Saltgrass Steaks, Saw's BBQ, Starbucks, Steak'n Shake, Stix Asian, Sumo Japanese, Taco Bell, Twin Peaks Rest., Wendy's, Courtyard, Days Inn, Embassy Suites, Hampton Inn, Holiday Inn, Hyatt Place, Hyatt Regency/Wynfrey Hotel, Mircotel, Barnes&Noble, Best Buy, Costco/gas, Dick's, GNC, Home Depot, Infiniti, JC Penney, Macy's, Mercedes, Michael's, Office Depot, PepBoys, PetSmart, Ross, Sam's Club/gas, Tuesday Morning, Verizon, Verizon, Walgreens, World Mkt

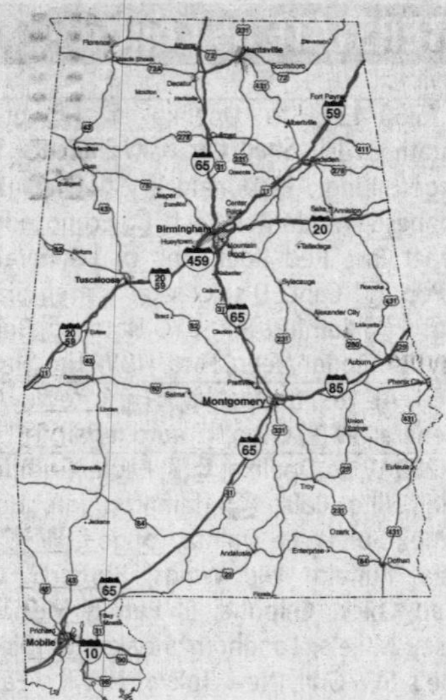

BESSEMER

10 AL 150, Waverly, **N** Beef o Brady's, Chick-fil-A, Freddy's, Frontera Mexican Grill, Jimmy John's, McDonald's, Starbucks, Taco Bell, Waffle House, $Tree, Express Oil Change, Kohl's, Marshall's, PetCo, Sprouts Mkt, Target, URGENT CARE, **S** Circle K/dsl, Shell, Arby's, Chipotle, LongHorn Steaks, Hyatt Place, Ford/Lincoln, Publix/deli, Toyota, Walgreens

6 AL 52, to Bessemer, **N** Circle K/dsl, Jack's, **S** Chevron/dsl, Circle K, Texaco/DQ, Arby's, China Wok, Domino's, McDonald's, Papa John's, Subway, Waffle House, Wendy's, Sleep Inn, $General, AutoZone, CVS Drug, RV Camping, Winn-Dixie

1 AL 18, Bessemer, **N** Exxon/dsl, Shell/Dunkin'/dsl, Burger King, Chick-fil-A, Firehouse Subs, Full Moon BBQ, Habanero's Mexican, Logan's Roadhouse, Marco's Pizza, McAlister's Deli, Taco Bell, AAA, AT&T, GNC, Michaels, PetSmart, Publix, Ross, Target/Starbucks, URGENT CARE, **S** Sunoco/dsl, Bojangles, China King, McDonald's, Meineke, San Antonio Grill, Subway, Takoyaki Sushi, Zaxby's, Holiday Inn Express, Advance Parts, CVS Drug, Piggly Wiggly, to Tannehill SP, U-Haul, Verizon

0mm I-459 begins/ends on I-20/59, exit 106

NOTES

AL

ARIZONA

INTERSTATE 8

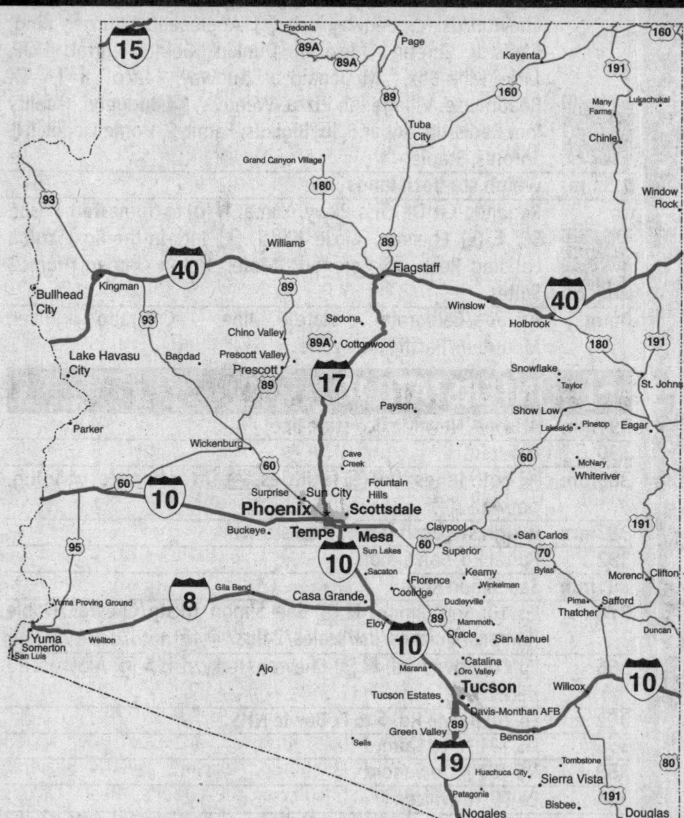

Exit #	Services
178b a	I-10, E to Tucson, W to Phoenix, I-8 begins/ends on I-10, exit 199.
174	Trekell Rd, to Casa Grande
172	Thornton Rd, to Casa Grande
171mm	Santa Cruz River
169	Bianco Rd, N to Francisco Grade Resort
167	Montgomery Rd, N to Francisco Grande Resort, Rover's Roost RV Camping
163mm	Santa Rosa Wash
161	Stanfield Rd
151	AZ 84 E, Maricopa Rd, to Stanfield, S Saguaro RV Park
151mm	**picnic area wb, , litter barrels**
149mm	**picnic area eb, , litter barrels**
144	Vekol Rd
140	Freeman Rd
119	Butterfield Trail, to AZ 85, I-10, Gila Bend, N Pilot/Subway/dsl/scales/24hr, Shell/Subway/dsl/scales/RV Park/24hr, Humberto's Mexican, Little Italy, Space Rest., America's Choice Inn, Best Western, Gila Bend Lodge, Palms Inn, $General, Sonoran Desert RV Park
117mm	Sand Tank Wash
115	AZ 85, to Gila Bend, N Chevron/dsl, Circle K, Love's/Taco Bell/dsl/scales/24hr, Tesla EVC, Burger King, Carl's Jr, Humberto's Mexican, Little Italy Pizza, McDonald's, Sofia's Mexican, Space Age Rest., Best Western, Palms Inn, Family$, NAPA, tire repair, visitors ctr/museum
111	Citrus Valley Rd
106	Paloma Rd
102	Painted Rock Rd, N Painted Rock Petroglyph Site
87	Aqua Caliente Rd, Sentinel Rd, Sentinel, Hyder, N Chevron/Conde's Store/dsl, RV Camping
85mm	**wb, full facilities, , litter barrels, vending, petwalk,**
84mm	**eb, full facilities, , litter barrels, vending, petwalk,**
78	Spot Rd
73	Aztec
67	Dateland, S Chevron/EVC/dsl, Dateland RV Park, Oasis RV Park/dump
56mm	**both lanes, full facilities, , litter barrels, vending, petwalk,**
54	Ave 52 E, Mohawk Valley
42	Ave 40 E, to Tacna, N Chevron/dsl, Jac's Whistlestop Cafe, USPO, S Shell/Subway/dsl, Copper Mtn RV Park
37	Ave 36 E, to Roll
30	Ave 29 E, Wellton, N Circle K/dsl, Geronimo's Mexican, Desert Motel, $General, Family$, Green Acres RV Park, NAPA, Tier Drop RV Park, USPO, S Chevron/dsl, Desert Penguin Grill, Jack-in-the-Box, Microtel
24mm	Ligurta Wash
23mm	Red Top Wash
22mm	**parking area/litter barrels both lanes**
21	Dome Valley
17mm	**insp sta eb**
15mm	Fortuna Wash
14	Foothills Blvd, N Fortuna De Oro RV Park, Sundance RV Park, S Domino's, Jimmy K's, Mr Fish Fish, auto/RV care/lube ctr, Family$, Foothills RV Park
12	Fortuna Rd, to US 95 N, N Chevron/dsl, Flying J/Giant/dsl/scales/24hr, DayBreakers Cafe, Jack-in-the-Box, Jersey Mike's, Las Palapas Tacos, McDonald's, Pizza Hut, Starbucks, Taco Bell, Comfort Inn, Courtesy Inn, Caravan RV Park, Shangri La RV Park, S Chevron/dsl, Circle K/Burger King/dsl, A&W/KFC, Applebee's, Baskin-Robbins, Carl's Jr, Daboyz Pizza, Denny's, Dunkin', Dutch Bros, Little Caesar's, Papa John's, Subway, Best Western+, $General, $Tree, AT&T, AutoZone, Big O Tire, Blue Sky RV Park, CVS Drug, Fry's Foods/dsl, O'Reilly Parts, USPO, Verizon, Walgreens
9	32nd St, to Yuma, S Del Taco, Domino's, Panda Express, Starbucks, Wendy's, Verizon, Walmart/McDonald's
7	AZ 195, Araby Rd, N Circle K/dsl, H, to AZWU, S Circle K/dsl, Jack-in-the-Box, Country Club RV, RV World, tires
3	AZ 280 S, Ave 3E, N Arby's, Candlewood Suites, Holiday Inn Express, Sheraton, S Love's/Subway/dsl/scales/24hr, Maverik, CarQuest, Harley-Davidson, to Marine Corp Air Sta
2	US 95, 16th St, Yuma, N Circle K, Ah-So Steaks, Black Bear Diner, Broken Yolk Cafe, Buffalo Wild Wings, Chick-fil-A, Chili's, Chipotle Mexican, ChuckeCheese, Coldstone Creamery, Cracker Barrel, Del Taco, Denny's, Famous Dave's BBQ, Five Guys, Freddy's, Hooters, In-N-Out, Jack-in-the-Box, Kneaders, Lin's Chinese, Olive Garden, Panda Express, Penny's Diner, Raising Cane's, Red Lobster, Starbucks, Best Western, Days Inn, Fairfield Inn, Hampton Inn, Holiday Inn, Homewood Suites, La Fuente Inn, Motel 6, Shilo Inn, SpringHill Suites, TownePlace Suites, Travelodge, Wingate Inn, AT&T, Best Buy, Dillard's, Discount Tire, Hobby Lobby, JC Penney, Kohl's, Marshall's, Michaels, Old Navy, PetSmart,

GILA BEND

AZTEC

DOME VALLEY

YUMA

AZ

YUMA

INTERSTATE 8 Cont'd

2 Continued
Ross, Sam's Club/gas, Target, Verizon, **S** [gas] Arco/dsl, Chevron/dsl, Speedway/dsl, [food] Applebee's, Burger King, Carl's Jr, Chretin's Mexican, Dunkin', Golden Corral, IHOP, Jack-in-the-Box, McDonald's, Subway, Taco Bell, TX Roadhouse, Village Inn Pizza, Wendy's, [lodging] Budgetel, Quality Inn, Radisson, Super 8, [other] BigLots, Family$, Home Depot, [H], Sprouts, Staples

1.5mm **weigh sta both lanes**

1 Redondo Ctr Dr, Giss Pkwy, Yuma, **N** [other] to Yuma Terr Prison SP, **E** [gas] Chevron, Circle K/dsl, [food] Jack-in-the-Box, Yuma Landing Rest., [lodging] Coronado Motel, Hilton Garden, Home2 Suites

0mm Arizona/California state line, Colorado River, Mountain/Pacific time zone

INTERSTATE 10

SAN SIMON

391mm Arizona/New Mexico state line

390 Cavot Rd

389mm **[rest stop] both lanes, full [handicapped] facilities, [picnic], litter barrels, vending, petwalk, [phone]**

383mm **weigh sta both lanes, insp sta wb**

382 Portal Rd, San Simon

381mm San Simon River

378 Lp 10, San Simon, **N** [gas] San Simon Trkstp/Chevron/Noble Romans/Quiznos/dsl/scales/24hrs/@, [other] auto/dsl/RV repair

366 Lp 10, Bowie Rd, **N** [gas] Chevron/Jerky/dsl, **S** [other] Alaskan RV park

362 Lp 10, Bowie Rd, **S** to Ft Bowie NHS

355 US 191 N, to Safford

352 US 191 N, to Safford

344 Lp 10, to Willcox

WILLCOX

340 AZ 186, to Rex Allen Dr, **N** [gas] Love's/Arby's/24hr, TA/Shell/Popeyes/Subway/dsl/scales/24hr/@, [lodging] Holiday Inn Express, Super 8, [other] Apple Annie's Country Store, RV/Truckwash, Wilcox KOA, **S** [gas] Chevron/dsl/rest., Circle K, Texaco/dsl, [food] Adolfo's Tacos, Burger King, Carl's Jr, Double S Steaks, McDonald's, Pizza Hut, R&R Pizza, [lodging] Days Inn, Motel 6, Wilcox Inn, [other] $General, Ace Hardware, AutoZone, Beall's, Family$, Grande Vista RV Park, [H], Lifestyle RV Park, Medicine Shoppe, Safeway, to Chiricahua NM, Verizon

336 AZ 186, Willcox, **S** [gas] Chevron/dsl/LP, [other] Cattlerest RV Park, Ft Willcox RV Park

331 US 191 S, to Sunsites, Douglas, **S** [other] to Cochise Stronghold

322 Johnson Rd, **S** [gas] Shell/DQ/dsl/gifts

320mm **[rest stop] both lanes, full [handicapped] facilities, [picnic], litter barrels, vending, petwalk, [phone]**

318 Triangle T Rd, to Dragoon, **S** [other] Amerind Museum

312 Sibyl Rd

309mm Adams Peak Wash

BENSON

306 AZ 80, Pomerene Rd, Benson, **S** [gas] Circle K, [food] 86 Cafe, [other] El Rio RV Park, NAPA, Pato Blanco Lakes RV Park

305mm San Pedro River

304 Ocotillo St, Benson, **N** [food] Denny's, Dickey's BBQ, Wing Boss, [lodging] Copper Stay Inn, [other] Benson RV Park, KOA, Red Barn RV Park, **S** [gas] Chevron, [food] Adolfo's Taco, Benson Donuts, Burger King, Farmhouse Rest, Jack-in-the-Box, Little Caesar's, Magaly's Mexican, Mi Casa Mexican, Pablo's Steaks, Subway, Wendy's, [lodging] Quality Inn, QuarterHorse Inn/RV Park, [other] $General, Ace Hardware, Butterfield RV Resort, Dillon RV Ctr, [H], Pardners RV Park, Safeway, Walmart

303 US 80(eb only), to Tombstone, Bisbee, **S** [food] Burger King, Farmhouse Rest., Little Caesar's, Mi Casa Mexican, Pablo's Steaks, Subway, [lodging] Quarter Horse Motel/RV Park, [other] Medicine Shoppe, O'Reilly Parts, Pardners RV Park,

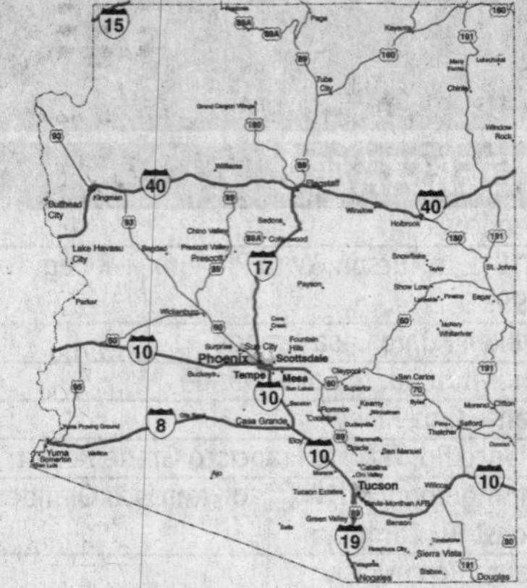

303 Continued
to Tombstone Courthouse SHP(26mi), Verizon, Walmart

302 AZ 90 S, to Ft Huachuca, Benson, **S** [gas] Love's, Love's/Chester's/Subway/dsl/scales/24hr, [food] KFC/Taco Bell, McDonald's, [lodging] Comfort Inn, Motel 6, [other] AZ Legends RV Resort, CT RV Park, Ft Huachuca NHS(25mi)

299 Skyline Rd

297 Mescal Rd, J-6 Ranch Rd, **N** [gas] Chevron/dsl, [other] $General, auto/RV repair

292 Empirita Rd

291 Marsh Station Rd

288mm Cienega Creek

281 AZ 83 S, to Patagonia

279 Colossal Cave Rd, Wentworth Rd, **N** [gas] Chevron/dsl, [food] AZ Pizza Co, DQ, Fito's Tacos, Montgomery's Grill, [other] Colossal Caves, USPO

275 Houghton Rd, **N** [food] Arby's, Denny's, Dunkin', Dutch Bros, Filiberto's Mexican, Freddy's Burgers, Jersey Mike's, McDonald's, MOD Pizza, Native Grill, Panda Express, Papa Murphy's, Popeye's, Rancho Rustico, Taco Bell, [other] AutoZone, Cactus Country RV Resort, Discount Tire, Petco, Saguaro NP, Verizon, Walmart, **S** Pima County Fairgrounds

273 Rita Rd, **N** [gas] Pilot/Subway/scales/dsl, [food] Burger King, [lodging] Hampton Inn, **S** [other] Pima County Fairgrounds

270 Kolb Rd, **S** [other] Bay RV Resort, Voyager RV Resort

269 Wilmot Rd, **N** [gas] Chevron/A&W/dsl, [lodging] Travel Inn, [other] $General, [H], **S** [gas] Shell/dsl

268 Craycroft Rd, **N** [gas] Circle K, Pilot/Subway/Taco Bell/dsl/lp/scales/24hr/@, TTT/rest/dsl/scales/24hr, [other] Crazy Horse RV Park, **S** dsl repair

267 Valencia Rd, **N** [gas] Speedway/Jack-in-the-Box, [food] Whataburger, [other] Pima Air&Space Museum, **S** [gas] Circle K/dsl, [other] Tuscon Intl [airport]

265 Alvernon Way, **N** [other] Davis-Monthan AFB

264b a Palo Verde Rd, **N** [gas] Chevron/Wendy's/dsl, Circle K/dsl, [food] Waffle House, [lodging] Comfort Inn, Days Inn, Red Roof Inn, Siegel Select, [other] Camping World RV Ctr, Freedom RV Ctr, **S** [food] Arby's, McDonald's, [lodging] Quality Inn, Studio 6, [other] KOA, La Mesa RV Ctr, Lazy Days RV Ctr, Pedata RV Ctr

263b Kino Pkwy N, **N** [gas] Chevron/dsl, Circle K, [food] Cane's, Chipotle, Culver's, Einstein Bagels, First Watch, In-N-Out, Jimmy John's, Panda Express, Rudy's BBQ, Starbucks, Wendy's, [other] AT&T, Costco/gas, Discount Tire, [H], Verizon

263a Kino Pkwy S, **N** [other] [H], **S** [gas] Arco/dsl, Circle K, QT, [food] Burger King, Eegee's, Famous Sam's Grill, Filiberto's Mexican, Little Caesars Pizza, McDonald's, Mi Pueblo Mexican, Papa John's, Peter Piper Pizza, Starbucks, Subway, Taco Bell, [other] $Tree, Ace Hardware, AutoZone, Food City, Fry's Foods, Tucson Intn'l [airport], Walgreens

262 Benson Hwy, Park Ave, **N** [gas] QT/dsl, [food] Arby's, Dave & Buster's, Lin's Buffet, McDonald's, Planet Sub, Popeyes,

INTERSTATE 10 Cont'd

262 Continued
Smoothie King, Taco Bell, Whataburger, Walmart/auto, S Arco/dsl, Circle K/dsl, Best Value Inn, Extended Stay, Super Inn, Mack/Volvo Trucks, USPO

261 6th/4th Ave, N Little Caesar's, Wingstop, Food City, tires, S Circle K/dsl, Church's TX Chicken, Domino's Food, Jack-in-the-Box, Los Beto's Mexican, Panda Express, Pizza Hut, Silver Saddle Steaks, Starbucks, Economy Inn, Oyo Rooms, Big O Tire, El Super Foods, Family$, H, Jiffy Lube, Midas, O'Reilly Parts, U-Haul

260 I-19 S, to Nogales

259 22nd St, Starr Pass Blvd, N Circle K/dsl, S Kettle, Waffle House, Quality Inn, Super 8, Travel Inn

258 Congress St, Broadway St, N Circle K, Double Tree, S Carl's Jr, Howard Johnson, Ramada, Red Lion Inn, Travelodge, Tuxon Hotel

257a St Mary's Rd, N Ace Hardware, vet, S Chevron/dsl, Betos Mexican, Buffalo Wings, Burger King, Denny's, Domino's, Eegee's Cafe, Jack-in-the-Box, Little Caesar's, Papa John's, Pizza Hut, St. Mary's Mexican, Starbucks, Wendy's, Whataburger, Country Inn&Suites, Days Inn, $Tree, 7-11, Family$, Food City, H, O'Reilly Parts, Pima Comm Coll, Safeway

257 Speedway Blvd, N Circle K, Eegee's, Popeyes, Starbucks, Best Western, EconoLodge, Red Roof Inn, University Inn, H, U of AZ, S Arco/dsl, museum, Old Town Tucson

256 Grant Rd, N Circle K, Circle K, Burger King, Dunkin, Jack-in-the-Box, McDonald's, Sonic, Hyatt Place, BrakeMax, CVS Drug, tires, U-Haul, URGENT CARE, S Chevron/dsl, Circle K, QT/dsl, Arby's, Beto's Mexican, Eegee's, IHOP, Waffle House, Comfort Inn, Grand Luxe, Holiday Inn Express, Super 8, Ace Hardware, Safeway, Walgreens

255 AZ 77 N, to Miracle Mile

254 Prince Rd, N Circle K, Valero/dsl, Cactus RV, O'Reilly Parts, Walgreens, S golf, Kenworth, Prince of Tucson RV Park

252 El Camino del Cerro, Ruthrauff Rd, N Pac Pride, QT/dsl, Synergy Petroleum

251 Sunset Rd

250 Orange Grove Rd, N Arco/dsl, Circle K/dsl, Culver's, Dave's Chicken, Domino's, Firehouse Subs, Golden Corral, Little Caesar's, Popeyes, Smoothie King, Subway, Wendy's, auto repair, Big O Tire, BrakeMax, Costco/gas, Home Depot, Michaels, PetSmart/vet, RV repair, South Forty RV Park, Sprouts Mkt, URGENT CARE, vet

248 Ina Rd, N Circle K/dsl, Speedway/dsl, Bisbee Breakfast Club, Carl's Jr, Chick-fil-A, Chickenuevo Mexican, Dickey's BBQ, DQ, Eegee's Cafe, Five Guys, Frankie's Philly Cheesesteaks, Jack-in-the-Box, Jade Garden, McDonald's, MOD Pizza, Molinito Mexican, Papa John's, Peter Piper Pizza, Pollo Loco, Starbucks, Subway, Taco Bell, Taco Rico, Wingstop, InTown Suites, Motel 6, Studio 6, $Tree, auto repair, auto repair, AutoZone, BigLots, CVS Drug, Discount Tire, Firestone/auto, Fry's Foods/dsl, Jiffy Lube, Lowe's, Midas, O'Reilly Parts, PepBoys, Target, tires, U-Haul, URGENT CARE, URGENT CARE, Walgreens, S QT/dsl, Denny's, Best Western, Red Roof Inn, Travelodge, Ace Hardware, Freedom RV Ctr, Harley-Davidson

246 Cortaro Rd, N Circle K/Arby's/dsl, QT/dsl, Arby's, Dutch Bros, Filiberto's Mexican, IHOP, Starbucks, Wendy's, S Chevron/dsl, Barro's Pizza, Burger King, Chili's, Chipotle, Cracker Barrel, Dunkin, Eegee's Rest., In-N-Out, Jersey Mike's, Jimmy John's, KFC, Little Caesar's, McDonald's, Nana's Mexican, Native Grill, New Town Asian,

MARANA ARIZONA CITY

246 Continued
Panda Express, Starbucks, Taco Bell, TX Roadhouse, Comfort Inn, Days Inn, Holiday Inn Express, La Quinta, Super 8, Village Inn, $Tree, access to RV camping, Ace Hardware, AT&T, Baggin's Sandwiches, GNC, Kohl's, O'Reilly Parts, Petco, Ross, TJ Maxx, USPO, Verizon, Walmart

244 Twin Peaks Rd, N QuikTrip, Hampton Inn, Tucson Outlets/famous brands

242 Avra Valley Rd, S Saguaro NP

240 Tangerine Rd, to Rillito, N Maverik, A-A RV Park, S QuikTrip

236 Marana, S Chevron/dsl/LP, Circle K/dsl, Bisbee Breakfast, Dutch Bros, Jack-in-the-Box, McDonald's, Nico's Mexican Food, R&R Pizza, Starbucks, Taco Bell, Family$, NAPA

232 Pinal Air Park Rd, S Pinal Air Park

228mm to frontage rd, wb pulloff

226 Red Rock, S $General, USPO

219 Picacho Peak Rd, N Shell/DQ, Shell/Subway/dsl, S Ostrich Ranch, Pichaco Peak RV Park, to Picacho Peak SP

211 AZ 87 N, AZ 84 W, to Coolidge, S KOA

208 Sunshine Blvd, to Eloy, N Pilot/Subway/DQ/dsl/scales/24hr, S Flying J/Denny's/dsl/scales/24hr, Blue Beacon

203 Toltec Rd, to Eloy, N Chevron/McDonald's/playplace/24hr, Circle K/dsl, Xpress/scales/dsl, Carl's Jr, McDonald's, Best Value Inn, Happy Smart Inn, dsl/tire repair, Silverado RV Park, S TA/A&W/Taco Bell/dsl/RV dump/scales/24hr/@, Pizza Hut, truckwash

200 Sunland Gin Rd, Arizona City, N Petro/Iron Skillet/dsl/scales/24hr/@, Pride/Subway/dsl/24hr, Burger King, Blue Beacon, Las Colinas RV Park, tire repair, S Love's/Arby's/Baskin-Robbins/dsl/24hr, Golden 9 Rest, Motel 6, Speedco Lube

199 I-8 W, to Yuma, San Diego

198 AZ 84, to Eloy, Casa Grande, N Robson Ranch Rest./golf

194 AZ 287, Florence Blvd, to Casa Grande, N Tesla EVC, Barro's Pizza, Buffalo Wild Wings, Cane's, Chick-fil-A, Culver's, Filiberto's, Hideout Steaks, In-N-Out, Krispy Kreme, Los Plebes Mexican, Olive Garden, $Tree, Chrysler/Dodge/Jeep, Dillard's, JC Penney, Kohl's, Marshall's, Michael's, PetSmart, Ross, Sunscape RV Park(7mi), Verizon, Walgreens, S 76/DQ, Arco/dsl, Chevron/dsl, Circle K, Circle K, QT, Angry Crab Shack, Arby's, Burger King, Carl's Jr, Chili's, China King, Chipotle, Church's TX Chicken, Cracker Barrel, Denny's, Dunkin, Dutch Bros, Eegee's, Filiberto's Mexican, Firehouse Subs, Freddy's, IHOP, Jack-in-the-Box, Jimmy John's, Lin's Buffet, LJ Silver/Taco Bell, McDonald's, Nico's Mexican, Panda Express, Papa John's, Papa Murphy's, Peter Piper Pizza, Popeyes, Sonic, Starbucks, Subway, TX Roadhouse, Wendy's, Whataburger, Baymont, Best Western+, Holiday Inn Express, Mainstay Suites, Quality Inn, Siegel Select, Super 8, $Tree, AT&T, AutoZone, Batteries+, Big Lots, Big O Tire, CVS Drug, Discount Tire, Encore Camping(2mi), Fiesta Grande RV Resort, Firestone, Food City, Fry's Food/drug/dsl, Home Depot, H, Jiffy Lube, Lowe's, O'Reilly Parts, tires, U-Haul, URGENT CARE, Verizon, vet, Walgreens, Walmart/McDonalds

190 McCartney Rd, S Circle K/dsl

185 AZ 387, to Casa Grande, Casa Grande Ruins NM, S Eva's Mexican(6mi), Francisco Grande(6mi), Holiday Inn(6mi), Fry's Food/gas(6mi), hwy patrol, to Casa Grande Ruins NM, Val Vista RV camping(3mi)

183mm **wb, full facilities, litter barrels, vending, petwalk,**

181mm **eb, full facilities, litter barrels, vending, petwalk,**

= gas = food = lodging = other = rest stop

INTERSTATE 10 Cont'd

Exit #	Services
175	AZ 587 N, Casa Blanca Rd, Chandler, Gilbert, S Chevron/dsl
173mm	Gila River
167	Riggs Rd, to Sun Lake, N Gulf/dsl, Akimel Smoke Shop
164	AZ 347 S, Queen Creek Rd, to Maricopa, N to Chandler
162b a	Wild Horse Pass Rd, Sundust Rd, N Love's/Arby's/dsl/scales/24hr, McDonald's, Best Western+, S Chevron/dsl, Sheraton Grand, Sheraton Resort, Wildhorse Pass Hotel/Casino, Firebird Sports Park, Gila River Casino, Phoenix Outlets/famous brands
161	AZ 202 E, Pecos Rd
160	Chandler Blvd, to Chandler, N Chevron/dsl, Circle K, Circle K/dsl, Can't Stop Smokin' BBQ, Denny's, Dunkin/Baskin-Robbins, Filiberto's Mexican, Firehouse Subs, McDonald's, Rudy's BBQ, Starbucks, Subway, US Egg Cafe, Wendy's, Whataburger, Wingstop, Comfort Inn, DoubleTree, Hampton Inn, Homewood Suites, Motel 6, Quality Inn, Super 8, Wingate, Aamco, Advance Parts, CVS, Firestone/auto, Harley-Davidson, Jiffy Lube, to Compadre Stadium, U-Haul, vet, Williams AFB, S Chevron/dsl, Circle K/dsl, Shell/dsl, Bell Italian Pizza, Carl's Jr, Cracker Barrel, Del Taco, Dunkin, El Jefe Tacos, Hong Kong Buffet, Jersey Mike's, Spinato's Pizzaria, Starbucks, Tukee's Grille, Waffle House, Wendy's, Extended Stay America, Fairfield Inn, InTown Suites, La Quinta, AutoZone, Discount Tire, H, Kohl's
159	Ray Rd, N Circle K, Bisbee Breakfast, Buca Italian, Carrabba's, Chipotle Mexican, Fleming's Steaks, Galeto Brazilian, In-N-Out, Jasons Deli, Jimmy John's, Longhorn Steaks, McDonald's, Outback Steaks, Pei Wei Asian, Red Lobster, Roy's Hawaiian, Smokin Fins, Starbucks, Tejas, WooWoo Burgers, Sonesta Select, AJ's Fine Foods, BMW, Chevrolet, Ford, Home Depot, Land Rover/Jaguar, Lexus, Lowe's Whse, Mercedes, REI, Sam's Club/gas, Verizon, S Circle K/dsl, Barro's Pizza, Chick-Fil-A, El Pollo Loco, Five Guys, Gus's Fried Chicken, Honeybaked Ham, IHOP/24hr, Jack-in-the-Box, Kneaders Cafe, Native Grill, On-the-Border, Peter Piper Pizza, Subway, The Hub Grill, Wendy's, Extended Stay America, $Tree, AT&T, auto repair, Best Buy, Big 5, Big Lots, Hobby Lobby, HomeGoods, JC Penney, Marshall's, Michael's, PetCo, PetSmart, Ross, Sprouts Mkt, Target
158	Warner Rd, N Circle K/dsl, Shell, Filiberto's, Flame Broiler, Forefathers Cheesteaks, King of Gyros, Panera Bread, Topical Smoothie, TX Roadhouse, White Castle, Drury Inn, Dick's, IKEA, S Circle K, Circle K/dsl, Andy's Fro-Yo, Burger King, DQ, Hillside Spot Cafe, Macayo's Mexican, Marco's Pizza, McDonald's, Nello's Pizza, Panda Garden, Starbucks, Taco Bell, Zesty Pizza, Zipp's Grill, Ace Hardware, Basha's Foods, Big O Tire, Jiffy Lube, vet
157	Elliot Rd, N Chevron/dsl, Circle K, QT/dsl, Shell/Circle K, Arby's, Black Bear Diner, Burger King, Chipotle, Crackers Cafe, Firehouse Subs, Jimmy John's, Kobe Japanese, McDonald's, Olive Garden, Oregano's Italian, Panda Express, Popeyes, Red Robin Rest., Sonic, Starbucks, Subway, Taco Bell, Wendy's, Whataburger, YC Mongolian Grill, Motel 6, $Tree, Acura, AutoZone, Buick, Cadillac/GMC, Chrysler/Dodge/Jeep, Costco/gas, Discount Tire, Fiat, Honda, Hyundai, Kia, Mazda, Midas, Mini, NAPA, Nissan, PetSmart, Ram, Ross, Staples, Toyota/Scion, Walmart, S Circle K/Dsl, Circle K/dsl, Biscuits, Cactus Jack's, Niros Gyros, Original Burrito, Starbucks, Subway, auto repair, O'Reilly Parts, Safeway, vet, Walgreens
155	Baseline Rd, Guadalupe, N Circle K, Circle K/dsl, Shell/Circle K/Popeyes/dsl, Carl's Jr, Ell Pollo Loco,

GUADALUPE

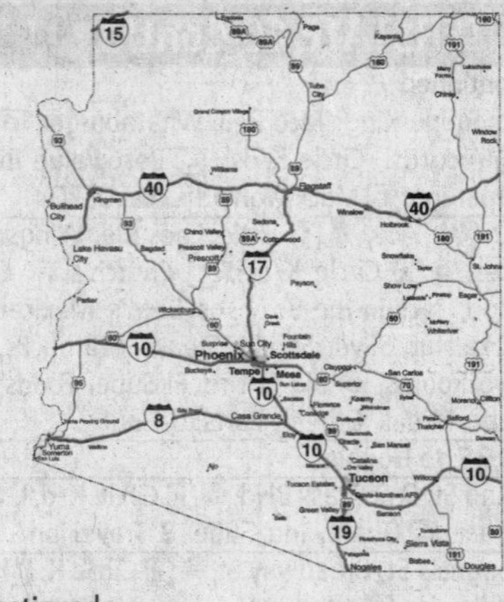

GUADALUPE

Exit #	Services
155	Continued Joe's Crabshack, KFC, McDonald's, Poliberto's Mexican, Rainforest Cafe, Subway, Taco Bell, Waffle House, Wendy's, Holiday Inn Express, Ramada, Sonesta, Sonesta Suites, SpringHill Suites, TownePlace Suites, AutoZone, AZ Mills/Famous Brands, Food City, Home Depot, Marshall's, Parts Authority, Ross, Walgreens, S Arco/dsl, QT, Aunt Chilada's Mexican, Burger King, Denny's, In-N-Out, Little Caesar's, Sonic, Starbucks, Subway, AZ Grand Resort, Sedona, Studio 6, Fry's Foods, URGENT CARE, water park
154	US 60 E, AZ 360, Superstition Frwy, to Mesa
153b	Broadway Rd E, N Denny's, Filiberto's Mexican, Jack-in-the-Box, McDonald's, Starbucks, The Burger Den, Comfort Suites, DoubleTree, Extended Stay America, Fairfield Inn, Hampton Inn, La Quinta, Motel 6, Red Roof+, Wyndham, Ace Hardware, CarMax, to Diablo Stadium, S Chevron/dsl, Shell/Circle K/Del Taco/24hr, Chipotle, Jimmy John's, Panda Express, Papa John's, Pizza Hut, Port of Subs, Taco Bell, Whataburger, GreenTree Inn, Home2 Suites, Homewood Suites, Marriot, $Tree
153a	AZ 143 N, N The Burger Den, Country Inn & Suites, Courtyard, Hilton, Holiday Inn, La Quinta, Phoenix Bridge, to Diablo Stadium, S same as 153b
152	40th St, N Shell/Pilot/Subway/dsl, Peppersauce Cafe, U Phoenix, U-Haul, S Shell/Circle K, Burger King, Burger King, Quiznos
151mm	Salt River
151b a	28th St, 32nd St, University Ave, N Waffle House, Drury Inn, Extended Stay America, Hilton Garden, Holiday Inn Express, AZSU, S Circle K/dsl, QT/dsl, Senergy Petroleum, Cookin On BBQ, McDonald's, Wendy's
150b	24th St E(from wb), N Motel 6, S Extend-a-Suites
150a	I-17 N, to Flagstaff
149	Buckeye Rd, N tires, S Shell, Burger King, Subway
148	Washington St, Jefferson St, N Chevron/dsl, Shell, Tiemco/dsl, McDonald's, Panchitas Mexican, Motel 6, to Sky Harbor, S Circle K, Jack-in-the-Box, H
147b a	AZ 51 N, AZ 202 E, to Squaw Peak Pkwy
146	16th St(from sb), N Shell/Circle K, Filiberto's Mexican, S Circle K, Shamrock/dsl, Church's TX Chicken, Jack-in-the-Box, Little Caesar's, Salsita's Mexican, H, O'Reilly Parts, Ranch Mkt
145	7th St, N Einstein Bagels, McDonald's, Sonic, Starbucks, Subway, Taco Bell, Whataburger, AT&T, H, Safeway Foods, Walgreens, S Chevron/dsl, Circle K, Jimmy John's, Best Western, Hyatt, Sheraton, Springhill Suites, to Chase Field
144	7th Ave, N Circle K, Chipotle, Five Guys, Habit Burger, Little O's, Peiwei Asian, Potbelly, Rubios, Wingstop, S Circle K, Chick-fil-A, El Norteno, Starbucks, central bus dist

INTERSTATE 10 Cont'd

Exit #	Services
143c	US 60, 19th Ave (from wb) Downtown
143b a	I-17, N to Flagstaff, S to Phoenix
142	27th Ave(from eb, no return), N Arco, Comfort Inn, S Senergy Petroleum
141	35th Ave, N Jack-in-the-Box, Rita's Mexican, S Circle K
140	43rd Ave, N Arco, Filberto's Mexican, KFC, Little Caesar's, Pizza Hut, Salsita's Mexican, Subway, Subway, Wingstop, Extended Stay, AutoZone, Food City, Fry's Mercado/gas, tires, Walgreens, S Arco
139	51st Ave, N Chevron/dsl, Circle K, Burger King, Domino's, El Pollo Loco, Los Armanos Mexican, McDonald's, Papa John's, Poliberto's Mexican, Subway, American Inn, Budget Inn, Days Inn, GreenTree Hotel, HomeTowne Studios, InTown Suites, La Quinta, Motel 6, Red Roof+, $Tree, 7-11, 99c Store, AutoZone, Food City, O'Reilly Parts, URGENT CARE, Walgreens, S Chevron/dsl, QT/dsl/scales, Carl's Jr, Filiberto's Mexican, IHOP, Jack-in-the-Box, Port of Subs, Taco Bell, Baymont Inn, Comfort Inn, Travelers Inn, Discount Zone
138	AZ 202
137	67th Ave, N Circle K/dsl, Mobil/dsl, QT/dsl, Church's TX Chicken, Dunkin', Starbucks, 99c Store, S Circle K/dsl, Flying J/Denny's/dsl/LP/24hr/scales, Jack-in-the-Box, O'Reilly Parts, truck repair
136	75th Ave, N Chevron/dsl, Circle K, Circle K, Applebee's, Carl's Jr, Chili's, Chipotle, Denny's, El Pueblo Mexican, Filiberto's, Hawaiian BBQ, Hooters, IHOP, Lin's Buffet, Longhorn Steaks, McDonald's, Olive Garden, Panda Express, Red Lobster, Starbucks, Subway, Taco Bell, TX Roadhouse, Wendy's, Whataburger, Wing Stop, $Tree, AT&T, Big Lots, Big O Tire, Dillard's, Home Depot, La Mesa RV Ctr, Lowe's, Ross, Target, URGENT CARE, Walmart, S Arco, Penske
135	83rd Ave, N Circle K, QT/dsl, Burger King, Dutch Bros, Jack-in-the-Box, Mr Leno, Waffle House, Best Western, Premier Inn, Victory Inn, Sam's Club/gas, S Loves/Subway/24hr/dsl/scales, Kenworth, Speedco
134	91st Ave, Tolleson, N Circle K/dsl, QT/dsl, Fairfield, S QT/dsl, McDonald's, Starbucks
133b	Lp 101 N
133a	99th Ave, N Chevron/Dunkin'/dsl, #1 Buffet, Blaze Pizza, Cafe Zupas, Cane's, Carrabba's, Chick-fil-A, Chipotle Mexican, Coldstone, Dickey's BBQ, El Pollo Loco, Firehouse Subs, Habit Burger, HoneyBaked Ham, Island's Burgers, Jack-in the-Box, Jamba Juice, Jimmy John's, Kneaders Cafe, Macayo's Mexican, McDonald's, Panda Express, Panera Bread, Peter Piper Pizza, Pieology, Pier 88, Pita Kitchen, Potbelly, Red Robin, Smashburger, Taco Bell, Tokyo Joe's, Village Inn, Waba Grill, World of Sourdough, Courtyard, Holiday Inn Express, Best Buy, Costco/gas, Discount Tire, Hobby Lobby, Marshall's, NAPA, Old Navy, PetCo, Ross, URGENT CARE, Verizon, S Circle K, Pilot/Wendy's/dsl/scales/24hr, CarMax, Chevrolet
132	107th Ave, N QT/dsl, Arby's, Barrio Queen, First Watch, Jersey Mike's, Popeyes, Walgreens, S EVC, Camping World RV Ctr, Chrysler/Jeep, Dodge/Ram, Freedomroads RV, Honda, Hyundai, Kia, Mazda, Nissan, Toyota, VW
131	Avondale Blvd, to Cashion, N Circle K/dsl, S QT, Casa De Plata, Culver's, Dutch Bros, Jack-in-the-Box, Panda Express, Starbucks, Hilton Garden, Homewood Suites, My Place Hotel, Residence Inn, CVS Drug, ISM Raceway
129	Dysart Rd, to Avondale, N Chevron/dsl, Circle K/dsl, Buffalo Wild Wings, Cane's, Chick-fil-A, ChuckECheese, Einstein Bros, El Pollo Loco, Fiesta Mexican, Fired Pie,
129	Continued In-N-Out, Jack-in-the-Box/24hr, Jersey Mike's, Manuel's Mexican, Nakama Japanese, NYPD Pizza, Ono Hawaiian BBQ, Panda Express, Pei Wei Asian, Rosati's Pizza, Rosie's Tacos, Starbucks, Subway, Taco Bell, Tomo Japanese, Holiday Inn, $Tree, AT&T, AutoZone, Discount Tire, Fry's Foods, Greulich's Auto Repair, JC Penney, Jo-Ann Fabrics, Kohl's, Lowe's, PetSmart, Sprouts Mkt, Verizon, vet, Walmart, S QT/dsl, Baskin-Robbins, Black Bear Diner, Country Griddle, Crepella, Del Taco, Golden Corral, IHOP, KFC, Krispy Kreme, McDonald's, Peter Piper Pizza, Pizza Hut, Red Dragon, Subway, Waffle House, Whataburger, Quality Inn, Super 8, Big Brand Tires/repair, Brakemasters, Food City, Home Depot, Pepboys, Sam's Club/gas, Walgreens
128	Litchfield Rd, N Circle K/dsl, Applebee's, Black Angus Steaks, Cafe Rio, Chili's, Chipotle, Cracker Barrel, Denny's, Five Guys, Freddy's Steakburgers, Gus' NY Pizza, Hayashi Japanese, Haymaker BBQ, Jimmy John's, Macayo's Mexican, McDonald's, MOD Pizza, Old Chicago Pizza, Raul&Theresa's Mexican, Starbucks, Wendy's, Wildflower Bread Co., Hampton Inn, Red Lion Inn, Residence Inn, Barnes&Noble, Best Buy, H, Luke AFB, Michael's, Ross, Target, URGENT CARE, Wigwam Resort/rest, S Circle K, Angry Crab Shack, Arby's, Burger King, Goodcents Sandwiches, Little Caesars Pizza, Ramiro's Mexican, Rudy's BBQ, Schlotsky's, Starbucks, Taco Bell, Best Western, TownePlace Suites, $Tree, AutoZone, BigLots, Buick/GMC, Ford, O'Reilly Parts
127	Bullard Ave, N QT, BJs Rest., Cheddar's Kitchen, Donatos Pizza, PF Chang's, Red Robin, SpringHill Suites, Tru
126	PebbleCreek Pkwy, to Estrella Park, N Circle K, Rubio's, Ah-So Steaks, Arriba Mexican, Barro's Pizza, Burger King, Del Taco, Jamba Juice, Olive Garden, Oregano's Pizza, Panera Bread, Popeyes, Popo's Mexican, Red Lobster, Starbucks, Taco Bell, TX Roadhouse, $Tree, CAL Ranch, Firestone/auto, GNC, Hobby Lobby, Old Navy, PetCo, Staples, T-Mobile, TJ Maxx, Valvoline, Walgreens, S QT/dsl, Augie's Grill, AZ Pizza Co., Chick-fil-A, Dutch Bros, Filiberto's Mexican, Firehouse Subs, Henry's HI Grill, Jack-in-the-Box, Jimmy John's, McDonald's, Panda Express, Papa Murphy's, Pizza Hut, Robeks Juice, Sammy's Burgers, Sandwich Masterz, Senor Taco, Starbucks, Starbucks, Subway, Two Hands Corn Dogs, Yan's Chinese, Comfort Suites, Ace Hardware, Aldi, Firestone, Safeway Foods/dsl, URGENT CARE, Verizon, vet, Walgreens, Walmart
125	Sarival Ave, Cotton Lane (from wb)
125mm	Roosevelt Canal
124	AZ 303
123	Citrus Rd, to Cotton Ln, S Destiny RV Park, UHaul
122	Perryville Rd
121	Jackrabbit Trail, N Chevron/dsl, $General, S Circle K/dsl, CarQuest
120	Verrado Way, N Shell/dsl, Barro's Pizza, Culver's, Starbucks, Taco Bell, Wingstop, Fairfield Inn, Verizon, S Costco/gas
117	Watson Rd, S Circle K/dsl, Burger King, Carl's Jr, Chipotle Mexican, Cracker Barrel, Denny's, Dunkin', El Pollo Loco, Federico's Mexican, Firehouse Subs, Jack-in-the-Box, Jimmy John's, KFC, Little Caesar's, McDonald's, Palermo's Pizza, Panda Express, Papa John's, Peter Piper Pizza, Pizza Hut, Robeks Juice, Subway, Taco Bell, Wendy's, Wingstop, Holiday Inn Express, Home2 Suites, My Place Hotel, $Tree, ALDI, AT&T, AutoZone, Discount Tire, Firestone, Fry's Foods/dsl, Lowe's, PetSmart, URGENT CARE, Verizon, vet, Walgreens, Walmart/McDonald's/auto
114	Miller Rd, to Buckeye, S Chevron/Sam's Deli/dsl/e85/LP/24hr, Love's/Chester's/Subway/dsl/scales/24hr, QT/dsl,

TOLLESON

= gas = food = lodging = other = rest stop

AZ

INTERSTATE 10 Cont'd

GILA BEND

Exit	Services
114	Continued Burger King, Days Inn, Ford, Leaf Verde RV Park
112	AZ 85, to I-8, Gila Bend
109	Sun Valley Pkwy, Palo Verde Rd, N AJ's Tire/auto repair
104mm	Hassayampa River
103	339th Ave, S TA/Country Pride/Pizza Hut/Shell/Subway/Taco Bell/dsl/scales/LP/24hr/@
98	Wintersburg Rd
97mm	Coyote Wash
95.5mm	Old Camp Wash
94	411th Ave, Tonopah, S Chevron/dsl, Mobil/dsl, Pilot/Subway/dsl/LP/24hr, USPO
86mm	**both lanes, full facilities, litter barrels, vending, petwalk,**
81	Salome Rd, Harquahala Valley Rd
69	Ave 75E, N Snowbird West RV Park
53	Hovatter Rd
52mm	**both lanes, full facilities, litter barrels, vending, petwalk,**
45	Vicksburg Rd, N Pilot/Subway/dsl/scales/parking/LP/24hr, S Pride/Pizza Hut/dsl/scales/24hr, J&K repair/towing, Kofa NWR, tires
31	US 60 E, to Wickenburg
26	Gold Nugget Rd, S parking area
19	Quartzsite, to US 95, Yuma, N 76/dsl, Arco/dsl, Chevron/dsl, Crawford's RV Park, Family$, Quartzite RV Park, Roadrunner Foods, S BLM tent camping, Gold Star RV Park
18mm	Tyson Wash
17	US 95, AZ 95, Quartzsite, N Mobil/Burger King/LP/dsl, Pilot/dsl/scales/24hr, Tesla EVC, Carl's Jr, McDonald's, Outback Pizza, Quartzsite Yacht Grill, Stagecoach Motel/rest., $General, tires/repair, S Love's/Chester's/Subway/scales/parking/dsl/24hr/@, Super 8, Desert Gardens RV Park
11	Dome Rock Rd
5	Tom Wells Rd, N Chevron/dsl/scales/24hr
4.5mm	**both lanes, full facilities, litter barrels, vending, petwalk,**
3.5mm	AZ Port of Entry, **weigh sta**
1	Ehrenberg, to Parker, N 76/dsl, Arizona Oasis RV Resort, Family$, River Sands RV Camping, S Flying J/Wendy's/dsl/LP/scales/lube/repair/tires/24hr, Best Western
0mm	Arizona/California state line, Colorado River, mountain/pacific time zone

QUARTZSITE

INTERSTATE 15

CEDAR POCKET

Exit	Services
29.5mm	Arizona/Utah state line
27	Black Rock Rd
21mm	turnout sb
18	Cedar Pocket, S Virgin River Canyon RA/camping
16mm	no services
15mm	truck parking nb
14mm	truck parking nb
10mm	truck parking nb
9	Desert Springs, N Pilot/dsl/scales/24hr, Desert Springs RV Camping
8.5mm	Virgin River
8	Littlefield, Beaver Dam, E Anasazi Palms RV Park, Four Seasons RV Park, W TA Express/Sunoco/scales/dsl, RV park/tent camping
0mm	Arizona/Nevada state line, mountain/pacific time zone

INTERSTATE 17

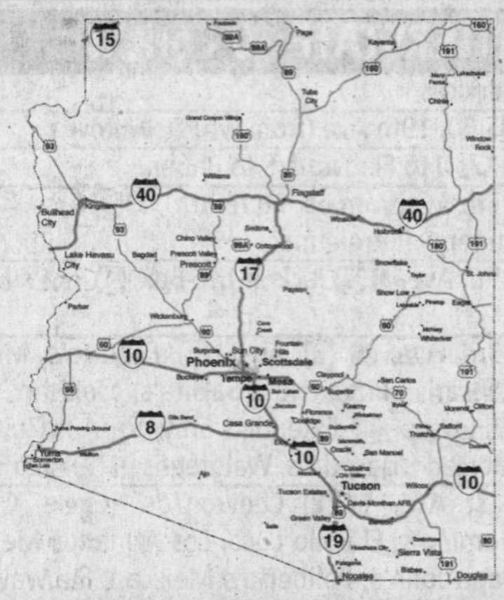

MORMON LAKE

Exit	Services
341	McConnell Dr, I-17 begins/ends, N Chevron/dsl, Circle K, Marathon/Wendy's/dsl, Mobil/dsl, Speedway/dsl, Arby's, Baskin-Robbins, Buffalo Wild Wings, Burger King, Cafe Rio, Cane's, Chick-fil-A, Chili's, Chipotle, Coco's, Del Taco, Denny's, Domino's, DQ, Dunkin', Freddy's Steakburgers, Jack-in-the-Box, Jersey Mike's, Jimmy John's, La Casita Mexican, McDonald's, My Pita Wrap, Ni Marco's Pizza, Olive Garden, Panda Express, Papa John's, Peter Piper Pizza, Pizza Hut, Quiznos, Red Lobster, Sizzler, Starbucks, Subway, Taco Bell, The Habit Burger, Your Pie Pizza, Baymont Inn, Best Western, Canyon Inn, Comfort Inn, Country Inn&Suites, Courtyard, Days Inn, DoubleTree, Drury Inn, Embassy Suites, GreenTree Inn, Hampton Inn, High Country Lodge, Hilton Garden, Howard Johnson, La Quinta, Motel 6, Sleep Inn, SpringHill Suites, Super 8, $Tree, AT&T, AutoZone, Basha's Foods, Big O Tires, Chevrolet, Discount Tire, H, Jiffy Lube, Kohl's, Michael's, O'Reilly Parts, PetSmart, Ross, Safeway, Sprouts Mkt, Staples, Target, Valvoline, Verizon, Verizon, vet, Walgreens, Walmart
340b a	I-40, E to Gallup, W to Kingman
339	Lake Mary Rd(from nb), Mormon Lake, access to same as 341, E Circle K/dsl, AZ Mtn Inn
337	AZ 89A S, to Sedona, Ft Tuthill RA, E Swift TC/Chevron/dsl, W camping
333	Kachina Blvd, Mountainaire Rd, E Mountainaire Rest. (1mi), W Shell/dsl, $General, county park
331	Kelly Canyon Rd
328	Newman Park Rd
326	Willard Springs Rd
322	Pinewood Rd, to Munds Park, E Shell/dsl, Pinewood Rest., golf, Motel in the Pines, W Chevron/dsl, Agee's BBQ, Munds RV Park
322mm	Munds Canyon
320	Schnebly Hill Rd
317	Fox Ranch Rd
316mm	Woods Canyon
315	Rocky Park Rd
313mm	scenic view sb, litter barrels, scenic view
306	Stoneman Lake Rd
300mm	runaway truck ramp sb
298	AZ 179, services in Sedona, to Sedona, Oak Creek Canyon, W Chevron, Circle K, EVC, Bell Rock Inn, Betos Mexican, Butterfly Burger, Cucina Rustica Italian, Dellepiane Grill, Maria's Mexican, Miley's Cafe, Pago's Italian, Pizza Lisa, Rotten Johnny's Pizza, Subway, Tortas de Fuego Mexican, Canyon Villa B&B, Desert Quail Inn, Element Sedona, Hilton, Holiday Inn, Kokopelli Inn, Las Posadas, Red Agave Resort, Sedona Village Lodge, Views Inn, Wildflower Inn

AZ

INTERSTATE 17 Cont'd

CAMP VERDE

Exit #	Services
297mm	**both lanes, full facilities, litter barrels, vending, petwalk,**
293mm	Dry Beaver Creek
293	Cornville Rd, McGuireville Rd, to Rimrock, E 76, OutPost Rest., antiques, W Conoco/Beaver Hollow/dsl, El Patio Grill
289	Middle Verde Rd, Camp Verde, E Chevron/dsl, Sonic, Cliff Castle Hotel/casino/rest., W Distant Drums RV Park
288mm	Verde River
287	AZ 260, to AZ 89A, Cottonwood, Payson, E Shell/Subway/dsl/RV dump/LP/24hr, Burger King, Denny's, DQ, Filiberto's Mexican, Gabriela's Mexican, McDonald's, Starbucks, Taco Bell, Comfort Inn, Days Inn, The Copper Hotel, Fort Verde RV Ctr, Territorial RV Park(1mi), Trails End RV Park, Zane Grane RV Park(9mi), W Chevron/Wendy's/dsl/24hr, RV camping, to Jerome SP
285	Camp Verde, Gen Crook Tr, E Rio Verde Mexican, Territorial Town Inn, to Ft Verde SP, Trail End RV Park, Zane Gray RV Park(9mi)
281mm	safety pullout area nb
278	AZ 169, Cherry Rd, to Prescott
269mm	Ash Creek
268	Dugas Rd, Orme Rd
265.5mm	Agua Fria River
263b a	AZ 69 N, Cordes Jct Rd(262 from nb), to Prescott, E Chevron, Love's/Arby's/dsl/scales/24hr/@, Pilot/Subway/dsl/LP/24hr, McDonald's, $Tree, Family$, Speedco
259	Bloody Basin Rd, to Crown King, Horse Thief Basin RA
256	Badger Springs Rd
252	Sunset Point, rest area/scenic view both lanes, full facilities, litter barrels, vending
248	Bumble Bee, W Horse Thief Basin RA
244	Squaw Valley Rd, Black Canyon City, E Chilleen's on 17 BBQ/Steaks, W Beni's Pizza, Two Brother's Kitchen, Mountain Breeze Motel, Black Canyon RV Resort, Family$, Ron's Mkt
243.5mm	no services
242	Rock Springs, Black Canyon City, E Black Canyon Campground, W Rock Springs/dsl, Beni's Pizza, Rock Springs Cafe, Mtn Breeze Motel
239.5mm	Little Squaw Creek
239mm	Mulch Gulch
236	Table Mesa Rd
232	New River, E Shell, RoadRunner Rest.
231.5mm	New River
229	Anthem Way, Desert Hills Rd, E Circle K, Barro's Pizza, McDonald's, Mr. Gyro, Rosati's Pizza, Starbucks, Subway, Sweethearts Donuts, Taco Bell, Wendy's, $Tree, Ace Hardware, Safeway, URGENT CARE, W Chevron/dsl, Circle K, Circle K/dsl, Charley's Cheesesteaks, Del Taco, Denny's, Firehouse Subs, Fresca's Mexican, Gio's Pizza, Ray's Pizza, Ruby's Express, Subway, TN Grill, Hampton Inn, Anthem Outlets/famous brands/food court, auto repair, Discount Tire, Meineke, O'Reilly Parts, tires, U-Haul, Walmart
227	Daisy Mtn Dr, E Circle K/dsl, Domino's, Freddy's, Jack-in-the-Box, Jersey Mike's, Starbucks, Tortas Mexican, Tru Burger, CVS Drug, Fry's Foods, GNC, Verizon, vet
227mm	Dead Man Wash
225	Pioneer Rd, W Pioneer AZ Museum, Pioneer RV Park
223	AZ 74, Carefree Hwy, to Wickenburg, E Chevron, AZool Grill, Chili's, Desert Donuts, First Watch, Hong Kong Chinese, In-N-Out, Jimmy John's, McDonald's, Subway, Taco Bell, Albertson's, Home Depot, Kohl's, Sprouts Mkt
222	Dove Valley
221	AZ 303, Senora Desert Dr
220	Dixileta(from nb)
219	Jomax Rd
218	Happy Valley Rd, E Circle K/dsl, Shell, Bento Box, Buffalo Wild Wings, Burger King, Cafe Rio, Carl's Jr, Carlos O'Brien's Mexican, Chipotle, Firehouse Subs, IHOP, Jack-in-the-Box, Jamba Juice, Jersey Mike's, L&L Hawaiian BBQ, Mellow Mushroom Pizza, Olive Garden, Panda Express, Panera Bread, PF Chang's, Pita Jungle, Rays Pizza, Red Robin, Sauce Pizza, Shane's Ribshack, Starbucks, Streets of NY Pizza, The Stillery Rest., TX Roadhouse, Best Western+, Courtyard, Hampton Inn, Holiday Inn Express, Home2 Suites, Homewood Suites, Residence Inn, Woodspring Suites, $Tree, Barnes&Noble, Best Buy, Big O Tire, Dick's, Discount Tire, Lowe's, O'Reilly Parts, PetCo, Ross, Staples, TJ Maxx, Verizon, vet, Walmart/auto, World Mkt, W QT/dsl, Shell/Circle K, Burger King, Dutch Bros, First Watch, Humble Pie, Safeway, Valvoline
217	Pinnacle Peak Rd, E QT, Angie's Grill, Corridors Cafe, Drury Inn, Hilton Garden, Phoenix RV Park
215a	Rose Garden Ln, same as 215b
215b	Deer Valley Rd, E Shell/Circle K, Arby's, Armando's Mexican, Culvers, Da Valley Grill, Del Taco, Dunkin', Jack-in-the-Box, Jimmy John's, McDonald's, Sonic, Subway, Taco Bell, Wendy's, Port of Subs, Little Dealer RV Ctr, W Arco/dsl, Circle K/dsl, Cracker Barrel, Denny's, Times Square Italian, Waffle House, Days Inn, Extended Stay America, H, U-Haul
214c	AZ 101 loop
214b	Yorkshire Dr, W 7-11, Barro's Pizza, Chick-fil-A, Chili's, Chipotle, In-N-Out, Jack-in-the-Box, Jersey Mike's, Jimmy John's, Macaroni Grill, Panda Express, Starbucks, Wendy's, Wingstreet, Budget Suites, $Tree, AT&T, Costco/gas, H, Michael's, PetSmart, Ross, Target
214a	Union Hills Dr, E Circle K/dsl, Shell, W Arco/dsl, Sleep Inn, Studio 6
212b a	Bell Rd, Scottsdale, to Sun City, E Chevron/dsl, QT, Burger Mania, Caramba Mexican, Jack-in-the-Box, LJ Silver, Manuel's Mexican, McDonald's, Naked BBQ, Schlotzsky's, Starbucks, Sullivan Rest., Waffle House, Wingstop, Comfort Inn & Suites, Extend A Suites, Motel 6, Chevrolet, Chrysler/Jeep/Dodge, Discount Tire, Fiat, Ford, Honda, Hyundai, Kohl's, Lincoln, Mazda, Nissan, O'Reilly Parts, Sam's Club/gas, Toyota/Scion, U-Haul, Volvo, Walmart, W QT, Cane's, Denny's, Eegee's Rest., Santisi Bros Grill, US Egg Breakfast, Red Roof Inn, Fry's Foods/dsl
211	Greenway Rd, E La Quinta, 7-11
210	Thunderbird Rd, E Circle K/dsl, Barro's Pizza, Jack-in-the-Box, Juliobertos Mexican, Lucky Donuts, Lucky's Burgers, Pizza Hut/Taco Bell, Starbucks, Subway, Wendy's, CVS Drug, Home Depot, Jiffy Lube, Walgreens, W QT, Jamba Juice, McDonald's, Port of Subs, Whataburger, Econolodge, Best Buy, Lowe's
209	Cactus Rd, W 7-11, QT/dsl, Anzio's Italian, China Harvest, DQ, Julioberto's Mexican, Rainbow Donuts, Stackers Rest., Family$
208	Peoria Ave, E First Watch, Native Grill, Pappadeaux, Seoul KBBQ, Wings N Things, Baymont, HomeTowne Studios, Homewood Suites, Hyatt Place, Sonesta Suites, W QT/dsl, Buffalo Wild Wings, Burger King, Cane's, Chick-fil-A, Chili's, Chipotle Mexican, Coldstone, Dickey's BBQ, Filiberto's Mexican, Harbor Seafood, Hooters, In-N-Out, Jason's Deli, Longhorn Steaks, Mi Pueblo, MOD Pizza, Mongolian BBQ, Olive Garden, Panera Bread, Peter Piper Pizza, Red Lobster, Red Robin, Smashburger, Starbucks, Subway, TX Roadhouse, Wendy's, Wingstop, DoubleTree, Premier Inn, $Tree, Barnes&Noble, Dillard's, Discount Tire, Firestone/auto,

BLACK CANYON CITY

= gas = food = lodging = other = rest stop

AZ

INTERSTATE 17 Cont'd

Exit	Services
208	Continued Macy's, Michael's, PetCo, PetSmart, Ross, Tire Pros/repair, URGENT CARE, Verizon, Walmart
208.5mm	Arizona Canal
207	Dunlap Ave, E Circle K, QuikTrip, Shell/dsl, Domino's, First Watch, Jack-in-the-Box, Subway, Taco Bell, Best Western, Courtyard, Sheraton, SpringHill Suites, Firestone, URGENT CARE, W Chevron/dsl, Bobby-Q's Rest., Denny's, Jack-in-the-Box, Subway, Taco Boy's, Extended Stay, Midas, repair, U-Haul
206	Northern Ave, E Circle K/dsl, Burger King, Del Taco, Dunkin', El Pollo Loco, IHOP, McDonald's, Ms. Martha's, Starbucks, Albertson's, AutoZone, Big O Tires, URGENT CARE, Walgreens, W Arco, QT, DQ, Motel 6, Super 8, $General, auto repair
205	Glendale Ave, E 7-11, QT, Filiberto's, Panda Express, Pizza Patron, Starbucks, Subway, Ace Hardware, auto repair, Fry's Foods/dsl, transmissions, URGENT CARE, W Circle K/dsl, Jack-in-the-Box, Lenny's Burger, 7-11, Walgreens
204	Bethany Home Rd, E Arco, Circle K/dsl, Shell/dsl, Carl's Jr, Chick-fil-A, Chipotle, Dunkin', Jersey Mike's, KFC, Mandarin Buffet, McDonald's, Olive Garden, Pizza Hut, Subway, Taco Bell, Whataburger, $Tree, BigLots, H, PetSmart, Ross, Target, URGENT CARE, Walgreens, Walmart, W 76, Super Gasoline, Burger King, Fruitlandia Creamery, Loritos Mexican, Lunch Box Cafe, Tacos Kissi Mexican, Royal Inn, auto repair, Food City, Jiffy Lube, Savers, tires
203	Camelback Rd, E BoSa Donuts, Church's TX Chicken, Country Boy's Rest., Filiberto's Mexican, Little Caesars, Popeyes, $General, Chrysler/Dodge/Jeep, Discount Tire, Family$, Wendy's, W Circle K/dsl, QT, Jack-in-the-Box, McDonald's, Grand Canyon Hotel, AutoZone, to Grand Canyon U, USPO
202	Indian School Rd, E Arco/dsl, Buffalo Wild Wings, Burger King, Chihuahua Seafood, Domino's, Federico's Mexican, Pizza Hut, Subway, Ace Hardware, CVS Drug, Food City, Verizon, W 76, Motel 6, Super 8, Travel Inn
201	Thomas Rd, E Chevron/McDonald's/playplace, Arby's, Denny's, Dunkin', Jack-in-the-Box, Starbucks, La Quinta, Vacation Inn, W QT, Carl's Jr, Subway, NAPA
200b	McDowell Rd, Van Buren, E Purcell's Tire, U-Haul, W Arco, Knights Inn
200a	I-10, W to LA, E to Phoenix
199b	Jefferson St(from sb), Adams St(from nb), Van Buren St(from nb), E Circle K, Jack-in-the-Box, $General, W Circle K/gas, Burger Shoppe, Filiberto's Mexican, La Canasta Mexican, Pete's Fish&Chip, Family$, Food City, PepBoys
199a	Grant St
198	Buckeye Rd(from nb), E Horseshoe Mexican, W 76, Circle K
197	US 60, 19th Ave, Durango St, E Jack-in-the-Box, Whataburger, $General, AutoZone
196	7th St, Central Ave, E Super Oscar's, H, W Chevron/dsl
195b	7th St, Central Ave, E Circle K/dsl, Pacific Pride, Jack-in-the-Box, McDonald's, Taco Bell, EZ 8 Motel, H, NAPA
195a	16th St(from sb, no EZ return), E Sky Harbor, Shell/Subway/dsl, Burger King
194	I-10 W, to AZ 151, to Sky Harbor Airport. I-17 begins/ends on I-10, exit 150a

VAN BUREN

INTERSTATE 19

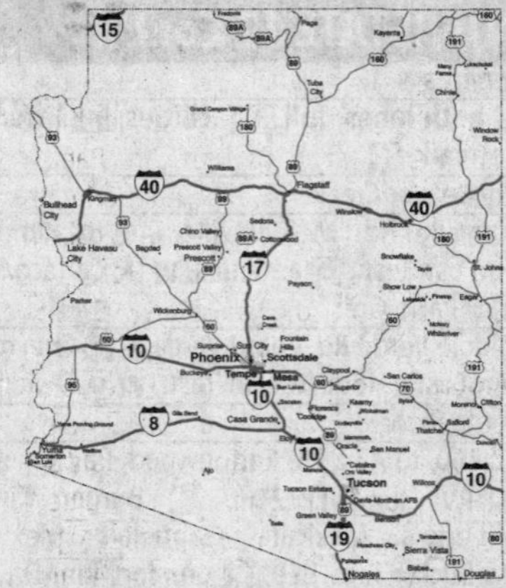

INTERSTATE 19

Exit #	Services
101b a	I-10, E to El Paso, W to Phoenix. I-19 begins/ends on I-10, exit 260. I-19 uses kilometers (km), W to Phoenix
99	AZ 86, Ajo Way, E Circle K, Speedway, Eegee's Cafe, Filiberto's, Hamburger Stand, Peter Piper Pizza, Subway, Big Brand Tire, Fry's Foods, H, vet, Walgreens, W QT/dsl, Burger King, Church's TX Chicken, Jack-in-the-Box, Little Caesar's, Los Betos Mexican, McDonald's, $General, city park, Family$, Food City, Jiffy Lube, museum, to Old Tucson
98	Irvington Rd, E Arco/dsl, TX Roadhouse, AutoZone, W Circle K/dsl, Marathon, Speedway, Buffalo Wild Wings, Chick-fil-A, Chipotle, Cold Stone, Cupbop BBQ, Dutch Bros, Eegee's, El Pollo Loco, Firehouse Subs, First Watch, Five Guys, In-N-Out, Krispy Kreme, McDonald's, MOD Pizza, Olive Garden, Oregano's Italian, Panda Express, Peter Piper Pizza, Red Lobster, Red Robin, Taco Bell, The Habit, $Tree, AT&T, Batteries+, Best Buy, Discount Tire, Family$, Food City, Hobby Lobby, Home Depot, JC Penney, Marshall's, Michael's, Old Navy, PetSmart, Ross, Sprouts Mkt, Target, URGENT CARE, URGENT CARE, Verizon
95b a	Valencia Rd, E Circle K, Speedway, Chickenuevo, Church's TX Chicken, Dominos, Donut Wheel, Eegee's Cafe, Jack-in-the-Box, Little Caesar's, McDonald's, Peter Piper Pizza, Sonic, Subway, Viva Burrito, Whataburger, Yokohama Asian, $Tree, AutoZone, Brake Masters, Family$, Food City, Jiffy Lube, Midas, O'Reilly Parts, Tuscon Intl', USPO, Walgreens, W Circle K/dsl, QT/dsl, Arby's, Blake's, Burger King, Cane's Chicken, Carl's Jr, Casa Valencia, Chili's, Cuver's, Denny's, DQ, Dunkin', Dutch Bros, Golden Corral, Grand Buffet, IHOP, Little Caesar's, Panda Express, Papa John's, Papa Murphy's, Pizza Hut, Starbucks, Subway, Taco Bell, Wendy's, Wienerschnitzel, Big O Tire, CVS Drug, Fry's Foods/gas, Lowe's, NAPA, repair, transmissions, URGENT CARE, Verizon, Walgreens, Walmart
92	San Xavier Rd, W to San Xavier Mission(2mi)
91.5km	Santa Cruz River
87	Papago Rd
80	Pima Mine Rd, E Agave Rest., Diamond Casino
75	Helmut Peak Rd, to Sahuarita, E Fry's Fuel, Speedway/dsl/e85, Arby's, Dunkin'/Baskin Robbins, EVC, McDonald's, Panda Express, Starbucks, Subway, Taco Bell, Fry's Foods/drug, USPO, vet
69	US 89 N, Duval Mine Rd., Green Valley, E Circle K, Carl's Jr., Chipotle, Culver's, Denny's, Dutch Bros, Eegee's, Jersey Mike's, Little Caesar's, Longhorn BBQ, MOD Pizza, Panda House, Pizza Hut, Popeyes, Rigoberto's, Starbucks, Subway, Ace Hardware, AutoZone, BigLots, Firestone, O'Reilly Parts, Petco, PetSmart, Ross, Sprouts Mkt, TJ Maxx, URGENT CARE, Verizon, Walgreens, Walmart/Subway,

GREEN VALLEY

GREEN VALLEY

INTERSTATE 19 Cont'd

Exit	Services
69	Continued Chevron, Circle K, [food] Arby's, Burger King, Domino's, DQ, Jerry Bob's Rest., Manuel's Mexican, Papa John's, Papa John's, Starbucks, Taco Bell, [lodging] Vagabond Inn, [other] Ford/Hyundai, Green Valley RV Resort, Safeway/dsl, Titan Missile Museum, Total Car Care, U-Haul, U-Haul, vet
65	Esperanza Blvd, to Green Valley, **E** [gas] Shell/repair/dsl, **W** [food] AZ Family Rest., El Rodeo Mexican, McGee's Pizza, [lodging] Best Western/rest., Comfort Inn, [other] Ace Hardware, vet, Walgreens
63	Continental Rd, Green Valley, **E** [other] golf, USPO, **W** [gas] Chevron, [food] KFC, Mama's Kitchen, McDonald's, [other] $Tree, CVS Drug, Safeway, to Madera Cyn RA, TrueValue, Verizon, Walgreens
56	Canoa Rd, **W** [food] Grill on the Green, [lodging] Canoa Resort
54km	**[rest stop] both lanes, full [handicapped] facilities, [picnic], litter barrels, vending, petwalk, [phone]**
48	Arivaca Rd, Amado, **E** [other] DeAnza RV Resort(2mi), Mtn View RV Park, **W** [food] Longhorn Grill, [other] $General, Amado Mkt/gas
42	Agua Linda Rd, to Amado, **E** [other] Mtn View RV Park
40	Chavez Siding Rd, Tubac, **E** [other] Tubac Golf Resort
34	Tubac, **E** [gas] El Mercado, [food] Elvira's Cafe, Habaneros Mexican, Italian Peasant, Tubac Deli, Tubac Jack's Rest., [other] to Tubac Presidio SP, Tubac Golf Resort, Tubac Mkt, USPO
29	Carmen, Tumacacori, **E** [other] to Tumacacori Nat Hist Park, USPO
25	Palo Parado Rd
22	Pec Canyon Rd
17	Rio Rico Dr, Calabasas Rd, **W** [gas] Chevron/dsl/LP, [food] Hua Mei Chinese, Joe's Place Mexican, La Bocanita Mexican, Little Caesars, Nickles Diner, Subway, [other] IGA Foods, USPO
12	AZ 289, to Ruby Rd, **E** [gas] Love's/McDonald's/dsl/scales/24hr, Pilot/Wendy's/dsl/scales/24hr, [other] Speedco, **W** to Pena Blanca Lake RA
8	AZ 82(exits left from sb, no return), Nogales, **E** [gas] Chevron, Circle K, [other] Mi Casa RV Park
4	AZ 189 S, Mariposa Rd, Nogales, **E** [gas] FasTrip/dsl, Jumpin' Jack, [food] Chipotle, Chuyitos Hotdogs, City Salads, Dragon Buffet, Dunkin, Jack-in-the-Box, KFC, Little Caesar's, McDonald's, Panda Express, Pizza Pollis, Ragazzi Italian, Starbucks, Subway, Tacos & Taros, Tito's Pizza, [lodging] Mariposa Hotel, Motel 6, [other] $Tree, AT&T, AutoZone, Buick/GMC, Ford, Hobby Lobby, Home Depot, JC Penney, Marshall's, Old Navy, O'Reilly Parts, PetSmart, Ross, Safeway, URGENT CARE, Walgreens, Walmart/Domino's, **W** [gas] Circle K/dsl, [food] Carl's Jr, IHOP, [lodging] Best Western, Candlewood Suites, Holiday Inn Express
1b	Western Ave, Nogales
1a	International St (from sb)
0km	I-19 begins/ends in Nogales, Arizona/Mexico Border, **N** [gas] Circle K, Express Fuel Depot/dsl, Shell, [food] Burger King, Church's TX Chicken, Denny's, McDonald's, Peter Piper Pizza, Pizza Hut, [lodging] Hotel Americana, Siesta Hotel, [other] AutoZone, Family$, Food City, museum, NAPA, O'Reilly Parts, PepBoys, U-Haul

NOGALES

INTERSTATE 40

Exit	Services
359.5mm	Arizona/New Mexico state line
359	Grants Rd, to Lupton, **Welcome Ctr/[rest stop] both lanes, full [handicapped] facilities, [phone], [picnic], litter barrels, petwalk, N** [gas] Speedy's/dsl/rest./24hr, [other] Tee Pee Trading Post/rest., YellowHorse Indian Gifts
357	AZ 12 N, Lupton, to Window Rock, **N** [other] USPO
354	Hawthorne Rd
351	Allentown Rd, **N** [other] Chee's Indian Store, Indian City Gifts
348	St Anselm Rd, Houck, **N** [other] Ft Courage Food/gifts
347.5mm	Black Creek
346	Pine Springs Rd

HOUCK

CEDAR POINT

Exit	Services
345mm	Box Canyon
344mm	Querino Wash
343	Querino Rd
341	Ortega Rd, Cedar Point, **N** [gas] Indian Ctr/gas/gifts
340.5mm	insp/weigh sta both lanes
339	US 191 S, to St Johns, **N** [food] Pizza Edge, [other] Bashas Groceries, **S** [gas] Speedway/dsl, [other] Family$, USPO
333	US 191 N, Chambers, **N** [other] to Hubbell Trading Post NHS, USPO, **S** [gas] Mobil/dsl/parking, [lodging] SureStay
330	McCarrell Rd
325	Navajo, **S** [gas] Shell/Subway/Navajo Trading Post/dsl/24hr
323mm	Crazy Creek
320	Pinta Rd
316mm	Dead River
311	Painted Desert, **N** [other] Painted Desert, Petrified Forest NP
303	Adamana Rd, **N** [other] Stewarts/gifts, **S** Painted Desert Indian Ctr
302.5mm	Big Lithodendron Wash
301mm	Little Lithodendron Wash
300	Goodwater
299mm	Twin Wash
294	Sun Valley Rd, **N** [lodging] Sun Valley RV camping, **S** [other] Knife City
292	AZ 77 N, to Keams Canyon, **N** [gas] One9/Burger King/dsl/24hr, [other] dsl repair
289	Lp 40, Holbrook, **N** [gas] Chevron/dsl, Hatch's/dsl, [food] Mesa Rest., [lodging] Best Western, Days Inn, GreenTree Inn, Howard Johnson, Motel 6, Quality Inn, Sahara Inn, Travelodge, [other] Goodyear
286	Navajo Blvd, Holbrook, **N** [gas] 76/dsl, Circle K, Maverik/dsl, [food] 66 Rest., Aliberto's Mexican, Burger King, Carl's Jr, McDonald's, Taco Bell, Tom & Suzie's, [lodging] 66 Motel, Baymont Inn, Econolodge, Super 8, [other] $General, KOA, O'Reilly Parts, OK RV Park, **S** [gas] Chevron/dsl, Hatch's Gas, Super Fuels, [food] A&W Rest., DQ, Little Caesars, Mr Maestas Mexican, Romo's Mexican, [lodging] El Rancho Motel/rest., [other] [H], museum, Pow Wow Trading Post, Scotty & Son Repair, SW Transmissions
285	US 180 E, AZ 77 S, Holbrook, **S** [rest stop]/[picnic]/litter barrels, [gas] Speedway/dsl, [food] Butterfield Steaks, Wayside Soda Shop, [lodging] Economy Inn, Wigwam Motel, [other] $General, Best Hardware, Family$, Safeway, to Petrified Forest NP
284mm	Leroux Wash
283	Perkins Valley Rd, Golf Course Rd, **N** [other] golf, **S** [gas] TA/Shell/Popeyes/dsl/scales/24hr/@
280	Hunt Rd, Geronimo Rd, **N** [other] Geronimo Trading Post
277	Lp 40, Joseph City, **N** [gas] Love's/Chester's/Subway/scales/dsl/24hr/@, **S** [other] to Cholla Lake CP
274	Lp 40, Joseph City, **N** [food] MR. G's Pizza, [other] RV Camping
269	Jackrabbit Rd, **S** [other] Jackrabbit Trading Post
264	Hibbard Rd
257	AZ 87 N, to Second Mesa, **N** [other] to Homolovi Ruins SP, **S** trading post
256.5mm	Little Colorado River
255	Lp 40, Winslow, **N** [food] Chang Thai, [lodging] Best Western+, **S** [gas] Flying J/Denny's/dsl/LNG/scales/RV Dump/24hr, [food] Sonic, [other] Goodyear
253	N Park Dr, Winslow, **N** [gas] Chevron, Maverik/dsl, ONE9/dsl/24hr, [food] Capt Tony's Pizza, Carl's Jr, El Gordo Mexican, Pizza Hut, [other] $General, AutoZone, Ford, O'Reilly Parts, tires/lube, Walmart, **S** [food] Alfonso's Mexican, China Town, LJ Silver/Taco Bell, McDonald's, Subway, [lodging] Clarion Pointe, Motel 6, [other] Family$, [H], Safeway
252	AZ 87 S, Winslow, **S** [gas] 76/dsl, [food] Entre Chinese, Mi Pueblo, [lodging] Quality Inn, Rodeway Inn, [other] Eagle RV Park, [H]
245	AZ 99, Leupp Corner
239	Meteor City Rd, Red Gap Ranch Rd
235mm	**[rest stop] both lanes, full [handicapped] facilities, [picnic], litter barrels, petwalk, [phone]**

HOLBROOK

WINSLOW

= gas = food = lodging = other = rest stop

AZ

INTERSTATE 40 Cont'd

TWIN ARROWS

Exit #	Services
233	Meteor Crater Rd, S Mobil/Meteor Crater RV Park/dump, museum, to Meteor Crater NL
230	Two Guns
229.5mm	Canyon Diablo
225	Buffalo Range Rd
219	Twin Arrows, N Navajo Travel Plaza, Twin Arrows Resort/Casino
218.5mm	Padre Canyon
211	Winona, N Shell/dsl/repair, U-Haul
207	Cosnino Rd
204	to Walnut Canyon NM
201	US 89, Flagstaff, to Page, N 76/dsl, Chevron/dsl, Circle K/dsl, Maverik/dsl, VP/dsl, Burger King, Carlillos Cocina, Chipotle, Del Taco, Dunkin, Jack-in-the-Box, McDonald's, NiMarco's Pizza, Panda Express, Pizza Hut, Starbucks, Taco Bell, Tacos Los Altos, Wendy's, Best Western, Country Inn Suites, Days Inn, Mtn View Inn, Super 8, $Tree, Barnes&Noble, Best Buy, Chrysler/Dodge/Jeep/Fiat, CVS Drug, Dillard's, Discount Tire, Family$, Family$, Home Depot, Honda, H, JC Penney, KOA, Marshall's, Mercedes, Nissan/Subaru, O'Reilly Parts, Old Navy, Pepboys, PetCo, Safeway/dsl, Subaru, tires, Toyota/Scion, Valvoline, Verizon, World Mkt, S Mobil/dsl, Speedway/dsl, Oregano's Pizza, Toasted Owl Brunch, Fairfield Inn, Hampton Inn, Sonesta Suites, Wyndham Resort

FLAGSTAFF

Exit #	Services
198	Butler Ave, Flagstaff, N Chevron, Marathon, Pacific Pride/dsl, Speedway/dsl, Agave Mexican, Cracker Barrel, Culver's, Denny's, Filiberto's Mexican, McDonald's, Outback Steaks, Sonic, Starbucks, Subway, Taco Bell, Comfort Inn, Days Hotel, Econolodge, Flagstaff Hotel, Holiday Inn Express, La Quinta, Motel 6, Quality Inn, Ramada, Studio 6, Travelers Inn, Jiffy Lube, NAPA, Sam's Club/gas, U-Haul, vet, Walmart, S Mobil, Sinclair/Little America/dsl/motel/@, Black Bart's Steaks/RV Park, Little America
197.5mm	no services
195b	US 89A N, McConnell Dr, Flagstaff, N Chevron, Chevron/dsl, Circle K, Marathon/Wendy's/dsl, Mobil/dsl, Shell, Speedway/dsl, Arby's, Baskin-Robbins, Buffalo Wild Wings, Burger King, Cafe Rio, Cane's, Carl's Jr, Chick-fil-A, Chili's, Chipotle Mexican, Coco's, Coldstone, Del Taco, Denny's, Domino's, DQ, Dunkin', Firehouse Subs, Freddy's Steakburgers, In-N-Out, Jack-in-the-Box, Jersey Mike's, Jimmy John's, La Casita Mexican, Little Caesar's, Lone Spur Cafe, McDonald's, My Pita Wrap, Natural Grocers, NiMarco's Pizza, Olive Garden, Over Easy, Panda Express, Papa John's, Papa Murphy's, Peter Piper Pizza, Pizza Hut, Red Lobster, Sizzler, Starbucks, Subway, Taco Bell, Your Pie Pizza, Baymont Inn, Best Western, Budget Inn, Canyon Inn, Comfort Inn, Country Inn, Courtyard, Days Inn, Drury Inn, Embassy Suites, GreenTree Inn, Hampton Inn, Hilton Garden, Howard Johnson, La Quinta, Motel 6, Sleep Inn, SpringHill Suites, Super 8, $Tree, AT&T, AutoZone, Basha's Foods/Starbucks, Discount Tire, H, Kohl's, Michael's, O'Reilly Parts, PetSmart, Ross, Safeway, Sprouts Mkt, Staples, Subway, Target, URGENT CARE, URGENT CARE, Verizon, Verizon, vet, Walgreens, Walmart
195a	I-17 S, AZ 89A S, to Phoenix
192	Flagstaff Ranch Rd
191	Lp 40, to Grand Canyon, Flagstaff, N Chevron, Maverik, DoubleTree, Big O Tires, Home Depot, Kia, Kit Carson RV Park, Valvoline, vet, Woody Mtn Camping
190	A-1 Mountain Rd
189.5mm	Arizona Divide, elevation 7335

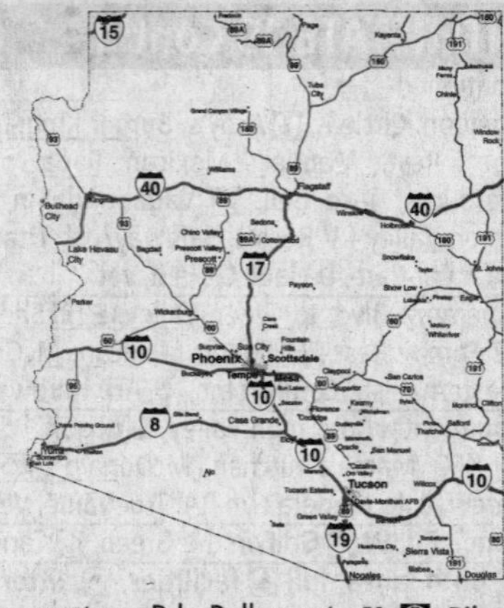

WILLIAMS

Exit #	Services
185	Transwestern Rd, Bellemont, N Pilot/McDonald's/dsl/scales/24hr/@, Best Western, S Harley-Davidson, RV Country
180mm	both lanes, full facilities, litter barrels, vending
178	Parks Rd, N Texaco/dsl, Mustang River Grill
171	Pittman Valley Rd, Deer Farm Rd
167	Garland Prairie Rd, Circle Pines Rd, N KOA
165	AZ 64, to Williams, Grand Canyon, N to Grand Canyon, S Super 8(1mi)
163	same as 161, Williams, N Chevron/dsl/U-Haul, Love's/Subway/dsl/scales/24hr, Maverik, Quality Inn, Canyon Gateway RV Park, S Circle K, Exxon/dsl, Mustang/dsl, Shell/dsl, KFC/Taco Bell, La Casita, McDonald's, Pine Country Rest., Pizza Factory, Pizza Hut, American Regency Inn, Best Value, Canyon Motel/RV Park, Drover's Inn, Econo Lodge, El Rancho Motel, Grand Canyon Railway Hotel, Historic Grand Canyon Hotel, Howard Johnson, Ramada Inn, Rodeway Inn, Star Hotel, The Lodge Motel, Travelodge, $General, tires, USPO
161	Lp 40, Golf Course Dr, Williams, S 76/dsl/LP, Circle K, Shell, DQ, Jessica's Rest., AZ 9 Hotel, Best Western+, Buffalo Pointe Inn, Canyon Country Inn, Comfort Inn, Days Inn, Grand Canyon Hotel, Grand Canyon Hotel, Highlander Motel, Holiday Inn Express, La Quinta, Motel 6, Motel 6, Super 8, Westerner Motel, Family$, Grand Canyon RV Park, public restrooms, Safeway, to Grand Canyon Railway
157	Devil Dog Rd

ASH FORK

Exit #	Services
155.5mm	safety pullout wb, litter barrels
151	Welch Rd
149	Monte Carlo Rd, N dsl repair
148	County Line Rd
146	AZ 89, to Prescott, Ash Fork, N ONE9/dsl/scales/24hr, Shell/dsl, Lulu Belle's BBQ, Ranch House Cafe, Canyon's Hotel, Family$
144	Ash Fork, N Canyon's Edge Rte 66, Grand Canyon RV Park, museum/info, USPO, S Hillside/U-Haul, Shell/Piccadilly's/dsl, auto/RV repair
139	Crookton Rd, to Rte 66
123	Lp 40, to Rte 66, to Grand Canyon Caverns, (same as 121), Seligman, N Shell/dsl, S Chevron/Subway/dsl
121	Lp 40, to Rte 66, (same as 123), Seligman, N 76/dsl, Chevron/A&W, Lilo's Rest., Roadkill Cafe, Canyon Lodge, Route 66 Motel/pizza, Supai Motel, Family$, KOA(1mi), tires, USPO
109	Anvil Rock Rd
108mm	Markham Wash
103	Jolly Rd
96	Cross Mountain Rd
91	Fort Rock Rd
87	Willows Ranch Rd
86mm	Willow Creek

AZ

INTERSTATE 40 Cont'd

Exit #	Services
79	Silver Springs Rd
75.5mm	Big Sandy Wash
73.5mm	Peacock Wash
71	US 93 S, to Wickenburg, Phoenix
66	Blake Ranch Rd, N Petro/Iron Skillet/dsl/scales/24hr/@, Blake Ranch RV Park, SpeedCo Lube, Verizon
60mm	Frees Wash
59	DW Ranch Rd, N Love's/Subway/dsl/scales/24hr, S Chevron/dsl, Rosati's Pizza, Hualapai Mtn Park(9mi)
57mm	Rattlesnake Wash
53	AZ 66, Andy Devine Ave, to Kingman, N Chevron/dsl, Flying J/Denny's/dsl/LP/scales/24hr, Maverik/dsl, Terrible's/dsl, Texaco/dsl, Arby's, Burger King, Denny's, Jack-in-the-Box, McDonald's, Pizza Hut, Starbucks, Taco Bell, Baymont, Days Inn, Motel 6, Silver Queen Inn, Super 8, Travelodge, $General, Basha's Foods, Blue Beacon, Freightliner, Harley-Davidson, KOA(1mi), Sunshine RV Park, S Mobil/dsl, Shell/dsl/repair, La Catrina Mexican, Oyster's Mexican, Sonic, Best Western+, Clarion, Days Inn, High Desert Inn, Holiday Inn Express, Mohave Inn, OYO Hotel, Ramada Inn, SpringHill Suites, Chrysler/Dodge/Jeep, Kia, NAPA, Penske, Sunrise RV Park, tires, Uptown Drug
51	Stockton Hill Rd, Kingman, N Arco/dsl, Chevron, Circle K/dsl, Asian Star Chinese, Carl's Jr, Chili's, Chipotle Mexican, Cracker Barrel, Culver's, Del Taco, Domino's, Dunkin', Dutch Bros, Five Guys, IHOP, In-N-Out, Jersey Mike's, Jimmy John's, KFC, Kingman Chophouse, McDonald's, Panda Express, Papa Murphy, Sonic, Starbucks, Subway, Subway, Taco Bell, Hampton Inn, La Quinta, $General, $Tree, AutoZone, BigLots, BrakeMasters, Buick/Chevrolet, CVS Drug, Discount Tire, Ford/Lincoln, Home Depot, Honda, H, Hyundai, O'Reilly Parts, PetCo, PetSmart, Ross, Safeway/gas, Smith's Foods/dsl, Staples, Tire Works, TrueValue, U-Haul, Valvoline, Verizon, vet, Walgreens, Walmart, S Circle K, DQ, Little Caesar's, Pizza Hut, Home2 Suites, $Tree, CarQuest, Safeway/dsl
48	US 93 N, Beale St, Kingman, N 76/Little Caesar's/dsl, Chevron/dsl, Conoco, Mobil/dsl, Shell/dsl, TA/Sinclair/Black Bear Diner/dsl/scales/24hr/@, USA/Subway/dsl, Filiberto's, Wendy's, Budget Inn, Economy Inn, auto repair, Best Tire Pros, S Chevron/dsl, Tesla EVC, Calico's Rest., Carl's Jr, Frey's Mexican, AZ Inn, Motel 6, $General, city park, Ft Beale RV Park, Mohave Museum
46.5mm	Holy Moses Wash
44	AZ 66, Oatman Hwy, McConnico, to Rte 66, S Canyon West RV Camping(3mi), truckwash
40.5mm	Griffith Wash
37	Griffith Rd
35mm	Black Rock Wash
32mm	Walnut Creek
28	Old Trails Rd, N Flying J/dsl/24hr, tires
26	Proving Ground Rd
25	Alamo Rd, to Yucca, N USPO, S Pride TC/Subway/dsl/scales/24hr/showers
23mm	**both lanes, full facilities, litter barrels, vending, petwalk,**
21mm	Flat Top Wash
20	Santa Fe Ranch Rd
18.5mm	Illavar Wash
15mm	Buck Mtn Wash
13.5mm	Franconia Wash
13	Franconia Rd
9	AZ 95 S, to Lake Havasu City, Parker, London Br, S Chevron/Starbucks/dsl, Love's/Carl's Jr/Subway/dsl/scales/24hr, Pilot/Wendy's/dsl/scales/24hr, RV Fuel, Havasu RV Park, Prospectors RV Resort
4mm	weigh sta both lanes
2	Needle Mtn Rd
1	Topock Rd, to Bullhead City, Oatman
0mm	Arizona/California state line, Colorado River, Mountain/Pacific time zone

KINGMAN

NOTES

ARKANSAS

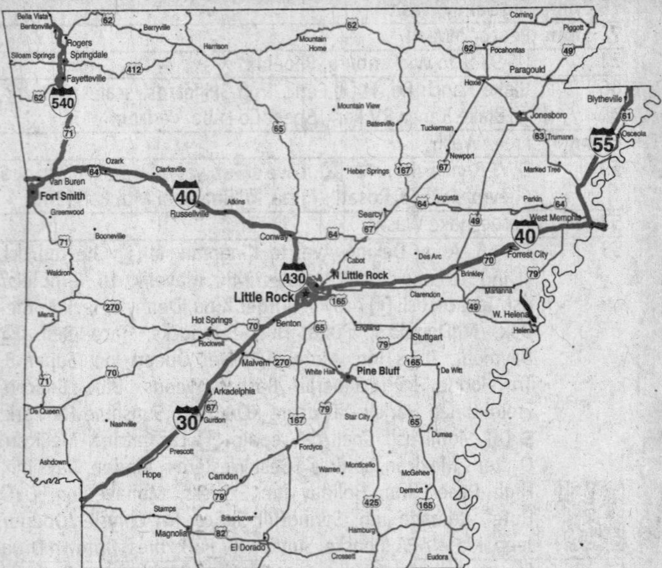

INTERSTATE 30

Exit #	Services
143.5mm	I-30 begins/ends on I-40, exit 153b
143b a	I-40, E to Memphis, W to Ft Smith
142	15th St, S Valero/dsl
141b	US 70, Broadway St, downtown, N Exxon, Starbucks, Burger King, Simmons Bank Arena, U-Haul, S Circle K, Shell/Super Stop/dsl, Magnolia Skillet, McDonald's, Popeyes, Taco Bell, Wendy's, Econolodge, Family$
141mm	Arkansas River
141a	AR 10, Cantrell Rd, Markham St(from wb), W to downtown
140	9th St, 6th St, downtown, N Shell, SuperStop, Pizza Hut, Holiday Inn, USPO, S SuperStop, Comfort Inn
139b	I-630, downtown
139a	AR 365, Roosevelt Rd, N Exxon, Sim's BBQ, AutoZone, O'Reilly Parts, S Shell, $Tree, Family$, Kroger
138b	I-530 S, US 167 S, US 65 S, to Pine Bluff
138a	I-440 E, to Memphis, S
135	W 65th St, N Exxon/dsl, Shell/dsl, Valero/dsl, Express Inn, S Magnuson Hotel
134	Scott Hamilton Dr, S Exxon/dsl, Best Value Inn, Red Roof Inn, Studio 6
133	Geyer Springs Rd, N Alon, Exxon, Mobil, Church's TX Chicken, Daily Donuts, Subway, S Citgo, Shell, Valero, Arby's, Burger King, El Herradero, KFC, Little Caesar's, McDonald's, Rally's, Sharks Fish, Shipley Donuts, Sonic, Starbucks, Taco Bell, Waffle House, Best Western, Days Inn, Red Roof Inn, Rest Inn, Family$, Goodyear/auto, Kroger/gas, Walgreens
132	US 70b, University Ave, N Circle K, RaceWay/dsl, SuperStop, Best Value Inn, NAPA, S Kum&Go/dsl, Phillips 66, O'Reilly Parts
131	McDaniel Dr, N U-Haul, S Economy Inn, Super 7 Inn, Crain RV Ctr
130	AR 338, Baseline Rd, Mabelvale, N Cimarron Inn, EconoLodge, S Murphy Express/dsl, Shell/dsl, Asian Buffet, McDonald's, Popeyes, Sonic, Taco Bueno, Wendy's, $Tree, Chevrolet, Crain RV Ctr, Home Depot, Pizza Hut, URGENT CARE, Walmart/Subway/EVC
129	I-430 N
128	Otter Creek Rd, Mabelvale West, N Love's/Hardee's/Subway/dsl/scales/24hr, QT/dsl, Tesla EVC, Chick-fil-A, Dave&Busters, Hooters, Saltgrass Steaks, Waldo's Chicken, Tru, AT&T, Bass Pro Shop, Cavender's, Harley Davidson, Little Rock Outlets/famous brands, S Exxon/dsl, Davids Burgers, Super 8, $General, Purcell Tire/auto
126	AR 111, County Line Rd, Alexander, N Shell/dsl, S Citgo, Cherokee RV Park/dump(4mi)
123	AR 183, Reynolds Rd, to Bryant, Bauxite, N Murphy USA/dsl, Shell, Arby's, Burger King, Casa Mexicana, Cracker Barrel, David's Burgers, Denny's, Dickey's BBQ, Firehouse Subs, IHOP, KFC, Papa John's, Pasta J's Italian, Popeyes, Subway, Ta Molly's, Waffle House, Whole Hog Cafe, Wingstop, Best Value Inn, Comfort Inn, Country Inn Suites, Econolodge, Hampton Inn, Home2 Suites, Hometown Hotel, La Quinta, $Tree, AT&T, AutoZone, CVS Drug, Take 5 Oil Change, URGENT CARE, vet, Walgreens, Walmart/gas, S Caseys/dsl, Exxon/dsl, Kum&Go/dsl/e85, Bryant Cafe, Chick-fil-A, Church's TX Chicken, Dunkin', Little Caesar's, Logan's Roadhouse, McDonald's, Mi Ranchito, Pizza Inn,
123	Continued Sonic, Taco Bell, Wendy's, Zaxby's, Super 8, $General, Food Giant, Jiffy Lube, Lowe's, O'Reilly Parts, USPO, vet
121	Alcoa Rd, N Pilot/Subway/dsl/scales/24hr/@, All Aboard Grill, Chicken Salad Chick, DQ, Freddy's, Hideaway Pizza, Jersey Mikes, McDonald's, Panda Express, Red Robin, Slim Chickens, Sonic, Taco Bell, Taco Bueno, Tacos 4Life, TX Roadhouse, Zaxby's, Chrysler/Dodge/Jeep, Discount Tire, Firestone/auto, Hobby Lobby, Infinity, Kroger/Starbucks/gas, NAPA, Nissan, PetSmart, TJ Maxx, S Buffalo Wild Wings, Chili's, McAlister's Deli, Moe's SW Grill, Sakura Japanese, Starbucks, Subway, Holiday Inn Express, AT&T, GNC, Kohl's, Old Navy, PetCo, Target, Verizon
118	Congo Rd, N Fairfield Inn, Relax Inn, Chevrolet, Williams Tire, S Kum&Go/dsl/e85, Burger King, Colton's Steaks, Popeyes, Taco Bell, Wendy's, Wood Grill, Eagle Suites, Advance Parts, Ford, Jayco RV, Kroger, RV City, USPO
117	US 64, AR 5, AR 35, N Shell, Olive Garden, Papa John's, Subway, Waffle House, Best Western, S Murphy USA/dsl, Shell, Valero, Arby's, Backyard Burger, Buffet City, Capt D's, Chicken Express, Colton's Steaks, KFC, La Hacienda Mexican, Little Caesar's, McDonald's, Pizza Hut, Rib Crib, Samurai Japanese, Sonic, Subway, Sumo Express, Taco Bell, Wendy's, Eagle Suites, $General, $Tree, Advance Parts, AutoZone, BigLots, H, Kroger/gas, O'Reilly Parts, Office Depot, URGENT CARE, USPO, Walgreens, Walmart/auto/gas
116	Sevier St, N Exxon, Mac's/dsl, Troutt Motel, S Alon/dsl, Hardee's, Capri Inn
114	US 67 S, Benton, S Valero/McDonald's/dsl
111	US 70 W, Hot Springs, N Valero, Cloud 9 RV Park(8mi), Oakhill RV Park(4mi), to Hot Springs NP
106	Old Military Rd, N Alon/JJ's Rest./dsl/scales/@, S JB'S RV Park
99	US 270 E, Malvern
98b a	US 270, Malvern, Hot Springs, N Valero/dsl, Super 8, S Circle K, Murphy USA/dsl, Phillips 66/dsl, Shell/dsl, Burger King, Cotija Mexican, Domino's, Great Wall Buffet, Larry's Pizza, McDonald's, Popeyes, Sonic, Subway, Taco Bell, Waffle House, Wendy's, Best Value Inn, Holiday Inn Express, Quality Inn, $Tree, AT&T, AutoZone, Chevrolet,

ALEXANDER

BAUXITE

BENTON

AR

CADDO VALLEY

INTERSTATE 30 Cont'd

98b a Continued
city park, H, O'Reilly Parts, Verizon, Walmart/gas

97 AR 84, AR 171, N Love's/Arbys/dsl/scales/24hr/@, Lake Catherine SP, RV camping

93mm **(both lanes exit left), full facilities, litter barrels, vending, petwalk,**

91 AR 84, Social Hill

83 AR 283, Friendship, S Exxon/dsl

78 AR 7, Caddo Valley, Days Inn, N Pilot/PJ Fresh/Dunkin/dsl/scales/24hr, Shell/dsl, Cracker Barrel, Flying Burger, Holiday Inn Express, Caddo Valley RV Park, DeGray SP, dsl repair, to Hot Springs NP, S Exxon/Subway/dsl, Valero, Fat Boys Cafe, McDonald's, Taco Bell, Waffle House, Baymont Inn, Best Value Inn, EconoLodge, Economy Inn, Hampton Inn, Motel 6, Quality Inn, Super 8, city park, Golden's Riverside RV Park

73 AR 8, AR 26, AR 51, Arkadelphia, N Phillips 66/dsl, Shell, Allen's BBQ, Chicken Express, Domino's, McDonald's, Taco Bell, Wendy's, $Tree, T-Mobile, to Crater of Diamond SP, Verizon, Walmart, S Exxon/dsl, Andy's Rest., Burger King, DQ, Dunkin, Great Wok, Hamburger Barn, Little Caesar's, Ranchito Mexican, Subway, Walk & Taco, Fairfield Inn, $General, Ace Hardware, AT&T, AutoZone, Brookshire's Foods, H, O'Reilly Parts, vet, Walgreens

69 AR 26 E, Gum Springs

63 AR 53, Gurdon, N South Fork Trkstp/Citgo/rest./dsl, Rodeway Inn, S Phillips 66/dsl, to White Oak Lake SP

PRESCOTT

56mm **both lanes, full facilities, litter barrels, vending, petwalk**

54 AR 51, Gurdon, Okolona

46 AR 19, Prescott, N Phillips 66/dsl/24hr, to Crater of Diamonds SP, S Love's/Hardee's/dsl/scales/24hr/@, Bojangles, Casa Carlos Mexican

44 AR 24, Prescott, N TA/Country Pride/Subway/Taco Bell/dsl/scales/24hr/@, S Norman's 44 Trkstp/rest/dsl/scales/@, Executive Inn & Suites, to S Ark U

36 AR 299, to Emmett

31 AR 29, Hope, N SuperStop/dsl, BigMac's BBQ, Relax Inn/Rest., Village Inn/RV park, st police, S Exxon/dsl, Valero/dsl, KFC, Best Value Inn, H

30 AR 4, Hope, N EVC, Murphy USA/dsl, Shell/dsl, Dos Loco Gringos, Best Western, Hampton Inn, Holiday Inn Express, Super 8, Millwood SP, Old Washington Hist SP, Verizon, Walmart/gas, S Exxon/Baskin-Robbins/Wendy's, Tesla EVC, Valero, Amigo Juan Mexican, Big Jake's BBQ, Burger King, Chicken Express, El Agave Mexican, McDonald's, Sheba's Rest., Subway, Taco Bell, Waffle House, Motel 6, $Tree, AT&T, AutoZone, Buick/Chevrolet/GMC, Bumper Parts, Ford, H, O'Reilly Parts, Super 1 Foods/gas, Walgreens

FULTON

26mm weigh sta both lanes

18 rd 355, Fulton, N Red River Trkstp/dsl

17mm Red River

12 US 67(from eb), Fulton

7mm **full facilities, info, litter barrels, petwalk, vending, Welcome Ctr eb**

7 AR 108, Mandeville, N Flying J/Denny's/Cinnabon/dsl/LP/24hr, Sunrise RV Park, truckwash

3 I-49, N to Ft Smith, S to Shreveport

2 Four States Fair Pkwy, Texarkana, N RoadRunner/dsl, Shell/Circle K/dsl, S Ferguson Fairpark, Greg Orr RV Ctr, Nick's RV Ctr

1 US 71, Jefferson Ave, Texarkana, N Best Western+, Comfort Suites, Hampton Inn, Holiday Inn, Holiday Inn Express, S Country Host Inn

0mm Arkansas/Texas State line

INTERSTATE 40

285mm Arkansas/Tennessee state line, Mississippi River

284mm weigh sta wb

281 AR 131, S to Mound City

280 Club Rd, Southland Dr, N Blu/dsl/LNG/24hr, Pilot/Wendy's/PJ Fresh/dsl/scales, S Flying J/Denny's/PJ Fresh/dsl/scales/LP/24hr, Love's/Subway/Godfather's/scales/dsl, Petro/Iron Skillet/dsl/24hr/@, KFC/Taco Bell, McDonald's, American Inn & Suites, Deluxe Inn, Express Inn, Super 8, Blue Beacon, SpeedCo Lube

279a Ingram Blvd, N Margaritas Mexican, Days Inn, Hallmarc Inn, HomeGate Inn, Red Roof Inn, Ford, Southland Casino, S Phillips 66, EconoLodge, Motel 6, New Hampshire Inn, Radisson, Ramada, Relax Inn, Rest Inn, Tru

279b I-55 S(from eb)

278 AR 77, 7th St, Missouri St, N **Welcome Ctr/, full facilities, litter barrels, petwalk**, Shell/dsl, S Exxon, MapCo, Shell, Shell/dsl, Applebee's, Burger King, Cracker Barrel, Domino's, Krystal, Lenny's Subs, Little Caesar's, McDonald's, Papa John's, Pizza Hut, Popeyes, Red Pier Rest., Subway, Taco Bell, Wendy's, Comfort Suites, Extend Suites, Holiday Inn Express, $Tree, Goodyear/auto, H, Kroger/dsl, Walgreens

277 I-55 N, to Jonesboro

276 AR 77, Rich Rd, to Missouri St(from eb, same as 278), S Exxon, Murphy Express/dsl, Shell, Shell/dsl, VF/dsl, Applebee's, Burger King, Chick-fil-A, Dixie Queen, Domino's, Fusion Buffet, Kelley's Chicken, Krystal, Lenny's Subs, Little Caesar's, McDonald's, Mi Pueblo Mexican, Papa John's, Popeyes, Rays BBQ, Shoney's, Subway, Taco Bell, Extend Suites, AT&T, Family$, Goodyear/auto, H, Kroger/dsl, Walgreens, Walmart

275 AR 118, Airport Rd, S Shell/DQ/dsl, city park, URGENT CARE

274mm weigh sta eb, parking area wb

271 AR 147, to Blue Lake, S Citgo, Exxon/Kwik Stop/dsl, Valero/dsl, Road Side BBQ, Horseshoe Lake, produce, tire repair

265 US 79, AR 218, to Hughes

260 AR 149, to Earle, N Citgo/Subway, Exxon/dsl, TA/Burger King/Taco Bell/dsl/scales/24hr/@, Relax Inn, S Citgo

256 AR 75, to Parkin, N to Parkin Archeological SP

FORREST CITY

247 AR 38 E, to Widener

245mm St Francis River

243mm **wb, full facilities, litter barrels, vending, petwalk,**

242 AR 284, Crowley's Ridge Rd, N H, to Village Creek SP

241b a AR 1, Forrest City, N Mobil/dsl, Shell/dsl, Don Jose Mexican, HoHo Chinese, Popeyes, Comfort Suites, Days Inn, Diamond Inn, Econolodge, Hampton Inn, Holiday Inn Express, Luxury Inn, Super 8, st police, S Exxon/dsl, Murphy USA/dsl, Phillips 66/dsl, Burger King, Domino's, Iguanas Mexican, KFC, McDonald's, Ole Sawmill Cafe, Pizza Hut, Sharks Seafood, Sonic, Subway, Taco Bell, Waffle House, Quality Inn, Red Roof Inn, $Tree, AT&T, Delta Ridge RV Park, O'Reilly Parts, Verizon, Walgreens, Walmart/gas/EVC

239 AR 1, to Wynne, Marianna

235mm **eb, full facilities, litter barrels, vending, petwalk,**

234mm L'Anguille River

233 AR 261, Palestine, N DK/Sbarro Pizza/dsl, Love's/Chester's/Subway/dsl/scales/24hr/@, Rest Inn, S Exxon/dsl, tire repair

221 AR 78, Wheatley, N dsl repair,

[gas] = gas [food] = food [lodging] = lodging [other] = other [Rs] = rest stop

AR

INTERSTATE 40 Cont'd

BRINKLEY

221 Continued
MapCo/Krispy Krunchy/dsl, Valero/Pitstop/diner/dsl

216 US 49, AR 17, Brinkley, N [gas] Exxon/dsl, ONE9/dsl, Phillips 66, Road Ranger/dsl, [food] KFC/Taco Bell, Los Piños Mexican, [lodging] Best Inn, Best Value, Brinkley RV Park, Days Inn, EconoLodge, Super8/RV Park, [other] dsl repair, S [gas] Exxon/Baskin-Robbins/dsl, Shell, Tesla EVC, Victory/dsl, [food] BBQ, McDonald's, New China, Pizza Hut, Sonic, Subway, Waffle House, [lodging] Motel 6, [other] $General, Bumper Parts, Family$, Food Giant, O'Reilly Parts

205mm Cache River

202 AR 33, to Biscoe

200mm White River

199mm **[Rs] both lanes, full [handicapped] facilities, [picnic], litter barrels, vending, no [phone]**

193 AR 11, to Hazen, N [gas] Exxon/dsl, S Love's/Chester's/Godfather's/Subway/dsl/scales/24hr/@, [food] El Amigo Mexican, [lodging] Super 8, Travel Inn

183 AR 13, Carlisle, S [gas] Exxon/Subway/dsl, Phillips 66/dsl, Valero/dsl, [food] Nick's BBQ, Sonic, [lodging] Days Inn, [other] $General

175 AR 31, Lonoke, N [gas] Phillips 66, Valero/dsl, [food] Burger King, Marachi Mexican, McDonald's, Waffle House, [lodging] Best Western, Days Inn, Economy Inn, Hampton Inn, Holiday Inn Express, [other] AT&T, Walmart, S [gas] Exxon/Subway, [food] KFC/Taco Bell, [lodging] Sonic, [other] $General, $Tree, O'Reilly Parts, vet

GALLOWAY

173 AR 89, Lonoke

169 AR 15, Remington Rd

165 Kerr Rd

161 AR 391, Galloway, N [gas] Love's/Chester's/Godfather's/dsl/scales/24hr, [other] Camping World RV Ctr, S [gas] IA-80 TruckOMat/dsl/scales, Petro/Iron Skillet/dsl/scales/24hr/@, Pilot/Subway/Pizza Hut/dsl/scales/24hr, [food] Burger King, [lodging] Galloway Inn, [other] Blue Beacon, Freightliner, Southern Tire Mart, SpeedCo

LITTLE ROCK AFB

159 I-440 W

157 AR 161, to US 70, S [gas] Hess, Mobil/dsl, Shell/dsl, [food] LA Fried Chicken, McDonald's, Sonic, Taco Bell, [lodging] Days Inn, EconoLodge, Quality Inn, Red Roof Inn, Regal Inn, Rest Inn, Super 8, [other] $General, Family$

156 Springhill Dr, N [gas] Caseys/dsl, Kum&Go/dsl, Murphy USA/dsl, [food] Arby's, Burger King, Cane's, Chick-fil-A, Cracker Barrel, Popeyes, Rally's, Rivera Italian, [lodging] Candlewood Suites, Fairfield Inn, Hilton Garden, Residence Inn, Tru, [other] [H], Lowe's, O'Reilly Parts, Walmart/gas

155 US 67 N, US 167, to Jacksonville (exits left from eb), Little Rock AFB, [food] IHOP, Waldo's Chicken, N [gas] Circle K/dsl, [food] BJ's Rest., Black Bear Diner, Buffalo Wild Wings, Cactus Jacks, Chili's, Chipotle, ChuckECheese, Chuy's TexMex, CiCi's Pizza, Corky's BBQ, David's Burgers, Fazoli's, Firehouse Subs, Five Guys, Franks, Freddy's, Golden Corral, Hideaway Pizza, Honey Baked, Hooters, Jason's Deli, Jersey Mikes, Jimmy John's, Kanpai Japanese, LongHorn Steaks, McDonald's, Mighty Crab, Olive Garden, Outback Steaks, Panera Bread, Purple Cow, Red Lobster, Sonic, Taco Bell, Taziki's Mediterranean, TGIFriday's, TX Roadhouse, US Pizza, Waffle House, Wendy's, Whole Hog Cafe, [lodging] Comfort Inn, Courtyard, Hampton Inn, La Quinta, Motel 6, Super 8, Wingate Inn, [other] $Tree, AutoZone, Barnes&Noble, Best Buy, BigLots, Buick/GMC, Chevrolet, Chrysler/Dodge/Jeep, Dick's, Dillard's, Discount Tire, Firestone/auto, Ford, Home Depot, Honda, [H], Hyundai, JC Penney, Kia, Kroger, Mazda, Michael's, Nissan, Office Depot, PetCo, PetSmart, Ross, Sam's Club/gas, Target, TJ Maxx, Toyota/Scion, URGENT CARE, Verizon, vet, VW, Walgreens

154 to Lakewood(from eb)

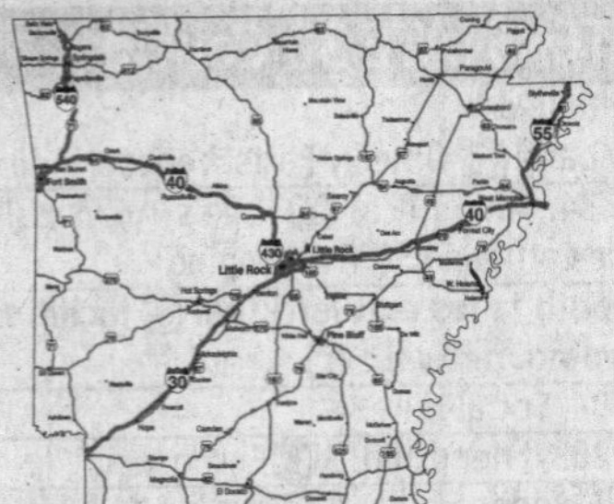

153b I-30 W, US 65 S, to Little Rock

153a AR 107 N, JFK Blvd, N [gas] Circle K, GS/dsl, Shell, [food] Schlotzsky's, [lodging] Hilltop Inn, [other] vet, S [gas] Exxon, Murphy Express/dsl, [food] Taco Bueno, [lodging] Baymont Inn, Best Western+, Country Inn & Suites, Motel 6, Quality Inn, Super Stay Inn, [other] USPO

LEVY

152 AR 365, AR 176, Camp Pike Rd, Levy, N [gas] Exxon, [food] Bamboo Hibachi, Blue Dolphin, Burger King, KFC, Little Caesar's McDonald's, Pizza Hut, Señor Tequila, Shark's Chicken, Sonic Subway, US Pizza, Waffle House, [other] $General, AutoZone Family$, Kroger/gas, O'Reilly Parts, S [gas] Shell, [food] Chicken King, [other] Family$, [H]

150 AR 176, Burns Park, Camp Robinson, S [other] camping

148 AR 100, Crystal Hill Rd, N [gas] Shell, S Exxon/dsl, Phillips 66 [other] KOA

147 I-430 S, to Texarkana

146 White Oak Crossing, to Maumelle

MAYFLOWER

142 AR 365, to Morgan, N [gas] QT/dsl, Shamrock, Valero/dsl, [lodging] Days Inn, [other] Bumper Parts, Trails End RV Park, S [gas] Kum&Go/dsl, Shell/dsl, [food] KFC, McDonald's, Razorbac Pizza, Smokeshack BBQ, Subway, Waffle House, [lodging] Best Value Inn, Holiday Inn Express, Quality Inn, [other] $Genera Autozone

135 AR 365, AR 89, Mayflower, N [gas] Hess/dsl, S Exxon/dsl, [food] Pizza Hut, Smachs Cafe, Sonic, Stoud's Diner, Subway, [other] D Mkt, Harps Foods

134mm truck parking both lanes

CONWAY

132 Baker-Wills Pkwy, S [gas] Shell, [food] Taylor's Made

129 US 65B, AR 286, Conway, N [food] David's Burgers, Denny Hideaway Pizza, Newk's, On the Border, Subway, Th Meltdown, TX Roadhouse, Walk-Ons Grill, [lodging] Courtyard, [other] $Tree, AT&T, BAM!, Buick/GMC, Discount Tire, Kia, Michael' Petco, Ross, Sam's Club/gas, S [gas] Caseys/dsl, Exxon/dsl, [other] Chevrolet, Chrysler/Dodge/Jeep, Honda, [H], to Toad Suck S Toyota/Scion, URGENT CARE

127 US 64, Conway, N [gas] Exxon/dsl, Gulf/dsl, Valero, [food] Arby' Blaze Pizza, Buffalo Wild Wings, Cane's, Chick-fil-A, Chili' Chipotle, Freddy's, Golden Corral, Jersey Mike's, Las Palma Mexican, Logan's Roadhouse, Mulan's Buffet, Olive Garde Outback Steaks, Panda Express, Pizza Hut, Popeyes, Soni Starbucks, Subway, TGIFriday's, Waffle House, [lodging] Be Western, Comfort Suites, Country Inn&Suites, Days In Hilton Garden, Home2 Suites, Motel 6, Simply Stay, [other] $General, AT&T, Belk, Best Buy, Dick's, Firestone/auto, For Goodyear/auto, Harley-Davidson, Home Depot, Hyunda Kohl's, Moix RV Ctr, NAPA, Nissan, O'Reilly Parts, Old Nav PetSmart, repair/transmissions, Staples, Target, TJ Max Verizon, vet, S [gas] Kum&Go, Shell/dsl, Tropical Smoothi Valero/dsl, [food] Andy's Frozen Custard, Bulgogi BBQ, Burg King, Colton's Steaks, LJ Silver, McDonald's, Rally's, Taco Be Tacos 4 Life, Taziki's Mediterranean, Wendy's, Whole H Cafe, [other] AutoZone, BigLots, CVS, Hobby Lobby, Jiffy Lub Kroger/gas, tire/auto repair, Walgreens

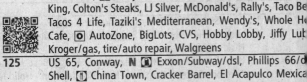

125 US 65, Conway, N [gas] Exxon/Subway/dsl, Phillips 66/d Shell, [food] China Town, Cracker Barrel, El Acapulco Mexica McDonald's, MktPlace Deli, Verona Italian, [lodging] Quality In

E INTERSTATE 40 Cont'd

CONWAY

125 Continued
$Tree, JC Penney, Office Depot, S Conoco, Mobil/dsl, Murphy USA/dsl, Sinclair, Burger King, Burgers, Pies & Fries, David's Burgers, Firehouse Subs, Fuji Steaks, IHOP, Los Potrillos Mexican, McAlister's Deli, Mighty Crab, Ol' Bart Rest., Sonic, Starbucks, Subway, The Purple Cow, Waffle House, Wendy's, ZAZA Pizza, Candlewood Suites, Comfort Inn, Eagle Suites, Fairfield Inn, Hampton Inn, Holiday Inn Express, La Quinta, Microtel, Super 8, Advance Parts, AT&T, H, Lowe's, tires, Walmart/auto/gas

124 AR 25 N, to Conway, S Alon/Hess/dsl, Kum&Go/dsl, Dominos, DQ, KFC, Popeyes, Sharks Chicken, H, vet

120mm Cadron Creek

117 to Menifee

112 AR 92, Plumerville, N Exxon/dsl, S Shell/dsl, $General, USPO

MORRILTON

108 AR 9, Morrilton, N Ford/Lincoln, S Casey's, Murphy USA, Shell/dsl, Valero, Arby's, Blue Diamond Cafe, Chopsticks Chinese, Colton's Steaks, Dominos, Elia's Mexican, McDonald's, Pizza Hut, Sonic, Subway, Taco Bell, Waffle House, Wendy's, Holiday Inn Express, Super 8, $General, $Tree, Ace Hardware, AutoZone, Chrysler/Dodge/Jeep, Harps, H, Jiffy Lube, NAPA, to Petit Jean SP(21mi), Verizon, vet, Walmart/gas

107 AR 95, Morrilton, N Sunoco/dsl, American Inn, Morrilton RV Park, S Love's/Godfathers Pizza/dsl/24hr, Morrilton Drive Inn, Yesterdays Rest., Morrilton Inn, Bumper Parts

101 Blackwell, N Blackwell TrkStp/Citgo/Chesters/dsl/scales/24hr

94 AR 105, Atkins, N Exxon/Subway/dsl, VP/McDonald's/dsl, El Parian Mexican, Sonic, $General, S Casey's/dsl, Cash Saver Foods

88 Pottsville, S $General, truck tire/repair

RUSSELLVILLE

84 US 64, AR 331, Russellville, N Flying J/Denny's/dsl/scales/LP/24hr, Shell/dsl, Ivys Cove RV Retreat, truck tire/repair/wash, S Phillips 66, Pilot/Subway/Wendy's/dsl/scales, Chick-fil-A, Hardee's, McDonald's, Mulan's Buffet, Sonic, Waffle House, Comfort Inn, Quality Inn, $Tree, Belk, Buick/Chevrolet/GMC, Chrysler/Dodge/Jeep, GNC, Hobby Lobby, Hyundai, JC Penney, Lowe's, Nissan, PetSmart, Ross, TJ Maxx, Toyota

83 AK 326, Weir Rd, S Chili's, Zaxby's, Phillips 66/dsl, Walmart Gas/dsl, Buffalo Wild Wings, DQ, McAlisters Deli, Popeyes, Starbucks, Steak'n Shake, Subway, Sumo, Taco Bell, Taco John's, Comfort Inn, $General, AutoZone, Firestone/auto, Ford/Lincoln, Mazda, NAPA, O'Reilly Parts, Verizon, Walmart/McDonald's

81 AR 7, Russellville, N CJ's Burgers, Courtyard, Motel 6, $General, Outdoor RV Ctr/Park, S Exxon/dsl, Phillips 66/dsl, Shell, Arby's, Burger King, Cagle's Mill Rest., Colton's Steaks, Cracker Barrel, Holiday Inn Express, IHOP, La Huerta Mexican, New China, Old Cafe, Subway, Waffle House, American Inn, Best Western, Clarion, Days Inn, Econolodge, Fairfield Inn, Hampton Inn, La Quinta, Super 8/EVC, H, RV camping, to Lake Dardanelle SP

80mm Dardanelle Reservoir

78 US 64, Russellville, S Darrell's Mkt, Fat Daddy's BBQ, H, Mission RV Park, to Lake Dardanelle SP

74 AR 333, London

72mm **full facilities, litter barrels, petwalk, wb, vending**

70mm overlook wb, litter barrels

68mm **full facilities, litter barrels, petwalk, eb, vending**

CLARKSVILLE

67 AR 315, Knoxville, S USPO

64 US 64, Clarksville, Lamar, S Valero/dsl, Lamar RV Park

58 AR 21, AR 103, Clarksville, N Casey's/dsl, Shell, Valero, DQ, KFC, La Chiquita Mexican, McDonald's, Pizza Hut, Subway, Taco Bell, Waffle House, Executive Inn, Quality Inn, Super 8, Buick/Chevrolet, DG Mkt, H, Verizon, S Murphy USA/dsl, Arby's, China Fun, South Park, Wendy's, $Tree, AT&T, Chrysler/Dodge/Jeep, Ford, Walmart/Subway/gas/EVC

57 AR 109, Clarksville, N Fuel Stop/dsl, Love's/dsl/scales/24hr/RV Hookup/@, Sonic, Subway, Harp's Mkt, S Shell/dsl, truckwash, TrueValue

55 US 64, AR 109, Clarksville, N Farmers Table Rest., Hardee's, Hampton Inn, Holiday Inn Express, Sunset Inn, S Valero/dsl, DG Mkt, st police

47 AR 164, Coal Hill

41 AR 186, Altus, S Wiederkehr Rest.(4mi), winery(4mi)

37 AR 219, Ozark, S Love's/Subway/dsl/scales/24hr/@, Valero/McDonald's/dsl, KFC/Taco Bell, Motel 6, H

36mm **both lanes, full facilities, , litter barrels, petwalk,**

DYER

35 AR 23, Ozark, N Valero/dsl/scales, S Oxford Inn, Ozark Inn, Aux Arc Park(5mi), H, to Mt Magazine SP(20 mi)

24 AR 215, Mulberry, S to Vine Prairie Park

20 Dyer, N Short Stop/dsl, S Phillips 66/dsl, Valero/dsl, Creekside Inn, $General

13 US 71 N, to Fayetteville, N Shell, Sunoco/dsl, Burger King, China Fun, Cracker Barrel, Domino's, KFC, La Fiesta Mexican, Subway, Taco Bell, Motel 6, Quality Inn, $General, Crabtree RV Ctr/Park, O'Reilly Parts, S Murphy USA/dsl, Valero/dsl, Workman's, Braum's, Geno's Pizza, McDonald's, Pizza Hut, Smiths Donuts, Sonic, The Pizza Place, Days Inn, $Tree, AT&T, Coleman Drug, Harps Foods, Walgreens, Walmart

12 I-49 N, to Fayetteville

9mm weigh sta both lanes

7 I-540 S, US 71 S, to Ft Smith, Van Buren

5 AR 59, Van Buren, N Citgo/dsl, Murphy USA/dsl, VP Fuels, Arby's, Burger King, Chick-fil-A, Chili's, Domino's, Firehouse Subs, Freddy's, Golden Wok, La Fiesta Mexican, Little Caesar's, McDonald's, Starbucks, Tropical Smoothie, Zaxby's, Best Western, Hampton Inn, $Tree, Advance Parts, ALDI, AutoZone, CVS Drug, Kenworth, Lowe's, O'Reilly Parts, USPO, Verizon, Walmart/Subway/gas, S Casey's/dsl, Conoco/dsl, Braum's, Colton's Steaks, Frank's Italian, Geno's Pizza, KFC/Taco Bell, La Fresas Mexican, Pizza Hut, Popeyes, Sonic, Subway, Waffle House, Wendy's, Whataburger, Comfort Inn, Holiday Inn Express, Super 8, Grizzle Tire, Harps Foods, Overland RV Park, truckwash, vet, Walgreens

3 Lee Creek Rd, N Sunoco/dsl, Park Ridge Camping

2.5mm **Welcome Ctr eb, full facilities, info, , , litter barrels, vending, petwalk**

1 to Ft Smith(from wb), Dora

0mm Arkansas/Oklahoma state line

N INTERSTATE 49 (Fayetteville)

BENTONVILLE

106mm Arkansas/Missouri state line

104 Highlands Blvd

102 AR 72, Gravette

97 AR 72, Centerton, E Hiwasse Store/dsl, Hiwasse Diner

93 AR 71, Bella Vista, Bentonville

88b a AR 72, E Central Ave, Bentonville, E Casey's, River Grille, Comfort Inn, Courtyard, W Kum&Go/dsl, Smokin' Joe's Ribs, Orchards Park, Walmart Visitors Ctr

87 8th St, Bentonville

86 US 62, AR 102, Bentonville, E Muse Burgers,

AR

INTERSTATE 49 (Fayetteville) Cont'd

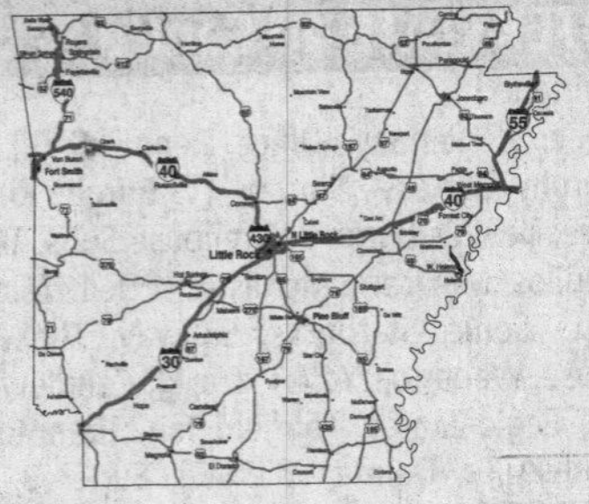

BENTONVILLE

86 Continued
Slim Chickens, Home2 Suites, TownePlace Suites, Pea Ridge NMP, Sam's Club/gas, URGENT CARE, Walmart Mkt, **W** Arby's, Dunkin', McDonald's, Sonic, Subway, Taco Bell, The Buttered Biscuit, Extended Stay

85 US 71B, AR 12, Bentonville, **E** Abuelo's, Applebee's, Arby's, Boar's Nest, Bossman Grill, Cane's, CAVA, Chick-fil-A, Chili's, Colton's Steaks, Freddy's Burgers, IHOP, JJ's Grill, McDonald's, Napoli's Italian, On-the-Border, Outback Steaks, Red Robin, Rick's Café, Sonic, Starbucks, Tokyo House, Affordable Suites, Candlewood Suites, Country Inn&Suites, Fairfield Inn, Hampton Inn, Homewood Suites, Hyatt Place, Residence Inn, AT&T, Barnes&Noble, Belk, Firestone/auto, Kohl's, Lowe's, Office Depot, PetCo, Ross, Staples, to Prairie Creek RA, Verizon, **W** Kum&Go/dsl, Murphy USA/dsl, Shell, Azul Tequila Mexican, Braum's, Buffalo Wild Wings, Chipotle, Cracker Barrel, Denny's, DQ, Firehouse Subs, First Watch, HoneyBaked Ham, Jonny Brusco's Pizza, Krispy Kreme, Lenny's Subs, Lin's Garden, McAlister's Deli, Panera Bread, Shogun Japanese, Smashburger, Starbucks, Subway, Taziki's Mediterranean Cafe, Village Inn, Waffle House, Zaxby's, Avid Hotel, Best Western+, Comfort Suites, Days Inn, DoubleTree Hotel, EconoLodge, Element Westin/EVC, Hilton Garden, Holiday Inn Express, La Quinta, Microtel, Quality Inn, Sheraton, SpringHill Suites, Super 8, BMW, Buick/GMC, Cadillac, Chevrolet, Christian Bros Auto, Chrysler/Dodge/Jeep, Discount Tire, Honda, H, Hyundai, Kia, Mazda, Mercedes, Nissan, Toyota, URGENT CARE

83 AR 94 E, Pinnacle Hills Pkway, **E** Phillips 66, After 5 Grill, Bariola's Pizza, ChuckECheese, Culver's, Dickey's BBQ, Einstein Bros., Firehouse Subs, Five Guys, Jimmy John's, Mojitos Mexican, Olive Garden, Panda Express, Qdoba, Red Lobster, Slim Chickens, Steak'n Shake, Taco Bell, TCBY, Courtyard, AT&T, Home Depot, H, to Horse Shoe Bend Park, URGENT CARE, Walgreens, **W** Bonefish Grill, Coldstone, Crabby's Seafood Grill, Domino's, First Watch, Grub's Grille, Ruth's Chris Steaks, Theo's, Tropical Smoothie, Aloft Hotel, Embassy Suites, Holiday Inn, Staybridge Suites

82 Promenade Blvd, **E** Fish City Grill, Longhorn Steaks, Mimi's Cafe, PF Chang's, Twin Peaks, Courtyard, Bass Pro Shops, Best Buy, Dillard's, Fresh Mkt, GNC, Gordman's, H, JC Penney, Old Navy, PetSmart, Target, TJMaxx, Verizon, **W** Chick-fil-A, Chuy's Mexican, Newk's Eatery, Pei Wei, Tacos 4 Life, Walmart Mkt/dsl

81 Pleasant Grove Rd, **E** Boss Man Tacos, Burger King, Chick-fil-A, China Cafe, Golden Corral, Gusano's Pizzaria, McDonald's, Moe's SW, Old Chicago, Papa Murphy's, Popeyes, Smoothie King, Starbucks, Subway, TX Roadhouse, Whataburger, Zaxby's, Burlington, Cavender's, Discount Tire, Duluth Trading, Firestone/auto, Ross, Valvoline Oil Change, Walgreens, Walmart/gas/EVC, **W** Casey's/dsl

78 AR 264, Lowell, Cave Sprgs, Rogers, **E** Kum&Go/dsl, Arby's, auto repair, Domino's, DQ, McDonald's, Sonic, Starbucks, Subway, Taco Bell, Tater's Grill, Super 8, $General, Camping World RV Ctr, **W** Kum&Go/dsl, Phillips 66/dsl/scales, Tesla EVC, Ozark Mtn Grill, Harps Foods

77 AR 612

76 Wagon Wheel Rd, **E** Shell/dsl, Kenworth/Volvo Trucks, to Hickory Creek Park

73 Elm Springs Rd, **E** Kum&Go/dsl, Azul Mexican, Boss Man Tacos, Eureka Pizza, Patrick's Burgers, Taco Bell, Whataburger, Woodspring Suites, Chevrolet, **W** Shell/dsl, Firehouse, McDonald's, MJ Pizzaria, Panda Express, Starbucks, Wienerschnitzel, H, URGENT CARE,

FAYETTEVILLE

73 Continued
Walmart/auto/gas

72mm weigh sta nb

72 US 412, Springdale, Siloam Springs, **E** Citgo/dsl, Kum&Go/dsl, Phillips 66, Angus Jack's Burgers, Applebee's, Blu Fin Sushi, Braum's, Denny's, Foghorn's Rest., Hawaiian Bros Grill, Little Caesar's, McDonald's, Mkt Place Rest., Sonic, Starbucks, Subway, Sunset Grill, Taco Bell, Waffle House, Wendy's, DoubleTree Hotel, Extended Stay America, Fairfield Inn, Hampton Inn, Holiday Inn, Home2 Suites, La Quinta, Quality Inn, Residence Inn, Royal Inn, Sleep Inn, Super 8, Big O Tire, Harp's Mkt, Kenworth/Volvo Trucks, Lowe's, O'Reilly Parts, Office Depot, URGENT CARE, Verizon, Walgreens, **W** Casey's/dsl, Murphy USA/dsl, Pilot/PJ Fresh/dsl/scales/24hr, Andy's Foyo, Arby's Buffalo Wild Wings, Burger King, Buttered Biscuit, Chick-filA Cracker Barrel, Freddy's, Gusano's Pizza, Jersey Mikes, La Palamas Mexican, McDonald's, Popeyes, RibCrib, Slim Chickens, Subway, Taco Bell, Tacos 4 Life, Tropical Smoothie Buick/GMC, Harp's Mkt/dsl, Hobby Lobby, Sam's Club gas

71mm weigh sta sb

70 Don Tyson Pkwy, **E** Casey's/dsl, Walmart Mkt/gas

69 Johnson Mill Blvd, Johnson, **E** Circle K, Pizzeria Ruby Inn at the Mill, TownePlace Suites

67 US 71B, Fayetteville, **E** Cane's Chicken, CAVA, Chilis Chipotle, Chuys Mexican, First Watch, Logan's Roadhouse Longhorn Steakhouse, Olive Garden, Wood Stone Pizza, Courtyard, Hyatt Place, La Quinta, Motel 6, Sleep Inn, Home Depot, H, Kohls, Target, Walmart/auto, Whole Foods

66 AR 112, Garland Ave, **E** Phillips 66/dsl, **W** Acura Chevrolet, Honda, Hyundai, Sam's Club/dsl, Toyota

65 Porter Rd, **W** Casey's/dsl, Subaru

64 AR 16 W, AR 112 E, Wedington Dr, **E** Casey's, **W** Murph Express/dsl, Phillips 66/McDonald's/dsl, AT&T, C Burgers, Dickey's BBQ, Dominos, El Matador, Freddy Burgers, Gusano's Pizza, Hunan Manor, IHOP, JJ's Gri Marco's Pizza, Sassy's BBQ, Slim Chickens, Sonic, Starbuck Subway, Taco Bell, Thai Spice, Walk-On's Grill, avid hote Comfort Inn, Hilton Garden, Holiday Inn Express, Homewo Suites, Harp's Foods/gas, Walmart Mkt

FARMINGTON

62 US 62, AR 180, Farmington, **E** Kum&Go, Phillips 66, She dsl, Andy's Custard, Arby's, Boss Man Tacos, Braum Burger King, Cane's, Chick-fil-A, Ginger Asian, KFC, Mang Mexican, McDonald's, Mexico Viejo, Morano's Grill, Oha Poke, Panda Express, Popeyes, Senior Munchies, Sli Chickens, Sonic, Starbucks, Subway, Taco Bell, Torchy's Tac Tropical Smoothie, Waffle House, Wendy's, Whataburg Wingstop, Zaxby's, Best Western, Candlewood Suit Quality Inn, Bumper Parts, to U of AR, **W** Circle Murphy USA/dsl, El Charro, Firehouse Subs, Jimmy's E Papa Murphy's, Pavilion Buffet, Serrano's, Baymont I Days Inn, Extended Stay, Hampton Inn, Regency 7 Mot Super 8, $Tree, ALDI, AT&T, AutoZone, Big O Tire, Lowe Verizon, Walgreens, Walmart/auto

61 US 71(from sb), to Boston Mtn Scenic Lp

CHESTER

INTERSTATE 49 (Fayetteville) Cont'd

Exit #	Services
60	AR 112, AR 265, Razorback Rd, E [lodging] Staybridge Suites, [other] Southgate RV Park
58	Greenland, W [gas] Phillips 66/McDonalds/dsl/scales/24hr, [food] Sonic, [other] Hog Valley RV Resort
53	AR 170, West Fork, E [gas] Harp's Mkt/dsl, [other] Winn Creek RV Resort(4mi)
45	AR 74, Winslow, W [other] to Devils Den SP
41mm	Bobby Hopper Tunnel
34	AR 282, to US 71, Chester, W [other] USPO
29	AR 282, to US 71, Mountainburg, E [other] $General, to Lake Ft Smith SP
24	AR 282, to US 71, Rudy, E [gas] Love's/Chester's/Subway/dsl/scales/24hr/@, Phillips 66/Rest./dsl, [other] Boston Mtns Scenic Lp, KOA
21	Collum Ln
20	to I-40(from sb). I-49 N begins/ends on I-40, exit 12.

INTERSTATE 49 (Texarkana)

Exit #	Services
42	I-49(Texarkana) begins/ends on US 59.
41	Sanderson Ln
37b a	I-30, E to Little Rock, W to Dallas
35	Arkansas Blvd, Four States Pkwy, E [other] [other], fairgrounds, W [food] Pelican Seafood, [other] $General
32	US 82, 19th St, 9th St, E [gas] Shell/dsl, [food] Subway, [other] CashSaver/gas
31	AR 196, Genoa Rd
29b a	US 71, Texarkana, US 59, to Houston, W [gas] Shell/dsl
26	AR 237
24	Rd 10, Ferguson
18	N Fouke Rd
16	US 71, Fouke
6	Rd 197, Spruell Rd
4	US 71, Doddridge
0mm	Arkansas/Louisiana state line

YARBRO

INTERSTATE 55

Exit #	Services
72mm	Arkansas/Missouri state line
72	State Line Rd, weigh sta sb
71	AR 150, Yarbro
68mm	Welcome Ctr sb, **full** [handicapped] **facilities, litter barrels, petwalk,** [phone], [picnic]
67	AR 18, Blytheville, E [gas] Mobil/dsl, Murphy Express/dsl, [food] Burger King, Hardee's, Las Brisas Mexican, Wendy's, Zaxby's, [lodging] Best Value Inn, Days Inn/RV park, [other] Chrysler/Dodge/Jeep, Lowe's, Verizon, Walmart/Subway/gas, W [gas] Citgo/dsl, Phillips 66/dsl, Shell, [food] $Tree, GreatWall Chinese, Grecian Steaks, Little Caesar's, McDonald's, Olympia Steaks, Perkins, Pizza Hut, Pizza Inn, Sonic, Subway, Taco Bell, Wendy's, [lodging] Comfort Inn, Fairview Suites, Hampton Inn, Holiday Inn, Quality Inn, Super 8, [other] $General, AT&T, AutoZone, Bumper Parts, Ford/Nissan, [H]
63	US 61, to Blytheville, E [gas] Love's/Bojangles/Godfather's/dsl/scales/24hr/@, [other] Shearins RV Park(2mi), W [gas] Dodge's Store/dsl, My Mkt/dsl, [lodging] Deerfield Inn, Relax Inn, [other] [H], Willow RV Park
57	AR 148, Burdette, E [other] NE AR Coll
53	AR 158, Victoria, Luxora
48	AR 140, to Osceola, E [gas] Exxon/Chesters/dsl, Shell/Baskin-Robbins/dsl, [food] Cielito Lindo Mexican, Huddle House, [lodging] Days Inn, Deerfield Inn, Roadside Inn, [other] [H]
45mm	truck parking nb, litter barrels
44	AR 181, Keiser
41	AR 14, Marie, E [other] to Hampson SP/museum
36	AR 181, to Wilson, Bassett

JOINER

Exit #	Services
35mm	truck parking sb, litter barrels
34	AR 118, Joiner
23b a	US 63, AR 77, to Marked Tree, Jonesboro, ASU, E [gas] BP/pizza
21	AR 42, Turrell, E [other] to Wapanocca NWR, W [gas] Valero/dsl/scales/24hr
17	AR 50, to Jericho
14	rd 4, to Jericho, E [gas] Citgo/dsl/scales/24hr, W [other] Chevrolet, KOA
10	US 64 W, Marion, E [gas] Shell/McDonald's, Shell/Subway/scales, [food] Arby's, Domino's, Sonic, Tacker's, Tops BBQ, Wendy's, [lodging] Comfort Inn, Hallmarc Inn, [other] $General, Family$, Mkt Place Foods, O'Reilly, USPO, W [gas] Exxon/dsl, Shamrock, [food] Andrey Grill, Burger King, Colton's Steaks, Mi Pueblo, Seafood Shack, Zaxby's, [lodging] Best Western, Dreamland Inn, Fairfield Inn, Hampton Inn, Journey Inn, [other] AutoZone, Parkin SP
9mm	truck parking nb, weigh sta sb
8	I-40 W, to Little Rock. I-55 and I-40 merge for 3mi. See I-40 AR, exits 278-279b.
5	(279 a from I-40) Ingram Blvd, E [lodging] Days Inn, Hallmarc Inn, Homegate Inn, Red Roof Inn, [other] Ford, Southland Racetrack, W [gas] Phillips 66/dsl, [lodging] EconoLodge, Hampshire Inn, Motel 6, Radisson Hotel, Ramada, Relax Inn, Rest Inn, Tru
4	King Dr, Southland Dr, E [gas] Flying J/Denny's/dsl/LP/scales/RV dump, LNG, Love's/Subway/dsl/scales/@, Petro/Iron Skillet/rest./dsl/24hr/@, Pilot/Subway/Wendy's/dsl/scales/24hr, Shell/dsl, [food] KFC/Taco Bell, McDonald's, [lodging] American Inn, Deluxe Inn, Express Inn, Super 8, [other] Blue Beacon, SpeedCo Lube, W [lodging] Sunset Inn
3b a	US 70, Broadway Blvd, AR 131, Mound City Rd(exits left from nb), W [lodging] Budget Inn
2mm	weigh sta nb
1	Bridgeport Rd
0mm	Arkansas/Tennessee state line, Mississippi River

MAUMELLE

INTERSTATE 430 (Little Rock)

Exit #	Services
13b a	I-40. I-430 begins/ends on I-40, exit 147.
12	AR 100, Maumelle, E [food] DQ, W [gas] Kum&Go/dsl/e85, Mobil, [other] auto repair, NAPA, O'Reilly Parts, vet
10mm	Arkansas River
9	AR 10, Cantrell Rd, W [other] to Maumelle Park, to Pinnacle Mtn SP
8	Rodney Parham Rd, E [gas] Hungry Howie's, Kroger/dsl, Shell, Super Stop, [food] Arby's, Baskin-Robbins, Dickey's BBQ, Dunkin', McDonald's, Sonic, Taco Bell, Terri Lynn's BBQ, Tropical Smoothie Cafe, US Pizza, [lodging] Eagle Suites, [other] $General, Advance Parts, AutoZone, Kroger, Midas, vet, Walgreens, W [gas] Exxon, [food] Burger King, Domino's, Gusano's Pizza, Homer's Kitchen, Jess's Chicken, Marco's Pizza, Olive Garden, Starbucks, Subway, The Pantry, Wendy's, [lodging] The Burgundy Hotel, [other] Cadillac, Firestone/auto, GNC, Jiffy Lube, Take 5 Oil Change, Volvo
6b	Kanis Rd, Markham St, to downtown, E [gas] Shell, [food] Subway, [lodging] Candlewood Suites, Motel 6, Quality Inn, SpringHill Suites, [other] Burlington Coats, Ross, W [gas] Exxon/dsl, [food] Applebee's, Back Yard Burgers, Bobby's Country Cookin', Butcher Shop Steaks, Chick-fil-A, Chilis, Corky's BBQ, David's Burgers, Denny's, Fazoli's, Freddy's Burgers, IHOP, Jason's Deli, KFC, Kobe Japanese, Lenny's Subs, McAlister's Deli, McDonald's, Mexico Cafe, On-the-Border, Outback Steaks, Popeyes, Purple Cow, Shotgun Dan's Pizza, Slim Chickens, Sonic, Taco Bell, The Mighty Crab, Tokyo House, Twin Peaks, Waffle House, Waffle House, Wendy's, Whole Foods Mkt, [lodging] Best Western, Courtyard, Embassy Suites, Extended Stay America, Holiday Inn, Marriott, Relax Inn, [other] $Tree, AutoZone, Barnes&Noble, Best Buy, Michael's, PetSmart, Sam's Club/gas, Trader Joes, Verizon, Walmart

= gas = food = lodging = other = rest stop

INTERSTATE 430 (Little Rock) Cont'd

Exit #	Services
6a	I-630, E to Little Rock, E
5	Kanis Rd, Shackleford Rd, E Arby's, BJ's Rest., ChuckECheese, Cracker Barrel, Longhorn Steaks, Main Event, Panda Garden, Samurai Steaks, Tacos 4 Life, TX Roadhouse, Comfort Suites, Home2 Suites, La Quinta, Towneplace Suites, JC Penney, Walmart, W Shell, Beef-A-Roo, Cheba Hut, Panera Bread, Starbucks, Zaxby's, Hampton Inn, Hilton Garden, MainStay Suites, Residence Inn, Wingate Inn, , Lexus
4	AR 300, Col Glenn Rd, E Circle K, American Pie Pizza, Domino's, Popeyes, Subway, Taco Bell, Wendy's, Extended Stay, Holiday Inn Express, Toyota, W Valero/Burger King/dsl, Sonic, Starbucks, BMW, Chrysler/Dodge/Jeep, Ford, Honda, Hyundai, Kia, Land Rover, Mazda, Mercedes, Nissan, Subaru, VW
1	AR 5, Stagecoach Rd, W Casey's/dsl, Exxon, Phillips 66, Domino's, Papa John's, Subway, $General, AutoZone, Walgreens
0mm	I-430 begins/ends on I-30, exit 129.

INTERSTATE 440 (Little Rock)

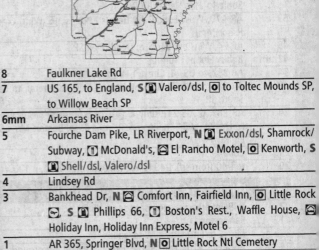

Exit #	Services
11	I-440 begins/ends on I-40, exit 159.
10	US 70, W Peterbilt
8	Faulkner Lake Rd
7	US 165, to England, S Valero/dsl, to Toltec Mounds SP, to Willow Beach SP
6mm	Arkansas River
5	Fourche Dam Pike, LR Riverport, N Exxon/dsl, Shamrock/Subway, McDonald's, El Rancho Motel, Kenworth, S Shell/dsl, Valero/dsl
4	Lindsey Rd
3	Bankhead Dr, N Comfort Inn, Fairfield Inn, Little Rock , S Phillips 66, Boston's Rest., Waffle House, Holiday Inn, Holiday Inn Express, Motel 6
1	AR 365, Springer Blvd, N Little Rock Ntl Cemetery
0mm	I-440 begins/ends on I-30, exit 138.

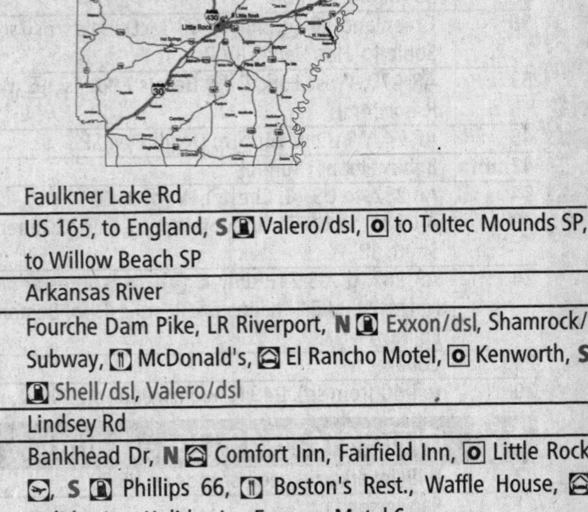

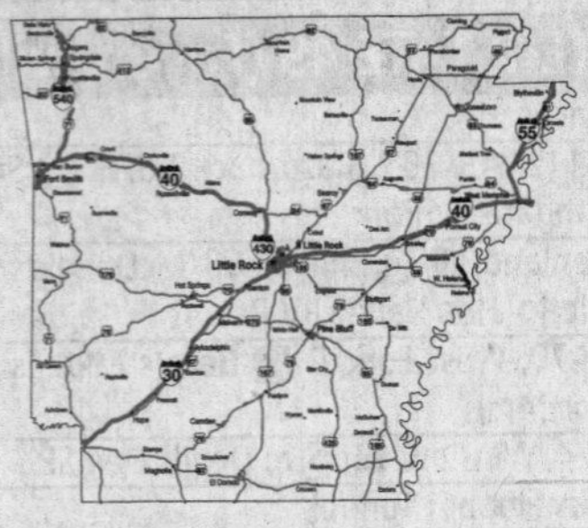

NOTES

CA

CALIFORNIA

INTERSTATE 5

HILT

CENTRAL YREKA

CENTRAL MT SHASTA

Exit #	Services
797mm	California/Oregon state line
796	Hilt
793	Bailey Hill Rd
791mm	inspection sta sb
790	Hornbrook Hwy, Ditch Creek Rd
789	A28, to Hornbrook, Henley, **E** Chevron/dsl/LP, Blue Heron RV Park/rest., to Iron Gate RA, USPO
786	CA 96, Klamath River Hwy, **wb, full facilities, info, , litter barrels, petwalk**
782mm	Anderson Summit, elevation 3067
780mm	no services
779mm	Shasta River
776	Yreka, Montague, **E** Holiday Inn Express, Yreka RV Park, **W** Puerto Vallarta, Mtn View Inn, Super 8, $General, Grocery Outlet
775	Miner St, Central Yreka, **W** 76/dsl, Chevron/dsl, Valero, Casa Ramo's Mexican, Gold Rush Burgers, RoundTable Pizza, Subway, Best Western, Budget Inn, EconoLodge, Jefferson Inn, Klamath Lodge, Relax Inn, Yreka Motel, Carquest, Dunn Automotive, G&G Hardware, museum, RiteAid, USPO
773	CA 3, to Ft Jones, Etna, **E** Les Schwab, tires, Waiiaka RV Park, **W** Chevron, Valero/dsl, Valero/dsl, Arby's, BlackBear Diner, Carl's Jr, Jefferson's Roadhouse, KFC, McDonald's, Starbucks, Taco Bell, Baymont Inn, Comfort Inn/Tesla EVC, Motel 6, $Tree, AutoZone, CHP, Ford, O'Reilly Parts, Raley's Foods, T-Mobile, Verizon, Walmart
770	Shamrock Rd, Easy St, **W** Fuel 24/7/dsl
766	A12, to Gazelle, Grenada, **E** Shell/dsl, **W** Chevron/dsl
759	Louie Rd
753	Weed Airport Rd, both lanes, full facilities, , litter barrels, , petwalk
751	Stewart Springs Rd, Edgewood
748	to US 97, to Klamath Falls, Weed, **E** Chevron, Spirit/dsl, Valero/dsl, Ellie's Cafe, Pizza Factory, Subway, Hi-Lo Motel/rest., Motel 6, Townhouse Motel, $General, auto repair, golf, NAPA, Ray's Foods, RV camping
747	same as 748, Central Weed, **W** Coll of Siskiyous
745	S Weed Blvd, **E** Chevron/dsl, Pilot/Subway/dsl/scales/24hr, Valero/dsl, McDonald's, Starbucks, Taco Bell, Comfort Inn, Sis-Q Inn, Friendly RV Park, Grocery Outlet
743	Summit Dr, Truck Village Dr
742mm	Black Butte Summit, elevation 3912
741	Abrams Lake Rd, **W** Abrams Lake RV Park
740	Mt Shasta City, **E** Pacific Pride/dsl/LP, Cold Creek Inn, , tires, vet
738	Central Mt Shasta, **E** 76/dsl, Chevron/dsl, Valero/dsl/LP, BlackBear Diner, Burger King, Starbucks, Subway, Best Western/Treehouse Rest., Mt Shasta Inn, Best Hardware, Carquest, CVS Drug, NAPA, O'Reilly Parts, Ray's Foods, RiteAid, USPO, visitors info, **W** Lake Siskiyou RV Park, Mt Shasta Resort/rest.
737	same as 738, from nb, Mt Shasta City, **E** Casa Ramos, La Perla Mexican, Lily's Rest., Alpine Lodge, Choice Inn, Evergreen Lodge, Shasta Inn, Strawberry Valley Inn, Swiss Holiday Lodge, McCloud RV Park
736	CA 89, to McCloud, to Reno, **E** Swiss Holiday Lodge
735mm	weigh sta sb
734	Mott Rd, to Dunsmuir, **E**
732	Dunsmuir Ave, Siskiyou Ave, **E** Penny's Diner,

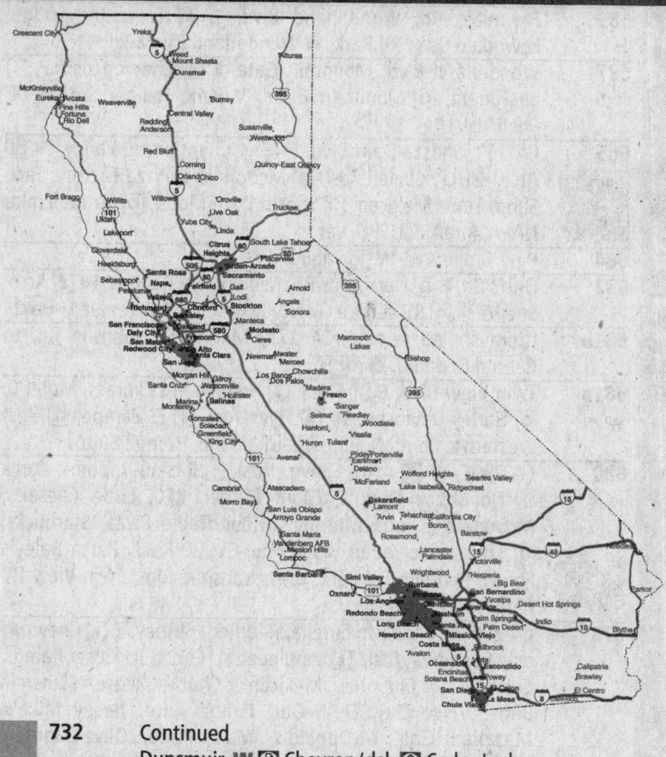

CASTELLA

Exit #	Services
732	Continued Dunsmuir, **W** Chevron/dsl, Cedar Lodge
730	Central Dunsmuir, **E** Burger Barn, Dunsmuir Brewery Rest., Pizza Factory, Dunsmuir Inn, Hotel Dunsmuir/Rest, $General, Dunsmuir Mkt, True Value, USPO, **W** Chevron/dsl/LP, Sten's Burger Strand, YAKS on the 5, Cave Springs Motel, city park
729	(from nb), Dunsmuir, **E** Valero/dsl/LP, Dunsmuir Lodge
728	Crag View Dr, Dunsmuir, Railroad Park Rd, **W** Railroad Park Motel/RV Park
727	Crag View Dr(from nb), **E** Cedar Pines RV Resort
726	Soda Creek Rd, to Pacific Crest Trail
724	Castella, **W** Chevron/dsl, Castle Crags SP, USPO
723mm	vista point nb
723	Sweetbrier Ave
721	Conant Rd
720	Flume Creek Rd
718	Sims Rd, **E** Sims Flat Campground, **W** Best in the West
714	Gibson Rd
712	Pollard Flat
710	Slate Creek Rd, La Moine
707	Delta Rd, Dog Creek Rd, to Vollmers
705mm	sb, full facilities, , litter barrels,
704	Riverview Dr, **E** Klondike Diner, Lake Shasta Lodge
702	Antlers Rd, Lakeshore Dr, to Lakehead, **E** Chevron/Subway/dsl, Lakehead Camping, Neu Lodge Motel, USPO, **W** Shell, Texaco/dsl, Bass Hole Rest./EVC, Lakeshore Mkt, Shasta Lake Motel/RV, Villa RV Park
698	Salt Creek Rd, Gilman Rd, **E** Lake Shasta RV Park, **W** Salt Creek Resort/RV Park, Trail In RV Park
695	Shasta Caverns Rd, to O'Brien, **E** camping/hiking, to Lake Shasta RA
694mm	**full facilities, litter barrels, petwalk, , , nb**
693	Packers Bay Rd(from sb)
692	Turntable Bay Rd
690	Bridge Bay Rd, **W** Huff's at Bridge Bay Rest.,

= gas = food = lodging = other = rest stop

CA

INTERSTATE 5 Cont'd

MOUNTAIN GATE

690 Continued
Bridge Bay Hotel

689 Fawndale Rd, Wonderland Blvd, E Fawndale Lodge, Fawndale Oaks RV Park, W Wonderland RV Park

687 Wonderland Blvd, Mountain Gate, E Chevron/dsl/LP, La Fogata, Mountain Gate RV Park, Ranger Sta, W Shell/dsl/LP

685 CA 151, Shasta Dam Blvd, Project City, Central Valley, W Arco/dsl/LP, Circle K/dsl, McDonald's, Pizza Factory, Taco Shop, Tinos Mexican, Shasta Dam Motel, farmers mkt, NAPA, RiteAid, USPO, vet

684 Pine Grove Ave, W Valero/dsl/LP

682 Oasis Rd, E Harrison's RV, Redding RV Rentals, W Arco, Shell/dsl, RV service, Towtally RV Ctr, truck repair, U-Haul

681b (from sb, no re-entry)CA 273, Market St, Johnson Rd, to Central Redding, W H

681a Twin View Blvd, E Shell, Holiday Inn Express, Motel 6, Harley-Davidson, W Flyers/dsl, El Zarape, Best Western+, Comfort Suites, Fairfield Inn, Home2 Suites

REDDING

680 CA 299E, W Arco, Chevron/dsl, Baskin-Robbins, Carl's Jr, Doughboy Donuts, Giant Burger, KFC, Little Caesar's, McDonald's, Papa Murphy's, RoundTable Pizza, Starbucks, $Tree, auto repair, AutoZone, CVS, O'Reilly Parts, Raley's Foods, Redding RV Park, tires, transmissions, Twin View RV Park, vet, Walgreens

678 CA 299 W, CA 44, to Eureka, Redding, Burney, E Chevron/dsl, Speedway/dsl, Applebee's, Carl's Jr, Casa Ramos, Chick-fil-A, Chipotle Mexican, ChuckeCheese, Einstein Bagels, Five Guys, In-N-Out, Jamba Juice, Jersey Mike's, Mazatlan Grill, McDonald's, MOD Pizza, Olive Garden, Outback Steaks, Panda Express, Panera Bread, Pete's Rest., Red Lobster, Red Robin, Starbucks, Taco Bell, Motel 6, Red Lion Inn, AT&T, Best Buy, Costco, Dick's, FoodMaxx, Hobby Lobby, Home Depot, JC Penney, Kohl's, Macy's, Michael's, O'Reilly Parts, Old Navy, PetCo, PetSmart, Schwab Tire, Target, TJ Maxx, Trader Joe's, Verizon, Walmart, WinCo Foods, World Mkt

677 Cypress Ave, Hilltop Dr, Redding, E Chevron/Circle K/dsl, Valero/dsl, Black Bear Diner, Burger King, Carl's Jr, Cattlemen's Rest., Chicken Shack, Del Taco, Denny's, Domino's, Donut House, Gibbs Grille, Grand Buffet, Hilltop Diner, IHOP, Jack-in-the-Box, Little Caesar's, Logan's Roadhouse, McDonald's, Niu Hawaiian, Papa Murphy's, Popeyes, Starbucks, Subarama, Subway, Taco Bell, Taco Shop, The Habit Burgers, Wendy's, Best Western+, Comfort Inn, Hampton Inn, Holiday Inn Express, La Quinta, Oxford Suites, Quality Inn, SureStay Plus, TownePlace Suites, 99c Store, AutoZone, BigLots, Buick/Cadillac/GMC, CVS Drug, Lowe's, Rite Aid, Ross, Safeway/gas, Verizon, vet, Walgreens, W Comets/dsl, Speedway/dsl, Burrito Bandito, CA Cattle Rest., Giff's Steakburger, Guadalajara Mexican, Humble Joe's Chophouse, Lucky Millers Deli, Lumberjack's Rest., Bridgeway Inn, Motel 6, Red Lion Inn, America's Tire, Big O Tire, Chevrolet, Dodge, Ford/Lincoln, Honda, Kia, Midas, Nissan, Office Depot, Subaru, Toyota, U-Haul, URGENT CARE

675 Bechelli Lane, Churn Creek Rd, E Arco/dsl, Chevron, Fast Track/dsl, In-N-Out, Jamba, MOD Pizza, Panda Express, Starbucks, Super 8, Petco, Ross, Save Mart, W Chevron/dsl, McDonald's, Hilton Garden, Costco/gas, Les Schwab Tire

673 Knighton Rd, E TA/Shell/Pizza Hut/Popeyes/dsl/LP/scales/24hr/@, W JGW RV Park(3mi), Sacramento River RV Park(3mi)

670 Riverside Ave, E Woodside Grill, Gaia Hotel, 7-11,

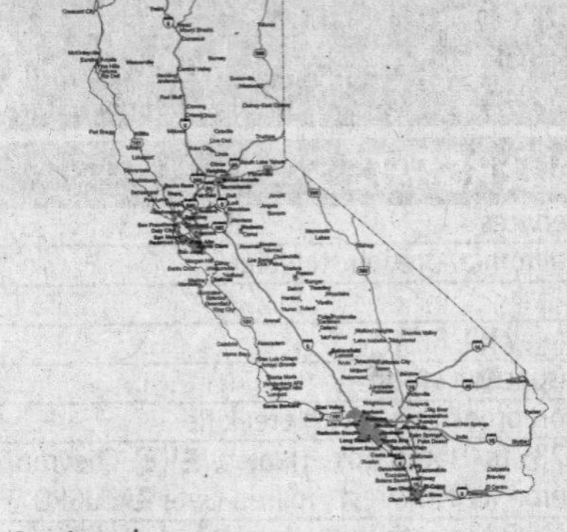

ANDERSON

670 Continued
TowTally RV, W Blue Compass RV, Camping World RV Ctr

668 Balls Ferry Rd, Anderson, E Marathon/dsl, Maverik, Speedway/dsl, Becca's Cafe, Burger King, Joe's Chophouse, Little Caesar's, McDonald's, Papa Murphy's, Peacock Chinese, Popeyes, Puerto Vallarta Mexican, RoundTable Pizza, Starbucks, Subway, Taco Bell, Best Western, Motel 6, $Tree, AutoZone, Les Schwab Tire, NAPA, Rite Aid, Safeway/dsl, URGENT CARE, W Players Pizza, O'Reilly Parts

667 CA 273, Factory Outlet Blvd, E vet, W Arco/dsl Chevron/dsl, Shell/dsl, Arby's, Jack-in-the-Box, Panda Express, Sonic, Starbucks, Westside Pizza, Baymont Inn $Tree, Dutch Bros, Grocery Outlet, Shasta Outlets/famous brands, Verizon, Walmart

665 (from sb), Cottonwood, E Kenny's Kitchen, Traveler Motel/RV Park, U-Haul, vet

664 Gas Point Rd, to Balls Ferry, E Chevron/dsl/LP, Alamo Motel, Alamo RV Park, auto repair, fireworks, NAPA USPO, W Circle K/dsl, Holiday/dsl/Tesla EVC, Eagle Nest Pizza, Ace Hardware, Holiday Mkt, vet

662 Bowman Rd, to Cottonwood, E Chevron/dsl

660mm weigh sta both lanes

659 Snively Rd, Auction Yard Rd, (Sunset Hills Dr from nb)

657 Hooker Creek Rd, Auction Yard Rd

656mm **full facilities, litter barrels, petwalk, both lanes**

653 Jellys Ferry Rd

652 Wilcox Golf Rd

RED BLUFF

651 CA 36W(from sb) same as 650, Red Bluff, W Arco/dsl, Holiday Inn Express, Home Depot, U-Haul

650 Adobe Rd, W Chevron/dsl, Burrito Bandito, Starbucks Hampton Inn, Holiday Inn Express, CHP, Chrysler Dodge/Jeep, Home Depot, Quick Lube, U-Haul

649 CA 36, to CA 99 S, Red Bluff, E Chevron/dsl, Red Bluff Ga Shell/dsl, Applebee's, Burger King, Del Taco, McDonald's Rockin' R Rest., Starbucks, Best Western/Tesla EV Comfort Inn, Motel 6, vistor ctr, W Mobil/dsl, Shell/ds Valero, Denny's, Los Mariachis, Luigi's Pizza, RoundTab Pizza, Shari's, Subway, Econolodge, Super 8, Travelodg Foodmaxx, O'Nite RV Park, Red Bluff KOA, River's Edge R Park, Tesla EVC, Verizon, vet

647a b S Main St, Red Bluff, E Valero/dsl, Days Inn, H, Arco/dsl, Chevron/dsl, Speedway/dsl, Arby's, Baski Robbins, China Doll, Domino's, Jack-in-the-Box, Litt Caesar's, Mike's Pizza, Papa Murphy's, Starbucks, Taco Be Best Value Inn, Crystal Motel, Gateway Inn, Red Bluff In Triangle Motel, $Tree, AutoZone, Big O Tires, CVS Dru Dutch Bros, Jiffy Lube, O'Reilly Parts, Raley's Food/drug, Tr Value, Verizon, vet, Walgreens, Walmart

642 Flores Ave, to Proberta, Gerber, E Walmart Dist Ctr

636 rd A11, Gyle Rd, to Tehama

633 Finnell Rd, to Richfield

INTERSTATE 5 Cont'd

CORNING

Exit #	Services
632mm	**both lanes, full facilities, litter barrels, petwalk**
631	A9, Corning Rd, Corning, E Chevron/dsl, Shell/dsl/LP, Tesla EVC, Valero/dsl, Burger King, Casa Ramos Mexican, Dutch Bros, Johnny Boys Tacos, Little Caesar's, Marco's Pizza, Olive Pit Rest., Papa Murphy's, Rancho Grande Mexican, RoundTable Pizza, Starbucks, Subway, Taco Bell, 7 Inn Motel, American Inn, Best Western+, Economy Inn, Super 8, $Tree, 7-11, AT&T, auto repair, AutoZone, Chevrolet, Ford, Heritage RV Park, Les Schwab Tire, NAPA, O'Reilly Parts, Safeway, tires, Verizon, W Giant Burger, Corning RV Park
630	South Ave, Corning, E Love's/Denny's/Godfather's/dsl/LP/RV dump/scales/24hr, Petro/Mobil/Iron Skillet/dsl/scales/24hr/@, TA/Shell/Arby's/dsl/scales/24hr/@, 2 Guys and A Grill, Amigos Mexican, Jack-in-the-Box, McDonald's, CA Inn, Econolodge, Holiday Inn Express, Ace Hardware, Blue Beacon, SpeedCo Lube, truck wash/lube, Woodson Br SRA/RV Park(6mi)
628	CA 99W, Liberal Ave, W Travel Center, Rolling Hills Hotel/Casino, Rolling Hills RV Park
621	CA 7

ARTOIS

Exit #	Services
619	CA 32, Orland, E Arco, Chevron/dsl, Burger King, Dutch Bros, Little Caesar's, McDonald's, Starbucks, $General, Ace Hardware, AutoZone, CVS Drug, Walgreens, W Maverik/dsl, Pilot/Wendy's/PJ Fresh/dsl/scales/24hr, Speedway/dsl, I-5 Cafe, Taco Bell, Parkway RV Park
618	CA 16, E Speedway/dsl, Orland Inn, $Tree, Grocery Outlet
614	CA 27
610	Artois
608mm	**both lanes, full facilities, litter barrels, petwalk, RV dump**
607	CA 39, Blue Gum Rd, Bayliss, E Blue Gum Motel
603	CA 162, to Oroville, Willows, E Arco, Chevron, Shell/dsl, Black Bear Diner, Burger King, Casa Ramos, KFC, La Taqueria, RoundTable Pizza, Starbucks, Subway, Taco Bell, The Tipsy Burro Mexican, Wong's Chinese, Best Western/RV parking, Holiday Inn Express, Motel 6, Quality Inn, Super 8, $Tree, CHP, H, O'Reilly Parts, W Walmart

MAXWELL

Exit #	Services
601	rd 57, E Chevron/dsl
595	Rd 68, to Princeton, to Sacramento NWR
591	Delevan Rd
588	Maxwell
586	Maxwell Rd, E Delevan NWR, W Chevron, Maxwell Inn/rest.
583	both lanes (sb), full facilities, litter barrels, petwalk

ARBUCKLE

Exit #	Services
578	CA 20, Colusa, E Love's/Arby's/ Godfather's/dsl/scales/24hr, CHP, W Shell/Orv's Cafe/dsl, H
577	Williams, E Arco/dsl, Shell/Baskin-Robbins/Togo's/dsl, Carl's Jr, Carl's Jr., Krispy Krunchy Chicken, Subway, Taco Bell, TOGO's Sandwiches, Ramada Inn, $General, Grocery Outlet, W 76/dsl, Chevron/dsl, Sinclair/dsl, Burger King, Granzella's Rest., McDonald's/RV parking, Starbucks, Straw Hat Pizza, Williams Chinese Rest., Granzella's Inn, Motel 6, StageStop Motel, SureStay, Travelers Inn, H, NAPA, Shop'n Save Foods, USPO
575	Husted Rd, to Williams
569	Hahn Rd, to Grimes
567	frontage rd(from nb), to Arbuckle, E truck repair, W Chevron/dsl
566	to College City, Arbuckle, E Ace Hardware, USPO, W Little Caesars, $General

WOODLAND

Exit #	Services
559	Yolo/Colusa County Line Rd
557mm	**both lanes, full facilities, littler barrels, petwalk**
556	E4, Dunnigan, E Chevron/dsl/LP, Dunnigan/dsl, EVC, Jack-in-the-Box, Best Value Inn/EVC, Super 8, Farmers Mkt Deli, USPO, W Camper's RV Park/golf(1mi)
554	rd 8, E Pilot/Wendy's/dsl/scales/24hr, Tesla EVC, Burger King, Starbucks, Taco Bell, California Motel, HappyTime RV Park, W Chevron/dsl
553	I-505(from sb), to San Francisco, callboxes begin sb
548	Zamora, E Shell/dsl
542	Yolo
541	CA 16W, Woodland, W H
540	West St, W Arco, Denny's
538	CA 113 N, E St, Woodland, E Valley Oaks Inn, W CFN/dsl, Chevron/dsl, Corabella's, Best Western, truck repair

W SACRAMENTO

Exit #	Services
537	CA 113 S, Main St, to Davis(same as 536), E Raise the Roost, 7-11, U-Haul, W Chevron/dsl, QT/dsl, Black Bear Diner, Carl's Jr, Denny's, Domino's, Dutch Bros, Jack-in-the-Box, McDonald's, RoundTable Pizza, Sonic, Starbucks, Subway, Taco Bell, The Habit, Days Inn, Motel 6, Quality Inn, $Tree, Ace Hardware, Food4Less, Ross, Sprouts Mrkt
536	rd 102(same as 537), E Arco, Chevron/dsl, Applebee's, Burger King, Crumbl Cookies, Dutch Bros, Jack-in-the-Box, Comfort Suites, Fairfield Inn, Hampton Inn, Holiday Inn Express, Chevrolet/Buick/GMC, Home Depot, Marshalls, Tesla EVC, Walmart, W Circle K/dsl, In-N-Out, Jimboy's Tacos, MOD Pizza, Panda Express, Red Robin, Starbucks, Subway, Best Buy, Costco/gas, Michael's, Target, URGENT CARE, Verizon
531	rd 22, W Sacramento
530mm	Sacramento River
529mm	**sb, full facilities, litter barrels, petwalk**
528	Airport Rd, E Arco
525b	CA 99, to CA 70, to Marysville, Yuba City
525a	Del Paso Rd, E Chevron, A&W/KFC, Chicken'n Waffles, Chipotle, Denny's, Dutch Bros, IHOP, In-N-Out, Jack-in-the-box, Jersey Mike's, Mas Fuego, Natomas Donuts, Panda Express, Panera Bread, Papa Murphy's, Sizzler, Sourdough & Co, Taco Bell, Teriyaki Maki, Wienerschnitzel, Hampton Inn, Hilton Garden/EVC, Holiday Inn Express, Homewood Suites, AT&T, Rite Aid, Safeway Foods/dsl, Sprouts Mkt, W Subway, Hyatt Place, Sheraton Four Points, Walgreens
524	Arena Blvd, E Chipotle, Huckleberry's, Papa John's, Starbucks, Wendy's, TownePlace Suites/EVC, Costco, URGENT CARE, W Menchie's, RoundTable Pizza, Starbucks, Jimboy's Tacos, Bel-Air Food/Drug/dsl
522	I-80, E to Reno, W to San Francisco
521b	W El Camino Ave(from nb, no return), West El Camino, W Speedway/dsl, Carl's Jr, Jack-in-the-Box, Jamba Juice, Starbucks, Subway, Togo's/Baskin-Robbins, Courtyard, Hilton Garden, Residence Inn, SpringHill Suites
521a	Garden Hwy, W Courtyard

BROADWAY

Exit #	Services
520	Richards Blvd, E Chevron/dsl, Denny's, McDonald's, Executive Inn, Governor's Inn, Surestay+, W Arco, Shell, Nena's Mexican, Best Western/EVC, Comfort Suites, Crossroads Inn, Howard Johnson, La Quinta, Motel 6, Quality Inn, museum, waterfront park
519b	J St, Old Sacramento, E Holiday Inn, Vagabond Inn, W Embassy Suites, Railroad Museum
519a	Q St , downtown, Sacramento, W Embassy Suites, to st capitol
518	US 50, CA 99, services downtown, Broadway
516	Sutterville Rd, E 76/dsl, Chevron/dsl, La Bou Cafe, Macau Cafe, Sprouts Mkt, Wm Land Park, zoo

CA

= gas = food = lodging = other = rest stop

CA

INTERSTATE 5 Cont'd

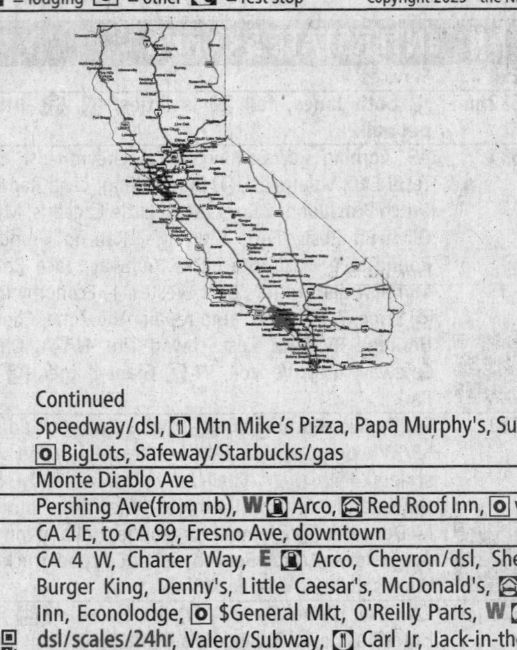

Exit #	Services
515	Fruitridge Rd, Seamas Rd
514	43rd Ave, Riverside Blvd(from sb), E Doubletime/7-11
513	Florin Rd, E Arco, Chevron/dsl, Carl's Jr, RoundTable Pizza, Starbucks, $Tree, Bel Air Foods, CVS Drug, O'Reilly Parts, W Burger King, Domino's, JimBoy's Tacos, L&L Hawaiian BBQ, Shari's, Starbucks, Subway, Marshall's, Nugget Mkt, Petco, Rite Aid
512	CA 160, Pocket Rd, Meadowview Rd, to Freeport, E Chevron/dsl, Shell/dsl, IHOP, KFC, McDonald's, Starbucks, Togo's, Wendy's, $Tree, AT&T, Home Depot, Les Schwab Tire, Staples, vet, W Starbucks, Vientos Mexican
510	Cosumnes River Blvd, E Chick-fil-A, Chipotle, Cold Stone, El Pollo Loco, In-N-Out, Jamba, Jersey Mike's, Menchie's, Noodles&Co, Panda Express, Panera Bread, Sonic, Starbucks, The Habit, AT&T, Dick's, Hobby Lobby, Old Navy, PetSmart, Ross, Verizon, Walmart, W dog park, golf
508	Laguna Blvd, E 76/Circle K/dsl/LP, Chevron/dsl, Shell, A&W/KFC, Starbucks, Wendy's, Extended Stay America, Hampton Inn/Tesla EVC, Jiffy Lube, tire repair, U-Haul
506	Elk Grove Blvd, E Arco/dsl, Chevron/dsl, Shell/Circle K/dsl, Carl's Jr, Huckleberry's, McDonald's, Oz Korean BBQ, Pete's Pizza, Wasabi Grill, Holiday Inn Express, vet
504	Hood Franklin Rd, W to Stone Lakes NWR
498	Twin Cities Rd, to Walnut Grove
493	Walnut Grove Rd, Thornton, E CFN/dsl, Chevron/Subway/dsl
490	Peltier Rd
487	Turner Rd
485	CA 12, Lodi, E Arco/dsl, Chevron/dsl, Flying J/Denny's/Subway/dsl/scales/24hr, Love's/Arby's/dsl/scales/24hr, Shell/dsl, Sinclair/Rocky's Rest./dsl/scales/24hr, CA Burrito, Carl's Jr, McDonald's, Starbucks, Best Western, Microtel, Blue Beacon, Discover RV Ctr, Flag City RV Resort, Profleet Trucklube, truck repair/wash, W KOA(5mi)
481	Eight Mile Rd, E Oak Grove Park, W Arco/dsl, Chevron/Jack-in-the-Box/dsl, Baskin-Robbins, Chipotle, El Pollo Loco, GK Mongolian BBQ, Huckleberry's, Jamba Juice, McDonald's, MooMoo's Burgers, Ono HBBQ, Panda Express, RoundTable Pizza, Sonic, Starbucks, Subway, Wendy's, Wingstop, $Tree, AAA, AT&T, AutoZone, Jo-Ann Fabrics, Kohl's, Lowe's, Mercedes, PetSmart, Ross, Target, URGENT CARE, Verizon, Walmart
478	Hammer Lane, Stockton, E 76/dsl, Sinclair, Adalberto's Mexican, Carl's Jr, KFC, Little Caesar's, McDonald's, Shirasoni Japanese, Subway, AutoZone, Food Source, URGENT CARE, Walgreens, W Chevron/dsl, QuikStop, 5 Star Burger, Jack-in-the-Box, Nations Burger, Taco Bell, Budget Inn
477	Benjamin Holt Dr, Stockton, E Arco, Chevron/dsl, QwikStop, Pizza Guys, Motel 6, golf, W 7-11, Eddie's Pizza, Lumberjack's Rest., Mandarin Villa, McDonald's, Starbucks, TCBY, Yogi KBBQ, Ace Hardware, Marina Foods, vet
476	March Lane, Stockton, E 7-11, Applebee's, Carl's Jr, Chick-fil-A, Denny's, Domino's, El Torito, GK Mongolian BBQ, Jack-in-the-Box, Matsuyama Sushi, McDonald's, Olive Garden, Red Lobster, Taco Bell, Wendy's, Hilton, CVS Drug, Marshall's, Save Mart Foods, W 76/dsl, Captain Crab, Habit Burger, IHOP, In-N-Out, Jamba Juice, Krispy Kreme, RoundTable Pizza, Starbucks, Subway, Wong's Chinese, Courtyard, Extended Stay America, La Quinta, Residence Inn, Home Depot
475	Alpine Ave, Country Club Blvd, same as 474 b
474b	Country Club Blvd(from nb), E Mobil/dsl, W 7-11,

LODI STOCKTON

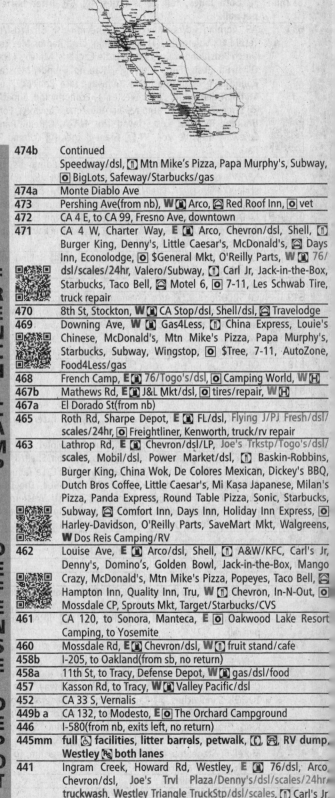

Exit #	Services
474b	Continued Speedway/dsl, Mtn Mike's Pizza, Papa Murphy's, Subway, BigLots, Safeway/Starbucks/gas
474a	Monte Diablo Ave
473	Pershing Ave(from nb), W Arco, Red Roof Inn, vet
472	CA 4 E, to CA 99, Fresno Ave, downtown
471	CA 4 W, Charter Way, E Arco, Chevron/dsl, Shell, Burger King, Denny's, Little Caesar's, McDonald's, Days Inn, Econolodge, $General Mkt, O'Reilly Parts, W 76/dsl/scales/24hr, Valero/Subway, Carl Jr, Jack-in-the-Box, Starbucks, Taco Bell, Motel 6, 7-11, Les Schwab Tire, truck repair
470	8th St, Stockton, W CA Stop/dsl, Shell/dsl, Travelodge
469	Downing Ave, W Gas4Less, China Express, Louie's Chinese, McDonald's, Mtn Mike's Pizza, Papa Murphy's, Starbucks, Subway, Wingstop, $Tree, 7-11, AutoZone, Food4Less/gas
468	French Camp, E 76/Togo's/dsl, Camping World, W H
467b	Mathews Rd, E J&L Mkt/dsl, tires/repair, W H
467a	El Dorado St(from nb)
465	Roth Rd, Sharpe Depot, E FL/dsl, Flying J/PJ Fresh/dsl/scales/24hr, Freightliner, Kenworth, truck/rv repair
463	Lathrop Rd, E Chevron/dsl/LP, Joe's Trkstp/Togo's/dsl/scales, Mobil/dsl, Power Market/dsl, Baskin-Robbins, Burger King, China Wok, De Colores Mexican, Dickey's BBQ, Dutch Bros Coffee, Little Caesar's, Mi Kasa Japanese, Milan's Pizza, Panda Express, Round Table Pizza, Sonic, Starbucks, Subway, Comfort Inn, Days Inn, Holiday Inn Express, Harley-Davidson, O'Reilly Parts, SaveMart Mkt, Walgreens, W Dos Reis Camping/RV
462	Louise Ave, E Arco/dsl, Shell, A&W/KFC, Carl's Jr, Denny's, Domino's, Golden Bowl, Jack-in-the-Box, Mango Crazy, McDonald's, Mtn Mike's Pizza, Popeyes, Taco Bell, Hampton Inn, Quality Inn, Tru, W Chevron, In-N-Out, Mossdale CP, Sprouts Mkt, Target/Starbucks/CVS
461	CA 120, to Sonora, Manteca, E Oakwood Lake Resort Camping, to Yosemite
460	Mossdale Rd, E Chevron/dsl, W fruit stand/cafe
458b	I-205, to Oakland(from sb, no return)
458a	11th St, to Tracy, Defense Depot, W gas/dsl/food
457	Kasson Rd, to Tracy, W Valley Pacific/dsl
452	CA 33 S, Vernalis
449b a	CA 132, to Modesto, E The Orchard Campground
446	I-580(from nb, exits left, no return)
445mm	**full facilities, litter barrels, petwalk, RV dump, Westley both lanes**
441	Ingram Creek, Howard Rd, Westley, E 76/dsl, Arco, Chevron/dsl, Joe's Trvl Plaza/Denny's/dsl/scales/24hr, truckwash, Westley Triangle TruckStp/dsl/scales, Carl's Jr, McDonald's, Subway, Days Inn, Executive Inn, Holiday Inn Express, Motel 6, W Valero/dsl, Krispy Krunchy Chicken, truck repair
434	Sperry Ave, Del Puerto, Patterson, E Arco/dsl, Chevron,

FRENCH CAMP DEFENSE DEPOT

INTERSTATE 5 Cont'd

CROWS LANDING

434 Continued
Flying J/Wendy's/PJ Fresh/dsl/scales/parking/24hr, Love's/Arby's/dsl/scales/24hr, Mobil/dsl, National/dsl, Valero/dsl, Almond Wood BBQ, Carl's Jr, Denny's, El Rosal Mexican, Golden Lion Chinese, Jack-in-the-Box, Starbucks, Best Western+, Hampton Inn, $Tree, Kit Fox RV Park, Walmart

430mm vista point nb

428 Fink Rd, Crows Landing

423 Stuhr Rd, Newman

422mm vista point sb

418 CA 140E, Gustine, E Chevron/dsl, Sinclair/dsl, auto repair

409 weigh sta both lanes

407 CA 33, Santa Nella, E Arco, Love's/Del Taco/dsl/scales/24hr, TA/Shell/Country Pride/Popeyes/dsl/scales/EVC//24hr/@, Andersen's Rest., Carl's Jr, Subway, Wendy's, Best Western/Andersen's, Quality Inn, W 76/dsl, Chevron, Rotten Robbie/dsl/scales, Valero/Circle K/dsl, Denny's, In-N-Out, McDonald's, Panda Express, Pizza Factory, Starbucks, Taco Bell, Hotel Mission de Oro, Motel 6, Santa Nella RV Park

403b a CA 152, Los Banos, E H, W EVC, Petro/Shell/diner/dsl/scales/24hr, Motel 6, KOA, tent camping

391 CA 165N, Mercy Springs Rd, E H, W Shell, fruit

388 vista point (from nb)

386mm **both lanes, full facilities, litter barrels, petwalk,**

385 Nees Ave, to Firebaugh, W Chevron/CFN/Subway/dsl/scales

379 Shields Ave, to Mendota

372 Russell Ave

368 Panoche Rd, W 76/dsl, Chevron/McDonald's, EVC, Mobil/Wayback Burger/dsl, Shell/dsl, Valero/Little Caesars/dsl, Subway, Best Western, country store

365 Manning Ave, to San Joaquin

357 Kamm Ave

349 CA 33 N, Derrick Ave

HURON

337 CA 33 S, CA 145 N, to Coalinga

334 CA 198, to Lemoore, Huron, E Shell/dsl/24hr, Tesla EVC, Harris Ranch Inn/rest., W 76/dsl, Arco/dsl, Chevron/EVC/dsl, Valero/Subway/Baja Fresh/dsl, Carl's Jr, Denny's, McDonald's, Starbucks, Taco Bell, Best Western, Motel 6, Travelodge, auto repair, H

325 Jayne Ave, to Coalinga, W Shell/Baja Fresh/dsl, Valero, Almond Tree RV Park/LP, H

320mm **both lanes, full facilities, litter barrels**

319 CA 269, Lassen Ave, to Avenal, W EZ Trip/Subway/dsl/scales/24hr

309 CA 41, Kettleman City, E 76/Subway, CFN/dsl, Chevron/McDonald's, Mobil/Starbucks/dsl/24hr, Shell/Baja Fresh/dsl, Valero/dsl, Carl's Jr, Denny's, In-N-Out, Jack-in-the-Box, Pizza Hut/Taco Bell, Best Western, Quality Inn, Bravo Farms Mercantile, EVC

LOST HILLS

305 Utica Ave

288 Twisselman Rd

278 CA 46, Lost Hills, E Buford Star Mart/dsl/LP, to Kern NWR, W 76, Arco/DQ/dsl, Chevron/dsl, Exxon/McDonald's/dsl/LP, Love's/Arby's/dsl/scales/dog park/24hr, Pilot/Wendy's/dsl/scales/24hr, Shell/Pizza Hut/Subway/Taco Bell/dsl, Valero/7-11/dsl, Carl's Jr, Denny's, Jack-in-the-Box, Days Inn, Motel 6, KOA, Royal Truck Wash/lube, tires, truck repair, truck wash

268 Lerdo Hwy, to Shafter

262 7th Standard Rd, Rowlee Rd, to Buttonwillow

259mm **Buttonwillow both lanes, full facilities,**

BUTTONWILLOW

259mm Continued
litter barrels, petwalk,

257 CA 58, to Bakersfield, Buttonwillow, E Arco/dsl, Chevron/dsl, EVC, EZ Trip/dsl, Sinclair/dsl, Speedy Fuel/dsl/wash, TA/Mobil/Taco Bell/dsl/scales/24hr/@, Carl's Jr, McDonald's, Starbucks, Subway, Taco Loco, Willow Ranch BBQ, Econolodge, Motel 6, National 9 Inn, Vagabond Inn, Castro's Tire/Truckwash, W Sinclair/dsl

253 Stockdale Hwy, E Chevron/Subway/dsl, EZ Trip/dsl/24hr, IHOP, Jack-in-the-Box, Best Western, W Tule Elk St Reserve

246 CA 43, to Taft, Maricopa, W to Buena Vista RA

244 CA 119, to Pumpkin Center, E Mobil/dsl, W Arco/dsl/scales/parking, Chevron/dsl/LP

239 CA 223, Bear Mtn Blvd, to Arvin, E Bear Mtn RV Resort, W to Buena Vista RA

234 Old River Rd

228 Copus Rd, E Murray Farms Mkt, W Shell

225 CA 166, to Mettler, W Chevron/Subway/dsl

221 I-5 and CA 99(from nb, exits left, no return)

GRAPEVINE

219b a Laval Rd, Wheeler Ridge, E Shell/dsl, TA/Shell/Popeyes/Subway/scales/@, Baja Fresh, Black Bear Diner, Burger King, Carl's Jr, Habit Burger, Jamba Juice, Pieology, Pizza Hut, Starbucks, Taco Bell, Hampton Inn, Microtel, Blue Beacon, Tejon Outlets/famous brands, W 76/Subway/dsl, EVC, Mobil/dsl, Petro/Iron Skillet/Subway/dsl/scales/24hr/@, Tesla EVC, Arby's, Baskin-Robbins, Chipotle Mexican, Del Taco, Denny's, IHOP, In-N-Out, McDonald's, Panda Express, Starbucks, Wendy's, Best Western

218 truck weigh sta sb

215 Grapevine, E Valero/dsl, Jack-in-the-Box, W Shell/dsl, Days Inn

210 Ft Tejon Rd, W to Ft Tejon Hist SP

209mm brake check area nb

207 Lebec Rd, W Grapevine RV/repair, towing, USPO

206mm **both lanes, full facilities, litter barrels, vending, petwalk**

206mm **full facilities, petwalk, litter barrels, both lanes, vending**

205 Frazier Mtn Park Rd, W Arco/dsl, Chevron/dsl, Flying J/Wendy's/dsl/LP/scales/24hr/@, Speedway/Subway/dsl/24hr, China Red, Jack-in-the-Box, Los Pinos Mexican, Holiday Inn Express, Motel 6, auto repair/towing, Carquest, EVC, to Mt Pinos RA

204 Tejon Pass, elev 4144, truck brake insp sb

202 Gorman Rd, to Hungry Valley, E Chevron/dsl/LP, Carl's Jr, W 76/dsl, McDonald's, auto repair

199 CA 138 E, Lancaster Rd, to Palmdale

198b a Quail Lake Rd, CA 138 E(from nb)

195 Smokey Bear Rd, Pyramid Lake, E Pyramid Lake RV Park, W tent camping

191 Vista del Lago Rd, W to Pyramid Lake RA, visitors ctr

186mm brake inspection area sb, motorist callboxes begin sb

184mm brake check sb

CASTAIC

183 Templin Hwy, W tent camping/hiking

176b a Lake Hughes Rd, Parker Rd, Castaic, E 7-11, Arco/dsl, Castaic Trkstp/dsl/24hr, Chevron, Pilot/PJ Fresh/dsl/scales/24hr/@, Shell/dsl, Cajun Chicken, Carl's Jr, Chabelo's Mexican, Denny's, Domino's, El Pollo Loco, Fosters Freeze, McDonald's, Panda Express, Red Dot Pizza, Starbucks, Subway, Tommie's Cafe, Vincenzo's Pizza, Waba Grill, Wok's Chinese, Castaic Inn, Days Inn, Rodeway Inn, $Tree, Castaic Lake RV Park, O'Reilly Parts, State Tire/repair, to Castaic Lake, vet, W Chargepoint EVC, Mobil, Shell/repair, Jack-in-the-Box, Taco Bell, Parkway RV Ctr, Walgreens

173 Hasley Canyon Rd, W Ameci Pizza, Las Delicias Mexican, Luv'n Donuts, Matsu Sushi, Pizza Hut, Subway, Wingstop,

CA

= gas = food = lodging = other = rest stop

CA

INTERSTATE 5 Cont'd

SAUGUS

173 Continued
Ralph's Foods

172 CA 126 W, to Ventura, E Courtyard, Embassy Suites, Homewood Suites

171mm no services

171 Rye Canyon Rd(from sb), W 7-11, Conserv/dsl, Del Taco, Jack-in-the-Box, Jimmy Dean's, Starbucks, Tommy's Burgers, Six Flags

170 CA 126 E, Magic Mtn Pkwy, Saugus, E Azul Tequila Mexican, Denny's, Sam's Grill, Starbucks, Yogi's Grill, Best Western, Holiday Inn Express, SpringHill Suites, W Chevron/dsl, Shell/dsl, Coffee Bean, In-N-Out, McDonald's, Red Lobster, Wendy's, Hilton Garden/EVC, Six Flags of CA

169 Valencia Blvd, W Fat Burger, Nashville Chicken, Panda Express, Robeks, Starbucks, Subway, The Road Pizza

168 McBean Pkwy, E H, W Cabo Cabana, Chili's, ChuckECheese's, Gyromania, Jersey Mikes Subs, MOD Pizza, Pick Up Stix, Starbucks, Subway, Urbane Cafe, Michael's, Old Navy, T-Mobile, Vons Foods, WorldMkt

PASADENA

167 Lyons Ave, Pico Canyon Rd, E 76/Circle K/dsl, Chevron/dsl, Shell/dsl, Burger King, Vincenzo's Pizza, Wendy's, W Arco, Shell/dsl, Carl's Jr, Del Taco, Denny's, El Pollo Loco, Fortune Express Chinese, IHOP, In-N-Out, Jack-in-the-Box, Jersey Mike's, McDonald's, Outback Steaks, Sandwich Spot, Spumoni Italian, Taco Bell, Wood Ranch BBQ, Yamato Japanese, Comfort Suites, Extended Stay America, Fairfield Inn, Hampton Inn, La Quinta, Residence Inn, AT&T, Camping World RV Ctr, EVC, Jiffy Lube, Marshall's, Old Navy, PetSmart, Ralph's Foods, Ross, Staples, Walmart/Domino's/auto

166 Calgrove Blvd

162 CA 14 N, to Palmdale

161b Balboa Blvd (from sb)

160a I-210, to San Fernando, Pasadena

159 Roxford St, Sylmar, E Chevron/dsl, Mobil/dsl, Denny's/24hr, McDonald's, Vagabond Inn

158 I-405 S(from sb, no return)

157b a SF Mission Blvd, Brand Blvd, E 76, Arco, Chevron/dsl, Exxon/dsl, Shell, Carl's Jr, Gallo Giro, In-N-Out, Little Caesar's, Popeyes, Subway, Subway, Taco Bell, Winchell's, Honda, Jiffy Lube, Vallarta Mkt

156b CA 118

156a Paxton St, Brand Ave(from nb), E Chevron/dsl, 7-11

155b Van Nuys Blvd(no EZ nb return), E Arco, Jack-in-the-Box, KFC/LJ Silver, McDonald's, Pizza Hut, Popeyes, Discount Parts, USPO, W Domino's, Joy HBBQ, Winchell's Donuts, auto repair

155a Terra Bella St(from nb), E USA, Birrieria Mexican

SUN VALLEY

154 Osborne St, to Arleta, E Arco, Chevron/dsl, Pizza Bayern, AutoZone, BigLots, Food4Less, Ross, Target, W 76, Mobil/Burger King, 7-11

153b CA 170(from sb), to Hollywood

152a Sheldon St, E Big Jim's Rest., 7-11, auto repair, H

152 Lankershim Blvd, Tuxford, E Superfine/dsl/scales, Donut Baker

151 Penrose St

150b Sunland Blvd, Sun Valley, E 76/dsl, Mobil, Carl's Jr, El Pollo Loco, Old Time Burger, Papa John's, Poke Moki, Subway, Town Café, Yoshinoya, Zest Grill, Economy Inn, $Tree, 7-11, Grocery Outlet, Sunland Produce, W Chevron/7-11, Shell, Chiguacle Mexican, Domino's Pizza, McDonald's, Raspado Xpress Juice, Starbucks, Sushi Dragon

150a GlenOaks Blvd(from nb), E Arco/dsl, Willows Motel

149 Hollywood Way, W Shell/dsl, The Ramp Rest.,

VERDUGO

149 Continued
U-Haul

148 Buena Vista St, E Hampton Inn, W 76/dsl, Jack-in-the-Box, Quality Inn, Ramada Inn

147 Scott Rd, to Burbank, E Sevan/dsl, Miracle Bakery, Sun Moon Chinese, tires, W Blaze Pizza, Dave's Hot Chicken, Hook Burger, Jamba Juice, Krispy Kreme, Olive Garden, Outback Steaks, Panda Express, Sharky's Mexican, Starbucks, Wendy's, Courtyard, Extended Stay America, Best Buy, Lowe's, Michael's, REI, Staples, T.J. Maxx, Target, Verizon

146b Burbank Blvd, E 76/repair, Alfredo's Mexican, Buffalo Wild Wings, CA Pizza Kitchen, Carl's Jr, Chipotle, Chop Stop, ChuckECheese's, Corner Cafe, El Pollo Loco, IHOP, In-N-Out, Jersey Mike's, McDonald's, Niko Sushi, Popeyes, Shakey's Pizza, Starbucks, Starbucks, Taco Bell, Tommy's Burgers, Wingstop, Yoshinoya, Zankou Chicken, Zono Sushi, Barnes&Noble, CVS Drug, IKEA, Macy's, Office Depot, Old Navy, Ralph's Foods, Ross, Sprouts Mkt, W El Criollo, McDonald's, Costco/gas, Discount Tire, Walmart

146a Olive Ave, Verdugo, E Ameci Pizza, BJ's Rest., Black Angus Steaks, Carving Board, Granville Cafe, Island Burger, Kabuki Japanese, Knight Greek, Moana HBBQ, Shake Shack, Slice House, Wild Carvery, Wokcano, Wood Ranch BBQ, Yard House, Hilton Garden, Hotel Burbank, Residence Inn, USPO, W Centanni Italian, Sub King, Subway, Portofino Inn, 7-11, Advance Parts, auto repair, Chevrolet, H, Jiffy Lube, Metro RV Ctr, Pep Boys

145b Alameda Ave, E Chevron, Habit Burger, Starbucks, CarMax, CVS Drug, EVC, Home Depot, IKEA, Ralph's Foods, Trader Joes, Walgreens, W 76/dsl, Arco, Shell, Baskin-Robbins, Burbank Inn, U-Haul

145a Western Ave, W Gene Autrey Museum

144b a CA 134, Ventura Fwy, Glendale, Pasadena

142 Colorado St

141a Los Feliz Blvd, E H, W Griffith Park, LA Zoo

140b Glendale Blvd, E 76, Shell, Crispy Crust Pizza, Dunkin', Subway, W Chevron

140a Fletcher Dr(from sb), W Arco, Chevron, Ivanhoe Rest., Rick's Drive In, vet

139b a CA 2, Glendale Fwy

138 Stadium Way, Figueroa St, E 76, Andy's Gas, Chevron, USA, Domino's, IHOP, McDonald's, Home Depot, W to Dodger Stadium

137b a CA 2, Glendale Fwy, W 76

136b Broadway St(from sb), W 76

136a Main St, E 76, Chevron/24hr, Jack-in-the-Box, Little Caesars, McDonald's, Tom's Jr. Burger, 7-11, H

135c I-10 W(from nb), Mission Rd(from sb), E Jack-in-the-Box, KFC, McDonald's

135b Cesar Chavez Ave, W H

135a 4th St, Soto St, E Shell/dsl, city park, W 76/dsl

134b Ca 60 E(from sb), Soto St(from nb)

INTERSTATE 5 Cont'd

Exit #	Services
134a	CA 60 W, Santa Monica Fwy
133	Euclid Ave(from sb), Grand Vista(from nb), W Exxon, China Gardern, El Pollo Loco, McDonald's, Subway, Winchell's Donuts
132	Calzona St, Indiana St
131b	Indiana St(from nb), E Arco/dsl, Valero/dsl,
131a	Olympic Blvd, E Arco, , W Jack-in-the-Box, King Taco
130c b	I-710 (exits left from nb), to Long Beach, Eastern Ave, E Arco, Alex Burgers, McDonald's
130a	Triggs St(from sb), E Winchell's Donuts, W Denny's/24hr, Destiny Inn
129	Atlantic Blvd N, Eastern Ave(from sb), E Carl's Jr, Chipotle, Cinnabon, Rocky Mtn Chocolate, Starbucks, Subway, Doubletree, Mitsubishi, outlets/famous brands, W Steven's Steaks
128b	Washington Blvd, Commerce, E Chevron/dsl/repair/24hr, Farmer Boys, McDonald's, Crowne Plaza Hotel/casino, Doubletree, Costco/gas, outlets/famous brands, W Arco, Del Taco
128a	Garfield Blvd, E Home Depot, W 76/7-11
126b	Slauson Ave, Montebello, E Chevron/dsl, Shell/dsl, Ozzie's Diner, Starbucks, Best Star Inn, Quality Inn, Travelodge, 7-11, W Arco, Best Western+, Ben's Mkt
126a	Paramount Blvd, Downey, E Shell/Jack-in-the-Box/dsl, Granny's Donuts, Teriyaki J's
125	CA 19 S, Lakewood Blvd, Rosemead Blvd, E Exxon, Speedway, Arthurs Cafe, Sam's Burgers, Starbucks, Mid City Inn, Pico Rivera Inn, 7-11, W Chris&Pitt's BBQ, Golden Corral, McDonald's, Poached, Subway, Taco Bell, city park, Ralph's Foods
124	I-605
123	Florence Ave, to Downey, E Mobil, Christine Donuts, W Giant RV Ctr, Honda, repair
122	Imperial Hwy, Pioneer Blvd, E Chevron, Applebee's, Habit Burgers, IHOP, Jack-in-the-Box, Jimmy John's, McDonald's, Panda Express, Pizza Hut, Rainbow Donuts, Subway, Wendy's, , O'Reilly Parts, Target, USPO, W 7-11, Alberts Mexican, Denny's, Jack in the Box, Panda King, Rally's, Shakey's Pizza, Wienerschnitzel, Imperial Inn, Keystone Motel, Motel 6, Norwalk Inn, Circle K, Toyota/Scion, Walmart
121	San Antonio Dr, to Norwalk Blvd, E Chevron, Applebee's, Chick-fil-A, IHOP, Jack-in-the-Box, Jersey Mike's, L&L HBBQ, McDonald's, Outback Steaks, Rainbow Donuts, SoCal Pizza, Subway, The Habit Burgers, Wendy's, Doubletree Inn, , Target, W Chevron, Burger Basket
120b	Firestone Blvd(exits left from nb)
120a	Rosecrans Ave, E 76/7-11/dsl, Casa Adelita, Jim's Burgers, KFC, Little Caesar's, Starbucks, Subway, W Arco/24hr, Guesthouse Inn, El Monte RV Ctr
119	Carmenita Rd, Buena Park, E Arco, Burger King, Taco Bell, The Burger Stop, Ford Trucks, Lowe's, W Dawa Japanese, Galaxy Burgers, Budget Inn, Dynasty Suites
118	Valley View Blvd, E Arco/dsl, In-N-Out, Laleh Creamery, Northwoods Inn, Starbucks, Subway, Wendy's, Extended Stay America, Holiday Inn, Residence Inn, W Thompson's RV Ctr
117	Artesia Blvd, Knott Ave, E Chevron, Hampton Inn, Extended Stay America, CarMax, Chrysler/Dodge/Jeep, W SC Fuels, Camping World RV Ctr, city park, Knotts Berry Farm
116	CA 39, Beach Blvd, E Chevron, Travelodge, BMW, Buick/GMC, CarMax, Chevrolet, Honda, Mercedes, Nissan, Tesla, Toyota/Scion, W Chevron, Arby's, Black Angus, Days Inn, Denny's, KFC, Pizza Hut, Subway, Wendy's, DoubleTree, Fairfield Inn, Stater Bros, Target/Pizza Hut/Starbucks/EVC, to Knotts Berry Farm, Verizon
115	Manchester(from nb), same as 116
114b	CA 91 E, Riverside Fwy, E to
114a	Magnolia Ave, Orangethorpe Ave, E Exxon/dsl, Burger King, Burger Town, Subway, Taco Bell, 7-11, Harley-Davidson
113c	CA 91 W(from nb)
113b a	Brookhurst St, LaPalma, E Chevron/dsl, Subway, auto care, W Arco, Chevron/dsl, Aloha HBBQ, Burger King, Carl's Jr, Starbucks, Home Depot
112	Euclid St, E Arco, Happy Dragon, IHOP, Jollibee Chicken, McDonald's, Rubio's, Starbucks, Subway, Taco Bell, Wendy's, 7-11, AAA, El Super, , Old Navy, PetCo, Ross, TJ Maxx, Verizon, Walmart, W 7-11, Mobil, Cane's Chicken, Charley's Subs, Denny's, KFC/LJ Silver, Pizza Hut, Subway, Wok Experience, Anaheim Executive Inn, AlLDI, Target
111	Lincoln Ave, to Anaheim, E La Villa Mexican, Mos 2 Japanese, Pizza Factory, Ruby's Diner, Starbucks, vet
110b	Ball Rd(from sb), E 7-11, 76, Chevron/dsl, Shell, Burger King, Carolina's Italian, El Pollo Loco, KFC, McDonald's, Pizza Dudes, Shakey's Pizza, Starbucks, Subway, Taco Bell, WaBa Grill, Astoria Inn, Days Inn, Frontier Inn, Hotel 414, Quality Inn & Suites, Sheraton, Anaheim Harbor RV Park, Anaheim RV, , Traveler's World RV Park, W Arco/24hr, Shell/dsl, Best Western, Budget Inn, Holiday Inn, Majestic Garden Hotel, Staybridge Suites, Super 8, Travelodge, Disneyland, USPO
110a	Harbor Blvd, same as 109, E Chevron, Shell, Shakey's Pizza, Starbucks, Taco Bell, Days Inn, Frontier, Sheraton, Solara Inn, Anaheim Harbor RV Park, W Del Sol Inn, Denny's, IHOP, McDonald's, Mimi's Cafe, Panera Bread, Tony Roma's, Alpine Inn, Anaheim Resort, Best Western+, Camelot Inn, Candy Cane Inn, Castle Inn Suites, Courtyard, Desert Palms Hotel, Fairfield Inn, Grand Legacy, Hilton Garden, Holiday Inn Express, Home2 Suites, Hotel Indigo, Howard Johnson, King's Inn, Park Place Inn, ParkVue Inn, Tropicana Inn, Wyndham Garden, multiple hotels & restaurants, to Disneyland
109	Katella Ave, Disney Way, E Arco, Carl's Jr, Chipotle, Dave's Hot Chicken, Denny's, McDonald's, Panda Express, Panera Bread, Starbucks, TownePlace Suites, Angels Stadium, W Chevron, Blaze Pizza, Bubba Gump Shrimp, CA Fish Grill, CA Pizza Kitchen, Cheesecake Factory, Denny's, Habit Burger, IHOP, McCormick&Schmick, Morton's Steaks, PF Chang's, Roy's, Starbucks, Starburger, Anaheim Islander Inn, Best Value Inn, Cambria, Candlewood Suites, Clarion, Comfort Inn, Desert Palms Hotel, Desert Palms Suites, DoubleTree, Extended Stay America, Hilton, Homewood Suites, Hotel Indigo, Hyatt House, Kings Inn, La Quinta, Little Boy Blue, Marriott, Marriott, Motel 6, Peacock Suites, Residence Inn, Riviera Motel, Sheraton, Sonesta Suites, SpringHill Suites, Worldmark, Wyndham Garden, 7-11, CVS, to Disneyland, Walgreens
107c	St Coll Blvd, City Drive, E Del Taco, Embassy Suites, Angels Stadium, W Chevron, Dave&Busters, Lucille's BBQ, Taco Bell, ALO Hotel, Ayres Hotel/EVC, Doubletree Hotel, Best Buy
107b a	CA 57 N, Chapman Ave, E 7-11, Jack-in-the-Box, Lee's Sandwiches, Pita Grill, W Bistro Box, BJ's Rest., Dave&Busters, Krispy Kreme, Starbucks, TGI Friday's, Wendy's, ALO Hotel, Ayres Inn, DoubleTree, Best Buy,

COMMERCE

LA PALMA

BUENA PARK

CA

INTERSTATE 5 Cont'd

107b a Continued
outlet/famous brands

106 CA 22 W(from nb), Garden Grove Fwy, Bristol St

105b N Broadway, Main St, E 7-11, Applebees, Baskin-Robbins, CA Pizza Kitchen, Carl's Jr, Chipotle, Corner Bakery Cafe, Habit Burger, Jamba Juice, Johnny Rocket's, Olive Garden, Papa Johns, Polly's Café, Rubio's Grill, Starbucks, Subway, Taco Bell, Togo's, Days Inn, Red Roof Inn, Barnes&Noble, CVS Drug, JC Penney, Macy's, mall, Verizon, W Golden West Motel, Bowers Museum

105a 17th St, E 76/dsl/24hr, IHOP, McDonald's, Chevrolet, CVS Drug, same as 104b, Walgreens, W Chevron, El Pollo Loco, YumYum Donuts, Travel Inn, 7-11

104b Santa Ana Blvd, Grand Ave, E Gavilan, Pollo Campero, Popeyes, Round Table Pizza, Starbucks, Taco Bell, WaBa Grill, Wingstop, AT&T, O'Reilly Parts, Target, vet, Walgreens

104a (103c from nb), 4th St, 1st St, to CA 55 N, E Shell, US Gas, Del Taco, Krispy Krunchy Chicken, W El Cortez Lodge, Holiday Inn Express, Motel 6, zoo

103b CA 55 S, to Newport Beach

103a CA 55 N(from nb), to Riverside

102 Newport Ave(from sb), E Gen Korean BBQ, Jack-in-the-Box, Taco Mesita, The Habit, Wahoo's Fish Tacos, W Arco, Shell, Carl's Jr, Domino's, Donuts King, Little Caesar's, American Tire Depot

101b Red Hill Ave, E Mobil/dsl, Shell/repair, Del Taco, Denny's, OB Square, Starbucks, Wendy's, Yang's Chicken, Key Inn, Orange Grove Inn, U-Haul, W Arco/24hr, Chevron/24hr, Habuya Japanese, Pizza Shack, Taco Bell, 7-11, Stater Bros

101a Tustin Ranch Rd, E McDonald's, Acura, Buick/GMC, Cadillac, Chrysler/Dodge/Jeep, Costco/gas, Ford/Lincoln, Hyundai, Infiniti, Lexus, Mazda, Nissan, Toyota/Scion

100 Jamboree Rd, E Shell, Baja Fresh, BJ's Rest., Burger King, CA Fish Grill, CA Pizza Kitchen, Cha Cha's Mexican, Chick-fil-A, Donut Star, DQ, El Pollo Loco, Fresh Bros Pizza, Hopdoddy Burgers, In-N-Out, Islands Burger, Lazy Dog Cafe, Macaroni Grill, Miguel's Mexican, Pacific Catch, Panda Express, Pick-up Stix, Rubio's, Snooze Eatery, Starbucks, Stearbucks, Subway, Taco Bell, Taco Rosa, Texas de Brazil, Which Wich, AAA, AT&T, Best Buy, Costco/gas, Dick's Sports, EVC, Home Depot, Old Navy, PetSmart, Ralph's Foods, REI, Ross, Sprouts Mkt, Target/CVS/Starbucks, TJ Maxx, Verizon

99 Culver Dr, E Shell/24hr, W Chevron, Baekjeong BBQ, Blaze Pizza, Boiling Point, Buffalo Wild Wings, Chan Chan, Domino's, Fire Wings, Habit Burger, Jamba Juice, Starbucks, The Kebab Shop, Wanderlust Creamery, Wendy's, Ralph's, Trader Joe's

97 Jeffrey Rd, E Arco, Honey Pig, Mokkoji, Pho Ha, Starbucks, Albertson's, EVC, Kohl's, W A&J Taiwanese, China Garden, Kaju Tofu, KFC, Shik Do Rak, Thai Cafe, 99 Ranch Mkt, vet

96 Sand Canyon Ave, Old Towne, W 76/dsl, Denny's, Jack-in-the-Box, Knowlwood Burgers, La Quinta, vet

95 CA 133 (toll), Laguna Fwy, N to Riverside, S Laguna Beach

94b Alton Pkwy, E Shell/Subway/dsl, Bruegger's Bagels, Carl's Jr, Del Taco, Extended Stay America, Starbucks, Wendy's, Residence Inn, Costco/gas, Walmart, W Brio, CA Pizza Kitchen, Capital Grill, Cheesecake Factory, Chipotle Mexican, Dave&Buster's, Habana Cuban, Javier's Mexican, Panda Express, PF Chang's, Pieology, Shake Shack, Starbucks, The Melt, Wahoo's Fish Tacos, Wood Ranch, Yardhouse Rest., Courtyard, Doubletree Inn, Marriott,

OLD TOWNE

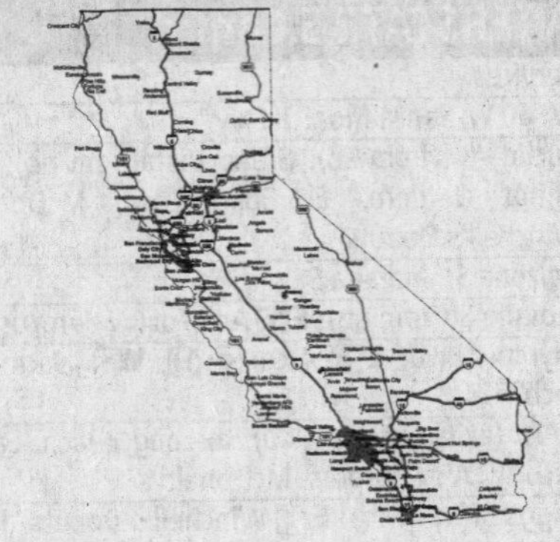

LAGUNA HILLS

MISSION VIEJO

94b Continued
Barnes&Noble, Nordstrom, Old Navy, Target

94a I-405 N(from nb)

92b Bake Pkwy, same as 92a, W CarMax, Toyota

92a Lake Forest Dr, Laguna Hills, E Chevron/24hr, Shell/dsl, Buffalo Wild Wings, DeLucia's Italian, IHOP, Ike's Sandwiches, Jack-in-the-Box, Krave Burger, McDonald's, Oh Poke, Panera Bread, RoundTable Pizza, Starbucks, Subway, Taco Bell, The Hat, Waba Grill, Best Western, Comfort Inn, Hampton Inn, Hilton Garden, SpringHill Suites, TownePlace Suites, America's Tire, Chevrolet, Chrysler/Dodge/Jeep, Ford/Lincoln, Honda, Hyundai, Mazda, Nissan, Subaru, VW, W Chevron/24hr, Shell, Baja Fish Tacos, Carl's Jr, Coco's, Del Taco, McDonald's, Pizza 900, Snooty Fox, Subway, Laguna Hills Inn, Sonesta, AZ Leather, Best Buy, BMW/Mini

91 El Toro Rd, E Chevron/dsl, Shell, Arby's, Asia Buffet, Baskin-Robbins, Brü Grill, CA Fish Grill, Cafe Rio, Chipotle Mexican, Corner Baker Cafe, Del Taco, Denny's, Dunkin', El Pollo Loco, Frank's Chinese, Habit Burger, Honeybaked Ham, Jack-in-the-Box, Jamba Juice, Jersey Mike's, Lucille's BBQ, Luna Grill, McDonald's, MOD Pizza, Panda Express, Peet's Coffee, Sizzler, Subway, Teriyaki Madness, Tommy's Burgers, 99c Store, AT&T, CVS Drug, Firestone/auto, Home Depot, PetSmart, Ralph's Foods, Ross, Staples, Verizon, W 76, Chevron/dsl, BJ's Rest., Cane's, Chick-fil-A, FarmerBoys, In-N-Out, King's Fishhouse, Rodrigo's Mexican, Ruby's Diner, Starbucks, Subway, Woody's Diner, Laguna Hills Lodge, CVS Drug, Just Tires, REI, Trader Joe's, USPO, Walgreens

90 Alicia Pkwy, Mission Viejo, E Dave's Chicken, Del Taco, Denny's, Five Guys, Flame Broiler, Mendocino Farms Sandwiches, Starbucks, Subway, $Tree, AT&T, CVS Drug, EVC, Target, W Chevron, Carl's Jr, Hafez Cafe, Little Caesar's, Togo's, Wendy's, AAA, BigLots, Dick's, to Laguna Niguel PK, vet

89 La Paz Rd, Mission Viejo, E Arco/24hr, Shell, Starbucks, Taco Bell, TK Burgers, vet, W 76, Dunkin', Flamingos Mexican, Ironwood Grill, McDonald's, Outback Steaks, Romano Cucina, Sushi Ramen, Villa Roma, Wienerschnitzel, Courtyard, Hills Hotel, 7-11, Best Buy, Petco, World Mkt

88 Oso Pkwy, Pacific Park Dr, E 76/dsl/repair, Chevron/repair, Carl's Jr, Starbucks, Subway, Fairfield Inn, Ace Hardware, golf, vet, W DQ, Jack-in-the-Box, Krispy Kreme, Midas, to Laguna Niguel PK

86 Crown Valley Pkwy, E 76, Arco, Chevron, Buffalo Wild Wings, CAVA, Cheesecake Factory, Chili's, Habit Grill, Island Grill, Jamba Juice, Panda Express, Ruby's Diner, Dick's Sports, Macy's, Nordstrom, vet, W Chevron/dsl, B+C Pizza, Costco/gas, to Laguna Niguel PK

85b Avery Pkwy, E Albertaco's Mexican, Broken Yolk, Del Taco, Jack-in-the-Box, Jimmy John's, Jk Burgers, Mr Pickle's Sandwiches, Starbucks, Sushi Plantation, Hampton Inn, America's Tire/auto, Audi/Infiniti, Burlington,

INTERSTATE 5 Cont'd

85b Continued
Jaguar/Land Rover, Kia, Lexus, Volvo, World Mkt, W Arco/dsl, A's Burgers, In-N-Out, Popeye's, Best Value Laguna Inn, Cadillac/GMC, Costco/gas, Hyundai, Mercedes

85a CA 73 N (toll)

83 Junipero Serra Rd, to San Juan Capistrano, W 76/7-11, Chevron

82 CA 74, Ortego Hwy, E Shell, Bad to the Bone BBQ, Ballpark Pizza, Bravo CA Fresh, Las Golondrinas, Subway, Best Western, vet, W Shell/dsl, Breezy, Carl's Jr, Chick-fil-A, Ciao Pasta Trattoria, Del Taco, Heritage BBQ, In-N-Out, KFC, L'Hirondelle Rest., McDonald's, Ramos Cafe, Starbucks, Sundried Tomato, Taco Bell, Trevor's, Inn at the Mission, $Tree, Ace Hardware, Capistrano Trading Post, GNC, Marshall's, O'Reilly Parts, Ross, San Juan Capistrano Mission, Target, Verizon

81 Camino Capistrano, Camino Capistrano, E VW, W Domino's, KFC, Pizza Amore, Ricardo's Mexican, Starbucks, Residence Inn, CHP, Chrysler/Dodge/Jeep, Ford, Goodyear/auto, Honda, Nissan, Ross, T-Mobile, Toyota/Scion, Trader Joe's, Verizon, Vons Foods

79 CA 1, Pacific Coast Hwy, Capistrano Bch, Capistrano, W Arco/24hr, Chevron/dsl, Costco/gas, A's Burgers, Carl's Jr, Del Taco, Denny's, El Pollo Loco, Jersey Mike's, McDonald's, Rib Joint, Starbucks, Best Western, DoubleTree, $Tree, AutoZone, PetSmart, Ralph's Foods, Staples, USPO

78 Camino de Estrella, San Clemente, Camino de Estrella, San Clemente, E 76/dsl, Cafe Rio, Flame Broiler, Habit Burger, Jersey Mike's, RoundTable Pizza, Rubio's, Starbucks, Subway, TJ's Pizza, Wahoo's Fish Taco, AAA, CVS Drug, Ralph's Foods, Stater Bros Foods, Trader Joe's, Verizon, vet, W Shell/7-11/dsl, Flights & Irons, Las Golondrinas, O'Reilly Parts, Sprouts Mkt, TJ Maxx

77 Ave Vista Hermosa, W Chick-fil-A

AVE PICO

76 Ave Pico, E Mobil/Circle K, Chipotle, Jersey Mike's, Juice it Up, McDonald's, Panda Express, Papa John's, SmashBurger, Starbucks, Wingstop, Albertson's/Sav-On, GNC, W Chevron, Burger Junkies, Del Taco, Denny's/24hr, In-N-Out, Pick-up-Stix, Stuft Pizza, Subway, Surfin' Chicken, Holiday Inn Express, $Tree, 99c Store, Outlets/famous brands, Staples, tires/repair, USPO, Valvoline, vet

75 Ave Palizada, Ave Presidio, Ave Palizada, Ave Presidio, W Valero, Mr. Pete's Burgers, Pizza Port, Rocco's Rest., Sonny's Pizza, South of Nick's, Starbucks, Subway, Vine Restaurant, Volare Hotel, 7-11, AutoZone, CVS Drug, TrueValue

74 El Camino Real, E Chevron/dsl, Hapa J's Hawaiian, Budget Lodge, Surfbreak Hotel, Tradewinds Motel, same as 75, W 76/dsl, Biggie's Burger, Guichos Eatery, Sancho's Tacos, Taco Bell, 7-11, O'Reilly Parts, Ralph's Foods

73 Ave Calafia, Ave Magdalena, E 76/dsl, Shell, Jack-in-the-Box, Molly Bloom's Cafe, Pedro's Tacos, Sugar Shack Cafe, C-Vu Inn, Calafia Beach Motel, Hampton Inn, Hotel Miramar, LaVista Inn, Travelodge, 7-11, repair/tires, W to San Clemente SP

72 Cristianitios Ave, E Carl's Jr., Valerie's Tacos, Comfort Suites, San Clemente Surf Inn, San Mateo RV Park/dump, W to San Clemente SP

71 Basilone Rd, W San Onofre St Beach

67mm weigh sta both lanes

66mm viewpoint sb

62 Las Pulgas Rd

59mm **Aliso Creek both lanes, full facilities, litter barrels, petwalk, , , RV dump, vending**

OCEANSIDE

54c Oceanside Harbor Dr, W Chevron, Mobil, Del Taco, Denny's/24hr, Days Inn, Harbor Inn, Holiday Inn, to Camp Pendleton

54b Hill St(from sb), to Oceanside, W Chevron, Mobil, Del Taco, Denny's/24hr, In-N-Out, WorldMark, Best Western+, Days Inn, Holiday Inn, Rodeway Inn

54a CA 76 E, Coast Hwy

53 Mission Ave, Oceanside, E 7-11/dsl, Arco/24hr, Mobil/dsl, Alberto's Mexican, Armando's Tacos, Burger King, Jack-in-the-Box, KFC, McDonald's, Starbucks, Ramada, Travelodge, Bussry's Automotive, El Super Mkt, Mission Donuts, W El Pollo Loco, Panda Express, Subway, Wendy's, 99c Store, Walmart Mkt

52 Oceanside Blvd, E Arco, Jiffy Lube, Alberto's Mexican, Cheesesteak Grill, Dunkin', Dutch Bros Coffee, IHOP, Marco's Pizza, McDonald's, Papa John's, Pizza Hut, Popeye's, Red Rooster Grill, Starbucks, Subway, Taco Bell, Wienerschnitzel, Big Lots, CVS Drug, Frazier Farms Mkt, W GM/dsl, Best Western

51c Cassidy St(from sb)

51b CA 78, Vista Way, Escondido, E Chevron/dsl, EVC, Shell, Applebee's, Buffalo Wild Wings, Cheesecake Factory, Chili's, Chipotle, ChuckECheese, Dave&Buster's, Domino's, Einstein Bros., Firehouse Subs, Gaja Korean BBQ, Jamba Juice, Krispy Kreme, Maui BBQ, McDonald's, Olive Garden, Panera Bread, QuikWok, TX Roadhouse, Yukiya Sushi, $Tree, Best Buy, Dick's, Firestone/auto, JC Penney, Macy's, Marshall's, Michael's, Old Navy, PetCo, T-Mobile, Target, Verizon, vet, Walmart, World Mkt, W Hunter Steaks

51a Las Flores Dr

CAR COUNTRY CARLSBAD

50 Elm Ave, Carlsbad Village Dr, E Shell, El Tejate, W 7-11, Chevron, Carl's Jr, El Puerto Mexican, Jack-in-the-Box, KFC/Taco Bell, Subway, Carlsbad Village Inn/EVC, Extended Stay America, Ace Hardware, verizon

49 Tamarack Ave, E Chevron, Mobil/dsl, Village Kitchen, Days Inn, Hyland Inn, Motel 6, Vons Foods/EVC, W Arco, Starbucks

48 Cannon Rd, Car Country Carlsbad, E Acura, Buick/GMC/Cadillac, Chevrolet, Chrysler/Dodge/Jeep, Ford, Honda, Hyundai, Jaguar/Land Rover, Kia, Lexus, Mazda, Mercedes, Subaru, Toyota, VW, W WestMart, Polo Steaks, Hyatt House, West Inn

47 Carlsbad Blvd, Palomar Airport Rd, E 7-11/EVC, Chevron, Mobil/dsl, BJ's Rest., Burger Lounge, Carl's Jr, Corner Bakery Cafe, Grand Pacific Resort, Green Dragon/Museum, Islands Burgers, Kings Fish House, Mainstream Grill, Panda Express, PF Chang's, Ruby's Diner, Starbucks, Subway, Taco Bell, Carlsbad by the Sea, Motel 6, AT&T, Carlsbad Ranch/Flower Fields, Chrysler/Dodge/Jeep, Costco/gas, Ford, Jiffy Lube, outlet mall, W Shell/dsl, In-N-Out, McDonald's, Miguel's Mexican, Hilton Garden, Toyota

45 Poinsettia Lane, W Shell/dsl, Benihana, El Pollo Loco, Jack-in-the-Box, Jersey Mike's, L'atelier de Paris, Pick-Up Stix, Starbucks, Best Western, Holiday Inn Express, La Quinta, Motel 6, Porsche/Volvo, Ralph's Foods/EVC, S Carlsbad St Bch

44 La Costa Ave, E vista point, W Chevron/dsl

43 Leucadia Blvd, E Quality Inn, W Chevron, Starbucks

42b Encinitas Blvd, E Chevron/dsl, Mobil, Valero, Crack Shack Chicken, HoneyBaked Ham, In-N-Out, Oggi's Pizza, CVS Drug, NAPA, Petco, to Quail Botanical Gardens, vet, W Shell, Little Caesar's, Subway, Wendy's, Best Western/rest., Days Inn, Lazy Acres Mkt

41a Santa Fe Dr, to Encinitas, E Shell, Carl's Jr, El Nopalito, 7-11, W Domino's, Plant Power, H, vet, Vons Foods

40 Birmingham Dr, E Chevron, Valero, El Pueblo, Hampton Inn, W Shell

= gas = food = lodging = other = rest stop

INTERSTATE 5 Cont'd

Exit #	Services
39mm	viewpoint sb
39	Manchester Ave, E 76, to MiraCosta College
37	Lomas Santa Fe Dr, Solana Bch, E Einstein Bros., Habit Burger, Jersey Mike's, Pizza Nova, Samurai Rest., Starbucks, Vons Foods, W Mobil, Carl's Jr, Crust Pizza, Jamba Juice, Panda Express, Panera Bread, Starbucks, CVS Drug, Discount Tire, Marshall's, Sprouts Mkt, Staples
36	Via de La Valle, Del Mar, E Chevron, Mobil, Cucina Italian, El Pueblo Mexican, McDonald's, Milton's Deli, Gelson's Mkt, PetCo, Verizon, Whole Foods Mkt, W Shell/dsl, Speedway, Denny's, FishMkt Rest., Red Tracton's Rest., Hilton, Pamplemousse Grille, Winners Circle Resort, minigolf, racetrack
34	Del Mar Heights Rd, E Shell/dsl, W 7-11, Broken Yolk Cafe, Bushfire Kitchen, Jack-in-the-Box, Jersey Mike's, Starbucks, AAA, CVS Drug, vet, Vons Foods
33	Carmel Mtn Rd, E Arco, Shell/repair, Ruth's Chris, Taco Bell, DoubleTree Hotel, Hampton Inn, Marriott, Residence Inn
32	CA 56 E, Carmel Valley Rd, E Hilton Garden, Homewood Suites, W Caliente Mexican Food, Mom's Pizza
31	I-805(from sb)
30	Sorrento Valley Rd
29	Genesee Ave, E H
28b	La Jolla Village Dr, E Embassy Suites, Hyatt/EVC, Marriott, H, to LDS Temple, W Mobil/dsl, BJ's Rest., CAVA, Chipotle Mexican, Dominos, Flame Broiler, Ike's Love Sandwiches, Rubio's, Starbucks, Sheraton, Best Buy, CVS Drug, Marshall's, Ralph's Foods, Ross, Trader Joe's, Verizon, Whole Foods Mkt
28a	Nobel Dr(from nb), E Hyatt, LDS Temple, W same as 28b
27	Gilman Dr, La Jolla Colony Dr
26b	CA 52 E
26a	La Jolla Rd(from nb)
23b	CA 274, Balboa Ave, E Del Taco, Costco/gas, H, W 7-11, In-N-Out, McDonald's, Rubio's, Starbucks, Wienerschnitzel, Fairfield Inn, GreenTree Inn, La Quinta, San Diego Motel, SureStay, auto repair, Discount Tire, Ford, Jiffy Lube, Mission Bay Pk, Nissan, Toyota/Scion
23a	Grand Ave, Garnet Ave, same as 23b
22	Clairemont Dr, Mission Bay Dr, E Shell, Speedway, Best Western, Chevrolet, Valvoline Oil Change, VW, W to Sea World
21	Sea World Dr, Tecolote Dr, E Bay Park Fuel, Shell, Aamco, NAPA, vet, W Hilton, Seaworld
20	I-8, W to Nimitz Blvd, E to El Centro, CA 209 S(from sb), to Rosecrans St
19	Old Town Ave, E Arco, Shell, Comfort Inn, Courtyard, Fairfield Inn, Western Inn, Old Town SP
18b	Washington St, E Chevron, Mobil, Holiday Inn Express, H
18a	Pacific Hwy Viaduct, Kettner St
17b	India St, Front St, Sassafras St, W
17a	Hawthorn St, Front St, W Mobil/dsl, Motel 6, Sheraton
16b	6th Ave, downtown
16a	CA 163 N, 10th St, E AeroSpace Museum, W Shell, Breuggers Bagels, Burger King, Del Taco, Jack-in-the-Box, McDonald's, Days Inn, Downtown Lodge, El Cortez Motel, Holiday Inn, Marriott, WorldMark
15c b	CA 94 E(from nb), Pershing Dr, B St, W civic ctr
15a	CA 94 E, J St, Imperial Ave(from sb),, E museum
14b	Cesar Chavez Pkwy
14a	CA 75, to Coronado, W toll rd to Coronado

NATIONAL CITY

CAMINO DE LA PLAZA

Exit #	Services
13b	National Ave SD, 28th St, E Jack-in-the-Box, Little Caesar's, Panda Express, Starbucks, Subway, AutoZone, W Shell, Burger King, Del Taco, El Pollo Loco, McDonald's
13a	CA 15 N, to Riverside
12	Main St, National City, E Shell, Sinclair, Quality Inn, W Chevron
11b	8th St, National City, E Arco, Jack-in-the-Box, Napoleone's Pizza, Howard Johnson, National City Inn, Ramada Inn, Rodeway Inn, Studio 6
11a	Harbor Dr, Civic Center Dr
10	Bay Marina, 24th St, Mile of Cars Way, E Chick-fil-A, Chipotle, Denny's, Freddy's, In-N-Out, Jersey Mike's, Starbucks, W Best Western+
9	CA 54 E
8b	E St, Chula Vista, E Arco, Black Angus, Denny's, La Quinta Mexican, Taco Bell, Wendy's, Holiday Inn Express, Howard Johnson, Motel 6, SureStay Hotel, AutoZone, Jiffy Lube, O'Reilly Parts, W The Rambler
8a	H St
7b	J St(from sb)
7a	L St, E 7-11, 76, Popeye's, China Vista Inn, NAPA, Valvoline Oil
6	Palomar St, E Arco, Buffet House Chinese, Carl's Jr., DQ, IHOP, Jack-in-the-Box, KFC, Little Caesar's, Mariscos La Perla Negra, McDonald's, Panda Express, Starbucks, Subway, Wingstop, Yoshinoya, Palomar Inn, $Tree, AutoZone, Costco/gas, Food4Less, Michael's, Petco, Ross, Target, Walmart, W Valero
5b	Main St, to Imperial Beach
5a	CA 75(from sb), Palm Ave, to Imperial Beach, E Arco, Armando's Mexican, Papa John's, Starbucks, 7-11, Discount Tire, Soto's Transmissions, W 7-11, Arco, Shell, Speedway, All American Sandwiches, Burger King, Burritos Luna, Carl's Jr, Coldstone Creamery, IHOP, Little Caesars, McDonald's, Popeye's, Rally's, Subway, Wienerschnitzel, 99c Store, AutoZone, CVS Drug, GNC, Home Depot, Jiffy Lube, Von's Foods, Walmart
4	Coronado Ave(from sb), E Chevron, Shell, In-N-Out, Taco Bell, 7-11, W Arco, Hollister/dsl, Denny's, Ed Fernandez Mexican, Motel 6, to Border Field SP
3	CA 905, Tocayo Ave, W 7-11
2	Dairy Mart Rd, E Arco/24hr, Carl's Jr, Mama Mia Pizza, McDonald's, Starbucks, Best Western/EVC, NAPA, Pacifica RV Resort, W Hotel Baja
1b	Via de San Ysidro, E Shell, W Chevron, Primera/Shell/dsl, Denny's, Motel 6, Studio 6
1a	I-805 N(from nb), Camino de la Plaza, E Burger King, Jack-in-the-Box, KFC, McDonald's, Subway, Holiday Motel, AutoZone, W Achiato Mexican, IHOP, Iron Wok, McDonald's, Starbucks, Sunrise Buffet, $Tree, Baja Duty-Free, border parking, factory outlet, Marshall's, Old Navy, Ross, TJ Maxx

CA

INTERSTATE 5 Cont'd

Exit #	Services
0mm	California state line, US/Mexico Border, customs, I-5 begins/ends.

INTERSTATE 8

ANDRADE

Exit #	Services
172.5mm	California/Arizona state line, Colorado River, Pacific/Mountain time zone
172	4th Ave, Yuma, **N** [other] Paradise Casino, **S** [gas] Chevron, Circle K/dsl, Tesla EVC, [food] Jack-in-the-Box, Yuma Landing Rest., [lodging] Coronado Motel, Hilton Garden, Home2 Suites, [other] to Yuma SP
170	Winterhaven Dr, **N** [other] Sans End RV Park, **S** Rivers Edge RV Park
166	CA 186, Algodones Rd to Mexico, Andrade, **S** [other] Cocopah RV Resort/golf, Quechan Hotel/Casino
165mm	CA Insp/weigh sta
164	Sidewinder Rd, **N** [other] st patrol, **S** [gas] Chevron/LP/dsl, [other] Pilot Knob RV Park
159	CA 34, Ogilby Rd, to Blythe
156	Grays Well Rd, [other] Imperial Dunes RA, **N** Imperial Dunes RA
155mm	rest area both lanes(exits left), full [handicapped] facilities, [picnic], litter barrels, petwalk
151	Gordons Well, **N** [food] Duner's Diner, [other] Gordon's Well RV Park
146	Brock Research Ctr Rd
143	CA 98, to Calexico, Midway Well
131	CA 115, VanDerLinden Rd, to Holtville
128	Bonds Corner Rd
125	CA 7 S, Orchard Rd, Holtville, **N** [other] food, gas/dsl
120	Bowker Rd
118b a	CA 111, to Calexico, **N** [other] Country Life RV Park
116	Dogwood Rd, **S** [gas] Arco/dsl, Tesla EVC, [food] Buffalo Wild Wings, Burger King, Carino's, Chili's, ChuckeCheese, Denny's, Famous Dave's BBQ, Fortune Garden, Jack-in-the-Box, Menchie's, Olive Garden, RoundTable Pizza, Sombrero Mexican, Starbucks, Subway, [lodging] Fairfield Inn, Hampton Inn/EVC, Home2 Suites, TownePlace Suites, [other] $Tree, 99c, AT&T, Best Buy, Dillard's, Discount Tire, JC Penney, Kohl's, Macy's, Marshall's, Michael's, PetCo, Ross, Staples
115	CA 86, 4th St, El Centro, **N** [gas] 7-11/dsl, Arco/dsl, Chevron/dsl, Gulf/dsl, Shell/dsl, [food] Jack-in-the-Box, Las Palmitas Tacos, Lucky Chinese, McDonald's, [lodging] Holiday Inn Express, Motel 6, [other] 99c, Family$, O'Reilly Parts, U-Haul, **S** [gas] 7-11/Subway, Anthem/dsl/scales, [food] Habit Burger, IHOP, In-N-Out, Johnny's Burritos, Korean BBQ, Panda Express, Starbucks, Taco Bell, [lodging] Best Value Inn, Best Western, Comfort Inn, MainStay Suites, [other] AutoZone, Buick/Chevrolet/GMC/Cadillac, Desert Trails RV Park, Home Depot, Honda, Hyundai
114	Imperial Ave, El Centro, **N** [gas] 7-11/dsl, Arco, Chevron, Chevron/dsl, Shell/dsl, [food] Applebee's, Broken Yolk Cafe, Burrito Factory, Carl's Jr, Chipotle, Church's TX Chicken, Coldstone, Del Taco, Del Taco, Denny's, Domino's, Donut Palace, El Pollo Loco, Farmer Boys, Hamburger Stand, Jack-in-the-Box, Jack-in-the-Box, KFC, Little Caesar's, Los Cabos, McDonald's, Papa John's, Pizza Hut, Rally's, Sizzler, Starbucks, Starbucks, Subway, Taco Bell, Wendy's, [lodging] Crown Motel, Days Inn, Ocotillo Inn, Quality Inn, Value Inn, [other] $General Mkt, $Tree, 99c Store, Ace Hardware, Advance Parts, ALDI, auto repair, AutoZone, Chrysler/Dodge/Jeep, Costco/gas, CVS Drug, Discount Tire, Food4Less, Ford, [H], Lowe's, Nissan, Nissan/EVC, O'Reilly Parts, PepBoys, PetSmart, Ross, st patrol, Target, Toyota, URGENT CARE, Verizon, Von's Foods, VW, Walgreens, Walmart
111	Forrester Rd, to Westmorland

EL CENTRO

CAMERON STATION

Exit #	Services
108mm	Sunbeam Rest Area both lanes, full [handicapped] facilities, [phone], [picnic], litter barrels, petwalk, RV dump
107	Drew Rd, Seeley, **N** [other] Sunbeam RV Park, to Sunbeam Lake, **S** Rio Bend RV Park
101	Dunaway Rd, elev 0 ft, Imperial Valley, **N** [other] st prison
89	Imperial Hwy, CA 98, Ocotillo, **N** [other] Red Feathers Mkt/Cafe, RV camping, USPO, **S** [gas] Chevron/dsl, [other] Desert Museum
87	CA 98(from eb), to Calexico
81mm	runaway truck ramp eb
80	Mountain Springs Rd
77	In-ko-pah Park Rd, **N** [phone], towing
75mm	brake insp area eb
73	Jacumba, **S** [gas] Chevron/dsl, Shell/Subway/dsl/24hr
65	CA 94, Boulevard, to Campo, **S** [gas] MtnTop/dsl, [lodging] Back Country Inn, [other] to McCain Valley RA(7mi), USPO
63mm	Tecate Divide, elev 4140 ft
62mm	Crestwood Summit, elev 4190 ft
61	Crestwood Rd, Live Oak Springs, **S** info, [gas] Golden Acorn Trkstp/casino/dsl
54	Kitchen Creek Rd, Cameron Station
51	rd 1, Buckman Spgs Rd, to Lake Morena, rest area both lanes, full [handicapped] facilities, [phone], [picnic], litter barrels, petwalk, RV dump
48	insp sta wb
47	rd 1, Sunrise Hwy, Laguna Summit, elev 4055 ft, **N** to Laguna Mtn RA
45	Pine Valley, Julian, **N** [gas] Valero, [food] Frosty Burger, [lodging] Pine Valley Inn, [other] city park, Mtn Mkt, to Cuyamaca Rancho SP, USPO, vet
44mm	Pine Valley Creek
42mm	elev 4000 ft
40	CA 79, Japatul Rd, Descanso, **N** [food] Descanso Rest., [other] to Cuyamaca Rancho SP
37mm	vista point eb, elev 3000 ft
36	E Willows, **N** [other] Alpine Sprs RV Park, casino, Viejas Indian Res
33	W Willows Rd, to Alpine, same as 36, **N** [other] Alpine Sprs RV Park, casino, Viejas Outlets/famous brands, **S** [food] Jack-in-the-Box, McDonald's, Pizza Hut, Starbucks, [other] $Tree, Albertsons, ranger sta
31mm	elev 2000 ft
30	Tavern Rd, to Alpine, **N** [gas] Chevron/dsl, Shell/dsl, **S** 76, Tesla EVC, [food] Carl's Jr, Jersey Mike's, La Carreta, Little Caesar's, Mananas Mexican, Mediterraneo Grill, Panda Machi Chinese, [lodging] Ayre's Lodge, [other] Ace Hardware, CVS Drug, NAPA, URGENT CARE
27	Dunbar Lane, Harbison Canyon, **N** [other] Flinn Sprgs CP, RV camping
25mm	elev 1000 ft
24mm	[phone]
23	Lake Jennings Pk Rd, Lakeside, **N** [gas] Mobil/Jack-in-the-Box/dsl/24hr, [other] RV camping, to Lake Jennings CP, **S** [gas] 7-11, [food] Marechiaro's Pizza, Starbucks
22	Los Coches Rd, Lakeside, **N** [gas] 7-11, Arco, Eagle/dsl/LP, [food] Albert's Mexican, Laposta Mexican, [other] RV camping/dump, **S** [gas] EVC, Shell/dsl, [food] Denny's, McDonald's, Panda Express, Starbucks, Subway, Taco Bell, [other] $Tree, Walmart
20b	Greenfield Dr, to Crest, **N** [gas] Chevron/dsl, Sky Fuel/dsl, [food] Domino's, Jack-in-the-Box, Marieta's Mexican, McDonald's, Menchie's, Panchos Tacos, Subway, [other] 7-11, 99c Store, Albertson's, auto repair, AutoZone, Ford, RV camping, st patrol, URGENT CARE, **S** [gas] Mobil/dsl/LP
20a	E Main St(from wb, no EZ return), **N** [lodging] Budget Inn, [other] Ford, RV repair, Vacationer RV Park, **S** [gas] Arco
19	2nd St, CA 54, El Cajon, **N** [gas] 76/dsl, Arco, Chevron/dsl, [food] Marechiaro's Italian, Pancake House, Starbucks, [other] CVS Drug, Genie Auto Ctr, USPO, **S** [gas] Golden State/dsl, Shell,

LAKESIDE

EL CAJON

INTERSTATE 8 Cont'd

19 Continued
Arby's, Baskin-Robbins, Carl's Jr, Chipotle, City Bistro, El Compadre Tacos, IHOP, Jack-in-the-Box, Jamba Juice, KFC, Little Caesar's, McDonald's, Papa John's, Popeyes, Rally's, Starbucks, Subway, Taco Bell, Tacos El Gallo, Wienerschnitzel, Wing Stop, Best Value Inn, Rancho Inn&Suites, $Tree, 7-11, CarQuest, Firestone/auto, Grocery Outlet, Jiffy Lube, PepBoys, PetCo, Sprouts Mkt, Valley Foods, Valvoline, Walgreens, Walmart Mkt

18 Mollison Ave, El Cajon, **N** Chevron, Denny's, Starbucks, Clarion Pointe, Days Inn, Quality Inn, **S** Arco, QuickTrip/dsl, Los Garcia's, EconoLodge

17c Magnolia Ave, CA 67(from wb), to Santee, **N** Arco, Black Angus Steaks, Del Taco, El Pollo Loco, Jack-in-the-Box, Jersey Mike's, L&L HI BBQ, Panda Express, Starbucks, AutoZone, Food4Less, O'Reilly Parts, Target, **S** EVC, Shell/service/dsl, Panda Express, Rubio's, Courtyard, Motel 6, Super 8, 7-11, Nudo's Drug, Ross

17b CA 67(from eb), same as 17 a&c

17a Johnson Ave(from eb), **N** EVC, Applebee's, Black Bear Diner, Burger King, Carl's Jr, Dunkin', Five Guys, Hacienda Mexican, In-N-Out, Jamba Juice, KFC, Little Caesar's, McDonald's, New Century Buffet, Panda Express, Panera Bread, Rubio's, Topfruit Juice, TX Roadhouse, Urban Cafe, Hampton Inn, $Tree, ALDI, Best Buy, CVS Drug, Dick's, Home Depot, Honda, JC Penney, Lexus, Marshall's, Mercedes, PetSmart, Subaru, Toyota, Walmart, **S** Aamco, Kenworth, Kia, Mazda, vet

16 Main St, **N** Arco, Denny's, Sombrero Mexican, Relax Inn, 7-11, **S** Chevron/dsl, Super Star, brakes/transmissions, Nissan

15 El Cajon Blvd(from eb), **N** Hotel Villa, **S** 76/dsl, UHaul, BMW

14c Severin Dr, Fuerte Dr(from wb), **N** Shell/dsl, Tesla EVC, Anthony's Fish Grotto, Charcoal House Rest., La Casa Blanca, Best Western+, **S** Brigantine Seafood Rest.

14b a CA 125, to CA 94

13b Jackson Dr, Grossmont Blvd, **N** Chevron, BJ's Rest., Burgers Fish & Fries, Casa de Pico, Chili's, ChuckeCheese, ClaimJumper, Olive Garden, Panda Express, Panera Bread, Red Lobster, Starbucks, Vallarta Express, $Tree, CVS Drug, Evan's Tire, H, Macy's, O'Reilly Parts, Office Depot, Petco, Target, Trader Joe's, USPO, Verizon, vet, Walmart, World Mkt, **S** 76, Honeybaked Ham, Jack-in-the-Box, Jersey Mike's, Discount Tire, Ford, Hobby Lobby, Lincoln, Ross, Walmart Mkt

13a Spring St(from eb), El Cajon Blvd(from wb), **S** Duke's Burgers, El Pollo Loco, El Torito, Subway, Hitching Post, 99c Store, AutoZone

12 Fletcher Pkwy, to La Mesa, **N** Shell/dsl, Carl's Jr, Chick-fil-A, Chipotle Mexican, Habit Burger, McDonald's, Pick Up Stix, Heritage Inn, Holiday Inn, 7-11, Costco, **S** Duke's Burgers, El Pollo Loco, El Torito, Subway, Motel 6, 99c Store, Chevrolet, San Diego RV Resort, Valvoline

11 70th St, Lake Murray Blvd, **N** Shell/dsl, Aromi Italian, Subway, **S** Shell/7-11/dsl, Akin's Deli, Burger Den, Denny's, Marie Callender's, auto repair, H, URGENT CARE

10 College Ave, **N** Chevron/dsl, Einstein Bros, Windmill Farms Mkt, **S** Habit Burgers, Jack in the Box, 7-11, H, to SDSU, Trader Joe's

9 Waring Rd, **N** Del's BBQ, Days Inn, Rodeway Inn, Navajo Canyon RA

8 Fairmount Ave(7 from eb), to Mission Gorge Rd, **N** 7-11, Chevron, Mobil, Sky/dsl, Carl's Jr, Chili's, Denny's, El Pollo Loco, In-N-Out, Jack-in-the-Box, Jamba Juice, Jersey Mike's,

8 Continued
McDonald's, Panda Express, Rolando's Tacos, Rubio's, San Diego Poke, Sombrero Mexican, Starbucks, Subway, Taco Fiesta, Wendy's, Admiral Baker RV Camping, AutoZone, CVS Drug, Discount Tire, Home Depot, Honda, H, Petco, Toyota, Vons Foods

7b a I-15 N, CA 15 S, to 40th St

6b I-805, N to LA, S to Chula Vista

6a Texas St, Qualcomm Way, same as 5, **N** Dave&Buster's

5 Mission Ctr Rd, **N** Chevron, Broken Yolk Cafe, Buffalo Wild Wings, CA Fish Grill, Chipotle Mexican, Corner Cafe, Dave's Hot Chicken, El Pollo Loco, Habit Burger, Hooters, In-N-Out, King's Fish House, Lazy Dog Rest., Mimi's Cafe, On The Border, Outback Steaks, Pei Wei, Pick-Up Stix, Puesto Mexican, Qdoba, Robek Juice, Rubio's, Sammy's Woodfired Pizza, Starbucks, Taco Bell, Marriott, Springhill Suites/EVC, AT&T, Best Buy, Chevrolet, Marshall's, Michael's, Nordstrom Rack, Old Navy, Staples, Target, Trader Joe's, **S** Benihana, Denny's, Wendy's, Hilton, Homewood Suites, Mission Inn, Ramada Suites, Sheraton/EVC, Worldmark, Buick/GMC/Cadillac, Chrysler/Dodge/Jeep, Mazda

4c b CA 163, Cabrillo Frwy, **S** to downtown, to SD Zoo

4a Hotel Circle Dr(from eb), CA 163 (from wb)

3a Hotel Circle, Taylor St, **N** Remy Steaks, Best Western, Handlery Hotel, Motel 6, Riverleaf Inn, Town&Country Motel, golf, **S** Tesla EVC, Atwood Hotel, Candlewood Suites, Courtyard, Days Inn, DoubleTree Inn, Extended Stay America, Hampton Inn, Holiday Inn Express, Homewood Suites, Hotel Iris, Howard Johnson, King's Inn/rest., Legacy Resort, Super 8, vet

2c Morena Blvd(from wb)

2b I-5, N to LA, S to San Diego

2a Rosecrans St(from wb), CA 209, **S** Shell, Burger King, Chipotle Mexican, ChuckECheese, Del Taco, In-N-Out, L&L HI BBQ, Panda Express, Starbucks, Starbucks, Subway, Comfort Inn, Old Town Inn, Staples, vet

1 W Mission Bay Blvd, Sports Arena Blvd(from wb), **N** to SeaWorld, **S** Arby's, Buffalo Wild Wings, Chick-fil-A, Chili's, Denny's, Habit Burgers, Ike's Sandwiches, In-N-Out, Jack-in-the-Box, McDonald's, Olive Garden, Phil's BBQ, Red Lobster, Sabor Brazillian, Wendy's, Holiday Inn Express, Wyndham Garden, Dick's, Home Depot, Ralph's, Target, U-Haul, Von's

0mm I-8 begins/ends on Sunset Cliffs Blvd, **N** Mission Bay Park, **W** 76, Shell/repair, Jack-in-the-Box, Kaiserhof Cafe, Dusty Rhodes Park

BLYTHE

INTERSTATE 10

245mm California/Arizona state line, Colorado River, pacific/mountain time zone

244mm inspection sta wb

243 Riviera Dr, **S** The Cove RV Park

241 US 95, Intake Blvd, to Needles, Blythe, **N** Exxon/dsl,

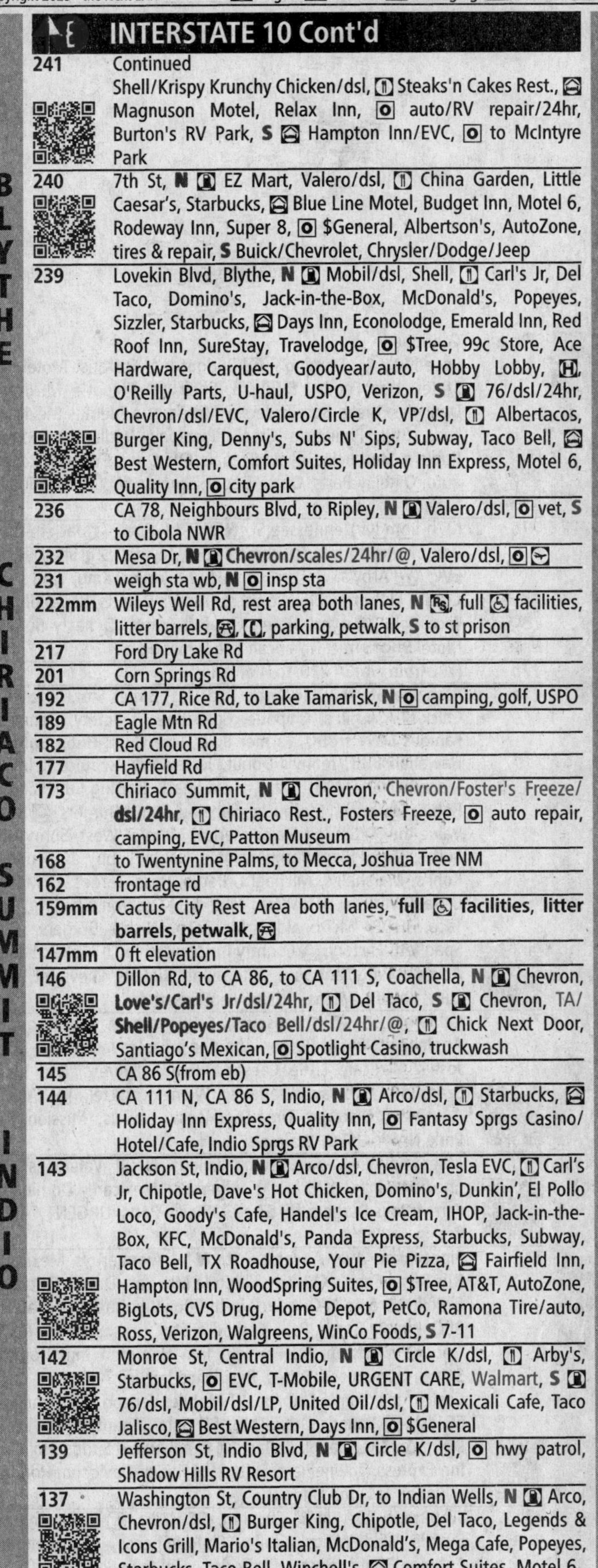

INTERSTATE 10 Cont'd

241 Continued
Shell/Krispy Krunchy Chicken/dsl, Steaks'n Cakes Rest., Magnuson Motel, Relax Inn, auto/RV repair/24hr, Burton's RV Park, **S** Hampton Inn/EVC, to McIntyre Park

BLYTHE

240 7th St, **N** EZ Mart, Valero/dsl, China Garden, Little Caesar's, Starbucks, Blue Line Motel, Budget Inn, Motel 6, Rodeway Inn, Super 8, $General, Albertson's, AutoZone, tires & repair, **S** Buick/Chevrolet, Chrysler/Dodge/Jeep

239 Lovekin Blvd, Blythe, **N** Mobil/dsl, Shell, Carl's Jr, Del Taco, Domino's, Jack-in-the-Box, McDonald's, Popeyes, Sizzler, Starbucks, Days Inn, Econolodge, Emerald Inn, Red Roof Inn, SureStay, Travelodge, $Tree, 99c Store, Ace Hardware, Carquest, Goodyear/auto, Hobby Lobby, H, O'Reilly Parts, U-haul, USPO, Verizon, **S** 76/dsl/24hr, Chevron/dsl/EVC, Valero/Circle K, VP/dsl, Albertacos, Burger King, Denny's, Subs N' Sips, Subway, Taco Bell, Best Western, Comfort Suites, Holiday Inn Express, Motel 6, Quality Inn, city park

236 CA 78, Neighbours Blvd, to Ripley, **N** Valero/dsl, vet, **S** to Cibola NWR

CHIRIACO SUMMIT

232 Mesa Dr, **N** Chevron/scales/24hr/@, Valero/dsl,

231 weigh sta wb, **N** insp sta

222mm Wileys Well Rd, rest area both lanes, **N** full facilities, litter barrels, , parking, petwalk, **S** to st prison

217 Ford Dry Lake Rd

201 Corn Springs Rd

192 CA 177, Rice Rd, to Lake Tamarisk, **N** camping, golf, USPO

189 Eagle Mtn Rd

182 Red Cloud Rd

177 Hayfield Rd

173 Chiriaco Summit, **N** Chevron, Chevron/Foster's Freeze/**dsl/24hr**, Chiriaco Rest., Fosters Freeze, auto repair, camping, EVC, Patton Museum

168 to Twentynine Palms, to Mecca, Joshua Tree NM

162 frontage rd

159mm Cactus City Rest Area both lanes, **full facilities, litter barrels, petwalk,**

147mm 0 ft elevation

INDIO

146 Dillon Rd, to CA 86, to CA 111 S, Coachella, **N** Chevron, **Love's/Carl's** Jr/dsl/24hr, Del Taco, **S** Chevron, TA/**Shell/Popeyes/Taco** Bell/dsl/24hr/@, Chick Next Door, Santiago's Mexican, Spotlight Casino, truckwash

145 CA 86 S(from eb)

144 CA 111 N, CA 86 S, Indio, **N** Arco/dsl, Starbucks, Holiday Inn Express, Quality Inn, Fantasy Sprgs Casino/Hotel/Cafe, Indio Sprgs RV Park

143 Jackson St, Indio, **N** Arco/dsl, Chevron, Tesla EVC, Carl's Jr, Chipotle, Dave's Hot Chicken, Domino's, Dunkin', El Pollo Loco, Goody's Cafe, Handel's Ice Cream, IHOP, Jack-in-the-Box, KFC, McDonald's, Panda Express, Starbucks, Subway, Taco Bell, TX Roadhouse, Your Pie Pizza, Fairfield Inn, Hampton Inn, WoodSpring Suites, $Tree, AT&T, AutoZone, BigLots, CVS Drug, Home Depot, PetCo, Ramona Tire/auto, Ross, Verizon, Walgreens, WinCo Foods, **S** 7-11

142 Monroe St, Central Indio, **N** Circle K/dsl, Arby's, Starbucks, EVC, T-Mobile, URGENT CARE, Walmart, **S** 76/dsl, Mobil/dsl/LP, United Oil/dsl, Mexicali Cafe, Taco Jalisco, Best Western, Days Inn, $General

139 Jefferson St, Indio Blvd, **N** Circle K/dsl, hwy patrol, Shadow Hills RV Resort

137 Washington St, Country Club Dr, to Indian Wells, **N** Arco, Chevron/dsl, Burger King, Chipotle, Del Taco, Legends & Icons Grill, Mario's Italian, McDonald's, Mega Cafe, Popeyes, Starbucks, Taco Bell, Winchell's, Comfort Suites, Motel 6,

137 Continued
Buick/GMC, Chrysler/Dodge/Jeep, Ford, Holland RV Ctr, Honda, Kia, Palm Springs RV Park, Stater Bros, Toyota, Toyota, VW, Walgreens, **S** 76, Mobil/Circle K/EVC, Carl's Jr, Carmen's Mexican, China Wok, Domino's, Goody's Cafe, La Casita Mexican, Subway, TJ's Steaks, Wendy's, Wingstop, Wrap Shack, Goodyear/auto, Ramona Tire

134 Cook St, to Indian Wells, **S** Arco, Mobil/Circle K/dsl, Applebee's, Billy Q's, Buccatini, Carl's Jr, Castenada's Mexican, Cold Stone, Firehouse Grill, Jack-in-the-Box, JT's Diner, Pueblo Viejo Grill, Starbucks, Subway, Courtyard, Fairfield Inn, Hampton Inn, Holiday Inn Express, Homewood Suites, Residence Inn, to Cal State U, URGENT CARE, vet

RANCHO MIRAGE

131 Monterey Ave, Thousand Palms, **N** Arco, Jack-in-the-Box, **S** EVC, Casteneda's Mexican, Chik-fil-A, Chipotle, Clark's Cafe/Food Mkt, Del Taco, El Pollo Loco, El Ranchito, Firehouse Subs, IHOP, Jersey Mike's, Juice It Up!, Krispy Kreme, Los Arcos Mexican, Maracas Cantina, McDonald's, Panda Express, Panera Bread, Red Robin, Starbucks, Subway, The Habit, Wendy's, $Tree, 99c Store, America's Tire, AutoZone, CarMax, Costco/gas, Home Depot, Kohl's, Lowe's, Mtn View Tire/auto, PetSmart, Sam's Club/gas, T-Mobile, Verizon, vet, Walmart

130 Ramon Rd, Bob Hope Dr, **N** Chevron/dsl, Flying J/dsl/LP/rest./24hr, Shell/dsl, Valero/dsl, Carl's Jr, Del Taco, Denny's, Denny's, Domino's, Goody's Cafe, In-N-Out, McDonald's, San Miguel Mexican, Starbucks, Starbucks, Taco Bell, The Meltdown, Best Western+, Rodeway Inn, truckwash, USPO, **S** Agua Caliente Casino/rest., H, Parkhouse Tire

126 Date Palm Dr, Rancho Mirage, **S** Arco/dsl, Mobil, U.S. Fuels, Denny's, DQ, GiGi's Crepes, Jack-in-the-Box, Starbucks, Subway, DoubleTree, CVS, Stater Bros. Mkt, Walgreens

123 Palm Dr, to Desert Hot Sprgs, **N** Arco/dsl, Chevron/Jack-in-the-Box/dsl, Caliente Springs Camping

120 Indian Ave, to N Palm Sprgs, **N** 76/Circle K, Arco/dsl, Shell/dsl, Denny's, Motel 6, Harley-Davidson, **S** Chevron, EVC, Pilot/Wendy's/dsl/scales/24hr, Del Taco, Jack-in-the-Box, H

117 CA 62, to Yucca Valley, Twentynine Palms, to Joshua Tree NM

114 Whitewater, many windmills

113mm rest area both lanes, full facilities, , , litter barrels

112 CA 111(from eb), to Palm Springs

110 Haugeen-Lehmann

106 Main St, to Cabazon, **N** Shell/dsl, **S** 76/Circle K/dsl, $General

104 Cabazon, same as 103

103 Fields Rd, **N** Chevron, EVC, Morongo/dsl, Tesla EVC, Alfonso's Ice Cream, Auntie Anne's, Blaze Pizza, Chipotle, Coldstone, Crazy Coyote Tacos, Five Guys, In-N-Out, Jersey Mike's, McDonald's, Panda Express, Sbarro, Starbucks, Taco Bell, Hadley Fruit Orchards, Morongo Reservation/casino, Premium Outlets/famous brands

BANNING

102.5mm Banning weigh sta both lanes

102 Ramsey St(from wb)

101 Hargrave St, Banning, **N** Daybreak, Mobil/Church's TX Chicken, Church's, Consuelo's Mexican, La Villa Burgers, Country Inn, Stagecoach Motel, tires, U-Haul, **S** auto repair

100 CA 243, 8th St, Banning, **N** Chevron/dsl, IHOP, Jack-in-the-Box, Subway

99 22nd St, to Ramsey St, **N** Arco/dsl, Shell/dsl, Carl's Jr, Del Taco, Fresh Burgers, KFC, Little Caesar's, McDonald's, Pizza Hut, Ramsey Burger, Russo's Italian, Sizzler, Starbucks, Taco Bell, Taqueria Orozco, Wall Chinese, Days Inn, Quality Inn, Travelodge, $General, Banning RV Ctr,

CA

CA

BANNING

INTERSTATE 10 Cont'd

99 Continued
Family$, Tire Choice

98 Sunset Ave, Banning, N Chevron/dsl, Domino's, Donut Factory, Gramma's Kitchen, Gus Jr #7 Burger, Holiday Inn Express, $Tree, AutoZone, Boyd's RV Ctr, Buick/Chevrolet/GMC, O'Reilly Parts, tires, vet

96 Highland Springs Ave, N 7-11, Arco, Chevron/dsl, Highland Fuel/dsl, Applebee's, Burger King, Denny's, Dutch Bros, FarmHouse Rest., Guy's Italian, Jack-in-the-Box, Little Caesar's, Papa John's, Subway, Thai Orchid, Wendy's, Hampton Inn, Food4Less, H, Stater Bros Foods, Walgreens, S Mobil/CircleK, Baskin-Robbins, Carl's Jr, Chili's, El Pollo Loco, FarmerBoys, Firehouse Subs, Good China, Hawaiian BBQ, In-N-Out, Jersey Mike's, La Casita, McDonald's, Panda Express, Panera Bread, Patsy's Country Kitchen, Pieology Pizza, Raising Cane's, Sonic, Starbucks, Taco Bell, Waba Grill, Wienerschnitzel, Wingstop, $Tree, Albertson's, ALDI, AT&T, Best Buy, Big Lots, EVC, Hobby Lobby, Home Depot, hwy patrol, Kohl's, Marshall's, PetCo, PetSmart, Ramona Tire/auto, Ross, Schwab Tire, Verizon, Walmart/Subway

BEAUMONT

95 Pennsylvania Ave (from wb), Beaumont, auto repair, N Shell/dsl, Rodeway Inn, AutoZone, Meineke, USPO

94 CA 79, Beaumont, N Mobil/dsl, USA, Baker's DriveThru, Beaumont Cafe, Casa Palacios, Cornerstone BBQ, East Wall Chinese, Juan Pollo, McDonald's, Popeyes, YumYum Donuts, Best Value Inn, Motel 6, auto repair, Family$, NAPA, O'Reilly Parts, S Arco/dsl, Chevron/dsl, Shell/Circle K/dsl, Alberto's Mexican, Del Taco, Jack-in-the-Box, Mr. Taco, Starbucks, Subway, vet

93 CA 60 W, to Riverside

92 San Timoteo Canyon Rd, Oak Valley Pkwy, N 76/Circle K, Chevron/dsl, Sand Trap Grill, Subway, Holiday Inn Express, golf, S golf

91mm rest area wb, full facilities, litter barrels, petwalk, N Cherry Valley RV Resort

90 Cherry Valley Blvd, N truck/tire repair, S Arby's, Del Taco, Fire Rock Burgers, Jack-in-the-Box, Juice It Up!, Panda Express, Starbucks, Stater Bros. Mkts

89 Singleton Rd(from wb), to Calimesa

88 Calimesa Blvd, N Arco/dsl, Chevron/dsl, Shell/Circle K/dsl, Aibeto's Mexican, Burger King, Carl's Jr, Denny's, Domino's, Donut House, McDonald's, NY Pizzaria, Rosie's Rest., Starbucks, Subway, Taco Bell, Calimesa Inn, $Tree, Stater Bros Mkts, Walgreens, S Jack-in-the-Box

OAK GLEN

87 County Line Rd, to Yucaipa, N FasTrip/dsl, Shell/dsl, Baker's DriveThru, Clarkie's Diner, Del Taco, Maria Pollo, Best Value, $General, 99c Store, Dinosaur Tire, NAPA, USPO, vet, S 76/dsl

86mm Wildwood Rest Area eb, full facilities, litter barrels, petwalk

85 Live Oak Canyon Rd, Oak Glen, N Arco/dsl, La Quinta

83 Yucaipa Blvd, N 7-11, Arco/dsl, Chevron/dsl, Mobil/Circle K, Baker's DriveThru, Chik-fil-A, Chipotle, Corky's Kitchen, Five Guys, Hawaiian BBQ, In-N-Out, Jack-in-the-Box, La Mexicana, Panera Bread, Starbucks, Taco Bell, The Crumb, tires, S Subway, antiques

82 Wabash Ave(from wb)

81 Redlands Blvd, Ford St, S La Volata, Starbucks

80 Cypress Ave, University St, N 7-11, to U of Redlands, S Arco, Abelinos Mexican, Baker's Drive-Thru, Baskin-Robbins, Del Taco, DQ, Jack-in-the-Box, KFC, McDonald's, Panera Bread, Taco Shack, Albertsons, auto repair, AutoZone, H

79b a CA 38, 6th St, Orange St, Redlands, N Chevron,

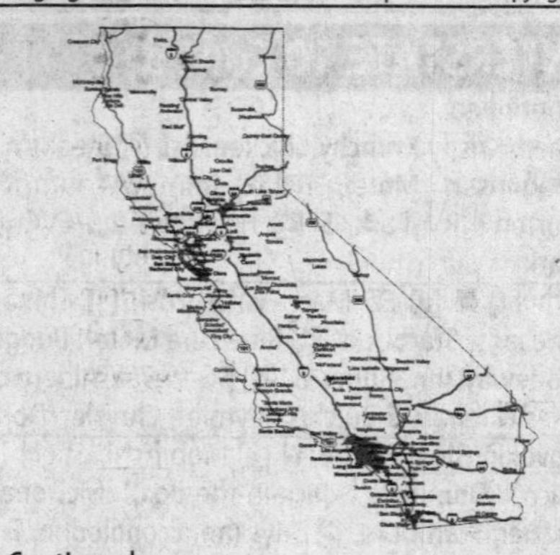

REDLANDS

79b a Continued
Speedway, Domino's, Budget Inn, Stardust Motel, Stater Bros Foods, S 76, Shell, Chipotle Mexican, Denny's, Eureka Burger, Jersey Mike's, Las Fuentes Mexican, Luna Grill, Phoenicia Greek, Pieology, Redlands Ramen, Rubio's, Starbucks, auto repair, CVS Drug, EVC, Firestone/auto, O'Reilly Parts, Office Depot, Sprouts Mkt, Trader Joe's, Verizon, Von's Foods

77c (77b from wb)Tennessee St, N 7-11, Shell, Jack-in-the-Box, Shakey's Pizza, Home Depot, Toyota, S Shell, Tesla EVC, Arby's, Bakers DriveThru, Burger King, Carl's Jr, Coco's, El Burrito, El Pollo Loco, Foster's Donuts, Papa John's, Taco Bell, Ayers Hotel, Comfort Suites, Dynasty Suites, Motel 6, $Tree, American Tire Depot, Ford

77b (77c from wb)CA 210, to Highlands

77a Alabama St, N 76/Circle K/dsl, Buffet Star, Cafe Rio, Chick-fil-A, Chili's, Chipotle, Coldstone Creamery, Denny's, Famous Dave's BBQ, Farmer Boys, Five Guys, Habit Burger, Hawaiian BBQ, Jenny's Donut, Jersey Mike's, Juice It Up! , Macaroni Grill, MOD Pizza, Pizza Shack, Raising Cane's, Red Robin, Starbucks, Starbucks, Subway, Tom's Burgers, Best Value Inn, Extended Stay America, Motel 7 West, SpringHill Suites, Super 8, Barnes&Noble, Hobby Lobby, JC Penney, Kohl's, Marshall's, Michael's, PetCo, Ross, Target, TJ Maxx, U-Haul, Verizon, vet, World Mkt, S Chevron, Shell, Del Taco, IHOP, McDonald's, Mr Taco, Nick's Burgers, Old Spaghetti Factory, Country Inn&Suites, 7-11, 99c Store, Advance Parts, antiques, auto repair, BigLots, Chevrolet, Jiffy Lube, Lowe's, Midas, Nissan, PepBoys, tires

LOMA LINDA

76 California St, N museum, S Anthem Oil, Arco, Applebee's, Bravo Burger, Cha-Cha's Tacos, Jack-in-the-Box, Jose's Mexican, Little Caesar's, Panda Express, Red Chili Szechuan, Subway, Wendy's, Wienerschnitzel, AT&T, AutoZone, Discount Tire, Food4Less, Lowe's, Mission RV Park, NAPA, USPO, Walmart

75 Mountain View Ave, Loma Linda, N Valero/dsl, S Chevron/Circle K/dsl, Alberto's Mexican, Domino's, FarmerBoys Burgers, $Tree, O'Reilly Parts, URGENT CARE, vet

74 Tippecanoe Ave, Anderson St, N Alanberto's Mexican, BJ's Rest., Cane's Chicken, Chipotle Mexican, Dave's Chicken, El Pollo Loco, In-N-Out, Jack-in-the-Box, Jamba Juice, Luau HI BBQ, Panera Bread, Pollo Campero, Starbucks, Subway, Tasty Goody, Wingstop, Fairfield Inn, Hampton Inn, Home2 Suites, Homewood Suites, Residence Inn, 7-11, Best Buy, Costco/gas, Sam's Club/gas, T-Mobile, Verizon, S Phillips 66/dsl, Baker's Drive-Thru, BK Subs, Chapter Two Thai, Del Taco, KFC, Napoli Italian, Candlewood Suites, Holiday Inn Express, TownePlace Suites, Harley-Davidson, Honda, Hyundai, to Loma Linda U

73b a Waterman Ave, N Chevron, G&M/dsl, Black Angus, Buffalo Wild Wings, Chili's, ChuckeCheese, ClaimJumper, Cutting Board Rest., El Torito, Golden Corral, IHOP,

INTERSTATE 10 Cont'd

73b a Continued
Kalaveras Mexican, King Buffet, Mimi's Café, Olive Garden, Outback Steaks, Panda Express, Red Lobster, Sizzler, Star Crab, Subway, Taco Bell, TGIFriday's, DoubleTree, Hilton Garden, Hity Inn, La Quinta, Quality Inn, Staybridge Suites, Super 8, SureStay+, 7-11, ALDI, Home Depot, PetSmart, S 7-11, Arco, Pilot/dsl/24hr/@, Burger King, Carl's Jr, Gus Jr Burger #8, McDonald's, Popeyes, Starbucks, Motel 6, El Monte RV Ctr, repair

72 I-215, CA 91

71 Mt Vernon Ave, Sperry Ave, N 7-11, Trkstp/dsl/LP, Alberto's Mexican, Colony Inn, Colton Motel, Comfort Inn, repair

70b 9th St, N Mobil, Denny's, Domino's, House of Eggs Cafe, McDonald's, P&G Burgers, PizzaDilly, Starbucks, Best Western+, NAPA, Stater Bros Foods, USPO

70a Rancho Ave, N Del Taco, Donut Star, Golden Pizza, Jack-in-the-Box, KFC/Taco Bell, Wienerschnitzel

69 Pepper Dr, N Arco/Chelo's/dsl, Chevron, Baker's DriveThru, Black Bear Diner, Blaze Pizza, Firehouse Subs, Jack-in-the-Box, Popeye's, Starbucks, The Habit Burgers, H

68 Riverside Ave, to Rialto, N Chevron/dsl, EVC, I-10 Trkstp/dsl/scales, USA, Burger King, Charley's Cheesesteaks, El Pollo Loco, IHOP, In-N-Out, Jack-in-the-Box, McDonald's, Panda Express, Panera Bread, Starbucks, Subway, Taco Joe's, Wingstop, American Inn, Days Inn, Welcome Inn, Woodspring Suites, American Tire Depot, AutoZone, dsl repair, Pepboys, T-Mobil, S Shell/Circle K/dsl

66 Cedar Ave, to Bloomington, N Arco, Valero/dsl, Baker's DriveThru, Burger King, Domino's, DQ, FarmerBoys Burgers, Taco Bell, S 7-11, Chevron, Pilot/Jack-in-the-Box/Del Taco/dsl/24hr, $Tree

64 Sierra Ave, to Fontana, N 76/dsl, Arco, Mobil, Shell, Billy J's Rest., ChuckeCheese, Dave's Chicken, Del Taco, Denny's, Dunkin', El Gallo Giro, IHOP, In-N-Out, Jack-in-the-Box, KFC, McDonald's, Ono HI BBQ, Pancho Villa's, Panda Express, Papa John's, Popeyes, Star Crab, Starbucks, Subway, Taco Bell, Thai Garden, The Habit Burger, Wendy's, Wienerschnitzel, Winchell's Donuts, Yoshinoya, Best Value Inn, Motel 6, Valley Motel, $Tree, American Tire Depot, AutoZone, Cardenas Foods, CVS Drug, Food4Less, H, PepBoys, Verizon, S Chevron/dsl, Blazin' Crab, Brandon's Diner, Chipotle, Circle K, Del Taco, Five Guys, National Buffet, Pizza Hut, Shakey's Pizza, Starbucks, Subway, Tasty Goody, Hilton Garden, AutoZone, O'Reilly Parts, Ross, Target, TJ Maxx

63 Citrus Ave, N 76, Chevron, Baker's Drive-Thru, Freddy's Burgers, Subway, Ford, S 7-11/dsl, Arco/dsl

61 Cherry Ave, N Arco, Chevron, Fontana Trkstp/dsl/24hr, One Stop/dsl, Carl's Jr, Del Taco, Jack-in-the-Box, Mack/Volvo, truck sales, S 3 Sisters Trkstp/dsl/@, 76/Circle K, North American Trkstp/dsl/scales, Farmer Boy's Rest., La Chiquita, Peterbilt

59 Etiwanda Ave, Valley Blvd

58b a I-15, N to Barstow, S to San Diego

57 Milliken Ave, N 76/dsl, Arco/24hr, Chevron, EVC, Mobil/Cherony's/dsl, Shell/7-11, Applebee's, Baskin-Robbins, BJ's Rest., Blaze Pizza, Boiling World, Bone&Broth Vietnamese, Burger King, Cane's Chicken, Carl's Jr, Chick-fil-A, Chipotle, Culichi Town, Dave&Buster's, Dave's Hot Chicken, Del Taco, Denny's, El Pollo Loco, Famous Dave's BBQ, Fat Burger, Flame Broiler, Fourth and Mill, Hero's Rest., Hooters, IHOP, In-n-Out, Jack-in-the-Box, Jamba Juice, Jersey Mike's, KFC, Krispy Kreme, Lazy Dog Rest., Luxe Buffet,

RANCHO CUCAMONGA

UPLAND

MONTE VISTA

57 Continued
McDonald's, Mkt Broiler, Norms Rest., Olive Garden, Outback Steaks, Panda Express, Panera Bread, Rainforest Cafe, Red Lobster, Rubio's, Sonic, Starbucks, Subway, Taco Bell, Tokyo Wako, Wendy's, Wienerschnitzel, Wingstop, Best Western, Country Inn&Suites, Courtyard, Fairfield Inn, Hampton Inn, Hilton Garden, Holiday Inn Express, Homewood Suites, Hyatt Place, TownePlace Suites, $Tree, 7-11, America's Tire, Big Lots, CarMax, Costco/gas, Jiffy Lube, Kohl's, Marshall's, Ontario Mills Mall, PetSmart, Ross, Sam's Club/gas, Staples, Target, Verizon, S Petro/Popeye's/dsl/scales/24hr/@, TA/Shell/Pizza Hut/Subway/Taco Bell/dsl/EVC/rest./24hr/@, Farmer Boys, Rodeway Inn, CarQuest

56 Haven Ave, Rancho Cucamonga, N Mobil, Benihana, Black Angus, El Torito, Hamburger Mary's, Jikan Japanese, Aloft Hotel, Comfort Inn & Suites, Extended Stay America, Hotel d'Lins, La Quinta, Ontario Hotel, S Panda Chinese, Starbucks, Embassy Suites, SpringHill, SureStay, Mercedes

55b a Holt Blvd, to Archibald Ave, N Arco, Mobil/dsl, Baker's Drive-thru, Burgertown USA, Starbucks, Weinerschnitzel, city park

54 Vineyard Ave, N 76/Circle K, Del Taco, El Pollo Loco, Freddy's Tacos, NY Pizza, Pizza Hut/Taco Bell, Popeyes, Subway, AutoZone, Stater Bros Foods, S 76/dsl/EVC, Mobil, Quick Gas/dsl, Denny's, In-N-Out, Jack-in-the-Box, KFC, Porter's Steaks, Spires Rest., Starbucks, Subway, Wendy's, Yoshinoya Japanese, Azure Suites, Best Western, Candlewood Suites, Comfort Suites, DoubleTree Inn, Folk Inn, Holiday Inn, Motel 6, Ontario Inn, Quality Inn, Ramada Inn, Residence Inn, Sheraton, Buick/Cadillac/Chevrolet/GMC, to

53 San Bernardino Ave, 4th St, to Ontario, N 7-11, Arco, Golden Corral, Shell, Carl's Jr, Domino's, Jack-in-the-Box, Tam's Burgers, Wingstop, Baymont, Motel 6, Target, S Arco/24hr, Chevron, McDonald's, United Bros Fuel, Denny's, Little Caesar's, Subway, Waba Grill, YumYum Donuts, Days Inn, Express Inn & Suites, city park

51 CA 83, Euclid Ave, to Ontario, Upland, N Arco, IHOP, H

50 Mountain Ave, to Mt Baldy, N Chevron, Mobil/Circle K/dsl, Shell/dsl, Chick-fil-A, Corky's Kitchen, Dunkin', HoneyBaked Ham, Jersey Mike's, Ono HI BBQ, Panda Express, Petrilli's Pizza, San Biagio's Pizza, Subway, Wendy's, Super 8, $Tree, AT&T, CVS Drug, Hobby Lobby, Home Depot, Michaels, Staples, T-Mobil, S 76/dsl, B's Chicken & Waffles, Cane's Chicken, Carl's Jr, Casa Jimenez, Coldstone, Juice it Up, Ontario Pizza, Sonic, Starbucks, vet, Walmart/Subway

49 Central Ave, to Montclair, N Carl's Jr., Chipotle Mexican, Clyde's Hot Chicken, El Pollo Loco, Flaming Buffet, John's Incredible Pizza, Lazy Dog Rest., McDonald's, Paradise Buffet, Ramen Ichiraku, Rodrigo's Mexican, Taco Bell, Waba Grill, $Tree, 99c Store, America's Tire, AutoZone, Barnes&Noble, Best Buy, Firestone/auto, Giant RV Ctr, JC Penney, Just Tires, Macy's, mall, PepBoys, PetCo, Ross, same as 48, Target, vet, S Chevron, USA, Burger King, Dos Amigos, Jack-in-the-Box, Jersey Mike's, Starbucks, Tommy's Burgers, Wienerschnitzel, 7-11, Acura/Honda/Infiniti/Nissan, AT&T, Costco/gas, Stater Bros

48 Monte Vista, N Applebee's, Black Angus, Buffalo Wild Wings, Chilis, Olive Garden, Pier 88 Seafood, Red Lobster, Sushi 1, Macy's, mall, Nordstrom's, same as 49, S H

47 Indian Hill Blvd, to Claremont, N Shell/dsl, Round Table Pizza, Sammys Cafe, Claremont Lodge, S 76/dsl, Chevron/McDonald's, Carl's Jr, Chipotle, Denny's, In-N-Out, Norm's Rest., Popeyes, Starbucks, Subway, Waba Grill,

CA

= gas = food = lodging = other = rest stop

INTERSTATE 10 Cont'd

VIA VERDE

Exit	Services
47	Continued Motel 6, Chrysler/Dodge/Jeep, Super King Mkt, Toyota/Scion, Verizon
46	Towne Ave, N 7-11, Chevron/dsl, Jack-in-the-Box, Jelly Donut
45b	Garey Ave, to Pomona, N USA/dsl, Golden Wok, H, tire repair, vet, S Chevron, Shell/dsl, Del Taco
45	White Ave, Garey Ave, to Pomona, S Bravo Burgers, Subway
44	(43 from eb)Dudley St, Fairplex Dr, N Arco/dsl, Coco Palm, Denny's, Pamona Valley Mining Rest., Starbucks, LemonTree Motel, Travelodge, S Chevron/24hr, Jack-in-the-Box, McDonald's, Starbucks, 7-11
42b	CA 71 S(from eb), to Corona
42a	to I-210, CA 57 S
41	Kellogg Dr, S to Cal Poly Inst
40	Via Verde, N Vons Foods
38b	Holt Ave, to Covina, N Hamiltons Steaks, Vanllee Suites
38a	Grand Ave, N 76, Arco/dsl, Da Han MBBQ, Denny's, Misky Misky Peruana, Best Western+, Fairfield Inn, Holiday Inn, 7-11
37b	Barranca St, Grand Ave, same as 37a, N 76, Chevron, BJ's Rest., Carl's Jr, Chick-fil-A, Chili's, Chipotle Mexican, El Torito, Habit Burgers, Islands Rest., Jollibee Chicken, Marie Callender, Menchie's, Ono HI BBQ, Starbucks, Waba Grill, Fairfield Inn, Hampton Inn, Holiday Inn, $Tree, CVS Drug, Dick's, Hobby Lobby, IKEA, Marshalls, PetSmart, Ross, Target, Verizon, S In-N-Out, McDonald's, 5 Star Inn, Days Inn
37a	Citrus Ave, to Covina, same as 37b, N Mobil, AHI BBQ, Buckboard BBQ, Buffalo Wild Wings, Burger King, Del Taco, IHOP, Jack-in-the-Box, Jersey Mike's, Millie's Rest., Popeyes, Starbucks, Subway, TGIFriday's, Yum Yum Donuts, Acura, AT&T, Baja Ranch Foods, Buick/GMC, Chevrolet, CVS Drug, Hobby Lobby, Kia, Marshall's, Office Depot, Sprouts, VW, Walmart, S 76/7-11, Classic Burger, Dave's Hot Chicken, 5 Star Inn, Days Inn, Cadillac, park
36	CA 39, Azusa Ave, to Covina, N 76/dsl, Arco/24hr, Denny's, L&L HI BBQ, McDonald's, Norm's Rest., Papa John's, Rio Picanha Brazillian, Subway, Wingstop, $Tree, 7-11, American Tire Depot, AutoZone, Chrysler/Dodge/Jeep, Food4Less, Mercedes, Stater Bros, S Mobil/Circle K, Tacos Gavilan, Audi, Ford, Honda, Mercedes, Tesla, Toyota
35	Vincent Ave, Glendora Ave, N Chevron, auto repair, S 76, Blaze Pizza, Chick-fil-A, Chipotle, Del Taco, El Pollo Loco, Gen Korean BBQ, Jamba Juice, Lazy Dog Rest., Lucille's BBQ, McDonald's, Panda Express, Panera Bread, Pizza Hut, Red Robin, Sizzler, Starbucks, Best Buy, CVS, EVC, Firestone/auto, JC Penney, Macy's, mall, Michael's, PetCo, USPO, Von's Foods
34	Pacific Ave, N 76, S Shell, mall, same as 35, tire repair
33	Puente Ave, N Chevron, Denny's, Farmer Boy's, Guadalajara Grill, McDonald's, Panda Express, Starbucks, Courtyard, AT&T, Home Depot, T-Mobil, Verizon, Walmart, S Jack-in-the-Box, Harley-Davidson
32b	Francisquito Ave, to La Puente, N Valero, 7-11, In-N-Out Burger Museum, S 76, Carl's Jr, Dunkin', In-N-Out, La Fogota, Wienerschnitzel, Grand Park Inn, hwy patrol, oil change/car wash
32a	Baldwin Pk Blvd, N Chevron/McDonald's, Cane's Chicken, Habit Burger, IHOP, Jack-in-the-Box, Papa Johns, Pizza Hut/Taco Bell, Starbucks, Subway, Wendy's, Wingstop, Yum Yum Donuts, CVS Drug, Food4Less, Target, transmissions, S H
31c	(31b from wb)Frazier St, N 7-11
31b a	(31a from wb)I-605 N/S, to Long Beach

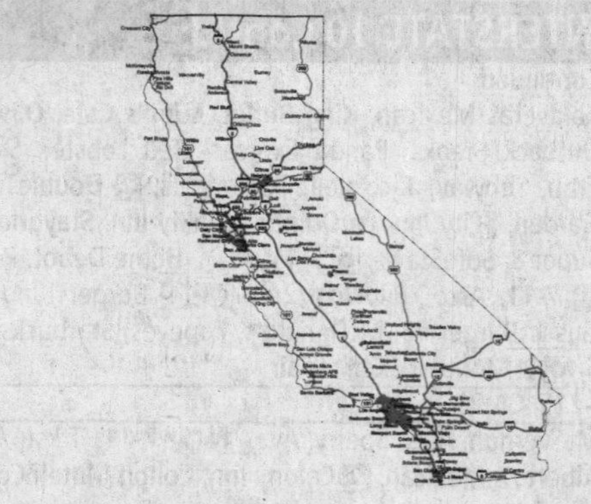

MONTEREY PARK

Exit	Services
30	Garvey Ave, S Rte 66
29b	Valley Blvd, Peck Rd, N Chevron, auto repair, Baskin-Robbins, Burger King, Carl's Jr., Jamba Juice, KFC, Shakey's Pizza, Subway, Taco Bell, Wendys, Yoshinoya, Motel 6, Honda, Hyundai, Lexus, Nissan, Toyota/Scion, Walgreens, S McDonald's, Tommy's Burgers, Waba Grill
29a	S Peck Rd(from eb)
28	Santa Anita Ave, to El Monte, S Sinclair/dsl, 7-11
27	Baldwin Avenue, Temple City Blvd, N USA, Holiday Inn, S Arco/24hr, Denny's, same as 26b a
26b	CA 19, Rosemead Blvd, Pasadena, Panda Express, N Boiling Crab, CA Fish, Chipotle, Coldstone, Dave's Hot Chicken, Habit Burger, IHOP, Jamba Juice, Subway, TGI Fridays, $Tree, GNC, PetSmart, Target, Uhaul, S Del Taco, Starbucks
26a	Walnut Grove Ave
25b	San Gabriel Blvd, N Shell, Carl's Jr, Popeyes, Taco Bell, Budget Inn, S 7-11, auto repair
25a	Del Mar Ave, to San Gabriel, N Arco, Mobil, Hilton, Sheraton, The Jordan Hotel, auto repair, S Chevron, Shell/dsl, Studio 6, Garvy Park
24	New Ave, to Monterey Park, N KFC, to Mission San Gabriel, S H
23b	Garfield Ave, to Alhambra, S 76, Arco, Grand Inn, H
23a	Atlantic Blvd, Monterey Park, N 76, Pizza Hut, Popeyes, Starbucks, H, T-Mobile, S Courtyard, Holiday Inn, Ralph's Foods/EVC
22	Fremont Ave, N H, S King Donuts, Papa Johns, 7-11
21	I-710, Long Beach Fwy, Eastern Ave(from wb)
20b a	Eastern Ave, City Terrace Dr, N Granny's Donuts, S Chevron/service, Mobil, Burger King, McDonald's
19c	Soto St(from wb), N 76, Shell/dsl, China Express, Green Grill, McDonald's, Popeyes, Starbucks, city park, H, S Mobil, Sinclair, Hugo's Pizza, Neris Tacos, Que Ricos
19b	I-5(from wb), US 101 S, N to Burbank, S to San Diego
19a	State St, N H
17	I-5 N
16b	I-5 S(from eb)
16a	Santa Fe Ave, San Mateo St, S 76/dsl, Mobil, El Pollo Loco, McDonald's, Subway, Penske
15b	Alameda St, N 76/dsl, Shell, Jack-in-the-Box, Starbucks, to downtown, S Blue Beacon Truckwash
15a	Central Ave, N Shell/repair, S Shell/7-11
14b	San Pedro Blvd, S industrial
14a	LA St, N Jack-in-the-Box, conv ctr, S El Pollo Loco, McDonald's, 99c Store, O'Reilly Parts, URGENT CARE
13	I-110, Harbor Fwy
12	Hoover St, Vermont Ave, N Chevron, Burger King, Dominos, McDonald's, Subway, Yum Yum Donuts, Advance Parts, AutoZone, CVS Drug, Uhaul, S 76, Arco, Chevron, Caveman Peruvian, Jack-in-the-Box, Mariscos Seafood, Papa Johns, Yoshinoya, Ralph's Foods
11	Normandie Ave, Western Ave

INTERSTATE 10 Cont'd

CULVER CITY

Exit #	Services
10	Arlington Ave, N [gas] 76, Chevron, [other] tire repair
9	Crenshaw Blvd, N [gas] Mobil, [food] Jack-in-the-Box, Starbucks, S [gas] 76, Chevron, Thrifty, [food] El Pollo Loco, Little Caesars, McDonald's, Panda Express, Phillips BBQ, Subway, Taco Bell, Yoshinoya, [other] U-Haul
8	La Brea Ave, N [gas] Valero/dsl, [other] USPO, S [gas] Chevron, [other] AutoZone
7b	Washington Blvd, Fairfax Ave, N [other] auto repair, S [gas] Arco, Mobil, same as 8, [other] Jiffy Lube, vet
7a	La Cienega Blvd, Venice Ave(from wb), N [gas] Chevron/24hr, Mobil, [food] Chick-fil-A, Del Taco, El Pollo Loco, McDonald's, Yum Yum Donuts, [other] $Tree, Aamco, CVS, Firestone/auto, [H], Ross, Target, S [food] Subway
6	Robertson Blvd, Culver City, N [gas] Shell/dsl, Valero, [food] Domino's, Taco Bell, [other] Valvoline, S [gas] EVC, [food] CAVA, Del Taco, In-N-Out, MOD Pizza, Shake Shack, The Jerk Jamaican, Wendy's, [lodging] The Culver Hotel, [other] CVS Drug, Honda, museum, park, Ross, Rubio's, Sprouts, Toyota, Trader Joe's, URGENT CARE, Wingstop
5	National Blvd, N [gas] Sinaco, [food] Papa John's, Starbucks, Subway, Taco+, [other] auto repair, Von's Foods, S [gas] Arco, [food] The Coop Pizza
4	Overland Ave, N [other] park, S [gas] Mobil/dsl, [food] Starbucks, [other] Jiffy Lube
3b a	I-405, N to Sacramento, S to Long Beach
2c b	Bundy Dr, N [gas] Chevron, Shell/dsl, [food] Jersey Mike's, Taco Bell, [other] Ace Hardware, Staples
2a	Centinela Ave, to Santa Monica, N [food] Taco Bell, S McDonald's, Upper West, [lodging] Best Western, [other] Trader Joe's
1c	20th St(from wb), Cloverfield Blvd, 26th St(from wb), N [gas] 76/dsl, Chevron/EVC, Shell/repair, [other] [H], S [food] Burger King, Burger King, [other] Pep Boys, to Virginia Avenue Park, Whole Foods
1b	Lincoln Blvd, CA 1 S, N [food] Denny's, McDonald's, Subway, [lodging] Hampton Inn, [other] BrakeMasters, Target, Toyota, Trader Joe's, Tuesday Morning, USPO, S [gas] Chevron/dsl, Shell, [food] Chick-fil-A, Dominos, El Pollo Loco, Jack-in-the-Box, Starbucks, Subway, Sushi Hanashi, [lodging] Doubletree Suites, Ocean Park, Rest Haven, [other] 7-11, Firestone/auto, O'Reilly Parts, U-Haul, U-Haul, Valvoline, Walgreens
1a	4th, 5th,(from wb), N [lodging] Courtyard, Hampton Inn, [other] mall, Trader Joe's, S [lodging] Hilton
0	Santa Monica Blvd, to beaches, I-10 begins/ends on CA 1.

INTERSTATE 15

YERMO / BARSTOW

Exit #	Services
298	California/Nevada state line, services in NV
291	Yates Well Rd
289	weigh sta sb
286	Nipton Rd, E Mojave Nat Preserve, to Searchlight NV
281	Bailey Rd
276mm	truck brake check area
272	Cima Rd, E [gas] Shell/cafe/dsl/towing
270mm	Valley Wells [RS] both lanes, full [handicap] facilities, [phone], [picnic], litter barrels, petwalk, EVC
265	Halloran Summit Rd
259	Halloran Springs Rd
248	to Baker(from sb), same as 246
246	CA 127, Kel-Baker Rd, Baker, to Death Valley, E [other] to Mojave Nat Preserve, W [gas] 76/dsl, Arco, Chevron/A&W/Pizza Hut/Subway/dsl, Chevron/KFC/Fatburger/Pizza Hut/dsl/EVC, Chevron/Taco Bell, EVC, Mobil, Shell/DQ/Jersey Mike's/dsl, Shell/Jack-in-the-Box/dsl, [food] Arby's, Burger King, Carl's Jr, Del Taco, Denny's, Mad Greek Café, [other] Alien Fresh Jerky, auto repair, Country Store, EVC, USPO,
246	Continued World's Tallest Thermometer
245	to Baker(from nb), same as 246
239	Zzyzx Rd
233	Rasor Rd, E [gas] Shell/Rasor Sta/dsl/towing/24hr
230	Basin Rd
221	Afton Rd, to Dunn
217mm	[RS] both lanes, full [handicap] facilities, [phone], [picnic], litter barrels, petwalk, EVC
213	Field Rd
206	Harvard Rd, to Newberry Springs, W [gas] 76/A&W/dsl, Mobil/Circle K
198	Minneola Rd, W [gas] Shell/dsl
196	Yermo Rd, Yermo
194	Calico Rd, E [gas] Eddie World/Peet's/Jed's Jerky/dsl, EVC, Tesla EVC
191	Ghost Town Rd, E [gas] Arco/24hr, Vegas Trkstp/dsl/24hr, [food] Jack-in-the-Box, Peggy Sue's 50s Diner, Penny's Diner, [lodging] Travelodge, [other] RV Camping, W [gas] Chevron/dsl, Shell/Subway/DQ/dsl/24hr, [other] KOA, to Calico GhostTown
189	Ft Irwin Rd
186	CA 58 W, to Bakersfield, W [other] RV camping, to Skyline Drive-in Theater
184	E Main, Barstow, Montera Rd(from eb), to I-40, E [gas] 76/dsl, Chevron, [food] Grill It, McDonald's, Panda Express, Popeyes, Starbucks, Subway, Tom's Burgers, [lodging] Arco, Best Western, Travelodge, [other] Walmart, W [gas] Circle K, Mobil/dsl, USA/dsl, Valero, [food] Barstow Burger, Burger King, Carl's Jr, Del Taco, Denny's, DiNapoli's Italian, IHOP, Jack-in-the-Box, Jenny's Grill, KFC, Little Caesar's, Los Domingo's, Taco Bell, tire repair, Wienerschnitzel, [lodging] Astro Budget Motel, Best Motel, Budget Inn, CA Inn, Days Inn/EVC, Desert Inn, EconoLodge, Economy Inn, Motel 6, Quality Inn/rest., Ramada Inn, Rodeway Inn, Super 8, [other] $Tree, 99c Store, AutoZone, O'Reilly Parts, U-Haul/LP
184a	I-40 E(from nb), I-40 begins/ends
183	CA 247, Barstow Rd, E [gas] Circle K, Valero/7-11/dsl, [food] Jimenez Mexican, Pizza Hut, Subway, [other] $General, W [gas] Mobil, [food] Domino's, [other] Food4Less/gas, [H], Marshall's, Mojave River Valley Museum, st patrol
181	L St, W Main, Barstow, W [gas] Arco/dsl, Chevron, USA, [food] Foster's Freeze, Rte 66 Pizza Palace, [lodging] Baymont Inn, Motel 66, [other] Firestone/auto, Home Depot, NAPA, tires/towing
179	CA 58, to Bakersfield
178	Lenwood, to Barstow, E [gas] Arco/dsl, Chevron, EVC, Flying J/Denny's/dsl/24hr, Mobil/dsl, Shell/dsl, [food] Arby's, Burger King, Cane's Chicken, Carl's Jr, Chili's, Chipotle Mexican, Del Taco, Denny's, Dunkin', El Pollo Loco, Fatburger, Habit Burger, IHOP, In-N-Out, Jersey Mike's, Oggi's, Panda Express, Panera Bread, Starbucks, Starbucks, Subway, Tommy's Burgers, [lodging] Comfort Suites, Fairfield Inn, Hampton Inn, Holiday Inn & Suites, Holiday Inn Express, Home2, [other] Blue Beacon, Old Navy, PJ Fresh, Tanger Outlet/famous brands/food ct, W [gas] Chevron, Love's/Chester's/Godfather's/dsl/scales/24hr/@, Pilot/Subway/dsl/scales/24hr, TA/Shell/Country Fare/Subway/dsl/scales/24hr/@, [food] Freddy's Steakburgers, McDonald's, [lodging] Best Western, Motel 6, [other] repair, truckwash
175	Outlet Ctr Dr, Sidewinder Rd
169	Hodge Rd
165	Wild Wash Rd
161	Dale Evans Pkwy, to Apple Valley
157	Stoddard Wells Rd, to Bell Mtn
154	Stoddard Wells Rd, to Bell Mtn, E [other] Shady Oasis Camping/LP, W [gas] EVC, Mobil, [lodging] HillTop Inn, Motel 6
153.5mm	Mojave River
153b	E St

CA

= gas = food = lodging = other = rest stop

CA

INTERSTATE 15 Cont'd

VICTORVILLE

Exit #	Services
153a	CA 18 E, D St, to Apple Valley, E Shell/7-11, repair, Rte 66 Museum, W Arco/Subway/dsl
151b	Mojave Dr, Victorville, E Mobil/dsl, Days Inn, W Mojave Gas Mart/dsl, Little Caesars, Economy Inn, Quality Inn
151a	La Paz Dr, Roy Rogers Dr, E Chevron, Circle K/dsl, Burger King, Carl's Jr, El Pollo Loco, IHOP, Jack-in-the-Box, McDonald's, Starbucks, Subway, W Spoon Buffet, Wendy's, Wienerschnitzel, Yum Yum Donuts, $Tree, 99c Store, AutoZone, BigLots, Costco/gas, Fiat, Food4Less, Harley-Davidson, NAPA Autocare, Pepboys, Toyota/Scion, W Arco, Chevron, Domino's, Dutch Bros, Farmer Boys, Golden ChopStix, In-N-Out, Jamba Juice, Krispy Kreme, Panda Express, Papa John's, Starbucks, Subway, Waba Grill, Wingstop, Buick/GMC, Chrysler/Dodge/Jeep, Home Depot, Honda, Nissan, Stater Bros, Verizon, Walgreens, WinCo Foods
150	CA 18 W, Palmdale Rd, Victorville, E Baker's Drive-Thru, Denny's, Goody's Rest., KFC, Richie's Diner, Tams Burgers, GT Hotels/EVC, Red Roof Inn, W 76/dsl, Arco, Berri Bros, Circle K/Church's Chicken, Del Taco, El Tio Mexican, House of Joy, McDonald's, Pizza Hut, Raul's Mexican, Slice Pizza, Starbucks, Subway, Taco Bell, Tom's Rest., Budget Inn, Holiday Inn, Park Ave Inn, $General, AutoZone, CVS Drug, Ford, Hyundai, Mazda, O'Reilly Parts, Town&Country Tire, transmissions, U-Haul, vet
148	La Mesa Rd, Nisquali Rd, E Circle K, EVC, Shell, Hilton Garden, Red Roof Inn, Scandia Funpark, W Baskin-Robbins, Captains Fish Tacos, ChuckeCheese, Home2 Suites, AT&T, PetSmart
147	Bear Valley Rd, to Lucerne Valley, E 76/Circle K/dsl, Arco, Chevron, Mobil, A1 Teriyaki, Arby's, Baker's Drive-Thru, Brooklyn Italian, Carl's Jr, Chick-fil-A, DQ, Dunkin', Jersey Mike's, KFC, Los Alazanes Mexican, Los Toritos, Marisco's Seafood, McDonald's, Panda Express, Pizza Guys, Popeye's, Steak'n Shake, Steer'n Stein, Tacos Mexico, Tam's Burgers, Wienerschnitzel, Comfort Suites, Day&Night Inn, EconoLodge, Extended Studio Hotel, Fairfield Inn, La Quinta, SureStay, Travelodge, Affordable RV Ctr, America's Tire, AutoZone, Firestone/auto, Home Depot, Michael's, O'Reilly Parts, Range RV, Vallarta Foods, Valvoline Oil Change, vet, W 76, Arco, Chevron, EVC, Valero/dsl, Applebee's, Archibald's Drive-Thru, Baja Grill, BJ's Rest., Carino's, Chili's, Cracker Barrel, Del Taco, El Pollo Loco, Farmer Boy's Rest., Freddy's Burgers, Giuseppe's, Jack-in-the-Box, Jimmy John's, Juice It Up!, Little Caesar's, Mimi's Cafe, Olive Garden, Ono HI BBQ, Outback Steaks, Pancho Villa's, Panera Bread, Red Lobster, Red Robin, RoadHouse Grill, Shakey's Pizza, Sonic, Starbucks, Thai Dawn Bistro, The Habit Burger, Tokyo Steaks, Wendy's, Hawthorn Suites, $Tree, 99c Store, AAA, Barnes&Noble, Best Buy, Castrol Oil Change, CVS Drug, Dick's, Goodyear/auto, Hobby Lobby, JC Penney, Kohl's, Lowe's, Macy's, mall, Michaels, Stater Bros., Verizon, Walgreens

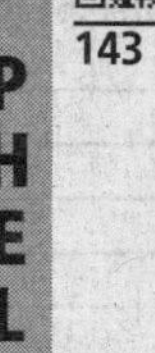

PHELAN

Exit #	Services
143	Main St, to Hesperia, Phelan, E Mobil/Alberto's, Shell/Popeyes/dsl, Arby's, Burger King, Cane's Chicken, Chipotle, Del Taco, Denny's, IHOP, In-N-Out, Jack-in-the-Box, Panda Express, Starbucks, The Habit Burger, TX Roadhouse, Wendy's, Wingstop, Courtyard, SpringHill Suites, $Tree, ALDI, O'Reilly Parts, Petco, Walmart/Subway/gas, W 7-11, 76/dsl, Baker's Drive-thru, Crumbl, Dominos, FarmerBoys, Five Guys, Golden Corral, Juice It Up!, Subway, Waba Grill, Holiday Inn Express, Motel 6, AT&T, Desert Willow RV Park, GNC, Marshall's, Ross, Target/Starbucks,

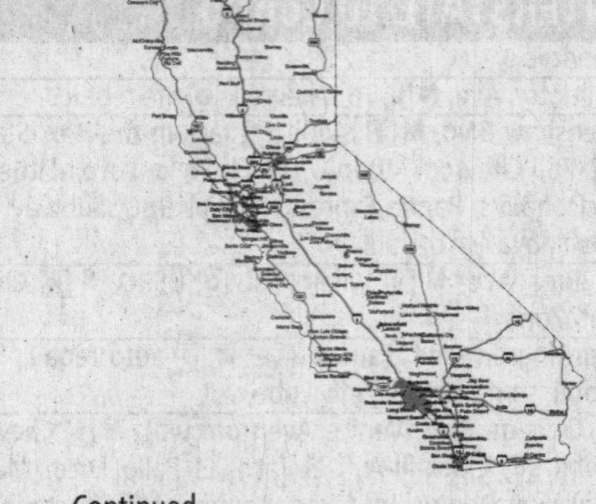

ADELANTO

Exit #	Services
143	Continued URGENT CARE, Verizon
141	US 395, Joshua St, Adelanto, W Arco/dsl, Pilot/Wendy's/dsl/scales/24hr, Outpost Café, Freightliner, repair, RV supply ctr, truck/RV wash/scales, Zippy Lube
140	Ranchero Rd, E 76/Circle K, Chevron/Fatburger, Starbucks
138	Oak Hill Rd, E Chevron/dsl, Summit Inn Café, W Oak Hills RV Village/LP
137mm	brake check sb, Cajon Summit, elevation 4260
131	CA 138, to Palmdale, Silverwood Lake, E Chevron, McDonald's, Silverwood SRA, W 76/Circle K/Del Taco/LP, Shell/Subway/dsl/LP, Cajon Inn
130mm	elevation 3000, weigh sta both lanes
129	Cleghorn Rd
124	Kenwood Ave
123	I-215 S, to San Bernardino, E Arco, to Glen Helen Park
122	Glen Helen Parkway
119	Sierra Ave, W 76/dsl, Arco/dsl, Chevron/dsl, Shell/Del Taco/dsl, Jack-in-the-Box, McDonalds, to Lytle Creek RA
118	Duncan Canyon Rd, W city park
116	Summit Ave, E 7-11, Chevron, Chili's, Coldstone, Del Taco, Five Guys, Jack-in-the-Box, Juice It Up, Little Caesar's, Ono HI BBQ, Panera Bread, Roundtable Pizza, Starbucks, Subway, Taco Bell, Wendy's, $Tree, AlLDI, CVS Drug, GNC, Kohl's, Marshall's, Michael's, Old Navy, PetSmart, Stater Bros, Target/Starbucks, Verizon
115b a	CA 210, Highland Ave, E Lake Arrowhead
113	Base Line Rd, E Speedway, Denny's, Jack-in-the-Box, Logans Roadhouse, Pizza Hut, Rosa Maria's, Starbucks, Comfort Inn
112	CA 66, Foothill Blvd, E Asia Buffet, In-N-Out, Ono Hawaiian BBQ, Panda Express, Pizza Guys, Subway, Taco Bell, Tropical Smoothie, Wienerschnitzel, Food4Less, Jiffy Lube, Walmart, W Arco, Chevron, Chevron/dsl, Shell, Buffalo Wild Wings, Carl's Jr., Cheesecake Factory, Chick-fil-A, Chipotle Mexican, Del Taco, Denny's, Dunkin, El Pollo Loco, Firehouse Subs, Flemings Steaks, Jack-in-the-Box, Joe's Crab Shack, Kings Fishouse, Lucille's BBQ, Mama Mexican, McDonald's, Old Spagetti Factory, PF Chang's, Popeyes, Red Robin, Richie's Diner, Shakey's Pizza, Shogun, Starbucks, Taco Hut, TGIFriday's, The Hat Grill, Hampton Inn, Sheraton 4 Points, AT&T, AutoZone, Bass Pro Shops, Best Buy, Home Depot, JC Penney, Macy's, Pep Boys, Ramona Tire, Verizon
110	4th St, E Arco/dsl, Baker's, Subway, W Arco, Chevron/dsl, Shell, Shell/7-11/dsl, Alberto's Mexican, Applebee's, Baskin-Robbins, BJ's Rest., Burger King, Carl's Jr, Chick-fil-A, Chipotle, Chop Sticks, Culichi Town Mexican, Daphne's Greek, Dave's Chicken, Del Taco, Denny's, El Pollo Loco, Famous Dave's BBQ, Fat Burger, Flame Broiler, Heroes Rest., Hooters, IHOP, In-N-Out, Jack-in-the-Box, Jamba Juice,

INTERSTATE 15 Cont'd

110 Continued
Jersey Mike's, Juice It Up, KFC, Krispy Kreme, Kudos Pizzeria, Lazy Dog Cafe, McDonald's, Mkt Broiler, Norm's Rest., Olive Garden, Outback Steaks, Panda Express, Panera Bread, Pita Street, Rain Forest Cafe, Raising Cane's, Red Lobster, Rubio's, Sonic, Starbucks, Starbucks, Subway, Taco Bell, The Habit, Tokyo Tokyo, WaBa Grill, Wendy's, Wienerschnitzel, Ayres Suites, Best Western, Country Inn&Suites, Courtyard, Fairfield Inn, Hampton Inn, Hilton Garden, Holiday Inn Express, Hyatt Place, TownePlace Suites, $Tree, America's Tire, Costco/gas, Kohl's, Marshall's, Ontario Mills Mall, PetSmart, Ross, Sam's Club/gas, Staples, Target, Tire Pros, TJ Maxx, Verizon

109b a I-10, E to San Bernardino, W to LA

108 Jurupa St, E Chevron/dsl, Del Taco, Jack-in-the-Box, La Bufadora Mexican, R Burger, Starbucks, Subway, BMW, Chrysler/Dodge/Jeep, Family RV, Honda, Hyundai, Hyundai, Lexus, Mini, Nissan, Subaru, Toyota, Toyota/Scion, Volvo, VW, W Arco, Carl's Jr, Ford, Kia

106 CA 60, E to Riverside, W to LA

105 Cantu-Galleano Ranch Rd, E 76/Circle K, Alvarado's Mexican, W Cafe Rio, Chick-fil-A, Devil's Kitchen, In-N-Out, MOD Pizza, Olive Garden, Pot on Fire, Starbucks, Zeppin Sushi, Costco/gas

103 Limonite Ave, E Asado Grill, Carl's Jr, Del Taco, Denny's, Five Guys, Flame Broiler, Golden Chopstix, Jamba Juice, Mt Mike's Pizza, Ono Hawaiian BBQ, The Burger Den, ALDI, Lowe's, Michael's, PetCo, Ross, W Chevron, Applebee's, Blaze Pizza, Buffalo Wild Wings, Carino's, Chipotle, Coldstone, Corky's Kitchen, Dickey's BBQ, Domino's, Farmer Boys, Fire Wings, Georgia's, Habit Burger, Jersey Mike's, Juice it Up, Little Caesar's, McDonald's, On-the-Border, Panda Express, Panera Bread, Starbucks, Subway, Taco Bell, Tio's Mexican, Tutti Frutti Yogurt, Waba Grill, Wabi Sabi, Wendy's, Wingstop, Zip Fusion, Best Buy, Home Depot, Kohl's, PetSmart, Ralph's Foods/gas, Staples, Target, TJ Maxx, Verizon, Vons Foods/gas, Walgreens

100 6th St, Norco Dr, Old Town Norco, E 76/dsl, Chevron, Jack-in-the-Box, McDonald's, Round Table Pizza, Taco Bell, W Arco, Sinclair/dsl, Big Boy, Dutch Bros Coffee, Norco's Burgers, Starbucks, Wienerschnitzel, Extended Stay, Fairfield Inn, Regency Inn, Brake Masters, Jiffy Lube, NAPA, USPO, vet

98 2nd St, W Mobil, Thrifty, VP/dsl, Baja Fish Tacos, Burger King, Carl's Jr, Del Taco, In-N-Out, Mi Hacienda Mexican, North Shore HI, Pancake House, Pizza Hut, Polly's Cafe, Seafood Boiler, Sports Nut Pizza, Subway, Sumabi Mexican, Tacos El Rancho, Tom's Jr, Howard Johnson, $Tree, Ace Hardware, Chrysler/Dodge/Jeep, Ford, Norco Tires, Schwab Tire, Stater Bros, vet

97 Yuma Dr, Hidden Valley Pkwy, E 7-11, Arco, Boil Daddy, Chick-fil-A, Menchie's FroYo, Pizza Guys, Starbucks, Subway, Yoshioishi Sushi, Kohl's, Stater Bros, W 76/dsl, Arco, Chevron, Shell/dsl, Alberto's Mexican, Badlands BBQ, Baskin-Robbins, Cane's Chicken, Carl's Jr, Chipotle, Denny's, Domino's, Fantastic Cafe, Fazoli's, Hanami Ramen, Jack-in-the-Box, Jamba Juice, Jersey Mike's, Jimmy John's, KFC, McDonald's, Miguel's Jr, Ono HI BBQ, Papa John's, Pieology, Popeyes, Rodrigo's Mexican, Rubio's, Taco Bell, The Habit Burger, Wahoos Fish Taco, Wingstop, Hampton Inn, America's Tire, AT&T, AutoZone, BigLots, GNC, Hobby Lobby, O'Reilly Parts, Staples, Target, URGENT CARE, Valvoline, Verizon, Walgreens, Winco

96b a CA 91, to Riverside, beaches

95 Magnolia Ave, E Chevron/Jack-in-the-Box/dsl, Islands Burgers, Luna Mexican, Round Table Pizza, Shamrock's Grill,

OLD TOWN NORCO

95 Continued
Residence Inn, AAA, auto repair, Lowe's, tire repair, W Mobil/Circle K, Shell, Al's Hot Chicken, Broken Yolk, Dalia's Pizza, Dhaka Kitchen, Fuze Pizza, Hon Sushi, Kalaveras, Little Caesar's, McDonald's, Red Ginger Chinese, Sizzler, Sonic, Starbucks, Subway, Waba Grill, Holiday Inn Express, $Tree, AT&T, El Super Mkt, O'Reilly Parts, Stater Bros Foods

93 Ontario Ave, to El Cerrito, E Shell/dsl, 7 Seas Thai, HI BBQ, Sombrero Mexican, Starbucks, Mtn View Tire, vet, W 76/Circle K, Arco, Chevron, Aloha Hawaiian BBQ, Cane's Chicken, Chipotle, Del Taco, Denny's, El Pollo Loco, Golden Chopstix, In-N-Out, Jack-in-the-Box, Jersey Mike's, Juice It Up, KFC, Magic Wok, Marui Sushi, McDonald's, Miguel's Jr, Papa John's, Porky's Pizza, Rubio's, Subway, Taco Bell, Tommy's Burgers, SpringHill Suites, Albertson's/Starbucks, America's Tire, AutoZone, CVS Drug, Home Depot, Sam's Club/gas, USPO, Walmart

92 El Cerrito Rd, W Circle K, Deli Delicious, Starbucks, The Habit Burger

91 Cajalco Rd, E Circle K/EVC, BJ's Rest., Buffalo Wild Wings, Chick-fil-A, Chili's, China Dragon, Chipotle, Coldstone, Con Amore Italian, Five Guys, Jamba Juice, King's Fish House, Macaroni Grill, Panera Bread, PizzaRev, Poki Cat Hawaiian, Rock Brews Rest., See's Candies, Starbucks, Taco Bell, Wendy's, Starbridge Suites, Woodspring Suites, AT&T, Barnes&Noble, Best Buy, EVC, Kohl's, Marshall's, Michael's, Old Navy, PetCo, Ross, Sportsman's Whse, Target, Verizon, W Mobil/dsl, Bucket Seafood, Corky's Kitchen, Jack-in-the-Box, NY Pizza, Starbucks, Subway, Stater Bros, vet

90 Weirick Rd, Dos Lagos Dr, E 76, Arco/dsl, Fatburger, Miguel's Mexican, Reunion Kitchen, Tap's Rest., TGIFriday's, Wood Ranch BBQ, Home2 Suites, Staybridge Suites, 7 Oaks Gen Store, Trader Joe's, W URGENT CARE

88 Temescal Cyn Rd, Glen Ivy, E Shell, W Arco/dsl, Carl's Jr, Tom's Farms/Burgers/BBQ

85 Indian Truck Trail, W Pizza Hut, Starbucks, Subway, CVS Drug, Von's Foods/gas/dsl

81 Lake St

78 Nichols Rd, W Arco/dsl, DQ, Outlets/famous brands

77 CA 74, Central Ave, Lake Elsinore, E Arco, Chevron, Mobil/Circle K/dsl, Burger King, Cane's Chicken, Chick-fil-A, Chili's, Chipotle, Del Taco, Douglas Burgers, Golden Corral, Juice It Up, Maui Hawaiian BBQ, Palm Thai, Panda Express, Starbucks, Submarina, Taco Bell, Wendy's, $Tree, AT&T, Costco/gas, EVC, Lowe's, PetSmart, Valvoline, Walmart/auto, W El Pollo Loco, Farmer Boys, Golden Chop Stix, IHOP, McDonald's, Miguel's Mexican, Ono HI BBQ, Panera Bread, Pho Ngon, Starbucks, Subway, Wienerschnitzel, 99c Store, ALDI, Home Depot, Marshall's, PetCo, Target/CVS/Starbucks, Walgreens

75 Main St, Lake Elsinore, W 7-11, tires/repair

73 Railroad Cyn Rd, to Lake Elsinore, E 76/7-11, Shell/dsl, Denny's, El Pollo Loco, In-N-Out, Jersey Mike's, KFC, Peony Chinese, Starbucks, Tijuana's Mexican, Holiday Inn Express, Jiffy Lube, O'Reilly Parts, URGENT CARE, Verizon, vet, Von's Foods, Waba Grill, Walmart, W Arco, Chevron, Mobil/Circle K/dsl, Annie's Cafe, Buddies Pizza, Carl's Jr, Del Taco, Emilios Mexican, Jack-in-the-Box, King Kabob, McDonald's, Pizza Hut, Starbucks, Subway, Taco Bell, Vincenzo's, Best Western+, Econolodge, Quality Inn, Travel Inn, $Tree, AutoZone, BigLots, Chevrolet, Chrysler/Dodge/Jeep, CVS Drug, Firestone/auto, Ford, Stater Bros, vet, Walgreens

71 Bundy Cyn Rd, E Shell/Circle K, W Arco, El Rey Mexican, Jack-in-the-Box, Popeyes

LAKE ELSINORE

CA

= gas = food = lodging = other = rest stop

INTERSTATE 15 Cont'd

Exit #	Services
69	Baxter Rd
68	Clinton Keith Rd, E Chevron, Shell, Chipotle, Denny's, Domino's, Los Jilbetos Tacos, Los Reyes Grill, McDonald's, Old Mkt Grill, Panda Express, Starbucks, Subway, 7-11, Ace Hardware, Albertsons/Sav-on, H, Jiffy Lube, vet, W 7-11, Arco/dsl, Del Taco, Dunkin, El Pollo Loco, Jack-in-the-Box, Jersey Mike's Subs, Stadium Pizza, Starbucks, Taco Bell, The Habit, Tresino's Italian, Yellow Basket Rest., Baron's Mkt, Stater Bros, URGENT CARE
65	California Oaks Rd, Kalmia St, E 76/Circle K/dsl, Chevron, Shell/7-11/dsl, Burger King, Carl's Jr, Chili's, Chipotle, DQ, Epic Wings, Jade Chinese, Jamba Juice, Jersey's Pizza, Jimenez Mexican, KFC, Little Caesar's, McDonald's, Papa John's, Starbucks, Subway, Comfort Inn, Holiday Inn Express, $Tree, Albertson's, AutoZone, Firestone, O'Reilly Parts, Target, Tuesday Morning, vet, Walgreens, W Arco/dsl, Chevron, Applebee's, Chick-fil-A, Farmer Boys, Jack-in-the-Box, Juice it Up, Raising Cane's, Sizzlin Steer, Taco Bell, America's Tire, Giant RV Ctr, Kohl's, Lowe's, Office Depot, PetCo, URGENT CARE
64	Murrieta Hot Springs Rd, to I-215, E 7-11, Shell/dsl, Alberto's Mexican, Buffalo Wild Wings, Carl's Jr, Dunkin, El Pollo Loco, Rise to Grind, Rubio's, Sizzler, Starbucks, The Habit, The Hat, Wendy's, $Tree, 7-11, Amazon Fresh, H, Marshalls, Ross, Sam's Club/gas, Walgreens, W 7-11, Shell, Shell/dsl, Arby's, Coldstone, Denny's, IHOP, Jersey Mike's Subs, McDonald's, Ocean Poke, Odalberto's Mexican, Starbucks, Toast Murrieta, Tom's Burgers, Wienerschnitzel, Courtyard, Residence Inn, 99c Store, AAA, American Tire Depot, AT&T, Best Buy, BigLots, CarMax, Home Depot, PetSmart, vet, Walmart
63	I-215 N(from nb), to Riverside
62	French Valley Pkwy(from sb, no return), E Audi, Mercedes, W BMW, O'Reilly Parts, VW
61	CA 79 N, Winchester Rd, E 76/dsl, Chevron, Shell, Baskin-Robbins/Togo's, Benihana, BJ's Rest., CA Pizza Kitchen, Cafe Rio, Chick-fil-A, China Chef, Chipotle, Coldstone, Corner Cafe, Del Taco, Del Taco, Dickey's BBQ, El Pollo Loco, Famous Dave's, Firehouse Subs, Five Guys, Islands Burgers, Jamba Juice, Jersey Mike's, Krispy Kreme, L&L Hawaiian BBQ, Lazy Dog Cafe, Lucille's BBQ, Macaroni Grill, McDonald's, Olive Garden, Original Pancake House, Outback Steaks, Panera Bread, Phil's BBQ, Raising Cane's, Red Ginger Chinese, Red Lobster, Red Robin, Rock n' Jenny's Italian, Shakey's Pizza, Shogun Chinese, Starbucks, Starbucks, Subway, Taco Bell, Wahoo's, Wingstop, $Tree, 99c Store, AAA, America's Tire, AT&T, auto repair, AutoZone, Barnes&Noble, Batteries+, Big O Tires, Costco/gas, CVS Drug, Dick's, Firestone, Food4Less, GNC, Hobby Lobby, Hyundai, JC Penney, Jiffy Lube, Jo-Ann Fabrics, Lowe's, Macy's, Nissan, Office Depot, Old Navy, PepBoys, PetCo, Ramona Tire, Roots Mkt, See's Candies, TJ Maxx, Trader Joe's, U-Haul, Verizon, WinCo Foods, World Mkt, W Arco, Chevron/dsl, Arby's, Banzai Japanese, Burger Lounge, Chin's Chinese, Farmer Boys, Guadalajara Mexican, Hibachi Buffet, In-N-Out, Jack-in-the-Box, Patsy Mae's Cafe, Serrano's Grill, Starbucks, Vero Mexican, Wendy's, Best Western, Extended Stay America, Fairfield Inn, Holiday Inn Express, La Quinta, Quality Inn, Staybridge Suites, Camping World, Meineke, NAPA, st patrol, tires/repair, U-Haul, URGENT CARE, vet
59	Rancho California Rd, E Arco, Mobil/Circle K/dsl, Shell/dsl, Black Angus, Chili's, Del Taco, Dragon Express, Jilberto's Mexican, Juice Bar, Little Caesar's,

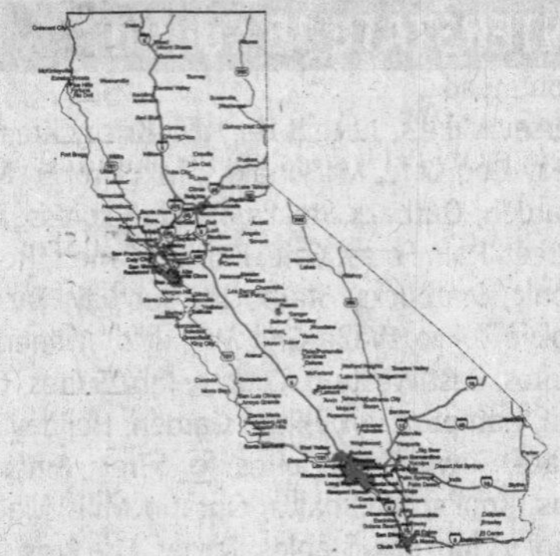

PALA

Exit #	Services
59	Continued LongHorn Steaks, Pat&Oscar's Rest., Peony Chinese, Rubio's, Subway, Times Square NY Pizza, Embassy Suites, Acura, ALDI, BigLots, Chevrolet/Buick/GMC, Chrysler/Dodge/Jeep, CVS Drug, Ford, Home Goods, Honda, Jiffy Lube, Kia, Mazda, Michael's, Midas, Nissan, Subaru, Target, Toyota, URGENT CARE, Verizon, vet, vet, Von's Foods, W 76/dsl, Chevron, Alberto's Mexican, Denny's, McDonald's, Mr Kabob Grill, Rosa's Café, Starbucks, Vince's Spaghetti, Best Western+, Hampton Inn, Motel 6, Rancho California Inn, Rodeway Inn, SpringHill Suites, to Old Town Temecula, USPO
58	CA 79 S, to Indio, Temecula, E 76/Circle K/Tesla EVC, Chevron/dsl, Mobil/Circle K/dsl, Sinclair/Circle K/dsl, 7-11, Carl's Jr, CVS Drug, Del Taco, Domino's, Francesca's Italian, Golden Bowl Asian, In-N-Out, Los Jilberto's, Mexican Food, Pizza Factory, Popeyes, Starbucks, Starbucks, America's Tire, U-Haul, Valvoline, W Shell/dsl, D'Sotos Mexican, Jack-in-the-Box, Lienzo Charro Mexican, Signature Temecula, Harley-Davidson
55mm	check sta nb
54	Rainbow Valley Blvd, W CA Insp Sta
51	Mission Rd, to Fallbrook
46	CA 76, to Oceanside, Pala, E fruit stand, W Mobil/Circle K, Nessy Burgers, Ribshack Que, Quality Inn, Pala Meas Mkt
44mm	San Luis Rey River
43	Old Hwy 395
41	Gopher Canyon Rd, Old Castle Rd, E Welk Resort, RV Park
37	Deer Springs Rd, Mountain Meadow Rd, E Circle K, W Arco
34	Centre City Pkwy(from sb)
33	El Norte Pkwy, E Arco, Shell/dsl, Del Taco, DQ, El Pollo Loco, IHOP, Papa John's, Starbucks, Best Western, Rodeway Inn, 7-11, CVS Drug, EVC, Firestone/auto, Jiffy Lube, Ross, RV Resort, vet, vet, Von's Foods, Vons Foods, W 76/7-11/dsl, Chevron, Jack-in-the-Box, Subway, Wendy's, Ace Hardware, vet, Von's Foods
32	CA 78, to Oceanside
31	Valley Pkwy, E Arco, Chili's, ChuckeCheese, Cocina del Charro, McDonald's, Olive Garden, Rock'N Jenny's Subs, Thai Kitchen, SpringHill Suites, Barnes&Noble, H, Jiffy Lube, Michael's, PetCo, URGENT CARE, W Express, Valero, Applebee's, Burger King, Carl's Jr, Chipotle Mexican, Dave's Hot Chicken, Del Taco, El Pollo Loco, In-N-Out, Jamba Juice, Mike's BBQ, Panera Bread, Pick Up Stix, Pieology, Primo's Mexican, Raising Cane's, Subway, Wendy's, Comfort Inn, Holiday Inn Express, 7-11, Albertson's, ALDI, AT&T, Audi, BMW, Chevrolet, Chrysler/Dodge/Jeep, CVS Drug, Dick's, Ford, GMC, Home Depot, Honda, Kia, Mazda, Mitsubishi, Ross, Staples, Target, TJ Maxx, Verizon, VW
30	9th Ave, Auto Parkway, E Mercedes, W same as 31

INTERSTATE 15 Cont'd

Exit #	Services
29	Felicita Rd
28	Centre City Pkwy(from nb, no return), E Escondido Lodge, vet
27	Via Rancho Pkwy, to Escondido, E Shell/7-11, Shell/dsl, BJ's Rest., Black Angus Steaks, Cheesecake Factory, On-the-Border, Red Robin, JC Penney, Macy's, Nordstrom, Target, W McDonald's, Starbucks, Subway
26	W Bernardo Dr, to Highland Valley Rd, Palmerado Rd
24	Rancho Bernardo Rd, to Lake Poway, E Arco, Mobil/Circle K, Cojita's Taco, Elmisa Cafe, Kangnam Korean BBQ, Pizza Hut, Starbucks, Stirfresh, Sub Marina, Hilton Garden, Barons Mkt, Von's Foods, W 76/Circle K, Chevron/7-11, Phil's BBQ
23	Bernardo Ctr Dr, E Chevron, Carl's Jr, Denny's, IHOP, Jack-in-the-Box, McDonald's, NY Bagels Cafe, Perfect Pizza, Rancho Viejo, Robeks Juice, Rubio's, Starbucks, Courtyard, 7-11, CVS Drug, Firestone/auto, USPO
22	Camino del Norte
21	Carmel Mtn Rd, E Chevron, Shell/7-11, Shell/dsl, Baskin-Robbins, Broken Yolk Cafe, CA Pizza Kitchen, Cafe Luna, CAVA, Chick-fil-A, China Fun, Chipotle Mexican, DQ, El Pollo Loco, Habit Burgers, In-N-Out, Islands Burgers, Jamba Juice, Krispy Kreme, McDonald's, O's American Kitchen, Olive Garden, Panda Express, Panera Bread, Robert's Jalepenos, Rubio's, Sombrero Mexican, Starbucks, Starbucks, Subway, Taco Bell, The Baked Bear, Which Wich?, Sonesta Suites, AT&T, Barnes&Noble, Best Buy, Costco/gas, Dick's, Home Depot, Marshall's, Michael's, PetCo, Ralph's Foods, Ross, See's Candies, Sprouts Mkt, Staples, TJ Maxx, Trader Joe's, USPO, Valvoline, Verizon, W Chevron, EVC, Jack-in-the-Box, tires
19	CA 56 W, Ted Williams Pkwy
18	Rancho Penasquitos Blvd, Poway Rd, E Arco, Burros & Fries Mexican, Papa John's, AAA, W 76/dsl, Mobil/dsl, Don Rios Mexican, McDonald's, Mi Ranchito Mexican, NY Pizza, Starbucks, La Quinta, 7-11, vet
17	Mercy Rd, Scripps Poway Pkwy, E Shell//7-11/dsl, Chili's, Wendy's, Yanni's Grill, Residence Inn, SpringHill Suites, W Chevron, KFC, Pernicano's Italian
16	Mira Mesa Blvd, to Lake Miramar, E ChuckeCheese, Denny's, Filippi's Pizza, Gyu-Kaku Japanese, Lucio's Mexican, Shozen Pizza, Holiday Inn Express, Homewood Suites, Trader Joe's, USPO, W Arco, Shell, Applebee's, Buca Italian, Cold Stone, Dave's Hot Chicken, Dunkin, El Patron, In-N-Out, Islands Burgers, Jack-in-the-Box, Jersey Mike's Subs, McDonald's, On the Border, Panera Bread, Pick Up Stix, Popeyes, Rubio's, Starbucks, Subway, AutoZone, Barnes&Noble, Best Buy, CVS Drug, Discount Tire, H Mart, Home Depot, Old Navy, Ross, USPO, Verizon, vet
15	Carroll Canyon Rd, to Miramar College, E Carl's Jr, Starbucks, Subway, Todo Sushi
14	Pomerado Rd, Miramar Rd, W Exxon, Shell, Shell/dsl, Speedway/dsl, Carl's Jr, Panda Express, Starbucks, Subway, Best Western, Comfort Inn, Courtyard, Audi, Audi/Porsche, Land Rover, Porsche, Subway, vet
13	Miramar Way, US Naval Air Station, E US Naval Air Sta, W Miramar
12	CA 163 S(from sb), to San Diego
11	to CA 52
10	Clairemont Mesa Blvd, E Mobil, Vons Foods, W Arco, Cali's & Fries, Carl's Jr, China Express, Denny's, Filiberto's Mexican, Firehouse Subs, Jack-in-the-Box, Jersey Mike's, Long Island Pizza, McDonald's, Panda Express, Panera Bread, Robeks, Rubio's, Starbucks, Sunny Donuts, Togo's, 7-11,
10	Continued H, vet
9	CA 274, Balboa Ave
8	Aero Dr, W Arco, Chevron/dsl, Einstein Bros., Jack-in-the-Box, McDonald's, Papa John's, Pick Up Stix, Starbucks, Starbucks, Taco Bell, Extended Stay America, Hilton, $Tree, AT&T, EVC, Firestone, PetSmart, Verizon, Von's Foods, Walmart/McDonald's
7b	Friars Rd W, W Cold Stone, Coldstone, Dragon Chinese, IHOP, Islands Burgers, Luna Grill, McDonald's, Oggi's Pizza, Starbucks, Costco/gas, IKEA, Lowe's, San Diego Stadium
7a	Friars Rd E
6b	I-8, E to El Centro, W to beaches
6a	Adams Ave, downtown, E Kensington Cafe, Starbucks, W Vons Foods
5b	El Cajon Blvd, E 76, Arco, Mobil, Pizza Hut, Subway, CVS Drug, U-Haul, W Chevron/dsl, United Oil, Church's TX Chicken, 7-11, PepBoys
5a	University Ave, E Chevron/dsl, Cali Fresh Mexican, Denny's, Jack-in-the-Box, Jamba, Little Caesars, McDonald's, Saigon Cafe, Starbucks, 7-11, O'Reilly Parts, Walgreens, W AutoZone, tires, Valvoline
3	I-805, N to I-5, S to San Ysidro
2b	(2c from nb)CA 94 W, downtown
2a	Market St, E Burger King, Costco/gas, W Taco Bell
1c	National Ave, Ocean View Blvd
1b	(from sb)I-5 S, to Chula Vista
1a	(from sb)I-5 N. I-15 begins/ends on I-5

NEEDLES

ESSEX

INTERSTATE 40

Exit #	Services
155	California/Arizona state line, Colorado River, pacific/mountain time zone
153	Park Moabi Rd, to Rte 66, N boating
149mm	insp both lanes
148	5 Mile Rd, to Topock, Rte 66(from eb)
144	US 95 S, E Broadway, Needles, N Chevron/dsl, Shell/dsl/LP, The Gas Station, Domino's, AutoZone, repair/towing
142	J St, Needles, N Valero/dsl, Jack-in-the-Box, McDonald's, Quality Inn/EVC, Rodeway Inn, Big O Tire, NAPA, S Days Inn, Motel 6, $General, dog park, H
141	W Broadway, River Rd, Needles, N River City Pizza, River City Pizza, Hampton Inn, River Valley Motel, S Chevron/Circle K/dsl, Mobil/dsl, Shell/DQ/Subway/dsl, Tesla EVC, Carl's Jr, Panda Garden, Wagon Wheel Rest., Best Western, Budget Inn, Red Roof Inn, Rio Del Sol Inn, auto/RV/tire/repair
139	River Rd Cutoff(from eb), N Hist Rte 66, rec area, Desert View RV Park, KOA
133	US 95 N, to Searchlight, to Rte 66
120	Water Rd
115	Mountain Springs Rd, Mountain Springs Summit, elev 2770, High Springs Summit, elev 2770
107	Goffs Rd, Essex, N Hist Rte 66, Chevron/dsl
106mm	rest area both lanes, full facilities, litter barrels, petwalk
100	Essex Rd, Essex, N Mitchell Caverns, to Providence Mtn SP
78	Kelbaker Rd, to Amboy, E Mojave Nat Preserve, Kelso, S to Hist Rte 66
50	Ludlow, N 76/DQ, S Chevron/dsl, Ludlow Cafe, Ludlow Motel
33	Hector Rd, to Hist Rte 66
28mm	rest area both lanes, full (hanicapped) facilities, litter barrels, petwalk
23	Ft Cady Rd, to Newberry Spgs, N Mobil/Circle K/dsl, S Newberry Mtn RV Park
18	Newberry Springs, N Chevron/cafe/dsl,

= gas = food = lodging = other = rest stop

CA

INTERSTATE 40 Cont'd

BARSTOW

18 Continued
Shell/Subway/dsl/LP

12 Barstow-Daggett Airport, N

7 Daggett, N RV camping, to Calico Ghost Town

5 Nebo St(from eb), to Hist Rte 66

2 USMC Logistics Base, N Oasis RV Park

1 E Main St, Montara Rd, Barstow, N 76/dsl, Circle K/dsl, Mobil/dsl, Travelodge, USA/dsl, Valero, Barstow Burger, Burger King, Carl's Jr, Del Taco, Denny's, DiNapoli's Italian, Domingos Mexican, Dutch Bros Coffee, Grill It, IHOP, Jack-in-the-Box, Jenny's Grill, KFC, Little Caesar's, Lola's Mexican, McDonald's, Panda Express, Popeyes, Rigoberto's, Southern Twistt, Starbucks, Subway, Taco Bell, Tom's Burgers, Wienerschnitzel, Astro Budget Motel, Best Motel, Best Western, Budget Inn, CA Inn, Days Inn/EVC, Desert Inn, EconoLodge, Economy Inn, Motel 6, Quality Inn/rest., Ramada Inn, Rodeway Inn, Super 8, $Tree, 99c Store, AutoZone, O'Reilly Parts, U-Haul/LP, S Arco, Jack-in-the-Box, Panda Express, Pit Stop Grill, Walmart/McDonald's

0mm I-40 begins/ends on I-15 in Barstow

INTERSTATE 80

FARAD

208 California/Nevada state line

201 Farad

199 Floristan

194 Hirschdale Rd, N to Boca Dam, to Stampede Dam, S RV Park

191 (from wb), inspection sta

190 Overland Trail

188 CA 89 N, CA 267, to N Shore Lake Tahoe, same as 186, N Coachland RV Park, S SpringHill Suites

186 Central Truckee(no eb return), S CA Welcome Ctr, 76/dsl, Valero/Beacon, Burger Me, Cottonwood Rest., El Toro Bravo Mexican, Jax Truckee Diner, Wagon Train Café, River Street Inn, USPO

185 CA 89 S, to N Lake Tahoe, N DQ, Golden Rotisserie, Panda Express, Port of Subs, Starbucks, Taco's Jalisco, Zano's Pizza, 7-11, Ace Hardware, Grocery Outlet, H, NAPA, New Moon Natural Foods, Safeway Foods, URGENT CARE, Verizon, S Shell/dsl, McDonald's, Starbucks, Village Pizzeria, The Inn, CVS Drug, O'Reilly Parts, SaveMart Foods, to Squaw Valley

184 Donner Pass Rd, Truckee, N Shell/dsl, Coffeebar, La Bamba Mexican, Smokey's Kitchen, S Chevron/dsl, Taco Bell, Truckee Donner Lodge, chain service, RV camp/dump, to Donner SP

181mm vista point both lanes

180 (from wb), Donner Lake, S Donner Lake Village Resort

177mm Donner Summit, elev 7239, **both lanes, full facilities, view area, litter barrels, petwalk**

CISCO GROVE

176 Castle Park, Boreal Ridge Rd, S skiing, skiing

174 Soda Springs, Norden, S Donner Summit, chain services, skiing

171 Kingvale, S Shell, Real Dough Pizza

168 Rainbow Rd, to Big Bend, S Rainbow Lodge/rest.

166 (from eb), Big Bend

165 Cisco Grove, S Chevron/dsl, Subway

164 Eagle Lakes Rd, South Yuba River

161 CA 20 W, to Nevada City, Grass Valley

160 Yuba Gap, N Lake Spaulding Campground, S vista point, Lodgepole Campground

158 Laing Rd, S Rustic Table, U-Haul, USPO

157mm brake check area, wb

158a Emigrant Gap(from eb), S USPO

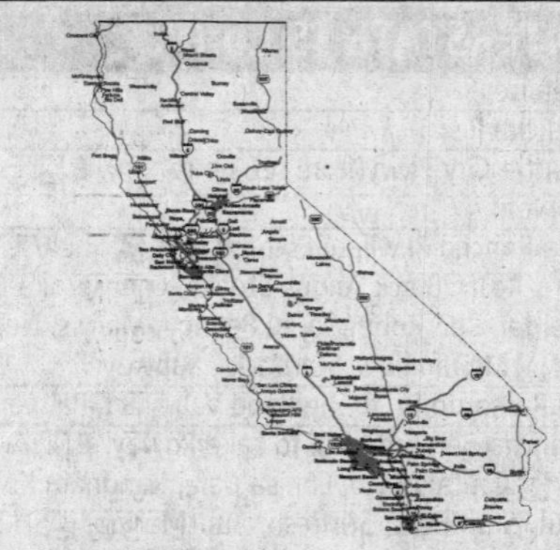

ALTA

156 Nyack Rd, Emigrant Gap, S snow park, Shell/dsl, Nyack Café, USPO

156mm N brake check area

155 Blue Canyon

150 Drum Forebay

148b Baxter

148a Crystal Springs

146 Alta

145 Dutch Flat, N Monte Vista Rest., S 76/dsl, Dutch Flat RV Resort, hwy patrol, truck repair

144 Gold Run(from wb)

143mm both lanes, full facilities, litter barrels, petwalk, N USPO

143 Magra Rd, Gold Run

140 Magra Rd, Rollins Lake Rd, Secret Town Rd

139 Rollins Lake Road(from wb)

APPLEGATE

135 CA 174, to Grass Valley, Colfax, N 76/dsl, Arco, Shell/dsl, McDonald's, Pizza Factory, Starbucks, Taco Bell, TJ's Roadhouse, Best Western, Colfax Motel, $General, NAPA, Sierra Mkt Foods, Tire & Brakes Ctr, S Chevron/dsl, Valero/dsl, Madi's Mexicali, Shang Garden Chinese, Subway, Sierra RV Ctr

133 Canyon Way, to Colfax, N U-Haul, S Dine'n Dash Cafe, Chevrolet, tires

131 Cross Rd, to Weimar

130 W Paoli Lane, to Weimar, S Weimar Store/dsl

129 Heather Glen, elev 2000 ft

128 Applegate, N Valero/dsl/LP, Applegate Inn, S truck repair, USPO

125 Clipper Gap, Meadow Vista, N Olivers

124 Dry Creek Rd

123 Bell Rd, N fruit stand, vet, S Auburn RV Resort

AUBURN

122 Foresthill Rd, Ravine Rd, Auburn, N Marriott, S Starbucks, same as 121

121 Lincolnway(from eb), Auburn, N EVC, Speedway/dsl, Valero/dsl, JimBoy's Tacos, Starbucks, Sweetpeas, Taco Bell, Wienerschnitzel, Foothills Motel, Motel 6, Red Lion Inn, Super 8, RV repairs, S Andy's, Arco, Chevron/dsl, Shell/dsl, Texaco/dsl, Awful Annie's Rest., Black Bear Diner, Brewsters Burger, Burrito Shop, El Portal Taqueria, Jack-in-the-Box, McDonald's, Starbucks, Szechuan, Taqueria El Burrito, Best Western, Rodeway Inn, Ikeda's Cafe, Raley's Foods

120 Russell Ave(from wb), same as 121, to Lincolnway from eb, S USPO

119c Elm Ave, Auburn, N 76/dsl, Shell/Circle K/dsl, Burger&Cream, Dutch Bros, Nancy's Cafe, Roundtable Pizza, Starbucks, Holiday Inn, CVS Drug, Grocery Outlet, SaveMart Foods, Staples, Verizon

119b CA 49, to Grass Valley, Auburn, N 76/dsl, Shell/dsl, In-N-Out, Holiday Inn, RV Connection

119a Maple St, Nevada St, Old Town Auburn, N antique, S Valero, Cafe Delicias, Old Town Grill,

NEWCASTLE

INTERSTATE 80 Cont'd

119a Continued
Pasquale's Risorante, Tio Pepe Mexican, Park Victorian, antiques

118 Ophir Rd (from wb)

116 CA 193, to Lincoln

115 Indian Hill Rd, Newcastle, N Newcastle Pizzeria, transmissions, USPO, S Speedway/dsl, Valero/dsl, Daily Grind, Denny's, hwy patrol

112 Penryn, N 76/dsl, Chevron/dsl, Subway, vet

110 Horseshoe Bar Rd, to Loomis, N RoundTable Pizza, Starbucks, Taco Bell, Raley's Food

109 Sierra College Blvd, N 7-11/dsl, Arco/dsl, Chevron/McDonald's/dsl, EVC, Carl's Jr, Chipotle, Jersey Mike's, Menchie's, Mooyah Burger, Noodles&Co, Panera Bread, Subway, Lemke RV Ctr, Ross, Target, Tesla, Trader Joe's, Verizon, S Shell/dsl, Baskin-Robbins, Buckhorn BBQ, Chick-fil-A, Cracker Barrel, Dutch Bros, In-N-Out, MOD Pizza, Panda Express, Starbucks, The Habit, AT&T, Bass Pro Shop, Les Schwab, PetSmart, TJ Maxx, Walmart

MARYSVILLE

108 Rocklin Rd, N 76/dsl, A&W/KFC, Adalberto's Mexican, Arby's, Fred's Burger, Jack-in-the-Box, Jamba Juice, Jing Jing Chinese, Mario's Early Toast, Milo's, Papa Murphy's, Starbucks, Taco Bell, Wienerschnitzel, Comfort Inn, Days Inn, SureStay Inn, CVS Drug, Land Rover, Mercedes, Porsche, Safeway Foods, S Arco, Little Caesar's, Starbucks, Rocklin Park Hotel, vet

106 CA 65, to Lincoln, Marysville, N 76, Arco, Chevron, Black Bear Diner, Buffalo Wild Wings, Carl's Jr, Cheesecake Factory, Dick's, Four Sisters Cafe, IHOP, Jack-in-the-Box, McDonald's, Olive Garden, PF Changs, Raising Cane's, Rubio's, Ruth's Chris Steaks, Togo's, Courtyard, Holiday Inn Express, Homewood Suites, Hyatt Place, AutoZone, Barnes&Noble, Best Buy, Costco/dsl, JC Penney, Macy's, Marshall's, Michael's, Nordstrom's, Old Navy, Ross, Staples, S Shell/7-11, BJ's Rest., Red Robin, AT&T, REI, Whole Foods, World Mkt

105b Taylor Rd, to Rocklin(from eb), N Cattlemen's Rest., S 76/Burger King/dsl, Chevron, Starbucks, Courtyard, Fairfield Inn, Hilton Garden, Holiday Inn Express, Larkspur Suites, Residence Inn, funpark, H

105a Atlantic St, Eureka Rd, S 76/7-11/dsl, Shell/Circle K, Brookfield's Rest., Chicago Fire Rest., In-N-Out, Taco Bell, Wendy's, Acura, America'sTire, Buick/GMC, Carmax, Chevrolet, Chrysler/Dodge/Jeep, Ford, Home Depot, Honda, H, Hyundai, Infiniti, Kia, Lexus, Mazda, Nissan, Subaru, Toyota/Scion

103b a Douglas Blvd, N Arco/dsl, Chevron, Exxon/dsl, Carolina's Mexican, DQ, McDonald's, Popeyes, Starbucks, Best Western, Extended Stay America, Heritage Inn, Ace Hardware, antique, Autozone, Big O Tire, Goodyear, Grocery Outlet, Midas, O'Reilly Parts, Trader Joe's, S Chevy's, Del Taco, Denny's, IHOP, Jack-in-the-Box, Lorenzo's Mexican, Outback Steaks, Panda Express, Panera, Rubio's, Starbucks, Subway, Togo's, Best Western+, Hampton Inn, Hobby Lobby, Hobby Lobby, H, Office Depot, Petco, Raley's Food, Ross, Sprouts, Target, TJ Maxx, U-Haul, Walmart

102 Riverside Ave, Auburn Blvd, to Roseville, N Arco/dsl, Chevron/dsl, Starbucks, auto repair, Meineke, S Chevron/7-11, EVC, Shell, Towne Mart, Back 40 TX BBQ, Baskin-Robbins, CA Burgers, Jack-in-the-Box, $General, auto repair, AutoZone, BMW Motorcycles, Camping World RV Ctr, NAPA, Schwab Tire

100 Antelope Rd, to Citrus Heights, N 76, CA Burrito, Carl's Jr, Dutch Bros, Extreme Hummus, Giant Pizza, McDonald's, Papa Murphy's, Popeyes, RoundTable Pizza, Subway,

SACRAMENTO

100 Continued
Taco Bell, Wendy's, $Tree, 7-11, O'Reilly Parts, Raley's Foods, vet

100mm weigh sta both lanes

98 Greenback Lane, Elkhorn Blvd, Orangedale, Citrus Heights, N Baskin Robbins, Carl's Jr, Little Caesar's, McDonald's, Pizza Hut, Starbucks, Subway, $General, CVS Drug, Safeway Foods, S Original Pizza House, Quiznos

96 Madison Ave, N Chevron/dsl, Speedway/dsl, Brookfield's Rest., Denny's, Hot Stone Pizza, Jack-in-the-Box, Little Caesars, Mongolian BBQ, Ninja Asian, Starbucks, Motel 6, Super 8, funpark, to McClellan AFB, S Arco, Shell/dsl, Burger King, CA Burrito, Chick-fil-A, Chipotle Mexican, Domino's, El Pollo Loco, IHOP, In-N-Out, Jack-in-the-Box, JJ's Hawaiian BBQ, McDonald's, Panda Express, Starbucks, Subway, Taco Bell, Wienerschnitzel, La Quinta, Wyndham, $Tree, 7-11, AT&T, Chevrolet, CHP, Firestone/auto, Ford, Jiffy Lube, PepBoys, Schwab Tire, Target, Verizon, Volvo

95 CA 99 S

94b Auburn Blvd

94a Watt Ave, N 76/dsl, Arco, Carl's Jr, El Parian Taqueria, Golden Corral, Jack-in-the-Box, KFC, Manna Thai, McDonald's, Panda Express, Popeyes, Starbucks, Subway, Taco Bell, Best Value Inn, $Tree, Firestone/auto, McClellan AFB, Walmart, S 76/dsl, Arco, Chevron, Shell, Denny's, Famous LA Chicken, Jerry's Phillies, Jimboy's Tacos, Starbucks, Wendy's, Sacramento Inn&Suites, AutoZone, Grocery Outlet, vet

93 Longview Dr

92 Winters St

91 Raley Blvd, Marysville Blvd, to Rio Linda, N Arco, Chevron/dsl, S Connie's Drive-In, Lucky Express, Q&R BBQ, $General, Hooten Tires, USPO, Valley Tire, Viva Mkt

90 Norwood Ave, N Arco/Jack-in-the-Box, Chevron, Little Caesar's, McDonald's, RoundTable Pizza, Starbucks, Subway, AutoZone, Family$, Viva Foods, S $General

89 Northgate Blvd, Sacramento, N 7-11, Cilantro's Mexican, Dutch Bros, Subway, Wendy's, U-Haul, S Arco, Shell, 524 Mexican, Carl's Jr, El Pollo Loco, IHOP, KFC, McDonald's/playplace, Original Pizza House, Subway, Taco Bell, Extended Stay America, Motel 6, Studio 6, $Tree, Advance Parts, Foodsco Foods, Jiffy Lube, O'Reilly Parts, PepBoys, Ross, Schwab Tire, tires

88 Truxel Rd, N Chevron/McDonald's, Shell/dsl, Applebee's, Baskin-Robbins, BJ's Rest, Buffalo Wild Wings, Chili's, Chipotle Mexican, Daikon Korean BBQ, Del Taco, Firehouse Subs, Hooters, In-N-Out, Logan's Roadhouse, Olive Garden, On the Border, Panera Bread, Rubio's, Starbucks, Starbucks, Togo's, Tokyo Steaks, Wingstop, Yue Huang Chinese, AT&T, Best Buy, Home Depot, HomeGoods, Michaels, Old Navy, PetSmart, Power Balance Pavilion, Ross, See's Candies, Staples, Target, TJ Maxx, Verizon, Walmart

86 I-5, N to Redding, S to Sacramento, to CA 99 N

85 W El Camino, N 49er Trkstp/dsl/scales/24hr/@, Chevron/dsl/24hr, Black Bear Diner, Burger King, Fairfield Inn, SureStay, S Arco, Dutch Bros, 7-11

83 Reed Ave, N Chevron/dsl, Jack-in-the-Box, Panda Express, Starbucks, Extended Stay America, Hampton Inn, SpringHill Suites, CHP, Peterbilt, truck repair, S Arco/24hr, Shell/McDonald's/dsl, Burger King, Chipotle, Dutch Bros, Five Guys, IHOP, In-N-Out, MOD Pizza, Taco Bell, America's Tire, Batteries+, EVC, Firestone/auto, Home Depot, IKEA, Petco, Ross, Walmart

82 US 50 E, W Sacramento

81 Enterprise Blvd, W Capitol Ave, W Sacramento, N Arco/dsl, Chevron, Granada Inn, S 7-11, EVC, EVC,

CA

= gas = food = lodging = other = rest stop

CA

INTERSTATE 80 Cont'd

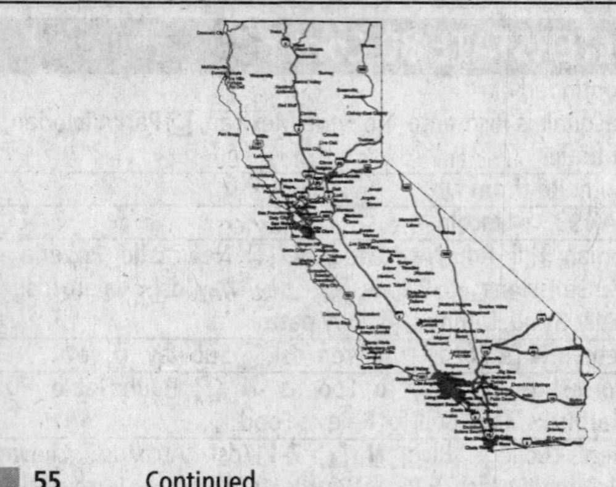

Exit	Services
81	Continued Maverik/24hr/scales, El Rancheros Mexican, Eppie's Diner, Starbucks, SacWest RV Park
78	Rd 32A, E Chiles Rd, S Fruit Stand
75	Mace Blvd, N Chevron, Residence Inn, Target, TJ Maxx, to Mace Ranch, Verizon, S 7-11/dsl, Arco/dsl, Chevron/dsl, Valero/dsl, Carl's Jr, Domino's, McDonald's, Stand Up Kabob, Starbucks, Subway, Taco Bell, Days Inn, Hi-Wheels Flats, auto repair, Chevrolet, Chrysler/Dodge/Jeep, Extreme RV Ctr, Honda, Kia, La Mesa RV Ctr, Nissan, Nugget Mkt Foods, Toyota/Scion, U-Haul
73	Olive Dr(from wb, no EZ return)
72b a	Richards Blvd, Davis, N Shell, Dutch Bros, In-N-Out, University Park Inn, NAPA, S Chevron/dsl, Carl's Jr, Four Seasons Chinese, IHOP, KFC, Starbucks, Holiday Inn Express, La Quinta, O'Reilly Parts
71	to UC Davis
70	CA 113 N, to Woodland, N H
69	Kidwell Rd
67	Pedrick Rd, N 76/LP, Chevron/dsl, Subway, produce
66b	Milk Farm Rd(from wb)
66a	CA 113 S, Currey Rd, to Dixon, S 76/dsl, Chevron/dsl, Shell/dsl, Cattlemen's Rest., Dutch Bros, Jack-in-the-Box, La Cocina, Panda Express, Popeyes, Starbucks, Wendy's, Country Inn Suites, $Tree, Ace Hardware, AutoZone, O'Reilly Parts, Schwab Tires, Verizon, Walmart
64	Pitt School Rd, to Dixon, S 76/dsl/24hr, Chevron/24hr, Baskin-Robbins, Burger King, Capital China, Denny's, Dutch Bros, Little Caesar's, McDonald's, Pizza Guys, Solano Bakery, Starbucks, Subway, Taco Bell, Taqueria Mexican, The Habit, Best Western+, Motel 6, Safeway/dsl
63	Dixon Ave, Midway Rd, N Truck Stp/dsl, S Arco/LP/lube, Chevron/dsl, Carl's Jr, Mr Taco, Wienerschnitzel, Super 8, Dixon Fruit Mkt
60	Midway Rd, Lewis Rd, Elmyra
59	Meridian Rd, Weber Rd
57	Leisure Town Rd, N Camping World, H, S 76/McDonald's, Arco, Arco/24hr/dsl, Chevron/dsl, QuikStop/24hr/dsl, Carl's Jr, Clay Oven Grill, Hideaway Grill, Jack-in-the-Box, King's Buffet, Popeyes, Starbucks, Subway, Taco Bell, Comfort Suites, Extended Stay America, Fairfield Inn, Holiday Inn Express, Hyatt Place, Motel 6, Quality Inn, Residence Inn, Buick/GMC, Chevrolet, Chrysler/Dodge/Jeep, Harley-Davidson, Home Depot, Honda, Hyundai, Kia, Kohl's, Mazda, Nissan, Toyota, VW
56	I-505 N, to Winters
55	Nut Tree Pkwy, Monte Vista Dr, Allison Dr, N 7-11, Chevron, Texaco, Boudin SF Sourdough, Buckhorn BBQ, Buffalo Wild Wings, Burger King, CA Burrito, Chipotle, Denny's, El Pollo Loco, Fenton's Creamery, Firehouse Subs, Five Guys, Food Court, Habit Burger, Hawaiian BBQ, Hoshi Japanese, IHOP, Jamba Juice, McDonald's, Murillo's Mexican, Nations Burger, Noodles&Co, Panda Express, Panera Bread, Pelayo's Mexican, Pieology Pizza, Starbucks, Taco Bell, Wendy's, Best Value Inn, Best Western, Super 8, America's Tire, Best Buy, Big O Tire, Firestone/auto, Jiffy Lube, Lowe's Whse, Michael's, Midas, Nugget Foods, O'Reilly Parts, Old Navy, PetSmart, See's Candies, U-Haul, Verizon, World Mkt, S Arco/24hr, Chevron/24hr, BJ's Grill, Carl's Jr, Chick-fil-A, Chili's, Coldstone Creamery, Freebirds Burrito, Grocery Outlet, In-N-Out, Jack-in-the-Box, Jamba Juice, Mel's Diner, Olive Garden, Pizza Twist, Popeyes, Raising Cane's, Starbucks, Togo's, Comfort Suites, Courtyard, Fairfield Inn, Holiday Inn Express, Motel 6, Residence Inn, $Tree, GMC, H, Marshall's, PetCo, Ross, Safeway, Sam's Club/dsl, 

DAVIS · ELMYRA · FAIRFIELD

Exit	Services
55	Continued Sprouts Mkt, Staples, Target, Vacaville Stores/famous brands, Walmart/McDonald's
54b	Mason St, Peabody Rd, N Chevron/7-11, Texaco/dsl, Little Caesars, Sonesta, Jiffy Lube, NAPA, O'Reilly Parts, Schwab Tire, S Speedway/dsl, CA Burrito, Del Taco, Dutch Bros, Starbucks, Wienerschnitzel, $Tree, 7-11, Costco/gas, Country Square Mkt, USPO
54a	Davis St, N Chevron/McDonald's, Outback Steaks, Starbucks, Hampton Inn, S DQ, Sonic, auto repair, WinCo Foods
53	Merchant St, Alamo Dr, N Chevron, Shell/dsl, Speedway/dsl, Baldo's Mexican, Black Bear Diner, RoundTable Pizza, Taco Bell, Alamo Inn, BigLots, vet, S 76/Starbucks, Alamo/dsl, Jack-in-the-Box, KFC, McDonald's, Subway, Walmart Mkt
52	Cherry Glen Rd(from wb)
51b	Pena Adobe Rd
51a	Lagoon Valley Rd, Cherry Glen
48	N Texas St, Fairfield, S Arco/24hr, Chevron/dsl, Shell, El Pollo Loco, Jimboy's Tacos, McDonald's, Panda Express, Starbucks, Subway, Texas Roadhouse, SureStay, CVS, Lowe's, Raley's Foods
47	Waterman Blvd, N Dynasty Chinese, RoundTable Pizza, Starbucks, Subway, Chevrolet, Safeway, Subaru, S Arco, Adalberto's Mexican, Carl's Jr, Hot Stone Korean, LJ Silver's/KFC, McDonald's, NY Pizza Express, Popeyes, Subway, Taco Bell, Wendy's, Gateway Inn, Quality Inn, $Tree, museum, Schwab Tires, tires, to Travis AFB, vet, Walgreens, Walmart
45	Travis Blvd, Fairfield, N 76, Chevron, EVC, Avalanche Fro-Yo, Baskin-Robbins, Burger King, Denny's, Domino's, Huckleberry's Cafe, In-N-Out, Mary's Pizza Shack, McDonald's, Peet's Coffee, Peking Rest., Subway, Taco Bell, Courtyard, Motel 6, $Tree, CHP, Jiffy Lube, Raley's Foods, S EVC, Travis/dsl, Buffalo Wild Wings, Carino's Italian, Chevy's Mexican, Chick-fil-A, Chipotle Mexican, Coldstone, Five Guys, Hibachi Grill, Jamba Juice, Jollibee, Mel's Diner, Mimi's Café, Ohana HI BBQ, Panda Express, Panera Bread, Pieology, Red Lobster, Red Robin, Starbucks, The Habit Burger, Wing Stop, Hilton Garden, AT&T, Barnes&Noble, Best Buy, Firestone/auto, H, JC Penney, Macy's, mall, Michael's, PetCo, Ross, Trader Joe's, Verizon
44	W Texas St, same as 45, Fairfield, N A&A/dsl, KwikServ/dsl, ChuckeCheese, Popeyes, Starbucks, Extended Stay America, Staples, S 76, Cenario's Pizza, Jack-in-the-box, McDonald's, Taco Exxpress, 99c Store, Acura/Honda, BMW, CarMax, Chrysler/Jeep/Dodge, Ford/Lincoln, Home Depot, Mercedes, Nissan, O'Reilly Parts, Target/CVS, Toyota/Scion, VW
43	CA 12 E, Abernathy Rd, Suisun City, S Holiday Inn Express, Budweiser Plant
42mm	weigh sta both lanes

INTERSTATE 80 Cont'd

Exit #	Services
41	Suisan Valley Rd, N H, S 7-11, Arco, Chevron/dsl, Shell/dsl, Sinclair/dsl, Arby's, Burger King, Carl's Jr, Cenario's Pizza, Del Taco, Denny's, Green Bamboo, Jersey Mike's, McDonald's, Mooyah Burgers, Starbucks, Subway, Taco Bell, Wendy's, Wienerschnitzel, Best Western, Comfort Inn, Fairfield Inn, La Quinta, Studio 6, Travelodge, Scandia FunCtr, vet
40	I-680(from wb)
39b	Green Valley Rd, I-680(from eb), N Happy Garden, Hawaiian BBQ, Hinata, Peloyas Mexican, RoundTable Pizza, Starbucks, Subway, Homewood Suites, Residence Inn, Staybridge Suites, Costco/gas, CVS, Safeway, TJ Maxx, S Arco, Cordeila RV Ctr
39a	Red Top Rd, N Chevron, Jack-in-the-Box
36	American Canyon Rd
34mm	**wb, full facilities, info, litter barrels, petwalk, vista parking**
33b a	CA 37, to San Rafael, Columbus Pkwy, N 7-11/dsl, Chevron/dsl, Courtyard, Hampton Inn, to Six Flags, S same as 32
32	Redwood St, to Vallejo, N Chevron, Denny's, Panda Garden, Econo Lodge, SureStay, H, S Shell, Valero, Applebee's, Black Bear Diner, Chevy's Mexican, Chick-fil-A, Chipotle, Coldstone, Daikon KBBQ, Habit Burger, IHOP, Ike's Sandwiches, In-N-Out, Jamba Juice, Little Caesar's, McDonald's, Menchie's, MOD Pizza, Mtn. Mike's Pizza, Olive Garden, Panda Express, Panera Bread, Red Lobster, Round Table Pizza, Starbucks, Subway, Wing Stop, Comfort Inn, Country Inn & Suites, $Tree, Advance Parts, AT&T, AutoZone, Best Buy, Cadillac/Chevrolet, Chrysler/Dodge/Jeep, Costco/gas, CVS, Home Depot, Honda, Kohl's, Lowe's, Marshall's, Mazda, Michael's, PepBoys, PetCo, Ross, Safeway, Target/Starbucks, Toyota/Scion, Verizon, vet
31b	Tennessee St, to Vallejo, S 76/dsl, Royal Gas, Jack-in-the-Box, Pacific Pizza, Pizza Guys, Motel 6, Scottish Inn, Travelodge, Grocery Outlet, USPO
31a	Solano Ave, Springs Rd, N Burger King, Cardinas Mkt, Church's TX Chicken, Subway, Szechuan, Taco Bell, Thrifty's Ice Cream, Solano Inn, Super 8, U-Haul, S Chevron, Exxon, Grand Gas, QuikStop, McDonald's, Popeye's, Sac's Hot Dogs, Express Inn, $Tree, AutoZone, Island Pacific Foods, O'Reilly Parts, vet
30c	Georgia St, Central Vallejo, N Safeway/gas, S California Motel
30b	Benicia Rd(from wb), S Chevron/dsl, Maggie's Burgers, McDonald's, Starbucks
30a	I-780, to Martinez
29b	Magazine St, Vallejo, N Gas&Shop/dsl, Starbucks, Subway, 7 Motel, Budget Inn, Discovery Inn, Economy Inn, El Rancho, Tradewinds RV Park, S McDonald's, Travel Inn, 7-11
29a	CA 29, Maritime Academy Dr, Vallejo, N Shell/dsl, Sinclair
28mm	toll plaza, pay from eb
27	Pomona Rd, Crockett, N Dead Fish Seafood, vista point, S Crockett Cocina, Lucia's Sandwiches
26	Cummings Skyway, to CA 4(from wb), to Martinez
24	Willow Ave, to Rodeo, N Subway, Warrior NY Pizza, auto repair, USPO, S 76/dsl, Burger King, Mazatlan, Mtn Mike's Pizza, Starbucks, Willow Garden Chinese
23	CA 4, to Stockton, Hercules, N Safeway, Shell, Jack-in-the-Box, Kinder's Meats BBQ, Pizza Twist, Starbucks, Safeway, S Dragon Terrace, L&L HI BBQ, McDonald's, RoundTable Pizza, Taco Bell, BigLots, Home Depot, Lucky Foods
22	Pinole Valley Rd, N Starbucks, The Habit Burger, Sprouts Mkt/EVC, S Arco/24hr, Chevron/dsl, Chipotle, Five Guys, Jack-in-the-Box, Jamba Juice, MOD Pizza, Red Onion Rest., Subway, 7-11, Trader Joe's, Walgreens
21	Appian Way, N Chevron, China Delights, McDonald's, CVS, Safeway, S Burger King, Carl's Jr, ChuckECheese, Coldstone, Due Rose Italian, Hawaiian BBQ, KFC, Mel'sOriginal Shakes, Mtn Mike's Pizza, Panda Express, Papa Murphy's, Sizzler, Starbucks, Taco Bell, Wendy's, Wing Stop, Days Inn, Motel 6, $Tree, AT&T, AutoZone, Best Buy, Goodyear/auto, Grocery Outlet, Lucky Foods
20	Richmond Pkwy, to I-580 W, N Chevron/dsl, IHOP, McDonald's, Me&Ed's Pizza, Subway, 99c Store, Buick/GMC, Chrysler/Dodge/Jeep, Ford, Hyundai, Kia, Nissan, Ross, Toyota/Scion, VW, S Shell/dsl, Applebee's, Cheese Steak, ChuckECheese, Ike's Sandwiches, In-N-Out, Mel's Original Shakes, Outback Steaks, Panera Bread, RoundTable Pizza, FoodMaxx, Michael's, O'Reilly Parts, PetSmart, Staples, Target/Starbucks, TJ Maxx
19b	Hilltop Dr, to Richmond, N Chevron, Courtyard, Extended Stay America, Firestone/auto, mall, Walmart, S Hilltop Fuel/dsl
19a	El Portal Dr, to San Pablo, S Shell, McDonalds, Mtn. Mike's Pizza, Pizza Twist, Starbucks, Subway, Dollar Tree, Raley's Foods, vet, Walgreens
18	San Pablo Dam Rd, N Chevron, Denny's, El Pollo Loco, Empire Buffet, Jack-in-the-Box, Jamba Juice, Jersey Mike's, Nations Burgers, Pizza Guys, Popeyes, RoundTable Pizza, Starbucks, Subway, Taco Bell, Holiday Inn Express, AutoZone, FoodMaxx, Ross, Walgreens
17	Macdonald Ave(from eb), McBryde Ave(from wb), Richmond, N Arco/24hr, Burger King
16	San Pablo Ave, to Richmond, San Pablo, N Panda Express, Target, S Chevron, KFC, LJ Silver, Wendy's, auto repair
15	Cutting Blvd, Potrero St, to I-580 Br(from wb), to El Cerrito, N Arco, S Valero/dsl, Brasil Bistro, Church's TX Chicken, Denny's, Frannie HI BBQ, IHOP, Jack-in-the-Box, McDonald's, Starbucks, Hotel Mira, Home Depot, Honda, Ross, Safeway, Walgreens
14b	Carlson Blvd, El Cerrito, N 40 Flags Motel, S Best Value Inn
14a	Central Ave, El Cerrito, S 76, Shell/dsl, Valero, Burger King, Chipotle, Nations Burgers, Popeyes, Barnes&Noble
13	to I-580(from eb), Albany
12	Gilman St, to Berkeley, E Target, W Golden Gate Fields Racetrack
11	University Ave, to Berkeley, E Chevron/dsl, Mobil, Valero/Circle K, Thai Table, La Quinta, Marina Inn, to UC Berkeley, vet, W Hana Japan Steaks, Seabreeze Seafood, Skates On The Bay, DoubleTree, walking/bike trails
10	CA 13, to Ashby Ave
9	Powell St, Emeryville, E 76, Black Bear Diner, Burger King, CA Pizza Kitchen, Denny's, Fogo de Chao, Starbucks, Togo's, Hyatt, Hyatt House, Sheraton, Sonesta, Barnes&Noble, Marshall's, Ross, Trader Joe's, Verizon, W Shell, Chevy's Mexican, Hilton Garden
8c b	Oakland, to I-880, I-580
8a	W Grand Ave, Maritime St
7mm	toll plaza wb
5mm	SF Bay
4a	Treasure Island (exits left)
2c b	Fremont St, Harrison St, Embarcadero(from wb), N Sandwich Boss, The Clancy Hotel, S Delancey Street Rest.
2a	4th st(from eb), S Shell
1	9th st, Civic Ctr, downtown SF
1b a	I-80 begins/ends on US 101 in SF

VALLEJO

EL CERRITO

CA

= gas = food = lodging = other = rest stop

INTERSTATE 110 (Los Angeles)

EXPO PARK

Exit #	Services
21	I-110 begins/ends on I-10.
20c	Adams Blvd, E Chevron, Audi, Chrysler/Dodge/Jeep, LA Convention Ctr., Mercedes, Nissan, VW
20b	37th St, Exposition Blvd, E Chichen Itza Mexican, Holbox Seafood, W Chick-fil-A, Chipotle, Starbucks, Wingstop, USC Hotel, Chevrolet
20a	MLK Blvd, Expo Park, W Chevron, McDonald's, Subway, 7-11
19b	Vernon Ave, E Mobil, Tacos El Gavilan, W 76/24hr, Shell, Burger King, Jack-in-the-Box, Tam's Burger, Ross
18b	Slauson Ave, E Mobil, W Arco, El Pollo Loco, Jack-in-the-box, KFC, McDonald's, Taco Bell, Tam's Burgers, CVS, Superior Mkt
18a	Gage Blvd, E 7-11, Arco, Church's Chicken, Hercules Burgers, The Family Rest.
17	Florence Ave, E Shell, Jack-in-the-Box, Louisiana Chicken, W Chevron, Valero, Burger King, Little Caesar's, McDonald's, Pizza Hut
16	Manchester Ave, E Arco, Burger Palace, El Pollo Loco, Little Caesar's, McDonald's, Roscoe's Chicken, Subway, Winchell's, AutoZone, W 76, Church's TX Chicken, Jack-in-the-Box, Krispy Krunchy Chicken, Popeyes, Tam's Burgers, Tumby's Pizza
15	Century Blvd, E Arco, Shell/Subway/dsl, Burger King, McDonald's, T-Mobil, W 76/dsl, Tam's Burgers
14b	Imperial Hwy, W Chevron/dsl, Jack-in-the-Box, McDonald's
14a	I-105
13	El Segundo Blvd, E Little Caesars Pizza, Subway, Taco Bell, W Shell, Hollywood Inn
12	Rosecrans Ave, E Arco/24hr, Chevron, W Chevron/McDonald's, Sinclair, Jack-in-the-Box, KFC/LJ Silver, Louisiana Fried Chicken, Pizza Hut, Popeyes, Rick's Drive-In, Starbucks, Subway, Yoshinoya, 7-11, casino
11	Redondo Beach Blvd, E K Pot Asian, McDonald's, W Mobil, FarmerBoys, Ono HI BBQ, Subway, casino, H, Ross, Staples
10b a	CA 91, 190th St, E Arco, Carl's Jr, Del Taco, El Pescador, Starbucks, Extended Stay, Hampton Inn, Motel 6, W Arco, Carl's Jr, Jack-in-the-Box, Krispy Kreme, Lee's Sandwiches, McDonald's, Subway, Taco Bell, Food4Less, Ranch Mkt, Sam's Club/gas
9	I-405, San Diego Fwy
8	Torrance Blvd, Del Amo, E BOSS Pizza, Burger King, Chile Verde, Starbucks, WaBa Grill, W Mobil, Shell/7-11/dsl
7b	Carson St, E KFC, Cali Inn, W Arco, Shell, Carl's Jr., Chick-fil-A, Golden Pheasant, In-N-Out, Jack-in-the-Box, La Cocina, Lee's Sandwiches, Louis Burgers IV, McDonalds, Pizza Hut, Starbucks, Wienerschnitzel, Autozone, Bella Vida Drug, H, O'Reilly Parts, Superior Mkt
5	Sepulveda Blvd, E L&L HI BBQ, McDonald's, Starbucks, Wendy's, Albertson's, Home Depot, Staples, Target, W Arco/24hr, Chevron, Exxon/dsl, Burger King, Carl's Jr, McDonald's, Popeyes, Starbucks, Taco Bell, Motel 6, $Tree, 99c Store, AT&T, Big Lots, Food4Less, Ross
4	CA 1, Pacific Coast Hwy, E Arco, Alberta's Mexican, Jack-in-the-Box, Pizza Hut, Wienerschnitzel, Crescent Inn, Red Roof Inn, W 76, Mobil, United/dsl, Bob's Burgers, Del Taco, Denny's, El Pollo Loco, Monarcas Mexican, Subway, Best Western, H, PepBoys, transmissions
3b	Anaheim St, E 76, Dunkin'
3a	C St
1b	Channel St, W Arco, Chevron, Big Nick's Pizza, Larry's Hamburgers, 7-11, Target/Starbucks
1a	CA 47, Gaffey Ave
0mm	I-110 begins/ends

DEL AMO

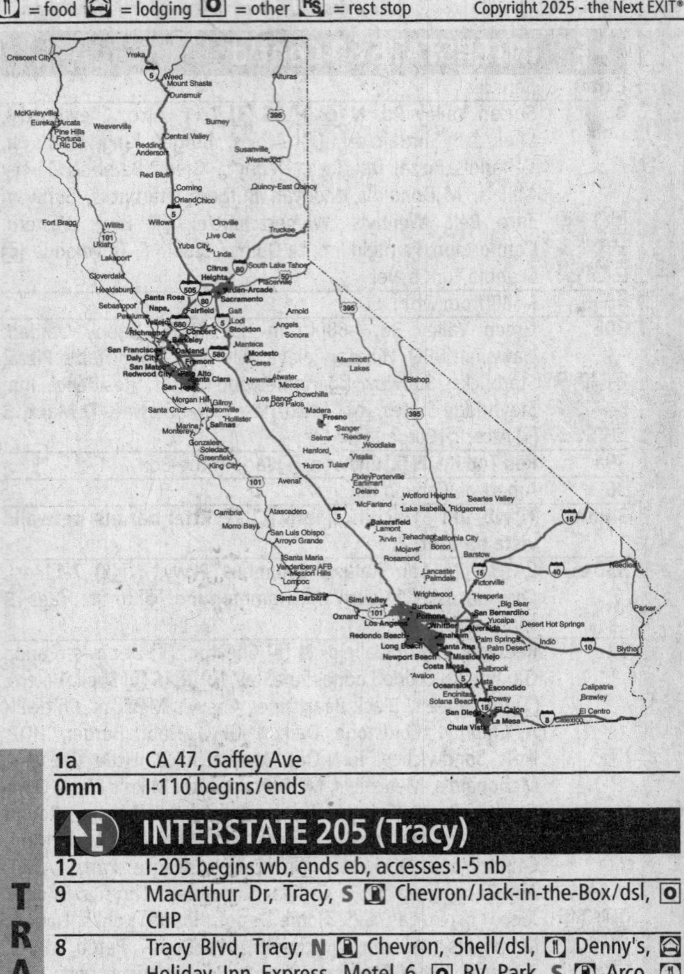

INTERSTATE 205 (Tracy)

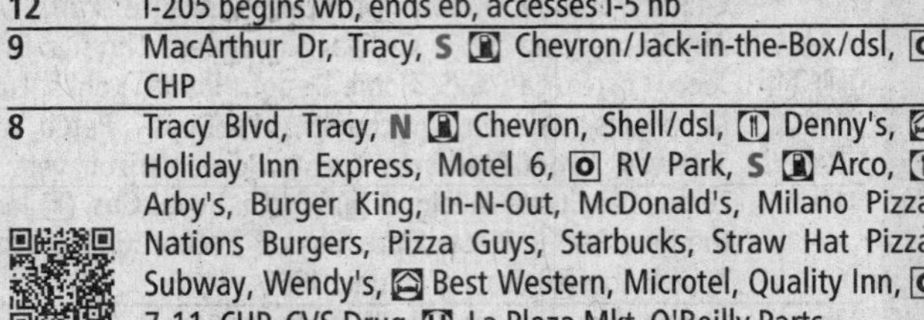

TRACY ANTIOCH

Exit #	Services
12	I-205 begins wb, ends eb, accesses I-5 nb
9	MacArthur Dr, Tracy, S Chevron/Jack-in-the-Box/dsl, CHP
8	Tracy Blvd, Tracy, N Chevron, Shell/dsl, Denny's, Holiday Inn Express, Motel 6, RV Park, S Arco, Arby's, Burger King, In-N-Out, McDonald's, Milano Pizza, Nations Burgers, Pizza Guys, Starbucks, Straw Hat Pizza, Subway, Wendy's, Best Western, Microtel, Quality Inn, 7-11, CHP, CVS Drug, H, La Plaza Mkt, O'Reilly Parts
6	Grant Line Rd, Antioch, N Chevron/dsl, Applebee's, BJ's Rest., Buffalo Wild Wings, Burger King, BurgerIM, El Pollo Loco, Five Guys, Golden Corral, IHOP, Jamba Juice, Jersey Mike's, Krispy Krunchy Chicken, MOD Pizza, Mongolian BBQ, Olive Garden, Ono Hawaiian BBQ, Panda Express, Panera Bread, Pizza Hut, RoundTable Pizza, Rubio's, Sonic, Starbucks, Subway, Taco Bell, The Habit, TX Roadhouse, Wienerschnitzel, Fairfield Inn, Hampton Inn, 99c, America's Tire, AT&T, Best Buy, Chevrolet, Chrysler/Dodge/Jeep, Costco/gas, Ford, Home Depot, Honda, Hyundai, Jiffy Lube, Les Schwab Tire, Macy's, mall, Marshall's, Michael's, Nissan, PetSmart, Ross, Staples, Target, Toyota/Scion, Verizon, VW, Walmart/auto, WinCo Foods, S 7-11, Arco, National/dsl, Shell/dsl, A&W/KFC, Black Bear Diner, Carl's Jr, Chili's, Hawaiian BBQ, Mtn Mike's Pizza, Popeyes, Home2 Suites, EVC, RV Ctr
4	11th St(from eb), to Tracy, Defense Depot
2	Mtn House Pkwy, to I-580 E
0mm	I-205 begins eb/ends wb, accesses I-580 wb.

INTERSTATE 210 (Pasadena)

Exit #	Services
85a	I-210 begins/ends on I-10, exit 77.
84	San Bernardino Ave, W Chipotle, Dutch Bros, Habit Burger, Miguel's Jr, MOD Pizza, ALDI, Barnes&Noble, Hobby Lobby, Kohls, Michaels, Old Navy, Ramona Tire, Ross, Target, TJ Maxx, World Mkt
83	W 5th St, Greenspot Rd, E Chevron/dsl, Del Taco,

INTERSTATE 210 (Pasadena) Cont'd

83 Continued
Dickey's BBQ, In-N-Out, Subway, Waba Grill, [O] AT&T, Lowe's, Staples

82 Base Line Rd, E [G] Arco, Valero, [F] Carl's Jr, KFC/Taco Bell, McDonald's, Subway, Wendy's, [O] Albertson's, CVS Drug, Walgreens, W [G] 76/dsl, [F] Baker's, Popeyes, Starbucks, [O] AutoZone, CVS Drug, Family$

81 CA 330 N, to Big Bear

79 Highland Ave, N [G] 76/Subway/dsl, Shell/dsl, [F] Baker's, Denny's, DQ, IHOP, Taco Bell, Wienerschnitzel, [O] 7-11, 99c, USPO, S [F] Chubzies, Del Taco, El Pollo Loco, KFC, Starbucks, WaBa Grill, Wendy's, [O] $Tree, 99c Store, AutoZone, Goodyear, O'Reilly Parts

78 Del Rosa Ave, N [G] 7-11, Shell, [F] Del Taco, S [G] Exxon, Quick Gas/Circle K, Valero, [F] Carl's Jr, Domino's, Jack-in-the-Box, Little Caesars, McDonald's, Wingstop, [O] CVS Drug, Stater Bros, USPO, Walgreens

76 Waterman Ave, S [G] Mobil/7-11/dsl, [O] [H]

75 CA 259(from wb), H St

74 I-215 N to Barstow S to San Bernardino

73 State St, University Pkwy, N [G] 76/7-11/dsl, Arco, USA, [O] $General, AutoZone, tires

71 Riverside Ave, N [G] Chevron, [F] Carl's Jr, Del Taco, Panda Paradise, Starbucks, Subway, [O] AutoZone, Verizon, S [G] Arco, [F] Chipotle, In-N-Out, Jack-in-the-Box, [O] 7-11, URGENT CARE, vet

70 Ayala Dr, N [G] 76/Circle K/McDonald's/dsl, S [F] Blaze Pizza, Chick-fil-A, Cracker Barrel, Dutch Bros, El Pollo Loco, Olive Garden, Panda Express, Panera Bread, Sonic, Starbucks, The Habit, TX Roadhouse, [L] Ayres Hotel, [O] 7-11, city park, Grocery Outlet, Old Navy, Ross

68 Alder Ave, N [G] Pilot/Arby's/24hr/dsl/scales, Shell/Subway/dsl, S 76/dsl, [O] U-Haul

67 Sierra Ave, N [G] 7-11, [F] Applebee's, Boston's, Carl's Jr, El Pollo Loco, Jamba Juice, McDonald's, Mimi's Cafe, MOD Pizza, Panda Express, Pizza Hut, Pollo Campero, Starbucks, Subway, Tio's Mexican, Waba Grill, Wendy's, Wendy's, [O] 7-11, [O] $Tree, Costco, Lowe's Whse, Petco, Schwab Tire, URGENT CARE, Verizon, S [F] Cane's, Dutch Bros, Jack-in-the-Box, [O] Chevrolet, Honda, Hyundai, Mountain View Tires, Nissan, Sprouts Mkt

66 Citrus Ave, N [F] Domino's, FarmerBoys Rest., Pick Up Stix, Pizza Guys, Popeyes, Taco Bell, [O] America's Tire, AT&T, AutoZone, Home Depot, Jiffy Lube, Ralph's Foods, Walgreens, S [G] Arco/dsl, [F] Habit Burger, Starbucks, [O] Chrysler/Dodge/Jeep, Kia, Sunrise Mkt

64 Cherry Ave

63 I-15 N to Barstow, S to San Diego

62 Day Creek Blvd, S [G] Arco/dsl, Shell, [F] Jack-in-the-Box, Menchies, Mr. You Chinese, Starbucks, Subway, Wendy's, [O] Ralph's Foods

60 Milliken Ave, S [G] Mobil/Circle K/dsl, [F] Subway, Taco Bell, [O] $Tree, Albertsons, CVS Drug, URGENT CARE, vet

59 Haven Ave, N [G] 7-11, 76, Exxon, [F] Corky's Kitchen, Del Taco, Domino's, Jack-in-the-Box, McDonald's, Subway, The Coffee Bean, Tio's Mexican, [O] Trader Joe's, vet, Vons Foods, Walgreens, Walgreens

58 Archibald Ave, S [F] Bamboo Garden, Barboni's Pizza, Carl's Jr, [O] Stater Bros, vet

57 Carnelion St, S [G] 76, [F] Del Taco, El Ranchero Mexican, Hills Kitchen, Juice It Up, Pizza Guys, Sal's Pizza, Starbucks, Subway, Terry's Burgers, [O] Sprouts, Vons Foods, Walgreens

56 Campus Ave, N [G] Arco/dsl, Shell, [F] In-N-Out, Starbucks, [O] Ford, S [F] Carl's Jr, Chick-fil-A, Chili's, Chipotle, El Pollo Loco, Golden Spoon Yogurt, Habit Burger, Hawaiian BBQ,

LAVERNE

56 Continued
Jersey Mike's, Panera Bread, Pick Up Stix, Starbucks, Wingstop, [O] Albertsons, AT&T, Dick's, Dick's, Home Depot, Kohl's, Mountain View Tire, Office Depot, Old Navy, PetSmart, Target, TJ Maxx, Verizon, Verizon

54 Mtn Ave, Mount Balde

52 Baseline Rd, N [F] RoundTable Pizza, Subway, [O] Vons Food, S [F] Chipotle, Cold Stone, Corky's Kitchen, Jersey Mike's, MOD Pizza, Starbucks, Waba Grill, Wendy's, [O] CVS Drug, Whole Foods Mkt

50 Towne Ave, N [O] museum, S park

48 Fruit St, Via Verde, S [G] Shell/7-11, [F] Blaze Pizza, Broken Yolk Cafe, Chili's, Chipotle, El Pollo Loco, Hawaiian BBQ, In-N-Out, Jersey Mike's, Jimmy John's, Little Caesars, McDonald's, Panda Express, Panera Bread, Robeks, Rubio's Grill, Subway, Wingstop, [O] ALDI, Big Lots, Kohl's, Marshall's, Michaels, Staples, Stater Bros. Mkt, Target, U of LaVerne, vet

47 Foothill Blvd, LaVerne, N [G] 7-11, Arco, Mobil, [F] Domino's, Mr D's, Subway, S [G] 76/dsl, [F] Carl's Jr, Del Taco, Don Baja Grill, IHOP, Jack-in-the-Box, Jamba Juice, Mi Ranchito, Starbucks, Taco Bell, The Grill House, The Habit, [O] $Tree, CVS Drug, Ross, Sprouts Mkt, URGENT CARE, vet, Vons Food/gas

46 San Dimas Ave, San Dimas, N [O] San Dimas Canyon CP

45 CA 57 S

44 Lone Hill Ave, Santa Ana, N [G] Shell, [F] Casa Jimenez, McDonalds, Panda Express, Szechuwan Garden, [O] Stater Bros. Mkt, vet, S [G] Chevron, [F] Blaze Pizza, Cane's Chicken, Chik-fil-A, Chili's, Chipotle, Coco's, Corner Bakery Cafe, In-N-Out, Krispy Kreme, Olive Garden, Starbucks, Subway, The Habit, Wendy's, Wingstop, [O] Barnes&Noble, Best Buy, Chevrolet, Chrysler/Dodge/Jeep, Costco/gas, Ford, Home Depot, Hyundai, Kohl's, Old Navy, PetSmart, Sam's Club/gas, Staples, Toyota, Verizon, Walmart/auto

43 Sunflower Ave

42 Grand Ave, to Glendora, N [G] Arco, Exxon, [F] Carl's Jr, Denny's, El Pollo Loco, Red Lantern, Wienerschnitzel, [L] Garden Inn&Suites, [O] America's Tire, [H], Sprouts Mkt, Walgreens

41 Citrus Ave, to Covina

IRWINDALE

40 CA 39, Azusa Ave, N [G] Arco/24hr, Chevron/dsl, Mobil/dsl, Shell/Del Taco, [F] Jack-in-the-Box, [L] Motel 6, Super 8, [O] auto repair, S [G] Arco, Chevron, [F] El Picoso, In-N-Out, McDonald's, [L] Best Value, Home2 Suites, [O] $Tree, 7-11, Family$

39 Vernon Ave (from wb), same as 38

38 Irwindale, N [G] Arco, EVC, Shell/7-11/dsl, [F] Carl's Jr, Chipotle, FarmerBoys Rest., Jersey Mike's, McDonald's, Starbucks, Taco Bell, WaBa Grill, [O] Costco/gas

36b Mt Olive Dr, N [G] Mobil/dsl, [F] Redwood Pizza, Subway, [O] CVS

36a I-605 S

35b a Mountain Ave, N [G] Arco, Chevron, [F] Church's TX Chicken, Del Taco, Denny's, Old Spaghetti Factory, Sonic, Taco Bell, Tommy's Hamburgers, Wienerschnitzel, [L] Oak Park Motel, [O] 7-11, Best Buy, BMW/Mini, Buick/Chevrolet, CarMax, Chrysler/Dodge/Jeep, Fiat, Ford, Goodyear/auto, Honda, Infiniti, Subaru, Target, Walgreens, S [F] IHOP, Panda Express, Subway, [O] Home Depot, Ross, Walmart/McDonald's

34 Myrtle Ave, N [F] Taco Bell, [L] TownePlace Suites, [O] Midas, PepBoys, S [G] 76, Chevron/dsl, [F] Jack-in-the-Box, [O] vet

33 Huntington Dr, Monrovia, N [G] Shell/dsl, [F] Burger King, Chili's, Chipotle, Dave's Hot Chicken, Domenico's Italian, Domino's, Hart House, Jack-in-the-Box, Jersey Mike's, Jimmy John's, LeRoy's Rest., McDonald's, Mimi's Cafe, Panda Express, Panera Bread, Papa Murphy's, Popeyes,

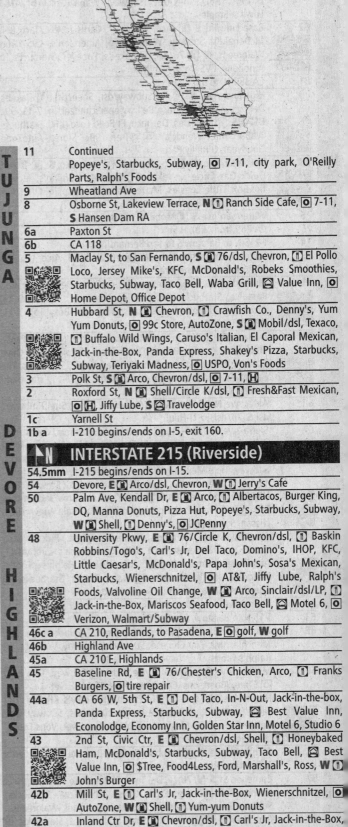

INTERSTATE 210 (Pasadena) Cont'd

Exit	Services
33	Continued RoundTable Pizza, Rubio's, Tacos Endenada, Courtyard, Baja Ranch Foods, Kohl's/EVC, Marshall's, PetSmart, Sprouts Mkt, Trader Joe's, vet, Walgreens, **S** 76, Baja Fresh, BJ's Grill, Burgerim, Cane's Chicken, Capital Seafood, Chick-fil-A, Derby Rest., Fatburger, Haru Ramen, MyDeli, Olive Garden, Outback Steaks, Pieology, Red Lobster, Robeks Juice, Soup Plantation, Starbucks, Taisho Rest., Tokyo Wako, DoubleTree, Embassy Suites, Extended Stay America, Hampton Inn, Hilton Garden, OakTree Inn, Residence Inn, SpringHill Suites, Verizon
ARCADIA 32	Santa Anita Ave, Arcadia, **N** 76, Arco, McDondald's, Pizza Hut, Subway, $Tree, **S** Chevron, Denny's, Goldstein's Bagel, In-N-Out, Jiffy Lube, Mercedes-Benz, REI
31	Baldwin Ave, to Sierra Madre
30b a	Rosemead Blvd, **N** 76/dsl, Arco, Baskin Robbins, CA Fish Grill, ChuckeCheese, Del Taco, Dominos, Einstein Bros, Habit Burger, Island Burger, Jamba Juice, Jersey Mikes, Maria's Italian, Panda Express, Panera Bread, Peet's Coffee, Pick Up Stix, Starbucks, Subway, AT&T, CVS Drug, Marshall's, Ralph's Foods, Toyota, Valvoline Instant Change, Verizon, Whole Foods Mkt, **S** Chevron, Jack-in-the-Box, Tops Rest., Best Value Inn, Best Western, Sprouts Mkt, Staples, tire repair, World Mkt
SIERRA MADRE 29b a	San Gabriel Blvd, Madre St, **N** 76, Chipotle Mexican, El Torito, Handel's Creamery, Pizza Rey, Starbucks, Best Buy, Dick's, Old Navy, PetSmart, Ross, **S** 76, KFC, Krispy Kreme, Mt Mike's Pizza, USPO, Astro Inn, Best Western, Holiday Inn Express, Hotel La Reve, Rodeway Inn, Super 8, Amazon Fresh, Buick/Chevrolet/GMC, Cadillac, Land Rover, Target
28	Altadena Dr, Sierra Madre, **N** Spirit, Super Burger, **S** Chevron, Exxon, Kalaveras, Just Tires
27b	Allen
27a	Hill Ave
26	Lake Ave, **N** Mobil/Circle K/dsl, AutoZone
25b	CA 134, to Ventura
25a	Del Mar Blvd, CA Blvd, CO Blvd (exits left from eb)
24	Mountain St
23	Lincoln Ave, **S** Lincoln Motel, tire service
22b	Arroyo Blvd, **N** Jack-in-the-Box, **S** to Rose Bowl
22a	Berkshire Ave, Oak Grove Dr
21	Gould Ave, **S** Arco, Chevron, Flintridge Pizza, Honeybird Rest., McDonald's, Panda Express, RoundTable Pizza, Subway, Firestone/auto, Just Tires, Petco, Ralph's Foods, Trader Joe's/Starbucks
20	CA 2, Angeles Crest Hwy, **S** 76, Shell, Berge's Sandwiches, Chipotle, Luna Grill, Panera Bread, Sakura Japanese, Taylor's Steaks, Target/Starbucks
19	CA 2, Glendale Fwy, **S** H
LA CRESCENTA 18	Ocean View Blvd, to Montrose, **N** Jack-in-the-Box, Starbucks, Taco Bell, Big Lots, Jiffy Lube
17b a	Pennsylvania Ave, La Crescenta Ave, La Crescenta, **N** 76, Mobil, Shell/7-11, Baja Fresh, Domino's, Juice It Up!, Subway, TOGO's Sandwiches, Wienerschnitzel, O'Reilly Parts, Office Depot, Ralph's Foods, Toyota/Scion, USPO, Verizon, vet, Vons Foods/Starbucks, Walgreens, **S** Gardenia Mkt/deli
16	Lowell Ave, **N** Aiden's Grill, Del Taco, In-N-Out, Sevan Chicken, Albertsons, Albertsons
14	La Tuna Cyn Rd
11	Sunland Blvd, Tujunga, **N** Chevron, Mobil/dsl, Shell, Alfred's Pizza, Baskin-Robbins, Burrito Factory, Hell's Chicken, Jack-in-the-Box, Panda Express, Pizza Hut,

Exit	Services
TUJUNGA 11	Continued Popeye's, Starbucks, Subway, 7-11, city park, O'Reilly Parts, Ralph's Foods
9	Wheatland Ave
8	Osborne St, Lakeview Terrace, **N** Ranch Side Cafe, 7-11, **S** Hansen Dam RA
6a	Paxton St
6b	CA 118
5	Maclay St, to San Fernando, **S** 76/dsl, Chevron, El Pollo Loco, Jersey Mike's, KFC, McDonald's, Robeks Smoothies, Starbucks, Subway, Taco Bell, Waba Grill, Value Inn, Home Depot, Office Depot
4	Hubbard St, **N** Chevron, Crawfish Co., Denny's, Yum Yum Donuts, 99c Store, AutoZone, **S** Mobil/dsl, Texaco, Buffalo Wild Wings, Caruso's Italian, El Caporal Mexican, Jack-in-the-Box, Panda Express, Shakey's Pizza, Starbucks, Subway, Teriyaki Madness, USPO, Von's Foods
3	Polk St, **S** Arco, Chevron/dsl, 7-11, H
2	Roxford St, **N** Shell/Circle K/dsl, Fresh&Fast Mexican, H, Jiffy Lube, **S** Travelodge
1c	Yarnell St
1b a	I-210 begins/ends on I-5, exit 160.

INTERSTATE 215 (Riverside)

Exit	Services
54.5mm	I-215 begins/ends on I-15.
DEVORE 54	Devore, **E** Arco/dsl, Chevron, **W** Jerry's Cafe
50	Palm Ave, Kendall Dr, **E** Arco, Albertacos, Burger King, DQ, Manna Donuts, Pizza Hut, Popeye's, Starbucks, Subway, **W** Shell, Denny's, JCPenny
48	University Pkwy, **E** 76/Circle K, Chevron/dsl, Baskin Robbins/Togo's, Carl's Jr, Del Taco, Domino's, IHOP, KFC, Little Caesar's, McDonald's, Papa John's, Sosa's Mexican, Starbucks, Wienerschnitzel, AT&T, Jiffy Lube, Ralph's Foods, Valvoline Oil Change, **W** Arco, Sinclair/dsl/LP, Jack-in-the-Box, Mariscos Seafood, Taco Bell, Motel 6, Verizon, Walmart/Subway
HIGHLANDS 46c a	CA 210, Redlands, to Pasadena, **E** golf, **W** golf
46b	Highland Ave
45a	CA 210 E, Highlands
45	Baseline Rd, **E** 76/Chester's Chicken, Arco, Franks Burgers, tire repair
44a	CA 66 W, 5th St, **E** Del Taco, In-N-Out, Jack-in-the-box, Panda Express, Starbucks, Subway, Best Value Inn, Econolodge, Economy Inn, Golden Star Inn, Motel 6, Studio 6
43	2nd St, Civic Ctr, **E** Chevron/dsl, Shell, Honeybaked Ham, McDonald's, Starbucks, Subway, Taco Bell, Best Value Inn, $Tree, Food4Less, Ford, Marshall's, Ross, **W** John's Burger
42b	Mill St, **E** Carl's Jr, Jack-in-the-Box, Wienerschnitzel, AutoZone, **W** Shell, Yum-yum Donuts
42a	Inland Ctr Dr, **E** Chevron/dsl, Carl's Jr, Jack-in-the-Box, Wienerschnitzel, AutoZone, Macy's, mall, O'Reilly Parts, **W** Arco/dsl

INTERSTATE 215 (Riverside) Cont'd

RIVERSIDE

Exit #	Services
41	Orange Show Rd, E Arco, World, Burger Mania, Jose's Mexican, Sundowners Rest., Viva Villa Grill, Orange Show Inn, Rodeway Inn, 7-11, 99c Store, BigLots, Carquest, Chrysler/Dodge/Jeep, Target, W AT&T, Kia, Nissan, Subaru, Toyota/Scion, VW
40b a	I-10, E to Palm Springs, W to LA
39	Washington St, Mt Vernon Ave, E Arco, Berri Bros/repair, Vred/Circle K, Baker's Drive-Thru, China Town, DQ, Dunkin', Juan Pollo, Nickelodeon Pizza, Starbucks, Colton Inn, Goodyear/auto, Jiffy Lube, W Carl's Jr, Church's TX Chicken, Cotijas Tacos, Del Taco, Denny's, El Pollo Loco, Jack-in-the-Box, McDonald's, Sayaka Japanese, Starbucks, Waba Grill, Rodeway Inn, 7-11, 99c Store, Ross, RV ctr, Walmart/auto
38	Barton Rd, E Arco, Mobil/Circle K/dsl, McDonald's, Miguel's Mexican, SoCal Subs, Taco Bell, Wingstop, Woody's Grill, AutoZone, Stater Bros., vet
37	La Cadena Dr, (Iowa Ave from sb), E Shell/dsl, Jack-in-the-Box, Starbucks, Holiday Inn Express, tire repair
36	Center St, to Highgrove, E Chevron/Subway/dsl, Chris' Burgers, W Arco, Shell/dsl
35	Columbia Ave, E Arco/dsl, W Del Taco, Jack-in-the-Box, 7-11
34b a	CA 91, CA 60, Main St, to beach cities, Riverside
33	Blaine St, 3rd St, E 76/Circle K, Arco, Shell, Baker's Drive-Thru, Duke's Grill, Farmer Boys, Jack-in-the-Box, My Hero Subs, Poke Bistro, Starbucks, Stater Bros., Valvoline Oil Change
32	University Ave, Riverside, E U of CA Riverside, W Arco, Mobil/dsl, Shell, Carl's Jr, Castaneda's Mexican, Del Taco, Denny's, Domino's, IHOP, Jack-in-the-Box, Jersey Mike's, Little Caesar's, Papa John's, Pizza Hut, R Burgers, Starbucks, Subway, Taco Bell, Wienerschnitzel, Winchell's, Wingstop, Courtyard, Dynasty Suites, Motel 6, Quality Inn, $Tree, AT&T, Food4Less, O'Reilly Parts, USPO, Walgreens
31	MLK Blvd, El Cerrito, E U of CA Riverside
30b	Central Ave, Watkins Dr, W to Sycamore Park
30a	Fair Isle Dr, Box Springs, E Marjon RV Ctr, W 76/Circle K/Subway/dsl, Jack-in-the-Box, Ford, Nissan
29	CA 60 E, to Indio, E Arco, Conserve/dsl, Baffalo Wild Wings, Baskin-Robbins, BJ's Rest., Boss Pizza, Burger Boss, Cane's Chicken, Carl's Jr, Chick-fil-A, Chili's, Chipotle Mexican, Del Taco, DQ, El Pollo Loco, Five Guys, HOGGS BBQ, Jade China, Jamba Juice, Jersey Mike's, John's Pizza, Kickin' Crab, Louisiana Seafood, McDonald's, Olive Garden, Ono Hawaiian BBQ, Panera Bread, R Burgers, Round Table Pizza, Rubio's, Starbucks, Subway, TX Roadhouse, Waba Grill, Wendy's, Wienerschnitzel, $Tree, 99c Store, Best Buy, Big Lots, JC Penney, Lowe's, Macy's, mall, Marshall's, Michael's, Old Navy, PetCo, PetSmart, Ross, Staples, Target, TJ Maxx, Verizon, Walmart
28	Eucalyptus Ave, Eastridge Ave, E 76, Alaska Crab, Applebee's, Baker's Drive-Thru, Bravos Rest., Miguel's Jr, Mimi's Cafe, Panda Express, Popeyes, Portillo's, The Habit Burger, Ayres Hotel, Fairfield Inn, Hampton Inn, Residence Inn, ALDI, Costco/gas, Sam's Club/gas, Winco Foods/EVC
27b	(27c from sb)Alessandro Blvd, E 7-11, Arco/dsl, auto repair, W Chevron, Farmer Boys
27a	Cactus Ave to March ARB, E 76/Circle K/dsl, Arco/dsl, Chevron/dsl, Angelo's Burgers, Carl's Jr, Donut Shop, Flaming Grill, Quik Stop Subs, Starbucks, Wendy's, truck stop, W URGENT CARE
25	Van Buren Blvd, E March Field Museum, W 76/Circle K/Sbarro/dsl, Chipotle, In-N-Out, Jersey Mike's, Starbucks,

HEMET

Exit #	Services
25	Continued Hampton Inn, Riverside Nat Cem
23	Harley Knox Blvd
22	Ramona Expswy, E Arco, Chevron/dsl, Mobil/Circle K, Shell/Subway/dsl, Farmer Boys, FarmerBoys Rest., Harry's Cafe, McDonald's, Papa John's, Playa Maya Mexican, Starbucks, Subway, Valentino's Pizza, W Arco/dsl/scales/24hr, Circle K/dsl/LP, Jack-in-the-Box
21	Placentia Ave, E Domino's, Jack-in-the-Box, KFC, La Bufadora, Little Caesars, Taco Bell, Wienerschnitzel, $General, $Tree, NAPA, Speedy Lube & Tire
19	Nuevo Rd, E Arco, Chevron/dsl, Mobil/Circle K, Alberto's Mexican, Baskin-Robbins, Burger King, Carl's Jr, Chick-fil-A, Chipotle, Del Taco, El Pollo Loco, IHOP, In-N-Out, Jamba Juice, Jersey Mike's, Juice It Up!, McDonald's, McDonald's, Mtn Mike's Pizza, Panda Express, Pizza Hut, Popeyes, Sizzler, Starbucks, Starbucks, Subway, WaBa Grill, Wendy's, Wingstop, American Inn, ALDI, AutoZone, Food4Less, Just Tires, O'Reilly Parts, Ross, Schwab Tire, Stater Bros Foods, U-Haul, URGENT CARE, URGENT CARE, Verizon, Walgreens, Walmart, Walmart
17	CA 74 W, 4th St, to Perris, Lake Elsinore, E Chevron, Shell, W 7-11, Chevron, Speedway, Del Taco, Denny's, Gus Jr, Jack-in-the-Box, Jimenez Mexican, La Mexicana, Los Jilbertos, Popeyes, Rose Donuts, Subway, Perris Hotel, AutoZone, Chrysler/Dodge/Jeep/Kia, Kia, vet
15	CA 74 E, Hemet, E Arco/dsl, Jack-in-the-Box, Sun Leisure Motel
14	Ethanac Rd, E Shell/Circle K, KFC/Taco Bell, Camping World, W 7-11, 76/dsl, Circle K/dsl, Carl's Jr, Corky's Kitchen, Del Taco, Ono Hawaiian BBQ, PanPan Wok, Starbucks, Subway, AutoZone, Home Depot, Jiffy Lube, Just Tires, WinCo Foods
12	McCall Blvd, Sun City, E 76/dsl, Gulf, Wendy's, Menifee Inn, Motel 6, H, W Chevron/dsl, Black Bear Diner, Castaneda's Mexican, Domino's, Jack-in-the-Box, McDonald's, Subway, $Tree, auto repair, Cherry Hills Farmers Mkt, Stater Bros, USPO, vet, Von's Foods, Walgreens
10	Newport Rd, Quail Valley, E Chevron/dsl, Shell/7-11/dsl, Blaze Pizza, Cafe Rio, Cane's Chicken, Cathay Chinese, Firehouse Subs, Jack-in-the-Box, Jamba Juice, Subway, Subway, Taco Bell, $Tree, AutoZone, Ralph's Foods, Ross, Valvoline, W Circle K/dsl, Applebee's, Baskin-Robbins, BJ's Rest., Buffalo Wild Wings, Chik-fil-A, Chipotle Mexican, El Pollo Loco, Hawaiian BBQ, In-N-Out, Krispy Kreme, Miguel's Mexican, Panda Express, Panera Bread, Red Robin, Rubios, Sonic, Starbucks, Subway, The Habit, TX Roadhouse, Yellow Basket Cafe, ALDI, America's Tire, AT&T, Best Buy, CVS Drug, Kohl's, Lowe's, Michael's, PetCo, PetSmart, See Candies, Staples, SuperTarget, TJ Maxx, URGENT CARE, Verizon, vet

LOS ALAMOS

Exit #	Services
7	Scott Rd, E 7-11, Chevron/dsl, Carl's Jr, Del Taco, Domino's, Jack-in-the-Box, Submarina, Albertson's/SavOn, vet, Walgreens, W Taco Bell
4	Clinton Keith Rd, E Albertos Mexican, Blaze Pizza, Cane's Chicken, Chik-fil-A, Chipotle, FarmerBoys Rest., Jamba Juice, ALDI, AutoZone, Costco/gas, Ramona Tire, URGENT CARE, W Arco/dsl, Del Taco, Jack-in-the-Box, Jersey Mike's, Juice It Up, Starbucks, Subway, $Tree, CVS Drug, Home Depot, Mtn View Tire, Target, URGENT CARE
2	Los Alamos, E 7-11, Shell, Board'z Grill, Chef K Chinese, Cojito's Mexican, Dickey's BBQ, El Gordito Mexican, In-N-Out, Miguel's Jr Mexican, Starbucks, Taco Bell, Grocery Outlet, USPO, W Mobil/Circle K/dsl, ChuckeCheese, El Ranchito Mexican, Jack-in-the-Box, McDonald's, Pizza Hut, Starbucks, Subway, Hampton Inn, CVS Drug, Stater Bros., vet

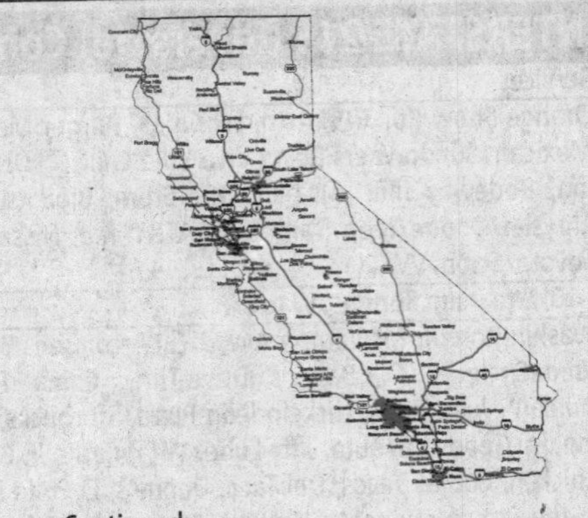

CA

INTERSTATE 215 (Riverside) Cont'd

Exit #	Services
1	Murrieta Hot Springs, E 7-11, Shell/dsl, Alberto's Mexican, Buffalo Wild Wings, Carl's Jr, Dunkin, El Pollo Loco, Habit Burger, Richie's Diner, Rise to Grind, Rubio's, Sizzler, Starbucks, The Hat, Wendy's, $Tree, Marshalls, Ross, Sam's Club/gas, URGENT CARE, Verizon, vet, Walgreens, W La Gordita Mexican, Richie's Diner, Starbucks, H
0mm	I-215 begins/ends on I-15.

INTERSTATE 280 (Bay Area)

DALY CITY · COLMA · MENLO PARK · PORTOLA VALLEY

Exit #	Services
58	4th St, I-280 begins/ends, N Whole Foods Mkt, S Shell
57	7th St, to I-80, downtown
56	Mariposa St, downtown
55	Army St, Port of SF
54	US 101 S, Alemany Blvd, Mission St, S Shell
52	San Jose Ave, Bosworth St(from nb, no return)
51	Geneva Ave
50	CA 1, 19th Ave, W Chevron, to SFSU
49	Daly City, Daly City, E Speedway, vet, W Valero, Canton Chinese, Carl's Jr, Domino's, IHOP, McDonald's, Hampton Inn
47a	Serramonte Blvd, Daly City(from sb), same as 47b
48	Eastmoor Ave, Sullivan Ave, from eb, E In-N-Out, Krispy Kreme, Hampton Inn, W 76/dsl/LP, Cbellas Pizza, Hi Drive-Inn, Keith's Chicken N Waffles, Wendy's, Toyota, Walgreens
47b	CA 1, Mission St (from nb), Pacifica, E Black Bear Diner, Chipotle, Panda Express, Poke Bowl, Popeyes, RoundTable Pizza, Sizzler, Starbucks, Wingstop, $Tree, Chevrolet, Chrysler/Jeep/Dodge, Ford, H, Lexus, Michael's, Target, vet, VW/Subaru, W Buffalo Wild Wings, Dave & Buster's, Ike's Love, Jollibee Chicken, MOD Pizza, Old Navy, Target
46	Hickey Blvd, Colma, E Chevron/dsl, Shell/dsl, W Shell/dsl/24hr, Celia's Rest., Habit Burger, In-N-Out, Koi Palace, Max's Filipino, McDonald's, Moonstar, Nick the Greek, Outback Steaks, Panera Bread, Starbucks, 7-11, CVS, PetSmart, Sprouts Mkt, Verizon
45	Avalon Dr (from sb), Westborough, W Arco/24hr, Fuel 24:7/dsl, Five Guys, McDonald's, Ng's Cooking, Subway, AT&T, Safeway, to Skyline Coll, Walgreens/24hr
44	(from nb), W same as 45
43b	I-380 E, to US 101, to SF Airport
43a	San Bruno Ave, Sneath Ave, E Baskin-Robbins, Big Mouth Burgers, Carl's Jr, Jamba Juice, Local Kitchens, Starbucks, The Melt, Ace Hardware, CVS, Mollie Stones Mkt, W Kwik Serv, 7-11
42	Crystal Springs (from sb), E county park
41	CA 35 N, Skyline Blvd(from wb, no EZ return), to Pacifica
40	Millbrae Ave, Millbrae, E Chevron
39	Trousdale Dr, to Burlingame, E H
36	Black Mtn Rd, Hayne Rd, W golf
36mm	Crystal Springs rest area wb, full (handicapped) facilities, phone, picnic table, litter barrels, petwalk
35	CA 35, CA 92W(from eb), to Half Moon Bay
34	Bunker Hill Dr
33	CA 92, to Half Moon Bay, San Mateo
32mm	vista point both lanes
29	Edgewood Rd, Canada Rd, to San Carlos, E H
27	Farm Hill Blvd, E Cañada Coll
25	CA 84, Woodside Rd, Redwood City, W Chevron/dsl, Buck's Rest., Firehouse Bistro, Robert's Mkt, USPO
24	Sand Hill Rd, Menlo Park, E Shell, Sandhill Rest., Starbucks, Rosewood Hotel, Stanford Hotel, CVS, Safeway
22	Alpine Rd, Portola Valley, E H, W Shell, Amigos Grill, Bianchi's Mkt
20	Page Mill Rd, to Palo Alto, E H, to Stanford U
16	El Monte Rd, Moody Rd, W to Foothill Coll
15	Magdalena Ave
13	Foothill Expswy, Grant Rd, E Chevron/24hr, Peet's, Red Pepper Grill, Starbucks, Subway, Trader Joe's, W to Rancho San Antonio CP
12b a	CA 85, N to Mtn View, S to Gilroy
11	Saratoga, Cupertino, Sunnyvale, E Chevron/dsl, Chipotle, Manley Donuts, Starbucks, Cupertino Inn, Goodyear/auto, Michael's, Ross, Safeway, W Chevron, Great Gas, Valero, BJ's Rest., Donut Wheel, The Habit, Aloft, Juniper Hotel, Marina Food, Target, Verizon
10	Wolfe Rd, E Gulf/dsl, Courtyard, Hilton Garden, Ranch Mkt, W 76, Benihana, Hyatt House, Residence Inn, Jiffy Lube
9	Lawrence Expswy, Stevens Creek Blvd(from eb), N Bill's Cafe, KAI Japanese, McDonald's, Panda Express, RoundTable Pizza, Wingstop, AT&T, Marshall's, Nissan, Safeway, URGENT CARE, S Rotten Robbie, Shell, Subway, Woodcrest Hotel, 7-11
7	Saratoga Ave, N 76/dsl, Arco/24hr, Chevron/24hr, Burger King, Lion Foods, McDonald's, Starbucks, Taco Bell, Wienerschnitzel, Yumi Yogurt, TownePlace Suites, 7-11, 7-11, Acura, BMW, Cadillac, Chevrolet, Chrysler/Jeep/Dodge, Ford, Honda, Hyundai, Inifiniti, Land Rover, Mazda, Mercedes, Mini, Nissan, PepBoys, Porsche, Toyota, Toyota, Volvo, VW, Walmart Mkt, S 76, Valero, Applebee's, Aloft Hotel
5c	Winchester Blvd, Campbell Ave(from eb), S Chevron/dsl, Valero, Dunkin, Honey Baked Ham, Starbucks, Wingstop
5b	CA 17 S, to Santa Cruz, I-880 N, to San Jose
5a	Leigh Ave, Bascom Ave, S Domino's, McDonald's, Mini Gourmet, Subway, Taco Bell, Wendy's, H
4	Meridian St(from eb), N Big O Tires, FoodMaxx, Harley Davidson, USPO, S Chevron, Subway
3b	Bird Ave, Race St, N 76/dsl, Chevron, auto repair
3a	CA 87, N Hilton, Marriott, Westin, museum
2	7th St, to CA 82, N conv ctr, S Chevron/dsl
1	10th St, 11th St, N 7-11, to San Jose St U
0mm	I-280 begins/ends on US 101.

INTERSTATE 405 (Los Angeles)

GRANADA HILLS

Exit #	Services
73	I-5, N to Sacramento, I-5, S to LA
72	Rinaldi St, Sepulveda, E Chevron/dsl, Presidente Mexican, H, W Shell, Granada Inn
71b a	S F Mission Blvd, CA 118 W, E Shell/7-11, Arby's, KFC, McDonald's, Starbucks, Nissan, Toyota
70	Devonshire St, Granada Hills, E 76, Arco, Sinclair/dsl, Buon Gusto Italian, Chipotle, Dunkin', Holiday Burger, Jamba Juice, Mandarin Island, Papa John's, Safari Room Rest, Starbucks, Subway, The Habit Burger, Vons Foods

INTERSTATE 405 (Los Angeles) Cont'd

RESEDA

Exit #	Services
69	Nordhoff St, E Mobil/dsl, China Wok, Coldstone, Del Taco, Panda Express, Pollo Campero, Starbucks, Subway, Hillcrest Inn, 7-11, Marshalls, Vallarta Foods, Walgreens, W 76/dsl, Arco, Jack-in-the-Box, Pizza Hut
68	Roscoe Blvd, to Panorama City, E Shell, Denny's, Domino's, Jack-in-the-Box, Kountry Folks Rest., Little Caesar's, Magma Grill, Mariscos Mexican, McDonald's, Panda Express, Taco Bell, The Burger Den, VW, Yoshinoya, Holiday Inn Express, Palm Tree Inn, Travel Inn, 7-11, AutoZone, Ford, Jaguar/Volvo, Lincoln, Mazda, U-Haul, W Chevron/dsl, Shell/dsl, Valero, Subway, Tommy's Burgers, Motel 6
66	Sherman Blvd, Reseda, E Chevron, Mobil/LP, McDonald's, Poke Rainbow, Starbucks, Teriyaki Plus, Hyland Inn, CVS Drug, H, Jon's Foods, W 76/dsl/24hr, Taco Bell, USPO
65	Victory Blvd, Van Nuys, E Carl's Jr, El Pollo Loco, Fatburger, Firehouse Subs, Jack-in-the-Box, Lido Pizza, Ono HI BBQ, Sam Woo Chinese, Subway, Wendy's, Zankou Chicken, $Tree, Costco/gas, CVS Drug, El Monte RV Ctr, H, Jiffy Lube, PepBoys, Staples, W Arco/24hr
64	Burbank Blvd, E Chevron, Shell, Denny's, Zankou Chicken, Best Western, Hampton Inn, Target, W golf, Lake Balboa Park
63b	US 101, Ventura Fwy
63a	Ventura Blvd(from nb), E Mobil, 8oz Poke, Blu Jam Cafe, Buffalo Wild Wings, Cheesecake Factory, El Pollo Loco, Mulberry Pizza, PF Chang's, Starbucks, mall, Whole Foods Mkt, W 76, CA Chicken Cafe, Corner Bakery Cafe, IHOP, IL Nido Italian, Mariachi Mexican, McDonald's, Valley Inn, Courtyard, vet
63a	Valley Vista Blvd(from sb)
61	Mulholland Dr, Skirvall Dr
59	Sepulveda Blvd, Getty Ctr Dr, W to Getty Ctr
57	Sunset Blvd, Morega Dr, E 76/dsl, Chevron/24hr, Allegro Pizza, Umberto's Italian, to UCLA, W Hotel Angeleno, Luxe Hotel
56	Waterford St, Montana Ave(from nb)
55c b	Wilshire Blvd, E downtown, H
55a	CA 2, Santa Monica Blvd, E Chevron, Mobil, Mobil, Shell, Al's Chicken, Fatburger, Green Olive Rest., Jack-in-the-Box, Jamba Juice, Pita Cafe, Sichuan Impression, Starbucks, Zankou Chicken, 7-11, Jiffy Lube, LDS Temple, Porsche, Tesla, World Mkt, W SK Gas, Nanbankan, Subway, Holiday Inn Express, vet
54	Olympic Blvd, Peco Blvd, E Pazzo Pizzeria, 7-11, USPO, W Big Tomy's Rest., Best Buy, Marshall's, Michael's, PetSmart
53	I-10, Santa Monica Fwy
52	Venice Blvd, E Chevron/service, Shell/dsl, Baskin-Robbins, Carl's Jr, Howard's Burgers, Maple Block BBQ, Papa John's, Subway, Ramada, 7-11, W SP/dsl, FatBurger
51	Culver Blvd, Washington Blvd, E Dear John's Café, Domino's, Fresh Pita, Taco Bell, vet, W Chevron
50b	CA 90, Slauson Ave, to Marina del Rey, E Arco/24hr, Capriotti's Sandwiches, Del Taco, El Pollo Loco, George Petrelli Steaks, HoneyBaked Ham, Shakey's Pizza, Winchell's, $Tree, BigLots, Goodyear/auto, Just Tires, Office Depot, Old Navy
50a	Jefferson Blvd(from sb), E Jack-in-the-Box, Menchie's Fro-yo, Panda Express, Panera Bread, Mayumi, Target, W to LA
49	Howard Hughes Pkwy, to Centinela Ave, E Chevron/dsl,

INGLEWOOD

Exit #	Services
49	Continued Mobil/dsl, BJ's Brewhouse, CA Fish Grill, Charley's Cheesesteaks, Chipotle, Five Guys, Jamba Juice, Lucille's BBQ, Mongolian BBQ, Olive Garden, Ono HI BBQ, Qdoba, Sizzler, Courtyard, Sheraton, Best Buy, CVS Drug, Ford, Honda, Macy's, Target, Tesla, Trader Joe's, W Chevron, Buffalo Wild Wings, Chick-fil-A, Dave & Buster's, Dinah's Rest., Hilton, Islands Burgers, Kabuki Japanese, Starbucks, Viva Fresh Mexican, Howard Hughes Ctr
48	La Tijera Blvd, E Mobil/sl, Burger King, Chipotle, Dave's Hot Chicken, Dunkin', El Pollo Loco, Fatburger, Jamba Juice, Jersey Mike's, KFC, McDonald's, Menchie's, Panda Express, Starbucks, Subway, Taco Bell, TGIFriday's, Wingstop, Best Western, CVS Drug, Marshalls, Ralph's Foods, Ross, Valvoline, W 76, Arco, Wendy's, USPO
47	CA 42, Manchester Ave, Inglewood, E 76/Circle K/dsl/24hr, Bravo's Charburgers, Carl's Jr, Jamba Juice, Roscoe's Chicken, Starbucks, Subway, Best Western, Economy Inn, 7-11, W 76, Arco, Mobil/7-11, Shell, 7 Nineteen Seafood, Arby's, Denny's, El Pollo Loco, Jack-in-the-Box, Papa John's, Pita Cafe, Randy's Donuts, Three Flames MBBQ, Tottino's Pizza, Tumby's Pizza, WaBa Grill, Days Inn, CarMax, Chrysler/Dodge/Jeep, Home Depot
46	Century Blvd, E El Pollo Loco, Little Caesar's, Panda Express, Starbucks, WaBa Grill, Best Western, Lyfe Inn, Motel 6, Quality Inn, 7-11, W 76, Arco/24hr, Chevron/dsl, Shell, Carl's Jr, Daily Grill, Denny's, McDonald's, Starbucks, Subway, Embassy Suites, Hilton, Holiday Inn, Hyatt, La Quinta, Marriott, Residence Inn, Sheraton, Sonesta, Westin Hotel, to LAX
45	I-105, Imperial Hwy, E 76/dsl, Arco, Shell, El Pollo Loco, Hampton Inn, Jack-in-the-Box, McDonald's, Starbucks, Wingstop, Candlewood Suites, Holiday Inn Express, Stadium Inn, W KFC, Winchell's
44	El Segundo Blvd, to El Segundo, E 76, Chevron/dsl, Thrifty, Cougars Burgers, Jack-in-the-Box, Subway, El Segundo Inn, transmissions, W Denny's, Ramada Inn

HERMOSA BEACH

Exit #	Services
43b a	Rosecrans Ave, to Manhattan Beach, E 76, Mobil, Denny's, El Pollo Loco, Pizza Hut, Starbucks, Subway, Best Buy, CVS Drug, Food4Less, Ford/Lincoln, Hobby Lobby, Home Depot, Marshall's, Michael's, Ross, TJ Maxx, Verizon, World Mkt, W Speedway, Blaze Pizza, Cafe Rio, Carl's Jr, Chipotle Mexican, Eddie V's Seafood, Flemings Rest., Fogo de Chao Brazillian, Fornaio Italian, Jamba Juice, Jimmy John's, Johnny Rockets, L&L HI BBQ, Lido Ristorante, McDonald's, Nomad Eatery, Pachanga Mexican, Robeks Juice, Sansai Japanese, Shake Shack, Starbucks, Union Pizza, Ayres Hotel, Hyatt, SpringHill Suites, TownePlace Suites, AT&T, Barnes&Noble, Bristol Mkt, Costco/gas, CVS Drug, Office Depot, Old Navy, Porsche, REI, Subaru, Trader Joe's, vet, VW
42b	Inglewood Ave, E Arco, Mobil, Denny's, Domino's, Flame Broiler Korean, In-N-Out, Mashawi Grill, Pizza Hut, Tarasco Mexican, CVS Drug, Marshall's, PetCo, Vons Foods, Walmart Mkt, W Chevron/dsl, Shell, Chile Verde Mexican, Subway, Tomboy's Chiliburgers, Homewood Suites, Residence Inn, 99c Store, Pep Boys, repair
42a	CA 107, Hawthorne Blvd, E Little Caesars, McDonald's, Panda Express, Papa John's, Rolling Zone Creamery, Spires Rest., Wingstop, Best Western, Days Inn, $Tree, El Super Foods, NAPA, URGENT CARE, vet, W Arco/24hr, USA/dsl, Chicken Chick, Pollo Campero, Taco Bell, URGENT CARE
40b	Redondo Beach Blvd (no EZ sb return), Hermosa Beach, E 76, Speedway, ChuckeCheese, Jack-in-the-Box, golf, W Coldstone, Dave's Hot Chicken, RoundTable Pizza, $Tree, auto repair, AutoZone, Walgreens

CA

= gas = food = lodging = other = rest stop

INTERSTATE 405 (Los Angeles) Cont'd

Exit #	Services
40a	CA 91 E, Artesia Blvd, to Torrance, W Chevron/service, Carl's Jr, Coldstone, Dave's Hot Chicken, Red Iron MBBQ, Red Robin, Sizzler, Union Pizza, YumYum Donuts, AutoZone, Kohl's, Macy's
39	Crenshaw Blvd, to Torrance, E Chevron, EVC, Coffee Bean, El Pollo Loco, McDonald's, Wingstop, T-Mobil, USPO, W Shell/dsl, Jiffy Lube
38b	Western Ave, to Torrance, E 76/dsl, Arco, Chevron, BB.Q Chicken, Bull KBBQ, Chipotle, Del Taco, Denny's, In-N-Out, Jersey Mike's, King's Hawaiian, Panda Express, Papa John's, Wendy's, Yorgos Burgers, Dynasty Inn, Albertson's, AT&T, GNC, Toyota/Scion, W Exxon, Sonesta
38a	Normandie Ave, to Gardena, E Sam's Club, W Shell/dsl, Aunty Maile's HI, Carl's Jr, Great Steak, Hong Kong Cafe, On + On Asian, Pizza Hut, Quiznos, Starbucks, Subway, Taco Bell, Wienerschnitzel, Extended Stay America, $Tree, AutoZone, URGENT CARE, Walmart
37b	Vermont Ave(from sb), W Holiday Inn
37a	I-110, Harbor Fwy
36	Main St(from nb)
36mm	weigh sta both lanes
35	Avalon Blvd, to Carson, E Chevron, Mobil, Buffalo Wild Wings, Cane's, Chick-fil-A, Chili's, Chipotle, ChuckeCheese, Denny's, Five Guys, Ike's Love & Sammies, Jack-in-the-Box, Jamba Juice, Jersey Mike's, McDonald's, Olive Garden, Panda Express, Panera Bread, Pieology, Pizza Hut, Pizza Hut, Shakey's Pizza, Sizzler, Smashburger, Starbucks, Starbucks, Subway, Tokyo Grill, WingStop, Motel 6, Advance Parts, ALDI, America's Tire, AT&T, Firestone/auto, IKEA, JC Penney, Just Tires, Old Navy, Ross, Target, U-Haul, Verizon, Walmart Mkt, W Arco, Mobil, Carl's Jr, IHOP, McDonald's, O'Reilly Parts, Ralph's Foods, USPO
34	Carson St, to Carson, E Rodeway Inn, W 76/dsl, Mobil/Circle K, Jack-in-the-Box, McDonald's, Starbucks, Subway, DoubleTree Inn
33b	Wilmington Ave, E Shell/dsl, Carson Burgers, Starbucks, W Chevron/Jack-in-the-Box/dsl, Shell/dsl, Del Taco, Spires Rest., Chevrolet/Hyundai, Honda, Nissan, Toyota/Scion
33a	Alameda St
32d	Santa Fe Ave(from nb), E SC Fuels, W 76, Chevron/24hr, Oasis/dsl, Fantastic Burgers, Tom's Burgers
32c b	I-710, Long Beach Fwy
32a	Pacific Ave(from sb)
30b	Long Beach Blvd, E Arco/dsl, Subway, 7-11, W United, H
30a	Atlantic Blvd, E 76, Arby's, Carl's Jr, Denny's/24hr, El Torito, Jack-in-the-Box, Polly's Cafe, CVS Drug, Staples, Target, vet, Walgreens, W Applebee's, Chipotle, In-N-Out, Starbucks, $Tree, Home Depot, H, PetCo, Ross
29c	Orange Ave(from sb)
29b a	Cherry Ave, to Signal Hill, E Mobil/Circle K/dsl, Fantastic Burgers, Pita Pitaki, Chevrolet, Ford, Hyundai, Lincoln, Mazda, Subaru, W 76/dsl, Black Bear Diner, Curley's Cafe, Del Taco, Golden Eagle, McDonald's, Starbucks, 99c, America's Tire, AT&T, Best Buy, BMW, Buick/GMC, Cadillac, Chrysler/Dodge/Jeep, Costco/gas, Food4Less, Home Depot, Honda, Mercedes, Office Depot, Tesla
27	CA 19, Lakewood Blvd, E Marriott, AAA, W Chevron, Shell, Jack-in-the-Box, Starbucks, Subway, Extended Stay America, Holiday Inn, Residence Inn, Staybridge Suites, American Tire, H

Exit #	Services
26b	Bellflower Blvd, E 76, Burger King, Carl's Jr, Denny's, Jamba Juice, KFC, Papa John's, Starbucks, Subway, Togo's, Ford, Lowe's, USPO, Verizon, W 76, Chevron, Mobil/dsl, Einstein Bagels, Hof's Hut, IHOP, McDonald's, Panera Bread, Pick-Up Stix, Pieology, Starbucks, Subway, Wendy's, AT&T, BigLots, CVS Drug, Goodyear/auto, H, See's Candies, Target, TJ Maxx, Trader Joe's, USPO
26a	Woodruff Ave(from nb)
25	Palo Verde Ave, W 76/Circle K, Del Taco, Domino's, Frozen Oasis, Simone's Donuts, Starbucks, Taco Bell
24b	Studebaker Rd (from sb)
24a	I-605 N
23	CA 22 W, 7th St, to Long Beach
22	Seal Beach Blvd, Los Alamitos Blvd, E 76/dsl, Chevron/repair/24hr, EVC, Exxon/dsl, Baja Fresh, Blaze Pizza, Bowlology, CA Pizza Kitchen, Chick-fil-A, Chipotle, Dave's Hot Chicken, Hof's Hut Rest., Hot Off the Grill, In-N-Out, Islands Burgers, Kobe Japanese, Panera Bread, Pick-Up Stix, Rubio's, Spaghettini Grill, Starbucks, Subway, The Habit, Ayres Hotel, CVS Drug, Kohl's, Marshall's, PetSmart, Ralph's Foods, Sprouts Mkt, Staples, Target, Verizon, W 76/dsl, Chevron, Carl's Jr, Del Taco, Domino's, Subway, Sunny Side Cafe, Hampton Inn
21	CA 22 E, Garden Grove Fwy, Valley View St, E Dillon RV Ctr
19	Westminster Ave, to Springdale St, E picnic table, restroom, playground, park, 76/dsl, Arco, Chevron, Shell, Baskin-Robbins, Carl's Jr, Del Taco, El Pollo Loco, Flame Boiler, In-N-Out, Jack-in-the-Box, Jamba Juice, KFC, L&L Hawaiian BBQ, McDonald's, Pizza Hut, Popeyes, Tommy's Burgers, Wienerschnitzel, Executive Inn, Motel 6, Quality Inn, $Tree, 7-11, Albertson's, ALDI, auto repair, AutoZone, Home Depot, O'Reilly Parts, Petco, Ross, tires, W Chevron/dsl/24hr, Freshco Mexican, Ham'nScram, Starbucks, Subway, Best Western, Courtyard Inn, Jiffy Lube
18	Bolsa Ave, Golden West St, E Harley-Davidson, W Mobil/dsl, Del Taco, Dunkin, El Torito, Ike's Love & Sammies, Jack-in-the-Box, Outback Steaks, Rodrigo's Mexican, Starbucks, Wendy's, $Tree, 7-11, CVS Drug, Grocery Outlet, JC Penney, Jons Foods, Macy's, Target, Wingstop
16	CA 39, Beach Blvd, to Huntington Bch, E Chevron, Jack-in-the-Box, Subway, Hotel 39, Princess Inn, H, Infiniti, PepBoys, tires, Toyota, U-Haul, W Mobil, Arby's, BJ's Rest., Brazilian Steakhouse, Buca Italian, Buffalo Wild Wings, Burger King, CA Pizza Kitchen, Carl's Jr, Cheesecake Factory, Cheesecake Factory, Chick-fil-A, Chipotle Mexican, Einstein Bagels, Hawaiian BBQ, In-N-Out, Islands Burgers, Jack-in-the-Box, Jamba Juice, King's Fish House, McDonald's, Olive Garden, Pieology, Rubio's, Starbucks, Starbucks, Subway, Wahoo's Fish Taco, Comfort Suites, SpringHill Suites, The Hotel, 99c, AAA, AT&T, AT&T, Barnes&Noble, Chrysler/Dodge/Jeep, Costco/gas, CVS Drug, Dick's, Grocery Outlet, 

INTERSTATE 405 (Los Angeles) Cont'd

FOUNTAIN VALLEY

16 Continued
Kohl's, Lowe's, Marshalls, Mazda, Michaels, Old Navy, REI, REI, See's Candies, Target, Verizon, vet, Whole Foods Mkt, World Mkt

15b a Magnolia St, Warner Ave, **E** [food] Del Taco, Little Caesars, Sizzler, [other] Sunrise Supermkt, Valvoline, **W** [gas] Chevron, Mobil/Circle K, [food] Magnolia Café, Starbucks, Tommy's Burgers, Winchell's, [lodging] Motel 6, Motel 6, [other] 7-11, ALDI, CVS Drug, Jiffy Lube, URGENT CARE

14 Brookhurst St, Fountain Valley, **E** [gas] Arco/24hr, Chevron, Shell, [food] Carl's Jr, Del Taco, Hot Off The Grill, KFC, Sabrosada Mexican, Taco Bell, The Habit, [lodging] Ayres Inn, Sonesta, [other] O'Reilly Parts, Sam's Club/gas, Thompson's RV Ctr, **W** [gas] Arco, Berri Bros/dsl, Shell/Circle K/dsl, Speedway/7-11/dsl, [food] Black Angus, CA Fish Grill, Coldstone, Islands Burgers, Jamba Juice, Jersey Mike's, Mimi's Cafe, Rubio's, Starbucks, Subway, Taste of Beauty, Wendy's, [other] Albertson's, [H], Ralph's Foods, TJ Maxx, Verizon, vet

12 Euclid Ave, **E** [gas] Tesla EVC, [food] Cancun Mexican, Hawaiian BBQ, Jimmy John's, McDonald's, Panda Express, Starbucks, Subway, Taco Bell, [other] $Tree, AT&T, Costco/gas, [H], PetSmart, Ross, Tire Mart

11b Harbor Blvd, to Costa Mesa, **E** [lodging] La Quinta, [other] AAA, IKEA/EVC, **W** [gas] Arco, Chevron, Mobil/Circle K/dsl, [food] Cane's, Chick-fil-A, Dave's Hot Chicken, Denny's, El Pollo Loco, Flame Broiler, IHOP, In-N-Out, McDonald's, Sonic, Starbucks, Subway, Taco Bell, [lodging] Motel 6, Vagabond Inn, [other] AutoZone, CarMax, Sprouts Mkt, Target

11a Fairview Rd, **E** [food] Starbucks, Subway, Zach's Chicken, [other] Best Buy, Marshall's, Old Navy, Verizon, **W** [gas] 76, Chevron, Shell, [food] Del Taco, Jack-in-the-Box, Round Table Pizza, Starbucks, [other] CVS Drug, O'Reilly Parts, Stater Bros

10 CA 73, to CA 55 S(from sb), Corona del Mar, Newport Beach

9b Bristol St, **E** [gas] Chevron/dsl, [food] Antonello's Italian, Baskin-Robbins, Black Bear Diner, Buffalo Wild Wings, Chick-fil-A, Chipotle Mexican, ClaimJumper, Corner Bakery, Corner Bakery, Hawaiian BBQ, In-N-Out, Jack-in-the-Box, Jersey Mike's, Maggiano's Rest., McDonald's, Morton's Steaks, Panera Bread, Pizza Hut, Red Robin, Starbucks, Subway, Wienerschnitzel, [lodging] Avenue Hotel, Marriott Suites, Westin Hotel, [other] $Tree, 7-11, AT&T, Bloomingdale's, CVS Drug, Firestone/auto, Hobby Lobby, Macy's, Michaels, PetCo, Ross, Staples, TJ Maxx, Trader Joe's, Vons Foods, World Mkt, **W** [gas] Chevron/dsl, [food] Del Taco, El Pollo Loco, McDonald's, Subway, TK Burgers, Wahoo's Fish Taco, [lodging] Crowne Plaza, Hilton, [other] 7-11, 7-11, PepBoys, vet

9a CA 55, Costa Mesa Fwy, to Newport Bch, Riverside

IRVINE

8 MacArthur Blvd, **E** [gas] Chevron, Mobil/Subway, [food] Carl's Jr, Jersey Mike's, McDonald's, Starbucks, [lodging] Embassy Suites, Homewood Suites, Sonesta, **W** [gas] Chevron, [food] Duck Donuts, El Torito, Gulliver's Ribs, IHOP, Subway, [lodging] Atrium Hotel, Hampton Inn, Hilton, Irvine Marriot, to [airport]

7 Jamboree Rd, Irvine, **E** [gas] Shell, [food] Andrei's Rest., Corner Bakery, Del Taco, Einstein Bros., Jamba Juice, Pick Up Stix, Rubio's, Starbucks, The Kebab Shop, [lodging] Courtyard, Hilton Garden, Hyatt, Hyatt(2), Residence Inn, [other] American Tire, Jiffy Lube, Ralphs Food, **W** [food] Houston's, North Italia, Panini Cafe, Ruth's Chris Steaks, Starbucks, Subway, Wahoo's Fish Taco, [lodging] Marriott, [other] Verizon

5 Culver Dr, **W** [gas] Chevron/dsl, [food] Carl's Jr, Starbucks, Subway, [other] Wholesome Choice Mkt

4 Jeffrey Rd, University Dr, **E** [gas] Chevron, Mobil, [food] CA Pizza Kitchen, El Pollo Loco, I Can Korean BBQ, McDonald's, Mooyah Burgers, Olive's Branch, Starbucks, [other] CVS Drug, Gelson's Mkt, [H], Ralph's Foods, Verizon, Walgreens,

LAKE FOREST

4 Continued
Speedway/dsl, [food] Starbucks, [other] vet, ZionMart

3 Sand Canyon Ave, **E** [other] [H], URGENT CARE, **W** [gas] Arco/dsl, [food] Dosirak Korean, Johnny's NY Pizza, Oliver's Italian, Starbucks, Thai Bamboo, [other] Albertson's, CVS Drug, vet

2 CA 133, to Laguna Beach, **E** [lodging] Courtyard, DoubleTree Inn

1c Irvine Center Dr, **E** [food] Cheesecake Factory, Chipotle Mexican, Panda Express, PF Chang's, Pieology, Shake Shack, Wahoo's Fish Tacos, [other] AT&T, Barnes&Noble, Macy's, Nordstrom, Old Navy, Target, Verizon, **W** [gas] 7-11, EVC, [food] Angelina's Pizza, Burger King, Puesto Mexican, Starbucks, [other] Big O Tire, Discount Tire, Harley Davidson, Jiffy Lube, URGENT CARE, Whole Foods Mkt

1b Bake Pkwy, **W** [other] Carmax, Toyota

1a Lake Forest

0mm I-405 begins/ends on I-5, exit 132.

INTERSTATE 505 (Winters)

33 I-5. I-505 begins/ends on I-5.

31 CR 12A

28 CR 14, Zamora

24 CR 19

21 CA 16, to Esparto, Woodland, **W** [gas] Guy's Food/fuel, [other] USPO

17 CR 27

15 CR 29A

11 CA 128 W, Russell Blvd, **W** [gas] Arco/Burger King/dsl, Chevron/24hr, [food] Krispy Krunchy, RoundTable Pizza, Starbucks, Subway, Togo, [lodging] Fairfield Inn, [other] $General, Lorenzo's Mkt

10 Putah Creek Rd, no crossover...same as 11

6 Allendale Rd

3 Midway Rd, **E** [other] RV camping, **W** [gas] Oates'

1c Vaca Valley Pkwy, **E** [other] [H], **W** [gas] Vaca Valley TC/Chevron/dsl, [food] Burger King, [lodging] Hyatt House, [other] U-Haul

1b I-80 E. I-505 begins/ends on I-80.

INTERSTATE 580 (Bay Area)

79 I-580 begins/ends, accesses I-5 sb.

76b a CA 132, Chrisman Rd, to Modesto, **N** [gas] 76/dsl, [other] RV camping

72 Corral Hollow Rd

67 Patterson Pass Rd, **N** [gas] Valero/dsl, [food] Subway, Wienerschnitzel, **S** [gas] Mobil

65 I-205(from eb), to Tracy

63 Grant Line Rd, to Byron

59 N Flynn Rd, Altamont Pass, elevation 1009, **S** brake check area, many wind turbines

57 N Greenville Rd, Laughlin Rd, Altamont Pass Rd, to Livermore Lab, **N** [other] CHP, **S** [gas] 76/7-11/dsl, Chevron, [food] Starbucks, [lodging] Best Western, La Quinta, [other] Harley-Davidson

56mm weigh sta both lanes

55 Vasco Rd, to Brentwood, **N** [gas] 7-11, Arco, Chevron/dsl, EVC, Gas&Shop/dsl, QuikStop/dsl, [food] A&W/KFC, China Pavillion, Country Waffles, Jimmy John's, McDonald's, Pizza Guys, Starbucks, Wienerschnitzel, [other] 88 Seafood Mkt, Toyota/Scion, **S** [gas] 7-11, 76/dsl, [food] Jack-in-the-Box, Ming's Garden, Starbucks, Taco Bell, Wendy's, [lodging] Quality Inn, [other] auto repair, Penske

54 CA 84, 1st St, Springtown Blvd, Livermore, **N** [gas] Springtown/dsl, [food] Can Am Pizza, Hidalgo's Mexican, Rancho Mexican, Wasabi Japanese, [lodging] DoubleTree, Motel 6, Rodeway Inn, [other] 7-11, **S** [gas] 76, Chevron, Exxon, Shell, [food] Baskin-Robbins, Chili's, Chipotle, Cinco TacoBar, IHOP, Jamba Juice, Kobe Japanese, McDonald's, Melo's Pizza, Panda Express, Panera Bread, Starbucks, Subway, Togo's, Wingstop, [other] $Tree, America's Tire, Big Lots, CVS Drug, Lowe's Whse, Petco, Ross, Safeway/gas, Target, TJ Maxx, vet

CA

INTERSTATE 580 (Bay Area) Cont'd

LIVERMORE

Exit #	Services
52	N Livermore Ave, S 7-11, Chevron, Baja Fresh, Chick-fil-A, Coldstone, Denica's Kitchen, In-N-Out, Jack-in-the-Box, Popeyes, Ta'Con Mexican, Hawthorn Suites, AT&T, Audi, Home Depot, Honda, Kohl's, Land Rover, OfficeMax, Porsche, Schwab Tire, Subaru, tires, Verizon, Walmart
51	Portola Ave, no EZ eb return, Livermore, S Ford/Lincoln
50	Airway Blvd, Collier Canyon Rd, Livermore, N Chevron/dsl, Wendy's, Courtyard, Hampton Inn, Hilton Garden, Holiday Inn Express, Home2 Suites, SureStay, Costco/gas, S Carl's Jr, Cattlemen's Rest., Corner Slice Pizza, Starbucks, Subway, Extended Stay America, 7-11, golf
48	El Charro Rd, O'Fallon Rd, N Chevron/dsl, EVC, 88 BaoBao Chinese, BBQ 85 Chinese, BJ's Rest., Coldstone, Crumbl, El Pollo Loco, Grand Cafe, Hawaiian Grill, Hawaiian Poke, Jersey Mike's, Panera Bread, Ramen 101, Seoul Jung KBBQ, Shabu King, Sourdough & Co, Starbucks, Taco Bell, Dick's, PetSmart, Target/Starbucks/Pizza Hut, vet, S Cali Kid Burgers, Denny's, Homewood Suites, Residence Inn, 99 Ranch Mkt, Chrysler/Dodge/Jeep, Ross, See's Candies, SF Outlets/famous brands

PLEASANTON

Exit #	Services
47	Santa Rita Rd, Tassajara Rd, N Armadillo Willy's BBQ, Buffalo Wild Wings, Coco Cabana, Dave's Hot Chicken, Mayflower Chinese, Peet's Coffee, Pikaso Pizza, Aloft, Buick/GMC, H, Kia, Lowe's, Nissan, Safeway, URGENT CARE, S EVC, Shell, Blaze Pizza, Kimona Japanese, Local Poke, McDonald's, Panda Express, Pizza Guys, Starbucks, Subway, Super Grill, Taco Bell, Wingstop, $Tree, Acura, AutoZone, BMW/Mini, Chevrolet/Cadillac, CVS Drug, EVC, Lexus, Ranch Mkt, tire/auto repair, Trader Joe's, vet
46	Hacienda Dr, Pleasanton, N EVC, Shell, Applebee's, Berevino Italian, Cherie's Southern Kitchen, Chipotle, Five Guys, Habit Burger, Ike's Love, Jamba Juice, Lazy Dog Rest., Market Tavern, Pacific Catch, Papa John's, Patxi's Pizza, Starbucks, Urban Plates, Extended Stay, Hyatt Place, Barnes&Noble, Best Buy, Old Navy, TJ Maxx, Toyota/Scion, Verizon, vet, Whole Foods Mkt, S EVC, Denica's Kitchen, L&L Hawaiian BBQ, H, Kohl's, Walmart
45	Hopyard Rd, Pleasanton, N 76, Chevron/dsl, Shell/dsl, Denica's Kitchen, IHOP, Subway, La Quinta, America's Tire, El Monte RV's, Honda, Hyundai, Mazda, O'Reilly Parts, Tire Choice, U-Haul, Volvo, VW, S Chevron/dsl, Shell/dsl, Black Bear Diner, Burger King, Chick-fil-A, Chili's, Denny's, Gobi Mongolian, Gotta Eatta Pita, In-N-Out, Nations Burgers, Starbucks, Taco Bell, Best Western, Courtyard, Doubltree, Extended Stay, Hyatt House, Larkspur Landing, Motel 6, Sheraton, Home Depot, Mercedes, USPO
44b	I-680, N to San Ramon, S to San Jose
44a	Foothills Rd, San Ramon Rd, N A & A, Chevron/dsl, Exxon/Circle K/dsl, Shell/dsl, Amakara Japanese, Baskin Robbins, Burger King, Casa Orozco, Chipotle Mexican, ChuckeCheese, Country Waffles, Domino's, Erik's Deli, Frankie Johnnie & Luigi's Too, Golden Sand Chinese, Habit Burger, Hana Japan, Korean BBQ, Outback Steaks, Panda Express, Panera Bread, Pieology, Pizza My Heart, Popeyes, Rigatoni's Italian, RoundTable Pizza, Starbucks, Taquiera Azteca, Togo's, Holiday Inn, $Tree, CVS Drug, Hobby Lobby, Marshall's, Michael's, O'Reilly Parts, PetCo, PetSmart, Ranch Mkt Foods, REI, Ross, Safeway/gas, Sprouts, Target, vet, S CA Pizza Kitchen, Cheesecake Factory, PF Chang's, Subway, AC Hotel, Marriott, Residence Inn, JC Penney, Macy's
39	Eden Canyon Rd, Palomares Rd
37	Center St, Crow Canyon Rd, N Panda Express, Subway,

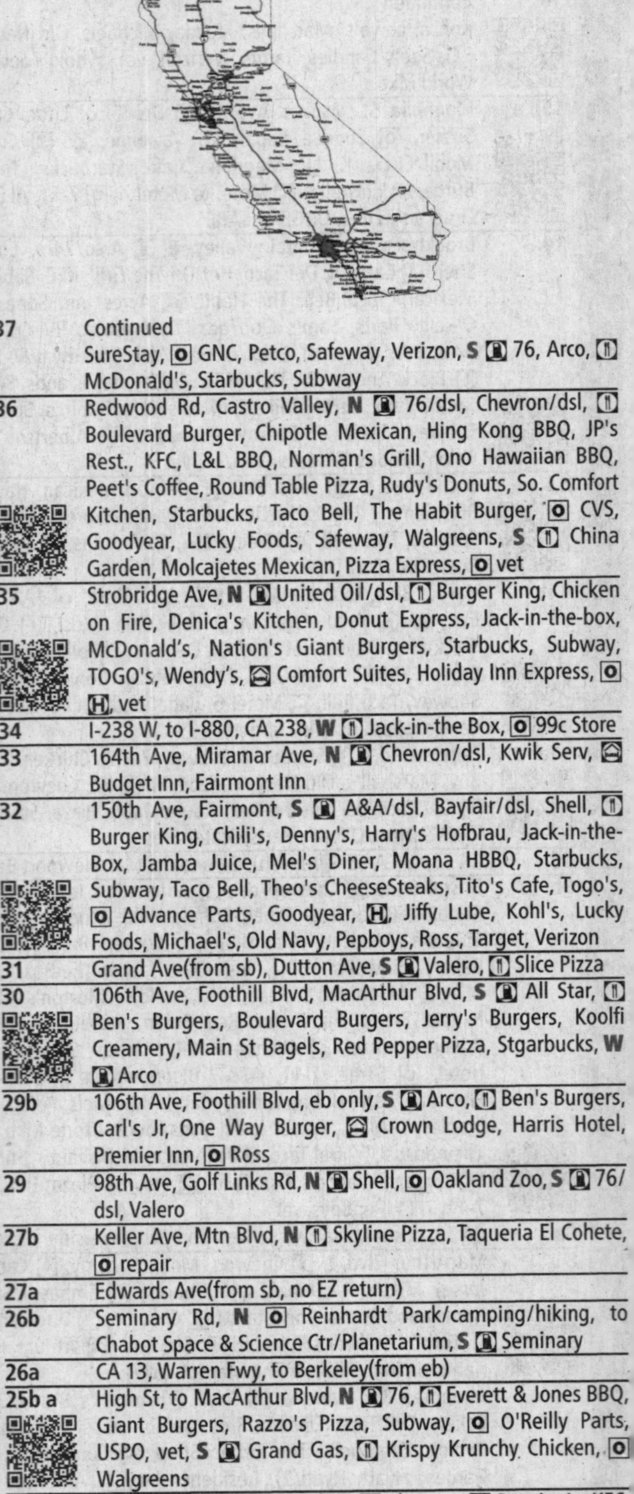

CASTRO VALLEY

Exit #	Services
37	Continued SureStay, GNC, Petco, Safeway, Verizon, S 76, Arco, McDonald's, Starbucks, Subway
36	Redwood Rd, Castro Valley, N 76/dsl, Chevron/dsl, Boulevard Burger, Chipotle Mexican, Hing Kong BBQ, JP's Rest., KFC, L&L BBQ, Norman's Grill, Ono Hawaiian BBQ, Peet's Coffee, Round Table Pizza, Rudy's Donuts, So. Comfort Kitchen, Starbucks, Taco Bell, The Habit Burger, CVS, Goodyear, Lucky Foods, Safeway, Walgreens, S China Garden, Molcajetes Mexican, Pizza Express, vet
35	Strobridge Ave, N United Oil/dsl, Burger King, Chicken on Fire, Denica's Kitchen, Donut Express, Jack-in-the-box, McDonald's, Nation's Giant Burgers, Starbucks, Subway, TOGO's, Wendy's, Comfort Suites, Holiday Inn Express, H, vet
34	I-238 W, to I-880, CA 238, W Jack-in-the Box, 99c Store
33	164th Ave, Miramar Ave, N Chevron/dsl, Kwik Serv, Budget Inn, Fairmont Inn
32	150th Ave, Fairmont, S A&A/dsl, Bayfair/dsl, Shell, Burger King, Chili's, Denny's, Harry's Hofbrau, Jack-in-the-Box, Jamba Juice, Mel's Diner, Moana HBBQ, Starbucks, Subway, Taco Bell, Theo's CheeseSteaks, Tito's Cafe, Togo's, Advance Parts, Goodyear, H, Jiffy Lube, Kohl's, Lucky Foods, Michael's, Old Navy, Pepboys, Ross, Target, Verizon
31	Grand Ave(from sb), Dutton Ave, S Valero, Slice Pizza
30	106th Ave, Foothill Blvd, MacArthur Blvd, S All Star, Ben's Burgers, Boulevard Burgers, Jerry's Burgers, Koolfi Creamery, Main St Bagels, Red Pepper Pizza, Stgarbucks, W Arco
29b	106th Ave, Foothill Blvd, eb only, S Arco, Ben's Burgers, Carl's Jr, One Way Burger, Crown Lodge, Harris Hotel, Premier Inn, Ross
29	98th Ave, Golf Links Rd, N Shell, Oakland Zoo, S 76/dsl, Valero
27b	Keller Ave, Mtn Blvd, N Skyline Pizza, Taqueria El Cohete, repair
27a	Edwards Ave(from sb, no EZ return)

FRUITVALE

Exit #	Services
26b	Seminary Rd, N Reinhardt Park/camping/hiking, to Chabot Space & Science Ctr/Planetarium, S Seminary
26a	CA 13, Warren Fwy, to Berkeley(from eb)
25b a	High St, to MacArthur Blvd, N 76, Everett & Jones BBQ, Giant Burgers, Razzo's Pizza, Subway, O'Reilly Parts, USPO, vet, S Grand Gas, Krispy Krunchy Chicken, Walgreens
24	35th Ave(no EZ sb return), N Chevron, Domino's, KFC, Taco Bell, S Energy, QuikStop
23	Coolidge Ave, Fruitvale, N Shell/dsl, 1/4 LB Burgers, Bombera Mexican, Diamond Slice Pizza, Flavor Brigade Ice Cream, Little Caesar's, Peet's Coffee, CVS, Farmer Joe's, Safeway/Starbucks, USPO, S Mobil
22	Park Blvd, S Arco, H
21b	Grand Ave, Lake Shore, N 76/24hr, Chevron/dsl, Cheese Steak Shop, Chipotle, Flipside Burgers,

LAKE SHORE · BERKELEY · SAN RAFAEL

INTERSTATE 580 (Bay Area) Cont'd

21b Continued
Gabriella's Pizza, Main Squeeze Juice, Modigliani Sandwiches, Peet's Coffee, Rico Rico Taco, Shakewell Rest., Starbucks, Top Dog Hotdogs, Wingstop, AT&T, T-Mobile, Trader Joe's, USPO, Walgreens, **S** Chevron, Ahn's 1/4 LB Burgers, Grand Ave Thai, Grand Lake Kitchen, Mama Italian, Round Table Pizza, city park

21a Harrison St, Oakland Ave, **N** 76, Quick Food&Gas, QuikStop, Mama's Royal Cafe, Piedmont Place, H, **S** Honda

19d c CA 24 E, I-980 W, to Oakland, **S** Chevron, Speedway

19b West St, San Pablo Ave, **N** Chick-fil-A, Rob Ben's Rest., Extended Stay America, Best Buy, Home Depot, Michael's, Office Depot, Safeway, Target/CVS

19a I-80 W

18c Market St, to San Pablo Ave, downtown

18b Powell St, Emeryville, **E** 76, Chevron, Black Bear Diner, Burger King, Denny's, Ike's Love, Starbucks, Togo's, Hyatt, Hyatt House, Sheraton, Sonesta, Marshalls, Old Navy, Trader Joe's, Verizon, **W** Shell, Hilton Garden

18a CA 13, Ashby Ave, Bay St, same as 18b

17 University Ave, Berkeley, **E** Chevron, Holiday Inn Express, Mobil, Valera/Circle K/Burger King, La Quinta, Marina Inn, Jiffy Lube, to UC Berkeley, vet, **W** Seabreeze

16 Gilman St, **E** Target, **W** Golden Gate Fields Race Track

13 Albany St, Buchanan St(from eb), **E** Starbucks, Toyota

12 Central Ave(from eb), El Cerrito, **N** Shell/dsl, Valero, **S** Costco/gas

11 Bayview Ave, Carlson Blvd

10b Regatta Blvd, **N** Golden Gate/dsl

10a S 23rd St, Marina Bay Pkwy, **N** Subway, **S** Artisan Kitchen, Starbucks

9 Harbour Way, Cutting Blvd, **N** 7-11, Central Gas, Richmond Gas, **S** Burger King

8 Canal Blvd, Garrard Blvd, **S** Chevron/dsl, SureStay

7b Castro St, to I-80 E, Point Richmond

7a Western Drive(from wb), Point Molate

5mm Richmond-San Rafael Toll Bridge

2a Francis Drake Blvd, to US 101 S, **N** Extended Stay America, BMW, Home Depot, Honda, Target

1b Francisco Blvd, San Rafael, **N** 76, Circle K, Valero, Burger King, El Quetzal Deli, La Croissant, Viking Subs, Motel 6, Travelodge, Big O Tire, H, Mazda, U-Haul, vet, **S** El Pollo Loco, Michael's Sourdough Sandwiches, Smoky's Deli, Subway, $Tree, AutoZone, Office Depot, USPO, **E** tires

1a US 101 N to San Rafael, I-580 begins/ends on US 101.

INTERSTATE 605 (Los Angeles)

27c Huntington Dr. I-605 begins/ends., Mobil/dsl, Subway, CVS Drug

27 I-210

26 Arrow Hwy, Live Oak, **E** Santa Fe Dam, **W** Irwindale Speedway

24 Lower Azusa Rd, LA St

23 Ramona Blvd, **E** Mobil, Del Taco/24hr, **W** Taco Burger Place, 7-11, auto repair, tires

22 I-10, E to San Bernardino, W to LA

21 Valley Blvd, to Industry, **E** 76, Chevron/Subway/dsl, El Jalisco Cafe, Krispy Krunchy Chicken, Taco Nazo, Tacos Gavilan, Winchell's Donuts, Valley Inn, auto repair, tires

19 CA 60, Pamona Fwy

18 Peck Rd, **E** Shell, **W** Truck Ctr

17 RoseHills Rd

16 Beverly Blvd

15 Whittier Blvd, **E** Egas, Carl's Jr, Carlos Tacos, Que Buena Taqueria, Taco Bell, YumYum Donuts, 7-11, **W** Arco, Chevron, Burger King, Cane's, Chick-fil-A, Chipotle, Clearman's Steaks, Coldstone, Denny's, El Pollo Loco, El Super Taco, In-N-Out, Jamba Juice, Little Caesars, McDonald's, Panda Express, Pizza Hut, Shakey's Pizza, Starbucks, Subway, Tommy's Burgers, Wa Wok, Yoshinoya, Howard Johnson, $Tree, 99c, AutoZone, O'Reilly Parts, Target

14 Washington Blvd, to Pico Rivera, **E** 76, Shell, Burger King, El Pollo Loco, IHOP, Jack-in-the-Box, Little Caesars, McDonald's, Rubi's Grill, Starbucks, Steak Rest., Subway, $Super Store, $Tree, CVS Drug, Firestone/auto, Food4Less, O'Reilly Parts, Pep Boys, Verizon

13 Slauson Ave, **E** Arco, Mobil, Denny's, H

12 Telegraph Rd, to Santa Fe Springs, **E** 76, Chevron, Casa Gazcon Mexican, Del Taco, Homestyle Donuts, Jersey Mike's, KFC, Starbucks, Subway, Yoshinoya, 99c, AutoZone, KFC, **W** Arco/dsl

12mm I-5

11 Florence Ave, to Downey, **E** Arco, Giant RV, Honda

10 Firestone Blvd, **E** Baskin-Robbins, ChuckeCheese, RC Burgers, Starbucks, Waba Grill, Best Western, 7-11, American's Tire, Audi/BMW/Porsche, AutoZone, BMW, Costco/gas, Verizon, Walgreens, **W** Chevron/repair, Chick-fil-A, Chrysler/Dodge/Jeep, Target

8 I-105, Imperial Hwy, **E** Chevron, Domino's, Golden Donuts, McDonald's, Taco Bell, **W** Arco, ABC Donuts, tires

9 Rosecrans Ave, to Norwalk, **E** Chevron, Mobil, Iguanas Mexican, Little Caesar's, McDonald's, Pizza Hut, Starbucks, Subway, Tacos Gavilan, $Tree, H, True Value, **W** Mobil, Carl's Jr, Denny's, Dunkin, Jack-in-the-Box, Johnny's Pilipino, Mr. Rosewood, Papa Johns, Popeyes, $Tree, AutoZone

7 Alondra Blvd, **E** 7-11, Chevron, Adalberto's Mexican, Frantone's Rest., In-N-Out, KFC, Starbucks, Toros Mexican, CVS Drug, Home Depot, Staples, **W** Shell, Del Taco

6 CA 91

5 South St, **E** 76, BJ's Rest., Blaze Pizza, Buffalo Wild Wings, Cane's, Cheesecake Factory, Chick-fil-A, Chipotle, ChuckeCheese, Dave's Hot Chicken, DQ, Five Guys, Four Seasons Buffet, Gen Korean BBQ, Jamba Juice, L&L Hawaiian BBQ, Lazy Dog Cafe, Lucille's BBQ, Moo BBQ, Olive Garden, Panda Express, Panera Bread, Panera Bread, Pizza Hut, Pizza Twist, Popeyes, Starbucks, Starbucks, The Habit, The Halal Guys, Wingstop, 99c, ALDI, Amazon Fresh, American Tire, AT&T, Dick's, Macy's, Nordstrom, O'Reilly Parts, Pep Boys, Sprouts Mkt, Target, TJ Maxx, Verizon, **W** Chevron, Shell/service, Acura, Buick/GMC, Chevrolet, Chrysler/Dodge/Jeep, Ford, Honda, Hyundai, Hyundai, Kia, Land Rover, Lexus, Mazda, Mitsubishi, Nissan, Toyota/Scion, VW

4 Del Amo Blvd, to Cerritos, **E** Caesar's Mongolian BBQ, Caribbean Mexican, Del Taco, Flame Broiler, Goody's Pizza, Loft Hawaiian, Omega Burgers, Starbucks, The Donut Palace, $Tree, **W** Mobil, 7-11

3 Carson St, **E** 76, Chevron, Jack-in-the-Box, Julian's Mexican, Little Caesar's, McDonald's, Popeyes, Starbucks, Subway, Wingstop, Lakewood Inn, LaQuinta, 7-11, antiques, AT&T, casino, CVS Drug, Food4Less, O'Reilly Parts, tires, vet, **W** Chevron/dsl, Carl's Jr, Chick-fil-A, Dave's & Bruster's, Del Taco, Denny's, El Pollo Loco, In-N-Out, Jack-in-the-Box, Lucille's BBQ, Roadhouse Grill, TGIFriday's, Barnes&Noble, IKEA, Lowe's, Michael's, Old Navy, PetSmart, Ross, Sam's Club/gas, Verizon, **Walmart/auto**

1 Katella Ave, Willow St, **E** Arco, Shell, Flame Boiler, Jack-in-the-Box, Jimmy John's, Madera's Steaks, McDonald's,

= gas = food = lodging = other = rest stop

INTERSTATE 605 (Los Angeles) Cont'd

1 Continued
Paul's Place, Polly's Cafe, Starbucks, Wendy's, antiques, CVS Drug, H, Jiffy Lube, Vons Food, **W** Eldorado Regional Park

0mm I-605 begins/ends on I-405., **E** st patrol

INTERSTATE 680 (Bay Area)

CONCORD

71b a I-80 E, to Sacramento, W to Oakland, I-680 begins/ends on I-80.

70 Green Valley Rd(from eb), Cordelia, **N** Arco, Starbucks, Costco/gas, CVS, Safeway, TJ Maxx, **W** Kia

68 Gold Hill Rd, **W** Chevron/dsl

65 Marshview Rd

63 Parish Rd

61 Lake Herman Rd, **E** Chevron/Jack-in-the-Box/dsl, **W** 76/Carl's Jr, Gas City/dsl, vista point

60 Bayshore Rd

58 I-780, to Benicia, toll plaza

56 Marina Vista, to Martinez

55mm Martinez-Benicia Toll Br

54 Pacheco Blvd, Arthur Rd, Concord, **W** Chevron/dsl, Shell/dsl

53 CA 4 E to Pittsburg, W to Richmond, Pittsburg

52 CA 4 E, Concord, Pacheco, **E** Buffalo Wild Wings, Dave & Buster's, Golden Corral, Habit Burger, Kebab Shop, MOD Pizza, Noodles&Co, Panda Express, Peet's Coffee, Starbucks, Taco Bell, Wingstop, Clarion, Concord Plaza, Barnes&Noble, Chrysler/Dodge/Jeep, Ford/Lincoln, Home Depot, Jiffy Lube, Kia, Mazda, Old Navy, Petco, Sam's Club, Seafood City Mkt, TJ Maxx, Toyota, Trader Joe's, USPO, vet, Whole Foods Mkt, **W** Chevron, Shell/24hr, Valero/dsl, A&W/KFC, Burger King, Chipotle, Denny's, In-N-Out, McDonald's, Mtn Mike's Pizza, Round Table Pizza, Taco Bell, Wendy's, 7-11, AutoZone, Batteries+, CarMax, Firestone/auto, Harley-Davidson, Nordstrom's, O'Reilly Parts, Pepboys, Ross, Safeway/dsl, Schwab Tire, Target, Verizon

51 Willow Pass Rd, Taylor Blvd, **E** Benihana Rest., Cajun Crackn, Chick-fil-A, Denny's, Fuddruckers, Gen Korean BBQ, Ike's Love Sandwiches, Jamba Juice, Krispy Kreme, Lazy Dog Rest., Longport Fish Co., MOD Pizza, Panera Bread, TX De Brazil, Yard House Rest., Hilton, Hobby Lobby, Old Navy, REI, Willows Shopping Ctr, World Mkt, **W** Dominos, McDonald's, Red Robin, Starbucks, Homewood Suites, Residence Inn, JC Penney, Macy's, See's Candies, URGENT CARE

50 CA 242(from nb), to Concord

49b Monument Blvd, Gregory Lane(from sb), **E** 76/dsl, Cheesesteak Shop, Hawaiian BBQ, Panda Express, Pieology, See's Candies, Starbucks, Wingstop, $Tree, AT&T, Dick's, Kohl's, Marshalls, **W** Chevron/dsl, Chipotle, ColdStone, Donut King, Five Guys, Jack's Rest., Jack-in-the-Box, Jamba Juice, L&L Hawaiian BBQ, McDonald's, Melo's Pizza, Mtn Mike's Pizza, My Thai Cuisine, Nations Burgers, Peet's Coffee, Sourdough & Co, Taco Bell, Togo, Zachary's Chicago Pizza, Hyatt, Sonesta, Big O Tire, EVC, Grocery Outlet, Michael's, Ross, Safeway Foods, Staples, USPO, Verizon

49a Contra Costa Blvd (from nb)

48 Treat Blvd, Geary Rd, **E** Chevron, Back 40 BBQ, Black Bear Diner, Heavenly Cafe, Noah's NY Bagels, Oak Road Cafe, Panera Bread, Starbucks, Starbucks, Subway, Embassy Suites, Extended Stay America, Renaissance, Best Buy, CVS Drug, Safeway, URGENT CARE, vet, **W** Chevron, Shell, Burger King, Chick-fil-A, China Palace, Habit Burger, IHOP, Manakish Grill, Pastapizzaprimavera, Starbucks, Wendy's, West Coast Sourdough,

OAKLAND DANVILLE SAN RAMON

48 Continued
Yan's China Bistro, Volvo, Walgreens

47 N Main St, to Walnut Creek, **E** Chevron, Chevron, Burger King, Jack-in-the-Box, Round Table Pizza, Taco Bell, Marriott, Motel 6, Residence Inn, Cadillac, Chrysler/Dodge/Jeep, Ford, Honda, Jaguar, Land Rover, Mercedes, Target, Toyota, URGENT CARE, VW, **W** Domino's, Holiday Inn Express, NAPA, OfficeMax, Porsche, Subaru

46b Ygnacio Valley Rd

46a SR-24 W

45b Olympic Blvd, Oakland, **E** CA Pizza Kitchen, Cheesecake Factory, Chipotle, Dunkin, Ike's Love & Sandwiches, Jersey Mike's, Original Hick'ry Pit, Ruth's Chris, The Habit, AT&T, CVS Drug, Macy's, mall, Nordstrom, PetCo, Ross, Safeway, Trader Joe's, Verizon, Whole Food Mkt

45a S Main St, Walnut Creek, **E** H

44 Rudgear (from nb)

43 Livorna Rd

42b a Stone Valley Rd, Alamo, **W** Chevron/dsl, Shell/dsl, Alamo Cafe, Alamo Palace, Bagel St Cafe, Coffee Shop, Five Guys, Great Donuts, Lever Cafe, Maguey Mexican, Panera Bread, Peet's Coffee, Round Table Pizza, Starbucks, Subway, Taco Bell, Xenia's, 7-11, Alamo Hardware, CVS, Safeway, USPO, vet, vet

40b El Pintado Rd, Danville

40 El Cerro Blvd

39 Diablo Rd, Danville, **E** Chevron, China Gourmet, Christy's Donuts, Taco Bell, Mt Diablo SP(12mi), **W** Ike's Love & Sandwiches, Jersey Mike's, Mtn Mike's Pizza, Panda Express, Starbucks, Taco Bell, The Melt, Trader Joe's

38 Sycamore Valley Rd, **E** Shell/Circle K, Amici's Pizzeria, Black Bear Diner, Esin, Starbucks, Best Western, vet, **W** Chevron/dsl, Expressway/dsl, Mobil, Forbes Steaks, Luna Loca, Melo's Pizza, Piatti, Round Table, Togo's, CVS, Lucky Foods, Walgreens

36 Crow Canyon Rd, San Ramon, **E** Shell/dsl, Baskin-Robbins, Burger King, Carl's Jr, Cheese Steak Shop, Chili's, Fat Maddie's Grille, Habit Burger, Ike's Love & Sandwiches, Jamba Juice, Menchie's, Panda Express, Panera Bread, Pizza My Heart, Primavera Ristorante, Starbucks(2), Sunrise Bagel Cafe, Thai Taste, The Kebab Shop, Extended Stay America, Ace Hardware, Big O Tire, Costco/gas, H, Jiffy Lube, Marshall's, Marshalls, PetCo, See's Candies, Sprouts, URGENT CARE, USPO, **W** Chevron/dsl, Shell/autocare, Best Donuts, Chipotle Mexican, Dainty Donuts, Erik's Cafe, Hula Wok BBQ, In-N-Out, McDonald's, Mtn Mike's Pizza, Orient Express, RoundTable Pizza, Sakura Japanese, Starbucks, Subway, Taco Bell, Wendy's, Wingstop, Hyatt House Hotel, 7-11, auto repair, CVS Drug, Home Depot, Safeway, Staples, Verizon, vet, vet, Windmill Farmers Mkt

34 Bollinger Canyon Rd, **E** Valero, Bagel St Cafe, Chipotle, Coldstone, MOD Pizza, Starbucks, Marriott, Residence Inn, AT&T, CVS Drug, mall, Target, Trader Joe's,

INTERSTATE 680 (Bay Area) Cont'd

PLEASANTON

Exit	Services
34	Continued Whole Foods Mkt, W Chevron/dsl, Clementine's Grill, Inchin's Asian, Extended Stay America, Sonesta, The Souk Mkt
31	Alcosta Blvd, to Dublin, E 76/dsl, Starbucks, 7-11, CVS Drug, URGENT CARE, Walmart, W Chevron, Shell/dsl, DQ, McDonalds, Peking Delight, Starbucks, Subway, $Tree, Lucky Foods
30	I-580, W to Oakland, E to Tracy
29	Stoneridge, Dublin, E DoubleTree, SpringHill Suites, TownePlace, W Cheesecake Factory, PF Chang's, AC Hotel, JC Penney, Macy's, mall
26	Bernal Ave, Pleasanton, E Chevron/Jack-in-the-Box/dsl, Bagel St Cafe, Chipotle, Habit Burger, Jersey Mike's, Lindo's Mexican, Panda Express, Parktown Pizza Co, Round Table Pizza, Sourdough & Co., Starbucks, CVS, Safeway/dsl, Verizon
25	Sunol Blvd, Pleasanton
21b a	CA 84, Calvaras Rd, Sunol, W to Dumbarton Bridge
20	Andrade Rd, Sheridan Rd(from sb), E Sunol Super Stp/dsl
19mm	weigh sta nb
19	Sheridan Rd(from nb)
18	Vargas Rd
16	CA 238, Mission Blvd, to Hayward, E Shell, McDonald's, W H
15	Washington Blvd, Irvington Dist, E QuikStop, Cantaritos Mexican, Mission Pizza
14	Durham Rd, to Auto Mall Pkwy, W 76/Subway/24hr, iniBurger, Jack-in-the-Box, Starbucks, Straw Hat Pizza, $Tree, Home Depot, Walmart
12	CA 262, Mission Blvd, to I-880, Warm Springs Dist, 7-11, W 76, Valero, Burger King, Carl's Jr, Donut House, Jack-in-the-Box, KFC, RoundTable Pizza, Starbucks, Subway, Taco Bell, Days Inn, Extended Stay America, Hilton, Motel 6, CVS, Ranch Mkt, Safeway
10	Scott Creek Rd
9	Jacklin Rd, E Bonfare Mkt, W Shell/dsl
8	CA 237, Calaveras Blvd, Milpitas, E 76, Shell/repair, Christy Donuts, Pizza Hut, RoundTable Pizza, Starbucks, Executive Inn, 7-11, Oceans SuperMkt, W Shell, CheeseSteaks Shop, Chick-fil-A, El Torito, Erik's Cafe, Giorgio's Italian, IHOP, Jamba Juice, McDonald's, Mikonos Grill, Mtn Mike's Pizza, Noah's NY Bagels, Panda Express, Red Lobster, Subway, Wingstop, Embassy Suites, CVS, Marina Grocery, Safeway, Staples
6	Landess Ave, Montague Expswy, E Arco, Chevron, Burger King, Dunkin, Jack-in-the-Box, McDonald's, Starbucks, Stuft Pizza, Subway, Taco Bell, $Tree, Firestone/auto, O'Reilly Parts, Target, vet, Walgreens, W Chevron/McDonald's, Olive Garden, Outback Steaks, Starbucks, Courtyard, TownePlace, Dick's, farmer's mkt, Home Depot, Kohl's, Legoland Discovery Ctr, mall, Trader Joe's
5	Capitol Ave, Hostetter Ave, E Shell, Popeyes, W 7-11
4	Berryessa Rd, E Arco/24hr, Speedway/dsl, Christy's Donut, Denny's, Jade China, Lee's Sandwiches, McDonald's, Round Table Pizza, Starbucks, Taco Bell, $Tree, AutoZone, CVS, Safeway
2b	McKee Rd, E 76, Chevron, Shell/dsl, Burger King, Chipotle, Five Guys, Jamba Juice, Panda Express, Popeyes, Starbucks, Togo's, Wienerschnitzel, $Tree, 7-11, AT&T, Grocery Outlet, Marshall's, Ross, Target, Walgreens, W World Gas, Baskin-Robbins, Lee's Sandwiches, McDonald's, RoundTable Pizza, Wendy's, Yum Yum Donuts, H
2a	Alum Rock Ave, E Shell/dsl/24hr, Jack-in-the-Box, Taco Bell, tires, vet, W Chevron, Valero, Chalateco, Domino's, The Pizza Box, AutoZone
1d	Capitol Expswy
1c	King Rd, Jackson Ave(from nb), E L&D Gas, Shell, El Pollo Loco, Jack-in-the-Box, King's Burger, Starbucks, Subway, Wingstop, AT&T, Target, Verizon, Walgreens
1b	US 101, to LA, SF
1a	(exits left from sb)I-680 begins/ends on I-280.

MILPITAS

INTERSTATE 710

COMMERCE

Exit	Services
23	I-710 begins/ends on Valley Blvd
22b a	I-10
20c	Chavez Ave
20b	CA 60, Pamona Fwy, E King Taco, Monterey Hill Rest., W Shell, Jack-in-the-Box, Pizza Hut, AutoZone
20a	3rd St
19	Whittier Blvd, Olympic Blvd, E Arco, Alex Burgers, W McDonald's
17b	Washington Blvd, Commerce, E 76, Jack-in-the-Box, Lucky Guy's Burgers, Starbucks, Xris Burgers, W Commerce Trkstp/dsl/rest.
17a	Bandini Blvd, Atlantic Blvd
15	Florence Ave, E Alfredo's Mexican, Applebee's, Coldstone, Dunkin', El Pescador Mexican, El Pollo Loco, Fosters Freeze, IHOP, Jack-in-the-Box, KFC, Kickin' Crab, Little Caesar's, McDonald's, Panda Express, Starbucks, Subway, Taco Bell, The Habit Burger, Wingstop, Quality Inn, $Tree, AT&T, casino, Food4Less, Marshall's, Ross, W 76, Chevron, Shell/service, Carl's Jr, ChuckECheese, La Barca Mexican, Popeye's, Diamond Bell Inn
13	CA 42, Firestone Blvd, E Arco, Buena Mesa, Chick-fil-A, Denny's, Golden Bowl, Hooters, McDonald's, Ono HI BBQ, Panda Express, Panera Bread, Pollo Campero, Soup Shop, Starbucks, Subway, Wendy's, Day's Inn, Guesthouse Inn, ALDI, El Super Foods, Ford, Sam's Club, Target, W Shell, CA Fish, Chipotle, Dunkin', In-N-Out, Jack-in-the-Box, Panda Express, Starbucks, TGI Fridays, The Habit Burger, Wingstop, Motel 6, AT&T, Walmart
12b a	Imperial Hwy, E GM/dsl, Carl's Jr., El Pollo Loco, Hercules Burgers, WaBa Grill, W Arco, Chevron/dsl, G&M, Angelo's Burgers, KFC, Las Islas Seafood, McDonald's, Panda Express, Starbucks, Subway, Taco Bell, Wienerschnitzel, Winchell's, AutoZone, El Super Mkt, Walgreens
11b a	I-105
10	Rosecrans Ave, W Arco
9b a	Alondra Ave, E Chevron/dsl, Jack-in-the-Box, Home Depot, W Arco, Pizza King, Ray's Drive-in
8b a	CA 91
7b a	Long Beach Blvd, E Sinclair, W Arco/24hr, Don's Fish, Jack-in-the-Box, Sal's Gumbo, Subway
6	Del Amo Blvd, E 76, Chevron, McDonald's, Travel King, CVS, W Rocco's Deli
4	I-405, San Diego Freeway
3b a	Willow St, E Arco, Chevron/dsl, Albertson's, Baskin-Robbins, Buono's Pizzeria, Domino's, Pizza Hut, Wienerschnitzel, Walgreens, W 76, Arco, KFC, Little Caesars, Poke Plus, Popeyes, Twins BBQ, AutoZone
2	CA 1, Pacific Coast Hwy, E 76/dsl, Arco/mart, Chevron, Mobil, KFC, Kickin' Crab, Mariscos Mexican, McDonald's, Beacon Hotel, La Mirage Inn, Tower Motel, Travel Eagle Inn, W Arco/service, Chevron/PCH Trkstp/dsl, Shell/Carl's Jr/dsl, Alberto's Mexican, Golden Star Rest., Jack-in-the-Box, McDonald's, Taco Bell, Tom's Burgers, Winchell's, Hiland Motel, SeaBreeze Motel
1d	Anaheim St, E Shell, Subway, W auto repair

= gas = food = lodging = other = rest stop

CA

INTERSTATE 710 Cont'd

Exit #	Services
1c	Ahjoreline Dr, Piers B, C, D, E, Pico Ave
1b	Pico Ave, Piers F-J, Queen Mary
1a	Harbor Scenic Dr, Piers S, T, Terminal Island, **E** Hilton, Golden Shore RV Camping
0mm	I-710 begins/ends in Long Beach

INTERSTATE 780 (Vallejo)

BENICIA

Exit #	Services
7	I-780 begins/ends on I-680.
6	E 5th St, Benicia, **N** Marathon, **S** 7-11, 76/dsl, Holiday Inn Express, Big O Tire
5	E 2nd St, Central Benicia, **N** 76/dsl, Best Western, **S** Kimono Steaks, McDonald's, Nations Burger, Subway, Safeway
4	Southampton Rd, Benicia, **N** Burger King, Ensenada Mexican, Huckleberry's, Jamba Juice, Panda Express, RoundTable Pizza, Starbucks, Subway, $Tree, Ace Hardware, Raley's Foods
3b	Military West, **S** to Benicia SRA
3a	Columbus Pkwy, **N** Chevron/dsl, Albertos Mexican, McDonald's, Mtn Mike's Pizza, Napoli Pizza, Palermos Italian, Papa Murphy's, Starbucks, CVS, Jiffy Lube, **S** to Benicia SRA
1d	Glen Cove Pkwy, **N** Hwy Patrol, **S** Domino's, Subway, Vons Chicken, Safeway
1c	Cedar St
1b a	I-780 begins/ends on I-80.

INTERSTATE 805 (San Diego)

Exit #	Services
28mm	I-5(from nb), I-805 begins/ends on I-5.
27.5	CA 56 E (from nb)
27	Sorrento Valley Rd, Mira Mesa Blvd
26	Vista Sorrento Pkwy, **E** bb.q Chicken, Chick-fil-A, Flame Broiler, Ike's Love & Sandwiches, McDonald's, Rubio's, Starbucks, Country Inn, Courtyard, Extended Stay America, Holiday Inn Express, Hyatt House, Residence Inn, EVC, U-Haul, URGENT CARE
25b a	La Jolla Village Dr, Miramar Rd, **E** Discount Tire, Firestone, **W** Corner Cafe, PF Chang's, RED O Mexican, Seasons 52, Embassy Suites, Marriott, H, Macy's, mall, Nordstom's
24	Governor Dr
23	CA 52
22	Clairemont Mesa Blvd, **E** 7-11/dsl, Chevron/dsl, Mega/dsl, Shell, Arby's, Carl's Jr, Castaneda's Mexican, Chipotle Mexican, Godfather Rest., Jersey Mike's, McDonald's, PT Eatery, Rubio's Grill, Starbucks, Starbucks, Subway, Tommy's Burgers, Camping World, Food4Less, Ford/Kia, Jiffy Lube, Mazda, NAPA, Nissan, Ranch Mkt, U-Haul, Verizon, Walmart, Zion Mkt, **W** 24/7 Gas&Food, Buga Korean BBQ, Havana Grill, Ma's House, CA Suites, Motel 6, Pleasant Inn
21	CA 274, Balboa Ave, **E** 7-11, 76, Arco/dsl, Chevron/dsl, Applebee's, Subway, CarMax, Chevrolet, Chrysler/Dodge/Jeep, Firestone, H Mart, VW, **W** Arco, Chevron, Circle K, Shell/7-11, Baskin-Robbins, Blaze Pizza, Burger King, Chick-fil-A, Dickey's BBQ, El Pollo Loco, Five Guys, Honey Baked Ham, IHOP, Jack-in-the-Box, Little Caesars, McDonald's, Mike's Red Tacos, Panda Express, Panera Bread, Starbucks, Subway, Taco Bell, AutoZone, CVS Drug, Discount Tire, Home Depot, Kohls, Marshalls, O'Reilly Parts, Ranch Mkt, Sprouts Mkt, Target, Valvoline, Vons Food
20	CA 163 N, to Escondido
20a	Mesa College Dr, Kearney Villa Rd, **W** H
18	Murray Ridge Rd, to Phyllis Place
17b	I-8, E to El Centro, W to beaches
16	El Cajon Blvd, **E** Arco, Ultra, Church's, Venice Pizza,

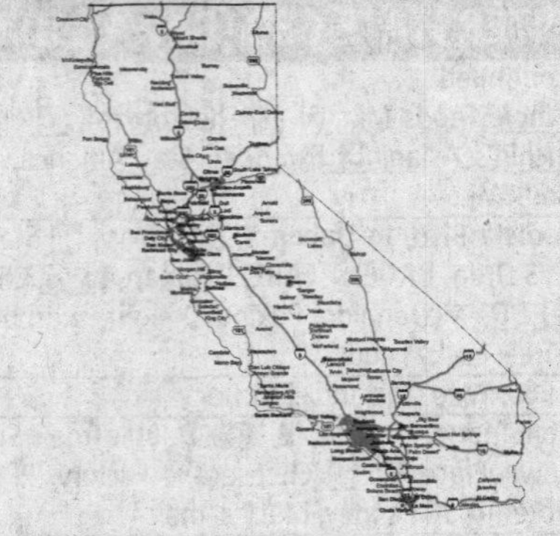

NATIONAL CITY

Exit #	Services
16	Continued 7-11, auto repair, Pancho Villa Mkt, **W** 76, Carl's Jr, Denny's, Jack-in-the-Box, Popeyes, Rudford's Rest., Sonic, Starbucks, Taco Bell, Wendy's, auto repair, O'Reilly Parts
15	University Ave, **E** Chevron, Filiberto's Mexican, SD Finest Donuts, Subway, 7-11, auto repair, tires, **W** 76/dsl, Speedway/dsl, Nomad Donuts, Panchita's Bakery, Starbucks, AT&T, Barons Mkt, CVS Drug
14	CA 15 N, 40th St, to I-15
13b	Home Ave, MLK Ave, **E** Arco, Shell/dsl, auto repair, **W** Capt. Sam's, 7-11
13a	CA 94
12b	Market St, **E** Sunrise, **W** Chula Tacos, Fresh Garden Mkt
12a	Imperial Ave, **E** Chevron/dsl, United, **W** Asia Wok, Burros Mexican, Domino's, KFC/LJ Silver, Sizzler, Subway, 99c Store, AT&T, Home Depot
11b	47th St
11a	43rd St, **W** Jack-in-the-Box, Jamba Juice, Sayulitas Mexican, AutoZone, CVS Drug, Northgate Mkt
10	Plaza Blvd, National City, **E** Dunkin, McDonald's, Pizza Hut, Popeyes, Starbucks, Subway, Winchell's, AutoZone, Firestone/auto, H, Vallarta Foods, vet, Walgreens, **W** Shell, Baskin-Robbins, BBQ Pit, Bistro City Chinese, Burger King, Carl's Jr, ChuckeCheese, Domino's, Epic Wings, Hawaiian BBQ, IHOP, In-N-Out, Jubilee Chicken/burgers, KFC, Little Caesar's, Panda Express, Papa John's, Starbucks, Subway, Sunny Donuts, Wingstop, Holiday Inn Express, Motel 6, Stardust Inn, 7-11, AT&T, AutoZone, BigLots, CA Produce, CVS Drug, Discount Tire, Firestone/auto, O'Reilly Parts, Walmart
9	Sweetwater Rd, **E** Applebee's, DQ, Outback Steaks, Panda Express, Pizza Hut, Red Robin, Starbucks, Super 8, 7-11, JC Penney, Macy's, mall, Target, **W** Chevron/7-11/dsl, Carl's Jr, Denny's, Hanaoka Japanese, Home Coffee, L&L Hawaiian BBQ, Mike's NY Pizza, Pizza Hut, Subway, Taco Bell, Toto's, TX Roadhouse, CVS Drug, Food4Less, Tire Choice, Verizon
8	CA 54
7c	E St, Bonita Rd, **E** Applebee's, GK Mongolian, Little Caesars, Manna BBQ, Outback Steaks, Panda Express, Red Robin, Starbucks, Victorinos Pizza, JC Penney, Macy's, mall, Target, **W** Chevron/dsl, Mobil/Circle K, San Diego Gas/dsl, Burger King, Denny's, Karina's Mexican, Comfort Inn, La Quinta
7b a	H St, **E** Shell, Bento & Noodles, Coldstone, D'Lish Pizza, Honey Baked Ham, Jack-in-the-Box, Knockout Korean Chicken, Robeks Juice, Subway, Taco Bell, CVS Drug, Dicks, Marshall's, Vons Foods, **W** Caffe Tazza, Einstein Bros
6	L St, Telegraph Canyon Rd, **E** Arco/dsl, Little Caesar's, Mandarin Chinese, McDonald's, Starbucks, Subway, 99 Ranch Mkt, H, Olympic Training Ctr, vet,

 = gas = food = lodging = other = rest stop

INTERSTATE 805 (San Diego) Cont'd

6 Continued
Chevron/Circle K/dsl, Shell, Lolita's Mexican, 7-11

4 Orange Ave, W Chevron, Wings Empire, 7-11

3 Main St, Otay Valley Rd, E Shell/dsl, In-N-Out, Panda Express, $Tree, ALDI, Ford/Kia, Honda, Kohl's, Nissan, PetSmart, Toyota/Scion, W Circle K/dsl, Asada Mexican, Best Western

2 Palm Ave, E Arco, Chevron, Baskin-Robbins, Carl's Jr, Chick-fil-A, Dominos, Jack-in-the-Box, Jamba Juice, Jersey Mike's, Manolo's Mexican, Paradise Buffet, Starbucks, Subway, Taco Bell, AT&T, Home Depot, Meineke, USPO, Von's Foods, Walmart/McDonald's/auto, W Chevron, Golden House Chinese, KFC, Little Caesar's, McDonald's

1b CA 905, E Brown Field, Otay Mesa Border Crossing

1a San Ysidro Blvd, E Shell/dsl, Valero, Church's TX Chicken, El Rincon Mexican, 99c Store, CVS Drug, Factory2U, O'Reilly Parts, W 76, Chevron, Mobil/dsl, Shell, Denny's, McDonald's, Motel 6

0 I-805 begins/ends on I-5.

INTERSTATE 880 (Bay Area)

EMBARCADERO

46b a I-80 W(exits left). I-80 E/580 W.

44 7th St, Grand Ave, downtown

42b a Broadway St, E KFC, McDonald's, Marriott, W La Santa Mexican, Nation's Giant Burgers, Waterfront Hotel, to Jack London Square

41a Oak St, Lakeside Dr, downtown

40 5th Ave, Embarcadero, E Burger King, W Ramen Sta., Starbucks, Best Western, Executive Inn, Homewood Suites, Motel 6

39b a 29th Ave, 23rd Ave, to Fruitvale, E Shell, DonutStar, Ono HI BBQ, Popeyes, Starbucks, The Habit Burger, AT&T, AutoZone, FoodMaxx, W 7-11

38 High St, to Alameda, E Go!/dsl, Bay Breeze Inn, W Shell/dsl, McDonald's, Home Depot

37 66th Ave, Zhone Way, E coliseum

36 Hegenberger Rd, E Arco/24hr, Shell/dsl, Burger King, Chubby Freeze, Jack-in-the-Box, McDonald's, Mt Mike's Pizza, Taco Bell, Day's Hotel, La Quinta, Radisson, Freightliner, GMC/Volvo, W 76/dsl, Chevron/dsl, Shell, Cane's Chicken, Chipotle, HegenBurger, Jamba Juice, Panda Express, SpringHill, Subway, Urgent Care, Wing Stop, Best Western, Courtyard, Hilton, Holiday Inn, Oakland Inn, Audi, Harley-Davidson, Lexus, T-Mobil, to Oakland, Toyota/Scion

35 98th Ave, W Hilton, Holiday Inn Express, to Oakland

CASTRO VALLEY

34 Davis St, W Shell/Burger King, Ohana HI BBQ, Togo's, $Tree, Costco/gas, Home Depot, Ross, Verizon, Walmart

33b a Marina Blvd, E Chevron/dsl, EVC, Valero, Five Guys, Jack-in-the-Box, La Salsa Mexican, Panda Express, Pieology, Starbucks, Taco Bell, Big O Tires, Chrysler/Dodge/Jeep, Ford/Lincoln, Honda, Hyundai, Marshall's, Nissan, Nordstrom's, Volvo, W Speedway/dsl, A&W/KFC, Denny's, H

32 Washington Ave(from nb), Lewelling Blvd(from sb), E $Tree, vet, W 76/dsl, Arco, Chevron, Fusion Delight, Jack-in-the-Box, McDonald's, Minami Sushi, Mtn Mike's Pizza, Papa Murphy's, Subway, Subway, 99c Store, Big O Tire, CVS, Food Maxx, GNC, Jo-Ann, Safeway, same as 30, Walgreens/24hr

31 I-238(from sb), to I-580, Castro Valley

30 Hesperian Blvd, E National, In-N-Out, Starbucks, Taco Bell, Teriyaki City, O'Reilly Parts, Walmart/Subway, W  Arco, Chevron, Classic Burger, Black Angus, Papa Murphy's, Peking Garden, Round Table Pizza, Starbucks,

SAN LORENZO

30 Continued
Hilton Garden, 99c Store, Big O Tires, CVS, Food Maxx, Lucky Foods, same as 32, USPO, vet, Walgreens

29 A St, San Lorenzo, E Mobile/dsl/e85, McDonald's, Best Western, Costco/gas, tires/repair, W 76/7-11/dsl, Chevron/dsl, Burger King, Carmen & Family BBQ, Five Guys, Jamba Juice, Ono HI BBQ, Rigatoni's Italian, Shell Shock Seafood, Starbucks, Sushi Ichimoto, Togo's, Wingstop, Days Inn, Heritage Inn, La Quinta, Rodeway Inn, Vagabond Inn, $Tree, Home Depot, T-Mobile, Target

28 Winton Ave, W Chevron, EVC, Applebee's, Buffalo Wild Wings, ChuckECheese, Famous Dave's BBQ, Hawaiian BBQ, Krispy Krunchy Chicken, Olive Garden, Panda Express, Panera Bread, Sizzler, Starbucks, Firestone/auto, Goodyear/auto, Hobby Lobby, JC Penney, Macy's, mall, O'Reilly Parts, Ross, Verizon

27 CA 92, Jackson St, E 76, DoubleTime/dsl, Annar Afghani, Asian Wok, Baskin-Robbins, Mtn Mike's Pizza, Naked Fish Japanese, Nations Burgers, Ohana HI BBQ, Popeyes, Round Table Pizza, South Smoking BBQ, Starbucks, Subway, Taco Bell, CVS, Grocery Outlet, Lucky Foods, Safeway, Walgreens, W San Mateo Br

26 Tennyson Rd, E All Star dsl, Mobil, Shell, Jack-in-the-Box, KFC, O'Reilly Parts, Walgreens, W 76, H

25 Industrial Pkwy(from sb), E Golden Gate/dsl, Industrial/dsl, Starbucks, Straw Hat Pizza, Subway, truck tires/service, W Red Roof Inn

24 Whipple Rd, Dyer St, E 76/dsl, Chevron/dsl/24hr, Denny's, Los Carnalitos, McDonald's, Ono HI BBQ, Panda Express, Starbucks, Taco Bell, Wingstop, Motel 6, SureStay Plus, FoodMaxx, Home Depot, PepBoys, Target, W Andersen Baker a Cafe, Backyard Bayou, Baskin-Robbins, Buffalo Wild Wings, Chevy's Mexican, Chili's, Chipotle, Coldstone, Dave's Hot Chicken, IHOP, Jamba Juice, Jollibee, Krispy Kreme, Lulu's Poke, Mtn Mike's Pizza, Ocean Oyster, Starbucks, Texas Roadhouse, TGIFriday, The Habit Burger, Togo's, Tomatina Italian, Tribu Grill, Extended Stay America, Hampton Inn, Holiday Inn Express, AT&T, GNC, Lucky Foods, Michael's, PetCo, Ross, Verizon, Walmart

23 Alvarado-Niles Rd, (same as 24), E Shell, Crowne Plaza, 7-11, W Chevron, Shell, Backyard Bayou, Burger King, Chili's, Dave's Hot Chicken, In-N-Out Burger, Jamba Juice, Jollibee, Krispy Kreme, Starbucks, Togo's, Hampton Inn, Holiday Inn Express, Lowe's Whse, Lucky Foods, playgound

FREMONT

22 Alvarado Blvd, Fremont Blvd, E Five Grains Noodle, Milk & Honey, Motel 6, Lucky Foods

21 CA 84 W, Decoto Rd to Dumbarton Br, E 7-11, McDonald's, Mt Mike's Pizza, Walgreens

19 CA 84 E, Thornton Ave, Newark, E U-Haul, W Chevron/dsl, Shell/Circle K, Carl's Jr, Mtn Mike's Pizza, My Cafe, Round Table Pizza, Subway, Taco Bell, 7-11, BigLots, Home Depot

17 Mowry Ave, Fremont, E 7-11, 76/Circle K, Chevron/dsl, QuikStop, Applebee's, Bill's Cafe, Chick-fil-A, Chili's, Country Way Rest., Denny's, Dunkin', Fremont Kabob, Jamba Juice, KFC, L&L Hi BBQ, Massimo's Italian, McDonald's, Ohana HI BBQ, Olive Garden, Papa Murphy's, Popeye's, Starbucks, T & D Sandwich, Trader Joe's, Best Western, Extended Stay America, Residence Inn, H, Lucky Foods, Michaels, Safeway, Target, W National, BJ's Rest., Jack's Rest., Jack-in-the-Box, Lazy Dog Rest., Little Caesar's, McDonald's, Papa John's, Ray's Crabshack, Starbucks, Taco Bell, Chase Suites, EZ 8 Motel, Homewood Suites, Wyndham Garden, Chrysler/Dodge/Jeep, Costco/gas, Firestone/auto, Ford, Jiffy Lube, Lion Mkt, Macy's, mall, Mazda, Pep Boys, VW

CA

= gas = food = lodging = other = rest stop

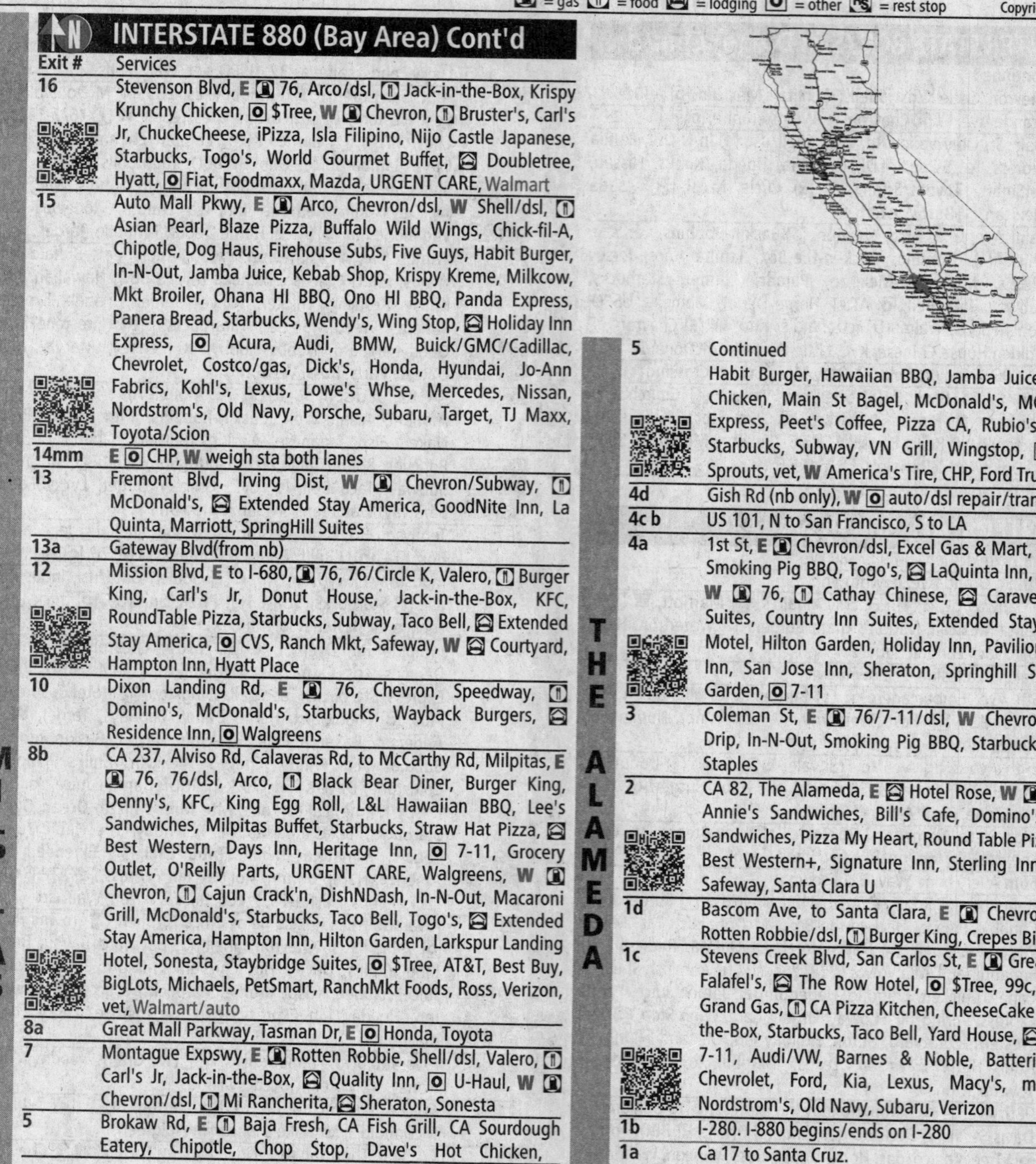

INTERSTATE 880 (Bay Area) Cont'd

Exit #	Services
16	Stevenson Blvd, E 76, Arco/dsl, Jack-in-the-Box, Krispy Krunchy Chicken, $Tree, W Chevron, Bruster's, Carl's Jr, ChuckeCheese, iPizza, Isla Filipino, Nijo Castle Japanese, Starbucks, Togo's, World Gourmet Buffet, Doubletree, Hyatt, Fiat, Foodmaxx, Mazda, URGENT CARE, Walmart
15	Auto Mall Pkwy, E Arco, Chevron/dsl, W Shell/dsl, Asian Pearl, Blaze Pizza, Buffalo Wild Wings, Chick-fil-A, Chipotle, Dog Haus, Firehouse Subs, Five Guys, Habit Burger, In-N-Out, Jamba Juice, Kebab Shop, Krispy Kreme, Milkcow, Mkt Broiler, Ohana HI BBQ, Ono HI BBQ, Panda Express, Panera Bread, Starbucks, Wendy's, Wing Stop, Holiday Inn Express, Acura, Audi, BMW, Buick/GMC/Cadillac, Chevrolet, Costco/gas, Dick's, Honda, Hyundai, Jo-Ann Fabrics, Kohl's, Lexus, Lowe's Whse, Mercedes, Nissan, Nordstrom's, Old Navy, Porsche, Subaru, Target, TJ Maxx, Toyota/Scion
14mm	E CHP, W weigh sta both lanes
13	Fremont Blvd, Irving Dist, W Chevron/Subway, McDonald's, Extended Stay America, GoodNite Inn, La Quinta, Marriott, SpringHill Suites
13a	Gateway Blvd(from nb)
12	Mission Blvd, E to I-680, 76, 76/Circle K, Valero, Burger King, Carl's Jr, Donut House, Jack-in-the-Box, KFC, RoundTable Pizza, Starbucks, Subway, Taco Bell, Extended Stay America, CVS, Ranch Mkt, Safeway, W Courtyard, Hampton Inn, Hyatt Place
10	Dixon Landing Rd, E 76, Chevron, Speedway, Domino's, McDonald's, Starbucks, Wayback Burgers, Residence Inn, Walgreens
8b	CA 237, Alviso Rd, Calaveras Rd, to McCarthy Rd, Milpitas, E 76, 76/dsl, Arco, Black Bear Diner, Burger King, Denny's, KFC, King Egg Roll, L&L Hawaiian BBQ, Lee's Sandwiches, Milpitas Buffet, Starbucks, Straw Hat Pizza, Best Western, Days Inn, Heritage Inn, 7-11, Grocery Outlet, O'Reilly Parts, URGENT CARE, Walgreens, W Chevron, Cajun Crack'n, DishNDash, In-N-Out, Macaroni Grill, McDonald's, Starbucks, Taco Bell, Togo's, Extended Stay America, Hampton Inn, Hilton Garden, Larkspur Landing Hotel, Sonesta, Staybridge Suites, $Tree, AT&T, Best Buy, BigLots, Michaels, PetSmart, RanchMkt Foods, Ross, Verizon, vet, Walmart/auto
8a	Great Mall Parkway, Tasman Dr, E Honda, Toyota
7	Montague Expswy, E Rotten Robbie, Shell/dsl, Valero, Carl's Jr, Jack-in-the-Box, Quality Inn, U-Haul, W Chevron/dsl, Mi Rancherita, Sheraton, Sonesta
5	Brokaw Rd, E Baja Fresh, CA Fish Grill, CA Sourdough Eatery, Chipotle, Chop Stop, Dave's Hot Chicken,

MILPITAS

Exit #	Services
5	Continued Habit Burger, Hawaiian BBQ, Jamba Juice, Krispy Krunchy Chicken, Main St Bagel, McDonald's, MOD Pizza, Panda Express, Peet's Coffee, Pizza CA, Rubio's, Sizzling Lunch, Starbucks, Subway, VN Grill, Wingstop, Lowe's, Ross, Sprouts, vet, W America's Tire, CHP, Ford Trucks
4d	Gish Rd (nb only), W auto/dsl repair/transmissions
4c b	US 101, N to San Francisco, S to LA
4a	1st St, E Chevron/dsl, Excel Gas & Mart, Jackie's Place, Smoking Pig BBQ, Togo's, LaQuinta Inn, O'Reilly Parts, W 76, Cathay Chinese, Caravelle Inn, Comfort Suites, Country Inn Suites, Extended Stay America, EZ 8 Motel, Hilton Garden, Holiday Inn, Pavilion Inn, Residence Inn, San Jose Inn, Sheraton, Springhill Suites, Wyndham Garden, 7-11
3	Coleman St, E 76/7-11/dsl, W Chevron/dsl, Chikin Drip, In-N-Out, Smoking Pig BBQ, Starbucks, Togo's, , Staples
2	CA 82, The Alameda, E Hotel Rose, W Shell/repair, Annie's Sandwiches, Bill's Cafe, Domino's, Ike's Love & Sandwiches, Pizza My Heart, Round Table Pizza, Taco Bell, Best Western+, Signature Inn, Sterling Inn, Valley Inn, Safeway, Santa Clara U
1d	Bascom Ave, to Santa Clara, E Chevron, W Platinum, Rotten Robbie/dsl, Burger King, Crepes Bistro, Starbucks
1c	Stevens Creek Blvd, San Carlos St, E Great Gas, Shell, Falafel's, The Row Hotel, $Tree, 99c, H, tires, W Grand Gas, CA Pizza Kitchen, CheeseCake Factory, Jack-in-the-Box, Starbucks, Taco Bell, Yard House, Studios Inn, 7-11, Audi/VW, Barnes & Noble, Batteries+, Best Buy, Chevrolet, Ford, Kia, Lexus, Macy's, mall, Mitsubishi, Nordstrom's, Old Navy, Subaru, Verizon
1b	I-280. I-880 begins/ends on I-280
1a	Ca 17 to Santa Cruz.

THE ALAMEDA

NOTES

COLORADO

INTERSTATE 25

FT COLLINS

Exit #	Services
299mm	Colorado/Wyoming state line
296mm	natural fort
293	to Carr, Norfolk
288	Buckeye Rd
281	Owl Canyon Rd, E KOA
278	CO 1 S, to Wellington, W Loaf'N Jug/dsl, Maverik/dsl, Sinclair/dsl, Burger King, Domino's, Les's BBQ, McDonald's, Papa's Table Italian, Subway, Taco Bell, Taco John's, Wellington Grill, Quality Inn, $General, Family$, O'Reilly Parts, Ridley's Mkt, USPO, vet
271	Mountain Vista Dr, W Budweiser Brewery
269b a	CO 14, to US 87, Ft Collins, E Maverik/dsl, McDonald's, Best Value Inn, WoodSpring Suites, W Loaf'N Jug, Shell/dsl, Denny's, Hacienda Real, Subway, Waffle House, 9 Motel, Baymont Inn, Clarion, Comfort Inn, Days Inn, La Quinta, Motel 6, Quality Inn, Super 8, CO St U, vet
268	Prospect Rd, to Ft Collins, Welcome Ctr/ both lanes, full facilities, litter barrels, petwalk, W
267mm	weight sta both lanes
266mm	Cache la Poudre River
265	Harmony Rd, Timnath, E Murphy USA/dsl, Chick-fil-A, Freddy's, Panda Express, Starbucks, Taco Bell, Wendy's, Costco/dsl, Schwab Tires, Walmart/Subway, W Sinclair/dsl, Austin's Grill, BJ's Rest., Carrabba's, Cheba Subs, Chipotle, Coldstone, Firehouse Subs, First Watch, Five Guys, Fuegos Mexican, Himalayan Bistro, Honey Baked Ham, IHOP, Jersey Mike's, Jimmy Johns, La Buena Vida Mexican, Old Chicago, Original Pancake House, Panera Bread, Papa John's, Potbelly, Qdoba, Red Robin, SmashBurger, Smoothie King, Sprouts Mkt, Starbucks, Tom+Chee, TX Roadhouse, Which Wich?, Cambria Suites, Comfort Suites, Courtyard, Fairfield Inn, Hampton Inn, Hilton Garden, Holiday Inn Express, Home2 Suites, Homewood Suites, Residence Inn, AT&T, Kohl's, Lowe's, Office Depot, Safeway/gas, Sam's Club, Staples, Target, Verizon, Walgreens, World Mkt
262	CO 392 E, to Windsor, E 7-11/dsl, Loaf'N Jug/Subway/dsl, Arby's, Pueblo Viejo, Taco John's, AmericInn, vet, W Maverik, CO Mtn RV Ctr
259	Crossroads Blvd, E 7-11/dsl, Maverik/dsl, Shell/dsl, Arby's, Boot Grill, Carl's Jr, Dominos, Fuzzy's Tacos, Nordy's, Palomino Mexican, Qdoba Mexican, Ruben's Grill, Starbucks, Subway, Taco Bell, Wendy's, Candlewood Suites, Embassy Suites, Extended Stay America, Holiday Inn Express, Microtel, My Place, W Hooters, BMW, Buick/GMC, CarMax, Chevrolet, Harley-Davidson, Hyundai, Mercedes, Mini, Subaru, to
257b a	US 34, to Loveland, E 7-11/dsl, Exxon/dsl, Arby's, Bad Daddy's Burger, Biaggi's Italian, BoneFish Grill, Culver's, Donata Pizza, East Coast Pizza, Kona Hawaiian, Lazy Dog Grill, MOD Pizza, On-the-Border, PF Chang's, Qdoba, Red Robin, Rock Bottom Rest., Starbucks, Urban Egg, Comfort Suites, Courtyard, Wingate, Barnes & Noble, Best Buy, Dick's, Duck Donuts, Macy's, See's Candies, URGENT CARE, Verizon, W Conoco/dsl, Buffalo Wild Wings, Chick-fil-A, Chili's, Chipotle Mexican, Cracker Barrel, IHOP, In-N-Out, Jimmy John's, KFC/Taco Bell, McDonald's, Noodles&Co, Old Chicago, Panera Bread, Starbucks, Wendy's, Best Western+, Fairfield Inn, Hampton Inn, Residence Inn, Jo-Ann Fabrics, Loveland Outlets/famous brands, Loveland RV Resort, Marshall's, Old Navy, PetSmart, Rocky Mtn NP,

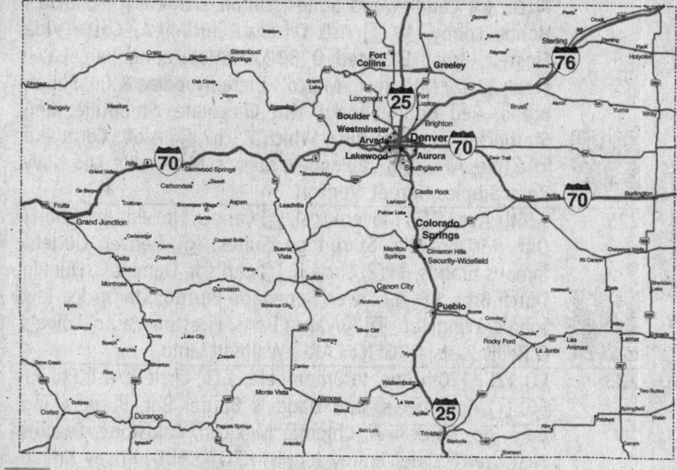

MILLIKEN

Exit #	Services
257b a	Continued Ross, Sportsman's Whse, Target
255	CO 402 W, to Loveland
254	to CO 60 W, to Campion, E Johnson's Corner/Sinclair/café/dsl/scales/motel/24hr, Budget Host, Lazydays RV Ctr/retreat, RV Retreat
252	CO 60 E, to Johnstown, Milliken, W Buc-ee's/dsl/EVC, Loaf'n Jug/Subway/dsl
250	CO 56 W, to Berthoud, W Love's/Subway/Taco John's/dsl/scales/24hr/@, Carter Lake
245	to Mead
243	CO 66, to Longmont, Platteville, E G&R/7-11/dsl, Maverik/dsl, Shell/7-11, Mead Pizza+, Rancheros Rest., Red Rooster Rest., Camping World, tires, vet, W Rocky Mtn NP
241mm	St Vrain River
240	CO 119, to Longmont, E Conoco/7-11/dsl, Murphy Express/dsl, Burger King, Carl's Jr, Del Taco, Good Times Grill, KFC, Pizza Hut, Popeyes, Qdoba, Starbucks, Teriyaki Madness, Wendy's, Best Western, Comfort Suites, Extended Stay, Holiday Inn Express, Century RV Ctr, Firestone, Home Depot, Kia, Windish RV Ctr, W 7-11/Subway/dsl, Phillips 66/dsl/scales/24hr, QT/dsl, Shell/Circle K/dsl, Arby's, McDonald's, Taco Bell, Waffle House, 1st Interstate Inn, Econolodge, Quality Inn, Super 8, Travelodge, Barbour Ponds SP, Blue Compass RV Ctr, truckwash, Windish RV Ctr
235	CO 52, Dacono, E Good2Go, Maverik/dsl, Burger King, Ford, Infiniti, Toyota, Transwest RV Ctr, W Exxon/dsl/LP, McDonald's, Starbucks, Eldora Ski Area, Harley-Davidson
232	to Erie, Dacono
229	CO 7, to Lafayette, Brighton, E Buffalo Wild Wings, Chick-fil-A, Chili's, Dutch Bros Coffee, Famous Dave's BBQ, Goodtimes Burgers, Gunther Toody's, Starbucks, Subway, Village Inn, Wapos Mexican, WoodSpring Suites, Costco/gas, Dick's, Discount Tire, Home Depot, PetSmart, Taste of Philly, W Conoco, Murphy Express/dsl, Beltran's Grill, Jimmy John's, McDonald's, MOD Pizza, Panda Express, Popeye's, Sonic, Starbucks, Taco Bell, Wendy's, AutoZone, King's Sooper/dsl, Les Schwab Tire
228	E-470(tollway), to Limon
226	144th Ave, E 7-11, Murphy Express/dsl, Arby's, Firehouse Subs, Five Guys, Freddy's, Johnny's Italian, Panda Express, Popeye's, Potbelly, Rosa Mexican,

BRIGHTON

INTERSTATE 25 Cont'd

226 Continued
Snarf's Sandwiches, Starbucks, Taco Bell, Wendy's, Your Pie Pizza, [lodging] Candlewood Suites, Hilton Garden, [other] Cabela's, Hobby Lobby, **W** [food] Asti D'Italia, Chick-fil-A, Costa Vida, Einstein Bros., Elevated Q BBQ, HuHot Mongolian, Law's Steaks, Lazy Dog Rest., Marco's Pizza, Noodles & Co, Panera Bread, Red Robin, Rocky Mtn Chocolate, Smoothie King, Starbucks, Sugarfire BBQ, Which Wich?, [lodging] Aloft, Courtyard, [other] $Tree, AT&T, [H], JC Penney, Macy's, Marshall's, Old Navy, Ross, Staples, Target, Verizon

225 136th Ave, **E** [gas] Maverik/dsl, [food] Cane's, Hot Pot Spot, In-N-Out, McDonald's, Starbridge Suites, [other] Denver Outlets/famous brands, **W** [gas] Circle K, [food] Carl's Jr, Domino's, Dunkin, Dutch Bros, KFC/LJ Silver, Renegade Burrito, Starbucks, Taco John's, Wingstop, [other] Advance Parts, Firestone/auto, Lowe's, O'Reilly Parts, URGENT CARE, Walmart/auto

223 CO 128, 120th Ave, to Broomfield, **E** [gas] Circle K/dsl, Phillips 66, [food] Applebee's, Bad Daddy's Burger Bar, Burger King, Café Rio, Chick-fil-A, Chipotle Mexican, Coldstone, Fazoli's, First Watch Cafe, Jimmy John's, KPOT KBBQ, Krispy Kreme, Longhorn Steaks, Los Dos Potrillos, Maverik, McDonald's, Olive Garden, Outback Steaks, Panda Express, Panera Bread, Pizza Hut, Smashburger, Sonic, Starbucks, Subway, Taziki's Cafe, Tequila's Mexican, [lodging] Baymont Inn, Delta Hotel, Denver North Hotel, DoubleTree, Holiday Inn Express, [other] $Tree, Advance Parts, AT&T, Barnes&Noble, Big O Tire, Brakes+, Discount Tire, GNC, Meineke, Michael's, O'Reilly Parts, PetCo, Safeway, Sprouts Mkt, Target, Verizon, Walgreens, **W** [gas] Circle K/dsl, Conoco/dsl, Valero/dsl, [food] Babbajoons Kabobs, Chili's, Cracker Barrel, DQ, Hooters, Menchie's, Qdoba, Rocky Fin, Scalzotto Italian, Tokyo Joe's, Village Inn Rest., Wendy's, [lodging] Comfort Suites, Extended Stay America, Fairfield Inn, La Quinta, Suburban Studios, Super 8

221 104th Ave, to Northglenn, **E** [gas] Shell, Sinclair, [food] Buffalo Wild Wings, Burger King, Cheddar's, Denny's, DQ, Firehouse Subs, Fuzzy's Tacos, Hungry Howie's, McDonald's, Old Chicago, Qdoba, Renegade Burrito, Subway, Taco Bell, Wendy's, [other] $Tree, GNC, Home Depot, [H], King Soopers, **W** [gas] 7-11, Circle K/dsl, [food] Applebee's, Blackeyed Pea, Carmen Kitchen, Cinzzetti's Italian, Dutch Bros, GoodTimes Burger, Gunther Toody's, Heidi's Deli, IHOP, McDonald's, Seoul BBQ, Starbucks, Taco Bell, TX Roadhouse, [other] Best Buy, Firestone/auto, Ford, Goodyear/auto, Jo-Ann Fabrics, Lowe's, Office Depot, PetSmart, Ross

220 Thornton Pkwy, **E** [food] Baskin-Robbins, Chipotle, Culvers, Golden Corral, Jack-in-the-Box, Jimmy John's, Kneaders, Popeyes, Rico Pollo, Starbucks, Taco John's, Wingstop, [other] AT&T, [H], Safeway, Sam's Club/gas, Thornton Civic Ctr, Valvoline, Walmart, **W** [gas] Circle K/dsl, Conoco/dsl, Shell, [food] Subway

219 84th Ave, to Federal Way, **E** [gas] Shell/dsl, Valero/dsl, [food] Arby's, McDonald's, Quiznos, Sonic, Starbucks, Subway, Taco Bell, Taco Star, Waffle House, [other] O'Reilly Parts, **W** [gas] Econogas, Valero/dsl, [food] Burger King, DQ, El Fogon, McDonald's, Popeyes, Santiago's Mexican, Village Inn Rest., [lodging] Motel 6, [other] AutoZone, CarQuest, Discount Tire, [H], Meineke, Save-A-Lot, vet

217 US 36 W(exits left from nb), to Boulder, **W** [gas] Conoco, [food] Ho Wei Chinese, [other] Chevrolet, Toyota

216b a I-76 E, to I-270 E

215 58th Ave, **E** [food] Burger King, McDonald's, Subway, Sugar Rush Donuts, Wendy's, [lodging] Comfort Inn, [other] URGENT CARE, **W** [gas] Circle K/dsl, Sinclair/dsl, [lodging] Super 8, [other] O'Reilly Parts

214c 48th Ave, **W** [lodging] Ramada

214b a I-70, E to Limon, W to Grand Junction

DENVER

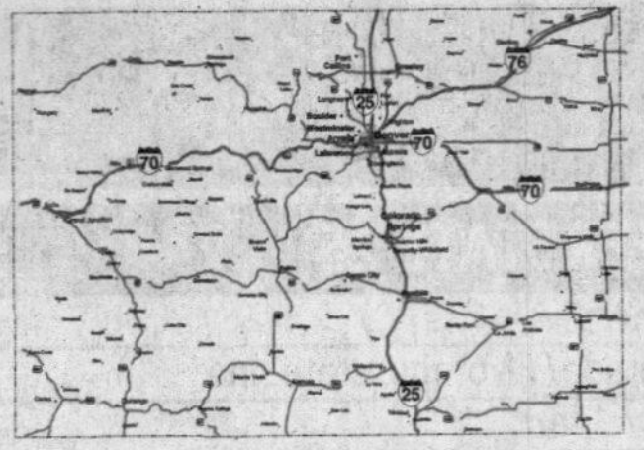

213 Park Ave, W 38th Ave, 23rd St, downtown, **E** [gas] Sinclair, [food] Domino's, Gomez Burritos, Starbucks

212c 20th St, downtown, Denver

212b a Speer Blvd, **E** downtown, [other] museum, museum, **W** [gas] Conoco/dsl, Shell/dsl, [food] Subway, [lodging] AutoZone, Fairfield Inn, Hampton Inn, Residence Inn, Super 8, [other] Walgreens

211 23rd Ave, **E** [other] aquarium, funpark

210c CO 33(from nb)

210b US 40 W, Colfax Ave, **W** [food] Denny's, KFC, [other] Mile High Stadium

210a US 40 E, Colfax Ave, **E** downtown, [other] civic ctr

209c 8th Ave

209b 6th Ave W, US 6, **W** [gas] Shell/dsl, [lodging] Comfort Suites

209a 6th Ave E, downtown, Denver

208 CO 26, Alameda Ave(from sb), **E** [gas] Circle K/dsl, Conoco, Maverik, [food] Denny's, McDonalds, [other] Home Depot, Safeway, same as 207b, **W** [gas] Sinclair/dsl, [food] Phillips 66/7-11

207b US 85 S, Santa Fe Dr, same as 208

207a Broadway, Lincoln St, **E** [food] Griff's Burgers, [other] USPO

206b Washington St, Emerson St, **E** [other] Whole Foods Mkt, **W** [H]

206a Downing St(from nb)

205b a University Blvd, **W** [other] [H], U of Denver

204 CO 2, Colorado Blvd, **E** [gas] Circle K, Loaf'n Jug, Mobil, Phillips 66/dsl, [food] Arby's, Beard Papap's, Cane's, Chili's, Crave Grill, Denver Panini, Domino's, GoodTimes Grill, IHOP, Jimmy John's, McDonald's, Noodles&Co, Pizza Hut, Qdoba, Smashburger, Starbucks, Taco Bell, Wahoo's, Zero Degrees, [lodging] Belcaro Motel, Courtyard, Fairfield Inn, Hampton Inn, Hyatt, [other] Barnes&Noble, Best Buy, Chevrolet, Home Depot, Kia, King Soopers, Mercedes/BMW, Old Navy, Petco, Ross, Safeway Foods, Staples, vet, Walgreens, Whole Foods Mkt, **W** [gas] Phillips 66, [food] A&W/KFC, Bonchon, CAVA, Crown Burgers, Dave&Buster's, Five Guys, McDonald's, Shawarma Shack, Which Wich, [lodging] La Quinta, [other] Natural Grocers, USPO, vet

203 Evans Ave, **E** [gas] Murphy USA, [other] vet, **W** Ford

202 Yale Ave, **E** [food] Starbucks, Taco Bell, **W** Chick-fil-A, Chipotle, Einstein Bros, Potbelly, Starbucks, Wendy's, [other] GNC, King Soopers, Michaels, Sprouts Mkt

AURORA

201 US 285, CO 30, Hampden Ave, to Englewood, Aurora, **E** [gas] Conoco/Circle K/LP, Shell, Valero, [food] Benihana, Cane's, Chick-fil-A, Chipotle Mexican, Coldstone, Domino's, Firehouse Subs, Jimmy John's, McDonald's, Noodles&Co, NY Deli, Qdoba, Starbucks, Subway, Sushi Train, Taziki's, Torchy's Tacos, Wahoos Fish Taco, Wingstop, [lodging] Embassy Suites, [other] Discount Tire, King's Sooper/dsl, Omaha Steaks, Petco, Target, URGENT CARE, Verizon, vet, Walgreens, Whole Food Mkt, **W** [gas] Conoco/7-11, [food] Birdcall, Starbucks, [other] Dunkin'

200 I-225 N, to I-70

199 CO 88, Belleview Ave, to Littleton, **E** [food] Bryan's Dumpling House, Chianti Italian, Chipotle Mexican, Eddie V's Seafood, Fiocchi's Pizzeria, Griffin Tavern, Jersey Mike's, Ocean Prime Seafood, Pancake House, Panera Bread, Qdoba, Shanahan's Steaks, Starbucks, Wendy's, Yayas Bistro, [lodging] Fairfield Inn, Hampton Inn, Hilton Garden, Hyatt, Hyatt Place, Marriott, **W** [gas] Ruth's Chris Steaks, Shamrock, [food] JING Denver, McDonald's, Pappadeaux Café, Pizza Hut/Taco Bell, [lodging] Extended Stay America, [other] Lexus

INTERSTATE 25 Cont'd

Exit #	Services
198	Orchard Rd, E Del Frisco's Steaks, Shepler's, Snarf's Sandwiches, Starbucks, city park, W Circle K/dsl, DoubleTree, city park
197	Arapahoe Blvd, E Circle K/dsl, Conoco/dsl, QT, 7-11, Anthony's Pizza, Bros BBQ, Cafe Rio, Chick-fil-A, Chipotle, Culver's, Del Taco, Dickie's BBQ, Dog Haus, Domino's, Dunkin', El Parral, Fire Bowl Asian, Hoong's Palace, Jabo's BBQ, Las Brisas Mexican, McDonald's, Nonna's Italian, Outback Steaks, Pat's Cheesesteaks, Pizza Hut, Pollo Limas, Qdoba, Schlotsky's, Sonic, Starbucks, Stefano's Pizza, Zig Zag Burgers, Courtyard, Embassy Suites, Extended Stay America, Hawthorn Suites, Holiday Inn, Hyatt House, LaQuinta, Motel 6, Parks Residential, Sleep Inn, Spark Hotel, AutoZone, Chrysler/Jeep, Discount Tire, Ford, Home Depot, Honda, Hyundai, Kia, Lowe's Whse, Mazda, Nissan, Subaru, Target, Toyota/Scion, USPO, Walmart, W Mobil/dsl, QT, Shell/dsl, Valero/dsl, Benedict's Rest., CAVA, Chipotle Mexican, Chuy's, Colonna's Pizza, DQ, Einstein Bros, El Karajo Mexican, Finn McCool's Grill, Five Guys, Goodtimes, Jersey Mikes, Jimmy John's, McDonald's, Mile H.I. Burritos, Qdoba, Red Robin, Shake Shack, Subway, Taco Bell, Torcy's Taco, Twin Peaks Grill, Wingstop, Yuan MBBQ, Residence Inn, SpringHill Suites, Wingate Inn, Advance Parts, Big O Tire, Brakes+, Firestone/auto, GNC, Goodyear/auto, Office Depot, Safeway, Sprouts Mkt, URGENT CARE, vet
196	Dry Creek Rd, E Eddie Marlot's Steaks, IHOP, Maggiano's Italian, Marco's Pizza, My Neighbor Mexican, Rodizio Brazilian, ViewHouse Grill, Comfort Suites, Even Hotel, Extended Stay, Extended Stay America, GreeTree Inn, La Quinta, Quality Inn, Sheraton, Staybridge Suites, H, W 7-11/dsl, Bono's BBQ, Drury Inn, TownePlace Suites
195	County Line Rd, E Fleming's, Courtyard, Homewood Suites, Residence Inn, W Phillips 66, Buffalo Wild Wings, CA Pizza Kitchen, Cheesecake Factory, Chick-fil-A, Chipotle Mexican, Cold Stone, Del Taco, Earl's Kitchen, Firehouse Subs, Fogo de Chao Brazillian, Genghis Grill, Hooters, In-N-Out, J Alexander's, Jason's Deli, Krispy Kreme, LongHorn Steaks, Panda Express, PF Changs, Popeyes, Potbelly, Red Llama, Red Robin, Seasons 52, Tokyo Joe's, Wahoo's Mexican, Which Which?, Yard House, Comfort Suites, Hyatt Place, AT&T, Barnes&Noble, Best Buy, Costco/gas, Dick's, Dillard's, Home Depot, JC Penney, Jo-Ann Fabrics, Macy's, Marshall's, Michaels, Nordstrom, Old Navy, PetSmart, REI, Ross, Verizon
194	CO 470 W, CO 470 E(tollway)
193	Lincoln Ave, to Parker, E 7-11/dsl, Circle K/dsl, Conoco, Phillips 66, Arby's, Carl's Jr, Hacienda Colorado, Starbucks, Subway, Hilton Garden, Holiday Inn, URGENT CARE, W Phillips 66/mkt/dsl, Chili's, Chipotle Mexican, Firehouse Subs, Five Guys, Heidi's, McDonald's, Noodles&Co, Papa John's, Qdoba, Starbucks, Starbucks, Subway, Hampton Inn, Marriott, Discount Tire, H, Safeway, Sprouts Mkt, Target, vet
192	Ridgegate Pkwy, W TownePlace Suites, Cabela's, H
191	no services
190	Surrey Ridge, Surrey Ridge
188	Castle Pines Pkwy, W Conoco, Phillips 66, Domino's, Duke's Steaks, Las Fajitas Mexican, Pino's Italian, Starbucks, Subway, Wendy's, Big O Tires, King's Sooper/dsl, URGENT CARE, vet, Walgreens
187	Happy Canyon Rd
185	Castle Rock Pkwy, W Phillips 66/7-11, Berry Blends Smoothies, Capriotti's, Chick-fil-A, Chipotle, Cuba Cuba, Del Taco, Fuzzy's Taco, In-N-Out, La Loma, Los Dos Potrillos,

SURREY RIDGE

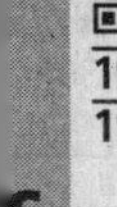

CASTLE ROCK

Exit #	Services
185	Continued Panda Express, Shake Shack, Starbucks, AT&T, Petco, Sam's Club/dsl, Schwab Tire, TJ Maxx, Verizon, Whole Foods Mkt
184	Founders Pkwy, Meadows Pkwy, to Castle Rock, E Circle K/dsl, Phillips 66, A&W/KFC, Applebee's, Burger King, Canes, Chick-fil-A, Chipotle Mexican, Coldstone, Dutch Bros, Five Guys, Jimmy John's, Little Caesar's, Noodles&Co, Outback Steaks, Panera Bread, Parry's Pizza, Qdoba, Red Robin, Sonic, Starbucks, Taco Bell, $Tree, Advance Parts, Brakes+, Discount Tire, Firestone/auto, Goodyear/auto, Grease Monkey, Home Depot, Just Brakes, King's Sooper, Kohl's, Michael's, Natural Grocers, O'Reilly Parts, Office Depot, Penske, PetSmart, Sprouts Mkt, Target, URGENT CARE, Verizon, vet, Walgreens, Walmart, W Loaf'n Jug/dsl, Arby's, Blackeyed Pea, Cafe Rio, CAVA, Chili's, Culver's, Food Court, Freddy's Steakburger, IHOP, Jersey Mike's, Kneaders, McDonald's, MOD Pizza, Popeyes, Potbelly, Rockyard Grill, Smashburger, Starbucks, Best Western+, Comfort Suites, Days Inn, Hampton Inn, Holiday Inn Express, AT&T, Castle Rock Outlet/famous brands, Hobby Lobby, King's Sooper/dsl, Lowe's, Midas, st patrol
182	CO 86, Castle Rock, Franktown, E 7-11/dsl, Dos Amigos Mexican, Castle Pines Motel, vet, W Circle K, Circle K/dsl, Burger King, Guadalajara Mexican, Jack-in-the-Box, McDonald's, Pollo Eats, Santiago's Mexican, Starbucks, Waffle House, Wendy's, Quality Inn, vet
181	CO 86, Wilcox St, Plum Creek Pkwy, Castle Rock, E Circle K, Conoco, Phillips 66, Phillips 66/7-11, DQ, El Meson Mexican, Jimmy John's, Papa John's, Papa Murphy's, Pizza Hut, Starbucks, Stumpy's Pizzaria, Taco Bell, Castle Rock Motel, AutoZone, Big O Tire, Buick/Chevrolet/GMC, Chrysler/Dodge/Jeep, Ford, Midas, Safeway/dsl, USPO, Walgreens
174	Tomah Rd, W Jellystone Park
173	Larkspur(from sb, no return), W Conoco/Larkspur Cafe/dsl/
172	Upper Lake Gulch Rd, Larkspur, W Conoco, Charrito's Mexican, Larkspur Pizza Cafe, Spur Grill, farmers mkt, USPO, vet
167	Greenland
163	County Line Rd
162.5mm	elev 7352, Monument Hill
162mm	weigh sta both lanes
161	CO 105, Woodmoor Dr, E Maverik, Sinclair/dsl, Back East Grill, Jimmy John's, Papa John's, Whataburger, vet, W 7-11, Phillips 66/dsl, Arby's, Domino's, Jarrito Loco, McDonald's, Rosie's Diner, Starbucks, Subway, Taco Bell, $Tree, Big O Tire, Safeway/dsl, USPO, vet, Walgreens
158	Baptist Rd, E Circle K/Popeyes, Murphy USA/dsl, Freddy's Steakburgers, Jersey Mike's, McDonald's, Papa Murphy's, Pizza Hut, Qdoba, Rodolfo's Mexican Grill, Starbucks, Subway, TX Roadhouse, Fairfield Inn, Advance Parts, AutoZone, Brakes+, Christian Bros. Auto, Discount Tire, Home Depot, Jiffy Lube, King's Sooper, Kohl's, Natural Grocers, O'Reilly Parts, PetSmart, Schwab Tire, Staples, Walgreens, Walmart, W Pilot/Arby's/dsl/scales/24hr, QT, Valero
156b	N Entrance to USAF Academy, E Loaf'n Jug, Bourbon Bros Kitchen, Carl's Jr, Chick-fil-A, Costa Vida, Domino's, Jimmy John's, Kneaders Cafe, MOD Pizza, Starbucks, Taco Bell, Vaqueros Mexican, Wendy's, My Place, 7-11, Bass Pro Shops, Sprouts Mkt
156a	Gleneagle Dr, E mining museum
155	new exit
153	InterQuest Pkwy, E Conoco, Maverik, Arby's, Burger King, Cheddar's, Chili's, Chipotle, CO Mtn Brewery/rest.,

CO

= gas = food = lodging = other = rest stop

CO

INTERSTATE 25 Cont'd

153 Continued
Dave's Hot Chicken, Dickey's BBQ, Dunkin, Dutch Bros, Five Guys, Freddy's, IHOP, In-N-Out, Jersey Mike's, Mission BBQ, Panda Express, Shake Shack, Slim Chickens, Sonic, Starbucks, Subway, Taco Bell, Whataburger, Wing Boss, Zoup!, Courtyard, Drury Inn, Great Wolf Lodge, Hampton Inn, Holiday Inn Express, Residence Inn, SpringHIll Suites, WoodSpring Suites, Firestone, Scheels

152 W scenic overlook on sb

151 Briargate Pkwy, E Conoco/7-11, Bad Daddy's, Biaggi's, Chuy's, Dave&Buster's, Marco's Pizza, Panera Bread, PF Changs, Qdoba, Starbucks, Ted's MT Grill, Ziggi's Coffee, Hilton Garden, Homewood Suites, AT&T, to Black Forest, Verizon

150b a CO 83, Academy Blvd, E Circle K/dsl, Valero, Applebee's, Buffalo Wild Wings, Cane's, Chick-fil-A, Chipotle Mexican, Coldstone, Cracker Barrel, Culver's, Del Taco, Dutch Bros, Einstein Bagels, Firehouse Subs, First Watch, Five Guys, IHOP, Jimmy John's, McDonald's, Mimi's Café, MOD Pizza, Noodles&Co, Olive Garden, On-the-Border, Panera Bread, Pei Wei, Red Robin, Salt Grass Steaks, Schlotzsky's, Subway, Tropical Smoothie, Wendy's, Academy Hotel, Baymont, EconoLodge, Hampton Inn, LaQuinta, Motel 6, Olympia Inn, Studio 6, Super 8, $Tree, AT&T, Barnes&Noble, Best Buy, Brakes+, Chevrolet, Dick's, Dillard's, Firestone/auto, Ford, Hobby Lobby, Home Depot, Hyundai, Jiffy Lube, Kia, King's Sooper, Macy's, Marshall's, Michael's, Midas, O'Reilly Parts, Office Depot, Old Navy, PepBoys, PetSmart, REI, Ross, Sam's Club/gas, to Peterson AFB, URGENT CARE, Verizon, VW, Walmart/Subway, Whole Foods Mkt, W S Entrance to USAF Academy

149 Woodmen Rd, E Maverik, Carl's Jr, Carraba's, ViewHouse, Nissan, W Circle K/dsl, Old Chicago Pizza, Outback Steaks, Best Western+, Comfort Inn, Embassy Suites, Fairfield Inn, Hilton, Holiday Inn Express, Staybridge Suites, U-Haul

148 Corporate Ctr Dr, Nevada Ave, E BJ's Rest., Bonefish Grill, Chipotle Mexican, Hacienda Colorado, Noodles&Co, Panera Bread, Smashburger, Starbucks, Tokyo Joe's Grill, The Lodges, BMW, Costco/gas, Harley-Davidson, H, Kohl's, Lexus, Lowe's, Petco, Trader Joe's, W Circle K, Extended Stay America, InTown Suites, Marriott, to Rodeo Hall of Fame

146 Garden of the Gods Rd, E Circle K/dsl, Conoco, Carl's Jr, Caspian Cafe, Drifter's Burgers, McDonald's, La Quinta, Aamco, W Conoco/7-11, Exxon/dsl, Arby's, Arceo's Mexican, Cane's, Chick-fil-A, Dutch Bros, Freddy's Steakburgers, Jimmy John's, Mollica's Italian, Qdoba, Taco Bell, Village Inn, Wendy's, Days Inn, Hyatt Place, Quality Inn, Super 8, $Tree, AutoZone, Discount Tire, URGENT CARE, vet

145 CO 38 E, Fillmore St, E Conoco/7-11, Valero, Aloha HA BBQ, Arby's, Burger King, DQ, Dunkin, Jersey Mike's, Jimmy John's, Lucky Dragon, McDonald's, Monica's Taco Shop, Sonic, Starbucks, Taco Bell, Budget Host, Advance Parts, AutoZone, Brakes+, H, O'Reilly Parts, U-Haul, Walgreens, W Kum&Go/dsl, Waffle House, Best Western+, Extended Stay, Motel 6, Super 8

144 Fontanero St

143 Uintah St, E 7-11, W Sinclair, 7-11, King Soopers, Petco, Walgreens

142 Bijou St, Bus Dist, E Hilton Garden, The Antlers Hotel, Firestone, W Holiday Inn Express

141 US 24 W, Cimarron St, to Manitou Springs, W Conoco, Shell, Sinclair/dsl, Arby's, Jersey Mike's, Joey's NY Pizza,

PETERSON AFB

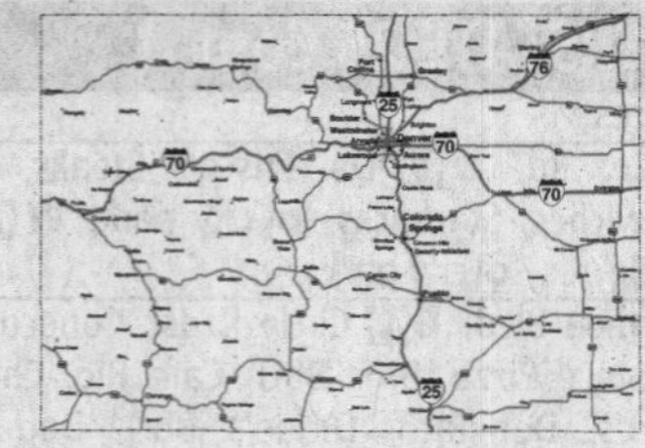

141 Continued
La Casita Mexican, McDonald's, Miguel's Mexican, Rocha' Mexican, Scooter's Coffee, Sonic, TX Roadhouse, Acura Audi, AutoZone, Brakes+, Buick/GMC, Cadillac, Chevrolet Chrysler/Dodge/Jeep, Discount Tire, Ford, Grease Monkey Hobby Lobby, Hyundai, Infiniti, Kia, Land Rover/Jagua Lincoln, Mazda, Meineke, Mercedes, NAPA, Office Depot Porsche, Subaru, Tesla, to Pikes Peak, Toyota/Scion, Volvo VW, Walmart

140b US 85 S, Tejon St, W Gas&Grass, Paris Crepe

140a Nevada Ave, E Maverik/dsl, Chateau Motel, Howar Johnson, repair, W 7-11, Valero, Angry Chicken Arceo's Mexican, Burger King, Chick-fil-A, Chipotle Mexican Dominos, Dunkin', Five Guys, Fuzzy's Tacos, IHOP, KFC McDonald's, Mexico Real, MOD Pizza, Noodles&Co, On th Border, Panda Express, Panera Bread, Qdoba, Red Robin Starbucks, Subway, Taco Bell, Wendy's, Rodeway Inn Travel Star Inn, $Tree, Advance Parts, Michael's, Midas Natural Grocers, O'Reilly Parts, PetSmart, Ross, Safeway Foods, Walgreens

139 US 24 E, to Lyman, Peterson AFB

138 CO 29, Circle Dr, E Phillips 66, Shell/Circle K/dsl, McDonald's, SPC, Kohl's, URGENT CARE, W Conoco/7-11, Arby's, Aspen Grill, Baskin-Robbins, Buffal Wild Wings, Carl's Jr, Carrabba's, Chili's, ChuckeCheese Culver's, Fazoli's, Macaroni Grill, Old Chicago Pizza, Outbac Steaks, Smoothie King, Subway, Best Western, Courtyard DoubleTree Hotel, Fairfield Inn, Hampton Inn, Home2 Suites La Quinta, Quality Inn, Residence Inn, AT&T, PetCo, Target

135 CO 83, Academy Blvd, E to, W Arby's, Freddy's Jersey Mike's, MOD Pizza, Panda Express, Qdoba, Starbucks Holiday Inn Express, Cheyenne Mtn SP, Ft Carson Sam's Club/gas, Verizon, Walmart

132 CO 16, Wide Field Security, E Love's/Subway/Godfathers dsl, Microtel, Camping World RV Ctr, KOA, Windish RV Ctr

128 to US 85 N, Fountain, Security, E 7-11, Loaf'n Jug Subway/dsl, Ute Hotel, Family$, USPO, W Tomahawk/Exxon/rest./dsl/24hr/@, Fountain Inn, Supe 8, Freightliner

125 Ray Nixon Rd

123 no services

122 to Pikes Peak Meadows, W Pikes Peak Intn'l Raceway

119 Rancho Colorado Blvd, Midway

116 county line rd

115mm **full facilities, litter barrels, petwalk, (picnic), nb**

114 Young Hollow

112mm **full facilities, litter barrels, petwalk, (picnic), sb**

110 Pinon, W atm

108 Purcell Blvd, Bragdon, E racetrack, W KOA

106 Porter Draw

104 Eden, W Love's/Chester's/Subway/dsl/scales/24hr, Peterbilt

102 Eagleridge Blvd, E Loaf'n Jug/dsl, Burger King Subway, TX Roadhouse, Candlewood Suites, Holiday Inn Express, Big O Tire, Home Depot, Sam's Club/gas, W Conoco/dsl, Buffalo Wild Wings, Cactus Flower Mexican Chili's, Cracker Barrel, Habanero's Grill, IHOP, Starbucks,

BRAGDON

 = gas = food = lodging = other = rest stop

INTERSTATE 25 Cont'd

102 Continued Village Inn, Wonderful Bistro, Best Western+, EconoLodge, Extended Stay, Hampton Inn, La Quinta, Quality Inn, Travelodge, Wingate Inn, Best Buy, Cavender's Boots, Dick's, frontage rds access 101, Harley-Davidson, Kohl's, PetCo

101 US 50 W, Pueblo, E Capt D's, Coldstone, Margaritas Mexican, Ruby Tuesday, Baymont Inn, Barnes&Noble, CO Tire, Dillard's, JC Penney, Jo-Ann, PetSmart, Ross, Target, TJ Maxx, U-Haul, Verizon, Walmart/Subway, W Circle K/dsl, Conoco/7-11, Loaf'n Jug/dsl, Shell/dsl, Applebee's, Arby's, Arriba Mexican, Blackeyed Pea, Carl's Jr, Chick-fil-A, Chipotle Mexican, Country Kitchen, DQ, Fazoli's, GG's BBQ, Golden Corral, Jack-in-the-Box, KFC, McAlister's Deli, McDonald's, Noodles&Co, Old Chicago, Olive Garden, Papa John's, Papa Murphy's, Pass Key Italian, Pizza Hut, Popeyes, Red Lobster, Rosario's Italian, Simple Simon Pizza, Starbucks, Subway, SW Grill, Taco Bell, The Firepit Rest., Wendy's, Wingstop, Clarion, Comfort Inn, Days Inn, Motel 6, Super 8, Aamco, Advance Parts, Albertson's, AT&T, AutoZone, Brakes+, Chevrolet, Chrysler/Dodge/Jeep, Discount Tire, EmergiCare, Ford/Lincoln, frontage rds access 102, Kia/Mazda, Lowe's, Midas, NAPA, Nissan, O'Reilly Parts, Staples, Topper RV, Toyota, Verizon, vet, Walgreens

100b 29th St, Pueblo, E Dominos, Los Girasoles Mexican, Mongolian Grill, $Tree, Hobby Lobby, King's Soopers, Natural Grocers, Peerless Tires, RNR Tire, W Conoco, Pueblo Dragon, Sonic, USA Motel, Family$, Grease Monkey

100a US 50 E, to La Junta, E Loaf'n Jug/dsl, Shell, Little Caesar's, Los Carnales Mexican, McDonald's, Pizza Hut, Spectators Grill, Wendy's, Advance Parts, AutoZone, Belmont Tire/repair, Save-A-Lot Foods, Walgreens

99b a Santa Fe Ave, 13th St, downtown, W Chelsey's Burgers, Subway, Taco Bell, Wendy's, Bramble Tree Inn, Santa Fe Inn, Buick/Cadillac/GMC, Honda, H

98b CO 96, 1st St, Union Ave Hist Dist, Pueblo, W Loaf'n Jug/dsl, Bingo Burger, Carl's Jr, Courtyard, SpringHill Suites, TownePlace Suites

98a US 50E bus, to La Junta, W El Pampano Mexican, Sonic

97b Abriendo Ave

97a Central Ave, W Alta/dsl, onoco, McDonald's, $General

96 Indiana Ave, W El Charro, H

95 Illinois Ave(from sb), W to dogtrack

94 CO 45 N, Pueblo Blvd, E Maverik, W Loaf'n Jug/dsl, Phillis 66/dsl, Culver's, Subway, Taco Bell, Hampton Inn, Microtel, Discount Tire, Forts RV Park, to Lake Pueblo SP

91 Stem Beach

88 Burnt Mill Rd

87 Verde Rd

83 no services

77 Hatchet Ranch Rd, Cedarwood

74 CO 165 W, Colo City, **full facilities, litter barrels, petwalk,** both lanes, **vending**, E Shamrock/deli/dsl/24hr, High Octane BBQ, KOA, W Exxon/Subway/dsl, Bolt Burgers, Three Sisters Grill, Days Inn/rest.

71 Graneros Rd

67 to Apache

64 Lascar Rd

60 Huerfano

59 Butte Rd

56 Redrock Rd

55 Airport Rd

52 CO 69 W, to Alamosa, Walsenburg, W Conoco/dsl, TA/Phillips 66/A&W/dsl, George's Rest., KFC/Taco Bell, Best Western, San Luis Valley, to Great Sand Dunes NM

50 CO 10 E, to La Junta, E TC's Diner, W Conoco/7-11, Loaf'n Jug/dsl, Carl's Jr, Subway, La Plaza, $General, CarQuest, H, O'Reilly Parts, Safeway, USPO

49 Lp 25, to US 160 W, Walsenburg, E Love's/Subway/Godfather's/dsl/scales/24hr, W Conoco, Loaf'n Jug/dsl, Carl's Jr., Corine's Mexican, La Plaza Hotel, Subway, $General, CarQuest, CarQuest, Cuchara Ski Valley, Lathrop SP, Safeway

42 Rouse Rd, to Pryor

41 Rugby Rd

34 Aguilar

30 Aguilar Rd, W Gears RV Park

27 Ludlow, W Ludlow Memorial

23 Hoehne Rd

18 El Moro Rd, **full facilities, litter barrels, petwalk,** both lanes

15 US 350 E, Goddard Ave, E Burger King, Pizza Hut, Super 8, AutoZone, Big R Ranch Store, Family$, H, W Shell/dsl, county fairgrounds

14 Commercial St, downtown, Trinidad, same as 13b

13b Main St, Trinidad, E **CO Welcome Ctr**, Exxon/dsl, Bella Luna Pizza, KFC/Taco Bell, McDonald's, Mission at the Bell Mexican, Moose's Grill, Sonic, Starbucks, Sunset Grille, The Sub Shop, Trinidad BBQ, Days Inn, Hilton Garden, Travelodge, CarQuest, H, Safeway Foods/dsl, W Conoco/dsl, Dominos, Habaneros Mexican, Monument Lake, Trinidad Lake

13a Santa Fe Trail, Trinidad, E Sunset Grille, Days Inn, Cawthon RV Park

11 Starkville, E Shell/Wendy's/dsl/24hr, Tequila's Mexican, Budget Host, Holiday Inn Express, Tower 64 Hotel, Summit RV Park, to Santa Fe Trail, weigh/check sta, W La Quinta, Quality Inn, Big O Tires, O'Reilly Parts, Walmart

8 Springcreek

6 Gallinas

2 Wootton

1mm scenic area pulloff nb

0mm Colorado/New Mexico state line, Raton Pass

INTERSTATE 70

450mm Colorado/Kansas state line

438 US 24, Rose Ave, Burlington, N Hi-Lo Motel, $General, Bomgaars, CarQuest, Family$, H, NAPA, O'Reilly Parts, Outback RV Park, S Sinclair/dsl/24hr, truck repair

437.5mm **full facilities, historical site, info, litter barrels, petwalk,** **Welcome Ctr wb**

437 US 385, Burlington, N Phillips 66/dsl, Arby's, Dish Room, McDonald's, Pizza Hut, Ziggi's Coffee, Burlington Inn, Burlington Stay Inn, Chaparral Motel, Quality Inn, Sloan's Hotel, Western Motel, CarQuest, Chevrolet/GMC, Family$, Ford, H, NAPA, Safeway, S Love's/Carl's Jr/dsl/scales/24hr@, Best Western+, Econolodge, Fairfield Inn

429 Bethune

419 CO 57, Stratton, N Cenex/dsl, Conoco/dsl, Handi's Burgers, Claremont Inn/café, Travelodge, Gypsy RV Camping, Marshall Ash Village Camping, USPO

412 Vona

405 CO 59, Seibert, N Shady Grove Camping/RV dump, S Valero/dsl, tire repair

395 Flagler, N Loaf'N Jug/dsl, I-70 Diner, Little England Motel, $General, Flagler SWA, NAPA, S Cenex/dsl

383 Arriba, **both lanes full facilities**, N DJ/dsl, S **litter barrels, petwalk,**

WALSENBURG · TRINIDAD · BURLINGTON · PUEBLO · CEDARWOOD · CO

= gas = food = lodging = other = rest stop

CO

LIMON

BENNETT

INTERSTATE 70 Cont'd

Exit #	Services
376	Bovina
371	Genoa, N Genoa RV Park
363	US 24, US 40, US 287, to CO 71, to Hugo, Limon
361	CO 71, Limon, N Ace Hardware, S Shell/Wendy's/dsl, Sinclair/dsl, Coyote Motel, KOA, NAPA
360.5mm	weigh/check sta both lanes
359	to US 24, to CO 71, Limon, N Flying J/IHOP/dsl/scales/LP/24hr, La Quinta, dsl repair, RV camping, S Cenex/dsl, Sinclair/dsl, TA/Phillips 66/Subway/Country Pride/dsl/scales/24hr/@, Arby's, McDonald's, Oscar's Grill, Taco Bell, Baymont Inn, Best Western, Comfort Inn, Holiday Inn Express, Motel 6, Quality Inn, Super 8, Chrysler/Dodge/Jeep, Romad RV Camp
354	no services
352	CO 86 W, to Kiowa
348	to Cedar Point
340	Agate, S USPO
336	to Lowland
332mm	**wb, full facilities, litter barrels, vending, petwalk, info**
328	to Deer Trail, N Deer Trail/dsl, Del Sol Mexican, S Conoco/dsl, USPO
325mm	East Bijou Creek
323.5mm	Middle Bijou Creek
322	Peoria
316	US 36 E, Byers, N Sinclair/dsl, Budget Host, Byers Gen. Store, S Shooters Grill, USPO
310	Strasburg, N Conoco/dsl, 7 Leguas Mexican, Denver BBQ, Pizza at Rookies, dsl/auto repair, KOA, NAPA, USPO, vet, Western Hardware
306	Kiowa, Bennett
305	Kiowa
304	CO 79 N, Bennett, N Love's/McDonald's/dsl/scales/24hr, QT/dsl, Bennett Asian, Carl's Jr, High Plains Diner, Sonic, Subway, Taco Bell, Comfort Inn, $General, Family$, King Soopers/gas, O'Reilly Parts, Schwab Tire, USPO, S Ace Hardware
299	CO 36, Manila Rd, S Circle K/dsl
295	Lp 70, Watkins, N Conoco, Shell/dsl/24hr/@, Lulu's Cafe, Country Manor Motel, USPO
292	CO 36, Airpark Rd
289	E-470 Tollway, 120th Ave, CO Springs
288	US 287, US 40, Lp 70, Colfax Ave(exits left from wb)
286	CO 32, Tower Rd, N Murphy Express/dsl, Chick-fil-A, Chili's, Chipotle Mexican, Del Taco, DQ, Firehouse Subs, Five Guys, Garibaldi Mexican, Mondo's Pizza, Noodles&Co, Panda Express, Starbucks, Wendy's, Wingstop, $Tree, AT&T, Best Buy, Brakes+, Discount Tire, GNC, Home Depot, Les Schwab Tire, O'Reilly Parts, PetCo, Walmart/Subway
285	Airport Blvd, N Denver Int, S Flying J/Denny's/dsl/scales/24hr, McDonald's, Quality Inn, SYLO Hotel, Harley-Davidson
284	I-225 N(from eb)
283	Chambers Rd, N Phillips 66, Shell/Circle K/Popeyes, A&W/KFC, Anthony's Pizza, Applebees, Einstein Bros, Jimmy John's, Outback Steaks, Pizza Hut, Qdoba, Sonic, Starbucks, Subway, Taco Bell, Ted's MT Grill, Urban Sombrero, Wendy's, Zume Asian, Aloft Hotel, Cambria Suites, Country Inn&Suites, Crowne Plaza, Econolodge, Hampton Inn, Hilton Garden, Homewood Suites, Hyatt Place, Marriott, Residence Inn, TownePlace Suites, Woolley's Suites, U-haul, S Circle K, Burger King, Jack-in-the-Box, Extended Stay, HomeTowne Suites, Lazy Days RV Ctr, URGENT CARE
282	I-225 S, to Colorado Springs
281	Peoria St, N Conoco/7-11, Phillips 66/dsl, Shell/dsl, Burger King, Chipotle, Domino's, Dutch Bros, El Patror GoodTimes Burgers, La Bocaza Mexican, McDonald's Popeyes, Real De Minas, Starbucks, Subway, Taco Bell, Tac Star, Tony Roma, Best Western, Comfort Inn, Holiday In Express, La Quinta, Big O Tire, Family$, S Phillips 66 dsl, Shamrock/dsl, Ay Cabron, Denny's, Ho Mei Chinese Motel 6, OYO, Star Hotel, auto/RV repair
280	Havana St, N Embassy Suites, S Conoco
279b	Central Ave, N Cane's Chicken, Chili's, Freddy's Burgers In-N-Out, MOD Pizza, Smoothie King, Drury Inn, Home Suites, Residence Inn, S QT, Cheba Hut, Fuzzy's Tacos Ike's Love Sandwiches, Wndy's
279	I-270 W, US 36 W(from wb), to Ft Collins, Boulder
278	CO 35, Quebec St, N Sapp Bros/Sinclair/Subway/dsl/@ TA/dsl/rest./24hr/@, Bar Louie, Bonchon Asian, Brother Grill, Coldstone, Cuba Cuba, Del Taco, Five Guys, HuHo MBBQ, Jim'N Nicks BBQ, Marco's Pizza, Menchie's, Oliv Garden, Qdoba, Starbucks, Subway, Tokyo Joe's, Torchy' Tacos, TX de Brazil, TX Roadhouse, Wahoo's, Waldo' Chicken, Best Western, Comfort Inn, Staybridge Suites, Bass Pro Shops, JC Penney, Macys, Old Navy, Target, S Walmart Gas, Arby's, Buffalo Wild Wings, Dominos Famous Dave's BBQ, Hook & Reel Seafood, IHOP, Jimm John's, La Mariposa, McDonald's, Panda Express, Paner Bread, Papa John's, Smashburger, Sonic, Subway, Bes Western, Courtyard, DoubleTree Hilton, Holiday Inr Renaissance Inn, Super 8, AT&T, Brakes+, GNC, Hom Depot, Office Depot, PetSmart, Ross, Sam's Club, Tires+, ve Walgreens, Walmart/Subway
277	to Dahlia St, Holly St, Monaco St, frontage rd
276b	US 6 E, US 85 N, CO 2, Colorado Blvd, S Phillips 66/dsl, Carl's Jr, Domino's, Neko Ramen, Popeyes, Qdoba, Starbucks
276a	Vasquez Ave, N Western Inn, Goodyear, S Conoco 7-11, Burger King, NAPA
275c	York St(from eb)
275b	CO 265, Brighton Blvd, Coliseum
275a	Washington St(from wb), N Conoco/7-11, Pizza Hut, Phillips 66/dsl, McDonald's, Best Western
274b a	I-25, N to Cheyenne, S to Colorado Springs
273	Pecos St, N Conoco/7-11/dsl, Family$, SavALot Foods S Conoco/7-11, Quiznos, Autocare
272	US 287, Federal Blvd, N Maverik, Phillips 66/dsl, Sinclai Burger King, Church's Chicken, Goodtimes Burgers, Littl Caesar's, McCoy's Rest., McDonald's, Rico Pollo, Subway Taco Bell, Viva Burrito, Wendy's, Winchell's, Motel 6, 7-11, Advance Parts, tires, S Conoco/Mkt/dsl, La Fuente Popeyes, Starbucks
271b	Lowell Blvd, Tennyson St(from wb)
271a	CO 95, S funpark
270	Sheridan Blvd, N Shell/dsl, S Murphy Express/dsl, Carl's Jr., Dominos, El Paraiso Mexican, Grammy's Italian Laredo Tacos, Popeyes, Wingstop, $Tree, Firestone/auto fun park, Schwab Tire, Walmart
269b	I-76 E(from eb), to Ft Morgan, Ft Collins
269a	CO 121, Wadsworth Blvd, N 7-11, Exxon/7-11, Shell/ds Applebee's, Bad Daddy Burger, BeauJo's, Bennet's BBQ CAVA, Chick-fil-A, Chipotle Mexican, Einstein Bros,

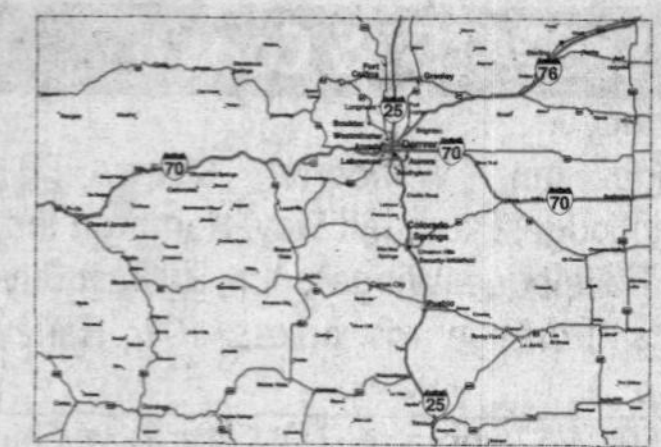

BOULDER

COLISEUM

INTERSTATE 70 Cont'd

Exit	Services
269a	Continued El Pollo Loco, El Tapatio Mexican, HuHot, IHOP, Jersey Mike's, King Buffet, Kokoro Japanese, Kona HBBQ, McDonald's/playplace, Menchie's, Noodles&Co, Parry's Pizza, Red Robin, Smashburger, Snarf Sandwiches, Snooze, Starbucks, Subway, Taco Bell, TX Roadhouse, Umai-Ya Japanese, Hilton Garden, Residence Inn, $Tree, Advance Parts, Big O Tire, Brakes+, city park, Costco/gas, Discount Tire, Home Depot, Lowe's, Midas, PetSmart, Sam's Club, URGENT CARE
267	CO 391, Kipling St, Wheat Ridge, N Circle K/dsl, Sinclair, Burger King, Denny's, Einstein Bros, Fat Shack, Jack-in-the-Box, Jersey Mike's, Lil Nick's Pizza, Luke's Steaks, Margarita's Mexican, Panda Express, Popeyes, Qdoba, Starbucks, Subway, American Inn, Motel 6, 7-11, AT&T, Cadillac/Chevrolet, GNC, NAPA, Natural Grocers, repair, Target, Verizon, vet, S Phillps 66/dsl, Shell, Joe Mama's, La Hopot, Taco Bell, Winchell's, Apple Inn, Best Value Inn, Comfort Inn, Holiday Inn Express, Super 8, Camping World RV Ctr
266	CO 72, W 44th Ave, Ward Rd, Wheat Ridge, N Mobil/dsl, transmissions, S TA/Country Pride/dsl/scales/24hr/@, Valero/dsl, Applewood RV Camping, Trailer Source RV Ctr
265	CO 58 W(from wb), to Golden, Central City
264	Youngfield St, W 32nd Ave, N Phillips 66/mkt, Denny's, GoodTimes Burgers, La Quinta, S Abrusci's Italian, Chick-fil-A, Chipotle, First Watch, Hacienda Mexican, Jersey Mike's, McDonald's, Noodles&Co, Starbucks, Taco Bell, Teriyaki Madness, Wendy's, Blue Compass RV Ctr, Hobby Lobby, King's Sooper/24hr, PetSmart, Valvoline, Walgreens
263	Denver West Blvd, N Marriott/rest., S BJ's Rest., Coldstone, Freddy's, Keg Steaks, Noodles&Co, Olive Garden, Qdoba, Red Robin, Tokyo Joe's, Twin Peaks, SpringHill Suites, Barnes&Noble, Best Buy, Old Navy, same as 262, Whole Foods Mkt
262	US 40 E, W Colfax, Lakewood, N Sinclair/dsl, El Tequileno Mexican, Jack-in-the-Box, Lil' Ricci's Cafe, Subway, Hampton Inn, Holiday Inn Express, Buick/GMC, Camping World RV Ctr, Chrysler/Jeep, Dodge, Home Depot, Honda, Hyundai, Kohl's, PetCo, Subaru, transmissions, U-Haul, S Circle K/dsl/LP, Bonefish Grill, Bono's Italian, Cafe Rio, Carrabba's, Chick-fil-A, Chipotle, Coriander Rest., Five Guys, Garbanzo Grill, Jimmy John's, Mod Mkt Eatery, Motomaki Sushi, Outback Steaks, Panera Bread, Pei Wei Asian, Qdoba, Tokyo Joe's, Wendy's, Which Wich?, Yard House, Aiden Hotel, Courtyard, Residence Inn, Chevrolet, Lexus, mall, Marshall's, Old Navy, same as 263, Target, Toyota, Verizon, World Mkt
261	US 6 E(from eb), W 6th Ave, to Denver
260	CO 470, to Colo Springs
259	CO 26, Golden, N Circle K/dsl, Maverik, Hampton Inn, Holiday Inn Express, Origin Hotel, Dakota Ridge RV Camping
257mm	runaway truck ramp eb
256	Lookout Mtn, N Buffalo Bill's Grave
254	Genesee, Lookout Mtn, S Conoco/Genesee Store, Chart House Rest., Genesee BBQ, Guido's Pizza
253	Chief Hosa, S Chief Hosa Lodge, RV Camping
252	(251 from eb), CO 74, Evergreen Pkwy, S Phillips 66, El Rancho Colorado, Illegal Burger, Jimmy John's, Kalaka Mexican, McDonald's/playplace, Qdoba, Smiling Moose, Comfort Suites, Big O Tire, Echo Mtn Ski Area, Home Depot, Jiffy Lube, King Sooper(2mi), Walmart
248	(247 from eb), Beaver Brook, Floyd Hill
244	US 6, to CO 119, to Golden, Central City , Eldora Ski Area, N 2 Bears Grill
243	Hidden Valley, N Sinclair/dsl
242mm	tunnel
241b a	rd 314, Idaho Springs West, N Conoco/dsl, Exxon/dsl, Phillips 66/McDonald's/dsl, Carl's Jr, Eric's Asian, Marion's Rest., Picci's Pizzaria, Smokin' Yards BBQ, Starbucks, Subway, 6&40 Motel, Argo Inn, Columbine Inn, H&H Motel, Idaho Springs Hotel, Lift Landing, Uplift Inn, CarQuest, NAPA, Safeway Foods/Drug, USPO
240	CO 103, Mt Evans, N Kum&Go/dsl, Shell/dsl, Sinclair/dsl, 2 Bros Deli, Azteca Mexican, Banana Leaf, Beau Jo's Pizza, Main St Rest., Pickaxe Pizza, Tommy Knocker Grill, vet, S to Mt Evans
239	Idaho Springs
238	Fall River Rd, to St Mary's Glacier
235	Dumont(from wb), N Conoco, S rafting
234	Downeyville, Dumont, weigh sta both lanes, N Sinclair/Subway/dsl, Taco Bell
233	Lawson(from eb), S Lawson Adventure Resort, Whitewater Park
232	US 40 W, to Empire
228	Georgetown, S Circle K/dsl, Exxon/dsl, Shell/dsl, Copper's on the Creek, Georgetown Lodge, Microtel Inn, chain up area, Family$, Georgetown Lake, park, visitors ctr
226.5mm	no services
226	Georgetown, Silver Plume Hist Dist, N USPO, S Georgetown Railroad & Mining park
221	Bakerville
220mm	no services
219	parking area (eb only)
218	no services
216	US 6 W, Loveland Valley, Loveland Basin
214mm	Eisenhower/Johnson Tunnel, elev 11013
213mm	parking area eb
205	US 6 E, CO 9 N, Dillon, Silverthorne, N Exxon, Kum&Go/dsl, Phillips66/7-11, Sinclair/dsl, Tesla EVC, Chipotle Mexican, Dunkin, Mint Cafe, Wendy's, Which Wich?, Days Inn, Hotel Indigo, La Quinta, Luxury Suites, Quality Inn, Silver Inn, Advance Parts, AutoZone, CarQuest, Chrysler/Dodge/Jeep, Ford, Lowe's, Murdoch's, Outlet Mall, Subaru, Target, S Conoco, Shell/dsl, Bamboo Garden, Blue Moon Deli, Chimayo Burrito, Dam Brewery/Rest., Einstein Bagels, Fiesta Mexican, McDonald's, Nick'n Willy's Pizza, Noodles&Co, Nozawa Japanese, Panera Bread, Qdoba, Red Mtn Grill, SmashBurger, Snarf's Sandwiches, Subway, Sunshine Cafe, Comfort Suites, Dillon Inn, Hampton Inn, Super 8, Ace Hardware, City Mkt Foods/gas, Outlets/famous brands, Petco, REI, TJ Maxx, Verizon, Walgreens
203.5mm	scenic overlook both lanes
203	CO 9 S, to Breckenridge, Frisco, S Conoco/7-11, Exxon/Wendy's/dsl, Kum&Go, Valero/Circle K/dsl, Cielo Mexican, Hacienda Real Mexican, KFC, Los Adobes Mexican, Starbucks, Starbucks, Subway, Szechuan Chinese, Taco Bell, Which Wich, AC Hotel Frisco, Alpine Inn, Ramada Ltd, Summit Inn, The Grand Hotel, auto repair, Big O Tire, NAPA, Natural Grocers, RV Resort(6mi), Safeway Foods, Utopia Tire/auto, Verizon, vet, Walmart, Whole Foods Mkt
201	Main St, Frisco, S Loaf N' Jug, Bagali's Italian, Butterhorn Cafe, Casa Sanchez, Frisco Emporium, Greco's Pastaria, Lost Cajun Rest., Moosejaw Cafe, Uptown on Main, Frisco Lodge, Hotel Frisco, Snowshoe Motel, museum/visitor info, RV camping, to Breckenridge Ski Area, USPO
198	Officers Gulch, restrooms
196mm	scenic area (wb only)
195	CO 91 S, to Leadville, S Conoco/dsl, Copper Lodging,

= gas = food = lodging = other = rest stop

INTERSTATE 70 Cont'd

Exit	Services
195	Continued to Copper Mtn Ski Resort
190	**full facilities, litter barrels, , , both lanes**
189mm	elev 10662 ft, parking area both lanes, Vail Pass Summit
180	Vail East Entrance, services 3-4 mi S
176	Vail, **S** , ski info/lodging
173	Vail Ski Area, **N** Phillips 66, Shell/dsl, May Palace, McDonald's, Qdoba, Starbucks, Westside Cafe, Double Tree, Ace Hardware, City Mkt Foods/deli, Safeway Food/Drug, USPO, **S** Conoco/dsl/LP, Marriott/Streamside Hotel
171	US 6 W, US 24 E, to Minturn, Leadville, **N** Ski Cooper ski area, **S** Shell, Crazy Chicken, Kirby Cosmo's BBQ, Magusto's Italian, Minturn Steaks, Rocky Mtn Taco, Thai Kitchen, Hotel Minturn, Minturn Inn, Minturn Mtn, RV Camping, USPO
169	Eaglevale, from wb
168	William J. Post Blvd, **N** Maverik, SpringHill Suites, **S** Shell, Sauce on the Creek, Home Depot, Verizon, Walmart/McDonald's
167	Avon, **N** Exxon/7-11/dsl, Shell, Northside Kitchen, vet, **S** Boxcar Rest., Burger King, Domino's, Fattoria Italian, Fiesta Jalisco Mexican, Gondola Pizza, Mazatlan Mexican, Montana's Smokehouse, Nozawa Sushi, Pazzo's Pizza, Starbucks, Subway, Avon Ctr Lodge, Beaver Creek, Christie Lodge, Comfort Inn, Sheraton, Westin, Wyndham, City Mkt/drugs, ski info, to Beaver Creek/Arrowhead Ski, URGENT CARE, USPO, Walgreens
163	Edwards, **full facilities, litter barrel, , both lanes, RV dump, S** Conoco/dsl, Shell/Wendy's/dsl, Boardroom Deli, Craftsman Brewery, Drunken Goat, Etown Colorado, Fiestas Cafe, Gashouse Rest., Henry's Chinese, il Mago Italian, Main St Grill, Marko's Pizza, Smiling Moose, Starbucks, Zino's Italian, Riverwalk Inn, AT&T, to Arrowhead Ski Area, Valvoline, vet, Village Mkt
162.5mm	parking area eb
162mm	parking area/toilets wb
159mm	Eagle River
157	CO 131 N, Wolcott
147	Eagle, **full facilities, info, both lanes, N** Kum&Go/dsl, Pizzaone, Ti Amigo, Quality Inn, Wingate, City Mkt Foods, **S** Conoco/dsl, Shell/dsl, Sinclair/Subway/dsl, Casa Mexico, Eagle Diner, Gourmet China, Grand Ave Grill, Moe's Original BBQ, Pazzo's Pizzaria, Primavera Mexican, Taco Bell, Wendy's, Best Western, Eagle Lodge&Suites, Extended Stay, AutoZone, Costco/dsl, NAPA, USPO, vet
140	Gypsum, **S** Kum&Go/dsl, Shell/dsl, Asian Fusion, Cowboy's Kitchen, Ehaki HI Grill, Mi Favorita, Tu Casa Mexican, , Down Valley Tire, Family$, O'Reilly Parts, Ridley's Mkt, River Dance RV Camping, USPO, vet
134mm	Colorado River
133	Dotsero, **N** camping, river tubing, truck parking
129	Bair Ranch, **full facilities, litter barrels, petwalk, , both lanes, S** UTV Tours
126mm	Hanging Lake Tunnel
125	to Hanging Lake(no return eb)
123	Shoshone(no return eb)
122.5mm	exit to river(no return eb)
121	to Hanging Lake, Grizzly Creek, **full facilities, litter barrels, , both lanes**
119	No Name, **full facilities, rafting, both lanes, RV camping, S** Glenwood Canyon Resort
118mm	No Name Tunnel
116	CO 82 E, to Aspen, Glenwood Springs, **N** Kum&Go/dsl,

VAIL · AVON · WOLCOTT · BAIR RANCH

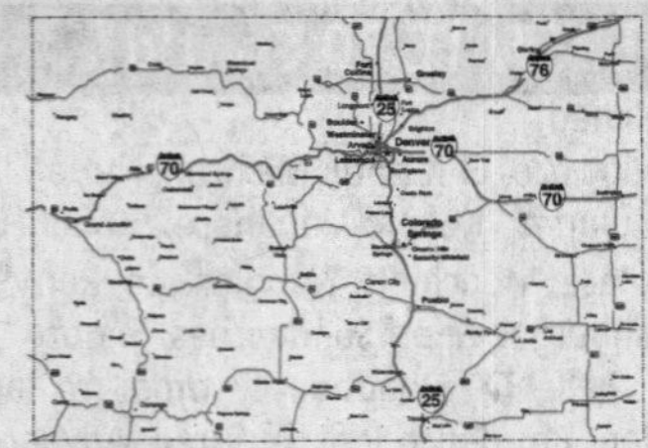

Exit	Services
116	Continued Chomps, Qdoba, Rosi's Bavarian, Tequilas Rest., Village Inn, Best Western, Glenwood Springs Inn, Glenwood Spring Lodge, Hampton Inn, Holiday Inn Express, Hotel Colorado, Hotel Glenwood Springs, La Quinta, Silver Spruce Motel, Starlight Motel, Hot Springs Bath, Land Rover, **S** Circle K/dsl, Conoco, Phillips 66, Sinclair, 19th St Diner, Bluebir Cafe, Brava Italian, Chocolate Moose Creamery, Daily Bread, Doc Holliday's Grill, Domino's, Frida Mexican, Grind Burgers, Italian Underground, Jimmy John's, Las Margaritas, McDonald's, Riviera Supper, Rocky Mtn Pizza, Smok Modern BBQ, Starbucks, Taco Bell, The Pullman, Uncle Pizza, Wendy's, Glewood Springs, Hotel Maxwell, Alpine Tire, AutoZone, B.Thornal DDS, Chrysler/Dodge/Jeep, City Mk Foods, city park, , Midas, NAPA, REI, Ski Sunlight, USPO, Verizon, vet, Walmart
114	W Glenwood Springs, **N** 7-11, Exxon/Arby's/dsl, Culver's, Jilberito's Mexican, Vicco's Charcoal Burger, Adventure Inn, Hanging Lake Inn, Ponderosa Motel, Ami' RV Camping, Big O Tire, Carquest, Chevrolet, Discount Tire, Ford, Honda, O'Reilly Parts, Ross, Subaru, Toyota, **S** Kum&Go/DQ/dsl, Chili's, Everest Neplanese, Russo' Pizza, Underbelly Burger, Zheng Asian, Comfort Inn, Courtyard, Quality Inn, Residence Inn, AT&T, Audi/VW, Bi 5 Sports, Harley-Davidson, Lowe's, Natural Grocers, PetCo, Target, TRUE auto repair, URGENT CARE, Verizon, whitewate rafting
111	South Canyon
109	no services
108mm	parking area eb
105	New Castle, **N** Conoco/dsl, Kum&Go/dsl, Hong' Garden, McDonald's, Tapatios, Wingate, City Mk Foods/deli, Elk Creek Campground, golf
97	Silt, **N** Kum&Go/dsl, Sinclair/dsl, Burning Mtn Subs, L Mora Pizza, Miner's Rest., Red River Inn, $General Family$, to Harvey Gap SP, **S** Golden Gate/dsl, Holida Inn Express, River Nest Resort, Heron's Nest RV Park, KOA
94	Garfield County Airport Rd
90	CO 13 N, Rifle, **full facilities, litter barrels, NF Info, both lanes, RV dump, N** Conoco/dsl, Kum&Go/dsl Wendy's, Brickhouse Pizza, Dickey's BBQ, Jalisco Mexican, Rama's Bistro, Tapatios Mexican, Thai Chili, Gatewa Lodge, Rifle Gap SP, USPO, **S** Kum&Go/dsl, Arby's, Culver's, Dunkin', Little Caesar's, McDonald's, Rib City BBQ, Sonic, Taco Bell, Wingchesters, Comfort Inn, Hampton Inn, La Quinta, Rodeway Inn, AutoZone, , O'Reilly Parts, Verizon, Walmart/auto
87	to CO 13, West Rifle
81	Rulison
75	Parachute, **full facilities, info, litter barrels, petwalk, , both lanes, N** CNG, Exxon/dsl, Sinclair/dsl, Tapatio Mexican, Hong's Garden Chinese, Nalini's Rest., Grand Vista, NAPA, USPO, vet, **S** Love's/Chester's scales/RV Hookup/dsl, Shell/Wendy's/dsl, Sinclair Domino's/dsl, Running Burrito, Shommy's Rest., Candlewood Suites, Grand River Hotel, Family$, R Park(4mi)
72	US 6, W Parachute

GLENWOOD SPRINGS · SILT · PARACHUTE

INTERSTATE 70 Cont'd

Exit #	Services
63mm	Colorado River
62	De Beque, N Kum&Go/dsl
50mm	Colorado River, parking area eb
49mm	Plateau Creek
49	CO 65 S, to CO 330 E, to Grand Mesa, S Powderhorn Ski Area
47	Island Acres St RA, N CO River SP, RV camping, S Exxon/dsl
46	Cameo
44	Lp 70 W, to Palisade, S food, gas, lodging
43.5mm	Colorado River
42	US 6, Palisade, S Golden Gate/dsl, Wine Country Inn, Fruitstand/store, wineries
37	to US 6, to US 50 S, Clifton, Grand Jct, S Conoco/dsl, Maverik/dsl, Shell/dsl, Sinclair/dsl, Arby's, Burger King, Chin Chin Oriental, China Jade, Chipotle, Denny's, Dos Hombres, Freddy's Burgers, Jimmy John's, KFC, McDonald's/playplace, Papa John's, Papa Murphy's, Pizza Hut, Popeyes, Qdoba, Randy's Diner, Sonic, Starbucks, Starvin Arvin's Steaks, Subway, Taco Bell, Taco John's, Wendy's, Best Western, Ace Hardware, AutoZone, City Mkt/dsl, Family$, Jiffy Lube, Murdoch's Store, O'Reilly Parts, repair, RV Ranch, URGENT CARE, USPO, vet, Walgreens
31	Horizon Dr, Grand Jct, N Shell/dsl, Blade and Bone Rest., Tepanyaki Rest., The Cutting Board, Wendy's, Best Value Inn, Clarion, Comfort Inn, Courtyard, Econolodge, Grand Vista Hotel, Holiday Inn, La Quinta, Motel 6, Ramada Inn, Residence Inn, Harley-Davidson, Horizon RV Park, Zarlingo's Repair, S Exxon/dsl, Shell/dsl, Applebee's, Aztecas, Denny's, Enzo's Pizza, Freddy's, Good Pastures Rest., PizzAmore, Sang Garden, Starbucks, Subway, Taco Bell, Days Inn, Days Inn, Doubletree Hotel, First Interstate Inn, Quality Inn, Studio 6, Super 8, golf, H, Mesa St Coll, Safeway Food/drug/gas, Shop'n Save, visitors ctr
28	Redlands Pkwy, 24 Rd, N Kenworth, S Arby's, Boston's Grill, Buffalo Wild Wings, Cafe Rio, Chili's, Chipotle Mexican, ChuckeCheese, Coldstone, Costa Vida, Culver's, Famous Dave's BBQ, Freddy's Burgers, IHOP, Jimmy John's, McDonald's/playplace, Mi Mexico, Mi Mexico, Mongolian Grill, Noodles&Co, Olive Garden, Outback Steaks, Panda Express, Red Lobster, Smokin' Oak Pizza, Starbucks, Subway, Taco Bell, Tequila's, Wendy's, Candlewood Suites, Holiday Inn Express, Home2 Suites, Woodspring Suites, $Tree, AT&T, AutoZone, Barnes&Noble, Best Buy, Big O Tire, Cabela's, City Mkt/dsl, city park, Firestone, Hobby Lobby, Home Depot, JC Penney, Kohl's, Lowe's, Mobile City RV Park, Natural Grocers, Office Depot, PetCo, PetSmart, Ross, Sam's Club/dsl, Sportsman's Whse, Sprouts Mkt, Subaru, Target, TJ Maxx, Verizon, VW, Walmart/McDonald's
26	US 6, US 50, Grand Jct, N Love's/Carl's Jr/dsl/scales/Lp/24hr/@, Pilot/PJ Fresh/dsl/scales/24hr, Hyundai, Jct W RV Park, S TA/Conoco/A&W/dsl, Red Roof Inn, Ford, Freightliner, Mobile City RV Park, Toyota
19	US 6, CO 340, Fruita, N Sinclair/dsl, Burger King, Fiesta Guadalajara, Balanced Rock Motel, City Mkt Foods/deli/24hr, city park, H, NAPA, USPO, Valvoline, Walgreens, S **full facilities, litter barrels, petwalk, RV dump, Welcome Ctr,** AMBest/dsl/scales/24hr, Exxon/dsl, Shell/Wendy's/dsl/24hr, DQ, Dragon Treasure Chinese, El Tapatio Mexican, Jimmy John's, McDonald's/playplace, Pablo's Pizza, Qdoba, Rib City Grill, Starbucks, Starvin Arvin's, Stayhorn Grill, Subway, Taco Bell, Comfort Inn, La Quinta, Super 8, dinosaur museum, Monument RV Park, Peterbilt, to CO NM, URGENT CARE, vet
17mm	Colorado River
15	CO 139 N, to Loma, Rangely, N to Highline Lake SP, S toilet
14.5mm	weigh/check sta both lanes
11	Mack
2	Rabbit Valley, N Trail Through Time
0mm	Colorado/Utah state line

CAMEO · FRUITA · MACK

INTERSTATE 76

Exit #	Services
185mm	I-76 begins/ends on NE I-80, exit 102.
184mm	Colorado/Nebraska state line
180	US 385, Julesburg, **Welcome Ctr/ both lanes, full facilities, info, RV dump,** N **RV dump,** Shell, Subway, Budget Host, H, S Conoco/dsl
172	Ovid
165	CO 59, to Haxtun, Sedgewick, N Lucy's Cafe
155	Red Lion Rd
149	CO 55, to Fleming, Crook, S Sinclair/dsl
141	Proctor
134	Iliff
125	US 6, Sterling, **both lanes full facilities, litter barrels, petwalk, vending, RV dump,** N Cenex, Cenex/dsl, Bamboo Garden, Burger King, Domino's, DQ, El Jacal Mexican, Forequarters BBQ, Jimmy John's, Little Caesar's, McDonald's, Papa Murphy's, Pizza Hut, Sonic, Starbucks, Subway, Taco Bell, Taco John's, Village Inn, Wendy's, 1st Interstate Inn, Best Western, Holiday Inn Express, $Tree, 7-11, Ace Hardware, AutoZone, Bomgaars, Buick/Chevrolet, Chrysler/Dodge/Jeep, Ford/Lincoln, Home Depot, H, museum, N Sterling SP, NAPA, O'Reilly Parts, st patrol, USPO, vet, vet, Walgreens, Walmart, S Reata/dsl, Budget Inn, Comfort Inn, Ramada Inn, Super 8, RV Camping
115	CO 63, Atwood, N Sinclair/dsl, S auto repair
102	Merino
95	Hillrose
92	to US 6 E, to US 34, CO 71 S
90b a	CO 71 N, to US 34, Brush, N Brush Trkstp/Shell/Subway/dsl/24hr, Tesla EVC, Tomahawk Truck Stop, Domino's, Wendy's, Rodeway Inn, S TA/Conoco/dsl, McDonald's, Boarders Inn
89	Hospital Rd, S Love's/Carl's Jr/dsl/scales/24hr, golf, H
86	Dodd Bridge Rd
82	Barlow Rd, N The Mav Grill, Best Western+, Comfort Inn, Rodeway Inn, Silver Spur Camping, S Reata/dsl/scales, Burger King, Fairfield Inn, $Tree, Walmart/Subway
80	CO 52, Ft Morgan, N City Park, Golf, GWSCX Locomotive 41, S Conoco/dsl, Maverik/dsl, Phillips 66/dsl, Sinclair/dsl, All About Smoke BBQ, Arby's, DQ, El Jacal Mexican, McDonald's, Sonic, Subway, Taco Bell, Taco John's, Wonderful House Chinese, Hampton Inn, Terrace Park Inn, AutoZone, Family$, H, Toyota, Verizon, Walgreens
79	CO 144, to Weldona, (no wb return)
75	US 34 E, to Ft Morgan, S Shell/pizza/dsl, Baymont Inn, Emerald RV Park
74.5mm	weigh sta both lanes
73	Long Bridge Rd
66b	US 34 W(from wb), to Greeley
66a	CO 39, CO 52, to Goodrich, **both lanes, full facilities, litter barrels, petwalk, vending,** N Shamrock/dsl, Jackson Lake SP, RV Camping, S Sinclair/cafe/dsl/e-85
64	Wiggins
60	to CO 144 E, to Orchard
57	rd 91
49	Painter Rd(from wb)
48	to Roggen, N Valero/dsl, S USPO
39	Keenesburg, N Maverik, S Shell/dsl, Keene Motel, CT Auto Service, Family$

CROOK · ATWOOD · FT MORGAN

CO

= gas = food = lodging = other = rest stop Copyright 2025 - the Next E

CO

BROMLEY

COMMERCE CITY

INTERSTATE 76 Cont'd

Exit #	Services
34	Kersey Rd
31	CO 52, Hudson, N Love's/Subway/Carl's Jr/scales/24hr/dsl/@, Ben's Pizza, Best Western+, S Conoco/dsl, Shell/dsl, Pepper Pod Rest., Pepper Pod Camping, USPO
25	CO 7, Lochbuie, N Exxon/dsl
22	Bromley, N Circle K/dsl, KFC, Wendy's, Hampton Inn, Lowe's, S Maverik/dsl, Barr Lake SP, Freightliner
21	144th Ave, Eagle Blvd, N Arby's, Buffalo Wild Wings, Chick-fil-A, Chili's, Chipotle, Donatos Pizza, Freddy's Burgers, McDonald's, Old Chicago, Panda Express, Popeyes, Red Robin, Smoothie King, Subway, Taco Bell, TX Roadhouse, Candlewood Suites, Comfort Inn, Holiday Inn Express, $Tree, AT&T, Dick's, GNC, Hobby Lobby, Home Depot, H, JC Penney, Kohl's, Michael's, Office Depot, PetSmart, Ross, Target, Verizon
20	136th Ave, N same as 21, Barr Lake RV Park
18	E-470 tollway, to Limon (from wb)
16	CO 2, Sable Blvd, Commerce City, S Denver Int
12	US 85 N, to Brighton (exits left from eb), Greeley
11	96th Ave, N dsl repair, S Buick/GMC
10	88th Ave, N Shell/dsl, La Quinta, Super 8, S Murphy USA, flea mkt
9	US 6 W, US 85 S(no EZ wb return), Commerce City, S Shell/dsl, Cliff's Transmissions
8	CO 224, 74th Ave(no EZ eb return), N NAPA, S Butcher Block Cafe
6b a	I-270 E, to Limon, to I-25 N, to airport
5	I-25, N to Ft Collins, S to Colo Springs
4	Pecos St
3	US 287, Federal Blvd, N Valero/dsl, S Maverik, McDonald's, Rico Pollo Mexican, Starbucks, Subway, Taco Bell, Advance Parts, vet
1b	CO 95, Sheridan Blvd
1a	CO 121, Wadsworth Blvd, N 7-11/gas, Exxon, Shell/dsl, Applebee's, Bad Daddy Burger, Beau Jo's Pizza, CAVA, Chick-fil-A, Chipotle Mexican, Einstein Bros, El Pollo Loco, El Tapatio Mexican, First Watch, IHOP, Jersey Mike's, King Buffet, Kona HBBQ, Kukoro Japanese, McDonald's/playplace, Menchie's, Noodles&Co, Parry's Pizza, Pier 8 Seafood, Red Robin, Smashburger, Snooze A.M., Starbucks, Subway, Taco Bell, TX Roadhouse, Umai-Ya Japanese, Hilton Garden, Residence Inn, $Tree, Advance Parts, Big O Tire, Costco/gas, Discount Tire, Home Depot, Lowe's Whse, Midas, PetSmart, Sam's Club, URGENT CARE
0mm	I-76 begins/ends on I-70, exit 269b.

INTERSTATE 225 (Denver)

Exit #	Services
12b a	I-70, W to Denver, E to Limon
10	US 40, US 287, Colfax Ave, E 7-11, Exxon, Murphy USA, Shell/dsl, Sinclair, Sinclair/dsl, Burger King, Carl's Jr, Del Taco, Domino's, Dutch Bros, El Camino Mexican, McDonald's, Starbucks, Subway, Taco Bell, Wendy's, Comfort Suites, Holiday Inn Express, Aamco, Advance Parts, Chevrolet, King Soopers/gas, Meineke, NAPA, Walgreens, W Circle K/dsl, Phillips 66/dsl, Chipotle Mexican, Firehouse, IHOP, Jersey Mikes, Noodles&Co, Panera Bread, Smashburger, Hyatt, Hyatt House, SpringHill Suites, H, U-Haul
9	Co 30, 6th Ave, E Conoco, Sinclair/dsl, Denny's, McDonald's, Extended Stay, W Shell/dsl, H
8	Alameda Ave, E Circle K/dsl, BJ's Rest., Cane's, Cheba Hut Subs, Chick-fil-A, Chili's, Coldstone, FatBurger, In-N-Out, Jamba Juice, Jimmy John's, L&L BBQ, Panda Express,

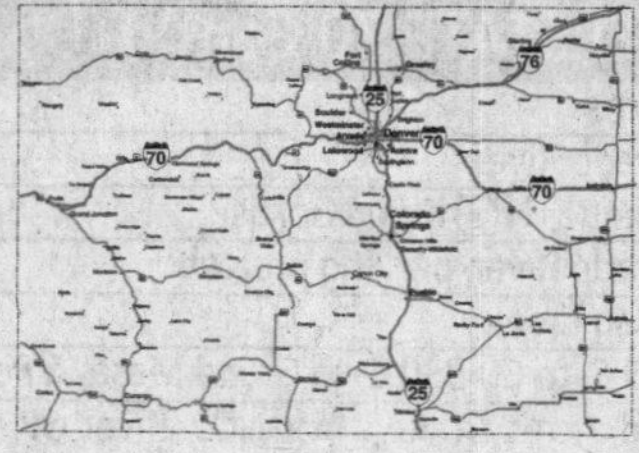

Exit #	Services
8	Continued Playa Bowls, Sabor Mexican, Wingstop, AT& Barnes&Noble, Dillards, Hobby Lobby, JC Penney, Macy Michael's, PetSmart, Ross, Target, W Circle K, Phillips 6 7-11/dsl, $Tree, Honda
7	Mississippi Ave, Alameda Ave, E Arby's, Burger Kin Chubby's Mexican, ChuckeCheese, CiCi's, Fazoli's, Fire Wing Guadalajara Mexican, La Morena Mexican, Sonic, Starbuck Subway, Tokyo Joe's, Best Western, La Quinta, Quali Inn, Batteries+, Best Buy, Big O Tires, Burlington Coat Home Depot, Sam's Club/gas, Verizon, Walmart, W Maverik, Cafe Paprika, Dominos, IHOP, McDonald Panda Buffet, Senor Ric's, Waffle House, 7-11, Advan Parts, AutoZone, H, Pepboys, Safeway
5	Iliff Ave, E Conoco, Applebee's, Black Bear Dine Carrabba's, Hibachi Japanese, McDonald's, Outback Steak Real de Minas Mexican, Rosie's Diner, TX Roadhouse, Comfort Inn, Crestwood Suites, Extended Stay Americ Extended Stay America(2), Fairfield Inn, Hampton In InTown Suites, Motel 6, Residence Inn, U-Haul, W Phillips 66, Dragon Boat, Legends Grill, Subway, DoubleTree, 7-11
4	CO 83, Parker Rd, E Cherry Creek SP, W Maverik, Shel dsl, DQ, IHOP, Little Caesar's, Popeyes, Starbucks, Ta Bell, Wendy's, $Tree, 7-11, King Soopers/gas
2b	Yosemite St
2	DTC Blvd, Tamarac St, W Phillips 66/7-11, Fel F Mediterranean, La Fogata Mexican, Sonic, South Garde Chinese, Subway, $Tree, Goodyear/auto
1b a	I-25. I-225 begins/ends on I-25, exit 200.

INTERSTATE 270 (Denver)

Exit #	Services
4	I-70
3	N TA/Burger King/Country Pride/Popeyes/Pizza Hut/ds 24hr/@, Staybridge Suites, S Sapp Bros/Sinclair/dsl/(
2b a	US 85, CO 2, Vasquez Ave, N Arby's, Carls Jr, Chipotl Jack-in-the-Box, KFC, Mama's Cafe, McDonald's, Pizza Hu Starbucks, Subway, Taco Bell, Wendy's, $Tree, Pomp Tire, Walmart
1b	York St
1a	I-76 E, to Ft Morgan
1c	I-25 S, to Denver

NOTES

CONNECTICUT

INTERSTATE 84

Exit #	Services
98mm	Connecticut/Massachusetts state line
74(97)	CT 171, Holland, S Traveler's Book Rest., Campers Inn RV Ctr
95mm	weigh sta wb
73(95)	CT 190, Stafford Springs, N motor speedway, Roaring Brook camping(seasonal)
72(93)	CT 89, Westford, N Ashford Motel, Roaring Brook camping(seasonal)
71(88)	CT 320, Ruby Rd, S TA/Shell/Burger King/Country Pride/dsl/scales/24hr/@, Dunkin', Rodeway Inn
70(86)	CT 32, Willington, N H, Wilderness Lake Camping, S Mobil/dsl, Sunoco/dsl
85mm	rest area both lanes, **campers, full facilities, info, litter barrels, petwalk, , vending**
69(83)	CT 74, to US 44, Willington, S food, gas, , RV camping, st police
68(81)	CT 195, Tolland, N Gulf/dsl, Mobil, Dunkin', Papa T's Rest., Subway, NAPA, S Citgo, Camille's Pizza, Lee's Garden, Big Y Foods, Verizon, vet
67(77)	CT 31, Rockville, N Mobil, Shell/dsl, Beni's Grill, Burger King, China Taste, Dunkin', McDonald's, Subway, H, S Nathan Hale Mon
66(76)	Tunnel Rd, Vernon
65(75)	CT 30, Vernon Ctr, N Cumberland/dsl, Mobil/dsl, Shell, Brick Oven Pizza, Burger King, Dunkin', KFC, Oki Asian, Rein's Deli, Simply Thai, Vernon Diner, Wang's Buffet, Days Inn, Red Roof Inn, Firestone/auto, Meineke, Stop&Shop/gas
64(74)	Vernon Ctr, N Sunoco, 99 Rest., Angellino's Italian, Anthony's Pizza, D'angelo's, Denny's, Dunkin', Friendly's, McDonald's, Moe's SW, Rita's Custard, Starbucks, Taco Bell, Wendy's, Wood'n Tap, Holiday Inn Express, $Tree, AutoZone, CVS Drug, GNC, Goodyear/auto, Staples, TJ Maxx, vet, S Motel 6, Chevrolet, VW
63(72)	CT 30, CT 83, same as 62, Manchester, S Windsor, N Azteca Mexican, BurgerIM, Chipotle Mexican, Dunkin', HomeTown Buffet, IHOP, Longhorn Steaks, McDonald's, Outback Steaks, Panera Bread, Red Robin, Smashburger, Starbucks, Subway, TGIFriday's, Courtyard, Residence Inn, AT&T, Best Buy, Marshall's, PetCo, Verizon, Walgreens, Walmart, S Best, BP/dsl, EVC, Shell/dsl, Sunoco/dsl, Xtra, Shea's Pizzaria, Best Value Inn, Extended Stay America, Motel 6, Big Y Mkt, H, Hyundai, Kohl's, Nissan, Subaru, Toyota, U-Haul, USPO
62(71)	Buckland St, same as 63, N Mobil/Dunkin'/dsl, Tesla EVC, Artisanal Burger, Boston Mkt, Burton's Grill, Chili's, Dave&Buster's, Five Guys, Friendly's, Hooters, Jersey Mike's, Maggie McFly's, Market Grille, Moe's SW Grill, Olive Garden, Panera Bread, Sakura Garden, Starbucks, Taco Bell, Ted's MT Grill, Fairfield Inn, Hampton Inn, Homewood Suites, $Tree, Barnes&Noble, BigLots, Dick's, Hobby Lobby, Home Depot, JC Penney, Jo-Ann Fabrics, LL Bean, Lowe's, Macy's, Michael's, Old Navy, PetSmart, Target, Town Fair Tire, Trader Joe's, Verizon, S Shell/dsl, Buffalo Wild Wings, Burger Fi, ChuckeCheese, EVC, Golden Dragon, Joey Garlic's, Kobe Asian, McDonald's, Sonic, Subway, TX Roadhouse, Wendy's, BJ's Whse/gas, Firestone/auto, GNC, Honda, USPO
61(70)	I-291 W, to Windsor
60(69)	US 6, US 44, Burnside Ave(from eb)
59(68)	I-384 E, Manchester
58(67)	Roberts St, Burnside Ave, N Margaritas Grill, Nolita Ristorante, Comfort Inn, S Mobil, Sunoco, Dunkin', Queen Pizza, Taco Bell, Cabela's, vet
57(66)	CT 15 S, to I-91 S, Charter Oak Br
56(65)	Governor St, E Hartford, S
55(64)	CT 2 E, New London, downtown
54(63)	Old State House, N Audi, Chevrolet, Chrysler/Dodge/Jeep, Ford, Kia, Lexus, Lincoln, S Hampton Inn
53(62)	CT Blvd(from eb), S Holiday Inn
52(61)	W Main St(from eb), downtown
51(60)	I-91 N, to Springfield
50(59.8)	to I-91 S(from wb), N Red Lion, S Hilton, Residence Inn
48(59.5)	Asylum St, downtown, N Red Lion, S Capitol Hotel, Homewood Suites, H
47(59)	Sigourney St, downtown, N Hartford Seminary, Mark Twain House
46(58)	Sisson St, downtown(from wb, exits left), N UConn Law School
45(57)	Flatbush Ave(from wb, exits left)
44(56.5)	Prospect Ave, N Mobil, Shell/dsl, Burger King, Goldroc Diner, Hibachi Grill, McDonald's, Prospect Pizza, Wendy's, ShopRite Foods
43(56)	Park Rd, W Hartford, N to St Joseph Coll
42(55)	Trout Brk Dr(exits left from wb), to Elmwood
41(54)	S Main St, Elmwood, N American School for the Deaf
40(53)	CT 71, New Britain Ave, S Sunoco/dsl, Tesla EVC, Brio Grille, Burger King, CA Pizza, Chili's, China Pan, Chipotle Mexican, McDonald's, Olive Garden, Panera Bread, PF Chang's, Red Robin, Starbucks, Subway, Wendy's, Courtyard, AT&T, Barnes&Noble, Best Buy, Costco/dsl, JC Penney, Macy's, Michael's, Nordstrom, Old Navy, PetCo, Target, TJ Maxx, Trader Joe's, Verizon
39a(52)	CT 9 S, to New Britain, Newington, S H
39(51.5)	CT 4, (exits left from eb), Farmington, N H
38(51)	US 6 W (from wb), same as 37, Bristol
37(50)	Fienemann Rd, to US 6 W, N Dunkin', Subway, Hampton Inn, Marriott, S Noble/Dunkin Donuts/dsl, Extended Stay America
36(49)	Slater Rd(exits left from eb), S H
35(48)	CT 72, to CT 9 (exits left from both lanes), New Britain, S H
34(47)	CT 372, Crooked St, N EVC, Gulf/dsl, Sunoco, Applebee's, Friendly's, McDonald's, Starbucks, Taco Bell/LJ Silver, Wendy's, Fairfield Inn, $Tree, AT&T, Big Y Mkt, Dick's, Ford/Lincoln, Kohl's, Lowe's, Marshall's, Old Navy, PetSmart, VW

WILLINGTON · VERNON CTR · MANCHESTER · E HARTFORD · BRISTOL

= gas = food = lodging = other = rest stop

INTERSTATE 84 Cont'd

Exit #	Services
33(46)	CT 72 W, to Bristol (exits left from eb)
SOUTHINGTON	
32(45)	Ct 10, Queen St, Southington, N Cumberland Farms, Exxon, Shell/dsl, Buffalo Wild Wings, Burger King, Chick-fil-A, Chili's, Chipotle, D'angelo, Denny's, Dunkin', Gobi Mongolian, IHOP, JD's Rest., KFC, Luen Hop Chinese, McDonald's, Moe's SW Grill, Noodles&Co, Outback Steaks, Puerto Vallarta, Smashburger, Starbucks, Subway, Taco Bell, Vivaldi Pizza, Motel 6, $Tree, 7-11, ALDI, AutoZone, BJ's/gas, CVS Drug, GNC, Home Depot, H, Jo-Ann, O'Reilly Parts, PetCo, ShopRite Foods, Staples, TJ Maxx, TownFair Tire, Verizon, S Gulf, Mobil, Sunoco, Aziagos Italian, Dunkin', Eddie's Sombrero, Friendly's, Nardelli's Cafe, Noble Japanese, Panera Bread, Rita's Custard, Subway, Tokyo Japanese, Wendy's, Wood'n Tap Grill, Days Inn, Holiday Inn Express, Advance Parts, AT&T, Firestone/auto, Midas, Monro, PriceChopper Foods, URGENT CARE, Walmart
31(44)	CT 229, West St, N EVC, Mobil/dsl, Sunoco/dsl, Chip's, Dunkin', Popeyes, Starbucks, Courtyard, Homewood Suites, Lowe's, Michael's, Target, S Citgo, Gulf/dsl, Dunkin', Giovanni's Pizza, Subway, Residence Inn
30(43)	Marion Ave, W Main, Southington, N ski area, S Mobil/dsl, H
MARION	
29(42)	CT 10, from wb, exits left from wb, Milldale
41.5mm	**full facilities, info, litter barrels, petwalk, eb**
28(41)	CT 322, Marion, S Fleet/dsl, Mobil, TA/Popeyes/Taco Bell/dsl/scales/24hr/@, Blimpie, Burger King, DQ, Dunkin', Manor Inn Rest., Subway, Young Young Chinese, Comfort Suites, EconoLodge, Home Depot
27(40)	I-691 E, to Meriden
26(38)	CT 70, to Cheshire, N Blackie's Cafe
25a(37)	Austin Rd, N Winzz/dsl, Asian Garden, Subway, Tiramisu Italian, Costco/gas, Kohl's
25(36)	Harper's Ferry Rd, Reed Dr, Scott Rd, E Main St, N Mobil/dsl, Dunkin', AT&T, NAPA, S Burger King, Dunkin', Golden Wok, McDonald's, Nino's Rest., Subway, TX Roadhouse, Quality Inn, AlLDI, BJ's Whse/gas, Cadillac/Chevrolet, CVS Drug, Super Stop&Shop/gas
23(33.5)	CT 69, Hamilton Ave, N Buffalo Wild Wings, Chili's, IHOP, McDonald's, Olive Garden, TGIFriday's, Barnes&Noble, H, JC Penney, Macy's, Michael's, Petco, Save-a-Lot Foods, TJ Maxx, S Shell, Dunkin'
22(33)	Baldwin St, same as 23, Waterbury, N Gulf, Courtyard, H, USPO
21(33)	Meadow St, Banks St, N 7-11, S Exxon/dsl, Home Depot, PetSmart
NAUGATUCK	
20(32)	CT 8 N(exits left from eb), to Torrington
19(32)	CT 8 S(exits left from wb), to Bridgeport
18(32)	W Main, Highland Ave, N ProFuel/dsl, Dunkin', Lena's Deli, Starbucks, Subway, Wayback Burger, Hampton Inn, CVS Drug, H
17(30)	CT 63, CT 64, to Watertown, Naugatuck, N Maggie McFly's Rest., S Mobil/dsl, Dunkin', Leo's Rest., Maples Rest., Subway
16(25)	CT 188, to Middlebury, N Mobil, Patty's Pantry Deli, Crowne Plaza
15(22)	US 6 E, CT 67, Southbury, N Citgo/deli, Mobil, Shell/repair, Dunkin', McDonald's, Panera Bread, Subway, Heritage Hotel, AT&T, Stop&Shop, TJ Maxx, Verizon, S to Kettletown SP
14(20)	CT 172, to S Britain, N Mobil, Dunkin', Maggie McFly's, S st police
20mm	motorist callboxes begin eb, end wb
13(19)	River Rd(from eb), to Southbury
11(16)	CT 34, to New Haven

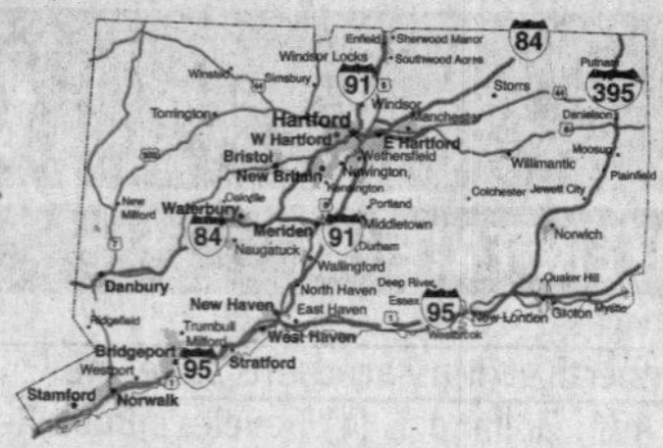

Exit #	Services
NEWTOWN	
10(15)	US 6 W, Newtown, N Fig's Rest., Foundry Kitche Subway, Villa Rest., S Citgo/dsl, Mobil/dsl, Blue Color Diner, Pizza Palace, Starbucks
9(11)	CT 25, to Hawleyville, N USPO
8(8)	Newtown Rd, N Global, Mobil/dsl, Applebee' Dunkin', Outback Steaks, La Quinta, Quality Inn, Be Buy, Harley-Davidson, Lowe's, Volvo, S Shell/dsl, Sunoc 99 Rest., Black Angus, Boston Mkt, Burger King, Chili' Denny's, Dunkin', Ichiro Steaks, Little Caesar's, McDonald' Popeyes, Puerto Vallarta, Rizzuto's, Starbucks, Subway, Tac Bell, TX Roadhouse, Wayback Burger, Best Wester Courtyard, Days Inn, Hampton Inn, Holiday Inn/rest Microtel, $Tree, AlLDI, Marshall's, Staples, Stop&Sho Subaru, Target, TJ Maxx, Town Fair Tire, Verizon, Walmart Subway
7(7)	US 7N/202E, to Brookfield(exits left from eb), New Milfor N Irving, Mobil, Sunoco, Arby's, Burger King, Chick-fi A, Dunkin', Five Guys, Jersey Mike's, KFC, McDonald's, Moe SW, Panera Bread, Starbucks, Wendy's, AT&T, Bj's Whse gas, Costco/gas, CVS Drug, Firestone/auto, Ford, GNC, Hom Depot, Jo-Ann Fabrics, Kohl's, Michael's, Petco, ShopRit Foods, Stew Leonards, Town Fair Tire, Toyota, Verizor Walgreens
DANBURY	
6(6)	CT 37(from wb), New Fairfield, N Gulf, Burger King Castello's Italian, Dunkin', Elmer's Diner, Grand Centur Buffet, McDonald's, Moon Star Chinese, Starbucks, $Tree CVS Drug, S Shell, KFC
5(5)	CT 37, CT 39, CT 53, Danbury, N Exxon/dsl, Shell, Bes Value Inn, S Mobil, Dunkin', Taco Bell, H, to Putnan SP
4(4)	US 6 W/202 W, Lake Ave, N Gulf/dsl, Orbit/dsl, Shell/ds Dunkin', McDonald's, Ethan Allen Hotel, Maron Hote Super 8, CVS Drug, Stop&Shop Foods, S Chuck' Steaks, Residence Inn, to mall
3(3)	US 7 S(exits left from wb), to Norwalk, S EVC, Mobil Burger King/dsl, Tesla EVC, Agave Mexican, Brio Grille Buffalo Wild Wings, Cheesecake Factory, Chipotle, Coldstone Olive Garden, Panera Bread, Red Lobster, AT&T Barnes&Noble, Dick's, JC Penney, LL Bean, Lord&Taylor Macy's, Petco, Whole Foods Mkt
2b a(1)	US 6, US 202, Mill Plain Rd, N Mobil/dsl, Chipotle, Rosy Tomorrows, Starbucks, Tuscanero's Pizza, Hilton Garden Holiday Inn Express, Staples, Trader Joe's, **S to Old Ridgebury, Welcome Ctr/weigh sta, full facilities, info, litter barrels, petwalk,** Crowne Plaza, Hotel Zerc Degrees, SpringHill Suites
1	Saw Mill Rd, N Hilton Garden, Holiday Inn Express, Maron Hotel
0mm	Connecticut/New York state line

INTERSTATE 91

Exit #	Services
58mm	Connecticut/Massachusetts state line
49(57)	US 5, to Longmeadow, MA, E Pride/dsl, Dunkin' McDonald's, Holiday Inn, Meineke, repair, W Sunoco/dsl, Baco's Pizza, Cloverleaf Café, DQ, Dunkin' Pizza Palace, $General, Chrysler/Dodge
48(56)	CT 220, Elm St(same as 47), E Mobil/Dunkin'/dsl, Burger King, Denny's, Dunkin', Figaro, First Wok, Friendly's,

INTERSTATE 91 Cont'd

WAREHOUSE POINT

48(56) Continued
Jason's Seafood, McDonald's, Outback Steaks, Panera Bread, Starbucks, TGIFriday's, Wendy's, $Tree, AutoZone, Best Buy, Costco/gas, Dick's, Firestone/auto, Home Depot, Honda, Hyundai, Jo-Ann Fabrics, Kohl's, Nissan, Target, TownFair Tire, Toyota, USPO, VW

47(55) CT 190, to Hazardville(same as 48), E 99 Rest., Acapulcos Mexican, Cheng's Garden, Chick-fil-A, Chipotle, D'angelo, Dunkin', Longhorn Steaks, McDonald's, Moe's SW Grill, Olive Garden, Red Robin, Starbucks, Subway, Taco Bell, Hampton Inn, Motel 6, Red Roof Inn, Advance Parts, AlLDI, AT&T, Barnes&Noble, Big Y Foods, CVS Drug, Ford, H, Marshall's, Michael's, NAPA, Old Navy, PetCo, PetSmart, ShopRite, Staples, Stop&Shop/gas, Suburban Tire/auto, URGENT CARE, Verizon, Walgreens

46(53) US 5, King St, to Enfield, E Mobil, Astro's Rest., W Enfield Inn

45(51) CT 140, Warehouse Point, E Shell, Burger King, Chen's Chinese, Cracker Barrel, Dunkin', Sofia's Rest., Subway, Wayback Burgers, Comfort Inn, to Trolley Museum, W Sunoco/dsl, Rodeway Inn, Advance Parts

44(50) US 5 S, to E Windsor, E Sunoco/dsl, Big Y Mkt, Dunkin', Elizabeth's Rest., KFC, Taco Bell, Wendy's, Baymont Inn, Walmart

49mm Connecticut River

42(48) CT 159, Windsor Locks, E Longview RV Ctr, W same as 41

41(47) Center St(exits with 39), W Ad's Pizzaria, HillPoint Hotel

40(46.5) CT 20, W Old New-Gate Prison

39(46) Kennedy Rd(exits with 41), Community Rd, E vet, W Shell/Dunkin'/dsl, Char Koon, Chili's, Starbucks, $Tree, AT&T, GNC, PetCo, Stop&Shop Foods, Target

38(45) CT 75, to Poquonock, Windsor Area, E Mobil/Circle K/dsl, Asian Bistro, Buffalo Wild Wings, Dunkin', Moe's SW, Pizzarama, Subway, PriceChopper Foods, to Ellsworth Homestead, W The Bistro, Courtyard, Hilton Garden, Hyatt House Suites, Marriott

37(44) CT 305, Bloomfield Ave, Windsor Ctr, E Mobil/dsl, McDonald's, W Sunoco, Residence Inn

36(43) CT 178, Park Ave, to W Hartford

35b(41) CT 218, to Bloomfield, to S Windsor, E food, gas/dsl

35a I-291 E, to Manchester

34(40) CT 159, Windsor Ave, E Sunoco/dsl, W Citgo/dsl, RanchHouse Rest., H

HARTFORD

33(39) Jennings Rd, Weston St, E Tesla EVC, Cadillac, Fiat, Jaguar, VW, W Mobil/dsl, Burger King, Dunkin', McDonald's, Subway, Super 8, Travel Inn, CarMax, Honda, Hyundai, Infiniti, Mazda, Mercedes, Midas, Nissan, Subaru, Toyota

32b(38) Trumbull St(exits left from nb), W to downtown, Hilton, Red Lion, Goodyear, H

32a (exit 30 from sb), I-84 W

29b(37) I-84 E, Hartford

29a(36.5) US 5 N, CT 15 N(exits left from nb), W capitol, civic ctr, downtown, H

28(36) US 5, CT 15 S(from nb), W Citgo, Burger King, Dunkin', Wendy's

27(35) Brainerd Rd, Airport Rd, E Mobil/Dunkin'/Subway/dsl, Shell/Dunkin'/dsl, McDonald's, USS Chowder Pot, Best Western, Days Inn, Regional Mkt

26(33.5) Marsh St, W CT MVD, Silas Deane House, Webb House

25(33) CT 3, Glastonbury, Wethersfield

24(32) CT 99, Rocky Hill, Wethersfield, E Phillips 66/dsl, Algarve Grill, Chuck's Steaks, Dakota Steaks, Dunkin', McDonald's, On-the-Border, Rita's Custard, Rockyhill Pizza,

CROMWELL

24(32) Continued
Saybrook Seafood, Subway, Holiday Inn Express, Howard Johnson, Super 8, AlLDI, Kohl's, Meineke, Monro, W Mobil, Shell/dsl, Valero/dsl, Buffalo Wild Wings, Burger King, Chipotle, Chip's Rest., D'Angelo, Denny's, Friendly's, Ginza Cuisine, KFC, Panera Bread, Red Lobster, Sake Japanese, Sofia's Pizzaria, Starbucks, Subway, Townline Diner, Wendy's, Wood-n-Tap Grill, Comfort Inn, Motel 6, $Tree, AT&T, CVS Drug, Goodyear/auto, Marshall's, Stop&Shop, TJMaxx, TownFair Tire, Verizon, Walgreens, Walmart/Subway

23(29) to CT 3, West St, Rocky Hill, Vet Home, E Sheraton, to Dinosaur SP, W Cumberland Farms/dsl, Exxon/dsl, Mobil, DeNovellis, Michelangeo's Pizza, Starbucks, Subway, Residence Inn, Westside Mktplace

22(27) CT 9, to New Britain, Middletown

21(26) CT 372, to Berlin, Cromwell, E Sunoco/dsl/repair, Quality Inn, Red Lion Inn, Krauszer's Foods, Lowe's, W Citgo/Subway/dsl, Mobil/dsl, Baci Grill, Burger King, Chili's, Cromwell Diner, Dunkin', McDonald's, Mizzu Asian, Nardelli's, Courtyard, Super 8, Firestone/auto, PriceRite Foods, URGENT CARE, Verizon, vet, Walmart

20(23) Country Club Rd, Middle St

22mm **full facilities, info, litter barrels, petwalk, rest stop/ weigh sta nb, RV dump, vending**

WALLINGFORD

19(21) Baldwin Ave(from sb)

18(20.5) I-691 W, to Marion, access to same as 16 & 17, ski area

17(20) CT 15 N(from sb), to I-691, CT 66 E, Meriden

16(19) CT 15, E Main St, E Gulf/dsl, Mobil/dsl, Valero, American Steaks, Gianni's Rest., Huxley's Cafe, Kings Garden Chinese, Olympos Diner, Subway, Extended Stay America, Hawthorn Inn, Red Roof Inn, The Meridan Inn, W Gulf/ repair, Shell/dsl, Boston Mkt, Boston Mkt, Burger King, Dunkin', KFC, Les' Dairy Bar, Little Caesar's, McDonald's, Nardelli's, Subway, Taco Bell, Wayback Burgers, Wendy's, Comfort Inn, CVS Drug, Hancock's Drug, H, Walgreens

15(16) CT 68, to Durham, E Hilton Garden, golf, W Courtyard, Fairfield Inn, Homewood Suites

15mm **full facilities, info, litter barrels, petwalk, rest stop sb**

14(12) CT 150(no EZ return), Woodhouse Ave, Wallingford

13(10) US 5(exits left from nb), services 2 mi W on US 5, Wallingford, W to Wharton Brook SP

12(9) US 5, Washington Ave, E Exxon, Sunoco, Valero, Boston Mkt, Burger King, D'angelo's, DQ, Dunkin', McDonald's, Popeyes, Starbucks, Subway, Verizon, CVS Drug, Stop&Shop Food, Town Fair Tire, USPO, Walgreens, W BP, Mobil, Shell/dsl, Arby's, Athena II Diner, Dunkin', Outback Steaks, Best Western+/Harry's Grill, Advance Parts, BigY Foods/drug, vet

11(7) CT 22(from nb), North Haven, same as 12

10(6) CT 40, to Cheshire, Hamden

FAIR HAVEN

9(5) Montowese Ave, W Gulf/dsl, Sunoco, Buffalo Wild Wings, Chick-fil-A, Dunkin', Friendly's, Longhorn Steaks, McDonald's, Olive Garden, Panera Bread, Red Lobster, Ruby Tuesday, Subway, Wendy's, $Tree, AT&T, Barnes&Noble, Best Buy, BigLots, BJ's Whse/gas, CVS, Dick's, GNC, Home Depot, Michael's, Nissan/Jeep, PetCo, PetSmart, Target, TJMaxx, URGENT CARE, Verizon

8(4) CT 17, CT 80, Middletown Ave, E 7-11, Global/dsl, Mercury/dsl, Popeyes, Shell, 91 Diner, Burger King, Dunkin', KFC, McDonald's, Seasons, Taco Bell, Days Inn, Advance Parts, AlLDI, AutoZone, Lowe's, vet, Walgreens, Walmart/Subway

7(3) Ferry St(from sb), Fair Haven, W Exxon/dsl, NAPA

6(2.5) Willow St(exits left from nb), Blatchley Ave, E repair

5(2) US 5(from nb), State St, Fair Haven

4(1.5) State St(from sb), downtown

CT

= gas = food = lodging = other = rest stop

NEW HAVEN

INTERSTATE 91 Cont'd

Exit #	Services
3(1)	Trumbull St, downtown, W Peabody Museum
2(.5)	Hamilton St, downtown, New Haven
1(.3)	CT 34W(from sb), New Haven, W downtown, H
0mm	I-91 begins/ends on I-95, exit 48.

INTERSTATE 95

94mm	Connecticut/Rhode Island state line
93(111)	CT 216, Clarks Falls, E Citgo/dsl/repair, Subway, to Burlingame SP, $General, W Mobil/dsl, Pilot/Shell/Stuckey's/Sbarro's/dsl/scales/24hr, Dunkin', Budget Inn, Stardust Motel
92(107)	CT 2, CT 49(no EZ nb return), rest area sb, full facilities, Pawcatuck, E Shell, Dunkin', McDonald's, La Quinta, H, Stop&Shop, W Cedar Park Suites, FoxWoods(8mi), KOA
91(103)	CT 234, N Main St, to Stonington, E H
90(101)	CT 27, Mystic, E Shell/Domino's/Dunkin/dsl, Tesla EVC, Friendly's, Go Fish, McDonald's, Mystic Diner, Peking Tokyo, Starbucks, Steak Loft, Hilton, Holiday Inn Express, Howard Johnson, Hyatt Place, Rodeway Inn, aquarium, Mystic Outlet Shops, W Mobil/Subway/dsl, Cristo's Pizza, Dunkin', Frank's Grille, Days Inn, Hampton Inn, Mystic River Inn, Quality Inn, Residence Inn, Chevrolet, Chrysler/Dodge/Jeep, Ford, TrueValue, VW
89mm	Mystic River, scenic overlook nb, scenic overlook
89(99)	CT 614, Mystic St, Allyn St, W camping(seasonal)
88(98)	CT 117, to Noank, E , W Octagon Steaks, Starbucks, Marriott
87(97)	Sharp Hwy(exits left from sb), Groton, E Applebee's, Hampton Inn, , to Griswold SP
86(96)	rd 184(exits left from nb), Groton, E 99 Rest., Applebee's, Olio Rest., Hampton Inn, Motel 6, Rodeway Inn, Walgreens, W Gulf/dsl, Mobil/dsl, Shell/dsl, Xpress Fuel, Chinese Kitchen, Domino's, Dunkin', Five Guys, Flanagan's Diner, Groton Rest., KFC, Moe's SW, Panera Bread, Pick Pockets Deli, Subway, Taco Bell, Days Inn, Groton Inn, Hilton Garden, Ramada, Super 8, Advance Parts, GNC, Honda, Kia, Kohl's, Midas, Stop&Shop, to US Sub Base, Verizon
85(95)	US 1 N, Groton, downtown, E Norms Diner, Sleep Inn
84(94)	CT 32(from sb), New London, downtown
83(92)	CT 32, New London, E to Long Island Ferry
82a(90.5)	frontage rd, same as 82, New London, E Mobil/dsl, Denny's, TX Roadhouse, Advance Parts, AutoZone, Goodyear/auto, NSA Foods, Staples, TownFair Tire, W Sunoco, Chili's, Outback Steaks, Panda Buffet, Clarion, Red Roof Inn, SpringHill Suites, Marshall's, PetSmart, ShopRite Foods
82(90)	CT 85, to I-395 N, New London, W Mobil/Dunkin', Buffalo Wild Wings, Coldstone, Jersey Mike's, Longhorn Steaks, Moe's SW, Olive Garden, Panera Bread, Ruby Tuesday, Smashburger, Starbucks, Subway, BAM, Best Buy, Dick's, Home Depot, JC Penney, Macy's, Michael's, PetCo, Target, Verizon
90mm	weigh sta both directions
81(89.5)	Cross Road, W Rodeway Inn, $Tree, BJ's Whse/gas, Lowe's, Walmart/McDonald's
80(89.3)	Oil Mill Rd(from sb), W Rodeway Inn
76(89)	I-395 N(from nb, exits left), to Norwich
75(88)	US 1, to Waterford
74(87)	rd 161, to Flanders, Niantic, E Citgo/dsl, Mobil, Niantic/dsl/repair, Burger King, Country Gourmet, Dunkin', Illiano's Grill, Starbucks, Days Inn, Motel 6, Niantic Inn, Sleep Inn, Ford, Monro Automotive, Stop&Shop/gas,

MYSTIC

NEW LONDON

NIANTIC

CLINTON

GUILFORD

74(87)	Continued Verizon, W Shell, Flanders Seafood, King Garden, McDonald's, Osaka Japanese, Shack Rest., Smokey O'Grady's BBQ, Subway, Yummy Yummy Pizza, CVS Drug, Tri Town Foods, TrueValue, Walgreens
74mm	rest area sb, **full facilities, st police**
73(86)	Society Rd
72(84)	to Rocky Neck SP, E food, lodging, RV camping, to Rocky Neck SP
71(83)	4 Mile Rd, River Rd, to Rocky Neck SP, beaches, E KOA(seasonal)
70(80)	US 1, CT 156, Old Lyme, W Shell/dsl, Dock 11 Cafe, Dunkin', Subway, Old Lyme Inn/dining, Big Y Foods, Griswold Museum, USPO, vet
69(77)	US 1, CT 9 N, to Hartford, W Otter Cove, Quality Inn
68(76.5)	US 1 S, Old Saybrook, E Mobil, Shell/dsl, Cloud 9 Deli, Mystic Mkt Kitchen, W Buick/GMC, Chevrolet, Chrysler/Dodge/Jeep, Hyundai, Kia, Nissan, VW
67(76)	CT 154, Elm St(no EZ sb return), Old Saybrook, E same as 68
66(75)	to US 1, Spencer Plain Rd, E Citgo/dsl, Alforno Trattoria, Cuckoo's Nest Mexican, Dunkin', Five Guys, Sal's Pizza, Samurai Japanese, Wayback Burgers, EconoLodge, Saybrook Motel, Super 8, Big Y Mkt, Kohl's, NAPA, transmissions, URGENT CARE, vet
65(73)	rd 153, Westbrook, E Mobil/Dunkin', Valero, Cafe Routier, Cristy's Rest., Denny's, Honda, H, Old Navy, Toyota, USPO, Walgreens, Westbrook Outlets/famous brands
64(70)	rd 145, Horse Hill Rd, Clinton
63(68)	CT 81, Clinton, E Shell, W Coldstone, Dunkin', AT&T, Clinton Crossing Premium Outlets/famous brands, PetCo
62(67)	E beaches, RV camping, to Hammonasset SP
66mm	service area both lanes, **Mobil/dsl(both)**, Dunkin'(nb), McDonald's(sb), Popeyes(sb), Subway(both), atm
61(64)	CT 79, Madison, E auto repair, Cumberland, Shell, Cafe Allegre, Starbucks, Subway, CVS Drug, Stop&Shop, USPO, Verizon
61mm	East River
60(63.5)	Mungertown Rd(from sb, no return), E food, lodging
59(60)	rd 146, Goose Lane, Guilford, E Citgo/dsl, Mobil/24hr, Shell/DQ/dsl, Avest Pizza, Dunkin', First Garden, McDonald's, Shoreline Diner, Wendy's, Whole Enchilada, Comfort Inn, Tower Motel, $Tree, Big Y Foods, NAPA, transmissions, Verizon, Walmart
58(59)	CT 77, Guilford, E Gulf/dsl, Mobil, Wave/dsl, Xpress, Dunkin', CVS Drug, to Henry Whitfield Museum, Walgreens, W vet
57(58)	US 1, Guilford, E Shell/Dunkin'/dsl, W Fresh Mkt, Michael's, Petco, Verizon, vet
56(55)	rd 146, to Stony Creek, E Rodeway Inn, W Mobil, Shell/dsl, TA/Popeyes/Starbucks/Subway/dsl/scales/24hr/@, 56 Diner, Dunkin', USS Chowderpot, American Inn, Baymont Inn, Freightliner, Stop&Shop Foods
55(54)	US 1, E Branford/repair, Cumberland, Shell/dsl, Carson's Rest., Dunkin', Hornet's Nest Deli, Lynn's Rest., Marco Pizzaria, Holiday Inn Express, Motel 6, Ford, vet, Walgreens, W Gulf, Mobil/Dunkin'/dsl, Brother's Deli, Cafe Fiore, Gourmet Wok, Parthenon Diner, Days Inn

INTERSTATE 95 Cont'd

Exit #	Services
54(53)	Cedar St, Branford, E Mobil, Stop&Shop Gas, Dragon East Chinese, Dunkin', La Luna Ristorante, Kia, Staples, Subaru, W Krauszer's Foods, NAPA
52mm	service area both lanes, Mobil/dsl(both), Dunkin'(sb), McDonald's(nb), Subway(nb)
52(50)	rd 100, North High St, E to Trolley Museum
51(49.5)	US 1, Easthaven, E Sunoco, Valero/dsl, Xpress/dsl, Boston Mkt, Chili's, Dunkin', Quality Inn, $Tree, Big Lots, Chevrolet, Hobby Lobby, Lexus, TJ Maxx, W Golden Dragon, Wendy's, AutoZone, CarMax, Home Depot, Hyundai
50(49)	Woodward Ave(from nb), E Shell, Ft Nathan Hale, US Naval/Marine Reserve
49(48.5)	Stiles St(from nb)
48(48)	I-91 N, to Hartford
47(47.5)	CT 34, New Haven, W Mobil/Dunkin'/dsl, Brazi's Italian, Greek Olive Diner, La Quinta, Ikea, Long Wharf Theater, same as 46
46(47)	Long Wharf Dr, Sargent Dr, E Lenny & Joe's Rest., W Mobil/Dunkin Donuts/dsl, Brazi's Italian, Greek Olive Diner, La Quinta, Ikea, Long Wharf Theater
44(46)	CT 10(from nb), Kimberly Ave, E Super 8, W DQ, Dunkin', McDonald's, Popeyes, same as 45, Townhouse Pizza
43(45)	CT 122, 1st Ave(no EZ return), West Haven, W 1st Fuel/dsl, Xtra, H, NAPA, to U of New Haven, vet
42(44)	CT 162, Saw Mill Rd, E Mobil/Dunkin', EconoLodge, W Shell, Chipotle, Denny's, Dunkin', McDonald's, Starbucks, Subway, TX Roadhouse, Best Western, Hampton Inn, AlLDI, Firestone/auto, Walmart/Subway
41(42)	Marsh Hill Rd, to Orange, E Homewood Suites, W Outback Steaks, Courtyard
41mm	service area both lanes, Mobil/dsl, Tesla EVC, Dunkin', McDonald's, Panda Express
40(40)	Old Gate Lane, Woodmont Rd, E Citgo/dsl, Pilot/Wendy's/dsl/scales/24hr, Shell, Sunoco, Cracker Barrel, Duchess Rest., Dunkin', Gipper's Rest., Popeyes, Hilton Garden, Holiday Inn Express, Hyatt Place, Mayflower Motel, Milford Inn, Midas
39(39)	US 1, to Milford, E $Tree, Cumberland Farms/dsl, Athenian Diner, Dunkin', Hooters, Mama Teresa's, Mexico Tipico, Howard Johnson, Super 8, CVS Drug, Firestone/auto, Mazda/Volvo, ShopRite Foods, vet, Walgreens, W Mobil, Tesla EVC, Boston Mkt, Buffalo Wild Wings, Burger King, Chili's, Chipotle Mexican, DiBella Subs, Domino's, Dunkin', Golden Corral, HoneyBaked Ham, McDonald's, Panera Bread, Rustica Rest., Smashburger, Sonic, Starbucks, Subway, Taco Bell, Acura, Advance Parts, AT&T, Barnes&Noble, BigLots, Chrysler/Dodge/Jeep, Costco/gas, Dick's, Jo-Ann Fabrics, Macy's, Marshall's, Michael's, Old Navy, PetCo, Shop&Shop/gas, Staples, Target, TownFair Tire, Walmart/Subway, Whole Foods Mkt
38(38)	CT 15, Merritt Pkwy, Cross Pkwy
37(37.5)	High St(no ez nb return), E Citgo, Gulf, Subway, 7-11, Toyota, vet
36	Plains Rd, E Cumberland Farms, EVC, Mobil, Dunkin', Gusto Italian, Hampton Inn, ALDI
35(37)	Bic Dr, School House Rd, E EVC, Wendy's, Motel 6, AutoZone, Chevrolet, CVS Drug, Dennis' Parts, Ford/Lincoln, Honda, Land Rover, Nissan, Stop&Shop Foods/gas, Subaru, Walgreens, W Red Roof Inn, Residence Inn, SpringHill Suites
34(34)	US 1, Milford, E Dunkin', McDonald's, Ming Feng Chinese, Subway, Taco Bell, Devon Motel, $Tree, Hyundai, Walgreens
33(33.5)	US 1(from nb, no EZ return), CT 110, Ferry Blvd, E Shell/dsl, Sunoco/dsl, Boathouse Cantina Grill, Danny's Drive-In, Riverview Bistro, Subway, $Tree, BJ's Whse, PetCo, W EVC, 99 Rest., McDonald's, Popeyes, Villa Pizza, Home Depot, Marshall's, ShopRite Foods, Stop&Shop/dsl, USPO, Walmart/Subway
32(33)	W Broad St, Stratford, E Sunoco/dsl, W Gulf/dsl, Acropolis Pizza, Dunkin'
31(32)	South Ave, Honeyspot Rd, E Gulf, HoneySpot Motel, Quality Suites, NAPA, W Citgo/dsl, TownFair Tire
30(31.5)	Lordship Blvd, Surf Ave, E Gulf/dsl, Shell/dsl, Dunkin', URGENT CARE, W Massey/dsl
29(31)	rd 130, Stratford Ave, Seaview Ave, same as 28, W H
28(30)	CT 113, E Main St, Pembrook St, E EVC, Chipotle, Starbucks, Uncle Buck's Grill, Bass Pro Shop
27(29.5)	Lafayette Blvd, downtown, W Dunkin', Barnum Museum, H
27a(29)	CT 25, CT 8, to Waterbury
26(28)	Wordin Ave
25(27)	CT 130(from sb, no EZ return), State St, Commerce Dr, Fairfield Ave, E Audi, Infiniti, Mercedes, Porsche, USPO, W McDonald's
24(26.5)	Black Rock Tpk, E Blackrock Oyster Bar, Fairfield Pizza, Rio Bravo, Sweet Basil, Best Western+, Audi, BJ's Whse/Subway, Lexus, Porsche, Staples, USPO, Verizon, W Gulf, Firestone/auto, Nissan
23(26)	US 1, Kings Hwy, E EVC, Sunoco/dsl, Chipotle, Five Guys, CVS Drug, Home Depot, Petco, Whole Foods Mkt
22(24)	Round Hill Rd, N Benson Rd
23.5mm	service area both lanes, Mobil/dsl, Dunkin', McDonald's, Qdoba, Subway
21(23)	Mill Plain Rd, E Citgo/dsl, Mobil/dsl, Avellino's Italian, DQ, Geronimo SW Grill, Rawley's Drive-In, Shu Chinese, Starbucks, Subway, Tequila Revolucion, Hemlock Hardware, Hyundai
20(22)	Bronson Rd(from sb)
19(21)	US 1, Center St, W Exxon, Shell/7-11/dsl, Athena Diner, Baskin-Robbins/Dunkin', Border Grill, Panera Bread, Shake Shack, Starbucks, Subway, Westport Inn, Balducci's Mkt, Honda, Michael's, Stop&Shop, TownFair Tire
18(20)	to Westport, E beaches, Sherwood Island SP, W Gulf, Angelina's Trattoria, Five Guys, Fresh Mkt, Little Barn, McDonald's, Sakura Japanese, Sherwood Diner, Starbucks, vet, Barnes&Noble, Marshall's, Toyota, URGENT CARE, Walgreens
17(18)	CT 33, rd 136, Westport
16(17)	E Norwalk, E Citgo, Mobil/Dunkin'/dsl, Shell/dsl, Baskin-Robbins, Mike's Deli, Penny's Diner, Subway
15(16)	US 7, to Danbury, Norwalk
14(15)	US 1, CT Ave, S Norwalk, E Shell, Walgreens, W Exxon, Global, Shell, Burger King, Dunkin', Post Road Diner, Silver Star Diner, Starbucks, Subway, Wendy's, $Tree, Best Buy, CVS Drug, GNC, H, Kohl's, PetSmart, REI, same as 13, ShopRite Foods, Stop&Shop, TJ Maxx, TownFair Tire
13(13)	US 1(no EZ return), Post Rd, Norwalk, W EVC, Mobil, Shell, Sunoco, American Steaks, Bertucci's, Blue Wave Taco, Chipotle Mexican, Darien Diner, Driftwood Diner, KFC, McDonald's, DoubleTree, AT&T, Costco, Home Depot, Mini, same as 14, vet, Walmart
12.5mm	service area nb, Mobil/dsl, Tesla EVC, McDonald's, Sbarro's, Subway, Taco Bell
12(12)	rd 136, Tokeneke Rd(from nb, no return), W SoNo Cafe
11(11)	US 1, Darien, E EVC, Exxon, Shake Shack, Chevrolet, Chevrolet/EVC, Land Rover/Jaguar, repair, vet, W Gulf, Dunkin', BMW, CVS, Whole Foods Mkt
10(10)	Noroton, W Mobil, Shell, Jake's Place, Subway, vet

MILFORD

STRATFORD

E NORWALK

DARIEN

CT

= gas = food = lodging = other = rest stop

GLENBROOK

INTERSTATE 95 Cont'd

Exit #	Services
9.5mm	service area sb, Mobil/dsl, Tesla EVC, Chipotle, Dunkin', McDonald's, Subway
9(9)	US 1, rd 106, Glenbrook, E Red Carpet Inn, W Gulf, Dunkin', McDonald's, Subway, Advance Parts, Meineke
8(8)	Atlantic Ave, Elm St, E Sunoco, Dunkin', W Marriott, H
7(7)	CT 137, Atlantic Ave, W Capital Grille, Hampton Inn, Marriott, Barnes&Noble, same as 8
6(6)	Harvard Ave, West Ave, E Stamford Diner, Starbucks, La Quinta, Advance Parts, PetSmart, Subaru, USPO, W Shell, Super 8, H
5(5)	US 1, Riverside, Old Greenwich, W Acme Mkt, BP, Mobil, Shell, Boston Mkt, Chipotle, Corner Deli, McDonald's, Starbucks, Taco Bell, Valbella Ristorante, Hyatt Regency, CVS Drug, GNC, Staples, USPO, Walgreens
4(4)	Indian Field Rd, Cos Cob, W Bush-Holley House Museum
3(3)	Arch St, Greenwich, E Bruce Museum, W Shell, Cadillac, H, Lexus
2mm	weigh sta nb
2(1)	Delavan Ave, Byram
0mm	Connecticut/New York state line

BYRAM

INTERSTATE 395

BALLOUVILLE

Exit #	Services
55.5mm	Connecticut/Massachusetts state line
53(54)	E Thompson, to Wilsonville
50(50)	rd 200, N Grosvenor Dale, W W Thompson Lake Camping(seasonal)
49(49)	to CT 12(from nb, exits left), Grosvenor Dale
47(47)	US 44, to E Putnam, E Dunkin', Empire Buffet, McDonald's, Subway, Wendy's, $Tree, Advance Parts, CVS Drug, Giant Pizza, GNC, Stop&Shop/gas, W Citgo/dsl/repair, Mobil, AutoZone, Walmart/Subway
46(46)	to CT 12, Putnam, W Best Value Inn, H
45(45)	Kennedy Dr, to Putnam, E Ford, W H
43(43)	Ballouville, W Comfort Inn
41(41)	CT 101, to Dayville, E Gulf, Shell/dsl, Burger King, China Garden, Dayville Mexican, Domino's, Dunkin', Subway, Yamato Japanese, Zip's Diner, Budget Inn, $General, $Tree, ALDI, Kohl's, O'Reilly Parts, Town Fair Tire, Walgreens, W Mobil/Taco Bell/dsl, Shell/dsl, 99 Rest., Dunkin', McDonald's, Railside Tavern, AT&T, city park, GNC, Lowe's, Michael's, PetCo, Staples, Stop&Shop, Target, TJ Maxx, Verizon
38(39)	to S Killingly, W Dunkin', Giant Pizza, st police
37(38)	US 6 W, to Danielson, to Quinebaug Valley Coll
35(36)	to US 6 E(from nb), to Providence
35mm	Plainfield Svc Plaza, **both lanes, full facilities**, E Dunkin', Subway, W Mobil/EVC/parking
32(32)	CT 14, to Sterling, Central Village, E Cumberland, T&S/repair, Edi's Place, Pizza Pizzaz, RV camping, USPO, Walgreens, W Citgo, Valero/dsl, Dunkin', Frank O's Pizza, Subway, Knights Inn, $General, transmissions
29(30)	CT 14A to Plainfield, W Mobil
28(28)	Lathrop Rd, to Plainfield, E Shell/Domino's/dsl, Dunkin', HongKong Star Chinese, Subway, Wendy's, La Quinta, Quality Inn, Big Y Foods, Ford, Hyundai/VW, Mazda, W Ardmore Fuel, Sunoco/dsl, Bakers Dozen Cafe, McDonald's, Mr Z's Rest., Advance Parts, CVS Drug
24(24)	rd 201, Hopeville, E Hopeville Pond SP, RV camping
22(23)	CT 164, CT 138, to Pachaug, Preston, E Exxon/Petro Max/Dunkin'/dsl, $Tree, Campers World, W AmericInn
21(21)	CT 12, Jewett City, E Chili's, Panera Bread, Ruby Tuesday, Starbucks, AlDI, AT&T, Dick's, GNC, Home Depot, Kohl's, Lowe's, PetCo, Target, Verizon, Walmart/Dunkin',

HOPEVILLE

NORWICH

Exit #	Services
21(21)	Continued Mobil/Dunkin'/dsl, Shell/dsl, McDonald's, Val-U Foo vet
19a(20)	CT 169(from nb), Lisbon, E Hidden Acres RV camping
18(18)	rd 97, Taftville, E Shell/dsl, W 7-11/dsl
14(14)	to CT 2 W, CT 32 N, Norwichtown, E Friendly's, tires, Global/Dunkin'/dsl, Mobil/dsl, Shell/dsl, Illiano's Gr Prime 82 Rest., Subway, Yantic River Inn, Courtya Rosemont Suites, Ace Hardware
13b a(14)	CT 2 E, CT 32 S, Norwich, E H
11(12)	CT 82, Norwich, E Mobil, Shell/dsl, 99 Rest., Burg King, Chinese Buffet, Dunkin', Five Guys, KFC/Taco Bell, Lit Caesar's, McDonald's, Popeyes, Starbucks, Subway, Wendy $Tree, AT&T, Jo-Ann Fabrics, ShopRite Foods, Staples, Maxx, TownFair Tire, Verizon, W Holiday Inn, Big Foods, Walmart
9a(10)	CT 2A E, to Ledyard, to Pequot Res
8.5mm	service plaza sb, Mobil/dsl(sb), Dunkin'(sb Subway(sb), st police(nb)
6(6)	rd 163, to Uncasville, Montville, E Mobil/dsl, Dunki Friendly Pizza, McDonald's, repair
5(5)	CT 32(from sb, exits left), to New London, RI Beaches
2(2)	CT 85, to I-95 N, Colchester, E Shell/dsl, Dunkin', Oakdell Motel
0mm	I-95. I-395 begins/ends on I-95, exit 76.

INTERSTATE 691

MERIDEN

Exit #	Services
12.5mm	I-691 begins/ends on I-91
12(12)	Preston Ave
11(11)	I-91 N, to Hartford
10(11)	I-91 S, to New Haven, CT 15 S, W Cross Pkwy
9	Berlin Tpk
8(10)	US 5, Broad St, N HH Gas, Irving, Shell/dsl, Do Gourmet Chinese Kitchen
7(9)	downtown (from wb, no ez wb return), Meriden
6(8)	Lewis Ave(from wb, no EZ return), to CT 71, N Rub Tuesday, Best Buy, Dick's, H, Macy's, Old Navy, Target, Maxx, S 7-11, Subway
5(7)	CT 71, to Chamberlain Hill(from eb, no EZ return), N Be Buy, H, Target, S 7-11/gas, Subway
4(4)	CT 322, W Main St(no re-entry from eb), N Sunoco, Dunkin', Hubbard Park Pizza, H
3mm	Quinnipiac River
3(1)	CT 10, to Cheshire, Southington, N Sam's Clams Rest Tony's Rest.
2(0)	I-84 E, to Hartford
1(0)	I-84 W, to Waterbury
0	I-691 begins/ends on I-84

NOTES

DELAWARE

INTERSTATE 95

Exit #	Services
23mm	Delaware/Pennsylvania state line, motorist callboxes for 23 miles sb
11(22)	to I-495 S, DE 92, Naamans Rd, E $General, Burlington Coats, Goodyear/auto, Jo-Ann Fabrics, SaveALot, WaWa, W Shell/Circle K/dsl, WaWa/dsl, CVS Drug, KFC/Taco Bell, Crowne Plaza, Home Depot
10(21)	Harvey Rd(no nb return)
9(19)	DE 3, to Marsh Rd, E Dunkin', Rockwood Museum, st police, to Bellevue SP
8b a(17)	US 202, Concord Pike, to Wilmington, E Home Depot, to Brandywine Park
7b a(16)	DE 52, Delaware Ave
6(15)	DE 4, MLK Blvd, E Joe's Crabshack, McDonald's, AAA, Fresh Grocer Foods, W Liberty, Family$
5c(12)	I-495 N, to Wilmington, to DE Mem Bridge
5b a(11)	DE 141, to US 202, to New Castle, Newport, E Sheraton
4b a(8)	DE 1, DE 7, to Christiana, E Bahama Breeze, Brio Tuscan Grille, CA Pizza Kitchen, Cheesecake Factory, Don Pablo, Foodcourt, JB Dawson's Rest., Panera Bread, Ted's MT Grill, Barnes&Noble, Cabela's, Costco, Dick's, JC Penney, Macy's, mall, Michael's, Nordstrom, PetCo, Target, W Applebee's, Dunkin', Firebird's Grill, Fuddrucker's, Jimmy John's, Marble Slab Creamery, Michael's Rest., Olive Garden, Red Lobster, Country Inn&Suites, Courtyard, Days Inn, Extended Stay America, Hampton Inn, Hilton, Quality Inn, Red Roof Inn, AAA, Best Buy, casino/racetrack, Home Depot, H, PetSmart, TJ Maxx, Verizon
3b a(6)	DE 273, to Newark, Dover, E BP, Exxon/dsl, Bertucci's, Bob Evans, Boston Mkt, Ciao Pizza, Famous Dave's BBQ, Olive Grill Italian, Red Robin, Shell Hammer's Grille, Wendy's, Ramada Inn, Residence Inn, Sheraton, Staybridge Suites, TownePlace Suites, Acme Foods, Boscov's, Jo-Ann Fabrics, Old Navy, Staples, Walgreens, W Getty, Shell/dsl, Denny's, Dunkin Donuts, Comfort Inn, Holiday Inn Express, Motel 6, 7-11
5mm	service area both lanes(exits left from both lanes), info, Sunoco/dsl, Baja Fresh, Burger King, Famiglia, Popeyes, Starbucks
1b a(3)	DE 896, to Newark, to U of DE, Middletown, W Exxon, Shell/dsl, Sunoco, Boston Mkt, China Garden, Dunkin', Friendly's, Jersey Mike's, Malin's Deli, Mario's Pizza, McDonald's, TGIFriday's, Baymont Inn, Candlewood Suites, Embassy Suites, Homewood Suites, Red Roof Inn, Rodeway Inn, DE Tire Ctr
1mm	toll booth, st police
0mm	Delaware/Maryland state line, motorist callboxes for 23 miles nb

INTERSTATE 295 (Wilmington)

Exit #	Services
15mm	Delaware/New Jersey state line, Delaware River, Delaware Memorial Bridge
14.5mm	toll plaza
14	DE 9, New Castle Ave, to Wilmington, E BP, Giovanni's Cafe, Advance Parts, CVS Drug, Family$, Firestone/auto, Harley-Davidson/rest., Super G Foods, W Shell, Super/dsl, Dunkin', McDonald's, Best Night Inn, Budget Inn, SuperLodge
13	US 13, US 40, to New Castle, E BP, Shell/dsl, Speedway/dsl, Sunoco/dsl, WaWa, Applebee's, Arby's, Arner's Rest, Burger King, Checkers, DogHouse, Dove Diner, Dunkin',

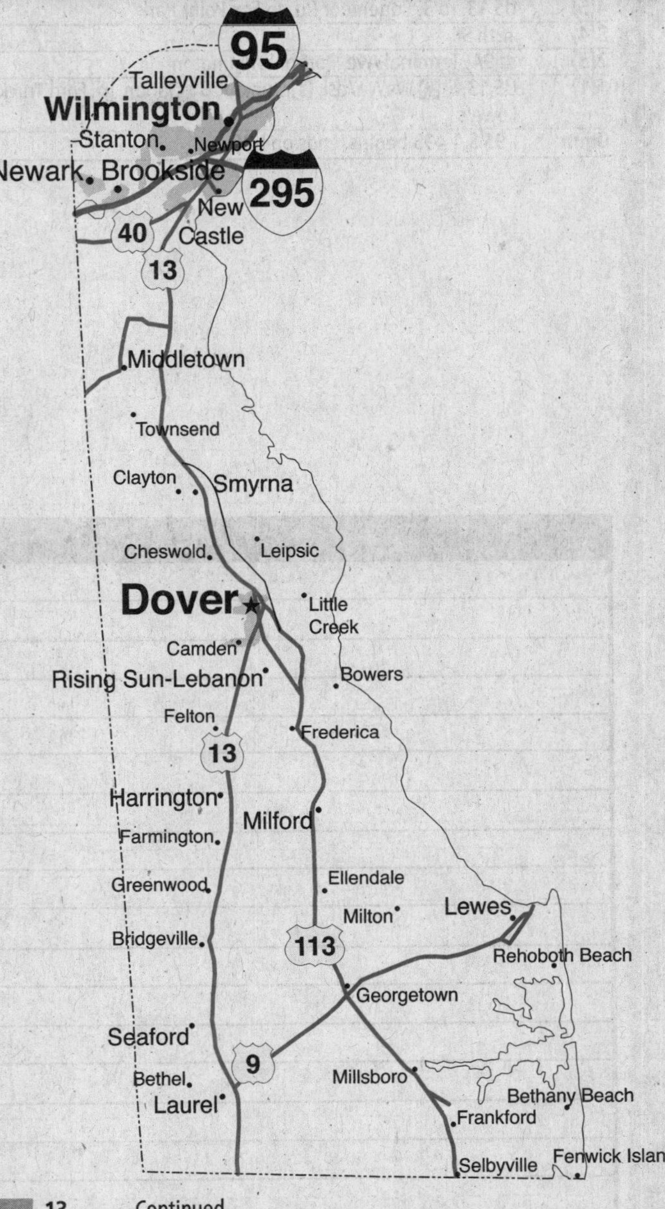

CLAYMONT

Exit #	Services
13	Continued Hooters, IHOP, KFC, Krispy Kreme, Little Caesar's, McDonald's, Popeyes, Season's Pizza, Taco Bell, TGIFriday's, Wendy's, Quality Inn, Super 8, $General, $Tree, Acura, AutoZone, Big Lots, BJ's Whse/gas, Chevrolet, Chrysler/Jeep/Dodge, Cottman Transmissions, Fiat, Ford, GNC, Home Depot, Hyundai, Lincoln, Mazda, Nissan, PepBoys, repair, Ross, Save-a-Lot, Staples, Toyota/Scion, URGENT CARE, Verizon, Walgreens, Walmart, W WaWa/dsl, Dunkin Donuts, Clarion, Fairfield Inn, Ford Trucks, Lowe's
12	I-495, US 202, N to Wilmington
11mm	I-295 begins/ends on I-95

INTERSTATE 495

Exit #	Services
11mm	I-95 N. I-495 begins/ends on I-95.
5(10)	US 13, Phila Pike, Claymont, W BP, Exxon/dsl, Sunoco/dsl, WaWa/dsl, Arby's, Boston Mkt, Burger King, Dunkin', McDonald's, Milan Motel, Aamco, Family$, Food Lion,

= gas = food = lodging = other = rest stop

CLAYMONT

DE

INTERSTATE 495 Cont'd

5(10)	Continued USPO
4(5)	US 13, rd 3, Edgemoor Rd, to Fox Point Park
3(4)	12th St
2(3)	rd 9A, Terminal Ave, Port of Wilmington
1(1)	US 13, E WaWa/dsl, Dunkin', Clarion, Ford Trucks, Lowe's
0mm	I-95 S. I-495 begins/ends on I-95.

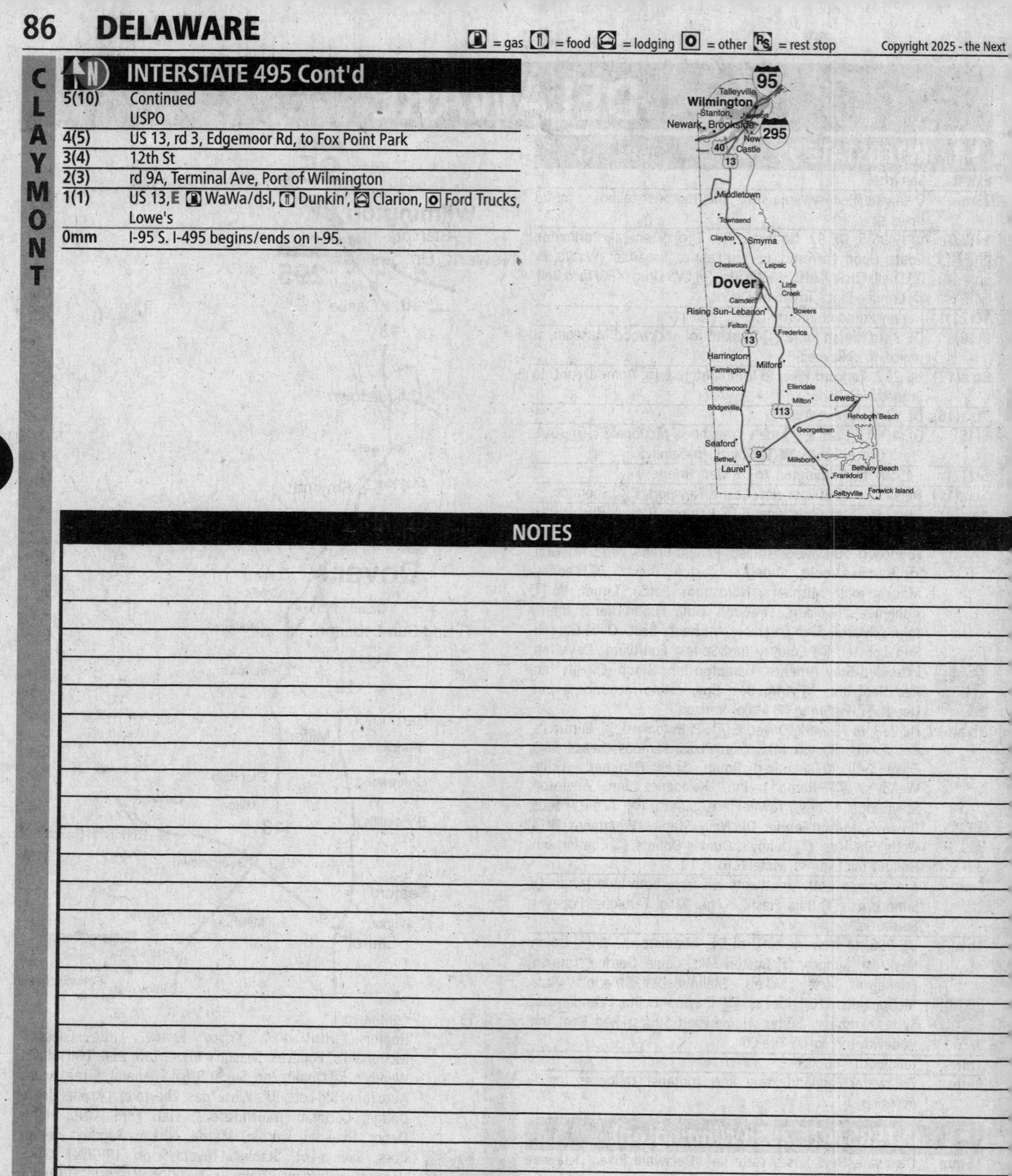

NOTES

FLORIDA

INTERSTATE 4

Exit #	Services
132	I-95, S to Miami, N to Jacksonville, FL 400. I-4 begins/ends on I-95, exit 260b
129	to US 92(from eb, exits left)
118	FL 44, to DeLand, N BP/dsl, Budget Inn,
116	Orange Camp Rd, Lake Helen
114	FL 472, to DeLand, Orange City, N Luna Sands Campground(1mi), Orange City Resort, to Blue Sprgs SP, S RaceTrac/dsl, Wawa, Burger King, Dunkin', McDonald's
111b a	Deltona, U-Haul, N RaceTrac/dsl, Shell/Circle K, Wawa/dsl, Applebee's, Baskin-Robbins/Dunkin', Chick-fil-A, Chili's, Colt's BBQ, Denny's, Five Guys, Fujiyama, Jersey Mike's Subs, Jimmy John's, KFC, Lelo's BBQ, Moe's SW, Olive Garden, Papa John's, Perkins, Pizza Hut, Popeyes, Saigon Vietnamese, Sonic, Sonny's BBQ, Starbucks, Steak'n Shake, Subway, Taco Bell, Tijuana Flats, TX Roadhouse, Woody's BBQ, Zaxby's, Holiday Inn Express, $General, Firestone/auto, Hobby Lobby, Home Depot, , Lowe's, Office Depot, Publix/deli, Save-A-Lot Foods, Target/Starbucks, Tire Kingdom, Tires+, URGENT CARE, Verizon, Walgreens, Walmart, S Citgo/repair, China Fun, Wendy's, Family$, Publix, Walgreens, W Jeremiah's Ice Cream
108	Dirksen Dr, DeBary, Deltona, N Burger King, IHOP, Hampton Inn, S RaceTrac/dsl, Valero, Hardee's, McDonald's, Subway(2mi), Waffle House, Travelodge, Publix(2mi)
104	US 17, US 92, Sanford, N La Mesa RV Ctr, S Circle K/Subway/dsl, Wavey's BBQ, Myers RV Ctr
101c	rd 46, to Mt Dora, Sanford, N 7-11, IHOP, Popeyes, Subway, Tijuana Flats, Ace Hardware, Audi, Ford, vet, S 7-11, Mobil, Murphy USA/dsl, RaceTrac/dsl, Wawa, Andy's Froyo, Buffalo Wild Wings, Burger King, Carrabba's, Cheddar's, Chianti's Pizza, Chick-fil-A, Chipotle, Cracker Barrel, Dominos, Dunkin', El Sol Mexican, Firehouse Subs, Habaneros, Honeybaked Ham, Hooters, LJ Silver/Taco Bell, Longhorn Steaks, McDonald's, Mellow Mushroom, Miller's Alehouse, Olive Garden, Outback Steaks, Panda Express, Panera Bread, PDQ Grill, Pollo Tropical, Red Lobster, Red Robin, Smokey Bones BBQ, Starbucks, Steak'n Shake, Subway, TX Roadhouse, Wendy's, Comfort Inn, Extended Stay America, Holiday Inn Express, SpringHill Suites, WoodSpring Suites, $Tree, AlLDI, AT&T, Beall's, Best Buy, Big Lots, BJ's Whse/gas, Books-A-Million, Chrysler/Dodge/Jeep, CVS Drug, Dick's, Dillard's, EVC, GNC, Goodyear/auto, Harley-Davidson, , JC Penney, Jo-Ann Fabrics, Laspada's Cheesesteaks, Macy's, mall, Marshall's, Michael's, Old Navy, PetCo, Ross, Target, Tire Kingdom, Tuesday Morning, URGENT CARE, Verizon, Walmart, World Mkt
101a b	rd 46a, FL 417(toll), FL 46, Sanford , Heathrow, N Blended Bistro, Coldstone, Duffy's Grill, F&D Cafe, FishBones, Friendly Confines Grill, Halal Guys, McDonald's, Menchie's, Papa Joe's Pizza, Ruth's Chris Steaks, Shula's 347 Grill, Terramia Pizza, Hampton Inn, Marriott, Residence Inn, Westin, Publix/Starbucks, URGENT CARE, Walgreens, S Dali's Thai, Giovanni's, Jersey Mike's, Marco's Pizza, Acura, CarMax, CVS Drug, Honda, Infiniti, Kohl's, Mercedes, Publix, Sam's Club/gas, Toyota/Scion
98	Lake Mary Blvd, Heathrow, N Shell, Broken Spoon, Casey's Grill, Panera Bread, Peach Valley Cafe, Stonewood Grill, Subway, Thai Cuisine, Courtyard, Hyatt Place,

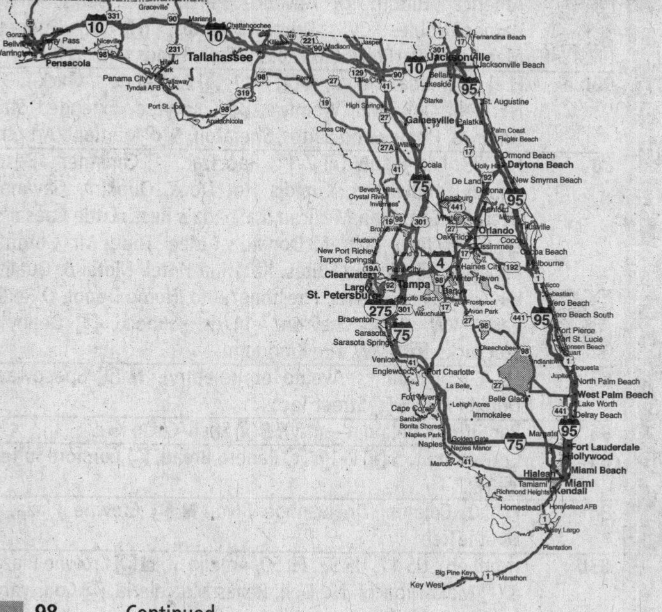

HEATHROW ALTAMONTE SPRINGS

Exit #	Services
98	Continued CVS Drug, Walgreens, Winn-Dixie, S 7-11, BP/24hr, Circle K/dsl, Mobil/dsl, Arby's, Baskin-Robbins/Dunkin', Boston Mkt, BurgerFi, Chick-fil-A, Chili's, China King, Chipotle Mexican, Chop Stix, Domino's, Firehouse Subs, First Watch, Gator's Dockside, Greek Village, Jason's Deli, Keke's Breakfast, Keller's BBQ, KFC, La Antioquena, Longhorn Steaks, McDonald's, Mikado Japanese, Noodles&Co, Panera Bread, Papa Joe's Pizza, Papa John's, Starbucks, Steak'n Shake, Subway, Taco Bell, Wendy's, Which Wich?, Zoes Mediterranean, Candlewood Suites, Extended Stay America, Hilton Garden, Homewood Suites, La Quinta, Advance Parts, AT&T, Fresh Mkt, GNC, Goodyear/auto, Home Depot, Office Depot, PetSmart, Publix, Ross, Staples, Target, Tires+, TJ Maxx, USPO, Verizon, Walgreens
95mm	**24hr security, full facilities, litter barrels, petwalk, , both lanes, vending**
94	FL 434, to Winter Springs, Longwood, N 7-11, Mobil/7-11/dsl, Burger King, China Gate, Fig's Steaks, First Watch, Hurricane Grill, Imperial Dynasty, Jeremiah's Italian Ice, Keke's Breakfast, Kobe Japanese, Melting Pot Rest., Panera Bread, Papa Joe's Pizza, Starbucks, Terramia Italian, Tijuana Flats, Wendy's, CVS Drug, Publix, vet, S 4 Rivers BBQ, Bonefish Grill, Chianti's Pizza, Pickle's NY, Starbucks,
92	FL 436, Altamonte Springs, N 7-11, Chevron/dsl, Shell/Circle K/dsl, Boston Mkt, Checkers, Chick-fil-A, Chipotle Mexican, ChuckeCheese, Cracker Barrel, Kobe Japanese, Little Caesar's, Longhorn Steaks, McDonald's, NY Best Pizza, Olive Garden, Perkins, Pollo Tropical, Popeyes, Red Lobster, Sweet Tomatoes, Taco Bell, Twin Peaks, Waffle House, WingHouse, Almonte Springs Inn, Days Inn, Hampton Inn, Hotel Elite, Opal Hotel, Ramada, Residence Inn, SpringHill Suites, TownePlace, Best Buy, CVS Drug, Family$, Firestone/auto, O'Reilly Parts, Tire Kingdom, U-Haul, Walgreens, S BP/Circle K, Chevron, Marathon/dsl, Mobil/dsl, Anthony's Pizza, Bahama Breeze, Burger King, Chili's, Coldstone, Denny's, Duffy's Grill, Dunkin', Firehouse Subs, Five Guys, Jason's Deli, Little Greek, Moe's SW Grill, Orlando Alehouse, Panda Express, Pei Wei, Pizza Hut, Seasons 52, Starbucks, Steak'n Shake, TooJay's Deli, Wendy's,

FL

ALTAMONTE SPRINGS

INTERSTATE 4 Cont'd

92 Continued
Yummy House Chinese, [lodging] Embassy Suites, Extended Stay America, Hilton, [other] Advance Parts, Albertson's, AT&T, Barnes&Noble, CVS Drug, Dillard's, [H], JC Penney, Marshall's, PetCo, Publix, Ross, Whole Foods Mkt

90b a FL 414, Maitland Blvd, **N** [gas] 7-11, [food] Applebee's, Chick-fil-A, NY Deli, Oak Grill, Wendy's, [lodging] Courtyard, Extended Stay America, Homewood Suites, Sheraton, **S** [other] Maitland Art Ctr

88 FL 423, Lee Rd, **N** [gas] 7-11, RaceTrac, [food] Christner's Rest., Cuban Sandwiches, Cupid's Hot Dogs, Dunkin', Gavanna Rest., La Campana Mexican, LaSpada's Rest., Little Caesar's, LJ Silver/Taco Bell, McDonald's, Mee Thai, Mi Gordita, Popeyes, [lodging] InTown Suites, Katerina Hotel, Motel 6, Quality Inn, [other] Advance Parts, Firestone/auto, Home Depot, O'Reilly Parts, VW, **S** [gas] Chevron/7-11/dsl, Sunoco, [food] Denny's, Starbucks, [other] BMW, Tire Kingdom

87 FL 426, Fairbanks Ave(no eb re-entry), **N** [gas] Speedway/Dunkin'/dsl, **S** [food] Street Tacos

86 Par St(from eb, no re-entry), **S** [gas] Shell/Circle K

85 Princeton St, **S** [gas] 7-11, [food] Panera Bread, [lodging] Comfort Suites, [other] [H]

84 FL 50, Colonial Dr, Ivanhoe Blvd, **N** [lodging] Crowne Plaza, **S** DoubleTree

83b (from eb), US 17, US 92, FL 50, Amelia St, **N** [lodging] Crowne Plaza, **S** [food] Maki Hibachi, NY Deli, Reyes Mezcaleria, [lodging] Courtyard, Residence Inn

83a FL 526(from eb), Robinson St

83 South St(from wb), downtown

82c Anderson St E, Church St Sta Hist Dist, downtown

82b Gore Ave(from wb), **S** downtown, [other] [H]

82a FL 408(toll), to FL 526

81b c Kaley Ave, **S** [gas] Mobil, [other] [H]

81a Michigan St(from wb), **N** [gas] Chevron/dsl

80b a US 17, US 441 S, US 92 W, **S** [gas] 7-11, BP, Chevron, Citgo, RaceTrac, Shell, [food] Checkers, McDonald's, Mr. Gyros, Mr. Snappers, Subway, Taqueria Mexican, [lodging] Days Inn, Lake Holden Inn, [other] $General, AlLDI, AutoZone, Save-A-Lot Foods, Walgreens

79 FL 423, 33rd St, John Young Pkwy, **N** [food] McDonald's, [other] Harley-Davidson, Toyota/Scion, **S** [gas] Chevron/dsl, Wawa/dsl, [food] IHOP, [lodging] Days Inn

78 Conroy Rd, **N** [gas] 7-11, [other] Audi, **S** [food] BJ's Rest., Bloomingdale's, Brio Grille, Burger 21, Cheesecake Factory, Chevy's Mexican, Chick-fil-A, Jimmy John's, Krispy Kreme, McDonald's, Moe's SW Grill, Olive Garden, Panda Express, Panera Bread, PF Chang's, Pollo Tropical, Subway, TGIFriday's, Wendy's, Zaxby's, [other] $Tree, AT&T, Best Buy, BJ's Whse/gas, Costco/gas, Dick's, Home Depot, Infiniti, Jaguar, Macy's, mall, Marshall's, Mercedes, Old Navy, PetCo, Ross, Super Target

77 FL 527, FL TPK(toll), **N** [food] Wendy's, [lodging] Best Western +, Extended Stay America, Fairfield, Residence Inn

75b a FL 435, International Dr(exits left from both lanes), **N** [gas] Chevron, Mobil, [food] Burger King, Carrabba's, TGIFriday's, [lodging] Clarion, Comfort Suites, DoubleTree, Extended Stay America, Fairfield Inn, Holiday Inn, Holiday Inn Express, Hyatt Place, InTowne Suites, La Quinta, [other] to Universal Studios, Walgreens, **S** [gas] 7-11, Chevron/dsl, Speedway/dsl, [food] Black Angus Steaks, Burger King, Del Taco, Denny's, IHOP, Red Lobster, Sonic, Subway, Sweet Tomatoes, [lodging] Avanti Palms, Best Western, Hampton Inn, Hilton Garden, Homewood Suites, La Quinta, Motel 6, multiple hotels & resorts, Quality Inn, Sheraton, Super 8, SureStay+, [other] Artegon/famous Brands, Bass Pro Shops, Walgreens

74b **N** [food] McDonald's, [other] Universal Studios(from wb),

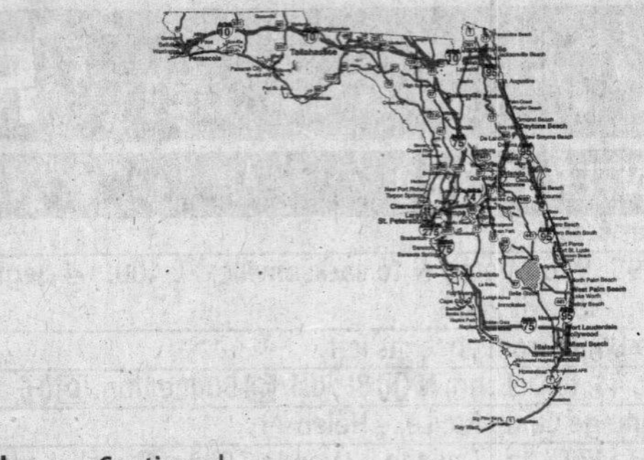

LAKE BUENA VISTA

74b Continued
Dunkin, [lodging] Home2 Suites

74a FL 482, Sand Lake Rd, **N** [gas] 7-11, Chevron, [food] Chick-fil-A, Dunkin, Eddie's Seafood, First Watch, Five Guys, Fres Italian, McDonald's, O'Charley's, Pei Wei, Wendy's, Zoe Kitchen, [lodging] Drury Inn, [other] $Tree, GNC, [H], Michael's, Publi Tire Kingdom, Walgreens, Walmart/McDonald's, Whole Foo Mkt, **S** [gas] BP/Circle K/dsl, Shell/Circle K/dsl, [food] Bahan Breeze, BJ's Rest., Boston Lobster, Boteco do Manolo, Buffa Wild Wings, Burger King, Cafe 34 Turkish, Cafe Tu Tu, Capit Grille, Carrabba's, Charley's Steaks, Checkers, Chili ChuckECheese, Chuy's Mexican, Cici's Pizza, CiCi's Pizz Coldstone, Dave&Buster's, Del Frisco's, Denny's, Domino Dunkin', Fish Bones Rest., Five Guys , Fogo de Chao Friendly's, Giordano's Pizza, Golden Corral, Hooters, IHO Joe's Crabshack, Juicy Crab, KAVAS Tacos, Kobe Japanes Longhorn Steaks, Maggiano's, MASH, McDonald's, Mia Italian, Miller's Alehouse, MOOYAH Burgers, Olive Garde Outback Steaks, Perkins, Pizza Hut, Pizza Hut, Popeyes, R Robin, Senor Frogs, Shake Shack, Sloppy Joe's, Starbuck Subway, Taco Bell, TGIFriday's, Tony Roma, Twin Peak Uncle Julio's, Uno, Vito's Chophouse, Yard House, Yardhous [lodging] Avanti Resort, Best Western/EVC, Castle Hotel/EV Clarion, CoCo Key Hotel, Comfort Inn, Courtya EconoLodge, Embassy Suites, Embassy Suites, Extended St America, Fairfield Inn, Hampton Inn, Hampton Inn, Holid Inn Express, Homewood Suites, Hyatt Place, Hyatt Regenc EVC, La Quinta, Quality Inn, Quality Suites, Ramada Inn, R Roof+, Residence Inn, Rosen Inn, Rosen Plaza, Sones Suites, Spring Hill , Springhill Suites, Wyndham Resort, Harley-Davidson, Ripley's Believe-it-or-not!, Walgreens

72 FL 528 E(toll, no eb re-entry), to Cape Canaveral, **N** [other] USP **S** [food] Cheddar's, Denny's, Dunkin', McDonald's, Red Lobst [lodging] Best Western, Days Inn, DoubleTree, Extended Sta Hilton, Sheraton, Tru, [other] to [airport]

71 Central FL Pkwy(from eb no re-entry), **S** [gas] 7-11/d Chevron, Mobil, Wawa/dsl, [food] Bonefish Grill, Buffalo W Wings, KFC, McDonald's, Mellow Mushroom, Panera Brea Starbucks, Taco Bell, TGIFridays, Wendy's, [lodging] Fairfield Ir Hampton Inn, Hilton Garden, Holiday Inn, Homewood Suit Renaissance Resort, Springhill Suites, Staybrid TownePlace Suites, [other] CVS, CVS, Publix, to SeaWor Walgreens

68 FL 535, Lake Buena Vista, **N** [gas] 7-11, Mobil/dsl, Shell/Cir K/dsl, Tesla EVC, Wawa, [food] AleHouse, Black Angus Steal Black Fire Brazilian Steaks, Burger King, Chili's, China Buff CiCi's Pizza, Crafty Crab, Denny's, Domino's, Dunkin', Patron, Giordano's, Hooters, IHOP, KFC, Kobe Japane Macaroni Grill, Olive Garden, Papa John's, Perkins, Pizza H Pizza Hut, Qdoba, Sofrito Latin Cafe, Steak'n Shake, Subw Twin Peaks, U & Me, Uno, Waffle House, [lodging] AC Hotel, Al Hotel, B Resort, Candlewood Suites, Clarion, Courtya Crowne Plaza, Delta Orlando, DoubleTree, Drury I Embassy Suites, Extended Stay America, Fairfield I Hampton Inn, Hawthorn Suites, Hilton, Hilton,

FL

INTERSTATE 4 Cont'd

LAKE BUENA VISTA

68 Continued
Hilton Garden, Holiday Inn, Holiday Inn Express, Homewood Suites, Hyatt Place, Quality Inn, Residence Inn, Sheraton, Sonesta Suites, SpringHill Suites, TownePlace Suites, Wyndham, Walgreens, Winn Dixie, **S** 7-11, Chevron/dsl, Applebee's, Bahama Breeze, BJ's Rest., Carrabba's, Chick-fil-A, CiCi's Pizza, Dunkin', Golden Corral, Landry's Seafood, Longhorn Steaks, Mexas Tacos, Pal Campo, Panera Bread, Pollo Tropical, Saltgrass Steaks, Starbucks, Subway, Wendy's, Blue Heron Resort, Buena Vista Suites, Courtyard, Fairfield Inn, Holiday Inn Resort, Residence Inn, Sheraton, SpringHill Suites, $Tree, CVS Drug, Orlando Premium Outlets, Verizon, Walgreens

67 Fl 536, to Epcot, **N** Marriott, Signia Hilton, Wyndham Grand/EVC, DisneyWorld, **S** 7-11, NY Pizza, Caribe Royale, Holiday Inn, Marriott, CVS Drug, multiple resorts, to

65 Osceola Pkwy, to FL 417(toll), **N** Animal Kingdom, Epcot, to DisneyWorld, Wide World of Sports

64b a US 192, FL 536, to FL 417(toll), to Kissimmee, **N** Hollywood Studios, Harley-Davidson, **S** 7-11, Mobil/dsl, RaceTrac/dsl, Boston Lobster Feast, Burger King, Charley's Steakhouse, Checkers, Chick-fil-A, Chinese Buffet, Chipotle, Cracker Barrel, Denny's, Domino's Pizza, Dunkin', Five Guys, Golden Corral, IHOP, Joe's Crabshack, KFC, Kobe Japanese, Little Italy, Logan's Roadhouse, Longhorn Steaks, Maple Street Breakfast, McDonald's, Mr. and Mrs. Crab, Panera Bread, Pei Wei, Pizza Hut, Pizza Press, Red Lobster, Senor Mannys, Starbucks, Tijuana Flats, Waffle House, Waffle House, Wendy's, Celebration Suites, Comfort Suites, Embassy Suites, Fairfield Inn, Holiday Inn, Magic Castle Inn, Motel 6, Parkway Resort, Quality Suites, Radisson, Rodeway Inn, Seralago Hotel, Super 8, Travelodge, CVS Drug, Publix, Sam's Club/dsl, T-Mobile, USPO, Walgreens

APOPKA

62 FL 417(toll, from eb), World Dr, Celebration, **N** to DisneyWorld, **S** to

60 Fl 429 N (toll), Apopka

58 FL 532, to Kissimmee, **N** 7-11, BP/Circle K/dsl, Chili's, Dunkin Donuts, First Watch, Huey Magoo's, Jersey Mike's, McDonald's, Millers Alehouse, Panera Bread, Pizzaria, Red Robin, Subway, Tijuana Flats, Wendy's, Championship Gate Resort, Publix, Walgreens, **S** 7-11, LongHorn Steaks, Olive Garden, Starbucks, Reunion Resort (2mi)

55 US 27, to Haines City, **N** 7-11, Chevron/dsl, Love's/Arby's/dsl/scales/24hr, RaceTrac, Sunoco/dsl, Burger King, Cracker Barrel, Denny's, McDonald's, Waffle House, Wendy's, Comfort Inn, Hampton Inn, Holiday Inn Express, Home Suites, Ford, **S** 7-11, Marathon/dsl, RaceTrac/dsl, Wawa/dsl, Bob Evans, Chick-fil-A, Chipotle, CiCi's Pizza, Davenport's Ale House, Dos Panza, Dunkin', First Watch, Five Guys, Panda Express, Popeyes, Starbucks, Subway, Taco Bell, Days Inn, Ramada Inn, $Tree, AT&T, Best Buy, Books-A-Million, Deer Creek RV Resort, Dick's, Family$, GNC, JC Penney, KOA, Michael's, PetSmart, Ross, Staples, Target, Theme World RV Park, to Cypress Gardens, tourist info

LAKE ALFRED

48 rd 557, to Winter Haven, Lake Alfred, **S** Marathon/dsl

46mm **24hr security, full facilities, litter barrels, petwalk, both lanes, vending**

44 FL 559, to Auburndale, **S** Love's/Arby's/dsl/scales/24hr, Shell/Subway/dsl/scales/24hr, McDonald's

41 FL 570 W toll, Auburndale, Lakeland

38 FL 33, to Lakeland, Polk City

33 rd 582, to FL 33, Lakeland, **N** 7-11, Exxon/dsl, Applebee's, Cracker Barrel, Five Guys, McDonald's, Starbucks, Subway, Wendy's, Baymont, Baymont Inn,

LAKELAND

33 Continued
Days Inn, Extended Stay, Hampton Inn, Holiday Inn Express, La Quinta, Sleep Inn, Stayable Suites, BMW/EVC, CVS Drug, GNC, Publix, **S** Marathon/dsl, Waffle House, Woodspring Suites, Harley-Davidson/EVC, Lakeland RV Resort, Mercedes, Nissan

32 US 98, Lakeland, Extended Stay, **N** 7-11, Marathon, Mobil/dsl, Murphy USA/dsl, Wawa/dsl, Arby's, Beef o' Brady's, BubbaQue's BBQ, Buffalo Wild Wings, Checkers, Chick-fil-A, Chili's, Chipotle, ChuckeCheese, Crafty Crab, Culver's, Domino's, DQ, Dunkin Donuts, Firehouse Subs, First Watch, Ford's Garage, Golden Corral, Hooters, Hungry Howie's, IHOP, Jersey Mike's, KFC, Krispy Kreme, Little Caesar's, Longhorn Steaks, McDonald's, Moe's SW Grill, Mr. Pollo Mexican, Olive Garden, Outback Steaks, Panda Express, Panera Bread, Papa John's, Pizza Hut, Red Lobster, Smokey Bones BBQ, Sonny's BBQ, Steak'n Shake, Subway, Taco Bell, Wendy's, Zaxby's, Comfort Inn, La Quinta, TownPlace Suites, Travelodge, $General, $Tree, Advance Parts, AlLDI, AT&T, AutoZone, Beall's, Best Buy, Big Lots, Chrysler/Dodge/Jeep, CVS Drug, Dick's, Dillard's, Discount Tire, Firestone/auto, Goodyear/auto, Hobby Lobby, JC Penney, JoAnn Fabrics, Lowe's, Michael's, O'Reilly Parts, Old Navy, PepBoys, PetCo, PetSmart, Publix, Ross, RV World, Sam's Club/gas, Save a Lot, Staples, Target/Starbucks, Tire Kingdom, Tires+, TJ Maxx, Toyota/Scion, Verizon, Walgreens, Walmart(2mi), **S** Chevron/dsl, Coastal, Exxon/7-11, Mobil/dsl, Bob Evans, Burger King, Denny's, Dunkin'/EVC, McDonald's, Nick&Moes, Popeyes, Waffle House, Wingstop, Howard Johnson, Motel 6, Ramada, $Tree, AutoZone, Beall's, Family$, Home Depot, NAPA, U-Haul

31 FL 539, to Kathleen, Lakeland, **N** Circle K/dsl, Marathon, Romeo's Pizza, Subway, Wendy's, Publix/dsl, Walgreens

28 FL 546, to US 92, Memorial Blvd, from eb re-entry, Lakeland, **S** Chevron, Mobil/Circle K/dsl, Burger King, Hardee's, Taco Bell

PLANT CITY

27 FL 570 E toll, Lakeland

25 County Line Rd, **S** Mobil/dsl, Shell/Circle K/Subway, McDonald's, Wendy's, Fairfield Inn, FL Air Museum

22 FL 553, Park Rd, Plant City, **N** Smokin Aces BBQ, Chevrolet, **S** Shell/Circle K/Subway, Arby's, Burger King, Culver's, Denny's, Popeyes, Holiday Inn Express, Quality Inn

21 FL 39, Alexander St, to Zephyrhills, Plant City, **S** BP/dsl, Mobil/dsl, Knights Inn

19 FL 566, to Thonotosassa, **N** Shell/Dunkin'/dsl, **S** RaceTrac/dsl, Wawa/dsl/Tesla EVC, Applebee's, BuddyFreddy's Rest., Burger King, Lin's Chinese, Little Caesar's, McDonald's, Mi Casa, Mr. & Mrs. Crab, OutBack Steaks, Pizza Hut/Taco Bell, Starbucks, Subway, Waffle House, Hampton Inn/EVC, $General, AT&T, GNC, Publix, Walgreens, **E** Carrabba's

17 Branch Forbes Rd, **N** Marathon/dsl, Shell/dsl, Dinosaur World, **S** Chevron, Citgo/dsl, Shell/Circle K/Subway/dsl, Advance Parts, AutoZone

14 McIntosh Rd, **N** Shell/Circle K/Dunkin', Camping World RV Ctr, Windward RV Park(2mi), **S** 7-11/dsl, ARCO, Marathon/dsl, RaceWay/dsl, Burger King, Hungry Howie's Pizza, McDonald's/playplace, General RV Ctr, Tampa East RV Park, Tampa RV Ctr

12mm both lanes, weigh sta

10 rd 579, Mango, Thonotosassa, **N** BP, Flying J/Denny's/dsl/LP/scales/24hr, TA/Arby's/Popeyes/dsl/scales/24hr/@, Texaco, Bob Evans, Cracker Barrel, Country Inn&Suites, Hampton Inn, Ford/Lincoln, Hillsboro River SP, Lazy Day's RV Ctr/Resort, Wade RV Ctr, **S** Shell/Circle K/dsl,

FL

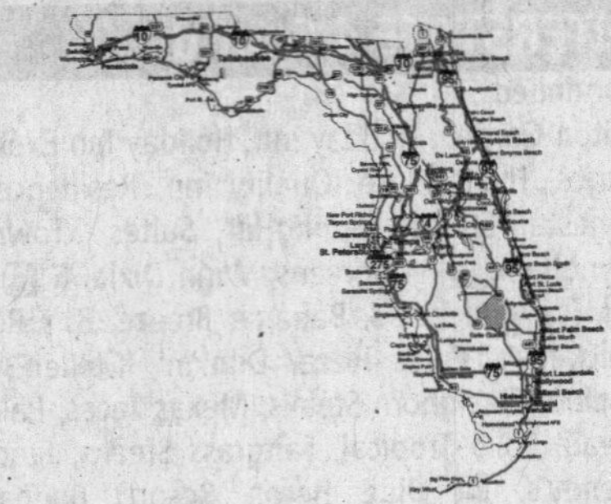

INTERSTATE 4 Cont'd

PORT OF TAMPA

10	Continued Hardee's, Subway, Wendy's, Masters Inn
9	I-75, N to Ocala, S to Naples
7	US 92W, to US 301, Hillsborough Ave, N Exxon/rest./dsl/scales/24hr, Mobil/dsl, Wawa/dsl, Waffle House, Extended Stay America, Hard Rock Hotel/casino, Roadway Inn, S Exxon, Speedway/dsl, Wawa/dsl, Five Guys, WingHouse, Comfort Suites, Holiday Inn Express, La Quinta, Red Roof Inn, FL Expo Fair
6	Orient Rd(from eb)
5	FL 574, MLK Blvd, N McDonald's, truck/rv wash, S Mobil, Shell, Sunoco/Subway, Wendy's, Fairfield Inn, Motel 6, Kenworth
3	US 41, 50th St, Columbus Dr(exits left from eb), N Chevron/dsl, Shell/Subway/dsl, Days Inn, Quality Inn, Rodeway Inn, $General, to Busch Gardens, S Marathon/dsl, Mobil, Wawa/dsl/Tesla EVC, Brocato's, Burger King, Checkers, Church's TX Chicken, Domino's, KFC, McDonald's, Salem's Subs, Subway, Taco Bell, Holiday Inn Express, Advance Parts, Family$, Save-A-Lot, URGENT CARE
1	FL 585, 22nd, 21st St, Port of Tampa, S Sunoco, Burger King, McDonald's, museum, USPO
0mm	I-4 begins/ends on I-275, exit 45b.

FL

INTERSTATE 10

MACCLENNY

363mm	I-10 begins/ends on I-95, exit 351b.
362	Stockton St, to Riverside, S BP, Gate, H
361	US 17 S(from wb)
360	FL 129, McDuff Ave, S Sunoco, Popeyes
359	Luna St, to Lenox Ave(from wb)
358	FL 111, Cassat Ave , N Shell/Subway/dsl, Sunoco/Godfather's/dsl, Burger King, McDonald's, Monroe BBQ, Popeyes, AutoZone, S BP/dsl, EVC, RaceWay/dsl, Domino's, Dunkin'/Baskin-Robins, Krispy Kreme, Pizza Hut, Royal Buffet, Taco Bell, Wendy's, $Tree, Advance Parts, Lowe's, Walgreens
357	FL 103, Lane Ave, N CNG, Speedway/dsl, Andy's Sandwiches, Knights Inn, Stars Rest Inn, S 76/dsl, Mobil/rest., Applebee's, Bono's BBQ, Cross Creek Steaks, Hardee's, KFC, Lee's Dragon, McDonald's, Executive Inn, Sleep Inn, CVS Drug, Firestone/auto, Home Depot, Office Depot, PepBoys
356	I-295, N to Savannah, S to St Augustine
355	Hammond Blvd, Marietta, S Speedway/Dunkin'/dsl, Domino's
351	FL 115, Chaffee Rd, to Cecil Fields, N Circle K/dsl, $General, Campers RV Ctr, S Shell/Subway/dsl, Valero, Cinco de Mayo, Cracker Barrel, King Wok, McDonald's, Mr Chubby's Wings, Subway, Wendy's, Best Western, Fairfield Inn, Hampton Inn, Holiday Inn Express, Family$, Winn-Dixie/Tesla EVC
350	FL 23, Cecil Commerce Ctr Pkwy
343	US 301, to Starke, Baldwin, N Love's/Bojangles/dsl/service/parking/scales/24hr/@, S Mobil/Circle K, Pilot/Subway/dsl/scales/24hr, TA/Shell/Arby's/dsl/scales/24hr/@, Burger King, McDonald's, Waffle House, Red Roof Inn
336	FL 228, to Maxville, Macclenny, N Murphy USA/dsl, Dunkin', Starbucks, fireworks, GNC, H, Walmart
335	FL 121, to Lake Butler, Macclenny, N Mobil, Shell/dsl, China Dragon, Crystal River Seafood, Domino's, Firehouse Subs, Hardee's, KFC, McDonald's, MotLee's, Pier 6, Pizza Hut, Popeyes, Sixth Street Steaks, Subway, Taco Bell, Waffle House, Wendy's, Woody's BBQ, Zaxby's, Hampton Inn,

SANDERSON

LEE

TALLAHASSEE

335	Continued Motel 6, $General, $Tree, Advance Parts, AutoZone, H, Save-A-Lot Foods, USPO, Verizon, vet, Walgreens, Winn-Dixie, S Exxon/dsl, Burger King, China Buffet, Havana Kitchen, Red Roof Inn, Travelodge
333	rd 125, Glen Saint Mary, N Mobil/dsl, Island Oaks RV Camping
327	rd 229, to Raiford, Sanderson
324	US 90, to Olustee, Sanderson, S Mobil/dsl, Osceola NF, to Olustee Bfd
318mm	**24hr security, full facilities, litter barrels, petwalk, , both lanes, vending**
303	US 441, Lake City, N Chevron/dsl, Lake City Camping(1mi), Lake City RV Resort, S Shell/dsl/EVC Sunoco/dsl, Huddle House, Days Inn, E Winn-Dixie
301	US 41, to Lake City, N Marathon/Busy Bee/dsl
296b a	I-75, N to Valdosta, S to Tampa
294mm	**24hr security, full facilities, litter barrels, petwalk, , both lanes, vending**
292	rd 137, to Wellborn
283	US 129, to Live Oak, N Busy Bee/Burger King/Dunkin' dsl/EVC/parking/24hr, S BP/Krystal, Chevron/dsl, Exxon/ds Murphy USA/dsl, Shell/dsl, Beef 'O'Brady's, China Buffe McDonald's, Moe's SW Grill, Papa John's, Subway, Taco Bel Waffle House, Wendy's, Zaxby's, EconoLodge, Holiday In Express, Quality Inn, $Tree, GNC, H, Lowe's, Verizo Walmart
275	US 90, Live Oak
271mm	truck insp sta both lanes
269mm	Suwannee River
265mm	**24hr security, full facilities, litter barrels, petwalk, , both lanes, vending**
264mm	weigh sta both lanes
262	rd 255, Lee, N to Suwannee River SP, S Jimmy's Sunoco/Red Onion Grill/dsl/scales/24hr/@, Love's/Arby's dsl/scales/24hr/@
258	FL 53, N Mobil/DQ/Subway/Wendy's/dsl/scales/24h Sunoco/McDonald's/dsl, Smackin' Lips Diner, Waff House, Best Western, Days Inn, Super 8, H, S Deerwood Inn, Madison Camping, Ragans RV Camping
251	FL 14, to Madison, N Mobil/Arby's/24hr, H
241	US 221, Greenville, N Mobil/DQ
234mm	**24hr security, full facilities, litter barrels, petwalk, , both lanes**
233	rd 257, Aucilla, N Shell/dsl
225	US 19, to Monticello, N Camper's World Camping, S B Chevron/McDonald's/dsl, Mobil/Arby's/parking/d Sunoco/dsl, Tokyo Grill, Days Inn, Super 8, A Ston Throw RV Park, KOA
217	FL 59, Lloyd, S Shell/Subway/dsl, EconoLodge
209b a	US 90, Tallahassee, N Lulu's Taqueria, Staybrid Suites, S Circle K/dsl, Shell/Subway/dsl, Backwoo Crossing, Eastern Chinese, Waffle House, Wendy's, R Roof Inn, auto museum, Publix, Tallahassee RV Park
203	FL 61, US 319, Tallahassee, N BP/dsl, Shell/Circle K

INTERSTATE 10 Cont'd

203 Continued
Shell/Circle K, Tesla EVC, Baskin-Robbins/Dunkin', Blaze Pizza, Bonefish Grill, Burger Bar, Chipotle, Dejavu Venezuelan, Firehouse Subs, Five Guys, Hungry Howie's, Island Fin Hawaiian, Jimmy John's, Kiku Japanese, Lofty Pursuits, McAlister's Deli, McDonald's, Moe's SW Grill, Newk's Eatery, Osaka Japanese, Panda Buffet, Panera Bread, Pepper's Cantina, Popeyes, Rock N Roll Sushi, Smashburger, Sonny's BBQ, Starbucks, Taco Bell, Tijuana Flats, Waffle House, Wendy's, Which Wich?, SpringHill Suites, $Tree, AT&T, Books-A-Million, CVS Drug, Discount Tire, Fresh Mkt Foods, GNC, Hobby Lobby, Petco, Publix, SteinMart/EVC, SuperLube, TJ Maxx, Trader Joe's, Walgreens, Walmart(3mi), **S** Citgo, Marathon/dsl, Bumpa's, Carrabba's, Chick-fil-A, El Jalisco, Outback Steaks, Steak'n Shake, Subway, Ted's MT Grill, TX Roadhouse, Village Inn, Walk-On's, Zaxby's, Comfort Inn, Courtyard, Extended Stay America, Hampton Inn, Hilton Garden, Holiday Inn Express, Residence Inn, Advance Parts, Goodyear/auto, Home Depot, H, O'Reilly Parts, Office Depot, PetSmart, U-Haul, URGENT CARE

199 US 27, Tallahassee, **N** Chevron/dsl, Citgo/dsl, Marathon/dsl, Burger King, China King, Country Kitchen, Domino's, Hungry Howies, Krispy Chicken, McDonald's, Papa John's, Pizza Hut, Starbucks, Subway, Taco Bell, Waffle House, Wahoo Seafood, Baymont Inn, Best Western, Country Inn&Suites, Fairfield Inn, Holiday Inn, Quality Inn, Sleep Inn, $General, Ace Hardware, Advance Parts, AutoZone, Big Oak RV Park(2mi), CVS Drug, Family$, USPO, vet, Walgreens, Walmart, Winn-Dixie, **S** Chevron/dsl, Shell/Circle K, Shell/KFC, Arby's, Bojangles, Boston Mkt, Chick-fil-A, China Buffet, ChuckECheese, Cracker Barrel, Crafty Crab, Crystal River Seafood, Culver's, Denny's, DQ, Dunkin', El Jalisco, Firehouse Subs, Golden Corral, Guthrie's, Hardee's, Hooters, IHOP, Kacey's Rest, Krispy Kreme, Lindy's Chicken, Little Caesar's, Longhorn Steaks, McDonald's, Melting Pot, Papa John's, Rankin Tacos, Red Lobster, Sado Mori Japanese, Sonic, Sonny's BBQ, Sonny's BBQ, Starbucks, Subway, Tour of Italy, Wendy's, Whataburger, Zaxby's, Candlewood Suites, Days Inn, EconoLodge, Howard Johnson, La Casa Inn, La Quinta, Motel 6, Red Roof Inn, Rodeway Inn, Seven Hills Suites, Suburban Hotel, Wingate, Advance Parts, AT&T, AutoZone, Barnes&Noble, Belk, city park, CVS Drug, PepBoys, Publix, Ross, Staples, Sun Tire, Tuffy Auto, U-Haul, Verizon, vet, Walgreens

196 FL 263, Tallahassee, **S** Chevron/dsl, Inland/dsl, Murphy USA/dsl, Shell/dsl, Stop'n Save Gas, Applebee's, DQ, Dunkin', Firehouse Subs, Great Wall Chinese, KFC, McDonald's, MCormick's Deli, Sonic, Steak'n Shake, Subway, Taco Bell, Waffle House, Wendy's, Zaxby's, Sleep Inn, Woodspring Suites, $Tree, Advance Parts, AutoZone, Chrysler/Dodge/Jeep, Harley-Davidson, Home Depot, Hyundai, Lowe's, Mazda, Office Depot, Toyota, Verizon, Walgreens, Walmart/Burger King

194mm **24hr security, full facilities, litter barrels, petwalk, both lanes, vending**

192 US 90, to Tallahassee, Quincy, **N** Exxon, Flying J/Denny's/dsl/LP/scales/24hr, Baymont, Comfort Inn, Camping World RV Ctr(2mi), **S** Pilot/Dunkin'/dsl/scales/24hr, Lindy's Chicken, Waffle House, Country Inn & Suites

181 FL 267, Quincy, **N** Murphy USA/dsl, Domino's, Mayflower Chinese, H, Walmart, **S** BP/dsl, Citgo/dsl, Hampton Inn, Holiday Inn Express, Quality Inn, to Lake Talquin SF

174 FL 12, to Greensboro, **N** Marathon/dsl, Shell/Burger King/dsl

BLOUNTSTOWN

166 rd 270A, Chattahoochee, **N** to Lake Seminole, **S** Marathon/dsl, CCC's RV Park(1mi), Flat Creek RV Park(1mi), to Torreya SP

161mm **24hr security, full facilities, litter barrels, petwalk, both lanes, vending**

160mm Apalachicola River, central/eastern time zone

158 rd 286, Sneads, **N** Lake Seminole, to Three Rivers SP

155mm weigh sta both lanes

152 FL 69, to Grand Ridge, Blountstown, **N** Exxon/dsl, Marathon/dsl

142 FL 71, to Marianna, Oakdale, **N** Murphy USA/dsl, Pilot/Arby's/dsl/scales/24hr, Beef'O'Brady's, Burger King, Dunkin', Firehouse Subs, Hong Kong Chinese, Pizza Hut, PoFolks, Ruby Tuesday, San Marco's Mexican, Sonny's BBQ, Waffle House, Baymont Inn, Comfort Inn, Days Inn, Econolodge, Fairfield Inn, Microtel, Quality Inn, Super 8, $Tree, AT&T, H, Lowe's, to FL Caverns SP(8mi), Walmart/Subway, **S** Marathon/dsl, TA/Pizza Hut/Popeyes/Taco Bell/dsl/scales/24hr/@, Dickey's BBQ, DQ, McDonald's, Best Value Inn, Dove Rest RV Park

136 FL 276, to Marianna, **N** to FL Caverns SP(8mi)

133mm **24hr security, full facilities, litter barrels, petwalk, both lanes**

130 US 231, Cottondale, **N** Hardee's, Subway, **S** Love's/Chester's/McDonald's/dsl/scales/24hr/@, Hitchinpost RV Camping(1mi)

120 FL 77, to Panama City, Chipley, **N** Exxon/Burger King/Stuckey's, Marathon/dsl, Murphy USA/dsl, Shell/dsl, Arby's, Bubba's BBQ, Cancun Mexican, Dominos, Dunkin', Hardee's, Hungry Howie's, Javier's Mexican, JinJin Chinese, KFC, McDonald's, Popeyes, Sonic, Subway, Taco Bell, Waffle House, Wendy's, Comfort Inn, Days Inn/rest., Quality Inn, Red Roof Inn, Super 8, Advance Parts, Brickyard Mkt, H, O'Reilly Parts, Walmart/EVC, **S** Falling Water SP

BONIFAY

112 FL 79, Bonifay, **N** Chevron, Shell/dsl, Tom Thumb/dsl, Burger King, Cancun Mexican, Castaway Cafe, Donutland, Hardee's, Hungry Howie, M&W BBQ, McDonald's, PHO Noodle, Pizza Hut, Subway, Waffle House, Bonifay Inn, Holiday Inn Express, Rodeway Inn, DG Mkt, FL Springs RV Camping, H, **S** Panama City Beach

104 rd 279, Caryville

96 FL 81, Ponce de Leon, **both lanes, full facilities, litter barrels, petwalk, 24hr security**, **N** $General, Ponce De Leon RV Park, to Ponce de Leon SRA, Vortex Spring Camping(5mi), **S** 76, 76/Subway/dsl, Shell/dsl, Ponce de Leon Motel

85 US 331, De Funiak Springs, **N** 76/dsl, Murphy USA/dsl, 4C BBQ, Arby's, Beef O'Brady's, Burger King, Domino's, Dunkin', Hungry Howie's, Larumba Mexican, Pizza Hut, Sonic, Subway, Taco Bell, Waffle House, Days Inn, Econolodge, Sundown Inn, Super 8, $General, AT&T, Buick/Chevrolet, Lowe's, Verizon, Walgreens, Walmart, winery, Winn-Dixie, **S** 76, 76/dsl, Sunoco/dsl, KFC, McDonald's, Whataburger, Zaxby's, Best Western, Holiday Inn Express, H

EGLIN AFB

70 FL 285, to Ft Walton Bch, Eglin AFB, **N** Love's/McDonald's/dsl/scales24hr, RaceWay/dsl, Waffle House, Sleep Inn, I-10 Truck Ctr, **S** Red Roof Inn, Great American RV Ctr

60mm **24hr security, full facilities, litter barrels, petwalk, both lanes, vending**

56 FL 85, Crestview, Eglin AFB, **N** Mobil/dsl, Shell/dsl, Tesla EVC, Applebee's, Bamboo Sushi, Burger King, Capt D's, Chick-fil-A, China 1, Dunkin', Firehouse Subs, Hot Head Burritos, Hunan Chinese, Hungry Howie's, Jimmy John's, Marco's Pizza, McAlister's Deli, McDonald's, Panera Bread, Pepper's Mexican, Pizza Hut, Starbucks, Taco Bell,

FL

INTERSTATE 10 Cont'd

MILTON

56 Continued
Voodoo BBQ, Country Inn&Suites, EconoLodge, Fairfield Inn, Hampton Inn, $General, Advance Parts, AT&T, AutoZone, BigLots, GNC, H, Lowe's, Publix, Staples, URGENT CARE, Verizon, Walgreens, Walmart, **S** Exxon/dsl, Tom Thumb/dsl, Tom Thumb/dsl, Arby's, Cracker Barrel, JC Seafood, LaRumba Mexican, Panda Express, Popeyes, Samuel's Roadhouse, Stewby's Seafood, Waffle House, Wendy's, Whataburger, Zaxby's, Baymont Inn, Best Value Inn, Comfort Inn, Hampton Inn, Holiday Inn Express, Home Town Inn, Quality Inn, Super 8, Buick/GMC, Chevrolet, Chrysler/Dodge/Jeep, Ford

45 rd 189, to US 90, Holt, **N** Marathon(1mi), Sheri's Diner, Susan's, Eagle's Landing RV Park, to Blackwater River SP, **S** River's Edge RV Park(1mi)

31 FL 87, to Ft Walton Beach, Milton, **N** Exxon/dsl, Waffle House, Holiday Inn Express, Blackwater River SP, KOA, **S** BP, Shell/dsl, Best Western, Blackwater Inn

31mm **24hr security, full facilities, litter barrels, petwalk, both lanes**

28 rd 89, Milton, **N** H, **S** Camp King Campground(1mi), Cedar Lakes RV Camping(3 mi)

27mm Blackwater River

26 rd 191, Bagdad, Milton, **N** Love's/Arbys/dsl/scales/24hr, Shell/Circle K/dsl, $General, H, **S** Chevron/DQ/Stuckey's, Pelican Palms RV Park

22 N FL 281, Avalon Blvd, **N** RaceTrac/dsl, Tom Thumb, McDonald's, **S** Shell/Circle K/Subway/dsl, Waffle House, Red Roof Inn, Avalon Landing RV Camping(1mi)

18mm Escambia Bay

PENSACOLA

17 US 90, Pensacola, **N** Marathon/dsl, $General, **S** Exxon/DQ, Quality Inn/rest.

13 FL 291, to US 90, Pensacola, **N** BP, Exxon, Shell/dsl, Arby's, Capt D's, Denny's, Dunkin', La Hacienda Mexican, Lupita's Mexican, McDonald's, Pho Real Vietnamese, Santino's Cafe, Taco Bell, Candlewood Suites, Comfort Inn, Holiday Inn, Home2 Suites, La Quinta, Queen Mary Inn, $Tree, CVS Drug, H, Ross, U-Haul, Walgreens, **S** Burger King, Cheddar's, ChuckECheese, Dickey's BBQ, Egg&I Cafe, HoneyBaked Ham, IHOP, Jimmy John's, Moe's SW, Pedros Tacos, Pho Golden Palace, Shrimp Basket Rest, Tu-Do Vietnamese, TX Roadhouse, Waffle House, Wendy's, Whataburger, Courtyard, Econolodge, Extended Stay America, Fairfield Inn, Hampton Inn, Mainstay Suites, Quality Inn, Red Roof Inn, Springhill Suites, Super 6 Inn, Sweet Dream Inn, TownePlace Suites, $General, Big Lots, Books-A-Million, Firestone/auto, GNC, Hobby Lobby, JC Penney, Jo-Ann Fabrics, Mr Transmission, PepBoys, PetSmart, TJ Maxx, Tuesday Morning, U-Haul, Verizon

12 I-110, to Pensacola, Hist Dist, Islands Nat Seashore

10b a US 29, Pensacola, **N** Murphy USA/dsl, Shell/dsl/scales, Chester's, Freddy's, Hardee's, La Cabana Mexican, Sonic, $Tree, Advance Parts, AT&T, AutoZone, Carpenter's RV Ctr, GNC, O'Reilly Parts, Office Depot, Walmart, **S** RaceWay/dsl, Shell/Circle K, Tom Thumb, Capt D's, Chicken'N The Egg, Founaris Greek, Lupita's Mexican, McDonald's, Miguel's Mexican, Pizza Hut, Smokey's BBQ, Subway, Waffle House, Wendy's, Whataburger, At Home Suites, Best Value Inn, Clarion Inn, Executive Inn, Extended Stay, Hotel Pensacola, Motel 6, Regency Inn, $General, Buick/Cadillac/GMC, Chevrolet, Chrysler/Dodge/Jeep, Ford, funpark, Harley-Davidson, Honda, Kia, Lincoln, Mazda, NAPA Autocare, Nissan, Subaru, Toyota/Scion

7b a Fl 297, Pine Forest Rd, **N** Chevron/Lupita's, Domino's, Dunkin', Great China, Philly's Cheesesteaks, Starbucks,

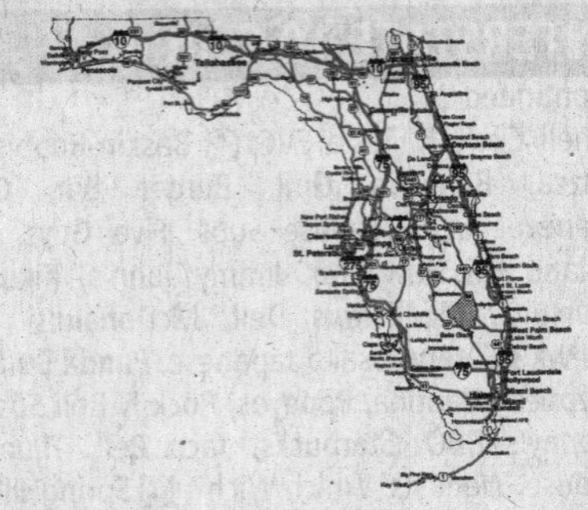

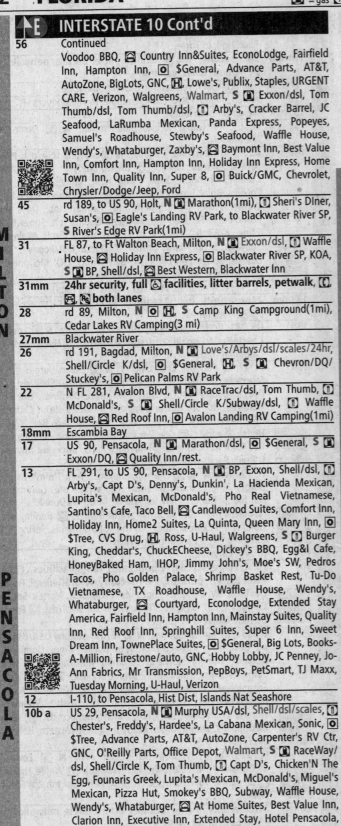

7b a Continued
Wendy's, Best Western, Garden Inn, Studio 6, Woodsprin Suites, Tall Oaks RV Park, transmissions, Walmart Mkt, Raceway/dsl, Shell, Tom Thumb, Burger King, Cracke Barrel, Hardee's, McDonald's, Ruby Tuesday, Sonny's BBC Subway, Waffle House, Wayne's Diner, Count Inn&Suites, Days Inn, Econolodge, Hampton Inn, Holiday In Express, Red Roof Inn, Big Lagoon SRA(12mi)

5 US 90 A, **N** Circle K/dsl, Shell/Circle K, Beef'O'Brady' BigOtes Mexican, Hot Head Burrito, Jersey Mike's, Pap Murphy's, Popeyes, Courtyard, AT&T, Publix/ga Verizon, Walgreens, **S** Leisure Lakes Camping

4mm **Welcome Ctr eb, full facilities, info, vending, litter barrels, petwalk, wi-fi, 24hr security**

3mm weigh sta both lanes

1mm inspection sta eb

0mm Florida/Alabama state line, Perdido River

INTERSTATE 75

JASPER

471mm Florida/Georgia state line

469mm **full facilities, info, litter barrels, petwalk, vending, Welcome Ctr sb**

467 FL 143, Jennings, **W** Shell/dsl, N Florida Inn, fireworks, Jennings Camping

460 FL 6, Jasper, **E** Indian River Fruit/gas, Marathon/Burg King/dsl, Marathon/Huddle House/dsl, Budget Inn, **W** Inland/dsl, Pilot/dsl/scales/24hr, American Inn, Suwanee River SP

451 US 129, Jasper, Live Oak, **E** Love's/Arby's/dsl/scale repair/24hr, Mobil/DQ/Subway/dsl, **W** Shell/Wendy's/d Suwanee Music Park(4mi), to FL Boys Ranch

448mm weigh sta both lanes

446mm insp sta both lanes

443mm Historic Suwanee River

LAKE CITY

439 to FL 136, White Springs, Live Oak, **E** Gate/dsl/e- Shell/dsl, McDonald's, Suwanee RV Camping(4mi), S Foster Ctr, **W** Quality Inn

435 I-10, E to Jacksonville, W to Tallahassee

427 US 90, to Live Oak, Lake City, **E** Chevron/dsl, Exx Murphy USA/dsl, Shell/dsl, Tesla EVC, Arby's, Buffalo W Wings, Burger King, Captain D's, Cedar River Seafood, Chi fil-A, Chili's, Chipotle, Cracker Barrel, Domino's, DQ, Dunk El Potro, Elliano's Coffee, Firehouse Subs, Five Guys, Gato GrilleHouse BBQ, Hardee's, IHOP, Jersey Mike's, Krys Longhorn Steaks, McDonald's, Moe's SW Grill, Ole Tin Buffet, Olive Garden, Panda Express, Panera Bread, Pa John's, Red Ginger Asian, Red Lobster, Ruby Tuesd Sonny's BBQ, Starbucks, Steak'n Shake, Subway, Taco B TX Roadhouse, Waffle House, Wendy's, Zaxby's, Best Days Inn, Dream Inn, Driftwood Inn, Holiday Inn, La Quin Quality Inn, Ramada Ltd, Regal Inn, Rodeway Inn, $T Advance Parts, ALDI, AT&T, AutoZone, Belk, BigLots, Drug, CVS Drug, Discount Tire, Ford/Lincoln, Hobby Lob Home Depot, H, JC Penney, Kia, Lowe's, Micha PetSmart, Publix, Tire Kingdom, TireMart, TJ Maxx, Toyo

FL

INTERSTATE 75 Cont'd

LAKE CITY

427 Continued
Verizon, Walgreens, Walmart, **W** Chevron/dsl, Circle K/dsl, Marathon/Subway, Bob Evans, China One, Denny's, Sal's Deli, Salsa's Mexican, Waffle House, Baymont Inn, Best Value Inn, Best Western+, Comfort Suites, EconoLodge, Fairfield Inn, Gateway Inn, Guest Inn, Hampton Inn, Home2 Suites, Tru Hilton, $General, Cadillac/Chevrolet, Camping World RV Ctr, Chrysler/Dodge/Jeep, Family$, Harvey's Foods, Honda, Nissan, vet

423 FL 47, to Ft White, Lake City, **E** Shell/dsl, Mack/Volvo Trucks, **W** Stop-N-Go/USPO, SunStop/dsl, Little Caesar's, Subway, Wendy's, Motel 6, Super 8, $General, Casey Jones RV Park, Freightliner

414 US 41, US 441, to Lake City, High Springs, **E** Chevron/dsl, Exxon, Love's/Hardee's/dsl/scales/24hr, Pitstop, Traveler's Inn, $General, **W** Marathon/dsl, Shell/Wendy's/dsl, Country Skillit, Subway, antiques, to O'Leno SP(5 mi)

413mm **24hr security, full facilities, litter barrels, petwalk, both lanes, vending**

409mm Santa Fe River

ALACHUA

404 rd 236, to High Springs, **E** Citgo/dsl, Marathon, Sunoco/fruits/gifts, **W** High Springs Camping

399 US 441, to High Sprs, Alachua, **E** BP, Kangaroo, Shell, Domino's, El Toro, McDonald's, Mi Apa Latin Cafe, Moe's SW Grill, NY Pizza, Pizza Hut, Sonny's BBQ, Subway, Taco Bell, Waffle House, EconoLodge, Quality Inn, $General, Advance Parts, AT&T, AutoZone, CVS Drug, Family$, Hitchcock's Foods, Lowe's, Traveler's Campground(1mi), Verizon, vet, Walgreens, **W** Kangaroo/Wendy's, Mobil/Dunkin'/dsl, RaceWay/dsl, Burger King, Hungry Howie's, KFC, Zaxby's, Best Value Inn, Royal Inn, Publix

390 FL 222, to Gainesville, **E** Circle K/McDonald's/dsl, Burger King, Chan's Chinese, La Fiesta Mexican, Pomodoro Cafe, Sonny's BBQ, Wendy's, H, Publix, Walgreens, **W** Shell/DQ/Dunkin'/dsl, Wahoo Grill, Best Western, Harley-Davidson, vet

387 FL 26, to Newberry, Gainesville, **E** Chevron/dsl, Sunoco, BJ's Rest., Bono's BBQ, Boston Mkt, Buffalo Wild Wings, Burger King, Dunkin', FoodCourt, HoneyBaked Ham, Jason's Deli, McAlister's Deli, McDonald's, Ocean Buffet, Panda Express, Panera Bread, Perkins, Red Lobster, Red Robin, Starbucks, Subway, Wendy's, Days Inn, La Quinta, AT&T, Belk, Books-A-Million, Dillard's, Hobby Lobby, H, JC Penney, mall, Office Depot, PetCo, to UF, Verizon, **W** BP, Chevron/dsl, Mobil/Circle K, Applebee's, Dunkin', Five Star Pizza, Krystal, Moe's SW Grill, Peppers Mexican, Pizza Hut, Taco Bell, Waffle House, Baymont Inn, Best Value Inn, Quality Inn, TownePlace Suites, $Tree, Advance Parts, Goodyear/auto, Home Depot, K-Mart, PepBoys, Publix, tires/repair, TJ Maxx, vet, Walgreens

384 FL 24, to Archer, Gainesville, **E** Exxon/dsl, Shell, Shell/Circle K, Arby's, Asian Wok, Blaze Pizza, BoneFish Grill, Burger King, BurgerFi, Carrabba's, Chick-fil-A, Chick-fil-A, Chili's, Chipotle Mexican, Chuy's Mexican, CiCi's Pizza, Coldstone, Domino's, DQ, Firehouse Subs, Five Guys, Hungry Howie's, KFC, McAlister's Deli, McDonald's, Moe's SW Grill, Olive Garden, Outback Steaks, Panda Express, Panera Bread, Papa John's, Pizza Hut, Pollo Tropical, Sonny's BBQ, Starbucks, Steak'n Shake, Subway, Taco Bell, Tijuana Flats, TX Roadhouse, Waffle House, Wendy's, Zaxby's, Zoe's Kitchen, Comfort Inn, Courtyard, Drury Inn, Extended Stay America, Hampton Inn, Hilton Garden, Homewood Suites, Red Roof Inn, Residence Inn, Sleep Inn, SpringHill Suites, Super 8, The Lodge, $Tree, AT&T, AutoZone, Best Buy,

GAINESVILLE

384 Continued
CVS Drug, Discount Tire, Firestone/auto, GNC, Jo-Ann, Kohl's, Lowe's, Michael's, Midas, Old Navy, PetSmart, Publix, Publix, Ross, Target, Trader Joe's, Tuesday Morning, Verizon, Walgreens, Walmart, **W** Mobil/Kangaroo, Cracker Barrel, Country Inn&Suites, hom hotel, to Bear Museum

382 FL 121, to Williston, Gainesville, **E** Marathon/dsl, Mobil/dsl, First Wok, Little Caesar's, McDonald's, Subway, Publix, USPO, **W** Chevron/dsl, Circle K/dsl, Shell/dsl, 43rd St Deli, Quality Inn, Rodeway Inn, Woodspring Suites

381mm **24hr security, full(handiacpped)facilities, litter barrels, petwalk, both lanes, vending**

374 rd 234, Micanopy, **E** Chevron/dsl, Exxon, antiques, to Paynes Prairie SP, **W** Micanopy Inn, repair

368 rd 318, Orange Lake, **E** Jim's/BBQ, Petro/BP/Iron Skillet/dsl/scales/24hr/@, Wendy's, Grand Lake RV Park(3mi), **W** Ocala N RV Camping

358 FL 326, **E** BP/FL Citrus Ctr/dsl, Mobil/McDonald's/dsl, Pilot/Arby's/dsl/scales/parking/24hr, Pilot/Wendy's/dsl/scales/24hr, auto/truck repair, Freightliner/repair, **W** Love's/Chester's/Subway/dsl/scales/24hr/@, Shell/Circle K/dsl, DQ

FL

354 US 27, to Silver Springs, Ocala, **E** CircleK/dsl, Marathon/dsl, RaceTrac/dsl, Burger King, Rascal's BBQ, Golden Palms Inn, **W** BP/dsl, Chevron/dsl, Shell/dsl, China Taste, Marco's Pizza, McDonald's, Murphy's Seafood, Pizza Hut, Roma Italian, Subway, Tokyo Sushi, Budget Host, Comfort Suites, Days Inn, Howard Johnson, Motel 6, $General, $Tree, AutoZone, Family$, Nelson's Trailers, Oaktree Village Camping, Publix, truck sales/service, Walgreens, Walgreens

352 FL 40, to Silver Springs, Ocala, **E** Chevron/dsl, Mobil/Circle K/dsl, RaceTrac, Sunoco/dsl, Wawa/dsl, Dunkin', McDonald's, Popeyes, Subway, Taco Bell, Waffle House, Wendy's, Zaxby's, Economy Inn, Motor Inn/RV, Studio 6, Family$, to Silver River SP(8mi), **W** Shell/dsl, Burger King, Denny's, Jerk Bowl, Candlewood Suites, Red Roof Inn, Super 8, Holiday Trav-L Park

OCALA

350 FL 200, to Hernando, Ocala, Eggs Up, **E** BP/dsl, RaceTrac, Shell/dsl, Texaco/dsl, Amrit Indian, Applebee's, Arby's, Asian Pop Sushi, Bob Evans, Boston Mkt, Burger King, Carrabba's, Checkers, Chick-fil-A, Chili's, Chipotle, ChuckECheese, Coldstone, Domino's, El Toreo Mexican, Firehouse Subs, First Watch, Five Guys, Freddy's, Golden Corral, Hardee's, Hungry Howie's, Jersey Mike's, KeKe's Breakfast, Logan's Roadhouse, Maddio's Pizza, McDonald's, Moe's SW Grill, Ocean Buffet, Olive Garden, Outback Steaks, Panda Express, Panera Bread, Papa John's, PDQ Grill, Pho Noodles, Pizza Hut, Red Crab, Red Lobster, Red Robin, Smoothie King, Sonic, Sonny's BBQ, Starbucks, Storming Crab Seafood, Subway, Taco Bell, Twistee Treat, TX Roadhouse, Yummy House, Zaxby's, Country Inn&Suites, Equus Inn, Hilton, La Quinta, $Tree, Acura, Advance Parts, AlLDI, Belk, Best Buy, Chevrolet/EVC, CVS Drug, Discount Tire, Goodyear/auto, Hobby Lobby, Home Depot, Honda, H, Hyundai, JC Penney, Lowe's, Macy's, Mazda, Michael's, Nissan, O'Reilly Parts, Office Depot, PepBoys, PetSmart, Ross, Staples, Target, Tire Kingdom, TJ Maxx, Toyota/Scion, Tuesday Morning, Tuffy Auto, URGENT CARE, Verizon, Walmart, **W** CircleK/dsl, Marathon, RaceTrac/dsl, Tesla EVC, WaWa/dsl, Bojangles, Bonefish Grill, Burger King, Cheddar's, Chicken Salad Chick, Cracker Barrel, Crazy Cucumber, Culver's, Dunkin', Edo Sushi, Five Star Pizza, Gator's, KFC, Las Margaritas, Marco's Pizza, McAlister's Deli, McDonald's, Mimi's Cafe, Panera Bread, Starbucks, Steak'n Shake, Tijuana Flats, Waffle House, Yamato Japanese,

= gas = food = lodging = other = rest stop

FL

INTERSTATE 75 Cont'd

OCALA

350 Continued
Best Western, Courtyard, Fairfield Inn, Hampton Inn, Holiday Inn, Homewood Suites, Residence Inn, SpringHill Suites, AT&T, Barnes&Noble, BMW, Buick/GMC, Cadillac, Dick's, Dillard's, H, Kohl's, Ocala RV Park, Old Navy, PetCo, Porsche, Sam's Club/gas, Tires+, Verizon, vet, VW, Walgreens

346mm 24hr security, full facilities, litter barrels, petwalk, both lanes, vending

341 rd 484, to Belleview, E BP/fruit, Exxon/dsl, RaceTrac/dsl, Shell/dsl, Cracker Barrel, Dunkin', KFC/Taco Bell, Sonny's BBQ, Tom's Cuban, Zaxby's, Microtel, Sleep Inn, FL Citrus Ctr, racing museum, W Pilot/DQ/Wendy's/dsl/scales/parking/24hr, Alrosti Peruvian, Burger King, McDonald's, Popeyes, Subway, Waffle House, Hampton Inn, Ocala Sun RV Resort, outlets

338mm weigh sta both lanes

LAKE PANASOFFKEE

329 FL 44, to Inverness, Wildwood, E Kangaroo/Exxon/dsl, Pilot/Steak'n Shake/dsl/scales/24hr, Sunoco, Burger King, Dunkin', M&M BBQ, McDonald's, Waffle House, Wendy's, Zaxby's, Holiday Inn Express, Willwood RV Park, W Mobil/dsl/repair/24hr, Pilot/dsl/scales/parking/24hr, TA/BP/Popeyes/Subway/dsl/scales/parking/24hr/@, Hardee's, IHOP, Taco Bell, Budget Inn, Days Inn, Motel 6, Red Roof Inn, truck repair, truckwash

328 FL TPK(from sb), to Orlando

321 rd 470, to Sumterville, Lake Panasoffkee, E Spirit/deli/dsl/scales/24hr, Coleman Correctional, W Mobil/Hardee's/Subway/dsl, Shell/Circle K/dsl, Countryside RV Park, Lake Pan RV Park

314 FL 48, to Bushnell, Burger King, E Citgo, Murphy USA/dsl, Shell/Circle K/Subway, Hong Kong Chinese, KFC/Taco Bell, Little Caesar's, McDonald's, Pico De Gallo Mexican, Wendy's, Rodeway Inn, $Tree, AutoZone, BlueBerry Hill RV Camp, Red Oaks Camp(1mi), Red Oaks RV Park, to Dade Bfd HS, Verizon, vet, Walmart, W Love's/Arby's/dsl/scales/service/24hr, Sunoco/dsl, Beef'O'Brady's, Fujiyama Japanese, Sonny's BBQ, Microtel, Optimum RV Ctr

309 rd 476, to Webster, E Breezy Oaks RV Park(1mi), Sumter Oaks RV Park(1mi)

307mm 24hr security, coffee, full facilities, litter barrels, petwalk, both lanes, vending

301 US 98, FL 50, to Dade City, E RaceTrac/dsl, Beef'O'Brady's, Cracker Barrel, Dunkin', El Sol Mexican, King's Wok, McDonald's, Subway, Taco Bell, Waffle House, Wendy's, Zaxby's, Days Inn, Holiday Inn Express, $General, Advance Parts, Winn-Dixie, W Burger King, Hampton Inn, Microtel, Quality Inn, 7-11, H

293 rd 41, to Dade City, E Citgo(2mi), to Sertoma Youth Ranch, W Travelers Rest Resort RV Park(3mi)

ZEPHYRHILLS

285 FL 52, to Dade City, New Port Richey, E Flying J/Denny's/dsl/LP/scales/parking/24hr, Burger King, Blue Beacon, H

279 FL 54, to Land O' Lakes, Zephyrhills, E Speedway/Dunkin'/dsl, Wawa, Applebee's, Burger King, Chick-fil-A, Chili's, China Wok, City Grill, Dominos, Dunkin', First Watch, Glory Days Grill, Gonna China, Las Vallartas, Papa's John's, Pizza Hut/Taco Bell, Popeyes, Sonny's BBQ, Starbucks, Twistee Treat, Waffle House, Wendy's, Ace Hardware, Advance Parts, Beall's, Beginning Point RV Park, Ducky's Day Off RV Park(5mi), Ford, Happy Days RV Camping(9mi), Kia, Leasure Days RV Camping(7mi), Lincoln, Nissan, Publix, to Hillsborough River SP(18mi), Toyota/Scion, Walgreens, Walmart, W 7-11, Marathon, Shell/Circle K/dsl, Shell/Dunkin', Beef'O'Brady's, Brooklyn Bagel, Chick'N Fun, ChuckeCheese, Cracker Barrel, DQ, Hot Wok,

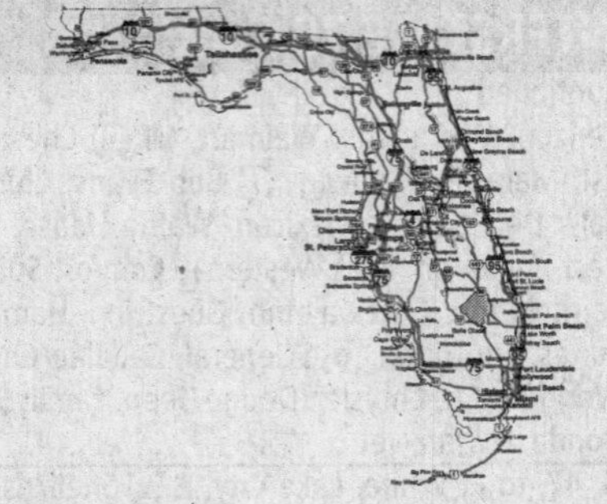

ST PETERSBURG

279 Continued
Hungry Howie's, Marco's Pizza, McDonald's, NY Pizz Outback Steaks, Winghouse, Best Western, EconoLodg Rodeway Inn, Sleep Inn, $General, $Tree, Advance Par Best Buy, Chevrolet, CVS Drug, Dick's, GNC, Goodyear/aut Honda, Hyundai, Mazda, Michael's, Old Navy, PetSma Quail Run RV Camping, Ross, Tire Kingdom, TJ Max Toyota/Scion, Tuffy Auto, URGENT CARE, Winn Dixie

277mm 24hr security, full facilities, litter barrels, petwalk, both lanes, vending

275 FL 56, Land O Lakes, Tarpon Springs, E Gate/d Marathon/Dunkin'/dsl, RaceTrac/dsl, Bubba's 33, Buffa Wild Wings, Capital Tacos, TX Roadhouse, Hampton In Hilton Garden, Holiday Inn Express, WoodSpring Suites, H(3mi), Mercedes, Mini, Publix(2mi), Sams Club(2mi), v W Shell/dsl, Wawa/EVC, Aussie's Grill, Bahan Breeze, BJ's, Blaze Pizza, Bonefish Grill, Burger Kin Carrabba's, Cheddar's, Chick-fil-A, Chuy's Tex-mex, Culver Ford's Garage, Longhorn Steaks, McDonald's, Mello Mushroom, Panda Express, Starbucks, Taco Bell, Wendy Zaxby's, Hyatt Place, ALDI, Costco/gas, Tampa Outle famous brands, Walgreens

274 I-275(from sb), to Tampa, St Petersburg

270 rd 581, Bruce B Downs Blvd, E 7-11, Mobil/Dunkin', She Circle K/Taco Bell/dsl, Baskin-Robbins/Dunkin', Chick-f A, Chili's, Chipotle, Coldstone, Glory Days Grill, Ko Japanese, Kobe Japanese, Liang's Asian Bistro, McDonald Minerva Indian, Moe's SW Grill, NY Pizzaria, Panera Brea Papa John's, Pizza Hut, Ruby Tuesday, Steak'n Sha Subway, TGIFriday's, Tijuana Flats, Wendy's, Holiday I Express, La Quinta, AT&T, Best Buy, CVS Drug, Hor Depot, Mavis Tire & Brakes, Michael's, Publix, Tires Verizon, vet, Walgreens, Walmart/Subway, W 7-11, McDonald's, Olive Garden, Red Lobster, Stonewood Grill, SpringHill Suites, $Tree, BJ's Whse/Subway/gas, C Drug, Lowe's, PetSmart, Ross, USPO

266 rd 582A, Fletcher Ave, W Shell/Circle K/dsl, Bask Robbins/Dunkin', Bob Evans, Desi Indian, Lenny's Su Starbucks, Wendy's, Courtyard, Extended Stay Ameri Fairfield Inn, Hampton Inn, Hilton Garden, Holiday I Express, Residence Inn, Sleep Inn, TownePlace Suit WoodSpring Suites, H

265 FL 582, Fowler Ave, Temple Terrace, E flea mkt, Hap Traveler RV Park, W 7-11/dsl, Marathon, Sunoco, IH Marco's Pizza, Ramada Inn, to Busch Gardens, to USF

BRANDON

261 I-4, W to Tampa, E to Orlando

260b a FL 574, to Mango, Tampa, E Mobil, Shell/Circle K/Subw Baskin-Robbins/Dunkin', Burger King, Domin Munchies Pizza, Waffle House, Walgreens, Winn Dixie, Mobil, Subway, Hilton Garden, Quality I Residence Inn, Sheraton, Staybridge Suites, Family$

257 FL 60, Brandon, E Winghouse, Mobil(2), Mobil/dsl, She Circle K, Tesla EVC, WaWa/dsl, Anthony's Pizza, Bab Pizza, Bahama Breeze, Bolay, Boston Mkt, Brando Burgers, Buffalo Wild Wings, Checkers, Cheesecake Facto

INTERSTATE 75 Cont'd

BRANDON

257 Continued
Chick-fil-A, Chili's, Chipotle, Chipotle, ChuckECheese, Corner Bakery Cafe, Denny's, DQ, Dunkin', Firehouse Subs, First Watch, Ford's Garage, Honeybaked Ham, Hungry Howie's, Jimmy John's, Keke's Breakfast, KFC, Kobe Japanese, Koizi Hibachi, Krispy Kreme, LJ Silver, Longhorn Steaks, Mama's Soul Food, McDonald's, McDonald's(2), Mellow Mushroom, Miller's Ale House, Mission BBQ, Moe's SW Grill, Olive Garden, Outback Steaks, P.F. Chang's, Panda Express, Panera Bread, Papa John's, PDQ Chicken, Poke Falls, Popeyes, Portillo's, Red Lobster, Sa Ri Korean, Salem's Fresh, Smokey Bones BBQ, Starbucks, Steak'n Shake, Steak'n Shake, Sushi Maru, Taco Bell/EVC, Tibby's NO Kitchen, Tijuana Flats, Tres Amigos Mexican, Tropical Smoothie, Waffle House, Wingstop, Extended Stay America, Holiday Inn Express, La Quinta, $General, $Tree, $Tree, Aamco, Advance Parts, AT&T, AutoZone, Barnes&Noble, Best Buy, Books-A-Million, Cadillac, Costco/gas, CVS Drug, Dick's, Dillard's, Fiat, Firestone/auto, H, JC Penney, Jo-Ann Fabrics, Kohl's, Lowe's, Macy's, mall, Marshall's, Michael's, Office Depot, PepBoys, PetCo, PetSmart, PetSmart(2), Publix, Publix(2), Ross, Sam's Club/gas, Staples, Target, Tires+, TJ Maxx, Verizon, Walgreens, Walmart, **W** Citgo/dsl, Shell, Bob Evans, Burger King, Dave&Busters, Hooters, McDonald's, Subway, Sushi Yama, Wendy's, Brandon Hotel, Comfort Suites, Country Inn&Suites, Courtyard, Embassy Suites, Fairfield Inn, Home2 Suites, Homewood Suites, La Quinta, Motel 6, Quality Inn, Red Roof Inn, SpringHill Suites, Bass Pro Shops, Buick/GMC, Chevrolet, Chrysler/Dodge/Jeep, Ford, Harley-Davidson, Home Depot, Honda, Hyundai, Kia, Mazda, Nissan, Office Depot, Toyota/Scion, VW

256 FL 618 W(toll), to Tampa

RIVERVIEW

254 US 301, Riverview, **E** RaceTrac, Thornton's/dsl, WaWa/dsl, Panda Express, Steak'n Shake, CVS Drug, Firestone/auto, Home Depot, Target/Starbucks, **W** 7-11/dsl, China 1, Crazy Cafe, Dunkin', Eggs Up Grill, McDonald's, Pizza Hut, Smokin' Pig BBQ, Starbucks, Subway, Wendy's, Hilton Garden, Uptown Suites, GNC, Publix

250 Gibsonton Dr, Riverview, **E** 7-11/dsl, RaceWay/dsl, Victory Lane/dsl, WaWa/dsl, Arby's, Beef'O'Brady's, Burger King, Hungry Howie's, Jola Pizza, Little Caesar's, McDonald's, New China, Pizza Hut, Ruby Tuesday, Subway, Taco Bell, Waffle House, Wendy's, $Tree, Alafia River RV Resort, Beall's, CVS Drug, Family$, Hidden River RV Resort(4mi), Lowe's, Rice Creek RV Camping(2mi), Save-a-Lot, USPO, Walgreens, **W** Circle K, Murphy USA/dsl, Cracker Barrel, Dunkin', Rosemary Grill, Extended Stay, Walmart/McDonald's

RUSKIN

246 rd 672, Big Bend Rd, Apollo Bch, **E** 7-11, Mobil/dsl, Tesla EVC, Thornton's/dsl, WaWa/dsl, Applebee's, Asian Yummy, Beef'O'Brady's, Buffalo Wild Wings, Burger King, Chick-fil-A, China Taste, Culver's, DQ, Dunkin Donuts, East Coast Pizza, Firehouse Subs, First Watch, Fried Flavor Wings, Little Caesars, McDonald's, Mi Casa, Moe's SW Grill, Outback, Panda Express, Panera Bread, Papa John's, PDQ Cafe, Pita's, Pizza Hut, Popeyes, Qdoba, Sakura Japanese, Sonic, Starbucks, Subway, Taco Bell, Tijuana Flats, Twistee Treat, TX Roadhouse, Village Inn, Wendy's, Fairfield Inn, $General, $Tree, Ace Hardware, Advance Parts, AT&T, AutoZone, Beall's, Firestone/auto, GNC, Goodyear/auto, H, Marshall's, Mavis Tire, Publix, Sam's Club/gas, Tire Choice, Tuffy Auto, URGENT CARE, Verizon, vet, Walgreens, Walmart Mkt, Winn Dixie, **W** Shell/Circle K/Dunkin'/dsl

240b a FL 674, Sun City Ctr, Ruskin, **E** Shell, Beef'O'Brady's, Bob Evans, BubbaQue's BBQ, Burger King, Checkers, China Star, Denny's, Dunkin Donuts, Hungry Howie's,

240b a Continued
Little Caesar's, Old Castle German, Pizza Hut, Popeyes, Subway, Taco Bell, Wendy's, Comfort Inn, AT&T, Beall's, GNC, Home Depot, H, to Little Manatee River SP, Verizon, **W** Circle K/dsl, RaceTrac/dsl, China Wok, Hot Tomato, KFC, McDonald's, Holiday Inn Express, Ruskin Inn, $General, BigLots, NAPA, SunLake RV Resort(1mi)

237mm **24hr security, full facilities, litter barrels, petwalk, both lanes, vending**

229 rd 683, Moccasin Wallow Rd, to Parrish, **E** Jet's Pizza, Little Manatee Sprs SRA(10mi), Publix, **W** Circle K, Mobil/dls, Fiesta Grove RV Park(3mi), Frog Creek RV Park(3mi), Terra Ceia RV Village(2mi), Winterset RV Park(3mi)

BRADENTON

228 I-275 N, to St Petersburg

224 US 301, to Bradenton, Ellenton, **E** 7-11, Shell/Circle K/dsl, Applebee's, Checkers, Chili's, Dunkin', Hungry Howie's, King's Wok, McDonald's, Peach's Rest., Ruby Tuesday, Starbucks, Subway, Taco Bell, Wendy's, Winghouse, Woody's River Grill, Hampton Inn, $General, $Tree, Ace Hardware, Beall's, Ellenton Gardens RV Camping(1mi), Ellenton Outlets/famous brands, GNC, TJ Maxx, USPO, Walgreens, **W** Pilot/dsl, Anna Maria's, Waffle House, Red Roof Inn, Super 8

223 Manatee River

220b a FL 64, to Zolfo Springs, Bradenton, **E** RaceTrac, DQ, Taco Bell, Costco/gas, Lake Manatee SRA, Timberlane RV Camping, **W** Marathon/dsl, RaceTrac/dsl, Shell/Circle K/dsl, Shell/Pizza Hut/dsl, Burger King, Cracker Barrel, Dunkin', IHOP, KFC/LJ Silver, McDonald's, Sonny's BBQ, Starbucks, Subway, Waffle House, Wendy's, Best Value Inn, Best Western+, Days Inn, Motel 6, Quality Inn, Sunrise Inn, Encore RV Resort(1mi), Gerzeny's RV Ctr, H, Toyota/Scion, Walmart

217b a FL 70, to Arcadia, **E** Speedway/dsl, Burger King, Culver's, Hungry Howie's, Jersey Mike's, Jet's Pizza, Menchie's, PDQ Chicken, Speaks Italian, Takos Cantina, TX Roadhouse, TX Roadhouse, Holiday Inn Express, GNC, Tire Choice/auto, Walmart/Subway/gas, **W** Marathon/Dunkin Donuts/dsl, RaceTrac/dsl, Shell/Circle K, Applebee's, Attardi's Pizza, Bob Evans, Breakfast Co., BubbaQue's BBQ, Chick-fil-A, DQ, Freddy's, Gecko's Grill, Jimmy John's, LJ Silver/Taco Bell, McDonald's, Papa John's, Parrot Patio, Peach's Rest., Petrosino's Italian, Poblanos Mexican, Rice Bowl, Shipley Do-Nuts, Starbucks, Zaxby's, Country Inn&Suites, Tru, WoodSpring Suites, $Tree, Beall's, CVS Drug, Horseshoe Cove RV Camping, Lowe's, Pleasant Lake RV Resort, Publix, Tire Kingdom, Tires+, Tuffy Auto, Verizon

213 University Parkway, to Sarasota, **E** Mobil/Subway/dsl, Broken Egg Cafe, Chili's, First Watch Cafe, Little Greek, Lucky Pelican Seafood, Papa Johns, Even Hotel, Fairfield Inn, Hyatt Place, GNC, H, Publix, URGENT CARE, Walgreens, **W** EVC, WaWa/dsl, Apollonian Mediterranean, Blaze Pizza, BoneFish Grill, Brio, Buffalo Wild Wings, BurgerFi, Capital Grille, Carrabba's, Chicken Kitchen, Chipotle Mexican, Five Guys, Ford's Garage, Glory Days, Jersey Mike's Subs, Jimmy John's, Keke's Breakfast, Mandarin Exps, Maple Street Breakfast, Mission BBQ, Moe's SW Grill, Newk's Eatery, Pascone's Ristorante, Pei Wei, Rusty Bucket Rest., Seasons Rest., Starbucks, Stonewood Grill, Sweet Tomatoes, Thai Seed, The Bistro, Tijuana Flats, Valentino's, Wendy's, Yaki Sushi BBQ, Zoe's Kitchen, Courtyard, Hampton Inn, Homewood Suites, $Tree, AT&T, Best Buy, BJ's Whse/gas, CVS Drug, Dillard's, Fresh Mkt Foods, Home Depot, Jo-Ann Fabrics, Kohl's, Macy's, Marshall's, Michael's, Old Navy, PetCo, Ross, Staples, SteinMart, Target, TJ Maxx, to Ringling Museum, Verizon, vet, Whole Foods Mkt

FL

[gas] = gas [food] = food [lodging] = lodging [other] = other [RS] = rest stop

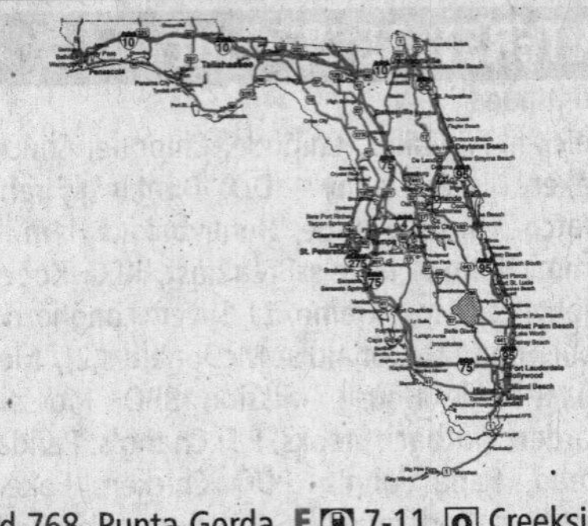

INTERSTATE 75 Cont'd

SARASOTA · NOKOMIS · PORT CHARLOTTE

Exit #	Services
210	FL 780, Fruitville Rd, Sarasota, E Cooper's, Sun-N-Fun RV Park(1mi), W Marathon/dsl, Mobil/7-11/dsl, RaceTrac/dsl, Shell/dsl, Applebee's, Bob Evans, Chick-fil-A, Chipotle, Coco's, Culver's, Daruma Japanese, Dunkin', Firehouse Subs, First Watch, Five Guys, Gecko's, Ginza Sushi, Jersey Mike's, Jets Pizza, KaCey's Seafood, L&L Hawaiian, Longhorn Steaks, McDonald's, Perkins, Pollo Tropical, Rodizio Grill, Starbucks, Subway, Super Buffet, Taco Bell, Amenti Bay, Comfort Inn, Homewood Suites(2mi), Magnolia Hotel/EVC, $Tree, Advance Parts, AT&T, CVS Drug, GNC, Lowe's, Office Depot, Publix, Sam's Club, Target, Tire Kingdom, Winn-Dixie
207	FL 758, Sarasota, E RaceTrac/dsl, W BP/Subway/dsl, Marathon/Dunkin', Arby's, Chili's, Domino's, First Watch Cafe, Jimmy John's, Joey D's Eatery, Madfish Grill, McDonald's, Miller's Alehouse, Panera Bread, Pizza Hut, Starbucks, Steak'n Shake, Taco Bell, Tequila Mexican, Hampton Inn, Beall's, Home Depot, [H], Publix, to Selby Botanical Gardens(8mi), Verizon, vet, Walgreens, Walmart
205	FL 72, to Arcadia, Sarasota, E Myakka River SP(9mi), W 7-11/dsl, Marathon/Jimmy John's/dsl, Mobil/7-11/dsl, Shell/Circle K, Applebee's, Burger King, Chick-fil-A, Dunkin', Gecko's Grill, McDonald's, Origin Craft, Pho 99, Starbucks, Subway, Waffle House, Wendy's, Comfort Suites/EVC, Days Inn, Holiday Inn Express, Quality Inn, Acura, Audi, Beall's, BMW/EVC, CVS Drug, Infiniti, Jaguar, Land Rover, Lexus, Mercedes/Smart, O'Reilly Parts, Publix, Tire Kingdom, Turtle Beach Camping(8mi), USPO, Walgreens, Walmart Mkt, Windward Isle RV Park
200	FL 681 S(from sb), to Venice, Osprey, Gulf Bchs
195	Laurel Rd, Nokomis, E Shell/USPO/dsl, Subway, $Tree, W Asaro's Pizza, McDonald's, Publix, Royal Coachman RV Park(2mi), Scherer SP(6mi)
193	Jaracanda Blvd, Venice, W RaceTrac/dsl, Shell, Speedway/dsl, WaWa/dsl, BrewBurgers, China Taste, Cracker Barrel, Culver's, Dunkin', McDonald's, Tomatillo's, Wendy's, Best Western+, Fairfield Inn, Holiday Inn Express, TownePlace Suites, CVS Drug, Publix, Verizon
191	rd 777, Venice Rd, to Englewood, W Mobil/7-11, Snook Haven(1mi), KOA(6mi), Meadows RV Park(6mi), Ramble Rest RV Park(3mi), to Myakka SF(9mi)
182	rd 771, Sumter Blvd, to North Port
179	rd 779, Toledo Blade Blvd, North Port, W Exxon/7-11, Mobil/Circle K/Subway/dsl, Shell/rest/dsl, Burger King, Empire Bagels, Little Caesars, Pizza Hut, Wings & Rings, $Tree, Publix
170	rd 769, to Arcadia, Port Charlotte, E 7-11/dsl, Murphy USA/dsl/EVC, RaceTrac/dsl, Applebee's, Culver's, Hampton Inn, Holiday Inn Express, Lettuce Lake Camping(7mi), Riverside Camping(5mi), Walmart/EVC, W Mobil/Circle K/DQ/dsl, Shell/Circle K/Dunkin Donuts, Speedway/dsl, Arbys, Burger King, Cracker Barrel, Domino's, DQ, Fin Sushi, Five Guys, Golden China, Jets Pizza, McDonald's, Papa John's, Pizza Hut, Popeyes, Starbucks, Subway, Taco Bell, Top China, Waffle House, Wendy's, Comfort Inn, Country Inn&Suites, Extended Stay, Sleep Inn, $General, $Tree, Ace Hardware, Advance Parts, AutoZone, Beall's, CVS Drug, Firestone, [H], Publix, vet, Walgreens, Winn-Dixie
167	rd 776, Port Charlotte
164	US 17, Punta Gorda, Arcadia, E 7-11/dsl, RaceWay/dsl, Shell/Circle K/dsl, King House Chinese, Peace River Seafood, Piccolo Italian, RV camping, Subway, $General, vet, Winn-Dixie, W Fisherman's Village Rest.(2mi), [H]

N FT MYERS · FT MYERS

Exit #	Services
161	rd 768, Punta Gorda, E 7-11, Creekside RV Park, W Marathon/DQ, Murphy USA/dsl, Pilot/Arby's/dsl/scales/parking/24hr, Shell/dsl, Wawa/EVC, Burger King, DQ, FK Your Diet, McDonald's, Subway, Waffle House, Wendy's, Baymont Inn, Holiday Inn Express, Knights Inn, Encore RV Park(2mi), Walmart
160mm	weigh sta both lanes
158	rd 762, Tropical Gulf Acres, Tuckers Grade, E Babcock-Wells Wildlife Mgt Area
143	FL 78, to Cape Coral, N Ft Myers, E Marathon/dsl, Seminole Camping(1mi), Up River Camping, W Love's/Subway/Wendy's/dsl/scales/repair/24hr, Encore RV Camping
141	FL 80, Palm Bch Blvd, Ft Myers, E Marathon, Sunoco/dsl, Cracker Barrel, Waffle House, Comfort Inn, Woodspring Suites, W Gulf, Mobil, Speedway/Dunkin'/dsl, Domino's, Hardee's, KFC, Papa John's, Popeyes, Subway, Taco Bell, $General, BigLots, CVS Drug, Family$, North Trail RV Ctr, Save-A-Lot, USPO, vet
139	Luckett Rd, Ft Myers, E Camping World RV Service/supplies, Cypress Woods RV Resort, W Pilot/Subway/dsl/scales/24hr/@
138	FL 82, to Lehigh Acres, Ft Myers, E 7-11/dsl, Hyatt Place, W Mobil/dsl, RaceTrac/dsl, Sunoco/dsl, Peterbilt
136	FL 884, Colonial Blvd, Ft Myers, Tesla, E 7-11/dsl, 3 Pepper Burrito, Buddyz Pizza, Buffalo Wild Wings, Domino's, Dunkin', Firehouse Subs, Five Guys, McAlister's Deli, Moe's SW, Pizza Hut, Poke Hawaii, Starbucks, Candlewood Suites, Holiday Inn Express, GNC, Home Depot, PetCo, Ross, Staples, Target/Pizza Hut, Winn Dixie, W 7-11/dsl, Murphy USA/dsl, RaceTrac/dsl, Shell/Circle K/dsl, Shell/dsl, Tesla EVC, Applebee's, Bellacino's, Bob Evans, Burger King, Chick-fil-A, Chilli's, Chipotle, Culver's, Dunkin', First Watch Cafe, Golden Corral, J&C Seafood, Jimmy John's, Keke's Breakfast, Kumo Japanese, LJ Silver/Taco Bell, McDonald's, Panda Express, Pollo Tropical, Steak'n Shake, Subway, TX Roadhouse, Wendy's, Woodspring Suites, $Tree, AT&T, Beall's, BJ's Whse/gas, Hobby Lobby, [H], Kohl's, Lowe's, PetSmart, Publix, Tire Choice/auto, Verizon, Walmart/McDonald's
131	rd 876, Daniels Pkwy, to Cape Coral, [RS] **both lanes, full facilities, [phone], vending, [picnic], litter barrels, petwalk, 24hr security,** E Mobil/Subway/dsl, RaceTrac/dsl, Cracker Barrel, Fat Katz, Comfort Inn, Dsys Inn, Sheraton, Audi, CVS Drug, Harley Davidson, Porsche, W 7-11, Exxon/Dunkin'/dsl, RaceTrac/dsl, Shell/Circle K/dsl, Arby's, Burger King, Da Vinci's Italian, Denny's, DQ, Fancy Southern Cafe, MAKS Sushi, McDonald's, New China, Origami Korean, Papa John's, Rusty's Grill, Starbucks, Taco Bell, Taco Bell, Two Meatballs Italian, Waffle House, Wendy's, Baymont Inn, Best Western, Hampton Inn, La Quinta, Quality Inn, SpringHill Suites, Travelodge, Artisián Eats, CVS Drug, [H], Publix, Tire Choice/auto, Tuffy Auto, Walgreens
128	Alico Rd, San Carlos Park, Adriatico Mediterranean, E 7-11, Arby's, Aurelio's Pizza, BJ's Rest., Brick Oven Pizza,

INTERSTATE 75 Cont'd

128 Continued
Carrabba's, Cheddar's, Chick-fil-A, Chili's, Chipotle, Connor's Steaks, Culver's, Famous Dave's BBQ, First Watch Cafe, Jason's Deli, Koto Sushi, Longhorn Steaks, McDonald's, Miller's Alehouse, Moe's SW Grill, Olive Garden, Outback Steaks, Panda Express, Panera Bread, Pei Wei, PF Chang's, Pincher's Crabshack, Pita Pit, Pollo Tropical, Red Robin, Starbucks, Taco Bell, Tijuana Flats, Twin Peaks, Zaxby's, Courtyard, Drury Inn, Hilton Garden, Holiday Inn, Homewood Suites, Residence Inn, $Tree, AT&T, Bass Pro Shop/Islamorada Fish Co, Belk, Best Buy, Costco/gas, Dick's, GNC, JC Penney, Jo-Ann Fabrics, Marshall's, PetCo, Ross, Staples, Target, Verizon, **W** 7-11/dsl, RaceTrac/dsl, Shell/Dunkin'/dsl, Family$

123 rd 850, Corkscrew Rd, Estero, **E** Marathon/7-11/dsl, Shell/Dunkin'/dsl, Bahia Bowl, China Gourmet, Domino's, Duffy's Grill, Dunkin', Ford's Garage, Marsala's Italian, McDonald's, Naples Flat Bread, Perkins, Pickled Onion, Subway, Wasabi Steaks, CVS Drug, Johnson Tire/auto, Miramar Outlet/famous brands, Publix, **W** 7-11, Marathon/dsl, Mobil/dsl, Applebees, Arby's, Culver's, Rib City, Embassy Suites, Hampton Inn, SpringHill Suites, $Tree, Chevrolet, Koreshan SHS(2mi), Lowe's, Tire Choice/auto, Woodsmoke RV Park(4mi)

116 Bonita Bch Rd, Bonita Springs, **E** 7-11, Mobil/7-11/dsl, RaceTrac/dsl, China A, Dolce Rita's, Subway, Advance Parts, Publix, Sanctuary RV Camping, Tire Choice/auto, **W** Chevron/dsl, Exxon/dsl, Marathon/dsl, Shell/McDonald's, Culver's, Dunkin', Five Guys, McDonald's, Peking Chinese, Starbucks, Teri's Diner, Waffle House, Days Inn, Fairfield Inn, CVS Drug, Home Depot, Imperial Bonita RV Park, Tire Kingdom, to Lovers Key SP(11mi), Walgreens

111 rd 846, Immokalee Rd, Naples Park, **E** 7-11, Mobil/dsl, Bob Evans, Burger King, Chili's, L'Appetito Pizza, La Santa Tacos, NY Baglels, Panera Bread, Hampton Inn/EVC, GNC, PetSmart/Tesla EVC, Staples, Target/Starbucks, World Mkt, **W** Shell/Circle K/dsl, McDonald's, Skillets, Subway, TownePlace Suites, H, Publix, to Delnor-Wiggins SP, Verizon, Walmart

107 rd 896, Pinebridge Rd, Naples, Home2 Suites, **E** BP/McDonald's/dsl, China Garden, Dominos, Giovanni Ristorante, Kwench Juice, H, Publix, vet, Walgreens, **W** RaceTrac/dsl, Shell/Circle K/dsl, Burger King, Fernandez Cuban, First Watch, Hooters, IHOP, Kraft Cafe, Napoli Pizza, Perkins, Senor Tequilas, Slicer's Hoagies, Sophia's, Starbucks, Waffle House, Best Western, Hawthorn Suites/EVC, Spinnaker Inn, Harley-Davidson, Johnson Tire/auto, Nissan, URGENT CARE, vet

105 rd 886, to Golden Gate Pkwy, Golden Gate, **E** Subway, CVS Drug, **W** to zoo

101 rd 951, to FL 84, to Naples, **E** Shell/Subway/dsl, Fairfield Inn, SpringHill Suites, Woodspring Suites, H, **W** Chevron/dsl, Marathon/Subway/dsl, Shell/dsl, Chili's, China Dragon, Cracker Barrel, Dunkin', McDonald's, Taco Bell, Waffle House, Comfort Inn, Holiday Inn Express/EVC, La Quinta, Super 8, $Tree, AT&T, Club Naples RV Resort, KOA(7mi), vet, Walmart/EVC

100mm toll plaza eb

80 FL 29, to Everglade City, Immokalee, **W** Big Cypress NR, Everglades NP, Smallwoods Store

71mm Big Cypress Nat Preserve, hiking, no security

63mm **24hr security, full facilities, litter barrels, petwalk, both lanes, vending**

49 rd 833, Snake Rd, Big Cypress Indian Reservation, **E** Miccosukee Service Plaza/deli/Dunkin'/Tesla EVC/dsl,

BIG CYPRESS INDIAN RESERVATION

49 Continued
museum, swamp safari

41mm litter barrels, rec area eb

38mm litter barrels, rec area wb

35mm **/rec area both lanes, W 24hr security, full facilities, litter barrels, petwalk, vending**

32mm litter barrels, rec area both lanes

25mm motorist callboxes begin/end, toll plaza wb

23 US 27, FL 25, , Miami, South Bay

22 FL 84 W, NW 196th, Glades Pkwy, **W** Publix, same as 21

21 FL 84 W(from nb), Indian Trace, **W** Exxon/dsl, Shell, Ceviche Peruvian, Las Rikuras, McDonald's, Papa John's, Spain's Cuisine, Subway, CVS Drug

19 I-595 E, FL 869(toll), Sawgrass Expswy

15 Royal Palm Blvd, Weston, Bonaventure, **W** Chevron, Mobil, Acquolina Italian, Argentine Steaks, Bellini Italian, BurgerFi, Carolina Ale House, Flanigan's Rest, Kokai Sushi, La Granja, Los Verdes, Lucille's Cafe, Mitch's Bagels, Moon Thai, Offerdahl's Grill, Pollo Tropical, Wendy's, Comfort Suites, Courtyard, Residence Inn, H, Meineke, Tires+, USPO, VW

13b a Griffin Rd, **E** Shell/dsl, Usave/dsl, Burger King, Donato's Rest., DQ, Outback Steaks, Waffle House, Goodyear/auto, LDS Temple, Porsche, Publix, vet, **W** 7-11/dsl, Tom Thumb/dsl, Anthony's Pizza, Bone Fish Grill, Ceviche Peruvian, Chick-fil-A, Chili's, Chipotle, Coldstone, Dunkin', HoneyBaked Ham, Jersey Mike's, McDonald's, Mission BBQ, Panera Bread, Pei Wei, Starbucks, Sushiato, Weston Diner, Fiat, Home Depot, Honda, Hyundai, Nissan/Volvo, Office Depot, Publix, T-Mobile, Toyota/Scion, vet, Walgreens

11b a Sheridan St, **E** Chevron, Cracker Barrel, Wendy's, Hampton Inn, Holiday Inn Express, Audi, BMW/EVC, Piccolo Park, **W** Shell/dsl, Blue Ginger Japanese, China One, Coldstone, Crazy Crab, Little Caesar's, McDonald's, Original Pancake House, Piola Pizza, Romeus Cuban, Starbucks, Subway, Sushi Sake, TGIFriday's, EVC, Firestone/auto, Lowe's, Publix, URGENT CARE, Verizon, vet, Walgreens

9b a FL 820, Pine Blvd, Hollywood Blvd, **E** Marathon, Shell, Agave Mexican, BJ's Rest., Boston Mkt, Brimstone Woodfire Grill, Brio Italian, Buffalo Wild Wings, Cheesecake Factory, Chick-fil-A, Chili's, Firebirds Steaks, First Watch Cafe, Fuddrucker's, Habit Burger, Havana 1957, HoneyBaked Ham, La Granja, Lime Mexican Grill, Longhorn Steaks, McDonald's, Miami Subs, Mikan Japanese, Olive Garden, Pembroke Pizza, Pieology Pizza, Pollo Tropical, RA Sushi, Sal's Italian, Sergio's Cuban, Starbucks, Taco Bell, TCBY, Tijuana Flats, Twin Peaks, Village Tavern, Wendys, Barnes&Noble, BJ's Whse/gas, Chrysler/Dodge/Jeep, Dick's, H, Mercedes, Old Navy, PetSmart, Publix, Target, Trader Joe's, USPO, Verizon, Walgreens, Walmart, **W** Chevron/dsl, Marathon/dsl, Mobil, Bolay, Burger King, BurgerFi, Cheddar's, Chipotle Mexican, Dough Boys Italian, Firehouse Subs, First Watch, Flanigan's Seafood, Hot Chicks Chicken, KFC/Taco Bell, La Granja, Las Vegas Cuban, Mazda Mediterranean, Menchie's FroYo, Nori Japanese, Panda Express, Russo's Italian, Sal's Italian, Starbucks, Sweet Tomatoes, Wendy's, Wingstop, Grand Palms Hotel, $Tree, Acura, Advance Parts, AT&T, AutoZone, Costco/gas, CVS Drug, GNC, Jiffy Lube, Lexus, Petco, Publix, Ross, Sedano's Foods, Subaru, Tires+, TJ Maxx, Tuesday Morning, vet, Walgreens, Whole Foods Mkt

7b a Miramar Pkwy, **E** Chevron, Blue Ginger Rest., Dunkin', Jimmy John's, La Carreta, McDonald's, Papa John's, Pollo Tropical, Sal's Italian, Starbucks, Subway, Tijuana Flats, Wendy's, Courtyard, Hilton Garden, Home2 Suites, Residence Inn, $Tree, Publix, USPO, vet, Walgreens,

FL

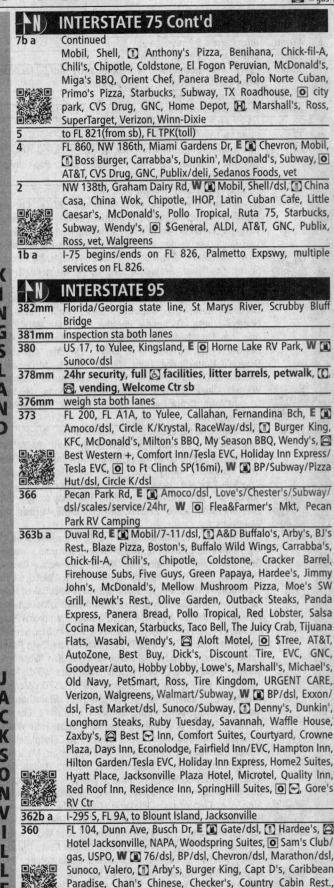

INTERSTATE 75 Cont'd

KINGSLAND

7b a Continued
Mobil, Shell, Anthony's Pizza, Benihana, Chick-fil-A, Chili's, Chipotle, Coldstone, El Fogon Peruvian, McDonald's, Miga's BBQ, Orient Chef, Panera Bread, Polo Norte Cuban, Primo's Pizza, Starbucks, Subway, TX Roadhouse, city park, CVS Drug, GNC, Home Depot, H, Marshall's, Ross, SuperTarget, Verizon, Winn-Dixie

5 to FL 821(from sb), FL TPK(toll)

4 FL 860, NW 186th, Miami Gardens Dr, E Chevron, Mobil, Boss Burger, Carrabba's, Dunkin', McDonald's, Subway, AT&T, CVS Drug, GNC, Publix/deli, Sedanos Foods, vet

2 NW 138th, Graham Dairy Rd, W Mobil, Shell/dsl, China Casa, China Wok, Chipotle, IHOP, Latin Cuban Cafe, Little Caesar's, McDonald's, Pollo Tropical, Ruta 75, Starbucks, Subway, Wendy's, $General, ALDI, AT&T, GNC, Publix, Ross, vet, Walgreens

1b a I-75 begins/ends on FL 826, Palmetto Expswy, multiple services on FL 826.

INTERSTATE 95

382mm Florida/Georgia state line, St Marys River, Scrubby Bluff Bridge

381mm inspection sta both lanes

380 US 17, to Yulee, Kingsland, E Horne Lake RV Park, W Sunoco/dsl

378mm **24hr security, full facilities, litter barrels, petwalk, , vending, Welcome Ctr sb**

376mm weigh sta both lanes

373 FL 200, FL A1A, to Yulee, Callahan, Fernandina Bch, E Amoco/dsl, Circle K/Krystal, RaceWay/dsl, Burger King, KFC, McDonald's, Milton's BBQ, My Season BBQ, Wendy's, Best Western +, Comfort Inn/Tesla EVC, Holiday Inn Express/Tesla EVC, to Ft Clinch SP(16mi), W BP/Subway/Pizza Hut/dsl, Circle K/dsl

JACKSONVILLE

366 Pecan Park Rd, E Amoco/dsl, Love's/Chester's/Subway/dsl/scales/service/24hr, W Flea&Farmer's Mkt, Pecan Park RV Camping

363b a Duval Rd, E Mobil/7-11/dsl, A&D Buffalo's, Arby's, BJ's Rest., Blaze Pizza, Boston's, Buffalo Wild Wings, Carrabba's, Chick-fil-A, Chili's, Chipotle, Coldstone, Cracker Barrel, Firehouse Subs, Five Guys, Green Papaya, Hardee's, Jimmy John's, McDonald's, Mellow Mushroom Pizza, Moe's SW Grill, Newk's Rest., Olive Garden, Outback Steaks, Panda Express, Panera Bread, Pollo Tropical, Red Lobster, Salsa Cocina Mexican, Starbucks, Taco Bell, The Juicy Crab, Tijuana Flats, Wasabi, Wendy's, Aloft Motel, $Tree, AT&T, AutoZone, Best Buy, Dick's, Discount Tire, EVC, GNC, Goodyear/auto, Hobby Lobby, Lowe's, Marshall's, Michael's, Old Navy, PetSmart, Ross, Tire Kingdom, URGENT CARE, Verizon, Walgreens, Walmart/Subway, W BP/dsl, Exxon/dsl, Fast Market/dsl, Sunoco/Subway, Denny's, Dunkin', Longhorn Steaks, Ruby Tuesday, Savannah, Waffle House, Zaxby's, Best Inn, Comfort Suites, Courtyard, Crowne Plaza, Days Inn, Econolodge, Fairfield Inn/EVC, Hampton Inn, Hilton Garden/Tesla EVC, Holiday Inn Express, Home2 Suites, Hyatt Place, Jacksonville Plaza Hotel, Microtel, Quality Inn, Red Roof Inn, Residence Inn, SpringHill Suites, Gore's RV Ctr

362b a I-295 S, FL 9A, to Blount Island, Jacksonville

360 FL 104, Dunn Ave, Busch Dr, E Gate/dsl, Hardee's, Hotel Jacksonville, NAPA, Woodspring Suites, Sam's Club/gas, USPO, W 76/dsl, BP/dsl, Chevron/dsl, Marathon/dsl, Sunoco, Valero, Arby's, Burger King, Capt D's, Caribbean Paradise, Chan's Chinese, Checker's, Country Cabin Rest., Dunkin', Firehouse Subs, Fuji Buffet, Jax Shrimp & Chicken,

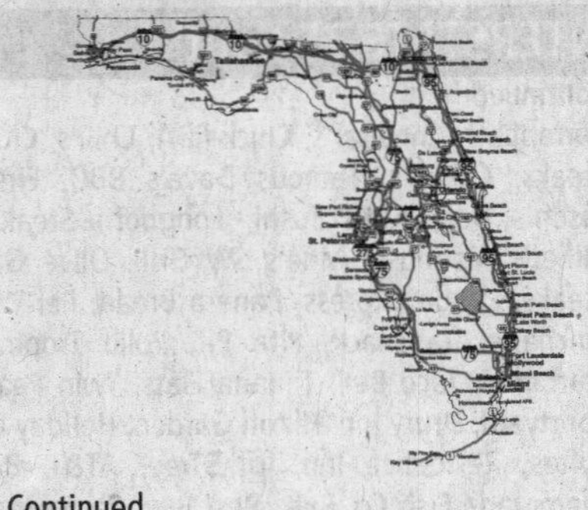

GOLFAIR BLVD

360 Continued
KFC, Krystal, Little Caesar's, McDonald's, New China, Papa Murphy's, Popeyes, Starbucks, Subway, Taco Bell, Wendy's, Knights Inn, Red Roof Inn, River City Inn, Stayable Suites, $Tree, Aamco, Advance Parts, Camping World RV Ctr, CVS Drug, Family$, PepBoys, Publix, Tires+, Walgreens

358b a FL 105, Broward Rd, Heckscher Dr, E zoo, W Extended Stay Jax, Motel Dunas

357mm Trout River

357 FL 111, Edgewood Ave, W BP/dsl, Texaco/dsl

356b a Fl 115, FL 117, Lem Turner Rd, Norwood Ave, E Blue Bo[x] Sandwiches, Hardee's, W BP/dsl, RaceWay/dsl, Speedway, Sunoco, Best Taste, Burger King, Checker's, G[...] Boy BBQ, Golden Egg Roll, Ho-Ho Chinese, Krystal, M[...] Cherry's Rest, Popeyes, Subway, Taco Bell, Advance Parts, Save-A-Lot, Tires+, Walgreens

355 Golfair Blvd, E 76, Pepper Pot, W RaceWay/dsl, Baron's Crab Stop, Wing Nation, Metro Inn

354b a US 1, 20th St, to Jacksonville, to AmTrak, MLK Pkwy

353d FL 114, to 8th St, E McDonald's, H, Walgreens

353c US 23 N, Kings Rd, downtown

353b US 90A, Union St, downtown, Sports Complex

353a Church St, Myrtle Ave, Forsythe St, downtown

352d I-10 W, Stockton St (from sb), Lake City

352c Monroe St(from nb), downtown

352b a Myrtle Ave(from nb), downtown

351d Stockton St, downtown, W H

351c Margaret St, downtown

351b I-10 W, to Tallahassee

351a Park St, College St, HOSPITAL, to downtown

351mm St Johns River

350b FL 13, San Marco Blvd, E H

350a Prudential Dr, Main St, Riverside Ave(from nb), downtown, E BP, Extended Stay America, Hampton Inn, W Bearded Pig BBQ, FL Cracker Kitchen, Good Doug[h] Doughnuts, Hightide Burritos, Hurricane Wings, Jimm[y] John's, Mayday Ice Cream, Nopalera Mexican, Olive Tre[e] Mediterranean, Panera Bread, Pizza & Sidecar, Sarah Bakery, Hilton Garden, Homewood Suites

349 US 90 E(from sb), to beaches, downtown, W Shell/dsl, Scottish Inn

348 US 1 S(from sb), Philips Hwy, W Scottish Inn, Super 8

347 US 1A, FL 126, Emerson St, E ChoppinCoppin Jamaica[n], Hot Wok, Mi Veracruz, Advance Parts, Advance Part[s], Family$, O'Reilly Parts, W BP/dsl, Gate/dsl, Speedway/dsl, Benchwarmers Cafe, McDonald's, Wendy's, Emerson Inn, $Tree, Chevrolet, Goodyear/auto

346b a FL 109, University Blvd, E 76, BP, Speedway/dsl, Sunoco/dsl, Beignets Caribbean, Bento Asian, Capt D's, Checker[s], DQ, Firehouse Subs, Hala's Eatery, Hibachi Japanese, Hung[...] Howie's, Korean BBQ, Krystal, Q Noodle, Tipicos Hondura[n], Ying's Chinese, Zaxby's, Ace Hardware, CVS Drug, Family$, Famous Tire & Auto, Freshfields Mkt, H, NAPA, Su[...] Tire, Tires+, Winn-Dixie, W BP/dsl, RaceTrac/dsl, Tesla EVC, Baskin-Robbins/Dunkin', Burger King, Chick-fil-A

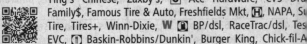

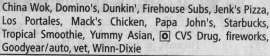

INTERSTATE 95 Cont'd

346b a Continued
Chipotle, Famous Amos, KFC, Little Caesars Pizza, McDonald's, Papa John's, Sonny's BBQ, Taco Bell, Wendy's, Woody's BBQ, Econolodge, Extended Stay, SureStay, $General, auto repair, AutoZone, U-Haul

345 FL 109, University Blvd(from nb), **E** Gate/dsl/24hr, Mobil/Subway/dsl, Speedway/dsl, Bono's BBQ, Selvino's Pizza, Subway, H

344 FL 202, Butler Blvd, **E** Gate/dsl, City Cafe, Dave&Buster's, JJ's Cafe, Kusina Rest., Best Western, Country Inn Suites, Extended Stay America, Holiday Inn Express, Marriott, Red Roof Inn, Sonesta Suites, Wyndham Garden, USPO, **W** BP/dsl, Shell, Applebee's, Arby's, Chick-fil-A, Cracker Barrel, Dunkin', Fresh Mex, Jimmy John's, McDonald's, Newk's, Sonic, Starbucks, Waffle House, Wendy's, Whataburger/24hr, Zaxby's, Baymont Inn, Courtyard, Extended Stay America, Extended Stay America(2), Fairfield Inn, Hampton Inn/Tesla EVC, Hometown Inn, La Quinta, Red Roof+, TownePlace Suites, WoodSpring Suites

341 FL 152, Baymeadows Rd, **E** BP/dsl, Gate/dsl, Shell/dsl, 5th Element Indian, Arby's, Athenian Owl, Chili's, First Watch, Four Rivers Smokehouse, Hardee's, Jimmy John's, Krystal, Las Tapatias, Mama's Pizza, Panda Express, Starbucks, Subway, Comfort Suites, Embassy Suites, Extended Stay America, Ramada Inn, Advance Parts, Autozone, Publix, Tires+, Walgreens, **W** Mobil/Kangaroo, RaceTrac, Shell, Al's Pizza, Cafe Kabob, Clara's Tidbits, Dunkin', Empanada's Factory, Full Circle, IHOP, Jersey Mike's, Karaikudi Indian, KFC, L&L Hawaiian, Maa Kitchen, McDonald's, Minerva Indian, Noom Thai, Nopalera Mexican, Pagoda Chinese, Red Lobster, Sakura Japanese, Taco Bell, Waffle House, Wendy's, Best Inn, Days Inn, InTown Suites, Knights Inn, Motel 6, Quality Inn, Sheraton, Sonesta Suites, Studio 6, $Tree, BJ's Whse/gas, CVS Drug, Discount Tire, EVC, Harley-Davidson, Lowe's, Office Depot, Pepboys, Verizon

340 FL 115, Southside Blvd(from nb), **E** Circle K, Five Guys, Longhorn Steaks, Newk's Eatery, Starbucks, ALDI, AT&T, Home Depot, Michael's, PetSmart, same as 339, Target

339 US 1, Philips Hwy, **E** BP/Circle K/dsl, Mobil/dsl, Arby's, Bono's BBQ, Burger King, Chick-fil-A, Chuck E. Cheese, Coldstone, Main Event, McDonald's, Mikado, Moe's SW Grill, Olive Garden, Starbucks, Taco Bell, $Tree, Belk, Best Buy, Chevrolet, Dillard's, EVC, EVC, Ford, JC Penney, mall, Nissan, Toyota, vet, Walmart, **W** BP/dsl, Benito's Italian, Salsa's Mexican, Steak&Shake, Subway

337 I-295 N, to rd 9a, Orange Park, Jax Beaches

335 Old St Augustine Rd, **E** Applebee's, Starbucks, Courtyard, H, **W** Gate/dsl, Shell/dsl, Bamboo Wok, Bono's BBQ, Brooklyn Pizza, Chili's, Chipotle, DQ, Duck Donuts, Dunkin', First Watch, Five Guys, Hurricane Grill, La Nopalera, McDonald's, Moe's SW, Panda Express, Panera Bread, PDQ Cafe, Red Bowl Asian, Subway, Sushi House, Tijuana Flats, Wendy's, Zaxby's, Zoe's Kitchen, Hampton Inn, Holiday Inn Express, Residence Inn, AT&T, GNC, Kohl's, Mavis Tires & Brakes, Publix, Tires+, vet, Walgreens

333 FL 9b, to US 1, I-295, N Jacksonville Beaches

331mm **24hr security, full facilities, litter barrels, petwalk, both lanes, vending**

329 rd 210, Green Cove Springs, Ponte Vedra Beach, **E** Pilot/McDonald's/PJ Fresh/dsl/scales/24hr, Sunoco/fruit, TA/Mobil/Popeyes/dsl/scales/service/24hr/@, Culver's, Dunkin', Grumpy's, Waffle House, **W** Circle K/dsl, Mobil/Subway/dsl/USPO, Shell/dsl, Tesla EVC, Burger King,

ST AUGUSTINE

FLAGLER BEACH

329 Continued
China Wok, Domino's, Dunkin', Firehouse Subs, Jenk's Pizza, Los Portales, Mack's Chicken, Papa John's, Starbucks, Tropical Smoothie, Yummy Asian, CVS Drug, fireworks, Goodyear/auto, vet, Winn-Dixie

323 International Golf Pkwy, **E** BP/dsl/USPO, EVC, Shell/Subway/dsl, St. mary's Seafood, Wendy's, Holiday Inn, **W** Buc-ee's/dsl, Gate/EVC, Burger King, King Wok, Legends Grille, MIO Kitchen, Murray Bros., Pirate Pizza, Renaissance Resort, vet, World Golf Village

318 FL 16, Green Cove Sprgs, St Augustine, **E** Chevron/DQ/dsl, EVC, Gate/dsl, Mobil/Circle K/dsl, Shell/dsl, Tesla EVC, Bojangles, Burger King, Chick-fil-A, Dunkin', McDonald's, Starbucks, Subway, Taco's Queen, Zaxby's, Comfort Inn, Courtyard, Fairfield Inn, Holiday Inn Express, Home2 Suites, La Quinta, Quality Inn, Smart Stay, Cadillac, Campers RV Ctr, Camping World RV Ctr, Ford/Lincoln, St Augustine Outlets/Famous Brands, **W** Exxon, RaceTrac/dsl, Cracker Barrel, Denny's, Giovanni's Italian, Hibachi Thai, KFC, Ruby Tuesday, Sonny's BBQ, Taco Bell, Waffle House, Wendy's, Best Western, Days Inn, Hampton Inn, Howard Johnson, Red Roof+, Scottish Inn, Super 8, Discount Tire, funpark, St Augustine Outlets

311 FL 207, St Augustine, **E** BP/Subway/dsl, RaceTrac/dsl, Burger King, Dunkin', Jeremy's Pizza, Wendy's, flea mkt, H, KOA (7mi), St Augustine RV Park, to Anastasia SP, **W** Quality Inn

305 FL 206, to Hastings, Crescent Beach, **E** Flying J/Denny's/Subway/dsl/LP/scales/24hr, to Ft Matanzas NM, truck repair, **W** truck repair

302mm **24hr security, full facilities, litter barrels, petwalk, both lanes, vending**

298 US 1, to St Augustine, **E** BP/dsl, Marathon/fruit, fruit/pecans, to Faver-Dykes SP, **W** Mobil/rest/dsl, Sunoco/dsl, truck repair

293 Matanzas Woods Pky

289 to FL A1A(toll br), to Palm Coast, **E** Exxon/Circle K, RaceTrac/dsl, Shell, Cantina Louie, Checkers, China Express, Cracker Barrel, Denny's, Dunkin', Fire In The Hole Pizza, IHOP, KFC, McDonald's, Metro Diner, Palm Harbor Grill, Salsas Mexican, Sonia's Brazilian, Starbucks, Stoner's Pizza, Thai By Thai, Wendy's, Econo Lodge, Fairfield Inn, Microtel, Red Roof+, Beall's, CVS Drug, Publix, Staples, Walgreens, **W** Exxon/Circle K/dsl, Exxon/Kangaroo, Shell/Circle K/dsl, Shell/dsl, A1 Burritos, Adette's Bistro, Baskin-Robbins/Dunkin', Bob Evans, Bruster's Creamery, Burger Bros, Carrabba's, Chick-fil-A, China King, China One, Dominics Deli, Golden Corral, Honey Baked Ham, Houligan's, Jimmy John's, Joe's NY Pizza, Mamaling Asian, McDonald's, Napoli Pizza, Outback Steaks, Pizza Hut, Purdee's Creamery, Ruby Tuesday, Sakura Japanese, Sonny's BBQ, Steak'n Shake, Subway, Taco Bell, TX Roadhouse, Wendy's, Zaxby's, Days Inn, $General, $Tree, Advance Parts, AutoZone, Beall's, Belk, CVS Drug, Ford, GNC, Home Depot, Kohl's, Lowe's, Publix, Tire Kingdom, Tuffy Auto, USPO, Verizon, Walgreens, Walmart, Winn-Dixie

286mm weigh sta both lanes

284 FL 100, to Bunnell, Flagler Beach, Chipotle, **E** Mobil/repair/dsl, RaceTrac, Shell/Circle K/dsl, Burger King, Domino's, Manny's Pizza, McDonald's, Oriental Garden, Popeyes, Subway, Woody's BBQ, Best Western+, Hampton Inn, Ace Hardware, Winn-Dixie, **W** Amoco, RaceTrac, McDonald's, Panda Express, Panera Bread, Pizza Hut, Subway, Hilton Garden, $Tree, AT&T, Chevrolet, Chrysler/Dodge/Jeep, Dunkin Donuts, H, Michael's, Olive Garden, PetSmart, Ross, Target, TJ Maxx, Verizon

FL

= gas = food = lodging = other = rest stop

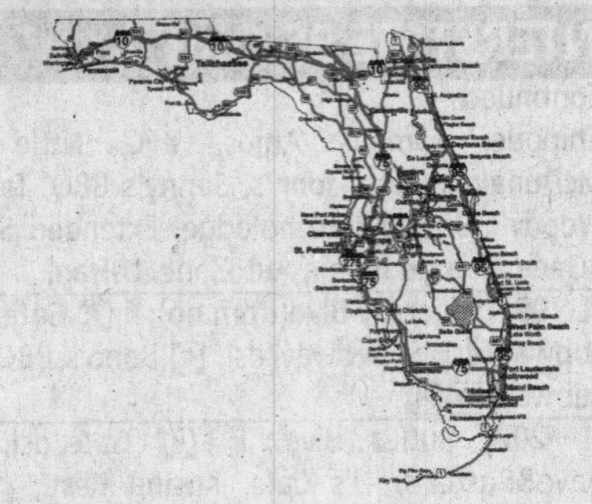

INTERSTATE 95 Cont'd

ORMOND BEACH · DAYTONA BCH

Exit #	Services
278	Old Dixie Hwy, E 7-11, Breakfast Station, Thai Elephant, Bulow RV Park (3mi), Publix, to Bulow Creek SP, vet, W BP/dsl, Holiday Travel Park, vet
273	US 1, E Mobil, RaceTrac/dsl, Sunoco/fruit, L'angolo Italian, McDonald's, Waffle House, Econo Inn, $General, Giant Rec RV Ctr, W Exxon/Burger King, Love's/Arby's/dsl/scales/24hr, Daytona Pig Stand BBQ, Houligan's, Days Inn, Econolodge, Extended Stay, Howard Johnson, Super 8, Encore RV Park, Harley-Davidson
268	FL 40, Ormond Beach, E Speedway/dsl, Sunoco/dsl, Agave Cantina, Applebee's, Boston Mkt, Bronx Pizza, Chick-fil-A, Chili's, Chipotle, Delcato's Pizza, Denny's, Dustin's BBQ, Mama Mia's Pizza, Panera Bread, Papa John's, Peach Valley Cafe, Red Bowl, Starbucks, Starbucks, Steak'n Shake, Subway, Taco Bell, Takeya Steaks, Wendy's, Wok&Roll, Zaxby's, Sleep Inn, $Tree, Beall's, Discount Tire, GNC, H, Love Whole Foods, Lowe's, Petco, Publix, Ross, Tire Kingdom, to Tomoka SP, USPO, Walmart/EVC, W 7-11, BP/Dunkin', RaceTrac/dsl, Texaco, Cracker Barrel, Fancy Sushi, Gourmet Kitchen, McDonald's, Baymont Inn, Extended Stay America, Hampton Inn, Walgreens
265	LPGA Blvd, Holly Hill, Daytona Beach, E 7-11, Buc-ee's/dsl, RaceTrac, Shell/Circle K/Dunkin'/dsl, Arby's, Blaze Pizza, Chipotle, Culver's, Dave & Buster's, Dominic's Deli, Dunkin', Ford's Garage, Salsas Conina, Stonewood Grill, Taco Bell, Wendy's, Wild Ginger Asian, CVS Drug, Sam's Club/gas, Tanger Outlets/famous brands, W Holiday Inn, BMW, Chrysler/Dodge/Jeep, EVC, EVC, Ford/Lincoln, Infiniti, Mazda, Mercedes, Nissan, VW
261b a	US 92, to DeLand, Daytona Bch, E 7-11, EVC, Sunoco, Sunoco/dsl, Tesla EVC, 4 Rivers BBQ, Applebee's, Arby's, Asian Grill, Bahama Breeze, BJ's Rest., Bonefish Grill, Buffalo Wild Wings, Burger King, Carrabba's, Checkers, Cheddar's, Chick-fil-A, Chili's, Chipotle Mexican, Cracker Barrel, Fancy Q Thai, Firehouse Subs, First Watch, Five Guys, Honeybaked Ham, Hooters, IHOP, Jersey Mike's Subs, Jimmy John's, Krystal, Longhorn Steaks, McDonald's, Miller's Ale House, Olive Garden, Outback Steaks, Panda Express, Panera Bread, Red Lobster, Starbucks, Subway, Taco Bell, Tijuana Flats, Waffle House, Wendy's, Winghouse, Baymont, Best Western, Courtyard, Extended Stay America, Fairfield Inn, Hampton Inn, Hilton Garden/Tesla EVC, Holiday Inn Express, Home2 Suites, Homewood Suites, Quality Inn, Residence Inn, $Tree, Barnes&Noble, Bass Pro Shops, Beall's, Best Buy, BigLots, Books-A-Million, Daytona RV Camping, Dick's, Dillard's, Firestone/auto, funpark, Home Depot, H, JC Penney, Jo-Ann Fabrics, mall, Michael's, Old Navy, PepBoys, PetSmart, Staples, SteinMart, Target/Starbucks, TJMaxx, to Daytona Racetrack, Tuesday Morning, Verizon, World Mkt, W BP/dsl, RaceTrac/dsl, McDonald's, Comfort Suites, Days Inn, Motel 6, WoodSpring Suites, Daytona Speedway RV Park, flea mkt
260b a	I-4, to Orlando, FL 400 E, to S Daytona, E Mobil/Circle K/dsl, RaceTrac/dsl/e85
256	FL 421, to Port Orange, Cinnamon Tree Cafe, E 76/dsl, BP/Circle K, EVC, Murphy USA/dsl, WaWa/dsl, Anthony's Pizza, Applebee's, Arby's, Bob Evans, Boston Mkt, Bronx House Pizza, Burger King, Chick-fil-A, Chicken Salad Chick, Chili's, China Star, Chipotle, Cici's, Culver's, Denny's, Domino's, Dominos, Dunkin', Dustin's BBQ, Firehouse Subs, First Watch, Five Star Pizza, Flo Greek, Ginza Japanese, Golden Corral, Half Wall, Herbert's Bakery, Houligan's, KFC, La Fiesta Mexican, McDonald's, McKenna's Seafood, Mellow Mushroom, Moe's SW, Monterrey Grill, Mulligans Grille,

NEW SMYRNA BEACH · TITUSVILLE · COCOA

Exit #	Services
256	Continued Panera Bread, Papa John's, Peach Valley Breakfast, Red Bowl Asian, Salsas Mexican, Sonny's BBQ, Starbucks, Subway, Sushi 99, Taco Bell, Thai Kitchen, Tijuana Flats, Wendy's, Yummy Rice Thai, Country Inn&Suites, La Quinta, BJ's/gas, CVS Drug, Daytona Beach RV Park, Home Depot, Lowe's, Publix, Super Target/Starbucks, Tuffy Auto, Verizon, vet, Walgreens, Walmart, W 7-11/dsl, Marathon/dsl, China Chef, ChuckECheese, Coldstone, Five Guys, Giovanni Italian, Malibu Beach Grill, McDonald's, Olive Garden, Panda Express, Popeyes, Red Robin, Subway, Takara Japanese, TX Roadhouse, Waffle House, Wendy's, $Tree, AT&T, Belk, Firestone/auto, GNC, Kohl's, Love Whole Foods, Marshall's, Michael's, PetCo, Publix, Walgreens
249b a	FL 44, to De Land, New Smyrna Beach, E Murphy Express, Dunkin', ALDI, Home Depot, New Smyrna RV Camp(3mi), SugarMill RV Park, W Chevron/dsl, RaceTrac, McDonald's, Popeyes, Walmart/Subway
244	FL 442, to Edgewater, E Marathon/dsl, truck repair
231	rd 5A, Scottsmoor, E BP/Stuckey's/dsl, Crystal Lake RV Park
227mm	**24hr security, full facilities, litter barrels, petwalk, sb, vending**
225mm	**24hr security, full facilities, litter barrels, petwalk, nb, vending**
223	FL 46, Mims, E McDonald's, W BP, Chevron/Dunkin'/dsl, Love's/dsl/repair/scales/24hr, $General, KOA/LP Seasons RV Park
220	FL 406, Titusville, E BP/dsl, Shell/Hungry Howie's/dsl, Beef O'Brady's, Dunkin', First Wok, Kelsey's Pizza McDonald's, Subway, Valentino's Rest., Wendy's, Executive Garden Inn, $General, $Tree, Advance Parts GNC, H, O'Reilly Parts, Publix, Tires+, to Canaveral Na Seashore, Walgreens
215	FL 50, to Orlando, Titusville, E BP/rest/dsl, Chevron Subway/dsl, EVC, Exxon/Circle K, Murphy USA/dsl, Shell Dunkin'/dsl, Tesla EVC, Bamboo Garden, Burger King Denny's, Humpavelli's Pizza, McDonald's, Panda Express Sonny's BBQ, Starbucks, Taco Bell, Waffle House, Wendy's, Best Western, Ramada Inn, AlLDI, AT&T, Firestone, Ford Home Depot, Lowe's, Marshall's, Pep Boys, PetCo, Staples Target/Starbucks, Tire Kingdom, to Kennedy Space Ct Walmart, W Cracker Barrel, Durango's Steaks, IHOP Popeyes, Days Inn, Extended Stay America, Fairfield Inn Hampton Inn, Holiday Inn, Quality Inn, TownePlace Suites, Christmas RV Park(8mi), Great Outdoors RV/golf Resort
212	FL 407, to FL 528 toll(no re-entry sb)
208	Port St John
205	FL 528(toll 528), to Cape Canaveral & Cape Port AFS, Cit Point
202	FL 524, Cocoa, E Flying J/Wendy's/dsl/scales/24hr, Shell dsl, Museum of History&Science, W BP/dsl, Days In
201	FL 520, to Cocoa Bch, Cocoa, E BP/dsl, Exxon/Circle K Pilot/Subway/dsl/scales/24hr, Dunkin', IHOP, Waffl House, Best Western, Budget Inn, fireworks, H,

INTERSTATE 95 Cont'd

COCOA

201 Continued
Sams Club/gas/EVC, **W** Chevron/dsl, Shell/Burger King, Sunoco/dsl, McDonald's, Holiday Inn Express, Camping World RV Ctr, JOY RV Park, Sonrise Palms RV Park

195 FL 519, Fiske Blvd, **E** 7-11, Mobil/dsl, Baci Pizza, Ruby Tuesday, Sushi Factory, Swiss Inn, Discount Tire, H, Lowe's, Space Coast RV Park

193 Viera Blvd, **E** Beef O Brady's, Brooklyn Pizza, Long Doggers, TX Roadhouse, Walgreens, Winn-Dixie/Tesla EVC, **W** Mobil/pizza, Chic-fil-A, Dunkin', El Leoncito, Kimbo Chinese, McDonald's, Pozzy Pizza, Publix, Slow&Low BBQ, Starbucks

VIERA

191 rd 509, to Satellite Beach, Viera, Fairfield Inn, **E** 7-11, BP/Pizza, Mobil/dsl, Sunoco/dsl, Bob Evans, Carrabba's, Celo's Shawarma, Chick-fil-A, Domino's, DQ, IHOP, Jimmy John's, McDonald's, Metro Diner, Mi Jalisco Mexican, Nature's Table, Papa John's, Perkins, Pizza Hut/Taco Bell, Sonny's BBQ, Subway, Time Square Pizza, Twisted Fin, Wendy's, Hampton Inn, Holiday Inn/EVC, CVS Drug, Publix, Tires+, to Patrick AFB, Tuffy Tire & Auto, URGENT CARE, Walgreens, zoo, **W** Murphy USA/dsl, Shell/dsl, Asian Wok, Bean Sprout Aisan, Blaze Pizza, Bonefish Grill, Buffalo Wild Wings, Burger King, Chili's, Chipotle, Coldstone, Cracker Barrel, Culver's, First Watch, Five Guys, Island IX, Jersey Mike's, Joella's Chicken, Longhorn Steaks, Melting Pot, Moe's SW Grill, Olive Tree Greek, Outback Steaks, Panera Bread, Pizza Gallery, Starbucks, Steak'nShake, Subway, Thai Hana, Tijuana Flats, Tuscany Grill, Walk-On Rest., La Quinta, $Tree, AT&T, Belk, Books-A-Million, GNC, Hobby Lobby, H, Kohl's, Lexus, Michael's, Old Navy, PetCo, PetSmart, Ross, SuperTarget/Starbucks, Tire Kingdom, TJ Maxx, Verizon, Walmart/McDonald's, World Mkt

188 FL 404, Patrick AFB, Satellite Beach, **W** Costco/gas

183 FL 518, Melbourne, Indian Harbour Beach, **E** BP/dsl, Marathon/Dunkin', RaceTrac/dsl, WaWa/dsl, Doghouse Pizza, art museum, AT&T, H, **W** Frankie's Italian, Flea Mkt

180 US 192, to Melbourne, **E** BP/dsl, Cumberland/dsl, Mobil/dsl, RaceTrac/dsl, Shell/Circle K, Sunoco/dsl, Bennigan's, ChuckECheese/EVC, CQ Pizza, Crispy Cone Ice Cream, Denny's, Dunkin'/EVC, Jimmy's Gyros, Zaxby's, Best Value Inn, Budget Inn, Comfort Inn, Days Inn, Fairfield Inn, Hampton Inn, Holiday Inn Express, Melbourne Suites/rest., Woodspring Suites, Ace Hardware, fireworks, H, Lowe's, Sam's Club/gas, Subaru, Volvo/Subaru/EVC

176 rd 516, to Palm Bay, **E** 7-11, Mobil, Murphy USA/dsl, RaceTrac/dsl, Wawa/dsl, Baskin Robbins/Dunkin Donuts, Chick-fil-A, Cracker Barrel, Denny's, Einstein Bagels, Golden Corral, Great Wall Chinese, IHOP, Little Asia, Melbourne Seafood, Popeyes, Smack Wings, Starbucks, Tijuana Flats, Extended Stay America, Hampton Inn, Home2 Suites, Hyatt Place, Quality Inn, AlLDI, Bass Pro Shops, BJ's Whse/gas, Harley-Davidson, Office Depot, Walgreens, Walmart, **W** 7-11, Mobil/dsl, Shell, Buffalo Wild Wings, Burger King, Chipotle, Firehouse Subs, Five Guys, Long Doggers, Longhorn Steaks, McDonald's, Michelli's Pizzeria, Moe's SW Grill, Panda Express, Panera Bread, Pollo Tropical, Subway, Thai Thai, Wendy's, Your Pie Pizza, $Tree, AT&T, CVS Drug, Discount Tire, Giant RV Ctr, Kohl's/EVC, Marshall's, Michael's, PetCo, Publix, Ross, Target, URGENT CARE, vet, Walgreens

173 FL 514, to Palm Bay, **E** RaceTrac/dsl, Shell, Sunoco/dsl, Twisty Cone Creamery, Holiday Inn Express, Firestone/auto, Ford, H, truck/RV repair, **W** Marathon, Mobil/dsl, Sunoco/dsl, Arby's, Brown's Jamaican, Burger King,

FELLSMERE

173 Continued
Chick-fil-A, Japanese Buffet, McDonald's/playplace, Panda Express, Somers Cafe, Sonic, Sonny's BBQ, Subway, Taco Bell, TX Roadhouse, Waffle House, Wendy's, Comfort Suites, Motel 6, $General, Advance Parts, CVS Drug, Gatto's Tire/auto, Home Depot, Lowe's, Publix, Tire Kingdom, URGENT CARE, USPO, Verizon, Walgreens, Walmart

168mm **24hr security, full facilities, litter barrels, petwalk, both lanes, vending**

166 St John's Heritage Pkwy

156 rd 512, to Sebastian, Fellsmere, **E** BP/DQ/Stuckey's/dsl, Chevron/McDonald's, RaceWay/dsl, H, Sebastian Inlet SRA, Sunshine RV Park, **W** St Sebastian SP

147 FL 60, Osceola Blvd, **E** Amoco/dsl, BP/deli/dsl, Citgo/dsl, Sunoco/Pizza, TA/BP/Popeyes/Subway/dsl/scales/24hr/@, WaWa/dsl, Dunkin', IHOP, McDonald's/EVC, Comfort Suites, Fairfield Inn, Howard Johnson, Knights Inn, Motel 6, Studio 6, Vero Beach Resort, Vero Beach Suites, H, Hyundai, USPO, vet, **W** Shell/dsl, Cracker Barrel, Steak'n Shake, Steak'n Shake, Country Inn&Suites, Hampton Inn, Holiday Inn Express, Vero Beach Outlets/famous brands

138 FL 614, Indrio Rd, **E** Oceanographic Institute

133mm **24hr security, full facilities, litter barrels, petwalk, both lanes, vending**

131b a FL 68, Orange Ave, **E** H, to Ft Pierce SP, **W** Flying J/Denny's/Subway/dsl/LP/scales/24hr, Love's/Hardee's/dsl/scales/24hr, Blue Beacon

129 FL 70, to Okeechobee, **E** Citgo, Murphy USA, RaceTrac/dsl, Sunoco/dsl, Wawa/Tesla EVC, Applebee's, Chick-fil-A, Cowboys BBQ, Golden Corral, Sonic, Starbucks, Waffle House, Advance Parts, AT&T, AT&T, Firestone/auto, Home Depot, H, URGENT CARE, Walgreens, Walmart/Subway, **W** Citgo, Love's/Arby's/dsl/24hr/@, Marathon/scales/dsl, Mobil/Dunkin'/Subway, Pilot/McDonald's/dsl/scales/24hr, Brisas Mexical, Burger King, Cracker Barrel, KFC, La Granja, LJ Silver, McDonald's, Pappy's Pizza, Red Lobster, Subway, Waffle House, Wendy's, 3 Palms Hotel, At Home Suites, Best Value Inn, Comfort Suites, Days Inn, Fairfield Inn, Hampton Inn, Holiday Inn Express, La Quinta, Motel 6, Quality Inn, Rodeway Inn, Sleep Inn, to FL TPK, Treasure Coast RV Park

126 rd 712, Midway Rd, **E** Marathon/Subway/dsl

121 St Lucie West Blvd, **E** 7-11, Mobil/Dunkin', Murphy USA/dsl, Arby's, Bob Evans, Burger King, Carrabba's, Cheddar's, Chick-fil-A, Chili's, China Wok, Chipotle Mexican, Denny's, First Watch, Five Guys, Frank&Al's Pizza, Hokkaido, Jersey Mike's, Jimmy John's, KFC, McDonald's, Moe's SW Grill, Outback Steaks, Panda Express, Panera Bread, Papa John's, Pollo Tropical, Spiro's Greek, Starbucks, Taco Bell, Tijuana Flats, TX Roadhouse, Wendy's, West End Grill, Hampton Inn/EVC, Holiday Inn Express, Residence Inn, SpringHill Suites, TownePlace Suites, $Tree, AT&T, Beall's, Carvel Creamery, CVS Drug, Outdoor Resorts Camping(2mi), PetCo, Publix/deli, Ross, Staples, SteinMart, Tire Kingdom, Tires+, USPO, Verizon, Walgreens, Walmart/EVC, **W** Chevron/BBQ/dsl, Park Ave. BBQ, Tutto Fresco, Hilton Garden, MainStay Suites, Sheraton Resort, PGA Village

120 Crosstown Pkwy

118 Gatlin Blvd, to Port St Lucie, **E** Mobil/Dunkin', RaceTrac, Shell/Dunkin'/Subway/dsl, Sunoco/e85, McDonald's, Starbucks, Taco Bell, Wendy's, AutoZone, Bass Pro Shops, Home Depot, Sam's Club/gas, Tire Kingdom, Tires+, vet, Walgreens, Walmart, **W** WaWa/dsl, Chipotle, Culver's, Great Greek, Longhorn Steaks, McDonald's, Meating Street Steaks, Olive Garden, Panda Express, Panera Bread, PDQ Chicken, Recovery Grill, Subway, Tropical Smoothie,

FL

FL

INTERSTATE 95 Cont'd

PALM CITY

118 Continued
Homewood Suites, TownePlace Suites, AT&T, GNC, H, Michael's, Old Navy, PetSmart, Publix, Target, TJ Maxx

114 Becker Rd

112mm weigh sta sb

110 FL 714, to Martin Hwy, Palm City, E H

106mm **24hr security, full facilities, litter barrels, petwalk, both lanes, vending**

102 Rd 713, High Meadow Ave, Palm City

101 FL 76, to Stuart, Indiantown, E Chevron/dsl, RaceTrac/dsl, Sunoco/dsl, Baskin-Robbins/Dunkin', Cracker Barrel, Galaxy Diner, La Forchetta Pizza, McDonald's, Popeyes, Wendy's, Courtyard, Holiday Inn Express, city park, H, Publix, Walgreens, W 7-11/dsl, Mobil/dsl

96 rd 708, to Hobe Sound, E Dickinson SP(11mi)

92mm weigh sta nb

JUPITER

87b a FL 706, to Okeechobee, Jupiter, E Mobil/dsl, Shell/dsl, Sunoco, Sunoco, Blaze Pizza, Carvel Ice Cream, Chipotle, CR Chicks, Domino's, Duffy's Rest., Dunkin', First Watch Cafe, Five Guys, Giuseppe's, Hurricane Grill, I Heart Mac & Cheese, IHOP, Jersey Mike's Subs, KFC, Lindburgers, McDonald's, Panera Bread, Park Ave Grill, Pollo Tropical, Rancho Chico, Starbucks, Subway, Taco Bell, Tijuana Flats, Uncle Mick's, Vinny's Pizza, YumYum, Comfort Inn, Fairfield Inn, Advance Parts, AT&T, BMW, GNC, Home Depot, PepBoys, PetSmart, Publix, Tire Kingdom, to Dickinson SP, URGENT CARE, vet, Walgreens, Walmart, Winn-Dixie, W Sunoco, CVS Drug, to FL TPK, West Jupiter RV Camping(3mi)

83 Donald Ross Rd, E Marathon/Subway, Shell/deli, Chipotle, Domino's Pizza, Dunkin', Firehouse Subs, Grande Italiano, Longhorn Steaks, McDonald's, Mrs. Smokey's BBQ, Panera Bread, Waxin's Rest., Hampton Inn(3mi), Holiday Inn Express(3mi), Homewood Suites, AT&T, CVS Drug, H, Publix, stadium, Walgreens

79c FL 809 S(from sb), Military Tr, W same services as 79b, to FL TPK

79a b FL 786, PGA Blvd, E Shell/dsl, Brio Italian, CheeseCake Factory, Chili's, Five Guys, Grimaldi's Pizza, Jimmy John's, Newk's Eatery, P.F. Chang's, The Capital Grille, Voodoo Bayou Rest., Yardhouse Rest., Hampton Inn, Hilton Garden, Marriott, Residence Inn, Best Buy, H, Michael's, PetCo, Whole Foods Mkt, W Shell/dsl, Blaze Pizza, Bonefish Grill, Chipotle Mexican, Christopher's Kitchen, Dunkin', Gyro's Greek, J. Alexanders, Lili's Cafe, Outback Steaks, Paddy Mac's, Panera Bread, Prezzo Italian, Prosecco Kitchen, Saito's Steaks, Spoto's Seafood, Starbucks, Taco Chula, Texas De Brazil, The Cooper, DoubleTree Hotel, Embassy Suites, CVS Drug, Publix

77 Northlake Blvd, to W Palm Bch, E Shell/dsl, Speedway, Arby's, Burger King, Checkers, Chicago Hot Dogs, Chick-fil-A, Dunkin', Giovanni's Rest., Habit Burger, Jersey Mike's, Jimmy John's, Jon Smith Subs, La Granja, McDonald's, Olive Garden, Panera Bread, Pollo Tropical, Starbucks, Taco Bell, $Tree, AT&T, Buick/Chevrolet/GMC, Chrysler/Dodge/Jeep, Costco/gas, CVS Drug, Ford, Ford, Hobby Lobby, Home Depot, H, Hyundai, Jo-Ann, Kia, Lowe's, PepBoys, Ross, Staples, Target, vet, VW, Walgreens, W Chevron, Mobil/dsl, Shell, Sunoco/dsl, CR Chicks, Domino's, Duffy's Grill, Dunkin', Lola's Seafood, Mansing Subs, One Thai, Original Pancakes, Papa John's, Papa Johns, Piknik Sandwiches, Pizza Hut, Souvlaki Greek, Subway, Wendy's, Inn of America, Advance Parts, CVS Drug, Publix, Tires+, vet, Winn-Dixie

76 FL 708, Blue Heron Blvd, E Marathon/dsl, Shell/dsl, WaWa/dsl, RNR Pizza, Wendy's, Travelodge, Honda, Nissan/EVC, tire/auto repair, W 7-11/dsl, Chevron/dsl,

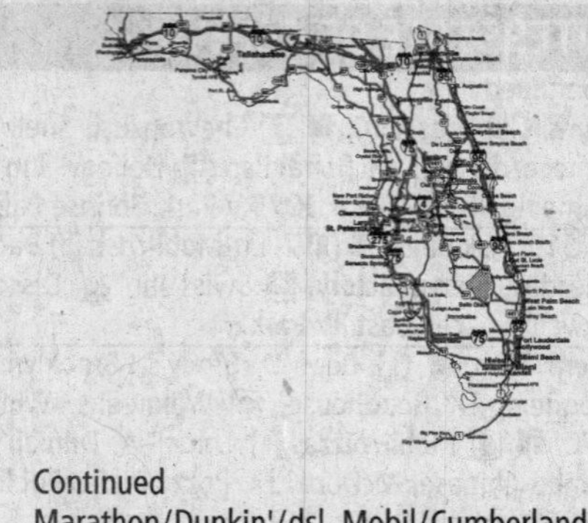

PALM BEACH

76 Continued
Marathon/Dunkin'/dsl, Mobil/Cumberland Farms, RaceTrac/dsl, Burger King, Denny's, McDonald's, Super 8, H

74 FL 702, 45th St, E 7-11/dsl, Citgo, McCray's Seafood, Pronto Pizza, Silentkitchen, Yaad Spice, Cadillac, H, URGENT CARE, Walgreens, W RaceTrac/dsl, Cracker Barrel, McDonald's, Pollo Tropical, Subway, Taco Bell, Wendy's, Courtyard, Extended Stay America, Holiday Inn Express, Homewood Suites, Red Roof Inn, Residence Inn, SpringHill Suites, FoodTown, Harley-Davidson, Sams Club/gas, Walmart

71 Lake Blvd, Palm Beach, E Marathon/Dunkin'/dsl, BJ's Rest., Clean Eatz, First Watch, Griot Hatian, McDonald's, Red Robin, Starbucks, TooJay's Deli, Wendy's, Best Western, Hawthorn Suites, Hilton Garden, Best Buy, Home Depot, H, Old Navy, PetSmart, Ross, Target/Starbucks, TJ Maxx/EVC, Whole Foods Mkt/EVC, W Texaco/dsl, Chick-fil-A, Chilli's, Chipotle Mexican, Dunkin Donuts, Hooters, Manzo's Italian, Park Ave BBQ, Raindancer Steaks, Red Lobster, Tijuana Flats, Twin Peaks, Your Greek, La Quinta, Ramada, URGENT CARE, vet, Walgreens

70b a FL 704, Okeechobee Blvd, E Ruth's Chris Steaks, Sweetgreen Steaks, Hilton/EVC, Marriott, W BP/Dunkin'/dsl, Chevron/dsl, Cumberland Farms, Marathon, Mobil/dsl, Shell, Valero/dsl, Anita's Mexican, Arby's, Bolay, Boston Mkt, Burger King, Checkers, ChuckECheese, De Pietros Pizza, Denny's, Einstein Bros., Firehouse Grill, IHOP, Jersey Mike's, King Crab, La Granja Preuvian, McDonald's, Mr. Mack's Rest., Okeeshobee Staks, PDQ Cafe, Pizza Hut, Pollo Tropical, Rama Thai, Starbucks, Taco Bell, Tiffin Box, $Tree, Advance Parts, ALDI, AT&T, Audi/Porsche, BMW/Mini, Chevrolet, Firestone/auto, GNC, Hyundai, Mercedes, Michael's, Office Depot, Staples, Verizon, VW

69b W to

69a Belvedere Rd, E BP, Churrasco Tacos, Dontee's Diner, El Tipico, McDonald's, Taco Bell, W Chevron, Shell, WaWa/dsl, Burger King, IHOP, Wendy's, Courtyard, DoubleTree, Embassy Suites, Hampton Inn, Hilton Garden, Holiday Inn/rest., Quality Inn, Studio 6

68 US 98, Southern Blvd, E Sunoco, W Palm Gas, Subway, Troy's BBQ, CVS Drug, Publix, W Hilton

66 Forest Hill Blvd, Four Bros. Italian, E Delicias Cuban, Forest Grill, Havana Rest., Economy Inn, W Chevron/dsl, Sunoco, Dunkin', Advance Parts

64 10th Ave N, W Marathon/Circle K/dsl, Mobil/dsl, Murphy USA/dsl, Orion, Chili's, Dunkin', Flanigan's Grill, Taco Bell, Wendy's, Woodspring Suites, CVS Drug, Ford, Presidente Foods, Ross, Tires+, Walgreens, Walmart/Subway

63 6th Ave S, E Checkers, Dunkin', Lake Worth Pizza, Taqueria Nopal, Sunshine Inn, Walgreens, W H

61 FL 812, Lantana Rd, E Shell, Domino's, Dunkin', KFC, Little Caesar's, McDonald's, Riggins Crabhouse, Subway, Motel 6, $General, 7-11, Ace Hardware, ALDI, AutoZone, CVS Drug, Publix, W Costco/gas, H

60 Hypoluxo Rd, E Chevron/dsl, Mobil/dsl, RaceTrac/dsl,

INTERSTATE 95 Cont'd

60 Continued
Shell/dsl, food: Popeyes, Subway, Taco Bell, Wendy's, lodging: Comfort Inn, Holiday Inn Express, Super 8, other: Family$, NAPA, Tire Kingdom, Tire Pros, Tires+, Winn-Dixie, **W** gas: Chevron, food: The Hive Rest., other: Advance Parts

59 Gateway Blvd, **W** gas: Mobil/7-11/dsl, food: Bonefish Grill, Boynton Alehouse, Bramer's Brazilian, BurgerFi, Carrabba's, Chili's, Cool Spot Ice Cream, Dunkin', Firehouse Subs, Happy Lavash, K&L HotPot, Marco's Pizza, McDonald's, PizzaRox, Starbucks, Subway, lodging: Hampton Inn, TownePlace Suites, other: $Tree, AT&T, CarMax, CVS Drug, Kohl's, Publix, Ross, Tuesday Morning, vet

57 FL 804, Boynton Bch Blvd, **E** gas: Marathon/dsl, food: Bud's Chicken, DJ's Grill, KFC, lodging: Boynton Beach Inn, other: [H], USPO, **W** gas: BP, Chevron/dsl, Mobil, Shell, food: Boynton Pizza, Burger King, Checkers, Chick-Fil-A, Crafty Crab, Dunkin', Golden Corral, KFC, Kimura Japanese, La Brasa, Little Caesars, LongHorn Steaks, Olive Garden, Panda Express, Panera Break, Red Lobster, Sonic, Starbucks, Steak'n Shake, Subway, TGIFriday's, Tijuana Flats, TX Roadhouse, Wendy's, Wing Wah Chinese, other: $Tree, 7-11, Barnes&Noble, BJ's Whse/gas, CVS Drug, Dick's, GNC, Office Depot, Old Navy, PetCo, PetSmart, Publix, SteinMart, TJ Maxx, USPO, vet, Walgreens, Walmart

56 Woolbright Rd, **E** gas: Marathon, Shell, food: McDonald's, Panera Bread, Starbucks, Subway, Wendy's, other: 7-11, Crumbl Cookies, [H], Jo-Ann Fabrics, Publix, vet, Walgreens, **W** gas: Marathon/McDonald's, RaceTrac/dsl, food: Burger King, Cracker Barrel, Dominos, Dunkin', Jupiter Donuts, other: Advance Parts, Home Depot, Lowe's, Staples, Walgreens

52b a FL 806, Atlantic Ave, **E** gas: Marathon, food: Nemo's Seafood, lodging: Fairfield Inn, FSuite#1, **W** gas: Chevron/dsl, Shell/dsl, food: Dunkin', Frankies Pizza, Sandwich Man, Silver Wok, Subway, other: [H], Tires+, transmissions/repair, Verizon, vet, Walgreens

51 rd 782, Linton Blvd, **E** gas: Shell, food: Arby's, Chick-fil-A, Chipotle Mexican, DQ, Duffy's Grill, First Watch, Five Guys, KFC, McDonald's, Outback Steaks, Pollo Tropical, Starbucks, Starbucks, Steak'n Shake, Subway, Taco Bell, Tijuana Flats, Wendy's, other: $Tree, BMW, Home Depot, Marshall's, Mercedes, Michael's, PetSmart, Publix, Ross, Target, Tire Kingdom, TJ Maxx, Whole Foods/EVC, **W** gas: Shell, food: Dunkin', Little Caesar's, other: AutoZone, [H], URGENT CARE

50 Congress Ave, **W** gas: Mobil, lodging: Extended Stay, Hilton Garden, Residence Inn, other: Costco/gas

48b a FL 794, Yamato Rd, **E** gas: Mobil, food: Big City Pizza, other: CVS Drug, **W** gas: BP/dsl, Mobil, food: Blue Fin, Bombay Cafe, Dunkin', Jersey Mike's Subs, Jimmy John's, McDonald's, Sal's Italian, Starbucks, The Grille, Wendy's, lodging: Embassy Suites, Hampton Inn, Holiday Inn, SpringHill Suites, TownePlace Suites, other: EVC

45 FL 808, Glades Rd, **E** gas: Mobil/dsl, food: J Alexander's Rest., Jamba Juice, PF Chang's, Shake Shack, lodging: Fairfield Inn, other: Barnes&Noble, CVS Drug, Whole Foods Mkt, **W** gas: Marathon, food: Abe & Louie's, CA Pizza Kitchen, Cafe Argento, Capital Grille, Cheesecake Factory, Chili's, Chipotle Mexican, Copperfish, Farmer's Table, Hooters, Houston's Rest., Maggiano's Italian, Moe's SW Grill, Morton Steaks, NY Prime, Season's Rest., Starbucks, lodging: Marriott, Renaissance, Sonesta, Wyndham Garden, other: Publix

44 Palmetto Park Rd, **E** gas: Valero/dsl, food: China One, Denny's, Dunkin', Taco Bell, Tomasso's Pizza, other: Publix, USPO

42b a FL 810, Hillsboro Blvd, **E** gas: Marathon, Shell/dsl, food: Dunkin', Hook Fish&Chicken, McDonald's, Popeyes, Wendy's, lodging: Doubletree, Fairfield Inn, Hampton Inn, La Quinta, other: Advance Parts, **W** gas: Chevron/dsl, Mobil/dsl,

FT LAUDERDALE

42b a Continued
WaWa/dsl/Tesla EVC, food: Checkers, Dunkin', Krispy Kreme, Subway, lodging: La Quinta, other: CVS Drug, Home Depot, Walgreens

41 FL 869(toll), SW 10th, to I-75, **E** gas: Mobil/7-11, food: Brazillian Depot, Cracker Barrel, Pizza Express, lodging: Extended Stay America, Woodspring Suites, **W** Best Western+, Quality Suites

39 FL 834, Sample Rd, **E** gas: Marathon/dsl, Shell/dsl, Speedway/dsl, food: Habaneros Mexican, Outback Steaks, Taco Bell, other: $General, [H], Save-A-Lot, U-Haul, **W** gas: Chevron, Citgo/dsl, Mobil, Mobil/dsl, Solo/dsl, Sunoco/dsl, WaWa/dsl, food: Burger King, Checkers, Feijao Com Arroz, IHOP, La Granja, McDonald's, Miami Subs, Subway, Unique Italian, other: CarMax, Costco/gas, CVS Drug, Family$, Seabra Foods, vet

38b a Copans Rd, **E** gas: Marathon/7-11, food: McDonald's, other: Land Rover, Mercedes, PepBoys, Porche/Audi, **W** gas: Chevron, Mobil/dsl, food: Sadie's Grill, lodging: Residence Inn, other: Home Depot, NAPA

36b a FL 814, Atlantic Blvd, to Pompano Beach, **E** gas: RaceTrac/dsl, food: KFC/Pizza Hut/Taco Bell, Miami Subs, **W** gas: Marathon, Mobil/dsl, Murphy USA/dsl, food: Baskin-Robbins/Dunkin', Burger King, Dimitri's Rest., Golden Corral, KFC/LJ Silver, McDonald's, Pollo Tropical, Tilapia Seafood, Wendy's, other: $Tree, Chevrolet/Mazda, CVS Drug, to FL TPK, USPO, Walmart/Subway

33b a Cypress Creek Rd, **E** gas: Speedway, food: Don King Taco, Downtown Grill, Fat Boyz BBQ, lodging: Extended Stay America, Hampton Inn, Westin Hotel, other: 7-11, Jiffy Lube, **W** gas: Shell/repair, food: Arby's, Blaze Pizza, Bread Shop, Burger King, Chili's, Chipotle, Five Guys, Gyroville Greek, Hooters, Jersey Mike's, Longhorn Steaks, Lucky Cat Rest., McDonald's, Moonlite Diner, Sal's Italian, Starbucks, Subway, Wendy's, lodging: Courtyard, La Quinta, Marriott, Sheraton Suites, other: AT&T, Jaguar, Office Depot, Tires+, URGENT CARE

32 FL 870, Commercial Blvd, Lauderdale by the Sea, Lauderhill, **E** food: Subway, **W** gas: Chevron, Circle K, Mobil/dsl, Shell, Sunoco/dsl, food: Dunkin', KFC, Major League Sandwich, McDonald's, Miami Subs, Waffle House, lodging: Best Western, Holiday Inn Express, Red Roof, Rodeway Inn, other: Advance Parts, auto repair, BJ's Whse/gas

31b a FL 816, Oakland Park Blvd, **E** gas: 7-11, Chevron, Mobil/dsl, food: Burger King, Denny's, Dunkin', Little Caesar's, McDonald's, Miami Subs, Subway, Wendy's, other: Lowe's, Publix, Walgreens, **W** gas: Chevron/dsl, Exxon, RaceTrac/dsl, Shell, Valero, food: Burger King, Dunkin', KFC, Subway, lodging: Days Inn, other: $General, Home Depot, USPO, Walgreens

29b a FL 838, Sunrise Blvd, **E** gas: Marathon/dsl, Mobil/dsl, Shell, Sunoco/dsl/e85, food: Burger King, Miami Subs, Popeyes, other: Advance Parts, auto repair/tires, AutoZone, Family$, to Birch SP, **W** gas: 7-11, BP, Exxon/dsl, Marathon, Valero, food: China Bowl, Church's TX Chicken, Dunkin', KFC, McDonald's, Snapper's Fish&Chicken, Subway, other: Family$, [H]

27 FL 842, Broward Blvd, Ft Lauderdale, **E** gas: Marathon, food: Burger King, Dunkin, lodging: Days Inn, other: [H], Walgreens, **W** gas: RaceTrac/dsl, WaWa/dsl, food: Charley's, Checkers, Chen's, Chipotle, McDonald's, other: T-Mobil, Walmart

26 I-595(from sb), FL 736(from nb), Davie Blvd, **E** other: to [airport]

25 FL 84, **E** gas: 7-11, Marathon, RaceTrac/dsl, Sunoco/dsl, Texaco, food: Dunkin', Li'l Red's BBQ, McDonald's, Ruby Chinese, Subway, Wendy's, lodging: Best Western, Candlewood Suites, Hampton Inn, Holiday Inn Express, Motel 6, Sky Motel, other: $Tree, BigLots, Firestone/auto, U-Haul, Walgreens, Winn-Dixie, **W** lodging: Ramada Inn, Red Carpet Inn, Rodeway Inn

24 I-595(from nb), to I-75

23 FL 818, Griffin Rd, **E** lodging: Ft Lauderdale Hotel, **W** gas: Mobil, food: Dunkin', Subway, Wendy's, lodging: Courtyard, Fairfield Inn, Homewood Suites, Residence Inn, other: Bass Pro Shops, Publix

FL

COOPER CITY

INTERSTATE 95 Cont'd

Exit #	Services
22	FL 848, Stirling Rd, Cooper City, E Mobil/Dunkin Donuts/dsl, AleHouse Grill, Burger King, Chipotle Mexican, Dave&Buster's, Firehouse Subs, McDonald's, Moonlite Diner, Red Lobster, Sal's Italian, Subway, Sweet Tomatoes, Taco Bell, TGIFriday's, Wendy's, Yum Berry Yogurt, Hampton Inn, Hilton Garden, Hyatt House, Hyatt Place, La Quinta, Quality Inn, SpringHill Suites, Advance Parts, BJ's Whse, GNC, Home Depot, Marshall's, Michael's, Old Navy, PetSmart, Ross, to Lloyd SP, W Las Vegas Cuban, Subway, Best Western, Cambria Suites, Comfort Suites, Home2 Suites, CVS Drug, PepBoys, Tire Kingdom, vet, Walgreens
21	FL 822, Sheridan St, E Chevron, Cumberland Farms/gas, Marathon/Dunkin Donuts/dsl, Domino's, W Shell, Denny's, McDonald's, GLo Best Western, Holiday Inn
20	FL 820, Hollywood Blvd, E Shell, Cliff's, Hollywood Donut, IHOP, Miami Subs, Hollywood Gateway Inn, Goodyear/auto, U-Haul, vet, W Chevron/dsl, Marathon, Boston Mkt, Burgers&Shakes, China Hollywood, Coldstone, First Watch, McDonald's, Offerdahl's Grill, Starbucks, Subway, Taco Bell, Wendy's, H, Publix, Target, Walgreens
19	FL 824, Pembroke Rd, E Orion/dsl, Shell, Family$, W Mobil/dsl, Rice N' Wings, Wendy's
18	FL 858, Hallandale Bch Blvd, E 7-11, Exxon, Shell, Baskin-Robbins/Dunkin Donuts, Burger King, Chapultepec Mexican, Denny's, IHOP, KFC, La Granja, Little Caesar's, Marco's Pizza, McDonald's, Pollo Tropical, Subway, Taco Bell, Wendy's, Won Ton Garden, Best Western+, Family$, Goodyear/auto, Tire Kingdom, vet, Walgreens, Winn-Dixie, W MOIL/dsl, RaceTrac/dsl, Advance Parts, H
16	Ives Dairy Rd, E H, mall, W Marathon/7-11, Subway
14	FL 860, Miami Gardens Dr, N Miami Beach, E H, Oleta River SRA, W Shell/dsl, Valero/dsl
12c	US 441, FL 826, FL TPK, FL 9, E 7-11, Chevron, Exxon/dsl, Marathon/dsl, Marathon/dsl, Speedway, Valero/dsl, Baskin-Robbins/Dunkin Donuts, Burger King, La Granja, McDonald's, Starbucks, Subway, Taco Bell/Pizza Hut, Wendy's, Rodeway Inn, PepBoys, Toyota
12b	US 441(from nb), same as 12c
12a	FL 868(from nb), FL TPK N
11	NW 151st (from nb), W Sunoco/dsl, McDonald's, Advance Parts, Family$, Winn-Dixie
10b	FL 916, NW 135th, Opa-Locka Blvd, W Chevron, Mobil/dsl, Checkers, Pizza Hut, Subway
10a	NW 125th, N Miami, Bal Harbour, W Shell, Burger King, Wendy's, $General
9	NW 119th(from nb), W 7-11/dsl, Marathon/McDonald's, KFC, Pollo Tropical, Popeyes, Advance Parts, AutoZone, CVS Drug, Family$, Walgreens, Winn-Dixie
8b	FL 932, NW 103rd, E Chevron, Shell, W Sunoco, Sunshine/dsl, $General, Baskin-Robbins/Dunkin Donuts, Bravo Foods
8a	NW 95th, E Chevron, Cuban Deli, W 7-11/dsl, Mobil/dsl, McDonald's, Advance Parts, H, Walgreens
7	FL 934, NW 81st, NW 79th, E Chevron/dsl, Mobil/dsl, W 7-11, Checkers
6b	NW 69th(from sb)
6a	FL 944, NW 62nd, NW 54th, W China Town, McDonald's, Subway, Family$, Presidente Mkt, Walgreens
4b a	I-195 E, FL 112 W(toll), Miami Beach, E downtown, W
3b	NW 8th St(from sb)
3a	FL 836 W(toll)(exits left from nb), W H, to
2d	I-395 E(exits left from sb), to Miami Beach

N MIAMI BEACH

MIAMI BEACH

FL

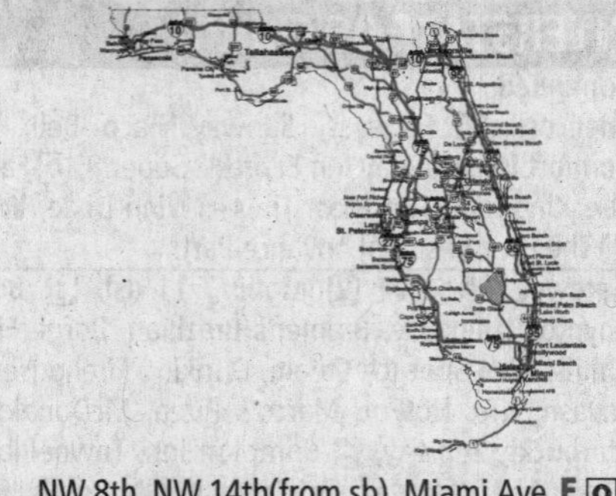

Exit #	Services
2c	NW 8th, NW 14th(from sb), Miami Ave, E Port of Miami
2b	NW 2nd(from nb), downtown Miami
2a	US 1(exits left from sb), Biscayne Blvd, downtown Miami
1b	US 41, SW 7th, SW 8th, Brickell Ave, E Chevron, Mobil, Burger King, Graziano's, McDonald's, Moxies Miami, Okeydokey Miami, Wendy's, YUZU Frozen Yogurt, Element Miami, Extended Stay America, Hampton Inn, Marriott, Smart Hotel, Starlite East, CVS Drug, GNC, Publix, vet, W Shell, Papa John's
1a	SW 25th(from sb), downtown, to Rickenbacker Causeway, E to Baggs SRA
0mm	I-95 begins/ends on US 1. , S Mobil

INTERSTATE 275 (Tampa)

Exit #	Services
59mm	I-275 begins/ends on I-75, exit 274.
53	Bearss Ave, E Citgo/dsl, Wawa/dsl, Culver's, Carmax, O'Reilly Parts, Tire Kingdom, Walmart, W Chevron/dsl, Marathon/Dunkin', Mobil, RaceTrac/dsl, Shell/dsl, Alfonso's Pizza, Burger King, Dominos, Golden Krust Carribean, Hibachi Japanese, Hungry Howies, IHOP, McDonald's, NY Pizza, Plato Latino, Popeyes, Subway, Vista Inn, AlLDI, BigLots, CVS Drug, Hibachi Japanese, Ross
52	Fletcher Ave, E Chevron, Chevron/dsl, Citgo/dsl, Exxon, Marathon, Mobil/dsl, Wawa/dsl, Arby's, Bruno's Pizza, Church's TX Chicken, DQ, El Senor Tacos, Krystal, Little Caesars, McDonald's, Popeyes, Salems Fresh, Palms Inn, AlLDI, Family$, H, to USF, Toyota/Scion, Walmart, W Citgo, Marathon, Mobil/BBQ, Hong King Chinese, Tom's Tavern, Americana Inn, Cadillac, Family$, Jaguar, Save-A-Lot
51	FL 582, Fowler Ave, E Marathon/dsl, Mobil/dsl, RaceTrac, Shell/Circle K, Tesla EVC, Texaco/dsl, A&W/LJ Silver, Boil Spot, Burger King, Checker's, Chili's, Chipotle Mexican, Crave Rest., Denny's, Dunkin', Firehouse Subs, Five Guys, Godavari, Jason's Deli, Jerk Hut, Jimmy John's, KFC, Longhorn Steaks, McDonald's, Miller's Ale House, Mr. & Mrs. Crab, Panda Express, Pizza Hut, Portillo's Hot Dogs, Saucy Crawfish, Shells Seafood, Sonic, Starbucks, Steak'n Shake, Subway, Taco Bell, Waffle House, Wendy's, Clarion, Embassy Suites, Home2 Suites/EVC, Hyatt Place, La Quinta, Red Roof+, Regency Inn, $General, $Tree, Advance Parts, AT&T, CVS Drug, O'Reilly Parts, Verizon, Walgreens, Winn Dixie, W Joe's NY Diner, Value Lodge, Audi, BMW, Chevrolet, NAPA, Porsche, VW
50	FL 580, Busch Blvd, E Citgo, Marathon/Circle K, Mobil, 1200 Cafe, Bruh Mans BBQ, Burger King, Dunkin', Four Brothers, Garden Gyros, McDonald's, Olive Garden, Popeyes, Red Lobster, Subway, Taco Bell, Budget Inn, Economy Inn, Hampton Inn/EVC, Holiday Inn Express, La Quinta, Rodeway Inn, Sunset Inn, Travelers Inn, $General, Advance Parts, AutoZone, Busch Gardens, Family$, Walgreens, W Burger King, $General, $Tree, Advance Parts, CVS Drug, Firestone/auto, Home Depot, Walmart Mkt 
49	Bird Ave(from nb), E Family$, W Checkers, KFC,

INTERSTATE 275 (Tampa) Cont'd

49 Continued
Krispy Kreme, McDonald's, Subway, Wendy's, [other] $General, K-Mart, Save-A-Lot

48 Sligh Ave, E [gas] Marathon, Shell, [lodging] Oasis, [other] USPO, W [gas] Sligh Petrol, [other] zoo

47b a US 92, to US 41 S, Hillsborough Ave, E [gas] Marathon, Mobil/dsl, Shell/Circle K, [food] Auntie's Soul Food, Burger King, Checkers, Hungry Howie's, Jerk Hut, Little Caesars, McDonald's, Popeyes, Subway, Taco Bell, Wendy's, Wingstop, Zeko's Grill, [other] $Tree, Advance Parts, Ross, vet, Walgreens, Walmart/Subway, W [gas] Mobil, Shell/Circle K, [food] Papa John's, Starbucks, [lodging] Dutch Motel

46b FL 574, MLK Blvd, E [gas] 7-11/dsl, BP, [other] Advance Parts, Walgreens, Winn Dixie, W [gas] Chevron/dsl, [food] McDonald's, [other] [H]

46a Floribraska Ave(from sb, no return)

45b I-4 E, to Orlando, I-75

45a Jefferson St, downtown E

44 Ashley Dr, Tampa St, downtown W

42 Howard Ave, Armenia Ave, W [gas] Marathon/dsl, Sunoco, [food] BBQ King, Popeyes, [other] USPO

41c Himes Ave(from sb), W [other] RJ Stadium

41b a US 92, Dale Mabry Blvd, E [gas] Marathon, Mobil/Dunkin'/dsl, Wawa/dsl, [food] Bonefish Grill, Brickhouse Grill, Burger King, Cali Rest., Carrabba's, Chick-Fil-A, Donatello Italian, Five Guys, IHOP, Izakaya Japanese, J.Alexanders Rest, Midtown Leathers Cafe, Sarione Korean, Shake Shack, Shells Rest., Subway, Village Inn, Yummy House Chinese, [lodging] Best Western, Courtyard, Quality Inn, Tahitian Inn/Cafe, [other] AT&T, Barnes&Noble, CVS Drug, Office Depot, Tire Kingdom, to MacDill AFB, Trader Joe's, Verizon, W [gas] Marathon/Dunkin', [food] Burger King, Chick-fil-A, Chili's, China 1, Chipotle, Denny's, Duffy's Grill, Jimmy John's, McDonald's, Moe's SW Grill, Riveters, Sonic, Subway, Sweet Tomatoes, WingHouse of Tampa, [lodging] Fairfield Inn, Hilton, Residence Inn, [other] Best Buy, Chrysler/Dodge/Jeep, Family$, Home Depot, Honda, PetSmart, Staples, Target, to RJ Stadium, Walmart, Whole Foods Mkt, Winn Dixie

40b Lois Ave, W [gas] Marathon/dsl, [food] Charley's Rest., [lodging] DoubleTree Hotel, Sheraton

40a FL 587, Westshore Blvd, E [gas] BP, Chevron/dsl, Citgo/Subway, [food] Burger King, Chipotle Mexican, Fresh Kitchen, Jimmy John's, Maggiano's Rest., McDonald's, Panera Bread, PF Chang's, Season's Grill, Starbucks, Taco Bell, Waffle House, [lodging] Crowne Plaza, Embassy Suites, [other] Firestone, JC Penney, Macy's, Old Navy, PetCo, Walgreens, W [gas] Shell/Subway, [food] First Watch, La Bamba Cuban, LongHorn Steakhouse, Olive Garden, Ruth's Chris, Starbucks, [lodging] Extended Stay, Hampton Inn, Holiday Inn, Hyatt Place, La Quinta, Marriott, Ramada Inn, SpringHill Suites

39b a FL 60 W, W [other] to [airport]

32 Fl 687 S, 4th St N, to US 92 (no sb re-entry)

31b a 9th St N, MLK St N(exits left from sb), info, [other] [airport]

30 FL 686, Roosevelt Blvd, E [food] Tijuana Flats, Yaya's Chicken, [other] Publix, W [gas] Rally, Shell, [food] Bascom's Chophouse, Burger King, Chil-fil-A, Cracker Barrel, Cuban Mexican, Dunkin', Jimmy John's, Korean BBQ, Laguna Girls Mexican, Little Greek, McDonald's, Panera Bread, Starbucks, Subway, Taco Bell, Wendy's, [lodging] Comfort Inn, Courtyard, Extended Stay America, Fairfield Inn, Hampton Inn, Hilton, Holiday Inn, La Quinta, Marriott, Red Roof Inn, Sleep Inn, SpringHill Suites, Super 8, SureStay, [other] CVS Drug, Publix

INDIAN SHORES

28 FL 694 W, Gandy Blvd, Indian Shores, W [gas] Citgo, Citgo, Murphy USA/dsl, Speedway/dsl, WaWa/dsl/EVC, [food] Applebee's, BJ's Brewhouse, Buffalo Wild Wings,

28 Continued
Burger King, Checkers, Cheddar's, Chick-fil-A, Chili's, Chipotle, Coldstone, Dunkin', Firehouse Subs, Five Guys, Honey Baked Ham, Huey Magoo's Chicken, IHOP, Jollibee Chicken, La Gloria, McDonald's, Moe's SW, Mr. and Mrs. Crab, Panda Express, Panera Bread, Pho Quyen, Pizza Hut/Taco Bell, Pollo Tropical, Sam's Sushi, Sonny's BBQ, Starbucks, Subway, Tijuana Flats, Wendy's, [lodging] Comfort Suites, Country Inn, Hampton Inn, La Quinta, [other] $Tree, Cadillac, GNC, Home Depot, Honda, Marshall's, Michael's, Office Depot, PetCo, Publix, Rolls Royce/Bently/McLaren, Target/Starbucks, U-Haul, Walgreens, Walmart

26b a 54th Ave N, E [food] Cracker Barrel, [lodging] Comfort Inn, Holiday Inn Express, W [gas] RaceTrac/dsl, [food] Waffle House, [lodging] Fairfield Inn, [other] Harley-Davidson, [H], NAPA

25 38th Ave N, to beaches, W [gas] Shell/dsl, Wawa/dsl, [food] Burger King, Hardee's, [other] Subaru, VW, Walgreens

24 22nd Ave N, W [gas] RaceTrac/dsl, Wawa/dsl, [food] Chile Verde, Dunkin', Grumpy Gringo, Little Caesar's, [other] Advance Parts, Home Depot, Lowe's

GULFPORT

23b FL 595, 5th Ave N, E [other] [H]

23a I-375, E downtown, [other] The Pier, Waterfront

22 I-175 E, Tropicana Field, E [other] [H]

21 28th St S, downtown

20 31st Ave(from nb), downtown

19 22nd Ave S, Gulfport, W [gas] Chevron, Citgo, Shell/dsl, [food] Church's TX Chicken, Domino's Pizza, Gators, KFC, King's Chicken, Salem's Gyros, [other] Family$

18 26th Ave S(from nb)

17 FL 682 W, 54th Ave S, Pinellas Bayway, W [gas] 7-11, Sunoco/dsl, [food] Beef'O'Brady's, Burger King, China Wok, Domino's, Dunkin', IHOP, McDonald's, Papa John's, Pizza Hut, Portofino Italian, Starbucks, Subway, Taco Bell, Wendy's, [lodging] Bayway Inn, Crystal Inn, [other] $Tree, AT&T, Beall's, CVS Drug, GNC, Publix, St Pete Beach, to Ft DeSoto Pk, vet, Walmart/McDonald's

16 Pinellas Point Dr, Skyway Lane, to Maximo Park, E [lodging] Magnuson Resort, W [other] marina

16mm toll plaza sb

13mm N Skyway Fishing Pier, **full [handicapped] facilities, litter barrels, petwalk, [phone], [picnic], [RS] both lanes, vending**

10mm Tampa Bay

7mm S Skyway Fishing Pier, **full [handicapped] facilities, litter barrels, petwalk, [phone], [picnic], [RS] both lanes, vending**

6mm toll plaza nb

5 US 19, Palmetto, Bradenton

2 US 41, (last nb exit before toll), Palmetto, Bradenton, E [other] $General, Fiesta Grove RV Resort, Frog Creek Campground, Terra Ceia Village Campground, Winterset RV Resort, W [gas] Shell/DQ/Subway/dsl

0mm I-275 begins/ends on I-75, exit 228.

INTERSTATE 295 (Jacksonville)

61b a I-295 begins/ends on I-95, exit 337

60 US 1, Philips Hwy, E [gas] RaceTrac/dsl, [food] Shane's Sandwiches, [other] Buick/GMC, Honda, Toyota/Scion, VW, W Chevrolet, Mazda/EVC, Tire Kingdom, Volvo

58 FL 9b(from sb)

56 FL 152, Baymeadows Rd, E [gas] Gate/dsl, Marcos Pizza, [food] McDonald's, [lodging] Holiday Inn, Woodspring Suites, [other] Chrysler/Dodge/Jeep, Fiat, W [gas] Shell, [food] Carrabba's, Chicken Salad Chick, China Wok, Hurricane Grill, Outback Steaks, St Marys Seafood, Tequila's Mexican, Tony D's Pizza, Wendy's, [lodging] Hampton Inn, [other] Publix, SteinMart, URGENT CARE, Walgreens, Winn Dixie

54 Gate Pkwy, W [food] Culver's, Melting Pot, Otaki Japanese Steaks, Pizza Point

FL

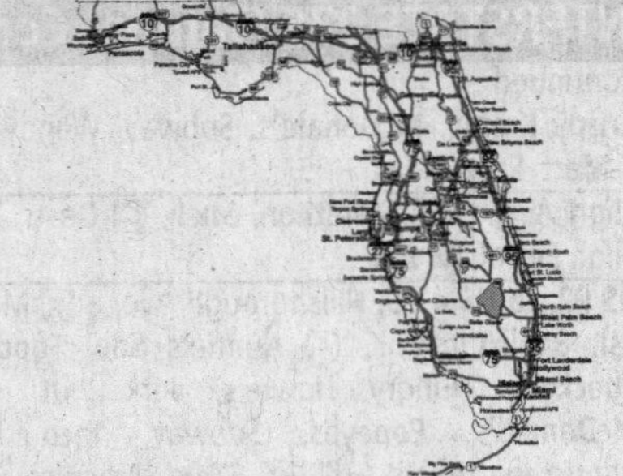

INTERSTATE 295 (Jacksonville) Cont'd

JACKSONVILLE

Exit #	Services
53	FL 202, Butler Blvd, E Fogo de Chao, W Shell/dsl, Arby's, Bahama Breeze, BJ's Rest, Blaze Pizza, Bono's BBQ, Brio Grille, Buffalo Wild Wings, BurgerFi, Cantina Laredo, Capital Grill, Cheddar's, Cheesecake Factory, Chick-fil-A, Chipotle Mexican, Chuy's, Cooper's Hawk, Firebird's, Firehouse Subs, Five Guys, Freddy's, J Alexander's, Maggiano's Italian, McDonald's, Mimi's Cafe, Mission BBQ, Moe's SW Grill, Noodles & Co., Ovinte, Panda Express, Panera Bread, Pei Wei, PF Chang's, Pollo Tropical, Prati Italia, Red Robin, Seasons Rest, Starbucks, Taco Bell, Ted's MT Grill, TX Roadhouse, Wasabi, Wendy's, Zaxby's, Zoe's Kitchen, Extended Stay, Homewood Suites, Sheraton, $Tree, ALDI, AT&T, Barnes&Noble, Best Buy, Costco, CVS Drug, Dick's, Dillard's, Jo-Ann, Nordstrom, Old Navy, PetSmart, REI, Ross, Staples, Target, Verizon
52	U of NF Dr, Town Center Pkwy, same as 53
51	US 90, Beach Blvd, E Burger King, Dunkin', Jimmy John's, Lubi's Subs, Tacos Azcatl, W Shell, Arby's, Checkers, KFC, Little Caesars, McDonald's, Pizza Hut, Sonic, Taco Bell, InTown Suites, InTown Suites, WoodSpring Suites, $Tree, Advance Parts, Sam's Club/gas, USPO, vet, Walgreens, Winn-Dixie
49	St John's Bluff Rd(from nb)
48	FL 10, to Atlantic Blvd, E BP, Shell, Dick's Wings, Papa John's, Holiday Inn Express, InTown Suites, $Tree, NAPA, Nissan, Pep Boys, Subaru, W Denny's, Dunkin', Hook Seafood, Waffle House
47	Monument Rd, E Marathon/Kangaroo/dsl, Domino's, Hong Kong Chinese, Larry's Subs, Southern Coast Seafood, vet, W Gate/dsl, Cantina Louie, Ruby Tuesday, Courtyard, Hampton Inn, Walmart/McDonald's
46	FL 116 E, Wonderwood Connector, Merrill Rd, E Speedway, Burger King, Dick's Wings, Golden Corral, Hardee's, Popeyes, Candlewood Suites, W RaceTrac, Bono's BBQ, KFC, Krystal, Woodspring Suites, RV One
44mm	St John's River
41	FL 105, Heckscher Dr, Zoo Pkwy, E Gate/dsl, W Pilot/Dunkin'/dsl/scales/24hr, Valero/Circle K/dsl, Wendy's, Holiday Inn Express, zoo
40	Alta Dr, E Capri Diner, Nopalera Mexican
37	Pulaski Rd, E Circle K/dsl
36	US 17, Main St, E Mobil/dsl, DQ, Happy Taco, Hungry Howie's, McDonald's, Winn-Dixie, W Subway
35b a	I-95, S to Jacksonville, N to Savannah
33	Duval Rd, W
32	FL 115, Lem Turner Rd, E 7-11/dsl, Burger King, China Wok, McDonald's(1mi), Subway, Waffle House, Wendy's, $Tree, Home Depot, Walmart/Deli, W Flamingo Lake RV Resort
30	FL 104, Dunn Ave, E 7-11/dsl, 76(1mi), Gate/dsl, Mobil(1mi), McDonald's(1mi), H, W Big Tree RV Park
28b a	US 1, US 23, to Callahan, Jacksonville, S Mobil/Circle K/Subway/dsl, E Circle K/dsl, W BP/DQ/dsl, RaceTrac/dsl, Waffle House, Wendy's, auto repair
25	Pritchard Rd, W Circle K/Subway/dsl/24hr, Pilot/Arbys/Mkt/dsl/24hr, dsl repair
22	Commonwealth Ave, E BP/dsl, Burger King, Hardee's, Waffle House, Zaxby's, Holiday Inn Express, Quality Inn, Stayable Suites, dogtrack, W Wendy's, Comfort Suites, Country Inn&Suites
21b a	I-10, W to Tallahassee, E to Jacksonville
19	FL 228, Normandy Blvd, E BP/dsl, Murphy USA/dsl, Burger King, Capt D's, El Potro, Firehouse Subs, Golden Corral, Hot Wok, McDonald's, Panda Express, Papa John's,

CECIL FIELD · ORANGE PARK

Exit #	Services
19	Continued Sonic, Waffle House, Wendy's, $Tree, AT&T, CVS Drug, Save-A-Lot, Walgreens, Walmart, W BP, Mobil/Dunkin', RaceTrac/dsl, Shell/dsl, Speedway/dsl, Famous Amos, Golden China, Hardee's, KFC, Larry's Subs, McDonald's, Pizza Hut, Popeyes, Sam's Seafood Rest., Whataburger, Advance Parts, CVS Drug, Family$, Publix, Walgreens, Winn-Dixie
17	FL 208, Wilson Blvd, E 7-11/dsl, BP/Subway/dsl, Speedway/Dunkin'/dsl, Wawa/dsl, China Wok, Hardee's, Wendy's, $General, Walmart Mkt, W Circle K
16	FL 134, 103rd St, Cecil Field, E BP/dsl, Gate/dsl, Murphy Express/dsl, RaceTrac/dsl, Speedway, Capt D's, Crafty Crab, Firehouse Subs, Krispy Kreme, Krystal, Leo Chimi, Marco's Pizza, Papa John's, Pizza Hut, Popeyes, Sonic, Wendy's, Wingstop, Hity Inn, $Tree, Advance Parts, AT&T, CVS Drug, GNC, Goodyear/auto, NAPA, Save-A-Lot Foods, Tires+, U-Haul, URGENT CARE, Walmart/McDonald's, W 76, BP/dsl, Exxon/dsl, Burger King, Checkers, DQ, Dunkin', Fat Mamaz, IHOP, KFC, Little Caesar's, McDonald's, Subway, Taco Bell, Waffle House, Aamco, AutoZone, Discount Tire, Family$, Goodyear/auto, Mavis Tires, O'Reilly Parts, Publix, vet, Walgreens
12	FL 21, Blanding Blvd, E Mobil, RaceTrac/dsl, Speedway/dsl, Wawa, Burger King, Dunkin', Juicy Crab, Larry's Subs, McDonald's, Philly Mike's, Pizza Hut, Subway, $General, Acura, Audi, Best Buy, BMW, Buick/GMC, Cadillac, CarMax, Chrysler/Dodge/Jeep, CVS Drug, Fiat, Ford, Honda, Hyundai, Infiniti, Lexus, Lincoln, Mazda, Mercedes/Smart, Nissan, Office Depot, Subaru, U-Haul, USPO, VW, Walgreens, W BP, ChuckeCheese, Circle K/dsl, Shell, Shell, Arby's, Buffalo Wild Wings, Burger King, Carabba's, Chick-fil-A, Chili's, China Buffet, Chipotle Mexican, Denny's, Dick's Wings, Dick's Wings, Firehouse Subs, HoneyBaked Ham, Hooters, KFC, Kyodai Steaks, Little Caesars, Longhorn Steaks, Miller's Ale House, Mission BBQ, No Manches, Olive Garden, Outback Steaks, Panda Express, Panera Bread, Papa John's, Red Lobster, Rocking Crab, Ruby Tuesday, Starbucks, Steak'n Shake, Sweet Tomatoes, Taco Bell, Ted's MT Grill, TGIFriday's, Thai Garden, Wendy's, Country Inn Suites, La Quinta, Motel 6, Quality Inn, Red Roof Inn, Stay Suites, Super 8, $Tree, AT&T, Belk, Books-A-Million, Dick's, Dillard's, Discount Tire, Firestone/auto, Goodyear/auto, Home Depot, H, JC Penney, Jo-Ann Fabrics, mall, Michael's, O'Reilly Parts, PepBoys, PetSmart, Publix, Sam's Club/gas, Tires+, TJMaxx, Toyota/Scion, Verizon, Walgreens, Walmart/dsl
10	US 17, FL 15, Roosevelt Blvd, Orange Park, E Best Western, W BP/dsl, Chevron/dsl, Exxon, RaceTrac/dsl, Speedway/dsl, 4 Rivers BBQ, Aron's Pizza, Cracker Barrel, Dunkin', Krystal, McDonald's, Subway, Waffle House, Wendy's, Courtyard, Days Inn, Extended Stay, Fairfield Inn, Hampton Inn, Hilton Garden, Holiday Inn, Wawa, General RV Ctr, Harley-Davidson, H, Sun Tire, vet
7mm	St Johns River, Buckman Br
5b a	FL 13, San Jose Blvd, E Speedway/dsl, Arby's,

FL

INTERSTATE 295 (Jacksonville) Cont'd

5b a Continued
Berndt Ends BBQ, Blue Bamboo Chinese, Bob Evans, Bono's BBQ, Carrabba's, Chick-fil-A, Domino's, Enza's Italian, Firehouse Subs, Five Guys, Five Star Pizza, HoneyBaked Ham, Jumpin Jax Seafood, Kim's BBQ, Krystal, McDonald's, Moe's SW Grill, Outback Steaks, Popeyes, Red Crab, Smoothie King, Starbucks, Steak'n Shake, The Loop Pizza, Zaxby's, Zoes Kitchen, La Quinta, Ramada Inn, Tru, Aamco, BigLots, CVS Drug, Firestone/auto, Office Depot, PepBoys, Publix, Save-A-Lot, Sun Tire, Target, Tire Kingdom, URGENT CARE, Verizon, Whole Foods Mkt, **W** BP, Mobil, Shell, Bonefish Grill, Bruster's, Chili's, Chipotle Mexican, Chophouse 13, Crumbl Cookies, Dunkin', First Watch, Hana Moon Japanese, Hardee's, Jersey Mike's, Jimmy John's, Kan-Ki Japanese,

5b a Continued
Krispy Kreme, La Nopalera, Mambos Cuban, McDonald's, Panera Bread, Papa John's, Papa Murphy's, Pollo Tropical, Starbucks, Subway, Taco Bell, Taziki's Cafe, Tijuana Flats, Waffle House, $Tree, Advance Parts, AT&T, AutoZone, Barnes&Noble, Goodyear/auto, Marshall's, Michael's, NAPA, PetCo, Publix, SteinMart, T-Mobile, Tire Kingdom, TJ Maxx, vet, Walgreens, Walmart, Winn-Dixie, World Mkt

3 Old St Augustine Rd, **E** BP/dsl, Shell/dsl, Burger King, Little Caesar's, Little China, McDonald's, Pizza Hut, Salento Steaks, St Mary's Seafood, Taco Bell, Wendy's, Holiday Inn Express, $General, $Tree, CVS Drug, GNC, Hobby Lobby, Publix/deli, Winn-Dixie, **W** Gate/dsl, Mobil/Circle K/dsl, Firehouse Subs, KFC, Rosy's Mexican, Subway, Vino's Pizza, Lowe's, vet, Walgreens

NOTES

FL

= gas = food = lodging = other = rest stop

GEORGIA

INTERSTATE 16

SAVANNAH

Exit #	Services
167b a	W Broad, Montgomery St, I-16 begins/ends in Savannah., Savannah, N Chevron, Enmarket, Parker's, Best Western, Courtyard, DoubleTree, Fairfield Inn, Hampton Inn, Hilton Garden, Holiday Inn, Quality Inn, Residence Inn, Springhill Suites, S Burger King, Popeyes, Wendy's, Family$
166	US 17, Gwinnet St, Savannah, Savannah Visitors Ctr
165	GA 204, 37th St(from eb), to Ft Pulaski NM, N Savannah College
164b a	I-516, US 80, US 17, GA 21
162	Chatham Pkwy, S Shell/dsl, KanPai Japanese, Katrina's Mexican, Larry's Subs, Sunrise Rest., Acura, Chrysler/Dodge/Jeep, Kia, Lexus, Subaru, Toyota
160	GA 307, Dean Forest Rd, N Mr. Fuel/Subway/dsl/scales, Parker's/dsl, Ronnie's Rest., S Holy Pie! Pizza, Sunshine RV Park
157b a	I-95, S to Jacksonville, N to Florence
155	Pooler Pkwy, N El Cheapo, EnMarket/EVC/dsl, Murphy USA/dsl, to , Dunkin', Jalapeno's Mexican, Papa John's, Subway, Sunrise Breakfast, Wasabi Fusion, Wendy's, Your Pie Pizza, Lowe's, Mavis Tire, Verizon, S BP/dsl, Parker's/Tesla EVC/dsl, Chick-fil-A, Noble Roots, Starbucks, Taco Stache, Costco, Publix

FT STEWART

Exit #	Services
152	GA 17, to Bloomingdale
148	Old River Rd, to US 80, N BP
144mm	weigh sta both lanes
143	US 280, to US 80, N Love's/dsl/scales/service/24hr/@, S BP/Subway/dsl, Marathon/dsl
137	GA 119, to Pembroke, Ft Stewart
132	Ash Branch Church Rd
127	GA 67, to Pembroke, Ft Stewart, N BP/dsl, EnMarket/dsl, Sallie Mae's Kitchen
116	US 25/301, to Statesboro, N Chevron/PoJo Diner/dsl/scales/24hr, Magnolia Springs SP(45 mi), to GA Southern U, S TA/dsl/service/scales/24hr, Patriot Inn
111	Pulaski-Excelsior Rd, S Citgo/Grady's Grill/dsl, Beaver Run RV Park, tires/repair
104	GA 22, GA 121, Metter, N info, BP/dsl/scales/24hr, Enmark, EVC, Parker's/dsl, Shell/dsl, Bevrick's Grille, Burger King, DQ, El Mariachi, Jomax BBQ, KFC/Taco Bell, McDonald's, Papa Buck's BBQ, Pizza Hut, Shogun, Subway, Waffle House, Zaxby's, American Inn, Days Inn, Garden Inn, Motel 6, Chevrolet, H, O'Reilly Parts, to Smith SP, Walgreens, S Chevron/dsl, Marathon/dsl, Ford

EAST DUBLIN

Exit #	Services
101mm	Canoochee River
98	GA 57, to Stillmore, S BP/dsl/24hr, Chevron/dsl, to Altahama SP
90	US 1, to Swainsboro, N bp/dsl, Chevron/Subway/dsl
88mm	Ohoopee River
84	GA 297, to Vidalia, N truck sales
78	US 221, GA 56, to Swainsboro
71	GA 15, GA 78, to Soperton, N Chevron/dsl
67	GA 29, to Soperton, S Marathon/dsl, Huddle House
58	GA 199, Old River Rd, East Dublin
56mm	Oconee River
54	GA 19, to Dublin, N Friendly Gus/dsl, S Chevron/dsl
51	US 441, US 319, to Dublin, N BP/Subway/dsl, Circle K, EVC, Exxon/dsl, Pilot/dsl/scales/24hr, Arby's, Burger King, Dunkin', Hunt Bros Pizza, KFC, McDonald's, Ruby Tuesday, Salsa's Mexican, Taco Bell, Wendy's, Baymont Inn,

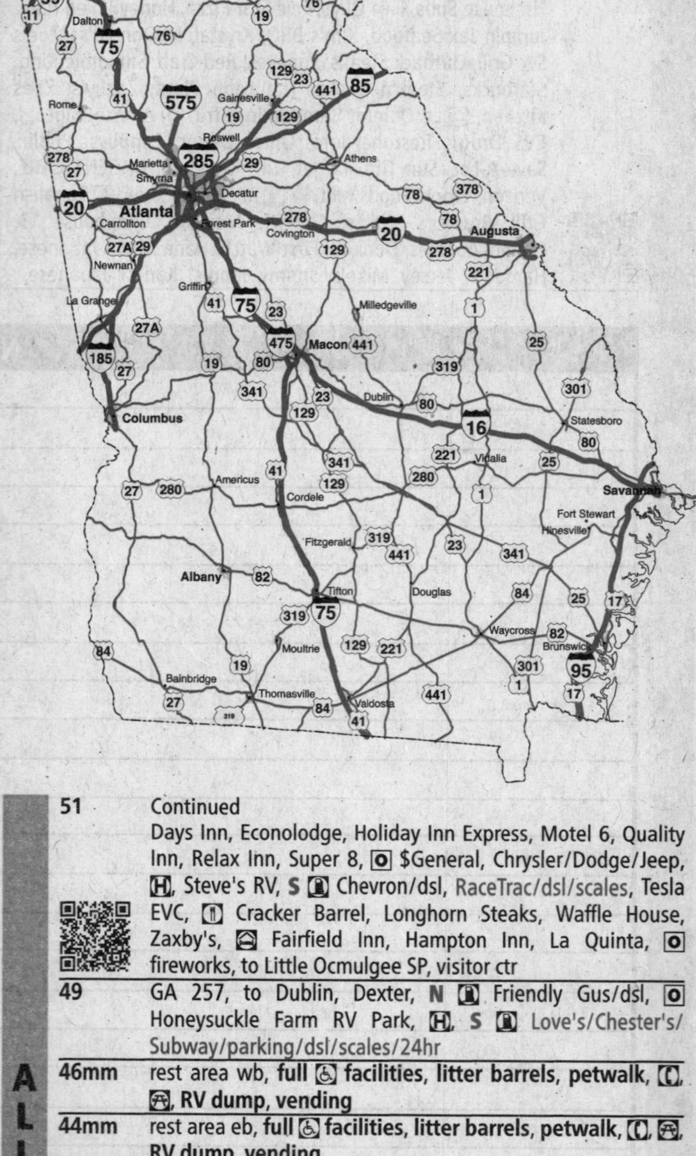

ALLENTOWN

Exit #	Services
51	Continued Days Inn, Econolodge, Holiday Inn Express, Motel 6, Quality Inn, Relax Inn, Super 8, $General, Chrysler/Dodge/Jeep, H, Steve's RV, S Chevron/dsl, RaceTrac/dsl/scales, Tesla EVC, Cracker Barrel, Longhorn Steaks, Waffle House, Zaxby's, Fairfield Inn, Hampton Inn, La Quinta, fireworks, to Little Ocmulgee SP, visitor ctr
49	GA 257, to Dublin, Dexter, N Friendly Gus/dsl, Honeysuckle Farm RV Park, H, S Love's/Chester's/Subway/parking/dsl/scales/24hr
46mm	rest area wb, **full facilities, litter barrels, petwalk, , , RV dump, vending**
44mm	rest area eb, **full facilities, litter barrels, petwalk, , , RV dump, vending**
42	GA 338, to Dudley
39	GA 26, to Cochran, Montrose
32	GA 112, Allentown, N 4 County RV Park (1.5mi), S Chevron/dsl
27	GA 358, to Danville
24	GA 96, to Jeffersonville, S Exxon/Huddle House/dsl/24hr, Suburban Inn, to Robins AFB
18	Bullard Rd, to Jeffersonville, Bullard
12	Sgoda Rd, Huber, N Marathon/dsl
6	US 23, US 129A, East Blvd, Ocmulgee, N Shell/Circle K/DQ, Texaco/dsl, McDonald's, Waffle House, to , S Chevron/Huddle House/dsl/scales/24hr, Friendly Gus, Subway
2	US 80, GA 87, MLK Jr Blvd, N Marriott, conv ctr, H, Ocmulgee NM, S Marathon/dsl, to Hist Dist
1b	GA 22, to US 129, GA 49, 2nd St(from wb), S H
1a	US 23, Gray Hwy(from eb), N Chevron/dsl, Exxon, Valero, Arby's, Burger King, Chen's Wok, DQ, Dunkin',

INTERSTATE 16 Cont'd

1a Continued
El Sombrero Mexican, Fincher's BBQ, Hong Kong Express, Krispy Kreme, Krystal, Little Caesars, McDonald's, Nu-Way Weiners, Subway, Taco Bell, Wendy's, Attaway Tire, CVS Drug, Family$, H, Kroger, O'Reilly Parts, Precision Tire & Auto, U-Haul, Walgreens, S Chevron, Exxon, Sunoco/dsl, American Feel & Wings, Burger King, Checker's, Hunt Bros Pizza, Krystal, Waffle House, Zaxby's

0mm I-75, S to Valdosta, N to Atlanta. I-16 begins/ends on I-75, exit 165 in Macon.

INTERSTATE 20

202mm Georgia/South Carolina state line, Savannah River

201mm **full facilities, litter barrels, petwalk, , , vending, Welcome Ctr wb**

AUGUSTA

200 GA 104, Riverwatch Pkwy, Augusta, N Pilot/Wendy's/dsl/scales/24hr, Waffle House, Baymont Inn, Best Western +, Candlewood Suites, Comfort Suites, Microtel, Sleep Inn, Suburban Studios, Woodspring Suites, Freightliner, S $Tree, Cabela's, Costco/gas

199 GA 28, Washington Rd, Augusta, Ephesus Greek&Turkish, N BP, BP, RaceWay, 2 Boys Pizza, Applebee's, Baskin-Robbins/Dunkin Donuts, Burger King, CA Dreaming, Capt D's, Checkers, Chick-fil-A, Diablo's Southwest Grill, Doc's Prochside, Domino's, DQ, Fujiyama Japanese, Krystal, Longhorn Steaks, Rhinehart's Seafood, Starbucks, Steakout, Veracruz Mexican, Waffle House, Wife Saver Rest, Clarion, Courtyard, Days Inn, Econolodge, Fairfield Inn, Hampton Inn, Hilton Garden, Holiday Inn Express, Homewood Suites, Rodeway Inn, Scottish Inn, Sheraton, Sunset Inn, Super 8, Travelodge, Acura, AutoZone, Buick/GMC, Chevrolet, Chrysler/Dodge/Jeep, Hyundai, Infiniti, Lexus, Mercedes, Nissan, Pep Boys, Toyota/Scion, Tuesday Morning, S Circle K, Exxon, Shell/Circle K/dsl, Arby's, BoneFish Grill, Carrabba's, Chicken Salad Chick, Crazy Turk's Pizza, Curry Hut, HoneyBaked Ham, Hooters, Jason's Deli, Jersey Mike's, Krispy Kreme, La Michoacana, McDonald's, Olive Garden, Outback Steaks, Red Lobster, Rocking Crab Seafood, Straw Hat Pizza, Subway, T-Bonz Steaks, Taco Bell, TX Roadhouse, Vallarta Mexican, Waffle House, Wendy's, Zaxby's, Agusta Best Inn, Best Western, Country Inn&Suites, Knights Inn, Magnolia Inn, Motel 6, Staybridge Suites, Westbank Inn, $Tree, AT&T, CVS Drug, Fresh Mkt Foods, Jiffy Lube, Kroger/dsl/EVC, Midas, Publix, SteinMart, Tire Kingdom, Verizon, Walgreens

196b GA 232 W, N Enmarket, EVC, Murphy Express/dsl, Checkers, Cheeseburger Bobby's, Five Guys, Golden Corral, Krystal, Mirin Asian, Pita Mediterranean, Salsa's Grill, Waffle House, Baymont Inn, Rodeway Inn, ALDI, Discount Tire, GNC, Home Depot, Lowe's, NTB, O'Reilly Parts, Sam's Club/dsl, Sprouts Mkt, URGENT CARE, Walgreens, Walmart

196a I-520, Bobby Jones Fwy, S Buffalo Wild Wings, Carolina Alehouse, Cheddar's Kitchen, Chick-fil-A, Chili's, Chipotle, Cold Stone, Dunkin', Logan's Roadhouse, Mandrino's Italian, McAliser's Deli, McDonald's, Panera Bread, Panera Bread, SmokeShow BBQ, Starbucks, Sticky Fingers, Tropical Smoothie Cafe, Waffle House, Days Inn, DoubleTree Hotel, Home2 Suites, Best Buy, Hobby Lobby, H, Jiffy Lube, Michael's, Office Depot, Old Navy, PetSmart, Staples, Target, Tires+, to , Verizon, vet, Walgreens

195 Wheeler Rd, N Sprint, Cicis Pizza, Farmhaus Burgers, Jersey Mike's, Hyatt Place, CarMax, Gander Outdoors, vet, S BP/dsl, Shell/Circle K, Guiseppe's Pizza, Sonic, Vic's Grill Puertorican, Zaxby's, Days Inn, Harley-Davidson, H, URGENT CARE, Walgreens

194 GA 383, Belair Rd, to Evans, N Circle K/dsl, Sprint, Bojangles, Burger King, Popeyes, Starbucks, Sun Kwong Chinese, Taco Bell, Waffle House, Wendy's, GA Inn, Family$, Food Lion, Fun Park, Jiffy Lube, S BP/DQ/dsl, Exxon, Pilot/Subway/dsl/scales/24hr, Tesla EVC, Cookout, Cracker Barrel, Hardee's, McDonald"s, Steak'n Shake, Waffle House, Baymont, Best Value Inn, Best Western, Comfort Inn, Days Inn, Econo Lodge, Hampton Inn, Holiday Inn, Holiday Inn, La Quinta, Quality Inn, Sleep Inn, Goodyear/auto, Kenworth

190 GA 388, to Grovetown, N Circle K, DQ, Dunkin', LongHorn Steaks, McDonald's, Popeyes, Starbucks, Waffle House, Wingstop, auto repair, AutoZone, Kroger, URGENT CARE, S Murphy Express/dsl, ALDI, Applebee's, Arby's, Chick-fil-A, Chicken Salad Chick, Culver's, Firehouse Subs, Five Guys, Jersey Mike's, KFC, McAlister's Deli, Mi Rancho, Shane's Ribs, Taco Bell, Avid Hotel, Home2 Suites, $Tree, Jiffy Lube, Walmart

189mm weigh sta both lanes

183 US 221, to Harlem, Appling, S Exxon/dsl, Sprint/dsl, to Laurel&Hardy Museum

182mm **full facilities, litter barrels, petwalk, , , both lanes, RV dump, vending**

THOMSON

175 GA 150, N Chevron/rest/dsl/24hr, OYO, to Mistletoe SP

172 US 78, GA 17, Thomson, N Love's/Chester's/Subway/dsl/scales/24hr, Sprint/dsl, Waffle House, Chrysler/Dodge/Jeep, Uhaul, S 76/dsl, BP/dsl, Circle K/dsl, RaceWay/dsl, Arby's, Bojangles, Bordeaux Seafood, Burger King, Checkers, Chick-fil-A, Domino's, Habaneros Mexican, Krystal, LJ Silver, Lucky Chinese, McDonald's, MingWah Chinese, Popeyes, Poppoa's BBQ, Starbucks, Taco Bell, Tasty Wings & Seafood, Waffle House, Wendy's, Zaxby's, Comfort Inn, Days Inn, Hampton Inn, Quality Inn, $General, Advance Parts, AutoZone, Family$, H, O'Reilly Parts, Verizon, Walgreens

169 Thomson

165 GA 80, Camak

160 E Cadley Rd, Norwood

154 US 278, GA 12, Barnett

148 GA 22, Crawfordville, N BP, to Stephens SP, S Molly's

138 GA 77, GA 15, Siloam, N Flying J/IHOP/dsl/LP/scales/24hr, S Chevron/dsl, $General

BUCKHEAD

130 GA 44, Greensboro, N BP/dsl, EVC, Valero/Subway, DQ, McDonald's, Pizza Hut, Waffle House, Wendy's, Zaxby's, Holiday Lodge, Quality Inn, $General, AutoZone, Buick/Chevrolet, Greensboro Tire/repair, S Chevron/dsl, Burger King, Chick-fil-A, Jackson Inn, Home Depot/gas, H

121 to Lake Oconee, Buckhead, S Sunoco/dsl, Museum of Art(3mi)

114 US 441, US 129, to Madison, N Chevron/dsl, Citgo/dsl, EVC, Pilot/IHOP/dsl/scales/24hr, RaceWay/dsl, Tesla EVC, Arby's, Bojangles, Burger King, Captain D's, Chick-fil-A, Cracker Barrel, Dos Amigos Mexican, Dunkin'/Baskin Robbins, KFC, Krystal, Little Caesars, McDonald's, Pizza Hut, Starbucks, Taco Bell, Waffle House, Wendy's, Yanmi Kitchen, Zaxby's, Hampton Inn, My Home&Suites, Quality Inn, $General, Advance Parts, AutoZone, Chrysler/Dodge/Jeep, H, Ingles Foods/gas, Lowe's, NAPA, O'Reilly Parts, Uhaul, Verizon, Walmart, S Circle K/dsl, Marathon, TA/BP/Country Pride/Popeyes/dsl/scales/24hr/@, Waffle House, Days Inn, Deerfield Inn, Holiday Inn Express, Rodeway Inn, Country Boys RV Park(1mi), truckwash/service

113 GA 83, Madison, N BP/dsl, Love's/Hardee's/Godfather/dsl/scales/24hr/@, Speedco, st patrol, S Exxon/dsl

GA

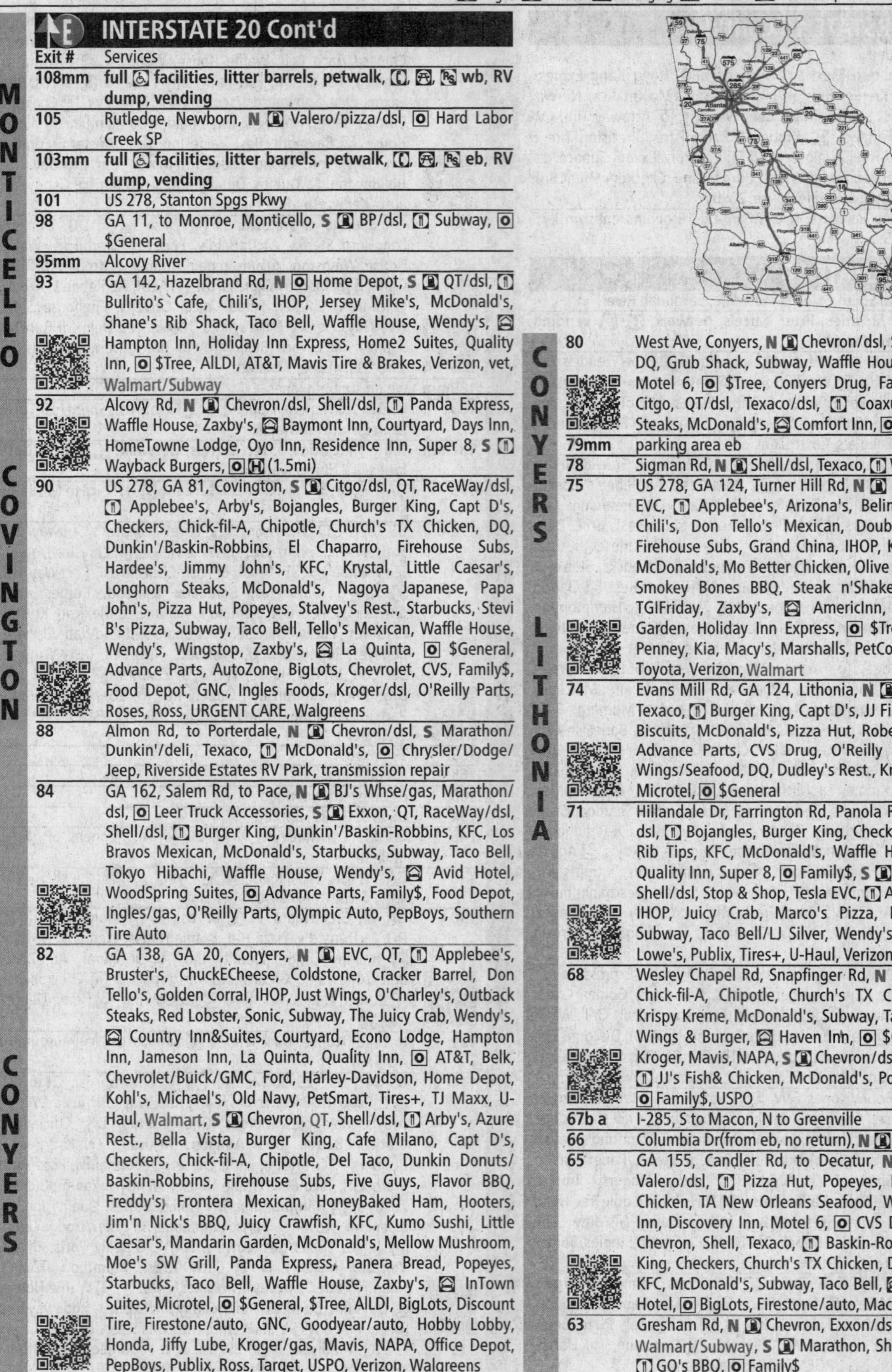

INTERSTATE 20 Cont'd

MONTICELLO

Exit #	Services
108mm	**full [handicapped] facilities, litter barrels, petwalk, [phone], [picnic], [RS] wb, RV dump, vending**
105	Rutledge, Newborn, **N** [gas] Valero/pizza/dsl, [other] Hard Labor Creek SP
103mm	**full [handicapped] facilities, litter barrels, petwalk, [phone], [picnic], [RS] eb, RV dump, vending**
101	US 278, Stanton Spgs Pkwy
98	GA 11, to Monroe, Monticello, **S** [gas] BP/dsl, [food] Subway, [other] $General
95mm	Alcovy River
93	GA 142, Hazelbrand Rd, **N** [other] Home Depot, **S** [gas] QT/dsl, [food] Bullrito's Cafe, Chili's, IHOP, Jersey Mike's, McDonald's, Shane's Rib Shack, Taco Bell, Waffle House, Wendy's, [lodging] Hampton Inn, Holiday Inn Express, Home2 Suites, Quality Inn, [other] $Tree, AlLDI, AT&T, Mavis Tire & Brakes, Verizon, vet, Walmart/Subway

COVINGTON

Exit #	Services
92	Alcovy Rd, **N** [gas] Chevron/dsl, Shell/dsl, [food] Panda Express, Waffle House, Zaxby's, [lodging] Baymont Inn, Courtyard, Days Inn, HomeTowne Lodge, Oyo Inn, Residence Inn, Super 8, **S** [food] Wayback Burgers, [other] [H] (1.5mi)
90	US 278, GA 81, Covington, **S** [gas] Citgo/dsl, QT, RaceWay/dsl, [food] Applebee's, Arby's, Bojangles, Burger King, Capt D's, Checkers, Chick-fil-A, Chipotle, Church's TX Chicken, DQ, Dunkin'/Baskin-Robbins, El Chaparro, Firehouse Subs, Hardee's, Jimmy John's, KFC, Krystal, Little Caesar's, Longhorn Steaks, McDonald's, Nagoya Japanese, Papa John's, Pizza Hut, Popeyes, Stalvey's Rest., Starbucks, Stevi B's Pizza, Subway, Taco Bell, Tello's Mexican, Waffle House, Wendy's, Wingstop, Zaxby's, [lodging] La Quinta, [other] $General, Advance Parts, AutoZone, BigLots, Chevrolet, CVS, Family$, Food Depot, GNC, Ingles Foods, Kroger/dsl, O'Reilly Parts, Roses, Ross, URGENT CARE, Walgreens
88	Almon Rd, to Porterdale, **N** [gas] Chevron/dsl, **S** Marathon/Dunkin'/deli, Texaco, [food] McDonald's, [other] Chrysler/Dodge/Jeep, Riverside Estates RV Park, transmission repair

CONYERS

Exit #	Services
84	GA 162, Salem Rd, to Pace, **N** [gas] BJ's Whse/gas, Marathon/dsl, [other] Leer Truck Accessories, **S** [gas] Exxon, QT, RaceWay/dsl, Shell/dsl, [food] Burger King, Dunkin'/Baskin-Robbins, KFC, Los Bravos Mexican, McDonald's, Starbucks, Subway, Taco Bell, Tokyo Hibachi, Waffle House, Wendy's, [lodging] Avid Hotel, WoodSpring Suites, [other] Advance Parts, Family$, Food Depot, Ingles/gas, O'Reilly Parts, Olympic Auto, PepBoys, Southern Tire Auto
82	GA 138, GA 20, Conyers, **N** [gas] EVC, QT, [food] Applebee's, Bruster's, ChuckECheese, Coldstone, Cracker Barrel, Don Tello's, Golden Corral, IHOP, Just Wings, O'Charley's, Outback Steaks, Red Lobster, Sonic, Subway, The Juicy Crab, Wendy's, [lodging] Country Inn&Suites, Courtyard, Econo Lodge, Hampton Inn, Jameson Inn, La Quinta, Quality Inn, [other] AT&T, Belk, Chevrolet/Buick/GMC, Ford, Harley-Davidson, Home Depot, Kohl's, Michael's, Old Navy, PetSmart, Tires+, TJ Maxx, U-Haul, Walmart, **S** [gas] Chevron, QT, Shell/dsl, [food] Arby's, Azure Rest., Bella Vista, Burger King, Cafe Milano, Capt D's, Checkers, Chick-fil-A, Chipotle, Del Taco, Dunkin Donuts/Baskin-Robbins, Firehouse Subs, Five Guys, Flavor BBQ, Freddy's, Frontera Mexican, HoneyBaked Ham, Hooters, Jim'n Nick's BBQ, Juicy Crawfish, KFC, Kumo Sushi, Little Caesar's, Mandarin Garden, McDonald's, Mellow Mushroom, Moe's SW Grill, Panda Express, Panera Bread, Popeyes, Starbucks, Taco Bell, Waffle House, Zaxby's, [lodging] InTown Suites, Microtel, [other] $General, $Tree, AlLDI, BigLots, Discount Tire, Firestone/auto, GNC, Goodyear/auto, Hobby Lobby, Honda, Jiffy Lube, Kroger/gas, Mavis, NAPA, Office Depot, PepBoys, Publix, Ross, Target, USPO, Verizon, Walgreens

CONYERS

Exit #	Services
80	West Ave, Conyers, **N** [gas] Chevron/dsl, Shell/dsl, [food] Domino's, DQ, Grub Shack, Subway, Waffle House, [lodging] Best Value Inn, Motel 6, [other] $Tree, Conyers Drug, Family$, Meineke, **S** [gas] Citgo, QT/dsl, Texaco/dsl, [food] Coaxum's Rest., Longhorn Steaks, McDonald's, [lodging] Comfort Inn, [other] Nissan, vet
79mm	parking area eb
78	Sigman Rd, **N** [gas] Shell/dsl, Texaco, [food] Waffle House
75	US 278, GA 124, Turner Hill Rd, **N** [gas] BP/dsl, QT/dsl, **S** Tesla EVC, [food] Applebee's, Arizona's, Belinda's Rest, Chick-fil-A, Chili's, Don Tello's Mexican, Double Scoop Ice Cream, Firehouse Subs, Grand China, IHOP, Kampai Sushi & Steak, McDonald's, Mo Better Chicken, Olive Garden, Panera Bread, Smokey Bones BBQ, Steak n'Shake, Subway, Taco Bell, TGIFriday, Zaxby's, [lodging] AmericInn, Fairfield Inn, Hilton Garden, Holiday Inn Express, [other] $Tree, AT&T, Dillard's, JC Penney, Kia, Macy's, Marshalls, PetCo, Ross, Staples, Tires+, Toyota, Verizon, Walmart

LITHONIA

Exit #	Services
74	Evans Mill Rd, GA 124, Lithonia, **N** [gas] BP/Circle K, Chevron, Texaco, [food] Burger King, Capt D's, JJ Fish & Chicken, Mamie's Biscuits, McDonald's, Pizza Hut, Robert's Rest., Subway, [other] Advance Parts, CVS Drug, O'Reilly Parts, **S** [food] Da-Bomb Wings/Seafood, DQ, Dudley's Rest., Krystal, Waffle House, [lodging] Microtel, [other] $General
71	Hillandale Dr, Farrington Rd, Panola Rd, **N** [gas] QT/dsl, Shell/dsl, [food] Bojangles, Burger King, Checkers, Cook Out, It's The Rib Tips, KFC, McDonald's, Waffle House, [lodging] Knights Inn, Quality Inn, Super 8, [other] Family$, **S** [gas] EVC, Murphy USA/dsl, Shell/dsl, Stop & Shop, Tesla EVC, [food] A-Town Wings, Dunkin', IHOP, Juicy Crab, Marco's Pizza, New China, Popeyes, Subway, Taco Bell/LJ Silver, Wendy's, [lodging] Red Roof Inn, [other] Lowe's, Publix, Tires+, U-Haul, Verizon, Walgreens, Walmart
68	Wesley Chapel Rd, Snapfinger Rd, **N** [food] Capt D's, Checkers, Chick-fil-A, Chipotle, Church's TX Chicken, Dunkin', KFC, Krispy Kreme, McDonald's, Subway, Taco Bell, Waffle House, Wings & Burger, [lodging] Haven Inn, [other] $General, Home Depot, Kroger, Mavis, NAPA, **S** [gas] Chevron/dsl, QT, Shell/dsl, Texaco, [food] JJ's Fish& Chicken, McDonald's, Popeyes, [lodging] Papa Johns, [other] Family$, USPO
67b a	I-285, S to Macon, N to Greenville
66	Columbia Dr(from eb, no return), **N** [gas] Chevron
65	GA 155, Candler Rd, to Decatur, **N** [gas] Chevron, Texaco, Valero/dsl, [food] Pizza Hut, Popeyes, Red Lobster, Spanky's Chicken, TA New Orleans Seafood, Wendy's, [lodging] Best Value Inn, Discovery Inn, Motel 6, [other] CVS Drug, U-Haul, **S** [gas] BP, Chevron, Shell, Texaco, [food] Baskin-Robbins/Dunkin', Burger King, Checkers, Church's TX Chicken, DQ, J&J Fish & Chicken, KFC, McDonald's, Subway, Taco Bell, [lodging] Economy Hotel, OYO Hotel, [other] BigLots, Firestone/auto, Macy's
63	Gresham Rd, **N** [gas] Chevron, Exxon/dsl, [food] American Deli, [other] Walmart/Subway, **S** [gas] Marathon, Shell, Texaco/dsl, Valero, [food] GQ's BBQ, [other] Family$

INTERSTATE 20 Cont'd

CYCLORAMA

Exit #	Services
62	Flat Shoals Rd(from eb, no return)
61b	GA 260, Glenwood Ave, N Chevron, Shell/dsl
61a	Maynard Terrace(from eb, no return)
60b a	US 23, Moreland Ave, N Texaco, Valero, Advance Parts, S Citgo/dsl, Shell, Buffalo China, Checkers, Cook Out, Krystal, McDonald's, Wendy's
59b	Memorial Dr, Glenwood Ave(from eb), S Kroger/gas
59a	Cyclorama, N Chevron/dsl, S BP/Subway, CVS
58b	Hill St(from wb, no return), N Shell, Mrs. Winners
58a	Capitol St(from wb, no return), downtown, N to GA Dome, S Capital Inn
57	I-75/85
56b	Windsor St(from eb)
56a	US 19, US 29, McDaniel St(eb only), N Chevron/dsl
55b	Lee St(from wb), Ft McPherson, S BP, Texaco, Church's TX Chicken, Little Caesars Pizza, Oak Street Rest., Popeyes, Taco Bell, West Inn Food Court
55a	Lowery Blvd, S Chevron, Little Caesars, NY Sandwich, Taste of Tropical, $Tree, CVS, Family$, U-Haul
54	Langhorn St(from wb), to Cascade Rd
53	MLK Dr, to GA 139, N Chevron, Shell/dsl, S Exxon, Texaco/dsl, auto repair
52b a	GA 280, Holmes Dr, High Tower Rd, S Chevron, Burger King, McDonald's, Wendy's, $General, AutoZone, CVS Drug
51b a	I-285, S to Montgomery, N to Chattanooga
49	GA 70, Fulton Ind Blvd, N Citgo/dsl, Boston Fish Supreme, The Seafood Social, Wendy's, Budgetel, Quality Inn, USA Economy Lodge, FleetPride Truck Parts, U-Haul, S BP/dsl, Chevron/dsl, Valero, Garian's, Grand Buffet, J&J Fish & Chicken, Economy Hotel, OYO
48mm	Chattahoochee River
47	Six Flags Pkwy(from wb), N BP, EconoLodge, S Guest Inn, Rodeway Inn, Wingate Inn, Six Flags Funpark
46b a	Riverside Parkway, N Citgo/Church's TX Chicken, Marathon, QT/dsl, Super 8, Family$, S Texaco, Wendy's, Guest Inn, Rodeway Inn, Wingate Inn, Six Flags Funpark
44	GA 6, Thornton Rd, to Lithia Springs, N BP, QT, RaceTrac/dsl, Shell/dsl, Tesla EVC, Valero, American Deli, Applebee's, Bojangles, Burger King, Checkers, Chick-fil-A, Chipotle, Domino's, Dunkin', Firehouse Subs, Fred's BBQ, Hardee's, IHOP, KFC, McDonald's, Moe's SW Grill, Olive Tree Rest., Popeyes, Sonic, Subway, Taco Bell, Waffle House, Waffle House, Wendy's, Zaxby's, Budget Inn, Budgetel, Holiday Inn Express, InTowne Suites, Knights Inn, Quality Inn, $General, AT&T, Atlanta West Camping(2mi), Autozone, Carmax, Chevrolet, Ford, Harley Davidson, Home Depot, Honda, Hyundai, Kroger/gas, Nissan, Tires+, vet, VW, Walgreens, S Shell, Beaver Creek Biscuit Co & BBQ, Bei Jin China, Cracker Barrel, Fiesta Mexican, Krispy Krunchy Chicken, Baymont Inn, Candlewood Suites, Country Inn&Suites, Courtyard, Extended Stay, Hampton Inn, Hilton Garden, Home2 Suites, My Place Hotel, Ramada, SpringHill Suites, Tru, Chrysler/Dodge/Jeep, Kia, Penske, to Sweetwater Creek SP, Toyota, Walmart/gas
42mm	weigh sta eb
41	Lee Rd, to Lithia Springs, N Marathon/Burger King/dsl, S Waffle House
37	GA 92, to Douglasville, N RaceTrac, Shell/dsl, Blimpie, Burger King, Carribbean Kitchen, Checker's, Chick-fil-A, Church's TX Chicken, DQ, Dunkin', Krystal, Longhorn Steaks, Los Tacos, Martin's Rest., McDonald's, Monterrey Mexican, Pizza Hut, Popeyes, Subway, Taco Bell, Waffle House,

VILLA RICA

Exit #	Services
37	Continued Wendy's, Baymont, Best Value Inn, Comfort Inn, Days Inn, EconoLodge, Quality Inn, Royal Inn, AutoZone, CVS Drug, Family$, Kroger/dsl, NAPA, O'Reilly Parts, Tires+, Walgreens, S Chevron/dsl, Marathon, QT, Texaco/dsl, Domino's, NaNum Chicken, Waffle House, $General, Aamco, Advance Parts, Ingles Foods
36	Chapel Hill Rd, N, S EVC, QT, Shell/dsl, Tesla EVC, Arby's, China Garden, Chipotle, Coldstone, Daruma, Firehouse Subs, Five Guys, Jason's Deli, Johnny's Subs, McDonald's, Olive Garden, Outback Steaks, Panda Express, Panera Bread, Shane's Rib Shack, Starbucks, Subway, TX Roadhouse, Waffle House, Hampton Inn, $Tree, AlLDI, Belk, BigLots, Dillard's, Firestone/auto, Hobby Lobby, JC Penney, Kohl's, Macy's, Marshall's, Michael's, Old Navy, PetSmart, Ross, Target
34	GA 5, to Douglasville, N RaceTrac/dsl, Texaco/dsl, Atlantic Grill, Cracker Barrel, Stevie B's Pizza, Waffle House, Williamson Bros BBQ, Zaxby's, Holiday Inn Express, La Quinta, Sleep Inn, $Tree, Kauffman Tires, Sam's Club, URGENT CARE, Walmart, S Circle K, Little Caesars, Applebee's, Bruster's, Buffalo Wild Wings, Burger King, Chick-fil-A, ChuckECheese, Del Taco, Dickey's BBQ, DQ, Dunkin, El Tio Mexican, Fiesta Mexican, Five Guys, Golden Corral, Golden Krust Carribean, HoneyBaked Ham, Hooters, IHOP, Jersey Mike's, Juicy Crab, KFC, La Salsa, McDonald's, Moe's SW Grill, Monterrey Mexican, Papa John's, Popeyes, Red Lobster, Sonic, Starbucks, Steak'n Shake, Subway, Taco Bell, Taco Mac, Tasty Crab House, Waffle House, Wasabi Japanese, Wendy's, InTown Suites, Advance Parts, AT&T, Batteries+, Best Buy, Discount Tire, Goodyear/auto, Home Depot, Jiffy Lube, Kroger/dsl, Lowe's, Mavis, Meineke, O'Reilly Parts, Office Depot, PepBoys, Publix, Tuesday Morning, U-Haul, vet, Walgreens
30	Post Rd, S Shell/dsl
26	Liberty Rd, Villa Rica, N BP/dsl, Shell/dsl, China Wok, Johnny's Pizza, McDonald's, Mex-Grill, Olive Tree Rest., Subway, Sumo Japanese, Taco Bell, Waffle House, $General, Family$, Publix, vet, vet, S Chevron, Pilot/Subway/dsl/scales/24hr, American Inn
24	GA 101, GA 61, Villa Rica, N BP/dsl, Chevron/dsl, RaceTrac/dsl, Arby's, Chick-fil-A, Hardee's, KFC/Taco Bell, Krystal, McDonald's, Pizza Hut, Sonic, Stix Grill, Subway, Wendy's, Comfort Inn, EconoLodge, Hometown Lodge, Super 8, Super 8, $Tree, Advance Parts, AT&T, AutoZone, CVS Drug, Ingles Foods, Walgreens, S EVC, QT, Bojangles, Burger King, Capt D's, Domino's, Dunkin, El Ranchito Mexican, La Chiquita Mexican, Papa John's, Popeyes, Starbucks, Thai Basil, Waffle House, Zaxby's, Holiday Inn Express, Chevrolet, Home Depot, to W GA Coll, URGENT CARE, Verizon, Walmart/Subway
21mm	Little Tallapoosa River
19	GA 113, Temple, N Flying J/dsl/scales/24hr, Pilot/Subway/Wendy's/dsl/scales/24hr/@, Bojangles, Burger King, El Tapatio Mexican, El Tapatio's, Fortune Star Chinese, Hardee's, Marco's Pizza, McDonald's, Waffle House, Ingles Foods/gas
15mm	weigh sta wb
11	US 27, Bremen, Bowdon, N Chevron/dsl, Murphy USA/dsl, Valero/Domino's/dsl, Arby's, butter'dudder Creamery, Capt D's, Chick-fil-A, Chopsticks Chinese, Cracker Barrel, DQ, Dunkin, Jack's, Juanito's, KFC/Taco Bell, Little Caesar's, Mama Deluca's, McDonald's, Papa John's, Popeyes, Waffle House, Wendy's, Zaxby's, Hampton Inn, Holiday Inn Express/EVC, Microtel, Motel 6, Quality Inn, $General, Advance Parts, Ford, Ingles Foods/gas, URGENT CARE, Verizon, Walmart/McDonald's, S BP/dsl, Circle K/dsl,

= gas = food = lodging = other = rest stop

GA

INTERSTATE 20 Cont'd

TALLAPOOSA

Exit	Services
11	Continued Subway, John Tanner SP
9	Waco Rd, N Love's/Chesters/Subway/dsl/scales/24hr/@, Jellystone RV Park(2mi)
5	GA 100, Tallapoosa, N Exxon/dsl, Robinson's/dsl/24hr, Waffle House, Big Oak RV park, S Newborn TrkStp/rest/dsl/scales/24hr/@, Pilot/Taco Bell/dsl/scales/24hr, Robinson & Son, DQ, GA Diner, Stateline BBQ, Super 8, to John Tanner SP, truck repair/wash
1mm	**Welcome Ctr eb, full facilities, litter barrels, vending, petwalk,**
0mm	Georgia/Alabama state line, Eastern/Central time zone

INTERSTATE 59

RISING FAWN

Exit	Services
20.5mm	I-59 begins/ends on I-24, exit 167. For I-24, turn to Tennessee Interstate 24.
20mm	I-24, W to Nashville, E to Chattanooga
17	Slygo Rd, to New England, W Citgo/dsl, KOA(2mi)
11	GA 136, Trenton, E Chevron/dsl, Mobil, Shell, Asian Garden, Guthrie's, Hardee's, McDonald's, Pizza Hut, Subway, Days Inn, $Tree, Advance Parts, CVS Drug, Ingles, O'Reilly Parts, to Cloudland Canyon SP, W BP, Citgo/dsl, Exxon/Circle K/dsl, Huddle House, Krystal, Little Caesar's, Taco Bell, Wendy's, $General, Food City, Food Outlet
4	Rising Fawn, E Marathon, camping (1mi), W BP/dsl, Pilot/Subway/dsl/scales/24hr
0mm	Georgia/Alabama state line, eastern/central time zone

INTERSTATE 75

RINGGOLD · DALTON · RESACA · ADAIRSVILLE

Exit	Services
355mm	Georgia/Tennessee state line
354mm	Chickamauga Creek
353	GA 146, Rossville, E Citgo, Cloud Springs Lodge, W Circle K, Shell/dsl, Costco/gas
352mm	Welcome Ctr sb, **full facilities, info, litter barrels, petwalk, vending**
350	GA 2, Bfd Pkwy, to Ft Oglethorpe, E Chevron/dsl, Mobil/Circle K/dsl, Farm to Fork, Hampton Inn, Hometown Inn, Springhill Suites, W RaceTrac/dsl, Subway, Battleground Camping, H, to Chickamauga NP
348	GA 151, Ringgold, E BP/Circle K/dsl, Mapco, Cracker Barrel, Hardee's, KFC, Little Caesar's, McDonald's, Pizza Hut, Sonic, Spencer B's BBQ, Taco Bell, Waffle House, Holiday Inn Express, Quality Inn, Super 8, Tru Hilton, $General, Advance Parts, AutoZone, Chevrolet, CVS Drug, Ingles, vet, Walgreens, W Exxon/dsl, Arby's, Bojangles, Burger King, Domino's, Krystal, New China, Wendy's, Ace Hardware, Chrysler/Dodge/Jeep, Dunlap RV Ctr, Family$, Food Lion, Hyundai, Northgate RV Ctr, Peterbilt, truck repair
345	US 41, US 76, Ringgold, E Exxon, W Circle K/Subway/dsl/scales/24hr, Cochran's TP/rest./dsl/scales/24hr/@, Shell, Waffle House
343mm	weigh sta both lanes
341	GA 201, to Varnell, Tunnel Hill, W BP/Mapco, Baby Hughy's Rest.
336	US 41, US 76, Dalton, Rocky Face, E Mapco, Murphy USA/dsl, RaceTrac/dsl, Burger King, Checkers, Mr Biscuit, Waffle House, Ford/Lincoln, Home Depot, H, Kohl's, PetCo, Verizon, Walmart/Subway, W Marathon/dsl, Victory Fuels, Flako's Mexican, Los Pablos, Wendy's, Baymont Inn, Econolodge, Extended Stay, Motel 6, Staylodge, carpet outlets
333	GA 52, Dalton, E BP/dsl, RaceTrac/dsl, Sexton's/dsl, Applebee's, Bruster's, Burger King, Chick-fil-A, CiCi's Pizza, Cracker Barrel, Five Guys, Fuji Japanese, IHOP, Jersey Mike's Subs, KFC, Krispy Kreme, Las Palmas Mexican,
333	Continued Longhorn Steaks, McDonald's, Olive Garden, Outback Steaks, Panda Express, Panera Bread, Schlotzsky's, Sonic, Starbucks, Steak'n Shake, Subway, Taco Bell, Waffle House, Days Inn, Hampton Inn, Holiday Inn Express, Red Roof Inn, Super 8, $Tree, AT&T, BigLots, Chevrolet, Chrysler/Dodge/Jeep, Food City, Harley-Davidson, Kroger/dsl, PetSmart, TJ Maxx, Tuesday Morning, Verizon, Walgreens, W Bojangles, Chili's, Red Lobster, Zaxby's, Comfort Inn, Country Inn Suites, Courtyard, Fairfield Inn, Hilton Garden, Howard Johnson, La Quinta, Quality Inn, Super 8, NW GA Trade/Conv Ctr
328	GA 3, to US 41, E Circle K/dsl, Pilot/Arby's/dsl/scales/24hr, Waffle House, Wendy's, Best Value Inn, W carpet outlets
326	Carbondale Rd, E LNG, Pilot/McDonald's/Subway/dsl/scales, W Circle K
320	GA 136, to Lafayette, Resaca, E Flying J/Denny's/dsl/LP/24hr, Dollar General Mkt, truck repair/parts
319mm	Oostanaula River, rest area sb, **full facilities, litter barrels, petwalk, vending**
318	US 41, Resaca, E Pilot/DQ/Wendy's/Dunkin'/scales/dsl/24hr, Hardee's, Days Inn, W BP/dsl, Marathon, Chuckwagon Rest., Budget Inn, Duffy's Motel, Econo Lodge, Executive Inn
317	GA 225, to Chatsworth, E New Echota HS, Vann House HS, W Circle K, OYO
315	GA 156, Redbud Rd, to Calhoun, E Circle K, Subway, Waffle House, AOK Camping (2mi), Food Lion, W BP/dsl, Arby's, Quality Inn, H, URGENT CARE, Walgreens
312	GA 53, to Calhoun, E Shell/Circle K/dsl, Applebee's, Cracker Barrel, Longhorn Steaks, Wendy's, Comfort Inn & Suites, EconoLodge, Fairfield Inn, Home2 Suites, La Quinta, Rodeway Inn, Calhoun Outlets/famous brands, W BP/Arby's, Circle K, Citgo, Exxon/dsl, Murphy USA, RaceTrac/dsl, Bojangles, Burger King, Capt D's, Checkers, Chick-fil-A, China Palace, Chipotle, Cook Out, DQ, Dunkin', El Nopal Mexican, Firehouse Subs, Five Guys, Gondolier Pizza, Hibachi Buffet, Huddle House, IHOP, KFC, Krystal, Little Caesar's, McDonald's, Panda Express, Peng's Pavilion Chinese, Pizza Hut, Popeyes, Ruby Tuesday, Starbucks, Subway, Taco Bell, Tokyo Steaks, Waffle House, Zaxby's, Baymont Inn, Holiday Inn Express, Motel 6, Red Roof Inn, Royal Inn, Scottish Inn, Super 8, $General, Advance Parts, ALDI, AT&T, AutoZone, GNC, Goodyear/auto, Home Depot, Kroger/dsl, NAPA, Verizon, vet, Walmart
310	Union Grove Rd, E Buc-ee's/dsl, Love's/Burger King/dsl/scales/24hr
308mm	**nb, full facilities, litter barrels, petwalk**
306	GA 140, Adairsville, E Marathon/dsl,

INTERSTATE 75 Cont'd

ADAIRSVILLE

306 Continued
Patty's Tkstp/rest./dsl, QT/dsl/scales/24hrs, Cracker Barrel, Wendy's, Hampton Inn, truck repair, **W** Chevron/dsl, RaceTrac, Shell/dsl, Burger King, Hardee's, McDonald's, Subway, Taco Bell, Waffle House, Zaxby's, Baymont Inn, Days Inn, Quality Inn, Advance Parts, AutoZone, Family$, Food Lion, Harvest Moon RV Park

296 Cassville-White Rd, **E** Mobil, Pilot/McDonald's/Subway/dsl/scales, TA/BP/Burger King/Taco Bell/IHOP/dsl/scales/24hr/@, Texaco/dsl, Baymont Inn, truckwash, **W** Chevron, Citgo/dsl, Exxon/dsl, Budgetel, KOA

293 US 411, to White, **E** Sunoco/dsl, Texaco/dsl, Quality Inn, **W** Chevron/dsl, Tesla EVC, Valero/Subway, Waffle House, Motel 6, Harley-Davidson, mineral museum

290 GA 20, to Rome, **E** Chevron/dsl, Circle K/dsl, Texaco/Subway/dsl, Arby's, Fire it Up BBQ, McDonald's, Wendy's, Best Value Inn, Best Western, Comfort Inn, EconoLodge, Motel 6, Red Roof Inn, Super 8, **W** Shell/dsl, Texaco/dsl, Burger King, Cracker Barrel, Waffle House, Zaxby's, Courtyard (1mi), Days Inn, Hampton Inn, Holiday Inn Express, $Tree (1.5mi), H, Lowe's (1.5mi), Walgreens (1.5mi), Walmart/McDonald's/gas (1.5mi)

288 GA 113, Cartersville, **W** EVC, Exxon/Circle K/dsl, RaceTrac/dsl, Shell/dsl, Applebee's, Bojangles, Bruster's, Burger King, Chick-Fil-A, Chicken Salad Chick, Chili's, CiCi's, Firehouse Subs, Five Guys, Freddy's, Gondolier Pizza, IHOP, Johnny's NY Pizza, KFC, Kobe Japanese, Krystal, Las Palamas, Longhorn Steaks, McDonald's, McDonald's, Ming Moon, Moe's SW Grill, Papa John's, Red Lobster, Shane's Ribshack, Starbucks, Steak'n Shake, Subway, Taco Bell, TX Roadhouse, Waffle House, Wendy's, Fairfield Inn, Hilton Garden, Home2 Suites, Knights Inn, $General, $Tree, AT&T, Belk, Big Lots, Chrysler/Dodge/Jeep, Discount Tire, GNC, Hobby Lobby, Honda, Kohl's, Kroger/gas, O'Reilly Parts, PetSmart, Publix, Staples, Target, TJ Maxx, to Etowah Indian Mounds(6mi), USPO, Verizon

EMERSON

286mm Etowah River

285 Emerson, **E** Sunoco, Red Top Mtn Lodge, to Red Top Mtn SP, **W** to Allatoona Dam

283 Allatoona Rd, Emerson, **W** Love's/McDonald's/Subway/dsl/scales/24hr, QT, Arby's, Chick-fil-A, St. Angelos Pizza, Starbucks, Taco Bell, Wendy's, Hampton Inn, MainStay Suites, Sleep Inn

280mm Allatoona Lake

ACWORTH

278 Glade Rd, to Acworth, **E** Chevron/dsl, Shell, Baymont, McKinney Camping(3mi), to Glade Marina, **W** RaceTrac/dsl, Bojangles, KFC, Krystal, Papa John's, Pizza Hut, Taco Bell, Waffle House, Red Roof Inn, AutoZone, Ingles/cafe, O'Reilly Parts

277 GA 92, Acworth, **E** BP/Dunkin'/dsl, RaceTrac/dsl, Culver's, Hardee's, Shoney's, Waffle House, Days Inn, Hampton Inn, Holiday Inn Express, Cabela's, **W** Chevron/dsl, Shell/dsl, Tesla EVC, Arby's, Bamboo Garden, Captain D's, China Chef, Domino's, DQ, La Bamba Mexican, McDonald's, Popeyes, Sonic, Subway, Waffle House, Wendy's, Zaxby's, Best Western, Deerfield Lodge, Econolodge, Fairfield Inn, Hometowne Lodge, Quality Inn, Super 8, $General, Advance Parts, CVS Drug, Family$, Goodyear/auto, Publix, Walgreens

273 Wade Green Rd, **E** BP/dsl, RaceTrac/dsl, Arby's, Burger King, Coldstone, Dunkin', Firehouse Subs, Happy Panda, Las Palmas Mexican, Marco's Pizza, McDonald's, Papa John's, QT/dsl, Starbucks, Taco Bell, Waffle House, Red Roof Inn, Sleep Inn, $Tree, BigLots, GNC, O'Reilly Parts, Pepboys, Publix, Tires+, **W** Shell, Texaco/dsl, Bojangles,

273 Continued
Domino's, First Watch, Jet's Pizza, Johnny's Pizza/Subs, Mandarin Cafe, Starbucks, Wendy's, Home Depot, Jiffy Lube, Kroger/gas, Mavis Tire, Publix, Verizon, Walgreens

271 Chastain Rd, to I-575 N, **E** Chevron/Circle K, Tesla EVC, Chick-Fil-A, Chipotle, Cookout, Cracker Barrel, Del Taco, Dunkin'/Baskin Robbins, Five Guys, Panda Express, Panera Bread, Ruth's Chris Steaks, Starbucks, Taco Mac, Taziki's, Tin Lizzy Cantina, Tropical Smoothie Cafe, Whataburger, Willy's Mexicana, Zaxby's, Comfort Suites, Embassy Suites, Extended Stay, Fairfield Inn, Hampton Inn, Kennesaw Inn, Residence Inn, **W** Shell/Circle K/dsl, Swifty Save, Taco Bell, Arby's, Jimmy John's, Mellow Mushroom, Waffle House, Wendy's, Baymont Inn, InTown Suites, SpringHill Suites, museum

MARIETTA

269 to US 41, to Marietta, **E** EVC, Shell/dsl, Anchor Grill, Applebee's, Honey Baked Ham, J Christopher's, Jimmy John's, McDonald's, Olive Garden, Penang Malaysian, Provino's, Red Lobster, Shogun Japanese, Smoothie King, Starbucks, Subway, Twin Peaks, Best Western, Comfort Inn, Holiday Inn Express, Belk, Firestone/auto, Home Depot, JC Penney, Macy's, Marshall's, Midas, Take 5 Oil Change, TJ Maxx, Verizon, **W** EVC, Shell/Circle K, Tesla EVC, Tesla EVC, Bahama Breeze, Carrabbas, CAVA, Chick-fil-A, Chili's, Chipotle, ChuckeCheese, Chuy's Mexican, Coldstone, Copeland's Grill, Crumbl Cookies, Del Taco, Five Guys, Golden Corral, IHOP, Jason's Deli, Jersey Mike's, KFC, Longhorn Steaks, Melting Pot, MOD Pizza, On-the-Border, Outback Steaks, Panera Bread, Sivas Tavern, Starbucks, Starbucks, Steak'n Shake, Taco Bell, Ted's MT Steaks, Weny's, Willy's Mexicana, Zama Mexican, Courtyard, Day's Inn, Hampton Inn, Hilton Garden, Homewood Suites, La Quinta, Quality Inn, TownPlace, Academy Sports, ALDI, AT&T, Best Buy, Buick/GMC, CarMax, Chevrolet, Costco/gas, DICK'S, Discount Tire, EVC, Ford/Lincoln, Hobby Lobby, Kia, Mavis Tires, Michael's, Nissan, Old Navy, PetSmart, REI, Subaru, Target, Tesla, to Kennesaw Mtn NP, Toyota, VW, Whole Foods, World Market

268 I-575 N, GA 5 N, to Canton

267b a GA 5 N, to US 41, Marietta

265 GA120, N Marietta Pkwy, **W** Chevron/dsl, Shell/dsl, Days Inn, Advance Parts, AutoZone, Enterpise, Family$, O'Reilly Parts, Office Depot

263 GA 120, to Roswell, **E** Chevron, QT, Shell, $General, **W** QT, Valero, ALDI, Applebee's, Arby's, Chikfila, China Kitchen, Cook Out, DQ, Haveli Rest., IHOP, Jimmy John's, KFC, Krispy Kreme, McDonald's, Piccadilly's, Popeyes, Sonny's BBQ, Subway, Taco Bell, Waffle House, Wendy's, Econolodge, Garden Plaza, Magnuson Hotel, Super 8, Wyndham Garden, AutoZone , U-Haul

261 GA 280, Delk Rd, to Dobbins AFB, **E** Chevron/Circle K/dsl, RaceTrac/dsl, Shell, Shell/dsl, J. Christopher's, KFC/Taco Bell, Little Caesar's, Marco's Pizza, McDonald's, Ruby Tuesday, Starbucks, Subway, Wendy's, Wings&Tings, Courtyard, Drury Inn, Fairfield Inn, Motel 6, Rodeway Inn, Sleep Inn, Jiffy Lube, Kroger, Publix, **W** BP, Chevron/dsl, Bojangles, Cracker Barrel, Dave&Busters, Baymont Inn, Days Inn, Economy Hotel, Hampton Inn, Holiday Inn Express, Home2 Suites, Hotel Weston, La Quinta, Quality Inn, FedEx

260 Windy Hill Rd, to Smyrna, **E** EVC, Jersey Mike's Subs, Mellow Mushroom, Pappadeaux Seafood, Pappasito's Cantina, Schlotzsky's, Best Western, Country Hearth , Extended Stay, Extended Stay America, Extended Stay America(2), Hilton Garden, Hyatt Regency, Marriott, SpringHill, CVS Drug, USPO, **W** Chevron, Conoco, Shell/Circle K, Texaco/dsl, Chick-fil-A, Chipotle, McDonald's,

GA

INTERSTATE 75 Cont'd

260 Continued
Panda Express, Popeyes, Starbucks, Starbucks, Waffle House, Wendy's, Budgetel Inns, Comfort Inn, Country Inn&Suites, Courtyard, Days Inn, DoubleTree, Red Roof Inn, Western Inn, H, Target, Walmart

259b a I-285, W to Birmingham, E to Greenville, Montgomery

258 Cumberland Pkwy, E Hyatt House, W Copeland's Rest., Moe's SW Grill, Shane's Ribshack, Subway, Embassy Suites, Homewood Suites, Kroger

257mm Chattahoochee River

256 to US 41, Northside Pkwy

255 US 41, W Paces Ferry Rd, E Chevron, Shell/dsl, Blue Ridge Grill, Chick-fil-A, Houston's Rest., McDonald's, OK Café, Pero's Pizza, Smoothie King, Starbucks, Starbucks, Whole Foods Mkt, Willy's Mexicana, Ace Hardware, CVS Drug, H, Publix, W Amoco

254 Moores Mill Rd

252b Howell Mill Rd, E Shell/auto, Chick-fil-A, Chipotle, Domino's, Fellini's Pizza, Flying Biscuit Cafe, Jersey Mike's, McDonald's, Willy's Mexicana, Goodyear/auto, Petco, Publix, USPO, USPO, Walgreens, W QT, Shell, Arby's, Chin Chin Chinese, Dunkin', La Parrilla Mexican, Starbucks, Subway, Taco Bell, Waffle House, Wendy's, Ace Hardware, Advance Auto, Firestone/auto, GNC, Kroger, Mavis Tires, Office Depot, Pep Boys, PetSmart, TJ Maxx, Verizon, Walmart

252a US 41, Northside Dr, E H, W Shell, Little Azio's, InTown Suites

251 I-85 N, to Greenville

250 Techwood Dr(from sb), 10th St, 14th St, Homewood Suites, E Chevron, Hilton Garden, Home2 Suites, Renaissance Inn, Publix

249d 10th St, Spring St(from nb), E EVC, Chick-fil-A, Starbucks, The Melting Pot, The Varsity, Courtyard, W Hampton Inn

249c Williams St(from sb), downtown, to GA Dome

249b Pine St, Peachtree St(from nb), downtown, E H, W Mellow Mushroom, Hilton, Marriott

249a Courtland St(from sb), downtown, W Hilton, Marriott, GA St U

248d Piedmont Ave, Butler St(from sb), downtown, W Hilton, Hyatt, Ritz-Carlton, downtown

248c GA 10 E, Intn'l Blvd, downtown, W Hilton, Hyatt, Marriott, Sheraton, downtown

248b Edgewood Ave(from nb), W hotels, downtown, H

248a MLK Dr(from sb), W st capitol, to Underground Atlanta, H

247 I-20, E to Augusta, W to Birmingham

246 Georgia Ave, Fulton St

245 Ormond St, Abernathy Blvd, E Comfort Inn, Country Inn & Suites

244 University Ave, E BP, Texaco, Chevron, NAPA

243 GA 166, Lakewood Fwy, to East Point

242 I-85 S, to

241 Cleveland Ave, E Chevron/Subway/dsl, Exxon, Checkers, Advance Parts, Piggly Wiggly, W Shell, Valero, Krystal

239 US 19, US 41, E Chevron/dsl, USPO, W Texaco, Chick-fil-A, IHOP, Junior's Pizza, McDonald's, Sombreros Mexican, Subway, Wendy's, Best Western, Holiday Inn Express, to

238b a I-285 around Atlanta

237a GA 85 S(from sb)

237 GA 331, Forest Parkway, E BP, Chevron/dsl, RaceTrac/scales/dsl, Shell/McDonald's, Burger King, Mr Taco, Waffle House, Econolodge, InTown Suites, Family$, Farmer's Mkt, W BP, Chevron/Subway/dsl, QT,

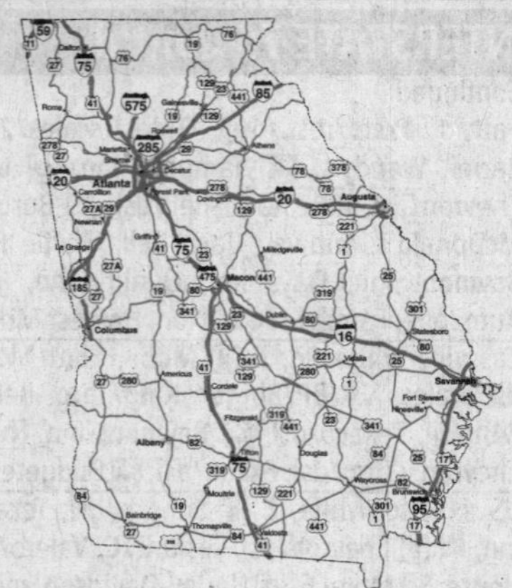

237 Continued
Knights Inn, Quality Suites, Lee Tires/repair

235 US 19, US 41, GA 3, Jonesboro, E BP/dsl, Shell/Subway/dsl, Texaco/dsl, Super 8, Travelodge, W Chevron/dsl, Shell, Texaco/dsl, Applebee's, Burger King, Checkers, ChuckeCheese, Dunkin, Hooters, Juicy Crab, Little Caesar's, McDonald's, Monterrey Mexican, Popeyes, Red Lobster, Starbucks, Waffle House, Zaxby's, Amercan Inn, Econolodge, Motel 6, $General, $Tree, H, Little Giant Farmers Mkt, O'Reilly Parts, Office Depot

233 GA 54, Morrow, E BP/dsl, Chevron, Citgo, Cold Stone, Cookout, Cracker Barrel, IHOP, Krystal, Popeyes, Taco Bell, Waffle House, Wendy's, Best Western, Comfort Suites, Days Inn, Drury Inn, Red Roof Inn, Walmart/McDonald's/gas, W Chevron/dsl, Exxon/dsl, QT/dsl, Bojangles, China Café, Del Taco, KFC, Oasis International, Olive Garden, Subway, Three$ Cafe, Wendy's, Hampton Inn, Quality Inn, Buick/GMC/Mazda, Burlington Coats, Cadillac, Costco/gas, Harley-Davidson, Kia, Macy's, Nissan, Sam's Club/gas, TJ Maxx, Toyota/Scion

231 Mt Zion Blvd, E QT, Chrysler/Dodge/Jeep, Ford/Lincoln, Honda, W BP/Circle K/Subway/dsl, Chevron/dsl, Shell, Arby's, Bruster's, Carrabba's, Chili's, Chipotle, Domino's, Golden Krust Caribbean, King Claw, Longhorn Steaks, McDonald's, Mo-Jo's Wings, Moe's SW Grill, Panda Express, Pizza Hut, Skyboxx Rest., Steak'n Shake, Taco Bell, TGIFriday, Truett's Rest., Waffle House, Wendy's, Wok Asian, Zaxby's, Best Value Inn, Country Inn&Suites, Extended Stay America, InTown Suites, $Tree, AT&T, Barnes&Noble, Best Buy, Home Depot, Mavis, PetSmart, Publix, Ross, Verizon

228 GA 54, GA 138, Jonesboro, E Raceway/dsl, Applebee's, Chick-fil-A, Frontera Mexican, Honeybaked Ham, IHOP, Krystal, Marco's Pizza, O'Charley's, Piccadilly's, Rockin' Crab, Stevi B's Pizza, Subway, Waffle House, Wing Nuts, Comfort Inn, Day's Inn, Express Inn, Hampton Inn, Holiday Inn, La Quinta, Red Roof Inn, WoodSpring Suites, H, Kroger/dsl, Lowes Whse, Office Depot, Tires+, URGENT CARE, Verizon, W Marathon, Mobil, Raceway/Wendy's/dsl, Dragon Garden Chinese, McDonald's, Ranchero's Mexican, Fairfield Inn, CarMax, CVS Drug, Kohl's

227 I-675 N, to I-285 E(from nb)

224 Hudson Bridge Rd, E Texaco/dsl, Chick-fil-A, Chicken Salad Chick, China Wok, DQ, Italian Oven, Jersey Mike's, Jimmy John's, Johnny's NY Pizza, KFC, La Hacienda, Moe's SW Grill, Outback Steaks, Pueblo Mio, Serafino Itlian, Starbucks, Sticky Cactus Mexican, Subway, Waffle House, Wendy's, Holiday Inn Express, Mircotel, Quality Inn, H, Mavis Tire, Publix, Walgreens, W EVC, QT, Arby's, Bojangles, China Cafe, Domino's, Dunkin, Firehouse Subs, Little Caesars, McDonald's, Mellow Mushroom, Popeyes, Scenic Burger, Taco Bell, Waffle House, Zaxby's, Super 8,

 = gas = food = lodging = other = rest stop

INTERSTATE 75 Cont'd

MCDONOUGH

Exit	Services
224	Continued $Tree, AutoZone, Discount Tire, Kroger/gas, O'Reilly Parts, Verizon, Walmart/gas
222	Jodeco Rd, E BP, Chevron, Exxon, QT/dsl, Hardee's, W U-Haul, Atlanta So. RV Camping
221	Jonesboro Rd, E Exxon/dsl, QT/dsl, Bojangles, Dunkin, Waffle House, Kroger/gas(2mi), Mavis, W American Deli, Arby's, Burger King, Cheddar's, Chili's, Firehouse Subs, Gezzo's Burritos, Golden Corral, Hong Kong Cafe, Hooters, La Parrilla, La Quinta, Logan's Roadhouse, Longhorn Steaks, Marble Slab Creamery, McDonald's, Mike's Burger, O'Charley's, Olive Garden, Red Lobster, Rocky's Pizza, Starbucks, Truett's Grill, Wendy's, Yuki Hibachi, Courtyard, Fairfield Inn, Home2 Suites/Tesla EVC, $Tree, AT&T, AutoZone, Belk, Best Buy, Books-A-Million, Dick's, Home Depot, Marshall's, Michael's, Old Navy, PetSmart, Ross, Sam's Club/gas, Target/Starbucks, Verizon
218	GA 20, GA 81, McDonough, E BP/dsl, Chevron, Murphy USA/dsl, QT, RaceTrac/dsl, American Deli, Applebee's, Arby's, Burger King, Cracker Barrel, Dominos, Fried Tomato Rest., IHOP, JJ Fish & Chicken, KFC, McDonald's, Mesquite Mexican, Moe's SW Grill, Popeyes, Sakura Hibachi, Supreme Fish, Taco Bell, Three $ Cafe, Wendy's, Zaxby's, Baymont Inn, Best Western+, Economy Inn, Super 8, Super 8, WoodSpring Suites, $General, $Tree, Aamco, Discount Tire, Goodyear, Lowe's Whse, Office Depot, URGENT CARE, Walmart/Subway, W RaceTrac/dsl, Shell, Tesla EVC, Chick-fil-A, Chicken Salad Chick, Cookout, Culver's, Dave & Busters, Del Taco, Dunkin, El Agave Mexican, Firehouse Subs, Freddy's, Hardee's, Ichiban Express, Jim'N Nick's BBQ, Jimmy John's, McAlister's Deli, Nana's Chicken, Panda Express, Panera Bread, Starbucks, Subway, Taco Mac, Waffle House, Comfort Suites, Econolodge, Extended Stay, FairBridge Inn, Hampton Inn, Hilton Garden, Holiday Inn Express, Motel 6, Residence Inn, Tru, Advance Parts, AT&T, BJ's Whse/gas, Hobby Lobby, Honda, Hyundai, JC Penney, Kia, Kohl's, Mavis, Nissan, O'Reilly Parts, TJ Maxx, Toyota/Scion, Verizon
216	GA 155, McDonough, Blacksville, E RaceTrac, Shell/dsl, Sunoco, Texaco/dsl, Honk Kong Express, Sonic, Best Value, Budget Inn, Hyundai, Motel 6, Chevrolet/Buick/GMC, Ford, GMC, Isuzu Trucks, Tire South, U-Haul, W BP, Chevron, EVC, Exxon/dsl/24hr, QT, Da Vinci's Pizza, Graffiti's Oizza, Krystal, Steve's Cafe, Subway, Waffle House, Country Inn&Suites, Quality Inn, Sleep Inn
212	to US 23, Locust Grove, E BP/McDonald's/dsl, Chevron/Burger King, Kangaroo/Circle K, Marathon/Dunkin/dsl, Murphy USA/dsl, QT/dsl, American Deli, Bojangles, Capt D's, Denny's, Gezzo's Burritos, IHOP, KFC/Taco Bell, Koji Japanese, Little Caesar's, Moe's SW Grill, Pizza Hut, San Diego Mexican, Shane's Ribshack, Starbucks, Steak'n Shake, Subway, Sunrise China, Waffle House, Wendy's, Zaxby's, Executive Inn, Fairfield Inn, Hampton Inn, Holiday Inn, Ramada, Red Roof Inn, $Tree, Advance Parts, AT&T, AutoZone, Ingles/gas, Tanger Outlet/famous brands, Verizon, Walmart, W Marathon/dsl, Shell/DQ/dsl, Chick-fil-A, DQ, Waffle House, Comfort Suites, La Quinta, Scottish Inn, Sundown Lodge, Super 8, Bumper Parts, U-Haul
205	GA 16, to Griffin, Jackson, E BP/Moe's SW Grill, Shell/Huddle House/Schlotzkys/dsl, W Marathon/Subway/Dunkin/Burger King/scales/parking/dsl, Zaxby's, Holiday Inn Express, Chrysler/Dodge/Jeep, Forest Glen RV Park
201	GA 36, to Jackson, Barnesville, E Love's/McDonald's/dsl/grill/scales/24hr, Pilot/DQ/Wendy's/dsl/scales/24hr/@,

BARNESVILLE

FORSYTH

Exit	Services
201	Continued TA/Subway/Taco Bell/dsl/scales/24hr/@, Blue Beacon, W BP/dsl, Flying J/dsl/LP/scales/24hr, Gulf, BBQ, Waffle House, Speedco Lube, truckwash
198	Highfalls Rd, E Marathon(2mi), Sunoco(1mi), High Falls BBQ, High Falls Lodge, $General(2mi), High Falls SP, HighFalls RV Park(1mi), Red Oaks RV Park (1mi), water park (1mi)
193	Johnstonville Rd, W Marathon/dsl
190mm	weigh sta both lanes
188	GA 42, E Shell, Quality Inn, Rodeway Inn, RV camping, to Indian Springs SP
187	GA 83, Forsyth, E BP, Huddle House, Shane's Rib Shack, Zaxby's, Best Value Inn, KOA, Travelodge, W Citgo/dsl, Exxon/Circle K, Marathon, Shell, Shell, Valero/dsl, Burger King, Capt D's, Dominos, DQ, Dunkin, Hardee's, McDonald's, Popeyes, Starbucks, Subway, Taco Bell, Waffle House, Wendy's, Day's Inn, La Quinta, $Tree, Advance Parts, Family$, H(1.5mi), O'Reilly Parts, Piggly Wiggly, Verizon, Walmart/EVC
186	Tift College Dr, Juliette Rd, Forsyth, E Hampton Inn, Jarrell Plantation HS(18mi), KOA, W BP/dsl, Chevron/dsl, Marathon, Waffle House, Holiday Inn Express, Red Roof, Super 8, CVS Drug, H(1.5mi), Ingles/Starbucks/Deli
185	GA 18, E BBQ, L&D RV Park(2mi), W Exxon/Circle K, QT/dsl, Shell/dsl, Shoney's, Clarion, Comfort Suites, Ford, st patrol
181	Rumble Rd, to Smarr, E BP/dsl
179mm	**full facilities, litter barrels, petwalk, , , sb, vending**
177	I-475 S around Macon(from sb)
175	Pate Rd, from nb, no re-entry, Bolingbroke
172	Bass Rd, E Chicken Salad Chick, J. Christopher's, McDonald's, Medi's Mediterranean, Tenmii Japanese, Zaxby's, Bass Pro Shop, Bealls, Marshalls, W Circle K/DQ/dsl, Citgo/dsl, Burger King, Chick-fil-A, Genghis Grill, Magarita's Mexican, Mellow Mushroom, Natalia's Rest., Subway, Taco Bell, Waffle House, Zheng's Wok, Holiday Inn Express, Homewood Suites, Microtel, Tru, Woodspring Suites, CVS, Publix, to Museum of Arts&Sciences
171	US 23, to GA 87, Riverside Dr, E BP, Marathon/dsl, Bonefish Grill, Chili's, Firehouse Subs, Jersey Mike's, La Parrilla, Olive Garden, Pig on a Pie, TX Roadhouse, Wild Wing Cafe, Zoe's Kitchen, SpringHill Suites, Acura, AT&T, Barnes&Noble, Belk, BMW, Dick's, Dillard's, GNC, Hobby Lobby, Jo-Ann, Mercedes, PetSmart, Subaru, Verizon, Volvo, W Shell, Lexus, Nissan, Toyota/Scion
169	to US 23, Arkwright Dr, E Shell/Circle K/24hr, Carrabba's, CowPies Pizza, Outback Steaks, Steve's Steak & Seafood, Waffle House, Wager's Grill, Avid Hotel, Candlewood Suites, Comfort Inn, Country Inn & Suites, Courtyard, Days Inn, Fairfield Inn, Hampton Inn, Holiday Inn, Home2 Suites, La Quinta, Residence Inn, Sleep Inn, Buick/Cadillac/GMC, W Chevron/dsl, Arby's, Buffalo Wild Wings, Burger King, Chick-fil-A, Chico & Chang, Chipotle, Cold Stone, Cookout, Cracker Barrel, Culvers, Dunkin, Five Guys, Fried Green Tomatoes, Guitarras Mexican, Hooters, IHOP, KFC, Krystal, Longhorn Steaks, Mandarin Chinese, McDonald's, Panda Express, Panera Bread, Papa John's, Starbucks, Steve B's Pizza, Subway, Taco Bell, Wendy's, Baymont Inn, Extended Stay America, Haven Inn, Motel 6, OYO, Quality Inn, Rodeway Inn, Wingate Inn, $General, $Tree, Ace Hardware, Chrysler/Jeep/Dodge, Goodyear/auto, H, Kia, Kroger/dsl, Mazda, O'Reilly Parts, Publix 
167	GA 247, Pierce Ave, E Studio Lodge, W 76/dsl, Chevron/dsl, Mobil, Shell/Circle K/dsl, Applebee's, Marco's Pizza, S&S Cafeteria, Shogun Japanese,

GA

= gas = food = lodging = other = rest stop

INTERSTATE 75 Cont'd

MACON

167 Continued
Waffle House, Best Western/rest., Red Carpet Inn, Red Roof Inn, Rodeway Inn, $General, Firestone/auto

165 I-16 E, to Savannah

164 US 41, GA 19, Forsyth Ave, Macon, E Sid's Rest., hist dist, H, W Citgo/dsl, museum

163 GA 74 W, Mercer U Dr, E Hilton Garden, TownePlace Suites, to Mercer U, W Citgo, U-Haul

162 US 80, GA 22, Eisenhower Pkwy, W Chevron/dsl, Exxon, Lo-lo Gas, Sunoco/dsl, Burger King, Capt D's, Checker's, Krispy Kreme, Krystal, McDonald's, Mrs Winners, Over Easy B-fast, Overtyme Grill, Wendy's, InTown Suites, $Tree, Family$, O'Reilly Parts, Save-A-Lot Foods

160 US 41, GA 247, Pio Nono Ave, E Flash/dsl, Shell/dsl, Bojangles, JJ Fish & Chicken, Waffle House, W Chevron, Marathon, Anderson's Diner, Arby's, DQ, KFC, Little Caesars, McDonald's, Shark's Fish & Chicken, Subway, $General, Advance Parts, Family$, Jiffy Lube, O'Reilly Parts, Piggly Wiggly, Raffield Tire, Roses, U-Haul

156 I-475 N around Macon(from nb)

155 Hartley Br Rd, E Shell/dsl, Domino's, Papa John's, Subway, Waffle House, Wendy's, Kroger/dsl, Verizon, W Circle K/DQ/scales/dsl, Citgo/dsl, McDonald's, Zaxby's, Motel 6, Advance Parts, CVS Drug

153 Sardis Church Rd, E Citgo/dsl, QT, W Love's/Chesters/scales/24hr/dsl/@

BYRON

149 GA 49, Byron, E Chevron/dsl, Circle K/dsl, Burger King, Casa Mexico, Chick-fil-A, Denny's, Dunkin, GA Bob's BBQ, Krystal, Marco's Pizza, McDonald's, Pizza Hut, Popeyes, Subway, Taco Bell, Waffle House, Wendy's, Zaxby's, Avid Hotel, Best Western, Comfort Suites, Holiday Inn Express, Super 8, Campers Inn RV Ctr, Mid-State RV Ctr, Peach Stores/famous brands, W Circle K/dsl, Gas N Go/dsl, Marathon/dsl, RaceWay/dsl, Texaco/Little Caesars/dsl, DQ, Hardee's, Sharks Fish & Chicken, Waffle House, Budget Inn, Days Inn, EconoLodge, Quality Inn, $General, Advance Parts, Camping World RV Ctr, Chevrolet, Interstate RV Ctr/park, O'Reilly Parts

146 GA 247, to Centerville, E Circle K/dsl, Exxon/dsl, QT, Shell, Subway, Comfort Lodge, EconoLodge, to Robins AFB, W Chevron/dsl, Pilot/Arby's/scales/dsl/24hr, Zaxby's, Royal Inn, H

144 Russel Pkwy, E Buc-ee's/dsl, Robins AFB, vet

142 GA 96, Housers Mill Rd, E Shell/dsl, $General, Ponderosa RV Park

PERRY

138 Thompson Rd, E Pacific Pride/LP/NG/dsl, H, Perry's Landing RV Park, W

136 US 341, Perry, E Marathon/dsl, Murphy Express/dsl, Shell/Circle K/dsl, Burger King, Capt D's, China House, Cookout, Firehouse Subs, George & Bob's BBQ, Hibachi Buffet, Jalisco Grill, Jamaican Jerk, KFC, Krystal, Little Caesar's, Longhorn Steaks, McDonald's, Pizza Hut, Red Lobster, Shane's RIbs, Sonny's BBQ, Subway, Waffle House, Wendy's, Zaxby's, Avid Hotel, Great Inn, Hampton Inn, Howard Johnson, Jameson Inn, Motel 6, Rodeway Inn, Super 8, $General, $Tree, Ace Hardware, Advance Parts, AT&T, Boland's RV Park, H, Kroger/dsl, NAPA, Verizon, Walmart, W Shell/Circle K/dsl, Chick-fil-A, Dunkin, Jersey Mike's, Popeyes, Taco Bell, Derby Inn, EconoLodge, FairBridge Inn, Holiday Inn Express, Quality Inn, Royal Inn, Super 8, Crossroads RV Park

135 US 41, GA 127, Perry, E Chevron/dsl, Circle K/dsl, Flash/dsl, Shell, Texaco/dsl, Cracker Barrel, DQ, Subway, Waffle House, Best Western, Budget Inn, Comfort Inn, Relax Inn, Scottish Inn, Travelodge, Chrysler/Dodge/Jeep, Kia,

GA

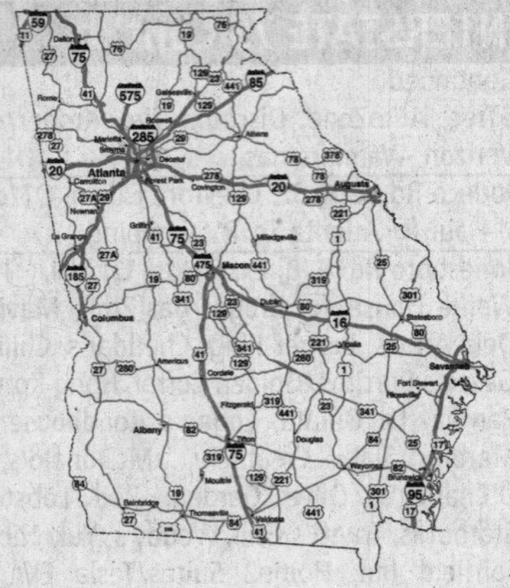

UNADILLA

135 Continued
Fair Harbor RV Park, st patrol

134 South Perry Pkwy, E GA Fairgrounds, W Microtel, Buick/Chevrolet/GMC, Ford, Waffle House

127 GA 26, Henderson, E Twin Oaks Camping, W Shell/dsl

122 GA 230, Unadilla, E Chevron/dsl, Chevrolet/Ford, W Travelodge

121 US 41, Unadilla, E Circle K/DQ/dsl, Shell, Sunoco, Subway, Scottish Inn, $General, NAPA, Southern Trails RV Resort, USPO, W Citgo/rest./dsl/scales/24hr

118mm **full facilities, litter barrels, petwalk, sb, RV dump, vending**

117 to US 41, Pinehurst, W GasnGo/Subway/dog park/dsl

112 GA 27, Vienna

109 GA 215, Vienna, E On 9 Trkstp/McDonalds/dsl/scales/24hr, W Chevron/Subway/dsl, Exxon, Shell/dsl, Huddle House, Popeyes, Vienna Travel Inn, $General Mkt, Cotton Museum

108mm **full facilities, litter barrels, petwalk, nb, RV dump, vending**

CORDELE

104 Farmers Mkt Rd, Cordele

102 GA 257, Cordele, E Sunoco/dsl, W Love's/Bojangles/scales/24hr/@, Smoakies BBQ, H, Love's RV Stop

101 US 280, GA 90, Cordele, E BP/dsl, Pilot/Arby's/dsl/scales/24hr, Shell, Denny's, Waffle House, FairBridge Inn, Fairfield Inn/Tesla EVC, Holiday Inn Express, OYO, Ford, st patrol, W Circle K/dsl, Exxon/Subway, Gas'n Go, Burger King, Capt D's, Chick-fil-A, Cookout, Cracker Barrel, DQ, Firehouse Subs, Hachi Japanese Grill, Hardee's, KFC, Krystal, Little Caesar's, Los Compadres, McDonald's, Pizza Hut, Sonic, Starbucks, Subway, Surcheros Fresh Mex, Taco Bell, Wendy's, Zaxby's, Ashburn Inn, Baymont Inn, Best Western, EconoLodge, Hampton Inn, Motel 6, Quality Inn, Travelodge, $General, $Tree, Advance Parts, AT&T, AutoZone, Belk, Harvey's Foods, Home Depot, J Carter HS, Mavis, O'Reilly Parts, to Veterans Mem SP, Verizon, Walgreens, Walmart/EVC, Winn-Dixie

99 GA 300, GA/FL Pkwy, E Marathon/DQ/Subway/dsl, W Comfort Inn, to Chehaw SP

97 to GA 33, Wenona, E dsl repair, W KOA, truckwash

ASHBURN

92 Arabi, W Citgo, Southern Gates RV Park, U-Haul

85mm **full facilities, litter barrels, petwalk, nb, vending**

84 GA 159, Ashburn

82 GA 107, GA 112, Ashburn, Tesla EVC, W BP, Circle K, Shell, Burger King, Carroll's Sausage & Country Store/RV Park, KFC, McDonald's, Shoney's, Subway, Waffle House, Zaxby's, Economy Inn, Quality Inn, Super 8, Buick/Chevrolet/GMC, O'Reilly Parts, to Chehaw SP, Walgreens

80 Bussey Rd, Sycamore, E Marathon/dsl, W Citgo/dsl, Allen's Tires

INTERSTATE 75 Cont'd

SUNSWEET

Exit #	Services
78	GA 32, Sycamore, E to Jefferson Davis Mem Pk(14mi)
76mm	rest area sb, **full facilities, litter barrels, petwalk,** **vending**
75	Inaha Rd
71	Willis Still Rd, Sunsweet, W Citgo/dsl
69	Chula-Brookfield Rd, E Marathon/dsl, W $General
66	Brighton Rd
64	US 41, Tifton, E BP/dsl, Shell, Chicken Salad Chick, Waffle House, Your Pie Pizza, $General, Harvey's Foods, H, W Marathon
63b	8th St, Tifton, E Circle K/dsl/e85, Firehouse Subs, Mavis, Publix, TJ Maxx, U-Haul, W Pit Stop BBQ, GA Museum of Agriculture
63a	2nd St, Tifton, E BP/dsl, Marathon, Arby's, Asahi Japanese, Checkers, Chicago Pizza, Cod Tail, El Metate, Hip Hop Seafood, JoJo's Rest., KFC, Krystal, McDonald's, Red Lobster, Subway, Surcheros Grill, Waffle House, Red Roof Inn, Super 8, $General, $Tree, Big Lots, W Bob's/dsl, El Cazadore Mexican, Motel 6, Quality Inn
62	US 82, to US 319, Tifton, E BP, Circle K/dsl, Applebee's, Bojangles, Charles Seafood, Chili's, Cracker Barrel, DQ, Golden Corral, Hardee's, King Buffet, Logan's Roadhouse, Sonic, Tokyo Japanese, Waffle House, Zaxby's, Comfort Inn, Country Inn&Suites, Fairfield Inn, Hampton Inn, Holiday Inn Express, Microtel, $Tree, Advance Parts, AutoZone, BigLots, Chrysler/Dodge/Jeep, Family$, Ford/Lincoln, NAPA, O'Reilly Parts, Pecan Outlet, Save-A-Lot, Staples, W Burger King, Circle K/dsl, Shell/dsl, Tesla EVC, Valero, Buffalo Wild Wings, Capt D's, Chick-fil-A, Cookout, HogBones BBQ, Jersey Mike's, Little Caesar's, Longhorn Steaks, McDonald's, Ojshi Japanese, Olive Garden, Panera Bread, Pizza Hut, Sonny's BBQ, Starbucks, Taco Bell, Waffle House, Wendy's, Days Inn, Hilton Garden, La Quinta/EVC, $General, AT&T, Chevrolet, Hobby Lobby, Honda, Lowe's, Toyota, URGENT CARE, Verizon, Walmart/Subway/gas
61	Omega Rd, E Nissan, W Exxon/dsl/24hr, Howard Johnson, Harley-Davidson, I-75 RV Park, The Pines RV Park
60	Central Ave, Tifton, E Sunoco, W Pilot/Steak'n Shake/Subway/dsl/scales/24hr, Blue Beacon, KOA
59	Southwell Blvd, to US 41, Tifton, E Love's/Hardee's/dsl/scales/24hr
55	to Eldorado, Omega, E Shell/Magnolia Plantation/dsl
49	Kinard Br Rd, Lenox, E 76/dsl, Lenox Inn, $General, W Chevron
47mm	rest area both lanes, **full facilities, litter barrels, petwalk,** **vending**
45	Barneyville Rd
41	Rountree Br Rd, E Citgo, W to Reed Bingham SP
39	GA 37, Adel, E Citgo/dsl, Dixie Gas, Marathon, Quick Gas, DQ, Hardee's, McDonald's, Pizza Hut, Subway, Waffle House, Zaxby's, Super 8, $General, $Tree, Ace Hardware, Advance Parts, Family$, H, O'Reilly Parts, Piggly Wiggly, W BP, Citgo/Huddle House/dsl/scales, Shell, Burger King, Capt D's, Don Julio's, Taco Bell, Wendy's, Western Sizzlin, Days Inn, Hampton Inn, to Reed Bingham SP, Verizon, Walmart
37	Adel, E BP/dsl, Citgo, Ford, GMC
32	Old Coffee Rd, Cecil, E Citgo/dsl, Rodeway Inn, Stagecoach Inn, $General, U-Haul, USPO, W Exxon/dsl, Cecil Bay RV Park
29	US 41 N, GA 122, Hahira, Sheriff's Boys Ranch, E Down Home Pizza, Huddle House, The Slice Pizza, Wendy's, $General, Food Lion, NAPA, NAPA, O'Reilly Parts, U-Haul,

TIFTON

LENOX

ADEL

VALDOSTA

Exit #	Services
29	Continued vet, W Citgo/dsl, Shell/Big Foot/cafe/dsl/24hr, Travelodge
23mm	weigh sta both lanes
22	US 41 S, to Valdosta, E Exxon, Shell/Subway/dsl, Jack's Steaks, Waffle House, Best Western+, Buick/Chevrolet/GMC, H, W Citgo/dsl, Burger King, La Quinta
18	GA 133, Valdosta, E Circle K, Mobil, Applebee's, Arby's, Beijing Cafe, Buffalo Wild Wings, Burger King, Chick-fil-A, Chili's, Chipotle, Chow Town, CiCi's Pizza, Cookout, Cracker Barrel, Denny's, Dick's Wings, El Toreo, Fazoli's, Firehouse Subs, Five Guys, Honeybaked Ham, Hooters, KFC, Krystal, Little Caesar's, Longhorn Steaks, McDonald's, Mellow Mushroom, Ole Times Country Buffet, Olive Garden, Outback Steaks, Panda Express, Panera Bread, Red Lobster, Sonny's BBQ, Southern Shores Seafood, Starbucks, Steak'n Shake, Subway, Taco Bell, TX Roadhouse, Waffle House, Wendy's, Zaxby's, Baymont Inn, Candlewood Suites, Comfort Suites, Country Inn&Suites, Courtyard, Drury Inn, Hilton Garden, Holiday Inn Express/Tesla EVC, Home2 Suites, InTown Suites, La Quinta, Motel 6, Quality Inn, $Tree, AT&T, Belk, Best Buy, Books-A-Million, Discount Tire, Family$, Goodyear/auto, Hobby Lobby, Home Depot, JC Penney, Kohl's, Lowe's, Michael's, Old Navy, PetSmart, Publix, Ross, Target, TJ Maxx, URGENT CARE, Verizon, Walgreens, W BP/dsl, QT, RaceWay/dsl, DQ, Days Inn, EconoLodge, Sleep Inn, Super 8, River Park Camping, Toyota
16	US 84, US 221, GA 94, Valdosta, E BP/dsl, Circle K, Citgo, Exxon/dsl, Shell/dsl, Sunoco, Bojangles, Bubba Jax Crab Shack, Burger King, Cajun Wild Crab, Cheddar's, IHOP, McDonald's, Pizza Hut, Sonic, Waffle House, Wendy's, Comfort Inn, Days Inn, Fairfield Inn, Hampton Inn, Holiday Inn, Hotel Valdosta, Motel 6, New Valdosta Inn, New Valdosta Inn, Super 8, Super Value Inn, Sam's Club/gas, Walmart/Subway/gas, W Inland/Moe's SW/dsl, RaceTrac/dsl/scales/24hr, Austin's Steaks, Briarwood Inn, Kinderlou Inn, Regency Inn
13	Old Clyattville Rd, Valdosta, W Wild Adventures Park
11	GA 31, Valdosta, E LNG, Pilot/Dunkin'/dsl/scales/24hr, Waffle House, Travelers Inn, truckwash, W Quick Gas, $General, tires/repair
5	GA 376, to Lake Park, E BP, Circle K/Stuckey's/dsl, RaceWay/dsl, Chick-fil-A, Cowboys Grill, Domino's, DQ, Farmhouse Rest., Krystal, Lin's Garden Chinese, Rodeo Mexican, Subway, Taco Bell, Waffle House, Zaxby's, Microtel, Motel 6, $Tree, antiques, Day Bros RV Ctr, Eagles Roost Camping, Family$, Horizon RV Ctr, USPO, Winn-Dixie, W Exxon/dsl, Shell, Cracker Barrel, McDonald's, Pizza Hut, Wendy's, Baymont Inn, Days Inn, Hampton Inn, Holiday Inn Express, Quality Inn, Camping World RV Ctr, Lake Park Camping
3mm	**Welcome Ctr nb, full facilities, litter barrels, vending, petwalk,**
2	Lake Park, Bellville, E TA/BP/Popeyes/dsl/scales/24hr/@, DQ, SpeedCo, W Flying J/Subway/dsl/LP/scales/24hr, lube/tires/wash
0mm	Georgia/Florida state line

INTERSTATE 85

Exit #	Services
179mm	Georgia/South Carolina state line, Tugaloo River, Lake Hartwell
177	GA 77 S, to Hartwell, E to Hart SP, W Tugaloo SP
176mm	full facilities, info, litter barrels, petwalk, vending, Welcome Ctr sb
173	GA 17, to Lavonia, E Raceway/dsl, Bojangles, Cracker Barrel, La Cabana Mexican, LongHorn Steaks, McDonald's, Southern Appalachian BBQ, Subway, Taco Bell,

GA

= gas = food = lodging = other = rest stop

INTERSTATE 85 Cont'd

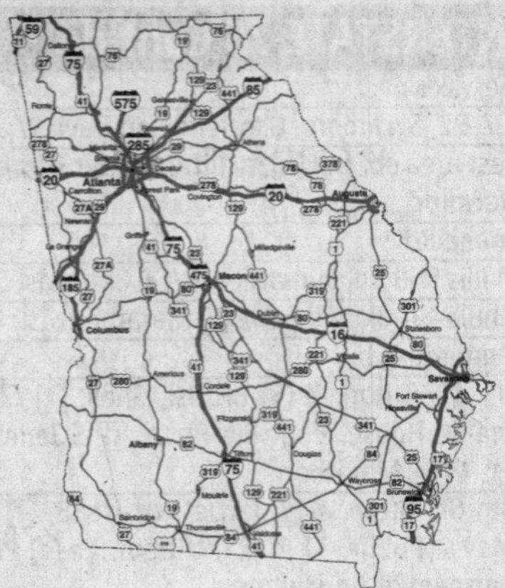

173 Continued
Waffle House, Days Inn, Red Roof Inn, $General, Walgreens, **W** EVC, Exxon/dsl, Burger King, Chick-fil-A, DQ, Dunkin, Hardee's, J Peters Grill, Jas-Sa Korean BBQ, Pizza Hut, Zaxby's, Hampton Inn, Holiday Inn Express, Super 8, to Tugaloo SP, U-Haul

171mm weigh sta nb

169mm weigh sta sb

166 GA 106, to Carnesville, Toccoa, **E** Exxon/dsl, Pilot/Dunkin/DQ/Wendy's/dsl/scales/24hr, Little Caesar's

164 GA 320, to Carnesville

160 GA 51, to Homer, **E** Chevron/Subway/dsl/24hr, to Russell SP, Ty Cobb Museum, Victoria Bryant SP, **W** Flying J/dsl/scales/24hr, Petro/BP/Iron Skillet/dsl/scales/24hr/@, Blue Beacon

154 GA 63, Martin Br Rd

149 US 441, GA 15, to Commerce, Homer, **E** EVC, QT/dsl, TA/Shell/Fuddruckers/dsl/scales/24hr/@, Bojangles, Capt D's, Chipotle, Dunkin, Firehouse, Koji Japanese, Krispy Kreme, Little Caesar's, Longhorn Steaks, Outback Steaks, Papa John's, Seoul Garden, Sonny's BBQ, Taco Bell, Waffle House, Zaxby's, Days Inn, Hampton Inn, Red Roof Inn, Scottish Inn, $Tree, AT&T, Chrysler/Dodge/Jeep, Funopolis, GNC, H, O'Reilly Parts, URGENT CARE, Walmart/Subway/gas, **W** Aamoco Express/dsl, BP/Krystal/dsl, RaceTrac/dsl, Applebee's, Arby's, Burger King, Chick-fil-A, Cracker Barrel, Culver's, DQ, Five Guys, IHOP, La Hacienda, McDonald's, Pizza Hut, Popeyes, Sonic, Starbucks, Subway, Wendy's, Baymont Inn, Best Western, Comfort Suites, Commerce Inn, Country Inn&Suites, Fairfield Inn, Holiday Inn Express, Howard Johnson, Motel 6, Quality Inn, Super 8, Travelodge, Home Depot, Pritchett Tires, Tanger Outlet/famous brands, Verizon

147 GA 98, to Commerce, **E** Citgo/dsl, Love's/Dunkin/dsl/scales/24hr/@, H, **W** Chevron

140 GA 82, Dry Pond Rd, **E** Circle K Trkstp/dsl/scales, Freightliner, **W** Truck Repair

137 US 129, GA 11 to Jefferson, **E** RaceTrac/dsl, Speedway/dsl, Arby's, Bojangles, El Jinete Mexican, KFC/Taco Bell, McDonald's, Waffle House, Zaxby's, Quality Inn, museum, **W** QT/dsl/scales/24hr, Burger King, Subway, Wendy's, flea mkt

129 GA 53, to Braselton, QT/dsl, **E** Chevron/dsl, Shell/Golden Pantry/dsl, Bojangles, La Hacienda Mexican, Waffle House, Best Western, USPO, **W** Pilot/McDonald's/dsl/scales/24hr, RaceTrac/dsl, Cracker Barrel, Domino's, DQ, Dunkin, El Centinela, Popeyes, Stonewall's BBQ, Subway, Taco Bell, Tea Garden Chinese, Wendy's, Zaxby's, La Quinta

126 GA 211, to Chestnut Mtn, **E** Circle K/Burger King/dsl, Circle K/dsl, RaceTrac/dsl, Jack's Rest., Waffle House, Country Inn&Suites, Holiday Inn Express, $General, **W** BP/dsl, EVC, Chateau Elan Winery/rest., China Garden, Papa John's, Tesla EVC, Baymont Inn, Hampton Inn, Publix, vet

120 to GA 124, Hamilton Mill Rd, **E** BP, Chevron, QT/dsl, Arby's, Buffalo's Café, Burger King, Cane's Chicken, Caprese Rest., Firehouse Subs, Five Guys, Iron Wok, J. Christopher's, McDonald's, Menchie's, Moe's SW Grill, Riverside Pizza, Starbucks, Waffle House, Wendy's, Wild Wing Cafe, Zaxby's, ALDI, auto repair, Home Depot, Kohl's, Petco, Publix/Deli, RV World of GA(1mi), vet, **W** Chevron, EVC, Murphy USA/dsl, Shell/dsl, Barberito's, Chick-fil-A, Chili's, Dunkin, El Molcajate, Italy's Pizza, Little Caesar's, Philly Bistro, Starbucks, Taco Bell, $Tree, Advance Parts, AT&T,

120 Continued
CVS Drug, O'Reilly Parts, Tires+, USPO, Verizon, Walmart/Subway

118 GA 324, Gravel Springs Rd, **E** QT/dsl

115 GA 20, to Buford Dam, **E** QT, Bubba's 33, Culver's, Five Guys, Gusto, JINYA Ramen, Mambo's Cafe, MOD Pizza, Popeyes, The Halal Guys, Waffle House, Whataburger, Pepboys, Sprouts Mkt, vet, **W** Tesla EVC, Atlanta Bread, Blaze Pizza, Bonefish Grill, Burger 21, Burger King, Cane's Chicken, CAVA, Cheesecake Factory, Chick-fil-A, Chicken Salad Chick, Chili's, Chipotle, ChuckeCheese, Del Taco, East Coast Wings, Einstein's Bagels, First Watch, Honeybaked Ham, Hooters, It's Just Wings, Kani House, Krispy Kreme, la Madeleine, Longhorn Steaks, Macaroni Grill, McDonald's, Moe's SW Grill, Olive Garden, On-the-Border, Panda Express, Panera Bread, Parma Tavern, PF Chang's, Provino's Italian, Red Lobster, Rockin Crab, Seasons 52, Shogun Japanese, Sonny's BBQ, Starbucks, Steak n' Shake, Subway, Tacos & Tequilas, Ted's MT Grill, TX Roadhouse, Waffle House, WEI Chinese, Wendy's, Which Wich?, Country Inn&Suites, Courtyard, Fairfield Inn, Hampton Inn, SpringHill Suites, $Tree, AT&T, Barnes&Noble, Belk, Best Buy, Buick/GMC, Costco/gas, Dick's, Dillard's, Discount Tire, Firestone, Firestone/auto, Honda, Hyundai, JC Penney, Lowe's, Macy's, Marshall's, Mazda, Michael's, Nissan, Nordstrom Rack, PetCo, PetSmart, REI, Ross, Sam's Club/gas, Staples, SteinMart, Target/Starbucks, TJ Maxx, to Lake Lanier Islands, Toyota, Tuesday Morning, U-Haul, Verizon, Volvo, Von Maur, VW, Walmart/gas

113 I-985 N(from nb), to Gainesville

111 GA 317, to Suwanee, **E** BP/dsl, Texaco/dsl, Arby's, Champs Chicken, Checker's, Cracker Barrel, Dunkin Donuts, Korean BBQ, Mandoo Korean, Outback Steaks, Philly Connection, Pizza Hut, Schlotsky's, Station Master Sushi, Taco Bell, Umaido Ramen, Waffle House, Wendy's, Comfort Suites, Courtyard, Fairfield Inn, InTown Suites, Motel 6, Quality Inn, GNC, O'Reilly Parts, **W** Chevron/dsl, QT/dsl, Raceway/dsl, Shell, Tesla EVC, Betos, Bonbon Chicken, Burger King, Chick-fil-A, Dunkin Donuts, HoneyBaked Ham, IHOP, Jimmy John's, KFC, Kyuramen - Suwanee, Main Event, McDonald's, Moe's SW Grill, Panda Express, Popeyes, Smoothie King, Sonic, Starbucks, Taco Mac, TODAM Asian, Two Cities Pizza, Your Pie Pizza, Zaxby's, Red Roof Inn, Super 8, $Tree, Advance Parts, Lowe's, Office Depot, Penn Sta Subs, Walmart/Subway/gas

109 Old Peachtree Rd, **E** QT, Bojangles, Fini's Pizza, Hong Kong Chinese, Kirin House Japanese, McAlister's, McDonald's, Hampton Inn, Home2 Suites, Homewood Suites, Bass Pro Shops, Publix, **W** BP, Carrabba's, Chick-fil-A, Cuts Steaks, Embassy Suites, Firehouse Subs, Five Guys, Jim&Nicks BBQ, Starbucks, Subway, Waffle House,

GA

INTERSTATE 85 Cont'd

109 Continued
Courtyard, Hilton Garden, Holiday Inn, Residence Inn, O AT&T, Home Depot

108 Sugarloaf Pkwy (from nb), E Hampton Inn, Home2 Suites, Homewood Suites, W Carrabba's, Chick-fil-A, Courtyard, Embassy Suites, Hilton Garden, Holiday Inn, Residence Inn, O Gwinnett Civic Ctr

107 GA 120, to GA 316 E, Athens, E EVC, Shell, Burger King, Dave&Busters, Dunkin, Fresh Bowl Thai, Pappadeaux Seafood, Pepe's Mexican, Red Crawfish, Zaxby's, Zuarepa Venezuelan, Aloft, Tru, O $Tree, Bass Pro Shops, Books-a-Million, Burlington Coats, CVS, Discount Tire, Ross, Saks 5th Ave, W BP/dsl, Chevron, Bojangles, China Gate, McDonald's, Subway, Waffle House, La Quinta, Suburban Lodge

106 Boggs Rd(from sb, no return), Duluth, W QT/dsl/24hr, O Mercedes

104 Pleasant Hill Rd, E Chevron/e85, QT/dsl, Shell/dsl, Valero/dsl, Bahama Breeze, Burger King, Chick-fil-A, Costas Nayaritas, East Pearl, GA Diner, Hibachi Buffet, Korean BBQ, Mariscos Mazatlan, McDonald's, Popeyes, Schlotsky's, Starbucks, Stevi B's Pizza, Subway, TGIFriday's, Volcano Steak & Sushi, Waffle House, Wendy's, Who's Got Soul, Best Western, Candlewood Suites, Clarion Suites, Fairfield Inn, Hampton Inn Suites, Holiday Inn Express, Residence Inn, Sonesta, O $General, $Tree, Advance Parts, Best Buy, Family$, Home Depot, PepBoys, Publix, URGENT CARE, Walgreens, W BP/Dunkin/dsl, Chevron/dsl, Texaco/dsl, Applebee's, Arby's, Burger King, Checker's, Chili's, Chipotle Mexican, Einstein Bros., Golden Corral, Hooters, IHOP, Jersey Mike's, Jimmy John's, KFC, Krispy Kreme, la Madeleine, McDonald's, Melting Pot, Olive Garden, Panda Express, Red Lobster, Starbucks, Subway, Taco Bell, Wendy's, Courtyard, Extended Stay America, Haven Hotel, Quality Inn, Sonesta Select, Wingate Inn, Wyndham Garden, O AT&T, Audi, BMW, Buick/GMC, Firestone/auto, Ford, Goodyear/auto, Honda, Hyundai, Infiniti, Kia, Macy's, Marshall's, Nissan, PetCo, Subaru, TJ Maxx, Toyota, Verizon

103 Steve Reynolds Blvd(from nb, no return), W QT/dsl, Shell, Dave&Buster's, Waffle House, InTown Suites, O $Tree, Big Lots, Costco/gas, Kohl's, PetSmart, Sam's Club, same as 104

102 GA 378, Beaver Ruin Rd, E QT, RaceTrac/dsl, Shell/dsl, Valero/dsl, Subway

101 Lilburn Rd, E QT, Shell/dsl, Bruster's, Burger King, Domino's, Jimmy John's, KFC, Krystal, Las Islitas, McDonald's/playplace, Smoothie King, Starbucks, Taco Bell, Waffle House, Guesthouse Inn, InTown Suites, Super 8, O Jones RV Park, W Chevron, Marathon/dsl, American Wings, Arby's, Dos Carlos Mexican, Papa John's, Pizza Plaza, Wendy's, Knights Inn, Red Roof Inn, O CarMax, Chrysler/Dodge/Jeep, Lowe's

99 GA 140, Jimmy Carter Blvd, E QT, Shell/dsl, Checker's, Chick-fil-A, Chipotle, Cracker Barrel, Denny's, Dunkin, McDonald's, Papa John's, Pollo Campero, Starbucks, Subway, Taco Bell, Wingstop, Araamda Inn, Baymont, Congress Suites, Extended Stay, Horizon Inn, Motel 6, Sonesta Hotel, O Advance Parts, U-Haul, Walgreens, W QT/dsl, Shell/Dunkin/dsl, Hibachi Grill, Juicy Crawfish, Pappadeaux Steak/seafood, Sonic, Waffle House, Wendy's, Country Inn&Suites, Days Inn, Hampton Inn, Microtel, O AutoZone, Mavis, O'Reilly Parts, PepBoys

96 Pleasantdale Rd, Northcrest Rd, E Burger King, Pleasantdale Chinese, W Exxon/dsl, QT/dsl, Subway,

CHATTANOOGA ATLANTA AIRPORT

96 Continued
Atlanta Lodge

95 I-285

94 Chamblee-Tucker Rd, E Chevron/Subway/dsl, Shell/dsl, Masters Inn, O to Mercer U, W QT/dsl, DQ, McDonald's, Waffle House, Extended Stay, Motel 6, Super 8

93 Shallowford Rd, to Doraville, E Shell, Hop Shing Chinese, Marco's Pizza, Subway, O Publix, U-Haul, W Shell/dsl, Quality Inn

91 US 23, GA 155, Clairmont Rd, E Chevron/dsl, QT/dsl, IHOP, Mo's Pizza, O URGENT CARE, W BP, McDonald's, Waffle House, Extended Stay America, Holiday Inn Express, Marriott, O NTB, Sam's Club/gas, U-Haul

89 GA 42, N Druid Hills, E Chevron/Subway/dsl, QT, Shell/dsl, Arby's, Boston Mkt, Burger King, CAVA, Chick-fil-A, Einstein Bros., El Torero, Hopdoddy Burger, Jersey Mike's, McDonald's, Moe's SW Grill, Panera Bread, Penn Sta Subs, Starbucks, Taco Bell, Tin Roof Cantina, Willy's Mexicana, Courtyard, O $Tree, Firestone/auto, GNC, Target, Walgreens, W Chevron/dsl, Exxon/dsl, HoneyBaked Ham, McDonald's, Waffle House, DoubleTree, Hampton Inn, Red Roof+, O CVS Drug

88 Lenox Rd, GA 400 N, Cheshire Br Rd(from sb), E Mobil, Valero/dsl, McDonald's, La Quinta

87 GA 400 N(from nb)

86 GA 13 S, Peachtree St, E BP, Chevron, Gino's Pizza, Mamas Mexican, Papa John's, Starbucks, Wendy's, O Sprouts Mkt, vet

85 I-75 N, to Marietta, Chattanooga

84 Techwood Dr, 14th St, E EVC, Shell, Einstein Bros Bagels, Farm Burger, Starbucks, Subway, Four Seasons, Hampton Inn, Marriott, O Whole Foods Mkt/EVC, W Crazy Cuban, Goodfellas, Jimmy Johns, Silver Skillet, Wagaya Japanese, Sonesta

77 I-75 S

76 Cleveland Ave, E Citgo/dsl, Burger King, Papa John's, O $General, $Tree, AutoZone, BigLots, Kroger, Walgreens, W Chevron/dsl, Chrvron/dsl, Chick-fil-A, Church's TX Chicken, Little Caesars, McDonald's, Popeyes, O H, O'Reilly Parts, Walmart/Subway/EVC/gas

75 Sylvan Rd, E Shell/dsl, InCity Suites

74 Loop Rd, O Aviation Commercial Center

73b a Virginia Ave, E Citgo/dsl, RaceTrac, Dunkin, Jimmy John's, Jonny's Pizza, Lickety Split, Malone's Grill, McDonald's, Moe's SW Grill, Ruby Tuesday, Schlotsky's, Skinny's, Spondivit's Rest., Waffle House, Wendy's, Willy's Mexican, Your Pie Pizza, Courtyard, Drury Inn, Hilton, La Quinta, Renaissance Hotel, Residence Inn, W Chevron/Subway, Shell, Arby's, BBQ Kitchen, Blimpie, Happy Buddha Chinese, KFC, La Fiesta Mexican, Louisiana Bistreaux Seafood, Mellow Mushroom, Waffle House, Country Inn&Suites, Crowne Plaza, DoubleTree, EconoLodge, Fairfield Inn, Hampton Inn, Hilton Garden, Holiday Inn, Holiday Inn, Home2 Suites, Homewood Suites, Hyatt Place, Motel 6, Sonesta, Staybridge Inn, TownePlace Suites/EVC

72 Camp Creek Pkwy, W Marriott, Renaissance, Tru

71 Riverdale Rd, Atlanta Airport, E Ruby Tuesday, Comfort Inn/EVC, Courtyard, Fairfield Inn, Hyatt Place, La Quinta, Microtel, Quality Inn, Sheraton/grill, Sleep Inn, Sonesta, W Days Inn, Embassy Suites, Hilton Garden, Holiday Inn Express, Marriott, Raddison, Westin Hotel

70 I-85 (from sb)

69 GA 14, GA 279, Red Snapper, E Chevron/dsl, Citgo, Shell/dsl, Valero, Bojangles, Burger King, Captain D's, Checker's, Chillz Grill, China Cafe, Church's TX Chicken, Cozumel, KFC, Krystal, McDonald's, Memphis Diva BBQ,

GA

INTERSTATE 85 Cont'd

69 Continued
Piccadilly Cafeteria, Taco Bell, Waffle House, Wendy's, Baymont Inn, Quality Inn, Ramada, Red Roof+, Super 8, Travelodge, AutoZone, Best America, Family$, U-Haul, URGENT CARE, **W** Chevron/dsl, Shell, Waffle House, EconoLodge, $General

68 I-285 Atlanta Perimeter (from nb)

66 Flat Shoals Rd, **E** Exxon, **W** BP/Circle K, Chevron/dsl, Shell, King's Rest., Waffle House, Motel 6, Family$

64 GA 138, to Union City, **E** BP/dsl, Exxon, Exxon, Exxon, RaceTrac/dsl, Waffle House, EconoLodge, Western Inn, BMW/Mini, Chevrolet, Chrysler/Dodge/Jeep, CVS Drug, EVC, Ford/Lincoln, Honda, Infiniti, Kia/Nissan, Lexus, Toyota, VW, **W** Chevron/dsl, EVC, QT, Shell/dsl, Arby's, Burger King, Capt D's, China Garden, Corner Cafe, Dunkin/Baskin Robbins, IHOP, KFC, Krystal, McDonald's, Papa John's, Pizza Hut, Popeyes, Sonic, Steak 'n Shake, Subway, Taco Bell, Wendy's, Zaxby's, Country Hearth Inn, Days Inn, Garden Inn, La Quinta, Quality Inn, Stay Express, $Tree, Advance Parts, ALDI, BigLots, Firestone/auto, Jiffy Lube, Kroger/dsl, Mavis Tires, O'Reilly Parts, Pep Boys, Take 5 Oil Change, vet, Walgreens, Walmart/Subway

61 GA 74, to Fairburn, **E** BP/dsl/scales/24hr, QT/dsl, RaceWay/dsl, Shell, Tesla Charger, Bojangle's, Chick-fil-A, Chipotle, Cracker Barrel, Dunkin, Krystal, Marco's Pizza, McDonald's, Starbucks, Subway, Taco Bell, Waffle House, Wendy's, Zaxby's, Best Western+, Country Inn&Suites, Fairfield Inn, Hampton Inn, Holiday Inn Express, Wingate Inn, AutoZone Parts, Fairburn Tires, URGENT CARE, vet, **W** Chevron/dsl, Sun Petro/dsl, Texaco, Efficiency Motel, AT&T

56 Collinsworth Rd, **W** Chevron/dsl, Shell, Frank's Rest., South Oaks Camping

51 GA 154, to Sharpsburg, **E** Marathon/dsl, Texaco/Subway/dsl, Hardee's, **W** Chevron/dsl, Shell/Circle K/dsl, Waffle House

47 GA 34, to Newnan, **E** Chevron/dsl, Marathon/dsl, QT, QT, Shell/dsl, Applebee's, Arby's, Bruster's Creamery, Capt D's, Chipotle, Dunkin, Fried Tomato Buffet, Hooters, La Hacienda, Longhorn Steaks, Marco's Pizza, Panda Express, Popeyes, Red Lobster, Starbucks, Steak'n Shake, TX Roadhouse, Waffle House, Wendy's, Country Inn&Suites, Hampton Inn, Quality Inn, Springhill Suites, WoodSpring Suites, ALDI, GNC, Goodyear/auto, Hobby Lobby, Home Depot, H, Kohl's, Lowe's, Mavis Tires, PetSmart, Walmart, **W** EVC, RaceTrac/dsl, Tesla Charger, Buffalo Wild Wings, Burger King, Chick-fil-A, Chicken Salad Chick, Coldstone, Cracker Barrel, Crumbl Cookies, Culver's, Dunkin, Einstein Bagels, Firehouse Subs, Five Guys, Goldberg's Deli, Golden Corral, HoneyBaked Ham, IHOP, Jimmy John's, KFC, Krystal, La Parrilla Mexican, Newk's Cafe, O'Charley's, Olive Garden, Panera Bread, Red Robin, Shane's BBQ, Starbucks, Subway, Taco Bell, Taco Mac, Tokyo Japanese, Zaxby's, Best Western, Candlewood Suites, Comfort Suites, Holiday Inn, Home2 Suites, La Quinta, Motel 6, Red Roof Inn, Sleep Inn, TownePlace Suites, $General, $Tree, AT&T, Barnes&Noble, Belk, Best Buy, BigLots, BJ's Whse/gas, Buick/Cadillac/GMC, Chevrolet, Dick's, Dillards, Ford/Lincoln, Honda, Hyundai, JC Penney, Michael's, Office Depot, Old Navy, Publix, Target, Tires+, TJ Maxx, Toyota, Verizon, vet, Walgreens

NEWNAN

44 Poplar Rd, **E** RaceTrac, Burger King, Chik-fil-A, Dunkin, H

41 US 27/29, Newnan, **E** Pilot/Wendy's/Subway/dsl/scales/24hr, Little White House NHS, Roosevelt SP, **W** BP/dsl, El Taquito Mexican, McDonald's, Waffle House,

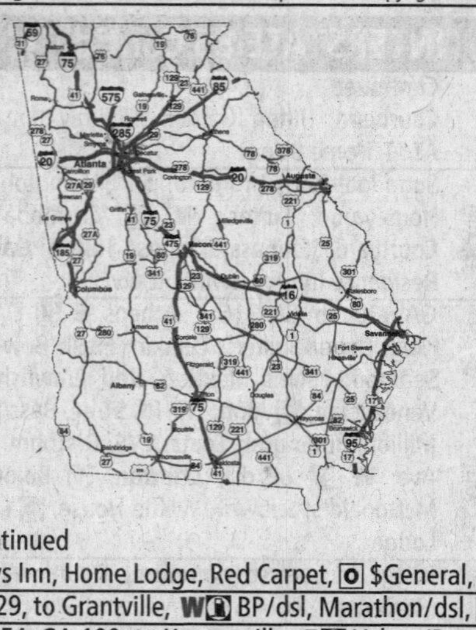

NEWNAN

41 Continued
Days Inn, Home Lodge, Red Carpet, $General, repair

35 US 29, to Grantville, **W** BP/dsl, Marathon/dsl, $Gene

28 GA 54, GA 100, to Hogansville, **E** Valero/Burger King/d **W** Love's/Arby's/dsl/scales/24hr, Marathon/dsl, Shell/ McDonald's, Roger's BBQ, Subway, Waffle Hou Wendy's, Garden Inn, Woodstream Inn, Ingles

23mm Beech Creek

22mm weigh sta both lanes

21 I-185 S, to Columbus

18 GA 109, to Mountville, **E** Marathon/Little Caesa Dunkin, Rodeway Inn, Wingate Inn, Little White Hou HS, to FDR SP, **W** BP/dsl, Exxon/Circle K/dsl, RaceTrac/d Valero, Banzai Japanese, Burger King, Chick-fil-A, Chick Salad Chick, Chipotle, Cracker Barrel, Firehouse Subs, IHC Juanito's Mexican, Longhorn Steaks, Los Nopal McDonald's, Moe's SW Grill, Popeyes, Sonic, Starbuc Subway, Taco Bell, Waffle House, Wendy's, Zaxby's, Baymont Inn, Comfort Inn, Holiday Inn Express, La Quin Lafayette Garden Inn, Motel 6, Quality Inn, AT&T, Be Chrysler/Dodge/Jeep, Ford/Lincoln, Hobby Lobby, Hon Depot, Honda, Hyundai, Pep Boys, TJ Maxx, Verizon

14 US 27, to La Grange, **W** Exxon, Marathon, Shell/Summ dsl, Waffle House, Hampton Inn

13 GA 219, to La Grange, **E** Exxon/dsl/scales/24hr, R Roof Inn, **W** Chevron/Circle K, Arbys, Dunki McDonald's, Waffle House, Wendy's Great Wolf Lodg Home2 Suites, H

10mm Long Cane Creek

6 Kia Blvd, **W** TA Express Travel Center

2 GA 18, to West Point, **E** Chevron/dsl, **Love's/Hardee' dsl/scales/24hr**, Shell/Summit/dsl, Red Roof Inn, **W** BP/dsl, Subway(1.5), camping, to West Point Lake

0.5mm **Welcome Ctr nb, full facilities, litter barre vending, petwalk, EVC**

0mm Georgia/Alabama state line, Chattahoochee River

INTERSTATE 95

113mm Georgia/South Carolina state line, Savannah River

111mm **full facilities, info, litter barrels, petwalk, vending, Welcome Ctr/weigh sta sb**

109 GA 21, to Savannah, Pt Wentworth, Rincon, **E** Enmark/d Pilot/McDonald's/Subway/dsl/scales/24hr, Waffle Hous Best Western, Country Inn&Suites, Fairfield Inn, Hampt Inn, Mulberry Grove Inn, Frieghtliner, **W** Fast Mkt/d Murphy Express/dsl, Shell/Circle K/Blimpie/dsl, Agav Mexican, Bojangles, Dunkin, El Ranchito, Happy Wok, Mila Grill, Taco Bell, Wendy's, Zaxby's, Baymont Inn, Comfo Suites, Days Inn, Holiday Inn Express, Home2 Suites, Re Roof Inn, Savannah Inn, Sleep Inn, Wingate Inn, Advan Parts, CVS Drug, Family$, Food Lion,

INTERSTATE 95 Cont'd

109 Continued
Whispering Pines RV Park(3mi)

107mm Augustine Creek

106 Jimmy DeLoach Pkwy

104 Savannah Airport, E BP, Shell/Wendy's/dsl, Sam Sneed's Grill, Waffle House, Candlewood Suites, Comfort Suites, Country Inn&Suites, DoubleTree, Fairfield Inn, Hampton Inn, Hilton Garden, Holiday Inn Express, Hyatt Place, SpringHill Suites, Staybridge Suites, TownePlace Suites, Tru, Wingate Inn, to, W Murphy USA, Shell/Subway, Applebee's, Arby's, Buffalo Wild Wings, Captain D's, Cheddar's, Chick-fil-A, Chicken Salad Chick, Chili's, Chipotle, Church's TX Chicken, CookOut, Culver's, DQ, El Mezcal Mexican, Firehouse Subs, First Watch, Five Guys, Hilliard's Rest., IHOP, Jalapeños, Jersey Mike's, Jim'N Nick's BBQ, Little Caesar's, Logan's Roadhouse, Longhorn Steaks, McAlister's Deli, McDonald's, Mellow Mushroom, Metro Diner, Moe's SW, Olive Garden, Panda Express, Panera Bread, Ruby Tuesday, Shane's Rib Shack, Sonic, Starbucks, Taco Bell, TX Roadhouse, Wild Wing Cafe, Zaxby's, Aloft, Courtyard, Embassy Suites, Holiday Inn, Homewood Suites, Red Roof Inn, Residence Inn, ALDI, AT&T, Chevrolet, Dick's, GNC, Goodyear, Hobby Lobby, Home Depot, Michael's, PetSmart, Publix, Ross, Sam's Club/gas, Savannah Tire, Tanger Outlets/famous brands, TJ Maxx, URGENT CARE, Verizon, Walmart/McDonald's

102 US 80, to Garden City, E Enmarket/dsl, Flash/Circle K/dsl, Shell, Bewon Korean BBQ, Bojangles, Carlito's Mexican, Cracker Barrel, Dickey's BBQ, Guerrero Mexican, KFC, Krystal, Los Bravos Mexican, McDonald's, Peking Chinese, Spanky's, Subway, Taco Bell, Terra Mia Italian, Waffle House, Baymont, Best Western, Microtel, Motel 6, Quality Inn, air force museum, Camping World RV Ctr, Family$, Food Lion, to Ft Pulaski NM, W Chevron, Gate/dsl, Marathon, Burger King, Domino's, El Potro Mexican, Hardee's, Lovezzola's Pizza, Omelette Cafe, Pizza Hut, Wendy's, Western Sizzlin, Best Western, Cottonwood Suites, La Quinta, Magnolia Inn, Sleep Inn, $General

99b a I-16, W to Macon, E to Savannah

94 GA 204, to Savannah, Pembroke, E 76/dsl/e85, BP/dsl, Exxon, Murphy USA/dsl(2mi), Shell/dsl, Applebee's, Cracker Barrel, Denny's, Hardee's, Houlihan's, IHOP, McDonald's, Perkins, Ruby Tuesday, Sonic, avid, Baymont Inn, Best Inn, Best Western, Clarion, Comfort Suites, Country Inn Suites, Econolodge, Fairfield Inn, Hampton Inn, Holiday Inn, Howard Johnson, Motel 6, OneWay, Quality Inn, San's Boutique Hotel, Scottish Inn, Sleep Inn, SpringHill Suites, Super 8, Wingate, Factory Stores/Famous Brands, GNC, H, Walmart(2mi), W Marathon/dsl, Sunoco, Flacos Mexican, Hooters, Shellhouse Rest, Subway, Waffle House, Days Inn, Red Roof+, Harley-Davidson, Indian Motorcycles, Savannah Oaks RV Park(2mi)

91mm Ogeechee River

90 GA 144, Old Clyde Rd, to Ft Stewart, Richmond Hill SP, E BP, Exxon/dsl, DQ, Jalapeno's, Pizza Hut, Starbucks, Taco Bell, Zaxby's, AT&T, Kroger/deli/dsl, URGENT CARE, Verizon, W Love's/McDonald's/dsl/scales/24hr, auto repair, Gore's RV Ctr, International

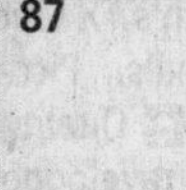

87 US 17, to Coastal Hwy, Richmond Hill, E BP/Subway/EVC, Chevron/dsl, RaceWay/dsl, Bubbas Bistro, China 1, Denny's, Domino's, Fuji Japanese, Papa Murphy's, Smokin' Pig BBQ, The Local Steaks, Days Inn, Motel 6, Royal Inn, Scottish Inn, Travelodge, Food Lion, URGENT CARE, W Marathon/McDonald's, Shell/dsl, Sunoco/dsl, TA/BP/Pizza Hut/Popeyes/dsl/scales/24hr/@, Arby's, Flacos Mexican,

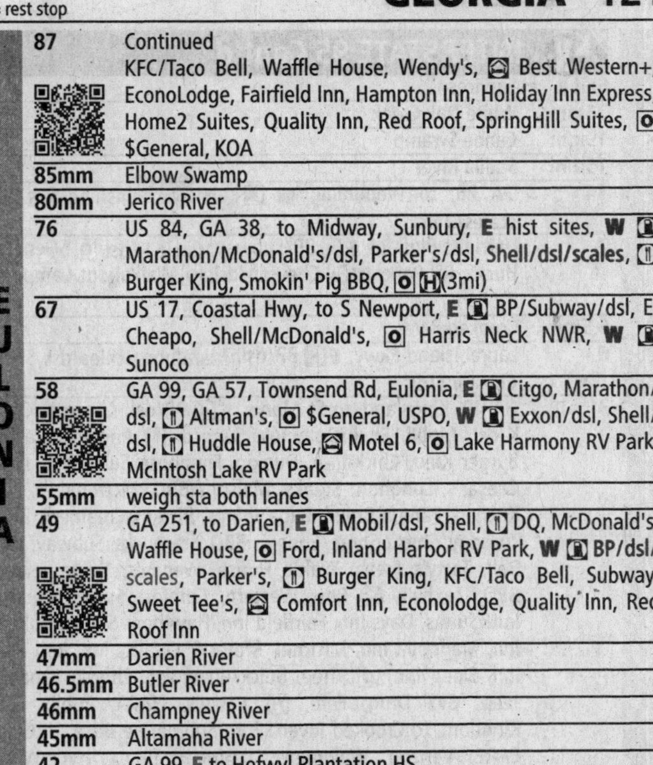

87 Continued
KFC/Taco Bell, Waffle House, Wendy's, Best Western+, EconoLodge, Fairfield Inn, Hampton Inn, Holiday Inn Express, Home2 Suites, Quality Inn, Red Roof, SpringHill Suites, $General, KOA

85mm Elbow Swamp

80mm Jerico River

76 US 84, GA 38, to Midway, Sunbury, E hist sites, W Marathon/McDonald's/dsl, Parker's/dsl, Shell/dsl/scales, Burger King, Smokin' Pig BBQ, H(3mi)

67 US 17, Coastal Hwy, to S Newport, E BP/Subway/dsl, El Cheapo, Shell/McDonald's, Harris Neck NWR, W Sunoco

EULONIA

58 GA 99, GA 57, Townsend Rd, Eulonia, E Citgo, Marathon/dsl, Altman's, $General, USPO, W Exxon/dsl, Shell/dsl, Huddle House, Motel 6, Lake Harmony RV Park, McIntosh Lake RV Park

55mm weigh sta both lanes

49 GA 251, to Darien, E Mobil/dsl, Shell, DQ, McDonald's, Waffle House, Ford, Inland Harbor RV Park, W BP/dsl/scales, Parker's, Burger King, KFC/Taco Bell, Subway, Sweet Tee's, Comfort Inn, Econolodge, Quality Inn, Red Roof Inn

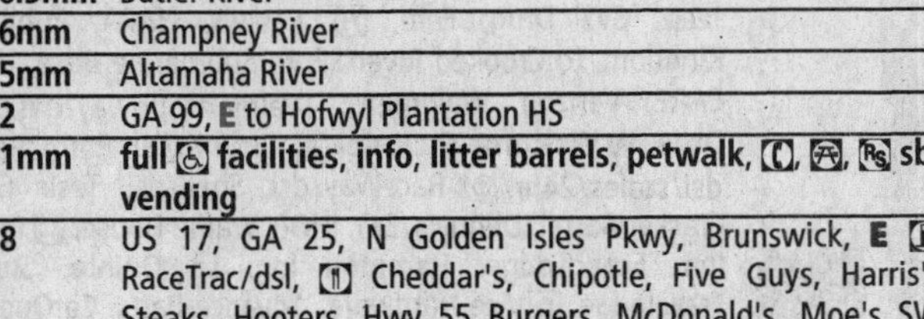

47mm Darien River

46.5mm Butler River

46mm Champney River

45mm Altamaha River

42 GA 99, E to Hofwyl Plantation HS

41mm **full facilities, info, litter barrels, petwalk, sb, vending**

38 US 17, GA 25, N Golden Isles Pkwy, Brunswick, E RaceTrac/dsl, Cheddar's, Chipotle, Five Guys, Harris's Steaks, Hooters, Hwy 55 Burgers, McDonald's, Moe's SW Grill, Panda Express, Panera Bread, Comfort Suites, Country Inn&Suites, Embassy Suites(2mi), Fairfield Inn, Holiday Inn, Microtel, Residence Inn, H, Nissan, Sam's Club/gas, W Flash/Circle K, Marathon/dsl, Parker's, Shell/dsl, China Town, Subway, Toucan's, Waffle House, Willie Jewell's BBQ, Best Western+, Courtyard/Tesla EVC, Guest Cottage Motel, Hampton Inn, Hilton Garden, Home2 Suites, La Quinta, Quality Inn, Sleep Inn, SureStay, $Tree, Toyota/Scion, Winn Dixie

BRUNSWICK

36b a US 25, US 341, to Jesup, Brunswick, E Chevron/Subway/dsl, Exxon/dsl, RaceWay/dsl, Cookout, Cracker Barrel, KFC, Krystal, McDonald's, Popeyes, Starbucks, Sunrise Diner, Taco Bell, Waffle House, Wendy's, Days Inn, Motel 6, Oneway Inn, Paragon, Pizza Hut, Red Roof Inn, Wingate, Jack's Tires, W Parker's/dsl, Shell/dsl, 1800 Mexican, Econolodge, Jay's Fish & Chicken, Larry's Subs, Minh Sun Chinese, Sonny's BBQ, Clarion, Comfort Inn, Economy Inn, Sheraton, Super 8, WoodSpring Suites, $General, Advance Parts, AutoZone, CVS Drug, Family$, URGENT CARE, Winn-Dixie

33mm Turtle River

30mm S Brunswick River

29 US 17, US 82, GA 520, S GA Pkwy, Brunswick, E Exxon/DQ/dsl, Flash, Love's/Godfather's/Subway/Chester's/dsl/scales/24hr, Mobil/dsl, QT/dsl, Jack's Mexican, Jay's Fish & Chicken, McDonald's, Zaxby's, Comfort Suites, Blue Beacon, SpeedCo, W Flying J/Denny's/dsl/LP/scales/24hr, Shell/Dunkin/dsl, TA/BP/Burger King/Starbucks/Subway/dsl/24hr, Domino's, Larry's Subs, Waffle House, Best Value, EconoLodge, Super 8, $General, Family$, Southern Retreat RV Park, TA Truck Service, Winn Dixie

27.5mm Little Satilla River

26 Dover Bluff Rd, E Mobil/Stuckey's/dsl

22 Horse Stamp Church Rd

GA

= gas = food = lodging = other = rest stop

INTERSTATE 95 Cont'd

Exit #	Services
21mm	White Oak Creek
19mm	Canoe Swamp
15mm	Satilla River
14	GA 25, to Woodbine, W Chevron/Sunshine/rest/dsl/scales/24hr
7	Harrietts Bluff Rd, E BP/Subway, Circle K/dsl, $General, Huck's RV Park, W Chevron/dsl, Walkabout Camping/RV Park
6.5mm	Crooked River
6	Laurel Island Pkwy, E BP/dsl, Marathon/scales/dsl, Shell/Chester's/dsl
3	GA 40, Kingsland, to St Marys, E BP/dsl, Chevron, Circle K/dsl, Mobil, Shell/Dominos, Sunoco, Angelo's Italian, Burger King, Chick-fil-A, Dunkin, Firehouse Subs, KFC, Little Caesar's, Longhorn Steaks, Malsons BBQ, McDonald's, OPS Kitchen, Panera Bread, Papa John's, Ritter's Creamery, Ruby Tuesday, Ship 2 Shore, Sonny's BBQ, Starbucks, Subway, Taco Bell, Tasty's Fresh, Waffle House, Wendy's, Willie Jewells BBQ, Zaxby's, Best Western, Comfort Suites, Country Inn&Suites, Days Inn, Fairfield Inn, Hawthorn Suites, Holiday Inn, Magnolia Inn, Microtel, Motel 6, Quality Inn, Red Roof Inn, Sleep Inn, $Tree, Buick/Chevrolet, Chrysler/Dodge/Jeep, CVS Drug, Ford, H, Lowe's, NAPA, Publix, Tire Kingdom, to Crooked River SP, to Submarine Base, URGENT CARE, Verizon, Walgreens, Walmart/Subway/gas, Winn-Dixie, W **Welcome Ctr/info**, Circle K/dsl, Petro/Popeyes/dsl/scales/24hr/@, RaceWay/dsl, Shell/dsl, Tesla EVC, Cracker Barrel, Denny's, DQ, IHOP, Waffle House, Baymont Inn, EconoLodge, Hampton Inn, La Quinta, Super 8, Travelodge, Ace Hardware, Advance Parts, CarQuest, Kiki RV Park
1	St Marys Rd, to Cumberland Is Nat Seashore, E **Welcome Ctr nb, full facilities, vending, litter barrels, petwalk**, Pilot/Subway/PJ Fresh/dsl/scales/24hr, South Link/dsl, W BP/dsl, Pilot/Dunkin/Wendy's/dsl/scales/24hr, Shell/dsl, Country Oaks RV Park, KOA
0mm	Georgia/Florida state line, St Marys River, Scrubby Bluff Bridge

INTERSTATE 185 (Columbus)

Exit #	Services
48	I-85. I-185 begins/ends on I-85.
46	Big Springs Rd, E Shell/dsl, W Citgo, tires
42	US 27, Pine Mountain, E Marathon/dsl, Shell/dsl, Little White House HS, Pine Mtn Camping, to Callaway Gardens
34	GA 18, to West Point, E Chevron, to Callaway Gardens
30	Hopewell Church Rd, Whitesville, W Shell/dsl, $General
25	GA 116, to Hamilton, W RV camping (3mi)
19	GA 315, Mulberry Grove, W Chevron/dsl, $General
14	Smith Rd
12	Williams Rd, W **Welcome Ctr/rest rooms**, Chevron, Summit/dsl, Country Inn&Suites, Microtel
10	US 80, GA 22, to Phenix City, W Springer Opera House
8	Airport Thruway, E Bojangles, $Tree, Home Depot, Walmart/Subway, W Circle K/dsl, Circle K/dsl, Applebee's, Baskin Robbins, Blue Iguana, Blue Iguana Grill, Burger King, Cafe Le Rue, Capt D's, Chicken Salad Chick, Country Road Buffet, Hardee's, Houlihan's, IHOP, McDonald's, Mikata Japanese, Taco Bell, Baymont, Comfort Suites, DoubleTree, Extended Stay America, Sleep Inn, BigLots, Office Depot, U-Haul
7	45th St, Manchester Expswy, E EVC, Applebee's, Burger King, Cook Out, Krystal, Ruby Tuesday, Sapo's Mexican, Courtyard, La Quinta, Super 8,

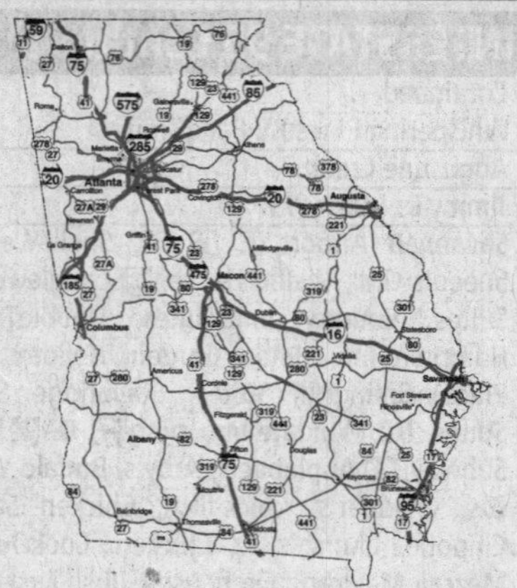

Exit #	Services
7	Continued Cadillac/Chevrolet, Dillard's, JCPenney, Macy's, mall, W BP/dsl, Chevron/dsl, Circle K, Circle K/dsl, Liberty, Liberty, Arby's, Chick-fil-A, Del Taco, Dunkin, Jersey Mike's, K Little Caesar's, McDonald's, Smoothie King, Sonic, Starbuc Subway, Waffle House, Fairfield Inn, Holiday I TownePlace Suites, $General, $General, Advance Pa auto repair, Big C Tire/repair, Civil War Naval Museum, Midas
6	GA 22, Macon Rd, E Chevron/dsl, Circle K/dsl, Burg King, DQ, Guthrie's Chicken, Marco's Pizza, Waffle House, Comfort Inn, Days Inn, Quality Inn, $General, U-Ha USPO, vet, Walgreens, W Chevron/dsl, Shell/dsl, Ca D's, Chipotle, ChuckeCheese, Cici's, Country's BBQ, Denny Dunkin'/Baskin Robbins, Firehouse Subs, Jimmy John Longhorn Steaks, McDonald's, Panera Bread, Smoothie Kir Starbucks, Subway, Taco Bell, Zaxby's, Efficiency Lodg Howard Johnson, ALDI, AT&T, CVS Drug, Family$, Ma Tires, Publix, Ross, TJ Maxx, Tuesday Morning, URGE CARE, Verizon
4	Buena Vista Rd, E 76, Chevron, Circle K, Liberty, Burg King, Capt D's, Church's TX Chicken, Domino's, Kryst McDonald's, Papa John's, Popeyes, Subway, Taco Bell, Waf House, Zaxby's, $General, AutoZone, O'Reilly Par Rainbow Foods, tires, USPO, vet, Walgreens, Walma Walmart, Winn-Dixie, W Chevron, Sunoco, Subway, Family$
3	St Marys Rd, E Sunoco, Microtel, Family$, W Marathon/dsl, Shell/dsl, Hardee's, $General, A Hardware, Advance Auto, Piggly Wiggly
1b a	US 27, US 280, Victory Dr, W 76, Chevron/dsl, Circle Exxon/Circle K, Liberty, Liberty, RaceWay/dsl, Bojangle Burger King, Capt D's, CC's Place, Checkers, Krystal, Lit Caesars, McDonald's, Papa John's, Subway, Taco Bell, Waf House, Wendy's, Budgetel Inn, Candlewood Suite EconoLodge, Hawthorn Suites, Holiday Inn Express, Motel $General, $Tree, Advance Parts, AutoZone, CVS Dru Family$, Family$, O'Reilly Parts, Verizon, Walmart
0mm	I-185 begins/ends on Victory Dr

INTERSTATE 285 (Atlanta)

Exit #	Services
62	GA 279, S Fulton Hwy, Old Nat Hwy, N Chevron/dsl, She Waffle House, Econolodge, $General, S Chevro Citgo, Exxon, Shell, Valero, American Deli, Bojangle Burger King, Checker's, China Cafeteria, Church's TX Chicke Cozumel Mexican, KFC, Krystal, McDonald's, Piccadi Cafeteria, Taco Bell, Waffle House, Wendy's, Quality In Ramada Plaza, Red Roof Inn, Super 8, Travelodge, AutoZone, Family$, Midas, O'Reilly Parts, U-Haul, URGE CARE
61	I-85, N to Atlanta, S to Montgomery

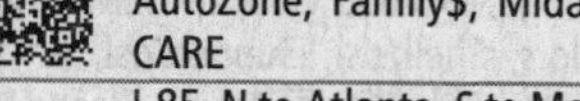

GA

PINE MOUNTAIN

INTERSTATE 285 (Atlanta) Cont'd

Exit #	Services
60	GA 139, Riverdale Rd, N [lodging] Fairfield Inn(2mi), Microtel(2mi), Wingate Inn(2mi), S [gas] QT/dsl, Shell/dsl, Valero/dsl, [food] Checkers, Church's TX Chicken, McDonald's, Papa John's, Waffle House, [lodging] Country Inn, Sky Point Hotel, [other] $General, Advance Parts, Family$, Family$
59	Clark Howell Hwy, N [other] air cargo
58	I-75, N to Atlanta, S to Macon(from eb), to US 19, US 41 , to Hapeville, S [gas] BP/dsl, Chevron/dsl, Exxon/dsl, QT, [food] American Deli, Jimmy John's, Subway, Waffle House, Wendy's, [lodging] Home Lodge Motel
55	GA 54, Jonesboro Rd, N [lodging] Super 8, [other] antiques, S [gas] Chevron/dsl, Exxon/dsl, Mobil/dsl, Texaco/dsl, [food] McDonald's, [other] Family$, Home Depot, repair, Volvo Trucks
53	US 23, Moreland Ave, to Ft Gillem, N [gas] 76/Champs Chicken, Chevron/dsl, Citgo/dsl, [other] auto parts, S [gas] Chevron/dsl, Citgo, [food] Wendy's, [lodging] HillTop Inn, [other] USPO
52	I-675, S to Macon
51	Bouldercrest Rd, N [gas] BP, Pilot/Wendy's/dsl/24hr, [food] Domino's, Hardee's, KFC, [other] Family$, Wayfield Foods, S [gas] Chevron/dsl, Exxon/dsl, Texaco/dsl
48	GA 155, Flat Shoals Rd, Candler Rd, N [gas] BP, Chevron, Chevron/dsl, Shell/dsl, Texaco/dsl, [food] Burger King, Checkers, Church's TX Chicken, DQ, Dunkin/BR, Family$, KFC, McDonald's, Subway, Taco Bell, Waffle King, [lodging] Budgetel Inns, Gulf American Inn, [other] $General, BigLots, Dollar$, Firestone Auto, Goodyear, S [gas] Chevron, Citgo, Exxon/dsl, QT, QT/dsl, [food] Burger King, China One, Sonic, Subway, Waffle House, [other] Family$, tires
46b a	I-20, E to Augusta, W to Atlanta
44	GA 260, Glenwood Rd, E [gas] Shell/dsl, [lodging] EconoLodge, W [gas] Chevron/dsl, Exxon/dsl, Texaco/dsl, Valero/dsl, [food] Hunt Bros Pizza, [other] U-Haul
43	US 278, Covington Hwy, E [gas] BP, Chevron/Subway, Texaco/dsl, [food] Waffle House, [other] U-Haul, W [gas] Circle K/dsl, Exxon/dsl, QT, Texaco/dsl, [food] HoneyBaked Ham, Wendy's, [lodging] Best Inn, [other] Advance Parts, Dollar$
42	(from nb), [other] Marta Station
41	GA 10, Memorial Dr, Avondale Estates, E [gas] QT, Valero, [food] Applebee's, Baskin-Robbins/Dunkin, Burger King, Church's TX Chicken, Domino's, IHOP, Pancake House, Subway, Taco Bell, Waffle House, Wendy's, [lodging] Best Value Inn, Budgetel, United Suites, [other] $General, $Tree, AutoZone, CVS, Firestone/auto, GNC, Pep Boys, Popeyes, Ross, Top Tire, U-Haul, USPO, Walgreens, W [gas] Citgo, EVC
40	Church St, to Clarkston, E [gas] Chevron, Marathon/dsl, Texaco, [other] auto repair, U-Haul, W [H]
39b a	US 78, to Athens, Decatu
38	US 29, Lawrenceville Hwy, E [gas] Citgo, QT/dsl, RaceTrac/dsl, [food] Bojangle's, Waffle House, [lodging] Best Value Inn, Knights Inn, [other] [H], W [gas] Citgo/dsl, [food] Dunkin, [lodging] Masters Inn, Motel 6, [other] auto repair, AutoZone, CVS Drug
37	GA 236, to LaVista, Tucker, E [gas] Exxon, [food] Bambinelli's Italian, Checkers, Del Taco, Einstein Bagel, Hudson Grille, IHOP, Jimmy John's, Newk's Eatery, Nothing Bundt Cakes, Piccadilly's, Waffle House, [lodging] Days Inn, Holiday Inn, [other] Bridgestone Firestone, DeKalb Tire/auto, EVC, Firestone/auto, Target, Zip Tire, W [gas] BP/Domino's, Chevron, EVC, Shell/dsl, [food] Blue Ribbon Grill, Bubble Creamery, Capt D's, Chick-fil-A, Chipotle, Dunkin, Eduardo's Mexican, Fork in the Road, Hibachi, HoneyBaked Ham, Jason's Deli, Kacey's Rest., Kobe Steaks, Lucky Key Chinese, Marlow's Tavern, McDonald's, Mellow Mushroom, Moe's SW, Monterrey Mexican, Panda Express, Panera Bread, Pizza Hut, Popeyes, Red Lobster, Smoothie King, Starbucks, Subway,
37	Continued Willy's Mexican, [lodging] Courtyard, DoubleTree, Holiday Inn, Quality Inn, [other] $Tree, ALDI, AT&T, Best Buy, Goodyear/auto, Kroger, Macy's, mall, Mavis Tires, Michael's, PetSmart, Publix, TJ Maxx, Verizon
36	Northlake Pkwy(from sb, no return), E [food] Old Hickory BBQ, [other] Dick's, Hobby Lobby, Ross, W [lodging] Hampton Inn, Hilton
34	Chamblee-Tucker Rd, E [gas] Chevron/Circle K/Dunkin, Shell, Texaco/dsl, [food] Hunan Inn, Jersey Mike's Subs, Moe's SW Grill, Taco Bell, Wendy's, Zaxby's, [other] Advance Parts, Goodyear/auto, Kroger, USPO, W [gas] Citgo, Exxon, [food] McDonald's, [other] BigLots, vet
33b a	I-85, N to Greenville, S to Atlanta
32	US 23, Buford Hwy, to Doraville, E [gas] BP/dsl, [food] Baldino's Subs, Bojangle's, Burger King/playland, Checkers, Chick-fil-A, Dunkin, McDonald's, Waffle House, White Windmill Café, Zaxby's, [other] Advance Parts, Firestone/auto, Marshalls, O'Reily Parts, PepBoys, USPO, W [gas] Exxon, QT/dsl, [food] McDonald's, Monterrey Mexican, Subway, [lodging] Clarion, [other] $Tree, Aamco
31b a	GA 141, Peachtree Ind, to Chamblee, E [gas] Shell, [food] Waffle House, [other] Home Depot, W [gas] 76 , QT, [food] Arby's, Baskin-Robbins/Dunkin, Chick-fil-A, IHOP, McDonald's, Pizza Hut, Smoothie King, Wendy's, [lodging] HomeTowne, [other] Acura, Advance Parts, AT&T, Audi, Brandsmart, Buick/GMC, Chevrolet, Chrysler/Dodge/Jeep, CVS Drug, Firestone/auto, Ford, Honda, Hyundai, Infiniti, Jiffy Lube, Kia, Lexus, Mini, Nissan, Office Depot, Porsche, Publix, TJ Maxx, Toyota, VW, VW, Walgreens
30	Chamblee-Dunwoody Rd, N Shallowford Rd, to N Peachtree Rd, N [gas] BP/dsl, BP/Dunkin, Chevron/dsl, EVC, Shell, [food] Bagel&Co. Deli, Burger King, Farm Burger, Marco's Pizza, McDonald's, Starbucks, Takorea, Waffle House, [other] Kroger, Tuesday Morning, S [gas] Amoco, Shell, Texaco, [food] La Botana Mexican, Mad Italian Rest., Papa John's, Taco Bell, Wendy's, Wild Ginger Thai, [lodging] DoubleTree, Holiday Inn, Sonesta
29	Ashford-Dunwoody Rd, N [gas] Exxon, QT, [food] Broken Egg, Capital Grille, Chick-fil-A, Chicken Salad Chick, Chopt Salad, Chuy's, First Watch, Fogo de Chao, J. Alexander's, Jason's Deli, Maggiano's Little Italy, McDonald's, Newk's Eatery, Olive Garden, Panda Express, Popeyes, Seasons 52 Grill, Shake Shack, Starbucks, [lodging] Crowne Plaza, Hampton Inn, [other] Barnes&Noble, Best Buy, Dillard's, Hobby Lobby, Macy's, mall, Marshalls, Nordstrom, Old Navy, Publix, Target, USPO, Walmart/Subway, S [lodging] Hyatt, [other] Hilton Garden
28	Peachtree-Dunwoody Rd(no EZ return wb), N [food] Arby's, Chuy's Mexican, Domino's, Einstein Bagels, Five Guys, Panera Bread, Starbucks, Willy's Mexican, [lodging] Courtyard, Extended Stay America, Extended Stay America (2), Fairfield Inn, Hampton Inn, Hilton Suites, Holiday Inn Express, Home2 Suites, La Quinta, Marriott, Sheraton, Westin, [other] Costco/gas, GNC, Home Depot, mall, Publix, Ross, Target, TJ Maxx, Walgreens, S [H]
27	US 19 N, GA 400, N [other] LDS Temple
26	Glenridge Dr(from eb), Johnson Ferry Rd
25	US 19 S, Roswell Rd, Sandy Springs, N [gas] BP, BP, Chevron, Shell/dsl, Shell/dsl, [food] Bruster's, Burger King, CAVA, Chick-fil-A, Chipotle Mexican, City BBQ, Domino's, Dunkin, Egg Harbor Café, El Azteca Mexican, Firehouse Subs, Five Guys, Flying Biscuit Cafe, Gyro Bros, Hardee's, Hudson Grille, IHOP, Jersey Mike's, Jet's Pizza, Jimmy John's, Longhorn Steaks, Maya Steaks, McDonald's, Mellow Mushroom, Napoli Pizza, Nothing Bundt Cakes, Papa John's, Roasters, Sonic, Starbucks, Taco Bell, The Select Rest., Waffle House, Willy's Mexican, Zafron, Zaxby's, [lodging] Comfort Inn, InTown Suites, [other] $Tree, AlLDI, AT&T, CVS Drug, Enterprise, Express Oil Change & Tires, Kroger, Lowe's, Marshalls, Mavis Tires, Mr Tire, NAPA, NAPA AutoCare, Pep Boys, PepBoys, PetCo, Publix,

AVONDALE ESTATES

TUCKER

SANDY SPRINGS

GA

= gas = food = lodging = other = rest stop

SANDY SPRINGS

INTERSTATE 285 (Atlanta) Cont'd

25 Continued
Take 5 Oil Change, Toyota, Trader Joe's, U-Haul, URGENT CARE, URGENT CARE, USPO, Verizon, Whole Foods Mkt, **S** Chevron/dsl, Citgo, Shell, Valero, Dunkin', El Taco Veloz, Panda Express, Sub Zero Ice Cream, Taco Mac, Waffle House, Publix, Target

24 Riverside Dr

22 New Northside Dr, to Powers Ferry Rd, **N** EVC, Shell/Subway/dsl, Extended Stay America, **S** Amoco, Chevron/dsl, McDonald's, Mojave, Ray's Rest., Starbucks, Waffle House, Sonesta, CVS Drug, Publix, UPS, vet

21 (from wb), **N** Chevron, Harry's Pizza, Extended Stay America, BMW/Mini, **S** Heirloom BBQ

20 I-75, N to Chattanooga, S to Atlanta(from wb), to US 41 N

19 US 41, Cobb Pkwy, to Dobbins AFB, **N** BP/dsl, Marathon, QT, Applebee's, Bruster's, Burger King, Carrabba's, ChuckeCheese, Del Taco, Dunkin, Golden Corral, IHOP, Jeni's Ice Cream, KFC, McDonald's, Olive Garden, Panda Express, Papa John's, Red Lobster, Scalini's Italian, Starbucks, Steak'nShake, Subway, Taco Bell, The Border Mexican, Thompson Bros BBQ, Waffle House, Wendy's, Wingate Inn, Zaxby's, DoubleTree, Extended Stay America, Hampton Inn, Holiday Inn Express, Hyatt, Residence Inn, $Tree, ALDI, Best Buy, Braves Stadium, Buick GMC, Cadillac, Chevrolet, Discount Tire, Honda, Kia, Lexus, Marshall's, Mavis Tires, Michael's, Pep Boys, PetSmart, Ross, Sprouts, Target, Ulta, Verizon, Walgreens, **S** Raceway/Starbucks, Buffalo Wild Wings, CAVA, Cheesecake Factory, Chick-fil-A, Chipotle, Cinco Mexican, Firehouse Subs, Honey Baked Ham, Hooters, Longhorn Steaks, Maggiano's Italian, PF Chang's, Pizza Hut, Snooze Eatery, Stoney River Steaks, Embassy Suites, Hampton Inn, Homewood Suites, Renaissance, Sheraton Suites, Sonesta, AT&T, Barnes&Noble, Costco/gas, Dick's, Macy's, OfficeMax, Old Navy, USPO, USPO

18 Paces Ferry Rd, to Vinings, **N** Panera Bread, Fairfield Inn, La Quinta, **S** QT/24hr, Chick-fil-A, Chicken Salad Chick, Chipotle , ColdStone, Einstein Bagels, Starbucks, Willy's Grill, Courtyard, Extended Stay America, Hotel Indigo, Home Depot, Mavis Tires, Publix, Walgreens , **E** Mellow Mushroom

16 S Atlanta Rd, to Smyrna, **N** Five Guys, Waffle House, H, **S** Chevron/Subway/dsl, Shell/dsl, Jersey Mike's, Kroger, **W** Zama Mexican

15 GA 280, S Cobb Dr, **E** Motel 6, U-Haul, **W** BP/Bojangles/Cinnabon/dsl, Exxon, Mobil, RaceTrac/dsl, Arby's, Chick-fil-A, Chipotle, Dollar Cafe, Dunkin', Jimmy John's, Krystal, McDonald's, Subway, Taco Bell, Wendy's, Zaxby's, Baymont Inn, Comfort Inn, Country Inn Suites, InTown Suites

14mm Chattahoochee River

13 Bolton Rd(from nb)

12 US 78, US 278, Bankhead Hwy, **E** Petro/Iron Skillet/dsl/scales/24hr/@, Shell/dsl/24hr, Valero/dsl, Burger King, Blue Beacon, **W** BP, Chevron

10b a I-20, W to Birmingham, E to Atlanta(exits left from nb), **W** to Six Flags

9 GA 139, MLK Dr, to Adamsville, **E** BP/Circle K, Quikmart, Family$, O'Reilly Parts, Wayfield Foods, **W** Chevron, Shell, Texaco/dsl, Checker's, Church's TX Chicken, Domino's, KFC/Taco Bell, McDonald's, Popeyes, $General, $Tree, Family$

7 Cascade Rd, **E** Exxon/dsl, Papa John's, Kroger, **W** BP/dsl, Shell, Applebee's, Chik-fil-A, China Express, KFC, McDonald's, Pizza Hut, Smoothie King, Starbucks, Subway,

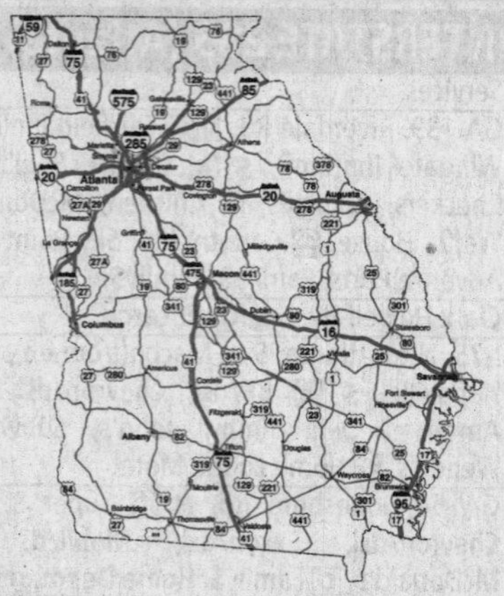

BOLINGBROKE

7 Continued
Wendy's, Wendy's, GNC, Home Depot, Publix, Tire
Walgreens, Walmart

5b a GA 166, Lakewood Fwy, **E** Chevron, Exxon, Exxon, Texa
Burger King, KFC, Subway, Wendy's, $Tree, CVS Dr
Family$, Firestone, Goodyear/auto, Kroger, Macy's, mall,
BP, Mobil/dsl, RaceWay/dsl, Texaco/dsl, Valero,
Church's TX Chicken, Church's TX Chicken, Deluxe Inn,
AutoZone, Family$, O'Reilly Parts

2 Camp Creek Pkwy, to airport, **E** Chevron, Exxon/d
Texaco, Checker's, Marco's, McDonald's, Sheraton,
RaceTrac/dsl, Carino's, Chick-fil-A, Chili's, Five Gu
Jason's Deli, Jimmy John's, LongHorn Steaks, Moe's S
Panda Express, Papa John's, Popeyes, Red Lobster, Ru
Tuesday, Smoothie King, Starbucks, Taco Bell, TGIFrida
Wendys, Zaxby's, Courtyard, Hampton Inn, Holiday I
Express, $Tree, BJ's Whse/gas, EVC, H, Lowes Wh
Marshall's, Old Navy, PetSmart, Publix, Ross, Staples, Targ
TJ Maxx, URGENT CARE, Verizon, Walgreens

1 Washington Rd, **E** Texaco/dsl, Family$, **W** Chevro
dsl, Days Inn, Regency Inn, U-Haul

INTERSTATE 475 (Macon)

16mm I-475 begins/ends on I-75, exit 177.

15 US 41, Bolingbroke, **E** Exxon/dsl/LP, Marathon/dsl,
USPO

9 Zebulon Rd, **E** Marathon/dsl, Shell/Circle K/24hr,
Applebee's, Buffalo's Café, Chick-fil-A, Fajitas Mexica
Fazoli's, Freddy's, Hong Kong, Johnny's NY Pizz, Kryst
Macon Pizza Co, McAlister's Deli, McDonald's, Moe's SW, N
Way Wieners, Pizza Hut, Sonny's BBQ, Subway, Taco Be
Taki Japanese, Waffle House, Wendy's, Baymont In
Comfort Suites, Fairfield Inn, SureStay, Goodyear/auto,
Kohl's, Kroger/dsl, Lowe's, UPS, URGENT CARE, USP
Verizon, Walgreens, Walmart/Subway, **W** Exxon/d
Shell/dsl, Marco's Pizza, Zaxby's, Advance Parts, C
Drug

MACON

8mm **full facilities, litter barrels, petwalk, , , n
vending**

5 GA 74, Macon, **E** RaceWay/dsl, Waffle House,
Harley-Davidson, to Mercer U, **W** BP/Church's TX Chicke
dsl, Circle K/Subway/dsl, Capt D's, Popeyes, Taco Bell,
$General, $Tree, Mavis Tires, O'Reily Parts, Publix, Tires+,
Lake Tobesofkee, UPS, vet

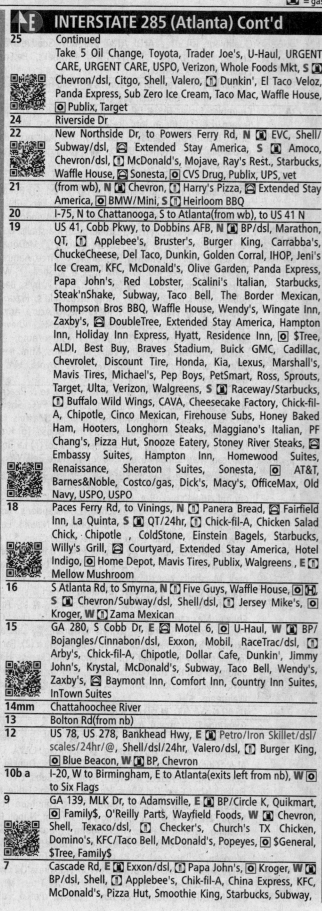

3 US 80, Macon, **E** Circle K/Subway, Marathon/dsl, Murph
USA/dsl, Applebee's, Burger King, Chick-fil-A, Chir
Buffet, Cook Out, Cracker Barrel, DQ, Fajita Mexica
Firehouse Subs, Golden Corral, KFC, Krystal, McAlister's De
McDonald's, Papa John's, Pizza Hut, S&S Cafeteria, Smoki
Pig BBQ, Taco Bell, Waffle House, Wendy's, Zaxby's, Be
Inn, Best Western, Bridgeview Inn, Comfort Suites,

INTERSTATE 475 (Macon) Cont'd

MACON

3 Continued
Country Inn, Days Inn, Discovery Inn, EconoLodge, Hampton Inn, Holiday Inn Express, Knights Inn, La Quinta, Quality Inn, Ramada Inn, Regency Inn, Rodeway Inn, Super 8, Super 8, Village Stay, Woodspring Suites, $Tree, ALDI, AutoZone, Best Buy, BigLots, CVS Drug, Discount Tire, Firestone/auto, Home Depot, Honda, Kroger/gas, Lowe's, mall, Mavis Tires, Ross, Sam's Club/gas, Staples, U-Haul, Verizon, vet, Walmart/Subway, W Sunoco/dsl, Burger King, Best Value Inn, Travelodge

1 Hartley Bridge Rd, same as I-75 exit 156

0mm I-475 begins/ends on I-75, exit 156.

INTERSTATE 575

30mm I-575 begins/ends on GA 5/515.

27 GA 5, Howell Br, to Ball Ground, E Chevron, Shell, Waffle House, O'Reily Parts

24 Airport Dr

CANTON

20 GA 5, to Canton, E Bojangles, Buffalo's Cafe, Chick-fil-A, Dos Margaritas Mexican, Stevi B's Pizza, Waffle Wouse, Wendy's, Homestead Inn, Motel 6, Quality Inn, Chevrolet, Chrysler/Dodge/Jeep, GNC, Toyota, URGENT CARE, Walmart/gas, W QT, RaceTrac/dsl, Applebee's, Arby's, Chick-fil-A, Cracker Barrel, Five Guys, Honeybaked Ham, Longhorn Steaks, McDonald's, Menchie's, O'Charley's, Okinawa Steaks, Outback Steaks, Panda Express, Provino's, Red Lobster, Seven Tequilas Mexican, Starbucks, Zaxby's, Comfort Inn, Country Inn, Hampton Inn, Belk, Home Depot, H, Michaels, Publix, Ross, UPS

19 GA 20 E, Canton, E Brooklyn Joe's, Chick-fil-A, Chipotle, Dunkin', Five Guys, IHOP, Jersey Mike's, Jimmy John's, La Parrilla Mexican, Maddio's Pizza, McDonald's, Newk's Eatery, Olive Garden, PITA, Starbucks, Taco Mac, Waffle House, Which Wich?, Your Pie Pizza, Zaxby's, AT&T, Best Buy, BooksAMillion, Dick's, Hobby Lobby, Kohl's, Lowe's, Mavis Tire, Mr. Tire/auto, PetSmart, RaceTrac, T-Mobile, Target, TJ Maxx, Verizon, W park

17 GA 140, to Roswell (from sb), Canton

16 GA 20, GA 140, E H, W Chevron, RaceTrac/dsl, Burger King, KFC, Papa John's, Subway, Taco Bell, Waffle House, Williamson Bros BBQ, $General, Advance Parts, Enterprise, NAPA, U-Haul

14 Holly Springs, E Shell/dsl, Domino's, Ichiban Buffet, Las Palmas Mexican, Pizza Hut, Saporitos Pizza, Pinecrest Motel, Nissan, USPO, Walmart/Subway, W $Tree, Chevron, EVC, Mobil/dsl, Dunkin', Eggs Up Grill, Golden China, McDonald's, Starbucks, Subway, Viva Mexico, Wendy's, Zaxby's, auto repair, Autozone, Kroger/dsl, Mavis Tires, park, Publix, Walgreens

WOODSTOCK

11 Sixes Rd, E Home Depot, QT, DQ, Jersey Mike's, Papa John's, Shane's Ribshack, Starbucks, Taco Bell, Wendy's, Zaxby's, Advance Parts, AT&T, Kroger, O'Reily Parts, Pep Boys, URGENT CARE, USPO, Verizon, W RaceTrac, URGENT CARE

9 Ridgewalk Pkwy, E RaceTrac, Applebee's, Chick-fil-A, Five Guys, McDonald's, Panda Express, Holiday Inn Express, outlets/famous brands

8 Towne Lake Pkwy, to Woodstock, E Shell/dsl, Waffle House, Ford, Ford, Quick Lane, W Chevron/Dunkin', QT, CAVA, Chili's, Longhorn Steaks, Sprouts, Walgreens

7 GA 92, Woodstock, E QT, Shell, Arby's, Bubba Q's Rest., Burger King, Capt D's, Checker's, Chick-fil-A, Chipotle, Del Taco, DQ, Dunkin', Firehouse Subs, Folk's Kitchen, Honeybaked Ham, McDonald's, Moe's SW Grill, Ninja Sushi, Popeyes, Resturante Mexico, Starbucks, Subway, Taco Bell,

7 Continued
Waffle House, Comfort Suites, Fairfield Inn, Hampton Inn, InTown Suite, Camping World, Firestone/auto, Goodyear/auto, Hertz, W Chevron/dsl, EVC, Atlanta Bread, Hacienda Vieja Mexican, IHOP, Jimmy John's, Schlotzky's, Smoothie King, Steak'n Shake, Taco Mac, Microtel, AT&T, BJ's Whse/gas, Chrysler/Dodge/Jeep, Discount Tire, Home Depot, Honda, Kohl's, Lowe's Whse, OfficeMax, Old Navy, PetSmart, Target, Verizon

4 Bells Ferry Rd, W QT, RaceTrac/dsl, Shell/dsl, Arby's, Burger King, Dunkin', Pizza Hut, Ralph's Grill, Starbucks, Subway, Waffle House, Pepboys, Publix, Walgreens

3 Chastain Rd, to I-75 N, W Chevron, Chikfila, Chipotle, Cookout, Cracker Barrel, Del Taco, Dunkin', Five Guys, Marlow's Tavern, Panda Express, Papa's Cuban, Ruth's Chris Steaks, Starbucks, Taco Mac, Taziki's, Tin Lizzy's, Tropical Smoothie, Whataburger, Zaxby's/Buffalo Wings, Best Western, Comfort Suites, Embassy Suites, Fairfield Inn, Hampton Inn, Sonesta Suites, Springhill Suites, to Kennesaw St Coll

1 Barrett Pkwy, to I-75 N, US 41, E Murphy USA/dsl, QT, Buffalo Wild Wings, Burger King, Cheeseburger Bobby's, Cozy Coop, Dunkin', Fuego Tortillo, Pacific Buffet, Starbucks, Texas Roadhouse, Twisted Kitchen, Waffle House, $Tree, AT&T, Barnes&Noble, CVS Drug, Mavis Tire, Petco, Publix, Ross, Tuesday Morning, Walmart/Subway, W Shell/dsl, Anchor Grill, Applebee's, Chicken Salad Chick, Honeybaked Ham, Jimmy John's, McDonald's, Olive Garden, Provino's Italian, Red Lobster, Shogun Japanese, Starbucks, Subway, Twin Peaks, Best Western, Comfort Inn, Holiday Inn Express, Red Roof Inn, Belk, Firestone/auto, Home Depot, Marshall's, Midas, Take 5 Lube, TJ Maxx, Verizon

0mm I-575 begins/ends on I-75, exit 268.

INTERSTATE 675

FT GILLEM

10mm I-285 W, to Atlanta Airport, E to Augusta. I-675 begins/ends on I-285, exit 52.

7 Anvil Block Rd, Ft Gillem, E Chevron/dsl, Murphy Express, Waffle House, Walmart/Subway, Wendy's, $Tree, W Chevron/dsl

5 Forest Pkwy, E Chevron/dsl, W BP/dsl, Chevron/dsl, QT/dsl/scales, McDonald's, Waffle House

2 US 23, GA 42, E Exxon, Marathon, Texaco, Valero/Dunkin'/Subway/dsl, El Granero Mexican, Waffle House, W Chevron/dsl, Citgo, $General, Family$, Food Depot, GoodTime/auto, USPO

1 GA 138, to I-75 N, Stockbridge, E Chevron/dsl, Exxon/dsl, Murphy USA/dsl, QT, Valero/dsl, Capt D's, Checker's, DQ, Dunkin', Golden Corral, KFC, Krispy Kreme, Little Caesar's, McDonald's, Olympia Pizza, Papa John's, Popeyes, Taco Bell, Waffle House, Wendy's, Zaxby's, Best Value, Magnolia Inn, Quality Inn, Royal Palms Inn, Sleep Inn, SleepWell, Stay Inn, Stockbridge Inn, $General, $Tree, Advance Parts, ALDI, BigLots, CVS Drug, Goodyear/auto, NAPA, Pepboys, Walmart, W Raceway/dsl, Applebee's, Chick-fil-A, Frontera Mexican, Honeybaked Ham, IHOP, Krystal, O'Charley's, Piccadilly's, Subway, Waffle House, Comfort Inn, Day's Inn, Hampton Inn, Holiday Inn, La Quinta, Motel 6, Red Roof Inn, Kroger/dsl, Lowes Whse, Office Depot, Tires+, URGENT CARE, Verizon

0 I-675 begins/ends on I-75, exit 227.

INTERSTATE 985 (Gainesville)

GAINESVILLE

24.5mm I-985 begins/ends on US 23, 25mm.

24 to US 129 N, GA 369 W, Gainesville, N EVC, QT/dsl, Chikfila, Chipotle, McAlister's Deli, McDonald's, Mr. Teriyaki, Papa John's, Shane's Rib Shack, Taco Bell, Autozone, H,

GA

= gas = food = lodging = other = rest stop

INTERSTATE 985 (Gainesville) Cont'd

GAINESVILLE

24 Continued
Kroger/dsl, **S** BP/dsl, Chevron/dsl, Subway, Double D Burger, Rabbittown Cafe

22 GA 11, Gainesville, **N** QT/dsl, RaceTrac, Burger King, **S** Chevron/dsl, Shell/dsl, Waffle House, Extended Stay, Motel 6, $General, U-Haul, USPO

20 GA 60, GA 53, Gainesville, **N** RaceTrac/dsl, **S** Circle K/Subway/dsl, Waffle House

17 GA 13, Gainesville, **N** Camping World

16 GA 53, Oakwood, **N** BP, Arby's, Burger King, Capt D's, Cook Out, DQ, Dunkin', El Sombrero Mexican, Firehouse Subs, Hardee's, Huey Magoo, KFC, McDonald's, Napoli's Pizza, Starbucks, Taco Bell, Waffle House, Wendy's, Zaxby's, Best Western, Jameson Inn, $Tree, ALDI, Camping World RV Ctr, Chrysler/Dodge/Jeep, Sam's Club/dsl, Verizon, Walmart/Subway, **S** QT/dsl, Big Burritos, Buffalo's Cafe, Chick-Fil-A, Cuban Cafe, Haydee's, Krystal, La Parilla Mexican, Quality Inn, Sonic, Waffle House, Quality Inn, AutoZone, Mavis Tires, NAPA, O'Reilly Parts, Pit Pass , Publix, Summit Ace Hardware, Toyota, Walgreens

12 Spout Springs Rd, Flowery Branch, **N** Exxon/dsl, **S** Chevron/dsl, Marathon/Subway/dsl, Baskin-Robbin, Burger&Shake, Chick-fil-A, Chili's, China Garden, CrossRoads Grill,. Domino's, El Sombrero Mexican, Little Caesar's, McDonald's, Napoli's Pizza, Shane's Ribshack, Shogun Japanese, Hampton Inn, AT&T, GNC, Home Depot, Kohl's, PetSmart, Publix, Ross, Target/Starbucks, TJ Maxx, Walgreens

8 GA 347, Friendship Rd, Lake Lanier, **N** Chevron/dsl, QT/dsl, Shell/dsl, Blimpie, Burger King, Cracker Barrel, Dunkin', McDonald's, Shazzy, Starbucks, Subway, Taco Guy,

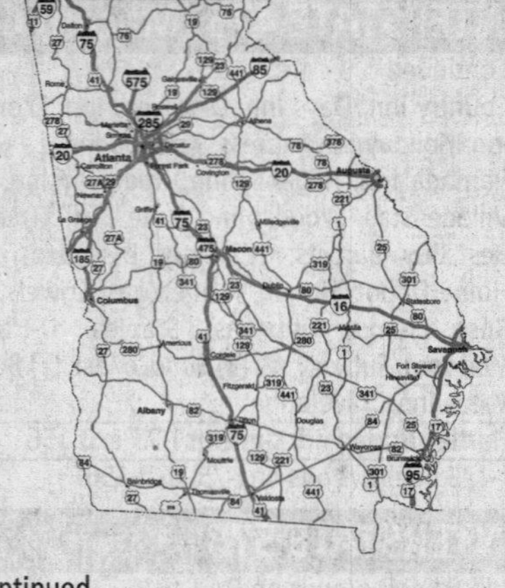

BUFORD

8 Continued
Vinny's NY Grill, Waffle House, Wendy's, Zaxby's, Holiday Inn Express, $General, Advance parts, O'Reilly Parts, Publix, URGENT CARE, Verizon, vet, **S** QT, Camper City RV Ctr, Harley Davidson

4 US 23 S, GA 20, Buford, **N** BP, QT, 985 Korean BBQ, Arby's, Bojangles, Burger King, Capt D's, Golden Buddah, Hardee's, IHOP, KFC, McDonald's, Pizza Hut, Subway, Taco Bell, Waffle House, Wendy's, Zaxby's, Holiday Inn Express, Travel Inn, Chrysler/Dodge/Jeep, Harbor Freight, Hobby Lobby, Home Depot, Kia, Mavis Tires, NAPA Autocare, **S** Chevron/dsl, Exxon/dsl, Murphy USA, Asia Buffet, Dunkin', First Watch, Sonny's BBQ, Texas Roadhouse, Viva Mexico, $Tree, Firestone/auto, Honda, Lowes Whse, Mavis Tires, Volvo, VW, Walmart/gas

0mm I-985 begins/ends on I-85.

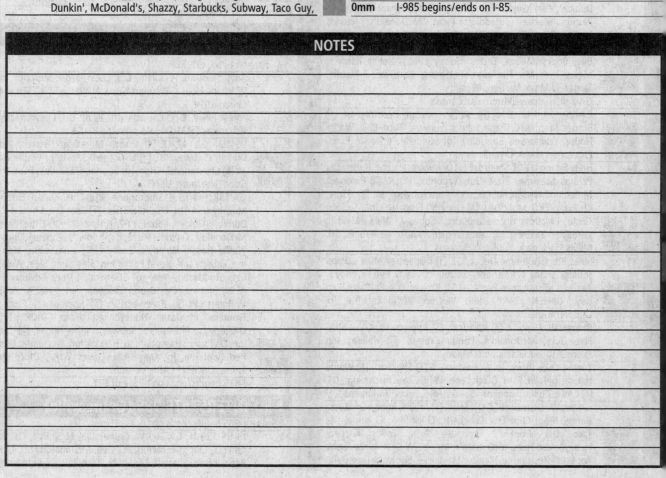

GA

NOTES

IDAHO

INTERSTATE 15

Exit #	Services
196mm	Idaho/Montana state line, Monida Pass, continental divide, elev 6870
190	Humphrey
184	Stoddard Creek Area, W Stoddard Creek Camping
180	Spencer, E Opal Country Café/gas, High Country Opal Store, W Spencer Grill/RV Park
172	no services
167	ID 22, Dubois, **both lanes, full facilities, , , litter barrels, petwalk,** E Phillips 66/dsl, city park, USPO, W Crates NM
150	Hamer, E USPO, W Camus NWR
143	ID 33, ID 28, to Mud Lake, Rexburg, weigh sta both lanes
142mm	hist site, roadside parking
135	ID 48, Roberts, E Phillips 66/cafe/dsl/LP
128	Osgood Area, E Osgood/dsl, camping(6mi)
119	US 20 E, to Rexburg, Idaho Falls, E Sinclair/dsl, Jaker's Steaks, Outback Steaks, Sandpiper Rest., Best Western+, Fairbridge Inn, Hilton Garden, LeRitz Hotel, Motel 6, Safari Inn, Shilo Inn/rest., Super 8, Tru Hilton, LDS Temple, same as 118, Snake River RV Park/camping, W Sinclair/dsl
118	US 20, Broadway St, Idaho Falls, E Phillips 66/dsl, Walmart/dsl, Applebee's, Arctic Circle, Buffalo Wild Wings, Carl's Jr, Cedric's Rest., Chili's, Culver's, Domino's, Don Alberto Mexican, Jalisco's Mexican, Jimmy John's, LongHorn Steaks, MacKenzie River Grill, Olive Garden, Panda Express, Shari's Rest., Smitty's Pancakes, Starbucks, Wendy's, Best Western, Candlewood Suites, Comfort Suites, Fairfield Inn, Hampton Inn, Hilton Garden, Residence Inn, SpringHill Suites, Tru, Ford, Harley-Davidson, H, LDS Temple, same as 119, URGENT CARE, Verizon, Walmart/Subway, W Phillips 66/dsl, Sinclair/McDonald's, Arby's, Burger King, Fiesta Ole, Homestead Pizza, Hong Kong Rest., Jack-in-the-Box, Los Adalaberto's Mexican, O'Brady's, Papa Murphy's, Pizza Hut, Subway, Comfort Inn, Econolodge, Motel West, Albertsons, AutoZone, Camping World RV Ctr, Jiffy Lube, O'Reilly Parts, Walgreens
116	US 26, Sunnyside Rd, Ammon, E Maverik, Burger Theory, Taco Bell, Holiday Inn, BMW, Chevrolet, Honda, H, Mazda, Sunnyside Acres RV Park, Toyota/Scion, VW, W Exxon/diesel, Sleep Inn
113	US 26, to Idaho Falls, Jackson, E Blu LNG/dsl, Chevron/Burger King/dsl, Flying J/dsl/24hr/@, Love's/McDonald's/dsl/scales/24hr, Subway, H, Jack's Tires, Peterbilt
108	Shelley, Firth Area
101mm	both lanes, full facilities, , , litter barrels, petwalk, geological site
98	Rose-Firth Area
94.5mm	Snake River
93	US 26, ID 39, Blackfoot, E Chevron/Jimmy John's/dsl, Maverik/dsl, Sinclair/Stinker/dsl, Arby's, Burger King, Burtos Mexican, Costa Vida, Domino's, DQ, Homestead Rest., Hong Kong Garden, Little Caesar's, McDonald's, Papa Murphy's, Subway, Taco Bell, Wendy's, Best Western, Super 8, $Tree, AutoZone, Chrysler/Dodge/Ford/Jeep, city park, Kesler's Foods, NAPA, O'Reilly Parts, Ridley's Mkt, Schwab Tire, URGENT CARE, Verizon, Walgreens, Walmart/Subway, W Sinclair/A&W/dsl
90.5mm	Blackfoot River
89	US 91, S Blackfoot, W Sinclair/Sage Cafe/dsl
80	Ft Hall, W Phillips 66/rest./dsl/casino,

DUBOIS

IDAHO FALLS

BLACKFOOT

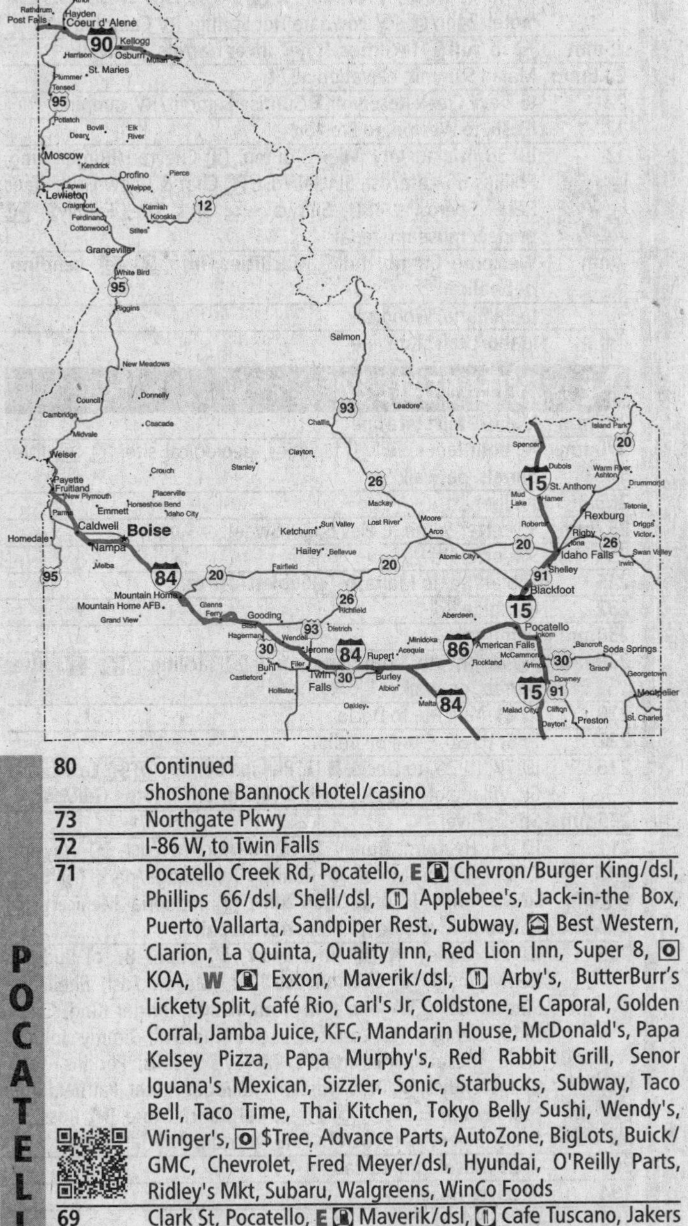

POCATELLO

Exit #	Services
80	Continued Shoshone Bannock Hotel/casino
73	Northgate Pkwy
72	I-86 W, to Twin Falls
71	Pocatello Creek Rd, Pocatello, E Chevron/Burger King/dsl, Phillips 66/dsl, Shell/dsl, Applebee's, Jack-in-the Box, Puerto Vallarta, Sandpiper Rest., Subway, Best Western, Clarion, La Quinta, Quality Inn, Red Lion Inn, Super 8, KOA, W Exxon, Maverik/dsl, Arby's, ButterBurr's Lickety Split, Café Rio, Carl's Jr, Coldstone, El Caporal, Golden Corral, Jamba Juice, KFC, Mandarin House, McDonald's, Papa Kelsey Pizza, Papa Murphy's, Red Rabbit Grill, Senor Iguana's Mexican, Sizzler, Sonic, Starbucks, Subway, Taco Bell, Taco Time, Thai Kitchen, Tokyo Belly Sushi, Wendy's, Winger's, $Tree, Advance Parts, AutoZone, BigLots, Buick/GMC, Chevrolet, Fred Meyer/dsl, Hyundai, O'Reilly Parts, Ridley's Mkt, Subaru, Walgreens, WinCo Foods
69	Clark St, Pocatello, E Maverik/dsl, Cafe Tuscano, Jakers Grill, Fairfield Inn, Hampton Inn, Holiday Inn Express, Home2 Suites, TownePlace Suites, H, W to ID St U
67	US 30/91, 5th St, Pocatello, E Exxon/dsl, W Shell/dsl, Elmer's Rest., Goody's Deli, Jimmy John's, McDonald's, Pizza Hut, Taco Bell, Days Inn, Thunderbird Motel, city park, dog park, Mountain View RV Park, museum, visitors info
63	Portneuf Area, W to Mink Creek RA
59mm	weigh sta both lanes
58	Inkom, W Sinclair/café/dsl, Muddy Moose, Bisharat's Mkt, Pebble Creek Ski Area, repair, USPO
57	Inkom(from nb), same as 58

= gas = food = lodging = other = rest stop

INTERSTATE 15 Cont'd

MCCAMMON

Exit #	Services
47	US 30, to Lava Hot Springs, McCammon, E Chevron/A&W/Taco Time/dsl, Flying J/dsl/scales/LP/RV dump/24hr, Subway, KOA, Lava Hot Springs RA, McCammon RV Park
44	Lp 15, Jenson Rd, McCammon
40	Arimo, E Sinclair, USPO
36	US 91, Virginia
31	ID 40, to Downey, Preston, E Shell/Flags West/café/dsl/motel/24hr/@, Downata Hot Springs RV Camping
25mm	**sb, full facilities, litter barrels, petwalk**
24.5mm	Malad Summit, elevation 5574
22	to Devil Creek Reservoir, E Sunrise Summit/RV camping
17	ID 36, to Weston, to Preston
13	ID 38, Malad City, W RV dump, Chevron/Burger King, Phillips 66/café/dsl, Sinclair/dsl, Chat & Chew Grill, Pines Rest., Sperow's BBQ, Subway, 3R's Tire, Family$, pioneer museum, repair
7mm	**Welcome Ctr nb, full facilities, info, vending, petwalk**
3	to Samaria, Woodruff
0mm	Idaho/Utah state line

WOODRUFF

INTERSTATE 84

TWIN FALLS

Exit #	Services
275mm	Idaho/Utah state line
270mm	both lanes, full facilities, geological site, litter barrels, petwalk
263	Juniper Rd
257mm	Sweetzer Summit, elev 5530, Sweetzer Summit
254	Sweetzer Rd
245	Sublett Rd, to Malta, N Sublett/dsl/café
237	Idahome Rd
234mm	Raft River
229mm	/weigh sta both lanes, full facilities, litter barrels, petwalk
228	ID 81, Yale Rd, to Declo
222	I-86, US 30, E to Pocatello
216	ID 77, ID 25, to Declo, N Phillips 66/dsl, to Walcott SP, Village of Trees RV Park, S Sinclair/Pit Stop Grill/dsl
215mm	Snake River
211	ID 24, Heyburn, Burley, N Sinclair/café/dsl, Wayside Cafe, Tops Motel, Country RV Village/park, S Love's/Carl's Jr./dsl/scales/24hr, Taqueria Mexican, Peterbilt, Riverside RV Park, truck repair
208	ID 27, Burley, N Sinclair/dsl, Super 8, Budget, Kenworth, S Chevron/dsl/24hr, Maverik/dsl, Shell/dsl, Sinclair/dsl, Aguila's Mexican, Arby's, Burger King, Costa Vida, Denny's, El Caporal, Jack-in-the-Box, Jimmy John's, Little Caesar's, McDonald's, Morey's Steaks, Perkins, Taco Bell, Wendy's, Best Western+, Budget Motel, Fairfield Inn, Holiday Inn Express, $Tree, Cal Ranch Store, Ross, to Snake River RA, URGENT CARE, Verizon, Walmart
201	ID 25, Kasota Rd, to Paul
194	ID 25, to Hazelton
188	Valley Rd, to Eden
182	ID 50, to Kimberly, Twin Falls, N Sinclair/dsl, Anderson Camp, Xtreme RV, S Shell/dsl/scales/24hr/@, Amber Inn, auto/truck/rv repair
173	US 93, Twin Falls, N Flying J/dsl/LP/24hr/@, Subway, Comfort Inn, Sleep Inn, Bish's RV Ctr, Blue Beacon, KOA, to Sun Valley, S Coll of S ID, LDS Temple, Shoshone Falls Scenic Area, visitors ctr
171mm	**/weigh sta eb, full facilities, vending, litter barrels, petwalk**
168	ID 79, to Jerome, N Chevron/dsl, Exxon/dsl, Shell/dsl, Arctic Circle, Burger King, Carl's Jr, Domino's,

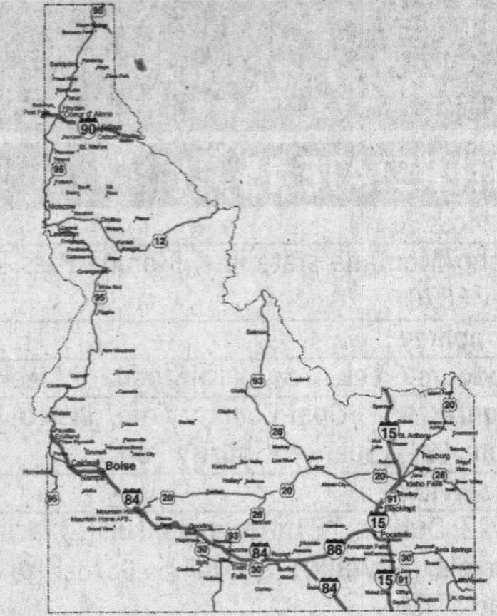

BLISS

HAMMETT

KUNA

Exit #	Services
168	Continued Jack-in-the-Box, Little Caesar's, McDonald's, Tabo Bell, Best Western, Crest Motel, $Tree, auto repair, AutoZone, Benito Tires, Les Schwab Tire, O'Reilly Parts, Verizon, Walmart/Subway, S Maverik, Jerome Pizza Factory, Subway, Chevrolet
165	ID 25, Jerome, N Sinclair/Mr. Gas/scales/dsl, Holiday Motel, vet
157	ID 46, Wendell, N Maverik, Artic Circle, Papa Kelsey's Pizza, Subway, CarQuest, Family$, John's Tire/lube, NAPA, Wilson's RV Park, S Phillips 66/dsl
155	ID 46, to Wendell, N Wilson's RV Park
147	to Tuttle, S Malad Gorge SP, Rest EZ RV Park
146mm	Malad River
141	US 26, to US 30, Gooding, S Love's/Subway/dsl/scales/24hr/@, Phillips 66/café/dsl, Sinclair/dsl, Amber Inn
137	Lp 84, to US 30, to Pioneer Road, Bliss, S Sinclair/Stinker/dsl/24hr, camping
133mm	both lanes, full facilities, info, litter barrels, petwalk
129	King Hill
128mm	Snake River
125	Paradise Valley, 125 Paradise Valley
122mm	Snake River
121	Glenns Ferry, S Sinclair/dsl, Veltex/dsl, Hansen Motel/cafe, 3 Island SP, Carmela Winery/rest., Family$, fudge factory, NAPA, tires, Trails Break RV camp/dump
120	Glenns Ferry(from eb), same as 121
114	ID 78(from wb), to Hammett
112	to ID 78, Hammett, S Bruneau Dunes SP
99	ID 51, ID 67, to Mountain Home
95	US 20, Mountain Home, N Chevron/KFC/dsl, Pilot/Arby's/dsl/scales/24hr, Jack-in-the-Box, Savory Layne Steaks, Subway, Wingers, Best Western, Hampton Inn, Mtn Home Inn, S Jade Palace, McDonald's, Smoky Mtn Pizza, Taco Bell, Wendy's, Hilander Motel(1mi), Towne Ctr Motel(1mi), $Tree, AT&T, Chrysler/Dodge/Jeep, Ford/Lincoln, Mtn Home RV Park, Verizon, visitors ctr, Walmart/Subway
90	to ID 51, ID 67, W Mountain Home, S Chevron/Burger King/dsl, McDonald's(4mi), Maple Cove Motel(4mi), to Hilander Motel(4mi), Towne Ctr Motel(4mi), KOA
74	Simco Rd
71	Orchard, Mayfield, S Sinclair/rest./StageStop Motel/dsl/24hr
66mm	weigh sta both lanes
64	Blacks Creek, Kuna
62mm	**both lanes, full facilities, OR Trail info, litter barrels, vending, petwalk**
59b a	S Eisenman Rd, Memory Rd, S Sinclair/dsl/scales

ID

INTERSTATE 84 Cont'd

Exit #	Services
57	ID 21, Gowen Rd, to Idaho City, N Sinclair, Domino's, Jack-in-the-Box, Mancino's Pizza, McDonald's, Subway, Taco Del Mar, Best Western/NW Lodge, Albertsons/Sav-On, Peterbilt, S Chevron/dsl, Burger King, ID Ice World
54	US 20/26, Broadway Ave, Boise, N Chevron/dsl, Flying J/dsl/LP/RV dump/24hr, Fred Meyer/dsl, Shell/dsl, A&W/KFC, Arby's, Dutch Bros, Fiesta Mexican, Freddy's Burgers, IHOP, Jack-in-the-Box, Jimmy John's, Sonic, Courtyard(3mi), Big O Tire, Boise St U, Firestone/auto, Fred Meyer, Goodyear/auto, Home Depot, Jo-Ann Fabrics, O'Reilly Parts, PetCo, Ross, Schwab Tire, Walgreens, S TA/Country Pride/Taco Bell/Subway/dsl/24hr/@, Hotel 28, Bretz RV Ctr, Mtn View RV Park
53	Vista Ave, Boise, N Shell, Shell/dsl, Applebee's, Spitfire Pizza, Best Value Inn, Comfort Inn, Comfort Suites, Extended Stay America, Fairfield Inn, Hampton Inn, Holiday Inn/rest., La Quinta, Ramada, Simple Suites, Super 8, museums, st capitol, st police, zoo, S Chevron/dsl, Inn, Best Western, InnAmerica, Motel 6, Quality Inn, Rodeway Inn,
52	Orchard St, Boise, N Maverik/dsl, Shell/dsl, Subway, Fiat, GMC
50b a	Cole Rd, Overland Rd, N Chevron/dsl, Shell, Sinclair, Cobby's Sandwiches, Eddie's Rest., Gyro Shack, McDonald's, Outback Steaks, Subway, Taco Bell, Taco Time, Grocery Outlet, LDS Temple, transmissions, S Phillips 66/dsl, Shell/dsl, A&W/KFC, Black Bear Diner, Burger King, Carl's Jr, Chapala Mexican, Chuck-a-Rama, Costa Vida, Country Bay Rest., Cracker Barrel, Del Taco, Domino's, El Tenampa, Goodwood BBQ, Jimmy John's, Lucky Palace Chinese, Panda Express, Sonic, Starbucks, Tortilla Factory, Tucano's Brazilian Grill, Twin Peaks, Wendy's, Westside Pizza, Hampton Inn, Hilton Garden, Homewood Suites, Howard Johnson's, Oxford Suites, Commercial Tire, Costco/gas, Dillon RV Ctr, Discount Tire, Les Schwab Tire, Lowe's, USPO, Valvoline, Verizon, vet, Walmart/auto
49	I-184(exits left from eb), to W Boise, N H
46	ID 55, Eagle, N Chevron/McDonald's/dsl, Buffalo Wild Wings, Del Taco, Gyro Shack, Ling&Louie's, Los Beto's, Mi Casa Mexican, Mo' Bettahs, Starbucks, Comfort Suites, Hampton Inn, Holiday Inn Express, La Quinta, H, S Chevron/dsl, Big Jud's Burgers, Chicago Connection, Dickey's BBQ, Dominos, Dutch Bros Coffee, Giggy D's Rest., Happy Teriyaki, Jack-in-the-Box, Jimmy John's, Joy Garden, Pita Pit, Qdoba, Rudy's Grill, Sakana Japanese, Sonic, Stella's Creamery, Subway, Taco Bell, The Griddle, Candlewood Suites, Courtyard, TownePlace Suites, Tru, Harley-Davidson, Indian Motorcycles, URGENT CARE, Valvoline, vet
44	ID 69, Meridian, N Chevron/dsl, Maverik/dsl, Sinclair, A&W/KFC, DQ, Jimmy John's, McDonald's, Panda Express, Shari's, Starbucks, Subway, Taco Bell, Taco Time, Wendy's, Best Western+, Motel 6, AT&T, Home Depot, Johnny's Autocare, Les Schwab Tire, Verizon, WinCo Foods, S Shell/dsl, Carl's Jr, Chipotle, KJ's Grille, Lovejoy's Ice Cream, Starbucks, Starbucks, Quality Inn, Camping World RV Ctr, Ford, Lowe's, O'Reilly Parts, Walgreens, Walmart, waterpark
42	Ten Mile Rd, N Maverik, Costa Vida, Dutch Bros, Johnny Bronx, Starbucks, Zupas, Grocery Outlet, Scheels, Valvoline, vet
38	Garrity Blvd, Nampa, N Chevron/dsl, Walmart Gas/dsl, Dutch Bros Coffee, Egg Factory, ID Pizza Co., Jack-in-the-Box, Krispy Krunchy Chicken, Los Betos, Port of Subs, Sonic, Everhome Suites, Hampton Inn, Home2 Suites,
38	Continued My Place Hotel, Buick/GMC, Cadillac/Chevrolet, Chrysler/Dodge/Jeep, Ford, Ford ID Conv Ctr, Hyundai, Infiniti, Nissan, O'Reilly Parts, Subaru, Toyota/Scion, Walmart/Subway, S McDonald's, Phillips 66/dsl, Shell/dsl, Chipotle, Fiesta Guadalajara, Freddy's, Jimmy John's, Mongolian BBQ, Noodles&Co, Panda Express, Papa Murphy's, Pizza Hut, Popeyes, Starbucks, Subway, Taco Bell, Wendy's, Holiday Inn Express, Garrity RV Park, H, JC Penney, Verizon, War Hawk Museum, Winco Foods
36	Franklin Blvd, Nampa, N Maverik/scales/dsl, Jack-in-the-Box, Shilo Inn/rest., S Chevron/dsl, Shell/Subway/dsl/RV dump/scales/4hr, Sleep Inn, Bretz RV Ctr, Freightliner, Honda, H, Mason Cr RV Park
35	ID 55, Nampa, S Maverik/dsl, Shell/dsl, Burger Den, Starbucks, Nampa Inn, Rodeway Inn, Super 8
33b a	ID 55 S, Midland Blvd, Marcine, N Chevron, Blaze Pizza, Chick-fil-A, Cracker Barrel, Dickey's BBQ, Dutch Bros, Five Guys, Habit Burger, In-N-Out, Krispy Krunchy Chicken, McDonald's, O Crab, Olive Garden, Panera Bread, Panera Bread, Qdoba Mexican, Sonic, Winger's, Fairfield Inn, Holiday Inn, AT&T, Batteries+, Best Buy, Costco/gas, Dick's, Discount Tire, Hobby Lobby, H, Kohl's, Michael's, Old Navy, PetCo, PetSmart, Sportsmans Whse, Target, TJ Maxx, Vavoline, Verizon, S Shell/dsl, Applebee's, Arby's, Blimpie, Buffalo Wild Wings, Carl's Jr, Coldstone, Costa Vida, Cupbop, DQ, Golden Corral, IHOP, Jack-in-the-Box, Jade Garden, Jalapeno's Grill, Jimmy John's, Mongolian BBQ, Outback Steaks, Papa Murphy's, Pizza Hut, Red Robin, Shari's Rest, Smashburger, Smokey Mtn Grill, Starbucks, Subway, Taco Bell, The Griddle, Tropical Smoothie, TX Roadhouse, Wendy's, Wingstop, Zupas Kitchen, $Tree, Big O Tire, Home Depot, Jiffy Lube, Lowe's, NAPA, O'Reilly Parts, Point S Automotive, Ross, Savers, Staples, U-Haul, Verizon, Verizon (2), vet, Walgreens, WinCo Foods
29	US 20/26, Franklin Rd, Caldwell, N Flying J/Denny's/dsl/LP/scales/24hr, Maverik, Ambassador RV camping, S Sage/Phillips 66/dsl/24hr, Burger King, Del Taco, Dutch Bros, Best Western+, La Quinta
28	10th Ave, Caldwell, N Maverik/dsl, city park, S Chevron/dsl, Shell/dsl, Carl's Jr, Fiesta Mexican, Jack-in-the-Box, McDonald's, Mr V's Rest., Pizza Hut, Subway, Wendy's, AutoZone, Bi-Mart, H, Point S Automotive, Walgreens
27	ID 19, to Wilder, S Chevron/dsl
26.5mm	Boise River
26	US 20/26, to Notus, N Caldwell Campground, fireworks, S Sinclair/dsl, RV Resort
25	ID 44, Middleton, N Chevron/dsl
17	Sand Hollow, N Sinclair/Sand Hollow Café/dsl, Country Corners RV Park
13	Black Canyon Jct
9	US 30, to New Plymouth
3	US 95, Fruitland, N Chevron/A&W/dsl, truck repair
1mm	Welcome Ctr eb, full facilities, info, litter barrels, petwalk
0mm	Idaho/Oregon state line, Snake River

INTERSTATE 86

Exit #	Services
63b a	I-15, N to Butte, S to SLC. I-86 begins/ends on I-15, exit 72.
61	US 91, Yellowstone Ave, Pocatello, N Exxon, Maverik/dsl, Shell/dsl, Arby's, Arctic Circle, Burger King, Chapala Mexican, Domino's, Jack-in-the-Box, Lei's BBQ, Papa Murphy's, Subway, Tres Hermanos, Wendy's, Extended Stay, Motel 6, $Tree, AutoZone, Bargain Tire, Family$, Jiffy Lube, O'Reilly Parts, Parris RV Ctr, Smith's Foods/dsl, vet, S Exxon/dsl, Phillips 66/dsl, Buffalo Wild Wings,

NAMPA MARCINE CALDWELL POCATELLO

ID

= gas = food = lodging = other = rest stop

ID

INTERSTATE 86 Cont'd

AMERICAN FALLS

Exit	Services
61	Continued Costa Vida, Firehouse Subs, Five Guys, Freddy's, Fuji Japanese, Great Wall, IHOP, Jimmy John's, Kingpot Korean, MacKenzie River Grill, McDonald's, MOD Pizza, Noodles&Co, Olive Garden, Panda Express, Panera Bread, Pizza Hut, Pizza Pie Café, Popeyes, Red Robin, Starbucks, TX Roadhouse, Wingstop, AT&T, Chrysler/Dodge/Jeep, Costco/gas, Dick's, Discount Tire, Ford/Lincoln, Hobby Lobby, Home Depot, Honda, JC Penney, Kia, Lowe's, NAPA, Nissan, Old Navy, PetCo, PetSmart, Ross, Schwab Tire, TJ Maxx, Toyota, U-Haul, Verizon, Verizon, Walgreens, Walmart
58.5mm	Portneuf River
58	US 30, W Pocatello, N Batise Springs RV Park/dump(1mi-seasonal)
56	N Pocatello Reg, S Sinclair/dsl/24hr
52	Arbon Valley, S Phillips 66/Bannock Peak/dsl, casino
51mm	Bannock Creek
49	Rainbow Rd
44	Seagull Bay
40	ID 39, American Falls, N Chevron, Sinclair, Sinclair/dsl(1mi), Arctic Circle, McDonald's, Subway, The Dam Pizza, Tres Hermanos Mexican, Family$(1mi), H, Jiffy Lube, NAPA, O'Reilly Parts, Schwab Tire, to Am Falls Dam, Willow Bay RV Park/dump, S Hillview Motel
36	ID 37, to Rockland, American Falls, N Shell/dsl, Falls Motel, H
33	Neeley Area
31mm	wb, full facilities, litter barrels, petwalk, vending, hist site
28	no services
21	Coldwater Area
19mm	eb, full facilities, litter barrels, petwalk, vending, hist site
15	Raft River Area
1	I-84 E, to Ogden. I-86 begins/ends on I-84, exit 222.

INTERSTATE 90

MULLAN / BIG CREEK

Exit	Services
74mm	Idaho/Montana state line, Pacific/Central time zone, Lookout Pass elev 4680
73mm	no services
72mm	scenic area/hist site eb
71mm	runaway truck ramp wb
70mm	runaway truck ramp wb
69	Lp 90, Mullan, N Sinclair/dsl, Harwood's Drug, museum, USPO
68	Lp 90(from eb), Mullan, same as 69
67	Morning District, Morning District
66	Gold Creek(from eb)
65	Compressor District
64	Golconda District
62	ID 4, Wallace, S Conoco, Pizza Factory, Brooks Hotel, Stardust Motel, Ace Hardware, Harvest Foods, museum, Wallace RV Park
61	Lp 90, Wallace, same as 62, S Conoco/dsl, Blackboard Cafe, Fainting Goat Rest., Pizza Factory, Trailside Cafe, Brooks Hotel/rest., Lux Rooms, The Stardust Motel, Wallace Inn, auto repair, info ctr, museum
60	Lp 90, Silverton, N USPO
57	Lp 90, Osburn, S 76/dsl, auto repair, Blue Anchor RV Park, USPO, Watson's Mkt
54	Big Creek, N hist site
51	Lp 90, Division St, Kellogg, N Conoco/dsl, Trail Motel, Buick/Cadillac/Chevrolet/GMC, Chrysler/Dodge/Jeep, H, Schwab Tire, vet, S Domino's, Wa Hing Chinese, La Maison B&B, USPO

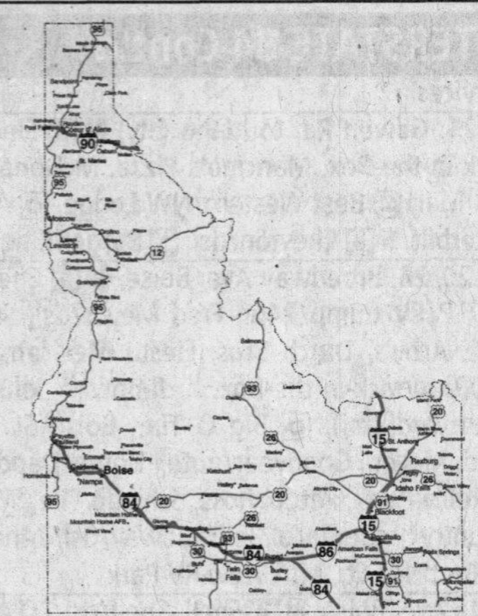

CATALDO / COEUR D' ALENE

Exit	Services
50	Hill St(from eb), Kellogg, N Casa De Oro Mexica[n], Humdinger Drive-In, Trail Motel, Ace Hardware, tires, [S] Conoco/dsl, museum, Silver Mtn Ski/summer resort rec area, Yoke's Foods
49	Bunker Ave, N 76/dsl, McDonald's, Sam's Drive-I[n], Subway, Silver Inn, H, S Silver Mtn Rest., Fairbridge Inn, Morning Star Lodge, city park, museum waterpark
48	Smelterville, S $Tree, auto repair, Dave Smith Tire, Grocer[y] Outlet, O'Reilly Parts, USPO, Walmart
45	Pinehurst, S Chevron/dsl/repair, Conoco, By-The-Wa[y] Camping, golf, Harvest Foods, Honda, True Value, U-Hau[l], USPO, vet
43	Kingston, N Conoco/dsl, S Exxon/dsl/rv dump, USPO
40	Cataldo, N Timbers Roadhouse, USPO, S CDA River RV Campground
39.5mm	Coeur d' Alene River
39	Cataldo Mission, S Nat Hist Landmark, Old Mission SP
34	ID 3, to St Maries, Rose Lake, S Conoco/dsl, Rose Lake dsl, Rose Lake Cafe
33	chain removal eb
32mm	chainup area/weigh sta wb
31.5mm	4th of July Cr, Panhandle NF eastern boundary
28	4th of July Pass, elevation 3069, Mullen Tree HS, turno[ut] both lanes, ski area, snowmobile area
24mm	chainup eb, removal wb
22	ID 97, to St Maries, L Coeur d' Alene Scenic ByWay, Wo[lf] Lodge District, Harrison, N Wolf Lodge Camping, S Lak[e] Coeur d'Alene RV Park
20.5mm	Lake Coeur d' Alene
17	Mullan Trail Rd
15	Lp 90, Sherman Ave, Coeur d' Alene, N forest info, Lak[e] Coeur D' Alene RA/HS, S Chevron, Exxon/dsl, Mobil/dsl LP, Jimmy's Cafe, Juniors Mexican, Michael D's Eater[y], Moontime Cafe, Roger's Burgers, Schmidty's Burgers, Th[e] Relic BBQ, Zip's Rest., Baymont Inn, Blackwel[l], BudgetSaver Motel, El Rancho Motel, Japan House Suite[s], North ID Inn, Two Lakes Motel, auto repair, Harvest Food[s], museum, tourist info
14	15th St, Coeur d' Alene, S TAJ Mart, Jordon's Grocery
13	4th St, Coeur d' Alene, N A&D/dsl, Atilano's Mexica[n], Baskin Robbins, Breaking Bread, Brunch Box, Carl's J[r], Denny's, Domino's, Jimmy John's, Little Caesar's, Origin[al] Mongolian BBQ, Panda Express, Roger's Burgers, Starbuck[s], Subway, Surf Shack, Wendy's, Ramada Inn, AutoZon[e], BigLots, Costco/gas, NAPA, same as 12, Schwab Tir[e], Tamarack RV Park & Cabins, Verizon, S Exxon/dsl, Maserati/Alfa Romeo, Thai Bamboo
12	US 95, to Sandpoint, Moscow, N Circle K, Exxon/ds[l], Holiday/dsl, Mobil/dsl, Walmart/dsl, Applebee's, Arby's

INTERSTATE 90 Cont'd

12 Continued
Buffalo Wild Wings, Cafe Rio, Capriotti's Sandwiches, Carl's Jr, Chili's, China Town, Del Taco, Dickey's BBQ, Elmer's, JB's Rest., Jimmy John's, Killer Burger, MacKenzie River Pizza, McDonald's, Olive Garden, Panda Express, Panera Bread, Pizza Hut, Qdoba, Red Lobster, Starbucks, Taco Bell, Tomato St., TX Roadhouse, Westside Pizza, Yummy Crab, Best Western+, Comfort Suites, Fairbridge Inn, Motel 6, Quality Inn, Rodeway Inn, Super 8, $Tree, Advance Parts, AT&T, Best Buy, Buick/GMC, Cadillac, Combs RV, Discount Tire, Ford/Subaru, Fred Meyer/dsl, Grocery Outlet, Home Depot, Jo-Ann Fabrics, Kia, Kohl's, Macy's, Natural Grocers, Nissan, O'Reilly Parts, PetCo, Pizza Factory, Ross, Safeway, Safeway/dsl, Super 1 Foods, Target, TireRama, TJ Maxx, Toyota/Scion, U-Haul, URGENT CARE, Verizon, Walgreens, Walmart/Subway, S Conoco/dsl, Mobil, Huhot, Jack-in-the-Box, Jamba Juice, Papa Murphy's, Qdoba Mexican, Starbucks, La Quinta, AT&T, GNC, H, Safeway, same as 13

11 Northwest Blvd, N 76/dsl, Cascadia Pizza, Cracker Barrel, Jack-in-the-Box, MOD Pizza, Starbucks, Subway, Lowe's, URGENT CARE, WinCo Foods, S 76/dsl, Chevron, Anthony's, Azteca Mexican, Dutch Bros, McDonald's, Red Robin, SF Sourdough, Starbucks, Days Inn, Hampton Inn, Holiday Inn Express, SpringHill Suites, Staybridge Suites, TownePlace Suites, Honda, H, Riverwalk RV Park

8.5mm both lanes, full facilities, info, litter barrels, petwalk, **Welcome Ctr/weigh sta eb**

7 ID 41, to Rathdrum, Spirit Lake, N 76/dsl, Maverik/dsl, Burger King, Del Taco, Domino's, Dutch Bros, El Ranchero, Embers Pizza, Jack-in-the-Box, Jimmy John's, Papa Murphy, Pita Pit, Popeyes, Sonic, Starbucks, Wendy's, Westside Pizza, $Tree, AT&T, auto repair, Chevrolet, Chrysler/Dodge/Jeep, Couer d'Alene RV Park, H, Hyundai, Nissan, URGENT CARE, VW, Walmart/Subway, S Chevron/dsl, Coleman/dsl, A&W/KFC, Capone's Grill, DQ, Quality Inn, Tommy's RV Ctr, truck repair, Verizon, vet

6 Seltice Way, N 7-11, La Cabana Mexican, Paul Bunyan Burgers, Pizza Hut, NAPA, Super 1 Foods, Walgreens, S 76/dsl/LP, Denny's, Fuki Japanese, Gross Donuts, Little Caesar's, McDonald's, Old European Cafe, Rancho Viejo Mexican, Taco Bell, Zip's Drive-In, Ace Hardware, Jiffy Lube, O'Reilly Parts, TireRama, USPO, vet, Yoke's Foods

5 Lp 90, Spokane St, Treaty Rock HS, N 76/dsl, Cenex, Exxon/dsl, Corner Cafe, Domino's, Golden Dragon, Papa John's, Rob's Seafood/burgers, Subway, Tilly's Rest., WhiteHouse Grill, AutoZone, Blue Compass RV Ctr, Family$, Perfection Tire/repair, Schwab Tire, S Handy Mart/Pacific Pride/dsl, Red Lion Inn, visitors ctr

2 Pleasant View Rd, N Flying J/dsl/LP/scales/24hr, Fuel&Snack, Love's/Carl's Jr/dsl/scales/24hr, McDonald's, Toro Viejo Mexican, Sure Stay+, antiques, RV/truckwash, Suntree RV Park, S Exxon/dsl, Zip's Drive-in, Red Lion Inn, Sleep Inn

1 Beck Rd, N Circle K/dsl, Maverik/dsl, Panda Express, Subway, Cabela's, NAPA, Post Falls RV Campground, Walmart, S greyhound track

0mm Idaho/Washington state line

INTERSTATE 184 (Boise)

6mm I-184 begins/ends on 13th St, downtown, Shell, Bonefish Grill, Chandler's Steaks, Five Guys, PF Chang's, Hampton Inn, Safari Inn, The Grove, Office Depot, USPO

5 River St(from eb), W Chevron, McDonald's, Red Lion

4.5mm Boise River

3 Fairview Ave, to US 20/26 E, W Joe's Crabshack, Tepanyaki Japanese, Boise Inn, Cottonwood Suites, Riverside Hotel, Commercial Tire

2 Curtis Rd, to Garden City, E Shell, H

1b a Cole Rd, Franklin Rd, E Chevron/Subway/dsl, Acura, Chrysler/Dodge/Jeep, Honda, Jaguar, Land Rover, Mercedes, Volvo, W Chevron/dsl, Sinclair/dsl, Applebee's, Cafe Ole, Cafe Rio, Carl's Jr, Cheesecake Factory, Chick-fil-A, Chili's, Chipotle, Dave&Buster's, Fujiyama Japanese, Golden Corral, IHOP, Jalapeno's, McDonald's, Noodles&Co, Old Chicago Pizza, Olive Garden, Port of Subs, Quiznos, Red Lobster, Red Robin, Rumbi Island Grill, Shari's, Sizzler, Smash Burger, Starbucks, Wendy's, Candlewood Suites, La Quinta, Residence Inn, AT&T, AT&T, Audi/VW, Best Buy, Cabela's, Dick's, Dillard's, JC Penney, Kohl's, Macy's, Michael's, Old Navy, PetCo, PetSmart, REI, Ross, Target, TJ Maxx, Tuesday Morning, Verizon

0mm I-184 begins/ends on I-84, exit 49.

ID

NOTES

ILLINOIS

INTERSTATE 24

VIENNA

Exit #	Services
38mm	Illinois/Kentucky state line, Ohio River
37	US 45, Metropolis, **[rest stop] both lanes, full [handicap] facilities, info, litter barrels, petwalk, [picnic], vending, S** [gas] BP/Quiznos/dsl, [food] Bill's BBQ, China House, El Tequila, Huddle House, McDonald's, Pizza Hut, Sonic, [lodging] Best Value Inn, Holiday Inn Express, Motel 6, Quality Inn, Super 8, [other] $General, Buick/Chrysler/Dodge/GMC/Jeep, camping, Chevrolet, Ft Massac SP, [H], O'Reilly Parts, Plaza Tire, to Riverboat Casino
27	to New Columbia, Big Bay
16	IL 146, Vienna, **S** [gas] BP/dsl, Citgo/dsl, FastStop, [food] DQ, McDonald's, Smokin Daddy's Grill, Subway, Vienna Diner, [lodging] Hotel 7, [other] vet
14	US 45, Vienna, **S** [other] camping
7	to Goreville, Tunnel Hill, **N** [other] winery(7mi), **S** camping, to Ferne Clyffe SP
1	I-57, N to Chicago, S to Memphis. I-24 begins/ends on I-57, exit 44.

INTERSTATE 39

SYCAMORE · EARLVILLE

Exit #	Services
122.5mm	I-39 and I-90 run together into Wisconsin. See Illinois Interstate 90.
122b a	US 20 E, Harrison Ave, to Belvidere(last nb exit before toll rd), **W** [gas] Fas Fuel/Subway/dsl, Mobil, Tesla EVC, [food] Arby's, Bergner's, Burger King, DQ, Granite City Rest., Lung Fung, Rosati's, Rosati's Pizza, Sonic, Taco Bell, TGIFriday's, [other] Barnes&Noble, BMW, Buick/Chevrolet/GMC, Collier RV Ctr, Goodyear/auto, Harley-Davidson, JC Penney, Macy's, mall, Menards, Schnuck's Foods/gas, Tires+, vet, VW, Walgreens
119	US 20 W, Alpine Rd, to Rockford
116.5mm	Kishwaukee River
115	Baxter Rd, **E** [gas] Shell/Subway/dsl/scales/24hr/@
111	IL 72, to Monroe Center, **E** [gas] BP/Sunrise Family Rest./dsl/24hr, Love's/dsl/scales/24hr, Marathon(1mi)
104	IL 64, to Oregon, Sycamore, **W** [food] Grubsteakers Rest/truck parking(2mi)
99	IL 38, to De Kalb, Rochelle, **E** [gas] Pilot/dsl/scales/24hr, **W** Murphy USA/dsl, Petro/Iron Skillet/dsl/scales/RV Dump/@, Phillips 66/Circle K/dsl, Road Ranger/Subway/dsl/scales/24hr, Shell/dsl, [food] Arby's, Butterfly Rest, China Wok, Culver's, Dunkin Donuts, Jimmy John's, Little Caesar's, McDonald's, New China, Pizza Hut, Subway, Taco Bell, Wendy's, [lodging] Comfort Inn, Country Hearth Inn, Holiday Inn Express, Super 8, [other] $General, $Tree, Blue Beacon, GNC, [H], O'Reilly Parts, Sullivan's Foods, Verizon, Walgreens, Walmart
97b a	I-88 tollway, to Moline, Rock Island, Chicago
93	Steward
87	US 30, to Sterling, Rock Falls, **E** [other] to Shabbona Lake SP, **W** Yogi Bear Camping(16mi)
84.5mm	**full [handicap] facilities, litter barrels, petwalk, [phone], [picnic], playground, [rest stop] both lanes, vending**
82	Paw Paw, **E** [gas] Casey's(3mi), **W** many wind turbines
72	US 34, to Mendota, Earlville, **W** [gas] BP/Cindy's/dsl/scales/24hr, Road Ranger/Subway/dsl/scales/24hr, [food] KFC/Taco Bell, McDonald's, [lodging] Quality Inn, Super 8/truck parking, [other] [H]
67.5mm	Little Vermilion River
66	US 52, Troy Grove, **E** [other] KOA(6mi)
62.5mm	Tomahawk Creek
59b a	I-80, E to Chicago, W to Des Moines
57	US 6, to Peru, La Salle, **W** [gas] Casey's, [lodging] Daniel's Motel,

IL

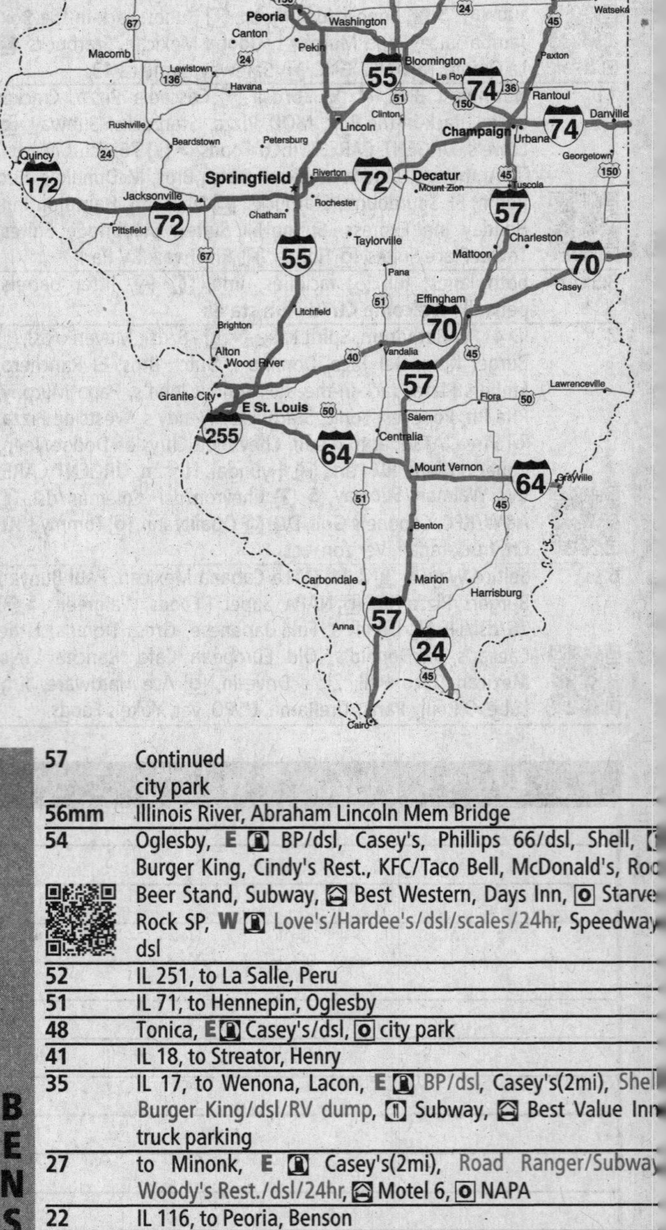

BENSON

Exit #	Services
57	Continued city park
56mm	Illinois River, Abraham Lincoln Mem Bridge
54	Oglesby, **E** [gas] BP/dsl, Casey's, Phillips 66/dsl, Shell, [food] Burger King, Cindy's Rest., KFC/Taco Bell, McDonald's, Roo Beer Stand, Subway, [lodging] Best Western, Days Inn, [other] Starve Rock SP, **W** [gas] Love's/Hardee's/dsl/scales/24hr, Speedway dsl
52	IL 251, to La Salle, Peru
51	IL 71, to Hennepin, Oglesby
48	Tonica, **E** [gas] Casey's/dsl, [other] city park
41	IL 18, to Streator, Henry
35	IL 17, to Wenona, Lacon, **E** [gas] BP/dsl, Casey's(2mi), Shel Burger King/dsl/RV dump, [food] Subway, [lodging] Best Value Inn truck parking
27	to Minonk, **E** [gas] Casey's(2mi), Road Ranger/Subway Woody's Rest./dsl/24hr, [lodging] Motel 6, [other] NAPA
22	IL 116, to Peoria, Benson
14	US 24, to El Paso, Peoria, **E** [gas] BP/Subway/dsl/24hr, Casey's dsl, Freedom/dsl, Speedway/dsl, [food] DQ, Hardee's McDonald's, Woody's Family Rest., [lodging] Days Inn, [other] Buick Chevrolet/GMC, city park, Ford, IGA Foods, USPO,

 = gas = food = lodging = other = rest stop

INTERSTATE 39 Cont'd

14 Continued Monical's Pizza, Super 8, $General, Hickory Hill Camping(4mi), PROMPT CARE
9mm Mackinaw River
8 IL 251, Lake Bloomington Rd, **E** Lake Bloomington, **W** Evergreen Lake, to Comlara Park
5 Hudson, **E** Casey's/dsl
2 US 51 bus, Bloomington, Normal
0mm I-39 begins/ends on I-55, exit 164.

INTERSTATE 55

295mm I-55 begins/ends on US 41, Lakeshore Dr, in Chicago.
293a to Cermak Rd(from nb)
292b a I-90/94, W to Chicago, E to Indiana
290 Damen Ave, Ashland Ave(no EZ nb return), **E** Marathon, Shell, Starbucks, Target
289 to California Ave (no EZ nb return), **E** Marathon, Road Ranger/Subway/dsl, Thornton's/dsl
288 Kedzie Ave, from sb, no ez return, **E** Citgo
287 Pulaski Rd, **E** BP/dsl, Shell, Burger King, Domino's, Dunkin Donuts, Subway, Wendy's, Advance Parts, AlLDI, AT&T, Dodge, Honda, Marshall's, Michael's, Pete's Mkt, PetSmart, Ross, Target, Walgreens
286 IL 50, Cicero Ave, **E** BP, Mobil/dsl, Shell/dsl, Dunkin Donuts, McDonald's, Starbucks, Subway, AutoZone, O'Reilly Parts, to
285 Central Ave, **E** BP/dsl, Grand Prix/Dunkin Donuts, Minuteman/Dunkin Donuts, Burger King, Donald's HotDogs
283 IL 43, Harlem Ave, **E** Shell, Baskin-Robbins/Dunkin Donuts, Burger King, Domino's, Little Caesar's, Portillo HotDogs, Potbelly's, Subway, ALDI, AT&T, AutoZone, Fannie May Candies, Walgreens
282b a IL 171, 1st Ave, **W** Brookfield Zoo
279b US 12, US 20, US 45, La Grange Rd, **W** BP, Mobil, Shell/Circle K, Andy's Custard, Applebee's, Arby's, Baskin-Robbins/Dunkin Donuts, Boston Mkt, Burger King, Chick-fil-A, Cocula Rest., Dragon Buffet, Dunkin Donuts, Hooters, JC Georges Rest., Jimmy John's, Ledo's Pizza, LoneStar Steaks, McDonald's, Nonno's Pizza, Panda Express, Pizza Hut, Popeyes, Starbucks, Subway, Taco Bell, Taco Tico, Time Out Grill, TX Roadhouse, Via Bella, Wendy's, White Castle, Best Western+, Holiday Inn, $Tree, AlLDI, Best Buy, Buick/Cadillac/GMC, Chevrolet, Chrysler/Dodge/Jeep, Discount Tire, Firestone/auto, Ford, GNC, Harley Davidson, Home Depot, Honda, Jo-Ann Fabrics, Kohl's, Mazda, Menards, NAPA, Nissan, NTB, O'Reilly Parts, PepBoys, PetCo, PetSmart, Sam's Club/gas, Subaru, Target, Toyota/Scion, Verizon, VW, Walmart
279a La Grange Rd, to I-294 toll, S to Indiana
277b I-294 toll(from nb), S to Indiana
277a I-294 toll, N to Wisconsin
276c Joliet Rd(from nb)
276b a County Line Rd, **E** Capri Rest., China King, Ciazza's Grill, Cooper's Hawk, Eddie Merlot's, Patti's Sunrise Cafe, Starbucks, Subway, Topaz Rest., Extended Stay America, Marriott, Quality Inn, Tuesday Morning, **W** SpringHill Suites
274 IL 83, Kingery Rd, **E** Shell, **W** BP/dsl, Mobil/dsl, Shell, Bakers Square, Buffalo Wild Wings, Chick-fil-A, Chipotle Mexican, Denny's, Dunkin Donuts, Jamba Juice, Jimmy John's, MOD Pizza, Panera Bread, Papa John's, Patio BBQ, Portillo's HotDogs, Potbelly's Rest., Starbucks, Wendy's, Econolodge, Holiday Inn, La Quinta, Red Roof Inn, Ford/KIA, GNC, Marshall's, Marshall's, Michael's, Staples, Target,

BOLINGBROOK AURORA . JOLIET BRAIDWOOD

274 Continued Verizon
273b a Cass Ave, **W** Shell, Al Chile Mexican, Chuck's Rest., Rosati's Pizza, Uncle Mao's Chinese
271b a Lemont Rd, **E** Extended Stay America, **W** Shell
269 I-355 toll, to W Suburbs
268 (from sb only), Joliet, same as 267
267 IL 53, Bolingbrook, **E** 55 Trkstp/rest./dsl/scales/24hr/@, BP/dsl, McDonald's, Ramada Ltd, Super 8, Chevrolet, **W** Shell/Circle K, Speedway/dsl, Burger King, Cheddar's, Denny's, Dunkin Donuts, El Burrito Loco, Family Square Rest., Golden Chopsticks, Golden Corral, McDonald's, Popeyes, Starbucks, Subway, Wendy's, White Castle, Hampton Inn, Hilton Garden, Holiday Inn, Quality Inn, Residence Inn, SpringHill Suites, $Tree, AlLDI, Fiesta Mkt, NAPA, Tony's Mkt, U-Haul, Walgreens, Walmart
266mm weigh sta both lanes
263 Weber Rd, **E** 7-11, BP/dsl, Speedway/Dunkin Donuts/dsl/e85, Burger King, Burrito's, Culver's, Doc Watson's Smokehouse, KFC, Little China, McDonald's, Michael's Pizza, Popeyes, Subway, Todake Steaks, White Castle, Days Inn, Holiday Inn Express, Ace Hardware, BB Rest., Discount Tire, GNC, Reba's Automotive, Walgreens, **W** Mobil/Jimmy John's/dsl, Shell/Circle K, Arby's, Cracker Barrel, Wendy's, Comfort Inn, Country Inn&Suites, Extended Stay America, Woodspring Suites
261 IL 126(from sb), to Plainfield
257 US 30, to Joliet, Aurora, **E** Shell/Circle K, Anthony's Rest., Applebee's, Baskin-Robbins/Dunkin Donuts, Burger King, Chipotle, ChuckeCheese, Denny's, Diamand's Rest., Five Guys, Fresh Thyme Mkt, Hooters, LoneStar Steaks, McDonald's, Outback Steaks, Panera Bread, Red Lobster, Steak'n Shake, Subway, Taco Bell, TGIFriday's, TX Roadhouse, Wendy's, Best Western+, Comfort Inn, Fairfield Inn, Hampton Inn, Home2 Suites, Motel 6, Super 8, $Tree, ALDI, AT&T, AutoZone, Barnes&Noble, Best Buy, Dick's, Discount Tire, Firestone/auto, Home Depot, Honda, JC Penney, Jo-Ann Fabrics, Macy's, Michael's, NTB, Old Navy, PetSmart, Ross, Target, Verizon, **W** Mobil/dsl, Blue's BBQ, Luigi's Pizza, Chevrolet, Ford
253b a US 52, Jefferson St, Joliet, **E** Citgo/dsl, Mobil/dsl, Shell, Freedom Automotive, Joe's Rest., McDonald's, Best Western, Econolodge, Elk's Motel, La Quinta, Wingate Inn, Ford, Freightliner, Harley-Davidson, H, Rick's RV Ctr, **W** BP/dsl, Shell, Burger King, Casa Maya, DQ, Rosati's Pizza, Starbucks, Subway, 7-11, Chrysler/Dodge/Jeep, Jewel-Osco, vet
251 IL 59(from nb), to Shorewood, access to same as 253 W
250b a I-80, W to Iowa, E to Toledo
248 US 6, Joliet, **E** Pilot/Dunkin Donuts/Subway/dsl/24hr, Speedway/dsl, Taco Burrito King, **W** BP/McDonald's, Thornton's/dsl/scales
247 Bluff Rd
245mm Des Plaines River
244 Arsenal Rd, **E** Exxon/Mobil Refinery
241 to Wilmington
241mm Kankakee River
240 Lorenzo Rd, **E** BP/dsl, **W** Mobil/pizza/dsl/scales/24hr, Petro/Shell/Iron Skillet/dsl/scales/24hr, Knights Inn
238 IL 129 S, to Wilmington (from nb), Braidwood
236 IL 113, Coal City, **E** EZ Living RV Ctr, Fossil Rock Camping, **W** Casey's, Shell/DQ/dsl, KFC/Taco Bell, Little Caesar's, Los 3 Burritos, WhistleStop Cafe
233 Reed Rd, **E** Marathon/dsl, Jones-sez BBQ
227 IL 53, Gardner, **E** Casey's, Gardner Rest., Subway, $General, truck/tire repair, **W** BP/dsl
220 IL 47, Dwight, **E** BP/Burger King/dsl,

IL

= gas = food = lodging = other = rest stop

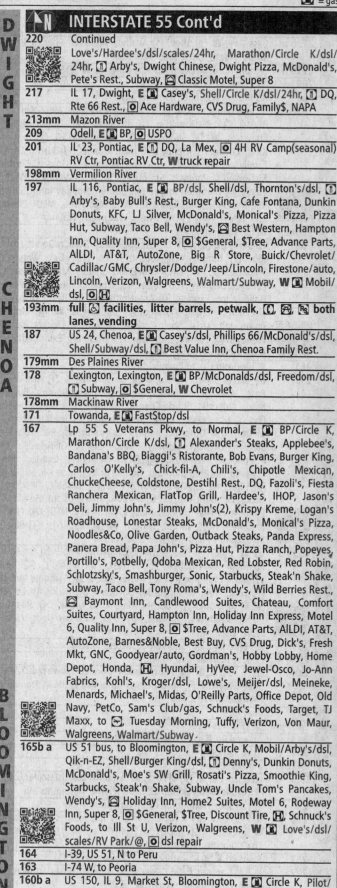

INTERSTATE 55 Cont'd

DWIGHT

220 Continued
Love's/Hardee's/dsl/scales/24hr, Marathon/Circle K/dsl/24hr, Arby's, Dwight Chinese, Dwight Pizza, McDonald's, Pete's Rest., Subway, Classic Motel, Super 8

217 IL 17, Dwight, E Casey's, Shell/Circle K/dsl/24hr, DQ, Rte 66 Rest., Ace Hardware, CVS Drug, Family$, NAPA

213mm Mazon River

209 Odell, E BP, USPO

201 IL 23, Pontiac, E DQ, La Mex, 4H RV Camp(seasonal) RV Ctr, Pontiac RV Ctr, W truck repair

198mm Vermilion River

CHENOA

197 IL 116, Pontiac, E BP/dsl, Shell/dsl, Thornton's/dsl, Arby's, Baby Bull's Rest., Burger King, Cafe Fontana, Dunkin Donuts, KFC, LJ Silver, McDonald's, Monical's Pizza, Pizza Hut, Subway, Taco Bell, Wendy's, Best Western, Hampton Inn, Quality Inn, Super 8, $General, $Tree, Advance Parts, AlLDI, AT&T, AutoZone, Big R Store, Buick/Chevrolet/Cadillac/GMC, Chrysler/Dodge/Jeep/Lincoln, Firestone/auto, Lincoln, Verizon, Walgreens, Walmart/Subway, W Mobil/dsl, H

193mm **full facilities, litter barrels, petwalk, both lanes, vending**

187 US 24, Chenoa, E Casey's/dsl, Phillips 66/McDonald's/dsl, Shell/Subway/dsl, Best Value Inn, Chenoa Family Rest.

179mm Des Plaines River

178 Lexington, Lexington, E BP/McDonalds/dsl, Freedom/dsl, Subway, $General, W Chevrolet

178mm Mackinaw River

171 Towanda, E FastStop/dsl

BLOOMINGTON

167 Lp 55 S Veterans Pkwy, to Normal, E BP/Circle K, Marathon/Circle K/dsl, Alexander's Steaks, Applebee's, Bandana's BBQ, Biaggi's Ristorante, Bob Evans, Burger King, Carlos O'Kelly's, Chick-fil-A, Chili's, Chipotle Mexican, ChuckeCheese, Coldstone, Destihl Rest., DQ, Fazoli's, Fiesta Ranchera Mexican, FlatTop Grill, Hardee's, IHOP, Jason's Deli, Jimmy John's, Jimmy John's(2), Krispy Kreme, Logan's Roadhouse, Lonestar Steaks, McDonald's, Monical's Pizza, Noodles&Co, Olive Garden, Outback Steaks, Panda Express, Panera Bread, Papa John's, Pizza Hut, Pizza Ranch, Popeyes, Portillo's, Potbelly, Qdoba Mexican, Red Lobster, Red Robin, Schlotzsky's, Smashburger, Sonic, Starbucks, Steak'n Shake, Subway, Taco Bell, Tony Roma's, Wendy's, Wild Berries Rest., Baymont Inn, Candlewood Suites, Chateau, Comfort Suites, Courtyard, Hampton Inn, Holiday Inn Express, Motel 6, Quality Inn, Super 8, $Tree, Advance Parts, AlLDI, AT&T, AutoZone, Barnes&Noble, Best Buy, CVS Drug, Dick's, Fresh Mkt, GNC, Goodyear/auto, Gordman's, Hobby Lobby, Home Depot, Honda, H, Hyundai, HyVee, Jewel-Osco, Jo-Ann Fabrics, Kohl's, Kroger/dsl, Lowe's, Meijer/dsl, Meineke, Menards, Michael's, Midas, O'Reilly Parts, Office Depot, Old Navy, PetCo, Sam's Club/gas, Schnuck's Foods, Target, TJ Maxx, to , Tuesday Morning, Tuffy, Verizon, Von Maur, Walgreens, Walmart/Subway

165b a US 51 bus, to Bloomington, E Circle K, Mobil/Arby's/dsl, Qik-n-EZ, Shell/Burger King/dsl, Denny's, Dunkin Donuts, McDonald's, Moe's SW Grill, Rosati's Pizza, Smoothie King, Starbucks, Steak'n Shake, Subway, Uncle Tom's Pancakes, Wendy's, Holiday Inn, Home2 Suites, Motel 6, Rodeway Inn, Super 8, $General, $Tree, Discount Tire, H, Schnuck's Foods, to Ill St U, Verizon, Walgreens, W Love's/dsl/scales/RV Park/@, dsl repair

164 I-39, US 51, N to Peru

163 I-74 W, to Peoria

160b a US 150, IL 9, Market St, Bloomington, E Circle K, Pilot/Wendy's/dsl/scales/24hr, Shell/repair,

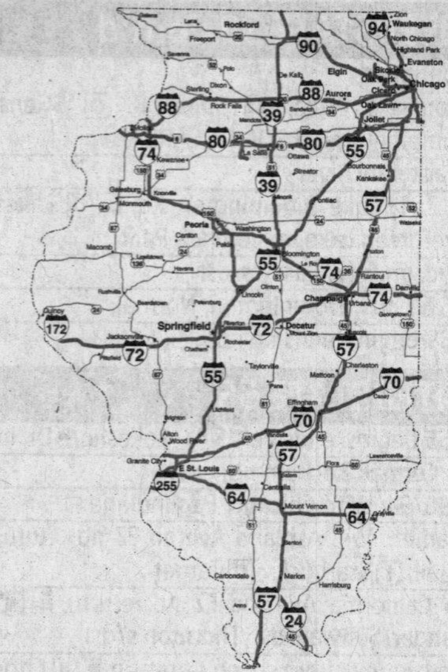

BLOOMINGTON

160b a Continued
TA/Country Pride/dsl/scales/24hr/@, Arby's, Crack Barrel, Culver's, KFC, McDonald's, Popeyes, Subway, Tac Bell, Days Inn, EconoLodge, Hawthorn Suites, Quality In Quality Suites, Red Roof Inn, Advance Parts, Blue Beaco Family$, H, Peterbilt, W Circle K/dsl, Murphy USA/dsl, Bob Evans, Fiesta Ranchera Mexican, Steak'n Shake, Comfort Suites, Country Inn&Suites, Fairfield Inn, Hampto Inn, Holiday Inn Express, Ramada Ltd, AlLDI, EV Farm&Fleet, Walmart

157b Lp 55 N, Veterans Pkwy, Bloomington, E H, to

157a I-74 E, to Indianapolis, US 51 to Decatur

154 Shirley

149 **full facilities, litter barrels, petwalk, playground, both lanes, vending**

145 US 136, E Quality RV Ctr, W Dixie/Road Range Subway/dsl/scales/24hr, Mobil/dsl, McDonald's, Rte 6 Drive Thru, Super 8

140 Atlanta, E RV camping(3mi), W Casey's/dsl, Country-Aire Rest., Atlanta Inn, $General, NAPA

LINCOLN

133 Lp 55, Lincoln, E Camp-A-While Camping, H

127 I-155 N, to Peoria

126 IL 10, IL 121 S, Lincoln, E BP/Arby's/dsl/24hr, Casey's/ds Thornton's/Pilot/dsl/scales/24hr, Bonanza Steaks, Burg King, Cracker Barrel, Culver's, Daphne's Rest., DQ, Dunki Donuts, El Mazatlan Mexican, Hardee's, McDonald's, Pizz Hut, Rio Grande Grill, Steak'n Shake, Subway, Taco Be Wendy's, EconoLodge, Hampton Inn, Holiday Inn Expres Super 8, $General, $Tree, AlLDI, AT&T, AutoZon Chrysler/Dodge/Jeep, CVS Drug, Ford/Lincoln, H, Kroge O'Reilly Parts, Russell Stover, Verizon, Walgreens, Walmart Subway

123 Lp 55, to Lincoln, E H

119 Broadwell

115 Elkhart

109 IL 123, Williamsville, E Casey's, Subway, W Love's McDonalds/dsl/scales/24hr, Huddle House, New Salem SHS

107mm weigh sta sb

105 Lp 55, to Sherman, W Casey's, Cancun Mexican, Chin King, Fairlane Diner, Fire&Ale Grill, Ricco's Pizza, Sam's To Pizza, Subway, Conv Ctr, County Mkt Foods, hist sites Military Museum, repair, Riverside Park Campground Verizon, vet, Walgreens

103mm **full facilities, litter barrels, petwalk, sb vending**

IL

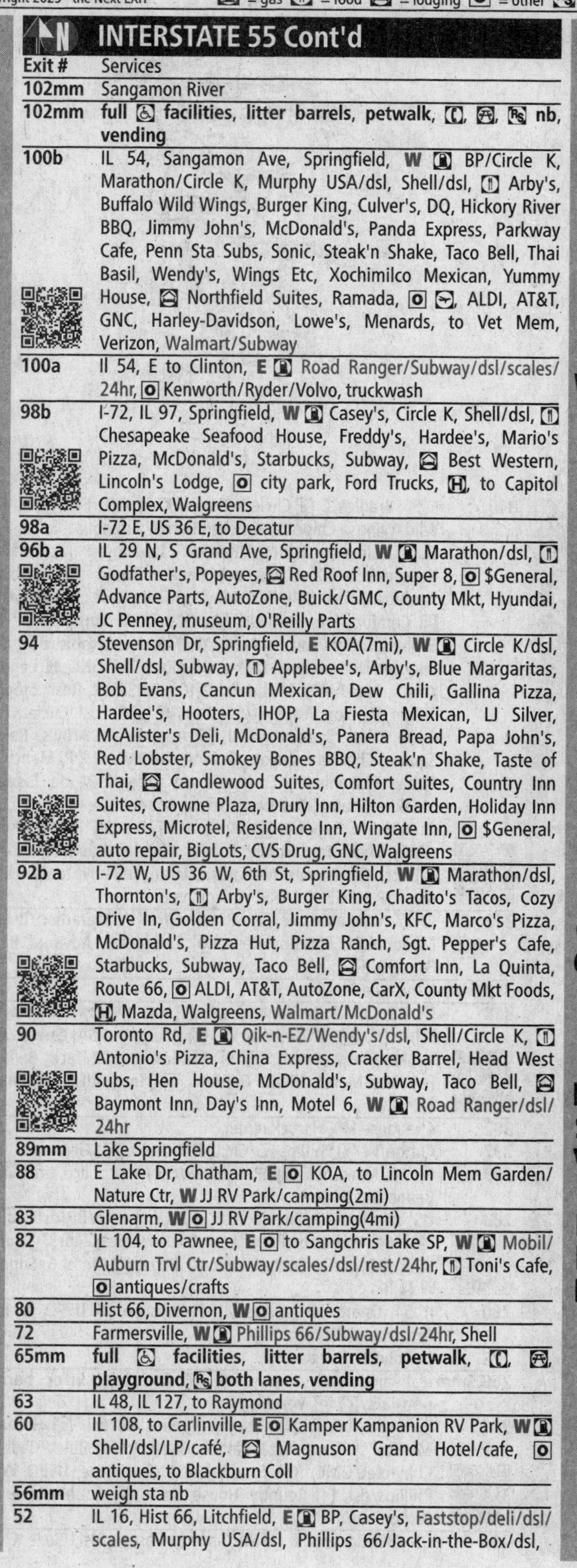

INTERSTATE 55 Cont'd

SPRINGFIELD

Exit #	Services
102mm	Sangamon River
102mm	**full [accessible] facilities, litter barrels, petwalk, [phone], [picnic], [rest stop] nb, vending**
100b	IL 54, Sangamon Ave, Springfield, **W** [gas] BP/Circle K, Marathon/Circle K, Murphy USA/dsl, Shell/dsl, [food] Arby's, Buffalo Wild Wings, Burger King, Culver's, DQ, Hickory River BBQ, Jimmy John's, McDonald's, Panda Express, Parkway Cafe, Penn Sta Subs, Sonic, Steak'n Shake, Taco Bell, Thai Basil, Wendy's, Wings Etc, Xochimilco Mexican, Yummy House, [lodging] Northfield Suites, Ramada, [other] [airport], ALDI, AT&T, GNC, Harley-Davidson, Lowe's, Menards, to Vet Mem, Verizon, Walmart/Subway
100a	Il 54, E to Clinton, **E** [gas] Road Ranger/Subway/dsl/scales/24hr, [other] Kenworth/Ryder/Volvo, truckwash
98b	I-72, IL 97, Springfield, **W** [gas] Casey's, Circle K, Shell/dsl, [food] Chesapeake Seafood House, Freddy's, Hardee's, Mario's Pizza, McDonald's, Starbucks, Subway, [lodging] Best Western, Lincoln's Lodge, [other] city park, Ford Trucks, [H], to Capitol Complex, Walgreens
98a	I-72 E, US 36 E, to Decatur
96b a	IL 29 N, S Grand Ave, Springfield, **W** [gas] Marathon/dsl, [food] Godfather's, Popeyes, [lodging] Red Roof Inn, Super 8, [other] $General, Advance Parts, AutoZone, Buick/GMC, County Mkt, Hyundai, JC Penney, museum, O'Reilly Parts
94	Stevenson Dr, Springfield, **E** KOA(7mi), **W** [gas] Circle K/dsl, Shell/dsl, Subway, [food] Applebee's, Arby's, Blue Margaritas, Bob Evans, Cancun Mexican, Dew Chili, Gallina Pizza, Hardee's, Hooters, IHOP, La Fiesta Mexican, LJ Silver, McAlister's Deli, McDonald's, Panera Bread, Papa John's, Red Lobster, Smokey Bones BBQ, Steak'n Shake, Taste of Thai, [lodging] Candlewood Suites, Comfort Suites, Country Inn Suites, Crowne Plaza, Drury Inn, Hilton Garden, Holiday Inn Express, Microtel, Residence Inn, Wingate Inn, [other] $General, auto repair, BigLots, CVS Drug, GNC, Walgreens
92b a	I-72 W, US 36 W, 6th St, Springfield, **W** [gas] Marathon/dsl, Thornton's, [food] Arby's, Burger King, Chadito's Tacos, Cozy Drive In, Golden Corral, Jimmy John's, KFC, Marco's Pizza, McDonald's, Pizza Hut, Pizza Ranch, Sgt. Pepper's Cafe, Starbucks, Subway, Taco Bell, [lodging] Comfort Inn, La Quinta, Route 66, [other] ALDI, AT&T, AutoZone, CarX, County Mkt Foods, [H], Mazda, Walgreens, Walmart/McDonald's
90	Toronto Rd, **E** [gas] Qik-n-EZ/Wendy's/dsl, Shell/Circle K, [food] Antonio's Pizza, China Express, Cracker Barrel, Head West Subs, Hen House, McDonald's, Subway, Taco Bell, [lodging] Baymont Inn, Day's Inn, Motel 6, **W** [gas] Road Ranger/dsl/24hr
89mm	Lake Springfield
88	E Lake Dr, Chatham, **E** [other] KOA, to Lincoln Mem Garden/Nature Ctr, **W** JJ RV Park/camping(2mi)
83	Glenarm, **W** [other] JJ RV Park/camping(4mi)
82	IL 104, to Pawnee, **E** [other] to Sangchris Lake SP, **W** [gas] Mobil/Auburn Trvl Ctr/Subway/scales/dsl/rest/24hr, [food] Toni's Cafe, [other] antiques/crafts
80	Hist 66, Divernon, **W** [other] antiques
72	Farmersville, **W** [gas] Phillips 66/Subway/dsl/24hr, Shell
65mm	**full [accessible] facilities, litter barrels, petwalk, [phone], [picnic], playground, [rest stop] both lanes, vending**
63	IL 48, IL 127, to Raymond
60	IL 108, to Carlinville, **E** [other] Kamper Kampanion RV Park, **W** [gas] Shell/dsl/LP/café, [lodging] Magnuson Grand Hotel/cafe, [other] antiques, to Blackburn Coll
56mm	weigh sta nb
52	IL 16, Hist 66, Litchfield, **E** [gas] BP, Casey's, Faststop/deli/dsl/scales, Murphy USA/dsl, Phillips 66/Jack-in-the-Box/dsl,

CHATHAM

EDWARDSVILLE

COLLINSVILLE

Exit #	Services
52	Continued Shell, [food] A&W/LJ Silver, Arby's, Ariston Café, Burger King, China Town, Denny's, DQ, El Rancherito Mexican, Huddle House, Jimmy John's, Jubelt's Rest., KFC, Maverick Steaks, McDonald's, Pizza Hut, Ruby Tuesday, Subway, Taco Bell, Wendy's, [lodging] Best Value Inn, Hampton Inn, Holiday Inn Express, Quality Inn, Super 8, [other] $General, $Tree, AlLDI, AT&T, Buick/Cadillac/Chevrolet/GMC, Ford, Goodyear/auto, [H], IGA Foods, NAPA, O'Reilly Parts, Rte 66 Museum, Verizon, vet, Walgreens, Walmart/Subway, **W** st police
44	IL 138, to Benld, Mt Olive, **E** [gas] Rte 138 Cafe, [food] Crossroads Diner, [other] Mother Jones Mon
41	to Staunton, **E** [other] Country Classic Cars, **W** [gas] Casey's, [food] DQ, [lodging] Super 8, [other] $General, Chrysler/Dodge/Jeep, [H]
37	Livingston, New Douglas, **W** [gas] Shell/dsl, [food] Gasperoni's Café, [lodging] Country Inn/cafe, [other] AutoCare, IGA Foods, USPO
33	IL 4, to Staunton, Worden
30	IL 140, Hamel, **E** [gas] Love's/McDonald's/Subway/dsl/scales/24hr, [lodging] Innkeeper Motel, **W** [gas] Shell, [food] Weezy's Grill
28mm	**full [accessible] facilities, litter barrels, petwalk, [phone], [picnic], [rest stop] both lanes, vending**
23	IL 143, Edwardsville, **E** [gas] Phillips 66/dsl
20b	I-270 W, to Kansas City
20a	I-70 E, to Indianapolis. I-55 and I-70 run together 15 mi.
19mm	I-55 S and I-70 W run together 15 mi
18	IL 162, to Troy, **E** [gas] Casey's/dsl, Phillips 66/Circle K/dsl, Pilot/Arby's/dsl/scales/24hr, TA/BP/Country Pride/dsl/scales/24hr/@, ZX, [food] Alfonzo's Pizza, Burger King, China King, Domino's, DQ, Dunkin Donuts, El Potro Mexican, Jack-in-the-Box, Little Caesar's, McDonald's/playplace, Pizza Hut, Subway, truckwash, [other] $General, Ace Hardware, [H], O'Reilly Parts, Schuette's Mkt, Speedco, USPO, vet, Walgreens, **W** [food] Cracker Barrel, Fire'n Smoke Kitchen, Joe's Pizza, Taco Bell, [lodging] Best Western, Holiday Inn Express, Motel 6, Red Roof Inn, Super 8, [other] Freightliner, Verizon
17	US 40 E, to Troy, to St Jacob
15b a	IL 159, Maryville, Collinsville, **E** [gas] Phillips 66/Circle K/dsl, VP/dsl, Zx Gas, [food] Asia Garden, Carisillo's Mexican, KFC, McDonald's, Sonic, Subway, [other] $General, Advance Parts, AlLDI, AutoZone, CVS Drug, Ford/Lincoln, O'Reilly Parts, vet, Walgreens, **W** [lodging] Loyalty Inn
14mm	weigh sta sb
11	IL 157, Collinsville, **E** [gas] Casey's, [food] A&W/LJ Silver, Denny's, Golden Corral, Little Caesar's, McDonald's, Penn Sta Subs, Qdoba Mexican, St Louis Bread Co, Starbucks, Waffle House, Wendy's, [lodging] Best Value Inn, [other] AT&T, Dobbs Tire, Gateway RV Ctr, GNC, Home Depot, Midas, Verizon, Walgreens, Walmart/Subway, **W** [gas] Motomart/dsl/24hr, [food] Applebee's, Arby's, Bandana's BBQ, Bob Evans, Burger King, Colton's Steaks, Culver's, DQ, Jimmy John's, Pizza Hut, Porter's Steaks, Ruby Tuesday, Steak'n Shake, White Castle/24hr, Zapata's Mexican, [lodging] Comfort Inn, Days Inn, DoubleTree Inn, Drury Inn, Fairfield Inn, Hampton Inn, La Quinta, Super 8, [other] Buick/GMC, st police
10	I-255, S to Memphis, N to I-270
9	Black Lane(from nb, no return), **E** Fairmount RaceTrack
6	IL 111, Great River Rd, Fairmont City, **E** [gas] Exxon, [lodging] Relax Inn, Royal Budget Inn, [other] auto repair, **W** Horseshoe SP
4b a	IL 203, Granite City, **E** [gas] BP/dsl, [lodging] Western Inn, **W** [gas] Pilot/Subway/Taco Bell/dsl/scales/24hr/@, [other] Gateway Int Raceway
3c	Exchange Ave
3b	I-70 W, to KC
3a	I-64 E, IL 3 N, St Clair Ave
2b	3rd St
2a	M L King Bridge, to downtown E St Louis
1	IL 3, to Sauget(from sb)

IL

INTERSTATE 55 Cont'd

Exit #	Services
0.5mm	I-55 N and I-70 E run together 15 mi
0mm	Illinois/Missouri state line, Mississippi River

INTERSTATE 57

Exit #	Services
358mm	I-94 E to Indiana, I-57 begins/ends on I-94, exit 63 in Chicago.
357	IL 1, Halsted St, **E** BP, Gulf/dsl, auto repair, **W** Shell/Dunkin', Supersave, McDonald's, Shark's
355	111th St, Monterey Ave, **W** BP, Citgo
354	119th St, **W** Citgo/Dunkin', Chili's, Panda Express, Subway, $Tree, AT&T, GNC, Jewel-Osco, PetCo, Pizza Hut
353	127th St, Burr Oak Ave, **E** Citgo, GoLo, Shell, Burger King, Dillinger's Drive-In, Dunkin', McDonald's, Wendy's, Days Inn, M Hotel, Plaza Inn, Ace Hardware, Advance Parts, Family$, Walgreens, **W** BP, Citgo/dsl, Egg Shack, H, JJ Fish&Chicken
352mm	Calumet Sag Channel
350	IL 83, 147th St, Sibley Blvd, **E** Marathon/dsl, Checkers, Domino's, Harold's Chicken, McDonald's, Subway, $General, AlLDI, Family$, O'Reilly Parts, **W** USPO
349	I-294(from nb)
348	US 6, 159th St, **E** BP/dsl, Clark, Marathon/dsl, Baskin-Robbins/Dunkin', Burger King, McDonald's, Popeyes, Subway, Taco Bell, White Castle, $Tree, AutoZone, U-Haul, **W** Shell/dsl
346	167th St, Cicero Ave, to IL 50, **E** BP, Shell/dsl, Tesla EVC, Baskin-Robbins/Dunkin', Harold's Chicken, Kenny's Ribs, McDonald's, Panda Express, Pizza Hut, Shark's Fish&Chicken, Sonic, Starbucks, Wendy's, Best Western, GNC, Walmart/Subway, **W** Shell, 7-11
345b a	I-80, W to Iowa, E to Indiana, to I-294 N toll to Wisconsin
342	Vollmer Rd, **E** Shell/Circle K/dsl, H
340b a	US 30, Lincoln Hwy, Matteson, **E** BP, Marathon/dsl, A Fusion Asian, A&W/LJ Silver, Bar Louie, Bocce's Grill, Burger King, Chipotle, ChuckeCheese, Culver's, Dunkin', Dusties Buffet, Five Guys, Fuddrucker's, Giordano's, Harold's Chicken, IHOP, Jimmy John's, KFC, McDonald's, Olive Garden, Panda Express, Panera Bread, Pepe's, Perros Bros Gyros, Pizza Hut, Potbelly, Red Lobster, Rosati's, Shark's, Starbucks, Subway, White Castle, Comfort Inn, Country Inn&Suites, Hampton Inn, Holiday Inn, Quality Inn, $Tree, AlLDI, Best Buy, Chrysler/Dodge/Jeep, Discount Tire, Firestone/auto, GNC, Home Depot, JC Penney, Marshall's, Menards, NTB, PepBoys, PetSmart, Ross, USPO, Verizon, Walgreens, **W** Buick/Cadillac/GMC, Ford/Lincoln, Honda, Hyundai, Kia, Nissan, Toyota, Walgreens
339	Sauk Trail, to Richton Park, **E** BP/dsl, Marathon/dsl, Blue Sharks, Domino's, McDonald's, Family$, Walgreens, **W** Walmart/dsl
337	Stuenkel Rd
335	Monee, **E** BP/Dunkin'/Subway/dsl, Petro/Iron Skillet/dsl/e85/scales/24hr/@, Pilot/McDonald's/dsl/scales/24hr, Burger King, Culver's, KFC/Taco Bell, Lucky Burrito, Pizza Hut, Schoops Rest., Country Host Motel, Quality Inn, Red Roof Inn, Super 8, Advance Parts, Blue Beacon
332mm	Prairie View Rest Area both lanes, **full facilities, info, litter barrels, petwalk,** **vending**
330mm	weigh sta both lanes
327	to Peotone, **E** Casey's, Circle K, McDonald's/RV parking
322	Manteno, **E** BP/McDonald's/dsl, Casey's/dsl, Phillips 66/Subway, DQ, Jimmy John's, KFC/Taco Bell, Monical's Pizza, Pizza Hut, Wendy's, Country Inn&Suites, Howard Johnson, Harley-Davidson, vet, **W** BP/Dunkin'/dsl
320	E. 6000N Rd

MATTESON

MONEE

IL

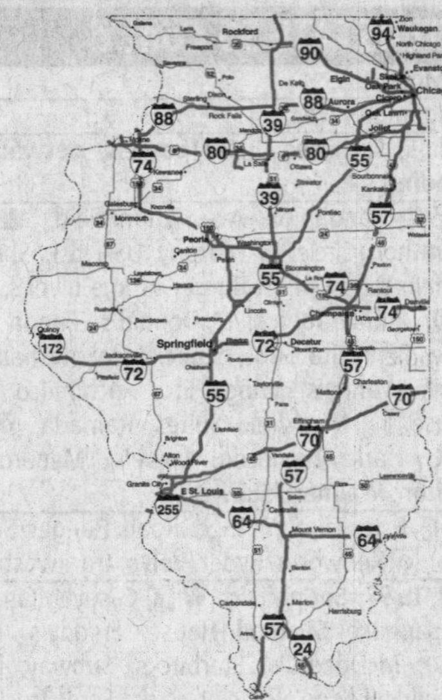

BRADLEY

ASHKUM

PAXTON

Exit #	Services
315	IL 50, Bradley, **E** Circle K/Burger King, EVC, F&F, Buffalo Wild Wings, Chipotle, Cracker Barrel, Firehouse Subs, Five Guys, Jimmy John's, KanSai Japanese, McDonald's, Noodles&Co, Olive Garden, Panera Bread, Red Lobster, Starbucks, Taco Bell, TGIFriday's, Tucci's Rest., White Castle, Comfort Inn, Fairfield Inn, Hampton Inn, Holiday Inn Express, Magnuson, ALDI, AT&T, Barnes&Noble, Best Buy, Chrysler/Dodge/Jeep, Dick's, Discount Tire, GNC, JC Penney, Kohl's, Marshall's, Michael's, PetCo, PetSmart, Ross, Staples, Target, Verizon, Walmart/Subway, **W** BP/dsl, Circle K/dsl, Circle K/dsl, Speedway/dsl, Applebee's, Arby's, Bakers Square, Checkers, Coyote Canyon, Denny's, IHOP, Mancino's Pizza, McDonald's, Oberweis Ice Cream, Panda Express, Steak'n Shake, Subway, Texas Roadhouse, Wendy's, Quality Inn, Super 8, $Tree, AT&T, Bradley RV Ctr, Buick/GMC, Chevrolet, Hobby Lobby, Honda, Hyundai, Jo-Ann Fabrics, Kia, Lowe's, Menards, Nissan, O'Reilly, to Kankakee River SP, URGENT CARE, Verizon, vet
312	IL 17, Kankakee, **W** BP/dsl, Circle K, Marathon/dsl, McDonald's, PoorBoy Rest., $ General, Advance Parts, Family$, H
310.5mm	Kankakee River
308	US 45, US 52, to Kankakee, **E** Love's/Arby's/dsl/scales/24hr, KOA(3mi), **W** Murphy USA, Speedway/Dunkin'/Subway/dsl, El Mexicano, KFC/Taco Bell, Fairview Motel, Hilton Garden, $Tree, AlLDI, Walmart/Subway
302	Chebanse, **W** truck repair
297	Clifton, **W** Phillips 66/Circle K/DQ/dsl, $General
293	IL 116, Ashkum, **E** BP/Subway/dsl, st police, tires, **W** Beans and Barley
283	US 24, IL 54, Gilman, **E** K&H Trkstp/BP/dsl/scales/24hr/@, Mobil/dsl, Pilot/Denny's/dsl/scales/24hr, Burger King, DQ, McDonald's, Monical's Pizza, Motel 6, Super 8, **W** BP/dsl
280	IL 54, Onarga, **E** Casey's, Phillips 66, USPO, **W** Lake Arrowhead RV camping
272	to Roberts, Buckley
268.5mm	rest area both lanes, **full facilities, litter barrels, petwalk,** **vending**
261	IL 9, Paxton, **E** Casey's, Phillips 66/dsl, Hardee's, Monical's Pizza, Pizza Palace, Subway, Buick/Cadillac/Chevrolet/GMC, IGA Foods, NAPA, TrueValue, USPO, **W** Phillips/dsl, Country House Rest., Cobblestone Inn, Paxton Inn
250	US 136, Rantoul, **E** BP/Circle K, Casey's/dsl, Circle K/dsl,

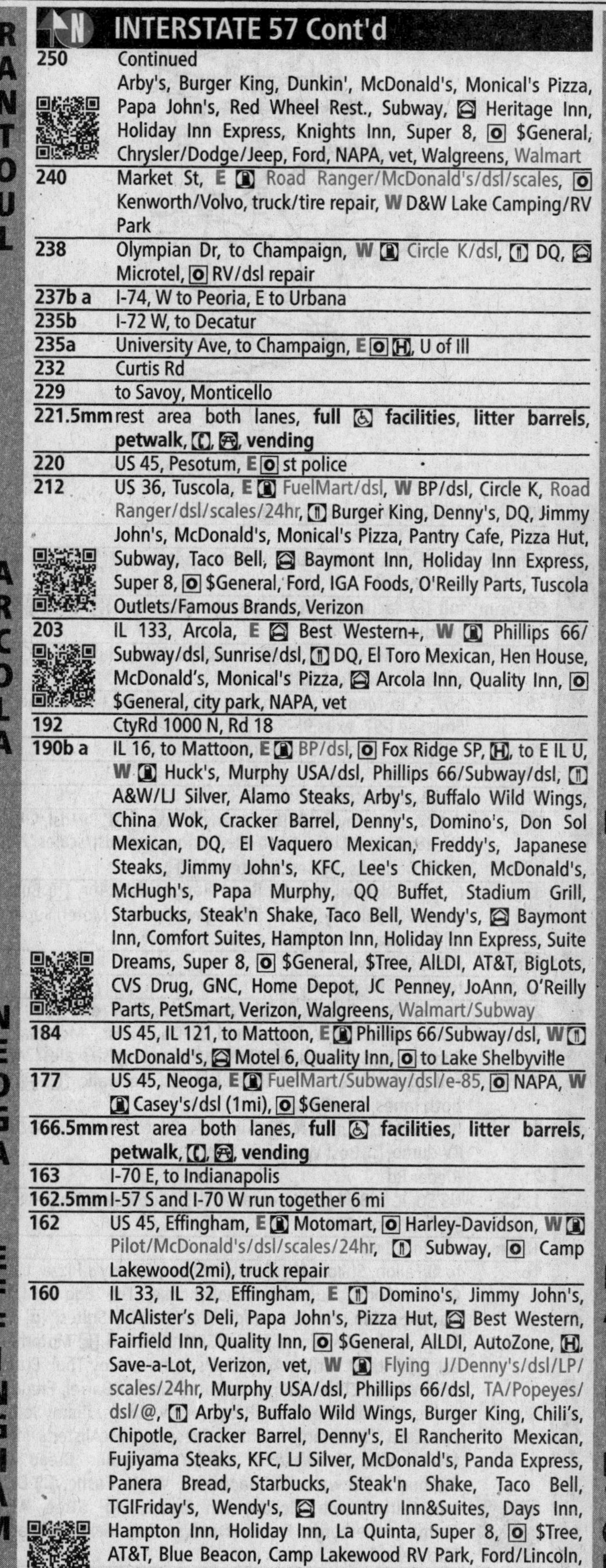

INTERSTATE 57 Cont'd

RANTOUL

250 Continued
Arby's, Burger King, Dunkin', McDonald's, Monical's Pizza, Papa John's, Red Wheel Rest., Subway, Heritage Inn, Holiday Inn Express, Knights Inn, Super 8, $General, Chrysler/Dodge/Jeep, Ford, NAPA, vet, Walgreens, Walmart

240 Market St, E Road Ranger/McDonald's/dsl/scales, Kenworth/Volvo, truck/tire repair, W D&W Lake Camping/RV Park

238 Olympian Dr, to Champaign, W Circle K/dsl, DQ, Microtel, RV/dsl repair

237b a I-74, W to Peoria, E to Urbana

235b I-72 W, to Decatur

235a University Ave, to Champaign, E H, U of Ill

232 Curtis Rd

229 to Savoy, Monticello

221.5mm rest area both lanes, **full facilities, litter barrels, petwalk, , , vending**

220 US 45, Pesotum, E st police

212 US 36, Tuscola, E FuelMart/dsl, W BP/dsl, Circle K, Road Ranger/dsl/scales/24hr, Burger King, Denny's, DQ, Jimmy John's, McDonald's, Monical's Pizza, Pantry Cafe, Pizza Hut, Subway, Taco Bell, Baymont Inn, Holiday Inn Express, Super 8, $General, Ford, IGA Foods, O'Reilly Parts, Tuscola Outlets/Famous Brands, Verizon

ARCOLA

203 IL 133, Arcola, E Best Western+, W Phillips 66/Subway/dsl, Sunrise/dsl, DQ, El Toro Mexican, Hen House, McDonald's, Monical's Pizza, Arcola Inn, Quality Inn, $General, city park, NAPA, vet

192 CtyRd 1000 N, Rd 18

190b a IL 16, to Mattoon, E BP/dsl, Fox Ridge SP, H, to E IL U, W Huck's, Murphy USA/dsl, Phillips 66/Subway/dsl, A&W/LJ Silver, Alamo Steaks, Arby's, Buffalo Wild Wings, China Wok, Cracker Barrel, Denny's, Domino's, Don Sol Mexican, DQ, El Vaquero Mexican, Freddy's, Japanese Steaks, Jimmy John's, KFC, Lee's Chicken, McDonald's, McHugh's, Papa Murphy, QQ Buffet, Stadium Grill, Starbucks, Steak'n Shake, Taco Bell, Wendy's, Baymont Inn, Comfort Suites, Hampton Inn, Holiday Inn Express, Suite Dreams, Super 8, $General, $Tree, AlLDI, AT&T, BigLots, CVS Drug, GNC, Home Depot, JC Penney, JoAnn, O'Reilly Parts, PetSmart, Verizon, Walgreens, Walmart/Subway

NEOGA

184 US 45, IL 121, to Mattoon, E Phillips 66/Subway/dsl, W McDonald's, Motel 6, Quality Inn, to Lake Shelbyville

177 US 45, Neoga, E FuelMart/Subway/dsl/e-85, NAPA, W Casey's/dsl (1mi), $General

166.5mm rest area both lanes, **full facilities, litter barrels, petwalk, , , vending**

163 I-70 E, to Indianapolis

162.5mm I-57 S and I-70 W run together 6 mi

EFFINGHAM

162 US 45, Effingham, E Motomart, Harley-Davidson, W Pilot/McDonald's/dsl/scales/24hr, Subway, Camp Lakewood(2mi), truck repair

160 IL 33, IL 32, Effingham, E Domino's, Jimmy John's, McAlister's Deli, Papa John's, Pizza Hut, Best Western, Fairfield Inn, Quality Inn, $General, AlLDI, AutoZone, H, Save-a-Lot, Verizon, vet, W Flying J/Denny's/dsl/LP/scales/24hr, Murphy USA/dsl, Phillips 66/dsl, TA/Popeyes/dsl/@, Arby's, Buffalo Wild Wings, Burger King, Chili's, Chipotle, Cracker Barrel, Denny's, El Rancherito Mexican, Fujiyama Steaks, KFC, LJ Silver, McDonald's, Panda Express, Panera Bread, Starbucks, Steak'n Shake, Taco Bell, TGIFriday's, Wendy's, Country Inn&Suites, Days Inn, Hampton Inn, Holiday Inn, La Quinta, Super 8, $Tree, AT&T, Blue Beacon, Camp Lakewood RV Park, Ford/Lincoln, Hodgson Mill Mercantile, Kohl's, Menards, Peterbilt,

160 Continued
SpeedCo, Verizon, Walmart/Subway

159 Fayette Ave, Effingham, E Phillips 66/dsl, Speedway/Speedy's Cafe/dsl/24hr, China Buffet, Culver's, Hardee's, Little Caesar's, Niemerg's Rest, Subway, Abe Lincoln Motel, Best Value Inn, Comfort Suites, EconoLodge, Lexington Inn, Honda, O'Reilly Parts, tires/repair, Walgreens, W Petro/Iron Skillet/dsl/24hr/@, Baymont Inn, Blue Beacon, Freightliner

158mm I-57 N and I-70 E run together 6 mi

157 I-70 W, to St Louis

151 Watson, E Percival Springs RV Park

150mm Little Wabash River, Little Wabash River

145 Edgewood, E Phillips 66/dsl, city park

SALEM

135 IL 185, Farina, E Shell/Subway/dsl, $General, Ford

127 to Kinmundy, Patoka

116 US 50, Salem, E Circle K/dsl, Huck's/dsl, Motomart, Tesla EVC, $General, Burger King, China King, Denny's, Domino's, Hardee's, La Cocina Mexican, McDonald's, Pizza Hut, Pizza Man, Subway, Taco Bell, Village Garden, Wendy's, Holiday Inn Express, AutoZone, Chrysler/Dodge/Jeep, CVS Drug, GMC, H, NAPA, O'Reilly Parts, Save-A-Lot, to Forbes SP, USPO, Verizon, W Murphy USA/dsl, Phillips 66/dsl, Applebee's, Arby's, El Rancherito, KFC, Mi Pueblo, Days Inn, Quality Inn, Super 8, $Tree, AT&T, Buick/Chevrolet, Carlisle Lake(23mi), Ford, Salem Tires, Walmart

114mm full(handicapped)facilities, **full facilities, litter barrels, petwalk, , , playground, vending**

DIX

109 IL 161, to Centralia, W Biggie's General Store/cafe/dsl

103 Dix, E Phillips 66/dsl, Red Carpet Inn

96 I-64 W, to St Louis

MT VERNON

95 IL 15, Mt Vernon, E Circle K/dsl, Hucks, Agave Mexican, Asian Buffet, Bandana's BBQ, Domino's, El Rancherito Mexican, Fazoli's, Hardee's, KFC, Little Caesar's, LJ Silver, McAlister's Deli, McDonald's, Moe's SW Grill, Panda Express, Panera Bread, Pizza Hut, Starbucks, Steak'n Shake, Subway, Taco Bell, The Grille, Waffle Co, Wendy's, Best Value Inn, Comfort Suites, Drury Inn, Motel 6, Super 8, AT&T, AutoZone, Big Lots, Chevrolet/Cadillac, CVS Drug, Harley-Davidson, Hobby Lobby, H, JC Penney, Kroger/dsl, Midas, O'Reilly Parts, Plaza Tire, Prompt Care, Ross, Verizon, Walgreens, W Circle K/dsl, Flying J/Hucks/Huddle House/dsl/scales/24hr, Pilot/Denny's/dsl/scales/24hr, TA/Country Pride/Popeyes/dsl/24hr/@, Tesla EVC, Applebee's, Arby's, Bob Evans, Buffalo Wild Wings, Burger King, Chili's, Cracker Barrel, Double Overtime Grill, Jimmy John's, McDonald's, Ryan's, Sonic, Subway, Days Inn, Doubletree, Fairfield Inn, Hampton Inn, Holiday Inn Express, Quality Inn, $Tree, Archway RV Park, Buick/GMC, Freightliner, Kohl's, Lowe's, NAPA, Staples, Toyota, truckwash, Walmart

94 Veteran's Memorial Dr, E Phillips 66/dsl, Culver's, H, W Menards

92 I-64 E, to Louisville

INA

83 Ina, E Love's/McDonald's/dsl/scales, Uncle Joe's BBQ, tire/trailer repair, W to Rend Lake Coll

79mm **full facilities, info, litter barrels, petwalk, , , playground, sb, vending**

BENTON

77 IL 154, to Whittington, E Phillips 66/dsl, Surestay Inn, Whittington Woods RV Park, W Seasons at Rend Lake Lodge/rest., golf, to Rend Lake, Wayne Fitzgerrell SP

74mm **full facilities, litter barrels, petwalk, , , playground, nb, vending**

71 IL 14, Benton, E Arby's, Hardee's, KFC/Taco Bell, Pizza Hut, Country Hearth Inn, Gray Plaza Motel, Phillips 66/dsl, AutoZone, CVS Drug, H, KOA(1.5mi), O'Reilly Parts, Plaza Tire, W Casey's/dsl, Circle K/dsl, Murphy USA/dsl, Applebee's, Burger King, McDonald's, Subway, $Tree,

IL

= gas = food = lodging = other = rest stop

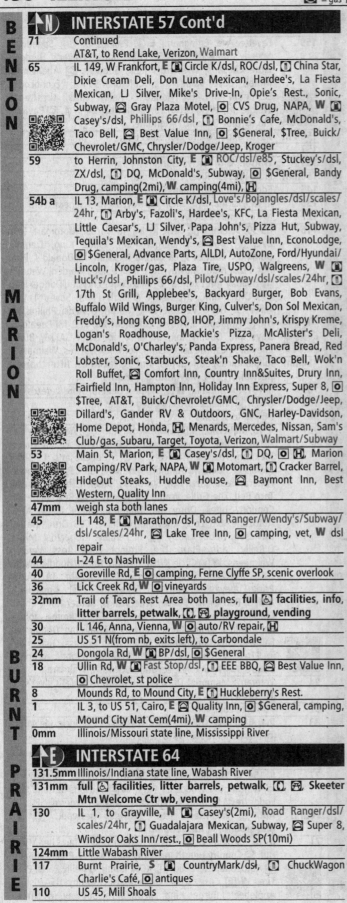

INTERSTATE 57 Cont'd

Exit	Services
71	Continued AT&T, to Rend Lake, Verizon, Walmart
65	IL 149, W Frankfort, E Circle K/dsl, ROC/dsl, China Star, Dixie Cream Deli, Don Luna Mexican, Hardee's, La Fiesta Mexican, LJ Silver, Mike's Drive-In, Opie's Rest., Sonic, Subway, Gray Plaza Motel, CVS Drug, NAPA, W Casey's/dsl, Phillips 66/dsl, Bonnie's Cafe, McDonald's, Taco Bell, Best Value Inn, $General, $Tree, Buick/Chevrolet/GMC, Chrysler/Dodge/Jeep, Kroger
59	to Herrin, Johnston City, E ROC/dsl/e85, Stuckey's/dsl, ZX/dsl, DQ, McDonald's, Subway, $General, Bandy Drug, camping(2mi), W camping(4mi), H
54b a	IL 13, Marion, E Circle K/dsl, Love's/Bojangles/dsl/scales/24hr, Arby's, Fazoli's, Hardee's, KFC, La Fiesta Mexican, Little Caesar's, LJ Silver, Papa John's, Pizza Hut, Subway, Tequila's Mexican, Wendy's, Best Value Inn, EconoLodge, $General, Advance Parts, AlLDI, AutoZone, Ford/Hyundai/Lincoln, Kroger/gas, Plaza Tire, USPO, Walgreens, W Huck's/dsl, Phillips 66/dsl, Pilot/Subway/dsl/scales/24hr, 17th St Grill, Applebee's, Backyard Burger, Bob Evans, Buffalo Wild Wings, Burger King, Culver's, Don Sol Mexican, Freddy's, Hong Kong BBQ, IHOP, Jimmy John's, Krispy Kreme, Logan's Roadhouse, Mackie's Pizza, McAlister's Deli, McDonald's, O'Charley's, Panda Express, Panera Bread, Red Lobster, Sonic, Starbucks, Steak'n Shake, Taco Bell, Wok'n Roll Buffet, Comfort Inn, Country Inn&Suites, Drury Inn, Fairfield Inn, Hampton Inn, Holiday Inn Express, Super 8, $Tree, AT&T, Buick/Chevrolet/GMC, Chrysler/Dodge/Jeep, Dillard's, Gander RV & Outdoors, GNC, Harley-Davidson, Home Depot, Honda, H, Menards, Mercedes, Nissan, Sam's Club/gas, Subaru, Target, Toyota, Verizon, Walmart/Subway
53	Main St, Marion, E Casey's/dsl, DQ, H, Marion Camping/RV Park, NAPA, W Motomart, Cracker Barrel, HideOut Steaks, Huddle House, Baymont Inn, Best Western, Quality Inn
47mm	weigh sta both lanes
45	IL 148, E Marathon/dsl, Road Ranger/Wendy's/Subway/dsl/scales/24hr, Lake Tree Inn, camping, vet, W dsl repair
44	I-24 E to Nashville
40	Goreville Rd, E camping, Ferne Clyffe SP, scenic overlook
36	Lick Creek Rd, W vineyards
32mm	Trail of Tears Rest Area both lanes, **full facilities, info, litter barrels, petwalk, , , playground, vending**
30	IL 146, Anna, Vienna, W auto/RV repair, H
25	US 51 N(from nb, exits left), to Carbondale
24	Dongola Rd, W BP/dsl, $General
18	Ullin Rd, W Fast Stop/dsl, EEE BBQ, Best Value Inn, Chevrolet, st police
8	Mounds Rd, to Mound City, E Huckleberry's Rest.
1	IL 3, to US 51, Cairo, E Quality Inn, $General, camping, Mound City Nat Cem(4mi), W camping
0mm	Illinois/Missouri state line, Mississippi River

BENTON

MARION

BURNT PRAIRIE

IL

INTERSTATE 64

Exit	Services
131.5mm	Illinois/Indiana state line, Wabash River
131mm	**full facilities, litter barrels, petwalk, , , Skeeter Mtn Welcome Ctr wb, vending**
130	IL 1, to Grayville, N Casey's(2mi), Road Ranger/dsl/scales/24hr, Guadalajara Mexican, Subway, Super 8, Windsor Oaks Inn/rest., Beall Woods SP(10mi)
124mm	Little Wabash River
117	Burnt Prairie, S CountryMark/dsl, ChuckWagon Charlie's Café, antiques
110	US 45, Mill Shoals

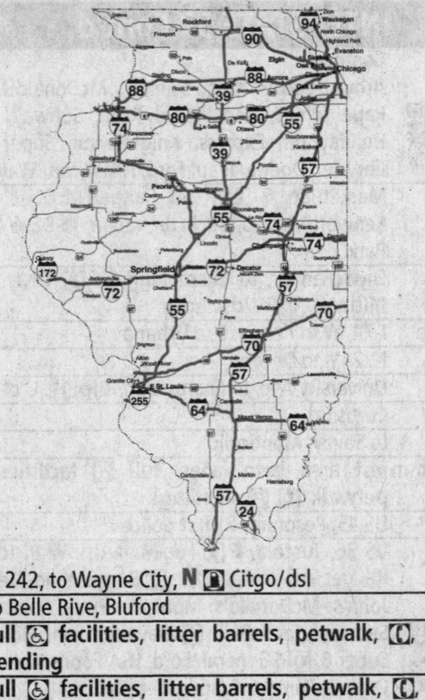

Exit	Services
100	IL 242, to Wayne City, N Citgo/dsl
89	to Belle Rive, Bluford
86mm	**full facilities, litter barrels, petwalk, , , wb, vending**
82.5mm	**full facilities, litter barrels, petwalk, , , eb, vending**
80	IL 37, to Mt Vernon, N Hucks/dsl/24hr, Phillips 66/Circle K/Burger King/dsl, $General
78	I-57, S to Memphis, N to Chicago. I-64 and I-57 merge for 5mi. See I-57, exits 95-94.
73	I-57, N to Chicago, S to Memphis
69	Woodlawn
61	US 51, to Centralia, Richview
50	IL 127, to Nashville, N to Carlyle Lake, S BP/dsl, Citgo/dsl/e85/rest., Little Nashville/Conoco/rest/dsl/scales/24hr, McDonald's, Best Western, H
41	IL 177, Okawville, S Road Ranger/dsl/24hr, Burger King, DQ, Subway, USPO, Original Springs Motel, Super 8, $General, tires/repair
37mm	Kaskaskia River
34	to Albers, N Casey's
27	IL 161, New Baden, N Casey's/dsl, Shell/dsl, A Fine Swine BBQ, China King, Good Ol Days Rest., McDonald's, Subway, $General, S Love's/Hardee's/dsl/scales/24hr
25mm	**full facilities, info, litter barrels, petwalk, , , both lanes, vending**
23	IL 4, to Mascoutah, N Domino's, Pilot/Huddle House/dsl/RV dump, Best Western+, S
21	Rieder Rd
19b a	US 50, IL 158, N Motomart/dsl, Subway, Super 8, H, S to Scott AFB
18mm	weigh sta eb
16	to O'Fallon, Shiloh, N Bella Milano, Dewey's Pizza, Lion's Choice, Sonic, Sugarfire Smokehouse, The Egg & I, Hampton Inn, Hilton Garden, TownePlace Suites, CVS Drug, Harley-Davidson, H, URGENT CARE, S Motomart/dsl, 54th St. Grille, Applebee's, Arby's, Aroy Thai, Buffalo Wild Wings, China King, Coldstone, Cracker Barrel, Freddy's, Golden Corral, Hop House Rest., Jersey Mike's, Jimmy John's, La Casa Mexicana, Little Caesar's, McAlister's Deli, McDonald's, Noodles&Co, Qdoba, St. Louis Bread Co., Starbucks, Subway, TX Roadhouse, White Castle, Drury Inn, Fairfield Inn, Holiday Inn Express, $Tree, AT&T, Carmax, Dierbergs Foods, Dobb's Tire, GNC, Menard's, Michael's, Target, vet
14	O'Fallon, N Circle K/dsl, Motomart, Shell/dsl, IHOP,

BLUFORD

NEW BADEN

O'FALLON

INTERSTATE 64 Cont'd

O'FALLON

14 Continued
Steak'n Shake, Subway, Best Western, Extended Stay America, HomeTowne Suites, La Quinta, Sleep Inn, Cadillac, Chevrolet, Ford, O'Reilly Parts, S Chevy's Mexican, Culver's, Hardee's, Jack-in-the-Box, KFC, McDonald's, O'Charley's, Panda Express, Papa Murphy's, Sake Grill, Starbucks, Syberg's Rest., Taco Bell, Baymont Inn, Candlewood Suites, Quality Inn, AlLDI, BMW, Home Depot, Honda, Hyundai, Kia, Mazda, Nissan, PetSmart, Sam's Club/gas, Toyota, VW, Walmart

12 IL 159, to Collinsville, N Circle K/dsl, Agostino's, Bob Evans, Crafty Crab, Ginger Buffet, Lotawata Creek Grill, Olive Garden, Red Lobster, Rio Grande, Shogun Japanese, TGIFriday's, Comfort Suites, Drury Inn, EconoLodge, Hampton Inn, Holiday Inn, Sheraton, Super 8, Wingate Inn, Fiat, Gordman's, S BP/dsl, Motomart/dsl, Arby's, Boston Mkt, Burger King, Capt D's, Cheddar's, Chick-fil-A, Chili's, Chipotle Mexican, ChuckECheese, Domino's, Dunkin Donuts, Fazoli's, Firehouse Subs, Five Guys, Honeybaked Ham, Hooters, Imo's Pizza, Jimmy John's, Krispy Kreme, Little Caesar's, LJ Silver, Longhorn Steaks, McAlister's Deli, McDonald's, Popeyes, Red Robin, Ruby Tuesday, St. Louis Bread, Subway, Taco Bell, Wasabi, Wendy's, White Castle, $General, $Tree, Aamco, ALDI, AT&T, Barnes&Noble, Best Buy, BigLots, Burlington Coats, CarX, Dick's, Dillard's, Dobb's Tire, Firestone/auto, Fresh Thyme Mkt, Hobby Lobby, JC Penney, Jo-Ann Fabrics, Kohl's, Lowe's, Macy's, Marshall's, Meineke, Midas, NTB, O'Reilly Parts, Old Navy, PetCo, Ross, Russell Stover, Schnuck's Foods, TJ Maxx, Verizon, vet, Walgreens

9 IL 157, to Caseyville, N Gulf/Subway, Huck's/dsl, Hardee's, Western Inn, S BP, Cracker Barrel, Domino's, DQ, McDonald's, Taco Bell, Best Inn, Fairbridge Inn, Motel 6, Quality Inn

7 I-255, S to Memphis, N to Chicago

BAUGH

6 IL 111, Kingshighway, N BP, Crown, Church's TX Chicken, Ray's Rest.

5 25th St

4 15th St, Baugh

3 I-55 N, I-70 E, IL 3 N, to St Clair Ave, to stockyards

2b a 3rd St, S gas

1 IL 3 S, E St Louis, N Casino Queen

0mm Illinois/Missouri state line, Mississippi River

INTERSTATE 70

156mm Illinois/Indiana state line

154 US 40 W

151mm weigh sta wb

149mm **full facilities, info, litter barrels, petwalk, wb, vending**

147 IL 1, Marshall, N Road Ranger/Church's TX Chicken/dsl/scales/24hr, Crossroads Rest., S Casey's(1mi), DQ, Marathon/Arby's/dsl, Phillips 66/dsl, Burger King, Los Tres Caminos, McDonald's, Pizza Hut, Sam's Steaks, Subway, Wendy's, Lincoln Suites, Relax Inn, Super 8, antiques, Ford, Lincoln Trail SP, Walmart

CASEY

136 to Martinsville, S Phillips 66/dsl/24hr

134.5mm N Fork Embarras River

129 IL 49, Casey, N KOA(seasonal), RV service, S Casey's, DQ, Marathon/Circle K/dsl, Phillips 66/dsl, Hacienda Mexican, McDonald's, Pizza Hut, Subway, Days Inn, $General, IGA Foods

GREENUP

119 IL 130, Greenup, S Casey's/dsl, Love's/Chester's/IHOP/dsl/scales/24hr, Phillips 66/dsl, Backyard BBQ, DQ, Subway, Budget Host, Greenup Motel, $General,

119 Continued
hist sites, NAPA

105 Montrose, N Spring Creek Camping(1mi), S BP/dsl, Phillips/dsl, Fairview Inn

98 I-57, N to Chicago. I-70 and I-57 run together 6 mi. See I-57, 159-162.

92 I-57, S to Mt Vernon. I-70 and I-57 run together 6 mi. See I-57, 159-162.

91mm Little Wabash River

87mm **full facilities, info, litter barrels, petwalk, playground, both lanes, RV dump, vending**

82 IL 128, Altamont, N Casey's/dsl, Phillips 66/Subway/dsl/24hr, Dairy Bar, Joe's Pizza/pasta, McDonald's, Altamont Motel, Cobblestone Inn, $General, city park, S Relax Inn

76 US 40, St Elmo, N Casey's, Waldorf Motel, Timberline Camping(2mi)

71mm weigh sta eb

68 US 40, Brownstown, N Okaw Valley Kamping, S truck repair

VANDALIA

63.5mm Kaskaskia River

63 US 51, Vandalia, N Chuck Wagon Cafe, LJ Silver, Best Value Inn, S Casey's, Phillips 66, Phillips 66/Burger King/24hr, Arby's, China Gate, DQ, McDonald's, Pizza Hut, Rancho Nuevo Mexican, Sonic, Subway, Wendy's, Economy Inn, Jay's Inn, AlLDI, city park, County Mkt Foods, hist site, H

61 US 40, Vandalia, N Fast Stop/Denny's/dsl/scales/24hr, S Murphy USA/dsl, China King, Embers Pizza, Huddle House, KFC/Taco Bell, Ponderosa, Holiday Inn Express, Ramada, $Tree, AT&T, AutoZone, Verizon, Walmart

52 US 40, Mulberry Grove, N Casey's/dsl, Timber Trail Camp-In(2mi), S Cedar Brook Camping(1mi)

45 IL 127, Greenville, N Love's/Subway/dsl/scales/24hr, Shell/dsl, Chang's Buffet, Domino's, Huddle House, KFC/Taco Bell, Los Amigos, Lu-Bob's Rest., McDonald's, EconoLodge, Red Carpet Inn, Super 8, H, S Comfort Inn, American Farm Heritage Museum, RV Service, to Carlyle Lake

41 US 40 E, to Greenville

36 US 40 E, Pocahontas, S BP/dsl, Phillips 66/dsl, Funderburk's Grill, Lighthouse Lodge, Powhatan Motel/rest., Tahoe Motel, truck/tire repair

MARINE

30 US 40, IL 143, to Highland, S Shell/dsl/wifi, Blue Springs Café, H, Tomahawk RV Park(7mi)

26.5mm **full facilities, litter barrels, petwalk, Silver Lake both lanes, vending**

24 IL 143, Marine, S H

21 IL 4, Troy

15b a I-55, N to Chicago, S to St Louis, I-270 W to Kansas City, **I-70 and I-55 run together 15 mi. Exits 3a-18.**

3 Louisville

2 to IL 3, Fairmount City Blvd, Sauget

0mm Illinois/Missouri state line, Mississippi River

INTERSTATE 72

183mm I-72 begins/ends, E Gas Depot, Thornton's/dsl, Arby's, Burger King, Dunkin', Garcia's Pizza, Jets Pizza, Jimmy John's, KFC, La Bamba Mexican, McDonald's, Monical's Pizza, Original Pancakes, Papa John's, Pizza Hut, Sonic, Subway, Taco Bell, TX Roadhouse, $General, Advance Parts, AutoZone, Big Lots, CVS Drug, O'Reilly Parts, Schnuck's Foods/e85, ValuCheck Mkt, Walgreens

182b a I-57, N to Chicago, S to Memphis, to I-74

176 IL 47, to Mahomet

172 IL 10, Lodge, Seymour

169 White Heath Rd

IL

= gas = food = lodging = other = rest stop

INTERSTATE 72 Cont'd

	Exit #	Services
	166	IL 105 W, Market St, N Ford, H, S Circle K/dsl, Red Wheel Rest., Best Western, Foster Inn, city park, railway museum
	165mm	Sangamon River
CISCO	164	Bridge St, S Circle K/dsl, DQ, Golden Kitchen, Hardee's, McDonald's, Monical's Pizza, Pizza Hut, Subway, $General, Buick/Chevrolet, Chrysler/Dodge/Jeep, H, USPO, vet
	156	IL 48, to Weldon, Cisco, N Friends Creek Camping(may-oct)(3mi)
	153mm	rest area both lanes, **full facilities, litter barrels, petwalk, , , vending**
	152mm	Friends Creek
	150	Argenta
	144	IL 48, Oreana, S Pilot/McDonald's/Subway/dsl/scales/24hr, Sleep Inn, Chrysler/Dodge/Jeep, Honda, H, Hyundai, Pressley RV Ctr(3mi)
DECATUR	141b a	US 51, Decatur, N Casey's/dsl, Circle K, Applebee's, Buffalo Wild Wings, Burger Theory, Cheddar's, Cracker Barrel, McDonald's, Panda Express, Penn Sta Subs, Pizza Hut, Red Lobster, Steak'n Shake, Subway, Taco Bell, TX Roadhouse, Baymont Inn, Country Inn&Suites, EconoLodge, Fairfield Inn, Hampton Inn, Homewood Suites, Quality Inn, Ramada Ltd, Residence Inn, $Tree, AT&T, Best Buy, Buick/Cadillac/GMC, GNC, Harley-Davidson, Hobby Lobby, Kohl's, Lowe's, Menards, PetSmart, Ross, Staples, TJ Maxx, Verizon, Von Maur, S Arby's, Burger King, El Rodeo Mexican, Fuji Japanese, La Fondita, Monical's Pizza, Olive Garden, Panera Bread, Papa Murphy's, Starbucks, H, Jo-Ann Fabrics, Sam's Club, Target, Verizon, Walgreens, Walmart/Subway
	138	IL 121, Decatur, S Love's/Hardee's/dsl/scales24hr, H
	133b a	US 36 E, US 51, Decatur, S Shell/Subway/dsl, Best Value Inn, Decatur Hotel/rest.
	128	Niantic
	122	to Mt Auburn, Illiopolis, N FastStop/dsl, $General
	114	Buffalo, Mechanicsburg, S Gas Depot/dsl, USPO
	108	Riverton, Dawson
	107mm	Sangamon River
	104	Camp Butler, N golf
	103b a	I-55, IL 97. I-72 and I-55 run together 6 mi. See I-55, exits 92-98., I-72 and I-55 run together 6 mi., **See Exits 92-98**
SPRINGFIELD	97b a	6th St, I-55 S, Loop 55 N(from eb), 6th St, I-55 S, N Road Ranger, Golden Corral, McDonald's, Pizza Ranch, Comfort Inn, La Quinta, Rte 66, ALDI, Lincoln, Mazda, Walmart
	96	MacArthur Blvd, N Tesla EVC, Engrained Brewing Co, Springhill Suites, Scheels
	93	IL 4, Springfield, N Hucks, Thorntons/dsl, Applebee's, Arby's, Bakers Square, Burger King, Casa Real, Chick-fil-A, Chili's, Chipotle Mexican, Cooper's Hawk Rest., Dew's Chili, Five Guys, Indigo, Jersey Mike's, Jimmy John's, Kiku Japanese, Longhorn Steaks, Los Rancheros Mexican, McDonald's, Noodles&Co, Olive Garden, Outback Steaks, Panda Express, Panera Bread, Pasta House, Penn Sta Subs, Popeyes, Qdoba, Red Robin, Sonic, Starbucks, Subway, Taco Bell, TGIFriday's, TX Roadhouse, Wendy's, Courtyard, Fairfield Inn, Quality Inn, Sleep Inn, ALDI, AT&T, Barnes&Noble, Best Buy, Big Lots, County Mkt Foods, Dick's, Discount Tire, Fannie May, Gordman's, Hobby Lobby, Jo-Ann Fabrics, Kohl's, Lowe's, Macy's, Marshall's, Michael's, Office Depot, Old Navy, PetCo, PetSmart, Ross, Sam's Club/gas, Target, TJ Maxx, Verizon, Walgreens, Walmart, S Meijer/dsl/e85, Bob Evans, Monical's Pizza, Steak'n Shake,
ALEXANDER	93	Continued Hampton Inn, Staybridge Suites, Cadillac, CarMax, Chevrolet, Chrysler/Jeep, Fiat, Ford, Honda, Menards
	91	Wabash Ave, to Springfield, N Qik-n- EZ/dsl, Bella Milano, Buffalo Wild Wings, Culver's, Freddy's, IHOP, McDonald's, Mimosa Thai, Papa Frank's Italian, Audi/VW, Dodge/Ram, Kia/Subaru, Nissan, Toyota, S Colmans RV Ctr
	82	New Berlin, S Road Ranger/Subway/dsl, $General
	76	IL 123, to Ashland, Alexander
	68	to IL 104, to Jacksonville, N Casey's/dsl, Circle K, H
	64	US 67, to Jacksonville, N Circle K/dsl, FastStop/dsl, Love's/IHOP/dsl/scales/24hr, Qik-n-EZ/Subway/dsl, KFC, Little Caesar's, McDonald's, Baymont Inn, Comfort Inn, Holiday Inn Express, Sleep Inn, $General, CVS Drug, Family$, Hopper RV Ctr, H, Walgreens
	60	to US 67 N, to Jacksonville, N food, gas, lodging, H
	52	to IL 106, Winchester, N golf, S food, gas, lodging
	46	IL 100, to Bluffs
	42mm	Illinois River
BARRY	35	US 54, IL 107, to Pittsfield, Griggsville, N food, gas, lodging, S H, Jellystone Camping(6mi), st police
	31	to Pittsfield, New Salem, S food, gas, lodging, H, Jellystone Camping
	20	IL 106, Barry, S FastStop/dsl/24hr, Shell/dsl, Wendy's, Ice House Inn, $General
	10	IL 96, to Payson, Hull
	4a	I-172, N to Quincy
	1	IL 106, to Hull
	0mm	Illinois/Missouri state line, Mississippi River. Exits 157 & 156 are in Missouri.
	157	to Hannibal, MO 179, S Ayerco, BP, Pickadilly, Shell/dsl, Mark Twain Dinette, Subway, Best Way Inn, Best Western, Country Hearth Inn, Hotel Mark Twain, auto repair, visitor info
	156	US 61, New London, Palmyra. I-72 begins/ends in Hannibal, MO on US 61., N BP, Casey's/dsl, Murphy USA/dsl, Arby's, Burger King, Country Kitchen, Domino's, Gabriella's Mexican, LJ Silver, McDonald's, Mi Mexico, Pizza Hut, Royal Garden, Rustic Oak Grill, Saints Ave Steaks, Sonic, Subway, Taco Bell, $General, $Tree, ALDI, BigLots, Ford, JC Penney, Lowe's, Walmart, S Ayerco, Shell/dsl, Cassano's Subs, China King, DQ, Gran Rio Mexican, Hardee's, Jimmy John's, KFC, Little Caesar's, Logue's Rest, Wendy's, Comfort Inn, Days Inn, Economy Inn, Hannibal Inn, Motel 6, Super 8, $General, AT&T, AutoZone, Buick/Chevrolet, Chrysler/Dodge/Jeep, County Mkt Foods, CVS Drug, O'Reilly Parts,

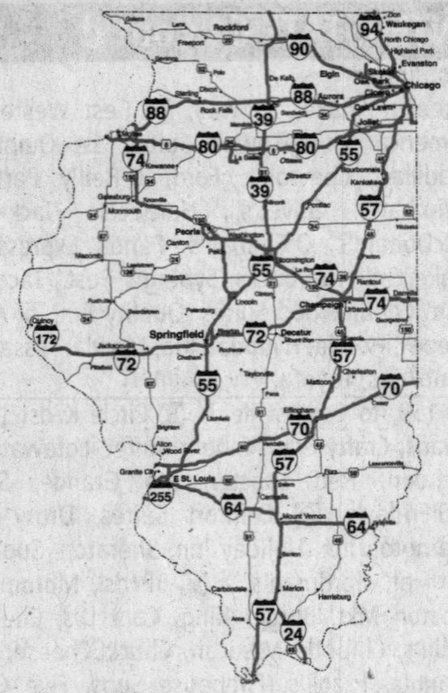

IL

INTERSTATE 72 Cont'd

Exit	Services
156	Continued Walgreens

INTERSTATE 74

DANVILLE

Exit	Services
221mm	Illinois/Indiana state line, Central/Eastern Time Zone
220	Lynch Rd, Danville, N [gas] Marathon/dsl/scales(1mi), Shell/dsl, [lodging] Best Western, Econo Lodge, Hampton Inn, Holiday Inn Express, Quality Inn, Red Roof Inn, Sleep Inn, Super 8, TownePlace Suites
216	Bowman Ave, Danville, N [gas] Mobil/Circle K/dsl, Phillips 66/dsl, [food] Burger King, McDonald's, [other] city park, Walgreens
215b a	US 150, IL 1, Gilbert St, Danville, N [gas] BP/dsl, [food] Arby's, El Toro, La Potosina, LJ Silver, McDonald's, Pizza Hut, Steak'n Shake, Subway, Taco Bell, [lodging] Best Western, Days Hotel, [other] AllDI, BigLots, [H], S [gas] Casey's/dsl, Marathon/Circle K/dsl, [food] Burger King, Green Jade Chinese, Mike's Grill, Monical's Pizza, Rich's Rest., [other] $General, $Tree, AutoZone, Buick/Chevrolet/GMC, County Mkt, Family$, Forest Glen Preserve Camping(11mi), Toyota/Scion
214	G St, Tilton
210	US 150, MLK Dr, N [gas] Marathon, [food] Little Nugget Steaks, [other] [H], to Kickapoo SP
206	Oakwood, N [gas] Love's/Hardee's/dsl/scales/24hr, S Casey's(1mi), Phillips 66/Subway/dsl/scales, Pilot/PJ Fresh/dsl/scales/24hr, Speedway/dsl, [food] Dunkin', McDonald's, [other] $General
200	IL 49 N, to Rankin
197	IL 49 S, Ogden, S [gas] Phillips 66/Godfather's/dsl, [food] Rich's Rest., [other] city park
192	St Joseph, S [gas] Casey's, Shell/dsl, [food] DQ, Monical's Pizza, Subway, [other] antiques

URBANA

Exit	Services
185	IL 130, University Ave, S [food] Casey's
184	US 45, Cunningham Ave, Urbana, N [gas] F&F, [other] Hyundai, Kia, Mazda, Toyota/Scion, VW, S [gas] Marathon/Circle K/dsl, Shell/dsl, [food] Arby's, Cracker Barrel, Hickory River BBQ, McDonald's, Steak'n Shake, Toro Loco, Wendy's, [lodging] Eastland Suites, Motel 6, [other] $General, auto repair, vet
183	Lincoln Ave, Urbana, S [gas] Circle K/dsl, Circle K/dsl, [food] Urbana Garden Rest., [lodging] Best Western Inn, Comfort Suites, Econo Lodge, Holiday Inn Express, Radisson, Rodeway Inn, [other] Harley-Davidson, [H], to U of IL

CHAMPAIGN

Exit	Services
182	Neil St(same as 181), Champaign, N [food] Alexander's Steaks, Bob Evans, Chick Shack Burgers, Food Court, McDonald's, Olive Garden, Panda Express, Panera Bread, Red Robin, Sweet Basil Cafe, Taco Bell, [lodging] Baymont Inn, La Quinta, Quality Inn, Red Roof Inn, Super 8, [other] Barnes&Noble, Cadillac/Chevrolet, Chrysler/Dodge/Jeep, Costco/gas, Dick's, Field&Stream, Hobby Lobby, Kohl's, Macy's, Mercedes/Volvo, TJ Maxx, Tuesday Morning, Verizon, S [gas] Circle K
181	Prospect Ave(same as 182), Champaign, N [gas] Meijer/dsl, Murphy USA/dsl, [food] Applebee's, Blaze Pizza, Buffalo Wild Wings, Burger King, Chili's, Chipotle, Culver's, Denny's, Fazoli's, Five Guys, Freddy's, Longhorn Steaks, McAlister's Deli, Oishi Asian, Outback Steaks, Panda Express, Penn Sta Subs, Portillo's, Red Lobster, Starbucks, Steak'n Shake, Subway, Wendy's, [lodging] Candlewood Suites, Country Inn&Suites, Courtyard, Drury Inn, Extended Stay America, Fairfield Inn, Quality Inn, Residence Inn, Woodspring Suites, [other] $Tree, Advance Parts, ALDI, AT&T, Best Buy, Ford/Lincoln, Jo-Ann, Lowe's, Menards, Michael's, Nissan, PetSmart, Sam's Club/gas, Staples, Target, Tires+, Verizon, Walmart/Subway, S [gas] Circle K/dsl, Mobil/Jimmy John's, Phillips 66/dsl, Shell/dsl, [food] Arby's, Dos Reales Mexican, Dunkin', LJ Silver, McDonald's, Popeyes, [lodging] Best Value Inn, Days Inn, [other] $General, CarX, Home Depot, NAPA, Tire Barn, Walgreens

MAHOMET

Exit	Services
179b a	I-57, N to Chicago, S to Memphis
174	Lake of the Woods Rd, Prairieview Rd, N [gas] BP, Casey's, Circle K/dsl, [other] $General, auto repair, Lake of the Woods SP, Tin Cup RV Park, S [gas] Marathon/Subway/dsl, [food] McDonald's
172	IL 47, Mahomet, N [other] R&S RV Sales, S [gas] Circle K/dsl, Exxon/Domino's/dsl, Mobil/dsl, [food] Arby's, DQ, HenHouse Rest., Jimmy John's, Los Zarapes, Monical's Pizza, Patricio's Pizza, Peking House, Subway, The Wok, YoYo's Frozen Yogurt, [lodging] Heritage Inn, [other] Ace Hardware, CVS Drug, NAPA, Schnucks, Walgreens
166	Mansfield, S [gas] Phillips 66/dsl, [other] Mansfield Gen. Store/Rest.
159	IL 54, Farmer City, S [gas] Casey's/dsl, Huck's/Godfather's/dsl, [food] $General, Imo's Cafe, Subway, [lodging] Budget Motel, Days Inn, [other] NAPA, to Clinton Lake RA, USPO
156mm	**full [handicapped] facilities, litter larrels, petwalk, [phone], [picnic], playground, [rest stop] both lanes, vending**

BLOOMINGTON

Exit	Services
152	US 136, to Heyworth
149	Le Roy, N [gas] Casey's/dsl, Love's/Arby's/dsl/scales/24hr, [food] Jack's Cafe, McDonald's, Roma Pizza, Subway, [lodging] Holiday Inn Express, [other] $General, IGA Foods, NAPA, to Moraine View SP, TrueValue, S [gas] Shell/Woody's Rest./dsl/scales/24hr, [lodging] Days Inn, [other] camping, Clinton Lake
142	Downs, N [gas] Mobil/Pizza/Subs/dsl/24hr, [other] USPO
135	US 51, Bloomington, N [gas] Circle K/dsl, Huck's/dsl, Pizza Hut, [food] McDonald's, [other] $General, S [gas] BP/dsl
134b[157]	Veterans Pkwy, to Bloomington, N [other] [H], to [airport]
134a	I-55, N to Chicago, S to St Louis, I-74 E, **I-74 and I-55 run together 6 mi. See I-55, exits 157b-160a.**
127[163]	I-55, N to Chicago, S to St Louis, I-74 W to Peoria
125	US 150, to Bloomington, Mitsubishi Motorway
123mm	weigh sta wb
122mm	weigh sta eb
120	Carlock, N [gas] BP/dsl/repair, [food] Carlock Rest., S [other] Kamp Komfort Camping (Apr-Oct)
114.5mm	**full [handicapped] facilities, litter barrels, petwalk, [phone], [picnic], [rest stop] both lanes, vending**
113.5mm	Mackinaw River
112	IL 117, Goodfield, N [gas] Shell/Subway/dsl, [food] Busy Corner Rest., [other] Eureka Coll, Jellystone Camping(1mi), Reagan Home, to Timberline RA, USPO
102b a	Morton, N [gas] Mobil/Arby's/dsl/scales/24hr, [food] Baskin Robins/Dunkin Donuts, Burger King, Cracker Barrel, Culver's, Steak'n Shake, Taco Bell, [lodging] Baymont Inn, Best Value Inn, Days Inn, Holiday Inn Express, Park Inn, Quality Inn, [other] Chrysler/Dodge/Jeep, Farm&Fleet, Freightliner, Walmart/Subway, S [gas] BP/Circle K, Casey's/dsl, Marathon/Circle K, Subway, [food] China Dragon, Domino's, Great Harvest Bread Co, Jimmy John's, La Fiesta, Lin's Buffet, McDonald's, Monical's Pizza, Pizza Hut, Pizza Ranch, [other] $Tree, Buick/GMC, CVS Drug, Ford, Kroger/dsl, O'Reilly Parts, Verizon

E PEORIA

Exit	Services
101	I-155 S, to Lincoln
99	I-474 W, [other] [airport]
98	Pinecrest Dr
96	95c(from eb), US 150, IL 8, E Washington St, E Peoria, N [gas] Fast Stop/dsl, [food] Subway, Super Gyros, [lodging] Super 8, [other] O'Reilly Parts
95b	(from eb) IL 116, to Metamora
95a	N Main St, Peoria, N [gas] Shell/dsl, [food] Burger King, [lodging] Hampton Inn, Paradice Hotel/Casino, S [gas] BP/Circle K, [food] A&W/LJ Silver, Bob Evans, Chick-fil-A, Chipotle Mexican, Firehouse Pizza, Hardee's, IHOP, Jason's Deli, Jersey Mike's, Jimmy John's, Johnny's Italian Steaks, McDonald's, Moe's SW, Noodles&Co, Panda Express, Papa Murphy's, Pizza Hut, Popeyes, Potbelly, Red Robin, Subway, Taco Bell, Tequilas Grill, Wendy's, [lodging] Best Value Inn, Best Western+, Fairfield Inn, Holiday Inn, [other] $Tree, Advance Parts, AllDI, AT&T,

IL

INTERSTATE 74 Cont'd

PEORIA

95a Continued
Costco/gas, CVS Drug, GNC, Goodyear/auto, Gordman's, Kohl's, Kroger, Ross, Target, Verizon, Walgreens

94 IL 40, RiverFront Dr, S Hucks/Godfather's/dsl, Arby's, Buffalo Wild Wings, Chili's, Culver's, Granite City Grill, Logan's Roadhouse, Lorena's Mexican, Panera Bread, Papa John's, Qdoba Mexican, Shogun, Slim Chickens, Steak'n Shake, TX Roadhouse, Uncle Buck's Grill, Embassy Suites, Holiday Inn Express, Bass Pro Shop, Lowe's, PetSmart, Verizon, Walmart/Subway

93.5mm Illinois River

93b US 24, IL 29, Peoria, N BP, S Mark Twain Hotel, civic ctr

93a Jefferson St, Peoria, N BP, S Two 25 Grill, Mark Twain Hotel, Marriott, Sheraton, to civic ctr

92b Glendale Ave, Peoria, S downtown, H

92a IL 40 N, Knoxville Ave, Peoria, S Sheraton, H

91 University St, Peoria

90 Gale Ave, Peoria, S $General, Marathon, to Bradley U

89 US 150, War Memorial Dr, Peoria, N BP/Circle K, Marathon/dsl, Burger King, Dunkin Donuts, Golden Corral, IHOP, McDonald's, Papa Murphy's, Perkins, Popeyes, Steak'n Shake, Wendy's, Baymont Inn, Comfort Suites, Courtyard, EconoLodge, Extended Stay America, Quality Inn, Red Roof Inn, Residence Inn, Super 8, ALDI, AT&T, AutoZone, Barnes&Noble, Best Buy, Chevrolet/Cadillac, Hobby Lobby, Lowe's, Midas, NAPA, PetSmart, Target, Tires+, U-Haul, vet, Walgreens, Walmart/Subway

88 to US 150, War Memorial Dr, N Shell, Arby's, Avanti's Rest., Baskin Robins/Dunkin Donuts, Biaggi's, Chick-fil-A, Chipotle, ChuckECheese, Firehouse Subs, Five Guys, Panda Express, Panera Bread, Portillo's, Red Lobster, Sonic, Motel 6, SpringHill Suites, $Tree, JC Penney, Michael's, Ross, Verizon, Walgreens

ELMWOOD

87b a I-474 E, IL 6, N to Chillicothe, S

82 Edwards Rd, Kickapoo, N Mobil/dsl/service, Shell/Subway/dsl, Jubilee Café, to Jubilee Coll SP, S USPO, Wildlife Prairie SP

75 Brimfield, Oak Hill, N Casey's/dsl

71 to IL 78, to Canton, Elmwood

62mm **full facilities, litter barrels, petwalk, both lanes, vending**

61.5mm Spoon River

54 US 150, IL 97, Lewistown, N TravL Park Camping(1mi), S Mobil/dsl(2mi), Alfano's Pizza(2mi)

51 Knoxville, S BP/dsl, Love's/Subway/Chester's/dsl/scales/24hr, Phillips 66/Charley's Subs/dsl/scales, Hardee's, McDonald's, Best Value Inn

48b a E Galesburg, Galesburg, N Best Western, Harley-Davidson, S BP/Circle K/dsl, HyVee/dsl, Phillps 66/Beck's/dsl, DQ, Hardee's, Jalisco Mexican, KFC, Marco's Pizza, McDonald's, Pizza Hut, Subway, Taco Bell, Baymont Inn, Holiday Inn Express, Family$, HyVee Foods, Lincoln-Douglas Debates, Sav-A-Lot Foods, to Sandburg Birthplace, Walgreens

WOODHULL

46b a US 34, to Monmouth, N Nichol's dsl Service, S Buffalo Wild Wings, Crazy Buffet, Mi Casa Mexican, Pizza Ranch, ALDI, AT&T, H, Kohl's, Menards, Toyota/Scion, Verizon, vet, Walmart/Subway

32 IL 17, Woodhull, N BP/dsl, Shell/dsl, Subway, $General, S Pilot/dsl/scales/24hr, Shady Lakes Camping(8mi)

30mm **full facilities, litter barrels, petwalk, playground, wb, RV dump, vending**

28mm **full facilities, litter barrels, petwalk,**

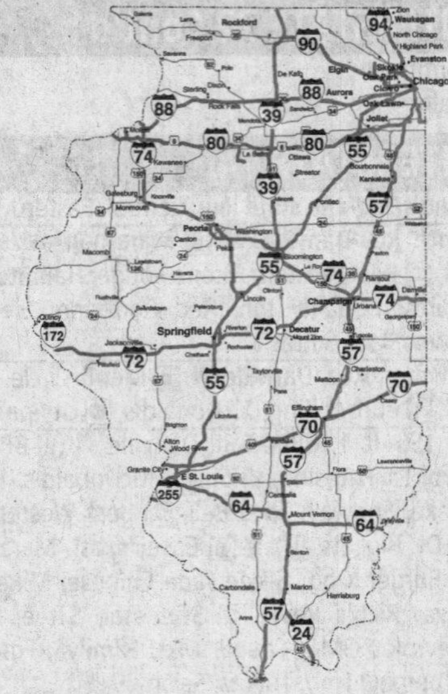

ANDOVER

28mm Continued
playground, eb, RV dump, vending

24 IL 81, Andover, N camping, Casey's(2mi)

14mm I-80, E to Chicago, I-80/I-280 W to Des Moines

8mm weigh sta wb

6mm weigh sta eb

MOLINE

5b US 6, Moline, S Shell/dsl, Bare Bones BBQ, McDonald's, MT Jack's, Best Inn, Country Inn&Suites, Hampton Inn, Holiday Inn Express, La Quinta, Motel 6, Quality Inn,

5a I-280 W, US 6 W, to Des Moines

4b a IL 5, John Deere Rd, Moline, N BP/7-11, Phillips 66, Shell/dsl, Applebee's, Burger King, Chipotle Mexican, Culver's, Hungy Hobo, Osaka Buffet, Panera Bread, Ryan's, Starbucks, Steak'n Shake, Subway, Wendy's, Residence Inn, $Tree, Cadillac, Farm&Fleet, Honda, Hyundai, Lowe's, Menard's, Staples, Subaru, Tires+, Toyota/Scion, Volvo, Walmart/Subway, S BP/7-11, A&W/LJ Silver, Arby's, Buffalo Wild Wings, China Cafe, Denny's, KFC, Los Agaves, McDonald's, New Mandarin Chinese, Qdoba Mexican, Taco Bell, Best Western, Comfort Inn, Fairfield Inn, Motel 6, $General, Best Buy, Buick/GMC, Chevrolet, Chrysler/Dodge/Jeep, Dillards, Firestone/auto, Ford/Lincoln, Goodyear/auto, Gordman's, JC Penney, Mazda, Nissan, PetCo, Von Maur, Walgreens, Younkers

3 23rd Ave, Moline, N Economy Inn

2 7th Ave, Moline, S QuikStop, La Casa Mexican, riverfront, to civic ctr, USPO

1 3rd Ave(from eb), Moline, S QuickStop, Stoney Creek Inn

0mm Illinois/Iowa state line, Mississippi River, Exits 4-1 are in Iowa.

BETTENDORF

4 US 67, Grant St, State St, Bettendorf, N BP/dsl, Hardee's, McDonald's, Subway, Waterfront Conv Ctr, CarQuest, S Village Inn Rest., City Ctr Motel, $General

3 Middle Rd, Locust St, Bettendorf, S BP/dsl, China Taste, Grinders Rest., Jimmy John's, McDonald's, Pizza Ranch, Red Ginger Asian, Starbucks, Subway, Hilton Garden, AT&T, Burlington Coats, Hobby Lobby, Home Depot, H, Marshall's, Schuck's Foods, Verizon, Walgreens

2 US 6 W, Spruce Hills Dr, Bettendorf, N BP/dsl, Phillips 66, Domino's, Old Chicago Pizza, Courtyard, EconoLodge, Ramada Inn, Super 8, The Lodge Hotel/rest., U-Haul, S Hyvee Gas, Applebee's, KFC, Panera Bread, Red Lobster, AmericInn, Days Inn, Holiday Inn, La Quinta,

BETTENDORF

INTERSTATE 74 Cont'd

2	Continued Buick/GMC, Gordman's, Kohl's, Lowe's, PetCo, Sam's Club/gas, st patrol
1	53rd St, Hamilton, N BP, Bad Boyz Pizza, Biaggi's Italian, Buffalo Wild Wings, Chili's, Coldstone, Granite City Rest., Los Agaves, Maggie Moo's, Moe's SW, Osaka Steaks, Panchero's Mexican, Red Lantern Chinese, Red Robin, TX Roadhouse, Hampton Inn, Homewood Suites, Staybridge Suites, GNC, Harley-Davidson, H, HyVee Foods, Michael's, Natural Grocers, Old Navy, TJ Maxx, Walgreens, S Murphy USA/dsl, Shell/dsl, Arby's, Azteca Mexican, Burger King, Chick-fil-A, China Cafe, Chipotle Mexican, DQ, Dynasty Buffet, Golden Corral, HuHot, Hungry Hobo, IHOP, La Rancherita, Noodles&Co., PepperJax Grill, Quiznos, Sonic, Starbucks, Steak'n Shake, Subway, Taco Bell, Village Inn Rest., Wendy's, Sleep Inn, $Tree, AlLDI, AT&T, Best Buy, Costco/dsl, Dick's, Discount Tire, Field&Stream, Meineke, PetSmart, Staples, Target, Verizon, Walmart
0mm	I-74 begins/ends on I-80, exit 298. Exits 1-4 are in Iowa.

INTERSTATE 80

OASIS

163mm	Illinois/Indiana state line
161	US 6, IL 83, Torrence Ave, N BP, Burger King, Chili's, Culver's, Dunkin', Hooters, IHOP, Kenny's Ribs, Liang's Garden, New China Buffet, Olive Garden, Outriggers, Ranch Grande, Subway, Wendy's, Comfort Suites, Extended Stay America, Holiday Inn Express, Red Roof Inn, Sleep Inn, Travelodge, $General, $Tree, AlLDI, Best Buy, CarX, Chrysler/Jeep/Dodge, Fannie May Candies, Firestone/auto, Home Depot, Honda, JustTires, PepBoys, Starway Inn, S Gas For Less, Marathon, Mobil, Burger King, Checkers, China Chef, DQ, Dunkin', Johnny K's Cafe, McDonald's, Popeyes, Round the Clock, Subway, AT&T, Auto Clinic, Chevrolet, O'Reilly Parts, Saab, SunRise Foods, vet, Walgreens, Walmart/Subway
160b	I-94 W, to Chicago, tollway begins wb, ends eb
160a	IL 394 S, to Danville
159mm	Lincoln Oasis, Oasis, EVC, Mobil/7-11/dsl, McDonald's, Panda Express, Starbucks, Subway
157	IL 1, Halsted St, N Quick Fuel, Maxwell St Grill, Clarion, Days Inn, Motel 6, Quality Inn, Red Carpet Inn, Super 8, Travelodge, S Delta Sonic, Shell, Speedway, Walmart/dsl, Boston Mkt, Buffalo Wild Wings, Burger King, Chick-fil-A, Chili's, Chipotle, Culver's, Dunkin', Freddy's, KFC, Krispy Kreme, McDonald's, Panda Express, Panera Bread, Popeyes, Portillo's Hot Dogs, Potbelly, Starbucks, Subway, Wendy's, White Castle, $Tree, AlLDI, Best Buy, Chevrolet, Fanny May Candies, Firestone/auto, GNC, Home Depot, Jewel-Osco, Kohl's, Menards, Old Navy, PepBoys, PetCo, Ross, Target, TJ Maxx, Walgreens, Walmart
156	Dixie Hwy(from eb, no return), S Mobil, Belagio, Dunkin', golf
155	I-294 N, Tri-State Tollway, toll plaza
154	Kedzie Ave(from eb, no return), N Speedway, S H
151b a	I-57(exits left from both directions), N to Chicago, S to Memphis
148b a	IL 43, Harlem Ave, N Speedway/dsl, Buffalo Wild Wings, Burger King, Cracker Barrel, Culver's, Dunkin', Hamada of Japan, Joy Yee Asian, Pop's Italian Beef, Side Street Tavern, Tin Fish Grill, Wendy's, Comfort Suites, Fairfield Inn, Hampton Inn, Holiday Inn, La Quinta, Sleep Inn, Wingate Inn, Woodspring Suites, AT&T, Tinley Park Convention Center, Verizon, S EVC, Arby's, Panera Bread, Subway, Taco Bell, TGIFriday's, ampitheater, Best Buy, CarMax, Dick's, GNC, Kohl's, Michael's, Old Navy,

NEW LENOX · MINOOKA · MORRIS

148b a	Continued PetSmart, Ross, SuperTarget, TJ Maxx
147.5mm	weigh sta wb
145b a	US 45, 96th Ave, N Arby's, Arrenello's Pizza, Baskin-Robbins/Dunkin', Tokyo Steaks, TX Roadhouse, Country Inn&Suites, Hilton Garden, Harley-Davidson, vet, S BP, Shell/Circle K/dsl/24hr, Beggar's Pizza, Chipotle, Denny's, Doc's Smokehouse, Domino's, DQ, Legends, Mindy's Ribs, Mobil, Rising Sun Chinese, Starbucks, Stoney Pt Grill, Subway, Wendy's, White Castle, Super 8, Firestone/auto, repair, vet
143mm	weigh sta eb
140	SW Hwy, I-355 N Tollway, US 6 S, N H
137	US 30, New Lenox, N Williamson's Rest., S Shell/Circle K/dsl, Speedway/dsl, Al's Hotdogs, Beggar's Pizza, Buffalo Wild Wings, Burger King, Keys's Chophouse, KFC, McDonald's, Paisano's Pizza, Subway, Taco Bell, Ace Hardware, Goodyear/auto, Jewel-Osco/dsl, Walgreens
134	Briggs St, N Speedway, S Mobil/dsl, Shell/dsl, Martin Camping
133	Richards St
132b a	US 52, IL 53, Chicago St, N BP, Shell, Dunkin', Shark Fish Chicken
131.5mm	Des Plaines River
131	US 6, Meadow Ave, N to Riverboat Casino
130b a	IL 7, Larkin Ave, N Delta Sonic/dsl, Marathon/24hr, Mobil/CircleK/dsl, Shell, Speedway, Baskin-Robbins/Dunkin', Bob Evans, Boston Mkt, Burger King, Checkers, Culver's, DQ, JJ Fish&Chicken, KFC, Little Caesar's, McDonald's, Subway, Taco Bell, Wendy's, White Castle, Budget Inn, Clarion, Joliet Inn, Motel 6, Quality Inn, Red Roof Inn, 7-11, AT&T, auto repair, Cadillac/Chevrolet, Discount Tire, Goodyear/auto, H, Meineke, Pepboys, Sam's Club/gas, to U of St Francis, USPO, S Mobil/dsl
127	Houbolt Rd, to Joliet, N 7-11, BP/deli, Burger King, Burger Theory, China Kitchen, Cracker Barrel, Dunkin', Heros Sports Grill, Jimmy John's, Jimmy K's, McDonald's, Subway, Comfort Inn, Fairfield Inn, Hampton Inn, Holiday Inn, TownePlace Suites, Riverboat Casino
126b a	I-55, N to Chicago, S to St Louis
125.5mm	Du Page River
122	Minooka, N Circle K/dsl, S BP, Pilot/Arby's/scales/dsl/24hr, 2-Fers Pizza, Baskin-Robbins/Dunkin', McDonald's, Rosati's Pizza, Subway, Taco Bell, Wendy's, Wings Etc, Hampton Inn, TownePlace Suites, $General, 7-11
119mm	rest area wb, **full facilities, litter barrels, petwalk, , playground, vending**
117mm	rest area eb, **full facilities, litter barrels, petwalk, , , playground, vending**
116	Brisbin Rd, CR 3000 E
112	IL 47, Morris, N Citgo/dsl, Pilot/Subway/dsl/scales/24hr, TA/BP/RPlace/scales/dsl/24hr/@, Bellacino's, Chili's, IHOP, Comfort Inn, Days Inn, Holiday Inn Express, Quality Inn, $General, Menards, S BP/dsl, Circle K/dsl, Shell, Buffalo Wild Wings, Burger King, Culver's, DQ, Dunkin', Hong Kong Chinese, KFC/LJ Silver, Maria's Ristorante, McDonald's, Morris Diner, Pizza Hut, Rosati's Pizza, Sherwood Oaks Rest., Subway, Taco Bell, Wendy's, Park Motel, Super 8, $Tree, AlLDI, AT&T, AutoZone, Big R Store, Buick/Cadillac/Chevrolet, Chrysler/Dodge/Jeep, Fisher Parts, Ford, GMC, GNC, H, Jewel-Osco, to Stratton SP, transmissions/repair, Verizon, Walgreens, Walmart/Subway
105	to Seneca
97	to Marseilles, S Shell/dsl, Four Star Camping(5mi), Glenwood Camping(4mi), to Illini SP
93	IL 71, Ottawa, N Pilot/Road Ranger/Subway/dsl/scales/24hr, Shell/rest./dsl, S Hank's Farm Rest., New Chiam,

IL

[gas icon] = gas [food icon] = food [lodging icon] = lodging [other icon] = other [RS icon] = rest stop

INTERSTATE 80 Cont'd

OTTAWA

93. Continued
H

92.5mm Fox River

90 IL 23, Ottawa, N BP/Subway, Arby's, Cracker Barrel, Fondita Mexican, Rosati's Pizza, Taco Bell, Comfort Inn, Hampton Inn, AT&T, F&F, GNC, Honda, Toyota, Verizon, Walmart/McDonald's, S BP/dsl/LP, Thornton's/dsl, China Inn, Culver's, DQ, Dunkin', Hardee's, KFC/LJ Silver, Sunfield Rest., Fairfield Inn, Holiday Inn Express, Quality Inn, Super 8, Surrey Motel, $Tree, AlLDI, Ford/Lincoln/Kia, Harley-Davidson, H, Kroger, O'Reilly Parts, USPO, Verizon

81 IL 178, Utica, N Love's/McDonald's/Subway/dsl/scales/24hr, KOA(2mi), S Casey's/dsl, Shell/Jimmy Johns/dsl, repair, to Starved Rock SP, visitor info

79b a I-39, US 51, N to Rockford, S to Bloomington

77.5mm Little Vermilion River

77 IL 351, La Salle, S Flying J/Denny's/dsl/scales/24hr, UpTown Grill(3mi), Daniels Motel(1mi), st police

PERU

75 IL 251, Peru, N Mobil, Shell/rest./dsl/24hr, Arby's, Four Star Rest., McDonald's, Olive Garden, Starbucks, Taco Bell, Holiday Inn Express, Quality Inn, Super 8, Kohl's, PetSmart, Walmart/Dunkin', S BP, Shell, Tesla EVC, Applebee's, Buffalo Wild Wings, Burger King, Culver's, DQ, IHOP, Jalepeno's Mexican, Jersey Mike's, Jimmy John's, Master Buffet, McDonald's, Pizza Hut, Red Lobster, Steak'n Shake, Subway, Wendy's, Fairfield Inn, Hampton Inn, La Quinta, $Tree, Advance Parts, AlLDI, AT&T, AutoZone, BigLots, Buick/GMC, Chevrolet, Chrysler/Dodge/Jeep, CVS Drug, Ford/Hyundai/Lincoln, Goodyear/auto, Hobby Lobby, Home Depot, H, HyVee Food/dsl, Jo-Ann Fabrics, Marshall's, Menards, Mercedes, Midas, NAPA, Nissan, O'Reilly Parts, Staples, Target, Verizon, Walgreens

IL

73 Plank Rd, N Sapp Bros/Burger King/Subway/dsl/scales/@, Speedway/Speedway Cafe/dsl, Big Apple Rest., Mack Trucks

70 IL 89, to Ladd, N Casey's, S Spring Valley Motel, golf, H

61 I-180, to Hennepin

56 IL 26, Princeton, N Road Ranger/scales/dsl/@, Super 8, S BP/Beck's/dsl, Casey's, Shell/dsl, Big Apple Rest., Burger King, Coffee Cup Rest., Culver's, McDonald's, Subway, Wendy's, AmericInn, Days Inn, EconoLodge, $General, AutoZone, Buick/Cadillac/Chevrolet, H, O'Reilly Parts, Sullivan's Food/gas/e85, vet, Walmart

ANNAWAN

51mm rest area both lanes, **full facilities, litter barrels, petwalk, playground, RV dump, vending**

45 IL 40, N antiques, to Ronald Reagan Birthplace(21mi), S Hennepin Canal SP

44mm Hennepin Canal

33 IL 78, to Kewanee, Annawan, N Shabbona RV Ctr/Camp(3mi), S Cenex/dsl, FS/dsl/e85, Shell/Subway/dsl, Best Western, to Johnson-Sauk Tr SP

27 to US 6, Atkinson, N Casey's(1mi), Love's/Chester's/Godfathers's/Subway/dsl/scales24hr

19 IL 82, Geneseo, N BP/dsl, Casey's/dsl, Culver's, DQ, Happy Joe's Pizza, Hardee's, McDonald's, New China, Pizza Hut, Subway, Sweet Pea's Grill, Best Western, $General, Ford, H, SaveALot Foods, Verizon, Walgreens, Walmart, S Los Ranchitos Mexican

10 I-74, I-280, W to Moline, E to Peoria

9 US 6, to Geneseo, N Lavender Crest Winery/Cafe, S Niabi Zoo

7 Colona, N Shell/dsl

5mm Rock River

4a IL 5, IL 92, W to Silvis, S Lundeen's Camping

E MOLINE

4b I-88, IL 92, E to Rock Falls

2mm weigh sta both lanes

1.5mm Welcome Ctr eb

1 IL 84, 20th St, Great River Rd, E Moline, N BP/dsl, Bros Rest., The Great River Rd, S camping

0mm Illinois/Iowa state line, Mississippi River

INTERSTATE 88

139.5mm I-88 begins/ends on I-290.

139 I-294, S to Indiana, N to Milwaukee

138mm toll plaza

137 IL 83 N, Cermak Rd, N Cheesecake Factory, Clubhouse Rest., Ditka's Rest., McDonald's, Marriott, Barnes&Noble, Lord&Taylor, Macy's, Nieman-Marcus

136 IL 83 S, Midwest Rd(from eb), N Shell/Circle K, Chipotle Mexican, Denny's, Devon Steaks, Giordano's Rest., Jamba Juice, Jimmy John's, McDonalds, Noodles&Co, Redstone Grill, Starbucks, Subway, Twin Peaks, Which Wich?, Courtyard, Holiday Inn, La Quinta, Staybridge, AT&T, Big Lots, Costco/gas, Home Depot, Nordstrom's, Old Navy, REI, TJ Maxx, Walgreens, World Mkt

134 Highland Ave(no EZ wb return), N Barbokoa, Benihana, Brick House, Brio Grille, Buca Italian, Burger King, Capital Grille, Chama Guacha Brazilian, Champps Grill, Chick-fil-A, Chipotle, Claimjumper Rest., Fuddruckers, Harry Caray's, Honey-Jam Cafe, Hooters, Kona Grill, Kyoto, McCormick & Schmick's, Melting Pot, Miller's Rest., Noodles&Co, Olive Garden, Olive Therapy Pizza, Panera Bread, PF Chang's, Portillo's Hotdogs, Potbelly, Red Lobster, Rockbottom Brewery, Ruby Tuesday, Starbucks, Starbucks, Subway, TGIFriday's, Tom&Eddie's Burgers, Uncle Julio's, Comfort Inn, Embassy Suites, Extended Stay America, Holiday Inn Express, Hyatt Place, Marriott, Red Roof Inn, Westin Hotel, $Tree, Best Buy, Dick's, Home Depot, H, JC Penney, Kohl's, Marshall's, Michael's, PetSmart, Ross, Target, Tuesday Morning, Verizon, Vonmaur, S Parkers Ocean Grill

132 I-355 N(from wb)

131 I-355 S(from eb)

130 IL 53(from wb), N BP, Mobil, McDonald's, Walmart

127 Naperville Rd, N Mullen's Grill, Hilton, Sheraton, S Mobil, Arby's, Buona Beef, Butterfield's Pancakes, Chipotle, Coopers Hawk, Fogo de Chao Brazilian, Granite City, HoneyBaked Ham, Jason's Deli, Maggiano's, McDonald's, Ming Hin, Morton's Steaks, Paisan's Pizza, Panera Bread, Pizza Hut, Subway, Tom & Eddie's Burgers, Uncle Julio's, Wendy's, White Chocolate Grill,

INTERSTATE 88 Cont'd

127 Continued
Best Western, Country Inn & Suites, Courtyard, Embassy Suites, Extended Stay America, Fairfield Inn, Hampton Inn, Marriott, Motel 6, Regency Inn, $Tree, CVS, Staples, Subaru

125 Winfield Rd, N BP, Mobil, Hyatt House, Hyatt Place, Resedence Inn, H, Walgreens, S Buffalo Wild Wings, CA Pizza Kitchen, Chipotle Mexican, Corner Bakery Cafe, Eddie Merlot, Masala, McDonald's, Potbelly, Red Robin, Rockbottom Brewery, Starbucks, Twin Peaks, Zoup, Hilton Garden, Springhill Suites, SuperTarget

123 IL 59, N CarMax, Speedway/dsl, S BP/Domino's, Delta Sonic, Speedway, Baskin Robbins/Dunkin Donuts, Cracker Barrel, Firehouse Subs, Jimmy John's, McDonald's, Oberweis, Starbucks, Subway, TX Roadhouse, Wendy's, Extended Stay America, Fairfield Inn, Red Roof Inn, Sleep Inn, Towneplace Suites, $Tree, 7-11, CVS Drug

119 Farnsworth Ave, N BP, Shell, Thornton's/dislike, Chipotle, McDonald's, Noodles&Co, Panera Bread, Papa Bear Rest., Quizno's, Sonic, Starbucks, Fox Valley Inn, Motel 6, Advance Parts, AT&T, Firestone/auto, GNC, Premium Outlets/Famous Brands, Verizon, Walgreens, Walmart/Subway, S Marathon, Moble, Shell, Speedway, Baskin-Robbins/Dunkin Donuts, Goody's, Little Caesar's, McDonald's, Mike&Denise's Pizza, Subway, Taco Bell, $General, 7-11, AutoZone, Family$, Walgreens

118mm toll plaza

117 IL 31, IL 56, to Aurora, Batavia, N BP/dsl, A&W, 7-11, S Mobil, Speedway/dsl, Thornton's/dsl, Baskin-Robbins/Dunkin Donuts, Burger King, Culver's, Denny's, McDonald's, Nikarry's, Popeyes, Subway, Taco Bell, Wendy's, White Castle, Baymont Inn, $General, $Tree, Ace Hardware, Advance Parts, AutoZone, Cermak Foods, Family$, Firestone, GNC, H, O'Reilly Parts, Ross, U-Haul, Walgreens

BATAVIA

115 Orchard Rd, N Dunkin Donuts, McDonald's, Subway, $Tree, Best Buy, Chrysler/Dodge/Jeep, Ford/Lincoln, Hyundai, JC Penney, Kia, Michaels, Nissan, PetCo, Subaru, Target, Verizon, Woodman's/dsl, S 7-11, Arby's, Buffalo Wild Wings, Chili's, Chipotle, IHOP, Jimmy John's, Panera Bread, Papa Saverio's, Pizza Hut, Starbucks, Wendy's, Candlewood Suites, Hampton Inn, Holiday Inn, AT&T, CVS Drug, Discount Tire, Home Depot, Office Depot

114 IL 56W, to US 30(from wb, no EZ return), to Sugar Grove

109 IL 47 (from eb), Elburn

ELBURN

94 Peace Rd, to IL 38, N H

93mm Dekalb Oasis/24hr both lanes, Mobil/dsl, McDonald's, Panda Express, Starbucks, Subway

92 IL 38, IL 23, Annie Glidden Rd, to DeKalb, N BP, Road Ranger/dsl, Shell, Baskin-Robbins, Burger King, Chipotle Mexican, Culver's, Dunkin Donuts, Fatty's, Happy Wok Chinese, IHOP, Jct Rest., Jersey Mike's, McDonald's, Miki MOto, Molly's Eatery, Panda Express, Papa John's, Pizza Hut, Pizza Pros, Pizza Villa, Potbelly, Starbucks, Subway, Taco Bell, Tom&Jerry's, Topper's Pizza, Baymont Inn, Hampton Inn, Red Roof Inn, Super 8, CVS, Ford, Illini Tire, Schnuck's Food/Drug, to N IL U, Walgreens

86mm toll plaza

78 I-39, US 51, S to Bloomington, N to Rockford

76 IL 251, Rochelle, N BP/dsl, Casey's, Shell, Ford, H, tires/repair, S Love's/Hardee's/dsl/scales/24hr

56mm toll plaza

DIXON

54 IL 26, Dixon, N Murphy USA/dsl, Road Ranger/dsl/24hr, Hardee's, Las Palmas, Panda Chinese, Pizza Hut, Comfort Inn, Super 8, $Tree, ALDI, GNC, H, to John Deere HS, to Ronald Reagan Birthplace, to St Parks, URGENT CARE,

54 Continued
Verizon, Walmart

DIXON

44 US 30(last free exit eb), N food, gas, lodging, Leisure lake RV Ctr(2mi)

41 IL 40, to Sterling, Rock Falls, N Mobil/dsl, Shell, American Grill, Arby's, Arthur's Deli, Burger King, Candlelight Rest., Culver's, Gazi's Rest., Hardee's, Jimmy John's, McDonald's/playplace, Perna's Pizza, Pizza Hut, Red Apple Rest., Subway, Country Inn&Suites, Days Inn, Holiday Inn Express, Super 8, $General, AutoZone, Harley-Davidson, H, O'Reilly Parts, Sav-a-Lot, Verizon, Walgreens, Walmart

36 to US 30, Rock Falls, Sterling

26 IL 78, to Prophetstown, Morrison, N to Morrison-Rockwood SP

18 to Albany, Erie

ERIE

10 to Port Byron, Hillsdale, S Phillips 66/dsl, Shell/Subway/scales/dsl/24hr

6 IL 92 E, to Joslin, N Jammerz Roadhouse(2mi), S Sunset Lake Camping(1mi)

2 Former IL 2

1b a I-80, W to Des Moines, E to Chicago

0mm IL 5, IL 92, W to Silvis. I-88 begins/ends on I-80, exit 4b., Lundeen's Camping, to Quad City Downs

INTERSTATE 90

0mm Illinois/Indiana state line, Chicago Skyway Toll Rd begins/ends

1mm US 12, US 20, 106th St, Indianapolis Blvd, N Mobil, Burger King, Starbucks, Taco Bell, AlLDI, AutoZone, casino, Jewel-Osco, S Citgo, Beggars Pizza, McDonald's, auto repair

2.5mm Skyway Oasis, McDonald's, toll plaza

3mm 87th St(from wb)

4mm 79th St, services on 79th St and Stoney Island Ave

5.5mm 73rd St(from wb)

6mm State St(from wb), S Citgo

7mm I-94 N(mile markers decrease to IN state line). I-90 and I-94 merge. See I-94 exits 43b - 59a.

84 I-94, Lawrence Ave, N BP/dsl

83b a Foster Ave(from wb), N BP, Elly's Pancakes, Subway, Advance Parts, Firestone/auto, Walgreens

82c Austin Ave, to Foster Ave

82b Byrn-Mawr(from wb)

82a Nagle Ave

81b Sayre Ave(from wb)

81a IL 43, Harlem Ave, S Gas Depot, Shell, Dunkin Donuts, Popeyes, Sally's Pancakes, Wendy's, $Tree, AutoZone

80 Canfield Rd(from wb), N Walgreens

79b a IL 171 S, Cumberland Ave(from wb), N 7-11, Mobil, Al's Burgers, Dunkin Donuts/Baskin Robbins, Hooters, McDonald's, Nancy's Pizza, Outback Steaks, Marriott, SpringHill Suites, Westin Hotel, Hampton Inn, Mariano's Mkt, S Bar Louie's, Starbucks, Holiday Inn, Hyatt, Renaissance

78 I-294, I-190 W, N Mobil, McDonald's, Hampton Inn, Westin, S Hyatt, to O'Hare

76 IL 72, Lee St(from wb), N Buona, Chili's, Chipotle, Culver's, IHOP, Jimmy John's, Longhorn Steaks, Panda Express, Steak'n Shake, Subway, Extended Stay America, Radisson, Residence Inn, Target, S McDonald's, Best Western, Holiday Inn Express, Holiday Inn Select, Sheraton Gateway

73 Elmhurst Rd(from wb), S Shell, Burger King, McDonald's, Subway, White Castle, Best Western, Days Inn, InTowne Suites, La Quinta, Motel 6, Super 8, Wyndham Garden

70 Arlington Hts Rd, BP/dsl, Shell/dsl, Arby's,

IL

INTERSTATE 90 Cont'd

70 Continued
Buona Beef, Chef Ping, Chipotle Mexican, Coopers Hawk, Denny's, Five Guys, Honey Baked Ham, Jimmy Johns, McDonald's, Noodles&Co, Panda Express, Panera Bread, Pie Five, Potbelly's, Steak'n Shake, Comfort Inn, Courtyard, DoubleTree, Holiday Inn Express, Red Roof Inn, Wingate Inn, AT&T, GNC, Lowe's Whse, Meijer/dsl, NTB, Staples, vet, Walmart, S Mobil, Shell, Subway, Sheraton, Chevrolet

68 I-290, IL 53, N Embassy Suites, Holiday Inn, Holiday Inn Express, Renaissance Inn, S CA Pizza Kitchen, Cheesecake Factory, Chevy's Mexican, Hooters, Joe's Crabshack, Longhorn Steaks, Maggiano's, Olive Garden, Panera Bread, Qdoba, Red Robin, Starbucks, Subway, TGI Friday's, Uno, Extended Stay America, Hyatt, Residence Inn, AT&T, Costco/gas, Firestone/auto, JC Penney, Lord&Taylor, Macy's, Marshall's, Michael's, Nordstrom, Old Navy, PetSmart, Trader Joe's

65 Roselle Rd(from wb, no return), N Medieval Times Funpark, S Mobil, Boston Mkt, Chipotle Mexican, Denny's, Fox&Hound, Jimmy John's, KFC, McDonald's, Melting Pot, Outback Steaks, Panda Express, Papa John's, Subway, Taco Bell, Wendy's, Country Inn&Suites, Extended Stay America, Extended Stay America(2), Holiday Inn Express, Radisson, 7-11, Buick/GMC, Carmax, Chrysler/Dodge/Jeep, Fiat, Firestone/auto, Jewel-Osco, Mazda, O'Reilly Parts, Office Depot, PetCo, TJ Maxx, Walgreens

62 Barrington Rd(from wb), N Apple Villa Pancake House, Gino's East, Hunan Beijing, Jersey's Grill, Jimmy John's, Lucky Monk, Hilton Garden, vet, S BP, Mobil/dsl, Buona Beef, Burger King, Chili's, Domino's, IHOP, Macaroni Grill, McDonald's, Moretti's, Starbucks, Steak'n Shake, Subway, Sweet Caroline's, Hampton Inn, Hawthorn Suites, Hyatt Place, La Quinta, Quality Inn, Red Roof Inn, U-Haul

59 IL 59, N Buffalo Wild Wings, Chipotle Mexican, Claim Jumper Rest., Cooper's Hawk Rest., Culver's, Dunkin Donuts, Firehouse Subs, Jersey Mike's, Jimmy John's, Moe's SW Grill, Noodles&Co, Panda Express, Panera Bread, Potbelly, Red Robin, Rookie's Grill, Ruth's Chris Steaks, Starbucks, Subway, Which Wich?, Marriott, Cabela's, CVS Drug, Duluth Trading, GNC, PetSmart, Ross, Target, TJ Maxx, Verizon, World Mkt

58 Beverly Rd(from wb)

56 IL 25, N Lexington Inn, S BP/dsl, Shell/dsl, Speedway/dsl, Arby's, Baker Hill Pancakes, Subway, Wendy's, Advance Parts, city park, NAPA AutoCare

54b a IL 31, N BP, Thornton's, Alexander's Rest., Baskin-Robbins/Dunkin Donuts, Courtyard, Hampton Inn, Holiday Inn, Quality Inn, Super 8, TownePlace Suites

53.5mm Elgin Toll Plaza, phone

52 Randall Rd, N Shell, Big Sammy's Hot Dogs, Burnt Toast, Cafe Roma, DQ, Jimmy John's, Jimmy's Charhouse, Mr Wok, Panera Bread, Rookies Grill, Starbucks, Village Pizza, Comfort Suites, Country Inn&Suites, Honda, VW, S 7-11, Candlewood Suites, H, Subaru

46 IL 47, to Woodstock, N Ford, General RV Ctr, Huntley Outlets/famous brands

42 US 20, Marengo, N Citgo/Mexican Grill/dsl/scales/24hr, Love's/Arby's/dsl/scales/24hr, Road Ranger/Subway/dsl/scales/24hr, Speedway/Speedy's Cafe/dsl/24hr, TA/BP/Country Pride/Burger King/Popeyes/dsl/scales/24hr/@, McDonald's, Wendy's, Super 8, access to services at exit 46(6mi), Ford, Huntley Outlets, to museums

MARENGO

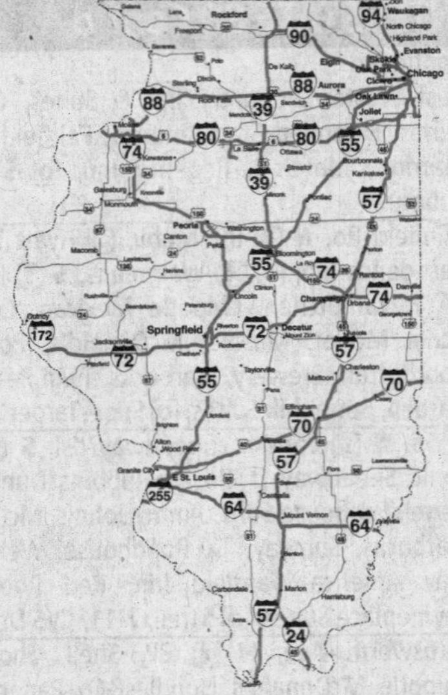

38mm Marengo Toll Plaza (from eb)

25 Genoa Rd, to Belvidere, N Murphy USA/dsl, Applebee's, Rosati's Pizza, Starbucks, Subway, Verizon, Walmart/Dunkin Donuts

24mm Belvidere Oasis both lanes, Mobil/7-11/dsl/24hr, Food Court, McDonald's, Panda Express, Sbarro, Starbucks, Subway

20 Irene Rd

18mm Kishwaukee River

17mm I-39 S, US 20, US 51, to Rockford, S funpark

15 US 20, State St, N Mobil/dsl, Phillips 66/Subway/dsl, Cracker Barrel, Baymont Inn, Clocktower Resort, Days Inn, S FasFuel/dsl, Mobil/dsl, Applebee's, Buffalo Wild Wings, Burger King, Chick-fil-A, Chili's, Chipotle Mexican, City Buffet, Coldstone, Culver's, Denny's, Dos Reales, Fiesta Cancun, Five Guys, Gerry's Pizza, Giovanni's Rest., Hoffman House Rest., Hooters, IHOP, Jason's Deli, Jersey Mike's, Jimmy John's, KFC/LJ Silver, Lino's Italian, LoneStar Steaks, Longhorn Steaks, Machine Shed Rest, McDonald's, Noodles&Co, Old Chicago Grill, Olive Garden, Outback Steaks, Panda Express, Panera Bread, Panino's Drive-Thru, Perkins, Pizza Hut/Taco Bell, PotBelly, Red Lobster, Red Robin, Ruby Tuesday, Starbucks, Steak'n Shake, Stone Eagle Tavern, Subway, ThunderBay Grille, TX Roadhouse, Wendy's, Candlewood Suites, Comfort Inn, Courtyard, Extended Stay America, Fairfield Inn, Hampton Inn, Hilton Garden, Holiday Inn, Motel 6, Quality Suites, Radisson, Red Roof Inn, Residence Inn, Sleep Inn, Staybridge Suites, Super 8, $Tree, Advance Parts, AlLDI, AT&T, Best Buy, BigLots, Burlington Coats, Cadillac, Chrysler/Dodge/Jeep, Dick's, Discount Tire, GNC, Gordman's, Hobby Lobby, Home Depot, H, Hyundai, JoAnn Fabrics, Kohl's, Lowe's, Marshall's, Mazda, Michael's, Nissan, Old Navy, Old Time Pottery, PetCo, PetSmart, Ross, Sam's Club/gas, Schnuck's Foods, Subaru, Target, Tuesday Morning, Valli Foods, Verizon, Walgreens, Walmart/McDonald's

12 E Riverside Blvd, Loves Park, N EVC, Burger King, Casey's, Costco/gas, H, S BP, Mobil/dsl, Phillips 66/dsl, Road Ranger/Subway/dsl, Shell/dsl, 2nd Cousin's Grill, Arby's, BeefARoo, Ciaobella, Culver's, DQ, Greenfire Rest., India House, Japanese Express, KFC, McDonald's, RBI Rest., Rosatti's Pizza, Sam's Ristorante, Singapore Grill, Subway, Taco Bell, Wendy's, Holiday Inn Express, Home2 Suites, Quality Inn, Audi/Honda/Mercedes, Autowerks, Farm&Fleet, funpark, Lexus, to Rock Cut SP, Toyota, Tuffy Auto, Walgreens

LOVES PARK

IL

INTERSTATE 90 Cont'd

S BELOIT

Exit #	Services
8	Il 173, S to Rock Cut SP
3.5mm	S Beloit Toll Plaza
3	Rockton Rd, S [gas] Love's/Hardee's/dsl/scales/24hr, Speedway/cafe/dsl/scales, Thorntons/Wendy's/dsl/scales, [food] Hardee's, [other] Camping World
1.5mm	**full [handicapped] facilities, info, litter barrels, petwalk, [phone], [picnic], playground, RV dump, Welcome Ctr/[rest stop] eb**
1	US 51 N, IL 75 W, S Beloit, N [gas] Fas Fuel/McDonald's/dsl, S Flying J/Denny's/dsl/scales/24hr, Road Ranger/Subway/dsl/E85/scales/24hr, [lodging] Best Western, Tollway Inn, [other] Finnegan's RV Ctr
0mm	Illinois/Wisconsin state line

INTERSTATE 94

BEAUBIEN WOODS

Exit #	Services
77mm	Illinois/Indiana state line. I-94 and I-80 run together for 3 miles. See I-80, Exit 161
74[160]b	I-80/I-294 W
74a	IL 394 S, to Danville
73b a	US 6,159th St, N [gas] Love's/Hardee's/dsl/scales/24hr, Mobil, [food] Applebee's, Buffalo Wild Wings, Continental Rest., Denny's, Outback Steaks, Panda Express, Sonic, Starbucks, Taco Bell, Tilly's, White Castle, [other] BigLots, Cadillac, Goodyear Commercial Tire, Hyundai, JC Penney, Kia, Lincoln, Macy's, Marshall's, Nissan, PetCo, Ross, Sam's Club, Toyota/Scion, USPO, vet, S [gas] BP, Marathon, [food] Checkers, Harold's Chicken, Little Caesar's, McDonald's, Papa John's, Popeyes, Shark's, Subway, [lodging] Holland Inn, [other] AlLDI, Family$, Jewel-Osco, O'Reilly Parts, Stanfa Tire/repair
71b a	Sibley Blvd, N [gas] BP/dsl, Citgo, Mobil/dsl, [food] $Tree, McDonald's, Nick's Gyros, Popeyes, Shark's, Subway, [lodging] Baymont Inn, [other] Family$, Pete's Mkt, S [gas] Circle K/Checkers/dsl, Marathon/dsl, Shell, [food] Baskin-Robbins/Dunkin Donuts, Burger King, KFC, Taco Bell, Wendy's, White Castle, [lodging] Best Motel, [other] $General, Advance Parts, AutoZone, Family$, Food4Less/gas, Menards, Walgreens
70b a	Dolton
69	(from eb), Beaubien Woods, Beaubien Woods Forest Preserve
68b a	130th St
66b	115th St, S [food] McDonald's
66a	111th Ave, S [gas] Citgo/dsl, Shell, [other] $Tree, Firestone/auto, [H], Ross, Walmart
65	103rd Ave, Stony Island Ave
63	I-57 S(exits left from wb)
62	Wentworth Ave(from eb), N [gas] Citgo, [food] Burger King, KFC, S McDonald's
61b	87th St, N [gas] BP, Shell/dsl, [food] Burger King, McDonald's, S Starbucks, Subway, [other] $Tree, AutoZone, Burlington Coats, Food4Less, Home Depot, Jewel-Osco, Marshall's, O'Reilly Parts, Staples, Verizon
61a	83rd St(from eb), N [gas] Shell, [food] Subway, [other] st police
60c	79th St, N [gas] Mobil, Shell, [other] Walgreens, S [gas] Falcon, [food] Church's TX Chicken, Subway
60b	76th St, N [gas] BP, Mobil, Shell, [other] Walgreens, S [food] KFC, Popeyes
60a	75th St(from eb), N [gas] BP, Shell, [other] AlLDI, S [food] KFC, Popeyes
59c	71st St, N [gas] BP, S [food] McDonald's
59a	I-90 E, to Indiana Toll Rd
58b	63rd St(from eb), N [gas] BP, S Mobil
58a	I-94 divides into local and express, 59th St, S [gas] Mobil
57b	Garfield Blvd, N [food] Checker's, [other] Family$, Walgreens, S [gas] Citgo, Mobil, Shell/24hr, [food] Wendy's
57a	51st St
56b	47th St(from eb)
56a	43rd St, S [gas] BP/Subway/dsl, Citgo/dsl
55b	Pershing Rd
55a	35th St, S [other] to New Comiskey Park
54	31st St
53c	I-55, Stevenson Pkwy, N to downtown, Lakeshore Dr
53b	I-55, Stevenson Pkwy, S to St Louis
52c	18th St(from eb), N [other] Whole Foods
52b	Roosevelt Rd, Taylor St(from wb), N [gas] Citgo, [food] Chipotle, [other] Best Buy, Home Depot, Walgreens, Whole Foods Mkt
52a	Taylor St, Roosevelt Rd(from eb), N [gas] Citgo
51h-i	I-290 W, to W Suburbs
51g	E Jackson Blvd, downtown
51f	W Adams St, downtown
51e	Monroe St(from eb), downtown, S [lodging] Crowne Plaza, [other] Walgreens, Whole Foods
51d	Madison St(from eb), downtown, S [lodging] Crowne Plaza, [other] Walgreens, Whole Foods
51c	E Washington Blvd, downtown
51b	W Randolph St, downtown
51a	Lake St(from wb)
50b	E Ohio St, downtown, S [gas] Marathon
50a	Ogden Ave
49b a	Augusta Blvd, Division St, N [other] Acura, Lexus, Mercedes, S [gas] BP, Shell
48b	IL 64, North Ave, N [gas] BP, S [other] Mercedes
48a	Armitage Ave, N [other] Best Buy, Kohl's, Lexus, S [gas] Shell, [other] Jaguar, Land Rover, Volvo
47c b	Damen Ave, N [gas] car/vanwash
47a	Western Ave, Fullerton Ave, N [gas] Mobil, [food] Burger King, Dunkin Donuts, Popeyes, Starbucks, Subway, [other] Costco/gas, Home Depot, Jo-Ann Fabrics, Pepboys, PetSmart, Staples, Target, S [gas] Marathon
46b a	Diversey Ave, California Ave, S [food] IHOP/24hr, Popeyes, [other] Walgreens
45c	Belmont Ave
45b	Kimball Ave, N [gas] Marathon/dsl, [other] CVS Drug, Home Depot, S [gas] Shell, [food] Dunkin Donuts, Subway, [other] AlLDI, Best Buy, Walgreens
45a	Addison St
44b	Pulaski Ave, Irving park Rd, N [gas] Mobil/Subway, Shell/dsl
44a	IL 19, Keeler Ave, Irving Park Rd, N [gas] Mobil/Subway, Shell/dsl, [other] to Wrigley Field
43c	Montrose Ave
43b	I-90 W
43a	Wilson Ave
42	W Foster Ave (from wb), S [gas] Marathon/service, Mobil, [food] Subway
41mm	Chicago River, N Branch
41c	IL 50 S, to Cicero, to I-90 W
41b a	US 14, Peterson Ave, N [other] Whole Foods Mkt
39b a	Touhy Ave, N [gas] BP/dsl, Shell/Circle K, [other] Cassidy Tire, Toyota/Scion, S [gas] BP, Citgo, Mobil, Shell, [food] Bar Louie's, Baskin-Robbins/Dunkin Donuts, Brickhouse Rest., Buffalo Wild Wings, Burger King, Chili's, Chipotle Mexican, ChuckeCheese, Corner Bakery Cafe, Jersey Mike's, Jimmy John's, McDonald's, Noodles&Co, Outback Steaks, Panda Express, Penn Sta Subs, Red Robin, Sander's Rest., Shallot's Bistro, Starbucks, Subway, Tilted Kilt, [lodging] Holiday Inn, [other] Barnes&Noble, Best Buy, Dick's, Fresh Farms Mkt, GNC, Jewel-Osco, Michael's, Nissan, PepBoys, PetSmart, Ross, Tuesday Morning, vet, Walgreens, Walmart
37b a	IL 58, Dempster St, N [gas] Shell, [food] Panda Express, Subway, S [gas] BP/dsl, Shell, [food] Pizza Hut, [other] Midas
35	Old Orchard Rd, N [gas] BP, Shell, [food] Bloomingdale's, Buffalo Wild Wings, CA Pizza Kitchen, CheeseCake Factory, [other] [H], Lord&Taylor, Macy's, Nissan, Nordstrom's, S [food] Ruby Tuesday, [lodging] Extended Stay America, Hampton Inn,

= gas = food = lodging = other = rest stop

INTERSTATE 94 Cont'd

Exit	Services
35	Continued Residence Inn
34c b	E Lake Ave, N BP/dsl, Corner Bakery Cafe, Five Guys, Panda Express, Starbucks, Subway, Fresh Mkt Foods, GNC, Walgreens, S Shell, DQ, Jimmy John's, Starbucks, auto repair
34a	US 41 S, Skokie Rd(from eb)
33b a	Willow Rd, S Shell, Dunkin Donuts, Starbucks, Mariano's Mkt, USPO, Walgreens
31	E Tower Rd, S BMW, Carmax, Infiniti, Land Rover, Mercedes, Toyota/Scion, vet, Volvo
30b a	Dundee Rd(from wb, no EZ return), S Citgo/dsl, Barnaby's Rest., Chipotle, Morton's Steaks, Noodles&Co, Panera Bread, Potbelly, Roti Mediterranean, Ruth's Chris Steaks, Starbucks, Renaissance, Mariano's Mkt
29	US 41, to Waukegan, to Tri-state tollway
28	IL 43, Waukegan Rd(from eb), N BP, Shell, Dunkin Donuts/Baskin Robbins, Mod Pizza, Noodles&Co, Starbucks, Courtyard, Embassy Suites, Red Roof Inn, Hobby Lobby, Home Depot, Jewel-Osco, Just Tires
25	I-294 S, Lake-Cook Rd (from sb), E Embassy Suites, Hyatt, W J Alexander's Rest.
24	Deerfield Rd (from nb), W Mobil, Marriott Suites
21	IL 22, Half Day Rd, E Leaf Cafe, La Quinta, W Homewood Suites
19	IL 60, Town Line Rd, E H, W Hilton Garden, Residence Inn, Costco/gas
18mm	Lake Forest Oasis both lanes, info, Mobil/7-11/dsl, KFC/Taco Bell, McDonald's, Panda Express, Starbucks, Subway
16mm	IL 176, Rockland Rd(no nb re-entry), E Harley-Davidson, to Lamb's Farm
14mm	IL 137, Buckley Rd, E Chicago Med School, to VA H
11mm	IL 120 E, Belvidere Rd(no nb re-entry), E H
10mm	IL 21, Milwaukee Ave(from eb, no eb re-entry), E H, Six Flags
8mm	IL 132, Grand Ave, E Speedway/dsl, Baskin-Robbins/Dunkin Donuts, Burger King, ChuckeCheese, Cracker Barrel, Cravings Red Hots, Culver's, Golden Corral, Ichibahn, IHOP, Jimmy John's, Joe's Crabshack, KFC/LJ Silver, Mama K's Zpizza, McDonald's, Oberweiss, Old Chicago Red Hots, Olive Garden, Outback Steaks, Rosati's Pizza, Starbucks, Subway, Baymont Inn, Country Inn&Suites, Extended Stay America, Hampton Inn, Key Lime Cove Resort, La Quinta, Super 8, Six Flags Park, W Shell/Circle K, Bakers Square, Boston Mkt, Buffalo Wild Wings, Chili's, Chipotle Mexican, Denny's, Five Guys, Giordano's Pizza, Jersey Mike's Subs, Jimano's Pizza, LoneStar Steaks, McDonald's, Noodles&Co, Panda Express, Panera Bread, Penn Sta Subs, Pizza Hut, Portillo's, Potbelly's, Red Lobster, Red Robin, Ruby Tuesday, Starbucks, Steak'n Shake, Taco Bell, TGIFriday's, Uno Grill, Wendy's, White Castle, Comfort Inn, Fairfield Inn, Holiday Inn, $Tree, AT&T, AutoZone, Bass Pro Shops, Best Buy, Buick/GMC, Chrysler/Dodge/Jeep, Goodyear, Gurnee Mills Outlet Mall/famous brands, Home Depot, Honda, Hyundai, Jewel-Osco, Kohl's, Macy's, Mariano's Mkt, Marshall's, Menards, Michael's, Old Navy, PetSmart, Ross, Sam's Club, Sears Grand/auto, Target, TJ Maxx, Tuesday Morning, Verizon, VW, Walgreens, Walmart
5mm	Waukegan toll plaza
2	IL 173(from nb, no return), Rosecrans Ave, E to IL Beach SP
1b	US 41 S, to Waukegan(from sb)
1a	Russell Rd, E I-94 RV Ctr, W Citgo/dsl/scales, Love's/dsl/scales/24hr/@, TA/Country Pride/dsl/scales/24hr/@,

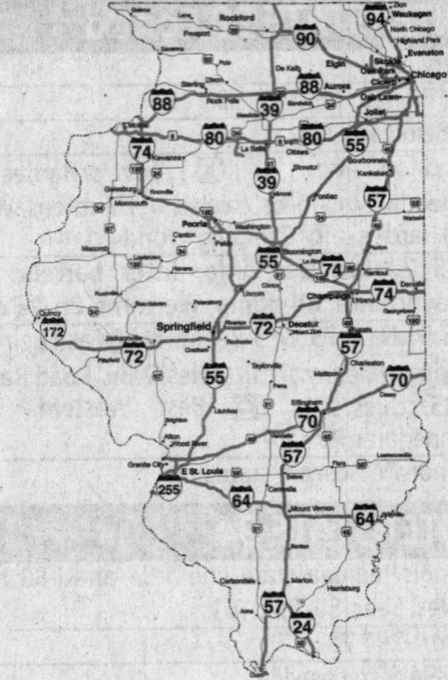

Exit	Services
1a	Continued Peterbilt
0mm	Illinois/Wisconsin state line

CENTREVILLE

INTERSTATE 255 (St Louis)

Exit	Services
30.5mm	I-255 begins/ends on I-270, exit 7.
30	I-270, W to Kansas City, E to Indianapolis
29	IL 162, to Glen Carbon, to Pontoon Beach, Granite City
26	Horseshoe Lake Rd, E st police
25b a	I-55/I-70, W to St Louis, E to Chicago, Indianapolis
24	Collinsville Rd, E BP, Jack-in-the-Box, Shop'n Save, W Fairmount Racetrack
20	I-64, US 50, W to St Louis, E to Louisville, services 1 mi E off I-64, exit 9.
19	State St, E St Louis, E Western Inn, W Holten SP
17b a	IL 15, E St Louis, to Belleville, Centreville, E Flying J/Denny's/dsl/scales/24hr, W Phillips 66, auto repair
15	Mousette Lane, E Love's/Chester's/Godfather's/Subway/dsl/scales/24hr/@, H, W Peterbilt
13	IL 157, to Cahokia, E Phillips 66, W BP, MotoMart, Capt D's, China Express, Classic K Burgers, Domino's, Hardee's, KFC, Little Caesar's, McDonald's, Pizza Hut, Rally's, Subway, Taco Bell, White Castle, Comfort Inn, $General, $Tree, Advance Parts, AllDI, AutoZone, Dobb's Tires, Family$, Schnuck's, Shop'n Save Foods, Walgreens, Walmart
10	IL 3 N, to Cahokia, E St Louis, W Fuelmart/Subway/dsl
9	to Dupo, W Hucks
6	IL 3 S, to Columbia (exits left from sb), E Phillips 66, Shell/dsl/24hr, Hampton Inn(2mi), Chevrolet
4mm	Missouri/Illinois state line, Mississippi River
3	Koch Rd, no facilities
2	MO 231, Telegraph Rd, N Conoco, Shell/Circle K, Great Wall, Little Caesar's, McDonald's, Pizza Hut/Taco Bell, Steak'n Shake, Waffle House, Advance Parts, AT&T, Jefferson Barracks Nat Cem, Petco, SaveALot, Walmart/Subway, S Phillips 66/dsl, QT, Shell/Circle K/dsl, China Wok, DQ, Dunkin Donuts, Verizon
1d c	US 50, US 61, US 67, Lindbergh Blvd, Lemay Ferry Rd, accesses same as I-55 exit 197 E, N Phillips 66, Applebee's, Arby's, Buffalo Wild Wings, ChuckeCheese, CiCi's Pizza, Dillard's, Hometown Buffet, HoneyBaked Ham, Hooters, IHOP, Imo's Pizza, Krispy Kreme, McAlister's Deli, Noodles&Co, Penn Sta Subs, Qdoba Mexican, Starbucks, Steak'n Shake, Subway, Taco Bell, Tucker's Place, Wendy's, Holiday Inn, AT&T, Best Buy, Chrysler/Dodge/Jeep, Costco/gas, CVS Drug, Dick's, Ford/Lincoln, Home Depot,

IL

INTERSTATE 255 (St Louis) Cont'd

1d c Continued
JC Penney, Macy's, mall, Marshall's, NTB, Verizon, vet, **S** Phillips 66, Jack-in-the-Box, Jimmy John's, McDonald's, Rich & Charlie's Italian, White Castle, $General, $Tree, BigLots, Firestone, Old Navy, PetSmart, Sam's Club/gas, Walgreens

1b a I-55 S to Memphis, N to St Louis. I-255 begins/ends on I-55, exit 196.

INTERSTATE 294 (Chicago)

5mm I-80 W, access to I-57. I-294 & I-80 merge for 5 mi. See I-80, exits 155-160.

5.5mm 167th St, toll booth, phones

6mm US 6, 159th St, **E** Citgo, Exxon/dsl, Marathon, Mobil/dsl, Shell/dsl, $Tree, AutoZone, Family$, **W** BP/dsl, Baskin-Robbins/Dunkin', Burger King, McDonald's, Popeyes, Subway, Taco Bell, White Castle, Chicago Inn&Suites, $Tree, AutoZone, U-Haul, Walgreens

11mm Cal Sag Channel

12mm IL 50, Cicero Ave, **E** BP, Shell/dsl, Dunkin', Subway, White Castle, Home Depot, O'Reilly Parts, **W** BP, Shell/dsl, Applebee's, Boston Mkt, Chipotle, Culver's, IHOP, Lone Star Steaks, Panda Express, Pizza Hut, Popeyes, Portillo's Dogs, Potbelly, Starbucks, Subway, Baymont Inn, Days Inn, DoubleTree, Holiday Inn Express, AT&T, Best Buy, GNC, Jo-Ann, Kohl's, NTB, PepBoys, PetSmart, Ross, Target, TJ Maxx, Ultra Foods, Walgreens, Walmart/Subway

18mm US 12/20, 95th St, **E** Marathon, Buffalo Wild Wings, Chick-fil-A, Starbucks, TX Corral, CarMax, Discount Tire, H, Mazda, **W** 7-11, BP, Shell, Speedway/dsl, Arby's, Baskin-Robbins, Burger King, Denny's, Dunkin', Jimmy John's, Les Bros Rest., McDonald's, Papa John's, Prime Time Rest., Subway, Taco Bell, The Pit Ribhouse, Wendy's, Motel 6, $Tree, AutoZone, Jewel-Osco, Walgreens

20mm toll booth, phones

22mm 75th St, Willow Springs Rd

23mm I-55, Wolf Rd, to Hawthorne Park

25mm Hinsdale Oasis both lanes, Mobil/7-11/dsl, KFC/Taco Bell, McDonald's, McDonald's, Panda Express, Sbarro, Subway

28mm US 34, Ogden Ave, **E** zoo, **W** BP, Shell/deli, Dunkin', McDonald's, Starbucks, Ferrari/Maserati, Firestone/auto, H, LandRover, Whole Foods Mkt

28.5mm Cermak Rd(from sb, no return)

29mm I-88 tollway

30mm toll booth,

31mm IL 38, Roosevelt Rd(no EZ nb return), **E** Shell/dsl, Hillside Manor Motel, vet

32mm I-290 W, to Rockford(from nb)

34mm I-290(from sb), to Rockford

38mm O'Hare Oasis both lanes, Mobil/7-11/dsl, KFC, McDonald's, Panda Express, Sbarro, Starbucks, Subway, Taco Bell, TCBY

39mm IL 19 W(from sb), Irving Park Rd, **E** Citgo, Marathon/dsl, Shell/dsl, Dunkin', McDonald's, Starbucks, Subway, Wendy's, Comfort Suites, 7-11, AlLDI, Walgreens, **W** BP/Subway/desk, Mirage Rest., Candlewood Suites, Hampton Inn, Sheraton

40mm I-190 W, **E** Mobil, Basil's Kitchen, McDonald's, Starbucks, Courtyard, Doubletree, Embassy Suites, Hampton Inn, Hilton, Hilton Garden, Holiday Inn, Hyatt, Hyatt Regency, Marriott, Rosemont Suites, Westin

41mm toll booth,

42mm Touhy Ave, **W** Mobil/service, Tiffany's Rest., Comfort Inn, Radisson

43mm Des Plaines River

44mm Dempster St(from nb, no return), **E** Wendy's, CVS Drug, H, **W** Dunkin', Subway

46mm IL 58, Golf Rd, **E** Mobil/Dunkin'/dsl, Shell/Subway/dsl, Omega Rest., Wyndham, Meijer, CVS Drug, Golf Mill Mall, Meineke, Target, **W** H

49mm Willow Rd, **W** BP/Subway/dsl, Chipotle, Jimmy John's, McDonald's, Pie Five Pizza, Starbucks, TGIFriday's, Best Western, Country Inn Suites, Courtyard, Motel 6, CVS Drug, Mariano's Mkt

53mm Lake Cook Rd(no nb re-entry), **E** Embassy Suites, Hyatt, **W** J Alexander's

0 I-294 begins/ends on I-94.

INTERSTATE 355 (Illinois)

31mm I-355 begins/end on I-290

30 US 20, W Lake St, **E** Marathon, Mobil/dsl, Baskin-Robbins/Dunkin Donuts, Burger King, Chipotle, Culver's, Famous Dave's BBQ, Firehouse Subs, IHOP, Jimmy John's, La Hacienda Mexican, Panda Express, Panera Bread, Ristorante de Marco's, Starbucks, Hampton Inn, Midas, Sam's Club/gas, Verizon, Walmart/Subway, **W** Shell, Dave&Buster's, Venuti's Rest.

29 Army Trail Rd, **E** Mobil/dsl, Shell/dsl, Serino's Deli, **W** BP/dsl, Mobil/dsl, Hilton Garden

27 IL 64, E North Ave, **E** BP/Subway/dsl, Burger King, Comfort Suites, Fairfield Inn, McDonald's, Shell/Circle K, Thornton's/dsl, Jimmy John's, **W** Speedway/dsl, Ramada, Art's RV Ctr, Suburban Tire/auto

24 Roosevelt, **E** Mobil, Dunkin Donuts, Subway, Crowne Plaza, Cadillac, Mariano's Mkt, Toyota/Scion, **W** Jimmy John's, NAPA, Pete's Mkt

22 IL 56, Butterfield Rd, **E** Arby's, Brick House Rest., Burger King, Chama Gaucha Brazilian, Chipotle Mexican, Fuddrucker's, Hooters, Melting Pot, Olive Garden, Panera Bread, Portillo's, Red Lobster, Ruby Tuesday, Starbucks, Subway, Zoup!, Comfort Inn, Extended Stay America, Holiday Inn Express, Marriott, Red Roof Inn, $Tree, Best Buy, Kohl's, Michael's, PetSmart, Ross, Verizon, **W** Carlucci Italian, DoubleTree Suites, 7-11, Home Depot

20mm I-88 E/I-355 run together

19 US 34, Ogden Ave, **E** Shell, Culver's, Jimmy John's, McDonald's, InTown Suites, AT&T, Buick/GMC, Chrysler/Dodge/Jeep, Ford, **W** Baskin-Robbins/Dunkin Donuts, Extended Stay America, Chevrolet, Speedway/dsl, vet

18 Maple Ave, **W** BP, Mobil, Shell/Circle K, KFC/Taco Bell, McDonald's, Jewel Osco, Walgreens

16 63rd St, Hobson Rd, **E** Mobil/dsl, Thornton's/McDonald's/dsl, Steven's Rest, Subway, AutoZone, Familia Fresh Mkt, GNC, Target, Walgreens

15 W 75th St, **E** Mobil, Arby's, Bakers Square Rest, Hobby Lobby, Home Depot, Sam's Club/gas, **W** Marathon, Dunkin', El Burro Loco, McDonald's, Pizza Italiano, Jewel-Osco

14 87th St, Baughton Rd, **E** BP, Shell, Al's Pizza, Dunkin', McDonald's, Oberweiss, Subway, Wendy's, Costco/gas, CVS Drug, **W** Mobil, Bar Louie, Buffalo Wild Wings, Famous Dave's BBQ, Five Guys, IHOP, Jimmy John's, Longhorn Steaks, Panda Express, Panera Bread, Potbelly, Starbucks, Ted's MT Grill, ALoft, AT&T, Barnes&Noble, Bass Pro Shops, Discount Tire, IKEA, Macy's, Meijer/gas, Verizon, Walgreens

12 I-55

8 127th St, **E** Burger King, Jimmy John's, KFC, McDonald's, Starbucks, Subway, Taco Bell, ALDI, AT&T, Firestone/auto, Jewel-Osco, Jiffy Lube, Pepper's Autocare, USPO, Verizon,

BAUGHTON RD

INTERSTATE 355 (Illinois) Cont'd

8	Continued Walgreens
6	IL 171, Archer Ave, 143rd St, **E** Kohl's, Target, vet
4	159th Ave, IL 7, Orland Park, Homer Glen, **E** Citgo/dsl, **W** URGENT CARE
3mm	toll booth both directions
1	US 6, **E** Rte 6 Food'n Fuel/Dunkin Donuts/dsl, **W**
0mm	I-80 E, W, I-355 begins/ends on I-80 exit 140

INTERSTATE 474 (Peoria)

BARTONVILLE

15	I-74, E to Bloomington, W to Peoria
9	IL 29, E Peoria, to Pekin, **N** Shell/Arby's/dsl, Thornton's, DQ, Driftwood Pizza, Taco John's, $General, Riverboat Casino(6mi), **S** BP/Subway/dsl, Casey's, Denny's, Domino's, Lian Wang, McDonald's, Rosati's Pizza, Chrysler/Dodge/Jeep, Toyota/Scion
8mm	Illinois River
6b a	US 24, Adams St, Bartonville, **S** BP/dsl, Mobil/dsl, Hardee's, KFC, McDonald's, Tyroni's Café
5	Airport Rd, **S** Mobil/e85/dsl,
3a	to IL 116, Farmington, **S** Wildlife Prairie Park
0b a	I-74, W to Moline, E to Peoria. I-474 begins/ends on I-74, exit 87.

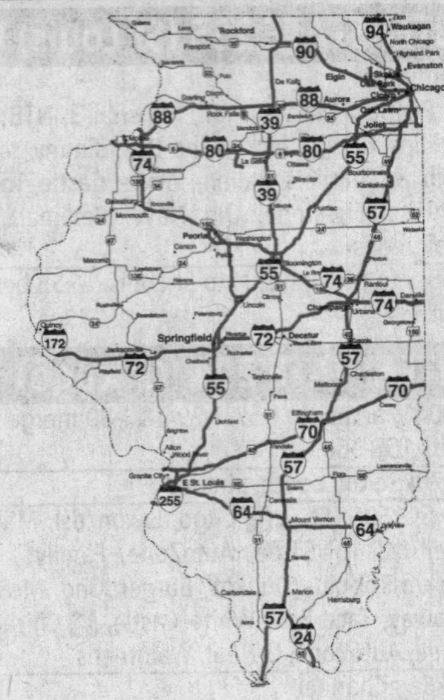

NOTES

INDIANA

INTERSTATE 64

Exit #	Services
124mm	Indiana/Kentucky state line, Ohio River
123	IN 62 E, New Albany, N [gas] Marathon/dsl, Shell/Circle K, [food] DQ, [other] Family$, Firestone/auto, [H], Save-A-Lot, S [gas] Shell/Circle K, Valero, [food] Daisy's Cafeteria, Subway, Waffle House, [lodging] Best Western, Holiday Inn Express
121	I-265 E, to I-65(exits left from eb), N access to [H]
119	US 150 W, to Greenville, N [gas] Marathon, [food] Bean St Cafe, Bearno's Buffet, Beef O'Brady's, Chillburger, China Cafe, Domino's, DQ, El Nopal, McDonald's, Papa John's, Sam's Family Rest., Subway, Taco Bell, Tumbleweed SW Grill, [other] AutoZone, JayC Foods, URGENT CARE, Walgreens
118	IN 62, IN 64W, to Georgetown, N [gas] Marathon/dsl/24hr, Shell/Circle K, [food] Korner Kitchen, McDonald's, [lodging] Red Roof Inn, [other] CashSaver Foods, Mr. Hardware, S [gas] Marathon/dsl
115mm	**full [handicap] facilities, litter barrels, [phone], [picnic], vending, Welcome Ctr wb**
113	to Lanesville
105	IN 135, to Corydon, N [gas] Marathon/dsl, Shell, [food] Big Boy, [lodging] Comfort Inn, S [gas] 5 Star, BP/dsl, [food] Alberto's Italian, Arby's, Beef O'Brady's, Burger King, Cracker Barrel, Culver's, Domino's, DQ, El Nopal Mexican, Hong Kong Buffet, Jimmy John's, KFC, Lee's Chicken, LJ Silver, McDonald's, O'Charley's, Papa John's, Papa Murphy's, Pizza Hut, Ryan's, Subway, Taco Bell, Waffle House, Wendy's, White Castle, [lodging] Baymont Inn, Hampton Inn, Holiday Inn Express, Super 8, [other] $Tree, Advance Parts, AT&T, AutoZone, Big O Tire, Buick/Chevrolet, Chrysler/Dodge/Jeep, CVS Drug, Family$, Ford, [H], Verizon, Walgreens, Walmart/Subway
100mm	Blue River
97mm	parking area both lanes
92	IN 66, Carefree, N [other] Marengo Caves, S [gas] Marathon/dsl/rest./24hr, Pilot/Subway/dsl/scales/24hr, [food] Big Dadd's Rest., Country Style Rest., [lodging] Red Carpet Inn, [other] Carefree Truckwash, Harrison Crawford SF, repair, to Wyandotte Caves
88mm	Hoosier Nat Forest eastern boundary
86	IN 37, to Sulphur, N to Patoka Lake, S food, gas, scenic route
79	IN 37, to Tell City, St Croix, S [gas] Marathon/Subshop/pizza/dsl, [other] to Hoosier NF, to OH River Br
76mm	Anderson River
72	IN 145, to Birdseye, N [other] to Patoka Lake, S gas, St Meinrad Coll, winery(2mi)
63	IN 162, to Ferdinand, N [gas] Sunoco/dsl, [food] China Garden, McDonald's, Subway, Taco Bell, Wendy's, [lodging] Comfort Inn, Red Roof Inn, [other] CVS Drug, Ferdinand SF, S Lake Rudolph RV Camping(8mi)
58mm	**full [handicap] facilities, info, litter barrels, [phone], [picnic], [rest stop] both lanes, vending**
57	US 231, to Dale, Huntingburg, N [other] [H], S [gas] Chuckles/dsl, [food] Denny's, Wendy's, [lodging] Baymont Inn, Motel 6, [other] Lincoln Boyhood Home, Lincoln SP
54	IN 161, to Holland,Tennyson
39	IN 61, Lynnville, N [gas] Marathon, [food] Monterrey Mexican, [other] USPO
32mm	N [other] Wabash & Erie Canal
29b a	I-69 N, IN 57 N&S, to Evansville
25b a	US 41, to Evansville, N [gas] Flying J/Denny's/dsl/scales/24hr, Love's/Wendy's/dsl/24hr, Pilot/Subway/Taco Bell/dsl/24hr, [lodging] Baymont Inn, [other] Blue Beacon, truck repair/lube, S [gas] Marathon/dsl, [food] Arby's, Denny's, McDonald's, Stoll's Amish Rest., [lodging] Holiday Inn Express, Quality Inn, Red Roof Inn,
25b a	Continued Super 8, [other] st police, to U S IN
18	IN 65, to Cynthiana, S [gas] Motomart/dsl/24hr
12	IN 165, Poseyville, S [gas] CountryMark/Subway/dsl, [food] Red Wagon Rest., [other] NAPA, New Harmonie Hist Area/SP
7mm	**Black River Welcome Ctr eb, full [handicap] facilities, [phone], [picnic], litter barrels, petwalk, full [handicap] facilities, litter barrels, petwalk, [phone], [picnic]**
5mm	Black River
4	IN 69 S, New Harmony, Griffin, N USPO, S Harmony St Park
2mm	Big Bayou River
0mm	Indiana/Illinois state line, Wabash River

MERRILLVILLE

INTERSTATE 65

Exit #	Services
262	I-90, W to Chicago, E to Ohio, I-65 begins/ends on US 12, US 20.
261	15th Ave, to Gary, E [other] Mack/Volvo Trucks, W [gas] Citgo
259b a	I-94/80, US 6W
258	US 6, Ridge Rd, E [gas] Luke/dsl, Marathon/dsl, [food] Diner's Choice Rest., W [gas] Citgo, Save Gas
255	61st Ave, Merrillville, E [gas] Family Express/dsl, Speedway/dsl, [food] Arby's, Cracker Barrel, McDonald's, Pizza Hut/Taco Bell, Wendy's, [lodging] Comfort Inn, Days Inn, [other] Chevrolet, [H], I-65 Repair, Menards, W [gas] Clark, [food] Burger King, Subway, [other] AutoZone, Walgreens

IN

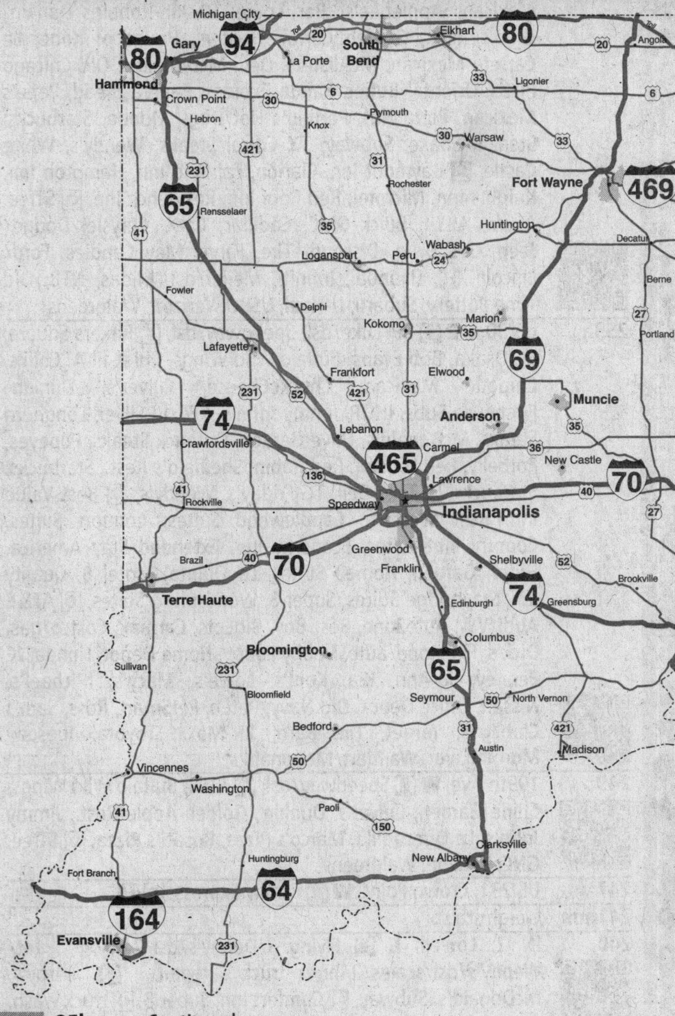

gas = food = lodging = other = rest stop

IN

INTERSTATE 65 Cont'd

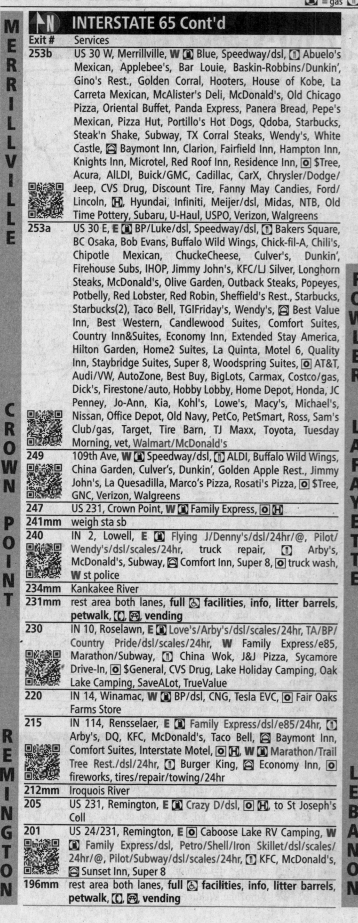

MERRILLVILLE · CROWN POINT · REMINGTON

Exit #	Services
253b	US 30 W, Merrillville, W Blue, Speedway/dsl, Abuelo's Mexican, Applebee's, Bar Louie, Baskin-Robbins/Dunkin', Gino's Rest., Golden Corral, Hooters, House of Kobe, La Carreta Mexican, McAlister's Deli, McDonald's, Old Chicago Pizza, Oriental Buffet, Panda Express, Panera Bread, Pepe's Mexican, Pizza Hut, Portillo's Hot Dogs, Qdoba, Starbucks, Steak'n Shake, Subway, TX Corral Steaks, Wendy's, White Castle, Baymont Inn, Clarion, Fairfield Inn, Hampton Inn, Knights Inn, Microtel, Red Roof Inn, Residence Inn, $Tree, Acura, AlLDI, Buick/GMC, Cadillac, CarX, Chrysler/Dodge/Jeep, CVS Drug, Discount Tire, Fanny May Candies, Ford/Lincoln, H, Hyundai, Infiniti, Meijer/dsl, Midas, NTB, Old Time Pottery, Subaru, U-Haul, USPO, Verizon, Walgreens
253a	US 30 E, E BP/Luke/dsl, Speedway/dsl, Bakers Square, BC Osaka, Bob Evans, Buffalo Wild Wings, Chick-fil-A, Chili's, Chipotle Mexican, ChuckeCheese, Culver's, Dunkin', Firehouse Subs, IHOP, Jimmy John's, KFC/LJ Silver, Longhorn Steaks, McDonald's, Olive Garden, Outback Steaks, Popeyes, Potbelly, Red Lobster, Red Robin, Sheffield's Rest., Starbucks, Starbucks(2), Taco Bell, TGIFriday's, Wendy's, Best Value Inn, Best Western, Candlewood Suites, Comfort Suites, Country Inn&Suites, Economy Inn, Extended Stay America, Hilton Garden, Home2 Suites, La Quinta, Motel 6, Quality Inn, Staybridge Suites, Super 8, Woodspring Suites, AT&T, Audi/VW, AutoZone, Best Buy, BigLots, Carmax, Costco/gas, Dick's, Firestone/auto, Hobby Lobby, Home Depot, Honda, JC Penney, Jo-Ann, Kia, Kohl's, Lowe's, Macy's, Michael's, Nissan, Office Depot, Old Navy, PetCo, PetSmart, Ross, Sam's Club/gas, Target, Tire Barn, TJ Maxx, Toyota, Tuesday Morning, vet, Walmart/McDonald's
249	109th Ave, W Speedway/dsl, ALDI, Buffalo Wild Wings, China Garden, Culver's, Dunkin', Golden Apple Rest., Jimmy John's, La Quesadilla, Marco's Pizza, Rosati's Pizza, $Tree, GNC, Verizon, Walgreens
247	US 231, Crown Point, W Family Express, H
241mm	weigh sta sb
240	IN 2, Lowell, E Flying J/Denny's/dsl/24hr/@, Pilot/Wendy's/dsl/scales/24hr, truck repair, Arby's, McDonald's, Subway, Comfort Inn, Super 8, truck wash, W st police
234mm	Kankakee River
231mm	rest area both lanes, **full facilities, info, litter barrels, petwalk, , vending**
230	IN 10, Roselawn, E Love's/Arby's/dsl/scales/24hr, TA/BP/Country Pride/dsl/scales/24hr, W Family Express/e85, Marathon/Subway, China Wok, J&J Pizza, Sycamore Drive-In, $General, CVS Drug, Lake Holiday Camping, Oak Lake Camping, SaveALot, TrueValue
220	IN 14, Winamac, W BP/dsl, CNG, Tesla EVC, Fair Oaks Farms Store
215	IN 114, Rensselaer, E Family Express/dsl/e85/24hr, Arby's, DQ, KFC, McDonald's, Taco Bell, Baymont Inn, Comfort Suites, Interstate Motel, H, W Marathon/Trail Tree Rest./dsl/24hr, Burger King, Economy Inn, fireworks, tires/repair/towing/24hr
212mm	Iroquois River
205	US 231, Remington, E Crazy D/dsl, H, to St Joseph's Coll
201	US 24/231, Remington, E Caboose Lake RV Camping, W Family Express/dsl, Petro/Shell/Iron Skillet/dsl/scales/24hr/@, Pilot/Subway/dsl/scales/24hr, KFC, McDonald's, Sunset Inn, Super 8
196mm	rest area both lanes, **full facilities, info, litter barrels, petwalk, , vending**

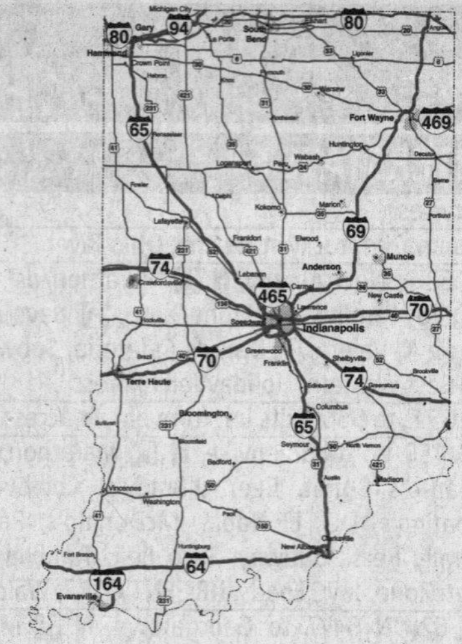

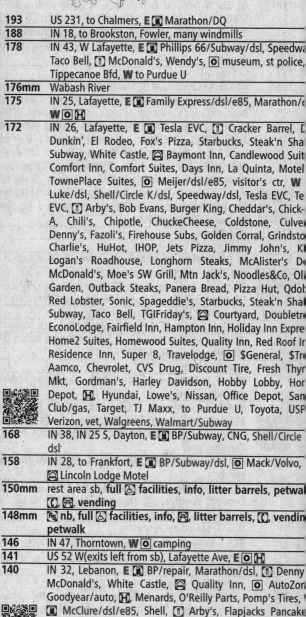

FOWLER · LAFAYETTE · LEBANON

Exit #	Services
193	US 231, to Chalmers, E Marathon/DQ
188	IN 18, to Brookston, Fowler, many windmills
178	IN 43, W Lafayette, E Phillips 66/Subway/dsl, Speedwa Taco Bell, McDonald's, Wendy's, museum, st police, Tippecanoe Bfd, W to Purdue U
176mm	Wabash River
175	IN 25, Lafayette, E Family Express/dsl/e85, Marathon/ W H
172	IN 26, Lafayette, E Tesla EVC, Cracker Barrel, D Dunkin', El Rodeo, Fox's Pizza, Starbucks, Steak'n Sha Subway, White Castle, Baymont Inn, Candlewood Suit Comfort Inn, Comfort Suites, Days Inn, La Quinta, Motel TownePlace Suites, Meijer/dsl/e85, visitor's ctr, W Luke/dsl, Shell/Circle K/dsl, Speedway/dsl, Tesla EVC, Te EVC, Arby's, Bob Evans, Burger King, Cheddar's, Chick-A, Chili's, Chipotle, ChuckeCheese, Coldstone, Culve Denny's, Fazoli's, Firehouse Subs, Golden Corral, Grindsto Charlie's, HuHot, IHOP, Jets Pizza, Jimmy John's, K Logan's Roadhouse, Longhorn Steaks, McAlister's De McDonald's, Moe's SW Grill, Mtn Jack's, Noodles&Co, Ol Garden, Outback Steaks, Panera Bread, Pizza Hut, Qdob Red Lobster, Sonic, Spageddie's, Starbucks, Steak'n Sha Subway, Taco Bell, TGIFriday's, Courtyard, Doubletr EconoLodge, Fairfield Inn, Hampton Inn, Holiday Inn Expre Home2 Suites, Homewood Suites, Quality Inn, Red Roof Ir Residence Inn, Super 8, Travelodge, $General, $Tr Aamco, Chevrolet, CVS Drug, Discount Tire, Fresh Thyr Mkt, Gordman's, Harley Davidson, Hobby Lobby, Hor Depot, H, Hyundai, Lowe's, Nissan, Office Depot, Sam Club/gas, Target, TJ Maxx, to Purdue U, Toyota, USP Verizon, vet, Walgreens, Walmart/Subway
168	IN 38, IN 25 S, Dayton, E BP/Subway, CNG, Shell/Circle dsl
158	IN 28, to Frankfort, E BP/Subway/dsl, Mack/Volvo, Lincoln Lodge Motel
150mm	rest area sb, **full facilities, info, litter barrels, petwal , vending**
148mm	**nb, full facilities, info, , litter barrels, , vendin petwalk**
146	IN 47, Thorntown, W camping
141	US 52 W(exits left from sb), Lafayette Ave, E H
140	IN 32, Lebanon, E BP/repair, Marathon/dsl, Denny McDonald's, White Castle, Quality Inn, AutoZor Goodyear/auto, H, Menards, O'Reilly Parts, Pomp's Tires, McClure/dsl/e85, Shell, Arby's, Flapjacks Pancake KFC, Steak'n Shake, Subway, Taco Bell, Best Value In EconoLodge, Holiday Inn Express, Motel 6, truckwash
139	IN 39, Lebanon, E Speedway/dsl, Penn Sta Subs

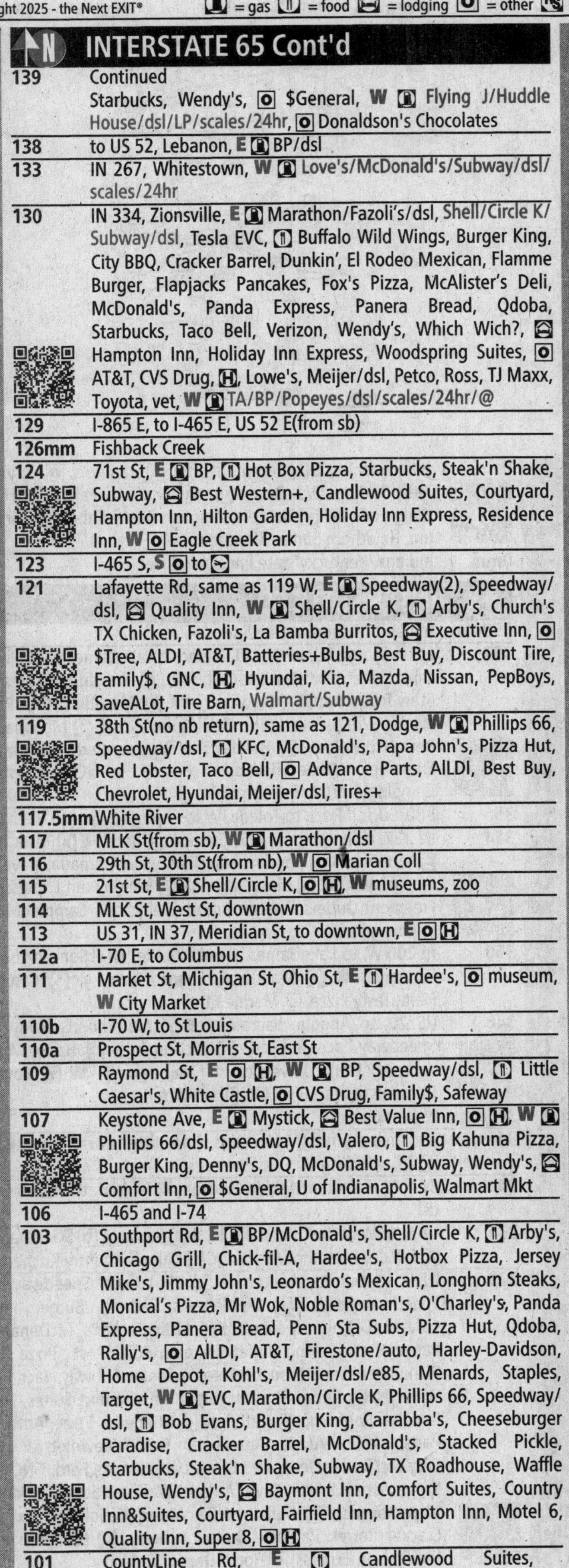

INTERSTATE 65 Cont'd

Exit	Services
139	Continued Starbucks, Wendy's, $General, W Flying J/Huddle House/dsl/LP/scales/24hr, Donaldson's Chocolates
138	to US 52, Lebanon, E BP/dsl
133	IN 267, Whitestown, W Love's/McDonald's/Subway/dsl/scales/24hr
130	IN 334, Zionsville, E Marathon/Fazoli's/dsl, Shell/Circle K/Subway/dsl, Tesla EVC, Buffalo Wild Wings, Burger King, City BBQ, Cracker Barrel, Dunkin', El Rodeo Mexican, Flamme Burger, Flapjacks Pancakes, Fox's Pizza, McAlister's Deli, McDonald's, Panda Express, Panera Bread, Qdoba, Starbucks, Taco Bell, Verizon, Wendy's, Which Wich?, Hampton Inn, Holiday Inn Express, Woodspring Suites, AT&T, CVS Drug, H, Lowe's, Meijer/dsl, Petco, Ross, TJ Maxx, Toyota, vet, W TA/BP/Popeyes/dsl/scales/24hr/@
129	I-865 E, to I-465 E, US 52 E(from sb)
126mm	Fishback Creek
124	71st St, E BP, Hot Box Pizza, Starbucks, Steak'n Shake, Subway, Best Western+, Candlewood Suites, Courtyard, Hampton Inn, Hilton Garden, Holiday Inn Express, Residence Inn, W Eagle Creek Park
123	I-465 S, S to
121	Lafayette Rd, same as 119 W, E Speedway(2), Speedway/dsl, Quality Inn, W Shell/Circle K, Arby's, Church's TX Chicken, Fazoli's, La Bamba Burritos, Executive Inn, $Tree, ALDI, AT&T, Batteries+Bulbs, Best Buy, Discount Tire, Family$, GNC, H, Hyundai, Kia, Mazda, Nissan, PepBoys, SaveALot, Tire Barn, Walmart/Subway
119	38th St(no nb return), same as 121, Dodge, W Phillips 66, Speedway/dsl, KFC, McDonald's, Papa John's, Pizza Hut, Red Lobster, Taco Bell, Advance Parts, AlLDI, Best Buy, Chevrolet, Hyundai, Meijer/dsl, Tires+
117.5mm	White River
117	MLK St(from sb), W Marathon/dsl
116	29th St, 30th St(from nb), W Marian Coll
115	21st St, E Shell/Circle K, H, W museums, zoo
114	MLK St, West St, downtown
113	US 31, IN 37, Meridian St, to downtown, E H
112a	I-70 E, to Columbus
111	Market St, Michigan St, Ohio St, E Hardee's, museum, W City Market
110b	I-70 W, to St Louis
110a	Prospect St, Morris St, East St
109	Raymond St, E H, W BP, Speedway/dsl, Little Caesar's, White Castle, CVS Drug, Family$, Safeway
107	Keystone Ave, E Mystick, Best Value Inn, H, W Phillips 66/dsl, Speedway/dsl, Valero, Big Kahuna Pizza, Burger King, Denny's, DQ, McDonald's, Subway, Wendy's, Comfort Inn, $General, U of Indianapolis, Walmart Mkt
106	I-465 and I-74
103	Southport Rd, E BP/McDonald's, Shell/Circle K, Arby's, Chicago Grill, Chick-fil-A, Hardee's, Hotbox Pizza, Jersey Mike's, Jimmy John's, Leonardo's Mexican, Longhorn Steaks, Monical's Pizza, Mr Wok, Noble Roman's, O'Charley's, Panda Express, Panera Bread, Penn Sta Subs, Pizza Hut, Qdoba, Rally's, AlLDI, AT&T, Firestone/auto, Harley-Davidson, Home Depot, Kohl's, Meijer/dsl/e85, Menards, Staples, Target, W EVC, Marathon/Circle K, Phillips 66, Speedway/dsl, Bob Evans, Burger King, Carrabba's, Cheeseburger Paradise, Cracker Barrel, McDonald's, Stacked Pickle, Starbucks, Steak'n Shake, Subway, TX Roadhouse, Waffle House, Wendy's, Baymont Inn, Comfort Suites, Country Inn&Suites, Courtyard, Fairfield Inn, Hampton Inn, Motel 6, Quality Inn, Super 8, H
101	CountyLine Rd, E Candlewood Suites,

EDINBURGH

COLUMBUS

SEYMOUR

Exit	Services
101	Continued Murphy USA/dsl, Shell/Circle K/dsl, Buffalo Wild Wings, Cheddar's, Culver's, El Meson Mexican, Freddy's, Leon Mexican, Lindo Mexico, McAlister's Deli, Newk's Eatery, Popeyes, Primanti Bros, Sonic, Taco Bell, Tokyo Buffet, Zaxby's, Hilton Garden, Holiday Inn Express, Home2 Suites, Residence Inn, Woodspring Suites, Costco/dsl, H, Kroger/dsl, Verizon, Walmart/Subway
99	Greenwood, E Road Ranger/Pilot/Subway/dsl/scales/24hr, W Marathon, Shell/Circle K, Arby's, China Wok, Denny's, Main St Grille, McDonald's, Papa John's, Puerto Vallarta, Starbucks, Subway, Taco Bell, Waffle House, White Castle, InTown Suites, La Quinta, Red Carpet Inn, Red Roof Inn, Camping World RV Ctr, H, Sam's Club, vet
97	Worthsville Rd, W Circle K/dsl
95	Whiteland, E Flying J/Denny's/scales/dsl/LP/RV dump/24hr, Blue Beacon, SpeedCo, tires, W Love's/Arby's/dsl/scales/24hr, Pilot/McDonald's/dsl/scales/24hr/@
90	IN 44, Franklin, W Marathon/Subway/dsl, Shell/Circle K, Burger King, McDonald's/RV Parking, Waffle House, Baymont Inn, EconoLodge, Motel 6, Quality Inn, golf, H
85mm	Sugar Creek
82mm	Big Blue River
80	IN 252, to Flat Rock, Edinburgh, W Marathon/dsl, Shell/dsl
76b a	US 31, Taylorsville, E Shell/Circle K/dsl, Speedway/dsl, A&W/KFC, Burger King, El Toreo Mexican, Waffle House, Red Roof Inn, $ General, H, Toyota, W EVC, GetGo/dsl, Marathon, Thornton's/café/dsl, Applebee's, Arby's, Cracker Barrel, Hardee's, Max&Erma's, McDonald's, MT Mikes, Ruby Tuesday, Snappy Tomato Pizza, Subway, Taco Bell, Best Western, Comfort Inn, Hampton Inn, Hilton Garden, Holiday Inn Express, antiques, Express Outlets/famous brands, Goodyear, Harley-Davidson, repair
73mm	rest area both lanes, **full facilities, info, litter barrels, petwalk, , vending**
68mm	Driftwood River
68	IN 46, Columbus, E Shell/Circle K, Speedway/dsl, Buffalo Wild Wings, Burger King, Culver's, IHOP, Jimmy John's, Lincoln Sq Rest., McAlister's Deli, McDonald's, Panda Express, RuYi Asian, Starbucks, Subway, TX Roadhouse, Waffle House, Wendy's, Fairfield Inn, Holiday Inn, Sleep Inn, Super 8, AutoZone, Belle Tire, Chevrolet, H, Menards, Sam's Club/gas, Verizon, Walgreens, Walmart/Subway, W BP, Arby's, Bob Evans, Chicago's Pizza, El Nopal Mexican, Freddy's, Marco's Pizza, Noble Roman's, Papa John's, Papa's Grill, Taco Bell, Courtyard, Days Inn, EconoLodge, La Quinta, Residence Inn, $General, CVS Drug, Jay-C Foods, to Brown Co SP, vet
64	IN 58, Walesboro, W Circle K/dsl, GetGo/dsl
55	IN 11, to Jonesville, Seymour
54mm	White River
51mm	weigh sta both lanes
50b a	US 50, Seymour, E Circle K/dsl, Sunshine Cafe/Waffle House, TA/BP/Country Pride/dsl/24hr/@, McDonald's, Allstate Inn, Days Inn, EconoLodge, Economy Inn, Motel 6, Travelodge, W Circle K/dsl, Murphy USA/dsl, Shell/Circle K/dsl, Speedway/dsl, Applebee's, Arby's, Bonanza, Buffalo Wild Wings, Buffet China, Burger King, Capt D's, Chili's, Cracker Barrel, Domino's, DQ, El Nopal Mexican, Freddy's, Hardee's, KFC, Little Caesar's, McDonalds, Papa John's, Pizza Hut, Popeyes, Rally's, Steak'n Shake, Subway, Taco Bell, Wendy's, White Castle, Fairfield Inn, Hampton Inn, Holiday Inn Express, Knights Inn, Quality Inn, $General, $Tree, Advance Parts, AlLDI, AT&T, AutoZone, BigLots, Buick/Cadillac/Chevrolet/GMC, Chrysler/Dodge/Jeep, CVS Drug, Ford, GNC, Home Depot, H, Jay-C Foods,

= gas = food = lodging = other = rest stop

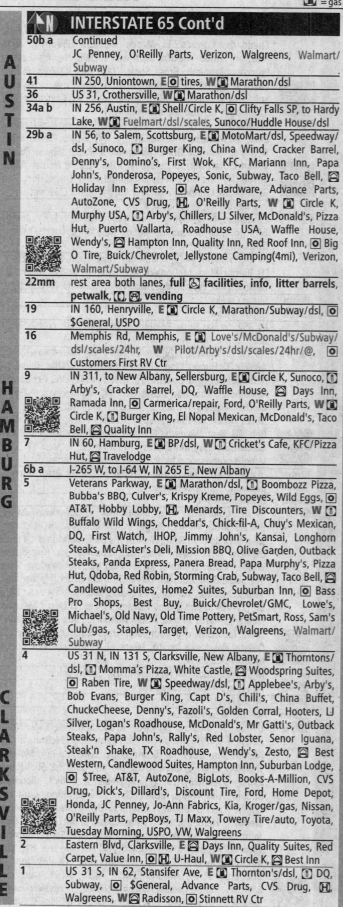

INTERSTATE 65 Cont'd

AUSTIN

Exit	Services
50b a	Continued JC Penney, O'Reilly Parts, Verizon, Walgreens, Walmart/Subway
41	IN 250, Uniontown, E tires, W Marathon/dsl
36	US 31, Crothersville, W Marathon/dsl
34a b	IN 256, Austin, E Shell/Circle K, Clifty Falls SP, to Hardy Lake, W Fuelmart/dsl/scales, Sunoco/Huddle House/dsl
29b a	IN 56, to Salem, Scottsburg, E MotoMart/dsl, Speedway/dsl, Sunoco, Burger King, China Wind, Cracker Barrel, Denny's, Domino's, First Wok, KFC, Mariann Inn, Papa John's, Ponderosa, Popeyes, Sonic, Subway, Taco Bell, Holiday Inn Express, Ace Hardware, Advance Parts, AutoZone, CVS Drug, H, O'Reilly Parts, W Circle K, Murphy USA, Arby's, Chillers, LJ Silver, McDonald's, Pizza Hut, Puerto Vallarta, Roadhouse USA, Waffle House, Wendy's, Hampton Inn, Quality Inn, Red Roof Inn, Big O Tire, Buick/Chevrolet, Jellystone Camping(4mi), Verizon, Walmart/Subway
22mm	rest area both lanes, **full facilities, info, litter barrels, petwalk, vending**
19	IN 160, Henryville, E Circle K, Marathon/Subway/dsl, $General, USPO
16	Memphis Rd, Memphis, E Love's/McDonald's/Subway/dsl/scales/24hr, W Pilot/Arby's/dsl/scales/24hr/@, Customers First RV Ctr
9	IN 311, to New Albany, Sellersburg, E Circle K, Sunoco, Arby's, Cracker Barrel, DQ, Waffle House, Days Inn, Ramada Inn, Carmerica/repair, Ford, O'Reilly Parts, W Circle K, Burger King, El Nopal Mexican, McDonald's, Taco Bell, Quality Inn
7	IN 60, Hamburg, E BP/dsl, W Cricket's Cafe, KFC/Pizza Hut, Travelodge
6b a	I-265 W, to I-64 W, IN 265 E , New Albany
5	Veterans Parkway, E Marathon/dsl, Boombozz Pizza, Bubba's BBQ, Culver's, Krispy Kreme, Popeyes, Wild Eggs, AT&T, Hobby Lobby, H, Menards, Tire Discounters, W Buffalo Wild Wings, Cheddar's, Chick-fil-A, Chuy's Mexican, DQ, First Watch, IHOP, Jimmy John's, Kansai, Longhorn Steaks, McAlister's Deli, Mission BBQ, Olive Garden, Outback Steaks, Panda Express, Panera Bread, Papa Murphy's, Pizza Hut, Qdoba, Red Robin, Storming Crab, Subway, Taco Bell, Candlewood Suites, Home2 Suites, Suburban Inn, Bass Pro Shops, Best Buy, Buick/Chevrolet/GMC, Lowe's, Michael's, Old Navy, Old Time Pottery, PetSmart, Ross, Sam's Club/gas, Staples, Target, Verizon, Walgreens, Walmart/Subway
4	US 31 N, IN 131 S, Clarksville, New Albany, E Thorntons/dsl, Momma's Pizza, White Castle, Woodspring Suites, Raben Tire, W Speedway/dsl, Applebee's, Arby's, Bob Evans, Burger King, Capt D's, Chili's, China Buffet, ChuckeCheese, Denny's, Fazoli's, Golden Corral, Hooters, LJ Silver, Logan's Roadhouse, McDonald's, Mr Gatti's, Outback Steaks, Papa John's, Rally's, Red Lobster, Senor Iguana, Steak'n Shake, TX Roadhouse, Wendy's, Zesto, Best Western, Candlewood Suites, Hampton Inn, Suburban Lodge, $Tree, AT&T, AutoZone, BigLots, Books-A-Million, CVS Drug, Dick's, Dillard's, Discount Tire, Ford, Home Depot, Honda, JC Penney, Jo-Ann Fabrics, Kia, Kroger/gas, Nissan, O'Reilly Parts, PepBoys, TJ Maxx, Towery Tire/auto, Toyota, Tuesday Morning, USPO, VW, Walgreens
2	Eastern Blvd, Clarksville, E Days Inn, Quality Suites, Red Carpet, Value Inn, H, U-Haul, W Circle K, Best Inn
1	US 31 S, IN 62, Stansifer Ave, E Thornton's/dsl, DQ, Subway, $General, Advance Parts, CVS Drug, H, Walgreens, W Radisson, Stinnett RV Ctr

HAMBURG

CLARKSVILLE

IN

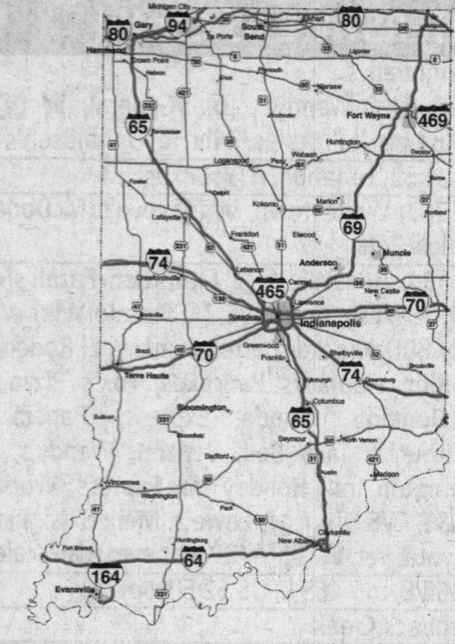

Exit	Services
0	Jeffersonville, E Thornton's/dsl, Hardee's, Chrys Jeep/Dodge, CVS Drug, H, Hyundai, to Falls of OH Walgreens, W Hooters, Kingfish Rest., Kobe, Fairf Inn, Hawthorn Suites, Sheraton
0mm	Indiana/Kentucky state line, Ohio River

INTERSTATE 69

CROOKED LAKE

Exit	Services
358mm	Indiana/Michigan state line
357	Lake George Rd, to IN 120, Fremont, Lake James, E Pe Iron Skillet/dsl/LP/scales/24hr/@, Freightliner/West Star Truck Repair, Kenworth, W Marathon/dsl, Pi Wendy's/dsl/scales/24hr, Shell/Subway/dsl, McDonal Red Arrow Rest., Holiday Inn Express, Redwood Inn, Freemont Outlets/Famous Brands, GNC, Jellyst Camping(5mi), to Pokagon SP
356	I-80/90 Toll Rd, E to Toledo, W to Chicago
354	IN 127, to IN 120, IN 727, Fremont, Orland, E Tesla E American Inn, Comfort Inn, Quality Inn, Ramada, Travel Inn, golf, W Marathon/dsl, Holiday Inn Express, Freemont Outlets/Famous Brands, Jellystone Camping(4 to Pokagon SP
350	rd 200 W, to Lake James, Crooked Lake, E Sunoco/dsl, fireworks, W Marathon, Sunoco/Subway, Carus Rest., Tasty Pizza, Marine Ctr
348	US 20, to Angola, Lagrange, E Marathon/Subway/ Speedway/Taco Bell/dsl, McDonald's, Happy Ac Camping(1mi), University Inn(2mi), H, W Love Hardee's/dsl/scales/24hr, KOA(2mi)
345mm	Pigeon Creek
344mm	rest area sb, **full facilities, info, litter barrels, petwa vending**
340	IN 4, to Hamilton, Ashley, Hudson, W Marathon/Subwa dsl
334	US 6, to Waterloo, Kendallville, E Subway, $General, BP/dsl, Marathon/dsl/24hr, Kathy's Kountry Kitchen
329	IN 8, to Garrett, Auburn, E BP, Lassus, Speedway/ Speedway/dsl(2), Applebee's, Arby's, Burger Ki Culver's, DQ, Jimmy John's, KFC, Little Caesar's, McDonal Papa John's, Peking Buffet, Penguin Point Rest., Pizza H Richard's Rest., Starbucks, Steak'n Shake, Subway, Taco B Wendy's, Auburn Inn, Baymont Inn, Comfort Suites, Da Inn, Red Roof Inn, Wingate Inn, $General, $Tree, Advan Parts, ALDI, AT&T, AutoZone, Buick/Chevrolet/RV C Chrysler/Dodge/Jeep, CVS Drug, Davis RV Ctr, Ford, GNC, Kroger/dsl, Monro, Save A Lot, Walmart/Subway, W Marathon/dsl, Buffalo Wild Wings, Cebolla's Mexica Cracker Barrel, Paradise Buffet, Subway, Hampton I Holiday Inn Express, Home Depot, Verizon

AUBURN

INTERSTATE 69 Cont'd

Exit #	Services
326	rd 11A, to Garrett, Auburn, E Auction Park, W Fireside Camping
324mm	rest area nb, **full facilities, info, litter barrels, , nb, vending**
317	Union Chapel Rd, E
316	IN 1 N, Dupont Rd, E Lassus/Elmo's/dsl, Phillips 66/ Burger King, Arby's, Arcos Mexicano, Culver's, Taco Bell, Comfort Suites, Hampton Inn, Holiday Inn Express, , W Speedway/dsl, Bagger Dave's Burgers, Bob Evans, Domino's, Jimmy John's, McDonald's, Panera Bread, Pine Valley Grill, Starbucks, Trolley Grill, Baymont Inn, La Quinta
315	I-469, US 30 E, W Woodspring Suites
312b a	Coldwater Rd, E BP/dsl, Marathon, Sunoco, Agaves Mexican, Arby's, Bill's Smokehouse, Buffalo Wings & Rings, Chili's, Cork'N Cleaver, Firehouse Subs, Hall's Factory Rest., IHOP, Jimmy John's, Koto Japanese, Mister Coney, Papa John's, Rally's, Red Lobster, Subway, Taco Bell, Wendy's, Wu's Fine Chinese, Hyatt Place, Ramada Plaza, $Tree, ALDI, Dick's, Hobby Lobby, Hyundai, JoAnn Fabrics, O'Reilly Parts, PetCo, Tuesday Morning, U-Haul, Walmart/Subway, W Marathon, Salsa Grille
311b a	US 27 S, IN 3 N, E Shell/dsl, Sunoco/dsl, Arby's, BJ's Rest., Cheddar's, Chick-fil-A, ChuckECheese's, DQ, Fazoli's, Golden Corral, Hall's Rest., Longhorn Steaks, McDonald's, Olive Garden, Starbucks, TGIFriday's, Tim Horton's, Candlewood Suites, Hawthorn Suites, TownePlace Suites, Tru Hilton, Barnes&Noble, Chevrolet, Chrysler/Dodge/Jeep, Costco/gas, Discount Tire, Fiat, Ford/Lincoln, Honda, Infiniti, JC Penney, Macy's, Nissan, Subaru, Toyota, Verizon, W BP/dsl, Lassus/Elmo's Pizza/dsl, Marathon/dsl, Applebee's, Burger King, Chipotle, Cracker Barrel, Culver's, Hardee's, IHOP, Logan's Roadhouse, McDonald's, Panda Express, Sapporo Japanese, Starbucks, Subway, Taco Bell, TX Roadhouse, Best Value Inn, Best Western+, Comfort Inn, Days Inn, EconoLodge, Extended Stay America, Fairfield Inn, Fairfield Inn, Guesthouse Motel, Hampton Inn, Quality Inn, Travelodge, Wyndham Garden, Belle Tire, CVS Drug, Home Depot, Lowe's, Meijer/dsl/e85, Sam's Club/gas, VW
309b a	US 33, Goshen Rd, Ft Wayne, E Phillips 66/dsl, Pilot/dsl/scales/24hr, Shell, Liberty Diner, McDonald's, Ft Wayne Inn, Knights Inn, Motel 6, Red Roof Inn, Rodeway Inn, Travel Inn, auto/dsl repair, Blue Beacon, , NAPA
305b a	IN 14 W, Ft Wayne, E Lassus, Murphy USA, Shell/Subway/dsl, Speedway/Speedy's Cafe/dsl, Arby's, Biaggi's, Chick-fil-A, Chipotle Mexican, Coldstone, Domino's, Eddy Merlot Rest., Firehouse Subs, Flat Top Grill, Great Wall Buffet, Little Caesar's, Logan's Roadhouse, McAlister's Deli, Noodles&Co., O'Charley's, Panda Express, Panera Bread, Penn Sta Subs, Smokey Bones BBQ, Starbucks, Steak'n Shake, Subway, Taco Bell, Tuscanos Brazilian, Wendy's, Klopfenstein Suites, $General, $Tree, Acura, Advance Parts, Audi/Porsche, Barnes&Noble, Belle Tire, Best Buy, BigLots, BMW, Buick/GMC, Cadillac, Chevrolet, Chrysler/Dodge/Jeep, Dick's, Ford/Lincoln, Gordman's, Harley-Davidson, , Kia, Kohl's, Lexus, Lowe's, Marshall's, Mazda, McMahon's Tire/auto, Meijer/dsl, Menards, Michael's, NAPA, Old Navy, PetSmart, Target, to St Francis U, Toyota, Tuesday Morning, Verizon, vet, Volvo, Walmart/Subway
302	US 24, to Jefferson Blvd, Ft Wayne, E Subway(1mi), Taco Bell(1mi), Extended Stay America, Fairfield Inn, Hampton Inn, Residence Inn, , IN Wesleyan Ft Wayne, W Lassus, Marathon/dsl, Applebee's, Arby's, Bob Evans, Buffalo Wild Wings, Coventry Tavern Rest., McDonald's,

FT WAYNE

Exit #	Services
302	Continued Naked Chopstix, Outback Steaks, Pizza Hut, Salsa Grille, Sara's Rest., Starbucks, Wendy's, Zesto Drive-In, Best Western, Comfort Suites, Hilton Garden, Holiday Inn Express, Homewood Suites, Staybridge Suites, Kroger/dsl, Meineke, st police, Walgreens
299	Lower Huntington Rd, E to
296b a	I-469, US 24 E, US 33 S, E to
286	US 224, to Huntington, Markle, E Marathon/dsl, Phillips 66/Subway/dsl, Sunoco/dsl, DQ, Guesthouse Inn, Heritage Place Inn, , repair/tires, W Roush Lake, to Huntington Reservoir
280mm	weigh sta sb/parking area nb
278	IN 5, to Warren, Huntington, E Huggy Bear Motel, W Marathon/Subway/dsl, Shell/Diner/dsl/scales/24hr, McDonald's, Ugalde's Rest., Arlington Inn, Comfort Inn, fireworks, , RV camping, to Salamonie Reservoir
276mm	Salamonie River
273	IN 218, to Warren
264	IN 18, to Marion, Montpelier, E Love's/McDonalds/dsl/scales/24hr, W BP/Subway/dsl, Flying J/Wendy's/dsl/scales/24hr, Arby's, Best Value Inn, Harley-Davidson, , Ram
260mm	Walnut Creek
259	US 35 N, IN 22, to Upland, E Shell/Subway, Burger King, Casa Grande Mexican, China 1, Cracker Barrel, Best Western+, Super 8, Mar-Brook Camping, Taylor U, W Marathon/dsl, McClure Trkstp/dsl/24hr, Phillips 66/dsl, Hardee's, Starbucks, Taco Bell, Holiday Inn Express, to IN Wesleyan
255	IN 26, to Fairmount
250mm	rest area both lanes, **full facilities, info, litter barrels, pet walk, , , vending**
245	US 35 S, IN 28, to Alexandria, Albany, E Petro/Shell/Iron Skillet/Subway/dsl/scales/24hr/@, RV Camping
241	IN 332, to Muncie, Frankton, E BP/Subway/dsl, , to Ball St U
234	IN 67, to IN 32, Chesterfield, Daleville, E Pilot/Subway/dsl/scales/24hr, Shell, Arby's, Pizza Hut, Smokehouse BBQ, Taco Bell, Waffle House, White Castle, Budget Inn, , W McClure/dsl/e85, Pilot/Denny's/dsl/scales/24hr, Speedway/dsl, McDonald's, Subway, Wendy's, Travel Inn, Timberline Valley Camping(3mi)
226	IN 9, IN 109, to Anderson, E A&W/KFC, Culver's, Golden Corral, MT Mike's, Fairfield Inn, Hampton Inn, Holiday Inn Express, Quality Inn, Red Roof Inn, Belle Tire, Meijer/dsl, Menards, visitors ctr, W BP, Marathon/dsl, Speedway/dsl, Applebee's, Arby's, Bob Evans, Buffalo Wild Wings, Burger King, Cracker Barrel, Fazoli's, IHOP, Jimmy John's, McDonald's, Olive Garden, Panda Express, Panera Bread, Papa Murphy's, Payless Mkt/dsl, Penn Sta Subs, Perkins, Pizza Hut, Ponderosa, Popeyes, Qdoba, Red Lobster, Riviera Maya, Ruby Tuesday, Starbucks, Steak'n Shake, Subway, Taco Bell, TX Roadhouse, Waffle House, Wendy's, White Castle, Baymont Inn, Best Value Inn, Best Western+, Comfort Inn, Days Inn, Motel 6, $Tree, AT&T, Big Lots, Cadillac/Chevrolet, Chrysler/Dodge/Jeep, GNC, Hobby Lobby, Honda, , Kohl's, Marshall's, Nissan, O'Reilly Parts, PetSmart, Tire Barn, to Anderson U, to Mounds SP, Verizon, vet, Walmart/Subway
222	IN 9, IN 67, to Anderson, W Speedway/dsl, Skyline Chili,
219	IN 38, Pendleton, E Ricker's/dsl, Burger King, McDonald's, Subway, W Pine Lakes Camping
214	IN 13, to Lapel, E BP/dsl, Love's/McDonald's/dsl/scales24hr, Waffle House, W Pilot/Subway/dsl/scales/24hr, camping

ALBANY

PENDLETON

INTERSTATE 69 Cont'd

FISHERS

Exit #	Services
210	IN 238, to Noblesville, Fortville, E BP/dsl, Arby's, Culver's, DQ, Starbucks, Subway, Taco Bell, Wendy's, H, W EVC, Shell/dsl, Aspen Grill, BJ's Rest., Chick-fil-A, Chuy's, Coldstone, Famous Dave's, Five Guys, Fresh to Order Cafe, Houlihan's, McAlister's Deli, McDonald's, Olive Garden, Panda Express, Perkins, Potbelly, Qdoba, Red Robin, Stone Creek Rest., Tuscano's, Cambria Suites, Embassy Suites, Holiday Inn Express, $Tree, AT&T, Cabela's, CVS Drug, Dick's, Duluth Trading, Earth Fare Foods, Firestone/auto, JC Penney, Old Navy, Sleepy Bear Camping, Steinmart, Verizon
205	IN 37 N, 116th St, to Noblesville, Fishers, E BP, Bent Cafe Asian, Penn Sta Subs, Sunrise Cafe, Kroger, W Shell/Circle K, Speedway, Brixx Pizzaria, Five Guys, Handel's Ice Cream, Happy Dragon, Jet's Pizza, Marco's Pizza, McAlister's Deli, McDonald's, Moe's SW Grill, O'Charley's, Original Pancakes, Pure Eatery, Qdoba, Starbucks, Steak'n Shake, Subway, Verde Mexican, Wendy's, Wild Ginger Asian, Hampton Inn, AT&T, CVS Drug, Firestone/auto, Target, URGENT CARE
204	E 106th St, W Fairfield Inn
203	96th St, E Marathon/dsl(2), Murphy USA/dsl, Shell/Circle K, Village Pantry/dsl, Applebee's, Bubba's Rest., Cracker Barrel, Donato's Pizza, Dunkin', Hot Box Pizza, IHOP, Jersey Mike's, Jimmy John's, McDonald's, Noodles&Co., Panda Express, Panera Bread, Qdoba, Red Habanero, Rita's, Ruby Tuesday, Sahm's Grill, Slimm's Pizza, Smoothie King, Starbucks, Steak'n Shake, Tijuana Flats, Wendy's, AmericInn, Baymont Inn, Hilton Garden, Holiday Inn Express, Studio 6, $Tree, AT&T, Fry's, GNC, Kohl's, Meijer/dsl, PepBoys, PetCo, Staples, Tuesday Morning, Verizon, Walmart, W Marathon/dsl, Arby's, Bob Evans, Burger King, Chicotes Mexican, Culver's, DJ's Hotdogs, Izakya Japanese, Journey Rest., Peterson's Steaks/seafood, Riviera Maya, Starbucks, Taco Bell, Tire Discounters, Wolfie's Grill, Comfort Suites, Residence Inn, SpringHill Suites, Staybridge Suites, AlLDI, Home Depot, Menards, NAPA, Sam's Club/gas, vet
201	82nd St, Castleton, E Boston Mkt, Burger King, Jet's Pizza, Red Robin, Drury Inn, Extended Stay America, Red Roof Inn, Super 8, CVS Drug, H, Lowe's, vet, Walgreens, W Speedway/Speedy's Cafe/dsl, Applebee's, Arby's, Burger King, Charleston's Rest., Dave & Buster's, Denny's, Domino's, Fazoli's, Firehouse Subs, Formosa Buffet, Hooters, Jimmy John's, Joe's Grill, KFC, LJ Silver, Longhorn Steaks, Los Cabos Mexican, McAlister's Deli, McDonald's, Olive Garden, Panda Express, Penn Sta Subs, Pizza Hut, Popeyes, Red Lobster, Skyline Chili, Starbucks, Subway, Taco Bell, Thai Orchid, Twin Peaks, Wendy's, Candlewood Suites, Days Inn, Hampton Inn, Suburban Suites, Surestay+, Aamco, Advance Parts, AutoZone, Best Buy, CarX, Dick's, Discount Tire, Firestone/auto, fireworks, Goodyear/auto, JC Penney, Macy's, Midas, O'Reilly Parts, Tire Barn
200mm	I-465 around Indianapolis. I-69 begins/ends on I-465, exit 37, at Indianapolis.

CASTLETON

IN

INTERSTATE 70

156.5mm	Indiana/Ohio state line, weigh sta
156b a	US 40 E, Richmond, N Petro/BP/Iron Skillet/dsl/24hr/@, Fairfield Inn, Blue Beacon, S Murphy USA/dsl, Shell/dsl, Speedway/dsl, Sunoco, A&W/LJ Silver, Applebee's, Arby's, Big Boy, Buffalo Wild Wings, Buffalo Wings&Rings, Burger King, Chili's, Chipotle Mexican, Cracker Barrel, El Rodeo Mexican, Fazoli's, Galo's Italian, Golden Corral, IHOP, Jade House Chinese, Jimmy John's, KFC, McAlister's Deli,

RICHMOND

156b a	Continued McDonald's, MCL Cafeteria, O'Charley's, Olive Garden, Pap Murphy's, Pizza Hut, Rally's, Red Lobster, Starbucks, Steak' Shake, Subway, Taco Bell, TX Roadhouse, Yamato Japanes Best Western, Days Inn, EconoLodge, Hampton In Holiday Inn, Motel 6, Quality Inn, $General, $Tre Advance Parts, AlLDI, AT&T, Best Buy, Big Lots, Buick/GM Chevrolet, Chrysler/Dodge/Jeep, Dick's, Dillard's, Firestone auto, Ford, Hobby Lobby, JC Penney, Jo-Ann Fabrics, Kohl' Kroger/dsl, Lowe's, Menards, O'Reilly Parts, Save-A-L Foods, Tires+, TJ Maxx, Toyota/Nissan, U-Haul, Verizo Walgreens, Walmart/Subway
153	IN 227, to Whitewater, Richmond, N Grandpa's Farm R Park(seasonal), KOA
151b a	US 27, to Chester, Richmond, N Fricker's Rest., Hond KOA, S Shell, Bob Evans, Burger Time, Carver's Rest., Bronco Mexican, Hardee's, McDonald's, Subway, Taco Be Wendy's, Comfort Inn, Red Roof Inn, CVS Drug, Harle Davidson, H, Meijer/dsl/E85
149b a	US 35, IN 38, to Muncie, N Love's/Hardee's/dsl/scale 24hr, S Shell/dsl, Camping World RV Ctr
148mm	weigh sta wb
145	Centerville, N Marathon/DQ/Godfather's/dsl, Super Goodyear/truck repair, S Warm Glow Candles/cafe
145mm	Nolands Fork Creek
144mm	**full facilities, info, litter barrels, petwalk, w vending**
141mm	Greens Fork River
137	IN 1, to Hagerstown, Connersville, N Amish Cheese, S BP/Arby's/dsl/24hr, Shell/Burger King, Speedway/dsl/e8 McDonald's
131	Wilbur Wright Rd, New Lisbon, S Shell/Pizza Hut/Ta Bell/dsl/scales/24hr/@, New Lisbon RV park
126mm	Flatrock River
123	IN 3, to New Castle, Spiceland, N All American Inn(3m Holiday Inn Express(3mi), H, S Flying J/Denny' Subway/dsl/LP/scales/24hr, Mr Fuel/rest./dsl/scales/24 Montgomery's Steaks, tires/repair
117mm	Big Blue River
115	IN 109, to Knightstown, Wilkinson, N Love's/McDonald' Subway/dsl/scales/24hr, Speedway/rest./dsl/scales/24 Burger King, Jellystone Camping
107mm	**full facilities, litter barrels, petwalk, bo lanes, vending**
104	IN 9, Greenfield, Maxwell, N Speedway/dsl, S Circle K/d Murphy USA/dsl, Shell/Circle K, Speedway/dsl, Applebee's, Arby's, Bamboo Garden, Bob Evans, Buffalo Wi Wings, Burger King, Chicago's Pizza, China Inn,

CONNERSVILLE

INTERSTATE 70 Cont'd

Exit	Services
104	Continued Cracker Barrel, Culver's, Firehouse Subs, Hardee's, Jimmy John's, KFC, Little Caesar's, McDonald's, Mi Casa Mexican, MT Mike's Steaks, O'Charley's, Papa John's, Papa Murphy's, Penn Sta Subs, Pizza Hut, Ponderosa, Popeyes, Qdoba, Starbucks, Steak'n Shake, Subway, Taco Bell, Waffle House, Wasabi, Wendy's, White Castle, Comfort Inn, Country Inn&Suites, Fairfield Inn, Greenfield Inn, Hampton Inn, Holiday Inn Express, Quality Inn, Super 8, $General, $Tree, Advance Parts, AllDI, AutoZone, Big Lots, CVS Drug, GNC, Home Depot, H, Kohl's, Kroger/dsl, PetSmart, Verizon, Walgreens, Walmart
96	Mt Comfort Rd, N Pilot/Pizza Hut/dsl/scales/24hr, Speedway/Subway/dsl, Burger King, Wendy's, S Shell/Circle K, McDonald's, KOA(seasonal), Mt Comfort RV Ctr
91	Post Rd, to Ft Harrison, N Mobil/Circle K, Cracker Barrel, Denny's, Outback Steaks, Steak'n Shake, Wendy's, InTown Suites, La Quinta, Lowe's, st police, S Admiral, BP/dsl, Shell/dsl, Speedway, Hardee's, Jack-in-the-Box, KFC/Taco Bell, Little Caesar's, Waffle House, Country Hearth Inn, Days Inn, CVS Drug, Family$, Home Depot
90	I-465(from wb)
89	Shadeland Ave, I-465(from eb), N Marathon/dsl, Bob Evans, Baymont Inn, Comfort Inn, Holiday Inn Express, Welcome Inn, Toyota, U-Haul, S Admiral/dsl, Circle K, Exxon/dsl, Marathon, Speedway/dsl, Arby's, Burger King, Damon's, Domino's, Four Seasons Diner, Jimmy John's, Lincoln Sq Rest., McDonald's, Papa John's, Penn Sta Subs, Rally's, Red Lobster, Starbucks, Subway, Taco Bell, TX Roadhouse, Wendy's, Always Inn, Best Value Inn, Candlewood Suites, Delta Hotel, Express Inn, Fairfield Inn, Marriott, Quality Inn, $General, CarX, Chevrolet, Chrysler/Dodge/Jeep, CVS Drug, Honda, Kia, Kroger/gas, Mazda, Nissan
87	Emerson Ave, N BP/McDonald's, Speedway/dsl, S Shell, H
85b a	Rural St, Keystone Ave, N Shell, Church's TX Chicken, fairgrounds, S Shell/dsl
83b(112)	I-65 N, to Chicago
83a(111)	Michigan St, Market St, downtown, S Hardee's
80(110a)	I-65 S, to Louisville
79b	Illinois St, McCarty St, downtown
79a	West St, N Speedway/dsl, Holiday Inn, Holiday Inn Express, Hyatt, JW Marriott, Staybridge Suites, Govt Ctr, H, Lucas Oil Stadium, zoo
78	Harding St, to downtown, S Marathon/Subway, Wendy's
77	Holt Rd, N Phillips 66/dsl, Rally's, Steak'n Shake, S Speedway/Speedy's Cafe/dsl, McDonald's
75	Airport Expswy, to Raymond St (no EZ wb return), N Marathon/dsl, Speedway/dsl, Indy's Rest., Jimmy John's, Library Rest., Subway, Waffle House, Candlewood Suites, Courtyard, Extended Stay America, Fairfield Inn, Hyatt Place, La Quinta, Ramada, Red Roof Inn, Residence Inn, Super 8, Wyndham, NAPA, to
73b a	I-465 N/S, I-74 E/W
69(only from eb)	to I-74 E, to I-465 S
68	Six Points Rd, N S Mobil/dsl, Burger Theory, Subway, Hampton Inn, Hilton Garden, Holiday Inn, Home2 Suites
66	IN 267, to Plainfield, Mooresville, N Blu/dsl, BP, Shell/Circle K, Speedway/dsl, Thornton's/dsl, Arby's, Bob Evans, Burger King, Coachman Rest., Cracker Barrel, Golden Corral,
66	Continued McDonald's, Narita Japanese, Nonna's Italian, Steak'n Shake, Subway, Taco Bell, Waffle House, White Castle, Baymont Inn, Best Western+, Budget Inn, Comfort Inn, Days Inn, Embassy Suites, Hampton Inn, Holiday Inn Express, Homewood Suites, Indianapolis Suites, La Quinta, Quality Inn, Staybridge Suites, Super 8, Wingate Inn, Woodspring Suites, Buick/GMC, Chateau Thomas Winery, Harley-Davidson
65mm	**full facilities, info, litter barrels, petwalk, both lanes, vending**
59	IN 39, to Belleville, N Love's/McDonald's/Subway/dsl/scales/24hr, S TA/Country Pride/dsl/scales/24hr/@, truckwash
51	rd 1100W, S Koger's/Sunoco/dsl/rest./24hr, repair/towing/24hr
41	US 231, to Greencastle, Cloverdale, S BP/dsl, Casey's(2mi), Marathon/dsl/scales/24hr, Arby's, Chicago's Pizza, El Cantarito, McDonald's, Subway, Taco Bell, Days Inn, EconoLodge, Holiday Inn Express, Motel 6, Super 8, $General, Family$, Jordan's Carcare, NAPA, Taylor's Hardware, to Lieber SRA, Value Mkt Foods
37	IN 243, to Putnamville, S Marathon/dsl, Misty Morning Campground(4mi), to Lieber SRA
23	IN 59, to Brazil, N Pilot/McDonald's/Subway/dsl/scales/24hr, Speedway/dsl, H, truck repair, S BP/dsl, Petro/Iron Skillet/dsl/scales/24hr/@, Road Ranger/Pilot/Subway/dsl/scales, Burger King, Family Table Rest., Best Western+, Travelodge
15mm	Honey Creek
11	IN 46, Terre Haute, N Pilot/Subway/dsl/scales/24hr, Thornton/dsl, Arby's, Burger King, Holiday Inn Express, McDonald's, Monical's Pizza, Real Hacienda, Sonic, Taco Bell, Home2 Suites, $Tree, ALDI, GNC, Meijer/dsl, Verizon, Walmart, S KOA
7	US 41, US 150, Terre Haute, N Casey's/dsl, Marathon/dsl, Sunoco/dsl, Thornton's/dsl, Applebee's, Bandana's BBQ, Bob Evans, Coyote's Mexican Hacienda, Cracker Barrel, Dunkin Donuts, East Star Buffet, Fazoli's, IHOP, Moe's SW Grill, NewDay Cafe, Pizza Hut, Real Hacienda Mexican, Starbucks, Steak'n Shake, Tokyo Japanese, TX Roadhouse, Comfort Suites, Days Inn, Drury Inn, Fairfield Inn, La Quinta, PearTree Inn, Super 8, AT&T, AutoZone, Chrysler/Jeep, O'Reilly Parts, URGENT CARE, S Speedway/dsl, Thornton's/dsl, Arby's, Baskin-Robbins, Buffalo Wild Wings, Burger King, Cheddar's, Chick-fil-A, Chili's, Denny's, DQ, Five Guys, Fuddrucker's, Golden Corral, Hardee's, Jimmy John's, KFC, LJ Silver, Longhorn Steaks, Los Tres Caminos, McDonald's, Monical's Pizza, Olive Garden, Outback Steaks, Panda Express, Panda Garden, Panera Bread, Papa John's, Penn Sta Subs, Popeyes, Qdoba, Rally's, Red Lobster, Ruby Tuesday, Starbucks, Subway, Taco Bell, TGIFriday's, Wendy's, White Castle, Hampton Inn, Holiday Inn, Motel 6, SpringHill Suites, $Tree, AllDI, AT&T, Best Buy, Big O Tire, BigLots, BooksAMillion, Buick/Cadillac/GMC, Burlington Coats, Chevrolet, Dodge, Ford, Fresh Thyme Mkt, Goodyear/auto, Harley-Davidson, Hobby Lobby, H, Hyundai, JC Penney, Jo-Ann Fabrics, Kohl's, Kroger/dsl, Lowe's, NAPA, Nissan, Old Navy, PetSmart, Ross, Sam's Club/gas, Staples, Tire Barn, TJ Maxx, Verizon, Walgreens, Walmart
5.5mm	Wabash River
3	Darwin Rd, W Terre Haute, N to St Mary of-the-Woods Coll
1.5mm	**Welcome Ctr eb, full facilities, info, litter barrels, vending, petwalk**
1	US 40 E(from eb, exits left), to Terre Haute, W Terre Haute
0.5mm	weigh sta eb
0mm	Indiana/Illinois state line

CLOVERDALE

TERRE HAUTE

MOORESVILLE

IN

= gas = food = lodging = other = rest stop

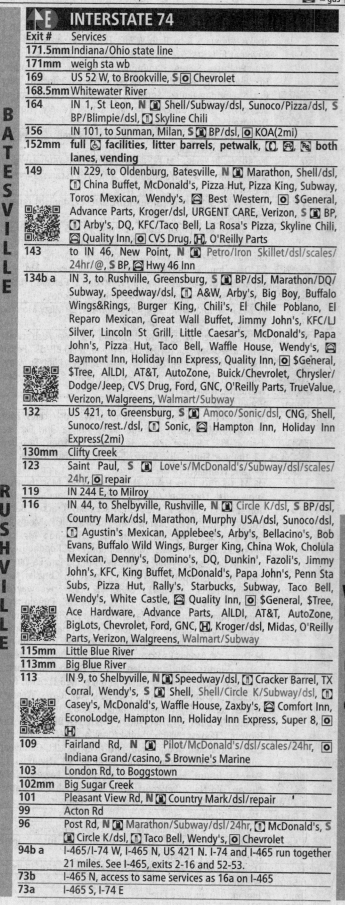

INTERSTATE 74

BATESVILLE

RUSHVILLE

Exit #	Services
171.5mm	Indiana/Ohio state line
171mm	weigh sta wb
169	US 52 W, to Brookville, S Chevrolet
168.5mm	Whitewater River
164	IN 1, St Leon, N Shell/Subway/dsl, Sunoco/Pizza/dsl, S BP/Blimpie/dsl, Skyline Chili
156	IN 101, to Sunman, Milan, S BP/dsl, KOA(2mi)
152mm	**full facilities, litter barrels, petwalk, both lanes, vending**
149	IN 229, to Oldenburg, Batesville, N Marathon, Shell/dsl, China Buffet, McDonald's, Pizza Hut, Pizza King, Subway, Toros Mexican, Wendy's, Best Western, $General, Advance Parts, Kroger/dsl, URGENT CARE, Verizon, S BP, Arby's, DQ, KFC/Taco Bell, La Rosa's Pizza, Skyline Chili, Quality Inn, CVS Drug, O'Reilly Parts
143	to IN 46, New Point, N Petro/Iron Skillet/dsl/scales/24hr/@, S BP, Hwy 46 Inn
134b a	IN 3, to Rushville, Greensburg, S BP/dsl, Marathon/DQ/Subway, Speedway/dsl, A&W, Arby's, Big Boy, Buffalo Wings&Rings, Burger King, Chili's, El Chile Poblano, El Reparo Mexican, Great Wall Buffet, Jimmy John's, KFC/LJ Silver, Lincoln St Grill, Little Caesar's, McDonald's, Papa John's, Pizza Hut, Taco Bell, Waffle House, Wendy's, Baymont Inn, Holiday Inn Express, Quality Inn, $General, $Tree, AlLDI, AT&T, AutoZone, Buick/Chevrolet, Chrysler/Dodge/Jeep, CVS Drug, Ford, GNC, O'Reilly Parts, TrueValue, Verizon, Walgreens, Walmart/Subway
132	US 421, to Greensburg, S Amoco/Sonic/dsl, CNG, Shell, Sunoco/rest./dsl, Sonic, Hampton Inn, Holiday Inn Express(2mi)
130mm	Clifty Creek
123	Saint Paul, S Love's/McDonald's/Subway/dsl/scales/24hr, repair
119	IN 244 E, to Milroy
116	IN 44, to Shelbyville, Rushville, N Circle K/dsl, S BP/dsl, Country Mark/dsl, Marathon, Murphy USA/dsl, Sunoco/dsl, Agustin's Mexican, Applebee's, Arby's, Bellacino's, Bob Evans, Buffalo Wild Wings, Burger King, China Wok, Cholula Mexican, Denny's, Domino's, DQ, Dunkin', Fazoli's, Jimmy John's, KFC, King Buffet, McDonald's, Papa John's, Penn Sta Subs, Pizza Hut, Rally's, Starbucks, Subway, Taco Bell, Wendy's, White Castle, Quality Inn, $General, $Tree, Ace Hardware, Advance Parts, AlLDI, AT&T, AutoZone, BigLots, Chevrolet, Ford, GNC, Kroger/dsl, Midas, O'Reilly Parts, Verizon, Walgreens, Walmart/Subway
115mm	Little Blue River
113mm	Big Blue River
113	IN 9, to Shelbyville, N Speedway/dsl, Cracker Barrel, TX Corral, Wendy's, S Shell, Shell/Circle K/Subway/dsl, Casey's, McDonald's, Waffle House, Zaxby's, Comfort Inn, EconoLodge, Hampton Inn, Holiday Inn Express, Super 8
109	Fairland Rd, N Pilot/McDonald's/dsl/scales/24hr, Indiana Grand/casino, S Brownie's Marine
103	London Rd, to Boggstown
102mm	Big Sugar Creek
101	Pleasant View Rd, N Country Mark/dsl/repair
99	Acton Rd
96	Post Rd, N Marathon/Subway/dsl/24hr, McDonald's, S Circle K/dsl, Taco Bell, Wendy's, Chevrolet
94b a	I-465/I-74 W, I-465 N, US 421 N. I-74 and I-465 run together 21 miles. See I-465, exits 2-16 and 52-53.
73b	I-465 N, access to same services as 16a on I-465
73a	I-465 S, I-74 E

IN

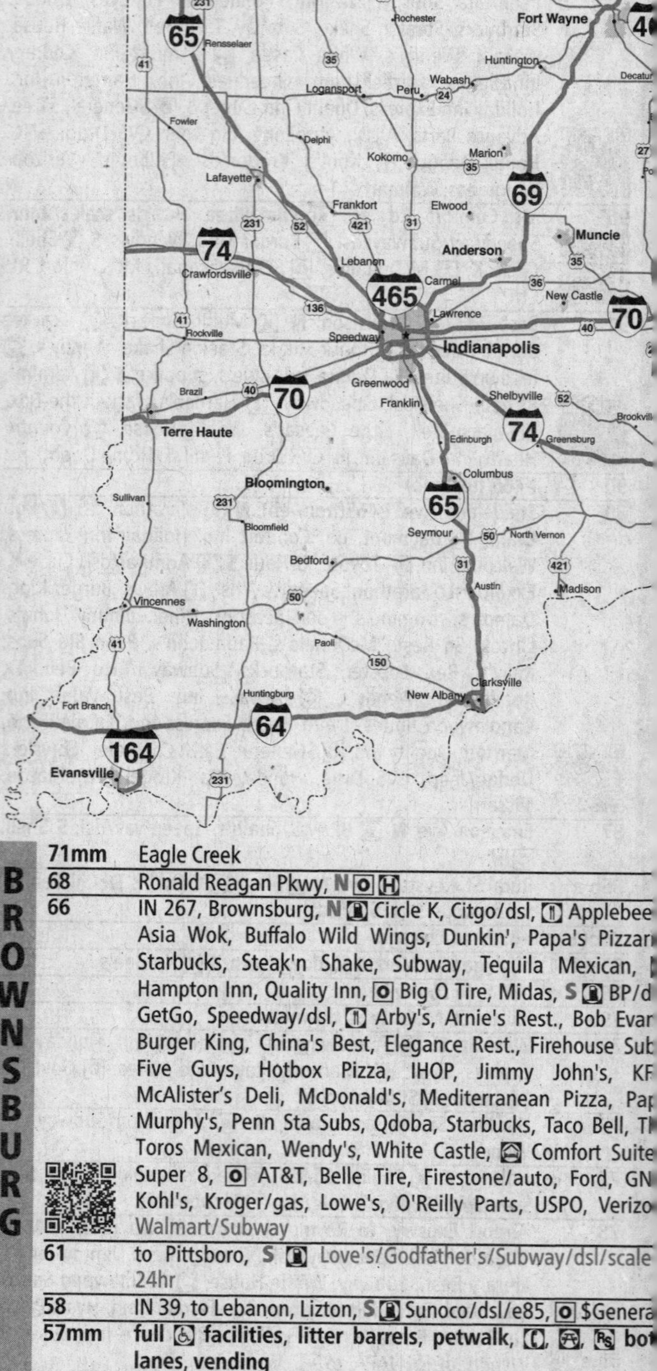

BROWNSBURG

Exit #	Services
71mm	Eagle Creek
68	Ronald Reagan Pkwy, N
66	IN 267, Brownsburg, N Circle K, Citgo/dsl, Applebee Asia Wok, Buffalo Wild Wings, Dunkin', Papa's Pizzar Starbucks, Steak'n Shake, Subway, Tequila Mexican, Hampton Inn, Quality Inn, Big O Tire, Midas, S BP/d GetGo, Speedway/dsl, Arby's, Arnie's Rest., Bob Evar Burger King, China's Best, Elegance Rest., Firehouse Sub Five Guys, Hotbox Pizza, IHOP, Jimmy John's, KF McAlister's Deli, McDonald's, Mediterranean Pizza, Pap Murphy's, Penn Sta Subs, Qdoba, Starbucks, Taco Bell, Th Toros Mexican, Wendy's, White Castle, Comfort Suite Super 8, AT&T, Belle Tire, Firestone/auto, Ford, GN Kohl's, Kroger/gas, Lowe's, O'Reilly Parts, USPO, Verizo Walmart/Subway
61	to Pittsboro, S Love's/Godfather's/Subway/dsl/scale 24hr
58	IN 39, to Lebanon, Lizton, S Sunoco/dsl/e85, $Genera
57mm	**full facilities, litter barrels, petwalk, bot lanes, vending**
52	IN 75, to Advance, Jamestown, S camping, food, gas
39	IN 32, to Crawfordsville, S Pilot/Subway/dsl/scales/24hr
34	US 231, to Linden, S Circle K/dsl, Marathon/dsl, McClure dsl, Speedway, Sunoco/dsl/cng, Cracker Barre McDonald's, Subway, Best Western+, Comfort Inn Hampton Inn, Holiday Inn Express, Knights Inn, Motel Super 8, KOA(1mi), Sugar Creek Campground(4mi)
25	IN 25, to Wingate, Waynetown
15	US 41, to Attica, Veedersburg, S BP/Subway, Casey's/dsl

INTERSTATE 74 Cont'd

15 Continued
Marathon/dsl, Suzie Q's, $General, camping, Family$, to Turkey Run SP

8 Covington, N Marathon/dsl, Valero/dsl, Benjamin's, Overpass Pizza, fireworks

7mm Wabash River

4 IN 63, to Newport, N One9/Arby's/dsl/scales/24hr, Beefhouse Rest.

1mm full facilities, info, litter barrels, **petwalk**, vending, **Welcome Ctr eb**

0mm Indiana/Illinois state line, Eastern/Central Time Zone

INTERSTATE 80/90

157mm Indiana/Ohio state line

153mm toll plaza, litter barrels

144 I-69, US 27, Angola, N Petro/Iron Skillet/dsl/scales/24hr/@, Pilot/Wendy's/dsl/scales, Shell/Subway/dsl, McDonald's, Red Arrow Rest., Redwood Inn, Freightliner/Western Star/truck repair, S Marathon/dsl, Comfort Inn, Holiday Inn Express, Quality Inn, Travelers Inn, Freemont Outlet Shops/famous brands, GNC, golf/rest, Jellystone Camping(5mi), to Pokagon SP

131.5mm Fawn River

126mm Ernie Pyle TP both lanes, Sunoco/dsl, Popeyes, Starbucks, RV dump

121 IN 9, to Lagrange, Howe, N Golden Buddha, Marathon, Murphy USA/dsl, Speedway/dsl, Applebee's, Buffalo Wild Wings, Burger King, Culver's, Fiesta Mexican, Hot'n Now, KFC, King Dragon, Little Caesar's, McDonald's, Pizza Hut, Subway, Taco Bell, Wendy's, American Inn, Best Western+, Hampton Inn, Travel Inn, Travelodge, $Tree, AT&T, CarQuest, Family$, Ford, GNC, H(4mi), Kroger, Meijer/dsl, Walgreens, Walmart/Subway, S Marathon/dsl, Holiday Inn Express, Super 8, H(8mi)

120mm Fawn River

108mm trucks only rest area both lanes

107 US 131, IN 13, to Middlebury, Constantine, N Marathon/dsl, Speedway/dsl, Country Table Rest., McDonald's, Patchwork Quilt Inn, Plaza Motel, $General, S BP/dsl, Yup's DairyLand, McKenzie House B&B, Dollar General, Eby's Pines RV Park, KOA(apr-nov)

101 IN 15, to Goshen, Bristol, S Mobil/7-11, Speedway/dsl, Subway, Eby's Pines Camping(3mi), USPO

96 Rd 1, E Elkhart, S BP/dsl, Marathon, Mobil/7-11, Arby's, China Star, DQ, McDonald's, Subway, Taco Bell, Ace Hardware, RV/MH Hall of Fame

92 IN 19, to Elkhart, N Marathon, Mobil/7-11/dsl, Phillips 66/Subway/dsl, Chubby Trout, Cracker Barrel, Perkins, Steak'n Shake, Best Western, Candlewood Suites, Comfort Suites, Country Inn&Suites, Diplomat Motel, EconoLodge, Fairfield Inn, Fairway Inn, Hampton Inn, Hilton Garden, La Quinta, Microtel, Quality Inn, Sheraton, Sleep Inn, Staybridge Suites, Turnpike Motel, $General, AlLDI, CVS Drug, Elkhart Campground(1mi), Martin's Foods, Montana RV Ctr, Walgreens, S Exxon, Marathon/dsl, Speedway/dsl, Arby's, Buffalo Wild Wings, Burger King, Callahan's, Culver's, DQ, Dunkin', El Camino Real, Jets Pizza, Jimmy John's, KFC, King Wha Chinese, LJ Silver, Marco's Pizza, McDonald's, MOD Pizza, Noodles&Co, North Garden Buffet, Olive Garden, Panda Express, Papa John's, Penn Sta Subs, Pizza Hut, Qdoba, Red Lobster, Subway, Taco Bell, TX Roadhouse, Wendy's, Wings Etc., Baymont Inn, Budget Inn, Daylite Inn, Garden Inn, Red Roof Inn, Super 8, $Tree, Advance Parts, AT&T, AutoZone, Belle Tire, CarQuest, Family$, Honda, H, Indian Motorcycles, Lowe's, Menards, O'Reilly Parts,

SOUTH BEND

VALPARAISO

BROADWAY

92 Continued
PetSmart, Ross, Verizon, Walmart/Subway

91mm Christiana Creek

90mm Schricker TP both directions, RV Dump, Sunoco/7-11/dsl, Starbucks, Z Mkt

83 to Mishawaka, N BP/dsl, Phillips 66/dsl, Phillips 66/Subway/dsl, Applebee's, Bar Louie, Five Guys, Granite City Grill, Longhorn Steaks, Olive Garden, Starbucks, Subway, Wendy's, Best Western+, Country Inn&Suites, Fairfield Inn, Hampton Inn, Holiday Inn Express, Quality Inn, Barnes&Noble, Best Buy, Costco/dsl, CVS Drug, JC Penney, KOA(mar-nov), Macy's, Martin's Foods/gas, Menards, Ross, Target, Verizon, Walgreens, S H

77 US 33, US 31B, IN 933, South Bend, N Admiral, Mobil/dsl, Murphy USA/dsl, Arby's, Burger King, DQ, Dunkin', Fazoli's, Hacienda Mexican, Jimmy John's, Jimmy John's, KFC, Little Caesar's, Marco's Pizza, McDonald's, McDonald's, Papa John's, Pizza Hut, Ponderosa, Sonic, Starbucks, Steak'n Shake, Subway, The Farmhouse, Comfort Suites, Hampton Inn, Rodeway Inn, Staybridge Suites, Suburban Lodge, Waterford Lodge, $Tree, Ace Hardware, AlLDI, AT&T, AutoZone, Belle Tire, BMW/Mazda, Meijer/dsl/24hr, NAPA, O'Reilly Parts, vet, Walgreens, Walmart/Subway, S Marathon, Phillips 66/Subway/dsl, American Pancake House, Bob Evans, HoPing House Chinese, King Gyros, Perkins, Pizza King, Taco Bell, Wendy's, Best Value Inn, Hilton Garden, Holiday Inn Express, Microtel, Quality Inn, St Marys Inn, CarX, H, to Notre Dame

76mm St Joseph River

72 US 31, to Niles, South Bend, N Pilot/Subway/dsl/scales/24hr, Speedway/Subway/dsl, Chivo's Pizza, El Arriero, Taco Bell, Super 8, S, to Potato Creek SP(20mi)

62mm Eastern Time Zone/Central Time Zone

56mm TP both lanes, Sunoco/dsl, Burger King, Starbucks

49 IN 39, to La Porte, N Hampton Inn, S Family Express, Phillips 66/dsl, DQ, El Bracero Mexican, Best Western+, Blue Heron Inn, Cassidy Inn & RV, Holiday Inn Express, Travelodge

39 US 421, to Michigan City, Westville, S Purdue U North Cent

38mm trucks only rest area both lanes, litter barrels

31 IN 49, to Chesterton, Valparaiso, N Family Express/dsl, Phillips 66, Speedway/dsl, AJ's Pizza, Bob Evans, Clock Rest., Culver's, Subway, Hilton Garden, CVS Drug, Dean's Tire/auto, Sand Creek RV Park(3mi, Apr-Oct), Strack&Van Til Mkt, to IN Dunes Nat Lakeshore, S Hampton Inn(8mi), Super 8(8mi)

24mm toll plaza

23 Portage, Port of Indiana, N Luke, Marathon, Denny's, Mark's Grill, Baymont Inn, Best Western+, Country Inn&Suites, Days Inn, Hampton Inn, Quality Inn, Rodeway Inn, Super 8, S BP, Speedway/dsl, Burger King, CiCi's Pizza, DQ, Dunkin', Jimmy John's, KFC, Little Caesar's, McDonald's, Rosewood Rest., Subway, Wendy's, Ace Hardware, Advance Parts, AutoZone, Family$, GNC, O'Reilly Parts, USPO, Walgreens

22mm TP both lanes, Sunoco/dsl, Ladson Grill

21mm I-90 and I-80 run together eb, separate wb. I-80 runs with I-94 wb. For I-80 exits 1 through 15, see Indiana Interstate 94.

21 I-94 E to Detroit, I-80/94 W, US 6, IN 51, Lake Station, S Flying J/Denny's/dsl/scales/24hr/@, Mr Fuel/dsl/scales/24hr, Pilot/Road Ranger/Subway/dsl/scales, TA/BP/Popeyes/dsl/scales/24hr/@, Blue Beacon, Blue Beacon

17 I-65 S, US 12, US 20, Dunes Hwy, to Indianapolis

14b IN 53, to Gary, Broadway, S Citgo

14a Grant St, to Gary, S H

10 IN 912, Cline Ave, to Gary, N, casino

5 US 41, Calumet Ave, to Hammond, S GoLo, Nice'n Easy,

IN

= gas = food = lodging = other = rest stop

INTERSTATE 80/90 Cont'd

5	Continued Speedway/dsl, Aurelio's Pizza, Dunkin', Gorditas, Johnel's Rest., KFC, McDonald's, Subway, Taco Bell, White Castle, EconoLodge, Ramada Inn, Super 8, AllDI, AutoZone, O'Reilly Parts, Walgreens
3	IN 912, Cline Ave, to Hammond, **N** to Gary Reg, **S** Shell
1.5mm	toll plaza
1mm	US 12, US 20, 106th St, Indianapolis Blvd, **N** BP, Citgo/ Dunkin', Luke/dsl, IHOP, Popeyes, Starbucks, $Tree, AT&T, casino, Ross, Walmart, **S** Burger King, KFC, McDonald's, Pizza Hut, Subway, AllDI, O'Reilly Parts
0mm	Indiana/Illinois state line

INTERSTATE 94

46mm	Indiana/Michigan state line
43mm	Welcome Ctr wb, **full facilities, info, litter barrels, petwalk, , , vending**
40b a	US 20, US 35, to Michigan City, **N**, **S** Speedway/dsl
34b a	US 421, to Michigan City, **N** BP/dsl, Family Express/e85, Marathon, Speedway/dsl, Speedway/White Castle/dsl, Arby's, Baskin-Robbins/Dunkin', Buffalo Wild Wings, Burger King, Chili's, Chipotle, Crawford's Eatery, Culver's, Denny's, El Bracero Mexican, Five Guys, Hardee's, IHOP, Jimmy John's, KFC, LJ Silver, McDonald's, Olive Garden, Panda Express, Panera Bread, Pizza Hut, Popeyes, Red Lobster, Sake Asian Fusion, Schoop's Rest., Sonic, Sophia's Pancakes, Starbucks, Subway, Taco Bell, TX Corral, Wendy's, ABC Motel, Baymont Inn, Comfort Suites, Country Inn&Suites, Dunes Inn, Hampton Inn, Holiday Inn Express, MI City Inn, Microtel, Quality Inn, Red Roof Inn, Super 8, Travel Inn, $General, $Tree, Advance Parts, AllDI, AT&T, AutoZone, Belle Tire, BigLots, Discount Tire, Family$, Fannie May Candies, Ford/ Lincoln, GNC, Hobby Lobby, Jo-Ann Fabrics, Kohl's, Lowe's, Meijer/dsl, Menards, Midas, PetSmart, Ross, Save-a-Lot, TJ Maxx, Verizon, Walgreens, Walmart/Subway, **S** Speedway/Subway/dsl/scales/24hr, Buick/Chevrolet/ GMC, Harley-Davidson
29mm	weigh sta both lanes
26b a	IN 49, to Valparaiso , Chesterton, **N** to IN Dunes SP, **S** BP/White Castle, Speedway/dsl, A&W/KFC, Arby's, Burger King, Domino's, DQ, Dunkin', El Salto Mexican, Gelsosomo's Pizza, Gino's Grill, Happy Wok, Jimmy John's, Lemon Tree Grill, Little Caesar's, McDonald's, Papa John's, Pizza Hut, Subway, Taco Bell, Tao Chen's, Third Coast Cafe, Wendy's, Best Western, EconoLodge, Hilton Garden(3mi), Lakeside Inn, Quality Inn, Advance Parts, AutoZone, Jewel-Osco, Sand Cr Camping(5mi), Verizon, Walgreens
22b a	US 20, Burns Harbor, **N** Shell/Subway/dsl/scales/LP, TA/ BP/Country Pride/Pizza Hut/Popeyes/Taco Bell/dsl/scales/ 24hr/@, Comfort Inn, fireworks, **S** Luke/dsl, Pilot/ McDonald's/Subway/dsl/scales/24hr, Camp-Land RV Ctr, Chevrolet, fireworks, Ford, Kia, Nissan, repair, Toyota
19	IN 249, to Port of IN, Portage, **N** Family Express/dsl/e85, DQ, El Salto, Hooters, Longhorn Steaks, McDonald's, Quaker Steak&Lube, Starbucks, Subway, Taco Bell, Affordable Suites, Country Inn&Suites, Bass Pro Shops, **S** Luke, Marathon/dsl, Denny's, Dunkin', Shenanigans Grill, Best Western+, Days Inn, Hampton Inn, Holiday Inn Express, Rodeway Inn, Super 8, Travel Inn
16	access to I-80/90 toll road E, I-90 toll road W, IN 51N, Ripley St, same as 15b a
15.7mm	I-94/I-80 run together wb
15b	US 6W, IN 51, **N** Flying J/Denny's/dsl/scales/24hr/@, Mr Fuel/dsl/scales/24hr,

BURNS HARBOR

IN

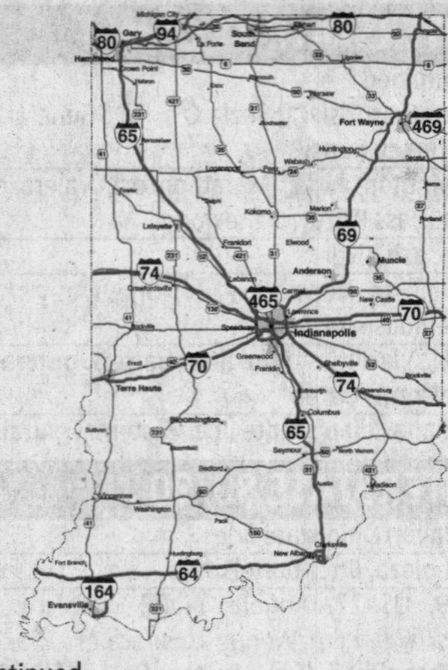

BROADWAY

15b	Continued TA/BP/Popeyes/Subway/dsl/scales/24hr/@, Wing Wah, Blue Beacon, Blue Beacon
15a	US 6E, IN 51S, to US 20, **S** GoLo, Road Ranger/Pilot/ Subway/dsl/scales/24hr, Shell/Luke, Burger King, DQ, Dunkin', LJ Silver, Papa John's, Ruben's Café, Wendy's, Ace Hardware, Walgreens
13	Central Ave(from eb)
12b	I-65 N, to Gary and toll road
12a	I-65 S(from wb), to Indianapolis
11	I-65 S(from eb)
10b a	IN 53, Broadway, **N** Clark, Tommy's Philly Steak, **S** GoLo, Checkers, DQ
9	Grant St, **N** Clark, $General, $Tree, Advance Parts, County Mkt Foods/gas, Walgreens, **S** Citgo, Love's/ Denny's/dsl/scales/LP/24hr/@, Petro/Iron Skillet/Pizza Hut/ dsl/scales/24hr, Speedway/dsl, Burger King, Dunkin', McDonald's, Subway, $Tree, AllDI, AutoZone, Firestone/ auto, Midas
6	Burr St, **N** Pilot/Subway/dsl/scales/24hr/@, TA/Country Pride/Pizza Hut/Taco Bell/dsl/scales/24hr/@, J&J Fish & Chicken, Philly Steaks, Rico's Pizza, SpeedCo, **S** GoLo, Mr Fuel/dsl/24hr
5	IN 912, Cline Ave, **S** BP, Speedway/dsl, Arby's, Culver's, DQ, Dunkin', Jedi's Garden Rest., KFC, McDonald's, Pizza Hut, Popeyes, Subway, Taco Bell, Wendy's, White Castle, Best Western, Hometowne Lodge, Motel 6, $Tree, Family$, Fannie May Candies
3	Kennedy Ave, **N** GoLo, Speedway, Burger King, Domino's, Dunkin'/Baskin Robbins, McDonald's, repair, Walgreens, **S** IN Welcome Ctr, Sixers, Buffalo Wild Wings, Cracker Barrel, Squigi's Pizza, Subway, Wendy's, Courtyard, Fairfield Inn, Hampton Inn, Holiday Inn Express, Residence Inn, USPO
2	US 41S, IN 152N, Indianapolis Blvd, **N** GoLo, Luke, SavAStop, Dunkin', House Of Pizza, Papa John's, Pepe's Mexican, Petros Rest., Pizza Hut, Popeyes, Rally's, Schoop's Burgers, Subway, Taco Bell, Wendy's, Wheel Rest., CarX, Chevrolet, Family$, Midas, vet, **S** Pilot/dsl/scales/24hr, JJ Fish, Starbucks, White Castle, Comfort Inn, AllDI, Cabela's, Walmart/Subway
1	US 41N, Calumet Ave, **N** Speedway/dsl, Baskin Robbins/Dunkin', Walgreens, **S** BP, CT Fuel, GoLo, Marathon, Arby's, Baskin-Robbins/Dunkin', Boston Mkt, Burger King, Canton House Chinese, Chipotle, Edwardo's Pizza, Five Guys, Fortune House, Munster Gyros, Panera Bread, Pizza Hut, Subway, Taco Bell, Wendy's, $Tree, AT&T, Jewel-Osco, Staples, Target, URGENT CARE, Verizon

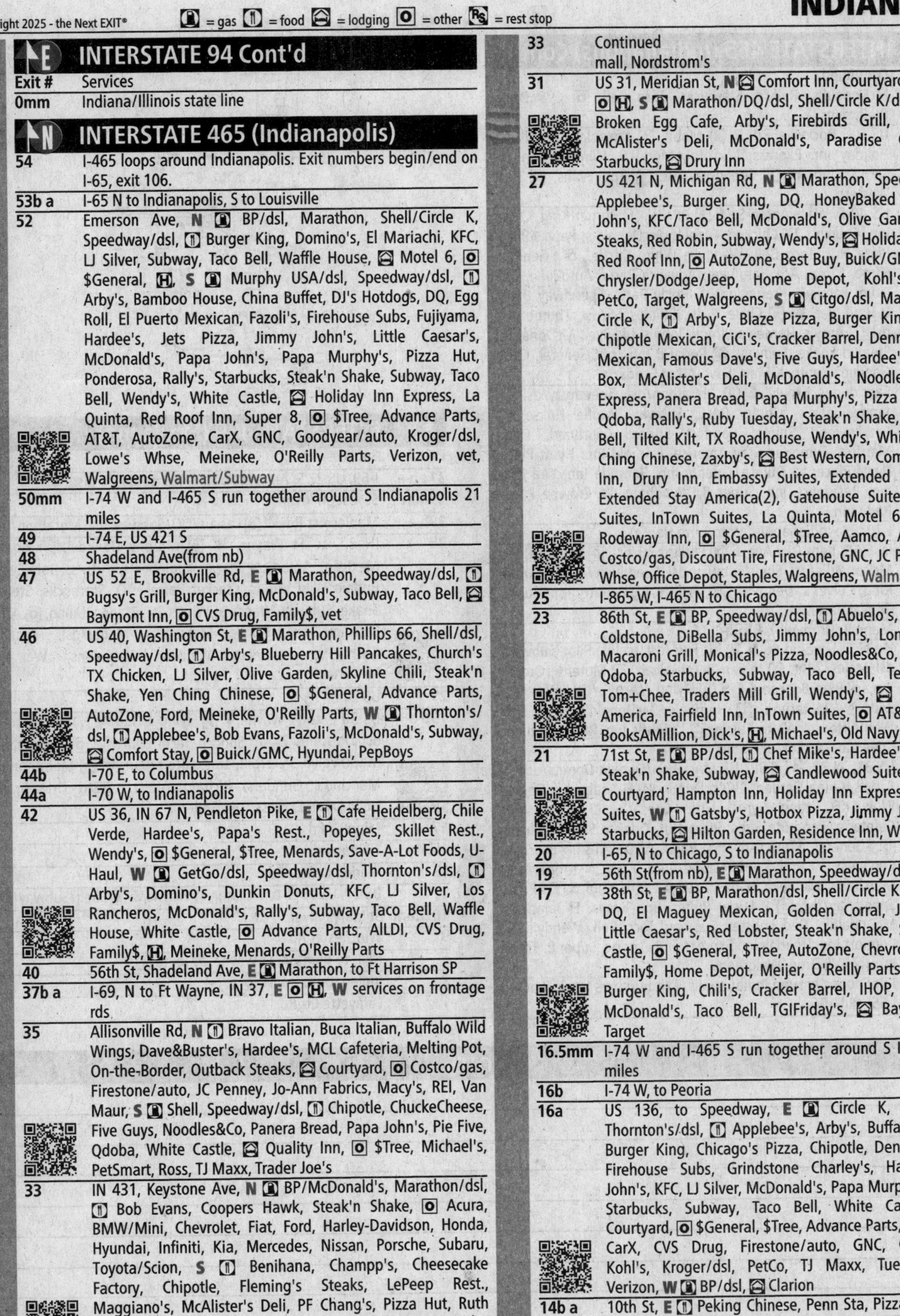

INTERSTATE 94 Cont'd

Exit #	Services
0mm	Indiana/Illinois state line

INTERSTATE 465 (Indianapolis)

Exit #	Services
54	I-465 loops around Indianapolis. Exit numbers begin/end on I-65, exit 106.
53b a	I-65 N to Indianapolis, S to Louisville
52	Emerson Ave, **N** [gas] BP/dsl, Marathon, Shell/Circle K, Speedway/dsl, [food] Burger King, Domino's, El Mariachi, KFC, LJ Silver, Subway, Taco Bell, Waffle House, [lodging] Motel 6, [other] $General, [H], **S** [gas] Murphy USA/dsl, Speedway/dsl, [food] Arby's, Bamboo House, China Buffet, DJ's Hotdogs, DQ, Egg Roll, El Puerto Mexican, Fazoli's, Firehouse Subs, Fujiyama, Hardee's, Jets Pizza, Jimmy John's, Little Caesar's, McDonald's, Papa John's, Papa Murphy's, Pizza Hut, Ponderosa, Rally's, Starbucks, Steak'n Shake, Subway, Taco Bell, Wendy's, White Castle, [lodging] Holiday Inn Express, La Quinta, Red Roof Inn, Super 8, [other] $Tree, Advance Parts, AT&T, AutoZone, CarX, GNC, Goodyear/auto, Kroger/dsl, Lowe's Whse, Meineke, O'Reilly Parts, Verizon, vet, Walgreens, Walmart/Subway
50mm	I-74 W and I-465 S run together around S Indianapolis 21 miles
49	I-74 E, US 421 S
48	Shadeland Ave(from nb)
47	US 52 E, Brookville Rd, **E** [gas] Marathon, Speedway/dsl, [food] Bugsy's Grill, Burger King, McDonald's, Subway, Taco Bell, [lodging] Baymont Inn, [other] CVS Drug, Family$, vet
46	US 40, Washington St, **E** [gas] Marathon, Phillips 66, Shell/dsl, Speedway/dsl, [food] Arby's, Blueberry Hill Pancakes, Church's TX Chicken, LJ Silver, Olive Garden, Skyline Chili, Steak'n Shake, Yen Ching Chinese, [other] $General, Advance Parts, AutoZone, Ford, Meineke, O'Reilly Parts, **W** [gas] Thornton's/dsl, [food] Applebee's, Bob Evans, Fazoli's, McDonald's, Subway, [lodging] Comfort Stay, [other] Buick/GMC, Hyundai, PepBoys
44b	I-70 E, to Columbus
44a	I-70 W, to Indianapolis
42	US 36, IN 67 N, Pendleton Pike, **E** [food] Cafe Heidelberg, Chile Verde, Hardee's, Papa's Rest., Popeyes, Skillet Rest., Wendy's, [other] $General, $Tree, Menards, Save-A-Lot Foods, U-Haul, **W** [gas] GetGo/dsl, Speedway/dsl, Thornton's/dsl, [food] Arby's, Domino's, Dunkin Donuts, KFC, LJ Silver, Los Rancheros, McDonald's, Rally's, Subway, Taco Bell, Waffle House, White Castle, [other] Advance Parts, AllDI, CVS Drug, Family$, [H], Meineke, Menards, O'Reilly Parts
40	56th St, Shadeland Ave, **E** [gas] Marathon, to Ft Harrison SP
37b a	I-69, N to Ft Wayne, IN 37, **E** [other] [H], **W** services on frontage rds
35	Allisonville Rd, **N** [food] Bravo Italian, Buca Italian, Buffalo Wild Wings, Dave&Buster's, Hardee's, MCL Cafeteria, Melting Pot, On-the-Border, Outback Steaks, [lodging] Courtyard, [other] Costco/gas, Firestone/auto, JC Penney, Jo-Ann Fabrics, Macy's, REI, Van Maur, **S** [gas] Shell, Speedway/dsl, [food] Chipotle, ChuckeCheese, Five Guys, Noodles&Co, Panera Bread, Papa John's, Pie Five, Qdoba, White Castle, [lodging] Quality Inn, [other] $Tree, Michael's, PetSmart, Ross, TJ Maxx, Trader Joe's
33	IN 431, Keystone Ave, **N** [gas] BP/McDonald's, Marathon/dsl, [food] Bob Evans, Coopers Hawk, Steak'n Shake, [other] Acura, BMW/Mini, Chevrolet, Fiat, Ford, Harley-Davidson, Honda, Hyundai, Infiniti, Kia, Mercedes, Nissan, Porsche, Subaru, Toyota/Scion, **S** [food] Benihana, Champp's, Cheesecake Factory, Chipotle, Fleming's Steaks, LePeep Rest., Maggiano's, McAlister's Deli, PF Chang's, Pizza Hut, Ruth Chris Steaks, Seasons 52, Starbucks, Sullivan's Steaks, TGIFriday's, [lodging] Hyatt Place, Marriott, Sheraton, [other] Kohl's,
33	Continued mall, Nordstrom's
31	US 31, Meridian St, **N** [lodging] Comfort Inn, Courtyard, Holiday Inn, [other] [H], **S** [gas] Marathon/DQ/dsl, Shell/Circle K/dsl, [food] Another Broken Egg Cafe, Arby's, Firebirds Grill, Granite City, McAlister's Deli, McDonald's, Paradise Cafe Bakery, Starbucks, [lodging] Drury Inn
27	US 421 N, Michigan Rd, **N** [gas] Marathon, Speedway/dsl, [food] Applebee's, Burger King, DQ, HoneyBaked Ham, Jimmy John's, KFC/Taco Bell, McDonald's, Olive Garden, Outback Steaks, Red Robin, Subway, Wendy's, [lodging] Holiday Inn Express, Red Roof Inn, [other] AutoZone, Best Buy, Buick/GMC, Chevrolet, Chrysler/Dodge/Jeep, Home Depot, Kohl's, Marshall's, PetCo, Target, Walgreens, **S** [gas] Citgo/dsl, Marathon, Shell/Circle K, [food] Arby's, Blaze Pizza, Burger King, Chick-fil-A, Chipotle Mexican, CiCi's, Cracker Barrel, Denny's, El Meson Mexican, Famous Dave's, Five Guys, Hardee's, Jack-in-the-Box, McAlister's Deli, McDonald's, Noodles&Co, Panda Express, Panera Bread, Papa Murphy's, Pizza Hut, Popeyes, Qdoba, Rally's, Ruby Tuesday, Steak'n Shake, Subway, Taco Bell, Tilted Kilt, TX Roadhouse, Wendy's, White Castle, Yen Ching Chinese, Zaxby's, [lodging] Best Western, Comfort Inn, Days Inn, Drury Inn, Embassy Suites, Extended Stay America, Extended Stay America(2), Gatehouse Suites, Homewood Suites, InTown Suites, La Quinta, Motel 6, Quality Inn, Rodeway Inn, [other] $General, $Tree, Aamco, AllDI, BigLots, Costco/gas, Discount Tire, Firestone, GNC, JC Penney, Lowe's Whse, Office Depot, Staples, Walgreens, Walmart
25	I-865 W, I-465 N to Chicago
23	86th St, **E** [gas] BP, Speedway/dsl, [food] Abuelo's, Arby's, Chili's, Coldstone, DiBella Subs, Jimmy John's, Longhorn Steaks, Macaroni Grill, Monical's Pizza, Noodles&Co, Panera Bread, Qdoba, Starbucks, Subway, Taco Bell, Ted's MT Grill, Tom+Chee, Traders Mill Grill, Wendy's, [lodging] Extended Stay America, Fairfield Inn, InTown Suites, [other] AT&T, Big-O Tires, BooksAMillion, Dick's, [H], Michael's, Old Navy, PetSmart
21	71st St, **E** [gas] BP/dsl, [food] Chef Mike's, Hardee's, McDonald's, Steak'n Shake, Subway, [lodging] Candlewood Suites, Clarion Inn, Courtyard, Hampton Inn, Holiday Inn Express, TownePlace Suites, **W** [food] Gatsby's, Hotbox Pizza, Jimmy John's, LePeep, Starbucks, [lodging] Hilton Garden, Residence Inn, Wingate Inn
20	I-65, N to Chicago, S to Indianapolis
19	56th St(from nb), **E** [gas] Marathon, Speedway/dsl
17	38th St, **E** [gas] BP, Marathon/dsl, Shell/Circle K, Speedway, [food] DQ, El Maguey Mexican, Golden Corral, Jack-in-the-Box, Little Caesar's, Red Lobster, Steak'n Shake, Subway, White Castle, [other] $General, $Tree, AutoZone, Chevrolet, CVS Drug, Family$, Home Depot, Meijer, O'Reilly Parts, **W** [food] Arby's, Burger King, Chili's, Cracker Barrel, IHOP, Jersey Mike's, McDonald's, Taco Bell, TGIFriday's, [lodging] Baymont Inn, [other] Target
16.5mm	I-74 W and I-465 S run together around S Indianapolis 21 miles
16b	I-74 W, to Peoria
16a	US 136, to Speedway, **E** [gas] Circle K, Shell/Circle K, Thornton's/dsl, [food] Applebee's, Arby's, Buffalo Wild Wings, Burger King, Chicago's Pizza, Chipotle, Denny's, El Rodeo, Firehouse Subs, Grindstone Charley's, Hardee's, Jimmy John's, KFC, LJ Silver, McDonald's, Papa Murphy's, Pizza Hut, Starbucks, Subway, Taco Bell, White Castle, [lodging] $Inn, Courtyard, [other] $General, $Tree, Advance Parts, AT&T, Big Lots, CarX, CVS Drug, Firestone/auto, GNC, Goodyear/auto, Kohl's, Kroger/dsl, PetCo, TJ Maxx, Tuesday Morning, Verizon, **W** [gas] BP/dsl, [lodging] Clarion
14b a	10th St, **E** [food] Peking Chinese, Penn Sta, Pizza Hut, Wendy's, [other] [H], Lowe's Whse, Walmart Mkt, **W** [gas] Shell/Circle K, Speedway/dsl, [food] Arby's, Fazoli's, Flapjacks, Marco's Pizza,

IN

= gas = food = lodging = other = rest stop

INTERSTATE 465 (Indianapolis) Cont'd

Exit	Services
14b a	Continued McDonald's, Rally's, Starbucks, Taco Bell, CVS Drug, Walgreens
13b a	US 36, Rockville Rd, E Mobil, Kazablanka Grill, Holiday Inn Express, Microtel, Motel 6, Wingate Inn, Sam's Club, W Speedway/dsl, Bob Evans, Best Western
12b a	US 40 E, Washington St, E BP/dsl, Burger King, China Inn, Church's TX Chicken, Fazoli's, McDonald's, Papa John's, Pizza Hut, Taco Bell, Wendy's, White Castle, $General, $Tree, $Tree, Ace Hardware, Advance Parts, AutoZone, CVS Drug, Family$, Kroger/gas, O'Reilly Parts, Speedway Parts, U-Haul, vet, W Circle K/dsl, Phillips 66/dsl, Thornton's/dsl, Arby's, Hardee's, Jimmy John's, LJ Silver, McDonald's, Steak'n Shake, Subway, Regal 8 Inn, $General, CarX, Goodyear/auto, K-Mart, Save-A-Lot Foods
11b a	Sam Jones Expwy, E Marathon/dsl, Speedway/dsl, Jimmy John's, Library Rest., Subway, Waffle House, Candlewood Suites, Comfort Suites, Courtyard, Delta Marriott, Extended Stay America, Fairfield Inn, Hyatt Place, Hyatt Place, La Quinta, Quality Inn, Ramada Inn, Red Roof Inn, Residence Inn, Super 8, Wyndham, W Crowne Plaza, Radisson
9b a	I-70, E to Indianapolis, W to Terre Haute
8	IN 67 S, Kentucky Ave, E Phillips 66/dsl, H, W BP/McDonald's/dsl, Shell/Subway/dsl, Speedway/dsl, Burger King, Culver's, Denny's, KFC, Rally's, Country Inn&Suites, Walmart Mkt
7	Mann Rd(from wb), E H
4	IN 37 S, Harding St, N Mr Fuel/dsl/scales, Pilot/Subway/dsl/scales/24hr, Indian & American, Motel 6, Quality Inn, Blue Beacon, H, S Flying J/Arby's/dsl/LP/scales/24hr/@, Marathon, Hardee's, McDonald's, Taco Bell, Waffle House, White Castle, Knight's Inn, Freightliner, SpeedCo, TruckoMat/scales
2b a	US 31, IN 37, N BP/dsl, Marathon/Dunkin Donuts/dsl, Arby's, China Garden, CiCi's, Domino's, El Azabache, Golden Wok, KFC, King Gyros, Little Caesar's, LJ Silver, MCL Cafeteria, Penn Sta Subs, Pizza Hut, Qdoba, Steak'n Shake, $General, $Tree, Advance Parts, AlLDI, AT&T, AutoZone, CarQuest, Family$, Firestone/auto, GNC, Kroger/gas, Marshall's, Meineke, Midas, Save-A-Lot, U-Haul, S BP/dsl, Speedway/dsl, 8 Lucky Buffet, Bob Evans, El Jalapeño, McDonald's, Red Lobster, Subway, Taco Bell, Wendy's, Comfort Inn, Holiday Inn Express, Indy Lodge, Super 8, Travel Inn, CVS Drug, Walgreens
0	I-465 loops around Indianapolis. Exit numbers begin/end on I-65, exit 106.

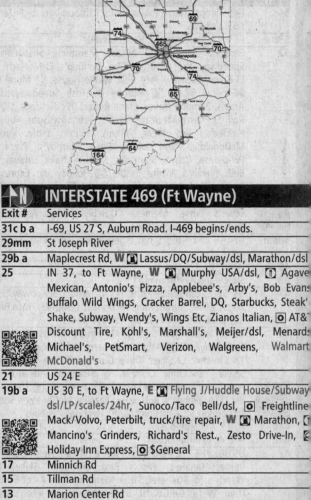

IN

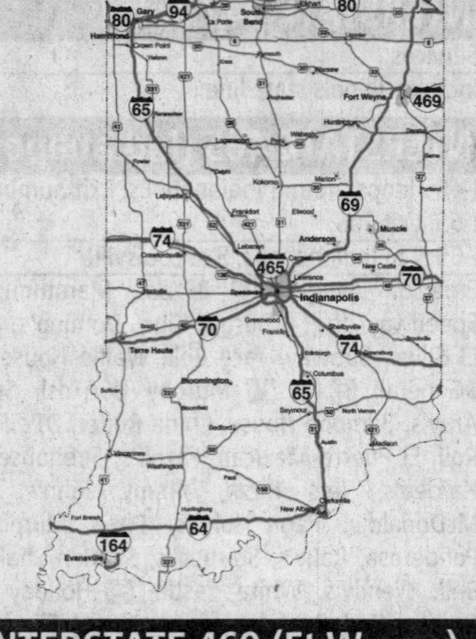

INTERSTATE 469 (Ft Wayne)

FT WAYNE

Exit #	Services
31c b a	I-69, US 27 S, Auburn Road. I-469 begins/ends.
29mm	St Joseph River
29b a	Maplecrest Rd, W Lassus/DQ/Subway/dsl, Marathon/dsl
25	IN 37, to Ft Wayne, W Murphy USA/dsl, Agave Mexican, Antonio's Pizza, Applebee's, Arby's, Bob Evans Buffalo Wild Wings, Cracker Barrel, DQ, Starbucks, Steak' Shake, Subway, Wendy's, Wings Etc, Zianos Italian, AT&T Discount Tire, Kohl's, Marshall's, Meijer/dsl, Menards Michael's, PetSmart, Verizon, Walgreens, Walmart McDonald's
21	US 24 E
19b a	US 30 E, to Ft Wayne, E Flying J/Huddle House/Subway dsl/LP/scales/24hr, Sunoco/Taco Bell/dsl, Freightline Mack/Volvo, Peterbilt, truck/tire repair, W Marathon, Mancino's Grinders, Richard's Rest., Zesto Drive-In, Holiday Inn Express, $General
17	Minnich Rd
15	Tillman Rd
13	Marion Center Rd
11	US 27, US 33 S, to Decatur, Ft Wayne, E Shell/Subway/dsl
10.5mm	St Marys River
9	Winchester Rd
6	IN 1, to Bluffton, Ft Wayne, W to
2	Indianapolis Rd, W to
1	Lafayette Ctr Rd

NOTES

IOWA

INTERSTATE 29

Exit #	Services
152mm	Iowa/South Dakota state line, Big Sioux River
151	IA 12 N, Riverside Blvd, **E** Casey's, $General, Ace Hardware, Fareway Foods, Pecaut Nature Ctr, Riverside Park, to Stone SP, War Eagle Park
149	Hamilton Blvd, **E** Sinclair, Horizon Rest., JiffyLube, to Briar Cliff Coll, **W Iowa Welcome Ctr sb, full facilities,** CRAVE Rest., Hilton Garden, Riverboat Museum
148	US 77 S, to S Sioux City, Nebraska, **W** Casey's, Conoco/dsl, Sam's, DQ, Jimmy John's, La Morena, McDonald's, Mi Familia, Mi Rancherita, Ostión Grill, Pizza Hut, Taco Bell, Budget Inn, Marriott, Regency Inn, Advance Parts, camping/picnic area, Family$, O'Reilly Parts
147b	US 20 bus, Sioux City, **E** Kum&Go/dsl, Arby's, Burger King, Chili's, Famous Dave's BBQ, Hardee's, IHOP, Perkins, avid hotel, Hard Rock Hotel, Holiday Inn, Stoney Creek Inn, Chevrolet, Speedy Lube, USPO, Walgreens
147a	Floyd Blvd, **E** Sinclair/dsl, Home Depot
146.5mm	Floyd River
144b	I-129 W, US 20 W, US 75 S
144a	US 20 E, US 75 N, to Ft Dodge, **E** Casey's, A&W/LJ Silver, Applebee's, Buffalo Wild Wings, Burger King, Chick-fil-A, Chipotle, Hardee's, HuHot Chinese, Japanese Steaks, Jimmy John's, McDonald's, Mr Stirfry, Old Chicago, Olive Garden, Outback Steaks, Panda Express, Panera Bread, Pizza Plaza, Qdoba, Red Lobster, Red Robin, Starbucks, TX Roadhouse, Wheelhouse Grill, Comfort Inn, Hampton Inn, Holiday Inn Express, Quality Inn, Staybridge Suites, Wingate Inn, AllDI, Barnes&Noble, Best Buy, Buick/Honda, Fareway Mkt, Hobby Lobby, Hy-Vee Foods/gas, JC Penney, Jiffy Lube, Kohl's, Lowe's, Marshall's, Michael's, PetSmart, Scheel's, Staples, Target, URGENT CARE, Verizon
143	US 75 N, Singing Hills Blvd, **E** Murphy USA/dsl, Pilot/Burger King/Subway/dsl/scales/24hr, Culver's, Fazoli's, Four Bros Grill, Hunan Palace, KFC, McDonald's, Monterrey Mexican, Popeyes, Taco Bell, Taco John's, AmericInn, Days Inn, Victorian Inn, $Tree, AT&T, Buick/Cadillac/GMC, Ford/Lincoln, Kia, Mazda, Nissan, Sam's Club/gas, Sgt Floyd Mon, Subaru, Toyota/Scion, URGENT CARE, VW, Walmart/auto, **W** Love's/Subway/dsl/scales/24hr, Wendy's, Super 8, Peterbilt, truckwash/repair
141	D38, Sioux Gateway Airport, **E** Cenex, Mike's Minimart, Shell/dsl, Aggies Rest., Pizza Ranch, Subway, Rodeway Inn, $General, Fareway Mkt, **W** Sioux City Inn, museum
139mm	**full facilities, info, litter barrels, both lanes, RV dump, wireless internet**
135	Port Neal Landing
134	Salix, **W** camping
132mm	weigh sta sb, rest area parking only nb, picnic tables, litter barrels
127	IA 141, Sloan, **E** Casey's/dsl, Kum&Go/Subway/dsl, Homestead Inn, WinnaVegas Inn, $General, RV park, **W** to Winnebago Indian Res/hotel/casino(3mi)
120	to Whiting, **W** camping
112	IA 175, Onawa, **E** Cenex/dsl, Phillips 66/Subway/dsl, DQ, McDonald's, Best Value Inn, DG Mkt, NAPA, On-Ur-Wa RV Park, repair, **W** Keel Boat Exhibit, KOA, Lewis&Clark SP
110mm	**full facilities, info, litter barrels, petwalk, both lanes, RV dump, wireless internet**

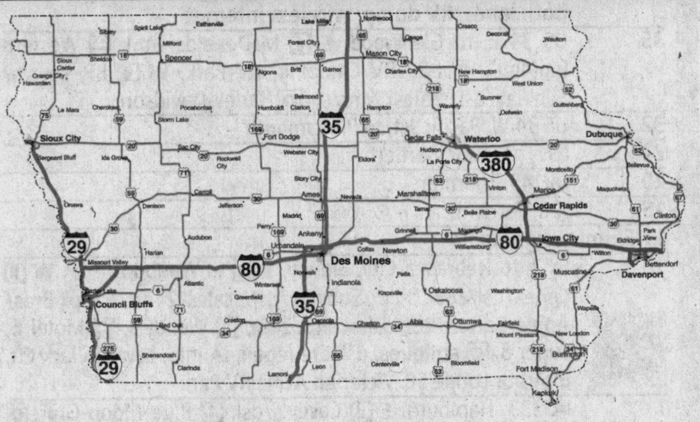

BLENCOE

Exit #	Services
105	E60, Blencoe
96mm	Little Sioux River
95	F 20, Little Sioux, **E** to Loess Hills SF, **W** Woodland RV Park
92mm	Soldier River
91.5mm	rest area both lanes, parking only, litter barrels
89	IA 127, Mondamin, **E** Jiffy Mart/dsl
82	F50, Modale, **W** Heartland/dsl
79mm	**full facilities, info, litter barrels, both lanes, RV dump, wireless internet**
75	US 30, Missouri Valley, **E** Shell/dsl/24hr, Arby's, McDonald's, Penny's Diner, Subway, Travelodge, farm museum, Steamboat Exhibit, **W** PetroMart/dsl, Burger King, Taco John's, Best Value Inn, Happy Valley Inn, Super 8, Buick/Chevrolet
72.5mm	Boyer River
72	IA 362, Loveland, **E** Desoto/dsl, **W** to Wilson Island SP(6mi)

COUNCIL BLUFFS

Exit #	Services
71	I-680 E, to Des Moines, **I-29 S & I-680 W run together 10 mi.**
66	Honey Creek , **E** Hitchcock Tent Camping
61b	I-680 W, to N Omaha, **I-29 N & I-680 E run together 10 mi, W** Mormon Trail Ctr
61a	IA 988, to Crescent, **E** Casey's/dsl
56	IA 192 S(sb only, exits left), Council Bluffs, **E** URGENT CARE, Walmart
55	N 25th, Council Bluffs, **E** Cenex/dsl, Shell, Mo Fish, URGENT CARE, Walmart/Subway
54b	N 35th St(from nb), Council Bluffs
54a	G Ave(from sb), Council Bluffs, **E** Kwik Shop
53b	I-480 W, US 6, to Omaha(exits left from nb)
53a	9th Ave, S 37th Ave, Council Bluffs, **E** Mega Saver, Shell, BridgePointe Inn, **W** Harrah's Hotel/Casino
52	Nebraska Ave, **E** Casey's/dsl, Home Team Cookout, Hooters, Quaker Steak, Comfort Suites, Courtyard, Holiday Inn Express, Microtel, My Place Hotel, SpringHill Suites, Woodspring Suites, Bass Pro Shops, **W** AmeriStar Hotel/casino, Hampton Inn, Holiday Inn
51	I-80 W, to Omaha
50mm	I-29 and I-80 run together 3 miles. See IA I-80 exits 1-3.
48	I-80 E(from nb), to Des Moines
47	US 275, IA 92, Lake Manawa, **E** Iowa School for the Deaf, **W** Tesla EVC, Buffalo Wild Wings, Firehouse Subs, Freddy's, Longhorn Steaks, McAlisters, Olive Garden, Panda Express, Panera Bread, Pepperjax Grill, Pizza Ranch, Qdoba, Red Anchor Seafood, Starbucks, $Tree, AT&T, Dick's, Hobby Lobby, Old Navy, PetSmart, Target, TJ Maxx, Verizon
42	IA 370, to Bellevue, **W** K&B Saddlery, to Offutt AFB, truck parts

= gas = food = lodging = other = rest stop

INTERSTATE 29 Cont'd

BARTLETT

Exit #	Services
38mm	**full facilities, info, litter barrels, petwalk, both lanes, RV dump, wireless internet**
35	US 34 E, to Glenwood, E McDonalds(4mi), Western Inn(4mi), I-29 RV Camping, RV Park, W BP, Love's/Subway/dsl/scales/24hr/@, Harley-Davidson
32	US 34 W, Pacific Jct, to Plattsmouth
24	L31, to Tabor, Bartlett
20	IA 145, Thurman
15	J26, Percival
11.5mm	weigh sta nb
10	IA 2, to Nebraska City, Sidney, E to Waubonsie SP, W Cenex/dsl/E85, Pilot/Subway/dsl/scales/24hr, Sapp Bros/Apple Barrel Rest/dsl/scales/24hr, Wendy's, Motel 6, Super 8, antiques, dsl/tire repair, IA Info, Lewis&Clark Ctr, to Arbor Lodge SP, Victorian Acres RV Park
1	IA 333, Hamburg, E Casey's/dsl, Blue Moon Grill, $General, H, NAPA
0mm	Iowa/Missouri state line

INTERSTATE 35

FOREST CITY · BELMOND · RANDALL

Exit #	Services
219mm	Iowa/Minnesota state line
214	rd 105, to Northwood, Lake Mills, **Welcome Ctr both lanes, full facilities, litter barrels, petwalk, RV dump, vending, wifi**, E Royal Motel(7mi), W BP/Burger King/dsl, Kum&Go/dsl, Country Inn&Suites, Holiday Inn Express, casino
212mm	weigh sta sb, rest area nb, picnic tables, litter barrels
208	rd A38, to Joice, Kensett, E windmills
203	IA 9, to Manly, Forest City, W to Pilot Knob SP
202mm	Winnebago River
197	rd B20, E to Lime Creek Nature Ctr
196mm	rest area both lanes, litter barrels, parking only
194	US 18, to Mason City, Clear Lake, E Kwik Star/dsl/24hr, Fairfield Inn, Chevrolet, Freightliner, H(8mi), W Casey's/dsl, Kum&Go/dsl, Pilot/Subway/dsl/scales, Arby's, Bennigan's, Culver's, DQ, KFC/Taco Bell, McDonald's, Perkins, Wendy's, AmericInn, Best Western, Best Western, Microtel, Ford
193	rd B35, to Mason City, Emery, E Kum&Go/Taco John's/dsl/e85, Super 8, truckwash, W Seven Stars Rest., to Clear Lake SP
190	US 18, rd 27 E, to Mason City
188	rd B43, to Burchinal, E Corn Patch RV Park
182	rd B60, to Rockwell, Swaledale
180	rd B65, to Thornton, W Cenex
176	rd C13, to Sheffield, Belmond
170	rd C25, to Alexander
165	IA 3, E Dudley's Corner/Rest./dsl
159	rd C47, Dows, **both lanes, full facilities, info, litter barrels, petwalk, RV dump, vending, wifi**, W BP/Arby's/Godfather's/dsl/24hr, Tesla EVC
155mm	Iowa River
151	rd R75, to Woolstock
147	rd D20, to US 20 E
144	rd D25, Williams, E Jay Bros Trkstp/cafe/dsl, Best Western, Circle S Motel, W Flying J/Subway/dsl/scales/24hr
142b a	US 20, to Webster City, Ft Dodge
139	rd D41, to Kamrar
133	IA 175, to Jewell, Ellsworth, W Kum&Go/Subway/dsl, Love's/dsl/scales/24hr/@
128	rd D65, to Stanhope, Randall, W to Little Wall Lake Pk
124	rd 115, Story City, E Kwik Star/dsl/scales/24hr, W Casey's, Kum&Go/dsl, DQ, McDonald's, Pizza Ranch, Subway,

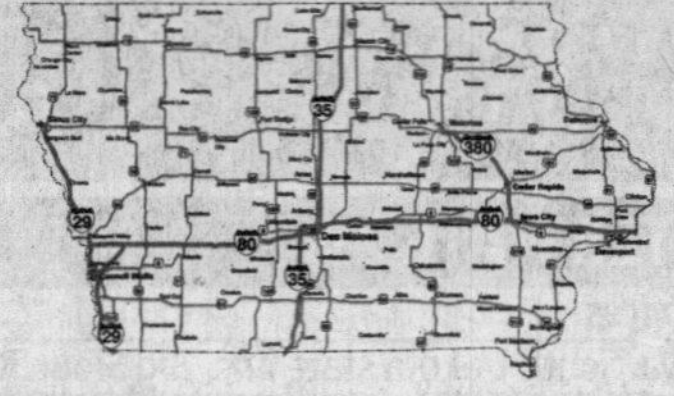

AMES · ANKENY

Exit #	Services
124	Continued Best Value, Comfort Inn, Super 8, $General, antiques, Ford, Wild Oak Camping
123	rd E18, to Roland, McCallsburg
121mm	prairie area sb
120mm	**full facilities, info, litter barrels, nb, RV dump/scenic prairie area sb, vending, wireless internet**
119mm	**full facilities, litter barrels, sb, RV dump, vending, wireless internet**
116	rd E29, to Story, W to Story Co Conservation Ctr
113	13th St, Ames, W Kum&Go/dsl/E85, Phillips 66/Arby's, Burger King, Jimmy John's, Pizza Ranch, Holiday Inn Express, Quality Inn, Harley-Davidson, H, to ISU, to USDA Vet Labs
111b a	US 30, to Nevada, Ames, E Twin Acres Campground(11mi), W Kum&Go/DQ/Subway/dsl/EVC, Kwik Star/dsl, Azteca Mexican, Flip'n Jacks, AmericInn, Baymont Inn, Country Inn&Suites, EconoLodge, Fairfield Inn, Hampton Inn, Microtel, Red Roof, SpringHill Suites, Super 8, TownePlace Suites, Chrysler/Dodge/Jeep, to ISU
109mm	S Skunk River
106mm	weigh sta sb, rest area nb, no restrooms
102	IA 210, to Slater, E Kum&Go/dsl, W Subway
100mm	**both lanes, full facilities, litter barrels, petwalk**
96	to Elkhart, W to Big Creek SP, to Saylorville Lake
94	NE 36th St, Ankeny, E Costco/gas, W Kum&Go/dsl, Subway, golf
92	1st St, Ankeny, W Casey's/dsl, Kum&Go, QT, Applebee's, Arby's, Cazador Mexican, Fazoli's, Guadalajara Mexican, Jimmy Johns, KFC, Krispy Kreme, Tokyo Steaks, Comfort Inn, Days Inn, Quality Inn, Super 8, Wyndham, NAPA/auto, O'Reilly Parts, Tires+
90	IA 160, Ankeny, E Casey's/dsl, Outback Steaks, Waterfront Seafood, AmericInn, Best Western/EVC, Country Inn&Suites, Courtyard, Econolodge, Homewood Suites, La Quinta, My Place Hotel, Sleep Inn, Buick/GMC, W Casey's/dsl, MurphyUSA/dsl, Alohana Hawaiian Grill, B-bops Rest., Buffalo Wild Wings, Burger King, Chick-fil-A, Chili's, China Buffet, Chipotle, Culver's, Five Guys, Fuzzy's Tacos, HuHot Chinese, IHOP, Los Charros Mexican, Maid Rite, Marble Slab, McDonald's, Old Chicago, Olive Garden, Other Place Pizza, Panchero's Mexican, Panda Express, Panera Bread, Pepperjax, Perkins, Starbucks, Subway, Taco Bell, Tasty Tacos, Wendy's, $Tree, AT&T, Best Buy, Big O Tires, Chevrolet, Chrysler/Dodge/Jeep, Duluth Trading, Ford, Home Depot, Kohl's, Menards, Michael's, PetSmart, Sportsman's Warehouse, Staples, Target/Starbucks, TJ Maxx, to Saylorville Lake, Tuffy Auto, Verizon, Walgreens, Walmart
89	Corporate Woods Dr, E Casey's/scales/dsl, Hampton Inn, W Woodspring Suites, F&F/dsl, Sam's Club/dsl
87b a	I-235, I-35 and I-80
86mm	I-35 and I-80 merge for 14 mi around NW Des Moines. See I-80, exits 124-136.
72c	University Ave, E Git'n Go/dsl, Bakers Square, Chick-fil-A, Chili's, Firehouse Subs, Huhot Mongolian, Jason's Deli, KFC, Laughing Crab, Little Caesars, McDonald's, Mi Mexico, Outback Steaks, Starbucks, Courtyard, Days Inn, Sheraton, Super 8, Wildwood Lodge, AT&T, Barnes&Noble, Best Buy, Home Depot, Kohl's, Lowe's, Marshall's, Office Depot,

IA

INTERSTATE 35 Cont'd

72c Continued
PetSmart, Target/Starbucks, Whole Foods Mkt, World Mkt, **W** Hy-Vee, Kum&Go/Burger King, Agave Grill, Biaggi's Rest, Capriotti's Sandwiches, Caribou Coffee, Cooper's Hawk Rest., Cracker Barrel, El Rodeo Mexican, Franka Pizza, Jersey Mike's, Jimmy John's, Other Place Grill, Panera Bread, Wendy's, Z'Marik's Cafe, Best Western, Country Inn&Suites, La Quinta, H, Walgreens

72b I-80 W

72a I-235 E, to Des Moines

70 Civic Pkwy, Mills , **E** Kum&Go/McDonald's, Fire Creek Grill, IHOP, Quiznos, Rosati's Pizza, Steak'n Shake, Sleep Inn, Hy-Vee Foods/gas/EVC, vet, Walgreens, **W** Casey's/dsl, Kum&Go, Abelardo's Mexican, Applebee's, B-Bop's Rest., Banana Leaf Thai, Bar Louie, Blaze Pizza, Bravo Italiana, Buffalo Wild Wings, Cane's, Cheesecake Factory, Chick-fil-A, Chipotle, El Fogon Mexican, Firebird's Grill, Fleming's Rest., Irina's Steaks, Iron Wok, Jimmy John's, McCaliser's Deli, Monterrey Mexican, Noodles&Co, On-the-Border, Panda Express, Panera Bread, PF Chang's, Red Robin, Smoothie King, Starbucks, Tasty Tacos, TX Roadhouse, Wellman's Grill, Courtyard, Drury Inn, Element Hotel, Hampton Inn, Hilton Garden, Homewood Suites, Residence Inn, The Rewind Hotel, TownePlace Suites, $Tree, ALDI, Barnes&Noble, Best Buy, Costco/gas, Dick's, Dillards, Firestone/auto, Kohl's, Lowe's, PetCo, REI, Scheel's Sports, Target/Starbucks, TJ Maxx, Trader Joe's, Verizon, Walmart

69b a Grand Ave, W Des Moines, **W** Kum&Go

68.5mm Racoon River

68 IA 5, **E** to , to Walnut Woods SP

65 G14, to Norwalk, Cumming

61mm North River

56 IA 92, to Indianola, Winterset, **W** Kum&Go, Hitchin Post Grill, Good Life RV Ctr

56mm Middle River

53mm rest area nb, litter barrels, no restrooms

52 G50, St Charles, St Marys, **W** Casey's/dsl, $General, to John Wayne Birthplace

51mm rest area sb, litter barrels, no restrooms

47 rd G64, to Truro

45.5mm South River

43 rd 207, New Virginia, **E** Kum&Go/Subway/dsl

36 rd 152, to US 69, **E** Blue Haven Motel, Evergreen Inn, **W** st patrol

34 Clay St, Osceola, **W** Pilot/Subway/dsl/scales/24hr, Lakeside Casino Resort/camping

33 US 34, Osceola, **E** Casey's/dsl/scales, McDonald's, Pizza Hut, Subway, Quality Inn, Super 8, Ford, Goodyear, H, Hy-Vee Foods, O'Reilly Parts, **W** BP/Arby's/dsl, KFC/Taco Bell, AmericInn, Harley-Davidson, Walmart

32mm **full facilities, litter barrels, petwalk, both lanes, RV dump, vending, wireless internet**

31mm parking area sb, weigh sta nb

29 rd H45

22 rd J14, Van Wert

18 rd J20, to Grand River

12 rd 2, Decatur City, Leon, **E** Ted's RV Camping, Little River Inn, H

7.5mm Grand River

7mm **full facilities, info, litter barrels, petwalk, both lanes, RV dump, vending, wireless internet**

4 US 69, to Davis City, Lamoni, **E** to 9 Eagles SP(10mi), **W** Casey's, Kum&Go/dsl/e85, Maid-Rite Cafe, Pizza Hut, Pizza Shack, Subway, Cobblestone Inn, Rodeway Inn,

4 Continued
$General, CarQuest, Hy-Vee Foods, Zoomers RV Ctr

0mm Iowa/Missouri state line

INTERSTATE 80

307mm Iowa/Illinois state line, Mississippi River

306 US 67, to Le Claire, **N** Kwik Star/dsl, Shell/dsl, Breakfast At Berries, Hungry Hobo, McDonald's, Steventon's Rest., Van's Pizza, Comfort Inn, Holiday Inn Express, Fareway Grocery, to Buffalo Bill Museum

301 Middle Rd, to Bettendorf, **N** golf, **S** Kwik Star/dsl, Tesla EVC, Cheesy Cow, Flips Pancakes, Subway, Cambria Hotel, Verizon

300mm **both lanes, full facilities, litter barrels, vending, petwalk, RV dump, wifi**

298 I-74 E, to Peoria, **S** H

295b a US 61, Brady St, to Davenport, **N** BP/dsl, to Scott CP, **S** BP, KwikStar/dsl, Shell, Azteca 1 Mexican, Costa Del Mar Mexican, Cracker Barrel, Freddy's, Happy Joe's Pizza, Hardee's, KFC, Lunardi's Italian, McDonald's, Mo Brady's Steaks, Olive Garden, Panchero's Mexican, Panera Bread, Papa John's, Popeyes, Tantra Asian Bistro, ThunderBay Grille, Baymont Inn, Best Western+, Country Inn&Suites, Holiday Inn Express, Motel 6, Quality Inn, Residence Inn, Super 8, $General, Advance Parts, AutoZone, Campers Inn RV Ctr, Dillard's, Firestone/auto, Honda, Hyundai, Lexus, Menards, NAPA, Nissan, Tires+, vet, Von Maur, VW

292 IA 130 W, Northwest Blvd, **N** Flying J/Denny's/dsl/LP/scales/24hr, Love's/Arby's/dsl/scales/24hr/@, Comfort Inn, Farm&Fleet, Interstate RV Park, Peterbilt, truckwash, **S** BP/McDonald's/dsl, Shell, Machine Shed Rest., Minh Chinese, Pizza Shack, Subway, I-80 Inn & Suites, Freightliner

290 I-280 E, to Rock Island

284 Y40, to Walcott, **N** Pilot/Arby's/dsl/24hr/scales, TA/IA 80/BP/DQ/Pizza Hut/Wendy's/dsl/scales/24hr/@, Tesla EVC, Checkered Flag Grille, Gramma's Rest., Comfort Inn, Blue Beacon, IA 80 Truck-o-Mat, IA 80 Trucking Museum, SpeedCo Lube, tires, **S** Pilot/Subway/dsl/24hr, McDonald's, Days Inn, Cheyenne Camping Ctr, Walcott CP

280 Y30, to Stockton, New Liberty

277 Durant, **S** 5th St Petro/dsl, Casey's/dsl, Subway

271 US 6 W, IA 38 S, to Wilton

270mm **full facilities, info, litter barrels, petwalk, both lanes, RV dump, vending, WiFi**

268mm parking areas

267 IA 38 N, to Tipton, **N** Kum&Go/dsl/e85, Cedar River Camping

266mm Cedar River

265 to Atalissa, **S** ONE9/diesel only/scales/24hr

259 to West Liberty, Springdale, **S** BP/dsl, Little Bear Camping

254 X30, West Branch, **N** BP/Subway/dsl, Hoover NHS, Jack&Jill Foods, USPO, **S** Kum&Go, Casa Tequila Mexican, McDonald's, Days Inn, Chrysler/Dodge/Jeep, vet

249 Herbert Hoover Hwy, **S** Wildwood Smokehouse, golf

246 IA 1, Dodge St, **N** BP/dsl, Jimmy John's, Joensy's, The Highlander, vet, **S** Amoco, Bob's Pizza, Starbucks, Travelodge, Hy-Vee Foods/gas

244 Dubuque St, Iowa City, **N** Coralville Lake, **S** H, to Old Capitol Museum

242 to Coralville, **N** Twelve 01 Kitchen, Hampton Inn, Radisson, **S** Kum&Go/dsl/EVC, 30 Hop Cafe, Applebee's, Blue Agave Tacos, Bruegger's Bagels, Burger King, Casa Azul, DQ, Dunkin', Edge Water Grill, Freddy's,

LAMONI OSCEOLA DURANT IOWA CITY IA

= gas = food = lodging = other = rest stop

INTERSTATE 80 Cont'd

Exit	
242	Continued Hardee's, IA Riverpower Rest., Jethro BBQ, Marquee Pizzaria, McDonald's, Monica's Rest., Panera Bread, Papa John's, Peking Buffet, Perkins, Subway, Wig&Pen Rest., Comfort Inn, Drury Inn, Heartland Inn, Homewood Suites, Hyatt, Quality Inn, Super 7, Super 8, SureStay+, H, Trader Joe's, vet, Von Maur
240	IA 965, to US 6, Coralville, N Liberty, N Casey's/dsl, Kum&Go, Buffalo Wild Wings, Cane's, Cheddar's, Culver's, Estela's Fresh Mex, Jimmy John's, McDonald's, Steak'n Shake, TX Roadhouse, Wendy's, AmericInn, Country Inn&Suites, Mainstay Suites, Costco/gas, Harley-Davidson, Kohl's, Michael's, PetCo, Ross, TJ Maxx, URGENT CARE, Walgreens, Walmart/Subway/auto, S Caribou Coffee, Chili's, Coldstone, Domino's, Five Guys, Food Court, Huhot Mongolian, IHOP, Jimmy John's, Longhorn Steaks, Mellow Mushroom, Noodles&Co, Olive Garden, Panchero's Mexican, Pizza Hut, Popeyes, Red Ginger Japanese, Red Lobster, Subway, Taco John's, Which Wich?, Comfort Suites, Fairfield Inn, Holiday Inn Express, Home2 Suites, Residence Inn, Advance Parts, Barnes&Noble, Best Buy, Dillard's, Discount Tire, Hobby Lobby, HyVee Foods/dsl, JC Penney, Lowe's, Old Navy, Scheel's, Target/Starbucks/CVS, Tires+, U-Haul
239b	I-380 N, US 218 N, to Cedar Rapids
239a	US 218 S
237	Tiffin, N Kum&Go/Subway/dsl, Jon's Rest(seasonal), S Sun& Fun RV Ctr
236mm	**full facilities, litter barrels, petwalk, both lanes, RV dump, vending, wireless internet**
230	W38, to Oxford, N Sleepy Hollow RV Camping, S to Kalona Historical Village
225	US 151 N, W21 S, N to Amana Colonies, AmericInn, S Amoco, Knights Inn
220	IA 149 S, V77 N, to Williamsburg, N BP, Casey's/Landmark Rest./dsl/EVC, Arby's, Bryant's Grill, McDonald's, Subway, Cozy House Inn, Crest Motel, factory outlets/famous brands, Old Navy, Rocky Mtn. Chocolate, S DG Mkt, Williamsburg Tire/auto
216	to Marengo, N Kum&Go/Subway/dsl, H(8mi)
211	to Ladora, Millersburg, S to Lake IA Park
208mm	**full facilities, litter barrels, petwalk, both lanes, RV dump, vending, wireless internet**
205	to Victor
201	IA 21, to Deep River, N Pilot/Subway/dsl/scales/24hr, Pleasant Stay Inn, S KwikStar/Denny's/dsl/scales/24hr/@, truck repair
197	to Brooklyn, N TA/Country Pride/dsl/scales/24hr/@
191	US 63, to Montezuma, S to Diamond Lake SP
182	IA 146, to Grinnell, N Casey's/dsl, Kum&Go/Subway/dsl/24hr, Tesla EVC, Margaritas Mexican, Pizza Ranch, AmericInn, Comfort Inn, Country Inn, Quality Inn, Super 8, $General, $Tree, Chrysler/Dodge/Jeep, HyVee Foods, Verizon, vet, Walmart
180mm	**full facilities, litter barrels, petwalk, playground, both lanes, RV dump(eb) wireless internet, vending, weather info**
179	IA 124, to Oakland Acres, Lynnville
175mm	N Skunk River, N Phillips 66/burgers, Kellogg RV Park
173	IA 224, Kellogg, N Phillips 66/Best Burger/dsl/24hr, Kellogg RV Park, Rock Creek SP(9mi), S Pella Museum
168	SE Beltline Dr, to Newton, N Casey's/dsl, Murphy USA/dsl, Arby's, Biaggio's Italian, Newton, Taco John's, $Tree, KOA(seasonal), Walmart/gas, S BP/dsl, Love's/Chester's/McDonald's/dsl/scales, AmericInn, Cobblestone Inn,

MILLERSBURG · KELLOGG · IA

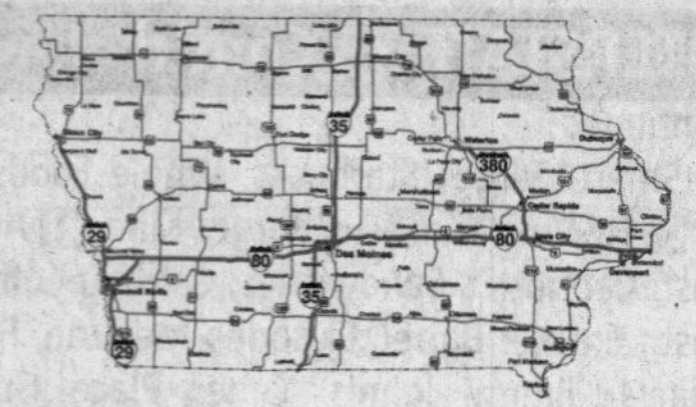

Exit	
168	Continued Iowa Speedway
164	US 6, IA 14, Newton, N Casey's/dsl, Phillips 66/Subwa dsl, Culver's, Hardee's, KFC/Taco Bell, MT Mikes, Okob Grill, Perkins, Pizza Ranch, Days Inn, EconoLodge, Quali Inn, Super 8, H, museum, S Cadillac/Chevrolet, Chrysle Jeep/Dodge, Ford/Lincoln, to Lake Red Rock
159	F48, to Jasper, Baxter
155	IA 117, Colfax, N Phillips 66/McDonald's/dsl, Subwa Colfax Inn, Microtel, S Casey's, Kum&Go/pizza/ds e85/24hr
153mm	S Skunk River
151	weigh sta wb
149	Mitchellville
148mm	**full facilities, litter barrels, petwalk, bo lanes, RV dump, vending, wireless internet**
143	Altoona, S Casey's/dsl/EVC, Kum&Go/dsl, Kwik Star, Tes EVC, Hampton Inn, Holiday Inn Express, RV One Ctr
142b a	US 65, Hubble Ave, Des Moines, S BP, Flying J/Cinnabo dsl/scales/24hr/@, Git'n Go, Tesla EVC, Big Steer Res Burger King, Culver's, Guadalajara, Jethro's BBQ, KFC/Ta Bell, McDonald's, Perkins, Scornovacca's Altoona, Subwa Taco John's, TX Roadhouse, Best Western+, Comfort In La Quinta, Motel 6, My Place, Quality Inn, Super 8, Adventureland Funpark, Blue Beacon, casino, Freightline Peterbilt
141	US 6 W, US 65 S, Pleasant Hill, Des Moines, S Burger She Johnny's Italian, Fairfield Inn, Hyatt Place, Bass P Shops
137b a	I-35 N, I-235 S, to Des Moines
136.5mm	I-80 W and I-35 S run together 14 mi.
136	US 69, E 14th St, Camp Sunnyside, N BP/dsl, Casey's/ds Kwik Star, Budget Inn, Motel 6, Quality Inn, Red Roof Inr antiques, Bauer Tire, S Casey's/dsl, QT/dsl/scales 24hr, Quick Star, Broken Spoke Grill, Chicken Shac Domino's, Fazoli's, Hardees, Iowa Beef Steaks, KF McDonald's, Pueblo Viejo Mexican, Subway, Taco John's, Baymont Inn, Super 8, $General, Advance Parts, AllD AutoZone, CarX, Family$, O'Reilly Parts, truck lube, USPO
135	IA 415, 2nd Ave, Polk City, N Kum&Go/dsl, Tesla EVC, Smokey D's BBQ, antiques, Harley-Davidson, Ryde Trucks, S Git'n Go, QT, NAPA/auto
133mm	Des Moines River
131	IA 28 S, NW 58th St, N Casey's, Hy-Vee/dsl, Bandi Burrito, Cactus Bob's BBQ, Charlotte's Kitchen, Chopsticks, E Mariachi Mexican, Greenbriar Rest., Jimmy John's, Marino' Italian, Pagliai's Pizza, Panera Bread, Sonic, Subway, AmericInn, Ace Hardware, Acura, Audi/VW, Car-X Aut Repair, Hy-Vee Food/dsl, USPO, vet, S Casey's, QT Tobacco Outlet/dsl/LP/24hr, Applebee's, Bennigan's Buffalo Wild Wings, Cajun Belle, Chick-fil-A, Chipotl Mexican, Dunkin, El Patron, Fazoli's, Hardee's, IHOP, KFC McAlister's Deli, McDonald's, McDonald's, Noodles&Co Perkins, Pita Pit, Popeyes, Starbucks, Taco Bell, Taco John's Tullpa Peruvian, Wendy's, Wingstop, EconoLodge, Holiday Inn, Quality Inn, Ramada/Rest., Super 8, $Tree, Advanc Parts, AT&T, Big Lots, Car-X, Discount Tire, Firestone/auto Ford, Goodyear/auto, Kia, Kia/Mitsubishi, Kohl's, Nissan Office Depot, Old Navy, Target/Starbucks, URGENT CARE,

BAXTER · DES MOINES · POLK CITY

CAMP DODGE

INTERSTATE 80 Cont'd

131 Continued Verizon, vet

129 NW 86th St, Camp Dodge, N Amigo Mexican, Cane's, Cozy Cafe, McDonald's, Panchero's Mexican, ShortE's BBQ, Starbucks, Tropical Smoothie, TX Roadhouse, Hilton Garden, Stoney Creek Inn, TownePlace Suites, S Casey's, Git N Go/dsl, Arby's, B-Bops Burgers, Culver's, Friedrich's Coffee, Papa Murphy's, Pizza Ranch, Ruby Tuesday, Subway, Viva Mexican, Fairfield Inn, Hampton Inn, Holiday Inn Express, Microtel, $General, Orange Leaf FoYo, Walgreens

128 NW 100th St, S Kwik Star

127 IA 141 W, Grimes, N QT/dsl, Sinclair/dsl, El Huapango Mexican, Rolling Wok, to Saylorville Lake, Toyota/Scion, S Kum&Go/dsl/e85, McDonald's, CVS Drug, Firestone/auto, Home Depot, Target

126 Douglas Ave, Urbandale, E Casey's/dsl, Kwik Star, EconoLodge, Extended Stay America, Chevrolet, W Kum&Go/dsl, Pilot/Subway/dsl/scales/24hr/@, Cancun Grill

125 US 6, Hickman Rd, E IA Machine Shed Rest., Starbucks, Subway, Clive Hotel, Hotel Renovo, Revel Hotel, CarMax, Honda, Hyundai, Living History Farm Museum, W Kum&Go/dsl, Love's/Denny's/dsl/scales/LP/24hr, Caribou Coffee, ProteinHouse, Chrysler/Dodge/Jeep, Menards

124 (72c from I-35 nb), University Ave, I-80 E and I-35 N run together 14 mi, E Git'n Go/dsl, Bakers Square, Chick-fil-A, Chili's, Firehouse Subs, Huhot Mongolian, Jason's Deli, KFC, Laughing Crab, Little Caesars, McDonald's, Mi Mexico, Outback Steaks, PepperJax, Starbucks, Courtyard, Days Inn, Sheraton, Super 8, Wildwood Lodge, AT&T, Barnes&Noble, Best Buy, Home Depot, Kohl's, Lowe's, Marshall's, Office Depot, PetSmart, Target/Starbucks, Verizon, Whole Foods Mkt, World Mkt, W Hy-Vee, Kum&Go/Burger King, Biaggi's Rest, Caprotti's Sandwiches, Caribou Coffee, Cooper's Hawk Rest., Cracker Barrel, El Rodeo Mexican, Franka Pizza, Jersey Mike's, Jimmy John's, Other Place Grill, Panera Bread, Wendy's, Z'Marik's Cafe, Best Western, Country Inn&Suites, La Quinta, H, Walgreens

123.5mm I-80 E and I-35 N run together 14 mi.

123b a I-80/I-35 N, I-35 S to Kansas City, I-235 to Des Moines

122 (from eb)60th St, W Des Moines, N H, same as 121

121 74th St, W Des Moines, N 5 Borough Bagels, Agave Grill, Biaggi's Rest., Capriotti's Sandwiches, Cooper's Hawk Rest., Jersey Mike's, Jimmy John's, Panera Bread, Starbucks, Z'Mariks Noodle Cafe, Comfort Inn, Hampton Inn, Staybridge Suites, golf, H, HyVee Food/gas, Walgreens, S Kum&Go/Burger King, Arby's, Burger King, Culver's, McDonald's, Perkins, Quiznos, Taco John's, Fairfield Inn, Marriott, Motel 6, Sonesta Suites, SpringHill Suites

118 Grand Prairie Pky, N Kum&Go/dsl, Sleep Inn, F&F/gas

117 R22, Booneville, Waukee, N Kum&Go/dsl/e85, Timberline Camping, S Rube's Steaks

115mm weigh sta eb

DESOTO

113 R16, Van Meter, S Casey's, 5th Quarter Rest., Veteran's Cemetary

112mm N Racoon River

111mm Middle Racoon River

110 US 169, to Adel, DeSoto, S Casey's/dsl, Kum&Go/dsl/e85, Kwik Star, Ambro's Roadhouse, Edgetowner Motel, $General, USPO

106 F90, P58, N KOA(apr-oct)

104 P57, Earlham, S Casey's/dsl

100 US 6, to Redfield, Dexter, N Casey's(2mi), $General(2mi)

97 P48, to Dexter, N camping, Casey's(2mi)

93 P28, Stuart, N Casey's/dsl/scales, Kum&Go/dsl/e85, McDonald's, Subway, AmericInn, Motel 6, Stuart Motor Lodge, $General, Chevrolet, city park, Hometown Foods, S Phillips 66/dsl, Economy Inn, NAPA

88 P20, Menlo

86 IA 25, to Greenfield, Guthrie Ctr, N to Spring Brook SP

85mm Middle River

ADAIR

83 N77, Casey, N Conoco

80.5mm **full facilities, litter barrels, petwalk, both lanes, RV dump, vending, wireless internet**

76 IA 925, N54, Adair, N Casey's/dsl, Kum&Go/Subway/dsl, Chuck Wagon Rest., Adair Budget Inn, Relax Inn, camping, city park, NAPA

75 G30, to Adair

70 IA 148 S, Anita, S to Lake Anita SP(6mi)

64 N28, to Wiota

61mm E Nishnabotna River

60 US 6, US 71, to Atlantic, Lorah, S Days Inn

57 N16, to Atlantic, N Nelsen RV Ctr, S H(7mi)

54 IA 173, to Elk Horn

51 M56, to Marne

46 M47, Walnut, N Sinclair/dsl, Backfield Grill, to Prairie Rose SP, S Kum&Go/dsl, EconoLodge/RV Park

AVOCA

44mm weigh sta wb/parking area eb

40 US 59, to Harlan, Avoca, N Flying J/Taco John's/Wendy's/dsl/24hr/scales, Subway, Cobblestone Inn, Motel 6, H(12mi), truckwash, S Casey's/dsl/EVC, Shell/dsl, Acova Inn, Capri Motel, $General, Avoca Foods, Nishna Museum

39.5mm W Nishnabotna River

34 M16, Shelby, N Shell/rest./dsl/e85, Tesla EVC, Shelby Country Inn/RV Park, S Love's/McDonald's/Chester's/dsl/scales/24hr/@

32mm **parking only, both lanes**

29 L66, to Minden, S Casey's/dsl/scales, Midtown Motel(2mi), winery(4mi)

27 I-680 W, to N Omaha

23 IA 244, L55, Neola, S Kum&Go/dsl/e85, to Arrowhead Park/camping

20mm **Welcome Ctr eb/ wb, full facilities, litter barrels, vending, petwalk, RV dump, wi-fi**

COUNCIL BLUFFS

17 G30, Underwood, N Cenex/Subway/dsl/24hr, Underwood Motel, truck/tire repair

8 US 6, Council Bluffs, N Casey's/dsl(1mi), $General, H(3mi), S st patrol

5 Madison Ave, Council Bluffs, N Casey's, Burger King, Great Wall Chinese, KFC, McDonald's, Papa Murphy's, Starbucks, Subway, Taco Bell, AmericInn, HyVee Foods/drug, Tesla, Walgreens, S DQ, 712 Eat + Drink, Village Inn Rest., Western Inn, Family Fare Mkt

4 I-29 S, to Kansas City

3 IA 192 N, Council Bluffs, N to Hist Dodge House, S Casey's/dsl, TA/Valero/Country Pride/dsl/scales/24hr/@, Applebee's, Burger King, Cracker Barrel, DQ, Fazoli's, Golden Corral, Hardee's, Huhot Mongolian, Jimmy John's, La Mesa Mexican, LJ Silver, McDonald's, Red Lobster, Taco Bell, Countryside Inn, Fairfield Inn, Motel 6, Red Roof Inn, Advance Parts, AlLDI, Buick/GMC/Cadillac, Chrysler/Dodge/Jeep, Ford, Freightliner, Home Depot, Hyundai/Subaru, Kia, Nissan, Outdoor Recreation RV, Sam's Club/gas, truck/dsl repair, U-Haul, Walmart/Subway

1b S 24th St, Council Bluffs, N Amoco, Casey's/dsl, Pilot/Arby's/scales/dsl/24hr, Sapp Bros/Burger King/dsl, Home Team Cookout, Hooters, Porch Rest., Quaker Steak&Lube,

IA

= gas = food = lodging = other = rest stop

COUNCIL BLUFFS

INTERSTATE 80 Cont'd

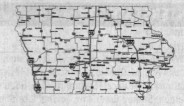

Exit	Services
1b	Continued
	Salty Dog Groll, American Inn, Best Western, Country Inn&Suites, Courtyard, Hilton Garden, Holiday Inn Express, Microtel, My Place Hotel, SpringHill Suites, Super 8, Bass Pro Shop, Blue Beacon, Camping World RV Ctr, Horseshoe Casino/RV Parking, Peterbilt, SpeedCo, S **Welcome Ctr, full facilities**, Culver's, TX Roadhouse, JC Penney, PetCo
1a	I-29 N, to Sioux City
0mm	Iowa/Nebraska state line, Missouri River

INTERSTATE 235 (Des Moines)

Exit	Services
15	I-80, E to Davenport
12	US 6, E Euclid Ave, E Casey's, Burger King, Dragon House Chinese, Papa John's, Perkins, Tasty Tacos, $Tree, HyVee Foods/drug, Walgreens, W QT/dsl, Midas, NAPA
11	Guthrie Ave, W Kum&Go/dsl, CarQuest
10b a	IA 163 W, E University Ave, Easton Dr
9	US 65/69, E 14th, E 15th, N Subway, Walgreens, S QT, McDonald's, Quiznos, Tasty Tacos, H, st capitol, URGENT CARE, zoo
8b	E 6th St, Penn Ave(from wb), N H
8a	3rd St, 5th Ave, N Holiday Inn, H, S Embassy Suites, Marriott, Quality Inn, Conv Ctr
7	Keo Way
6	MLK Blvd/31st St, N Drake U, S Governor's Mansion
5b	42nd St, Science & Art Ctr, N Git'n Go, Papa John's, Drake Automotive
5a	56th St(from wb), N golf
4	IA 28, 63rd St, to Windsor Heights, S Historic Valley Jct, zoo
3	8th St, W Des Moines, N Kum&Go, B-Bop's Café, Burger King, Papa Murphy's, Starbucks, HyVee Foods, PetCo, Sam's Club/gas, Walmart/Subway, S BP, Kum&Go/dsl/e85, Dunkin Donuts, Jimmy John's, Lemon Grass Thai, Tacos Andreas, Days Inn
2	22nd St, 24th St, W Des Moines, N BP, Casey's/dsl, Kum&Go/dsl, QT/dsl, Arby's, ChuckeCheese, Culver's, Famous Dave's BBQ, Hardee's, Hibachi Buffet, Jethro's BBQ, McDonald's, SmashBurger, Taco Bell, Village Inn, $Tree, CarX, Firestone/auto, Gordman's, Meineke, Michael's, Midas, Walgreens
1b	Valley West Dr, W Des Moines, N BP/dsl, Chipotle Mexican, Cozy Cafe, Hamilton's Rest., Hurricane Grill, Jimmy John's, La Hacienda, Noodles&Co, Olive Garden, Panda Express, Panera Bread, Red Lobster, Subway, Valley West Inn, AT&T, Best Buy, Home Depot, HyVee Foods, JC Penney, Marshall's, Target, Von Maur, Whole Foods Mkt
0mm	I-235 begins/ends on I-80, exit 123.

W DES MOINES

INTERSTATE 280 (Davenport)

Exit	Services
18b a	I-74, US 6, Moline, S Shell/dsl, Bare Bones BBQ, McDonald's, MT Jack's, Best Inn, Country Inn&Suites, Hampton Inn, Holiday Inn Express, La Quinta, Motel 6, Quality Inn
15	Airport Rd, Milan, N Hardee's, MaidRite Café, McDonald's, Subway, auto repair, Buick/Chevrolet, Firestone
11b a	IL 92, to Andalusia, Rock Island, S Jumer's Hotel/casino/rest., KOA Camping
9.5mm	Iowa/Illinois state line, Mississippi River
8	rd 22, Rockingham Rd, to Buffalo, E truck repair
6	US 61, W River Dr, to Muscatine, W Kwik Star/dsl/scales, Casey's, El Compita Mexican, Camping World, Lakeside RV Park
4	Locust St, rd F65, 160th St, E H, St Ambrose U,
4	Continued
	to Palmer Coll, W BP/Subway/dsl, Honda
1	US 6 E, IA 927, Kimberly Rd, to Walcott, E Murphy USA/dsl, Applebee's, Culver's, Harlan's Rest., $Tree, Discount Tire, Walmart
0mm	I-280 begins/ends on I-80, exit 290.

MILAN

IA

INTERSTATE 380 (Cedar Rapids)

Exit	Services
73mm	I-380 begins/ends on US 218, 73mm in Waterloo., E BP/dsl, W Clark, Chapala Mexican, Pizza Hut
72	San Marnan Dr, W Casey's, Kwik Star/Dallas/e85, Applebee's, Burger King, Carlos O'Kelly's, Chick-fil-A, Domino's, DQ, Freddy's, Hardee's, IHOP, Jimmy John's, Little Ceasar's, Lone Star, Longhorn Steaks, McDonald's, Noodles&Co, Olive Garden, Panchero's, Panda Express, Panera Bread, Red Lobster, Starbucks, Subway, Taco Bell, Taco John's, Tokyo Bay, Wendy's, Baymont Inn, Boarding Inn, Comfort Inn, Country Inn&Suites, Days Inn, Fairfield Inn, Hampton Inn, Holiday Inn Express, Motel 6, Suburban Studios, Advance Parts, ALDI, AT&T, Barnes & Noble, Best Buy, Chevrolet, Chrysler/Dodge/Jeep, CVS Drug, Dick's, Ford, Hobby Lobby, Home Depot, HyVee Foods, KIA, Menards, PetSmart, Staples, Target, Tires+, TJ Maxx, Verizon, Walmart
71	I-380, US 20, IA 27, Cedar Rapids, Cedar Falls, Dubuque, W Isle Hotel/Casino
70	River Forest Rd, E Casey's, Kwik Star, Famliy$
68	Elk Run Heights, Evansdale Dr, E Flying J/dsl/scales/24hr, Pilot/RR/Junie's/Subway/dsl/scales/24hr/@, Arby's, McDonald's, Days Inn, Freightliner, Ketelsen RV Ctr, truckwash/repair
66	Gilbertville, Raymond
65	US 20 E, Dubuque
62	rd d-38, Gilbertville
55	rd v-65, Jesup, La Port, W to Hickory Hills Park/camping
54mm	weigh sta sb
51mm	weigh sta nb
49	rd d-48, Brandon
43	IA 150, Independence, Vinton, E Casey's/dsl, Urbana Inn Suites, Bish's RV Ctr
41	Urbana, E Lazy Acres RV Park, W Casey's/dsl, $General
35	rd w-36, Center Point, E BP, Casey's/McDonald's/Subway/dsl/scales/24hr, $General, Chrysler/Dodge/Jeep/Ford, vet, W Pleasant Creek SRA(5mi)
28	rd e-34, Robins, Toddville, E BP/dsl, W Wickiup Outdoor Learning Ctr(5mi)
26	Tower Terrace Rd
25	Boyson Rd, Hiawatha, E Casey's, Culver's, Oscar's, Pita'z Mediterranean, Tomaso's, Buick/GMC/Cadillac, Ketelsen RV Ctr, Kia, Nissan, Subaru, W BP, Toyota/Mazda
24	IA 100, Blairs Ferry Rd, E Casey's, Buffalo Wild Wings, Burger King, Hardee's, Jimmy John's, KFC, Las Glorias Mexican, McDonald's, Moe's SW Grill, O's Pizza, Papa John's, Pedalers Fork, Scott Family Rest., Starbucks, Wendy's, Comfort Inn, Days Inn, Residence Inn, Staybridge Suites, Ace Hardware, Advance Parts, Chrysler/Dodge/Jeep, CVS Drug, Discount Tire, O'Reilly Parts, Target, vet, W Fas Fuel, Adelitas Mexican, Arby's, Burger King, Dunkin', Freddy's,

BLAIRS FERRY RD

INTERSTATE 380 (Cedar Rapids) Cont'd

CEDAR RAPIDS

24	Continued Pizza Hut, Starbucks, Subway, Taco Bell, O ALDI, AutoZone, Lowe's, Sam's Club/gas, Walmart
22	Glass Rd, 32nd St, E KwikShop/dsl, Casey's, Papa Murphys, The Blind Pig, O Hy-Vee Foods
21	H St, Cedar Rapids, downtown
20b	7th St E, Cedar Rapids, downtown, E O H
20a	US 151 Bus, E Barrel House Grill, Bricks Grill, Cobble Hill Rest., Need Pizza, Runts Munchies, The Map Room, DoubleTree, O art museum
19b	1st Ave W, W O NAPA
18	Wilson Ave, O museums, W FasMart/dsl
17	33rd ave SW, Hawkeye Downs, E Kwik Star/dsl, Pizza Hut, W Casey's, Burger King, Cancun, Los Compadres, McDonald's, Perkins, Taco Bell, Wendy's, American Inn, Aspen Inn, Baymont, Econolodge, Fairfield Inn,

ELY

17	Continued Hampton Inn, Holiday Inn Express, Motel 6, Motel 6, Quality Inn, Residence Inn, Super 8, SureStay
16	US 30 W, US 151 S, US 218 N, Tama
13	Ely, E Pilot/Arby's/dsl/scales/24hr, W Casey's/A&W/dsl, Casey's/dsl/scales, Kwik Star/dsl/e85, McDonald's, Subway, AmericInn, avid hotel, Comfort Inn, Country Inn&Suites, O
12mm	**littler barrels, petwalk, both lanes, RV Dump, vending, wireless internet**
10	rd f-12, Shueyville, Swisher, E BP/dsl, O to Lake Mcbride SP, W to Amana Colonies
8mm	Iowa River
4	rd f-28, North Liberty, E Casey's, Kum&Go/dsl/e85, Arby's, Sleep Inn
0b a	I-80 E to Iowa City, W to Des Moines, I-380 begins/ends on I-80

NOTES

IA

KANSAS

INTERSTATE 35

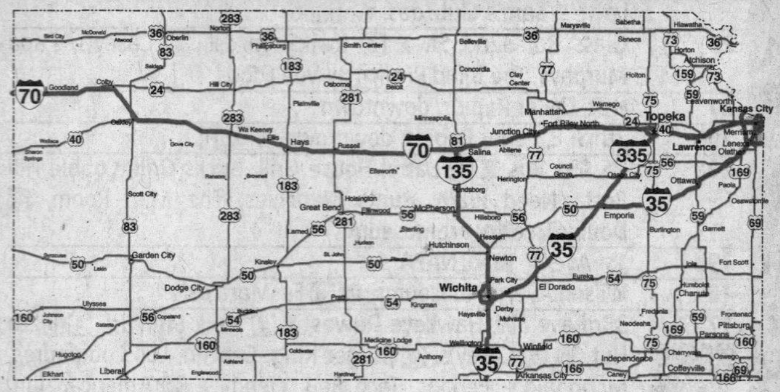

Exit #	Services
235mm	Kansas/Missouri state line
235	Cambridge Circle
234b a	US 169, Rainbow Blvd, E QT, Applebee's, Bohemio Mexican, Rosedale BBQ, Sonic, Subway, Taqueria Mexico, Home2 Suites, Oak Tree Inn, KU MED CTR, O'Reilly Parts, W Sinclair/dsl
233a	SW Blvd, Mission Rd
233b	37th Ave(from sb)
232b	US 69 N, E Phillips 66/dsl, QT, Burger King, China Star, Cici's, McDonald's, Starbucks, Taco Bell, ALDI, Lowe's, Price Chopper, Walgreens, Walmart
232a	Lamar Ave, E QT, WoodSpring Suites
231b a	I-635(exits left from sb)
230	Antioch Rd(from sb)
229	Johnson Dr, E QT/dsl, Chili's, China Garden, IHOP, Jack-in-the-Box, Jimmy John's, McDonald's, Starbucks, Subway, Taco Bell, AT&T, Dick's, GNC, Hen House Mkt, Hobby Lobby, Home Depot, IKEA, Marshall's, Old Navy, PetSmart, Verizon, Walgreens, W Cenex/dsl, El Pulgarcito Salvadoran
228b	US 56 E, US 69, Shawnee Mission Pkwy, E Shell, Caribou Coffee, Denny's, Krispy Kreme, Pegahs Rest., Extended Stay, Hotel Lotus, Quality Inn, BMW/Mini, W A&W, Applebee's, Arby's, Cane's, KFC, LJ Silver, McAlister's Deli, Panera Bread, Pizza Hut, Subway, Wendy's, AutoZone, Discount Tire, Family$, Firestone/auto, Ford, Goodyear/auto, Jo-Ann Fabrics, O'Reilly Parts, Russell Stover, Walgreens
228a	67th St, E Audi, CarMax, W Phillips 66/dsl, Hyundai, Infiniti, Jaguar, Land Rover, Lexus, Maserati, Mercedes, Porsche Smart, Toyota/Scion
227	75th St, E Dos Reales Mexican, McDonald's, Panera Bread, Extended Stay America, Acura, Audi, H, Walmart, W QT/dsl, Domino's, Sonic, Starbucks, Subway, Taco Bell, Wendy's, Hampton Inn, Hyundai, URGENT CARE
225b	US 69 S(from sb), Overland Pkwy
225a	87th St, E BP, Green Mill Rest, Wendy's, Holiday Inn, W Phillips 66/dsl, Dunkin Donuts, Taco Bell, Zarda BBQ
224	95th St, $Tree, E QT, Applebee's, Baskin-Robbins, BD Mongolian BBQ, Bibibop, Bo Lings, Cane's, Cava, Cheddar's, Chick-fil-A, Chipotle Mexican, Five Guys, Houlihan's, Jimmy John's, KFC, McDonald's, Noodles&Co, On-the-Border, Outback Steaks, Panda Express, Pie Five, Taco Bell, Candlewood Suites, Extended Stay, Holiday Inn Express, La Quinta, Motel 6, Quality Inn, Radisson Hotel, Super 8, Advance Parts, Barnes&Noble, Best Buy, Dillard's, Firestone/auto, Hobby Lobby, H, JC Penney, Macy's, Michaels, Nordstrom, PetCo, Ross, Sam's Club/gas, Target, Verizon, W Amoco, Mi Ranchito, Monkey King Chinese, Costco/gas, O'Reilly Parts, U-Haul
222b a	I-435 W & E
220	119th St, E Conoco/7-11, Minit Mart/Phillips 66/dsl, Phillips 66, 180 Room BBQ, Aoyama Ramen, Baskin-Robbins, Black Bear Diner, Buffalo Wild Wings, Chick-fil-A, Chipotle Mexican, Coldstone, Cracker Barrel, Firehouse Subs, First Watch, Five Guys, Freddy's, Hira's Steak, IHOP, Jimmy John's, KC Joe's BBQ, KC Super Buffet, Master Wok, McDonald's, Mo' Bettahs BBQ, Mr Gyros Greek, Noodles&Co, Old Chicago, Olive Garden, Panda Express, Panera Bread,
220	Continued Papa Murphy's, Pei Wei, Penn Sta Subs, Pie Five, Planet Sub, Popeyes, Red Lobster, Schlotzsky's, Smashburger, Starbucks, Steak'n Shake, Taco Bell, Torchy's Tacos, Twin Peaks, TX Roadhouse, Wahlburgers, Wendy's, Zaxby's, Courtyard, Fairfield Inn, Hampton Inn, Hilton Garden, Holiday Inn Express/EVC, Residence Inn, Wood Spring Suites, AT&T, Big O Tires, Chrysler/Dodge/Jeep, Dick's, Discount Tire, Fiat, GNC, Goodyear/auto, Home Depot, Honda, Marshall's, Michael's, Natural Grocers, Old Navy, PetSmart, Ross, Target/Starbucks, U-Haul, Verizon, Whole Foods Mkt/EVC, W Anejo Mexican, Jason's Deli, Longhorn Steaks, Main Event, Starbucks, Bass Pro Shops
218	135th, Santa Fe St, Olathe, E Phillips 66/dsl, QT, Applebee's, Arby's, Cane's, China Buffet, ChuckE.Cheese, Church's TX Chicken, Fuzzy's Tacos, Golden Corral, Johnathan's Wood-Fire, Jose Pepper's Mexican, La Pasadita, Los Compadres, McDonald's, Other Place Grill, Papa John's, Pizza St, Popeyes, Sonic, Starbucks, Subway, Taco Bell, $General, $Tree, Ace Hardware, Advance Parts, AlLDI, AutoZone, BigLots, Discount Foods, Ford/Lincoln, Hobby Lobby, Kohl's, Lowe's, Midas, Petco, Valvoline Oil Change, vet, Walgreens, W QT, Bonito Michoacán, Domino's, K-Macho's Mexican, KFC, Little Caesars, LJ Silver's, McDonald's, Sakura Japanese, Strip's Chicken, Subway, Taco Bell, Waffle House, SureStay, Aamco, Advance Parts, Buick/GMC, Chevrolet, Harley-Davidson, Hyundai, Kia, Meineke, Nissan, O'Reilly Parts, Subaru, Toyota/Scion, VW
217	Old Hwy 56(from sb), same as 215
215	US 169 S, KS 7, Olathe, E Phillips 66/dsl, QT/dsl, Chipotle Mexican, IHOP, Jimmy John's, MOD Pizza, Panera Bread, Red Robin, Candlewood Suites, Quality Inn, AlLDI, Big O Tires, Discount Tire, Home Depot, Jiffy Lube, Target/Starbucks, W Phillips 66/dsl/scales/24hr, 54th St Grill, Chapala Mexican, Chili's, McDonald's, Taco Bell, Best Western, Econolodge, eLODGE, La Quinta, Motel 6, Burlington Coats, H, Mazda
214	Lone Elm Rd, 159th St
213mm	weigh sta both lanes
210	US 56 W, Gardner, W Phillips 66/dsl, QT/dsl, Arby's, Burger King, Casey's, Daylight Donuts, DQ, Freddy's, Fronteras Mexican, Gambino's, Goodcents, KFC, McDonald's, Papa Johns, Perkins, Pizza Hut, Planet Sub, Sonic, Subway, Taco Bell, Hampton Inn, Super 8, AutoZone, Price Chopper, Walgreens, Walmart
207	US 56 E, Gardner Rd, E Olathe RV Ctr, W Phillips 66/dsl, QT/dsl
205	Homestead Lane, W TA/Dunkin'/dsl
202	Edgerton
198	KS 33, to Wellsville, W Casey's, Shell/dsl/scales

OLATHE

EDGERTON

KS

INTERSTATE 35 Cont'd

OTTAWA

Exit #	Services
193	Tennessee Rd, Baldwin
188	US 59 N, to Lawrence
187	KS 68, Ottawa, E Midwest RV Ctr, W Phillips 66/dsl, Central RV Ctr
185	15th St, Ottawa
183	US 59, Ottawa, E Love's/Hardee's/dsl/scales/24hr, dsl repair, Ottawa RV Ctr, W BP, Cenex/dsl, Phillips 66/dsl, Applebee's, Arby's, Burger King, Freddy's, McDonald's, Nagoya Japanese, Old 56 Rest., Pizza Hut, PrimeTime Grille, Sonic, Starbucks, Taco Bell, Wendy's, Comfort Inn, Days Inn, Holiday Inn Express, Knights Inn, Super 8, SureStay, $General, $Tree, Advance Parts, Ford, H, Walmart
182b a	US 50, Eisenhower Rd, Ottawa
176	Homewood, W RV camping
175mm	**full facilities, litter barrels, petwalk, both lanes, RV dump, vending, wireless internet**
170	KS 273, Williamsburg
162	KS 31 S, Waverly
160	KS 31 N, Melvern
155	US 75, Burlington, Melvern Lake, E Phillips 66/Subway/dsl, TA/Shell/Wendy's/dsl/scales/24hr/@, Lebo Inn, dsl repair
148	KS 131, Lebo, E Casey's/dsl, $General, W to Melvern Lake

EMPORIA

Exit #	Services
141	KS 130, Neosho Rapids, E NWR(8mi)
138	County Rd U
135	County Rd R1
133	US 50 W, 6th Ave, Emporia, E Casey's, Budget Host
131	KS 57, KS 99, Burlingame Rd, E Phillips 66/Circle K/dsl, Do-B's, Goodcents Subs, Hardee's, Peking Express, $General, Dillon's Food, tire repair
130	KS 99, Merchant St, E Phillips 66/dsl, Subway, CVS Drug, Emporia SU, Lyon Co Museum
128	Industrial Rd, E Tesla EVC, Bruff's Steaks, Burger King, Ichiban Japanese, Spangles, EconoLodge, Emporia Inn, $General, AlLDI, AT&T, H, JC Penney, Walgreens, W Phillips 66/Dunkin'/scales/dsl, Applebee's, Braum's, Domino's, IHOP, KFC, McDonald's, Panda Express, Pizza Hut, Pizza Ranch, Planet Sub, Starbucks, Taco Bell, Best Western, Comfort Inn, Hampton Inn, Holiday Inn Express, La Quinta, MainStay Suites, $Tree, Verizon, Walmart/Subway
127c	KS Tpk, I-335 N, to Topeka
127b a	US 50, KS 57, Newton, E Casey's/dsl, Flying J/Huddle House/dsl/LP/scales/24hr, Arby's, Gambino's Pizza, Golden Wok, Subway, Best Inn, Days Inn, Knights Inn, Super 8, Travel Inn, Buick/Chevrolet, Chrysler/Dodge/Jeep, dsl repair, Ford/Lincoln, Kenworth, NAPA, Nissan, PriceChopper Foods, tire repair, Toyota, W Emporia RV Park
127mm	I-35 and I-335 KS Tpk, I-35 S and KS tpk S run together, toll plaza

CASSODAY

Exit #	Services
126	I-35 S and KS Tpk S run together.
125mm	Cottonwood River
111	Cattle Pens
97.5mm	Matfield Green Service Area(both lanes exit left), **Phillips 66/dsl, Hardee's/Dunkin'**
92	KS 177, Cassoday, E Fuel'n Service
76	US 77, El Dorado N, E Casey's, Jump Start/dsl, Hibachi Express, Pizza Hut, Taco Bell, Stardust Motel, $General, Ace Hardware, city park, Dillon's Foods/dsl, El Dorado SP, Walgreens
71	KS 254, KS 196, El Dorado, E Casey's/dsl, Conoco/dsl, QT/dsl, 2 Bros BBQ, Arbys, Beijing Bistro, Braum's, Burger King, Freddy's, Gambino's Pizza, Hog Wild BBQ, Jimmy John's, Jimmy's Egg, KFC, LJ Silver, McDonald's, Pizza Hut,

ANDOVER

Exit #	Services
71	Continued Sonic, Spangles, Subway, Taco Tico, Baymont Inn, Days Inn, Heritage Inn, Holiday Inn Express, Sky-Palace Inn, Super 8, $General, AutoZone, Buick/Cadillac, Bumper Parts, Deer Grove RV Park, H, KS Oil Museum, O'Reilly Parts, tire repair, Verizon, Walmart
65mm	Towanda Service Area(both lanes exit left), Phillips 66/dsl, Hardee's/Dunkin'
62mm	Whitewater River
57	21st St, Andover

WICHITA

Exit #	Services
53	KS 96, Wichita
50	US 54, Kellogg Ave, Beijing Bistro, BJ's Rest., Bubba's Rest., Burger King, Carlos Kelly's, Chipotle Mexican, Firehouse Subs, Green Mill Rest., Hook&Reel, IHOP, LJ Silver, Longhorn Steaks, Mary's Kitchen, McDonald's, Old Chicago Pizza, Panda Express, Poblano's Mexican, Red Lobster, Starbucks, Taco Bell, Best Western+, Comfort Inn, Country Inn & Suites, Days Inn, Extended Stay America, Fairfield Inn, Hampton Inn, Hawthorn Suites, Holiday Inn, La Quinta, Marriott, Motel 6, Super 8, $Tree, Acura, AT&T, AT&T, Bosley Tires, Cadillac/Chevrolet, CarMax, Chrysler/Dodge/Jeep, Costco/dsl, Dillard's, Fiat, Firestone/auto, Ford, Honda, Infiniti, JC Penney, Lincoln, Lowe's, Mazda, Nissan, PetSmart, Ross, Subaru, TJ Maxx, Toyota/Scion, USPO, Verizon, Von Maur, VW, Walmart/Subway
45	KS 15, Wichita, E Spirit Aero Systems
44.5mm	Arkansas River
42	47th St, I-135, to I-235, Wichita, W JumpStart, QT/dsl, Angry Elephant BBQ, Applebee's, Arby's, Braum's, Burger King, Carlos O'Kelly's, Domino's, Dunkin', El Viejito Mexican, Godfather's, Goodcents Subs, Heritage Inn, Hog Wild BBQ, IHOP, Jalisco, KFC, Little Caesar's, McDonald's, New China, Pizza Hut, Sonic, Spangles Rest., Subway, Taco Bell, Wendy's, Best Western, Days Inn, Holiday Inn Express, Quality Inn, Springfield Inn, Super 8, Woodspring Suites, $General, $Tree, Air Capital RV Park, Dillon's Foods/Starbucks/dsl, K-Mart, O'Reilly Parts

HAYSVILLE

Exit #	Services
39	US 81, Haysville, W JumpStart, Sonic, Subway, Express Inn, Sleep Inn, U-Haul
33	KS 53, Mulvane, E Mulvane Hist Museum, W Hampton Inn, Kansas Star Casino/Hotel, Wyldewood Winery
26mm	Belle Plaine Service Area(both lanes exit left), **Phillips 66/dsl, McDonald's**
19	US 160, Wellington, W Casey's, Canelo's Mexican, McDonald's, Penny's Diner, Taco Bell, Sky-Palace Inn, Travelodge, $Tree, KOA, Walmart
17mm	toll plaza
16mm	I-35 N and KS TPK N run together.
4	US 166, to US 81, South Haven, E Jump Start/dsl, Motel 6, repair/tires, W Oasis RV Park
1.5mm	weigh sta nb
0mm	Kansas/Oklahoma state line

INTERSTATE 70

Exit #	Services
424mm	Kansas/Missouri State Line
423b	3rd St, James St
423a	5th St(from eb, exits left)
422d c	Central Ave, service rd
422b a	US 69 N, US 169 S
421b	I-670
421a	S railroad yard
420b a	US 69 S, 18th St Expswy, N Cenex/dsl, Sinclair/Subway/dsl, China Town, Jack-in-the-Box, Little Caesars, Tapatio Mexican, SunFresh Foods
419	38th St, Park Dr, access to 10 motels
418b	I-635 N(eb only)
418a	I-635 S

KS

= gas = food = lodging = other = rest stop

INTERSTATE 70 Cont'd

KANSAS CITY

Exit #	Services
417	57th St
415a	KS 32 E(from eb)
415b	to US 24 W, State Ave, Kansas City, N Papa John's, Taco Bell, Gables Motel, Lowe's
414mm	parking area both lanes, vehicle insp sta wb
414	78th St, N Phillips 66, QT/dsl, Arby's, Burger King, Capt D's, Chinese Buffet, Chipotle, CVS Drug, Domino's, Don Antonio, Go Chicken Go, Hardee's, Italian Delight, KFC, McDonald's, Papa John's, Pizza Hut, Sonic, Subway, Taco Bell, Wendy's, Days Inn, $Tree, Advance Parts, BigLots, Buick/GMC, Firestone/auto, H, Jiffy Lube, Marshall's, O'Reilly Parts, PetSmart, PriceChopper Foods, SavALot, Tires+, Walgreens, XPress/auto/tire, S BP, American Motel, Quality Inn
411b	I-435 N, access to Woodlands Racetrack, to KCI
411a	I-435 S
410	110th St, N Famous Dave's, Best Western, Chateau Avalon, Great Wolf Lodge, Hampton Inn, Cabela's, KS Speedway
225mm	I-70 W and KS TPK W run together
224	KS 7, to US 73(last free exit wb before KS TPK), Bonner Springs, Leavenworth, N Phillips 66/7-11/dsl, QT/dsl, El Potro Mexican, KFC/Taco Bell, Waffle House, Comfort Inn, Holiday Inn Express, museum, S BP, Arby's, Goodcents Subs, Lin's Chinese, McDonald's, Papa Murphy's, Pizza Hut, Taco John's, $Tree, Ace Hardware, AutoZone, Nachbar Automotive, PriceChopper Foods, Walgreens, Walmart/Subway
217mm	toll booth
212	Eudora, Tonganoxie
209mm	Lawrence Service Area(both lanes exit left) full facilities, **Phillips 66/dsl/EVC, McDonald's**
204	US 24, US 59, to E Lawrence, S Cenex/dsl, Phillips 66/Subway, Burger King, Motel 6, SpringHill Suites(1mi), $General, O'Reilly Parts
203mm	Kansas River
202	US 59 S, to W Lawrence, Conoco, Phillips 66/dsl, QT/dsl, Biemer's BBQ, Burger King, Casey's, Domino's, Dunkin', Henry T's, Jimmy John's, Kobe Japanese, McDonald's, Red Pepper Chinese, Sonic, Subway, Szechuan House, Taco Bell, Taco John's, Wendy's, Zoe's Noodle, Baymont Inn, Comfort Inn, Days Inn, DoubleTree, EconoLodge, Hampton Inn, Super 8, Virginia Inn, $General, Advance Parts, Dillon's Foods/gas, H, O'Reilly Parts, to Clinton Lake SP, to U of KS, vet, Walgreens
197	KS 10, Lecompton, Lawrence, N Perry Lake SP, S Clinton Lake SP
188mm	Topeka Service Area, full(handicapped)facilities, Phillips 66/dsl, Dunkin', Hardee's, Pizza Hut, Taco Bell
183	I-70 W(from wb), to Denver
367mm	toll plaza
366	I-470 W, to Wichita, I-70 E and KS TPK E run together
365	21st St, Rice Rd, access to Shawnee Lake RA
364b	US 40 E, Carnahan Ave, to Lake Shawnee
364a	California Ave, S BP/dsl, Phillips 66/dsl, Arby's, Baskin-Robbins, Burger King, Domino's, DQ, McDonald's, Pizza Hut, Subway, Tacos El Guitarron, Tacos Mexicano, $General, $Tree, Ace Hardware, Advance Parts, AutoZone, Dillon's Food/gas, O'Reilly Parts, repair, vet, Walgreens, Walmart/Subway
363	Adams St, S Phillips 66/dsl
362c	10th Ave(from wb), S st capitol
362b a	to 8th Ave, downtown, N Ramada Inn, S to st capitol
361b	3rd St, Monroe St

TOPEKA PAXICO

Exit #	Services
361a	1st Ave, S city park, Ryder Trucks
359	MacVicar Ave, S H, Kenworth
358b a	Gage Blvd
357b a	Fairlawn Rd, 6th Ave, S Amoco, Valero/dsl, Riegel's Grill, Best Western, Motel 6, $General, NAPACare, vet
356b a	Wanamaker Rd, N Red Robin, Hyatt Place, KS Museum of History, S BP, Murphy Express/dsl, Phillips 66/dsl, Applebee's, Arby's/Tesla EVC, AutoZone, Buffalo Wild Wings, Burger King, Chick-fil-A, Chili's, Chipotle Mexican, ChuckECheese, CiCi's Pizza, Coldstone, Cracker Barrel, Culver's, Denny's, Five Guys, Freddy's Steakburgers, Golden Corral, Hardee's, Hooters, HuHot Chinese, IHOP, Jason's Deli, Jersey Mike's Subs, Jimmy John's, Jose Pepper's, Longhorn Steaks, McAlister's, McDonald's, Mizu Sushi, Noodles&Co, Old Chicago, Olive Garden, On-the-Border, Panda Express, Panera Bread, Papa John's, Perkins, Pie Five Pizza, Pizza Hut, Qdoba, Red Lobster, Sonic, Spangles, Starbucks, Steak'n Shake, Taco Bell, TX Roadhouse, Wendy's, Baymont Inn, Candlewood Suites, Clubhouse Inn, Comfort Suites, Country Inn&Suites, Courtyard, Days Inn, Econolodge, Fairfield Inn, Hampton Inn, Hilton Garden, Holiday Inn Express, Homewood Suites, Quality Inn, Residence Inn, Sleep Inn, Super 8, Woodspring Suites, $Tree, AAA, AlLDI, AT&T, Barnes&Noble, Best Buy, Dick's, Dillard's, Goodyear/auto, Hobby Lobby, Home Depot, JC Penney, Jo-Ann, Kohl's, Lowe's, Menards, Michael's, Natural Grocers, Old Navy, Ross, Sam's Club/gas, Target, TJ Maxx, URGENT CARE, Verizon, Walmart/Subway
355	I-470 E, US 75 S, to VA MED CTR, Topeka, air museum, S same as 356
353	KS 4 W, to Auburn Rd
351	frontage rd(from eb), Mission Creek
350	Valencia Rd
347	West Union Rd
346	Carlson Rd, to Rossville, Willard
343	Ranch Rd
342	Keene-Eskridge Rd, access to Lake Wabaunsee
341	KS 30, Maple Hill, S 24-7/Subway/café/dsl/RV dump
338	Vera Rd, S Valero/Baskin-Robbins/dsl
336mm	**full facilities, litter barrels, petwalk, (exits left from both lanes), RV parking, wireless internet**
335	Snokomo Rd, Paxico, Skyline Mill Creek Scenic Drive
333	KS 138, Paxico, N Mill Creek RV Park, winery
332	Spring Creek Rd
330	KS 185, to McFarland
329mm	weigh sta both lanes
328	KS 99, to Alma, S Wabaunsee Co Museum
324	Wabaunsee Rd, N Grandma Horners Store&Factory
322	Tallgrass Rd
318	frontage rd
316	Deep Creek Rd
313	KS 177, to Manhattan, N Casey's, AJ's Pizza, ALDI, Cane's, Carlos O'Kelly's, Chick-fil-A, Chili's, Cox Bros BBQ, DQ, Dunkin', Firehouse Subs, Five Guys, Freddy's Burgers, Fridas Mexican, Hy-Vee Foods, IHOP, KFC, LongHorn Steaks, McAlister's Deli, McDonald's, Olive Garden, Panda Express, Pizza Hut, Sonic, Starbucks, Taco Bell, TX Roadhouse, UNI Japanese, Best Western, Candlewood Suites, Comfort Suites, Fairfield Inn, Hilton Garden, Holiday Inn Express, Quality Inn, Super 8, $Tree, AT&T, Chevrolet,

INTERSTATE 70 Cont'd

FT RILEY

Exit	Services
313	Continued Dick's Sports, Dillard's, Dillon Foods/gas, Hobby Lobby, JC Penny, to KSU, Verizon, Walgreens, Walmart/Subway
311	Moritz Rd
310mm	**full facilities, litter barrels, petwalk, both lanes, RV dump**
307	McDowell Creek Rd, scenic river rd to Manhattan
304	Humboldt Creek Rd
303	KS 18 E, to Ogden, Manhattan, N to KSU
301	Marshall Field, N Cavalry Museum, Custer's House, KS Terr Capitol, to Ft Riley
300	US 40, KS 57, Council Grove
299	Flinthills Blvd, to Jct City, Ft Riley, N Cenex/dsl, Stacy's Rest., Tyme Out Grill, Grandview Plaza Inn, Great Western Inn, Love Hotels, Smoky Hill RV Park
298	Chestnut St, to Jct City, Ft Riley, N Shell/dsl/24hr, ALDI, Arby's, Cracker Barrel, Family Buffet, Freddy's Steakburgers, JC's BBQ, La Fiesta, Pizza Hut, Qdoba, Starbucks, Taco Bell, Tokyo Steaks, Best Western, Candlewood Suites, Comfort Inn, Courtyard, Quality Inn, $General, $Tree, CVS Drug, Verizon, Walmart/Subway
296	US 40, Washington St, Junction City, N Casey's, Cenex/dsl, Phillips 66, Shell/dsl, El Patron Mexican, IHOP, McDonald's, Sonic, Subway, The Best Hamburger, Budget Host/RV park, Hampton Inn, Holiday Inn Express, Super 8, Travelodge, Woodspring Suites, Cadillac/Chevrolet, Haas Tire, Harley-Davidson, vet
295	US 77, KS 18 W, Marysville, to Milford Lake, N Sapp Bros/A&W/dsl/24hr, Motel 6, Ford/Lincoln/Kia/Chrysler/Dodge/Jeep, RV Ctr, S Owls Nest Camping, truckwash
290	Milford Lake Rd
286	KS 206, Chapman, S Casey's/dsl, La Hacienda Mexican, $General, Chapman Creek RV Park, KS Auto Racing Museum
281	KS 43, to Enterprise, N Phillips 66/dsl, 4 Seasons RV Ctr/Park
277	Jeep Rd

ABILENE

Exit	Services
275	KS 15, to Clay Ctr, Abilene, N Brookville Hotel/rest., Holiday Inn Express, S 24-7/Arby's/dsl, Cenex, KwikShop, Short Stop, Burger King, Ike's Grill, M&R Grill, McDonald's, Pizza Hut, Sonic, Subway, Budget Inn, Super 8, $General, AutoZone, Buick/Cadillac/Chevrolet, O'Reilly Parts, to Eisenhower Museum
272	Fair Rd, to Talmage, S Love's/Hardee's/dsl/scales/24hr, Russell Stover Candies
266	KS 221, Solomon, S $General
265mm	**full facilities, litter barrels, petwalk, both lanes, RV dump, vending**
264mm	Solomon River
260	Niles Rd, New Cambria
253mm	Saline River
253	Ohio St, N RV park, S Flying J/Huddle House/dsl/LP/scales/24hr, Kenworth

HEDVILLE

Exit	Services
252	KS 143, 9th St, Salina, N 24-7/Subway/dsl/24hr, Petro/Shell/Starbucks/Popeyes/dsl/24hr/@, IHOP, Iron Skillet, McDonald's, Budget Host, Days Inn, Holiday Inn Express, La Quinta, Motel 6, Rodeway Inn, Super 8, Blue Beacon, dsl repair, Freightliner, KOA, S Pilot/dsl/scales/24hr/@, Comfort Inn, Marifah Inn
250b a	I-135, US 81, N to Concordia, S to Wichita
249	Halstead Rd, to Trenton
244	Hedville, S Phillips 66/dsl, Rolling Hills Park(2mi), Sundown RV Park
238	to Brookville, Glendale, Tescott
233	290th Rd, Juniata
225	KS 156, to Ellsworth, S D&S/dsl, Ft Harker Museum, Ft Larned HS
224mm	**full facilities, litter barrels, petwalk, both lanes, RV dump**
221	KS 14 N, to Lincoln
219	KS 14 S, to Ellsworth, S Conoco/dsl
216	to Vesper
209	to Sylvan Grove
206	KS 232, Wilson, N Wilson Lake(6mi), S RV camping
199	Dorrance, N to Wilson Lake

RUSSELL

Exit	Services
193	Bunker Hill Rd, N Shell/dsl/24hr, to Wilson Lake WA
189	US 40 bus, Pioneer Rd, Russell
187mm	parking area both lanes, picnic tables, litter barrels
184	US 281, Russell, N 24-7/dsl, Cenex/Fossil Sta./dsl, A&W, McDonald's, Meridy's Rest., Peking Garden, Pizza Hut, Sonic, Subway, Days Inn, Fossil Creek Hotel, Quality Inn, Russell's Inn, $General, Bumper Parts, CarQuest, Fossil Creek RV Park, JJJ RV Park, Klema Mkt, st patrol
180	Balta Rd, to Russell
175	Gorham, N Co-Op/dsl(1mi), tire repair(1mi)
172	Walker Ave
168	KS 255, to Victoria, S to Cathedral of the Plains
163	Toulon Ave
161	Commerce Parkway, S Volvo/Mack Trucks

HAYS

Exit	Services
159	US 183, Hays, N Cenex/Taco Grande/dsl, EVC, Qwest/dsl, Tesla EVC, Applebee's, El Dos Mexican, Fuzzy's Tacos, IHOP, Old Chicago, Sims BBQ, Wendy's, Avid Hotel, Best Western+, Comfort Inn, Fairfield Inn, Hampton Inn, Hilton Garden, Holiday Inn Express, Sleep Inn, TownePlace Suites, AT&T, Chrysler/Dodge/Jeep, Ford/Lincoln, Harley-Davidson, Home Depot, Toyota, Verizon, Walmart/Subway, S 24-7/dsl, Love's, Phillips 66/dsl, Phillips 66/dsl/24hr, Sinclair/dsl, Arby's, China Garden, Domino's, Freddy's, Ft Hays Inn, Gambino's Pizza, Hickok's Steaks, Jimmy John's, La Curva Mexican, Lucky Buffet, McDonald's, Pheasant Run Pancakes, Qdoba, Sonic, Starbucks, Subway, Taco Bell, Taco Grande, Thirsty's Grill, Vernie's Hamburger House, Wendy's, Whiskey Creek Grill, Baymont Inn, Days Inn, EconoLodge, Quality Inn, Rodeway Inn, Super 8, $Tree, Ace Hardware, Advance Parts, Chevrolet, Dillon's Foods/gas, Hobby Lobby, JC Penney, O'Reilly Parts, Peerless Tires, Verizon, Walgreens
157	US 183 S byp, to Hays, N Peterbilt, S museum, st patrol, to Ft Hays St U, tourist info
153	Yocemento Ave
145	KS 247 S, Ellis, S Casey's, Love's/DQ/Subway/dsl/scales/24hr, Cancun Mexican, Days Inn, Railroad Museum, RV camping, to Chrysler Museum, USPO

WAKEENEY

Exit	Services
140	Riga Rd
135	KS 147, Ogallah, S to Cedar Bluff SP(13mi)
132mm	**full facilities, litter barrels, petwalk, both lanes, RV dump**
128	US 283 N, WaKeeney, N Super 8
127	US 283 S, WaKeeney, N Pizza Hut, Tropical Mexican, Best Western+, KS Kountry Inn, $General, S 24-7/McDonald's/dsl/24hr, Conoco/Subway/dsl, Brazen Bull, EconoLodge, KOA
120	Voda Rd
115	KS 198 N, Banner Rd, Collyer
107	KS 212, Castle Rock Rd, Quinter, N Sinclair/dsl, Castle Rock Inn, First Inn/rest., $General, S Conoco/dsl/24hr, DQ
99	KS 211, Park
97mm	**full facilities, litter barrels, petwalk, both lanes, RV dump, vending**
95	KS 23 N, to Hoxie
93	KS 23, Grainfield, N Sinclair/dsl

INTERSTATE 70 Cont'd

Exit #	Services
85	KS 216, Grinnell
79	Campus Rd
76	US 40, to Oakley, **S** TA/Shell/IHOP/Subway/dsl/e-85/scales/24hr/@, Rodeway Inn, Sleep Inn, Blue Beacon, Fick Museum, H
70	US 83, to Oakley, **N** Nostalgic Stay Inn, **S** Cenex/dsl, Tres Hermanos, antiques, Fick Museum, High-Plains RV Park, H
62	rd K, Mingo
54	Country Club Dr, Colby, **N** LNG, Pilot/Subway/dsl/scales/24hr, Hampton Inn, H
53	KS 25, Colby, **N** 24-7/Subway/dsl, Casey's, Arby's, Burger King, China Buffet, Jimmy John's, McDonald's, Pizza Hut, Sonic, Subway, Taco John's, Days Inn, Holiday Inn Express, Motel 6, Sleep Inn, Super 8, $General, $Tree, Dillon's Foods/dsl, Ford/Lincoln, H, O'Reilly Parts, Prairie Museum, Quilt Cabin, RV park/antiques, U-Haul, visitors ctr, Walmart/EVC, **S** Petro/Cenex/scales/dsl/dog park/@, Tesla EVC, City Limits Grill, Qdoba, Starbucks, Comfort Inn, Chrysler/Dodge/Jeep, truck repair
48.5mm	**full facilities, litter barrels, petwalk, both lanes, RV park/dump, vending**
45	US 24 E, Levant
36	KS 184, Brewster
35.5mm	Mountain/Central time zone
27	KS 253, Edson
19	US 24, Goodland, **N** Pizza Hut, $General, High Plains Museum, KOA
17	US 24, KS 27, Goodland, **N** Cenex/dsl, Phillips 66/dsl, Arby's, Maria's Mexican, McDonald's, Mom's Kitchen, Original Grande, Shiraz, Sonic, Subway, ASAM, Econolodge, Motel 6, Quality Inn, Super 8, CarQuest/Firestone, Chevrolet/GMC, Ford, H, Walmart, **S** 24-7/dsl/EVC/scales, Steak'n Shake, Comfort Inn, Holiday Inn Express, Mid-America Camping, Tesla EVP
12	rd 14, Caruso
9	rd 11, Ruleton
7.5mm	**full facilities, info, litter barrels, petwalk, RV dump, vending, Welcome Ctr eb/ wb, wireless internet**
1	KS 267, Kanorado, **N** food, gas
0.5mm	weigh sta eb
0mm	Kansas/Colorado State Line

COLBY · GOODLAND · SALINA

INTERSTATE 135 (Wichita)

Exit #	Services
95b a	I-70, E to KS City, W to Denver, US 81 N. I-135 begins/ends on I-70, exit 250., I-70, E to KS City, W to Denver.
93	KS 140, State St, Salina, **E** art ctr, museum
92	Crawford St, **E** 24-7/dsl, KwikShop, Shell, Sinclair, Arby's, Bayard's Cafe, Big Cheese Pizza, Braum's, Fresnillo Mexican, Great Wall Chinese, Hickory Hut BBQ, Jim's Chicken, KFC, La Casita, McDonald's, Russell's Rest., Seoul Korean, Spangles, Subway, Taco Bell, Ambassador Hotel, AmericInn, Baymont Inn, Days Inn, Salina Inn, Value Inn&Suites, $General, $Tree, Advance Parts, Dillon's Foods/gas, Kansas Land Tires, NAPA, O'Reilly Parts, Walgreens, **W** Phillips 66/dsl, Quality Inn
90	Magnolia Rd, **E** Casey's, Phillips 66/dsl, Buffalo Wild Wings, Burger King, Carlos O'Kelly's, Chick-fil-A, Chili's, Chipotle, Domino's, Freddy's Burgers, Gambino's Pizza, Hog Wild BBQ, Hong Kong Buffet, IHOP, Jalisco Mexican, Longhorn Steaks, McAlister's Deli, McDonald's, Panera Bread, Papa Murphy's, Qdoba, Schlotzsky's, Sonic, Spangles, Starbucks, Subway, Taco Bell, Candlewood Suites, $General, $General, $Tree, AllDI, AllDI, AutoZone, BigLots,
90	Continued Cadillac/Chevrolet, Dick's, Dillon's Foods/dsl, Hobby Lobby, Honda, JC Penney, Kohl's, Marshall's, O'Reilly Parts, Old Navy, PetCo, Ross, Subaru, T-Mobile, Toyota, **W** Cenex/dsl, Fairfield Inn, Menard's
89	Schilling Rd, **E** KwikShop/dsl, Applebee's, Arby's, Daimaru Steaks, Five Guys, Olive Garden, Pancho's Mexican, Perkins, Pizza Hut, Red Lobster, Taco John's, Tucson's Steaks, Wendy's, Country Inn&Suites, Courtyard, Hampton Inn, Hilton Garden, Holiday Inn, Lowe's, Sam's Club/gas, Target, URGENT CARE, Walmart/Subway, **W** Casey's, Best Western+, Comfort Suites, Super 8
88	Water Well Rd, **E** Rodeway Inn, Chrysler/Dodge/Jeep, Ford, Nissan
86	KS 104, Mentor, Smolan
82	KS 4, Falun Rd, Assaria, **E** RV Camping
78	KS 4 W, Lindsborg, **W** to Sandz Gallery/Museum
72	Lindsborg, **E** Maxwell WR, McPherson St Fishing Lake, **W** camping, food, gas, H, lodging, museum
68mm	**full facilities, litter barrels petwalk, (both lanes exit left), RV dump**
65	Pawnee Rd
62	Mohawk Rd
60	US 56, McPherson, Marion, **E** Love's/Hardee's/dsl/LP/scales/24hr, **W** 24/7/Burger King/EVC/dsl, Applebee's, Arby's, Braum's, Freddy's Burgers, General Star Chinese, La Fiesta Mexican, McDonald's, Pizza Hut, Slim Chickens, Subway, Taco Bell, The Fieldhouse Grill, Woodies BBQ, Executive Inn, Fairfield Inn, Hampton Inn, Holiday Inn Express, Holiday Manor, Knights Inn, AutoZone, Buick/Cadillac/GMC, Chrysler/Dodge/Jeep, Ford, H, Walgreens, Walmart
58	US 81, KS 61, to Hutchinson, McPherson
54	18th Ave, Comanche Rd, Elyria
48	KS 260 E, Moundridge, **W** gas
46	KS 260 W, Moundridge, **W** food, gas
40	Lincoln Blvd, Hesston, **E** Rodeway Inn, Cottonwood Grove RV Camping, **W** Casey's/dsl/24hr, El Cerrito Grill, Lincoln Perk Coffee, Pizza Hut, Sonic, Subway, Best Value Inn, city park
34	KS 15, N Newton, to Abilene, KS 15, **E** RV camping, **W** Billy Sims BBQ(1mi), Hangar 54 Pizza(1mi), Kiko's Burrito(1mi), Papa John's(1mi), Subway(1mi), Taco Bell(1mi), Kauffman Museum
33	US 50 E, to Peabody(from nb)
31	1st St, Broadway St, **E** JumpStart/dsl, Phillips 66/dsl/@, Applebee's, KFC, Coratel Inn, Holiday Inn Express, Newton Inn, Cadillac/Chevrolet, Chrysler/Dodge/Jeep, Ford/Lincoln, **W** Braum's, Comfort Inn, Red Coach Inn
30	US 50 W, KS 15(exits left from nb), to Hutchinson, Newton, **W** KwikShop/dsl, Arby's, Freddy's Burgers, Genova Italian, Panda Kitchen, Pizza Hut, Sonic, Subway, $Tree, AutoZone, Buick/GMC, Dillon's Foods, H, R Tires, Verizon, Walmart
28	SE 36th St, **W** Nusser/dsl, Burger King, Le-J's BBQ, Chisholm Trail Outlets/famous brands
25	KS 196, to Whitewater, El Dorado
23mm	**full facilities, litter barrels, petwalk, both lanes, RV dump, vending**
22	125th St

LINDSBORG · MOUNDRIDGE · EL DORADO

 = gas = food = lodging = other = rest stop

INTERSTATE 135 (Wichita) Cont'd

Exit #	Services
19	101st St, W RV Camping
17	85th St, Valley Ctr
16	77th St, E Wichita Greyhound Park
14	61st St, E QT/dsl, Applebee's, Chopstix, Cracker Barrel, Domino's Pizza, Masters of BBQ, Pizza Hut, Spangles Rest., Subway, Taco Bell, Wendy's, Coratel Inn, Sleep Inn, Chevrolet, Family$, W Phillips 66/dsl, KFC, McDonald's, Park City Inn, Super 8, Goodyear/auto
13	53rd St, E Freightliner, Harley-Davidson, Volvo/Mack Trucks, W JumpStart/dsl, Arby's, Best Western, Sky-Palace Inn
11b	I-235 W, KS 96, to Hutchinson
11a	KS 254, to El Dorado
10b	29th St, Hydraulic Ave
10a	KS 96 E
9	21st St, E Valero, Sonic, $General, Wichita St U
8	13th St, E $General, W Pig In Pig Out BBQ
7b	8th St, 9th St, Central Ave., E School of Medicine
7a	downtown
6b	1st St, 2nd St, downtown
5b	US 54, US 400, Kellogg Ave, E QT/dsl
5a	Lincoln St, E DQ, W QT/dsl
4	Harry St, E Arby's, Bionic Burger, Burger King,
4	Continued Chick'n Pop, Church's TX Chicken, Denny's, Hardee's, Jimmie's Diner, La Chona Tacos, LA Fried Chicken, Little Caesar's, McDonald's, NuWay Drive-Thru, Pho Ong, Shanghai Chinese, Spangles Rest., Subway, Taco Bell, Wendy's, BigLots, CVS Drug, Firestone/auto, H, W American Gas/dsl, Gorditas Express
3	Pawnee Ave, E QT, Los Mexican Burritos, Pho Special, Family$, O'Reilly Parts, W Jumpstart/dsl, Burger King, Pizza Hut, Spangles, $General, AutoZone
2	Hydraulic Ave, E KwikShop, Buster's Burgers, CheeZies Pizza, $General, W McDonald's, Subway
2mm	Arkansas River
1c	I-235 N, W Hilton
1b a	US 81 S, 47th St, E JumpStart, QT/dsl, Sonic, Days Inn, Holiday Inn Express, Quality Inn, Super 8, W Angry Elephant BBQ, Applebee's/Tesla EVC, Arby's, Braum's, Burger King, Carlos O'Kelly's, Domino's, Dunkin', Godfather's, Goodcents Subs, Heritage Inn, Hog Wild BBQ, IHOP, Jalisco Mexican, KFC, Little Caesar's, McDonald's, New China, Pizza Hut, Spangles Rest., Subway, Taco Bell, Wendy's, Best Western, Springfield Inn, Woodspring Suites, $General, $Tree, Air Capital RV Park, Dillon's Foods/Starbucks/dsl, O'Reilly Parts, RNR Tires
0mm	I-135 begins/ends on I-35, exit 42.

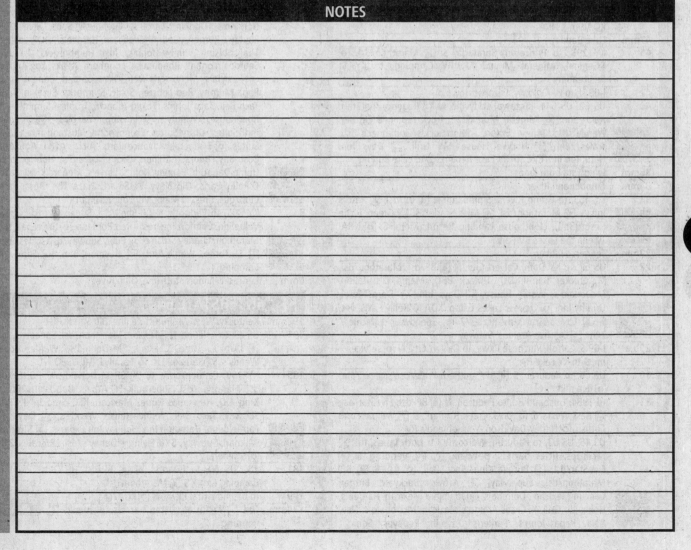

NOTES

= gas = food = lodging = other = rest stop

KENTUCKY

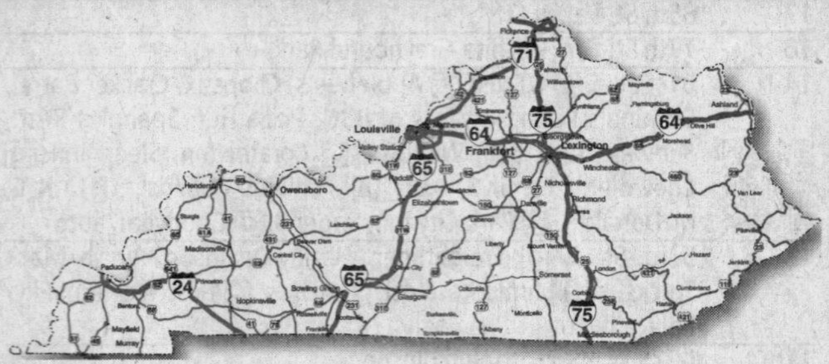

INTERSTATE 24

HOPKINSVILLE

Exit #	Services
93.5mm	Kentucky/Tennessee state line
93mm	**full facilities, litter barrels, petwalk, , , vending, Welcome Ctr wb**
91.5mm	Big West Fork Red River
89	KY 115, to Oak Grove, N to Jeff Davis Mon St HS, S Pilot/McDonald's/dsl/scales/24hr, Shell/Subway/dsl, Goodyear
86	US 41A, to Ft Campbell, Pennyrile Pkwy, Hopkinsville, N Love's/Hardee's/dsl/scales/24hr/@, Marathon/dsl/scales/24hr/@, S Exxon/dsl, Flying J/Denny's/dsl/LP/scales/24hr, Pilot/Subway/Wendy's/dsl/scales/24hr, McDonald's, Waffle House, Candlewood Suites, Days Inn, Hampton Inn, Holiday Inn Express, Quality Inn, Sleep Inn, H, truck wash
81	Pennyrile Pky N, to Hopkinsville
79mm	Little River
73	KY 117, to Gracey, Newstead
65	US 68, KY 80, to Cadiz, S BP/dsl, Marathon/dsl, Shell/dsl, Cracker Barrel, Harper House Rest., KFC, McDonald's, No Way Jose Mexican, Subway, Taco Bell, Triplets BBQ, Wendy's, Quality Inn, Red Roof Inn, Rodeway Inn, Super 7 Inn, Chevrolet, golf, H, to NRA
56	KY 139, to Cadiz, Princeton, S Marathon/dsl, $General, KOA(9mi), NRA
47mm	Lake Barkley
45	KY 293, to Princeton, Saratoga, S Marathon/dsl, $General, Mineral Mound SP, RV Camping, to KY St Penitentiary
42	I-69 N, to W KY Pkwy, Elizabethtown
40	US 62, US 641, Kuttawa, Eddyville, N Regency Inn(2mi), Relax Inn, Mineral Mound SP, truck repair, S BP/Wendy's/dsl/24hr, Exxon, Pilot/Huck's/Godfather's/dsl/scales/24hr, Huddle House, SW Grill, Days Inn, Hampton Inn/EVC, KY Lake Rec Areas, to Lake Barkley
36mm	weigh sta both lanes
34mm	Cumberland River
31	KY 453, to Grand Rivers, Smithland, N BP/dsl, Patti's Inn, S Marathon/dsl, Miss Scarlett's, Green Turtle Resort(3mi), Lighthouse Landing Resort, Motel 6, NRA, Tween the Lakes RV Park
29mm	Tennessee River
27	US 62, to KY Dam, Calvert City, N BP/dsl, Marathon/dsl, Cracker Barrel, DQ, J-Mack BBQ, Mama D's Italian, McDonald's, Waffle House, Days Inn, KY Dam Motel, Quality Inn, Cypress Lakes Camp, KOA, O'Reilly Parts, vet, S Love's/Arby's/dsl/scales/24hr, Speedway/dsl/scales/24hr, Los Tres Amigos, Subway
25b a	I-69 S, Carroll/Purchase Pkwy, to Calvert City, N services 1 mi, S to KY Lake RA
16	US 68, to Paducah, S BP/Southern Pride/dsl/scales/24hr, flea mkt
11	rd 1954, Husband Rd, to Paducah, N BP/dsl, FiveStar/dsl, Best Western, Duck Creek RV Park, S Willow Pond Catfish, Harley-Davidson, Youngblood's RV
7	US 45, US 62, to Paducah, **Welcome Ctr both lanes, full facilities, litter barrels, petwalk, , , vending,** N FiveStar/dsl, Burger King, Taco Bell, H, S BP, Marathon/dsl, Superway, Arby's, Backyard Burger, Cancun Mexican , Domino's, Guadalajara Mexican, Hardee's, Hokkaido Grill, KFC, Los Amigo's Mexican, McDonald's, New Asia, Papa John's, Parker's Drive-In, Popeyes, Sonic,

CALVERT CITY

Exit #	Services
7	Continued Subway, Waffle House, Wendy's, Travelers Inn, Banks Mkt/gas, CVS Drug, Family$, O'Reilly Parts, Plaza Tires, U-Haul, Verizon
4	US 60, to Paducah, N BP/dsl, Exxon/dsl, Applebee's, Bob Evans, Burger King, McDonald's, O'Charley's, Outback Steaks, Rafferty's, Auburn Place, Candlewood Suites, Comfort Inn&Suites, Courtyard, Days Inn, Drury Inn, Fairfield Inn, Hampton Inn, Holiday Inn Express, Homewood Suites, La Quinta, Residence Inn, Toyota, S BP, BP/dsl, Murphy USA/dsl, Arby's, Backwood BBQ, Bandanas BBQ, Boss Burrito, Buffalo Wild Wings, Capt D's, Cheddar's Kitchen, Chick-fil-A, Chicken Salad Chick, Chong's Chinese, ChuckeCheese, Cold Stone , Cracker Barrel, Culver's, Domino's, Dunkin, Fazoli's, Firehouse Subs, Five Guys, Freddy's Burgers, Godfather's Pizza, Hardee's, IHOP, Jasmine Thai Cuisine, Jimmy John's, Just Hamburgers, La Juicy Seafood, Logan's Roadhouse, Longhorn Steaks, Los Amigos, Los Garcia's, McAlister's Deli, Olive Garden, Panera Bread, Papa Murphy, Red Lobster, Sonic, Starbucks, Steak'n Shake, Taco Bell, Taco John's, Tokyo Hibachi, Tropical Smoothie, TX Roadhouse, Wendy's, Wingstop, Zaxby's, Country Inn&Suites, Drury Suites, EconoLodge, Mustang Inn, Quality Suites, $General, Advance Parts, AILDI, AT&T, AutoZone, Best Buy, Books-A-Million, Dick's, Dillard's, Hobby Lobby, Home Depot, JC Penney, Kohl's, Lowe's, Menard's, Michael's, O'Reilly Parts, Old Navy, PetSmart, Plaza Tire, Ross, Sam's Club/gas, tires, TJ Maxx, Verizon, Walmart
3	KY 305, to Paducah, N Shell/dsl, Superway/dsl, Best Value Inn, Comfort Inn/rest., Red Roof Inn, tire repair, S Marathon/Charley's/dsl/e85, Pilot/Subway/dsl/scales/24hr, El Torito, Waffle Hut, Baymont Inn, Fern Lake Camping
0mm	Kentucky/Illinois state line, Ohio River

INTERSTATE 64

CANNONSBURG

Exit #	Services
192mm	Kentucky/West Virginia state line, Big Sandy River
191	US 23, to Ashland, N Exxon, Marathon/dsl, Speedway/dsl, Arby's, Little Caesar's, McDonald's, Waffle House, Wendy's, Ramada Ltd, Family$, H, USPO
185	KY 180, Cannonsburg, N BP/McDonald's/USPO, Exxon/dsl, Marathon/dsl, Superquik, Arby's, Bob Evans, Burger King, DQ, Hermanos Nunez Mexican, KFC, Smokin' J's Ribs, Subway, Taco Bell, Waffle House, Wendy's, Days Inn, Fairfield Inn, Hampton Inn, Holiday Inn Express, $Tree, H, Walmart/Subway, S Flying J/Denny's/dsl/LP/scales/24hr, $General
181	181 US 60, to Princess, N BP/dsl, Oasis Point RV Camping (2mi), S Marathon/dsl
179	rd 67, Industrial Pkwy, N KOA/@
174mm	**full facilities, litter barrels, petwalk, , , eb, vending**

INTERSTATE 64 Cont'd

Exit #	Services
173mm	**full [handicapped] facilities, litter barrels, petwalk, [phone], [picnic], [RS] wb, vending**
172	rd 1, rd 7, Grayson, N [gas] Marathon/dsl, Superquik/dsl/scales/24hr, [food] A&W/LJ Silver, Hog's Trough BBQ, Huddle House, KFC, Pizza Hut, Subway, [lodging] Best Value Inn, Days Inn, The Inn, [other] $General, $Tree, Chrysler/Dodge/Jeep, Ford, Save-A-Lot Foods, URGENT CARE, S [gas] BP, Exxon/Hardees, Love's/Wendy's/scales/dsl/24hr, Marathon, Shell/dsl, Speedway/dsl, [food] Arby's, Burger King, China House, DQ, Little Caesar's, McDonald's, Taco Bell, Toro Loco, [lodging] Super 8, [other] Advance Parts, AT&T, AutoZone, Family$, Food Fair, Verizon, Walgreens
161	US 60, to Olive Hill, N [gas] BP, [lodging] Spanish Manor Motel, [other] to Carter Caves SP, S [gas] Marathon, [other] $General
156	rd 2, to KY 59, to Olive Hill, S [gas] BP, [food] $General
148mm	weigh sta wb
141mm	**full [handicapped] facilities, litter barrels, petwalk, [phone], [picnic], [RS] both lanes, vending**
137	KY 32, to Morehead, N [gas] Shell/dsl, Speedway/dsl, [food] $Tree, Cattleman's Roadhouse, DQ, Huddle House, McDonald's, [other] AT&T, Big Lots, Kroger/dsl, Lowe's, Walmart/Subway, S [gas] BP/McDonald's/dsl/24hr, Marathon/dsl, [food] China Star, Cracker Barrel, Domino's, Don Señor, Hardee's, Reno's Roadhouse, Starbucks, [lodging] Best Western, Days Inn, Hampton Inn, Motel 6, Red Roof Inn, [other] $General, Ace Hardware, auto repair, AutoZone, [H] (1.5mi), st police
133	rd 801, to Sharkey, Farmers, N [gas] Shell/dsl, [other] Chrysler/Dodge/Jeep/Ford, S [gas] BP/Subway/dsl, [lodging] Comfort Inn, [other] Outpost RV Park(4mi)
123	US 60, to Salt Lick, Owingsville, N [gas] Valero, S [other] farmers mkt
121	KY 36, to Owingsville, N [gas] BP/dsl, Exxon/dsl, Valero/dsl, [food] DQ, McDonald's, Subway, [other] DG Mkt, Family$, S Save-a-Lot Foods
113	US 60, to Mt Sterling, N [gas] Marathon, S Pilot/McDonald's/Subway/dsl/scales/24hr, [food] Rally's, [other] U-Haul
110	US 460, KY 11, Mt Sterling, N [gas] Shell/Krystal/Subway/dsl, Valero/dsl, [food] Cattleman's Roadhouse, Cracker Barrel, [lodging] Comfort Inn, Ramada Ltd, S [gas] BP/dsl, Exxon, Marathon, Murphy Express/dsl, Speedway/dsl, Sunoco/dsl, [food] Applebee's, Arby's, Burger King, Capt D's, City King Buffet, Dominos, Don Señor, Hardee's, KFC, Lee's Chicken, Little Caesar's, LJ Silver, McDonald's, Pizza Hut, Subway, Taco Bell, Waffle House, Wendy's, [lodging] Budget Inn, Days Inn, [other] $Tree, Advance Parts, AT&T, AutoZone, Chevrolet, Chrysler/Dodge/Jeep, CVS Drug, Family$, Ford, [H], JC Penney, Kroger, Lowe's, O'Reilly Parts, Petco, URGENT CARE, Verizon, Walmart/Subway
101	US 60
98.5mm	**full [handicapped] facilities, litter barrels, petwalk, [phone], [picnic], [RS] eb, vending**
98	KY 402(from eb), S [food] to Natural Bridge SP
96b a	KY 627, to Winchester, Paris, N [gas] 96 Truck Plaza/dsl/rest./scales, BP/dsl, S [lodging] Baymont Inn, Hampton Inn, Red Roof Inn, [other] Buick/Chevrolet/GMC
94	KY 1958, Van Meter Rd, Winchester, N [gas] Go Time, Marathon/dsl/24hr, Shell/scales/dsl, [lodging] Comfort Inn, Value Stay Inn, S [gas] BP/dsl, Marathon/dsl, Murphy Express/dsl, Shell/dsl, Speedway/dsl, [food] Applebee's, Arby's, Big Boy, Burger King, Capt D's, Cook Out, Domino's, Don Senor, DQ, El Camino Real, Fazoli's, Golden Corral, Great Wall Chinese, Hardee's, Jade Garden Chinese, Jimmy John's, KFC, Little Caesar's, McDonald's, Papa John's, Pizza Hut, Popeyes, Puerta Grande, Rally's, Sakura Express, Sir Pizza, Sonic,
94	Continued Starbucks, Subway, Taco Bell, Taste Of China, Waffle House, Wendy's, [lodging] Best Western, Holiday Inn Express, [other] $Tree, Advance Parts, AT&T, auto repair, AutoZone, Chrysler/Dodge/Jeep, [H], Kroger/dsl, Lowe's, O'Reilly Parts, Office Depot, Tire Discounters, to Ft Boonesborough Camping, Verizon, Walgreens, Walmart/Subway
87	KY 859, Blue Grass Sta
81	I-75 S, to Knoxville
80mm	**I-64 and I-75 run together 7 mi. Exits 113-115.**
75	I-75 N, to Cincinnati, N [other] to KY Horse Park
69	US 62 E, to Georgetown, N [other] Georgetown College
65	US 421, Midway, S [gas] BP/dsl, McDonald's, Shell/dsl, [food] Holly Hill Inn, Subway
60mm	**full [handicapped] facilities, litter barrels, petwalk, [RS] both lanes, vending**
58	US 60, Frankfort, N [gas] BP/dsl, Five Star/dsl, Shell/dsl, Speedway/dsl, [food] Arby's, Buffalo Wild Wings, Burger King, Capt. D's, Cattleman's Roadhouse, DQ, Jersey Mike's, Jimmy John's, KFC, McDonald's, Miguel's Mexican, Penn Sta Subs, Pizza Inn, Shelby's Diner, Starbucks, Taco Bell, Waffle House, White Castle, Zaxby's, [lodging] Best Western, Bluegrass Inn, Fairfield Inn, Home2 Suites, [other] $General, $Tree, Buick/Chevrolet/GMC, Chrysler/Dodge/Jeep, Dick's, ElkHorn Camping(5mi), Ford/Lincoln, Honda, Kohl's, Kroger/gas, KYSU, Michael's, Nissan, TireDiscounters, TJMaxx, to KY St Capitol, to Viet Vets Mem, Toyota/Scion, Walgreens, S [gas] Racetrac/dsl, Shell, [food] Cracker Barrel, Sonny's BBQ
55mm	Kentucky River
53b a	US 127, Frankfort, N [gas] Marathon, Speedway/dsl, Speedway/dsl, [food] Applebee's, Beef O'Brady's, Big Boy, Bojangles, Capt D's, Carino's Italian, Chick-fil-A, Chili's, China Buffet, CookOut, Domino's, DQ, Fazoli's, Ginza Japanese, Hardee's, Johnny Carinos, KFC, La Fiesta Grande, Longhorn Steaks, McDonald's, My Guadalajara, Panera Bread, Penn Sta Subs, Qdoba Mexican, Sonic, Starbucks, Staxx BBQ, Steak'n Shake, Taco Bell, Wendy's, Wings and Rings, [lodging] Days Inn, Hampton Inn, Holiday Inn Express, [other] $General, Advance Parts, ALDI, Ancient Age Tour, AT&T, AutoZone, Big Lots, Big-O Tire, CVS Drug, Family$, Goodyear/auto, [H], JC Penney, Kroger/gas, Lowe's, Midas, Petco, st police, Staples, to KY St Capitol, USPO, Verizon, Walgreens, Walmart/Subway, S [gas] Shell/dsl
48	KY 151, to US 127 S, S [gas] Valero/dsl
43	KY 395, Waddy, N [gas] Flying J/Denny's/dsl/LP/scales/24hr, S Love's/McDonald's/Subway/dsl/scales/24hr/@, Speedway/dsl
38.5mm	weigh sta eb
35	KY 53, Shelbyville, N [gas] Circle K/dsl, Speedway/dsl, [food] Cracker Barrel, Hometown Pizza, Ken-Tex BBQ, Waffle House, Wings and Rings, [other] Ford, Lake Shelby Camping(3mi), S [gas] Huck's/White Castle/dsl, Valero/dsl, [lodging] Holiday Inn Express, [other] golf
32b a	KY 55, Shelbyville, N [gas] Murphy USA/dsl, Valero/dsl, [food] Arby's, Asian Buffet, Bojangle's, Burger King, El Nopal, McDonald's, Subway, Taco Bell, Waffle House, Wendy's, [lodging] Best Western, Econolodge, Red Roof Inn, [other] $Tree, AutoZone, Big O Tire, Buick/Chevrolet/GMC, Chrysler/Dodge/Jeep, CVS Drug, [H], Lowe's, Rolling Hills Camping(16mi), Verizon, Walgreens, Walmart, S [food] Cattleman's Roadhouse, [lodging] Comfort Inn & Suites, [other] Taylorsville Lake SP
28mm	**full [handicapped] facilities, info, litter barrels, petwalk, [phone], [picnic], [RS] eb, vending**
28	KY 1848, Veechdale Rd, Simpsonville, N [gas] Pilot/Wendy's/dsl/scales/24hr, [food] DQ, Subway, [lodging] Hampton Inn, [other] golf, S [food] Culver's, El Nopal, McDonald's, [other] Blue Grass Outlets/famous brands

GRAYSON

FARMERS

PARIS

MIDWAY

FRANKFORT

SHELBYVILLE

KY

[gas] = gas [food] = food [lodging] = lodging [other] = other [RS] = rest stop

INTERSTATE 64 Cont'd

SBLANKENBAKER LOUISVILLE

Exit #	Services
19b a	I-265, Gene Snyder Fwy, N [other] to Tom Sawyer SP
17	S Blankenbaker, N [gas] Circle K/dsl, [food] Impellizzeri's Pizza, Zaxby's, [lodging] Staybridge Suites, S [gas] Marathon, Speedway/dsl, Thornton's/dsl, [food] Arby's, Burger King, Chick-fil-A, Cracker Barrel, El Caporal Mexican, El Nopal, KFC, Las Palamas, LJ Silver/Taco Bell, Logan's Roadhouse, McDonald's, Penn Sta Subs, Qdoba, Starbucks, Waffle House, Wendy's, Yoki Buffet, [lodging] Comfort Suites, Country Inn&Suites, Extended Stay America, Fairfield Inn, Hampton Inn, Hilton Garden/EVC, Holiday Inn Express, La Quinta, MainStay Suites, Microtel, Quality Inn, Sleep Inn, Tru, Wingate Inn/EVC, Woodspring Suites, [other] BMW, Lexus, Sam's Club/gas
15	Hurstbourne Pkwy, Louisville, N [gas] Shell/Circle K/dsl, Speedway, Thorton's/dsl, [food] Arby's, Bob Evans, Bonefish Grill, Brownie's Grill, Carrabba's, Chili's, Chipotle, City BBQ, Firehouse Subs, First Watch, Gustavo's Mexican, IHOP, Jimmy John's, Louisville Pizza Kitchen, McDonald's, Momma's BBQ, Noodles&Co, Olive Garden, Panda Express, Panera Bread, Papa John's, PF Changs, Starbucks, Subway, Vallarta Mexican, Waffle House, [lodging] Baymont Inn, Courtyard, Drury Inn, Econolodge, Holiday Inn, Hyatt Place, Red Roof Inn, Residence Inn, [other] Barnes&Noble, Kroger/gas, Lowe's, Towery's Auto, Walgreens, S [gas] Kroger/gas, [food] BoomBozz Pizza, Buca Italian, Buffalo Wild Wings, Burger King, Cane's Chicken, Chick-fil-A, ChuckeCheese, Coldstone, DQ, El Torazo Mexican, Famous Daves, Happy China, Jersey Mikes, Jumbo Buffet, Kyushu Japanese, Longhorn Steaks, McAlister's Deli, McDonald's, Melting Pot, Milantoni Italian, Moe's SW Grill, Mussel & Burger, O'Charley's, Penn Sta. Subs, Pizza Hut, Qdoba, Shogun Japanese, Smokey Bones BBQ, Starbucks, Steak'n Shake, Taco Bell, White Castle, Yen Ching, [lodging] Best Western, Marriott, Ramada, Red Carpet Inn, Suburban Studios, [other] $Tree, AutoZone, BMW, Buick/GMC, Cadillac, Carmax, Chevrolet, Discount Tire, Home Depot, Honda, Infiniti, Michael's, Petco, Subaru, Target, Valvoline, Verizon, Volvo/EVC, VW, Walgreens
12b	I-264 E, Watterson Expswy, N [food] Blaze Pizza, Buffalo Wild Wings, Cheesecake Factory, Chuy's Mexican, J. Alexander's, Jason's Deli, Red Robin, Taco Bell, [lodging] Hawthorn Suites, Hilton, Residence Inn, [other] Acura, AT&T, Best Buy, Dillard's, Ford, JC Penney, Kia/EVC, Kohl's, tire/auto repair, Whole Foods Mkt
12a	I-264 W, N [other] access to [H], S [lodging] DuPont Suites
10	Cannons Lane
8	Grinstead Dr, Louisville, S [food] Le Moo, [other] Cherokee Park
7	US 42, US 62, Mellwood Ave, Story Ave, S [gas] Valero
6	I-71 N(from eb), to Cincinnati
5a	I-65, S to Nashville, N to Indianapolis
5b	3rd St, Louisville, N [food] Joe's CrabShack, S [lodging] Galt House Hotel, Marriott, [other] [H]
4	9th St, Roy Wilkins Ave, S downtown, [other] KY Arts Ctr, KY Science Center, museum
3	US 150 E, to 22nd St, S [gas] Circle K, Marathon/dsl, [food] DQ, Little Caesars, McDonald's, Subway, [other] Family$
1	I-264 E, to Shively, S [other] [airport], Kroger/gas, zoo
0mm	Kentucky/Indiana state line, Ohio River

INTERSTATE 65

LOUISVILLE SHEPHERDSVILLE

Exit #	Services
138mm	Kentucky/Indiana state line, Ohio River
137	I-64 W, I-71 N, I-64 E, W downtown, [other] to Galt House
136c	Jefferson St, Louisville, E [other] $General, CVS, Firestone, [H], W [gas] Shell, [food] Jimmy John's, Los Azteca Mexican, McDonald's, White Castle, Wild Eggs, [lodging] Aloft, Cambria Hotel, Courtyard, EconoLodge, Embassy Suites, Fairfield Inn, Hampton Inn,
136c	Continued Hilton Garden, Holiday Inn, Hyatt, Marriott, Omni, Residence Inn, SpringHill Suites, [other] Tires+
136b	Broadway St, Chestnut St (from nb), E [other] [H], NAPA, Walgreens, W [gas] Shell, Thornton's, [food] McDonald's, Subway, White Castle, [lodging] Courtyard, Fairfield Inn, Hampton Inn, Hyatt, Marriott, Springhill Suites, [other] same as 136c, Tires+
135	W St Catherine, E [gas] Valero, [other] U-Haul
134b a	KY 61, Jackson St, Woodbine St, W [gas] Shell/Circle K, [lodging] Quality Inn, [other] Harley-Davidson
133b	US 60A, Eastern Pkwy, Taylor Blvd, E [food] Bandido Mexican, Denny's, W [gas] Speedway/dsl, [food] Cracker Barrel, McDonald's, Papa John's, [other] Churchill Downs, museum, U of Louisville
133a	Crittenden Dr(132from sb), E [food] same as 133, W [gas] BP, [food] Arby's, Burger King, Cracker Barrel, El Nopal Mexican, [lodging] Comfort Inn, Country Inn&Suites, Hilton Garden, Holiday Inn, Home2 Suites, Sheraton, Staybridge Suites, Super 8, [other] U-Haul
131b a	I-264, Watterson Expswy, E [gas] Circle K, Marathon/dsl, [food] Craft Pizza, Mirage Mediterranean, [lodging] SureStay, [other] ALDI, W [lodging] Courtyard , Crowne Plaza, Fairfield Inn, Hampton Inn, Howard Johnson, Residence Inn, SpringHill Suites, Tru, [other] [airport] Cardinal Stadium, Expo Center
130	KY 61, Preston Hwy, [lodging] EconoLodge, E [gas] Shell/Circle K, Thornton's, [food] Domino's, Dunkin, KFC, McDonald's, Popeyes, Waffle House, Wendy's, [lodging] Red Roof Inn, Super 8, [other] $General, Chevrolet/Kia, Danny's Tires, O'Reilly Parts, Save-A-Lot, U-Haul, URGENT CARE, W [food] Papa John's
128	KY 1631, Fern Valley Rd, E [gas] BP, Marathon/Circle K, Thornton's/dsl, [food] Dunkin Donuts, El Nopal Mexican, Hardee's, Indi's Rest., McDonald's, Outback Steaks, Shoney's, Subway, Taco Bell, Waffle House, Wendy's, White Castle, White Castle, [lodging] Baymont Inn, Comfort Suites, Days Inn, Holiday Inn, InTown Suites, TownePlace, [other] Sam's Club/gas, W UPS Depot
127	KY 1065, outer loop, E [food] Cheddar's, TX Roadhouse, W McDonald's/RV Parking
125b a	I-265 E, KY 841, Gene Snyder Fwy
121	KY 1526, Brooks Rd, E [gas] BP, Marathon, [food] Burger King, Cracker Barrel, McDonald's, Subway, Tumbleweed Grill, [lodging] Best Western, Comfort Inn, Fairfield Inn, Holiday Inn Express, Home2 Suites, Tru, [other] fireworks, [H], W [gas] BP/dsl, Pilot/Subway/dsl/scales/24hr, [food] El Maguey Mexican, Taco Bell, Waffle House, [lodging] Baymont Inn, EconoLodge, Hampton Inn, Quality Inn, [other] $General
117	KY 44, Shepherdsville, E [gas] BP/dsl, Valero, [food] Denny's, [lodging] Best Western/rest., Garden Inn, [other] KOA(2mi), vet, W [gas] EVC, Marathon, Speedway/dsl, [food] Arby's, Big Boy, Bojangles, Burger King, Cattlemans Roadhouse, China Buffet, Domino's, Donut Express, DQ, El Nopal, El Tarasco, Fazoli's, Fish House, Freddy's Burgers, KFC, Little Caesar's, LJ Silver, McDonald's/playplace, Mr Gatti's, Panda Express, Panera Bread, Papa John's, Penn Sta Subs, Pizza Hut, Sonic, Starbucks, Subway, Taco Bell, Waffle House, Wendy's, White Castle, Zaxby's, [lodging] Country Inn&Suites, Motel 6, Sleep Inn, Super 8, [other] $General, $Tree, Ace Hardware, Advance Parts, AT&T, auto repair, AutoZone, BigLots, CVS Drug, Kroger/dsl, Lowe's, NAPA, O'Reilly Parts, Price Less Foods, Towery Tire/auto, Walgreens, Walmart/dsl
116.5mm	Salt River

INTERSTATE 65 Cont'd

Exit #	Services
116	KY 480, to KY 61, E [gas] Love's/Chester's/Subway/dsl/scales/24hr, RaceTrac/dsl, Valero/dsl, [food] El Burrito Loco, [other] Speedco, truck wash, W [gas] BP/dsl, [other] antiques, flea mkt, Grandma's RV Park/flea mkt
114mm	**full [hc] facilities, litter barrels, petwalk, [phone], [picnic], [RS] sb, vending**
112	KY 245, Clermont, E [gas] Valero/dsl, [other] Bernheim Forest, Jim Beam Outpost, to My Old Kentucky Home SP(15mi), W $Genereak, Bullitt Supermkt
105	KY 61, Lebanon Jct, W [gas] Pilot/McDonald's/Subway/dsl/scales/24hr/@, Speedway/dsl, [food] Little Rick's Grill
102	KY 313, to KY 434, Radcliff
94	US 62, Elizabethtown, E [gas] BP/dsl, Marathon/dsl, [food] Denny's, Waffle House, White Castle, [lodging] Best Western+, Days Inn, Quality Inn, Super 8, [other] $General, W [gas] BP/dsl, Shell/dsl, Speedway/dsl, [food] Arby's, Burger King, Chalupa's Mexican, Cracker Barrel, Culver's, Dewster's Ice Cream, Gatti's Pizza, Hardee's, HoneyBaked Ham, KFC/Taco Bell, La Paloma Mexican, Papa John's, Pizza Hut, Ruby Tuesday, Shogun Japanese, Shoney's, Starbucks, Subway, TX Outlaw Steaks, TX Roadhouse, Wendy's, [lodging] Baymont Inn, Comfort Suites, Country Inn, Fairfield Inn, Hampton Inn, Hilton, Holiday Inn Express, La Quinta, Motel 6, Ramada Inn, Springhill Suites, Wingfield Inn, [other] $General, $Tree, Advance Parts, AutoZone, Crossroads Camping, [H], Kroger/gas, Skagg's RV Ctr, st police, USPO, Walgreens
93	to Bardstown, to BG Pky, E [other] Maker's Mark Distillery(27mi), to My Old KY Home SP(25mi)
91	US 31 W, KY 61, WK Pkwy, Elizabethtown, E [gas] Marathon/dsl, RaceTrac/dsl/scales/24hr/@, Tesla EVC, [food] LJ Silver, [lodging] Best Value Inn, Royal Inn, [other] $General, $General, to Lincoln B'Place, W [gas] Marathon, [other] [H]
90mm	weigh sta sb only
86	KY 222, Glendale, E [gas] Pilot/McDonalds/dsl/scales/24hr, [other] Glendale Camping, Royal Oak RV Park, trk repair, W [gas] Marathon/dsl, Petro/Iron Skillet/dsl/scales/24hr/@, [other] truck wash
83mm	Nolin River
81	KY 84, Sonora, E [gas] ONE9/Subway/dsl/scales/24hr, [other] to Lincoln B'Place, W [gas] Five Star/dsl, [food] Cheezie's Cafe, [other] $General, auto repair, U-Haul, USPO
76	KY 224, Upton, E [gas] Marathon/dsl, W [other] $General, to Nolin Lake
75mm	eastern/central time zone
71	KY 728, Bonnieville, W [gas] Marathon/dsl, [other] $General, USPO
65	US 31 W, Munfordville, E [gas] FiveStar/dsl, [food] DQ, El Mazatlan, King Buffet, McDonald's, Pizza Hut, Sonic, Subway, Taco Bell, [lodging] Super 8, [other] $General, Ace Hardware, Advance Parts, Family$, IGA Foods, Save-A-Lot, W [gas] Shell, Valero/dsl, [food] to Nolin Lake, [other] U-Haul
61mm	**full [hc] facilities**, Green River, **info, litter barrels, petwalk, [phone], [picnic], [RS] both lanes, vending**
58	KY 218, Horse Cave, E [gas] Love's/McDonald's/dsl/scales/24hr/@, [food] Farmwald's Dutch Bakery, [other] [H], KY RV Park, Speedco, zoo, W [gas] Shell/dsl, [lodging] Holiday Inn Express, Quality Inn, [other] KOA, to Mammoth Cave NP
53	KY 70, KY 90, Cave City, E Cave City Welcome Ctr, [gas] BP/Five Star/dsl, Shell/Subway/Sonic/dsl, [food] A&W/LJ Silver, Bucky Bees BBQ, Cave City Creamery, Cracker Barrel, El Mazatlan Mexican, KFC, McDonald's, Pizza Hut, Taco Bell, Wendy's, [lodging] Baymont Inn, Comfort Inn, Days Inn/rest., Econolodge, Hampton Inn, Red Roof Inn, Sleep Inn, [other] Barren River Lake SP(24mi), Cave Country RV Camping, DG Mkt, [H], museum, W [food] Watermill Rest., [lodging] Jellystone Park, [other] Dinosaur World,
53	Continued Mammoth Cave NP, Onyx Cave, playground/restrooms, Rock Cabin Camping(1.5mi), Singing Hills RV Park(1mi)
48	KY 255, Park City, E [gas] Shell/Subway/dsl, [food] Miss Betty's, [lodging] Grand Victorian Inn, [other] $General, Family$, Park Mammoth Resort, USPO, W Diamond Caverns Resort, Mammoth Cave NP
43	Nun/Cumberland Pky, E [other] to Barren River Lake SP
38	KY 101, Smiths Grove, E [gas] Buc-ees/dsl, W BP/Taco Bell/dsl/scales, Marathon/Subway/dsl, Shell/Schlotsky's/dsl, Speedyway/dsl, [food] Cinco De Mayo, McDonald's, Wendy's, [other] $General, city park, IGA Foods, vet
36	US 68, KY 80, Oakland, (no nb return)
31	to Bristol Rd
28	rd 446, to US 31 W, Bowling Green, E [gas] Mobil/dsl, W Huck's/dsl, Shell/dsl, [food] Hardee's, McDonald's, Starbucks, Wendy's, [lodging] Country Hearth Inn, MainStay/Sleep Inn, Super 8, SureStay, Value Lodge, [other] antiques, Corvette Museum/cafe/EVC, [H], to WKYU
26	KY 234, Bowling Green, W [gas] Shell/dsl, [food] Subway, [lodging] Embassy Suites, [other] Crossroads IGA, [H], IGA Foods
22	US 231, Bowling Green, E [gas] Marathon/Godfather's, Shell/dsl, Shell/Subway/IGA/dsl, [food] Cracker Barrel, Culver's, Domino's, El Maguey, El Mazatlan, Hardee's, Motor City Grill, Sonic, Waffle House, Zaxby's, [lodging] Baymont Inn, Best Western+, Days Inn, InTown Suites, La Quinta, Microtel, Quality Inn, Ramada Inn, Super 8, Wingate, [other] $General, Camping World, Harley-Davidson, O'Reilly Parts, USPO, W [gas] Marathon/dsl, Speedway/dsl, Speedway/dsl, [food] Arby's, Beijing Chinese, Bruster's, Buffalo Wild Wings, Burger King, Capt D's, Chick-fil-A, Chick-fil-A, Chipotle, ChuckeCheese, Chuy's Mexican, Corner Bakery Cafe, Fazoli's, Firehouse Subs, Five Guys, Freddy's, Honeybaked Ham, IHOP, Jimmy John's, KFC, Krystal, Kyoto Steaks, Longhorn Steaks, McDonald's, O'Charley's, Olive Garden, Outback Steaks, Panera Bread, Penn Sta Subs, Puerto Vallarta, Qdoba, Rafferty's, Raising Cane's, Red Lobster, Roosters, Ruby Tuesday, Smokey Bones BBQ, Sonic, Sonny's BBQ, Starbucks, Subway, Subway, Taco Bell, Toots Rest., TX Roadhouse, Waffle House, Wendy's, White Castle, Zaxby's, [lodging] Best Value, Candlewood Suites, Comfort Suites, Country Inn&Suites, Courtyard, Drury Inn, Hampton Inn, Hilton Garden, Holiday Inn, Holiday Inn Express, Home2 Suites, Red Roof Inn, [other] $General, $Tree, Advance Parts, AT&T, auto/tire repair, AutoZone, Barnes&Noble, Best Buy, BMW/Mercedes, Buick/GMC/Cadillac, Cabela's, Chevrolet, Chrysler/Dodge/Jeep, Crossroads IGA, CVS Drug, Dick's, Dillard's, Ford/Lincoln, Home Depot, Honda, [H], [H], Hyundai, JC Penney, Kia, KOA, Kohl's, Kroger/gas, Lowe's, Meijer, Michael's, Nissan, Old Navy, PetCo, PetSmart, Sam's Club/gas, Staples, Target, TJ Maxx, Toyota, U-Haul, vet, Walgreens, Walmart/McDonald's
20	WH Natcher Toll Rd, to Bowling Green, access to W KY U, W [other] st police
6	KY 100, Franklin, E [gas] Shell/dsl/24hr, [other] truckwash, W [gas] ONE9/Subway/dsl/scales/24hr, Pilot/Wendy's/dsl/scales/24hr, [food] El Potrero, [lodging] Comfort Inn, Days Inn, Red Roof Inn, [other] Bluegrass RV Park, [H], SpeedCo, TA Truck Service, truck&tires/repair, truckwash, Volvo Trucks
4mm	weigh sta nb
2	US 31 W, to Franklin, E [gas] Flying J/Denny's/dsl/LP/scales/24hr, Keystop/Marathon/Burger King/dsl/24hr, W BP/dsl, [food] Colorado Grill, Cracker Barrel, Franklin Steakhouse, McDonald's, Sol Azteca, Waffle House, [lodging] Baymont Inn, EconoLodge, Hampton Inn/EVC, Holiday Inn Express, Quality Inn, Super 8, [other] antiques, antiques, [H]
1mm	**full [hc] facilities, litter barrels, petwalk, [phone], [picnic], vending, Welcome Ctr nb**

ELIZABETHTOWN BONNIEVILLE CAVE CITY BOWLING GREEN FRANKLIN

KY

= gas = food = lodging = other = rest stop

INTERSTATE 65 Cont'd

Exit #	Services
0mm	Kentucky/Tennessee state line

INTERSTATE 71

100	Kentucky/Ohio state line, Ohio River. I-71 and I-75 run together 19 miles. Exits 175-192.
77[173]	I-75 S, to Lexington
75mm	weigh sta sb
72	KY 14, to Verona, E Shell/dsl, $General, Oak Creek Camping
62	US 127, to Glencoe, E 62 TrkPlaza/rest./dsl, W Valero/dsl, 127 Motel
57	KY 35, to Sparta, E Marathon/dsl, Speedway Inn, Eagle Valley Camping(10mi), Sparta RV Park(3mi), W BP/dsl, Ramada, KY Speedway
55	KY 1039, W Love's/McDonald's/Subway/dsl/scales/24hr, Hog Wild BBQ, Edge of Speedway, casino, NAPA truck repair
44	KY 227, to Indian Hills, W Marathon/dsl, Murphy USA/dsl, Sunoco, Valero/dsl, Arby's, El Nopal, Hometown Pizza, KFC, McDonald's, Mi Viejo Mexican, Subway, Taco Bell, Waffle House, Wendy's, Hampton Inn, Holiday Inn, Quality Inn, Red Roof Inn, $General, $Tree, AutoZone, Chevrolet, Ford, Gen. Butler SP, H, Kroger/gas, tire/auto repair, Verizon, vet, Walmart
43.5mm	Kentucky River
43	KY 389, to KY 55, English, E tire/auto repair
34	US 421, New Castle, Campbellsburg, E $General, st police, W Marathon/dsl, Valero/Subway/dsl, st police
28	KY 153, KY 146, to US 42, Pendleton, E Pilot/Subway/Dunkin/dsl/scales/24hr/@, Valero/dsl, W Pilot/McDonald's/scales/dsl/24hr, $General, Speedco, USPO
22	KY 53, La Grange, E Murphy USA/dsl, Speedway/dsl, Applebee's, Burger King, Cattleman's Roadhouse, Freddy's, Gustavo's Mexican, Jersey Mike's, Jumbo Buffet, Papa John's, Subway, Waffle House, Wendy's, Best Western, Comfort Inn, $General, AT&T, Big-O Tire, H, Kroger/gas, O'Reilly Parts, Towery's Tire/auto, URGENT CARE, Walgreens, Walmart/Subway, W Marathon/dsl, Arby's, Cracker Barrel, Domino's, DQ, El Nopal, Hometown Pizza, KFC, LJ Silver, McDonald's, Pizza Hut, Taco Bell, Holiday Inn Express, Quality Suites, Super 8, $Tree, Advance Parts, AutoZone, Buick/Chevrolet/GMC, NAPA, USPO, vet
18	KY 393, Buckner, W Marathon/dsl, McDonald's, Ford, Kroger/gas
17	KY 146, Buckner, W Thornton's/dsl/24hr, Mi Tierra Mexican, Subway, U-Haul, USPO
14	KY 329, Crestwood, Pewee Valley, Brownsboro, E BP/dsl, Gustavo's Mexican, Starbucks, Taco Bell, The Cottages, $General, LDS Temple, Walmart Supercenter
13mm	**full facilities, litter barrels, petwalk**, both lanes, **vending**
9b a	I-265, KY 841, Gene Snyder Fwy, E Speedyway/dsl, Arby's, Big Bad Breakfast, Blaze Pizza, DQ, Drake's, Martini Italian, McDonald's, Mitchell's Seafood, Olive Garden, Potbelly, Qdoba, Red Robin, Starbucks, Stoney River Steaks, Drury Inn, Hilton Garden, Cabela's, Costco/gas, H, LDS Temple, Lowe's, mall, Sawyer SP, Verizon, Walgreens
5	I-264, Watterson Expswy (exits left from sb), E Sawyer SP
2	Zorn Ave, E VA H, W Shell/dsl, Valero, River House Rest., River Road BBQ, Candlewood Suites
1b	I-65, S to Nashville, N to Indianapolis

CAMPBELLSBURG

BUCKNER

INTERSTATE 75

193mm	Kentucky/Ohio state line, Ohio River
192	5th St(from nb), Covington, park, E BP/dsl, Circle K, Speedway/dsl, Big Boy, Burger King, Chipotle, GoldStar Chili, McDonald's, Popeyes, Riverfront Pizza, Skyline Chili, Taco Bell, Waffle House, Wendy's, White Castle, Courtyard, Extended Stay America, Holiday Inn, Radisson, Lexus, Riverboat Casino, W Holiday Inn Express
191	12th St, Covington, E Sunoco, H, Kroger, same as 192, Walgreens, W museum
189	KY 1072, Kyles Lane, W BP/dsl, Shell/dsl, Big Boy, Skyline Chili, Rodeway Inn, same as 188, Walgreens
188	US 25, US 42, Dixe Hwy, E Sunoco, Starbucks, Subway, Kroger/dsl, W Fort Mitchell Rest., Rodeway Inn, Infiniti, Mercedes, same as 189
186	KY 371, Buttermilk Pike, Covington, E Marathon/dsl, Shell/dsl, Graeter's Ice Cream, Oriental Wok, Papa John's, Super 8, W BP, Speedway/dsl, Sunoco/dsl, Arby's, Baskin-Robbins/Dunkin, Bonefish Grill, Burger King, Cancun Mexican, Chipotle Mexican, Domino's, Empire Buffet, GoldStar Chili, Jimmy John's, Joella's Chicken, La Rosa's Pizza, McDonald's, Miyako Steaks, Panera Bread, PeeWee's Place, Penn Station Subs, Skyline Chili, Subway, Sweet Basil Thai, Taco Bell, Tropical Smoothie, $Tree, AutoZone, Home Depot, Petco, Remke Foods, Verizon, Walgreens
185	I-275 E and W, W to ✈
184	KY 236, Donaldson Rd, to Erlanger, E BP, Sunoco/Dunkin, W Marathon/dsl, Speedway/dsl, Waffle House, Candlewood Suites, Country Inn, EconoLodge, Red Roof Inn, Wingate Inn, auto/tire, URGENT CARE
182	KY 1017, Turfway Rd, E BP/dsl, Shell/dsl, Big Boy, Chipotle, Dunkin, Lee's Chicken, McDonald's, Papa John's, Subway, Taco Bell, Courtyard, Days Inn, Extended Stay, Quality Inn, BigLots, CVS Drug, Remke Foods, USPO, W Applebee's, Burger King, Chick-fil-A, Chili's, CiCi's Pizza, Cracker Barrel, Golden Corral, Longhorn Steaks, McAlister's, O'Charley's, Potbelly, Rafferty's, Skyline Chili, Steak'n Shake, Subway, TX Roadhouse, Wendy's, Comfort Inn, Extended Stay, Extended Stay America, Hampton Inn, Hilton, Hyatt Place, La Quinta, SpringHill Suites, TownePlace, ALDI, Best Buy, Dick's, Home Depot, H, Kohl's, Lowe's, Meijer, Michael's, PetSmart, Sam's Club/gas, Target
181	KY 18, Florence, E Speedway/dsl, TA/Marathon/Popeyes/Subway/dsl/24hr/@, Waffle House, Best Value Inn, Best Western, Motel 6, Chevrolet, W BP/dsl, Speedway/dsl, Buffalo Wild Wings, Cheddar's, Chipotle Mexican, Chuy's Mexican, City BBQ, Dunkin, El Rio Grande, Fazoli's, Firehouse Subs, Fuji Steaks, Hooters, IHOP, Jersey Mike's, La Rosa's, Miyoshi Japanese, Panda Express, Panera Bread, Raising Cane's, Red Robin, Tropical Smoothie, Twin Peaks Rest., Comfort Suites, Fairfield Inn, Holiday Inn Express/EVC, Home2 Suites, Homewood Suites, Microtel, Tru, Buick/GMC, Chrysler/Jeep/Dodge, Ford, Honda, Hyundai, Mazda, Nissan/EVC, Tire Discounters, Toyota/Scion, URGENT CARE, Verizon, VW, Walmart/Subway
180a	Mall Rd(from sb), W Asian Buffet, BJ's Rest., Buca Italian, ChuckeCheese, GoldStar Chili, HoneyBaked Ham, Jimmy John's, Olive Garden, Pizza Hut, Qdoba, Skyline Chili, Smokey Bones BBQ, Starbucks, Subway, Taco Bell, Which Wich?, $General, $Tree, AT&T, Barnes&Noble, Harley Davidson, Hobby Lobby, JC Penney, Kroger/dsl, Macy's, Old Navy, same as 180, Staples, TJ Maxx, Tuesday Morning
180	US 42, US 127, Florence, Union, E BP/dsl, Speedway/dsl,

COVINGTON

FLORENCE

KY

INTERSTATE 75 Cont'd

RICHWOOD

180 Continued
Big Boy, Bob Evans, Capt D's, Chipotle Mexican, El Nopal Mexican, Mai Thai, McDonald's, Penn Sta Subs, Rally's, Red Lobster, Subway, Wendy's, Holiday Inn, Howard Johnson, Quality Inn, Rodeway Inn, Super 8, Cadillac/EVC, funpark, Subaru, **W** Marathon/dsl, Murphy USA/dsl, Speedway/dsl, Acapulco Mexican, Arby's, Chick-fil-a, Dave&Buster's, Little Caesar's, LJ Silver, outback, Waffle House, White Castle, SureStay, Travelodge, Costco/dsl, Midas, O'Reilly Parts, PepBoys, Tire Discounters, Tires+, Walgreens

178 KY 536, Mt Zion Rd, **E** Marathon/Rally's/dsl, Speedway/dsl, Sunoco/Subway/dsl, Buffalo Bob's, El Rio Grande, GoldStar Chili, Hot Head Burritos, Jersey Mike's Subs, La Rosa's Pizza, Smokin' This & That BBQ, Sonic, Steak'n Shake, Taco Bell, AutoZone, Goodyear/auto, Kroger/dsl

177mm **full facilities, litter barrels, , , RV dump, vending, Welcome Ctr sb/ nb**

175 KY 338, Richwood, **E** Mr. Fuel/Subway/dsl/24hr/scales, Burger King, Domino's, White Castle, Motel 6, **W** BP/dsl, Pilot/Wendy's/dsl/scales/24hr, Shell/dsl, Dunkin, GoldStar Chili, McDonald's, Penn Station Subs, Skyline Chili, Snappy Tomato Pizza, Waffle House, Wendy's, Hampton Inn, Holiday Inn Express, Red Roof Inn, to Big Bone Lick SP

173 I-71 S, to Louisville

171 KY 14, KY 16, to Verona, Walton, **E** Marathon/Wendy's/dsl, Shell/dsl, Arbys, Burger King, China Moon, El Toro Mexican, McDonald's, Pizza Hut, Starbucks, Starbucks, Subway, Taco Bell, Waffle House, Advance Parts, AT&T, AutoZone, Kohl's, Kroger/gas, Tire Discounters, URGENT CARE, Walton Drug, **W** Flying J/Denny's/dsl/scales/24hr, Blue Beacon, Delightful Days RV Ctr, Oak Creek Camping(1mi), to Big Bone Lick SP, vet

CRITTENDEN

168mm weigh sta/rest haven sb

166 KY 491, Crittenden, **E** BP/dsl, Sunoco/dsl, McDonald's, auto/tires, Chrysler/Dodge/Jeep, Family$, Northern KY RV Camping(2mi), **W** Marathon/dsl, Shell/Gold Star Chili, Wendy's, $General, Grant Co Drugs, U-Haul, URGENT CARE

159 KY 22, to Owenton, Dry Ridge, **E** BP, Shell/dsl, Speedway/dsl, Arby's, Casa Martini, Dunkin, Happy Dragon Chinese, KFC/Taco Bell, La Rosa's, McDonald's, Papa Johns, Penn Sta. Subs, Skyline Chili, Starbucks, Subway, Waffle House, Wendy's, Microtel, Red Roof Inn, $General, Buick/Chevrolet, O'Reilly Parts, Verizon, Walmart/gas, **W** Marathon/dsl, Speedway/dsl, Big Boy, Cracker Barrel, Comfort Suites, Hampton Inn, Holiday Inn Express, Quality Inn, $Tree, Camper Village, Tire Discounters, Toyota/Scion

156 Barnes Rd, **E**

CORINTH

154 KY 36, Williamstown, **E** Marathon/dsl, Shell/dsl, $General, to Kincaid Lake SP, **W** Sunoco/dsl, El Jalisco Mexican, Best Value Inn, Sunrise Inn

144 KY 330, to Owenton, Corinth, **E** Noble's Trk Plaza/rest./dsl, Sunoco/dsl, $General, Three Springs Camping, **W** BP, North Star Inn

136 KY 32, to Sadieville, **E** Love's/Hardee's/dsl/scales/24hr

130.5mm weigh sta nb

129 rd 620, Cherry Blossom Wy, **E** Pilot/Wendy's/dsl/scales/24hr/@, Waffle House, Days Inn, Motel 6, **W** Pilot/McDonald's/dsl/scales/24hr, Shell, Whispering Hills RV Park(3mi)

127mm **full facilities, litter barrels, petwalk, , , both lanes, vending**

127 Georgetown, **N** , full facilities, , litter barrels, vending,

126 US 62, to US 460, Georgetown, **E** EVC, Marathon/dsl,

GEORGETOWN

126 Continued
Murphy USA/dsl, Applebee's, Big Boy, Buffalo Wild Wings, Burger King, Hibachi Grill, Jimmy John's, McDonald's, O'Charley's, Papa John's, Penn Sta Subs, Pepe's Mexican, Qdoba, Starbucks, Steak'n Shake, Holiday Inn Express, TownePlace Suites, AT&T, auto repair, Kohl's, Lowe's, T-Mobile, Tire Discounters, URGENT CARE, Verizon, Walmart/Subway, **W** Shell/Subway, Speedway/dsl, Cane's, Cattleman's Roadhouse, Chick-fil-A, Cracker Barrel, Culver's, Dunkin, Fazoli's, First Watch, KFC, Panera Bread, Skyline Chili, Waffle House, Baymont Inn, Best Western, Comfort Suites, Country Inn&Suites, Fairfield Inn, Hampton Inn, Hilton Garden, Home2 Suites, Microtel, Super 8, Buick/Chevrolet, Chrysler/Dodge/Jeep, , same as 125, to Georgetown Coll

125 US 460(from nb), Georgetown, **E** BP, Shell, FatKats Pizza, Red Roof Inn, **W** Marathon/dsl, Valero/dsl, Arby's, DQ, Little Caesar's, Taco Bell, TX Roadhouse, Wendy's, Winner's Circle Motel, $Tree, Advance Parts, BigLots, Camping World, Midas, Outlets/Famous Brands, same as 126

120 rd 1973, to Ironworks Pike, KY Horse Park, **E** KY Horse Park, KY Horse Park Camping, **W** BP/dsl, Shell/dsl,

118 I-64 W, to Frankfort, Louisville

115 rd 922, Lexington, **E** Shell/Subway/dsl, Cracker Barrel, McDonald's, Fairfield Inn, Glo Best Western, La Quinta, Quality Inn, **W** Marathon/dsl, Clarion, Embassy Suites, Marriott/rest./Tesla EVC

113 US 27, US 68, to Paris, Lexington, **E** BP/dsl, Speedway/dsl, Waffle House, Ramada Inn, $General, Peterbilt, **W** Lex Express, Marathon/dsl, Shell/dsl, Arby's, Burger King, Capt D's, Chick-fil-A, Donato's Pizza, Golden Corral, Hardee's, KFC, Little Caesar's, McDonald's, Panda Express, Penn Sta Subs, Popeyes, Rally's, Sir Pizza, Subway, Taco Bell, Wendy's, Zaxby's, Catalina Motel, Days Inn, Red Roof Inn, Advance Parts, ALDI, AutoZone, Blue Compass RV Ctr, Chevrolet, CVS Drug, Family$, Family$, O'Reilly Parts, Rupp Arena, to UK, United RV Ctr, Walmart

LEXINGTON

111 I-64 E, to Huntington, WV

110 US 60, Lexington, **W** Murphy USA/dsl, Shell/dsl, Speedway/dsl, Thorntons/dsl, A&W Rest., Arby's, Cane's Chicken, Cracker Barrel, First Watch, Jersey Mikes, McDonald's, MOD Pizza, Smashing Tomato, Sonny's BBQ, Starbucks, Wendy's, Best Western, Comfort Inn, Country Inn&Suites, Fairfield Inn, Guesthouse Inn, Hampton Inn, Holiday Inn Express, Microtel, Motel 6, Quality Inn, Red Roof Inn, Super 8, $Tree, Hobby Lobby, (1.5mi), Lowe's, Walmart/Subway/gas

108 Man O War Blvd, **E** Shell, Freddy's, Cabela's, Costco/gas, **W** Marathon/dsl, Shell/KFC/Pizza Hut/Wendy's/dsl, Arby's, BD Mongolian Grill, Big Boy, Big City Pizza, BoneFish Grill, Carino's, Carrabba's, Cheddar's, Chick-fil-A, Chipotle Mexican, Chuy's, Coldstone, Culver's, Fazoli's, GoldStar Chili, Joella's Chicken, Local Taco, Logan's Roadhouse, Malone's, McDonald's, Old Chicago, Outback Steaks, Qdoba, Rafferty's, Red Lobster, Starbucks, Steak'n Shake, Subway, Taco Bell, Ted's MT Grill, Tekka Japanese, Waffle House, avid hotel, Courtyard, Holiday Inn, Home2 Suites, Homewood Suites, Hyatt Place, Residence Inn, Sleep Inn, TownePlace Suites, $Tree, AT&T, Audi, Barnes&Noble, Best Buy, BigLots, Dick's, GNC, Harley-Davidson, , Kohl's, Marshall's, Meijer/dsl/EVC, Michael's, Old Navy, PetSmart, Ross, Staples, Target/Starbucks, Tire Discounters, Verizon, Walgreens, World Mkt

104 KY 418, Lexington, **E** BP/dsl, Shell/McDonald's, Comfort Inn, Days Inn, EconoLodge, Hotel LEX, La Quinta, **W** BP/dsl, Marathon, Speedway/dsl, Wendy's,

KY

= gas = food = lodging = other = rest stop

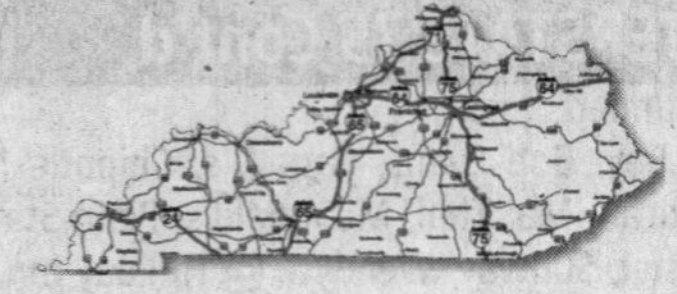

INTERSTATE 75 Cont'd

Exit #	Services
99mm	US 25 N, US 421 N, Clays Ferry
98mm	Kentucky River
97	US 25 S, US 421 S, Clay's Ferry, W BP/WOW/pizza/dsl/scales/24hr
95	rd 627, to Boonesborough, Winchester, E Love's/Arby's/dsl/scales/24hr/@, camping, Ft Boonesborough SP, W Shell/dsl

RICHMOND

Exit #	Services
90	US 25, US 421, Richmond, E Shell, Cracker Barrel, Clarion Pointe, Red Roof Inn, Relax Inn, Super 7, W BP, Gulf/dsl, Marathon, Shell, Valero, DQ, El Charro, El Mamut, Hardee's, McDonald's, Pizza Hut, Subway, Taco Bell, Waffle House, Wendy's, Days Inn, Super 8, $General, vet
87	rd 876, Richmond, E BP/dsl, Marathon/dsl, Shell, Shell/dsl, Speedway/dsl, Arby's, Baskin-Robbins, Casa Fiesta Mexican, Cook Out, Domino's, Dunkin, Fazoli's, Hardee's, Hooters, King Buffet, Little Caesar's, McAlister's Deli, McDonald's, Papa John's, Penn Sta. Subs, Qdoba, Rally's, Taco Bell, Tokyo Express, Waffle House, Wendy's, Best Western, Country Hearth Inn, Quality Quarters Inn, $General, Aamco, Ace Hardware, AT&T, BigLots, Goodyear/auto, H, to EKU, W Circle K, Shell/Jimmy John's/dsl, Buffalo Wild Wings, Burger King, Cane's, Chick-fil-A, Culver's, Firehouse Subs, First Watch, Golden Corral, IHOP, Koto Japanese, Logan's Roadhouse, Olive Garden, Panda Express, Panera Bread, Starbucks, Steak'n Shake, Subway, TX Roadhouse, Comfort Suites, Hampton Inn, Holiday Inn Express, Quality Inn, TownePlace Suites/EVC, Tru, Belk, Dick's, GNC, JC Penney, Meijer/dsl, Michaels, PetSmart, Tire Discounters, TJ Maxx, Verizon
83	to US 25, rd 2872, Duncannon Ln, Richmond, E Buc-ees/dsl/EVC

BEREA

Exit #	Services
77	rd 595, Berea, E KY Artisan Ctr/Cafe/Travelers Ctr, W BP/Subway/dsl, Shell/dsl, Smokehouse Grill, Motel 6, Quality Inn, $General, vet
76	KY 21, Berea, E BP, Marathon/Circle K, Shell/Burger King, Speedway/dsl, A&W/LJ Silver, Arby's, Cracker Barrel, Dinner Bell Rest., Gold Star Chili, Hong Kong Buffet, McDonald's, Old Town Amish Rest., Papa John's, Pizza Hut, Subway, Taco Bell, Wendy's, Yamato Japanese, Best Value Inn, Holiday Motel, Knights Inn, $General, $Tree, H, URGENT CARE, Walmart, W Casa Amigos, 76 Fuel/dsl, BP/dsl, Marathon/dsl, KFC, Lee's Chicken, Comfort Inn, EconoLodge, Holiday Inn Express, Oh! Kentucky Camping, tires, Walnut Meadow RV Park

LIVINGSTON

Exit #	Services
62	US 25, to KY 461, Renfro Valley, E Derby City/rest./dsl, Shell, Hardee's, Little Caesar's, Baymont Inn, $General, KOA(2mi), Renfro Valley RV Park/rest, W BP, Marathon/dsl, Marathon/Wendy's/dsl, Shell, Arby's, El Dorado Mexican, KFC, Limestone Grill, McDonald's, Mi Mexico, Taco Bell, Haven Hotel, Rodeway Inn, H(2mi), Walgreens
59	US 25, to Livingston, Mt Vernon, E Mt Vernon Fuel/dsl, Shell, Pizza Hut, Kastle Inn, W BP
51mm	Rockcastle River
49	KY 909, to US 25, Livingston, E Camp Wildcat Bfd, W 49er/dsl/24hr/RV Parking, truck/tire repair

LONDON

Exit #	Services
41	rd 80, to Somerset, London, E Speedway/dsl, Arby's, Burger King, Gondolier Italian, KFC, McDonald's, Subway, White Castle, EconoLodge, Motel 6, Quality Inn, Red Roof Inn, $General, Advance Parts, AutoZone, CVS Drug, H, Kroger, Parsley's Tire/repair, st police, W BP/Home Cooker/dsl/24hr, Marathon/McDonald's/EVC, Shell, Sunoco/dsl, Valero/dsl, Buffalo Wings&Rings, Cheddar's,
41	Continued Cracker Barrel, Habanero Mexican, LJ Silver, Old Town Grill, Shiloh Roadhouse, Subway, Taco Bell, Waffle House, Wendy's, Budget Host, Fairfield Inn, Hampton Inn, Dog Patch Ctr
38	rd 192, to Rogers Pkwy, London, E BP/dsl, Marathon, Murphy USA/dsl, Shell/McAlisters Deli/dsl, Speedway/dsl, Big Boy, Burger King, Capt D's, Dino's Italian, Domino's, Dunkin/Baskin Robins, El Dorado Mexican, Fazoli's, Fiesta Mexican, Golden Corral, Great Wall Chinese, Hardee's, Huddle House, Krystal, Penn Sta Subs, Pizza Hut, Slim Chickens, Starbucks, Subway, Taco Bell, TX Roadhouse, Baymont Inn, Comfort Suites, Country Inn&Suites, Holiday Inn Express, Microtel, $Tree, Advance Parts, AT&T, Ford/Lincoln, Kroger/gas, Lowe's, Nissan, Office Depot, Peterbilt, USPO, Verizon, Walgreens, Walmart/Subway/gas, W H
34mm	truck haven, weigh sta both lanes
30.5mm	Laurel River

CORBIN

Exit #	Services
29	US 25, US 25E, Corbin, E Marathon, Murphy USA, Pilot/McDonald's/Subway/dsl/scales/24hr, Spur Oil, Arbys, David's Steaks, DQ, Huddle House, Little Caesars, Mi Jalisco Mexican, Moes SW Grill, Taco Bell, Super 8, AlLDI, Blue Beacon, Lowe's, McKeever RV Ctr, Walmart/Subway/gas, W Love's/Hardee's/dsl/scales/24hr/@, Shell/dsl, Spur Oil/dsl, Cracker Barrel, Sonny's BBQ, Baymont Inn, Comfort Inn, Corbin Inn, Hampton Inn, Quality Suites, KOA, tires/repair, to Laurel River Lake RA
25	US 25W, Corbin, E Speedway/dsl, Applebee's, Arby's, Bojangle's, Brooklyn Bros Pizza, Burger King, McDonald's, Santa Fe Mexican, Taco Bell, Wendy's, EconoLodge, Holiday Inn Express, Motel 6, Red Roof Inn, H, W Shell, Bubby's BBQ, Mi Casa Mexican, Subway, Waffle House, Best Western, to Cumberland Falls SP
15	US 25W, to Williamsburg, Goldbug, W Shell, Xpress/dsl, Cumberland Falls SP
14.5mm	Cumberland River
11	KY 92, Williamsburg, E BP, Exxon, Shell, Arby's, El Dorado Mexican, Hardee's, KFC, Little Caesar's, McDonald's, Pizza Hut, Subway, Cumberland Inn, Holiday Inn Express, Super 8, $General, Advance Parts, O'Reilly Parts, Sav-A-Lot, Windham Drug, W Pilot/Wendy's/dsl/scales/24hr, Shell, Burger King, Cook Out, DQ, Huddle House, LJ Silver, Taco Bell, Torres Mexican, Hampton Inn, $Tree, EVC, to Big South Fork NRA, Walmart
1.5mm	**full facilities, litter barrels, petwalk, vending, Welcome Ctr nb**
0mm	Kentucky/Tennessee state line

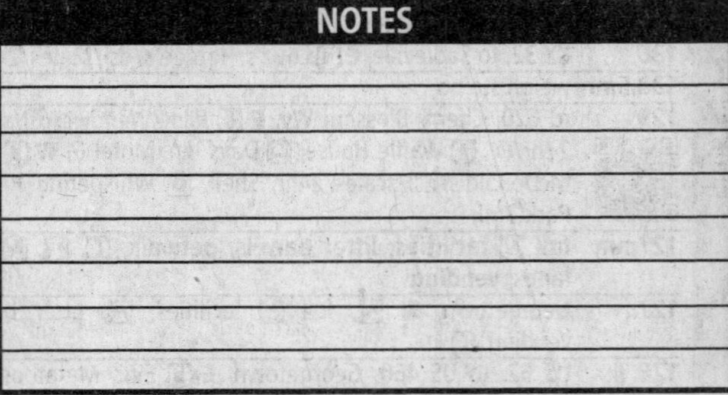

LOUISIANA

INTERSTATE 10

Exit #	Services
274mm	Louisiana/Mississippi state line, Pearl River
272mm	West Pearl River
270mm	**full facilities, info, litter barrels, petwalk, , , RV dump, Welcome Ctr wb, N** Pearl River Camprgrounds
267b	I-12 W, to Baton Rouge
267a	I-59 N, to Meridian
266	US 190, Slidell, **N** Exxon/dsl, RaceTrac/dsl, TA/Country Pride/dsl/scales/24hr/@, Baskin-Robbins, Cane's, Chick-fil-A, Chicken Salad Chick, Copeland's Rest., DQ, Firehouse Subs, Golden Dragon Chinese, Los Tres Amigos, McDonald's, NOLA Southern Grill, Panda Express, Rotolo's Pizza, Sonic, Subway, Taco Bell, Best Value Inn, Best Western, Comfort Inn, Country Inn Suites, Motel 6, Red Roof Inn, $Tree, Batteries+, CVS Drug, Firestone/auto, Harley-Davidson, Hobby Lobby, H, O'Reilly Parts, Office Depot, PepBoys, Petco, Rouse's Mkt, U-Haul, **S** Chevron/dsl, Murphy USA/dsl, RaceTrac/dsl, Applebee's, Big Easy Diner, Cracker Barrel, Fuji Yama Hibachi, Hooters, McAlister's Deli, Outback Steaks, Popeyes, Sonic, Starbucks, TX Roadhouse, Waffle House, Days Inn, La Quinta, Wingate Inn, $General, $Tree, AT&T, auto repair, CVS, Home Depot, H, Lowe's, tires, vet, Walgreens, Walmart/Subway
265	US 190, Fremaux Ave, **N** Circle K/dsl, RaceTrac/dsl, BJ's Rest., Cheddar's, Chipotle, Five Guys, Habanero's Mexican, Longhorn Steaks, Marble Slab, Panera Bread, Pizza Platoon, Red Robin, Smoothie King, Starbucks, Which Wich?, TownePlace Suites, auto repair, BAM, Best Buy, Dick's, Dillard's, Goodyear/auto, H, Kohl's, Michael's, Old Navy, PetSmart, tires, TJ Maxx, Verizon, **S** tires
263	LA 433, Slidell, **N** Exxon/Circle K/dsl, Shell/dsl, Valero, Waffle House, Hampton Inn, Super 8, repair, **S** Circle K/Subway/scales/dsl, Exxon/Circle K/dsl, McDonald's, Taco Bell, Wendy's, Holiday Inn, $General, Buick/GMC, Chevrolet/Cadillac, Chrysler/Dodge/Jeep, Ford, Honda, Hyundai, Kia, Nissan, Pinecrest RV Park, Toyota
261	Oak Harbor Blvd, Eden Isles, **N** Exxon/Circle K/dsl, Waffle House, Sleep Inn, **S** Shell/Subway/dsl
255mm	Lake Pontchartrain
254	US 11, to Northshore, Irish Bayou
251	Bayou Sauvage NWR, **S** swamp tours
248	Michoud Blvd
246b a	I-510 S, LA 47 N, S to Chalmette, N to Little Woods
245	Bullard Ave, **N** Chevron/dsl, Shell/dsl, Bullard Diner, Waffle House, Comfort Suites, Holiday Inn Express, Family$, Honda, **S** Chevron/dsl, Shell, Baskin-Robbins, Burger King, IHOP, KFC/Taco Bell, McDonald's, NO Rest., Papa John's, Subway, Super Cajun Seafood, Wendy's, Siegel Select, Trident Inn & Suites, Chrysler/Dodge/Jeep, Goodyear, Home Depot, Nissan, PepBoys, Toyota, Walgreens, Walmart
244	Read Blvd, **N** Shell/dsl, Burritos Grill, Cajun Seafood, McDonald's, Family$, O'Reilly Parts, Walgreens, **S** EVC, EZ Stop/dsl, Popeyes, Subway, Waffle House, Wendy's, Best Western, Country Inn, Quality Inn, CVS Drug, H, NAPA, park
242	Crowder Blvd, **N** Chevron, **S** Crowder Ctr, Exxon/dsl, Little Caesars, Pizza Hut, Subway, Sunrise Inn&Suites, $General, Walgreens
241	Morrison Rd, **N** Big E-Z/dsl, FuelXpress/dsl
240b a	US 90 E, Chef Hwy, Downman Rd, **N** Shell/dsl, Domino's, Ramada, Super 8, auto repair, Chevrolet, U-Haul, USPO, **S** Chevron, Pelican Fuel, Delta Tires
239b a	Louisa St, Almonaster Blvd, **N** Chevron/dsl, FuelZone/dsl, Burger King, Cane's, Church's TX Chicken, McDonald's, Popeyes, Rally's, Taco Bell, Waffle House, Wendy's, Wingstop, Days Inn, Motel 6, New Orleans Inn, Rodeway Inn&Suites, Royal Inn, $General, $Tree, AT&T, AutoZone, Family$, Goodyear/auto, tires, Walgreens, Walmart, **S** Day&Night/dsl
238b	I-610 W(from wb)
237	Elysian Fields Ave, **N** Mardi Gras Trkstp/Subway/dsl, Lowe's
236c	St. Bernard Ave
236b	LA 39, N Claiborne Ave
236a	Esplanade Ave, downtown
235a	Orleans Ave, to Vieux Carre, French Qtr, **S** Chevron/dsl, Marriott, Sheraton
235b	Poydras St, **N** H, **S** downtown, to Superdome
234a	US 90A, Claiborne Ave, to Westbank, **S** Superdome
232	US 61, Airline Hwy, Tulane Ave, **N** Chick-fil-A, $Tree, **S** Exxon, Shell, Valero, Cane's, Chick-fil-A, Domino's, IHOP, McDonald's, Mikimoto Japanese, Popeyes, Rallys, Subway, Wendy's, AT&T, Costco/gas, CVS Drug, Family$, Firestone/auto, NTB, to Xavier U, USPO, vet
231b	Florida Blvd, WestEnd
231a	Metairie Rd
230	I-610 E(from eb), to Slidell
229	Bonnabel Blvd, **N** Chevron/dsl, Giorlando's, Pho Bang Vietnamese, Pizza Hut, Popeyes, Starbucks, Taco Bell, AutoZone, Trader Joe's
228	Causeway Blvd, **N** Exxon/Circle K/dsl, Shell/dsl, Applebee's, Arby's, Atomic Burger, Buffalo Wild Wings, Carrabba's, Cheesecake Factory, Chick-fil-A, Chipotle, Firehouse, Honey Baked Ham, McDonald's, Outback Steaks, Panda Express, PF Chang's, Ruth's Chris Steaks, Shake Shack, Smoothie King, Sonic, Starbucks, Wendy's, Comfort Inn&Suites, Country Inn, Fairfield Inn, Hampton Inn,

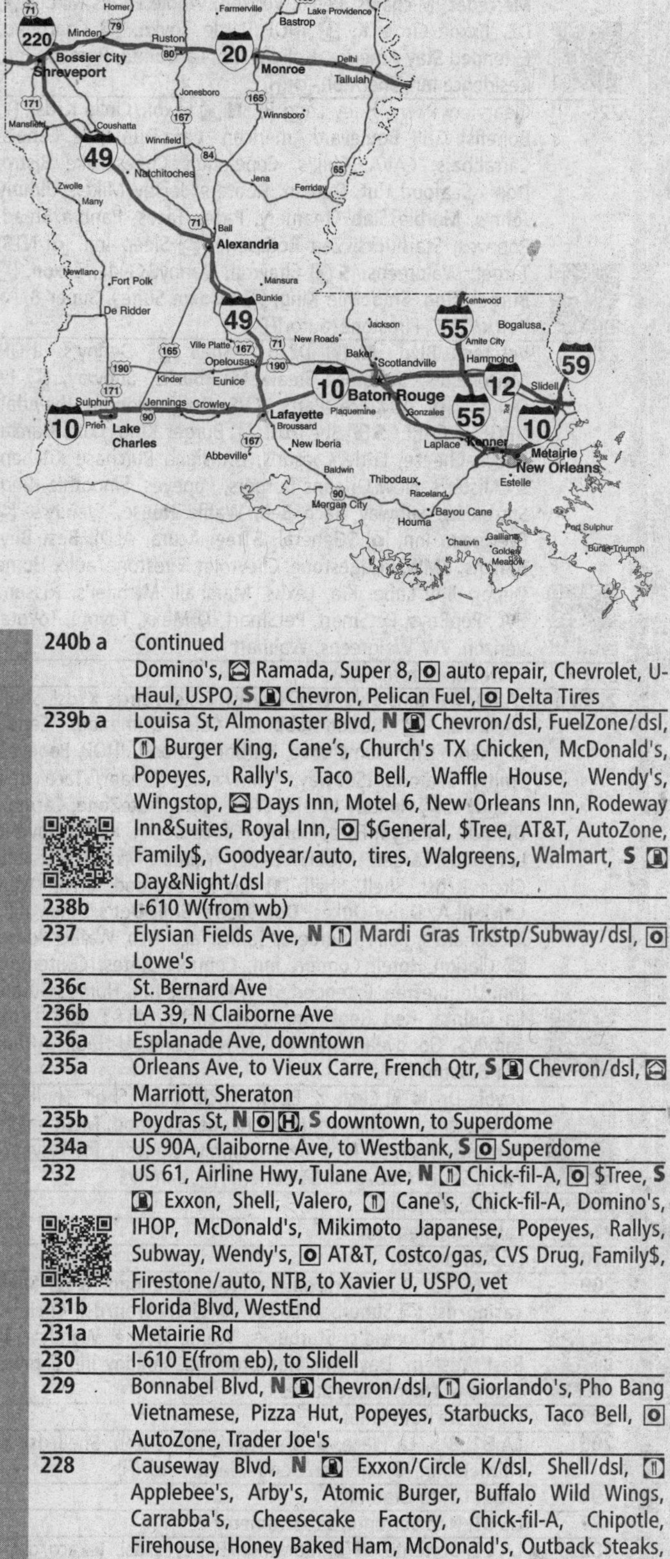

= gas = food = lodging = other = rest stop

INTERSTATE 10 Cont'd

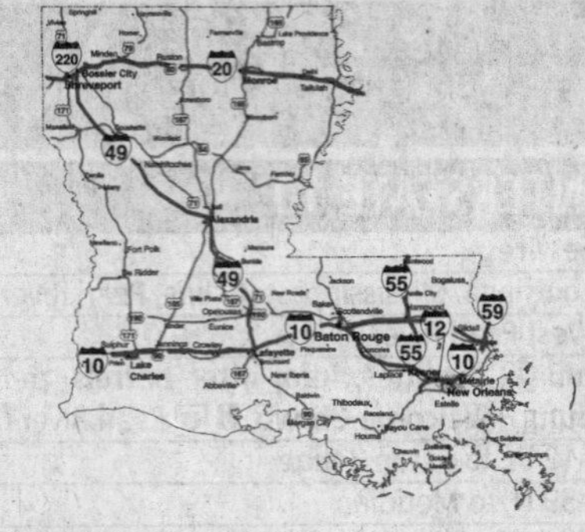

228 Continued
Homewood Suites, $General, Barnes&Noble, Dick's, Dillard's, Firestone, Goodyear, JC Penney, Lowe's, Macy's, Mercedes, Michaels, Petco, Verizon, Whole Foods Mkt, **S** DZ, Exxon/Circle K, IHOP, Little Toyko, Courtyard, Extended Stay America, Holiday Inn, La Quinta, Ramada Inn, Residence Inn, Sheraton, H

226 Clearview Pkwy, Huey Long Br, **N** Exxon/Circle K/dsl, Bonefish Grill, Boulevard American , Cafe Dumonde, Cane's, Carrabba's, CAVA, Chili's, Copeland's Cheesecake Bistro, Don's Seafood Hut, Dunkin, Hooters, Jersey Mike's, Jimmy John's, Marble Slab Creamery, Pacos Tacos, Panera Bread, Popeyes, Starbucks, Zea Rotisserie, Sleep Inn, NTB, Target, Walgreens, **S** Chevron, Danny&Clyde, Exxon, Burger King, Smoothie King, InTown Suites, Super 8, Buick/GMC, Firestone/auto, H

225 Veterans Blvd, **N** DZ/dsl, Shell, Denny's, IHOP, McDonald's, Saltgrass Steaks, Starbucks, Subway, La Quinta, Advance Parts, CVS Drug, Honda, Hyundai, URGENT CARE, **S** Shell/dsl, Burger King, Casa Garcia, ChuckeCheese, Little Caesar's, Louisiana Purchase Kitchen, McAlister's, New Orleans Burgers, Popeyes, Smoothie King, Starbucks, Subway, Taco Bell, Waffle House, Wendy's, Evergreen Inn, $General, $Tree, Acura, ALDI, Best Buy, BigLots, BMW, Bridgestone, Chevrolet, Firestone/auto, Home Depot, Jiffy Lube, Kia, Lexus, Marshall, Michael's, Nissan/EVC, PepBoys, PetSmart, PetSmart, TJ Maxx, Toyota, Toyota, Verizon, VW, Walgreens, Walmart

224 Power Blvd(from wb)

223b a LA 49, Williams Blvd, **N** DZ/dsl, Exxon/Circle K/dsl, Shell, Shell/dsl, Baskin-Robbins, Cafe Dumonde, Cane's Chicken, Fisherman's Cove, Harbor Seafood, IHOP, Popeyes, Smitty Seafood, Subway, Sunny's Ice Cream, Taco Bell, Wendy's, Holiday Inn, $Tree, auto, AutoZone, Carmax, Dillards, Family$, Ford, Lincoln, Office Depot, PetCo, Save-a-Lot Foods, Target, URGENT CARE, Walmart Mkt, **S** Exxon/Circle K/dsl, Shell, Shell, Big EZ Seafood, Brick Oven, Chick-fil-A, Daisy Dukes, Don Jose's Grill, Dot's Diner, KFC, McDonald's, Pollo Campero, Sonic, Taco Tico, Waffle House, Clarion Hotel, Comfort Inn, Comfort Suites, Contempra Inn, DoubleTree, Extended Stay, Holiday Inn, Home2 Suites, La Quinta, Red Roof Inn, $General, AT&T, CVS Drug, Family$, Goodyear/auto, NAPA, NTB, tires, U-Haul, U-Haul, USPO, Winn-Dixie

221 Loyola Dr, **N** Circle K, Exxon/Circle K/dsl, Shell, Shell/dsl, Church's TX Chicken, IHOP, Kenner Seafood, McDonald's, Popeyes, Rally's, Taco Bell, Yummy Chinese, Advance Parts, Sam's Club/gas, **S** $General, Family$

220 I-310 S, to Houma

214mm Lake Pontchartrain

210 I-55N(from wb)

209 I-55 N, US 51, to Jackson, LaPlace, Hammond, **N** Shell/casino/dsl, Suburban Lodge, **S** Chevron/dsl, Circle K/dsl, McDonald's, Starbucks, Waffle House, Wendy's, Best Western, Days Inn, Hampton Inn, Holiday Inn Express, Studio 6, TownePlace Suites

207mm weigh sta both lanes

206 LA 3188 S, La Place, **S** Circle K/dsl, Exxon, Shell/dsl, Fairfield Inn, Chrysler/Dodge/Jeep, Ford, H

194 LA 641 S, to Gramercy

187 US 61, N to Sorrento, S to Gramercy

182 LA 22, Sorrento, **N** Marathon/Popeyes/dsl, Texaco/dsl, **S** Marathon/Subway/dsl/scales/24hr, RaceTrac/dsl, SJ/dsl, McDonald's, Waffle House, antiques, tourist info

179 LA 44, Gonzales, **N** Exxon/Popingo's Cafe/dsl,

GONZALES

179 Continued
Murphy USA/dsl, Alabasha Cafe, Chicken Salad Chic Domino's, Smoothie King, Subway, Topical Smoothie, $General, $Tree, Buick/GMC, Chabill's Automotiv Walgreens

177 LA 30, Gonzales, **N** BP/Circle K/dsl, Shell/dsl, Tesla EV Buffalo Wild Wings, Burger King, Chick-fil-A, Days Inn, Paso Mexican, Jack-in-the-Box, McDonald's, Outback Steal Taco Bell, Waffle House, Zaxby's, Best Value Inn, Budg Inn, Clarion, Highland Inn, Western Inn, Home Depot, Mavis Tires, O'Reilly Parts, **S** Marathon/dsl, RaceTrac/d Checkers, Chili's, Chipotle, Cracker Barrel, Don's Seafo Hut, Fiery Crab Seafood, Firehouse Subs, KFC, Mooy Burger, Olive Garden, Popeyes, Salad Station, Son Starbucks, Tang Buffet, Wendy's, Candlewood Suit Comfort Suites, Holiday Inn Express, Holiday Inn Expre Home2 Suites, La Quinta, Quality Inn, SpringHill Suit TownePlace Suites, Cabela's, Tanger/famous bran Vesta RV Park

173 LA 73, to Geismar, Prairieville, **N** Circle K/dsl, Maratho dsl, Starbucks, vet, **S** Exxon/dsl, Mobil/McDonald dsl, RaceTrac/dsl, Burger King, DQ, Griffin Grill, Jo Michael's Rest., Las Palmas Mexican, Mission Street, Piz Hut, Popeyes, Sonic, Subway, Mainstay Suites, Sleep I O'Reilly Parts, repair, Twin Lakes RV Park(1mi)

166 LA 42, LA 427, Highland Rd, Perkins Rd, **N** Circle Church's TX Chicken/Tesla EVC/dsl, Exxon/Circle K/ RaceTrac, CAVA, City Pork BBQ, Las Palmas Mexica Popeyes, Ruffino's Italian, Sonic, Starbucks, Waffle House, Alexander's Mkt, Goodyear/auto, Home Depot, Mavis Tir **S** Chevron/dsl, Shell/Circle K/dsl, Subway, Th Heavenly Doughnut

163 Siegen Lane, **N** Circle K/dsl, Marathon/dsl, RaceTrac/ Blaze Pizza, Burger King, Cane's, CC's Coffee, Chick-fil CiCi's Pizza, Crumbl Cookies, Firehouse Subs, Fredd Hooters, IHOP, Jason's Deli, McDonald's, Mooyah Burge Olive Garden, PoBoy Express, Ribs Chophouse, Smoot King, Sonic, Subway, Taco Bell, Twin Peaks Rest., Wa House, Whataburger, Best Value Inn, Hampton I Heritage Inn, Holiday Inn Express, Home2 Suites, Motel Siegen Inn, Super 8, Trident Inn, Tru, $Tree, Advance Pa ALDI, AT&T, Batteries+, BigLots, Cadillac, CarMax, CVS Dr Firestone/auto, Harley-Davidson, Hobby Lobby, Honda, K PetCo, Ross, Target, Verizon, **S** Chili's, ChuckeChee Honey Baked Ham, TX Roadhouse, Courtyard, Reside Inn, Kohl's, Lowe's/Subway, Old Navy, PetSmart, Sa Club/gas, TJ Maxx, Walmart/Subway, World Mkt

162 Bluebonnet Rd, **N** Circle K/dsl, Albasha Rest., Cadi Cafe, Comfort Suites, vet, **S** BJ's Brewhou Copeland's Cheesecake Bistro, J Alexander's, King Buf Longhorn Steaks, Menchie's FroYo, Pluckers Wing Bar, R Lobster, Shake Shack, Shake Shack, Hyatt Pla Renaissance, Best Buy, Dick's, Dillard's, H, JC Penn Macy's

GONZALES

LA

INTERSTATE 10 Cont'd

Exit #	Services
160	LA 3064, Essen Lane, S Exxon/Circle K/dsl, RaceTrac, RaceTrac/dsl, Baskin-Robbins, Burger King, Cheng's Chinese, Domino's, Gatti's Pizza, India's Rest., Jimmy John's, McDonald's, Piccadilly, Popeyes, Taco Bell, Wendy's, Best Western, Drury Inn, Springhill Suites, $General, Albertson's, auto repair, H, NTB, O'Reilly Parts, Tire Choice, URGENT CARE, Walgreens
159	I-12 E, to Hammond
158	College Dr, Baton Rouge, N Speed Zone, Broken Egg Cafe, Hooters, Izzo's Grill, Jason's Deli, Mansurs Rest., Marble Slab Creamery, Sullivan's Rest., Waffle House, Wendy's, Candlewood Suites, Extended Stay America, Home2 Suites, Homewood Suites, Marriott, Richmond Inn/Tesla EVC, Tru Hilton, Barnes&Noble, H, Meineke, S Circle K, Exxon/Circle K/dsl, Chick-fil-A, Chili's, Gino's Rest., IHOP, McDonald's, Panda Express, Ruth's Chris Steaks, Starbucks, Taco Bell, Tio Javi's Mexican, Comfort Inn, Comfort Suites, Crowne Plaza, DoubleTree, Econolodge, Embassy Suites, Hampton Inn, Holiday Inn, $Tree, Albertson's, AutoZone, Hobby Lobby, Office Depot, USPO, Verizon, Walgreens, Walmart/Subway
157b	Acadian Thwy, N Chevron/dsl, Mestizo Grill, TJ Ribs BBQ, La Quinta, H, S Circle K/dsl, Acme Oyster House, Juban's Rest., Outback Steaks, Saltgrass Steaks, Smoothie King, Courtyard, AT&T, Trader Joe's, Trader Joe's
157a	Perkins Rd (from eb), same as 157b
156b	Dalrymple Dr, S to LSU
156a	Washington St
155c	Louise St(from wb)
155b	I-110 N, to Baton Rouge bus dist, N
155a	LA 30, Nicholson Dr, Baton Rouge, N Chevron, McDonald's, Sonic, Starbucks, Belle Hotel, Courtyard, Hilton, Watermark, S Shell/Circle K/dsl, to LSU
154mm	Mississippi River
153	LA 1, Port Allen, Cou-yon's Cajun BBQ, N Chevron, Circle K/dsl, Church's TX Chicken, Pizza Hut, AutoZone, Family$, Kenworth, NAPA, O'Reilly Parts, repair, tires, Walgreens, S LA 1S TP/Exxon/Casino/dsl/scales/24hr, RaceTrac/dsl, Sunoco, Domino's, Hardee's, Waffle House, Red Roof Inn, $Tree, Verizon, Walmart/Subway
151	LA 415, to US 190, N Cash's Trk Plaza/dsl/scales/casino, Chevron/dsl, Circle K/dsl, Exxon/dsl, Nino's/dsl/casino, Texaco/Emerald Plaza Trkstp/dsl, Burger King, KFC/Taco Bell, McDonald's, Popeyes, Subway, Waffle House, Wendy's, Comfort Suites, Hampton Inn, Holiday Inn Express, La Quinta, Quality Inn, Red Roof Inn, TownePlace Suites, West Inn, $General, S Love's/Arby's/dsl/scales/24hr, truck stop, Audubon Inn, Motel 6, OYO, Studio 6
139	LA 77, Grosse Tete, N Shell/dsl, visitor center, S auto repair/@, truck stop
135	LA 3000, to Ramah
127	LA 975, to Whiskey Bay
126.5mm	Pilot Channel of Whiskey Bay
122mm	Atchafalaya River
121	Butte La Rose, **both lanes, N full facilities, litter barrels, petwalk, visitors ctr/, tourist info, vending,** S Lazy Cajun Grill(2mi), Frenchman's Wilderness Camground(.5mi)
115	LA 347, to Cecilia, Henderson, N Citgo/dsl, Exxon/dsl/24hr, Texaco/dsl, Chicken on the Bayou, Holiday Inn Express, casinos, S Chevron/dsl, Exxon/Subway/dsl, Shell/McDonald's/dsl, Texaco/dsl, Valero/dsl, Popeyes, Waffle House, $General, Family$
109	LA 328, to Breaux Bridge, N Shell/dsl, Texaco/dsl/casino, Motel 6, Camping World, S Exxon/Domino's/dsl, Murphy USA/dsl, Pilot/Arby's/dsl/scales/24hr, Sunoco/Popeyes/dsl, Burger King, Checkers, City Buffet, Crazy Bout Cajun, Hacienda Real, McDonald's, Pizza Hut, Sonic, Taco Bell, Waffle House, Wendy's, Motel 6/EVC, Super 8, $General, $Tree, AT&T, AutoZone, Chrysler/Dodge/Jeep, city park, Family$, Ford/Lincoln, Great American RV, O'Reilly Parts, Super 1 Foods, USPO, Walgreens, Walmart/Subway
108mm	weigh sta both lanes
104	Louisiana Ave, S RaceTrac/dsl, Tesla EVC, Chick-fil-A, McDonald's, Subway, Taco Bell, ALDI, AT&T, JC Penney, PetCo, Ross, Target
103b	I-49 N, to Opelousas
103a	US 167 S, to Lafayette, S Circle K, Shell/dsl, Waffle House, Baymont Inn, Best Value Inn, Best Western, Fairfield Inn, Holiday Inn, Howard Johnson, La Quinta, Motel 6, Quality Inn, Super 7, $Tree, Home Depot, H, tires, transmissions
101	LA 182, to Lafayette, Valero/dsl, N Circle K/dsl, Phillips/TA/Boston Mkt/dsl/scales/24hr/@, Burger King, McDonald's, Waffle House, Whataburger, Red Roof Inn, $General, Honda, S Chevron/dsl, Citgo, Exxon, Church's TX Chicken, Cracker Barrel, Drury Inn, Hilton Garden(2mi), Kings Motel, Smart Stay Inn, Travelodge, Advance Parts, Family$, H, O'Reilly Parts
100	Ambassador Caffery Pkwy, N Exxon/dsl, Family$, Gauthier's RV Ctr, Peterbilt, Ryder Trucks, vet, S Chevron/dsl, RaceTrac/dsl, Shell/dsl, Burger King, McDonald's, Sonic, Taco Bell, Waffle House, Wendy's, Ambassador Inn, Hampton Inn, Microtel, Sleep Inn, Goodyear, H, Southern Tire Mart, tires
97	LA 93, to Scott, N Shell/dsl, La Rumba Mexican, Super 1 Foods/dsl, S Chevron/McDonald's, Shell/Church's TX Chicken/dsl, Billy's Cracklings, Domino's, Don's BBQ, Fezzo's Seafood, Huddle House, Legends Scott, Popeyes, Rochetto's Pizza, Smoothie King, Subway, Comfort Inn, Holiday Inn Express, Howard Johnson, Harley-Davidson, KOA
92	LA 95, to Duson, N Exxon/dsl/casino/RV dump/scales/24hr, Love's/Bojangles/Wendy's/dsl/scales/24hr, S Chevron/dsl, Marathon/Subway/dsl/casino, Roady's/cafe/dsl/casino, Super 8, flea mkt/antiques, Frog City RV Park
87	LA 35, to Rayne, N Chevron/dsl, Shell/Subway/casino/dsl, Burger King, Chef Roy's Rest., McDonald's, Taco Bell, Days Inn, $General, S Circle K/dsl, Frog City/Exxon/dsl, Candyland Ice Cream, DQ, Gabe's Café, Popeyes, Sonic, Best Western, Advance Parts, O'Reilly Parts, Super 1 Foods, Walgreens
82	LA 1111, to E Crowley, S Chevron/dsl, Murphy USA, Chili's, Wendy's, AT&T, H, Lowe's, Walgreens, Walmart/Subway
80	LA 13, to Crowley, N Conoco/dsl/rest./24hr, DQ, La Rumba Mexican, Waffle House, Best Western, Days Inn, Buick/Chevrolet, vet, S Chevron/dsl, Exxon, Raceway/dsl, Valero/dsl, Asian Buffet, Burger King, Cajun Way, El Dorado Mexican, Gatti's Pizza, McDonald's, Pizza Hut, PJ's Coffee, PJ's Grill, Popeyes, Sonic, Starbucks, Subway, Taco Bell, $General, $Tree, AutoZone, O'Reilly Parts, Super 1, U-Haul, Verizon
76	LA 91, to Iota, S Petro/Shell/Subway/dsl/scales/24hr
72	Egan, N Shell/dsl, Cajun Haven RV Park
65	LA 97, to Jennings, S Shell/dsl/casino
64	LA 26, to Jennings, N Los Tres Potrillos, Budget Inn, LA Oil & Gas Park, S Circle K/dsl, Exxon/dsl, EZ Mart, Jennings Travel Plaza/dsl/casino, Murphy USA/dsl,

EGAN

LA

INTERSTATE 10 Cont'd

CAMERON

64 Continued
Burger King, Domino's, Domino's, Gatti's Pizza, General Wok Chinese, King Buffet, La Rumba Mexican, McDonald's, Pizza Hut, Popeyes, Shoney's, Sonic, Subway, Taco Bell, Waffle House, Wendy's, Days Inn, Hampton Inn, Motel 6, $General, $Tree, AT&T, AutoZone, CVS Drug, H, O'Reilly Parts, Verizon, Walgreens, Walmart/Subway

59 LA 395, to Roanoke, N Peto's TrvlCtr/Chevron/dsl/scales/24hr

54 LA 99, Welsh, S Chevron/dsl, Citgo, Exxon/dsl/24hr, Valero/dsl, DQ, Subway, auto repair

48 LA 101, Lacassine, S Exxon

44 US 165, to Alexandria, N Lacassine RV Park(10mi), S Rabideaux's Cajun

43 LA 383, to Iowa, N Love's/Hardee's/dsl/scales/24hr, Pilot/Arby's/PJ Fresh/dsl/scales/24hr, Burger King, Best Western, Fairway Inn, auto/tires, truck repair, S Citgo/dsl, Shell/McDonald's/dsl, Texaco, La Rumba Mexican, Sonic, Subway, $General, Cypress Bend RV Park

36 LA 397, to Creole, Cameron, N Jean Lafitte RV Park(2mi), S Cash Magic/Citgo/dsl, Chevron/dsl, Los Ponchos, Red Roof Inn, Country Oaks RV Park

34 I-210 W, to Lake Charles

33 US 171 N, N RaceWay/dsl/E85, Shell/dsl, Time/dsl, Burger King, Church's TX Chicken, Happy Donuts, Subway, Taco Bell, Best Western, Comfort Suites, El Tapatio Mexican, Motel 6, Super 8, $General, AutoZone, O'Reilly Parts, to Sam Houston Jones SP, S EconoLodge, Holiday Inn Express

32 Opelousas St

31b US 90 E, Shattuck St, to LA 14, S Save&Go/dsl

31a US 90 bus, Enterprise Blvd, S Valero/dsl, Popeyes

30b downtown

30a LA 385, N Lakeshore Dr, Ryan St, N Citgo, Steamboat Bill's Rest., Waffle House, Days Inn, Oasis Inn, S Wendy's, Quality Suites

29 LA 385(from eb), same as 30a, N Valero, Days Inn, Steamboat Bill's, Waffle House, S visitor ctr

28mm Calcasieu Bayou, Lake Charles

COLUMBIA

27 LA 378, to Westlake, N Chevron/dsl, Citgo, Phillips 66/dsl, Shell, Burger King, Dino's Donuts, Dunkin, El Tapatio Mexican, McDonald's, Pizza Hut, Popeyes, RoundTop Burger, Sonic, Extended Stay, La Quinta, $General, $Tree, auto/tires, Bumper Parts, MarketBasket, O'Reilly Parts, tires, to Sam Houston Jones SP(6mi), S Horseshoe Hotel

26 US 90 W, Southern Rd, Columbia, N Exxon/dsl

25 I-210 E, to Lake Charles

23 LA 108, to Sulphur, N Chevron/Dunkin/Baskin-Robbins/dsl, Circle K, Exxon/dsl, Murphy USA/EVC, Burger King, Cane's, Checkers, Chili's, China Wok, Firehouse Subs, Kyoto, Maria's Cocina, McDonald's, Popeyes, Subway, Taco Bell, Wendy's, Whataburger, $General, $Tree, AT&T, Bumper Parts, Jeep/Dodge/Chrysler, Lowe's, URGENT CARE, Verizon, Walgreens, Walmart/Subway, S Citgo/Cash Magic/dsl, Sulphur Trkstp/Subway/dsl/casino, Cracker Barrel, Waffle House, Best Western+, Comfort Suites, Days Inn, Holiday Inn Express, HomeTowne Studios, Studio 6, Super 8, WoodSpring Suites, Southern Tire Mart

21 LA 3077, Arizona St, N Phillips 66/dsl, Shell, Boiling Point Cajun, China Taste, Papa John's, Smoothie King, Starbucks, $General, AT&T, Chevrolet, CVS Drug, Ford, GNC, H, Kroger/gas, NAPA, Walgreens, S Chevron/dsl, Shell/dsl, Valero/dsl/casino, $General, Hidden Ponds RV Park

20 LA 27, to Sulphur, N Chevron/dsl, Circle K, Conoco/dsl,

VINTON

20 Continued
Burger King, Casa Ole Mexican, Checkers, Gatti's Pizz Hollier's Cajun, Hong Kong Chinese, Joe's Pizza/pasta, Rumba Mexican, LeBleu's Landing Cajun, Little Caesa McDonald's, Popeyes, Subway, Taco Bell, Wendy's, Be Value, Hampton Inn, HomeTel Inn, Motel 6, Brookshi Bros/gas, H, Jiffy Lube, tires, S Chevron/dsl, Exxon, Brick House Creamery, Navrosky's Burgers, Pizza Hut, Soni Waffle House, Candlewood Suites, Clarion Pointe, Da Inn, Double Tree, Fairfield Inn, La Quinta, Red Roof In Wingate Inn, $Tree, Maplewood Place RV Park, O'Rei Parts, Stine, to Creole Nature Trail, U-Haul

8 LA 108, Vinton, N Chevron/dsl, Exxon/dsl, V RV Park

7 LA 3063, Vinton, N Burger King, Sonic, Cobblesto Inn, $General, S Love's/Arby's/dsl/scales/24hr

4 US 90, LA 109, Toomey, N Cash Magic/Shell/dsl/gri casino, Chevron/dsl, truck repair, S Exxon/dsl, Sunoc dsl, Valero/dsl/rest., Subway, Best Western, casino

2.5mm weigh sta wb lanes

1.5mm full facilities, litter barrels, petwalk, , , Welcon Ctr eb

1 (from wb), Sabine River Turnaround

0mm Louisiana/Texas state line, Sabine River

INTERSTATE 12

85c I-10 E, to Biloxi. I-12 begins/ends on I-10, exit 267.

85b I-59 N, to Hattiesburg

85a I-10 W, to New Orleans

83 US 11, to Slidell, N Circle K/dsl, Citgo/Circle K/dsl, Exxo dsl, Burger King, McDonald's, Sonic, Waffle House, S RaceTrac/dsl, Shell/dsl, H

80 Airport Dr, North Shore Blvd, N Circle K/Krystal/dsl, Dickey's BBQ, IHOP, Sonic, Quality Inn, AT&T, Ross, S Chevron, Shell/dsl, Burger King, Cane's, Chili's, Domino Koi's Asian, McDonald's, Olive Garden, Pedro's Mexica Starbucks, Subway, Taco Bell, Waffle House, Wendy's, Candlewood Suites, Holiday Inn Express, Homewood Suit La Quinta, $Tree, AlLDI, AutoZone, Dillard's, Home Dep Marshalls, Sam's Club/gas, Walgreens, Walmart

74 LA 434, to Lacombe, N Exxon/Subway/dsl, H, Stev RV Ctr, S Big Branch Marsh NWR

68 LA 1088,, to Mandeville,, Arkansas River

65 LA 59, to Mandeville, N Chevron/dsl, Exxon/dsl, Shell/d Domino's Pizza, Popeyes, Smoothie King, Son Starbucks, Waffle House, Comfort Suites, S Circle K/c El Rancho Mexican, Liu's Wok, McDonald's, PJ's Coff Quiznos, $General, camping, to Fontainebleau SP, v Winn-Dixie

63b a US 190, Covington, Mandeville, N Chevron/dsl, Circle dsl, Exxon, Murphy USA, RaceTrac, Burger King, Can Chick-fil-A, Copeland's Grill, Don's Seafood, Dunk Firehouse Subs, Four Seasons Chinese, Golden Koi, Gol Wok, HoneyBaked Ham, IHOP, Johnny's Pizza, La Carre Lee's Hamburgers, McAlister's Deli,

INTERSTATE 12 Cont'd

63b a Continued
North Shore Empress Asian, Osaka Japanese, Outback Steaks, PJ's Coffee, Smoothie King, Sonic, Starbucks, Subway, Taco Bell, Thai Spice, Waffle House, Wendy's, Zea Rotisserie, Best Western, Clarion, Comfort Inn, Country Inn&Suites, Courtyard, Hampton Inn, Hilton Garden, Holiday Inn, Residence Inn, Super 8, WeStay Suites, AAA, Ace Hardware, AT&T, AutoZone, CarMax, Chevrolet, Chrysler/Dodge/Jeep, CVS Drug, Home Depot, Honda, Lowe's, Nissan, Office Depot, PetSmart, Subaru, Tire Choice, Toyota/Scion, Verizon, Walmart/McDonald's, S H, st police, to New Orleans via toll causeway

60 Pinnacle Pkwy, to Covington, same as 59

59 LA 21, to Covington, Madisonville, N Circle K, Shell/dsl, Shell/dsl, Buffalo Wild Wings, Cafe Du Monde, Carreta's Grill, Chili's, Cracker Barrel, Crumbl Cookies, Five Guys, Isabella's Pizza, Izzo's Burrito, Jimmy John's, McDonald's, Olive Garden, Panda Buffet, Panera Bread, PJ's Coffee, PJ's Coffee, Smoothie King, Starbucks, Steak'n Shake, Subway, Theo's Pizza, Tropical Smoothie, TX Roadhouse, $Tree, AT&T, auto repair, AutoZone, CVS Drug, Hobby Lobby, H, Kohl's, Petco, Walgreens, Winn-Dixie, S Circle K, Chick-fil-A, ChuckECheese, Dickey's BBQ, Habaneros Mexican, Jersey Mike's, Pedro's Mexican, Taco Bell, Wendy's, Holiday Inn Express, Belk, Best Buy, Fairview Riverside SP, JC Penney, Marshall's, Michael's, Ross, Sam's Club/dsl, Target, Verizon

57 LA 1077, to Goodbee, Madisonville, N Shell/dsl, Lit Pizza, McDonald's, Rouses Mkt, S Marathon/QuickWay/dsl, Best Wok, Pizza Hut, PJ's Coffee, Subway, to Fairview Riverside SP, vet

47 LA 445, to Robert, N Sonic, Jellystone Camping, Sun Outdoors Camping, to Global Wildlife Ctr, S Chevron/dsl

42 LA 3158, to Airport, N Chevron/Quiznos/dsl/24hr, Texaco/dsl, Burger King, McDonald's, Popeyes, Waffle House, Stay Express Inn, S Shell/Subway/dsl, Berryland RV Ctr, H

40 US 51, to Hammond, N RaceTrac/dsl, Shell/Circle K, Burger King, Cane's, Chick-fil-A, Chipotle, Church's TX Chicken, Don's Seafood, DQ, East of Italy, Five Guys, Golden Corral, IHOP, Jersey Mike's, Jimmy John's, Lit Pizza, McDonald's, Nagoya Rest., Olive Garden, PJ's Coffee, Santa Fe Steaks, Smoothie King, Sonic, Starbucks, Subway, Taco Bell, Wendy's, Best Western, Courtyard, Holiday Inn, Home2 Suites, Quality Inn, AT&T, Best Buy, Books-A-Million, Dillard's, Firestone, Home Depot, JC Penney, Michaels, Target/EVC, TJ Maxx, U-Haul, Verizon, Walgreens, S Petro/Mobil/dsl/scales/24hr/@, Pilot/Arby's/dsl/scales/24hr, Waffle House, Colonial Inn, Days Inn, La Quinta, $General, Blue Beacon, H, SpeedCo, Tire Choice

38b a I-55, N to Jackson, S to New Orleans

37mm weigh sta both lanes

35 Pumpkin Ctr, Baptist, N $General, Great American RV, S Chevron/Subway/dsl

32 LA 43, to Albany, N Chevron/Subway/dsl, Exxon/Circle K/dsl, Shell/Big River/dsl, McDonald's, S $General, to Tickfaw SP(11mi), tourist info

29 LA 441, to Holden, N Chevron/dsl, Sunoco/dsl, Berryland Campers

22 LA 63, to Frost, Livingston, N Shell/dsl, Burger King, Taco Bell, Family$, O'Reilly Parts, S Chevron/dsl, Lakeside RV Park(1mi)

19 to Satsuma, Colyell, N Exxon/dsl, $General

15 LA 447, to Walker, N Chevron/dsl, Murphy USA/dsl, Shell/Subway/dsl, Arby's, Burger King, Cane's, China Wok,

ESSEN LANE

15 Continued
Domino's, Foochow Buffet, Jack-in-the-Box, Little Caesars, McDonald's, Pizza Hut, Popeyes, Sherwood PoBoy's, Smoothie King, Sombrero Mexican, Sonic, Taco Bell, Waffle House, Wendy's, Best Western+, La Quinta, AT&T, AutoZone, Carter's Mkt, CVS Drug, O'Reilly Parts, URGENT CARE, Verizon, vet, Walgreens, Walmart/Subway, S H

12 LA 1036, Juban Rd, N Chevron/Taco Bell/dsl, RaceTrac/dsl, Verizon, Burger King, Chicken Salad Chick, Crumbl Cookies, Jersey Mike's, Marble Slab, Moe's SW, Panda Express, Starbucks, TX Roadhouse, AT&T, Belk, Hobby Lobby, Kia/Nissan, Michael's, Old Navy, PetSmart, Ross, Rouse's Mkt, TJ Maxx, S Shell/dsl, DQ, Smoothie King

10 LA 3002, to Denham Springs, N Chevron, Circle K/dsl, RaceTrac/dsl, Rushing Corner/dsl, Arby's, Baskin-Robbins, Burger King, Cane's, CC's Coffee, Chili's, Church's TX Chicken, Domino's, Don's Seafood, Gatti's Pizza, IHOP, McDonald's, Papa John's, Pizza Hut, Ron's Seafood, Ryan's, Sonic, Starbucks, Taco Bell, Uno Dos Tacos, Waffle House, Wendy's, Best Value Inn, Candlewood Suites, Carom Inn, Comfort Suites, Hampton Inn, $General, $Tree, Advance Parts, Albertsons, AT&T, AutoZone, CVS Drug, Home Depot, Mavis Tires, NTB, O'Reilly Parts, Office Depot, PetCo, Walgreens, Walmart/Subway, S Circle K, Pilot/Subway/dsl/scales/24hr, Duke's Seafood, El Rancho Mexican, Firehouse Subs, Hooters, Longhorn Steaks, Mooyah Burgers, Days Inn, Highland Inn, Advance Parts, Bass Pro Shops, Cavender's, Chrysler/Dodge/Jeep, Ford, KOA, Sam's Club/dsl, Walgreens

8.5mm Amite River

7 O'Neal Lane, N RaceTrac/dsl, La Quinta, Quality Inn, Toyota, S Murphy USA/dsl, Shell/dsl, McDonald's, Popeyes, Rice & Roux, Sonic, Starbucks, Taco Bell, Waffle House, $Tree, ALDI, auto repair, AutoZone, H, O'Reilly Parts, Walgreens, Walmart/Subway

6 Millerville Rd, N Circle K/dsl, Chick-fil-A, Chili's, Crust Pizza, Freddy's, Golden Corral, Zaxby's, Best Buy, CVS Drug, Honda, Lowe's, Office Depot, PetSmart, Super Target, Verizon, S Shell/Circle K/dsl, Rotolo's Pizza, Subway, Ace Hardware

4 Sherwood Forest Blvd, N Exxon/Circle K, Shell/Circle K/dsl, Burger King, Jack-in-the-Box, McDonald's, Pizza Hut, Popeyes, Sonic, Subway, Taco Bell, Waffle House, Baymont, FairBridge Inn, Siegel Select, Super 8, WoodSpring Suites, $General, tires, S RaceTrac/dsl, Shell/dsl, Arby's, Cane's, DQ, Piccadilly, Podnuh's BBQ, Volcano Japanese, Travelodge, AT&T, auto care

2b US 61 N, N Chevron/dsl, Circle K, Mobil/dsl, Murphy USA/dsl, Tesla EVC, Applebee's, Cracker Barrel, Little Caesar's, Taco Bell, Days Inn, Holiday Inn, Microtel, Motel 6, Quality Inn, Regency Inn, Sleep Inn, Albertsons/gas, Burlington Coats, GNC, Marshall's, Michael's, Mitsubishi, Nissan, O'Reilly Parts, PepBoys, Toyota/Scion, Walgreens, Walmart Mkt, S Exxon/Circle K, Burger King, CC's Coffee, McDonald's, Waffle House, $Tree, Costco/gas, Home Depot, NTB

2a US 61 S, N Chevron/dsl, Tesla EVC, Applebee's, Cracker Barrel, Taco Bell, Holiday Inn, Motel 6, Quality Inn, Regency Inn, Sleep Inn, Albertsons, Pep Boys, S Citgo/Circle K, Exxon/Circle K/dsl, Burger King, CC's Coffee, China 1, Jimmy John's, McDonald's, Old School BBQ, Subway, Waffle House, $Tree, Costco/gas, Home Depot, NTB, Volvo

1b LA 1068, to LA 73, Essen Lane, N Shell/Circle K/dsl, Cane's, McDonald's, Philly Me Up, Family$, Rouses Mkt, URGENT CARE, S H

1a I-10(from wb). I-12 begins/ends on I-10, exit 159 in Baton Rouge

LA

INTERSTATE 20

Exit #	Services
DELTA	
189mm	Louisiana/Mississippi state line, Mississippi River
187mm	weigh sta both lanes
186	US 80, Delta, S Chevron/dsl/24hr
184mm	**full facilities, litter barrels, petwalk, wb, RV dump**
182	LA 602, Mound
173	LA 602, Richmond
171	US 65, Tallulah, N Chevron/Subway/dsl, Circle K/dsl, Chopsticks Buffet, McDonald's, Wendy's, Days Inn, Super 8, H, S Exxon/dsl/scales, Love's/Arby's/dsl/scales/24hr, Marathon/TA/dsl/scales/24hr/@, Texaco
164mm	Tensas River
157	LA 577, Waverly, N Waverly Trkstp/Diner/dsl/24hr, S Central Station/dsl/24hr, Chevron/dsl/24hr, to Tensas River NWR
DELHI	
155mm	Bayou Macon
153	LA 17, Delhi, N Chevron/Subway, Exxon/dsl, Texaco/dsl, Bestz Donuts, Burger King, La Fonda Mexican, Pizza Hut, Sonic, $General, Brookshire's Foods, Delhi Farmers Mkt, Family$, H, USPO, S Central/dsl, Delhi Little Grill, Best Western, Executive Inn, C&S RV Park, Delhi RV Park
148	LA 609, Dunn
145	LA 183, rd 202, Holly Ridge
141	LA 583, Bee Bayou Rd
138	US 425, Rayville, N Pilot/Wendy's/dsl/scales/24hr, Fox's Pizza, McDonald's, Sonic, Days Inn, $General, $Tree, AT&T, auto repair, AutoZone, Brookshire's Foods, Buick/Chevrolet, Family$, H, O'Reilly Parts, repair, Verizon, Walmart, S Chevron/Subway/dsl/24hr, Circle K/dsl, RaceWay/dsl, Big John's Rest., Crispy Donuts, KFC, Popeyes, Waffle House, Super 8
MILLHAVEN	
135mm	Boeuf River
132	LA 133, Start, N Exxon/dsl
128mm	Lafourche Bayou
124	LA 594, Millhaven, N Love's/Subway/dsl/scales/24hr/@, Shell/dsl, st police, to Sage Wildlife Area
120	Garrett Rd, Pecanland Mall Dr, N Chevron/dsl, Applebee's, ChuckECheese, IHOP, Longhorn Steaks, McAlister's, Olive Garden, Panda Express, Red Lobster, Ronin Habachi, Sonic, The Mighty Crab, Courtyard, Residence Inn, TownePlace/Tesla EVC, $Tree, AT&T, Belk, Dick's, Dillard's, Home Depot, JC Penney, Kohl's, Michael's, Old Navy, PetSmart, Ross, Target, TJ Maxx, U-Haul, Verizon, S Circle K/dsl, Best Western, Days Inn, Hampton Inn, Harley-Davidson, Lowe's, Ouachita RV Park, Pecanland RV Park, RV Center, Sam's Club/gas
MONROE	
118b a	US 165, N Fast Stop/dsl, Motel 6, Red Roof Inn, Kia, Nissan/EVC, to NE LA U, S 76, Circle K/dsl, Burger King, Capt D's, Church's TX Chicken, Haskell Donuts, KFC, McDonald's, Popeyes, Shaw Nuff BBQ, Sonic, Subway, Taco Bell, Wendy's, Comfort Suites, Quality Inn, Studio 6, Super 8, AutoZone, Family$
117b	LA 594, Texas Ave, N 76/dsl
117a	Hall St, Monroe, N H
116b	US 165 bus, LA 15, Jackson St, N H
116a	5th St, Monroe
115	LA 34, Mill St, N Chevron
114	LA 617, Thomas Rd, N Murphy USA, RaceWay/dsl, Cane's, Capt D's, Chick-fil-A, Chick-fil-A, El Paso Mexican, Hibachi Grill, IHOP, KFC, McAlister's, McDonald's, McDonald's, Popeyes, Subway, Taco Bell, Waffle House, Wendy's, Best Value Inn, Super 8, Wingate Inn, Woodspring Suites, AT&T, BigLots, Family$, Hobby Lobby, H, O'Reilly Parts, Office Depot, URGENT CARE, Walgreens,

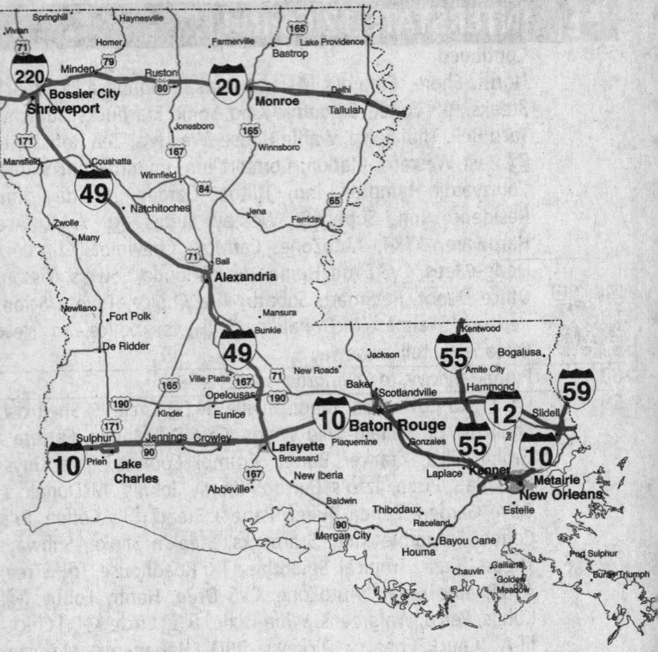

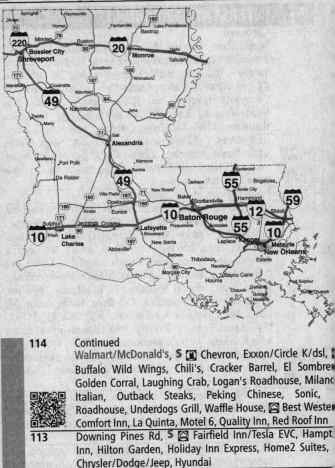

Exit #	Services
114	Continued Walmart/McDonald's, S Chevron, Exxon/Circle K/dsl, Buffalo Wild Wings, Chili's, Cracker Barrel, El Sombre[ro], Golden Corral, Laughing Crab, Logan's Roadhouse, Milanc[...] Italian, Outback Steaks, Peking Chinese, Sonic, Roadhouse, Underdogs Grill, Waffle House, Best Weste[rn], Comfort Inn, La Quinta, Motel 6, Quality Inn, Red Roof Inn
CHENIERE	
113	Downing Pines Rd, S Fairfield Inn/Tesla EVC, Hampt[on] Inn, Hilton Garden, Holiday Inn Express, Home2 Suites, Chrysler/Dodge/Jeep, Hyundai
112	Well Rd, N 76/dsl, Circle K/dsl, QT/dsl, Burger Ki[ng], Denny's, DQ, McDonald's, Sonic, Subway, Taco Bell, T[...] Burger Den, Waffle House, Zaxby's, Comfort Suites, Advance Parts, CVS Drug, Walgreens, Walmart, S Pil[ot/] Subway/dsl/scales/24hr
108	LA 546, to US 80, Cheniere, N Mobil/Central/dsl, Sma[...] dsl, $General, S Exxon/Subway/dsl
107	Camp Rd, rd 25, Cheniere
103	US 80, Calhoun, N Exxon/USA/dsl/24hr, Motel 103
101	LA 151, to Calhoun, S Chevron/Huddle House/Subwa[y/] dsl, Exxon, Sonic, $General, 101 RV Park, USPO
97mm	**full facilities, litter barrels, petwalk, wb, dump**
95mm	**full facilities, litter barrels, petwalk, eb, dump**
RUSTON	
93	LA 145, Choudrant, S Soul Food Kitchen, Subway, $General, camping, Jimmie Davis SP(28mi)
86	LA 33, Ruston, N Circle K/dsl, Murphy USA, RaceWay/[...] Tesla EVC, Texaco/dsl, Arby's, Avocados Ruston, Can[e's], Chili's, Don Chuy , El Jarrito Mexican, Hot Rod BBQ, Hud[dle] House, Log Cabin Grill, McAlister's Deli, McDonald's, Pa[nda] Express, PJ's Coffee, Popeyes, Sonic, Taco Bell, Whatabur[ger], Days Inn, Holiday Inn Express, Quality Inn, $Tree, AT[&T], Ford/Lincoln, GNC, Lowe's, Ruston's, Toyota, vet, Walm[art], Subway, S Exxon, Spirit/dsl, Waffle House, [Best] Western, Comfort Inn, Fairfield Inn
85	US 167, Ruston, N Chevron/Subway, Circle K, Exxon, Burger King, Capt D's, Chick-fil-A, Chicken Salad Chick, Li[ttle] Caesar's, McDonald's, Peking Chinese, Wendy's, Courtyard, Hampton Inn, auto repair, Office Depot, Su[per] 1 Foods, Walgreens, S QT/dsl, Sleep Inn, Adva[nce] Parts, H, Verizon

LA

 = gas = food = lodging = other = rest stop

E INTERSTATE 20 Cont'd

Exit #	Services
84	LA 544, Ruston, N Brister's BBQ, DQ, Hobby Lobby, TJ Maxx, S Chevron/dsl, Exxon, Flying Burger, Johnny's Pizza, Smoothie King, Starbucks, Subway, Waffle House, Zaxby's, Super 8
83	LA 818, Tarbutton Rd
81	LA 149, Grambling, S Exxon, $Tree, Spring Mkt, to Grambling St U
78	LA 563, Industry, S Texaco/dsl
77	LA 507, Simsboro, S Antique Village RV Park, USPO
69	LA 151, Arcadia, N Chevron/dsl, Mobil/Burger King/dsl, La Fogata Mexican, Ford, S Exxon/dsl, Texaco/dsl, Valero/dsl, El Jarrito Mexican, McDonald's, Sonic, Subway, Days Inn, $General, Brookshire Foods, Bumper Parts, H, outlet mall, tires/repair
67	LA 9, Arcadia, N tires, to Lake Claiborne SP
61	LA 154, Gibsland, N to Lake Claibourne SP
55	US 80, Ada
52	LA 532, to US 80, Dubberly, N ONE9/dsl, Shell/dsl
49	LA 531, Minden, N Exxon/dsl/24hr, Love's/Arby's/dsl/scales/24hr, Murphy USA(3mi), QuickDraw/Subway/dsl, KFC(3mi), Pizza Hut(3mi), Taco Bell(3mi), Walmart(3mi), S truck/tire repair
47	US 371 S, LA 159 N, Minden, N Chevron/dsl, Exxon/dsl, Valero/dsl, Best Western, Exacta Inn/rest., Holiday Inn Express, Southern Inn, Ford, H, S camping, to Lake Bistineau SP
44	US 371 N, Cotton Valley, N Exxon/Huddle House/dsl, Crawfish Hole #2, Los Compas Mexican, Sonic, Minden Motel(2mi), Cinnamon Creek RV/camping, Family$, Lakeside RV Camping
38	Goodwill Rd, S Valero/dsl/24hr, Ammo Plant, truck/trailer repair
33	LA 157, Fillmore, S Exxon, Pilot/Arby's/dsl/scales/24hr, Pizza Hut, PJ's Coffee, Sonic, Stacked & Tossed, Waffle House, $General, Family$, Lake Bistineau SP, USPO
26	I-220 , Shreveport, N Nickys Mexican, Comfort Suites, Holiday Inn, Springhill Suites, Casino
23	Industrial Dr, N Chevron/dsl, Circle K, QT, Valero/dsl, McDonald's, Taco Bell, Wendy's, O'Reilly Parts, RV Repair, st police, S Camping World
22	Airline Dr, N Circle K, Arby's, Burger King, Chili's, IHOP, Johnny's Pizza, Notini's Italian, Popeyes, Red Lobster, Shogun Steaks, Smoothie King, Sonic, Starbucks, Subway, Taco Bell, TX Street Steaks, Waffle House, Motel 6, Siegel Select, Super 8, BigLots, CVS Drug, Dillard's, Firestone/auto, H, JC Penney, mall, Office Depot, PepBoys, Walgreens, S Gulf/dsl, Church's TX Chicken, Griff's Burgers, Outback Steaks, Comfort Inn, Crown Inn, Microtel, AutoZone, Family$, Super1 Foods, to Barksdale AFB
21	LA 72, to US 71 S, Old Minden Rd, N Shell/Circle K/dsl, Denny's, Johnny's Pizza, McDonald's, Podnah's BBQ, Posado's Mexican, Ralph&Kacoo's, Subway, TX Roadhouse, Whataburger, Econolodge, Extended Studio Suites, Hampton Inn, Hilton Garden, Homewood Suites, La Quinta, TownePlace Suites, Bayou RV Ctr, O'Reilly Parts, USPO, VW, S RaceWay, Waffle House, Wendy's, Extended Stay America, Super 7 Inn
20c	to US 71 S, to Barksdale Blvd
20b	LA 3, Benton Rd, same as 21
20a	Hamilton Rd, Isle of Capri Blvd, N Circle K, Quality Inn, Wingate Inn, antiques, auto repair, S Chevron, Bossier Inn, Hamilton Inn
19b	Traffic St, Shreveport, downtown, N ColdStone, Fuddruckers, Courtyard, Courtyard, Horseshoe Hotel,
19b	Continued Residence Inn, Bass Pro Shop, casino, Chevrolet, S casino
19a	US 71 N, LA 1 N, Spring St, Shreveport, N Hilton, Holiday Inn Express, Shreveport Hotel, USPO
18b-d	Fairfield Ave(from wb), downtown Shreveport, S H
18a	Line Ave, Common St(from eb), downtown, S H
17b	I-49 S, to Alexandria
17a	Lakeshore Dr, Linwood Ave
16b	US 79/80, Greenwood Rd, N H, S Valero/dsl, Travelodge
16a	US 171, Hearne Ave, N Mobil/dsl, Subway, H, tires, vet, S Raceway/dsl, Wendy's, Cajun Inn
14	Jewella Ave, Shreveport, N Shell/dsl, Burger King, McDonald's, Pizza Hut, Popeyes, Sonic, Subway, Whataburger, AutoZone, County Mkt Foods, Family$, O'Reilly Parts, Super 1 Foods, tires, Walgreens
13	Monkhouse Dr, Shreveport, N Joe G's, Best Western+, Economy Inn, OYO Hotel, Residence Inn, Super 8, Family$, S Chevron/dsl, Exxon/dsl, Valero/dsl, Waffle House, Clover Inn, Country Inn, Hampton Inn, Holiday Inn Express, Merryton Inn, Quality Inn, Regency, Shreveport, to
11	I-220 E, LA 3132 E, to I-49 S
10	Pines Rd, N Chevron/dsl, Domino's, Johnny's Pizza, Kumo Japanese, Popeyes, Sam's Eatery, Subway, U-Haul, S Exxon/dsl, Murphy USA/dsl, Shell/Circle K/dsl, Burger King, Cane's, CiCi's Pizza, Cracker Barrel, Dragon Chinese, KFC, McDonald's, Nicky's Mexican, Papa John's, Pizza Hut, Taco Bell, Waffle House, Wendy's, Whataburger, Comfort Suites, Courtyard, Hilton Garden, Holiday Inn, Homewood Suites, La Quinta, Sleep Inn, Wingate, Woodspring Suites, $Tree, AT&T, AutoZone , CVS Drug, Family$, GNC, Home Depot, Mavis Tires, O'Reilly Parts, USPO, Walmart/Subway
8	US 80, LA 526 E, N Red Roof Inn, repair, tires, S Petro/Shell/dsl/scales/@, QT/dsl/scales/24hr, Wendy's, Blue Beacon, Blue Beacon, Camper's RV Ctr/park, Tall Pines RV Park(1mi)
5	US 79 N, US 80, to Greenwood, N Sinclair/dsl, TA/Shell/dsl/scales/24hr/@, Country Inn, Mid Continent Motel, RV park, S Pizza Hut, $General
3	US 79 S, LA 169, Mooringsport, N Gator's RV Park(4mi), S Flying J/Denny's/dsl/LP/scales/24hr, Love's/Arby's/dsl/scales/24hr, Sonic, Goodyear, SpeedCo
2mm	**full facilities, litter barrels, petwalk, RV dump**, Welcome Ctr eb
1mm	weigh sta both lanes
0mm	Louisiana/Texas state line

ARCADIA · FILLMORE · SHREVEPORT · SHREVEPORT · MOORINGSPORT

N INTERSTATE 49

Exit #	Services
246.5mm	Louisiana/Arkansas state line
245	LA 168, Ida, Rodessa
241	Rd 16, Mira Myrtis Rd, to Mira, E Exxon/dsl, U-Haul
237	LA 2, Plain Dealing, Hosston
234	US 71, Gilliam, Hosston
231	LA 170, Gilliam, Vivian, W H
228	LA 530, Belcher, Oil City
223	LA 169, Mooringsport
221	LA 173, Dixie, Blanchard
215	LA 1, N Market St, E Family$, vet, W Exxon/dsl, Walmart/dsl, China Wok, Johnny's Pizza, McDonald's, Popeyes, Sonic, Subway, Taco Bell, Trejo's Mexican, Wendy's, Zaxby's, Verizon, Walmart
211	LA 3194, MLK JR Dr, E Chevron/dsl, Exxon, Checkers, Domino's, Pizza Hut, Sonic, Subway, Waffle House, Whataburger, Brookshire's/gas, Walgreens
210b a	I-220, I-49 begins/ends

LA

INTERSTATE 49 Cont'd

KINGSTON

Exit #	Services
206	I-20, E to Monroe, W to Dallas. I-49 begins/ends in Shreveport on I-20, exit 17.
205	King's Hwy, E Tesla EVC, Cane's, Dunkin, McDonald's, Piccadilly, Taco Bell, Dillard's, Walgreens, W Circle K/dsl, Burger King, Sleep Inn, H
203	Hollywood Ave, Pierremont Rd, E Circle K, Another Broken Egg, Jason's Deli, McDonald's, Papa Murphy's, Sonic, Starbucks, Subway, Brookshire's, W Shell/dsl
202	LA 511, E 70th St, E RaceWay/dsl, Advance Parts, W Circle K, SC Chicken, Family$
201	LA 3132, to Dallas, Texarkana
199	LA 526, Bert Kouns Loop, E Chevron/dsl/24hr, Circle K, Burger King, KFC, Taco Bell, Wendy's, Comfort Inn, Home Depot, W RaceWay/dsl, Walmart Mkt, McDonald's, Sonic, Starbucks, Subway, Waffle House, Audi/Porsche, Brookshire's, Verizon
196	Southern Loop
196mm	Bayou Pierre
191	LA 16, LA 3276, to Stonewall, W Chevrolet
186	LA 175, to Frierson, Kingston, W Relay Sta./casino/dsl/scales
177	LA 509, to Carmel, E Shell/Eagles Trkstp/casino/dsl, W Hwy 509 RV Park(4mi)
172	US 84, to Grand Bayou, Mansfield, W Love's/Subway/dsl/24hr, Civil War Site, Glorey RV Park(4mi)
169	Asseff Rd
162	US 371, LA 177, to Evelyn, Pleasant Hill
155	LA 174, to Ajax, Lake End, W Cowboys/dsl
148	LA 485, Powhatan, Allen, W Plantation RV Park
142	LA 547, Posey Rd, E St Luke RV Park, The Cabins Camping, to Alligator Park
138	LA 6, to Natchitoches, E French Mkt/cafe/dsl, RaceWay/dsl, IHOP, Popeyes, Wendy's, Whatburger, Best Western, Comfort Suites, Days Inn, Fairfield Inn, Holiday Inn Express, Chevrolet/Buick, Dogwood Ridge RV Park, H, Jeep/Chrysler/Dodge/Ram, W Chevron/dsl, Exxon, Texaco/dsl, Burger King, DQ, El Patio, Huddle House, McDonald's, Subway, EconoLodge, Hampton Inn, Quality Inn, Nakatosh RV Park, to Kisatchie NF
132	LA 478, rd 620
127	LA 120, to Cypress, Flora, E Exxon/dsl, RV Park, to Cane River Plantations
119	LA 119, to Derry, Cloutierville, E to Cane River Plantations, Cane River Plantations
113	LA 490, to Chopin, E Exxon/dsl
107	to Lena, E USPO
103	LA 8 W, to Flatwoods, E Chevron/dsl, W RV camping, to Cotile Lake
99	LA 8, LA 1200, to Boyce, Colfax, E $General, USPO, W Cotile Lake RV Camping
98	LA 1(from nb), to Boyce
94	rd 23, to Rapides Sta Rd, E truck stop, W Love's/Arby's/dsl/scales/24hr, $General(1mi), Alexandria RV Park(2mi), I-49 RV Ctr
90	LA 498, Air Base Rd, W Chevron/dsl/24hr, Exxon/Subway/dsl, Shell/dsl, Texaco/dsl, Burger King, Cracker Barrel, McDonald's, Comfort Suites, Hampton Inn, La Quinta, Rodeway Inn, SureStay, Cabana RV Park
86	US 71, US 165, MacArthur Dr, E tire repair, W Conoco/dsl, Exxon/dsl, Mobil/dsl, Shell/Circle K/dsl, Texaco/dsl, Valero, Valero/dsl, Applebee's, Burger King, Cane's, Chick-fil-A, Church's TX Chicken, CiCi's Pizza, Dominos, DQ, Eddie's BBQ, El Paso Mexican, El Reparo Mexican, Firehouse Subs, Golden Corral, Little Caesar's, McDonald's,

CLOUTIERVILLE

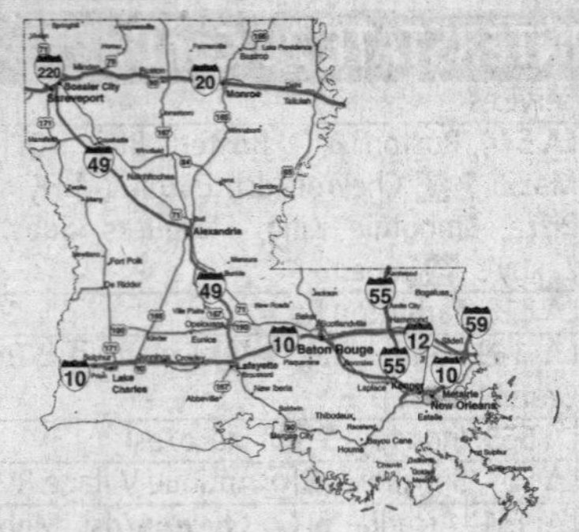

ALEXANDRIA

Exit #	Services
86	Continued Outlaw's BBQ, Pedros Mexican, Piccadilly, Popeye Schlotzsky's, Sonic, Subway, Taco Bell, TX Roadhouse, Alexandria Inn, Avalon Hotel, Best Value Inn, Best Wester Candlewood Suites, Holiday Inn Express, Macarthur In Motel 6, Quality Inn, Red Roof Inn, Red Roof Inn, $General, $Tree, Advance Parts, AutoZone, Buick/GMC, Ki Kroger/gas, NAPA, O'Reilly Parts, Office Depot, Petco, RV C Super 1 Foods, Tuesday Morning, USPO, Verizon
85b	Monroe St, Medical Ctr Dr(from nb), E Holiday Inn, H
85a	LA 1, 10th St, MLK Dr, downtown
84	US 167 N, LA 28, LA 1, Pineville Expswy(no EZ nb return)
83	Broadway Ave, E Fuel+, $General, tires, W Murp USA/dsl, Capt. D, Checker's, Chilli's, Little Caesar's, Soni Taco Bell, Wendy's, Courtyard, Home2 Suites, TownePla Suites, $Tree, Albertson's/gas, AutoZone, Books-Million, Hobby Lobby, Lowe's, mall, O'Reilly Parts, Targe Verizon, Walgreens, Walmart
81	US 71 N, LA 3250, Sugarhouse Rd, MacArthur Dr(from sb), same as 80 and 83
80	US 71 S, US 167, MacArthur Dr, Alexandria, W Chevro dsl, Exxon/dsl, Mobil, Valero/dsl, Buffalo Wild Wing Burger King, Carino's Italian, Huddle House, IHOP, KF Logan's Roadhouse, McDonald's, Outback Steaks, Pan Express, Pizza Hut, Popeyes, Rosie's Crawfish, Son Whataburger, Fairfield Inn, TownePlace Suites, $General, $General, Best Buy, Ford/Lincoln, Hyundai, O Navy, PetSmart, Sam's Club/gas, U-Haul
73	LA 3265, rd 22, to Woodworth, W Chevron/dsl, Indian Creek RA
66	LA 112, to Lecompte, E Chevron/dsl, Burger King, W Exxon/dsl, museum(10mi)
61	US 167, to Meeker, Turkey Creek
56	LA 181, Cheneyville
53	LA 115, to Bunkie, E Sammy's/Chevron/dsl/casin 24hr/@, Knights Inn
46	LA 106, to St Landry, E Bayou RV Park, W USPO
40	LA 29, to Ville Platte, E Pilot/dsl/scales/24hr
35mm	/ rec area both lanes, E full facilities, litter barre petwalk, , RV dump, vending
27	LA 10, to Lebeau
25	LA 103, to Washington, Port Barre, W Citgo, Family Ponderosa RV Park
23	US 167 N, LA 744, to Ville Platte, E Chevron/dsl/scale casino, Valero/dsl/casino, W Texaco/dsl/casino, visit ctr
19b a	US 190, to Opelousas, E Evangeline Downs Racetrack, Chevron/dsl, Exxon/dsl, RaceTrac/dsl, Valero, C Drug, H, Lowe's, USPO
18	LA 31, to Cresswell Lane, E Murphy USA/dsl, Waf House, Evangeline Downs Hotel/casino, Hampton In Holiday Inn, Quality Inn, $Tree, Chrysler/Dodge/Jee Ford/Lincoln, Verizon, Walmart/Subway, W Chevron/d Shell/dsl, Valero/Circle K/dsl, Burger King, Cane's

PORT BARRE

LA

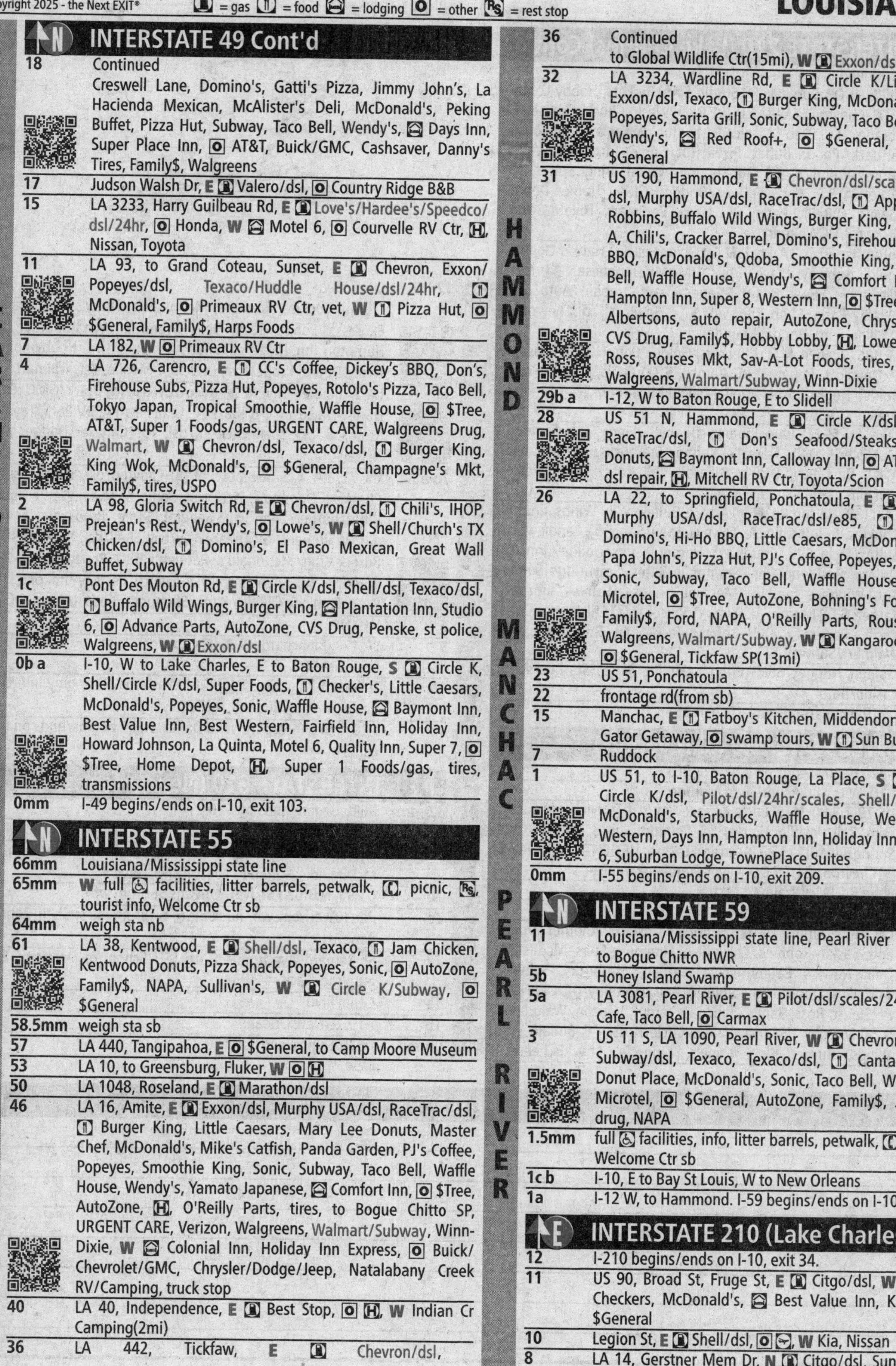

INTERSTATE 49 Cont'd

18 Continued
Creswell Lane, Domino's, Gatti's Pizza, Jimmy John's, La Hacienda Mexican, McAlister's Deli, McDonald's, Peking Buffet, Pizza Hut, Subway, Taco Bell, Wendy's, Days Inn, Super Place Inn, AT&T, Buick/GMC, Cashsaver, Danny's Tires, Family$, Walgreens

17 Judson Walsh Dr, **E** Valero/dsl, Country Ridge B&B

15 LA 3233, Harry Guilbeau Rd, **E** Love's/Hardee's/Speedco/dsl/24hr, Honda, **W** Motel 6, Courvelle RV Ctr, H, Nissan, Toyota

CARENCRO

11 LA 93, to Grand Coteau, Sunset, **E** Chevron, Exxon/Popeyes/dsl, Texaco/Huddle House/dsl/24hr, McDonald's, Primeaux RV Ctr, vet, **W** Pizza Hut, $General, Family$, Harps Foods

7 LA 182, **W** Primeaux RV Ctr

4 LA 726, Carencro, **E** CC's Coffee, Dickey's BBQ, Don's, Firehouse Subs, Pizza Hut, Popeyes, Rotolo's Pizza, Taco Bell, Tokyo Japan, Tropical Smoothie, Waffle House, $Tree, AT&T, Super 1 Foods/gas, URGENT CARE, Walgreens Drug, Walmart, **W** Chevron/dsl, Texaco/dsl, Burger King, King Wok, McDonald's, $General, Champagne's Mkt, Family$, tires, USPO

2 LA 98, Gloria Switch Rd, **E** Chevron/dsl, Chili's, IHOP, Prejean's Rest., Wendy's, Lowe's, **W** Shell/Church's TX Chicken/dsl, Domino's, El Paso Mexican, Great Wall Buffet, Subway

1c Pont Des Mouton Rd, **E** Circle K/dsl, Shell/dsl, Texaco/dsl, Buffalo Wild Wings, Burger King, Plantation Inn, Studio 6, Advance Parts, AutoZone, CVS Drug, Penske, st police, Walgreens, **W** Exxon/dsl

0b a I-10, W to Lake Charles, E to Baton Rouge, **S** Circle K, Shell/Circle K/dsl, Super Foods, Checker's, Little Caesars, McDonald's, Popeyes, Sonic, Waffle House, Baymont Inn, Best Value Inn, Best Western, Fairfield Inn, Holiday Inn, Howard Johnson, La Quinta, Motel 6, Quality Inn, Super 7, $Tree, Home Depot, H, Super 1 Foods/gas, tires, transmissions

0mm I-49 begins/ends on I-10, exit 103.

INTERSTATE 55

66mm Louisiana/Mississippi state line

65mm **W** full facilities, litter barrels, petwalk, picnic, tourist info, Welcome Ctr sb

64mm weigh sta nb

61 LA 38, Kentwood, **E** Shell/dsl, Texaco, Jam Chicken, Kentwood Donuts, Pizza Shack, Popeyes, Sonic, AutoZone, Family$, NAPA, Sullivan's, **W** Circle K/Subway, $General

58.5mm weigh sta sb

57 LA 440, Tangipahoa, **E** $General, to Camp Moore Museum

53 LA 10, to Greensburg, Fluker, **W** H

50 LA 1048, Roseland, **E** Marathon/dsl

AMITE

46 LA 16, Amite, **E** Exxon/dsl, Murphy USA/dsl, RaceTrac/dsl, Burger King, Little Caesars, Mary Lee Donuts, Master Chef, McDonald's, Mike's Catfish, Panda Garden, PJ's Coffee, Popeyes, Smoothie King, Sonic, Subway, Taco Bell, Waffle House, Wendy's, Yamato Japanese, Comfort Inn, $Tree, AutoZone, H, O'Reilly Parts, tires, to Bogue Chitto SP, URGENT CARE, Verizon, Walgreens, Walmart/Subway, Winn-Dixie, **W** Colonial Inn, Holiday Inn Express, Buick/Chevrolet/GMC, Chrysler/Dodge/Jeep, Natalabany Creek RV/Camping, truck stop

40 LA 40, Independence, **E** Best Stop, H, **W** Indian Cr Camping(2mi)

36 LA 442, Tickfaw, **E** Chevron/dsl,

36 Continued
to Global Wildlife Ctr(15mi), **W** Exxon/dsl

HAMMOND

32 LA 3234, Wardline Rd, **E** Circle K/Little Caesars/dsl, Exxon/dsl, Texaco, Burger King, McDonald's, PJ's Coffee, Popeyes, Sarita Grill, Sonic, Subway, Taco Bell, Waffle House, Wendy's, Red Roof+, $General, Tony's Tire, **W** $General

31 US 190, Hammond, **E** Chevron/dsl/scales/24hr, Exxon/dsl, Murphy USA, RaceTrac/dsl, Applebee's, Baskin-Robbins, Buffalo Wild Wings, Burger King, Cane's, Chick-fil-A, Chili's, Cracker Barrel, Domino's, Firehouse Subs, Hi-Ho 1 BBQ, McDonald's, Qdoba, Smoothie King, Starbucks, Taco Bell, Waffle House, Wendy's, Comfort Inn, Econolodge, Hampton Inn, Super 8, Western Inn, $Tree, Advance Parts, Albertsons, auto repair, AutoZone, Chrysler/Dodge/Jeep, CVS Drug, Family$, Hobby Lobby, H, Lowe's, Office Depot, Ross, Rouses Mkt, Sav-A-Lot Foods, tires, URGENT CARE, Walgreens, Walmart/Subway, Winn-Dixie

29b a I-12, W to Baton Rouge, E to Slidell

28 US 51 N, Hammond, **E** Circle K/dsl, Citgo, Exxon, RaceTrac/dsl, Don's Seafood/Steaks, Doughlicious Donuts, Baymont Inn, Calloway Inn, AT&T, Buick/GMC, dsl repair, H, Mitchell RV Ctr, Toyota/Scion

26 LA 22, to Springfield, Ponchatoula, **E** Marathon/dsl, Murphy USA/dsl, RaceTrac/dsl/e85, Burger King, Domino's, Hi-Ho BBQ, Little Caesars, McDonald's/playplace, Papa John's, Pizza Hut, PJ's Coffee, Popeyes, Smoothie King, Sonic, Subway, Taco Bell, Waffle House, Wendy's, Microtel, $Tree, AutoZone, Bohning's Foods, CVS Drug, Family$, Ford, NAPA, O'Reilly Parts, Rouse's Mkt, tires, Walgreens, Walmart/Subway, **W** Kangaroo/Domino's/dsl, $General, Tickfaw SP(13mi)

23 US 51, Ponchatoula

22 frontage rd(from sb)

MANCHAC

15 Manchac, **E** Fatboy's Kitchen, Middendorf's Manchac, Gator Getaway, swamp tours, **W** Sun Buns Bar & Grill

7 Ruddock

1 US 51, to I-10, Baton Rouge, La Place, **S** Chevron/dsl, Circle K/dsl, Pilot/dsl/24hr/scales, Shell/casino/dsl, McDonald's, Starbucks, Waffle House, Wendy's, Best Western, Days Inn, Hampton Inn, Holiday Inn Express, Motel 6, Suburban Lodge, TownePlace Suites

0mm I-55 begins/ends on I-10, exit 209.

INTERSTATE 59

PEARL RIVER

11 Louisiana/Mississippi state line, Pearl River Turnaround, to Bogue Chitto NWR

5b Honey Island Swamp

5a LA 3081, Pearl River, **E** Pilot/dsl/scales/24hr, **W** Halo Cafe, Taco Bell, Carmax

3 US 11 S, LA 1090, Pearl River, **W** Chevron/dsl, Circle K/Subway/dsl, Texaco, Texaco/dsl, Cantaritos Mexican, Donut Place, McDonald's, Sonic, Taco Bell, Waffle House, Microtel, $General, AutoZone, Family$, Jubilee Foods/drug, NAPA

1.5mm full facilities, info, litter barrels, petwalk, RV dump, Welcome Ctr sb

1c b I-10, E to Bay St Louis, W to New Orleans

1a I-12 W, to Hammond. I-59 begins/ends on I-10/I-12.

INTERSTATE 210 (Lake Charles)

12 I-210 begins/ends on I-10, exit 34.

11 US 90, Broad St, Fruge St, **E** Citgo/dsl, **W** Exxon/dsl, Checkers, McDonald's, Best Value Inn, Knights Inn, $General

10 Legion St, **E** Shell/dsl, **W** Kia, Nissan

8 LA 14, Gerstner Mem Dr, **N** Citgo/dsl, Sunoco/7-11/dsl,

LA

= gas = food = lodging = other = rest stop

INTERSTATE 210 (Lake Charles) Cont'd

8 Continued
Chili's, IHOP, Subway, Studio 6, BigLots, Hobby Lobby, **S** Chevron, Shell/dsl, BBQ West, ChuckECheese, El Dorado, El Paso Mexican, Kyoto, Logan's Roadhouse, Outback, Panda Buffet, Pizza Hut, Sonic, Taco Bell, Waffle House, Wendy's, Quality Inn, WoodSpring Suites, $Tree, AT&T, Chrysler/Jeep/Dodge, GMC, Home Depot, Lowe's, O'Reilly Parts, Old Navy, PetSmart, Toyota/Scion, Verizon, VW, Walmart

7b Enterprise Blvd, LA Blvd, **N** Exxon/dsl, Hank's Donuts, Sonic, Subway, Taco Bell, UMAMI Japanese, Best Western+, Super 8, $General, auto repair, AutoZone, O'Reilly Parts, Shop Rite, vet, **S** Shell/dsl, Chevrolet/Cadillac, Ford, Honda, Hyundai

6a LA 385, Ryan St, **N** Checkers, Golden Corral, Little Caesars, McDonald's, Popeyes, Aamco, **S** CiCi's, Gatti's Pizza, Golden Hooks, Jason's Deli, Mellow Mushroom, $General, Firestone/auto

5 Lake St, **N** Blue Iguana, Denny's, Fiery Crab Seafood, McAlister's Deli, Nawal's Kebab, Starbucks, Wendy's, AT&T, Best Buy, Dick's, Dillard's, H, Kohl's, mall, Petco, Verizon

4 LA 1138, Nelson Rd, **N** Arby's, Buffalo Wild Wings, Crumbl Cookies, Jo Jo's Chinese, Olive Garden, Sonic, Candlewood Suites/Tesla EVC, Courtyard, Hampton Inn, Holiday Inn, La Quinta, Residence Inn, Springhill Suites, Staybridge Suites, Tru, Wingate Inn, Marshall's, Ross, Sam's Club/gas, Target, **S** Murphy USA/dsl, Tobacco+, Chick-fil-A, Crust Pizza, Panera Bread, Torchy Tacos, TX Roadhouse, Walmart/Subway

3 Golden Nugget Blvd, Prien Lake Rd, **N** Starbucks, casino/hotel

1b a I-210 begins/ends on I-10, exit 25.

INTERSTATE 220 (Shreveport)

18mm I-220 begins/ends on I-20, exit 26.

17b I-20, W to Shreveport, E to Monroe

17a US 79, US 80, **N** Circle K, RaceWay/dsl, Nickys Mexican, Taco Bell, Waffle House, Comfort Suites, Holiday Inn, SpringHill Suites, racetrack/casino, URGENT CARE, vet, **S** Chevron/dsl, DQ, Silver Star Smokehouse

15 Shed Rd, **N** Walmart Mkt

13 Swan Lake Rd, **N** Honda

12 LA 3105, Airline Dr, **N** Andy's Custard, Another Broken Egg, Baskin-Robbins, Chick-fil-A, Firehouse Subs, McAlister's Deli, Newk's Eatery, Olive Garden, Starbucks, Subway, TaMolly's, Tropical Smoothie, Belk, Best Buy, H, Old Navy, PetSmart, Ross, Sam's Club/gas, Target, Verizon, Walgreens, **S** Murphy USA/dsl, Valero/Circle K/dsl, Buffalo Wild Wings, Burger King, Cane's, Chipotle, ChuckECheese,

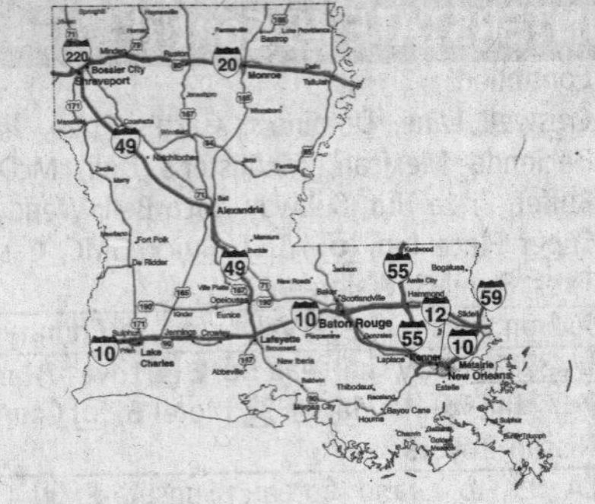

ELYSIAN FIELDS

12 Continued
Crumbl Cookies, Freddy's, McDonald's, Nicky's Rest., Panda Express, Sonic, Taco Bell, Wendy's, Whataburger, Hampton Inn, $Tree, AT&T, Discount Tire, Hobby Lobby, Home Depot, Kroger/dsl, Lowe's, T-Mobile, vet, Walmart

11 LA 3, Bossier City, **N** RaceWay/dsl, Buick/GMC, Ford, Harley-Davidson, H, Kia/EVC, Lexus, NAPA, RV Park, Toyota/Scion, **S** Shell/Circle K/dsl, Chrysler/Dodge/Jeep, Nissan

7b a US 71, LA 1, Shreveport, **N** Chevron/dsl, Exxon/dsl, Checkers, Domino's, Pizza Hut, Sonic, Subway, Waffle House, Whataburger/24hr, $General, $Tree, Brookshire Foods/gas, Walgreens, **S** RaceWay/dsl, Shell/dsl, Valero/dsl, Burger King, McDonald's, Podnuh's BBQ, Popeyes, Taco Bell Wendy's, Royal Inn, Advance Parts, AutoZone, CVS Drug, Family$, O'Reilly Parts, Shoppers Foods, U-Haul

6 I-49 N

5 LA 173, Blanchard Rd, **N** Citgo/dsl

2 Lakeshore Dr

1a Jefferson Paige Rd, **S** Best Western+, Economy Inn, OYO Residence Inn, Super 8, Family$

1b c I-20, E to Shreveport, W to Dallas. I-220 begins/ends on I-20 exit 11.

INTERSTATE 610 (New Orleans)

4.5mm I-610 begins/ends on I-10

4 Franklin Ave(from eb)

3 Elysian fields, **S** Exxon/dsl, Shell, Burger King McDonald's, Sammy's Food, H, Lowe's

2b US 90, N Broad St, New Orleans St (from wb)

2c Paris Ave(from wb, no return), **S** Jimmy's, Shell/24hr, Popeyes

2a St Bernard Ave(from eb), to LSU School of Dentistry, **S** auto racetrack

1a Canal Blvd

1b I-10, to New Orleans

0mm I-610 begins/ends on I-10

NOTES

MAINE

INTERSTATE 95

Exit #	Services
305mm	US/Canada border, Maine state line, US Customs. I-95 begins/ends.
305	US 2, to Houlton, S Houlton
303mm	Meduxnekeag River
302	US 1, Houlton, **full facilities, litter barrels, petwalk,** , S $Tree, E Irving/dsl/24hr, Domino's, McDonald's, Pizza Hut, Tang's Chinese, IGA Foods, Marden's, O'Reilly Parts/VIP Service, W Citgo/Subway/dsl, Irving/Circle K/dsl/scales/@, Shell/Dunkin'/dsl, Tim Hortons/Coldstone, Ivey's Motel, Shiretown Motel, Arrowstook SP, Family$, Ford, Hannaford Mkt, NAPA, Toyota, Walmart
301mm	B Stream
291	US 2, to Smyrna, E Brookside Motel/rest.
286	Oakfield Rd, to ME 11, Eagle Lake, Ashland, W Irving/Circle K/dsl, Sunoco/dsl, A Place To Eat, USPO
277mm	Mattawamkeag River, W Branch
276	ME 159, Island Falls, E Islands Falls Onestop, Porter's/rest., Bishop's Mkt, USPO, W Baxter SP(N entrance), vet
264	to ME 11, Sherman, E Shell/dsl/LP/rest., W Irving/Circle K/dsl, Katahdin Valley Motel, Baxter SP(N entrance)
259	Benedicta(from nb, no re-entry)
252mm	scenic view Mt Katahdin, nb
247mm	Salmon Stream
244	ME 157, to Medway, E Millinocket, W Irving/Circle K/dsl, Gateway Inn, Baxter SP(S entrance), city park, Katahdin Shadows Camping, USPO
244mm	Penobscot River
243mm	**full facilities, litter barrels, petwalk,** , , **both lanes**
227	to US 2, ME 6, Lincoln, E food, gas, lodging, RV camping
219mm	Piscataquis River
217	ME 6, Howland, E Citgo/95 Diner/dsl, Chubby's Ice Cream, Hometown Cafe
201mm	Birch Stream
199	ME 16(no nb re-entry), to LaGrange
197	ME 43, to Old Town
196mm	Pushaw Stream
193	Stillwater Ave, to Old Town, E Citgo/dsl, Irving/Circle K/dsl, China Garden, Dunkin', Dunkin', Governor's Rest., McDonald's, Riverside Pizza, Subway, Wendy's, Black Bear Inn, $Tree, IGA Foods, O'Reilly Parts/VIP Service, Stillwater River Reservoir, W vet
191	Kelly Rd, to Orono
187	Hogan Rd, Bangor Mall Blvd, to Bangor, E Citgo, Denny's, Courtyard, Hampton Inn, Hilton Garden, TownePlace Suites, Audi/VW, Buick/GMC, Cadillac/Chevrolet, Chrysler/Dodge/Jeep, Ford, Honda, Hyundai/Mitsubishi, Mazda, Mercedes, NAPA, Nissan, Sam's Club/gas, Subaru, Volvo, W Citgo/dsl, Irving/Circle K/dsl, Applebee's, Buffalo Wild Wings, Chick-fil-A, Chili's, Chipotle, Dunkin', Firehouse Subs, Five Guys, Green Tea Japanese, Happy China, Harvest Moon Deli, Jersey Mike's, Kobe Japanese, Las Palapas, Longhorn Steaks, McDonald's, Miguel's Mexican, Olive Garden, Papa Johns, Starbucks, Subway, Taco Bell, TX Roadhouse, UNO Pizzeria, Wendy's, Bangor Motel, Comfort Inn, Country Inn, Quality Inn, $Tree, AT&T, AutoZone, Best Buy, BJ's/gas, Books-A-Million, Dick's, Hannaford Foods, Hobby Lobby, Home Depot,

BANGOR

Exit #	Services
187	Continued JC Penney, Kia, Kohl's, LL Bean, Lowe's, Michaels, Old Navy, PetCo, PetSmart, Staples, Sullivan Tire/auto, Target, Town Fair Tire, URGENT CARE, Verizon, Verizon, VIP Service, Walmart
186	Stillwater Ave, same as 187
185	ME 15, to Broadway, Bangor, E Irving/Circle K/dsl, Tri-City Pizza, , W China Wok, Coldstone/Tim Hortons, DQ, Governor's Rest., KFC, McDonald's, Moe's BBQ, Pizza Hut, Starbucks, Subway, Taco Bell, Advance Parts, Hannaford Foods, TJ Maxx, URGENT CARE, Walgreens
184	ME 222, Union St, to Ohio St, Bangor, E Trade Winds, auto repair, Walgreens, W auto repair, Mobil, Shell/dsl, Burger King, Dunkin', McDonald's, Wendy's, Sheraton, $Tree, Hannaford Foods, Marshall's, Midas, to
183	US 2, ME 2, Hammond St, Bangor, E Citgo, Gulf, Angelo's Pizza, Papa Gambino's Pizza, Corner Store, Fairmont Hardware, Fairmont Mkt, NAPA, W
182b	US 2, ME 100 W, W Irving/Circle/Subway/dsl, Shell/dsl, Dunkin', Pete & Larry's, Tim Hortons, Bangor Grande Hotel, Best Value Inn, Fairfield Inn, Holiday Inn, Home2 Suites, Howard Johnson, Quality Inn, Queen City Inn, Super 8, O'Reilly Parts/VIP Service, Pumpkin Patch RV Resort, Tire Whse, U-Haul
182a	I-395, to US 2, US 1A, downtown, Bangor
180	Cold Brook Rd, to Hampden, E Citgo, Angler's Rest. (1mi), W Citgo/dsl/24hr/@, Dysarts Fleet Fuel/dsl, Best Western, dsl repair, Volvo
178mm	**full facilities, info, litter barrels, petwalk,** , , **sb, vending, wireless internet**

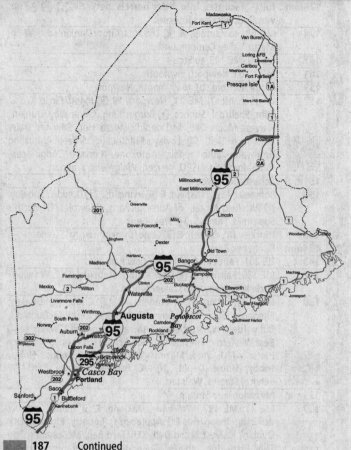

INTERSTATE 95 Cont'd

PLYMOUTH

Exit #	Services
177mm	Soudabscook Stream
176mm	**full facilities, info, litter barrels, petwalk, nb, vending, wireless internet**
174	ME 69, to Carmel, **E** Dysart's/Citgo/Dunkin'/dsl, **W** Mystic Valley Campground
167	ME 69, ME 143, to Etna
161	ME 7, to E Newport, Plymouth
159	Ridge Rd(from sb), to Plymouth, Newport
157	to US 2, ME 7, ME 11, Newport, **W** Irving/Circle K/dsl/24hr, Shell/dsl, Sunoco, Burger King, China Way, Dunkin', Harvest Moon Deli, McDonald's, Pizza Hut, Sawyers Dairy Bar, Taco Bell, Lovley's Motel, $Tree, Aubuchon Hardware, auto repair, AutoZone, Chrysler/Dodge/Jeep, Hannaford Mkt, USPO, Verizon, Walgreens, Walmart

FAIRFIELD

Exit #	Services
151mm	Sebasticook River
150	Somerset Ave, Pittsfield, **E** Irving/dsl, Dunkin', Subway, Pittsfield Motel, Advance Parts, Chevrolet, Danforth's Supermkt, Family$, H, Walgreens
138	Hinckley Rd, Clinton, **E** Citgo/Dunkin'/dsl, $General
134mm	Kennebec River
133	US 201, Fairfield, **E** Purple Cow Pancakes
132	ME 139, Fairfield, **E** Dow's Quick Stopt/dsl, EVC, **W** Irving/Circle K/Subway/dsl/scales/24hr
130	ME 104, Main St, Waterville, **E** Citgo, Dunkin', Firehouse Subs, Five Guys, Governor's Rest., McDonald's, Ruby Tuesday, Starbucks, Subway, Taco Bell, Wendy's, Best Western+, Fireside Inn, Holiday Inn Express, Advance Parts, AT&T, Audi/Mazda/VW, Hannaford Foods, Hobby Lobby, Home Depot, H, JC Penney, O'Reilly Parts/VIP Service, Staples, Walmart

SIDNEY

Exit #	Services
129mm	Messalonskee Stream
127	ME 11, ME 137, Waterville, Oakland, **E** Irving/Circle K/dsl/24hr, Irving/dsl, Applebee's, Country Kitchen, DQ, Dunkin', Harvest Moon Deli, KFC/Taco Bell, McDonald's, Pad Thai, Pizza Hut, Subway, Budget Host, Hampton Inn, The Elmwood, AutoZone, Buick/Chevrolet, Chrysler/Dodge/Jeep/Fiat, CVS Drug, Freightliner, Hannaford Foods, H, Jiffy Lube, Marden's, Shaw's Foods/Osco Drug, Tire Whse, TJ Maxx, Toyota, Verizon, **W** Shell/dsl, Dunkin', Aubuchon Hardware, Ford/Lincoln, NAPA
120	Lyons Rd, Sidney, **E** tires
117mm	weigh sta both lanes

AUGUSTA

Exit #	Services
113	ME 3, Augusta, Belfast, **W** H
112	ME 27, ME 8, ME 11, Augusta, **E** Citgo, Tesla EVC, Asian Noodle Bowl, Denny's, Dunkin', El Agave Mexican, IHOP, Jersey Mike's, Kume Japanese, Longhorn Steaks, Olive Garden, Panera Bread, Red Robin, Sam's Italian, Best Western+, AT&T, Barnes&Noble, Dick's, Home Depot, Kohl's, Old Navy, Sam's Club, TJ Maxx, TownFair Tire, U of Maine, Verizon, Walmart, **W** Irving/Circle K/dsl/24hr, 99 Rest., Great Wall Chinese, KFC/Taco Bell, Wendy's, Comfort Inn, Fairfield Inn, Advance Parts
109	US 202, ME 11, ME 17, ME 100, Augusta, **E** Citgo/dsl, Irving/Circle K/dsl, Amazing Garden, Applebee's, Arby's, Augusta Pancakes, Burger King, Damon's Italian, Domino's, Dunkin', Five Guys, McDonald's, Pizza Hut, Starbucks, Subway, Sunrise Bagel, Taco Bell, Wendy's, Senator Inn, $Tree, auto repair, AutoZone, Best Buy, BigLots, Lowe's, Michaels, O'Reilly Parts/VIP Service, PetSmart, Shaw's Foods/Osco Drug, Staples, Target, U-Haul, URGENT CARE, USPO, vet, Walgreens, **W** Gas For Less, Margarita's Mexican, TX Roadhouse, Days Inn, Hampton Inn, Homewood Suites, Maine Evergreen Hotel, Super 8, Chrysler/Dodge, Hannaford Foods, Honda, Hyundai, Kia,
109	Continued PetCo, Subaru, Toyota, URGENT CARE
103	to I-295 S(from sb), ME 9, ME 126, to Gardiner, service pla **Citgo, Dunkin, Popeyes**
102	to I-295 S(from nb), rd 9, rd 106, service plaza, Dunkin'/@, **E Citgo, Popeyes**
100mm	toll plaza
99mm	Cobbosseecontee Stream
86	to ME 9, Sabattus
84mm	Sabattus Creek
80	ME 196, Lewiston, **W** Coast Fuels, Domino's, Gendron dsl, Shell/dsl, XPress/dsl, Burger King, Canton Wok, Chi A-Dee, D'Angelo, Dunkin', Fast Breaks Rest., Govern Rest., KFC/Taco Bell, McDonald's, Papa John's, Sam's Itali Starbucks, Subway, Ramada Inn, Super 8, SureStay, $General, Advance Parts, H

FREEPORT

Exit #	Services
78mm	Androscoggin River
75	US 202, rd 4, rd 100, to Auburn, **E** Citgo/Subway/ Irving/Circle K/dsl, Peking Chinese, Econolod Quality Inn, **W** H
71mm	Royal River
66mm	toll plaza
63	US 202, rd 115, rd 4, to ME 26, Gray, **E** Citgo, Cumberla Farms/dsl, Mobil, Sunoco, China Gray, Dunk Fishermen's Net, Jess'n Nic's Pizza, Manee Thai, McDonal Subway, Tailgate Grill, Two Mums Kitchen, $Gene $Tree, Ace Hardware, NAPA, Shop'n Save Mkt, **W** Walgree
59mm	service plaza both lanes, **Citgo/dsl,** Burger King
55mm	Piscataqua River
53	to ME 26, ME100 W, N Portland, **E** Irving/Circle Subway/dsl, Dunkin', Hannaford Foods, H
52	to I-295, US 1, Freeport
48	ME 25, to Portland, **E** Applebee's, Asian Bistro, Pa Garden, Tasty Fried Chicken, Hampton Inn, Inn Portland, $Tree, BigLots, BJ's Whse/gas, Chevrolet, Drug, Fiat, Lowe's, Sullivan Tire, vet, **W** Irving/Circle K/ Mobil, Amato's Rest., Burger King, Chick-fil-A, Chipo Dunkin', Dunkin', KFC/Taco Bell, McDonald's, Panera Bre Pizza Hut, Rio Bravo Mexican, Stacks Pancake Co., Starbu Wendy's, Fireside Inn, Motel 6, Ramada, Super 8, Advance Parts, AT&T, Chrysler/Dodge/Jeep, Ford, Har Davidson, Home Depot, Hyundai, Jiffy Lube, Kohl's, Lex Toyota, Lincoln, Midas, NAPA, Tire Whse, vet
47	to ME 25, Rand Rd
47mm	Stroudwater River
46	to ME 22, Congress St, same as 45
45	to US 1, Maine Mall Rd, S Portland, **E** Citgo/dsl, Suno dsl, Tesla EVC, Amato's Italian, Burger King, Chipo Mexican, Cracker Barrel, Dunkin', Five Guys, Food Co Friendly's, Heidi's Brooklyn Deli, IHOP,

ME

INTERSTATE 95 Cont'd

45	Continued Jaffa Mediterranean Grill, Kobe Steakhouse, Longhorn Steaks, McDonald's, Olive Garden, OTTO Pizza, Panda Express, Panera Bread, Popeyes, Sebago Brewing Rest., Starbucks, Tuscan Table, UNO Pizzaria, Wendy's, [lodging] Casco Bay Hotel, Comfort Inn, Courtyard, Days Inn, DoubleTree, Fairfield Inn, Hampton Inn, Home2 Suites, Homewood Suites, TownePlace Suites, Tru Hilton, [other] $Tree, Best Buy, BooksAMillion, Carmax, Dick's, Hannaford Foods, Honda, JC Penney, Macy's, Michael's, Nissan, Old Navy, PetCo, Staples, TJ Maxx, TownFair Tire, Verizon, **W** [food] Applebee's, [lodging] Holiday Inn Express, Sheraton, [other] Target
44	I-295 N(from nb), to S Portland, Scarborough, **E** [gas] Cumberland Farms, EVC, [food] Chia Sen Chinese, Jersey Mike's, KFC/Taco Bell, Little Caesar's, Red Robin, Subway, TX Roadhouse, [lodging] Candlewood Suites, Courtyard, Extended Stay America, Fairfield Inn, Homewood Suites, Residence Inn, [other] AT&T, Hannaford Mkt, [H], Lowe's, Marshall's, NAPA, O'Reilly/VIP Parts/service, PetSmart, Sam's Club/gas, Walmart
42mm	Nonesuch River
42	to US 1, **E** [gas] Irving/Dunkin'/dsl, [food] Portland Pie, [other] Cabela's, fireworks, Scarborough Downs Racetrack(seasonal), URGENT CARE
36	I-195 E, to Saco, Old Orchard Beach, **E** [gas] Shell, [lodging] Comfort Inn, Ramada, [other] KOA, Paradise Park Resort RV
33mm	Saco River
32	ME 111, to Biddeford, **E** [gas] Irving/Circle K/dsl, [food] 99 Rest., Amato's Sandwiches, Burger King, D'Angelo Sandwiches, Dunkin', McDonald's, OTTO Pizza, Starbucks, Tropical Smoothie, Valerie's Kitchen, Wendy's, [lodging] Best Value Inn, Holiday Inn Express, [other] AAA, Advance Parts, AutoZone, CVS Drug, [H], O'Reilly/VIP Parts/Service, Walgreens, Walmart, **W** [gas] Cumberland Farms/dsl, [food] Applebee's, Firehouse Subs, Five Guys, Kobe Japanese, Longhorn Steaks, Panera Bread, [other] Home Depot, Kohl's, MarketBasket Foods, Michael's, PetSmart, Staples, Target, TJ Maxx, TownFair Tire, Verizon
25mm	Kennebunk River
25	ME 35, Kennebunk Beach, service plaza both lanes, Kennebunk Beach, [gas] Citgo/dsl, EVC(nb&sb), [food] Burger King(sb), Starbucks(nb&sb), **E** [other] vet, **W** [gas] Shell, [lodging] Hampton Inn, Kennebunk Lodge
24mm	Mousam River
19.5mm	Merriland River
19	ME 9, ME 109, to Wells, Sanford
7	ME 91, to US 1, The Yorks, (last exit before toll rd nb), **E** [gas] Irving/Circle K/dsl, Mobil/dsl, Shell, [food] Bamboo Garden, Moose Burger, Nick's Steaks, Norma's Rest., Ruby's Grill, Wild Willy's Burgers, York 54 Pizza, [lodging] Best Western, Microtel, [other] $Tree, Ace Hardware, Hannaford Foods, [H], vet, Walgreens
5.5mm	weigh sta nb
5mm	York River
4mm	weigh sta sb
3mm	**full [handicapped] facilities, info, litter barrels, petwalk,** [phone], [picnic], **vending**, Welcome Ctr nb, [other] wireless
2	(2 & 3 from nb), US 1, to Kittery, **E** [gas] 7-11/dsl, Irving/Circle K/dsl/scales, Mobil, [food] Bagel Caboose, Bob's Clam Hut, Burger King, La Casita Mexican, McDonald's, Robert's Maine Grill, Siam Mellow, Spruce Creek Pizza, Subway, Sunrise Grill, Weathervane Seafood Rest., [lodging] Hampton Inn, Kittery Inn, Northeaster Hotel, Ramada Inn, [other] Naval Museum, Outlets/Famous Brands, vet
1	ME 103(from nb, no re-entry), to Kittery
0mm	Maine/New Hampshire state line, Piscataqua River

OLD ORCHARD BEACH SANFORD

BOWDOINHAM BATH YARMOUTH

INTERSTATE 295 (Portland)

Exit #	Services
52mm	I-295 begins/ends on I-95 exit 103.
51	ME 9, ME 126, to Gardiner, Litchfield, toll plaza, service plaza, Litchfield, **W** [gas] Citgo, [food] Dunkin', Popeyes
49	US 201, to Gardiner
43	ME 197, to Richmond, **E** [gas] Irving/dsl, [food] Dunkin', Subway, **W** [other] KOA
37	ME 125, Bowdoinham, **W** [other] USPO
31b a	ME 196, to Lisbon, Topsham, **E** [gas] EVC, Irving/Circle K/Dunkin'/Subway, Mobil, Mobil/dsl, [food] 99 Rest., Arby's, Buffalo Wild Wings, Fairground Cafe, Firehouse Subs, Jersey Mike's, Kopper Kettle, Kume Japanese, McDonald's, Panera Bread, Romeo's Pizza, Sam's Italian, Starbucks, Wendy's, [other] $Tree, AT&T, Dick's, Hannaford Foods, Home Depot, Lee's Tire, Meineke, Nissan, O'Reilly Parts/VIP Service, PetCo, Target, Tire Whse, Town Fair Tire, Toyota, Verizon, Volvo, Walgreens, **W** [gas] Shell/dsl
30mm	Androscoggin River
28	US 1, Bath, **E** [gas] Cumberland/dsl, Irving/dsl, Shell, [food] Amato's, Brunswick Diner, Dunkin', McDonald's, Pancho Villa, Pat's Pizza, Subway, [lodging] Comfort Inn, Fairfield Inn, Moonlight Inn, Relax Inn, Travelers Inn, [other] Chevrolet/Mazda, Chrysler/Dodge/Jeep, [H]
24	to Freeport(from nb)
22	ME 125, to Pownal, **E** [gas] Irving/Circle K, [food] Brickyard Pizza, Derosier's Pizza, Domino's, Jameson Rest., Linda Bean's ME Kitchen, Lobster Cooker Seafood, McDonald's, Sam's Italian, Starbucks, Tuscan Bistro, [lodging] Brewster B&B, Candlebay Inn, Harraseeket Inn, Hilton Garden, James Place Inn, [other] CVS Drug, LL Bean, outlets/famous brands, USPO, **W** Bradbury Mtn SP
20	Desert Rd, Freeport, **E** [gas] Irving/Circle K, [food] Antonia's Pizza, Buck's BBQ, Dunkin', Thai Garden Rest., [lodging] Econolodge, Freeport Hotel, Hampton Inn, Holiday Inn Express, [other] Shaw's Foods
17	US 1, Yarmouth, **full [handicapped] facilities, [RS] both lanes, E** [food] Day's Seafood, Muddy Rudder Rest., [lodging] Best Western, [other] Delorme Mapping, Ford, **W** [gas] Citgo/Dunkin'/dsl, Cumberland/dsl, [food] Binga's Wings, Honeycone Creamery, Pat's Pizza, [other] Ace Hardware, Hannaford Mkt, O'Reilly Parts/VIP Service, Tire Whse
15	US 1, to Cumberland, Yarmouth, **W** [gas] Mobil, Sunoco/dsl, [food] Maggie Mae's, OTTO Pizza, Romeo's Pizza, Subway, Yarmouth Rice & Noodle
11	to I-95, ME Tpk (from sb)
10	US 1, to Falmouth, **E** [gas] Citgo/dsl, Irving/dsl, [food] Bernie's Foreside Rest., Dunkin', Foreside Rest., Fuego Mexican, Leavitt & Sons Deli, McDonald's, Orchid Thai, Portland Pie Co., Sicillian Table, Starbucks, Subway, [lodging] Falmouth Inn, [other] Ace Hardware, Audi/VW, Mazda, Shaw's Foods, Staples, Sullivan Tire/auto, vet, Walmart
9mm	Presumpscot River
9	US 1 S, ME 26, to Baxter Blvd
8.5mm	Tuckeys Bridge
8	ME 26 S, Washington Ave, **E** [other] U-Haul
7	US 1A, Franklin St, **E** [food] Miss Portland Diner, [other] Tire Whse, Trader Joe's, Verizon, Walgreens, Whole Foods Mkt
6b a	US 1, Forest Ave, **E** [gas] Citgo, EVC, [food] Bayside Cafe, Chipotle, Coals Bayside Pizza, Leavitt & Son Deli, [other] city park, CVS Drug, [H], Trader Joe's, USPO, **W** [gas] Mobil/dsl, [food] Burger King, Crown Fried Chicken, Leonardo's Pizza, [other] Hannaford Foods, U of So ME, Walgreens
5b a	ME 22, Congress St, **E** [food] Amato's Rest., Crown Fried Chicken, D'Angelos Sandwiches, Dunkin', McDonald's, Pizza Villa, Subway, [lodging] Inn at St John, La Quinta, [other] [H], Sullivan Tire,

ME

= gas = food = lodging = other = rest stop

INTERSTATE 295 (Portland) Cont'd

5b a	Continued Gulf, Mobil/dsl, Anania's Italian, Dunkin', Maria's Italian, Tony's Donuts, Clarion, Advance Parts, CVS Drug, Shaw's Mkt
3mm	Fore River
4	US 1 S, to Main St, to S Portland, services on US 1
3	ME 9, to Westbrook St, no sb return, **E** golf, **W** Citgo/dsl, Irving/Circle K/dsl, Big Fin HBBQ, Buffalo Wild Wings, El Rodeo Mexican, Guerrero Maya, Moe's BBQ, Olive Garden, OTTO Pizza, Seadog Brew Co., Subway, Tropical Smoothie, Casco Bay Hotel, Hampton Inn, Chevrolet, Home Depot
2	to US 1 S, S Portland
1	to I-95, to US 1, multiple services E on US 1
0mm	I-295 begins/ends on I-95, exit 44.

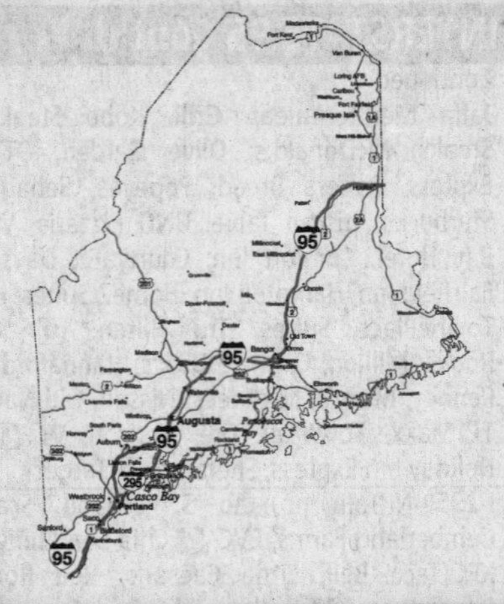

NOTES

MARYLAND

INTERSTATE 68

Exit #	Services
82c	I-70 W, to Breezewood. I-68 begins/ends on I-70, exit 1.
82b	I-70 E, US 40 E, to Hagerstown
82a	US 522, Hancock, **S** [gas] Sheetz/dsl, Sunoco, [food] Food Lion, Hardee's, Krazy Rayz Smokehouse, Pizza Hut, [lodging] Hancock Motel, Super 8, [other] Chevrolet, EVC, Happy Hills Camping, NAPA, Save-A-Lot Foods
77	US 40, MD 144, Woodmont Rd
75mm	runaway truck ramp eb
74mm	full [handicapped] facilities, Sideling Hill [RS]/exhibit both lanes
74	US 40, Mountain Rd(no return from eb)
73mm	Sideling Hill Creek
72mm	no services
72	US 40, High Germany Rd, Swain Rd, **S** [gas] Citgo/dsl, [food] Oak Barrel Cafe
68	Orleans Rd, **N** [gas] Exxon/dsl, [other] Town Hill B&B
67mm	Town Hill, elevation 940 ft, Town Hill
64	MV Smith Rd, **S** [other] scenic overlook, elevation 1040 ft, to Green Ridge SF HQ
62	US 40, 15 Mile Creek Rd, **N** [other] Billmeyer Wildlife Mgt Area
58.7mm	Polish Mtn, elevation 1246 ft
57mm	Town Creek
56mm	Flintstone Creek
56	MD 144, National Pike, Flintstone, **N** [other] $General, **S** [lodging] Seven C's Lodge, [other] USPO
52	MD 144, Pleasant Valley Rd (from eb), National Pike
50	Pleasant Valley Rd, **N** [lodging] Rocky Gap Resort/golf/rest., [other] to Rocky Gap SP
47	US 220 N, MD 144, Dehaven Rd(from wb), Old National Pike, Bedford, **S** [gas] Love's/McDonald's/Subway/dsl/scales/24hr, [lodging] Sleep Inn
46	US 220 N, Dehaven Rd, Baltimore Pike, Naves Crossroads, **N** [gas] Sheetz/dsl, [lodging] Cumberland Motel, [other] $General, Fisher Auto Parts, **S** [food] Puccini's Rest.
45	Hillcrest Dr, **S** [gas] Sunoco/dsl
44	US 40A, Baltimore Ave, Willow Brook Rd, to Allegany Comm Coll, **N** [lodging] Hampton Inn, **S** [other] [H], to Allegany Comm Coll
43d	Maryland Ave, **N** [lodging] Ramada, [other] USPO, **S** [gas] Gulf/7-11/Subway, [food] Chick-fil-A, Papa John's, [other] AT&T, AutoZone, [H], Martin's Foods/gas
43c	downtown, same as 43b
43mm	Youghiogheny River
43b	MD 51, Industrial Blvd, **N** [food] McDonald's, [lodging] Ramada, [other] Family$, Save-A-Lot, **S** [gas] Sunoco/dsl, [food] Chick-fil-A, Papa John's, Roy Rogers, Taco Bell, Wendy's, [lodging] Fairfield Inn, [other] Martin's Mrkt/gas
43a	to WV 28A, Beall St, Industrial Blvd, to Cumberland, Johnson St, **N** [gas] Sheetz
42	US 220 S, Greene St, Ridgedale
41	Seton Dr(from wb, no directory turn)
41mm	Haystack Mtn, elev 1240 ft
40	US 220 S, to US 40A, Vocke Rd, La Vale, **N** [gas] BP/dsl, Sheetz/dsl, Sunoco/Little Caesars/dsl, Tesla EVC, [food] Arby's, Bob Evans, Burger King, Cracker Barrel, D'Atri Rest., Denny's, DQ, Dunkin, Fro-Yo Factory, KFC, Ledo Pizza, LJ Silver, McDonald's, New Orient, Rio Grande Mexican, Ruby Tuesday, Starbucks, Subway, Taco Bell, TX Grill, Wendy's, [lodging] Best Western, Comfort Inn, Holiday Inn Express, Super 8, [other] $General, Advance Parts, AT&T, AutoZone, CVS Drug, Harley-Davidson, Lowe's, Mr Tire, NAPA, st police, Staples, URGENT CARE, **S** [food] Applebee's, Buffalo Wild Wings, Chick-fil-A,

HANCOCK

NATIONAL PIKE

JOHNSON ST

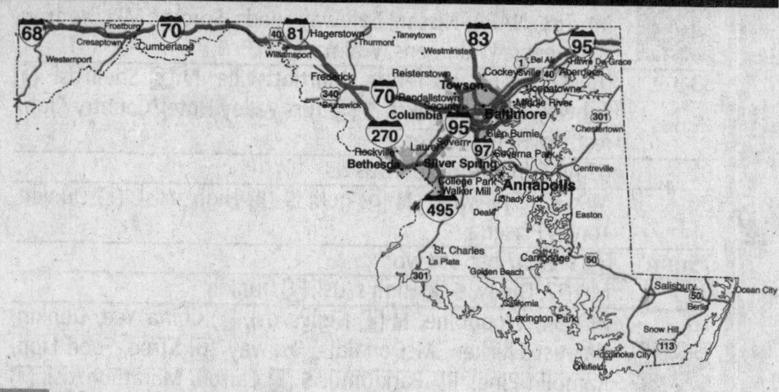

Exit #	Services
40	Continued Wasabi Japanese, [lodging] Suburban Studios, [other] $Tree, ALDI, Kohl's, Martin's Foods/gas, PetSmart, TJ Maxx, Walmart/McDonald's
39	US 40A(from wb), same as 40
34	MD 36, to Westernport, Frostburg, **N** [gas] Sheetz/dsl, Valero/dsl, [food] Burger King, Mario's Italian, McDonald's, Subway, Yamato Japanese, [lodging] Hampton Inn, Quality Inn, [other] $General, park, Save-A-Lot, Walgreens, Weis Mkt, **S** to Dans Mtn SP
33	Midlothian Rd, to Frostburg
31mm	weigh sta eb
30mm	Big Savage Mtn, elevation 2800 ft
29	MD 546, Finzel, **N** [food] Hen House Rest.(2mi), **S** [lodging] Savage River Lodge/rest.(4mi)
25.8mm	eastern continental divide, elevation 2610 ft
24	Lower New Germany Rd, to US 40A, **S** [other] to New Germany SP
23mm	Meadow Mtn, elevation 2780 ft
22	US 219 N, to Meyersdale, **N** [gas] Pilot/Arby's/dsl/scales/24hr, Sunoco/dsl, [food] Burger King, IHOP, Little Caesar's, Penn Alps Rest., [other] $General, Ford, Hilltop Fruit Mkt, NAPA, Walgreen, **S** [gas] Valero/dsl, [food] Katie's Ice Cream, [lodging] Comfort Inn, [other] New Germany SP, Savage River SF
20mm	Casselman River
19	MD 495, to US 40A, Grantsville, **N** [gas] Exxon/Subway/dsl, Sunoco/dsl, [food] Hey Pizza, High Country Creamery, [lodging] Casselman Motel/rest., [other] museum, park, USPO
15mm	Mt Negro, elevation 2740 ft
14mm	Keyser's Ridge, elevation 2880 ft
14b a	US 219, US 40 W, Oakland, **N** [gas] Sunoco/76/dsl, [food] McDonald's, repair, [other] Keyser's Truck Stop
6mm	**full [handicapped] facilities, info, litter barrels, petwalk, [phone], [picnic], vending, Welcome Ctr eb**
4.5mm	Bear Creek
4	MD 42, Friendsville, **N** [gas] Exxon/dsl, Marathon/dsl, [other] USPO, **S** [lodging] Sunset Inn, [other] to Deep Creek Lake SP
0mm	Maryland/West Virginia state line

FINZEL

OAKLAND

INTERSTATE 70

Exit #	Services
94.5mm	I-70 begins/ends in Baltimore at Cooks Lane.
94	Security Blvd N, **S** [gas] Shell
91b a	I-695
87b a	US 29(exits left from wb)to MD 99, Columbia, **S** [gas] BP/dsl, Exxon/dsl, Mobil/7-11, Shell/dsl, Sunoco, [food] Arby's, Baskin-Robbins/Dunkin, Bon Appetit, Boston Mkt, Burger King, Cafe EZ, Checkers, Domino's, Einstein Bagels, Honey Pig Korean, Jimmy John's, McDonald's, Mi Casa Mexican, Mission BBQ, Papa John's, Petco, Qdoba, Sonic, Starbucks, Subway, [other] Acura, Advance Parts, AT&T, Cadillac/Chevrolet, Carmax, CVS Drug, Dick's, EVC, Goodyear/auto, H Mart Foods,

COLUMBIA

INTERSTATE 70 Cont'd

COLUMBIA

87b a Continued
Home Depot, Honda, Infiniti, Jiffy Lube, Kia, Midas, Mr Tire, Mr. Tire, NAPA, Nissan, Safeway Foods, Sprouts Mkt, Verizon, Walgreens, Walgreens, Walmart/EVC

83 US 40, no EZ wb return, Marriottsville, **N** Shell/dsl, Subway, Weis Mkts, **S** Turf Valley Hotel/Country Club/rest., Harris Teeter

82 US 40 E(from eb), same as 83

80 MD 32, Sykesville, **N** golf, **S** High's/dsl, Dunkin, Tony's Pizzeria

79mm weigh/insp sta wb

76 MD 97, Olney, **S** High's/dsl, Dunkin

73 MD 94, Woodbine, **N** High's/dsl, China Yee, Dunkin, Harvest Chicken, McDonald's, Subway, $Tree, Food Lion, Ramblin Pines RV Park(6mi), **S** Carroll, Marathon/dsl, The Grill, auto repair

LIBERTYTOWN

68 MD 27, Mt Airy, **N** 7-11, Carroll/dsl, Arby's, Baskin-Robbns/Dunkin Donuts, Burger King, CarterQue BBQ, Chick-fil-A, Chipotle, Chong Yet Yin Chinese, Five Guys, J&P Pizza, Jersey Mike' Subs, Jimmie Cone, KFC/Taco Bell, Ledo's Pizza, McDonald's, Mommy Magic Cakes, Mount Airy Inn, Papa John's, Rita's Ice Cream, Starbucks, Subway, Ace Hardware, Advance Parts, Food Lion, Mr Tire, Safeway, Tire Choice, vet, Walgreens, Walmart, **S** Exxon/dsl, Shell/dsl, Budget Inn

66mm truckers parking area eb

64mm weigh/insp sta eb

62 MD 75, Libertytown, **N** Falcon Fuels, High's/dsl, Asian Bistro, Baskin Robbins, Burger King, Domino's, Dunkin, McDonald's, Morgan's Grill, Popeyes, CVS Drug, Food Lion, Verizon, vet

59 MD 144

57mm Monocacy River

56 MD 144, **N** BP, Sheetz, Beef'nBuns Burgers, Beijing, Burger King, Roy Rogers, Taco Bell, Wendy's, NAPA, to Hist Dist, **S** Chesaco RV Ctr

55 South St, **N** same as 56

BRADDOCK

54 Market St, to I-270, **N** Costco/gas, Super 8, **S** 7-11, EVC, Sheetz/dsl, Sheetz/dsl/Tesla EVC, Shell/dsl, SouStates/dsl, Wawa/dsl, Applebee's, Arby's, BJ's Rest., Blue BBQ, Burger King, CAVA, Checker's, Chick-fil-A, ChuckeCheese, Cracker Barrel, Golden Corral, Jersey Mike's, KFC/Taco Bell, Longhorn Steaks, Mariachi Mexican, McDonald's, Olive Garden, Panera Bread, Papa John's, Peking Gourmet, Popeyes, Red Robin, Ruby Tuesday, Sonic, Starbucks, Waffle House, Clarion, Country Inn Suites, Courtyard, Days Inn, EconoLodge, Extended Stay America, Fairfield Inn, Hampton Inn, Hilton Garden, Residence Inn, Sleep Inn, $Tree, AAA, Aamco, ALDI, AT&T, Audi, AutoZone, Barnes&Noble, Best Buy, Buick/GMC, Chrysler/Dodge/Jeep, Dick's, Food Lion, Home Depot, Honda, Hyundai, JC Penney, Kia, Kohl's, Lincoln, Lowe's, Macy's, Michael's, Mr Tire, Nissan/EVC, PetSmart, Ross, Sam's Club/dsl, Staples, Target, Tires+, TJMaxx, Toyota, Verizon, Volvo, Walgreens, Walmart

HEIGHTS

53b a I-270 S, US 15 N, US 40 W, to Frederick

52b a US 15 S, US 340 W, Leesburg

49 US 40A, Braddock Heights, Exxon/dsl, Home Depot, H, Mr Tire, **N** 7-11, Carroll/dsl, Citgo/dsl, GetGo, Shell/dsl, Sunoco, WaWa/dsl, Arby's, Bob Evans, Burger King, Casa Rico Mexican, Chipotle, Denny's, Domino's, Dunkin Donuts, Fajita Grande, Flaming Grill, HoneyBaked Ham, KFC, Little Caesars, Los Trios, McDonald's, McDonald's, Mtn View Diner, Outback Steaks, Popeyes, Red Horse Rest., Red Lobster, Roy Rogers, Starbucks, Subway, Taco Bell, Wendy's, Comfort Inn, Motel 6, Motel 6, $General, $Tree, 7-11,

HAGERSTOWN

49 Continued
Advance Auto, AlLDI, AT&T, auto repair, AutoZone, BigLots, Boscov's, CVS Drug, Giant Eagle Foods, H Mart, Jiffy Lube, Lidl Foods, NTB, PepBoys, PetCo, Subaru, U-Haul, Verizon, Walgreens, Weis Foods, **S** camping, to Washington Mon SP

48 US 40 E, US 340(from eb, no return), **N** same as 49

42 MD 17, Myersville, **N** Exxon, Sunoco/dsl, Burger King, JB Seafood, McDonald's, Greenbrier SP(4mi), Martin's Farm Mkt, to Gambrill SP(6mi), **S** Crown/dsl, Subway, EVC

39mm **full facilities, litter barrels, petwalk, both lanes, vending**

35 MD 66, to Boonsboro, **S** Sheetz/dsl(1mi), camping, to Greenbrier SP

32b a US 40, Hagerstown, Martin's Mkt, **N** BP, Exxon/dsl, Bob Evans, Checkers, Chipotle, Denny's, El Ranchero Mexican, Jimmy John's, McDonald's, Paradise NY Pizza, Sonic, TX Roadhouse, Comfort Suites, Fairfield, Hampton Inn, AT&T, Cadillac/Chevrolet, Chrysler/Dodge/Jeep, CVS Drug, H, Martin's Foods, Mercedes, Nissan, Tires+, Toyota, URGENT CARE, Volvo, Walgreens, **S** Buick/GMC, Honda, Kia, Subaru/Mazda/VW

29b a MD 65, to Sharpsburg, **N** EVgo EVC, Exxon/Subway/dsl, Sheetz/dsl, Tesla EVC, FoodCourt, Longhorn Steaks, H, Prime Outlets/famous brands, **S** EVC, Liberty/dsl, Sheetz/dsl, Arby's, Baskin-Robbins, Burger King, Chick-fil-A, Cracker Barrel, Dunkin, Jimmy John's, McDonald's, McDonald's/playplace, Taco Bell, Waffle House, Wendy's, Sleep Inn, ALDI, Jellystone Camping, st police, to Antietam Bfd, Walmart

28 MD 632, Hagerstown

26 I-81, N to Harrisburg, S to Martinsburg

24 MD 63, Huyett, **N** Pilot/Subway/dsl/24hr, Sheetz/dsl(2mi), **S** KOA(2mi)

18 MD 68 E, Clear Spring, **N** BP/dsl, Liberty, Al's Grill, McDonald's, Holiday Inn Express, **S** $General

12 MD 56, Indian Springs, **S** Exxon/dsl, Ft Frederick SP

9 US 40 E(from eb, exits left), Indian Springs

5 MD 615(no immediate wb return), **N** Log Cabin Rest.(2mi

3 MD 144, (exits left from wb), Hancock, **S** Exxon/dsl, Burger King, IHOP, Hilltop Inn, Blue Goose Mkt

1b US 522(exits left from both lanes), Hancock, **S** EVC, Sheetz/dsl, Sunoco, Hardee's, Krazy Rayz BBQ, Pizza Hut, Hancock Motel, Super 8, Chevrolet, Food Lion, Happy Hills Camp, NAPA, Save-A-Lot Foods

1a I-68 W, US 40, W to Cumberland

0mm Maryland/Pennsylvania state line, Mason-Dixon Line

INTERSTATE 81

HAGERSTOWN

12mm Maryland/Pennsylvania state line

10b a Showalter Rd, **E** Love's/Wendy's/Subway/dsl/scales/24hr/@,

9 Maugans Ave, **E** BP/dsl, Sheetz/dsl, Domino's, McDonald's, Subway, Taco Bell, Waffle House, Hampton Inn, $General, auto/tire repair, AutoZone, CVS Drug, Martin's Foods/gas, Meineke, Penske, URGENT CARE, vet, Walgreens, **W** Burger King, Dunkin, Microtel, tires, U-Haul

7b a MD 58, Hagerstown, same as 6

6b a US 40, Hagerstown, **E** Shell, Cafe De Sol,

MD

HAGERSTOWN

INTERSTATE 81 Cont'd

6b a Continued
Foster's on the Point, H, W Arby's, Chipotle Mexican, Five Guys, IHOP, Jersey Mike's Subs, KFC, McDonald's, Number One Chinese, Panera Bread, Starbucks, TGIFriday's, Tropical Smoothie, Wendy's, $Tree, AT&T, Best Buy, Dick's, Home Depot, Marshall's, PetSmart, Verizon, Walmart

5b a Halfway Blvd, E AC&T/dsl, Big Papi's Tacos, BJ's Rest., Buffalo Wild Wings, Burger King, Chick-fil-A, Chili's, ChuckECheese's, CiCi's Pizza, El Ranchero Mexican, Fireside Rest., Golden Corral, Home2 Suites, Hub City Diner, McDonald's, Mexicali Cantina, Nikko Japanese, Noodles&Co, Olive Garden, Outback Steaks, Papa John's, Popeyes, Red Lobster, Red Robin, Roy Rogers, Sakura Steaks, Silk Thai, Starbucks, Subway, Taco Bell, Wendy's, Country Inn&Suites, Courtyard, Holiday Inn Express, Homewood Suites, Motel 6, Ramada, SpringHill Suites, $Tree, BigLots, Firestone/auto, Ford, Hobby Lobby, Hyundai, JC Penney, Jiffy Lube, Kohl's, Lowe's/EVC, mall, Martin's Foods/gas, Michael's, NTB, PetCo, Ross, Sam's Club/gas, Staples, Target, URGENT CARE, W ACT/dsl/scales/24hr, Pilot/McDonald's/Subway/dsl/scales/24hr, Super 8, Freightliner

WILLIAMSPORT

4 I-70, E to Frederick, W to Hancock, to I-68

2 US 11, Williamsport, E ACT/dsl, W Sunoco/Waffle House/dsl, Marco's Pizza, McDonald's, Subway, Red Roof Inn

1 MD 63, MD 68, Williamsport, E Bowman/dsl, Elmwood Farm B&B, Jellystone Camping, Save-A-Lot, to Antietam Bfd, W $General, auto/tire, KOA, NAPA

0mm Maryland/West Virginia state line, Potomac River

INTERSTATE 83

38mm Maryland/Pennsylvania state line, Mason-Dixon Line

37 to Freeland(from sb)

36 MD 439, Bel Air, E The Farmyard, W Filler-Up, Maryland Line Inn Grill, StoneBridge Grille, Holiday Travel Park(5mi), Merry Meadows Camping(5mi)

35mm weigh/insp sta sb

33 MD 45, Parkton, E USPO

31 Middletown Rd, to Parkton, E golf

27 MD 137, Mt Carmel, Hereford, E Exxon/dsl, Michael's Pizza, Subway, 7-11, Graul's Foods, Hereford Drug, Mt Carmel Drug, USPO, vet

24 Belfast Rd, to Butler, Sparks

COCKEYSVILLE

20 Shawan Rd, Hunt Valley, E Exxon/Subway/dsl, Mobil, Shell, Barrett's Grill, Burger King, CA Pizza, Carrabba's, Chick-fil-A, Chipotle Mexican, Coal Fire Cafe, Iron Rooster, Jersey Mike's, Ledo Pizza, McDonald's, Mission BBQ, Nalley Fresh, Noodles&Co, Outback Steaks, Panera Bread, Sakura Hibachi, Starbucks, TX Roadhouse, Courtyard, Delta Hotels, Embassy Suites, Holiday Inn Express, Residence Inn, Burlington Coats, Dick's, Giant Foods/EVC, Marshall's, tire/auto, vet, Wegman's Foods

18 Warren Rd(from nb, no return), Cockeysville, services E on York Rd

17 Padonia Rd, Deereco Rd, E 7-11, Carroll, Marathon/dsl, Marathon/dsl, Bob Evans, Charcoal Deli, Chick-fil-A, Chili's, Domino's, Dunkin, Five Guys, IHOP, Macaroni Grill, Mother's North Grille, Popeyes, Ryleigh's Oyster, Seasons Pizza, Starbucks, Taco Bell, The Corner Stable, Tutti Frutti Frozen Yogurt, Wawa, Wendy's, Extended Stay America, Hampton Inn, Holiday Inn, Audi/VW, auto repair, AutoZone, Buick/GMC, Chevrolet, Food Lion, Home Depot, Honda, Lidl, Lowe's Whse, NTB, Sam's Club, **services E on York Rd**, Subaru, Target, tire/auto repair, USPO, Volvo, Walmart, W Cold Stone Creamery, Starbucks,

17 Continued
Graul's Mkt

16b a Timonium Rd, E Amoco, Carroll Fuel, Exxon/dsl, Shell, Sunoco/dsl, Baja Fresh, Burger King, CAVA, Chipotle, Dunkin, Firehouse Subs, First Watch, Honey Baked Ham, Jersey Mike's, McDonald's, Michael's Cafe, Panera, Pizza Hut, Smoothie King, Sonic, Starbucks, SweetFrog FroYo, TCBY, Tropical Smoothie, Red Lion Hotel, Red Roof Inn, $Tree, ALDI, Giant Food, Infiniti/Nissan, Jiffy Lube, Kia, Kohl's, Old Navy, PetSmart, REI, services E on York Rd, ShopRite Foods, Verizon, Walgreens

14 I-695 N

13 I-695 S, Falls Rd, W Exxon

12 Ruxton Rd(from nb, no return)

10b a Northern Parkway, E Exxon, Shell, W H

9b a Cold Spring Lane

8 MD 25 N(from nb), Falls Rd

7b a 28th St, E Burger King, Subway, H, W Baltimore Zoo, Wilson House B&B

6 US 1, US 40T, North Ave, downtown, E Carroll Fuels/dsl, Popeyes, Firestone, Jiffy Lube, Mr. Tire, Save-A-Lot Foods, W Subway

5 MD Ave(from sb), downtown, W BP/dsl, Chipotle, Dunkin, Potbelly, Starbucks

3 Chase St, Gilford St, downtown

2 Pleasant St(from sb), downtown

1 Fayette St, downtown Baltimore, I-83 begins/ends., downtown Baltimore

INTERSTATE 95

110mm Maryland/Delaware state line

109b a MD 279, to Elkton, Newark, E Carroll Fuels/dsl, Flying J/Golden Corral/dsl/scales/24hr/@, Cracker Barrel, Dunkin, KFC/Taco Bell, McDonald's, Waffle House, Elkton Lodge, Hampton Inn, La Quinta, Motel 6, Red Carpet Inn, Sunrise Inn, Blue Beacon, H, truck repair, W TA/dsl/scales/24hr/@, WaWa/dsl, BnB Seafood, SmoQ-N-Meat BBQ, Holiday Inn Express, Family$, to U of DE, U-Haul

100 MD 272, to North East, Rising Sun, E Flying J/Denny's/dsl/scales/24hr, Sunoco/dsl, AT&T, Burger King, Forge Southern Comfort, Frank's Pizza, Little Caesar's, McDonald's, Wendy's, Comfort Inn, Holiday Inn Express, $General, $Tree, Advance Parts, auto repair, AutoZone, Food Lion, Lowe's, PetCo, st police, to Elk Neck SP, Verizon, Walgreens, Walmart/Subway, W High's/dsl, Hunan Wok, Pizza Hut, Best Western, zoo

96mm Chesapeake House service area(exits left from both lanes), Sunoco/dsl, Tesla EVC, Auntie Anne's, Earl of Sandwich, KFC, Wendy's

93 MD 275, to Rising Sun, US 222, to Perryville, E Exxon/dsl, ONE9/Subway/dsl/scales/24hr, Denny's, H, W Dunkin, Jumbo Jimmy's Crab Shack, Great Wolf Lodge, casino

92mm weigh sta/toll booth, W st police

91.5mm Susquehanna River

89 MD 155, to Havre de Grace(last nb exit before toll), E BP/dsl, Crown , Burger King, Chesapeake Grill, Dunkin, Maria's Pizza, McDonald's, Pizza Hut, Subway, Waffle House, Best Budget Inn, Super 8, $General, auto parts, CVS, Family$, H, Verizon, Weis Mkt/gas, W to Susquehanna SP

85 MD 22, to Aberdeen, E 7-11, Royal Farms/dsl, Shell/dsl, Sunoco/dsl, Applebee's, Bob Evans, Burger King, Chap's Pit Beef, Chick-fil-A, Dunkin, Great American Grill, IHOP, KFC, La Tolteca Mexican, Ledo Pizza, Little Caesar's, McDonald's, Olive Tree Italian, Panera Bread, Papa John's, Rita's Custard, Starbucks, Subway, Taco Bell, Wendy's, Comfort Inn, Days Inn, Fairfield Inn, Hampton Inn, Hilton Garden,

= gas = food = lodging = other = rest stop

INTERSTATE 95 Cont'd

JOPPATOWNE

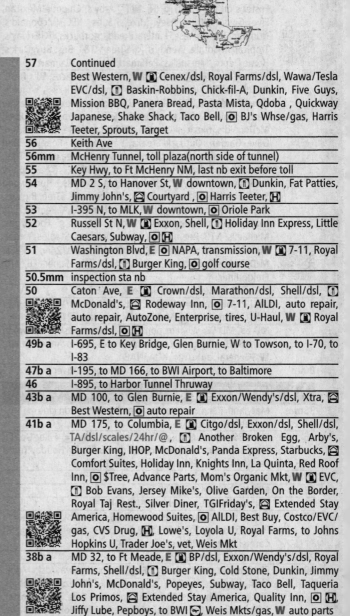

85 Continued
Holiday Inn Express, La Quinta, Red Roof Inn, Super 8, Travelodge, $General, $Tree, 7-11, Firestone/auto, Home Depot, ShopRite Foods, Target, U-Haul, Verizon, Walgreens, Walgreens, **W** EVC, Royal Farms/Tesla EVC/dsl, All American Steaks, Courtyard, Residence Inn

81mm MD House service area(exits left from both lanes), A+, EVC, Sunoco/Tesla EVC/dsl

80 MD 543, to Riverside, Churchville, **E** BP/Burger King, Shell/dsl, Sunoco, Arby's, Cracker Barrel, Lee's Asian Bistro, McDonald's, Pizza Hut, Plaza Mexican, Riverside Grille, Riverside Pizzeria, Subway, Waffle House, Candlewood Suites, Country Inn&Suites, Extended Stay America, Hilton, Holiday Inn, SpringHill Suites, TownePlace, 7-11, Bar Harbor RV Park(4mi), ShopRite Foods, Walgreens, **W** Royal Farm/dsl

77b a MD 24, to Edgewood, Bel Air, **E** Exxon/dsl, Royal Farms/dsl, Sunoco/dsl, Denny's, Dunkin, Island Spice Grille, My 3 Sons Rest., Subway, Tacos Tijuana, Waffle House, Hampton Inn, Holiday Inn Express, La Quinta, Motel 6, Quality Inn, Ramada, Red Roof Inn, Wingate, Old Navy, **W** EVC, Exxon/dsl, WaWa/Tesla EVC/dsl, Abingdon Grill, Bacco Italian, Bacco Pizzeria, Chick-fil-A, Conrad's Seafood, Dunkin, KFC/Taco Bell, Lemon N Ginger Asian, McDonald's, Panda Express, Panera Bread, Rita's Custard, Starbucks, $Tree, 7-11, AAA, BJ's Whse, Buick/GMC, Giant Food/gas, Goodyear, Hobby Lobby, H, Lowe's, PetSmart, Target, USPO, Walgreens, Walmart/Subway/EVC, Wegman's Foods

74 MD 152, Fallston, Joppatowne, **E** Carroll Fuels/dsl, Exxon/dsl, Royal Farms/dsl, WaWa/dsl, La Tolteca, Papa John's, Popeyes, Super 8, Advance Parts, ALDI, AutoZone, Chrysler, CVS Drug, Toyota(1mi), **W** Royal Farms/dsl

70mm Big Gunpowder Falls, **E** 7-11

67b a MD 43, to White Marsh Blvd, US 1, US 40, **E** BP/dsl, Royal Farms/Tesla EVC/dsl, Applebee's, CAVA, Chick-fil-A, Chipotle, Crumbl Cookies, Duck Donuts, Edorrito Asian, Five Guys, Jimmy John's, Ledo Pizza, McDonald's, Noodles&Co, Panda Express, Panera Bread, Pie Five, Qdoba, Starbucks, Subway, Subway, Taco Bell, Holiday Inn Express, Home2 Suites, Best Buy, Carmax, Chevrolet, Dick's, Lowe's, Michael's, Nissan, Petco, Target, TJ Maxx, Volvo, **W** 7-11, EVC, Exxon/dsl, Buffalo Wild Wings, BurgerFi, Chili's, China Wok, Coldstone, Dunkin, Kobe Japanese, Konoko Japanese, McDonald's, Olive Garden, PF Chang's, Red Brick Sta., Red Lobster, Red Robin, Starbucks, TGIFriday's, Tilted Kilt, TX Roadhouse, Fairfield Inn, Hampton Inn, Hilton Garden, Residence Inn, Woodspring Suites, AAA, AT&T, Barnes&Noble, Giant Foods, IKEA, JC Penney, Macy's, Mr Tire, Old Navy, to Gunpowder SP, URGENT CARE, USPO, Verizon

64b a I-695(exits left), E to Essex, W to Towson

62 to I-895(from sb)

61 US 40, Pulaski Hwy, **E** Rosario's Italian, Wawa, auto repair, **W** Carroll Fuels/McDonald's/dsl, Royal Farms, Shell/dsl, Dunkin, vet

60 Moravia Rd

59 Eastern Ave, **W** Carroll Fuels/dsl, Exxon, Royal Farms, Broadway Diner, Chipotle, Dunkin, El Habanero, Jersey Mike's, McDonald's, Panda Express, Shawarma Pizza, Starbucks, Subway, Wawa, Wendy's, Hampton Inn, 7-11, Firestone, Home Depot, H, Savemart Supermkt, tires, Toyota, USPO, vet

58 Dundalk Ave, from nb, **E** Citgo, auto/tire

57 O'Donnell St, Boston St, **E** TA/Buckhorn/Country Pride/Subway/dsl/scales/motel/@, McDonald's,

COLLEGE PARK

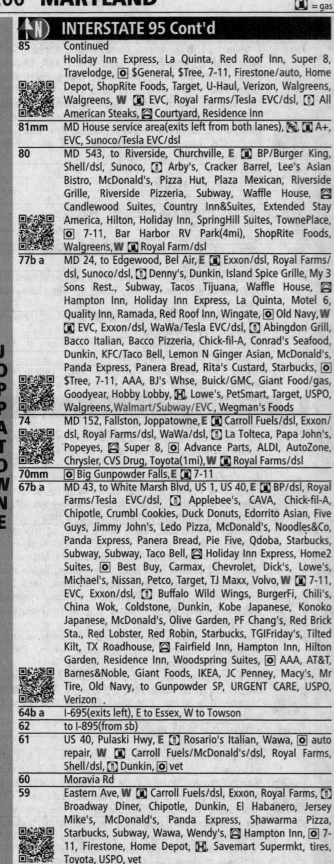

57 Continued
Best Western, **W** Cenex/dsl, Royal Farms/dsl, Wawa/Tesla EVC/dsl, Baskin-Robbins, Chick-fil-A, Dunkin, Five Guys, Mission BBQ, Panera Bread, Pasta Mista, Qdoba, Quickway Japanese, Shake Shack, Taco Bell, BJ's Whse/gas, Harris Teeter, Sprouts, Target

56 Keith Ave

56mm McHenry Tunnel, toll plaza(north side of tunnel)

55 Key Hwy, to Ft McHenry NM, last nb exit before toll

54 MD 2 S, to Hanover St, **W** downtown, Dunkin, Fat Patties, Jimmy John's, Courtyard, Harris Teeter, H

53 I-395 N, to MLK, **W** downtown, Oriole Park

52 Russell St N, **W** Exxon, Shell, Holiday Inn Express, Little Caesars, Subway, H

51 Washington Blvd, **E** NAPA, transmission, **W** 7-11, Royal Farms/dsl, Burger King, golf course

50.5mm inspection sta nb

50 Caton Ave, **E** Crown/dsl, Marathon/dsl, Shell/dsl, McDonald's, Rodeway Inn, 7-11, AlLDI, auto repair, auto repair, AutoZone, Enterprise, tires, U-Haul, **W** Royal Farms/dsl, H

49b a I-695, E to Key Bridge, Glen Burnie, W to Towson, to I-70, to I-83

47b a I-195, to MD 166, to BWI Airport, to Baltimore

46 I-895, to Harbor Tunnel Thruway

43b a MD 100, to Glen Burnie, **E** Exxon/Wendy's/dsl, Xtra, Best Western, auto repair

41b a MD 175, to Columbia, **E** Citgo/dsl, Exxon/dsl, Shell/dsl, TA/dsl/scales/24hr/@, Another Broken Egg, Arby's, Burger King, IHOP, McDonald's, Panda Express, Starbucks, Comfort Suites, Holiday Inn, Knights Inn, La Quinta, Red Roof Inn, $Tree, Advance Parts, Mom's Organic Mkt, **W** EVC, Bob Evans, Jersey Mike's, Olive Garden, On the Border, Royal Taj Rest., Silver Diner, TGIFriday's, Extended Stay America, Homewood Suites, AlLDI, Best Buy, Costco/EVC/gas, CVS Drug, H, Lowe's, Loyola U, Royal Farms, to Johns Hopkins U, Trader Joe's, vet, Weis Mkt

38b a MD 32, to Ft Meade, **E** BP/dsl, Exxon/Wendy's/dsl, Royal Farms, Shell/dsl, Burger King, Cold Stone, Dunkin, Jimmy John's, McDonald's, Popeyes, Subway, Taco Bell, Taqueria Los Primos, Extended Stay America, Quality Inn, H, Jiffy Lube, Pepboys, to BWI, Weis Mkts/gas, **W** auto parts

37mm **full facilities, info, litter barrels, petwalk, RV Dump, vending, Welcome Ctr both lanes**

35b a MD 216, to Laurel, **E** Exxon, Shell/dsl, McDonald's, Subway, Weis Food/drug

34mm Patuxent River

33b a MD 198, to Laurel, **E** Exxon/dsl/24hr, H, **W** Exxon/dsl, Shell, Double Tree

31 MD 200 (toll), to I-270

29 MD 212, to Beltsville, **E** Cherry Hill RV Resort, **W** Exxon/dsl, Baskin-Robbins, Danny's Subs, KFC, McDonald's, Taco Bell, The Villa Rest., Wendy's, Comfort Inn, Wyndham, CVS Drug

27 I-495 S around Washington

25b a US 1, Baltimore Ave, to Laurel, College Park, **E** 7-11, Exxon/dsl, Liberty/dsl, Shell, Shell, Sunoco, Tesla EVC, Wawa, Wawa/dsl, Arby's, Buffalo Wild Wings, Burger King, Chipotle, Domino's, Dunkin, McDonald's, Panera Bread, Pizza Hut/Taco Bell, Popeyes, Potbelly's, Starbucks, Wendy's,

 = gas = food = lodging = other = rest stop

INTERSTATE 95 Cont'd

COLLEGE PARK

25b a Continued
Holiday Inn, $Tree, Advance Parts, AlLDI, AutoZone, Cherry Hill RV Resort, Costco/gas, IKEA/EVC, URGENT CARE, US Agri Library, Verizon, Walgreens, **W** Exxon, Shell, Xtra, Azteca, College Park Diner, Denny's, Dunkin, IHOP, Mamma Lucia, McDonald's, Pizza Hut, Sakura Seafood Buffet, Starbucks, Taco Bell, Best Western, Cambria Hotel, Days Inn, Hampton Inn, Holiday Inn Express, Howard Johnson, Red Carpet Inn, Super 8, TownePlace, 7-11, CVS Drug, Home Depot, Hyundai, Jiffy Lube, Lidl, NAPA, Nissan, Rita's Custard, Shoppers Foods, to U of MD, U-Haul, USPO, vet

24 (from sb), to metro

23 MD 201, Kenilworth Ave, **E** EVC, Colette's Cafe, Crowne Plaza, **W** Shell, Shell/dsl, 3 Brothers Italian, Baskin-Robbins, Checker's, Chipotle, Domino's, Dunkin, Hook & Reel Seafood, Jersey Mike's, KFC, Little Caesars, McDonald's, Mission BBQ, Popeyes, Silver Diner, Subway, TGIFriday's, Wendy's, Hilton Garden, Residence Inn, Sonesta, ALDI, AutoZone, CVS Drug, Giant Food, Honda, T-Mobile, Target/CVS Drug, URGENT CARE

22 Baltimore-Washington Pkwy, **E** Exxon, Chevy's Mexican, IHOP, Starbucks, Wendy's, Holiday Inn, WoodSpring Suites, $Tree, Advance Parts, CVS Drug, H, PetSmart, to NASA, USPO, **W** Safeway

LANHAM

20b a MD 450, Annapolis Rd, Lanham, **E** Sunoco/7-11/dsl, Burger King, Just Jerk, McDonald's, Pizza Hut, Red Lobster, Best Western, Days Inn/rest., Red Roof Inn, $Tree, Ford/KIA, NTB, **W** 7-11/dsl, BP, Exxon, Shell, Sunoco, Bojangles, Chipotle, Domino's , King Pollo, Pancake House, Papa John's, Popeyes, Starbucks, Subway, T-Mobile, Wendy's, Metro Points Hotel, 7-11, Advance Parts, AutoZone, Chrysler/Dodge/Jeep, CVS Drug, Family$, Foodway Foods, H, JustTires, Lowe's, Lube Center, Meineke, police, Shoppers Foods, Staples

19b a US 50, to Annapolis, Washington, **W** Courtyard, Giant Food

17 MD 202, Landover Rd, to Upper Marlboro, **E** Royal Farms/dsl, CAVA, Chipotle, Cold Stone, Copper Canyon, Firehouse, Jasper's Rest., Kobe Japanese, Ledo Pizza, Outback Steaks, Ruby Tuesday, Silver Diner, Doubletree, Hampton Inn, Holiday Inn Express, Homewood Suites, Best Buy, Costco/gas, Old Navy, Wegman's, **W** Chick-fil-A, FedEx Center

16 Arena Dr, **E** Carolina Kitchen, Chick-fil-A, ChuckeCheese, Golden Corral, Longhorn Steaks, TGIFriday's, Courtyard, Residence Inn, H, **W** WoodSpring Suites, to FedEx Field

CAPITOL HGTS

15 MD 214, Central Ave, **E** Comfort Inn, Extended Stay America, to Six Flags, **W** BP, Exxon/dsl, Shell, Checker's, Dunkin, IHOP, KFC, McDonald's, McDonald's, Panda Express, Wendy's, Country Inn, La Quinta, Motel 6, 7-11, Goodyear/auto, Home Depot, Jiffy Lube, Midas, NTB, tires, U-Haul

13 Ritchie-Marlboro Rd, Capitol Hgts, **E** Royal Farms, **W** WaWa/EVC/dsl, Buffalo Wild Wings, Chick-fil-A, Chipotle, Dave&Buster's, Five Guys, Jersey Mike's, Ledo Pizza, McDonald's, mezeh, Olive Garden, Panda Express, Popeyes, Sonic, Starbucks, Tropical Cafe, Residence Inn, $Tree, Ace Hardware, Advance Parts, ALDI, AT&T, Big Lots, BJ Whse/gas, Hobby Lobby, Honda, Hyundai, Tires+, TJ Maxx, URGENT CARE, VW

11 MD 4, Pennsylvania Ave, to Upper Marlboro, **E** Marathon/dsl, Ford, park, **W** 7-11/dsl, Exxon, Royal Farms/dsl, Shell, Sunoco, Applebee's, Arby's, Chipotle,

MARLOW HGTS

11 Continued
Golden Skillet, Honey Baked Ham, IHOP, Ledo Pizza, Lidl, LJ Silver, Papa John's, Raising Cane's, Starbucks, Subway, Taco Bell, Wendy's, $Tree, auto repair, CVS Drug, JC Penney, Marshall's, NAPA, PetCo, Save-A-Lot, Shoppers Foods, Target, tires, U-Haul, vet

9 MD 337, to Allentown Rd, **E** Exxon, Shell/7-11, Checker's, Dunkin, McDonald's, Popeyes, Days Inn, Quality Inn, Rodeway Inn, Super 8, Ffamily$, to Andrews AFB, U-Haul

7 MD 5, Branch Ave, to Silver Hill, **E** Citgo, Sunoco, Wawa, Domino's, Dunkin, Wendy's, WoodSpring Suites, **W** Exxon, Royal Farms/dsl, Royal Farms/dsl, Shell/dsl, Valero, Blue Waters, Chipotle, Red Lobster, Topolino Rest., Country Inn Suites, Hampton Inn, Holiday Inn Express, ALDI, BMW, Chrysler/Dodge/Jeep, Family$, Ford, H, Infiniti, KIA, Mazda, Nissan, Toyota/Scion

4b a MD 414, St Barnabas Rd, Marlow Hgts, **E** Citgo/dsl, Mobil, Bojangle's, Burger King, Checker's, Five Guys, IHOP, Jersey Mike's, KFC, McDonald's, Outback Steaks, Panda Express, Quiznos, Subway, Wendy's, Wingstop, Red Roof Inn, $Tree, CVS Drug, Home Depot, PetSmart, Ross, Safeway Foods, Staples, Target, **W** Exxon/7-11/dsl, Shell/autocare, McDonald's, Subway, AutoZone, Family$, Global Food, Jiffy Lube, URGENT CARE

3b a MD 210, Indian Head Hwy, to Forest Hgts, **S** Exxon/dsl, Charley's, Pizza Hut, Marshall's, **E** EVC, Marathon, Sunoco, Chipotle, Popeyes, Taco Bell, Comfort Inn, Harborside, Advance Parts, AlLDI, Family$, MGM Casino, Sav-A-Lot Foods, Tanger Outlets/famous brands, tires, USPO, **W** BP/dsl, Citgo, Shell, 7-11, Burger King, Giant Foods, Goodyear/auto, McDonald's, Papa John's, Popeyes, $General, $Tree, EVC

2b a I-295, N to Washington

0mm Maryland/Virginia state line, Potomac River, Woodrow Wilson Bridge

INTERSTATE 97

17 I-695. I-97 begins/ends on I-695.

16 MD 648, Ferndale, Glen Burnie, **E** Dunkin, McDonald's, Rita's Custard, $General, Roses, U-Haul, **W** U-Haul

15b a MD 176 W, Dorsey Rd, Aviation Blvd, **W** tires, to BWI

14b a MD 100, Ellicott City, Gibson Island

13b a MD 174, Quarterfield Rd, **E** Gulf, Liberty/dsl, Squisito Pizza, Subway, The Grill, Tijuana Taco, 7-11, vet, **W** Shell/dsl, WaWa/dsl, Chick-fil-A, Ichiban, Pizza Hut, AT&T, Kohl's, Lowe's, Sam's Club/dsl, Walgreens, Walmart/Subway

CROWNSVILLE

12 MD 3, New Cut Rd, Glen Burnie, **E** Crown, Exxon, Royal Farms, Sunoco, Burger King, Dunkin, Fortune Cooky, Hardee's, KFC, McDonald's, Popeyes, Starbucks, Subway, Taco Bell, Wendy's, auto repair, auto/tire, CVS Drug, Giant Foods, H, Jiffy Lube, Shoppers, Target/EVC, vet, Walgreens

10b a Benfield Blvd, Severna Park, **E** Exxon/dsl, High's, Baskin-Robbins/Dunkin, Ledo's Pizza, Smoothie King, 7-11, access to same as 12

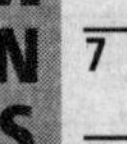

7 MD 3, MD 32, Bowie, Odenton, **E** White Gables Motel, **W** KOA

5 MD 178(from sb, no EZ return), Crownsville

0mm I-97 begins/ends on US 50/301.

INTERSTATE 270 (Rockville)

32 I-270 begins/ends on I-70, exit 53.

31b a MD 85, **N** 7-11, Sheetz/24hr, Sheetz/dsl, Shell/dsl, Tesla EVC, Wawa/dsl, Applebee's, Arby's, BJ's Rest., Blues BBQ, Burger King, CAVA, Checker's, Chick-fil-A, ChuckeCheese, Golden Corral, Jersey Mike's, KFC/Taco Bell,

= gas = food = lodging = other = rest stop

INTERSTATE 270 (Rockville) Cont'd

Exit	Services
31b a	Continued Longhorn Steaks, Mariachi Mexican, McDonald's, Olive Garden, Panera Bread, Papa John's, Peking Gourmet, Popeyes, Red Robin, Roy Rogers, Ruby Tuesday, Sonic, Starbucks, sweet frog, UNO Grill, Waffle House, Clarion Inn, Country Inn Suites, Days Inn, EconoLodge, Sleep Inn, Super 8, $Tree, AAA, Aamco, AllDI, AT&T, Audi, Audi, auto repair, AutoZone, Barnes&Noble, Best Buy, Buick/GMC, CarMax, Chrysler/Dodge/Jeep, Costco/gas, Dick's, Harley-Davidson, Home Depot, Hyundai, JC Penney, Kohl's, Lincoln, Lowe's, Macy's, mall, Michael's, Mr Tire, Nissan/EVC, PetSmart, Ross, Sam's Club/dsl, Staples, Target, Tires+, TJ Maxx, U-Haul, Verizon, Walmart/EVC, S Royal Farms/dsl, Sheetz/dsl, Cafe Rio, Chipotle Mexican, Cici's, Cracker Barrel, Domino's, Dunkin, Firebirds, Firehouse Subs, Five Guys, Gran Azteca Mexican, IHOP, Jimmy John's, Krispy Kreme, McDonald's, Mission BBQ, MOD Pizza, Noodles&Co, Panda Express, Silver Diner, Starbucks, TGIFriday's, TX Roadhouse, Wendy's, Comfort Inn, Courtyard, Extended Stay America, Fairfield Inn, Hampton Inn, Hilton Garden, Home2 Suites, Homewood Suites, MainStay Suites, Residence Inn, TownePlace Suites, Food Lion, Honda, Toyota/Scion, Walgreens
30mm	Monocacy River
28mm	scenic view wb, no rest rooms
26	MD 80, Urbana, N 7-11, Exxon, Royal Farms/dsl/Tesla EVC, Shell/dsl, Black Hog BBQ, Buffalo Wild Wings, Burger King, Chipotle, Domino's, Dunkin, Ledo's Pizza, McDonald's, Panera Bread, Papa Johns, Popeyes, Starbucks, Tropical Smoothie, Waffle House, Advance Parts, AutoZone, CVS Drug
22	MD 109, to Barnesville, Hyattstown, N Carroll/dsl, Dunkin, Laurienzo Cafe
21mm	weigh/insp sta both lanes
18	MD 121, to Clarksburg, Boyds, N Little Bennett Pk, S Blackhill Pk, Clarksburg Outlets/famous brands
16	MD 27, Father Hurley Blvd, to Damascus, N 7-11/dsl/24hr, Exxon, Free State/dsl, Shell, Washington Express, Applebee's, Burger King, Chipotle, Crumbl Cookies, Jersey Mike's Subs, McDonald's, Noodles&Co, Panera Bread, Potbelly, Starbucks, Extended Stay America, ALDI, Best Buy, Giant Foods, Home Depot, Kohl's, Michael's, PepBoys, PetSmart, Target, TJ Maxx, URGENT CARE, Verizon, Walmart, Wegmans 
15b a	MD 118, to MD 355, N Hilton, S 7-11, BP/dsl, Exxon, Exxon/Circle K, Sunoco/dsl, Burger King, Carrabba's, CAVA, Chick-fil-A, Chipotle, Cold Stone, Domino's, Firehouse Subs, Five Guys, IHOP, Longhorn Steaks, McDonald's, mezeh, Mi Rancho, Mission BBQ, Panda Express, Panera Bread, Red Robin, Royal Bagel, Senor Tequilas, Starbucks, Sushi Legend, Taco Bell, Tropical Smoothie, Wendy's, Extended Stay America, Fairfield Inn/EVC, Giant Foods, Honda, Mercedes/Smart Car/EVC, Nissan, Petco, Safeway Foods, Walgreens
13b a	Middlebrook Rd(from wb), N 7-11, Sunoco, KFC, McDonald's, Popeyes, CVS Drug, GW Supermkt, H
11	MD 124, Quince Orchard Rd, N Exxon, Exxon, Chipotle, McDonald's, Panera Bread, Popeyes, Potbelly, Subway, The Habit, DoubleTree, Hampton Inn, Holiday Inn, Homewood Suites, TownePlace Suites, Acura, AT&T, Costco, CVS Drugs, Ford, Hyundai/Subaru, Lincoln, mall, Mazda, Mini, Ross, Sam's Club, Tires+, Toyota, Verizon, VW/Kia, S Shell, Buffalo Wild Wings, Dunkin, Five Guys, Jimmy John's, McDonald's, McDonald's, Starbucks, Motel 6, Advance Parts, ALDI, Chevrolet, Chrysler/Dodge/Jeep/EVC,

BOYDS

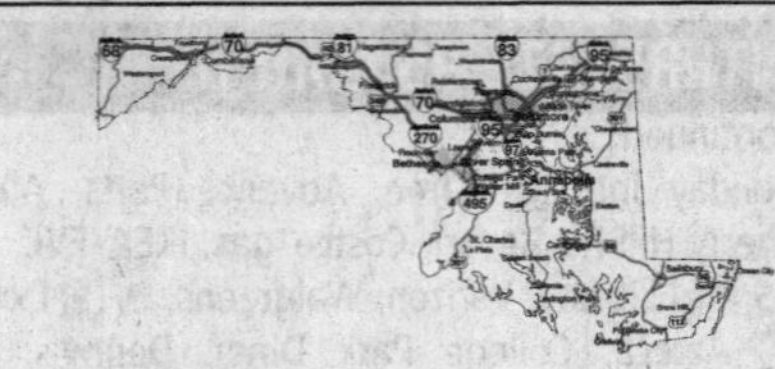

Exit	Services
11	Continued Fiat, Giant Foods, Seneca Creek SP, Staples, Walgreens
10	MD 117, Clopper Rd(from wb), same as 11
9b a	I-370, to Gaithersburg, Sam Eig Hwy, S Copper Canyon Grill, Corner Cafe Bakery, Joe's Crabshack, Uncle Julio's, Courtyard, Barnes&Noble, Dick's, Kohl's, Target
8	Shady Grove Rd, N Shell/dsl, Burger King, CAVA, Farmsook Thai, Five Guys, Red Lobster, Subway, Red Roof Inn, Sheraton, 7-11, Best Buy, CVS Drug, Home Depot, Mom's Mkt, vet, S That's Amore, Courtyard, Marriott, Residence Inn, Sleep Inn, SpringHill Suites, The Rockville, H
6b a	MD 28, W Montgomery Ave, S Shell, Chadol Korean BBQ, Chick-fil-A, Best Western
5b a	MD 189, Falls Rd
4b a	Montrose Rd, S Baskin-Robbins, Domino's, Starbucks, Harris Teeter, Walgreens
2	I-270/I-270 spur diverges eb, converges wb
1b a	MD 187, Old Georgetown Rd, S Exxon, Chipotle, Not Your Joe's, Subway, Balducci's Foods, Giant Foods, H, Verizon
1	(I-270 spur)Democracy Blvd, E Marriott, W Exxon/dsl, Shell/dsl, Macy's, mall, Nordstrom
0mm	I-270 begins/ends on I-495, exit 35.

INTERSTATE 495 (DC)

Exit	Services
27	I-95, N to Baltimore, S to Richmond. I-495 & I-95 S run together. See MD I-95, exits 25b a-2b a.
28b a	MD 650, New Hampshire Ave, N BP, Exxon, Shell, Cheesesteak Mikes, Chipotle, Domino's, Safeway Foods, Starbucks, Home2 Suites
29b a	MD 193, University Blvd
30b a	US 29, Colesville, N Citgo, Shell, Chipotle, Dunkin', McDonald's, Papa John's, Pizza Hut, Starbucks, 7-11, Safeway Foods
31b a	MD 97, Georgia Ave, Silver Spring, S Exxon, 7 Starr Wings, La Casa del Mofongo, Meleket Ethiopian, Silvestre Chicken, ALDI, CVS Drug, Snider's Foods
33	MD 185, Connecticut Ave, N LDS Temple, S Carroll/repair, Giant/dsl, Einstein Bros., Manoli Canoli, Starbucks, CVS
34	MD 355, Wisconsin Ave, Bethesda
35	(from wb), I-270
36	MD 187, Old Georgetown Rd, S H
38	I-270, to Frederick
39	MD 190, River Rd, Washington, Potomac
40	Cabin John Pkwy(no trucks), Glen Echo
41	Clara Barton Pkwy(no trucks), Carderock, Great Falls

BETHESDA

INTERSTATE 695 (Baltimore)

Exit	Services
48mm	Patapsco River, Francis Scott Key Br
44	Broening Ave(from nb)
43	MD 157, S Royal Farms/dsl
42	MD 151 S, Sparrows Point(last exit before toll sb), E Mickey's Carrol/dsl, Pizza Roma
41	MD 20, Cove Rd, W Royal Farms/dsl, WaWa, Burger King, Dunkin, McDonald's, Grand Lodge, North Point SP, tires
40	MD 150, MD 151, North Point Blvd, (nb only)
39	Merritt Blvd, W Crown, Burger King, Dunkin,

MD

 = gas = food = lodging = other = rest stop

INTERSTATE 695 (Baltimore) Cont'd

ESSEX

39 Continued
McDonald's, $Tree, AlLDI, Ford, Giant Foods, Honda, Hyundai, JC Penney, Mr Tire, Mr. Tire, NAPA, Walmart

38b a MD 150, Eastern Blvd, to Baltimore, E Royal Farms, W Arby's, Checker's, Chick-fil-A, Dunkin, Hibachi Buffet, Hip Hop Fish&Chicken, AT&T, auto/tire, JC Penney, Kia/Nissan, Staples

36 MD 702 S(exits left from sb), Essex

35 US 40, N Sunoco, WaWa/dsl, Arby's, Checkers, Chipotle Mexican, DQ, Dunkin, IHOP, Longhorn Steaks, McDonald's, Panda Express, Panera Bread, Popeyes, Sonic, $Tree, AlLDI, AutoZone, Harley-Davidson, Home Depot, Marshall's, Mr Tire, NTB, Office Depot, PetCo, Sam's Club/gas, same as 34, U-Haul, Verizon, Walmart/EVC, S Kenworth

34 MD 7, Philadelphia Rd, N McDonald's, Panda Express, Popeyes, La Quinta, $General, $Tree, Giant Foods, Goodyear/auto, H, Marshall's, S Exxon/dsl, Liberty, Fiesta Mexicana, Family$, same as 35, Walgreens

BEL AIR

33b a I-95, N to Philadelphia, S to Baltimore

32b a US 1, Bel Air, N Exxon, Arby's, Bob Evans, Burger King, Dunkin, Eato's Pizza, Golden Corral, IHOP, McDonald's, Taco Bell, $Tree, 7-11, BJ's Whse/gas, Giant Foods, Mr Tire/auto, Nissan, NTB, T-Mobile, Toyota/Scion, Walmart, Weis Mkt/gas, S Shell, Baskin-Robbins/Dunkin, Carrabba's, Diablo Doughnuts, Papa John's, Rita's Custard, Skipjacks Crab House, Venus Pizza, Waterman's Pride Seafood, 7-11, Goodyear/auto, Verizon

31c MD 43 E(from eb, exits left)

31b a MD 147, Harford Rd, N 7-11/dsl, BP, CF/dsl, Sunoco, Das Bierhalle, Dunkin, Pauly's Pizza, The Bowman, Wendy's, Chrysler/Dodge/Jeep, Honda, VW, Walgreens, Weis Mkt

30b a MD 41, Perring Pkwy, N Shell, Burger King, Charley's Cheesesteaks, Checker's, Chick-fil-A, Chuck E. Cheese, Denny's, Dunkin, Five Guys, Hibachi Buffet, Kabuto Japanese, Mamma Lucia, McDonald's, Pete's Seafood, Popeyes, Remo's Italian, Starbucks, Subway, Taco Bell, Urban Crab Shack, Wayback Burgers, $Tree, Advance Parts, Chevrolet, Ford/Lincoln, Goodyear/auto, Home Depot, Jiffy Lube, Mitsubishi, NTB, Ross, Safeway Foods, Shoppers Foods, Verizon

29b MD 542, Loch Raven Blvd, S CF, Marathon, Marathon, Royal Frms, Cheezy's Pizza, Chicken Paul, Dunkin, McDonald's, Mo's Seafood, Papa John's, Pastore's Italian, Raven Inn, Sonic, Suya Spot, Comfort Inn, Days Inn, Welcome Inn, Mr Tire, PepBoys

29a Cromwell Bridge Rd, S Holiday Inn Express

28 Providence Rd, S Sunoco

27b a MD 146, Dulaney Valley Rd, N Hampton NHS, S Exxon, Bonefish Grill, Cheesecake Factory, PF Changs, Starbucks, Stoney River Steaks, TGI Fridays, Sheraton, Fresh Mkt, Macy's, mall

BALTIMORE

26b a MD 45, York Rd, Towson, N CF, Citgo, Exxon/dsl, Oceanic, Sunoco/dsl, Dunkin/Baskin-Robbins, GT Pizza, Ocean Pride Rest., Rita's Custard, Subway, The Peppermill, Best Buy, fire museum, Firestone/auto, Kia, Mazda, Mr Tire, NTB, Petco, S Exxon, Shell, Burger King, Five Guys, McDonald's, Mission BBQ, MOD Pizza, The Habit Burger, Towson Diner, CVS Drug, EVC, Fresh Mkt, Goodyear/auto, Hyundai, Hyundai, Lexus, Midas, Safeway Foods/Starbucks, Verizon, vet, Walgreens

25 MD 139, Charles St, S H(2mi)

24 I-83 N, to York

23b MD 25, Falls Rd, Baltimore, N Exxon/Circle K/dsl

23a I-83 S, MD 25 N, Baltimore

22 Greenspring Ave, S Chipotle, Playa Bowls,

PIKESVILLE

22 Continued
Rita's Ice Cream, Starbucks, Fresh Mkt, Walgreens

21 MD 129, to Stevenson Rd, Park Hghts Rd

20 MD 140, Reisterstown Rd, Pikesville, N Exxon/7-11/dsl, Chipotle Mexican, Cold Stone Creamery, Good Guys Pizza, MOD Pizza, Panera Bread, Ruth's Chris, Starbucks, Tropical Smoothie, AT&T, Barnes&Noble, Barnes&Noble, Trader Joe's, URGENT CARE, vet, Walgreens, S CF/dsl, Shell/dsl, Sunoco/Subway, Baskin-Robbins, Dunkin, First Watch, Ledo Pizza, McDonald's, Doubletree, Ramada Inn, Advance Parts, Giant Food, Staples, Target/CVS Drug, Walgreens

19 I-795, NW Expswy

18b a MD 26, Randallstown, Lochearn, E Shell/dsl, Sunoco/dsl, Baskin-Robbins/Dunkin, KFC, Popeyes, Subway, $General, Family$, W Exxon/dsl, Liberty, Shell/dsl, Burger King, Dunkin, Good Times Seafood, Liberty Seafood, McDonald's, Sonic, Subway, Taco Bell, 7-11, Firestone/auto, Giant Foods, H, Shoppers Foods, vet, Walgreens

17 MD 122, Security Blvd, E CF, Shell, City View Grill, Dunkin, Little Caesar's, McDonald's, Subway, Taco Bell, Rodeway Inn, Super 8, Chevrolet, Family$, Jiffy Lube, Nissan, PriceRite Foods, W Exxon/dsl, Sunoco/dsl, Arbys, Burger King, Chick-fil-A, Chipotle, Five Guys, Ledo Pizza, McDonald's, Panera Bread, Popeyes, Hampton Inn, Hampton Inn, Quality Inn, Ford, Macy's, mall, Weis Mkt

16b a I-70, E to Baltimore, W to Frederick

CATONSVILLE

15b a US 40, Ellicott City, Baltimore, E Sunoco, Addy's BBQ, Burger King, Checker's, Chick-fil-A, ChuckECheese, IHOP, KFC, McDonald's, Panda Express, Shirley's Diner, Subway, Holiday Inn Express, Studio 6, $Tree, Advance Parts, AutoZone, BigLots, CVS Drug, EVC, Firestone/auto, Lowe's, Marshall's, Mr Tire, Ross, Safeway Foods/gas, Sam's Club/gas, Shoppers Foods, Walgreens, W Crown/dsl, Exxon/dsl, Shell, Shell, Applebee's, Bob Evans, Double T Diner, Dunkin, Golden Krust Caribbean, Iron Age Korean, KPOT Korean, Krispy Kreme, Loafers Seafood, McDonald's, Panera Bread, Popeyes, Starbucks, Taco Bell, Wendys, Ramada, $Tree, Aamco, AlLDI, Autozone, Chrysler/Jeep, Firestone/auto, Five Below, Giant Foods/EVC, Goodyear/auto, Home Depot, Hyundai, Lidl, Mr. Tire, NTB, PepBoys, PetSmart, Toyota/Scion, Verizon, Walgreens, Walmart/Subway

14 Edmondson Ave, E Crown, Grilled Cheese&Co, Royal Farms, W Carroll, Papa John's

13 MD 144, Frederick Rd, Catonsville, E El Patron Mexican Grill, Pizza Hut, Thai Heaven, Salai Auto Repair, Walgreens, W BP, CF, Gas+, Baskin-Robbins/Dunkin, GL Shacks Grill, McDonald's, Ritas Custard, Subway, 7-11, Jiffy Lube

12c b MD 372 E, Wilkens, E H(2mi)

11b a I-95, N to Baltimore, S to Washington

10 US 1, Washington Blvd (from wb only), E Royal Farms/dsl, WaWa, 3 Bros Pizza, Chick-fil-A, Dunkin, IHOP, Panda Express, Wendy's, Beltway Motel/rest., Home Depot, PetCo, Walmart/auto, W Burger King

9 Hollins Ferry Rd, Lansdowne, E CF/Circle K/Subway, Sunoco/7-11/dsl, Victor's Deli, Royal Farms

8 MD 168, Nursery Rd, N Exxon, Shell, Dunkin, Hardee's, KFC, McDonald's, Taco Bell, Motel 6, Volvo/Mack Trucks, S CF/dsl, Sunoco, Bubbakoo's Burritos, G&M Rest., Happy Garden Chinese, Rita's Custard, Seasons Pizza

7b a MD 295, N to Baltimore, S BWI

6b a Camp Mead Rd(from eb), N Shell, Antonios Pizza, Checkers, Dunkin, Clarion Hotel, Sleep Inn, NAPA

5 MD 648, Ferndale, N Exxon/7-11/dsl, Shell/dsl, Checker's, Dunkin, Clarion Hotel, Sleep Inn, NAPA, W Hot Wok

M

INTERSTATE 695 (Baltimore) Cont'd

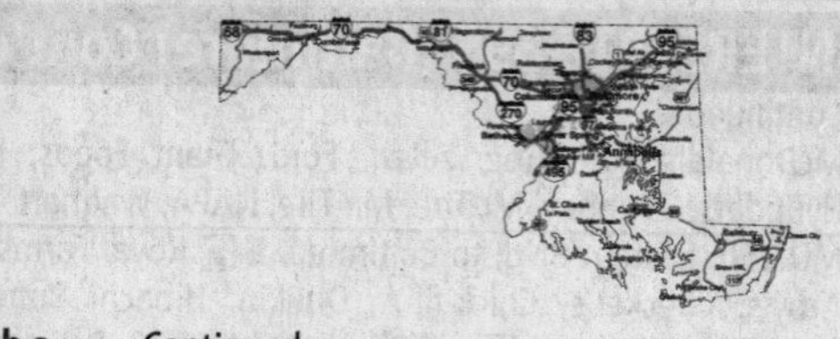

Exit #	Services
4b a	I-97 S, to Annapolis
3b a	MD 2, Brooklyn Park, S Exxon, Royal Farms/dsl, Shell/dsl, BoneFish Grill, Chaps Pit BBQ, Checker's, Chick-fil-A, ChuckECheese, Coldstone, Denny's, First Watch, Five Guys, Hibachi Buffet, HipHop Fish&Chicken, Hook&Reel Seafood, Jersey Mike's, Ledo Pizza, McDonald's, MOD Pizza, Noodles&Co, Panda Express, Panera Bread, Pappas Rest., Pizza Hut, Qdoba, Romanos Grill, Starbucks, Subway, Taco Bell, Tropical Smoothie, Wendy's, Extended Stay America, Hampton Inn, La Quinta, Red Roof Inn, $Tree, Advance Parts, AlLDI, AT&T, Autozone, Best Buy, BigLots, Buick/GMC,
3b a	Continued Dick's, Hyundai, Lowe's, PetCo, ShopRite Foods, Subaru, Target/CVS Drug, tire/auto repair, Verizon, Walgreens, Walmart
2	MD 10, Glen Burnie, S McDonald's, Costco/gas, Home Depot, PetSmart
1	MD 174, Hawkins Point Rd, S Citgo/deli/dsl

NOTES

MD

MASSACHUSETTS

INTERSTATE 84

STURBRIDGE

Exit #	Services
4(11)	I-84 begins/ends on I-90, Exit 9.
3b a(9)	US 20, Sturbridge, **N** Citgo, Cumberland Farms, EVC, Burger King, CVS Drug, Dunkin', Empire Village, Friendly's, McDonald's, Panera Bread, Sturbridge Coffeehouse, Sturbridge Seafood, Subway, Village Pizza, EconoLodge, Hampton Inn, Holiday Inn Express, La Quinta, Old Sturbridge Lodges, Super 8, USPO, **S** S&S, Shell/Dunkin'/Subway, Applebee's, Cracker Barrel, Uno Pizzaria, Wendy's, Comfort Inn, Marshall's, Michael's, Petco, Staples, Stop&Shop, Verizon, vet, Walmart/Subway
2(5)	MA 131, to Old Sturbridge Village, Sturbridge, **S** Publick House, RV camping
4mm	picnic area wb, litter barrels
1(3)	Mashapaug Rd, to Southbridge, **S** Mobil/dsl, Pilot/deli/dsl/scales/24hr/@, Days Inn, H
2mm	weigh sta both lanes
0.5mm	picnic area eb
0mm	Massachusetts/Connecticut state line

INTERSTATE 90

NEWTON

FRAMINGHAM

Exit #	Services
140mm	I-90 begins/ends near Logan Airport
25	to I-93, to downtown Boston
24	to I-93, to downtown Boston
22(134)	Presidential Ctr, downtown
20(132)	MA 28, Alston, **N** Courtyard, Doubletree Inn, H, **S** Mobil
131mm	toll plaza
18(130)	MA Ave(from eb), **N** IHOP, Starbucks
17(128)	Centre St, Newton, **N** Bertucci's, Starbucks, Crowne Plaza, Honda, Walgreens
16(125)	MA 16, W Newton, **N** Shell/repair, Blue Ribbon BBQ, CVS Drug
15(124)	I-95, **N** Marriott, Speedway
123mm	toll plaza
14(122)	MA 30, Weston
117mm	Natick Travel Plaza eb, EVC, **Gulf/dsl**, **Dunkin'**, **McDonald's**, Papagino's/d'Angelo's
13(116)	MA 30, Natick, **S** Cumberland, EVC, Mobil, Shell, Tesla EVC, Boston Mkt, Burger King, Chick-fil-A, Dunkin', Five Guys, Lotus Flower Chinese, McDonald's, Panera Bread, Stop&Shop, Courtyard, Monticello Inn, Red Roof+, Best Buy, BJ's Whse, Home Depot, Kia, Kohl's, Lowe's, Marshall's, REI, Target, TJ Maxx, USPO, Walmart
114mm	Framingham Travel Plaza wb, **Gulf/dsl**, **Boston Mkt**, **McDonald's**, Starbucks, **S** EVC
12(111)	MA 9, Framington, **N** BP, Speedway, Dunkin', Godavari Framingham, Wendy's, Motel 6, Sheraton, **S** China Gourmet, Toyota
11a(106)	I-495, N to NH, S to Cape Cod
105mm	Westborough Travel Plaza wb, **Gulf/dsl**, **Boston Mkt**, **D'angelo**, **Dunkin'**, **Papagino's**
11(96)	MA 122, to Millbury, **N** UMA Med Ctr
10a(95)	MA 146
94mm	Blackstone River
10(90)	I-395 S, to Auburn, I-290 N, Worcester, **N** Outback, Papa Gino's, Comfort Inn, La Quinta, **S** Shell, Shell/repair/24hr, Applebee's, D'angelo, Dunkin', Friendly's, Wendy's, Fairfield Inn, Hampton Inn, Holiday Inn Express, CVS Drug, Hyundai, Park'n Shop, TJ Maxx
84mm	Charlton Travel Plaza wb, Gulf/dsl, McDonald's,

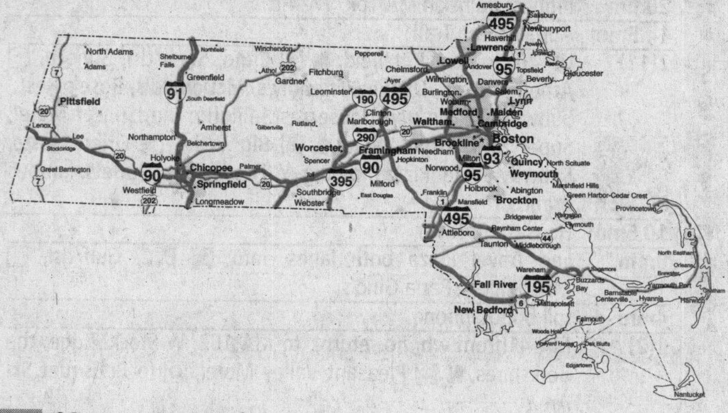

HARTFORD CT

Exit #	Services
84mm	Continued Papa Gino's/d'Angelo's
80mm	Charlton Travel Plaza eb, **Gulf/dsl**, **McDonald's**, Papa Gino's, **st police**
79mm	toll plaza
9(78)	I-84, to Hartford, NYC, Sturbridge, access to same services as I-84, exit 3., **S** access to H
67mm	Quaboag River
8(62)	MA 32, to US 20, Palmer, Pride, Shell/dsl, vet, Domino's, Dunkin', McDonald's, Subway, Wendy's, Big Y Foods, Chevrolet, CVS Drug, H, repair/transmissions
58mm	Chicopee River
56mm	Ludlow Travel Plaza wb, **Gulf/dsl**, Papa Gino's, Starbucks
55mm	Ludlow Travel Plaza eb, **Gulf/dsl**, **McDonald's**, Starbucks
7(54)	MA 21, to Ludlow, **N** Cumberland Farms, Pride/dsl, Sunoco, Burger King, Dunkin', McDonald's, Starbucks, Subway, Ace Hardware, Big Y Foods, CVS Drug, **S** Shell/dsl, Dominos, Taco Bell, Holiday Inn Express
6(51)	I-291, to Springfield, Hartford CT, **N** Pride/50's Diner/Subway/dsl, Dunkin', McDonald's, Mercedes, Po's Chinese, Motel 6, Basketball Hall of Fame, H, to Bradley Int
5(49)	MA 33, to Chicopee, Westover AFB, **N** Tesla EVC, 99 Rest., Applebee's, Arby's, Buffalo Wild Wings, Chick-fil-A, Chipotle Mexican, Denny's, Dunkin', Five Guys, Friendly's, Little Caesar's, McDonald's, Panera Bread, Popeyes, Royal Buffet, Starbucks, Subway, Wendy's, Hampton Inn, Quality Inn, Residence Inn, $Tree, AlLDI, Big Y Foods, BJ's Whse/gas, Chrysler/Dodge/Jeep, Home Depot, Honda, Marshall's, Monro, Nissan, PetSmart, Staples, Staples, Stop&Shop/gas, TownFair Tire, U-Haul, Verizon, Walmart/Subway, **S** Pride/Dunkin'/Subway/dsl, Buick/GMC
46mm	Connecticut River
4(46)	I-91, US 5, to Holyoke, W Springfield, **N** Shell, Dunkin', Welcome Inn, **S** Pride/dsl, Donut Dip, Five Guys, Hooters, On the Border, Outback Steaks, Subway, Hampton Inn, Red Roof+, Residence Inn, Springfield Inn, Super 8, BMW, Honda/Lexus/Toyota
41mm	st police wb
3(40)	US 202, to Westfield, **N** Mobil, Alessio's Pizza, **S** Citgo/Subway/dsl, Shell/dsl, Dunkin', Friendly's, McDonald's, Wendy's, Hampton Inn, Quality Inn, H, repair, vet
36mm	Westfield River
35.5mm	runaway truck ramp eb
29mm	Blandford/Ludlow TP both lanes, info, Gulf/dsl,

INTERSTATE 90 Cont'd

PITTSFIELD

29mm Continued McDonald's

20mm highest point on MA Tpk, 1724 ft

14.5mm Appalachian Trail

2(11) US 20, to Lee, Pittsfield, **N** Citgo, Shell/dsl, Sunoco, Athena's Rest., Dunkin', Friendly's, McDonald's, Rose's Rest., Subway, Morgan House/rest., Pilgrim Inn, Sunset Motel, Super 8, True Value, **S** Big Y/dsl, Orient Taste, Subway, Villa Pizza, Big Y Foods, Lee Outlets/famous brands

10.5mm Hoosatonic River

8mm Lee Travel Plaza both lanes, info, EVC, Gulf/dsl, McDonald's, Papa Gino's

4mm toll booth, phone

1(2) MA 41(from wb, no return), to MA 102, W Stockbridge, the Berkshires, **N** Pleasant Valley Motel, to Bousquet Ski Area

0mm Massachusetts/New York state line

INTERSTATE 91

GREENFIELD

55mm Massachusetts/Vermont state line

54mm parking area both lanes, picnic tables

28(51) US 5, MA 10, Bernardston, **E** Fox Inn, **W** Sunoco, Antonio's II Ristorante, Four-leaf Clover Rest., Hillside Organic Pizza, Country Corner Store, USPO

27(45) MA 2 E (exits left from sb), Greenfield, Cumberland Farms, Speedway, Stop&Shop, Sunoco/dsl, Denny's Pantry, Domino's, Dunkin', McDonald's, Subway, $General, AT&T, Aubuchon Hardware, AutoZone, Chrysler/Dodge/Jeep, Honda, H, O'Reilly Parts, Walgreens

26(43) MA 2 W, MA 2A E, Greenfield, **E** Mobil/dsl, Planet/dsl, Shell/dsl, Applebee's, Athens Pizza, China Gourmet, D'Angelo, Dunkin Donuts, Chevrolet, Ford/Lincoln, H, Toyota, **W** Shell, 99 Rest., Friendly's, KFC/Taco Bell, Kobe Asian, McDonald's, Subway, Days Inn, Hampton Inn, $General, $Tree, Big Y Foods, BJ's Whse, Home Depot, Staples, to Mohawk Tr, Verizon

39mm Deerfield River

37mm weigh sta both lanes

25(36) MA 116(from sb), S Deerfield, camping, hist dist, same as 24

24(35) US 5, MA 10, MA 116, no EZ return, Deerfield, **E** Irving/Circle K/Dunkin Donuts/Subway/dsl, Red Roof+, vet, Yankee Candle Co, **W** Roady's Trkstp/diner/dsl/24hr, 24hr Diner

34.5mm parking area both lanes

NORTHAMPTON

23(34) US 5(from sb), **E** Tom's Hot Dog, Orchard Trailers, Rainbow Motel/camping

22(30) US 5, MA 10(from nb), N Hatfield, **W** Diamond RV Ctr

21(28) US 5, MA 10, Hatfield, **W** Sunoco/dsl, Subway, Hatfield Inn, st police

20(26) US 5, MA 9, MA 10(from sb), Northampton, **W** Pride/dsl, Speedway/dsl, Burger King, D'angelo's, Domino's, KFC, McDonald's, Moe's SW, Taco Bell, AutoZone, Big Y Food/Drug, BigLots, Chevrolet, Chrysler/Dodge/Jeep, CVS Drug, Firestone/auto, Ford, Goodyear/auto, Honda, H, Hyundai, Stop&Shop/gas, TownFair Tire, Toyota, U-Haul, Verizon, VW, Walgreens, Walmart/Subway

19(25) MA 9, to Amherst, Northampton, **E** Big Y/dsl, Cumberland Farms, Phillips 66, Pride/Subway/dsl, Primo Pizza, Hampton Inn, Nissan, to Elwell SP, vet

18(22) US 5, Northampton, **W** Shell/Dunkin', Fairfield Inn, Quality Inn, to Smith Coll

18mm scenic area both lanes

17b a(16) MA 141, S Hadley, **E** Mobil/dsl, Shell/dsl, Dunkin', Real China, Subway, Motel 6, Meineke, Walgreens

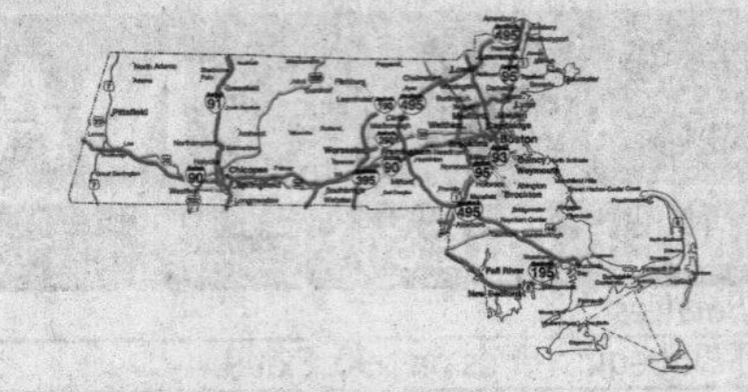

HOLYOKE

16(14) US 202, Holyoke, **W** Soldier's Home

15(12) to US 5, Ingleside, **E** Shell/Dunkin', Applebee's, Chicago Grill, Chipotle, Cracker Barrel, JP's Rest., McDonald's, Red Robin, Fairfield Inn, Barnes&Noble, Best Buy, CVS Drug, Hobby Lobby, H, JC Penney, Macy's, Old Navy, PetCo, Target, TJ Maxx, **W** Homewood Suites

14(11) to US 5, to I-90(Mass Tpk), E to Boston, W to Albany, **E** H

13b a(9) US 5 N, W Springfield, **E** Pride/dsl, Donut Dip, Five Guys, Hooters, On-the-Border, Outback Steaks, Shallot Thai, Subway, Tap House Grill, Express Inn, Red Roof+, Residence Inn, Springfield Inn, Super 8, BMW, Lexus/Toyota, **W** Pride/dsl, Shell/dsl, Tesla EVC, 99 Rest., Burger King, Cal's Grill, Carrabba's, Chili's, D'angelo's, Dunkin', Friendly's, IHOP, KFC, Longhorn Steaks, McDonald's, Nippon Grill, Olive Garden, Panera Bread, Pizza Hut, Tokyo Cuisine, Wendy's, Bel Air Inn, Best Western, Candlewood Suites, Clarion, Courtyard, EconoLodge, Hampton Inn, Quality Inn, Red Carpet Inn, Travel Inn, $Tree, ALDI, AT&T, Chrysler/Dodge/Jeep, Costco, CVS Drug, Dick's, Fiat, GNC, Home Depot, Honda, Kohl's, Mazda, Michael's, Nissan, Staples, Stop&Shop, Subaru, TownFair Tire, Verizon

SPRINGFIELD

12(8.5) I-391 N, to Chicopee

11(8) Birnie Ave(from sb), **E** Mobil, H

10(7.5) Main St(from nb), Springfield, **E** Mobil

9(7) US 20 W, MA 20A E(from nb), **E** McDonald's, **W** Pride/Subway/dsl

8(6.5) I-291, US 20 E, to I-90, **E** downtown

7(6) Columbus Ave(from sb), **E** Pride/Subway/dsl, Sheraton, Tower Square, **W** to Basketball Hall of Fame

6(5.5) Springfield Ctr, **E** Pride/Dunkin Donuts/Subway/dsl, Starbucks, **W** Coldstone, Plan B Burger, Basketball Hall of Fame

5(5) Broad St, same as 4, **E** Shell/dsl, Hampton Inn, Hyundai, **W** Sunoco/dsl, Chicago Grill, Subway, Hilton Garden, Buick/GMC

4(4.5) MA 83, Broad St, Main St, same as 5, **E** Shell/dsl, Antonio's Grinders, Hyundai, **W** Sunoco/dsl, Chicago Grill, Subway, Buick/GMC, Chevrolet, Hilton Garden

3(4) US 5 N, to MA 57, Columbus Ave, W Springfield, **E** Sunoco, Antonio's Pizza, **W** Chevrolet

2(3.5) MA 83 S(from nb), to E Longmeadow

1(3) US 5 S(from sb)

0mm Massachusetts/Connecticut state line, callboxes begin/end

INTERSTATE 93

METHUEN

47mm Massachusetts/New Hampshire state line, callboxes begin/end

48(46) MA 213 E, to Methuen, **E** H

47(45) Pelham St, Methuen, **E** Sunoco, Dunkin', Heavenly Donuts, McDonald's, Outback Steaks, **W** BP, Irving/Circle K/Subway/dsl, Fireside Rest., Day's Hotel/rest., Chrysler/Dodge/Jeep

46(44) MA 110, MA 113, to Lawrence, **E** BP/repair, Mobil, Shell, Burger King, Dunkin', KFC/Taco Bell, McDonald's, Pizza Hut, $Tree, H, MktBasket Foods, **W** Super, Anthony's Roast Beef, Dunkin', Irish Cottage, Royal Roast Beef, Passport Inn

45(43) Andover St, River Rd, to Lawrence, **E** Courtyard,

INTERSTATE 93 Cont'd

ANDOVER

45(43) Continued
Doubletree, Homewood Suites, W Mobil/Dunkin', Chateu Italian, Chili's, La Quinta, Residence Inn, Sonesta Suites, SpringHill Suites, vet

44b a(40) I-495, to Lowell, Lawrence, E H

43(39) MA 133, N Tewksbury, E Mobil/Dunkin', W 99 Rest.

42(38) Dascomb Rd, East St, Tewksbury, W Citgo/dsl, Dunkin', Luna Rossa Italian, Subway, 7-11

41(35) MA 125, Andover, E EVC, Dunkin', Hampton Inn, Target

40(34) MA 62, Wilmington

39(33) Concord St, E Dunkin', Mona's Kitchen, Shriners Auditorium, URGENT CARE

38(31) MA 129, Reading, W Mobil/Dunkin'/Subway/dsl, Burger King, Pacific Grove Chinese, Red Heat Tavern

37c(30) Commerce Way, Atlantic Ave, W Chipotle Mexican, Firehouse Subs, Starbucks, Red Roof+, Residence Inn, PetCo, PetSmart, Target, Verizon

37b a(29) I-95, S to Waltham, N to Peabody

36(28) Montvale Ave, E Mobil/Circle K, Deli Works, Dunkin', Courtyard, W BP, Gulf, Speedway/dsl, Bickford's Grille, Dunkin', McDonald's, Polcari's Italian, Wendy's, Best Western+, Comfort Inn, H

35(27) Winchester Highlands, Melrose, E H(no EZ return to sb)

34(26) MA 28 N(from nb, no EZ return), Stoneham, E Mobil/Circle K/dsl, Friendly's, W H

33(25) MA 28, Fellsway West, Winchester, W H

SOMERVILLE

32(23) MA 60, Salem Ave, Medford Square, W Hyatt Place, H, to Tufts U

31(22) MA 16 E, to Revere(no EZ return sb), W Fred's Gas, Mobil/dsl, Mr. C's/dsl, Avellino's Italian, Burger King, Dunkin', AutoZone, Chrysler/Dodge/Jeep, Infiniti, Nissan

30(21) MA 28, MA 38, Mystic Ave, Somerville, W Mr. C's/dsl, Burger King, AutoZone, VW

29(20) MA 28(from nb), same as 30, Somerville, E 99 Rest., Dunkin', Starbucks, La Quinta, Home Depot, Staples, TJ Maxx, Trader Joe's, W Gulf, Speedway, Dunkin', Stop&Shop

28(19) Sullivans Square, Charles Town, downtown

27 US 1 N(from nb)

26(18.5) MA 28 N, Storrow Dr, North Sta, downtown

25 Haymarket Sq, Gov't Center

24(18) Callahan Tunnel, E

23(17.5) High St, Congress St, W Harborside Inn

22(17) Atlantic Ave, Northern Ave, South Sta, Boston World Trade Ctr

21(16.5) Kneeland St, ChinaTown

20(16) I-90 W, to Mass Tpk

19(15.5) Albany St(from sb), W H

18(15) Mass Ave, to Roxbury, W H

17(14.5) E Berkeley(from nb)

16(14) S Hampton St, Andrew Square, W Applebee's, Chipotle, Olive Garden, Panera Bread, Wahlburgers, Courtyard, Holiday Inn Express, Best Buy, Home Depot, Marshall's, Old Navy, Stop&Shop/gas, Target, TJ Maxx

QUINCY

15(13) Columbia Rd, Everett Square, E DoubleTree, JFK Library, to UMA, W Gulf, Speedway

14(12.5) Morissey Blvd (from nb no return), E JFK Library, W Shell

13(12) Freeport St, to Dorchester, from nb, W 7-11, Citgo, Deadwood Cafe, Dunkin', Ruritan Pizza, Subway, Comfort Inn, Ramada, CVS Drug, Honda, Lambert's Mkt, Stop&Shop, Toyota

12(11.5) MA 3A S(from sb, no EZ return), Quincy, E Express, tires, Best Western, W Gulf/Dunkin', Speedway/dsl,

BRAINTREE

12(11.5) Continued
PapaGino's, AutoZone, CVS Drug, Staples, Verizon, Walgreens

11b a(11) to MA 203, Granite Ave, Ashmont

10(10) Squantum Ave(from sb), Milton, W H

9(9) Adams St, Bryant Ave, to N Quincy, E House of Pizza, Dunkin', W Shell/repair, USPO

8(8) Brook Pkwy, to Quincy, Furnace, E Gulf/dsl, Mobil/dsl

7(7) MA 3 S, to Cape Cod(exits left from sb), Braintree, E Marriott

6(6) MA 37, to Holbrook, Braintree, E EVC, Mobil/dsl, 99 Rest., Buffalo Wild Wings, CA Pizza Kitchen, Cheesecake Factory, Chicago Grill, Chipotle, D'angelo, Dave&Buster's, Five Guys, Legal Seafood, Potbelly, Qdoba, Red Robin, Starbucks, TGIFriday's, Tokyo Japanese, Hyatt Place, AT&T, Lord&Taylor, Macy's, Nordstrom's, Sullivan Tire/auto, Target, URGENT CARE, W Citgo, Best Western, Candlewood Suites, Extended Stay America, Hampton Inn, Barnes&Noble, Ford, VW

5b a(4) MA 28 S, to Randolph, Milton, E Mobil/dsl, Shell/dsl, Domino's, Dunkin', La Scala, Lombardo's, Randolph Cafe, Wong's Chinese, Comfort Inn, AT&T

4(3) MA 24 S(exits left from sb), to Brockton

3(2) MA 138 N, to Ponkapoag Trail, Houghtons Pond

2b a(1) MA 138 S, to Stoughton, Milton, E golf, W BlueHill/dsl, Mobil/dsl, Shell/dsl, Blue Hills Grill, Dunkin', Homewood Suites

1(0) I-95 N, S to Providence. I-93 begins/ends on I-95, exit 12.

INTERSTATE 95

SALISBURY

89.5mm Massachusetts/New Hampshire state line, Welcome Ctr/rest area sb, **full facilities, litter barrels,**

60(89) MA 286, to Salisbury, beaches, E Mobil/dsl, Cosmos Rest., Dunkin', Lena's Seafood Rest., Black Bear Camping(seasonal)

59(88) I-495 S(from sb)

58b a(87) rd 110, to I-495 S, to Amesbury, Salisbury, E Sunoco/Dunkin'/Subway/dsl, China Buffet, Niko's Place, Sylvan St Grille, Winner's Circle Rest., $Tree, Ford, U-Haul, vet, W EVC, Irving Gas/Circle K, Mobil, Sunoco/dsl, Tesla EVC, Acapulco's Mexican, Burger King, Dunkin', Friendly's, McDonald's, Subway, Fairfield Inn, Hampton Inn, AT&T, Chevrolet, Stop&Shop, Verizon

57(85) MA 113, to W Newbury, E Mobil/dsl, Shell/dsl/repair, Sunoco, China Wok, Dunkin', Giuseppe's Italian, Hana Japan, McDonald's, Moe's SW, Panera Bread, Wendy's, 7-11, CVS Drug, GNC, H, Marshall's, Midas, MktBasket Foods, Shaw's Foods, Verizon, Walgreens

BOXFORD

56(83) Scotland Rd, to Newbury, E st police

55(82) Central St, to Byfield, E Rusty Can, W Prime/dsl/repair

54b a(78) MA 133, E to Rowley, W to Groveland, E vet

77mm weigh sta both lanes

53b a(76) MA 97, S to Topsfield, N to Georgetown

52(74) Topsfield Rd, to Topsfield, Boxford

51(72) Endicott Rd, to Topsfield, Middleton

50(71) US 1, to MA 62, Topsfield, E Gulf/dsl, Mobil/dsl, Honda, W S&S, Break Away Rest., Supino's Rest., TX Roadhouse, DoubleTree, Knights Inn, CVS Drug, st police, Staples, Stop&Shop, USPO

49(70) MA 62(from nb), same as 50, Danvers, Middleton

48(69) Hobart St(from sb), W Calitri's Italian, Best Western+, Comfort a Inn, Motel 6, Home Depot

47b a(68) MA 114, to Middleton, Peabody, E Gulf/Dunkin', Sunoco, Dunkin', Honey Dew Donuts, McDonald's, Olive Garden, Outback Steaks, Pizza Hut, Audi, CarMax, Chevrolet, Chrysler/Dodge/Jeep, Infiniti, Lexus, Lowe's, NTB, PetSmart, Subaru, TJ Maxx, Toyota, Trader Joe's, Verizon, vet, VW,

= gas = food = lodging = other = rest stop

INTERSTATE 95 Cont'd

47b a(68) Continued
Walmart/Subway, **W** Cumberland Farms, Speedway/dsl, Chili's, Hardcover Rest., TGIFriday's, Motel 6, Residence Inn, TownePlace Suites, Costco/gas, Home Depot, Land Rover, Mazda, Meineke, NAPA

46(67) to US 1, **W** Best, Gulf/dsl, Mobil, Sunoco/dsl, Dunkin', Dunkin'(2), Honey Dew Donuts, auto repair

LYNNFIELD

45(66) MA 128 N, to Peabody

44b a(65) US 1 N, MA 129, **E** H, **W** 7-11, Gulf, Shell, Bertucci's, Bros Kouzina Rest., Dunkin', Marco's Italian, Santarpio's Pizza, Sonic, Wendy's, Hampton Inn, Holiday Inn, Homewood Suites, Plaza Inn, SpringHill Suites

43(61) Walnut St, Lynnfield, **E** 99 Rest., golf, to Saugus Iron Works NHS(3mi), **W** Panera Bread, Starbucks, Yardhouse, Sheraton, EVC, Whole Foods

42(62) Salem St, Montrose, **E** Irving/Circle K/Subway, Sunoco, Dunkin', **W** Sheraton

41(60) Main St, Lynnfield Ctr, **E** Shell, **W** vet

40(59) MA 129, Wakefield Ctr, N Reading, **E** Bellino's Italian, Honey Dew Donuts, city park, vet, **W** Cumberland Farms, Dunkin', Mandarin Chinese, Chevrolet, Mazda, REI

39(58) North Ave, Reading, **E** Lakeside Inn, city park, Subaru, **W** Shell/dsl, Anthony's Pizza, Bertucci's, Chili's, Chipotle, Fuddrucker's, Longhorn Steaks, Oye's Rest., Starbucks, Home Depot, Honda, Mkt Basket Foods, Staples, Stop&Shop Foods, URGENT CARE, Verizon

38b a(57) MA 28, to Reading, **E** Gulf/repair, Mobil, Speedway/dsl, 99 Rest., Burger King, D'Angelo's/PapaGino's, Dunkin', Five Guys, Loui Loui, Subway, Advance Parts, AutoZone, Ford, GNC, Marshall's, Michael's, Stop&Shop/gas, Target, Verizon, Walgreens, **W** Citgo, Mobil/dsl, Shell, Anthony's Roast Beef, Burger King, Calareso's Farm Stand, China Moon, Domino's, Dunkin', Harrow's Chicken Pies, McDonald's, Starbucks, Meineke

37b a(56) I-93, N to Manchester, S to Boston

36(55) Washington St, to Winchester, **E** BP, Dunkin', B Good, Chick-fil-A, Red Robin, Sal's Pizza, Starbucks, Subway, Hilton, BJ's Whse/gas, Hogan Tire/auto, Nissan, Staples, Toyota, **W** Sunoco, 99 Rest., Bertucci's, China Pearl, Dave&Buster's, Dunkin', Joe's Grill, On the Border, Qdoba, Courtyard, Fairfield Inn, Holiday Inn Express, Red Roof+, $Tree, AT&T, CVS Drug, Kohl's, Lowe's, Mkt Basket Foods, NTB, TJ Maxx, Town Fair Tire, USPO

WOBURN

35(54) MA 38, to Woburn, **E** Scoreboard Grill, Crowne Plaza, H, **W** Mobil/dsl, Applebee's, Dunkin', Sichuan Garden, Extended Stay America, city park, CVS Drug, Stop&Shop Foods

34(53) Winn St, Woburn

33b a(52) US 3 S, MA 3A N, to Winchester, **E** Bickford's Grille, Café Escadrille, Capital Grille, Coldstone, Dunkin', NYA Joe's Grill, Panera Bread, Potbelly, Seasons 52 Grill, Starbucks, Subway, Hyatt House, CVS Drug, Honda, LL Bean, Marshall's, Michael's, **W** EVC, Prime, Speedway, Chopps Grill, Marriott, Audi/Porsche, H, Kia, Mercedes, repair

32b a(51) US 3 N, MA 2A S, to Lowell, **E** Mobil/dsl, Shell, Burger King, Burton's Grill, Chateau Italian, Dunkin', Five Guys, McDonald's, Hilton Garden, Sonesta Suites, Best Buy, Jo-Ann, Midas, Mkt Basket Foods, Nordstrom, Old Navy, PetCo, Trader Joe's, **W** Border Cafe, Buffalo Wild Wings, Cheesecake Factory, Chipotle, Del Frisco's Grill, Legal Seafoods, Macaroni Grill, Wendy's, Candlewood Suites, Extended Stay America, AT&T, Barnes&Noble, Kohl's, Lord&Taylor, Macy's, Nordstrom, Staples, URGENT CARE, Verizon

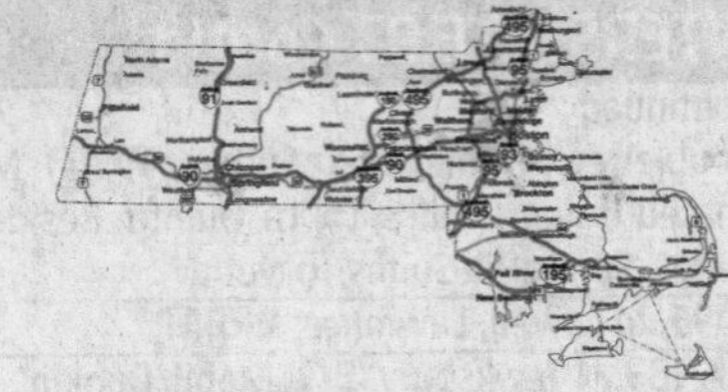

LEXINGTON

31b a(48) MA 4, MA 225, Lexington, **E** Gulf, Mobil/dsl/repair, Alexander's Pizza, Qdoba, Starbucks, Stop&Shop, Walgreens, **W** Gulf, Shell, Chipotle, Dunkin', Great Wall, Margarita's, McDonald's, Minuteman Diner, Bedford Plaza Hotel, Quality Inn, Stop&Shop, TJ Maxx, vet

30b a(47) MA 2A, Lexington, **E** Sunoco/Dunkin'/dsl, H, **W** ALoft, Element Hotel, Hanscom AFB, to MinuteMan NP

46.5mm travel plaza nb, Gulf/dsl/CNG, Honey Dew Donuts, McDonald's, Original Boston Pizza

29b a(46) MA 2 W, Cambridge

28b a(45) Trapelo Rd, Belmont, **E** Gulf/dsl, Mobil/dsl, Boston Mkt, Burger King, Dunkin', Panera Bread, Papa Gino's, Starbucks, Subway, Verizon, city park, Star Mkt/Osco Drugs

27b a(44) Totten Pond Rd, Waltham, **E** Shell, Copper House, D'Angelo, Dunkin', Osteria Posto, Ruth's Chris, Best Western+, Courtyard, Extended Stay America, Extended Stay America(2), Hilton Garden, Holiday Inn Express, Home Suites, Hyatt, Westin Hotel, **W** Bertucci's Rest., Green Papaya Thai, Embassy Suites/The Grille, Hampton Inn, AT&T, Costco, Home Depot

26(43) US 20, to MA 117, to Waltham, **E** Sunoco/dsl, **W** Mobil/dsl, Dunkin', NTB, vet

25(42) I-90, MA Tpk

24(41) MA 30, Newton, Wayland, **E** Speedway, Marriott/rest.

23(40) Recreation Rd(from nb), to MA Tpk

22b a(39) Grove St, **E** Hotel Indigo, golf

38.5mm travel plaza sb, Gulf/dsl, McDonald's

21b a(38) MA 16, Newton, Wellesley, **E** H, **W** Sunoco, Dunkin', North End Pizza, Papa Razzi, Starbucks, CVS Drug

20b a(36) MA 9, Brookline, Framingham

19(35) Highland Ave, Newton, Needham, **E** EVC, Speedway, Anthony's Pizza, Chef Mike's, Chipotle Mexican, Five Guys, Mandarin Cuisine, Mighty Subs, Panera Bread, PetSmart, Starbucks, Residence Inn, Sheraton/rest., AAA, Advance Parts, CVS Drug, Marshall's, Michael's, PetCo, Staples, TJ Maxx, **W** Three Squares Rest., Chevrolet, Ford

DEDHAM

18(34) Great Plain Ave, W Roxbury

33.5mm parking area sb

17(33) MA 135, Needham, Wellesley

32mm truck turnout sb

16b a(31) MA 109, High St, Dedham, **W** Mobil/dsl

15b a(29) US 1, MA 128, **E** Gulf, Dunkin', Harrow's Chicken Pies, Hooters, Joe's Grill, Panera Bread, PapaGino's, PF Chang's, Qdoba, Starbucks, Subway, TGI Friday's, Victory Grille, Yard House Rest., Fairfield Inn, Holiday Inn, Residence Inn, AT&T, AutoZone, Best Buy, BJ's Whse, Costco/gas, CVS Drug, LL Bean, NTB, PepBoys, PetCo, Staples, Star Mkt, Tesla, Verizon, vet, Whole Foods Mkt, **W** Irving/dsl, Shell/dsl, Burger King, Dunkin', Jade Chinese, McDonald's, Budget Inn, AAA, Acura, AT&T, Audi, Buick/GMC, Chevrolet, Chrysler/Dodge/Jeep, Fiat, Honda, Hyundai, Kia, Mercedes, Porsche, Toyota

14(28) East St, Canton St, **E** Hilton

27mm rest area sb, **full facilities, litter barrels,**

13(26.5) University Ave, **W** EVC, Anthony's Pizza, Chipotle, De Frisco's, Joe's Grill, Panda Express, Panera Bread Smashburger, Starbucks, Which Wich?, GNC, Michael's,

INTERSTATE 95 Cont'd

BOSTON

13(26.5) Continued PetSmart, Target, Verizon, Wegman's Mkt
12(26) I-93 N, to Braintree, Boston, motorist callboxes end nb
11b a(23) Neponset St, to Canton, **E** Citgo/repair, Sunoco/dsl, Dunkin', **W** Gulf/dsl, Sunoco, Jake&Joe's, The Chateau, Hampton Inn, Chevrolet, Ferrari, Ford, Honda, H, Hyundai, Maserati, Nissan, Toyota, Volvo
22.5mm Neponset River
10(20) Coney St(from sb, no EZ return), to US 1, Sharon, Walpole, **W** BJ's Gas, Mobil, 99 Rest., Bertucci's, Chili's, Chipotle Mexican, Dunkin', Five Guys, Friendly's, IHOP, McDonald's, Panda Express, Panera Bread, Starbucks, Subway, Taco Bell, TX Roadhouse, Wendy's, Courtyard, Holiday Inn Express, Residence Inn, Sheraton, Advance Parts, Barnes&Noble, CarMax, Home Depot, Jo-Ann, Kohl's, O'Reilly Parts, Old Navy, PetCo, PetSmart, Staples, Stop&Shop, TownFair Tire, VW, Walgreens

SHARON

9(19) US 1, to MA 27, same as 10, Walpole, **W** Gulf, Mobil/dsl, Applebee's, Dunkin', Starbucks, Best Western+, EconoLodge, BigY Foods/drug, Lexus, Walmart
8(16) S Main St, Sharon, **E** Dunkin', Starbucks, Shaw's Foods
7b a(13) MA 140, to Mansfield, **E** 99 Rest., Jake'nJoe's Grille, Comfort Inn, Courtyard, Holiday Inn, Red Roof+, Residence Inn, Stop&Shop/gas, **W** Shell/HoneyDew Donuts/dsl, Dunkin', PapaGino's, $Tree
6b a(12) I-495, S to Cape Cod, N to NH
10mm Welcome Ctr/rest area nb, **full facilities, info, litter barrels, petwalk**
9mm truck parking area sb

ATTLEBORO

5(7) MA 152, Attleboro, **E** H, **W** Gulf/dsl, Barett's Alehouse, Wendy's, Shaw's Foods/Osco Drug
4(6) I-295 S, to Woonsocket
3(4) MA 123, to Attleboro, **E** Shell/dsl, Dunkin', H, zoo
2.5mm parking area/weigh sta both lanes, litter barrels, no restrooms
2b a(1) US 1A, Newport Ave, Attleboro, **E** Mobil/dsl, McDonald's, Olive Garden, Hobby Lobby, Home Depot, Market Basket Foods, TJ Maxx, Verizon, **W** Grampy's/dsl, Kia
1(.5) US 1(from sb), **E** Attleboro Inn, Volvo, **W** Speedway/dsl
0mm Massachusetts/Rhode Island state line

INTERSTATE 195 MA

22(41) I-495 N, MA 25 S, to Cape Cod. I-195 begins/ends on I-495, exit 1.
21(39) MA 28, to Wareham, **N** BB's Rest., Casa Cancun, Cosi, Gourmet Garden, Longhorn Steaks, Qdoba Mexican, Red Robin, ALDI, AutoZone, GNC, JC Penney, LL Bean, Lowe's, Michael's, Old Navy, PetCo, Staples, Target, TJ Maxx, Verizon, Walmart/Subway, **S** Gateway Star/dsl, Mobil/Dunkin/Subway/dsl, 99 Rest., Five Guys, Saga Fusion, TownPlace Suites, H
37mm parking area eb, **boatramp, info**
36mm Sippican River
20(35) MA 105, to Marion, **S** RV camping(seasonal)
19b a(31) to Mattapoisett, **S** Mobil, Dunkin', Nick's Pizza, Ying Dynasty, USPO
18(26) MA 240 S, to Fairhaven, **S** 7-11, 99 Rest., Burger King, Frontera Grill, Jake's Diner, McDonald's, PapaGino's, Pasta House, Riccardi's Italian, Subway, Taco Bell, Wendy's, Hampton Inn, $Tree, AutoZone, Brahmin Handbags, Buick/GMC, GNC, Marshall's, Mazda, Staples, Stop&Shop/gas, Sullivan Tire, TownFair Tire, Walgreens, Walmart/Subway

25.5mm Acushnet River

NEW BEDFORD

17(24) Coggeshall St, from wb only, same as 16, New Bedford, **N** 7-11/gas, Petro/dsl, Sunoco, HoneyDew Donuts, Little Caesar's, McDonald's, Popeyes, Subway, Taco Bell, GNC, Market Basket Foods, URGENT CARE
16(23) Washburn St(from eb), **N** Sunoco, McDonald's
15(22) MA 18 S, New Bedford, **S** Mutual, hist dist, to downtown, Whaling Museum
14(21) Penniman St(from eb), New Bedford, downtown
13b a(20) MA 140, **N** **S** Sunoco, Buttonwood Park/zoo, CVS Drug, H, Shaw's Foods, Walgreens
12b a(19) N Dartmouth, **S** Mobil/dsl, Mobil/Subway/dsl, Speedway, 99 Rest., Applebee's, Azuma Asian, Buffalo Wild Wings, Burger King, Chipotle, ChuckeCheese, Coldstone, Dunkin', Five Guys, Friendly's, IHOP, Jimmy's Pizza, McDonald's, Olive Garden, Panera Bread, Peking Garden, Starbucks, Subway, Taco Bell, TGIFriday's, Tropical Smoothie, TX Roadhouse, Wendy's, Residence Inn, $Tree, AT&T, Barnes&Noble, Best Buy, BJ's Whse/gas, Chevrolet, Dick's, Firestone/auto, Home Depot, JC Penney, Jo-Ann, Kia, Kohl's, Lowe's, Macy's, Michael's, Nissan, Old Navy, PetCo, Stop&Shop/gas, Target, TJ Maxx, TownFair Tire, Toyota, USPO, Walgreens, Walmart
11b a(17) Reed Rd, to Dartmouth, **S** Shell, Dunkin'
10(16) MA 88 S, to US 6, same as 9, Westport, **S** Cumberland, CVS Drug

FALL RIVER

9(15.5) MA 24 N(from nb), Stanford Rd, Westport, **S** Rte 6 Gas, Supreme, Valero, Dunkin', Galley Grill, Hampton Inn, White's H ity
8b MA 24 N, (exits left from eb)
8a(15) MA 24 S, Fall River, Westport
7(14) MA 81 S, Plymouth Ave, Fall River, **N** Speedway, 99 Rest., Boston Mkt, Burger King, Dunkin', HoneyDew Donuts, KFC, Subway, Wendy's, CVS Drug, H, Hyundai, **S** Gulf, Shell, Applebee's, McDonald's, Stop&Shop, Sullivan Tire, Walgreens
6(13.5) Pleasant St, Fall River, downtown
5(13) MA 79, MA 138, to Taunton, **S** 7-11, Speedway/dsl, Dunkin'
12mm Assonet Bay
4b a(10) MA 103, to Swansea, Somerset, **N** Wilbur's, Rogers Rest., repair, vet, **S** Shell, Jillian's Grill, Riverview Inn
3(8) US 6, to MA 118, Swansea, Rehoboth, **N** Mobil/Dunkin', Speedway, Five Guys, Friendly's, McDonald's, Subway, Thai Taste, Wendy's, $Tree, AT&T, BigLots, Firestone/auto, Jo-Ann Fabrics, Marshall's, PetSmart, Price Rite Foods, Target, Verizon, Walmart/Subway, **S** Cumberland Farms/dsl, Umi Japanese, Holiday Inn Express, Rodeway Inn, Kia, NAPA, USPO
5.5mm parking area wb
2(5) MA 136, to Newport, **S** Mobil/24hr, Shell/24hr, Dunkin', McDonald's, Subway, CVS Drug, Toyota
3mm weigh sta eb
1(1) MA 114A, to Seekonk, **N** Exxon, Global/Subway/dsl, Shell/dsl, 99 Rest., Dunkin', Newport Creamery, Motel 6, vet, **S** Mobil/24hr, Speedway/dsl, Stop&Shop Gas/repair, Sunoco, Applebee's, Buffalo Wild Wings, Burger King, Chick-fil-A, Chili's, Chipotle, Dunkin', Five Guys, Ichigo Ichie Japanese, IHOP, Joe's Kitchen, Longhorn Steaks, McDonald's, Moe's SW, Outback Steaks, Panera Bread, Papa John's, PapaGino's, Rebeco Mexican, Starbucks, Subway, Taco Bell, TGIFriday's, Wendy's, Best Western, Clarion, Extended Stay America, Hampton Inn, Knights Inn, Mary's Motel, Quality Inn, $Tree, Acura, Advance Parts, AT&T, Best Buy, BigLots, BJ's/gas, Bob's Stores, Dick's, Firestone/auto, GNC, Hobby Lobby, Home Depot, Kohl's, Lowe's, Michael's, PepBoys, Petco, Staples, Stop&Shop Foods,

= gas = food = lodging = other = rest stop

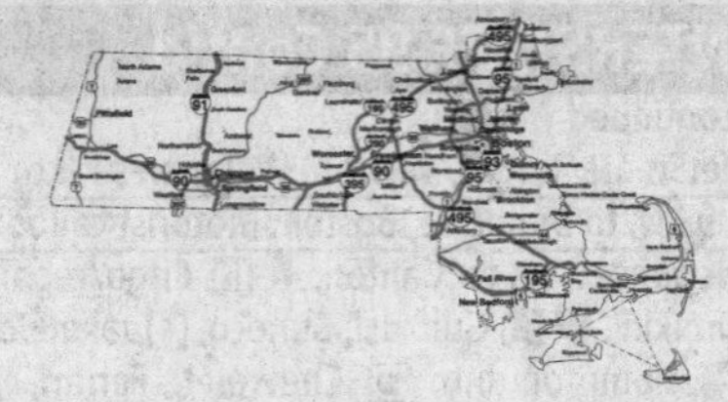

INTERSTATE 195 MA Cont'd

Exit	Services
1(1)	Continued Target, TJMaxx, TownFair Tire, Verizon, Walmart
0mm	Massachusetts/Rhode Island state line. Exits 8-1 are in RI.
8(5)	US 1A N, Pawtucket, S Mobil/dsl, Dunkin', Subway, CVS Drug, Walgreens
7(4)	US 6 E, CT 114 S, to Barrington, Seekonk
6(3)	Broadway Ave, N Monro
5(2.5)	RI 103 E, Warren Ave
4(2)	US 44 E, RI 103 E, Taunton Ave, Warren Ave
3(1.5)	Gano St, S EVC, Hilton Garden
2(1)	US 44 W, Wickenden St, India Pt, downtown , N Shell/dsl, S EVC, Hilton Garden
1(.5)	Providence, downtown
0mm	I-195 begins/ends on I-95, exit 20 in Providence, RI. Exits 1-8 are in RI.

INTERSTATE 290

Exit	Services
26b a(20)	I-495. I-290 begins/ends on I-495, exit 25.
25b a(17)	Solomon Pond Mall Rd, to Berlin, N EVC, Bertucci's, Olive Garden, TGIFriday's, Quality Inn, Residence Inn, Best Buy, JC Penney, Macy's, Old Navy, Target, S Cafe Norma
24(15)	Church St, Northborough
23b a(13)	MA 140, Boylston, N Gulf/Dunkin'/dsl, Shell/dsl
22(11)	Main St, Worchester, N Dunkin'
21(10)	Plantation St(from eb), N Dunkin', same as 20
20(8)	MA 70, Lincoln St, Burncoat St, N Gulf/Subway/dsl, Shell/dsl, Crown Chicken, Denny's, Dunkin', Five Guys, KFC, Kyoto, McDonald's, PapaGino's/D'Angelo, Ruby Tuesday, Subway, Taco Bell, TX Roadhouse, Wendy's, Quality Inn, Suburban Inn, $Tree, AlLDI, AT&T, AutoZone, Barnes&Noble, CVS Drug, Dick's, Kohl's, Lowe's, Staples, Stop&Shop, Target, URGENT CARE, USPO, Walgreens
19(7)	I-190 N, MA 12
18	MA 9, Framington, Ware, N Worcester, S H
16	Central St, Worcester, N 99 Rest., Starbucks, Hilton Garden, Holiday Inn Express, USPO
14	MA 122, Barre, Worcester, downtown
13	MA 122A, Vernon St, Worcester, downtown
12	MA 146 S, to Millbury
11	Southbridge St, College Square, N Shell/dsl, Culpepper's Cafe, Family$, Wendy's
10	MA 12 N(from wb), Hope Ave
9	Auburn St, to Auburn, E Shell, Arby's, Auburn Town Pizza, Dunkin', McDonald's, Outback, PapaGino's, Starbucks, Subway, Yong Shing, Comfort Inn, Holiday Inn Express(1mi), La Quinta, Acura, AutoZone, Big Lots, Firestone/auto, Macy's, Midas, Monro, Petco, Shaw's Foods, Staples, TownFair Tire, USPO, Verizon
8	MA 12 S(from sb), Webster, W Shell, Holiday Inn Express
7	I-90, E to Boston, W to Springfield. I-290 begins/ends on I-90.

INTERSTATE 395

Exit	Services
12.5mm	I-395 begins/ends on I-290, exit 10.
7(12)	to I-90(MA Tpk), MA 12, same as 6b, E Holiday Inn Express, W Shell, Bentley Cafe
6b a(11)	US 20, E Cumberland, Major League Roast Beef, Tiny Tim's, NAPA, truck tires/repair, VW, W Shell, Applebee's, Chuck's Steakhouse, D'angelo, Dunkin', Friendly's, Wendy's, Fairfield Inn, Hampton Inn, BJ's Whse/dsl, Buick/Cadillac/GMC, Chevrolet, CVS, Ford, Home Depot, Hyundai, Nissan, TJ Maxx
5(8)	Depot Rd, N Oxford
4b a(6)	Sutton Ave, to Oxford, E Shell/Dunkin'/dsl, $Tree, Home Depot, MktBasket Foods, URGENT CARE, W Cumberland Farms, Mobil/dsl, Dunkin', McDonald's, NE Pizza, Subway, CVS Drug
3(4)	Cudworth Rd, to N Webster, S Oxford
2(3)	MA 16, to Webster, E RV Camping, Subaru, W BP/repair, Gulf, Sunoco, Burger King, D'angelo, Dunkin', Empire Wok, Friendly's, HoneyDew Donuts, KFC/Taco Bell, Little Caesar's, McDonald's, Mexicali Grill, Panera Bread, PapaGino's, Wendy's, $Tree, Advance Parts, AutoZone, Big Lots, CVS Drug, Ford, GNC, H, O'Reilly Parts, PriceChopper Foods, Verizon, Walgreens
1(1)	MA 193, to Webster, E H, W Mobil/dsl, Golden Greek Rest., Wind Tiki Chinese, Goodyear/auto
0mm	Massachusetts/Connecticut state line

INTERSTATE 495 MA

Exit	Services
119	I-495 begins/ends on I-95, exit 59.
55(119)	MA 110(from nb, no return), to I-95 S, E EVC, Irving/Circle K, Mobil, Sunoco/dsl, Acapulco Mexican, Burger King, Dunkin', Friendly's, McDonald's, Subway, Fairfield Inn, Hampton Inn, AT&T, Chevrolet, Stop&Shop, Verizon, W Cumberland Farms/dsl, CVS, NAPA
54(118)	MA 150, to Amesbury, W RV camping
53(115)	Broad St, Merrimac, W Osaka, Dunkin'
114mm	parking area sb, **litter barrels (6AM-8PM)**, **restrooms**
52(111)	MA 110, to Haverhill, E H, W Mobil, Racing Mart, Biggart Ice Cream, Dunkin'
110mm	parking area nb, litter barrels
51(109)	MA 125, to Haverhill, E Gulf, Mobil, Bros Pizza, China King, Dunkin', H, W Mobil/dsl, Applebee's, Burger King, Dunkin', Five Guys, Friendly's, Li's Asian, Longhorn Steaks, Lucky Corner Chinese, McDonald's, Mr Mikes Grill, Starbucks, Taco Bell, Wendy's, Monro Service
50(107)	MA 97, to Haverhill, W Starbucks, Ford, Target
49(106)	MA 110, to Haverhill, E Cumberland Farms, Sunoco, 99 Rest., Athens Pizza, Dunkin', McDonald's, Oriental Garden, PapaGino's, Best Western, Hampton Inn, Buick/Chevrolet/GMC, Chrysler/Dodge/Jeep, CVS Drug, Marshall's, MktBasket Foods, Tire Whse, Walgreens
105.8mm	Merrimac River
48(105.5)	MA 125, to Bradford, E BJ's Whse/Subway/gas
47(105)	MA 213, to Methuen, W EVC, Haffner's, Shell, Burger King, Chick-fil-A, Chipotle, ChuckeCheese, Joe's Grill, Margaritas Mexican, McDonald's, Olive Garden, Starbucks, TGIFriday's, Wendy's, Home Depot, H, Marshall's, MktBasket Foods, Old Navy, Stop&Shop, Target, The Mann Orchards/Bakery, Walmart/Subway
46(104)	MA 110, E Giovanni's Deli, Sunoco, Tekila's Mexican, W H
45(103)	Marston St, to Lawrence, W Chevrolet, Honda, Kia, Nissan, VW
44(102)	Merrimac St, to Lawrence
43(101)	Mass Ave, W Mobil
42(100)	MA 114, E Gulf, Mobil, Wave, Bollywood Grill, Boston Mkt, Burger King, Burtons Grill, Chipotle Mexican, Dunkin', Friendly's, Lee Chin Chinese, Panera Bread, Holiday Inn Express, Ace Hardware, AT&T, CVS Drug, Kohl's, MktBasket Foods, PetCo, Staples, TJ Maxx, Walgreens,

INTERSTATE 495 MA Cont'd

CHELMSFORD

42(100) Continued
Gas'n Go, Dunkin', KFC, Little Caesar's, Starbucks, Subway, Taco Bell, Wendy's, Advance Parts, America's Food Basket, Family$, H, Marshall's, Monro Service, O'Reilly Parts/VIP Service, vet

41(99) MA 28, to Andover, E Dunkin', Cadillac/Chevrolet

40b a(98) I-93, N to Methuen, S to Boston

39(94) MA 133, to Dracut, E Speedway, Longhorn Steaks, McDonald's, Extended Stay America, W Mobil/Circle K/dsl, Cracker Barrel, Wendy's, Fairfield Inn, Holiday Inn/rest., Residence Inn, TownePlace Suites

38(93) MA 38, to Lowell, E Cumberland Farms/dsl, EVC, Petroil/dsl, 99 Rest., Applebee's, Burger King, Dunkin', Harrow's Chicken Pie, IHOP, Jade East, Vic's Waffle House, Motel 6, AT&T, Home Depot, Honda, TownFair Tire, Toyota, URGENT CARE, Verizon, Walmart, W Citgo, Mobil, NTB, Sunoco, Dunkin', Jillie's Rest., McDonald's, Milan Pizza, Wendy's, Buick/GMC, Chevrolet, Chrysler/Dodge/Jeep, CVS Drug, Hannaford Foods, Hogan Tire/auto, Marshall's, Mazda, MktBasket Foods

37(91) Woburn St, to S Lowell, W Gulf/Dunkin'/Subway

35c(90) to Lowell SP, Lowell ConX, W Chili's, Outback Steaks, Courtyard, Kia/VW, Lincoln, Shop&Save, Target, Walgreens

35b a(89) US 3, S to Burlington, N to Nashua, NH

34(88) MA 4, Chelmsford, E Ampet, EVC, Mobil, Sunoco, 110 Grill, Domino's, Dunkin', Jimmy's Pizza, PapaGino's, Radisson, CVS Drug, USPO, Walgreens, W Shell, Moonstone's Rest., Best Western+

33 MA 4, from nb, N Chelmsford

87mm rest area both lanes, **(8AM-8PM)**, **full facilities**, **litter barrels**, **vending**

32(83) Boston Rd, to MA 225, E Cumberland Farms, EVC, Gulf, Mobil, British Beer Co, Burton's Grill, Chili's, Chipotle, Dunkin', Evviva Trattoria, Five Guys, GNC, McDonald's, Panera Bread, Starbucks, Subway, Hampton Inn, Regency Inn, Residence Inn, CVS Drug, Jo-Ann Fabrics, Marshall's, MktBasket Foods, Petco, to Nashoba Valley Ski Area, Verizon, vet, Walgreens, Whole Foods Mkt

HARVARD

31(80) MA 119, to Groton, E Gulf, Mobil/dsl, Shell/Dunkin', Dunkin', Littleton Subs, Subway, Yangtze River Chinese, Aubuchon Hardware, CVS Drug, Donelan's Foods, Toyota, Verizon, vet, W Anthony's Pizza, Moe's SW, Starbucks, Courtyard, AT&T, Market Basket, Town Fair Tire

30(78) MA 110, to Littleton, E EVC, Littleton Cafe, W Mobil/Dunkin', vet, H

29b a(77) MA 2, to Leominster, E to Walden Pond St Reserve

28(75) MA 111, to Boxborough, Harvard, E Gulf/Dunkin', Bravo Pizza, Boxboro Regency, W vet

27(70) MA 117, to Bolton, E Mobil/dsl, Dunkin', Subway, W vet

26(68) MA 62, to Berlin, E Gulf/Dunkin', Tesla EVC, 110 Grill, Panera Bread, Qdoba, Subway, Holiday Inn Express, BJ's Whse/gas, Cabela's, GNC, Lowe's, Market Basket, Michael's, PetSmart, TJ Maxx, URGENT CARE, Verizon, W Mobil/dsl

66mm Assabet River

25b(64) I-290, to Worchester

25a to MA 85, Marlborough, E Cumberland Farms, Mobil/dsl, Stop&Shop Gas, 99 Rest., Applebee's, Burger King, Checkerboards Rest., Dunkin', HoneyDew Donuts, KFC/Taco Bell, McDonald's, PapaGino's, $Tree, AutoZone, Chevrolet, CVS Drug, GMC Trucks, Hogan Tire/auto, PetCo, Shaw's Foods, Stop&Shop, Verizon, Walgreens, Walmart/Subway, W Residence Inn

MARLBOROUGH

24b a(63) US 20, to Northboro, Marlborough, E Mobil/dsl, D'angelo, Dunkin', Lake Williams Pizza, Holiday Inn, W EVC, EVC, Gulf/Dunkin', Shell, 99 Rest., Boston Mkt, Chick-fil-A, China Taste, Chipotle Mexican, Five Guys, Friendly's, Japan 1, Jersey Mike's, Longhorn Steaks, McDonald's, Panera Bread, Qdoba, Starbucks, Subway, Wendy's, Best Western, Courtyard, Embassy Suites, Extended Stay America, Fairfield Inn, Hampton Inn, Hyatt Place, $Tree, AT&T, Hannaford Foods, Sullivan Tire/auto, URGENT CARE

23c(60) Simrano Dr, Marlborough

23b a(59) MA 9, to Shrewsbury, Framingham, E Cumberland/Dunkin', Gulf, Wendy's, Red Roof Inn, Cadillac, Volvo, W Mobil/dsl, Shell, Bertucci's, Chateau Rest., Chipotle Mexican, Dunkin', Harry's Rest., Mandarin, McDonald's, Starbucks, Subway, Courtyard, Doubletree Inn, Extended Stay America, Extended Stay America(2), Extended Stay America(3), Hampton Inn, Residence Inn, Buick/GMC, CarMax, Chrysler/Dodge/Jeep, H, Marshall's, Staples, Stop&Shop, VW

22(58) I-90, MA TPK, E to Boston, W to Albany

21b a(54) MA 135, to Hopkinton, Upton, E Cumberland, Mobil/Dunkin', 110 Grill, Dynasty Chinese, Hiller's Pizza, Starbucks, Verizon

20(50) MA 85, to Milford, E Dunkin', W Gulf/dsl/LP, Mobil/dsl, 99 Rest., Pizza 85/deli, TGIFriday's, Wendy's, Best Western, Courtyard, Fairfield Inn, Holiday Inn Express, Best Buy, H, Lowe's, PetCo, Staples, Target, Toyota

19(48) MA 109, to Milford, W Mobil/Circle K/dsl, Shell, Applebee's, Burger King, Chipotle, Dunkin', Five Guys, IHOP, KFC, McDonald's, Panera Bread, PapaGino's, Red Heat Tavern, Starbucks, Subway, Doubletree, La Quinta, $General, $Tree, AutoZone, Big Y Foods, CVS Drug, Jo-Ann Fabrics, Kohl's, Stop&Shop, TJ Maxx, TownFair Tire

BELLINGHAM

18(46) MA 126, to Bellingham, E Chili's, McDonald's, Moe's SW, Barnes&Noble, Michael's, MktBasket Foods, Old Navy, Staples, Verizon, Walmart/Subway, Whole Foods Mkt, W Mobil, Speedway/dsl, Sunoco/dsl, Chicago Grill, Dunkin', Outback Steaks, Home Depot, PetSmart

17(44) MA 140, to Franklin, Bellingham, E BP/7-11, Mobil/dsl, Shell/dsl, URGENT CARE, 3 Rest., British Beer Co, Burger King, Chipotle, Dunkin', Firehouse Subs, Five Guys, HoneyDew Donuts, Longhorn Steaks, Panera Bread, PapaGino's, Pepper Terrace Thai, Starbucks, Subway, Taco Bell, Wendy's, AT&T, AutoZone, Buick/GMC, CVS Drug, GNC, Marshall's, Midas, Stop&Shop, Verizon, W Stop&Shop Gas, 99 Rest., Ichigo Ichie Hibachi, Residence Inn, BJ's Whse/Subway/gas

16(42) King St, to Franklin, E BP/7-11, Dunkin', King St Cafe, Spruce Pond Creamery, Hampton Inn, W Hawthorn Suites

15(39) MA 1A, to Plainville, Wrentham, E repair, Assisi Pizza, W Mobil/dsl, Chicago Grill, Cracker Barrel, Dunkin', Ruby Tuesday, Premium Outlets/famous brands

14b a(37) US 1, to N Attleboro, E Shell/dsl, Luciano's Rest., Arbor Motel, Bass Pro Shops(4mi), W Mobil, Chili's, Dunkin', Panera Bread, Holiday Inn Express, casino, Lowe's, NTB, Pete's RV Ctr, Stop&Shop, Target, TJ Maxx, vet

13(32) I-95, N to Boston, S to Providence, W H

12(30) MA 140, to Mansfield, E Tesla EVC, Bertucci's Italian, Buffalo Wild Wings, Chipotle Mexican, Coldstone, Dunkin', Longhorn Steaks, Papa Gino's, Qdoba Mexican, Sake Japanese, TGIFriday's, AT&T, Best Buy, Firestone/auto, GNC, Home Depot, Kohl's, LL Bean, Michael's, PetCo, Shaw's Foods, Staples, Verizon

11(29) MA 140 S(from sb), W Cumberland, Mobil, Best Sandwich, Dunkin', Fiesta Mexican, Mandarin Chinese, McDonald's, $Tree, Roche Bros Mkt

10(26) MA 123, to Norton, E Dunkin', QuickStop, W H

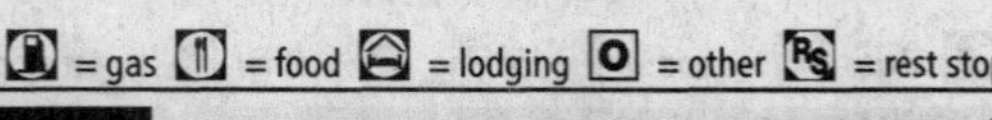

BOSTON

INTERSTATE 495 MA Cont'd

Exit #	Services
9(24)	Bay St, to Taunton, E Chateau Rest., W Dunkin', Jaybo Cafe, Ruby Tuesday, Subway, Wendy's, Extended Stay America, Holiday Inn, $Tree, BJ's Whse, Tadeschi Foods, Watson Pond SP
8(22)	MA 138, to Raynham, E Mobil/dsl, Speedway/dsl, HoneyDew Donuts, W AARC/dsl/repair, Gulf/Dunkin', Stop'n Go/dsl, Brothers Pizza, Cape Cod Cafe, D'angelo, HoneyDew Donuts, Lucky Corner Chinese, McDonald's, PieZoni's Pizza, Ace Hardware, H, Mkt Basket Foods, O'Reilly Parts, USPO, Walmart
7b a(19)	MA 24, to Fall River, Boston, E Mobil/dsl, Burger King
18mm	weigh sta both lanes
17mm	Taunton River
6(15)	US 44, to Middleboro, E Super/dsl, Burger King, Dunkin', Friendly's, PapaGino's, Subway, W Irving/Circle K/Dunkin'/dsl, Fairfield Inn, Holiday Inn Express
5(14)	MA 18, to Lakeville, E Shell, Super/dsl, D'Angelo, Dave's Diner, Harry's Grille, Lorenzo's Rest, PapaGino's, Persy's Place Cafe, CVS Drug, Kelly's Tire, Trucchi's Mkt,

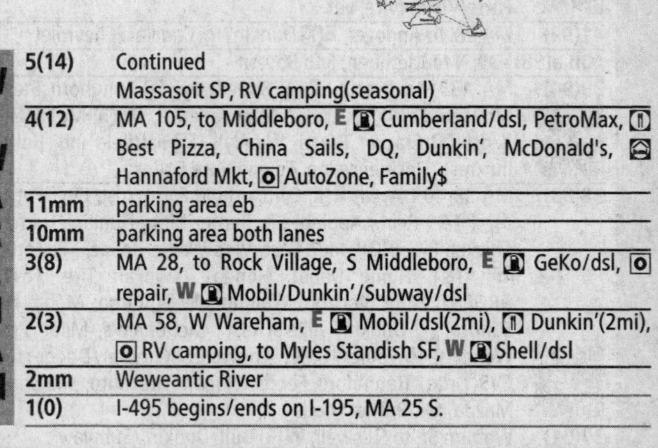

WAREHAM

Exit #	Services
5(14)	Continued Massasoit SP, RV camping(seasonal)
4(12)	MA 105, to Middleboro, E Cumberland/dsl, PetroMax, Best Pizza, China Sails, DQ, Dunkin', McDonald's, Hannaford Mkt, AutoZone, Family$
11mm	parking area eb
10mm	parking area both lanes
3(8)	MA 28, to Rock Village, S Middleboro, E GeKo/dsl, repair, W Mobil/Dunkin'/Subway/dsl
2(3)	MA 58, W Wareham, E Mobil/dsl(2mi), Dunkin'(2mi), RV camping, to Myles Standish SF, W Shell/dsl
2mm	Weweantic River
1(0)	I-495 begins/ends on I-195, MA 25 S.

NOTES

MA

MICHIGAN

INTERSTATE 69

Exit #	Services
199	Lp 69(from eb, no return), to Port Huron, S [gas] Mobil/dsl, Speedway, [food] $General, Arby's, Burger King, Jimmy John's, KFC, Little Caesar's, McDonald's, Subway, Taco Bell, Tim Horton's, Wendy's, [other] Advance Parts, AutoZone, Kroger/gas, repair, Sam's Club/gas, to Port Huron, USPO
198.5mm	I-69 E and I-94 E merge, see I-94 exits 274-275mm.
198	I-94, to Detroit and Canada
196	Wadhams Rd, N [gas] BP/Wendy's, Marathon, Speedy Q/dsl, [food] Hungry Howie's, McDonald's, Peking Kitchen, Subway, Taco Bell, [other] KOA(1mi), Vinckier Foods, Wadham's Drugs, S [gas] Pilot/Subway/dsl/scales/24hr, [other] golf
194	Taylor Rd, N [other] Goodells CP, RV camping
189	Wales Center Rd, to Goodells, S [other] golf
184	MI 19, to Emmett, N [gas] Sunoco/dsl/scales/24hr, [other] repair, USPO, S [gas] Marathon/dsl/24hr
180	Riley Center Rd, N [other] KOA
	IMLAY CITY
176	Capac Rd, N [gas] BP/dsl/scales, Love's/Chester's/McDonald's/dsl/scales/24hr
174mm	**full [handicap] facilities, litter barrels, petwalk, [phone], [picnic], [RS] wb, vending**
168	MI 53, Imlay City, N [gas] BP/dsl, Speedway/dsl, [food] Big Boy, Burger King, DQ, Hungry Howie's, Jet's Pizza, John's Country Kitchen, Little Caesar's, Lucky's Steaks, McDonald's, New China, Taco Bell, Wah Wong Chinese, Wendy's/Tim Horton, [lodging] Days Inn, M53 Motel, Super 8, [other] AutoZone, Chevrolet, Chrysler/Dodge/Jeep, CVS Drug, Ford, GNC, Kroger/dsl, NAPA, O'Reilly Parts, Verizon
163	Lake Pleasant Rd, to Attica
160mm	**full [handicap] facilities, litter barrels, petwalk, [phone], [picnic], [RS] eb, vending**
159	Wilder Rd
158mm	Flint River
	LAPEER
155	MI 24, Lapeer, N [gas] Speedy Q/dsl, Sunoco/dsl, [food] Apple Tree Rest., Applebee's, Arby's, Blind Fish Rest., Brian's Rest., Buffalo Wild Wings, Burger King, Checkers, DQ, Jet's Pizza, Jimmy John's, KFC, Leo's Coney Island, Little Caesar's, Mancino's, McDonald's, Nick's Grill, Sonic, Starbucks, Subway, Taco Bell, Tim Horton, Wah Wong Chinese, Wendy's, [lodging] Best Western, Holiday Inn Express, [other] $Tree, ALDI, AT&T, AutoZone, Belle Tire, Home Depot, Honda, [H], Kohl's, Kroger/gas, Marshall's, Meijer/dsl, Michael's, O'Reilly Parts, Office Depot, st police, URGENT CARE, Verizon, vet, Walgreens, S [gas] Mobil/dsl, [other] Chrysler/Dodge/Jeep, Harley Davidson
153	Lake Nepessing Rd, S [other] camping, golf, to Thumb Correctional
	DAVISON
149	Elba Rd, N [other] Torzewski CP, S Country Mkt, RV/truck repair
145	MI 15, Davison, N [gas] Marathon, Speedway/dsl, Sunoco/dsl, [food] Apollo Rest., Applebee's, Arby's, Big Boy, Burger King, Chee Kong Chinese, Flag City Diner, Hungry Howie's, Italia Gardens, Jimmy John's, KFC, Little Caesar's, Lucky's Steaks, McDonald's, Pizza Hut, Senor Lucky, Subway, Taco Bell, Tim Horton, Tropical Smoothie, [lodging] Best Western, [other] AutoValue Parts, Buick/GMC, Davison Automotive, GNC, Monro Tire, Verizon, Walgreens, YaYa Chicken, S [gas] Mobil/dsl, [food] Sicilian Pizza, [other] vet
143	Irish Rd, N [gas] Speedway/dsl, [other] Menard's, S [gas] Sunoco/McDonald's/24hr, [other] Meijer/dsl/e85
	FLINT
141	Belsay Rd, Flint, N [gas] Marathon/Wendy's/dsl/24hr, Mobil, [food] Halo Burger, KFC, McDonald's, Subway, Taco Bell, [other] $Tree,

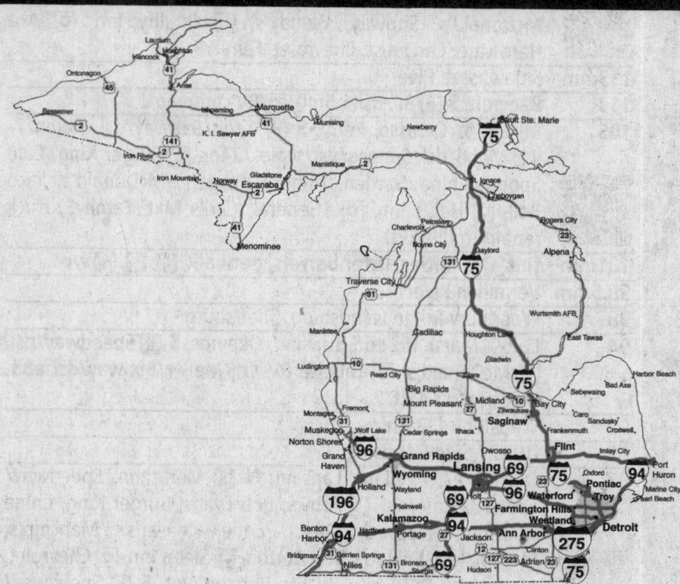

Exit #	Services
141	Continued Walmart/Subway, S [gas] Sunoco/Tubby's/dsl, [food] Little Caesar's
139	Center Rd, Flint, N [gas] Speedway/dsl, [food] Applebee's, Domino's, El Cozumel Mexican, Empire Wok, Halo Burger, Leo's Coney Island, Starbucks, Subway, Tim Horton, [other] AlLDI, Big Lots, Discount Tire, GNC, Home Depot, JC Penney, Jo-Ann Fabrics, Staples, S [food] China 1, Coney Island, DQ, Hungry Howie's, McDonald's, Red Baron Rest., Subway, [lodging] Burton Inn, [other] $Tree, AT&T, Belle Tire, Meijer/dsl, TJ Maxx, Verizon
	FLINT
138	MI 54, Dort Hwy, N [gas] BP/dsl, Speedway/dsl, Sunoco/dsl, [food] Big John's Rest., Little Caesar's, Rally's, Tom's Coney Island, YaYa's Chicken, [other] $General, [H], KanRock Tires, Save-a-Lot, Walgreens, S [gas] Marathon, Marathon, Sunoco, [food] American Diner Coney Island, Arby's, Big John Steak, Burger King, Church's TX Chicken, Empress of China, KFC, McDonald's, Taco Bell, The Coney Grill, [lodging] Travel Inn, [other] $General, Advance Parts, AutoZone, Burton Tire/auto, Family$, O'Reilly Parts, Tuffy Auto, U-Haul, Walgreens
137	I-475, UAW Fwy, to Detroit, Saginaw
136	Saginaw St, Flint, N [gas] Sunoco/dsl, [other] [H], U MI at Flint
135	Hammerberg Rd, industrial area
133b a	I-75, S to Detroit, N to Saginaw, US 23 S to Ann Arbor
	DURAND
131	MI 121, to Bristol Rd, N [food] Bar Louie, BD Mongolian BBQ, Buffalo Wild Wing, Casa Real, Chili's, Chipotle, ChuckeCheese, Famous Dave's BBQ, Golden Corral, Golden Moon Chinese, Halo Burger, Hooters, Jimmy John's, Leo's Coney Island, LJ Silver, Logan's Roadhouse, Olive Garden, Osaka Buffet, Outback Steaks, Panda Express, Panera Bread, Red Robin, Subway, Taco Bell, Telly's Coney Island, TX Roadhouse, [other] $Tree, AT&T, Barnes&Noble, Belle Tire, Best Buy, BigLots, Hobby Lobby, JC Penney, Jo-Ann Fabrics, Kohl's, Macy's, Michael's, Old Navy, PetCo, PetSmart, Target, TJ Maxx, USPO, Valley Tire, Verizon
129	Miller Rd, S [food] Arby's, Burger King, McDonald's, Subway, Taco Bell, Wendy's, [other] Kroger/gas, O'Reilly Parts
128	Morrish Rd, N [other] Meijer/dsl/e85, S [gas] Admiral, Mobil/dsl, [food] Hungry Howie's
126mm	**full [handicap] facilities, info, litter barrels, petwalk, [phone], [picnic], [RS] eb**
123	MI 13, to Saginaw, Lennon, N [gas] Speedway/dsl, [other] USPO
118	MI 71, to Corunna, Durand, N [other] Durand Automotive,

INTERSTATE 69 Cont'd

BANCROFT

118 Continued
Shell/dsl, Valero, China House, Hungry Howie's, McDonald's, Subway, Wendy's, Quality Inn, Ace Hardware, CarQuest, Chevrolet, Family$, golf

115mm Shiawassee River

113 Bancroft, S BP/dsl(1.5mi), RV camping

105 MI 52, to Owosso, Perry, S Citgo/Subway/dsl, Exxon/7-11, Mobil/dsl, Sunoco/dsl/scales/24hr, Burger King, Cafe Sports, China Garden, Hungry Howie's, McDonald's, Taco Bell, Heb's Inn, $General, Carl's Mkt, Family$, truck repair(1mi), USPO

101mm full facilities, litter barrels, petwalk, wb

98.5mm Vermilion River

98 Woodbury Rd, to Laingsburg, Shaftsburg

BATH

94 Lp 69, Marsh Rd, to E Lansing, Okemos, S Speedway/dsl, McDonald's, Gillette RV Ctr, Meijer/Subway/dsl/e85, Monticello's Mkt

92 Webster Rd, Bath

89 US 127 S, to E Lansing

87 Old US 27, to Clare, Lansing, N Marathon, Speedway/Speedy's Café/dsl, Arby's, Bob Evans, Burger King, China Gourmet, FlapJack Rest., Little Ceasar's, Mancino's, McDonald's, Subway, Tim Horton, Sleep Inn, Chevrolet, Meijer/dsl, Price Rite RV Ctr, Verizon, vet, S Speedway/dsl, American Inn

85 DeWitt Rd, to DeWitt

84 Airport Rd

81 I-96(from sb), W to Grand Rapids, Grand River Ave, Frances Rd, W Flying J/Denny's/dsl/24hr, Love's/Hardee's/Subway/dsl/scales/24hr

93b a MI 43, Lp 69, Saginaw Hwy, to Grand Ledge, N Shell, Speedway/dsl, Applebee's, Buffalo Wild Wings, Burger King, Carrabba's, Cheddar's, Chick-fil-A, Chipotle, Denny's, Finley's Grill, Frank's Grill, Hibachi Grill, Honeybaked Ham, Houlihan's, Logan's Roadhouse, Longhorn Steaks, McDonald's, Outback Steaks, Panera Bread, Qdoba, Red Robin, Subway, Comfort Inn, Fairfield Inn, Hampton Inn, Motel 6, Quality Inn, Ramada Inn, Red Roof Inn, Residence Inn, $Tree, ALDI, AT&T, Barnes&Noble, Best Buy, BigLots, Chrysler/Dodge/Jeep, Hobby Lobby, H, JC Penney, Kohl's, Kroger/dsl, Macy's, Meijer/dsl/24hr, Target, TJ Maxx, vet, Walgreens, S QD, Shell/Dunkin', Sunoco/McDonald's, Arby's, Biggby Coffee, Bob Evans, Cancun Mexican, Cracker Barrel, Culver's, Steak'n Shake, SpringHill Suites, Belle Tire, Buick/GMC, Discount Tire, Lowe's, Mazda/Volvo, Menards, Michael's, PetSmart, Staples, Walmart/Subway

95 I-496, to Lansing

72 I-96, E to Detroit, W to Grand Rapids

70 Lansing Rd

68mm full facilities, litter barrels, petwalk, nb, vending

CHARLOTTE

66 MI 100, to Grand Ledge, Potterville, W BP/dsl, Shell/Subway/dsl, Charlie's Grill, McDonald's, to Fox Co Park

61 Lansing Rd, E Murphy USA/dsl, Applebee's, Comfort Inn, $Tree, AT&T, AutoZone, Buick/Chevrolet/GMC, Verizon, Walmart/Subway, W QD, Speedway/dsl, Arby's, Big Boy, Biggby Coffee, Burger King, Jersey Subs, Jet's Pizza, KFC, Little Caesar's, McDonald's, Pizza Hut, Rally's, Taco Bell, Tasty Twist, Top Chinese, Wendy's, Ace Hardware, Advance Parts, Family$, Ford, H, NAPA, O'Reilly Parts, Tire City, vet

60 MI 50, Charlotte, E Holiday Inn Express, Meijer/dsl, URGENT CARE, W Admiral, Best Value Inn, H

57 Lp 69, Cochran Rd, to Charlotte

51 Ainger Rd, E gas, food, RV camping

OLIVET

48 MI 78, to Bellevue, Olivet, E Cenex/Subway/dsl, to Olivet Coll

42 N Drive N, Turkeyville Rd, W Osprey Grille

41mm full facilities, litter barrels, petwalk, sb

38 I-94, E to Detroit, W to Chicago

36 Michigan Ave, to Marshall, E Admiral, Citgo/dsl/e85, Shell/Subway/dsl, Applebee's, Arby's, Biggby Coffee, Little Caesar's, McDonald's, Pizza Hut, Speedy Chick, Starbucks, Taco Bell, Wendy's, Yin Hai Chinese, Quality Inn, $General, $Tree, Ace Hardware, AT&T, AutoZone, Chevrolet, Family Fare Mkt/gas, K-Mart, NAPA, O'Reilly Parts, Save-A-Lot, Tuffy Auto, Verizon, W Arbor Inn, Chrysler/Dodge/Jeep, H

32 F Drive S, E Shell/dsl, RV Camping

25 MI 60, to Three Rivers, Jackson, E BP/dsl, Sunoco/dsl, TA/Shell/Country Pride/dsl/scales/24hr/@, McDonald's, Subway, $General, Auto Value Parts, RV camping

COLDWATER

23 Tekonsha, W access to RV camping

16 Jonesville Rd, W Waffle Farm Camping(2mi)

13 US 12, to Quincy, Coldwater, E Speedway/dsl, Applebee's, Biggby Coffee, Bob Evans, Buffalo Wild Wings, Grand Buffet, Hampton Inn, Holiday Inn Express, Red Roof Inn, $Tree, AlLDI, AT&T, AutoZone, Belle Tire, BigLots, Buick/Chevrolet/GMC, GNC, Haylett RV Ctr, Home Depot, Meijer/dsl, Verizon, Walmart/Subway, W Citgo/dsl, Speedway/dsl, Arby's, Burger King, Coldwater Garden Rest., Cottage Inn Pizza, Culver's, Dickey's BBQ, Jimmy John's, KFC, Little Caesar's, McDonald's, Pizza Hut, Subway, Taco Bell, Best Western+, Quality Inn, auto repair, Ford/Lincoln, H, O'Reilly Parts, st police, Walgreens

10 Lp 69, Fenn Rd, to Coldwater, W Harbor Cove RV Park(4mi)

8mm weigh sta nb

6mm full facilities, litter barrels, petwalk, vending, Welcome Ctr nb

3 Copeland Rd, Kinderhook, W BP/dsl

0mm Michigan/Indiana state line

INTERSTATE 75

SAULT STE MARIE

395mm US/Canada Border, Michigan state line, I-75 begins/ends at toll bridge to Canada

394 Easterday Ave, E Citgo/Krist/dsl, Holiday Inn Express, Ramada Inn(2mi), H, to Lake Superior St U, W info, Welcome Ctr/, Admiral/dsl, Holiday/dsl/currency exchange

392 3 Mile Rd, Sault Ste Marie, E Admiral/dsl, Holiday/dsl, Marathon/dsl, Shell/dsl, Sunoco/dsl, Applebee's, Arby's, Asian Buffet, Buffalo Wild Wings, Burger King, Domino's, DQ, Fuji Steaks, Great Wall Chinese, Indo China Garden, Jimmy John's, Little Caesar's, McDonald's, Pizza Hut, Subway, Taco Bell, Wendy's, Best Value Inn, Best Western, Comfort Inn, Days Inn, Hampton Inn, Plaza Motel, Skyline Motel, Super 8, $Tree, Advance Parts, AT&T, AutoZone, BigLots, Buick/Chevrolet/GMC, Family$, Goodyear/auto, H, Jo-Ann Fabrics, Kohl's, NAPA, O'Reilly Parts, Save-a-Lot, Soo Locks Boat Tours, st police, TJ Maxx, Verizon, Walgreens,

INTERSTATE 75 Cont'd

Exit	Services
392	Continued Walmart/Subway, W Meijer/dsl
389mm	**full facilities, info, litter barrels, petwalk, nb**
386	MI 28, W to Brimley SP
379	Gaines Hwy, E to Barbeau Area
378	MI 80, Kinross, E BP/dsl, golf, to Kinross Correctional
373	MI 48, Rudyard, W gas/dsl, food, lodging
359	MI 134, to Drummond Island, W National Forest Camping
352	MI 123, to Moran, Newberry
348	H63, to Sault Reservation, St Ignace, E Jose's Cantina, Bavarian Haus, Baymont Inn, Bayview Motel, Bear Cove Inn, Best Value Inn, Birchwood Motel, Breakers Resort, Cedars Motel, Evergreen Motel, Great Lakes Motel, Holiday Inn Express, NorthernAire Motel, Pines Motel, Quality Inn, casino, Castle Rock Camping, H, st police, to Mackinac Trail, W Castle Rock Gifts
346mm	rest area/scenic turnout sb, **full facilities, litter barrels, petwalk,**
345	Portage St(from sb), St Ignace
344b	US 2 W, W BP/dsl, Holiday/dsl, Shell/dsl, Big Boy, Burger King, Clyde's Drive-In, McDonald's, Subway, Suzy's Pasties, Quality Inn, Sunset Motel, Super 8, Ford, golf, KOA, Lakeshore RV Park
344a	Lp 75, St Ignace, E Shell, BC Pizza, Bentley's Cafe, Galley Rest., Mackinac Grille, MI Patio Grill, Aurora Borealis Motel, Boardwalk Inn, Cedar Hill Lodge, Colonial House, Moran Bay Motel, Normandy Motel, Thunderbird Motel, Village Inn/rest., Voyager Motel, $General, Ace Hardware, Bay Drug, Family Fare Mkt, Family$, H, NAPA, public marina, st police, Straits SP, to Island Ferrys, TrueValue, USPO
343mm	toll booth to toll bridge, E **full facilities, litter barrels,** **Welcome Ctr nb,** W museum
341mm	toll bridge, Lake Huron, Lake Michigan
339	US 23, Jamet St, E Audie's Rest., Days Inn, Knights Inn, LightHouse View Motel, Parkside Motel, Riviera Motel, Super 8, W Shell, Bridgeview Diner, Darrow's Rest., Mackinaw Cookie Co, Holiday Inn Express, Vindel Motel, Wilderness SP
338	US 23(from sb), same as 337, E Marathon/dsl, BC Pizza, Burger King, DQ, KFC, Mama Mia's Pizza, Pancake Chef, Subway, Wienerlicious, Baymont Inn, Court Plaza Hotel, Mackinaw Mkt, Mackinaw Outfitters, USPO, W Holiday Inn Express
337	MI 108(from nb, no EZ return), Nicolet St, Mackinaw City, E **Welcome Ctr/**, Citgo/dsl/LP, Tesla EVC, Bell's Melody Motel, Blue Water Grill, Lighthouse Rest., Mackinaw Pastie&Cookie Co., Starbucks, Bayside Inn, Beach House Cottages, BeachComber Motel, Best Value Inn, Best Western, Bridge Vista Beach Motel, Bridgeview Motel, Budget Inn, Capri Motel, Clarion, Clearwater Lakeshore Motel, Comfort Inn, Crown Choice Inn, Days Inn, EconoLodge, Fairview Inn, Great Lakes Inn, Hamilton Inn, Mackinaw Inn, North Winds Motel, Quality Inn, Rainbow Motel, Ramada Ltd, Sundown Motel, Sunrise Beach Motel, Super 8, Thunderbird Inn, Waterfront Inn, Harley-Davidson, Old Mill Creek SP, Tee Pee Camping, to Island Ferrys, W KOA, Wilderness SP
336	US 31 S(from sb), to Petoskey
328mm	**full facilities, info, litter barrels, petwalk, sb**
326	C66, to Cheboygan, E Andy's/dsl, H, Sea Shell City/gifts
322	C64, to Cheboygan, E H, LP, st police
317mm	**full facilities, info, litter barrels, petwalk, / scenic turnout nb**
313	MI 27 N, Topinabee, E Indian River RV Resort/Camping, Topinabee Motel
311mm	Indian River
310	MI 33, MI 68, E Hometown Inn, Michigan Oaks Camping(3mi), W Marathon, Shell/McDonald's, Burger King, Subway, Wilson's Rivers Edge Rest., Coach House Motel, Indian River Motel, auto repair, Family$, Ken's Mkt/gas, to Burt Lake SP, to Indian River Trading Post/RV Resort
301	C58, Wolverine, E Marathon/dsl, Whistle Stop Rest., Elkwood Campground(5mi), W Sturgeon Valley Campground(3mi)
297mm	Sturgeon River
290	Vanderbilt, E Marathon/dsl/LP/RV dump, Spirit/dsl, Elk Horn Grill, USPO, Village Mkt Foods, W Mobil/dsl, Black Bear Golf Resort(2mi)
287mm	**full facilities, info, litter barrels, sb**
282	MI 32, Gaylord, E Family Fare/dsl, Holiday, Speedway/dsl, Arby's, Arlene's Diner, Big Buck Steaks, Burger King, DQ, Jet's Pizza, KFC, La Senorita Mexican, McDonald's, Qdoba Mexican, Subway, Wendy's, Alpine Lodge, Baymont Inn, Fairfield Inn, Quality Inn, Advance Parts, Family FareMkt, Harley-Davidson, H, st police, W Marathon/dsl, Marathon/dsl(2), Mobil/dsl, Murphy USA/dsl, Shell/dsl, Applebee's, BC Pizza, Big Boy, Biggby Coffee, Bob Evans, Buffalo Wild Wings, China Buffet, Coldstone/Tim Horton, Culver's, El Rancho Mexican, Five Guys, Jimmy John's, Little Caesar's, Mancino's Pizza, Panera Bread, Ponderosa, Ruby Tuesday, Starbucks, Taco Bell, Best Western, Hampton Inn, Holiday Inn Express, $Tree, ALDI, AT&T, BigLots, Chrysler/Dodge/Jeep, GNC, Hobby Lobby, Home Depot, Kenworth, Kohl's, Lowe's, Meijer/dsl, Northern MI RV Ctr, O'Reilly Parts, PetSmart, Save-A-Lot Foods, TJ Maxx, Verizon, Walgreens, Walmart/Subway
279mm	45th Parallel...halfway between the equator and North Pole
279	Old US 27, Gaylord, E Marathon/Subway/dsl, Mobil/dsl, Shell, Burger King, Mama Leone's, Best Value Inn, Ace Hardware, auto repair, Buick/GMC, Chevrolet, Ford/Lincoln, st police, W Bennethum's Rest., Porter Haus, KOA(3mi)
277mm	**full facilities, info, litter barrels, petwalk, nb**
270	Waters, E Marathon/dsl, Hilltop Rest., W BP/dsl, Waters Inn, Freeway RV Ctr, to Otsego Lake SP, USPO
264	Lewiston, Frederic, W access to food, camping
262mm	**full facilities, litter barrels, petwalk, sb**
259	MI 93, E Hartwick Pines SP
256	(from sb), to MI 72, Grayling, access to same as 254
254	MI 72(exits left from nb, no return), Grayling, W Admiral/dsl, Marathon/dsl, Shell, Speedway/dsl, Burger King, DQ, Keg'O'Nails, Little Caesar's, McDonald's, Pizza Hut, Subway, Taco Bell, Wendy's, Days Inn, Ramada, $General, 7-11, Ace Hardware, AT&T, Auto Value Parts, Family Fare Mkt, Family$, Ford, H, K-Mart, NAPA, O'Reilly Parts, Save-A-Lot Foods, Verizon, Walgreens
251mm	**full facilities, info, litter barrels, petwalk, nb, vending**
251	4 Mile Rd, E Jellystone RV Park(5mi), W Marathon/Arby's/dsl/scales/RV Dump/24hr, Super 8
249	US 127 S(from sb), to Clare
244	MI 18, Roscommon, E Shell/dsl, McDonald's, W Valero/dsl, Higgins Lake SP, KOA(1mi)
239	MI 18, Roscommon, S Higgins Lake SP, E Shell/McDonald's/dsl, camping, W camping, Higgins Lake SP
235mm	**full facilities, info, litter barrels, petwalk, sb, vending**
227	MI 55 W, rd F97, to Houghton Lake, W food
222	Old 76, to St Helen, E food, lodging, camping

= gas = food = lodging = other = rest stop

INTERSTATE 75 Cont'd

Exit #	Services
215	MI 55 E, West Branch, E Shell/dsl,
212	MI 55, West Branch, E Mobil/dsl, Murphy USA/dsl, Shell/Subway/dsl, Applebee's, Arby's, Big Boy, Burger King, KFC, Lumberjack Rest., McDonald's, Ponderosa, Rally's, Taco Bell, Tim Hortons, Wendy's, Quality Inn, Super 8, Home Depot, st police, Walmart/Subway, West Branch Outlets/famous brands, W Marathon/dsl
210mm	**full facilities, info, litter barrels, petwalk, nb, vending**
202	MI 33, to Rose City, Alger, E Marathon/Narski's Mkt/jerky, Mobil/jerky outlet/dsl, Shell/Subway/dsl, Greenwood Camping
201mm	**full facilities, litter barrels, petwalk, sb, vending**
195	Sterling Rd, to Sterling, E gas, Riverview Camping(seasonal)
190	MI 61, to Standish, E W Marathon, Mobil/jerky/dsl
188	US 23, to Standish, E gas, food, camping
181	Pinconning Rd, E Shell/McDonald's/dsl, Cheesehouse Diner, Pinconning Inn(2mi), W BP/pizza/dsl/24hr
175mm	**full facilities, litter barrels, petwalk, nb, vending**
173	Linwood Rd, to Linwood, E Mobil/dsl/jerky, Arby's(2mi)
171mm	Kawkawlin River
168	Beaver Rd, to Willard, E to Bay City SRA, W Mobil/jerky
166mm	Kawkawlin River
164	to MI 13, Wilder Rd, to Kawkawlin, E Cracker Barrel, Lucky Steaks, Ponderosa, Uno Pizzaria, AmericInn, Holiday Inn Express, KanRock Tire, Meijer/dsl, Menards
162b a	US 10, MI 25, to Midland
160	MI 84, Delta, E Mobil, Shell/Subway/dsl, W Econolodge, Speedway/dsl, Berger's Rest., Burger King, KFC/Taco Bell, McDonald's, RV World Super Ctr, to Saginaw Valley SU
158mm	**full facilities, litter barrels, petwalk, sb, vending**
155	I-675 S, to downtown Saginaw, W Outback Steaks, Hampton Inn
154	to Zilwaukee
153mm	Saginaw River
153	MI 13 E Bay City Rd, Saginaw
151	MI 81, to Reese, Caro, E BP/McDonald's/dsl, Volvo Trucks, W Flying J/Wendy's/dsl/LP/24hr
150	I-675 N, to downtown Saginaw, W Outback Steaks, Hampton Inn
149b a	MI 46, Holland Ave, to Saginaw, W BP, Speedway/dsl, Arby's, Big John's Steaks, McDonald's, Popeyes, Subway, Taco Bell, Red Roof Inn, Welcome Inn, Advance Parts, USPO
144b a	Bridgeport, E Love's/Hardee's/dsl/scales/24hr, Speedway/dsl, Jellystone Camping(9mi), W Mobil/dsl/e85, TA/Country Pride/dsl/scales/24hr/@, Arby's, Big Boy, Cracker Barrel, Hungry Howie's, McDonald's, Subway, Taco Bell, Wendy's, Baymont Inn, Knights Inn, $General, Family$, Kroger/gas, st police, USPO
143mm	Cass River
138mm	pull off both lanes
136	MI 54, MI 83, Birch Run, E Mobil/dsl/24hr, Halo Burger, KFC, Subway, Best Value Inn, Best Western, Comfort Inn, Hampton Inn, Holiday Inn Express, Advance Parts, General RV Ctr, Mejier/dsl/e85, Totten Tires, W BP, Citgo/7-11, Marathon, A&W, Applebee's, Arby's, Bagger Dave's Burgers, Beijing Express, Bob Evans, Buffalo Wild Wings, Culver's, DQ, Dunkin', Jimmy John's, Leo's Coney Island,

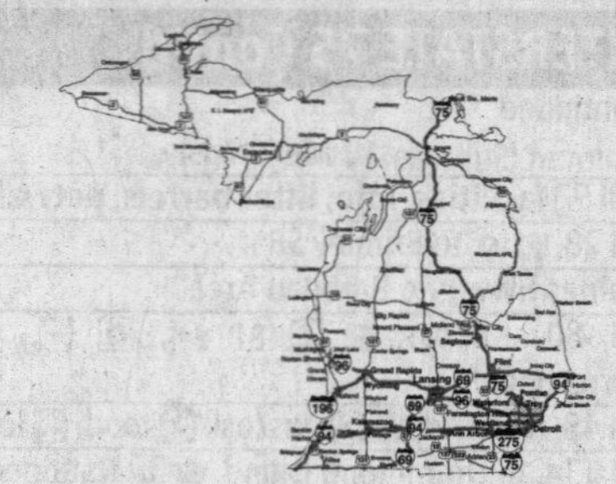

Exit #	Services
136	Continued Little Caesar's, McDonald's, Sonic, Starbucks, Taco Be Tony's Rest., Uno Grill, Victor&Merek's Pizza, Wendy's, Country Inn&Suites, Birch Run Outlet/famous branc Buick/Chevrolet, Family$, GNC, Old Navy, USPO
131	MI 57, to Montrose, E BP, Arby's, Big John's Steal Burger King, DQ, KFC, McDonald's, Oriental Expre Subway, Taco Bell, Tim Hortons, Twins Pizza, Wendy's, AutoZone, Chevrolet, Chrysler/Dodge/Jeep, K-Mart, KanRo Tire, Tradewinds RV Ctr, vet, W Mobil/Rally's/dsl, Murp USA/dsl, Applebee's, Big Boy, Lucky Steaks, Tropic Smoothie Cafe, $Tree, auto repair, Menards, Verizo Walmart/Subway
129mm	**full facilities, litter barrels, petwalk, bo lanes, vending**
126	to Mt Morris, E B&B/A&W/dsl/scales/24hr, W BP/dsl
125	I-475 S, UAW Fwy, to Flint
122	Pierson Rd, to Flint, E BP/dsl, Marathon/dsl, McDonald's, Papa's Coney's, Subway, Family$, O'Rei Parts, Tuffy Auto, W Citgo/dsl, ClicMart/dsl, Arby's, B John's, Cracker Barrel, Domino's, Halo Burger, Red Lobst Taco Bell, Tim Hortons, YaYa Chicken, Baymont Inn, $General, $Tree, AlLDI, AT&T, Belle Tire, Discount Tire, Hon Depot
118	MI 21, Corunna Rd, E BP, Badawest Lebanese, B John's Steaks, Burger King, Church's TX Chicken, Hung Howie's, Little Caesar's, Taco Bell, Wing Fong Chinese, Ya Chicken, Advance Parts, Family$, Kroger/gas, W BP/dsl, Marathon/Wendy's, Mobil, Speedway/dsl, Valero, Burger King, KFC, Mega Diner, Rally's, Tim Horton, Whi Castle, Economy Motel, $General, AlLDI, AutoZon Buick, Chevrolet, GMC, Home Depot, KanRock Tire, Kroge gas, O'Reilly Parts, Sam's Club/gas, st police, Verizo Walgreens, Walmart
117b	Miller Rd, to Flint, E Speedway/dsl, Applebee's, Arby Cottage Inn Pizza, Domino's, Fuddrucker's, McDonald Popeyes, Qdoba, Sonic, Subway, Vehicle City Diner, We Side Diner, Knights Inn, Quality Inn, Rodeway Inn, Harley Davidson, Tuffy Auto, W Mobil, Bar Louie, BD Mongolian BBQ, Bob Evans, Buffalo Wild Wings, Casa Rea Chili's, Chipotle, ChuckeCheese, Famous Dave's BBQ, Fiv Guys, Golden Corral, Golden Moon, Halo Burge HoneyBaked Ham, Hooters, IHOP, Italia Garden, Jimm John's, Logan's Roadhouse, Olive Garden, Outback Steak Panda Express, Panera Bread, Pizza Hut, Red Robi Starbucks, Subway, Taco Bell, Telly's Coney Island, Ti Horton, TX Roadhouse, Red Roof Inn, Super 8, AT& Barnes&Noble, Belle Tire, Best Buy, Big Lots, Hobby Lobb JC Penney, Jo-Ann Fabrics, Macy's, Michael's, Midas, Offic Depot, Old Navy, PetSmart, Target, U-Haul, Valley Tir Verizon, vet
117a	I-69, E to Lansing, W to Port Huron
116	MI 121, Bristol Rd, E Mobil, Speedway/dsl, Capit Coney Island, KFC, McDonald's, Subway, Advance Part AutoZone, W Marathon/dsl,
115	US 23(from sb), W Citgo, Mobil, Arby's, Hill Rd Grille

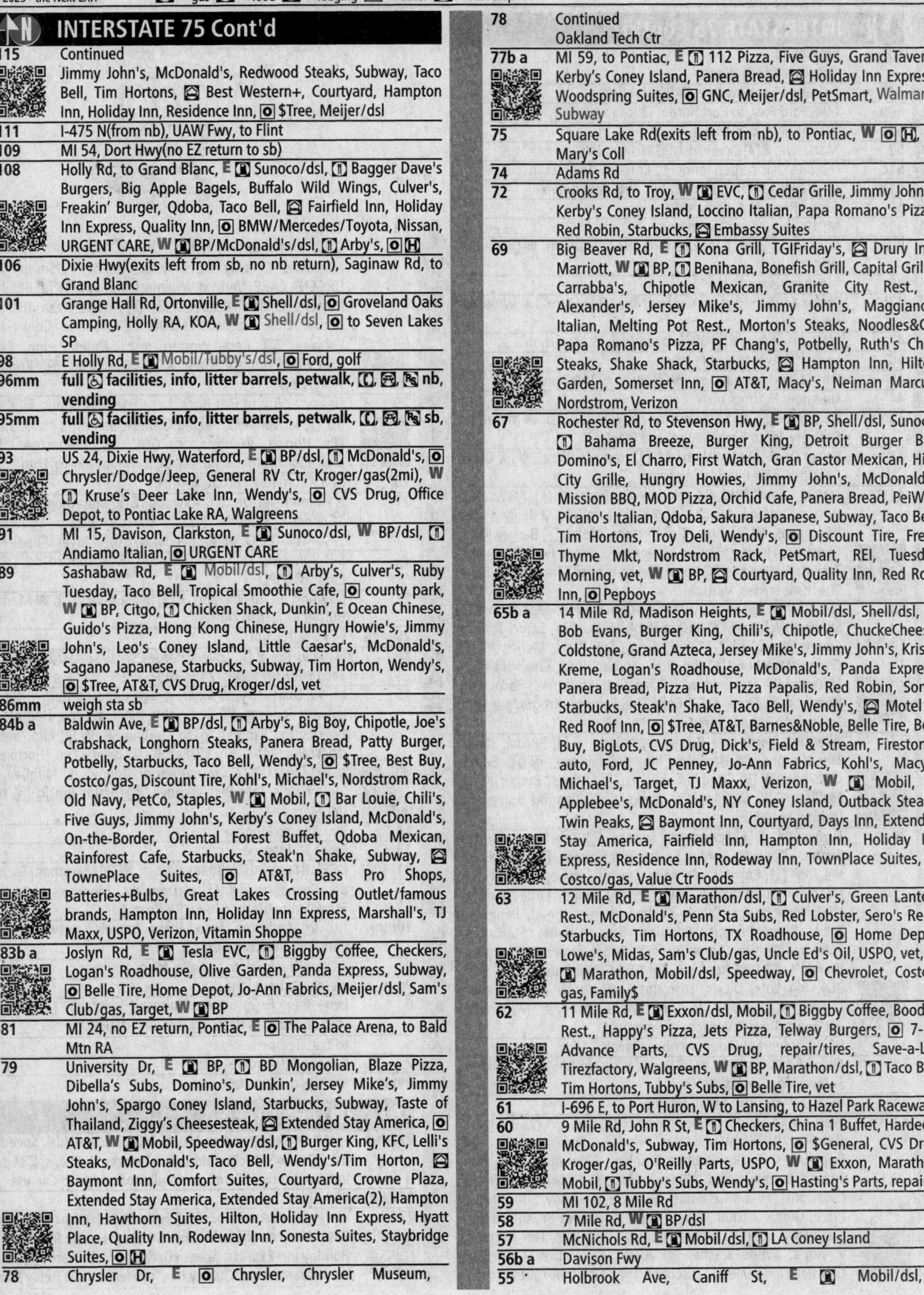

INTERSTATE 75 Cont'd

115 Continued
Jimmy John's, McDonald's, Redwood Steaks, Subway, Taco Bell, Tim Hortons, Best Western+, Courtyard, Hampton Inn, Holiday Inn, Residence Inn, $Tree, Meijer/dsl

111 I-475 N(from nb), UAW Fwy, to Flint

109 MI 54, Dort Hwy(no EZ return to sb)

108 Holly Rd, to Grand Blanc, E Sunoco/dsl, Bagger Dave's Burgers, Big Apple Bagels, Buffalo Wild Wings, Culver's, Freakin' Burger, Qdoba, Taco Bell, Fairfield Inn, Holiday Inn Express, Quality Inn, BMW/Mercedes/Toyota, Nissan, URGENT CARE, W BP/McDonald's/dsl, Arby's, H

106 Dixie Hwy(exits left from sb, no nb return), Saginaw Rd, to Grand Blanc

101 Grange Hall Rd, Ortonville, E Shell/dsl, Groveland Oaks Camping, Holly RA, KOA, W Shell/dsl, to Seven Lakes SP

98 E Holly Rd, E Mobil/Tubby's/dsl, Ford, golf

96mm **full facilities, info, litter barrels, petwalk, nb, vending**

95mm **full facilities, info, litter barrels, petwalk, sb, vending**

93 US 24, Dixie Hwy, Waterford, E BP/dsl, McDonald's, Chrysler/Dodge/Jeep, General RV Ctr, Kroger/gas(2mi), W Kruse's Deer Lake Inn, Wendy's, CVS Drug, Office Depot, to Pontiac Lake RA, Walgreens

91 MI 15, Davison, Clarkston, E Sunoco/dsl, W BP/dsl, Andiamo Italian, URGENT CARE

89 Sashabaw Rd, E Mobil/dsl, Arby's, Culver's, Ruby Tuesday, Taco Bell, Tropical Smoothie Cafe, county park, W BP, Citgo, Chicken Shack, Dunkin', E Ocean Chinese, Guido's Pizza, Hong Kong Chinese, Hungry Howie's, Jimmy John's, Leo's Coney Island, Little Caesar's, McDonald's, Sagano Japanese, Starbucks, Subway, Tim Horton, Wendy's, $Tree, AT&T, CVS Drug, Kroger/dsl, vet

86mm weigh sta sb

84b a Baldwin Ave, E BP/dsl, Arby's, Big Boy, Chipotle, Joe's Crabshack, Longhorn Steaks, Panera Bread, Patty Burger, Potbelly, Starbucks, Taco Bell, Wendy's, $Tree, Best Buy, Costco/gas, Discount Tire, Kohl's, Michael's, Nordstrom Rack, Old Navy, PetCo, Staples, W Mobil, Bar Louie, Chili's, Five Guys, Jimmy John's, Kerby's Coney Island, McDonald's, On-the-Border, Oriental Forest Buffet, Qdoba Mexican, Rainforest Cafe, Starbucks, Steak'n Shake, Subway, TownePlace Suites, AT&T, Bass Pro Shops, Batteries+Bulbs, Great Lakes Crossing Outlet/famous brands, Hampton Inn, Holiday Inn Express, Marshall's, TJ Maxx, USPO, Verizon, Vitamin Shoppe

83b a Joslyn Rd, E Tesla EVC, Biggby Coffee, Checkers, Logan's Roadhouse, Olive Garden, Panda Express, Subway, Belle Tire, Home Depot, Jo-Ann Fabrics, Meijer/dsl, Sam's Club/gas, Target, W BP

81 MI 24, no EZ return, Pontiac, E The Palace Arena, to Bald Mtn RA

79 University Dr, E BP, BD Mongolian, Blaze Pizza, Dibella's Subs, Domino's, Dunkin', Jersey Mike's, Jimmy John's, Spargo Coney Island, Starbucks, Subway, Taste of Thailand, Ziggy's Cheesesteak, Extended Stay America, AT&T, W Mobil, Speedway/dsl, Burger King, KFC, Lelli's Steaks, McDonald's, Taco Bell, Wendy's/Tim Horton, Baymont Inn, Comfort Suites, Courtyard, Crowne Plaza, Extended Stay America, Extended Stay America(2), Hampton Inn, Hawthorn Suites, Hilton, Holiday Inn Express, Hyatt Place, Quality Inn, Rodeway Inn, Sonesta Suites, Staybridge Suites, H

78 Chrysler Dr, E Chrysler, Chrysler Museum,

78 Continued
Oakland Tech Ctr

77b a MI 59, to Pontiac, E 112 Pizza, Five Guys, Grand Tavern, Kerby's Coney Island, Panera Bread, Holiday Inn Express, Woodspring Suites, GNC, Meijer/dsl, PetSmart, Walmart/Subway

75 Square Lake Rd(exits left from nb), to Pontiac, W H, St Mary's Coll

74 Adams Rd

72 Crooks Rd, to Troy, W EVC, Cedar Grille, Jimmy John's, Kerby's Coney Island, Loccino Italian, Papa Romano's Pizza, Red Robin, Starbucks, Embassy Suites

69 Big Beaver Rd, E Kona Grill, TGIFriday's, Drury Inn, Marriott, W BP, Benihana, Bonefish Grill, Capital Grille, Carrabba's, Chipotle Mexican, Granite City Rest., J Alexander's, Jersey Mike's, Jimmy John's, Maggiano's Italian, Melting Pot Rest., Morton's Steaks, Noodles&Co, Papa Romano's Pizza, PF Chang's, Potbelly, Ruth's Chris Steaks, Shake Shack, Starbucks, Hampton Inn, Hilton Garden, Somerset Inn, AT&T, Macy's, Neiman Marcus, Nordstrom, Verizon

67 Rochester Rd, to Stevenson Hwy, E BP, Shell/dsl, Sunoco, Bahama Breeze, Burger King, Detroit Burger Bar, Domino's, El Charro, First Watch, Gran Castor Mexican, Hills City Grille, Hungry Howies, Jimmy John's, McDonald's, Mission BBQ, MOD Pizza, Orchid Cafe, Panera Bread, PeiWei, Picano's Italian, Qdoba, Sakura Japanese, Subway, Taco Bell, Tim Hortons, Troy Deli, Wendy's, Discount Tire, Fresh Thyme Mkt, Nordstrom Rack, PetSmart, REI, Tuesday Morning, vet, W BP, Courtyard, Quality Inn, Red Roof Inn, Pepboys

65b a 14 Mile Rd, Madison Heights, E Mobil/dsl, Shell/dsl, Bob Evans, Burger King, Chili's, Chipotle, ChuckeCheese, Coldstone, Grand Azteca, Jersey Mike's, Jimmy John's, Krispy Kreme, Logan's Roadhouse, McDonald's, Panda Express, Panera Bread, Pizza Hut, Pizza Papalis, Red Robin, Sonic, Starbucks, Steak'n Shake, Taco Bell, Wendy's, Motel 6, Red Roof Inn, $Tree, AT&T, Barnes&Noble, Belle Tire, Best Buy, BigLots, CVS Drug, Dick's, Field & Stream, Firestone/auto, Ford, JC Penney, Jo-Ann Fabrics, Kohl's, Macy's, Michael's, Target, TJ Maxx, Verizon, W Mobil, Applebee's, McDonald's, NY Coney Island, Outback Steaks, Twin Peaks, Baymont Inn, Courtyard, Days Inn, Extended Stay America, Fairfield Inn, Hampton Inn, Holiday Inn Express, Residence Inn, Rodeway Inn, TownPlace Suites, Costco/gas, Value Ctr Foods

63 12 Mile Rd, E Marathon/dsl, Culver's, Green Lantern Rest., McDonald's, Penn Sta Subs, Red Lobster, Sero's Rest., Starbucks, Tim Hortons, TX Roadhouse, Home Depot, Lowe's, Midas, Sam's Club/gas, Uncle Ed's Oil, USPO, vet, W Marathon, Mobil/dsl, Speedway, Chevrolet, Costco/gas, Family$

62 11 Mile Rd, E Exxon/dsl, Mobil, Biggby Coffee, Boodles Rest., Happy's Pizza, Jets Pizza, Telway Burgers, 7-11, Advance Parts, CVS Drug, repair/tires, Save-a-Lot, Tirezfactory, Walgreens, W BP, Marathon/dsl, Taco Bell, Tim Hortons, Tubby's Subs, Belle Tire, vet

61 I-696 E, to Port Huron, W to Lansing, to Hazel Park Raceway

60 9 Mile Rd, John R St, E Checkers, China 1 Buffet, Hardee's, McDonald's, Subway, Tim Hortons, $General, CVS Drug, Kroger/gas, O'Reilly Parts, USPO, W Exxon, Marathon, Mobil, Tubby's Subs, Wendy's, Hasting's Parts, repair

59 MI 102, 8 Mile Rd

58 7 Mile Rd, W BP/dsl

57 McNichols Rd, E Mobil/dsl, LA Coney Island

56b a Davison Fwy

55 Holbrook Ave, Caniff St, E Mobil/dsl,

= gas = food = lodging = other = rest stop

INTERSTATE 75 Cont'd

CHICAGO

Exit	Services
55	Continued Grandy's Coney Island
54	E Grand Blvd, Clay Ave, W Mobil/dsl
53b	I-94, Ford Fwy, to Port Huron, Chicago
53a	Warren Ave, E Mobil, W BP
52	Mack Ave, E Exxon/dsl, McDonald's
51c	I-375 to civic center, tunnel to Canada, downtown
51b	MI 3(exits left from nb), Gratiot Ave, downtown
50	Grand River Ave, downtown
49b	MI 10, Lodge Fwy, downtown
49a	Rosa Parks Blvd, E Firestone, Tiger Stadium, W Mobil/dsl
48	I-96 begins/ends
47b	Porter St, E bridge to Canada, DutyFree/24hr, MI Welcome Ctr
47a	MI 3, Clark Ave, E BP/Subway/dsl, W Marathon
46	Livernois Ave, to Hist Ft Wayne
45	Fort St, Springwells Ave, W Mobil, McDonald's
44	Deerborn St (from nb)
43b a	MI 85, Fort St, to Schaefer Hwy, E Exxon/dsl, W Marathon Refinery, to River Rouge Ford Plant
42	Outer Dr, E Marathon/dsl, Happy's Pizza, W Quick Fuel/dsl, Family$, truck tires
41	MI 39, Southfield Rd, to Lincoln Park, E A&W, Tim Hortons, White Castle, AlLDI, Family$, O'Reilly Parts, Walgreens, W Citgo/Tim Hortons, Mobil, Burger King, Checkers, Hungry Howie, McDonald's, Pizza Hut, Starbucks, Taco Bell, Wendy's, Royal Choice Inn, $Tree, AT&T, Belle Tire, Kroger/gas, Verizon
40	Dix Hwy, E AAA/A&W/dsl, China Bowl, Marathon/dsl, Sunoco, Welcome, Baskin-Robbins/Dunkin', Sonic, Toma's Coney Island, 7-11, CVS Drug, Dix Parts, Meijer, W Citgo, Marathon, Big Boy, Burger King, Checkers, DQ, McDonald's, Papa John's, Pizza Hut, Starbucks, Taco Bell, Wendy's, $Tree, AT&T, Belle Tire, Family$, Kroger/gas, Tire Traxx Auto/repair, Verizon
37	Allen Rd, North Line Rd, to Wyandotte, E BP/dsl, Shell/Tim Hortons, Hampton Inn, Holiday Inn, H, Sam's Club/gas, W Citgo/dsl, Sunoco, Arby's, Burger King, Mallie's Grill, McDonald's, Wendy's, Comfort Suites, La Quinta, Motel 6
36	Eureka Rd, E Speedway, Sunoco, Bob Evans, Burrito Express, Denny's, Golden Corral, Tim Hortons, Super 8, vet, W Culver's, Famous Dave's, HoneyBaked Ham, Hooters, Jimmy John's, Leo's Coney Island, Little Daddy's Grill, McDonald's, Olga's Kitchen, Panera Bread, Penn Sta Subs, Pizza Papalis, Primanti Bros, Qdoba, Starbucks, Subway, Tropical Smoothie, TX Roadhouse, Wahlburgers, Wendy's, Red Roof Inn, $Tree, AT&T, Belle Tire, Best Buy, Big Lots, Dick's, Discount Tire, Hobby Lobby, Home Depot, JC Penney, Jo-Ann, Kohl's, Macy's, Meijer/dsl, PetSmart, Target, Verizon, Walgreens
35	US 24, Telegraph Rd, from nb, exits left
34b	Sibley Rd, Riverview, W Sunoco/Baskin-Robbins/Dunkin'/Subway, General RV Ctr
34a	to US 24(from sb), Telegraph Rd
32	West Rd, to Trenton, Woodhaven, E EVC, EVC(2), Flying J/Detroiter/IHOP/dsl/LP/scales/24hr/@, Speedway/dsl, Applebee's, Baskin-Robbins/Dunkin', Blue Margarita, Bob Evans, Buffalo Wild Wings, Chipotle, Christoff's Rest., Coldstone, Firehouse Subs, Five Guys, Jersey Subs, MOD Pizza, Olga's Kitchen, Panda Express, Panera Bread, Qdoba, Starbucks, Steak'n Shake, Subway, Taco Bell, Tim Hortons, Wendy's, White Castle, AlLDI, Belle Tire, Chevrolet, Chrysler/Dodge/Jeep, Discount Tire, Firestone/auto, Ford,

RIVERVIEW

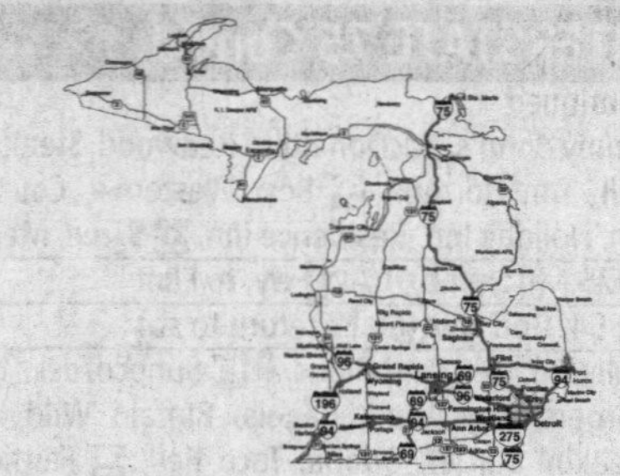

LAKE ERIE METROPARK

Exit	Services
32	Continued GNC, Home Depot, Kohl's, Lowe's, Marshall's, Meijer/d Michael's, O'Reilly Parts, Office Depot, PetSmart, Targ URGENT CARE, Verizon, Walmart/Subway, W BP, BP/T Hortons, Circle K/Hardee's/dsl, Andy's Pizza, DQ, Jim John's, Little Caesar's, McDonald's, Sparta Coney Islar Subway, Best Western/rest., Holiday Inn Expre Westwood Inn, $Tree, AT&T, CVS Drug, H, Kroger/d Walgreens
29	Gilbralter Rd, to Flat Rock, Lake Erie Metropark, E Citg dsl, McDonald's, Peking Chinese, Sammy's Pizza, Subwa Tim Horton, Wendy's, GNC, H, Kroger/gas, W Marathon/Burger King/dsl, Baymont Inn, Ford
28	rd 85(from nb), Fort St, E H
27	N Huron River Dr, to Rockwood, E Marathon/7-11/dsl, $General, Benito's Pizza, Marco's Pizza, Subway, SaveALot, USPO, W Speedway/dsl, River Village Rest.
26	S Huron River Dr, to S Rockwood, E Sunoco/dsl, Dix Cafe, USPO
21	Newport Rd, to Newport, E BP/Subway/dsl, W Maratho Burger King/dsl/24hr
20	I-275 N, to Flint
18	Nadeau Rd, E Love's/Hardee's/dsl/scales/24hr, W Pilo Taco Bell/dsl/scales/24hr, H
15	MI 50, Dixie Hwy, to Monroe, E Citgo, Burger King, Re Lobster, Subway, Best Value Inn, Days Inn, Hampton In Holiday Inn Express, to Sterling SP, W Pilot/Subwa dsl/scales/24hr, TA/BP/Fazoli's/Popeyes/Tim Hortons/ds scales/24hr/@, Cracker Barrel, Denny's, El Maguey, IHO McDonald's, Taco Bell, Wendy's, Quality Inn, H, to Vi Vet Mem
14	Elm Ave, to Monroe
13	Front St, Monroe
11	La Plaisance Rd, to Bolles Harbor, W Marathon/Taco Be dsl, Speedway/dsl, McDonald's, Monroe's Hotdogs, Econolodge, Harbor Town RV Resort
10mm	**full facilities, info, litter barrels, petwalk, vending, Welcome Ctr nb**
9	S Otter Creek Rd, to La Salle, W antiques
7mm	weigh sta both lanes
6	Luna Pier, E Sunoco/Subway/dsl/scales, Beef Jerk UnLtd., Ganders Rest., Pier Inn, USPO
5	to Erie, Temperance
2	Summit St(no nb re-entry)
0mm	Michigan/Ohio state line

LUNA PIER

INTERSTATE 94

Exit	Services
275mm	I-69/I-94 begin/end on MI 25, N BP, Shell/dsl, Speedway dsl, Arby's, McDonald's, Tim Horton, Wendy's, Comfo Inn, Days Inn, Family$, Honda, tollbridge to Canada
274.5mm	Black River
274	Water St, Port Huron, N Tesla EVC, Cracker Barrel, Best Western, Lake Port SP, Port Huron RV Park, S Holiday Inn Express, SpeedyQ/dsl, Bob Evans, Fairfiel Inn, Hampton Inn, Quality Inn, Menard's, O'Reilly Parts

INTERSTATE 94 Cont'd

Exit #	Services
273mm	**Welcome Ctr/ eb, full facilities, , litter barrels, petwalk**
271	I-69 E and I-94 E run together eb, Lp I-69, S Mobil/dsl, Speedway, $General, Arby's, Burger King, Jimmy John's, KFC, Little Caesar's, McDonald's, Subway, Taco Bell, Tim Horton's, Wendy's, Advance Parts, AutoZone, Kroger/gas, repair, Sam's Club/gas, to Port Huron, USPO
269	Dove St, Range Rd, N Speedway/dsl, Theo's Rest., Baymont Inn
266	Gratiot Rd, Marysville, S BP, Marathon/dsl/scales/24hr, Speedway/dsl, Arby's, Big Boy, Burger King, China Lite, Dairy Boy, Daliono's, Four Star Grille, Hungry Howie's, Jets Pizza, Jimmy John's, KFC, Little Caesar's, McDonald's, Mr Pita, Pelican Café, Subway, Taco Bell, Tim Horton, Super 8, $General, $Tree, Advance Parts, AutoZone, CVS Drug, H, Meijer/dsl, O'Reilly Parts, Verizon, vet, Wally's Mkt
262	Wadhams Rd, N Love's/Subway/dsl/scales/24hr, S Mobil/dsl
257	St Clair, Richmond, N Sunoco/dsl, S BP/dsl
255mm	**full facilities, info, litter barrels, petwalk, , , eb**
251mm	**full facilities, info, litter barrels, petwalk, , , wb**
248	26 Mile Rd, to Marine City, N McDonald's(2mi), S Mobil/7-11, Shell, Subway, Taco Bell, Tim Horton, Mejier/dsl
247mm	Salt River
247	MI 19(no eb return), New Haven
243	MI 29, MI 3, Utica, New Baltimore, N BP/Dunkin', EVC, Marathon/dsl, Sunoco/dsl, Applebee's, Arby's, Buffalo Wild Wings, Burger King, Chapo's Tacos, Chipotle, Chophouse, Coldstone, Coney Island, Dave's Pizza, Del Taco, Detroit Wings, Dimitri's Rest., Eagles Grill, Happy's Pizza, Jersey Mike's, Little Caesar's, McDonald's, MOD Pizza, Noodles&Co, Olga's Kitchen, Panda Express, Panera Bread, Potbelly, Qdoba, Ruby Tuesday, Starbucks, Tim Horton, TX Roadhouse, Wendy's, White Castle, $Tree, AutoZone, Belle Tire, Best Buy, Big Jim's Automotive, Big Lots, Dick's, Discount Tire, GNC, Hobby Lobby, Home Depot, JC Penney, Jo-Ann Fabrics, Kohl's, Lowe's, Meijer/Subway/dsl, Michael's, NAPA, O'Reilly Parts, Old Navy, PetCo, PetSmart, Staples, Target, TJ Maxx, URGENT CARE, Verizon, Walgreens, S Marathon/dsl/24hr, Speedway/dsl/24hr, Big Boy, Buscemi's Pizza, Checkers, Taco Bell, LodgeKeeper, Chevrolet
241	21 Mile Rd, same as 240, Selfridge, N Exxon/dsl/e85, Speedway/dsl, China King, Hungry Howie's, Jets Pizza, Jimmy John's, Advance Parts, AT&T, CVS Drug, Verizon, vet
240	to MI 59, N 7-11/gas, BP, Mobil, Arby's, Bob Evans, Burger King, Coney Island, Culver's, KFC, McDonald's, Taco Bell, Twisted Rooster, Fairfield Inn, Hampton Inn, Holiday Inn Express, $Tree, Ford, Harley-Davidson, Kia, Menard's, Subaru, Toyota, Walmart
237	N River Rd, Mt Clemens, N BP/dsl, Mobil/Subway/dsl, Clinton River Cruise Co, McDonald's, General RV Ctr, H
236.5mm	Clinton River
236	Metro Parkway, S Big Apple Bagels, Empire Chinese, Little Caesar's, McDonald's, Subway, CVS Drug, H, Kroger, URGENT CARE, Verizon
235	Shook Rd(from wb)
234b a	Harper Rd, 15 Mile Rd, N BP/McDonald's, Marathon/dsl, SpeedyQ, Sunoco/dsl, Domino's, Gina's Cafe, Tim Horton's, Family$, vet, S Shell, China Moon, Subway, Travis Rest., Winners Grill
232	Little Mack Ave(from wb only), same as 231, N Marathon, Mobil, Shell, Sunoco, Chipotle, Coldstone, Denny's, Hooters, McDonald's, Pizza Hut, Potbelly, Red Robin, Hampton Inn, Holiday Inn Express, Red Roof Inn, Relax Inn, Super 8, Victory Inn, Advance Parts, AlLDI, AT&T, Belle Tire, Discount Tire, Firestone/auto, O'Reilly Parts, Sam's Club/gas, Target, Tuesday Morning, S Kroger/dsl, Speedway/dsl, Cracker Barrel, Culver's, IHOP, Baymont Inn, Home Depot, Jo-Ann Fabrics, Kroger, Meijer/dsl/24hr, PetSmart, URGENT CARE
231	(from eb), MI 3, Gratiot Ave, N Exxon/dsl, Marathon, Applebee's, Arby's, Bob Evans, Burger King, Chili's, Chipotle, ChuckeCheese, Del Taco, Denny's, Famous Dave's BBQ, Huddle Grill, Jersey Mike's, Logan's Roadhouse, McDonald's, National Coney Island, Panera Bread, PetCo, Pizza Hut, Potbelly, Qdoba, Ruby Tuesday, Starbucks, Subway, Tim Horton, TX Roadhouse, Days Inn, Extended Stay America, Hampton Inn, Microtel, Belle Tire, Best Buy, Dick's, Discount Tire, Firestone/auto, Honda/Acura, Kia, Kohl's, Kroger, Michael's, Nissan, Sam's Club/gas
230	12 Mile Rd, N Mobil/dsl, Sunoco/dsl, Jimmy John's, Outback Steaks, Starbucks, Taco Bell, $Tree, AT&T, CVS Drug, Marshall's, Verizon, Walmart/Subway, S Marathon
229	I-696 W, Reuther Fwy, to 11 Mile Rd, S Shell/dsl, Speedway/dsl, $General, 7-11
228	10 Mile Rd, N 7-11, BP, Baskin-Robbins, Donna's Rest., Eastwind Chinese, Jet's Pizza, Little Italy Pizza, Sugarbush Rest., $General, Save Mor Drugs, URGENT CARE
227	9 Mile Rd, N BP, Metro, Mobil/dsl, Speedway/dsl, DQ, McDonald's, Milestone Grill, Popeyes, Subway, Taco Bell, Tim Horton's, Wendy's, $Tree, AlLDI, CVS Drug, Family$, Fresh Choice Mkt, Office Depot, TrueValue, vet, S Mobil/dsl, Shore Pointe Motel, Cadillac, Mercedes
225	MI 102, Vernier Rd, 8 Mile Rd, S BP/Subway, Mobil, Sunoco/dsl, Coney Island, KFC, Taco Bell, Wendy's, Kroger, Walgreens
224b	Allard Ave, Eastwood Ave
224a	Moross Rd, S Citgo, Family Foods Mkt, H
223	Cadieux Rd, S BP/Subway, Marathon/dsl, Mobil, Sunoco, Checkers, Papa's Pizza, Popeyes, Tubby's Subs, Wendy's, White Castle, Family$
222b	Harper Ave(from eb), S Hastings Auto Parts
222a	Chalmers Ave, Outer Dr, N 76, BP/Subway/dsl, Coney Island, KFC, Little Caesar's, Family$
220b	Conner Ave, N BP, Sunoco
220a	French Rd, S Mobil
219	MI 3, Gratiot Ave, N 76, Marathon/Subway, Coney Island, McDonald's, $General, Farmer John's Foods, USPO, S Citgo, Burger King
218	MI 53, Van Dyke Ave, N BP, Mobil/dsl
217b	Mt Elliott Ave, S Citgo, Mobil/dsl, Royal BBQ
217a	E Grand Blvd, Chene St, S Marathon
216b	Russell St(from eb), to downtown
216a	I-75, Chrysler Fwy, to tunnel to Canada
215c	MI 1, Woodward Ave, John R St
215b	MI 10 N, Lodge Fwy
215a	MI 10 S, tunnel to Canada, downtown
214b	Trumbull Ave, N to Ford H
214a	(from wb)Grand River Ave
213b	I-96 W to Lansing, E to Canada, bridge to Canada, to Tiger Stadium
213a	W Grand(exits left from eb)
212b	Warren Ave(from eb)
212a	Livernois Ave, S BP/dsl, Marathon/Subway/dsl
211b	Cecil Ave(from wb), Central Ave
211a	Lonyo Rd, S Sunoco, Ford
210	US 12, Michigan Ave, Wyoming Ave, N Mobil/dsl,

INTERSTATE 94 Cont'd

MELVINDALE

210 Continued
BP/dsl, Checkers, Sunoco/dsl

209 Rotunda Dr(from wb)

208 Greenfield Rd, Schaefer Rd, N Mobil/dsl, Senate Coney Island, Wendy's/Tim Horton, 7-11, S River Rouge Ford Plant

207mm Rouge River

206 Oakwood Blvd, Melvindale, N EVC, Marathon, Shell, Applebee's, Biggby Coffee, Chili's, Chipotle, Coldstone, Coney Island, Five Guys, Jimmy John's, Little Caesar's, Longhorn Steaks, Olga's Kitchen, On-the-Border, Panda Express, Panera Bread, Potbelly, Qdoba, Starbucks, Subway, Taco Bell, AAA, Barnes&Noble, Best Buy, GNC, Greenfield Village Museum, Home Depot, Jo-Ann Fabrics, Lowe's, Meijer, Michael's, Old Navy, PetCo, Staples, Target, TJ Maxx, USPO, Verizon, S BP/dsl, Burger King, McDonald's, Ming Sun Chinese, Mr Steve's Pizza, Sabina's, Tim Horton's, Best Western, Comfort Inn, $General, $Tree, 7-11, CVS Drug, O'Reilly Parts

205mm Largest Uniroyal Tire in the World

204b a MI 39, Southfield Fwy, Pelham Rd, N Mobil, Valero/dsl, 7-11, to Greenfield Village, S Exxon/dsl, Marathon/dsl, Marathon/dsl, Walgreens

202b a US 24, Telegraph Rd, N Citgo, Mobil, Sunoco, Burger King, Checkers, Dunkin', Jets Pizza, KFC, McDonald's, Papa John's, Pizza Hut, Ram's Horn Rest., Subway, Taco Bell, Wendy's, Advance Parts, AlLDI, Walgreens, S BP, Citgo/dsl, Marathon/dsl, Valero/dsl, Arby's, Big Boy, Burger King, Dunkin', Hungry Howie's, Jersey Mike's, Jimmy John's, KFC, Leo's Coney Island, Leon's Rest., Little Caesar's, Lucky Star Buffet, Marina's Pizza, McDonald's, New Hong Kong, Pancho's Mexican, Pizza Hut, Popeyes, Subway, Taco Bell, Teppanyaki, Tim Horton's/Coldstone, Tubby's, Wendy's, Comfort Inn, $Tree, AT&T, AutoZone, Family$, Firestone/auto, Home Depot, H, st police, U-Haul, Verizon, vet, Walgreens, Walmart/Burger King

200 Ecorse Rd,(no ez eb return), to Taylor, N Marathon/Subway/dsl/scales, Tim Horton's, S Citgo/dsl, Rich

ROMULUS

199 Middle Belt Rd, S BP/dsl, Checkers, McDonald's, Wendy's, Days Inn, Knights Inn, Quality Inn

198 Merriman Rd, N Citgo/dsl, Marathon, Speedway/Speedy Cafe/dsl, Big Boy, Bob Evans, Capitol Bistro, Fortune Chinese, Leonardo's Italian, McDonald's, Merriman St Grill, Subway, Urban Steak, Baymont Inn, Best Value Inn, Clarion, Comfort Inn, Courtyard, Delta Hotel, Embassy Suites, Extended Stay America, Fairfield Inn, Hampton Inn, Hilton Garden, Holiday Inn, Holiday Inn Express, Howard Johnson, La Quinta, Magnuson Hotel, Marriott, Rodeway Inn, Sheraton, Sheraton Four Points, SpringHill Suites, Travelodge, Wyndham Garden Hotel, S Wayne Co

197 Vining Rd

196 Wayne Rd, Romulus, N Shell/dsl, Little Caesar's, McDonald's, Taco Bell, $General, S Mobil/dsl, Burger King, Jimmy John's, Subway

194b a I-275, N to Flint, S to Toledo

192 Haggerty Rd, N BP/Tubby's/dsl, Mobil/dsl, S Lower Huron Metro Park

190 Belleville Rd, to Belleville, N EVC, Marathon, Mobil/dsl, Applebee's, Arby's, Asian Garden, Coney Island, Cracker Barrel, Culver's, Dunkin', Hampton Inn, Happy's Pizza, Hungry Howie's, McDonald's, Qdoba, Starbucks, Taco Bell, Tim Horton, Twisted Rooster, Wendy's, Holiday Inn Express, Red Roof Inn, $Tree, ALDI, AT&T, AutoZone, Belle Tire, Camping World RV Ctr, CVS Drug, Firestone/auto, Ford, Meijer/dsl, Menards, National RV Ctr, O'Reilly Parts, Verizon,

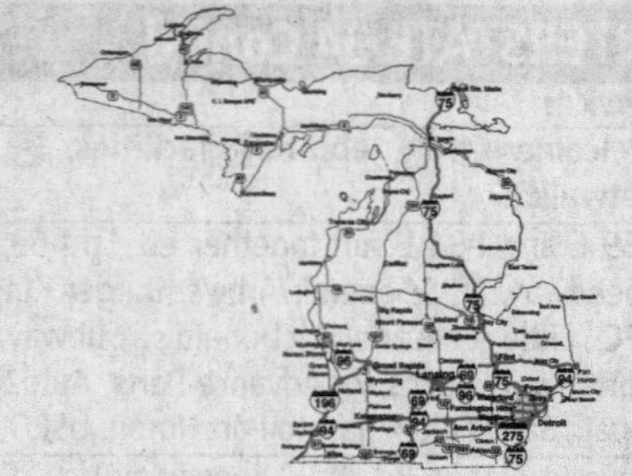

YPSILANTI

190 Continued
Walgreens, Walmart, S Shell, Burger King, China C China King, Dos Pesos Mexican, Subway, Baymont I Super 8, URGENT CARE, USPO

189mm **full facilities, info, litter barrels, petwalk, w vending**

187 Rawsonville Rd, N Freightliner, S Mobil/d Speedway/dsl, Burger King, Denny's, KFC, Little Caesa McDonald's, Pearl River Chinese, Pizza Hut, Taco Bell, T Horton, Wendy's, $General, $Tree, Detroit Greenfield Park

185 US 12, Michigan Ave(from eb, exits left, no return), frontage rds, N

184mm S Ford Lake

183 US 12, Huron St, Ypsilanti, N Citgo/dsl, H, to E MI U, Shell, Buffalo Wild Wings, Coney Island, Jet's Pizz McDonald's, Tim Horton's, Fairfield Inn, Marriott, Kroger/dsl, USPO

181b a US 12 W, Michigan Ave, Ypsilanti, N Speedway/dsl, Dunkin', Hong Kong Chinese, Koney Island, Popeyes, Ta Bell, Tim Horton/Wendy's, Aamco, BigLots, GNC, Walmart/Subway, S Mobil/Circle K, Shell/Subway/d Sunoco/dsl, Harvest Moon Cafe, McDonald's, Sam Club/gas

180b a US 23, to Toledo, Flint

177 State St, N BP, Mobil, Shell/dsl, Bravo Italiana, Buffa Wild Wings, Burger King, CA Pizza, Chipotle, Los Amigo Macaroni Grill, Mediterrano Rest, Olive Garden, Pan Express, PF Chang's, Red Robin, Relish Rest., Wendy's, Comfort Inn, Courtyard, Extended Stay America, Extend Stay America, Fairfield Inn, Hampton Inn, Hilton Garde Holiday Inn, Holiday Inn Express, Kensington Court Inn, R Roof Inn, Sheraton, Sonesta Suites, TownePlace Suites, Firestone/auto, Honda, JC Penney, Macy's, Porsche, to UN URGENT CARE, Von Maur, VW, World Mkt, S Citg Subway/dsl, Speedway/dsl, Black Rock Grill, Con Island, Jimmy John's, McDonald's, Taco Bell, Tim Horton's, Motel 6, Staybridge Suites, Belle Tire, Costco/gas, U-Hau

175 Ann Arbor-Saline Rd, N Shell/Tim Horton's, Applebee's, Blaze Pizza, Dibella Subs, Moe's SW Grill, Pane Bread, Potbelly, Tropical Smoothie, Zamaan Cafe, Candlewood Suites, REI, to UMI Stadium, vet, Who Foods Mkt, S Tesla EVC, Bob Evans, Buddy's Pizz ChuckECheese's, Five Guys, Jets Pizza, McDonald's, Nick Pancakes, Outback Steaks, Panchero's, Starbucks, Subwa TGIFriday's, TX Roadhouse, AT&T, Best Buy, BigLot Dick's, Jo-Ann Fabrics, Kohl's, Meijer/dsl/e85, PetSma Target

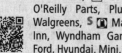

172 Jackson Ave, to Ann Arbor, Marathon, Shell/dsl, Cottage Inn Pizza, DQ, Jersey Mike's, McDonald' Noodles&Co, Quarter Rest., Subway, Taco Bell, Zingerman Roadhouse, CVS, Goodyear/auto, H, Kroger, Mida O'Reilly Parts, Plum Mkt, Staples, TJ Maxx, Verizo Walgreens, S Marathon, Weber's Rest., Hampto Inn, Wyndham Garden, Belle Tire, Chevrolet/Cadilla Ford, Hyundai, Mini, Nissan, Subaru, Toyota

INTERSTATE 94 Cont'd

Exit #	Services
171	MI.14(from eb, exits left), Ann Arbor, to Flint by U.S. 23
169	Zeeb Rd, N BP/dsl, Grand Traverse Pies Co, Kathy's Pancakes, McDonald's, Metzger's Rest., Holiday Inn Express, S Citgo/dsl, Arby's, Burger King, Culver's, Domino's, Panera Bread, Standard Grill, Subway, Taco Bell, Wendy's, AutoZone, CVS Drug, Discount Tire, Lowe's, Meijer/dsl, Menard's, vet
167	Baker Rd, Dexter, N Pilot/Subway/scales/dsl/24hr, S Pilot/Arby's/dsl/scales/24hr, TA/BP/Popeyes/dsl/scales/24hr/@, McDonald's, Blue Beacon
162	Jackson Rd, Fletcher Rd, S Marathon/Krispy Chicken/dsl/24hr, Stiver's Rest.
161mm	**full facilities, litter barrels, petwalk, eb, vending**
159	MI 52, Chelsea, N Shell/dsl, Speedway/dsl, Sunoco/dsl, Big Boy, Biggby Coffee, China Garden, Chinese Tonite, Jimmy John's, KFC/Taco Bell, McDonald's, Subway, Uptown Coney Island, Wendy's, Baymont Inn, Comfort Inn, $Tree, Ace Hardware, AutoZone, Chrysler/Dodge/Jeep, Country Mkt Foods/drug, CVS Drug, H, Travel Land RV Ctr, USPO, Verizon, S Buick/Chevrolet
157	Jackson Rd, Pierce Rd, N Gerald Eddy Geology Ctr
156	Kalmbach Rd, N to Waterloo RA
153	Clear Lake Rd, N Marathon/dsl
151.5mm	weigh sta both lanes
150	to Grass Lake, S Mobil/Dunkin'/Subway/dsl
150mm	**full facilities, litter barrels, petwalk, wb, vending**
147	Race Rd, N Hideaway RV Park, to Waterloo RA, S Joy Motel, Holiday RV Camp
145	Sargent Rd, S BP, Marathon/145 Auto Trk Plaza, McDonald's, Wendy's, Colonial Inn, $General
144	Lp 94(from wb), to Jackson
142	US 127 S, to Hudson, S Meijer/dsl, Speedway/dsl, Arby's, Bob Evans, KFC, McDonald's, Taco Bell, Wendy's, $General, $Tree, Advance Parts, AT&T, to MI Speedway, Verizon, Walgreens
141	Elm Rd, N Travelodge, Chevrolet, Chrysler/Dodge/Jeep, Ford/Lincoln, Honda, Nissan, S H
139	MI 106, Cooper St, to Jackson, N st police/prison, S Citgo/Subway, H, Meekhof Tire
138	US 127 N, MI 50, to Lansing, Jackson, N Red Lobster, Yen King Chinese, Baymont Inn, Comfort Inn, Fairfield Inn, Hampton Inn, Super 8, vet, S Admiral, BP/dsl, Shell/dsl, Arby's, Bob Evans, Buffalo Wild Wings, Burger King, Dunkin', Fazoli's, IHOP, KFC, LJ Silver, Los Tres Amigos, McDonald's, Outback Steaks, Panda Express, Panera Bread, Papa John's, Potbelly, Qdoba, Rally's, Starbucks, Subway, TX Roadhouse, Wendy's, Best Value Inn, $Tree, Advance Parts, AlLDI, AT&T, AutoZone, Belle Tire, Best Buy, BigLots, Discount Tire, Home Depot, JoAnn Fabrics, Kohl's, Kroger/gas, Lowe's, Michael's, Midas, O'Reilly Parts, PetSmart, Target, TJ Maxx, Verizon, Walgreens
137	Airport Rd, N Marathon/dsl, Shell/Taco Bell, Burger King, Denny's, McDonald's, Steak'n Shake, Subway, Wendy's, Holiday Inn, 7-11, Meijer/dsl, S BP/dsl, Cracker Barrel, Culver's, Olive Garden, Holiday Inn Express, Sam's Club/gas, Save-A-Lot Foods
136	Lp 94, MI 60, to Jackson
135mm	**full facilities, litter barrels, petwalk, eb, vending**
133	Dearing Rd, Spring Arbor, S to Spring Arbor U
130	Parma, S $General
128	Michigan Ave, N BP/Burger King/scales/dsl/24hr,
128	Continued Marathon/deli/dsl, Zephyr Hill Farms
127	Concord Rd
124	MI 99, to Eaton Rapids
121	28 Mile Rd, to Albion, N Mobil/Subway/dsl, Arby's, Days Inn, S Marathon/dsl, Speedway/dsl, Sunoco/dsl, Frosty Dan's, KFC, La Casa Mexican, McDonald's, Pizza Hut, Taco Bell, Super 9 Inn, $General, AutoZone, Buick/Chevrolet, Family Fare Foods, Family$, Ford, H, O'Reilly Parts, Tire City/auto
119	MI 199, 26 Mile Rd
115	22.5 Mile Rd, N Citgo/115 Rest./dsl/24hr
113mm	**full facilities, litter barrels, petwalk, wb, vending**
112	Partello Rd, S Love's/Hardee's/scales/dsl/24hr, Schuler's Rest.(2mi)
110	Old US 27, Marshall, N Shell/Country Kitchen/Subway/dsl/24hr, S Citgo/dsl, Tesla EVC, Denny's, Schuler's Rest. (2mi), Hampton Inn, Holiday Inn Express, H, sheriff
108	I-69, US 27, N to Lansing, S to Ft Wayne
104	11 Mile Rd, Michigan Ave, N Pilot/McDonald's/dsl/scales/24hr, TA/Country Pride/dsl/scales/24hr/@, S Citgo/Subway/dsl/e85, Quality Inn/rest., casino
102mm	Kalamazoo River
100	rd 294, Beadle Lake Rd, N Moonraker Rest., S Citgo/dsl/repair, Binder Park Zoo
98b	I-194 N, to Battle Creek
98a	MI 66, to Sturgis, same as 97, S Citgo/Tim Horton/dsl, Chili's, Los Aztecas, McDonald's, Ruby Tuesday, Schlotzsky's, Starbucks, Steak'n Shake, Courtyard, Holiday Inn, TownePlace Suites, AT&T, Best Buy, Discount Tire, Kohl's, Lowe's, Meijer/dsl, Menards, Michael's, PetCo, Sam's Club/gas, Staples, TJ Maxx, Verizon, Walgreens, Walmart/Subway
97	Capital Ave, to Battle Creek, N BP, Marathon, Arby's, Domino's, Lux Cafe, McDonald's, Old China, Red Lobster, Knights Inn, Quality Inn, S BP/Subway, Shell/dsl, Applebee's, Bob Evans, Buffalo Wild Wings, Burger King, Cracker Barrel, Culver's, Denny's, Fazoli's, Hibachi Steaks, Jimmy John's, La Cocina, Panera Bread, Pizza Hut, Qdoba, Taco Bell, Baymont Inn, Best Value Inn, Best Western, Fairfield Inn, Hampton Inn, Red Roof Inn, Rodeway Inn, Travelodge, $Tree, AAA, Barnes&Noble, Belle Tire, BigLots, Firestone/auto, Harley Davidson, Hobby Lobby, Jo-Ann Fabrics, Target, Uncle Ed's Oil Shoppe, URGENT CARE, vet
96mm	**full facilities, litter barrels, petwalk, eb, vending**
95	Helmer Rd, N Citgo/dsl, Arby's, Big Boy, Meijer/dsl/e85
92	Lp 94, rd 37, to Battle Creek, Springfield, N BP/Arlene's Trkstp/dsl/rest./24hr, Shell, to Ft Custer RA
88	Climax, N Galesburg Speedway
85	35th St, Galesburg, N Shell/dsl, McDonald's, Subway, Galesburg Speedway, River Oaks CP, to Ft Custer RA, S Colebrook CP, Scott's Mill CP
85mm	**full facilities, litter barrels, petwalk, wb, vending**
81	Lp 94(from wb), to Kalamazoo
80	Cork St, Sprinkle Rd, to Kalamazoo, N Marathon/dsl, Speedway/dsl, Sunoco/dsl, Arby's, Burger King, Crew Rest., Denny's, Godfather's, Taco Bell, Baymont Inn, Clarion, Holiday Inn Express, Red Roof Inn, Sheraton, Monro, vet, S BP/dsl, Speedway/dsl, McDonald's, Michelle's Rest., Nob Hill Grill, Subway, Wendy's, Candlewood Suites, EconoLodge, Fairfield Inn, Motel 6, Quality Inn
78	Portage Rd, Kilgore Rd, N Mobil/Circle K, China Hut,

CHELSEA

JACKSON

PARMA

MARSHALL

CLIMAX

MI

= gas = food = lodging = other = rest stop

INTERSTATE 94 Cont'd

Exit	Services
78	Continued Summer Thyme Cafe, Comfort Inn, Residence Inn, H, repair, S Marathon/dsl, Shell, Speedway, Angelo's Italian, Biggby Coffee, Bravo Rest., Brewster's Jct., Café Meli, McDonald's, Pizza King, Subway, Taco Bell, Travelers Cafe, Country Inn&Suites, Days Inn, Hampton Inn, AutoValue Parts, Fields Fabrics
76	Westnedge Ave, N Meijer/dsl, Speedway/dsl, Grand Traverse Pie Co, Hibachi Buffet, IHOP, Jersey Giant Subs, Lee's Chicken, McDonald's, Old Chicago Grill, Outback Steaks, Papa Murphy's, Pizza Hut, Qdoba, Riviera Mayo, Root Beer Stand, Steak'n Shake, Subway, Taco Bell, Theo&Stacy's Rest., Courtyard, Homewood Suites, $Tree, Advance Parts, Discount Tire, Earth Fare, Firestone/auto, Goodyear/auto, Lowe's, Midas, Walgreens, S Shell, Antique Kitchen Rest., Applebee's, Biggby Coffee, Blaze Pizza, Bob Evans, Brann's Steaks, Burger King, Carrabba's, Chick-fil-A, Chili's, ChuckECheese's, Coldstone, CoreLife Eatery, Culver's, Five Guys, HoneyBaked Ham, Jimmy John's, KFC, Little Caesar's, Logan's Roadhouse, Los Amigos Mexican, McDonald's, Moe's SW Grill, Noodles&Co, Olive Garden, Panera Bread, Penn Sta Subs, Qdoba Mexican, Red Lobster, Red Robin, Schlotzsky's, Starbucks, Subway, Taco Bell, Tim Horton, TX Roadhouse, Wendy's, Zoup!, Holiday Motel, $Tree, ALDI, AT&T, AutoZone, Barnes&Noble, Belle Tire, Best Buy, BigLots, Buick/Cadillac/GMC, Dick's, Fannie May Candies, Firestone/auto, Harding's Mkt, Hobby Lobby, Home Depot, JC Penney, JoAnn Fabrics, Kohl's, Macy's, Michael's, Monro, O'Reilly Parts, Old Navy, PepBoys, Petco, Sam's Club/gas, Target, TJMaxx, Tuesday Morning, Tuffy Auto, Verizon, Walgreens, World Mkt
75	Oakland Dr
74b a	US 131, to Kalamazoo, N Kalamazoo Coll, to W MI U
72	9th St, Oshtemo, N Citgo/dsl, Speedway/dsl, Arby's, Culver's, McDonald's, Starbucks, Taco Bell, Wendy's, Hampton Inn, S Fairfield Inn, Microtel, Towne Place Suites
66	Mattawan, N Citgo/dsl, Speedway/Subway/dsl/scales/24hr, Chinn Chinn, Mancino's Italian, $General, Family$, Freightliner, R&S RV Service, vet, S Shell/dsl, Pizza Hut, Subway, USPO, Wagoner's Foods
60	MI 40, Paw Paw, N Citgo, Speedway/dsl, Arby's, Biggby Coffee, Burger King, Chicken Coop, Copper Grille, McDonald's, Pizza Hut, Red's Root Beer, Subway, Taco Bell, Wendy's, Comfort Inn, EconoLodge, Travelodge, Advance Parts, AT&T, Buick/Chevrolet/GMC, Chrysler/Dodge/Jeep, Family Fare Mkt, Ford, H, O'Reilly Parts, St Julian Winery, Walgreens, S Walmart/Subway
56	MI 51, to Decatur, N st police, S Citgo/dsl, Marathon/dsl
52	Lawrence
46	Hartford, N Shell/dsl, McDonald's, Panel Room Rest., Subway
42mm	**full facilities, litter barrels, petwalk, wb, vending**
41	MI 140, to Niles, Watervliet, N Casey's/dsl, Citgo, Marathon/dsl, Shell/dsl, Burger King, Chicken Coop, Frosty Boy, Mill Creek Charlie's Rest., Subway, Taco Bell, Fairfield Inn, H, KOA(Apr-Oct)(7mi)
39	Millburg, Coloma, Deer Forest, N BP/dsl, Shell/dsl, Speedway/dsl, Wesco/dsl, DQ, El Asadero Mexican, Friendly Grill, McDonald's, Subway, Family$, Krenek RV Ctr, S fruit mkt, wine tasting
34	I-196 N, US 31 N, to Holland, Grand Rapids
33	Lp I-94, to Benton Harbor, N

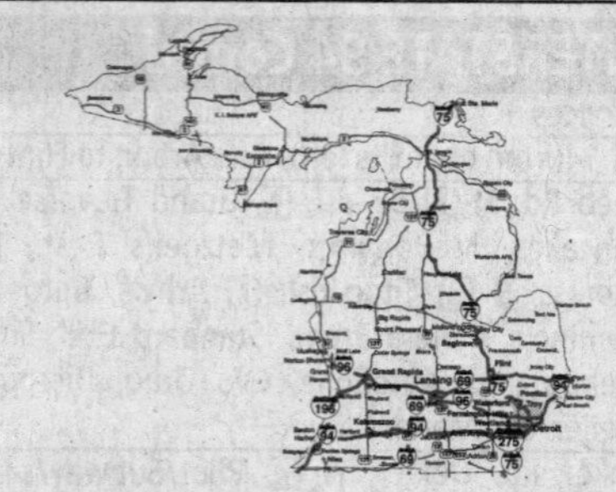

Exit	Services
30	Napier Ave, Benton Harbor, N Pilot/Wendy's/dsl/L 24hr/@, Shell/dsl, American Inn, Blue Beacon, H
29	Pipestone Rd, Benton Harbor, N Applebee's, Asian Gri Burger King, El Rodeo Mexican, IHOP, McDonald's, Popey Sophia's Pancake House, Steak'n Shake, Super Buffet, Corral, Best Western, Days Inn, Hilton Garden, Red Ro Inn, Travelodge, ALDI, Best Buy, Big Lots, Chrysler/Dodg Jeep, Home Depot, JC Penney, Jo-Ann Fabrics, Lowe Meijer/dsl, Staples, USPO, Walmart/Subway, S BP/dsl, Bob Evans, Comfort Suites, Holiday Inn Express
28	US 31 S, MI 139 N, Scottdale Rd, to Niles, N Citgo/d Marathon/dsl, Burger King, Chicken Coop, Coun Kitchen, Henry's Burgers, Jimmy John's, Joey C Pizza, KF Little Caesar's, Pizza Hut, Sonic, Subway, Taco Bell, Wendy Best Value Inn, Loyalty Inn, $General, $Tree, AutoZor Belle Tire, Chevrolet/Buick/GMC, Family$, H, Kohl's, M& Tire, Michael's, Midas, NAPA, O'Reilly Parts, PetSma radiators/repair/transmissions, Save-A-Lot, TJ Maxx, U-Ha vet, Walgreens
27mm	St Joseph River
27	MI 63, Niles Ave, to St Joseph, N Citgo, Nye's App Barn, S Tesla EVC, Five Guys, Moe's SW Grill, Pane Bread, Goodyear
23	Red Arrow Hwy, Stevensville, N Admiral, BP/Taco John Marathon/dsl, Mobil/Dunkin', Shell/dsl, Big Boy, Burg King, Coach's Grill, Cracker Barrel, Crimson Cafe, Culver DQ, LJ Silver, McDonald's, Papa John's, Baymont In Candlewood Suites, Comfort Suites, Fairfield Inn, Super 8, Honda, Walgreens, S Hampton Inn, Meijer/dsl
22	John Beers Rd, Stevensville, N Chalet on the Lake, Grand Mere SP, S Marathon/dsl
16	Bridgman, N BP/Quiznos/dsl, camping, to Warre Dunes SP, S Citgo, Early Bird Eatery, Lydia's Res McDonald's, Pizza Hut, Roma Pizza, Subway, Bridgma Inn, auto repair, Chevrolet, Chrysler/Dodge/Jeep, For Mazda, vet
12	Sawyer, N Marathon/deli/dsl/scales/24hr, truck was S TA/Burger King/Popeyes/Taco Bell/scales/dsl/24hr/ Family$, Greenbush Brewing, Super 8, USPO
6	Lakeside, Union Pier, N Round Barn Winery, St Julia Winery, S RV camping
4b a	US 12, to Three Oaks, New Buffalo, N Pizza Hu Redamak's Hamburgers, Roma Pizza
2.5mm	weigh sta both lanes
1	MI 239, to Grand Beach, New Buffalo, N Shell/Subway dsl, Brewster's Italian, Casey's Grille, McDonald Nancy's, Rosie's Rest., Stray Dog Grill, Subway, Baymo Inn, Fairfield Inn, Holiday Inn Express, Quality Inn, Super In $General, S Days Inn, casino
0.5mm	**full facilities, info, litter barrels, petwalk, vending, Welcome Ctr eb**
0mm	Michigan/Indiana state line

INTERSTATE 96

Exit	Services
191.5mm	I-96 begins/ends on I-75, exit 48 in Detroit.

INTERSTATE 96 Cont'd

Exit #	Services
191	I-75, N to Flint, S to Toledo, US 12, to MLK Blvd, to Michigan Ave
190b	Warren Ave, N BP/dsl
190a	I-94 E to Port Huron
189	W Grand Blvd, Tireman Rd, N Citgo/dsl, Mobil
188b	Joy Rd, N Church's TX Chicken
188a	Livernois, N Exxon/Subway, Mobil, Burger King, KFC, McDonald's, Wendy's
187	Grand River Ave(from eb)
186b	Davison Ave, I-96 local and I-96 express divide, no exits from express
186a	Wyoming Ave
185	Schaefer Hwy, to Grand River Ave, N Citgo, Mobil, Coney Island, McDonald's, CVS Drug, S Sunoco/dsl
184	Greenfield Rd
183	MI 39, Southfield Fwy, exit from expswy and local
182	Evergreen Rd
180	Outer Dr, N BP/dsl/lube
180mm	I-96 local/express unite/divide
179	US 24, Telegraph Rd, N BP, Marathon/dsl, Arby's, Baskin-Robbins/Dunkin', China King, Little Caesar's, McDonald's, Tim Horton's, White Castle, AutoZone, Chevrolet, Family$, Family$, O'Reilly Parts, URGENT CARE, S Marathon/dsl, Shell/dsl
178	Beech Daly Rd, N Sunoco
177	Inkster Rd, N BP/Tim Horton, Best Value Inn, $General, 7-11, URGENT CARE
176	Middlebelt Rd, N Bob Evans, IHOP, Olive Garden, Comfort Inn, ALDI, H, S Applebee's, Chili's, Culver's, Del Taco, Five Guys, Jimmy John's, Leo's Coney Island, Logan's Roadhouse, McDonald's, MOD Pizza, Noodles&Co, Outback, Panda Express, Panera Bread, Pizza Hut, Popeyes, Potbelly, Qdoba, Red Lobster, Starbucks, Hampton Inn, Holiday Inn Express, Hometowne Suites, Jo-Ann Fabrics, $Tree, AT&T, AutoZone, BigLots, Costco/gas, Dick's, Firestone/auto, GNC, Goodyear/auto, Home Depot, Marshall's, Meijer, Menard's, Michael's, Office Depot, PetSmart, Target, URGENT CARE, Verizon, Walgreens, Walmart
175	Merriman Rd, N Mobil/dsl, Speedway/dsl, S Exxon/dsl, Prime Grill
174	Farmington Rd, N Mobil/dsl, Sunoco, Looney Baker, S BP, KFC, vet
173b	Levan Rd, N H, to Madonna U
173a	Newburgh Rd
171mm	I-275 and I-96 run together 9 miles
170	6 Mile Rd, N Bar Louie, Big Boy, Buffalo Wild Wings, Jersey Mike's, Jimmy John's, Johnny's Italian, Panera Bread, Qdoba, Red Robin, Best Western, Courtyard, Holiday Inn, Marriott, Ace Hardware, AT&T, Busch's Foods, GNC, H, O'Reilly Parts, Verizon, Walgreens, S Marathon, Mobil, Applebee's, Brann's Steaks, Bravo Italian, Buca Italian, Charlie's Grille, Claddagh Rest., Fleming's, Hyde Park Steaks, Leo's Coney Island, McDonald's, Mitchell's Fish Mkt, Noodles&Co, Panchero's, PF Chang, Potbelly, Tahini Grill, Tim Horton, Wendy's, Fairfield Inn, Residence Inn, TownePlace Suites, Barnes&Noble, CVS, Kroger, Office Depot, PetSmart, REI
169b a	7 Mile Rd, N Dave&Buster's, Los Amigos, Embassy Suites, S EVC, Andiamo's Cafe, Bahama Breeze Rest., BJ's Rest., Burger Fi, Chipotle, Gaucho Brazilian, Granite City Grill, J Alexander's Rest., Jimmy John's, Macaroni Grill, MOD Pizza, Rusty Bucket Rest., Trader Joe, Hyatt Place, AT&T, Home Depot
167	8 Mile Rd, to Northville, S BP/dsl, Speedway/dsl, Benihana, Big Boy, Chili's, Five Guys, Kerby's Koney Island, McDonald's, Mission BBQ, On-the-Border, Panera Bread, Qdoba, Starbucks, Taco Bell, Twin Peaks, Zoup!, Country Inn Suites, Extended Stay America, Hampton Inn, Holiday Inn Express, Sheraton, Best Buy, Costco/gas, Dick's, Firestone/auto, Kohl's, Meijer/dsl, Target, to Maybury SP, Verizon
165	I-696, I-275, MI 5, Grand River Ave. I-275 and I-96 run together 9 miles
163	I-696(from eb)
162	Novi Rd, to Walled Lake, Novi, N BP, Bar Louie, Black Rock Rest., Buddy's Pizzaria, Buffalo Wild Wings, CA Pizza, Carrabba's, Cheesecake Factory, ChuckECheese's, Coldstone, McDonald's, Novi Chophouse, Red Lobster, Starbucks, Subway, Taco Bell, Hilton Garden, Renaissance, Residence Inn, BigLots, Dick's, JC Penney, JoAnn Fabrics, Kohl's, Lord&Taylor, Macy's, Marshalls, Michael's, Midas, Nordstrom, Old Navy, S Mobil/dsl, Sunoco/dsl, Athenian Coney Island, Bagger Dave's Burgers, BD Mongolian BBQ, Blaze Pizza, Bonefish Grill, Boston Mkt, Chipotle, Famous Dave's, Genji Japanese, Honeybaked Express, IHOP, Jersey Mike's, Maisano's Italian, Noodles&Co, Olive Garden, Panda Express, Panera Bread, Pei Wei, Pizza Hut, Potbelly, Primanti Bros, Qdoba, Red Robin, Steve&Rocky's, TGIFriday's, Tony Sacco Pizza, Wasabi, Wendy's, Courtyard, DoubleTree, Homewood Suites, Towne Place Suites, Advance Parts, AT&T, Belle Tire, Better Health Mkt, Chevrolet, Discount Tire, Hobby Lobby, H, Kia, Monro/auto, NAPA, O'Reilly Parts, TJ Maxx, URGENT CARE, Verizon, Walmart
160	Beck Rd, 12 Mile Rd, S EVC, Shell/Tim Horton, Applebee's, China King, Guido's Pizza, La Herraduro Mexican, Leo's Coney Island, Olga's Kitchen, Outback Steaks, Starbucks, Subway, Zoup!, Hyatt Place, Staybridge Suites, GNC, Home Depot, H, Kroger, Staples, to Maybury SP
159	Wixom Rd, Walled Lake, N Marathon/dsl, Sunoco/dsl, Culver's, Denise's Grill, Quiznos, Wendy's, Holiday Inn Express, My Place, Springhill Suites, ALDI, General RV Ctr, Meineke, Menard's, to Proud Lake RA, S Exxon, Mobil/dsl, Valero/dsl, A&W/KFC, Arby's, Baskin-Robbins/Dunkin', Burger King, Dickey's BBQ, Grand Diner, Jimmy John's, McDonald's, Red Olive Rest., Shakers Grill, Stinger's Grill, Taco Bell, Tropical Cafe, Comfort Suites, AutoZone, Lincoln, Meijer/dsl, Sam's Club/gas, Target
155b a	to Milford, New Hudson, N Camp Dearborn(5mi), Ford, to Lyon Oaks CP, S Sunoco, Applebee's, Arby's, Biggby Coffee, Jet's Pizza, Jimmy John's, Kensington Grill, Leo's Coney Island, McDonald's, Starbucks, Subway, Tim Horton's, AAA, AT&T, Belle Tire, Chevrolet, Discount Tire, Hyundai, Lowe's, URGENT CARE, Verizon, Walmart
153	Kent Lake Rd, N Kensington Metropark, S BP/dsl, Country Meadows Inn(3mi)
151	Kensington Rd, N Kensington Metropark, S Island Lake RA
150	Pleasant Valley Rd(no return wb)
148b a	US 23, N to Flint, S to Ann Arbor
147	Spencer Rd, N Mobil/dsl, Cheryl's Cafe, st police, S to Brighton St RA
145	Grand River Ave, to Brighton, N BP, Shell/dsl, Arby's, Baskin-Robbins/Dunkin', Cracker Barrel, Outback Steaks, Pizza Hut, Courtyard, $General, Buick/GMC, Ford, Honda, H, Mazda, URGENT CARE, vet, S Marathon/Subway, Big Boy, Burger King, Chili's, Chipotle, Firehouse Subs, Five Guys, Gourmet Garden, IHOP, Jimmy John's, Leo's Coney Island, Lil Chef, McDonald's, MOD Pizza, Olga's Kitchen, Panda Express, Panera Bread, Pi's Asian, Potbelly,

LIVERNOIS · NOVI · NEW HUDSON

= gas = food = lodging = other = rest stop

INTERSTATE 96 Cont'd

Exit	Services
145	Continued Red Robin, Starbucks, Taco Bell, Tim Horton, Wendy's, Homewood Suites, Wingate Inn, $Tree, AAA, Advance Parts, AlLDI, AT&T, Belle Tire, Best Buy, Bob's Tire, CVS Drug, Home Depot, JoAnn Fabrics, Marshalls, Meijer/dsl, Michael's, O'Reilly Parts, PetSmart, Staples, Target, to Brighton Ski Area, USPO, Verizon, Walgreens
141	Lp 96(from wb, return at 140), to Howell,, **N** BP/dsl, Shell/Tim Horton/dsl, Speedway, Sunoco/dsl, Applebee's, Arby's, Asian Fusian Buffet, Aubree's Pizzaria, Biggby Coffee, Bluefin Steaks, Bob Evans, Buffalo Wild Wings, Jimmy John's, KFC, Leo's Coney Island, Little Caesar's, Los Tres Amigos, McDonald's, Panera Bread, Qdoba, Subway, Taco Bell, White Castle, $Tree, AT&T, Belle Tire, Big Lots, Chevrolet, Discount Tire, GNC, Home Depot, Kohl's, Lowe's, Meijer, O'Reilly Parts, PetSmart, URGENT CARE, Walmart
140	S Latson Rd, same as 141
137	D19, to Pinckney, Howell, **N** Marathon, Mobil/dsl, Speedway/dsl, Sunoco/Baskin-Robbins/Dunkin'/dsl, All Star Coney Island, Block Brewing Co, Joanna's 2 Go, Taco Bell, Wendy's, Kensington Inn, H, Parts+, Spartan Tire, True Value, USPO, **S** Wooly Bully's Rest., Magnuson Hotel
FOWLERVILLE	
135mm	**full facilities, litter barrels, petwalk, eb, vending**
133	MI 59, Highland Rd, **N** Marathon/McDonald's/dsl, Arby's, Jersey Giant Subs, Leo's Coney Island, Baymont, Holiday Inn Express, Tanger Outlets/famous brands
129	Fowlerville Rd, Fowlerville, **N** BP/dsl, Marathon/dsl, Sunoco/dsl, Great Lakes Rest., McDonald's, Pizza Hut/Taco Bell, Wendy's, Magnuson Hotel, Chevrolet, O'Reilly Parts, Walmart, **S** Mobil/dsl, Subway, Chysler/Dodge/Jeep, Ford
126mm	weigh sta both lanes
122	MI 43, MI 52, Webberville, **N** Mobil/dsl/24hr, McDonald's
117	to Dansville, Williamston, **N** Marathon/Jersey's Giant Subs/dsl, **S** Sunoco/dsl
111mm	**full facilities, litter barrels, petwalk, wb, vending**
110	Okemos, Mason, **N** Jimmy John's, Marathon/dsl, Sunoco/Dunkin', Applebee's, Arby's, Backyard BBQ, Big John's Steaks, Biggby Coffee, Coldstone/Tim Horton, Cracker Barrel, Culver's, Grand Traverse Pie Co., Hibachi Grille, Leaf Salad Bar, Little Caesar's, Lucky's Steaks, McDonald's, Ozzy Mediterranean, Panchero's Mexican, Starbucks, Stillwater Grill, Subway, Taco Bell, Comfort Inn, Fairfield Inn, Hampton Inn, Holiday Inn Express, Staybridge Suites, 7-11, BMW/Porsche, Mercedes, to stadium, Verizon
106b a	I-496, US 127, to Jackson, Lansing, **N** St Police
LANSING	
104	Lp 96, Cedar St, to Holt, Lansing, **N** Admiral, Speedway/dsl, Applebee's, Arby's, Asia's Finest, Big John's, Biggby Coffee, Blimpie, Bob Evans, Boston Mkt, Burger King, China King, Domino's, Fazoli's, Happy's Pizza, Hooters, Jet's Pizza, KFC, Los Tres Amigos, Mikado Grill, Panda Gourmet, Pizza Hut, Steak'n Shake, Taco Bell, TX Roadhouse, Wendy's, Zeus Coney Island, Best Value Inn, $Tree, ALDI, AT&T, auto repair, Belle Tire, Cadillac, Chevrolet, Chrysler/Dodge/Jeep, Discount Tire, Family$, GNC, H, Kia, Lexus, Meijer/dsl, Menards, Target, Toyota, Tuffy Auto, Verizon, vet, **S** Speedway/dsl, Aldaco's Taco Bar, Burger King, Champion's Grill, China East Buffet, Dairy Dan, Hungry Howie's, McDonald's, Starbucks, Subway, Taco Bell, Causeway Bay Hotel, Advance Parts, AutoZone, Budget Tire, CVS Drug, Family$, Kroger/gas, Lowe's, NAPA,

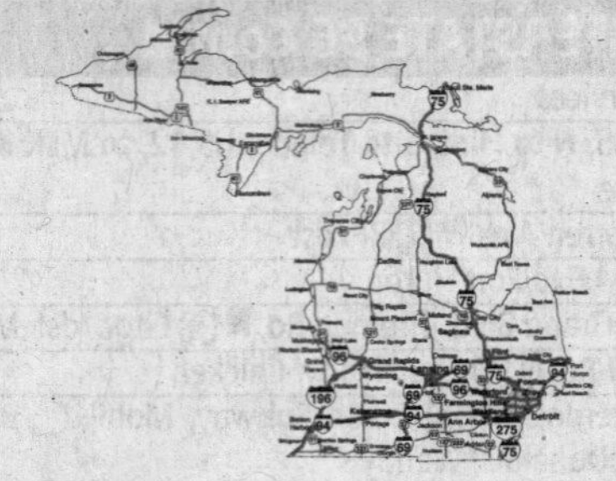

Exit	Services
LANSING	
104	Continued O'Reilly Parts, URGENT CARE, Verizon
101	MI 99, MLK Blvd, to Eaton Rapids, **N** QD, **S** Mobil/Tim Horton, Speedway/Subway/dsl, Coach's Grill, McDonald's, Wendy's
98b a	Lansing Rd, to Lansing, **N** Arby's, Wendy's, Comfort Inn, Holiday Inn Express, Harley-Davidson, **S** st police
97	I-69, US 27 S, S to Ft Wayne, N to Lansing
95	I-496, to Lansing
92mm	Grand River
91	I-69 N(from wb), US 27 N, to Flint
90	Grand River Ave, to airport(from wb), **N** Love's/Hardee's/Subway/dsl/scales/24hr, **S** Flying J/Denny's/dsl/24hr, E Love's/Hardee's/dsl/scales/24hr/@
89	I-69 N, US 27 N(from eb), to Flint
87mm	**full facilities, litter barrels, petwalk, eb vending**
86	MI 100, Wright Rd, to Grand Ledge, **S** Mobil/McDonald's/dsl, Speedway/Subway/24hr
PORTLAND	
84	to Eagle, Westphalia
79mm	**full facilities, info, litter barrels, petwalk, wb vending**
77	Lp 96, Grand River Ave, Portland, **N** Citgo/dsl, Shell/Subway, Speedway/dsl, Arby's, Biggby Coffee, Burger King, Little Caesar's, McDonald's, New China Buffet, Red Tomato Pizza, American Heritage Inn, CarQuest, Family$, Tom's Foods, Verizon, **S** Tom's/dsl, Wendy's
76	Kent St, Portland
76mm	Grand River
73	to Lyons-Muir, Grand River Ave
69mm	weigh sta both lanes
67	MI 66, to Ionia, Battle Creek, **N** Pilot/Subway/dsl/scales/24hr, Corner Landing Grill, Midway Motel, Super 8, Alice Springs RV Park(3mi), H, Lakeside Camping, Meijer/dsl(4mi), Walmart(4mi)
64	to Lake Odessa, Saranac, **N** Ionia St RA, **S** I-96 Speedway
63mm	**full facilities, litter barrels, petwalk, eb vending**
59	Clarksville
52	MI 50, to Lowell, **N** Mobil/Subway/dsl, **S** Marathon/dsl(2mi)
46mm	Thornapple River
46	rd 6, to rd 37
44	36 St, **S**
CASCADE	
43b a	MI 11, 28th St, Cascade, **N** Bagger Dave's, Biggby Coffee, Brann's Steaks, Culver's, Dan's Diner, Dunkin'/Baskin Robbins, Firehouse Subs, Freddy's, Gipper's Grill, Jet's Pizza, Jimmy John's, Korean BBQ, Leo's Coney Island, New Beginnings Rest., Panera Bread, Pit Stop BBQ, Pizza Hut, Qdoba, Starbucks, Subway, Sundance Grill, Taco Bell, Baymont Inn, Best Western, Country Inn&Suites, Crowne Plaza, EconoLodge, Holiday Inn Express, Ace Hardware, AT&T, Audi/Porsche/Subaru, Fresh Mkt, GNC, Meijer/dsl, Mercedes/Volvo/VW, Verizon, Walmart, **S** Citgo, Shell, Speedway/dsl, Applebee's, Arby's, Arby's, Arnie's Rest., Bob Evans, Buddy's Pizza, Burger King, Cantina Mexican,

INTERSTATE 96 Cont'd

CASCADE

43b a Continued
Chick-fil-A, Chipotle Mexican, ChuckeCheese, Dave&Buster's, Denny's, Five Guys, Grand Coney, Grand Traverse Pie Co, Honey Baked Ham, IHOP, Jersey Mike's, Jimmy John's, Krispy Kreme, Longhorn Steaks, McDonald's, Moe's SW Grill, Noodles&Co, Old Chicago, Olive Garden, Osaka Japanese, Outback Steaks, Panera Bread, Pizza Hut, Pizza Ranch, Potbelly, Red Lobster, Smokey Bones, Starbucks, Steak'n Shake, Subway, Taco Bell, Tropical Cafe, TX Roadhouse, Wendy's, lodging Clarion, Comfort Inn, Courtyard, Delta Marriott, DoubleTree, Drury Inn, Extended Stay America, Fairfield Inn, Hampton Inn, Hawthorn Suites, Homewood Suites, Motel 6, Red Roof Inn, Residence Inn, Sleep Inn, SpringHill Suites, Tru Hilton, Wyndham Garden, other $General, $Tree, Advance Parts, ALDI, Belle Tire, Best Buy, Big Lots, Costco/gas, Dick's, Ford/Mazda, Hobby Lobby, Home Depot, Honda, Hyundai/Kia, Jo-Ann Fabrics, Lowe's, Michael's, Monro Auto, Nissan, Old Navy, PetSmart, Sam's Club/gas, Staples, Target, TJ Maxx, Trader Joe's, Tuesday Morning, U-Haul, World Mkt

40b a Cascade Rd, N gas BP/dsl, Forest Hills Fuel, food Biggby Coffee, Forest Hills Mkt, Great Harvest, Jets Pizza, Little Bangkok, Little Caesar's, Manna Cafe, Noco Provisions, Subway, other vet, Walgreens, S gas Shell/dsl, Speedway/dsl, food Bonefish Grill, Jimmy John's, Zoup!, other H

39 MI 21(from eb), to Flint

38 E Beltline Ave, to MI 21, MI 37, MI 44, N gas BP, food Applebee's, Fuji Yama Japanese, Red Hot Inn Rest., Wendy's, other Meijer/dsl, URGENT CARE, Verizon, S food Gravity Grille, lodging Country Inn&Suites, other H

37 I-196(from wb, exits left), Gerald Ford Fwy, to Grand Rapids

36 Leonard St, S food Arby's, Jimmy John's, McDonald's

33 Plainfield Ave, MI 44 Connector, N gas Citgo/dsl, Speedway/dsl, food Anna's House, Arby's, Biggby Coffee, Charlie's Grille, Cheers Grill, Fred's Italian, Freddy's, Jimmy John's, KFC, Little Caesar's, Loco Taco, McDonald's, Pizza Hut, Rice Wok, Russ' Rest., Subway, Taco Bell, Tim Horton's, Wendy's, lodging Lazy T Motel, Motel 6, other $Tree, AAA, AutoZone, Belle Tire, BigLots, Chevrolet, Chrysler/Jeep/Dodge, CVS, Discount Tire, Firestone/auto, Ford, Kia, Lowe's, Meijer/dsl, Midas, NAPA, Nissan/VW, O'Reilly Parts, Quality/auto, Toyota, U-Haul, vet, Walgreens, S gas BP, food Denny's

31mm Grand River

31b a US 131, N to Cadillac, S to Kalamazoo, N gas Speedway/Subway/dsl, food McDonald's

GRAND RAPIDS

30b a Alpine Ave, Grand Rapids, N gas BP/dsl, Marathon/dsl, Mobil, food Applebee's, Buffalo Wild Wings, Checkers, ChuckeCheese, Culver's, El Burrito Mexican, Empire Buffet, Firehouse Subs, First Wok, Five Guys, Freddy's, Golden Corral, Hibachi Grill, IHOP, Jersey Mike's, Jimmy John's, Little Caesar's, Logan's Roadhouse, McDonald's, MOD Pizza, Olive Garden, Outback Steaks, Panda Express, Panera Bread, Qdoba, Russ' Rest., Sonic, Starbucks, Steak'n Shake, Subway, Taco Bell, TGIFriday's, Three Happiness Chinese, lodging Hampton Inn, Holiday Inn Express, SpringHill Suites, other $Tree, ALDI, AT&T, AutoZone, Belle Tire, Best Buy, Discount Tire, Ford, GNC, Hobby Lobby, Jo-Ann, Kohl's, Marshall's, Menards, Michael's, NAPA, PepBoys, PetCo, Sam's Club/gas, Target, TJ Maxx, Verizon, Walgreens, Walmart, S gas Admiral/dsl, Speedway/dsl, food Arby's, Burger King, Fazoli's, Jimmy John's, KFC, LJ Silver, McDonald's, Papa John's, Wendy's, lodging Best Value Inn, other Goodyear/auto, Home Depot, Meijer/dsl, Midas, O'Reilly Parts, U-Haul, URGENT CARE

28 Walker Ave, S gas Meijer/dsl/24hr, food Bob Evans, McDonald's, lodging Baymont Inn, Quality Inn

26 Fruit Ridge Ave, N gas Citgo/dsl, S Marathon/deli/dsl

EASTMANVILLE

25mm **full facilities, litter barrels, petwalk, phone, picnic, rest stop eb**

25 8th Ave, 4Mile Rd(from wb), S gas Marathon/dsl, lodging Wayside Motel

24 8th Ave, 4Mile Rd(from eb), S gas Marathon/dsl, lodging Wayside Motel

23 Marne, N other tires, S food Depot Café, Rinaldi's Café, other Ernie's Mkt, fairgrounds/raceway, USPO

19 Lamont, Coopersville, S other LP

16 B-35, Eastmanville, N gas Citgo/Subway/dsl, Shell/Burger King/dsl, Speedway/dsl/24hr, food #1 Chinese, Arby's, Biggby Coffee, Hungry Howie's, Little Caesar's, McDonald's, New Beginnings Rest., Taco Bell, lodging Rodeway Inn, other Buick/Chevrolet, Chrysler/Dodge/Jeep, Family Fare Foods, Family$, Ford, Fun 'N Sun RV Ctr, vet, S gas Pacific Pride/dsl, other RV camping

10 B-31(exits left from eb), Nunica, N food Turk's Rest., S other Conestoga RV camping, golf course/rest.

9 MI 104(from wb, exits left), to Grand Haven, Spring Lake, S gas Marathon/dsl, other to Grand Haven SP, vet

8mm **full facilities, litter barrels, petwalk, phone, picnic, rest stop wb, vending**

GRAND HAVEN

5 Fruitport(from wb, no return)

4 Airline Rd, S gas Speedway/dsl, Wesco/dsl, food Burger Crest Diner, McDonald's, Norm's Ice Cream, Subway, Village Inn, other $General, Grover Drug, Orchard Mkt Foods, to PJ Hoffmaster SP, USPO

1c Hile Rd(from eb), S gas Tesla EVC, food Arby's, Asian Buffet, Bob Evans, Brann's Grille, Buffalo Wild Wings, Burger King, ChuckeCheese, Five Guys, Golden Corral, Grand Traverse Pie Co, Kazumi Steaks, KFC/Taco Bell, Logan's Roadhouse, McDonald's, Olive Garden, Qdoba, Red Lobster, Red Robin, Starbucks, Subway, TX Roadhouse, lodging Baymont Inn, Fairfield Inn, Hampton Inn, other $Tree, ALDI, AT&T, Barnes&Noble, Belle Tire, Best Buy, Dick's, Hobby Lobby, JC Penney, Jo-Ann Fabrics, Kohl's, Meijer/dsl, Menards, Old Navy, PetCo, Target, TJ Maxx, Verizon, VW/Audi/Nissan/Subaru/Toyota

1b a US 31, to Ludington, same as 1c, Grand Haven, N food Applebee's, Arby's, Fazoli's, Los Amigos, McDonald's, Panera Bread, Pizza Ranch, Red Wok, Subway, Taco Bell, Tim Horton, Wendy's, lodging Airline Motel, Alpine Motel, Bel-aire Motel, Quality Inn/rest., other $Tree, All Seasons RV Ctr, Big Lots, GNC, H, Lowe's, Marathon/dsl, Norton Automotive, PetSmart, Sam's Club/gas, Staples, Walmart

0mm I-96 begins/ends on US 31 at Muskegon.

INTERSTATE 196 (Grand Rapids)

81mm I-196 begins/ends on I-96, 37mm in E Grand Rapids.

79 Fuller Ave, N other sheriff, S gas Shell/dsl, Speedway/dsl, food Biggby Coffee, Bill's Rest., Checkers, Elbow Room, KFC, Subway, Taco Bell, Wendy's, other Ace Hardware, Family$, H, Verizon, Walgreens

78 College Ave, S gas Mobil/Circle K, food McDonald's, Omelette Shop, other Ford Museum, H

77c Ottawa Ave, downtown, S other Gerald R Ford Museum

77b a US 131, S to Kalamazoo, N to Cadillac

76 MI 45 E, Lane Ave, S other Gerald R Ford Museum, John Ball Park&Zoo

75 MI 45 W, Lake Michigan Dr, S other to Grand Valley St U

74mm Grand River

73 Market Ave, N other to Vanandel Arena

72 Lp 196, Chicago Dr E(from eb)

70 MI 11(exits left from wb), Grandville, Walker, S gas Citgo/dsl, Shell, food New Beginnings, lodging Best Western+, other USPO, vet

69c Baldwin St (from wb)

69b a Chicago Dr, N gas Speedway, food Biggby Coffee, Culver's, Dickey's BBQ, Domino's, Fazoli's, Jimmy John's, KFC, McDonald's, Peppino's Pizza, Subway, Taco Bell, other $Tree,

INTERSTATE 196 (Grand Rapids) Cont'd

ZEELAND · GANGES

Exit	Services
69b a	Continued Advance Parts, ALDI, AutoZone, Meijer/dsl, O'Reilly Parts, USPO, Walgreens, S Admiral, Speedway/dsl, Adobe Mexican, Arby's, Brann's Steaks, Little Caesar's, Rainbow Grill, Russ' Rest., Wings&More, Grand Village Inn, Holiday Inn Express, NAPA
67	44th St, N Mobil/dsl, Burger King, Cracker Barrel, Panera Bread, Steak'n Shake, Comfort Suites, Honda, Walmart/Subway, S Anna's House, Applebee's, Big Boy, Carrabba's, China One, Famous Dave's, IHOP, Jimmy John's, Logan's Roadhouse, Noodles&Co, Olive Garden, On the Border, Qdoba, Red Lobster, Red Robin, Sakura Japanese, Starbucks, Subway, TGIFriday's, Tropical Smoothie, TX Roadhouse, Uccello's Ristorante, Wendy's, Residence Inn, $Tree, Barnes&Noble, Best Buy, Chrysler/Dodge/Jeep, Costco/gas, Dick's, Discount Tire, Family Fare Foods, Fiat, Gordman's, Hobby Lobby, Home Depot, JC Penney, Kohl's, Lowe's, Macy's, Marshall's, Meijer/zeal, Michael's, Old Navy, PetSmart, Verizon, World Mkt
64	MI 6 E, to Lansing(exits left from wb)
62	32nd Ave, to Hudsonville, N BP/dsl, Citgo/dsl, Arby's, Biggby Coffee, Burger King, Hudsonville Grille, Little Caesar's, McDonald's, Quality Inn, Chevrolet, S Mobil/Subway/dsl/24hr, Tesla EVC, Rainbow Grill, Wendy's, Travelodge, Harley-Davidson, Harvest Foods, Meijer/dsl
58mm	**full facilities, litter barrels, petwalk, eb, vending**
55	Byron Rd, Zeeland, N Citgo/7-11, Blimpie, McDonald's, H, to Holland SP
52	16th St, Adams St, N Speedway/dsl, Burger King, Jimmy John's, Papa Murphy's, Pizza Ranch, Wendy's, H, Meijer/dsl/e85, S Love's/Hardee's/dsl/scales/24hr, Mobil/Subway/dsl
49	MI 40, to Allegan, N BP/McDonald's/dsl, Residence Inn, S Pilot/Arby's/dsl/scales/24hr, Tulip City/Marathon/Subway/dsl/scales/24hr, truck repair, truck wash
44	US 31 N(from eb), to Holland, N food, gas, H
43mm	**full facilities, info, litter barrels, petwalk, wb, vending**
41	rd A-2, Douglas, Saugatuck, N Marathon/dsl, Marathon/dsl, Shell/Subway/dsl, Burger King, Dairy Dayz, Spectators Grill, Best Western(1mi), $General, NAPA, to Saugatuck SP, S Belvedere Inn/Rest.
38mm	Kalamazoo River
36	rd A-2, Ganges, N Shell, Christo's Rest., Pizza Mambo, Saugatuck Brewing Co, AmericInn, Blue Star Motel
34	MI 89, to Fennville, N to West Side CP, S Shell, Cranes Pie Pantry(4mi), Lyons Farm Mkt
30	rd A-2, Glenn, Ganges, N to Westside CP(4mi)
28mm	**full facilities, litter barrels, petwalk, eb, vending**
26	109th Ave, to Pullman, N Dutch Farm Mkt
22	N Shore Dr, N Cousin's RV Camping/rest., to Kal Haven Trail SP
20	rd A-2, Phoenix Rd, N BP/dsl, Marathon/dsl, Arby's, China Buffet, Taco Bell, $Tree, AutoZone, H, Meijer/dsl, Walgreens, S Murphy USA/dsl, Shell/dsl, Big Boy, McDonald's, Sherman's Dairybar, Wendy's, Baymont Inn, Comfort Suites, Hampton Inn, Holiday Inn Express, $General, ALDI, Menards, Walmart
18	MI 140, MI 43, to Watervliet, N Shell/dsl, Burger King, Little Caesar's, McDonald's, Pizza Hut, Great Lakes Inn, LakeBluff Motel, auto repair, AutoValue Parts, Buick/Cadillac/GMC, Chevrolet, Chrysler/Dodge/Jeep,

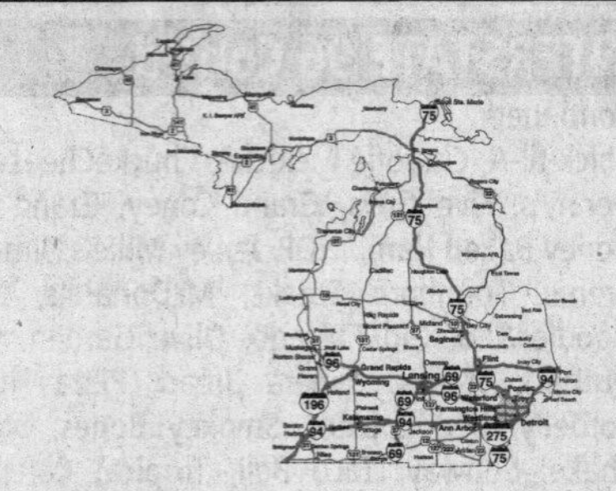

RIVERSIDE

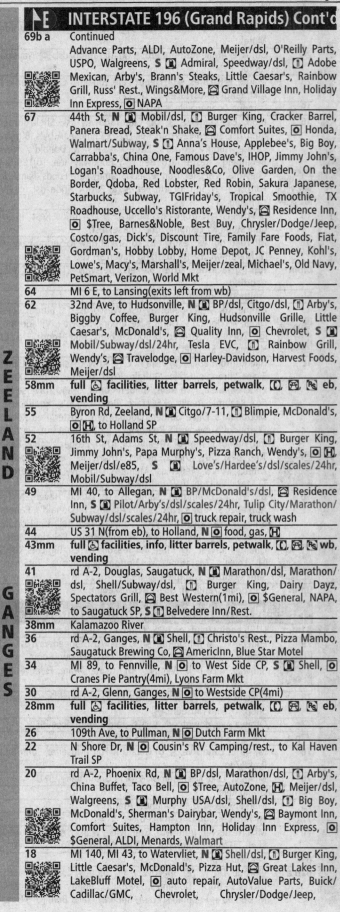

Exit	Services
18	Continued Ford/Lincoln, H, Village Mkt Foods, S KOA(Apr-Oct)
13	to Covert, N RV camping, to Van Buren SP
7	MI 63, to Benton Harbor, N DiMaggio's Pizza
4	to Coloma, Riverside, S Shell/dsl, KOA(Apr-Oct)
2mm	Paw Paw River
1	Red Arrow Hwy, N SW Michigan
0mm	I-94, E to Detroit, W to Chicago. I-196 begins/ends on I-94 exit 34 at Benton Harbor.

INTERSTATE 275 (Livonia)

GARDEN CITY · NEW BOSTON

Exit	Services
37mm	I-275 and I-96 run together 9 miles. See I-96, exits 165-170.
29	I-96 E, to Detroit, MI 14 W, to Ann Arbor
28	Ann Arbor Rd, Plymouth, E BP/Dunkin', Mobil, Shell/dsl, Little Caesar's, Los Tres Amigos, McDonald's, Red Roof Inn, $Tree, Verizon, W Burger King, Firehouse Subs, Grand Traverse Pie Co., Lee's Coney Island, Tropical Smoothie, Comfort Inn, Cadillac, CVS Drug, Lincoln, vet
25	MI 153, Ford Rd, Garden City, E Sam's Club, Logan Roadhouse, Parthenon Coney Island, Starbucks, Subway, Walmart, Home Depot, W BP, Speedway, Sunoco/dsl, Applebee's, Arby's, Basement Burger Bar, BD Mongolian BBQ, Black Rock Grill, Bob Evans, Boston Mkt, Bowery Grill, Buffalo Wild Wings, Burger King, Carrabba's, Carvel Ice Cream, Chili's, Chipotle, Chopstick House, ChuckeCheese, Coldstone, Dunkin'/Baskin-Robbins, Five Guys, Jersey Mike's, Jimmy John's, KFC, Little Caesar's, McDonald's, Mexican Fiesta, MOD Pizza, Olga's Kitchen, Outback Steak, Panera Bread, Potbelly, Qdoba, Starbucks, Subway, Taco Bell, TGIFriday's, Tim Hortons, Wendy's, White Castle, Baymont Inn, Comfort Suites, Extended Stay America, Fairfield Inn, Hampton Inn, La Quinta, TownePlace Suites, Advance Parts, ALDI, CVS Drug, Discount Tire, Firestone/auto, GNC, Hobby Lobby, IKEA, JC Penney, Jo-Ann, Kohl's, Lowe's, Marshall's, Meijer/dsl, Michael's, Midas, PetCo, Target, Tuesday Morning, URGENT CARE, Verizon, vet, Walgreens
23	**full facilities, info, litter barrels, nb**
22	US 12, Michigan Ave, to Wayne, E BP/dsl, Mobil/dsl, Shell, Valero/dsl, Arby's, Jonathan's Rest., McDonald's, Quiznos, Subway, Wendy's, EconoLodge, Fellows C Motel, Holiday Inn Express, Super 8, Willo Acres Motel, W Marathon/dsl, Jimmy John's, Kia, Nissan, vet
20	Ecorse Rd, to Romulus, E Mobil/7-11, Shell/Tubby's/dsl, W BP/Burger King/scales/dsl/24hr
17	I-94 E to Detroit, W to Ann Arbor, E
15	Eureka Rd, E Shell/Subway/dsl,
13	Sibley Rd, New Boston, W Mobil/Subway/dsl, to Lower Huron Metro Park
11	S Huron Rd, W Sunoco/Burger King/dsl, Iron Mike Rest.
8	Will Carleton Rd, to Flat Rock
5	Carleton, South Rockwood, W Speedway/dsl, Sunoco/Subway/dsl, $General, USPO
4mm	**full facilities, litter barrels, sb**
2	US 24, to Telegraph Rd, W BP/dsl, Marathon/Subway/dsl, $General

= gas = food = lodging = other = rest stop

MI

INTERSTATE 275 (Livonia) Cont'd

Exit #	Services
0mm	I-275 begins/ends on I-75, exit 20.

INTERSTATE 475 (Flint)

Exit #	Services
17mm	I-475 begins/ends on I-75, exit 125.
15	Clio Rd, W BP, Chevrolet
13	Saginaw St, E BP, Hungry Howie's, KFC, McDonald's, Taco Bell, Advance Parts, Kroger/gas, O'Reilly Parts, W Marathon, Burger King, Little Caesar's
11	Carpenter Rd
10	Pierson Rd
9	rd 54, Dort Hwy, Stewart Ave, E BP/dsl, McDonald's
8mm	Flint River
8b	Davison Rd, Hamilton Ave
8a	Longway Blvd, W Holiday Inn Express, H, USPO
7	rd 21, Court St, downtown Flint
6	I-69, W to Lansing, E to Port Huron
5	Atherton Rd(from sb), E Marathon/dsl
4	Hemphill Rd, Bristol Rd, E Speedway/dsl, Rally's, Subway, W Speedway/dsl, Little Caesar's, Tim Horton/Wendy's, $General, Kroger/dsl, vet
2	Hill Rd, E Speedway, Applebee's, Bob Evans, Wingate Inn, vet, W Mobil, Speedway/dsl, Arby's, Burger King, Burger St Grill, Little Caesar's, McDonald's, Starbucks, Taco Bell, Wendy's
0mm	I-475 begins/ends on I-75, exit 111.

INTERSTATE 696 (Detroit)

ROSEVILLE

Exit #	Services
28.5mm	I-696 begins/ends on I-94.
28	I-94 E to Port Huron, W to Detroit, 11 Mile Rd, E 7-11, Shell/dsl, Speedway/dsl, $General
27	MI 3, Gratiot Ave, N BP, Marathon, Valero, Checkers, Firehouse Subs, McDonald's, National Coney Island, Tubby's Subs, Costco/gas, S Marathon, Mobil/McDonald's/dsl, Shell, Biggby Coffee, Burger King, JW Ice Cream, KFC, Subway, Taco Bell, Tim Horton's, White Castle, Belle Tire, Chrysler/Dodge/Jeep, Family$, Firestone/auto, GNC, Kroger/gas, Sav-A-Lot Foods, TJ Maxx
26	MI 97, Groesbeck Ave, Roseville, N BP/dsl, S Tim Horton
24	Hoover Rd, Schoenherr Rd, N BP, Burger King, KFC, S BP/dsl, Mobil/7-11, Boston Mkt, Del Taco, DQ, Grubhouse, Little Caesar's, Popeyes, Red Lobster, Subway, Taco Bell, Tim Horton, Wendy's, Holiday Inn Express, $Tree, Advance Parts, CVS Drug, GNC, Home Depot, Kroger
23	MI 53, Van Dyke Ave, N BP, Marathon, Mobil/dsl, Applebee's, Arby's, Baskin-Robbins/Dunkin', McDonald's, Simple Palate Rest., Subway, $General, Cadillac, Dodge/Ram, Toyota, Walmart, S Luca's Coney Island, Chevrolet/Buick/GMC, Discount Tire, Ford, USPO, vet
22	Mound Rd, N BP/Burger King, Mobil/dsl
20	Ryan Rd, Dequindre Rd, N Citgo, Mobil/7-11, Sunoco, Knights Inn, Red Roof Inn, auto repair, BigLots, vet, S Church's TX Chicken, LA Coney Island, McDonald's, Best Inn, Victory Suites, transmissions
19	Couzens St, 10 Mile Rd, S Hazel Park Racetrack
18	I-75 N to Flint, S to Detroit
17	Campbell Ave, Hilton Ave, Bermuda, Mohawk, S Marathon/dsl
16	MI 1, Woodward Ave, Main St, N zoo, S Sunoco
14	Coolidge Rd, 10 Mile Rd, S Speedway, Hungry Howie's, Jade Palace Chinese, Little Caesar's, Sahara Grill, Subway, CVS Drug, Family$, URGENT CARE
13	Greenfield Rd, N Marathon, Mobil, L George Coney Island, McDonald's, Popeyes, Subway, White Castle, $Tree, ALDI, Family$, Save a Lot Foods, Sol's Automotive, URGENT CARE, S Shell, Sunoco, Baskin-Robbins/Dunkin', Front Page Deli, Pita Cafe, Starbucks
12	MI 39, Southfield Rd, 11 Mile Rd, N Panera Bread, Discount Tire, S Shell, Happy's Pizza, AT&T
11	Evergreen Rd, S Mobil, Speedway/dsl, Benito's Pizza, China Gourmet, Chipotle, Coldstone/Tim Horton's, Fuddrucker's, Jimmy John's, Potbelly, Qdoba, Subway, TGIFriday's, Hawthorn Suites, Holiday Inn Express
10	US 24, Telegraph Rd, N Marathon, Mobil, Sunoco, Chipotle, DiBella Subs, Five Guys, Jimmy John's, Mezzanine Mediterranian, Noodles&Co, Panera Bread, Popeyes, Potbelly, Qdoba, Starbucks, Wendy's, Extended Stay America, Red Roof Inn, Springhill Suites, AT&T, Belle Tire, Best Buy, Buick/GMC, Chevrolet, Chrysler/Dodge/Jeep, Ford, Honda, Hyundai, Kia, Lexus, Lincoln, Lowe's, Meijer/dsl, Michael's, Mini, Nissan, Office Depot, PetSmart, Subaru, Verizon, S Mobil/7-11, Sunoco, Kerby's Koney Island, Starbucks, Tim Horton's, Best Western, Candlewood Suites, Courtyard, Holiday Inn Express, Marriott, Quality Inn, AutoZone, Family$
8	MI 10, Lodge Fwy
7	American Dr (from eb), S Extended Stay America, Hilton Garden
5	Orchard Lake Rd, Farmington Hills, N BP/dsl, Marathon, Mobil/dsl, Sunoco, Arby's, Burger King, Camelia's Mexican, Hong Hua Chinese, Jet's Pizza, Jimmy John's, Kabuki Japanese, Marie's Scrambler, Roberto's, Ruby Tuesday, Starbucks, Subway, Wendy's, Comfort Inn, Extended Stay America, Fairfield Inn, Radisson, CVS, Discount Tire, Holocaust Museum, Petco, to St Mary's Coll, Verizon
1	(from wb), I-96 W, I-275 S, to MI 5, Grand River Ave

FARMINGTON HILLS

NOTES

= gas = food = lodging = other = rest stop

MN

MINNESOTA

INTERSTATE 35

NORTH SHORE

Exit #	Services
260mm	I-35 begins/ends on MN 61 in Duluth.
259	MN 61, London Rd, to Two Harbors, North Shore, E Beacon Pointe Hotel, W Holiday/dsl, Beijing Chinese, Blackwoods Grill, Burger King, Caribou Coffee, Dunn Bros Coffee, Einstein Bagels, McDonald's, Papa Murphys, Perkins, Subway, Taco John's, Days Inn, Edgewater Inn, H, vet
258	21st Ave E(from nb), to U of MN at Duluth, same as 259, W H
256b	Mesaba Ave, Superior St, E DQ, 310 Grill, Bellisio's, Caribou Coffee, Grandma's Grill, Greenmill Rest., Little Angie's Cantina, Love Creamery, Old Chicago, Red Lobster, Smokehouse Rest., Twisted Tenders, Canal Park Lodge, Hampton Inn, Inn at Lake Superior, Lift Bridge Lodge, Suites Hotel, W LuLus Pizza, Starbucks, Vitta Pizza, Holiday Inn, Hostel du Nord, Radisson, Sheraton, railroad museum
256a	Michigan St, E aquarium, W downtown, H
255a	US 53 N (exits left from nb), downtown, W Mobil, Hungry Hippie Tacos, Love Creamery, OMC Smokehouse, children's museum, Kia
255b	I-535 spur, to Wisconsin
254	27th Ave W, W Holiday/Burger King/dsl, KwikTrip/dsl, Clyde Iron Works, Duluth Grill, Little Caesar's, Subway, Motel 6, USPO
253b	40th Ave W, W Holiday/dsl/CNG, Perkins, Vintage Italian Pizza, Comfort Inn, Super 8
253a	US 2 E, US 53, to Wisconsin
252	Central Ave, W Duluth, W Holiday/dsl, Mobil/Charley's/dsl, China King Buffet, Domino's, KFC, McDonald's, Mr. D's Grill, Papa Murphy's, Pizza Hut, Sammy's Pizza, Subway, Taco Bell, Taco John's, $Tree, Advance Parts, CVS Drug, H, Menards, O'Reilly Parts, Super 1 Foods, USPO, Walgreens
251b	MN 23 S, Grand Ave
251a	Cody St, E Allyndale Motel, zoo
250	US 2 W(from sb), to Grand Rapids, W Holiday/dsl, Kwik Trip/dsl, Blackwoods Grill, AmericInn

NOPEMING

Exit #	Services
249	Boundary Ave, Skyline Pkwy, **both lanes, full facilities, litter barrels, vending, info,** E Holiday/dsl, McDonald's, Duluth Inn, to ski area, to Spirit Mtn RA, W Exxon/Subway/dsl, Blackwoods Grill, AmericInn, Best Value Inn, Mack/Volvo
246	rd 13, Midway Rd, Nopeming, W Dry Dock Rest.
245	rd 61, E Buffalo House Rest./camping
242	rd 1, Esko, Thomson, E Caywood Country Store, W USPO
239.5mm	St Louis River

CARLTON

Exit #	Services
239	MN 45, to Cloquet, Scanlon, E to Jay Cooke SP, W Holiday, KwikTrip/dsl/e85, dsl repair, River Inn Grill, Trapper Pete's Steaks, H(4mi), Knife Island Campground
237	MN 33, Cloquet, E city park/playground, KOA, W BP/dsl, Mobil, ALDI, Arby's, Burger King, DQ, Erbert&Gerberts, Little Caesar's, McDonald's, Papa Murphy's, Perkins, Pizza Hut, Subway, Taco Bell, Taco John's/Steak Escape, AmericInn, Super 8, $Tree, AT&T, AutoZone, Chrysler/Dodge/Jeep, Ford, H(4.5), NAPA, O'Reilly Parts, Super 1 Foods, Verizon, Walgreens, Walmart
236mm	weigh sta both lanes
235	MN 210, to Cromwell, Carlton, E Kiwk Trip/dsl/24hr, AmericInn, Royal Pines Motel, to Jay Cooke SP, W Black Bear Casino/Hotel/rest.
235mm	Big Otter Creek

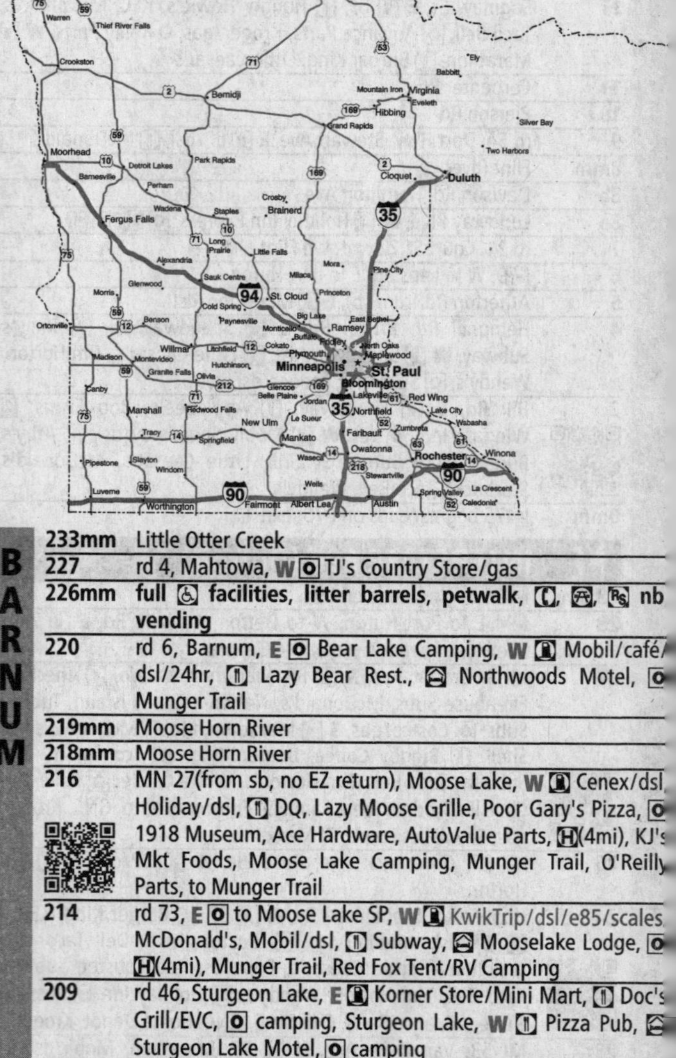

BARNUM

Exit #	Services
233mm	Little Otter Creek
227	rd 4, Mahtowa, W TJ's Country Store/gas
226mm	**full facilities, litter barrels, petwalk, nb vending**
220	rd 6, Barnum, E Bear Lake Camping, W Mobil/café/dsl/24hr, Lazy Bear Rest., Northwoods Motel, Munger Trail
219mm	Moose Horn River
218mm	Moose Horn River
216	MN 27(from sb, no EZ return), Moose Lake, W Cenex/dsl, Holiday/dsl, DQ, Lazy Moose Grille, Poor Gary's Pizza, 1918 Museum, Ace Hardware, AutoValue Parts, H(4mi), KJ's Mkt Foods, Moose Lake Camping, Munger Trail, O'Reilly Parts, to Munger Trail
214	rd 73, E to Moose Lake SP, W KwikTrip/dsl/e85/scales, McDonald's, Mobil/dsl, Subway, Mooselake Lodge, H(4mi), Munger Trail, Red Fox Tent/RV Camping
209	rd 46, Sturgeon Lake, E Korner Store/Mini Mart, Doc's Grill/EVC, camping, Sturgeon Lake, W Pizza Pub, Sturgeon Lake Motel, camping
209mm	**full facilities, litter barrels, petwalk, sb vending**
206.5mm	Willow River
205	rd 43, Willow River, E North Country RV Camping, W BP/cafe/dsl, $General
198.5mm	Kettle River

HINCKLEY

Exit #	Services
198mm	**full facilities, litter barrels, petwalk, nb vending**
195	rd 18, rd 23 E, to Askov, E Cenex/Banning Jct/cafe/dsl, Banning Jct Cafe, Quality Inn, camping, to Banning SP, W Banning RV Camping
191	MN 23, rd 61, Sandstone, E Casey's/dsl, Victory/dsl, Sandstone 61 Motel, Chris' Food Center/Subway/dsl, to Robinson's Ice Cave
184mm	Grindstone River
183	MN 48, Hinckley, E Holiday/Hardee's/dsl, **KwikTrip/dsl** Minnoco/Caribou Coffee/dsl/E-85, DQ, McDonald's, Subway, Taco Bell, Tobie's Rest., Days Inn, Grand Hinckley Inn, Grand Northern Inn, casino/RV park, to St Croix SP,

MN

INTERSTATE 35 Cont'd

PINE CITY

183	Continued Mobil/White Castle/dsl, Best Value Inn, Family$, Hinckley Fire Museum
180	MN 23 W, rd 61, to Mora
175	rd 14, Beroun, E Marathon/dsl
171	rd 11, Pine City, E Speedway/dsl, McDonald's, Ace Hardware, Chrysler/Dodge/Jeep, Verizon, W camping
170mm	Snake River
169	MN 324, rd 7, Pine City, E BP/dsl, Don Julio's Mexican, Holiday/dsl, A&W, DQ, KFC, Pizza Hut, Subway, $Tree, Campbell Auto/tire, EVC, Ford, O'Reilly Parts, USPO, vet, Walmart/Subway/auto, W to NW Co Fur Post HS
165	MN 70, to Grantsburg, Rock Creek, E Marathon/dsl
159	MN 361, rd 1, Rush City, E Holiday/Burger King/dsl, Kwik Trip/dsl, $General, World's Largest Walleye, W golf, to camping
154mm	**full facilities, litter barrels, petwalk, nb, vending**
152	rd 10, Harris, E Harris 61/dsl, Kaffe Stuga Caffe, $General
147	MN 95, to Cambridge, North Branch, E Casey's, Holiday/dsl, Tesla EVC, Cairbou Coffee, China Taste, Domino's, DQ, McDonald's, Muddy Cow Rest., Subway, Taco Bell, AmericInn, Budget Host, Family$, Fisk Tire, NAPA, O'Reilly Parts, to Wild River SP, vet, W Holiday/dsl/e85, Burger King, Denny's, Dickey's BBQ, Don Julio Mexican, KFC, Chevrolet, County Mkt Foods, Ford, North Branch Outlets/famous brands, Verizon

STACY

143	rd 17, W Marathon/dsl, tire repair
139	rd 19, Stacy, E Casey's, Stacy Grill, Subway, The Fort Rest., $General, city park, USPO, W KwikTrip/dsl/e85
135	US 61 S, rd 22, Wyoming, E Casey's, Cornerstone Rest., DQ, Linwood Pizza, Subway, Tasty Asia, Bruce Foods, CarQuest, H, WY Drug, W Holiday/dsl, McDonald's, Village Inn Rest., vet
132	US 8(from nb), to Taylors Falls
131	rd 2, Forest Lake, E Holiday/dsl, Speedway/dsl, Starbucks, Applebee's, Arby's, Burger King, Chipotle, Culver's, Joy Garden, KFC, McDonald's, Papa John's, Perkins, Quack's Cafe, Subway, Taco Bell, White Castle, AmericInn, ALDI, AutoZone, O'Reilly Parts, RV/Auto repair, Target, Tires+, Verizon, Walgreens, Walmart/Subway, W Holiday/dsl, Famous Dave's BBQ, Jimmy John's, Papa Murphy's, Taco John's, Wendy's, Country Inn&Suites, Buick/GMC, Cadillac/Chevrolet, Chrysler/Dodge/Jeep, Cub Foods, Home Depot, Jiffy Lube, Menards
131mm	**full facilities, litter barrels, petwalk, sb, vending**

CENTERVILLE

129	MN 97, rd 23, E Kwik Trip/dsl/e85, W Holiday/dsl, Camping World, casino
128mm	weigh sta both lanes
127	I-35W, S to Minneapolis. See I-35W.
123	rd 14, Centerville, E Kwik Trip, Blue Heron Grill, Dunn Bros Coffee, Jersey Mike's, McDonald's, Papa Murphy's, Red's Pizza, Festival Foods, vet, White Bear RV Ctr, W Mobil, Shell, DQ, Fiesta Cancun, WiseGuys Pizza, auto repair
120	rd J(from nb, no return), W Holiday, Lucy's Burgers, Orchid Vietnamese, Tria Rest.
117	rd 96, E Speedway/dsl, Burger King, Carbone's Pizza, AmericInn, Goodyear/auto, NAPA, W Holiday, Applebee's, Arby's, Caribou Coffee, Culver's, McDonald's, Noodles&Co, Punch Pizza, Ricardo's Pizza, Subway, Zen Asia, AutoZone, Cub Foods, Tires+, USPO, Walgreens
115	rd E, E Holiday/repair, Speedway/dsl, Jimmy's Rest.,
115	Continued Perkins, Savoy Pizza, Country Inn&Suites, Fairfield Inn, Holiday Inn Express, URGENT CARE, W CherryBerry FroYo, Chipotle Mexican, Jersey Mike's, KFC, Panera Bread, Papa Murphy's, $Tree, AT&T, Fresh Thyme Mkt, Target/Starbucks, Walmart/auto
114	I-694 E(exits left from sb)
113	I-694 W
112	Little Canada Rd, E BP, W Caribou Coffee, Porterhouse Rest.
111a/b	MN 36 E, to Stillwater/MN 36 W, to Minneapolis
110b	Roselawn Ave
110a	Wheelock Pkwy, E Arco, BP, Casa Azul Mexican, Subway
109	Maryland Ave, E Speedway/dsl, W Wendy's
108	Pennsylvania Ave, downtown
107c	University Ave, downtown, E Speedway/dsl, W H, to st capitol
107b a	I-94, W to Minneapolis, E to St Paul. I-35 and I-94 run together.
106c	11th St(from nb), Marion St, downtown
106b	Kellogg Blvd(from nb), downtown, E Cossetta Italian, Zamboni's Pizza, Courtyard, Holiday Inn, H
106a	Grand Ave, E Hope Breakfast, Mobil, H
105	St Clair Ave
104c	Victoria St, Jefferson Ave
104b	Ayd Mill Rd(from nb)
104a	Randolph Ave, E Rooster's BBQ, W Papa John's, Trader Joe's
103b	MN 5, W 7th St, E vet, W Speedway/dsl, Midas, USPO
103a	Shepard Rd(from nb)
102mm	Mississippi River
102	MN 13, Sibley Hwy, W BP, Holiday/Subway
101b a	MN 110 W, E BP/dsl, Caribou Coffee, Cold Stone, McDonald's, Subway, Teresa's Mexican, Tommy Chicago's Pizza, Verizon, Walgreens, W Speedway/dsl/e85, Copperfield Rest.
99b a	I-494 W/I-494 E
98	Lone Oak Rd, E Extended Stay America, Microtel, Sam's Club/gas, URGENT CARE, USPO, W Shell, Farmer Grandson's Eatery, Hampton Inn, Sonesta Suites
97b	Yankee Doodle Rd, E Applebee's, Arby's, Bonchon Asian, Buffalo Wild Wings, Burger King, Caribou Coffee, Chick-fil-A, Chipotle, Coldstone, Culver's, Domino's, El Nuevo Mexican, Houlihan's, Jersey Mike's, KFC, Kyoto Sushi, Kyuramen Ramen, Mad Cow, Noodles&Co, Panda Express, Panera Bread, Papa John's, Perkins, Pizza Man, Popeyes, Potbelly, Qdoba, Red's Pizza, Taco Bell, Taco John's, $Tree, Barnes&Noble, Best Buy, Home Depot, Kohl's, Lunds&Byerly's Mkt, Michael's, O'Reilly Parts, Old Navy, PetSmart, TJ Maxx, Verizon, Walgreens, Walmart/Subway, W Speedway/dsl, Bruegger's Bagels, Dunkin, El Loro Mexican, Granite City, Ichiddo Ramen, Olive Garden, Starbucks, Subway, Zupas, Best Western, Extended Stay America, Holiday Inn Express, Hobby Lobby, HyVee Foods/EVC, Marshall's, NAPA
97a	Pilot Knob Rd, same as 97b, E Holiday, Speedway, Chili's, McDonald's, Wendy's, SpringHill Suites, TownePlace Suites, Car-X, Discount Tire, Firestone/auto, Jiffy Lube, Kohl's, Tires+, Walmart/Subway, W Speedway/dsl, Bruegger's Bagels, Dunkin', Best Western+, Holiday Inn Express
94	rd 30, Diffley Rd, to Eagan, E Holiday/dsl, Andiamo Italian, CVS Drug, Kowalski's Mkt, URGENT CARE, W BP/dsl, Heartland Tire
93	rd 32, Cliff Rd, E Holiday/dsl, Mason Jar Kitchen,

= gas = food = lodging = other = rest stop

MN

INTERSTATE 35 Cont'd

Exit	Services
93	Continued Sarpino's Pizza, Ace Hardware, W Holiday/dsl, Anadari's Mediterranean, Baskin-Robbins, Brueggers Bagels, Burger King, Casper's Cherokee, Chipotle Mexican, Dolittle's Grill, DQ, Jersey Mike's, Jimmy John's, Leeann Chin, Noodles&Co, Papa John's, Papa Murphy's, Pizza Hut, Rack Shack BBQ, Southern Social, Starbucks, Taco Bell, Wendy's, Candlewood Suites, Hilton Garden, Norwood Inn, $Tree, Cub Foods, Target/Starbucks, Trader Joe's, USPO, Valvoline, Walgreens
92	MN 77, Cedar Ave, E Zoo, W access to Cliff Rd services
90	rd 11, E KwikTrip, Pizza Man, Valley Natural Foods, vet, W Speedway/dsl
88b	rd 42, Crystal Lake Rd, E Chianti Grill, Lund's&Byerly's Mkt, PetSmart, W BP, Holiday, Holiday/dsl, Speedway/dsl, Arby's, Blue Ox Sandwiches, Burger Jones, Burger King, Cam Ranh Bay, Cane's, Caribou Coffee, Chick-fil-A, Chili's, Chipotle Mexican, ChuckECheese, HoneyBaked Ham, IHOP, Jimmy John's, KFC, LeeAnn Chin, Little Caesar's, McDonald's, Noodles&Co, Olive Garden, Original Pancake House, Outback Steaks, Panera Bread, Papa Murphy's, Pizza Hut, Porter Creek Grill, Red Lobster, Royal Buffet, Shogun Japanese, Smashburger, Starbucks, Taco Bell, Taco John's, TGIFriday's, Wendy's, AmericInn, Best Western, Fairfield Inn, Hampton Inn, InTown Suites, $Tree, Advance Parts, Barnes&Noble, Best Buy, Costco/gas, Cub Foods, Dick's, Discount Tire, Home Depot, H, JCPenney, Kohl's, Macy's, mall, Michael's, Old Navy, PetCo, Target/Starbucks, Tires+, Verizon, VW, Walgreens
88a	I-35W(from nb), N to Minneapolis. **See I-35W.**
87	Crystal Lake Rd(from nb), W Kwik Trip/dsl, Honda/Nissan, Hyundai, Mazda, Subaru, Toyota/Scion
86	rd 46, E KwikTrip/dsl, Speedway/dsl, KFC, Starbucks, Harley-Davidson, W McDonald's, O'Reilly Parts
85	MN 50, E F&F/dsl, Speedway/dsl, Chipotle, Culver's, Domino's, DQ, Eddie Cheng, Gerbert's Sandwiches, Green Mill Rest., Jimmy John's, Lakeville Chinese, Papa John's, Pizza Hut, Red's Pizza, Starbucks, Subway, Taco Bell, Tak Ching Chinese, Wendy's, Quality Inn, $Tree, Caribou Coffee, Cub Foods, CVS Drug, Goodyear/auto, Verizon, Walgreens, W Holiday/dsl, Cracker Barrel, Perkins, Pizza Ranch, Baymont Inn, Camping World
84	185th St W, Orchard Trail, E Speedway/dsl, Buffalo Wild Wings, Cane's, Caribou Coffee, SawaJapan, Marshall's, Target/Starbucks
81	rd 70, Lakeville, N Hampton Inn, E Holiday/dsl, Baldy's BBQ, Goodfella's Pizza, McDonald's, Porterhouse Steaks, Subway, Holiday Inn/rest., Motel 6, W Speedway/dsl, Gary's Supper, Candlewood Suites, ALDI, Walmart
76	rd 2, Elko, W Endzone Grill, Elko Speedway
76mm	**full facilities, litter barrels, petwalk, sb, vending**
69	MN 19, to Northfield, New Prague, E Carleton Coll, H, St Olaf Coll, W Flying J/Subway/dsl/scales/24hr
68mm	**full facilities, litter barrels, petwalk, nb, vending**
66	rd 1, to Dundas, W Boonie's Grill
59	MN 21, Faribault, S Ford/Lincoln, E Speedway/Diner/dsl/scales/24hr, Hardee's, Pizza Hut, Boarders Inn, Days Inn, Faribault Inn & Suites, Grandstay, Satakah St Trail, vet, W Harley-Davidson
56	MN 60, Faribault, E Holiday/dsl, KwikTrip, A&W, Arby's, Asian Buffet, Burger King, Caribou Coffee, DQ, Jimmy John's, KFC, McDonald's, Perkins, Subway, Taco Bell,

FARIBAULT

Exit	Services
56	Continued Taco John's, $Tree, ALDI, AutoZone, Buick/Chevrolet/GMC, Chrysler/Dodge/Jeep, H, Hy-Vee Foods/dsl, NAPA, PetSmart, tire repair, Walmart/auto, W DQ, Regency Inn, Sakatah Lake SP
55	rd 48, from nb, no return, E Mobil/dsl, Broaster Rest., Carbones Pizza, El Tequila Mexican
48	rd 12, rd 23, Medford, E Casey's/dsl, W McDonald's, Outlet Mall/famous brands, zoo
45	rd 9, Clinton Falls, W KwikTrip/dsl/scales, Caribou Coffee, El Loro Mexican, Famous Dave's BBQ, TimberLodge Steaks, Wendy's, Comfort Inn, Buick/Chevrolet/Cadillac, Cabela's Sporting Goods, Russell-Stover Candies
43	rd 34, 26th St, Owatonna, E Camping World, W H
42b a	US 14 W, rd 45, to Waseca, Owatonna, E Grace's TexMex, Hardee's, Kernel Rest., Valu Stay Inn, AutoZone, CashWise Foods, Chrysler/Dodge/Jeep, Ford/Lincoln, O'Reilly Parts, repair, vet, W KwikTrip/dsl, Buffalo Wild Wings, Culver's, Don Juan Cantina, East Wind Buffet, McDonald's, Olivia's Rest., Panda Express, Perkins, Best Budget Inn, Super 8, $Tree, Aldi, Kohl's, Lowe's, Verizon, Walmart/auto
41	Bridge St, Owatonna, E Holiday/dsl, Applebee's, Arby's, Burger King, Caribou Coffee, DQ, Jimmy John's, KFC, Papa Murphy's, Red&Green Burrito, Starbucks, Subway, Taco Bell, Baymont Inn, Country Inn&Suites, Verizon, W F&F/dsl, Quality Inn, Target
40	US 14 E, US 218, Owatonna
38mm	Turtle Creek
35mm	**full facilities, litter barrels, petwalk, both lanes, vending**
34.5mm	Straight River
32	rd 4, Hope, E Hope Oak Knoll Camping
26	MN 30, to Blooming Prairie, Ellendale, E Crystal Springs RV Resort, W Casey's/dsl/scales
22	rd 35, to Hartland, Geneva
18	MN 251, to Hollandale, Clarks Grove, W BP/dsl/LP, Pour House Grill
17mm	weigh sta both lanes
13b a	I-90, W to Sioux Falls, E to Austin, W H
12	US 65 S(from sb), Lp 35, Albert Lea, same as 11
11	rd 46, Albert Lea, E Love's/Wendy's/dsl/scales/24hr, Petro/Iron Skillet/McDonald's/Pizza Hut/dsl/scales/24hr/@, Comfort Inn, Holiday Inn Express, dsl repair, to Myre-Big Island SP, W Casey's, KwikTrip, Al's Burgers, Burger King, Casa Zamora Mexican, GreenMill Rest., KFC, MineAgain's Bar and Grill, Perkins, Taco John's, Taco King, Wok'n Roll, Country Inn&Suites, Countryside Inn, Econolodge, Motel 6, Quality Inn, Ramada, $Tree, Advance Parts, AutoValue Parts, AutoZone, CarQuest, Chrysler/Dodge/Jeep, Ford, Home Depot, Honda, H(4mi), NAPA, Nissan/VW, O'Reilly Parts, Volvo Trucks, Walmart/auto
9mm	Albert Lea Lake
8	US 65, Lp 35, Albert Lea, W tire/auto repair

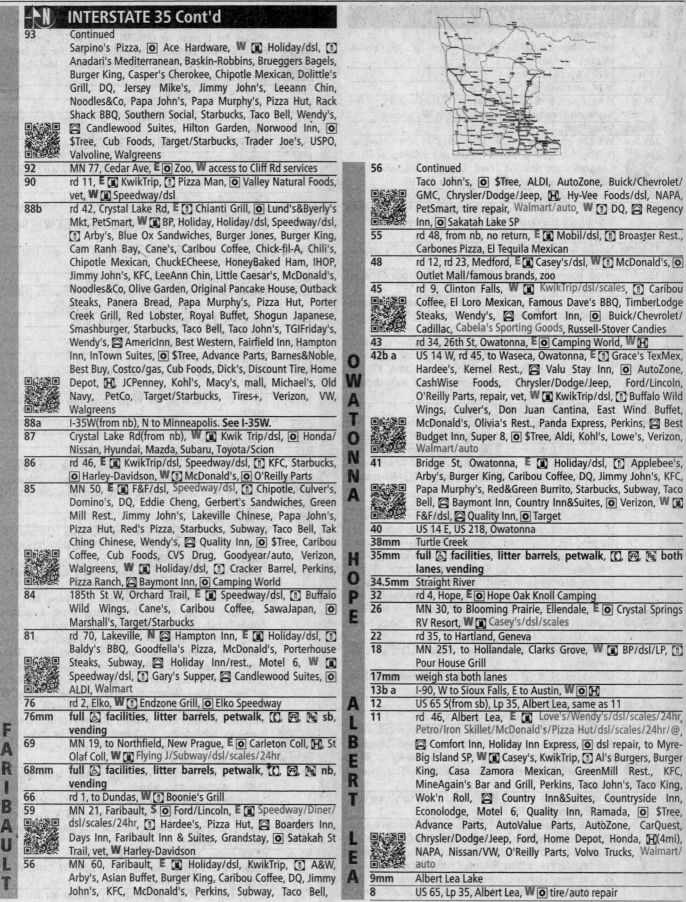

OWATONNA

HOPE

ALBERT LEA

INTERSTATE 35 Cont'd

Exit #	Services
5	rd 13, to Glenville, Twin Lakes, W to camping
2	rd 5
1mm	**full facilities, litter barrels, petwalk, , , vending, Welcome Ctr nb**
0mm	Minnesota/Iowa state line

INTERSTATE 35 West

CIRCLE PINES

Exit #	Services
41mm	I-35W begins/ends on I-35, exit 127.
36	rd 23, E Holiday/dsl, W Casey's/dsl, Caribou Coffee, Don Julio, DQ, El Zocalo Grill, Mac Kitchen, McDonald's, Subway, Hampton Inn, Discount Tire, Kohl's, Target/Starbucks, Verizon
33	rd 17, Lexington Ave, E F&F/dsl, Holiday/dsl, Burger King, ALDI, Walmart/Subway, W Kwik Trip/dsl, Applebee's, Arby's, Caribou Coffee, Culver's, Jersey Mike's, Lucy's Burgers, Starbucks, Taco Bell, Wendy's, $Tree, AT&T, Cub Foods, Home Depot, Michael's, URGENT CARE, Walgreens
32	95th Ave NE, to Lexington, Circle Pines, W Nat Sports Ctr
31b a	Lake Dr, E Kwik Trip/dsl, Speedway/dsl, Caribou Coffee, El Norte Mexican, Quizno's, Red Ginger Asian, Country Inn&Suites, W tires
30	US 10 W, MN 118, to MN 65
29	rd I, W Marathon/dsl
28c b	rd 10, rd H, W BP, McDonald's, Mermaid Café, Popeyes, RJ Ritches, Taco Bell, AmericInn, Days Inn
28a	MN 96, E Holiday/dsl, W Homewood Suites/EVC
27b a	I-694 E and W
26	rd E2, W Circle K/dsl, Domino's, DQ, Jimmy John's, Limu Coffee, Pho 400 Vietnamese, USPO
25b	MN 88, to Roseville(no EZ return to sb), same as 25a
25a	rd D(from nb), E BP/dsl, Original Grill, Avid Hotel, Courtyard, Fairfield Inn, Residence Inn, W Holiday, Marathon/dsl, Speedway/dsl, Big Louie's, Caribou Coffee, McDonald's, New Hong Kong, Perkins/24hr, Sarpino's Italian
24	rd C, E BP, Applebees, Buffalo Wild Wings, Burger King, Cane's, Caribou Coffee, Chili's, Denny's, Dunkin, India Palace Rest., La Casito Mexican, Panda Express, Red Lobster, Starbucks, Wendy's, Double Tree, Home2 Suites, Key Inn, Motel 6, Norwood Inn, $Tree, Advance Parts, ALDI, Hobby Lobby, REI, U-Haul, USPO, Walmart, W Holiday Inn Express, Buick/GMC, Chevrolet, Chrysler/Dodge/Jeep, Norm's Tires
23b	Cleveland Ave, MN 36
23a	MN 280, Industrial Blvd(from sb)
22	MN 280, Industrial Blvd(from nb), E Holiday, Wendy's, Marriott
21b a	Broadway St, Stinson Blvd, E Holiday/dsl, auto parts, W Burger King, Caribou Coffee, Leeann Chin, McDonald's, Taco Bell, Cub Foods, GNC, Home Depot, Office Depot, PetSmart, Target/Starbucks

HIAWATHA

Exit #	Services
19	E Hennepin(from nb)
18	US 52, 4th St SE, University Ave, to U of MN, E University Inn, W Maxwell's Cafe
17c	11th St, Washington Ave, E Courtyard, W Mobil, H, US Bank Stadium
17b	I-94 W(from sb)
17a	MN 55, Hiawatha
16b a	I-94(from nb), E to St Paul, W to St Cloud, to MN 65
15	31st St(from nb), Lake St, E Gordita's Mexican, Taco Bell, AutoZone, H, W StopNShop/Subway, Chinese Express, Hibachi Buffett, $Tree, USPO, Walgreens
14	35th St, 36th St, W Speedway, Hola Arepa, U-Haul
13	46th St, W BP, Caribou Coffee, Papa John's, Pepitos Mexican, Subway, auto repair
13mm	Minnehaha Creek
12b	Diamond Lake Rd
12a	60th St(from sb), W Mobil, Cub Foods
11b	MN 62 E, to airport, to
11a	Lyndale Ave(from sb)
10b	MN 62 W, 58th St
10a	rd 53, 66th St, E Speedway, Burger King, Caribou Coffee, Firehouse, McDonald's, My Burger, Popeyes, Wendy's, $Tree, Marshalls, Michaels, Petco, vet, Walgreens, W BP, Dunkin, Subway, Tazzah, CVS Drug
9c	76th St(from sb)
9b a	I-494, MN 5, to airport, to
8	82nd St, E BMW, W Applebee's, Bruegger's, Caribou Coffee, Chick-fil-A, Hunan, Jimmy John's, McDonald's, Panda Express, Red Lobster, Sonic, Subway, Wendy's, Embassy Suites, Chevrolet, Chrysler/Dodge/Jeep, Fresh Thyme Mkt, Hobby Lobby, Infiniti, Kia, Kohl's, Petco, Target/Starbucks, TJ Maxx, Verizon, Walgreens
7b	90th St, E CVS Drug, W BP, Holiday, Burger King, Gyropolis, $Tree
7a	94th St, E Arby's, DQ, Popeyes, Taco Bell, AutoZone, Goodyear/auto, Midas, tires, W Holiday Inn
6	rd 1, 98th St, E Applebee's, Domino's, Golden Wok, Jimmy John's, Leeann Chin, McDonald's, Starbucks, Subway, Wendy's, White Castle, Batteries+, Bloomington Drug, Festival Foods, Ford, URGENT CARE, Walgreens, W Speedway/dsl, Snuffy's Malt Shop
5	106th St
5mm	Minnesota River
4b	113th St, Black Dog Rd
4a	Cliff Rd, E Dodge, Walmart
3b a	MN 13, Shakopee, Canterbury Downs

CRYSTAL LAKE RD

Exit #	Services
2	Burnsville Pkwy, E BP, Carbone's Pizza, W Holiday, Clive's Roadhouse, Denny's, Gourmet Chinese, Burnsville Inn, LivInn, Motel 6, Prime Rate Motel, auto repair, vet
1	rd 42(from sb), Crystal Lake Rd, E BP, Holiday, Arby's, Burger King, Caribou Coffee, Chianti Grill, HoneyBaked Ham, McDonald's, Original Pancake House, Taco Bell, Taco John's, AmericInn, Best Western, Fairfield Inn, Hampton Inn, Home Depot, H, Lunds&Byerly's Mkt, PetSmart, W Holiday/dsl, Speedway/dsl, Blue Ox Sandwiches, Cam Ranh Bay, Cane's, Caribou Coffee, Chick-fil-A, Chili's, Chipotle, ChuckECheese, Dragon Star Buffet, Five Guys, IHOP, Jimmy John's, KFC, Leann Chin, Little Caesar's, Lucky's 13, Noodles&Co, Olive Garden, Panera Bread, Papa Murphy's, Pizza Hut, Porter Creek Grill, Red Lobster, Shogun Japanese, Smashburger, Starbucks, TGIFriday's, Wendy's, InTown Suites, $Tree, Advance Parts, ALDI, Barnes&Noble, Best Buy, Costco/gas, Cub Foods, Dick's, Discount Tire, Hobby Lobby, JC Penney, Kohl's, Macy's, mall, Michael's, Old Navy, PetCo, Target/Starbucks/CVS, Tires+, Verizon, VW, Walgreens
0mm	I-35W begins/ends on I-35, exit 88a.

INTERSTATE 90

Exit #	Services
278mm	Minnesota/Wisconsin state line, Mississippi River
276	US 14, US 61, to MN 16, La Crescent, N **Welcome Ctr wb, full facilities, info, , , litter barrels, vending, petwalk,** S Kwik Trip, Best Western+
273b a	Dresbach
271	Dakota
270	US 14, US 61, to Winona(from wb), N to OL Kipp SP/camping, S USPO

= gas = food = lodging = other = rest stop

INTERSTATE 90 Cont'd

Exit #	Services
NODINE	
267	rd 12, Nodine, N Great River Bluffs SP, S Kwik Trip/Hearty Platter Rest./dsl/e-85/scales/24hr/@
261mm	weigh sta both lanes, N The Shed
258	MN 76, to Houston, Ridgeway, Witoka
252	MN 43 N, to Winona, N (7mi), S vet
249	MN 43 S, to Rushford
244mm	**eb, full facilities, , , litter barrels, vending, petwalk**
242	rd 29, Lewiston
DOVER	
233	MN 74, to Chatfield, St Charles, N Kwik Trip/LP/24hr, Love's/Hardee's/dsl/scales/24hr, Cabin Coffee, Cenex/A&W Rest/dsl, Subway, Chrysler/Dodge/Jeep/Ram, Whitewater SP, S Sinclair/Amish Oven/truck repair/RVdump/dsl
229	rd 10, Dover
224	MN 42, rd 7, Eyota, N KwikTrip/dsl/e85(3mi), Country Cafe(3mi)
222mm	**wb, full facilities, , , litter barrels, vending, petwalk**
218	US 52, to Rochester, S Minnoco/dsl, KOA(Mar-Oct), U-Haul
209b a	US 63, MN 30, to Rochester, Stewartville, N , S Casey's/dsl, KwikTrip/dsl/EVC, DQ, Pizza Ranch, Taco Bell, America Stay Inn, Verizon
BROWNSDALE	
205	rd 6
202mm	**eb, full facilities, , , litter barrels, vending, petwalk**
193	MN 16, Dexter, N VP/dsl
189	rd 13, to Elkton
187	rd 20, S Adventure Bound Camping
183	MN 56, to Rose Creek, Brownsdale, S Freeborn County Co-op/dsl/LP
181	28th St NE
180b a	US 218, 21st St NE, to Austin, Oakland Place, S Marathon, Rodeway Inn
179	11th Dr NE, to Austin, N KwikTrip/dsl/scales/24hr
178b	6th St NE, to Austin
178a	4th St NW, N Caribou Coffee, Culver's, Jimmy John's, Perkins, Pizza Hut, Qdoba, AmericInn, Cobblestone Hotel, Days Inn, Holiday Inn, Marshalls, vet, S KwikTrip/dsl, Burger King, Hardee's, Subway, , vet
177	US 218 N, to Owatonna, Austin, Mapleview, N Applebee's, Arby's, China Star, El Patron Mexican, KFC, Pizza Hut, Pizza Ranch, $Tree, ALDI, AT&T, AutoZone, EVC, Hobby Lobby, Hy-Vee Foods, O'Reilly Parts, Verizon, Walmart/Subway, S Kwik Trip/dsl, Sinclair/McDonald's/dsl, Super 8
175	MN 105, rd 46, to Oakland Rd, S BP/dsl, Minnoco/dsl, Chrysler/Dodge/Jeep, Ford/Lincoln, vet
ALBERT LEA	
171mm	wb, full facilities, , , litter barrels, petwalk
166	rd 46, Oakland Rd, N KOA/LP
163	rd 26, Hayward, S Freeborn County Co-op/dsl, Myre-Big Island SP
161.5mm	**eb, full facilities, , , litter barrels, petwalk**
159b a	I-35, N to Twin Cities, S to Des Moines
157	rd 22, Albert Lea, S HyVee/dsl, KwikTrip/dsl, Applebee's, Arby's, Caribou Coffee, DQ, Jersey Mike's Subs, McDonald's, Pizza Ranch, Plaza Morina Mexican, Qdoba, AmericInn, Best Western+, $Tree, Ace Hardware, auto repair, BigLots, Chevrolet, Harley-Davidson, , Hy-Vee, Hy-Vee Foods, Riverland Comm. Coll., Verizon
154	MN 13, to US 69, to Manchester, Albert Lea, N Speedway/dsl
146	MN 109, to Wells, Alden, S Cenex/dsl/rest.,

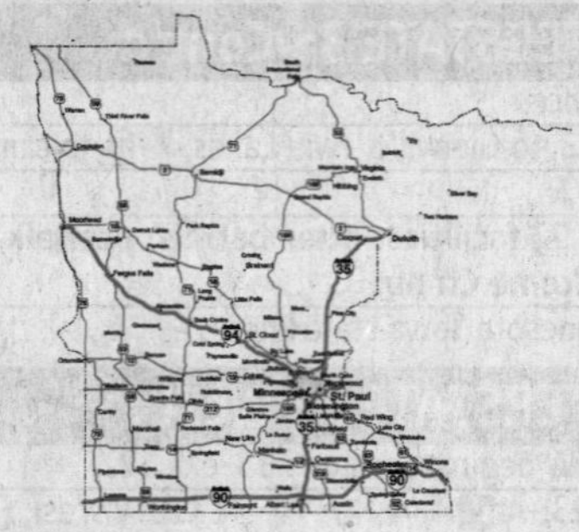

Exit #	Services
ALDEN	
146	Continued Freeborn Co-Op Gas/dsl/E-85
138	MN 22, to Wells, Keister, N Casey's
134	MN 253, rd 21, to Bricelyn, MN Lake
128	MN 254, rd 17, Frost, Easton
119	US 169, to Winnebago, Blue Earth, S Shell/dsl, Cabin Coffee, DQ, Farmer's Kitchen, McDonald's, Pizza Hut, Subway, AmericInn, Super 8, $General, Bomgaars, , Jolly Green Giant
119mm	both lanes, full facilities, , , litter barrels, petwalk, playground
113	rd 1, Guckeen
FAIRMONT	
107	MN 262, rd 53, to East Chain, Granada, S camping(May-Oct)
102	MN 15, to Madelia, Fairmont, N Verizon, Walmart/Subway, Walmart, S Cenex/dsl, Speedway/dsl/24hr, Bean Town a Grill, Green Mill Rest., Hardee's, McDonald's, Perkins, Pizza Ranch, Ranch Family Rest., Taco Bell, Best Western, Budget Inn, Hampton Inn, Quality Inn, Super 8, Advance Parts, auto repair, Chrysler/Dodge/Jeep, F&F, Freightliner, Goodyear/auto,
99	rd 39, Fairmont
93	MN 263, rd 27, Welcome, S Casey's/dsl, camping
87	MN 4, Sherburn, N Fox Lake Camping(3mi), S Casey's/dsl, Kum&Go/Subway/dsl/E-85/Tesla EVC, $General
80	rd 29, Alpha
73	US 71, Jackson, N Speedway/dsl, Burger King, EconoLodge, Super 8, KOA, to Kilen Woods SP, S BP/DQ, Casey's/dsl, Pizza Ranch, Santee Rest., Subway, AmericInn, Earth Inn, Ace Hardware, Chrysler/Dodge/Jeep, city park, Family$, , Sunshine Foods, to Spirit Lake
72.5mm	Des Moines River
72mm	full facilities, , info, , litter barrels, petwalk
69mm	eb, full facilities, , , litter barrels, vending, petwalk
WORTHINGTON	
64	MN 86, Lakefield, N to Kilen SP(12mi)
57	rd 9, to Heron Lake, Spafford
50	MN 264, rd 1, to Brewster, Round Lake
47	rd 3(from eb, no return)
46mm	weigh sta eb
45	MN 60, Worthington, N Cenex/Blueline Cafe/dsl/scales, S Holiday/dsl/scales/24hr, dsl repair, truckwash
43	US 59, Worthington, N Casey's/dsl, Comfort Suites, Norwood Inn, S Cenex/dsl, Holiday, Kwik Trip, Kwik Trip, Arby's, Burger King, Caribou Coffee, Domino's, DQ, Jimmy John's, KFC, McDonald's, New City Buffet, Perkins, Pizza Ranch, Subway, Taco John's, AmericInn, Holiday Inn Express, Ace Hardware, CarQuest, Chrysler/Dodge/Jeep, Fareway Foods, Ford, , Hy-Vee Foods/dsl, NAPA, O'Reilly Parts, U-Haul, Verizon, Walgreens, Walmart/Subway
42	MN 266, rd 25, to Reading, S Days Inn, Super 8
33	rd 13, to Wilmont, Rushmore
26	MN 91, Adrian, S Cenex/dsl, Kum&Go/Subway/dsl/E-85/24hr, $General, Adrian Camping, city park
25mm	wb, full facilities, , , litter barrels, petwalk
24mm	**wb, full facilities, , , litter barrels, petwalk**

INTERSTATE 90 Cont'd

Exit #	Services
18	rd 3, Kanaranzi, Magnolia, N Magnolia RV Park
12	US 75, Luverne, N BP/dsl/E-85, Casey's/dsl, Holiday/dsl, Los Bravos Mexican, McDonald's, Taco John's, Cozy Rest Motel(1mi), Econolodge, GrandStay Hotel, $General, Buick/Cadillac/Chevrolet/GMC, Chrysler/Dodge/Jeep, Ford, H, Lewis Drugs, NAPA, Pipestone NM, Sturdevant's Parts, to Blue Mounds SP, S Howling Dog Saloon, Subway, Super 8
5	rd 6, Beaver Creek, N Local/dsl
3	rd 4 (from eb), Beaver Creek
1	MN 23, rd 17, to Jasper, N to Pipestone NM
0mm	Minnesota/South Dakota state line, Welcome Ctr eb, full facilities, info, litter barrels

BEAVER CREEK

INTERSTATE 94

Exit #	Services
259mm	Minnesota/Wisconsin state line, St Croix River
258	MN 95 N, to Stillwater, Hastings, Lakeland, N Bungalow Rest.
257mm	weigh sta wb, Welcome Ctr wb, full facilities, litter barrels, vending, petwalk
253	MN 95 S, rd 15, Manning Ave, N StoneRidge Golf, S to Afton Alps SP
251	rd 19, Keats Ave, Woodbury Dr, S EVC, KwikTrip, Speedway/dsl, Arby's, Burger King, Caribou Coffee, Chili's, Chipotle Mexican, ChuckECheese, Culver's, Dino's Rest., Dunn Bros Coffee, Jersey Mike's, Little Chopstix, McDonald's, Noodles&Co, Quiznos, Ray J's Grill, Starbucks, Extended Stay America, Holiday Inn Express, AT&T, AutoZone, Discount Tire, Hobby Lobby, Michael's, Sam's Club/gas, Target/Starbucks, Trader Joe's, Verizon, Walmart/Subway, Woodbury Lakes Outlets/famous brands
250	rd 13, Radio Dr, Inwood Ave, N Buffalo Wild Wings, Five Guys, Machine Shed Rest., Olive Garden, Red Lobster, Hampton Inn, Hilton Garden, Holiday Inn, Best Buy, S Holiday/e85, Cane's, Crumbl Cookies, Domino's, DUC Vietnamese, Jamba Juice, Pei Wei, Piada Italian, Potbelly, Qdoba, Taco Bell, Tamarack Rest., TX Roadhouse, Wendy's, Wild Bill's Grill, Zupas, Courtyard, Residence Inn, ALDI, Barnes&Noble, Cabela's, Cub Foods, CVS Drug, Dick's, Heppner's Auto Ctr, Home Depot, JC Penney, LandsEnd Inlet, OfficeMax, Old Navy, PetSmart, Tires+, TJ Maxx, Verizon, vet, Whole Foods Mkt
249	I-694 N & I-494 S
247	MN 120, Century Ave, auto repair, N Denny's, LivInn, Harley-Davidson, S Speedway/dsl, Caribou Coffee, GreenMill Rest., Country Inn/rest., Chevrolet
246c b	McKnight Ave, N 3M, S Double Tree
246a	Ruth St(from eb, no return), N BP, Bruegger's Bagels, Culver's, Domino's, Hoho Chinese, Jimmy John's, Leeann Chin, $Tree, Cub Foods, Firestone/auto, S vet
245	White Bear Ave, N Speedway/dsl, Subway, Motel 6, Jiffy Lube, Walgreens, S BP, Arby's, Davanni's Pizza/subs, Los Ocampo, McDonald's, Papa John's, Popeyes, Sonic, Taco Bell, Wendy's, $General, ALDI, NAPA, O'Reilly Parts, Target
244	US 10 E, US 61 S, S Mounds/Kellogg
243	US 61, Mounds Blvd, S River Centre
242d	US 52 S, MN 3, 6th St, (exits left from wb), N Holiday/dsl, Subway
242c	7th St, S Speedway
242b a	I-35E N, US 10 W, I-35E S(from eb)
241c	I-35E S(from wb)
241b	10th St, 5th St, to downtown
241a	12th St, Marion St, Kellogg Blvd, N Radisson Hotel,
241a	Continued St Paul's Cathedral, vet
240	Dale Ave
239b a	Lexington Pkwy, Hamline Ave, N BP, Speedway, Hardee's, Jersey Mike's, Noodles&Co, Popeyes, White Castle, $Tree, ALDI, AutoZone, Cub Foods, Discount Tire, O'Reilly Parts, Target/Starbucks/CVS, Verizon, S H
238	MN 51, Snelling Ave, N Culver's, Denny's, McDonald's, same as 239, S Holiday/dsl, Dunkin, Starbucks, Tires+, Whole Foods Mkt
237	Cretin Ave, Vandalia Ave, to downtown
236	MN 280, University Ave, to downtown
235b	Huron Blvd, N Holiday, Papa John's, Hampton Inn, Hilton, Fresh Thyme Mkt
235mm	Mississippi River
235a	Riverside Ave, 25th Ave, N Arco, H
234c	Cedar Ave, downtown
234b a	MN 55, Hiawatha Ave, 5th St, N Courtyard, to downtown
233b	I-35W N, I-35W S(exits left from wb)
233a	11th St(from wb), N downtown
231b	Hennepin Ave, Lyndale Ave, N downtown
231a	I-394, US 12 W, N downtown
230	US 52, MN 55, 4th St, 7th St, Olson Hwy, N US Bank Stadium, S H, Int Mkt Square
229	W Broadway, Washington Ave, N Holiday/dsl, S Winner, Little Caesar's, McDonald's, Subway, Taco Bell, Wendy's, $General, AutoZone, Cub Foods, Family$, W Popeyes
228	Dowling Ave N
226	53rd Ave N, 49th Ave N
225	I-694 E, MN 252 N, to Minneapolis. I-94 & I-494 run together. See I-494 exits 28-34.
216	I-94 & I-494.
215	rd 109, Weaver Lake Rd, N Speedway/dsl, Angeno's, Arby's, Burger King, Caribou Coffee, ChuckECheese's, Domino's, DQ, Dunkin, El Rodeo Mexican, Famous Dave's BBQ, Frankie's Pizza, Golden Corral, Great Harvest Bread Co., Jimmy John's, McDonald's, Papa Murphy's, Starbucks, Subway, Taco Bell, Taco John's, Wendy's, Hampton Inn, Staybridge Suites, AT&T, auto repair, Barnes&Noble, Batteries+, Best Buy, Cub Foods, Kohl's, Lund&Byerly's Foods, Michael's, Midas, Old Navy, PetCo, same as 28, Tires+, USPO, Verizon, Walgreens, S Applebee's
214mm	eb, full facilities, litter barrels
213	rd 30, 95th Ave N, Maple Grove, N Speedway/dsl, Cane's, Chipotle Mexican, Subway, Cambria Suites, ALDI, Home Depot, H, Target/Starbucks, URGENT CARE, S Holiday/dsl, Caribou Coffee, Culver's, Jersey Mike's, Jets Pizza, Jimmy John's, Leeann Chin, McDonald's, Starbucks, Teresa's Mexican, Which Wich?, White Castle, $Tree, Discount Tire, Firestone/auto, Goodyear/auto, Hobby Lobby, KOA(2mi)(Apr-Oct), Menards, Sam's Club/gas, Verizon, Walgreens, Walmart/Subway
212	101st Ave(from eb)
207	MN 101, to Elk River, Rogers, N Holiday/dsl, Speedway/dsl, TA/Shell/Country Pride/dsl/scales/24hr/@, Arby's, Caribou Coffee, China Kitchen, Chipotle, Culver's, Davanni's Pizza, Denny's, Domino's, DQ, El Loro, Hardee's, Jimmy John's, Maynard's, McDonald's, Noodles&Co, Papa Murphy's, Starbucks, Subway, Taco Bell, Wendy's, Hampton Inn, Holiday Inn Express, Super 8, AT&T, auto repair, Cabela's, Cub Foods, Discount Tire, Discount Tire, Kohl's, NAPA, O'Reilly Parts, Target/Starbucks, Tires+, Verizon, vet, Walgreens, S BP/Dunkin/dsl, Holiday, Freddy's, Guadalajara Mexican, Jersey Mike's, Linda's Cafe, AmericInn, Chevrolet, CVS Drug, TrueValue, USPO
205.5mm	Crow River

MAPLE GROVE

INTERSTATE 94 Cont'd

ALBERTVILLE

Exit #	Services
205	MN 241, rd 36, St Michael, S KwikTrip/dsl, Speedway/dsl, Caribou Coffee
202	rd 37, Albertville, N Shell/dsl, Emma Krumbee's Rest., S BP/dsl, same as 201, Speedway/dsl, Taco John's, auto repair
201	rd 19(from eb), Albertville, N EVC, Kwik Trip/dsl, Andy's Pizza, Burger King, Five Guys, Michael B's Grill, Starbucks, Country Inn&Suites, Albertville Outlets/famous brands, Old Navy, S Casey's, Speedway/Circle K, Caribou Coffee, Caribou Coffee, China Dragon, Culver's, Hong Thai, Jersey Mike's, Papa John's, Papa Murphy's, Space Aliens Grill, Subway, Taco Bell, Ton Ramen, Willy McCoy's, $Tree, Ace Hardware, Coburn's/dsl, Goodyear/auto, Verizon, vet
194	rd 18, rd 39, Monticello, N KwikTrip/dsl, Caribou Coffee, Little Caesar's, AT&T, Home Depot, H, Marshall's, PetSmart, Target, Verizon
193	MN 25, to Buffalo, Monticello, Big Lake, N Holiday/dsl, Burger King, Caribou Coffee, KFC, Pancho Mexican, Papa Murphy's, Perkins, Rancho Grande Mexican, Scooter's Coffee, Taco Bell, AmericInn, AutoValue Parts, Cub Foods, USPO, Walgreens, S Holiday/dsl, Kwik Trip/dsl, Speedway/dsl, Applebee's, Arby's, Bluestone Grill, Buffalo Wild Wings, Culver's, DQ, Jimmy John's, McDonald's, Papa John's, Pizza Ranch, Subway, Taco John's, Best Western, Days Inn, Super 8, $Tree, ALDI, AutoZone, Buick/GMC, Chevrolet, Jiffy Lube, Lake Maria SP, O'Reilly Parts, tires, Verizon, Walmart/Subway
187mm	eb, full facilities, litter barrels, vending, petwalk
183	rd 8, to Silver Creek, Hasty, Maple Lake, S Speedway/rest./dsl/scales/24hr/@, camping, to Lake Maria SP
178	MN 24, to Annandale, Clearwater, N Holiday/Petro/dsl/scales/24hr/@, Burger King, DQ, Jimmy John's, Subway, Taco Gringo, HomeTown Inn, Clearwater Hardware, Coburn's Foods/gas, Parts City, repair, USPO, S Kwik Trip/dsl/scales/24hr, A-J Acres RV Camping(Apr-Oct), Recreation Outdoor RV Ctr
178mm	wb, full facilities, litter barrels, petwalk, vending
173	Opportunity Dr
171	rd 7, rd 75, St Augusta, N Pilot/dsl/scales/24hr, Shell/Burger King/dsl, McDonald's, RJ's Grill, Subway, AmericInn, Holiday Inn Express, Travelodge, H, tires, S BP, Freightliner, Pleasureland RV Ctr
167b a	MN 15, to St Cloud, Kimball, Discount Tire, N Country Inn&Suites, Days Inn, Fairfield Inn, Hampton Inn, Hilton Garden, Holiday Inn, Homewood Suites, Quality Inn, Residence Inn, Super 8, AT&T, Costco/gas, O'Reilly Parts, Subaru, USPO, Walgreens, Walmart
164	MN 23, to St Cloud, Rockville, N Coratel Inn, Discount Tire, Grande Depot Gourmet Foods, Honda, Hyundai, Kia, same as 167, S Love's/Hardees/RV Hookup/dsl/24hr/@
162.5mm	Sauk River
160	rd 2, to Cold Spring, St Joseph, N Kwik Trip/dsl, Speedway, Kay's Kitchen, Subway, Coll of St Benedict
158	rd 75(from eb exits left), to St Cloud, N same as 160
156	rd 159, St Joseph, S St Johns U
153	rd 9, Avon, N Casey's/dsl, Tesoro/McDonald's/dsl, Subway, Budget Host, city park, USPO, S El Rancho Manana Camping(10mi)
152mm	both lanes, full facilities, litter barrels, vending, petwalk
147	MN 238, rd 10, Albany, N Holiday/dsl, Shell/Godfather's/dsl, A&W/Subway, DQ, Baymont Inn, CVS Drug, golf, H(2mi), S Chrysler/Dodge/Jeep, NAPA

CLEARWATER · ST JOSEPH · SAUK CENTRE · FERGUS FALLS

Exit #	Services
140	rd 11, Freeport, N Cenex/dsl, Sinclair/dsl, Ackie's Pioneer Rest., Charlie's Café, tire repair, vet
137	MN 237, rd 65, New Munich
137mm	Sauk River
135	rd 13, Melrose, N Sinclair/dsl/repair, Victory/Subway/dsl, Burger King, $General, H(2mi), S Casey's/dsl, DQ, El Portal Mexican, Super 8, TrueValue, vet
132.5mm	Sauk River
131	MN 4, to Paynesville, Meire Grove
128mm	Sauk River
127	US 71, MN 28, Sauk Centre, N Casey's, Holiday/dsl, Caribou Coffee, DQ, Four Seas Buffet, Hardee's, McDonald's, Subway, Taco Bell, AmericInn, Best Value Inn, Gopher Prairie Inn, Ace Hardware, Coborn's Foods, Ford, H(3mi), NAPA, O'Reilly Parts, to Sinclair Lewis Home, Verizon, Walmart/Subway, S Shell/café/dsl/scales/24hr/@, Buick/Chevrolet/Chrysler/Dodge/Jeep, Kenworth
124	Sinclair Lewis Ave(from eb), Sauk Centre
119	rd 46, West Union
114	MN 27, rd 3, to Westport, Osakis, N auto repair
105mm	wb, full facilities, litter barrels, vending, petwalk
103	MN 29, to Glenwood, Alexandria, N F&F/dsl, Holiday/dsl, Simonson/dsl/EVC, Tesla EVC, Arby's, Caribou Coffee, China Buffet, Culver's, El Loro Mexican, Great Hunan, Hardee's, Jimmy John's, KFC, Longtrees Grill, McDonald's, Perkins, Qdoba, Starbucks, Subway, Taco Bell, AmericInn, Best Western, Fairfield Inn, Hampton Inn, Relax Inn, Super 8, $Tree, ALDI, AutoZone, Cadillac/Chevrolet/Mazda, Cub Foods, Goodyear/auto, Harley-Davidson, H, Mazda, Menards, Target/Starbucks, Verizon, Walmart/Subway, S Holiday/dsl, Country Inn&Suites, Holiday Inn, Buick/GMC, Hilltop RV Ctr
100	MN 27, N Pilot/Subway/dsl/scales/24hr/@, Alexandria RV Park(2mi), H, S camping
100mm	Lake Latoka
99mm	eb, full facilities, litter barrels, vending, petwalk
97	MN 114, rd 40, to Lowry, Garfield
90	rd 7, Brandon, N to camping, S camping
82	MN 79, rd 41, to Erdahl, Evansville, N BP/dsl, H, S camping
77	MN 78, rd 10, to Barrett, Ashby, N camping
69mm	**wb, full facilities, litter barrels, petwalk, vending**
67	rd 35, Dalton, S camping
61	US 59 S, rd 82, to Elbow Lake, N Marathon/dsl/LP/24hr
57	MN 210 E, rd 25, Fergus Falls, N golf, H(3mi)
55	rd 1, to Wendell, Fergus Falls, N antiques
54	MN 210 W, Lincoln Ave, Fergus Falls, N Arco/dsl, Cenex/dsl, F&F/dsl, Applebee's, Arby's, Caribou Coffee, Family Diner, Hardee's, Hunan Spring Buffet, Jimmy John's, McDonald's, Papa Murphy's, Perkins, Pizza Ranch, Subway, Taco Bell, AmericInn, Comfort Inn, Country Inn, Fergus Inn, Hotel 8, $Tree, ALDI, Chrysler/Dodge/Jeep, Ford/Lincoln, GMC, Home Depot, H(3mi), museum, NAPA, O'Reilly Parts, Thrifty White Drug, tire repair, Toyota, USPO,

 = gas = food = lodging = other = rest stop

INTERSTATE 94 Cont'd

BARNESVILLE

- **54** Continued
  Mabel Murphy's Rest., Walmart
- **50** rd 88, rd 52, to US 59, to Fergus Falls, Elizabeth
- **38** rd 88, Rothsay, S Tesoro/cafe/dsl/24hr, Powerhouse Grill, Comfort Zone Inn, tires
- **32** MN 108, rd 30,to Pelican Rapids, Lawndale, N to Maplewood SP
- **24** MN 34, Barnesville, N Renee's Drive-in, to golf, S Arco/dsl, Cenex/dsl, DQ, Subway, $General, city park, Wagner Park Camping(May-Oct)
- **22** MN 9, Barnesville, S Arco/dsl, Cenex/dsl, DQ, Subway, $General
- **15** rd 10, Downer
- **8mm** Buffalo River
- **6** MN 336, rd 11, to US 10, Dilworth, N to Buffalo River SP
- **5mm** Red River weigh sta eb
- **2b** 34th St, Moorhead, N Casey's/dsl, Holiday/dsl/e-85, Arby's, El Torro Mexican, Fry'n Pan, Hardee's, McDonald's, Pizza Ranch, Starbucks, Subway, $Tree, ALDI, CVS Drug, H, Menards, Target/CVS, Tires+, Walmart
- **2a** no services
- **1mm** **full facilities, info, litter barrels, vending, Welcome Ctr eb**
- **1b** 20th St, Moorhead(from eb, no return), S Casey's
- **1a** US 75, Moorhead, N Cenex/dsl, Altony's Italian, Burger King, Jimmy John's, Newroz Kebab, Noodles&Co, Papa Murphy's, Qdoba, Starbucks, Village Inn, Courtyard, Verizon, S Casey's, Holiday/dsl, DQ, Snapdragon Asian, Speak Easy Rest., Subway, Bison Plains Lodge, Grand Inn, Microtel, Hornbacher's Mkt, Subaru, vet, Walgreens
- **0mm** Minnesota/North Dakota state line, Red River

INTERSTATE 494/694

HASTINGS

- **71.5mm** I-494/I-694 loops around Minneapolis/St Paul.
- **71** rd 31, Pilot Knob Rd, N Courtyard, Extended Stay, Fairfield Inn
- **70** I-35E, N to St Paul, S to Albert Lea
- **69** MN 149, MN 55, Dodd Rd, S Caribou Coffee, Dickey's BBQ, Jimmy John's, McDonald's, Taco Bell, Country Inn&Suites, Omni, museum
- **67** MN 3, Roberts St, N Exxon, Holiday, Applebee's, Arby's, Cane's, Caribou Coffee, Chick-fil-A, Chipotle Mexican, Culver's, Hamburguesas El Gordo, Jersey Mike's, KFC, Noodles&Co, Panda Express, Panera Bread, Papa Murphy's, Pizza Hut, Pollo Campero, Taco Bell, White Castle, Zupas, $Tree, ALDI, AT&T, Buick/GMC, Chevrolet, Cub Foods, Discount Tire, Ford, Home Depot, Honda, Hyundai, Kia, Lincoln, Lowe's, Mazda, NAPA, Nissan, O'Reilly Parts, Petco, Target, Toyota/Scion, Verizon, VW, Wagreens, Walmart/Subway
- **66** US 52, S Speedway, Applebee's, B-52 Burger, Caribou Coffee, Los Portales, Mallard's Rest., Outback Steaks, AmericInn, Holiday Inn Express, Microtel, auto repair, Valvoline Oil Change
- **65** 7th Ave, 5th Ave
- **64b a** MN 56, Concord St, N KwikTrip/dsl/scales, Stockmens/dsl, Burger King, Stockyards ChopHouse, Subway, Envision Hotel, Goodyear, Peterbilt, S Holiday/dsl, Chrysler/Jeep/Dodge
- **63mm** Mississippi River
- **63c** Maxwell Ave
- **63b a** US 10, US 61, to St Paul, Hastings, S Speedway, Burger King, Cloverleaf Grill, North Pole Rest., Subway, Tinucci's, Boyd's Motel, NAPA
- **60** Lake Rd, E Speedway/dsl, W H
- **59** Valley Creek Rd, E Holiday/repair, Speedway/dsl/LP, Applebee's, Chipotle Mexican, Coldstone, DQ, Jersey Mike's, Jimmy John's, Noodles&Co, Panda Express, Papa Murphy's, Potbelly, Red's Savoy Pizza, Ronnally's Pizza, Starbucks, Yang's Chinese, Chick-fil-A, $Tree, Kohl's, Lunds&Byerly's Mkt, Marshall's, PetCo, Target/Starbucks, USPO, Walgreens, W BP, Andiamo Italian, Burger King, Dunkin', Joey C's Pizza, Keys Cafe, McDonald's, Pizza Hut, Subway, Hampton Inn, Goodyear, H
- **58c** Tamarack Rd, E Tavern Grill, Woodbury Cafe, La Quinta, Sheraton, W Extended Stay, Costco/gas, URGENT CARE
- **58b a** I-94, E to Madison, W to St Paul. **I-494 S begins/ends, I-694 N begins/ends**
- **57** rd 10, 10th St N, E Speedway/dsl, Cajun Crave, D-Spot, IHOP, Pizza Man, Sgt Peppers Grill, Taco Bell, Wild Boar Grill, Comfort Inn, W Holiday/dsl, Bambu Kitchen, Burger King, Caribou Coffee, Hardee's, KFC, Starbucks, $Tree, Cub Foods, HyVee/dsl
- **55** MN 5, E Speedway/dsl, McDonald's, AutoZone, Target/CVS, W Holiday/dsl, KwikTrip/dsl, Subway, Menards, st patrol
- **52b a** MN 36, N St Paul, to Stillwater, W F&F/dsl, Burger King, Caribou Coffee, DQ, Shar'els Cafe
- **51** MN 120, E Speedway/dsl, Bella Ciao Italian, QC Pizza, Quinny's Grill, W The Corner/gas
- **50** White Bear Ave, N Speedway/dsl, Culver's, Cub Foods, Sam's Club/gas, S Acapulco, Arby's, Buffalo Wild Wings, Cane's, Caribou Coffee, Chick-fil-A, Chili's, Chipotle, Great Moon Buffet, IHOP, J Pot, Jimmy John's, McDonald's, Meltdown, Million's Crab, Noodles&Co, Olive Garden, Osaka, Outback Steaks, Panera Bread, Perkins, Pizza Hut, Popeyes, Red Lobster, Taco Bell, TGI Friday, Tono Pizza, Wendy's, Emerald Inn, Aamco, Barnes&Noble, Best Buy, Firestone/auto, Hobby Lobby, JC Penney, Kohl's, Macy's, mall, Michael's, Midas, Tires+, Verizon, Walgreens
- **48** US 61, N KwikTrip/dsl, Black Sea Rest., Acura, Chrysler/Dodge/Jeep, Ford, Honda, Hyundai, Kia, Lincoln, Mitsubishi, Subaru, S Dunkin', McDonald's, Million's Crab, Olive Garden, Outback Steaks, Audi/Porsche, CarMax, Costco/gas, H, Lexus, Mercedes, Nissan, Volvo
- **47** I-35E, N to Duluth
- **46** I-35E, US 10, S to St Paul
- **45** rd 49, Rice St, N Holiday, Oliver's Rest., Taco Bell, S Caribou Coffee, Taco John's
- **43b** Victoria St
- **43a** Lexington Ave, N Greenmill Rest., Red Robin, Best Western+, Hilton Garden, S Exxon/Circle K/dsl, Arby's, Cane's, Caribou Coffee, Chick-fil-A, Chipotle, Davanni's Pizza, Five Guys, Jimmy John's, Noodles&Co, Old Southern BBQ, Starbucks, Subway, Wendy's, Quality Inn, SpringHill Suites, AT&T, Cub Foods, Target, Trader Joe's
- **42b** US 10 W(from wb), to Anoka
- **42a** MN 51, Snelling Ave, S Holiday/dsl, Flaherty's Grill, Lindey's Steaks, McDonald's, vet
- **41b a** I-35W, S to Minneapolis, N to Duluth
- **40** Long Lake Rd, 10th St NW
- **39** Silver Lake Rd, N BP, Alicia's Mexican, Cowboy Jack's, McDonald's, Subway, Ford, U-Haul
- **38b a** MN 65, Central Ave, N Holiday/dsl, Kings Korean, Subway, URGENT CARE, S Speedway, $Tree, A&W/KFC, Applebee's, Big Marina Deli, Chipotle, Crafty Crab, Domino's, Flameburger Rest., Jimmy John's, La Casita Mexican, Little Caesar's, McDonald's, Noodles&Co, Papa John's, Pizza Hut, Sonic, Starbucks, Subway, Taco Bell, Wendy's, White Castle, LivInn Hotel, Advance Parts, ALDI, AT&T, AutoZone, Discount Tire, PetCo, Target/Starbucks, Tasty , vet, Walgreens

= gas = food = lodging = other = rest stop

INTERSTATE 494/694 Cont'd

OSSEO

Exit #	Services
37	rd 47, University Ave, N Holiday, Speedway/dsl, Burger King, McDonald's, Panchero's, Papa Murphy's Pizza, Teppanyaki Grill, Zantigo's Rest., Extended Stay, Big O Tires, Cub Foods, Home Depot, Valvoline Oil Change, S Bona Bros/repair
36	E River Rd
35mm	I-494 W begins/ends, I-694 E begins/ends
35c	MN 252, N Holiday, SA
35b a	I-94 E to Minneapolis
34	to MN 100, Shingle Creek Pkwy, N Casey's, BB's Grille, Denny's, Best Western+, Country Inn&Suites, Extended Stay America, Motel 6, Quality Inn, Super 8, Travelodge, A-Abco Parts, S Rose Garden, Embassy Suites, Fairfield Inn, New King Chinese
33	rd 152, Brooklyn Blvd, N Speedway/dsl, Culver's, Slim's Café, Subway, Buick/GMC, Chevrolet, Honda, Toyota/Scion, USPO, VW, S BP, $Tree, AutoZone, Sun Foods, Walgreens
31	rd 81, Lakeland Ave, N Speedway/dsl, Angelea's Kitchen, Chipotle Mexican, Hooks Fish, Panda Express, Panda Garden, Wagner's Drive-In, Wendy's, CarMax, Petco, Target, U-Haul, S Northstar Inn
30	Boone Ave, N La Quinta, Marriott, S Home Depot
29b a	US 169, to Hopkins, Osseo
28	rd 61, Hemlock Lane, N Arby's, Benihana, Biaggi's Italian, Buca Italian, Chick-fil-A, Chipotle Mexican, Coldstone, Dave&Buster's, Dickey's BBQ, Firehouse Subs, Five Guys, Freddy's, Granite City Rest., Leeann Chin, Malone's Grill, Mongo's Grill, Noodles&Co, Olive Garden, Panda Express, Panera Bread, Patrick's Cafe, PF Chang's, Pittsburgh Blue, Potbelly's, Red Lobster, Redstone Grill, Starbucks, Subway, TGIFriday's, Wild Bill's Café, Zupas, Courtyard, Hampton Inn, Holiday Inn, Staybridge Suites, $Tree, Best Buy, Costco/gas, Dick's, Jo-Ann Fabrics, Lowe's, Marshalls, PetSmart, REI, Trader Joe's, Verizon, Whole Foods Mkt, World Mkt, S BP, Perkins, Asteria Suites
27	I-94 W to St Cloud, I-94/694 E to Minneapolis
26	rd 10, Bass Lake Rd, E Holiday, Caribou Coffee, Culver's, McDonald's, Subway, Extended Stay America, vet, W BP, Holiday/dsl, Bruegger's Bagels, Jimmy John's, Pancake House, Pizza Hut, Rusty Taco, Hilton Garden, auto repair, CVS Drug
23	rd 9, Rockford Rd, $Tree, E Holiday, Chili's, Domino's, Five Guys, Sunshine Factory Grill, AT&T, Kohl's, O'Reilly Parts, PetSmart, Target, TJ Maxx, Walgreens, W Amoco/dsl, Bruegger's Bagels, Cowboy Jack's, DQ, Oyama Sushi, Starbucks, Toppers Pizza
22	MN 55, E Holiday/dsl, Broadway Pizza, Caribou Coffee, Green Mill Rest., Jimmy John's, McDonald's, Red Robin, Solos Pizza, Crowne Plaza, Ramada, Red Roof Inn, Residence Inn, H, W Holiday/dsl, Arby's, Burger King, Chick-fil-A, Davanni's Rest., Firehouse Subs, Lucky's 13, Perkins, Wendy's, Holiday Inn Express, Goodyear/auto, Tires+
21	rd 6, E KwikTrip, Discount Tire, Home Depot
20	Carlson Pkwy, E Holiday/dsl, Pizza Hut, Subway, W Country Inn&Suites
19b a	I-394 E, US 12 W, to Minneapolis, Wendy's, JC Penney, Subaru, Tires+, E Bacio Italian, Caribou Coffee, Jimmy John's, Barnes&Noble, Best Buy, Ford, Hobby Lobby, Lunds&Byerly's Foods, Mazda, Mercedes, Office Depot, Petco, Target/Starbucks, Whole Foods, W BP, Holiday, Chipotle, McDonald's, My Burger, Starbucks, BMW, Chevrolet, Goodyear/auto, Lexus, Nissan

Exit #	Services
17b a	Minnetonka Blvd, E Holiday, DQ, Station Pizzeria
16b a	MN 7, W Marathon, Davanni's Rest., Duke's, Famous Dave's BBQ, Taco Bell, Goodyear
13	MN 62, rd 62, E Home2 Suites
12	Valleyview Rd, rd 39(from sb)
11c	MN 5 W, same as 11 a b
11b a	US 169 S, US 212 W, N Jets Pizza, Pizza Luce, TequeArepa, Eden Prarie, Fairfield Inn, Hyatt Place, Residence Inn, Sonesta, S Holiday, Mobil, Baker's Ribs, Caribou Coffee, Champp's, CRAVE, Davanni's Rest., Leeann Chin, McDonald's, Old Chicago, Osaka Japanese, Popeyes, Qdoba, Redstone Rest., Smashburger, Starbucks, vet, Wildfire Steaks, Best Western, Discount Tire, Extended Stay America, Hampton Inn, SpringHill Suites, TownePlace Suites, Walgreens, $Tree, Barnes&Noble, Best Buy, Costco/gas, Cub Foods, JC Penney, Office Depot, Petco, Scheels, Target/Starbucks, Walmart
10	US 169 N, to rd 18
8	rd 28(from wb, no return), E Bush Lake Rd, same as 7 a b
7b a	MN 100, rd 34, Normandale Blvd, N Shell/dsl, Burger King, Caribou Coffee, Domino's, DQ, Jimmy John's, Starbucks, Subway, TGIFridays, Doubletree, Sheraton, S Holiday/dsl, Olive Garden, Hampton Inn, Hilton Garden, Holiday Inn, La Quinta, Renaissance, Staybridge Inn
6b	rd 17, France Ave, N Mobil, Ciao Bella, Perkins, Smack Shack, Courtyard, Holiday Inn Express, Residence Inn, H(3mi), Marshall's, Michael's, Trader Joe's, World Mkt, S Denny's, Olive Garden, Best Western, Hilton, Buick/GMC, Hyundai, Mercedes, Toyota/Scion
6a	Penn Ave(no EZ eb return), S Applebee's, Brueggers Bagels, Caribou Coffee, Charley Cat Chicken, Home2 Suites, Itton Ramen, Jimmy John's, Mallard's, McDonald's, Red Lobster, Sonic, Subway, Wendy's, Embassy Suites, Chrysler/Jeep/Dodge, Fresh Thyme Mkt, Hobby Lobby, Kohl's, Lucky 13, Target/Starbucks, TJ Maxx, Walgreens
5b a	I-35W, S to Albert Lea, N to Minneapolis
4b	Lyndale Ave, N BP, Speedway, Blaze Pizza, Chipotle Mexican, DQ, Eddie Cheng's, Noodles&Co, Panera Bread, Papa John's, Potbelly, Sarpino's Pizza, Starbucks, Sheraton, Sonesta Suites, Best Buy, Honda, Lands End, PetSmart, S Extended Stay America, Acura/Subaru, Lincoln, REI
4a	MN 52, Nicollet Ave, N Speedway/dsl, Taco Bell, Menards, S Holiday/dsl, Culver's, McDonald's, La Quinta, Super 8, Home Depot, Sam's Club
3	Portland Ave, 12th Ave(from eb), N Arby's, Baymont, S Jimmy John's, Outback Steaks, Pizza Hut, Subway, Toppers Pizza, Comfort Inn, Courtyard, Hilton Garden, Holiday Inn Express, Microtel, Quality Inn, Residence Inn, $Tree, Walgreens, Walmart/Subway
2c b	MN 77, N SA, S Outback Steaks, Pizza Hovara, AC Hotel, Comfort Inn, Courtyard, Element Hotel, Fairfield Inn, Great Wolf Lodge, Hampton Inn, Hilton Garden, JW Marriott, Marriott, Northwood Inn, Residence Inn, SpringHill Suites, TownePlace Suites, IKEA, Macy's, Mall of America,

 [gas] = gas [food] = food [lodging] = lodging [other] = other [RS] = rest stop

INTERSTATE 494/694 Cont'd

2c b	Continued Nordstrom's
2a	24th Ave, same as 2c b
1b	34th Ave, Nat Cemetary, N [gas] Holiday/dsl,
1b	Continued Crowne Plaza, Embassy Suites, Hilton, Hyatt Place, Hyatt Regency
1a	MN 5 E, N [other] [airport]
0mm	Minnesota River. I-494/I-694 loops around Minneapolis/St Paul.

NOTES

MISSISSIPPI

INTERSTATE 10

Exit #	Services
77mm	Mississippi/Alabama state line, weigh sta wb
75	Franklin Creek Rd
75mm	**full facilities, litter barrels, petwalk, , , RV dump, Welcome Ctr wb, weigh sta eb**
74mm	Escatawpa River
69	MS 63, to E Moss Point, N Circle K/Domino's/dsl/24hr, Raceway/dsl, Waffle House, La Quinta, Motel 6, Super 8, S Chevron/dsl, Exxon/Subway/dsl, Pilot/Moe's SW/dsl/scales/24hr, Shell, Arby's, Burger King, Captain D's, Cracker Barrel, Hardee's, McDonald's, Ruby Tuesday, San Miguel Mexican, Taco Bell, Waffle House, Wendy's, Best Western, Comfort Inn, Days Inn, EconoLodge, Hampton Inn, Holiday Inn Express, Quality Inn, Honda, H, Toyota
68	MS 613, to Moss Point, Pascagoula, N Chevron/dsl, Texaco/dsl, Coco Loco Mexican, Tugus' Rest., Red Roof Inn, S Marathon/dsl, H, Pelican Landing Conf Ctr
64mm	Pascagoula River
63.5mm	**24hr security, full facilities, litter barrels, petwalk, , , both lanes, RV dump**
61	to Gautier, N MS Nat Golf Course, S Marathon/dsl, Hardee's, KFC, McDonald's, Pizza Hut, Sonic, Wendy's, Best Western, Suburban Lodge, Sandhill Crane WR, Shephard Camping
57	MS 57, to Vancleave, N Chevron/dsl, Shed BBQ, Journey's End Camping, tires/repair, S Texaco
50	MS 609 S, Ocean Springs, N Shell/Circle K/Domino's/dsl, Waffle House, Baymont, Best Western, Country Inn&Suites, Motel 6, Red Roof Inn, Super 8, Wingate Inn, Martin Lake Camping(1mi), tires/repair, S Chevron/McDonald's, Circle K/Subway/dsl, Marathon/dsl, RaceTrac/dsl, Denny's, Pizza Hut, Taco Bell, Waffle House, Wendy's, Comfort Suites, Days Inn, Hampton Inn, Holiday Inn Express, Quality Inn, $General, $Tree, Nat Seashore
46b a	I-110, MS 15 N, to Biloxi, N Chevron/dsl, Murphy USA/dsl, Asian Fusion Cafe, Buffalo Wild Wings, Chick-fil-A, Chicken Salad Chick, Chili's, Dickey's BBQ, Five Guys, Ichiro Japanese, IHOP, Moe's SW Grill, Newk's Cafe, Olive Garden, Osaka Japanese, Outback Steaks, Panda Palace, Papa John's, Pedro's Taco, Red Lobster, Ruby Tuesday, Samurai Japanese, Sonic, Starbucks, Subway, T-Mobile, Tiantian Chinese, Twin Peaks, Waffle House, Wendy's, Whataburger, Which Wich?, Comfort Inn, Courtyard, Hampton Inn, Home2 Suites, Regency Inn, AT&T, Best Buy, CVS, Dick's, Firestone, GNC, Kohl's, Lowe's, Marshall's, Mercedes, Michaels, Office Depot, PetSmart, Ross, Target/CVS, URGENT CARE, Verizon, vet, VW, Walgreens, Walmart/gas, S Walk-On's Grill, BMW, Buick/GMC, to beaches
44	Cedar Lake Rd, to Biloxi, N Love's/Subway/dsl/scales/24hr/@, Chevrolet, S Circle K/dsl, Shell/dsl, Applebee's, Dunkin, El Saltillo, KFC/LJ Silver, McDonald's, Pop's Pizza, Slim Chickens, Sonic, Subway, Taco Bell, Waffle House, La Quinta, AutoZone, Biloxi Nat Cem, Cedar Lake Drug, Harley-Davidson, Home Depot, H, O'Reilly Parts
41	MS 67 N, to Woolmarket, N Chevron/dsl, Texaco/dsl, Subway, golf(6mi), S Camping World, Freightliner, Mazalea RV Prk, Parkers Landing RV Prk, Southern Tire Mart
39.5mm	Biloxi River
38	Lorraine-Cowan Rd, N Chevron/dsl, Exxon/Subway, Shell/Circle K/dsl, Domino's, McDonald's, Sonic, Chrysler/Dodge/Jeep, Toyota, S RaceTrac/dsl, to beaches

OCEAN SPRINGS

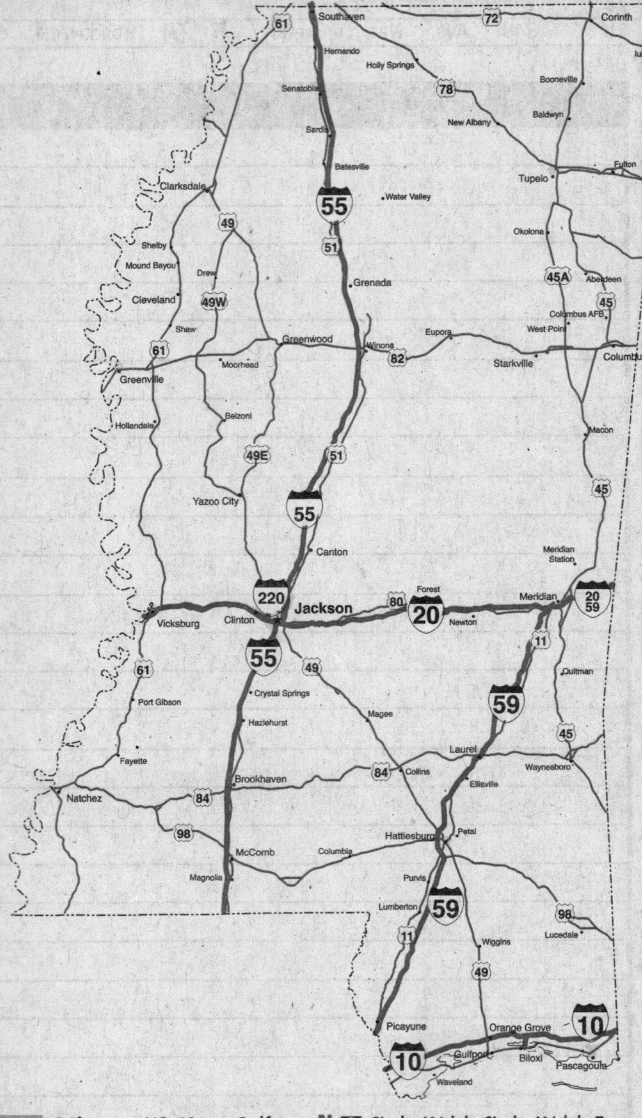

Exit #	Services
34b a	US 49, to Gulfport, N Circle K/dsl, Circle K/dsl, Exxon, Bop's Foyo, Buffalo Wild Wings, Cane's, Chick-fil-A, Chicken Salad Chick, Chili's, ChuckeCheese, Cracker Barrel, Dickey's BBQ, Firehouse Subs, Five Guys, Hardee's, Jersey Mikes, Logan's Roadhouse, Longhorn Steaks, Marble Slab, Mugshots Grill, Newk's Cafe, Panda Palace, Salad Station, Sicily's Italian Buffet, Starbucks, TGIFridays, TX Roadhouse, Waffle House, Hampton Inn, Home2 Suites, Sleep Inn, SpringHill Suites, $Tree, Advance Parts, AT&T, Barnes&Noble, Belk, Best Buy, Buick/Cadillac/Chevrolet, CVS Drug, Foley's RV Ctr, Hobby Lobby, Honda, H, Michael's, NTB, Office Depot, Old Navy, PetSmart, Ross, Sam's Club/gas, TJ Maxx, URGENT CARE, USPO, Walgreens, Winn-Dixie, S Circle K/dsl, Murphy USA, RaceWay/dsl, Shell/dsl, Applebee's, Arby's, Aztecas Mexican, Burger King, Claw Daddy's, Food Court, Hibachi Express, Hooters, IHOP, Jimmy John's, Krispy Kreme, McAlister's Deli, McDonald's, Mr. & Mrs. Crab, Shrimp Basket, Sonic, Subway, Taco Bell, Waffle House, Wendy's, Best Western, Comfort Suites, Days Inn, EconoLodge, Extended Stay, Fairfield Inn, Hilton Garden, Holiday Inn, InTown Suites, Motel 6, Quality Inn,

MS

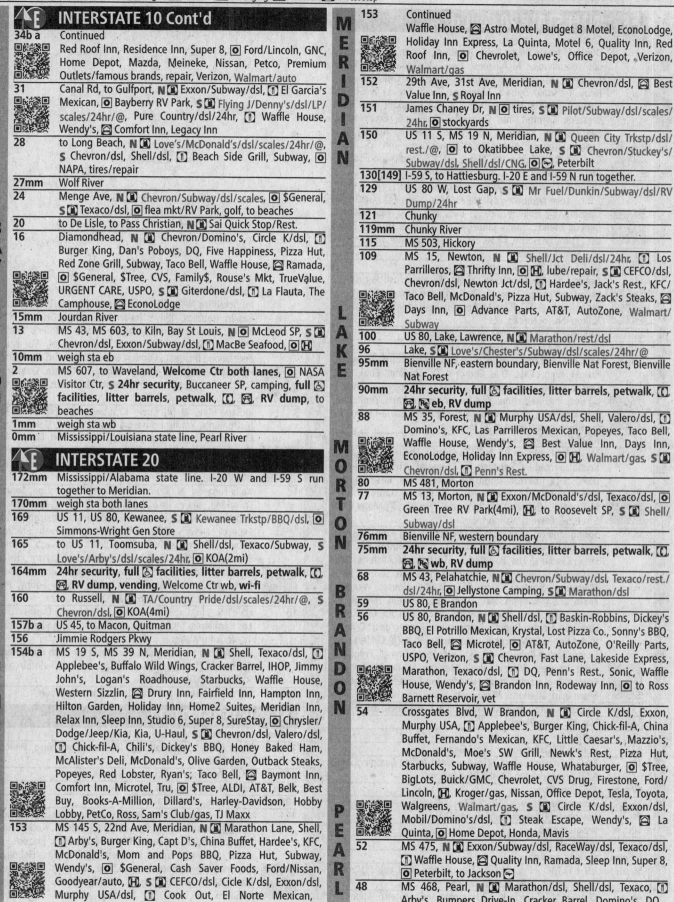

INTERSTATE 10 Cont'd

34b a Continued
Red Roof Inn, Residence Inn, Super 8, Ford/Lincoln, GNC, Home Depot, Mazda, Meineke, Nissan, Petco, Premium Outlets/famous brands, repair, Verizon, Walmart/auto

31 Canal Rd, to Gulfport, N Exxon/Subway/dsl, El Garcia's Mexican, Bayberry RV Park, S Flying J/Denny's/dsl/LP/scales/24hr/@, Pure Country/dsl/24hr, Waffle House, Wendy's, Comfort Inn, Legacy Inn

28 to Long Beach, N Love's/McDonald's/dsl/scales/24hr/@, S Chevron/dsl, Shell/dsl, Beach Side Grill, Subway, NAPA, tires/repair

27mm Wolf River

24 Menge Ave, N Chevron/Subway/dsl/scales, $General, S Texaco/dsl, flea mkt/RV Park, golf, to beaches

20 to De Lisle, to Pass Christian, N Sai Quick Stop/Rest.

BAY ST LOUIS

16 Diamondhead, N Chevron/Domino's, Circle K/dsl, Burger King, Dan's Poboys, DQ, Five Happiness, Pizza Hut, Red Zone Grill, Subway, Taco Bell, Waffle House, Ramada, $General, $Tree, CVS, Family$, Rouse's Mkt, TrueValue, URGENT CARE, USPO, S Giterdone/dsl, La Flauta, The Camphouse, EconoLodge

15mm Jourdan River

13 MS 43, MS 603, to Kiln, Bay St Louis, N McLeod SP, S Chevron/dsl, Exxon/Subway/dsl, MacBe Seafood, H

10mm weigh sta eb

2 MS 607, to Waveland, **Welcome Ctr both lanes,** NASA Visitor Ctr, S **24hr security,** Buccaneer SP, camping, **full facilities, litter barrels, petwalk,** **RV dump,** to beaches

1mm weigh sta wb

0mm Mississippi/Louisiana state line, Pearl River

INTERSTATE 20

172mm Mississippi/Alabama state line. I-20 W and I-59 S run together to Meridian.

170mm weigh sta both lanes

169 US 11, US 80, Kewanee, S Kewanee Trkstp/BBQ/dsl, Simmons-Wright Gen Store

165 to US 11, Toomsuba, N Shell/dsl, Texaco/Subway, S Love's/Arby's/dsl/scales/24hr, KOA(2mi)

164mm **24hr security, full facilities, litter barrels, petwalk,** **RV dump, vending,** Welcome Ctr wb, **wi-fi**

160 to Russell, N TA/Country Pride/dsl/scales/24hr/@, S Chevron/dsl, KOA(4mi)

157b a US 45, to Macon, Quitman

156 Jimmie Rodgers Pkwy

MERIDIAN

154b a MS 19 S, MS 39 N, Meridian, N Shell, Texaco/dsl, Applebee's, Buffalo Wild Wings, Cracker Barrel, IHOP, Jimmy John's, Logan's Roadhouse, Starbucks, Waffle House, Western Sizzlin, Drury Inn, Fairfield Inn, Hampton Inn, Hilton Garden, Holiday Inn, Home2 Suites, Meridian Inn, Relax Inn, Sleep Inn, Studio 6, Super 8, SureStay, Chrysler/Dodge/Jeep/Kia, Kia, U-Haul, S Chevron/dsl, Valero/dsl, Chick-fil-A, Chili's, Dickey's BBQ, Honey Baked Ham, McAlister's Deli, McDonald's, Olive Garden, Outback Steaks, Popeyes, Red Lobster, Ryan's, Taco Bell, Baymont Inn, Comfort Inn, Microtel, Tru, $Tree, ALDI, AT&T, Belk, Best Buy, Books-A-Million, Dillard's, Harley-Davidson, Hobby Lobby, PetCo, Ross, Sam's Club/gas, TJ Maxx

153 MS 145 S, 22nd Ave, Meridian, N Marathon Lane, Shell, Arby's, Burger King, Capt D's, China Buffet, Hardee's, KFC, McDonald's, Mom and Pops BBQ, Pizza Hut, Subway, Wendy's, $General, Cash Saver Foods, Ford/Nissan, Goodyear/auto, H, S CEFCO/dsl, Cicle K/dsl, Exxon/dsl, Murphy USA/dsl, Cook Out, El Norte Mexican,

153 Continued
Waffle House, Astro Motel, Budget 8 Motel, EconoLodge, Holiday Inn Express, La Quinta, Motel 6, Quality Inn, Red Roof Inn, Chevrolet, Lowe's, Office Depot, Verizon, Walmart/gas

152 29th Ave, 31st Ave, Meridian, N Chevron/dsl, Best Value Inn, S Royal Inn

151 James Chaney Dr, N tires, S Pilot/Subway/dsl/scales/24hr, stockyards

150 US 11 S, MS 19 N, Meridian, N Queen City Trkstp/dsl/rest./@, to Okatibbee Lake, S Chevron/Stuckey's/Subway/dsl, Shell/dsl/CNG, Peterbilt

130[149] I-59 S, to Hattiesburg. I-20 E and I-59 N run together.

129 US 80 W, Lost Gap, S Mr Fuel/Dunkin/Subway/dsl/RV Dump/24hr

121 Chunky

119mm Chunky River

115 MS 503, Hickory

109 MS 15, Newton, N Shell/Jct Deli/dsl/24hr, Los Parrilleros, Thrifty Inn, H, lube/repair, S CEFCO/dsl, Chevron/dsl, Newton Jct/dsl, Hardee's, Jack's Rest., KFC/Taco Bell, McDonald's, Pizza Hut, Subway, Zack's Steaks, Days Inn, Advance Parts, AT&T, AutoZone, Walmart/Subway

LAKE

100 US 80, Lake, Lawrence, N Marathon/rest/dsl

96 Lake, S Love's/Chester's/Subway/dsl/scales/24hr/@

95mm Bienville NF, eastern boundary, Bienville Nat Forest, Bienville Nat Forest

90mm **24hr security, full facilities, litter barrels, petwalk,** **eb, RV dump**

MORTON

88 MS 35, Forest, N Murphy USA/dsl, Shell, Valero/dsl, Domino's, KFC, Las Parrilleros Mexican, Popeyes, Taco Bell, Waffle House, Wendy's, Best Value Inn, Days Inn, EconoLodge, Holiday Inn Express, H, Walmart/gas, S Chevron/dsl, Penn's Rest.

80 MS 481, Morton

77 MS 13, Morton, N Exxon/McDonald's/dsl, Texaco/dsl, Green Tree RV Park(4mi), H, to Roosevelt SP, S Shell/Subway/dsl

76mm Bienville NF, western boundary

75mm **24hr security, full facilities, litter barrels, petwalk,** **wb, RV dump**

BRANDON

68 MS 43, Pelahatchie, N Chevron/Subway/dsl, Texaco/rest./dsl/24hr, Jellystone Camping, S Marathon/dsl

59 US 80, E Brandon

56 US 80, Brandon, N Shell/dsl, Baskin-Robbins, Dickey's BBQ, El Potrillo Mexican, Krystal, Lost Pizza Co., Sonny's BBQ, Taco Bell, Microtel, AT&T, AutoZone, O'Reilly Parts, USPO, Verizon, S Chevron, Fast Lane, Lakeside Express, Marathon, Texaco/dsl, DQ, Penn's Rest., Sonic, Waffle House, Wendy's, Brandon Inn, Rodeway Inn, to Ross Barnett Reservoir, vet

PEARL

54 Crossgates Blvd, W Brandon, N Circle K/dsl, Exxon, Murphy USA, Applebee's, Burger King, Chick-fil-A, China Buffet, Fernando's Mexican, KFC, Little Caesar's, Mazzio's, McDonald's, Moe's SW Grill, Newk's Rest, Pizza Hut, Starbucks, Subway, Waffle House, Whataburger, $Tree, BigLots, Buick/GMC, Chevrolet, CVS Drug, Firestone, Ford/Lincoln, H, Kroger/gas, Nissan, Office Depot, Tesla, Toyota, Walgreens, Walmart/gas, S Circle K/dsl, Exxon/dsl, Mobil/Domino's/dsl, Steak Escape, Wendy's, La Quinta, Home Depot, Honda, Mavis

52 MS 475, N Exxon/Subway/dsl, RaceWay/dsl, Texaco/dsl, Waffle House, Quality Inn, Ramada, Sleep Inn, Super 8, Peterbilt, to Jackson

48 MS 468, Pearl, N Marathon/dsl, Shell/dsl, Texaco, Arby's, Bumpers Drive-In, Cracker Barrel, Domino's, DQ,

= gas = food = lodging = other = rest stop

MS

INTERSTATE 20 Cont'd

PEARL

48	Continued Dunkin', Jose's Rest., Kobe Japanese, Logan's Roadhouse, Los Parrilleros, McAlister's Deli, McDonald's, Mikado Japanese, Moss Creek Fishouse, Mugshots Grill, Popeyes, Ruby Tuesday, Salsa's Mexican, Sonic, Steak 'n Shake, Subway, Waffle House, Wendy's, Baymont Inn, Best Western, Comfort Inn, Courtyard, Days Inn, Econolodge, Fairfield Inn, Hampton Inn, Hilton Garden, Holiday Inn Express, Home2 Suites, Motel 6, Residence Inn, AT&T, CarCare, S Exxon/dsl, Mobil/dsl, Candlewood Suites, Country Inn&Suites, La Quinta, $General, Family$
47b a	US 49 S, Flowood, N Flying J/Denny's/dsl/LP/RV dump/ 24hr, Love's/Subway/dsl/scales/24hr, QT, Godfrey's Flagship, Holiday Inn, Bass Pro Shop, MS Outlets/ famous brands, Sam's Club/gas, SpeedCo, S RaceWay/ dsl, Waffle House, SureStay, Freightliner, tires
46	I-55 N, to Memphis
45b	US 51, State St, to downtown
45a	Gallatin St, to downtown, N Marathon/dsl, Petro/Iron Skillet/dsl/scales/24hr/@, Shell, Blue Beacon, tires/truck repair, vet, S Pilot/McDonald's/dsl/scales/24hr/@, Hilltop Inn, Nissan, vet
44	I-55 S(exits left from wb), to New Orleans
43b a	Terry Rd, N Jasco, Apache RV Ctr
42b a	Ellis Ave, Belvidere, N Gas Plus, Marathon/Subway, Burger King, Capt D's, Church's TX Chicken, Cook Out, Crechale's Steaks, McDonald's, Pizza Hut, Popeyes, Wendy's, Best Inn, Relax Inn, $Tree, Advance Parts, AutoZone, Firestone/auto, Jackson Zoo, O'Reilly Parts, Sav-a-Lot Foods, transmissions, U-Haul, S Midwest
41	I-220 N, US 49 N, to Jackson
40b a	MS 18 W, Robinson Rd, N Exxon/dsl, Shell/dsl, Arby's, Krystal, Piccadilly, Popeyes, $General, AT&T, tire repair, USPO, S Chevron, Citgo/dsl, Murphy USA, RaceWay/dsl, Shell/Church's TX Chicken/dsl, Chan's Garden, IHOP, McDonald's, Subway, Waffle House, Wendy's, Motel 6, $Tree, H, Lowe's, Walmart/gas
36	Springridge Rd, Clinton, N Chevron/Burger King, DTR/dsl, Murphy USA/dsl, Shell, Capt D's, China Buffet, DQ, KFC, Little Ceasar's, Los Parrilleros, Mazzio's, McAlister's Deli, McDonald's, Newk's Cafe, Picantes, Pizza Hut, Sonny's BBQ, Starbucks, Subway, Taco Bell, Waffle House, Wendy's, Zaxby's, Comfort Inn, Days Inn, Fairfield Inn, Hilton Garden, $Tree, Advance Parts, AT&T, BigLots, CVS Drug, Family$, Home Depot, Kroger/gas, Kroger/gas, O'Reilly Parts, Verizon, Walgreens, Walmart(2mi), S Circle K/dsl, Exxon/Baskin-Robbins/dsl, Applebee's, Bonsai, Froghead Grill, Popeyes, QT/dsl, Salsa's Mexican, Best Value Inn, Econolodge, Hampton Inn, Holiday Inn Express, Quality Inn, Super 8, $General, Mavis, vet
35	US 80 E, Clinton, N Chevron, Circle K/dsl, Shell/dsl, vet
34	Natchez Trace Pkwy
31	Norrell Rd
27	Bolton, S Chevron/dsl, $General
19	MS 22, Edwards, Flora, N Askew's Landing Camping(2mi), S Exxon/dsl, Shell/dsl, Relax Inn
17mm	Big Black River
15	Flowers, N Love's/Arby's/Chester's/dsl/scales/24hr/@
11	Bovina, N Texaco/Subway/dsl/24hr
10mm	weigh sta wb
8mm	weigh sta eb
6.5mm	parking area eb
5b a	US 61, MS 27 S, N Chevron/dsl, Shell/dsl, Sonic, Toney's Grill, H, S same as 4a
4b a	Clay St, N Circle K, Hampton Inn, Motel 6, Super 8,

BELVIDERE

CLINTON

BOVINA

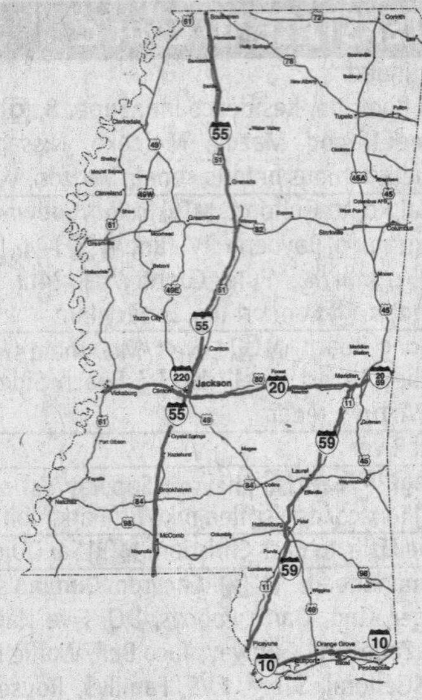

VICKSBURG

4b a	Continued to Vicksburg NP, S Circle K/Little Caesars/dsl, Texaco, Baskin Robbins, Billy's Italian, Bumper's Drive-In, China Buffet, Cracker Barrel, McAlister's deli, Palmer's Seafood, Pizza Inn, Subway, Taco Casa, Waffle House, Wendy's, Beechwood Inn/rest., Comfort Suites, Courtyard, Econolodge, Holiday Inn Express, Home2 Suites, La Quinta, Quality Inn, Scottish Inn, $General, Outlet Mall/famous brands, same as 5
3	Indiana Ave, N Circle K/Subway/dsl, China King, McDonald's, Waffle House, Best Western, Deluxe Inn, Chevrolet, Chrysler/Dodge/Jeep, Corner Mkt Foods, Ford/ Lincoln, Honda, Nissan, Toyota, S Circle K, Goldie's BBQ, Honey Baked Ham, KFC, Best Inn, Buick/Cadillac/ GMC, Family$
1c	Halls Ferry Rd, N Chevron/dsl, Burger King, Sonic, Travel Inn, CVS Drug, H, S Shell/dsl, Asian Kitchen, Captain D's, Chick-fil-A, DQ, El Sombrero Mexican, Goldie's Express, Newk's Eatery, Pizza Hut, Popeyes, Starbucks, Subway, Superior Crab, Taco Bell, Taco Casa, Wendy's, Whataburger, Candlewood Suites, Holiday Inn, Howard Johnson, Red Roof Inn, Rodeway Inn, $General, Advance Parts, AT&T, Belk, BigLots, Dillard's, Hobby Lobby, Home Depot, Kroger/gas, TJ Maxx, USPO, Walgreens
1b	US 61 S, S Circle K/Domino's/dsl, Murphy Express/dsl, Los Parrilleros, McDonald's, Waffle House, $Tree, same as 1c, Verizon, Walmart
1a	Washington St, Vicksburg, **Welcome Ctr both lanes, full facilities,** N Circle K/dsl, AmeriStar Hotel/Casino/ RV Park, S Waffle House
0mm	Mississippi/Louisiana state line, Mississippi River

INTERSTATE 22

118mm	Alabama/Mississippi State Line
115mm	**litter barrels, petwalk, , RV dump, vending, Welcome Ctr/ wb**
113	rd 23, Tremont, Smithville
108	rd 25 N, Belmont, Iuka
106mm	both lanes, weigh sta
104	rd 25 S, Fulton, Amory, N Shell/cafe/dsl/scales, Texaco/ dsl, American's Inn, Burger King, Hardee's, Huddle House, Jack's Rest., Little Caesars Pizza, McDonald's, Piezons Pizza, Sonic, Subway, Yamato Japanese, Days Inn, Holiday Inn Express, $General, AutoZone, Brown's Auto Repair, Family$, Food Giant/gas, O'Reilly Parts, RV camping, Whitten HS, S Murphy USA/dsl, KFC,

INTERSTATE 22 Cont'd

Exit	Services
104	Continued Los Compadres Mexican, Peking Palace, Pizza Hut, Taco Bell, Wendy's, [other] AT&T, Walmart/gas
104mm	Tombigbee River/Tenn-Tom Waterway
101	rd 178, rd 363, Peppertown, Mantachie, N [gas] Marathon, [food] auto/truck repair, Do Right BBQ, Dynasty 78 Rest., Peppertown Rest., S [gas] Dorsey Fuel/dsl(2mi)
97	Fawn Grove Rd
94	rd 371, Mantachie, Mooreville, N [gas] Woodchuck's/dsl, [food] Bishops BBQ
90	Auburn Rd, N [gas] Chevron/dsl
87	Veterans Blvd, N [gas] Shell/dsl, [food] Huddle House, [lodging] Wingate Inn, [other] $General, E. Presley Campground/Park, S Tombigbee SP
86	US 45 N, Tupelo, to Corinth, N [gas] Shell/dsl, Texaco, Valero, [food] ALDI, Applebees, Baskin Robbins, Buffalo Wild Wings, Burger King, Cane's, Cantina Del Sol, Capt D's, Chick-fil-A, Chicken Salad Chick, Chipotle, ChuckeCheese, Cracker Barrel, Crossroads Rib Shack, Five Guys, IHOP, Just Wings, Kyoto Japanese, Lobster King, Lone Star Grill, Longhorn Steaks, McDonald's, New China Buffet, Newk's Eatery, O'Charley's, Olive Garden, Panda Express, Papa John's, Red Lobster, Slim Chickens, Sonic, Starbucks, Waffle House, Wendy's, [lodging] Best Inn, Best Western, Comfort Suites, Econolodge, Fairfield Inn, Hampton Inn, [other] $Tree, AT&T, AutoZone, Barnes&Noble, Belk, Best Buy, CarMax, Chrysler/Dodge/Jeep, Dick's, Firestone, Ford, Hobby Lobby, Home Depot, [H], Hyundai, JC Penney, Kia, Kohl's, Kroger, Lowe's, Midas, NAPA, Nissan, Old Navy, PetSmart, Ross, Sam's Club/gas, TJ Maxx, URGENT CARE, Verizon, VW, Walmart
85	Natchez Trace Pkwy
82	Barnes Crossing Rd, Coley Rd, S [gas] Shell/dsl, [food] Bishops BBQ, [other] Penske
81	rd 178, McCullough Blvd, N [gas] Love's/McDonald's/dsl/scales/24hr/@, [lodging] Best Value Inn, [other] Freightliner, S [gas] Exxon/dsl, Shamrock, [food] King Chicken, Sonic, [lodging] Super 8, [other] $General, USPO
76	rd 9 S, Sherman, Pontotoc, N [gas] Wild Bill's/dsl, [other] Adventure Campers RV Ctr
73	rd 9 N, to Magnolia Way, Blue Springs, N [other] Lakeview RV Park, USPO
64	rd 15, rd 30 E, Pontotoc, Ripley, N [gas] 76/dsl, S Circle K/dsl, Pilot/Arby's/scales/dsl/24hr
63	New Albany, N [gas] Dee's Oil/dsl, [other] Buick/Chevrolet/GMC, Ford
62mm	Tallahatchie River
61	rd 30 W, W New Albany, N [gas] Dee's, [food] Cracker Barrel, McAlister's Deli, McDonald's, Popeyes, Subway, Waffle House, Wendy's, [lodging] Hampton Inn, [other] [H], Walgreens, S [gas] Exxon, Murphy USA/dsl, Shell, [food] Burger King, Capt D's, Domino's, El Agave Mexican, Hacienda Mexican, Huddle House, KFC, Little Caesars, Pizza Hut, Taco Bell, Zaxby's, [lodging] Best Western, Economy Inn, Hallmarc Inn, Holiday Inn Express, [other] $Tree, AT&T, Lowe's, Verizon, Walmart/gas
60	Glenfield, to Oxford, N [gas] Pure, [lodging] Budget Inn, [other] Tire Pros, S to U of MS
55	Myrtle, N [other] $General
48	rd 178, Hickory Flat, S [gas] Exxon/Trkstp/rest/dsl/24hr
41	rd 346, Potts Camp, S [gas] Flicks/dsl, [other] $General, NAPA
41mm	Tippah River
37	Lake Center, N [other] Chewalla Lake/RV camping
30	rd 7, rd 4, Holly Springs, Oxford, N [gas] Circle K/BBQ/dsl, URGENT CARE, [food] Burger King, Domino's, El Nopalito, Huddle House, KFC, Little Caesar's, McDonalds, Panda Buffet, Popeyes, Sonic, Subway, Taco Bell, Wendy's,
30	Continued Magnolia Inn, [other] $General, $Tree, AT&T, AutoZone, CVS Drug, O'Reilly Parts, S [gas] Circle K/dsl, Love's/Arby's/dsl/scales/24hr/RV, Murphy USA/dsl, [lodging] Best Value Inn, Quality Inn, [other] Walmart/gas
26	W Holly Springs
21	Red Banks, N [gas] Dee's Oil/dsl, Valero/dsl, [food] Clancy's Cafe, [other] $General
18	Victoria, E Byhalia, N [gas] Exxon/dsl, S Victoria/dsl
14	rd 309, Byhalia, N [gas] BP/Baskin-Robbins/dsl, Exxon/dsl, [lodging] Best Value Inn, [other] Autozone
12	I-269, MS 304
10	W Byhalia, N [gas] Exxon/dsl
6	Bethel Rd, Hacks Crossroad, N [gas] Exxon/Baskin Robbins/dsl, Flying J/Subway/dsl/scales/LP/RV dump/24hr, Valero, [food] JR's Grill, Rancho Grande, Tops BBQ, [lodging] Best Western+, Super 8, [other] truck repair, S [H]
4	rd 305, Olive Branch, Independence, N [gas] Valero, [food] DQ, Flava Seafood, Old Style BBQ, Pizza Hut, [lodging] Holiday Inn Express, Hotel DeSoto, [other] $General, Piggly Wiggly, USPO, S [gas] BP/dsl, QT, [other] CVS Drug
3.5mm	weigh sta both lanes
2	rd 302, Olive Branch, N [gas] Murphy Express/dsl, [food] Abbay's Rest., Baskin-Robbins, Buffalo Wild Wings, Chick-fil-A, Chili's, Chipotle, Colton's Steaks, Freddy's, Guthrie's Chicken, Huey's Burgers, IHOP, Krystal, Little Caesars, McAlisters Deli, Mis Pueblos Mexican, O'Charley's, Starbucks, Wendy's, [lodging] Best Western+/EVC, Comfort Suites, Hilton Garden, TownePlace Suites, [other] $Tree, Ford, Home Depot, Lowe's, Verizon, Walmart/gas, S [gas] Shell/Circle K, [food] Applebees, Burger King, Casa Mexicana, Dunkin, Honeybaked Ham, Hunan Chinese, McDonald's, Panera Bread, Papa John's, Taco Bell, Waffle House, Zaxby's, [lodging] Hampton Inn, Holiday Inn & Suites, Home2 Suites, Quality Inn, [other] AutoZone, CVS Drug, Kroger/gas, Pep Boys, Petco
1	Craft Rd, N [lodging] Candlewood Suites, [other] Camping World RV Ctr, Chevrolet, Hyundai, S [gas] Shell
0mm	Mississippi/Tennessee state line, I-22 begins/ends. US 78 continues wb.

INTERSTATE 55

Exit	Services
291.5mm	Mississippi/Tennessee state line
291	State Line Rd, Southaven, E [gas] Exxon, RaceWay/dsl, Shell/dsl, [food] Dixie Queen, Interstate BBQ, Southaven Pizza, Subway, Tops BBQ, [lodging] Days Inn, Quality Inn, Southern Inn, Super 8, [other] $Tree, Firestone/auto, Kroger/dsl, Pep Boys, Southaven RV Park, Walgreens, W [food] Checker's, Dale's Rest., Lucky China, Sonic, Taco Bell, Wendy's, [other] BigLots, Valvoline Oil Change, Walgreens
289	MS 302, to US 51, Horn Lake, E [gas] BP/Circle K, Shell/Circle K, [food] Abbays Rest., Backyard Burger, Baskin-Robbins, Buffalo Wild Wings, Burger King, Chick-fil-A, Chili's, Chipotle, Dunkin', Fazoli's, Firehouse Subs, Five Guys, Fox&Hound, Huey's Rest., IHOP, Jimmy John's, Krystal, Kublai Khan, Longhorn Steaks, McDonald's, Naru Japanese, Olive Garden, On-the-Border, One & Only BBQ, Outback Steaks, Red Lobster, Sonic, Starbucks, Subway, Taco Felix, Wendy's, Whataburger, [lodging] avid hotel, Candlewood Suites, Comfort Suites, Courtyard, Fairfield Inn, Hampton Inn, Hilton Garden, Holiday Inn, Holiday Inn Express, Home2 Suites, Homewood Suites, Residence Inn, [other] $Tree, Advance Parts, ALDI, AT&T, Best Buy, Books-A-Million, Buick/GMC, Chevrolet, Chrysler/Dodge/Jeep, CVS Drug, Dillard's, Discount Tire, Firestone, Ford, [H], JC Penney, Lowe's, Marshall's, Midas, Nissan, Office Depot, Old Navy, PetCo, Sam's Club/gas, Tuesday Morning, URGENT CARE, Valvoline, Verizon, Walmart/Subway, W [gas] Circle K, Exxon/dsl, Shell/Circle K/dsl, [food] Applebee's, Arby's, 

[gas] = gas [food] = food [lodging] = lodging [other] = other [RS] = rest stop

MS

INTERSTATE 55 Cont'd

HORN LAKE

289 Continued
ChuckECheese, Crab Island, Cracker Barrel, Crazy Lu Seafood, Golden Corral, Grand Buffet, Hardee's, Hooters, KFC, McDonald's, Memphis BBQ, Papa John's, Popeyes, Starbucks, Taco Bell, TX Roadhouse, Waffle House, Wendy's, Zaxby's, [lodging] Best Value Inn, Best Western, Comfort Inn, Drury Inn, EconoLodge, La Quinta, Sleep Inn, Wingate, [other] Gateway Tires/repair, Home Depot, Jiffy Lube, Kroger, Meineke, Target, Walgreens

287 Church Rd, **E** [gas] Citgo/dsl, [food] Domino's, Krispy Krunchy, Starbucks, [other] AutoZone, Tanger Outlets/famous brands, **W** [gas] Circle K/dsl, Citgo/dsl, Exxon, Mapco/dsl/deli, [food] Burger King, Casa Mexicana, Dixie Queen, McDonald's, Red Pier Seafood, Sonic, Subway, Taco Bell, Three Guys Pizza, Waffle House, Wendy's, [lodging] Magnolia Inn, [other] El Daze RV Camping, Family$, Harley-Davidson, Jellystone Camping, Southaven RV Ctr, Walgreens

285mm weigh sta both lanes

284 to US 51, Nesbit Rd, **W** [gas] Shell, [food] Happy Daze Dairybar, [other] USPO

283 I-69, MS 304, Tunica

280 MS 304, US 51, Hernando, **E** [gas] Exxon, Murphy USA/dsl, [food] Arby's, Buon Cibo, Domino's, El Paraiso, Guadalajara Mexican, KFC, Sonic, Steak Escape, Taco Bell, Yellowfin Hibachi, Zaxby's, [lodging] Days Inn, Hampton Inn, [other] $Tree, AT&T, Ultimate Tires/repair, URGENT CARE, Walgreens, Walmart/Subway, **W** [gas] BP, Circle K/dsl, [food] Blue Agave, Brick Oven Rest., Lenny's Subs, McDonald's, Mi Pueblo, Mr Chen's, Papa John's, Parish Oyster, Starbucks, Taco Felix, Waffle House, Wendy's, [lodging] Super 8, [other] AutoZone, Bryant Repair, Desoto Museum, Kroger/gas, NAPA, to Arkabutla Lake, USPO, vet

COLDWATER

279mm **24hr security, full [handicap] facilities, litter barrels, petwalk, [phone], [picnic], RV dump, Welcome Ctr sb**

276mm **24hr security, full [handicap] facilities, litter barrels, petwalk, [phone], [picnic], [RS] nb, RV dump**

273mm Coldwater River

271 MS 306, Coldwater, **W** [gas] Shell, [food] Subway, [other] Lake Arkabutla, Memphis S RV Park

265 MS 4, Senatobia, **W** [gas] Marathon/dsl, Pilot/Huddle House/dsl/scales/24hr, Shell/dsl, [food] Applebee's, Coleman's BBQ, Domino's, Dunkin, KFC, McDonald's, New China Buffet, Popeyes, Rio Lindo Mexican, Sonic, Subway, Taco Bell, Wendy's, Zaxby's, [lodging] Days Inn, Dreamland Inn, [other] Fred's, [H], Kaye Mkt, USPO

263 rd 740, S Senatobia

257 MS 310, Como, **E** [other] N Sardis Lake, **W** [gas] Citgo/dsl, Exxon/Baskin-Robbins, [food] Windy City Grille(1mi), [other] $General

252 MS 315, Sardis, **E** [gas] Chevron/dsl, Local/dsl, [food] McDonald's, [lodging] Lake Inn, Rodeway Inn, [other] repair, RV camping, Sardis Dam, to Kyle SP, **W** [gas] BP/Subway/dsl, [food] Sonic, [other] $General, Family$

246 MS 35, N Batesville, **E** [other] to Sardis Lake, **W** [gas] Love's/McDonald's/Subway/dsl/scales/24hr/@, Spirit/dsl

243b a MS 6, to Batesville, **E** [gas] Marathon/dsl, Mobil/dsl, Murphy USA/dsl, RaceWay/dsl, [food] Backyard Burger, Chili's, KC Steaks, Mi Pueblo Mexican, Zaxby's, [lodging] Comfort Suites, Home2 Suites, [other] $Tree, [H], Lowe's, to Sardis Lake, to U of MS, Walmart, **W** [gas] Circle K, Exxon/dsl, Shell/dsl, Sunoco/dsl, [food] Burger King, Cafe Ole, Capt D's, Costa Mexican, Cracker Barrel, Dodge's Rest., Domino's, Hardee's, Huddle House, Jack's Rest., KFC, Little Caesar's, McDonald's, New China, Popeyes, Sonic, Subway, Taco Bell, Waffle House, Wendy's, Yamato Hibachi, [lodging] Days Inn, Fairfield Inn, Hampton Inn, Holiday Inn, Quality Inn, Ramada Ltd, [other] $General, AT&T, AutoZone, Family$, Kroger/gas,

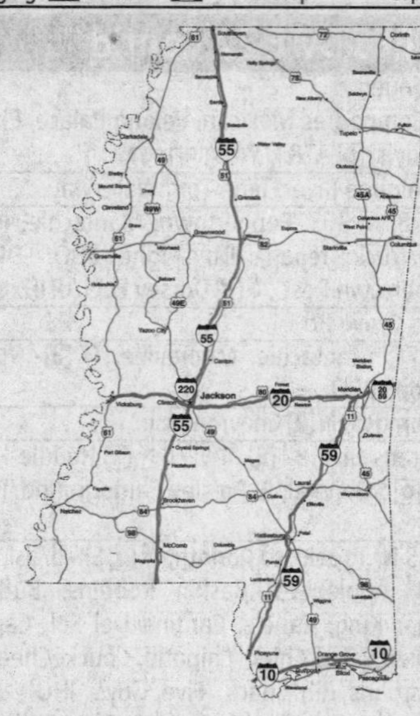

COURTLAND

243b a Continued
O'Reilly Parts, Piggly Wiggly, Save-a-Lot, URGENT CARE, USPO, Walgreens

240mm **24hr security, full [handicap] facilities, litter barrels, petwalk, [phone], [picnic], [RS] both lanes, RV dump**

237 to US 51, Courtland, **E** [gas] BP/dsl, **W** [other] $General

233 to Enid Dam, **E** [other] RV camping, to Enid Lake

227 MS 32, Oakland, **E** [gas] Citgo, [other] Sunrise Retreat RV Resort, to Cossar SP, **W** [gas] Sayle/Baskin Robbins/dsl, Shell/dsl, [food] Country Catfish, [other] $General

220 MS 330, Tillatoba, **E** [gas] Exxon/dsl

211 MS 7 N, to Coffeeville, **E** [other] Frog Hollow RV Park, **W** [gas] Exxon/dsl, Marathon/dsl

208 Papermill Rd, **E** [gas] Monroe's/Chester's/dsl/scales, [other] $General, Grenada [airport]

DUCK HILL

206 MS 8, MS 7 S, to Grenada, **E** [gas] Exxon/dsl, Shell/dsl, Sprint, [food] Applebee's, Burger King, Captain D's, Carmella's Italian, Domino's, Grand Palace, Great Wall Chinese, Jake&Rip's Catfish, La Cabana Mexican, Lost Pizza Co., McAlister's Deli, McDonald's, No Way Jose, Pizza Hut, Pizza Inn, Taco Bell, Wendy's, Yamato Steaks, Zaxby's, [lodging] Baymont Inn, Best Value Inn, Budget Inn, EconoLodge, Hampton Inn, Holiday Inn Express, [other] $General, $Tree, Advance Parts, AT&T, AutoZone, Chevrolet, CVS Drug, [H], O'Reilly Parts, to Grenada Lake/RV camping, Walmart, **W** [gas] Exxon/Huddle House, Sayle/Baskin Robbins/dsl, [food] Waffle House, [lodging] Comfort Inn, [other] Ford/Lincoln, Nissan, Toyota

199 Troutt Rd, S Grenada, **E** [other] to Camp McCain

195 MS 404, Duck Hill, **E** [other] to Camp McCain, **W** [gas] Conoco/dsl

185 US 82, Winona, **E** [gas] Circle K/dsl, Exxon, [food] Burger King, KFC, McDonald's, Sonic, Subway, Waffle House, [lodging] Best Value Inn, Holiday Inn Express, Magnolia Lodge, Relax Inn, [other] [H], **W** [gas] Pilot/Taco Bell/dsl/scales/24hr/@

DURANT

174 MS 35, MS 430, Vaiden, **E** [gas] 35-55 Trkstp/Chester's/dsl/scales/24hr, Chevron/dsl, Shell, [food] S&S Burger, [other] $General, Vaiden Camping, **W** [gas] Exxon/dsl, [food] La Terraza Mexican

173mm **24hr security, full [handicap] facilities, litter barrels, petwalk, [phone], [picnic], [RS] sb, RV dump**

164 to West, **W** [gas] West Trkstp/dsl

163mm **24hr security, full [handicap] facilities, litter barrels, petwalk, [phone], [picnic], [RS] nb, RV dump**

156 MS 12, Durant, **E** [gas] Shell/pizza/dsl, [lodging] Oak Tree Inn, [other] $General, **W** [H]

150 **E** [other] Holmes Co SP

146 MS 14, Goodman, **W** [other] to Little Red Schoolhouse

INTERSTATE 55 Cont'd

Exit #	Services
144	MS 17, to Pickens, W Marathon/Baskin-Robbins/dsl/24hr, Shell/dsl, to Little Red Schoolhouse
139	MS 432, to Pickens
133	Vaughan
128mm	E to Jackson Zoo, W RaceWay, Shell, McDonald's, Popeyes, Sonic, Family$
124	MS 16, to N Canton
119	MS 22, to MS 16 E, Canton, E Burger King, Exxon, Kangaroo, Shell, Valero/dsl, El Patio Mexican, McDonald's, Popeyes, Sonic, Waffle House, Wendy's, Best Western, Econolodge, Hampton Inn, Holiday Inn Express, La Quinta, Relax Inn, Rodeway Inn, Super 8, Family$, H, O'Reilly Parts, to Ross Barnett Reservoir, W Chevron/KFC/dsl, Citgo, Love's/Arby's/dsl/scales/24hr/@, Texaco/dsl, Old Town Mexican, Two Rivers Steaks, Walmart/auto
118a b	Nissan Parkway
114a b	Sowell Rd, W Shell/Sun Trkstp/dsl
112	US 51, Gluckstadt, E Exxon/Krystal/dsl, Shell/dsl, Angelo's Italian, Sonic, Wendy's, Super 8, NAPA AutoCare, W Shell/Pizza Hut/dsl, Sprint/dsl, Burger King, Dominos, Jersey Mike's, Waback Burgers, vet
108	MS 463, Madison, E Circle K/dsl, Shell/dsl, Applebee's, Burger King, Cane's, Chick-Fil-A, Chicken Salad Chick, Chili's, Chipotle, Full Moon BBQ, Ichiban Buffet, Karibé Potrillo, La Guadalupe Mexican, Longhorn Steaks, Menchie's, Moe's SW Grill, OEC Japanese, Pizza Shack, Taco Bell, Zaxby's, $Tree, AT&T, Best Buy, Dick's, Lowe's, Marshalls, Michael's, Office Depot, PetCo, T-Mobile, Verizon, Walmart, W Circle K, BoneFish Grill, Gator Jr's BBQ, Georgia Blue Rest., Nagoya Japanese, Papito's Grill, Salad Station, Schlotsky's, Starbucks, Subway, Wendy's, Courtyard, Hilton Garden, CVS Drug, Home Depot, Kroger, Walgreens
107	Colony Park Blvd, Madison Ave, E Sam's Club/gas, W Soulshine Pizza, Newk's Eatery, Sombra Mexican, AC Hotel, Embassy Suites, Hampton Inn, SpringHill Suites, TownePlace Suites
105c b	Old Agency Rd, E Chevron/dsl, Red Samurai Japanese, Holiday Inn Express, Home2 Suites, Honda, Hyundai, W Enzo Osteria, Five Guys, Koestler Prime, Panera Bread, Smoothie King, Starbucks, Hyatt Place/EVC, Barnes&Noble, Costco/gas, Fresh Mkt Foods
105a	Natchez Trace Pkwy
104	I-220, to W Jackson
103	County Line Rd, E Chevron/Circle K, Exxon/dsl, Murphy Express/dsl, Asian Kitchen, Bop's Custard, Breaux Bridge, Cane's, Chick-fil-A, ChuckECheese, Denny's, Drago's Rest., Grand China, HoneyBaked Ham, KFC, Krispy Kreme, Popeyes, Smoothie King, Taco Bell, Wendy's, Whataburger, Zaxby's, Chipotle, Courtyard, Days Inn, Extended Stay America, Hilton, Homewood Suites, Red Roof Inn, Residence Inn, Staybridge Suites, $Tree, Belk, BigLots, Cadillac, Dillard's, Ford, JC Penney, Lowe's, Old Navy, Ross, TJ Maxx, to Barnett Reservoir, Toyota, Verizon, Walmart, W Olive Garden, Drury Inn, Motel 6, Wingate, Home Depot, Mavis, PetSmart, Target/Starbucks
102b	Beasley Rd, Adkins Blvd, E QT, Super 8, Advance Parts, Chevrolet, W Shell/dsl, Texaco/dsl, Burger King, Chili's, China King, IHOP, McDonald's, Waffle House, Baymont Inn, Comfort Inn, Extended Stay America, InTown Suites, La Quinta, Quality Inn, AutoZone, CarMax, Chrysler/Dodge/Jeep, frontage rds access 102a, Mazda
102a	Briarwood, E Buick/GMC, W Capt D's, Popeyes, Clarion, Chrysler/Dodge/Jeep, Porsche
100	North Side Dr W, E Chevron, Marathon/dsl, Sprint,
100	Continued Aplos Simple Mediterranean, BRAVO Italian, Burger King, Capitol Grill, Char Rest., McAlister's Deli, Papa John's, Pizza Hut, Starbucks, Subway, Wendy's, Extended Stay America, $Tree, Audi, Books-A-Million, CVS Drug, Firestone/auto, Goodyear/auto, Jaguar/LandRover, Kroger/gas, Office Depot, Verizon, vet, Walgreens, Whole Foods Mkt, W Exxon/dsl, FastLane, Shell, Domino's
99	Meadowbrook Rd, Northside Dr E(from nb), E Newk's Eatery
98c b	MS 25 N, Lakeland Dr, E Shell/dsl, Crawdad Hole, Imperial Suites, LaFleur's Bluff SP, MS Agriculture Museum, W Homewood Suites, H
98a	Woodrow Wilson Dr(exits left from nb), downtown
96c	Fortification St, E Extended Studio Suites, W Bellhaven College, H
96b	High St, Jackson, E BMW, Chevrolet, Infiniti, Lexus, W Circle K/dsl, Shell/Subway/dsl, Arby's, Cook Out, Domino's, Taco Bell, Waffle House, Wendy's, Whataburger, Best Western, Days Inn, Hampton Inn, Holiday Inn Express, Red Roof Inn, fairgrounds, Honda, H, museum, st capitol, Subaru/Volvo
96a	Pearl St(from nb), Jackson, W access to same as 96b, downtown
94	(46 from nb), I-20 E, to Meridian, US 49 S
45b[I-20]	US 51, State St, to downtown, N Marathon, Petro/dsl/scales/24hr, Shell, Valero, S Pilot/McDonald's/dsl/scales/24hr/@, Nissan, vet
45a	Gallatin St(from sb), N Marathon, Petro/Iron Skillet/dsl/scales/24hr, Shell, S Pilot/McDonald's/scales/dsl/@, Nissan, W Blue Beacon
92c	(44 from sb), I-20 W, to Vicksburg, US 49 N
92b	US 51 N, State St, Gallatin St
92a	McDowell Rd, E Petro/Iron Skillet/dsl/scales/24hr, W Marathon/dsl, Shell, Advance Parts, Family$, Food Depot
90b	Daniel Lake Blvd(from sb), W Shell, Harley-Davidson
90a	Savanna St, E transmissions, W Marathon
88	Elton Rd, W Marathon/dsl, Shell/Subway/dsl, Camping World RV Ctr
85	Byram, E Blue Sky/dsl, Hungry Jack's/dsl, QT/gas, Caporales Mexican, El Sombrero Grill, Krystal, Comfort Inn, Extended Stay, Swinging Bridge RV Park, W Byram/dsl, Chevron/dsl, Circle K/dsl, Exxon/dsl, Burger King, Cane's, Capt D's, Domino's, KFC, McAlister's Deli, McDonald's, New China, Newk's Eatery, Papa John's, Popeyes, Sonic, Starbucks, Steak Escape, Subway, Taco Bell, Waffle House, Wendy's, Best Value Inn, Holiday Inn Express, $General, AutoZone, NAPA, O'Reilly Parts, T-Mobile, Tire Depot, Walgreens, Walmart/Subway
81	Wynndale Rd, W CEFCO/dsl
78	Terry, E Citgo/dsl, Texaco/dsl, Buick/Chevrolet/GMC(1mi), DG Mkt, USPO, W Shell
72	MS 27, Crystal Springs, E Exxon/Subway/dsl, Shell/dsl, Louise's Pit BBQ, McDonald's, Popeyes, Ford
68	to US 51, S Crystal Springs, E Red Barn Produce, vet
65	to US 51, Gallman
61	MS 28, Hazlehurst, E 76/dsl, Exxon/Circle K/Subway/dsl, Murphy Express/dsl, Burger King, Duke's Rest., KFC/Taco Bell, Little Caesars Pizza, Los Parilleros, McDonald's, Pizza Hut, Popeyes, Stark's Rest., Waffle House, Wendy's, Quality Inn, Rodeway Inn, Western Inn, $General, Advance Parts, AutoZone, Bumpers Parts, Family$, URGENT CARE, Verizon, Walgreens, Walmart/auto
59	to S Hazlehurst
56	to Martinsville
54mm	**24hr security, full facilities, litter barrels, petwalk, both lanes, RV dump, vending**

CANTON MADISON JACKSON BYRAM GALLMAN

MS

INTERSTATE 55 Cont'd

Exit #	Services
51	to Wesson, E Lake Lincoln SP, W Texaco/Country Jct Trkstp/dsl/rest.
48	Mt Zion Rd, to Wesson
42	to US 51, N Brookhaven, E Exxon/Subway, Shell/dsl/scales/24hr, H, W Super 8
40	to MS 550, Brookhaven, E Blue Sky, Exxon/Subway, Marathon/Domino's/dsl, Murphy USA/dsl, Shell/dsl, Bowie BBQ, Burger King, China Buffet, Cracker Barrel, DQ, El Dorado Mexican, KFC, Krystal, Little Caesar's, Little Tokyo, Los Parrilleros, McDonald's, Pizza Hut, Popeyes, Rallys, Sonic, Taco Bell, Tropical Smoothie, Waffle House, Wendy's, Zaxbys, Best Value Inn, Hampton Inn, Holiday Inn Express, Motel 6, Quality Inn, Spanish Inn, $General, $Tree, AT&T, AutoZone, Buick/Cadillac/Chevrolet/GMC, Ford/Lincoln, Honda, H, Nissan, O'Reilly Parts, Save-A-Lot Foods, tire repair, Toyota, Walgreens, Walmart, W Home Depot
38	US 84, S Brookhaven, W Chevron/dsl, tire repair
30	Bogue Chitto, Norfield, Bogue Chitto, Norfield, E Shell/dsl, $General
24	Johnston Station, E to Dixie Springs Lake, W Crossroads Quickstop
20b a	US 98 W, to Natchez, Summit, E Marathon/BBQ/dsl, Shell/dsl, Stop'n Shop/dsl, W Exxon/Subway/dsl, ShawnMart/dsl
18	MS 570, Smithdale Rd, N McComb, E Marathon/BBQ, Murphy USA/dsl, Burger King, Chick-fil-A, Juicy Seafood, McDonald's, Starbucks, Holiday Inn Express, AT&T, Belk, Hobby Lobby, Kia, Lowe's, Ross, Walgreens, Walmart, W Chevron/dsl, Applebee's, Arby's, El Dorado Mexican, Santa Fe Steaks, Comfort Inn, Deerfield Inn, Hampton Inn, Ford/Lincoln
17	Delaware Ave, McComb, E Blue Sky, Chevron/dsl, Exxon/Penn's Rest., Marathon/Subway/dsl, Pump&Savor, Burger King, China Palace, Domino's, Golden Corral, Little Caesar's, McCalister's Deli, Pizza Hut, Popeyes, Smoothie King, Sonic, Taco Bell, Tortillo Soup, Waffle House, Wendy's, Zaxby's, Baymont, Quality Inn, $General, AutoZone, Buffalo Express, Chrysler/Dodge/Jeep, H, McComb Mkt, O'Reilly Parts, Verizon, Walgreens, W Days Inn
15b a	US 98 E, MS 48 W, McComb, E Citgo/dsl, Exxon/Subway, Market Max/dsl, Presley QuikStop/dsl, Pure, Church's TX Chicken, KFC, Vine's 2.0, Wendy's, Camellian Motel, $General, $Tree, Advance Parts, Family$, Kia, tire repair, vet, W Marathon/dsl, $General
13	Fernwood Rd, W Love's/Chester's/McDonald's/dsl/scales/24hr/@, golf, to Percy Quin SP
10	MS 48, Magnolia, E Exxon/Subway/dsl, Marathon, Marathon, Shell/dsl, Family$, RV camping
8	MS 568, Magnolia
4	Chatawa
3mm	**24hr security, full facilities, litter barrels, petwalk, , RV dump, Welcome Ctr nb**
2mm	weigh sta nb
1	MS 584, Osyka, Gillsburg
0mm	Mississippi/Louisiana state line

BROOKHAVEN · N MCCOMB · MAGNOLIA

INTERSTATE 59

Exit #	Services
149mm	I-59 and I-20 merge for 22 mi. See I-20, exits 172mm-150.
142	to US 11, Dunns Falls, Savoy
137	to N Enterprise, to Stonewall
134	MS 513, S Enterprise, E FastStop
126	MS 18, to Rose Hill, Pachuta, E Alliance/dsl, Pachuta TP/dsl, $General
118	to Vossburg, Paulding

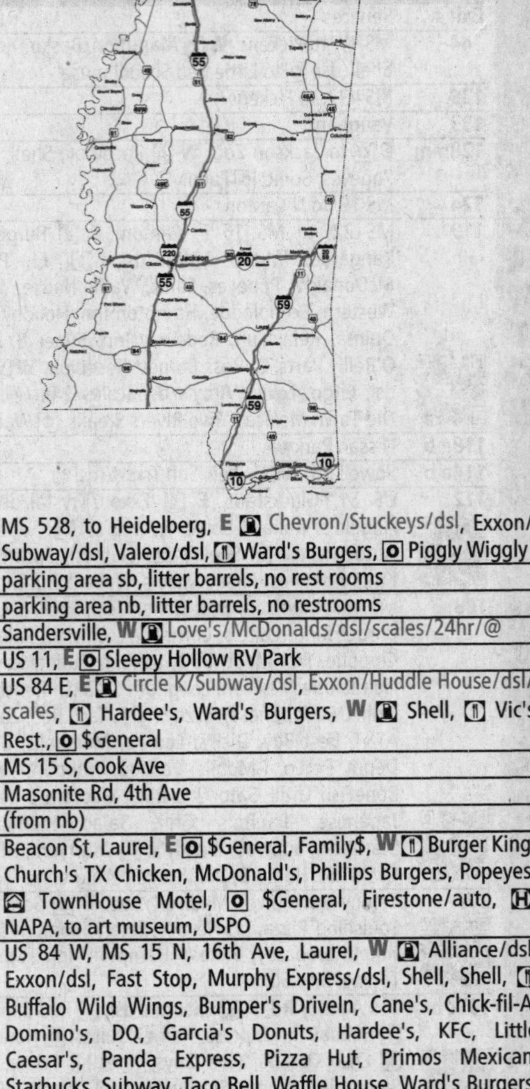

Exit #	Services
113	MS 528, to Heidelberg, E Chevron/Stuckeys/dsl, Exxon/Subway/dsl, Valero/dsl, Ward's Burgers, Piggly Wiggly
109mm	parking area sb, litter barrels, no rest rooms
106mm	parking area nb, litter barrels, no restrooms
104	Sandersville, W Love's/McDonalds/dsl/scales/24hr/@
99	US 11, E Sleepy Hollow RV Park
97	US 84 E, E Circle K/Subway/dsl, Exxon/Huddle House/dsl/scales, Hardee's, Ward's Burgers, W Shell, Vic's Rest., $General
96b	MS 15 S, Cook Ave
96a	Masonite Rd, 4th Ave
95d	(from nb)
95c	Beacon St, Laurel, E $General, Family$, W Burger King, Church's TX Chicken, McDonald's, Phillips Burgers, Popeyes, TownHouse Motel, $General, Firestone/auto, H, NAPA, to art museum, USPO
95b a	US 84 W, MS 15 N, 16th Ave, Laurel, W Alliance/dsl, Exxon/dsl, Fast Stop, Murphy Express/dsl, Shell, Shell, Buffalo Wild Wings, Bumper's DriveIn, Cane's, Chick-fil-A, Domino's, DQ, Garcia's Donuts, Hardee's, KFC, Little Caesar's, Panda Express, Pizza Hut, Primos Mexican, Starbucks, Subway, Taco Bell, Waffle House, Ward's Burgers, Baymont Suites, Best Western, EconoLodge, Hampton Inn, Holiday Inn Express, Motel 6, Super 8, $General, Advance Parts, auto tech, AutoZone, CVS Drug, H, Lowe's, Piggly Wiggly, Roses, Verizon, Walgreens, Walmart/gas
93	US 11, S Laurel, W Exxon/dsl, Shell/dsl, Hardee's, Southern Tires
90	US 11, Ellisville Blvd, E Marathon/dsl, Charlie's Seafood, W Valero/dsl
88	MS 588, MS 29, Ellisville, E Chevron/dsl, Fast Mkt/dsl, Keith's/dsl, Burrito Express, Domino's, Jack's, KFC, Little Caesar's, McDonald's, Pizza Hut, Sonic, Subway, Ward's Burgers, $General, AutoZone, CashSaver, Family$, NAPA, O'Reilly Parts, Walgreens, W Shell/dsl, Millennium Inn
85	MS 590, to Ellisville, W Texaco/dsl
80	to US 11, Moselle, E Chevron/Keith's/dsl
78	Sanford Rd, E Driver's RV Park
76	W to Hattiesburg-Laurel Reg
73	Monroe Rd, to Monroe
69	MS 42 E, Gandy Pkwy, to Petal, Eatonville
67b a	US 49, Hattiesburg, E Clark's/dsl, Exxon/dsl/scales, Shell, Texaco/Dandy Dan's, Burger King, Burger Theory, Cracker Barrel, DQ, Krystal, McDonald's, Popeyes, Waffle House, Executive Inn, Holiday Inn, Howard Johnson, Magnolia Inn, Motel 6, Quality Inn, Sleep Inn, Super 8, University Inn,

LAUREL · HATTIESBURG

MS

INTERSTATE 59 Cont'd

HATTIESBURG

67b a Continued
$General, Hattiesburg Cycles, W Chevron/Keith's, Dandy Dan's, Marathon/Maple's/dsl, Shell, Stuckey's Express/dsl, Texaco/Dandy Dan's, Valero, Sonic, Ward's Burgers, Wendy's, Candlewood Suites, DoubleTree Inn, Northgate Inn

65b a US 98 W, Hardy St, Hattiesburg, E Exxon, Shell/dsl, Valero, Baskin Robbins, Buffalo Wild Wings, Cane's, Checkers, Chicken Salad Chick, Cookout, Crab House, Crescent City Grill, Domino's, Ed's Burger Joint, Front Porch BBQ, Fuzzy's Tacos, IHOP, Lenny's Subs, Little Caesar's, McDonald's, Papa John's, Pizza Hut, Qdoba, Smoothie King, Starbucks, Subway, Tabella Italian, Topher's, Ward's Burgers, Wingstop, avid hotel, Courtyard, Days Inn, Fairfield Inn, Holiday Inn Express, Hotel Indigo, La Quinta, Residence Inn, Super 8, TownePlace Suites, Western Motel, CVS Drug, Goodyear/auto, Home Depot, H, to USM, URGENT CARE, Verizon, vet, Walgreens, W Chevron, Exxon, Mobil/Circle K, Shell/Jimmy John's/dsl, Burger King, Chesterfield's Rest., Chick-fil-A, Chili's, China Buffet, ChuckECheese, City Buffet, Dickey's BBQ, Five Guys, Fuji Yama Japanese, Golden Corral, Hardee's, HoneyBaked Ham, Krispy Kreme, Logan's Roadhouse, Longhorn Steaks, Lost Pizza Co., Marble Slab, Mario's Italian, McAlister's Deli, McDonald's, Newk's Eatery, Olive Garden, Outback Steaks, Panda Express, Panera Bread, Pizza Hut, Popeyes, Qdoba, Red Lobster, Steak'n Shake, Super King Asian, Taco Bell, Underground Chuck's, Waffle House, Walk-On's Grill, Ward's Burgers, Wendy's, Which Wich?, Yamato Japan, Zaxby's, Best Western, Comfort Suites, Hampton Inn, Hilton Garden, Home2 Suites, InTown Suites, Microtel, Wingate Inn, $Tree, Aamco, Advance Parts, AT&T, AutoZone, Belk, Best Buy, BigLots, Books-A-Million, Dick's, Dillard's, Firestone/auto, Goodyear/auto, Hobby Lobby, H, Jo Ann, Kohl's, Lowe's, Michael's, Nissan, Office Depot, Office Depot, Old Navy, PetCo, PetSmart, Ross, Sam's Club/gas, Target, TJ Maxx, Verizon, Walgreens, Walmart, Winn-Dixie

MS GULF COAST

60 US 11, S Hattiesburg, E Marathon/BBQ/dsl, W Circle K/Subway/dsl/24hr, Texaco/Dandy Dan's, Valero/dsl, Guanatos Mexican, Sully's Steaks, Freightliner, Peterbilt

59 US 98 E, to US 49, Lucedale, MS Gulf Coast

56mm litter barrels, no restrooms, parking area both lanes

51 rd 589, to Purvis, W Chevron/Keith's/dsl, to Little Black Cr Water Park

48mm Little Black Creek

41 MS 13, to Lumberton, W Marathon/Keith's/dsl, Los Cabos Mexican, $General, to Little Black Cr Water Park

35 Hillsdale Rd, E to Kings Arrow Ranch

32mm Wolf River

29 rd 26, to Poplarville, W Love's/Arby's/dsl/scales/24hr/@, Shell/dsl, Popeyes, NAPA, tires/repair

CARRIERE

27 MS 53, to Poplarville, Necaise, W Chevron/Keith's/dsl, McDonald's

19 to US 11, Millard

15 to McNeill

10 to US 11, Carriere, E Texaco/Keith's/dsl, Clearwater RV Camp

6 MS 43 N, N Picayune, E Mi Sol Azteca, Paul's Pastries, W Chevron/dsl, DQ, McDonald's, Sonic, Subway, Waffle House, Super 8, Claiborne Hill Mkt, CVS Drug, Family$, H, Walgreens

4 MS 43 S, to Picayune, E Murphy USA/dsl, RaceTrac/dsl, Atchafalaya Seafood, McDonald's, Rio Grande Mexican, $Tree, Buick/Cadillac/Chevrolet/GMC, Chrysler/Dodge/Jeep, Home Depot, Nissan, Sunroamers RV Park, Verizon, Walgreens, Walmart, W Exxon/Circle K/dsl, Shell/dsl, Applebee's, Arby's, Burger King, Domino's, Hardee's, Ichiban Japanese, IHOP, Lester's Seafood, Little Caesar's, Logan's Chicken, New Buffet City, Papa John's, Pizza Hut, Popeyes, Subway, Taco Bell, Tokyo Grill, Waffle House, Wendy's, Days Inn, EconoLodge, Heritage Inn, Holiday Inn Express, $General, Advance Parts, AutoZone, Family$, Ford/Lincoln, Gene's Tire/auto, O'Reilly Parts, Paw Paw's RV Ctr, URGENT CARE

3mm **full facilities, litter barrels, petwalk, RV dump, vending, Welcome Ctr nb**

1.5mm weigh sta both lanes

1 US 11, MS 607, E NASA, W Pit Stop, Shell/dsl, $General

0mm Mississippi/Louisiana state line, Pearl River

INTERSTATE 220 (Jackson)

11mm I-220 begins/ends on I-55, exit 104.

9 Hanging Moss Rd, County Line Rd, E Marathon/dsl, W Shell/dsl, Costco/gas

8 Watkins Dr, E Exxon/Subway, Shell/dsl, $General

5b a US 49 N, Evers Blvd, to Yazoo City, E KFC, Sonic, Wing Guys, Star Motel, $General, Family$, W Exxon/Burger King, Marathon/Subway/dsl, Shell/Baskin Robbin/dsl, $General, Penske

3 Industrial Dr

2b a Clinton Blvd, Capitol St, E Fuel Time, W Shell, McDonald's, Popeyes, Sonic, $General, Family$

1b a US 80, E Arco/Subway/dsl, Gas+/dsl, Texaco/dsl, Burger King, Capt D's, Cook Out, Country Fisherman, Crechale's Steaks, DQ, KFC, McDonald's, Pizza Hut, Popeyes, Taco Bell, Wendy's, Best Inn, Relax Inn, AutoZone, Firestone/auto, Mr Transmission, UHaul, W Citgo/dsl, Exxon/dsl, Arby's, Krystal, $General

0mm I-220 begins/ends on I-20, exit 41.

NOTES

MO

MISSOURI

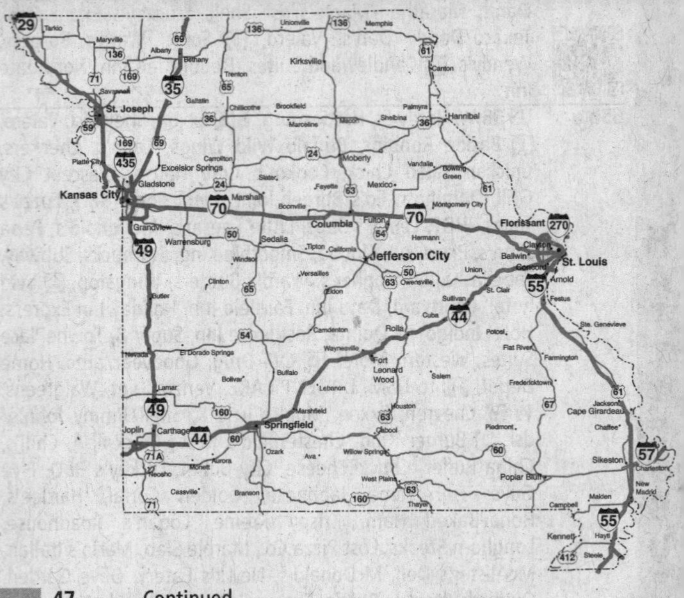

INTERSTATE 29

Exit #	Services
CORNING	
124mm	Missouri/Iowa state line
123mm	Nishnabotna River
121.5mm	weigh sta both lanes
116	rd A, rd B, to Watson
110	US 136, Rock Port, Phelps City, E Sinclair/dsl, to NW MO St U, W BP/dsl/24hr, Phillips 66/Subway/dsl/24hr, McDonald's, Trails End Rest., Super 8, All American Campground & RV Park, fireworks, tires, truck wash
109.5mm	W full facilities, info, littler barrels, petwalk, Welcome Ctr sb
107	MO 111, to Rock Port
106.5mm	Rock Creek
102mm	Mill Creek
99	rd W, Corning
97mm	Tarkio River
92	US 59, to Fairfax, Craig, W Sinclair/dsl
90.5mm	Little Tarkio Creek
86.5mm	Squaw Creek
84	MO 118, Mound City, E Schoonover Oil, Sinclair/Subway/dsl, Casey's, McDonald's, Quacker's Steaks, Shakers Icecream, Audrey's Motel, Super 8, $General, U-Haul, USPO, W Shell/dsl, Big Lake SP(12mi)
82mm	truck parking both lanes, limited facilities
79	US 159, Rulo, E Phillips 66 Trkstp/dsl/rest/RV dump/@, Garden Inn RV Park, W to Big Lake SP(12mi), to Squaw Creek NWR(3mi)
AMAZONIA	
78mm	Kimsey Creek
75	US 59, to Oregon
67	US 59 N, to Oregon
66.5mm	Nodaway River
65	US 59, rd RA, to Fillmore, Savannah, E Trex/dsl, antiques, fireworks, park
60	rd K, rd CC, Amazonia
58.5mm	Hopkins Creek
56b a	I-229 S, US 71 N, US 59 N, to St Joseph, Maryville
55mm	Dillon Creek
53	US 59, US 71 bus, to St Joseph, Savannah, E AOK Camping, W Phillips 66/dsl, antiques
ST JOSEPH	
50	US 169, St Joseph, King City, E fireworks, W Casey's, Cenex/dsl, Conoco, EVC, Sinclair/Subway/dsl, 54th St Grill, Buffalo Wild Wings, Cheddar's, Chili's, Chipotle Mexican, Culver's, Hardee's, IHOP, KFC, McDonald's, Olive Garden, Panda Express, Smoothie King, Sonic, Starbucks, Subway, Taco Bell, Wendy's, Candlewood Suites, Fairfield Inn, Holiday Inn Express, Advance Parts, ALDI, AT&T, AutoZone, CVS Drug, Dick's, Home Depot, Kohl's, Lowe's, Michael's, Petco, PetSmart, Sam's Club/gas, Target, Tires+, TJ Maxx, URGENT CARE, vet, Walgreens, Walmart/Subway
47	MO 6, Frederick Blvd, to Clarksdale, St Joseph, E Phillips 66/dsl, Bandana's BBQ, Best Value Inn, Drury Inn, H, W Sinclair/dsl, Tesla EVC, Abelardo's Mexican, Applebee's, Arby's, Burger King, Cracker Barrel, Dunkin, El Maguey Mexican, Fazoli's, Five Guys, Freddy's, LJ Silver, McAlister's Deli, McDonald's, New China Super Buffet, Panera Bread, Papa John's, Papa Murphy's, Perkins, Red Lobster, RibCrib, Sonic, Starbucks, Subway, Taco Bell, Taco John's, TX Roadhouse, Wendy's, Budget Inn, Hampton Inn, Motel 6, Quality Suites, Stoney Creek Inn, $General, auto/tire, BigLots, Buick/GMC, Chevrolet, CVS Drug, Discount Tire, Firestone/auto, Hobby Lobby, Honda/Ford,
47	Continued HyVee Foods/dsl, JC Penney, NAPA, Nissan/EVC, Office Depot, Ross, Toyota/Scion, U-Haul, U-Haul, Verizon, vet, Walgreens
46b a	US 36, to Cameron, St Joseph, E to MWSU, W BP/dsl, Cenex/dsl, Conoco/dsl, Phillips 66/dsl, Sinclair/dsl, Burger King, Jimmy John's, KFC, Pizza Hut, Taco John's, Wendy's, $General, Ace Hardware, Advance Parts, AT&T, CVS Drug, KIA, Klein RV Ctr, Mitsubishi, O'Reilly Parts, Walgreens
44	US 169, to Gower, St Joseph, E Love's/Arby's/dsl/scales/24hr, Phillips 66, Nelly's Mexican, Subway, Guesthouse Inn, dsl repair, W Casey's/dsl/24hr, Murphy USA/dsl, DQ, El Maguey, Goodcents Subs, McDonald's, McDonald's, San Jose Steaks, Sonic, Taco Bell, Waffle House, $Tree, ALDI, Chrysler/Dodge/Jeep, Harley-Davidson, Menards, Walmart/Subway
43	I-229 N, to St Joseph
LEAVENWORTH	
39.5mm	Pigeon Creek
35	rd DD, Faucett, W Pilot/Taco Bell/dsl/scales/24hr/@
33.5mm	Bee Creek
30	rd Z, rd H, Dearborn, New Market, E Trex/Subway/dsl/24hr, $General
29.5mm	Bee Creek
27mm	full facilities, litter barrels, petwalk, both lanes, vending
25	rd E, rd U, to Camden Point, E Phillips 66/Trex/dsl
24mm	weigh sta nb/truck parking sb
20	MO 92, MO 273, to Atchison, Leavenworth, W Trex/Dunkin'/dsl, antiques, to Weston Bend SP
19.5mm	Platte River
19	rd HH, Platte City(sb returns at 18), W Casey's, Platte-Clay Fuel/dsl, DQ, Pizza Hut, Rapidos Mexican, Red Dragon Chinese, Roxanne's Cafe, Suburban Studios, Travelodge, $General, CarQuest, O'Reilly Parts, same as 18, USPO, Verizon
18	MO 92, Platte City, E auto repair, Basswood RV Park(5mi), vet, W Phillips 66/Jimmy John's, QT/dsl, Arby's, Burger King, China Wok, Culver's, DQ, El Maguey, McDonald's, Pizza Hut/Taco Bell, Pizza Shoppe, Sonic, Starbucks, Subway, Wendy's, Ramada, Super 8, Buick/Chevrolet, Chrysler/Dodge/Jeep, CVS Drug, Ford, PriceChopper Foods,

INTERSTATE 29 Cont'd

PLATTE CITY

Exit	Services
18	Continued same as 19, tires, TrueValue, Verizon, Walgreens
17	I-435 S, to Topeka
15	Mexico City Ave, W Marriott,
14	I-435 E(from sb), to St Louis
13	to I-435 E, E Extended Stay America/EVC, Fairfield Inn, Holiday Inn, Microtel, Orangewood Inn&Suites, Quality Suites, Sheraton, Super 8, Towneplace Suites, W Marriott, KCI
12	NW 112th St, E BP, Phillips 66/dsl, Best Western+, Candlewood Suites, Days Inn, Extended Stay America, Hampton Inn, Hilton, Hilton Garden, W KCI Lodge
10	Tiffany Springs Pkwy, E Phillips 66/dsl, SmokeBox BBQ, Embassy Suites, Holiday Inn Express, Home2 Suites, Homewood Suites, Residence Inn, W Cracker Barrel, LongHorn Steaks, Waffle House, Wendy's, Chase Suites, Drury Inn, Extended Stay America, Sleep Inn, Sonesta, Wyndham Garden, Buick/GMC, Harley-Davidson, Honda, Lexus, Nissan, Toyota/Scion, vet
9b a	MO 152, to Liberty, Topeka
8	MO 9, rd T, NW Barry Rd, E Phillips 66/dsl, Big Biscuit, Burger King, Cane's, Chick-fil-A, Chilli's, China Wok, Chipotle Mexican, ChuckeCheese, Crumbl Cookies, Dickey's BBQ, Firehouse Subs, First Watch, Five Guys, Freddy's, Godfather's, Golden Corral, Honey Baked Ham, Hong's Buffet, Hooters, Jason's Deli, Panda Express, Panera Bread, Papa Murphy's, Sheridan's Custard, Starbucks, Subway, Taco Bell, TX Roadhouse, Wendy's, $Tree, ALDI, AutoZone, Best Buy, Big O Tires, Discount Tire, Ford, Hobby Lobby, Home Depot, H, HyVee/dsl, JC Penney, Lowe's, PetSmart, Ross, Target, USPO, Verizon, Walmart/EVC, W Phillips 66/dsl, 54th St Grill, Arby's, BoLings Chinese, Bravo Italian, Buffalo Wild Wings, Granite City, Hereford House, In-A-Tub, Jimmy John's, McDonald's, Minsky's Pizza, Outback Steaks, Popeyes, Rainbow Oriental, Red Robin, Smokehouse BBQ, Smoothie King, Sonic, Starbucks, Subway, La Quinta, Motel 6, SpringHill Suites, Super 8, AT&T, Barnes&Noble, CVS Drug, Dick's, Dillard's, Jiffy Lube, Michael's, Old Navy, Staples, Tires+, U-Haul

PLATTE WOODS

Exit	Services
6	NW 72nd St, Platte Woods, E Sinclair/dsl, vet, W Phillips 66, Big Bowl Pho, Iron Wok, Papa John's, Tasty Thai
5	MO 45 N, NW 64th St, W Shell/dsl, Bonefish Grill, Caribou Coffee, Casey's Pizza, Chipotle, Culver's, Dominic's Italian, Dunkin, Em Chamas Grill, Luna Azteca, McDonald's, Smoothie King, Spin! Pizza, Starbucks, Subway, Taco Bell, The Peanut, Tropical Smoothie, Wendy's, $General, $Tree, ALDI, CVS Drug, HyVee/gas, Sprouts Mkt, vet
4	NW 56th St(from nb), W Phillips 66
3c	rd A(from sb), Riverside, W QT/dsl, Corner Café, Sonic, Rverside Automotive, USPO
3b	I-635 S
3a	Waukomis Dr, rd AA(from nb)
2b	US 169 S(from sb), to KC
2a	US 169 N(from nb), to Smithville
1e	US 69, Vivion Rd, E Sinclair/dsl, Arby's, Freddy's, Panda Express, Starbucks, Steak'n Shake, Wendy's, ALDI, Chevrolet, Discount Tire, Fiat, Home Depot, Lincoln/EVC, Lowe's, Petco, Sam Club/gas, Subaru, Verizon
1d	MO 283 S, Oak Tfwy(from sb), W Shell/dsl, McDonald's, Subway, $General, CVS Drug, O'Reilly Parts
1c	Gladstone(from nb), E Phillips 66, Arby's, Freddy's, Panda Express, Pizza Ranch, Taco Bueno, Wendy's, BigLots, Discount Tire, H, Lowe's, Petco, PriceChopper Foods, Sam's Club/dsl
1b	I-35 N(from sb), to Des Moines
1a	Davidson Rd
8mm	I-35 N. I-29 and I-35 run together 6 mi. Exits 3-8a., see Missouri Interstate 35.

INTERSTATE 35

BETHANY

Exit	Services
114mm	Missouri/Iowa state line
114	US 69, to Lamoni, W Conoco/dsl/24hr
113.5mm	Zadie Creek
112mm	W full facilities, litter barrels, MO Welcome Ctr sb, petwalk, wireless internet
110	weigh sta both lanes
106	rd N, Blythedale, E Phillips 66/dsl/scales/24hr/EVC/@, Eagles Landing Motel, camping, fireworks, W Love's/Subway/dsl/scales/24hr, Eagle Ridge RV Park(2mi), fireworks, Speedco
99	rd A, to Ridgeway
94mm	E Fork Big Creek
93	US 69, Bethany
92	US 136, Bethany, E Casey's/dsl/scales, Sinclair/Subway/dsl, KFC/Taco Bell, McDonald's, Budget Inn, NAPA, W Casey's/dsl, EVC, Kum&Go/dsl, MFA, Shell/dsl, DQ, Nopal Mexican, Pizza Hut, Sonic, TootToot Rest., Quality Inn, Super 8, $General, $Tree, H, Peterbilt, Walmart
90mm	Pole Cat Creek, Pole Cat Creek
88	MO 13, to Bethany, Gallatin
84	rds AA, H, to Gilman City, E Crowder SP(24mi)
81mm	truck parking sb/nb, weigh sta
80	rds B, N, to Coffey
78	rd C, Pattonsburg, W BP/dsl, gas/dsl, USPO
74.5mm	Grand River
72	rd DD
68	US 69, to Pattonsburg, E Lake Viking
64	MO 6, to Maysville, Gallatin
61	US 69, Winston, Gallatin, E Trex/dsl/24hr

CAMERON

Exit	Services
54	US 36, Cameron, E EVC, Phillips 66/dsl, Shell/Wendy's/dsl/scales/24hr, McDonald's, Subway, Motel 6, Quality Inn, SureStay, H, truck repair, W Valero/dsl, China Garden Buffet, DQ, El Maguey Mexican, KFC/Taco Bell, Pizza Hut, Sonic, Days Inn, Econolodge, Red Roof Inn, Super 8, $Tree, Advance Parts, Cameron Mkt, Chevrolet/Buick/GMC, Chrysler/Dodge/Jeep, O'Reilly Parts, Twin Creeks Tire, USPO, Verizon, Walmart
52	rd BB, Lp 35, to Cameron, E Love's/Arby's/dsl/scales/24hr, H, RV Hookup, W Casey's, same as 54, $General
49mm	Brushy Creek
48.5mm	Shoal Creek, Shoal Creek
48	US 69, Cameron, E to Wallace SP(2mi)
40	MO 116, Lathrop, E Trex/Country Cafe/dsl, antiques

HOLT

Exit	Services
34.5mm	full facilities, littler barrels, both lanes, vending
33	rd PP, Holt, E auto repair, U-Haul, W BP/dsl, Conoco/dsl, Betty's Place, American Eagle Inn, $General
30mm	Holt Creek
26	MO 92, Kearney, E Kwik, Phillips 66/dsl, QT/dsl, Casey's Pizza, Domino's, DQ, Jimmy John's, La Fuente Mexican, McDonald's, Papa Murphy's, Pizza Hut, Sonic, Starbucks, Comfort Inn, Holiday Inn Express, SureStay+, CVS, fireworks, Price Chopper, to Watkins Mill SP, True Value, Verizon, W Pilot/Taco Bell/dsl/scales/24hr, Arby's, Burger King, Hunan Garden Chinese, Pizza Shoppe, Subway, EconoLodge, Quality Inn, $Tree, auto repair, Goodyear, O'Reilly Parts, to Smithville Lake
22mm	parking area sb, weigh sta nb
20	US 69, MO 33, to Excelsior Springs, E H
17	MO 291, rd A, E Best Western, Home2 Suites,

MO

MO

INTERSTATE 35 Cont'd

LIBERTY

17 Continued
Microtel Inn&Suites, Chevrolet, Liberty RV Ctr, same as 16, W Phillips 66/dsl, QT, DQ, Masabi Japanese, McDonald's, Nicky's Pizza, Sonic, Starbucks, Subway, Zaxby's, Sleep Inn, ValuePlace Inn, Price Chopper Foods, to KCI, URGENT CARE, vet, Walgreens

16 MO 152, Liberty, E Phillips 66, Tesla EVC, Baskin-Robbins, Cane's, Chick-fil-A, CiCi's Pizza, Culver's, Domino's, El Potro Mexican, Five Guys, IHOP, Jimmy John's, Margarita's, McAlister's Deli, MOD Pizza, Olive Garden, Red Robin, Starbucks, TX Roadhouse, Wendy's, Days Inn, Red Lion Inn, TownePlace Suites, Advance Parts, AutoZone, CVS Drug, Discount Tire, Hobby Lobby, H, Hy-Vee/gas, Lowe's, Petco, Walgreens, W Murphy USA/dsl, Phillips 66/dsl, 54th St Grill, Arby's, Buffalo Wild Wings, Burger King, Chili's, Chipotle Mexican, Corner Cafe, Cracker Barrel, First Watch, Freddy's Burgers, Joy Wok, KFC, LongHorn Steaks, McDonald's, Noodles&Co, Old Chicago Pizza, Panda Express, Panera Bread, Smoothie King, Steak'n Shake, Subway, Taco Bell, Waffle House, Comfort Suites, Fairfield Inn, Hampton Inn, Holiday Inn Express, ALDI, Best Buy, Big O Tires, Christian Bros Auto, Ford, Home Depot, JC Penney, Jiffy Lube, Kohl's, Michael's, NAPA, Office Depot, PetSmart, Sam's Club/dsl, Sprouts Mkt, Target, TJ Maxx, URGENT CARE, Verizon, Walmart/Subway

14 US 69(exits left from sb), Liberty Dr, to Glenaire, Pleasant Valley, E Amoco/dsl/24hr, Casey's, W QT/dsl/scales/24hr

13 US 69(from nb), to Pleasant Valley, E Phillips 66, Sinclair/dsl, W QT/dsl/scales/24hr

12b a I-435, to St Louis

11 US 69 N, Vivion Rd, E Church's TX Chicken, W QT/dsl, Sonic, Stroud's Rest., Subway, CVS Drug, O'Reilly Parts, USPO, vet

10 N Brighton Ave(from nb)

9 MO 269 S, Chouteau Trfwy, E Phillips 66, IHOP, McDonald's, Ming Garden, Papa Murphy's, Subway, Wing Stop, Harrah's Casino/rest., Target

8c MO 1, Antioch Rd, E Conoco/7-11, Domino's, Best Western, auto repair, W Casey's, QT, Dickey's BBQ, Waffle House, AT&T, Walgreens

8b I-29 N, US 71 N, KCI airport

8mm I-35 S and I-29 S run together 6 mi.

8a Parvin Rd, E BP/dsl, Shell/dsl, Subway, O'Reilly Parts

6b a Armour Rd, E Phillips 66/dsl, Arby's, Burger King, Denny's, McDonald's, Old Chicago, Quiznos, Starbucks, Subway, EconoLodge, La Quinta, H, repair, to Riverboat Casino, W Phillips 66, QT/dsl/24hr, Sinclair/dsl, DQ, First Watch, Jimmy John's, Lucky Dragon Chinese, Taco Bell, Wendy's, American Inn, Holiday Inn Express, URGENT CARE, USPO

BROADWAY

5b 16th Ave, industrial district

5a Levee Rd, Bedford St

4.5mm Missouri River

4b Front St, E Isle of Capri Riverboat Casino/rest.

4a US 24 E, Independence Ave

3 I-70 E, US 71 S, to St Louis

2g I-35 N and I-29 N run together 6 mi

2e Oak St, Grand-Walnut St, E Phillips 66, Marriott

2d Main-Delaware, Wyandotte St, downtown

2a I-70 W, to Topeka

2y US 169, Broadway, to downtown

2w 12th St, Kemper Arena, to downtown

2v 14th St, to downtown

2u I-70 E, to Broadway

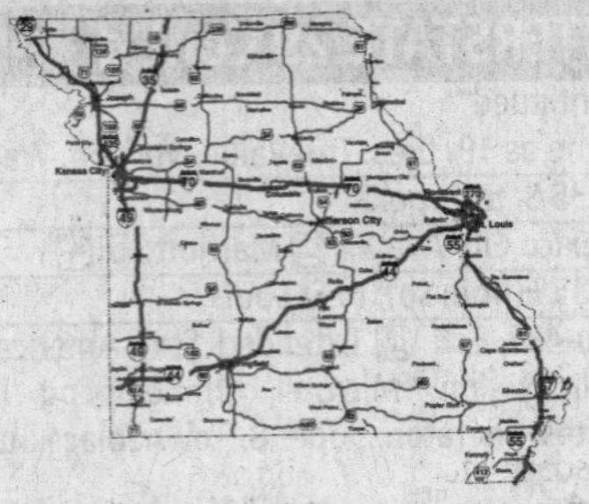

1e US 69, Vivion Rd, E Sinclair/dsl

1d 20th St(from sb), E Sinclair

1c 27th St, SW Blvd, W Pennway(from nb), E H

1a SW Trafficway(from sb)

0mm Missouri/Kansas state line

INTERSTATE 44

ST LOUIS

293mm I-44 begins/ends on I-70, exit 249 in St Louis.

290a I-55 S, to Memphis

290c Gravois Ave(from wb), 12th St

290b 18th St(from eb), downtown

289 Jefferson Ave, St Louis, N Phillips 66, Subway, Residence Inn, Family$, SaveALot, S Conoco, Lee's Chicken, McDonald's, $General, USPO, vet

288 Grand Blvd, St Louis, N BP, H, vet, S Domino's, Jack-in-the-Box, Starbucks, Subway, Fleur-de-Lys Mansion, Family$, TG Farmers' Mkt

287b a Kingshighway, Vandeventer Ave, St Louis, N BP, QT/dsl, Subway, H, Jiffy Lube, U-Haul, S antiques, auto/tire repair, Chevrolet, to MO Botanical Garden, U-Haul, Walgreens

286 Hampton Ave, St Louis, N BP, Circle K, Phillips 66, Shell, Courtesy Diner, McDonald's, Steak'n Shake, Subway, Taco Bell, Toyota, zoo, S Circle K/dsl, QT/dsl/24hr, Bartolino's Rest., Hardee's, Wendy's, Drury Inn, Forest Park, Red Roof Inn, URGENT CARE

285 SW Ave(from wb, no EZ return)

284b a Arsenal St, Jamieson St

283 Shrewsbury(from wb), some services same as 282

282 Laclede Sta Rd, Murdock Ave(from eb), St Louis, N BP, Phillips 66/dsl, Big Sky Cafe, DQ, Dunkin, Einstein Bagels, Frisco Cafe, Front Row Grill, Hwy 61 Roadhouse, Imo's Pizza, McDonald's, MeYou Thai, Racanelli's Pizza, Starbucks, Subway, auto/tires, vet

280 Elm Ave, St Louis, N BP, Schnuck's Foods, S Shell/Circle K, Steak'n Shake, Walgreens

279 (from wb), Berry Rd

278 Big Bend Rd, St Louis, N Culver's, H, Sam's Club/gas, S Mobil/dsl, QT

S MEMPHIS

277b US 67, US 61, US 50, Lindbergh Blvd, N Buffalo Wild Wings, Cane's, Chili's, Chipotle Mexican, Dunkin, Sonic, TX Roadhouse, White Castle, Best Western, $Tree, ALDI, AT&T, AutoZone, Harley-Davidson, Hobby Lobby, Lowe's Whse, Office Depot, Target, TJ Maxx, Verizon, Walmart, S Circle K/dsl, Phillips 66/dsl, Burger King, Chick-fil-A, Denny's, El Agave Mexican, Five Guys, Helen Fitzgerald' Grill, Lion's Choice, Longhorn Steaks, Mellow Mushroom, Panda Express, Smoothie King, St Louis Bread, Starbucks, Steak'n Shake, Subway, Walnut Grill, Days Inn/rest., Holiday Inn, LaQuinta, Bass Pro, Dobb's Auto/Tire, Home Depot, Marshall's, Midas, Old Navy, PetSmart

277a MO 366 E, Watson Rd, access to same as 277b S

276b a I-270, N to Chicago, S Memphis

275 N Highway Dr(from wb), Soccer Pk Rd, N Road Ranger/Subway/dsl

274a b Bowles Ave, N Road Ranger/Subway/dsl/scales/24hr

INTERSTATE 44 Cont'd

274a b Continued
Wally's/dsl/24hr/EVC, **S** Phillips 66/dsl, QT/dsl, Bandana's BBQ, Cracker Barrel, Krispy Kreme, McDonald's, White Castle, Drury Inn, Economy Inn, Extended Stay America, Fairfield Inn, Holiday Inn Express, Motel 6, PearTree Inn, tires

BEAUMONT

272 MO 141, Fenton, Valley Park, **N** Motomart, **S** Phillips 66/dsl, ZX, Bob Evans, Hardee's, Psghettis Italian, Ruby Tuesday, Starbucks, Subway, Sugarfire BBQ, Taco Bell, Drury Inn, Hampton Inn

269 Antire Rd, Beaumont

266 Lewis Rd, **N** golf, Rte 66 SP, West Tyson Park

266mm Meramec River

265 Williams Rd(from eb)

264 MO 109, rd W, Eureka, **N** Phillips 66/dsl, Arby's, Burger King, Culver's, Domino's, Jimmy John's, Pizza Hut, Poor Richard's, St Louis Bread, Taco Bell, White Castle, AT&T, Byerly RV Ctr, O'Reilly Parts, Schnuck's Foods, to Babler SP, Valvoline, **S** QT/dsl, Walgreens

261 Lp 44, to Allenton, **N** Motomart/McDonald's/dsl, China King, Imo's Pizza, Lion's Choice, Steak'n Shake, Subway, Best Inn, Holiday Inn, Super 8, $Tree, AutoZone, Jellystone RV Camping, same as 264, to Six Flags, Walmart, **S** Circle K/dsl, KOA

PACIFIC

257(256 from eb) Lp 44, Pacific, **N** Phillips 66/dsl, Pilot/Subway/dsl/scales/24hr, Comfort Inn, fireworks, **S** BP/dsl, Mobil/dsl, Motomart, Domino's, El Agave Mexican, Hardee's, KFC, McDonald's, New China, Pizza Hut, Taco Bell, Quality Inn, $General, B&H Foods, Chrysler/Dodge/Jeep, CVS Drug, O'Reilly Parts, SaveALot, st police

253 MO 100 E, to Gray Summit, Guffey's Pizza, **N** Phillips 66/dsl, $General, **S** Mobil/dsl, fireworks, Shaw Nature Preserve

251 MO 100 W, to Washington, **N** BP/dsl, Conoco/dsl/scales/24hr, Phillips 66/Burger King/dsl, $General, **S** fireworks

247 US 50 W, rd AT, rd O, to Union, **N** Pin Oak Creek RV Park, **S** to Robertsville SP

247mm Bourbeuse River, **N** flea mkt

242 rd AH, to Hist Rte 66

ST CLAIR

240 MO 47, St Clair, **N** Phillips 66/Taco Bell/dsl, Burger King, tire/auto, **S** Mobil/dsl, Domino's, Gibby's, McDonald's, Subway, Pinemark Inn, Super 8, $General, $Tree, Country Mart Foods, NAPA, O'Reilly Parts, Save-A-Lot Foods, USPO

239 MO 30, rds AB, WW, St Clair, **S** Phillips 66/dsl, Tres Toritos, antiques

238mm weigh sta both lanes

235mm full facilities, litter barrels, petwalk, (both lanes exit left), vending

230 rds W, Stanton, **N** $General, **S** Amstar/fireworks, KOA, Meramec Caverns Camping(3mi), USPO

SULLIVAN

226 MO 185 S, Sullivan, **N** Flying J/Denny's/dsl/LP/scales/24hr, truck repair, Verizon, vet, **S** same as 225, Circle K/dsl, EVC, Applebee's, Arby's, China Buffet, DQ, Imo's Pizza, KFC, Little Caesar's, McDonald's, Sonic, Starbucks, Subway, Taco Bell, $General, $Tree, Ace Hardware, ALDI, AT&T, AutoZone, O'Reilly Parts, tires, to Meramec SP, Walmart

225 MO 185 N, rd D, Sullivan, **N** Mobil, Phillips 66/dsl, Domino's, Jimmy John's, Rich's Famous Burgers, Baymont Inn, Best Value Inn, Motel 6, Super 8, Chevrolet/Buick/GMC, Chrysler/Dodge/Jeep, Ford, **S** BP/Fas-Trip/dsl/café, ZX, Cracker Barrel, El Nopal Mexican, Jack-in-the-Box, Lion's Choice, Pizza Hut, Comfort Inn, city park, H, same as 226, Valvoline

BOURBON

218 rds N, C, J, Bourbon, **N** ZX/dsl, Budget Inn, antiques, **S** Mobil/dsl, $General, Planet Sub, Subway, Blue Sprgs Camping(6mi), Bourbon RV Ctr, Riverview Ranch Camping(8mi), Sinks Drug, Town&Country Mkt

214 rd H, Leasburg, **N** Exxon/dsl, outlet, **S** Skippy's Rte 66 Rest., antiques, to Onandaga Cave SP(7mi)

210 rd UU, **N** Meremac Valley Resort, **S** MO Hick BBQ(3mi)

208 MO 19, Cuba, **N** Phillips 66/Dottie's Rest./dsl/scales/24hr/@, Huddle House, Pearls Creamery, Pizza Hut, Cuba Inn, Super 8, antiques, Blue Beacon, **S** Mobil/dsl, East Sun Chinese, Hardee's, Jack-in-the-Box, McDonald's, Sonic, Subway, Taco Bell, Days Inn, $General, $Tree, auto, Mace Foods, O'Reilly Parts, Walmart

203 rds F, ZZ

195 MO 8, MO 68, St James, Maramec Sprg Park, **N** BP/Circle K/dsl, Mobil/dsl, China King, McDonald's, Pizza Hut, Ruby's Ice Cream, Sonic, Subway, Economy Inn, Greenstay Inn, DG Mkt, Family$, Ford, Goodyear, O'Reilly Parts, Ray's Tires, tires, to Maremac Winery, tours ctr, **S** Casey's/dsl, Phillips 66/dsl, Burger King, Finn's Motel, CountryMart Foods

HYPOINT

189 rd V, Industrial Park Dr, Hypoint, **N** Love's/McDonald's/Subway/dsl/scales/24hr, QT/dsl, U-Haul, **S** Mule Trading Post

186 US 63, MO 72, Rolla, Ay Caramba Mexican, **N** Sinclair/dsl, Steak'n Shake, Days Inn, Hampton Inn, Motel 6, Big O Tire, Kia, Kohl's, Lowe's, Nissan, Plaza Tire, **S** BreakTime/dsl, Mobil/dsl, Phillips 66/dsl, Buffalo Wild Wings, Colton's Steaks, Domino's, IHOP, Koi Chinese, Lee's Chicken, Panera Bread, Piscotti's Pizza, Starbucks, Taco Co, Budget Motel, H

185 rd E, to Rolla, **N** hwy patrol, **S** ZX, Chick-fil-A, Jimmy John's, Jimmy John's, Papa John's, Taco Bell, CVS Drug, Havener Ctr, H, Kroger, NAPA, O'Reilly Parts, UMO at Rolla

184 US 63 S, to Rolla, **N** Comfort Suites, Fairfield Inn, Holiday Inn Express, Discount Tire, Menards, PetSmart, Ross, TJ Maxx, **S** MotoMart, Arby's, Bandana's BBQ, Burger King, Denny's, Dickey's BBQ, Little Caesar's, LJ Silver, Lucky House Chinese, Maid-Rite, McAlister's Deli, McDonald's, Penelope's Rest., Pizza Hut, Sirloin Stockade, Subway, Waffle House, Wendy's, Baymont Inn, Best Western, EconoLodge, Quality Inn, Regency Inn, Sunset Inn, Super 8, ALDI, Batteries+, Buick/Cadillac/GMC, Chevrolet, city park, Ford/Lincoln, H, O'Reilly Parts, Walgreens, Walmart

JEROME

179 rds T, C, to Doolittle, Newburg, truck parking both lanes, **N** antiques, Doolittle RV Park/Campground, **S** Phillips 66/Dunkin/dsl, $General

178mm truck parking both lanes, restrooms

176 Sugar Tree Rd

172 rd D, Jerome

169 rd J, **S** Camp Elim RV Park/Campground

166 to Big Piney

164mm Big Piney River

163 MO 28, to Dixon, **N** Road Ranger/Chesters/Subway/dsl/scales/24hr, **S** Phillips 66/dsl, Best Western, Days Inn, Motel 6, $General, RV Park, Uranus Fudge Factory

161b a rd Y, to Ft Leonard Wood, **N** Mobil/dsl, Murphy USA/dsl, Burger King, Cracker Barrel, Domino's, DQ, Jimmy John's, Mama Mia Mediterranean, Ocean Buffet, Pizza Hut, Rte 66 Diner, Ruby Tuesday, Wendy's, Baymont Inn, Best Value Inn, Candlewood Suites, Comfort Inn, Fairfield Inn, Hampton Inn, Hawthorn Suites, Mainstay Suites, Red Roof Inn, Lowe's, Toyota, visitors ctr, Walmart/Subway, **S** Cenex/dsl, Kum&Go/dsl, Agave Mexican, Arby's, Buffalo Wild Wings, Casey's Pizza, Colton's Steaks, Culver's, El Jimador Mexican, Freddy's, Ichiban Japanese, Little Caesar's, McDonald's, Panera Bread, Papa John's, Starbucks, Subway,

= gas = food = lodging = other = rest stop

INTERSTATE 44 Cont'd

ST ROBERT

161b a Continued
Taco Bell, Waffle House, Budget Inn, EconoLodge, Extended Stay, Holiday Inn Express, Quality Inn, ZLoft Hotel, $General, $Tree, AT&T, AutoZone, Chrysler/Dodge/Jeep, Family$, Ford/Lincoln, NAPA, O'Reilly Parts, U-Haul, USPO, Valvoline, Verizon

159 Lp 44, to Waynesville, St Robert, N Sonic, All Star Motel, Super 8, auto repair, O'Reilly Parts, S Cenex/Godfather's/dsl, El Cabrito, Sleep Inn, auto repair, Big O Tire, U-Haul

158mm N Roubidoux Creek

156 rd H, Waynesville, N EX Stop, Gulf/dsl, Kum&Go/dsl, Shell/dsl/24hr, Master Donuts, McDonald's, Subway, Taco Bell, $General, Chevrolet, Price Cutter+

153 MO 17, to Buckhorn, S Cenex/dsl, $General, Glen Oaks RV Park

150 MO 7, rd P to Richland

SLEEPER

145 MO 133, rd AB, to Richland, N Sinclair/Oasis/cafe/dsl/24hr, tires, S antiques

143mm Gasconade River, S Eden Park

140 rd N, to Stoutland, S Cenex/pizza/dsl, Ozark RV Park

139mm Bear Creek

135 rd F, Sleeper

130 rd MM, N Cenex/dsl, Express Stop/Taco John's/dsl, Andy's Rest., Taylor's Dairy Joy, Best Western, Budget Inn, Munger Moss Inn, auto repair, Route 66 Farmers' Mkt, S Kum&Go/dsl, H

LEBANON

129 MO 5, MO 32, MO 64, to Hartville, Lebanon, N Applebee's, Arby's, Bamboo Garden, Bandana's BBQ, Burger King, El Charro Mexican, Elm St Eatery, Jimmy John's, KFC, Little Caesar's, McDonald's, Papa Murphy's, Sonic, Steak'n Shake, Subway, Taco Bell, Wendy's, ALDI, AT&T, AutoZone, Chevrolet, Ford, King Cashsaver, O'Reilly Parts, repair, Rte 66 Museum, to Bennett Sprgs SP, to Lake of the Ozarks, Verizon, Walgreens, S Cenex/dsl, Phillips 66/dsl, Capt D's, Denny's, Domino's, Hardee's, La Tolteca, Pizza Hut, $Tree, BigLots, H, Lowe's, NAPA, O'Reilly Parts, Sawyer Tire/auto, Walmart/Subway

127 Lp 44, Lebanon, N Cenex/dsl, Gulf/B&D/dsl/scales/24hr, Dowd's Catfish&BBQ, El Sombrero Mexican, Slim Chickens, Subway, Waffle House, Best Value Inn, Budget Host Inn, Hampton Inn, Holiday Inn Express, Maple Tree Inn, Rte 66 Motel, Super 8, $General, Chrysler/Dodge/Jeep, Shepherd Hills Outlets, S Cenex/McDonald's/dsl, Taco Bell, antiques, Buick/GMC

123 County Rd, S Pizza City, antiques, Happy Trails RV Ctr, Rustic Trails RV Park

CONWAY

118 rds C, A, Phillipsburg, S Phillip 66/dsl, Phillips 66, Large Gift shop, Redmon's Candy Factory, tourist info

113 rds J, Y, Conway, N Phillips 66/dsl, Rockin Chair Café, Budget Inn, to Den of Metal Arts, S Sinclair/dsl, $General, Price Cutter, tires, USPO.

111mm full facilities, litter barrels, petwalk, playground, both lanes, vending

108mm Bowen Creek

107 Sparkle Brooke Rd, Sampson Rd

106mm Niangua River

100 MO 38, rd W, Marshfield, N Murphy USA/dsl, Phillips 66, $Tree, Ace Hardware, auto repair, Chevrolet, Chrysler/Dodge/Jeep, Ford, tires, Walmart/Subway, S Casey's/dsl, Cenex/dsl, Shell/dsl, Burger King, Domino's, DQ, Golden China, Grillos Cafe, Hucklebuck BBQ, Hunan Chinese, KFC/Rib Crib, McDonald's, Pizza Hut, Sonic, Subway, Taco Bell, Tokyo Japanese, Wendy's, Holiday Inn Express, $General, antiques, auto, AutoZone,

FEDALIA

100 Continued
Marshfield Farmer's Mkt, O'Reilly Parts, Price Cutter, RV Express RV Park, Verizon, Walgreens

96 rd B, Northview, N Rustic Meadows RV Park(2mi)

89mm weigh sta both lanes

88 MO 125, to Fair Grove, Strafford, N Love's/Hardee's/dsl/scales/rv dump/24hr, ONE9/dsl/scales/24hr, Sinclair/dsl TA/Subway/Taco Bell/dsl/scales/24hr/@, McDonald's, Camping World RV Ctr, Speedco, truckwash, vet, S Breaktime/dsl, Phillips 66/dsl, El Paraiso Mexican, Fat Ca Pizza, Joe's Diner, Pizza Hut, Super 8, $General O'Reilly Parts, Strafford RV Park

84 MO 744, S Peterbilt

82b a US 65, to Branson, Fedalia, S Conoco/dsl, Kum&Go/dsl, Welcome Inn, Bull Shoals Lake, Chrysler/Dodge/Jeep Kenworth, st patrol, to Table Rock Lake

80b a rd H to Pleasant Hope, Springfield, N Conoco/dsl/scales 24hr, Kum&Go/dsl, Shell/dsl, Sinclair, Tesla EVC, Tropica Smoothies, Days Inn, Holiday Inn Express, Red Roof Inn Super 8, S Casey's, Kum&Go/dsl, Phillips 66/dsl, Shell, Andy's Custard, Applebee's, Braum's, Burger King Cantonese Chinese, Cracker Barrel, Culver's, El Mague Mexican, Farm House Cafe, Fazoli's, Freddy's, Hardee's, Hong Kong Inn, Ichiban Buffet, King's Asian Chef, Little Tokyo, L Silver, McDonald's, Panda Express, Ruby Tuesday Schlotzsky's, Shanghai Inn, Sonic, Steak'n Shake, Subway Taco Bell, Whole Hog Cafe, Ziggies Cafe, Baymont Inn Best Western, Campus Inn, Candlewood Suites, Comfort Inn Dogwood Park Inn, Doubletree Hotel, Drury Inn, EconoLodge Economy Inn, Fairfield Inn, Flagship Motel, Hampton Inn Holiday Inn, Home2 Suites, Lamplighter Hotel, Motel 6, Plaz Inn, Quality Inn, Springhill Suites, ALDI, AT&T, AutoZone Big O Tire, Honda, H, Tire Express, U-Haul, Walmart/Subwa

SPRINGFIELD

77 MO 13, KS Expswy, N Kum&Go/dsl/e85, Lowe's, zoo, Casey's/dsl, Phillips 66/dsl, Braum's, Five Guys, Golde Corral, Goodcents, IHOP, Jimmy John's, McAlister's Del McDonald's, New China, Panera Bread, Papa Murphy's, Pizz Hut, Starbucks, Subway, Wingstop, $Tree, AT&T Batteries+, BigLots, Goodyear/auto, Hobby Lobby PriceCutter Foods, Verizon, Walgreens, Walmart

75 US 160 W byp, to Willard, Stockton Lake, S Kum&Go/ds Wendy's, Courtyard, La Quinta

72 MO 266, to Chesnut Expwy, S Casey's, Cenex, Flying J Wendy's/PJ Fresh/dsl/scales/24hr, Kum&Go/dsl/e85, Shell dsl/24hr, Alli's Rest., Arby's, Bubba's BBQ, Burger King China Wok, Hardee's, KFC, LJ Silver, McDonald's, Pizza Hu Plaza Mexico, Sonic, Subway, Taco Bell, Waffle House, Best Budget Inn, Best Western+, Redwood Motel, $General, AutoZone, city park, PriceCutter Foods, Verizon

70 rds MM, B, N fireworks, S KOA(1mi), Wilson's Creek Na Bfd(5mi)

69 to US 60, Springfield

67 rds N, T, Bois D' Arc, to Republic, S Conoco/dsl, antqiues

66mm Pond Creek

64.5mm Dry Branch

INTERSTATE 44 Cont'd

Exit #	Services
64.5mm	Pickerel Creek, N LaFayette Mansion
61	rds K, PP, N Cenex/Hoods/dsl/scales/LP/24hr, Phillips 66, Hood I-44 Motel, S MO Berries
58	MO 96, rds O, Z, to Carthage, Halltown, S Shell/dsl
57	to rd PP(from wb)
56.5mm	Turnback Creek
56mm	Goose Creek
52.5mm	truck parking both lanes
49	MO 174E, rd CCW, Chesapeake
46	MO 39, MO 265, Mt Vernon, Aurora, N Casey's/dsl, Gulf/dsl, Kum&Go/dsl, TA/Conoco/dsl/scales/24hr/@, El Azteca Mexican, KFC/LJ Silver, McDonald's, Pizza Hut, Sonic, Subway, Taco Bell, Best Western, USA Inn, $General, $Tree, O'Reilly Parts, tires, True Value, U-Haul, S Cenex/dsl, TA/Phillips 66/dsl, Quality Inn, to Table Rock Lake
44	rd H, to Monett, Mt Vernon, N EVC, Subway(1mi), auto repair, Mid-America Dental/Hearing, Walmart
43.5mm	Honey Creek, Spring River
38	MO 97, to Stotts City, Pierce City, N gas/dsl/repair/tires, S U of MO SW Ctr(4mi)
33	MO 97 S, to Pierce City
29	rd U, to La Russell, Sarcoxie, N Beagle Bay RV Camping, Ozarkland Gifts, S Kum&Go/Subway/dsl, antiques
29mm	Center Creek
26	MO 37, to Reeds, Sarcoxie, N tires, S MFA/dsl
22	rd 100 N, N Colaw RV Ctr
21mm	Jones Creek
18b a	I-49 N, US 71 N, MO 59 S, to Carthage, Neosho, N Coachlight RV Ctr/Camping, S Ballard's RV Park/Campground
15	MO 66 W, Lp 44(from wb), Joplin, N Tara Motel
15mm	Grove Creek
14mm	Turkey Creek
13	Prigmore Ave, S Phillips 66/EVC/dsl/scales/24hr, Road Ranger/dsl, Wendy's
11b a	I-49 S, US 71 S, MO 249 N, to Neosho, Ft Smith, S Flying J/Conoco/Denny's/dsl/LP/scales/24hr/@, QT/dsl/24hr, Speedco, Blue Beacon, fireworks, Kenworth, Penske, Speedco, truck repair
8b a	US 71, to Neosho, Joplin, N Cenex/dsl, Kum&Go/dsl, Shell/dsl, Andy's Custard, Applebee's, Arby's, Braum's, Burger King, Cheddar's, Chick-fil-A, Chick-fil-A, CiCi's, Denny's, Domino's, Firehouse Subs, First Watch, Five Guys, Freddy's, Golden Corral, HuHot, IHOP, Jersey Mike's, Jimmy's Egg, Little Caesar's, Longhorn Steaks, McAlister's, McDonald's, Old Chicago, Olive Garden, Olive Garden, Outback Steaks, Panda Express, Pizza Hut, Popeyes, Red Lobster, Rib Crib, Smoothie King, Sonic, Starbucks, Steak'n Shake, Subway, TX Roadhouse, Waffle House, Wendy's, Best Western, Candlewood Suites, Comfort Inn, Days Inn, Drury Inn, EconoLodge, Fairfield Inn, Hampton Inn, Hilton Garden, Holiday Inn, Home2 Suites, Homewood Suites, La Quinta, Quality Inn, Residence Inn, Super 7, Super 8, ALDI, AT&T, Chrysler/Dodge/Jeep/RAM, Discount Tire, Food4Less, Goodyear/auto, Hobby Lobby, Home Depot, Honda, Hyundai, Joplin RV, Lowe's, Nissan/EVC, O'Reilly Parts, Office Depot, Sam's Club/gas, Subaru, Toyota, Valvoline, Verizon, Walgreens, Walmart/Subway, S Casey's, Cracker Barrel, Fazoli's, Microtel, TownePlace Suites, vet, Wheelen RV Ctr
6	MO 86, MO 43 N, to Racine, Joplin, N Phillips 66, Jimmy John's, Moe's SW Grill, Schlotzsky's, Sonic, CVS Drug, Walgreens, S Kum&Go/dsl/e15/Tesla EVC, Goodyear, Harley-Davidson, H
5.5mm	Shoal Creek
4	MO 43 to Seneca, N Love's/Hardee's/dsl/scales/24hr, S Conoco/Subway/dsl, Petro/Iron Skillet/Pizza Hut/Taco Bell/dsl/scales/24hr/@, Pilot/Wendy's/dsl/scales/24hr, Blimpie, McDonald's, Sleep Inn, $General, 4 State Trucks, fireworks, IA 80 Truckomat, KOA, tires
3mm	weigh sta both lanes
2mm	litter barrels, full facilities, restrooms, vending, Welcome Ctr eb
1	US 400, US 166W, to Baxter Springs, KS, N Downstream/dsl, Downstream Casino/RV Park, Downstream RV Park
0mm	Missouri/Oklahoma state line

Margin labels: HALLTOWN · SARCOXIE · FT SMITH · JOPLIN · BELTON · MO

INTERSTATE 49

Exit #	Services
184	I-435, I-470. I-49 begins/ends, continues N as US 71.
182	Red Bridge Rd, Longview Rd, E Sinclair/dsl, McDonald's, Taco Bell, auto repair, W Phillips 66/dsl, Extended Stay America
181	Blue Ridge Blvd, E Shell/dsl, Church's TX Chicken, Best Value Inn, NAPA, U-Haul, W BP/dsl, Conoco/dsl, Arby's, Chipotle, IHOP, KFC, McAlister's Deli, Panda Express, Papa John's, Petco, Starbucks, Wendy's, Wing Street, Wingstop, $Tree, Advance Parts, AutoZone, Burlington Coats, CVS, Price Chopper, TJ Maxx, True Value
180	(from sb), same as 181 w, W Jerry's Auto Repair
179	Main St, E Conoco, Burger King, Capestre Mexican, DQ, Manila Bay Filipino, Popeyes, Providence Pizzeria, $General, Firestone/auto, Holiday Inn Express, to Longview Lake CP, W Phillips 66/dsl, Holt's Donuts, Taco Bell, transmissions, USPO, Walgreens
178	140th St, W Phillips 66/dsl, Pizza Hut, $General
177	MO 150, E EVC, Phillips 66/dsl, QT/dsl, Sonic, Subway, W True Value
176	155th St, Belton, W Fast Gas N Sacks/dsl, $General
175	rd Y, 163rd St, Belton, E Cracker Barrel, Hampton Inn, H, W Fazoli's, Kneader's, Hobby Lobby, Marshall's, Menards, Petco, Ross
174	MO 58, Belton, E QT/dsl, Shell/dsl, Burger King, China Star, Church's TX Chicken, Firehouse Subs, KFC, MOD Pizza, Panda Express, Papa John's, Qdoba, Taco Bell, The Big Biscuit, Tokyo Japanese, Waffle House, Wendy's, Whataburger, Quality Inn, Advance Parts, AT&T, Big O Tire, Chrysler/Dodge/Jeep, Firestone/auto, H, Lowe's, Sam's Club/dsl, Transwest RV Ctr, U-Haul, Walmart/Subway, W Casey's/dsl, Popeyes, QT/dsl, Applebee's, Arby's, Buffalo Wild Wings, Cane's, Casa Mexico, Chipotle, Domino's, Dutch Bros, Five Guys, Freddy's, Hawaiian Bros, IHOP, Jimmy John's, Jose Pepper's, Longhorn Steaks, McDonald's, Panera Bread, Papa Murphy's, Pepper Jax Cafe, Royal Gyros, Starbucks, Subway, TX Roadhouse, EconoLodge, Fairfield Inn, $Tree, ALDI, auto repair, AutoZone, CVS Drug, Discount Tire, GNC, Home Depot, HyVee/dsl, Kohl's, O'Reilly Parts, PetSmart, Price Chopper, Target, URGENT CARE, USPO, Verizon, Walgreens
172	N Cass Pkwy
168	Peculiar Way
167	MO C, J, Peculiar, E Casey's, Flying J/Denny's/dsl/Lp/scales/24hr, Subway, Highland Inn, Peculiar RV Park, W Cenex, Sonic, Price Chopper, USPO
160	MO 291 N, Harrisonville , E Casey's/dsl, Murphy USA, QT/dsl, Applebee's, Arby's, Branding Iron BBQ, Capt D's, Culver's, El Maguey Mexican, Jimmy John's, KFC, McDonald's, Scooter's Coffee, Starbucks, Subway, Sunrise Chinese, Taco Bell, Wendy's, Whataburger, Best Value Inn, Harrisonville Inn, $Tree, AT&T, H, tires, U-Haul, vet, Walmart, W Ford
159	MO 2 W, 7 N, Mechanic St, Harrisonville, E BP,

⛽ = gas 🍴 = food 🏨 = lodging ⓞ = other RS = rest stop

MO

INTERSTATE 49 Cont'd

159 Continued
Casey's/dsl, EVC, Phillips 66/dsl, 🍴 Burger King, China Wok, DQ, Papa Murphy's, Pizza Hut, Starbucks, ⓞ $General, ALDI, CVS, Price Chopper, tire/auto, Verizon, vet, Walgreens

158 MO 2 E, Commercial Blvd, Harrisonville, E ⛽ Conoco/dsl, Phillips 66, 🍴 Best Burrito, Peniku Japanese, 🏨 Comfort Inn, ⓞ $General, Sutherland's, W ⛽ Love's/McDonald's/Subway/dsl/scales/24hr

157mm weigh sta both lanes, weigh sta both sb/nb

157 MO 7 S, to Clinton, E ⓞ, W ⛽ BP/dsl, Sapp Bros/dsl/scales/24hr, 🍴 Apple Barrel, Dunkin, 🏨 Slumber Inn, ⓞ fireworks, truck repair

153 307th St

148mm S Grand River

147 MO A, B, Archie, Drexel, S ⓞ $General, W ⛽ Phillips 66, 🍴 Fishing Dock, Mama's Kitchen, ⓞ Archie RV Park, tires

144 MO E, AA, Crescent Hill

141 MO 18, Adrian, to Clinton, W ⛽ Casey's/dsl, Phillips 66/dsl, 🍴 Byrd's Delights, Gray's Cafe, ⓞ $General, auto repair, NAPA

136 rds D, F, Passaic, to Butler, W ⓞ McBee's Bratwurst/BBQ, Rest RV Park

131 MO 52 W, Butler, Amoret, E ⛽ Conoco, 🍴 Burger King, McDonald's, Pizza Hut, Sonic, Steiner's Rest., Subway, Taco Bell, Taco Bell, 🏨 Days Inn, ⓞ $General, Chrysler/Dodge/Jeep/Ford, H, NAPA, O'Reilly Parts, Walmart, W tires

130 US 71 Bus(from nb), to Butler

129 MO 52 E, Appleton City, ⓞ 3 Mile RV Park

120 rds B, A, Rich Hill, to Osceola, W ⛽ Phillips 66/dsl, 🍴 Swope's Drive In, ⓞ $General, Food Fair Mkt/drug

116 Rd TT, to Panama

112 Horton

110 Rd D, Stotesbury

107 Rd M, Compton Jct, E ⓞ J&K RV Park

103 Highland Ave, to Nevada, E ⓞ auto, W $General, Chevrolet/GMC/Buick, Osage Prairie RV Park

NEVADA

102b 49 Bus, Nevada, W ⓞ same as 103

102a US 54, to El Dorado Springs, Nevada, W ⛽ MFA/dsl/e85, 🍴 54 Cafe, ⓞ Centennial Park, Highly Tires, Kate Allen Lake

101 Rd K, to Camp Clark, Nevada, W ⛽ Hot Spot/dsl, Murphy USA/dsl, Pilot/dsl/scales/24hr, 🍴 Burger King, Buzz's BBQ, Freddy's, Sonic, Subway, Taco Bell, 🏨 Best Value Inn, Country Inn&Suites, Holiday Inn Express, Nevada Inn, Super 8, ⓞ $Tree, AutoZone, Chrysler/Dodge/Jeep/Ford, Sutherlands, Verizon, Walmart/Subway, Wilson Tire

95 Rd E, Milo

91 Rds DD, BB, to Bellamy

88 Rds B, N, Sheldon, Bronaugh, E ⓞ to Stockton Lake(33 mi)

83 Rds C, V, Irwin

80 Rds EE, DD

77 US 160, Lamar, Mindenmines, E ⛽ Phillips 66, Sinclair/dsl/scales/24hr, 🍴 Bamboo House, McDonald's, Pizza Hut, Sonic, Subway, Taco Bell, Taco Palace, 🏨 Blue Top Inn, Super 8, ⓞ $Tree, Blue Top Quilt Shop, O'Reilly Parts, truckwash, W ⛽ Murphy USA/dsl, Phillips 66/Roady's/dsl, 🍴 DQ, ⓞ H, Lamar Truck/tire, Walmart

74 30th Rd

70 MO 126, Golden City, Pittsburg

66 Rds K, H, Jasper, W ⛽ Judy's Trkstp/Cafe/dsl, Phillips 66/dsl, ⓞ $General

63 Rds N, M

56 Garrison Ave(from sb), to Carthage

55 Civil War Rd, to Carthage

53 MO 571 S, MO 96, MO 171 N, Central Ave, Carthage, E ⛽ Casey's/dsl, Phillips 66/dsl, 🍴 Arby's, Boomer's BBQ,

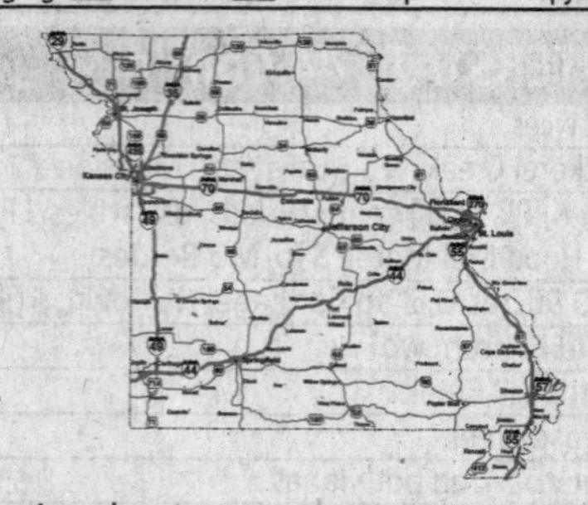

53 Continued
Burger King, LJ Silver, McDonald's, Sirloin Stockade, Son
Subway, 🏨 Days Inn, ⓞ $General, King Cashsaver

51 Fairview Ave, to Carthage

50 Rd HH, Fir Rd, E ⛽ Murphy USA, Phillips 66/McDonald's/d
🍴 Big Ben's BBQ, Dunkin, El Charro, Iggy's Diner, KFC, Lit
Caesar's, Taco Bell, Tropical Smoothie, Wendy's, 🏨 Qual
Inn, Super 8, ⓞ $General, $Tree, ALDI, Chrysler/Dodge/Jee
Ford, Lowe's, Verizon, Walgreens, Walmart/Subway, W H

49 MO 571, Garrison Ave, to Carthage(from nb)

47 Cedar Rd, W ⓞ Coachlight RV Ctr/Park, Mid America RV Ct

46mm I-44, E to Springfield, W to Joplin. I-49 and I-44 run togeth
7 mi. See I-44, exit 15.

39b I-44, E to Springfield, W to Joplin. I-49 and I-44 run togeth
7 mi. See I-44, exit 15.

39a Rd FF, 32nd St, E ⛽ QT/dsl/scales/24hr, ⓞ Kenwort
Penske, truck repair, W ⛽ Flying J/Conoco/Denny's/dsl/L
scales/24hr, ⓞ Blue Beacon, fireworks, Goodyear Tire
repair, Speedco, U-Haul

35 Rd V, Diamond, E ⓞ G Washington Carver NM

33 MO 175, Gateway Dr, E ⓞ $General, W ⛽ Casey's/dsl,
Shoal Creek RV Park

30 Iris Rd

27 MO 86, to Neosho, Racine, E ⛽ Love's/McDonald's/Subwa
dsl/scales/24hr, W ⓞ truck repair

24 US 60, to Neosho, Seneca, E ⛽ Kum&Go/dsl/e85, Murp
USA, 🍴 Burger King, Denny's, El Charro, KFC, LJ Silver, Ta
Bell, 🏨 Best Western, Super 8, ⓞ $Tree, ALDI, Lowe
Verizon, Walmart, W Whispering Woods RV Park(12 mi)

20 Rd AA

17 Rds C, B, to Goodman, E 🍴 Casey's, Tammy's Cafe,
$General, Goodman Mini Mart, truck repair

16 MO 59(from sb), Kelley Springs

10 MO 76, to Anderson, W ⛽ Conoco/Subway/dsl,
EconoLodge, ⓞ Harps/dsl, O'Reilly Parts

7 Rd EE, to Pineville, Lanagan, E 🍴 Burger Time, ⓞ Sug
Island Camping

5 Rd H, to Pineville, E ⓞ $General, W Lazy Days Camping

2 AR 90, Jane

0mm Missouri/Arkansas state line

INTERSTATE 55

209mm Missouri/Illinois state line at St. Louis, Mississippi River

209b to I-70 W to Kansas City

BROADWAY

209a W ⓞ Busch Stadium, to Arch

208 Park Ave, 7th St, W ⛽ BP, ZX, 🍴 Broadway Oyster Bar, Imo
Pizza, Taco Bell, White Castle, ⓞ Meineke, tires

207c b I-44W, Truman Pkwy, to Tulsa

207a Gravois St(from nb)

206c Arsenal St, E ⓞ Anheuser-Busch Tour Ctr, W ⛽ BP/dsl

206b Broadway(from nb), Broadway

206a Potomac St(from nb)

205 Gasconade, W ⓞ H

204 Broadway, E ⛽ Phillips 66, W Conoco/dsl, Phillips 66/dsl,
Subway, ⓞ Family$, O'Reilly Parts, Walgreens

203 Bates St, Virginia Ave, W ⛽ BP

INTERSTATE 55 Cont'd

Exit #	Services
202c	Loughborough Ave, W Burger King, China King, Little Caesar's, Starbucks, AT&T, AutoZone, Firestone/auto, Lowe's Whse, Ross, Schnuck's Foods
202b	Germania(from sb)
202a	Carondelet(from nb), Carondelet
201b	Weber Rd
201a	Bayless Ave, E BP, McDonald's, W Mobil/dsl, Phillips 66/7-11/gas, DQ, Jack-in-the-Box, Subway, Taco Bell, auto repair
200	Union Rd(from sb)
199	Reavis Barracks Rd, E Circle K, QT/dsl, $General, auto repair
197	US 50, US 61, US 67, Lindbergh Blvd, E Phillips 66, Arby's, Buffalo Wild Wings, Chick-fil-A, ChuckeCheese, CiCi's, Dillard's, Five Guys, HoneyBaked Ham, Hooters, IHOP, KFC, Krispy Kreme, McAlister's, Panera Bread, Penn Sta Subs, Qdoba, Starbucks, Taco Bell, Tucker's Place, Wendy's, Aviator Hotel, AT&T, Best Buy, Chrysler/Dodge/Jeep, CVS Drug, Dick's, Dobbs Tire, Ford/Lincoln, Home Depot, JC Penney, Macy's, mall, Marshall's, Verizon, vet, W QT/dsl, Bob Evans, Culvers, Denny's, Golden Corral, McDonald's, Panda Express, Pasta House, Best Value Inn, ALDI, AT&T, CarMax, Chevrolet, Costco/gas, Hobby Lobby, Honda, Hyundai, Kia, Mazda, Nissan, Target, VW
196b	I-270 W, to Kansas City
196a	I-255 E, to Chicago
195	Butler Hill Rd, E BP/dsl, Phillips 66, Popeyes, Hampton Inn, Holiday Inn Express, Advance Parts, Walgreens, W Phillips 66, Burger King, Frailey's Grill, Hardee's, Starbucks, Subway, Taco Bell, Fairfield Inn, Schnuck's Foods, tires/repair
193	Meramec Bottom Rd, E QT/dsl, Cracker Barrel, Best Western, Midwest RV Ctr
191	MO 141, Arnold, E QT, Applebee's, Arby's, Bandana's BBQ, Cane's, Capt D's, Chick-fil-A, China King, Denny's, Dunkin/Baskin Robbins, Fazoli's, Five Guys, Jack-in-the-Box, Las Fuentes, Lee's Chicken, Lion's Choice, LJ Silver, McDonald's, Panda Express, Papa John's, Rally's, Starbucks, Steak'n Shake, Syberg's Arnold, Taco Bell, Wendy's, Drury Inn, Pear Tree Inn, ALDI, AT&T, CVS Drug, Dobbs Tire, Hobby Lobby, Jiffy Lube, Kohl's, NAPA, O'Reilly Parts, PetCo, vet, Walgreens, Walmart/Subway, W Circle K/dsl, Chili's, Miyabi, Pasta House, Penn Sta Subs, Qdoba, St Louis Bread, Sunny St Cafe, TX Roadhouse, Woodspring Suites, $Tree, Dierberg's Foods, Lowe's, Office Depot, PetSmart, Ross, URGENT CARE
190	Richardson Rd, E BP/McDonald's, Circle K/dsl, Hucks, Phillips 66/dsl, Culver's, Domino's, DQ, Pizza Hut, Ponderosa, Shamrock Donuts, Taco Bell, White Castle, $Tree, Advance Parts, Firestone, Save-A-Lot Foods, Tire Choice, URGENT CARE, W 7-11, Mobil/dsl/24hr, Shell/Circle K/dsl, Burger King, Front Row Grill, Happy Wok, Imo's Pizza, McDonald's/playplace, Mr. Goodcents Subs, Waffle House, Waffle House, Quality Inn, Aamco, AutoZone, Home Depot, Plaza Tire, Schnuck's Foods, Target, vet, Walgreens
186	Imperial, Kimmswick, E Circle K, Mobil, Blue Owl(1mi), auto repair, W Phillips 66/Jack-in-the-Box/dsl, China Wok, Domino's, Frankie's Grill, Papa John's, Subway, to Mastodon SP, USPO
185	rd M, Barnhart, Antonia, W Mobil/dsl/24hr, Phillips 66, Hunt Brothers Pizza, AutoZone, fireworks, Karsch's Mkt, USPO, Walgreens
180	rd Z, to Hillsboro, Pevely, E Mobil/dsl, Burger King,
180	Continued Domino's, Las Brisas Mexican, Pizza Hut, Subway, Taco Bell, $General, O'Reilly Parts, Save-A-Lot, W Mr Fuel/dsl, Phillips 66/McDonald's/dsl/scales, Super 8, auto repair, rv camping
178	Herculaneum, E Little Caesar's, Circle K, QT/dsl/scales, Cracker Barrel, DQ, Imo's Pizza, Jack-in-the-Box, La Pachanga Mexican, Tokyo Japanese, Toyota/Scion, W Buick/GMC, Cadillac/Chevrolet, Ford, vet
175	rd A, Festus, E Mobil, Murphy USA/dsl, Phillips 66/dsl, Arby's, Bob Evans, Burger King, Capt D's, China 1, Fazoli's, Hibachi Grill, Imo's Pizza, Jack-in-the-Box, Krabby Daddy's, McDonald's, McDonald's/playplace, Oriental Buffet, Panda Express, Papa John's, Sonic, St. Louis Bread Co, Starbucks, Steak'n Shake, Subway, Taco Bell, White Castle, La Quinta, Quality Inn, $Tree, Advance Parts, ALDI, AT&T, AutoZone, CVS Drug, Dobbs Tire, Home Depot, Plaza Tire, Schnuck's Foods/gas, URGENT CARE, Verizon, Walgreens, Walmart, W Phillips 66/7-11/dsl, Phillips 66/Domino's/dsl, Hardee's, Jimmy John's, Ruby Tuesday, Waffle House, Whittaker's Pizza, Comfort Inn, Holiday Inn Express, Chrysler/Dodge/Jeep, Lowe's
174b a	US 67, Lp 55, Festus, Crystal City, E Phillips 66/dsl, H
170	US 61, E $General, W BP/dsl
165	rd TT(from sb)
162	rds DD, OO
160mm	full facilities, litter barrels, petwalk, nb/weigh sta sb, vending
157	rd Y, Bloomsdale, E Phillips 66/Subway, $General, W Love's/McDonald's/dsl/scales/24hr
154	rd O, to St Genevieve
150	MO 32, rds B, A, to St Genevieve, E BP, DQ, Hist Site(6mi), H, W Phillips 66/dsl, Hawn SP(11mi)
143	rds J, M, N, Ozora, W Exxon/dsl, truckwash
141	rd Z, St Mary
135	rd M, Brewer
129	MO 51, to Perryville, E MotoMart/McDonald's/dsl, Chin, KFC, Taco Bell, Ford, H, W Rhodes/IMO's/dsl, Arby's, Burger King, Five Star Chinese, Los Primos, Subway, Days Inn, Holiday Inn, Quality Inn, Super 8, AT&T, Buick/Chevrolet, Chrysler/Dodge/Jeep, Walmart
123	rd B, Biehle, W Rhodes/dsl
119mm	Apple Creek
117	rd KK, to Appleton
111	rd E, Oak Ridge
110mm	rest area sb/full facilities, truck parking nb, rest both nb/sb
105	US 61, Fruitland, E Casey's, Phillips 66/dsl, Rhodes/dsl, Las Brisas Mexican, Subway, $General, Purcell Tires/repair, Trail of Tears SP(11mi), W Mobil/D-Mart/dsl, Bavarian Halle, DQ, Pizza Inn, Drury Inn
102	LaSalle Ave, E Main St
99	US 61, MO 34, to Jackson, Phillips 66/dsl/Tesla EVC, E RV camping, W Delmonico's Steaks, Comfort Suites, La Quinta, McDowell South RV Ctr
96	rd K, to Cape Girardeau, E Phillips 66/dsl, Asian Yummy Chinese, AT&T, Burger King, Chick-fil-A, Chili's, Cracker Barrel, El Acapulco, Firehouse Subs, Golden Corral, Honey Baked Ham, Logan's Roadhouse, McAlister's, Olive Garden, Panera Bread, Popeyes, Qdoba, Red Lobster, Starbucks, Steak'n Shake, Subway, Taco Bell, TX Roadhouse, Auburn Place, Drury Plaza/Rest., Hampton Inn, Holiday Inn Express, PearTree Inn, AT&T, Barnes&Noble, Best Buy, H, JC Penney, Old Navy, to SEMSU, Verizon, W Mobil, McDonald's/playplace, Outback Steaks, Panda Express, Penn Sta Subs, White Castle, Drury Suites, Pear Tree Inn, $Tree, Chrysler/Dodge/Jeep, Honda, Hyundai, Kohl's, Lowe's, Mazda, Nissan, PetCo, Plaza Tire, Sam's Club,

ARNOLD

PEVELY

FESTUS

BIEHLE

MO

= gas = food = lodging = other = rest stop

MO

INTERSTATE 55 Cont'd

96 Continued
Staples, Target, TJ Maxx, Toyota, Walmart/Subway

95 MO 74 E, E Mercato/dsl, Candlewood Suites, Fairfield Inn, URGENT CARE, W Menard's

93a b MO 74 W, Cape Girardeau

91 rd AB, to Cape Girardeau, E Rhodes/IMO's/dsl, Goodyear, Harley-Davidson, W , Youngblood's RV Ctr

89 US 61, rds K, M, Scott City, E Phillips 66/dsl, Rhodes, Berghoff's Cafe, Burger King, Ice Cream Corner, Las Brisas Mexican, Pizza Hut, Subway, MediCtr Drug, NAPA, Plaza Tire/auto

87 MO PP

80 MO 77, Benton, E Express/dsl, U-Haul, W Exxon/McDonald's/dsl/fireworks, Subway, antiques, winery(8mi)

MINER

69 rd HH, to Sikeston, Miner, E Peterbilt, W H

67 US 60, US 62, Miner, E Breaktime/dsl, Best Western+, Country Yard, Days Inn, Hinton RV Park, W Hucks, Larry's Pitstop, Mobil, QuickCheck, Bo's BBQ, Buffalo Wild Wings, Burger King, Dexter BBQ, El Tapatio Mexican, Lambert's Rest., Little Caesars, McDonald's, Pizza Inn, Rally's, Sonic, Subway, Taco John's, Wendy's, Comfort Inn, Drury Inn, PearTree Inn, Super 8, Travel Inn, $General, AutoZone, Buick/Chevrolet, Cadillac/GMC, CVS Drug, Family$, Food Giant, Food Giant, Goodyear, H, Sikeston Outlets/famous brands, Walgreens

66b US 60 W, to Poplar Bluff, W Breaktime/E-85, Love's/Dunkin Donuts/dsl/scales/24hr, A&W/LJ Silver, Applebee's, Arby's, China Buffet, Colton's Steaks, DQ, El Bracero Mexican, Hardee's, La Ruleta Mexican, McDonald's, Sonic, Taco Bell, Watami, Zaxby's, Days Inn, Hampton Inn, Holiday Inn Express, $Tree, ALDI, AT&T, Chrysler/Dodge/Jeep, Ford/Lincoln, GNC, JC Penney, Lowe's, O'Reilly Parts, Walmart/Subway

66a I-57 E, to Chicago, US 60 W

59mm St Johns Bayou

NEW MADRID

58 MO 80, Matthews, E Speedway/dsl, TA/Taco Bell/dsl/scales/24hr/@, to Big Oak Tree SP(24mi), truck repair, W Flying J/dsl/LP/RV dump/scales/24hr, Love's/Chester's/Subway/dsl/scales/24hr, repair

52 rd P, Kewanee, E Mobil/BJ Travel Center/dsl

49 US 61, US 62, New Madrid, E Hunter-Dawson HS(3mi)

44 US 61, US 62, Lp 55, New Madrid, E Casey's, Pizza Hut, Pro Pizza, Subway, $General, Chevrolet, Family$, Higgerson School Hist Site, NAPA, Riverbend RV Park

42mm rest area sb/full facilities, truck parking nb, parking nb, playground, RS, Welcome Ctr

40 rd EE, St Jude Rd, Marston, E ONE9/Subway/dsl/scales/24hr, Red Roof Inn, NAPA, W Phillips 66, Travel Inn

32 US 61, MO 162, Portageville, W Casey's, Phillips 66/dsl, China King, McDonald's, Sonic, Subway, $General

27 rds K, A, BB, to Wardell, W Delta Research Ctr

20mm **full facilities, litter barrels, petwalk, , picnic table, RS nb, vending**

HAYTI

19 MO 84, Hayti, E Double Nickel/dsl, Pilot/Arby's/dsl/scales/24hr, Shell, Burger King, McDonald's, Pizza Hut, Quality Inn, Regency Motel, Lady Luck Casino/camping, W Exxon/dsl, Chubby's BBQ, Los Portales, Drury Inn, $General, CarQuest, Hay's Foods, H, tires, USPO

17b a I-155 E, US 412, to TN

14 rds J, H, U, to Caruthersville, Braggadocio

10mm weigh sta nb

8 US 61, MO 164, Steele, E truck repair, W Shell/Subway/dsl/scales, Deerfield Inn

4 rd E, to Holland, Cooter

3mm truck parking both lanes, truck parking sb/nb

1 US 61, rd O, Holland, E Phillips 66/dsl/24hr, W Shell/dsl/24hr

0mm Missouri/Arkansas state line

INTERSTATE 57

CHARLESTON

22mm Missouri/Illinois state line, Mississippi River

18.5mm RS nb, weigh sta both lanes

12 US 62, MO 77, Charleston, E Flying J/Huddle House/dsl/scales/24hr, Eagle Inn, JSH Towing/repair, W Casey's/dsl, Cenex/dsl, Las Brisas Mexican, Waffle&Pancake House, Super 8, tires, vet

10 MO 105, Charleston, E Exxon/Boomland/dsl, McDonald's, Wally's Eatery, Boomland RV Park, W Casey's, Pizza Hut, Quality Inn, $General, city park

4 rd B, Bertrand

1b a I-55, N to St Louis, S to Memphis. I-57 begins/ends on I-55

0mm I-57 begins/ends on I-55, exit 66.

INTERSTATE 64

FOREST PARK

41mm Mississippi River, Missouri/Illinois state line

40b a Broadway St, to Stadium, to the Arch, N Drury, Hilton, Hyatt Regency, stadium, S BP/dsl/24hr, ZX/dsl, Imo's Pizza, Taco Bell, White Castle, Dobbs Tire Ctr

40c (from wb), I-44 W, I-55 S

39c 11th St(exits left), downtown

39b 14th St, downtown, S BP

39a 21st St, Market St(from wb), N Drury Inn, Hampton Inn

38d Chestnut at 20th St, N Courtyard, Fairfield Inn

38c Jefferson Ave, St Louis Union Sta, N BP/dsl, Starbucks, S Residence Inn, Advance Parts, CarQuest

38a Forest Park Blvd(from wb), N BP, S NAPA

37b a Market St, Bernard St, Grand Blvd, N Circle K, Chipotle, Jimmy John's, Starbucks, IKEA, S H

36d Vandeventer Ave, Chouteau Ave

36b a Kingshighway, N First Watch, Shake Shack, DoubleTree, Holiday Inn Express, H, Whole Foods, S BP, BP, Subway, Home2 Suites

34d c Hampton Ave, Forest Park, N museums, zoo, S BP, Phillips 66, Shell, Imo's Pizza, McDonald's, Slim Chicken, Starbucks, Steak'nShake, Subway, Taco Bell, Mercedes, Toyota

34a Oakland Ave, N Chinese Express, Einstein Bagels, Qdoba, Starbucks, H, Office Depot, Schnucks, Walgreens

33d McCausland Ave

33c Bellevue Ave, N H

33b Big Bend Blvd, N Mobil, ZX, Office Depot, S tires

32b a Eager Rd, Hanley Rd, S Circle K, QT/dsl/24hr, Tesla EVC, Andy's FroYo, Bonefish Grill, Buffalo Wild Wings, Chick-fil-A, Chipotle, Dunkin, First Watch, Five Guys, Lion's Choice, McDonald's, Panda Express, Qdoba, Red Lobster, Red Robin, Starbucks, Subway, Trader Joe's, Courtyard, Drury Inn, SpringHill Suites, TownePlace, AT&T, Best Buy, Dierberg's Foods, Dobbs Tire, Home Depot, Lowe's, PetSmart, REI, Sam Club/gas, Target, vet, Walmart, Whole Foods Mkt

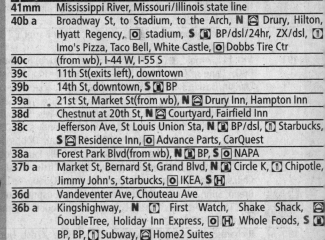

 = gas = food = lodging = other = rest stop

INTERSTATE 64 Cont'd

Exit #	Services
31b a	I-170 N, N Burger King, CA Pizza Kitchen, Cheesecake Factory, Dillard's, Five Guys, IHOP, Maggiano's, PF Chang's, St Louis Bread, Homewood Suites, CVS Drug, Macy's, mall, Nordstrom, Verizon, S Drury Inn, Bonefish Grill, Chick-fil-A, Subway, Dierberg's Foods, Michael's, Target
30	McKnight Rd
28b	Clayton Rd(from wb)
28a	US 67, US 61, Lindbergh Blvd, N Honda, S Bricktops, Brio Grill, Fleming's Rest., Starbucks, Hilton, mall, Shnuck's Foods/EVC
27	Spoede Rd
26	rd JJ, Ballas Rd, N H, S H
25	I-270, N to Chicago, S to Memphis
24	Mason Rd, N Lion's Choice, LDS Temple
23	Maryville Centre Dr(from wb), N Marriott
22	MO 141, N H, to Maryville U, S BP, Phillips 66, Dave's Rest., First Watch, Global Quesadilla , Jimmy John's, McDonald's, Melting Pot, Napoli 2, Qdoba, Starbucks, Subway, Yellowstone Cafe, Ace Hardware, REI, Schnucks, Target, USPO, vet, Whole Foods
21	Timberlake Manor Pkwy
20	Chesterfield Pkwy(from wb), same as 19b a
19b a	MO 340, Chesterfield Pkwy, Olive Blvd, N BP/dsl, Circle K, Parkway Fuels/dsl, Daylight Donuts, First Watch, Mellow Mushroom, Starbucks, DoubleTree Hotel, Fairfield Inn, Hampton Inn, Homewood Suites, Sonesta ES, Dobb's Tire, park/playground, USPO, Walgreens, S Mobil, Billy G's Diner, Cheesecake Factory, Chipotle, Crumbl Cookies, Duck Donuts, Edgewild Rest., Noodles & Co, Papa John's, PF Chang's, Smashburger, Starbucks, Which Wich, Drury Plaza Hotel, Hyatt Place, Barnes&Noble, Dierbergs Mkt, mall, Trader Joe's
17	Boones Crossing, Long Rd, Chesterfield Airport Rd, N Residence Inn, mall, S Mobil, 54th St Grill, Annie Gunn's, Bar Louie, Brickhouse Tavern, Cane's, Chick-fil-A, Chicken Salad Chick, Culver's, East Coast Pizza, Five Guys, Hardee's, IHOP, Kaldi's Coffee, Lion's Choice, McDonald's, Mimi's Cafe, Old Spaghetti Factory, Olive Garden, Original Pancakes, Panda Express, Qdoba Mexican, Red Lobster, Red Robin, Shake Shack, Sonic, St Louis Bread, Starbucks, Subway, Syberg's Grill, Taco Bell, Tropical Smoothie, Walnut Grill, Wendy's, Courtyard, Hampton Inn, Hilton Garden, Holiday Inn Express, $Tree, ALDI, AT&T, AutoZone, Best Buy, Dick's, Dobb's Tire, Firestone/auto, Ford, Home Depot, Land Rover/Jaguar, Lowe's, Michael's, Old Navy, PetSmart, Ross, Sam's Club, Target, Tesla, Tire Choice, Verizon, Walgreens, Walmart, WorldMkt
16	Long Rd(from wb)
14	Chesterfield Airport Rd(from eb), S BP/dsl, Phillips 66/dsl, Comfort Inn, TownePlace Suites, Premium Outlets/famous brands
13mm	Missouri River
11	Research Park Ctr Dr, S Research Park
10	MO 94(from wb), N Mercedes
9	rd k, O'Fallon, N BP, Mobil, QT/dsl, Cracker Barrel, Culver's, Las Margaritas, Lion's Choice, McDonald's, Popeyes, Starbucks, Subway, Taco Bell, Walnut Grill, Wendy's, Holiday Inn Express, Residence Inn, Sleep Inn, Staybridge Suites, Chevrolet, Honda, H, Jiffy Lube, URGENT CARE, Walgreens
6	rd DD, Wing Haven Blvd, N Mobil/dsl, Phillips 66, Bayon Bistro, Bristol Seafood, Outback Steaks, Subway, Sugarfire BBQ, Hilton Garden, GMC, U-Haul, vet, Walgreens, S Exxon/dsl, MotoMart/dsl
4	rd N, N ZX, Qdoba Mexican, Red Robin, JC Penney, Petco, Schnucks, Target, S Murphy USA/dsl, Phillips 66, Arby's, Cold Stone, El Maguay, Freddy's, Jack-in-the-Box, Jimmy John's, McDonald's, Panda Express, Panera Bread, Sonic, Starbucks, Steak'n Shake, Subway, Taco Bell, Wendy's, $Tree, ALDI, AutoZone, Discount Tire, Dobb's Tire, Firestone/auto, Lowe's, TJ Maxx, U-Haul, Walmart
2	Lake St. Louis Blvd, N Hucks/dsl, BC's Rest., Imo's Pizza, Old Navy, Schnuck's Foods, Von Maur, Walgreens
1	Prospect Rd
0mm	I-70 E to St Louis, W to Kansas City

O'FALLON

MO

INTERSTATE 70

Exit #	Services
251.5mm	Missouri/Illinois state line, Mississippi River
251a	I-55 S, to Memphis, to I-44, to downtown/no return
249b	Tucker Blvd, downtown St Louis, S Mobil/dsl
249a	I-44 W, I-55 S
248b	St Louis Ave, Branch St
248a	Salisbury St, McKinley Br, S BP, Phillips 66
247	Grand Ave, N BP, Phillips 66/Subway/dsl, Western Inn, S tires
246b	Adelaide Ave
246a	N Broadway, O'Fallon Park, N Love's/McDonald's/Subway/dsl/scales/24hr, Mobil/dsl, Super 8, Freightliner, Goodyear, truck tires
245b	W Florissant
245a	Shreve Ave, S BP
244b	Kingshighway, S BP, Burger King, Church's TX Chicken, Lee's Chicken, McDonald's, Rally, Subway, Taco Bell, White Castle, Walgreens
244a	Bircher Blvd, Union Blvd, N BP/dsl, Mobil/dsl
243b	(243c from eb)Bircher Blvd
243a	Riverview Blvd
243	Goodfellow Blvd, N BP, Conoco/dsl, S tires
242b a	Jennings Sta Rd, N White Castle, Family$, S Western Inn
241b	Lucas-Hunt Rd, N Circle K, S Church's TX Chicken, Domino's, Imo's Pizza, Lee's Chicken, McDonald's, Penn Sta Subs, Wingstop, O'Reilly Parts, Save-A-Lot, Walgreens
241a	Bermuda Rd, S H
240b a	Florissant Rd, N BP, BP/McDonald's, Shell/Circle K, $Tree, Family$, Save-A-Lot
239	N Hanley Rd, N Hilton Garden, S BP
238c b	I-170 N, I-170 S, no return
238a	N Lambert-St Louis, S Renaissance Hotel
237	Natural Bridge Rd(from eb), S Phillips 66, Church's TX Chicken, Jack-in-the-Box, Rally's, Steak'n Shake, Waffle House, Renaissance, St Louis, Travelodge
236	Lambert-St Louis Airport, S BP/dsl, Bandana's BBQ, Golden Pancake, Lombardo's Café Rafferty's Rest., Subway, Best Value Inn, Best Western+, DoubleTree, Drury Inn, Drury Inn, Hilton, Holiday Inn Express, Marriott/Tesla EVC, Peartree Inn, Quality Inn, Wingate
235c	Cypress Rd, rd B W, N to
235b a	US 67, Lindbergh Blvd, N SureStay+, S QT, IHOP, Lion's Choice Rest., Comfort Inn, Crowne Plaza, Embassy Suites, Extended Stay America, $Tree, Home Depot, Menard's, Schnucks Foods
234	MO 180, St Charles Rock Rd, N Phillips 66/dsl, Applebee's, Arby's, Chimi's Mexican, Chipotle, Fazoli's, Five Guys, Imo's Pizza, Jack-in-the-Box, Jimmy John's, McAlister's, New China Buffet, Ponderosa, Qdoba, Red Lobster, St Louis Bread, Starbucks, Subway, Taco Bell, Wendy's, White Castle, $Tree, ALDI, AT&T, AutoZone, CVS Drug, Hobby Lobby, H, Jiffy Lube, Kohl's, Meineke, NTB, Office Depot, PetSmart, Target, URGENT CARE , Walgreens, Walmart/Burger King, S QT, Chrysler/Dodge/Jeep,

MO

INTERSTATE 70 Cont'd

ST CHARLES

234 Continued
tire/auto repair, Walgreens

232 I-270, N to Chicago, S to Memphis

231b a Earth City Expwy, **N** Motomart, Phillips 66/Jack-in-the-Box/dsl, Courtyard, Extended Stay America, Holiday Inn, Residence Inn, Sonesta Suites, SpringHill Suites, **S** Mobil/Subway/Burger King, Dave&Buster's, Holiday Inn Express, Homewood Suites, La Quinta, Hollywood Casino/Hotel, St Louis Ampitheatre

230mm Missouri River

229b a 5th St, St Charles, **N** Mobil/dsl, Motomart/dsl, Bellacino's Italian, Buffalo Wild Wings, China House Buffet, Denny's, Dunkin', Firehouse Subs, Lee's Chicken, McDonald's, Qdoba, Smoothie King, Starbucks, TX Roadhouse, Waffle House, Best Value Inn, Best Western, Comfort Suites, Hampton Inn, ALDI, Ameristar Casino, Bass Pro Shops, URGENT CARE, Walgreens, **S** QT/dsl, Tesla EVC, Bar Louie, Cracker Barrel, Dewey's Pizza, Firebirds, First Watch, Five Guys, Mission Taco, PF Chang's, Tuscanos Brazilian, Drury Suites, Embassy Suites, Fairfield Inn, Tru

228 MO 94, to Weldon Springs, access to 227, St Charles, URGENT CARE, **N** Mobil/dsl, QT/dsl, Burger King, DQ, Imo's Pizza, Leo's Grill, Papa John's, Starbucks, Steak'n Shake, Advance Parts, CVS Drug, NAPA, Schnuck's, Valvoline, **S** Mobil/dsl, QT, ChuckECheese, Fazoli's, Gingham Homestyle, Grappa Grill, Jimmy John's, McAlister's Deli, Pizza Hut, Yummy House, Intown Suites, $General, Dobb's Tire

227 Zumbehl Rd, access to 228, **N** Phillips 66/dsl, ZX, Culpepper's Grill, Super 8, Ford, Lowe's, Sav-A-Lot Foods, **S** BP, Hucks/dsl, Applebee's, Big Woody's BBQ, Black Bear, Bob Evans, Capt D's, Chick-fil-A, Chipotle, El Mariachi Mexican, Fratelli's Ristorante, Hardee's, Hoho Chinese, McDonald's, Panda Express, Panera Bread, Penn Sta Subs, Shogun, Smashburger, Taco Bell, Candlwood Suites, $Tree, ALDI, Dierberg's Foods, Jiffy Lube, Michael's, Petco, PetSmart, Sam's Club/gas, Schnuck's Foods, URGENT CARE, URGENT CARE, Walgreens, Walmart/EVC

ST PETERS

225 Truman Rd, to Cave Springs, **N** Phillips 66/dsl, Hampton Inn, Relax Inn, Buick/GMC, Cadillac, Harley Davidson, Indian Motorcycles, Mazda, U-Haul, VW, **S** Conoco, QT, Abelardos Mexican, Advance Parts, Bandanas BBQ, Chicken Coop, Chimi's Mexican, Culver's, Denny's, Freddy's, Hooters, IHOP, Jack-in-the-Box, KFC, Lion's Choice Rest., LJ Silver, Longhorn Steaks, Mario's Donut, McDonald's, Pasta House, Red Lobster, Subway, Taco Bell, Viet-Thai, Wendy's, White Castle, Country Inn&Suites, Courtyard, $Tree, AT&T, AutoZone, Batteries+, Chrysler/Dodge/Jeep, Firestone, Hobby Lobby, Home Depot, H, Kia, Office Depot, Target, TJ Maxx, URGENT CARE, Verizon

224 MO 370 E

222 Mid-Rivers Mall Dr, rd C, St Peters, **N** QT/dsl/24hr, Burger King, Outback Steaks, CarMax, Chevrolet, Discount Tire, Honda, Lincoln, Old Navy, Ross, Toyota, **S** Mobil/dsl, Arby's, Buffalo Wild Wings, Chili's, China Wok, Domino's, First Watch, HoneyBaked Ham, McDonald's/playplace, Olive Garden, Red Robin, Ruby Tuesday, Smoothie King, St Louis Bread, Taco Bell, Wendy's, Drury Inn, Extended Stay America, ALDI, AT&T, Barnes&Noble, Best Buy, BigLots, Costco/gas, Dick's, Dillard's, Hyundai/Nissan/VW, JC Penney, Jo-Ann Fabrics, Kia, Macy's, Midas, NTB

220 MO 79, to Elsberry, **S** Phillips 66/7-11/gas, Phillips 66/dsl, El Mezon, Gettemeier's Rest., McDonald's/playplace, Pirrone's Pizzaria, Popeyes, Sonic, Subway, Days Inn,

O'FALLON

220 Continued
Holiday Inn Express, Dierberg's Foods, O'Reilly Parts, Walgreens

219 T R Hughes Blvd, **S** QT, Comfort Inn

217 rds K, M, O'Fallon, **N** Hucks/dsl, Baskin-Robbins, Burger King, Jack-in-the-Box, Pizza Hut/Taco Bell, Rally's, Waffle House, $General, Firestone, Jiffy Lube, O'Reilly Parts, **S** Mobil/dsl, Phillips 66/dsl, QT, Applebee's, Arby's, Culver's, Domino's, Dunkin, Fazoli's, Golden Corral, Jimmy John's, KFC, La Maria's, Lion's Choice Rest., McAlister's, McDonald's/playplace, Pantera's Pizza, Papa John's, Pizza Hut, Qdoba, Red Robin, Smoothie King, St Louis Bread, Stefanina's Pizza, Subway, TX Roadhouse, Wendy's, Wingstop, Advance Parts, ALDI, AutoZone, CVS Drug, Home Depot, Lowe's, Meineke, Midas, Schnuck's Foods, tire/auto repair, Verizon, Walgreens, Walmart

216 Bryan Rd, **N** Super 8, Ford, Peterbilt, St Louis RV Ctr, **S** Mobil/dsl, Phillips 66/dsl, QT, DQ, Little Caesar's, Mr. Goodcents, Starbucks, Wendy's

214 Lake St Louis, **N** Phillips 66/McDonald's/dsl, El Mezon Mexican, Jimmy John's, Pizza Hut, **S** Circle K, Phillips 66/dsl, Asabi Bistro, Denny's, El Maguey, Hardee's, Subway, Lakeview Inn, H

NEW MELLE

212 rd A, **N** Budget Inn, Economy Inn, Camping World, **S** Mobil, Chrysler/Dodge/Jeep

210b a I-64, US 40 E, US 61 N, **S** H

209 rd Z, Church St, New Melle, **N** DQ, Parlor Doughnuts, Holiday Inn Express, **S** Mobil/dsl, Burger King, Marco's Pizza, Soulard Gyro, Stone Summit Steaks, Hampton Inn

WRIGHT CITY

208 Pearce Blvd, Wentzville Pkwy, Wentzville, **N** Mobil/dsl, QT/dsl, 54th St Grill, 88 China, Applebee's, Arby's, Bob Evans, Buffalo Wild Wings, Chick-fil-A, China Buffet, Crumbl Cookies, Culver's, Domino's, El Maguey, Fritz's Custard, Hardee's, Imo's Pizza, Jack-in-the-Box, Jimmy John's, KFC, Lion's Choice, Little Caesar's, McDonald's, MOD Pizza, Olive Garden, Panda Express, Panera Bread, Papa John's, Penn Sta., Smoothie King, Starbucks, Steak'n Shake, Stefanina's Pizzeria , Sunny St Cafe, Syberg's Wentzville, Taco Bell, Waffle House, Wendy's, White Castle, Fairfield Inn, $General, ALDI, AutoZone, Chevrolet, Dick's, Dierberg's Foods, Dobb's Tire, Home Depot, H, Jiffy Lube, Kohl's, Lowe's, Michael's, Midas, O'Reilly Parts, PetSmart, Ross, Sam's Club/dsl, Save-A-Lot, Schnuck's Food, Target, URGENT CARE, Walgreens, Walmart, **S** BP/dsl, Bandana's BBQ, Chimi's FreshMex, IHOP, TX Roadhouse, Hyundai, Thomas RV Ctr

206 new exit

204mm weigh sta both lanes

203 rds W, T, Foristell, **N** Mr Fuel/dsl/scales, TA/BP/Pizza Hut/Popeyes/Taco Bell/dsl/scales/24hr/@, Quality Inn, **S** Phillips 66/McDonald's/dsl, $General, dsl repair

200 rds J, H, F (from wb), Wright City, **N** Phillips 66/dsl, Domino's, **S** BP, Ball's BBQ, New China, Subway, Super 7 Inn, USPO, vet

199 rd J, H, F, Wright City, **N** Shell/McDonald's/dsl, Wright Way Diner, $General

INTERSTATE 70 Cont'd

Exit #	Services
198mm	rest area both lanes, full facilities, litter barrels, petwalk
193	MO 47, Warrenton, N Phillips 66/dsl, Applebee's, Burger King, China House, Domino's, DQ, Jack-in-the-Box, Little Asia, McDonald's, Pizza Hut, Subway, Waffle House, Wendy's, Extended Stay, Holiday Inn Express, Super 8, ALDI, Jay's RV, Mosers Foods, Walmart, S Mobil/dsl, Phillips 66/dsl, Denny's, Imo's Pizza, Imo's Pizza, Papa John's, Taco Bell, Two Dudes BBQ, Baymont Inn, Relax Inn, antiques, AT&T, AutoZone, CarQuest, Chevrolet, NAPA, O'Reilly Parts, Schnucks Foods, tires, Valvoline, Walgreens
191	W Warrenton Blvd
188	rds A, B, to Truxton, N truck/tire repair, S Flying J/Conoco/Denny's/dsl/LP/RV Dump/scales/24hr
183	rds E, NN, Y, Jonesburg, N Jonesburg Campground, S Phillips 66/dsl, $General, USPO
179	rd F, High Hill, S Motel 70, Tree Farm Inn
175	MO 19, New Florence, N BP/dsl, Shell/dsl/24hr, McDonald's, Brady, Grandview Lodge, Knights Inn, S Love's/Arby's/Speedco/dsl/scales/24hr/@
170	MO 161, rd J, Danville, N Sinclair/dsl, Hickory Ridge Campground, to Graham Cave SP, S Lazy Day RV Park
169.5mm	truck parking
168mm	Loutre River
167mm	truck parking eb
161	rds D, YY, Williamsburg, N Cranes/mkt, Crane's Museim, USPO
155	rds A, Z, to Calwood, N antiques, I-70 RV Ctr
148	US 54, Kingdom City, N Phillips 66/Burger King/dsl, Yesway, Taco Bell, MO Tourism Ctr, to Mark Twain Lake, S Fast Lane/DQ/dsl, Petro/Mobil/Iron Skillet/dsl/scales/24hr/@, Phillips 66/Gasper's/dsl/scales/@, Phillips 66/Subway/dsl/scales/24hr, Denny's, McDonald's, Amerihost Inn, Days Inn, Frontier, Holiday Inn Express, Motel 6, Quality Inn, Ozarkland Gifts, Wheeler's Truckwash
144	rds M, HH, to Hatton
137	rds DD, J, to Millersburg, Stephens, S antiques, Freightliner, to Little Dixie WA(4mi)
133	rd Z, to Centralia, N Camping World RV, S antiques, Kenworth
131	Lake of the Woods Rd, N BP, Phillips 66/Subway/dsl, George's Rest, Jake's Grill, Las Margaritas, Sonic, Super 8, Harley-Davidson, O'Rellly Parts, S Phillips 66/dsl, Jimmy John's, Holiday Inn/Tesla EVC
128a	US 63, to Jefferson City, Columbia, N Mobil/dsl, QT, Bandanas BBQ, Bob Evans, Burger King, Casey's, China Garden, Cracker Barrel, El Jimador Mexican, Hooters, KFC, McDonald's, Pizza Hut, Steak'n Shake, Taco Bell, Wendy's, White Castle, Best Western+, Candlewood Suites, Fairfield Inn, Hampton Inn, Hilton Garden, Residence Inn, Springhill Suites, Super 8, $General, Bass Pro Shop, Home Depot, Menard's, Pine Grove RV Park, S MFA Oil/dsl, Andy's Frozen Yogurt, Applebee's, Big Mama's Cafe, Chicken Salad Chick, Chili's, Chipotle Mexican, CiCi's, Crumbl Cookies, Culver's, Firehouse Subs, Five Guys, Freddy's, IHOP, Kobe Japanese, La Tolteca, Little Caesar's, Longhorn Steaks, Med Mex Cafe, MOD Pizza, Noodles & Co, Panda Express, Panera Bread, Quickway Japanese, Sonic, Starbucks, Subway, TGIFriday's, Walk-On's, Wingstop, Country Inn&Suites, Drury Plaza, Motel 6, Quality Inn, Ramada, Staybridge Suites, Suburban Inn, Wingate Inn, $Tree, ALDI, Firestone, H, HyVee Foods, Lowe's/Subway, Moser's Foods, Sam's Club, Staples, Walmart/McDonald's
128	Lp 70(from wb), same as 128a, Columbia, N Phillips 66,
128	Continued Domino's, Lee's Chicken, Sonic, Honda, O'Reilly Parts, S Abelardo's Mexican, Big Daddy's BBQ, Ace Hardware, Big O Tire, H, H, NAPA
127	MO 763, to Moberly, Columbia, N Waffle House, $General, auto repair, Chrysler/Dodge/Jeep, Dobbs Tires, Fiat, Hyundai, Mazda, Toyota, transmissions, VW, S Phillips 66/dsl, Super 7 Motel
126	MO 163, Providence Rd, same as 127, Columbia, N Cenex/dsl, JJ's Cafe, Red Roof Inn, Welcome Inn, CarQuest, flea mkt, tires, S BreakTime/dsl, Big Daddy's BBQ, Burger King, Carlito's Mexican, Church's TX Chicken, DQ, LJ Silver, McDonald's, Popeyes, Subway, Taco Bell, AutoZone, Buick/Cadillac/Chevrolet/GMC, Nissan, O'Reilly Parts
125	Lp 70, West Blvd, same as 124, Columbia, N Comfort Suites, S Phillips 66/dsl, Agave Mexican, Cheddar's, Fazoli's, Fazoli's, Imo's Pizza, Just Jeff's, Mugs Up, Olive Garden, Red Lobster, Syrian Kitchen, ALDI, BMW, Firestone/auto, Food Bank Mkt, Kia, Mercedes, Subaru, U-Haul, vet
124	MO 740, rd E, Stadium Blvd, same as 125, Columbia, N Extended Stay America, S Phillips 66, Phillips 66/dsl, Applebee's, AutoZone, Chick-fil-A, Chipotle, Culver's, Five Guys, Jazz Kitchen, KFC, McDonald's, Pancheros, Panera Bread, Pizza Hut, Smokehouse BBQ, Steak'n Shake, Subway, Taco Bell, TX Roadhouse, Wendy's, Drury Inn, Holiday Inn, La Quinta, $Tree, Ace Hardware, AT&T, auto repair, Barnes&Noble, Best Buy, Dick's, Dillard's, Ford, Hobby Lobby, JC Penney, Jiffy Lube, Marshalls, Michael's, O'Reilly Parts, Old Navy, Petco, PetSmart, Target, to U of MO, URGENT CARE, Verizon
122mm	Perche Creek
121	US 40, rd UU, Midway, N Midway/dsl/rest., Budget Inn, $General, fireworks, S golf
117	rds J, O, to Huntsdale, Harrisburg
115	rd BB N, Rocheport, N to Katy Tr SP, winery
114.5mm	Missouri River
111	MO 98, MO 179, to Wooldridge, Overton, N Peach Tree Farm, S Cenex/dsl/repair
106	MO 87, Bingham Rd, to Boonville, N tires, S Cenex/dsl, Northwood Diner, The 87 Diner, auto repair
104mm	rest area both lanes, full facilities, litter barrels, petwalk, vending
103	rd B, Main St, Boonville, N Breaktime, Casey's/dsl, Murphy USA/dsl, China One Buffet, La Hacienda Mexican, McDonald's, Pizza Hut, Sonic, Subway, Taco Bell, Days Inn, Super 8, H, NAPA, RV Express Camping, to Katy Tr SP, Walmart/Subway, S Cenex/dsl, Rte B Cafe, QT Inn, Buick/Chevrolet/GMC
101	US 40, MO 5, to Boonville, N Pilot/Dunkin/dsl/scales/24hr, Arby's, Holiday Inn Express, Isle of Capri Hotel(3mi), Quality Inn, Chrysler/Dodge/Jeep/Ram, Ford, Goodyear, S Love's/Hardee's/scales/dsl/24hr, to Lake of the Ozarks, Speedco
98	MO 41, MO 135, Lamine, N auto repair, to Arrow Rock HS(13mi), S Cenex/dsl, truck repair
93mm	Lamine River
89	rd K, to Arrow Rock, N to Arrow Rock HS
84	rd J, N Cooper's Coffee, DQ, truck repair
78b a	US 65, to Marshall, N Phillips 66/dsl, fireworks
77mm	Blackwater River
74	rd YY, N Cenex/Betty's/cafe/dsl/repair/24hr, Betty's
71	rds EE, K, to Houstonia
66	MO 127, Sweet Springs, N EVC, S BreakTime/dsl, Casey's/dsl, Sherry Lynn's Diner, Night Inn, Super 8, $General

= gas = food = lodging = other = rest stop

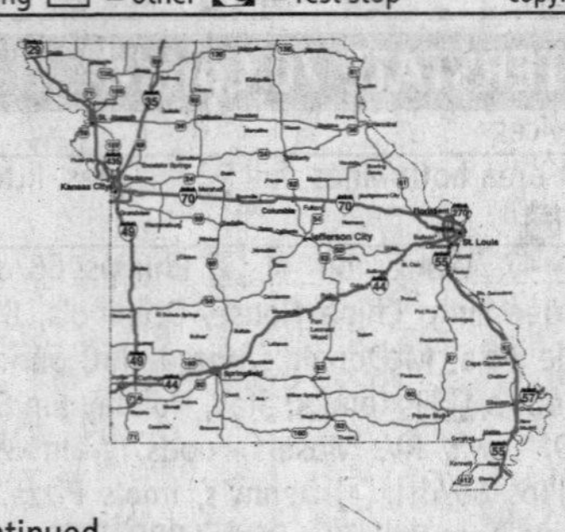

CONCORDIA ODESSA OAK GROVE BLUE SPRINGS

INTERSTATE 70 Cont'd

Exit #	Services
65.5mm	Davis Creek
62	rds VV, Y, Emma
58	MO 23, Concordia, N TA/Shell/Country Pride/Subway/dsl/scales/24hr/@, El Patron Mexican, McDonald's, Seven Days Diner, $General, Bratchers Mkt, S Casey's/dsl/Tesla EVCz, Cenex/dsl, Cree-Mee Freeze, Dempsey's BBQ, Budget Inn, Days Inn, Econolodge, Bumper Parts, tires
57.5mm	rest area both lanes, full facilities, litter barrels, petwalk, , vending
52	rd T, Aullville
49	MO 13, to Higginsville, N Casey's/dsl, Pilot/McDonald's/Subway/dsl/scales/24hr, Sure Stay Inn, to Confederate Mem, S Super 8, Great Escape RV Park
45	rd H, to Mayview
43mm	weigh sta both lanes
41	rds O, M, to Lexington, Mayview, S Surplus Grocery
38	MO 131(from wb), same as 37, Odessa, S BP/dsl, Shell, Sinclair/dsl, El Tucan Mexican, McDonald's, Pizza Hut, Sonic, Taco John's, Parkside Inn, $General, NAPA, O'Reilly Parts
37	MO 131, same as 38, Odessa, N Owl Creek RV Park, S El Camino Real, Chrysler/Dodge/Jeep/Ram, fireworks, truck repair
35mm	truck parking both lanes
31	rds D, Z, to Bates City, Napoleon, N Love's/Subway/RV Hookup/dsl/scales/24hr, Bates City RV Camping, S Valero/dsl, Baskin-Robbin's, Bate's City Cafe, Bates City BBQ, antiques, fireworks
29.5mm	Horse Shoe Creek
28	rd H, rd F, Oak Grove, N Shell/TA/Popeyes/dsl/scales/24hr/@, Oak Grove Inn, Blue Beacon, KOA, S Casey's, Petro/BP/DQ/Wendy's/scales/dsl/@, QT/dsl, China Buffet, KFC/Taco Bell, McDonald's, OG Donut, Pizza Hut, PT's Rest., Scooter's Coffee, Subway, Tepoz Mexican, Waffle House, EconoLodge, Holiday Inn Express, $Tree, Hy-Vee Foods, O'Reilly Parts, SpeedCo Lube, Walgreens, Walmart
24	US 40, rds AA, BB, to Buckner, N Casey's/dsl, QT/dsl, Burger King, Culver's, Panda Express, Papa Murphy's, Starbucks, Starbucks, Taco Bell, Best Value Inn, Comfort Inn, Camping World RV, KC RV, LifeStyle RV Ctr, Price Chopper, vet, S Temp Stop/Amoco/dsl, McDonald's, Sonic, Advance Parts, antique, Trailside RV Park/Ctr
21	Adams Dairy Pkwy, S Murphy USA/dsl, Phillips 66/Burger King/dsl, Arby's, Cane's, Chick-fil-A, Chipotle Mexican, Five Guys, Hawaiian Bros, IHOP, MOD Pizza, Olive Garden, Panda Express, Panera Bread, Sonic, Taco Bell, TX Roadhouse, Wingstop, Courtyard, AT&T, Big O Tires, Home Depot, Kohl's, Michael's, Old Navy, PetCo, Ross, Target, TJ Maxx, URGENT CARE, Verizon, Walmart
20	MO 7, Blue Springs, N Casey's/dsl, Phillips 66/dsl, QT/dsl, Backyard Burger, Casa Mexico, China 1, Custard's, Dunkin', Goodcents Subs, Minsky's Pizza, Rancho Grande, Scooter's Coffee, Sonic, Subway, The Pizza Place, Days Inn, Extended Stay, Super 8, $General, Ace Hardware, CVS Drug, NAPA, O'Reilly Parts, PriceChopper Foods, Valvoline, Walgreens, Walmart Mkt, S BP/dsl, Conoco/dsl, Andy's Custard, Applebee's, Big Biscuit, Domino's, Firehouse Subs, Jack-in-the-Box, Jimmy John's, KFC, Marco's Pizza, McDonald's, Mo Bettahs Hawaiian, Popeyes, Ranchos Mexican, Smoothie King, Starbucks, Subway, Tacos 4 Life, Tropical Smoothie, Vito's Pizza, Wendy's, Whataburger, Zarda's BBQ, Hampton Inn, Sure Stay+, Advance Parts, ALDI, auto repair, Chevrolet, Firestone/auto, Hobby Lobby,
20	Continued H, Jiffy Lube, Midas, Office Depot, transmissions
18	Woods Chapel Rd, same as 20, N Casey's/dsl, La Quinta, Motel 6, Quality Inn, Welcome Inn, Harley-Davidson, S Phillips 66/dsl, QT/dsl, China Kitchen, KFC/Taco Bell, La Fuente Mexican, Las Playas Mexican, McDonald's, Pizza Hut, Scooter's Coffee, Sonic, Subway, Taco John's, Waffle House, $Tree, CVS Drug, Ford, Hyundai
17	Little Blue Pkwy, 39th St, N QT/dsl, Black Bear Diner, Buffalo Wild Wings, Coldstone, DQ, Dutch Bros Coffee, Hereford House, Lion's Choice, On the Border, Saints Grill, Sonic, Twin Peaks, Wendy's, Hilton Garden, H, Menard's, World Mkt, S QT, Arby's, BD Mongolian, Carrabba's, Chipotle Mexican, Corner Cafe, Crumbl Cookies, Culver's, Golden Corral, Hooters, IHOP, Kobe Steaks, McDonald's, Panera Bread, Red Robin, Shawarmar, Subway, Whataburger, Comfort Suites, Drury Inn, Holiday Inn Express, My Place, auto/tires, Candlewood Suites, Carmax, Costco/gas, Lowe's
16mm	Little Blue River, Little Blue River
15b	MO 291 N, Independence, Starbucks, Staybridge Suites, AT&T, H, N Casey's, EVC, QT, Chick-fil-A, Chili's, ChuckECheese, Fazoli's, Longhorn Steaks, McDonald's, Perkins, Smokehouse BBQ, Smoothie King, Sonic, Starbucks, Taco Bell, Best Western, Residence Inn, $Tree, AutoZone, Best Buy, Dick's, Dillard's, Kohl's, mall, Marshalls, PetSmart, Ross, Sam's Club/gas, Target, URGENT CARE, Walmart
15a	I-470 S, MO 291 S, to Lee's Summit, same as 14
14	Lee's Summit Rd, S Sunoco/dsl, Tesla EVC, Cheddar's, Cracker Barrel, Los Cabos, Old Chicago, Pizza Ranch, Slim Chickens, Twisted Tenders, Stoney Creek Hotel, Bass Pro Shops, Duluth Trading, Hobby Lobby, Home Depot
12	Noland Rd, Independence, N Conoco/dsl, QT, Andy's Custard, Batteries+, Denny's, Goodcents, Hacienda Vieja, Hardee's, Hawaiian Bros, Jimmy John's, Little Caesars, Pizza St, Sonic, The Lunch Box , Clarion Pointe, Super 8, $General, Advance Parts, AutoZone, Bridgestone, Buick, GMC/Cadillac, Chevrolet, Chrysler/Jeep, CVS Drug, Firestone/auto, Ford, Office Depot, to Truman Library, Walgreens, Walmart Mkt, S $General, Arby's, Baskin-Robbins, Burger King, Five Guys, HoneyBaked Ham, Jack-in-the-Box, KFC/Taco Bell, Ma Ma Garden, McDonald's, Olive Garden, Panda Express, Red Lobster, Scooter's Coffee, Taco John's, Wendy's, Best Value Inn, Countryside Suites, Days Inn, Quality Inn, BigLots, HyVee Foods/gas, Petco, PriceChopper Mkt, Tires+, U-Haul
11	US 40, Blue Ridge Blvd, Independence, N QT/dsl, A&W/LJ Silver, La Fuentes, Rosie's Cafe, Sonic, Subway, V's Italian, ALDI, S 7-11, BP, Murphy USA/dsl, Sinclair, Big Boy Burgers, Church's TX Chicken, Firehouse Subs, IHOP, McDonald's, Papa John's, Starbucks, AT&T, Family$, Lowe's, O'Reilly Parts, Thai Spice, Verizon, vet, Walmart, Subway
10	Sterling Ave(from eb), same as 11
9	Blue Ridge Cutoff(from wb), N Extended Stay,

BLUE SPRINGS INDEPENDENCE

INTERSTATE 70 Cont'd

Exit	Services
9	Continued Hotel Lotus, **S** [gas] BP, Casey's/Subway, [food] Taco Bell, [lodging] Best Western, [other] Sports Complex
8b a	I-435, N to Des Moines, S to Wichita
7b	Manchester Trafficway, **S** [lodging] Arrowhead Inn
7mm	Blue River
7a	US 40 E, 31st St
6	Van Brunt Blvd, **N** [gas] Conoco/7-11, Phillips 66/dsl, [food] Golden Seafood, **S** [gas] BP, [food] McDonald's, Yummy's Donut Palace, [other] $General, auto repair, tires, VA [H]
5c	Jackson Ave(from wb)
5b	31st St(from eb)
5a	27th St(from eb)
4c	23rd Ave
4b	18th St
4a	Benton Blvd(from eb), Truman Rd, **N** [gas] Super Stop/ Wendy's/dsl, [food] Subway, [other] Advance Parts, Save-A-Lot Foods
3c	Prospect Ave, **N** [gas] BP, [food] Church's TX Chicken, **S** McDonald's, Taco Bell
3b	Brooklyn Ave(from eb), **N** [gas] BP, [food] Church's TX Chicken, **S** McDonald's
3a	Paseo St, **S** [gas] BP/dsl, [other] tires
2m	US 71 S, downtown
2l	I-670, to I-35 S
2j	11th St, downtown
2g	I-29/35 N, US 71 N, to Des Moines
2h	US 24 E, downtown
2e	MO 9 N, Oak St, **S** [gas] Phillips 66, [lodging] Marriott
2d	Main St, downtown
2c	US 169 N, Broadway, **S** [gas] Phillips 66, [lodging] Marriott
2b	Beardsley Rd
2a	I-35 S, to Wichita
0mm	Missouri/Kansas state line, Kansas River

BROADWAY

INTERSTATE 270 (St Louis)

Exit	Services
15b a	I-55 N to Chicago, S to St Louis. I-270 begins/ends in Illinois on I-55/I-70, exit 20.
12	IL 159, to Collinsville, **N** [gas] QT/dsl, ZX/dsl, [food] Annie's Custard, Applebee's, Culver's, Denny's, Hardee's, Jack-in-the-Box, Jimmy John's, KFC, Little Caesar's, Papa John's, Scooter's Coffee, [other] ALDI, AT&T, Chrysler/Dodge/Jeep, Home Depot, Lowe's, Midas, PetSmart, Sam's Club/dsl, Target, Walgreens, Walmart, **S** [H]
9	IL 157, to Collinsville, **N** [food] Comfort Inn, **S** [gas] BP/dsl, [lodging] Hampton Inn
7	I-255, to I-55 S to Memphis
6b a	IL 111, **N** [gas] Flying J/Denny's/dsl/scales/24hr, Speedway/ dsl, [food] Burger King, Hen House Rest., [lodging] Hotel Camelot, [other] Blue Beacon/scales, Speedco, truck/trailer repair, **S** [gas] Mobil/dsl, [food] McDonald's/playplace, Rosati's Pizza, Taco Bell, Taco Shack, [lodging] Best Western+, Days Inn, Fairfield Inn, La Quinta, Super 8, [other] to Pontoon Beach
4	IL 203, Old Alton Rd, to Granite City
3b a	IL 3, **N** [other] Riverboat Casino, **S** [food] Hardee's, Waffle House, [lodging] Budget Motel, EconoLodge, Economy Inn, Sun Motel, [other] KOA, Trails End RV
2mm	Chain of Rocks Canal Bridge
0mm	Illinois/Missouri state line, Mississippi River
34	Riverview Dr, to St Louis, **Welcome Ctr/[RS] both lanes, full [handicapped] facilities, info, litter barrels, [phone], litter barrels, [picnic]**, **N** [gas] Mobil, Moto Mart/Subway
33	Lilac Ave, **N** [other] USPO, **S** [gas] Phillips 66/Jack-in-the-Box/dsl, QT/dsl/scales/24hr, [food] Hardee's
32	Bellefontaine Rd, **N** [gas] Circle K, [food] Burger King, China King, McDonald's, Steak'n Shake, [lodging] Budget Inn, [other] $Tree,
32	Continued Advance Parts, Schnuck's Foods, **S** [gas] BP, [food] White Castle, [other] ALDI
31b a	MO 367, **N** [gas] BP, QT/dsl/24hr, [food] Imo's Pizza, McDonalds, Taco Bell, [other] $General, CVS Drug, Family$, [H], U-Haul, Walgreens
30b a	Hall's Ferry Rd, rd AC, **N** [gas] Conoco/dsl, QT/dsl, Shell/dsl, [food] Applebee's, Capt. D's, Donut Delight, White Castle, [lodging] Knights Inn, [other] Ford/Lincoln, Kia, **S** [gas] Phillips 66, Phillips 66, [food] China Wok, Church's TX Chicken, Steak'n Shake, Subway, [other] AutoZone, Family$, Home Depot, Meineke, O'Reilly Parts
29	W Florissant Rd, **N** [food] China Moon, Jack-in-the-Box, [other] ALDI, Dobb's Tire/auto, Family$, Ross, **S** [gas] Phillips 66/dsl, QT/dsl, [food] Arby's, Burger King, Domino's, Krispy Kreme, Little Caesar's, McDonald's, Starbucks, [other] $General, $Tree, AT&T, NTB, Sam's Club/gas, Walmart
28	Elizabeth Ave, Washington St, **N** [gas] Phillips 66/dsl, [food] Jack-in-the-Box, Taco Bell, [other] Chevrolet, Schnuck's Foods, Walgreens
27	New Florissant Rd, rd N, **N** [gas] CVS Drug, Shell/Circle K
26b	Graham Rd, N Hanley, **N** [gas] Phillips 66/7-11/dsl, [food] A&W Rest., Arby's, Starbucks, [lodging] Quality Inn, Red Roof Inn, [other] $Tree, [H], **S** [food] McDonald's, [lodging] Days Inn, Extend A Stay, [other] $General
26a	I-170 S
25b a	US 67, Lindbergh Blvd, **N** [gas] Capt D, Phillips 66, Phillips 66, QT/dsl, [food] Bandana's BBQ, Church's TX Chicken, Domino's, Dunkin, Five Guys, IHOP, Imo's Pizza, Jimmy John's, Kelly's Donut, McDonald's, Panda Express, Penn Sta Subs, Smoothie King, Starbucks, Subway, Taco Bell, Waffle House, Wendy's, [lodging] Best Western, Comfort Inn, InTown Suites, La Quinta, [other] $General, $Tree, AT&T, AutoZone, Batteries+, Dierberg's Deli, Discount Tire, EVC, Family$, Firestone/auto, Ford, Hyundai, Midas, Nissan, O'Reilly Parts, RV Ctr, Sav-a-Lot Foods, Schnuck's Foods, Toyota, U-Haul, Walgreens, Walgreens, **S** [gas] Phillips 66, [food] Jimmy John's, [lodging] Budget Inn, HomeTowne, [other] Honda, VW
23	McDonnell Blvd, **N** [food] Burger King, **E** Denny's, La Nortena Mexican, [lodging] Motel 6, **W** [gas] Mobil/dsl, QT/dsl, [food] Arby's, Jack-in-the-Box, Lion's Choice, McDonald's, Subway, Taco Bell, Tony's Donuts
22b a	MO 370 W, to MO Bottom Rd
20c	MO 180, St Charles Rock Rd, **E** [gas] Phillips 66/dsl, [food] Applebees, Arby's, Chick-fil-A, Chimi's Mexican, Chipotle, Fazoli's, Five Guys, Imo's Pizza, Jack-in-the-Box, Jimmy John's, McAlister's, New China Buffet, Qdoba, Red Lobster, St Louis Bread, Starbucks, Subway, Taco Bell, Wendy's, White Castle, [other] $Tree, ALDI, AT&T, AutoZone, Best Buy, CVS Drug, Hobby Lobby, [H], Kohl's, NTB, Office Depot, PetSmart, Target, URGENT CARE, Walgreens, Walmart, **W** [gas] QT, [food] Bob Evans, Olive Garden, Waffle House, [lodging] Quality Inn, The Lodge
20b a	I-70, E to St Louis, W to Kansas City
17	Dorsett Rd, **E** [food] Bandana's BBQ, Papa John's, Syberg's Grill, Waffle House, [lodging] Best Western+, Hampton Inn, [other] Schnucks, **W** [gas] Circle K, Mobil, Phillips 66/dsl, [food] Denny's, Firehouse Subs, McDonald's, MOD Pizza, [lodging] Motel 6, [other] Schnuck's Mkt, Walgreens
16b a	Page Ave, rd D, MO 364 W, **E** [gas] BP, Circle K/dsl, QT, [food] Hooters, McDonald's, Spazio Café, St Louis Bread, Starbucks, [lodging] Comfort Inn, Courtyard, Craigshire Suites, Days Inn, DoubleTree, Extended Stay America, Extended Stay America (2), Extended Stay America (3), Fairfield Inn, La Quinta/EVC, Red Roof Inn, Residence Inn, Sheraton, Sheraton, Sonesta Suites, Staybridge Suites, [other] USPO
14	MO 340, Olive Blvd, **E** [gas] CVS Drug, Phillips 66/dsl, [food] Applebee's, Bristol Cafe, Chipotle, First Watch, Five Guys, Imo's Pizza, Lion's Choice Rest., McDonald's, Pasta House,

N HANLEY

MO

MO

INTERSTATE 270 (St Louis) Cont'd

14 Continued
Pei Wei, Pizza Hut, Potbelly, Qdoba, Sauce on the Side, Starbucks, Courtyard, Drury Inn, ALDI, BMW/Audi/Infiniti, Chevrolet, Dierberg's Mkt, Land Rover/Jaguar/EVC, Lexus, Mercedes, Trader Joe's, URGENT CARE, Verizon, W Buffalo Wild WIngs, Burger King, Chicken Salad Chick, Coldstone, Gulf Shores Rest., HuHot Grill, Ichiban Japanese, IMO's Pizza, Jersey Mike's Sub, Jet's Pizza, La Bonne Cafe, McAlister's, Penn Sta Subs, Pizza World, Santa Fe Bistro, Shack, Subway, Holiday Inn Express, $Tree, Batteries+, Dierberg's Foods, H, Kohl's, Marshalls, Office Depot, Petco, Schnuck's Mkt, TJ Maxx, vet, Walgreens

13 rd AB, Ladue Rd

12b a I-64, US 40, US 61, E to St Louis, W to Wentzville, E H

9 MO 100, Manchester Rd, E Cane's, Casa de Tres Reyes, Chick-fil-A, Chick-fil-A, Five Guys, Imo's Pizza, J Gilbert's Rest., Jersey Mike's Subs, Jimmy John's, McAlister's Deli, McDonald's, Village Bar, Wan Fu Chinese, ALDI, Barnes&Noble, JCPenney, Lion's Choice, Macy's, Michaels, Nordstrom, Schnuck's, TJ Maxx, USPO, Walgreens, W Circle K, Chipotle, Crumbl Cookies, Red Robin, Rosalita's Cantina, St Louis Bread, Sam's Club, Trader Joe's

8 Dougherty Ferry Rd, S H

7 Big Ben Rd

5b a I-44, US 50, MO 366, E to St Louis, W to Tulsa

3 MO 30, Gravois Rd, N Amoco, Bandana BBQ, Ford

2 MO 21, Tesson Ferry Rd, N BP, Mobil, 54th St Grill, Baskin Robbins, Church's TX Chicken, Coldstone, El Maguey Mexican, Freddy's, Jersey Mike's Subs, Jimmy John's, Joey B's, McDonald's, Olive Garden, Outback Steaks, Panda Chinese, Red Lobster, Shogun Japanese, TGIFriday's, Waffle House, White Castle, Acura, AutoZone, Buick/GMC, Dobb's Auto, Honda, O'Reilly Parts, Schnuck's Foods, Toyota, Walgreens, S Circle K/dsl, Chevy's Mexican, Crumbl Cookies, Dierberg's Foods, Firehouse Subs, Jack-in-the-Box, St Louis Bread, Starbucks, $Tree, AT&T, Firestone, H, URGENT CARE, Walgreens

1b a I-55 N to St Louis, S to Memphis

INTERSTATE 435 (Kansas City)

OVERLAND PARK

83 I-35, N to KS City, S to Wichita

82 Quivira Rd, Overland Park, N H, S Domino's, Freddy's, Hawaiian Bros, McDonald's, Panera Bread, Scooter's Coffee, Starbucks, Starbucks, Subway, Taco Bell, Extended Stay America, MainStay Suites, Ace Hardware, CVS Drug, Hen House Mkt, tires, Valvoline, vet

81 US 69 S, to Ft Scott, S DoubleTree

80 Antioch Rd

79 Metcalf Ave, N Conoco, Conoco/7-11, Phillips 66/dsl, Buffalo Wild Wings, Carrabba's, Chartroose Caboose, ChuckECheese, D'Bronx Pizza, Denny's, Fox&Hound, Hardee's, Hooters, Jack-in-the-Box, Jose Pepper's, Krispy Kreme, Lion's Choice, Scooter's Coffee, Subway, Days Inn, Embassy Suites, Extended Stay America, Hampton Inn, Homewood Suites, Motel 6, Quality Inn, Savai Hotel/EVC, Staybridge Suites, H, Office Depot, vet, Walmart Mkt, S Applebee's, McDonald's, Panera Bread, Drury Inn, Marriott

77b a Nall Ave, Roe Ave, N QT, Brobeck's BBQ, Crushed Red, Freddy's, Goodcents, McLain's Mkt, Scooter's Coffee, Sonic, Winstead's Grill, SpringHill Suites, USPO, S Wendy's, Courtyard, Extended Stay America, Hilton Garden, Holiday Inn, Hyatt Place, Overland Conv Ctr

75b State Line Rd, N Casey's, Gate's BBQ, Jimmy John's, McDonald's, Taco Bell, Buick/GMC/Cadillac/EVC,

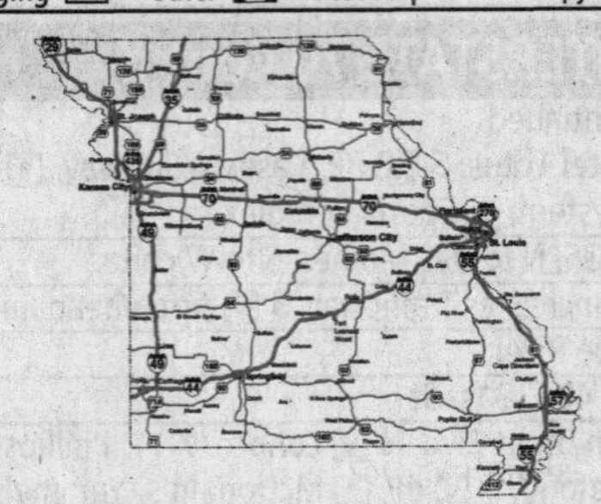

75b Continued
Chrysler/Dodge/Jeep/Ram, Goodyear/auto, Midas, O'Reilly Parts, PriceChopper Foods, S QT/dsl, city park, H

75a Wornall Rd, N QT, Dunkin', Fuzzy's Taco Shop, Pizza Hut, Acura, Audi, Chevrolet, Honda, Nissan, Price Chopper, Toyota, VW

74 Holmes Rd, N Phillips 66/dsl, Lamar's Donuts, Thai House, H, S Extended Stay America, Sonesta

73 103rd St(from wb)

71b a I-470/US 50 E, I-49/US 71S

70 Bannister Rd, E Minit Mart, Phillips 66, Church's TX Chicken, Hardee's, Pizza Hut, Taco Bell, Wendy's, Hampton Inn, Family$, Price Chopper, Walgreens, W Big Momma's, Chick-In Waffle, Firestone/auto, Home Depot

69 87th St., E Phillips 66/dsl, QT, Little Caesars, Luna's, McDonald's, New China, $General, Advance Parts, Family$, Save-A-Lot, W Days Inn

67 Gregory Blvd(same as 66a b), W Nature Ctr, zoo

66 MO 350 E, 63rd st

65 Eastwood Tfwy, W Phillips 66, Charlie D's, McDonald's, New Wok, Peachtree Rest.

63c Raytown Rd, Stadium Dr(nb only), E to Sports Complex

63b a I-70, W to KC, E to St Louis

61 MO 78, E Fisca/dsl, W tires

60 MO 12 E, Truman Rd, 12th St, E Phillips 66/dsl, fireworks, W QT

59 US 24, Independence Ave, E Conoco, tires, tires, to Truman Library, W Hardee's, Ace Hardware, Advance Parts, ALDI, Family$, vet

57 Front St, E Flying J/dsl/scales/24hr, Blue Beacon, Kenworth, W Phillips 66/dsl, QT, Sinclair/dsl, Denny's, McDonald's, Waffle House, Howard Johnson Plaza, Quality Inn, URGENT CARE

56mm Missouri River

55b a MO 210, E Phillips 66/dsl, Pilot/PJ Fresh/dsl/scales/24hr, Subway, Ameristar Hotel/Casino, Motel 6, Ford, Volvo/GMC/Mercedes Trucks

54 48th St, Parvin Rd, E Panda Express, W QT, Burger King, Taco Bell, Waffle House, Wendy's, Best Western, Candlewood Suites, Comfort Inn, Hampton Inn, Holiday Inn, Hometowne, Springhill Suites, Super 8, Wingate

52a US 69, E Phillips 66/dsl, W Aberlado's, McDonald's, Pizza Hut, Subway, $General, $Tree

52b I-35, S to KC

51 Shoal Creek Dr, W LDS Temple

49b a MO 152 E, to I-35 N, Liberty, E Starbucks, W Casey's

47 NE 96th St

46 NE 108th St

45 MO 291, NE Cookingham Ave, to I-35 N

42 N Woodland Ave

41b a US 169, Smithville

40 NW Cookingham

37 NW Skyview Ave, rd C, N Conoco, S golf(3mi)

36 to I-29 S, to KCI Airport, N Cenex, S Scott's BBQ, Extended Stay America/EVC, Fairfield Inn, Holiday Inn,

LIBERTY

INTERSTATE 435 (Kansas City) Cont'd

Exit	Services
36	Continued Marriott, Microtel, Orangewood Inn, Quality Suites, Sheraton, Super 8, TownePlace
31	I-29 N, to St Joseph, S to KC, Prairie Creek
29	rd D, NW 120th St
24	MO 152, rd N, NW Berry Rd
22	MO 45, Weston, Parkville, E The Station/DiBella's Pizza/dsl, Plaza Mariachi, Taco Bell, W Burger King, Creekside/EVC, Holiday Inn Express
20mm	Missouri/Kansas state line, Missouri River
18	KS 5 N, Wolcott Dr, E to Wyandotte Co Lake Park
16	Donohoo Rd
15b a	Leavenworth Rd, E Casey's/dsl, Comfort Suites, vet
14b a	Parallel Pkwy, E Phillips 66/dsl, Freddy's, Chrysler/Dodge/Jeep/Ram, Ford, Honda, H, Nissan, Toyota, W Phillips 66/Subway/dsl, Applebee's, Bob Evans, Burger King, Chili's, Chipotle Mexican, Culver's, Danny's Grill, Dave&Buster's, Dutch Bros Coffee, El Toro Loco, Five Guys, Granite City Rest, Hooters, IHOP, Jack-in-the-Box, La Fuente Mexican, Longhorn Sreaks, McDonald's, Olive Garden, Panda Express, Panera Bread, Pizza Hut, Red Lobster, Starbucks, Stix Asian, Taco Bell, Wendy's, Whatburger, Candlewood Suites, Country Inn&Suites, Holiday Inn Express, Homewood Suites, Residence Inn, ALDI, AT&T, Big O TIres, JC Penney, Kohl's, Old Navy, Sam's Club/dsl, Target/Starbucks, TJ Maxx, Verizon, Walmart
13b a	US 24, US 40, State Ave, E Camping World RV, W Famous Dave's BBQ, Best Western, Great Wolf Lodge, Hampton Inn, Bass Pro Shops, KS Speedway,

BONNER SPRINGS

Exit	Services
13b a	Continued Russell Stovers
12b a	I-70, KS Tpk, to Topeka, St Louis
11	Kansas Ave
9	KS 32, KS City, Bonner Springs, W Conoco/dsl
8b	Woodend Rd, E Peterbilt, W Shell/Subway/dsl/scales
8.8mm	Kansas River
8a	Holliday Dr, to Lake Quivira
6c	Johnson Dr
6b a	Shawnee Mission Pkwy, E Chili's, IHOP, Jersey Mike's, McDonald's, Pizza Hut, ALDI, AT&T, Batteries+, Big O Tires, Home Depot, Kohl's, Lowe's, Michael's, PetSmart, Ross, Target/Starbucks, Walmart/Subway
5	Midland Dr, Shawnee Mission Park, E Conoco, Phillips 66/7-11/dsl, Barley's Brewhaus, Eggtc, Jose Pepper's Grill, Minsky's Pizza, Paulo&Bill's Ristorante, Wendy's, Yos Donuts, Comfort Inn&Suites, Fairfield Inn, Hampton Inn, W Hereford House, Courtyard, Holiday Inn Express
3	87th Ave, E Phillips 66/dsl, Chick-fil-A, Chipotle, Culver's, Daylight Donuts, Freddy's, Hawaiian Bros, Lucky Wok Grill, McDonald's, MOD Pizza, Panera Bread, Papa John's, Papa Murphy's, Red Door Grill, Rudy's Mexican, Sonic, Starbucks, Taco Bell, The Big Biscuit, Ace Hardware, ALDI, Sprouts Mkt, URGENT CARE, vet, Walgreens, W Grand St Cafe, Hen House Mkt, Jack Stack BBQ, Hyatt Place, SpringHIll Suites
2	95th St, W Casey's, Jimmy John's
1b	KS 10, to Lawrence
1a	Lackman Rd, N QT/dsl, Studio 6
0mm	I-435 begins/ends on I-35.

MO

NOTES

MONTANA

INTERSTATE 15

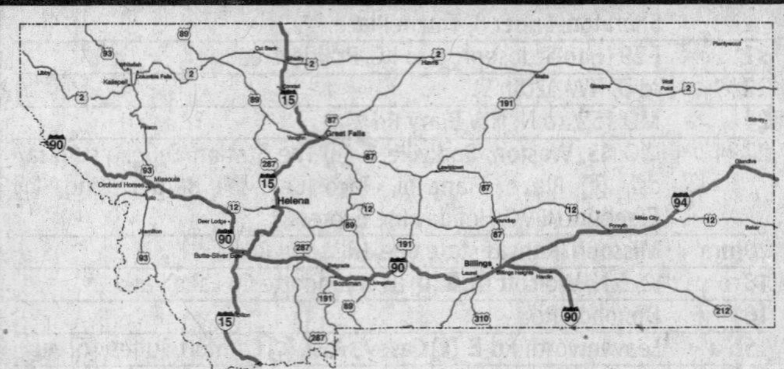

Exit #	Services
398mm	Montana/US/Canada Border, Sweetgrass
397	Sweetgrass, **full facilities, litter barrels, petwalk,** [rest stop] **both lanes,** W [gas] Duty Free, [other] Duty Free
394	ranch exit
389	MT 552, Sunburst, W [gas] Sunburst/dsl, [other] J&S RV Park, Sunburst Mercantile, USPO
385	Swayze Rd
379	MT 215, MT 343, to Kevin, Oilmont, W [food] Four Corners Café
373	Potter Rd
369	Bronken Rd
366.5mm	weight sta sb
364	Shelby, E [other] Lake Sheloole Camping, Lewis&Clark RV Park, W
363	US 2, Shelby, to Cut Bank, Shelby, E [gas] Cenex, Conoco, Pilot/Exxon/dsl/scales/parking/24hr, Sinclair/dsl, [food] Dash Drive-In, Dixie Inn Steaks, Pizza Hut, Shelby Wok'N Roll, Subway, The Griddle, [lodging] Comfort Inn, Glacier Motel/RV Park, [other] Albertsons, CarQuest, city park, [H], Mark's Tire, TrueValue, USPO, visitor info, W [lodging] Best Western, [other] Family$, Glacier NP, Trails West RV Park
361mm	parking area nb
358	Marias Valley Rd, to Golf Course Rd, E [other] camping
357mm	Marias River
352	Bullhead Rd
348	rd 44, to Valier, W [other] Lake Frances RA
345	MT 366, Ledger Rd, E [other] Tiber Dam
339	Conrad, [rest stop]**/weigh sta both lanes, full facilities, litter barrels, petwalk,** W [gas] Cenex/dsl, Conoco, Conoco/dsl, Exxon/Subway/dsl, Tom's/dsl, [food] Home Cafe, Keg Family Rest., Main Drive-In, [lodging] Northgate Motel, Super 8, [other] Buick/Chevrolet/GMC, Conrad Transportation Museum, Ford, [H], IGA Foods, NAPA, Olson's Drug, Pondera RV Park, USPO, vet, Village Drug, Westco RV Ctr
335	Midway Rd, Conrad
328	MT 365, Brady, W [gas] Mtn View Co-op/dsl, [other] USPO
321	Collins Rd
319mm	Teton River, **full facilities, litter barrels, petwalk,** [rest stop] **both lanes**
313	MT 221, MT 379, Dutton, W [gas] Cenex/dsl, [food] Golden Harvest Cafe, [other] city park
302	MT 431, Power
297	Gordon
290	US 89 N, rd 200 W, to Choteau, W [gas] Conoco/dsl, Sinclair/dsl/LP/RV dump, [food] Silver Spur Grill, [other] USPO
288mm	parking area both lanes
286	Manchester
282	US 87 N(from sb), NW bypass, E [gas] Circle K/dsl, Conoco/dsl, [food] Arby's, Buffalo Wild Wings, Burger King, Dominos, Jimmy John's, McDonald's, Starbucks, Subway, Taco Bell, Taco John's, Taco Treat, [lodging] Days Inn, [other] $Tree, Ace Hardware, Albertsons/Osco, O'Reilly Parts, Sam's Club/gas, Staples, Tire-Rama, TJ Maxx, Valvoline, Walgreens, Walmart
280	US 87 N, Central Ave W, Great Falls, E [gas] Loaf 'N Jug/dsl, [food] A&K Diner, A&W/KFC, Ford's Drive-In, Kobe Japanese, Papa John's, [lodging] Alberta Inn, Central Motel, Days Inn, Staybridge Suites, [other] city park, Giant Sprgs SP, Pomp's Tire, U-Haul/LP, vet
280mm	Sun River
278	US 89 S, rd 200 E, 10th Ave, Great Falls, E [gas] Conoco/dsl, Conoco/dsl, Exxon/dsl, Holiday/Subway/dsl, Mobil/dsl,
278	Continued Sinclair/dsl, Town Pump/dsl, [food] Applebee's, Arby's, Best Wok, Burger King, Café Rio, Cattlemen's Steaks, Chili's, Chipotle, Classic 50s Diner/casino, Coldstone, DQ, Firehouse Subs, Five Guys, Fuddrucker's, Hardee's, Jaker's Rest., Jimmy John's, MacKenzie River Pizza, McDonald's, McDonald's, MOD Pizza, Papa Murphy's, Pita Pit, Pizza Hut, Roadhouse Diner, Sonic, Starbucks, Stone House Deli, Street Burgers, Subway, Taco Bell, Taco Del Mar, Taco John's, Taco Treat, Wendy's, Wheat MT, [lodging] Best Western, Comfort Inn, Comfort Inn(2), Extended Stay America, Hampton Inn, Heritage Inn, Hilton Garden, Holiday Inn, Holiday Inn Express, MainStay Suites, Motel 6, Plaza Inn, Super 8, Western Motel, Wingate, [other] $Tree, Ace Hardware, Albertsons/Osco, AT&T, AT&T, AutoZone, Barnes&Noble, Big O Tire, BigLots, Cadillac/Chevrolet/Toyota, CarQuest, Chrysler/Dodge/Jeep, CVS Drug, Firestone/auto, Ford, golf, Great Falls RV Park, Harley-Davidson, Home Depot, [H], JC Penney, Malmstrom AFB, Michael's, Midas, O'Reilly Parts, Old Navy, PetCo, Pierce RV Ctr, Ross, Scheels Sports, Smith's/gas, Super 1 Foods, Target, Tire-Rama, USPO, Verizon, Walgreens
277	Airport Rd, E [gas] Flying J/Denny's/dsl/scales/24hr, Pilot/Conoco/Subway/casino/dsl/scales/24hr, [lodging] Crystal Inn, W [gas] Love's/Godfathers/dsl/scales/dog park/24hr, [other]
275mm	weigh sta nb
270	MT 330, Ulm, E [other] USPO, W [food] Beef'n Bone Steaks, [other] Buffalo Jump SP
256	rd 68, Cascade, E [gas] Sinclair, [food] Angus Bear Cafe, [lodging] Trout Flyshop Motel, [other] USPO
254	rd 68, Cascade, E same as 256
250	local access
247	Hardy Creek, W [other] Prewett Creek RV Park, Tower Rock SP
246.5mm	Missouri River
245mm	scenic overlook sb
244	Canyon Access, W [lodging] Hidden Canyon Lodge, Jumping Rainbow Lodge, [other] Prewett Creek Camping, Prewett Creek RV Park
240	Dearborn, E [lodging] MO Cliffs Lodge, [other] Canyon RV park
239mm	**full facilities, litter barrels, petwalk,** [rest stop] **both lanes**
238mm	Stickney Creek
236mm	Missouri River
234	Craig, E [food] Izaak's Cafe, Trout Shop Café/lodge, [other] boating, Wegner RV Park
228	US 287 N, to Augusta, Choteau
226	MT 434, Wolf Creek, E [gas] Exxon/dsl, [food] Oasis Café, [other] camping, Frenchy's RV Camping, Holter Lake, Wolf Creek Angler, W USPO
222mm	parking area both lanes, toilets both lanes
219	Spring Creek, Recreation Rd(from nb), Spring Creek
218mm	Little Prickly Pear Creek

INTERSTATE 15 Cont'd

Exit #	Services
216	Sieben
209	E Gates of the Mtns RA
202mm	weigh sta sb
200	MT 279, MT 453, Lincoln Rd, W Sinclair/Bob's Mkt/dsl, GrubStake Rest., Ace Hardware, Family$, KOA
194	Custer Ave, E Conoco/dsl, Chili's, Nagoya Japanese, Qdoba, Comfort Suites, Residence Inn, Costco/gas, Discount Tire, Hobby Lobby, Home Depot, Staples, Super 1 Foods, TJ Maxx, W Cenex/dsl, Conoco/dsl, Exxon/dsl, Applebee's, Arby's, Buffalo Wild Wings, Burger King, DQ, Jade Garden, Mackenzie River Pizza, McDonald's, Panda Express, Papa Murphy's, Pizza Ranch, Rib Shack, Smashburger, Steve's Cafe, Subway, Suds Hut, Taco Bell, Holiday Inn Express, Home2, $Tree, Albertson's, AutoZone, CVS Drug, Helena RV Park, Jo-Ann, Lowe's, Murdoch's, Natural Grocers, PetCo, PetSmart, Ross, Target, Verizon
193	Cedar St, Helena, E W Conoco/dsl, Conoco/dsl, Exxon/dsl, Little Caesar's, Shellie's Cafe, Steffano's Pizza, Subway, Taco John's, Fairfield Inn, Helena Inn, Ace Hardware, Chevrolet/Buick/GMC, NAPA, O'Reilly Parts, Tire-Rama, USPO, vet
192b a	US 12, US 287, Helena, Townsend, E Conoco/dsl, Fiesta Mexicana, Burger King, Pizza Hut, Hampton Inn, Big Lots, Chrysler/Dodge/Jeep, D&D RV Ctr, Ford/Lincoln, Honda, Nissan, NW Automotive Repair, Schwab Tire, Walmart/Subway, W Exxon/dsl, Sinclair/dsl, DQ, Golden Chinese, Jimmy John's, McDonald's, Overland Express Rest., Papa John's, Slim Chickens, Smashburger, Steve's Cafe, Taco Treat, Village Inn Pizza, Wendy's, Baymont Inn, Best Value, Best Western, Days Inn, Delta Hotels, Fairfield Inn, Howard Johnson, Jorgenson's Inn, La Quinta, Shilo Inn, Super 8, Albertson's, CVS Drug, H, J&J Tire/auto, Safeway/dsl, Verizon, Walgreens
190	S Helena, W H
187	MT 518, Montana City, Clancy, E Hugo's Pizza/casino, W Conoco/dsl, Hardware Cafe, Jackson Creek Cafe, MT City Grill, Elkhorn Inn
182	Clancy, E Alhambra RV Park, W Chubby's Grill, Legal Tender Rest., USPO
178mm	**full facilities, litter barrels, petwalk, , , both lanes**
176	Jefferson City, W USPO
174.5mm	chain up area both lanes
168mm	chainup area both lanes
164	rd 69, Boulder, E Conoco/dsl/casino, Dave's Grill, Mtn Good Rest., Ace Hardware, L&P Grocery, USPO
161mm	parking area nb
160	High Ore Rd
156	Basin, E camping, Merry Widow Health Mine/RV camping, W Silver Saddle Grill, USPO
154mm	Boulder River
151	to Boulder River Rd, Bernice, W Ladysmith Campground, picnic area, Whitehouse Campground/picnic area
148mm	chainup area both lanes
143.5mm	chainup area both lanes
138	Elk Park, W Lowland Campground, Sheepshead Picnic Area
134	Woodville
133mm	continental divide, elev 6368
130.5mm	Butte Scenic Overlook sb
129	I-90 E, to Billings
128	I-15 S and I-90 W run together 8 mi
127	Harrison Ave, Butte, S $Tree, E Cenex/dsl, Conoco/dsl,
127	Continued Exxon/dsl, A&W/KFC, Arby's, Asia Buffet, Buffalo Wild Wings, Burger King, Hwy 55 Burgers, MacKenzie River Pizza, McDonald's, MT Club Rest., Perkins, Pizza Hut, Pizza Ranch, Silver Bow Pizza, Starbucks, Subway, Taco Bell, Three Amigos, Wendy's, Best Western, Comfort Inn, Hampton Inn, Super 8, American Car Care, Bretz RV Ctr, Buick/Chevrolet/GMC, CarQuest, Chrysler/Dodge/Jeep, Ford, Honda, Murdoch's, Petco, Rocky Mtn RV Ctr, Staples, Subaru, Toyota/Scion, Verizon, vet, Walmart/auto, W Cenex/dsl, Conoco/dsl, Derby Steaks, Dickey's BBQ, Domino's, DQ, El Taco Mexican, Hanging 5 Rest., John's Rest., Mr. Hot Dogs, Papa John's, Papa Murphy's, Quiznos, Royse's Burgers, Fairfield Inn, Holiday Inn Express, La Quinta, Ramada, Wingate, Ace Hardare, AutoZone, Lisac's Tires, O'Reilly Parts, Safeway, Walgreens
126	Montana St, Butte, E Conoco/dsl, Exxon/dsl, W Bonanza Freeze, Shebrews Coffee, H, Safeway, Schwab Tire
124	I-115(from eb), to Butte City Ctr
123mm	weigh sta sb
122	Rocker, E Pilot/Conoco/McDonald's/Subway/dsl/scales/24hr, Red Lion Inn, casino, W Flying J/Exxon/rest./dsl/LP/24hr, Rocker Inn, 2 Bar Lazy-H RV Camping
121.5mm	I-15 N and I-90 E run together 8 mi
121	I-90 W, to Missoula
119	Silver Bow, drive-in movie theater
116	Buxton
112mm	Continental Divide, elevation 5879
111	Feely
109mm	**full facilities, litter barrels, petwalk, , , /weigh sta both lanes**
102	rd 43, to Wisdom, Divide, W David Bridge Campground
99	Moose Creek Rd, W Maidenrock Campground
93	Melrose, W Hitchin Post Rest., Melrose Café/grill/dsl, Pioneer Mtn Cabins, Sportsman Motel/RV Park, Sunrise Flyshop, USPO
85.5mm	Big Hole River
85	Glen, E Willis Sta RV camping, W FishOn Cabins, Browne's Bridge Campground
74	Apex, Birch Creek
64mm	Beaverhead River
63	Lp 15, rd 41, Dillon, Twin Bridges, E Cenex/dsl/LP/RV Dump, Exxon/dsl, 4B's Rest., China Garden, Fiesta Mexicana, McDonald's, Pizza Hut, Subway, The Den Steaks, Beaverhead Lodge, Best Western, Fairbridge Inn, Quality Inn, Sundowner Motel, Super 8, Buick/Chevrolet, CarQuest, city park, Family$, H, KOA, Les Schwab Tire, Murdoch's, museum, NAPA, O'Reilly Parts, Safeway/dsl, W MT U
62	Lp 15, Dillon, E Domino's, DQ, Pita Pit, Sparky's Rest., Angler Village Inn, H, KOA, Southside RV Park, to W MT U, Van's/IGA Foods, vet
60mm	Beaverhead River
59	MT 278, to Jackson, W Bannack SP, Countryside RV Park/LP
56	Barretts, E Barretts Park, W Chevron/RV Park/dsl
55mm	parking area sb, litter barrels, hist site
52	Grasshopper Creek
51	Dalys(from sb, no return)
50mm	Beaverhead River
46mm	Beaverhead River
45mm	Beaverhead River
44	MT 324, E Buffalo Lodge, Armstead Campground, W Clark Cyn Reservoir/RA, RV camping
38.5mm	Red Rock River
37	Red Rock

MT

INTERSTATE 15 Cont'd

DELL

Exit #	Services
34mm	parking area both lanes, litter barrels, restrooms
29	Kidd
23	Dell, E Cenex/dsl, EVC, USPO
16.5mm	weigh sta both lanes
15	Lima, E **both lanes, full facilities, litter barrels, petwalk**, Exxon/dsl, Tesla EVC, The Homestead Cafe, Mtn View Motel/RV Park, Big Sky Tire/auto, USPO

ABERDEEN

Exit #	Services
9	Snowline
0	Monida, E Red Rock Lakes
0mm	Montana/Idaho state line, Monida Pass, elevation 6870

INTERSTATE 90

Exit #	Services
554.5mm	Montana/Wyoming state line
549	Aberdeen
544	Wyola
530	MT 463, Lodge Grass, S Farmers Union, Greasy Mouth Grill
517.5mm	Little Bighorn River
514	Garryowen, N Custer Bfd Museum, S 7th Ranch RV camp
511.5mm	Little Bighorn River

HARDIN

Exit #	Services
510	US 212 E, N Conoco/café/dsl/gifts, Little Bighorn Bfd
509.2mm	Little Bighorn River
509	Crow Agency, N Conoco, S Bighorn Canyon NRA
503	Dunmore
498mm	Bighorn River
497	MT 384, 3rd St, Hardin, N fireworks, S Bighorn Cty Museum, H
495	MT 47, City Ctr, Hardin, N Cenex/dsl, Love's/Hardee's/dsl/scales/RV Hookup/24hr, KOA, S Cenex/dsl, Exxon/dsl, Flying J/Conoco/Subway/dsl/LP/24hr, DQ, McDonald's, Pizza Hut, Subway, Taco John's, Homestead Inn, Super 8, Western Motel, Chevrolet, Grandview Camping/RV Park, H, Sunset Village RV Park
484	Toluca
478	Fly Creek Rd
477mm	**full facilities, litter barrels, petwalk, both lanes**
469	Arrow Creek Rd
462	Pryor Creek Rd

BILLINGS

Exit #	Services
456	I-94 E, to Bismarck, ND
455	Johnson Lane, N Pilot/Conoco/McDonald's/dsl/scales/24hr, S Exxon/A&W/dsl, Flying J/dsl/LP/scales/24hr, Burger King, Domino's, DQ, Jin's Chinese, Subway, Holiday Inn Express, Bretz RV Ctr, Pomp's Tire, Verizon
452	US 87 N, City Ctr, Billings, N Conoco, Conoco/dsl/LP, Exxon, Holiday/dsl, Applebee's, Arby's, Burger King, Chipotle, Domino's, DQ, Godfather's, Jersey Mike's, Jimmy John's, MacKenzie River Pizza, McDonald's, MT Jack's, Panda Express, Papa John's, Papa Murphy's, Pizza Hut, Pizza Ranch, Sonic, Starbucks, Subway, Taco Bell, Taco John's, TopZ Sandwiches, Wendy's, Boothill Inn, Country Inn&Suites, Heights Motel, Ace Hardware, Albertsons/Osco, American Spirit RV Ctr, AT&T, AutoZone, BigLots, CarQuest, CVS Drug, Jiffy Lube, Metra RV Ctr, O'Reilly Parts, PetSmart, Target, Tire Rama, U-Haul, Verizon, vet, Walgreens, Walmart/auto, S Cenex/dsl, RV Camping
451.5mm	Yellowstone River
450	MT 3, 27th St, Billings, N Conoco/dsl, Pizza Hut, Sandee's Drive-In, Doubletree, Vegas Motel, CarQuest, city park, H, USPO, visitor ctr, S J&M Tire, KOA, Yellowstone River Camping
447	S Billings Blvd, N Circle K/dsl, Conoco/Subway/dsl, 4B's Rest., Domino's, DQ, Fiddlers Green Grill, McDonald's,
447	Continued Starbucks, Taco Bell, Taco John's, Wendy's, Best Western/Kelly, Comfort Suites, Days Inn, Extended Stay America, Hampton Inn, Ledgestone Hotel, My Place, Sleep Inn, Super 8, Cabela's, NAPA, Sam's Club/dsl, S Freightliner, Kenworth
446	King Ave, Billings, N Conoco/dsl, Holiday/dsl, Mobil, Phillips 66/dsl, Applebee's, Arby's, Asian Sea Grill, Buffalo Wild Wings, Burger King, Café Rio, Carverss Brazilian Steaks, Chick-fil-A, ChuckECheese's, City Brew Coffee, Coldstone, Denny's, DQ, Emporium Rest., Famous Dave's, Fiesta Mexicana, Fuddrucker's, Gusicks Rest., Hardee's, HuHot Mongolian, IHOP, Jake's Grill, KFC, Little Caesars Pizza, McDonald's, MooYah Burgers, Old Chicago, Olive Garden, Outback Steaks, Panera Bread, Papa John's, Papa Murphy's, Perkins, Pie Guys Pizza, Pizza Hut, Pizza Ranch, Qdoba, Red Lobster, Rendezvous Grill, Starbucks, Subway, Taco Bell, TX Roadhouse, Wendy's, Baymont Inn, C'Mon Inn, Fairfield Inn, Hilton Garden, Quality Inn, Residence Inn, SpringHill Suites, SureStay+, TownePlace Suites, Western Executive Inn, $Tree, Albertsons, AT&T, AutoZone, Barnes&Noble, Best Buy, Chevrolet, Chrysler/Dodge/Jeep, Dillards, Discount Tire, Firehouse Subs, Ford, Hobby Lobby, Home Depot, JC Penney, Lisac's Tire, Lowe's, Mercedes, Michael's, Midas, Natural Grocers, O'Reilly Parts, Office Depot, Old Navy, PetCo, PetSmart, Ross, Subaru, USPO, Verizon, vet, Walmart, World Mkt, S Circle K, Conoco/dsl, Cracker Barrel, Billings Hotel, EconoLodge, Howard Johnson, Kelly Inn, La Quinta, Montana Trailhead Inn, Motel 6, Motel 6(2), Volvo/Mack Trucks

E LAUREL

Exit #	Services
443	Zoo Dr, to Shiloh Rd, N Holiday/dsl, Five Guys, MT Rib/Chophouse, Avid Hotel, Bighorn Resort/waterpark, Hampton Inn, Holiday Inn Express, Homewood Suites, Honda, H, Hyundai/Volvo/Buick, Pierce RV Ctr, Scheels, zoo, S Harley-Davidson, vet
439mm	weigh sta both lanes
437	E Laurel, S TA/Sinclair/cafe/dsl/scales/RV Park/24hr, antiques, vet
434	US 212, US 310, to Red Lodge, Laurel, N Cenex/dsl, Conoco/dsl, Exxon/dsl, City Brew Coffee, Fiesta Mexicana, Jimmy John's, McDonald's, Pizza Hut, Subway, Taco Bell, Wendy's, Your Pie Pizza, Best Western, Fairfield Inn, Locomotive Inn, Ace Hardware, Albertsons, AutoZone, Chevrolet, CVS Drug, Ford, NAPA, O'Reilly Parts, Rapid Tire, Verizon, Walmart, S Riverside Park/RV Camping, to Yellowstone NP

COLUMBUS

Exit #	Services
433	Lp 90(from eb), same as 434
426	Park City, S Cenex, KwikStop, USPO
419mm	**full facilities, litter barrels, petwalk, both lanes**
408	rd 78, Columbus, N Mtn Range RV Park, truck repair, S Conoco, Pilot/Exxon/dsl/24hr, Bearstone Cafe, McDonald's, Subway, Big Sky Motel, Super 8, auto repair, Family$, Ford, H, IGA Foods, NAPA, O'Reilly Parts, tires/repair, to Yellowstone, E city park
400	Springtime Rd
398mm	Yellowstone River
396	ranch access
392	Reed Point, N Cenex, Old West RV Park, USPO
384	Bridger Creek Rd
381mm	**full facilities, litter barrels, petwalk,**

BIG TIMBER

INTERSTATE 90 Cont'd

381mm Continued
both lanes

377 Greycliff, S KOA, Prairie Dog Town SP

370 US 191, Big Timber, N Sinclair/dsl, Grand Hotel, Lazy J Motel, H, Spring Creek RV Ranch(4mi), USPO

369mm Boulder River

367 US 191 N, Big Timber, N Exxon/dsl, River Valley Inn, Super 8, CarQuest, Family$, fishing, H, Spring Creek Camping(3mi)

362 De Hart

354 MT 563, Springdale

352 ranch access

350 East End access

343 Mission Creek Rd

340 US 89 N, to White Sulphur Sprgs, S

337 Lp 90, to Livingston

333mm Yellowstone River

333 US 89 S, Livingston, N DQ, Homemade Kitchen, Hungry Mexican, Los Pinos Mexican, Mark's In&Out, Pizza Hut, Taco John's, Econo Lodge, Fairfield Inn, Home2 Suites, Livingston Inn, Travelodge, Yellowstone Park Inn, Ace Hardware, Town&Country Foods, Verizon, Western Drug, S Cenex/dsl, Exxon/dsl, McDonald's, Starbucks, Subway, Taco Bell, Super 8, Yellowstone Inn, Albertsons/Osco, KOA(10mi), to Yellowstone, URGENT CARE, vet

330 Lp 90, Livingston, N Cenex/Yellowstone Trkstp/dsl/rest./24hr

326.5mm chainup/chain removal area both lanes

324 ranch access

323mm chain/chain removal area wb

322mm Bridger Mountain Range

321mm no services

319 Jackson Creek Rd

319mm no services

316 Trail Creek Rd

313 Bear Canyon Rd, S Bear Canyon Camping

BOZEMAN

309 US 191 S, Main St, Bozeman, N Audi, Bozeman Trail RV Park, fireworks, Subaru, VW, S Cenex/dsl, Conoco/dsl, Exxon/dsl, MT AleWorks, Ranch House Motel, Residence Inn, H, Tire Rama, to Yellowstone

306 MT 205, N 7th, to US 191, Bozeman, N Cenex, McDonald's, Baymont, La Quinta, Microtel, Motel 6, Quality Inn, Super 8, Murdoch's, Pomp's Tire, ski area, S Conoco/dsl, Exxon, Applebee's, Audrey's Pizza, Dominos, DQ, Papa John's, Taco John's, Best Western, Bozeman Inn, Comfort Inn, Days Inn, Hampton Inn, Homewood Suites, RSVP, Sapphire, Big O Tire, Firestone/auto, Museum of the Rockies, Price Drug, U-Haul, Verizon, vet, Walmart/McDonald's

BELGRADE

305 MT412, N 19th Ave, N Exxon, Mountainview Inn, Schwab Tire, vet, S **full facilities, petwalk**, Conoco/dsl, A&W/KFC, Buffalo Wild Wings, City Brew Coffee, Five Guys, IHOP, Jimmy John's, Mongolian BBQ, Montana Steaks, Noodles&Co, Old Chicago Pizza, Olive Garden, Outback Steaks, Papa Murphy's, Starbucks, Super Chix, Taco Bell, Wasabi Grill, Wendy's, C'mon Inn, Comfort Suites, Country Inn Suites, Hilton Garden, Holiday Inn Express, My Place Extended Stay, Residence Inn, SpringHill Suites, AT&T, Costco/gas, Ford/Lincoln/RV Ctr, Home Depot, Lowe's, Michael's, PetSmart, **/litter barrels**, REI, Ross, Smith's Foods/dsl, Staples, Target, TJMaxx, USPO, Verizon, WinCo Foods, World Mkt

299 Airway Blvd, N Holiday,

298 MT 291, rd 85, Belgrade, N Cenex, Exxon, Burger King, DQ, Heros Sandwiches, Jersey Mike's, McDonald's,

298 Continued
Papa Murphy's, Rosa's Pizza, Starbucks, Taco Bell, Taco Time, Holiday Inn Express, Albertson's, NAPA, Pomp's Tire, Town&Country Foods, Verizon, S Pilot/Conoco/dsl/scales/24hr, Fiesta Mexicana, Mackenzie Pizza, La Quinta, Quality Inn, Super 8, Ace Hardware, Freightliner, Harley-Davidson, Interwest Tire Point, repair, to Yellowstone NP, E Wendy's

292.5mm Gallatin River

288 MT 288, MT 346, Manhattan, N Conoco/Subway/dsl, Ace Hardware, RV camping

283 Logan, S Madison Buffalo Jump SP(7mi)

279mm Madison River

278 MT 205, rd 2, Three Forks, Trident, N Missouri Headwaters SP, S Conoco, 3 Forks Cafe, Iron Horse Cafe, Peking Chinese; Stageline Pizza, T-Rex BBQ, Broken Spur Motel, Lewis&Clark Motel, Sacajawea Hotel, antiques, CarQuest, golf

277.5mm Jefferson River

CARDWELL

274 US 287, to Helena, Ennis, N Conoco/dsl, Wheat MT Bakery/deli, Travelodge, dsl repair, to Canyon Ferry SP, S Pilot/Exxon/Subway/dsl/scales/24hr, Camp 3 Forks, Lewis&Clark Caverns SP, to Yellowstone NP

267 Milligan Canyon Rd

261.5mm chain-up area

257mm Boulder River

256 MT 359, Cardwell, S Cenex/dsl/RV Park, Lewis&Clark Caverns SP, to Yellowstone NP

249 rd 55, to rd 69, Whitehall, S Exxon/dsl, A&W/KFC, Subway, Jefferson Inn, casino, Cliff's Tire/auto

241 Pipestone

240.5mm chainup/chain removal area both lanes

238.5mm runaway ramp eb

237.5mm pulloff eb

235mm truck parking both lanes, litter barrels, restrooms

233 Continental Divide, elev 6393, Homestake

230mm chain-up area both lanes

RAMSAY

228 MT 375, Continental Dr, S Conoco/dsl, Harley-Davidson, Three Bears Foods

227 I-15 N, to Helena, Great Falls

226 I-90 and I-15 run together 8 mi. See MT I-15, Exits 122-127.

123mm weigh sta wb

219 I-15 S, to Dillon, Idaho Falls

216 Ramsay

211 MT 441, Gregson, S Fairmont RV Park(Apr-Oct), food, lodging

210.5mm parking area wb, Pintlar Scenic route info

208 rd 1, Pintler Scenic Loop, Georgetown Lake RA, Opportunity, Anaconda, **full facilities, litter barrels, petwalk**, **both lanes**

DEER LODGE

201 Warm Springs

197 MT 273, Galen

195 Racetrack

187 Lp 90, Deer Lodge(no wb return), same as 184, S H, Old MT Prison/auto museum

184 Deer Lodge, S Conoco/dsl, Exxon/dsl, Sinclair/Subway/dsl, 4B's Rest., McDonald's, Travel Inn/casino, Western Big Sky Inn, city park, Deer Lodge Campground/RV, Family$, Grant-Kohrs Ranch NHS, H, Indian Creek Camping, Safeway/deli, Schwab Tire, USPO

179 Beck Hill Rd

175 US 12 E, Garrison, N RiverFront RV Park

175mm Little Blackfoot River

174 US 12 E(from eb), S same as 175

170 Phosphate

166 Gold Creek, S Camp Mak-A-Dream, USPO

162 Jens

M

MT

INTERSTATE 90 Cont'd

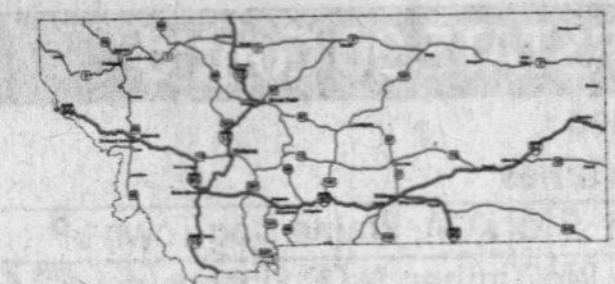

CLINTON

Exit #	Services
154	to MT 1(from wb), Drummond, **S** Cenex/dsl, Conoco/dsl, Parker's Rest., Drummond Motel, city park, Georgetown Lake RA
153	MT 1(from eb), **S** same as 154
150.5mm	weigh sta both lanes
143mm	**full facilities, litter barrels, petwalk, both lanes**
138	Bearmouth Area, **N** Bearmouth RV Park/rest.
130	Beavertail Rd, **S** to Beavertail Hill SP
128mm	parking area both lanes, litter barrels/restrooms
126	Rock Creek Rd
120	Clinton, **N** Conoco/dsl, Poor Henry's Café(1mi W on frtg rd), Clinton Market, **S** USPO
113	Turah, **S** Turah RV Park/gas
109.5mm	Clark Fork
109mm	Blackfoot River
109	MT 200 E, Bonner, **N** Pilot/Exxon/Arby's/Subway/dsl/scales/casino/LP/24hr, River City Grill, park, USPO
108.5mm	Clark Fork

MISSOULA

Exit #	Services
107	E Missoula, **N** Cenex, Ole's/Conoco/dsl, Reno Cafe, Aspen Motel, dsl repair
105	US 12 W, Missoula, **S** Cenex/dsl, Conoco/dsl, Sinclair, Sinclair/dsl, 5 Guys, Burger King, McDonald's, Pizza Hut, Taco Bell, Comfort Inn, Days Inn, DoubleTree, Goldsmith's Inn, Motel 6, Thunderbird Motel, Travelodge, Ace Hardware, Albertson's, Jiffy Lube, Kingfisher Flyshop, O'Reilly Parts, U of MT, Verizon
104	Orange St, Missoula, **S** Conoco/dsl, Pagoda Chinese, Taco John's, Red Lion Inn, H, TireRama, to City Ctr
101	US 93 S, Reserve St, **N** Conoco/dsl, Cracker Barrel, MacKenzie River Pizza, Starbucks, Best Western+, C'Mon Inn, Motel 6, My Place, ski area, **S** Cenex/dsl/LP, Conoco/dsl, Exxon, Exxon/Subway/dsl, Arby's, Buffalo Wild Wings, Burger King, Cafe Rio, Chick-fil-A, Chipotle, Coldstone, DQ, Famous Dave's BBQ, Firehouse Subs, Freddy's, Frugals, IHOP, Jersey Mike's, Jimmy John's, Little Caesar's, McDonald's, MOD Pizza, MT Club Rest./casino, Old Chicago, Outback Steaks, Panda Express, Panera Bread, Pizza Hut, Popeyes, Stone Of Accord, Taco Bell, Taco Time, Wendy's, Comfort Inn, Courtyard, EconoLodge, Hilton Garden, Holiday Inn Express, Homewood Suites, La Quinta, Quality Inn, Staybridge Suites, Super 8, TownePlace Suites, WoodSpring Suites, Albertson's, AT&T, AT&T, Barnes&Noble, Best Buy, Bretz RV/Marine, Chevrolet/Cadillac, Costco/gas, dsl repair, Firestone/auto, Home Depot, Jiffy Lube, Lowe's, NAPA, Old Navy, PetSmart, REI, Target, TJ Maxx, Verizon, VW, Walgreens, Walmart
99	Airway Blvd, **S** Mobil/dsl/24hr, Sinclair/dsl, Fairfield Inn, Stone Creek Lodge, Chrysler/Dodge/Jeep, Harley-Davidson, Kia, Peterbilt

CLARK FORK

Exit #	Services
96	US 93 N, MT 200W, Kalispell, **N** Conoco/rest./dsl/scales/24hr/@, Flying J/Exxon/McDonald's/dsl/scales/24hr, Taco Bell, Days Inn/rest., Granite Peak RV Park(1mi), Jim&Mary's RV Park(1mi), to Flathead Lake&Glacier NP, **S** Love's/Hardee's/dsl/scales/24ht, Sinclair/dsl, TA/dsl/scales/24hr, Motel 6, Harlow Truck Ctr, Kenworth
92.5mm	inspection sta both lanes
89	Frenchtown, **N** to Frenchtown Pond SP, **S** Conoco/dsl/café, Sinclair, Alcan Grill, Gammy's Cafe, Broncs Grocery/gas, Granite Drug, USPO
85	Huson, **S** Larry's 6 Mile
82	Nine Mile Rd
81.5mm	Clark Fork
80mm	Clark Fork

CLARK FORK

Exit #	Services
77	MT 507, Petty Creek Rd, Alberton
75	Alberton, **N** Cenex/dsl, antiques, USPO, **S** River Edge Steaks, River Edge Rest.
73mm	parking area wb, litter barrels
72mm	parking area eb, litter barrels
70	Cyr
70mm	Clark Fork
66	Fish Creek Rd
66mm	Clark Fork
61	Tarkio
59mm	Clark Fork River, Clark Fork
58mm	**full facilities, litter barrels, NF camping(seasonal), petwalk, both lanes**
55	Lozeau, Quartz, **N** Lozeau Lodge, whitewater rafting
53.5mm	Clark Fork
49mm	Clark Fork
47	MT 257, Superior, **N** Cenex, Conoco/dsl, Durango's, Big Sky Motel, Hilltop Motel, Darlow's Foods, H, Mineral Drug, USPO, **S** Pilot/Exxon/dsl/casino/24hr
45mm	Clark Fork
43	Dry Creek Rd
37	Sloway Area
34mm	Clark Fork
33	MT 135, St Regis, **N** Exxon, Sinclair, Huck's Grill, Jasper's Rest., Winks Diner, Little River Motel, Super 8, city park, Nugget Camground, St Regis Campground(seasonal), to Glacier NP, USPO

DEBORGIA

Exit #	Services
30	Two Mile Rd
29mm	fishing access wb
26	Ward Creek Rd(from eb)
25	Drexel
22	Camels Hump Rd, Henderson, **N** camping (seasonal), **S** scenic view
18	DeBorgia, **N** Hideout Grill, Black Diamond Guest Ranch, fireworks, USPO
16	Haugan, **N** Exxon/dsl/24hr, 50000 Silver $/motel/rest./casino/RV park, Savenac Cottage
15mm	weigh sta both lanes, exits left from both lanes
10	Saltese, weigh sta, **N** Mangold's Motel
10mm	St Regis River
5	Taft Area
4.5mm	**chainup/removal, full facilities, litter barrels, petwalk, both lanes**
0	Lookout Pass, access to Lookout Pass ski area/lodge, info
0mm	Montana/Idaho state line, Central/Pacific time zone, Lookout Pass elev 4680

INTERSTATE 94

WIBAUX

Exit #	Services
250mm	Montana/North Dakota state line
248	Carlyle Rd
242	MT 7(from wb), Wibaux, **full facilities, litter barrels, both lanes**, **S** Cenex/dsl/service, Tastee Hut, Rodeway Inn
241	MT 261(from eb), to MT 7, Wibaux, **S** same as 242
240mm	weigh sta both lanes
236	ranch access
231	Hodges Rd
224	Griffith Creek, frontage road
222.5mm	Griffith Creek
215	MT 335, Glendive, City Ctr, **N** Cenex/dsl, C's Family Café, Penny's Diner, Astoria Suites, Baymont Inn,

INTERSTATE 94 Cont'd

GLENDIVE

Exit	Services
215	Continued FairBridge Inn, Glendive Lodge, Holiday Inn Express, SureStay, Yellowstone River Inn, Glendive Camping(apr-oct), museum, Running's Hardware, S Exxon/dsl, Holiday/dsl, Subway, El Centro Motel, La Quinta, H, Makoshika SP, Verizon
215mm	Yellowstone River
213	MT 16, to Sidney, Glendive, N Town Pump/dsl/scales, S Cenex/dsl, Sinclair/dsl, Pizza Hut, Riverside Inn, $Tree, Albertson's, Ford, NAPA, Reynolds Mkt
211	MT 200S(from wb, no EZ return), to Circle
210	Lp 94, to rd 200 S, W Glendive, S Cenex/dsl, Exxon/dsl, Buick/Chevrolet, Makoshika SP, Tire Rama
206	Pleasant View Rd
204	Whoopup Creek Rd
198	Cracker Box Rd
192	Bad Route Rd, **/weigh sta both lanes, S camping, full facilities, litter barrels, petwalk, , , weather info**
187mm	Yellowstone River
185	MT 340, Fallon
184mm	O'Fallon Creek

MILES CITY

Exit	Services
176	MT 253, Terry, N Cenex/dsl, Four Corners/dsl, Dizzy Diner, Kempton Hotel, H, Smal Towne RV, Terry RV Oasis, USPO
170mm	Powder River
169	Powder River Rd
159	Diamond Ring
148	Valley Access
141	US 12 E, Miles City, N Big Sky RV Park
138	rd 59, Miles City, N Cenex/dsl, Conoco/dsl, Pilot/Exxon/dsl/24hr, 4B's Rest., Arby's, Black Iron Grill, City Brew Coffee, DQ, Gallagher's Rest., KFC, Little Caesar's, McDonald's, Mexico Lindo, Pizza Hut, Subway, Taco John's, Uncle Mike's BBQ, Wendy's, Best Western, EconoLodge, Sleep Inn, Travelodge, Ace Hardware, Albertsons/Osco, Buick/Chevrolet, casinos, H, Murdoch's, O'Reilly Parts, Schwab Tire, Verizon, Walmart, S Cenex/dsl, Tesla EVC, New Hunan Chinese, FairBridge Inn, Miles City, Super 8
137mm	Tongue River
135	Lp 94, Miles City, N KOA(Apr-Oct)
128	local access
126	Moon Creek Rd
117	Hathaway
114mm	**full facilities, litter barrels, petwalk, , , eb**
113mm	**full facilities, litter barrels, overlook, petwalk, , , wb**

FORSYTH

Exit	Services
106	Butte Creek Rd, to Rosebud, N food,
103	MT 446, MT 447, Rosebud Creek Rd
98.5mm	weigh sta both lanes
95	Forsyth, N Six Gun Pizza, Family$, Ford, H, NAPA, to Rosebud RA, S LoneWolf RV Park, Wagon Wheel Camping
93	US 12 W, Forsyth, N Exxon/dsl, Forsyth Watering Hole, DQ, Fitzgerald's Rest., Speedway Diner, Top That Eatery, Rails Inn, Restwel Inn, Sundowner Inn, WestWind Motel, antiques, CarQuest, H, IGA Foods
87	rd 39, to Colstrip
82	Reservation Creek Rd
72	MT 384, Sarpy Creek Rd

CUSTER

Exit	Services
67	Hysham
65mm	**full facilities, litter barrels, petwalk, , , both lanes**
63	ranch access
53	Bighorn
52mm	Bighorn River
49	MT 47, to Hardin, Custer, S Ft Custer Café
47	Custer, S Cenex, Jct City Saloon/café, USPO
41.5mm	**full facilities, litter barrels, petwalk, , , wb**
38mm	**full facilities, litter barrels, petwalk, , , eb**
36	frontage rd, Waco
23	Pompeys Pillar, N Pompeys Pillar Nat Landmark
14	Ballentine, Worden, N Tiger Town, USPO, S Long Branch Café/casino
6	MT 522, Huntley, N Pryor Creek Café/casino, S golf
0mm	I-90, E to Sheridan, W to Billings, I-94 begins/ends on I-90, exit 456.

MT

NOTES

NEBRASKA

INTERSTATE 80

Exit #	Services
455mm	Nebraska/Iowa state line, Missouri River
454	13th St, N Caseys/dsl, Midtown, Valero, Burger King, Jimmy John's, Los Portales Mexican, McDonald's, Smoking Jay's BBQ, Comfort Inn, Family$, tire/lube, S King Kong Burgers, Doorly Zoo
453	24th St(from eb)
452b	I-480 N, US 75 N, N Eppley Airfield
452a	US 75 S
451	42nd St, N Casey's/dsl, H, S Phillips 66, Burger King, McDonald's, Taco Bell, Pitstop Lube
450	60th St, N Mega Saver, NAPA, to U of NE Omaha, S Casey'/dsl, transmissions
449	72nd St, to Ralston, N Casey's, QT, Burger King, Spezia Italian, Comfort Inn, DoubleTree, Home2 Suites, Super 8, Tru Hotel, H, Walmart, S Cenex/dsl
448	84th St, N Casey's/dsl, 402 Bbq, Arby's, BBQ Hot Pot, Denny's, Farmhouse Café, Great Wall Chinese, Hip Bao, Jimmy John's, La Casa, Little Caesar's, McDonald's, Pizza Ranch, RTG Grill, Taco Bell, Motel 6, Ace Hardware, Advance Parts, CVS Drug, Jensen's Tire/auto, Mangelson's Crafts, USPO, S Kum&Go/dsl/e85, QT/atm, Shell/dsl/mart, Costa El Sol, Cruiser's Grill, Kolache Factory, Wendy's, Chevrolet, Kia, Lyle's Tire Repair
446	I-680 N, to Boystown
445	US 275, NE 92, I thru L St, N Buffalo Wings&Rings, Candlewood Suites, Cheddar's, Hardee's, Jason's Deli, Noodles&Co, Pickleman's Cafe, Pita Pit, Qdoba, Starbucks, Wendy's, Book-A-Million, Buick/GMC, Holiday Inn Express, Home Depot, Michael's, Nelsen's RV Ctr, PetCo, Sam's Club/gas, Target, Verizon, Walmart, S Casey's, QT/dsl, Abelardo's Mexican, Arby's, Burger King, Hog Wild BBQ, LJ Silver, Subway, Village Inn, Best Western, La Quinta, Motel 6, Super 8, Travel Inn, Victorian Inn, Jensen Automotive, URGENT CARE
444	Q St, N Shell/dsl, S Cane's, Dunkin', Hunan Garden, Jimmy John's, Jimmy's Egg, Little King Sandwiches, McDonald's, Rib Shack BBQ, Runza Rest., T&T Rest., Taco Bell, Valvoline Oil Change
442	126th St, Harrison St, N Subaru, Toyota/Scion, VW/charging sta, S Casey's/dsl, Amigo's Mexican, Burger King, Coldstone, Dunkin Donuts, Hooters, Houston's, Jimmy John's, Osaka Steaks, Pizza West, Runza, Sonic, Summer Kitchen, Courtyard, Embassy Suites, Hampton Inn, My Place Hotel, Cabela's, Costco/gas
440	NE 50, to Springfield, N Casey's/dsl, Phillips 66/dsl, Sapp Bros/Subway/dsl/24hr/@, Azteca Mexican, Cracker Barrel, Hardee's, McDonald's, Baymont, Countryside Suites, Home-towne Lodge, Motel 6, Quality Inn, Super 8, Ford, tires, S BP, Love's/Wendy's/dsl/scales/24hr/@, to Platte River SP, El Bees, H
439	439 NE 370, to Gretna, N Kum&Go/dsl, QT/dsl, Arby's, Taco Bell, Taco John's, Holiday Inn Express, Walmart, S H, Kenworth Trucks, Volvo Trucks
432	US 6, NE 31, to Gretna, N Pump&Pantry/dsl/24hr, McDonald's, Super 8, KOA, Nebraska X-ing/famous brands, S Flying J/Denny's/dsl/LP/scales/24hr, to Schramm SP
431mm	**full facilities, info, litter barrels, petwalk, wb**
427mm	Platte River
426	NE 66, to Southbend, N museum, rv camping, Continued to Mahoney SP
425.5	**full facilities, litter barrels, petwalk, eb, vending**
420	NE 63, Greenwood, N Cenex/cafe/dsl/scales/24hr, I-80 Speedway, May Trucking Co., Pine Grove RV Park, S Shell/dsl, antiques, to Platte River SP
416mm	weigh sta both lanes
409	US 6, to E Lincoln, Waverly, N Casey's(2mi), Cenex/dsl(2mi), McDonald's(2mi), Runza Rest.(2mi)
405	US 77 N, 56th St, Lincoln, S Phillips 66, Camping World, Freightliner, H(6mi), Peterbilt, truck service/wash/tires
403	27th St, Lincoln, S Mobil, Phillips 66/Subway/dsl, Phillips 66/Wendy's/dsl, Shell, Amigos/King's Classic Mexican, Applebee's, Arby's, Asian Buffet, Blessing Thai, Burger King, Cane's, Casey's Rest., China Inn, CiCi's Pizza, Cocky's Chicken, Cracker Barrel, Culver's, daVinci's Italian, DQ, Freddy's Burgers, Goodcents Subs, Honest Abe's Rest., IHOP, Jimmy John's, King Kong Burger, Mazatlan Mexican, McDonald's, Oishii Japanese Steaks, PepperJax Cheesesteaks, Perkins, Pizza Hut, Popeyes, Ruby Tuesday, Runza, Sonic, Starbucks, Subway, Taco Bell, Taco John's, Taste of LA, Villa Amore, AmericInn, Best Western+, Comfort Suites, Country Inn&Suites, Countryside Suites, Fairfield Inn, Hampton Inn, Holiday Inn Express, La Quinta, MainStay Suites, Microtel, Motel 6, Quality Inn, Red Roof Inn, Sleep Inn, Super 8, TownePlace Suites, Woodspring Suites, $Tree, AutoZone, BMW, BMW, Buick/Chevrolet/GMC, Chrysler/Dodge/Jeep, Ford/Lincoln, Haas Tire, Home Depot, HyVee Foods, Mazda, Menards, Mercedes, Mitsubishi, PetSmart, Sam's Club/dsl, Super Saver Foods, Tesla Supercharger, to U NE, URGENT CARE, URGENT CARE, Verizon, Walmart/McDonald's
401b	US 34 W, S RV camping
401a	I-180, US 34 E, to 9th St, Lincoln
399	NW 12th St, Lincoln, Lincoln, N Gulf/FatDogs/dsl, Phillips 66/dsl, McDonald's, Best Value Inn, Comfort Inn, Country Inn Suites, Fairfield Inn, Hampton Inn, Holiday Inn Express, Horizon Inn, Luxury Inn, Motel 6, OYO, Studio 6, Sunset Inn, Travelodge, to ✈, S Casey's/dsl, Abelardo's Mexican, EconoLodge
397	US 77 S, to Beatrice, S D'Leon's Mexican, Rodeway Inn, Super 8, SureStay Hotel
396	US 6, West O St(from eb), S Rodeway Inn, Super 8
395	US 6, NW 48th St, S Shell/Shoemaker's/dsl/scales/@, Harley-Davidson, truck repair
388	NE 103, to Crete, Pleasant Dale
382	US 6, Milford, S Phillips 66/dsl
381mm	**full facilities, litter barrels, petwalk, eb, vending**
379	NE 15, to Seward, N Buick/Chevrolet/GMC, H(3mi),

GREENWOOD LINCOLN MILFORD

INTERSTATE 80 Cont'd

Exit	Services
379	Continued Shell/dsl
375mm	truck parking(wb)
373	80G, Goehner
369	80E, Beaver Crossing, S Smith Creek RA
366	80F, to Utica, S Smith Creek RA
360	93B, to Waco, N Phillips 66/dsl/24hr, S Double Nickel Camping, golf
355mm	**full facilities, info, litter barrels, petwalk, wb, vending**
353	US 81, to York, N Conoco/dsl, Pump-N-Pantry/Cinnabon/e85, SappBros/Sinclair/scales/dsl, Shell/dsl, $Tree, Arby's, Burger King, DQ, Golden Gate Chinese, Jimmy John's, KFC/Taco Bell, McDonald's, Runza, Starbucks, Taco John's, The Kitchen, Wendy's, Best Value Inn, Days Inn, Hampton Inn, Holiday Inn Express, New Victorian Inn, Quality Inn, Super 8, Yorkshire Motel, AutoZone, Buick/GMC, Chevrolet, Ford, H, Kenworth, RV Camp, Walmart, S Petro/Phillips 66/Iron Skillet/Pizza Hut/dsl/24hr/@, **Shell/Huddle House/dsl**, Applebee's, Best Western+, Motel 6, Blue Beacon, Freightliner, tires/wash/lube
351mm	**full facilities, info, litter barrels, petwalk, eb, vending**
348	93E, to Bradshaw
342	93A, Henderson, N Prairie Oasis Camping, S Henderson Trkstp/dsl, Subway, Sun Motel, H
338	41D, to Hampton
332	NE 14, Aurora, N Casey's/dsl(2mi), McDonald's(2mi), Subway(2mi), Budget Host(2mi), $General(2mi), Ford, H(2mi), Plainsman Museum(1.5mi), S Love's/Arby's/dsl/scales/repair/24hr/@
324	41B, to Giltner
318	NE 2, to Grand Island, S KOA(seasonal)
317mm	**full facilities, info, litter barrels, petwalk, wb, vending**
315mm	**full facilities, info, litter barrels, petwalk, eb, vending**
314mm	Platte River
314	Locust Street, to Grand Island
312	US 34/281, to Grand Island, N Bosselman/Pilot/Arby's/grill/scales/dsl/24hr/@, Gulf, Tesla EVC, Motel 6, USA Inn, H, Mormon Island RA, to Stuhr Pioneer Museum, truck wash, S Phillips 66/dsl, Days Inn, Suburban Studios/EVC, Hastings Museum(15mi), Peterbilt
305	40C, to Alda, N Sinclair/dsl, TA/Country Pride/dsl/scales/24hr/@, S Crane Meadows Nature Ctr/
300	NE 11, Wood River, N Cheyenne SRA, S Pilot/Subway/dsl/scales/24hr, motel/RV park
291	10D, Shelton, N War Axe SRA
285	10C, Gibbon, N Petro Oasis/dsl, Windmill SP, S Country Inn, auto repair
279	NE 10, to Minden, N Conoco/dsl, S Pioneer Village Camping(13mi)
275	NE 10, Kearney, N Archway Mon
275mm	The Great Platte River Road Archway Monument
272	NE 44, Kearney, N Casey's, Casey's, Casey's/dsl, Cenex/dsl, Phillips 66/Subway/dsl, Pump&Pantry/dsl, Amigo's, Angus Burger, Arby's, B's BBQ, Billy Jack's Pizza, Burger King, Coppermill Steaks, Dunkin', Egg&I, Firehouse Subs, Freddy's, Good Evans, Gourmet House Japanese, Hunan's Rest., King's Buffet, Kyoto Japanese, LJ Silver, Margaritas Mexican, McDonald's, PepperJax Grill, Perkins, Red Lobster, Runza, Starbucks, Taco Bell, Wendy's, Whiskey Creek BBQ, AmericInn, Candlewood Suites, Comfort Inn, Country Inn&Suites, Crowne Plaza/EVC, Crystal Inn, Days Inn,
272	Continued EconoLodge, Fairfield Inn, Hampton Inn, Holiday Inn, La Quinta, Microtel, Midtown Inn/rest., Motel 6, New Victorian Inn, Quality Inn, Ramada Inn, Rodeway Inn, Super 8, Western Inn, antiques, Bish's RV Ctr, Boogaart's, Buick/Cadillac/GMC, Chrysler/Dodge/Jeep, Ft Kearney Museum, H, H(2mi), Kearney RV Park/camping, NAPA, O'Reilly Parts, to Archway Mon, U NE Kearney, Verizon, vet, Walmart(3mi), S Conoco/dsl, Skeeter's BBQ, Best Western+, Holiday Inn Express
271mm	**full facilities, info, litter barrels, petwalk, wb**
269mm	**full facilities, info, litter barrels, petwalk, eb**
263	Rd 10 b, Odessa, N Sapp Bros./Apple Barrel Rest./dsl, truck repair, Union Pacific RA
257	US 183, Elm Creek, N One 9 Fuel Stop/Subway/dsl/scales/24hr, Sunset Inn, The 4 Seasons RV Camping, S Nebraska Prairie Museum(9mi)
248	Overton
237	US 283, Lexington, N Casey's, Cenex/dsl, Gulf/dsl, Phillips 66/dsl, Arby's, Belen Pupuseria, Burger King, Delight Donuts, DQ, El Rancho Viejo, Hong Kong Buffet, Little Caesar's, McDonald's, Runza, Comfort Inn, Days Inn, Econolodge, Holiday Inn Express, Minute Man Motel, $General, $Tree, Buick/Chevrolet, Military Vehicle Museum, O'Reilly Parts, Plum Creek Foods, Verizon, Walmart/Subway/EVC, S Sinclair/dsl/@, Kirk's Café, Super 8, to Johnson Lake RA(6mi)
231	Darr Rd
227mm	**full facilities, info, litter barrels, petwalk, both lanes, vending**
222	NE 21, Cozad, N Casey's/dsl/scales, Cenex/dsl, Burger King, DQ, El Paradiso, Mickies Rest., Pizza Hut, Runza, Subway, Cobblestone Inn, Rodeway Inn, $General, Firestone/auto, H, museum
211	NE 47, Gothenburg, N Cenex/dsl, Sinclair/dsl/24hr, Tesla EVC, Lasso Espresso, McDonald's, Mi Ranchito Mexican, NE Grill, Pizza Hut, Runza, Comfort Suites, Howard Johnson, Travel Inn, Buick/Chevrolet, Carquest, H, Pony Express Sta Museum(1mi), S Blue Heron Camping/Gas
199	Brady
194mm	**full facilities, litter barrels, petwalk, both lanes, vending**
190	Maxwell, N gas/dsl, S RV camping, to Ft McPherson Nat Cemetary(2mi)
181mm	weigh sta both lanes
179	to US 30, N Platte, N Pump&Pantry/dsl, Comfort Inn, La Quinta, Motel 6, Studio 6, Tru Hilton, RV camping, S Flying J/Denny's/dsl/scales/LP/RV dump/24hr/@, Love's/McDonald's/Subway/dsl/scales/24hr, tire/lube/repair, truckwash
177	US 83, N Platte, N Cenex/dsl, Gulf/PepperJax Grill, Phillips 66, Sinclair, Sinclair/dsl, Tesla EVC, Amigo's Rest., Applebee's, Arby's, Burger King, Cane's, Coldstone, DQ, Dunkin', Jimmy John's, KFC, King Buffet, Little Caesar's, Luigi's Italian, McDonald's, Noel's Tacos, Perkins, Qdoba, Royal Wok, Ruby Tuesday, Runza, Runza, San Pedro Mexican, Sonic, Starbucks, Subway, Szechuan Buffet, Wendy's, Blue Spruce Motel, Fairfield Inn, Hampton Inn, Hity Inn, North Platte Inn, Ramada, Travelodge, $General, $Tree, Advance Parts, Goodyear/auto, Harley-Davidson, Holiday RV Park, H, museum, O'Reilly Parts, Staples, Tire Pros, to Buffalo Bill's Ranch, Verizon, visitor ctr, Walgreens, Walmart/Subway, S Cenex, Gulf/Hardee's/dsl/24hr, Phillips 66/dsl/RV dump, Taco John's, Best Western+, Candlewood Suites, Days Inn, Holiday Inn Express, Quality Inn, Super 8, Chevrolet/Cadillac, dsl repair, Ford/Lincoln, Hobby Lobby, Honda, Menards, Nissan,

BEAVER CROSSING · AURORA · GIBBON · ELM CREEK · BRADY · N PLATTE

NE

NE

INTERSTATE 80 Cont'd

HERSHEY

177	Continued Seevers Tire/auto, to Lake Maloney RA, Toyota, vet, veterans memorial/info
164	56C, Hershey, N Shell/Western Cafe/dsl/scales/24hr/@, KJ's Ranch Store
160mm	**full facilities, info, litter barrels, petwalk, both lanes**
158	NE 25, Sutherland, N Park Motel(1mi); RV camping, S Sinclair/Godfather's Pizza/dsl, RV camping
149mm	Central/Mountain time zone
145	51C, Paxton, N Shell/dsl/24hr, Days Inn
133	51B, Roscoe
132mm	**full facilities, info, litter barrels, petwalk, wb**
126	US 26, NE 61, Ogallala, N Casey's/dsl, Cenex/dsl, Pump & Pantry/dsl, Sapp Bros/Shell/dsl/24hr, Sinclair, 3 Margarita's, Arby's, Front Street Steaks, Golden Village Chinese, McDonald's, Peking Chinese, Pizza Hut, Runza, Valentino's, Americinn/Tesla EVC, Days Inn, Quality Inn, Travelodge, $General, Buick/Chevrolet/GMC, CarQuest, Chrysler/Dodge/Jeep, Firestone/auto, Ford/Lincoln, Homemade Heaven Sandwiches, H, NAPA, O'Reilly Parts, Ogallala Nature Park, Sinclair, to Lake McConaughy, USPO, S Gulf/Subway/dsl, TA/Country Pride/dsl/scales/24hr/@, DQ, Mi Ranchito Mexican, Noel's Tacos, Wendy's, Best Western+, Holiday Inn Express, Super 8, Ace Hardware, KOA, truck repair, Walmart/dsl/EVC/parking
124mm	**full facilities, info, litter barrels, petwalk, eb**
117	51A, Brule, N Conoco/dsl, Riverside RV camping
107	25B, Big Springs, N Flying J/Max's Diner/dsl/scales/24hr/@, Sinclair/dsl, Motel 6, S McGreer's Camping
102	I-76 S, to Denver
102mm	S Platte River
101	US 138, to Julesburg, S truck parking
99mm	scenic turnout eb
95	NE 27, to Julesburg
85	25A, Chappell, N Pump&Pantry/dsl, Shell/dsl, Rusty Bucket Rest., CarQuest, Creekside RV Camping, Super Foods, USPO, wayside park
76	17F, Lodgepole, N gas/dsl(2mi)
69	17E, to Sunol
61mm	**full facilities, litter barrels, petwalk, wb, vending**
59	US 385, 17J, Sidney, N Gulf/dsl, Sapp Bros/Shell/dsl/24hr, Tesla EVC, Applebee's, Arby's, DQ, McDonald's, Mi Ranchito Mexican, Pit BBQ, Pizza Hut, Runza, Subway, Best Western+, Days Inn, Fairfield Inn, Hampton Inn, Motel 6, Quality Inn, auto/dsl repair, Cabela's Outfitters/RV Park, Chrysler/Dodge/Jeep, Verizon, visitor ctr, Walmart, S Love's/Taco John's/dsl/scales/24hr/@, Comfort Inn & Suites, Country Inn Suites, auto tire/truck repair, truckwash
55	NE 19, to Sterling, Sidney
51.5mm	**full facilities, litter barrels, petwalk, /hist marker eb, vending**
48	to Brownson
38	rd 17 b, Potter, N FVC/dsl/LP, Point of Rocks RV Camping(2mi)
29	53A, Dix, N gas, food
22	53E, Kimball, N Days Inn, Motel Kimball, Sleep4Less Motel, city park, Main St Mkt, NAPA, Rook RV Park(seasonal)
20	NE 71, Kimball, N Conoco/dsl, FVC/dsl, Kwik Stop, O'Henry's Diner, Pizza Hut, Subway, 1st Interstate Inn, Days Inn, Motel Kimball, Sleep4Less Motel, Super 8, city park, Main St Mkt, NAPA, Rook RV Park(seasonal)

BIG SPRINGS · SIDNEY · KIMBALL

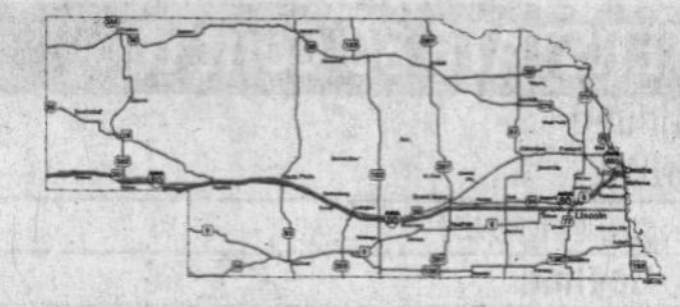

8	53C, to Bushnell
1	53B, Pine Bluffs, N RV camping
0mm	Nebraska/Wyoming state line

INTERSTATE 680 (Omaha)

BEEBEETOWN

29b a	I-80, W to Omaha, E to Des Moines. I-680 begins/ends on I-80, exit 27.
28	IA 191, to Neola, Persia
21	L34, Beebeetown
19mm	**full facilities, info, litter barrels, petwalk, wb**
16mm	**full facilities, info, litter barrels, petwalk, eb**
15mm	scenic overlook
71	I-29 N, to Sioux City
66	Honey Creek, E Hitchcock Tent Camping
3b a	(61 b a from wb) I-29, S to Council Bluffs, IA 988, to Crescent, E Casey's/dsl, to ski area
1	County Rd
14mm	Nebraska/Iowa state line, Missouri River, Mormon Bridge
13	US 75 S, 30th St, Florence, E Shell/dsl, Burger King(1mi), Domino's Pizza(1mi), Holy Smokes BBQ(1mi), KFC(1mi), McDonald's(1mi), OJ's Mexican, Ramona's Mexican, Taco Bell(1mi), Zesto Diner, $Fresh Mkt, LDS Temple, Mormon Trail Ctr, tire repair, Walgreens(1mi), W Mega Saver
12	US 75 N, 48th St, E Cenex/dsl, Tussey's Grill
9	72nd St, E Kwikshop, Burger King, Chick-fil-A, El Muchacho Mexican, Golden Corral, Jimmy John's, KFC, Panda Express, Taco Bell, Big Lots, H, Marshall's, PetSmart, Target/Starbucks, Walgreens, W Cunningham Lake RA
6	NE 133, Irvington, E Casey's, MurphyUSA/dsl, Burger King, Jimmy John's, $Tree, Salween Thai, Walmart/Subway/drugs/24hr, W Legend's Grill, Villagio Pizzeria, Zesto Cafe, Fairfield Inn, Holiday Inn Express
5	Fort St, W KwikShop, QT, Beach House Grill, Dunkin', CVS Drug, HyVee Foods, Walgreens
4	NE 64, Maple St, E Casey's, Valentino's, W Kum&Go/dsl, Megasaver, Burger King, China 1, Godfather's Pizza, Jimmy John's, La Mesa Mexican, McDonald's, Pizza Hut, Runza, Taco Bell, Taco John's, Comfort Suites, La Quinta, $General, Family Fare, O'Reilly Parts, vet
3	US 6, Dodge St, E Bonefish Grill, Cheesecake Factory, Chipotle, Fleming's Steaks, Granite City Rest., JC Mandarin Chinese, PF Chang's, Sickies Burgers, AmericInn, Marriott, AAA, Dick's, JC Penney, Von Maur, Whole Foods Mkt, W QT, Burger King, Chick-fil-A, China Buffet, Domino's, DQ, Fernando's Mexican, Grand China, Jerico's Steaks, Jimmy John's, McDonald's, Panera Bread, Starbucks, Swine Dining BBQ, Best Western, Hampton Inn, Super 8, TownPlace Suites, Wyndham, Cadillac, Chevrolet, Costco/gas, Discount Tire, Menard's
2	Pacific St, E Runza, Subway, W BP, Mega Saver, Big Fred's Pizza, Bronco's, Schucks Seafood, Sebastian's Steaks
1	NE 38, W Center Rd, E Cenex/dsl, Don Carmelo's, Don&Millie's Rest., W Baker's Fuel, Phillips 66, Arby's, Burger King, Chippy's, DeLeon's, Dickey's BBQ, IHOP, Krispy Kreme, Krispy Kreme, Starbucks, Subway, Taco Bell, $Tree, Baker's Foods/dsl, Office Depot, TJ Maxx, Tuesday Morning
0mm	I-680 begins/ends on I-80, exit 446.

IRVINGTON

NEVADA

INTERSTATE 15

MESQUITE ELGIN BYRON

Exit #	Services
123mm	Nevada/Arizona state line, Pacific/Mountain time zone
122	Lp 15, Mesquite, NV Welcome Ctr both lanes, **E full facilities, petwalk,** Arco, Maverik/dsl, Shell/DQ/dsl, Cafe Rio, Cucina Italiana, Dominos, Dutch Bros, Golden West Rest./casino, Jack-in-the-Box, KFC, Los Lupes, Los Moritas Mexican, Peggy Sue's Cafe, Taco Bell, Thai House, Best Western, Rising Star, $General, Ace Hardware, AutoZone, Big O Tire, city park, museum, NAPA, Smith's/Subway/dsl, Sun Resort RV Park, USPO, Walgreens, **W** 76/dsl/LP/RV park, McDonald's, Sierra's Buffet, Eureka Motel/casino, Virgin River Hotel/casino
120	Lp 15, Mesquite, Bunkerville, **E** Chevron, Conoco, Shell/dsl, Sinclair/dsl, Chipotle, McDonald's, Panda Express, Casablanca Resort/casino/RV Park, Grand Destinations Hotel, Oasis Resort RV Park, Mesquite Trails RV Camping, USPO, **W** Chevron/dsl, Shell, Del Taco, Pancho's Tacos, Pizza Hut, Holiday Inn Express, $Tree, Ford/RV Ctr, H, Thai Bistro, Verizon, Walmart/Subway
118	Lower Flat Top Dr, **W** Flying J/Wendy's/dsl/scales/24hr
112	NV 170, Riverside, Bunkerville
110mm	truck parking both lanes
100	to Carp, Elgin
96mm	truck parking both lanes
93	NV 169, to Logandale, Overton, **E** Shell, Pirates Landing Pizza, Lake Mead RA, Lost City Museum
91	NV 168, Glendale, **E** Chevron, **W** Arco/dsl, Muddy River Rest., USPO
90.5mm	Muddy River
90	NV 168(from nb), Glendale, Moapa, **W** Moapa Indian Res.
88	Hidden Valley
88mm	parking area both lanes
84	Byron
80	Ute
75	Valley of Fire SP, Lake Mead NRA, **E** Chevron/dsl
64	US 93 N, Great Basin Hwy, to Ely, Great Basin NP, **W** Love's/Subway/Godfather's/dsl/scales/24hr/@
60mm	weigh sta sb
58	NV 604, Las Vegas Blvd, to Apex, Nellis AFB
54	Speedway Blvd, Hollywood Blvd, **E** Petro/Sinclair/dsl/scales/24hr/@, Lisa Marie's Kitchen, Las Vegas Speedway, **W** Speedee Mart/dsl, Motel 6
52	rd 215 W, **E** Maverik/dsl/scales
50	Lamb Ave, **E** Arco, Shell, Taco Bell, Comfort Inn, **W** Chevron, H
48	Craig Rd, **E** 7-11, Arco, Pilot/KFC/Pizza Hut/dsl/scales/24hr, Shell, Sinclair/Subway/dsl, Burger King, Farmer Boys, Jack-in-the-Box, Saborr Mexican, Taco Bell, Zapata's Cantina, Comfort Inn, Firestone/auto, Freightliner, O'Rielly Parts, to Nellis AFB, **W** 7-11, 7-11, Chevron, BJ's Rest., Blaze Pizza, Cafe Rio, Cane's, Carl's Jr, Chili's, Chipotle Mexican, Cracker Barrel, Del Taco, Dutch Bros, El Pollo Loco, Famous Dave's BBQ, Five Guys, In-N-Out, Jamba Juice, Jersey Mike's, Jimmy Johns, L&L HBBQ, Marble Slab, McDonald's, Mo Bettahs HBBQ, Old School Pizza, Olive Garden, Panda Express, Panera Bread, Poke Sushitto, Sonic, Starbucks, Subway, Taco Bell, The Habit Burger, TX Roadhouse, Best Western, Cannery Casino, Hampton Inn, My Place Hotel, Springhill Suites, AutoZone, Lowe's, Sam's Club/gas, truck repair
46	Cheyenne Ave, **E** Hamburger Hut, Panda Express,

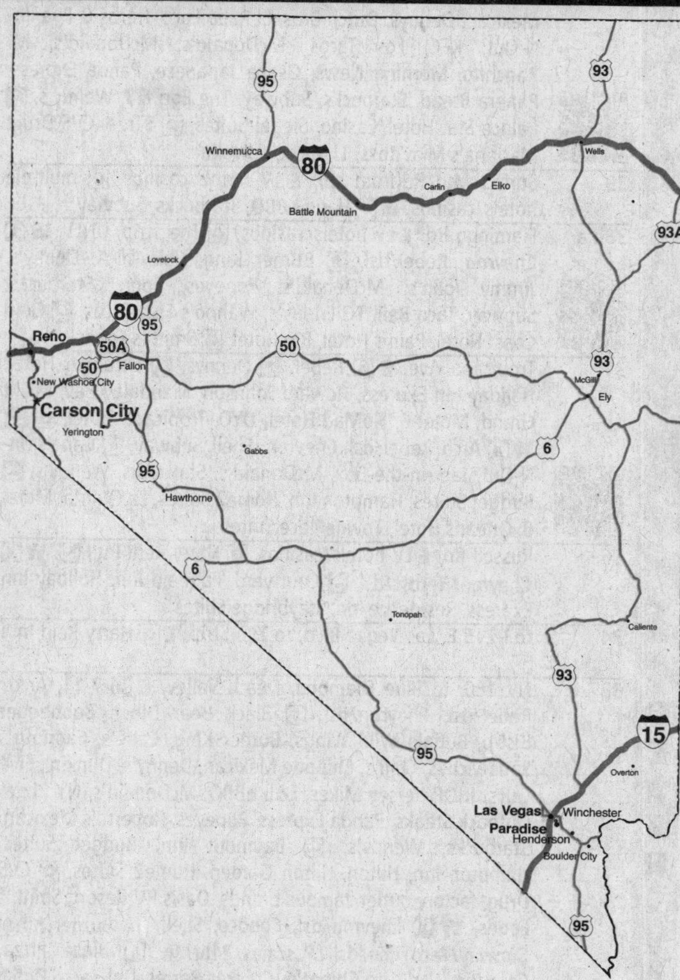

Exit #	Services
46	Continued Subway, Taco Bell, Teriyaki Boy, 7-11, Family$, Marianna's Mkt, NAPA, vet, **W** 7-11, Sinclair/Mortons/Subway/dsl/LP24hr, Denny's, Mariscos Mexican, McDonald's, Tacos El Gordo, Sunrise Inn, Aamco, Blue Beacon, dsl repair, Kenworth, SpeedCo, tires
45	Lake Mead Blvd, **E** Arco/Rebel/dsl, Chevron/McDonald's, Arby's, Burger King, CaliBombs, Carl's Jr, Chipotle, Denny's, Dunkin', El Cazador, El Pollo Loco, Jack-in-the-Box, McDonald's, Popeye's, Starbucks, Taco Bell, Wingstop, 7-11, PepBoys, **W** Arco/dsl, Maverik, Del Taco, El Pollo Loco, Jack-in-the-Box, McDonald's, Panda Express, Starbucks, West Side Oasis
44	Washington Ave(from sb), **E** museum
43	D St(from nb), same as 44
42b a	I-515 to LV, US 95 N to Reno, US 93 S to Phoenix
41b a	NV 159, Charleston Blvd, **E** 7-11, Arco/dsl, Cheesecake Factory, Shake Shack, Bungalows Hotel, Super 8, Premium Outlets/famous brands, Walgreens, **W** Arco/Rebel/dsl, Chevron, Del Taco, Jimmy John's, McDonald's, Omelet House, Poppy's Donuts, Port of Subs, Wendy's, 7-11, CVS Drug, H, Smith's Foods
40	Sahara Ave, **E** Golden Steer Steaks, Circus Circus, Hilton Grand, Sahara Hotel, The Lexi Hotel, The Strat Hotel, Westgate, multiple casinos/hotels, The Strip, **W** 7-11, Arco/dsl, Chevron, Rebel/dsl, Shell, Sinclair/7-11,

NV

INTERSTATE 15 Cont'd

40 Continued
Biwon KBBQ, Cafe Rio, Carl's Jr, Chick-fil-A, Chipotle Mexican, Dennys, Dutch Bros, El Pollo Loco, Herbs & Rye, In-N-Out, KFC, Los Tacos, McDonald's, McDonald's, Mi Ranchito, Morning News, Osaka Japanese, Panda Express, Panera Bread, Starbucks, Subway, The Egg & I, Wendy's, Palace Sta. Hotel/Casino, Siegel Suites, $Tree, CVS Drug, Mariana's Mkt, Ross, TJ Maxx, Valvoline

39 Spring Mtn Rd(from sb), E LV hotels/casinos, multiple hotels/casinos, W Hanu KBBQ, Starbucks, Subway

38b a Flamingo Rd, E LV hotels/casinos, The Strip, UNLV, W Chevron, Rebel/dsl, Burger King, Chick-fil-A, Denny's, Jimmy John's, McDonald's, Popeyes, Sonic, Starbucks, Subway, Taco Bell, TGIFriday's, Wahoo's Fish Tacos, Gold Coast Hotel, Palms Hotel, Rio Hotel, Smith's Foods

37 Tropicana Ave, E Rebel, Dennys, Excaliber Hotel, Holiday Inn Express, Howard Johnson, Mandalay Bay, MGM Grand, Motel 6, NoMad Hotel, OYO, Tropicana Hotel, W Arco/Rebel/dsl, Chevron, Shell/Subway, Cane's, In-N-Out, Jack-in-the-Box, McDonald's, Starbucks, Wendy's, Budget Suites, Hampton Inn, Home2 Suites, La Quinta, Motel 6, Orleans Hotel, TownePlace Suites

36 Russell Rd, E LV hotels/casinos, Harry Reid Int'l, W Chevron/Herbst/dsl, Courtyard, Fairfield Inn, Holiday Inn Express, Residence Inn, Staybridge Suites

34 to I-215 E, Las Vegas Blvd, to The Strip, E Harry Reid Int'l

DEATH VALLEY

33 NV 160, to Blue Diamond, Death Valley, E 7-11, Arco/Rebel/dsl, Chevron/dsl, Black Bear Diner, Bootlegger Bistro, Buffalo Wild Wings, Burger King, Cane's, Capriotti's Sandwiches, Chili's, Chipotle Mexican, Denny's, Dunkin', Five Guys, IHOP, Jersey Mikes, L&L HBBQ, McDonald's, NY Pizza, Outback Steaks, Panda Express, Popeyes, Roberto's Mexican, Starbucks, Wendy's, Baymont Inn, Budget Suites, Hampton Inn, Hilton, Hilton Garden, Home2 Suites, CVS Drug, factory outlet/famous brands, Oasis RV Resort, Smith's Foods, W Chevron/dsl, Conoco, Shell, TA/Burger King/Subway/TacoTime/dsl/LP/scales/24hr/@, Blaze Pizza, Cafe Rio, Carl's Jr, Chipotle, Cracker Barrel, Del Taco, Dutch Bros, El Pollo Loco, Famous Dave's BBQ, In-N-Out, Jack-in-the-Box, Jersey Mike's, McDonald's, Ohana HBBQ, Panda Express, Panera Bread, Papa Murphy's, Subway, The Habit Burger, Zupas, Silverton Lodge/Casino, The Berkley Hotel, $Tree, 99c Store, Albertson's, AT&T, Bass ProShops, BigLots, Discount Tire, GNC, Kohl's, Meineke, PetCo, Ross, Verizon, Walgreens, WorldMkt

31 Silverado Ranch Blvd, E Chevron, Shell, Capriotti's Sandwiches, Del Taco, Denny's, Don Vito's, McDonald's, Vikings Seafood, South Point Hotel/Casino, The Granview

30 W Cactus Ave, E Chevron, Shell, W Chevron/dsl, Circle K, Domino's, Dutch Bros, KFC, Starbucks

29 Starr Ave

27 NV 146, to Henderson, Lake Mead, Hoover Dam, E 7-11, Arco, Shell, Burger King, Jack-in-the-Box, Camping World, casino, Costco/gas, W vet

JEAN

25 NV 161, Sloan, E Camping World

24mm bus/truck check sta nb

12 NV 161, to Goodsprings, Jean, E Chevron/dsl, NV Correctional, skydiving, USPO, W Chevron/White Castle/dsl, Starbucks

1 Primm, E Chevron/dsl, Chevron/dsl, Alex's Mexican, Carl's Jr, Denny's, McDonald's, McDonald's, Pony Express Pizza, Taco Bell, Buffalo Bill's Resort/casino, factory outlets, Primm Valley Resort/casino, W Flying J/DQ/dsl/scales, Whiskey Pete's Hotel/casino

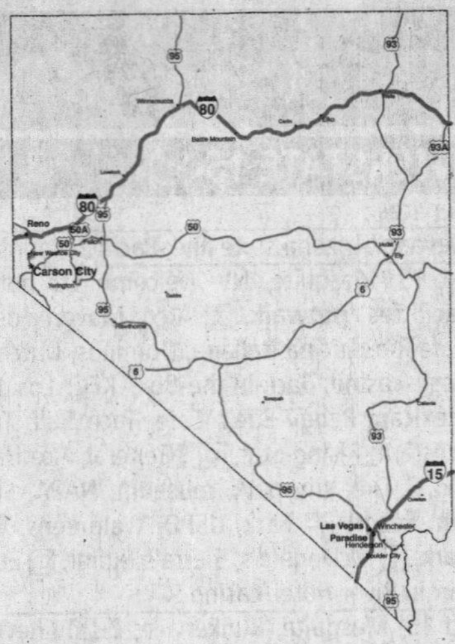

0mm Nevada/California state line

INTERSTATE 80

411mm Nevada/Utah state line

410 US 93A, to Ely, W Wendover, N Maverik, S **full facilities, NV Welcome Ctr/info**, Chevron/dsl, EVC, Pilot/Arby's/dsl/scales/24hr, ShellAM Best/dsl, Sinclair, Burger King, Fratelli Pizza, McDonald's, Pizza Hut, Rolberto's Mexican, Subway, Bonneville Inn, Knights Inn, Montego Bay Hotel/casino, Motel 6, Nugget Hotel/casino, Peppermill Hotel/casino/RV parking, Quality Inn, Rainbow Hotel/casino, Red Garter Hotel/casino, A & I Hardware, city park, KOA, Smith's Foods/fuel

407 Ola, W Wendover

405mm Pacific/Mountain time zone

OASIS

398 to Pilot Peak

390mm Silverzone Pass, elevation 5940

387 to Shafter

378 NV 233, to Montello, Oasis

376 to Pequop

373mm Pequop Summit, elev 6967, **both lanes**, **litter barrels**

365 to Independence Valley

360 to Moor

354mm parking area eb

352b a US 93, Great Basin Hwy, E Wells, N Chevron/dsl/LP, Conoco/dsl, Petro/Sinclair/Dunkin/dsl/café/casino, Burger King/Subway, Motel 6, Sharon Motel, Super 8, SureStay Hotel, Crossroads RV Park, repair, tires, S Flying J/dsl/scales/LP/casino/RV Dump/24hr, LNG, Love's/McDonalds/dsl/scales/24hr, Hampton Inn

351 W Wells, N Wells/dsl/LP, Family$, Mtn Shadows RV Park, NAPA, Roy's Foods, USPO, Well's Hardware, S Maverik/dsl, Angel Lake RV Park, to Angel Lake RA

DEVILS GATE

348 to Beverly Hills

343 to Welcome, Starr Valley, N Welcome RV Park

333 Deeth, Starr Valley

328 to River Ranch

321 NV 229, Halleck, Ruby Valley

318mm N Fork Humboldt River

317 to Elburz

314 to Ryndon, Devils Gate, N Sinclair/cafe/dsl, S Elk RV Park

312mm check sta both lanes

310 to Osino, S Valley View RV Park

303 E Elko, N Flyers/CFN/dsl, Sinclair/Arctic Circle/dsl/24hr, Wingers, Holiday Inn Express, Home2 Suites, Ledgestone Hotel, TownePlace Suites, Harley-Davidson, S Chevron/dsl, Maverik/dsl, Sinclair/dsl,

INTERSTATE 80 Cont'd

ELKO

303 Continued
Blue Moon Rest., Burger King, Chef Cheng's Chinese, Domino's, DQ, Garibaldi's Mexican, McDonald's/playplace, Pizza Barn, Pizza Hut, Subway, Taco Time, Teppanyaki, Thai Cafe, Toki Ona Diner, Wendy's, Best Western, Comfort Inn, Days Inn, Elkotel, Gold Country Inn/casino, Holiday Motel, Maverick Hotel/casino, Motel 6, Quality Inn, Shutters Hotel, Stay Express Inn, Super 8, Travelers, Travelodge, $Tree, Albertson's, AT&T, Big O Tires, Buick/Cadillac/Chevrolet/GMC, city park, Double Dice RV Park, Ford, H, Iron Horse RV Park, JC Penney, NAPA, NE NV Museum, Purcell Tires, Valley View RV Park

301 NV 225, Elko, N Maverik/dsl, 9 Beans & A Burrito, Arby's, Burger King, Chipotle, Greatwall Chinese, Jack-in-the-Box, Mattie's Grill, McDonald's/playplace, Papa Murphy's, Port of Subs, RoundTable Pizza, Baymont Inn, Shilo Inn Suites, Home Depot, Kohl's, Marshall's, Petco, Raley's Foods, Ross, Tesla EVC, Verizon, Walmart, S Flyers, Shell, Shell/dsl, BJ Bull Bakery, Costa Vida, Dos Amigos, KFC, Little Caesar's, Luciano's, Starbucks, Subway, Taco Bell, American Inn, Centre Motel, Economy Inn, Esquire Inn, Hampton Inn, Key Inn, Manor Inn, Midtown Motel, Ramada, Rodeway Inn, Stampede Motel, Stockmen's Hotel/casino, Super 8, Thunderbird Motel, Travelodge, Advance Parts, AutoZone, Cimarron West RV Park, CVS Drug, Family$, H, O'Reilly Parts, OfficeMax, Smith's Foods/dsl, USPO, Verizon

298 W Elko, S Sinclair/Port of Subs/dsl

292 to Hunter, N CA Trail Interpretive Ctr

CARLIN

285mm Humboldt River, S Carlin Tunnel

282 NV 221, E Carlin

280 NV 766, Carlin, N Pizza Factory, S Chevron/dsl, Flyers, ONE9/dsl/scales/24hr, Build A Burger, Chin's Cafe, Rigobertos Mexican, State Café/casino, Traveler's Inn, Ace Hardware, Family$, Fresh Mkt, tires, USPO

279 NV 278(from eb), to W Carlin

271 to Palisade

270mm Emigrant Summit, elevation 6114, truck parking both lanes, litter barrels

268 to Emigrant

BATTLE MOUNTAIN

261 NV 306, to Beowawe, Crescent Valley

259mm **both lanes, full facilities, litter barrels, petwalk**

257mm Humboldt River

254 to Dunphy, N Bunny Trails RV

244 to Argenta

233 NV 304, to Battle Mountain, N Conoco/dsl, Mama's Pizza/deli, Comfort Inn, FoodTown, Hardware Store, H, S Golden Gate Petro, Krispy Krunchy Chicken

231 NV 305, Battle Mountain, N Chevron/dsl, Flying J/76/dsl/casino/24hr, Maverik/dsl, El Aguila Real, Hide-a-way Steaks, McDonald's, Ming Dynasty, Owl Rest., Pizza Factory, Subway, Big Chief Motel, Super 8, Carquest, city park, Family$, fireworks, H, Mills Drug, NAPA, tires, USPO

229 NV 304, W Battle Mountain, N Flying J/76/dsl/casino/scales/24hr, Shell/dsl, Colt Rest./casino, Colt RV camping

222 to Mote

216 Valmy, **both lanes, full facilities, litter barrels, petwalk, RV dump**, N Chevron/USPO/dsl, S Valmy RV Park

212 to Stonehouse

205 to Pumpernickel Valley

203 to Iron Point

200 Golconda Summit, elevation 5159, truck parking both lanes, litter barrels

GOLCONDA

194 Golconda, N USPO

187 to Button Point, **both lanes, full facilities, litter barrels, petwalk, RV dump**

180 NV 794, E Winnemucca Blvd

178 NV 289, Winnemucca Blvd, Winnemucca, N Wagon Wheel RV Park, S Chevron/dsl, Maverik, Korean Cuisine, Candlewood Suites, Frontier Motel, Valu Motel, carwash, H, vet

176 US 95 N, Winnemucca, N Love's/Carl's Jr./Speedco/dsl/24hr, Pacific Pride/dsl, S Chevron/dsl/24hr, Conoco/dsl, Flyers, Flying J/dsl/LP/RV dump/24hr, G Gas, Silver State Gas, Burger King, China Garden, Dos Amigos Mexican, Dotty's, Griddle Rest., Jack-in-the-Box, KFC/LJ Silver, McDonald's/playplace, Pig BBQ, Port of Subs, Rolbertos, RoundTable Pizza, Sid's Rest., Subway, Taco Bell, Best Western, Days Inn, Econo Lodge Inn, Holiday Inn Express, Holiday Motel, Model T Motel/casino/RVPark, Motel 6, Regency Inn, Rodeway Inn, Scott Motel, Scottish Inns, Super 8, Town House, Winnemucca Inn/casino, Winners Hotel/casino, $Tree, Ace Hardware, AutoZone, Ford, H, NAPA, O'Reilly Parts, Ridley's Foods, RV camping, Schwab Tire, Tesla EVC, Walmart

MILL CITY

173 W Winnemucca, N Pilot/dsl/scales/24hr, S

168 to Rose Creek, prison area

158 to Cosgrave, **both lanes, full facilities, litter barrels, petwalk**

151 Mill City, N TA/Mobil/Taco Bell/dsl/casino/24hr/@

149 NV 400, Mill City, S Star Point Gen. Store/RV camping

145 Imlay, N USPO, S Star Peak RV Park

138 Humboldt

129 Rye Patch Dam, N Rye Patch State Park, S Chevron/Rye Patch Trkstp/dsl

119 to Rochester, Oreana

112 to Coal Canyon, S to correctional ctr

107 E Lovelock(from wb), same as 106

106 Main St, Lovelock, N Chevron/dsl/LP, PJ's Gas/subs/dsl, Black Rock Grill, McDonald's, Cadillac Inn, Covered Wagon Motel, Punch Inn/casino, Royal Inn, Sunset, Super 10 Motel, Sure Stay, auto care, Candy Beach Camping, city park/playground/restrooms, Family$, H, Safeway Foods, U-Haul, USPO, S Conoco/Port of Subs/dsl/24hr

105 W Lovelock(from eb), N Shop'n Go/dsl, Valero/dsl, Mendoza's Mexican, Pizza Factory, H, museum, NAPA, same as 106, tires

93 to Toulon, S

83 US 95 S, to Fallon, **both lanes, full facilities, litter barrels**

FERNLEY

78 to Jessup

65 to Hot Springs, Nightingale

50 NV Pacific Pkwy, Fernley

48 US 50A, US 95A, to Fallon, E Fernley, N Flying J/Denny's/dsl/scales/Lp/24hr, S Chevron/dsl, Shell/dsl, Burger King, Domino's, Dotty's Grill, Jack-in-the-Box, KFC, McDonald's, Papa Murphy's, Pizza Factory, Pizza Hut, Port of Subs, Ranch House Rest./casino, Starbucks, Taco Bell, Best Western, Super 8, $Tree, AutoZone, Chrysler/Dodge/Jeep, Grocery Outlet, Lowe's, O'Reilly Parts, Raley's Mkt, tires, to Great Basin NP, URGENT CARE, Verizon, Walgreens, Walmart/Subway

46 US 95A, W Fernley, N Love's/Arby's/dsl/scales/24hr, S Pilot/Wendy's/dsl/scales/24hr, Las Palmas Mexican, Comfort Suties, Blue Beacon, SpeedCo

45mm Truckee River

43 to Pyramid Lake, Wadsworth, N Pyramid Lake/dsl/RV camping

42mm N wb, full facilities, litter barrels, petwalk, wireless internet, check sta eb

= gas = food = lodging = other = rest stop

NV

DERBY DAM — SPARKS — RENO — BOOMTOWN

INTERSTATE 80 Cont'd

Exit #	Services
40	Painted Rock
38	Orchard
36	Derby Dam
32	USA Pkwy, Tracy, Clark Station, S Golden Gate/Port of Subs/dsl/scales, ONE9/dsl/24hr, Burger King, Philly's, Shanghai Express, Taco Bell, Studio 6, URGENT CARE
28	NV 655, Waltham Way, Patrick
27mm	scenic view eb
25mm	check sta wb
23	Mustang, S Chevron/dsl, Kenworth
22	Lockwood
21	Vista Blvd, Greg St, Sparks, N Chevron/McDonald's, QuikStop, Del Taco, Wendy's, Fairfield Inn, Woodspring Suites, H, S Petro/Mobil/Iron Skillet/dsl/24hr/@, Super 8, Peterbilt, Verizon
20	Sparks Blvd, Sparks, N 7-11, Shell/dsl, BJ's Rest., Buffalo Wild Wings, Buffalo Wild Wings, Burrito Bandito, Carl's Jr, Chick-fil-A, Chipotle, Dunkin, Jimmy John's, L&L HA BBQ, Olive Garden, Outback Steaks, Panda Express, Papa John's, Peg's Ham'N Eggs, Popeyes, Taco Bell, The Habit, Hampton Inn, Residence Inn, AAA, AT&T, Lowe's, mall, Old Navy, Petco, Scheel's Sports, Schwab Tire, Target, Tires+, TJ Maxx, Verizon, water funpark, S Petro/Mobil/Iron Skillet/dsl/24hr/@, Super 8, Freightliner, Verizon, Volvo
19	E McCarran Blvd, Sparks, N Arco, Chevron/dsl, Sinclair/dsl, TA/Fuddrucker's/dsl/scales/@, Applebee's, Baskin-Robbins, BJ's BBQ, Black Bear Diner, Burger King, Cane's, Domino's, El Pollo Loco, El Pulgarcito, Firehouse Subs, Jack-in-the-Box, KFC, Little Caesar's, McDonald's, Pizza+, Port Of Subs, Siu Korean, Starbucks, Taco Bell, Wendy's, Wienerschnitzel, Aloha Inn, Extended Stay, Sunrise Motel, Western Village Inn/casino, Windsor Inn, $Tree, 99c Store, AutoZone, CVS Drug, Family$, Foodmaxx Foods, O'Reilly Parts, Pep Boys, Ross, Victorian RV Park, S Denny's, Super Burrito, Best Western+
18	NV 445, Pyramid Way, Sparks, N 7-11, Blind Onion Pizza, Bourbon Square Casino, In-N-Out, S Nugget Hotel/casino
17	Rock Blvd, Nugget Ave, Sparks, N Arco, Chevron, V/dsl, Safari Motel, Victorian Inn, Wagon Train Motel, casinos, O'Reilly Parts, S Nugget Hotel/casino
16	B St, E 4th St, Victorian Ave, N Arco, Quick Mart, Jack's Cafe, Motel 6, Rail City Casino, S Chevron/repair
15	I-580 S, US 395, to Carson City, Susanville, S Best Western, Holiday Inn Express, Hyatt Place, La Quinta, Costco/gas, Grand Sierra Resort, USPO, Walmart
14	Wells Ave, Reno, N Motel 6, S Chevron/dsl, Denny's, Jack's Coffee, America's Best Inn, Ramada Inn, auto repair, Tire Pros, vet
13	US 395, Virginia St, Reno, N Shell/dsl, Capriotti's Sandwiches, Taco Shop, S Chevron, Jimmy John's, Circus Circus, Travelodge, H, to downtown hotels/casinos, to UNVReno, Walgreens
12	Keystone Ave, Reno, N Arco, Bighorn Tavern,
12	Continued Pizza Hut, Starbucks, Gateway Inn, 7-11, CVS Drug, Jiffy Lube, Raley's Foods, USPO, S Chevron/dsl, Maverik/dsl, Burger King, Chipotle, Cracker Barrel, Domino's, Firehouse Subs, Gold'N Silver Rest., In-N-Out, Jack-in-the-Box, KFC, McDonald's, Mt Mike's Pizza, Pizza Baron, Port of Subs, Starbuks, Taco Bell, Wendy's, casinos, Keystone RV Park, NAPA, O'Reilly Parts, SaveMart/drug
10	McCarran Blvd, Reno, N 7-11/dsl, Arco, Baskin-Robbins, Bully's Grill, Burger King, Carl's Jr, Chili's, Chipotle, Del Taco, El Pollo Loco, IHOP, Jack-in-the-Box, KFC, L&L HBBQ, McDonald's, Papa Murphy's, Pizza+, Poke King, Popeyes, Qdoba Mexican, RoundTable Pizza, Saladworks, Silver Chop Chinese, Starbucks, Subway, Sushi Rose, Taco Bell, Tacos el Rey, Wingstop, $Tree, AT&T, AutoZone, Big O Tires, Discount Tire, Kohl's, O'Reilly Parts, PetSmart, Ross, Safeway/dsl, SaveMart Foods, Staples, Tires+, Walgreens, Walmart, S 7-11, Home Depot, URGENT CARE, vet
9	Robb Dr, N Chevron/dsl, Maverik/dsl, Bully's Grill, Burger Me!, Casa Grande, China Kitchen, Domino's, Inclined Burgers, Jimmy John's, Moxie's Cafe, Pizza Guys, Port Of Subs, Rita's Custard, Starbucks, Hampton Inn, CVS Drug, Raley's Foods/dsl, URGENT CARE
8	W 4th St(from eb), Robb Dr, Reno
7	Mogul
6.5mm	truck parking/hist marker
5	to E Verdi(from wb no return), N Maria's Mexican
4.5mm	scenic view eb
4	Garson Rd, Boomtown, N Chevron/dsl/casino, Best Western Plus, Boomtown Hotel, Cabela's, KOA/RV dump
3.5mm	check sta eb
3	(from wb), Verdi
2.5mm	Truckee River
2	Lp 80, to Verdi, N Sinclair/dsl/24hr, Jack-in-the-Box, Port of Subs, Gold Ranch RV Resort/casino
0mm	Nevada/California state line

NOTES

NEW HAMPSHIRE

INTERSTATE 89

W LEBANON

Exit #	Services
61mm	New Hampshire/Vermont state line, Connecticut River
20(60)	NH 12A, W Lebanon, E Sunoco, 99 Rest., Chili's, Dunkin', KFC/Taco Bell, Lui Lui Pizza, Subway, GNC, Hannaford Foods, Jo-Ann Fabrics, K-Mart, LL Bean, Shaw's Foods, TJ Maxx, Town Fair Tire, USPO, W Tesla EVC, 110 Grill, Applebee's, D'angelo's, Denny's, Five Guys, Koto Japanese, McDonald's, Moe's SW Grill, Panera Bread, Starbucks, Weathervane Seafood, Wendy's, Baymont Inn, Fireside Inn, $Tree, AT&T, Best Buy, BJ's Whse/dsl, CVS Drug, Home Depot, JC Penney, Kohl's, Michael's, Midas, Old Navy, PetSmart, PriceChopper Foods, Staples, Verizon, Walgreens, Walmart
19(58)	US 4, NH 10, W Lebanon, E Gulf/dsl, Mobil, China Station, AutoZone, Family$, Ford, Harley-Davidson, Honda, Pricechopper Foods, W Sunoco/Maplewoods/dsl, O'Reilly Parts
57mm	**full facilities, litter barrels, petwalk, , , vending, weigh sta nb, Welcome Ctr/ /weigh sta sb**
18(56)	NH 120, Lebanon, E Irving/dsl/scales, Courtyard(3mi), Hilton Garden, Quality Inn, Residence Inn(2mi), Chrysler/Dodge/Jeep, Freightliner, H, Nissan, to Dartmouth Coll, Volvo/VW, Wilson Tire/repair, W Mobil/Subway/dsl, Shell/dsl, U-Haul
17(54)	US 4, to NH 4A, Enfield, E vet
16(52)	Eastman Hill Rd, E Gulf/Subway/dsl, W Mobil/Dunkin Donuts/dsl, Whaleback Ski Area
15(50)	Montcalm
14(47)	NH 10(from sb), N Grantham
13(43)	NH 10, Grantham, E Irving/Gen Store/dsl, W Irving/Circle K, Dunkin', Pizza Chef, vet
40mm	**full facilities, info, litter barrels, petwalk, ; picnic table, nb, vending**
12A(37)	Georges Mills, W , food, lodging, RV camping, to Sunapee SP
12(34)	NH 11 W, New London, E Irving/dsl, McKenna Rest., Maple Hill Country Inn, New London Inn, H
11(31)	NH 11 E, King Hill Rd, New London, E Fairway Motel, New London Inn
10(27)	to NH 114, Sutton, E to Winslow SP, W to Wadleigh SP
26mm	**full facilities, info, litter barrels, petwalk, , , sb, vending**
9(19)	NH 103, Warner, E Irving/Circle K/Dunkin Donuts/dsl, Shell/Subway/pizza, McDonald's, Aubuchon Hardware, MktBasket Foods, Rollins SP, W to Sunapee SP
8(17)	NH 103(from nb, no EZ return), Warner, W gas, food, museum, to Rollins SP
15mm	Warner River
7(14)	NH 103, Davisville, W Pleasant Lake Camping
12mm	Contoocook River
6(10)	NH 127, Contoocook, E Sunoco, Everyday Cafe, vet, W Elm Brook Park, Sandy Beach Camping(3mi)
5(8)	US 202 W, NH 9(exits left from nb), Hopkinton, W food, RV camping(seasonal)
4(7)	NH 103, from nb, no EZ return, Hopkinton, E gas
3(4)	Stickney Hill Rd(from nb)
2(2)	NH 13, Clinton St, Concord, E H, W NH Audubon Ctr
1(1)	Logging Hill Rd, Bow, E Mobil, Chen Yang Li Chinese, Hampton Inn
0mm	I-93 N to Concord, S to Manchester, I-89 begins/ends on I-93, 36mm.

NEW LONDON

BOW

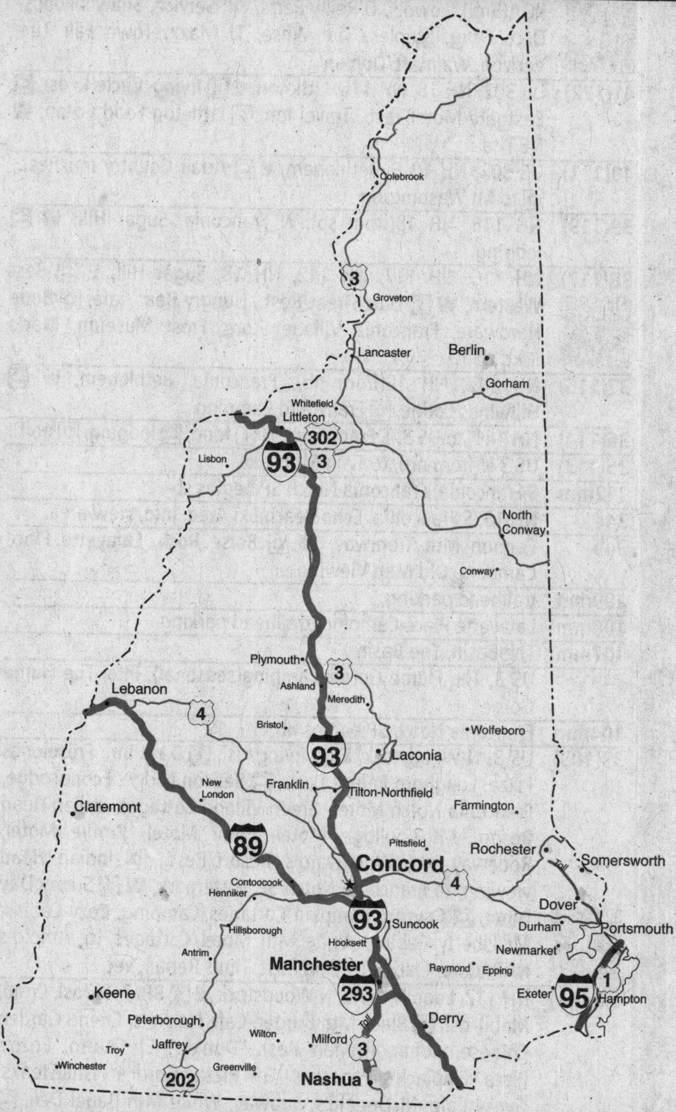

NH

INTERSTATE 93

LITTLETON

Exit #	Services
2(11)	I-91, N to St Johnsbury, S to White River Jct. I-93 begins/ends on I-91, exit 19.
1(8)	VT 18, to US 2, to St Johnsbury, E gas, food, camping, lodging
1mm	**full facilities, info, litter barrels, petwalk, , , vending, Welcome Ctr nb, WiFi**
131mm	Vermont/New Hampshire state line, Connecticut River, exits 1-2 are in VT
44(130)	NH 18, NH 135, **Welcome Ctr(8am-8pm)/scenic vista both lanes, W full facilities, info, litter barrels, petwalk, ,**
43(125)	NH 135(from sb), to NH 18, Littleton, W same as 42, H
42(124)	US 302 E, NH 10 N, Littleton, E Citgo/Quiznos, Cumberland Farms, Sunoco/dsl, Burger King, Deluxe Pizza, Dunkin', Littleton Diner, Pizza Hut, Subway, Littleton Motel, Family$, USPO, Walgreens, W Cumberland Farms/dsl, Mobil, 99 Rest., Applebee's, Domino's, McDonald's, Hampton Inn, $Tree,

INTERSTATE 93 Cont'd

42(124) Continued
Buick/Chevrolet, Chrysler/Dodge/Jeep/Fiat, Home Depot, KOA(5mi), Lowe's, O'Reilly Parts/VIP Service, Shaw's Foods/Osco Drug, Staples, Tire Whse, TJ Maxx, Town Fair Tire, Verizon, Walmart/Dunkin'

41(122) US 302, NH 18, NH 116, Littleton, **E** [gas] Irving/Circle K/dsl, [lodging] Eastgate Motel/rest., Travel Inn, [other] Littleton Food Co-op, **W** NE Tire

40(121) US 302, NH 10 E, Bethlehem, **E** [lodging] Adair Country Inn/Rest., [other] to Mt Washington

39(119) NH 116, NH 18(from sb), N Franconia, Sugar Hill, **W** [lodging] lodging

S FRANCONIA

38(117) NH 116, NH 117, NH 142, NH 18, Sugar Hill, **E** [lodging] Best Western, **W** [food] DutchTreat Rest., Hungry Bear Café, [other] Bode Hardware, Franconia Village Store, Frost Museum, Mac's Mkt, USPO

37(115) NH 142, NH 18(from nb), Franconia, Bethlehem, **W** [lodging] Hillwinds Lodge, [other] Franstead Camping

36(114) NH 141, to US 3, S Franconia, **W** [food] food, [lodging] lodging, [other] golf

35(113) US 3 N(from nb), to Twin Mtn Lake

112mm S Franconia, Franconia Notch SP begins sb

34c NH 18, S Franconia, Echo Beach Ski Area, info, view area

34b Cannon Mtn Tramway, **W** [other] Boise Rock, Lafayette Place Camping, Old Man Viewing

109mm trailhead parking

108mm Lafayette Place Camping, trailhead parking

107mm The Basin, The Basin

34a US 3, The Flume Gorge, camping(seasonal), info, The Flume Gorge

104mm Franconia Notch SP begins nb

N WOODSTOCK

33(103) US 3, N Woodstock, **E** [gas] Irving/dsl, [food] Days Inn, Fresolones Pizza, Longhorn Palace Rest., [lodging] Beacon Lodge, EconoLodge, Franconia Notch Motel, Green Village Cottages, Indian Head Resort, Mt Coolidge Motel, Pemi Motel, Profile Motel, Rodeway Inn, Woodward's Resort/Rest., [other] Indian Head viewing, to Franconia Notch SP, waterpark, **W** [food] Sunny Day Diner, [lodging] Country Bumpkin Cottages/Camping, Cozy Cabins, Mt Liberty Cabins, White Mtn Motel/Cottages, [other] Arnold's NAPACare, Clark's Trading Post, Tim's Repair, vet

32(101) NH 112, Loon Mtn Rd, N Woodstock, **E** [gas] BP/7-11/dsl, Citgo, Mobil/dsl, [food] Black Mtn Burger, Cafe Nacho's, Cheng Garden Chinese, Common Man Rest., Dunkin', El Charro, Enzo's Pizza, Flapjack's Pancakes, GH Pizza, Gordi's Fish&Steaks, Gypsy Cafe, McDonald's, Subway, White Mtn Bagel Deli, [lodging] Holiday Inn Express, Kancamagu's Lodge, Lincoln Sta. Lodge, Nordic Inn, South Mtn Resort, [other] Aubuchon Hardware, Family$, NAPA, PriceChopper Foods, USPO, **W** [gas] Citgo, [food] Imperial Chinese, Lafayette Dinner Train, Landmark II Rest., Peg's Café, Truant's Rest., Woodstock Inn Rest., [lodging] Alpine Lodge, Cascade Lodge, [other] USPO

31(97) to NH 175, Tripoli Rd, **W** [other] KOA(2mi)

CAMPTON

30(95) US 3, Woodstock, **E** [food] Lanterns End Grill, [lodging] Jack-O-Lantern Inn/rest., [other] golf

29(89) US 3, Thornton, **E** [other] Pemi River RV Park/LP, **W** [lodging] Gilcrest Motel

28(87) NH 49, Campton, **E** [gas] Gulf, Mobil, [food] Dunkin', Exit 28 Pizza, [other] Handy Man Hardware, USPO, **W** [gas] Irving/dsl, [food] Sunset Grill, [other] Branch Brook Camping, Chelsey's Pizza, Mtn Vista RV Park, repair

27(84) Blair Rd, Beebe River, **E** [food] Covered Bridge Farm Table, [lodging] Days Inn, Red Sleigh Condos

26(83) US 3, NH 25, NH 3A, Tenney Mtn Hwy, **W** [lodging] Common Man Inn, EconoLodge, Pilgrim Inn, [other] [H]

25(81) NH 175(from nb), Plymouth, **W** [gas] Citgo/dsl, Irving/Circle K/dsl, [food] Downtown Pizza, Fracher's Diner, HongKong Garden,

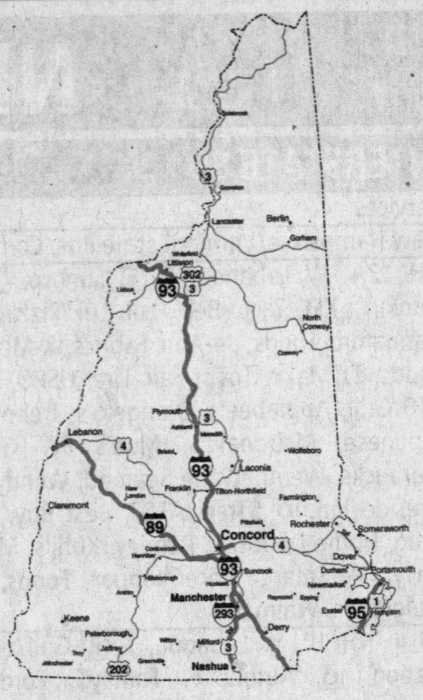

ASHLAND

25(81) Continued
Lucky Dog Grill, Thai Smile, [other] Chase St Mkt, [H], Plymouth State U, USPO

24(76) US 3, NH 25, Ashland, **E** [gas] Irving/Circle K/dsl, Mobil, Racing Mart, [food] Ashland Pizza, Burger King, Common Man Diner, Dunkin', La Catrina, Lucky Dragon Chinese, Village Grill, [lodging] Comfort Inn, [other] $General, Bob's Mkt, Jellystone RV Camp(4mi), repair, USPO

23(71) NH 104, NH 132, to Mt Washington Valley, New Hampton, **E** [gas] Irving/Circle K/dsl, Mobil/dsl, [food] Dunkin', Rossi Italian, Subway, [other] Jellystone, USPO

22(62) NH 127, Sanbornton, **W** [phone], [other] food, gas/dsl, [H]

61mm **full [handicapped] facilities, info, litter barrels, petwalk, [phone], [picnic], [rest stop] sb, vending**

TILTON

20(57) US 3, NH 11, NH 132, NH 140, Tilton, **E** [gas] Irving/Circle K/dsl/24hr, Shell/Subway/dsl, [food] 99 Rest., Applebee's, Burger King, Dunkin', Five Guys, Green Ginger Chinese, KFC, McDonald's, Starbucks, Taco Bell, Thai Cuisine, Tilt'n Diner, UNO, UpperCrust Pizza, Wendy's, [lodging] Hampton Inn, Holiday Inn Express, Super 8, [other] BJ's Whse/gas, Hobby Lobby, Home Depot, Kia, O'Reilly Parts/VIP Service, Old Navy, Staples, Subaru, Tanger Outlet/famous brands, Verizon, Walgreens, **W** [food] Chili's, Pizza Hut, [other] Chrysler/Dodge/Jeep, Ford, Kohl's, Lowe's, MktBasket Foods, Nissan, USPO, VW, Walmart/Subway

56mm Winnipesaukee River

19(55) NH 132(from nb no ez return), Franklin, **W** [gas] Gulf, [food] Ciao Italian, [other] [H], NH Vet Home

51mm **full [handicapped] facilities, info, litter barrels, petwalk, [phone], [picnic], [rest stop] nb, vending**

18(49) to NH 132, Canterbury, **E** [other] to Shaker Village HS

17(46) US 4 W, to US 3, NH 132, Boscawen, **W** [gas] Mobil/Dunkin'

CONCORD

16(41) NH 132, E Concord, **E** [gas] Mobil/dsl, [other] Quality Cash Mkt

15W(40) US 202 W, to US 3, N Main St, Concord, **W** [gas] Citgo, Cumberland/Dunkin', Speedway, [food] Domino's, Friendly's, [lodging] Courtyard/café

15E I-393 E, US 4 E, to Portsmouth

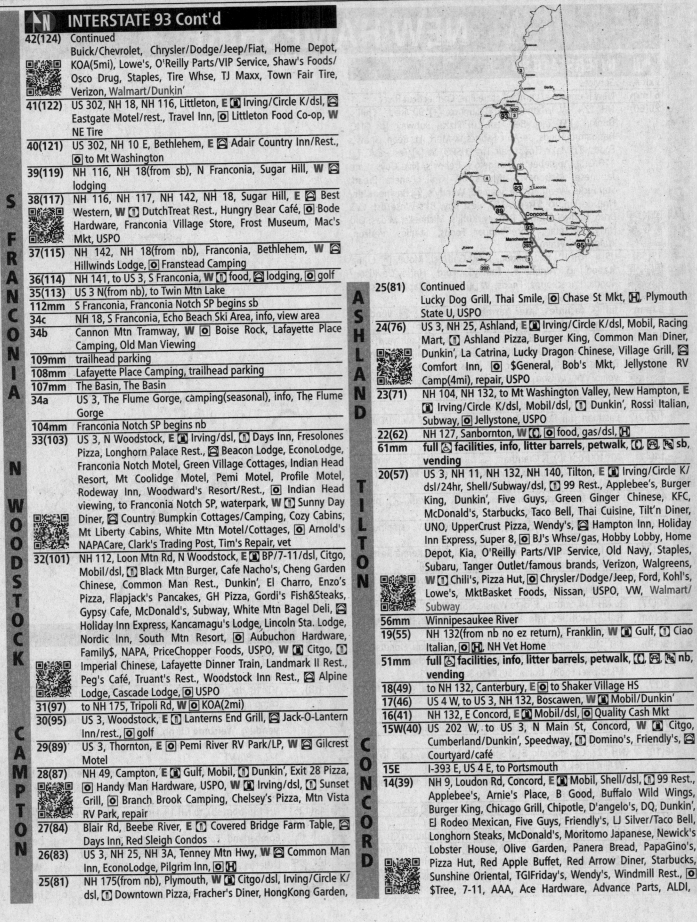

14(39) NH 9, Loudon Rd, Concord, **E** [gas] Mobil, Shell/dsl, [food] 99 Rest., Applebee's, Arnie's Place, B Good, Buffalo Wild Wings, Burger King, Chicago Grill, Chipotle, D'angelo's, DQ, Dunkin', El Rodeo Mexican, Five Guys, Friendly's, LJ Silver/Taco Bell, Longhorn Steaks, McDonald's, Moritomo Japanese, Newick's Lobster House, Olive Garden, Panera Bread, PapaGino's, Pizza Hut, Red Apple Buffet, Red Arrow Diner, Starbucks, Sunshine Oriental, TGIFriday's, Wendy's, Windmill Rest., [other] $Tree, 7-11, AAA, Ace Hardware, Advance Parts, ALDI,

NH

INTERSTATE 93 Cont'd

CONCORD

14(39) Continued
AutoZone, Best Buy, BonTon, BooksAMillion, city park, CVS, Dick's, GNC, Hannaford Foods, Home Depot, Irving/Circle K/Subway/dsl, JC Penney, LLBean, Lowe's, Meineke, Michael's, Midas, Mkt Basket Foods, PetCo, PetSmart, Sam's Club/gas, Shaw's Foods(2), Shaws Foods, Shell/dsl, Staples, Target, TJ Maxx, TownFair Tire, URGENT CARE, USPO, Verizon, Walgreens, Walmart, W Citgo, Cumberland, Speedway, Domino's, Tea Garden Rest., Holiday Inn, hist sites, Jo-Ann, Marshall's, MktBasket, museum, to state offices

13(38) to US 3, Manchester St, Concord, E Cumberland, Sunoco/dsl/deli, Beefside Rest., Brookside Pizza, Dunkin', Ichiban Japanese, Red Blazer Rest., Veano's Italian, Buick/GMC, Cadillac/Chevrolet, Chrysler/Dodge/Jeep, Harley-Davidson, Kia, Nissan, O'Reilly Parts/VIP Service, Outdoor RV Ctr Subaru, Stratham's Tire, Subaru, Tire Whse, Volvo, W Mobil/dsl, Speedway/dsl, Burger King, Common Man Diner, D'angelo's, Dunkin', KFC, McDonald's, Best Western, Comfort Inn, Fairfield Inn, Residence Inn, Aubuchon Hardware, CVS Drug, Firestone, Goodyear/auto, H

12N(37) NH 3A N, S Main, E 7-11, Irving/Subway/dsl/24hr, Dunkin Donuts, Tru Hilton, Ford, Honda, Hyundai, Mazda, Toyota, W H

12S NH 3A S, Bow Junction, E 7-11, Irving/Circle K/Subway/dsl, Dunkin', Tru Hilton, Ford/Mazda, Honda, Hyundai, Toyota

36mm I-89 N to Lebanon, toll road begins/ends

HOOKSETT

31mm Welcome Ctr both lanes, full facilities, Irving/dsl, Hi-Way Diner, General Store

11(28) NH 3A, to Hooksett, toll plaza, E Pilot/dsl/rest.

28mm I-293, Everett Tpk

10(27) NH 3A, Hooksett, E Irving/Circle K/dsl, Dunkin', Subway, Wendy's, Home Depot, Kohl's, Petco, Target, Verizon, W Irving/Circle K/Dunkin'/dsl, Mr Gas, Bass Pro Shop, MktBasket Foods, Walmart/Subway

26mm Merrimac River

9N S(24) US 3, NH 28, Manchester, E Irving/Dunkin Donuts/Circle K/dsl, Fairfield Inn, W Sunoco/dsl, Burger King, Cheng Du Chinese, Happy Garden Chinese, La Carreta Mexican, Lusia's Italian, Mr Mac's Cafe, PapaGino's, Puritan Rest., Shorty's Mexican, Subway, Villaggio Ristorante, Chrysler/Dodge/Jeep, city park, Hannaford Foods, Lincoln, O'Reilly Parts/VIP Service, U-Haul

8(23) to NH 28a, Wellington Rd, W Currier Gallery, H

7(22) NH 101 E, to Portsmouth, Seacoast

6(21) Hanover St, Candia Rd, Manchester, E Dunkin', Wendy's, vet, W Citgo, Mobil/dsl, Shell, Dunkin', McDonald's, GNC, Granite State Tire/auto, Hannaford Foods, H

19mm I-293 W, to Manchester (from nb), to ✈

5(15) NH 28, to N Londonderry, E Irving/Dunkin'/dsl, Sunoco/dsl, Poor Boy's Diner, W Shell/dsl, Subway, Sleep Inn

DERRY

4(12) NH 102, Derry, E Mobil/dsl, Mutual, Rte 102, Shell/Dunkin'/dsl, Sunoco/dsl, Burger King, Cracker Barrel, Derry Rest., Juliano's Pizza, Subway, Advance Parts, H, R. Frost Farm, W 7-11, Global, Speedway, 99 Rest., Dunkin', KFC/Taco Bell, La Carreta Mexican, McDonald's, PapaGino's, Starbucks, Wendy's, AT&T, Ford, GNC, Hannaford Foods, Home Depot, Mkt Basket Foods, O'Reilly Parts/VIP Service, Shaw's Foods, Staples, TJ Maxx, Town Fair Tire, USPO, Verizon

7mm weigh sta both lanes

SALEM

3(6) NH 111, Windham, E Mobil/McDonald's, House of Pizza, Windham Rest., URGENT CARE, vet, W B&H, 33 Hilltop, Dunkin', Klemm's Bakery, Castleton Conference Ctr, CVS Drug, Osco Drug, Shaw's Foods, USPO

2(3) to NH 38, NH 97, Salem, E Tuscan Kitchen, Red Roof Inn, W Blackwater Grill, Dunkin', Margarita's Cafe, Michael's Flatbread, Holiday Inn, La Quinta, URGENT CARE

1(2) NH 28, Salem, E Citgo/dsl, Gulf, 99 Rest., Chili's, LJ Silver, Mary Ann's Diner, McDonald's, Panera Bread, PapaGino's, T-Bones, Taco Bell, Verizon, Park View Inn, AT&T, Best Buy, Dick's, Home Depot, JC Penney, K-Mart, Kohl's, Lord&Taylor, Macy's, Marshall's, Meineke, Michael's, MktBasket Foods, NTB, PetCo, PetSmart, Staples, Target, TJ Maxx, TownFair Tire, vet, Walgreens

1mm Welcome Ctr nb, **full facilities, info, litter barrels, petwalk, , vending**

0mm New Hampshire/Massachusetts state line

INTERSTATE 95

17mm New Hampshire/Maine state line, Piscataqua River

7(16) Market St, Portsmouth, Port Authority, waterfront hist sites, E Hampton Inn, Hilton Garden, Residence Inn, Sheraton, W BP, Mobil, Applebee's, D'Angelo, Dunkin', Panera Bread, Qdoba, Starbucks, Wendy's, Courtyard, Homewood Suites, $Tree, AutoZone, BJ's Whse/gas, Marshall's, MktBasket Foods, PepBoys, PetCo, TJ Maxx, Verizon, vet

NH

6(15) Woodbury Ave(from nb), Portsmouth, E Howard Johnson, W same as 7

GREENLAND

5(14) US 1, US 4, NH 16, The Circle, Portsmouth, E Bypass Gas, Shell/dsl, Roudabout Diner, Anchorage Inn, Best Western+, Fairfield Inn, Holiday Inn, Howard Johnson, Port Inn, Buick/Cadillac/GMC, Chevrolet, H, U-Haul, W Chipotle, Longhorn Steaks, McDonald's, Hampton Inn, Motel 6, Residence Inn, Barnes&Noble, Best Buy, Dick's, Ford/Lincoln, Home Depot, Kohl's, Mazda, Michael's, Nissan, Old Navy, Staples, Trader Joe's

4(13.5) US 4(exits left from nb), to White Mtns, Spaulding TPK, E H, W to Pease Int Trade Port

3a(13) NH 33, Greenland

3b(12) NH 33, to Portsmouth, E H, W Sunoco/dsl, TA/Country Pride/dsl/scales/24hr/@, Dunkin', McDonald's, Starbucks, Lowe's, Mercedes, Target, VW

6.5mm toll plaza

2(6) NH 101, to Hampton, W H

4mm Taylor River

1(1) NH 107, to Seabrook, toll rd begins/ends, E BP, Irving/Circle K/dsl, Mobil/dsl, Prime, Richdale, Shell, Sunoco/Subway/dsl, 99 Rest., Applebee's, Burger King, Chili's, Dunkin', Five Guys, IHOP, KFC/Taco Bell, McDonald's, Outback Steaks, Panera Bread, Pizza Hut, Starbucks, Wendy's, Best Western Hampshire Inn, Holiday Inn Express, $Tree, Advance Parts, AutoZone, CVS Drug, Dick's, GNC, Hobby Lobby, Home Depot, Jo-Ann Fabrics, Kohl's, Lowe's, Meineke, MktBasket Foods, NTB, PetSmart, Staples, Sullivan Tire, TJ Maxx, TownFair Tire, Verizon, Walmart, W Citgo, McGrath's Dining, Seabrook Inn, NAPA

0.5mm Welcome Ctr nb, **full facilities, litter barrels, petwalk, , vending**

0mm New Hampshire/Massachusetts state line

INTERSTATE 293 (Manchester)

8(9) I-93, N to Concord, S to Derry. I-293 begins/ends on I-93, 28mm.

7(6.5) NH 3A N, Dunbarton Rd(from nb)

6(6) Amoskeag Rd, Singer Park, Manchester, E Sunoco/dsl,

 = gas = food = lodging = other = rest stop

INTERSTATE 293 (Manchester) Cont'd

6(6) Continued
La Quinta, **W** Mobil, Shell/dsl, Dunkin', Hot Stone Pizza, H

5(5) Granite St, from nb, no EZ return, Manchester, **E** The Foundry, DoubleTree, **W** 7-11, Gulf, Dunkin', Subway, H, tires, Walgreens

4(4) US 3, NH 3A, NH 114A, Queen City Br, **E** 7-11, Elliott H, **W** Mobil/dsl, Rapid Refill/dsl, Speedway/dsl, Applebee's, Burger King, Chen's Garden, D'angelo's, DQ, Dunkin', KC's Rib Shack, KFC, KFC, Little Caesar's, McDonald's, Panera Bread, Taco Bell, Wendy's, Comfort Inn, EconoLodge, $Tree, Family$, Subaru, Walmart

3(3) NH 101, **W** Carrabba's, Dunkin Donuts, IHOP, Panera Bread, Chipotle, Outback Steaks, Starbucks, T-Bones, Whole Foods Mkt, Country Inn& Suites, Hampton Inn, CVS Drug, Hannaford's, Kohl's, Lexus, Lowe's, Marshall's, Mini, O'Reilly Parts/VIP Service, Staples, Target, Trader Joe's, URGENT CARE, vet

2.5mm Merrimac River

2(2) NH 3A, Brown Ave, **S** Mobil/dsl, Shell/Subway/dsl, Diner, Dunkin', McDonald's, Holiday Inn, Homewood Suites, Springhill Suites, Super 8, Manchester

1(1) NH 28, S Willow Rd, **N** Mobil/dsl, Sunoco/dsl, Boston Mkt, Burger King, Chipotle Mexican, CJ's Grill, Coldstone, Dunkin', Firehouse Subs, Five Guys, Friendly's, McDonald's, Panera Bread, Papa John's, Pizza Hut, Sal's Pizza, Starbucks, Subway, Taco Bell, Wendy's, Yee Dynasty Chinese, Fairfield Inn, Holiday Inn Express, Quality Inn, $Tree, ALDI, AT&T, AutoZone, Batteries+Bulbs, BJ's Whse, Buick/GMC, Chevrolet, CVS Drug, Hannaford Foods, Harley-Davidson, Home Depot, H, Kia, Mazda, Mercedes, Michael's, PepBoys,

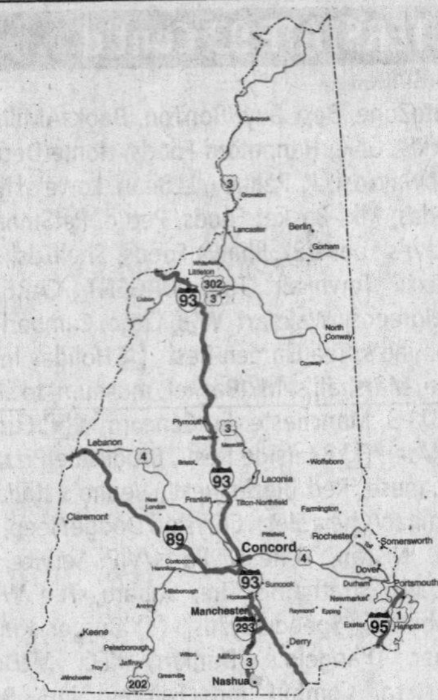

1(1) Continued
PetCo, PetSmart, Sullivan Tire/repair, TJ Maxx, TownFair Tire, U-Haul, URGENT CARE, Verizon, vet, VW, Walmart, **S** Shell, 99 Rest., Bertucci's, Buffalo Wild Wings, ChuckeCheese, D'angelo's, FoodCourt, Great Buffet, La Carreta, Longhorn Steaks, Masa Japanese Steaks, Olive Garden, Red Robin, TGIFriday's, TX Roadhouse, Courtyard, TownePlace Suites, Barnes&Noble, Best Buy, BMW, CarMax, Ford, Hobby Lobby, Honda, Hyundai, JC Penney, Macy's, Nissan, NTB, Old Navy, Staples, Toyota

0mm I-93, N to Concord, S to Derry. I-293 begins/ends on I-93.

NH

NOTES

NEW JERSEY

INTERSTATE 78

Exit #	Services
58b a	US 1N, US 9N, NJ Tpk
57	US 1S, US 9S, N Doubletree, Howard Johnson, Ramada Inn, S Courtyard, Fairfield Inn, SpringHill Suites, to Newark
56	Clinton Ave (exits left from eb)
55	Irvington(from wb), N Speedway/dsl, Burger King, Dunkin', Wendy's, White Castle, AutoZone
54	(from eb), Hillside, Irvington, N Speedway/dsl, Burger King, Dunkin', Wendy's, White Castle, AutoZone
52	Garden State Pkwy
50b a	(from wb), Millburn, N BP, Exxon, Lukoil, Manny's Wieners, Best Buy, Firestone/auto, Ford/Lincoln, Home Depot Superstore, Target, USPO, Whole Foods Mkt
49b a	NJ 124(from eb), to Maplewood, same as 50b a
48	to NJ 24, to I-287 N, (exits left from eb), Springfield
48mm	I-78 eb divides into express & local
45	NJ 527(from eb), Glenside Ave, Summit
44	(from eb), to Berkeley Heights, New Providence
43	to New Providence, Berkeley Heights
41	to Berkeley Heights, Scotch Plains
40	NJ 531, The Plainfields, S
36	NJ 651, to Warrenville, Basking Ridge, N Exxon, Tesla EVC, Dunkin', S Exxon
33	NJ 525, to Martinsville, Bernardsville, N 3West Rest., LingLing Chinese, Starbucks, Courtyard, USGA Golf Museum, S Exxon/7-11, Chipotle, Panera Bread, Mavis Tire, Verizon
32mm	scenic overlook wb
29	I-287, to US 202, US 206, I-80, to Morristown, Somerville, S
26	NJ 523 spur, to North Branch, Lamington
24	NJ 523, to NJ 517, to Oldwick, Whitehouse, S Exxon/dsl, Gulf/dsl, Readington Diner, Starbucks, Subway, Kings Mkt, Walgreens
20b a	NJ 639(from wb), to Cokesbury, Lebanon, S Exxon, Sunoco, Dunkin', Janina Bistro, Kirsten's Italian, Courtyard, to Round Valley RA, vet
18	US 22 E, Annandale, N same as 17, S Honda
17	NJ 31 S, Clinton, N Exxon, Speedway, Valero/dsl, Baskin-Robbins/Dunkin', Finnigel's, McDonald's, Mavis Tire/auto, to Voorhees SP
16	NJ 31 N(from eb), Clinton, N same as 17
15	NJ 173 E, to Pittstown, Clinton, N Express/repair, Shell/dsl, Subway, Holiday Inn, S Cracker Barrel, Frank's Italian, Hunan Wok, Hampton Inn, GNC, ShopRite Foods, TJ Maxx, Verizon, Walmart/Dunkin'
13	NJ 173 W(from wb), same as 12, N Clinton Sta Diner
12	NJ 173, to Jutland, Norton, N Clinton/dsl, Exxon/Dunkin'/dsl, Pilot/Subway/dsl/scales/24hr, to Spruce Run RA, vet, S Shell, Bagelsmith Deli
11	NJ 173, West Portal, Pattenburg, N Mobil, Shell/pizza/dsl, American Spirits Rest., Chalet Rest., Jugtown Camping, st police
8mm	rest area both lanes, **litter barrels, no restrooms,**
7	NJ 173, to Bloomsbury, West Portal, N RV camping, S Citgo/deli, Pilot/Subway/dsl/scales/24hr, TA/Burger King/Country Pride/dsl/scales/24hr/@
6mm	weigh sta both lanes
6	(from eb), Warren Glen, Asbury
4	Warren Glen, Stewartsville(from wb)
3	US 22, NJ 173, to Phillipsburg, N BP/dsl, Penn Jersey Trkstp/dsl/scales/24hr, Speedway/dsl, US/dsl, Wawa, Applebee's, Chick-fil-A, Dunkin', Frank's Trattoria, IHOP, Key City Diner, McDonald's, Panera Bread, Pizza Hut, Quaker Steak, Ruby Tuesday, Starbucks, Taco Bell, Teppanyaki, White Castle, Best Value, $Tree, Advance Parts, ALDI, AutoZone, Best Buy, Hobby Lobby, Home Depot, Honda, Kohl's, Lowe's, Marshall's, Meineke, Michael's, Old Navy, PetCo, ShopRite Foods, Stop&Shop, Target, Verizon, Walmart/Subway
0mm	New Jersey/Pennsylvania state line, Delaware River

BASKING RIDGE

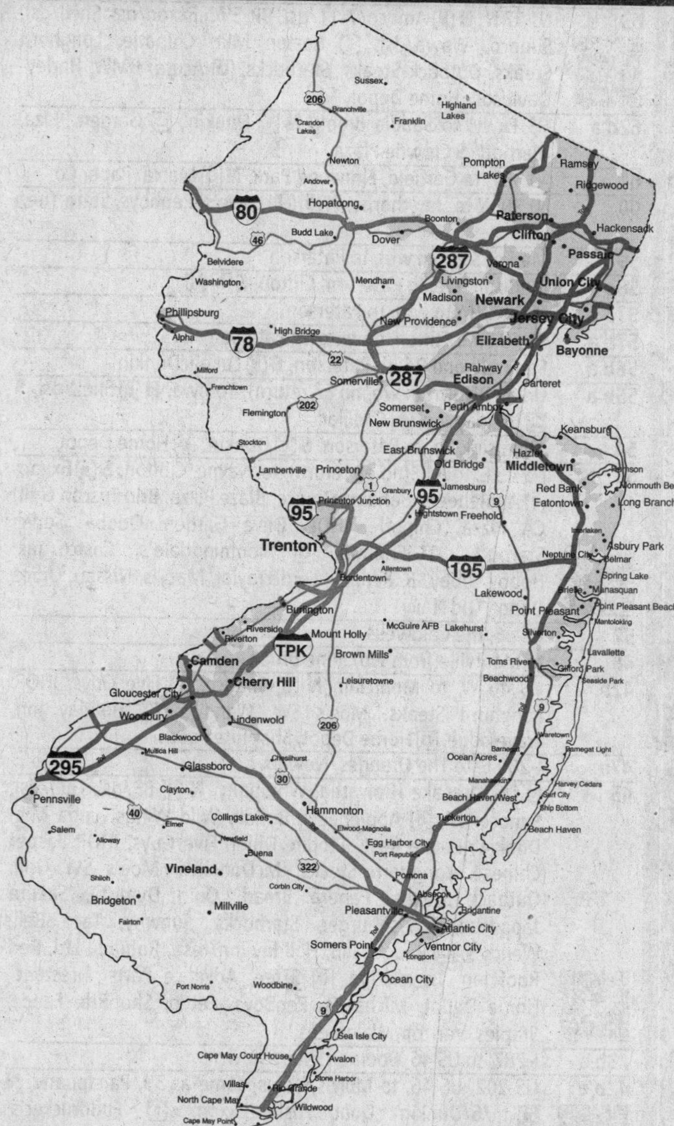

S HACKENSACK

INTERSTATE 80

Exit #	Services
68mm	I-80 begins/ends on I-95, exit 69., Leonia, Teaneck, N Marriott, Starbucks, Hampton Inn,
68b a	I-95, N to New York, S to Philadelphia, to US 46
67	to Bogota(from eb)
66	Hudson St, to Hackensack
65	Green St, S Hackensack
64b a	NJ 17 S, to US 46 E, Newark, Paramus, S BP/dsl,

= gas = food = lodging = other = rest stop

INTERSTATE 80 Cont'd

CLIFTON

Exit	Services
64b a	Continued Crow's Nest Rest., Hilton, Stop&Shop
63	NJ 17 N, **N** Amoco/7-11/dsl, BP, EVC, Exxon/dsl, Shell/dsl, Sunoco, Wawa/dsl, Boston Mkt, Chipotle, Longhorn Steaks, Outback Steaks, Starbucks, Acura, BMW, Harley-Davidson, Home Depot, H
62b a	GS Pkwy, to Saddle Brook, **N** Dunkin', Garden Plaza, Marriott, **S** Crowne Plaza
61	NJ 507, to Garfield, Elmwood Park, **N** Marcal Paper Co
60	NJ 20, N to Hawthorne, **N** H, Lowe's, Pepboys, Stern Tire/auto
59	Market St(from wb), to Paterson
58b a	Madison Ave, to Paterson, Clifton, **S** H
57c	Main St(from wb), to Paterson
57b a	NJ 19 S, to Clifton, downtown Paterson
56b a	Squirrelwood Rd, to Paterson, **S** Lukoil/Dunkin'
55b a	Union Blvd(from wb, no EZ return), Totowa, **N** Shell/dsl, **S** Holiday Inn, Cadillac
54	Minnisink Rd, to Paterson, **S** Dunkin', Home Depot
53	US 46 E, to NJ 3(no eb return), to Wayne, Cliffton, **S** Exxon, Applebee's, Bahama Breeze, Blaze Pizza, Brio Tuscan Grill, CA Pizza, Chipotle, IHOP, Olive Garden, Qdoba, Sonic, Starbucks, TGIFriday's, Bloomingdale's, Costco/gas, Hobby Lobby, JC Penney, Lord&Taylor, Macy's, Nissan, Office Depot, Old Navy

NEWARK

Exit	Services
52	US 46, the Caldwells
48	to Montville(from wb), Pine Brook
47b	US 46 W, to Montclair, **N** Sunoco, Five Guys, IHOP, Longhorn Steaks, Moe's SW, Wendy's, Holiday Inn, Travelodge, Home Depot, ShopRite Foods
47a	I-280 E, to The Oranges, Newark
45	to US 46, Lake Hiawatha, Whippany, **N** BP/dsl, Gulf/dsl, Sunoco/dsl, Applebee's, Buffalo Wild Wings, Cuba Mia, Dunkin', Eccola Rest., Empire Diner, Five Guys, IHOP, Jasper Chinese, Longhorn Steaks, McDonald's, Moe's SW Grill, Outback Steaks, Panera Bread, Quin Dynasty, Sakura Japanese, Smashburger, Starbucks, Subway, Taco Bell, Wendy's, Budget Inn, Holiday Inn/rest., Ramada Ltd, Red Roof Inn, Travelodge, $Tree, Advance Parts, Firestone, Home Depot, Michael's, PepBoys, PetCo, ShopRite Foods, Staples, Verizon, Walgreens
43b a	I-287, to US 46, Boonton, Morristown

DENVILLE

Exit	Services
42b a	US 202, US 46, to Morris Plains, same as 39, Parsippany, **N** 76/Dunkin Donuts/dsl, Exxon, Fuddrucker's, McDonald's, TGIFriday's, Wendy's, Courtyard, Days Inn, Fairfield Inn, Hampton Inn, Marshall's, Subaru
39	(38 from eb), US 46 E, to NJ 53, Denville, **N** Citgo/dsl, Enrite Gas, Exxon, Speedway/Dunkin', Sunoco, Burger King, Casa Bella Italian, Charlie Brown's Steaks, Dunkin', Moe's SW Grill, Paul's Diner, Summit West Diner, Chevrolet, H, Verizon, Walgreens, **S** Delta, Verizon
37	NJ 513, to Hibernia, Rockaway, **N** Exxon/dsl, Shell, Dunkin', Hibernia Diner, River Barn Rest., Hampton Inn, **S** BP, H
35b a	to Dover, Mount Hope, **S** Exxon, Buffalo Wild Wings, Chipotle, Coldstone, Dunkin', Olive Garden, Red Robin, Riviera Mexican, Hilton Garden, Homewood Suites, TownePlace Suites, Best Buy, H, JC Penney, Lord&Taylor, Macy's, Michael's, Verizon
34b a	NJ 15, to Sparta, Wharton, **N** Exxon/dsl, Fortune Buffet, USPO, **S** Dunkin', Five Guys, Frank's Pizza, Panera Bread, Qdoba, Starbucks, Townsquare Diner, $Tree, Big Lots, Costco/gas, Dick's, Home Depot, H, PetSmart, ShopRite Foods, Target, Walmart/Subway
32mm	truck rest area wb

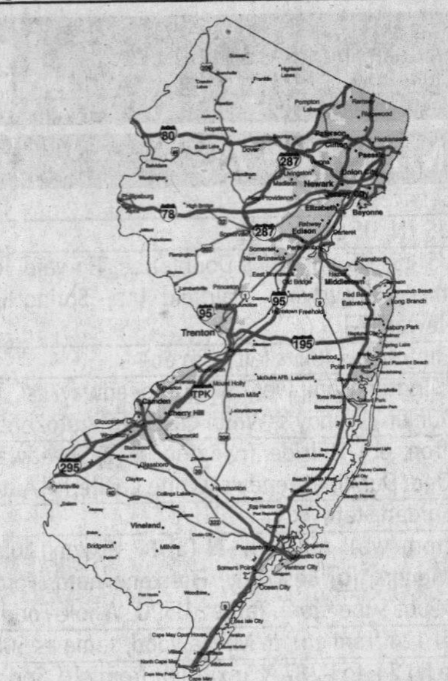

ANDOVER

Exit	Services
30	Howard Blvd, to Mt Arlington, **N** Exxon/dsl, Quickche Gas, Blossom Asian, Cracker Barrel, Davy's Hotdog Dunkin', Frank's Pizza, Courtyard, Holiday Inn Express, $Tree
28	US 46, to NJ 10, to Ledgewood, Lake Hopatcong, **S** Speedway/dsl, Sunoco/dsl, Boston Mkt, Domino' Dunkin', Fuddruckers, KFC, McDonald's, Muldoons Dine Outback Steaks, Panera Bread, Red Lobster, Taco Be TGIFriday's, Wendy's, White Castle, AutoZon Barnes&Noble, BJ's Whse, CVS Drug, Home Depot, Jo-An Kohl's, Petco, ShopRite Foods, Toyota, Walgreens, Walmart
27	US 206 S, NJ 182, to Netcong, Somerville, **N** Dunkin', Ford, **S** Shell/dsl, Applebee's, Chili's, Longhorn Steak McDonald's, Panera Bread, Subway, Wendy's, Extende Stay America, $Tree, Lowe's, Michael's, Old Nav PetSmart, TJMaxx, Verizon, Walmart
26	US 46 W(from wb, no EZ return), to Budd Lake, same as 27, Conoco, Shell/dsl
25	US 206 N, to Newton, Stanhope, **N** Exxon/dsl, Shell/d Bellas Pizza, Blackforest Rest., Byram Diner, Dunki Empire Buffet, Frank's Pizza, McDonald's, Subway, Holiday Inn, Residence Inn, CVS Drug, Mavis Tire, Nissa ShopRite Foods, to Waterloo Village, vet
23.5mm	Musconetcong River
21mm	**litter barrels, petwalk,** , **scenic overlook(eb),** **picn area both lanes**
19	NJ 517, to Hackettstown, Andover, **N** Shell/dsl, **S** She dsl/repair, Terranova Pizza, 7-11, H, Stephen's USPO
12	NJ 521, to Blairstown, Hope, **N** Dunkin', Harle Davidson, st police, **S** US Gas, Hope Mkt Deli, Jen Jump SF, Land of Make Believe, RV camping(5mi), USPO
7mm	rest area eb, **full facilities, info, litter barrels, petwa** , **vending**
6mm	scenic overlook wb, no trailers
4c	to NJ 94 N(from eb), to Blairstown
4b	to US 46 E, to Buttzville
4a	NJ 94, to US 46 E, to Portland, Columbia, **N** TA/Pizza H Taco Bell/dsl/scales/24hr/@, McDonald's, camping, **S** Columbia Inn Rest., USPO
3.5mm	Hainesburg Rd(from wb), accesses services at 4
2	weigh sta eb
1mm	**N** **Worthington SF**
1	to Millbrook(from wb), **N** Worthington SF
0mm	New Jersey/Pennsylvania state line, Delaware River

NJ

FT LEE

INTERSTATE 95

Exit #	Services
124mm	New Jersey/New York state line, Hudson River, Geo Washington Br
123mm	Palisades Pkwy(from sb)
73	NJ 67, Lemoine Ave, **W** [gas] Sunoco, [food] Five Guys, McDonald's, [other] A&P Mkt, GNC, Verizon, Walgreens
72(122)	US 1, US 9, US 46, Ft Lee, **E** [lodging] Doubletree, **W** [gas] Sunoco, [food] McDonald's
71(121)	Broad Ave, Leonia, Englewood, **E** [gas] Lukoil, **W** Speedway, [lodging] Holiday Inn
70(120)	to NJ 93, Leonia, **W** [lodging] Hampton Inn, Marriott
69(119)	I-80 W(from sb), to Paterson
68(118)	US 46, Challenger Blvd, Ridgefield Park, **E** [gas] Exxon, [food] Lan Garden Chinese, [lodging] Day's Inn, Hampton Inn, Hilton Garden
117mm	I-95 and NJ Turnpike run together sb

LAKEWOOD

INTERSTATE 195

Exit #	Services
36	Garden State Parkway N. I-195 begins/ends on GS Pkwy, exit 98.
35b a	NJ 34, to Brielle, GS Pkwy S., Pt Pleasant, **S** [gas] Exxon/dsl, Getty/dsl, Lukoil/dsl, [food] Legends Japanese
31b a	NJ 547, NJ 524, to Farmingdale, **N** [other] to Allaire SP
28b a	US 9, to Freehold, Lakewood, **N** [gas] LukOil/7-11/dsl, WaWa/dsl, [food] Ivy League Grill, Lino's Pizza, Stewart's Drive-In, [lodging] At 9 Motel, **S** [gas] Exxon, Gulf, LukOil, QuickChek/dsl, WaWa, [food] Applebee's, Arby's, Baskin-Robbins/Dunkin Donuts, Boston Mkt, Chick-fil-A, China Moon, Chipotle, Dunkin Donuts, Five Guys, IHOP, Jersey Mike's Subs, Longhorn Steaks, Luigi's Pizza, McDonald's, Panera Bread, Pizza Hut, Ruby Tuesday, Sonic, Starbucks, Subway, Taco Bell, [other] $Tree, Advance Parts, AT&T, Barnes&Noble, Best Buy, BJ's/dsl, CVS Drug, GNC, Hobby Lobby, Kohl's, Lowe's, Michael's, PepBoys, PetCo, PetSmart, repair, ShopRite Foods, Staples, Stop&Shop, Target, TJ Maxx, USPO, Verizon, vet, Walgreens, Walmart/McDonald's
22	to Jackson Mills, Georgia, **N** [other] to Turkey Swamp Park, **S** [food] McDonald's, [other] ShopRite Foods
21	NJ 526, NJ 527, to Jackson, Siloam
16	NJ 537, to Freehold, **N** [gas] Citgo/dsl, Sunoco, [food] FoodCourt, GianMarco's Pizza, [other] [H], Jackson Outlets/famous brands, **S** [gas] WaWa/dsl, [food] Burger King, Chicken Holiday, Dunkin Donuts, KFC/LJ Silver, McDonald's, McGinns Pizzaria, Rio Grande Mexican, Tommy's Rest., [other] Six Flags
11	NJ 524, Imlaystown, **N** [other] to Horse Park of NJ
8	NJ 539, Hightstown, Allentown, **S** [gas] Shell(1mi), Valero/repair, [food] Sam's Deli, [other] vet
7	NJ 526, Robbinsville, Allentown, **N** [lodging] Hampton Inn, **S** [food] La Piazza Ristorante
6	NJ Tpk, N to NY, S to DE Memorial Br
5b a	US 130, **N** [gas] Delta/dsl/repair, Valero/dsl, [food] Domino's, Dunkin Donuts, Rusert's Deli, ShrimpKing Rest., Taco Bell, [lodging] Homewood Suites, [other] AAA, vet, **S** [gas] GS Fuel/dsl, WaWa/dsl, [food] Chick-fil-A, Chili's, China Grill, Cracker Barrel, DQ, Jersey Mike's Subs, Longhorn Steaks, McDonald's, Outback Steaks, Panchero's, Panera Bread, Red Robin, Ruby Tuesday, Subway, TGIFriday's, Wendy's, [lodging] Hilton Garden, Residence Inn, [other] $Tree, AT&T, Barnes&Noble, BJ's Whse, GNC, Harry's Army Navy, Home Depot, Honda, Kohl's, Lowe's, Michael's, Old Navy, PetSmart, Ross, ShopRite Foods, Staples, to state aquarium, USPO, Verizon, Walmart
3b a	Hamilton Square, Yardville, **N** [other] [H]
2	US 206 S, S Broad St, Yardville, **S** [gas] BP, Shell/dsl, [food] Subway, [other] $Tree, 7-11, CVS Drug
1b a	US 206 (eb only), **N** [food] Circle Deli, Taco Bell, [other] Advance Parts, Midas, **S** [food] Papa John's, [other] ShopRite Foods
0mm	I-295, I-195 begins/ends.

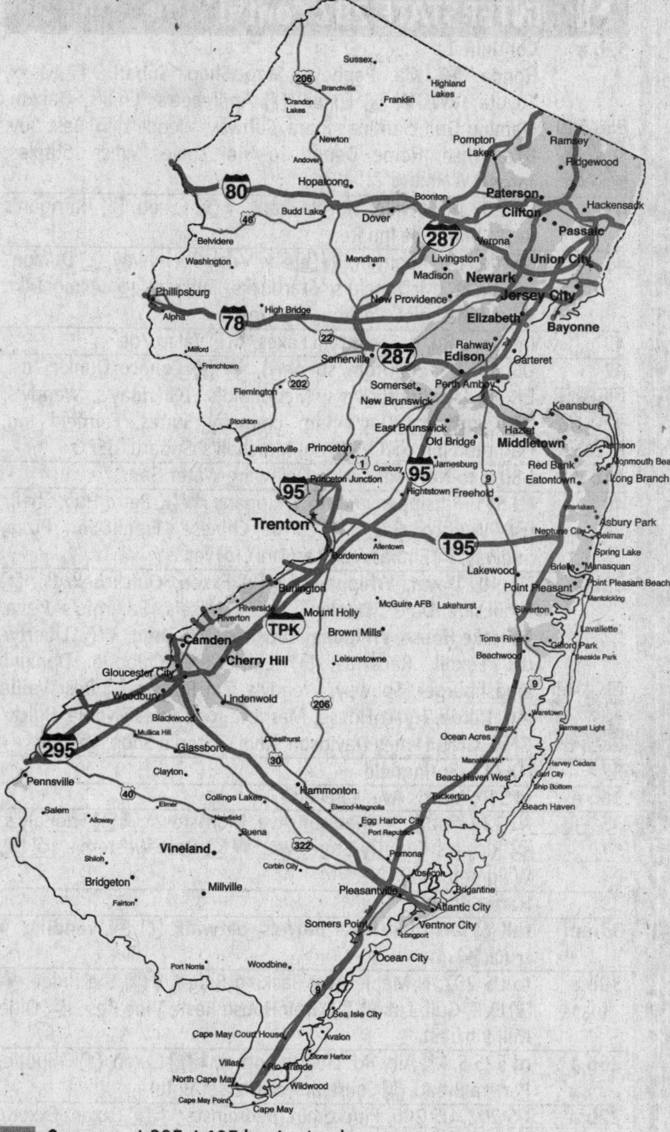

FRANKLIN LAKES

INTERSTATE 287

Exit #	Services
68mm	New Jersey/New York state line
66	NJ 17 S, Mahwah, **E** [gas] Amoco/dsl, BP, Liberty/dsl, Pilot/dsl, Sunoco/dsl, Valero/Subway/dsl, [food] Boston Mkt, Burger King, Dunkin', McDonald's, [lodging] Comfort Suites, Courtyard, Doubletree, Hampton Inn, Homewood Suites, Sheraton, Super 8, [other] Buick/GMC, Cadillac, Chrysler/Dodge/Jeep, Home Depot, Honda, Hyundai
59	NJ 208 S, Franklin Lakes
58	US 202, Oakland, **E** [gas] Lukoil/dsl, [food] Jr's Pizza, Luca Pizza, Mike's Doghouse, Pizza Hut, Starbucks, Subway, [other] $Tree, Staples, USPO, Walgreens, **W** [gas] Exxon
57	Skyline Dr, Ringwood
55	NJ 511, Pompton Lakes, **E** [food] Frank's Pizza, Starbucks, Thatcher McGhee Eatery, Wendy's, **W** [gas] Gulf/dsl, [food] Baskin-Robbins, Burger King, Dunkin', [lodging] Holiday Inn Express, [other] CVS Drug, Stop'n Shop
53	NJ 511A, rd 694, Bloomingdale, Pompton Lakes, **E** [gas] Sunoco, Valero, [food] Dunkin', Karen's Country Kitchen, [other] USPO
52b a	NJ 23, Riverdale, Wayne, Butler, **E** [gas] Amoco/dsl, Delta, Shell, Sunoco, [food] 23 Buffet, Dunkin', Jersey Mike's, Moe's SW Grill, Pompton Queen Diner, Stefano's Pizza, [other] 7-11, GNC,

NJ

INTERSTATE 287 Cont'd

BOONTON

52b a Continued
Honda, H, Kia, Pepboys, Stop&Shop, Subaru, TJ Maxx, Toyota, VW, W Lukoil, Applebee's, Chili's, Dunkin, Flaming Grill, Santinas Pizza, Subway, Wendy's, Best Buy, BJ's Whse, Home Depot, Jo-Ann, Lowes Whse, Staples, Target, Walmart

47 US 202, Montville, Lincoln Park, E Exxon, Harrigan's Rest., Montville Inn Rest.

45 Myrtle Ave, Boonton, W Shell/dsl, Speedway, Dunkin', Jr's Pizza, McDonald's, Starbucks, Subway, Acme Mkt, Buick/Chevrolet, Verizon, Walgreens

43 Intervale Rd, to Mountain Lakes, E Valero/dsl

42 US 46, US 202(from sb only), W Conoco/Dunkin'/dsl, Exxon, Fuddrucker's, McDonald's, TGIFriday's, Wendy's, Courtyard, Day's Inn, Embassy Suites, Fairfield Inn, Hampton Inn, CVS Drug, Marshall's, Subaru, USPO

41b a I-80, E to New York, W to Delaware Water Gap

40 NJ 511, Parsippany Rd, to Whippany, W Petro Hub, Shell/dsl, Woroco Gas, Carrot Chinese, Frank&Son Pizza, Subway, Embassy Suites(1mi), vet

39b a NJ 10, Dover, Whippany, E Exxon, Quickchek/dsl, Brookside Diner, Dunkin', Jersey Mike's, Palermo's Pizza, Pancake House, Whippany Diner, CVS Drug, W Liberty/dsl, Lukoil, Raceway, Chick-fil-A, Chipotle, Dunkin', Smashburger, Subway, Wendy's, Zin Burger, Best Value Inn, Hilton, Hyatt House, Marriott, Barnes&Noble, Buick/GMC, GNC, Harley Davidson, Kohl's, Stop'n Shop, Verizon

NJ

BASKING RIDGE

37 NJ 24 E, Springfield

36b a rd 510, Morris Ave, Lafayette

35 NJ 124, South St, Madison Ave, Morristown, E Friendly's, Richie's Country Store, vet, W Best Western+, H, Walgreens

33 Harter Rd

33mm full facilities, litter barrels, petwalk, vending, E truck nb

30b a to US 202, N Maple Ave, Basking Ridge, E The Ridge, W EVC, Gulf, Lukoil, GrainHouse Rest., Vine Rest., Olde Mill Inn/rest.

26b a rd 525 S, Mt Airy Rd, Liberty Corner, E Exxon, Chipotle, Panera Bread, Courtyard, Somerset Hotel

22b a US 202, US 206, Pluckemin, Bedminster, E Exxon, Exxon/dsl, Coldstone, Dunkin', Golden Palace, Panchero's, Rocco's Pizza, Starbucks, Subway, CVS Drug, Fresh Mkt, King's Foods, URGENT CARE, Verizon

21b a I-78, E to NY, W to PA

BOUND BROOK

17 US 206(from sb), Bridgewater, W Exxon, Buffalo Wild Wings, CA Pizza, Cheesecake Factory, Chipotle Mexican, Dunkin', KFC, Maggiano's Italian, McDonald's, Redstone, Seasons 52 Grill, Taco Bell, TGIFriday, Wendy's, Marriott, Best Buy, Bloomingdale's, Lord&Taylor, Macy's

14b a US 22, to US 202/206, E Speedway/dsl, Chevrolet/Lexus, W BP, Sunoco/dsl, Valero/dsl, Houlihan's, Red Lobster, Hampton Inn, Acura, Chrysler/Dodge/Jeep, Fiat, Ford, Infiniti, Kia, Mercedes, Nissan, Volvo

13b a NJ 28, Bound Brook, E 76/dsl, BP/dsl, 30 Burgers, Burger King, Dunkin', Frank's Pizza, Girasole Rest., Little Caesar's, 7-11, AT&T, AutoZone, QuickChek Mkt, ShopRite Foods, Walgreens, W WaWa/dsl, Applebee's, ChuckeCheese, McDonald's, Panchero's, Hilton Garden, 7-11, Costco, Home Depot, H, Marshall's, Michael's, Old Navy, PepBoys, PetSmart, Target

12 Weston Canal Rd, Manville, E USPO, W Hooters, Clarion

10 NJ 527, Easton Ave, New Brunswick, E Hotel Somerset, W Exxon, Dunkin', Ichiban, Ruby Tuesday, Subway,

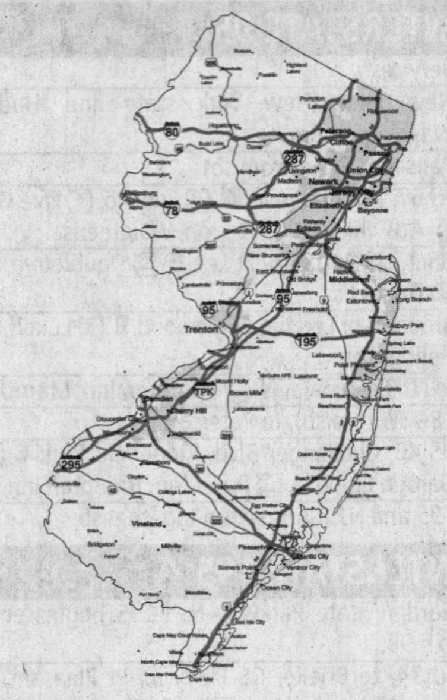

PISCATAWAY

10 Continued
Wild Ginger Asian, Candlewood Suites, Comfort In Courtyard, Doubletree, Extended Stay America, Fairbrid Inn, Fairfield Inn, Homewood Suites, Residence Inn, Sones Suites, Springhill Suites, Garden State Conv Ctr, H

9 NJ 514, River Rd, W Delta, Dunkin', Embassy Suite Radisson

8.5mm weigh sta nb

8 Possumtown Rd, Highland Park

7 S Randolphville Rd, Piscataway, E Lukoil/dsl

6 Washington Ave, Piscataway, E Shell/7-11/dsl, Popeyes, AutoZone, W Applebee's, Chand Palac Gourmet Pizza, Healthy Garden, Longhorn Steaks, Oli Garden, Panera Bread, Piscataway Pizza, Smashburg Starbucks, Subway, TGIFriday's, Thai Basil, 99c Dep ALDI, GNC, Lowes Whse, PetCo, same as 5, ShopRite Foo Walmart/McDonald's

5 NJ 529, Stelton Rd, Dunellen, E BP/dsl, Gulf/dsl, Luko dsl, Enzo's Pizza, KFC, Red Carpet Inn, Advan Parts, Goodyear/auto, Home Depot, Meineke, Stop'n Sho W Exxon, WaWa/dsl, Brickhouse Rest., Burger Kin Chipotle, Dunkin', El Toro Loco, Five Guys, Fontainbleu Din Gabrieles Grill, Gianni Pizza, IHOP, Joe's Crabshack, Pan Express, Pizza Hut, Red Lobster, Red Robin, Taco Bell, Vi Pizza, Wendy's, White Castle, Garden Executive Hot Hampton Inn, Holiday Inn, Motel 6, Woodspring Suites, $Tree, Burlington Coats, Dick's, Kohl's, Marshall's, Mav Tire, NAPA, Pep Boys, Staples, Target, Tuesday Mornin Verizon

4 Durham Ave(from nb, no EZ return), S Plainfield, E FuelOne/dsl, McDonald's, Subway, Firestone/auto, H

3 New Durham Rd(from sb), E Shell, W Dunkin', R Onion Chinese, Fairfield Inn, Home2 Suites, Red Roof In Walgreens

2b a NJ 27, Metuchen, New Brunswick, E Brownstone Grill, BP, Lukoil, Dunkin', Costco/gas, PetSmart, USP Walmart/Subway

1b a US 1, N Exxon/dsl, Raceway/dsl, Shell, Tesla EVC, Benihana, Cheesecake Factory, Dunkin', Famous Dave's BB Houlihan's, IHOP, Little Italy, Macaroni Grill, McDonal Menlo Park Diner, Panera Bread, Seasons 52 Grill, Sor White Castle, Barnes&Noble, Firestone/auto, Goodye auto, Macy's, Midas, Nordstrom's, Target, S Shell/7-1 dsl, Applebee's, Boston Mkt, ChuckeCheese, Jers Mike's, McDonald's, Starbucks, Zinburger, Comfort In

INTERSTATE 287 Cont'd

1b a Continued
Quality Inn, $Tree, AT&T, BJ's Whse, Home Depot, Infiniti, Land Rover/Jaguar/Porche, Mercedes, Office Depot, PepBoys, PetCo, Sam's Club/gas, Stop&Shop Foods, Volvo

0mm I-287 begins/ends on NJ 440. I-95/NJ Tpk

INTERSTATE 295

77mm New Jersey/Delaware state line, Delaware River, Delaware Memorial Bridge

76 1 NJ 29, to Trenton, W st police museum

75 NJ 579, to Harbourton, E LukOil(1mi), Dunkin Donuts, Red Star Pizza, 7-11, W BP

73b a Scotch Rd, E Courtyard, W

72b a NJ 31, to Ewing, Pennington, E Citgo/repair, Exxon/repair, LukOil/Dunkin Donuts/dsl, SpringHill Suites, Robbins Drug, W Exxon, LukOil/Blimpie/dsl, Mizuki Asian, Starbucks, ShopRite Foods, Stop&Shop Foods

71b a Federal City Rd(sb only)

69b a US 206, W LukOil/dsl, Fox's Pizza, Starbucks

68b a NJ 583, NJ 546, to Princeton Pike

67b a US 1, to Trenton, New Brunswick, E Shell, WaWa/McDonald's/dsl, Michael's Diner, Howard Johnson, Sleepy Hollow Motel, Acura, W LukOil/dsl, Applebee's, Bahama Breeze, Big Fish Bistro, Bonefish Grill, Brick House Tavern, Brio Grille, Buffalo Wild Wings, Cheesecake Factory, Chipotle, ChuckECheese's, Corner Bakery Cafe, Dunkin Donuts, Firehouse Subs, Hooters, Houlihan's, Jersey Mike's, Joe's Crabshack, Olive Garden, On-the-Border, Outback Steaks, Panera Bread, Pei Wei, PF Chang's, Red Lobster, Seasons 32, Smashburger, Starbucks, Subway, TGIFriday's, Wendy's, Clarion, Comfort Inn, Extended Stay America, Hyatt Place, Hyatt Regency, Red Roof Inn, Residence Inn, $Tree, AT&T, Barnes&Noble, Best Buy, Buick/Cadillac/GMC, Chevrolet, Dick's, Firestone/auto, Hobby Lobby, Home Depot, JC Penney, Jo-Ann Fabrics, Kohl's, Lord&Taylor, Lowe's, Macy's, malls, Marshall's, Michael's, Mini, NTB, Old Navy, PepBoys, PetCo, PetSmart, REI, Ross, ShopRite Foods, Staples, Target, TJ Maxx, Trader Joe's, Verizon, Walmart, Wegman's Foods, Whole Foods Mkt

65b a Sloan Ave, E Exxon, Burger King, DeLorenzo's Pizza, Dunkin Donuts, Five Guys, New China Buffet, Subway, Taco Bell, Uno Grill, Goodyear/auto, Risoldi's Mkt

64 NJ 535 N(from sb), to NJ 33 E, same as 63

63b a NJ 33 W, rd 535, Mercerville, Trenton, E Lukoil, Speedway/dsl, Valero, Applebee's, Lucky Star Buffet, McDonald's, Pizza Hut, Popeyes, Stewart's Rootbeer, Subway, Vincent's Pizza, Ace Hardware, auto repair, CVS Drug, Ford/Subaru, USPO, W Exxon, Dunkin Donuts, White Horse Diner, Advance Parts, Family$, transmissions, Walgreens, Walmart, WaWa

62 Olden Ave N(from sb, no return), W Delta, Exxon

61b a Arena Dr, White Horse Ave, W 7-11

60b a I-195, to I-95, W to Trenton, E to Neptune

58mm scenic overlook both lanes

57b a US 130, to US 206, E Amera, Valero, Denny's, Dunkin Donuts, McDonald's, Rosario's Pizza, Best Western, Days Inn, Ramada Inn, ALDI, W Starbucks, Candlewood Suites, Acme Foods, st police, Verizon

56 to US 206 S(from nb, no return), to NJ Tpk, Ft Dix, McGuire AFB, E Love's/Wendy's/dsl/scales/24hr, Petro/Iron Skillet/dsl/scales/24hr/@, Days Inn, Hampton Inn, same as 57, Blue Beacon, W Candlewood Suites, st police

52b a rd 656, to Columbus, Florence, E Love's/Wendy's/dsl/scales/24hr, Petro/Iron Skillet/dsl/scales/24hr/@

47b a NJ 541, to Mount Holly, NJ Tpk, Burlington, E BP,

BURLINGTON

47b a Continued
Exxon/dsl, Valero/dsl, Applebee's, Burger King, China House, Cracker Barrel, Dunkin Donuts, IHOP, Recovery Grill, TGIFriday's, Best Western, Courtyard, Hampton Inn, Hilton Garden, Holiday Inn Express, Motel 6, Quality Inn, $Tree, AT&T, Dick's, Home Depot, Kohl's, mall, Target, W BP, Citgo/dsl, Gulf/dsl, WaWa/dsl, Checker's, Chick-fil-A, Dunkin Donuts, Kum Fong, Subway, Villa Pizza, Wendy's, AutoZone, Marshall's, ShopRite, Walmart/Subway

45b a to Mt Holly, Willingboro, W LukOil/dsl, auto repair,

43b a rd 636, to Rancocas Woods, Delran, W Exxon, Carlucci's Rest.

40b a NJ 38, to Mount Holly, Moorestown, E Ruby Tuesday, Residence Inn, W Amera/dsl, WaWa/dsl, Anthony 's Pizza, Arby's, Chick-fil-A, Chipotle, Dunkin Donuts, Jimmy John's, Naf Naf Grill, Panera Bread, Qdoba, Starbucks, Subway, TGIFriday's, Wendy's, SpringHill Suites, Costco/gas, GNC, Jo-Ann Fabrics, PetSmart, Target, TJ Maxx, UHaul, Wegman's Foods

36b a NJ 73, to NJ Tpk, Tacony Br, Berlin, E LukOil/dsl, Bob Evans, Miller's Alehouse, Starbucks, aLoft, Courtyard, EconoLodge, Fairfield Inn, Hotel ML, Red Roof Inn, Super 8, TownePlace Suites, Westin, W Citgo, Shell, WaWa/dsl, Bertucci's, Boscov's, Boston Mkt, Buffalo Wild Wings, Burger King, Chick-fil-A, Chipotle Mexican, Corner Cafe, Don Pablo, Dunkin Donuts, Five Guys, Friendly's, Jersey Mike's, Old Town Buffet, Panera Bread, Pei Wei, Perkins, PJ Whelahin's, Popeyes, The Melting Pot, Uno Grill, Wendy's, Crossland Suites, Homewood Suites, Motel 6, Quality Inn, $Tree, Acura, Advance Parts, AT&T, AutoZone, Barnes&Noble, Best Buy, Dick's, Fiat, Ford/Lincoln, Home Depot, Infiniti, Lord&Taylor, Lowe's, mall, Marshall's, Michael's, Mr Tire, Old Navy, PepBoys, PepBoys, PetSmart, Ross, ShopRite Foods, Staples

BERLIN

34b a NJ 70, to Camden, Cherry Hill, E BP, Exxon, WaWa, Burger King, Dunkin Donuts, PJ Whelihans, Rock Hill Rest., Stacy's Korean BBQ, Extended Stay America, Residence Inn, Mavis Tire, Tires+, W Jersey Gas, LukOil, US Gas, Dunkin Donuts, Famous Dave's BBQ, Han Dynasty, McDonald's, Norma's Rest., Ponzio's Rest, Qdoba, Rita's, Salad Works, Seasons Pizza, Starbucks, Whole Foods Mkt, Woodspring Suites, $Tree, AT&T, CVS Drug, Goodyear/auto, Mom's Mkt, vet, WaWa

32 NJ 561, to Haddonfield, Voorhees, E LukOil/dsl, Herman's Deli, Hunan Wok, Tucchi's Pizza, Vito's Pizza, Trio Tire, $Tree, USPO, W Pioneer/dsl, Burger King, Dunkin Donuts, Subway, Tutti Toscani, 7-11, Ford

31 Woodcrest Station

30 Warwick Rd(from sb)

29b a US 30, to Berlin, Collingswood, E Astro/dsl, Citgo/dsl, Valero/dsl, WaWa/dsl, Arby's, Church's TX Chicken, Dunkin Donuts, McDonald's, Popeyes, Wendy's, Wild Wing Cafe, AutoZone, Home Depot, Lowe's, PetSmart, ShopRite

COLLINGSWOOD

28 NJ 168, to NJ Tpk, Belmawr, Mt Ephraim, E Riggins, Shell/dsl, Valero/dsl, Burger King, Club Diner, Dunkin Donuts, Vero Pizzaria, Wendy's, Bellmawr Motel, EconoLodge, Howard Johnson, Red Roof Inn, Super 8, W BP, Conoco, Speedway/dsl, WaWa/dsl, Applebee's, Arby's, Black Horse Diner, Chick-fil-A, Da Vinci'sRest., Domino's, Dunkin Donuts, Little Caesar's, McDonald's, Pizza Hut/Taco Bell, Sonic, Acme Foods, AutoZone, Chrysler/Dodge, CVS Drug, Firestone/auto, Harley-Davidson, Meinke, Midas, Mr Tire, PepBoys, URGENT CARE, USPO, Walgreens, Walmart/Subway

26 I-76, NJ 42, to I-676 (exits left from sb), Walt Whitman Bridge, Walt Whitman Bridge

25b a NJ 47, to Westville, Deptford

24b a NJ 45, NJ 551(no EZ sb return), to Westville, E AutoZone,

INTERSTATE 295 Cont'd

GIBBSTOWN

Exit	Services
24b a	Continued H, W Chevrolet, Family$
23	US 130 N, to National Park
22	NJ 644, to Red Bank, Woodbury, E Citgo, Dunkin Donuts, W Crown Point Trkstp/dsl/@
21	NJ 44 S, Paulsboro, Woodbury, W WaWa, Wendy's, Westwood Motor Lodge
20	NJ 44, rd 643, to National Park, Thorofare, E Best Western, W Red Bank Inn
19	to NJ 44, rd 656, Mantua
18b a	rd 667, to rd 678, Clarksboro, Mt Royal, E Exxon/dsl, TA/Shell/Country Pride/dsl/scales/@, Dragon Nest Chinese, Dunkin Donuts, McDonald's, RV camping, W Valero, WaWa/dsl
17	rd 680, to Mickleton, Gibbstown, W Burger King, Domino's, Dunkin Donuts, Mr Bee's Deli, $General, Advance Parts, Family$, GNC, ShopRite Foods
16b	rd 551, to Gibbstown, Mickleton
16a	rd 653, to Paulsboro, Swedesboro
15	rd 607, to Gibbstown
14	rd 684, to Repaupo
13	US 130 S, US 322 W, to Bridgeport(from sb, no return)
11	US 322 E, to Mullica Hill
10	Ctr Square Rd, to Swedesboro, E Citgo/dsl, WaWa/dsl, Applebee's, Ciconte's Pizza, Dunkin Donuts, McDonald's, Wendy's, Hampton Inn, Holiday Inn, TownePlace Suites, Acme Foods/Sav-On, Firestone/auto, URGENT CARE, Verizon, W Camping World RV Supplies/service

DEEPWATER

Exit	Services
7	to Auburn, Pedricktown
4	NJ 48, Woodstown, Penns Grove
3mm	weigh sta nb
2mm	**full facilities, info, litter barrels, picnic table, nb, rv dump, vending**
2c	to US 130(from sb), Deepwater, E same as 2b, W Flying J/Denny's/dsl/scales/LP/24hr, Sunoco/Dunkin Donuts/dsl/scales/24hr
2b	US 40 E, to NJ Tpk, E Gulf, Pilot/Subway/dsl/scales/24hr, Comfort Inn, Friendship Motor Inn, Holiday Inn Express, Red Carpet Inn, W same as 2c
2a	to Delaware Bridge, US 40 W(from nb)
1c	NJ 551 S, Hook Rd, to Salem, E White Oaks Motel
1b	US 130 N(from nb), Penns Grove
1a	NJ 49 E, to Pennsville, Salem, E WaWa/dsl, Applebee's, Burger King, Cracker Barrel, Dunkin Donuts, KFC/Taco Bell, McDonald's, Hampton Inn, Super 8, Peterbilt, W Coastal/dsl, Seaview Motel
0mm	New Jersey/Delaware state line, Delaware River, Delaware Memorial Bridge

NJ Turnpike

BAYONNE

Exit	Services
18(117)	US 46 E, Ft Lee, Hackensack, last exit before toll sb
17(116)	Lincoln Tunnel
115mm	Vince Lombardi Service Plaza nb, W **Sunoco/rest./dsl**
114mm	toll plaza,
112mm	Alexander Hamilton Service Area sb, **Sunoco/dsl, Roy Rogers, gifts**
16E(112)	NJ 3, Secaucus, E Lincoln Tunnel
15W(109)	I-280, Newark, The Oranges
15E(107)	US 1, US 9, Newark, Jersey City, E Lincoln Tunnel
14c	Holland Tunnel
14b	Jersey City
14a	Bayonne
102mm	Halsey Service Area, **other services in Elizabeth, Sunoco/dsl, Roy Rogers**

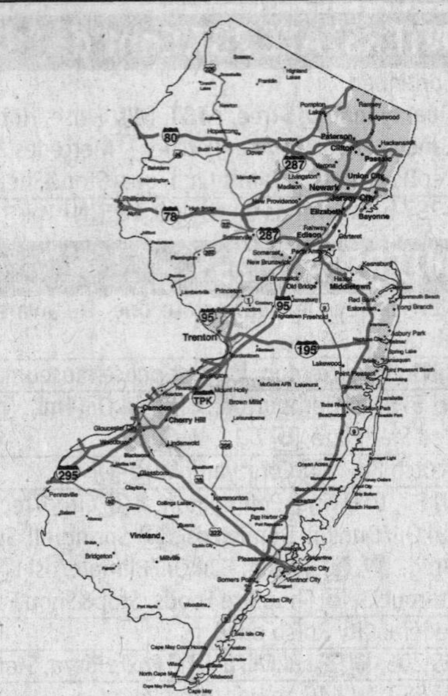

CRANBURY

Exit	Services
93mm	Cleveland Service Area nb, T Edison Service Area sb, W Sunoco/dsl
8a(74)	to Jamesburg, Cranbury, W Courtyard, Crowne Plaza
72mm	Pitcher Service Area, **Sunoco/dsl, Cinnabon, Di Clark's AB Grill, Nathan's, Roy Rogers, Starbucks**
59mm	**Richard Stockton Service Area sb...gas: Sunoco/d Woodrow Wilson Service Area nb...gas: Sunoco, Burger King, Nathan's, Pizza Hut, Quiznos, Roy Roge Starbucks, TCBY**
7(54)	US 206, to Bordentown, to Ft Dix, McGuire AFB, to I-29 Trenton, W AmeriGas, Delta/dsl, Exxon, Gulf, Love' Wendy's/dsl/scales/24hr, Petro/Iron Skillet/dsl/scale 24hr/@, Sunoco, Valero/dsl, Denny's, Dunkin Donu McDonald's, Best Western, Comfort Inn, Days In Hampton Inn, Ramada Inn, WaWa
6(51)	I-276, to PA Tpk
5(44)	to Mount Holly, Willingboro, E AJ's Gas/dsl, Applebee's, Charlie Brown's Steaks, Cracker Bar McDonald's, Recovery Grill, Best Western, Hampton I Hilton Garden, Quality Inn, vet, W BP, Exxon/d Valero/dsl, Burger King, China House, Dunkin Donu IHOP, TGIFriday's, Courtyard, Holiday Inn Express, $Tree, AT&T, Dick's, Home Depot, Kohl's, Motel 6, Target

CAMDEN

Exit	Services
39mm	James Fenimore Cooper Service Area nb, **Sunoco/dsl, Burger King, Cinnabon, Popeyes, Roy Rogers, TCBY, gifts**
4(34)	NJ 73, to Philadelphia, Camden, E US Gas, WaWa/dsl, Applebee's, Chili's, Cracker Barrel, Dunkin Donuts, Kazu McDonald's, On-the-Border, Sage Rest., TGIFriday Wendy's, Candlewood Suites, Comfort Inn, Extended S America, Hampton Inn, Hilton Garden, Holiday Inn Expre Hyatt House, Hyatt Place, Knights Inn, La Quinta, Rodev Inn, Staybridge Suites, Wyndham Hotel, BMW, Cadill Lexus, Mini, Toyota/Scion, Verizon, Whole Foods Mkt, W Lukoil, Bob Evans, Miller's Alehouse, Starbucks, aL Courtyard, Fairfield Inn, Hotel ML, Red Roof Inn, Super Westin 
30mm	Walt Whitman Service Area sb, Walt Whitman Service Ar **Sunoco, Cinnabon, Nathan's, Roy Rogers, TCBY, gifts**
3(26)	NJ 168, Atlantic City Expwy, Walt Whitman Br, Camd Woodbury, E Pioneer, WaWa/dsl, Antonietta's, Lui Pizza, Pat's Pizza, Phily Diner, Rita's Custard, Days Inn, Quinta, Advance Parts, CVS Drug, Toyota/Sci Walgreens, W Riggins, Shell/dsl, Valero/dsl

NJ Turnpike Cont'd

3(26)	Continued Burger King, Club Diner, Dunkin Donuts, Vero Pizzaria, Wendy's, Bellmawr Motel, EconoLodge, Howard Johnson, Red Roof Inn, Super 8
2(13)	US 322, to Swedesboro, **W** Shell/Dunkin Donuts/dsl
5mm	Barton Service Area sb, Fenwick Service Area nb, **Sunoco/dsl**, **Burger King, Nathan's, Pizza Hut, Starbucks, TCBY**
1(1.2)	Deepwater, **W** Gulf, Pilot/Subway/dsl/scales/24hr,
1(1.2)	Continued Comfort Inn, Friendship Motor Inn, Holiday Inn Express, Red Carpet Inn
1mm	toll road begins/ends
2(I-295)	I-295 N divides from toll road, I-295 S converges with toll road
1(I-295)	NJ 49, to Pennsville, **E** WaWa/dsl, Applebee's, Burger King, Cracker Barrel, Dunkin Donuts, KFC/Taco Bell, McDonald's, Hampton Inn, Super 8, Peterbilt, **W** Coastal, Seaview Motel

NOTES

NJ

= gas = food = lodging = other = rest stop

NEW MEXICO

INTERSTATE 10

ANTHONY

Exit #	Services
164.5mm	New Mexico/Texas state line
164mm	litter barrels, petwalk, **Welcome Ctr wb**
162	NM 404, Anthony, **N** fireworks, **S** Circle K/dsl, El Paso West RV Park, Family$
160mm	weigh sta wb
155	NM 227 W, to Vado, **N** Western Sky's RV Park, **S** NTS/Valero/dsl/scales/24hr/@, **Shell/dsl/scales/24hr,** Mi Casa Cafe, $General
151	Mesquite
144	I-25 N, to Las Cruces

LAS CRUCES

Exit #	Services
142	Rd 188, Rd 101, Valley Dr, Las Cruces, **N** Shell/dsl, Burger King, Chick-fil-A, Chilito's Mexican, Dick's Cafe, IHOP, Matteo's Mexican, Starbucks, Whataburger, Best Western, Courtyard, EconoLodge, Holiday Inn Express, Motel 9, Quality Inn, Ramada Inn, Super 8, Teakwood Inn, Cadillac/Chevrolet, Dalmont's RV Camping, Ford/Lincoln, H, Hyundai, Nissan, vet, **S** Circle K/dsl, USPO
140	NM 28, to Mesilla, Las Cruces, **N** Circle K/dsl, Applebee's, Blake's Lotaburger, Cracker Barrel, Domino's, Dunkin, Dutch Bros, Golden Corral, Lucy's Mexican, McDonald's, Murry Express, Ricardo's Mexican, Starbucks, Subway, Village Inn, Days Inn, Drury Inn, Hampton Inn, La Quinta, La Quinta, SpringHill Suites, Buick-GMC, NAPA, Toyota, URGENT CARE, VW, **Walmart/McDonald's**, **S** LunaRossa Pizza, Comfort Inn, Holiday RV Ctr, Holiday World RV Ctr, Siesta RV Park
139	NM 292, Amador Ave, Motel Blvd, Las Cruces, **N** Pilot/Subway/dsl/scales/24hr, **TA/Shell/Pizza Hut/Taco Bell/dsl/24hr/scales/@**, **S** PitStop Café, Coachlight Inn/RV Park
138mm	Rio Grande River, Rio Grande River
135.5mm	**eb, full facilities, litter barrels, petwalk, scenic view**
135	US 70 E, to W Las Cruces, Alamogordo, **N** KOA
132	**N** to, **S** Love's/dsl/scales/24hr, fairgrounds

AKELA

Exit #	Services
127	Corralitos Rd, **N** Bowlin's Trading Post
120.5mm	insp sta wb
116	NM 549
111mm	parking area wb, litter barrels
102	Akela, **N** Marathon/dsl/gifts, dog park/truck parking

DEMING

Exit #	Services
85	East Motel Dr, Deming, **S** Chevron/dsl, Hampton Inn, Holiday Inn Express, La Quinta, Motel 6, Quality Inn, Buick/Cadillac/Chevrolet/GMC, Chrysler/Dodge/Jeep, Dreamcatcher RV Park
82b	Railroad Blvd, Deming, **N** Chevron/dsl, **S** Valero/dsl, Golden Star Chinese, IHOP, KFC, Little Caesar's, Wendy's, Baymont, Days Inn, $Tree, AutoZone, Big O Tire, Deming Visitors Ctr, Little Vineyard RV Park, O'Reilly Parts, Roadrunner RV Park, st police, Sunrise RV Park, to Rock Hound SP, Verizon, Wagon Wheel RV Park, **Walmart/Subway**
82a	US 180, NM 26, NM 11, Deming, **N** Chevron/dsl, Blake's Lotaburger, **S** Arby's, Burger King, China Rest., Denny's, KFC, Pizza Hut, Popeyes, Si Senor, Butterfield Stage Motel, Budget Tire, CarQuest, H, museum, Rockhound SP, to Pancho Villa SP, Walgreens, Walgreens
81	NM 11, W Motel Dr, Deming, **S** Circle K/dsl, CNG, Benji's Rest, El Camino Real, McDonald's, Sonic, Subway, Taco Bell, Best Western, Comfort Inn, Deming Motel, Super 8, Western Motel, 81 Palms RV Park, city park, H, Rock Hound SP, to Pancho Villa SP

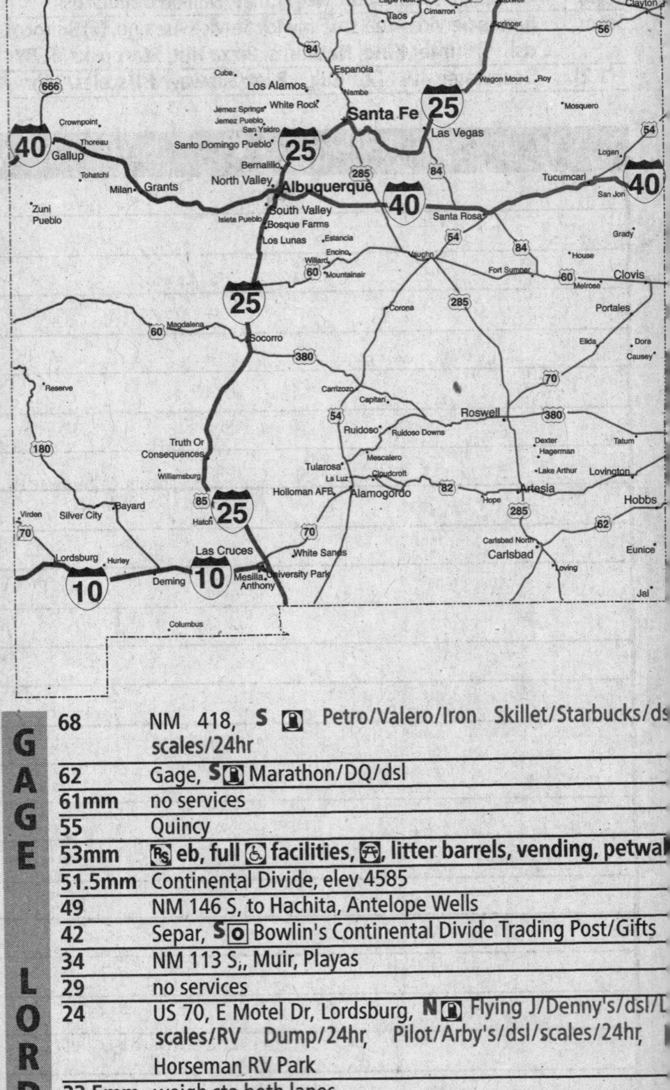

GAGE

Exit #	Services
68	NM 418, **S** Petro/Valero/Iron Skillet/Starbucks/ds scales/24hr
62	Gage, **S** Marathon/DQ/dsl
61mm	no services
55	Quincy
53mm	**eb, full facilities, litter barrels, vending, petwal**
51.5mm	Continental Divide, elev 4585
49	NM 146 S, to Hachita, Antelope Wells
42	Separ, **S** Bowlin's Continental Divide Trading Post/Gifts

LORDSBURG

Exit #	Services
34	NM 113 S,, Muir, Playas
29	no services
24	US 70, E Motel Dr, Lordsburg, **N** Flying J/Denny's/dsl/L **scales/RV Dump/24hr**, Pilot/Arby's/dsl/scales/24hr, Horseman RV Park
23.5mm	weigh sta both lanes
22	NM 494, Main St, Lordsburg, **N** McDonald's, Comf Inn, Hampton Inn, $General, Family$, NAPA, Sauced Foods, USPO, **S** Circle K/dsl, Ramona's Cafe, EconoLodge, Motel 10, Motel 6, Plaza Inn, KOA
20b a	W Motel Dr, Lordsburg, **N** Love's/Subway/scales/dsl, Days Inn, fireworks, Speedco, **S Visitors Ctr/, full facilities,** Chevron/dsl, **info**
15	to Gary
11	NM 338 S, to Animas
5	NM 80 S, to Road Forks, **S** Conserv Fuel/truckstop/dsl, fireworks
3	Steins
0mm	New Mexico/Arizona state line

INTERSTATE 25

RATON

Exit #	Services
460.5mm	New Mexico/Colorado state line
460	Raton Pass Summit, elev 7834, weigh sta sb, **E** Raton P Camping
454	2nd St, Lp 25, Raton, **W** Crossroads, Budget Ho

NM

INTERSTATE 25 Cont'd

Exit	Services
454	Continued CarQuest, Ford
452	NM 72 E, Raton, E [other] to Sugarite Canyon SP, W [gas] Conoco, [lodging] Budget Host, [other] city park
RATON	
451	US 64 E, US 87 E, Raton, E [gas] 87 Express/dsl, Chevron/dsl, Raton Trkstp/dsl/24hr, [food] Subway, [other] Summerlan RV Park, to Capulin Volcano NM, W [gas] Conoco, Conoco/dsl, CR/dsl, Loaf'n Jug/dsl, Shamrock, [food] Arby's, Denny's, Domino's, JRs Burritos, K-Bob's Steaks, McDonald's, Pappa's Sweets, Sonic, [lodging] Best Western+, Casa Lemus, Microtel, Peak Inn, Quality Inn, Robin Hood Motel, Super 8, Travelodge, [other] Ace Hardware, AutoZone, KOA, O'Reilly Parts, Super Save Foods, Visitor's Ctr/info
450	Lp 25, Raton, W [gas] Shamrock, [lodging] Holiday Inn Express, Oasis Motel/rest., [other] AutoZone, [H], KOA, vet
446	US 64 W, to Cimarron, Taos, W [other] NRA Whittington Ctr
440mm	Canadian River
435	Tinaja
434.5mm	[rest stop] both lanes, full [handicapped] facilities, [picnic], litter barrels, petwalk, weather info
426	NM 505, Maxwell, W [gas] Maxwell Station/dsl, [other] to Maxwell Lakes, USPO
SPRINGER	
419	NM 58, to Cimarron, E [gas] **Chevron/Russell's/Subway/dsl/scales/24hr/@**
414	US 56, Springer, E [gas] Conoco/dsl, Crossroads/dsl, [food] Zayra's Cafe, [lodging] Broken Arrow Motel, Oasis Motel, [other] Old Santa Fe Trail RV Park
412	US 56 E, US 412 E, NM 21, NM 468, Springer, E [gas] Alon, [lodging] Springer Sta. Hotel/cafe, [other] CarQuest, Family$, Springer Foods, USPO
404	NM 569, Colmor, Charette Lakes
393	Levy
387	NM 120, to Roy, Wagon Mound, E [gas] Conoco/dsl, Phillips 66/dsl, [other] USPO
376mm	[rest stop] sb, full [handicapped] facilities, [picnic], litter barrels, petwalk, [phone], RV camp
374mm	[rest stop] nb, full [handicapped] facilities, [picnic], litter barrels, petwalk, [phone], RV camp
366	NM 97, NM 161, Watrous, Valmora
364	NM 97, NM 161, Watrous, Valmora
361	no services
360mm	parking area both lanes
356	Onava, Onava
LAS VEGAS	
352	E [other] [airport]
347	to NM 518, Las Vegas, W [gas] **Love's/Subway/dsl/scales/24hr**, Pino/dsl/rest., [lodging] Best Western+, Comfort Inn, Days Inn, Regal Motel, Super 8, [other] [H], Storrie Lake SP
345	NM 65, NM 104, University Ave, Las Vegas, E [other] to Conchas Lake SP, W [gas] Allsups, Crossroads/dsl, [food] Arby's, Buffalo Hall BBQ, Burger King, Dave's Diner, Domino's, DQ, Hillcrest Rest., KFC, Little Caesars, McDonald's, Olivia's Cafe, Phillips 66, Pizza Hut, Sonic, Starbucks, Taco Bell, Wendy's, [lodging] Econolodge, El Fidel, Knights Inn, Travelodge, [other] Hist. Old Town Plaza, museum, Verizon, Walgreens
343	to NM 518 N, Las Vegas, E [other] Garcia Tires, W [gas] Valero/Allsup's, [food] Smiling Faces Mexican, [lodging] Holiday Inn Express, Thunderbird Motel, [other] auto repair
339	US 84 S, to Santa Rosa, Romeroville, E [other] KOA, W [gas] Speedway/Subway/dsl
335	Tecolote
330	Bernal
325mm	parking area both lanes, no rest rooms
323	NM 3 S, Villanueva, E [other] to Villanueva SP/rv camping, USPO
319	San Juan, San Jose, W [gas] Pecos River Sta.
307	NM 63, Rowe, Pecos
299	NM 50, Glorieta, Pecos, W [other] Glorieta Conf Ctr
297	Valencia
294	Apache Canyon, W [other] KOA, Rancheros Camping(Mar-Nov)
290	US 285 S, to Lamy, S to Clines Corners, E [gas] Phillips 66/dsl, W [food] Cafe Fina, [other] Rancheros Camping(Mar-Nov)
284	NM 466, Old Pecos Trail, Santa Fe, W [food] Harry's Roadhouse, [lodging] Pecos Trail Inn/Cafe, [other] [H], museums
282	US 84, US 285, St Francis Dr, W [gas] Maverik, Speedway/dsl, [food] Church's TX Chicken
SANTA FE	
278	NM 14, Cerrillos Rd, Santa Fe, W [gas] Murphy Express/dsl, Shell, Speedway/dsl, Speedway/dsl, [food] Applebee's, Buffalo Wild Wings, Burger King, Dion's Pizza, Five Guys, Flying Tortilla, Jersey Mike's, Jimmy Johns, McDonald's, Olive Garden, Outback Steaks, Panda Express, Panera Bread, Pizza Hut, Ranch House Steaks, Red Lobster, Rustica Italian, Sonic, Starbucks, Subway, Taco Bell, [lodging] Best Western, Comfort Inn, Doubletree, EconoLodge, Fairfield Inn, Hampton Inn, Hyatt Place, La Quinta, Ramada, Santa Fe Inn, Tranquilla Inn, [other] AAA, Albertson's, AT&T, Best Buy, BigLots, BMW, Buick/GMC, Cadillac/Chevrolet, CVS Drug, Dillard's, Discount Tire, Firestone/auto, Ford/Lincoln, Harley-Davidson, Home Depot, JC Penney, Jo-Ann Fabrics, Kohl's, Land Rover, Lexus, Los Campos RV Park, Lowe's, Mazda, Mecedes/Smart, Meineke, Michaels, PetSmart, Ross, Sam's Club/gas, Santa Fe Outlets/famous brands, Sprouts Mkt, Target, TJ Maxx, Verizon, Walgreens, Walmart
276b a	NM 599, to NM 14, to Madrid, E [gas] Phillips 66/Allsup's, [other] Santa Fe Skies RV Park
271	CR 50F, La Cienega
269mm	**full [handicapped] facilities, litter barrels, petwalk, [phone], [picnic], [rest stop] nb**
267	Waldo Canyon Rd
ALGODONES	
264	NM 16, Pueblo, W [other] to Cochiti Lake RA
263mm	Galisteo River
259	NM 22, to Santo Domingo Pueblo, W [gas] Phillips 66/cafe/dsl, [other] to Cochiti Lake RA(11mi)
257	Budaghers, W Mormon Battalion Mon.
252	San Felipe Pueblo, E [gas] **Black Mesa TC/dsl**, [other] San Felipe Casino/rest.
248	Rte 66, Algodones, W [other] Family$, vet
242	US 550, NM 44 W, NM 165 E, to Farmington, Aztec, W [gas] Chevron/dsl, **Circle K/dsl**, Phillips 66/dsl, Speedway, Speedway/dsl, [food] Applebees, Church's Chicken, Del Taco, Denny's, Dunkin', Dutch Bros, Filaberto's Mexican, Guang Dong Chinese, KFC, Little Caesars, Lotaburger, McDonald's, Sonic, Starbucks, Starbucks, Subway, Taco Bell, Twisters, Wendy's, Whataburger, [lodging] Days Inn, Holiday Inn Express, Motel 6, Super 8, [other] $General, AutoZone, Casino, Coronado Campground, Home Depot, KOA, O'Reilly Parts, vet, Walgreens, **Walmart**
240	NM 473, to Bernalillo, W [gas] Phillips 66/dsl, [food] Abuelita's Mexican, Range Café, [other] KOA, to Coronado SP, USPO
234	NM 556, Tramway Rd, E [gas] Valero/Subway/dsl, [lodging] Sandia Resort/casino, W [gas] Phillips 66/dsl
233	Alameda Blvd, E [gas] Chevron, [food] Burger King, Whataburger, [lodging] Comfort Suites, Motel 6, Staybridge Suites, [other] Audi/Porsche, Lincoln, Mercedes, Toyota/Scion, Volvo, W [gas] Phillips 66/Circle K/dsl, [food] Carl's Jr, [lodging] Holiday Inn Express, Quality Inn, [other] Balloon Fiesta Park, CarMax
232	Paseo del Norte, Paseo del Norte, E [food] Blaze Pizza, Chick-fil-A, China Luck, Chipotle Mexican, Cocina Azul Mexican, Domino's, Firehouse Subs, Five Guys, Freddy's Steakburgers, Jason's Deli, McDonald's, Panda Express, Panera Bread, Starbucks, Subway, Tomato Cafe, Wendy's, [lodging] GreenTree Inn, SpringHill Suites, [other] Aloha RV Ctr, AutoZone, Discount Tire, Kohl's, Lowe's, Office Depot, Target, Verizon, Walgreens, W [gas] Shell/Circle K, [food] Restoration Pizza, [lodging] Courtyard, Marriott, [other] Cabela's
231	San Antonio Ave, E [gas] Alon/7-11, [food] Cracker Barrel,

NM

INTERSTATE 25 Cont'd

231 Continued
Denny's, Lotaburger, Comfort Suites, GreenTree Inn, Hilton Garden, Homewood Suites, La Quinta, H, USPO, **W** Days Inn, LaQuinta, Siegel Select, Mazda, VW

230 San Mateo Blvd, Osuna Rd, Albuquerque, **E** Giant/dsl, Speedway, Applebee's, Arby's, Bob's Burgers, Burger King, Hayashi Japanese, KFC, McDonald's, Olive Garden, Royal Buffet, Schloztsky's, Starbucks, Taco Bueno, Taco Cabana, Teriyaki Chicken, TX Roadhouse, Village Inn, Wendy's, Wienerschnitzel, Nativo Lodge, $Tree, AT&T, Cadillac, Firestone, Midas, PetCo, Sprouts Mkt, Subaru, **W** Circle K/dsl, Valero/dsl, Einstein Bros, McDonald's, Sterbucks, Subway, Weck's Breakfast/lunch, Whataburger, Studio 6, BMW/Mini

ALBUQUERQUE

229 Jefferson St, **S** Tru, **E** Marverik, Azuma Japanese, Duke City BBQ, Golden Corral, LJ Silver, Mariscos La Playa, Outback Steaks, Sonic, Storming Crab Seafood, Subway, Taco Bell, Holiday Inn, same as 230, Valvoline, **W** Boston's Pizza, Chama River Rest., Cheddar's, Chile Rio, Coldstone, Dickey's BBQ, Fox&Hound, Fuddrucker's, Genghis Grill, Mimi's Café, Nick&Jimmy's Grill, Pappadeaux, Pars Cuisine, PF Chang's, Plum Cafe Asian, Red Robin, Subway, Twin Peaks Rest., TX Land&Cattle Steaks, Drury Inn, Hampton Inn, Hampton Inn, Residence Inn, TownePlace Suites, Lexus

228 Montgomery Blvd, **E** Alon/7-11/dsl, Chevron, Chevron/dsl, Conoco/dsl, Cane's Chicken, Chick-fil-A, Chipotle, Cici's Pizza, Cocina Azul, Del Taco, Domino's, Fiestas Cantina, Firehouse Subs, Lotaburger, Starbucks, Best Western, $Tree, Albertsons, Discount Tire, **W** Circle K, Arby's, Carl's Jr, IHOP, McDonald's, Panda Express, Pizza 9, Starbucks, Wendy's, InTown Suite, Acura, Costco/gas, Ford, Home Depot, Infiniti, Office Depot, PetSmart, REI, Sam's Club/gas, Sportsman's Whse

227b Comanche Rd, Griegos Rd, **E** Maverik

227a Candelaria Rd, Albuquerque, **E** Circle K/dsl, Maverik, Shell, TA/Phillips 66/Country Pride/dsl/scales/24hr/@, Applebee's, Stripes Burrito, Twisters Burgers, Crowne Plaza, Holiday Inn Express, La Quinta, Motel 76, Ramada, Red Rood Inn, Siegel Select, Sonesta Suites, The Querque Hotel, Tree Inn, Chevrolet, **W** Chevron/dsl, Days Inn, SureStay, Penske

226b a I-40, E to Amarillo, W to Flagstaff

225 Lomas Blvd, **E** Howard Johnson, **W** Shell/Circle K/McDonald's, Taqueria Mexican, Carl's Jr, Starbucks, Embassy Suites, H

224 Lead Ave, Coal Ave, Grand Ave, Central Ave, **E** Alon/7-11, 66 Diner, Crossroads Motel, SpringHill Suites, H, **W** Holy Cow Burger, Days Inn, EconoLodge, Hotel Parq Central

223 Chavez Ave, **E** Motel 6, sports arena, **W** Texaco, Little Caesars, Nexus Blue BBQ

222b a Gibson Blvd, **E** Alon/dsl, Applebee's, Buffalo Wild Wings, Burger King, Cane's Chicken, Chick-fil-A, Chili's, Del Taco, Denny's, Dion's Pizza, Dutch Bros, Fuddrucker's, Little Caesars, Lotaburger, Subway, Subway, Village Inn, Waffle House, Wienerschnitzel, Baymont, Best Western, Comfort Inn, Courtyard, Days Inn, Extended Stay America, Fairfield Inn, Hawthorn Suites, Hilton Garden, Holiday Inn Express, La Quinta, Quality Suites, Ramada Inn, Residence Inn, Sleep Inn, Super 8, TownePlace Suites, Albuquerque Int, Family$, museum, vet, **W** Alon/7-11/dsl, Church's TX Chicken, El Botanero Mexican

221 Sunport, **E** Comfort Suites, Hampton Inn, Holiday Inn, Home2 Suites, Homewood Suites, Hyatt Place,

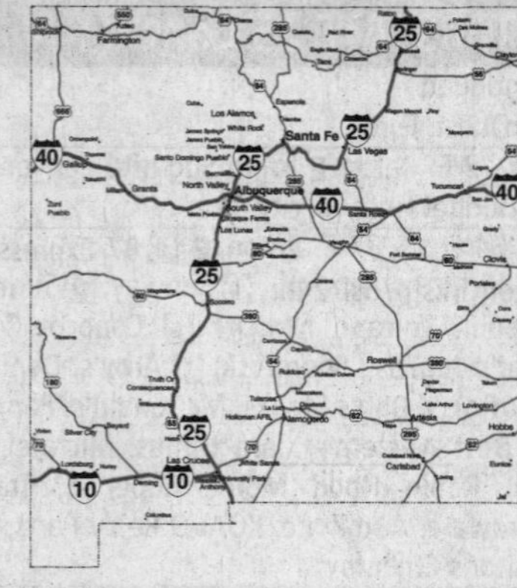

221 Continued
Albuquerque Int, USPO

MOUNTAIN VIEW

220 Rio Bravo Blvd, Mountain View, **E** golf, **W** Circle K/dsl Maverik, Speedway/dsl, Bob's Burgers, Burger King Church's TX Chicken, Dominos, KFC/Taco Bell, Little Caesars LJ Silver, McDonald's, Wingstop, Albertsons/Sav-On Family$, O'Reilly Parts, vet, Walgreens

215 NM 47, **E** Isleta One Stop/dsl, Phillips 66/Subway/dsl, golf, Isleta Lakes RA/RV Camping, Isleta Resort Casino, **W** Pilot/McDonalds/dsl/scales/24hr

214mm Rio Grande

213 NM 314, Isleta Blvd, **W** Chevron/dsl, $General, vet

209 NM 45, to Isleta Pueblo

203 NM 6, to Los Lunas, **E** Circle K/dsl, Circle K/Wendy's/dsl 24hr, Murphy USA/dsl, Applebee's, Buffalo Wild Wings Burger King, Del Taco, Denny's, IHOP, Jersey Mike's McDonalds, Pizza 9, Sonic, Starbucks, Subway Wienerschnitzel, Days Inn, Quality Inn, AutoZone, Bi O Tire, Chevrolet, Chrysler/Dodge/Jeep, Ford, Home Depot Lowe's, O'Reilly Parts, Valvoline, Verizon, Walgreens, **W** Phillips 66/dsl, Carl's Jr, Chili's, Coldstone, Dominos, KFC Mariscos Altamar, Panda Express, Wingstop, Western Skies Inn, Buick/GMC, Discount Tire, Walmart/auto

BELEN

195 Lp 25, Los Chavez, **E** Roadrunner/grill/dsl, Taco Bell, Walmart

191 NM 548, Belen, **E** Love's/Arby's/dsl/scales/24hr, Circl T Burger, Dominos, Greg's BBQ, Little Caesars, McDonald's Pizza Hut, Starbucks, Subway, Varela's Steaks, Super 8, $General, $Tree, Autozone, Family$, USPO, vet, Walgreens **W** Rio Grande Diner, Baymont, RV park, Travelodge

190 Lp 25, Belen, **E** Phillips 66, A&W/LJ Silver

175 US 60, Bernardo, **W** Kiva RV Park

174mm Rio Puerco

169 **W** Sevilleta NWR

167mm both lanes, full facilities, litter barrels, vendin petwalk

166mm Rio Salado

165mm weigh sta/parking area both lanes

SOCORRO

163 San Acacia

156 Lemitar, **W** Marathon/dsl/24hr

152 Escondida, **W** to st police

150 US 60 W, Socorro, **W** Alon/7-11/dsl, Chevron/dsl, Circle Valero/dsl, Burger King, China Best, Dominos, El Camin Rest., Jackson Ranch Steaks, Lotaburger, McDonald's, RJ Chick-Inn, Sofia's Kitchen, Sonic, Subway, Yo Mama's Gri Baymont, Best Western, Comfort Inn, Days In EconoLodge, Economy Inn, Holiday Inn Express, San Migu Inn, Super 8, $General, Ace Hardware, AutoZone, Brook Foods, GPS Tire, NAPA, NM Tech Institute, O'Reilly Parts, ve Walmart

147 US 60 W, Socorro, **W** Chevron/dsl, Circle K/dsl, Conoco dsl/LP, Arby's, $Tree, H, Socorro RV Park

NM

INTERSTATE 25 Cont'd

Exit #	Services
139	US 380 E, to San Antonio, E Bosque Del Apache NWR
124	to San Marcial, E Bosque del Apache NWR
115	NM 107, E Fort Craig HS
114mm	**both lanes, full facilities, littler barrels, petwalk, RV parking, vending**
107mm	Nogal Canyon
100	Red Rock
92	Mitchell Point
90mm	La Canada Alamosa, La Canada Alamosa
89	NM 181, to Cuchillo, to Monticello, E Monticello RV Park
83	NM 52, NM 181, to Cuchillo, E Elephant Butte Inn/rest., Cedar Cove RV Park, Elephant Lake Butte SP
82mm	insp sta nb
79	Lp 25, to Truth or Consequences, E Chevron/dsl, Circle K, Shell/dsl, Del Taco, Johnny B's, La Cocina Mexican, Los Arcos Steaks, McDonald's, Pizza Hut, Sonic, Subway, Sunset Grill, Ace Lodge, Comfort Inn, Desert View Motel, Holiday Inn Express, Motel 6, Travelodge, AutoZone, Elephant Butte SP, O'Reilly Parts, USPO, Walmart
76	(75 from nb)Lp 25, to Williamsburg, E Arco/dsl, Conoco/dsl, Marathon/dsl, Tony's Mexican, Rio Grande Motel, $General, Cielo Vista RV Park, city park, Reeds Tire, Rio Grande RV Park, RJ RV Park, USPO, Windmill RV Park
71	Las Palomas
63	NM 152, to Hillsboro, Caballo, E Lakeview RV Park/dsl/LP
59	rd 187, Arrey, Derry, E Caballo-Percha SPs, Riverside Camping
58mm	Rio Grande
51	rd 546, to Arrey, Garfield, Derry
41	NM 26 W, Hatch, W Circle K/Subway/dsl, B & E Burritos, Sparky's Cafe, Grajeda's Hotel, Chile Pepper Outlets, USPO
35	NM 140 W, Rincon
32	Upham
27mm	scenic view nb, litter barrels
26mm	insp sta nb
23mm	both lanes, full facilities, litter barrels, vending, petwalk
19	Radium Springs, W Family$, Fort Selden St Mon, Leasburg SP, RV camping, USPO
9	Dona Ana, W Chucky's/dsl, Circle K/dsl, Chachi's Mexican, $General, Family$, O'Reilly Parts, RV camping, USPO
6	US 70, to Alamogordo, Las Cruces, E Circle K/dsl, Speedway, Cold Stone Creamery, Domino's, IHOP, Outback Steaks, Papa Johns, Peter Piper Pizza, Ruby Tuesday, Rudy's Country Store and BBQ, Starbucks, Subway, Sushi Freak, Fairfield Inn, Holiday Inn Express, Home2 Suites, Motel 6, Staybridge Suites, Super 8, Towneplace Suites, AT&T, Sam's Club/gas, Sportsman's Whse, USPO, vet, Walmart, W Circle K/dsl, Shell, Shell/dsl, Valero/dsl, Burger King, China Express, Domino's, DQ, Dunkin', KFC, Little Caesar's, Lotaburger, McDonald's, Sonic, Spanish Kitchen, Subway, Taco Bell, Whataburger/24hr, Wienerschnitzel, Century 21, $Tree, Albertson's, AutoZone, CVS Drug, Family$, Kohl's, Lowe's, O'Reilly Parts, Verizon, vet, Walgreens
3	Lohman Ave, Las Cruces, E Circle K/dsl, Shell, Applebee's, Bubbas 33, Buffalo Wild Wings, Burger King, Butter Smith Kitchen, Cane's Chicken, Cattle Baron Steaks, Chili's, Chipotle, ChuckeCheese, Dunkin', Farley's Grill, Fidencio's Mexican, Five Guys, Freddy's Burgers, Genghis Grill, Hooters, Jack-in-the-Box, KFC, McAlister's Deli, Olive Garden, Pecan Grill, Red Lobster, Smokey Sensations BBQ,
3	Continued Sonic, Starbucks, Sushi Freak, Whataburger, Comfort Inn, Hotel Encanto, Albertsons, AutoZone, Barnes&Noble, Dick's, Dillard's, Discount Tire, Home Depot, JC Penney, mall, Marshalls, PetCo, Ross, Target, W Circle K/dsl, Speedway/dsl, Arby's, Carl's Jr, Chick-fil-A, Corner Bakery Cafe, McDonald's, Subway, Taco Bell, TX Roadhouse, Wendy's, Hampton Inn, AT&T, Best Buy, Big Lots, Brake Masters, Hobby Lobby, Old Navy, PepBoys, PetSmart, Sprouts Mkt, Staples, Verizon, vet, Walgreens, Walmart
1	University Ave, Las Cruces, E Circle K/dsl, Maverik, Hilton Garden, golf, H, NM Farm Museum, W Speedway/dsl, Dominos, Lorenzo's Italian, McDonald's, Weck's, Comfort Suites, Extended Stay, Sleep Inn, $Tree, Jo-Ann Fabrics, NMSU
0mm	I-25 begins/ends on I-10, exit 144 at Las Cruces.

INTERSTATE 40

Exit #	Services
373.5mm	New Mexico/Texas state line, Mountain/Central time zone
373mm	full facilities, litter barrels, petwalk, Welcome Ctr wb
369	NM 93 S, NM 392 N, Endee, N Phillips66//Russell's Truck&Travel/Subway/dsl/scales/24hr
361	Bard
358mm	weigh sta both lanes
356	NM 469, San Jon, N to Ute Lake SP, truck repair, S Valero/dsl, Zoni Burger, city park, USPO
343	no services
339	NM 278, N
335	Lp 40, E Tucumcari Blvd, Tucumcari, N Conoco/dsl, EconoLodge, Motel 6, Quality Inn, Rodeway Inn, Sunset Inn, Super 8, to Conchas Lake SP, S KOA
333	US 54 E, Tucumcari, N Flying J TC/Phillips 66/dsl/LP/scales/repair/24hr, Love's/Arby's/dsl/scales, Fairfield Inn, city park, Mtn Rd RV Park, truck repair, truck repair, truckwash
332	NM 209, NM 104, 1st St, Tucumcari, N Circle K, Valero, Blake's Lotaburger, McDonald's, Pizza Hut, Sonic, Stone Ranch Steaks, Taco Bell, Best Western, Days Inn, Desert Inn, Holiday Inn Express, La Quinta/EVC, $General, Ace Hardware, Dinosaur Museum, Family$, H, Lowe's Foods, to Conchas Lake SP, S ONE9 TC
331	Camino del Coronado, Tucumcari
329	US 54, US 66 E, W Tucumcari Ave, S golf
321	Palomas
311	Montoya
302mm	both lanes, full facilities, litter barrels, petwalk, RV dump
300	NM 129, Newkirk, N Newkirk, to Conchas Lake SP, USPO
291	to Rte 66, Cuervo, N Cuervo Gas/repair
284	no services
277	US 84 S, to Ft Sumner, N Phillips 66/dsl, Pilot/dsl/scales/24hr, DQ, Silver Moon Café, Best Western, Budget Inn, Comfort Inn, Hampton Inn, Holiday Inn Express, Hotel Blue 66, Motel 6, NAPACare, S Love's/Carl's Jr/dsl/24hr, TA/Shell/Subway/dsl/24hr/@, truck/tire repair
275	US 54 W, Santa Rosa, N Valero/Allsup's, McDonald's, Days Inn, Econolodge, La Quinta, Rodeway Inn, Santa Rosa Camping, st police, S Shell/Circle K/dsl, Joseph's Grill, Laloma Motel/RV Park, Route 66 Inn, Sun&Sand Motel/rest., Super 8, Tower Motel, $General, CarQuest, city park, Family$, H, NAPA, USPO
273.5mm	Pecos River
273	US 54 S, Santa Rosa, N Santa Rosa Lake SP, S Phillips 66/dsl, Best Value Inn, auto repair, to Carlsbad Caverns NP

LAS CRUCES · BARD · TUCUMCARI · SANTA ROSA

NM

= gas = food = lodging = other = rest stop

INTERSTATE 40 Cont'd

COLONIAS

Exit #	Services
267	Colonias, N Sinclair/dsl
263	San Ignacio
256	US 84 N, NM 219, to Las Vegas
252	no services
251.5mm	N both lanes, full facilities, , , litter barrels, petwalk, RV dump
243	Milagro, N Phillips 66/dsl
239	no services
234	N Bowlin's Ranch/DQ/dsl/gifts
230	NM 3, to Encino, N to Villanueva SP
226	no services
220mm	parking area both lanes, litter barrels
218b a	US 285, Clines Corners, N Cline's TC/Chevron/dsl/24hr, Phillips 66/dsl, Subway, Clines Corners RV Park, USPO
208	Wagon Wheel, N U-Haul
207mm	wb, full facilities, , litter barrels, petwalk
203	N Zia RV Park, S Longhorn Ranch RV Park

MORIARTY

Exit #	Services
197	to Rte 66 (same as 196), Moriarty, S Glider Museum
196	NM 41, Howard Cavasos Blvd, N Pilot/Subway/dsl/scales/24hr, La Hacienda, S Lisa's TC/Conoco/dsl, Phillips 66/Circle K/dsl, Blakes Lotaburger, Quality Inn, Sunset Motel, $General, auto repair, city park, Family$, Sal & Inez's Service, to Salinas NM(35mi), USPO
194	NM 41, Moriarty, S Alon, TA/Shell/Burger King/Country Pride/Pizza Hut/dsl/24hr/scales/@, Arby's, Chili Hills Mexican, KFC/Taco Bell, Nachos, Best Western, Motel 6, Ponderosa Motel, Rodeway Inn, Super 8, $General, Chevrolet/GMC, fireworks, Happy Trails RV, Moriarty Foods, RV Ctr
187	NM 344, Edgewood, N Marathon/DQ, Tony's auto repair, Blake's Lotaburger, Denny's, Taco Zone, Walmart, S Phillips 66/dsl, Chili Hills Mexican, China Chef, Domino's, McDonald's, Pizza Barn, Sonic, Comfort Inn, $Tree, auto/rv repair, AutoZone, Ford, O'Reilly Parts, Rte 66 RV Park, RV Camping, Smith's Foods/dsl, USPO, Walgreens

NM

CARNUEL

Exit #	Services
181	NM 217, Sedillo, S Route 66/dsl
178	Zuzax, S Chevron, Albuquerque RV Park, Leisure Mtn RV Park
175	NM 337, NM 14, Tijeras, N to Cibola NF, Turquoise Trail RV Park, S Subway, USPO
170	Carnuel
167	Central Ave, to Tramway Blvd, S Alon, Alon, Phillips 66/Circle K/dsl, Blakes Lotaburger, Domino's, Einstein Bagel, Happy Garden, KFC, McDonald's, Papa Murphy's, Subway, Taco Bell, Desert Sands Inn, EconoLodge, Motel 6, Rodeway Inn, Woodspring Suites, Rocky Mtn RV/marine, Smith's/gas, Sprouts Mkt, to Kirtland AFB, Valvoline, Verizon
166	Juan Tabo Blvd, N Maverik, Phillips 66/Circle K, Burger King, Chipotle, Domino's, Donut Mart, Dutch Bros, McDonald's, Olive Garden, Pack Your Maxx, Starbucks, Subway, Taco Bell, Twisters Diner, Wendy's, Wreck's, Guest Gate Inn, Quality Inn, $General, Albertson's, Big O Tires, Discount Tire, Family$, Hobby Lobby, Midas, U-Haul, Valvoline, vet, S Sonic, Wienerschnitzel, $General, KOA/LP, Myer's RV Ctr, repair
165	Eubank Blvd, N Chevron, Phillips 66/Circle K, Applebee's, Owl Cafe, Panda Express, Sonic, Days Inn, Econolodge, $Tree, Best Buy, city park, Office Depot, PetCo, Target, S Circle K/dsl, Speedway/dsl, Burger King, Chick-fil-A, Chili's, Church's TX Chicken, Del Taco, Dutch Bros, Freddy's, Jack-in-the-Box, Jimmy John's, Little Caesars, Starbucks, Taco Bell, Taco Cabana, Twister's Burritos, Wendy's, Wingstop, Holiday Inn Express, $Tree, Advance Parts, AutoZone, Costco/gas, Home Depot,

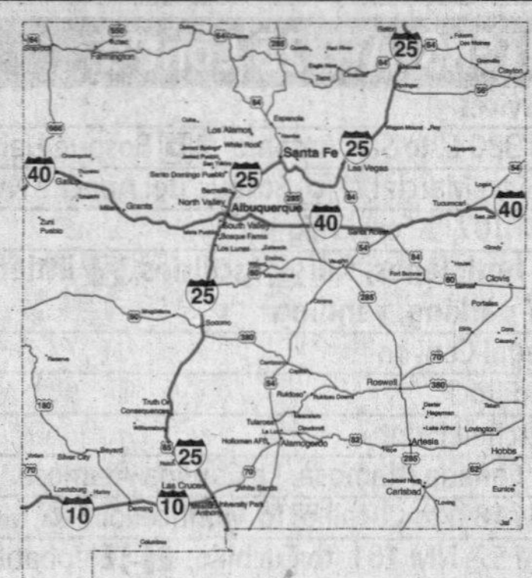

ALBUQUERQUE

Exit #	Services
165	Continued O'Reilly Parts, Peerless Tires, PetSmart, repair, Ross, Sam Club/gas, Toyota, Walgreens, Walmart/McDonald's
164	Lomas Blvd, Wyoming Blvd, N Maverik, Murphy US Phillips66/Circle K/dsl, Shwan, Baskin-Robbins, Blac Angus, Cane's, Chick-fil-A, Dickey's BBQ, Dominos, Krisp Kreme, Subway, Village Inn, Wendy's, $Tree, H, Jif Lube, Walgreens, Walmart, S Chrysler/Dodge/Jeep, For Ford, Honda, Hyundai, Kirtland AFB, Mazda, transmission VW
162b a	Louisiana Blvd, N Valero, Arby's, BJ's Rest., Blaze Pizz Bravo Italian, Buca Italian, CA Pizza Kitchen, Cheesecak Factory, Chili's, Chipotle, Dave & Buster's, Firehouse Sub Five Guys, Fuddrucker's, Genghis Grill, Honey Baked Ha Japanese Teppanyaki, Jasons Deli, Jimmy John's, L Madeleine, Longhorn Steaks, McAlister's Deli, McDonald' Melting Pot, Ojos Locos, Panera Bread, Red Robin, Ruth Chris, Seasons Grill 52, Starbucks, Hilton Garde Homewood Suites, Hyatt Place, Marriott, Sheraton, Barnes&Noble, Big O Tire, Dick's, Dillard's, Discount Tir Firestone/auto, JC Penney, Macy's, Midas, Target, TJ Max Trader Joe's, Valvoline, Verizon, S Circle K, Shwan, Blake Lotaburger, Burger King, Barcelona Suites, atomic museum, Chevrolet, GMC, Jaguar, Kia, Mitsubish Nissan, Subaru, URGENT CARE
161b a	San Mateo Blvd, Albuquerque, N Speedway, Ziggi Coffee, Bob's Burgers, Burger King, Denny's, Domino' KFC, Pizza Hut, Scooter's Coffee, Starbucks, Taco Bell, $Tree, Office Depot, Walmart Mkt, S Chevron/dsl, Starbucks
160	Carlisle Blvd, Albuquerque, N Circle K/gas, Maveri Murphy Express/dsl, Shell, TA/Phillips66/Country Pride/ds scales/24hr, Applebee's, Blakes Lotaburger, Daily Grin Jack-in-the-Box, McDonald's, Papa Murphy's, Rudy's BB Sonic, Starbucks, Stripes Burrito, Subway, Twisters Gri Whataburger, Best Value Inn, Crowne Plaza, Hampto Inn, Holiday Inn Express, La Quinta, Motel 6, Ramada Plaz Red Roof Inn, Siegel Select, Sonesta Suites, Suburban Mote The Querque, AutoZone, Firestone/auto, USP Walgreens, Walmart, S Chevron/dsl, Circle K, Burge King, Home2 Suites, Motel 6, H, Whole Foods Mkt
159b c	I-25, S to Las Cruces, N to Santa Fe
158	6th St, 8th St, 12th St, Albuquerque, N Love's/Subway dsl, $General, U-Haul, S Chevron/dsl
157b	12th St(from eb), N Four Winds/Burrito Co/dsl, Domino's, Laguna Burgers, McDonald's, Starbucks, Holiday Inn Express, TownePlace Suites, Lowe' Walgreens
157a	Rio Grande Blvd, Albuquerque, N Chevron, Range Caf S Speedway/dsl, Ben Michaels, Blakes Lotaburge Burger King, Little Anita's, Seasons Rotisserie Gri Starbucks, Best Western+/grill, Hotel Albuquerque,

INTERSTATE 40 Cont'd

ALBUQUERQUE

157a Continued
auto parts

156mm Rio Grande River

155 Coors Rd, Albuquerque, N Circle K, Speedway/dsl, Valero/dsl, Applebee's, Arby's, Blake's Lotaburger, Burger King, Chick-fil-A, Chili's, Chipotle, Cracker Barrel, Golden Corral, Hibachi Japanese, IHOP, Jersey Mike's, Krispy Kreme, Little Caesar's, McDonald's, Panda Express, Panera Bread, Sal's Italian, Sonic, Starbucks, Stripes Burrito, Taco Cabana, Wendy's, Wienerschnitzel, Wing Stop, $Tree, AutoZone, Brake Masters, Family$, Firestone, Home Depot, Jiffy Lube, Jiffy Lube, U-Haul, Verizon, Walgreens, Walmart/Subway, S Chevron/dsl, Circle K, Phillips 66/Circle K/dsl, Shell, Blakes Lotaburger, Buffalo Wild Wings, Del Taco, Denny's, Dutch Bros, Little Caesars, McDonald's, Papa John's, Pizza Hut/Taco Bell, Starbucks, Subway, Days Inn, EconoLodge, Extend-A-Suites, Hampton Inn, La Quinta, Motel 6, Quality Inn, Rodeway Inn, Super 8, Travelodge, BigLots, Discount Tire, KC Tires, O'Reilly Parts

154 Unser Blvd, N Circle K, Walmart/dsl, Burger King, McDonald's, Starbucks, Taco Bell, to Petroglyph NM, Verizon, Walmart Mkt

153 98th St, S Circle K/dsl, Clean Energy, Flying J/Denny's/dsl/LP/24hr, Maverik, Burger King, Church's TX Chicken, Dutch Bros, Jack-in-the-Box, Little Caesars, McDonald's, Starbucks, Subway, The Burger Den, Whataburger, Wing Stop, Microtel, $Tree, AT&T, AutoZone, truckwash/tire/lube

149 Central Ave, Paseo del Volcan, N Camping World, Enchanted Trails RV Camping, Freightliner, S Love's/Carl's Jr/dsl/scales/24hr/dog park, Las Victorias, American RV Park, High Desert RV Park

140.5mm Rio Puerco River, N The 66 Pit Stop

140 Rio Puerco, N 66 Pit Stop, S Rte 66 TC/Phillips66/DQ/hotel/casino/dsl/@

131 Canoncito

126 NM 6, to Los Lunas

120mm Rio San Jose

117 Mesita

114 NM 124, Laguna, N Laguna Burger

113.5mm scenic view both lanes, litter barrels

ACOMITA

108 Casa Blanca, Paraje, S Rte 66 TC/DQ/dsl/24hr, casino, Dancing Eagle Mkt, RV park, USPO

104 Cubero, Budville, N USPO

102 Sky City Rd, Acomita, **both lanes, full facilities, , , litter barrels, petwalk**, N Sky City/Phillips66/McDonald's/dsl, Family$, RV Park/laundry, Sky City Hotel/casino

100 San Fidel, N USPO, S Burger Barn

96 McCartys

89 NM 117, to Quemado, N Sky City/Phillips66/Subway/dsl/gifts, S El Malpais NM

GRANTS

85 NM 122, NM 547, Grants, N Chevron/dsl, Phillips 66/dsl, Valero/dsl, Asian Buffet, Blakes Lotaburger, Canton Cafe, Denny's, El Cafecito, Pizza 9 Grants, Pizza Hut, Subway, Surf Shack Pizza, Taco Bell, Best Western, Days Inn, Holiday Inn Express, Motel 6, Quality Inn, Sands Motel, Super 8, SureStay, $Tree, AutoZone, Delta Tire, H, O'Reilly Parts, repair/transmissions/towing, Walgreens, Walmart, S Lavaland RV Park

81b a NM 53 S, Grants, N Phillips 66/dsl, Domino's, KFC, McDonald's, Rosie's Cafe, Sonic, Ford, H, USPO, S Blue Spruce RV Park, El Malpais NM, KOA/Cibola Sands RV Park

79 NM 122, NM 605, Milan, N Chevron/dsl, Love's/Chester's/Subway/dsl/scales/24hr, $General,

BLUEWATER VILLAGE

79 Continued
Bar-S RV Park, NAPA, S Petro/Shell/dsl/scales/24hr/@, Senergy Petroleum, Gabby's Diner, dsl repair, Speedco Lube

72 Bluewater Village, N DQ, S USPO

63 NM 412, Prewitt, S to Bluewater Lake SP(7mi)

53 NM 371, NM 612, Thoreau, N Speedway/dsl, $General, Family$, NAPA, USPO

47 Continental Divide, elevation 7275, N Phillips 66, Continental Divide Trdg Post, S USPO

44 Coolidge

39 Refinery, N Flying J/Subway/Dennys/dsl/scales/24hr/@

36 Iyanbito

33 NM 400, McGaffey, Ft Wingate, N RV camping, to Red Rock SP

GALLUP

26 E 66th Ave, E Gallup, N Speedway/dsl, Denny's, Comfort Suites, Holiday Inn Express, La Quinta, Sleep Inn, TownePlace Suites, museum, Red Rock Camping, st police, to Red Rock SP, S Maverik/dsl, Pronto Express, Speedway/dsl/24hr, Valero, Blakes Lotaburger, Dickey's BBQ, KFC, Days Inn, Fairfield Inn, Hacienda Motel, La Quinta, $Tree, Family $, H

22 Montoya Blvd, Gallup, **both lanes**, S Duke City/dsl, Gas Up, Phillips 66, Speedway/dsl, Avalon Chinese, Baskin-Robbins, Big Cheese Pizza, Burger King, Domino's, DQ, Earl's Rest., Hong Kong Buffet, La Barraca, LJ Silver, McDonald's, Papa John's, Pizza Hut, Sonic, Starbucks, Subway, Taco Bell, Wendy's, El Rancho Motel/rest., $General, Albertson's, Auto Care Express, Eagle Tires, O'Reilly Parts, Shop'n Save, U-Haul, Verizon, Walgreens

20 US 491, to Shiprock, Gallup, N Maverik, Shell/dsl, Speedway/dsl, Speedway/dsl, Applebee's, Big Cheese Pizza, Blakes Lotaburger, Burger King, CA Chinese, Carl's Jr., Church's TX Chicken, Cracker Barrel, Del Taco, Denny's, Golden Corral, KFC, King Dragon Chinese, Little Caesars, Mama's Kitchen, McDonald's, Oasis Mediterranean, Panda Express, Pizza Hut, Popeyes, Sizzler, Sonic, Starbucks, Subway, Taco Bell, Wendy's, Comfort Inn, Hampton Inn, Hilton Garden, Quality Inn, SpringHill Suites, $Tree, AT&T, AutoZone, Big Lots, CarQuest, Family$, Hobby Lobby, Home Depot, JC Penney, O'Reilly Parts, Safeway, Verizon, Walmart/McDonald's, S Phillips66/dsl, Blakes Lotaburger, Don Diego's, El Charrito, El Sombrero Mexican, Garcia's Rest., McDonald's, Sonic, Days Inn, Golden Desert Motel, Knights Inn, Royal Holiday Motel, Super 8, Ford/Lincoln, H, tires

16 NM 118, W Gallup, Mentmore, N Love's/Chester's/Subway/dsl/24hr, Navajo/dsl/24hr, TA/Country Pride/dsl/scales/24hr/@, USave Trkstp/dsl, Ace Truck/dsl Service, Blue Beacon, NKS Truck Repair, S ONE9/dsl/24hr, Shell/dsl, Speedway/dsl, Valero/Allsup's, Taco Bell, Virgie's Mexican, Budget Inn, EconoLodge, Hampton Inn, Howard Johnson, Knights Inn, Microtel, Motel 6, Red Roof Inn, Rodeway Inn, Family $, USA RV Park

12mm inspection/weigh sta eb

8 to Manuelito

3mm full facilities, , , litter barrels, petwalk, Welcome Ctr eb

0mm New Mexico/Arizona state line

NOTES

NEW YORK

INTERSTATE 81

ISLANDS PARKS

Exit #	Services
184mm	US/Canada border, New York state line. I-81 begins/ends.
183.5mm	US Customs(sb)
52(183)	Island Rd, to De Wolf Point, last US exit nb, last US exit nb
51(180)	Island Rd, to Fineview, Islands Parks, E USPO, W Wellesley Island Mkt, Thousand Islands Park
179mm	St Lawrence River
178.5mm	Thousand Islands Toll Bridge Booth, NY Welcome Ctr/rest area sb, **full facilities, litter barrels, petwalk,**
50NS(178)	NY 12, E to Alexandria Bay, W to Clayton, Thousand Island Region, E Sunoco/dsl, Kountry Kottage Rest., Subway, PineHurst Motel, $General, Chrysler/Dodge/Jeep, PriceChopper Mkt, st police, W **NY Welcome Ctr/**, EVC, Valero, Bridgeview Motel, AutoShack Parts, vet
174mm	**nb, full facilities, vending, litter barrels, petwalk**
49(171)	NY 411, to Theresa, Indian River Lake, W The Flying Spatula
168mm	parking area sb, picnic table
161mm	parking area nb
48a	I-781, CR 16, to Ft Drum, parking eb,
48(158)	US 11, NY 37, E Circle K/dsl, Mobil/Dunkin'/dsl, Celest Jamaican Cafe, Allen's Budget Motel, Royal Inn, golf course, Long-Park Tire, U-Haul
156.5mm	parking area both lanes

WATERTOWN

Exit #	Services
47(155)	NY 12, Bradley St, Watertown, E Sunoco/7-11/Subway/dsl, Valero, Frosty Dairy Bar, auto repair, General Store, Honda, Speedco, W Love's/McDonald's/Godfather's/RV hookup/dsl/scales/24hr
154.5mm	Black River
46(154)	NY 12F, Coffeen St, Watertown, E Mobil/Dunkin/dsl, Cracker Barrel, Shorty's Diner, Home Depot, URGENT CARE, W Sunoco/Tim Horton/dsl
45(152)	NY 3, to Arsenal St, Watertown, E Mobil, Sunoco, Tesla EVC, Applebee's, Arby's, Buffalo Wild Wings, Burger King, Chick-fil-A, Chipotle Mexican, Daily Buffet, Dunkin', Five Guys, Hacienda Mexican, IHOP, Jreck Subs, KFC, Lotus Rest., McDonald's, Moe's SW Grill, Sonic, Starbucks, Taco Bell, Comfort Inn, EconoLodge, Fairfield Inn, Hampton Inn, Hilton Garden, Holiday Inn Express, Travelodge, $General, $Tree, Advance Parts, ALDI, AT&T, AutoZone, BigLots, Goodyear, Mavis Discount Tire, Midas, Monro, Mr Tire, PriceChopper Foods/24hr, Staples, URGENT CARE, USPO, Valvoline, Walgreens, W Fastrac, Olive Garden, Panera Bread, Pizza Hut, Popeyes, Red Robin, Super Wok, TX Roadhouse, Ramada Inn, Best Buy, Burlington Coats, Dick's, Hannaford Foods, JC Penney, Kohl's, Lowe's, Michael's, Old Navy, PetCo, Sam's Club, Target, TJ Maxx, to Sackets Harbor, Verizon, Walmart
149mm	parking area nb
44(148)	NY 232, to Watertown Ctr, E
147mm	rest area sb, **full facilities, litter barrels, petwalk,** , **vending**

ADAMS

Exit #	Services
43(146)	US 11, to Kellogg Hill
42(144)	NY 177, Adams Center, E Sunoco/7-11/dsl, Honeyville Manor, Harley Davidson, Tugger's Camping(12mi)
41(140)	NY 178, Adams, E Sunoco/dsl, China Wok, Dunkin', Gram's Diner, Jreck Subs, McDonald's, $General, Chrysler/Jeep/Dodge, Ford, Freeway Grocery, Kinney Drug, NAPA, tires, Tops Friendly Mkt, USPO, vet, Willows on the Lake RV Park, W KOA, st police

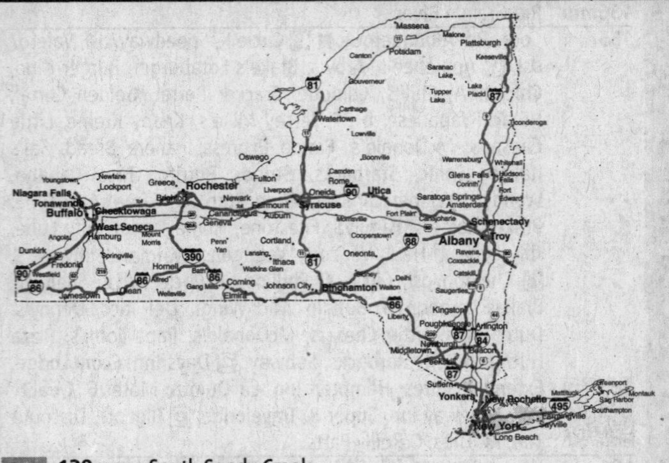

MANNSVILLE

Exit #	Services
138mm	South Sandy Creek
40(135)	NY 193, to Ellisburg, Pierrepont Manor
134mm	parking area/picnic tables both lanes
39(133)	Mannsville
38(131)	US 11
37(128)	Lacona, Sandy Creek, E Huckleberry Cafe, Harris Lodge, USPO, W Mobil/dsl, Creekside Pizza, New China One, The Martin Inn, Pink House Inn B&B, $General, Colonial Court Camping(3mi), Sandy Island Beach SP, Tops/dsl, USPO
36(121)	NY 13, Pulaski, E Byrne Dairy/dsl, Valero, Red Carpet Inn, Buick/Chevrolet, Ford, NAPA, W FasTrac/dsl, KwikFill/dsl, Sunoco, Arby's, Burger King, Dragon Garden, Dunkin', Endzone, Little Caesars, McDonald's, Mill House Mkt, Paulanjo's Pizza, River House Rest., Stefano's Rest., Steph's Place, 1880 House B&B, Super 8, $General, $Tree, Advance Parts, ALDI, BigLots, Family$, Kinney Drug, Mavis Tire, to Selkirk Shores SP, Top's Foods, URGENT CARE, USPO, Verizon
35(118)	to US 11, Tinker Tavern Rd, E Streamside RV Park
34(115)	NY 104, to Mexico, E ONE9/Maple View Rest./dsl/scales, W Feeder Creek Lodge(5mi), Jellystone Camping(9mi)
33(111)	NY 69, Parish, E Sunoco/dsl/24hr, Tesla EVC, Grist Mill Rest., Parish Country Lodge, $General, W Mobile, Dunkin, Passarella Pizza, Subway, USPO

BREWERTON

Exit #	Services
32(103)	NY 49, to Central Square, E Mirabito/dsl, Good Golly's Rest., Murphy's Automotive, W Fastrac/gas, Burger King, Dunkin', McDonald's, Taco Bell, $Tree, Advance Parts, Ford, NAPA, O'Reilly Parts, URGENT CARE, Verizon Walmart/Subway
31(99)	to US 11, Brewerton, E Oneida Shores Camping, W Circle K/dsl, Mirabito/dsl, Dunkin', Little Caesars, Little Caesar's, McDonald's, Subway, Days Inn, $General, AT&T, Kinney Drugs, USPO, vet
30(96)	NY 31, to Cicero, E Fastrac/dsl, Speedway/dsl, Arby's, Cracker Barrel, Dunkin', McDonald's, Rancho Viejo, Comfort Suites, Holiday Inn Express, $Tree, ALDI, Camping World, W Kwik FIll, Cicero Pizza, Seven O's RV Ctr
29(93)	I-481 S, NY 481, to Oswego, Syracuse, W EVC, Speedway, Buffalo Wild Wings, Burger King, Chick-fil-A, Chipotle, Copper Top Tavern, Dave's Chicken, Denny's, DQ, DQ, Dunkin', Firehouse, KFC, Little Caesar's, McDonald's, Moe's SW Grill, Panera Bread, Pizza Hut, Starbucks, Taco Bell, Tropical Smoothie, Tully's Rest., Vietnamese Noodles, Wendy's, Budget Inn, $General, $Tree, Advance Parts, Audi/Porsche/VW, AutoZone, BMW, Buick/GMC, Chevrolet,

NY

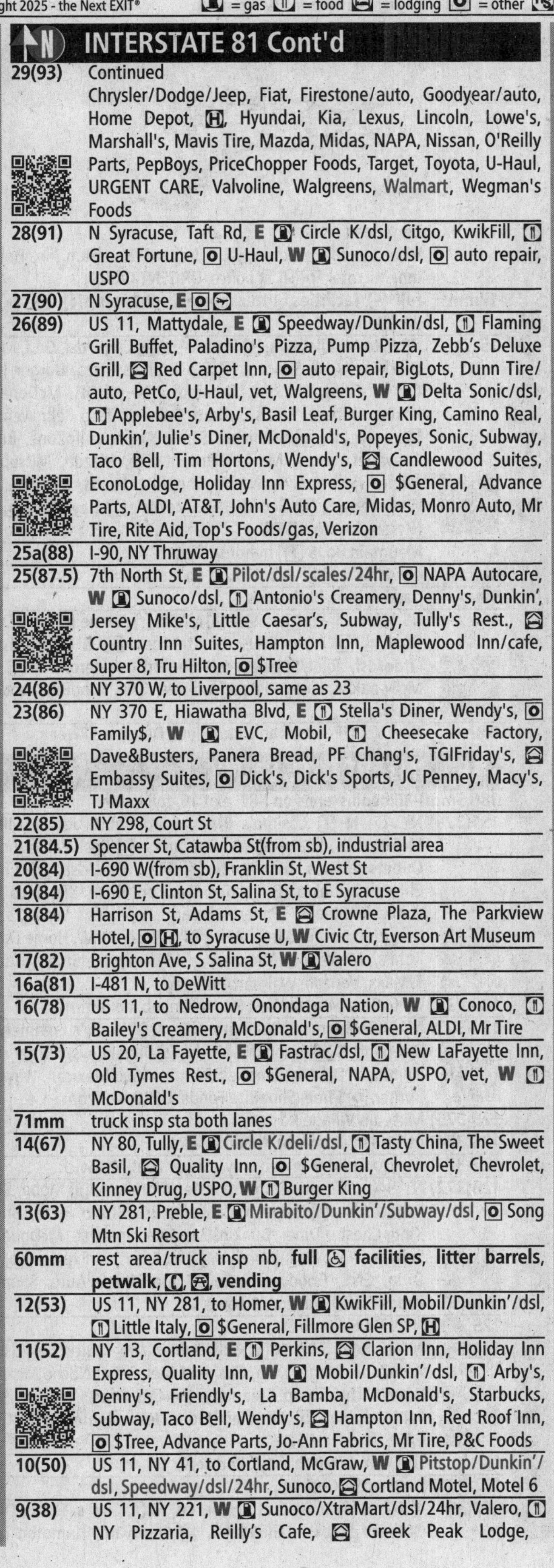

INTERSTATE 81 Cont'd

29(93) Continued
Chrysler/Dodge/Jeep, Fiat, Firestone/auto, Goodyear/auto, Home Depot, H, Hyundai, Kia, Lexus, Lincoln, Lowe's, Marshall's, Mavis Tire, Mazda, Midas, NAPA, Nissan, O'Reilly Parts, PepBoys, PriceChopper Foods, Target, Toyota, U-Haul, URGENT CARE, Valvoline, Walgreens, Walmart, Wegman's Foods

28(91) N Syracuse, Taft Rd, E Circle K/dsl, Citgo, KwikFill, Great Fortune, U-Haul, W Sunoco/dsl, auto repair, USPO

27(90) N Syracuse, E

26(89) US 11, Mattydale, E Speedway/Dunkin/dsl, Flaming Grill Buffet, Paladino's Pizza, Pump Pizza, Zebb's Deluxe Grill, Red Carpet Inn, auto repair, BigLots, Dunn Tire/auto, PetCo, U-Haul, vet, Walgreens, W Delta Sonic/dsl, Applebee's, Arby's, Basil Leaf, Burger King, Camino Real, Dunkin', Julie's Diner, McDonald's, Popeyes, Sonic, Subway, Taco Bell, Tim Hortons, Wendy's, Candlewood Suites, EconoLodge, Holiday Inn Express, $General, Advance Parts, ALDI, AT&T, John's Auto Care, Midas, Monro Auto, Mr Tire, Rite Aid, Top's Foods/gas, Verizon

MATTYDALE

25a(88) I-90, NY Thruway

25(87.5) 7th North St, E Pilot/dsl/scales/24hr, NAPA Autocare, W Sunoco/dsl, Antonio's Creamery, Denny's, Dunkin', Jersey Mike's, Little Caesar's, Subway, Tully's Rest., Country Inn Suites, Hampton Inn, Maplewood Inn/cafe, Super 8, Tru Hilton, $Tree

24(86) NY 370 W, to Liverpool, same as 23

23(86) NY 370 E, Hiawatha Blvd, E Stella's Diner, Wendy's, Family$, W EVC, Mobil, Cheesecake Factory, Dave&Busters, Panera Bread, PF Chang's, TGIFriday's, Embassy Suites, Dick's, Dick's Sports, JC Penney, Macy's, TJ Maxx

22(85) NY 298, Court St

21(84.5) Spencer St, Catawba St(from sb), industrial area

20(84) I-690 W(from sb), Franklin St, West St

19(84) I-690 E, Clinton St, Salina St, to E Syracuse

18(84) Harrison St, Adams St, E Crowne Plaza, The Parkview Hotel, H, to Syracuse U, W Civic Ctr, Everson Art Museum

17(82) Brighton Ave, S Salina St, W Valero

16a(81) I-481 N, to DeWitt

16(78) US 11, to Nedrow, Onondaga Nation, W Conoco, Bailey's Creamery, McDonald's, $General, ALDI, Mr Tire

15(73) US 20, La Fayette, E Fastrac/dsl, New LaFayette Inn, Old Tymes Rest., $General, NAPA, USPO, vet, W McDonald's

71mm truck insp sta both lanes

14(67) NY 80, Tully, E Circle K/deli/dsl, Tasty China, The Sweet Basil, Quality Inn, $General, Chevrolet, Chevrolet, Kinney Drug, USPO, W Burger King

13(63) NY 281, Preble, E Mirabito/Dunkin'/Subway/dsl, Song Mtn Ski Resort

60mm rest area/truck insp nb, **full facilities, litter barrels, petwalk**, , , **vending**

12(53) US 11, NY 281, to Homer, W KwikFill, Mobil/Dunkin'/dsl, Little Italy, $General, Fillmore Glen SP, H

11(52) NY 13, Cortland, E Perkins, Clarion Inn, Holiday Inn Express, Quality Inn, W Mobil/Dunkin'/dsl, Arby's, Denny's, Friendly's, La Bamba, McDonald's, Starbucks, Subway, Taco Bell, Wendy's, Hampton Inn, Red Roof Inn, $Tree, Advance Parts, Jo-Ann Fabrics, Mr Tire, P&C Foods

10(50) US 11, NY 41, to Cortland, McGraw, W Pitstop/Dunkin'/dsl, Speedway/dsl/24hr, Sunoco, Cortland Motel, Motel 6

CORTLAND

9(38) US 11, NY 221, W Sunoco/XtraMart/dsl/24hr, Valero, NY Pizzaria, Reilly's Cafe, Greek Peak Lodge,

9(38) Continued
Three Bear Inn/rest., city park, Country Hills Camping, NAPA, Robinson's Repair, USPO

33mm **full facilities, litter barrels, petwalk**, , , sb, **vending**

8(30) NY 79, to US 11, NY 26, NY 206(no EZ return), Whitney Pt, E Kwikfill, Mobil, Sunoco, Aiello's Ristorante, Arby's, Dominic's Pizza, Dunkin', McDonald's, Steve's BBQ, Subway, Whitney Point Kitchen, $General, Auto Parts+, Dorchester Park, Gregg's Mkt, NAPA, USPO, Walgreens

7(21) US 11, Castle Creek, W Mirabito/Subway/Tim Hortons/dsl

6(16) US 11, to NY 12, I-88E, Chenango Bridge, E Mirabito/dsl, Mirabito/dsl, Arby's, Burger King, Cheesesteak Boss, Denny's, Dunkin', Grande Pizza, Moe's SW Grill, Spiedie BBQ, Subway, Wendy's, Advance Parts, AutoZone, Big E Tire/auto, Chrysler/Dodge/Jeep, CVS Drug, Lowe's, Mavis Tire, Monro Tire, Mr Tire, Valvoline, Verizon, Weis Foods, W KwikFill, SNK/dsl, Tesla EVC, China Star, El Pulpo, Nirchi's Pizza, Pinkie's BBQ, Sonic, Spot Diner, Starbucks, Comfort Inn, Motel 6, Quality Inn, ALDI, Harley Davidson

15mm I-88 begins eb

5(14) US 11, Front St, W Mirabito/dsl, Speedway/McDonald's/dsl, Tesla EVC, Applebee's, Cracker Barrel, PK Thai, Starbucks, EconoLodge, Fairfield Inn, Red Roof Inn, Cutler Botanical Garden

BINGHAMTON

4(13) NY 17, Binghamton

3(12) Broad Ave, Binghamton, W Mirabito, KFC, CVS Drug, Weis Mkt

3(10) Industrial Park, same as 2

2(8) US 11, NY 17, W Love's/Wendy's/EVC/dsl/scales/24hr, Mirabito/Dunkin'/dsl, TA/Country Pride/dsl/scales/24hr/@, Burger King, Christy's Diner, McDonald's, Michaelangelo's Pizza, Subway, Taco Bell, Del Motel, Clements Tire & Auto

1(4) US 11, NY 7, Kirkwood, W Citgo/dsl

2mm Welcome ctr nb, **full facilities, litter barrels, petwalk**, , , **vending**, Welcome ctr nb

1mm truck insp sta nb

0mm New York/Pennsylvania state line

INTERSTATE 84

71.5mm New York/Connecticut state line

69 US 6, US 202, NY 121(from wb), N Salem, same as 20

68N NY 22, Palling, N Mobil, Shell/dsl, Valero, Carvel Creamery, Dunkin', Pizza & Pasta 22, Ford, Honda

68S I-684, to NYC

65 NY 312, Carmel, S Applebee's, Dunkin', Eveready Diner, Gaetano's Deli, Tilly's Table, DeCicco's Mkt, Home Depot, Kohl's, Marshall's, Michael's, URGENT CARE, Verizon, vet

CARMEL

61 NY 311, Lake Carmel, S La Famiglia, Lake Carmel Gen. Store

58 Ludingtonville Rd, N Metric Motors Shop, S Mobil/dsl, Sunoco/7-11/dsl, 3 Bros Pizza, Cutillo's Rest., Dunkin', Gappy's Pizza, Lou's Rest.

56mm elevation 965 ft

55mm **full facilities, litter barrels, petwalk**, , , both lanes, **vending**

52 Taconic Parkway, N to Albany, S to New York

50 CR 27, Lime Kiln NY, N Shell, Dunkin', Plated American Bistro, Arbor Ridge Inn

46 US 9, to Poughkeepsie, N Mobil, Sunoco/Dunkin'/dsl, 18 N Grill, A&W/KFC, Chipotle, Coldstone, Cracker Barrel, Domino's, Dunkin', Five Guys, Hudson Buffet, Izla of Fishkill, Jersey Mike's, Panera Bread, Red Line Diner, Starbucks, Subway, Taco Bell, Wendy's, Best Western, Courtyard, Extended Stay America, Extended Stay America, Hampton Inn, Hilton Garden, Holiday Inn Express, Hyatt House,

NY

INTERSTATE 84 Cont'd

FISHKILL

46 Continued
Springhill Suites, Wingate, AT&T, Sam's Club, URGENT CARE, Verizon, Walmart, S Speedway/dsl, Maya Cafe, McDonald's, Home Depot

44 NY 52 E, Fishkill, N Valero/dsl, Golden Buddha, Sal's Pizza, CVS Drug, USPO, S Mobil, Sunoco/dsl, 84 Diner, Hometown Deli, Comfort Suites, Quality Inn

41 NY 9D, to Wappingers Falls, N Gulf/dsl, Mobil/dsl

41mm toll booth

40mm Hudson River

NEWBURGH

39 US 9W, NY 32, to Newburgh, N BP, Sunoco, Alexis Diner, Burger King, Domino's, Dunkin', Green Garden Chinese, KFC, McDonald's, Papa John's, Pizza Hut, Planet Pizza, $Tree, Advance Parts, Family$, Firestone/auto, Monro, PriceChopper Foods, URGENT CARE, Verizon, Walgreens, S Citgo/dsl, Mobil, Sunoco, Dunkin', H

37 NY 52, to Walden, N Mobil/dsl

36b NY 300, Newburgh, N Mobil, Buffalo Wild Wings, DQ, Dunkin', Flaming Grill Buffet, Leo's Pizzaria, McDonald's, Perkins, Taco Bell, Wendy's, $Tree, AT&T, AutoZone, CVS Drug, Marshall's, Mavis Tire, Midas, Stop&Shop Foods, Valvoline, S BJ's, Exxon/dsl, Gulf/dsl, Mobil, Sunoco/7-11/dsl, Tesla EVC, Applebee's, Burger King, Chili's, China City, Cosimo's Pizza, Denny's, Five Guys, IHOP, Ikaros Diner, Jersey Mike's, Longhorn Steaks, Orange Hill Bistro, Panera Bread, Pizza Mia, Smoothie King, Sonic, Starbucks, Subway, TGIFriday's, Wingstop, Yobo Asian, Hampton Inn, Howard Johnson, Hudson Valley Hotel, Ramada Inn, Red Roof Inn, Super 8, $General, Adam's Farm Mkt, ALDI, AT&T, Barnes&Noble, Buick/GMC, Cadillac/Chevrolet, Chrysler/Dodge/Jeep, Ford/Lincoln, Home Depot, Honda, Kia, Kohl's, Lowe's, Michael's, Nissan, PetSmart, Target, Verizon, Walmart

36a I-87, NY Thruway, Albany, to NYC

34 NY 17K, to Newburgh, N Mobil/dsl, Pilot/Arby's/dsl/scales/24hr, Diner, The Crossroads Hotel, Petebilt, S Shell/dsl, Courtyard, Toyota

MAYBROOK

32 NY 747, International Blvd, S to Stewart

28 NY 208, Maybrook, N Mobil/dsl, Sunoco/dsl, Blazing Bagels, Burger King, Cascarino's Pizza, Dunkin', McDonald's, Taco Bell, Holiday Inn Express, fireworks, NAPA, Rite Aid, ShopRite Foods, Verizon, Walgreens, Winding Hills Camping, S Speedway/dsl, TA/Shell/Country Pride/Pizza Hut/dsl/scales/24hr/@, Super 8, Advance Parts, Blue Beacon, Freightliner, Penske, st police

24mm rest area wb, **full facilities, litter barrels, petwalk**, , **vending**

19 NY 17, Middletown, N Mobil/24hr, Tesla EVC, Americana Diner, Applebee's, Buffalo Wild Wings, Burger King, Chipotle, Colandrea Pizza, Cosimo's Pizza, Denny's, Dunkin', Five Guys, Fuji Japanese, Hook & Reel Seafood, Jersey Mike's, KFC, McDonald's, Olive Garden, Panera Bread, Pizza Hut, Pizza Star, Popeyes, Red Lobster, Ruby Tuesday, Smoothie King, Sonic, Starbucks, Starbucks, Taco Bell, TX Roadhouse, Wendy's, Wingstop, Youyou Asian, Home2 Suites, La Quinta, Middletown Motel, Residence Inn, Super 8, Tru, $General, $Tree, ALDI, AT&T, AutoZone, Best Buy, Big Lots, CVS Drug, Dick's, Firestone/auto, Hannaford Foods, Hobby Lobby, Home Depot, Honda, JC Penney, Kohl's, Lowe's, Macy's, Marshall's, Mavis Tire/auto, Michael's, Midas, Old Navy, PetCo, PetSmart, PriceChopper Foods, Red Berry Farm, Ross, Sam's Club/dsl, ShopRite/gas, Staples, Target, Tire Discount, TJ Maxx, U-Haul, URGENT CARE, Valvoline, vet, Walmart/Subway, S Sunoco/Dunkin', Chili's, D lux Diner, Outback Steaks, TGIFriday,

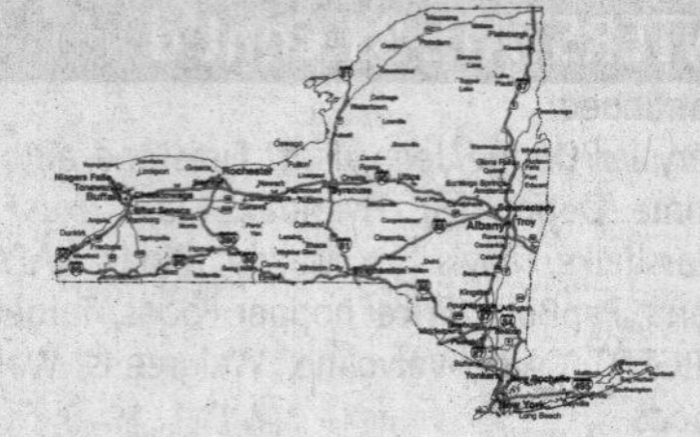

MIDDLETOWN

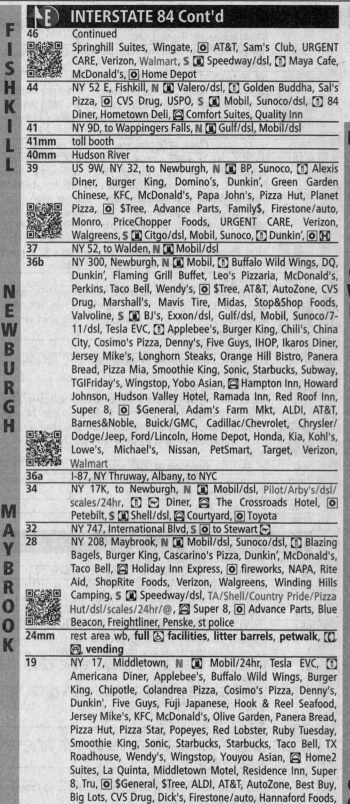

19 Continued
Viva Bandido Mexican, Courtyard, Hampton Inn, Holida Inn, Microtel, H, st police, URGENT CARE

17mm **full facilities, litter barrels, petwalk**, , , eb **vending**

15 US 6, to Middletown, Dunkin', N Citgo/dsl, Gulf, Mobi QuickChek/dsl, Sunoco, Bro Bruno's Pizza, Burger King Crown Fried Chicken, Dominos, DQ, IHOP, McDonald's Peking Chinese, Rita's Custard, Subway, Taco Bell, Wendy's Sleep Inn, $General, $Tree, Acura, AutoZone, Buick Chevrolet, Lexus, Mavis Discount Tire, Mazda, Mitsubishi Monro Automotive, NAPA, ShopRite Foods, Verizon, VW Walgreens, S Geo/dsl, Sunoco/dsl, Days Inn, Kia Nissan, Toyota, USPO

4 Mountain Rd, S Firehouse Deli

4mm elevation 1254 ft wb, 1272 ft eb

3mm parking area both lanes

1 US 6, NY 23, Port Jervis, N Mobil, Arlene'n Tom's Dine Dunkin', Alpin Haus RV Ctr, Ford, H, S BP/dsl/LF Citgo/dsl, Pilot/Subway/dsl, Shell/dsl, Valero/dsl, DQ McDonald's, Village Pizza, $Tree, GNC, ShopRite Foods, T Maxx

0mm New York/Pennsylvania state line, Delaware River

INTERSTATE 86 NY

386.5mm I-86 begins/ends on I-87, exit 16, toll booth

131(379) NY 17, N Cosimo's Pizza, Food Court, Jersey Mike's McDonald's, Shake Shack, Starbucks, Best Value Inn, Outlets/famous brands, S EVC, Gulf/dsl, Chili's Chipotle, Dunkin', El Castillo Mexican, IHOP, KFC/Taco Bel Outback Steaks, Panera Bread, Popeye's, Wendy's, Hampton Inn, $Tree, ALDI, BJ's Whse, BMW, Home Depot Kohl's, Mercedes, Michael's, Old Navy, PetSmart, Target TJMaxx, Verizon, Walmart/Subway

130a(378) US 6, Bear Mtn, to West Point(from eb, no return)

130(377) NY 208, Monroe, Washingtonville, N Wally's Creamery, Sleep Inn, S Exxon, Mobil/dsl, Bagel Boys, Burger King Domino's, Dunkin', Empire Diner, Tulcingo Mexican, Waybac Burger, $Tree, ShopRite Foods, USPO, Verizon

129(375) Museum Village Rd

128(374) rd 51(only from wb), Oxford Depot

127(373) Greycourt Rd(from wb only), Sugar Loaf, Warwick

126(372) NY 94(no EZ wb return), Chester, Florida, N Mobil, Shell Sunoco/dsl, Bagel Girls Cafe, Bro Bruno Pizza, Burge King, Chester Diner, Dunkin', Magoya Japanese, McDonald's Subway, Taco Bell, Wendy's, Holiday Inn Express, CV Drug, GNC, Goodyear/auto, Monro Tire & Auto, ShopRite Foods, USPO, Verizon, S Lowe's

GOSHEN

125(369) NY 17M E, South St

124(368) NY 17A, NY 207, N Gulf/Dunkin'/dsl, QuickChek/dsl, AutoZone, Burger King, Goshen Diner, Super Nacho Mexican What's The Scoop Creamery, CVS Drug, Verizon, S Fairfield Inn, Chrysler/Dodge/Jeep, Hyundai, URGEN CARE

123 US 6, NY 17M(wb only), Port Jervis

122a(367) Fletcher St, Goshen

122(364) rd 67, E Main St, Crystal Run Rd, N Chili's, D Lux Dine Outback Steaks, TGIFriday's, Courtyard, Hampton Inn,

INTERSTATE 86 NY Cont'd

BLOOMINGBURG

122(364) Continued Holiday Inn, Microtel, URGENT CARE, S El Bandido Rest., H

121(363) I-84, E to Newburgh, W to Port Jervis

120(363) NY 211, N Mobil, Tesla EVC, Buffalo Wild Wings, Cosimo's Ristorante, Fuji Japanese, Olive Garden, Home2 Suites, La Quinta, Middletown Motel, Residence Inn, Super 8, Best Buy, Dick's, Hannaford's Foods, Honda, JC Penney, Lowe's, Macy's, Mavis Discount Tire, PetCo, Sam's Club/dsl, Target, vet, S Americana Diner, Applebee's, Burger King, Chipotle, Colandrea Pizza, Denny's, Dunkin', El Tapatio, Five Guys, Franco Di Roma Italian, Frank's Pizza, Hook & Reel Seafood, Indira's Carribean, KFC, McDonald's, Panera Bread, Pizza E Birra, Pizza Hut, Pizza Star, Planet Wings, Popeyes, Red Lobster, Ruby Tuesday, Smoothie King, Sonic, Starbucks, Taco Bell, TX Roadhouse, Wendy's, Wingstop, You You Chinese, Holiday Inn Express, Tru Hotel, $General, $Tree, ALDI, AT&T, AutoZone, BigLots, CVS Drug, Firestone/auto, GNC, Hobby Lobby, Home Depot, Jo-Ann, Kohl's, Marshall's, Michael's, Midas, Old Navy, PetSmart, PriceChopper, ShopRite/gas, Staples, Tire Discount Ctr, TJMaxx, U-Haul, Verizon, Walmart/Subway

119(360) NY 302, Circleville, to Pine Bush, Pine Bush, N golf, S Exxon/Dunkin'/dsl, Sunoco/dsl, Subway, Ace Hardware

118a(358) NY 17M, Fair Oaks

118(358) Fair Oaks, Circleville, S Exxon/dsl, Mobil/dsl

116(355) NY 17K, Bloomingburg, N Mtn View Rest., S Citgo/dsl, Quickway Diner

115 Burlingame Rd

114 Wurtsboro

113(350) US 209, Wurtsboro, Ellenville, N Mobil/dsl, Stewarts/gas, Danny's Steaks, Days Inn, G-Mart Foods, S Giovanni's Café

112(347) Masten Lake, Yankee Lake, S Yankee Lake

111(344) (eb only), Wolf Lake, S Sunoco/dsl

110(343) Lake Louise Marie

109(342) Rock Hill, Woodridge, N Citgo/dsl, EVC, Dunkin', Dutch's Cafe, Pizza Rock, Rock Bistro, Hamaspik Resort, $General, Hilltop Farms Camping(6mi), Rock Hill Trading Post, USPO, vet, S Mobil/dsl, Windsong B&B

108(341) Bridgeville, same as 109

107(340) Thompsonville, S Chevrolet, Chrysler/Dodge/Jeep

106(339) East Broadway, E. Broadway, N Ford/Lincoln, S Exxon/dsl, GMC Trucks

105(337) NY 42, Monticello, N Mobil/dsl, Phillips 66, Burger King, China City, Dunkin', Giovanni's Rest, KFC, McDonald's, Popeyes, Subway, Hampton Inn, AutoZone, Home Depot, ShopRite Foods, Walmart, S Citgo/dsl, Sunoco/dsl, La Fondita Mexican, Monticello Diner, Taco Bell, Wendy's, Yanni's Gyros, Montecello Inn, Super 8, Upstate Inn, Advance Parts, Family$, J&J Grocery, NAPA, Walgreens

HARRIS

104(336) NY 17B, Raceway, Monticello, S Citgo/dsl, Mobil/Subway/dsl, Albella Rest., Colosseo Rest., Dunkin', Tilly's Diner, Best Western, LUX Hotel, AT&T, Swinging Bridge RA

103 Rapp Rd (wb only)

102(332) Harris, N H, S USPO

101(327) Ferndale, Swan Lake, S Exxon/dsl

100(327) NY 52 E, Liberty, N Citgo/dsl, EVC, Sam's, Sunoco, Burger King, Casi's Diner, Chick E BBQ, Dunkin', Liberty Diner, McDonald's, Pancho's Pizza, Pizza Hut, Stella Pizza, Subway, Yiasou Greek, Days Inn, Knights Inn, $General, $Tree, Ace Hardware, Advance Parts, AutoZone, ShopRite Foods, USPO, Verizon, S El Chinchorro, Lincoln Motel,

LIBERTY

100(327) Continued K&K Pharmacy, NAPA

100a NY 52 W(no wb return), Liberty, S st police

99(325) NY 52 W, to NY 55, Liberty, S Sunoco, Catskill Motel

98(321) Cooley, Parksville, N Sunoco/dsl, USPO

97(319) Morsston

96(316) Livingston Manor, S Citgo, Sunoco, Robin Hood Diner, Smoke Joint BBQ, The Kaatskeller Pizza, Covered Bridge, Covered Bridge Camping, Mongaup Pond Camping, Peck's Mkt, USPO

313mm **full facilities, litter barrels, petwalk, eb, vending**

94(311) NY 206, Roscoe, Lew Beach, N Mobil/dsl, Sunoco/dsl, Tesla EVC, Raimondo's Diner, Roscoe Diner, Reynolds House Motel, Rockland House Motel, Roscoe Motel, Trout Town B&B, Beaverkill St Camping, Roscoe Mkt, st police, USPO, S Exxon/dsl

93(305) to Cooks Falls(from wb)

92(303) Horton, Cooks Falls, Colchester, S Sunoco/dsl, Riverside Café/lodge, Russell Brook Camping

90(297) NY 30, East Branch, Downsville, N Sunoco, Beaver-Del Camping, Oxbow Camping, Peaceful Valley Camping

295mm **full facilities, litter barrels, petwalk, wb, vending**

89(293) Fishs Eddy

87a(288) NY 268(from wb, no ez-return), same as 87

87(284) NY 97, to NY 268, to NY 191, Hancock, Cadosia, S Mirabito/Subway/dsl, Sunoco, Valero, Little Italy, McDonald's, New China, Hancock House Hotel, Upper Delaware Inn, Auto+ Parts, NAPA, Tops Foods

276mm parking area wb

DAMASCUS

84(274) Deposit, N Mirabito/dsl, BC Pizza, Honey's Cafe, Wendy's, Deposit Motel, Family$, st police

83(272) Deposit, Oquaga Lake

82(270) NY 41, McClure, Sanford, N Cozy Brook Cafe, Kellystone Park, Oquaga Creek SP, S Chestnut Inn

265mm parking area eb/ /litter barrels

81(263) E Bosket Rd

80(261) Damascus, N Mirabito/dsl, auto repair, Forest Hill Lake Park Camping(3mi)

79(259) NY 79, Windsor, N Big M Mkt, Mirabito/dsl, China Star, Pizza Wings, Subway, USPO, S Halal Pizza & Gyro, Windsor Diner, $General, Lakeside Camping(8mi)

78(256) Dunbar Rd, Occanum

77(254) W Windsor, N Speedway/dsl, McDonald's, $General, S Schoolhouse Creamery

76(251) Haskins Rd, to Foley Rd

75(250) I-81 S, to PA(exits left from wb)

JOHNSON CITY

3 Colesville Rd(from eb). I-86/I-81 run together 4 miles, S Love's/Wendy's/dsl/scales/24hr, Mirabito/Dunkin'/dsl, Subway, TA/Country Pride/dsl/scales/24hr

3 Broad Ave(from wb, no return)

4s NY 7, I-86/I-81 run together 4 miles

72(244) I-81 N, US 11, Front St, Clinton St, (no wb re-entry)

71(242) Airport Rd, Johnson City, S Mirabito, Microtel, Walmart

70(241) NY 201, Johnson City, N Mirabito, Speedway/dsl, ALDI, Carvel Creamery, Chipotle, Cinnabon, Dave&Busters, Dunkin', Food&Fire BBQ, McDonald's, Oakdale Pizza, Panera Bread, Papa John's, Pizza Hut, Taco Bell, Comfort Inn, Hampton Inn, La Quinta, Red Roof Inn, $Tree, JC Penney, Mavis Tire, Mr Tire, PetCo, Wegman's Foods, S Speedway, Applebees, Bao Bao Hibachi, Blaze Pizza, Chipotle, ChuckECheese, Denny's, Dunkin', Five Guys, Greek House Rest., IHOP, Jimmy John's, Man Nam Korean, Moe's SW Grill, Nirichi's Pizza, Panera Bread, Red Chili Rest., Spiedie Ribs, Subway, Tapatios, TX Roadhouse, Wendy's,

NY

INTERSTATE 86 NY Cont'd

70(241) Continued
Candlewood Suites, Courtyard, Holiday Inn Express, Homewood Suites, Quality Inn, Residence Inn, Tru Hotel, Home Depot, Honda, H, Monro Tire & Auto

69(239) NY 17C

238mm Susquehanna River

68(237) NY 17C, Old Vestal Rd, from eb, no re-entry

67(236) NY 26, NY 434, Vestal, Endicott, S Gulf, Mirabito/dsl, Arby's, Burger King, CA Grill, Chili's, Dunkin', Kampai Japanese, McDonald's, Olive Garden, Olive Garden, Outback Steaks, Pudgie's Pizza, Red Lobster, Red Robin, Sliderz Bar & Grill, Subway, Taco Bell, Take-A-Break, TGIFriday's, Parkway Motel, University Inn, $Tree, ALDI, AT&T, Barnes&Noble, Best Buy, Big E Tire/auto, BigLots, Chrysler/Dodge/Jeep, CVS Drug, Dick's, Firestone, Ford/Lincoln, Kohl's, Lowe's, Mavis Tire, Michael's, Mr Tire, Nissan, Old Navy, PetSmart, Price Rite Foods, Sam's Club, Target, TJ Maxx, USPO, Valvoline, Verizon, vet, Volvo, VW, Walmart/Dunkin', Wies Foods

66(231) NY 434, Apalachin, S KwikFill, Big Dipper Drive-In, Blue Dolphin Diner, Chat-A-Wyle Rest., Donoli's Italian, Dunkin', McDonald's, Subway, Comfort Inn, Dollar General

65(225) NY 17C, NY 434, Owego, N Speedway, A&W/KFC, Arby's, McDonald's, Panda Wok, River Rock Diner, Subway, Wendy's, Best Western, Hampton Inn, Quality Inn, $General, Buick/GMC, Grand Union Mkt, Hickories Park Camping, Mr Tire, Verizon, S st police

64(223) NY 96, Owego, N Dunkin', AutoZone, CVS Drug, USPO

222mm **full facilities, litter barrels, petwalk,** wb, **vending**

63(218) Lounsberry, S Sunoco/Burger King/dsl/24hr

62(214) NY 282, Nichols, S Citgo/pizza/dsl, Tioga Downs Race Track, Wilkin's RV Ctr

212mm **full facilities, litter barrels, petwalk,** eb, **vending**

208mm Susquehanna River

61(206) NY 34, PA 199, Waverly, Sayre, N $General, Goodyear/gas, S Dandy, Alliger's Chicken, Best Western/rest., Chrysler/Dodge/Jeep, Meyer's RV Ctr, Nissan

60(204) US 220, to Sayre, Waverly, N Becky's Diner, Coaches Pizza, Vinny's Pizza, golf, S Citgo/dsl, Mirabito/Dunkin'/dsl, Tesla EVC, Wendy's, Candlewood Suites, Comfort Inn, Hampton Inn, Microtel, Advance Parts, ALDI, Lowe's, Mavis, Tire Choice, Top's Foods, Toyota, Walmart

59a(202) Wilawana, S Sunoco/Subway/dsl

59(200) NY 427, Chemung, N Dandy/dsl, USPO

58a(197) to CR 60, Lowman

57(195) rd 2, Lowman, Wellsburg, N Gardner Hill Campground, USPO

56(190) Jerusalem Hill, N Hilltop Rest., S Citgo/dsl, Sunoco/Dandy Pizza/Subway/dsl, Dunkin', McDonald's, Clarion Inn, Mark Twain Motel(3mi), H, Save-A-lot Foods

54(186) NY 13, to Ithaca

53(185) Horseheads, S Speedway/dsl, Burger King, Domino's, Dunkin', Guiseppe's Pizza, KFC, Lin Buffet, McDonald's, Postal Pizza, Rico's Pizza, Subway, Wendy's, Best Value Inn, Budget Inn, Advance Parts, Family$

52b(184) NY 14, to Watkins Glen, N Best Western, Quality Inn, Travel Inn, S Arby's, Dunkin', Rita's Custard, Young's Tire

52a(183) Commerce Ctr, S Buffalo Wild Wings, Cracker Barrel, Jersey Mike's, Red Robin, Starbucks, TX Roadhouse, Fairfield Inn, ALDI, AT&T, Dick's, Jo-Ann Fabrics, Kohl's, Mavis, PetSmart, Toyota, Walmart

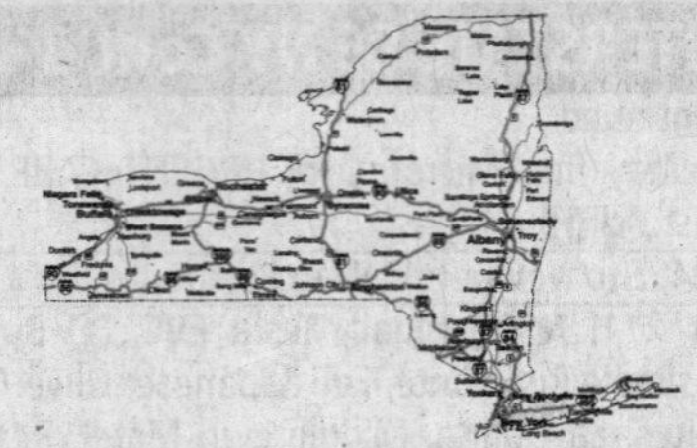

51a(182) Chambers Rd, N Speedway/dsl, Chili's, Dunkin', McDonald's, Mooney's Rest., Olive Garden, Outback Steaks, Red Lobster, Ruby Tuesday, Candlewood Suites, Country Inn&Suites, Courtyard, Hampton Inn, JC Penney, Nissan, S Applebee's, Charley's Subs, DQ, Five Guys, Kyoto Japanese, Moe's SW, Panera Bread, Popeyes, Taco Bell, Wendy's, EconoLodge, Relax Inn, Barnes&Noble, Best Buy, Buick/GMC/Cadillac, Field&Stream, Hobby Lobby, Honda, Hyundai, Kia, Lowe's, Michael's, Mr Tire, Old Navy, PetCo, Sam's Club, Staples, Subaru, Target, TJ Maxx, Top's Foods, URGENT CARE, Verizon

50(180) Kahler Rd, N

49(178) Olcott Rd, Canal St, Big Flats, N antiques, S Sunoco, Picnic Pizza, USPO

48(171) NY 352, E Corning, N Citgo, Budget Inn, Gate House Motel, H

47(174) NY 352, Gibson, E Corning, N Budget Inn, Gatehouse Motel, golf

46(171) NY 414, to Watkins Glen, Corning, N Ferenbaugh Camping, KOA, S Sunoco, Hilton Garden, Quality Inn, Radisson, Staybridge Suites, Corning Glass Museum

45(170) NY 352, Corning, S Fastrac, Bob Evans, En En Chinese, Original Italian Pizza, Subway, Wendy's, Fairfield Inn, $General, Advance Parts, AutoZone, Monro Tire & Auto, Tops/gas, Walgreens

44a I-99 S, US 15 S, NY 417 W, Gang Mills, N Mobil, KFC, McDonald's, S Sunoco, Applebee's, Arby's, Taco Bell, Best Value Inn, Corning Inn, EconoLodge, Hampton Inn, Red Roof Inn, $Tree, ALDI, Chevrolet, Home Depot, Verizon, Walmart

43(167) NY 415, Painted Post, N Sunoco, Burger King, $General, Big Lots, Firestone/auto, S 7-11, Dunkin', Holiday Inn Express

167mm litter barrels, parking area wb/litter barrels

42(165) Coopers Plains

41(161) rd 333, Campbell, N Sunoco/Subway/dsl, Champs Pizza, Camp Bell Camping, S Sunoco, $General, Cardinal Campground

160mm **full facilities, litter barrels, petwalk,** eb, **vending**

40(156) NY 226, Savona, N Mobil/dsl, $General, King's Mkt

39(153) NY 415, Bath, S Jellystone Camping

38(150) NY 54, to Hammondsport, Bath, N Exxon/dsl, KwikFill, Mobil, Angry Oven Pizza, Arby's, Burger King, Chat-A-Whyle Rest., Dunkin', KFC, Ling Ling Chinese, McDonald's, Rico's Pizza, Stephanie's Family Rest., Subway, Taco Bell, Budget Inn, Days Inn, Microtel, Old National Hotel, Super 8, $General, Advance Parts, AT&T, Campers Haven Camping, Family$, Keuka Lake, KOA, Meyer's RV Ctr, Monro, museum, SaveALot, st police, Top's Foods/gas, Verizon, Walgreens

147mm rest area wb, **full facilities, litter barrels, petwalk,** **vending**

37(146) NY 53, to Prattsburg, Kanona, S Love's/Wendy's/dsl/scales/24hr/@, Pilot/Subway/dsl/scales/24hr/@, Twin Kiss Creamery, USPO, Wilkin's RV Ctr

36(145) I-390 N, NY 15, to Rochester

35(138) Howard, S Lake Demmon Campground, Lake Demmon RA

34(130) NY 36, Hornell, Arkport, S KwikFill, Marathon/dsl,

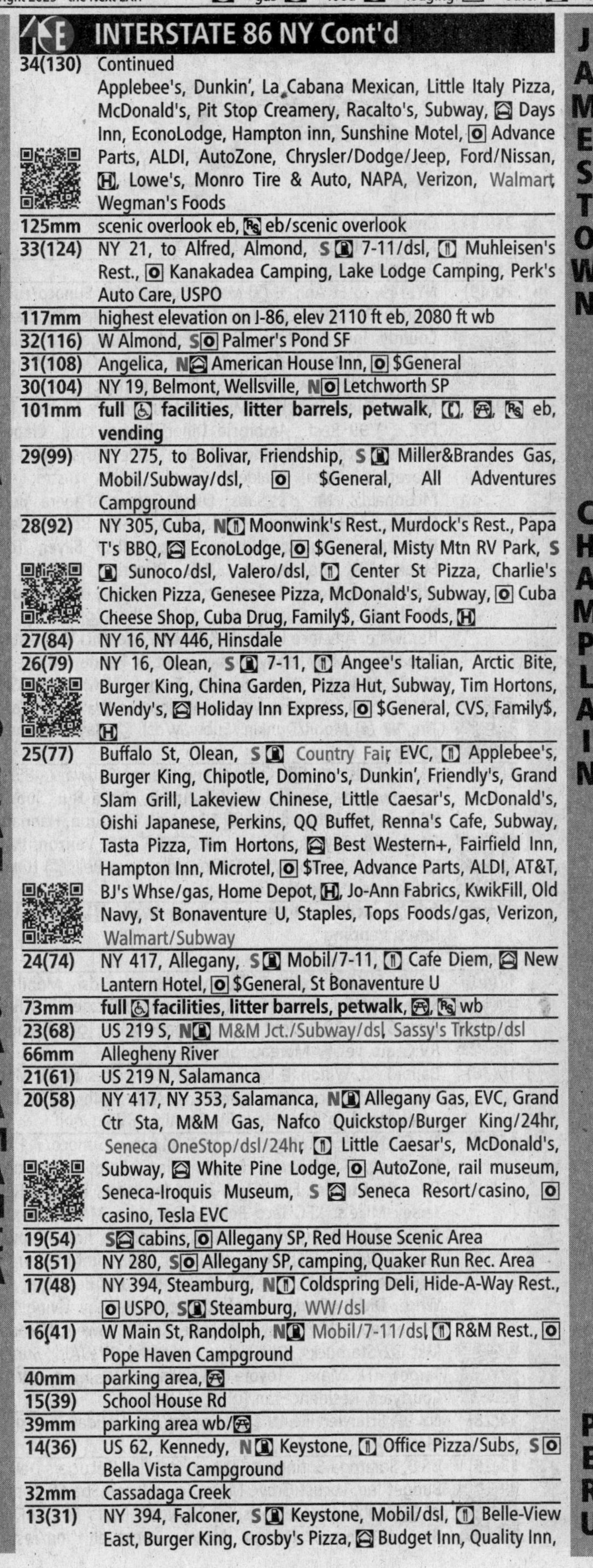

INTERSTATE 86 NY Cont'd

34(130) Continued
Applebee's, Dunkin', La Cabana Mexican, Little Italy Pizza, McDonald's, Pit Stop Creamery, Racalto's, Subway, Days Inn, EconoLodge, Hampton inn, Sunshine Motel, Advance Parts, ALDI, AutoZone, Chrysler/Dodge/Jeep, Ford/Nissan, H, Lowe's, Monro Tire & Auto, NAPA, Verizon, Walmart, Wegman's Foods

125mm scenic overlook eb, eb/scenic overlook

ANGELICA

33(124) NY 21, to Alfred, Almond, S 7-11/dsl, Muhleisen's Rest., Kanakadea Camping, Lake Lodge Camping, Perk's Auto Care, USPO

117mm highest elevation on I-86, elev 2110 ft eb, 2080 ft wb

32(116) W Almond, S Palmer's Pond SF

31(108) Angelica, N American House Inn, $General

30(104) NY 19, Belmont, Wellsville, N Letchworth SP

101mm **full facilities, litter barrels, petwalk**, , , eb, **vending**

29(99) NY 275, to Bolivar, Friendship, S Miller&Brandes Gas, Mobil/Subway/dsl, $General, All Adventures Campground

28(92) NY 305, Cuba, N Moonwink's Rest., Murdock's Rest., Papa T's BBQ, EconoLodge, $General, Misty Mtn RV Park, S Sunoco/dsl, Valero/dsl, Center St Pizza, Charlie's Chicken Pizza, Genesee Pizza, McDonald's, Subway, Cuba Cheese Shop, Cuba Drug, Family$, Giant Foods, H

27(84) NY 16, NY 446, Hinsdale

OLEAN

26(79) NY 16, Olean, S 7-11, Angee's Italian, Arctic Bite, Burger King, China Garden, Pizza Hut, Subway, Tim Hortons, Wendy's, Holiday Inn Express, $General, CVS, Family$, H

25(77) Buffalo St, Olean, S Country Fair, EVC, Applebee's, Burger King, Chipotle, Domino's, Dunkin', Friendly's, Grand Slam Grill, Lakeview Chinese, Little Caesar's, McDonald's, Oishi Japanese, Perkins, QQ Buffet, Renna's Cafe, Subway, Tasta Pizza, Tim Hortons, Best Western+, Fairfield Inn, Hampton Inn, Microtel, $Tree, Advance Parts, ALDI, AT&T, BJ's Whse/gas, Home Depot, H, Jo-Ann Fabrics, KwikFill, Old Navy, St Bonaventure U, Staples, Tops Foods/gas, Verizon, Walmart/Subway

24(74) NY 417, Allegany, S Mobil/7-11, Cafe Diem, New Lantern Hotel, $General, St Bonaventure U

SALAMANCA

73mm **full facilities, litter barrels, petwalk**, , wb

23(68) US 219 S, N M&M Jct./Subway/dsl, Sassy's Trkstp/dsl

66mm Allegheny River

21(61) US 219 N, Salamanca

20(58) NY 417, NY 353, Salamanca, N Allegany Gas, EVC, Grand Ctr Sta, M&M Gas, Nafco Quickstop/Burger King/24hr, Seneca OneStop/dsl/24hr, Little Caesar's, McDonald's, Subway, White Pine Lodge, AutoZone, rail museum, Seneca-Iroquis Museum, S Seneca Resort/casino, casino, Tesla EVC

19(54) S cabins, Allegany SP, Red House Scenic Area

18(51) NY 280, S Allegany SP, camping, Quaker Run Rec. Area

17(48) NY 394, Steamburg, N Coldspring Deli, Hide-A-Way Rest., USPO, S Steamburg, WW/dsl

16(41) W Main St, Randolph, N Mobil/7-11/dsl, R&M Rest., Pope Haven Campground

40mm parking area,

15(39) School House Rd

39mm parking area wb/

14(36) US 62, Kennedy, N Keystone, Office Pizza/Subs, S Bella Vista Campground

32mm Cassadaga Creek

13(31) NY 394, Falconer, S Keystone, Mobil/dsl, Belle-View East, Burger King, Crosby's Pizza, Budget Inn, Quality Inn,

JAMESTOWN

13(31) Continued
CVS Drug, Harley-Davidson

12(28) NY 60, Jamestown, N KwikFill/dsl, Moonbrook Golf, st police, S Mobil/McDonald's/dsl, Bob Evans, Tim Hortons, Clarion, Hampton Inn, Holiday Inn Express, H

11(25) to NY 430, Jamestown, S Beef Boss, Hiller Tire

22mm **full facilities, litter barrels, petwalk**, , **vending**, welcome ctr/ eb

10(21) NY 430 W, Bemus Point

9(20) NY 430 E(no EZ eb return), N Mobil/dsl, Bemus Point Rest., Bemus Point Lodge

19mm Chautauqua Lake

8(18) NY 394, Mayville, N Keystone, USPO, vet

7(15) Panama

6(9) NY 76, Sherman, N Keystone Gas, $General, city park, NAPA, Sherman Drug, USPO

4(1) NY 430, Findley Lake, S Alexander's Rest., Peek'n Peak Resort, $General, Peek'n Peak Ski Area, U-Haul

0mm New York/Pennsylvania state line. Exits 3-1 are in PA.

3 PA 89, North East, Wattsburg

1b a I-90, W to Erie, E to Buffalo. I-86 begins/ends on I-90, exit 37. I-390 begins/ends on I-86, exit 36.

INTERSTATE 87

CHAMPLAIN

176mm US/Canada Border, NY state line, I-87 begins/ends

43(175) US 9, Champlain, E Duty Free America, W Peterbilt Trkstp/deli/dsl/scales/24hr/@, repair

42(174) US 11 S, to Rouse's Point, Champlain, E Irving/dsl/scales, Sunoco/Subway, $General, $Tree, Ace Hardware, Chevrolet(3mi), Kinney Drug, PriceChopper, USPO, W Mobil/dsl, Valero/dsl, Dunkin', McDonald's

41(167) NY 191, Chazy, E Whistle Stop BBQ, $General, W Miner Museum

162mm **full facilities, info, litter barrels, petwalk**, , , **both lanes**

40(160) NY 456, Beekmantown, E Mobil/dsl, Pt Auroche Lodge, Stonehelm Motel/café, W Twin Ells Camping

39(158) NY 314, Moffitt Rd, Plattsburgh Bay, E Mobil/dsl, Stewarts, Dunkin', Gus' Rest, Rip van Winkle Motel, Super 8, $General, Plattsburgh RV Park, VT Ferry, W Shady Oaks Camping, to Adirondacks

38(154) NY 22, NY 374, to Plattsburgh, S Sunoco, E Mobil/dsl, Mickey's Rest., NY Pizza, Subway, $Tree, Kinney Drug

37(153) NY 3, Plattsburgh, E Stewarts, #1 Chinese, Buffalo Wild Wings, Burger King, Chick-fil-A, Chipotle, Domino's, Dunkin', Five Guys, Giuseppe's Pizza, Jade Buffet, Jersey Mike's, KFC, Koto Japanese, McDonald's, Michigans+ Rest., Panera Bread, Perkins, Pizza Hut, Starbucks, Subway, Taco Bell, TX Roadhouse, Wendy's, Comfort Inn, Days Inn, ALDI, BigLots, Buick/GMC, Family$, Ford, GNC, H, Kinney Drug, Michael's, O'Reilly Parts, PetSmart, Sam's Club/dsl, Staples, TJ Maxx, TrueValue, Verizon, Walgreens, Walmart, W Mobil/dsl, Shell, Sunoco, Sunoco/Lambo's Subs, Tesla EVC, 99 Rest., Anthony's Rest., Applebee's, Armitto's Pizza, Butcher Block Steaks, Dino's, Dunkin', Fairfield Inn, Little Caesars Pizza, McSweeney Red Hots, PriceChopper Mkt, Subway, Best Value Inn, Best Western+, Hampton Inn, Holiday Inn Express, La Quinta, Microtel, Quality Inn, $Tree, Advance Parts, AT&T, AutoZone, Best Buy, Hannaford Foods, Harley-Davidson, Hobby Lobby, Honda, JC Penney, Kinney Drug, Lowe's, Mitsubishi, Target, Town Fair Tire, vet

PERU

151mm Saranac River

36(150) NY 22, Plattsburgh AFB, E Mobil/dsl, st police, W Shell/Dunkin'/dsl

146mm **litter barrels**, **petwalk**, , nb **full facilities**, truck insp sta both lanes

35(144) NY 442, to Port Kent, Peru, E Iroquois Campground,

NY

INTERSTATE 87 Cont'd

PERU

35(144) Continued
VT Ferry, **W** Mobil/repair, Mobil/Subway/dsl, Dunkin', Livingood's Rest., McDonald's, Pasquale's Rest., Aubuchon Hardware, Tops Foods, USPO

143mm emergency phones at 2 mi intervals begin sb/end nb

34(137) NY 9 N, Ausable Forks, **E** Sunoco/dsl, Giuseppes Pizza, Pleasant Corner Rest., **W** Ausable River RV Camping, auto repair

136mm Ausable River

33(135) US 9, NY 22, to Willsboro, **E** Essex Ferry

125mm N Boquet River

32(124) Lewis, **W** Beavers, st police

120mm Boquet River

31(117) NY 9 N, to Elizabethtown, Westport, Mobil/dsl

SCHROON LAKE

30(104) US 9, NY 73, Keene Valley

99mm **full facilities, litter barrels, petwalk, both lanes, trk insp sta**

29(94) N Hudson, **E** EVC, Sunoco, Frontier Ghost Town/ Camping, Spacious Skies Campground, USPO, **W** Blue Ridge Falls Camping

28(88) NY 74 E, to Ticonderoga, Schroon Lake, **E** Sunoco/dsl, Maple Leaf Motel, Schroon Lake B&B, On The River Camping, st police

83mm parking area nb

27(81) US 9(from nb, no EZ return), Schroon Lake

26(78) US 9(from sb, no EZ return), Pottersville, Schroon Lake, **E** Lee's Corner Motel, Ideal Campground, Schroon Lake RV Park, Wakonda Camping, **W** Sunoco/dsl, Black Bear Diner, USPO

25(73) NY 8, Chestertown, **E** Crossroads Country Store, Country Haven Camping, **W** Stewart's/dsl, $General

24(67) Bolton Landing, **E** parking area, RV camping, **W** Lake George Campground

67mm Schroon River

66mm parking area sb, picnic tables

64mm parking area nb, picnic tables

LAKE GEORGE

23(58) to US 9, Diamond Point, Warrensburg, **W** Citgo/dsl, Cumberland, Mobil/Dunkin'/dsl, Stewarts, Sunoco, Brunetto's Italian, Dragon Lee Chinese, George Henry's Rest., McDonald's, Subway, Tommy Guns Pizza, Super 8, Family$, Ford, Grand Union Mkt, PriceChopper Foods, Riverview Camping, Schroon River Camping, ski area, ski area

22(54) US 9, NY 9 N, to Diamond Pt, Lake George, parking area both lanes, **E** Ali Bab Express, Breakfast Spot, Guiseppe's Pizza, Mario's Italian, Mezzaluna Italian, Moose Tooth Grill, Number 1, Oasis Vietnamese, 7 Dwarfs Motel, Admiral Motel, Balsam Motel, Barberry Ct, Baymont, Best Value Inn, Blue Moon Motel, Brookside Motel, Courtyard, Georgian Lakeside Resort, Heritage Motel, Lake Crest Inn, Lake George Inn, Lake Haven Motel, Lake Motel, Marine Village Resort, Motel Montreal, Nordick's Motel, O'Sullivan's Motel, Oasis Motel, Park Lane Motel, Pinebrook Motel, Sundowner Motel, Surfside Motel, PriceChopper Foods

21(53) NY 9 N, Lake Geo, Ft Wm Henry, **E** Exxon, Stewarts, Sunoco/dsl, A&W, Adirondack Brewery, Barnsider BBQ, Caldwell House Rest., Lobster Pot, Mama Riso's Italian, McDonald's, Prospect Diner, Saluti Italian, Best Western, Comfort Inn, Cozy Nook Cottages, Doray Hotel, Ft William Henry Inn, Hampton Inn, Holiday Inn Resort, Howard Johnson, Lake View Inn, Legacy Inn, Lincoln Log Motel, Lyn Aire Motel, Quality Inn, Super 8, The Harbor Hotel, Tiki Hotel, Travelodge, Windsor Hotel, Wingate Inn, city park, Jo Ti Asian, King Phillip Camping, Lake George Amusement Park, Lake George Camping, Walgreens, **W** Mobil/dsl/LP,

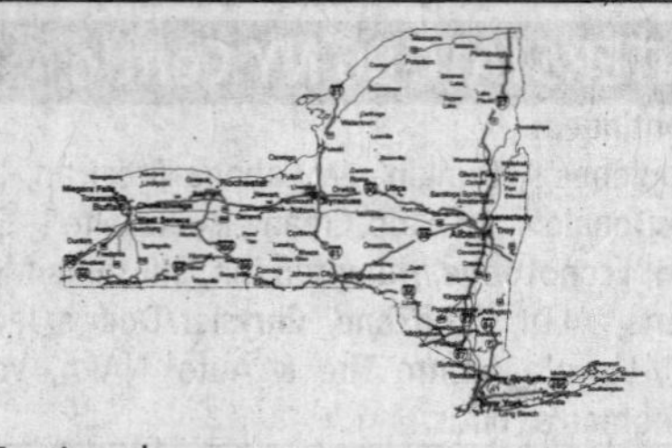

GLENS FALLS

21(53) Continued
Kathy's Cottages

51mm Adirondack Park

20(49) NY 149, to Ft Ann, **E** Mobil/Dunkin'/dsl, Sunoco/dsl, Johnny Rocket's, Log Jam Steaks, Starbucks, Clarion, Country Inn & Suites, Great Escape Lodge, La Quinta, Mohican Motel, Rodeway Inn, Factory Outlets/famous brands, Ledgeview RV Park, Six Flags Funpark

19(47) NY 254, Glens Falls, **E** Mobil/dsl, Speedway, Sunoco, Tesla EVC, 99 Rest., Ambrosia Diner, Burger King, Chipotle, Dave's Chicken, Dominos, Dunkin', Five Guys, Friendly's, Giavano's Pizza, Golden Corral, Jack's Bistro, KFC, McDonald's, Mr B's Subs, Olive Garden, Panera Bread, Queen of Harts Pizza, Red Lobster, Silo Rest., Spargel German, Starbucks, Subway, Taco Bell/LJ Silver, Tokyo Steaks, TX Roadhouse, UNO Pizzeria, Wendy's, Alpenhouse Motel, Budget Inn, EconoLodge, Home2 Suites, Northway Inn, Quality Inn, Sleep Inn, $Tree, Ace Hardware, Advance Parts, AT&T, AutoZone, Dick's, Firestone, Goodyear, Hobby Lobby, Home Depot, JC Penney, Market 32, Mavis, Meineke, Petco, Staples, Target, TJ Maxx, URGENT CARE, USPO, Valvoline, Verizon, Walgreens, Walmart, Warren Tire, **W** Mobil/Dunkin'/Subway/dsl, Baymont Inn, st police

18(45) Glens Falls, **E** Cumberland Farms/Subway/e-85/dsl, Speedway/dsl, Sunoco/dsl, Dunkin', Pizza Hut, Subway, Days Inn, Fairfield Inn, $General, CVS Drug, Hannaford Foods, H, Toyota, U-Haul, URGENT CARE, Verizon, **W** Fastrac/dsl, Stewarts, McDonald's, Taco Bell, Holiday Inn Express, Super 8

43mm **full facilities, litter barrels, petwalk, both lanes, vending**

42mm Hudson River

SARATOGA SPRINGS

17(40) US 9, S Glen Falls, **E** Exxon/Subway/dsl, Mobil/dsl, Speedway/dsl, Stewarts/dsl, Dunkin', Fitzgerald's Rest., Pizza Shack, Budget Inn, Landmark Motel, Adirondack RV Camp, vet, **W** Moreau Lake SP

16(36) Ballard Rd, Wilton, **E** Coldbrook Campsites, **W** Mobil, Stewart's, Sunoco/Scotty's Rest./dsl/scales/24hr, Mt View Acres Motel, Alpin Haus RV Ctr, Alpin RV Ctr, golf

15(30) NY 50, NY 29, Saratoga Springs, **E** Exxon, Sunoco/7-11, 99 Rest., Applebee's, Burger King, Chipotle Mexican, Denny's, Dunkin', Five Guys, Haru Japanese, Hattie's Rest., Jersey Mike's, KFC/Taco Bell, McDonald's, Moe's SW Grill, Osaka, Panera Bread, Red Robin, Smoothie King, Subway, Sunny Wok, TGIFriday's, Wendy's, Comfort Inn, Advance Parts, ALDI, AT&T, Barnes&Noble, Best Buy, BJ's Whse, Dick's, Ford, Hannaford Foods, Healthy Living Mkt, Home Depot, JC Penney, Jiffy Lube, Kohl's, Lowe's, Michaels, Mkt 32/Starbucks, Old Navy, PetSmart, Rite Aid, Subaru, Target, TJ Maxx, Toyota, Walgreens, Walmart, **W** Courtyard, Residence Inn, H, U-Haul

14(28) NY 9P, Schuylerville, **W** Hampton Inn, Holiday Inn, H, racetrack

13(25) US 9, Saratoga Springs, **E** Andy's Grille, DeLucia's Deli, Budget Inn, Locust Grove Motel, Ballston Spa SP, Nissan, **W** Mobil/dsl, Stewarts, 13 North Rest., PJ's BBQ, Best Western+, Design Motel, Roosevelt Inn/rest.,

INTERSTATE 87 Cont'd

MALTA

13(25) Continued
Top Hill Hotel, Saratoga SP

12(21) NY 67, Malta, E Citgo/dsl, Cumberland Farms/dsl, Sunoco/dsl, 5Guys, Bentley's Rest., Dunkin', Jersey Mike's, Jimmy's Pizza, KFC/Taco Bell, McDonald's, Panera Bread, Starbucks, Subway, The Ugly Rooster Cafe, Fairfield Inn, Home2 Suites, CVS Drug, Mkt 32, st police, Stewart's, USPO, Verizon, W Hyatt Place, Chevrolet, URGENT CARE

11(18) Round Lake Rd, Round Lake, W Citgo/dsl, Stewarts/dsl, Dunkin, Hannaford Foods, U-Haul, Walgreens

10(16) Ushers Rd, E Speedway/dsl, Xtra/dsl, auto repair, W Stewarts

14mm **full facilities, info, litter barrels, petwalk, , , nb, vending,** E Dunkin, Primavera Pizza, La Quinta, Chrysler/Dodge/Jeep, USPO

CLIFTON PARK

9(13) NY 146, Clifton Park, E Speedway/dsl, Stewarts, USA, Burger King, Caputo's Pizza, Chili's, Clifton Pizza Shop, Cracker Barrel, Delmonico's Steaks, Peddler's Grill, Pizza Hut, Popeyes, Red Robin, Snyder's Rest., Subway, Wheatfields Bistro, Holiday Inn Express, Residence Inn, Advance Parts, ALDI, AutoZone, BigLots, Goodyear/auto, Home Depot, Jiffy Lube, Kohl's, Lowe's, Michael's, Midas, Petco, Red Roof Inn, Target, Trader Joe's, URGENT CARE, Valvoline, Valvoline, W Mobil, Sunoco/dsl, Blaze Pizza, Buffalo Wild Wings, Chick-fil-A, Chipotle Mexican, Dunkin', East Wok, Five Guys, Friendly's, IHOP, Jersey Mike's, La Fiesta, McDonald's, Menchie's, Moe's SW Grill, Olive Garden, Outback Steaks, Panera Bread, Pasta Pane, Salad Creations, Smoothie King, Starbucks, Subway, Taco Bell, TGIFriday's, Wendy's, Best Western, Courtyard, Hampton Inn, Hilton Garden, Homewood Suites, $Tree, AT&T, Chevrolet, CVS Drug, Firestone/auto, Hannaford Foods, JC Penney, Marshall's, Mkt 32, NAPA, PetSmart, st police, Staples, Verizon, Walgreens

8a(12) Grooms Rd, to Waterford

8(10) Crescent, Vischer Ferry, E Speedway/dsl, Fortune Cookies, Mama's Pizza, McDonald's, USPO, W Stewart's/dsl, Sunoco, bb.q Chicken, Dunkin', Pancho's Mexican, CVS Drug

TROY

8mm Mohawk River

7(7) NY 7, Troy, N Exxon, NY Pizza, Century House, Comfort Inn, Holiday Inn Express, $General, Acura, Chrysler/Dodge/Jeep, Infiniti, Lexus, Nissan, Walgreens, S Sunoco, BurgerFi, Dunkin', McDonald's, New Panda, Red Robin, Subway, AutoZone, Hobby Lobby, Marshall's, E vet

6(6) NY 2, to US 9, same as 7, Schenectady, E Exxon, Mobil, Applebee's, ChuckeCheese, Circle Diner, Domino's, Duck Donuts, Jersey Mike's, Moe's SW Grill, Mr Subb, Panera Bread, Popeyes, Starbucks, Wendy's, Golden Circle Inn, La Quinta, $Tree, Audi, CVS Drug, Dick's, Hannaford Foods, Home Depot, Lowe's, Mavis Discount Tire, PetSmart, Sam's Club, Staples, Toyota, Valvoline, VW, Walmart/Subway, W Mobil/dsl, Stewart's, Chipotle Mexican, Sake Japanese, Sonic, Starbucks, Subway, Microtel, Quality Inn, Super 8, TownePlace Suites, H, Michael's, Target, TJ Maxx, Warren Tire

LATHAM

5(5) NY 155 E, Latham, E DeeDee's Rest., Philly's Grill, Latham Inn, USPO

4(4) NY 155 W, Wolf Rd, E Mobil, Speedway/dsl, Sunoco, 99 Rest., Albany Wasabi, Arby's, Barnsider, Chipotle Mexican, Dunkin', Honeybaked Ham, Jersey Mike's, Jimmy John's, Longhorn Steaks, Maxie's Grill, McDonald's, Olive Garden, Outback Steaks, Pizza Hut, Red Lobster, Ruth's Chris, Samurai, Starbucks, Ted's Fishfry, TX Roadhouse,

4(4) Continued
Courtyard, Fairfield Inn, Hampton Inn, Home2 Suites, Homewood Suites, Marriott, Red Roof Inn, Staybridge Suites, antiques, Chevrolet, CVS Drug, Firestone/auto, Hannaford Foods, Trader Joe's, W Blu Stone Bistro, Koto Japanese, Desmond Hotel, Hotel Indigo, to Heritage Park

2(2) NY 5, Central Ave, E Mobil/Dunkin/dsl, Sunoco, Tesla EVC, BJ's Rest., Buca Italian, Cheesecake Factory, Chili's, Five Guys, Honeybaked Ham, Hooters, IHOP, Mission BBQ, Panera Bread, PF Chang's, Taco Bell, Wendy's, Holiday Inn Express, Scottish Inn, SpringHill Suites, Staybridge Suites, Super 8, Travelodge, Barnes&Noble, BJ's Whse/gas, Goodyear/auto, Hobby Lobby, LL Bean, Lowe's, Macy's, Marshall's, Mr Tire, O'Reilly Parts, Staples, Target, Whole Foods Mkt, W Cumberland Farms/dsl, Mobil, Stewart, USA/dsl, Delmonico's Steaks, DQ, Dunkin', La Fiesta Mexican, McDonald's, Midas, Moe's SW Grill, Mr Subb, Smokey Bones BBQ, Wendy's, Days Inn, EconoLodge, Howard Johnson, Motel 6, Quality Inn, AT&T, AutoZone, Buick/GMC, Cadillac, Jiffy Lube, Kohl's, Krause's Candy, Mazda, PepBoys, Price Chopper Foods, Subaru, Verizon, Walgreens

1W(1) NY State Thruway(from sb), I-87 S to NYC, I-90 W to Buffalo

1E(1) I-90 E(from sb), to Albany, Boston

1S(1) to US 20, Western Ave, E Blaze Pizza, Burger King, Chipotle Mexican, Coldstone, Dave's Chicken, Five Guys, J&A Italian, Jersey Mike's, Starbucks, Days Inn, Hampton Inn, Verizon, CVS Drug, USPO, W Mobil, USA, Dunkin', Hana Grill, McDonald's, Homewood Suites, Tru Hilton, Adirondack Tires, Mkt 32

BOSTON

1N(1) I-87 N(from nb), to Plattsburgh

149 NY State Thruway goes west to Buffalo(I-90), S to NYC(I-87), I-87 N to Montreal

24(148) I-90 and I-87 N

23(142) I-787, to Albany, US 9 W, E Speedway, Sunoco/Dunkin/dsl, Five Guys, Panera Bread, Popeyes, Sonic, Taco Bell, Wendy's, Comfort Inn, Sheraton, Lowe's, PetSmart, transmissions, Verizon, Walmart, W Stewarts, Quality Inn

139mm parking area sb,

22(135) NY 396, to Selkirk

21a(134) I-90 E, to MA Tpk, Boston

CATSKILL

127mm New Baltimore Travel Plaza both lanes, Mobil/dsl, Chick-fil-A, Panera Bread, Shake Shack, Starbucks

21b(124) US 9 W, NY 81, to Coxsackie, W 21B Travel Plaza/rest./dsl/scales/24hr, Sunoco/dsl, Dunkin', McDonald's, Best Western, Holiday Inn Express, Camping World, vet

21(114) NY 23, Catskill, E Stewart's, Sunoco/dsl, Pelokes Motel(2mi), Home Depot, to Rip van Winkle Br, visitors ctr, W Anthony's Banquet Hall, Casa Susanna, Camptown, to Hunter Mtn/Windham Ski Areas

103mm Malden Service Area nb, Exxon, Mobil/McDonald's/dsl

20(102) NY 32, to Saugerties, E Citgo, Mobil/dsl, Stewart's, Bleu Collar Sammies, Buns Burgers, Dunkin', McDonald's, Pizza Star, Starbucks, Subway, Advance Parts, AutoZone, Big Lots, Chrysler/Dodge/Jeep, CVS Drug, Family$, NAPA, PriceChopper Foods, Sawyer Ice Cream, True Value, Verizon, vet, W Speedway/dsl, Sunoco/dsl, Abby's Rest., Comfort Inn, Holiday Inn Express, Howard Johnson/rest., Blue Mtn Campground(5mi), Brookside Campground(10mi), KOA(2mi), Rip Van Winkle Campground(3mi), to Catskills

99mm parking area nb, , , litter barrels

96mm Ulster Travel Plaza sb, , **Sunoco/dsl,** **Burger King, Nathan's, Pizza Hut, Starbucks, TCBY,** **atm, wi-fi**

19(91) NY 28, Rhinecliff Br, Kingston, E QC Express, QuickChek/dsl/EVC, Advance Parts, Moonburger, Picnic Pizza, Savona's Pizza, Stadium Diner, Super Bowl Chinese,

INTERSTATE 87 Cont'd

KINGSTON

Exit	Services
19(91)	Continued Best Western+, Super 8, access to I-587 E, Advance Parts, CVS Drug, Hannaford Foods, Kia, Walgreens, W Sky View Mexican, Kingston Inn, Motel 19, access to US 209, Camping World RV Ctr, Chrysler/Dodge/Jeep/Fiat, Ford, Nissan
18(76)	NY 299, to Poughkeepsie, New Paltz, E Mobil, Shell/dsl, BestInn, Rodeway Inn, Lowe's, to Mid-Hudson Br, W EVC, Sunoco, Burger King, Dunkin', Gadaletos Seafood, McDonald's, Pasquale's Pizza, Plaza Diner, Rino's Pizza, Rococo's Pizza, Ruby Rest., Twistee Cone, Best Value Inn, Hampton Inn, Advance Parts, KOA(10mi), Midas, ShopRite Foods, Tops Mkt, Verizon, Walgreens
66mm	Modena service area sb, W Sunoco/EVC
65mm	Plattekill Travel Plaza nb, E Sunoco, Auntie Anne's, Burger King, Chick-fil-A, Panera Bread, Starbucks
17(60)	I-84, NY 17K, to Newburgh, N Mobil, Buffalo Wild Wings, DQ, Dunkin', Flaming Grill, Joe's Deli, McDonald's, Perkins, Taco Bell, Wendy's, $Tree, AT&T, AutoZone, Marshall's, Mavis Tire, Midas, Stop&Shop, Valvoline, Verizon, S Exxon, Gulf, Mobil, Sunoco/dsl, Tesla EVC, Applebee's, Burger King, Chili's, China City, Cosimos Ristorante, Denny's, Five Guys, IHOP, Ikaros Diner, Jersey Mike's, Longhorn Steaks, Panera Bread, Pizza 300, Pizza Mia, Smoothie King, Starbucks, Subway, TGIFriday's, Wingstop, Yobo Asian, Hampton Inn, Howard Johnson, Hudson Valley Hotel, Ramada Inn, Red Roof Inn, Super 8, $General, Adam's Food Mkt, ALDI, Barnes&Noble, BJ's/gas, Buick/GMC, Cadillac/Chevrolet, Chrysler/Dodge/Jeep, Ford, Home Depot, Honda, Kia, Kohl's, Lowe's, Michael's, Mkt Fresh, Nissan, PetSmart, Target, U-Haul, Verizon, Walmart
16(45)	US 6, NY 17, to West Point, Harriman, W Gulf/dsl, Chili's, Chipotle, Dunkin', IHOP, KFC, Outback Steaks, Panera Bread, Popeyes, Shake Shack, Starbucks, Wendy's, Hampton Inn, $Tree, ALDI, Best Buy, BJ's Whse, BMW, Home Depot, Kohl's, Mercedes, Michaels, Old Navy, PetSmart, st police, Target, TJ Maxx, Verizon, Walmart/Subway, Woodbury Outlet/famous brands
34mm	Ramapo Service Area sb
33mm	Sloatsburg Travel Plaza nb, E Sunoco/dsl, Auntie Anne's, W McDonald's, Starbucks
15a(31)	NY 17 N, NY 59, Sloatsburg
15(30)	I-287 S, NY 17 S, to NJ. I-87 S & I-287 E run together.

CHESTNUT RIDGE

Exit	Services
14b(27)	Airmont Rd, Montebello, E Crowne Plaza, W Gulf/Dunkin'/dsl, AJ's, Bagel Boys Cafe, Burger King, Dunkin, Le Brick, Panera Bread, Starbucks, Sutter's Mill Rest., AutoZone, H, ShopRite Foods, Tallman Tires, Walgreens, Walmart
14a(23)	Garden State Pkwy, to NJ, Chestnut Ridge
14(22)	NY 59, Spring Valley, Nanuet, E 76/dsl, Citgo/dsl, Exxon, Shell/dsl, Burger King, Domino's, IHOP, McDonald's, Popeyes, Quality Inn, Sonesta, BMW, Costco/gas, Lowe's, Maserati/Ferrari, Target, W Gulf, Valero, BJ's Rest., Buffalo Wild Wings, ChuckeCheese, Dunkin, Dunkin, Franco's Pizza, Jersey Mike's, KFC/Taco Bell, Nanuet Diner, Panera Bread, PF Chang's, Playa Bowls, Red Lobster, Shake Shack, Smashburger, White Castle, Days Inn, Hampton Inn, Hilton Garden, $Tree, AT&T, Barnes&Noble, Home Depot, Kohl's, Marshall's, Mavis Tires, Midas, Staples, Stop&Shop, Verizon, VW
13(20)	Palisades Pkwy, N to Bear Mtn, S to NJ, S ALDI, W Mobil, 5Guys, Chili's, Moe's SW Grill, Pizza Hut, Wendy's, DoubleTree, 7-11, AutoZone, Cadillac, Chrysler/Buick/GMC, Ford, Honda, JT's Auto, Kohl's, Mavis Tire, Mercedes, Michaels, vet

W NYACK

Exit	Services
12(19)	NY 303, Palisades Ctr Dr, W Nyack, E Kia, W Mobil, Cheesecake Factory, Chipotle, Dave&Buster's, Dunkin, Popeyes, Wendy's, Tappan Zee Hotel, Barnes&Noble, Best Buy, BJ's Whse, Home Depot, Macy's, Mavis Tire/repair, Old Navy, Staples, Target, Verizon
11(18)	US 9W, to Nyack, E Exxon, Shell/dsl, West Gate Inn, H, Walgreens, W Shell/dsl, Dunkin', McDonald's, Nyack Diner, Supreme Grill, Taco Boys, Fairbridge Inn, Audi, J&L Repair/tire, Mazda, Midas, Old World Food Mkt, Valvoline
10(17)	Nyack(from nb), same as 11
14mm	Hudson River, Tappan Zee Br
13mm	toll plaza, E Stewart's, Nissan, W Mobil, Stewart's, Roosevelt Inn
9(12)	to US 9, to Tarrytown, E Mobil/dsl, Shell, Harvest Field Mkt, URGENT CARE, W BP, EVC, Sleepy Hollow, Honda, Mavis Tire

ARDSLEY

Exit	Services
8(11)	I-287 E, to Saw Mill Pkwy, White Plains, E BP, Dunkin, Days Inn, Extended Stay America, Hampton Inn, Marriott, Motel 6, Sheraton, Shop&Stop
7a(10)	Saw Mill River Pkwy S, to Saw Mill River SP
7(8)	NY 9A(from nb), Taconic SP, Ardsley, W Ardsley Acres Motel
6mm	Ardsley Travel Plaza nb, E Sunoco/dsl, Burger King, Starbucks, Starbucks
5.5mm	toll plaza
6ba (5)	Stew Leonard Dr, to Ridge Hill, W Costco, Home Depot, Stew Leonard's Farmfresh Foods

WESTCHESTER FAIR

Exit	Services
6(4.5)	Tuckahoe Dr, Yonkers, E BP, McDonald's, Subway, Hampton Inn, ShopRite Foods/drug, Staples, W Gulf, Mobil/dsl, Domino's, Dunkin', Kim Wei Chinese, Royal Regency Hotel
5(4.3)	NY 100 N(from nb), Central Park Ave, White Plains
4(4)	Cross Country Pkwy, Mile Sq Rd, E Applebee's, Chipotle, Cinnabon, LongHorn Steaks, Olive Garden, Panda Express, Panera Bread, Red Lobster, Shake Shack, Starbucks, Hyatt Place, Ford/Mazda/Subaru, Macy's, Old Navy, Stop&Shop, Target, TGIFridays, Verizon, W BP, Shell/dsl, Shell/Dunkin'/dsl, Burger King, Mavis Tire
3(3)	Mile Square Rd, E Dunkin, W Citgo, Chevrolet, True Value
2(2)	Yonkers Ave(from nb), Westchester Fair, E Yonkers Speedway
1(1)	Hall Place, McLean Ave
0mm	New York St Thruway and I-87 N run together to Albany
14(11)	McLean Ave, E Acme/dsl
13(10)	E 233rd , NE Tollway, service plaza both lanes, Gulf/Dunkin', W Mobil
12(9.5)	Hudson Pkwy(from nb), Sawmill Pkwy
11(9)	Van Cortlandt Pk S, W Mobil, Domino's, McDonald's, Wendy's, Chrysler/Jeep/Dodge, Rite Aid
10(8.5)	W 230th St(from sb), W 240th(from nb), E Citgo, W Applebee's, Chick-fil-A, Dunkin, IHOP, KFC, Pick Up Six, Pizza Hut, Starbucks, Taco Bell, Wingstop, ALDI, H, Marshall's, Target, USPO, Walgreens
9(8)	W Fordham Rd, E Dallas BBQ, H, Toyota
8(7)	W 179th (from nb), W Roberto Clemente SP
7(6)	I-95, US 1, S to Trenton, NJ, N to New Haven, CT

 = gas = food = lodging = other = rest stop

INTERSTATE 87 Cont'd

Exit #	Services
6(5)	E 153rd t, River Ave, Stadium Rd, E Dunkin, McDonald's, Pizza Hut, Subway, Best Western, Family$, Yankee Stadium
5(5)	E 161st, Macombs Dam Br, (exit 4 from nb), E Ramada, Target, Yankee Stadium
3(3)	E 138th St, Madison Ave Br, E BP/dsl
2(2)	Willis Ave, 3rd Ave Br, E Amoco, 99c Store, W McDonald's
1(1)	Brook Ave, Hunts Point, E BP, Citgo, $Tree, W Shell, Speedway, Dunkin, Best Western+
0mm	I-87 begins/ends on I-278.

INTERSTATE 88 NY

MIDDLEBURGH

25a	I-90/NY Thruway. I-88 begins/ends on I-90, exit 25a.
117mm	toll booth (to enter or exit NY Thruway)
25(116)	NY 7, to Rotterdam, Schenectady, N Frosty Acres Camping, S Mobil/dsl, Pilot/Dunkin'/Subway/dsl/scales/24hr, Wendy's
24(112)	US 20, NY 7, to Duanesburg, N Stewart's, Valero/Dunkin'/dsl, Duanesburg Diner, S USPO
23(101)	NY 30, to Schoharie, Central Bridge, N Citgo/dsl, Hide-A-Way Campground, S Mobil/Subway/dsl, Apple Barrel Cafe, Dunkin', Quality Inn, Old Stone Fort Museum
22(95)	NY 7, NY 145, to Cobleskill, Middleburgh, N Speedway/dsl, Stewart's/dsl, Sunoco, Dunkin', Rubbin Butts Bar-B-Q, Super 8, $Tree, AT&T, Buick/Chevrolet/GMC, Chrysler/Dodge/Jeep, golf, H, Howe Caverns, Monro Tire & Auto, PriceChopper Foods, Walmart, S Twin Oaks Camping
21(90)	NY 7, NY 10, to Cobleskill, Warnerville, N Mobil/dsl, Speedway/dsl, Stewart's/dsl, Arby's, Bull's Head Rest., Burger King, Chieftans Rest., KFC/Taco Bell, Little Deb's Creamery, Little Italy Pizza, McDonald's, Pizza Shack, Red Apple Buffet, Subway, $General, Ace Hardware, Advance Parts, AutoZone, CVS Drug, H, Mavis Tire, NAPA, O'Reilly Parts, PriceChopper Foods, Walmart/McDonald's
20(87)	NY 7, NY 10, to Richmondville, S Mobil/dsl, Sunoco/dsl, Countryside Inn, USPO
79mm	**full facilities, litter barrels, petwalk**, wb, **vending**
19(76)	to NY 7, Worcester, N Stewart's, Sunoco/dsl, Ardy's Rest., $General
73mm	eb, full facilities, litter barrels
18(71)	to Schenevus, N Mirabito/dsl
17(61)	NY 7, to NY 28 N, Colliersville, Cooperstown, N Mirabito, Cabin Pizza, Redwood Inn, $General, Baseball Hall of Fame
16(59)	NY 7, to Emmons, N Arby's, Brooks BBQ, Plaza Diner, Rainbow Inn, PriceChopper Foods

ONEONTA

15	NY 28, NY 23, Oneonta, N Speedway, Dunkin', KFC, Advance Parts, H, to Soccer Hall of Fame, USPO, S Mirabito, Speedway/dsl, Applebee's, Buffalo Wild Wings, Burger King, Denny's, Five Guys, Jersey Mike's, McDonald's, Moe's SW, Mt Fuji Japanese, Panera Bread, Subway, Taco Bell, Tim Horton, Wendy's, Budget Inn, Courtyard, Holiday Inn Express, Quality Inn, Super 8, $Tree, ALDI, AT&T, BJ's Whse/gas, Dick's, Ford, Hannaford Foods, Home Depot, JC Penney, Lowe's, Mr Tire, Petco, TJ Maxx, Verizon, Walmart
14(55)	Main St(from eb), Oneonta, N Stewart's, Sunoco, Alfresco's Italian, Guernsey Creamery, Advance Parts
13(53)	NY 205, N Mirabito, Speedway, Stewart's, Valero/dsl, Dante's Pizza, DQ, Dunkin', Jay's Steaks, McDonald's, Pizzaland, Sloan's NY Grill, Star Mix Grill, Celtic Motel, Hampton Inn, Motel 88, Buick/Cadillac/Chevrolet/GMC,

DELHI

13(53)	Continued Gilbert Lake SP, Honda, NAPA, Nissan, repair, st police, Subaru, Susquehanna RV Camping
12(47)	NY 7, to Otego, S Mirabito/dsl/24hr, Sunoco/dsl
42	wb, facilities, tables, litter barrels
11(40)	NY 357, to Unadilla, Delhi, S KOA
39mm	**full facilities, litter barrels, petwalk**, eb, **vending**
10(38)	NY 7, to Unadilla, N KwikFill, Mirabito, Unadilla Diner, Family$, USPO
9(33)	NY 8, to Sidney, N Mirabito, Little Caesar's, McDonald's, Pizza Hut, Super 8, $General, Advance Parts, AutoZone, H, PriceChopper Foods, Tall Pines Camping, USPO
8(29)	NY 206, to Bainbridge, N Citgo/dsl, Sunoco, Bob's Family Diner, China Star, Dunkin', Jerry's Grill, S&S Cafe, Algonkin Motel, Susquehanna Motel, Auto Parts+, Bainbridge B&B, Chevrolet/GMC, Family$, Riverside RV Park, USPO, S Oquage Creek Park

PORT CRANE

7(22)	NY 41, to Afton, N Mirabito, Sunoco/dsl, Henry's Drive-In, Main St Grill, RiverClub Rest., Afton Golf/rest., Kellystone Park
6(16)	NY 79, to NY 7, Harpursville, Ninevah, S Mirabito/Subway/dsl, Pantheon Rest., Family$, Nathanial Cole Park
5(12)	Martin Hill Rd, to Belden, N Sunoco, Belden Hill Camping, golf
4(8)	NY 7, to Sanitaria Springs, S Speedway/dsl
3(4)	NY 369, Port Crane, N Chenango Valley SP, S Fastrac/dsl, KwikFill, Fat Cowboy BBQ
2(2)	NY 12a W, to Chenango Bridge, N Mirabito, Guiseppe's Pizza, golf, USPO
1(1)	NY 7 W(no wb return), to Binghamton
0mm	I-81, N to Syracuse, S to Binghamton. I-88 begins/ends on I-81.

INTERSTATE 90

DEFREESTVILLE

0mm	New York/Massachusetts state line
0(B23)	NY 22, to Austerlitz, New Lebanon, W Stockbridge, N Love's/Dunkin'/Subway/dsl/scales/24hr/@, Mobil/dsl/scales/24hr, S Sunoco/dsl, Berkshire Travel Lodge, Woodland Hills Camp(3mi)
0(B17)	toll plaza
0(B15)	NY 295, Taconic Pkwy
0(B7)	US 9, NY Thruway W, to I-87
12(20)	US 9, to Hudson, N Pilot/Subway/dsl/scales/24hr, Skyview, S Van Buren NHS
18.5mm	rest area/weigh sta wb, **full facilities, litter barrels, petwalk**, **vending**
11(15)	US 9, US 20, E Greenbush, Nassau, N Speedway/dsl, Stewarts/dsl, Dunkin', st police, S Hawaii Poke, My Place, Four Seasons Motel, USPO, vet, Walgreens
10(10)	Miller Rd, to E Greenbush, S Mobil/dsl, Stewart's, Dunkin', Goomba's Pizza, Castle Inn, Comfort Inn
9(9)	US 4, to Rensselaer, Troy, N Mobil/dsl, Applebee's, Bruegger's Bagels, Chipotle, Dunkin', Five Guys, Gene's Seafood, Jersey Mike's, McDonald's, OffShore Pier Rest., Panera Bread, Recovery Sports Grill, Starbucks, Holiday Inn Express, Residence Inn, $Tree, AT&T, Home Depot, Mavis Tire/auto, PetSmart, Staples, Target, Walmart/auto, S Mobil/dsl, Stewart's, Cracker Barrel, Denny's, Dunkin', Golden Grain Pizza, Fairfield Inn, Hampton Inn
8(8)	NY 43, Defreestville, N Stewarts/dsl, Chick-fil-A, Chili's, Route Four Pizza, Taco Bell, The Bunker Grill, Upstate Cookie Shack, Wendy's, ALDI, AutoZone, CVS, Micheals, ShopRight Foods, TJ Maxx

= gas = food = lodging = other = rest stop

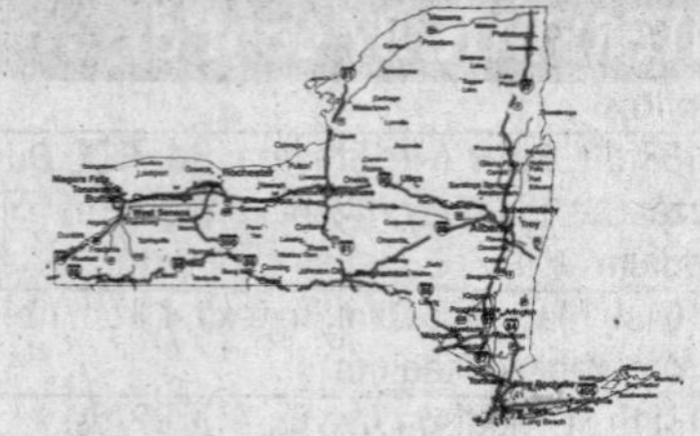

INTERSTATE 90 Cont'd

RENSSELAER

Exit #	Services
7(7)	Washington Ave(from eb), Rensselaer, S Nelson's Steak Out, Lucky Times Foods
6.5mm	Hudson River
6a	I-787, to Albany
6(4.5)	US 9, Northern Blvd, to Loudonville, N Stewart's, Cafe Madison, Dunkin', Risotto Rest., H
5a(4)	Corporate Woods Blvd
5(3.5)	Everett Rd, to NY 5, N Sunoco, Albany Auto, S Exxon/Dunkin', Mobil, Speedway/dsl, Dunkin, Gateway Diner, Hokkaido Asian, Little Caesar's, McDonald's, Popeyes, Subway, Taco Bell, Wingstop, Motel 6, Ramada, $Tree, Advance Parts, AutoZone, Chevrolet, Chrysler/Dodge/Jeep, CVS Drug, Fiat, Ford, Hannaford's Foods, Home Depot, H, Hyundai, Kia, Mavis Tire, Mazda, Midas, Mkt 32, Monro, Nissan, PepBoys, PriceChopper Foods, Valvoline
4(3)	NY 85 S, to Slingerlands
3(2.5)	S State Offices
2(2)	Fuller Rd, Washington Ave, same as 1S, same as 1S, S Sunoco/7-11, Dunkin', Courtyard, Hilton Garden, Hotel Luna, U of Albany
1N(1)	I-87 N, to Montreal, to Albany Airport
1S(1)	US 20, Western Ave, S Mobil, Dave&Buster's, Dunkin, McDonald's, Panera Bread, Residence Inn, Tru, Dick's, Home Depot, JC Penney, Macy's, Michael's, Old Navy, PetSmart, Walmart
24(149)	I-87 N to Albany, Montreal, S to NYC
153mm	Guilderland Service Area eb, Mobil/dsl, Burger King, McDonald's

AMSTERDAM

Exit #	Services
25(154)	I-890, NY 7, NY 146, to Schenectady
25a(159)	I-88 S, NY 7, to Binghamton
26(162)	I-890, NY 5 S, Schenectady
168mm	Pattersonville Service Area wb, Exxon
172mm	Mohawk Service Area eb, Exxon
27(174)	NY 30, Amsterdam, N Exxon/Dunkin'/dsl, Mobil/dsl, Knight Inn, Microtel, Super 8, Alpin Haus RV Ctr
28(182)	NY 30A, Fonda, N Mobil/Burger King/dsl/motel/24hr, Pilot/Taco Bell/dsl/scales/24hr, Sunoco/dsl, TA/Country Pride/dsl/motel/scales/24hr/@, Dunkin', McDonald's, Riverside Motel, st police, truck repair
184mm	parking area/truck insp area both lanes
187mm	wb, full facilities, living history site
29(194)	NY 10, Canajoharie, N Citgo, Stewart's/dsl, Budget Inn, McDonald's, Subway, $General, BigLots, Riverfront Park, USPO, Walgreens, S America Gas, Beavers/dsl, Village Rest., USPO

HERKIMER

Exit #	Services
210mm	Indian Castle Service area eb, Iroquois Service Area wb, EVC, Mobil, Burger King, Chick-fil-A, Popeyes, Starbucks
29a(211)	NY 169, to Little Falls, N Herkimer Home, H
30(220)	NY 28, to Mohawk, Herkimer, N FasTrac/dsl, Stewart's, Sunoco/Subway/dsl, Applebee's, Burger King, Denny's, Dominos, Dunkin', KFC/Taco Bell, McDonald's, Tony's Pizzaria, Vinny's Pizza, Budget Motel, Inn Towne Motel, Red Roof Inn, $General, $Tree, Advance Parts, AutoZone, Mavis Tire/auto, Verizon, vet, Walgreens, Walmart, S FasTrac, Little Caesar's, Paesano's Pizza, Red Apple Chinese, Tren De Villa Mexican, Cooperstown(Baseball Hall of Fame), Family$
227mm	Schuyler Service Area wb, Mobil, Dunkin', McDonald's
31(233)	I-790, NY 8, NY 12, to Utica, N Citgo/dsl, Fastrac, Applebee's, Bella Regina, Burger King, Franco's Pizza, It's A Utica Thing!, $Tree, ALDI, Bass Pro Shop, BigLots, BJ's Whse/gas, Lowe's, PriceChopper Foods, Walmart, S Speedway/dsl, Babe's Grill, Delmonico's Steaks, Denny's, Dunkin', KFC, McDonald's, Starbucks, Taco Bell, Wendy's,

CHITTENANGO

Exit #	Services
31(233)	Continued Wingstop, Best Western, Days Inn, EconoLodge, Fairfield Inn, Hampton Inn, Holiday Inn Epress, Home2 Suites, Red Roof Inn, Utica Happy Journey, Utica Rest Inn, AT&T, Monro Auto/Tire
236mm	I-790(from eb), to Utica
237.5mm	Erie Canal
238mm	Mohawk River
32(243)	NY 232, Westmoreland, S Circle K, Stewart's, Franco's Pizza, $General, USPO
244mm	Oneida Service Area eb, Sunoco, Burger King, Panera Bread, Starbucks
250mm	parking area eb, litter barrel
33(253)	NY 365, to Vernon Downs, Verona, N Maple Leaf Mkt/Dunkin/dsl, Inn at Turning Stone, S SavOn Gas/LP/repair, Dunkin', Recovery Grill, Fairfield Inn, Hampton Inn, Sandstone Hollow Inn, H, Turning Stone Casino
256mm	parking area wb, litter barrel
34(262)	NY 13, to Canastota, N Verona Beach SP Camping, S SavOn/dsl, Dunkin', McDonald's, Prevo's, Days Inn, Boxing Hall of Fame
266mm	Chittenango Service Area wb, Sunoco/dsl, Chick-fil-A, Starbucks
34a(277)	I-481, to Syracuse, Chittenango
35(279)	NY 298, The Circle, Syracuse, S Speedway, Burger King, Denny's, Dunkin', East Wok, Joey's Italian, Lala Lu Italian, McDonald's, Mr. Kabob, Nick's Pizza, Patty's Subs, Ruby Tuesday, Taco Bell, Best Value Inn, Candlewood Suites, Comfort Inn, Courtyard, Cresthill Suites, Days Inn, Doubletree Inn, Embassy Suites, Extended Stay America, Fairfield Inn, Hampton Inn, Hilton Garden, Home Town Inn, Homewood Suites, Hotel Concord, Motel 6, Quality Inn, Red Roof Inn, Residence Inn, Rodeway Inn, SpringHill Suites, Syracuse Inn, Midas, Stevenson's Tire/auto, U-Haul, Valvoline, Verizon, Verizon

SYRACUSE

Exit #	Services
280mm	Dewitt Service Area eb, Sunoco/dsl, McDonald's
36(283)	I-81, N to Watertown, S to Binghamton
37(284)	7th St, Electronics Pkwy, to Liverpool, N Byrne Dairy & Deli, Best Western+, S Speedway, KFC/Taco Bell, Days Inn, Homewood Suites, Staybridge Suites, Kinney Drug
38(286)	NY 57, to Liverpool, Syracuse, N Fastrac/dsl, KwikFill, Speedway, Bangkok Thai, Dunkin', Pizza Hut, Super 8, $General, $Tree, ALDI, Mavis Tire, Midas, NAPA, URGENT CARE, Walgreens
39(290)	I-690, NY 690, Syracuse, N Comfort Inn/rest., Camping World RV Ctr, S Holiday Inn Express
292mm	Warners Service Area wb, N Chick-fil-A, McDonald's, Mobil/dsl
40(304)	NY 34, to Owasco Lake, Weedsport, N Riverforest RV Park, S Fastrac, KwikFill, Marathon/dsl, Arby's, Arnold's Rest., Cj's Rest., DB's Drive-In, Dunkin', NY Pizzeria, Red Roof Inn, Rodeway Inn, $General, Ace Hardware, Kinney Drug, NAPA, USPO, Weedsport Foods
310mm	Port Byron Service Area eb, Mobil/dsl
318mm	parking area wb, litter barrels
41(320)	NY 414, to Cayuga Lake, Waterloo, S Byrne Dairy/dsl, Circle K/dsl, Exxon, Love's/Subway/dsl/scales/24hr,

NY

INTERSTATE 90 Cont'd

41(320) Continued
Petro/Iron Skillet/dsl/scales/24hr/@, Dunkin, Monterrey Mexican, Cayuga Lake SP/camping, Speedco, Waterloo Outlets/famous brands(3mi)

LYONS

324mm Junius Ponds Service Area wb, Sunoco/dsl, Shake Shack, Starbucks

42(327) NY 14, to Geneva, Lyons, S Mobil/7-11/dsl/scales, Junius Ponds RV Camping, Waterloo Outlets/famous brands(3mi)

337mm Clifton Springs Service Area eb, Sunoco/dsl, Chick-fil-A, Shake Shack

43(340) NY 21, to Palmyra, Manchester, N Hill Cumorah LDS HS(2mi), S Sunoco/dsl, Dunkin', McDonald's, Rodeway Inn, KOA(6mi)

44(347) NY 332, Victor, S 7-11/dsl, Crosby's/Subway, Exxon, Sunoco, Burger King, Dunkin', KFC, McDonald's, Park Place Rest., Taco Bell, Best Value, Budget Inn, Comfort Inn, Microtel, Travelodge, $General, $Tree, ALDI, AutoZone, casino, CVS Drug, KOA(4mi), st police, Top's Foods

350mm Seneca Service Area wb, Exxon, Dunkin, Popeyes

45(351) I-490, NY 96, to Rochester, N Mobil/dsl, Adelita's Mexican, Champp's Grill, Chipotle, Distillery Rest., Five Guys, Longhorn Steaks, McDonald's, Moe's SW Grill, Old Pueblo Grill, Olive Garden, Panera Bread, PF Chang's, Pi Craft Pizza, Ross, Starbucks, Subway, Umi Japanese Steaks, Hampton Inn, $Tree, AT&T, Best Buy, BJ's Whse/gas, Dick's, Hobby Lobby, Home Depot, JC Penney, Kohl's, Macy's, Michael's, Old Navy, PetSmart, Staples, Target, TJ Maxx, U-Haul, Verizon, Von Maur, Walmart, S KwikFill/dsl, Burger King, Chili's, Taco Bell, Wendy's, Best Western+, Holiday Inn Express, Homewood Suites, Microtel, Valvoline, vet

353mm parking area eb, litter barrels

46(362) I-390, to Rochester, W Mobil/Dunkin/dsl, Speedway/dsl, Sunoco/dsl, Burger King, Fire Crust, McDonald's, Peppermint's Rest., Tim Hortons, Wendy's, Fairfield Inn, Microtel, Red Roof Inn, Super 8, Buick/GMC

366mm Scottsville Service Area eb, Mobil/dsl, Dunkin

376mm Ontario Service Area wb, Sunoco, McDonald's

47(379) I-490, NY 19, to Rochester, N 490 Truckstop/dsl, Timberline Camping

48(390) NY 98, to Batavia, N Fairbridge Inn, Fairfield Inn, Hampton Inn, Holiday Inn Express, S Citgo, Quicklees/Tim Hortons/dsl/EVC, Alex's Steaks, Applebee's, Chipotle, Five Guys, Fortune's Italian, Jersey Mike's, Starbucks, Subway, Taco Bell, Tim Horton's, Tropical Smoothie, Yume Asian Bistro, Best Western, Budget Inn, Hotel Batavia, La Quinta, Quality Inn, Red Roof Inn, Relax Inn, AT&T, AutoZone, BJ's Whse, Dick's, Home Depot, Kohl's, Marshall's, Michael's, PetCo, Target, Tops Foods, Verizon, Walmart/Subway

397mm Pembroke Service Area eb, Sunoco, Burger King, Dunkin, Panera Bread, Popeye's

48a(402) NY 77, Pembroke, S Flying J/Denny's/Subway/dsl/LP/scales/24hr, Speedway, TA/Mobil/Country Pride/dsl/scales/24hr/@, Subway, Darien Lake Lodge/camping, EconoLodge, Sleepy Hollow Camping

412mm Clarence Service Area wb, Sunoco, Burger King, Tim Hortons

DEPEW

49(417) NY 78, Depew, N Mobil/dsl, Sunoco, Tesla EVC, Andale Cantina, Arby's, Burger King, Carmine's Italian, Chili's, Cielito Lindo Mexican, Cracker Barrel, DiBella's Subs, DQ, Duff's Wings, Dunkin', Fuji Grill, King Crab, La Tolteca, Mighty Taco, Olive Garden, Pesci's Pizza, Picasso's Pizza, Pita Gourmet, Russel's Steaks, Salsarita's, Starbucks, Subway, Ted's HotDogs, Tim Horton, Tully's Rest., Wendy's,

49(417) Continued
Best Western, Fairbridge Inn, Hawthorn Suites, Home2 Suites, Motel 6, Salvatore's Hotel, Springhill Suites, Tru Hilton, Acura, Advance Parts, Advance Parts, ALDI, Barnes&Noble, BigLots, Chrysler/Dodge/Jeep, Dunn Tire, Firestone/auto, Ford, Goodyear/auto, Hobby Lobby, Home Depot, JC Penney, Mavis Tire, Monro Tire & Auto, Office Depot, PetCo, TJ Maxx, Verizon, S Kwikfill, Speedway/dsl, China 1, Italian Village, John&Mary's Cafe, McDonald's, Pan Pizza Co, Salvatore's Italian, Subway, Tim Hortons, Delavan Hotel, Garden Place Hotel, Hity Inn, La Quinta, Red Roof Inn, $Tree, Mavis Tire, Top's Foods/gas

BUFFALO

419mm toll booth

50(420) I-290 to Niagara Falls

50a(421) Cleveland Dr(from eb)

51(422) NY 33 E, Buffalo, S Buffalo Intl, st police

52(423) Walden Ave, to Buffalo, N Applebee's, Burger King, Chick-fil-A, Chipotle, Don Patron Mexican, IHOP, King Crab, McDonald's, Papa John's, Starbucks, Taco Bell, Tim Horton, Hampton Inn, Holiday Inn Express, Residence Inn, $Tree, ALDI, AT&T, AutoZone, Firestone/auto, Ford, Home Depot, Michael's, Office Depot, PetSmart, PriceRite Mkt, Target, Top's Foods, S Delta Sonic/Dunkin', Jim's Trk Plaza/Sunoco/dsl/rest./scales/24hr, KwikFill, Aloha Krab Seafood, Alton's Rest., Anderson's Custard, Cheesecake Factory, Dave & Busters, Five Guys, Longhorn Steaks, McDonald's, Melting Pot, Mighty Taco, Moe's SW, Olive Garden, Panera Bread, PF Chang's, Popeyes, Rachels Grill, Santora's Pizza, Smokey Bones BBQ, Sonic, Taco Bell, Ted's Hot Dogs, Texas de Brazil Steaks, Tim Horton, TX Roadhouse, Zahng's Buffet, Baymont Inn, Home2 Suites, M Hotel Buffalo, Best Buy, Burlington Coats, Cabela's, Dick's, JC Penney, Lord&Taylor, Macy's, Marshall's, Mavis Tire, Sam's Club, Verizon

E AURORA

52a(424) William St

53(425) I-190, to Buffalo, Niagara Falls, N Best Western+

54(428) NY 400, NY 16, to W Seneca, E Aurora

55(430) US 219, Ridge Rd, Orchard Park, N Tim Hortons, S Delta Sonic, Mobil, Burger King, Connor's, Denny's, Ferro's NY Pizza, Mighty Taco, Subway, Tim Horton, Wendy's, Country Inn&Suites, Hampton Inn, Staybridge Suites, $General, ALDI, ALDI, Goodyear/auto, Home Depot, Monro Tire & Auto, Mr Tire, Pepboys, Petco, Tops Foods/gas, Verizon, Wegman's Foods

431mm toll gantry

56(432) NY 179, Mile Strip Rd, N BJs Gas, Marathon/dsl, Mobil, Sunoco, Blasdell Pizza, China King, DiPaolo's Rest., Odyssey Rest., EconoLodge, $General, Advance Parts, CVS Drug, SaveALot Foods, USPO, S Applebee's, Chick-fil-A, Chipotle, ChuckeCheese, El Canelo Mexican, Firehouse Subs, Five Guys, Ichiban Japanese, Jersey Mike's, McDonald's, Mongolian Buffet, Olive Garden, Outback Steaks, Panera Bread, Popeyes, Rachels Grill, Starbucks, Wendy's, $Tree, ALDI, Barnes&Noble, Best Buy, BJ's Whse, Firestone/auto, Hobby Lobby, Home Depot, JC Penney, Old Navy, PepBoys, TJ Maxx, Wegman's Foods

57(436) NY 75, to Hamburg, N Mobil/Dunkin'/dsl, Arby's, Blasdell Pizza, Denny's, McDonald's, Moe's SW Grill, Starbucks, Taco Bell, Tim Horton, Uncle Joe's Diner, Waterstone Grill, Wendy's, Comfort Inn, Holiday Inn Express, Motel 6, Red Roof Inn, Chevrolet, Chrysler/Dodge/Jeep, Ford, Honda, Lowe's, Pepboys, transmissions, Walmart/Subway, S Hi-Quality Gas, Kwikfill/dsl, Marathon, NAPA, Burger King, Mexico City, Papa's Pizza, Pita Gourmet, Savory Cafe, Subway, Tim Hortons, Hampton Inn, $General, Advance Parts, AutoZone, Camping World, Goodyear/auto, Monro Automotive, USPO,

NY

[gas] = gas [food] = food [lodging] = lodging [other] = other [RS] = rest stop

INTERSTATE 90 Cont'd

ANGOLA

57(436) Continued vet

442mm parking area both lanes

57a(445) to Eden, Angola, **N** [gas] Mobil/dsl

447mm Angola Service Area both lanes, [gas] Sunoco, [food] McDonalds

58(456) US 20, NY 5, to Silver Creek, Irving, **N** [gas] Kwikfill, Native Pride Trkstp/dsl/scales, Seneca Hawk Trkstp/dsl, [food] Burger King, Colony Rest., McDonald's, Millie's Rest., Sunset Bay, Sunset Grill, Tim Hortons, Tom's Rest., [lodging] Lighthouse Inn, [other] auto repair, Evangola SP, [H], USPO

WESTFIELD

59(468) NY 60, Fredonia, Dunkirk, **N** [lodging] Clarion, Dunkirk Motel, [other] Lake Erie SP/camping, **S** [gas] Citgo/Country Fair/dsl, Kwikfill/dsl, [food] Applebee's, Arby's, Azteca Cantina, Burger King, Denny's, Dominos, Dunkin', KFC/Taco Bell, Little Caesar's, McDonald's, Subway, Tim Horton, Tim Hortons, Tuscany Deli, Wendy's, [lodging] Best Western, Econolodge/Suburban Lodge, Quality Inn, Suburban Studios, [other] $General, $Tree, Advance Parts, ALDI, AT&T, auto repair, AutoZone, BigLots, Chrysler/Dodge/Jeep, Ford/Lincoln, GMC, Home Depot, Monro Tire&Auto, PetSmart, TJ Maxx, Tops Foods/gas, Verizon, Walmart

60(485) NY 394, Westfield, **N** [other] Barcelona Lighthouse, KOA, Lake Erie SP/camping, **S** [lodging] Holiday Motel, Webb's Resort, [other] [H]

489mm toll gantry

61(495) Shortman Rd, to Ripley, **N** [other] Lakeside RV Camping, **S** [gas] Love's/Hardee's/dsl/scales/24hr/@

496mm New York/Pennsylvania state line

INTERSTATE 95

CO-OP CITY BLVD

32mm New York/Connecticut state line

22(30) Midland Ave(from nb), Port Chester, Rye, **W** [food] Coyote Flaco, Dunkin', Michael's Pizza, [lodging] Courtyard, [other] Home Depot, Target, Whole Foods Mkt

21(29) I-287 W, US 1 N, to White Plains, Port Chester, Tappan Zee

20(28) US 1 S(from nb), Port Chester, **E** [gas] Shell, [food] Averna Steaks, Bareburger, Fogama Japanese, Frankie & Johnnie's Steaks, Granola Bar, Ruby's Bistro, Rye Grill, Starbucks, Sunrise Pizza, [other] CVS Drug, Subaru, USPO, Verizon

19(27) Playland Pkwy, Rye, Harrison

18b(25) Mamaroneck Ave, to White Plains, **E** [gas] Shell, Speedway, [food] Chipotle, Domino's, Duck Donuts, Jimmy's Pizza, [other] Mavis Tire, Valvoline, Verizon

18a(24) Fenimore Rd(from nb), Mamaroneck, **E** [gas] Conoco, Gulf, [food] Fenimore Deli

17(20) Chatsworth Ave(from nb, no return), Larchmont

19.5mm toll plaza

16(19) North Ave, Cedar St, New Rochelle, **E** [food] Applebee's, Buffalo Wild Wings, Starbucks, Subway, Taco Bell, TX Roadhouse, [lodging] NoMa Hotel, Residence Inn, [other] Chevrolet, CVS, ShopRite, Toyota, USPO, **W** [H]

15(16) US 1, New Rochelle, The Pelhams, **E** [gas] BP/dsl, Conoco, SuperGas, [food] Dubrovnik Croatian, Dunkin', Mexico Alegre, New China, New Rochelle Diner, Pizza La Rosa, [other] AutoZone, Costco/gas, CVS, Harley-Davidson, Home Depot, Land Rover, NAPA, **W** auto repair

14(15) Hutchinson Pkwy(from sb), to Whitestone Br

13(16) Conner St, to Mt Vernon, **E** [gas] Shell/dsl, [food] Taco Bell, [lodging] Ramada Inn, **W** [gas] BP, [food] McDonald's, [lodging] Holiday Motel, [other] Co-Op City Tire/auto, [H], Kia

12(15.5) Baychester Ave(exits left from nb)

11(15) Bartow Ave, Co-op City Blvd, **E** [food] Buffalo Wild Wings, Burger King, Chipotle, Dallas BBQ, Dragon City Chinese, Dunkin', KPOT KBBQ, McDonald's, Olive Garden, Panera Bread, Pizza Chop, Popeyes, Red Lobster, Shake Shack, Starbucks, [other] $Tree, AT&T, JC Penney, K-Mart, Macys, Marshall's, Staples,

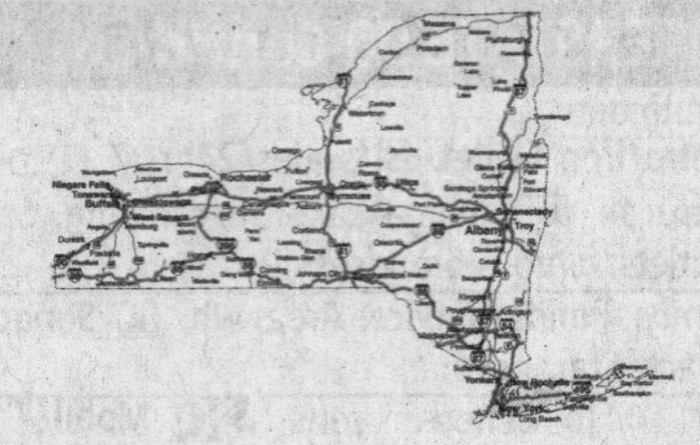

11(15) Continued Stop & Shop, Verizon, **W** [gas] Bartow Gas/dsl, Mobil/dsl, Shell/Dunkin', [food] ChuckeCheese, Dunkin', Joyful Dragon, Pizza Hut, [other] ALDI, Home Depot

10(14.5) Gun Hill Rd(exits left from nb), **W** [lodging] Pelham Garden

9(14) Hutchinson Pkwy

8c(13.5) Pelham Pkwy W

8b(13) Orchard Beach, City Island

8a(12.5) Westchester Ave(from sb)

7c(12) Pelham Bay Park(from nb), Country Club Rd

7b(11.5) E Tremont, **W** [other] Super FoodTown

7a(11) I-695(from sb), to I-295 S, Throgs Neck Br

6b(10.5) I-278 W(from sb), I-295 S(from nb)

6a(10) I-678 S, Whitestone Bridge

5b(9) Castle Hill Ave, **E** [food] Circle Pizza, [other] Family$, vet, **W** [gas] Sunoco, [food] Halalbee's Burgers, McDonald's, Pizza Hut, [lodging] Hotel Ninety Five, [other] $Tree, USPO

5a(8.5) Westchester Ave, White Plains Rd

4b(8) Bronx River Pkwy, Rosedale Ave, **E** [gas] BP/Dunkin'

4a(7) I-895 S, Sheridan Expsy

3(6) 3rd Ave, **W** [other] [H]

2b(5) Webster Ave, **W** [other] [H]

2a(4) Jerome Ave, to I-87

1c(3) I-87, Deegan Expswy, to Upstate

1b(2) Harlem River Dr

1a(1) US 9, NY 9A, H Hudson Pkwy, 178th St, downtown

0mm New York/New Jersey state line, Hudson River, Geo Washington Br

INTERSTATE 190 (Buffalo)

LEWISTON

25.5mm US/Canada Border, US Customs

25b a R Moses Pkwy, NY 104, NY 265, Lewiston, **E** [other] [H]

24 NY 31, Witmer Rd, **E** [other] st police

23 NY 182, Porter Rd, Packard Rd, **E** [gas] EVC, Speedway, Sunoco/dsl, [food] Applebee's, Burger King, Chili's, Chipotle, DQ, Five Guys, Jersey Mike's, Jet Port Rest., Longhorn Steaks, Mighty Taco, Mom's Rest., Olive Garden, Panera Bread, Subway, Tim Horton, [other] $Tree, Advance Parts, Big Lots, Chrysler/Dodge/Jeep, Fashion Outlets/famous brands, Firestone/auto, Goodyear/Auto, Hobby Lobby, Mavis Tire, Mr Tire, NAPA, Sam's Club/gas, Save-A-Lot, U-Haul, Verizon, Walmart/Subway, Wegman's, **W** [gas] Quicklees/dsl, [food] Wendy's, [other] ALDI

22 US 62, Niagara Falls Blvd, **E** [gas] Delta Sonic, EVC, Sunoco, [food] Arby's, Bob Evans, Broadway Pizza, Burger King, Buzzys Pizza, Denny's, Duff's Wings, Dunkin', Fuji Sushi, KFC, Mandalay Rest., McDonald's, Niagra Falls Buffet, Popeyes, Starbucks, Subway, Taco Bell, Wagon Wheel, Wendy's, [lodging] Aarya Hotel, Hampton Inn, Mircotel, Moonlite Motel, Pelican Motel, Quality Inn, Red Carpet Inn, Red Roof, Super 8, Swiss Cottage Inn, Woodland Inn, [other] $Tree, Advance Parts, AT&T, Dunn Tire, Ford, Target, TJ Maxx, Top's Foods/gas, Walgreens, **W** [food] Tim Hortons, [lodging] Comfort Inn, Econolodge, La Quinta, [other] Bundy's Tire & Auto, Home Depot

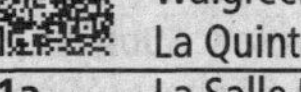

21a La Salle Expswy

21 NY 384, Buffalo Ave, R Moses Pkwy, **E** [lodging] Aashram Hotel, Niagra Riverside Hotel, **W** [gas] Niagra Fuel, [other] American Falls, casino, Niagra Falls

NY

INTERSTATE 190 (Buffalo) Cont'd

Exit #	Services
20.5mm	Niagara River East, toll booth sb
20b a	Long Rd, E Budget Motel, Kelly's Country Store
19	Whitehaven Rd, E Speedway/dsl, John's Pizza, McDonald's, $Tree, funpark, KOA, Top's Foods/gas, W Chevrolet, Hyundai, Toyota, vet
18b a	NY 324 W, Grand Island Blvd, E Burger King, Tim Horton, Wendy's, Chateau Motel, W Beaver Island SP
17.5mm	Niagara River East
17	NY 266, last free exit nn
16	I-290 E, to I-90, Albany
15	NY 324, Kenmore Ave, E 7-11, Economy Inn, city park, W U-Haul
14	Ontario St, E KwikFill, Faso's Italian, McDonald's, River Rock Cafe, Tim Horton, Advance Parts, W dog park
13	(from nb), same as 14
12	Amherst St, from nb, downtown
11	NY 198, Buffalo, E First Line
9	Porter Ave, to Peace Bridge, Ft Erie
8	NY 266, Niagara St, E downtown, Hilton, Embassy Suites, Hilton Garden, Hyatt
7	NY 5 W, Church St, Buffalo, E downtown
6	Elm St, E downtown, H, W Courtyard, KeyBank Center
5	Louisiana St, Buffalo, E downtown
4	Smith St, Fillmore Ave, Buffalo, E downtown
3	NY 16, Seneca St, from sb, W Tim Hortons
2	US 62, NY 354, Bailey Ave, Clinton St
1	Ogden St, E Sunoco, Wendy's, Best Western, Quality Inn, Big Lots, CVS Drug, Family$
0mm	I-90. I-190 begins/ends on I-90, exit 53.

INTERSTATE 287 (NYC)

Exit #	Services
12	I-95, N to New Haven, S to NYC. I-287 begins/ends on I-95, exit 21.
11	US 1, Port Chester, Rye, N BP, Mobil, Shell, Sunoco, Burger King, Domino's, Dunkin, Dunkin, McDonald's, Popeyes, Port Chester Diner, Subway, Taco Bell, Courtyard, Goodyear, Home Depot, Kohl's, Mavis Tire, Midland Truck & Auto, Nissan, Old Navy, Staples, Target, Verizon, Whole Foods Mkt
10	Bowman Ave, Webb Ave
9N S	Hutchinson Pkwy, Merritt Pkwy, to Whitestone Br
9a	I-684, Brewster
8	Westchester Ave, to White Plains, S Mobil, Buffalo Wild Wings, Cheesecake Factory, Chipotle, Five Guys, Morton's Steaks, PF Chang's, Cambria Hotel, Sonesta, Neiman Marcus, Nordstrom, Stop&Shop Foods, Target, URGENT CARE, vet, Westchester Mall Place, Whole Foods Mkt
7	Taconic Pkwy(from wb), to N White Plains
6	NY 22, White Plains
5	NY 100, Hillside Ave, S BP, Lukoil, Duck Donuts, Dunkin, Panera Bread, Planet Pizza, Smashburger, Subway, Aamco, AutoZone, BJ Optical, BMW, Infiniti, Kia, Lexus, PetSmart, Tesla, vet, VW
4	NY 100A, Hartsdale, N Shell, H, S Mobil, Bamboo Garden Chinese, Burger King, Popeyes, Starbucks, BMW/Mini, Jaguar/Subaru, Land Rover, Lincoln, Staples, Volvo
3	Sprain Pkwy, to Taconic Pkwy, NYC
2	NY 9A, Elmsford, N BP, Citgo, Mobil, Dunkin, Subway, Taco Bell, Mavis Tire, NAPA, Sam's Club, S Shell, Wendy's
1	NY 119, Tarrytown, N Shell/dsl, Tesla EVC, Marriott, Sheraton, SpringHill Suites, S BP/dsl, Dunkin,
1	Continued El Dorado Diner, Days Inn, Extended Stay America, Hampton Inn, Motel 6
0	I-287 runs with I-87 N.

INTERSTATE 290 (Buffalo)

Exit #	Services
8	I-90, NY Thruway, I-290 begins/ends on I-90, exit 50.
7b a	NY 5, Main St, N Mobil/dsl, Sunoco, Giancarlo's Steaks, Hampton Inn, La Nova Pizza/Wings, McDonald's, Panera Bread, Starbucks, Tim Horton, Wendy's, Mosey Hotel, Tops Foods, Verizon, Walgreens, S Valero, Hyatt Place
6	NY 324, NY 240, N Marathon/dsl, Courtyard, Cadillac, S McDonald's, Pizza Hut, Sheridan Rest., Tim Hortons, 7-11, CVS Drug, Hyundai, Kia/Mazda, Lexus, Mr Tire, Nissan, Subaru, URGENT CARE, Valvoline, Walgreens
5b a	NY 263, to Millersport, N Sunoco, bb.q Chicken, Candlewood Suites, Comfort Inn, DoubleTree, Marriott, Residence Inn, S Mobil, Homewood Suites, Jaguar/Land Rover, Mr Tire, Toyota, VW, Walgreens
4	I-990, to St U
3b a	US 62, to Niagara Falls Blvd, N Mobil/7-11, Valero, Anderson's Rest., Bob Evans, Checkers, Dunkin', Just Pizza, Pancake House, Ted's Hot Dogs, Tom Hortons, Amherst Inn, Blue Falls, CarMax, Extended Stay America, Holiday Inn Express, La Quinta, Route 62, Sleep Inn, AutoZone, Chrysler/Dodge/Jeep, Home Depot, Honda, NAPA, Rite Aid, URGENT CARE, Valvoline, vet, S Delta Sonic, Sunoco/dsl, Applebee's, AT&T, Blaze Pizza, Brother BBQ, Buffalo Wild Wings, Burger King, Carrabba's, Cheeburger, Chili's, Chipotle, Denny's, Dibella's Subs, Domino's, El Toro Mexican, Five Guys, Jersey Mike's, John's Pizza, McDonald's, Moe's SW Grill, Olive Garden, Outback Steaks, Panera Bread, Papa John's, Starbucks, TGIFriday, Tim Horton, Tim Hortons, Tropical Smoothie, Tulley's, White Rabbit, Days Inn, Home2 Suites, Royal Inn, $General, $Tree, ALDI, Barnes&Noble, Best Buy, BJ's/gas, Dick's, Firestone/auto, Goodyear/auto, JC Penney, Lowes Whse, Macy's, Michael's, Michaels, Office Depot, Office Max, Old Navy, Pepboys, PetCo, PetSmart, Target, TJ Maxx, Trader Joe's, Verizon
2	NY 425, Colvin Blvd, N Athena's Rest., KFC, McDonald's, Texas Roadhouse, Tim Horton, Wendy's, Big Lots, Family$, H, Top's Foods/gas, S KwikFill, Just Pizza, Pepboys
1b a	Elmwood Ave, NY 384, NY 265, N KwikFill, Franco's Pizza, John's Pizza/Subs, Subway, Touch of Italy, Center Way Motel, $Tree, auto repair, H, Rite Aid, S Sunoco/dsl, Arby's
0mm	I-190. I-290 begins/ends on I-190 in Buffalo.

INTERSTATE 390

Exit #	Services
20b a	I-490. I-390 begins/ends on I-490 in Rochester
19(75)	NY 33a, Chili Ave, N KwikFill, Chili Diner, El Latino Mexican, Zoc's Burgers, AutoZone, S Sunoco, Burger King, KFC, Little Caesar's, Subway, Motel 6, Red Roof Inn
18b a	NY 204, Brooks Ave, S Best Western, Fairfield Inn,
17(73)	NY 383, Scottsville Rd, N Campi's Rest., S 7-11/dsl, Fastrac/dsl
16(71)	NY 15a, to E Henryetta, N KwikFill, Burger King, Chipotle, Chuy's Mexican, Country Sweet Chicken, Dominos, Dunkin', McDonald's, Moe's SW Grill, Texas de Brazil, Wendy's, Hilton Garden, $Tree, Costco/gas, H, REI, S Delmonico's Rest., TGI Friday's, Courtyard, Holiday Inn Express, Spark Hotel
15(70)	I-590, Rochester
14(68)	NY 15a, NY 252, E Mobil, Dunkin', Gray's Cafe, Jeremiah's, Residence Inn, Super Crab, Tully's Rest., Extended Stay America, $Tree, NAPA, Top's Foods/gas,

NY

INTERSTATE 390 Cont'd

DANSVILLE

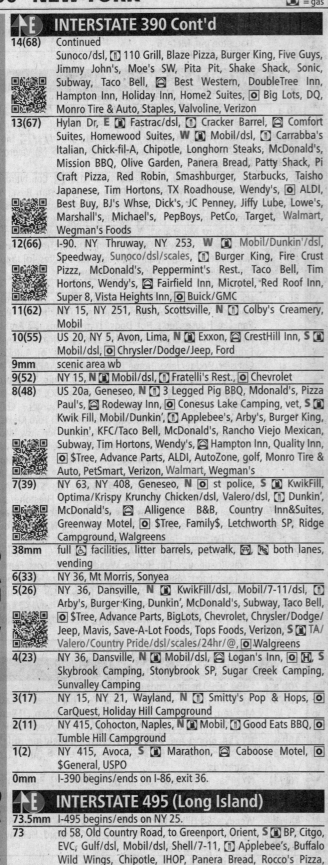

14(68) Continued
Sunoco/dsl, 110 Grill, Blaze Pizza, Burger King, Five Guys, Jimmy John's, Moe's SW, Pita Pit, Shake Shack, Sonic, Subway, Taco Bell, Best Western, DoubleTree Inn, Hampton Inn, Holiday Inn, Home2 Suites, Big Lots, DQ, Monro Tire & Auto, Staples, Valvoline, Verizon

13(67) Hylan Dr, E Fastrac/dsl, Cracker Barrel, Comfort Suites, Homewood Suites, W Mobil/dsl, Carrabba's Italian, Chick-fil-A, Chipotle, Longhorn Steaks, McDonald's, Mission BBQ, Olive Garden, Panera Bread, Patty Shack, Pi Craft Pizza, Red Robin, Smashburger, Starbucks, Taisho Japanese, Tim Hortons, TX Roadhouse, Wendy's, ALDI, Best Buy, BJ's Whse, Dick's, JC Penney, Jiffy Lube, Lowe's, Marshall's, Michael's, PepBoys, PetCo, Target, Walmart, Wegman's Foods

12(66) I-90. NY Thruway, NY 253, W Mobil/Dunkin'/dsl, Speedway, Sunoco/dsl/scales, Burger King, Fire Crust Pizzz, McDonald's, Peppermint's Rest., Taco Bell, Tim Hortons, Wendy's, Fairfield Inn, Microtel, Red Roof Inn, Super 8, Vista Heights Inn, Buick/GMC

11(62) NY 15, NY 251, Rush, Scottsville, N Colby's Creamery, Mobil

10(55) US 20, NY 5, Avon, Lima, N Exxon, CrestHill Inn, S Mobil/dsl, Chrysler/Dodge/Jeep, Ford

9mm scenic area wb

9(52) NY 15, N Mobil/dsl, Fratelli's Rest., Chevrolet

8(48) US 20a, Geneseo, N 3 Legged Pig BBQ, Mdonald's, Pizza Paul's, Rodeway Inn, Conesus Lake Camping, vet, S Kwik Fill, Mobil/Dunkin', Applebee's, Arby's, Burger King, Dunkin', KFC/Taco Bell, McDonald's, Rancho Viejo Mexican, Subway, Tim Hortons, Wendy's, Hampton Inn, Quality Inn, $Tree, Advance Parts, ALDI, AutoZone, golf, Monro Tire & Auto, PetSmart, Verizon, Walmart, Wegman's

7(39) NY 63, NY 408, Geneseo, N st police, S KwikFill, Optima/Krispy Krunchy Chicken/dsl, Valero/dsl, Dunkin', McDonald's, Alligence B&B, Country Inn&Suites, Greenway Motel, $Tree, Family$, Letchworth SP, Ridge Campground, Walgreens

38mm full facilities, litter barrels, petwalk, both lanes, vending

6(33) NY 36, Mt Morris, Sonyea

5(26) NY 36, Dansville, N KwikFill/dsl, Mobil/7-11/dsl, Arby's, Burger King, Dunkin', McDonald's, Subway, Taco Bell, $Tree, Advance Parts, BigLots, Chevrolet, Chrysler/Dodge/Jeep, Mavis, Save-A-Lot Foods, Tops Foods, Verizon, S TA/Valero/Country Pride/dsl/scales/24hr/@, Walgreens

4(23) NY 36, Dansville, N Mobil/dsl, Logan's Inn, H, S Skybrook Camping, Stonybrook SP, Sugar Creek Camping, Sunvalley Camping

3(17) NY 15, NY 21, Wayland, N Smitty's Pop & Hops, CarQuest, Holiday Hill Campground

2(11) NY 415, Cohocton, Naples, N Mobil, Good Eats BBQ, Tumble Hill Campground

1(2) NY 415, Avoca, S Marathon, Caboose Motel, $General, USPO

0mm I-390 begins/ends on I-86, exit 36.

INTERSTATE 495 (Long Island)

ORIENT

73.5mm I-495 begins/ends on NY 25.

73 rd 58, Old Country Road, to Greenport, Orient, S BP, Citgo, EVC, Gulf/dsl, Mobil/dsl, Shell/7-11, Applebee's, Buffalo Wild Wings, Chipotle, IHOP, Panera Bread, Rocco's Pizza, Starbucks, Taco Bell, TGIFriday's, Wendy's, Hilton Garden, Holiday Inn Express, Residence Inn, AT&T, AutoZone, Best Buy, Buick/GMC, Chevrolet, Costco/gas, CVS Drug, Dick's,

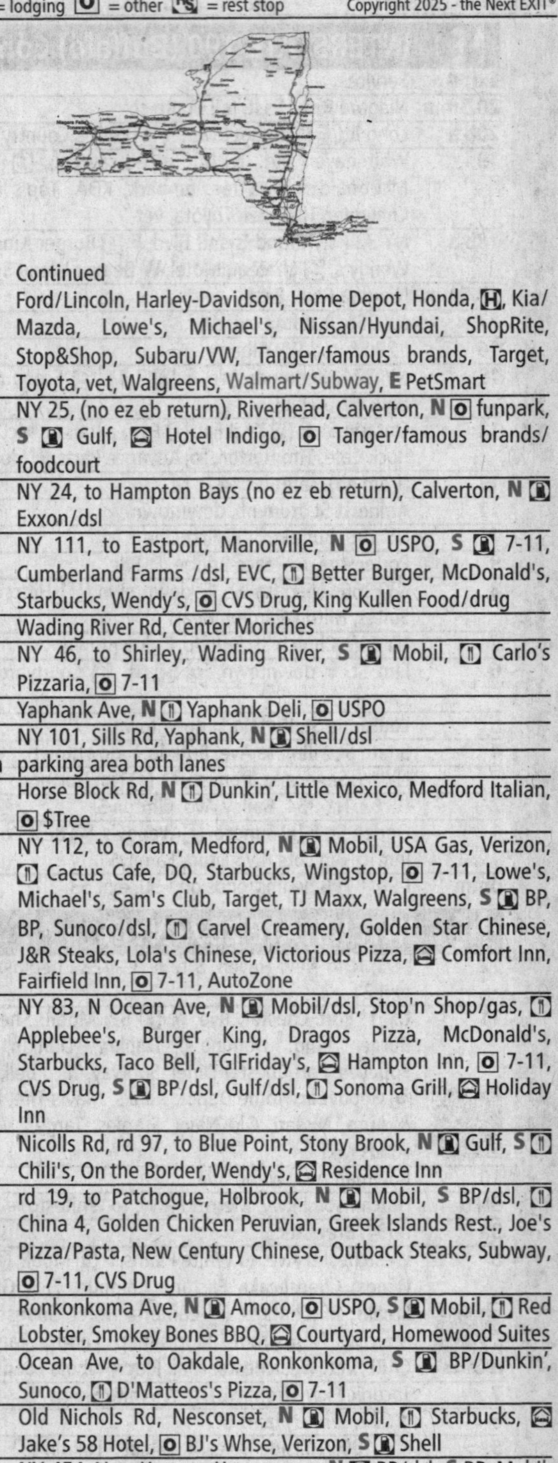

CALVERTON

73 Continued
Ford/Lincoln, Harley-Davidson, Home Depot, Honda, H, Kia/Mazda, Lowe's, Michael's, Nissan/Hyundai, ShopRite, Stop&Shop, Subaru/VW, Tanger/famous brands, Target, Toyota, vet, Walgreens, Walmart/Subway, E PetSmart

72 NY 25, (no ez eb return), Riverhead, Calverton, N funpark, S Gulf, Hotel Indigo, Tanger/famous brands/foodcourt

71 NY 24, to Hampton Bays (no ez eb return), Calverton, N Exxon/dsl

70 NY 111, to Eastport, Manorville, N USPO, S 7-11, Cumberland Farms /dsl, EVC, Better Burger, McDonald's, Starbucks, Wendy's, CVS Drug, King Kullen Food/drug

69 Wading River Rd, Center Moriches

68 NY 46, to Shirley, Wading River, S Mobil, Carlo's Pizzaria, 7-11

MEDFORD

67 Yaphank Ave, N Yaphank Deli, USPO

66 NY 101, Sills Rd, Yaphank, N Shell/dsl

65.5mm parking area both lanes

65 Horse Block Rd, N Dunkin', Little Mexico, Medford Italian, $Tree

64 NY 112, to Coram, Medford, N Mobil, USA Gas, Verizon, Cactus Cafe, DQ, Starbucks, Wingstop, 7-11, Lowe's, Michael's, Sam's Club, Target, TJ Maxx, Walgreens, S BP, BP, Sunoco/dsl, Carvel Creamery, Golden Star Chinese, J&R Steaks, Lola's Chinese, Victorious Pizza, Comfort Inn, Fairfield Inn, 7-11, AutoZone

63 NY 83, N Ocean Ave, N Mobil/dsl, Stop'n Shop/gas, Applebee's, Burger King, Dragos Pizza, McDonald's, Starbucks, Taco Bell, TGIFriday's, Hampton Inn, 7-11, CVS Drug, S BP/dsl, Gulf/dsl, Sonoma Grill, Holiday Inn

62 Nicolls Rd, rd 97, to Blue Point, Stony Brook, N Gulf, S Chili's, On the Border, Wendy's, Residence Inn

61 rd 19, to Patchogue, Holbrook, N Mobil, S BP/dsl, China 4, Golden Chicken Peruvian, Greek Islands Rest., Joe's Pizza/Pasta, New Century Chinese, Outback Steaks, Subway, 7-11, CVS Drug

CENTRAL ISLIP

60 Ronkonkoma Ave, N Amoco, USPO, S Mobil, Red Lobster, Smokey Bones BBQ, Courtyard, Homewood Suites

59 Ocean Ave, to Oakdale, Ronkonkoma, S BP/Dunkin', Sunoco, D'Matteos's Pizza, 7-11

58 Old Nichols Rd, Nesconset, N Mobil, Starbucks, Jake's 58 Hotel, BJ's Whse, Verizon, S Shell

57 NY 454, Vets Hwy, to Hauppauge, N BP/dsl, S BP, Mobil, Shell, Sunoco/Burger King, Dave&Buster's, Dunkin, Islandia Buffet, Subway, Hampton Inn, $Tree, 7-11, AT&T, Mavis Tire, Penske, TJ Maxx, Verizon, Walgreens, Walmart

56 NY 111, Smithtown, Islip, N BP/Dunkin', Tropical Smoothie, S Sunoco/dsl, Steve's Italian, Holiday Inn Express

55 rd 67, Motor Pkwy, Central Islip, N Mobil, Albert's Pizza, Burger King, Chipotle, Dunkin', IHOP, Jersey Mike's, Just Salad, Qdoba, Smoothie Hut, Starbucks, Subway, Tim Hortons, S Shell/dsl, 7-11

54 Wicks Rd

INTERSTATE 495 (Long Island) Cont'd

BABYLON

Exit #	Services
53	Sagkitos Pkwy, Bay Shore, Kings Park, Bayshore, N BP/7-11, Sunoco/Pizza Hut, Applebee's, Radisson, S Mobil
52	rd 4, Commack Rd, N Babylon, Commack, N BP, Cumberland Farms, Shell/dsl, Chick-fil-A, Dunkin, McDonald's, Premier Diner, Starbucks, Starbucks(2), Hampton Inn, Costco, Home Depot, Kohl's, Lowe's, Marshall's, ShopRite Mkt, Verizon, Walmart
51.5mm	LI Welcome Ctr eb, full facilities/parking area wb, litter barrels
51	NY 231, to Northport, Babylon
50	Bagatelle Rd, to Wyandanch
49N	NY 110 N, to Huntington, N Marriott
49S	NY 110 S, to Amityville
48	Round Swamp Rd, Old Bethpage, S Cumberland Farms/dsl, Starbucks, Hilton Garden, Homewood Suites, Sheraton, ShopRite, USPO
46	Sunnyside Blvd, Plainview, N Holiday Inn, S 7-11
45	Manetto Hill Rd, Plainview, Woodbury
44	NY 135, to Seaford, Syosset
43	S Oyster Bay Rd, to Syosset, Bethpage, N BP
42	Northern Pkwy, rd N, Hauppauge
41	NY 106, NY 107, Hicksville, Oyster Bay, N Buffalo Wild Wings, Starbucks, Whole Foods Mkt, CVS Drug, Marshalls, URGENT CARE, USPO, S BP, Mobil, Sunoco, Arby's, Blaze Pizza, Broadway Diner, Chick-fil-A, Chipotle, Cold Stone, Dunkin', Five Guys, McDonald's, On The Border, Red Lobster, Starbucks, Tikka Grill, $Tree, AT&T, Goodyear, IKEA, Mavis Tire, Target, Verizon
40	NY 25, Mineola, Syosset, S Gulf, Speedway/dsl, Burger King, DD Hibachi, Dunkin', Gyrolicious, KFC, McDonald's, Wendy's, Edgewood, Jericho Inn, 7-11, BMW, Chrysler/Dodge/Jeep, Home Depot, Kohl's, U-Haul
39	Glen Cove Rd, N Mobil, Kitchen Kabaret, CVS Drug
38	(from eb)Northern Pkwy E, Meadowbrook Pkwy, to Jones Beach
37	Willis Ave, to Roslyn, Mineola, N BP, Shell, Dunkin', Green Cactus Mexican, Skinny Pizza, Verizon, S Mobil/dsl
36	Searingtown Rd, to Port Washington, N H

MINEOLA

MANHASSET

Exit #	Services
35	Shelter Rock Rd, Manhasset
34	New Hyde Park Rd
33	Lakeville Rd, to Great Neck, N H
32	Little Neck Pkwy, N Shell/Burger King, Centre Pizza, Chipotle, Five Guys, Panera Bread, Starbucks, Petco
31	Douglaston Pkwy, S BP/service, Jade Asian, Joe's Pizza, USPO, vet
30	E Hampton Blvd, Cross Island Pkwy
29	Springfield Blvd, S BP/Dunkin', GNC, Starbucks
27	I-295, Clearview Expswy, Throgs Neck, N 7-11, Barney's, Blue Bay Diner
26	Francis Lewis Blvd
25	Utopia Pkwy, 188th St, N Citgo, Gas Sale, Mobil, Courtyard, Fairfield Inn, S Gas Sale/dsl, Mobil, Sunoco, Applebee's, Arby's, Blaze Pizza, Brother's Pizza, Burger King, Dunkin', Five Guys, Pizza Hut, Qdoba, Red Mango, Starbucks, Tim Hortons, Wyndham Garden, CVS Drug, Kohl's, USPO
24	Kissena Blvd, N BP/dsl, Dunkin', Subway, S Mobil
23	Main St, N Lake Pavilion, H
22	Grand Central Pkwy, to I-678, College Pt Blvd, N Gulf, Holiday Inn Express
21	108th St, N BP/7-11, Mobil, Dunkin, Holiday Inn Express, Louvre Hotel, S Exxon, D'Angelo's Pizza, Pizza Palace, Taco King
19	NY 25, Queens Blvd, Woodhaven Blvd, to Rockaways, N Applebee's, Cheesecake Factory, Dunkin, Haagen Daz, Halal Eats, KFC, Longhorn Steaks, Lulu's Pizza, Olive Garden, Popeyes, Shake Shack, White Castle, JC Penney, Macy's, Target, Verizon, S Mobil, Burger King, Chipotle, Dallas BBQ, Dunkin, Panera Bread, Starbucks, Starbucks, Subway, ALDI, Costco, CVS, Marshall's, PetCo, TJ Maxx, USPO
18.5	69th Ave, Grand Ave(from wb), S Dunkin, True Value, Walgreens
18	Maurice St, N Exxon/Dunkin'/dsl, Comfort Inn, dsl repair, S BP, Jersey Mike's, McDonald's, Smashburger, Super Bowl Chinese, Holiday Inn Express, Home Depot
17	48th St, to I-278, N Mobil, City View Inn, S Dunkin
16mm	I-495 begins/ends in NYC.

NY

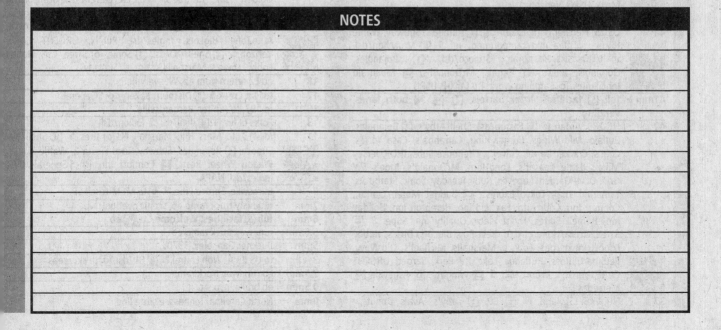

NORTH CAROLINA

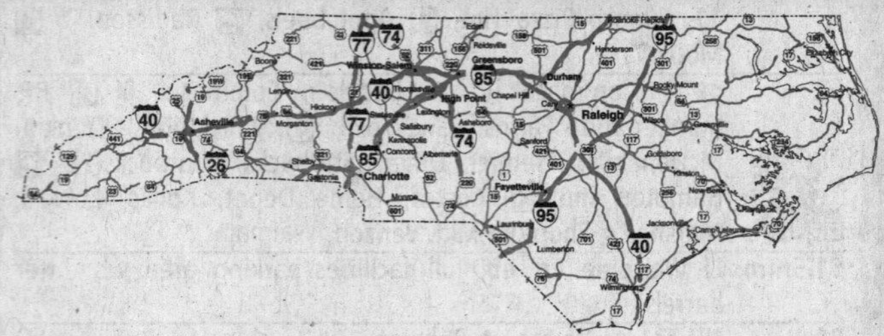

INTERSTATE 26

SALUDA / HENDERSONVILLE / ARDEN

Exit #	Services
71mm	North Carolina/South Carolina state line
69mm	N Pacolet River
67.5mm	**full facilities, litter barrels, , , Welcome Ctr wb**
67	US 74 E, to NC 108, Columbus, Tryon, N Shell/Fuji Express/dsl, Vgo/dsl, Bojangles, Cocula Mexican, Joy Wok, McDonald's, Subway, Taco Bell, Waffle House, Wendy's, Advance Parts, CVS Drug, Family$, Food Lion, URGENT CARE, S Exxon/dsl, KFC/Taco Bell, Mtn View Deli, Openroad Coffee, Columbus Inn, $General, H
59	Saluda, S BP/dsl, Marathon/Subway/EVC/dsl, AppleMill Outlet, Saluda Rest., Orchard Inn B&B(2mi), $General, Atkins Fruit, camping, repair, vet
56mm	Green River
54	US 25(from eb), to Greenville, E Flat Rock, to Carl Sandburg Home
53.5mm	2130 ft, Eastern Continental Divide
53	Upward Rd, Hendersonville, Dickey's, N Marathon/Dunkin/dsl, Waffle House, Zaxby's, Fairfield Inn, Mtn Inn&Suites, The Lodge, Bloomfields Giftshop, Lakewood RV Park, Wildflower RV Park, S Exxon/McDonald's, Shell/pizza, Bojangles, Boo Choo Thai, Cracker Barrel, Holiday Inn Express, Quality Inn, repair, to Carl Sandburg Home
49b a	US 64, Hendersonville, N Marathon/dsl, Shell/dsl, Sunoco/dsl, Chick-fil-A, Chipotle, CookOut, Dunkin, Golden Corral, Jack-in-the-Box, Kin's Kitchen, O'Charley's, Starbucks, Waffle House, Zaxby's, Best Western, Hampton Inn, Quality Inn, Ramada Inn, $Tree, Advance Parts, AutoZone, Ingles/gas, PetCo, Sam's Club/gas, Staples, Walmart, World of Clothing, S Exxon/dsl/LP, Shell/dsl, Applebee's, Arby's, Binion's Roadhouse, Bojangles, Burger King, China Buffet, Denny's, Hardee's, HoneyBaked Ham, KFC, Lon Sen Chinese, McDonald's, Outback Steaks, Panera Bread, Piggy's Ice Cream, Pizza Hut, Starbucks, Subway, Taco Bell, Tequila's Grill, Wendy's, Days Inn, EconoLodge, Red Roof Inn, ALDI, Belk, BigLots, Chrysler/Dodge/Jeep, CVS Drug, Home Depot, H, Lowe's, Mr. Tire/auto, NAPA, TJ Maxx, USPO, Verizon
46mm	weigh sta both lanes, ,
44	US 25, Fletcher, N Exxon/dsl, Hardee's, Subway, Waffle House, flea mkt/campground, vet, S Marathon/dsl, Shell/DQ/dsl/scales/24hr, Sunoco/dsl, Bojangles, Domino's, Joey's NY Bagels, McDonald's, Mountain Inn&Suites, Camping World RV Ctr, H, USPO
41mm	**full facilities, litter barrels, , , both lanes, vending**
40	NC 280, Arden, N Fastop/dsl, Shell/Arby's, Bojangles, Buffalo Wild Wings, Burger King, Carrabba's, Casa Torres, Chili's, Cracker Barrel, Culver's, Firehouse Subs, IHOP, Jersey Mike's, Little Caesar's, LongHorn, McDonald's, Moe's SW Grill, Olive Garden, Popeyes, Ruby Tuesday, Sonic, Starbucks, Tamarind Thai, Tokyo Express, Budget Motel, Clarion, Comfort Inn, Courtyard, Fairfield Inn, Hampton Inn, Holiday Inn, Home2 Suites, Hyatt Place, Quality Inn, Super 8, $Tree, Acura/Honda, ALDI, Best Buy, BigLots, Dick's, Hobby Lobby, Ingles/gas, Lowe's, Marshalls, Michael's, Old Navy, PetSmart, Ross, Rutledge Lake RV Park, Target, URGENT CARE, Verizon, World Mkt, S Wingate, Asheville , Mercedes
37	NC 146, Skyland, N BP, Arby's, Ava's Donuts,

SKYLAND / BARNARDSVILLE

Exit #	Services
37	Continued Bojangles, Brixx Pizza, Broken Egg Cafe, Coldstone, Fork Lore, Hickory Tavern, Luella's BBQ, McDonald's, PF Chang's, Starbucks, Waffle House, Which Wich, Yum Poke, Hilton, Barnes&Noble, BMW, CVS Drug, Ingles/gas, Lake Julian, REI, S Chevrolet
34mm	French Broad River
33	NC 191, Brevard Rd, N Asheville Farmers Mkt, Bear Creek RV Camp, Toyota, S HotSpot/dsl, Shell, Tesla EVC, Apollo Flame, Chipotle, Harbor Inn Seafood, LJ Silver, McDonald's, Papa's Mexican, Popeyes, Shogun Buffet, Stoneridge Grill, Taco Bell, Waffle House, Comfort Suites, Country Inn&Suites, Fairfield Inn, Hampton Inn, Hilton Garden/EVC, Holiday Inn Express, Rodeway Inn, Asheville Outlets, Dillards, Ingles Foods/dsl, Kia, PetCo, to Blue Ridge Pkwy, Verizon
31b a	I-40, E to Statesville, W to Knoxville
27mm	I-240 E, Patton Ave, I-26 and I-240 run together 3 mi. See NC I-240 exits 1-4
25	rd 251, N to UNCA
24	Elk Mtn Rd, Woodfin
23	Merrimon Ave, N Asheville, N EVC, Gulf/dsl, HotSpot, Bellagio Bistro, Bojangles, Frank's Pizza, LaRumba Mexica, Moe's BBQ, Days Inn, camping, vet
21	New Stock Rd, N Citgo/dsl, Shell, Domino's, Granny's Kitchen, Pizza Hut, Stoney Knob Cafe, $General, Campfire Lodge RV Park, CVS, Ingles/gas
19b a	N US 25, W US 70, Marshall, N Shell/dsl, Arby's, Bojangles, Burger King, Chapala Mexican, Firehouse Subs, Golden Wok, Hardee's, KFC, La Carreta Mexican, Little Caesars, McDonald's, Papa John's, Subway, Waffle House, Wendy's, Zaxby's, Fairfield, Advance Parts, ALDI, AutoZone, BigLots, Ingles/dsl, Publix, URGENT CARE, Verizon, S Shell/DQ/dsl, Sonic, $Tree, CVS, Hobby Lobby, Lowe's, Marshalls, Walmart/Subway
18	no EZ return from eb, Weaverville
17	to Flat Creek, S Discount Bakery, $General
15	rd 197, to Jupiter, Barnardsville
13	Forks of Ivy, N Shell/dsl, S Exxon/dsl
11	rd 213, to Mars Hill, Marshall, N tires, S Shell/dsl, Sunoco, Bojangles, Subway, Taco Fiesta 2, Waffle House, Wagon Wheel Rest., Comfort Inn, $General, CVS, Ingles/dsl, NAPA
9	Burnsville, Spruce Pine, N to Mt Mitchell SP
7mm	runaway truck ramp eb, scenic overlook wb
6mm	**full facilities, Welcome Ctr/ eb**
5.5mm	runaway truck ramp eb
5mm	Buckner Gap, elev. 3370
3	to US 23 A, Wolf Laurel, N BP/dsl, to ski areas
2.5mm	eb runaway truck ramp
0.5mm	eb brake insp sta
0mm	North Carolina/Tennessee state line

INTERSTATE 40

Exit #	Services
420mm	I-40 begins/ends at Wilmington, Carolina Ale House, Chili's, Jersey Mike's, Comfort Inn, Courtyard, Holiday Inn Express, $Tree, Chevrolet, Chrysler/Dodge/Jeep, Lowe's Foods, TJ Maxx, **N** Buffalo Wild Wings, Cici's Pizza, Clean Eatz, Cookout, CookOut, Crumbl Cookies, Domino's, Hiro Japanese Steaks, HoneyBaked Ham, Jimmy John's, Mission BBQ, Smoothie King, TX Roadhouse, Fairfield Inn, Hampton Inn, Home2 Suites, Suburban Studios, TownePlace, Best Buy, CarQuest, Home Depot, Hyundai, Kohl's, Land Rover, Nissan, Subaru, Suzuki, Toyota, Volvo, **S** BP/dsl, Exxon, Exxon/dsl, Murphy USA/dsl, Applebee's, Arby's, Bojangles, Bojangles, Capt'n Bill's Grill, Carrabba's, Checker's, Chick-fil-A, Church's TX Chicken, Cracker Barrel, Dunkin, Elizabeth's Pizza, Golden Corral, Hieronymus Seafood Co, Hooters, IHOP, Jason's Deli, Kickback Jack's, Little Caesar's, McAlister's Deli, McDonald's, McDonald's, Okami Japanese, Olive Garden, Outback Steaks, Panda Express, Sonic, Subway, Taco Bell, Taco Bell, Waffle House, Wendy's, Baymont Inn, Baymont Inn, Best Western+, Comfort Suites, Country Inn Suites, Days Inn, Extended Stay America, Hilton, Holiday Inn, MainStay Suites, Quality Inn, Red Roof Inn, Rodeway Inn, Sleep Inn, Staybridge Suites, Travel Inn, Wingate Inn, Academy, Advance Parts, AT&T, AutoZone, Batteries+, Black's Tires/auto, Buick, Cadillac, Costco/gas, Discount Tire, Food Lion, Harris-Teeter, Lowe's Whse, Old Navy, PetCo, PetSmart, Porsche/BMW, Ross, Sam's Club/gas, Staples, Target, to UNCW, URGENT CARE, Verizon, VW, Walgreens, Walmart
420b a	Gordon Rd, NC 132 N, **N** Shell/dsl, Tesla EVC, KOA(4mi), **S** BP/dsl, Circle K/dsl, Go Gas/dsl, Dunkin, McDonald's, Subway, Taco Bell, $General, Family$, Lowe's Foods, Walgreen
416b a	I-140, US 17, to Topsail Island, New Bern, Myrtle Beach
414	Holly Shelter Rd, to Brunswick Co beaches, Castle Hayne, **S** Circle K/dsl, GoGas/dsl, Buen Dia Mexican, Domino's, Hardee's, Hwy 55 Cafe, Subway, $General, CVS Drug, Fresh Foods IGA, USPO
413mm	NE Cape Fear River
408	NC 210, **N** Mack/Volvo/Isuzu, **S** Amoco/Freshway Cafe/dsl, Phoenix TC/Exxon/Subway/dsl/scales, Speedway/Wendy's/dsl, Hardee's, McDonald's, Advance Parts, Family$, Food Lion, to Moore's Creek Nat Bfd/camping, U-Haul, USPO
398	NC 53, Burgaw, **S** GOGAS/dsl, Shell/dsl, Bojangles, Hardee's, KFC, McDonald's, Subway, Taco Bell, Burgaw Motel, $Tree, Advance Parts, AutoZone, Food Lion, H, Walmart/gas
390	to US 117, Wallace
385	NC 41, Wallace, **N** Exxon/Village Subs, Tesla EVC, Bojangles, Mad Boar Rest., The Inn, Lake Leamon Camping, **S** Murphy USA/dsl, Speedway/dsl, Burger King, Domino's, McDonald's, Sensation Farmhouse Rest., Subway, Taco Bell, Wendy's, Zaxby's, $General, $Tree, Food Lion, O'Reilly Parts, Verizon, Walgreens, Walmart/Subway
384	NC 11, Wallace
380	Rose Hill, **S** BP/Subway/dsl(1mi), Marathon(1mi), Pure, Speedway, Family$
373	NC 24 E, NC 903, Magnolia, **N** BP/dsl, Exxon/dsl/e85, Cowan Museum, H
369	US 117, Warsaw
364	NC 24, to NC 50, Clinton, **full facilities, litter barrels, petwalk, both lanes, vending, N** Pilot/Arby's/Dunkin Donuts/dsl/24hr, **S** BP/dsl, Citgo, Tesla EVC,

CASTLE HAYNE

WALLACE

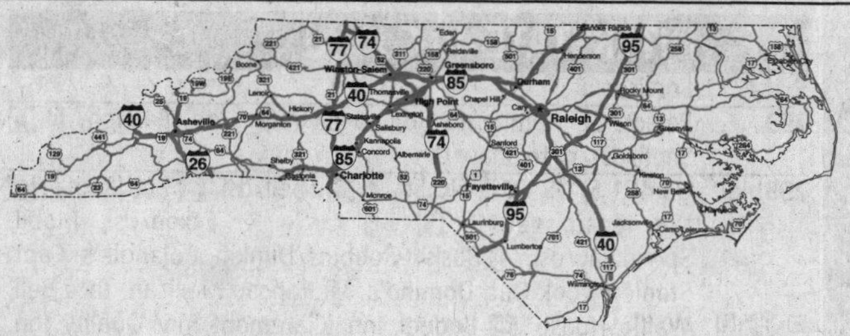

NEWTON GROVE

Exit #	Services
364	Continued Bojangles, Cookout, Jersey Mike's, KFC, McDonald's, Smithfield's BBQ, Starbucks, Taco Bell, Waffle House, Wendy's, Quality Inn, VIP Inn
355	NC 403, to US 117, Goldsboro, Faison, **N** Exxon
348	Suttontown Rd
343	US 701, Newton Grove, **N** Exxon/dsl, to Bentonville Bfd, Hardee's, Taco Rico, The Farm House Cafe, NAPA, USPO
341	NC 50, NC 55, to US 13, Newton Grove, **N** Exxon/dsl, Hardee's, Food Lion, **S** BP/McDonald's, Shell/Subway/dsl, Smithfield BBQ, Family Auto/tire
334	NC 96, Meadow, **S** Citgo/dsl, Meadow Village Rest., $General
328b a	I-95, N to Smithfield, S to Benson
325	NC 242, to US 301, to Benson, **S** Marathon/dsl
324mm	**full facilities, litter barrels, no overnight parking, petwalk, both lanes, vending**
319	NC 210, McGee's Crossroads, **N** BP/BBQ/dsl, Shell/Dunkin/dsl, Hardee's, McDonald's, Ms. B's Bake Shop, Waffle House, H, vet, **S** Mobil/dsl, Sheetz/dsl, Big Steve's Bagels, Bojangles, China Star, Domino's, Hwy 55 Burgers, KFC/Taco Bell, La Piazza, Subway, Wendy's, $General, AutoZone, CVS Drug, Food Lion, O'Reilly Parts
312	NC 42, to Clayton, Fuquay-Varina, **N** Murphy Express/dsl, Speedway/Wendy's/dsl, Tesla EVC, China King, Cookout, Cracker Barrel, Divano's Pizza, Domino's , Fiesta Mexicana, Hibachi&Co, Hwy 55 Burger, Jersey Mike's Subs, King Chinese, Panera Bread, Ruby Tuesday, Smithfield BBQ, Comfort Inn, Holiday Inn Express, Super 8, Woodspring Suites, $Tree, ALDI, JustTires, Lowe's, O'Reilly Parts, URGENT CARE, Verizon, Walmart/McDonald's, **S** 76/dsl, BP/Subway/dsl, Shell/dsl, Biscuitville, Bojangles, Dunkin, Jumbo China, KFC/Taco Bell, Little Caesar's, McDonald's, Snoopy's Hotdogs, Waffle House, Yummi Japan, Hampton Inn, Sleep Inn, Advance Parts , AutoZone, AutoZone, CVS Drug, Firestone, Food Lion, vet, Walgreens
309	US 70 E, Goldsboro, Smithfield
306b a	US 70 E bus, to Smithfield, Garner, Goldsboro, **N** Circle K/dsl, Citgo/dsl, Chrysler/Dodge/Jeep, **S** Sheetz/dsl, Alpaca Chicken, Blaze Pizza, Buffalo Bros Pizza, Buffalo Wild Wings, Carolina Alehouse, Chick-fil-A, Chili's, Chipotle, City BBQ, Coldstone, Demarios, Five Guys, La Cocina Mexican, Logan's Roadhouse, Longhorn Steaks, McDonald's, Mia Bistro, Moe's SW Grill, New Japan Express, Panera Bread, Red Robin, Starbucks, TGIFriday's, Tropical Smoothie, Wendy's, Zaxby's, $Tree, AT&T, Best Buy, BJ's Whse/gas, Burlington, Cabela's, Dick's, GNC, Kohl's, Michael's, PetSmart, Ross, Staples, Target, TJ Maxx, URGENT CARE, Verizon
303	Jones Sausage Rd, **N** Sheetz/dsl, Speedway/dsl, Bojangles, Burger King, Cookout, Smithfield BBQ, Subway, **S** Speedway/dsl
301	I-440 E, US 64/70 E, to Wilson
300b a	Rock Quarry Rd, **S** Exxon, Valero/dsl, Burger King, Domino's, Subway, Wang's Kitchen, Wingstop, Family$, Food Lion

= gas = food = lodging = other = rest stop

INTERSTATE 40 Cont'd

RALEIGH

Exit #	Services
299	Person St, Hammond Rd, no EZ return eb, Raleigh, N Shell/dsl, to Shaw U
298b a	US 401 S, US 70 E, NC 50, N Shell/dsl, Red Roof+, tire repair, vet, S BP, Circle K, Exxon/dsl, Mobil, Speedway/dsl, Baskin-Robbins/Dunkin, Bojangle's, Capt. Stanley, Cook Out, Domino's, Mi Rancho Mexican, Taco Bell, Waffle House, Budget Inn, Claremont Inn, Quality Inn, Super 8, AutoZone, Family$, Jiffy Lube, Meineke, O'Reilly Parts, Sam's Club/gas
297	Lake Wheeler Rd, N Exxon, Farmer's Mkt, S Marathon
295	Gorman St, N Exxon/dsl, Kangaroo, Hardee's, Subway, Holiday Inn Express, TownePlace, Family$, Food Lion, to NCSU, U-Haul, Walgreens, S Circle K
293	to I-440, US 1, US 64 W, Raleigh, S Exxon, Shell, Baker's Dozen, BJ's Rest., Carolina Ale, CAVA, Chick-fil-A, Chipotle, Coldstone, Cook-Out, First Watch, Good Harvest, HoneyBaked Ham, Jasmin, Jason's Deli, Jersey Mike's Subs, McDonald's, Moe's SW Grill, Noodle Boulevard, Noodles&Co, Olive Garden, Panera Bread, Red Lobster, Red Robin, Rey's, Seol Grille, Starbucks, Subway, Taco Addicts, Taco Bell, Thai Villa, The Shiny Diner, Topical Smoothie, Waffle House, Yopop Frozen Yogurt, Best Western, Courtyard, DoubleTree, Fairfield Inn, Hilton Garden, Holiday Inn, Homewood Suites, MainStay, Motel 6, Red Roof Inn, SpringHill Suites, Best Buy, BJ's Whse, Dick's, GNC, Hobby Lobby, Home Depot, Jiffy Lube, Kohl's, Lincoln, Lowe's, Marshalls, Mazda, Michael's, Office Depot, Old Navy, PetCo, PetSmart, REI, Ross, Target, Verizon, World Mkt
291	Cary Towne Blvd, Cary, S Mobil, Andia's Ice Cream, Dave & Buster's, DQ, Jersey Mike's, McDonald's, On-the-Border, Outback Steakhouse, Penn Sta Subs, Primo Pizza, Starbucks, AT&T, Firestone, Harris Teeter, vet, vet
290	NC 54, Cary, N Sheetz/dsl, McDonald's, Ole Time BBQ, Home2 Suites, Hyatt Place, Wingate Inn, S Quality Mart, Valero, Bojangles, Hampton Inn, Patel Brothers
289	to I-440, Wade Ave, to Raleigh, N Carter-Finley Stadium, H, museum, to fairgrounds
287	Harrison Ave, Cary, N to Wm B Umstead SP, S Circle K/dsl, Tesla EVC, Bonefish Grill, Burger King, BurgerFi, Chick-fil-A, Dame's Chicken & Waffle, First Watch, La Victoria Mexican, Lucky Chicken, McDonald's, Moe's SW Grill, NY Pizza, Ruth's Chris Steaks, Starbucks, Subway, Tropical Smoothie, Wendy's, YUMYUM Thai, Embassy Suites, Extended Stay America, TownePlace Suites, Umstead Hotel, Bass Pro Shops, Jiffy Lube, Mr Tire
285	Aviation Pkwy, to Morrisville, N Shell, Wayback Burgers, Hilton Garden, Raleigh/Durham
284	Airport Blvd, N Capital City Chophouse, Cambria Suites, Country Inn&Suites, Holiday Inn, Hyatt Place, Tru, to RDU, S Circle K/dsl, Mobil, Bojangles, Carmen's, Cracker Barrel, Hooters, Jersey Mike's, Los Tres Magueyes, TX Steaks, Waffle House, Wendy's, Days Inn, Extended Stay America, Fairfield Inn, Hampton Inn, Holiday Inn, Holiday Inn Express, La Quinta, Microtel, Quality Inn, Residence Inn, Sheraton, Sonesta, Staybridge Suites
283	I-540 E, toll I-540 W, to US 70, Aviation Pkwy, S Wayback Burgers, Home2 Suites, URGENT CARE, Walmart Supercenter
282	Page Rd, S Arby's, Bojangles, Burger King, Chipotle, Farmside Kitchen, Firehouse Subs, First Watch, Jimmy John's, McDonald's, Mez Cafe, Page Road Grill, Panera Bread, Starbucks, Comfort Suites, DoubleTree, Sheraton,
282	Continued Sleep Inn, SpringHill Suites, Wingate Inn, EVC, Office Depot, Office Depot
281	Miami Blvd, N Extended Stay America, Hilton Garden, Marriott, S BP, Shell/dsl, Carolina Donuts, Randy's Pizza, Subway, Tropical Smoothie, Wendy's, Zaxby's, Extended Stay America, Holiday Inn Express, Homewood Suites
280	Davis Dr, N to Research Triangle
279b a	NC 147 N, Triangle Expwy, to Durham, N H
278	NC 55, to NC 54, Apex, Foreign Trade Zone 93, N 76, Jimmy's Hotdogs, Mexicali Mexican, Waffle House, Comfort Inn, DoubleTree, EconoLodge, La Quinta, Red Roof Inn, S BP, EVC, Exxon/dsl, Mobil/dsl, Anissa's Spot, Arby's, BBQ Pit, Bojangles, Brigs Rest., Capt D's, Chick-fil-A, CookOut, El Dorado Mexican, Favor Desserts, Golden Corral, Hardee's, Little Caesar's, McDonald's, Papa John's, Pizza Hut, Popeyes, Starbucks, Subway, Taco Bell, Thai 55, Wendy's, William's Kitchen, Candlewood Suites, Extended Stay America, HomeTowne, Residence Inn, Sonesta, $Tree, AutoZone, BigLots, CVS Drug, Firestone/auto, Food Lion, Jiffy Lube, Morgan auto/tire, NAPA, O'Reilly Parts, Pep Boys, vet, Walgreens
276	Fayetteville Rd, N Circle K/dsl, Exxon, Exxon/Circle K/dsl, City BBQ, McDonald's, Melting Pot, Orient Garden, Waffle House, Wendy's, Harris Teeter/gas, Roses, Sprouts, to NC Central U, URGENT CARE, vet, Walgreens, S Barnes&Noble, Bufflo Wild Wings, CA Pizza Kitchen, Cheesecake Factory, Chili's, Chipotle, Cold Stone, Firebird's, First Watch, Fork-in-the-Road Cafe, Jersey Mike's, Los Tres Mexican, Maggiano's, Moe's SW Grill, Panera Bread, PF Chang's, Potbelly, Ruth's Chris Steaks, Starbucks, Ted's MT Grill, Hilton Garden, Acura, AT&T, Belk, Best Buy, Buick/Cadillac/GMC, Chevrolet/EVC, JC Penney, Macy's, Mercedes, Nordstrom, Old Navy, Porsche, REI, Subaru, World Mkt
274	NC 751, to Jordan Lake, N Circle K, EVC, Sheetz/dsl, Shell, Asian Kitchen, Burger King, Char Grill, Dunkin, Jimmy John's, KFC, Marco's Pizza, Menchie's, Salt N Cocoa, Taco Bell, Which Wich, Wing Stop, Advance Parts, CVS Drug, Food Lion, Harris Teeter, Honda, Lexus, URGENT CARE, vet, Volvo, Walgreens, S Circle K, Bonefish Grill, Bruster's, Chick-fil-A, Harvest 18, Jake's Pizzeria, Penn Sta Subs, Rise, Town Hall Burger, Fairfield Inn, Hyatt/EVC, ALDI, Michael's, PetCo, Target
273	NC 54, to Durham, UNC-Chapel Hill, N BP/dsl, S Circle K, Shell/dsl, Amante Pizza, Hardee's, Jersey Mike's, Nantucket Grill, New China, Courtyard(2mi), Hampton Inn, Holiday Inn Express
270	US 15, US 501, Chapel Hill, Durham, N Tesla EVC, Applebee's, Bella Italian, Bob Evans, Carrabba's, Chipotle, Duck Donuts, First Watch, Five Guys, Freddy's, Frozy, Jason's Deli, Jersey Mike's, Kanki Japanese, Moe's SW Grill, Namu, Noodle 501, NY Pizza, Outback Steaks, Panera Bread, Papa John's, PDQ, Peony Asian, Philly Steaks, Red Robin, Sister Liu's, Starbucks, Tandoori Bites, Comfort Inn, Home2 Suites, Homewood Suites/Tesla EVC, SpringHill Suites, Staybridge Suites, $Tree, AT&T, Barnes&Noble, Best Buy, Big Lots, Dick's, Ford, Home Depot, HS, Kia, Kohl's, Marshalls, Michael's, Old Navy, PetSmart, to Duke U, Verizon, vet, Walmart/Subway, S Exxon, Exxon, Alpaca Chicken, Bruegger's Bagel, Chipotle, Chopt Salad,

RALEIGH · CARY · UNC-CHAPEL HILL

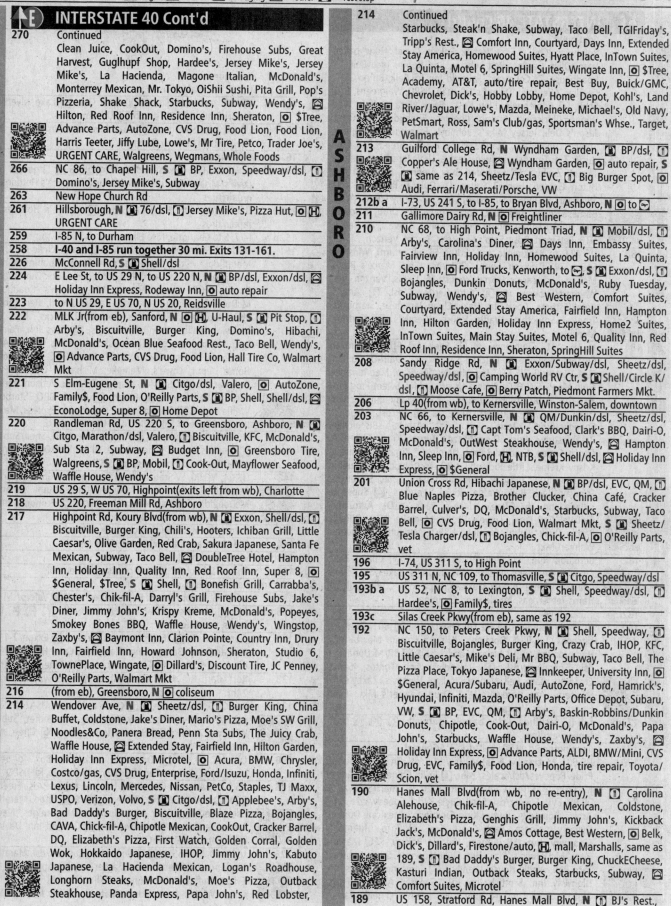

INTERSTATE 40 Cont'd

270 Continued
Clean Juice, CookOut, Domino's, Firehouse Subs, Great Harvest, Guglhupf Shop, Hardee's, Jersey Mike's, Jersey Mike's, La Hacienda, Magone Italian, McDonald's, Monterrey Mexican, Mr. Tokyo, OiShii Sushi, Pita Grill, Pop's Pizzeria, Shake Shack, Starbucks, Subway, Wendy's, Hilton, Red Roof Inn, Residence Inn, Sheraton, $Tree, Advance Parts, AutoZone, CVS Drug, Food Lion, Food Lion, Harris Teeter, Jiffy Lube, Lowe's, Mr Tire, Petco, Trader Joe's, URGENT CARE, Walgreens, Wegmans, Whole Foods

266 NC 86, to Chapel Hill, S BP, Exxon, Speedway/dsl, Domino's, Jersey Mike's, Subway

263 New Hope Church Rd

261 Hillsborough, N 76/dsl, Jersey Mike's, Pizza Hut, H, URGENT CARE

259 I-85 N, to Durham

258 **I-40 and I-85 run together 30 mi. Exits 131-161.**

226 McConnell Rd, S Shell/dsl

224 E Lee St, to US 29 N, to US 220 N, N BP/dsl, Exxon/dsl, Holiday Inn Express, Rodeway Inn, auto repair

223 to N US 29, E US 70, N US 20, Reidsville

222 MLK Jr(from eb), Sanford, N H, U-Haul, S Pit Stop, Arby's, Biscuitville, Burger King, Domino's, Hibachi, McDonald's, Ocean Blue Seafood Rest., Taco Bell, Wendy's, Advance Parts, CVS Drug, Food Lion, Hall Tire Co, Walmart Mkt

221 S Elm-Eugene St, N Citgo/dsl, Valero, AutoZone, Family$, Food Lion, O'Reilly Parts, S BP, Shell, Shell/dsl, EconoLodge, Super 8, Home Depot

220 Randleman Rd, US 220 S, to Greensboro, Ashboro, N Citgo, Marathon/dsl, Valero, Biscuitville, KFC, McDonald's, Sub Sta 2, Subway, Budget Inn, Greensboro Tire, Walgreens, S BP, Mobil, Cook-Out, Mayflower Seafood, Waffle House, Wendy's

219 US 29 S, W US 70, Highpoint(exits left from wb), Charlotte

218 US 220, Freeman Mill Rd, Ashboro

217 Highpoint Rd, Koury Blvd(from wb), N Exxon, Shell/dsl, Biscuitville, Burger King, Chili's, Hooters, Ichiban Grill, Little Caesar's, Olive Garden, Red Crab, Sakura Japanese, Santa Fe Mexican, Subway, Taco Bell, DoubleTree Hotel, Hampton Inn, Holiday Inn, Quality Inn, Red Roof Inn, Super 8, $General, $Tree, S Shell, Bonefish Grill, Carrabba's, Chester's, Chik-fil-A, Darryl's Grill, Firehouse Subs, Jake's Diner, Jimmy John's, Krispy Kreme, McDonald's, Popeyes, Smokey Bones BBQ, Waffle House, Wendy's, Wingstop, Zaxby's, Baymont Inn, Clarion Pointe, Country Inn, Drury Inn, Fairfield Inn, Howard Johnson, Sheraton, Studio 6, TownePlace, Wingate, Dillard's, Discount Tire, JC Penney, O'Reilly Parts, Walmart Mkt

216 (from eb), Greensboro, N coliseum

214 Wendover Ave, N Sheetz/dsl, Burger King, China Buffet, Coldstone, Jake's Diner, Mario's Pizza, Moe's SW Grill, Noodles&Co, Panera Bread, Penn Sta Subs, The Juicy Crab, Waffle House, Extended Stay, Fairfield Inn, Hilton Garden, Holiday Inn Express, Microtel, Acura, BMW, Chrysler, Costco/gas, CVS Drug, Enterprise, Ford/Isuzu, Honda, Infiniti, Lexus, Lincoln, Mercedes, Nissan, PetCo, Staples, TJ Maxx, USPO, Verizon, Volvo, S Citgo/dsl, Applebee's, Arby's, Bad Daddy's Burger, Biscuitville, Blaze Pizza, Bojangles, CAVA, Chick-fil-A, Chipotle Mexican, CookOut, Cracker Barrel, DQ, Elizabeth's Pizza, First Watch, Golden Corral, Golden Wok, Hokkaido Japanese, IHOP, Jimmy John's, Kabuto Japanese, La Hacienda Mexican, Logan's Roadhouse, Longhorn Steaks, McDonald's, Moe's Pizza, Outback Steakhouse, Panda Express, Papa John's, Red Lobster,

214 Continued
Starbucks, Steak'n Shake, Subway, Taco Bell, TGIFriday's, Tripp's Rest., Comfort Inn, Courtyard, Days Inn, Extended Stay America, Homewood Suites, Hyatt Place, InTown Suites, La Quinta, Motel 6, SpringHill Suites, Wingate Inn, $Tree, Academy, AT&T, auto/tire repair, Best Buy, Buick/GMC, Chevrolet, Dick's, Hobby Lobby, Home Depot, Kohl's, Land River/Jaguar, Lowe's, Mazda, Meineke, Michael's, Old Navy, PetSmart, Ross, Sam's Club/gas, Sportsman's Whse., Target, Walmart

213 Guilford College Rd, N Wyndham Garden, BP/dsl, Copper's Ale House, Wyndham Garden, auto repair, S same as 214, Sheetz/Tesla EVC, Big Burger Spot, Audi, Ferrari/Maserati/Porsche, VW

212b a I-73, US 241 S, to I-85, to Bryan Blvd, Ashboro, N to

211 Gallimore Dairy Rd, N Freightliner

210 NC 68, to High Point, Piedmont Triad, N Mobil/dsl, Arby's, Carolina's Diner, Days Inn, Embassy Suites, Fairview Inn, Holiday Inn, Homewood Suites, La Quinta, Sleep Inn, Ford Trucks, Kenworth, to , S Exxon/dsl, Bojangles, Dunkin Donuts, McDonald's, Ruby Tuesday, Subway, Wendy's, Best Western, Comfort Suites, Courtyard, Extended Stay America, Fairfield Inn, Hampton Inn, Hilton Garden, Holiday Inn Express, Home2 Suites, InTown Suites, Main Stay Suites, Motel 6, Quality Inn, Red Roof Inn, Residence Inn, Sheraton, SpringHill Suites

208 Sandy Ridge Rd, N Exxon/Subway/dsl, Sheetz/dsl, Speedway/dsl, Camping World RV Ctr, S Shell/Circle K/dsl, Moose Cafe, Berry Patch, Piedmont Farmers Mkt.

206 Lp 40(from wb), to Kernersville, Winston-Salem, downtown

203 NC 66, to Kernersville, N QM/Dunkin/dsl, Sheetz/dsl, Speedway/dsl, Capt Tom's Seafood, Clark's BBQ, Dairi-O, McDonald's, OutWest Steakhouse, Wendy's, Hampton Inn, Sleep Inn, Ford, H, NTB, S Shell/dsl, Holiday Inn Express, $General

201 Union Cross Rd, Hibachi Japanese, N BP/dsl, EVC, QM, Blue Naples Pizza, Brother Clucker, China Café, Cracker Barrel, Culver's, DQ, McDonald's, Starbucks, Subway, Taco Bell, CVS Drug, Food Lion, Walmart Mkt, S Sheetz/Tesla Charger/dsl, Bojangles, Chick-fil-A, O'Reilly Parts, vet

196 I-74, US 311 S, to High Point

195 US 311 N, NC 109, to Thomasville, S Citgo, Speedway/dsl

193b a US 52, NC 8, to Lexington, S Shell, Speedway/dsl, Hardee's, Family$, tires

193c Silas Creek Pkwy(from eb), same as 192

192 NC 150, to Peters Creek Pkwy, N Shell, Speedway, Biscuitville, Bojangles, Burger King, Crazy Crab, IHOP, KFC, Little Caesar's, Mike's Deli, Mr BBQ, Subway, Taco Bell, The Pizza Place, Tokyo Japanese, Innkeeper, University Inn, $General, Acura/Subaru, Audi, AutoZone, Ford, Hamrick's, Hyundai, Infiniti, Mazda, O'Reilly Parts, Office Depot, Subaru, VW, S BP, EVC, QM, Arby's, Baskin-Robbins/Dunkin Donuts, Chipotle, Cook-Out, Dairi-O, McDonald's, Papa John's, Starbucks, Waffle House, Wendy's, Zaxby's, Holiday Inn Express, Advance Parts, ALDI, BMW/Mini, CVS Drug, EVC, Family$, Food Lion, Honda, tire repair, Toyota/Scion, vet

190 Hanes Mall Blvd(from wb, no re-entry), N Carolina Alehouse, Chik-fil-A, Chipotle Mexican, Coldstone, Elizabeth's Pizza, Genghis Grill, Jimmy John's, Kickback Jack's, McDonald's, Amos Cottage, Best Western, Belk, Dick's, Dillard's, Firestone/auto, H, mall, Marshalls, same as 189, S Bad Daddy's Burger, Burger King, ChuckECheese, Kasturi Indian, Outback Steaks, Starbucks, Subway, Comfort Suites, Microtel

189 US 158, Stratford Rd, Hanes Mall Blvd, N BJ's Rest.,

INTERSTATE 40 Cont'd

WINSTON-SALEM

189 Continued
Bojangles, Chili's, First Watch, Golden Corral, Honeybaked Ham, Olive Garden, Red Lobster, Red Robin, Taco Bell, TX Roadhouse, Courtyard, Fairfield Inn, Belk, Buick/GMC, Cadillac, Chevrolet, Dillard's, H, mall, USPO, Walgreens, S Shell, Applebee's, Bleu Rest., Brixx Pizza, Buffalo Wild Wings, Chick-fil-A, Crumbl Cookies, Firebirds, Five Guys, Jason's Deli, Jersey Mike's, Johnny's Farmhouse, Longhorn Steaks, Luna Playa, Mario's Pizza, Panera Bread, Red Crab Juicy, Tin Tin Asian, Twin Peaks, Umi Japanese, Village Tavern, Zaxby's, Extended Stay America, Hampton Inn, Hilton Garden, Home2 Suites, La Quinta, Residence Inn, Sleep Inn, SpringHill Suites, $Tree, Academy Sports, AT&T, Barnes&Noble, Best Buy, Costco/gas, CVS Drug, Discount Tire, Hobby Lobby, Home Depot, Kohl's, Lowe's, Michael's, NTB, PetSmart, Ross, Sam's Club/gas, Target, Verizon

188 US 421, to Yadkinville, to WFU(no EZ wb return), Winston-Salem, N Exxon, Shell, Burger King, Marco's Pizza, McDonald's, Zack's Frozen Yogurt, Lexus, Verizon, vet, Walmart/Subway, S Citgo/Circle K/dsl, Arby's, Breakfasttime, Cook-Out, HakkaChow Japanese, Starbucks, Tropical Smoothie, Waffle House, Wendy's, CarMax, Mercedes

184 to US 421, Clemmons, N Shell, Abbott's Frozen Custard, Applebee's, Chicken Salad Chick, Dairi-O, Dunkin, First Watch, IHOP, KFC, Los Muelles Mexican, Mediterraneo Grill, Moe's SW Grill, Panera Bread, Publix, Sweet Frog Fro-Yo, The Habit, Toyko Hibachi , Holiday Inn Express, Quality Inn, URGENT CARE, S BP/dsl, Circle K, Speedway/dsl, Tesla EVC, Arby's, Biscuitville, Breakfastime, Brick Oven Pizza, Burger King, Chik-fil-A, Clutch Coffee, Cracker Barrel, Domino's, Kimono Japanese, Krispy Kreme, Little Richard's BBQ, McDonald's, Mi Pueblo Mexican, Ruby Tuesday, Sam's Ice Cream, Sonic, Starbucks, Subway, Taco Bell, Waffle House, Wendy's, Super 8, Village Inn, $Tree, Advance Parts, ALDI, AutoZone, BigLots, CVS Drug, Lowe's Foods, Meineke, NTB, O'Reilly Parts, Qwik Lube, Staples, USPO, Verizon, Walgreens, Walmart Mkt

NC

TANGLEWOOD

182 Bermuda Run, Tanglewood, N H, S Chang Thai, Cindy's Creamery, Jersey Mike's, Joe's Take Out, Lee's Chinese, Monte De Rey Mexican, Papa John's, Villa Grill, Harris-Teeter/gas, Tanglewood Camping

182mm Yadkin River

180 NC 801, Tanglewood, N Sheetz/dsl, 801 Southern Kitchen, Chik-fil-A, Domino's, KJ's, La Carreta Mexican, Hampton Inn, H, Lowe's Foods/dsl, S BP/McDonald's/dsl, Speedway/dsl, Bojangles, Los Toritos, Sam's Creamery, Taco Bell, Venezia Italian, Wendy's, Zaxby's, $General, Ace Hardware, CVS Drug, Farmer's Mkt., Food Lion, tires, vet, Walgreens

177mm full facilities, litter barrels, petwalk, both lanes, vending

174 Farmington Rd, N Shell/dsl, $General

170 US 601, Mocksville, N Murphy USA/dsl, TA/Shell/Country Pride/Popeyes/dsl/scales/24hr, JinJin Chinese, La Carreta Mexican, $Tree, Campers Inn RV Ctr, Walmart/Subway, S BP, EVC, Sheetz/dsl, Shell/Circle K/dsl, Speedway/dsl, Arby's, Bojangles, Burger King, Domingo's Mexican, Dunkin, Dynasty Chinese, East Coast Grill, El Taco, Huffman's Creamery, Hwy 55 Burgers, Ketchie Bakery, KFC, Marco's Pizza, McDonald's, Pizza Hut, Shiki Japanese, Sonic, Subway, Taco Bell, Waffle House, Wendy's, Comfort Inn, Days Inn, HighWay Inn, Scottish Inn, $General, Advance Parts, BigLots, Food Lion, H, Jiffy Lube, Lowe's, O'Reilly Parts,

COOL SPRINGS

170 Continued
USPO, vet, Walgreens

168 US 64, to Mocksville, N Pure Gas, Lake Myers RV Resort(3mi), S BP/dsl, H, U-Haul

162 US 64, Cool Springs, N Lake Myers RV Resort(5mi), S Shell/dsl, Midway Camping

161mm S Yadkin River

154 to US 64, Old Mocksville Rd, N H, S Citgo/dsl, EVC, Love's/McDonald's/dsl/scales/24hr, Jaybee's Hotdogs, repair/tires

153 US 64(from eb), S Citgo/dsl, Jaybee's Hotdogs, repair/tires

152b a I-77, S to Charlotte, N to Elkin

151 US 21, E Statesville, N 7-11, EVC, Exxon/Circle K/DQ/dsl, Marathon, Applebee's, Baskin-Robbins/Dunkin', Bojangles, Chick-fil-A, Chili's, Chipotle, Cook-Out, Cracker Barrel, IHOP, Jersey Mike's, KFC, Logan's Roadhouse, McDonald's, Mi Pueblo Café, Panera Bread, Red Lobster, Shiki Japanese, Sorrento's Italian, Starbucks, Taco Bell, Vesuvio's Italian, Wendy's, Zaxby's, Days Inn, Fairfield Inn, Sleep Inn, $Tree, Advance Parts, ALDI, AT&T AutoZone, BigLots, Chevrolet, CVS Drug, GNC, Hobby Lobby, Home Depot, Lowe's, Meineke, Michael's, O'Reilly Parts, PetSmart, Publix, Staples, Staples, TJ Maxx, Verizon, Verizon Walmart/Subway, S Exxon, Greg's BBQ, Starbucks Waffle House, Clarion Pointe, Holiday Inn Express, Master Inn, $General, H, Ingles/gas, URGENT CARE

150 NC 115, Statesville, N BP/dsl, Sheetz/dsl, Shell/Subway Amalfi's Italian, Coffee House, Ol'Bob's BBQ, $General CVS Drug, Food Lion, museum, S $Tree

148 US 64, NC 90, W Statesville, N Citgo/dsl, Shell, Arby's Bojangles, BoxCar Grille, Burger King, Katana Japanese McDonald's, Subway, Village Inn Pizza, Economy Inn, $General, CVS Drug, Ingles Foods

146 Stamey Farm Rd, N truck repair, U-Haul

144 Old Mountain Rd, S BP/dsl, Shell/dsl

143mm weigh sta both lanes

CLAREMONT

141 Sharon School Rd, N Citgo/dsl, $General

140mm Catawba River

138 NC 10 W, Oxford School Rd, to Catawba, N Valero/dsl

136mm full facilities, litter barrels, petwalk, both lanes, vending

135 Claremont, N 76, Marley's Pizza, S Exxon/7-11, BoxCar Grille, Burger King, Claremont Cafe, Hannah's BBQ Hardee's, Subway, Claremont Inn, $General, RV Ctr, tir

133 Rock Barn Rd, N Shell/dsl, S Pilot/Subway/dsl/scales 24hr

132 to NC 16, Taylorsville, N Circle K, Murphy USA/dsl, Shel dsl, Burger King, Hwy 55 Cafe, Jin's Buffet, Subwa Wendy's, Zaxby's, Holiday Inn Express, $Tree, AT& AutoZone, Walmart

130 Old US 70, N Domino's, Jack-in-the-Box, repa Verizon, S Citgo, Pure, 1877 Pub & Grub, USPO

128 US 321, Fairgrove Church Rd, Hickory, N BP/dsl, Freedo McDonald's, Waffle House, H, S Citgo, Maratho dsl, Sheetz, Casa Azul Mexican, Dos Amigos, Naga Japanese, Souper Bites, Wendy's, Comfort Inn, Days In to Catawba Valley Coll

126 to US 70, NC 155, S Circle K/Little Caesars/dsl, Maratho Dunkin/dsl, Sheetz/Tesla Charger/dsl, Applebee's, B Evans, Buffalo Wild Wings, Chili's, Crumbl Cookies, E Coast Wings, Harbor Inn Seafood, IHOP, Jason's Deli

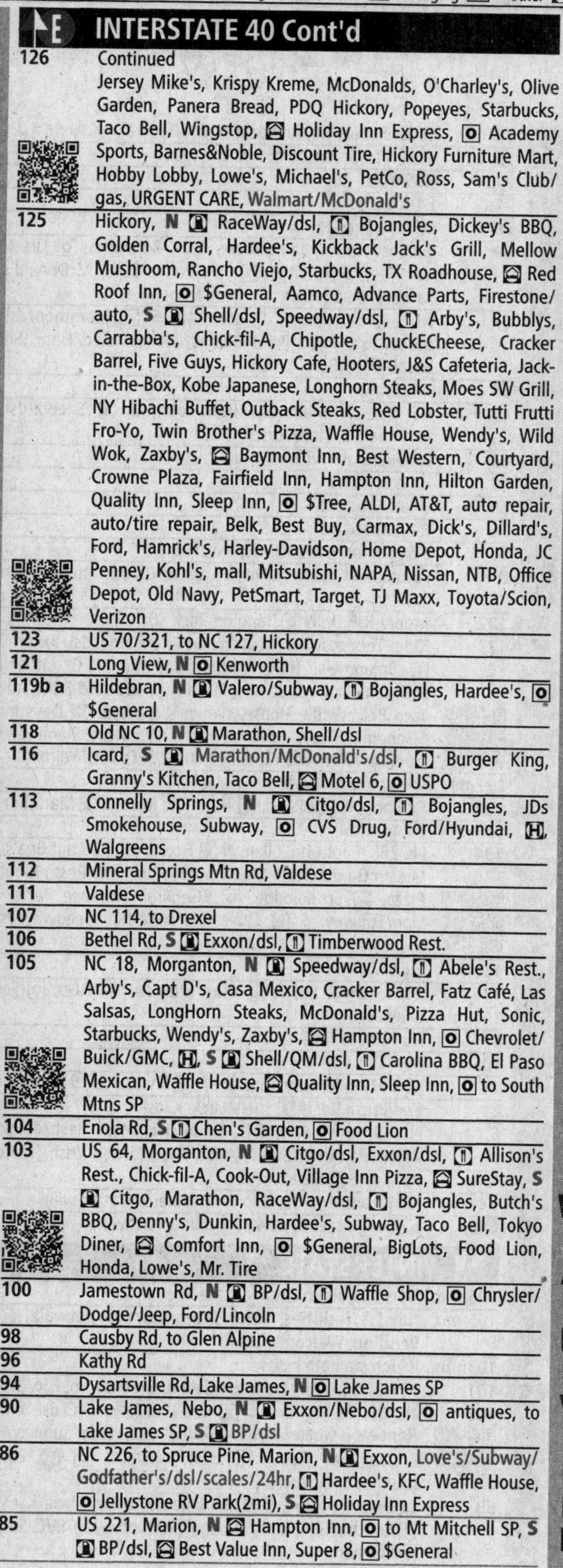

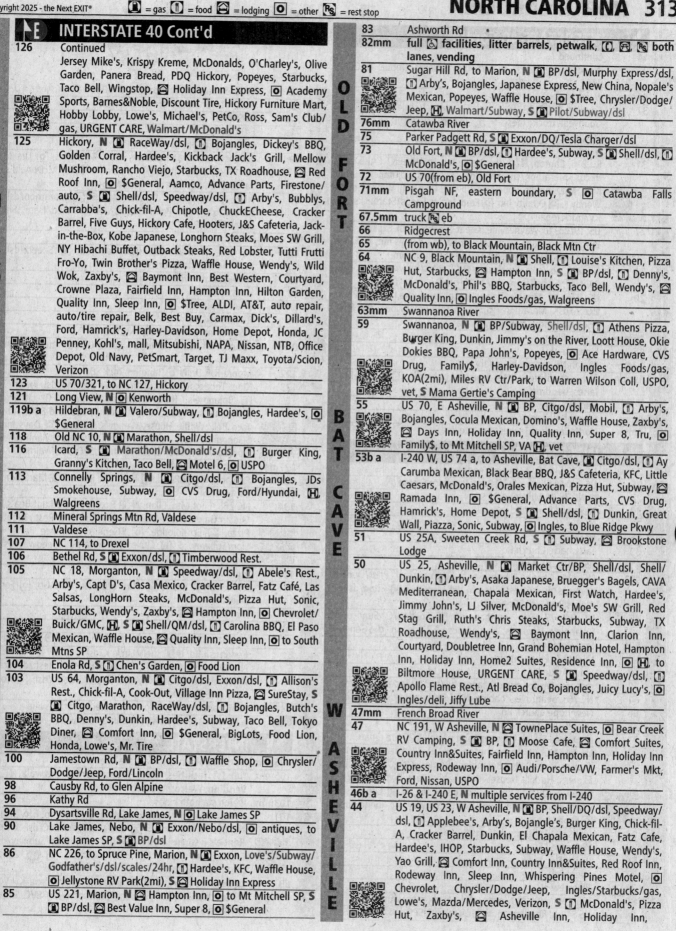

INTERSTATE 40 Cont'd

HICKORY

126 Continued
Jersey Mike's, Krispy Kreme, McDonalds, O'Charley's, Olive Garden, Panera Bread, PDQ Hickory, Popeyes, Starbucks, Taco Bell, Wingstop, Holiday Inn Express, Academy Sports, Barnes&Noble, Discount Tire, Hickory Furniture Mart, Hobby Lobby, Lowe's, Michael's, PetCo, Ross, Sam's Club/gas, URGENT CARE, Walmart/McDonald's

125 Hickory, N RaceWay/dsl, Bojangles, Dickey's BBQ, Golden Corral, Hardee's, Kickback Jack's Grill, Mellow Mushroom, Rancho Viejo, Starbucks, TX Roadhouse, Red Roof Inn, $General, Aamco, Advance Parts, Firestone/auto, S Shell/dsl, Speedway/dsl, Arby's, Bubblys, Carrabba's, Chick-fil-A, Chipotle, ChuckECheese, Cracker Barrel, Five Guys, Hickory Cafe, Hooters, J&S Cafeteria, Jack-in-the-Box, Kobe Japanese, Longhorn Steaks, Moes SW Grill, NY Hibachi Buffet, Outback Steaks, Red Lobster, Tutti Frutti Fro-Yo, Twin Brother's Pizza, Waffle House, Wendy's, Wild Wok, Zaxby's, Baymont Inn, Best Western, Courtyard, Crowne Plaza, Fairfield Inn, Hampton Inn, Hilton Garden, Quality Inn, Sleep Inn, $Tree, ALDI, AT&T, auto repair, auto/tire repair, Belk, Best Buy, Carmax, Dick's, Dillard's, Ford, Hamrick's, Harley-Davidson, Home Depot, Honda, JC Penney, Kohl's, mall, Mitsubishi, NAPA, Nissan, NTB, Office Depot, Old Navy, PetSmart, Target, TJ Maxx, Toyota/Scion, Verizon

123 US 70/321, to NC 127, Hickory

121 Long View, N Kenworth

119b a Hildebran, N Valero/Subway, Bojangles, Hardee's, $General

ICARD

118 Old NC 10, N Marathon, Shell/dsl

116 Icard, S Marathon/McDonald's/dsl, Burger King, Granny's Kitchen, Taco Bell, Motel 6, USPO

113 Connelly Springs, N Citgo/dsl, Bojangles, JDs Smokehouse, Subway, CVS Drug, Ford/Hyundai, H, Walgreens

112 Mineral Springs Mtn Rd, Valdese

111 Valdese

107 NC 114, to Drexel

106 Bethel Rd, S Exxon/dsl, Timberwood Rest.

MORGANTON

105 NC 18, Morganton, N Speedway/dsl, Abele's Rest., Arby's, Capt D's, Casa Mexico, Cracker Barrel, Fatz Café, Las Salsas, LongHorn Steaks, McDonald's, Pizza Hut, Sonic, Starbucks, Wendy's, Zaxby's, Hampton Inn, Chevrolet/Buick/GMC, H, S Shell/QM/dsl, Carolina BBQ, El Paso Mexican, Waffle House, Quality Inn, Sleep Inn, to South Mtns SP

104 Enola Rd, S Chen's Garden, Food Lion

103 US 64, Morganton, N Citgo/dsl, Exxon/dsl, Allison's Rest., Chick-fil-A, Cook-Out, Village Inn Pizza, SureStay, S Citgo, Marathon, RaceWay/dsl, Bojangles, Butch's BBQ, Denny's, Dunkin, Hardee's, Subway, Taco Bell, Tokyo Diner, Comfort Inn, $General, BigLots, Food Lion, Honda, Lowe's, Mr. Tire

100 Jamestown Rd, N BP/dsl, Waffle Shop, Chrysler/Dodge/Jeep, Ford/Lincoln

98 Causby Rd, to Glen Alpine

96 Kathy Rd

MARION

94 Dysartsville Rd, Lake James, N Lake James SP

90 Lake James, Nebo, N Exxon/Nebo/dsl, antiques, to Lake James SP, S BP/dsl

86 NC 226, to Spruce Pine, Marion, N Exxon, Love's/Subway/Godfather's/dsl/scales/24hr, Hardee's, KFC, Waffle House, Jellystone RV Park(2mi), S Holiday Inn Express

85 US 221, Marion, N Hampton Inn, to Mt Mitchell SP, S BP/dsl, Best Value Inn, Super 8, $General

OLD FORT

83 Ashworth Rd

82mm **full facilities, litter barrels, petwalk, both lanes, vending**

81 Sugar Hill Rd, to Marion, N BP/dsl, Murphy Express/dsl, Arby's, Bojangles, Japanese Express, New China, Nopale's Mexican, Popeyes, Waffle House, $Tree, Chrysler/Dodge/Jeep, H, Walmart/Subway, S Pilot/Subway/dsl

76mm Catawba River

75 Parker Padgett Rd, S Exxon/DQ/Tesla Charger/dsl

73 Old Fort, N BP/dsl, Hardee's, Subway, S Shell/dsl, McDonald's, $General

72 US 70(from eb), Old Fort

71mm Pisgah NF, eastern boundary, S Catawba Falls Campground

67.5mm truck eb

66 Ridgecrest

BAT CAVE

65 (from wb), to Black Mountain, Black Mtn Ctr

64 NC 9, Black Mountain, N Shell, Louise's Kitchen, Pizza Hut, Starbucks, Hampton Inn, S BP/dsl, Denny's, McDonald's, Phil's BBQ, Starbucks, Taco Bell, Wendy's, Quality Inn, Ingles Foods/gas, Walgreens

63mm Swannanoa River

59 Swannanoa, N BP/Subway, Shell/dsl, Athens Pizza, Burger King, Dunkin, Jimmy's on the River, Loott House, Okie Dokies BBQ, Papa John's, Popeyes, Ace Hardware, CVS Drug, Family$, Harley-Davidson, Ingles Foods/gas, KOA(2mi), Miles RV Ctr/Park, to Warren Wilson Coll, USPO, vet, S Mama Gertie's Camping

55 US 70, E Asheville, N BP, Citgo/dsl, Mobil, Arby's, Bojangles, Cocula Mexican, Domino's, Waffle House, Zaxby's, Days Inn, Holiday Inn, Quality Inn, Super 8, Tru, Family$, to Mt Mitchell SP, VA H, vet

53b a I-240 W, US 74 a, to Asheville, Bat Cave, Citgo/dsl, Ay Carumba Mexican, Black Bear BBQ, J&S Cafeteria, KFC, Little Caesars, McDonald's, Orales Mexican, Pizza Hut, Subway, Ramada Inn, $General, Advance Parts, CVS Drug, Hamrick's, Home Depot, S Shell/dsl, Dunkin, Great Wall, Piazza, Sonic, Subway, Ingles, to Blue Ridge Pkwy

51 US 25A, Sweeten Creek Rd, S Subway, Brookstone Lodge

W ASHEVILLE

50 US 25, Asheville, N Market Ctr/BP, Shell/dsl, Shell/Dunkin, Arby's, Asaka Japanese, Bruegger's Bagels, CAVA Mediterranean, Chapala Mexican, First Watch, Hardee's, Jimmy John's, LJ Silver, McDonald's, Moe's SW Grill, Red Stag Grill, Ruth's Chris Steaks, Starbucks, Subway, TX Roadhouse, Wendy's, Baymont Inn, Clarion Inn, Courtyard, Doubletree Inn, Grand Bohemian Hotel, Hampton Inn, Holiday Inn, Home2 Suites, Residence Inn, H, to Biltmore House, URGENT CARE, S Speedway/dsl, Apollo Flame Rest., Atl Bread Co, Bojangles, Juicy Lucy's, Ingles/deli, Jiffy Lube

47mm French Broad River

47 NC 191, W Asheville, N TownePlace Suites, Bear Creek RV Camping, S BP, Moose Cafe, Comfort Suites, Country Inn&Suites, Fairfield Inn, Hampton Inn, Holiday Inn Express, Rodeway Inn, Audi/Porsche/VW, Farmer's Mkt, Ford, Nissan, USPO

46b a I-26 & I-240 E, N multiple services from I-240

44 US 19, US 23, W Asheville, N BP, Shell/DQ/dsl, Speedway/dsl, Applebee's, Arby's, Bojangle's, Burger King, Chick-fil-A, Cracker Barrel, Dunkin, El Chapala Mexican, Fatz Cafe, Hardee's, IHOP, Starbucks, Subway, Waffle House, Wendy's, Yao Grill, Comfort Inn, Country Inn&Suites, Red Roof Inn, Rodeway Inn, Sleep Inn, Whispering Pines Motel, Chevrolet, Chrysler/Dodge/Jeep, Ingles/Starbucks/gas, Lowe's, Mazda/Mercedes, Verizon, S McDonald's, Pizza Hut, Zaxby's, Asheville Inn, Holiday Inn,

NC

= gas = food = lodging = other = rest stop

INTERSTATE 40 Cont'd

CANTON

Exit	Services
44	Continued Woodspring Suites, CVS Drug, Home Depot, URGENT CARE
41mm	weigh sta both lanes
37	Candler, N BP, TA/Country Pride/dsl/scales/24hr/@, Goodyear/truck tires, S Exxon/dsl, Days Inn, $General, KOA
33	Newfound Rd, to US 74, S Exxon
31	Rd 215, Canton, N Best Value Inn, URGENT CARE, S BP/dsl, Marathon/DQ, Shell/dsl, Arby's, Bojangles, Burger King, McDonald's, Popeyes, Subway, Taco Bell, Waffle House, Wendy's, Quality Inn, Ford, Ingles Foods/Starbucks/dsl, RV/truck repair
27	US 19/23, to Waynesville, Great Smokey Mtn Expswy, S Burger King, Coffee Cup Cafe, Subway, Days Inn, $Tree, $Tree, Food Lion, GNC, H, Lowe's, to WCU(25mi)
24	NC 209, to Lake Junaluska, N Pilot/Subway/dsl/scales/24hr/@, S Shell/cafe/dsl/24hr, H
20	US 276, to Maggie Valley, Lake Junaluska, S BP/dsl, Exxon/dsl, Marathon, $General, Creekwood RV Park, Pride RV Resort, Winngray RV Park

HARMON DEN

Exit	Services
16mm	Pigeon River
15	Fines Creek
13mm	Pisgah NF eastern boundary
10mm	**full facilities, litter barrels, petwalk, both lanes, vending**
7	Harmon Den
4mm	tunnel both lanes
0mm	North Carolina/Tennessee state line

INTERSTATE 74

Exit	Services
23	US 220 S, I-70/73 begins/ends
25	US 220 N, Ellerbe, N Berry Patch Ice Cream
28	to NC 73 W, Millstone Rd
30	Haywood Parker Rd
33	NC 73
35	Norman
39	Tabernacle Church Rd
41	US 220 S, US 220 A N, Candor
44	NC 211, Candor, Pinehurst, N Exxon/dsl, Pilot/Dunkin/Wendy's/dsl/scales/24hr, dsl repair, S Citgo/dsl, Blakes Rest., $General
49	NC 24, 27, Troy, Carthage, S Shell/EVC, Sunoco, Bojangle's, Hardee's, Waffle House, Day Inn, $General
52	Star, Robbins
56	US 220 A, Ether, Steeds
58	Black Ankle Rd
60	rest area/visitor ctr both lanes, full(handicapped)facilities
61	NC 705, Seagrove, Robbins, N Sunoco/Hardee's/dsl
66	New Hope Church Rd
68	US 220, NC 134, Ulah, Troy
71	McDowell Rd, N Exxon, st patrol, S tire repair
72b a	US 64, NC 49, To Lexington , N BP, Speedway/dsl, Arby's, Biscuitville, Bojangles, Burger King, Dairi-O, Dixie Express, Huddle House, McDonald's, Taco Bell, Wendy's, Motel 6, Quality Inn, Lowe's Foods, S Citgo/dsl, Coach's Grill, Glaze King Donuts, Subway, Randolph Inn, Food Lion
74	(exits left)Salisbury St, Sunset Ave
75	W Presnell St
76	Vision Dr
77	Spero Rd
79	Pineview St
86	(80 from wb)I-73 N(exits left from eb, runs with I-74)
84	US 311 S, Randleman, S Citgo, USPO
79	Cedar Square Rd, Archdale, S $General
75	I-85, N to Greensboro, S to Charlotte
71b	I-85BR, US 29
71a	E Green St
70	MLK Dr, S H
69	Greensboro Rd, Jamestown, N Bojangles, Tire Max/auto, vet, S Citgo, Five Points Subs, McDonald's, Family$, Pineda Tire
67	NC 68, Eastchester Dr, to I-40, S Marathon/dsl, Barbarito's, High Point Bagles, Honeybaked Ham, Shinko Sushi, URGENT CARE
66	Johnson St
65	US 311, N Main St, High Point, S Sheetz/dsl, McDonald's, Starbucks, ALDI
63	NC 66, Kernersville
60	High Point Rd
59	Union Cross Rd
56	Ridgewood Rd
55	I-74 begins/ends on I-40, exit 196
0	Future I-74 connects via US 52 to US 311 around Winston Salem
122	Moore-RJR Dr, N Hanging Rock SP
123	King, Tobaccoville, N Circle K/Kangaroo/dsl, Exxon/7-11 Bojangle's, Burger King, CookOut, KFC, Little Italy McDonald's, Papa John's, Pizza Hut, Stratford BBQ, Subway Taco Bell, Waffle House, Wendy's, Zaxby's, Days Inn, $General, $Tree, Advance Parts, CVS Drug, Family$, Food Lion, Lowe's Foods, O'Reilly Parts, USPO, vet, Walmart
127mm	scenic overlook wb
129	Pinnacle, N BP/dsl, Trails End Rest., S Marathon
131	Pilot Mtn SP
134	NC 268, Pilot Mtn, Elkin, N Exxon/dsl, Aunt Bea's BBQ Cousin Gary's Rest., McDonald's, Mtn View Rest., Rigatoni Pizza, Econolodge, $General, Advance Parts, Food Lion/Subway, S Circle K/dsl/scales, Speedway/dsl, Wendy's
135	Pilot Mtn
136	Cook School Rd, N Blue Mtn/dsl, Gas&Go, Ford, $General
17	US 52 N, to Mt Airy
13	Park Dr
11	US 601, to Mt Airy, Dobson, N Sheetz/dsl, S $General
8	Red Brush Rd, N Shell/Circle K/dsl
6	NC 89, to Mt Airy, S Flying J/Brintle's Rest./dsl/scales/24hr, Marathon/Subway/dsl, Shell/Circle K/dsl, Copper Pot Rest., Best Western
5	(101 from eb) I-77, N to Wytheville, S to Statesville
0mm	I-74 begins/ends at NC state line, runs with I-77

GREENSBORO

INTERSTATE 77

Exit	Services
105mm	North Carolina/Virginia state line
105mm	**full facilities, info, litter barrels, petwalk, vending, Welcome Ctr sb**
103mm	weigh sta both lanes
101	I-74 E, to Mt Airy, Winston-Salem, Greensboro, E H(12mi)
100	NC 89, to Mt Airy, E Circle K/Tesla EVC/dsl, Flying J/Brintle's Rest./dsl/scales/24hr/@, Marathon/Subway/dsl, Copper Pot Rest., Best Western, H(12mi), International Trucks
93	to Dobson, Surry, E BP/DQ/dsl, Exxon/Circle K/EVC/dsl, Coach's Grill, Surry Diner, Hampton Inn/EVC, Surry Inn, $General

NC

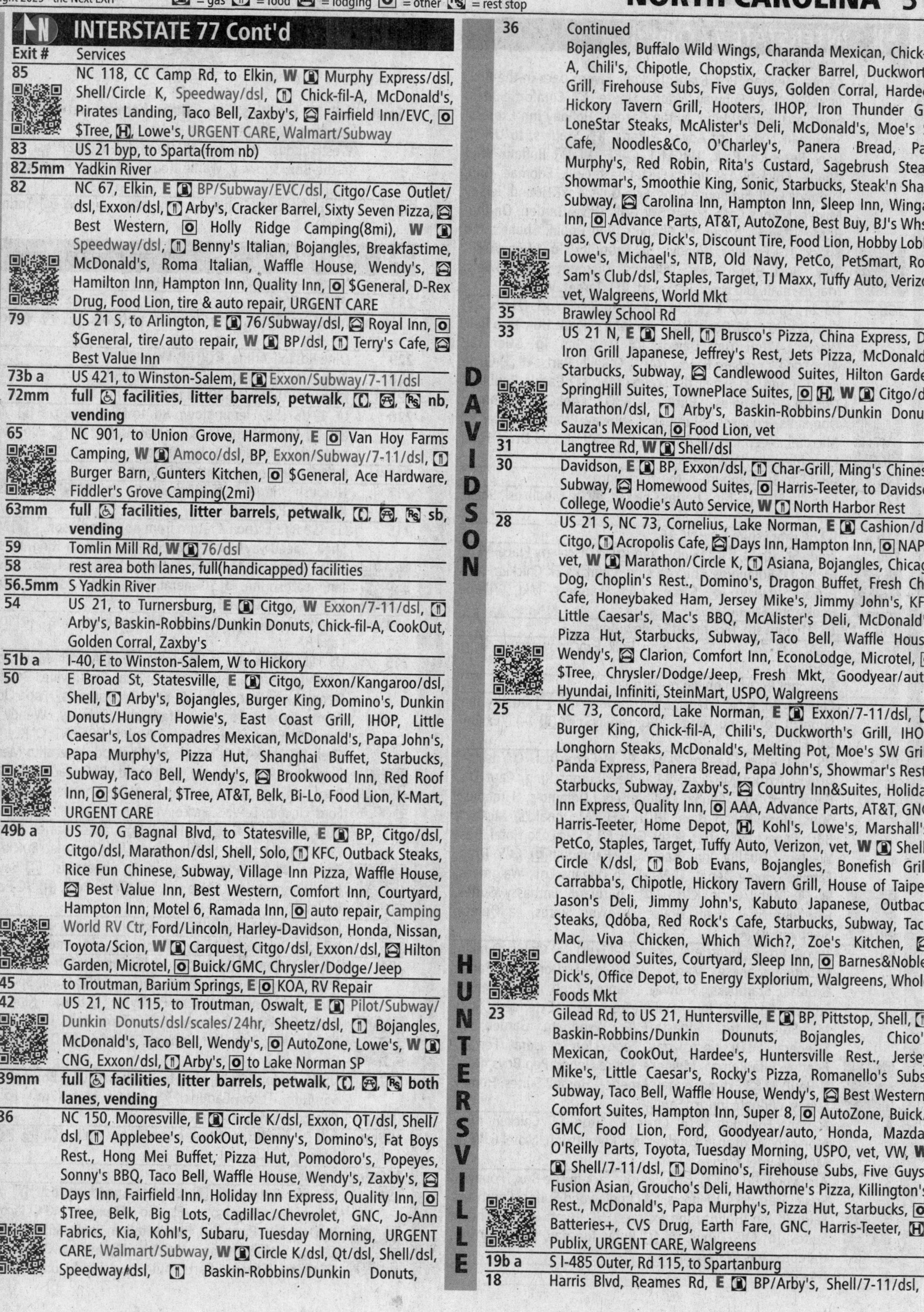

INTERSTATE 77 Cont'd

Exit #	Services
85	NC 118, CC Camp Rd, to Elkin, **W** [gas] Murphy Express/dsl, Shell/Circle K, Speedway/dsl, [food] Chick-fil-A, McDonald's, Pirates Landing, Taco Bell, Zaxby's, [lodging] Fairfield Inn/EVC, [other] $Tree, [H], Lowe's, URGENT CARE, Walmart/Subway
83	US 21 byp, to Sparta(from nb)
82.5mm	Yadkin River
82	NC 67, Elkin, **E** [gas] BP/Subway/EVC/dsl, Citgo/Case Outlet/dsl, Exxon/dsl, [food] Arby's, Cracker Barrel, Sixty Seven Pizza, [lodging] Best Western, [other] Holly Ridge Camping(8mi), **W** [gas] Speedway/dsl, [food] Benny's Italian, Bojangles, Breakfastime, McDonald's, Roma Italian, Waffle House, Wendy's, [lodging] Hamilton Inn, Hampton Inn, Quality Inn, [other] $General, D-Rex Drug, Food Lion, tire & auto repair, URGENT CARE
79	US 21 S, to Arlington, **E** [gas] 76/Subway/dsl, [lodging] Royal Inn, [other] $General, tire/auto repair, **W** [gas] BP/dsl, [food] Terry's Cafe, [lodging] Best Value Inn
73b a	US 421, to Winston-Salem, **E** [gas] Exxon/Subway/7-11/dsl
72mm	**full [handicap] facilities, litter barrels, petwalk, [phone], [picnic], [RS] nb, vending**
65	NC 901, to Union Grove, Harmony, **E** [other] Van Hoy Farms Camping, **W** [gas] Amoco/dsl, BP, Exxon/Subway/7-11/dsl, [food] Burger Barn, Gunters Kitchen, [other] $General, Ace Hardware, Fiddler's Grove Camping(2mi)
63mm	**full [handicap] facilities, litter barrels, petwalk, [phone], [picnic], [RS] sb, vending**
59	Tomlin Mill Rd, **W** [gas] 76/dsl
58	rest area both lanes, full(handicapped) facilities
56.5mm	S Yadkin River
54	US 21, to Turnersburg, **E** [gas] Citgo, **W** Exxon/7-11/dsl, [food] Arby's, Baskin-Robbins/Dunkin Donuts, Chick-fil-A, CookOut, Golden Corral, Zaxby's
51b a	I-40, E to Winston-Salem, W to Hickory
50	E Broad St, Statesville, **E** [gas] Citgo, Exxon/Kangaroo/dsl, Shell, [food] Arby's, Bojangles, Burger King, Domino's, Dunkin Donuts/Hungry Howie's, East Coast Grill, IHOP, Little Caesar's, Los Compadres Mexican, McDonald's, Papa John's, Papa Murphy's, Pizza Hut, Shanghai Buffet, Starbucks, Subway, Taco Bell, Wendy's, [lodging] Brookwood Inn, Red Roof Inn, [other] $General, $Tree, AT&T, Belk, Bi-Lo, Food Lion, K-Mart, URGENT CARE
49b a	US 70, G Bagnal Blvd, to Statesville, **E** [gas] BP, Citgo/dsl, Citgo/dsl, Marathon/dsl, Shell, Solo, [food] KFC, Outback Steaks, Rice Fun Chinese, Subway, Village Inn Pizza, Waffle House, [lodging] Best Value Inn, Best Western, Comfort Inn, Courtyard, Hampton Inn, Motel 6, Ramada Inn, [other] auto repair, Camping World RV Ctr, Ford/Lincoln, Harley-Davidson, Honda, Nissan, Toyota/Scion, **W** [gas] Carquest, Citgo/dsl, Exxon/dsl, [lodging] Hilton Garden, Microtel, [other] Buick/GMC, Chrysler/Dodge/Jeep
45	to Troutman, Barium Springs, **E** [other] KOA, RV Repair
42	US 21, NC 115, to Troutman, Oswalt, **E** [gas] Pilot/Subway/Dunkin Donuts/dsl/scales/24hr, Sheetz/dsl, [food] Bojangles, McDonald's, Taco Bell, Wendy's, [other] AutoZone, Lowe's, **W** [gas] CNG, Exxon/dsl, [food] Arby's, [other] to Lake Norman SP
39mm	**full [handicap] facilities, litter barrels, petwalk, [phone], [picnic], [RS] both lanes, vending**
36	NC 150, Mooresville, **E** [gas] Circle K/dsl, Exxon, QT/dsl, Shell/dsl, [food] Applebee's, CookOut, Denny's, Domino's, Fat Boys Rest., Hong Mei Buffet, Pizza Hut, Pomodoro's, Popeyes, Sonny's BBQ, Taco Bell, Waffle House, Wendy's, Zaxby's, [lodging] Days Inn, Fairfield Inn, Holiday Inn Express, Quality Inn, [other] $Tree, Belk, Big Lots, Cadillac/Chevrolet, GNC, Jo-Ann Fabrics, Kia, Kohl's, Subaru, Tuesday Morning, URGENT CARE, Walmart/Subway, **W** [gas] Circle K/dsl, Qt/dsl, Shell/dsl, Speedway/dsl, [food] Baskin-Robbins/Dunkin Donuts,
36	Continued Bojangles, Buffalo Wild Wings, Charanda Mexican, Chick-fil-A, Chili's, Chipotle, Chopstix, Cracker Barrel, Duckworth's Grill, Firehouse Subs, Five Guys, Golden Corral, Hardee's, Hickory Tavern Grill, Hooters, IHOP, Iron Thunder Grill, LoneStar Steaks, McAlister's Deli, McDonald's, Moe's SW Cafe, Noodles&Co, O'Charley's, Panera Bread, Papa Murphy's, Red Robin, Rita's Custard, Sagebrush Steaks, Showmar's, Smoothie King, Sonic, Starbucks, Steak'n Shake, Subway, [lodging] Carolina Inn, Hampton Inn, Sleep Inn, Wingate Inn, [other] Advance Parts, AT&T, AutoZone, Best Buy, BJ's Whse/gas, CVS Drug, Dick's, Discount Tire, Food Lion, Hobby Lobby, Lowe's, Michael's, NTB, Old Navy, PetCo, PetSmart, Ross, Sam's Club/dsl, Staples, Target, TJ Maxx, Tuffy Auto, Verizon, vet, Walgreens, World Mkt
35	Brawley School Rd
33	US 21 N, **E** [gas] Shell, [food] Brusco's Pizza, China Express, DQ, Iron Grill Japanese, Jeffrey's Rest, Jets Pizza, McDonald's, Starbucks, Subway, [lodging] Candlewood Suites, Hilton Garden, SpringHill Suites, TownePlace Suites, [other] [H], **W** [gas] Citgo/dsl, Marathon/dsl, [food] Arby's, Baskin-Robbins/Dunkin Donuts, Sauza's Mexican, [other] Food Lion, vet
31	Langtree Rd, **W** [gas] Shell/dsl
30	Davidson, **E** [gas] BP, Exxon/dsl, [food] Char-Grill, Ming's Chinese, Subway, [lodging] Homewood Suites, [other] Harris-Teeter, to Davidson College, Woodie's Auto Service, **W** [food] North Harbor Rest
28	US 21 S, NC 73, Cornelius, Lake Norman, **E** [gas] Cashion/dsl, Citgo, [food] Acropolis Cafe, [lodging] Days Inn, Hampton Inn, [other] NAPA, vet, **W** [gas] Marathon/Circle K, [food] Asiana, Bojangles, Chicago Dog, Choplin's Rest., Domino's, Dragon Buffet, Fresh Chef Cafe, Honeybaked Ham, Jersey Mike's, Jimmy John's, KFC, Little Caesar's, Mac's BBQ, McAlister's Deli, McDonald's, Pizza Hut, Starbucks, Subway, Taco Bell, Waffle House, Wendy's, [lodging] Clarion, Comfort Inn, EconoLodge, Microtel, [other] $Tree, Chrysler/Dodge/Jeep, Fresh Mkt, Goodyear/auto, Hyundai, Infiniti, SteinMart, USPO, Walgreens
25	NC 73, Concord, Lake Norman, **E** [gas] Exxon/7-11/dsl, [food] Burger King, Chick-fil-A, Chili's, Duckworth's Grill, IHOP, Longhorn Steaks, McDonald's, Melting Pot, Moe's SW Grill, Panda Express, Panera Bread, Papa John's, Showmar's Rest., Starbucks, Subway, Zaxby's, [lodging] Country Inn&Suites, Holiday Inn Express, Quality Inn, [other] AAA, Advance Parts, AT&T, GNC, Harris-Teeter, Home Depot, [H], Kohl's, Lowe's, Marshall's, PetCo, Staples, Target, Tuffy Auto, Verizon, vet, **W** [gas] Shell/Circle K/dsl, [food] Bob Evans, Bojangles, Bonefish Grill, Carrabba's, Chipotle, Hickory Tavern Grill, House of Taipei, Jason's Deli, Jimmy John's, Kabuto Japanese, Outback Steaks, Qdoba, Red Rock's Cafe, Starbucks, Subway, Taco Mac, Viva Chicken, Which Wich?, Zoe's Kitchen, [lodging] Candlewood Suites, Courtyard, Sleep Inn, [other] Barnes&Noble, Dick's, Office Depot, to Energy Explorium, Walgreens, Whole Foods Mkt
23	Gilead Rd, to US 21, Huntersville, **E** [gas] BP, Pittstop, Shell, [food] Baskin-Robbins/Dunkin Dounuts, Bojangles, Chico's Mexican, CookOut, Hardee's, Huntersville Rest., Jersey Mike's, Little Caesar's, Rocky's Pizza, Romanello's Subs, Subway, Taco Bell, Waffle House, Wendy's, [lodging] Best Western, Comfort Suites, Hampton Inn, Super 8, [other] AutoZone, Buick/GMC, Food Lion, Ford, Goodyear/auto, Honda, Mazda, O'Reilly Parts, Toyota, Tuesday Morning, USPO, vet, VW, **W** [gas] Shell/7-11/dsl, [food] Domino's, Firehouse Subs, Five Guys, Fusion Asian, Groucho's Deli, Hawthorne's Pizza, Killington's Rest., McDonald's, Papa Murphy's, Pizza Hut, Starbucks, [other] Batteries+, CVS Drug, Earth Fare, GNC, Harris-Teeter, [H], Publix, URGENT CARE, Walgreens
19b a	S I-485 Outer, Rd 115, to Spartanburg
18	Harris Blvd, Reames Rd, **E** [gas] BP/Arby's, Shell/7-11/dsl,

ELKIN · HARMONY · BARIUM SPRINGS · DAVIDSON · HUNTERSVILLE

NC

INTERSTATE 77 Cont'd

DOWNTOWN

18 Continued
Azteca Mexican, Bob Evans, Hickory Tavern, Jack-in-the-Box, Jimmy John's, Subway, Waffle House, Comfort Suites, Courtyard, Fairfield Inn, Hilton Garden, Holiday Inn Express, Suburban Lodge, Advance Parts, H, Staples, to UNCC, Univ Research Park, URGENT CARE, **W** Buffalo Wild Wings, Chick-fil-A, Chili's, East Coast Grill, Edomae Grill, Firebirds Grill, Firehouse Subs, Five Guys, Fox&Hound, Jersey Mike's, Mimi's Cafe, Moe's SW Grill, Olive Garden, On-the-Border, Panera bread, PF Chang's, Red Robin, Shane's Rib Shack, TGI Friday's, Wendy's, Drury Inn, $Tree, AT&T, Belk, Best Buy, Dick's, Dillard's, Discount Tire, Lowe's, Macy's, mall, Old Navy, PetSmart, REI, Target, Verizon

16b a US 21, Sunset Rd, **E** Circle K, Exxon/7-11/dsl, QT/dsl, Capt D's, KFC, McDonald's, Papa John's, Pizza Hut, Taco Bell, Wendy's, Yum Yum Dawgs, Days Inn, $General, AutoZone, Compare Foods, NAPA, O'Reilly Parts, **W** Circle K/dsl, Citgo/dsl, Shell/dsl/scales/24hr, Baskin-Robbins/Dunkin, Bojangles, Bubba's BBQ, CookOut, Denny's, Domino's, Popeyes, Starbucks, Subway, Waffle House, Microtel, Sleep Inn, Advance Parts, ALDI, CVS Drug, Food Lion, Meineke, Walgreens

13b a I-85, S to Spartanburg, N to Greensboro

12 La Salle St, **E** Mr. Charles Chicken, **W** Mobil/dsl, Shell/dsl

11b a I-277, Brookshire Fwy, NC 16

10b Trade St, 5th St, **E** DoubleTree, to Discovery Place, **W** Mobil, Bojangles, Chicken King, Church's TX Chicken, Jet's Pizza, Subway, $Tree, 7-11, Farmers Mkt, Village Bookstore/Starbucks

10a US 21(from sb), Moorhead St, downtown

9 I-277, US 74, to US 29, John Belk Fwy, downtown, **E** stadium

8 Remount Rd(from nb, no re-entry)

7 Clanton Rd, **E** QT/dsl, Shell/Circle K/dsl, Quality Inn, Super 8, Econo Lodge, EVC, Family$, **W** 7-11/Exxon/dsl, Citgo

6b a US 521, Billy Graham Pkwy, **E** Exxon/dsl, QT/dsl, Arby's, Azteca Mexican, Bojangles, Burger King, Capt D's, Carribean Hut, Chubz Chiliburgers, Domino's, Firehouse Subs, HoneyBaked Ham, IHOP, KFC, McDonald's, McKoy's BBQ, Papa John's, Tres Pesos Grill, 315@Loso Hotel, Best Western, Quality Inn, Radisson, Ramada, CVS Drug, Family$, Home Depot, TJ Maxx, to Queens Coll, Walgreens, **W** Mobil/Circle K/dsl, Courtyard, Embassy Suites, Extended Stay, Hyatt House, InTowne Suites, La Quinta, Sleep Inn,

5 Tyvola Rd, **E** Circle K, Exxon/7-11/dsl, Chili's, Dunkin, Kabuto Japanese, Maria's Mexican, McDonald's, Panda Express, Starbucks, Subway, Yummy Crab, Cloverleaf Suites, Comfort Inn, DoubleTree Inn, Extended Stay, MainStay Suites, Sonesta/EVC, Wyndham Garden, $General, ALDI, Costco/gas, Food Lion, Maserati/Ferrari/Bentley/Alfa Romeo, Meineke, Office Depot, Pep Boys, Ross, U-Haul, **W** Extended Stay America, Home2 Suites, Home2 Suites, Wingate Inn, Family$

4 Nations Ford Rd, **E** Circle K, Citgo, Chicken King, Morazan Mexican, Budget Inn, Knights Inn, Motel 6, **W** Mobil/Burger King

3 Arrowood Rd, **E** Cafe South, Jack-in-the-Box, Popeyes, Sonic, Starbucks, Wendy's, Candlewood Suites, Courtyard, Fairfield Inn, Holiday Inn Express/EVC, Hyatt Place, Sonesta Suites, CVS Drugs, **W** Ruby Tuesday, Drury Inn, Hampton Inn, Waterwalk

2 I-485

1.5mm **full facilities, info, litter barrels, petwalk, vending, Welcome Ctr nb**

1 Westinghouse Blvd, to I-485(from nb), **E** BP/dsl, Jack-in-the-Box, Subway, Waffle House, Super 8, **W** Mobil/7-11/dsl

0mm North Carolina/South Carolina state line, **W** Springhill Suites

INTERSTATE 85

HENDERSON

234mm North Carolina/Virginia state line

233 US 1, to Wise

231mm **full facilities, litter barrels, petwalk, Welcome Ctr sb**

229 Oine Rd, to Norlina, **E** BP, **W** SRA

226 Ridgeway Rd, **W** to Kerr Lake, to SRA

223 Manson Rd, **E** USPO, **W** to Kerr Dam

220 US 1, US 158, Flemingtown Rd, to Middleburg, **E** Mobil/dsl, Middleburg, $General, USPO, **W** Sunoco/dsl/scales/truck wash, Chex Trkstp/motel/rest.

218 US 1 S(from sb exits left), to Raleigh

217 Nutbush Bridge, **E** Mitchell's RV Ctr, **W** Exxon/dsl, Kerr Lake RA

215 US 158 BYP E, (no EZ return from nb), Henderson, **E** Mobi Shell, Speedway/dsl, 220 Seafood, Burger King, Forsyth' BBQ, Habanero Mexican, Subway, Budget Host, Qualit Inn, Scottish Inn, $General, Food Lion, Roses, services o US 158, tires, U-Haul

214 NC 39, Henderson, **E** BP, **W** Mobil/dsl, Shell, to Ke Lake RA

213 US 158, Dabney Dr, to Henderson, **E** Amoco, Marathon, Bamboo Garden, Big Cheese Pizza, Biscuitville, Bojangle Denny's, Ichibar Chinese, KFC, McDonald's, Papa John' Pino's Italian, Popeyes, Starbucks, Subway, Wendy's, Family$, Food Lion, Roses, T-Mobil, URGENT CARE, **W** Shell, Chick-fil-A, Mayflower Seafood, Mezcalito Mexica Pizza Hut, Ruby Tuesday, Smithfields BBQ, Taco Bell, Re Roof Inn, Advance Parts, ALDI, Chrysler/Dodge/Jee Ford/Lincoln, Lowe's, Petco, Verizon

212 Ruin Creek Rd, **E** Shell/dsl, Cracker Barrel, Mazatla Mexican, Ribeye's, Waffle House, Chevrolet/Buick/GM Toyota, **W** Exxon/Burger King, Sheetz/dsl, Baymo Inn, Hampton Inn, Sleep Inn, $Tree, Belk, H, JC Penne Walmart

OXFORD

209 Poplar Creek Rd, **W** Vance-Granville Comm Coll

206 US 158, Oxford, **E** Citgo, **W** BP/dsl, $General,

204 NC 96, Oxford, **E** Exxon/dsl, Comfort Inn, King's Inn, Buick/Chevrolet/GMC, Ford, Honda, **W** Shell, Speedwa dsl, Speedway/dsl, Valero/Popeyes, Burger King, Chi Wok, CookOut, Domino's, KFC/Taco Bell, Little Caesa McDonald's, Pizza Hut, Subway, Wendy's, Days Inn, Roses

202 US 15, Oxford, **W** Murphy Express/dsl, Bojangles, H 55 Cafe, Toros Cantina, Crown Motel(2mi), Te Charger, Verizon, Walmart

199mm **full facilities, litter barrels, petwalk, bo lanes**

198mm Tar River

191 NC 56, Butner, **E** BP/dsl, Speedway/dsl, Arby Bojangles, Domino's, El Rio Mexican, KFC/Taco B McDonald's, Pizza Hut, Rino's Italian, Sonic, Subway, Taste China, Waffle House, Wendy's, Inn at Creedmoor, $General, Advance Parts, AutoZone, Food Lion, M&H Tire

NC

BUTNER

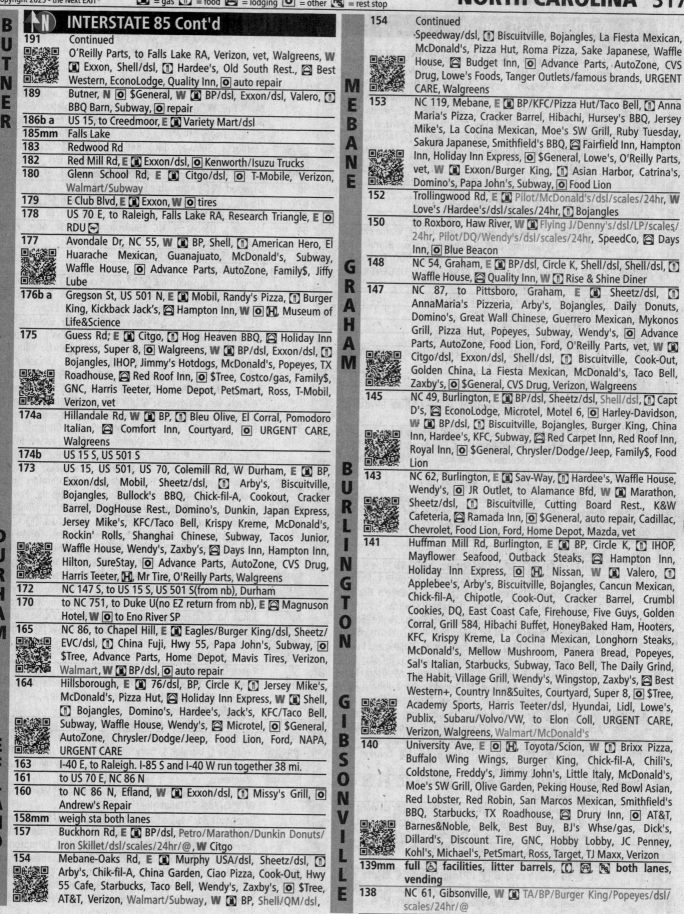

INTERSTATE 85 Cont'd

191 Continued
O'Reilly Parts, to Falls Lake RA, Verizon, vet, Walgreens, **W** Exxon, Shell/dsl, Hardee's, Old South Rest., Best Western, EconoLodge, Quality Inn, auto repair

189 Butner, **N** $General, **W** BP/dsl, Exxon/dsl, Valero, BBQ Barn, Subway, repair

186b a US 15, to Creedmoor, **E** Variety Mart/dsl

185mm Falls Lake

183 Redwood Rd

182 Red Mill Rd, **E** Exxon/dsl, Kenworth/Isuzu Trucks

180 Glenn School Rd, **E** Citgo/dsl, T-Mobile, Verizon, Walmart/Subway

179 E Club Blvd, **E** Exxon, **W** tires

178 US 70 E, to Raleigh, Falls Lake RA, Research Triangle, **E** RDU

177 Avondale Dr, NC 55, **W** BP, Shell, American Hero, El Huarache Mexican, Guanajuato, McDonald's, Subway, Waffle House, Advance Parts, AutoZone, Family$, Jiffy Lube

176b a Gregson St, US 501 N, **E** Mobil, Randy's Pizza, Burger King, Kickback Jack's, Hampton Inn, **W** H, Museum of Life&Science

175 Guess Rd, **E** Citgo, Hog Heaven BBQ, Holiday Inn Express, Super 8, Walgreens, **W** BP/dsl, Exxon/dsl, Bojangles, IHOP, Jimmy's Hotdogs, McDonald's, Popeyes, TX Roadhouse, Red Roof Inn, $Tree, Costco/gas, Family$, GNC, Harris Teeter, Home Depot, PetSmart, Ross, T-Mobil, Verizon, vet

174a Hillandale Rd, **W** BP, Bleu Olive, El Corral, Pomodoro Italian, Comfort Inn, Courtyard, URGENT CARE, Walgreens

174b US 15 S, US 501 S

DURHAM

173 US 15, US 501, US 70, Colemill Rd, W Durham, **E** BP, Exxon/dsl, Mobil, Sheetz/dsl, Arby's, Biscuitville, Bojangles, Bullock's BBQ, Chick-fil-A, Cookout, Cracker Barrel, DogHouse Rest., Domino's, Dunkin, Japan Express, Jersey Mike's, KFC/Taco Bell, Krispy Kreme, McDonald's, Rockin' Rolls, Shanghai Chinese, Subway, Tacos Junior, Waffle House, Wendy's, Zaxby's, Days Inn, Hampton Inn, Hilton, SureStay, Advance Parts, AutoZone, CVS Drug, Harris Teeter, H, Mr Tire, O'Reilly Parts, Walgreens

172 NC 147 S, to US 15 S, US 501 S(from nb), Durham

170 to NC 751, to Duke U(no EZ return from nb), **E** Magnuson Hotel, **W** to Eno River SP

165 NC 86, to Chapel Hill, **E** Eagles/Burger King/dsl, Sheetz/EVC/dsl, China Fuji, Hwy 55, Papa John's, Subway, $Tree, Advance Parts, Home Depot, Mavis Tires, Verizon, Walmart, **W** BP/dsl, auto repair

164 Hillsborough, **E** 76/dsl, BP, Circle K, Jersey Mike's, McDonald's, Pizza Hut, Holiday Inn Express, **W** Shell, Bojangles, Domino's, Hardee's, Jack's, KFC/Taco Bell, Subway, Waffle House, Wendy's, Microtel, $General, AutoZone, Chrysler/Dodge/Jeep, Food Lion, Ford, NAPA, URGENT CARE

EFLAND

163 I-40 E, to Raleigh. I-85 S and I-40 W run together 38 mi.

161 to US 70 E, NC 86 N

160 to NC 86 N, Efland, **W** Exxon/dsl, Missy's Grill, Andrew's Repair

158mm weigh sta both lanes

157 Buckhorn Rd, **E** BP/dsl, Petro/Marathon/Dunkin Donuts/Iron Skillet/dsl/scales/24hr/@, **W** Citgo

MEBANE

154 Mebane-Oaks Rd, **E** Murphy USA/dsl, Sheetz/dsl, Arby's, Chik-fil-A, China Garden, Ciao Pizza, Cook-Out, Hwy 55 Cafe, Starbucks, Taco Bell, Wendy's, Zaxby's, $Tree, AT&T, Verizon, Walmart/Subway, **W** BP, Shell/QM/dsl,

154 Continued
Speedway/dsl, Biscuitville, Bojangles, La Fiesta Mexican, McDonald's, Pizza Hut, Roma Pizza, Sake Japanese, Waffle House, Budget Inn, Advance Parts, AutoZone, CVS Drug, Lowe's Foods, Tanger Outlets/famous brands, URGENT CARE, Walgreens

153 NC 119, Mebane, **E** BP/KFC/Pizza Hut/Taco Bell, Anna Maria's Pizza, Cracker Barrel, Hibachi, Hursey's BBQ, Jersey Mike's, La Cocina Mexican, Moe's SW Grill, Ruby Tuesday, Sakura Japanese, Smithfield's BBQ, Fairfield Inn, Hampton Inn, Holiday Inn Express, $General, Lowe's, O'Reilly Parts, vet, **W** Exxon/Burger King, Asian Harbor, Catrina's, Domino's, Papa John's, Subway, Food Lion

152 Trollingwood Rd, **E** Pilot/McDonald's/dsl/scales/24hr, **W** Love's /Hardee's/dsl/scales/24hr, Bojangles

150 to Roxboro, Haw River, **W** Flying J/Denny's/dsl/LP/scales/24hr, Pilot/DQ/Wendy's/dsl/scales/24hr, SpeedCo, Days Inn, Blue Beacon

GRAHAM

148 NC 54, Graham, **E** BP/dsl, Circle K, Shell/dsl, Shell/dsl, Waffle House, Quality Inn, **W** Rise & Shine Diner

147 NC 87, to Pittsboro, Graham, **E** Sheetz/dsl, AnnaMaria's Pizzeria, Arby's, Bojangles, Daily Donuts, Domino's, Great Wall Chinese, Guerrero Mexican, Mykonos Grill, Pizza Hut, Popeyes, Subway, Wendy's, Advance Parts, AutoZone, Food Lion, Ford, O'Reilly Parts, vet, **W** Citgo/dsl, Exxon/dsl, Shell/dsl, Biscuitville, Cook-Out, Golden China, La Fiesta Mexican, McDonald's, Taco Bell, Zaxby's, $General, CVS Drug, Verizon, Walgreens

BURLINGTON

145 NC 49, Burlington, **E** BP/dsl, Sheetz/dsl, Shell/dsl, Capt D's, EconoLodge, Microtel, Motel 6, Harley-Davidson, **W** BP/dsl, Biscuitville, Bojangles, Burger King, China Inn, Hardee's, KFC, Subway, Red Carpet Inn, Red Roof Inn, Royal Inn, $General, Chrysler/Dodge/Jeep, Family$, Food Lion

143 NC 62, Burlington, **E** Sav-Way, Hardee's, Waffle House, Wendy's, JR Outlet, to Alamance Bfd, **W** Marathon, Sheetz/dsl, Biscuitville, Cutting Board Rest., K&W Cafeteria, Ramada Inn, $General, auto repair, Cadillac, Chevrolet, Food Lion, Ford, Home Depot, Mazda, vet

141 Huffman Mill Rd, Burlington, **E** BP, Circle K, IHOP, Mayflower Seafood, Outback Steaks, Hampton Inn, Holiday Inn Express, H, Nissan, **W** Valero, Applebee's, Arby's, Biscuitville, Bojangles, Cancun Mexican, Chick-fil-A, Chipotle, Cook-Out, Cracker Barrel, Crumbl Cookies, DQ, East Coast Cafe, Firehouse, Five Guys, Golden Corral, Grill 584, Hibachi Buffet, HoneyBaked Ham, Hooters, KFC, Krispy Kreme, La Cocina Mexican, Longhorn Steaks, McDonald's, Mellow Mushroom, Panera Bread, Popeyes, Sal's Italian, Starbucks, Subway, Taco Bell, The Daily Grind, The Habit, Village Grill, Wendy's, Wingstop, Zaxby's, Best Western+, Country Inn&Suites, Courtyard, Super 8, $Tree, Academy Sports, Harris Teeter/dsl, Hyundai, Lidl, Lowe's, Publix, Subaru/Volvo/VW, to Elon Coll, URGENT CARE, Verizon, Walgreens, Walmart/McDonald's

GIBSONVILLE

140 University Ave, **E** H, Toyota/Scion, **W** Brixx Pizza, Buffalo Wing Wings, Burger King, Chick-fil-A, Chili's, Coldstone, Freddy's, Jimmy John's, Little Italy, McDonald's, Moe's SW Grill, Olive Garden, Peking House, Red Bowl Asian, Red Lobster, Red Robin, San Marcos Mexican, Smithfield's BBQ, Starbucks, TX Roadhouse, Drury Inn, AT&T, Barnes&Noble, Belk, Best Buy, BJ's Whse/gas, Dick's, Dillard's, Discount Tire, GNC, Hobby Lobby, JC Penney, Kohl's, Michael's, PetSmart, Ross, Target, TJ Maxx, Verizon

139mm **full facilities, litter barrels, both lanes, vending**

138 NC 61, Gibsonville, **W** TA/BP/Burger King/Popeyes/dsl/scales/24hr/@

NC

= gas = food = lodging = other = rest stop

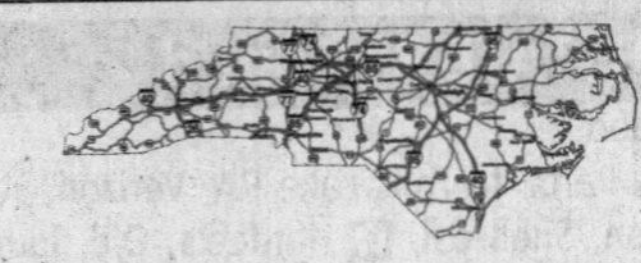

INTERSTATE 85 Cont'd

CHARLOTTE

Exit #	Services
135	Rock Creek Dairy Rd, E Fairfield Inn, W BP, Circle K, Biscuitville, Bojangles, China 1, Ciao Italian, Domino's, Guacamole Mexican, Jersey Mike's, McDonald's, Osaka Japanese, Pizza Hut/Taco Bell, Starbucks, Subway, Waffle House, Zaxby's, Comfort Suites, $General, Ace Hardware, CVS Drug, Food Lion, O'Reilly Parts, Verizon
132	Mt Hope Church Rd, E Shell/Subway/dsl, McDonald's, Pascali's Pizza, W Liberty/dsl, Pilot/Wendy's/dsl/24hr, Hampton Inn
131	to I-85 S, to I-73 N, to US 421, Highpoint, Charlotte
129	Youngsmill Rd, W KOA(4mi)
128	Alamance Church Rd, E Citgo/Subway/dsl
126b a	US 421, to Sanford, E Hagan Stone Park Camping
124	S Elm, Eugene St, E Murphy Express/dsl, Waffle House, W EVC, Bamboo Grill, Bojangles, Cracker Barrel, Hwy 55 Cafe, McDonald's, Pizza Hut, Smithfield's BBQ, Starbucks, Taco Bell, Wendy's, Zaxby's, AT&T, Lowe's, URGENT CARE, Verizon, Walmart/McDonald's
122c b a	US 220, to Greensboro, Asheboro(from sb)
121	I-40 W, I-73 N, to Winston-Salem
120	N US 29, E US 70, to I-40 W
119	Groometown Rd, from nb, W Citgo/dsl
118	US 29 S, US 70 W, to High Point, Jamestown, W Grandover Resort, H
115mm	Deep River
113c	I-74, US 311, Ashboro, to Winston-Salem
113a	NC 62, Archdale, E Citgo/dsl, Valero/dsl, W BP/dsl, Red Roof Inn
111	US 311, to High Point, Archdale, E Sheetz/Tesla Charger/dsl, Bamboo Garden, Bojangles, Carolina's Diner, Dairi-O, Hibachi Express, Starbucks, Subway, Taco Bell, Wendy's, Zaxby's, Days Inn, $General, antiques, CVS Drug, Food Lion, Lowes Food, Walmart Mkt, W Circle K/dsl, Citgo, McDonald's, Mobil/dsl, Valero/dsl, Biscuitville, Cabo Grill, Rancho Rest., Waffle House, Comfort Inn, Fairfield Inn, Hampton Inn, Holiday Inn Express, Quality Inn, H, O'Reilly Parts, USPO, vet
108	Hopewell Church Rd, Trinity
106	Finch Farm Rd, E BP/dsl, W Sheetz/dsl, BBQ Joe's
103	NC 109, to Thomasville, E Exxon/dsl, Mobil/dsl, Murphy USA/dsl, Sheetz/Tesla EVC/dsl, Arby's, Chen's Kitchen, CookOut, Dairi-O, Domino's, Elizabeth's Pizza, Subway, Zaxby's, Staylodge, $Tree, CVS Drug, Ingles Foods, Walmart/McDonald's, W Exxon/dsl, Fast Fuels/dsl, Shell, Speedway/dsl, BBQ Shack, Biscuitville, Bojangles, Burger King, Captain's Table, China Garden, Denny's, E Coast Grill, Granny Donuts, Hardee's, KFC, La Carreta Mexican, Little Caesar's, Mazatlan Mexican, McDonald's, Papa John's, Pizza Hut, Ruby Tuesday, Sonic, Sunrise Diner, Waffle House, Wendy's, Davidson Lodge, Quality Inn, $General, Advance Parts, ALDI, AutoZone, Family$, Food Lion, NAPA, NTB, O'Reilly Parts, Peebles, UHaul, Verizon, Walgreens
102	Lake Rd, W Exxon/dsl, Sunoco/dsl, Comfort Inn, Microtel, $General, H
100mm	**full facilities, litter barrels, petwalk, both lanes, vending**
96	US 64, to Asheboro, Lexington, E BP/dsl, Modern Tire, NC Zoo, W Exxon/dsl, Gulf/dsl, Randy's Rest., $General, auto repair, tires, to Davidson Co Coll
94	Old US 64, E Marathon/dsl, W BP/dsl, Timberlake Gallery
91	NC 8, to Southmont, E BP/dsl, Mobil, Biscuit King, Bojangle's, Christo Rest., CookOut, KFC, McDonald's, Ocean View Seafood, Subway, Waffle House, Wendy's, Days Inn,

ARCHDALE

LEXINGTON

HIGH POINT

SALISBURY

CHINA GROVE

Exit #	Services
91	Continued Red Roof Inn, Food Lion, High Rock Lake Camping(7mi), Mock Tire, W Amoco/dsl, Shell/dsl, Applebee's, Arby's, Burger King, Cagney's Kitchen, Chick-fil-A, Cracker Barrel, Dunkin, Jersey Mike's, La Carreta Mexican, Mavis Tires(1mi), Starbucks, Subway, Taco Bell, Zaxby's, Country Inn, Hampton Inn, Quality Inn, $Tree, Belk, EVC, GNC, H, Lowe's(1mi), PetSmart, Walgreens, Walmart
88	Linwood, W Affordable Suites, H
87	US 29, US 70, US 52(from nb), High Point, W H
86	Belmont Rd, W Bill's Trkstp/dsl/scales/24hr/@
84	US 29 S, US 70 W, NC 150(from nb), to Spencer, W $General, auto repair
82	US 29, US 70(from sb), to Spencer
81.5mm	Yadkin River
81	Long Ferry Rd, Spencer, E BP/dsl, Exxon/7-11/dsl/scales
79	Spencer Shops SHS, Spencer, E Spencer, W Citgo, Bojangles, Garden Chinese, $General, Food Lion
76b a	US 52, to Albemarle, Salisbury, E 7-11, BP, Exxon/dsl, Applebee's, Buffalo Wild Wings, Capriano's, Chipotle, ColdStone, Domino's, E Coast Grill, IHOP, Pancho Villa, Top China, Which Wich?, Zaxby's, Days Inn, Economy Inn, Sleep Inn, $Tree, ALDI, AT&T, CVS Drug, Food Lion, GNC, Lowe's, Marshall's, NTB, Old Navy, PetSmart, Staples, Verizon, vet, Walgreens, W Circle K/dsl, Murphy Express/dsl, Speedway/dsl, Blue Bay Seafood, Bojangles, Burger King, Capt D's, Chick-fil-A, China Buffet, Christo's Rest., Cookout, Cracker Barrel, Dunkin, Hardee's, Jersey Mike's, KFC, Marco's Pizza, McDonald's, O'Charley's, Outback Steaks, Panera Bread, Papa John's, Starbucks, Taco Bell, Tokyo Express, Waffle House, Wendy's, Comfort Suites, Courtyard, Advance Parts, AutoZone, BigLots, Family$, Firestone/auto, Goodyear/auto, H, USPO, Walmart/Subway
75	US 601, Jake Alexander Blvd, E Sheetz/dsl, Arby's, Breakfastime, Econolodge, Home2 Suites, to Da Nicholas Park, W BP, Exxon/dsl, Tesla Charger, Casa Grande Mexican, Culver's, Ichiban Japanese, Nyosh Japanese, Waffle House, Wendy's, Hampton Inn, Holiday Inn, Quality Inn, Buick, Cadillac/Chevrolet, Chrysler, Dodge/Jeep, Ford, GMC, Honda, Kia, Nissan, Toyota/Scion
74	Julian Rd, E Honeybaked Ham, Salsarita's, TX Roadhouse, Affordable Suites, Dick's, Hobby Lobby, W Longhor Steaks, Los Arcos, Olive Garden, Starbucks, $Tree, Belk Kohl's, Michael's
72	Peach Orchard Rd
71	Peeler Rd, E Love's/Chester's/McDonald's/dsl/scales 24hr, W Pilot/Dunkin/Subway/dsl/scales/24hr, Bojangle's, dsl repair
70	Webb Rd, E flea mkt, W Shell/dsl, st patrol
68	US 29, US 601, to Rockwell, China Grove, W BP, Bojangle's, Domino's, Gary's BBQ, Hardee's, Jimmie's Rest Pizza Hut, Subway, Taste of China, $General, AutoZon Walgreens
63	Kannapolis, E Pilot/Subway/dsl/scales, Waffle Hous W QT/dsl, Bojangles
60	Earnhardt Rd, Copperfield Blvd, E Circle K/dsl, Exxon/ds Bojangles, Breakfast Time Rest., Charros Mexican, Cracke Barrel, Waffle House, Country Inn&Suites, Hampton In Sleep Inn, H, URGENT CARE, W Casa Grande Mexica Dunkin, East Coast Wings, Firehouse Subs, Little Caesar' Logan's Roadhouse, McDonald's, Steak'n Shake, Taco Be Wendy's, Holiday Inn Express, AT&T, Hobby Lobby

NC

INTERSTATE 85 Cont'd

CONCORD

60 Continued
Kohl's, Lowe's, Petco, Sam's Club/gas, Walmart

59mm **full facilities, litter barrels, petwalk, both lanes, vending**

58 US 29, US 601, Concord, **E** Marathon/dsl, Applebee's, Chik-fil-A, Chili's, Chipotle, Five Guys, Golden Corral, Hibachi Pit, Honey Baked Ham, Jimmy John's, Mayflower Seafood, McDonald's, Moe's SW Grill, Mr C's Rest., O'Charley's, Panera Bread, Popeyes, Starbucks, Subway, Tropical Smoothie, Wendy's, Cabarrus Inn, Quality Inn, Belk, Harris Teeter, H, JC Penney, Staples, Verizon, Walgreens, **W** BP, QT/dsl, Speedway/dsl, CiCi's, IHOP, Comfort Inn, InTown Suites, Microtel, $General, Ford, Home Depot, Rose's, st patrol

55 NC 73, to Davidson, Concord, **E** Shell, McDonald's, **W** Shell/Circle K/dsl, Rodeway Inn, Blue Compass RV

54 Kannapolis Pkwy, George W Lyles Pkwy, **E** Amoco/dsl, QT/dsl, Afton Pizza, Bojangles, China Garden, E Noodle Asian, Marco's Pizza, Off-the-Grill, Village Kitchen , Advance Parts, AutoZone, CVS Drug, Firestone/auto, Food Lion, Harris Teeter, URGENT CARE, vet, Walgreens, **W** Circle K/dsl, Arby's, Asian Cafe, Buffalo Wild Wings, Chick-fil-A, Chipotle, Dunkin, Jersey Mike's, L&L Hawaiian Grill, McDonald's, Mi Pueblo, Showmar's Rest., Starbucks, Wendy's, Zaxby's, $Tree, Goodyear/auto, Marshall's, PetSmart, Super Target, Verizon

52 Poplar Tent Rd, **E** Mobil/7-11/dsl, R&R BBQ, to Lowe's Speedway, **W** Exxon/dsl

49 Bruton Smith Blvd, Concord Mills Blvd, **E** BP/McDonalds, Mobil/7-11/dsl, Bojangles, ChuckECheese, Cinco de Mayo Mexican, Cookout, Cracker Barrel, Firehouse Subs, Hooters, Jack-in-the-Box, KFC/Taco Bell, Ruby Tuesday, Sonic, Sonny's BBQ, Starbucks, Subway, Taco Bell, TX Roadhouse, Waffle House, Wendy's, Zaxby's, Comfort Suites, Courtyard, Embassy Suites, Great Wolf Lodge, Hampton Inn, Hilton Garden, Holiday Inn Express, Home Towne Suites, Homewood Suites, Residence Inn/EVC, Sleep Inn, SpringHill Suites, Wingate Inn, BJ's Whse/gas, Camping World, Camping World Resort(1.5mi), Chrysler/Dodge/Jeep, Harley-Davidson, Honda, Kia, to Lowe's Motor Speedway, Toyota/Scion, VW, **W** Circle K/dsl, Circle K/dsl, QT/dsl, Andy's Frozen Yogurt, Bad Daddy's, Biscuitville, BJ's Rest., Bonefish Grill, Burger King, Carolina Alehouse, CAVA, Charanda Mexican, Chick-fil-A, Chipotle, Crafty Crab, Crumbl Cookies, Dave&Buster's, Dunkin, First Watch, Freddy's, Jason's Deli, Jersey Mike's, Jimmy John's, Jim'n Nick's BBQ, Kohl's, Krispy Kreme, Mac's BBQ, McAlisters Deli, McDonald's, Olive Garden, On-the-Border, Outback Steaks, Panda Express, Panera Bread, PDQ Cafe, Razzoo's Cafe, Red Lobster, Steak'n Shake, Tacos 4 Life, TGI Friday's, Twin Peaks, Viva Chicken, $General, $Tree, AT&T, BassPro Shops, Best Buy, BooksAMillion, Concord Mills Mall, Dick's, Discount Tire, Firestone/auto, Lowe's, Old Navy, PetCo, Ross, TJ Maxx, URGENT CARE, Verizon, Walmart/Subway

48 I-485, to US 29, to Rock Hill

46 Mallard Creek Church Rd, **E** Circle K, Exxon/7-11, Mobil/dsl, Giacomos Pizza, Jack-in-the-Box, Research Park, vet, **W** Shell/Circle K, Capital Tacos, Great Harvest, Rita's, Sofia's Steaks, Starbucks, Toyama Express, Trader Joe's

45b a Harris Blvd, **E** Office Depot, Applebee's, Blaze Pizza, Bojangles, Burger King, CAVA, Cheddar's, Chick-fil-A, Chili's, China Buffet, China Palace, Chipotle, City BBQ, Dunkin, Five Guys, IHOP, Jersey Mike's Subs, Jimmy John's, McDonald's, Mezeh, Nakato Steaks, Noodles&Co, Panera Bread,

45b a Continued
Papa John's, Picasso's Pizza, Qdoba, Showmar's Rest., Starbucks, Taco Bell, TGIFriday's, Tropical Cafe, Costa Maya Mexican, Country Inn&Suites, Drury Inn, Extended Stay America, Hampton Inn, Hilton, Holiday Inn, Home2 Suites, Hyatt Place, Microtel, Sleep Inn, Sonesta, Food Lion, H, Michaels, Ross, Sam's Club, to Miz Scarlett's, to UNCC, U Research Park, Verizon, Walgreens, Walmart/McDonald's, **W** Longhorn Steaks, Red Robin, Tony's Pizza, Fairfield Inn, SpringHill Suites, $Tree, Food Lion

43 University City Blvd, **E** Circle K/dsl, Circle K/Subway/dsl, Chipotle, Culver's, Golden Corral, Honeybaked Ham, Jasons Deli, KFC/Taco Bell, Mi Pueblo Mexican, Outback Steaks, Starbucks, Zaxby's, Comfort Suites, Extended Stay America, Holiday Inn Express, InTown Suites, InTowne Suites, AutoZone, Chevrolet, Discount Tire, Firestone/auto, GNC, Hobby Lobby, IKEA/EVC, Marshall's, Old Navy, PetSmart, TJ Maxx, Volvo, Walmart/EVC, World Mkt

42 US 29(nb only)

41 Sugar Creek Rd, **E** Exxon/7-11/gas, Shell/dsl, Bojangles, KFC, McDonald's, Wendy's, Brookwood Inn, Continental Inn, Economy Inn, Motel 6, Travel Inn, Family$, **W** Shell/Circle K/dsl, Chicken Box Rest., Cookout, DQ, La Riviera Mexican, Baymont, Charlotte Speedway Inn, Quality Inn, Red Roof Inn, Rodeway Inn, Super 8

40 Graham St, **E** Exxon/7-11/dsl, Budget Inn, NAPA, Penske, UPS, Volvo, Western Star, **W** Circle K/dsl, QT/dsl/scales, truck tire/repair

39 Statesville Ave, **E** Pilot/Subway/dsl/scales/24hr, Advance Parts, repair, **W** Citgo/dsl, Shell/dsl, Bojangles, Family$, U-Haul

38 I-77, US 21, N to Statesville, S to Columbia

37 Beatties Ford Rd, **E** Exxon/7-11/dsl, Burger King, McDonald's, Tops China, CVS Drug, Family$, Food Lion, USPO, **W** Citgo

36 NC 16, Brookshire Blvd, **E** Rodeway Inn, **W** Exxon/7-11/dsl, Mobil/dsl, QT/dsl, RaceWay/dsl, Burger King, Jack-in-the-Box, Starbucks, Subway, Family$, Griffin Tire

35 Glenwood Dr, **E** Exxon, Econolodge, **W** Shell/dsl

34 NC 27, Freedom Dr, **E** Circle K, Shell, Beauregard's Rest., Bojangles, Capt D's, Cookout, Domino's, KFC, McDonald's, Pizza Hut, Po Boy's Seafood, Showmar's, Taco Bell, Wendy's, $Tree, Advance Parts, ALDI, AutoZone, Family$, Goodyear/auto, URGENT CARE, Walgreens, **W** Charlotte Express

33 US 521, Billy Graham Pkwy, **E** Shell/dsl, Bojangles, KFC/Taco Bell, McDonald's, Mobil/dsl, Wendy's, Baymont Inn, Comfort Suites, Royal Inn, Sheraton, SpringHill Suites, USPO, **W** Exxon/dsl, Cracker Barrel, Ichiban, Waffle House, EconoLodge, Holiday Inn Express, La Quinta, Microtel, Quality Inn, Studios & Suites, Super 8

32 Little Rock Rd, **E** Mobil/7-11/dsl, Inn, Courtyard, Hampton Inn, Holiday Inn, **W** BP/dsl, Citgo/dsl, Mobil/7-11, Arby's, Showmar's Rest., Country Inn&Suites, Day's Inn, Wingate Inn/EVC, Family$, Food Lion, Griffin Tire, Walgreens

MT HOLLY

30b a I-485, to 1-77, Pineville

29 Sam Wilson Rd, **S** camping, **W** Love's/Chester's/dsl/scales/24hr/@, Shell/dsl

28mm weigh sta both lanes

27.5mm Catawba River

27 NC 273, Mt Holly, **E** BP/Dunkin/dsl, Murphy USA/dsl, Arby's, Captain's Cap Seafood, Chick-fil-A, Culvers, KFC, Pizza Hut, Sake Japanese, Starbucks, Subway, Taco Bell, Waffle House, Wendy's, Home2 Suites, Big Lots, CVS Drug, Family$, Firestone/auto, Lowe's, NAPA, Walgreens,

NC

= gas = food = lodging = other = rest stop

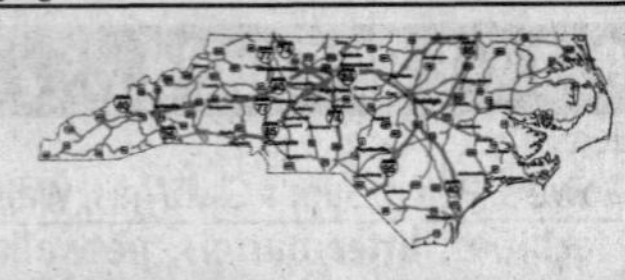

MCADENVILLE

INTERSTATE 85 Cont'd

27 Continued
Walmart/Subway, W BP/dsl, Fairfield Inn, Holiday Inn Express

26 NC 7, E BP/dsl, Marathon/Circle K/dsl, Bojangles, Estia's Kouzina Greek, Famous Toastery, Hardee's, McDonald's, New China, Papa John's, Hampton Inn, $Tree, Advance Parts, ALDI, AT&T, AutoZone, Ford, Verizon, W Belmont Abbey Coll

24mm South Fork River

23 NC 7, McAdenville, W Exxon/dsl, Shell/Subway/dsl, Hardee's

22 Cramerton, Lowell, E Circle K/dsl, Speedway/dsl, Bubba's 33, CiCi's, Hooters, Jack-in-the-Box, Jersey Mike's Subs, Juicy Crab, Moe's SW, Popeyes, Portofino's, Sakura Japanese, Schlotzsky's, Shane's Ribshack, Showmar's, Zaxby's, Books-A-Million, Buick/Cadillac/Chevrolet/GMC, Kia, Kohl's, Lowe's, Old Navy, PetSmart, Sam's Club/gas, U-Haul

21 Cox Rd, E Shell, Akropolis Cafe, Buffalo Wild Wings, Cheddar's, Chili's, Chipotle, ChuckeCheese, Cookout, Dynasty Buffet, Firehouse Subs, Five Guys, Golden Corral, Jimmy John's, Krispy Kreme, La Fuente, Logan's Roadhouse, Longhorn Steaks, McAlister's Deli, McDonald's, Noodles&Co, Olive Garden, On the Border, Panera Bread, Peking Garden, Qdoba, Ruby Tuesday, Starbucks, Steak'n Shake, Hilton Garden, $Tree, AT&T, Best Buy, Chrysler/Dodge/Jeep, Dick's, Discount Tire, Ford/Subaru, GNC, Hobby Lobby, Home Depot, Michael's, Nissan, NTB, O'Reilly Parts, Office Depot, PepBoys, Petco, Ross, Target, TJ Maxx, Verizon, vet, Walgreens, Walmart/Subway, W Shell/dsl, Arby's, Brixx Pizza, IHOP, Super 8, $General, H, Medical Ctr Drug

20 NC 279, New Hope Rd, E World, Agave Mexican, Capt D's, Dunkin, Los Arcos Mexican, Lucky Samurai, McDonald's, Red Lobster, Taco Bell, Wendy's, Gaston Inn, Advance Parts, AutoZone, Belk, Family$, Firestone/auto, vet, W Bojangles, Cracker Barrel, Honeybaked Ham, KFC, Outback Steaks, TX Roadhouse, Waffle House, Best Western, Comfort Suites, Courtyard, Fairfield Inn, Hampton Inn, Tru, CarMax, H

19 NC 7, E Gastonia, E Shell

17 US 321, Gastonia, E Exxon/dsl/LP, Los Arcos Mexican, Pancake House, Quality Inn, Woodspring Suites, Family$, W Circle K/dsl, QT/dsl, Dunkin, Hardee's, Papa John's, Taco Bell, Wendy's, Zaxby's, Econolodge, Holiday Inn Express, Motel 6

14 NC 274, E Bessemer, E Citgo/dsl, Murphy USA/dsl, Walmart, W Citgo/dsl, Shell/Subway, Bojangles, Waffle House, Affordable Suites, Express Inn

KINGS MTN

13 Edgewood Rd, Bessemer City, E to Crowders Mtn SP, W Exxon/dsl

10b a US 74 W, US 29, Kings Mtn

8 NC 161, to Kings Mtn, E Holiday Inn Express, camping, W BP/dsl, Biscuitville, Los Tarascos, McDonald's, Starbucks, Taco Bell, Waffle House, Wendy's, Comfort Inn, Quality Inn, $General, Campers Inn RV Ctr, H

5 Dixon School Rd, E Trkstp/dsl/24hr, truck/tire repair

4 US 29 S(from sb)

2.5mm **full facilities, info, litter barrels, petwalk, vending, Welcome Ctr nb**

2 NC 216, Kings Mtn, E to Kings Mtn Nat Military Park

0mm North Carolina/South Carolina state line

INTERSTATE 95

181mm North Carolina/Virginia state line, **full facilities,**

PLEASANT HILL

INTERSTATE 95

181mm Continued
litter barrels, petwalk, vending, Welcome Ctr sb

180 NC 48, to Gaston, to Lake Gaston, Pleasant Hill, W ONE9/Subway/dsl/scales/24hr

176 NC 46, to Garysburg, W Shell/dsl, Super 8

174mm Roanoke River

173 US 158, Roanoke Rapids, Weldon, E BP/dsl, Shell/dsl, Ralph's BBQ, Waffle House, Days Inn, Econolodge, W BP/dsl, Exxon/DQ/Stuckey's, Murphy USA/dsl, Sheetz/dsl, Shell/dsl, Applebee's, Arby's, Biscuitville, Bojangles, Burger King, Carolina BBQ, Chick-fil-A, China Lin, Chipotle, Cookout, Cracker Barrel, Don Juan Mexican, Dunkin, Hardee's, Hwy 55 Burger, Ichiban, Jersey Mike's, KFC, Little Caesar's, Logan's Roadhouse, Mayflower Seafood, McDonald's, New China, Papa John's, Pino's Pizza, Pizza Hut, Popeyes, Ruby Tuesday, Starbucks, Subway, Taco Bell, Waffle House, Wendy's, Zaxby's, Baymont Inn, Country Inn, Hampton Inn, Holiday Inn Express, Quality Inn, Red Roof Inn, $General, $Tree, Advance Parts, AutoZone, Belk, BigLots, Firestone/auto, Food Lion, GNC, Harley-Davidson, Honda, H, Lowe's, O'Reilly Parts, Save a Lot Foods, Staples, Toyota, URGENT CARE, Verizon, Walgreens, Walmart

171 NC 125, Roanoke Rapids, E Hilton Garden, Carolina Crossroads RV Resort, Roanoke Rapids Theater, W Shell/dsl, SureStay Plus, st patrol

168 NC 903, to Halifax, E Exxon/Subway/dsl, Shell/Burger King/dsl, W Mobil/Dunkin/LP/dsl/EVC

BATTLEBORO

160 NC 561, to Brinkleyville, E Exxon, W Shell/dsl/EVC

154 NC 481, to Enfield, W KOA

151mm weigh sta both lanes

150 NC 33, to Whitakers, W BP/Subway/DQ/Stuckey's/dsl

145 NC 4, to US 301, Battleboro, E BP/dsl, Exxon/dsl, Shell, Denny's, Hardee's, Waffle House, 121 Motel, Baymont, EconoLodge, Quality Inn, Red Carpet Inn, Red Roof Inn, Super 8

142mm **full facilities, litter barrels, petwalk, both lanes, vending**

141 NC 43, Red Oak, E Circle K/dsl, Exxon/dsl/LP, $General Smith's Foods

138 US 64, E Speedway/dsl, Bojangles, Cracker Barrel Outback Steaks, TX Steaks, Waffle House, Candlewood Suites, Country Inn&Suites, Courtyard, Doubletree, Hampton Inn, Holiday Inn, Holiday Inn, Residence Inn, Buick/GMC Harley-Davidson, Honda, H, to Cape Hatteras Nat Seashore URGENT CARE

132 to NC 58, E Pitstop/dsl, W BP/dsl, $General

128mm Tar River

127 NC 97, to Stanhope

WILSON

121 US 264a, Wilson, E BP, Kangaroo/dsl/LP, Murphy USA/dsl Shell, Speedway/dsl, Applebee's, Arby's, Buffalo Wild Wings, Burger King, Chick-fil-A, Chili's, Chopstix, Cookout Denny's, El Tapatio, Golden Corral, Hardee's, Hibachi Buffet Jersey Mike's, KFC/LJ Silver, Kobe Express, Mama Mia' Pizzaria, McDonald's, Moe's SW Grill, Olive Garden Quizno's, Red Chileez Grill, Ruby Tuesday, San Jose Mexican Sonic, Starbucks, Subway, Teppanyaki, TX Steaks, Waffle House, Wendy's, Zaxby's's, Candlewood Suites, Hampton Inn, Quality Inn, $General, $Tree, ALDI, AT&T AutoZone, Belk, Best Buy, Big Lots, Chevrolet, Chrysler Dodge/Jeep, Ford/Lincoln, GNC, Harris-Teeter, Hobby Lobby

NC

INTERSTATE 95 Cont'd

WILSON

121 Continued
Honda, H, Lowe's, Marshall's, Mr Tire, Nissan, O'Reilly Parts, PetSmart, Ross, Staples, Target, Toyota/Scion, URGENT CARE, Verizon, vet, Walmart, White's Tires, W BP, Best-N-Burgers, Bojangles, Burger King, Chick-fil-A, Cracker Barrel, McDonald's, Pino's Pizza, Starbucks, Comfort Suites, Country Inn&Suites, Fairfield Inn, Hampton Inn, Holiday Inn Express, Microtel, Red Roof Inn, Sleep Inn, to Country Dr Museum

119b a I-795 S, US 264, US 117

116 NC 42, to Clayton, Wilson, E Shell/dsl, H, W Exxon/dsl

KENLY

107 US 301, Kenly, E BP/Circle K/dsl, Citgo, Exxon/McDonald's/dsl, PitStop, Golden China, Hwy 55 Burgers, Nik's Pizza, Norman's BBQ, Subway, Budget Inn, Deluxe Inn, Quality Inn, $General, $Tree, CarQuest, Food Lion, Ford, O'Reilly Parts, Piggly Wiggly, Tobacco Museum

106 Truck Stop Rd, Kenly, E Flying J/Denny's/dsl/LP/scales/24hr/@, W Kenly 95/Petro/DQ/Subway/Wendy's/dsl/scales/24hr/@, Pilot/Arby's/dsl/scales/24hr, Waffle House, Motel 6, Red Roof, Blue Beacon, Speedco Lube, Truck-o-Mat

105.5mm Little River

105 Bagley Rd, Kenly, E Big Boys/Shell/105 Pizza/dsl/scales/24hr, Lowell Mill Rest.

102 Micro, E repair, W Marathon, Old Towne Steaks, $General, city park, USPO

101 Pittman Rd

99mm **full facilities, hist marker, litter barrels, petwalk, both lanes, vending**

98 to Selma, E North Pointe RV Camping

SMITHFIELD

97 US 70 A, to Pine Level, Selma, E Mobil/dsl, Robbins Nest Rest., Denny's, Days Inn, J&R Outlet, W BP, Citgo/dsl, Exxon/Dunkin/dsl, Shell/dsl, Bojangles, Cookout, Don Beto's Tacos, KFC, McDonald's, Popeyes, Waffle House, Wendy's, EconoLodge, Knights Inn, La Quinta, Masters Inn, Quality Inn, H

95 US 70, Smithfield, E Best Value Inn, Village Motel, W Sheetz/dsl/Tesla EVC, Speedway/dsl, Arby's, Bob Evans, Buffalo Wild Wings, Burger King, Checker's, CiCi's Pizza, Coldstone, Cracker Barrel, Golden Corral, Outback Steaks, Panera Bread, San Marcos Mexican, Starbucks, Subway, TX Steaks, Waffle House, Zaxby's, Baymont Inn, Best Western, Comfort Inn, Country Inn & Suites, Fairfield Inn, Hampton Inn, Holiday Inn Expres, Sleep Inn, Super 8, Tru, Ava Gardner Museum, Carolina Premium Outlets/famous brands, EVC, Harley-Davidson, H

93 Brogden Rd, Smithfield, W Citgo, $General

91.5mm Neuse River

90 US 301, US 701, to Newton Grove, E BP/dsl, Sunoco/dsl, Travelers Inn, Happy Trails RV Park, Raleigh Oaks RV Resort, to Bentonville Bfd(14mi), W Exxon/dsl, Four Oaks Motel/RV Park

87 NC 96, Four Oaks, W BP/dsl, Speedway/dsl, Hwy 55 Burgers, McDonald's, Subway, $General, AutoZone, NAPA, O'Reilly

81b a I-40, E to Wilmington, W to Raleigh

79 NC 50, to NC 27, to NC 242, Benson, Newton Grove, E Citgo/dsl, Short Stop/dsl, Char-Grill, Daddy D's BBQ, Jordana's Italian, Waffle House, Hampton Inn/EVC, auto repair, W Exxon/Burger King/dsl, China 8, Domino's, Fiesta Mexicana, Gabriella's Peruvian, McDonald's, Pizza Hut, Subway, Taco Bell, Days Inn, Advance Parts, Family$, Food Lion, Walgreens

78mm Neuse River

CLINTON

77 Hodges Chapel Rd, E Love's/Subway/dsl/scales/RV dump/24hr, tire/auto repair

75 Jonesboro Rd, W Exxon/Milestone Diner, Pilot/Shell/DQ/Quiznos/dsl/scales/24hr/@

73 US 421, NC 55, to Dunn, Clinton, E Cracker Barrel, Jersey Mikes, Mama Ruths, McDonald's, Panda House Chinese, Chevrolet, Chrysler/Dodge/Jeep, Family$, Food Lion, W Exxon/dsl, Shell, Speedway/dsl, Bojangles, Burger King, El Charro Mexican, Hot Dog&Hamburger Heavan, Sagebrush Steaks, Starbucks, Subway, Taco Bell, Triangle Waffle, Baymont Inn, Country Inn, Hampton Inn, Quality Inn, Super 8, Charlie C's IGA, museum, to Campbell U.

72 Pope Rd, E Comfort Inn, W BP, Pure/dsl, Fairfield Inn, Cadillac/GMC

71 Longbranch Rd, E Pilot/Circle K/Hardee's/dsl/EVC/scales/24hr, W to Averasboro Bfd

70 SR 1811, E Relax Inn

65 NC 82, Godwin, E Falcon Children's Home, W Godwin Mart/dsl

61 to Wade, E Fayetteville RV Resort Cottages, W Lucky 7/Exxon/dsl

FAYETTEVILLE

58 US 13, to Newton Grove, I-295 to Fayetteville, E Shell/Subway/dsl/scales, DQ, Waffle House

56 Lp 95, to US 301(from sb), Fayetteville, W Pope AFB, to Ft Bragg

55 NC 1832, Murphy Rd, W Circle K/dsl, Epco/dsl, Eastover Inn

52 NC 24, Fayetteville, W botanical gardens, museum, Pope AFB, to Ft Bragg

49 NC 53, NC 210, Fayetteville, E BP/dsl, Circle K, Exxon/dsl, Burger King, Jersey Mikes, McDonald's, Pizza Hut, Taco Bell, Waffle House, Days Inn, Deluxe Inn, Travelodge, Tru Hilton, $General, W BP/Subway/dsl, Exxon/dsl, Sunoco/dsl, Bojangles, Cracker Barrel, Ruby Tuesday, Starbucks, Best Night Inn, Comfort Inn, Country Inn, Doubletree/EVC, EconoLodge, Holiday Inn Express, La Quinta, Red Roof Inn, Sleep Inn, Super 8, SureStay Inn

48mm **full facilities, litter barrels, petwalk, both lanes, vending**

47mm Cape Fear River

46b a NC 87, to Fayetteville, Elizabethtown

44 Claude Lee Rd, W Lazy Acres Camping, to

41 NC 59, to Hope Mills, Parkton, E Circle K/Subway/dsl, Bojangles, $General, W Circle K/dsl, Grandsons Buffet, Camping World RV Ctr, Lake Waldo's Camping, Spring Valley RV Park

RAEFORD

40 Lp 95, to US 301(from nb), to Fayetteville, services on US 301(5-7mi)

33 US 301, St Pauls, E BP/dsl

31 NC 20, to St Pauls, Raeford, E BP, Marathon/dsl, Mobil/McDonald's, Valero, Burger King, Hardee's, Days Inn, AutoZone, Volvo Trucks, Walgreens, Walmart Mkt, W BP/dsl, Taco Bell, Food Lion

25 US 301, E Sun-Do/dsl

24mm weigh sta both lanes

22 US 301, E BP, Exxon, Shell/DQ, Tesla EVC, Burger King, Chick-fil-A, China Wok, Cold Stone, Denny's, Firehouse Subs, Golden Corral, Hardee's, IHOP, McDonald's, Outback Steaks, Panera Bread, Pizza Hut, Ruby Tuesday, San Jose Mexican, Smithfield BBQ, Starbucks, The Wing Co., TX Steaks, Waffle House, Wendy's, Zaxby's, Best Western, Comfort Suites, Hampton Inn, Holiday Inn, Holiday Inn Express, Quality Inn, $Tree, AT&T, Black's Tire & Auto, Chrysler/Dodge/Jeep, Honda, Lowe's, Lowe's Foods, Toyota, URGENT CARE, Verizon, Walmart/Subway, W Mobil, Sun-Do/dsl, Sunoco/dsl, Bojangles, Your Pie Pizza, Springhill Suites, Ford/Lincoln, Kia

NC

INTERSTATE 95 Cont'd

Exit #	Services
20	NC 211, to NC 41, Lumberton, E BP/dsl, Shell/dsl, Arby's, Arnold's Rest., Bojangles, Capt D's, CiCi's Pizza, Cook Out, Dunkin Donuts, Hardee's, Hong Kong Chinese, Hwy 55 Cafe, Jersey Mike's, Kami Japanese, KFC, McDonald's, Popeyes, Sonic, Subway, Taco Bell, Tokyo Express, Waffle House, Red Roof Inn, Travelodge Inn, Advance Parts, AutoZone, Belk, city park, CVS Drug, Food Lion/deli, H, Nissan, O'Reilly Parts, Verizon, Walgreens, W Marathon/dsl, Sun-do/dsl, Cracker Barrel, San Jose Mexican, Best Value, Comfort Inn, Country Inn&Suites, Fairfield Inn, Knights Inn, Lumberton Inn
19	Carthage Rd, Lumberton, E BP, Econolodge, W Sunoco, Motel 6, Royal Inn
18mm	Lumber River
17	NC 72, Lumberton, Pembroke, E Atkinson's/dsl, BP/dsl, Go-Gas/dsl, Mobil/dsl, Burger King, China Garden, Dominos, Hardee's, Huddle House, McDonald's, Pizza Hut, Subway, Waffle House, Atkinson Inn, Budget Inn, Economy Inn, Southern Inn, $General, $Tree, Advance Parts, AutoZone, CVS Drug, Food Lion, O'Reilly Parts, W KOA(3mi)
13	I-74, US 74, Rockingham, Wilmington, E to SE NC Beaches, to U.S.S. Wilmington
10	US 301, to Fairmont
7	to McDonald, Raynham
5mm	**full facilities, litter barrels, petwalk, , , vending, Welcome Ctr nb**
2	NC 130, to NC 904, Rowland
1b a	US 301, US 501, Dillon, E Sunoco/EVC, Burrito Loco, Peddler Steaks, Pedro's Trkstp, Budget Motel, South-of-the-Border Motel, Pedro's Campground, W Shell/dsl, Waffle House
0mm	North Carolina/South Carolina state line

LUMBERTON

DILLON

NC

INTERSTATE 240 (Asheville)

Exit #	Services
9mm	I-240 begins/ends on I-40, exit 53b a.
8	Fairview Rd, N Shell/dsl, Ay Carumba, Cheddar's, China Buffet, Coldstone, J&S Cafeteria, KFC, Little Caesar's, McDonald's, Papa John's, Subway, Ramada Inn, $General, Advance Parts, ALDI, Bi-Lo Foods, CVS Drug, Discount Tire, Hamrick's, Kohl's, PetSmart, U-Haul, Walmart/McDonald's, S Citgo, Pizza Hut, Home Depot
7.5mm	Swannanoa River
7	US 70, N Enmark, Best Western, Hyundai, Kia, Subaru, S Shell/dsl, Applebee's, Bonefish Grill, Buffalo Wild Wings, Burger King, Carrabba's, Chick-fil-A, Chili's, ChuckeCheese, Cici's Pizza, Cook Out, Cornerstone Rest., Cracker Barrel, DQ, Firehouse Subs, IHOP, Jersey Mike's Subs, Longhorn Steaks, McAlister's Deli, McDonald's, McDonald's, Mikado Japanese, O'Charley's, Olive Garden, Outback Steaks, Papa's Mexican, Red Lobster, Starbucks, Subway, Taco Bell, Waffle House, Wild Wok, Country Inn&Suites, Courtyard, Days Inn, EconoLodge, Extended Stay America, Hampton Inn, Holiday Inn, Homewood Suites, InTown Motor Inn, Mountaineer Inn, SpringHill Suites, Super 8, $Tree, AT&T, Barnes&Noble, Belk, Best Buy, BigLots, Clark Tire/auto, Dick's, Dillards, Firestone/auto, Ingles Foods/gas, JC Penney, Jo-Ann, Lowe's, Michael's, Midas, Office Depot, Old Navy, Ross, Target, TJ Maxx, Walgreens, Whole Foods Mkt
6	Tunnel Rd(from eb), same as 7
5b	US 70 E, US 74A, Charlotte St, N Exxon, Shell, Charlotte St. Grill, Fuddruckers, Starbucks, Two Guys Hogi, B&B, vet, S Chop House Rest., Renaissance Hotel, Sheraton, Civic Ctr
5a	US 25, Merrimon Ave, N Enmark, Exxon/dsl, Shell/dsl, Bojangles, Chick-fil-A, Green Life Foods, Harris Teeter, Staples, Trader Joe's
4c	Haywood St(no EZ return to eb), Montford, S Carmel's Rest., Isa's Bistro, Roman's Deli, B&B, Hotel Indigo, downtown
4b	Patton Ave(from eb), downtown
4a	US 19 N, US 23 N, US 70 W, to Weaverville
3b	Westgate, N Green Sage Cafe, Jason's Deli, Oriental Pavillion, Country Inn Suites, Crowne Plaza, CVS Drug, EarthFare Foods, Mr Transmission, Sam's Club/gas, Tuesday Morning
3a	US 19 S, US 23 S, W Asheville, N Shell/dsl, A&W/LJ Silver, Bojangles, Burger King, CookOut, Denny's, Dragon China, El Que Pasa Mexican, Firehouse Subs, Green Tea Japanese, Jersey Mike's, KFC, Krispy Kreme, Little Caesar's, McDonald's, Neo Burrito, New 1 China, Papa John's, Pizza Hut, Sonic, Subway, Taco Bell, Wendy's, Yoshida Japanese, Zingers Cafe, $General, Advance Parts, ALDI, AT&T, AutoZone, Clark Tire/auto, Ingles Foods, Sav-Mor Foods, URGENT CARE, vet, Walgreens
2	US 19, US 23, W Asheville, N Haywood Quickstop/dsl, Zia Mexican, S B&B Drug
1c	Amboy Rd(from eb)
1b	NC 191, to I-40 E, Brevard Rd, S camping, farmers mkt
1a	I-40 W, to Knoxville
0mm	I-240 begins/ends on I-40, exit 46b a.

W ASHEVILLE

INTERSTATE 440 (Raleigh)

Exit #	Services
16	I-40. I-440 begins/ends on I-40.
15	Poole Rd, E BP, Exxon, W 76, Circle K, Valero/dsl, Burger King, KFC/Taco Bell, McDonald's, Subway, Wang' Kitchen, Food Lion
14	I-495, US 64/264, to Wilson, to Rocky Mount
13b a	US 64 bus, New Bern Ave, to Wilson, E BP, Circle K, Exxon dsl, Marathon, Murphy USA/dsl, Shell/dsl, Bojangles Burger King, Domino's, El Tapatio, McDonald's, Papa John's Pizza Hut, Popeyes, Starbucks, Subway, Waffle House Wendy's, Budgetel, Comfort Suites, Econo Lodge, Holida Inn Express, Microtel, Advance Parts, AutoZone, CVS Drug Firestone/auto, Food Lion, O'Reilly Parts, Plemmons RV Ct U-Haul, vet, Wal-Mart, Walgreens, W H
12	Yonkers Rd, Brentwood Rd
11b a	US 1, US 401, Capital Blvd N, N BP, BP, Exxon, Mobi Valero/dsl, Baskin-Robbins/Dunkin Donuts, Buffalo Bro Pizza, Burger King, ChuckeCheese, Cookout, Golden Corra IHOP, Mayflower Seafood, McDonald's, Popeyes, Starbuck Taco Bell, Vallerta Mexican, Waffle House, Best Value In Best Western, Clarion Pointe, DoubleTree, La Quint MainStay Suites, Motel 6, Quality Inn, $Tree, Advanc Parts, AutoZone, Food Lion, U-Haul
10	Wake Forest Rd, N Bahama Breeze, Denny's, Days In Extended Stay America, Hilton, Hyatt Place, CVS Drug, S BP, Applebee's, Arby's, BurgerFi, CAVA, First Watc Jimmy John's, Jumbo China, McDonald's, Melting Pot Res Papa John's, Starbucks, Torchys Tacos, Tropical Smoothie, Comfort Inn, Courtyard, Extended Stay America, Advanc Parts, AutoZone, Buick/GMC, Costco/gas, Discount Tir Hyundai, Mazda, NAPA, Ross, Staples, Subaru, Trader Joe's
8b a	6 Forks Rd, North Hills, N Exxon/repair, Tesla EVC, Bonefish Grill, Capital Grille, Chick-fil-A, Chipotle, Chuy Cowfish Burgers, Firebirds Grill, Five Guys,

NORTH HILLS

CRABTREE VALLEY

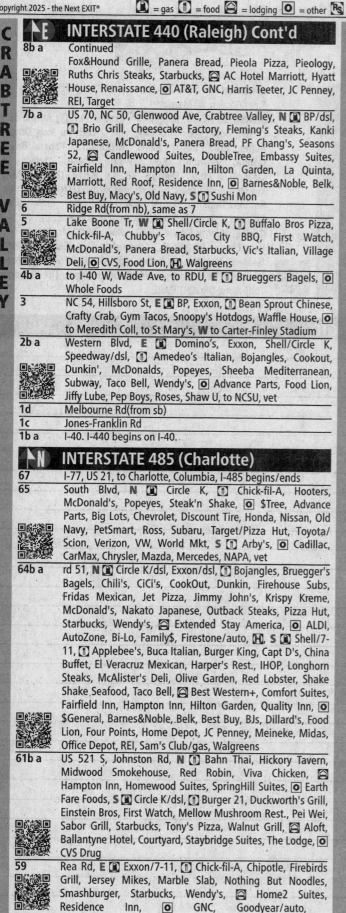

INTERSTATE 440 (Raleigh) Cont'd

8b a Continued
Fox&Hound Grille, Panera Bread, Pieola Pizza, Pieology, Ruths Chris Steaks, Starbucks, AC Hotel Marriott, Hyatt House, Renaissance, AT&T, GNC, Harris Teeter, JC Penney, REI, Target

7b a US 70, NC 50, Glenwood Ave, Crabtree Valley, N BP/dsl, Brio Grill, Cheesecake Factory, Fleming's Steaks, Kanki Japanese, McDonald's, Panera Bread, PF Chang's, Seasons 52, Candlewood Suites, DoubleTree, Embassy Suites, Fairfield Inn, Hampton Inn, Hilton Garden, La Quinta, Marriott, Red Roof, Residence Inn, Barnes&Noble, Belk, Best Buy, Macy's, Old Navy, S Sushi Mon

6 Ridge Rd(from nb), same as 7

5 Lake Boone Tr, W Shell/Circle K, Buffalo Bros Pizza, Chick-fil-A, Chubby's Tacos, City BBQ, First Watch, McDonald's, Panera Bread, Starbucks, Vic's Italian, Village Deli, CVS, Food Lion, H, Walgreens

4b a to I-40 W, Wade Ave, to RDU, E Brueggers Bagels, Whole Foods

3 NC 54, Hillsboro St, E BP, Exxon, Bean Sprout Chinese, Crafty Crab, Gym Tacos, Snoopy's Hotdogs, Waffle House, to Meredith Coll, to St Mary's, W to Carter-Finley Stadium

2b a Western Blvd, E Domino's, Exxon, Shell/Circle K, Speedway/dsl, Amedeo's Italian, Bojangles, Cookout, Dunkin', McDonalds, Popeyes, Sheeba Mediterranean, Subway, Taco Bell, Wendy's, Advance Parts, Food Lion, Jiffy Lube, Pep Boys, Roses, Shaw U, to NCSU, vet

1d Melbourne Rd(from sb)

1c Jones-Franklin Rd

1b a I-40. I-440 begins on I-40.

INTERSTATE 485 (Charlotte)

67 I-77, US 21, to Charlotte, Columbia, I-485 begins/ends

65 South Blvd, N Circle K, Chick-fil-A, Hooters, McDonald's, Popeyes, Steak'n Shake, $Tree, Advance Parts, Big Lots, Chevrolet, Discount Tire, Honda, Nissan, Old Navy, PetSmart, Ross, Subaru, Target/Pizza Hut, Toyota/Scion, Verizon, VW, World Mkt, S Arby's, Cadillac, CarMax, Chrysler, Mazda, Mercedes, NAPA, vet

64b a rd 51, N Circle K/dsl, Exxon/dsl, Bojangles, Bruegger's Bagels, Chili's, CiCi's, CookOut, Dunkin, Firehouse Subs, Fridas Mexican, Jet Pizza, Jimmy John's, Krispy Kreme, McDonald's, Nakato Japanese, Outback Steaks, Pizza Hut, Starbucks, Wendy's, Extended Stay America, ALDI, AutoZone, Bi-Lo, Family$, Firestone/auto, H, S Shell/7-11, Applebee's, Buca Italian, Burger King, Capt D's, China Buffet, El Veracruz Mexican, Harper's Rest., IHOP, Longhorn Steaks, McAlister's Deli, Olive Garden, Red Lobster, Shake Shake Seafood, Taco Bell, Best Western+, Comfort Suites, Fairfield Inn, Hampton Inn, Hilton Garden, Quality Inn, $General, Barnes&Noble, Belk, Best Buy, BJs, Dillard's, Food Lion, Four Points, Home Depot, JC Penney, Meineke, Midas, Office Depot, REI, Sam's Club/gas, Walgreens

61b a US 521 S, Johnston Rd, N Bahn Thai, Hickory Tavern, Midwood Smokehouse, Red Robin, Viva Chicken, Hampton Inn, Homewood Suites, SpringHill Suites, Earth Fare Foods, S Circle K/dsl, Burger 21, Duckworth's Grill, Einstein Bros, First Watch, Mellow Mushroom Rest., Pei Wei, Sabor Grill, Starbucks, Tony's Pizza, Walnut Grill, Aloft, Ballantyne Hotel, Courtyard, Staybridge Suites, The Lodge, CVS Drug

59 Rea Rd, E Exxon/7-11, Chick-fil-A, Chipotle, Firebirds Grill, Jersey Mikes, Marble Slab, Nothing But Noodles, Smashburger, Starbucks, Wendy's, Home2 Suites, Residence Inn, GNC, Goodyear/auto,

59 Continued
Harris Teeter/Starbucks, Michaels, Target, vet

57 Providence Rd, rd 16, E Circle K/Wendy's, Arbys, CAVA, Chick-fil-A, Chipotle, First Watch, Hickory Tavern, Ilios Noche, McDonalds, Panera Bread, Starbucks, Taziki, The Wok, Viva Peruvian, YAMA, Bojangles, Courtyard, CVS, Harris Teeter, USPO, W Exxon/7-11, Shell, Buffalo Wild Wings, Inizio Pizza, Queen City Rest., Showmars Rest., Starbucks, The Q Shack, CVS Drug, Harris-Teeter, Home Depot, Lowes Whse, Staples, SteinMart, vet

52 E John St, to Matthews

51b a US 74, to Charlotte, Monroe, E Hinsons Burgers, InTown Suites, Quality Inn, Wingate, Toyota, W Citgo/dsl, Exxon/7-11, Shell, Bojangles, Bonefish Grill, Bruegger's Bagels, Chipotle, DQ, Golden Corral, MOD Pizza, Panera Bread, South 21 Matthews, Wendy's, Courtyard, EconoLodge, Extended Stay, Microtel, AutoZone, Best Buy, Black's Auto/tire, Costco/gas, Firestone/auto, Harris Teeter/Starbucks, Home Depot, H, Lowe's Whse, Sam's Club/gas, Target/Starbucks

49 Idlewild Rd, E Exxon/7-11/dsl, China Cafe, Cornerstone Grill, Moochie's Tavern, $Tree, Harris Teeter, Mavis

47 Lawyers Rd, E Gate/dsl, Best China, Carnita's Mexican, Domino's, Fresh Chef, McDonald's, Subway, CVS Drug, Firestone/auto, Harris Teeter, vet

44 rd 218, to Mint Hill, E O'Reilly Parts, tires, W BP/dsl, Exxon/7-11, J-Birds, $General, ALDI, city park, CVS, Food Lion

43 rd 51, to Mint Hill

41 rd 24, rd 27, to Albemarle, E BP/EVC, Speedway/dsl, Arby's, Bojangles, McDonalds, Waffle House, H, W Wendy's

39 Harrisburg Rd, W BP/EVC, China Garden, Papa John's, Wendy's, Food Lion

36 Rocky River Rd, E BP/dsl, Gate/dsl, Best China, Bojangles, Capriccio Pizza, Chick-fil-A, Dunkin, Subway, CVS Drug, Discount Tire, Harris Teeter/Starbucks, H, Tuffy Auto

33 rd 49, to Harrisburg, E Mobil/dsl, Cici's Pizza, Food Lion, USPO, W BP, Circle K/dsl, Exxon/7-11, Exxon/7-11/dsl, Arby's, Chopsticks, Domino's, Hungry Howie's, Jimmy Johns, Little Caesar's, Wendy's, Family$

32 US 29, N QT/dsl, CVS Drug, Walmart Mkt, S Circle K, Exxon/7-11/dsl, Mobil/dsl, Jack-in-the-Box, H

30b a I-85, N to High Point, S to Charlotte

28 Mallard Creek Rd

26 Benfield Rd, Prosperity Church Rd, Prosperity Ridge Rd, N BP/EVC/dsl, Bojangles, Chick-fil-A, Hunan Park, IHOP, Jersey Mike's, Little Big Burger, Papa Johns, Starbucks, $Tree, ALDI, Harris Teeter, Mavis, Publix, S Circle K/dsl, Due Amici Pizza

23c rd 115, to Huntersville, N Shell/7-11/dsl, Bojangles, McDonald's, Audi, BMW, Firestone, Lexus, Mercedes, Walmart

23b a I-77, to Charlotte, Statesville

21 rd 24, Harris Blvd, N Exxon/7-11, QT, Popeyes, $General, Food Lion, Jiffy Lube, S Buffalo Wild Wings, Chick-fil-A, Chili's, Chipotle, East Coast Grill, Edomae Grill, Firebirds Grill, Firehouse Subs, Five Guys, Jersey Mike's, McDonald's, Olive Garden, On-the-Border, Panera bread, PF Chang's, Red Crab, Red Robin, TGI Friday's, Wendy's, Drury Inn, Hampton Inn, $Tree, AT&T, Belk, Best Buy, Dick's, Dillard's, Discount Tire, Lowe's Whse, Macy's, mall, Old Navy, PetSmart, REI, Target, Verizon

16 rd 16, to Newton, Brookshire Blvd, E city park, W Exxon, QT/dsl, Bojangles, Chick-fil-A, Chick-fil-A, Chicken Salad Chick, Domino's, First Watch, Freddys,

NC

= gas = food = lodging = other = rest stop

INTERSTATE 485 (Charlotte) Cont'd

16 Continued
Johnny Brusco's Pizza, McDonald's, Papa John's, Pizza Hut, Red Bowl Asian, Taco Bell, Wendy's, AT&T, AutoZone, Harris-Teeter/Starbucks/gas, O'Reilly Parts, vet, Walgreens, Walmart/Subway

14 rd 27, to Mt Holly Rd

12 Moores Chapel Rd, **E** Jin Jin Chinese, Subway, Advance Parts, CVS Drug, Food Lion

10b a I-85, to Spartanburg, Greensboro

9 US 29, US 74, Wilkinson Blvd, **S** Mobil, rv camping

6 West Blvd

4 rd 160, to Fort Mill, **N** Exxon/7-11/dsl, Waffle House, CVS Drug, **S** BP/dsl, Mobil, Arbys, Bojangles, Chicken Salad Chick, First Watch, Longhorn Steaks, McAlisters Deli, McDonalds, Olive Garden, Outback Steaks, Smithfields BBQ, Starbucks, Wendys, Zaxby's, Courtyard, Hampton Inn, Residence Inn/EVC, Charlotte Premium Outlets/famous brands, Harris Teeter/gas, Walgreens

3 Arrowood Rd, **N** Holiday Inn Express, **S** Quizno's,

3 Continued
Siam Garden, Marriott

1 S Tryon St, NC 49, **N** Citgo, Exxon/7-11, Arby's, Blue Orchid, Bojangles, Chick-fil-A, Chili's, Crab Du Jour, Dragon Buffet, IHOP, Jimmy Johns, McDonald's, Panera Bread, Qdoba, Showmars Rest., Waffle House, Zaxby's, Carmella's Pizza, Family$, Lowe's Whse, O'Reilly Parts, Walgreens, Walmart, **S** Kangaroo/dsl, QT/dsl, Baskin-Robbins/Dunkin, Burger King, Chipotle, Clean Eatz, Domino's, Don Pedro Mexican, Firehouse Subs, Fortune Cookie, Hungry Howie's, KFC, Mac's BBQ, McAlister's Deli, Pan China, Portofino's, Starbucks, Taco Bell, Hilton Garden, Homewood Suites, $Tree, AT&T, AutoZone, Discount Tire, Food Lion, NAPA, Office Depot, Tire Kingdom, Tuffy Auto, URGENT CARE

NOTES

NC

NORTH DAKOTA

INTERSTATE 29

BOWESMONT GRAND FORKS

Exit #	Services
218mm	US/Canada border, North Dakota state line
217mm	US Customs sb
216mm	historical site nb, tourist info sb
215	ND 59, rd 55, Pembina, E Gastrak/dsl/scales/24hr, Gastrak/DutyFree Store/dsl, Pembina State Museum/info
212	no services
208	rd 1, to Bathgate
203	US 81, ND 5, to Hamilton, Cavalier, weigh sta both lanes, W to Icelandic SP(25 mi)
200	no services
196	rd 3, Bowesmont
193	no services
191	rd 11, to St Thomas
187	ND 66, to Drayton, E Arco/dsl, Cenex/dsl/E-85, Hastings Landing Rest., Motel 66, city park, USPO, W Love's/Taco John's/dsl/scales/RV hookup/24hr
184	to Drayton
180	rd 9
179mm	**full facilities, litter barrels, petwalk, both lanes(both lanes exit left), vending**
176	ND 17, to Grafton
172	65th St NE
168	rd 15, to Minto, Warsaw
164	57th St NE
161	ND 54, rd 19, to Ardoch, Oslo
157	32nd Ave
152	US 81, to Gilby, Manvel, W Manvel/dsl/food
145	US 81 bus, N Washington St, to Grand Forks
141	US 2, Gateway Dr, Grand Forks, E Casey's/dsl, Cenex, Loaf'N Jug/dsl, Burger King, Far East Buffet, Little Caesar's, McDonald's, Papa Murphy's, Taco John's, Wake'N Bake Cafe, Best Value Inn, EconoLodge, Ideal Inn, Ramada Inn, Super 8, Freightliner, Hugo's Foods, O'Reilly Parts, Peterbilt, Subaru, to U of ND, transmissions, U-Haul, visitors ctr, W Simonson/café/dsl/EVC/24hr, StaMart/dsl/RV dump/scales/24hr/@, Hardee's, Knights Inn, Budget RV Ctr, dsl repair, Mack/Volvo, NW Tire, to AFB, vet, Walmart
140	DeMers Ave, E Cenex/dsl, Loaf'N Jug/dsl, Marathon/Valley Dairy, Red Pepper Cafe, Baymont Inn, Canada Inn, Expressway Suites, Hilton Garden, La Quinta, My Place Suites, Sleep Inn, Staybridge Suites, Alerus Ctr, H, to U of ND
138	US 81, 32nd Ave S, E Cenex, Holiday/dsl, Telsa EVC, Applebee's, Arby's, Buffalo Wild Wings, Burger King, Charras Mexican, Cherry Berry Yogurt, Chick-fil-A, China Garden, Coldstone, Culver's, DQ, Erbert&Gerbert's, Firehouse Subs, Five Guys, Ground Round, IHOP, Jimmy John's, McDonald's, Noodles&Co, Olive Garden, Panera Bread, Papa Murphy's, Pizza Ranch, Qdoba Mexican, Red Lobster, Sakura Japanese, Starbucks, Subway, TX Roadhouse, Wendy's/EVC, Best Western, C'mon Inn, Country Inn&Suites, Days Inn, Fairfield Inn, Hampton Inn, Holiday Inn Express, Quality Inn, Rodeway Inn, SpringHill Suites, $Tree, ALDI, Best Buy, Chrysler/Dodge/Jeep, CVS Drug, Ford/Lincoln, Gordman's, Hobby Lobby, Hugo's Foods, JC Penney, Kohl's, Lowe's, Menards, Michael's, Natural Grocers, Old Navy, PetCo, Sam's Club/gas, Scheel's, Target, Tire 1, Tires+, TJ Maxx, Toyota/Scion, Verizon, vet, Walmart/Subway, White Drug, W Flying J/Subway/dsl/LP/scales/RV dump/24hr, Hangar 54 Pizza,

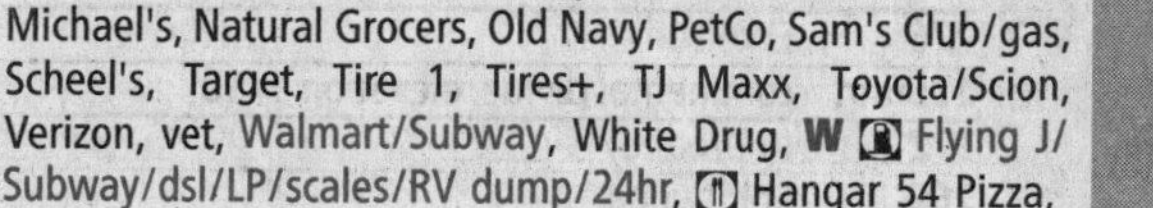

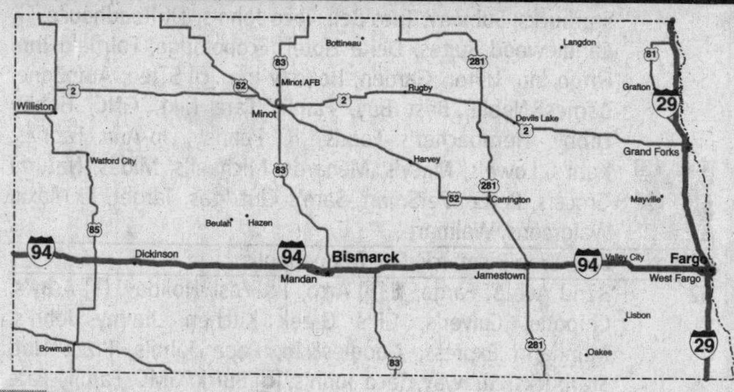

ARGUSVILLE FARGO

Exit #	Services
138	Continued Grand Forks Camping(1mi)
130	ND 15, rd 81, Thompson
123	to Reynolds
120	truck insp sb
118	to Buxton
111	ND 200 W, to Cummings, Mayville, W Big Top Fireworks, to Mayville St U
104	Hillsboro, E Casey's/EVC, Cenex/Burger King/dsl/LP/24hr, Subway, Hillsboro Inn, Hillsboro Camping, H, U-Haul, USPO
100	ND 200 E, ND 200A, to Blanchard, Halstad
99mm	**full facilities, litter barrels, petwalk, both lanes, vending**
92	rd 11, Grandin, E tire repair
86	Gardner
78	Argusville
74.5mm	Sheyenne River
72	rd 17, rd 22, Harwood, E Cenex/dsl/LP/café/24hr, W USPO
69	rd 20
67	US 81 bus, 19th Ave N, E Casey's, Holiday, Applebee's, Buffalo Wild Wings, Burger King, Chipotle, Little Caesars, McDonald's, Red Pepper Mexican, Subway, Taco Bell, Candlewood Suites, Days Inn, Homewood Suites, CVS Drug, Hector Int, to ND St U, VA H
66	12th Ave N, E StaMart/dsl/scales/24hr, Woodspring Suites, H, to ND St U, tuck repair, W Cenex/dsl, Arby's, Super 8, tire repair
65	US 10, Main Ave, W Fargo, E Petro Serve/dsl, CarQuest, NAPA, OK Tire, vet, W Cenex/Subway/dsl, Simonson/dsl, Hardee's, Biltmore on Main Inn, Camping World, CarQuest, Honda, Kia, Lincoln, Mac's Hardware, Mazda, Mercedes, O'Reilly Parts, Toyota/Scion, VW
64	13th Ave, Fargo, E Casey's, Exxon, Marathon/Don's, PetroServe/dsl, Acapulco Mexican, Applebee's, Arby's, Buck's Rest, Burger King, ChuckeCheese, DQ, Erbert&Gerbert's Subs, Perkins, Schlotzsky's, Sickie's Garage, Subway, Taco John's, Wendy's, AmericInn, Best Value, Bison Inn, Country Inn&Suites, Days Inn, Grand Inn, Motel 6, Quality Suites, Ramada Inn, Travelodge, CashWise Foods/drug/gas, CVS Drug, Family$, Goodyear/auto, Jiffy Lube, O'Reilly Parts, Tires+/transmissions, Tuesday Morning, Verizon, White Drug, W Casey's, Exxon/dsl, Arby's, Blaze Pizza, Boston's Rest, Buffalo Wild Wings, Chick-fil-A, Chili's, Coldstone, Culver's, Denny's, Domino's, DQ, Five Guys, Giant Panda Chinese, Hardee's, Izumi Hibachi, KFC, Kobe Japanese, Kroll's Diner, La Fiesta Mexican, Longhorn Steaks, McDonald's, Noodles & Co, Olive Garden, Osaka Japanese, Pancheros Mexican, Panera Bread,

ND

INTERSTATE 29 Cont'd

64 Continued
Paradiso Mexican, Pizza Hut, Porter Creek BBQ, Red Lobster, Starbucks, Subway, Taco Bell, Taco John's, TX Roadhouse, Candlewood Suites, Delta Hotel, Econolodge, Fairfield Inn, Fargo Inn, Hilton Garden, Holiday Inn, $Tree, AutoZone, Barnes&Noble, Best Buy, Family Fare Mkt, GNC, Hobby Lobby, Hornbacher's Foods, JC Penney, Jo-Ann Fabrics, Kohl's, Lowe's, Macy's, Menards, Michael's, Midas, Natural Grocers, PetCo, PetSmart, Sam's Club/gas, Target, TJ Maxx, Walgreens, Walmart

63b a I-94, W to Bismarck, E to Minneapolis

62 32nd Ave S, Fargo, E Arco, F&F/dsl, Holiday, Arby's, Chipotle, Culver's, GP's Greek Kitchen, Jimmy John's, Mandarin Express, Noodles&Co, Papa John's, Pizza Hut, Starbucks, Subway, Taco John's, Buick/GMC, Family Fare Mkt, Ford, Freightliner, H, JiffyLube, Verizon, W Flying J/Huddle House/dsl/LP/scales/24hr/@, Love's/McDonald's/Subway/dsl/scales/24hr, Motel 6, Elite Auto Repair, Mack/Volvo, Peterbilt

60 52nd Ave S, to Fargo, E Casey's/dsl/e85, Marathon/Don's/Hot Stuff Pizza, Burger King, DQ, Jersey Mike's, W Panda Express, AutoZone, Walmart

56 to Wild Rice, Horace

54 rd 16, to Oxbow, Davenport

50 rd 18, Hickson

48 ND 46, to Kindred

44 to Christine

42 rd 2, to Walcott, E gas

37 rd 4, to Abercrombie, Colfax, E to Ft Abercrombie HS, W gas(1.5mi)

31 rd 8, Galchutt

26 to Dwight

24mm weigh sta both lanes exit left

23b a ND 13, to Wahpeton, Mooreton, E H, ND St Coll of Science

15 rd 16, to Mantador, Great Bend

8 ND 11, to Hankinson, Fairmount, E Marathon/dsl, W camping

3mm **full facilities, litter barrels, petwalk, Welcome Ctr nb**

2 rd 22

1 rd 1E, E Dakota Magic Casino/Hotel/rest./gas/dsl

0mm North Dakota/South Dakota state line

INTERSTATE 94

352mm North Dakota/Minnesota state line, Red River

351 US 81, Fargo, N Casey's, Loaf'n Jug, CJ's Kitchen, Domino's, Duane's Pizza, Great Harvest Breads, Great Wall Chinese, Taco Shop, Hornbacher's Foods, H, Medicine Shoppe, vet, S Cenex/dsl, Burger King, Marcos Pizza, McDonald's, Pepper's Café, Randy's Diner, Subway, Taco Bell, Baymont, Rodeway Inn, K-Mart

350 25th St, Fargo, N Casey's, S Casey's/dsl, Loaf'n Jug/dsl, Dolittle's Grill, Ruby Tuesday

349b a I-29, N to Grand Forks, S to Sioux Falls, services 1 mi N, exit 64

348 45th St, **N Visitor Ctr/, full facilities, litter barrels,** Holiday/dsl, Petro/Popeyes/dsl/Lp/24hr, Carino's, Chipotle, Coldstone, Culver's, Denny's, HuHot Mongolian, IHOP, Kroll's Diner, Little Caesar's, Longhorn Steaks, McDonald's, Noodles&Co, Olive Garden, Panda Express, Papa Murphy's, Pizza Hut, Porter Creek BBQ, Potbelly, Qdoba, Smashburger, Space Aliens Grill, Subway, TX Roadhouse, Wendy's, Wild Bill's, Best Western+, C'Mon Inn, Delta Inn, Expressway Suites, Hilton Garden,

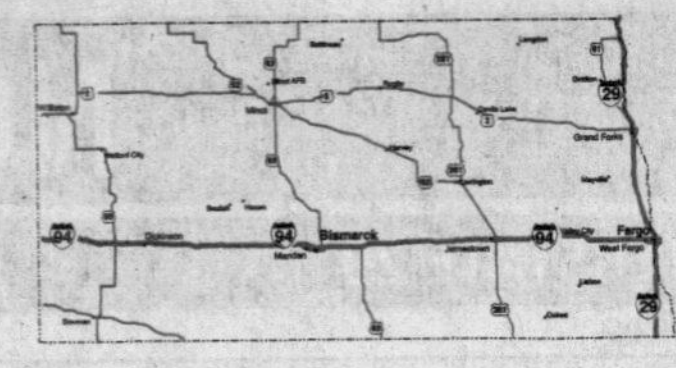

348 Continued
Holiday Inn Express, Home2 Suites, MainStay Suites, Red Roof Inn, Staybridge Suites, Wingate Inn, Blue Beacon, Hobby Lobby, Home Depot, Kohl's, NAPA, Sam's Club, Scheel's Sports, Target, Tuffy Auto, Verizon, Walmart/Subway, S Casey's/DQ/dsl, Holiday, Applebee's, Freddy's Burgers, Hardee's, Korean BBQ, Mexican Village, Mi Familia, Old Chicago Pizza, Pizza Ranch, Slim Chickens, Smiling Moose Sandwiches, Sonic, Starbucks, Taco John's, AmericInn, Comfort Suites, Hampton Inn, La Quinta, Residence Inn, Sheraton, Sleep Inn, AT&T, Red River Zoo

347 9th St E, Veterans Blvd, N Jojo's Italian, DoubleTree, Element Hotel, Homewood Suites, S Casey's/dsl, Tesla EVC, Barcode Grill, Burger King, Firehouse Subs, Izumi Japanese, Jersey Mikes, Jimmy John's, MacKenzie River Pizza, McAlister's Deli, McDonald's, Oasis Rest., Papa John's, Plaza Azteca, Say Cheese Mac, Spicy Pie Pizza, Subway, Taco Bell, Wurst Bier Hall, Courtyard, Microtel, My Place Hotel, Costco/gas, H, O'Reilly Parts

346b a to Horace, W Fargo, S Tesoro/dsl, Harley Davidson, repair

343 US 10, Lp 94, W Fargo, N Cenex/dsl, Adventure RV Ctr

342 38th St NE

342mm weigh sta wb

340 to Kindred

338 Mapleton, N Arco

337mm truck parking wb, litter barrels

331 ND 18, to Leonard, Casselton, N Marathon/Subway/dsl, Country Kitchen, Days Inn/RV park

328 to Lynchburg

327mm truck parking eb, litter barrels

324 Wheatland, to Chaffee

322 Absaraka

320 to Embden

317 to Ayr

314 ND 38 N, to Alice, Buffalo

310 36th St SE

307 to Tower City, N Cenex/café/dsl/RV Park/24hr

304mm **full facilities, info, litter barrels, petwalk, both lanes(both lanes exit left), vending**

302 ND 32, to Fingal, Oriska

298 123rd Ave SE

296 121st Av SE

294 Lp 94, to Kathryn, Valley City, N H

292 Valley City, N PetroServe/Marathon/café/dsl, Sabir's Rest., AmericInn, Econolodge, Grand Stay Hotel, Super 8, Ford, H, to Bald Hill Dam, S Love's/scales/24hr/@, Ft Ransom SP(35mi)

291 Sheyenne River

290 Lp 94, Valley City, N Casey's/dsl, Budget Burger, Burger King, Chinese Palace, Dakota Dogs, Kirin House Chinese, Maria! Maria!, Pizza Ranch, Subway, Buick/Chevrolet, GMC, Family$, Firestone/auto, H, NAPA, O'Reilly Parts

288 ND 1 S, to Oakes, S Fort Ransom SP(36 mi)

283 ND 1 N, to Rogers

281 to Litchville, Sanborn

276 Eckelson

275mm continental divide, elevation 1490

272 to Urbana

269 Spiritwood

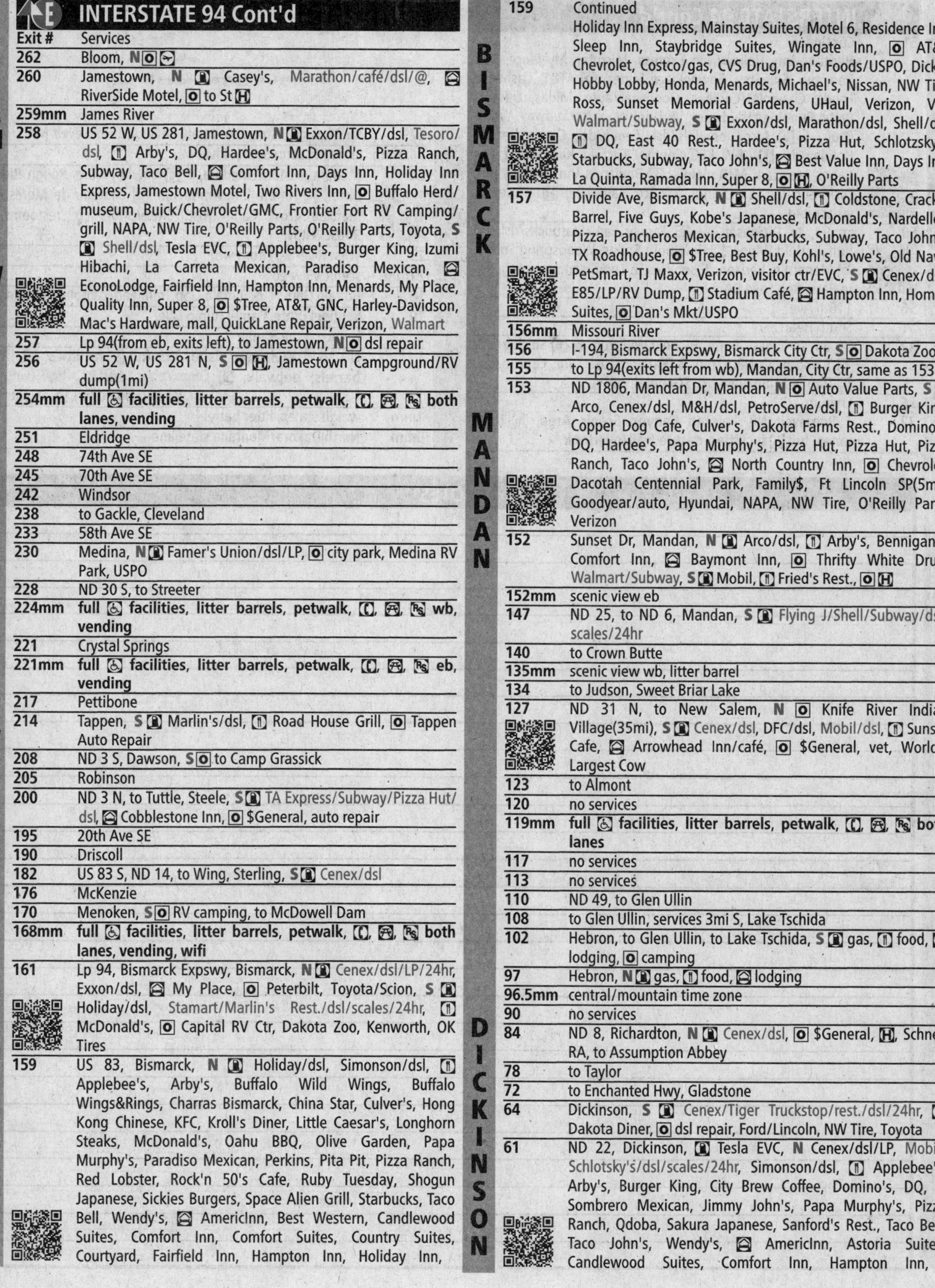

INTERSTATE 94 Cont'd

Exit #	Services
262	Bloom, N
260	Jamestown, N Casey's, Marathon/café/dsl/@, RiverSide Motel, to St
259mm	James River
258	US 52 W, US 281, Jamestown, N Exxon/TCBY/dsl, Tesoro/dsl, Arby's, DQ, Hardee's, McDonald's, Pizza Ranch, Subway, Taco Bell, Comfort Inn, Days Inn, Holiday Inn Express, Jamestown Motel, Two Rivers Inn, Buffalo Herd/museum, Buick/Chevrolet/GMC, Frontier Fort RV Camping/grill, NAPA, NW Tire, O'Reilly Parts, O'Reilly Parts, Toyota, S Shell/dsl, Tesla EVC, Applebee's, Burger King, Izumi Hibachi, La Carreta Mexican, Paradiso Mexican, EconoLodge, Fairfield Inn, Hampton Inn, Menards, My Place, Quality Inn, Super 8, $Tree, AT&T, GNC, Harley-Davidson, Mac's Hardware, mall, QuickLane Repair, Verizon, Walmart
257	Lp 94(from eb, exits left), to Jamestown, N dsl repair
256	US 52 W, US 281 N, S Jamestown Campground/RV dump(1mi)
254mm	**full facilities, litter barrels, petwalk, both lanes, vending**
251	Eldridge
248	74th Ave SE
245	70th Ave SE
242	Windsor
238	to Gackle, Cleveland
233	58th Ave SE
230	Medina, N Famer's Union/dsl/LP, city park, Medina RV Park, USPO
228	ND 30 S, to Streeter
224mm	**full facilities, litter barrels, petwalk, wb, vending**
221	Crystal Springs
221mm	**full facilities, litter barrels, petwalk, eb, vending**
217	Pettibone
214	Tappen, S Marlin's/dsl, Road House Grill, Tappen Auto Repair
208	ND 3 S, Dawson, S to Camp Grassick
205	Robinson
200	ND 3 N, to Tuttle, Steele, S TA Express/Subway/Pizza Hut/dsl, Cobblestone Inn, $General, auto repair
195	20th Ave SE
190	Driscoll
182	US 83 S, ND 14, to Wing, Sterling, S Cenex/dsl
176	McKenzie
170	Menoken, S RV camping, to McDowell Dam
168mm	**full facilities, litter barrels, petwalk, both lanes, vending, wifi**
161	Lp 94, Bismarck Expswy, Bismarck, N Cenex/dsl/LP/24hr, Exxon/dsl, My Place, Peterbilt, Toyota/Scion, S Holiday/dsl, Stamart/Marlin's Rest./dsl/scales/24hr, McDonald's, Capital RV Ctr, Dakota Zoo, Kenworth, OK Tires
159	US 83, Bismarck, N Holiday/dsl, Simonson/dsl, Applebee's, Arby's, Buffalo Wild Wings, Buffalo Wings&Rings, Charras Bismarck, China Star, Culver's, Hong Kong Chinese, KFC, Kroll's Diner, Little Caesar's, Longhorn Steaks, McDonald's, Oahu BBQ, Olive Garden, Papa Murphy's, Paradiso Mexican, Perkins, Pita Pit, Pizza Ranch, Red Lobster, Rock'n 50's Cafe, Ruby Tuesday, Shogun Japanese, Sickies Burgers, Space Alien Grill, Starbucks, Taco Bell, Wendy's, AmericInn, Best Western, Candlewood Suites, Comfort Inn, Comfort Suites, Country Suites, Courtyard, Fairfield Inn, Hampton Inn, Holiday Inn,
159	Continued Holiday Inn Express, Mainstay Suites, Motel 6, Residence Inn, Sleep Inn, Staybridge Suites, Wingate Inn, AT&T, Chevrolet, Costco/gas, CVS Drug, Dan's Foods/USPO, Dick's, Hobby Lobby, Honda, Menards, Michael's, Nissan, NW Tire, Ross, Sunset Memorial Gardens, UHaul, Verizon, VW, Walmart/Subway, S Exxon/dsl, Marathon/dsl, Shell/dsl, DQ, East 40 Rest., Hardee's, Pizza Hut, Schlotzsky's, Starbucks, Subway, Taco John's, Best Value Inn, Days Inn, La Quinta, Ramada Inn, Super 8, O'Reilly Parts
157	Divide Ave, Bismarck, N Shell/dsl, Coldstone, Cracker Barrel, Five Guys, Kobe's Japanese, McDonald's, Nardello's Pizza, Pancheros Mexican, Starbucks, Subway, Taco John's, TX Roadhouse, $Tree, Best Buy, Kohl's, Lowe's, Old Navy, PetSmart, TJ Maxx, Verizon, visitor ctr/EVC, S Cenex/dsl/E85/LP/RV Dump, Stadium Café, Hampton Inn, Home2 Suites, Dan's Mkt/USPO
156mm	Missouri River
156	I-194, Bismarck Expswy, Bismarck City Ctr, S Dakota Zoo
155	to Lp 94(exits left from wb), Mandan, City Ctr, same as 153
153	ND 1806, Mandan Dr, Mandan, N Auto Value Parts, S Arco, Cenex/dsl, M&H/dsl, PetroServe/dsl, Burger King, Copper Dog Cafe, Culver's, Dakota Farms Rest., Domino's, DQ, Hardee's, Papa Murphy's, Pizza Hut, Pizza Hut, Pizza Ranch, Taco John's, North Country Inn, Chevrolet, Dacotah Centennial Park, Family$, Ft Lincoln SP(5mi), Goodyear/auto, Hyundai, NAPA, NW Tire, O'Reilly Parts, Verizon
152	Sunset Dr, Mandan, N Arco/dsl, Arby's, Bennigan's, Comfort Inn, Baymont Inn, Thrifty White Drug, Walmart/Subway, S Mobil, Fried's Rest.,
152mm	scenic view eb
147	ND 25, to ND 6, Mandan, S Flying J/Shell/Subway/dsl/scales/24hr
140	to Crown Butte
135mm	scenic view wb, litter barrel
134	to Judson, Sweet Briar Lake
127	ND 31 N, to New Salem, N Knife River Indian Village(35mi), S Cenex/dsl, DFC/dsl, Mobil/dsl, Sunset Cafe, Arrowhead Inn/café, $General, vet, World's Largest Cow
123	to Almont
120	no services
119mm	**full facilities, litter barrels, petwalk, both lanes**
117	no services
113	no services
110	ND 49, to Glen Ullin
108	to Glen Ullin, services 3mi S, Lake Tschida
102	Hebron, to Glen Ullin, to Lake Tschida, S gas, food, lodging, camping
97	Hebron, N gas, food, lodging
96.5mm	central/mountain time zone
90	no services
84	ND 8, Richardton, N Cenex/dsl, $General, Schnell RA, to Assumption Abbey
78	to Taylor
72	to Enchanted Hwy, Gladstone
64	Dickinson, S Cenex/Tiger Truckstop/rest./dsl/24hr, Dakota Diner, dsl repair, Ford/Lincoln, NW Tire, Toyota
61	ND 22, Dickinson, Tesla EVC, N Cenex/dsl/LP, Mobil/Schlotsky's/dsl/scales/24hr, Simonson/dsl, Applebee's, Arby's, Burger King, City Brew Coffee, Domino's, DQ, El Sombrero Mexican, Jimmy John's, Papa Murphy's, Pizza Ranch, Qdoba, Sakura Japanese, Sanford's Rest., Taco Bell, Taco John's, Wendy's, AmericInn, Astoria Suites, Candlewood Suites, Comfort Inn, Hampton Inn,

JAMESTOWN CLEVELAND DAWSON BISMARCK BISMARCK MANDAN DICKINSON ND

DICKINSON

INTERSTATE 94 Cont'd

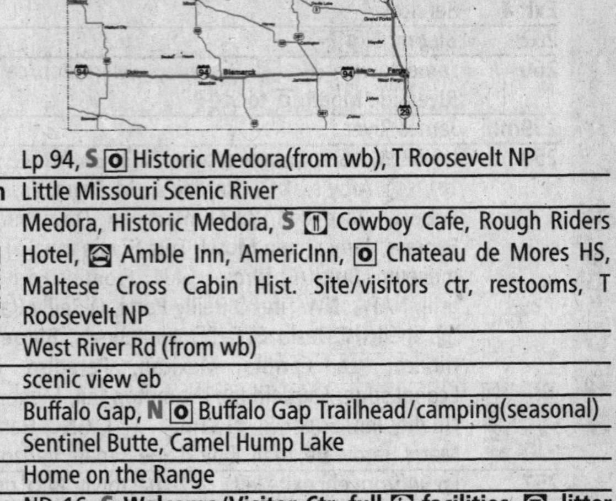

61 Continued
Heritage Inn, Holiday Inn Express, Microtel, My Place, Red Roof Inn, SureStay, TownePlace Suites, AT&T, Cashwise Foods, Chevrolet/Cadillac, Goodyear/auto, Midas, O'Reilly Parts, Runnings Hardware, Verizon, Walmart/Subway, White Drug, S Arco/Domino's/dsl, Cenex/dsl, Conoco/repair, Holiday/dsl, A&W/KFC, Country Kitchen, King Buffet, Los Cabos Mexican, McDonald's, Badlands Inn, Budget Inn, Dickinson Inn, La Quinta, Ace Hardware, H, museum, visitor info

59 Lp 94, to Dickinson, N Family Fare/Starbucks/dsl, Buffalo Wild Wings, Hawthorn Suites, Woodspring Suites, Menard's, Verizon, S services in Dickinson, camping, H, to Patterson Lake RA

56 116th Ave

51 South Heart

42 US 85, to Grassy Butte, Belfield,Williston, N Sinclair/dsl, T Roosevelt NP(52mi), S Cenex/dsl/24hr, Conoco/dsl, Trapper's Inn/Rest., $General, NAPA

36 Fryburg

32 T Roosevelt NP, **Painted Canyon Scenic Area, both lanes, full facilities, nature trail/overlook**

27 Lp 94, S Historic Medora(from wb), T Roosevelt NP

24.5mm Little Missouri Scenic River

24 Medora, Historic Medora, S Cowboy Cafe, Rough Riders Hotel, Amble Inn, AmericInn, Chateau de Mores HS, Maltese Cross Cabin Hist. Site/visitors ctr, restooms, T Roosevelt NP

23 West River Rd (from wb)

22mm scenic view eb

18 Buffalo Gap, N Buffalo Gap Trailhead/camping(seasonal)

10 Sentinel Butte, Camel Hump Lake

7 Home on the Range

1 ND 16, **S Welcome/Visitor Ctr, full facilities, litter barrels, petwalk,** Cenex/pizza/dsl/LP/24hr, Flying J/ Subway/dsl/scales/LP/24hr, Buckboard Inn, $General

1mm weigh sta eb, litter barrel

0mm North Dakota/Montana state line

NOTES

 = gas = food = lodging = other = rest stop

OHIO

INTERSTATE 70

BRIDGEPORT · FLUSHING · CAMBRIDGE

Exit #	Services
225.5mm	Ohio/West Virginia state line, Ohio River
225	US 250 W, OH 7, Bridgeport, N Marathon, Marathon, Sunoco/dsl, DQ, Papa John's, Pizza Hut, Sha Nay Nay's Pizza, Extended Stay, Advance Parts, AutoZone, Family$, Meineke, S Clark, Gulf, Domino's
220	US 40, rd 214, N Sunoco/dsl, U-Haul, Comfort Inn, S Exxon/dsl, Days Inn, vet
219	I-470 E, to Bel-Aire, from eb, Washington PA
218	Mall Rd, to US 40, to Blaine, N BP, Exxon/dsl, Sheetz/dsl, Applebee's, Arby's, Burger King, DeFelice Pizza, Denny's, Eat'n Park, HoneyBaked Ham, Kirke's Creamery, Little Caesar's, Outback Steaks, Pizza Hut, Red Lobster, Steak'n Shake, Taco Bell, Tlaquepaque Mexican, W Texas Steaks, Wendy's, Best Value Inn, Best Western, Hawthorn Suites, Knights Inn, Microtel, Red Roof Inn, Super 8, Wingate Inn, $General, Advance Parts, ALDI, AT&T, AutoZone, Buick/Cadillac/Chevrolet, CVS Drug, Kroger, Lowe's, Sam's Club, Staples, URGENT CARE, Verizon, Walmart, S Bob Evans, Buffalo Wild Wings, Chick-fil-A, Chipotle, Coaches Burgers, Cracker Barrel, KFC/LJ Silver, Longhorn Steaks, McDonald's, Osaka Steaks, Panera Bread, Starbucks, Candlewood Suites, Fairfield Inn, Hampton Inn, Residence Inn, Boscov's, Jo-Ann Fabrics, Marshall's, NTB
216	OH 9, St Clairsville, N Marathon
215	National Rd, N Burger King, Domino's, WenWu Chinese, Riesbeck's Foods, USPO
213	OH 331, Flushing, S Arco, Marathon/Subway/dsl, Sunoco/dsl
211mm	**full facilities, litter barrels, petwalk, , , both lanes, vending**
208	OH 149, Morristown, N Exxon/McDonald's/dsl, DiCarlo's Pizza, Schlepp's Rest., Arrowhead Motel, Days Inn, $General, Ford/Lincoln, S Marathon/dsl, Pilot/Subway/dsl/scales/24hr, Sleep Inn, Barkcamp SP
204	US 40 E(from eb, no return), National Rd
202	OH 800, to Barnesville, S Sunoco/dsl,
198	rd 114, Fairview
193	OH 513, Middlebourne, N BP, FuelMart/dsl, fireworks
189mm	**full facilities, litter barrels, petwalk, , , eb, vending**
186	US 40, OH 285, to Old Washington, N Marathon/dsl, $General, S GoMart/dsl, Speedway/dsl/scales/24hr
180b a	I-77 N, to Cleveland, to Salt Fork SP, I-77 S, to Charleston
178	OH 209, Cambridge, N Marathon/dsl, Sheetz/dsl, Bob Evans, Cracker Barrel, Denny's, DQ, Dunkin', Forum Rest., KFC, McDonald's, Papa John's, Pizza Hut, Ruby Tuesday, Subway, Tim Hortons, Wendy's, Best Western, Comfort Inn, Days Inn, Hampton Inn, Holiday Inn Express, Microtel, Quality Inn, Southgate Hotel, $General, Advance Parts, AutoZone, BigLots, Cash Saver Foods, Ford, O'Reilly Parts, S Murphy USA/dsl, Pilot/Subway/dsl/scales/24hr, Arby's, Buffalo Wild Wings, Burger King, Chipotle, Little Caesar's, Starbucks, Taco Bell, Tlaquepaque Mexican, Baymont Inn, Fairfield Inn, $Tree, ALDI, Chevrolet, Chrysler/Dodge/Jeep, golf, Shogun Japanese, Spring Valley RV Park, T-Mobile, Verizon, Walmart/Subway
176	US 22, US 40, to Cambridge, N Sunoco/dsl, Budget Inn, st patrol, vet
169	OH 83, to Cumberland, New Concord, N Sheetz/dsl, Garland Hotel, $General, John&Annie Glen Historic Site,

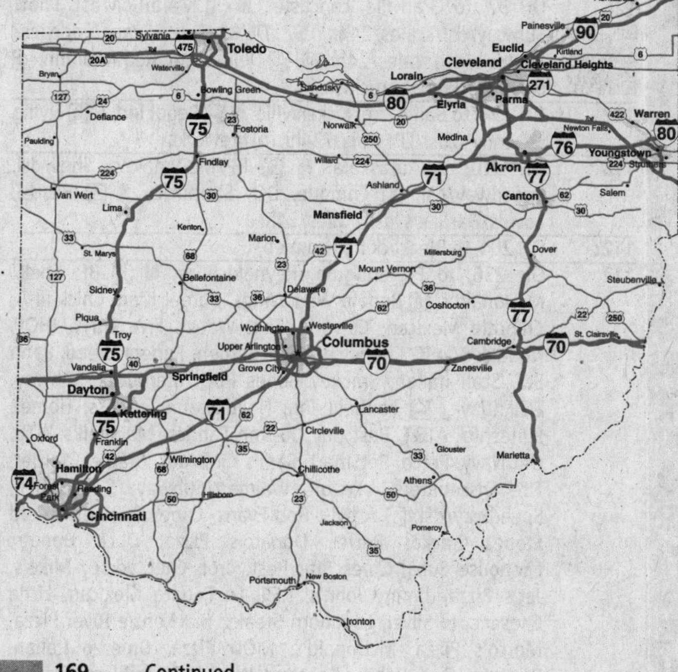

ZANESVILLE · HEBRON

Exit #	Services
169	Continued Muskingum U
164	US 22, US 40, Norwich, N BP, Baker's Motel, Zane Gray Museum, S antiques, pottery
163mm	**full facilities, litter barrels, petwalk, , , wb, vending**
160	OH 797, Airport Rd, N Love's/Arby's/dog park/dsl/scales/24hr, Peterbilt, S BP, Marathon/Subway/dsl, Burger King, Denny's, Earl's Pizza, McDonald's, Wendy's, Best Western, Rodeway Inn, st patrol
157	OH 93, Zanesville, N BP, S Marathon, Shell/dsl, National Road Camping, st patrol
155	OH 60, OH 146, Underwood St, Zanesville, N Bob Evans, Chipotle, Olive Garden, Oriental Buffet, Red Lobster, Starbucks, Steak'n Shake, Tumbleweed Grill, TX Roadhouse, Comfort Inn, Hampton Inn, Holiday Inn Express, Quality Inn, city park, , Riesbeck's Mkt, USPO, Wolfie's RV Camping, S Marathon/dsl, Cracker Barrel, Wendy's, Baymont Inn, EconoLodge, Travel Inn, $General
154	5th St(from eb)
153b	Maple Ave(no EZ return from wb), N BP, DQ, Papa John's, Tee Jaye's Rest., CVS Drug, Family$, , Monro Tire&Auto
153a	State St, N Speedway/dsl, Dillon SP, USPO
153mm	Licking River
152	US 40, National Rd, N BP/A&W/Subway/dsl, Shell/dsl, McDonald's, Super 8
142	US 40(from wb, no EZ return), Gratiot, N $General
141	OH 668, US 40(from eb, no return), to Gratiot, same as 142
132	OH 13, to Thornville, Newark, N Dawes Arboretum, S BP, Marathon
131mm	**full facilities, litter barrels, petwalk, , , both lanes, vending**
129b a	OH 79, to Buckeye Lake, Hebron, N Burger King, Starbucks, Subway, Best Western, Advance Parts, Bowman Tire, Kroger/gas, Vance Sporting Goods, S BP, Blue Heron Grill, Donato's Pizza, McDonald's, Subway,

OH

HEBRON

INTERSTATE 70 Cont'd

129b a Continued
Taco Bell, Wendy's, Motel 6, CarQuest, KOA, Ritterberger Mkt

126 OH 37, to Granville, Lancaster, N Marathon/dsl, Pilot/Subway/dsl/scales/24hr, S TA/BP/Bob Evans/Popeyes/Sbarro's/dsl/scales/24hr/@, Deluxe Inn, Red Roof Inn, IA 80 Truckomat/truckwash

122 OH 158, to Baltimore, Kirkersville, N Regal Inn, S Flying J/Denny's/dsl/LP/scales/24hr, fireworks

118 OH 310, to Pataskala, N BP/McDonald's, Shell/dsl, Speedway/dsl, Chipotle, DQ, Starbucks, S BP/dsl, Love's/Hardee's/dsl/scales/24hr

REYNOLDSBURG

112c OH 204, to Blecklick Rd (from eb)

112 OH 256, to Pickerington, Reynoldsburg, N BP, Shell/McDonald's, Buffalo Wild Wings, Burger King, Chick-fil-A, Chipotle Mexican, Culver's, First Watch, Five Guys, IHOP, Noodles&Co, O'Charley's, Olive Garden, Panera Bread, Penn Sta, Scali Italian, Smokey Bones BBQ, Starbucks, Subway, TGIFriday's, Fairfield Inn, Holiday Inn Express, Home2 Suites, AT&T, Best Buy, Jo-Ann Fabrics, Marshall's, NTB, Old Navy, Petco, PetSmart, Sam's Club/gas, Staples, Target, Tire Discounters, Verizon, Walmart/Subway, S Shell, Speedway/dsl, Arby's, Bob Evans, Cane's, Chipotle, Cold Stone, Cracker Barrel, Donato's Pizza, Duck Donuts, Firehouse Subs, Greek Star Rest., Iron Chef, Jersey Mike's, Jet's Pizza, Jimmy John's, KFC, La Fogata Mexican, Little Caesar's, LJ Silver, Longhorn Steaks, MacKenzie River Pizza, Marco's Pizza, McDonald's, MOD Pizza, Omezzo Italian, Popeyes, Red Robin, Roosters Wings, Scramblers, Skyline Chili, SmokeOut BBQ, Smoothie King, Starbucks, Steak'n Shake, Thai Paradise, Wendy's, Wendy's, Zapatas, Comfort Inn, Executive Suites, Hampton Inn, Advance Parts, ALDI, AT&T, AutoZone, Barnes&Noble, CVS, Giant Eagle, Kohl's, Kroger/E85, Valvoline, Verizon, Walgreens

110 Brice Rd, to Reynoldsburg, N Speedway/dsl, Sunoco, Donato's, Golden China, Munchie's Rest., Popeyes, Subway, Tim Horton's, Waffle House, Days Inn, La Quinta, Quality Inn, Red Roof Inn, Suburban Studios, BigLots, Family$, Goodyear/auto, Home Depot, O'Reilly Parts, S BP, Sheetz/dsl, Speedway/dsl, Applebee's, Arby's, Asian Star, Cajun Boil Seafood, Chipotle Mexican, Crispy Cook Chicken, KFC, McDonald's, Starbucks, Subway, Taco Bell, Waffle House, Comfort Suites, Loyalty Inn, Motel 6, Acura, Advance Parts, Family$, Firestone/auto, Gordon Foods, Jiffy Lube, Lowe's, Mar Azul Mexican, Michael's, Toyota, Walgreens

108b a I-270 N to Cleveland, access to HOSPITAL, I-270 S to Cincinnati

BEXLEY

107a OH 317, Hamilton Rd, to Whitehall, S Shell/dsl, Ichiban Japanese, J Lemon Pepper Chicken, McDonald's, Papa John's, Popeyes, Red Lobster, Taco Bell, Tim Hortons, Hampton Inn, InTown Suites, $General, AT&T, PepBoys

105a US 33, to Lancaster

105b US 33, James Rd, Bexley, N McDonald's, TAT Italian, Walgreens

103b a Livingston Ave, to Capital University, N Exxon, Speedway/dsl, Mr Hero Subs, Peking Dynasty, Popeyes, Starbucks, Subway, Taco Bell, Tim Horton's, Wendy's, auto repair, Katz Tires, Tire Choice, S Marathon, Shell, M&M Chicken & Fish, McDonald's, Rally's, White Castle, Family$, U-Haul

102 Kelton Ave, Miller Ave

101a I-71 N, to Cleveland

100b US 23, to 4th St, downtown

99c Rich St, Town St(exits left from wb)

99b OH 315 N, downtown

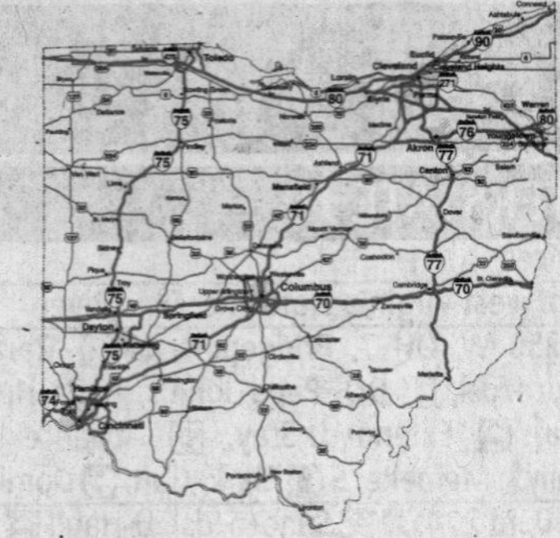

NEW ROME

99a I-71 S, to Cincinnati

98b Mound St(from wb, no EZ return), S Speedway, Sunoco, China King, Downtown Tabby's, Little Caesar's, McDonald's, Rally's, Tim Hortons, ALDI, Buckeye Tire, Family$, R&J Tire, Save-A-Lot

98a US 62, OH 3, Central Ave, to Sullivant, same as 98b

97 US 40, W Broad St, N Arby's, McDonald's, Popeyes, Savvy Sliders, Subway, Taco Bell, Tim Horton's, $General, Aamco, U-Haul, USPO, Verizon

96 I-670(exits left from eb)

95 Hague Ave(from wb), S Exxon

94 Wilson Rd, N Circle K/dsl, UDF, Minelli's Pizza, S BP, Pilot/Wendy's/dsl/scales/24hr, Speedway, McDonald's, Waffle House, EconoLodge, vet

93b a I-270, N to Cleveland, S to Cincinnati

91b a to Hilliard, New Rome, N Shell, Speedway/dsl, Applebee's, Arby's, Bibibop Asian Grill, Buffalo Wild Wings, Burger King, Chick-fil-A, Chipotle, Cracker Barrel, Culver's, Donato's Pizza, El Vaquero Mexican, Fazoli's, Firehouse Subs, Five Guys, Golden Chopsticks, Hot Head Burrito, IHOP, KFC, Krispy Kreme, McDonald's, Olive Garden, Outback Steaks, Panda Express, Panera Bread, Red Robin, Rooster's Rest., Sakura Japanese, Scramblers, Skyline Chili, Starbucks, Subway, Supreme Buffet, Taco Bell, Tim Horton's, TX Roadhouse, Wendy's, White Castle, Wild Ginger Asian, Comfort Suites, Fairfield Inn, Hampton Inn, Hawthorn Inn, Holiday Inn, La Quinta, Motel 6, Red Roof Inn, Rodeway Inn, $Tree, Advance Parts, ALDI, AT&T, Dick's, Discount Tire, Firestone/auto, Ford, Hobby Lobby, Kohl's, Marshall's, Meijer/dsl, Michael's, Midas, OfficeMax, Old Navy, PetSmart, Ross, Sam's Club/gas, Target, URGENT CARE, Verizon, Walmart, S BP/dsl, Marathon/dsl, Bob Evans, Handel's Ice Cream, Steak'n Shake, Best Western, Country Inn&Suites, Home2 Suites, Super 8, Take5 Oil Change

85 OH 142, to Plain City, W Jefferson, N Freightliner, Prairie Oaks SP, S Battelle Darby SP

SPRINGFIELD

80 OH 29, to Mechanicsburg

79 US 42, to London, Plain City, N Pilot/Arby's/dsl/scales/24hr, Sheetz/dsl, Waffle House, truck/auto repair, S Speedway/dsl, TA/BP/Popeyes/dsl/scales/24hr/@, McDonald's, Wendy's, Fairbridge Inn, Holiday Inn Express, H

72 OH 56, to London, Summerford, N Marathon/dsl, S H

71mm **full facilities, litter barrels, petwalk**, both lanes, **vending**

66 OH 54, to Catawba, South Vienna, N Fuelmart/dsl/scales, S Speedway/dsl, Main Street Pizza, $General, USPO

62 US 40, Springfield, N Harmony Motel, antiques, auto repair, Harmony Farm Mkt, H, to Buck Creek SP, S Tomorrow's Stars RV Resort

59 OH 41, to S Charleston, N H, st patrol, S BP/dsl, Love's/Subway/Wendy's/dsl/scales/24hr, Sheetz/dsl, antiques

54 OH 72, to Cedarville, Springfield, N Amoco, BP/dsl, Shell,

OH

INTERSTATE 70 Cont'd

54 Continued
Speedway/dsl, food A&W/LJ Silver, Arby's, Bob Evans, Bourbon St Cafe, Burger King, Cassano's Pizza, Chipotle, Cracker Barrel, Domino's, Dunkin, El Toro Mexican, Lee's Chicken, McDonald's, Panda Chinese, Popeyes, Rally's, Rudy's Smokehouse, Subway, Taco Bell, lodging Baymont Inn, Comfort Suites, Hampton Inn, Holiday Inn Express, Motel 6, Quality Inn, Red Roof Inn, other $Tree, Advance Parts, BigLots, Family$, Groceryland, H, Schuler's Bakery, Walgreens, **S** gas Marathon/dsl, other U-Haul

52b a US 68, to Urbana, Xenia

48 OH 4(from wb), to Enon, Donnelsville, **N** other camping, **S** gas Speedway

47 OH 4(from eb), to Springfield

44 I-675 S, Spangler Rd, to Cincinnati

43mm Mad River

41b a OH 4, OH 235, to Dayton, New Carlisle, **N** gas Buc-ee's, Shell/dsl, food Casey's, McDonald's, Taco Bell, Wendy's, other Ace Hardware, Freightliner, Kenworth

38 OH 201, Brandt Pike, **N** gas Marathon/dsl, Sheetz/dsl, food TJ Chumps, lodging Tru, other Meijer/Subway/dsl/E85, **S** gas Shell, UDF/dsl, food Bob Evans, Classic Pizza, Hardee's, Sonic, Tim Horton's, Waffle House, Wendy's, lodging Comfort Inn, Red Roof Inn, other Take5 Oil, vet, Walmart

36 OH 202, Huber Heights, **N** gas Speedway/dsl, food Applebee's, Big Boy, Chick-fil-A, Dragon City, El Toro Grill, Fazoli's, Firehouse Subs, Steak'n Shake, Taco Bell, Waffle House, lodging Baymont Inn, other $Tree, AAA, AT&T, Big Lots, Dick's, Hobby Lobby, H, Jiffy Lube, Kia, Kohl's, Lowe's, Marshall's, PetSmart, Staples, Target, Verizon, vet, **S** gas BP/dsl, Marathon/dsl, Sheetz/dsl, food 5Guys, Arby's, Bibibop Asian Grill, Burger King, Cane's Chicken, Chipotle Mexican, Dunkin, IHOP, Jersey Mike's, McDonald's, Panera Bread, Penn Sta Subs, Rooster's Rest., Skyline Chili, Starbucks, Submarina House, Subway, Super Subby's, TX Roadhouse, lodging Days Inn, Hampton Inn, Holiday Inn Express, other Discount Tire, Kroger/gas, Valvoline

33b a I-75, N to Toledo, S to Dayton

32 to US 40, Vandalia, **N** other to Dayton Intn'l airport

29 OH 48, to Dayton, Englewood, **N** gas BP, Drive Thur & Gas, Speedway/dsl, Sunoco/dsl, food Arby's, Big Boy, Buffalo Wild Wings, China Star, Company BBQ, Domino's, Dunkin, Firehouse Subs, Fox's Pizza Den, Hot Head Burrito, Jersey Mike's, Lee's Chicken, Perkins, Popeyes, Skyline Chili, Subway, Taco Bell, Tim Horton's, TJ Chumps, Tony's Italian, Wendy's, Yen Ching Chinese, lodging Hampton Inn, Quality Inn, The Hotel, other $Tree, Advance Parts, ALDI, AutoZone, Family$, Grismer/auto, Jiffy Lube, Midas, O'Reilly Parts, Petco, Precision Auto Care, Verizon, vet, **S** food Chipotle, El Toro, Huey Magoo's Chicken, McDonald's, Panera Bread, Starbucks, Waffle House, lodging Comfort Inn, Motel 6, other AT&T, H, H, Meijer/dsl/E85, URGENT CARE

26 OH 49 S, **N** gas Murphy USA/dsl, food Bob Evans, El Rancho Grande, Subway, other Walmart, **S** gas Shell/dsl, food Wendy's

24 OH 49 N, to Greenville, Clayton, **N** other KOA(seasonal)

21 Arlington Rd, Brookville, **N** gas Speedway/dsl, **S** BP, OM Oil, Speedway/dsl, food Arby's, Brookville Grille, El Bronco Mexican, Great Wall Chinese, Hardee's, KFC/Taco Bell, Lee's Chicken, McDonald's, Pizza Hut, Rob's Rest., Subway, Waffle House, Wendy's, lodging Brookville Inn, Holiday Inn Express, other $General, Advance Parts, Chevrolet, Family$, IGA Foods, O'Reilly Parts

14 OH 503, to West Alexandria, Lewisburg, **N** gas Marathon/Subway/dsl, other $General, **S** gas Sunoco/dsl

10 US 127, to Eaton, Greenville, **N** gas TA/BP/Burger King/dsl/scales/24hr/@, **S** Pilot/Subway/dsl/scales/24hr, lodging Budget Inn

3mm **full handicapped facilities, litter barrels, petwalk, phone, picnic, vending,** Welcome Ctr eb/rest stop both lanes

1 US 35 E(from eb), to Eaton, New Hope

0mm Ohio/Indiana state line, Welcome Arch, weigh sta eb

INTERSTATE 71

247b I-90 W, I-490 E. I-71 begins/ends on I-90, exit 170 in Cleveland.

247a W 14th, Clark Ave, **E** food Applebee's, Burger King, Five Guys, IHOP, Panda Express, Penn Sta. Subs, Starbucks, Steak'n Shake, Taco Bell, other $Tree, ALDI, Home Depot, Old Navy, Petco, Target, Walmart

246 Denison Ave, Jennings Rd(from sb)

245 US 42, Pearl Rd, **E** gas BP/7-11, Gas&Go, other zoo, **W** H

244 W 65th, Denison Ave(exits left from nb)

242b a W 130th, to Bellaire Rd, **E** other city park, **W** gas Race Fuel, food Georgio's Pizza, other city park

240 W 150th, **E** gas Speedway/dsl, Sunoco, food Burger King, Canary's Rest., Denny's, Happy's Pizza, lodging Wyndham, other AutoZone, Goodyear/auto, Marc's Foods, Take5 Oil Change, **W** gas BP/Subway/7-11/dsl, food Conzumel Mexican, lodging La Quinta

239 OH 237 S(from sb), **W** other Cleveland Intl airport

238 I-480, Toledo, Youngstown, **W** other airport

237 Snow Rd, Brook Park, **E** gas GetGo, Marathon/Circle K, Shell, food Arby's, Bob Evans, Dunkin', Garden Rest., Goody's Rest., KFC, Kicker's Pizza, Little Caesar's, McDonald's, Rally's, Savvy Sliders, Subway, Taco Bell, lodging Best Western, Holiday Inn Express, other $General, $Tree, Advance Parts, AutoZone, Conrad Tire/repair, CVS Drug, Giant Eagle, Midas, O'Reilly Parts, vet, **W** Cleveland Intl airport

235 Bagley Rd, **E** food Bob Evans, other Mr Tire, vet, **W** gas BP/dsl, Marathon, Speedway/dsl, food Aladdin's Eatery, Baskin-Robbins/Dunkin', Brown Derby Steak, Cane's Chicken, Capri Pizza, Chipotle, Craft Brew Garden, First Watch, Five Guys, IHOP, Jersey Mike's, Jimmy John's, Little Hong Kong, Max&Erma's, McDonald's, Olive Garden, Panera Bread, Penn Sta Subs, Perkins, Pizza Hut, Starbucks, Taco Bell, Tropical Smoothie Cafe, Z!Eats, lodging Comfort Inn, Courtyard, Crowne Plaza, Days Inn, Extended Stay America, Hampton Inn, Home2 Suites, MainStay Suites, Motel 6, Red Roof Inn, Sonesta Inn, other ALDI, H, Take5 Oil Change, Verizon

234 US 42, Pearl Rd, **E** gas Shell/dsl, Sunoco/dsl, food Hunan Chinese, Jet's Pizza, Katherine's Rest., Mr Hero, Santo's Italian, Torito Tacos, other Audi/Porsche, Honda, **W** gas Mobil/dsl, Sheetz/dsl, Tesla EVC, food Arby's, Buffalo Wild Wings, Culver's, Gordon's Mkt, McDonald's, Starbucks, lodging Kings Inn, other Home Depot, Lowe's, Walmart/Subway

233 I-80 and Ohio Tpk, to Toledo, Youngstown

231 OH 82, Strongsville, **E** gas Shell, lodging Best Western+, Super 8, other Chevrolet, **W** gas BP/7-11/dsl, Marathon/dsl, food Applebee's, Buca Italian, Chick-fil-A, Chipotle, Chipotle, City BBQ, DiBella's Subs, Firehouse Subs, Houlihan's, Longhorn Steaks, Outback Steaks, Panera Bread, Rosewood Grill, Samurai Japanese, Starbucks, TGIFriday, Tropical Smoothie, other $Tree, AAA, AT&T, Best Buy, Costco/gas, Dick's, Dillard's, Heinen's Mkt, JC Penney, Kohl's, Macy's, Michael's, Midas, Old Navy, PetCo, Take5 Oil Change, Target, TJ Maxx, URGENT CARE, Verizon

226 OH 303, Brunswick, **E** gas Sheetz/dsl, Shell/dsl, food Antonio's Pizza, other Chrysler/Dodge/Jeep, Hyundai, Mazda, Subaru, Toyota, vet, VW, **W** Comfort Suites, gas GetGo Mkt, Shell/dsl, Speedway/dsl, food Applebee's, Arby's, Bob Evans, Burger King, Chick-fil-A, Chipotle, First Watch, Georgio's Pizza,

BRUNSWICK

INTERSTATE 71 Cont'd

226 Continued
Jersey Mike's, KFC, McDonald's, Mission BBQ, Muchos Buenos Mexican, Panera Bread, Panini's Grill, Starbucks, Steak'n Shake, Subway, Taco Bell, Wendy's, Quality Inn, Ford, Giant Eagle Mkt, GNC, Home Depot, Marc's Mkt, Verizon

225mm rest area nb, full facilities, **litter barrels, petwalk**,

224mm rest area sb, full facilities, **litter barrels, petwalk**,

222 OH 3, Medina, Hinckley, W st patrol

220 I-271 N, to Erie, Pa, from nb

218 OH 18, to Akron, Medina, E BP/dsl, Marathon/dsl, Sunoco/dsl, Baskin-Robbins/Dunkin', Culver's, DQ, Master Pizza, Holiday Inn Express, Quality Inn, Super 8, antique, Kia, Nissan, Verizon, W GetGo, Shell, Speedway/dsl, Arby's, Bob Evans, Brown Derby, Buffalo Wild Wings, Denny's, McDonald's, Starbucks, Taco Bell, Waffle House, Wendy's, Fairfield Inn, Hampton Inn, Motel 6, Red Roof Inn, Ace Hardware, ALDI, Buehler's Foods, Buick/Cadillac/GMC, Chrysler/Dodge/Jeep, Firestone/auto, Harley-Davidson, Honda, H, Valvoline

209 I-76 E, to Akron, US 224 , W Pilot/Subway/dsl/scales/24hr, TA/BP/Burger King/Starbucks/Popeyes/dsl/scales/24hr/@, Arby's, McDonald's, Starbucks, Super 8, Blue Beacon, SpeedCo

W SALEM

204 OH 83, Burbank, E BP/dsl, Duke/dsl, Love's/Hardee's/dsl/scales/24hr, $General, W Pilot/Wendy's/dsl/scales/24hr, Sheetz/dsl, Arby's, Bob Evans, McDonald's, Taco Bell, H, OH Sta Outlets/famous brands

198 OH 539, W Salem, W fireworks

196mm rest area both lanes, full facilities, **litter barrels, petwalk**, , **vending**

196 OH 301(from nb, no re-entry), W Salem

186 US 250, Ashland, E Marathon, Grandpa's Village/cheese/gifts, Perkins, Hickory Lakes Camping, W Goasis/BP/Popeyes/Pizza Hut/dsl/24hr, Marathon/Subway/dsl, Bob Evans, Buffalo Wild Wings, Burger King, Chipotle, Dunkin', Jersey Mike's, McDonald's, Taco Bell, Wendy's, Wingstop, Hampton Inn, Motel 6, Quality Inn, Super 8, SureStay, $Tree, ALDI, Buehler's Foods, Home Depot, H, Kenworth, st patrol, to Ashland U, U-Haul, URGENT CARE, Verizon, Walmart/Subway

MANSFIELD

176 US 30, to Mansfield, E Heritage Inn, fireworks

173 OH 39, to Mansfield, W H

169 OH 13, Mansfield, E BP, EVC, Marathon/7-11/dsl, Murphy USA/dsl, Applebee's, Chipotle, Cracker Barrel, Steak'n Shake, Wendy's, Best Western, La Quinta, Mohican SP, Walmart/Subway, W BP/7-11, Arby's, Bob Evans, Burger King, El Charrito Mexican, McDonald's, Taco Bell, Hampton Inn, Red Roof Inn, Travelodge, H, st patrol

165 OH 97, to Bellville, E Amoco/Dunkin'/EVC/dsl, BP, Speedway/dsl, Buckeye Express Diner, Burger King, Der Dutchman, McDonald's, Panchos Tacos, Comfort Inn, Days Inn, Motel 6, Quality Inn, to Mohican SP, W Love's/Subway/Taco John's/dsl/scales/24hr, Wendy's

151 OH 95, to Mt Gilead, E Duchess, Marathon, 8 Sisters Cafe, McDonald's, Wendy's, Best Western, st patrol, W Shell/dsl, Subway, H, Mt Gilead SP

149mm truck parking both lanes

140 OH 61, Mt Gilead, E Pilot/Arby's/dsl/scales/24hr, Sheetz/dsl, Shell/dsl, W BP/Taco Bell, Marathon/Subway, OH Pizza, Cardinal Ctr Camping

131 US 36, OH 37, to Delaware, E Flying J/Denny's/dsl/LP/scales/24hr/@, Pilot/Subway/dsl/scales/24hr, Burger King, Harley-Davidson, Tanger Outlets/Famous Brands, W BP/dsl, Shell, Arby's, Bob Evans, Chipotle,

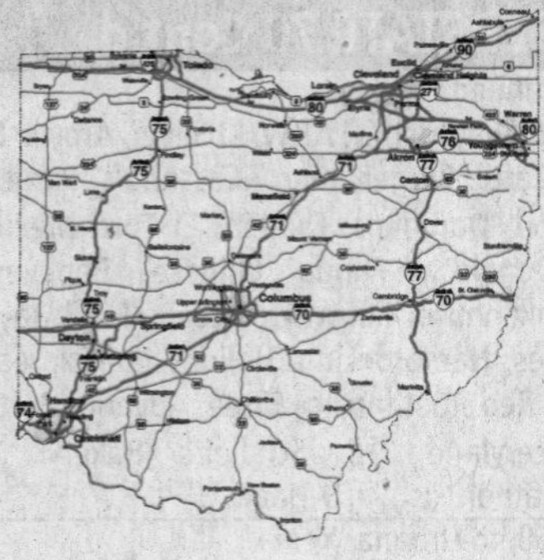

WHEELING

131 Continued
Cracker Barrel, KFC/LJ Silver, McDonald's, Starbucks, Taco Bell, Waffle House, Wendy's, White Castle, Hampton Inn, Holiday Inn Express, Microtel, Alum Cr SP, Cross Creek Camping, H

128mm rest area both lanes, full facilities, **litter barrels, petwalk**, , **vending**

121 Polaris Pkwy, to Gemini Pl, E Marathon, Sheetz/dsl, Shell/dsl, UDF, Bonefish Grill, Buffalo Wild Wings, Cane's, Chicken Salad Chick, Firehouse Subs, First Watch, Five Guys, Giordano's, Jimmy John's, McDonald's, Pancake House, Panera Bread, Polaris Grill, Skyline Chili, Smoothie King, Starbucks, Steak'n Shake, Tim Horton's, Drury Inn, Fairfield Inn, Four Points Sheraton, Hampton Inn, Holiday Inn Express, Homewood Suites, Hyatt Place, Firestone/auto, IKEA, Mr Tire, Valvoline, W BP/Duchess, Circle K, Applebee's, Benihana, Bibibop Asian, BJ's Rest., Brio Grille, Burger King, CA Pizza, Carrabba's, Charley Subs, CheeseCake Factory, Chick-fil-A, Chili Verde Mexican, Chipotle, Chuy's, City BBQ, Coldstone, Dave&Buster's, Domino's, Eddie's Steaks, Firebird's Grill, Greek Express, Honey Baked Ham, House of Japan, Jason's Deli, Jersey Mike's, Jet's Pizza, Jimmy John's, KPOT KBBQ, Krispy Kreme, Marcella's Italian, McDonald's, Mimi's Cafe, Mitchell's Steaks, Molly Woo's, Olive Garden, Panda Express, Poke Bros, Potbelly's, Qdoba, Quaker Steak, Red Lobster, Red Robin, Rooster's Grill, Scramblers Breakfast, Shake Shack, Sonic, Starbucks, Sushi En, Sushi Factory, Taco Bell, Torchy's Tacos, TX Roadhouse, Waffle House, Wendy's, Cambria Suites, Candlewood Suites, Comfort Inn, Extended Stay America, Hilton, Hilton Garden, Home2 Suites, Residence Inn, Staybridge Suites, AT&T, AutoZone, Barnes&Noble, Best Buy, Cabela's, Costco/gas, Hobby Lobby, JC Penney, Kroger/gas, Lowe's, Macy's, NTB, Old Navy, PetSmart, Target, TireDiscounters, TJ Maxx, Valvoline, Verizon, Von Maur, Walgreens, World Mkt

119b a I-270, to Indianapolis, Wheeling

117 OH 161, to Worthington, E BP/dsl, Shell, Speedway/dsl, Burger King, Casa Mescal Mexican, Chipotle, Dunkin', El Barco Mexican, KFC, Massey's Pizza, McDonald's, Penn Sta Subs, Popeyes, Rally's, Subway, Super Seafood Buffet, Taco Bell, Wendy's, White Castle, Columbus Grand Hotel, M Star Hotel, Norwood Inn, Red Roof Inn, $General, auto repair, CVS Drug, Family$, Walgreens, W Sheetz/dsl, Shell, Speedway/dsl, Asian Kitchen, Bob Evans, China Jade, McDonald's, Pizza Hut, Subway, Tim Hortons, Waffle House, Candlewood Suites, Crowne Plaza, Hawthorn Suites, Hometowne Studios, Motel 6, Super 8, Advance Parts, AutoZone, Chevrolet, Family$, Premier Tire, USPO

116 Morse Rd, Sinclair Rd, E BP/Duchess, Shell/dsl, Speedway/dsl, Turkey Hill/dsl, Arby's, Burger King, Charley's, Chipotle, Dunkin', Little Caesar's, Little Dragons, McDonald's, Papa John's, Subway, Taco Bell, Tim Horton's, Wendy's, Wingstop, Baymont Inn, $General, $General, $Tree, $Tree, Advance Parts, ALDI, AutoZone, Buick/GMC,

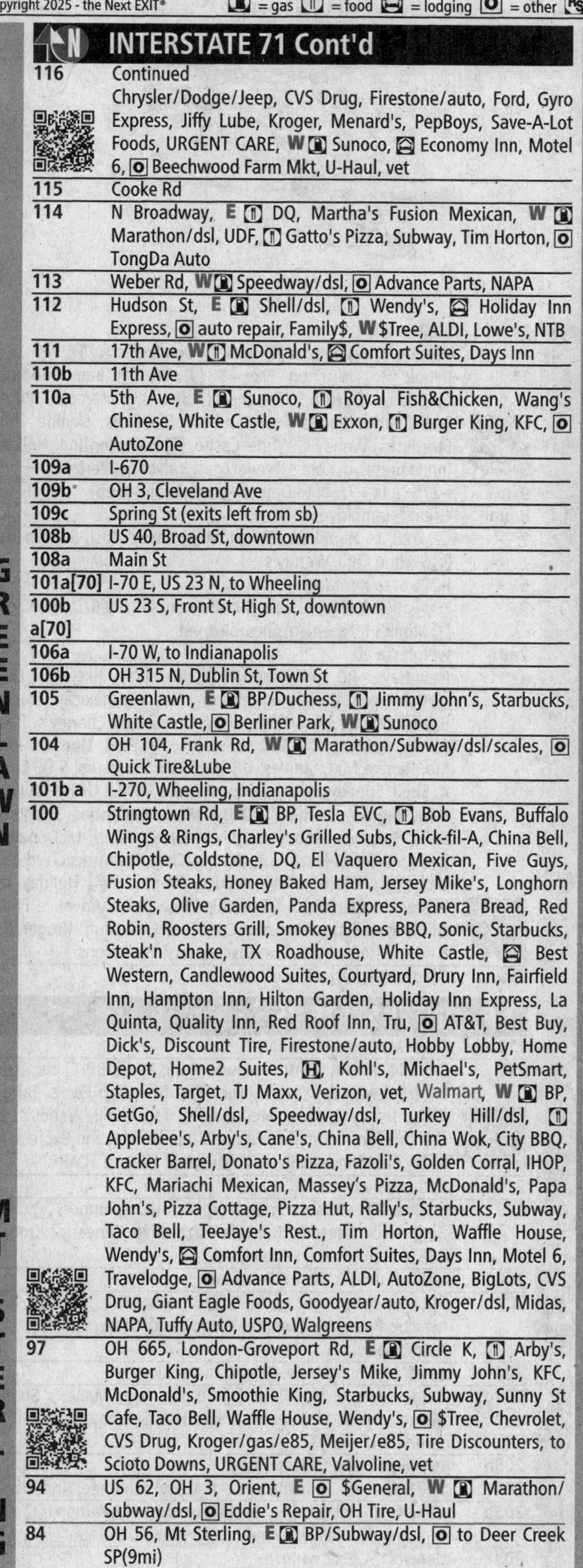

INTERSTATE 71 Cont'd

GREENLAWN

116 Continued
Chrysler/Dodge/Jeep, CVS Drug, Firestone/auto, Ford, Gyro Express, Jiffy Lube, Kroger, Menard's, PepBoys, Save-A-Lot Foods, URGENT CARE, W Sunoco, Economy Inn, Motel 6, Beechwood Farm Mkt, U-Haul, vet

115 Cooke Rd

114 N Broadway, E DQ, Martha's Fusion Mexican, W Marathon/dsl, UDF, Gatto's Pizza, Subway, Tim Horton, TongDa Auto

113 Weber Rd, W Speedway/dsl, Advance Parts, NAPA

112 Hudson St, E Shell/dsl, Wendy's, Holiday Inn Express, auto repair, Family$, W $Tree, ALDI, Lowe's, NTB

111 17th Ave, W McDonald's, Comfort Suites, Days Inn

110b 11th Ave

110a 5th Ave, E Sunoco, Royal Fish&Chicken, Wang's Chinese, White Castle, W Exxon, Burger King, KFC, AutoZone

109a I-670

109b OH 3, Cleveland Ave

109c Spring St (exits left from sb)

108b US 40, Broad St, downtown

108a Main St

101a[70] I-70 E, US 23 N, to Wheeling

100b a[70] US 23 S, Front St, High St, downtown

106a I-70 W, to Indianapolis

106b OH 315 N, Dublin St, Town St

105 Greenlawn, E BP/Duchess, Jimmy John's, Starbucks, White Castle, Berliner Park, W Sunoco

104 OH 104, Frank Rd, W Marathon/Subway/dsl/scales, Quick Tire&Lube

101b a I-270, Wheeling, Indianapolis

100 Stringtown Rd, E BP, Tesla EVC, Bob Evans, Buffalo Wings & Rings, Charley's Grilled Subs, Chick-fil-A, China Bell, Chipotle, Coldstone, DQ, El Vaquero Mexican, Five Guys, Fusion Steaks, Honey Baked Ham, Jersey Mike's, Longhorn Steaks, Olive Garden, Panda Express, Panera Bread, Red Robin, Roosters Grill, Smokey Bones BBQ, Sonic, Starbucks, Steak'n Shake, TX Roadhouse, White Castle, Best Western, Candlewood Suites, Courtyard, Drury Inn, Fairfield Inn, Hampton Inn, Hilton Garden, Holiday Inn Express, La Quinta, Quality Inn, Red Roof Inn, Tru, AT&T, Best Buy, Dick's, Discount Tire, Firestone/auto, Hobby Lobby, Home Depot, Home2 Suites, H, Kohl's, Michael's, PetSmart, Staples, Target, TJ Maxx, Verizon, vet, Walmart, W BP, GetGo, Shell/dsl, Speedway/dsl, Turkey Hill/dsl, Applebee's, Arby's, Cane's, China Bell, China Wok, City BBQ, Cracker Barrel, Donato's Pizza, Fazoli's, Golden Corral, IHOP, KFC, Mariachi Mexican, Massey's Pizza, McDonald's, Papa John's, Pizza Cottage, Pizza Hut, Rally's, Starbucks, Subway, Taco Bell, TeeJaye's Rest., Tim Horton, Waffle House, Wendy's, Comfort Inn, Comfort Suites, Days Inn, Motel 6, Travelodge, Advance Parts, ALDI, AutoZone, BigLots, CVS Drug, Giant Eagle Foods, Goodyear/auto, Kroger/dsl, Midas, NAPA, Tuffy Auto, USPO, Walgreens

MT STERLING

97 OH 665, London-Groveport Rd, E Circle K, Arby's, Burger King, Chipotle, Jersey's Mike, Jimmy John's, KFC, McDonald's, Smoothie King, Starbucks, Subway, Sunny St Cafe, Taco Bell, Waffle House, Wendy's, $Tree, Chevrolet, CVS Drug, Kroger/gas/e85, Meijer/e85, Tire Discounters, to Scioto Downs, URGENT CARE, Valvoline, vet

94 US 62, OH 3, Orient, E $General, W Marathon/Subway/dsl, Eddie's Repair, OH Tire, U-Haul

84 OH 56, Mt Sterling, E BP/Subway/dsl, to Deer Creek SP(9mi)

BLOOMINGBURG

75 OH 38, Bloomingburg, E fireworks, W Sunoco/dsl

69 OH 41, OH 734, Jeffersonville, E Flying J/Denny's/dsl/scales/LP/24hr, H, Walnut Lake Camping, W Buckeye RV Ctr, Buckeye RV Ctr, BP, Sheetz/dsl, Shell/Subway/dsl, Arby's, Wendy's, Quality Inn, Family$

68mm no services

65 US 35, Washington CH, E EVC, EVC, Shell/dsl, Speedway/Speedy Cafe/dsl, TA/BP/Pizza Hut/Popeyes/dsl/scales/24hr/@, Bob Evans, Chipotle Mexican, KFC, McDonald's, Starbucks, Subway, Taco Bell, Waffle House, Wendy's, Werner's BBQ, Baymont Inn, Fairfield Inn, Hampton Inn, H, Tanger Outlets/famous brands, W Love's/Hardee's/dsl/scales/24hr, Rodeway Inn

58 OH 72, to Sabina

50 US 68, to Wilmington, E H, W BP/DQ/dsl, ONE9/Subway/dsl/scales/24hr, Shell/dsl, McDonald's, Ralph's American Grill, Wendy's, Holiday Inn, repair/tires

49mm weigh sta nb

45 OH 73, to Waynesville, E Arco, Shell/dsl, 73 Grill, H, vet, W Buckeye RV, Caesar Creek Camping(3mi), Caesar Creek SP(5mi), flea mkt

36 Wilmington Rd, E Olive Branch Camping, to Ft Ancient St Mem

MORROW

35mm Little Miami River

34mm rest area both lanes, full facilities, **litter barrels, petwalk**, **scenic view, vending**

32 OH 123, to Lebanon, Morrow, E Flying J/Wendy's/dsl/scales/24hr, Marathon, Sunoco, Country Kitchen, Morgan's Riverside Camping

28 OH 48, S Lebanon, E Marathon, Speedway/dsl, Chipotle, Dickey's BBQ, McDonald's, Starbucks, Waffle House, White Castle, $Tree, Firestone, Kohl's, Lowe's, PetSmart, Target, Verizon, vet, W hwy patrol

25 OH 741 N, Kings Mills Rd, E Shell/Popeyes/Dunkin', Speedway/dsl, Buffalo Wings&Rings, Chipotle, El Rancho Nuevo, Jimmy John's, McDonald's, Outback Steaks, Taco Bell, Tokyo Grill, Wendy's, Comfort Suites, Great Wolf Lodge, Residence Inn, Harley-Davidson, USPO, W BP, Marathon, Arby's, Big Boy, Dunkin, El Trompo Mexican, Panera Bread, Perkins, Pizza Hut, Skyline Chili, Starbucks, Subway, Tenji Sushi, TX Roadhouse, Waffle House, Baymont Inn, Hampton Inn, Microtel, Quality Inn, Tru Hilton, auto repair, CVS Drug, Jiffy Lube, Kroger/dsl

24 Western Row, King's Island Dr(from nb), E Sunoco, Eli's Grill, Fantastic Wok, King's Island Resort, URGENT CARE, W TownePlace Suites

19 US 22, Mason-Montgomery Rd, E Speedway/dsl, UDF, Arby's, Big Boy, Burger King, Cane's, Ccs Empanadas, Chipotle, Cracker Barrel, Dunkin', Flipdaddy's Burgers, Freddy's, Fricker's, HoneyBaked Ham, Hurts Donuts, KFC, Longhorn Steaks, McDonald's, Olive Garden, Potbelly, Taco Bell, Tony's Steaks, Wendy's, Comfort Inn, Hawthorn Hotel, King's Suites, Red Roof Inn, $Tree, ALDI, AT&T, AutoZone, Best Buy, Buick/GMC, Chevrolet, Chrysler/Dodge/Jeep, Costco/gas, Discount Tire, Firestone/auto, Ford, GNC, Honda, Honda, Infiniti, Jiffy Lube, Kia, Kohl's, Kroger, Lexus, Mazda, Meijer/dsl, Michael's, Nissan, O'Reilly Parts, Old Navy, Petco, Porsche, Ross, Subaru, Target, Tire Discounters, Tires+, Toyota, Tuffy Auto, USPO, Valvoline, Verizon, VW, Walgreens, W Shell/Dunkin', Bibibop Grill, Blaze Pizza, Bravo Italian, Carrabba's, Chick-fil-A, Firebirds Grill, First Watch, Five Guys, Graeter's Cafe, IHOP, Jimmy John's, Joella's Hot Chicken, Kirkwood's Kitchen, Korean Hotpot, McAlister's Deli, Mission BBQ, Noodles&Co, Panda Express, Panera Bread, Piada Italian, Popeyes, Qdoba, Red Robin, Rusty Bucket, Skyline Chili, Taziki's Cafe, Truva Mediterranean, Waffle House, Wendy's, Wingstop,

= gas = food = lodging = other = rest stop

INTERSTATE 71 Cont'd

BLUE ASH

Exit	Services
19	Continued WNB Burgers, Best Western, Candlewood Suites, Drury Inn, Hampton Inn, Hilton Garden, Holiday Inn Express, Homewood Suites, La Quinta, Marriott, Mason Inn, Dick's, Hobby Lobby, Home Depot, Lowe's, Marshall's, NAPA, Staples, vet, Walmart/Subway, Whole Foods Mkt
17b a	I-275, to I-75, OH 32
15	Pfeiffer Rd, E H, W BP, Shell/dsl, Sunoco/dsl, Bob Evans, Buffalo Wild Wings, City BBQ, Firehouse Grill, Comfort Inn, Courtyard, Embassy Suites, Extended Stay, Holiday Inn Express, MainStay Suites, Quality Hotel, Red Roof Inn, Springhill Suites, Wingate Inn
14	OH 126, Reagan Hwy, Blue Ash
12	US 22, OH 3, Montgomery Rd, E BP/dsl, Shell/Dunkin'/Subway, Sunoco, Arby's, Bob Evans, Chipotle Mexican, Chuy's, Coopers Hawk, Delicio Pizza, El Rancho Grande, Ember's, First Watch, Fusian, Graeter's Creamery, Jimmy John's, Outback Steaks, Panera Bread, Penn Sta Subs, Red Lobster, Truva Turkish; Hampton Inn, W BP, BIBIBOP, Buffalo Wild Wings, Cheesecake Factory, Chick-fil-A, Chipotle, Honeybaked Ham, Jersey Mike's, Maggiano's, McAlister's Deli, McDonald's, Popeyes, Potbelly, Taziki's Grill, TX Roadhouse, Verizon, Wendy's, Best Western+, AT&T, Dick's, Dillard's, Firestone/auto, Fresh Mkt Foods, H, Macy's, Marshall's, Staples, TJ Maxx, Trader Joe's, Valvoline
11	Kenwood Rd, from nb, same as 12, W H
10	Stewart Rd(from nb), to Silverton, E BMW/Mini, W Marathon/dsl
9	Redbank Rd, to Fairfax, (no ez sb return), E UDF, Rally's
8	Kennedy Ave, Ridge Ave W, E Meijer/dsl, Cane's Chicken, Chick-fil-A, IHOP, Pardon My Cheesesteak, Steak 'n Shake, Motel 6, Kroger/dsl, PetSmart, Target, W Marathon/dsl, Shell/Subway/Dunkin'/dsl, Gold Star Chili, Hooligan's, Jack-in-the-Box, LJ Silver, McDonald's, Wendy's, Quality Inn, $General, ALDI, Buick/GMC, Home Depot, Lowes Whse, Sumeral Tire

NORWOOD

Exit	Services
7	(from sb) OH 562, Ridge Ave E, Norwood
6	Edwards Rd, E BP, Shell/Popeyes/Dunkin', Speedway/dsl, BIBIBOP Asian, BJ's Rest., Bonefish Grill, Buca Italian, Capital Grille, Donato's, First Watch, Five Guys, J Alexander's Rest., Jason's Deli, Longhorn Steaks, Marco's Pizza, Penn Sta Subs, PF Chang's, Pilot Inn Grill, Potbelly, Qdoba, Rusty Bucket, Seasons 52 Grill, The Pub, Courtyard, Hampton Inn, AT&T, GNC, Old Navy, REI, TJ Maxx, URGENT CARE, Valvoline, Whole Foods Mkt, W Shell
5	Dana Ave, Montgomery Rd, W Xavier Univ, Zoo
3	Taft Rd(from sb), W U of Cincinnati
2	US 42, Reading Rd, Gilbert ave(from sb), E art museum, downtown, W ballpark stadium arena, H
1k j	I-471 S
1d	Main St, downtown
1c b	Pete Rose Way, Fine St, Bengals Stadium, downtown
1a	I-75 N, US 50, to Dayton
1mm	I-71 S and I-75 S run together

OH

INTERSTATE 74

CHEVIOT

Exit	Services
20	I-75(from eb), N to Dayton, S to Cincinnati, I-74 begins/ends on I-75.
19	Gilmore St, Spring Grove Ave
18	US 27 N, Colerain Ave
17	Montana Ave(from wb), N Sunoco
14	North Bend Rd, Cheviot, N Shell, Speedway/dsl, Big Boy, Chipotle, Dunkin', Jersey Mike's, McDonald's, Papa John's, Skyline Chili, Subway, Taco Bell, Wendy's, Family$, Kroger, Petco, Sam's Club/gas, Tire Discounters, Valvoline,

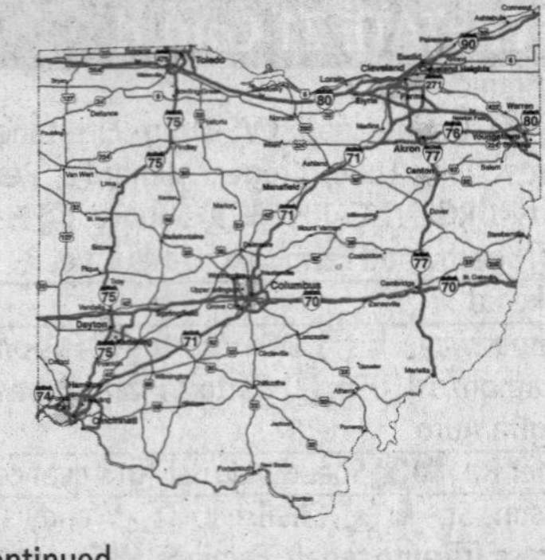

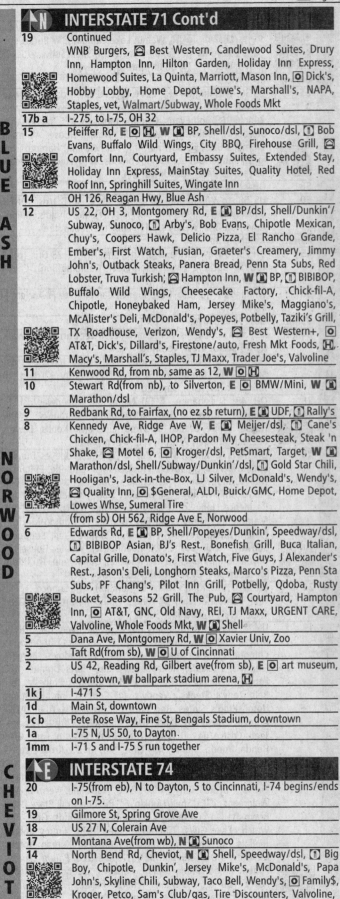

Exit	Services
14	Continued Verizon, Walgreens, S Shell, Bob Evans, H, vet
11	Rybolt Rd, Harrison Pike, S BP, BambooHouse, Chipotle, Dunkin, Longhorn Steaks, Marco's Pizza, McDonald's, Panda Express, Penn Sta Subs, Skyline Chili, Starbucks, Wendy's, White Castle, Hampton Inn, Holiday Inn Express, Kohl's, Meijer/gas, Valvoline, Verizon
9	I-275 N, to I-75, N to Dayton, (exits left from eb)
8mm	Great Miami River
7	OH 128, to Hamilton, Cleves, N Casey's/dsl, Sunoco/dsl, Skyline Chili, Wendy's
5	I-275 S, to Kentucky
3	Dry Fork Rd, N BP/dsl, S Marathon/dsl, Shell/Dunkin'/dsl, Monk's Kitchen, Chevrolet, vet
2mm	weigh sta eb
1	New Haven Rd, to Harrison, N BP/Jersey Mike's/dsl, UDF, Bob Evans, Buffalo Wild Wings, Chipotle Mexican, Cracker Barrel, Dunkin', Five Guys, Little Caesar's, O'Charley's, Papa John's, Subway, Best Western+, Ford, Home Depot, Kia, Remke Mkt, Staples, URGENT CARE, Verizon, S Circle K, Shell, Speedway/dsl, Sunoco/White Castle, UDF/Mobil, A&W, Big Boy, Domino's, DQ, El Mariachi Cantina, Firehouse Subs, Freddy's, Happy Garden, Marco's Pizza, McDonald's, Penn Sta Subs, Pizza Hut, Skyline Chili, Starbucks, Taco Bell, Valle Escondidos, Waffle House, Wendy's, Holiday Inn Express, Super 8, $General, $Tree, AAA, Advance Parts, AT&T, AutoZone, Big Lots, C&C Tire, CVS Drug, Kroger/dsl, NAPA, O'Reilly Parts, Tire Discounters, Walgreens
0mm	Ohio/Indiana state line

INTERSTATE 75

ANN ARBOR

Exit	Services
211mm	Ohio/Michigan state line
210	OH 184, Alexis Rd, to Raceway Park, W BP/Circle K/dsl, Pilot/Subway/dsl/scales/24hr, Arby's, Bob Evans, Burger King, Jersey Mike's, McDonald's, Taco Bell, Wendy's, Comfort Inn, Courtyard, Fairfield Inn, Holiday Inn Express, ALDI, AutoZone, Meijer/dsl, Menards, URGENT CARE
210mm	Ottawa River
209	Ottawa River Rd(from nb), E Marathon, Sunoco, China King, Little Caesar's, Marco's Pizza, River Diner, Kroger/e85, O'Reilly Parts, Verizon, vet
208	I-280 S, to I-80/90, to Cleveland
207	Stickney Ave, Lagrange St, E BP, Stop&Go, Arby's, KFC, Marco's Pizza, McDonald's, Wendy's, $Tree, Family$, Save A Lot Foods
206	to US 24, Phillips Ave, W transmissions
205b	Berdan Ave, E H, W Burger King, Mancy's Steaks, Marco's Pizza, McDonald's, Pizza Hut, Subway, Taco Bell, $General, Family$
205a	to Willys Pkwy, to Jeep Pkwy
204	I-475 W, to US 23 (exits left fom nb), to Maumee, Ann Arbor
203b	US 24, to Detroit Ave, W Arco/dsl, Marathon, KFC, McDonald's, Rally's, Wendy's, Family$, U-Haul
203a	Bancroft St, E downtown

INTERSTATE 75 Cont'd

Exit #	Services
202	Washington St, Collingwood Ave(from sb, no EZ return), **E** Art Museum, Family$, H, **W** China Star, Happy's Pizzz, McDonald's, $General
201b a	OH 25, Collingwood Ave, **W** Toledo Zoo
200	South Ave, Kuhlman Dr
200mm	Maumee River
199	OH 65, Miami St, to Rossford, **E** Days Inn
198	Wales Rd, Oregon Rd, to Northwood, **E** Mobil/Subway/dsl, S&G/dsl, Arby's, Arturo's Kitchen, Coney Island, Fried Rice, Jimmy John's, Baymont Inn, BlissPoint Inn
197	Buck Rd, to Rossford, **E** Shell/dsl, Tim Horton's, Wendy's, **W** Amoco/dsl, BP, McDonald's, Subway, The Meltdown, Knights Inn, Motel 6
195	to I-80/90, OH 795, OH Tpk(toll), Perrysburg, **E** BP/Subway/dsl, Country Inn&Suites, Courtyard, Hampton Inn, Staybridge Suites, Tru Hotel, Bass Pro Shops, Camping World RV Ctr
193	US 20, US 23 S, Perrysburg, **E** ALDI, BP/dsl, Arby's, Bob Evans, Burger King, Chick-fil-A, Chili's, China City, Chipotle, Cocina de Carlos, Cracker Barrel, Culvers, Dickey's BBQ, First Watch, Five Guys, Fricker's, IHOP, Jimmy John's, KFC, McDonald's, Panda Express, Panera Bread, Sonic, Starbucks, Taco Bell, Tim Horton's, Wendy's, Wendy's, Yum Yummy Chinese, Baymont Inn, Candlewood Suites, Comfort Suites, Days Inn, Holiday Inn, Quality Inn, $Tree, Belle Tire, Discount Tire, GNC, Hobby Lobby, Home Depot, KOA, Kohl's, Kroger/gas/e85, Lowe's, Meijer/dsl, Michael's, PetSmart, Target, TJ Maxx, Tuffy, Valvoline, Walgreens, Walmart/Subway, **W** Speedway/dsl, Cane's Chicken, La Quinta, AutoZone, Harley-Davidson
192	I-475, US 23 N(exits left from nb), to Maumee, Ann Arbor
187	OH 582, to Luckey, Haskins
181	OH 64, OH 105, to Pemberville, Bowling Green, **E** Holiday Inn Express, Meijer/dsl/e85, **W** Circle K/dsl, Speedway/dsl, Bob Evans, Buffalo Wild Wings, Burger King, Chipotle, El Zarape Mexican, Fricker's Rest., Jimmy John's, McDonald's, Panera Bread, Starbucks, Subway, Taco Bell, Tim Horton's, Waffle House, Wendy's, Best Western, Days Inn, Fairfield Inn, Hampton Inn, Home2 Suites, Bowling Green State U, H, USPO, Verizon
179	US 6, to Fremont, Napoleon, **E** museum
179mm	**full facilities, litter barrels, petwalk,** both lanes, **vending**
175mm	weigh sta nb
171	OH 25, Cygnet
168	Eagleville Rd, Quarry Rd, **E** FuelMart/dsl
167	OH 18, to Fostoria, North Baltimore, **E** Petro/BP/Iron Skillet/dsl/scales/24hr/@, McDonald's, **W** Love's/Arby's/dsl/scales/24hr, Sunoco, $General, Great Scot Mkt
165mm	Rocky Ford River
164	OH 613, to McComb, Fostoria, **E** RV camping, Van Buren SP, **W** Pilot/Subway/Taco Bell/dsl/scales/24hr
162mm	weigh sta sb
161	rd 99, **E** Shell/Subway/dsl, Speedway/Speedy Cafe/dsl, Comfort Suites, Ford/Lincoln, hwy patrol, Hyundai, Kia, URGENT CARE, **W** antiques
159	US 224, OH 15, Findlay, **E** Marathon/dsl, S&G/dsl, Speedway/dsl, Beckett's Burgers, Burger King, Cancun Mexican, Culver's, Jimmy John's, KFC/LJ Silver, McDonald's, Ming's Great Wall, Ralphie's, Starbucks, Steak'n Shake, Subway, Taco Bell, Take 5 Oil Change, Wendy's, Drury Inn, Red Roof Inn, Rodeway Inn, Super 8, Advance Parts, **W** Murphy USA/dsl, Shell/dsl, Bob Evans, China Garden, Chipotle, Cracker Barrel, Jac&Do's Pizza, Penn Sta Subs,
159	Continued Tim Horton's, Tony's Rest., TX Roadhouse, Waffle House, Country Inn&Suites, Hampton Inn, Hilton Garden, Holiday Inn Express, Quality Inn, AutoZone, Best 1 Tires/repair, Chrysler/Dodge/Jeep, Peterbilt, Verizon, Walmart/Subway
158mm	Blanchard River
157	OH 12, Findlay, **E** Marathon/dsl, **W** Fricker's Rest., Pilgrim, SureStay, vet
156	US 68, OH 15, to Carey, **E** H
153mm	**full facilities, litter barrels, petwalk,** both lanes, **vending**
145	OH 235, to Ada, Mount Cory, **E** KOA
142	OH 103, to Arlington, Bluffton, **E** Fairway Inn, **W** Marathon/Circle K/dsl, Shell, Arby's, Dunkin, McDonald's/rv parking, Subway, Taco Bell, Wendy's, Bluffton Inn, $General, Bluffton U, vet
140	Bentley Rd, to Bluffton, **W** H
135	OH 696, to US 30, to Delphos, Beaverdam, **E** Speedway/Speedy's Cafe/dsl/24hr, **W** Flying J/Denny's/dsl/scales/LP/24hr/@, Pilot/McDonald's/Subway/dsl/24hr/@, $General, Blue Beacon, SpeedCo, tire repair, truck repair
134	Napolean Rd(no nb re-entry), to Beaverdam
130	Bluelick Rd, **E** Clark
127b a	OH 81, to Ada, Lima, **W** Fuelstop/dsl, Red Carpet Inn, Subway, Waffle House, Comfort Inn
126mm	Ottawa River
125	OH 309, OH 117, Lima, **E** Murphy USA/dsl, Speedway/Speedy's Cafe/dsl, Applebee's, Asian Buffet, Bob Evans, Burger King, Capt D's, China Buffet, Chipotle, Cracker Barrel, El Cazadore, Hunan Garden, McDonald's, Olive Garden, Panera Bread, Red Lobster, Skyline Chili, Starbucks, Subway, Taco Bell, TX Roadhouse, Wendy's, Wings & Rings, Courtyard, Hampton Inn, Holiday Inn Express, Howard Johnson, Motel 6, $Tree, ALDI, AT&T, BigLots, Ford/Lincoln, Sam's Club/gas, Verizon, Walgreens, Walmart, **W** Arby's, Kewpee Hamburger's, Yamato Steaks, Country Inn&Suites, Holiday Inn, TownePlace Suites, Travelodge, $General, Advance Parts, Best 1 Tires/repair, H, O'Reilly Parts, Save-A-Lot Foods
124	4th St, **E** Ford/Lincoln, hwy patrol
122	OH 65, Lima, **E** Speedway/Speedy Cafe/dsl, **W** Marathon/dsl, Family$, Freightliner, Volvo
120	Breese Rd, Ft Shawnee, **W** Shawnee Fuelstop/dsl, Harley-Davidson
118	to Cridersville, **W** Casey's/dsl, Fuelmart/Subway/dsl, Speedway/dsl, Community Mkt, $General, vet
114mm	rest area both lanes, **facilities, litter barrels, pet walk,** **vending**
113	OH 67, to Uniopolis, Wapakeneta
111	Bellefontaine St, Wahpakeneta, **E** TA/Hub Room Rest./dsl/scales/@, Red Roof Inn, KOA, truck tires, **W** BP/dsl, Murphy USA/dsl, Shell, Arby's, Bob Evans, Burger King, Capt D's, DQ, Dunkin', El Azteca, McDonald's, Subway, Taco Bell, Waffle House, Wendy's, Best Western, Holiday Inn Express, Super 8, Advance Parts, ALDI, CVS Drug, Lowe's, Neil Armstrong Museum, O'Reilly Parts, st patrol, URGENT CARE, Valvoline, Verizon, Walmart
110	US 33, to St Marys, Bellefontaine, **E** hwy patrol
104	OH 219, v, **W** Circle K/Subway/dsl, Marathon, Sunoco/dsl, Budget Host, $General
102	OH 274, to Jackson Ctr, New Breman, **E** air stream tours, **W** bicycle museum
99	OH 119, to Minster, Anna, **E** 99/dsl, Marathon/dsl, **W** Shell, Speedway/Taco Bell/dsl, Subway, Wendy's, Family$, truck lube/wash/repair
94	rd 25A, Sidney, **E** Marathon/deli
93	OH 29, to St Marys, Sidney, **W** Camp Qtokee,

INTERSTATE 75 Cont'd

SIDNEY

93 Continued
Lake Loramie SP

92 OH 47, to Versailles, Sidney, E Speedway/dsl, Arby's, Coldstone, Fuji Steakhouse, Little Caesar's, Subway, Time Horton's, Wendy's, Advance Parts, AutoZone, CVS Drug, H, NAPA, O'Reilly Parts, Walgreens, W Murphy USA/dsl, VP, Applebee's, Big Boy, Bob Evans, Buffalo Wild Wings, Burger King, Cazadores Mexican, Chipotle, Culver's, Firehouse Subs, Fricker's, Hong Kong Buffet, KFC, McDonald's, Perkins, Pizza Hut, Smokin Jo's BBQ, Taco Bell, Waffle House, Days Inn, Holiday Inn Express, Motel 6, Quality Inn, TownePlace Suites, Travel Inn, $Tree, ALDI, Buick/Cadillac/Chevrolet/GMC, Chrysler/Dodge/Jeep, Ford/Lincoln, Kroger/dsl, Lowe's, Menards, Valvoline, Verizon, Verizon, Walmart/Subway

90 Fair Rd, to Sidney, E Sunoco/dsl, W Love's/Chester's/Godfather's/Hardee's/dsl/scales/RV Hookup/24hr/@, Marathon/DQ/dsl, Hampton Inn

88mm Great Miami River

PIQUA

83 rd 25A, Piqua, E $General, W Sunoco/dsl, Camping World, Chrysler/Dodge/Jeep, to Piqua Hist Area

82 US 36, to Urbana, Piqua, E Clark, Murphy USA/dsl, A&W/LJ Silver, Arby's, China East, DQ, KFC, Starbucks, Subway, Taco Bell, Waffle House, Wendy's, $Tree, ALDI, AT&T, BigLots, Harley-Davidson, Home Depot, st patrol, Valvoline, Verizon, vet, Walmart/Subway, W Speedway, Bob Evans, Buffalo Wings&Rings, Cracker Barrel, McDonald's, Red Lobster, Baymont, Comfort Inn, Elder Beerman

81mm rest area both lanes, full facilities, **litter barrels**, **vending**

78 rd 25A, E H

TROY

74 OH 41, to Covington, Troy, E BP/dsl, Al's Pizza, Golden Bowl, Jersey Mike's, Little Caesar's, McDonald's, Pizza Hut, Subway, Taco Bell, to Hobart Arena, URGENT CARE, vet, W Circle K/dsl, Shell, Speedway/dsl, Applebee's, Big Boy, Bob Evans, Buffalo Wild Wings, Burger King, Chick-fil-A, Chipotle Mexican, Culver's, Fazoli's, Fricker's, Jimmy John's, J's Cuisine, KFC, Los Pitayos Mexican, Marion's Pizza, Outback Steaks, Panera Bread, Penn Sta Subs, Sakai Japanese, Skyline Chili, Starbucks, Steak'n Shake, Tim Horton, Tropical Smoothie, TX Roadhouse, Comfort Suites, Hampton Inn, Holiday Inn Express, Home2 Suites, Residence Inn, Super 9, $General, $Tree, ALDI, AT&T, AutoZone, Grismer Auto Service, Kohl's, Lowe's, Meijer/dsl, Peak Foods, Petco, Staples, Tire Discounters, Verizon, Walmart/Subway

73 OH 55, to Ludlow Falls, Troy, E BP, Shell, Asian Cottage, Boston Stoker Coffee House, Honeybaked Ham, Hot Head Burrito, La Catrina Mexican, Lincoln Sq Rest., Papa John's, Starbucks, Subway, Waffle House, Wendy's, Budget Inn, Motel 6, Royal Inn, $General, Kroger/e85, Verizon, W Casey's, Speedway/dsl

TIPP CITY

69 rd 25A, E Casey's/dsl, Circle K/dsl, Shell/dsl, $General, Arbogast RV Ctr, Buick/GMC, Chrysler/Dodge/Jeep, Ford

68 OH 571, to West Milton, Tipp City, E BP/dsl, Shell, Speedway/dsl, Burger King, Cassano's Pizza, Domino's, Dos Lunas Mexican, Fridas Mexican, Hickory River BBQ, Hot Head Burritos, McDonald's, Subway, AT&T, CVS Drug, Family$, Goodyear/auto, Honda, O'Reilly Parts, W Marathon, Speedway/dsl, Arby's, Big Boy, Bob Evans, Taco Bell, Wendy's, Comfort Inn & Suites, Holiday Inn Express, Lee's Garage, Menards

64 Northwoods Blvd, E El Toro Mexican, Fu Ying, Starbucks, $Tree, Kroger/dsl, W Flying J/Subway/dsl/scales/RV dump/24hr

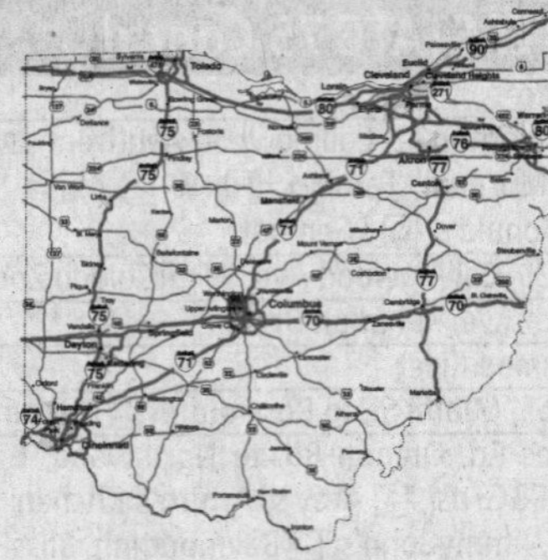

VANDALIA

63 US 40, to Donnelsville, Vandalia, E Speedway/dsl, Bunker's Grill, Dragon China, Fricker's, AutoZone, O'Reilly Parts, repair, W BP/dsl, Shell, Speedway/dsl, Arby's, Chipotle, Domino's, Hot Head Burrito, Jim's Donut Shop, KFC/LJ Silver, McDonald's, Pizza Hut, Subway, Taco Bell, Waffle House, Wendy's, Super 8, USPO, vet

61b a I-70, E to Columbus, W to Indianapolis, to Dayton Int Airport

59 Wyse Rd, Benchwood Rd, E Little York Pizza, Shen's, Hawthorn Suites, Knights Inn, BMW/Volvo/VW, W Speedway/dsl, Sunoco/dsl, Tesla EVC, Arby's, Asian Buffet, Big Boy, Bob Evans, Burger King, Cassano's Pizza, Chick-fil-A, Chipotle Mexican, City BBQ, Coldstone, Cracker Barrel, Culver's, El Toro Mexican, Fricker's, Golden Corral, IHOP, Longhorn Steaks, McAlister's Deli, McDonald's, Olive Garden, Outback Steaks, Panera Bread, Popeyes, Red Lobster, Red Robin, Sake Japanese, Skyline Chili, SmashBurger, SmokeyBones BBQ, Subway, Taco Bell, Baymont, Comfort Inn, Courtyard, Days Inn, Drury Inn, Extended Stay America, Fairfield Inn, Hampton Inn, Home2 Suites, Motel 6, Quality Inn, Red Roof Inn, Residence Inn, Springhill Suites, TownePlace Suites, Wingate, WoodSpring Suites, ALDI, Batteries+, Office Depot, Sam's Club/gas, Tire Discounters, Walmart

DAYTON

58 Needmore Rd, to Dayton, E BP/dsl, Shell/McDonald's, Valero, Hardee's, Goodyear/auto, to AF Museum, W Marathon/dsl, Speedway, Sunoco/dsl, A&W/LJ Silver, Church's TX Chicken, Domino's, Little Caesar's, Subway, Waffle House, Wendy's, $General, $Tree, Advance Parts, auto repair, AutoZone, Family$, Family$, Jiffy Lube, Midas, O'Reilly Parts, USPO, vet

57b Wagner Ford Rd, Siebenthaler Rd, Dayton

57a Neva Rd

56 Stanley Ave, Dayton, E Shell, W Dragon City Chinese, McDonald's, Taco Bell, Victor's Taco Shop, Dayton Motel

55b a Keowee St, downtown, Dayton

54c OH 4 N, Webster St, to Springfield, downtown

54mm Great Miami River

54b OH 48, Main St, Dayton, E Chevrolet, Honda, W Family$, H

54a Grand Ave, Dayton

53b OH 49, 1st St, Salem Ave, downtown, Dayton

53a OH 49, 3rd St, downtown

52b a US 35, E to Dayton, W to Eaton

51 Edwin C Moses Blvd, Nicholas Rd, E Courtyard, Marriott, H, to U of Dayton, W BP/dsl, Love's/Hardee's/dsl/scales/24hr, QT/dsl, McDonald's, Wendy's, Holiday Inn Express, SunWatch Indian Village

50b a OH 741, Kettering St, Dryden Rd, E H, vet, W Marathon/dsl, Red Roof Inn

47 Dixie Dr, W Carrollton, Moraine, E Shell/dsl, Domino's, Waffle House, $General, U-Haul, W Shell/dsl, Speedway/dsl, Speedway/dsl, El Meson, KFC, McDonald's, Pizza Hut, Taco Bell, Wendy's, Wing Zone, $General, USPO

OH

INTERSTATE 75 Cont'd

Exit #	Services
44	OH 725, to Centerville, Miamisburg, E [gas] BP/dsl, Speedway/dsl, [food] Applebee's, Big Boy, Bonefish Grill, Bravo Italiana, Chick-fil-A, ChuckeCheese, Dunkin'/Baskin-Robbins, El Toro Mexican, First Watch, Fricker's, Fuji Grill, Godfather's, Hardee's, Jimmy John's, KFC, KPOT Korean BBQ, Marion's Pizza, McDonald's, Mission BBQ, Olive Garden, Outback Steaks, Penn Sta Subs, PF Chang's, Red Lobster, Rusty Bucket Grill, Sake Japanese, Skyline Chili, SmashBurger, Starbucks, Steak'n Shake, Subway, Taco Bell, Waffle House, Wendy's, Wingstop, [lodging] Comfort Suites, Courtyard, DoubleTree Suites, Extended Stay America, Extended Stay America, Hampton Inn, Homewood Suites, InTowne Suites, Motel 6, SpringHill Suites, Studio 6, [other] $Tree, Advance Parts, ALDI, AT&T, Audi/VW/Porsche/Jaguar, Batteries+, Best Buy, Burlington Coats, Dick's, Discount Tire, Grismer Auto Service, Hobby Lobby, Home Depot, Honda/Nissan/Mazda, [H], JC Penney, Kia, Lowe's, Menard's, Michael's, Midas, Monro, Office Depot, PepBoys, PetSmart, Target, Tire Discounters, Toyota, Valvoline, Verizon, vet, Walmart, W [gas] BP, Marathon, Shell/dsl, [food] Bob Evans, Donatos Pizza, LJ Silver, Perkins, Tim Horton's, [lodging] Quality Inn, Red Roof Inn, Rodeway Inn, Super 8, [other] $General, CarMax, Chevrolet, Ford, [H], transmissions
43	I-675 N, to Columbus
41	Austin Blvd, E [food] BJ's Rest., Broken Egg Cafe, Buffalo Wild Wings, Chipotle, Chuy's, Cold Stone, Coldstone, Dewey's Pizza, Firebirds, Five Guys, Noodles&Co, Panera Bread, [lodging] Hilton Garden, Staybridge Suites, [other] AT&T, Dick's, Kohl's, Kroger/dsl, TJ Maxx, W [lodging] Home2 Suites
38	OH 73, Springboro, Franklin, E [gas] Sheetz/dsl, Shell, Speedway/dsl, Thornton's/dsl, [food] Applebee's, Arby's, Bob Evans, Burger King, China Garden, Chipotle Mexican, KFC, McDonald's, Papa John's, Pizza Hut, Popeyes, Skyline Chili, Starbucks, Subway, Taco Bell, Tim Horton's, Waffle House, Wendy's, [lodging] Hampton Inn, Quality Inn, [other] Jiffy Lube, Kroger, O'Reilly Parts, Tire Discounters, URGENT CARE, USPO, vet, W [gas] Murphy USA/dsl, Speedway/dsl, Sunoco, [food] A&G Pizza, Big Boy, El Vaquero Mexican, GoldStar Chili, Lee's Chicken, McDonald's, [lodging] EconoLodge, Holiday Inn Express, Skylight Motel, [other] $General, $Tree, auto repair, AutoZone, NAPA, URGENT CARE, USPO, Walgreens, Walmart
36	OH 123, to Lebanon, Franklin, E [gas] Pilot/Subway/Dunkin/dsl/scales/24hr/@, Shell/Wendy's/dsl, [food] McDonald's, Mom's Rest., Waffle House, [lodging] Motel 6, W [gas] Marathon/White Castle/dsl, Sheetz/dsl, Sunoco
32	OH 122, Middletown, E [gas] BP, [food] McDonald's, Waffle House, [lodging] Days Inn, Red Roof Inn, Super 8, [other] [H], W [gas] Shell, [food] Applebee's, Arby's, Big Boy, Bob Evans, Buffalo Wild Wings, Cancun Mexican, China King Buffet, Chipotle, Cracker Barrel, Domino's, El Rancho Grande, Fricker's, GoldStar Chili, Hot Head Burritos, KFC, La Rosa's Pizza, O'Charley's, Olive Garden, Sonic, SteakNShake, Wendy's, White Castle, [lodging] Comfort Inn&Suites, Drury Inn, Fairfield Inn, Hampton Inn, Quality Inn, [other] $General, $Tree, ALDI, AT&T, AutoZone, BigLots, DQ, Jiffy Lube, Kohl's, Kroger/dsl, Lowe's, Meijer/dsl, Petco, Save-A-Lot, Staples, Tire Discounters, URGENT CARE, Verizon, Walmart/Subway
29	OH 63, to Hamilton, Monroe, E [gas] Shell/dsl, [food] Burger King, Chipotle, Culver's, DQ, Dunkin', El Trompo Mexican, Jersey Mike's, Popeyes, Skyline Chili, Taco Bell, Tim Horton/Wendy's, Waffle House, [lodging] Holiday Inn Express, Tru by Hilton, [other] Premium Outlets/Famous Brands, Tire Discounters, Trader's World, U-Haul, W [gas] Speedway/Speedy Cafe/dsl, [food] Arby's, Froggy's, Jimmy John's, McDonald's, Prime BBQ Smokehouse, Richard's Pizza, Subway, [lodging] Baymont,
29	Continued Motel 75, [other] flea mkt, Honda
27.5mm	rest area both lanes, full [handicapped] facilities, **info**, **litter barrels**, **petwalk**, [phone], [picnic], **vending**
24	OH 129 W, to Hamilton, E [lodging] Holiday Inn Express, [other] Costco/gas, W [gas] Shell, Tesla EVC, UDF, [food] Bibibop Asian, Brio Italian Grille, Buffalo Wings & Rings, Burger King, Caporal Mexican, Chick-fil-A, China Wok, Coopers Hawk, Donato's Pizza, First Watch, Five Guys, Freddy's, Grand Peking, Hot Head Burritos, Jets Pizza, Kona Grill, McDonald's, MOD Pizza, Outback Steaks, Potbelly, Rusty Bucket Rest., Shake Shack, Skyline Chili, Starbucks, Starbucks, Subway, Taco Bell, The Donut Dude, Torchy's Tacos, [lodging] AC Hotel, Hampton Inn, Home2 Suites, [other] $Tree, CVS, Dick's, Dillard's, [H], Kroger/gas, Old Navy, Verizon, vet
22	Tylersville Rd, to Mason, Hamilton, E [gas] Marathon, Thornton's/dsl, [food] Arby's, Bob Evans, BoneFish Grill, Broken Egg Cafe, Burger King, Cane's, Chick-fil-A, Chipotle, City BBQ, Dewey's Pizza, Dunkin, Firehouse Subs, Graeter's Grill, Hooks Fish&Chicken, IHOP, Jack-in-the-Box, Jimmy John's, KFC, Krispy Kreme, Longhorn Steaks, McAlister's Deli, McDonald's, Miyako Grill, Noodles&Co, Panda Express, Panera Bread, Skyline Chili, SmashBurger, Soho Japanese, Starbucks, Taco Bell, Taziki Grill, TGIFriday's, Twin Dragon, TX Roadhouse, Waffle House, Wayback Burger, Wendy's, [other] AAA, AT&T, Batteries+, Big Lots, Discount Tire, Fresh Mkt, Home Depot, [H], Kohl's, Kroger, Michael's, Office Depot, PetSmart, Ross, Target, TJ Maxx, URGENT CARE, Walgreens, W [gas] Speedway/dsl, [lodging] Holiday Inn, [other] ALDI, CarX, Lowe's, Meijer/dsl, Tire Discounters
21	Cin-Day Rd, N [other] AAA, E [food] Big Boy, [lodging] Quality Inn, W [gas] EVC, Shell/dsl, Speedway/dsl, UDF/dsl, [food] Arby's, Domino's, Dunkin', El Rancho Nuevo, LaRosa's Pizza, Papa John's, Sonic, Taco's John's, Waffle House, Wendy's, [other] Ace Hardware, AutoZone, Christian Bros Automotive, USPO, Valvoline, Walgreens, Walmart/Subway
19	Union Centre Blvd, to Fairfield, E [food] Bravo Italiana, Chuy's, Original Pancakes, Panera Bread, PF Chang's, Red Robin, Smokey Bones BBQ, [other] Barnes&Noble, Verizon, W [gas] BP/dsl, Circle K, Shell, [food] Aladdin's Eatery, Applebee's, Bob Evans, Buffalo Wild Wings, Burger King, Chipotle Mexican, Dingle House, First Watch, Jag's Steaks, Jimmy John's, McDonald's, Mellow Mushroom, Rancho Nuevo, Skyline Chili, Smoothie King, Starbucks, Subway, Tom+Chee, Tropical Smoothie, Wendy's, [lodging] Aloft, avid hotel, Comfort Inn, Courtyard, Fairfield Inn, Hampton Inn, Hilton Garden, Holiday Inn, Home2 Suites, Homewood Suites, Marriott, Residence Inn, Staybridge Suites, [other] IKEA, Mercedes
16	I-275 to I-71, to I-74
15	Sharon Rd, to Sharonville, Glendale, E [gas] Shell, Thornton's/dsl, [food] Big Boy, Bob Evans, Cracker Barrel, Rally's, Ruby Tuesday, Skyline Chili, Waffle House, [lodging] Baymont Inn, Drury Inn, Hawthorn Suites, Hilton Garden, Holiday Inn Express, La Quinta, Quality Inn, Red Roof Inn, Travel Inn, Tru Hilton, W [food] Tokyo Japanese, [lodging] Chester Inn&Suites, Home Towne Studios, Hyatt Place Conv Ctr, LivInn Suites, Marriot
14	OH 126, to Woodlawn, Evendale, W [gas] Sunoco/dsl
13	Shepherd Lane, to Lincoln Heights, W [food] Wendy's
12	Wyoming Ave, Cooper Ave, to Lockland, W [gas] Marathon/dsl
10a	OH 126, Ronald Reagan Hwy
10b	Galbraith Rd(exits left from nb), Arlington Heights
9	OH 4, OH 561, Paddock Rd, Seymour Ave, W [other] fairgrounds
8	Towne St, Elmwood Pl(from nb)
7	OH 562, to I-71, Norwood, Cincinnati Gardens
6	Mitchell Ave, St Bernard, S [other] AutoZone, E [gas] Amoco, Shell, Sunoco, [food] Popeyes, White Castle, [lodging] Comfort Inn, [other] to Cincinnati Zoo, to Xavier U, Walgreens, W [gas] BP/dsl,

MIAMISBURG FRANKLIN MONROE MONROE HAMILTON ARLINGTON HEIGHTS

INTERSTATE 75 Cont'd

ST BERNARD

6 Continued
Gold Star Chili, McDonald's, Rally's, Advance Parts, Ford, Honda, Hyundai, Kia, Kroger, Tires+

4 I-74 W, US 52, US 27 N, to Indianapolis

3 to US 27 S, US 127 S, Hopple St, E White Castle, Budget Host, H, U of Cincinnati, W Shell, Wendy's, Family$

2b Harrison Ave, W BP, Family$

2a Western Ave, Liberty St(from sb)

1g Ezzard Charles Dr((from sb), W Quality Inn

1f US 50W, Freeman Ave(from sb), W Marathon/dsl, Shell/Subway, Big Boy, Taco Bell, Wendy's, White Castle, Quality Inn, Ford, NAPA, USPO

1e 7th St(from sb), downtown

1c 5th St, downtown, E Courtyard, Hilton, Hyatt, Westin, to Duke Energy Center

1a I-71 N, to Cincinnati, downtown

0mm Ohio/Kentucky state line, Ohio River

INTERSTATE 76

65 Ohio/Pennsylvania state line. See OH TPK, exits 232-234.

234 I-680(from wb), to Youngstown

232 OH 7, to Boardman, Youngstown, N Marathon/dsl, Sheetz, DQ, Los Gallos Mexican, Rita's Custard, Steamer's Stonewall Tavern, Budget Inn, Holiday Inn Express, Quality Inn, Skylight Inn, $General, antiques, S Pilot/McDonald's/dsl/scales/24hr, Davis Motel, Liberty Inn

LAKE MILTON

60mm I-76 eb joins Ohio TPK(toll)

57 to OH 45, Bailey Rd, to Warren, N Sheetz/dsl, S Shell/dsl, Dunkin'

54 OH 534, to Newton Falls, Lake Milton, N KOA, S Sunoco/dsl, Berlin Lake

52mm Lake Milton

48 OH 225, to Alliance, N Love's/Godfathers/Subway/dsl/scales/24hr/@, W Branch SP, S Berlin Lake, Lake Milton SP

45mm rest area both lanes, **full facilities, litter barrels, petwalk, both lanes**

43 OH 14, to Alliance, Ravenna, N W Branch SP, S Marathon/Subway/dsl, fireworks

KENT

38b a OH 5, OH 44, to Ravenna, N BP/dsl, Speedway/dsl, Arby's, McDonald's/rv parking, Wendy's, vet, S Circle K, China Dragon, Cracker Barrel, Dunkin', Romeo's Pizza, $General, auto parts, Giant Eagle Foods, H, RV camping

33 OH 43, to Hartville, Kent, N BP/dsl, Marathon, Los Girasoles Mexican, Days Inn, EconoLodge, Hampton Inn, Holiday Inn Express, Super 8, Kent St U, S Circle K, Speedway/dsl, Brimfield Rest., Gionino's Pizza, Joe's BBQ, McDonald's, Pizza Hut, Subway, Wendy's, $General, tire repair, vet

BRITTAIN

31 rd 18, Tallmadge, N Murphy USA/dsl, #1 Chinese, Applebee's, Arby's, Burger King, Chipotle, DQ, La Terraza Mexican, Panda Express, Panera Bread, Taco Bell, $Tree, ALDI, AT&T, Kohl's, Lowe's, Marshall's, Meijer/gas, Petco, Verizon, Walmart/Subway

29 OH 532, Tallmadge, Mogadore

27 OH 91, Canton Rd, Gilchrist Rd, N Bob Evans, S Marathon/Subway/dsl, Royal Inn, NAPA

26 OH 18, E Market St, Mogadore Rd, N Marathon/dsl, Azteca Mexican, S Arby's, Dunkin', Lamp Post Rest., McDonald's, Subway, Wendy's, $General

25b a Martha Ave, General St, Brittain, N Circle K/dsl, Hilton Garden, Mercedes, Toyota, S Goodyear HQ

24 Arlington St, Kelly Ave, S Goodyear HQ

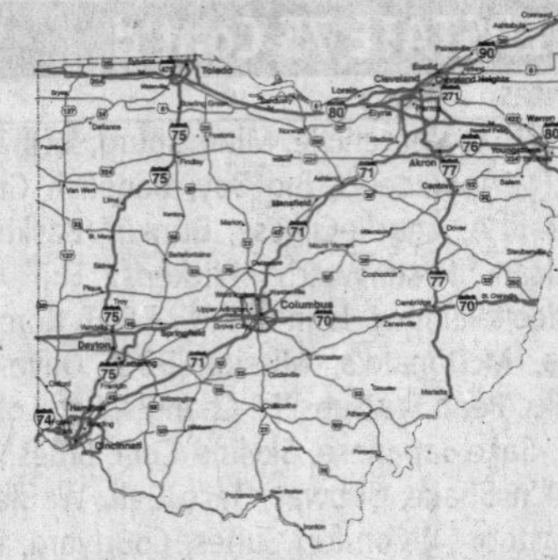

BARBERTON

23b OH 8, Buchtell Ave, to Cuyahoga (exits left from eb), U of Akron

23a I-77 S, to Canton

22a Main St, Broadway, N downtown, ALDI

21c OH 59 E, Dart Ave, N H

21b Lakeshore St, Bowery St(from eb)

21a East Ave(from wb)

20 I-77 N(from eb), to Cleveland

19 Battles Ave, Kenmore Blvd

18 I-277, US 224 E, to Canton, Barberton

17b OH 619, Wooster Rd, S Sunoco/dsl, H, tires/repair

17a (from eb, no return) State St, to Barberton, N Arlene's Cuisine, Caravan House, LJ Silver's, Taco Bell, S Papa John's, Papa Roni's Pizza, H, Walgreens

16 Barber Rd, S Rocky's/dsl/e85, Sheetz, DQ, Willey's Grill, Chrysler/Dodge/Jeep

14 Cleve-Mass Rd, to Norton, S BP/dsl, Circle K/dsl, Arby's, Casa Del Mar Mexican, Chipotle, Marco's Pizza, McDonald's, Pizza Hut, Subway, Wendy's, Wingstop, $General, Ace Hardware, Acme Fresh Mkt, Advance Parts, CVS Drug, O'Reilly Parts, USPO, Verizon

13b a OH 21, N to Cleveland, S to Massillon

WADSWORTH

11 OH 261, Wadsworth, N Speedway/dsl, S GetGo/e85, Giant Eagle, Antonio's Pizza, Wayback Burger, AAA, American Auto & Tire, Jiffy Lube, Kohl's, Lowe's, PetCo, Target, Verizon

9 OH 94, to N Royalton, Wadsworth, N Circle K, GetGo, Applebee's, Arby's, Bob Evans, Burger King, China Express, Chipotle Mexican, El Rincon Mexican, Galaxy Rest., Marie's Cafe, McDonald's, Panera Bread, Pizza Hut, Romeo's Pizza, Starbucks, Subway, Taco Bell, Wendy's, Whitehouse Chicken, Comfort Inn, Holiday Inn Express, $Tree, ALDI, BigLots, Buehler's Foods, DrugMart, Goodyear/auto, Home Depot, NTB, Verizon, Walmart/Subway, S Marathon/DQ/dsl, Sunoco, Casa Del Rio, Dunkin', Gionino's Pizza, KFC, Papa John's, Advance Parts, auto repair, AutoZone, CVS Drug, vet

7 OH 57, to Rittman, Medina, N Marathon/dsl, S H

6mm weigh sta eb

2 OH 3, to Medina, Seville, N Marathon/Circle K/dsl, Boscos Pizza, DQ, Hardee's, Subway, Hawthorn Suites, Quality Inn, Maple Lakes Camping(seasonal), S Sheetz, Shell/dsl, #1 Chinese, El Patron Mexican, Romeo's Pizza, $General

1 I-76 E, to Akron, US 224, W Pilot/Subway/dsl/scales/24hr, TA/BP/Burger King/Popeyes/dsl/scales/24hr/@, Arby's, McDonald's, Super 8, Blue Beacon, SpeedCo

0mm I-76 begins/ends on I-71, exit 209.

INTERSTATE 77

TOWER CITY

163.7mm I-77 begins/ends on I-90, exit 172 in Cleveland.

163c I-90, E to Erie, W to Toledo

163b E 9th St, Tower City

162b E 22nd St, E 14th St(from nb)

INTERSTATE 77 Cont'd

Exit #	Services
162a	E 30th St, Woodland Ave, Broadway St(from nb), W USPO
161b	I-490 W, to I-71, E 55th, E
161a	OH 14(from nb), Broadway St
160	Pershing Ave(from nb)
159b	Fleet Ave, E BP/dsl
159a	Harvard Ave, Newburgh Heights, E Mr Hero, CVS Drug, Family$, Save-A-Lot, W BP/Subway/dsl, Shell/dsl, 49 St Tavern
158	Grant Ave, Cuyahoga Heights
157	OH 21, OH 17(from sb), Brecksville Rd
156	I-480, to Youngstown, Toledo
155	Rockside Rd, to Independence, E Shell, Sunoco/dsl, Aladdin's, Bob Evans, Bonefish Grill, Chipotle, Delmonico's Steaks, Denny's, DiBella's Subs, Hibachi Japanese, Jimmy John's, LA Pete's, McDonald's, Outback Steaks, Panera Bread, Potbelly, Red Robin, Starbucks, The Sanctuary, Wendy's, Winking Lizard Grill, Zoup!, Comfort Inn, DoubleTree, Embassy Suites, Holiday Inn, La Quinta, Red Roof Inn, Springhill Suites, AT&T, Drugmart, NTB, to Cuyahoga Valley NP, Verizon, Walgreens, W Applebee's, Longhorn Steaks, Wasabi Steaks, Courtyard, Extended Stay America, Hampton Inn, Home2 Suites, Ramada, Residence Inn
153	Pleasant Valley Rd, to Independence, 7 Hills
151	Wallings Rd
149	OH 82, to Broadview Heights, Brecksville, E Shell/dsl, Austin's Grille, Burger Fresh, Courtyard Cafe, Panera Bread, Simon's Rest., Starbucks, CVS Drug, Marc's Foods, Verizon, Walgreens, W BP, GetGo/dsl, Bubbakoo's Burritos, Chipotle, McDonald's, Wayback Burgers, Wild Eagle Steaks, Giant Eagle Foods
147	to OH 21, Miller Rd(from sb)
146	I-80/Ohio Tpk, to Youngstown, Toledo
145	OH 21(from nb), E Pilot/Wendy's/dsl/scales, Cozumel Mexican, Subway, Comfort Inn, Holiday Inn Express, Motel 6, Quality Inn, Super 8
144	I-271 N, to Erie
143	OH 176, to I-271 S, W Shell, McDonald's, Ocelot Cafe, Panda Chinese, Subway, Teresa's Pizza
141mm	rest area both lanes, full facilities, **litter barrels, petwalk**, **vending**
138	Ghent Rd, W Circle K/dsl, Gasoline Alley, Lanning's Rest.
137b a	OH 18, to Fairlawn, Medina, S Panera Bread, E Circle K, GetGo, Shell, Speedway, Akron's Burgers, Applebee's, Arby's, BJ's Rest., Bob Evans, Bruegger's Bagels, Burntwood Tavern, Chick-fil-A, Chili's, Chipotle Mexican, Coldstone, Cracker Barrel, Donato's Pizza, First Watch, Five Guys, Fleming's Steaks, Gionino's Pizza, HoneyBaked Ham, Jimmy John's, Macaroni Grill, McDonald's, Olive Garden, Pad Thai, Penn Sta Subs, PF Chang's, Red Lobster, Robeck's FruitJuice, Starbucks, Steak'n Shake, Subway, Swensons Drive-In, Taco Bell, Vicious Biscuit, Wendy's, Winking Lizard Grill, Courtyard, DoubleTree, EconoLodge, Fairfield Inn, Hampton Inn, Holiday Inn, Holiday Inn Express, Homewood Suites, Motel 6, Quality Inn, $Tree, Acme Fresh Mkt, ALDI, AT&T, Barnes&Noble, Best Buy, Dick's, Dillard's, Earth Fare Foods, Flynn's Tire, Ford, Giant Eagle Foods, Goodyear/auto, Hobby Lobby, Home Depot, JC Penney, Jo-Ann Fabrics, Lowe's, Macy's, Michael's, NTB, Old Navy, PetSmart, Sam's Club, Staples, TJ Maxx, Verizon, Walmart, World Mkt, W Sunoco, DQ, Kingfish Rest., Longhorn Steaks, Tres Potrillos, Wasabi Grill, Baymont Inn, Best Western+, Extended Stay America 2, Fairbridge Suites, Radisson,
137b a	Continued Residence Inn, Suburban Studio, Super 8,
136(exits left from nb)	OH 21S, to Massillon
135	Cleveland-Massillon Rd(from nb, no return)
133	Ridgewood Rd, Miller Rd, E Circle K/dsl, W Master Pizza, Old Carolina BBQ, Tiffany's Bakery, Conrad's Automotive
132	White Pond Dr, Mull Ave
131	OH 162, Copley Rd, E Circle K, China Star, Gino's Pizza, Little Caesar's, Copley Tire, CVS, Save-A-Lot Foods, Walgreens, W BP/dsl, McDonald's, Pizza Hut, vet
130	OH 261, Wooster Ave, E Circle K, Sunoco/dsl, Burger King, Church's TX Chicken, Domino's, McDonald's, Nephew's BBQ, New Ming Chinese, Rally's, Subway, Advance Parts, AutoZone, O'Reilly Parts, W Chevrolet, Toyota, U-Haul
129	I-76 W, to I-277, to Kenmore Blvd, Barberton
125b	I-76 E, to Youngstown. I-77 and I-76 merge. See I-76 exits 21a-22b.
125a	OH 8 N, to Cuyahoga Falls, U of Akron
124b	Lover's Lane, Cole Ave
124a	Archwood Ave, Firestone Blvd(from sb)
123b	OH 764, Wilbeth Rd, E DQ, Akron Fulton
123a	Waterloo Rd(from sb), W BP, GetGo, Burger King, Charlie's Cheesesteaks, Chipotle, House of Hunan, Hyde Out Japanese, Mi Casa, Papa John's, Rally's, Waterloo Rest., $General, $Tree, Big Lots, Giant Eagle Foods, Marc's Mkt, Walgreens
122b a	I-277, US 224 E, to Barberton, Mogadore
120	Arlington Rd, to Green, E Speedway/dsl, Applebee's, Denny's, Golden Corral, IHOP, Mr Hero, Pulp Juice, Shogun, Starbucks, Waffle House, Quality Inn, Red Roof Inn, AT&T, AutoZone, Home Depot, Kohl's, O'Reilly Parts, Staples, Walmart/Subway, W BP, Bob Evans, Burger King, Chipotle Mexican, Circle K, East of Chicago Pizza, El Fogon Mexican, Five Guys, Freddy's Burgers, Latino Grill, Maki House Japanese, McDonald's, Panera Bread, Skyway Burgers, Subway, Taco Bell, Tommy's Chicken, Wendy's, Comfort Inn, Extended Stay, Hampton Inn, Holiday Inn Express, Residence Inn, $Tree, Acura, Buick/GMC, Camping World RV Ctr, Chevrolet, Goodyear/auto, Honda, Hyundai, Infiniti, Lexus, Lowe's, Nissan, Subaru, T-Mobile, Target, Valvoline, Verizon
118	OH 241, to OH 619, Massillon, E Speedway/dsl, Gionino's Pizza, Handel's Ice Cream, Mr. Cheng's Chinese, Subway, W Circle K/dsl, GetGo, Tesla EVC, 35 Brix Rest., Antonio's Pizza, Arby's, Chipotle, DQ, Dunkin', Hungry Howie's, Jimmy John's, Kasai Japanese, Lucky Star Chinese, McDonald's, Menches Rest., Pizza Hut, Starbucks, Subway, Cambria Suites, Super 8, $General, Acme Fresh Mkt, Advance Parts, ALDI, Conrad Automotive, CVS Drug, Giant Eagle Foods,
113	W Hilton Garden, Akron-Canton, General RV Ctr
112	Shuffel St, E Embassy Suites
111	Portage St, N Canton, E Amoco/dsl, Circle K, TA/Country Pride/dsl/scales/24hr/@, Burger King, Casa Tlaquepaque, Flavorfuel, KFC, Palombo's Italian, Quaker Steak, Subway, Sylvester's Italian, Mr Tire, TrueValue, W BP/dsl, Speedway/dsl, Aladdin's Eatery, BJ's Rest., Bonefish Grill, Carrabba's, Charlie's Cheesesteaks, ChuckeCheese, Coldstone, Cracker Barrel, Dunkin'/Baskin-Robbins, Five Guys, IHOP, Longhorn Steaks, McDonald's, Outback Steaks, Panera Bread, Red Robin, Rockne's Cafe, Romeo's Pizza, Samantha's Rest., Starbucks, Taco Bell, Wasabi Japanese, Wendy's, Best Western+, Microtel, Rodeway Inn, AAA, AT&T, Best Buy, BJ's Whse,

TOLEDO 7 HILLS MEDINA BARBERTON MASSILLON

OH

INTERSTATE 77 Cont'd

N

CANTON

111 Continued
Books A Million, Chevrolet, DrugMart, Giant Eagle Foods, Goodyear/auto, Home Depot, Lowe's, Marshall's, Michael's, Old Navy, Sam's Club/gas, Walgreens, Walmart/Subway

109b a Everhard Rd, Whipple Ave, E Marathon/Subway/dsl, Speedway/dsl, Caribou Coffee, Fat Head's Brewery, Fazoli's, Freddy's Burgers, Fuji Sushi, Jersey Mike's, Waffle House, Baymont Inn, Comfort Inn, Fairfield Inn, Hampton Inn, Home2 Suites, Hyatt Place, Residence Inn, Staybridge Suites, Buick/GMC, Ford, W Marathon, A1 Japanese Steaks, Applebee's, Arby's, BIBIBOP Asian, Blaze Pizza, Bob Evans, Bojangles, Bravo Italiana, Brown Derby, Buffalo Wild Wings, Burnt Wood Tavern, Cane's, Chick-fil-A, Chili's, Chipotle Mexican, Cluver's, DiBella Subs, Dunkin', Firehouse Subs, First Watch, Golden Corral, HoneyBaked Ham, Jerzees Grille, Katana Buffet, KFC, La Loma Mexican, Lucia's Steaks, McAlister's Deli, McDonald's, Mission BBQ, Mr Hero, Mulligan's, Olive Garden, Panda Express, Panera Bread, Papa Bear's, Papa Gyros, Penn Sta Subs, Red Lobster, Robek's, Sakura Japanese, Smoothie King, Starbucks, Steak'n Shake, Subway, Sukho Thai, Taco Bell, TGIFriday's, Tropical Smoothie, TX Roadhouse, Wendy's, Wingstop, Courtyard, Holiday Inn, Knights Inn, Quality Inn, Ramada, Red Roof Inn, Springhill Suites, $Tree, ALDI, AT&T, AutoZone, Dick's, Dillard's, Firestone/auto, Goodyear/auto, Hobby Lobby, Kohl's, Macy's, Magnuson, Marc's Foods, NTB, PetSmart, Target, Valvoline, Verizon, World Mkt

107b a US 62, OH 687, Fulton Rd, to Alliance, E Circle K, Italo's Pizza, Jerzee's Grille, city park, W Circle K, Don Shula's Kitchen, Pizza Oven, Pro Football Hall of Fame

106 13th St NW, E [other] [H]

105b OH 172, Tuscarawas St, E Sunoco, McDonald's, W KFC, Subway, Taco Bell, AutoZone, CVS

105a 6th St SW(no EZ return from sb), E Sunoco, McDonald's, Ford, W Subway, AutoZone, [H]

104b a US 30, US 62, to E Liverpool, Massillon

103 OH 800 S, E Marathon/Subway/dsl, Speedway, Arby's, DQ, Dunkin', Gionino's Pizza, Italo's Pizza, McDonald's, Peking Chinese, Taco Bell, Waffle House, $Tree, Advance Parts, Family$, Goodyear/auto, O'Reilly Parts, Save-A-Lot Foods, W Firestone

BOLIVAR

101 OH 627, to Faircrest St, E Pilot/Subway/Dunkin'/dsl/scales/24hr, Speedway, Speedway/McDonald's, Wendy's, Fairfield Inn, W fireworks

99 Fohl Rd, to Navarre, E KOA, W Marathon

93 OH 212, to Zoar, Bolivar, E Speedway/dsl, McDonald's, Wendy's, Sleep Inn, $General, Giant Eagle Foods, Lake Atwood, Zoar Historic Village, W Marathon/DQ/Subway/dsl

87 US 250W, to Strasburg, W BP/Taco Bell/dsl, Marathon/dsl, Hardee's, Malcuit's Tavern, McDonald's, Subway, Ramada Ltd, Family$, Verizon

DOVER

85 Schneiders Crossing Rd, to Dover, E Marathon, Freddy's, Grinders, Starbucks, Subway, Buehler's Mkt/gas, Discount Drug

83 OH 39, OH 211, to Sugarcreek, Dover, E BP/dsl, Speedway/Speedy's Cafe/dsl, Bob Evans, KFC, McDonald's, Shoney's, Wendy's, Dover Inn, AutoZone, Chrysler/Dodge/Jeep, Flynn's Tires, Ford, Honda, [H], Lincoln, Nissan, Ziegler Tire, W Country Inn&Suites, Quality Inn, vet

81 US 250, to Uhrichsville, OH 39, New Philadelphia, E Sheetz/dsl, Speedway, Arby's, Buffalo Wild Wings, Burger King, Chipotle, Denny's, El San Jose Mexican, Hog Heaven BBQ, LJ Silver, Starbucks, Taco Bell, TX Roadhouse,

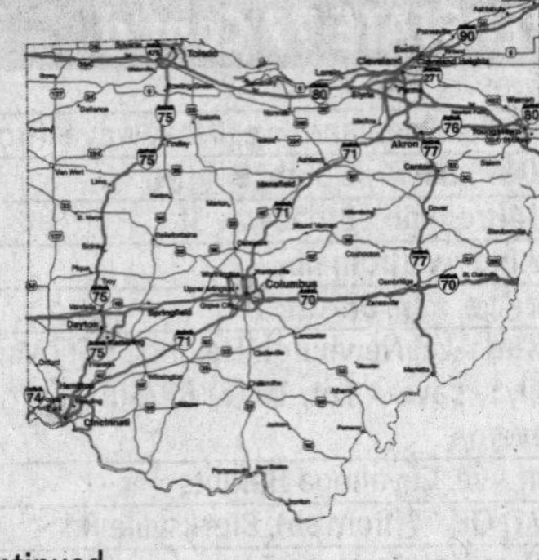

CAMBRIDGE

81 Continued
Best Western, Days Inn, Hampton Inn, Holiday Inn Express, Schoenbrunn Inn, TownePlace Suites, Travelodge, $General, $Tree, Advance Parts, ALDI, BigLots, O'Reilly Parts, Verizon, Walmart/Subway, W Eagle TP/rest./dsl/scales/24hr, Harley-Davidson

73 OH 751, to rd 53, Stone Creek, W Marathon/dsl

65 US 36, Port Washington, Newcomerstown, W BP, Speedway/Wendy's, McDonald's, Taco Bell, Spark Hotel, Super 8

64mm Tuscarawas River

54 OH 541, rd 831, to Plainfield, Kimbolton, E Rod's RV Camping, W Marathon

47 US 22, to Cadiz, Cambridge, E Salt Fork SP, W BP, Glass Museum, [H]

46b a US 40, to Old Washington, Cambridge, W Marathon/Wendy's/dsl, Speedway/dsl, Burger King, Hunan Chinese, Lee's Rest., LJ Silver, McDonald's, Taco Bell, Wally's Pizza, Family$, Riesbeck's Mkt

44b a I-70, E to Wheeling, W to Columbus

41 OH 209, OH 821, Byesville, W Circle K, Clark, EVC, Marathon, Galaxy Pizza, McDonald's, Rasor's DriveIn, Subway, Tommy's Pizza, $General, U-Haul

39mm **full facilities, litter barrels, petwalk**, [phone], [picnic], [RS] nb, **vending**

37 OH 313, Buffalo, E BP, Dough Boys Pizza, Subway, Senecaville Lake, UPSO, W $General

CALDWELL

36mm **full facilities, litter barrels, petwalk**, [phone], [picnic], [RS] sb, **vending**

28 OH 821, Belle Valley, E Sunoco/dsl, Liberty Mkt, RV camping, USPO, Wolf Run SP

25 OH 78, Caldwell, E Pilot/Arby's/dsl/scales/24hr, Sunoco/Subway/dsl, DQ, Lori's Rest., McDonald's, Taco Bell, Best Western, Days Inn, Quality Inn, W Comfort Inn

16 OH 821, Macksburg

6 OH 821, to Devola, E BP/Subway/dsl, W Marathon/dsl/LP, [other] [H]

MARIETTA

3mm **full facilities, info, litter barrels, petwalk**, [phone], [picnic], [RS], **vending**, Welcome Ctr nb

1 OH 7, to OH 26, Marietta, E GoMart/dsl/24hr, DQ, Gran Rev Mexican, IHOP, Subway, TX Roadhouse, Wings Etc, Baymont Inn, Comfort Suites, Fairfield Inn, Holiday Inn Express, Red Roof Inn, Wingate Inn, $Tree, ALDI, Cadillac/Chevrolet, Chrysler/Dodge/Jeep, Ford/Lincoln, GNC, Lowe's, Toyota, Walmart/McDonald's, W BP/dsl, GetGo/dsl, Marathon/dsl, Speedway/dsl, Applebee's, Arby's, Biscuit World, Bob Evans, Burger King, Capt D's, China Fun, Donatos Pizza, E Chicago Pizza, Empire Buffet, Jersey Mike's, KFC, Las Trancas Mexican, Little Caesar's, LJ Silver, McDonald's, Napoli's Pizza, Papa John's, Pizza Hut, Qdoba, Shogun Hibachi, Subway, Taco Bell, Wendy's, Hampton Inn, Microtel, Super 8, Advance Parts, AT&T, AutoZone, Big Lots, CVS Drug, Family$, Kroger, TrueValue, Valvoline, Walgreens

INTERSTATE 77 Cont'd

Exit #	Services
0mm	Ohio/West Virginia state line, Ohio River

INTERSTATE 80

HUBBARD

Exit #	Services
237mm	Ohio/Pennsylvania state line
237mm	**full facilities, info, litter barrels, petwalk**, , , **vending**, Welcome Ctr wb
234b a	US 62, OH 7, Hubbard, to Sharon, PA, Hubbard, N Flying J/dsl/LP/scales/24hr, Shell/rest./dsl/scales/motel/24hr/@, Arby's, Burger King, Dunkin', McDonald's, Waffle House, Best Western, Travelodge, $General, Blue Beacon, tire/dsl repair, S Love's/Chester's/Subway/dsl/scales/24hr/@, Chevrolet
232mm	weigh sta wb
229	OH 193, Belmont Ave, to Youngstown, N GetGo, Speedway/dsl, Chipotle, Coaches Burgers, Dunkin', Fortune Garden, Handel's Ice Cream, Sta Square Italian, Starbucks, Subway, Comfort Suites, Hampton Inn, Motel 6, Super 8, Giant Eagle Foods, S BP/dsl, Shell, Arby's, Bob Evans, Bull & Bear Rest., C's Waffles, Denny's, El Tapatio, Golden Hunan Chinese, Happy Buffet, Jimmy's Italian, KFC, Little Caesar's, LJ Silver, McDonald's, Papa Johns, Pizza Hut, Pizza Joe's, Popeyes, Rally's, Señor Jalapeño Mexican, Taco Bell, Uptown Pizza, Wendy's, Baymont Inn, Days Inn, $General, $Tree, Advance Parts, ALDI, Firestone/auto, Goodyear/auto, O'Reilly Parts, SaveALot Foods, Valvoline, vet, Walgreens, Walmart/Subway

ASHTABULA

Exit #	Services
228	OH 11, to Warren(exits left from eb), Ashtabula
227	US 422, Girard, Youngstown, N Shell/dsl, Sunoco, Burger King, Cocca's Pizza, DQ, El Hefe, Hibachi Japanese, JibJab Hotdogs, Marco's Pizza, Pizza Joe's, Subway, NAPA
226	Salt Springs Rd, to I-680(from wb), N BP/Dunkin'/dsl, Sheetz/dsl, McDonald's, Waffle House, vet, S Mr Fuel/Road Rocket Diner/dsl/24hr, Petro/Shell/Iron Skillet/dsl/scales/24hr/@, Pilot/dsl/scales/24hr, Blue Beacon, Peterbilt, Quality Truckwash, SpeedCo
224b	I-680(from eb), to Youngstown
224a	OH 11 S, to Canfield
223	OH 46, to Niles, N Citgo/dsl, Pilot/McDonald's/dsl/scales/24hr, Sheetz, Bob Evans, Dunkin', IceHouse Rest., Los Girasoles, Candlewood Suites, Days Inn, Holiday Inn Express, S BP/Subway/dsl, Sunoco, TA/Counry Pride/dsl/scales/24hr/@, Arby's, Chipotle, Cracker Barrel, LJ Silver/Taco Bell, Perkins, Quaker Steak&Lube, Starbucks, Wendy's, Fairfield Inn, Hampton Inn, Home2, Quality Inn, Sleep Inn, Super 8, Wingate, Freightliner, Harley-Davidson
221mm	Meander Reservoir
219mm	I-80 wb joins Ohio Tpk(toll)
218.5mm	For I-80 exits 2-218, see Ohio Turnpike.

INTERSTATE 90

CONNEAUT

Exit #	Services
244mm	Ohio/Pennsylvania state line
242mm	**full facilities, info, litter barrels, petwalk**, , , /weigh sta wb
241	OH 7, to Andover, Conneaut, N McDonald's, Days Inn, AutoZone, Evergreen RV Park, H, S Love's/McDonald's/Subway/dsl/scales/24hr, Shell/Burger King/dsl
235	OH 84, OH 193, to Youngstown, N Kingsville, N Circle K, Grab&Go/gas, Dav-Ed Motel, Village Green Camping, S Circle K/Subway/dsl, TA/BP/Burger King/dsl/scales/24hr/@, Kay's Place Diner, Kingsville Motel, towing/repair
228	OH 11, to Ashtabula, Youngstown, N H
223	OH 45, to Ashtabula, N Flying J/Denny's/Shell/dsl/LP/scales/24hr, Best Value Inn, Holiday Inn Express, Red Roof Inn, Sleep Inn, golf, S Pilot/Subway/Dunkin'/dsl/scales/24hr, SpeedCo, Burger King, Clay St Grill, McDonald's, Taco Bell, Waffle House, Fairfield Inn, Hampton Inn, $General, auto repair, Family$, Honda, Hyundai, Toyota

CHARDON

Exit #	Services
218	OH 534, Geneva, N GetGo, Best Friend's Grill, Chop's Grille, McDonald's, Pizza Roto, Wendy's, TownePlace Suite, Geneva SP, H, Willow Lake Camping, S KwikFill/dsl/scales/24hr, Kenisse's Camping
212	OH 528, to Thompson, Madison, N McDonald's, Sheetz, Hampton Inn, Holiday Inn Express, Mentor RV Ctr, S Love's/Arby's/dsl/scales/dog park/RV Hookup, Marathon/dsl, KOA
205	Vrooman Rd, N Indian Point Park, Masons Landing Park, S Mobil/dsl, Shell/Subway/dsl, Capps Pizza
200	OH 44, to Painesville, Chardon, S BP/7-11/dsl, Shell/dsl, B2B Burgers, Chipotle, Marys Diner, McDonald's, Nouveau Bistro, Paninis Grill, Pizza Roto, Red Hawk Grille, Starbucks, Sunny St Cafe, Waffle House, Comfort Inn, Holiday Inn Express, golf, H, URGENT CARE, Verizon
198mm	**full facilities, litter barrels, petwalk**, , , both lanes, **vending**

WILLOUGHBY

Exit #	Services
195	OH 615, Center St, Kirtland Hills, Mentor, N Best Western+
193	OH 306, to Mentor, Kirtland, N BP/7-11/dsl, Shell, McDonald's, Mentor Home Inn, H, S Marathon/dsl, Sheetz, Red Roof Inn, golf, Kirtland Temple LDS Historic Site
190	Express Lane to I-271(from wb)
189	OH 91, to Willoughby, Willoughby Hills, N BP/7-11/dsl, Shell/dsl, Applebee's, Big Cheese Pizza, Bob Evans, Bruegger's Bagels, Café Europa, Cracker Barrel, Subway, TX Roadhouse, Wendy's, Courtyard, Extended Stay, SkyLight Inn, CVS Drug, H, Walgreens, S BMW/Mini, golf, Lexus
188	I-271 S, to Akron
187	OH 84, Bishop Rd, to Wickliffe, Willoughby, S BP/7-11/dsl, Sheetz, Shell, Shell, Dunkin', Golden Mtn Chinese, McDonald's, Subway, Tony's Pizza, Fairbridge Inn, $Tree, ALDI, Chevrolet, CVS Drug, H, Marc's Foods, Mazda/VW, NTB, O'Reilly Parts
186	US 20, Euclid Ave, N Sunoco, GreenRidge, Ford, Subaru, S Shell, Arby's, Five Star Subs, KFC, Popeyes, R-Ribs BBQ, Taco Bell, Advance Parts, Family$, Firestone/auto, Save-a-Lot Foods
185	OH 2 E(exits left from eb), to Painesville
184b	OH 175, E 260th St, N Shell, USPO, S auto/tire repair
184a	Babbitt Rd, N Buick/GMC, S BP
183	E 222nd St, N repair, China Sea, Panini's Grill, S BP, Sunoco/dsl, Boardwalk Grill, vet
182b a	185 St, 200 St, N BP/7-11/dsl, Subway, Home Depot, Honda, Hyundai, S Marathon/dsl, Shell/dsl, Speedway/dsl
181b a	E 156th St, S BP/Mr Hero
180b a	E 140th St, E 152nd St
179	OH 283 E, to Lake Shore Blvd
178	Eddy Rd, to Bratenahl
177	University Circle, MLK Dr, N Cleveland Lake SP, S H
176	E 72nd St
175	E 55th St, Marginal Rds
174b	OH 2 W, to Lakewood, downtown, N Browns Stadium, Rock&Roll Hall of Fame
174a	Lakeside Ave
173c	Superior Ave, St Clair Ave, downtown, N BP
173b	Chester Ave, S BP
173a	Prospect Ave(from wb), downtown
172d	Carnegie Ave, downtown, S Shell/dsl, KFC,

OH

INTERSTATE 90 Cont'd

ROCKY RIVER

Exit	Services
172d	Continued McDonald's, Cadillac
172c b	E 9th St, S, to Cleveland St U
172a	I-77 S, to Akron
171b a	US 422, OH 14, Broadway St, Ontario St, N BP, Hilton Garden
171	Abbey Ave, downtown
170c b	I-71 S, to I-490
170a	US 42, W 25th St, S **Royal**
169	W 44th St, W 41st St, N
167b a	OH 10, West Blvd, 98th St, to Lorain Ave, N, S BP/dsl, CVS Drug
166	W 117th St, N BP/dsl, GetGo/dsl, Shell, Penn Sta Subs, Advance Parts, AutoZone, Giant Eagle Foods, Home Depot, Staples, Target, S Gas USA, Dunkin', Tire Choice
165	W 140th St, Bunts Rd, Warren Rd, S
164	McKinley Ave, to Lakewood
162	Hilliard Blvd(from wb), to Westway Blvd, Rocky River, S BP, Shell, Bucci's Italian, Ferris Steaks, Joe's Rest., USPO, vet
161	OH 2, OH 254(from eb, no EZ return), Detroit Rd, Rocky River
160	Clague Rd(from wb), same as 159, S Panini's
159	OH 252, Columbia Rd, N EVC, Carrabba'a, Cozumel Mexican, Dave&Busters, Outback Steaks, Courtyard, TownePlace Suites, WestSpring Inn, BMW, S BP, Chipotle, Clean Eats, Domino's, Dunkin, Houlihan's, Jets Pizza, Lehman's Deli, McDonald's, Panera Bread, Penn Sta Subs, Subway, Taco Bell, Urban Grill, Chevrolet, NTB
156	Crocker Rd, Bassett Rd, Westlake, Bay Village, N BP, Shell, DoubleTree, Extended Stay America, Holiday Inn Express, Red Roof Inn, Sonesta Suites, S BP, Speedway, Aladdin's Eatery, Another Broken Egg, Bar Louie, Bob Evans, Bonefish Grill, Bruegger's Bagels, Cabin Club, Cheesecake Factory, Chick-fil-A, Chipotle, Dave's Cosmic Subs, Don Ramon Mexican, First Watch, Five Guys, Jersey Mike's, Jimmy John's, Leo's Italian, McDonald's, Mission BBQ, Pizza by Robert, Robeks, Starbucks, Starbucks, Tropical Smoothie, TX de Brazil, Wendy's, Yard House, Hampton Inn, Hyatt Place, ALDI, AT&T, Barnes & Noble, CVS Drug, Dick's, Fresh Thyme Mkt, Mkt District Supermkt, Mr Tire, OfficeMax, Trader Joe's, Verizon, World Mkt
155	Nagel Rd, Avon Lake, N GetGo/dsl, Chipotle, Starbucks, Residence Inn, S Dunkin', Slim Chickens, Drugmart, Jiffy Lube, Meijer/dsl
153	OH 83, Avon Lake, N GetGo/dsl, Marathon/Circle K/dsl, Arby's, Cane's, City BBQ, Culver's, Fujiyama, King Yuan, Longhorn Steaks, McAlister's Deli, Panda Express, Panera Bread, Perkins, Rush Inn Grille, Swensons Drive-In, Wendy's, ALDI, ALDI, AutoZone, Best Buy, Cabela's, Discount Tire, Duluth Trading, Firestone/auto, Hobby Lobby, JC Penney, Lowe's, Menard's, O'Reilly Parts, PetCo, Walmart, S Antonio's Pizza, Applebee's, Barry Bagels, Bob Evans, Burger King, Chipotle, Firehouse Subs, Jimmy John's, Mesquite Mexican, Moe's SW Grill, Moe's SW Grill, Penn Sta Subs, Red Robin, Starbucks, Subway, Taco Bell, Winking Lizard Tavern, Zoup!, Wyndham, AT&T, Costco/gas, CVS Drug, Heinen's Mkt, Home Depot, Kohl's, Marc's Foods, Marshall's, Michael's, PetSmart, Target, URGENT CARE, USPO, Verizon
151	OH 611, Avon, N BP/dsl, Pilot/dsl/24hr/scales, Speedway/Speedy Cafe/dsl, Fiesta Habaneros Mexican, McDonald's, Extended Stay America, Fairfield Inn, Buick/GMC, Chevrolet, NAPA, S BJ's Whse/gas, Dunkin', Mulligan's Grille, auto repair, Mr. Tire
148	OH 254, Sheffield, Avon, N Homewood Suites,

AVON

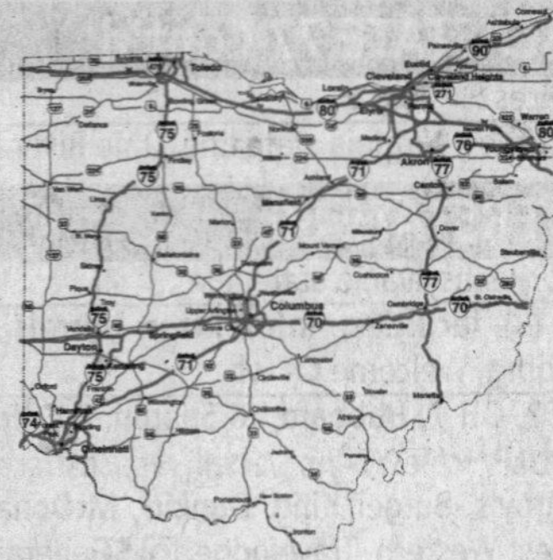

CINCINNATI

Exit	Services
148	Continued Flea Mkt, Ford, Kenworth, Kia, Mazda, Nissan, S GetGo, Sheetz/dsl, Speedway/dsl, Arby's, China Star, Chipotle, Cracker Barrel, Domino's, Jimmy John's, KFC, Marco's Pizza, McDonald's, Panera Bread, Pizza Hut, Ruby Tuesday, Sorrento Pizzaria, Starbucks, Steak'n Shake, Subway, Sugarcreek Rest., Taco Bell, Wendy's, $General, $Tree, ALDI, AutoZone, Drug Mart, Giant Eagle Mkt, Sam's Club/gas
147mm	Black River
145	OH 57, to Lorain, I-80/Ohio Tpk E, Elyria, N Burger King, George's Rest., $General, Save-a-Lot, U-Haul, S Speedway/dsl, Applebee's, Bob Evans, Buffalo Wild Wings, Chipotle Mexican, Denny's, Golden Corral, Jimmy John's, McDonald's, Olive Garden, Red Lobster, Taco Bell, TX Roadhouse, Wasabi Grill, Wendy's, Best Western, Camelot Inn, Courtyard Cleveland, Hampton Inn, Holiday Inn Express, Knights Inn, Quality Inn, $General, $Tree, AT&T, Conrad's Automotive, Firestone/auto, Giant Eagle Mkt, Home Depot, Honda, Hyundai, Lowe's, Marc's Foods, PetSmart, Staples, Target, Tuffy Repair, Verizon
144	OH 2 W(from wb, no return), to Sandusky
143	I-90 wb joins Ohio Tpk
142.5mm	WB exits to Ohio/Indiana state line are on Ohio Turnpike. Exits 142-0.

INTERSTATE 270 (Columbus)

Exit	Services
55	I-71, to Columbus, Cincinnati
52b a	US 23, High St, Circleville, N Circle K, Speedway/dsl, Turkey Hill/dsl, Arby's, Bob Evans, Burger King, China City, Chipotle, Down Yonder Rest., Gyro City, Hardee's, KFC, Little Caesar's, Los Mariachis, McDonald's, Ponderosa, Popeye's, Skyline Chili, Smoothie King, Subway, Taco Bell, Tim Hortons, Waffle House, Wendy's, White Castle, Wingstop, Kozy Inn, $Tree, Advance Parts, ALDI, AutoZone, CVS Drug, Firestone/auto, Kroger/gas, Lowe's, NAPA, O'Reilly Parts, Walgreens, Walmart, S BP/dsl, Marathon/dsl, Scioto Downs
49	Alum Creek Dr, N $Tree, BP, Sheetz, Shell/dsl, Thornton's/dsl, Donato's Pizza, Subway, $General, S BP/dsl, Sheetz, Arby's, Chipotle, McDonald's, Taco Bell, Wendy's, Holiday Inn, Quality Inn
46b a	US 33, Bexley, Lancaster
43b a	I-70, E to Cambridge, W to Columbus
41b a	US 40, E Shell, Speedway, City BBQ, DQ, Hibachi Express, Honeybaked Ham, McDonald's, Outback Steaks, Rally's, Sakura HBBQ, Steak'n Shake, Taco Bell, Texas Roadhouse, $Tree, auto repair, AutoZone, Kroger, Mr. Tire, NAPA, Verizon, W Shell/dsl, Speedway, Sunoco, UDF, Del Taco, El Puerto Mexican, El Pulgarcito, Golden Corral, LJ Silver/A&W, Main St Grill, McDonald's, MCL Rest., Mi Mexico, Poblanos Mexican, Str8 Out The Kitchen, Walgreens
39	OH 16, Broad St, E BP, GetGo, Speedway/dsl, Arby's,

INTERSTATE 270 (Columbus) Cont'd

39 Continued
BIBIBOP, Bob Evans, Buckeye Hibachi, Cane's, Cazuelas Mexican, Chick-fil-A, Chipotle, Donato's Pizza, Five Guys, Jersey Mike's, Jets Pizza, Jimmy John's, Krispy Kreme, McDonald's, Panera Bread, Penn Sta Subs, Sababa Grill, Skyline Chili, Smoothie King, Sonic, Starbucks, Subway, Sunny St Cafe, Taco Bell, Tim Hortons, Waffle House, Wendy's, White Castle, Wingstop, Comfort Suites, Holiday Inn Express, Home2 Suites, Tru Hotel, AAA, Discount Tire, Giant Eagle Mkt, Goodyear/auto, Grismer Auto Service, H, Jiffy Lube, Kroger, Menard's, URGENT CARE, Verizon, Walgreens, W Shell, Chevrolet, golf

37 OH 317, Hamilton Rd, E BP/dsl, Speedway/dsl, Arby's, Bob Evans, Burger King, Chicken Takeover, Chinese Express, Chipotle, Donatos Pizza, DQ, Dunkin', Firehouse Subs, Gatsby's Grill, Hickory House Steaks, Jersey Mike's, Jimmy John's, McDonald's, MOD Pizza, Moe's SW Grill, Panera Bread, Penn Sta Subs, Pulp Juice, Rusty Bucket, Starbucks, Taco Bell, Tim Hortons, Holiday Inn Express, Sonesta Suites, SpringHill Suites, TownePlace Suites, Firestone/auto, Kroger/dsl, W Fairfield Inn, Hampton Inn, Hilton Garden, Residence Inn, Buick/GMC, Subaru/Jaguar/Porsche, Volvo, VW/Audi

35b a I-670W, US 62, E Speedway/dsl, City BBQ, Little Caesar's, McDonald's, Tim Hortons, $Tree, Advance Parts, AutoZone, CVS Drug, Family$, O'Reilly Parts, W I-670

33 Easton Way

32 Morse Rd, E Marathon, Speedway/dsl, UDF, Gauchos Mexican, SuperChef's Breakfast, CVS Drug, Mazda, Nissan, Toyota/Scion, W BP, EVC, Shell, UDF/dsl, Applebee's, BD's Mongolian Grill, BJ's Rest., Brio Italian, Charley's Cheesesteaks, Cheesecake Factory, Chick-fil-A, Chicken Takeover, ChuckECheese, Chuy's TexMex, Donato's Pizza, Dos Hermanos, Jimmy John's, Kona Grill, Logan's Roadhouse, McDonald's, Mitchell's Seafood, On-the-Border, Panera Bread, Papa John's, PF Chang's, Red Robin, Rusty Bucket, Sakura Japanese, Shake Shack, Smokey Bones, Steak'n Shake, Taco Bell, Ted's MT Grill, Tropical Smoothie, TX De Brazil, Wendy's, Z!Eats, Zupas, Aloft Hotel, Courtyard, Extended Stay America, Hampton Inn, Hilton, Hilton Garden, Holiday Inn Express, Residence Inn, SpringHill Suites, WoodSpring Suites, AT&T, Best Buy, Cadillac, Carmax, Costco/gas, Dick's, Discount Tire, Infiniti, Jaguar, Land Rover, Lexus, Lowe's Whse, Macy's, mall, Mercedes, Michael's, Nordstrom's, Old Navy, PetSmart, REI, Sam's Club, Staples, Target, TJ Maxx, Trader Joe's, Verizon, Verizon, Walmart/McDonald's/auto, Whole Foods Mkt, World Mkt

30 OH 161 E to New Albany, W to Worthington

WESTERVILLE

29 OH 3, Westerville, N BP/dsl, Shell, Arby's, Bob Evans, Burger King, Chipotle Mexican, City BBQ, Dunkin', Fazoli's, First Watch, Gionino's Pizza, KFC, Lucky House Chinese, McDonald's, Pancake House, Papa John's, Pizza Hut, Smashburger, Starbucks, Steak Escape, Taco Bell, Tim Horton's, Wendy's, Wingstop, Aloft Hotel, Red Roof Inn, $Tree, Advance Parts, Big Lots, Firestone/auto, Honda, Kohl's, Kroger, Petco, T-Mobil, Verizon, vet, Walmart, S Clark/dsl, Sheetz, Speedway/dsl, Carsonie's Italian, China House, Delaney's Diner, Domino's, Subway, Tim Hortons, ALDI, Family$, Grismer Tire/auto, Midas, Mr. Tire, USPO, W Rita's Custard

27 OH 710, Cleveland Ave, N Bamboo Garden Chinese, Kuya Ian's, OX-B's Chicken, Subway, Tim Hortons, Zapata's Mexican, Ramada Inn, $General, CVS Drug, NAPA Autocare, Tuffy Tire, S Turkey Hill/dsl, Don Tequila Mexican, McDonald's, Yanni's Greek, Embassy Suites,

WORTHINGTON

27 Continued
Home Depot

26 I-71, S to Columbus, N to Cleveland

23 US 23, Worthington, N Sheetz, Bob Evans, El Acapulco, J Alexander's, J Gilbert's Steaks, Lotus Grill, Salateen Grill, Starbucks, Subway, Sushiko Japanese, Courtyard, Days Inn, DoubleTree, Extended Stay America, Holiday Inn Express, Hyatt Place, Quality Inn, Red Roof+, Revi Inn, Sheraton, StayBridge Suites, WoodSpring Suites, golf, S BP, Aladdin's Eatery, Buca Italian, First Watch, Five Guys, Huey Magoo's Chicken, J Liu Rest., Jimmy John's, Maple Street Biscuits, McDonald's, Panera Bread, Piada Italian, Starbucks, Tropical Smoothie, Wings over Columbus, Econolodge, AAA, Kroger

22 OH 315, N BP/dsl, Marathon/dsl, Massey's Pizza, Rusty Bucket

20 Sawmill Rd, N BP, Marathon/dsl, Duck Donuts, IHOP, Jersey Mike's, McAlisters Deli, McDonald's, Menchies, Olive Garden, Papa John's, Pizza Hut, Popeye's, Roosters Rest., Swensons Drive-In, Taco Bell, Tim Hortons, Wendy's, Wing Snob, Fairfield Inn, $Tree, Buick/Chevrolet/GMC, CVS Drug, Ford, Ford/Lincoln, Hyundai, Kroger/gas, Mazda, NTB, Subaru, Valvoline, vet, Walmart, S Shell, Speedway, Speedway, Arby's, bd Mogolian, BIBIBOP, Blue Ginger Asian, Burger King, Cane's, Charlie's Subs, Chick-fil-A, Chili's, Chipotle, ChuckeCheese, Dave's Chicken, Einstein Bros, El Vaquero Mexican, Firehouse Subs, First Watch, Five Guys, HoneyBaked Cafe, Jimmy John's, KFC, Krispy Kreme, Kyoto Japanese, McDonald's, MOD Pizza, Moretti'a Italian, Ohana Grill, Piada Italian, Red Lobster, Shake Shack, Starbucks, Steak'n Shake, Subway, Tim Hortons, Torchy's Tacos, Vicenzos Italian, Hampton Inn, Quality Inn, Suburban Studios, $Tree, Advance Parts, AT&T, AutoZone, Barnes&Noble, Big Lots, CarMax, Dick's, Discount Tire, Firestone/auto, GNC, Hobby Lobby, Home Depot, Honda, Infiniti, Kohl's, Lexus, Lowe's Whse, Meijer/gas, Michael's, Old Navy, PetSmart, Ross, Sam's Club/gas, Staples, Target, Toyota/Scion, Trader Joe's, Verizon, vet, Whole Foods Mkt

17b a US 33, Dublin-Granville Rd, E Marathon, Shell, Graeter's Creamery, Hyde Park Steaks, Jason's Deli, McDonald's, Romeo's Pizza, Subway, Courtyard, DoubleTree, Embassy Suites, Extended Stay America, Hilton Garden, Home2 Suites, Red Roof+, Residence Inn, Sonesta Suites, TownePlace Suites, CVS Drug, Kia, Kroger, Mr Tire, USPO, W BMW, Chrysler/Dodge/Jeep, H, Land Rover, Porsche, VW

15 Tuttle Crossing Blvd, E BP, UDF, AT&T, BJ's Rest., Bob Evans, Chick-fil-A, Chipotle Mexican, DiBella's Subs, Five Guys, House of Japan, Longhorn Steaks, McDonald's, Noodles&Co, Panera Bread, PF Chang's, Popeyes, Starbucks, Taco Bell, Wendy's, Drury Inn, Homewood Suites, Hyatt Place, La Quinta, Marriott, JC Penney, mall, vet, W Shell, Turkey Hill/dsl, Luna Pizza, Steak'n Shake, Extended Stay, Holiday Inn Express, Staybridge Suites, Best Buy, NTB, Walmart/Subway, World Mkt

13 Cemetery Rd, Fishinger Rd, E Shell, Speedway, Carrabba's, Chipotle Mexican, Crazy Burrito, Daruma Japanese, Dave&Buster's, Donato's Pizza, First Watch, Grandad's Pizza, Habaneros Mexican, Moon Pizza, Panera Bread, Popeyes, Pulp Juice, Skyline Chili, Starbucks, Steak&Shake, Tim Horton's, Best Western, Homewood Suites, $Tree, CVS Drug, Discount Tire, Home Depot, Lowe's Whse, NTB, Staples, Tire Choice, Tire Dicounters, URGENT CARE, W GetGo/dsl, Sheetz, Speedway, Arbys, Bob Evans, Dickey's BBQ, Jersey Mike's, McDonald's, Rusty Bucket Rest., Scramblers Breakfast, Subway, Taco Bell, Tim Hortons, Wendy's, Avid Hotel, Hampton Inn,

OH

= gas = food = lodging = other = rest stop

INTERSTATE 270 (Columbus) Cont'd

GEORGESVILLE

13 Continued
Hillard Motor Lodge, TownePlace Suites, Advance Parts, ALDI, Giant Eagle Mkt, Kroger, Nissan

10 Roberts Rd, **E** Marathon, Thornton's/dsl, Subway, Tim Hortons, Wendy's, Woodspring Suites, **W** Sheetz, Speedway/dsl, Tim Hortons, Waffle House, Courtyard, Quality Inn, Royal Inn, CVS Drug, Family$, O'Reilly Parts, Penske, URGENT CARE, Valvoline

8 I-70, E to Columbus, W to Indianapolis

7 US 40, Broad St, **E** BP, Sheetz, Speedway/dsl, 3 Amigos Mexican, Baskin-Robbins, Bob Evans, ChuckeCheese, Dunkin', King Taco, McDonald's, Popeyes, Sparano's Pizza, TeeJay's, White Castle, York Steaks, $Tree, Advance Parts, Big Lots, Buick/GMC, Chevrolet, Kroger/gas, **W** GetGo, Marathon, Speedway/dsl, Thornton's, A&W/LJ Silver, Arby's, Canes, Chipotle, Dunkin', El Barco Mexican, Joseppi's Pizza, KFC, McDonald's, Papa John's, Roosters Chicken, Save A Lot, Taco Nice, Tim Hortons, Waffle House, Red Roof Inn, $Tree, CVS Drug, Family$, Giant Eagle Foods, Goodyear/auto, Home Depot, H, O'Reilly Parts, URGENT CARE

5 Georgesville, **E** Marathong/dsl, Shell/dsl, UDF/dsl, Domino's, Jimmy John's, Starbucks, Walmart, **W** Applebee's, Arby's, Bob Evans, Buffalo Wild Wings, Chipotle Mexican, DQ, Fiesta Mexican, Hibachi Japanese, Ichiban Japanese, KFC/LJ Silver, McDonald's, Red Lobster, Steak'n Shake, Subway, Taco Bell, Wendy's, White Castle, Advance Parts, AT&T, Chrysler/Dodge/Jeep, Honda, Hyundai/Subaru, Kia, Kroger/gas, Lowe's Whse, Nissan, NTB, Subaru, TireDiscounters, Toyota/Scion, Valvoline, VW

2 US 62, OH 3, Grove City, **N** Turkey Hill/dsl, WoodSpring Suites, **S** Marathon, Shell, Speedway, Speedway/dsl, Big Boy, Burger King, Domino's, Donato's Pizza, DQ, Jet's Pizza, Jimmy John's, Little Caesar's, Marco's Pizza, McDonald's, Subway, Taco Bell, Tim Hortons, Waffle House, Wendy's, Zanzis Pizza, $General, CVS Drug, O'Reilly Parts, URGENT CARE

0mm I-71

INTERSTATE 271 (Cleveland)

MAYFIELD

39mm I-271 begins/ends on I-90, exit 188

36 Wilson Mills Rd, Highland Hts, Mayfield, **E** Shell, Aladdin's Eatery, Austin's Steaks, Jersey Mike's, Piza Roma, Yours Truly Rest., Hilton Garden, Holiday Inn, Chrysler/Dodge/Jeep, Heinen's Mkt, vet, **W** Marathon/dsl, Burgers 2 Beer, Chipotle, Denny's, Dunkin', La Fiesta Mexican, Panini's Grill, Big Lots, DrugMart, Home Depot, Kohl's, Verizon, vet

34 US 322, Mayfield Rd, **E** BP/7-11, Circle K, BIBIBOP, Charley's Subs, Chipotle, DiBella's Subs, First Watch, Five Guys, Honey Baked Ham, Jimmy John's, Juicy Seafood, Master Pizza, Panera Bread, Piccolo Italian, Scramblers, Starbucks, Wendy's, Wingstop, ALDI, CVS Drug, Hobby Lobby, H, Marc's Foods, Michael's, Mr Tire, Old Navy, Take 5 Oil Change, Target, Tire Pros, **W** Amoco, Marathon, Sheetz, Shell, Applebees, Arby's, Arrabiata's Italian, Bob Evans, Burger King, Cane's Chicken, Cheesesteak Whizard, Chick-fil-A, ChuckECheese, Crafty Crab, Don Ramon Mexican, DQ, Dunkin', Firehouse Subs, Krispy Kreme, Marco's Pizza, McDonald's, Moe's SW Grill, Otani Japanese, Panera Bread, Penn Sta Subs, Piada Italian, Primoz Pizza, Pulp Juice, Subway, Taco Bell, Teresa's Pizza, Comfort Inn, $Tree, AT&T, AutoZone, Best Buy, Costco/gas, CVS Drug, Ford/Lincoln, Fresh Thyme Mkt, Giant Eagle Mkt, JoAnn Fabrics, Marshall's, Midas, Nissan, NTB, O'Reilly Parts, PetSmart, Staples, URGENT CARE, World Mkt

OH

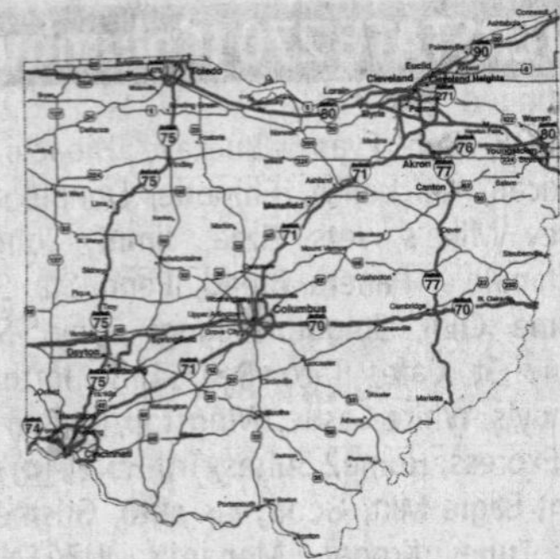

CLEVELAND

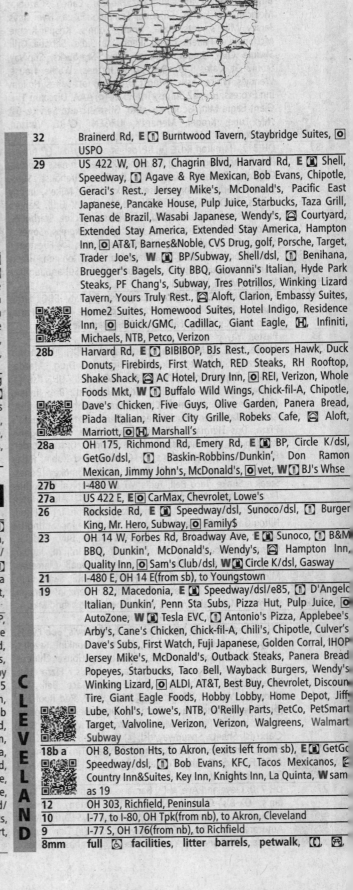

32 Brainerd Rd, **E** Burntwood Tavern, Staybridge Suites, USPO

29 US 422 W, OH 87, Chagrin Blvd, Harvard Rd, **E** Shell, Speedway, Agave & Rye Mexican, Bob Evans, Chipotle, Geraci's Rest., Jersey Mike's, McDonald's, Pacific East Japanese, Pancake House, Pulp Juice, Starbucks, Taza Grill, Tenas de Brazil, Wasabi Japanese, Wendy's, Courtyard, Extended Stay America, Extended Stay America, Hampton Inn, AT&T, Barnes&Noble, CVS Drug, golf, Porsche, Target, Trader Joe's, **W** BP/Subway, Shell/dsl, Benihana, Bruegger's Bagels, City BBQ, Giovanni's Italian, Hyde Park Steaks, PF Chang's, Subway, Tres Potrillos, Winking Lizard Tavern, Yours Truly Rest., Aloft, Clarion, Embassy Suites, Home2 Suites, Homewood Suites, Hotel Indigo, Residence Inn, Buick/GMC, Cadillac, Giant Eagle, H, Infiniti, Michaels, NTB, Petco, Verizon

28b Harvard Rd, **E** BIBIBOP, BJs Rest., Coopers Hawk, Duck Donuts, Firebirds, First Watch, RED Steaks, RH Rooftop, Shake Shack, AC Hotel, Drury Inn, REI, Verizon, Whole Foods Mkt, **W** Buffalo Wild Wings, Chick-fil-A, Chipotle, Dave's Chicken, Five Guys, Olive Garden, Panera Bread, Piada Italian, River City Grille, Robeks Cafe, Aloft, Marriott, H, Marshall's

28a OH 175, Richmond Rd, Emery Rd, **E** BP, Circle K/dsl, GetGo/dsl, Baskin-Robbins/Dunkin', Don Ramon Mexican, Jimmy John's, McDonald's, vet, **W** BJ's Whse

27b I-480 W

27a US 422 E, **E** CarMax, Chevrolet, Lowe's

26 Rockside Rd, **E** Speedway/dsl, Sunoco/dsl, Burger King, Mr. Hero, Subway, Family$

23 OH 14 W, Forbes Rd, Broadway Ave, **E** Sunoco, B&M BBQ, Dunkin', McDonald's, Wendy's, Hampton Inn, Quality Inn, Sam's Club/dsl, **W** Circle K/dsl, Gasway

21 I-480 E, OH 14 E(from sb), to Youngstown

19 OH 82, Macedonia, **E** Speedway/dsl/e85, D'Angelo Italian, Dunkin', Penn Sta Subs, Pizza Hut, Pulp Juice, AutoZone, **W** Tesla EVC, Antonio's Pizza, Applebee's Arby's, Cane's Chicken, Chick-fil-A, Chili's, Chipotle, Culver's Dave's Subs, First Watch, Fuji Japanese, Golden Corral, IHOP Jersey Mike's, McDonald's, Outback Steaks, Panera Bread Popeyes, Starbucks, Taco Bell, Wayback Burgers, Wendy's Winking Lizard, ALDI, AT&T, Best Buy, Chevrolet, Discoun Tire, Giant Eagle Foods, Hobby Lobby, Home Depot, Jiff Lube, Kohl's, Lowe's, NTB, O'Reilly Parts, PetCo, PetSmart Target, Valvoline, Verizon, Verizon, Walgreens, Walmart Subway

18b a OH 8, Boston Hts, to Akron, (exits left from sb), **E** GetGo Speedway/dsl, Bob Evans, KFC, Tacos Mexicanos, Country Inn&Suites, Key Inn, Knights Inn, La Quinta, **W** same as 19

12 OH 303, Richfield, Peninsula

10 I-77, to I-80, OH Tpk(from nb), to Akron, Cleveland

9 I-77 S, OH 176(from nb), to Richfield

8mm full facilities, litter barrels, petwalk,

INTERSTATE 271 (Cleveland) Cont'd

8mm Continued
[RS] both lanes

3 OH 94, to I-71 N, Wadsworth, N Royalton, W [gas] PetroUSA/dsl

0mm I-271 begins/ends on I-71, exit 220.

INTERSTATE 275 (Cincinnati)

84 I-71, I-75, N to Cincinnati, S to Lexington, Louisville

83 US 25, US 42, US 127, S [gas] Circle K/dsl, Thornton's/dsl, [food] Buffalo Wings&Rings, Burger King, Carrabba's, Chicken Salad Chick, Chipotle, Coldstone, Dewey's Pizza, Donato's Pizza, First Watch, Gold Star Chili, Jimmy John's, KFC, MacKenzie River, McAlister's Deli, McDonald's, Moe's SW Grill, Panera Bread, Starbucks, Subway, Taco Bell, Taste of Belgium, The Pub, Wendy's, [other] $Tree, Dillard's, Trader Joe's, Valvoline, Verizon, Walgreens, Xpress Pro Tire

82 rd 1303, Turkeyfoot Rd, S [food] Applebee's, TGIFriday's, [other] [H]

80 KY 17, Independence, N [gas] Speedway/dsl, United/dsl, [food] Arby's, Big Boy, Bob Evans, Buffalo Wild Wings, Burger King, Chick-fil-A, Chipotle, DQ, Guthrie's Chicken, Harmon's BBQ, Hot Head Burrito, Jet's Pizza, Penn Sta Subs, Penn Sta Subs, Snappy Tomato Pizza, Subway, Taco Bell, TX Roadhouse, Wendy's, White Castle, [other] AAA, AT&T, AutoZone, TireDiscounters, URGENT CARE, vet, Walmart, S [gas] Thornton's/dsl, [food] McDonald's, Waffle House

79 KY 16, Taylor Mill Rd, N [gas] BP, Marathon, Speedway/dsl, [food] Domino's, Goldstar Chili, McDonald's, Peking Chinese, Starbucks, Subway, Wendy's, [other] $General, $Tree, Big Lots, CVS Drug, Kroger/gas, URGENT CARE, Walgreens, S [gas] Shell/dsl, [food] Dunkin, El Jinete Mexican, Graeter's Creamery, KFC/Taco Bell, La Rosa's Pizza, Marco's Pizza, McDonald's, Original Wok, Skyline Chili, Subway, [other] Remke's Mkt, Verizon, vet

ALEXANDRIA

77 KY 9, Maysville, Wilder, N [lodging] Hampton Inn, Holiday Inn Express, S [gas] Speedway/dsl, Thorntons/dsl, UDF/dsl, [food] DQ, McDonald's, Mellow Mushroom Pizza, Subway, Waffle House, [lodging] Comfort Inn Suites

76 Three Mile Rd

74a Alexandria, (exits left from sb), to US 27

74b I-471 N, Newport, Cincinnati, N [other] [H]

73mm OH State Line, Ohio River

72 US 52 W, Kellogg Ave, E [gas] Marathon/dsl(2mi)

71 US 52 E, New Richmond

69 5 Mile Rd, W [gas] BP/dsl, [food] Arby's, Big Boy, Buffalo Wild Wings, Carrabba's, Chipotle, Don Rigo Mexican, First Watch, IHOP, La Rosa's Mexican, Marco's Pizza, McDonald's, Moe's SW Grill, Outback Steaks, Starbucks, [other] CVS, [H], Kroger/gas, Petco, TireDiscounters, Valvoline, vet

AMELIA

65 OH 125, Beechmont Ave, Amelia, E [gas] Shell, Speedway, UDF/dsl, [food] King Buffet, Los Cazadores, Red Lobster, Tender Towne, [lodging] Beechmont Motel, [other] CarX, Discount Tire, Family$, Ford, Lowe's, Tires+, Walgreens, W [gas] Speedway/dsl, Sunoco, [food] Big Boy, Bob Evans, Burger King, Butterbee's Grille, Chick-fil-A, Chipotle Mexican, Dragon City, Graeter's Ice Cream, McDonald's, Olive Garden, Panera Bread, Skyline Chili, Starbucks, Swensons Drive-In, Taziki's, Tropical Smoothie, Waffle House, Wendy's, White Castle, [lodging] Best Western, Days Inn, Red Roof Inn, [other] $Tree, AAA, ALDI, Audi, AutoZone, BigLots, Home Depot, Honda, Kroger/gas, O'Reilly Parts, Staples, Target, TireDiscounters, TJ Maxx, Toyota/Scion, Verizon, vet

63b a OH 32, Batavia, Newtown, E [gas] UDF, [food] Arby's, Big Boy, Bob Evans, Burger King, Chick-fil-A, China Buffet, Chipotle, ChuckECheese, Cici's Pizza, City BBQ, Dunkin, Everything Bagels, Firehouse Subs, Five Guys, Fuji Steaks,

HILLSBORO

63b a Continued
Golden Corral, Jersey Mike's, Jimmy John's, KFC, LaRosa's Pizza, LJ Silver, Longhorn Steaks, McDonald's, Michaels, O'Charley's, Outback Steaks, Panera Bread, Penn Sta Subs, Popeyes, Raising Cane's, Skyline Chili, Sonic, Starbucks, Steak'n Shake, Taco Bell, Waffle House, White Castle, [lodging] Comfort Inn, Fairfield Inn, Hampton Inn, Holiday Inn, Home2 Suites, [other] $Tree, Advance Parts, ALDI, AT&T, Best Buy, Big Lots, Dick's, Dillard's, Firestone/auto, Hobby Lobby, JC Penney, Jiffy Lube, Jungle Jim's Mkt, Kohl's, Kroger/dsl, Marshall's, Meijer/dsl, OfficeMax, PepBoys, PetSmart, Sam's Club/gas, Tire Discounters, URGENT CARE, Valvoline, Walmart, W [gas] Casey's, Marathon, Speedway/dsl, Sunoco, [food] Gold Star Chili, Gramma's Pizza, [other] Midas

59 OH 452, US 50, Milford Pkwy, Hillsboro, S [gas] UDF/dsl, [food] Buffalo Wild Wings, Cracker Barrel, Dos Amigos, El Rancho Mexican, Goldstar Chili, Mint Bistro, Quaker Steak&Lube, Red Robin, Roney's Rest., Starbucks, Subway, Taco Bell, TX Roadhouse, Wendy's, [lodging] Homewood Suites, Staybridge Suites, Tru, [other] $Tree, PetSmart, Target, U-Haul, Verizon, Walmart

57 OH 28, Blanchester, Milford, N [gas] Marathon/Circle K/McDonald's, [food] Arby's, Burger King, Butterbee's Grille, Chick-fil-A, Chipotle Mexican, Donato's Pizza, DQ, Dunkin, Freddy's Steakburgers, Goldstar Chili, IHOP, Jersey Mike's, Jimmy John's, KFC, LJ Silver's, Marco's Pizza, O'Charley's, Panera Bread, Papa John's, Skyline Chili, Sonic, Starbucks, Taco Bell, Tropical Smoothie, Waffle House, Wendy's, White Castle, Wings Rings, [other] ALDI, Firestone, Home Depot, Kroger/dsl, Lowe's, Meijer/dsl, Tire Discounters, URGENT CARE, URGENT CARE, Valvoline, S [gas] Thornton's/dsl, [food] Bob Evans, Cazadore's Mexican, Roosters Grill, Tokugawa Japanese, [lodging] Holiday Inn Express, [other] auto repair, USPO, vet

54 Wards Corner Rd, N [gas] BP, S UDF/dsl, [food] Big Boy, Goldstar Chili, Shanghai Bistro, [lodging] Hilton Garden, [other] vet

53mm Little Miami River

52 Loveland, Indian Hill, N [gas] Circle K/dsl, Shell, Speedway/dsl, [food] Arby's, Chipotle, Penn Sta Subs, Skyline Chili, Starbucks, Taco Bell, Tropical Smoothie, Wendy's, [other] $Tree, CVS Drug, URGENT CARE, Walgreens

BLUE ASH

50 US 22, OH 3, Montgomery, N [gas] Shell, [food] Buffalo Wild Wings, Chili's, deSha's Tavern, Dewey's Pizza, DQ, First Watch, Johnny Chan's, Melting Pot, Menchie's, Smoothie King, Subway, [other] Acura, Fresh Thyme Mkt, Hyundai, Kroger/dsl, TJ Maxx, S [gas] BP/dsl, Shell/Dunkin, [food] El Jinete, McDonald's, Merlot's Rest., Skyline Chili, Wendy's, [other] [H]

49 I-71 N to Columbus, S to Cincinnati

47 Reed Hartman Hwy, Blue Ash, S [food] Chick-fil-A, Chipotle, J. Gumbo's, Jersey Mike's, McDonald's, Starbucks, Tropical Cafe, [lodging] Blu Hotel, DoubleTree, Home2 Suites, Hyatt Place, Sonesta Suites

46 US 42, Mason, N [gas] BP, [food] Arby's, Burger King, Chipotle, KFC, McDonald's, Rodeway Inn, Scrambler, Skyline Chili, Starbucks, Taco Bell, Wendy's, White Castle, [lodging] Clarion Hotel, Extended Stay, [other] $Tree, Advance Parts, CVS Drug, Kroger/dsl, UDF/dsl, Walgreens, S [gas] Speedway/dsl, UDF/dsl, [food] El Rancho Grande, Mi Ranchito, Popeyes, Szechuan House, Waffle House, [lodging] Days Inn, [other] KOI Auto Parts, Midas, Mr Transmission, Tire Discounters

44 Mosteller Rd, N [food] Subway, S [lodging] Sonesta ES Suites

43b a I-75, N to Dayton, S to Cincinnati, S [gas] Sunoco/dsl, [food] Burger King, Chick-fil-A, Five Guys, LJ Silver's, McDonald's, Panda Express, Panda Wok, Penn Sta Subs, Raising Cane's, Taco Bell, [lodging] Motel 6, Sonesta ES Suites, Travel Inn, Welcome Suites, [other] AT&T, Chuck E Cheese, Kwik-Stop, Nissan, Sam's Club, Target, Valvoline

42 OH 747, Springdale, Glendale, N [gas] Sunoco/dsl,

INTERSTATE 275 (Cincinnati) Cont'd

42 Continued
$General, S Shell/Dunkin'/dsl, Arby's, Benihana, Chipotle, Culver's, Dave & Buster's, First Watch, Graeter's Ice Cream, Hibachi Japanese, Jade Buffet, Jersey Mike's, La Rosa's Pizza, McDonald's, Noodles&Co, Outback, Skyline Chili, Starbucks, ALDI, BigLots, BMW, Chevrolet, Chrysler/Dodge/Jeep, Ford, Hobby Lobby, Lowe's, Mazda, Office Depot, PetSmart, Ross, TJ Maxx, Verizon

41 OH 4, Springdale Pkwy, N Eagles Fuel, Shell, Speedy Cafe/dsl, Sunoco/dsl, Burger King, Dunkin, Home2 Suites, Olive Garden, Pappadeaux, Roosters, Skyline Chili, Wendy's, La Quinta, Midas, Tire Discounters, S BP, UDF/dsl, DQ, Goldstar Chili, Penn Sta Subs, Subway, Waffle House, White Castle, Wingstop, Days Inn, Extended Stay America, Super 8, CVS Drug, Family$, O'Reilly Parts

39 Winton Rd, Winton Woods, N BP, Asian Buffet, Bob Evans, Burger King, Chick-fil-A, Chipotle, Dunkin', Freddy's Burgers, IHOP, McDonald's, Old Spaghetti Factory, Red Lobster, Comfort Suites, Hampton Inn, CarMax, Home Depot, Kohl's, Meijer/dsl/EVC, Tire Discounters, S Shell/dsl, Speedyway/dsl, UDF/dsl, Big Boy, Cracker Barrel, El Asadero Mexican, El Nopal Mexican, Izzy's Cafe, KFC, La Fiesta Mexican, Papa John's, Park Place, Penn Sta Subs, Popeyes, Skyline Chili, Starbucks, Subway, Taco Bell, Wendy's, Quality Inn, SpringHill Suites, $Tree, AAA, AutoZone, Jiffy Lube, Kroger/gas, Tires+, vet

36 US 127, Hamilton, Mt Healthy, N Circle K/dsl, Speedway, Wendy's, CVS Drug, S Shell/dsl, Sunoco, UDF, Big Boy, La Rosa's, Little Caesars, McDonald's, Mike's Seafood, Tacana Mexican, Taco Bell, Advance Parts, O'Reilly Parts

33 US 27, US 126, Colerain Ave, N Speedway/dsl, Burger King, Skyline Chili, Steak'n Shake, Wendy's, $Tree, AutoZone, Dick's, Lowe's, PetSmart, TireDiscounters, Walmart, S Shell, Arby's, Big Boy, Bob Evans, Bubbakoo's Burritos, Buffalo Wild Wings, Burger King, Cheddar's, Chick-fil-A, Chipotle, Domino's, DQ, Dunkin, First Watch, Five Guys, Honey Baked Ham, IHOP, La Rosa's Pizza, Logan's Roadhouse, Longhorn Steaks, McDonald's, Noodles&co, Olive Garden, Outback Steaks, Panda Express, Panera Bread, Pizza Hut, Popeyes, Potbelly, Quaker Steak, Raising Cane's, Red Lobster, Starbucks, Taco Bell, TGIFriday's, White Castle, AAA, ALDI, AT&T, Batteries+, Best Buy, BigLots, Hobby Lobby, JC Penney, Kroger/gas, Marshalls, Meijer/dsl, Michael's, Old Navy, Ross, URGENT CARE, Valvoline, Walgreens

31 Ronald Reagan Hwy, Blue Rock Rd

28 I-74, US 52, E to Cincinnati, W to Indianapolis

25 I-74, E to Cincinnati, W to Indianapolis

21 Kilby Rd, Indian Springs Camping(3mi), S Shell

18mm Ohio/Indiana State Line

16 US 50, Greendale, Lawrenceburg, W Ameristop/dsl, Circle K, Sinclair/dsl, Burger King, Dunkin, El Nopal Mexican, La Rosa's Pizza, McDonald's, Taco Bell, Waffle House, White Castle, Will's Grill, Wings&Rings, Baymont Inn, Comfort Inn, Quality Inn, Red Roof Inn, auto repair, Chevrolet, Chrysler/Dodge/Jeep, Ford, TireDiscounters, Walgreens

14mm Kentucky/Indiana state line, Ohio River

11 Petersburg, S museum

8 Worldwide Blvd

6b a KY 237, Hebron, N Shell/DQ/dsl, UDF/dsl, Agave Mexican, China Wok, Hebron Grille, Jimmy John's, Longnecks Grill, Lucky Dragon, Papa John's, Pizza Hut, Wendy's, $Tree, S Speedway/Subway/dsl, Burger King, Chipotle, Domino's, Skyline Chili, Waffle House

4a b KY 212, KY 20, N Shell/dsl, Comfort Suites,

WINTON WOODS

HEBRON

OH

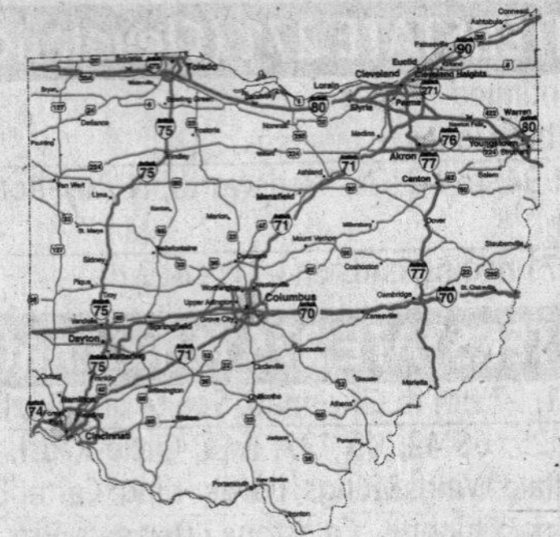

4a b Continued
Country Inn&Suites, Hampton Inn, Marriott, S DoubleTree,

2 Mineola Pike, N Marathon/Rally's/Subway/dsl, Holiday Inn, Quality Inn, S Shell/dsl, Guthries Chicken, Hot Head Burrito, Subway, Courtyard Inn/EVC, Residence Inn

INTERSTATE 280 (Toledo)

13 I-280 begins/ends on I-75, exit 208.

12 Manhattan Blvd, E Sunoco, W Sunoco/dsl

11 OH 25 S, Eerie St, W Huntington Ctr

10mm Maumee River

9 OH 65, Front St, E Sunoco, Tony Packo's Hot Dogs, Subway, W Sunoco/dsl

8 Starr Ave, from sb only

7 OH 2 , Oregon, E Circle K/dsl, Sunoco, Arby's, Azteca Mexican, Bob Evans, Buffalo Wild Wings, Burger King, Chipotle, Coldstone/Tim Horton's, Culver's, Deet's BBQ, Dunkin', Firehouse Subs, McDonald's, Penn Sta Subs, Pizza Hut, Ralphie's, Sonic, Star Diner, Starbucks, Subway, Taco Bell, Wendy's, Wingstop, Comfort Inn, Hampton Inn, Holiday Inn Express, TownePlace Suites, AutoZone, Belle Tire, Ford, Kroger, O'Reilly Parts, to Maumee Bay SP, URGENT CARE, Valvoline, Verizon, Walgreens

6 OH 51, Woodville Rd, Curtice Rd, E Circle K, Shell, Speedway, Bob Evans, Burger King, Marco's Pizza, Menards, W Speedway/dsl, Applebee's, Arby's, Big Boy, Biggby Coffee, Domino's Pizza, Don's Donuts, KFC, Mancino's Pizza, McDonald's, Paddy Joe's, Subway, Taco Bell, Sleep Inn, $General, $Tree, Advance Parts, Meijer/gas, Midas, O'Reilly Parts

4 Walbridge, E Adler's Parts

2 OH 795, Perrysburg, W Sunoco/dsl, 795 Tire Repair

1b Bahnsen Rd, E Flying J/Denny's/dsl/LP/scales/24hr, Regency Inn, W Love's/Arby's/dsl/scales/24hr/@, Petro/BP/Iron Skillet/dsl/scales/24hr/@, Budget Inn, Red Roof Inn, Super 8, Blue Beacon, SpeedCo

1a I-280 begins/ends on I 80/90, OH Tpk, exit 71., S FuelMart/Subway/dsl/scales, Pilot/McDonald's/dsl/scales/24hr, TA/BP/Taco Bell/dsl/scales/24hr/@, KOA

CURTICE RD

INTERSTATE 475 (Toledo)

20 I-75. I-475 begins/ends on I-75, exit 204.

19 ProMedica Pky, Central Ave, S Burger King, Gino's Pizza, Subway,

18b Douglas Rd(from wb)

18a OH 51 W, Monroe St

17 Secor Rd, N Shell/dsl, Valero, Value America, Applebee's, Bambino's Pizza, Baskin-Robbins, Bob Evans, Burger King, Famous Dave's BBQ, Jersey Mike's, KFC, Monroe St Diner, Netty's, Penn Sta Subs, Red Robin, Rudy's Hot Dogs, Tim Horton's, Toledo Thai, $Tree, Advance Parts, AT&T, Barnes&Noble, Best Buy, Kohl's, Kroger/dsl

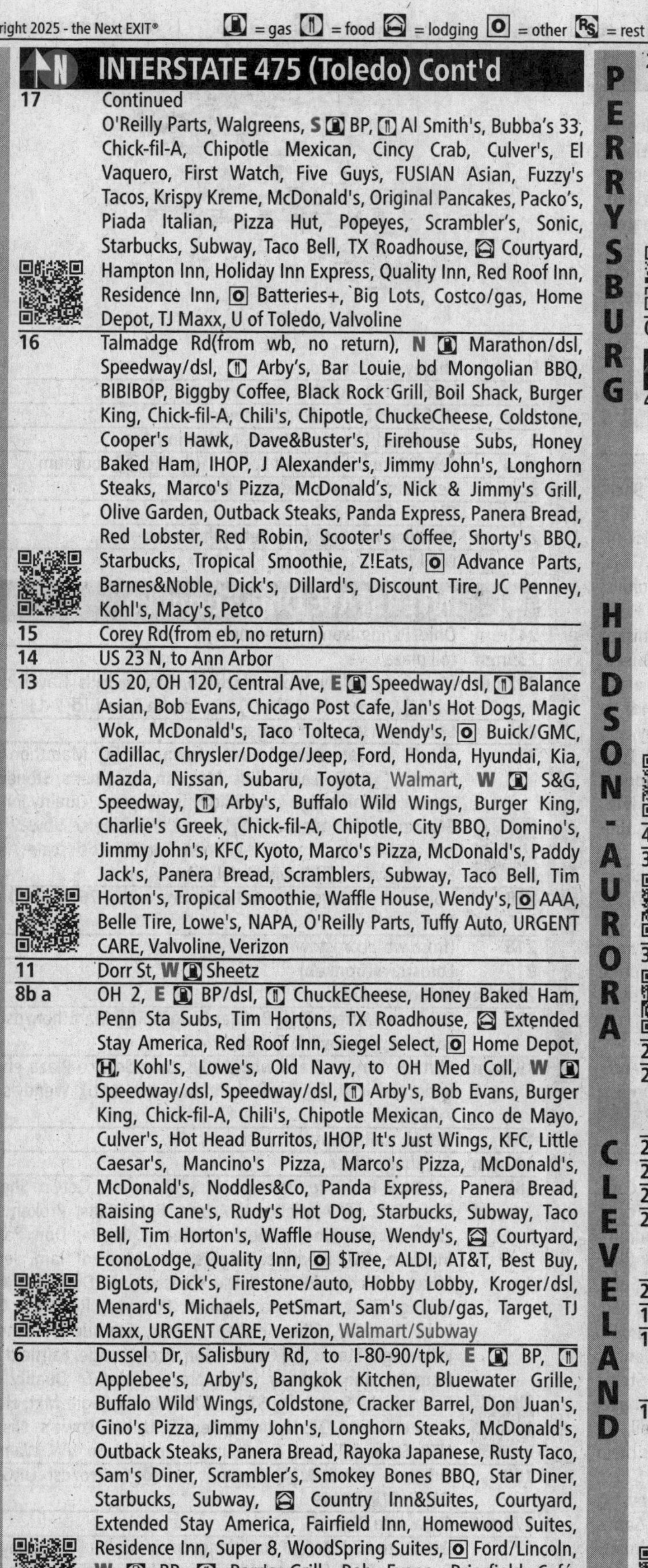

INTERSTATE 475 (Toledo) Cont'd

17 Continued O'Reilly Parts, Walgreens, S BP, Al Smith's, Bubba's 33, Chick-fil-A, Chipotle Mexican, Cincy Crab, Culver's, El Vaquero, First Watch, Five Guys, FUSIAN Asian, Fuzzy's Tacos, Krispy Kreme, McDonald's, Original Pancakes, Packo's, Piada Italian, Pizza Hut, Popeyes, Scrambler's, Sonic, Starbucks, Subway, Taco Bell, TX Roadhouse, Courtyard, Hampton Inn, Holiday Inn Express, Quality Inn, Red Roof Inn, Residence Inn, Batteries+, Big Lots, Costco/gas, Home Depot, TJ Maxx, U of Toledo, Valvoline

16 Talmadge Rd(from wb, no return), N Marathon/dsl, Speedway/dsl, Arby's, Bar Louie, bd Mongolian BBQ, BIBIBOP, Biggby Coffee, Black Rock Grill, Boil Shack, Burger King, Chick-fil-A, Chili's, Chipotle, ChuckeCheese, Coldstone, Cooper's Hawk, Dave&Buster's, Firehouse Subs, Honey Baked Ham, IHOP, J Alexander's, Jimmy John's, Longhorn Steaks, Marco's Pizza, McDonald's, Nick & Jimmy's Grill, Olive Garden, Outback Steaks, Panda Express, Panera Bread, Red Lobster, Red Robin, Scooter's Coffee, Shorty's BBQ, Starbucks, Tropical Smoothie, Z!Eats, Advance Parts, Barnes&Noble, Dick's, Dillard's, Discount Tire, JC Penney, Kohl's, Macy's, Petco

15 Corey Rd(from eb, no return)

14 US 23 N, to Ann Arbor

13 US 20, OH 120, Central Ave, E Speedway/dsl, Balance Asian, Bob Evans, Chicago Post Cafe, Jan's Hot Dogs, Magic Wok, McDonald's, Taco Tolteca, Wendy's, Buick/GMC, Cadillac, Chrysler/Dodge/Jeep, Ford, Honda, Hyundai, Kia, Mazda, Nissan, Subaru, Toyota, Walmart, W S&G, Speedway, Arby's, Buffalo Wild Wings, Burger King, Charlie's Greek, Chick-fil-A, Chipotle, City BBQ, Domino's, Jimmy John's, KFC, Kyoto, Marco's Pizza, McDonald's, Paddy Jack's, Panera Bread, Scramblers, Subway, Taco Bell, Tim Horton's, Tropical Smoothie, Waffle House, Wendy's, AAA, Belle Tire, Lowe's, NAPA, O'Reilly Parts, Tuffy Auto, URGENT CARE, Valvoline, Verizon

11 Dorr St, W Sheetz

8b a OH 2, E BP/dsl, ChuckECheese, Honey Baked Ham, Penn Sta Subs, Tim Hortons, TX Roadhouse, Extended Stay America, Red Roof Inn, Siegel Select, Home Depot, H, Kohl's, Lowe's, Old Navy, to OH Med Coll, W Speedway/dsl, Speedway/dsl, Arby's, Bob Evans, Burger King, Chick-fil-A, Chili's, Chipotle Mexican, Cinco de Mayo, Culver's, Hot Head Burritos, IHOP, It's Just Wings, KFC, Little Caesar's, Mancino's Pizza, Marco's Pizza, McDonald's, McDonald's, Noddles&Co, Panda Express, Panera Bread, Raising Cane's, Rudy's Hot Dog, Starbucks, Subway, Taco Bell, Tim Horton's, Waffle House, Wendy's, Courtyard, EconoLodge, Quality Inn, $Tree, ALDI, AT&T, Best Buy, BigLots, Dick's, Firestone/auto, Hobby Lobby, Kroger/dsl, Menard's, Michaels, PetSmart, Sam's Club/gas, Target, TJ Maxx, URGENT CARE, Verizon, Walmart/Subway

6 Dussel Dr, Salisbury Rd, to I-80-90/tpk, E BP, Applebee's, Arby's, Bangkok Kitchen, Bluewater Grille, Buffalo Wild Wings, Coldstone, Cracker Barrel, Don Juan's, Gino's Pizza, Jimmy John's, Longhorn Steaks, McDonald's, Outback Steaks, Panera Bread, Rayoka Japanese, Rusty Taco, Sam's Diner, Scrambler's, Smokey Bones BBQ, Star Diner, Starbucks, Subway, Country Inn&Suites, Courtyard, Extended Stay America, Fairfield Inn, Homewood Suites, Residence Inn, Super 8, WoodSpring Suites, Ford/Lincoln, W BP, Barr's Grill, Bob Evans, Briarfield Café, Carrabba's, Best Western, Churchill's Mkt

4 US 24, to Maumee, Napolean, N H, Toledo Zoo

3mm Maumee River

NAPOLEAN

PERRYSBURG

2 OH 25, to Bowling Green, Perrysburg, N BP/dsl, Circle K/dsl, Shell, American Table Rest., Arby's, Biggby Coffee, Dunkin', El Vaquero, Lee's Garden, Marco's Pizza, McDonald's, Starbucks, Subway, Wendy's, Chevrolet, Churchill's Mkt, Costco/dsl, GMC, Hyundai, Midas, URGENT CARE, Volvo, VW, S S&G, Speedway/dsl, Agave&Rye Rest, Bar Louie's, Biaggi's, Blue Pacific Grill, Bob Evans, Nagoya Japanese, Scrambler's, Starbucks, Taco Bell, Tea Tree Asian, Waffle House, Economy Inn, Hilton Garden, Holiday Inn Express, Home2 Suites, AAA, AT&T, Belle Tire, Books-A-Million, Mytee Automotive, URGENT CARE, Verizon, vet

0mm I-475 begins/ends on I-75, exit 192.

INTERSTATE 480 (Cleveland)

HUDSON-AURORA CLEVELAND

42 I-80, PA Tpk, I-480 begins/ends, S Circle K, EVC, GetGo, Marathon/Circle K, Sheetz/24hr, Tesla EVC, Another Broken Egg, Applebee's, Arby's, Baskin Robbins/Dunkin', Bob Evans, Brown Derby Roadhouse, Buffalo Wild Wings, Burger King, China Chef, Chipotle, Don Patron Mexican, DQ, El Campesino, Freddy's Burgers, Honeybaked Ham, Jersey Mike's, Jimmy John's, KFC, Little Caesar's, McDonald's, Mr Hero, New Peking Chinese, Panda Express, Popeyes, Raising Cane's, Rita's Custard, Rockne's Grill, Ruby Tuesday, Slim Chickens, Sonic, Starbucks, Taco Bell, Wendy's, Comfort Inn, Econolodge, Fairfield Inn, Hampton Inn, Holiday Inn Express, Motel 6, Quality Inn, TownePlace Suites, $General, $Tree, ALDI, All Seasons RV Ctr, AT&T, AutoZone, Giant Eagle Mkt, Home Depot, Honda, H, Hyundai, Kia, Lowes Whse, Midas, NAPA, Nissan, NTB, O'Reilly Parts, Staples, Target, Tire Source/auto, to Kent St U, U-Haul, URGENT CARE, USPO, Van's Tires, Verizon, vet, VW, Walgreens, Walmart

41 Frost Rd, Hudson-Aurora

37 OH 91, Solon, Twinsburg, N Arby's, Brewster's, Chinese Buffet, Chipotle, DQ, Mr. Chicken, Panera Bread, Panini's Grill, Pizza Hut, Starbucks, Taco Bell, Comfort Suites, Giant Eagle Mkt, S BP, H

36 OH 82, Aurora, Twinsburg, N BP/Circle K, Sheetz/dsl, Burger King, Dunkin', McDonald's, Super 8, S Blue Canyon Rest., Get'n Go, Wendy's, Cracker Barrel, Hilton Garden

26 I-271, to Erie, PA

25a b c OH 8, OH 43, Northfield Rd, Bedford, S Marathon, Shell, Sunoco, Papa John's, Wendy's, Giant Eagle Mkt, Home Depot

24 Lee Rd(from wb), S Marathon/dsl

23 OH 14, Broadway Ave, N Marathon, H, S Freightliner

22 OH 17, Garanger, Maple Hts, Garfield Hts

21 Transportation Blvd, to E 98th St, N H, S GetGo, Applebee's, Chipotle, Penn Sta Subs, Starbucks, Giant Eagle Foods, Verizon

20b a I-77, Cleveland

17 OH 176, OH 17, Cleveland

16 OH 94, to OH 17 S, State Rd, N auto repair, Convenient Mart, transmissions, S BP/7-11, Sunoco/dsl, Fiesta Vallarta, Kia

15 US 42, Ridge Rd, N Applebee's, Baskin-Robbins/Dunkin', Coldstone Creamery, Kintaro Hot Pot, McDonald's, Mr Hero, Penn Sta Subs, Pizza Hut, Plaza Nueva, Red Crab Rest., Starbucks, TX Roadhouse, $General, Giant Eagle Mkt, Lowe's, Marc's Foods, Michael's, Ross, TJ Maxx, URGENT CARE, USPO, S Advance Parts, GetGo, Sheetz/dsl, Speedway/dsl, Arby's, DQ, Firehouse Subs, Little Caesars, Rally's, Swenson's Drive-In, Taco Bell, Wendy's, $Tree, AT&T, AutoZone, Best Buy, Hyundai, Meineke, Walgreens

13 Teideman Rd, Brooklyn, S BP/dsl, Sheetz/dsl, Speedway/dsl, Buffalo Wild Wings, Carrabba's, Chipotle Mexican,

BROOKLYN

INTERSTATE 480 (Cleveland) Cont'd

13 Continued
Cracker Barrel, El Palenque Mexican, Golden Corral, Hooley House Grill, Hungry Howie's, Ice House Grill, IHOP, LJ Silver, McDonald's, Panera Bread, Raising Cane's, Starbucks, Subway, TGIFriday's, Extended Stay America, Fairfield Inn, Hampton Inn, ALDI, Home Depot, LandRover/Jaguar, Sam's Club/gas, Volvo, Walmart

12b W 150th, W130th, Brookpark, S Marathon/dsl, Shell/dsl, Big Boy, Bob Evans, Charley's, Travelodge, Acura, Chevrolet, Chrysler/Dodge/Jeep, Lexus, Mazda, Toyota

11 I-71, Cleveland, Columbus

10 S Rd 237, Airport Blvd(wb only)

9 OH 17, Brookpark Rd, N Graytown Rd Tavern, Steaks & Hoagies, Extended Stay America, Hilton Garden, H, S

7 (wb only)Clague Rd, to WestLake

6 OH 252, Great Northern Blvd, to N Olmsted, N Shell, Speedway/dsl, Applebee's, Arby's, Biggby Coffee, BJ's Rest., Bob Evans, Buffalo Wild Wings, Burger King, Chick-fil-A, Chili's, ChuckeCheese, Dunkin', Famous Dave's, Five Guys, Frankie's Italian, Harry Buffalo, Jersey Mike's, Jimmy John's, Little Caesar's, Macaroni Grill, McAlister's Deli, Mr. Hero, Olive Garden, Panera Bread, Penn Sta Subs, Popeyes, Raising Cane's, Red Lobster, Red Robin, Sarku Japan, Scrambler's, Wendy's, Wingstop, Courtyard, Extended Stay America, Extended Stay America, Hampton Inn, Hotel Cleveland, La Quinta, Sonesta Suites, $Tree, ALDI, AT&T, Best Buy, Big Lots, Buick/GMC/Cadillac, Chipotle Mexican, Conrad's Tire/auto, Dick's, Dillard's, Firestone/auto, Home Depot, Honda, Hyundai/VW, JC Penney, Macy's, Marc's Foods, NTB, PetSmart, Subaru, Target, Tire Choice, TJ Maxx, Toyota, Uni-Mart, Verizon, Walmart, S Aloft Cleveland

OBERLIN

3 Stearns Rd, N H, S Lily's Chinese, Mi Rancho Mexican, Razzle's Cafe(2 mi), Steaks & Hoagies, CVS Drug(2 mi), H, Shaker's MktPlace

2 OH 10, Lorain Rd, to OH Tpk, S BP, Sheetz/dsl, Speedway/dsl, Burger King, Chipotle, Culver's, Dunkin', Gourme Rest., Lone Tree Tavern, McDonald's, Panera Bread, Starbucks, Taco Bell, Motel 6, South Ridge Inn

1 OH 10 W, to US 20(from wb), Oberlin

0mm OH 10, OH Tpk, I-480 begins/ends on exit 151, to Cleveland

INTERSTATE 680 (Youngstown)

16 OH TPK, I-680 begins/ends

14 OH 164, to Western Reserve Rd, I-680 begins/ends on OH Tpk, exit 234, S Shell/dsl, Cafe 422, Carmella's Cafe, Coney's, Dunkin', Ely's, McDonald's, Taco Bell, Wendy's, H

STRUTHERS

11b a US 224, S GetGo, McAlister's Deli, Shell/dsl, Aladdin's Eatery, Applebee's, Burger King, Cane's Chicken, Chick-fil-A, Chipotle, Condado Tacos, Domino's, Dunkin', Firehouse Subs, Honeybaked Ham, IHOP, Izumi Japanese, Jersey Mike's, KFC, Longhorn Steaks, McDonald's, O'Charley's, Olive Garden, Outback Steaks, Panda Express, Panera Bread, Papa John's, Perkins, Popeyes, Primanti Bros, Pulp Juice, Quaker Steak, Red Lobster, Springfield Grill, Starbucks, Steak'n Shake, Storming Crab, Subway, Swensons Drive-In, Taco Bell, TX Roadhouse, Wendy's, Baymont, Best Western+, Fairfield Inn, Hampton Inn, Holiday Inn, Residence Inn, $Tree, ALDI, AT&T, Best Buy, Big Lots, Giant Eagle, Hobby Lobby, H, Lowe's, Marc's Foods, Marshall's, NTB, PetSmart, Ross, Sam's Club/gas, URGENT CARE, Valvoline, Verizon, Walmart/Subway

9b a OH 170, Midlothian Blvd, Struthers, N BP, Dunkin', Marco's Pizza, Pizza Hut, S Shell/dsl, Speedway/dsl, McDonald's, $General

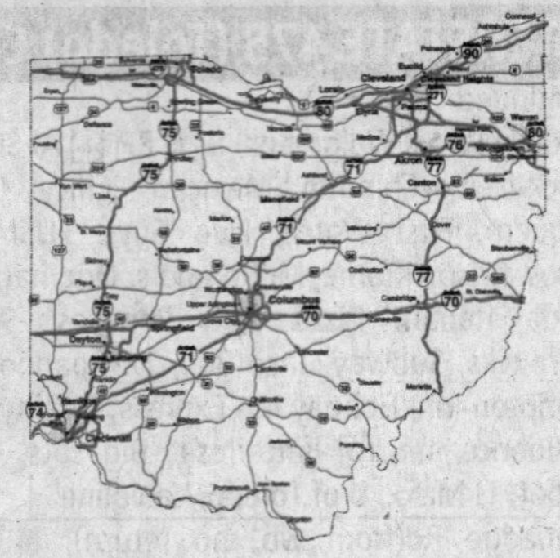

8 Shirley Rd, downtown

7 US 62, OH 7, South Ave, downtown

6b a US 62, OH 7, Mkt St, downtown

5 Glenwood Ave, downtown, Mahoning Ave

4b a OH 193, to US 422, Salt Springs Rd, N H, museum

3c b Belle Vista Ave, Connecticut Ave

3a OH 711 E, to I-80 E

2 Meridian Rd, S Ford/Peterbilt Trucks

1 OH 11

LORDSTOWN

INTERSTATE Ohio Turnpike

241mm Ohio/Pennsylvania state line

239mm toll plaza

237mm Mahoning Valley Travel Plaza eb, Glacier Hills Travel Plaza wb, Sunoco/dsl/24hr, DQ, Panera Bread, 7-11

234 I-680(from wb), to Youngstown

232 OH 7, to Boardman, Youngstown, N Marathon/dsl, Sheetz, DQ, Los Gallos Mexican, Steamer's Stonewall Tavern, FairBridge Inn, Holiday Inn Express, Quality Inn, $General, antiques, S Love's/Hardee's/Subway/dsl/scales/24hr/@, Pilot/McDonald's/dsl/scales/24hr, Speedway/dsl, Davis Motel, Liberty Inn

218 I-80 E, to Youngstown. OH Tpk runs with I-76 eb, I-80 wb, Niles

216 (from wb), Lordstown

215 Lordstown(from eb)

210mm Mahoning River

209 OH 5, to Warren, N Budget Lodge, S Marathon/dsl, Falls Inn, Holiday Inn Express

197mm Portage Service Plaza wb, Bradys Leap Service Plaza eb, Sunoco/dsl/24, Dunkin', Jimmy John's(wb), Wendy's, 7-11(wb)

193 OH 44, to Ravenna

192mm Cuyahoga River

187 OH 14 S, I-480, to Streetsboro, S Circle K, GetGo, Sheetz, Tesla EVC, Applebee's, Arby's, Bob Evans, Broken Egg Cafe, Burger King, Cane's Chicken, Chipotle, Don Patron Mexican, DQ, Freddy's Burgers, Honeybaked Ham, Jersey Mike's, Jimmy John's, Little Caesar's, McDonald's, New Peking Chinese, Panda Express, Popeyes, Rockne's Grill Ruby Tuesday, Slim Chickens, Sonic, Starbucks, Wendy's Wild Eagle Steaks, Comfort Inn, EconoLodge, Fairfield Inn Hampton Inn, Holiday Inn Express, Motel 6, Quality Inn TownePlace Suites, $Tree, AT&T, Giant Eagle Mkt, Home Depot, Honda, H, Hyundai, Kent St U, Kia, Lowe's, Nissan NTB, Staples, Target, Tire Source/auto, Verizon, VW, Walmar

180 OH 8, to I-90 E, N Baymont Inn, Costco/dsl, URGEN CARE, S BP/dsl

177mm Cuyahoga River

173 OH 21, to I-77, N Pilot/Wendy's/dsl/scales, Holiday In Express, S Cozumel Mexican, Subway, Comfort Inn Quality Inn, Super 8

170mm Towpath Service Plaza eb, Great Lakes Service Plaza wb, Sunoco/dsl/24hr, Burger King, Popeyes, Starbucks

INTERSTATE Ohio Turnpike Cont'd

CLEVELAND

Exit #	Services
161	US 42, to I-71, Strongsville, **N** Mobil/dsl, Sheetz/dsl, Tesla EVC, Arby's, Buffalo Wild Wings, Culver's, Dunkin', McDonald's, Starbucks, Kings Inn, Home Depot, Lowe's, vet, Walmart/Subway, **S** DQ, Freddy's Burgers, J-Bella Rest., KFC, Marco's Pizza, Mr Hero, Elmhaven Motel, Fiat, Staples, vet
152	OH 10, to Oberlin, I-480, Cleveland, **N** BP, Sheetz/dsl, Speedway/dsl, Burger King, Chipotle, Culvers, Dunkin', Gourme Rest., Lone Tree Tavern, McDonald's, Panera Bread, Starbucks, Taco Bell, Motel 6, South Ridge Inn, Super 8, **S** Pizza Pan
151	I-480 E(from eb), to Cleveland
146mm	Black River
145	OH 57, to Lorain, to I-90, Elyria, **N** Speedway/dsl, Applebee's, Biggby Coffee, Bob Evans, Buffalo Wild Wings, Chipotle Mexican, Denny's, Giant Eagle Mkt, Golden Corral, Hunan King, IHOP, Jimmy John's, Knights Inn, McDonald's, Olive Garden, Red Lobster, Taco Bell, TX Roadhouse, Uncle Bo's BBQ, Wasabi Grill, Wendy's, Best Western, Camelot Inn, Courtyard, Hampton Inn, Holiday Inn & Suites, Quality Inn, $General, $Tree, AT&T, Conrad's Automotive, Dick's, Firestone/auto, Home Depot, Honda, Hyundai, JC Penney, Lowe's, Marc's Foods, PetSmart, Staples, Target, Tuffy, Verizon, **S** Shell, Speedway/dsl, Sprucewood Inn
142	I-90(from eb, exits left), OH 2, to W Cleveland
140	OH 58, Amherst, **N** Shell, DQ, Moosehead Grill, $General, Chrysler/Dodge/Jeep, **S** Ford
139mm	Service Plaza both lanes, **Burger King, Popeyes, Starbucks**
135	rd 51, Baumhart Rd, to Vermilion
132mm	Vermilion River
118	US 250, to Norwalk, Sandusky, **N** Circle K/dsl, Marathon/dsl, McDonald's, Subway, Country Inn Suites, Days Inn, Hampton Inn, Holiday Inn Express, Motel 6, Quality Inn, Red Roof Inn, Milan RV Park, **S** Edison's Birthplace
110	OH 4, to Bellevue
100mm	Service Plaza both lanes, **Sunoco/dsl/24hr**, Burger King, Sbarro
93mm	Sandusky River
91	OH 53, to Fremont, Port Clinton, **N** Days Inn, **S** Murphy USA/dsl, Shell/dsl/24hr, Applebee's, Bob Evans, Buffalo Wild Wings, Burger King, Chipotle, Fricker's, Jimmy John's, McDonald's, Subway, Taco Bell, Tropical Smoothie, Comfort Inn, Delux Inn, Hampton Inn, Holiday Inn Express, Quality Inn, $Tree, ALDI, AT&T, AutoZone, Ford/Lincoln, H, Lowe's, Marshalls, Rutherford B. Hayes Library, URGENT CARE, USPO, Verizon, vet, Walmart
81	OH 51, Elmore, Woodville, Gibsonburg
80.5mm	Portage River

AMHERST

PERRYSBURG

Exit #	Services
77mm	Service Plaza both lanes, Sunoco/dsl/24hr, Hardee's(eb)
71	I-280, OH 420, to Stony Ridge, Toledo, **N** Flying J/Denny's/dsl/scales/LP/24hr, Love's/Arby's/dsl/scales/24hr, Petro/BP/dsl/scales/24hr/@, Budget Inn, Red Roof Inn, Regency Inn, Super 8, Blue Beacon, **S** FuelMart/Subway/dsl/scales, Pilot/McDonald's/dsl/scales/24hr, TA/BP/Taco Bell/dsl/scales/24hr/@, KOA
64	I-75 N, to Toledo, Perrysburg, **S** BP/Subway/dsl, Country Inn&Suites, Courtyard, Hampton Inn, Staybridge Suites, Tru Hotel, Bass Pro Shops, Camping World RV Ctr
63mm	Maumee River
59	US 20, to I-475, Maumee, Toledo, **N** Shell/dsl, Speedway/dsl, Bob Evans, Golden Lily, Marco's Pizza, McDonald's, Nick's Cafe, Olive Garden, Steak'n Shake, Waffle House, Motel 6, $Tree, Goodyear/auto, Jo-Ann Fabrics, NAPA, O'Reilly Parts, to Toledo Stadium, Walgreens, **S** Shell/dsl, Speedway/dsl, Big Boy, Chipotle Mexican, Deet's BBQ, Dunkin', Five Guys, Fricker's, La Fiesta Mexican, Packo's, Pizza Hut, Red Lobster, Schlotzsky's, Steak Escape, Taco Bell, Tim Horton's, Tropical Smoothie, Best Value Inn, Comfort Inn, Comfort Inn, Days Inn, Hampton Inn, Holiday Inn, Home2 Suites, Red Roof Inn, antiques, AT&T, Honda, Kroger/dsl, Meijer/dsl, Toyota, Verizon, vet
52	OH 2, to Toledo, **N** Loma Linda Mexican, **S** Baymont Inn, RV/truck repair
39	OH 109, **S** Country Corral/Valero/Winchester's Rest./dsl/scales/24hr
34	OH 108, to Wauseon, Circle K, Marathon, Murphy USA/dsl, Burger King, DQ, El Jarro Mexican, McDonald's, Pizza Hut, Subway, Taco Bell, Wendy's, Ace Hardware, AutoZone, Walmart, **S** Sunoco/dsl/24hr, Blue Ribbon Diner, Days Inn, Holiday Inn Express, Rodeway Inn, H
25	OH 66, Burlington, **N** Harrison Lake SP, **S** Sauder Village Museum/Inn
24.5mm	Tiffen River
20	Indian Meadow wb/Tiffen River eb Service Plaza, **Sunoco/7-11/dsl**, **Burger King(eb), Sbarro, Starbucks**
13	OH 15, to Bryan, Montpelier, **S** Marathon/dsl, Four Seasons Rest., Holiday Inn Express, Quality Inn, Rainbow Motel, Rodeway Inn, Suburban Studios, Hutch's Dsl Repair
11.5mm	St Joseph River
3mm	toll plaza, phone
2	OH 49, to US 20, **N** Flying J/dsl/24hr/scales, Love's/Arby's/dsl/24hr/scales/@, Calli's BBQ, truck repair, truck wash
0mm	Ohio/Indiana state line

BURLINGTON

OH

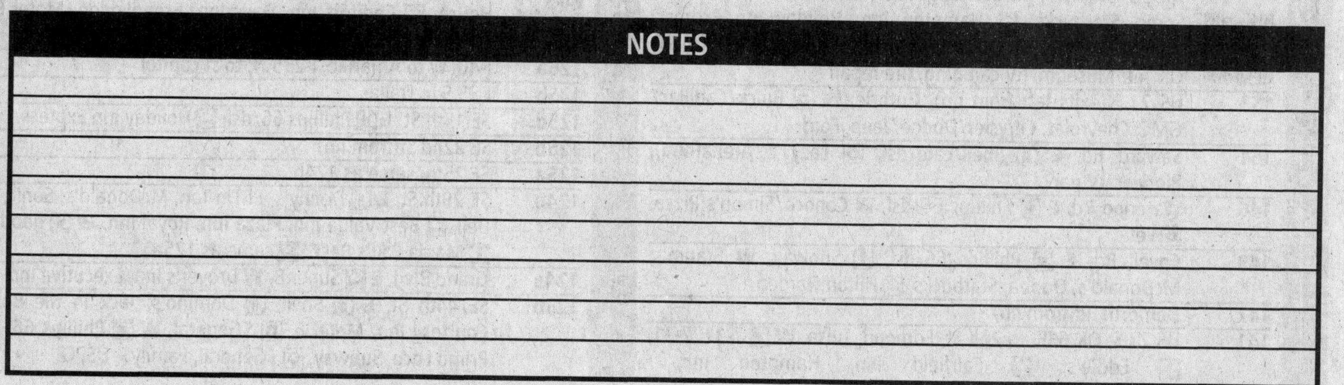

= gas = food = lodging = other = rest stop

OKLAHOMA

INTERSTATE 35

Exit #	Services
236mm	Oklahoma/Kansas state line
235	weigh sta sb
231	US 177, Braman, E Conoco/deli/dsl, casino
230	Braman Rd
229mm	Chikaskia River
225mm	**full facilities, litter barrels, petwalk, , vending, Welcome Ctr sb**
222	OK 11, to Blackwell, Medford, Alva, Newkirk, E Casey's/dsl/EVC, Sunoco/dsl, Braum's, Los Potros Mexican, McDonald's, Subway, Baymont, Best Way Inn, Holiday Inn Express, Sleep Inn, SureStay,
218	Hubbard Rd
217mm	weigh sta both lanes
214	US 60, to Tonkawa, Lamont, Ponka City, N OK Coll, E Valero/Papa John's/dsl, W Pilot/Taco Bell/dsl/scales/24hr, Tonkawa Hotel, casino
213mm	Salt Fork of Arkansas River
211	Fountain Rd, E Love's/Chester's/Subway/dsl/scales/24hr/RV Dump
209mm	parking area, litter barrels
203	OK 15, to Marland, Billings, E Phillips 66/DQ/dsl/CNG/scales/24hr, dog park
199mm	Red Rock Creek
195mm	litter barrels, parking area both lanes
194b a	US 412, US 64 W, Cimarron Tpk, to Cimarron, Enid
193	airport Rd (from nb, no return)
191mm	Black Bear Creek
186	US 64 E, to Fir St, Perry, E Love's/dsl/scales/24hr, Phillips 66/dsl, Tesla EVC, Braum's, Mariachi Mexican, McDonald's, Super 8, EVC, , museum, W Shell/dsl, Comfort Suites, Holiday Inn Express, Microtel, Chevrolet/Buick/GMC
185	US 77, to Covington, Perry, E American Inn, W Phillips 66/rest./motel/dsl/24hr
180	Orlando Rd
174	OK 51, to Stillwater, Hennessee, E Phillips 66/dsl, Fairfield Inn(12mi), Hampton Inn(12mi), La Quinta(12mi), Residence Inn(12mi), Lake Carl Blackwell RV Park, to OSU
173mm	litter barrels, parking area sb, parking only
171mm	litter barrels, parking area nb, parking only
170	Mulhall Rd
166mm	Cimarron River
157	OK 33, to Cushing, Guthrie, E Love's/Carl's Jr/dsl/scales/24hr/RV hookup, Valero/Golden Chick/dsl, Langston U, W Love's/Subway/dsl, Road Star, Shell/dsl, Valero, Arby's, Braum's, Burger King, El Rodeo Mexican, Pizza Hut, Sonic, Starbucks, Hampton Inn, Holiday Inn Express, Interstate Motel, La Quinta, Sleep Inn, Territorial Inn, , OK Terr Museum, RV camping, tire repair
153	US 77 N(exits left from nb), Guthrie, W Buick/Cadillac/GMC, Chevrolet, Chrysler/Dodge/Jeep, Ford
151	Seward Rd, E Shell/cafe/dsl, Lazy E Arena(4mi), Pioneer RV park
146	Waterloo Rd, E Phillips 66/dsl, W Conoco/Simon's Pizza, vet
143	Covell Rd, E Phillips 66/dsl, Subway, W Braum's, McDonald's, Qdoba, Starbucks, Hilton Garden
142	Danforth Rd(from nb)
141	US 77 S, OK 66E, to 2nd St, Edmond, Tulsa, W 7-11, 7-11, Eddie's, Fairfield Inn, Hampton Inn,

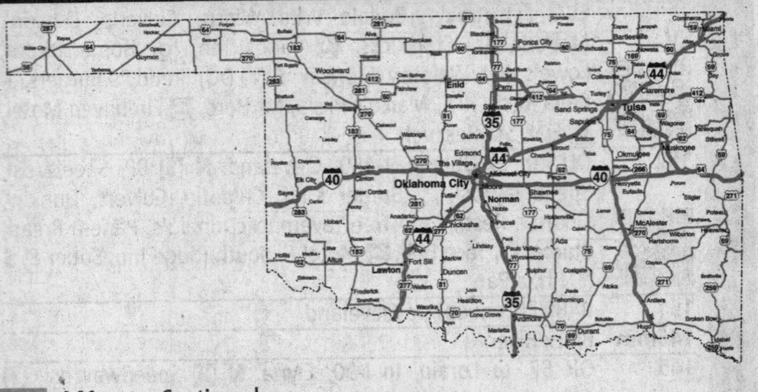

Exit #	Services
141	Continued Holiday Inn Express, Home2 Suites, La Quinta, SureStay+, , vet
140	SE 15th St, Spring Creek, Arcadia Lake, Edmond Park, E , W Phillips 66/Circle K/Casey's/dsl, Braum's, Buffalo Wild Wings, Chick-fil-A, Taco Bell, Whataburger, Sam's Club/dsl, Walmart
139	SE 33rd St
138d	Memorial Rd
138c	Sooner Rd(from sb)
138b	Kilpatrick Tpk
138a	I-44 Tpk E to Tulsa
137.5mm	I-35 S and I-44 W run together 8 mi.
137	NE 122nd St, to OK City, E Conoco/dsl, Mama Lety Mexican, Hampton Inn, Sleep Inn, W Flying J/Huddle House/dsl/scales/LP/24hr, Love's/Godfathers/Subway/dsl/scales/24hr, Phillips 66, Valero/dsl/scales, Cracker Barrel, McDonald's, Sonic, Waffle House, Baymont Inn, Best Value, Days Inn, Econo Lodge, Economy Hotel, Economy Inn, Holiday Inn Express, Motel 6, Super 8, Abe's RV Park, Frontier City Funpark, Oklahoma Visitors Ctr/info/restrooms
136	Hefner Rd, W same as 137
135	Britton Rd
134	Wilshire Blvd, W Executive Inn, Blue Beacon
133.5	I-35 N and I-44 E run together 8 mi
133	I-44 W, to Amarillo, W Cowboy Hall of Fame, st capitol
132b	NE 63rd St(from nb), E Conoco/dsl, Braum's, Remington Inn
132a	NE 50th St, Remington Pk, W funpark, museum, zoo
131	NE 36th St, W Casey's/Circle K/dsl, 45th Inf Division Museum
130	US 62 E, NE 23rd St, W to st capitol
129	NE 10th St, E Family$
128	I-40 E, to Ft Smith
127	Eastern Ave, OK City, N Valero, W Checkers/Subway/dsl/scales/24hr/@, Petro/Iron Skillet/dsl/24hr/@, Waffle House, Comfort Inn, Days Inn, EconoLodge, Motel 6, Lewis RV Ctr
126a	I-40, W to Amarillo, I-235 N, to st capitol
126b	I-35 S to Dallas
125d	SE 15th St, E Phillips 66/dsl, Holiday Inn Express
125b	SE 22nd St(from nb)
125a	SE 25th, same as 124b
124b	SE 29th St, E Denny's, El Tin-Tan, McDonald's, Sonic, Taco Bell, Best Value Inn, Plaza Inn, Royal Inn, W goodstop Mama Lou's Rest., same as 125a
124a	Grand Blvd, E Super 8, W Drover's Inn, Executive Inn
123b	SE 44th St, E Shell, Domino's, Jack in the Box, Courtesy Inn, Motel 6, $General, W Phillips 66, Primo Loco, Subway, $General, Family$, USPO

INTERSTATE 35 Cont'd

Exit #	Services
123a	SE 51st St, E [lodging] Best Western+, Comfort Inn & Suites
122b	SE 59th St, E [gas] Phillips 66/dsl, W Valero/dsl, [other] U-Haul
122a	SE 66th St, E [food] Burger King, TX Roadhouse, [lodging] Residence Inn, Wingate, W [gas] 7-11, [food] Arby's
121b	US 62 W, I-240 E
121a	SE 82nd St, from sb, W [lodging] Days Inn, Hemp Inn
120	SE 89th St, E [other] Ford, W [gas] Love's/Subway/dsl/24hr, [other] Classic Parts
119b	N 27th St, E [gas] Casey's, [food] Starbucks
119a	Shields Blvd(exits left from nb)
118	N 12th St, E [food] Boomerang Diner, Mazzio's, Sonic, [lodging] Super 8, W [gas] 7-11, Valero, [food] Arby's, Braum's, Del Rancho, Grandy's, KFC, McDonald's, Papa John's, Pickles Grill, Subway, Taco Bell, Wendy's, [lodging] Best Western, Candlewood Suites, Comfort Inn, Hampton Inn, Holiday Inn Express, Quality Inn, SpringHill Suites, [other] $General, AutoZone
117	OK 37, S 4th St, W [gas] 7-11, Phillips 66/dsl, [food] Dunkin', [other] [H], USPO
116	S 19th St, E [gas] Sam's Club/dsl, Shell, [food] Braum's, Garage Burgers, Genghis Grill, Jimmy John's, McDonald's, Ricky's Cafe, Slim Chickens, Taco Bell, Taco Bueno, Waffle House, Whataburger, Zaxby's, [other] American Automotive, AT&T, Best Buy, Firestone/auto, GNC, Hobby Lobby, JC Penney, Old Navy, PetSmart, Ross, URGENT CARE, W [gas] Murphy USA, [food] Alfredo's Mexican, Applebee's, Arby's, Black Bear Diner, Black Rifle Coffee, Buffalo Wild Wings, Cane's, Carl's Jr, Chick-fil-A, Chicken Express, Chicken Salad Chick, Chili's, China House, Chipotle, Crumbl, Del Taco, DQ, Firehouse Subs, Five Guys, Freddy's Custard, Hildago's Mexican, IHOP, Jack-in-the-Box, Jersey's Mike's Subs, Jimmy's Egg, Louie's Grill, Mazzio's, McAlister's Deli, Oliveto's Italian, Panda Express, Qdoba Mexican, Schlotzsky's, Sonic, Starbucks, Taco Casa, The Catch, Tropical Cafe, [lodging] La Quinta, [other] $Tree, ALDI, AT&T, AutoZone, Costco/gas, Dick's, Discount Tire, Harley-Davidson, Home Depot, Kohl's, Lowe's, Target, Tires+, Verizon, Walmart
114	Indian Hill Rd, E [lodging] WoodSpring, W [food] Double Dave's Pizza, [other] Cadillac
113	US 77 S(from sb, exits left), Norman
112	Tecumseh Rd, E [food] El Huevo Mexi-Diner, Land Run Grill, W McDonald's, Pizza Hut, Sonic, Wendy's, [lodging] Best Western, [other] CVS Drug, [H], Nissan, Toyota/Scion, URGENT CARE
110b a	Robinson St, E [food] Carl's Jr, CAVA, Cheddar's, Chili's, Chipotle, ChuckECheese, Crumbl, Five Guys, Logan's Roadhouse, Marco's Pizza, Panda Express, Pei Wei, Ranch Steakhouse, Sonic, Starbucks, Swig, Taco Bell, Wing Stop, [lodging] Embassy Suites, Hampton Inn, Holiday Inn Express, Motel 6, Residence Inn, [other] $Tree, AT&T, Buick/GMC, Crest Mkt, Discount Tire, Ford, Homeland Foods/gas, Honda, [H], Hyundai, Kohl's, Mazda, Michael's, Office Depot, PetCo, Target, TJ Maxx, Verizon, VW, W [food] Arby's, Braum's, Cafe Escondido, Chuy's Mexican, Cracker Barrel, Domino's, Jersey Mike's, Outback Steaks, Saltgrass Steaks, Waffle House, Yamato Steaks, [lodging] Comfort Inn, Courtyard, Delta Hotels, Hilton Garden, [other] Kia
109	Main St, E [gas] Murphy USA/dsl, Sinclair, [food] Arby's, Chick-fil-A, DQ, Golden Corral, Jimmy's Egg, La Baguette Bakery, Little Caesar's, Panera Bread, Subway, Waffle House, Wendy's, Whataburger, [lodging] Best Value, Days Inn, Super 8, Travelodge, [other] ALDI, AT&T, AutoZone, Best Buy, BigLots, Chrysler/Dodge/Jeep, Hobby Lobby, Lowe's, Tires+, Walmart/McDonald's, W [gas] Goodstop by Casey's, [food] BJ's Brewhouse, Cane's, Charleston's, Denny's, Gaberino's Italian, McDonald's, Olive Garden, Red Lobster, [lodging] Fairfield Inn, La Quinta, SureStay+,
109	Continued Barnes&Noble, JC Penney, Jo-Ann, Old Navy, Sam's Club
108b a	OK 9 E, Norman, E [gas] Casey's, [food] Braum's, Del Rancho Steaks, Taco Bell, [other] O'Reilly Parts, to U of OK, W [food] IHOP, Jason's Deli, Red Robin, [lodging] Country Inn&Suites, La Quinta, [other] Chevrolet, Home Depot, PetSmart, Ross
107mm	Canadian River
106	OK 9 W, to Chickasha, E [other] Casino, W [gas] Love's/Subway/dsl/24hr, Shell, [food] Burger King, McDonald's, Sonic, Taco Bueno, [lodging] Sleep Inn, [other] casino, URGENT CARE, vet
104	OK 74 S, Goldsby, E [other] Floyd's RV Ctr, W [gas] CNG, Valero/dsl, [food] Libby's Cafe
101	Ladd Rd
98	Johnson Rd
95	US 77(exits left from sb), Purcell, E [gas] Phillips 66/dsl, [food] Mazzio's, [other] $General, AutoZone, Ford, [H]
91	OK 74, to OK 39, Maysville, E [gas] Conoco/dsl, Murphy USA/dsl, Phillips 66/dsl, [food] Braum's, Domino's, McDonald's, Sonny's Cafe, Subway, Taco Mayo, Wendy's, [lodging] EconoLodge, Executive Inn, Holiday Inn Express, Ruby's Inn/rest., [other] AT&T, Walmart/Subway, W [gas] Shell/dsl, [food] A&W/LJ Silver, Taco Bell, [other] RV park
86	OK 59, Wayne, Payne, E [other] Family$
79	OK 145 E, Paoli, E [gas] Phillips 66/EVC/dsl
76mm	Washita River
74	Kimberlin Rd, to OK 19, W [other] RV park
72	OK 19, Paul's Valley, E [gas] Murphy USA/dsl, Phillips 66/dsl, Sunoco/dsl/rest/24hr, [food] Arby's, Braum's, Chicken Express, Green Tea Chinese, Happy Days Diner, KFC, McDonald's, Riviera Maya, Sonic, Subway, Taco Bell, The Grille, Tio's Mexican, [lodging] Best Value Inn, Best Western, Comfort Inn, Days Inn, Hampton Inn, Holiday Inn Express, Relax Inn, Rodeway Inn, [other] AT&T, Buick/Cadillac/GMC, Chrysler/Dodge/Jeep, URGENT CARE, Walmart, W [gas] Phillips 66/dsl/24hr, Shell/dsl, [food] Papa John's, [other] Ford/Lincoln, truckwash
70	Airport Rd, E [gas] Love's/Burger King/dsl/LP/scales/24hr/@, [other] [H], W T&R RV Resort
66	OK 29, Wynnewood, E [lodging] Kent's Motel, W [gas] Valero/dsl
64	OK 17A E, to Wynnewood, E [other] RV park
60	Ruppe Rd
59mm	**full [handicapped] facilities, litter barrels, petwalk, [phone], picnic table, [RS] both lanes, RV dump**
55	OK 7, Davis, E [gas] Conoco/dsl, Phillips 66/A&W/dsl/24hr, [food] IHOP, [other] to Chickasaw NRA, Treasure Valley Casino/Inn, W Chickasaw Nation Welcome Ctr, [gas] Conoco/dsl, [other] to Arbuckle Ski Area
54.5mm	Honey Creek Pass
53mm	weigh sta both lanes
51	US 77, Turner Falls, E [lodging] Arbuckle Mtn Motel, Mtnview Inn(3mi), [other] RV camping, to Arbuckle Wilderness, W [gas] Sinclair/rv park
49mm	scenic turnout both lanes
47	US 77, Turner Falls Area
46mm	scenic turnout both lanes
42	OK 53 W, Springer, Comanche, W [gas] Exxon/Subway/dsl
40	OK 53 E, Gene Autry, E [gas] Valero/dsl/café/24hr, [other] $General, Gene Autry Museum
33	OK 142, Ardmore, E [gas] Shell, Valero/dsl, [food] IHOP, Jimmy's Egg Cafe, [lodging] Best Value Inn, Courtyard, Holiday Inn, La Quinta, Nissan, Red Roof Inn, SpringHill Suites, Super 8, [other] Honda, regional park, tires, W [gas] Flying J/Huddle House/dsl/LP/scales/24hr
32	12th St, Ardmore, E [gas] Phillips 66/dsl, Shell, [food] Arby's, Braum's, Chick-fil-A, Chili's, Freddy's, Rib Crib, Sakura Hibachi, Santa Fe Steaks, Starbucks, Whataburger, Wingstop, [lodging] Holiday Inn Express, La Quinta, Quality Inn, [other] $Tree, AT&T, Chevrolet, Hilton Garden, Hyundai, Lowe's, PetCo,

NORMAN GOLDSBY PAOLI DAVIS ARDMORE

OK

INTERSTATE 35 Cont'd

ARDMORE

32 Continued
Ross, Toyota, W Love's/Godfather's/Subway/dsl/24hr/@, McDonald's, Microtel

31b a US 70 W, OK 199 E, Ardmore, E Shell/dsl, Valero/dsl, Applebee's, Burger King, El Chico, El Tapatio, Interurban Grill, KFC, McDonald's, Papa John's, Pizza Hut, Prairie Kitchen, Two Frogs Grill, Best Western+, Boarders Inn, Comfort Inn, Days Inn, Hampton Inn, Motel 6, Quality Hotel, AutoZone, Econolodge, Kia, O'Reilly Parts, W Phillips/dsl, Ardmore RV Park, Chrysler/Dodge/Jeep, Ford/Lincoln, vet

29 US 70 E, Ardmore, E to Lake Murray SP/lodge(8mi), W Hidden Lake RV Park

24 OK 77 S, E By the Lake RV Park, to Lake Murray SP

22.5mm Hickory Creek

21 Oswalt Rd, W Valero/dsl, Oswalt RV Park

15 OK 32, Marietta, E Valero/dsl/24hr, Carl's Jr, Homeland Foods, La Roca Mexican, McDonald's, Robertson's Sandwiches, Sonic, Subway, $General, H, to Lake Texoma SP, W Phillips/dsl, Shell/dsl

5 OK 153, Thackerville, W $General, Red River Ranch RV Park, Shorty's Foods/gas

3.5mm **full facilities, litter barrels, petwalk, vending, Welcome Ctr nb**

3 Winstar Blvd, E casino, same as 1

FT SMITH

1 US 77 N, E Phillips 66/dsl/CNG, Sonic, Best Western, Red River Suites, The Inn, RV park, Winstar Casino, W Red River RV Resort(3mi)

0mm Oklahoma/Texas state line, Red River

INTERSTATE 40

331mm Oklahoma/Arkansas state line

330 OK 64D S(from eb), Ft Smith

329mm weigh sta wb

325 US 64, Roland, Ft Smith, N Cherokee Trkstp/Valero/Subway/dsl/scales/24hr, 4 Star Diner, Cherokee Hotel, Walnut Inn, casino, S Phillips 66/dsl/scales, Pilot/Wendy's/dsl/scales/24hr, QS/dsl, Arby's, El Celaya Mexican, Mazzio's, McDonald's, Pizza Hut, Sonic, Subway, Taco Bell, Interstate Inn, $General, Harps Foods, O'Reilly Parts

321 OK 64b N, Muldrow, N Phillips 66, S Arena/dsl, Executive Inn, truck parts/svc

316mm **full facilities, info, litter barrels, petwalk, eb, vending**

313mm **full facilities, info, litter barrels, petwalk, wb, RV dump, vending**

SALLISAW

311 US 64, Sallisaw, N Phillips 66/dsl, Sunoco/dsl, El Toro Mexican, Hardee's, KFC/Taco Bell, Pizza Hut, Sherry's Kitchen, Simple Simon's Pizza, Motel 6, Sallisaw Inn, $General, AutoZone, Brushy Lake SP(10mi), H, O'Reilly Parts, Sequoya's Home(12mi)

308 US 59, Sallisaw, N Murphy USA/dsl, Sunoco/dsl, A&W/LJ Silver, Arby's, Asian Star, Braum's, Cazadore Mexican, China Harbor, Domino's, Mazzio's, McDonald's, Roma Italian, Sonic, Subway, Taco Bueno, Blue Ribbon Inn, Economy Inn, Golden Spur Motel, Quality Inn, Super 8, $Tree, AT&T, casino, H, Verizon, Walmart/Subway, S Shell/dsl, Olde Feed Barn, Buick/Chevrolet/GMC, Chrysler/Dodge/Jeep, Ford, KOA, to Kerr Lake, truck/tire repair

303 Dwight Mission Rd

297 OK 82 N, Vian, N FL/dsl, Love's/Subway/dsl/24hr/@, Rustic Cantina, Simple Simon, Subway, Cherokee Landing SP(24 mi), Harps Foods, to Tenkiller Lake RA(12 mi), USPO,

VIAN

297 Continued
Sequoia NWR

291 OK 10 N, to Gore, N Greenleaf SP(10mi), Tenkiller SP(21mi)

290mm Arkansas River

287 OK 100 N, to Webbers Falls, N Love's/Burger King/Subway/dsl/scales/24hr/@, Cox's Buffet, Greenleaf SP, Tenkiller SP

286 Muskogee Tpk, to Muskogee

284 Ross Rd

CHECOTAH

283mm parking area both lanes, litter barrels

278 US 266, OK 2, Warner, N Conoco, Sinclair/dsl(2), Sinclair/McDonald's/dsl, El Jaracho Mexican, Simple Simon's Pizza, Sonic, Subway, Ambassadors Inn & RV, $General

270 Texanna Rd, to Porum Landing, S Campbell's/BBQ

265 US 69 bus, Checotah, N Kwik'n Easy, Pizza Hut, Sonic, S Phillips 66/dsl, Chevrolet/Chrysler/Dodge/Jeep

264b a US 69, to Eufaula, N Casey's/dsl, Flying J/Denny's/dsl/LP/scales/24hr, Phillips 66/dsl/24hr, Charlie's Chicken, McDonald's, Sallie's Cafe, Simple Simon's Pizza, Taco Bell, Walnut Inn, $General, AT&T, O'Reilly Parts, repair, Walmart/Subway

262 to US 266, Lotawatah Rd

261mm Lake Eufaula

259 OK 150, to Fountainhead Rd, S Shell/dsl, Lake Eufaula Inn, to Lake Eufaula SP

HENRYETTA

255 Pierce Rd, N KOA

251mm both lanes

247 Tiger Mtn Rd

240b a US 62 E, US 75 N, Henryetta, N Conoco/dsl, Love's/dsl, Phillips 66, QT, Arby's, Braum's, Braum's, Burger King, CheeZies Pizza, Classic Diner, KFC, Mazzio's, McDonald's, New China, Rustler's BBQ, Shoney's, Sonic, Subway, Taco Bell, Taco Bueno, Days Inn, Relax Inn, Chrysler/Dodge/Jeep, Ford, O'Reilly Parts, tires/repair, Walmart, S Indian Nation Tpk

237 US 62, US 75, Henryetta, N Shell/dsl, Green Country Inn, Trail Motel, Henryetta RV Park(2mi), H, tires/repair, S Super 8

231 US 75 S, to Weleetka, N Sinclair/dsl, Cowpoke's Cafe

227 Clearview Rd, S casino

221 US 62, OK 27, Okemah, N Express/Subway/dsl/24hr, Phillips 66/McDonald's, Pepino's Mexican, Simple Simon's Pizza, Sonic, Days Inn, Chevrolet, Homeland Foods, NAPA, Pine Tree RV Park (3mi), TrueValue, S Love's/Chester Fried/dsl/24hr, John's BBQ, casino, H, truck repair

EARLSBORO

217 OK 48, to Bristow, Bearden, S gas/dsl

216mm N Canadian River

212 OK 56, to Cromwell, Wewoka, S to Seminole Nation Museum(16mi), Valero/Chester's/dsl

208mm Gar Creek

202mm Turkey Creek

200 US 377, OK 99, to Little, Prague, N Stuckey's/Shell/Dunkin'/dsl/RV park, S Conoco/dsl, Love's/Subway/dsl/24hr, Sinclair/dsl, Robertson's Ham Sandwiches, Roundup Rest/RV Park, H, tire repair

197mm **full facilities, litter barrels, petwalk**

192 OK 9A, Earlsboro, N Rolling Stones RV Park (2mi), S Valero/dsl

OK

INTERSTATE 40 Cont'd

Exit #	Services
189mm	N Canadian River
186	OK 18, to Shawnee, N Phillips 66, Sinclair, American Inn, Baymont, Comfort Inn, Days Inn, Fairfield Inn, Holiday Inn Express, La Quinta, Super 8, Chrysler/Dodge/Jeep, Happy Acres RV Park, Shawnee RV Park, S Shell/dsl, Sinclair/dsl, Carl's Jr, Cazadorez, Chicken Express, Marco's Pizza, Roma's Italian, Sonic, Van's BBQ, Colonial Inn, Homeland Foods
185	OK 3E, Shawnee Mall Dr, to Shawnee, N Murphy USA/dsl, Buffalo Wild Wings, Chili's, Garage Burgers, KFC, Panda Express, Red Lobster, Santa Fe Steaks, Taco Bueno, Wendy's, $Tree, AT&T, Chevrolet, Dillard's, Ford, JC Penney, Kohl's, Ross, Walgreens, Walmart, S Circle K/dsl, Braum's, Burger King, Chick-fil-A, Cracker Barrel, Delta Cafe, Freddy's, IHOP, Marble Slab Creamery, Mazzio's, McAlister's Deli, McDonald's, Papa John's, Popeyes, Qdoba, RibCrib BBQ, Schlotzky's, Sonic, Starbucks, Subway, Taco Bell, Whataburger, Hampton Inn, ALDI, CVS Drug, Discount Tire, Hobby Lobby, Lowe's, O'Reilly Parts, PetSmart, Staples, TJ Maxx, Verizon
181	US 177, US 270, to Tecumseh, S Shell/dsl, Rosa's Mexican, dsl repair, Prestige RV Ctr
180mm	N Canadian River
178	OK 102 S, Dale, N Grand TC/hotel/casino/dsl
176	OK 102 N, McLoud Rd, S Love's/Subway/Godfather's/dsl/24hr, Sinclair/dsl, Curtis Watson Rest.
172	Newalla Rd, to Harrah
170	Kickapoo Turnpike to Tulsa
169	Peebly Rd
166	Choctaw Rd, to Woods, N Love's/McDonald's/Subway/dsl/scales/24hr/@, KOA, S Pilot/Wendy's/dsl/scales/24hr, Sonic, to Lake Thunderbird SP(11mi)
165	I-240 W(from wb), to Dallas
162	Anderson Rd, N Camping World, LP
159b	Douglas Blvd, N Casey's, OnCue/dsl, A&W/LJ Silver, Denny's, Freddy's, Jimmy John's, KFC, McDonald's, Pizza Hut, Sonic, Subway, Taco Bell, Whataburger, Eastland Hills RV Park, S [H], Tinker AFB
159a	Hruskocy Gate, N Chrysler/Dodge/Jeep, same as 157, U-Haul, S Tinker AFB, Gate 7
157c	Eaker Gate, same as 159
157b	Air Depot Blvd, N Casey's, Blaze Pizza, Bricktown Brewery, Cane's, Cheddar's, Chick-fil-A, Chili's, Flatbread Pizza, Jack-in-the-Box, Logans Roadhouse, McAlister's Deli, Panda Express, Panera Bread, Pei Wei, Qdoba, Santa Fe Steaks, Seafood Party, Starbucks, Taco Bell, Wingstop, AT&T, Best Buy, Dick's, Firestone/auto, GNC, JC Penney, Kohl's, Lowe's, Marshall's, O'Reilly Parts, Office Depot, Old Navy, PetSmart, Target, Verizon, S Tinker AFB, Gate 1
157a	SE 29th St, Midwest City, N Casey's/Circle K, On the Border, Swadley's BBQ, The Surf Bar, Best Western+, Traveler's Inn, O'Reilly Parts, S Ford, Sam's Club/gas
156b a	Sooner Rd, N Conoco/Circle K, Gulf, Black Bear Diner, Chick-fil-A, Feast Korean BBQ, Fuzzy's Tacos, Golden Corral, Meiji Experience, Olive Garden, Seoul Garden, Waffle House, Econo Lodge, Hampton Inn, Hawthorn Suites, Holiday Inn Express, Home2 Suites, La Quinta, Sheraton, Studio 6, Hobby Lobby, Home Depot, Walmart/Subway, S Buffalo Wild Wings, Carl's Jr, Garage Grill, Off The Hook Seafood, Ted's Mexican, Candlewood Suites, SpringHill Suites, Super 8, AT&T, Chevrolet/GMC, Discount Tire, Tires+, Toyota/Scion, Verizon
155b	SE 15th St, Del City, N Valero/dsl, Family$, [H], Nissan
155a	Sunny Lane Rd, Del City, N Conoco/Subway/dsl,

DALE

EAKER GATE

DEL CITY

155a	Continued Hyundai, U-Haul, S Braum's, Church's TX Chicken, Dunkin', Luigi's Pizza, Sonic, $General, $Tree
154	Reno Ave, Scott St, N Woodspring Suites, S 7-11
152	(153 from wb)I-35 N, to Wichita
127	Eastern Ave(from eb), Okla City, N Checkers/Subway/dsl/scales/24hr, Petro/Iron Skillet/dsl/scales/@, Valero, Waffle House, Comfort Inn, Days Inn, Econolodge, Motel 6, Lewis RV Ctr
151b c	I-35, S to Dallas, I-235 N, to downtown, N to st capitol
151a	Lincoln Blvd, N Casey's/Subway/Circle K/dsl, Earl's Rib Palace, Fuzzy's Taco Shop, McDonald's, Hampton Inn, Homewood Suites, Residence Inn, Bass Pro Shop, Bricktown Stadium
150c	Robinson Ave(from wb), OK City, N Abuelo's Mexican, Bob's Steaks, Pearl's Crabtown, Spark, Starbucks, Texadelphia, Yucatan Tacos, Courtyard, Hilton Garden, Residence Inn, Sheraton, SpringHill, U-Haul
150b	Harvey Ave(from eb), downtown, N Casey's Pizza, McDonald's, Starbucks, Courtyard, Fairfield Inn, Hilton, Hilton Garden, Renaissance Hotel, Sheraton, SpringHill Suites, Staybridge Suites, American Banjo Museum, Bass Pro Shops
150a	Shields Blvd(from eb), N to downtown
149b	Classen Blvd(from wb), same as 149a, to downtown
149a	Western Ave, Reno Ave, N Conoco/dsl, VP/Subway/dsl, McDonald's, Sonic, Sweis Gyros, Taco Bell, S Wheeler Park
148c	Virginia Ave(from wb), to downtown
148b	Penn Ave(from eb), N Valero/dsl, Holt Truck Repair, tire repair
148a	Agnew Ave, Villa Ave, N VP/dsl
147c	May Ave
147b a	I-44, E to Tulsa, W to Lawton
146	Portland Ave(from eb, no return), N Phillips 66/Subway/dsl, Taqueria Mexican, diesel repair
145	Meridian Ave, OK City, N Casey's/Circle K/dsl, Casey's/Circle K/dsl, Denny's, Earl's Ribs, Gopuram Indian, McDonald's, On the Border, Shiki Japanese, Trapper's Rest., Best Western, Biltmore Hotel, Courtyard, Days Inn, Extended Stay America, Hawthorn Suites, Howard Johnson, Red Roof Inn, Studio 6, Super 8, S Phillips 66/Circle K/dsl, BiBi Mediterranean, Billy Sims BBQ, Brielle's Bistro, Bunny's Burgers, Burger King, Charleston Rest., Chili's, Cracker Barrel, Frosted Mug Grill, Golden Palace Chinese, IHOP, Mackie's Steaks, Maple Korean BBQ, San Marcos Mexican, Sonic, Subway, Taco Bell, Waffle House, Whataburger, Zapata's, Zio's Italian, avid hotel, Baymont Inn, Clarion, Comfort Suites, Comfort Suites(2), Country Inn&Suites, Courtyard, DoubleTree, Econo Lodge, Embassy Suites, Fairfield Inn, Governors Suites, Hampton Inn, Hilton Garden, Holiday Inn, Holiday Inn Express, Home2 Suites, La Quinta, Meridian Inn, Motel 6, Oak Tree Inn, Ramada, Residence Inn, Sheraton, Sonesta, Staybridge Suites, The Douillet, TownePlace Suites, Tru, Wingate Inn, Woodspring Suites, Wyndham Garden, Boot Barn
144	MacArthur Blvd, N Casey's/Circle K/dsl, Phillips 66/dsl, Applebee's, Arby's, Bubba's 33, Cane's Chicken, Chick-fil-A, China One, Coldstone, Del Taco, Firehouse Subs, Five Guys, Freddy's, Golden Corral, Hook & Reel Cajun, Jack-in-the-Box, Jimmy John's, KFC, McDonald's, Olive Garden, Panda Express, Panera Bread, Qdoba, Schlotzsky's, Sonic, Starbucks, Taco Bueno, Twin Peaks, TX Roadhouse, SpringHill Suites, $Tree, AT&T, Hobby Lobby, PetSmart, Ross, Verizon, Walmart/McDonald's, S 7-11, Wendy's, BestWay Inn, Comfort Inn, Green Carpet Inn, Microtel, Travelers Inn, Sam's Club/gas
143	Rockwell Ave, N 7-11/dsl, Buffalo Wild Wings,

DEL CITY

OK CITY

OK

= gas = food = lodging = other = rest stop

INTERSTATE 40 Cont'd

MUSTANG

YUKON

Exit	Services
143	Continued Jersey Mike's, S&B's Burgers, Taco Bell, Best Western, Homewood Suites, Best Buy, Dick's, Discount Tire, Harley Davidson, Home Depot, McClain's RV Ctr, Tires+, S Sands Motel/RV Park/LP, Kenworth, Rockwell RV Park
142	Council Rd, N On Cue/dsl/CNG, Tesla EVC, BJ's Rest., Braum's, Garage Burgers, Golden Burrito, Jimmy's Egg, McDonald's, Starbucks, Subway, Taco Mayo, Ted's Mexican, Whataburger, Super 40 Inn, dsl repair, S TA/Country Pride/dsl/scales/24hr/@, Econo Inn, Council Rd RV Park, Ford/Peterbilt, truckwash
140	Morgan Rd, N Pilot/McDonald's/dsl/24hr/@, TA/Popeyes/Fazoli's/dsl/24hr/@, Blue Beacon, S Flying J/Huddle House/dsl/LP/scales/24hr, Love's/Subway/dsl/scales/24hr, Braum's Ice Cream, Sonic, Speedco
139	Kilpatrick Tpk
138	OK 4, to Yukon, Mustang, N Catfish Cove, Best Value Inn, Comfort Suites, Studio 6, Chrysler/Dodge/Jeep, vet, S Casey's Pizza, All American Pizza, Braum's, Burger King, Golden Chick, IHOP, Interurban Grill, McDonald's, Sonic, Subway, Taco Bell, Thai Orchid, Best Western+, Home2 Suites, La Quinta, Aamco, CVS Drug, Homeland Food/drug, Mustang Run RV Park, URGENT CARE
137	Cornwell Dr, Czech Hall Rd, N OnCue/dsl, Homeland Food/drug, URGENT CARE, S Mo' Bettahs, Sleep Inn
136	OK 92, Garth Brooks Blvd, Yukon, N Casey's, Murphy USA/dsl, A&W/LJ Silver, Braum's, Cane's, Chelino's Mexican, CiCi's Pizza, KFC, McDonald's, Popeyes, Primo's Italian, Subway, Waffle House, Wendy's, Hampton Inn, $Tree, AutoZone, Big O Tire, NAPA, repair, Sprouts Mkt, T-Mobile, Tuesday Morning, USPO, Walgreens, Walmart, S Shell/dsl, Alfredo's Mexican, Arby's, Buffalo Wild Wings, Carino's Italian, Cheddar's, Chick-fil-A, Chicken Express, Chili's, Del Taco, DQ, Freddy's, Hawaiian Bros, Hideaway Pizza, Hooters, Jersey Mike's, Jimmy's Egg Café, Logan's Roadhouse, LongHorn Steaks, Louie's Grill, McAlister's Deli, Panda Express, Pauline's Kitchen, Pizza Hut, RibCrib, Sapporo Japanese, Schlotzsky's, Sonic, Starbucks, Taco Bueno, Taco Casa, Tokyo Moon, Avid Hotel, Fairfield Inn, Holiday Inn Express, Sleep Inn, ALDI, AT&T, Big Lots, Discount Tire, Ford, GNC, Hobby Lobby, H, Kohl's, Lowe's, lube & service, Marshall's, Petco, PetSmart, Ross, Staples, Target/Starbucks, tire repair
135	Frisco Rd
132	Cimarron Rd, S
130	Banner Rd
129mm	weigh sta both lanes
127	S Radio Rd, S Love's/Carl's Jr/dsl/scales/24hr
125	US 81, to El Reno, N Love's/Subway/dsl, Phillips 66/dsl, Shell/dsl, Chelino's Mexican, China King, Swadley's BBQ, Taco Mayo, Wendy's, Hotel 81, Ranger Motel, $General, Buick/GMC, Chevrolet, Chrysler/Dodge/Jeep, Ford, Ford/Lincoln, URGENT CARE
123	Country Club Rd, to El Reno, N Casey's, Murphy USA/dsl, Shell/dsl, Valero/dsl, Arby's, Braum's, Burger King, Domino's, Greatwall Chinese, KFC, McDonald's, Pizza Hut, Pizza Xpress, Subway, Taco Bell, Ume Japanese, Fairfield Inn, Hampton Inn, Home2 Suites, Motel 6, AT&T, AutoZone, H, Walgreens, Walmart, S Mama Cha Cha's, MT Mikes Steaks, Baymont Inn, Best Western/RV Park, Days Inn, Holiday Inn Express, Regency Motel
119	Lp 40, to El Reno
115	US 270, to Calumet
111mm	picnic area eb, picnic tables, litter barrels
108	US 281, to Geary, N Shell/Subway/dsl/24hr,

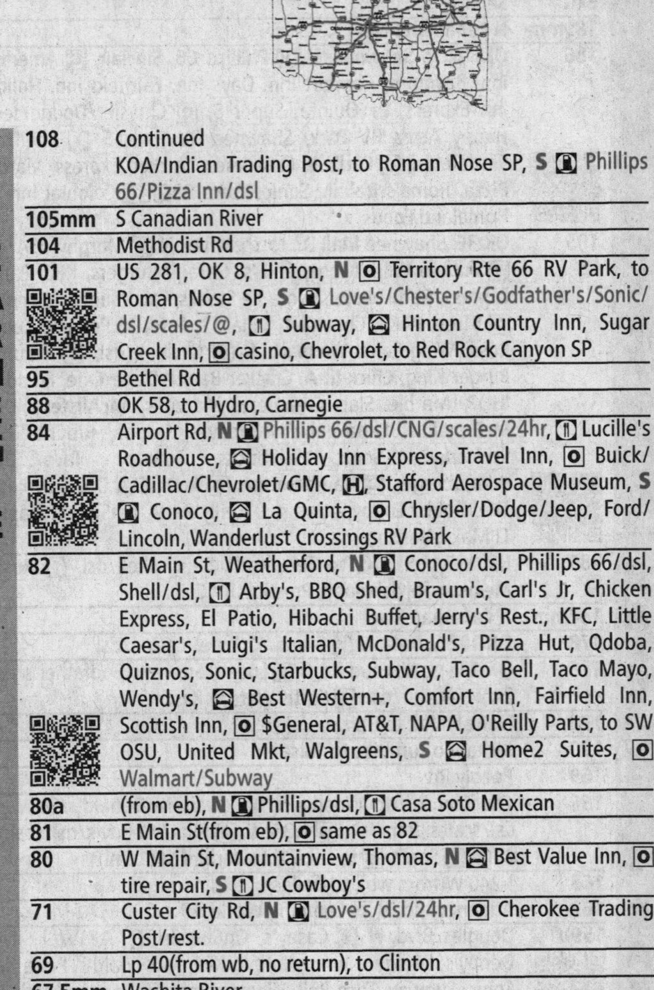

CARNEGIE

CLINTON

ELK CITY

Exit	Services
108	Continued KOA/Indian Trading Post, to Roman Nose SP, S Phillips 66/Pizza Inn/dsl
105mm	S Canadian River
104	Methodist Rd
101	US 281, OK 8, Hinton, N Territory Rte 66 RV Park, to Roman Nose SP, S Love's/Chester's/Godfather's/Sonic/dsl/scales/@, Subway, Hinton Country Inn, Sugar Creek Inn, casino, Chevrolet, to Red Rock Canyon SP
95	Bethel Rd
88	OK 58, to Hydro, Carnegie
84	Airport Rd, N Phillips 66/dsl/CNG/scales/24hr, Lucille's Roadhouse, Holiday Inn Express, Travel Inn, Buick/Cadillac/Chevrolet/GMC, H, Stafford Aerospace Museum, S Conoco, La Quinta, Chrysler/Dodge/Jeep, Ford/Lincoln, Wanderlust Crossings RV Park
82	E Main St, Weatherford, N Conoco/dsl, Phillips 66/dsl, Shell/dsl, Arby's, BBQ Shed, Braum's, Carl's Jr, Chicken Express, El Patio, Hibachi Buffet, Jerry's Rest., KFC, Little Caesar's, Luigi's Italian, McDonald's, Pizza Hut, Qdoba, Quiznos, Sonic, Starbucks, Subway, Taco Bell, Taco Mayo, Wendy's, Best Western+, Comfort Inn, Fairfield Inn, Scottish Inn, $General, AT&T, NAPA, O'Reilly Parts, to SW OSU, United Mkt, Walgreens, S Home2 Suites, Walmart/Subway
80a	(from eb), N Phillips/dsl, Casa Soto Mexican
81	E Main St(from eb), same as 82
80	W Main St, Mountainview, Thomas, N Best Value Inn, tire repair, S JC Cowboy's
71	Custer City Rd, N Love's/dsl/24hr, Cherokee Trading Post/rest.
69	Lp 40(from wb, no return), to Clinton
67.5mm	Washita River
66	US 183, Clinton, S Shell/dsl, Ford
65a	10th St, Neptune Dr, Clinton, N Branding Iron Rest., Canelo's Mexican, China King, Picante Grille, Days Inn, Relax Inn, Super 8, United Foods, S Phillips 66/dsl, EconoLodge, Hargus RV Park
65	Gary Blvd, Clinton, N Hutch/dsl, Braum's, KFC/Taco Bell, Lucille's Roadhouse, Mazzio's, McDonald's, Palacios Mexican, Pizza Hut, Sleep's Bakery, Subway, T C's Kitchen, Taco Mayo, Hampton Inn, Motel 6, Tradewinds Inn, $General, $Tree, H, K-Mart, Rte 66 Museum, S Holiday Inn Express, La Quinta
62	Parkersburg Rd, N Jiggs BBQ, S Matt's RV Ctr
61	Haggard Rd
57	Stafford Rd
53	OK 44, Foss, S Conoco
50	Clinton Lake Rd, N KOA/LP/dsl
47	Canute, S Shell/dsl
41	OK 34(exits left from eb), Elk City, N Love's/Subway/dsl, Phillips 66/dsl, Econo Lodge, Hiway Inn, La Quinta, Motel 6, Red Carpet Inn, Sleep Inn, Super 8, Elk Run RV Park, H
40	E 7th St, Elk City, N Holiday Inn Express, Chrysler/Dodge/Jeep, S Hutch's/dsl/CNG, Burger King, Huddle House, Rib Crib, Starbucks, Wendy's, Hampton Inn, Hobby Lobby, same as 41, Walmart/McDonald's
38	OK 6, Elk City, N Conoco/dsl, Phillips 66/dsl, Arby's, Boomtown Grill, China Super Buffet, Fred's Steakhouse, Janice's Cafe, McDonald's, Bedford Inn, Best Value,

OK

INTERSTATE 40 Cont'd

Exit	Services
38	Continued Ace Hardware, Elk Creek RV Park, tires, S Phillips 66/dsl, Best Western+, Comfort Inn, Elks Inn, Elk City RV Ctr, to Quartz Mtn SP
34	Merritt Rd
32	OK 34 S(exits left from eb), Elk City
26	Cemetery Rd, N I-40 Travel Plaza/dsl, dsl repair, S TA/Taco Bell/Subway/dsl/scales/24hr/@
25	Lp 40, Sayre, N Hutch's/dsl/CNG, Western Motel, Bobcat Creek RV Park, Chevrolet/GMC, Ford
23	OK 152, Sayre
22.5mm	N Fork Red River
20	US 283, Sayre, N Flying J/Denny's/dsl/LP/RV dump/scales/24hr, McDonald's, AmericInn, Sayre RV Park, to Washita Bfd Site(25mi), truck lube, truckwash
14	Hext Rd
13.5mm	check sta both lanes, litter barrels
11	Lp 40, to Erick, Hext
10mm	**full facilities, litter barrels, petwalk, RV dump, Welcome Ctr eb/**
7	OK 30, Erick, S Love's/Subway/dsl/scales/EVC, Simple Simon's Pizza, Days Inn, $General
5	Lp 40, Honeyfarm Rd
1	weigh Sta eb
1	Texola, S RV camping
0mm	Oklahoma/Texas state line

INTERSTATE 44

Exit	Services
329mm	Oklahoma/Missouri state line
321mm	Spring River
314mm	Oklahoma Welcome Ctr wb, full facilities
313	OK 10, Miami, N Love's/dsl, Phillips 66, Phillips 66/dsl, Donut Palace, Subway, Days Inn, Deluxe Inn, Hampton Inn, Holiday Inn Express, Microtel, OYO, Woodridge Inn, auto repair, H, Miami RV Park, to NE OK A&M Coll, S Chrysler/Dodge/Jeep
312mm	Neosho River
302	US 59, US 69, Afton, S Buffalo Ranch/Simple Simon/dsl, Rte 66 Motel, $General
289	US 60, Vinita, N Murphy USA/dsl, Braum's, Cesar's Place, Clanton's Cafe, Goodfellas Pizza, McDonald's, Pizza Hut, Ropin' Flamingo, Sonic, Subway, Taco Bell, Woodshed Deli, Holiday Inn Express, Vinita Inn, $General, $Tree, Ace Hardware, Chevrolet, H, O'Reilly Parts, st patrol, USPO, Walmart
288mm	service plaza both lanes, **Kum&Go/dsl**, McDonald's, Subway
286mm	toll plaza
283	US 69, Big Cabin, N Love's/Carl's Jr/dsl/scales/24hr, Phillips 66/Simon's Pizza/dsl/scales/24hr/@, Super 8, Cabin RV Park, trk repair
269	OK 28(from eb, no re-entry), to Adair, Chelsea
255	OK 20, to Pryor, Claremore, N Kum&Go/dsl/e85, Murphy USA/dsl, QT/dsl, Boomerang Diner, Carl's Jr, Chick-fil-A, Domino's Pizza, New Star Chinese, Pizza Hut, Hampton Inn, Holiday Inn Express, La Quinta, Super 8, Travel Inn, Will Rogers Inn, $General, AT&T, H, museum, O'Reilly Parts, to Rogers U, Walgreens, Walmart, Will Rogers Memorial
248	to OK 266, Port of Catoosa, N QT/dsl, Microtel(2mi), Lazydays RV Ctr
244mm	Kerr-McClellan Navigation System
241mm	Will Rogers Tpk begins eb, ends wb
241b	US 412 E(34 from wb), Choteau
241	(35 from wb)OK 66 E, to Catoosa
240a	OK 167 N, 193rd E Ave, N Freddy's, IHOP, McDonald's,
240a	Continued OK Joe's BBQ, Olive Garden, Panda Express, Taco Bell, Taco Bueno, Waffle House, Wendy's, Cherokee Inn/Casino, Fairfield Inn, Hampton Inn, Hardrock Hotel/Casino, Homewood Suites, La Quinta, AT&T, Petco, Ross, Walgreens, Walmart, S QT, China Bowl, Flo's Burgers, Mazzio's, Port City Diner, Sonic, Comfort Suites, Motel 6, Rodeway Inn, $General, Hall Of Fame RV Park, O'Reilly Parts, tires/repair
238	161st E Ave, N **Cherokee Nation Welcome Ctr**, QT/dsl/scales/24hr, truckwash, S Arby's, Burger King, Microtel, truckwash
236b	I-244 W, to downtown Tulsa, N
236a	129th E Ave, N Flying J/Denny's/dsl/LP/24hr, Southern Tire Mart, S McDonald's
235	E 11th St, Tulsa, N QT/dsl, Mazzio's, Molcajetes Mexican, Sonic, Subway, Economy Inn, Executive Inn, Nights Stay, OYO, $General, O'Reilly Parts, Walgreens, S Braum's, Price Mart
234b	same as 235
234a	US 169, N to Owasso, S to Broken Arrow, to airport
233	E 21st St, N Golden Corral, Camping World RV Ctr, S El Chico, vet
231	US 64, OK 51, to Muskogee, E 31st St, Memorial Dr, N QT/dsl, D'oro Pizza, Speedy Gonzales Mexican, Delux Inn, Hometown Inn & Suites, OYO, Ramada Inn, Walgreens, S Phillips 66, Cracker Barrel, IHOP, McDonald's, Pizza Hut, Ruby Tuesday, Best Value Inn, Best Western+, Clarion, Comfort Suites, Courtyard, Days Inn, Embassy Suites, Extended Stay America, Fairfield Inn, Hampton Inn, Motel 6, Quality Suites, Sleep Inn, Cavender's Boots, Chevrolet, Harley-Davidson, Nissan
230	E 41st St, Sheridan Rd, N Carl's Jr, Chick-fil-A, Desi Wok, Jimmy John's, On-the-Border, Panera Bread, Schlotzsky's, Smoothie King, Starbucks, Top That! Pizza, Whatburger, AT&T, Barnes&Noble, Cartec Automotive, Firestone, Jo-Ann Fabrics, Michael's, Old Navy, Petco, PetSmart, Reasor's Foods, Ross, Verizon, S Buffalo Wild Wings, Shawkat's Mediterranean, La Quinta, Best Buy, Home Depot
229	Yale Ave, Tulsa, N Carl's Jr., McDonald's, Dillard's, Firestone/auto, S Kum&Go/dsl/e85, QT, Andy's Custard, Applebee's, Arby's, Braum's, Cane's, Delta Kitchen, Jack-in-the-Box, Outback Steaks, Qdoba, Red Lobster, Saltgrass Steaks, Sonic, Taco Bell, The Bros. Houligan, Village Inn, Waffle That!, Comfort Inn, Extended Stay, Hilton Garden, Holiday Inn Express, Red Roof Inn, Residence Inn, H, Kia, vet
228	Harvard Ave, Tulsa, N QT/dsl, Casa Tequila Mexican, McDonald's, NYC Pizza, Tradewinds Motel, S A&W/LJ Silver, Bodean Seafood, Chili's, Jamil's Rest, Mario's Pizza, Papa John's, Starbucks, Sushi Train, Wingate Inn, $Tree, Hobby Lobby
227	Lewis Ave, Tulsa, S QT/dsl, Walgreens
226b	Peoria Ave, Tulsa, N QT/dsl, Arby's, Biga Italian, Brookside Diner, Burger St., China Wok, CiCi's, Egg Roll Express, Fajitas Mexican, KFC, Little Caesar's, Mazzio's, Subway, Super Wok, Taco Bell, Taco Bueno, Peoria Inn, $Tree, Harley-Davidson, O'Reilly Parts, Robertson Tire, Verizon, Walmart Mkt, Whole Foods Mkt, S Braum's, Sin Fronteras Mexican, $General, AutoZone, Family$, Walgreens
226a	Riverside Dr
225mm	no services
225	Elwood Ave, N Chevrolet, Ford, S Budget Inn
224b a	US 75, to Okmulgee, Bartlesville, N QT/dsl, KFC, Linda-Mar, Mazzio's, Sonic, Taco Bell, $General, vet, Whse Mkt, S Royal Inn, Hurley RV Ctr, Warrior RV Park

= gas = food = lodging = other = rest stop

INTERSTATE 44 Cont'd

Exit #	Services
223c	33rd W Ave, Tulsa, N Braum's, Domino's, S Conoco, Rib Crib BBQ
223b	51st St(from wb)
223a	I-244 E, to Tulsa, downtown
222c	(from wb), S Value Inn
222b	55th Place, N Crystal Motel, Rest Inn, S Best Value Inn, Winston's Inn
222a	49th W Ave, Tulsa, N Carl's Jr, Monterey Mexican, Subway, Gateway Motel, Interstate Inn, Motel 6, $General, BigLots, Mack Trucks, S QT/Kitchens/dsl/scales/24hr, Arby's, Freeway Cafe, McDonald's, Taco Bueno, Waffle House, Comfort Inn, Super 8, Buick/GMC, Freightliner, Kenworth
221a	57th W Ave, from wb, S Buick/GMC
221mm	Turner Tkp begins wb, ends eb
218	Creek Tpk E(from eb)
215	OK 97, to Sand Sprgs, Sapulpa, N QT, $General, S Kum&Go/dsl/e85, Freddie's Rest., La Margarita Mexican, Super 8, H, Hunter RV Ctr, Route 66 RV Park, Whispering Oaks RV Camping
211	OK 33, to Kellyville, Drumright, S Phillips 66, Heyburn Lake SP
207	no services
196	OK 48, Bristow, S Kenny's/dsl, Phillips 66/dsl, Boomerang Diner, Los Arcos Mexican, McDonald's, Patrona Mexican, Pizza Hut, Sonic, Steak'nEgg Rest, Subway, Taco Mayo, Carolyn Inn, $General, $Tree, Ford, O'Reilly Parts, train museum, Walmart
182mm	toll plaza
179	OK 99, to Drumright, Stroud, N Ranch House Rest., Cattle Country Lodge, S Kids/dsl, Phillips 66/Subway/dsl, 5Star BBQ, Cozumel Mexican, McDonald's, Sonic, Hampton Inn, Skyliner Motel, Sooner Motel, auto/tire repair, H, USPO
178mm	Hoback Plaza both lanes(exits left), Phillips 66/dsl, McDonald's
167mm	service plaza(from eb), Phillips 66/dsl
166	OK 18, to Cushing, Chandler, S Phillips 66/dsl, Sonic, Lincoln Motel, Chandler Tire, Chevrolet/GMC, Ford
158	OK 66, to Wellston, N Phillips 66/Subway/dsl/24hr, Butcher BBQ, $General
147	N Luther Rd
146	Luther-Jones
138d	to Memorial Rd, to Enterprise Square
138a	I-35, I-44 E to Tulsa, Turner Tpk
135mm	Turner Tpk begins eb, ends wb
130	I-35 S, to Dallas, access to services on I-35 S
129	MLK Ave, Remington Park, N Park Hill Inn, Cowboy Museum, S McDonald's, Sonic, Subway, Family$
128b	Kelley Ave, OK City, N Conoco, VP/Subway/dsl, Gabriella's Italian
128a	Lincoln Blvd, S Lincoln Mart/dsl, Lincoln Inn Express, Oxford Inn, st capitol
127	I-235 S, US 77, City Ctr, Broadway St, N Conoco/Circle K, Shell/Circle K, Holiday Inn, Surestay, URGENT CARE
126	Western Ave, S Sleep Inn
125c	NW Expressway(exits left from sb)
125	Classen Blvd, (exits left from wb), OK City, N Cheesecake Factory, Chili's, Freebirds Burrito, Jamba Juice, Olive Garden, Pei Wei, Smashburger, Subway, Whiskey Cake Kitchen, AT&T, Dillard's, JC Penney, Macy's, Old Navy, Ross, Verizon, Walmart/McDonald's, S IHOP, McDonald's, Milagro Mexican, Courtyard, Hyatt Place
125a	OK 3A, Penn Ave, to NW Expswy, S Valero, Braum's, Casey's, OYO, auto/tire repair, Family$
124	N May, N Shell/Circle K/Subway, Azteca Mexican, Days Inn, Motel 6, Super 8, O'Reilly Parts, Sam's Club/dsl, S Phillips 66, Dunkin', Patty Wagon Burgers, Starbucks, Wendy's, Aamco, Advance Parts, Family$, Ford, Lowe's
123b	OK 66 W, NW 39th, to Warr Acres, N 7-11, Phillips 66/dsl, Shell, Arby's, Braum's, Carl's Jr, Dunkin', Jimmy's Egg, KFC, McDonald's, Sonic, Taco Bell, Wingstop, Hity Inn, Family$, U-Haul, URGENT CARE, WinCo
123a	NW 36th St, S Woodspring Suites
122	NW 23rd St, N 7-11, Church's TX Chicken, EggRoll King, Tires+, S Arby's, Sonic, Family$
121b a	NW 10th St, N OnCue/dsl, Taqueria Mexican, S 7-11, Shamrock, $General, fairgrounds, Family$, Whittaker's Foods
120b a	I-40, W to Amarillo, E to Ft Smith
119	SW 15th St
118	OK 152 W, SW 29th St, OK City, E 7-11, Citgo, Burger King, CiCi's Pizza, El Tarasco, Jimmy's Egg, KFC, McDonald's, Pizza Hut, Sonic, Starbucks, $General, $Tree, Advance Parts, AT&T, AutoZone, Buy-4-Less Foods, city park, O'Reilly Parts, Walgreens, W Alon/dsl, El Majahual Salvadoran, Taqueria Durango, Budget Inn, city park, transmissions, U-Haul/LP
117	SW 44th St, E Gorditas Mexican
116b	Airport Rd (exits left from nb), W
116a	SW 59th St, E Caseys/Circle K, Las Palamas, Sonic, Subway, Trompudo's Tacos, Waffle House, $General, Family$, W Will Rogers
115	I-240 E, US 62 E, to Ft Smith
114	SW 74th St, OK City, E Nova, Braum's, Burger King, Perry's Rest., Cambridge Inn, Motel 6, $General
113	SW 89th St, E 7-11, Love's/Subway/dsl, Valero/dsl, Buffalo Wild Wings, Cajun Corner, Sonic, CVS Drug, H
112	SW 104th St, E Valero, Arby's, Krave, McDonald's, Salad & Go, Starbucks, Subway, Taco Bell, Victoria's Italian, $General, Crest Mkt/EVC, Firestone/auto, Verizon, Walmart
111	SW 119th St, E 7-11, On Cue/dsl, Little Caesar's, Sonic
110	OK 37 E, to Moore, E H
109	SW 149th St, E JR's Grill
108mm	S Canadian River
108	OK 37 W, to Tuttle, W Conoco/dsl, Phillips 66/dsl, Arby's, Braum's, Carlito's Mexican, Creek Bottom Burgers, Domino's, Jimmy's Egg, KFC/Taco Bell, Little Caesar's, Luigi's Bistro, McDonald's, New China, Sonic, The Pizza Shop, $General, AT&T, AutoZone, O'Reilly Parts, RV General Store, Walgreens, Walmart/Subway
107	US 62 S(no wb return), to Newcastle, E Love's/Subway/Dunkin'/dsl/scales/24hr, Boomerang Diner, Pizza Hut, Comfort Inn, Newcastle Motel, casino, Newcastle RV
99	H E Bailey Spur, rd 4, to Blanchard, Tuttle, Norman
97mm	toll booth
85.5mm	service plaza, both lanes exit left, **Phillips 66/dsl**, **McDonald's**
83	US 62, Chickasha, W Jay's/dsl, Valero/dsl, Best Western+, Southern Plains Indian Museum(18mi)
80	US 81, Chickasha, E Casey's/dsl, Shell/dsl, Jake's Ribs, La Fiesta Mexican, Castle Inn, Fairfield Inn, Hampton Inn,

OK

INTERSTATE 44 Cont'd

CHICKASHA

Exit	Services
80	Continued Holiday Inn Express, Maverick Inn, Super 8, Buick/GMC, Cadillac/Chevrolet, Chrysler/Dodge/Jeep, Pecan Grove RV Camping, vet, **W** Love's/dsl, Murphy USA/dsl, Valero, Arby's, Boomerang Diner, Braum's, Chicken Express, China Dream, China Moon, Cotton Patch Cafe, Domino's, Interurban of Chickasha, KFC, Little Caesar's, Mama Carol's, McDonald's, Napoli's Italian, Paw Paw's Burgers, Pizza Hut, Sims BBQ, Sonic, Subway, Taco Bell, Taco Mayo, Tropical Cafe, Wendy's, Budget Inn, Burger King, Quality Inn, Regency Inn, $General, $Tree, Ace Hardware, ALDI, AT&T, AutoZone, Chickasha RV Park, CVS Drug, Ford, Griffith's Repair, H, O'Reilly Parts, Ralph&Son's Tires/repair, URGENT CARE, Verizon, Walgreens, Walmart/Subway
78	no services
66mm	toll plaza both lanes
62	to Cyril(from wb)
53	US 277, Elgin, Lake Ellsworth, **E** Sunoco, Billy Sim's BBQ, Braum's, China Garden, McDonald's, Sonic, Subway, $General, Family$, tires
46	US 62 E, US 277, US 281, to Elgin, Apache, Comanche Tribe, last free exit eb
45	OK 49, to Medicine Park, **W** Love's/Subway/dsl/24hr, Burger King, Sonic, $General, Wichita NWR
41	to Ft Sill, Key Gate, **W** Ft Sill Museum
40c	Gate 2, to Ft Sill
40a	to Cache
39	US 62 W, to Cache, **E** Alon/dsl, **W** Castle Inn
39b	US 281(from sb), same as 39a
39a	US 281, Cache Rd (exits left from nb), Lawton, **E** Alon/dsl, $General, **W** Stripes/dsl, Valero/dsl, Castle Inn, $General
38	Cache Rd(exits left from nb)
37	Gore Blvd, Lawton, **E** Apache/dsl, Braum's, Los Tres Amigos, Marco's Pizza, Sonic, Taco Mayo, URGENT CARE, Apache Casino/Hotel, Extended Stay, SureStay+, casino, USPO, **W** Cracker Barrel, Mike's Grille, Salas Cantina, Comfort Suites, Fairfield Inn, Hilton Garden/EVC, Holiday Inn Express, Homewood Suites, MySuites, Sleep Inn, $Tree, AT&T, Chrysler/Dodge/Jeep, Dick's, Harley-Davidson, Jo-Ann, Kohl's, Nissan, Petco
36a	OK 7, Lee Blvd, Lawton, **E** Mark's/dsl, **W** Alon/dsl/repair, Barefoot/dsl, Stripes/dsl, Valero/dsl, Braum's, Burger King, Leo&Ken's Rest., McDonald's, Nana's Grill, Tu Familia Mexican, Wright's Diner, Lawton Inn, Motel 6, $General, $Tree, Advance Parts, CVS Drug, H, vet
33	US 281, 11th St, Lawton, **W**
30	OK 36(last free exit sb), Geronimo
20.5mm	Elmer Graham Plaza(both lanes exit left), **info**, **Phillips 66/dsl**, **Back 40 BBQ**
20	OK 5, to Walters
19.5mm	toll plaza
5	US 277 N, US 281, Randlett, last free exit nb, **E** Love's/Subway/dsl/scales/24hr
1	OK 36, to Grandfield, **E** Comanche Nation TP/dsl, **W** Kiowa Hotel/casino
0mm	Oklahoma/Texas state line, Red River

KEY GATE · LAWTON

INTERSTATE 240 (Okla City)

SANTA FE

Exit	Services
16mm	I-240 begins/ends on I-40.
14	Anderson Rd, **S** Conoco/dsl
11b a	Douglas Blvd, **N** Tinker AFB
9	Air Depot Blvd
8	OK 77, Sooner Rd, **N** OnCue/dsl/CNG/e85, Sonic, URGENT CARE, **S** McDonald's, Phillips 66/Popeyes/dsl, H
7	Sunnylane Ave, **S** Valero/Subway/dsl, Woodspring Suites
6	Bryant Ave
5	S Eastern Ave
4c	Pole Rd, **N** Burger King, TX Roadhouse, Residence Inn, Wingate
4b a	I-35, N to OK City, S to Dallas, US 77 S, US 62/77 N
3b	S Shields, **N** Valero/dsl, Braum's, Home Depot, **S** Discount Tire, Fun Town RV, Nissan
3a	S Santa Fe, **N** Chrysler/Dodge/Jeep, Kia, **S** Murphy USA/dsl, Chili's, IHOP, Jersey Mike's, Panda Express, Lowe's, Staples, Walmart/McDonald's
2b	S Walker Ave, **N** 7-11, Casey's/Circle K, RibCrib, **S** Burger Joint, Carino's, ChuckeCheese, City Bites, Jimmy's Egg Grill, Holiday Inn Express, PepBoys
2a	S Western Ave, **N** 7-11, Braum's, Burger King, CiCi's Pizza, House of Szechwan, Taste of China, $General, Advance Parts, Hyundai, Tires+, vet, **S** 7-11, VP, A&W/LJ Silver, Chick-fil-A, Garage Burgers, Grandy's, Hibachi Buffet, Jimmy John's, KFC, McDonald's, Popeyes, Red Lobster, Best Western+, Comfort Inn, Hampton Inn, Home2 Suites, Super Inn, Chevrolet, Honda, Office Depot
1c	S Penn Ave, **N** Cane's, Charleston's Rest., Denny's, Golden Corral, Hooters, Olive Garden, Outback Steaks, Pier 88 Seafood, SaltGrass Steaks, Schlotsky's, AT&T, Best Buy, BigLots, GNC, Green Acres Mkt, Hobby Lobby, Marshall's, Michaels, Old Navy, PetSmart, Ross, Verizon, **S** Goodstop, Crawfish Pot, Del Taco, Mazzio's, Papa John's, Starbucks, Taco Bueno, $Tree, Family$, URGENT CARE
1b	S May Ave, **N** 7-11/gas, Phillips 66, Jack-in-theBox, Taco Bell, Taqueria Express, Grand Mart, O'Reilly Parts, **S** Nova, Braum's, Burger King, Perry's Rest., Cambridge Inn, Motel 6, $General, auto/tire repair
1a	I-44, US 62, I-240 begins ends on I-44.

OK

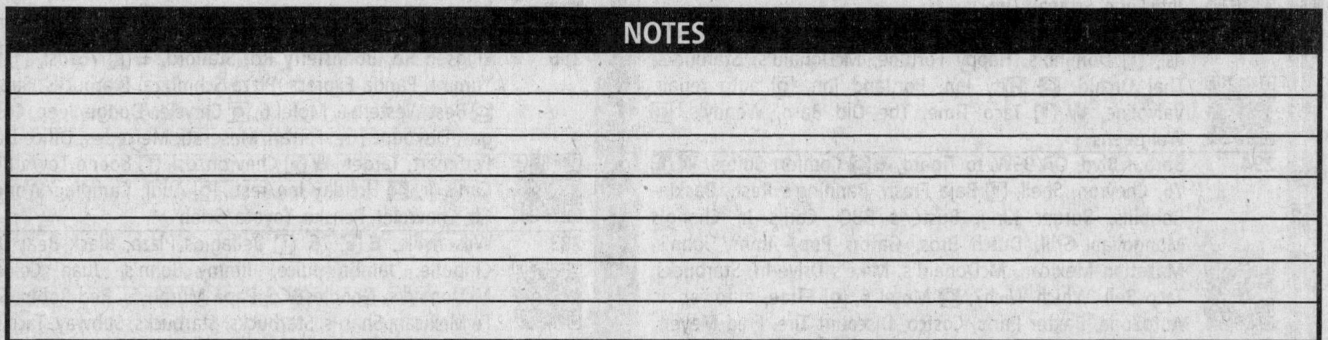

OREGON

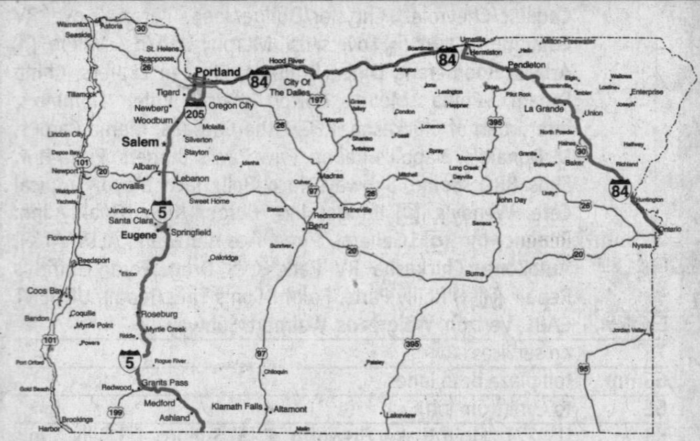

INTERSTATE 5

DELTA PARK

Exit #	Services
308.5mm	Oregon/Washington state line, Columbia River
308	Jansen Beach Dr, E Chevron/dsl, Burger King, JayBee's Palace, La Quebrada Mexican, Taco Bell, Holiday Inn, Oxford Suites, W Boomers, Denny's, Jersey Mike's, Jimmy John's, McDonald's, Panera Bread, Starbucks, Holiday Inn Express, Rodeway Inn, Best Buy, Burlington Coats, Home Depot, Jansen Beach RV Park, Michael's, PetCo, Ross, Staples, Target, TJ Maxx
307	OR 99E S, MLK Blvd, Union Ave, Marine Dr (sb only), E 76/dsl, Jubitz Trvl Ctr/rest/dsl/@, Doughboys, Heavy Plays Rest., Portland Cascade Grill, Courtyard, Fairfield Inn, Portlander Inn, Residence Inn, auto repair, Blue Beacon, tires, truck repair, W Expo Ctr
306b	Interstate Ave, Delta Park, E Chevron, Burger King, Shari's, Country Inn & Suites, Inn at the Meadows, Motel 6, $Tree, Baxter Parts, Dick's, Lowe's, vet
306a	same as 306b, from nb, Columbia, E U-Haul
305b a	US 30, Lombard St(from nb, no return), E Little Caesar's, Mi Burrito Mexican, W Astro/dsl, Chevron, Shell/dsl, Heavenly Donuts, Northside Rest., Panda Express, Wendy's, 7-11, Fred Meyer
304	Rosa Parks Way, E Peninsula Park, W 76/dsl, Arco, Nite Hawk Cafe, Viking Motel, New Seasons Mkt, U of Portland
303	Alberta St, Swan Island, E H, W Taco Bell, Monticello Motel, Westerner Motel, park, URGENT CARE
302b	I-405, US 30 W, W to ocean beaches
302a	Rose Qtr, City Ctr, E 76/dsl, Shell, Shell/dsl, Burger King, Chipotle Mexican, Five Guys, Habaneros Mexican, Jimmy Johns, McDonald's, Qdoba Mexican, Starbucks, Subway, Taco Bell, Wendy's, Courtyard, Crowne Plaza, Shiloh Inn, $Tree, 7-11, AT&T, H, Safeway, Schwab Tire, Toyota/Scion, U-Haul, Verizon, Walgreens, W coliseum
301	I-84 E, US 30 E, services E off I-84 exits
300	US 26 E(from sb), Milwaukie Ave, W Courtyard, Embassy Suites, Hilton, Marriott, The Nines Hotel, The Royal Sonesta, Powell's Books
299b	I-405, US 26 W
299a	US 26 E, OR 43(from nb), City Ctr, to Lake Oswego
298	Corbett Ave
297	Terwilliger Blvd, W Baja Fresh, KFC, Starbucks, Taco Bell, Fred Meyer, H, to Lewis and Clark Coll., to OR Health & Science U, Verizon
296b	Multnomah Blvd (from sb) same as 296a, W Safeway
296a	(from sb), Barbur, W Chevron/dsl, Bellagio's Pizza, El Jalisco, Muchas Gracias, Subway, The Pancake House, Aladdin Inn, Budget Lodge, Capitol Hill Motel, 7-11, AT&T, Jiffy Lube, Schwab Tire
295	Capitol Hwy(from sb), Taylors Ferry Rd(from nb), E Shell/dsl, Domino's, Happy Fortune, McDonald's, Starbucks, Thai Orchid, Hity Inn, Portland Inn, auto repair, Valvoline, W Taco Time, The Old Barn, Wendy's, Walgreens
294	Barbur Blvd, OR 99W, to Tigard, E Comfort Suites, W 76, Chevron, Shell, Baja Fresh, Banning's Rest., Baskin-Robbins, Burger King, Buster's BBQ, Carl's Jr, Chang's Mongolian Grill, Dutch Bros, Gators Pub, Jimmy John's, Mazatlan Mexican, McDonald's, Mike's Drive-In, Starbucks, Taco Bell, Which Wich?, Motel 6, $Tree, auto repair, AutoZone, Baxter Parts, Costco, Discount Tire, Fred Meyer,
294	Continued PetCo, PetSmart, Schwab Tire, transmissions, U-Haul, URGENT CARE, Verizon, vet, Walmart/Subway, Winco Foods
293	Haines St, W Hampton Inn
292	OR 217, Kruse Way, Lake Oswego, E Shell/dsl, Applebee's, Chipotle, Killer Burger, Olive Garden, Oswego Grill, Pizzicato, Stanford's Rest., Starbucks, Best Western, Crowne Plaza, Fairfield Inn, Hilton Garden, Residence Inn, AAA, LDS Temple, W Extended Stay America, Lowe's
291	Carman Dr, Carman Dr, E Trader Joe's, W 76/dsl, Chevron, Burgerville, El Sol De Mexico, Munch, Starbucks, Subway, Courtyard, Holiday Inn Express, Home Depot, Office Depot, vet
290	Lower Boonsferry Rd, Lake Oswego, E Chevron/dsl, Space Age/dsl/LP, Baja Fresh, Baskin-Robbins, Burger King, Cafe Yumm, Carl's Jr., Miller's Rest., Panda Express, See's Kitchen, Starbucks, Starbucks, Subway, Taco Bell, Motel 6, Dick's, Jiffy Lube, Safeway Foods, U-Haul, Walgreens, Walgreens, W CA Pizza Kitchen, Claim Jumper, Einstein Bros., Jamba Juice, Jimmy John's, McCormick&Schmick's, MOD Pizza, Pastini Pastaria, PF Chang's, Qdoba Mexican, Royal Panda, Shake Shack, Grand Hotel, Barnes&Noble, Verizon, Whole Foods Mkt
289	Tualatin, E 76, Shell/dsl, Chipotle Mexican, Domino's, El Sol De Mexico, Famous Dave's BBQ, Five Guys, Jamba Juice, McDonald's, Panera Bread, Starbucks, 7-11, Best Buy, H, Old Navy, PetSmart, Valvoline, vet, W Bellagios, Buffalo Wild Wings, Carl's Jr, Dave's Chicken, Donutland, Dutch Bros, Grab A Gyro, Jack-in-the-Box, Jersey Mike's, Las 4 Lunas, McDonald's, Outback Steaks, Papa Murphy's, Pieology Pizzaria, Red Robin, Shari's, Starbucks, Starbucks, Subway, Taco Bell, Wendy's, Century Hotel, Comfort Inn, Batteries+, Cabela's, Fred Meyer, Michael's, New Seasons Mkt, O'Reilly Parts, PetCo, Staples, TJ Maxx, Valvoline, vet, vet
288	I-205, to Oregon City
286	Elligsen Rd, Boonsferry Rd, Stafford, E 76/dsl, Cafe Yumm!, Panda Express, Pizza Schmizza, Starbucks, Subway, Best Western+, Motel 6, Chrysler/Dodge/Jeep, Costco/gas, Discount Tire, Ferrari/Maserati, Mercedes, Office Depot, PetSmart, Target, W Chevron/dsl, Boone Town Bistro, Carl's Jr, Holiday Inn/rest., Audi, Camping World RV Ctr, Chevrolet, Penske, Toyota/Scion
283	Wilsonville, E 76, Bellagios Pizza, Black Bear Diner, Chipotle, Jamba Juice, Jimmy John's, Juan Colorado, McDonald's, Noodles&Co, Papa Murphy's, Red Robin, Santa Fe Mexican, Shari's, Starbucks, Starbucks, Subway, Taco Bell,

CITY CTR

BARBUR

LAKE OSWEGO

STAFFORD

OR

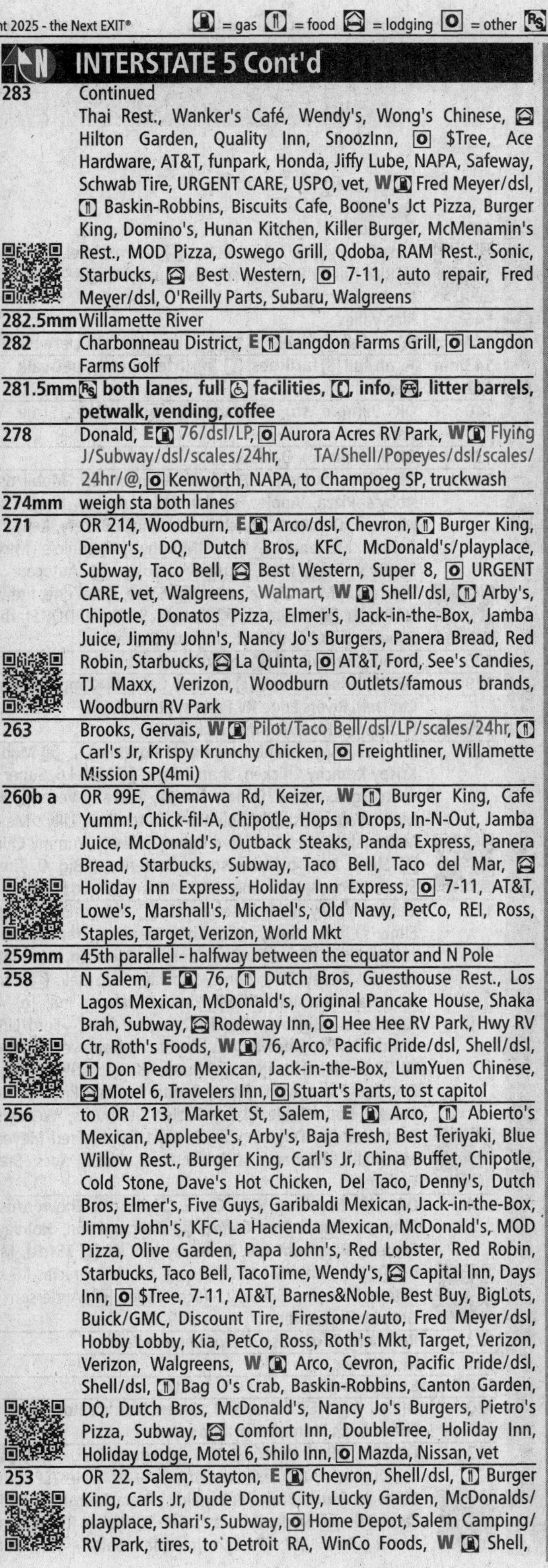

INTERSTATE 5 Cont'd

CHARBONNEAU DISTRICT

283 Continued
Thai Rest., Wanker's Café, Wendy's, Wong's Chinese, Hilton Garden, Quality Inn, SnoozInn, $Tree, Ace Hardware, AT&T, funpark, Honda, Jiffy Lube, NAPA, Safeway, Schwab Tire, URGENT CARE, USPO, vet, W Fred Meyer/dsl, Baskin-Robbins, Biscuits Cafe, Boone's Jct Pizza, Burger King, Domino's, Hunan Kitchen, Killer Burger, McMenamin's Rest., MOD Pizza, Oswego Grill, Qdoba, RAM Rest., Sonic, Starbucks, Best Western, 7-11, auto repair, Fred Meyer/dsl, O'Reilly Parts, Subaru, Walgreens

282.5mm Willamette River

282 Charbonneau District, E Langdon Farms Grill, Langdon Farms Golf

281.5mm **both lanes, full facilities, info, litter barrels, petwalk, vending, coffee**

278 Donald, E 76/dsl/LP, Aurora Acres RV Park, W Flying J/Subway/dsl/scales/24hr, TA/Shell/Popeyes/dsl/scales/24hr/@, Kenworth, NAPA, to Champoeg SP, truckwash

274mm weigh sta both lanes

271 OR 214, Woodburn, E Arco/dsl, Chevron, Burger King, Denny's, DQ, Dutch Bros, KFC, McDonald's/playplace, Subway, Taco Bell, Best Western, Super 8, URGENT CARE, vet, Walgreens, Walmart, W Shell/dsl, Arby's, Chipotle, Donatos Pizza, Elmer's, Jack-in-the-Box, Jamba Juice, Jimmy John's, Nancy Jo's Burgers, Panera Bread, Red Robin, Starbucks, La Quinta, AT&T, Ford, See's Candies, TJ Maxx, Verizon, Woodburn Outlets/famous brands, Woodburn RV Park

263 Brooks, Gervais, W Pilot/Taco Bell/dsl/LP/scales/24hr, Carl's Jr, Krispy Krunchy Chicken, Freightliner, Willamette Mission SP(4mi)

KEIZER

260b a OR 99E, Chemawa Rd, Keizer, W Burger King, Cafe Yumm!, Chick-fil-A, Chipotle, Hops n Drops, In-N-Out, Jamba Juice, McDonald's, Outback Steaks, Panda Express, Panera Bread, Starbucks, Subway, Taco Bell, Taco del Mar, Holiday Inn Express, Holiday Inn Express, 7-11, AT&T, Lowe's, Marshall's, Michael's, Old Navy, PetCo, REI, Ross, Staples, Target, Verizon, World Mkt

259mm 45th parallel - halfway between the equator and N Pole

SALEM

258 N Salem, E 76, Dutch Bros, Guesthouse Rest., Los Lagos Mexican, McDonald's, Original Pancake House, Shaka Brah, Subway, Rodeway Inn, Hee Hee RV Park, Hwy RV Ctr, Roth's Foods, W 76, Arco, Pacific Pride/dsl, Shell/dsl, Don Pedro Mexican, Jack-in-the-Box, LumYuen Chinese, Motel 6, Travelers Inn, Stuart's Parts, to st capitol

256 to OR 213, Market St, Salem, E Arco, Abierto's Mexican, Applebee's, Arby's, Baja Fresh, Best Teriyaki, Blue Willow Rest., Burger King, Carl's Jr, China Buffet, Chipotle, Cold Stone, Dave's Hot Chicken, Del Taco, Denny's, Dutch Bros, Elmer's, Five Guys, Garibaldi Mexican, Jack-in-the-Box, Jimmy John's, KFC, La Hacienda Mexican, McDonald's, MOD Pizza, Olive Garden, Papa John's, Red Lobster, Red Robin, Starbucks, Taco Bell, TacoTime, Wendy's, Capital Inn, Days Inn, $Tree, 7-11, AT&T, Barnes&Noble, Best Buy, BigLots, Buick/GMC, Discount Tire, Firestone/auto, Fred Meyer/dsl, Hobby Lobby, Kia, PetCo, Ross, Roth's Mkt, Target, Verizon, Verizon, Walgreens, W Arco, Cevron, Pacific Pride/dsl, Shell/dsl, Bag O's Crab, Baskin-Robbins, Canton Garden, DQ, Dutch Bros, McDonald's, Nancy Jo's Burgers, Pietro's Pizza, Subway, Comfort Inn, DoubleTree, Holiday Inn, Holiday Lodge, Motel 6, Shilo Inn, Mazda, Nissan, vet

253 OR 22, Salem, Stayton, E Chevron, Shell/dsl, Burger King, Carls Jr, Dude Donut City, Lucky Garden, McDonalds/playplace, Shari's, Subway, Home Depot, Salem Camping/RV Park, tires, to Detroit RA, WinCo Foods, W Shell,

253 Continued
Shell/dsl, Burger Basket, Carl's Jr, Denny's, DQ, Dutch Bros, Jack-in-the-Box, Panda Express, Popeyes, Starbucks, Best Western+, Comfort Suites, Hampton Inn, Home2 Suites, Howard Johnson, La Quinta, Residence Inn, AAA, AT&T, Chrysler/Jeep, H, Hyundai, Lowe's, Schwab Tire, Walmart

ANKENY HILL

252 Kuebler Blvd, W Chick-fil-A, Killer Burger, Starbucks, Costco/gas, Walmart

249 to Salem, W Domino's, Little Caesars, Popeye's, Stonefront Grill, Subway, Taco Bell, Safeway/gas

248 Sunnyside, E Enchanted Forest Themepark, Willamette Valley Vineyards, W Pacific Pride/dsl

244 to N Jefferson, E Emerald Valley RV Park

243 Ankeny Hill

242 Talbot Rd

241mm **both lanes, full facilities, info, litter barrels, petwalk**

240.5mm Santiam River

239 Dever-Conner, Dever-Conner

238 S Jefferson, Scio, W Love's/Arby's/dsl/scales/24hr

237 Viewcrest

235 Millersburg

ALBANY

234 OR 99E, Albany, E Cascade Grill, Comfort Suites, Holiday Inn Express, Knox Butte Camping/RV dump, W Chevron, Burger King, Carl's Jr, Domino's, DQ, McDonald's, Panera Bread, Subway, Taco Bell, Thai Express, Victorico's Mexican, Budget Inn, Motel 6, Quality Inn, Super 8, Costco/gas, H, Kohl's, NAPA, Valvoline, WinCo

233 US 20, Albany, E Chevron/dsl/LP, Denny's, Best Western+, Phoenix Inn, Rodeway Inn, Albany RV Ctr, Blue Ox RV Park, Home Depot, Honda, Peterson Trucks, st police, Toyota/Scion, Walmart, W Shell/dsl, Space Age/dsl, Abby's Pizza, Applebee's, Arby's, BJ's Ice Cream, Burger King, Burgerville, Carl's Jr, Chipotle, Cork's Donuts, Del Taco, Dutch Bros, El Palenque Mexican, Elmer's, Jack-in-the-Box, Little Caesars, Los Dos Amigos, Los Tequilas Mexican, Panda Express, Pizza Hut, Red Robin, Sizzler, Starbucks, Sweetwaters Rest., Tony's Taco Shop, Wendy's, Studio 6, $Tree, Advance Parts, Bi-Mart, Chrysler/Dodge/Hyundai/Jeep/Subaru, Discount Tire, Fred Meyer/dsl, Grocery Outlet, Hobby Lobby, H, Hyundai, Lowe's, Marshalls, O'Reilly Parts, Old Navy, PetCo, Ross, Safeway/gas, Schwab Tires, Staples, Target, Verizon, Walgreens

228 OR 34, to Lebanon, Corvallis, E Leather's/dsl, Pacific Pride/dsl/24hr/scales, W Arco/dsl, Chevron/CFN/A&W/dsl, Circle K/dsl, VP Fuels/dsl, Subway, to OSU

222mm Butte Creek

216 OR 228, Halsey, Brownsville, E 76/Pioneer Villa TrkStp/deli/dsl/24hr/@, Travelodge, W Shell/dsl

209 to Jct City, Harrisburg, E RV repair, W Diamond Hill RV Park

COBURG

206mm **both lanes, full facilities, info, litter barrels, petwalk**

199 Coburg, E Pacific Pride/dsl, Taco El Paisa, Eugene RV Resort, W Shell/McDonald's/dsl, TA/dsl/scales/24hr/@, Coburg Crossing Cafe, antiques, Camping World, Coburg RV Ctr, Eugene Kamping RV Park, Freightliner, Kenworth, Marathon RV Ctr, Penske, RV Ctr

197mm McKenzie River

195b a N Springfield, E Arco, Chevron/dsl, Applebee's, Bao Bao House, Buffalo Wild Wings, Cafe Yummi, Carl's Jr, China Sun, Chipotle, Denny's, Dutch Bros, FarMan Chinese, Five Guys, Hacienda Amigo Mio, Hop Valley Rest., IHOP, Jimmy John's, KFC, Master Donut, McDonald's, Outback Steaks, Panda Express, Panera Bread, Roadhouse Grill, Shari's, Sizzler, Starbucks, Subway, Taco Bell, Victorico's, Best Western, Comfort Suites, Courtyard, Hilton Garden,

INTERSTATE 5 Cont'd

N

SPRINGFIELD

Exit	Services
195b a	Continued Holiday Inn, La Quinta, Motel 6, Quality Inn, Super 8, $Tree, AT&T, Best Buy, Cabela's, Hobby Lobby, H, Kohl's, Michael's, PetCo, Ross, Schwab Tire, st police, Target, USPO, Valvoline, Walmart Mkt, W Taco Bell, Costco/gas, Office Depot, PetSmart, to WinCo
194b a	OR 126 E, I-105 W, Springfield, Eugene, E Baja Fresh, Chipotle, Vitality Bowls, Verizon, W 76, Chevron, Speedway, Cafe Yumm!, Carl's Jr, Killer Burger, MOD Pizza, Mucho Gusto, Newman's Grotto, Pastini, Pegasus Pizza, PF Chang's, Starbucks, Even Hotel, Hyatt Place, La Quinta, Residence Inn, Albertson's, BMW, Mercedes, Natural Grocers, Nissan, Old Navy, See's Candies, Subaru, TJ Maxx, Trader Joe's, U Of O
193mm	Willamette River
192	OR 99(from nb), to Eugene, E Candlewood Suites, Fairfield Inn, Hilton, W 76, Dutch Bros, Little Big Burger, Starbucks, Subway, Track Town Pizza, Wild Duck Cafe, Wild Goats Grill, Best Western, Hayward Inn, Holiday Inn Express, The Maverick, University Inn, Mkt Of Choice, to U of O
191	Glenwood, W 76/dsl, Shell/dsl/LP, Denny's, Comfort Suites, Motel 6
189	30th Ave S, Eugene, E Shell/dsl/LP, Harley-Davidson, NW RV Supply, Shamrock RV Park, W Chevron/dsl, SeQuntial/dsl
188b	OR 99 S(nb only), Goshen
188a	OR 58, OR 99 S to Oakridge, E Deerwood RV Park, W Pacific Pride/dsl, tires
186	Dillard Rd, to Goshen(from nb)
182	Creswell, E Blue Valley Bistro, DQ, My Boys Pizza, Subway, Comfort Inn, $General, Bi-Mart, golf, OR RV Ctr, vet, W 76/dsl, Arco/dsl, Eduardo's Mexican, Figaro's Pizza, Joe's Diner, TJ's Rest., $Tree, Creswell Automotive, Dari Mart, Farmlands Mkt, Fast Mart, Meadowlark RV Park, NAPA
180mm	Coast Fork of Willamette River
178mm	**both lanes, full facilities, litter barrels, petwalk, coffee**
176	Saginaw
175mm	Row River
174	Cottage Grove, Cottage Grove, E Chevron/dsl/repair, Pacific Pride/dsl, Arby's, Chalerm Thai, Taco Bell, AutoZone, Chevrolet/GMC, Chrysler/Dodge/Jeep, H, Walmart, W Chevron/dsl/LP, Mobil/dsl, Shell/dsl, Burger King, Carl's Jr, Domino's, Dutch Bros, Hacienda Mexican, KFC, McDonald's/RV parking, Papa Murphy's, Pinocchio's Pizza, Popeyes, Subway, Szechuan Chinese, Torero's Mexican, Victorico's Mexican, Vintage Rest., Best Western, Cottage Grove Inn, Relax Inn, $Tree, Bi-Mart Foods, Family$, Grocery Outlet, O'Reilly Parts, Safeway/dsl, URGENT CARE, Walgreens
172	6th St (from sb), Cottage Grove Lake, W Cottage Grove RV Village
170	to OR 99, London Rd(nb only), Cottage Grove Lake, W Cottage Grove RV Village
163	Curtin, E Shell, W Lucky Duck Campground, Pass Creek Park/camping
162	OR 38, OR 99, to Drain, Elkton
161	Anlauf(from nb)
160	Salt Springs Rd
159	Elk Creek, Cox Rd
154	Yoncalla, Elkhead, N Rooster Rock SP
150	OR 99, to OR 38, Yoncalla, Red Hill, W Eagle Valley RV Park
148	Rice Hill, E Arco/LP, Pacific Pride/dsl,

EUGENE

COTTAGE GROVE LAKE

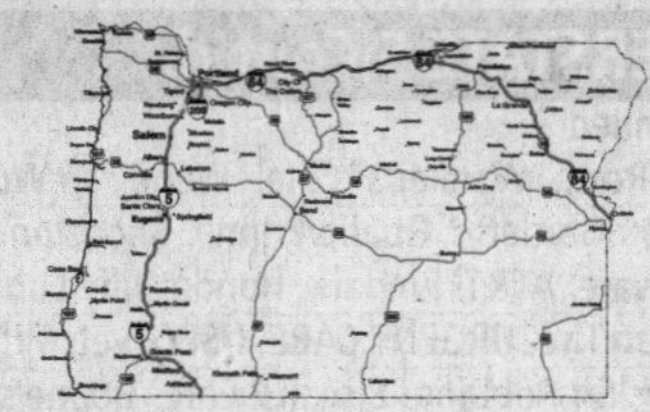

OAKLAND

ROSEBURG

WINSTON

Exit	Services
148	Continued Pilot/Denny's/dsl/scales/24hr, Ranch Motel, Rice Hill Inn, Rice Hill RV Park, towing/dsl repair, W K&R Drive-In, truck repair
146	Rice Valley
144mm	**sb, full facilities, litter barrels, petwalk**
143mm	**nb, full facilities, litter barrels, petwalk**
142	Metz Hill
140	OR 99(from sb), Oakland, E antiques, True Value Hardware
138	OR 99(from nb), Oakland
136	OR 138W, Sutherlin, E 76, Chevron/dsl, Mobil/dsl, Abby's Pizza, Apple Peddler Rest., Burger King, Cancun Mexican, Domino's, Dutch Bros, Henry's Bakery, Kelly's Cozy Corner, McDonald's, Papa Murphy's, Romulo's Mexican, Smitty's Food Mart, Yummy House, Autocare, Best Western+, Motel 6, Relax Inn, $Tree, AutoZone, fireworks, NAPA, W Shell/dsl, Dakota St Pizza, DQ, Starbucks, Subway, KOA, U-Haul, Umpqua RV Park
135	Wilbur, Sutherlin, E Shell/dsl/LP, vet
129	OR 99, Winchester, E Del Ray Cafe, Kamper Korner RV Ctr(1mi), Rivers Edge RV Park, st police, USPO
129mm	N Umpqua River, N Umpqua River
127	Stewart Pkwy, Edenbower Rd, N Roseburg, E Mobil, Krispy Krunchy Chicken, Shari's Rest., Motel 6, Super 8, Costco/gas, Home Depot, Honda, Lowe's, Verizon, W Mobil, Valero/dsl, Applebee's, Dutch Bros, Lilly's Mexican, McDonald's/playplace, Red Robin, Subway, Yummy Chinese, Sleep Inn, Albertson's, Batteries+, Big O Tire, H, Sherm's Foods, Valvoline, vet, Walmart, WinCo Foods
125	Garden Valley Blvd, Roseburg, E Abby's Pizza, Casey's, Elmer's, Five Guys, Gilberto's Mexican, Jack-in-the-Box, Jersey Lilly, KFC, Los Dos Amigo's Mexican, McDonald's, Smokin' Friday BBQ, Sonic, Subway, Taco Bell, Comfort Inn, Hampton Inn, Quality Inn, Roseburg Inn, AT&T, AutoZone, BigLots, Buick/Chevrolet/GMC, Ford/Lincoln, Honda, NAPA, Safeway/gas, Toyota, U-Haul, vet, Walgreens, W Sinclair/LP/repair, Burger King, Carl's Jr, Chipotle, Fox Den Pizza, MOD Pizza, Panda Express, Pita Pit, Rodeo Steaks, RoundTable Pizza, Sizzler, Starbucks, Wendy's, Best Western, Days Inn, Bi-Mart Foods, Fred Meyer/dsl, Marshall's, Michael's, O'Reilly Parts, PetCo, Ross, Staples, Walgreens
124	OR 138, Roseburg, City Ctr, E 76/dsl, Chevron/dsl, Denny's, Dutch Bros Coffee, Baymont Inn, Holiday Inn Express, Riverfront Inn, Rodeway Inn, W 76/dsl, Mobil/dsl, Domino's, MT Mike's Pizza, Muchas Gracias Mexican, Pete's Drive-In, Subway, Taco Time, Anderson Mkt, Grocery Outlet, vet
123	Roseburg, E museum, to Umpqua Park
121	McLain Ave
120.5mm	S Umpqua River
120	OR 99 N(no EZ nb return), Green District, Roseburg, E Shady Oaks Motel, W auto repair
119	OR 99 S, OR 42 W, Winston, E Ingram Dist. Ctr, W 76/dsl, Chevron/A&W/dsl, Love's/Arby's/dsl/scales/LP/24hr, Carl's Jr, Dutch Bros, McDonald's, Papa Murphy's, Subway, Taco Bell, $General, Ray's Foods, Rising River RV Park, South Fork RV Park, Umpqua Safari RV Park,

OR

INTERSTATE 5 Cont'd

DILLARD

Exit	Services
119	Continued Western Star RV Park
113	Clarks Branch Rd, Round Prairie, W Quikstop Motel, On the River RV Park
112.5mm	S Umpqua River, S Umpqua River
112	OR 99, OR 42, Dillard, E Rivers West RV Park
111mm	weigh sta both lanes
110	Boomer Hill Rd
108	Myrtle Creek, E Chevron, Abby's Pizza, Armando's Mexican, El Azteca Mexican, golf, Subway, Tommy's Cafe, city park, Millsite RV Park, NAPA, Ray's Foods
106	Weaver Rd
103	Tri City, Myrtle Creek, E $Tree, Tri-City RV Park, W Chevron/A&W/dsl, Pacific Pride, McDonald's
102	Gazley Rd, E Surprise Valley RV Park
101.5mm	S Umpqua River, S Umpqua River
101	Riddle, Stanton Park
99	Canyonville, E Burger King, El Paraiso, 7 Feathers Hotel/casino, city park, W **Jordan Creek**, 7 Feathers Trkstp/café/dsl/scales/24hr/@, Creekside Hotel, 7 Feathers RV Resort
98	OR 99, Canyonville, Days Creek, E 76/dsl, Chevron/dsl, Penny Pincher, Ken's Cafe, Papa Morgan's Rest., Subway, USPO, Travelodge, $General, auto repair, Canyon Mkt, Canyonville Hardware, NAPA, Ray's Foods, vet, W museum

AZALEA

Exit	Services
95	Canyon Creek
90mm	Canyon Creek Pass, elevation 2020
88	Azalea
86	Barton Rd, Quine's Creek, E Quines Creek/dsl, Heaven on Earth Rest.
83	Barton Rd(from nb), E Applegate RV Camping
80	Glendale, W Cow Creek/Lp/Rest.
79.5mm	Stage Road Pass, elevation 1830
78	Speaker Rd (from sb)
76	Wolf Creek, W 76/deli/dsl, Pacific Pride/dsl, Shell/dsl, Wolf Creek Inn/rest., Creekside RV park, USPO
74mm	Smith Hill Summit, elevation 1730

HUGO

Exit	Services
71	Sunny Valley, E Covered Bridge Store/gas, Grave Creek Covered Bridge, W Sunny Valley RV Park/motel
69mm	Sexton Mtn Pass, elevation 1960
66	Hugo, E KOA, W Pottsville Museum
63mm	**both lanes, full facilities, info, litter barrels, vending, petwalk**
61	Merlin, W 76/dsl, Dutch Bros, $General, Almeda RV Park, Beaver Creek RV Resort, OR RV Ctr, Ray's Foods
58	OR 99, to US 199, Grants Pass, W 76/Circle K/dsl, CFN/dsl, Chevron, Mobil/dsl, Shell/dsl/repair, TownePump Gas, Black Bear Diner, Carl's Jr, China Hut, Denny's, DQ, Dutch Bros, In-N-Out, Krispy Krunchy Chicken, McDonald's, Muchas Gracias Mexican, Papa Murphy's, Sizzler, Subway, Taco Bell, Uptown Grill, Wendy's, Best Way Inn, Buona Sera Inn, Hampton Inn, Hawks Inn, La Quinta, Motel 6, Quality Inn, Red Lion Inn, Redwood Motel, Sunset Inn, Super 8, SweetBreeze Inn, Travelodge, $Tree, AutoZone, Chevrolet, Chrysler/Dodge/Jeep, Jack's RV Resort, Nissan, repair, Rouge Valley RV Park, Schwab Tire, st police, towing
55	US 199, Redwood Hwy, E Grants Pass, W Arco/dsl, Speedway/dsl, Abby's Pizza, Applebee's, Arby's, Carl's Jr, Dutch Bros, Elmer's, Jersey Mike's, KFC, La Burrita, McDonald's, MOD Pizza, Mt Mike's, Panda Express, Pita Pit, Shari's, Si Casa Flores Mexican, Starbucks, Starbucks, Subway, Taco Bell, Best Western, Holiday Inn Express, $Tree, AT&T, BigLots, Fred Meyer/dsl, Grocery Outlet, Home Depot, H, Jo-Ann, Moon Mtn RV Park, O'Reilly Parts, Petco, RiverPark RV Park, Ross, Staples, Verizon, Walmart,
55	Continued Winco Foods
48	Rogue River, E 76/dsl, Chevron/Circle K/dsl, Abby's Pizza, BeeGees Diner, Homestead Rest., Paisano's Italian, Subway, $General, Ace Hardware, auto repair, Ray's Foods, Rogue River RA, USPO, vet, W La Guayacama, Mkt Basket Deli, Best Western, Bridgeview RV Park, Chinook Winds RV Park, visitors ctr/info, Whispering Pines RV Park
45b	Valley of the Rogue SP/ both lanes, W **full facilities, litter barrels, petwalk, camping**
45mm	Rogue River
45a	OR 99, Savage Rapids Dam, E Cypress Grove RV Park

CENTRAL POINT

Exit	Services
43	OR 99, OR 234, to Crater Lake, Gold Hill, E Rock Point RV Park
40	OR 99, OR 234, Gold Hill, E Figaro's Pizza, Patti's Kitchen, Willy's Burgers, $General, KOA, Lazy Acres Motel/RV Park, Ray's Food Place, W Dardanelle's/gas, Gold Hill RV Park
35	OR 99, Blackwell Rd, Central Point
33	Central Point, E Chevron, Pilot/Taco Bell/dsl/scales/24hr, Burger King, KFC, Shari's Rest., Sonic, Sweet Tea Express, Courtyard(2mi), Holiday Inn Express, La Quinta, SpringHill Suites(2mi), Super 8, Costco/dsl, Firestone, funpark, Schwab Tire, vet, W Chevron/Circle K/dsl, Shell/dsl, Abby's Pizza, Domino's, Dutch Bros, Hawaiian Hut, Little Caesar's, Mary's BBQ, Mazatlan Grill, McDonald's, Schmizza Pizza, Albertson's, USPO

MEDFORD

Exit	Services
30	OR 62, to Crater Lake, Medford, E Chevron/dsl, Towne Pump, Abby's Pizza, Applebee's, Arby's, Baskin Robbins, Buffalo Wild Wings, Burger King, Carl's Jr, Carl's Jr, Del Taco, DQ, Dutch Bros, Elmer's, McDonald's, McDonald's, Olive Garden, Outback Steaks, Panda Express, Papa Murphy's, Pita Pit, Sonic, Starbucks, Subway, Subway, Taco Bell, Taco Delite, TX Roadhouse, Wayback Burger, Wendy's, Comfort Inn, Hampton Inn, Motel 6, Quality Inn, Rogue Regency Hotel, $Tree, AutoZone, Barnes&Noble, Batteries+, Best Buy, Bi-Mart, BigLots, Chevrolet/Buick/GMC, Discount Tire, Food4Less, Ford/Lincoln, Fred Meyer/dsl, Hobby Lobby, H, Johnson RV, Lowe's, Mazda, Mercedes, Michael's, O'Reilly Parts, Office Depot, Old Navy, PetSmart, Ross, Safeway, Schwab Tire, st police, Subaru, Verizon, vet, Walmart/Subway, W Chevron/dsl, Mobil/dsl, Shell, Chick-fil-A, Chipotle, Dutch Bros, Five Guys, In-n-Out, Jack-in-the-Box, Jamba Juice, Kaleidoscope Pizza, Killer Burger, Luigi's Italian Sandwiches, MOD Pizza, Red Lobster, Starbucks, Subway, Wendy's, Dick's, JC Penney, Jiffy Lube, Kohl's, Macy's, mall, Marshalls, Natural Grocers, Petco, REI, Target, Toyota/Scion, Trader Joe's, Verizon

PHOENIX

Exit	Services
27	Barnett Rd, Medford, E Black Bear Diner, DQ, Best Western, Days Inn/rest., Hilton Garden, Homewood Suites, Motel 6, Travelers Inn, H, W Chevron/dsl, Shell, Shell/Circle K/dsl, Abby's Pizza, Arby's, Burger King, Carl's Jr, Chipotle, Del Tacos, Domino's, Dragon Chinese, Dutch Bros, El Arriero Mexican, Elmer's Rest., Five Guys, IHOP, Jack-in-the-Box, Jersey Mike's, Jimmy John's, KFC, Luna Mexican, McDonald's, MOD Pizza, New China, Panda Express, Pizza Hut, Rooster's Rest., Shari's, Starbucks, Subway, Taco Bell, Victorico's, Clarion Pointe, Comfort Inn, Fairfield Inn&Suites, Holiday Inn Express, Rodeway Inn, Royal Crest Motel, Sovana Inn, SpringHill Suites, TownePlace Suites, $Tree, AT&T, Discount Tire, Family Mart, Fred Meyer/dsl, Grocery Outlet, Harry&David's, O'Reilly Parts, Staples, Verizon, Walmart, WinCo Foods
24	Phoenix, E Petro/Iron Skillet/dsl/scales/RV dump/24hr/@, Shell/dsl, Best Value, Home Depot, Peterbilt, U-Haul, W Chevron/Circle K/dsl, Angelo's Pizza,

OR

= gas = food = lodging = other = rest stop

INTERSTATE 5 Cont'd

Exit	Services
24	Continued Dutch Bros, Lucy's Taco Shop, McDonald's, auto repair, Harley Davidson, Holiday RV Park, Ray's Foods, vet
22mm	sb, full facilities, , , litter barrels, vending, petwalk
21	Talent, W Chevron/dsl, Shell/Circle K/dsl, Pump House Burgers, $General, Ashland Talent RV Resort, Ray's Food, restroom/park, vet
19	Valley View Rd, Ashland, W 76/dsl, Pacific Pride/dsl, Shell/dsl/LP, Dutch Bros, El Tapatio Mexican, Ashland Valley Inn, Comfort Inn, Lithia Springs Resort, Acura, Chevrolet, Ford, U-Haul, vet
18mm	weigh sta both lanes
14	OR 66, to Klamath Falls, Ashland, E 76, Chevron/dsl, Mobil/dsl/LP, El Paraiso Mexican, OakTree Rest., Ashland Hills Inn & Suites, Best Western, Holiday Inn Express, Relax Inn, W Arco, Shell, Dutch Bros, Starbucks, Subway, Taco Bell, Wendy's, Wild Goose Cafe, Scottish Inn, $Tree, Albertson's, AT&T, Bi-Mart, H, NAPA, Schwab Tire, Shop'n Kart, vet, vet
12mm	rest area nb, full (handicapped) facilities, picnic tables, litter barrels, petwalk
11	OR 99, Siskiyou Blvd(nb only, no return)
6	to Mt Ashland, E Callahan's Siskiyou Lodge/rest., W ski area
4mm	Siskiyou Summit, elevation 4310, brake check both lanes
1	to Siskiyou Summit(from nb, no return)
0mm	Oregon/California state line

ASHLAND

INTERSTATE 84

Exit	Services
378mm	Oregon/Idaho state line, Snake River
377.5mm	Welcome Ctr wb, full facilities, info, , , litter barrels, vending, petwalk
376b a	US 30, to US 20/26, Ontario, Payette, N Chevron/dsl, A&W/KFC, Burger King, Carl's Jr, China Buffet, Chipotle, Country Kitchen, DQ, Dutch Bros Coffee, Little Caesar's, McDonald's, Panda Express, Papa Murphy's, Starbucks, Subway, Wingers, Best Western, Motel 6, Quality Inn, Red Lion Inn, Sleep Inn, $Tree, AT&T, Home Depot, st police, Staples, Toyota/Scion, Verizon, Walgreens, Walmart/Subway, Waremart, S Pilot/Arby's/dsl/scales/24hr, Sinclair/dsl, Far East Chinese, Rusty's Pancakes, Taco Bell, Tacos El Zarape, Budget Inn, Holiday Inn Express, OR Trail Motel, Super 8, American Tire, H, Les Schwab Tire, NAPA
374	US 30, OR 201, to Ontario, N to Ontario SP, S Love's/Chester's/Subway/dsl/scales/24hr/@, Pacific Pride, truck repair
373.5mm	Malheur River
371	Stanton Blvd
362	Moores Hollow Rd
356	OR 201, to Weiser, ID, N Oasis RV Park
354.5mm	weigh sta eb
353	US 30, to Huntington, N Chevron/Champ's/dsl/parking/@, RV camping, to Farewell Bend SP, weigh sta wb
351mm	Pacific/Mountain time zone
345	US 30, Lime, Huntington, N gas, lodging, to Snake River RA, Van Ornum BFD
342	(from eb), Lime
340	Rye Valley
338	Lookout Mountain, N Lost Dutchmans Camping
337mm	Burnt River
335	to Weatherby, both lanes, full facilities, Oregon Trail Info, , litter barrels, vending, petwalk
330	Plano Rd, to Cement Plant Rd, S cement plant

LIME

OR

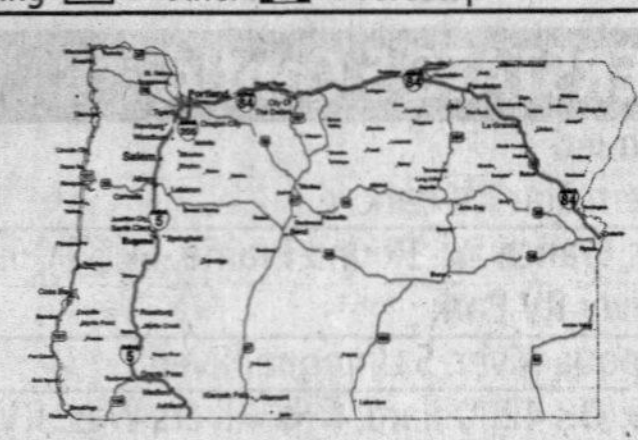

Exit	Services
329mm	pulloff eb
327	Durkee
325mm	no services
321mm	Alder Creek
317	to Pleasant Valley(from wb)
315	to Pleasant Valley(from wb)
313	to Pleasant Valley(from eb)
306	US 30, Baker, S Baker City Motel, same as 304
304	OR 7, Baker, N Pacific Pride/dsl, Motel 6, Super 8, Grocery Outlet, S Maverik/dsl, Shell/dsl, Sinclair/dsl/rest./scales/24hr, Golden Crown, McDonald's, Mother Lode, Papa Murphy's, Pizza Hut, Starbucks, Subway, Taco Bell, Taco Time, Best Western, Eldorado Inn, Geiser Grand Motel, Rodeway Inn, $Tree, Albertson's/gas, Bi-Mart, Carquest, city park, H, Mtn View RV Park/LP(3mi), museum, O'Reilly Parts, Paul's Transmissions/repair, Safeway Foods, to hist dist, Verizon
302	OR 86 E to Richland, S A Frame RV Park/LP, H, st police
298	OR 203, to Medical Springs
297mm	Baldock Slough, Baldock Slough
295mm	both lanes, full facilities, info, , , litter barrels, vending, petwalk
289mm	Powder River
287.5mm	45th parallel...halfway between the equator and north pole
286mm	N Powder River
285	US 30, OR 237, North Powder, N 76, North Powder Motel/cafe, Wagon Tracks RV Camping, S to Anthony Lakes, to ski area
284mm	Wolf Creek, Wolf Creek
283	Wolf Creek Lane
278	Clover Cr., Clover Creek
273	Frontage Rd
270	Ladd Creek Rd(from eb, no return)
269mm	both lanes, full facilities, info, , , litter barrels, vending, petwalk
268	Foothill Rd, N Eagles Hot Lake RV Park
265	OR 203, LaGrande, N , S Flying J/dsl/scales/24hr, Freightliner
261	OR 82, LaGrande, N Chevron/dsl, Arby's, Denny's, Lucky's Grill, Panda Express, Starbucks, Taco Bell, LaGrande Inn, Chrysler/Dodge/Jeep, Ford, Grocery Outlet, Legacy RV Ctr, NAPA, URGENT CARE, Verizon, Walmart/Subway, S Chevron/dsl, Exxon/Subway/dsl, Gasco/dsl, Cinco de Mayo, Cock&Bull Italian, Domino's, DQ, Dutch Bro's Coffee, KFC, La Fiesta Mexican, McDonald's, Moy's Dynasty, Nell's Steakburger, Papa Murphy's, SmokeHouse Rest., Taco Time, Wendy's, Best Western+, Royal Motel, Sandman Inn/Best Value, Super 8, The Landing Hotel, $Tree, Ace Hardware, CarQuest, E OR U, H, O'Reilly Parts, Safeway/dsl, Schwab Tire, Wallowa Lake
260mm	Grande Ronde River
259	US 30 E(from eb), to La Grande, S Chevron/dsl, Mobil/dsl, Greenwell Motel/rest., Rodeway Inn, Royal Motel, same as 261, city park
257	Perry(from wb), Perry
256.5mm	weigh sta eb
256	Perry(from eb)
255mm	Grande Ronde River
254mm	scenic wayside

BAKER · NORTH POWDER · LAGRANDE · PERRY

INTERSTATE 84 Cont'd

MEACHAM

Exit #	Services
252	OR 244, to Starkey, Lehman Springs, S Bird Track Spgs camping, Hilgard SP/restrooms
251mm	Wallowa-Whitman NF
248	Spring Creek Rd, to Kamela, N OR Trail Visitors Park, S Spring Creek Campground
246mm	western boundary, Wallowa-Whitman NF
243	Summit Rd, Mt Emily Rd, to Kamela, N Emily Summit SP
241mm	Summit of the Blue Mtns, elevation 4193
238	to Meacham, Meacham
234	Meacham, S Emigrant Sprs SP
231.5mm	eastern boundary, Umatilla Indian Reservation
228mm	Deadman Pass, both lanes, full facilities, picnic table, litter barrel, petwalk, vending, RV Dump(wb), OR Trail info
227mm	weigh sta wb, brake check area
224	Poverty Flats Rd, Old Emigrant Hill Rd, to Emigrant Springs SP
223mm	no restrooms, wb viewpoint
221.5mm	eb viewpoint, no restrooms
220mm	wb runaway truck ramp
216	Mission, McKay Creek, N Arrowhead Trkstp/Pacific Pride/McDonald's/dsl/24hr, DQ, Subway, golf, Wildhorse Casino/RV Park
213	US 30(from wb), Pendleton
212mm	Umatilla Indian Reservation western boundary
210	OR 11, Pendleton, N MotoLodge, museum, st police, S Chevron/Circle K/dsl, Sinclair/dsl/LP, Shari's/24hr, Best Western, Hampton Inn, Holiday Inn Express, Motel 6, Red Lion Inn/rest., Super 8, KOA
209	US 395, Pendleton, N Space Age, Domino's, DQ, Jack-in-the-Box, KFC, Little Caesar's, Pizza Hut, Taco Bell, Oxford Suites, $Tree, AT&T, Grocery Outlet, NAPA, O'Reilly Parts, Safeway/dsl, T-Mobile, Verizon, Walmart/Subway/auto, S Astro/dsl, Sinclair/dsl, Abby's Pizza, Burger King, Denny's, McDonald's, Rooster's Rest, Smoked BBQ, Starbucks, Subway, Wendy's, Motel 6, H, Les Schwab, Thompson RV Ctr
208mm	Umatilla River
207	US 30, W Pendleton, N Sinclair/dsl/LP, Lookout RV Park
202	Barnhart Rd, to Stage Gulch, N truck repair
199	Stage Coach Rd, Yoakum Rd
198	Lorenzen Rd, McClintock Rd, N trailer/reefer repair
193	Echo Rd, to Echo
188	US 395 N, Hermiston, N Pilot/Subway/McDonald's/dsl/24hr/RV park, H
187mm	both lanes, full facilities, info, litter barrels, petwalk
182	OR 207, to Hermiston, N Space Age/A&W/dsl/LP/24hr, Comfort Inn, Panelview RV Park
180	Westland Rd, to Hermiston, McNary Dam, N trailer repair, S Chevron/dsl, Freightliner
179	I-82 W, to Umatilla, Kennewick, WA
177	Umatilla Army Depot
171	Paterson Ferry Rd, to Paterson
168	US 730, to Irrigon, N Green Acres RV Park, Oregon Trail RV Park
165	Port of Morrow, S Pacific Pride/dsl
164	Boardman, N Chevron/Circle K/dsl, Sinclair/dsl, C&D Drive-In, Smiley's Cafe, Sunrise Cafe, Village Rest., Best Value Inn, Knights Inn, Boardman RV/Marina Park, city park, USPO, S Subway, Rodeway Inn, Sleep Inn, Harvest Town Mkt, NAPA, Oregon Trail Library
161mm	rest area both lanes, full (handicapped) facilities, phone, picnic tables, litter barrels, vending, petwalk
159	Tower Rd, S Love's/Carl's Jr/dsl/scales/24hr/@
151	Threemile Canyon
147	OR 74, to Ione, Blue Mtn Scenic Byway, Heppner, S OR Trail Site
137	OR 19, Arlington, S Shell/Circle K/dsl, Happy Canyon Cafe, Rodeway Inn, Arlington Hardware, city park, Port of Arlington, Thrifty Foods, USPO
136.5mm	viewpoint wb, picnic tables, litter barrels
131	Woelpern Rd(from eb, no return)
129	Blalock Canyon
123	Philippi Canyon
114.5mm	John Day River, John Day River
114	S LePage Park
112	parking area both lanes, litter barrels, N John Day Dam
109	Pendleton, N John Day Visitor Ctr, S Sinclair/dsl, Bob's T-Bone, Bull Dog Diner, Hillview Motel, Tyee Motel, Ed's RV Park, Family Mkt/deli, Rufus RV Park, USPO
104	US 97, Biggs, N fruit stand, Maryhill Museum, Maryhill SP, S 76/Circle K/Noble Roman's/dsl/24hr, Pilot/McDonald's/dsl/scales/24hr, Shell/Subway/dsl, TA Express/Chevron/dsl, Dinty's Motel, Three Rivers Inn, Dinty's Mkt, dsl/tire repair
100mm	Columbia River Gorge Scenic Area, Deschutes River
97	OR 206, Celilo, N Celilo SP, S Deschutes River SRA, Indian Village
92mm	pull off eb
88	N to The Dalles Dam
87	US 30, US 197, to Dufur, N Chevron/dsl, Sinclair/dsl/24hr, McDonald's, Portage Grill, Columbia River Hotel, Comfort Inn, Columbia Hills RV Park, S Big Jim's Drive-In, Celilo Inn, Schwab Tire
85	The Dalles, N **litter barrels**, **playground, restrooms, Riverfront Park**, **marina**, S 76/dsl, Shell, Sinclair, Burgerville, Canton Wok, Domino's, Petite Patisserie, River Tap Rest., Budget Inn, Dalles Inn, Ace Hardware, Dalles Parts, H, USPO
83	(84 from wb), W The Dalles, N Pacific Pride, Casa El Mirador, Holiday Inn Express, S-Point Automotive, S Astro/dsl, Chevron/dsl, Fred Meyer/dsl, Burger King, Denny's, DQ, Dutch Bro's Coffee, Ixtapa Mexican, Jack-in-the-Box, KFC, McDonald's, Papa Murphy's, Pizza Hut, Shari's Rest., Starbucks, Subway, Taco Bell, Taco Time, The BBQ, Cousin's Inn/rest., Fairfield Inn, Motel 6, Super 8, $Tree, AutoZone, Buick/Chevrolet/GMC, Chrysler/Dodge/Jeep, Ford, Fred Meyer, Grocery Outlet, Honda, Jo-Ann Fabrics, Nissan, O'Reilly Parts, PetCo, Safeway/dsl, Subaru, Toyota/Scion, Verizon, Walgreens
82	Chenowith Area, S Sinclair/dsl, Spooky's Pizza, Bi-Mart Foods, Columbia Discovery Ctr, Home Depot, museum, same as 83
76	Rowena, Rowena, N Mayer SP, windsurfing, S viewpoint
73mm	N Memaloose SP/
69	US 30, Mosier, S USPO
66mm	N Koberg Beach SP/
64	US 30, OR 35, to White Salmon, Hood River, N Chevron/dsl, Shell, McDonald's, Riverside Grill, Starbucks, Best Western, marina, museum, st police, visitors info
63	Hood River, City Ctr, N Sinclair/dsl, Hampton Inn/EVC, S Astro, 3 River's Grill, Andrew's Pizza, Hood River Rest., Pietro's Pizza, Hood River Hotel, Oakstreet Hotel, H, USPO
62	US 30, Westcliff Dr, W Hood River, N Columbia Cliff Villas, Columbia Gorge Hotel, Westcliff Lodge, S 76/dsl, Chevron/dsl/LP, Domino's, DQ, Egg River Cafe, Ixtapa Mexican, McDonald's, Pelinti Cafe, Red Carpet Cafe, Subway, Taco Bell, Holiday Inn Express, Riverview Lodge, AT&T, H, Les Schwab Tire, Safeway/Starbucks, Verizon, Walmart
61mm	pulloff wb

Side labels: MEACHAM; PENDLETON; BOARDMAN; ARLINGTON; CELILO; CHENOWITH AREA

INTERSTATE 84 Cont'd

HERMON CREEK

Exit #	Services
60	no services
58	S Mitchell Point Overlook(from eb)
56	N Viento SP, S RV camping
55	Starvation Peak Tr Head(from eb), S restrooms, Starvation Creek Falls
54mm	weigh sta wb
51	Wyeth, S camping/hiking
49mm	pulloff eb
47	Forest Lane, from wb, Hermon Creek
45mm	weigh sta eb
44	US 30, to Cascade Locks, N Chevron/dsl, Shell/dsl, Bridgeside Rest., Cascade Inn Rest., Eastwind Drive-In, Waterfront Cafe, Best Western+, Bridge of the Gods Motel, Cascade Motel, Columbia Gorge Inn, Columbia Mkt, KOA, museum, Stern Wheeler RV Park, to Bridge of the Gods
41	N Eagle Creek RA(from eb), S fish hatchery
40	N Bonneville Dam NHS, to fish hatchery
37	(from wb), Warrendale, S to falls area
35	Historic Hwy, (exits left from both lanes), Multnomah, S Ainsworth SP, Fishery RV Park, scenic loop highway, waterfall area
31	exits left from both lanes, Multnomah Falls, S Multnomah Falls Lodge/Rest.(hist site)
30	S Benson SRA(from eb)
29	Dalton Point(from wb)
28	to Bridal Veil(7 mi return from eb)
25	no services
23mm	N viewpoint wb
22	Corbett, S Corbett Mkt, Crown Point RV Camping
19mm	Columbia River Gorge scenic area
18	S Lewis & Clark SP, to Oxbow SP
17.5mm	Sandy River
17	Marine Dr, Troutdale, N DQ, Comfort Inn, S Chevron/dsl, Love's/Chester's/dsl/LP/scales/24hr/@, TA/Shell/Country Pride/Popeyes/Subway/dsl/scales/24hr/@, Arby's, McDonald's, Shari's/24hr, Starbucks, Subway, Taco Bell, Taco Bell, Holiday Inn Express, Motel 6, Premium Outlets/famous brands, Sandy Riverfront RV Resort
16	238th Dr, Fairview, N Arco/dsl/24hr, Jack-in-the-Box, Starbucks, Travelodge, Camping World, Walmart/Subway, S Chevron, Gyro King, Best Western, H
14	207th Ave, Fairview, N Shell/dsl, Parkway Grill, auto repair, Portland RV Park, Rolling Hills RV Park
13	181st Ave, Gresham, N Chevron/dsl, Courtyard, Hampton Inn, S 76, Arco, Shell, Burger King, Carl's Jr, Elmer's, McDonald's, Pizza Hut, Shari's, Subway, Wendy's, Bridgeway Inn, Extended Stay America, Sheraton, $Tree, 7-11, vet
10	122nd Ave(from eb), S WinCo Foods
9	I-205, S to Salem, N to Seattle, to airport, (to 102nd Ave from eb)
8	I-205 N(from eb), N to
7	Halsey St(from eb)
6	I-205 S(from eb)
5	OR 213, to 82nd Ave(eb only), N Portland Value Inn, S Eastern Cathay
4	68th Ave(from eb), to Halsey Ave
3	58th Ave(from eb), S 76, Shell/dsl, Fred Meyer, H, PetCo
2	43rd Ave, 39th Ave, Halsey St, N 76, Honey Spicy Korean, Trader Joe's, S H, same as 1
1	33rd Ave, Lloyd Blvd(eb only), downtown, same as 2, N Blind Onion Pizza, Shell/dsl, Burger King, AT&T,

FAIRVIEW

DOWNTOWN

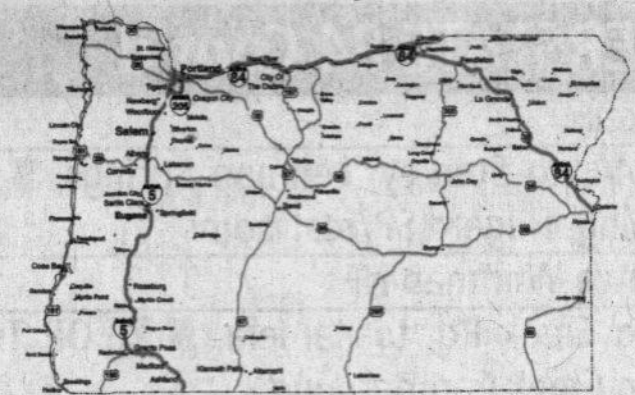

Exit #	Services
1	Continued Dave's Hot Chicken, Schwab Tire
1	to downtown(wb only), N Five Guys, Doubletree, $Tree, Nordstrom, Ross, Safeway, S Cadillac
0mm	I-84 begins/ends on I-5, exit 301.

INTERSTATE 205 (Portland)

BATTLE GROUND

Exit #	Services
37mm	I-205 begins/ends on I-5. Exits 36-27 are in Washington.
36	NE 134th St(from nb), E Chevron/dsl, Domino's, Holiday Inn Express, H, Walgreens, W 7-11, 76, Shell, Applebee's, Baskin-Robbins, Billygan's Roadhouse, Black Rock Coffee, Bruchi's, Burger King, Burgerville, Creekside BBQ, Freshii, Jack-in-the-Box, McDonald's, Muchas Gracias, Panda Express, Papa Murphy's, Round Table Pizza, Subway, Taco Bell, La Quinta, Quality Inn, Red Lion, 99 RV Park, Fred Meyer, Safeway/dsl, Verizon
32	NE 83rd St, Andreson Rd, Battle Ground, W Shell/dsl/24hr, Black Rock Coffee, Burger King, Krispy Kreme, Panda Express, Starbucks, Subway, Taco Bell, Taste of China, Wendy's, Costco/gas, Home Depot, vet
30c b a	WA 500, Orchards, Vancouver, E Megabite Pizza, Mobil, Shell, Shell, Applebee's, Blind Onion Pizza, Burger King, Burgerville, DQ, Dutch Bros Coffee, KFC, McDonald's, Papa Murphy's, Pita Pit, Shen Chang, Starbucks, Subway, Wendy's, 7-11, GNC, Jo-Ann Crafts, Midas, Office Depot, PetCo, repair, Sportsman's Whse, Toyota, Vancouver RV Ctr/Park, Walgreens, W 7-11/dsl, 76/dsl, Chevron/dsl, Champ Pizza, Chick-fil-A, Chipotle, ChuckeCheese, Dutch Bros Coffee, Fiesta Bonita Mexican, Five Guys, Great Taste Chinese, Hometown Buffet, IHOP, Jack-in-the-Box, Jamba Juice, Olive Garden, Outback Steaks, Popeyes, Red Lobster, Red Robin, RoundTable Pizza, Shari's, Starbucks, Taco Bell, Best Western, Comfort Suites, Day's Inn, Heathman Lodge, Holiday Inn Express, Sonesta Inn, $Tree, Americas Tire, auto repair, Barnes&Noble, Dodge/Ram, GNC, Honda, JC Penney, Jeep, Kia, Macy's, Nissan, Old Navy, PetSmart, Ross, Subaru, Target, TJ Maxx, URGENT CARE, Verizon, VW
28	Mill Plain Rd, E 76, Chevron, Applebee's, Baskin-Robbins, Breakfast At Valerie's, Burger King, Burgerville, DQ, Elmer's Rest., Irishtown Grill, Jimmy John's, Kings Buffet, McDonald's, McGrath's Fish House, Muchas Gracias Mexican, Pizza Hut, Shari's, Starbucks, Sweet Tomatoes, Taco Bell, Yummy Mongolian, Best Western, DoubleTree Hotel, Extended Stay America, The Guesthouse Motel, $Tree, 7-11, Fred Meyer/dsl, O'Reilly Parts, PetCo, Schwab Tire, Trader Joe's, W 7-11, 76, Arby's, Jack-in-the-Box, Little Caesar's, Subway, auto/tire repair, H, Walgreens, Walmart/McDonald's
27	WA 14, Vancouver, Camas, E to Columbia River Gorge
25mm	Oregon/Washington state line. Columbia River. Exits 27-36 are in Washington.
24	122nd Ave, Airport Way, E 7-11/dsl, Burger King, China Wok, Dutch Bros Coffee, Jack-in-the-Box, Jimmy John's, McDonald's, Shari's, Starbucks, Best Western+, Candlewood Suites, Clarion, Comfort Suites, Courtyard, Fairfield Inn, Hilton Garden, Homewood Suites, La Quinta, Shilo Inn/rest., SpringHill Suites, Staybridge Suites, Super 8, Home Depot, Michael's, W Buffalo Wild Wings, Famous Dave's, Fuller's Burgers, Jersey Mike's, Red Robin,

INTERSTATE 205 (Portland) Cont'd

Exit	Services
24	Continued Starbucks, Subway, Aloft Hotel, Country Inn&Suites, Embassy Suites, Hampton Inn, Holiday inn Express, Home2 Suites, Hyatt Place, Red Lion Hotel, Residence Inn, Sheraton/rest., Tru, Best Buy, Marshall's, Old Navy, PetSmart, Ross, Target
23b a	US 30 byp, Columbia Blvd, E Leather's Fuel/dsl, Shell/dsl, Bill's Steaks, Elmer's Rest., Jim Dandy Burgers, Sandy-O's, Subway, Best Western, Econolodge, W Holiday Inn, Radisson, Studio 6
22	I-84 E, US 30 E, to The Dalles
21b	I-84 W, US 30 W, to Portland
21a	Glisan St, 76, Arco, Applebee's, Carl's Jr, Jamba Juice, Subway, Wingstop, Fred Meyer, Kohl's, Office Depot, Ross, WinCo Foods
20	Stark St, Washington St, E 76/7-11, Chevron/dsl, Arby's, Burger King, Chipotle, Denny's, Elmer's Rest., Fujiyama, Jack-in-the-Box, McMenamin's Rest., Mi Cava Mexican, Olive Garden, Panda Express, Red Robin, Sayler's, Soy Grill Japanese, Ramada, $Tree, AT&T, Home Depot, H, Target, Verizon, W Stark St Pizza, Taco Bell, Motel 6, 7-11
19	US 26, Division St, E Space Age/dsl, W Shell, McDonald's, Jiffy Lube
17	Foster Rd, E 7-11, W Humdinger
16	Johnson Creek Blvd, W 76, Chevron, Applebee's, Arawan Thai, Arbys, Bajio, Birrieria Tacos, Burger King, Carl's Jr, Dutch Bros Coffee, Five Guys, Hog Wild BBQ, Jack-in-the-Box, Krispy Kreme, McDonald's, MOD Pizza, Panda Express, RoundTable Pizza, Roxy's Grill, Starbucks, Starbucks, Taco Bell, 7-11, Best Buy, Dick's, Firestone/auto, Fred Meyer/dsl, Home Depot, O'Reilly Parts, PetSmart, Trader Joe's, Walgreens, Walmart/Subway
14	Sunnyside Rd, E Chevron/dsl, A&W/KFC, Dave's Hot Chicken, Domino's, Jersey Mike's, McMenamin's, Papa John's, Starbucks, Wingstop, Quality Inn, Sunnyside Inn, AAA, H, Office Depot, W Astro/dsl, Burger King,
14	Continued Cheesecake Factory, Chipotle, Claim Jumper, Dave&Buster's, Denny's, DQ, Jimmy John's, Little Caesars, McDonald's, Noodles&Co, Old Spaghetti Factory, Olive Garden, Panera Bread, Red Robin, Stanford's Rest., Taco Bell, Victorico's Mexican, Wendy's, Courtyard, Monarch Hotel/rest., Barnes&Noble, Costco/gas, Discount Tire, Food Depot, Hobby Lobby, JC Penney, Kohl's, Macy's, Michaels, Midas, Old Navy, PetCo, REI, Ross, Target, tires, TJ Maxx, U-Haul, Verizon, WinCo Foods, World Mkt
13	OR 224, to Milwaukie, E NAPA, W CarMax, Lowe's
12	OR 213, to Milwaukie, E Chevron/dsl, Pacific Pride, Shell, Elmer's, McDonald's, New Cathay Chinese, Taco Bell, Wendy's, Clackamas Inn, Hampton Inn, $Tree, 7-11, Fred Meyer, USPO, vet, W Comfort Suites
11	82nd Dr, Gladstone, W 76, Chevron, High Rocks Rest., McDonald's, Starbucks, Subway, Holiday Inn Express, Harley-Davidson, park/restroom, Safeway
10.5mm	Clackamas River
10	OR 213, Park Place, E Chevron/dsl, Pacific Pride, Discount Tire, Home Depot, H, to Oregon Trail Ctr
9	OR 99E, Oregon City, E 76, Chevron/dsl, KFC, H, Subaru, W McDonald's, Rivershore Grill, Shari's, Starbucks, Subway, Best Western+, $Tree, AT&T, Michael's, Ross, URGENT CARE
8.5mm	Willamette River
8	OR 43, W Linn, Lake Oswego, E Space Age, W Astro Express/dsl, Shell/dsl, Starbucks, Mkt of Choice, Verizon, vet
7mm	viewpoint nb, hist marker, vista point nb
6	10th St, W Linn St, E Chevron/LP, Bellagio's Pizza, Five Guys, McDonald's, McMenamin's Rest., Papa Murphy's, Les Schwab, Valvoline, W Biscuit's Cafe, Dutch Bros, Subway, U-Haul
4mm	Tualatin River
3	Stafford Rd, Lake Oswego, W Wanker's Country Store, H
0mm	I-205 begins/ends on I-5, exit 288.

GLADSTONE

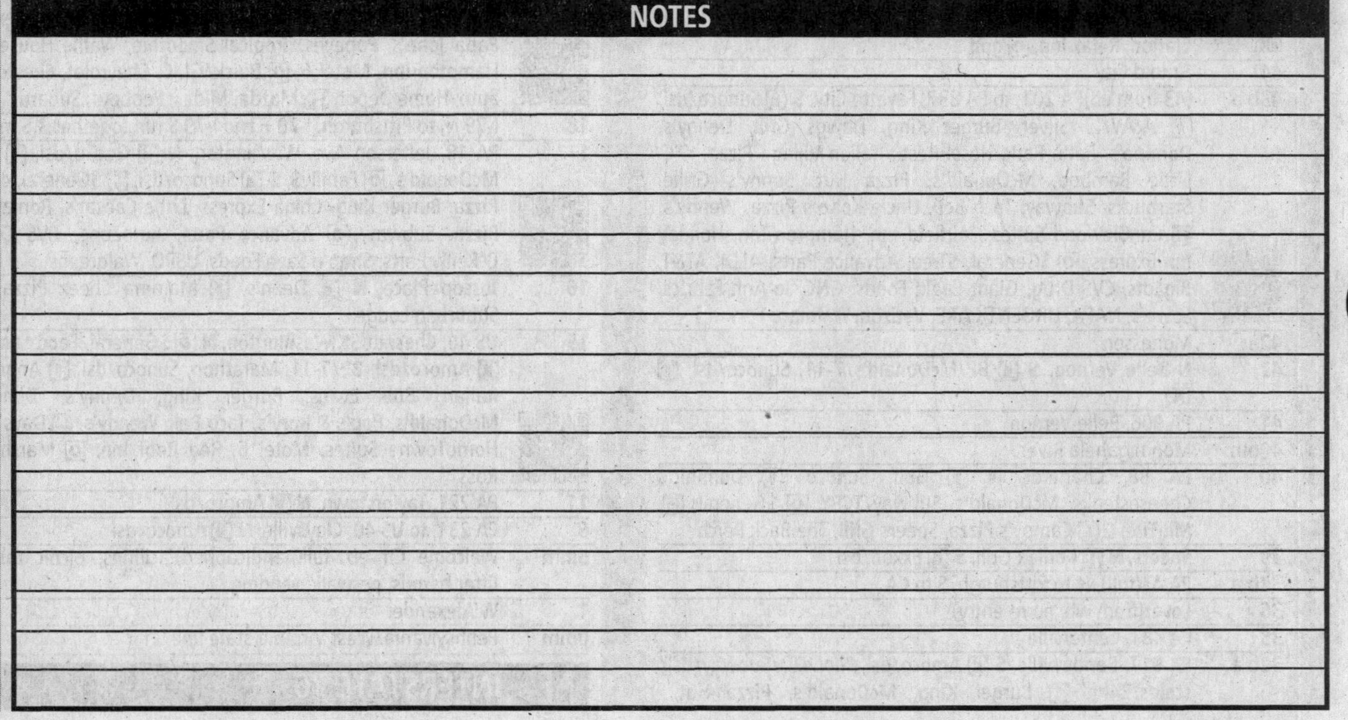

NOTES

OR

PENNSYLVANIA

INTERSTATE 70

AMARANTH · ARNOLD CITY · SPEERS

Exit #	Services
171mm	Pennsylvania/Maryland state line, **full facilities, info, litter barrels, petwalk, , , vending, Welcome Ctr wb**
168	US 522 N, Warfordsburg, S fireworks
163	PA 731 S, Amaranth
156	PA 643, Town Hill
153mm	**full facilities, litter barrels, petwalk, , , eb, vending**
151	PA 915, Crystal Spring, N auto repair, S Country Store/ USPO
149	US 30 W, to Everett, S Breezewood(no immediate wb return)
147	US 30, Breezewood, Exxon/Arbys/dsl, Flying J/Perkins/ dsl/scales/24hr, Marathon, Mobil/Dunkin'/dsl, Sheetz/dsl, Shell, Sunoco/Chesters/dsl, TA/Valero/Gateway Rest./ Subway/dsl/scales/24hr/@, Bob Evans, McDonald's, Pizza Hut, Starbucks, Subplicity, Budget Inn, Days Inn, Holiday Inn Express, Wiltshire Motel, Blue Beacon
146.5mm	I-70 and I-76/PA TPK merge for 71 mi. See I-76 PA/TPK exits 148mm-75.
77	I-70 merges with 1-76/PA Turnpike eb
58	PA Tpk. I-70 E and I-76/PA Turnpike E run together.
57	Hunker, New Stanton, N Sheetz/dsl, BBG Grill, Bob Evans, Eat'n Park, McDonald's, Subway, Taco Bell, Wendy's, Budget Inn, Fairfield Inn, Hampton Inn, Motel 6, Ramada, Red Roof Inn, Super 8, Wingate, S Marathon/dsl, Sunoco/ dsl, Cracker Barrel, La Tavola Ristorante, $General, USPO
54	Madison, N KOA, S truck repair
53	Yukon
51b a	PA 31, West Newton, S $General, Volvo/Mack
49	Smithton, N Citgo/rest./dsl/scales/@, Flying J/Denny's/ dsl/LP/scales/24hr/@, Speedway/dsl
48mm	Youghiogheny River
46b a	PA 51, Pittsburgh, N Sunoco/dsl, Burger King, Comfort Inn, Buick/Cadillac/Chevrolet, Ford/Kia, Honda, S GetGo/dsl, PP/dsl, Clubhouse Grille, Budget Inn, Clarion, Relax Inn, golf
44	Arnold City
43b a	(43 from eb)PA 201, to PA 837, Fayette City, S Sunoco/dsl, A&W/LJ Silver, Burger King, Dawgs Grill, Denny's, Domino's, Eat'n Park, Hoss' Rest., Italian Village Pizza, KFC, Little Bamboo, McDonald's, Pizza Hut, Sonny's Grille, Starbucks, Subway, Taco Bell, Uncle KoKo's Pizza, Wendy's, Candlewood Suites, Fairfield Inn, Hampton Inn, Holiday Inn Express, $General, $Tree, Advance Parts, ALDI, AT&T, BigLots, CVS Drug, Giant Eagle Foods, GNC, Jo-Ann Fabrics, Lowe's, NAPA, URGENT CARE, Verizon, Walmart
42a	Monessen
42	N Belle Vernon, S BP/McDonald's/7-11, Sunoco/dsl, DQ
41	PA 906, Belle Vernon
40mm	Monongahela River
40	PA 88, Charleroi, N Gulf, Sunoco, Dominic's Cheesesteaks, McDonald's, Subway/TCBY, $General, H, Mr. Tire, S Campy's Pizza, Speers Grill, The Back Porch
39	Speers, N Kodiax Grill, S Exxon/dsl
37b a	PA 43(toll), N to Pittsburgh, S to CA
36	Lover(from wb, no re-entry)
35	PA 481, Centerville
32b a	PA 917, Bentleyville, S Amoco/dsl, Pilot/DQ/Subway/dsl/ scales/24hr, Burger King, McDonald's, Pizza Hut,

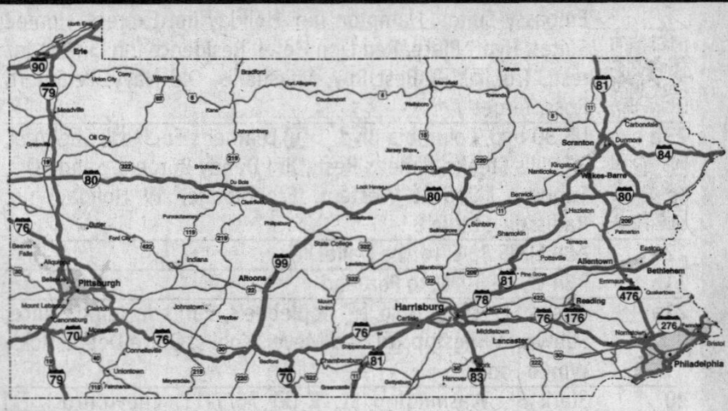

BENTLEYVILLE · CLAYSVILLE

Exit #	Services
32b a	Continued Taco Bell, Best Western, $General, $Tree, Advance Parts, AutoZone, Blue Beacon, Giant Eagle Foods
31	to PA 136, Kammerer
27	Dunningsville
25	PA 519, to Eighty Four, S Amoco/dsl, BP/7-11/dsl/24hr
21	I-79 S, to Waynesburg. I-70 W and I-79 N run together 3.5 mi.
20	PA 136, Beau St, S to Washington&Jefferson Coll
19b a	US 19, Murtland Ave, N Amoco/dsl, GetGo, Applebee's, Arby's, Asahi Buffet, Buffalo Wild Wings, Charleys Cheesesteaks, Chick-fil-A, Chipotle, Cracker Barrel, Dickey's BBQ, Five Guys, Fusion Steaks, Italian Village Pizza, Jersey Mike's, Jimmy John's, Krispy Kreme, Longhorn Steaks, McDonald's, Moe's SW Grill, Olive Garden, Outback Steaks, Panera Bread, Penn Sta Subs, Plaza Azteca, Red Lobster, Red Robin, Rita's Custard, Starbucks, Subway, Taco Bell, TX Roadhouse, Walnut Grill, SpringHill Suites, ALDI, AT&T, Dick's, Field&Stream, Ford, Giant Eagle Foods, GNC, Hobby Lobby, Honda, Hyundai, Kohl's, Lowe's, Mercedes, Michael's, Nissan, PetCo, PetSmart, Sam's Club/gas, Target, Toyota, URGENT CARE, Walmart/McDonald's, S Amoco/dsl, Exxon/dsl, Sunoco, Sunoco/dsl, Bob Evans, Dominos, Dunkin Donuts, Eat'n Park, Grand China, KFC, Old Mexico, Papa John's, Popeyes, Tropical Smoothie, Waffle House, Hampton Inn, Motel 6, Buick/GMC, Chevrolet, Firestone/ auto, Home Depot, H, Mazda, Midas, Pepboys, Subaru
18	I-79 N, to Pittsburgh. I-70 E and I-79 S run together 3.5 mi.
17	PA 18, Jefferson Ave, Washington, N GetGo/dsl, DQ, McDonald's, Family$, S Sunoco/dsl, $General, 4Star Pizza, Burger King, China Express, Little Caesar's, Romano's Pizza, Subway, Advance Parts, AutoZone, CVS Drug, O'Reilly Parts, Shop'n Save Foods, USPO, Walgreens
16	Jessop Place, N Dean's, Mamma Cheez Pizza, Suburban Lodge
15	US 40, Chesnut St, Washington, N $General, Food Land, S Amoco/dsl, BP/7-11, Marathon, Sunoco/dsl, Angelo's Italian, Bob Evans, Burger King, Denny's, Dunkin', McDonald's, Pop's & Rory's, Taco Bell, Wendy's, Days Inn, HomeTowne Suites, Motel 6, Red Roof Inn, Marshalls, Ross
11	PA 221, Taylorstown, N Amoco/dsl
6	PA 231, to US 40, Claysville, N Amoco/dsl
5mm	Welcome Ctr eb, full(handicapped)facilities, picnic tables, litter barrels, petwalk, vending
1	W Alexander
0mm	Pennsylvania/West Virginia state line

INTERSTATE 76

PA

INTERSTATE 76

CONSHOHOCKEN

Exit #	Services
354mm	Pennsylvania/New Jersey state line, Delaware River, Walt Whitman Br
351	Front St, I-95(from wb), N to Trenton, S to Chester
350	Packer Ave, 7th St, to I-95(from eb), S Hotel Philadelphia, sports complex
349	to I-95, PA 611, Broad St
348	PA 291, W to Chester (exits left from wb)
347a	to I-95 S (exits left from wb)
347b	Passyunk Ave, Oregon Ave, N Burger King, Gulf Seafood, KFC, Little Caesar's, McDonald's, Taco Bell, BJ's Whse, Home Depot, Ross, ShopRite, S FDR Park
346c	28th St, Vare Ave, Mifflin St(from wb)
346b	Grays Ferry Ave, University Ave, N Day Break Breakfast, McDonald's, Fresh Grocer, H, USPO, S Conoco, Exxon/dsl, Dunkin'
346a	South St(exits left from wb)
345	30th St, Market St, downtown, N downtown
344	I-676 E, US 30 E, to Philadelphia(no return from eb), N LDS Temple
343	Spring Garden St, Haverford
342	US 13, US 30 W, Girard Ave, N E Fairmount Park, S Philadelphia Zoo
341	Montgomery Dr, W River Dr, W Fairmount Park, S W Fairmount Park
340b	US 1 N, Roosevelt Blvd, to Philadelphia
339	US 1 S, S Chick-fil-A, Chipotle, Longhorn Steaks, Olive Garden, Panera Bread, Starbucks, TGIFriday's, Courtyard, Hilton, HomeWood Suites, Philly Inn, Target, Verizon
340a	Lincoln Dr, Kelly Dr, to Germantown
338	Belmont Ave, Green Lane, N Lucky's Burgers, Manayunk Gues House, S Sunoco/7-11, La Collina Italian, Rock Hill Pizza, CVS, UHaul, WaWa
337	Hollow Rd(from wb), Gladwyne
332	PA 23(from wb), Conshohocken, N Sunoco, Hotel West & Main, McDonald's, Tomato Shack, Wawa, Marriott, Residence Inn
331b a	I-476, PA 28(from eb), to Chester, Conshohocken
330	PA 320, Gulph Mills, S Villanova U
329	Weadley Rd (from wb), N Exxon
328b a	US 202 N, to King of Prussia, N Exxon/dsl, Global, Lukoil, Sunoco, Sunoco, WaWa, Azteca Mexican, Bahama Breeze, Bonefish Grill, Burger King, Capital Grille, Cheesecake Factory, Chili's, Chipotle, Eddie V's Seafood, Five Guys, Gaucho's Steaks, Hooters, J. Alexander's, KPOT KBBQ, Maggiano's, Melting Pot, Morton's Steaks, Panera Bread, Red Lobster, Seasons 52, Shake Shack, Sullivan's Steaks, Taku Japanese, Yard House Rest., Best Western, Doubletree, Fairfield Inn, Hampton Inn, Holiday Inn Express, Home2 Suites, Hyatt, Motel 6, Sheraton, Costco, Dick's, Dick's, Home Depot, Lord&Taylor, Macy's, Macy's, mall, Neiman Marcus, Nordstrom, Old Navy, S Crowne Plaza
327	US 202 S, to US 420 W, Goddard Blvd, Valley Forge Park, E Valley Forge Park
326	I-76 wb becomes I-76/PA Tpk to Ohio
325.5	**For I-76 westbound to Ohio, see I-76/PA Turnpike.**

INTERSTATE 76/Turnpike

Exit #	Services
6mm	PA Tpk runs wb as I-276/I-95, eb ends on NJ Tpk.
6a(I-95)	US 130 exit is in NJ, to Bordentown, N $Tree, S Conoco/dsl, WaWa/dsl, Burger King, Dunkin Donuts
355mm	PA Tpk/I-276 merges with I-95 N
352.5mm	toll plaza
352	PA 132, Street Rd, EZ tag only, from eb
351	US 1, to I-95, to Philadelphia, N Cane's Chicken,

FT WASHINGTON

POTTSTOWN

Exit #	Services
351	Continued Chick-fil-A, Chipotle, Cracker Barrel, Longhorn Steaks, McDonald's, On The Border, Panda Express, Red Robin, Starbucks, Uno, Wendy's, Crowne Plaza, ALDI, Barnes&Noble, Buick/GMC, CVS Drug, Home Depot, Lowes Whse, mall, Target, Walmart, S 7-11/dsl, Shell, Sunoco/dsl, Dunkin', Best Western+, Candlewood Suites, Comfort Inn, Courtyard, Hampton Inn, Inn of Dover, Knights Inn, Quality Inn, Radisson, Red Roof Inn, Sleep Inn, Indian Motorcycles, Toyota/Scion
343	PA 611, Willow Grove, N Liberty/dsl, Sunoco, Carrabba's, Dunkin', Grandma's Grotto Pizza, Olive Garden, Sonic, Courtyard, Fairfield Inn, SpringHill Suites, Home Depot, Homewood Suites, H, Lexus, Sams Club, Verizon, Walmart, S Bonefish Grill, China Garden, Domino's, Dunkin', Ooka Japanese, Tony Roni's Pizza, Hampton Inn, Advance Parts, Audi/Infiniti, Best Buy, PepBoys, repair, Staples, transmissions
340	to VA Dr, EZ tag only, from wb, no trucks, N Chipotle, Dunkin', McDonald's, Wendy's, WaWa/dsl
339	PA 309, Ft Washington, N LukOil/dsl, Dunkin', Best Western, Hilton Garden, Holiday Inn Express, BMW, Mercedes, Volvo, WaWa
334	PA Tpk NE Extension, I-476, S to Philadelphia, N to Allentown
333	Germantown Pike, to Norristown, N Lukoil, Sunoco, Azteca Mexican, Benihana, Bertucci's, California Pizza Kitchen, CAVA, Chipotle, Dave&Buster's, Dunkin Donuts, Papa John's, PF Chang's, Redstone Grill, Shake Shack, Starbucks, Courtyard, DoubleTree, Extended Stay America, SpringHill Suites, Boscov's, Verizon, vet, Whole Foods, S LukOil, Extended Stay, Homewood Suites
328mm	King of Prussia Service Plaza wb, Sunoco/dsl/24hr, Auntie Annes, Burger King, 7-11
326.5mm	PA Tpk runs eb as I-276, wb as I-76.
326	I-76 E, to US 202, I-476, Valley Forge, N SpringHill Suites, S Exxon, Gulf, LukOil, Sunoco, WaWa, Bahama Breeze, Burger King, CA Pizza Kitchen, Capital Grille, Cheesecake Factory, Chili's, Chipotle, Eddie V's Seafood, Gaucho's Steaks, Hooters, KPOT KBBQ, Maggiano's, Panera Bread, Seasons 52, Shake Shack, Sullivan Steaks, Taku Japanese, Best Western+, Crowne Plaza, Hampton Inn, Holiday Inn Express, Homewood Suites, Hyatt, Motel 6, Sheraton, Costco, Dick's, Dick's, Home Depot, Macy's, mall, Neiman Marcus, Nordstrom, Walmart, Wegman's
325mm	Valley Forge Service Plaza eb, Sunoco/dsl/24hr, Starbucks
312	PA 100, to Downingtown, Pottstown, N WaWa/dsl, S Sunoco/dsl, WaWa, Wawa, Chick-fil-A, Dominos, McDonald's, Nudy's, O2 KBBQ, Starbucks, Taco Maya, Timothy's Lionville, Wendy's, Extended Stay America, Exton, Fairfield Inn, Hampton Inn, Hilton Garden, Residence Inn, Spark Hotel, SpringHill Suites, $Tree, Advance Parts,

PA

INTERSTATE 76/Turnpike Cont'd

EPHRATA

312 Continued
AutoZone, Giant Foods, Target

305mm Camiel Service Paza wb, Sunoco/dsl/24hr, Baskin-Robbins, Dunkin', Roy Rogers

298 I-176, PA 10, to Reading, Morgantown, N AJs Pizza, Arby's, Dominos, Dunkin', Heritage Rest., Popeyes, Sonic, Starbucks, Subway, Taco Fest, Wendy's, USA Inn, AutoZone, Lowe's, Mavis Tire, T-Mobil, Verizon, Walmart, S Exxon, Sheetz/dsl, Clair's Rest., McDonald's, Nurse's Deli, Rita's Custard, Holiday Inn, Red Carpet Inn, Chevrolet, USPO

290mm Bowmansville Service Plaza eb , EVC, Sunoco/dsl/24hr, Baskin-Robbins, 7-11

286 US 322, PA 272, to Reading, Ephrata, N Sunoco/dsl, Turkey Hill, Baskin-Robbins/Dunkin Donuts, Park Place Diner, Procopio's Pizza, Subway, Zia Maria's Eatery, Penn Amish Motel, Verizon, Weaver Foods, S Turkey Hill, Comfort Inn, Hampton Inn(11mi), HomeTowne, Red Roof Inn, Tru

266 PA 72, to Lebanon, Lancaster, N Exxon/Krispy Krunchy, Speedway/dsl, Comfort Inn, Penns Woods Inn, auto repair, Harley-Davidson, H, Pinch Pond Camping

259mm Lawn Service Plaza wb , Sunoco/dsl/24hr, Baskin-Robbins, Burger King, Dunkin

250mm Highspire Service Plaza eb , Sunoco/dsl/24hr, Roy Rogers

247 I-283, PA 283, to Harrisburg, Harrisburg East, Hershey, N Exxon/dsl, Sheetz/dsl, Sunoco, Capitol Diner, Chick-fil-A, Chili's, El Rancho Mexican, El Sol Mexican, Five Guys, Friendly's, Gilligan's Steaks, Harbour House Seafood, Leeds Seafood, McDonald's, Moe's SW, Panera Bread, Subway, Taco Bell, Tropical Smoothie, Wendy's, Best Western, Courtyard, Econolodge, Holiday Inn, Hotel Indigo, La Quinta, Red Lion, Red Roof Inn, Sheraton, Super 8, GNC, Harrisburg East Camping, JC Penney, Kia, Petco, Target, Verizon

246mm Susquehannah River

242 I-83, Harrisburg West, N Exxon, Shell/dsl, Sunoco, John's Diner, McDonald's, Pizza Hut, Best Western, Budget Inn, Budget Inn, Fairfield Inn, Holiday Inn Express, La Quinta, Motel 6, Scottish Inn, Super 8, vet, S Rutter's/dsl, Days Inn, Red Carpet Inn

236 US 15, to Gettysburg, Gettysburg Pike, Harrisburg, N Exxon, Gulf/dsl, Ferrante's Italian, Marzoni's, McDonald's, Papa John's, Peppermill Rest, Comfort Inn, Country Inn&Suites, Courtyard, EconoLodge, Hampton Inn, Holiday Inn Express, Homewood Suites, TownePlace Suites, U-Haul, vet, S Sheetz, Arby's, Cracker Barrel, Dominos, Dunkin', Starbucks, Subway, Vito's Pizza, Wendy's, Wingate Inn, $Tree, Giant Food/gas

CARLISLE

226 US 11, to I-81, to Harrisburg, Carlisle, N Flying J/Denny's/dsl/LP/scales/24hr/@, Gulf/dsl, Gulf/dsl, Love's/Wendy's/dsl/scales/24hr, Petro/Iron Skillet/dsl/scales/24hr/@, Sheetz, Sunoco/Subway/dsl, Arby's, Burger King, Dunkin', McDonald's, Middlesex Diner, Moonlight Diner, Popeye's, Royal Kitchen, Waffle House, Best Value, Best Value Inn, Days Inn, EconoLodge, Larkspur Landing Motel, Quality Inn, Residence Inn, Rodeway Inn, Super 8, Blue Beacon, S Rutter's/dsl, American Inn, Best Western, Comfort Inn, Holiday Inn Express, H, vet

219mm Plainfield Service Plaza eb , Sunoco/dsl/24hr, Auntie Anne's, Roy Rogers, Starbucks, 7-11

203mm Blue Mtn Service Plaza wb , Sunoco/dsl/24hr, Auntie Anne's, Hershey's Ice Cream, Roy Rogers, Starbucks, Starbucks, 7-11

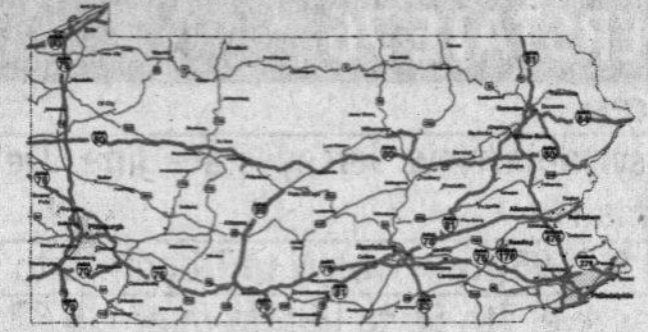

WILLOW HILL

201 PA 997, to Shippensburg, Blue Mountain, S McKinney Station, auto/truck repair, Kenmar Motel

199mm Blue Mountain Tunnel

197mm Kittatinny Tunnel

189 PA 75, Willow Hill, S Double Dip Drive-In, Willow Hill Motel/rest.

187mm Tuscarora Tunnel

180 US 522, Mt Union, Ft Littleton, N Martin/dsl, Park Pitstop/dsl, The New Fort, Downes Motel

172mm Sideling Service Plaza both lanes, Sunoco/dsl/24hr, Baskin-Robbins, Burger King, Dunkin', Famiglia Pizza, Hershey's Ice Cream, Popeyes

BEDFORD

161 US 30, Breezewood, N Flying J/dsl/scales/24hr, Marathon/dsl, Mobil/Dunkin'/dsl, Sheetz/dsl, Shell, Sunoco/dsl, TA/Exxon/Gateway Rest./Dunkin'/Arby's/dsl/scales/24hr/@, Bob Evans, McDonald's, Pizza Hut, Starbucks, Subplicity, Days Inn, Holiday Inn Express, Wiltshire Motel, Blue Beacon

161mm I-70 W and I-76/PA Turnpike W run together

148mm Midway Service Plaza both lanes, Sunoco/dsl/24hr, Roy Rogers, Starbucks, 7-11

146 I-99, US 220, Bedford, N GetGo/McDonald's/dsl, Sheetz/dsl/24hr, Shell/Subway/Champ's Chicken/dsl, Arby's, Denny's, Hoss' Rest., Pizza Hut, Rte 220 Diner, Taco Bell, Wendy's, Budget Host, Fairfield Inn, Quality Inn, Rodeway Inn, Super 8, Blue Knob SP(15mi), to Shawnee SP(10mi), S Hampton Inn

141.3mm parking area wb

123mm Allegheny Tunnel

112mm Somerset Service Plaza both lanes, Sunoco/dsl/24hr, Auntie Annes, Burger King, Dunkin', Popeyes, Roy Rogers, Sbarro, 7-11

DONEGAL

110 PA 601, to US 219, Somerset, N KwikFill/dsl, Sheetz, BFS/Burger King/dsl, Chipotle, Pizza Hut, $Inn, Economy Inn, Advance Parts, AT&T, Ford, Midas, NAPA, S Somerset TravelCtr/dsl/@, Tesla EVC, Turkey Hill, Arby's, Azteca Mexican, DQ, Eat'n Park, KFC, LJ Silver, McDonald's, Pine Grill, Ruby Tuesday, Starbucks, Subway, Summit Diner, Wendy's, Budget Inn, Comfort Inn, Days Inn, Hampton Inn, Holiday Inn Express, Knights Inn, Quality Inn, Red Roof Inn, Wingate, Harley-Davidson, Verizon

91 PA 711, PA 31, to Ligonier, Donegal, S Amoco/McDonald's, Sheetz, Sumoco/dsl, DQ, Days Inn, Holiday Inn Express, Donegal Campground, golf, Laurel Highlands Camping

78mm New Stanton Service Plaza wb , pet, EVC, Sunoco/dsl/24hr, Burger King, Starbucks, 7-11

75.5mm I-70 E merges with I-76/PA Turnpike eb

IRWIN

75 I-70 W, US 119, PA 66(toll), New Stanton, S Marathon/dsl, Sheetz, Sunoco, BBG Grill, Bob Evans, CJs Korner, Cracker Barrel, Eat'n Park, La Tavola Risorante, McDonald's, Subway, Taco Bell, Wendy's, Budget Inn, Fairfield Inn, Hampton Inn, Motel 6, Ramada, Red Roof Inn, Super 8, Wingate, Dollar General, USPO, vet

67 US 30, to Greensburg, Irwin, N BP/7-11/dsl, Sheetz/dsl, DQ, Ford, Goodyear, H, Mr Tire, S GetGo, Marathon/7-11/dsl, Sheetz/dsl, Sunoco/24hr, Acapulco Mexican, Applebee's, Arby's, Bob Evans, Burger King, Conforti's Pizza, Denny's, Dunkin', Eat'n Park, Fire Pit Grill, Five Guys, KFC, Little Caesar's, Mama Pepino's, McDonald's,

INTERSTATE 76/Turnpike Cont'd

IRWIN

67 Continued
Mr. Mike's Pizza, Panera Bread, Pizza Hut, Starbucks, Subway, Taco Bell, Wendy's, Hampton Inn, Holiday Inn Express, $Tree, Advance Parts, ALDI, AT&T, AutoZone, Giant Eagle Foods/24hr, GNC, Jiffy Lube, Kohl's, NTB, Target, Valvoline, Verizon, Walgreens, Walmart

61mm parking area eb

57 I-376, US 22, to Pittsburgh, Monroeville, S Marathon, Sheetz, Sunoco, Arby's, Blaze Pizza, Chick-fil-A, China Palace, Chipotle, Denny's, El Campesino, Esta Esta Italian, Five Guys, Mad Mex Mexican, Max&Erma's, McDonald's, Meadows Fro-Yo, Mission BBQ, Outback Steaks, Panda Express, Panera Bread, Penn Sta Subs, Primanti Bros, Red Lobster, Starbucks, Starbucks, Subway, Taco Bell, Wendy's, Comfort Suites, Courtyard, Extended Stay America, Hampton Inn, Holiday Inn Express, Red Roof Inn, Rodeway Inn, SpringHill Suites, Acrisure Stadium, ALDI, AT&T, Big Lots, CVS Drug, GNC, Honda, H, Lowes Whse, Marshall's, NTB, Old Navy, Pet Land, PetCo, URGENT CARE

49mm Oakmont Service Plaza eb, EVC, Sunoco/dsl/24hr, Auntie Ann's, Burger King, Starbucks

48.5mm Allegheny River

48 PA 28, to Pittsburgh, Allegheny Valley, N Exxon, Sunoco, S GetGo, Marathon/dsl, Sheetz/dsl, Bob Evans, Burger King, Denny's, Dunkin Donuts, Jersey Mike's, KFC, McDonald's, Popeyes, Primanti Bros, Wendy's, Day's Inn, Hampton Inn, Holiday Inn Express, Quality Inn, TownePlace Suites, Valley Motel, Advance Parts, AutoZone, Ford, Target

BUTLER VALLEY

41mm parking area/call box eb

39 PA 8, to Pittsburgh, Butler Valley, N GetGo, Marathon, Sheetz/dsl, Sunoco, Applebee's, Bruno's Pizza, Buffalo Wild Wings, Eat'n Park, Emiliano's Mexican, Emily's Turkish Rest., McDonald's, Penn Sta Subs, Starbucks, Taco Bell, Tequila Jalisco, Wendy's, Quality Inn, $Tree, Advance Parts, Chrysler/Dodge/Jeep, Dunkin', Giant Eagle Foods, GNC, Kohl's, Lowes Whse, Petco, Shop'n Save Foods, Target, TJ Maxx, USPO, Valvoline, Verizon, Walmart/auto, S BP, Sunoco/dsl, Arby's, Bob's Subs, Bruster's, Chipotle, Domino's, Jersey Mike's, KFC, McDonald's, Panera Bread, Pasquales Pizza, Pizza Hut, Primanti Bros, Simply Subs, Starbucks, Subway, Thai Kitchen, Vocelli Pizza, $General, $Tree, ALDI, AT&T, AutoZone, CVS Drug, Firestone/auto, Home Depot, Midas, Monro Tire & Auto, Mr. Tire, NTB, O'Reilly Parts, Pepboys, USPO, Verizon

31mm Toll Plaza wb

28 to I-79, to Cranberry, Pittsburgh, N BP/dsl, GetGo, Sheetz/dsl, Sunoco/dsl, Arby's, Blaze Pizza, Bob Evans, Bravo Italian, Buffalo Wild Wings, Burger King, Capriotti's Sandwiches, Chipotle, Condado Tacos, Denny's, Domino's, Dunkin', Eat'n Park, Einstein Bros, Emiliano's, Firehouse Subs, First Watch, Five Guys, HotDog Shoppe, Ichiban Steakhouse, Jason's Deli, Jersey Mike's, Jimmy John's, Mad Mex, McDonald's, Monte Cello's Grill, Panda Express, Panera Bread, Pizza Hut, Pizza Roma, Primanti Bros, Saga Steaks, Tepache Mexican, Vocelli Pizza, Wendy's, Candlewood Suites, Clarion, Clarion, Comfort Inn, Doubletree, Extended Stay, Extended Stay America, Quality Inn, Red Roof Inn, Residence Inn, Super 8, Wingate Inn, $Tree, ALDI, AT&T, AutoZone, Barnes&Noble, Best Buy, Costco/gas, Firestone/auto, Giant Eagle Foods, Home Depot, Marshall's, Michael's, Monro Tire & Auto, O'Reilly Parts, PepBoys, Toyota/Scion, USPO, Valvoline, Walgreens, Walmart

23.5mm pulloff eb

17mm parking area eb

13.4mm parking area eb

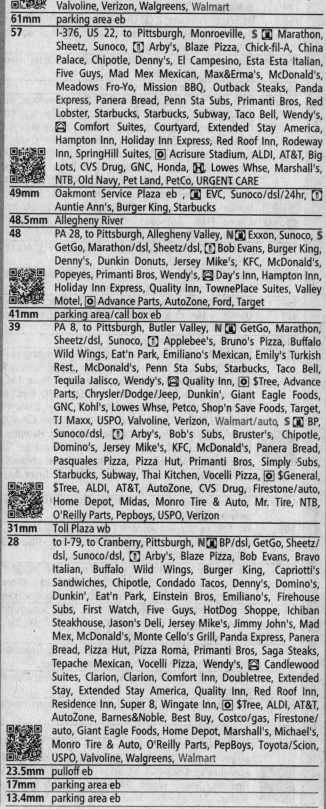

BEAVER VALLEY

13mm Beaver River

13 PA 8, to Ellwood City, Beaver Valley, N Al's Corner, Subway, Beaver Falls Motel, Lark Motel, Ramada, $General, S Super 8

10 PA 60(toll), to New Castle, Pittsburgh

6mm pulloff eb

2mm pulloff eb

1mm toll plaza eb, toll plaza eb

0mm Pennsylvania/Ohio state line

INTERSTATE 78

77mm Pennsylvania/New Jersey state line, Delaware River

76mm Welcome Ctr wb, toll booth wb, **full facilities, litter barrels, petwalk, , vending**

75 to PA 611, Easton, N TurkeyHill/dsl, Dunkin', McDonald's(1mi), Pino's Pizzeria, Subway, auto repair, Crayola Factory, CVS Drug, S Marathon/dsl, Pop's Kitchen, fireworks

71 PA 33, to Stroudsburg, N Chipotle, Duck Donuts, Frank's Pizza, Kung Fu Chinese, MOD Pizza, Panera Bread, Ruby Tuesday, Starbucks, Subway, TGIFriday's, TX Roadhouse, Wayback Burgers, Courtyard, Fairfield, $Tree, Barnes&Noble, Best Buy, Dick's, H, Lowe's, Michael's, Pet Supplies+, Ross, ShopRite Mkt, Staples, Verizon

QUAKERTOWN

67 PA 412, Hellertown, N TurkeyHill/gas, WaWa/dsl, Wendy's, Comfort Suites(3mi), Chevrolet, H, S Exxon/dsl, Fill & Fly, Sunoco, Sunoco, Aloha Jay's Donuts, Dunkin', Hellertown Pizza, Papa John's, Rita's Custard, Roma Pizza, Taste of Italy, Vassi's Drive-In, Waffle House, Holiday Inn Express, 7-11, antiques, auto repair, CVS Drug, Penske

60b a PA 145 N, PA 309 S, South Fort St, Quakertown

59 to PA 145(from eb), Summit Lawn

58 Emaus St(from wb), N Primo Pizza, S Papa John's, $General

57 Lehigh St, N Sunoco/dsl, WaWa/dsl, Arby's, China House, Dunkin', IHOP, Palumbo Pizza, Subway, Red Roof Inn, Rodeway Inn, $Tree, AAA, BigLots, CVS Drug, Family$, Ford/Lincoln, Home Depot, Infiniti, Kia, Mavis Tires/repair, Monro Tire, Penske, Redner's Whse, Toyota, VW, S Sheetz, Sunoco, TurkeyHill, Valero, Dunkin, Lee's Hoagies, McDonald's, Perkins, Plaza Azteca, Rossi's Pizza, Starbucks, Taco Bell, Tijuana Tacos, Wendy's, Yocco's Hot Dog, Acura, antique, AT&T, AutoZone, Batteries+, Buick/GMC, Cadillac/Chevrolet, Chrysler/Dodge/Jeep, Honda, Hyundai, Kost Tire, Mavis Tire, Mazda, Mercedes, Midas, Mitsubishi, PetCo, Ross, Staples, Verizon, Volvo

FOGELSVILLE

55 PA 29, Cedar Crest Blvd, N Shell, S H

54b a US 222, Hamilton Blvd, N Speedway, WaWa/dsl, Bamboo Asian, Carrabba's, Dunkin', Gourmet Buffet, Ice Cream World, McDonald's, Menchie's, Perkins, Pizza Hut, TGIFriday's, Wendy's, Holiday Inn Express, Howard Johnson, Sheraton, ALDI, Dorney Funpark, USPO, Weis Foods, S WaWa, BJ's Rest, Cane's, Chick-fil-A, Dunkin, Dunkin', Hunan Springs, Outback Steaks, Panera Bread, Papa John's, Rita's Custard, Smashburger, Taco Bell, TX Roadhouse, Wawa, Holiday Inn, ALDI, AT&T, Audi, AutoZone, Costco/gas, CVS, Dick's, Firestone, Home Depot, PetSmart, Subaru, Target, vet, Walgreens, Walmart, Whole Foods Mkt

53 PA 309(wb only)

51 to I-476, US 22 E, PA 33 N(eb only), Whitehall

49b a PA 100, Fogelsville, N Arby's, Cracker Barrel, Domino's, Old School Sandwich, Panda&Fish Chinese, Pizza Hut, Rita's Custard, Windsor Deli, Comfort Inn, Hawthorn Inn, KOA(7mi), Mavis Tire/repair, URGENT CARE, S Sunoco/7-11, US Gas, WaWa/dsl, Burger King, Starlite Diner,

PA

FOGELSVILLE

INTERSTATE 78 Cont'd

49b a Continued
Taco Bell, Yocco's Hotdogs, [lodging] Allentown Park Hotel, Delta Hotels, Fairfield Inn, Hilton Garden, Homewood Suites, Sleep Inn, Staybridge Suites, [other] Clover Hill Winery, st police, Toyota, vet

45 PA 863, to Lynnport, **N** [gas] Sheetz/dsl, Sunoco/New Smithville Diner/dsl, [food] Piccadilly Pizza, [other] truck service, **S** [food] Demarco's Italian, Dunkin, [lodging] Super 8

40 PA 737, Krumsville, **N** [other] Pine Hill Campground, Robin Hill RV Park(4mi)

35 PA 143, Lenhartsville, **S** [other] Robin Hill Park

30 Hamburg, **S** [food] Hamburg Mkt, [other] USPO

29b a PA 61, to Reading, Pottsville, **N** [gas] Shell/dsl, WaWa/dsl, [food] Burger King, Cracker Barrel, Dunkin', Five Guys, JA Buffet, LJ Silver/Taco Bell, Logan's Roadhouse, McDonald's, Red Robin, Starbucks, Wendy's, [lodging] Microtel, [other] $Tree, Advance Parts, ALDI, AT&T, AutoZone, Cabela's Outdoor, Camping World, Harley-Davidson(8mi), Hyundai, Lowe's, Pet Supplies+, Russell Stover, Toyota, Verizon, Walmart/Subway

23 Shartlesville, **N** [gas] Chromeshop/dsl, Love's/McDonald's/Subway/dsl/scales/24hr, [food] Dunkin', [lodging] Dutch Motel, [other] Appalachian Campsites, Kenworth, **S** [food] Blue Mtn Family Rest., [lodging] Motel 6, [other] $General, antiques, camping, USPO

BETHEL

19 PA 183, Strausstown, **S** [gas] Power/dsl

17 PA 419, Rehrersburg, **N** [gas] US Gas, [other] truck/tire repair

16 Midway, **N** [gas] Exxon/dsl, Sunoco/dsl, [food] J&S Pizza, Midway Diner, [lodging] Quality Inn

15 Grimes

13 PA 501, Bethel, **N** [gas] Sunoco/dsl, [food] Burger King, **S** [gas] Bethel/dsl, Sheetz/dsl, [other] dsl repair, USPO

10 PA 645, Frystown, **S** [gas] Flying J/Huddle House/Subway/dsl/scales/24hr/@, [lodging] Travel Inn

6 (8 from wb, US 22)PA 343, Fredricksburg, **S** [gas] PP/dsl, Redner's Whse/mkt, [food] Esther's Rest., [other] KOA(5mi)

1 I-81. I-78 begins/ends on I-81, exit 89.

ERIE

INTERSTATE 79

183b a PA 5, 12th St, Erie, **E** [other] [H], Valley Tire, **W** [gas] Country Fair/dsl, Speed Check/dsl, [food] Applebee's, Arby's, Bob Evans, Chick-fil-A, Chipotle, Domino's, Dunkin', El Canelo Mexican, Firehouse Subs, Five Guys, Hibachi Japanese, Jersey Mike's, Jimmy John's, KFC, McDonald's, Moe's SW Grill, Panera Bread, Pizza Hut, Popeyes, Roma's Italian, Starbucks, Taco Bell, Tim Hortons, Wendy's, [lodging] Lake Eerie Lodge, [other] $General, $Tree, Advance Parts, ALDI, BigLots, CVS Drug, Family$, Giant Eagle Foods, Save-a-Lot Foods, Tires-4-Less, to Presque Isle SP, Tuesday Morning, U-Haul, vet

182 US 20, 26th St, **E** [gas] Citgo/Country Fair/dsl, KwikFill, [food] Subway, [other] CVS Drug, Family$, [H], **W** [gas] Country Fair/dsl, [food] Arby's, Burger King, Dunkin, Hong Kong Chinese, Hungry Howie's, Little Caesar's, LJ Silver, McDonald's, Pizza Pete's, Subway, Tim Hortons, [lodging] Glass House Inn, [other] $General, AT&T, AutoZone, Ford, Monro, O'Reilly Parts, TrueValue, URGENT CARE, USPO, vet, Volvo

180 US 19, to Kearsarge, **E** [food] Arby's, Buffalo Wild Wings, Cheddar's, Coldstone, Dunkin, Firebirds Grill, KFC, Mad Mex, Max&Erma's, McDonald's, Moe's SW Grill, O'Charley's, Olive Garden, Outback Steaks, Primanti Bros, Smokey Bones BBQ, Sonic, Starbucks, Wendy's, [lodging] Candlewood Suites, Fairfield Inn, Homewood Suites, SpringHill Suites, TownePlace Suites, [other] Audi/Cadillac, Barnes&Noble, Chrysler/Dodge/Jeep, Firestone/auto, Giant Eagle Mkt, [H], JC Penney, Macy's, Michael's, Petco, Ross, TJ Maxx, Toyota, Verizon, **W** [gas] Citgo/Country Fair/dsl

178b a I-90, E to Buffalo, W to Cleveland

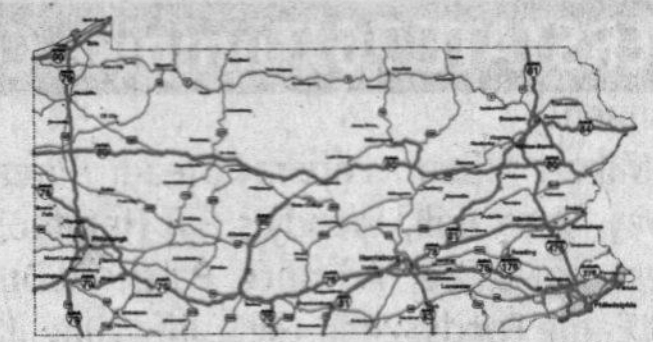

174 to McKean, **W** [other] KOA

166 US 6N, to Edinboro, **E** [gas] Citgo/Country Fair/dsl, Sheetz, [food] Dunkin, Wendy's, [lodging] Comfort Suites, [other] Advance Parts, O'Reilly Parts, vet, Walmart

163mm rest area both lanes, **full [handicapped] facilities, litter barrels, petwalk, [phone], [picnic], vending**

154 PA 198, to Saegertown, Conneautville

147b a US 6, US 19, US 322, to Meadville, **E** [gas] All American, Citgo/Country Fair/dsl, GetGo, Sheetz/dsl, [food] Applebee's, Arby's, Cracker Barrel, DQ, Dunkin, Hoss's Rest., Jersey Mike's, KFC, Perkins, Pizza Hut, Starbucks, Subway, Super China, Taco Bell, Tim Hortons, [lodging] EconoLodge, Holiday Inn Express, [other] Advance Parts, AT&T, Family$, Giant Eagle Foods, Home Depot, [H], Verizon, **W** [gas] Sheetz/dsl, [food] Burger King, Compadres Mexican, McDonald's, Red Lobster, Subway, Tim Hortons, Yuen's Garden, [lodging] Hampton Inn, Quality Inn, [other] $Tree, ALDI, AutoZone, Chevrolet, O'Reilly Parts, to Pymatuning SP, Toyota, URGENT CARE, Verizon, Walmart

141 PA 285, to Geneva, **E** [other] to Erie NWR(20mi), **W** [gas] Aunt Bee's Rest./dsl, Citgo/dsl

135mm rest area/weigh sta both lanes, **full [handicapped] facilities, litter barrels, petwalk, [phone], [picnic], vending**

130 PA 358, to Sandy Lake, **W** [other] [H](13mi), to Goddard SP

121 US 62, to Mercer, **E** [gas] Sunoco, [food] DQ, [other] $General, Valley Tire, **W** st police

116b a I-80, E to Clarion, W to Sharon

113 PA 208, PA 258, to Grove City, **E** [gas] Citgo/Country Fair/dsl, Marathon/dsl, [food] Compadres Mexican, [other] [H], Seivers Farm Mkt, **W** [gas] KwikFill/Subway, Sheetz/dsl, Tesla EVC, [food] Blackout Burger Bar, Eat'n Park, Fat Eddy's BBQ, Hoss' Rest., Margarita King Mexican, McDonald's, My Bro's Place, Navarro's Grill, Primanti Bros, Taco Bell, Timber Creek Rest., Wendy's, [lodging] Best Western, Candlewood Suites, Hampton Inn, Holiday Inn Express, Quality Inn, Super 8, TownePlace Suites, Wingate, [other] KOA(3mi), Premium Outlets/famous brands

110mm rest area/weigh sta sb, **full [handicapped] facilities, litter barrels, petwalk, [phone], [picnic], vending**

PORTERSVILLE

107mm rest area/weigh sta nb, **full [handicapped] facilities, litter barrels, petwalk, [phone], [picnic], vending**

105 PA 108, to Slippery Rock, **E** [food] Subway, [lodging] Evening Star Motel, [other] $General, Slippery Rock Camping, to Slippery Rock U, **W** [gas] Love's/Subway/dsl/scales24hr

99 US 422, to New Castle, **E** [other] to Moraine SP, **W** [gas] Pilot/McDonald's/Subway/dsl/scales/24hr, [food] Duke's Diner, [other] Coopers Lake Camping, to Rose Point Camping, Truckstop

96 PA 488, Portersville, **E** [other] Moraine SP, **W** [gas] Sunoco/dsl, [food] Brown's Country Kitchen, McConnell's Mill SP(3mi), [other] antiques, Cal's General Store, USPO

88 (87 from nb) US 19, PA 68, Zelienople, **W** [gas] Exxon/dsl, [food] Burger King, DQ, Fox's Pizza, Log Cabin Inn Rest.

85 (83 from nb), PA 528(no quick return), to Evans City, **W** [other] Buick/GMC

83 PA 528, Evans City, **W** [gas] Sunoco, [food] Meadows Fro-Yo, [other] Penske

80mm weigh sta both lanes

78 (76 from nb, exits left from nb), US 19, PA 228, to Mars, access to I-76, PA TPK, **E** [gas] GetGo/dsl, Sheetz/dsl, [food] Applebee's, Chick-fil-A, Cracker Barrel, DiBella's Subs, Firebirds, Jimmy Wan's Chinese, Juniper Grill, Longhorn Steaks, McDonald's, Moe's SW Grill, Noodles&Co,

PA

INTERSTATE 79 Cont'd

78 Continued
Olive Garden, Patron Mexican, Red Robin, River City Grille, Smokey Bones BBQ, Starbucks, Subway, Best Western+, Courtyard, Hilton Garden, Home2 Suites, Marriott, TownePlace Suites, Dick's, Kohl's, Lowe's, PetSmart, Staples, Target, TJ Maxx, Verizon, **W** BP/dsl, Sheetz/dsl, Sunoco/7-11/dsl, Aladdin's Eatery, Arby's, Blaze Pizza, Bob Evans, Bravo Italian, Buffalo Wild Wings, Burger King, Chipotle Mexican, Denny's, Domino's, Dunkin', Eat'n Park, Emiliano's Mexican, Firehouse Subs, First Watch, Five Guys, HotDog Shoppe, Ichiban Steakhouse, Jason's Deli, Jersey Mike's, Jimmy John's, Mad Mex, McDonald's, Monte Cello's Grill, Panda Express, Panera Bread, Pizza Hut, Pizza Roma, Primanti Bros, Saga Steaks, Starbucks, Vocelli Pizza, Wendy's, Candlewood Suites, Clarion Inn, Comfort Inn, DoubleTree, Extended Stay America, Extended Stay America, Quality Inn, Red Roof Inn, Residence Inn, Super 8, Wingate, $Tree, ALDI, AT&T, AutoZone, Barnes&Noble, Best Buy, Costco/gas, Firestone/auto, GetGo, Giant Eagle Foods, Home Depot, H, Marshall's, Michael's, NAPA, NTB Tire, O'Reilly Parts, PepBoys, Rite Aid, Toyota, USPO, Valvoline, Verizon, Walgreens, Walmart

77 I-76/Tpk, to Youngstown

75 US 19 S(from nb), to Warrendale, services on US 19

73 PA 910, to Wexford, **E** BP, Eat'n Park, Starbucks, EconoLodge, **W** Exxon/dsl, Sheetz/dsl, Tesla EVC, Hampton Inn

72 I-279 S(from sb, exits left), to Pittsburgh

68 Mt Nebo Rd, **E** Sheetz/dsl

66 to PA 65, Emsworth

65 to PA 51, Coraopolis, Neville Island, **E** Speedway/Speedway Cafe, Fairfield Inn, Penske Trucks

64.5mm Ohio River

64 PA 51(from nb), to Coraopolis, McKee's Rocks

60 PA 60, Crafton, **E** GetGo/dsl, Primanti Bros, Comfort Inn, Hilltop Motel, Motel 6, H, **W** Juliano's Rest., Meineke

59b I-376 W, US 22 W, US 30(from nb), **W**

59a I-376 E, to Pittsburgh

57 to Carnegie

55 PA 50, to Heidelberg, **E** Marathon/dsl, Sunoco/7-11, Arby's, Bob Evans, ChuckeCheese, Domino's, Dunkin, El Paso Mexican, Golden Dragon, Jersey Mike's, LJ Silver, McDonald's, Moe's SW, Panera Bread, Pizza Hut, Smoothie King, Sonic, Starbucks, Starbucks, Taco Bell, TX Roadhouse, Wendy's, Wingstop, $Tree, Advance Parts, Big G Tire, BigLots, Firestone/auto, Ford, Giant Eagle Foods, Home Depot, Lowe's, Mr Tire, Pepboys, Shop'n Save, TJ Maxx, Valvoline, Walgreens, Walmart

54 PA 50, to Bridgeville, **E** GetGo, Chipotle, Jimmy John's, McDonald's, Starbucks, Holiday Inn Express, ALDI, Chevrolet, H, Midas, Monro, NAPA, URGENT CARE, USPO, **W** Sunoco/dsl, Blaze Pizza, Cane's, Dunkin, Firebirds Grill, First Watch, Five Guys, Primanti Rest., Taco Bell, Tropical Smoothie, Hampton Inn

50mm rest area/weigh sta both lanes, **full facilities, litter barrels, petwalk, , , vending**

48 South Pointe, **W** Jackson's Rest., Subway, Hilton Garden, Holiday Inn Express, Homewood Suites

45 to PA 980, Canonsburg, **E** Sheetz, Jaguar/Land Rover, Toyota, **W** BP, Marathon, Dunkin', KFC/Taco Bell, Little Caesar's, McDonald's, Papa John's, Pizza Hut, Starbucks, Subway, WaiWai Grill, Wendy's, Super 8, $General, Advance Parts, auto/transmission repair, AutoZone, Walgreens

43 PA 519, Houston, **E** Amoco/dsl, H, vet, **W** Sunoco, Freightliner

41 Race Track Rd, **E** Sheetz/dsl, Burger King, Dunkin', Maxwell's, McDonald's, Primanti Rest., Starbucks, Waffle House, Wendy's, Candlewood Suites, Comfort Inn, Country Inn&Suites, Courtyard, DoubleTree, Fairfield Inn, Hampton Inn, Holiday Inn Express, Hyatt Place, Audi, Old Navy, racetrack, Tanger Outlets/famous brands, **W** BP/dsl, Microtel, Trolley Museum

40 Meadow Lands, **W** golf, racetrack, Trolley Museum(3mi)

38 I-70 W, to Wheeling

34 I-70 E, to Greensburg

33 US 40, to Laboratory, **W** KOA

31mm weigh sta sb

30 US 19, to Amity, **W** Exxon/dsl

23 to Marianna, Prosperity

19 US 19, to PA 221, Ruff Creek, **W** Coen Mkt

14 PA 21, to Waynesburg, **E** Amoco/Coen Mkt, Sheetz, Arby's, Bob Evans, Microtel, Quality Inn, Walmart/Subway, **W** BP/dsl, Exxon/dsl, GetGo, Marathon, Sheetz, Sunoco, Burger King, DQ, Fat Angelo's, Golden Wok, Hardee's, KFC, Little Caesar's, McDonald's, McDonald's, Scotty's Pizza, Subway, Taco Bell, Wendy's, EconoLodge, Hampton Inn, Residency Inn, Super 8, $General, $Tree, Advance Parts, ALDI, AutoZone, BigLots, Cadillac/Chevrolet/Subaru, Chrysler/Dodge/Jeep, CVS Drug, Giant Eagle Foods, H, Monro Tire, NAPA, Verizon, Watson's RV Park

7 to Kirby

6mm Welcome Ctr/weigh sta nb, **full facilities, litter barrels, petwalk, , , vending**

1 Mount Morris, **E** Sunoco/Huddle House/dsl/scales/24hr, Meyer's RV, **W** Marathon/Subway/dsl

0mm Pennsylvania/West Virginia state line

INTERSTATE 80

311mm Pennsylvania/New Jersey state line, Delaware River

310.5mm toll booth wb

310 PA 611, Delaware Water Gap, Welcome Ctr/rest area, **S** Gulf, Sunoco, Apple Pie Bakery, Doughboys Pizza, Joe Bosco BBQ, Sycamore Grille, Fairmont Inn, Glenwood Inn, USPO,

309 US 209 N, PA 447, to Marshalls Creek, **N** Gulf, DQ, Dunkin', Staybridge Suites, H

308 East Stroudsburg, **N** Sunoco, Dunkin, Groberg's Cafe, H, WaWa, **S** Roasted Tomato Grill, Quality Inn, Super 8

307 PA 191, Broad St, **N** Burger King, Domino's, McDonald's, Panda Kitchen, Starbucks, Tacos Los Morros, Hampton Inn, $Tree, Giant Foods/gas, H, USPO, Valvoline, Walmart/gas, **S** Sunoco, Compton's Rest., Red Roof Inn

306 Dreher Ave(from wb, no EZ return), **N** WaWa

305 US 209, Main St, **N** Sunoco, Perkins, Pocono Plaza Inn, **S** Exxon/dsl, Holiday Inn Express, Kost Tire & Auto

304 US 209, to PA 33, 9th St (from wb)

303 9th St, from eb, **N** Burger King, Dunkin', Five Guys, Five Star, McDonald's, Momento Italian, Olive Garden, Panera Bread, Popeyes, TX Roadhouse, Wendy's, $Tree, Best Buy, BJ's/gas, Buick/GMC, Chevrolet, Chrysler/Dodge/Jeep, CVS Drug, Home Depot, Hyundai, JC Penney, Kia, Michael's, Midas, Old Navy, Penske, PetSmart, Staples, Target, TJ Maxx, Walgreens, Weis Foods/gas

302 PA 611, to Bartonsville, **N** Exxon/dsl, Giant, Chik-fil-A, Chili's, Duck Donuts, Dunkin', East Gourmet Buffet, Frank's Pizza, Ichiban Steaks, Jersey Mike's, La Tolteca Mexican, Longhorn Steaks, Moe's SW Grill, Red Lobster, Red Robin,

INTERSTATE 80 Cont'd

BLAKESLEE

302 Continued
Sonic, Springhill Suites, Taco Bell, Baymont Inn, Fairfield Inn, Hampton Inn, Advance Parts, AT&T, Dick's, Giant Foods/gas, H, Kohl's, Lowe's, Mavis Tire, Verizon

299 PA 715, Tannersville, N BP/dsl, Mobil/Burger King/dsl, Tesla EVC, Turkey Hill, Domino's, DQ, Dunkin', FoodCourt, Friendly's, NY Pizza, Pocono Diner, Volare Ristorante, Wawa, Wendy's, Best Western+, Scotrun Motel, Ace Hardware, CVS Drug, The Crossing Factory Outlet/famous brands, Weis Foods, S Sunoco/dsl, Days Inn, to Big Pocono SP, to Camelback Ski Area

298 PA 611(from wb), to Scotrun, N Gulf/dsl, Brick Oven Pizza, Eats 'N Sweets, Great Wolf Lodge, Scotrun Diner/motel, to Mt Pocono, U-Haul, USPO

295mm rest area eb, **full facilities, litter barrels, petwalk,** **vending**

293 I-380 N, to Scranton, (exits left from eb)

284 PA 115, to Wilkes-Barre, Blakeslee, N Citgo, Sunoco, WaWa/dsl, Dunkin', Best Western, $General, CVS, Family$, st police, USPO, S Conoco/dsl, fireworks, Jimmy's Auto Services, Pocono Farmers Mkt, to Pocono Raceway, U-Haul

277 PA 940, to PA Tpk(I-476), to Pocono, Lake Harmony, Allentown, N WaWa, Arby's, Burger King, McDonald's, Comfort Inn, Country Place Inn, EconoLodge, Holiday Inn Express, Mtn Laurel Resort, Pocono Inn/Resort, Pocono Resort

274 PA 534, N Exxon/IHOP/dsl/scales/24hr, Sunoco/dsl/24hr, towing/repair, S to Hickory Run SP(6mi)

273mm Lehigh River

CONYNGHAM

273 PA 940, PA 437, to Freeland, White Haven, N Exxon, Fuel One, S Powerhouse Eatery

270mm rest area eb, **full facilities, info, litter barrels, petwalk,** **vending**

262 PA 309, to Hazleton, Mountain Top, N Sunoco/Dunkin', Mary's Rest., Wendy's, EconoLodge, auto/truck repair, Nescopeck SP(5mi), S Valero/dsl, Holiday Inn Express

260b a I-81, N to Wilkes-Barre, S to Harrisburg

256 PA 93, to Nescopeck, Conyngham, N Pilot/Subway/dsl/scales/24hr, Freightliner, S Hampton Inn(4mi), Motel 6, H, towing/truck repair

251mm Nescopeck River

246mm rest area/weigh sta both lanes, **full facilities, litter barrels, petwalk,** **vending, weather info**

242 PA 339, to Mainville, Mifflinville, N Love's/Arby's/dsl/scales/24hr, Sunoco/Burger King/Subway/dsl, McDonald's, Super 8, $General, S Fuelway/dsl, Red Roof Inn

241mm Susquehanna River

BUCKHORN

241b a US 11, to Berwick, Lime Ridge, Bloomsburg, N Red Maple Inn(2mi), H, S Sheetz/dsl, Sunoco/dsl, Applebee's, Arby's, Burger King, China Queen, Domino's, Dunkin', Fish-N-Rib, Little Caesar's, Marley's Grill, McDonald's, Morris Rest., Oliran Japanese, Pizza Hut, Rita's Custard, Subway, Taco Bell, Taste of Italy, Wendy's, Motel 6, Relax Inn, $General, $Tree, AAA, Ace Hardware, Advance Parts, auto repair, BigLots, Buick/GMC, Cadillac/Chevrolet, CVS Drug, Ford/Honda, Giant Foods/gas, Kost Tire, Mr. Tire, Staples, U-Haul, Verizon, Weis Foods/gas

236 PA 487, to Bloomsburg, Lightstreet, N Tesla EVC, Fairfield Inn, S Sunoco, Denny's, Hampton Inn, Turkey Hill Inn, H, to Bloomsburg U

232 PA 42, Buckhorn, N Exxon/Papa John's, TA/Shell/Subway/dsl/scales/24hr/@, Burger King, Cracker Barrel, KFC, Perkins, Quaker Steak&Lube, Ruby Tuesday, Starbucks,

BUCKHORN

232 Continued
Wendy's, Holiday Inn Express, Quality Inn, ALDI, AT&T, Home Depot, S Sheetz/dsl, Gourmet Buffet, Moe's SW Grill, Olive Garden, Panera Bread, Comfort Suites, $Tree, auto repair, Indian Head Camping(3mi), Lowe's, Marshall's, PetCo, Verizon, Walmart/McDonald's

224 PA 54, to Danville, N Exxon/Subway/dsl, S Mobil/dsl, Friendly's, McDonald's, Best Western, Hampton Inn, Red Roof Inn, Super 8, H

219mm rest area both lanes, **full facilities, info, litter barrels, petwalk,** **vending**

215 PA 254, Limestonevill, S Sunoco/dsl/@, Eagle Truckwash

212b a I-180 W, PA 147 S, to Muncy, Williamsport, S Sunoco(1mi), Fairview Country Farm

210.5mm Susquehanna River

210b a US 15, to Williamsport, Lewisburg, N Penske, S Sunoco/dsl, Bonanza, Holiday Inn Express, Quality Inn, H, KOA(5mi)

199 Mile Run

194mm rest area/weigh sta both lanes, full facilities, **litter barrels, petwalk,** **vending**

192 PA 880, to Jersey Shore, N Sunoco/dsl, H, S Valero/dsl

185 PA 477, Loganton, N Valero, S RB Winter SP(12mi), Twilight Diner

LAMAR

178 US 220, Lock Haven, N KwikFill/dsl, Sheetz/dsl, Little Caesar's, Original Italian Pizza, Ruby Tuesday, $General, $Tree, Advance Parts, AT&T, H, Lowe's, NAPA, Walmart, Weis Foods

173 PA 64, Lamar, N Pilot/Subway/dsl/scales/24hr, Cottage Rest., McDonald's, Hampton Inn, Quality Inn/rest., S Flying J/Dunkin'/dsl/LP/scales/24hr, TA/BP/Country Pride/dsl/scales/24hr/@, Valero

161 I-99, US 220 S, PA 26, to Bellafonte, N Bellefonte Camping, KOA, S PSU

158 US 220 S, PA 150, to Altoona, Milesburg, N Amoco/Subway, TA/Country Pride/dsl/scales/24hr/@, Valero/dsl, McDonald's

147 PA 144, to Snow Shoe, N Phillips 66/dsl/repair/24hr, Sunoco/dsl/24hr, Snow Shoe Sandwich Shop, $General, Family$

146mm rest area both lanes, full facilities, **litter barrels, petwalk,** **vending**

138mm Moshannon River

CLEARFIELD

133 PA 53, to Philipsburg, Kylertown, N Exxon, KwikFill/hotel/dsl/scales, Bradley Street Cafe, $General, Mtn View Mkt, USPO, S Black Moshannon SP(9mi)

123 PA 970, to Shawville, Woodland, N Woodland Camping, S Gio's BBQ/dsl(2mi), PP/dsl, st police, USPO

120mm Susquehanna River, W Branch

120 PA 879, Shawville, Clearfield, N Sapp Bros/rest./dsl/scales/24hr/@, Hunter Truck, S BP/dsl, Sheetz, Snappy's, Arby's, Burger King, Dunkin', Dutch Pantry, KFC, McDonald's, Best Western+, Hampton Inn, Holiday Inn Express, Red Roof Inn, Super 8, Wingate, H, Lowe's, Verizon, Walmart/Subway

111mm highest point on I-80 east of Mississippi River, 2250 ft

111 PA 153, to Penfield, N to Parker Dam, to SB Elliot SP, S H

101 PA 255, Du Bois, N Snappy's/dsl, Silverwoods Hotel,

INTERSTATE 80 Cont'd

DU BOIS

101 Continued
camping, KOA, S Sheetz/dsl, A&W/LJ Silver, Buck's Pizza, Burger King, Dunkin, Eat'n Park, Fusion Buffet, Jersey Mike's, McDonald's, Napoli Pizzeria, Perkins, Pizza Hut, Red Lobster, Ruby Tuesday, Station 101 Grill, Subway, Taco Bell, Wendy's, Fairfield Inn, Hampton Inn, Homewood Suites, $General, $Tree, ALDI, AT&T, BigLots, Hobby Lobby, H, JC Penney, Lowe's, Micahels, Monro Tire, O'Reilly Parts, Old Navy, PetCo, Ross, Staples, TJ Maxx, Verizon, Walmart/Subway

97 US 219, to Brockway, Du Bois, S Pilot/Arby's/dsl/scales/24hr, Sheetz/dsl/24hr, Dutch Pantry Rest., Hoss' Rest. (2mi), Best Western(2mi), Holiday Inn Express, Hotel Veranda, Advance Parts(2mi), AutoZone(2mi), Freightliner, H

90 PA 830 E, N Du Bois Regional

87.5mm rest area both lanes, full facilities, **litter barrels, petwalk,** **vending**

BROOKVILLE

86 PA 830, to Reynoldsville

81 PA 28, to Brookville, Hazen

78 PA 36, to Sigel, Brookville, N Flying J/Denny's/dsl/LP/scales/24hr, TA/BP/Taco Bell/dsl/scales/24hr/@, McDonald's, Pizza Hut, Super 8, NAPA, to Cook Forest SP, Verizon, S GetGo/dsl, Marathon/DQ, Sheetz/dsl, A&M, Arby's, Burger King, Moon Palace, Subway, Rodeway Inn, $General, Chrysler/Dodge/Jeep, Family$, truckwash

73 PA 949, Corsica, N to Clear Creek SP, S USPO

70 US 322, to Strattanville

64 PA 66 S, to New Bethlehem, Clarion, N to Clarion U, S CNG

62 PA 68, to Clarion, N BP, KwikFill/dsl, Applebee's, Arby's, Burger King, Eat'n Park, Hunan King, McDonald's, Perkins, Pizza Hut, RRR Roadhouse, Sakura Buffet, Subway, Taco Bell, Clarion, Hampton Inn, Holiday Inn Express, Motel 6, Quality Inn, ALDI, AutoZone, H, Monro Tire, NAPA, Verizon, vet, Walmart/Subway, S Jimmy John's, Microtel

61mm Clarion River

60 PA 66 N, to Shippenville, N Jiffy/dsl, $Tree, Rustic RV/camping, to Cook Forest SP

56mm weigh sta both lanes

53 to PA 338, to Knox, N Big Country Rest., S Dunkin, antiques, Good Tire Service

45 PA 478, to St Petersburg, Emlenton

44.5mm Allegheny River

42 PA 38, to Emlenton, N Amoco/Coen Mkt/Subway/dsl, Pilot/rest./dsl/scales/24hr, Emlenton Motel, Gaslight RV Park, truck/RV repair

BARKEYVILLE

35 PA 308, to Clintonville, N Anchors Away, Family$, Kenworth

30.5mm rest area both lanes, full facilities, **litter barrels, petwalk,** **vending**

29 PA 8, to Franklin, Barkeyville, N Speedway/dsl, Arby's, Burger King, Motel 6, Freightliner, S Heath/dsl, KwikFill/dsl/scales/motel/24hr, TA/BP/dsl/scales/24hr/@, Subway, $General, to Slippery Rock U, truckwash

24 PA 173, to Grove City, Sandy Lake, S Grove City Coll, H

19b a I-79, N to Erie, S to Pittsburgh

15 US 19, to Mercer, N Automated Fueling, PP/dsl, Shell, Burger King, Margarita King Mexican, Rodeway Inn, S Iron Bridge Rest., KOA(4mi)

4b a I-376, PA 60, to PA 18, to Sharon-Hermitage, New Castle, N Sheetz/dsl, Sunoco/Subway/dsl, EconoLodge, Hampton Inn, Holiday Inn Express, Park Inn, Quality Inn,

4b a Continued
Red Roof Inn, Super 8, S DQ, MiddleSex Diner, $General, NAPA

2.5mm Shenango River

1mm Welcome Ctr eb, full facilities, **litter barrels, petwalk,** **vending**

0mm Pennsylvania/Ohio state line

INTERSTATE 81

GREAT BEND

233mm Pennsylvania/New York state line

232mm Welcome Ctr/weigh sta sb, full facilities, **litter barrels, petwalk,**

230.3mm Susquehanna River

230 PA 171, Great Bend, E Kwik Fill, Chrysler/Dodge/Jeep, Lakeside Camping, W Exxon/Tim Hortons/dsl, Sunoco/dsl, Bluestone Pizza, Burger King, Dobb's Country Kitchen, Dunkin', McDonald's, Subway, Tedeschi's Pizza, Colonial Brick Motel, Family$, Rob's Foods

223 PA 492, New Milford, E East Lake Camping/RV Park, W Citgo/dsl, Gulf/dsl, Green Gables Rest., Uncle Charlie's Pizza, Blue Ridge Motel, Parkview Hotel, USPO

219 PA 848, to Gibson, E Sunoco/Burger King/dsl, Armetta's Pizza, W Exxon/McDonald's/dsl/24hr, Flying J/Denny's/dsl/scales/24hr, Holiday Inn Express, st police

217 PA 547, Harford, E Exxon/Subway/dsl/24hr, Mobil/dsl/24hr

211 PA 92, Lenox, E Elk Mtn Ski Area, Shady Rest Camping, W Citgo/dsl, Shell/dsl, Bingham's Rest., Lenox Creamery, Rustic Roost Cafe, Lenox Drug

209mm rest area sb, full facilities, **litter barrel, petwalk,** **vending**

206 PA 374, to Glenwood, Lenoxville, E Sunoco/dsl, Elk Mountain Ski Resort

203mm rest area nb, full facilities, **litter barrels, petwalk,** **vending**

CLARKS SUMMIT

202 PA 107, to Fleetville, Tompkinsville

201 PA 438, East Benton, W Duchniks/dsl/repair, B&B Rest.

199 PA 524, Scott, E Gulf/dsl, golf, W Exxon/Subway, La Rosa Italian, Motel 81, Lackawanna SP

197 PA 632, Waverly, E Weis Foods, W Sunoco/Doc's Deli, Camelot Inn/rest

194 US 6, US 11, to I-476/PA Tpk, Clarks Summit, W Exxon/dsl, Sheetz/dsl, Sunoco/dsl, Valero, Abbiocco Italian, Burger King, Dino&Francesco's, Domino's, DQ, Dunkin', Jimmy John's, Krispy Kreme, Kyoto Japanese, McDonald's, Moe's SW Grill, Ninas Wings, Starbucks, Subway, Sunny Chinese, Taco Bell, Tully's Rest., Waffle House, Wendy's, EconoLodge, Hampton Inn, Ramada Inn, Spark Hotel, Ace Hardware, Advance Parts, Kost Tire, Valvoline, Verizon, Weis Mkt

191b a US 6, US 11, to Carbondale, E Sheetz/dsl, Sunoco, A&W/LJ Silver, Anthony's Italian, Applebee's, Basilico's Pizza, Buffalo Wild Wings, Burger King, Burrito loco, Chick-fil-A, China Palace, Chipotle, ChuckECheese, Denny's, DQ, Dunkin', Five Guys, Harbor Crabs, HoneyBaked Ham, Jersey Mike's, La Tonalateca, McDonald's, Olive Garden, Panera Bread, Perkins, Primanti Bros, PrimoHoagies Sandwiches, Red Lobster, Red Robin, Rita's Custard, Roma Pizza, Royal Buffet, Starbucks, Subway, Taco Bell, TGIFriday's, Tokyo Japanese, TX Roadhouse, Viewmont Diner, Days Inn, Holiday Inn Express, Home2 Suites, $Tree, ALDI, AT&T, Books-A-Million, Dick's, Discount Tire, Firestone/auto, Harley-Davidson, Hobby Lobby, Home Depot, Hyundai, JC Penney, Kohl's, Macy's, Marshall's, Mavis, Michael's, Old Navy, PepBoys, PetSmart, Target, TJ Maxx, URGENT CARE, Verizon, Walmart, Wegmans Foods, W Anthracite Museum

190 Main Ave, Dickson City, E Colarusso's Pizza, Wendy's,

= gas = food = lodging = other = rest stop

INTERSTATE 81 Cont'd

DICKSON CITY

190 Continued
Fairfield Inn, Microtel, Residence Inn, auto repair, Best Buy, Ford, Lowe's, Sam's Club/gas, Staples, vet, W Dunkin', Schiff's Mkt, Toyota

188 PA 347, Throop, E Sheetz/dsl, Sunoco/dsl, Joey's Pizza, McDonald's, Starbucks, Wendy's, Baymont Inn, Dunmore Inn, Rodeway Inn, Sleep Inn, Advance Parts, BigLots, Kost Tire, Nissan, PriceChopper Foods, st police, Tire Choice, URGENT CARE, W Exxon/Subway/dsl, Burger King, Dunkin', Yummy Bowl

187 to I-84, I-380, US 6(no return from nb)

186 PA 435, Drinker St (from nb), E Sunoco/dsl, W Exxon/dsl, Drinker Pizza

185 Central Scranton Expwy (exits left from nb), W H

184 to PA 307, River St, W Exxon/Subway/dsl, Vamco, Asian Taste, Anz Hotel, $Tree, CVS Drug, Fresh Grocer, H

182 Davis St, Montage Mtn Rd, E EVC, Exxon/Coldstone/Subway/dsl, Tesla EVC, Akita Japanese, Burger King, Chipotle, Dave&Busters, Duck Donuts, Food&Fire BBQ, Harvest Seasonal Grill, Jersey Mike's, Longhorn Steaks, Nonno's Pizza, Panchero's Mexican, Panchero's Mexican, Panera Bread, Starbucks, Comfort Suites, Courtyard, Fairfield Inn, Hampton Inn, Springhill Suites, TownePlace Suites, W Sunoco, Dunkin', Taco Bell, Waffle House, Wendy's, EconoLodge, CVS Drug, USPO

AVOCA

180 to US 11, PA 502, to Moosic, (exits left from nb), W Citgo/dsl, Sunoco, 50s Diner

178b a to US 11, Avoca, E Best Western+, W Petro/Shell/Iron Skillet/dsl/scales/24hr/@

175b a PA 315 S, to I-476, Dupont, E Exxon/Subway/dsl, Sunoco/dsl, Arby's, McDonald's, Knights Inn, Volvo, W Pilot/Wendy's/dsl/scales/24hr, Burger King, Denny's, Star Asia Buffet, Taco Bell, Uncle Joe's Pizza, Candlewood Suites, Holiday Inn Express, truck repair, Verizon, Walmart

WILKES-BARRE

170b a PA 115, PA 309, Wilkes-Barre, E Exxon/Subway/dsl, Sunoco/dsl, Tesla EVC, Holiday Inn, W Sheetz, Sunoco/dsl, Bettelli's Villa Italian, Buffalo Wild Wings, Burger King, Denny's, Dough Co. Pizza, Dunkin', El Azteca Mexican, Friendly's, Grotto Pizza, Harvest Buffet, IHOP, Jersey Mike's, Longhorn Steaks, McDonald's, Moe's SW Grill, Red Lobster, Sonic, TGIFriday's, Wendy's, Days Inn, Extended Stay America, Fairfield Inn, Holiday Inn Express, Host Inn, Red Roof Inn, Wilkes Barr Inn, Woodlands Inn, Woodspring Suites, $General, AutoZone, Chevrolet, H, JC Penney, Lexus, Macy's, Mavis, Mercedes, Pocono Downs, Toyota

168 Highland Park Blvd, Wilkes-Barre, W Sheetz/dsl, Sunoco/Subway/dsl, Tesla EVC, Applebee's, Blaze Pizza, Bob Evans, Chick-fil-A, Chipotle, ChuckeCheese, Cracker Barrel, King's Buffet, La Tolteca Mexican, Miller's Alehouse, Mirakuya Japanese, Mizu Steaks, Nello's Pizza, Olive Garden, Outback Steaks, Panera Bread, Popeyes, Red Robin, Smokey Bones BBQ, Starbucks, TX Roadhouse, Wendy's, Courtyard, Hampton Inn, Hilton Garden, Motel 6, $Tree, AT&T, Barnes&Noble, Best Buy, Dick's, Firestone/auto, Hobby Lobby, Home Depot, Kohl's, Kost Tire/auto, Lowe's, Marshall's, Michael's, Nissan, Old Navy, PepBoys, PetCo, PetSmart, PriceChopper, Ross, Sam's Club/gas, Staples, Target, TJ Maxx, U-Haul, URGENT CARE, Verizon, Walgreens, Walmart/Subway, Wegman's Foods

165b a PA 309 S, (exits left from nb), Wilkes-Barre, W Burger King, Citgo/dsl, Dunkin', McDonald's, Perkins, Taco Bell, Comfort Inn, Quality Inn, $Tree

164 PA 29, to Nanticoke, Ashley

159 Nuangola, W Valero/dsl, $General

PA

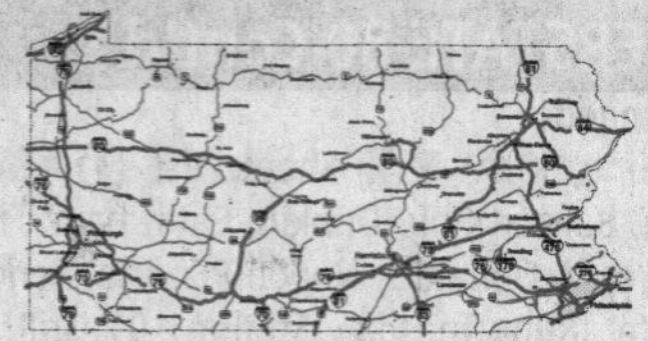

MAHANOY CITY

157mm rest area/weigh sta sb, full facilities, **litter barrels, petwalk**, **vending**

156mm rest area/weigh sta nb, full facilities, **litter barrels, petwalk**, **vending**

155 to Dorrance, E Sunoco/dsl, W Blue Ridge Plaza/dsl

151b a I-80, E to Mountaintop, W to Bloomsburg

145 PA 93, W Hazleton, E Sunoco/Dunkin'/dsl, TurkeyHill/dsl, Applebee's, Arby's, Chipotle, Damon's, Denny's, Five Stars Chinese, McDonald's, Panera Bread, Perkins, Pizza Hut, Popeyes, Subway, Taco Bell, Wendy's, Comfort Inn, Fairfield Inn, Forest Hill Inn, Advance Parts, ALDI, AT&T, Big Lots, Boscov's, Buick/Cadillac/GMC, Chrysler/Dodge/Jeep, H, Lowe's, Michael's, Old Navy, Penske, PetSmart, st police, TJ Maxx, Verizon, Walmart/McDonald's, Weis Foods, W Citgo, Damenti's, Top of the 80's, Candlewood Suites, Hampton Inn

143 PA 924, to Hazleton, W Fuelon/Citgo/dsl/scales, Sunoco/Subway, TurkeyHill/dsl, Burger King, Sonic, Residence Inn

141 PA 424, S Hazleton Beltway, E Mt Laurel Motel

138 PA 309, to McAdoo, E Sunoco

134 to Delano

132mm parking area/weigh sta both lanes

131b a PA 54, Mahanoy City, E Tuscarora/Locust Lake SP, W Conoco/dsl, Sunoco/dsl, Comfort Inn & Suites

124b a PA 61, to Frackville, E Cracker Barrel, McDonald's, Holiday Inn Express, BigLots, W Exxon, Gulf/dsl, Speedway, Anthony's Pizza, Dutch Kitchen, Subway, EconoLodge, Granny's Motel, Motel 6, st police

119 High Ridge Park Rd, to Gordon, E Country Inn&Suites

116 PA 901, to Minersville

112 PA 25, to Hegins, W camping

107 US 209, to Tremont

104 PA 125, Ravine, E Exxon/Burger King/dsl/scales/24hr, Echo Valley Campground

GRANTVILLE

100 PA 443, to Pine Grove, E Sunoco/dsl, Arby's, McDonald's, Baymont, Comfort Inn, Knights Inn, $General, W Pilot/dsl/scales/24hr, Pine Grove Diner, Hampton Inn, truckwash, vet

90 PA 72, to Lebanon, E Exxon/Subway, Love's/McDonald's/dsl/scales/24hr/@, Speedway/dsl, Burger King, Wendy's, Fairfield Inn, Holiday Inn Express, auto repair, Freightliner, KOA, st police, W SureStay+

89 I-78 E, to Allentown

85b a PA 934, to Annville, W Funck's Rest., IndianTown Gap Nat Cem

80 PA 743, Grantville, E Sheetz, Shell/dsl, Fabio's Italian, Days Inn, Hampton Inn, Mainstay Suites, Tru Hotel, W Exxon/dsl, Italian Delight, Best Western, Holiday Inn, racetrack

79mm rest area/weigh sta both lanes, full facilities, **litter barrels, petwalk**, **vending**

77 PA 39, to Hershey, E ONE9/Pizza Hut/dsl/scales/24hr, Sheetz/dsl, Manda Hill Diner, Avid Hotel, Country Inn&Suites, EconoLodge, La Quinta, Motel 6, Super 8, WildWoods Inn, Hershey Attractions, st police, W Flying J/Perkins/dsl/24hr/@, TA/Country Pride/dsl/scales/24hr/@, McDonald's, Holiday Inn Express, Goodyear, SpeedCo, truck repair

72 to US 22, Linglestown, E Marathon/dsl, Sunoco/dsl,

INTERSTATE 81 Cont'd

LINGLESTOWN

72 Continued
Burger King, Chick-fil-A, Chipotle Mexican, Coldstone, Five Guys, McDonald's, Mission BBQ, Noodles&Co, Olive Garden, Red Robin, Starbucks, Subway, Wendy's, Baymont Inn, Quality Inn, $Tree, Advance Parts, Chrysler/Dodge/Jeep, Costco/gas, CVS Drug, Dick's Sports, Harley-Davidson, Hobby Lobby, Karn's Foods, Kohl's, Lidl Foods, Target, Toyota, U-Haul, W Turkey Hill, Shangrila Japanese, Subway, Candlewood Suites, Ramada Inn, Woodspring Suites, $G Mkt, Ace Hardware

70 I-83 S, to York,

69 Progress Ave, E Cracker Barrel, Dunkin', Harvest Grill, Macaroni Grill, Tonino's Grill, Home2 Suites, AT&T, CVS Drug, Susquehanna Shoppes, W Turkey Hill/dsl, Arby's, Burger King, Plaza Azteca, Best Western, Hampton Inn, Red Roof Inn, Residence Inn, SpringHill Suites, vet

67b a US 22, US 322 W, PA 230, Cameron St, to Lewistown

66 Front St, E Sunoco, Dunkin', W Exxon, Sunoco, Front St Diner, McDonald's, Pizza Hut, Simply Turkey, Two Guys Pizza, Wendy's, Days Inn, Motel 6

65 US 11/15, to Enola, E Sunoco/dsl, Al's Pizza, China Taste, Domino's, DQ, Dunkin', McDonald's, Squeaky Rail Diner, Subway, Wendy's, Quality Inn, $Tree, Advance Parts, Fischer Parts

61 PA 944, to Wertzville, E Burger King, Taco Bell, Tonino's Pizza, Valley Bistro, Holiday Inn Express, AT&T, Giant/dsl, H, Weiss Mkt, W Turkey Hill/dsl, Best Western+

59 PA 581, to US 11, to I-83, Harrisburg

57 PA 114, to Mechanicsburg, E Sheetz/dsl, Alfredo's Pizza, Arby's, Dickey's BBQ, Great Wall Chinese, Isaac's Rest., KFC/LJ Silver, McDonald's, Olive Garden, Pizza Hut, Red Robin, Silver Spring Diner, Subway, Taco Bell, Home2 Suites, La Quinta, CarMax, Giant Foods/gas, Sam's Club/gas, Walmart

MIDDLESEX

52b a US 11, to I-76/PA Tpk, Middlesex, E Flying J/Denny's/dsl/scales/24hr/@, I-81/dsl, Sheetz/dsl, Tesla EVC, Dunkin', Middlesex Diner, Moonlight Diner, Motel 6, Quality Inn, Super 8, H, W Gulf, Love's/Wendy's/dsl/24hr, Petro/Iron Skillet/dsl/24hr/@, Rutters/dsl, Sunoco/Subway/dsl, Arby's, Burger King, Happy Chen Chinese, McDonald's, Popeyes, Royal Kitchen, Waffle House, American Inn, Best Value, Best Western, Comfort Inn, Days Inn, EconoLodge, Holiday Inn Express, Larkspur Landing Hotel, Residence Inn, Rodeway Inn, Blue Beacon, H, Speedco, vet

49 PA 74(no EZ sb return), same as 48, E Sheetz/dsl, Hardee's, W Super Mart, Trindle Grill, AAA

48 PA 74, York Rd(no EZ nb return), E Sheetz, Asian Cafe, Hardee's, Red Robin, Starbucks, Subway, Microtel, $Tree, ALDI, antiques, Kohl's, Michael's, PetSmart, Target, Verizon, W Gulf/dsl, Speedway, Burger King, Dunkin', El Rodeo Mexican, McDonald's, Pizza Hut, Southside Deli, Taco Bell, $Tree, Ford, Harry's Kwik Stop, Lowe's, Midas, Valvoline, Weis Mkt

47 PA 34, Hanover St, E 7-11, Chili's, Cracker Barrel, Sleep Inn, Home Depot, W Applebee's, Bruster's/Nathan's, Chick-fil-A, China Palace, Chipotle, DQ, Five Guys, Panera Bread, Papa John's, Rita's Custard, Super Buffet, Vinny's Rest., Wendy's, AT&T, CVS Drug, Staples, TJ Maxx, Walmart

45 College St, E Gulf/dsl, Alfredo Pizza, Arby's, Hoss's Rest., McDonald's, Best Western, Super 8, Giant Food Mkt, H, Monro, Tire Pros, Verizon

44 PA 465, Allen Rd, to Plainfield, E Country Inn&Suites, Fairfield Inn, Holiday Inn Express, MainStay Suites, H, st police, W Sheetz/dsl, Burger King, vet

38.5mm rest area both lanes, full facilities, **litter barrels**, **petwalk**,

SCOTLAND

37 PA 233, to Newville, E Pine Grove Furnace SP, W Col Denning SP

29 PA 174, King St, E Sunoco/dsl, Rodeway Inn, W Gulf, Rutter's/dsl, Bros Pizza, Burger King, China House, Domino's, El Mariachi Mexican, Jersey Mike's, KFC, Starbucks, Subway, Taco Bell, Wendy's, Best Western, Holiday Inn Express, Theo's Motel, $General, Advance Parts, ALDI, Cadillac/Chevrolet, CVS Drug, Ford, Verizon, vet, Walmart

24 PA 696, Fayette St, E Sheetz/dsl, W Pacific Pride/dsl, Maplewood Farm Mkt

20 PA 997, Scotland, E Citgo/dsl, McDonald's, Comfort Inn, Super 8, $General, W Pit Stop, Sunoco, Quality Inn

17 Walker Rd, W Sheetz/dsl, Aki Japanese, Bruster's/Nathan's, Buffalo Wild Wings, Cafe del Sol, Chick-fil-A, Chipotle Mexican, Five Guys, Jersey Mike's, Longhorn Steaks, MOD Pizza, Naruto Asian, Olive Garden, Panera Bread, Primanti Bros, Red Robin, Sonic, Starbucks, Subway, TX Roadhouse, Candlewood Suites, Country Inn&Suites, Springhill Suites, ALDI, AT&T, BJ's/dsl, Buick/Chevrolet/GMC, Ford, Giant Foods/gas, Kohl's, Mr Tire, PetSmart, Staples, Target, URGENT CARE

16 US 30, to Chambersburg, E Sheetz/dsl, Arby's, Bonanza, Bro's Pizza, Domino's, DQ, Dunkin', Hoss's Rest., KFC, Ledo Pizza, Little Caesar's, Perkins, Popeyes, Wendy's, Sleep Inn, $Tree, AAA, Dick's, Harley-Davidson, Hobby Lobby, Lowe's, NAPA, Nissan/Toyota, TJ Maxx, U-Haul, vet, Walmart/gas, W Big Oak Cafe, Burger King, Copper Kettle, Domino's, Hardee's, McDonald's, Pizza Hut, Sunrise Diner, Taco Bell, Best Western, La Quinta, Travelodge, Tru, Advance Parts, AutoZone, H, Lincoln

GREENCASTLE

14 PA 316, Wayne Ave, E Sheetz/dsl, Bob Evans, Cracker Barrel, Baymont Inn, Hampton Inn, Red Carpet Inn, W KwikFill, Sunoco, Applebee's, Arby's, China Wok, Dunkin, Mario's Italian, Montezuma Mexican, Papa John's, Red Lobster, Starbucks, Stoner's Rest., Subway, Twin Dragon Chinese, Volcano Japanese, Wendy's, Econolodge, Holiday Inn Express, Red Roof Inn, $Tree, CVS Drug, Giant Foods/gas, Jiffy Lube, Mr Tire, Verizon, Weis Mkt

12mm weigh sta sb

10 PA 914, Marion

7mm weigh sta nb

5 PA 16, Greencastle, E BP/dsl, Sheetz/dsl, Sunoco/dsl, TA/Country Pride/dsl/scales/24hr/@, Burger King, Godfather's, McDonald's, Subway, Taco Bell, Super 8, truckwash, vet, Whitetail Ski Resort, W Exxon/Dunkin'/dsl, Green Motel, AutoZone, H

3 US 11, E Bro's Pizza, La Plazita Mexican, Holiday Inn Express, Bowers Tire/auto, W Sheetz/dsl, Chevrolet, URGENT CARE

2mm Welcome Ctr nb, full facilities, **litter barrels**, **petwalk**, **vending**

1 PA 163, Mason-Dixon Rd, W Hoffman's Grill, State Line Inn, Keystone RV Ctr

0mm Pennsylvania/Maryland state line, Mason-Dixon Line

INTERSTATE 83

51b a I-83 begins/ends on I-81, exit 70.

50b a US 22, Jonestown Rd, Harrisburg, E Liberty, Sunoco/7-11/dsl, Blaze Pizza, Buffalo Wild Wings, Chick-fil-A, Chipotle Mexican, Cold Stone, Domino's, El Rodeo Mexican, Five Guys, Gilligan's Grill, Hibachi Grill, LJ Silver, Longhorn Steaks, McAlister's, McDonald's, Mission BBQ, Noodles&Co, Olive Garden, Panera Bread, Pizza Hut, Red Lobster,

PA

= gas = food = lodging = other = rest stop

INTERSTATE 83 Cont'd

HARRISBURG

50b a Continued
Red Robin, Shogun Asian, Starbucks, Subway, Taco Bell, Wendy's, $Tree, Advance Parts, ALDI, AT&T, AutoZone, Batteries+, Best Buy, BooksAMillion, Boscov's, Costco/gas, CVS Drug, Dick's, Ford, Hobby Lobby, Home Depot, Kohl's, Marshall's, Mavis Tire, Meineke, Michael's, NTB, Old Navy, PepBoys, PetCo, Ross, Shannon Tire/auto, Target, Tires+, U-Haul, Verizon, vet, W Sunoco/dsl, DQ, Dunkin', Gabriella's Italian, Johnstown Diner, KFC, Jiffy Lube

48 Union Deposit Rd, E Sunoco, Sunoco, Arby's, Burger King, Dunkin', Panera Bread, Best Western, Hampton Inn, $Tree, Giant Foods/gas, H, Staples, URGENT CARE, W Gulf/dsl, Sheetz/dsl, Tesla EVC, Chipotle, ChuckeCheese, Great Wall Chinese, HFC Pizza, IHOP, Jimmy John's, Little Caesars, McDonald's, Naples Pizza, New China, Rita's Ice Cream, Starbucks, Subway, TX Roadhouse, Waffle House, Wendy's, Comfort Inn, Country Inn&Suites, EconoLodge, Fairfield Inn, Holiday Inn Express, $General, $Tree, BigLots, Lowe's, PriceRite Foods, Weis Foods

47 (46b from nb), US 322 E, to Hershey, Derry St, E Papa John's, Home Depot, PetSmart/vet

46b a I-283 S, to I-76/PA Tpk, Sheetz/dsl, Sunoco/dsl, Capitol Diner, Chick-fil-A, Chili's, El Rancho Mexican, El Sol Mexican, Five Guys, Friendly's, Lancaster Brewing Rest., Leeds Rest., McDonald's, Panera Bread, Subway, Tropical Smoothie, Courtyard, EconoLodge, Hotel Indigo, Howard Johnson, La Quinta, Red Lion Inn, Red Roof Inn, Residence Inn, Sheraton, Sleep Inn, Super 8, $General, JC Penney, Kia, Monro, Petco, Target, Verizon

45 Paxton St, E Sheetz/dsl, Applebee's, Burger King, Dunkin', Fiesta Mexico, Lin He Buffet, McDonald's, Melting Pot, Papa Joe's Pizza, Pizza Hut, Ruby Tuesday, Tomato Pie Cafe, Hilton Garden, Homewood Suites, Towneplace Suites, $Tree, Advance Parts, AutoZone, Bass Pro Shops, Honda, Meineke, Nissan, Subaru

44b 17th St, 19th St, E Sunoco, Turkey Hill, Dunkin', El Patron Mexican, Hardee's, Kajimachi Japanese, McDonald's, Advance Parts, AutoZone, Buick/GMC, Firestone/auto, Hyundai, Midas, Tires+

44a PA 230, 13th St, Harrisburg, downtown, E Family$, W Chevrolet, VW

43 2nd St, downtown, Harrisburg, W Crowne Plaza, Hilton, H, st capitol

42.5mm Susquehanna River

42 Lemoyne

41b Highland Park, E Burger King, KFC, W VP Racing Fuels, Vito's Italian, Ace Hardware, Weis Foods

FISHING CREEK

41a US 15, PA 581 W, to Gettysburg

40b New Cumberland, W Sheetz/dsl, Cedar Cliff Pizza, Chipotle, Jersey Mike's, Joey's Chicken Shack, McDonald's, New China, Starbucks, Subway, CVS Drug

40a Limekiln Rd, to Lewisberry, E Shell/dsl, Sunoco, John's Diner, McDonald's, Pizza Hut, Budget Inn, Fairfield Inn, Holiday Inn Express, La Quinta, Super 8, W Exxon, Best Western+, Motel 6, Scottish Inn, vet

39b I-76/PA Tpk

39a PA 114, Lewisberry Rd, E Rutter's/dsl, Days Inn, Highland Inn, Red Carpet Inn

38 Reesers Summit

36 PA 262, Fishing Creek, E Speedway, Culhane's Steaks, Mamma's Pizza, CVS Drug

35 PA 177, Lewisberry, E Patriot Pizza/subs, W Exxon, Francesco's Pizza, Summit Rest.

34mm parking area/weigh sta sb

34 same as 33, from nb, Valley Green

PA

EMIGSVILLE

33 PA 392, Yocumtown, E Rutter's, Speedway/dsl, Brothers Pizzaria, Burger King, KFC/Taco Bell, Maple Donuts, McDonald's, New China Buffet, Starbucks, Subway, Xing Xing Buffet, Value Inn, $Tree, Advance Parts, AutoZone, Verizon, Walmart

33mm parking area/weigh sta nb

32 PA 382, Newberrytown, E Rutter's/dsl/24hr, Sunoco/dsl, Dunkin, W Exxon/dsl

28 PA 295, Strinestown, W Rutter's/24hr, Sheetz/dsl, 83 Diner, Wendy's

24 PA 238, Emigsville, W Sunoco/dsl

22 PA 181, N George St, same as 21b, E Rutter's, Comfort Inn, Homewood Suites

21b a US 30, Arsenal Rd, to York, E Sheetz/dsl, Cheddar's, Clock Diner, Qdoba, Starbucks, Days Inn, Inn at York, MainStay, Motel 6, Sheraton, Sleep Inn, Tru Hilton, Buick/GMC, W Royal Farms/dsl, Rutter's/dsl, Sheetz/dsl, Arby's, Bob Evans, Buffalo Wild Wings, Burger King, Burger King, Chick-fil-A, Chili's, China Buffet, Chipotle, Denny's, Domino's, DQ, Dunkin', El Rodeo Mexican, Friendly's, Fujihana Japanese, Great Wall, Hardee's, Hoss's, Infinito's, Jersey Mike's, KFC, Little Caesar's, LJ Silver, Lyndon Diner, Maple Donuts, McDonald's, Mission BBQ, MOD Pizza, Olive Garden, Panera Bread, Pizza Hut, Plaza Azteca Mexican, Quaker Steak, Rita's Custard, Smokey Bones BBQ, Smoothie King, Starbucks, Subway, Taco Bell, Tropical Smoothie, Wendy's, Wendy's, Best Western, La Quinta, Motel 6, Ramada, Wingate Inn, Wyndham, $General, Advance Parts, ALDI, AutoZone, BigLots, BJ's Whse/gas, BMW, Cadillac/Chevrolet, Chrysler/Dodge/Jeep, CVS Drug, Giant Foods/gas, Harley-Davidson, Hobby Lobby, Honda, Kia, Kohl's, Lowe's, Mavis Tire, Mitsubishi, Monro, Nissan, NTB, Old Navy, PetCo, PetSmart, Ross, Staples, Subaru, Taco Bell, Target, TJ Maxx, URGENT CARE, Verizon, Verizon, Walmart, Weis Foods/gas, Weis Mkt

19 PA 462, Market St, E Giant/dsl, Rutter's/dsl, Applebee's, Arby's, Aroma Buffet, Buffalo Wild Wings, Chick-fil-A, ChuckECheese's, DQ, Dunkin', Fiesta Mexican Firehouse Subs, KFC, Little Caesars, Memory Lane Pizza MOD Pizza, Moe's SW, Panera Bread, Papa John's, Popeyes Red Lobster, Rita's Custard, Smoothie King, Starbucks, Taco Bell, Taco Bell, Village Green, Wendy's, Yummy Yummy, Quality Inn, $General, $Tree, Advance Parts, ALDI AutoZone, Burlington Coats, Firestone/auto, Giant Foods/gas, Goodyear/auto, Home Depot, Lowe's, Mavis Tire Mazda, Meineke, NTB, Petco, Sam's Club/gas, Valvoline Verizon, Volvo, Walgreens, Walmart, Weis Mkt, W H

18 PA 124, Mt Rose Ave, Prospect St, E Rutters, Arooga's Grille, Burger King, Five Guys, Nino's Pizza, Parma Pizza Grill Pizza Hut, $Tree, Grocery Outlet, Nello Tire

16b a PA 74, Queen St, E Sunoco, Baskin-Robbins/Dunkin Cracker Barrel, IHOP, Imperial Gourmet, Isaac's Rest., J Panda, Maple Donuts, MOD Pizza, Primanti Bros, Starbucks Stone Grille, Country Inn&Suites, Hampton Inn, Home Suites, Giant Foods/gas, W Sheetz/dsl, Chipotle Infinito's Pizza, Jersey Mike's, Jimmy John's, McDonald's Noodles&Co, Panera Bread, Pizza Hut/Taco Bell, Starbucks Subway, Wendy's, $General, $Tree, AT&T, CVS Drug Monro, Price Rite Foods, vet, Walgreens, Weis Mkt

15 S George St, I-83 spur into York, W H

INTERSTATE 83 Cont'd

GLEN ROCK

Exit #	Services
14	PA 182, Leader Heights, **E** Sheetz/dsl, Tesla EVC, Arby's, Domino's, First Wok, vet, **W** Rutter's, McDonald's, Best Western+
10	PA 214, Loganville, **W** Rutter's/dsl, Mamma's Pizza, $General
8	PA 216, Glen Rock, **W** Shrewsbury Mkt(2mi)
4	PA 851, Shrewsbury, **E** Burger King, Cracker Barrel, Papa John's, Ruby Tuesday, Hampton Inn, Home Depot, **W** Exxon/dsl, Arby's, Chick-fil-A, Chipotle, Coachlight Rest., Emerald Garden Chinese, Five Guys, Jersey Mike's, KFC/Taco Bell, McDonald's, Panera Bread, Rita's Custard, Sons of Italy Pizzaria, Starbucks, Subway, Wendy's, $Tree, Advance Parts, antiques, Giant Foods, Mr Tire, NAPA, Saubel's Foods, URGENT CARE, Verizon, vet, Walmart
2mm	Welcome Ctr nb, full facilities, **litter barrels**, **petwalk**, **vending**
0mm	Pennsylvania/Maryland state line

INTERSTATE 84

DINGMANS FERRY

Exit #	Services
54mm	Pennsylvania/New York state line, Delaware River
53	US 6, PA 209, Welcome Ctr/both lanes, Matamoras, **N** full facilities, **full** **facilities**, **litter barrels**, PA Welcome Ctr, **petwalk**, **vending**, Shell, Sunoco, TurkeyHill/dsl, The Grill, Two Rivers Grille, AutoZone, fireworks, Market 32, **S** Sunoco/dsl, Dunkin', Goodfella's Italian, Luna Rossa Pizza, McDonald's, Peking Garden, Perkins, Popeyes, Subway, Taco Bell, Village Diner, Wayback Burger, Wendy's, Best Western, Hampton Inn, Scottish Inn, $Tree, Advance Parts, Home Depot, Lowe's, Mavis Tire/auto, ShopRite Foods, TJ Maxx, Tristate RV Park, Verizon, Walmart/auto
46	US 6, to Milford, **N** Mirabito/dsl, **S** Exxon/dsl, Gulf, TurkeyHill, Apple Valley Rest., Chang Mao Chinese, China Buffet, Dimmick Inn Steaks, John's Pizza, Rodeway Inn, Key Food Mkt, NAPA, U-Haul, USPO
34	PA 739, to Lords Valley, Dingmans Ferry, **S** Mirabito/dsl, Sunoco/Dunkin'/dsl, Bruno's Pizza, Hunter Valley Rest., McDonald's, Panda Chinese, Family$, Walgreens, Weis Foods
30	PA 402, to Blooming Grove, **N** Lake Wallenpaupack, st police, White Deer Campground
26	PA 390, to Tafton, **N** Exxon/dsl, Lake Wallenpaupack, Tanglewood Ski Area, **S** Promised Land SP
26mm	**full** **facilities**, **litter barrels**, **petwalk**, /weigh sta both lanes, **vending**
20	PA 507, Greentown, **N** Exxon/dsl, Sunoco/Subway, John's Italian, Claws'n Paws Animal Park
17	PA 191, to Newfoundland, Hamlin, **N** Exxon/dsl/scales/24hr, IHOP, Comfort Inn, dsl repair
8	PA 247, PA 348, Mt Cobb, **N** Mobil/dsl, Sunoco/Burger King/Tim Hortons/dsl, Isabella's Eatery, $General
4	I-380 S, to Mount Pocono
2	PA 435 S, to Elmhurst
1	Tigue St, **N** The Bistro Grill, Holiday Inn, **S** Sunoco/dsl
0mm	I-84 begins/ends on I-81, exit 54.

INTERSTATE 90

NORTH EAST

Exit #	Services
46mm	Pennsylvania/New York state line, **full** **facilities**, **litter barrels**, **petwalk**, **vending**, Welcome Ctr/weigh sta wb
45	US 20, to State Line, **N** KwikFill/dsl/scales, McDonald's, **S** Citgo/dsl, Red Carpet Inn, fireworks
41	PA 89, North East, **N** New Harvest Rest., Continued Holiday Inn Express, **S** Creekside Camping, golf
37	I-86 E, to Jamestown
35	PA 531, to Harborcreek, **N** TA/IHOP/Pizza Hut/Subway/dsl/scales/24hr/@, Blue Beacon, dsl repair
32	PA 430, PA 290, to Wesleyville, **N** Country Fair, GetGo/dsl, John's Pizza, Cobblestone Hotel
29	PA 8, to Hammett, **N** Country Fair, Wendy's, **S** Days Inn, dsl repair
27	PA 97, State St, Waterford, **N** Country Fair/dsl, Kwik Fill, Arby's, Barbato's Italian, Doc Holiday's Grill, McDonald's, Clarion, La Quinta, Motel 6, Red Roof Inn, **S** Pilot/Subway/dsl/scales/24hr, Sheetz/dsl, Shell/Tim Hortons/dsl, Taco Bell, Baymont Inn, Quality Inn, Super 8, $General, casino
24	US 19, Peach St, to Waterford, **N** Country Fair/dsl, Delta Sonic/Subway, GetGo/dsl, KwikFill, Tesla EVC, Applebee's, Blaze Pizza, Burger King, Chick-fil-A, Chipotle, ChuckeCheese, Cracker Barrel, Dunkin', Eat'n Park, Five Guys, Golden Corral, Jersey Mikes, KFC, Krispy Kreme, Longhorn Steaks, McDonald's, Olive Garden, Panera Bread, S&S Buffet, Starbucks, Storming Crab, Taco Bell, TGIFriday's, Tim Hortons, Torero's Mexican, TX Roadhouse, Courtyard, Hilton Garden, Holiday Inn, $Tree, Advance Parts, ALDI, AT&T, Best Buy, Hobby Lobby, Home Depot, Jo-Ann Fabrics, Kohl's, Lowe's, Marshall's, Old Navy, PetSmart, Sam's Club/gas, Staples, Target, URGENT CARE, Verizon, Walmart, Wegman's Foods, **S** Country Fair, Shell/Subway, Bob Evans, IHOP, Quaker Steak & Lube, Best Western, Comfort Inn, Country Inn&Suites, Hampton Inn, Hawthorn Suites, Home2 Suites, Sleep Inn, Spark Hotel, Wingate Inn, Wyndham Garden, waterpark
22b a	I-79, N to Erie, S to Pittsburgh
18	PA 832, Sterrettania, **N** Marathon/dsl, Coney Island, Presque Isle SP, Presque Passage RV Park, Waldameer Park, **S** Quality Inn, golf, KOA, West Haven RV Park/camping
16	PA 98, to Franklin Center, Fairview, **S** Follys Camping
9	PA 18, to Girard, Platea, **N** Fiesler's Service/repair/tires, st police, **S** Green Roof Inn
6	PA 215, to Albion, East Springfield
3	US 6N, to Cherry Hill, West Springfield
2.5mm	**full** **facilities**, **info**, **litter barrels**, **petwalk**, /weigh sta eb, **vending**, welcome center
0mm	Pennsylvania/Ohio state line

FAIRVIEW

INTERSTATE 95

BRISTOL PARK

Exit #	Services
42.5mm	Pennsylvania/New Jersey state line, Delaware River. I-276 runs eb to NJ TPK.
42(I-95)	US 13, Delaware Valley, **N** BP, McDonald's, Dallas Diner, Under the Pier, Motel 6, 7-11, auto repair, U-Haul, **S** G Fuel, Sunoco/dsl, Valero/dsl, WaWa/dsl, Burger King, Dunkin', Golden Eagle Diner, Italian Family Pizza, Porfirio's Pizza, Knights Inn, Village Lodge, $General, Meineke
40	(from nb)I-295 N, to NJ. I-95 N merges with PA Tpk/276 to NJ Tpk
39	PA 413, I-276, to Bristol Bridge, Burlington
37	PA 132, to Street Rd, **W** Karco/dsl, Liberty, Sunoco/dsl, Burger King, Chick-fil-A, China Sun Buffet, Crafty Crab, Dunkin', Golden Corral, McDonald's, Philly Pretzels, Popeyes, Sakura Japanese, TX Roadhouse, Wendy's, $General, Advance Parts, ALDI, AutoZone, Firestone, GNC, Jiffy Lube, PepBoys, U-Haul, Walgreens, WaWa
35	PA 63, to US 13, Woodhaven Rd, Bristol Park, **W** Conoco/Dunkin', Sunoco/dsl, Apple Pizza, Arby's, Burger King, Charley's Cheesesteaks, Dunkin', Dunkin', Grand China Buffet, KFC, McDonald's, McDonald's, Nick's Rest.,

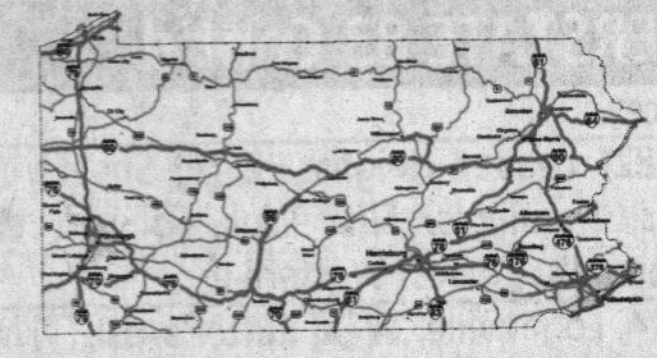

INTERSTATE 95 Cont'd

Exit	Services
35	Continued Old Haven Pizza, Pho Nam, Rainbow Sandwiches, Rayaki Ramen, Rita's Custard, Sbarro Pizza, Taco Bell, Wendy's, Holiday Inn Express, WoodSpring Suites, Acme Foods, CVS Drug, Dick's, Home Depot, Marshall's, Mavis, TJ Maxx, Verizon, vet, Walmart, WaWa
32	Academy Rd, W 7-11, Lukoil, Dominos, Dunkin', McDonald's, Popeyes, Smoothie King, AutoZone, PJP Mkt, Wawa
30	PA 73, Cottman Ave, W Sunoco, Sunoco, Dunkin', Popeyes
27	Bridge St, W Citgo/dsl, Exxon, Lukoil, Sunoco, Dunkin'
26	to NJ 90, Betsy Ross Br, W Speedway, Sunoco/dsl, Sunoco/Dunkin', WaWa/dsl, Applebee's, Boston Mkt, Burger King, Chick-fil-A, KFC, McDonald's, Taco Bell, Wendy's, $Tree, Advance Parts, Home Depot, Lowe's, ShopRite Foods, Target, Walmart
25	Allegheny Ave, W Sunoco/dsl, M&M Breakfast, The Pizza Store,
23	Lehigh Ave, Girard Ave, E casino, W Karco, Applebee's, Brunchaholics, Coldstone, Dunkin', Nifty Fifty Diner, Pizza Hut, Rita's Custard, Starbucks, Wendy's, Wingstop, $Tree, AutoZone, CVS Drug, GNC, PepBoys, WaWa/dsl
22	I-676, US 30, to Central Philadelphia, Independence Hall
20	Columbus Blvd, Penns Landing, E Liberty/dsl, Burger King, Chart House Seafood, Chick-fil-A, Chipotle, ChuckECheese, Dunkin', Hook & Reel, IHOP, Longhorn Steaks, McDonald's, Moshulu Rest., Ruby Buffet, Shank's Sandwiches, Wendy's, Hilton, Holiday Inn Express, $Tree, Acme Mkt, AT&T, Best Buy, Giant Foods, Home Depot, IKEA, Independence Seaport Museum, Lowe's, Michaels, Old Navy, PepBoys, Staples, Target, Walmart, Wawa, W Marriott
19	I-76 E, to Walt Whitman Bridge, E U-Haul, W BP, Liberty, Sunoco/dsl, Boyd's Steaks, Dunkin', Dunkin', McDonald's, Popeyes, Royal Buffet, Tony $ Nick's Steaks, $General, ALDI, AutoZone, Citizen's Bank Ballpark, ShopRite
17	PA 611, to Broad St, Pattison Ave, E Courtyard, Naval Shipyard, W Citizen's Bank Ballpark, FDR Park,
15mm	Schuykill River
15	Enterprise Ave, Island Ave(from sb)
14	Bartram Ave, Essington Ave(from sb)
13	PA 291, to I-76 W(from nb), to Central Philadelphia, E Aloft, Doubletree, Extended Stay, Marriott, Renaissance Inn, Sheraton, Sheraton Four Points, W Embassy Suites, Extended Stay, Fairfield Inn, Hampton Inn, Mircotel, Residence Inn, Sonesta
12	Philadelphia Intl Airport, E Philadelphia Intl, W Ruby Tuesday, Embassy Suites, Extended Stay, Fairfield Inn, Hampton Inn, Mircotel, Sonesta Select, WaWa/dsl
10	PA 291, Bartrom Ave, from nb, Cargo City, E Delta Hotel, Marriott, Motel 6, Philadelphia Int, W Ruby Tuesday, Embassy Suites, Extended Stay America, Fairfield Inn, Hampton Inn, Microtel, Sonesta Select, Heinz NWR
9b a	PA 420, to Essington, Prospect Park, E Sunoco/dsl, Valero/dsl, Big Joe's Sandwiches, Denny's, Lehmans Rest., Miller's Cafe, Clarion, La Quinta, Red Roof+, SpringHill Suites, Travelodge, Wyndham Garden, USPO, WaWa, W Heinz NWR,
8	to Chester Waterfront, Ridley Park, E Royal Farms, Cracker Barrel, Clarion, Home2 Suites, Microtel, SpringHill Suites, W Stargate Diner,
7	I-476 N, to Plymouth, Meeting
6	PA 352, PA 320, to Edgmont Ave, E Chester Pizza, McDonald's, Popeyes, Portobello Cafe, Systahs Soulfood, Zac's Burgers, Candlewood Suites, $General, $Tree, AT&T, AutoZone, Shoprite, Walmart/Subway, W Days Inn, W
5	Kerlin St(from nb), E Chester Gas, Gulf/Krispy Krunchy Chicken, Sunoco, Lee Seafood, NY Fried Chicken
4	US 322 E, to NJ, to Barry Bridge, E Family$, W Highland Motel
3	(from nb, no EZ return)US 322 W, Highland Ave, E Sunoco/dsl, $General, Ford, Goodyear, Penske, W U-Haul
2	PA 452, to US 322, Market St, E Corner Pizza, Di Costanza Sanwiches, Richman's Creamery, Family$, Wawa, W Exxon/dsl, Royal Farms/dsl, Dunkin', McDonald's
1	Chichester Ave, E Sunoco, Linwood Pizza, fireworks, W Dunkin', transmissions
0.5mm	full facilities, littler barrels, petwalk, Welcome Ctr/weigh sta nb
0mm	Pennsylvania/Delaware state line

INTERSTATE 99

Exit	Services
85	I-99 begins/ends on I-80, exit 161
83	PA 350, Bellefonte, Bellafonte, E Tesla EVC, Weis Foods/gas, Wendy's, RV repair, W Lyken's Mkt, Burger King, TrueValue
81	PA 26 S, to PA 64, to Pleasant Gap
80	Harrison Rd(from nb, no re-entry)
78b a	PA 150, to Bellafonte, W Rutters/dsl/scales, Sheetz/dsl, Dunkin', McDonald's, EconoLodge, auto repair, Ford, Giant Foods
76	Shiloh Rd, E Sheetz/dsl, McDonald's, Perkins, Quaker Steak, Rey Azteca, Taco Bell, Best Western+, $Tree, AAA, Advance Parts, ALDI, Barnes&Noble, BigLots, Chevrolet, Jo-Ann Fabrics, Ross, Sam's Club/gas, Subaru, Valvoline, vet, Walmart/Subway
74	Innovation Park, , Beaver Stadium, Penn State U
73	US 322 E, Lewiston, State College
71	Woodycrest, Tofftrees, E Sheetz/dls, Sheetz/dsl, Applebee's, Chick-fil-A, Chipotle, Cracker Barrel, Dunkin' Hoss's Steaks, McDonald's, Moe's SW Grill, Monro Tire & Auto, Olive Garden, Panda Express, Panera Bread, Qdoba Red Lobster, Starbucks, Taco Bell, TX Roadhouse, Wendy's Hampton Inn, Holiday Inn Express, SpringHill Suites, $Tree, Advance Parts, ALDI, Best Buy, Best Buy, Dick's Kohl's, Michael's, PetCo, Target, Tire Town, TJ Maxx, Trade Joe's, Verizon, Walmart, Wegman's Foods, Weis Foods, W Carnegie Inn, Toftrees Golf Resort
69	US 322 E, Valley Vista Dr, E Sheetz/dsl, Fairfield Inn, Home Depot, Lowe's, Midas, NAPA
68	Skytop Mtn Rd, Grays Woods, Waddle, E, W Exxon
62	US 322 W, to Phillipsburg(from sb)
61	to US 322 W, Port Matilda, E Lykens Mkt/Sub Express/ds Brother's Pizza, Port Matilda Hotel, city park
52	PA 350, W Snappy's/dsl, Family Chill & Grill, Bal Eagle Campground
48	PA 453, Tyrone, W Exxon, Sheetz/dsl, Burger King Dottavio Italian, Ace Hardware, Advance Parts, Fishe Auto Parts, USPO
45	Tipton, Grazierville, W Rossi's, Pappy Fred's Pizza Tipton Creek Deli, DelGrosso's Funpark, Ford

PA

BELLWOOD ALTOONA LEVITTOWN

INTERSTATE 99 Cont'd

Exit #	Services
41	PA 865 N, Bellwood, E Ft Roberdeau HS, W Martin Gen Store/dsl, Sheetz/dsl, Relax Inn
39	PA 764 S, Pinecroft, W Comfort Inn, Days Inn, Martin's Foods
33	17th St, same as 32, Altoona, E Arby's, Chili's, Chipotle, Panera Bread, TX Roadhouse, Best Buy, Dick's Sports, Home Depot, W Sheetz/dsl, Microtel, ALDI, Lowe's, Railroader Museum, U-Haul
32	PA 36, Frankstown Rd, Altoona, E GetGo, Sheetz/dsl, Arby's, Chili's, Chipotle, Dino's Pizza, DQ, Panera Bread, TX Roadhouse, Barnes&Noble, Boscov's, Canoe Cr SP, Dick's, Giant Eagle Foods, GNC, Kohl's, Michael's, PetCo, Ross, Staples, Verizon, W Sheetz/dsl, ChuckeCheese, Dunkin', El Campesino Mexican, Five Guys, Honeybaked Ham, Jersey Mike's, Jimmy John's, La Fiesta Pizza, McDonald's, Olive Garden, Papa John's, Perkins, Popeyes, Red Lobster, Rita's Custard, Subway, Wendy's, Fairfield Inn, Horseshoe Lodge, Quality Inn, Super 8, TownePlace Suites, $Tree, AT&T, AutoZone, Chrysler/Dodge/Jeep, CVS Drug, H, H, Jo-Ann Fabrics, NAPA, Nissan, O'Reilly Parts, URGENT CARE, Walgreens
31	Plank Rd, Altoona, E Chick-fil-A, Dunkin', Jethro's Rest., Outback Steaks, Plaza Azteca, Primanti Bros, U-Haul, Altoona Grand Hotel, Courtyard, Holiday Inn Express, Firestone/auto, Petco, Sam's Club/gas, Sportsman's Whse, st police, Target, TJ Maxx, Walmart/McDonald's, W Applebees, Arby's, Burger King, Casa Valadez, Champs Grill, Chinese Gourmet, Cracker Barrel, Denny's, Eat'n Park, KFC, Little Caesar's, LJ Silver, Longhorn Steaks, Panda Express, Red Robin, Starbucks, Taco Bell, Hampton Inn, Rodeway Inn, Advance Parts, BigLots, Buick/GMC, Hobby Lobby, JC Penney, Macy's, Martin's/gas, Mitsubishi, Monro Tire&Auto, Verizon, Weis Foods
28	US 22, to Ebensburg, Holidaysburg
23	PA 36, PA 164, Roaring Spring, Portage, E GetGo/dsl, Sheetz/24hr, Best Way Pizza, Cony's Kitchen, Sipes BBQ, Taco Bell, H, truck repair, Walmart/Subway
15	Claysburg, King, Claysburg, King, E Olde Thyme Pizza, W Sheetz/dsl, Tesla EVC
10	to Imler, W Blue Knob SP
7	PA 869, Osterburg, St Clairsville, W Blue Knob SP
3	PA 56, Johnstown, Cessna, E st police, truck parts
1	I-70/76, E GetGo/McDonald's/dsl, Sheetz/dsl, Shell/Subway/Champ's/dsl, Arby's, Denny's, Hoss' Rest, Pizza Hut, Rte 220 Diner, Taco Bell, Wendy's, Budget Host, Fairfield Inn, Hampton Inn, Quality Inn, Rodeway Inn, Super 8, truck repair
0	I-99 begins/ends on US 220.

INTERSTATE 295

10mm	Pennsylvania/New Jersey state line, Delaware River
10	PA 32, to New Hope, W Washington Crossing Hist Park
9mm	Welcome Ctr sb, **full facilities, litter barrels, petwalk**, **vending**
8	PA 332, to Yardley, Newtown, W Dunkin', Uncle Dave's Creamery, Hampton Inn, CVS Drug, H, Tyler SP, Wegman's
5b a	US 1, W to I-276/PA TPK, Langhorne, Oxford Valley, W H
3	US 1 bus, to PA 413, Penndel, Levittown, E Shell/dsl, Arirang Hibachi Steaks, CA Tortilla Mexican, Duck Donuts, Dunkin', Friendly's, Hong Kong Pearl, Hubba Hubba Hoagies, MrBeast Burgers, Olive Garden, Panera Bread, Plum Tree Chinese, Popeye's, Red Lobster, Ruby Tuesday, Steve's Steaks, Uncle Bill's Homestyle, Wendy's, $Tree, Acura,
3	Continued ALDI, Chevrolet, Chrysler/Dodge/Jeep, Firestone/auto, Ford, Goodyear/auto, Harley-Davidson, Honda, Hyundai, Kia, Lowe's, Marshall's, Redner's Whse Mkt, Sam's Club, Subaru, Subaru, Target, vet, VW/Volvo, W Wawa/dsl, Burger Den, McDonald's, H, Toyota, U-Haul
0mm	I-295 begins/ends on I-276/I-95/PA Tpk

LEVITTOWN LANSDALE

INTERSTATE 476

131	US 11, US 6. I-476 begins/ends on I-81. Services same as I-81, exit 194.
122	Keyser Ave, Old Forge, Taylor
121mm	toll plaza
120.5mm	Lackawanna River
115	I-81, PA 315, Wyoming Valley, Pittston, W Exxon/Subway/dsl, Pilot/Wendy's/dsl/scales/24hr, Sunoco/dsl, Arby's, Burger King, Denny's, McDonald's, Taco Bell, Candlewood Suites, Holiday Inn Express, Knight's Inn, AT&T, truck repair, Verizon, Volvo, Walmart/Subway
112mm	toll plaza
105	PA 115, Wilkes-Barre, Bear Creek, E Exxon, Mobil, Dunkin'
95	I-80, PA 940, Pocono, Hazleton, W WaWa, Arby's, Burger King, McDonald's, Comfort Inn, EconoLodge, Holiday Inn Express, Mtn Laurel Resort, Split Rock Resort
87	PA 903, Jim Thorpe(tag holder only)
86mm	Hickory Run Service Plaza both lanes, Sunoco/dsl, Burger King, Starbucks, 7-11
74	US 209, Mahoning Valley, Lehighton, Stroudsburg, W Citgo, Shell/Subway/dsl, Country Inn&Suites, Hampton Inn, Pocono Point RV Camping
71mm	Lehigh Tunnel
56	I-78, US 22, PA 309, Lehigh Valley, E Tesla EVC, China House, Duck Donuts, Dunkin', Jersey Mike's, Moe's SW, Red Robin, Sal's Pizza, Subway, Trivet Diner, Wendy's, Zio's Pizza, Allenwood Inn, ParkView Inn, Red Carpet Inn, BMW/Mini, Lexus, Maserati, Staples, vet, W Exxon, Trexler Plaza, Chris Rest., Dunkin', Potsy Pizza, Holiday Inn Express, Motel 6, Woodspring Suites, CVS Drug, Jaguar, Land Rover, U-Haul
56mm	Allentown Service Plaza both lanes, Sunoco/dsl, Auntie Anne's, Cinnabon, Hershey's Ice Cream, Roy Rogers
44	PA 663, Quakertown, Pottstown, E Exxon/Subway/dsl, Sunoco, Wawa/dsl, Dunkin', Faraco's Pizza, Hampton Inn, Holiday Inn Express, Quality Inn, SpringHill Suites, H
31	PA 63, Lansdale, E Royal Farms, Asahi Japanese, Margaritas Mexican, Pudge's Steaks, The Mill Rest., Courtyard, Holiday Inn, H, USPO, Walgreens
20	Germantown Pike W, to I-276 W, PA Tpk W
19	Germantown Pike E
18b a	(18 from sb), Conshoshocken, Norristown, E Lukoil, Lukoil, Sunoco, Andy's Diner, Burger King, Cracker Barrel, Dunkin', Five Guys, Franzone's Pizza, Illiano's Pizza, McDonald's, Mezeh, Outback Steaks, Panera Bread, PrimoHoagies, Qdoba, Rita's Ice Cream, Salad Works, Starbucks, Tony Roni Pizza, Wingstop, Hampton Inn, Barnes&Noble, Best Buy, Giant Foods, Lowe's, Old Navy, PetSmart, REI, Ross, Target, Tony Roni's Pizza, Toyota, URGENT CARE, Verizon, vet, Weis Mkt, W Uno Pizzeria, Wendy's, ALDI, Audi, BJ's Whse, Ford, Home Depot, Honda, Hyundai, IKEA, Kia, Mazda, Nissan, Porsche
16b a	(16 from sb), I-76, PA 23, to Philadelpia, Valley Forge
13	US 30, E Liberty, Campus Pizza, Charlie's Chicken, First Watch Cafe, Goodness Bowls, Nova Grill, H, to Villanova U
9	PA 3, Broomall, Upper Darby, E Barnaby's Rest., Fairfield Inn, H, URGENT CARE

[gas] = gas [food] = food [lodging] = lodging [other] = other [RS] = rest stop

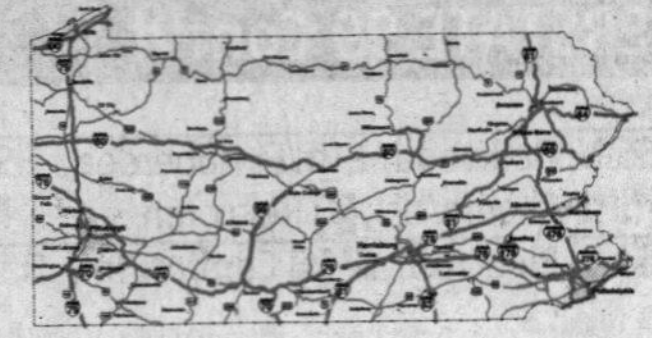

INTERSTATE 476 Cont'd

Exit #	Services
5	US 1, Lima, Springfield, E [food] Capriotti's Sandwiches, Chipotle, Crack Crab, Hibachi Japanese, Poke Bros, Smashburger, [other] AT&T, Giant Foods, Jo-Ann Fabrics, Marshall's, Old Navy, Staples, Verizon, Walmart
3	Baltimore Pike, Media, Swarthmore, E [gas] EVC, Mobil/dsl, [food] Bertucci's Italian, Dunkin', First Watch, LongHorn Steaks, Mission BBQ, Noodle 88 Chinese, Olive Garden, Outback Steaks, Panera Bread, Qdoba, Shake Shack, Starbucks, Tony Luke's Steaks, [other] Giant Foods, [H], Macy's, Swarthmore Coll, Target, vet, W [food] Double Decker Pizza, Dunkin, Starbucks,
3	Continued Hampton Inn, [other] Wawa
1	McDade Blvd, E [gas] Exxon, [food] Dunkin', McDonald's, Panda Chinese, Taco Bell, [other] $Tree, CVS Drug, W [gas] Lukoil, [food] Liberty Steaks, Ocean Buffet, Wing Hut, [other] Family$
0mm	I-476 begins/ends on I-95, exit 7.

NOTES

PA

RHODE ISLAND

INTERSTATE 95

Exit #	Services
43mm	Rhode Island/Massachusetts state line
30(42)	East St, to Central Falls, E Dunkin', Subway
29(41)	US 1, Cottage St, W d'Angelo
28(40)	RI 114, School St, E Sunoco, H, to hist dist, Yarn Outlet
27(39)	US 1, RI 15, Pawtucket, W EVC, Shell/repair/dsl, Sunoco/dsl/24hr, Burger King, Dunkin', Murphy's Law, Hampton Inn
26(38)	RI 122, Lonsdale Ave(from nb), E U-Haul
25(37)	US 1, RI 126, N Main St, Providence, E Shell/dsl, Speedway/dsl, Chili's, Dunkin', Gregg's Rest., $Tree, Firestone/auto, H, PepBoys, Walgreens, W Speedway, Burger King, Chelo's Rest., Aamco
24(36.5)	Branch Ave, Providence, downtown, W Stop&Shop/gas, Wendy's, Home Depot, Stop&Shop, URGENT CARE, Walmart/Subway
23(36)	RI 146, RI 7, Providence, E Mobil/dsl, Marriott, W H, USPO
22(35.5)	US 6, RI 10, Providence, E Cheesecake Factory, Dave&Buster's, Fleming's Steaks, Panera Bread, PF Chang's, CVS Drug, Macy's
21(35)	Broadway St, Providence, E Starbucks, Hilton
20(34.5)	I-195, to E Providence, Cape Cod
19(34)	Eddy St, Allens Ave, to US 1, W Dunkin', Wendy's, H
18(33.5)	US 1A, Thurbers Ave, W Shell/dsl, Burger King, H
17(33)	US 1(from sb), Elmwood Ave, W Dunkin', Tires Whse, USPO
16(32.5)	RI 10, Cranston, E Williams Zoo/park
15(32)	Jefferson Blvd, E Mobil, Dunkin', Shogun Steaks, Courtyard, La Quinta, Motel 6, W Ryder Trucks
14(31)	RI 37, Post Rd, to US 1, W Shell/dsl, Burger King, ALDI, CVS Drug, Ford/Lincoln, Mazda, Volvo
13(30)	TF Green Airport Connector Rd, E Shell, Sunoco/Dunkin', Bertucci's, Chelo's Grill, Chipotle, HoneyDew Donuts, IHOP, Subway, Tuscan Grille, Wendy's, Best Western, Extended Stay America, Fairfield Inn, Hampton Inn, Hilton Garden, Holiday Inn Express, Homewood Suites, Radisson, Sheraton, Sonesta Suites, TF Green
12b(29)	RI 2, I-295 N(from sb)
12a	RI 113 E, to Warwick, E Shell/Dunkin'/dsl, Crowne Plaza Hotel, Lowe's, Stop&Shop, W Sunoco, BJ's Rest., ChuckeCheese, On the Border, Wendy's, Kohl's, Walmart/Subway
11(29)	I-295 N(exits left from nb), to Woonsocket
10b a(28)	RI 117, to Warwick, W H
9(25)	RI 4 S, E Greenwich
8b a(24)	RI 2, E Greenwich, E Shell/dsl, Tesla EVC, Dunkin', McDonald's, Outback Steaks, Panera Bread, PieZone Pizza, TX Roadhouse, Extended Stay America, AT&T, CVS Drug, Dave's Mkt, W Sunoco/dsl, Applebee's, Carrabba's, Chick-fil-A, Chili's, Denny's, Dunkin', Five Guys, KFC, Moe's SW, Olive Garden, PapaGino's Pizza, Smokey Bones BBQ, Starbucks, TGIFriday's, Wendy's, SpringHill Suites, Acura, ALDI, Arlington RV Ctr, Audi/Bentley/BMW/Inifinti/Lexus/Mini/Porsche, Barnes&Noble, Best Buy, Cadillac, Home Depot, Honda, Jaguar, Jo-Ann Fabrics, Land Rover, Lowe's, Mercedes, Michael's, Nissan, PepBoys, Petco, PetSmart, Staples, Stop&Shop/gas, Subaru, Target, vet, VW
7(21)	to Coventry, E Mobil/dsl, W Cumberland/dsl, Applebee's, Cracker Barrel, Denny's, Dunkin', McDonald's, Wendy's, Hampton Inn, Holiday Inn Express,

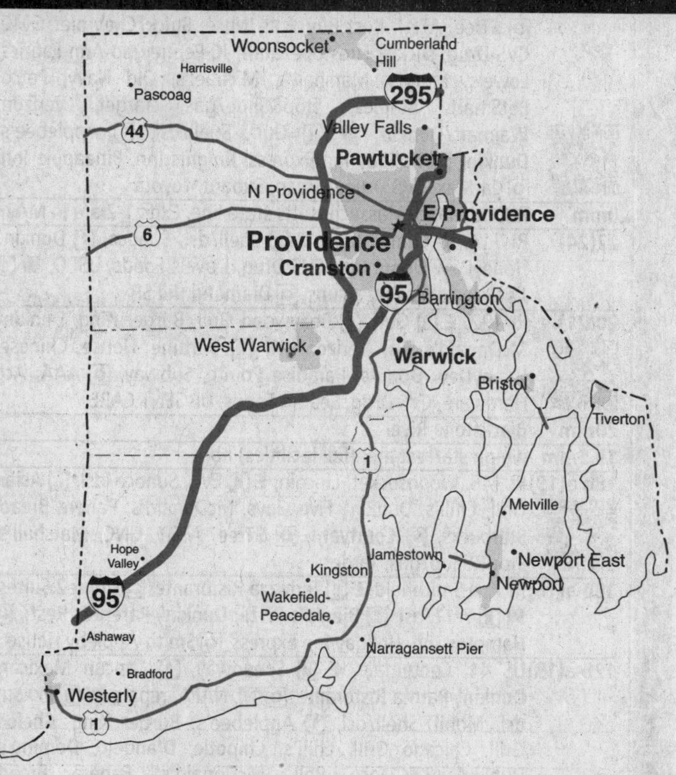

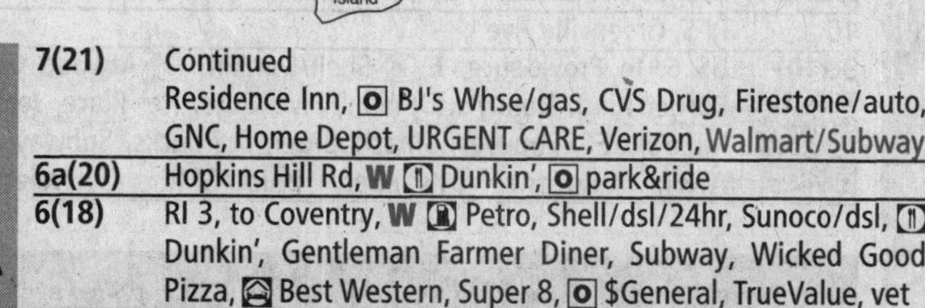

Exit #	Services
7(21)	Continued Residence Inn, BJ's Whse/gas, CVS Drug, Firestone/auto, GNC, Home Depot, URGENT CARE, Verizon, Walmart/Subway
6a(20)	Hopkins Hill Rd, W Dunkin', park&ride
6(18)	RI 3, to Coventry, W Petro, Shell/dsl/24hr, Sunoco/dsl, Dunkin', Gentleman Farmer Diner, Subway, Wicked Good Pizza, Best Western, Super 8, $General, TrueValue, vet
5b a(15)	RI 102, W TA/Shell/Popeyes/dsl/scales/24hr, Dan's Rest., Classic Motor Lodge
10mm	parking area both lanes
4(9)	RI 3, to RI 165(from nb), Arcadia, W Arcadia SP, camping
3b a(7)	RI 138 E, to Kingston, Wyoming, E Dunkin', McDonald's, Village Pizza, Wendy's, Stop&Shop/gas, vet, W Cumberland/dsl, Mobil/Dunkin', Bali Village Chinese, Dragon Palace, Subway, Wood River Inn Rest., Stagecoach House B&B, $General, CVS Drug, Family$, NAPA, USPO
6mm	Welcome Ctr/weigh sta nb, full facilities
2(4)	Hope Valley
1(1)	RI 3, to Hopkinton, Westerly, E beaches, H, RV camping, to Misquamicut SP
0mm	Rhode Island/Connecticut state line

INTERSTATE 295 (Providence)

Exit #	Services
4b a(4)	I-95, N to Boston, S to Providence. I-295 begins/ends on I-95, exit 4 in MA. Exits 2-1 are in MA.
2b a(2)	US 1, E Mobil/Dunkin'/dsl, 99 Rest., Chicago Grill, Chick-fil-A, Chipotle, ChuckeCheese, d'Angelo, Five Guys, Friendly's, Longhorn Steaks, Moe's SW, Panera Bread,

INTERSTATE 295 (Providence) Cont'd

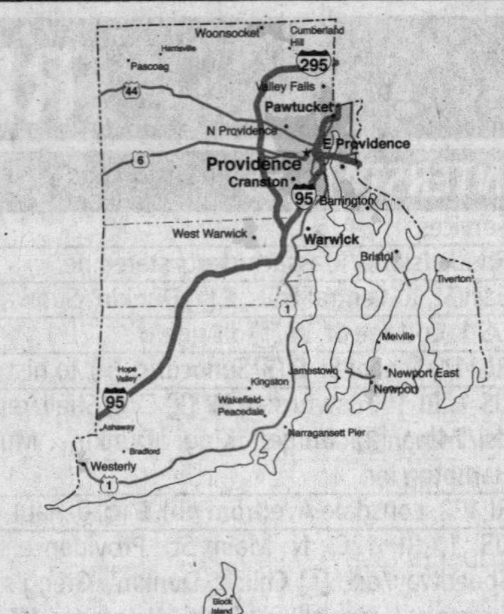

2b a(2) Continued
PapaGino's Italian, Ruby Tuesday, Smashburger, TGIFriday's, $Tree, AT&T, Best Buy, BJ's Whse, Buick/Chevrolet/GMC, CVS Drug, Dick's, Firestone/auto, JC Penney, Jo-Ann Fabrics, Lowe's, Macy's, Marshall's, Michael's, Old Navy, Petco, PetSmart, Staples, Stop&Shop/gas, Target, Verizon, Walmart/Dunkin', W Gulf, Shell/dsl, Applebee's, Dunkin', Holiday Inn Express, Knights Inn, Pineapple Inn, CarMax, CVS Drug, Nissan, Subaru, Toyota

0mm Rhode Island/Massachusetts state line. Exits 1-2 are in MA.

22(24) RI 114, to Cumberland, E Shell/dsl, Sunoco, Dunkin', HoneyDew Donuts, CVS Drug, Dave's Foods, USPO, W J's Deli, Saki's Pizza/subs, Diamond Hill SP

20(21) RI 122, E Gulf, Bollywood Grill, Burger King, Dunkin', McDonald's, Verizon, W Fortune House Chinese, HoneyDew Donuts, Paradise Pointe, Subway, AAA, Ace Hardware, CVS Drug, Seabra Foods, URGENT CARE

20mm Blackstone River

19.5mm weigh sta/rest area(full facilities) nb

18b a(19) RI 146, Woonsocket, Lincoln, E EVC, Sunoco/dsl, Asian Grill, Chili's, Dunkin', Five Guys, McDonald's, Panera Bread, Starbucks, Courtyard, $Tree, AT&T, GNC, Marshall's, Stop&Shop/gas, Target

15b a(16) RI 7, N Smithfield, E Terrazza Ristorante, Home2 Suites, W 7-11/dsl, Biagio's Pizza, Dunkin', Parentes Rest., Hampton Inn, Holiday Inn Express, Smith-Appleby House

CENTERDALE

12b a(13) US 44, Centerdale, E Speedway, Cancun Mexican, Dunkin', Parma Ristorante, H, NAPA, repair, W Exxon/dsl, Mobil, Shell/dsl, Applebee's, Burger King, Chelo's Grill, Chicago Grill, Chili's, Chipotle, D'angelo, Domino's, Dunkin', KFC/Taco Bell, McDonald's, Panera Bread, PapaGino's, Sonic, Starbucks, Subway, TinTsin Chinese, Yamato Steaks, $Tree, AT&T, Barnes&Noble, CVS Drug, Dave's Foods, Dick's, Home Depot, Kohl's, Michael's, Old Navy, Staples, Stop&Shop, Target, TJ Maxx, to Powder Mill Ledges WR, URGENT CARE, Verizon

10 RI 5, Greenville Ave

9c(10) US 6, to Providence, E Shell/Dunkin', Atwood Grill, Burger King, Denny's, Dunkin', Five Guys, Hei Place, Jersey Mike's, KFC, Popeyes, Smashburger, Starbucks, Subway, AT&T, AutoZone, BJ's Gas, Buick/GMC, Chevrolet,

9c(10) Continued
Chrysler/Dodge/Jeep, CVS Drug, Honda, Hyundai, Kia Stop&Shop/gas, Town Fair Tire, USPO

9a(9) US 6 E Expswy, E Chipotle, McDonald's, Taco Bell, $Tree, BJ's Whse, Home Depot, PetSmart

7(8) RI Resource Recovery Industrial Park

6(7) RI 14, Plainfield Pk, E Speedway/dsl, McDonald's, $Tree, Walmart/Subway, W Gulf, Mobil/dsl/24hr, Dunkin', Palmieri Pizza, Subway, CVS Drug, repair

3b a(4) rd 37, Phenix Ave, E TF Green

1b(2) RI 2 S, to Warwick, E EVC, Buffalo Wild Wings, Chicag Grill, Longhorn Steaks, Red Robin, Extended Sta America, $Tree, JC Penney, Macy's, Marshalls, Old Navy Target, Verizon, W Mobil, Sunoco/Subway, BJ's Rest Burger King, Chili's, Chipotle Mexican, ChuckeCheese Dunkin', McDonald's, Olive Garden, On-the-Border, Paner Bread, Smashburger, Smokey Bones, Sonic, Starbucks Subway, Taco Bell, Wendy's, AT&T, AutoZone Barnes&Noble, Best Buy, Chrysler/Dodge/Keep/Kia, Dick's Hobby Lobby, Home Depot, Jaguar, Kia, Kohl's, Petc PetSmart, Price Rite Foods, Staples, Target, TJMaxx, TownFa Tire, Trader Joe's, Verizon, Walmart/Subway

1a(1) RI 113 W, to W Warwick, same as 2

0mm I-295 begins/ends on I-95, exit 11.

NOTES

SOUTH CAROLINA

INTERSTATE 20

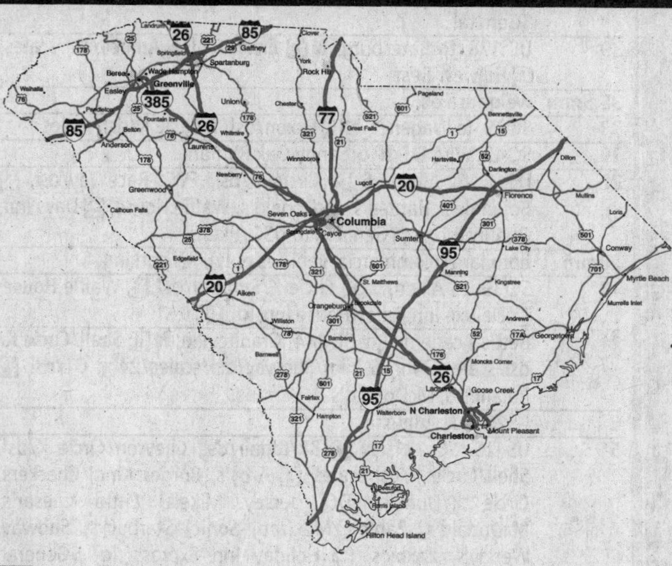

BISHOPVILLE

Exit #	Services
141b a	I-95, N to Fayetteville, S to Savannah. I-20 begins/ends on I-95, exit 160. See Interstate 95, exit 160a for services.
137	SC 340, to Timmonsville, Darlington, N BP/dsl(1mi), $General(1mi), S Marathon
131	US 401, SC 403, to Hartsville, Lamar, N Exxon/dsl, to Darlington Raceway, S Mobil/dsl
129mm	parking area both lanes, commercial vehicles only
123	SC 22, N camping, Lee SP
121mm	Lynches River
120	SC 341, Bishopville, Elliot, N BP/dsl, to Cotton Museum, S Exxon/dsl, Best Value Inn
116	US 15, to Sumter, Bishopville, N Shell/KFC/dsl/24hr, McDonald's, Pizza Hut, Waffle House, Zaxby's, Red Roof Inn, to Cotton Museum(1mi), S Pilot/DQ/Wendy's/dsl/scales/24hr, Shaw AFB
108	SC 34, to SC 31, Manville, N BP/dsl, Family$, S Exxon/dsl, truck parking
101	rd 329, Dr Humphries Rd
98	US 521, to Camden, N BP/dsl, Exxon/McDonald's, Mobil/Circle K/dsl, Shell/dsl, Fatz Cafe, Grouchos Deli, Popeyes, Waffle House, Comfort Suites, Hampton Inn, Holiday Inn Express, H, to Revolutionary War Park
96mm	Wateree River
93mm	**full facilities, litter barrels, petwalk, both lanes, vending**
92	US 601, to Lugoff, N Circle K, Pilot/DQ/DQ/dsl/scales/24hr, Shell/Bojangles/dsl, Hardee's, Waffle House, Days Inn, EconoLodge, $General
87	SC 47, to Elgin, N BP/dsl, Shell/dsl, S Love's/Hardee's/dsl/scales/24hr/@
82	SC 53, to Pontiac, N Bojangles, Burger King, Shell/Burger King, Egg Roll Express, Ratio, Starbucks, Taco Bell, Woodspring Suites, $General, Harley-Davidson, vet, S BP/dsl, Clothing World Outlet
80	Clemson Rd, N Circle K, Shell/Bojangles/dsl, China Garden, Dunkin, Groucho's Deli, Henry's, J.R. Cash's Grill, Julia's German, Krispy Kreme, Maurice's BBQ, McDonald's, Subway, Sumo Japanese, Travinia Italian, Waffle House, Zaxby's, Hampton Inn, Holiday Inn Express, CVS Drug, Firestone/auto, S Wendy's, Chevrolet, Ft Jackson Nat Cem
76b	Alpine Rd, to Ft Jackson, N Sesquicentennial SP
76a	(76 from eb), I-77, N to Charlotte, S to Charleston
74	US 1, Two Notch Rd, to Ft Jackson, N Mobil/dsl, Chick-fil-A, Chili's, Fazoli's, Hooters, IHOP, Lizard's Thicket, Outback Steaks, Waffle House, Best Western+, Comfort Suites, Fairfield Inn, Hampton Inn, Microtel, Motel 6, Red Roof Inn, Rodeway Inn, Wyndham Garden, Home Depot, to Sesquicentennial SP, USPO, vet, S Shell, Sunoco, Bojangles, Captain D's, China Garden, Church's TX Chicken, Crafty Crab, Harbor Inn Seafood, Honeybaked Ham, Jasmine Buffet, Kiki's Chicken, Longhorn Steaks, Maurice's BBQ, McDonald's, My House Rest., Substation II, Taco Bell, Magnuson Hotel, AT&T, AutoZone, Lowe's, Precision Auto, U-Haul
73b	SC 277 N, to I-77 N
73a	SC 277 S, to Columbia, S H
72	SC 555, Farrow Rd
71	US 21, N Main, to Blythewood, Columbia, N BP/dsl, Exxon/dsl, TA/Taco Bell/Dunkin/dsl/scales/24hr/@,

COLUMBIA

Exit #	Services
71	Continued McDonald's, Days Inn, tires/repair, truckwash, S Shell, Von's Diner
70	US 321, Fairfield Rd, S Exxon, Flying J/Denny's/dsl/LP/scales/24hr, Hardee's, Super 8, Blue Beacon, Keystone Auto Parts, truck repair
68	SC 215, Monticello Rd, to Jenkinsville, N Exxon/dsl, Shell/dsl, $General, S Shell/dsl
66mm	Broad River
65	US 176, Broad River Rd, to Columbia, N CK Mart, Exxon, Shell/Circle K, American Deli, Bojangles, Rush's BBQ, Sonic, Subway, Waffle House, Economy Inn, $Tree, Aamco, CVS Drug, Family$, U-Haul, Walgreens, S Murphy USA, Speedway/dsl, Arby's, Asian Express, Chick-fil-A, Chicki's Wings, Dunkin, KFC, Lizard's Thicket, McDonald's, Nick's, Ocean View Seafood, Taco Bell, Wendy's, Zaxby's, American Inn, InTown Suites, Ramada Ltd, Royal Inn, $General, Advance Parts, PepBoys, vet
64b a	I-26, US 76, E to Columbia, W to Greenville, Spartanburg
63	Bush River Rd, N Circle K, Burger King, Cracker Barrel, Real Mexican, Subway, Wings & Ale, Quality Inn, CVS Drug, S Marathon, Murphy USA/dsl, Sunoco, Baymont Inn, Best Western, DoubleTree, Hawthorn Suites, Knights Inn, Sleep Inn, AutoZone, Hamrick's, Walmart

W COLA

Exit #	Services
61	US 378, W Cola, N Murphy Express/dsl, Shell/7-11/Burger King, Chik-fil-A, Chili's, Jewell's BBQ, McDonald's, Starbucks, Substation II, Subway, Taco Bell, Wingate Inn, Honda, S BP/dsl, Shell/Burger King/dsl, Waffle House, $General
58	US 1, W Columbia, N Shell/Subway/dsl, Sunoco, Waffle House, S Murphy Express/dsl, Bojangles, San Jose Mexican, auto repair, County Tire
55	SC 6, to Lexington, N BP/Circle K/dsl, QT/dsl, Best Western +, S BP/Circle K/dsl, Circle K/DQ/dsl, Bojangles, Dunkin, Great Wall Chinese, Maurice's BBQ, McDonald's, Taco Bell, Waffle House, Wendy's, Days Inn, $General, CVS Drug
52.5mm	weigh sta wb
51	SC 204, to Gilbert, N Circle K/dsl, Shell/Subway/dsl/24hr, Burger King, John's RV Sales/Svc, S Love's/Chester's/McDonald's/dsl/scales/24hr, Shell/dsl, Arby's, Starbucks, $General

INTERSTATE 20 Cont'd

GRANITEVILLE

Exit #	Services
44	SC 34, to Gilbert, N 44Trkstp/rest./dsl/24hr, BP/dsl, $General
39	US 178, to Batesburg, N Exxon/dsl, S Amoco/dsl/scales, Hillview Rest.
35.5mm	weigh sta eb
33	SC 39, to Wagener, N Exxon/dsl, S Circle K/dsl/scales
29	SC 49, Wire Rd, N Sandy Oak RV Park
22	US 1, to Aiken, S Circle K/dsl, EVC, RaceWay/dsl, Bojangle's, Hardee's, McDonald's, Waffle House, Days Inn, Quality Inn, $General, to USC Aiken
20mm	both lanes(commercial vehicles only), /parking
18	SC 19, to Aiken, S Circle K/Subway/dsl, Waffle House, Deluxe Inn, GuestHouse Inn, H
11	Bettis Academy Rd, SC 144, Graniteville, N Shell/Circle K/dsl/scales/24hr, S Pilot/Subway/dsl/scales/24hr, QT/dsl, Bojangles, McDonald's
6	I-520 to N Augusta
5	US 25, SC 121, N BP/repair/dsl, Chevron/Circle K/dsl, Shell/Circle K/dsl/scales, Arby's, Burger King, Checkers, Circle K/Dunkin, DQ, Jersey Mike's, Little Caesar's, McDonald's, Pablo's Mexican, Sonic, Starbucks, Subway, Wendy's, Zaxby's, Holiday Inn Express, $General, $Tree, Advance Parts, Food Lion, Verizon, Walmart, S Eagle Express, Exxon, QT/dsl, Marco's Pizza, Waffle House, Sleep Inn, H, Jiffy Lube
1	SC 230, Martintown Rd, N Augusta, N Gas+/dsl, S Shell/Circle K/Subway/dsl, Waffle House, to Garn's Place
0.5mm	**full facilities, litter barrels, petwalk, , vending, Welcome Ctr eb**
0mm	South Carolina/Georgia state line, Savannah River

INTERSTATE 26

N CHARLESTON

Exit #	Services
221	Meeting St, Charleston, E Circle K, Church's TX Chicken, Starbucks, Courtyard, Courtyard , Embassy Suites, Hampton Inn, Hampton Inn, Homewood Suites, Hyatt Place, Family$
221.5mm	I-26 begins/ends on US 17 in Charleston, SC
221b	US 17 N, to Georgetown
221a	US 17 S, to Kings St, to Savannah
220	Romney St(from wb)
219b	Morrison Dr, East Bay St(from eb), N Exxon, E Santi's Mexican
219a	Rutledge Ave(from eb, no EZ return), to The Citadel
218	Spruill Ave(from wb), N Charleston
217	N Meeting St(from eb)
216b a	SC 7, Cosgrove Ave, to US 17 S
215	SC 642, Dorchester Rd, N Charleston, N Marathon, Mobil/Cheapway/dsl, S BP/dsl, Charleston Inn, auto repair, tires
213b a	Montague Ave, Mall Dr, N Cowboys Brazilian, Hello Deli, Red Lobster, Courtyard, Marriott, Woodspring Suites, Charles Towne Square, S BP/Circle K/dsl, EVC, Mobil, Spinx/dsl, Arby's, Big Billy's Burgers, Bonefish Grill, Bufflo Wild Wings, Chick-fil-A, Chipotle, CiCi's Pizza, Culver's, Domino's, Dunkin', Firehouse Subs, Five Guys, Golden Corral, Grand Buffet, IHOP, Jersey Mike's, Jim'N Nick's BBQ, La Hacienda, McAlister's Deli, McDonald's, Mellow Mushroom, Panda Express, Panera Bread, Sake Japanese, Starbucks, Taste of Tokyo, Tropical Smoothie, Waffle House, Zaxby's, ALoft, Comfort Inn, Crowne Plaza, Days Inn, EconoLodge, Embassy Suites, Extended Stay America, Extended Stay America(2), Fairfield Inn, Hampton Inn, Hilton Garden, Holiday Inn Express, Home2 Suites, Homewood Suites, Hyatt Place, InTown Suites, Quality Inn, Residence Inn,

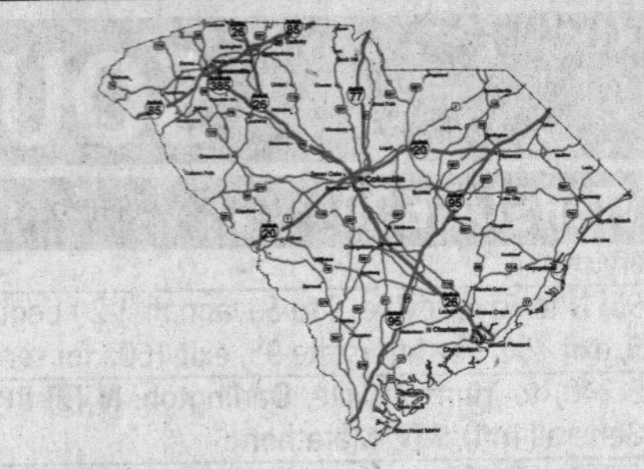

HANAHAN

Exit #	Services
213b a	Continued TownePlace Suites, Wingate Inn, $Tree, AT&T, Charleston Convention Center, Old Navy, Sam's Club/gas, Staples, Tanger Outlet/Famous Brands, Verizon, vet, Walmart/Subway
212c b	I-526, E to Mt Pleasant, W to Savannah, S
212a	Remount Rd, Hanahan, N Sunoco/dsl, KFC, Taco Bell, Advance Parts, AutoZone, Ford
211b a	Aviation Pkwy, N Amoco, Exxon, Exxon, Burger King, Capt D's, Church's TX Chicken, KFC, La Hacienda Mexican, McDonald's, Nick's Gyro's, Papa John's, Popeyes, Sonic, Subway, Super Buffet, Taco Bell, Stay Express Inn, O'Reilly Parts, PepBoys, U-Haul, USPO, S Circle K/dsl, Waffle House, Budget Inn
209	Ashley Phosphate Rd, to US 52, TownePlace, N CircleK/dsl, Exxon, Cane's, Carrabba's, Chick-fil-A, China Buffet, Chipotle Mexican, ChuckECheese, Coldstone, Dunkin, Firehouse Subs, Five Guys, Hooters, Jersey Mike's Subs, Jimmy John's, Longhorn Steaks, Los Reyes, Moe's SW Grill, O'Charley's, Olive Garden, Outback Steaks, Panda Express, Panera Bread, Smokey Bones BBQ, Starbucks, Subway, Taco Bell, Tropical Smoothie, Waffle House, Wendy's, Wild Wing Cafe, Candlewood Suites, Country Inn&Suites, DoubleTree, Extended Stay America, Hawthorn Inn, Holiday Inn Express, InTown Suites, Red Roof Inn, Rodeway Inn, URGENT CARE, $General, $Tree, ALDI, AT&T, Belk, Best Buy, BigLots, Books-A-Million, Dillard's, Discount Tire, Firestone/auto, Hobby Lobby, Home Depot, H, JC Penney, Lowe's, Michael's, Nissan, NTB, Old Navy, Petco, PetSmart, Pizza Hut, Ross, Target, Toyota, Verizon, Walgreens, Walmart/McDonald's, S BP, Shell/dsl, Speedway/dsl, Sunoco/76/dsl, Bojangles, Cracker Barrel, IHOP, McDonald's, Ruby Tuesday, Waffle House, Best Western, Comfort Suites, Courtyard, Extended Stay Suites, Fairfield Inn, Hampton Inn, Hyatt Place, InTown Suites, Quality Inn, Relax Inn, Residence Inn, Sleep Inn, SpringHill Suites, Staybridge Suites
209a	to US 52(from wb), to Goose Creek, Moncks Corner

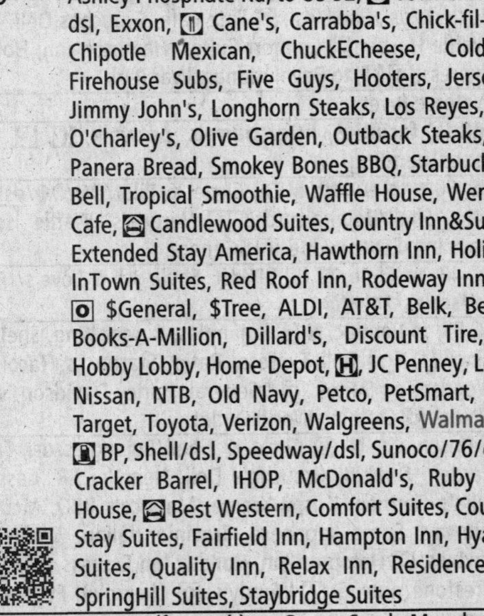

LADSON

Exit #	Services
205b a	US 78, to Summerville, N Circle K, Exxon/dsl, Sunoco/dsl Arby's, Cook Out, Dunkin, East Bay Deli, Firehouse Subs Fortune Garden, Jersey Mike's, Sonic, Starbucks, Subway Waffle House, Wendy's, Willie Jewells BBQ, Zaxby's, Fairfield Inn, Hampton Inn, Holiday Inn Express, Wingate Inn Charleston Southern U, CVS Drug, Family$, H, S BP Speedway/dsl, Spinx/EVC, Sunoco/7-11/dsl, Burger King KFC, Little Caesars, Subway, Taco Bell, Advance Parts, CVS Drug, KOA, O'Reilly Parts, Piggly Wiggly, USPO
204mm	**full facilities, litter barrels, petwalk, , , eb vending**
203	College Park Rd, Ladson, N BP, Sunoco/dsl, McDonald's, Waffle House, Best Western, Days Inn, S Spinx/dsl, Burger King, HonkyTonk, KFC, Little Caesars Subway, Taco Bell, CVS, KOA(2mi), O'Reilly Parts, Piggly Wiggly, vet
202mm	**full facilities, litter barrels, petwalk, , , wb vending**
199b a	US 17 A, to Moncks Corner, Summerville, N Circle K,

E INTERSTATE 26 Cont'd

SUMMERVILLE

199b a Continued
Circle K/dsl, Marathon, Mr. Fuel/McDonald's/dsl/scales/24hr, Speedway/dsl, Bad Daddys Burgers, Carolina Alehouse, China Chef, China Wok, Culvers, KFC, Pizza Hut, Poogan's Kitchen, Sangaree Pizza, Starbucks, Subway, Taco Boy, The CODfather, Vicious Biscuit, Viva Chicken, Waffle House, Courtyard, Hilton Garden, Holiday Inn Express, Residence Inn, $General, Advance Parts, AutoZone, Buick/GMC, CVS Drug, Family$, Food Lion, O'Reilly Parts, vet, **S** Circle K, Azul Mexican, Bojangles, Chick-fil-A, Chicken Salad Chick, China Token, Chipotle, Cracker Barrel, Domino's, Dunkin', El Patron, Firehouse, First Watch, Five Guys, Hardee's, IHOP, Jersey Mike's Subs, La Hacienda, Logan's Roadhouse, Marble Slab, McAlisters Deli, Moe's SW Grill, Newk's Eatery, O'Charleys, Panera Bread, Papa John's, Ruby Tuesday, Smashburger, Waffle House, Zaxby's, Avid Hotel, Comfort Inn, Comfort Inn, Country Inn&Suites, EconoLodge, Economy Inn, Hampton Inn, Hampton Inn, Home2 Suites, Quality Inn, Sleep Inn, Staybridge Suites, Wyndham Garden, ALDI, AT&T, Belk, Best Buy, BJs/tire/gas, Chrysler/Dodge/Jeep, Dick's, Earthfare Mkt, Home Depot, Kohl's, Lowe's, NTB, Petco, PetSmart, Ross, Staples, Target/Starbucks, TJ Maxx, Verizon, Walgreens, Walmart/McDonald's, World Mkt

197b a Nexton Pkwy

194 SC 16, to Jedburg, **N** Spinx/dsl, Arby's, Smokin' Gringos BBQ, **S** Flying J/PJ Fresh/Wendy's/dsl/scales/24hr, **E** access to Foreign Trade Zone 21

187 SC 27, to Ridgeville, St George, **N** Shell, **S** BP/dsl, Francis Beidler Forest(10mi)

177 SC 453, to Holly Hill, Harleyville, **S** Shell/dsl, Countryside Inn/RV park

174mm weigh sta both lanes

172b a US 15, to Santee, St George, **S** Enmarkey/Subway/dsl/e-85/scales/24hr

169b a I-95, N to Florence, S to Savannah

ORANGEBURG

165 SC 210, to Bowman, **N** Exxon/dsl, **S** BP/dsl

159 SC 36, to Bowman, **N** Pilot/McDonald's/dsl/scales/24hr/@, **S** Exxon

154b a US 301, to Santee, Orangeburg, **N** Days Inn, **S** Exxon, Love's/Chesters/Subway/dsl/scales/24hr, QT/dsl/scales, Shell/dsl, Waffle House

152mm **full facilities, litter barrels, petwalk, wb, vending**

150mm **full facilities, litter barrels, petwalk, eb, vending**

149 SC 33, to Cameron, to SC State Coll, Orangeburg, Claflin Coll

145b a US 601, to Orangeburg, St Matthews, **S** BP/dsl, Exxon, Shell/Burger King, Spinx/Tesla EVC/dsl, Bojangles, Chick-fil-A, Cracker Barrel, Fatz Café, Firehouse Subs, Hardee's, McDonald's, Ruby Tuesday, Sonic, Starbucks, Subway, Taco Bell, Waffle House, Wendy's, Zaxby's, Baymont Inn, Carolina Lodge, Comfort Inn, Country Inn&Suites, Days Inn, Fairfield Inn, Hampton Inn, Holiday Inn Express, Quality Inn, Sleep Inn, Southern Lodge, SpringHill Suites, Super 8, Tru, $General, H, Toyota

SWANSEA

139 SC 22, to St Matthews, **N** truck tires/repair, **S** Enmarket, Mobil, Pilot/Dunkin/Arby's/dsl/scales/24hr, $General, Sweetwater Lake Camping(2.5mi)

136 SC 6, to North, Swansea, **N** Exxon/dsl

129 US 21, **N** Shell/dsl

125 SC 31, to Gaston, **N** BP, Wolfe's Truck/trailer repair

123mm **full facilities, litter barrels, petwalk, both lanes, vending**

119 US 176, US 21, to Dixiana, **S** Circle K/Subway/dsl,

CAYCE

119 Continued
Shell/dsl

116 I-77 N, to Charlotte, US 76, US 378, to Ft Jackson

115 US 176, US 21, US 321, to Cayce, **N** Exxon, RaceWay, Shell/dsl, Pizza Hut, Waffle House, $General, $Tree, Advance Parts, CVS Drug, Family$, Food Lion, **S** Pilot/DQ/Cinnabon/dsl/scales/24hr, Shell/dsl, Bojangles, Carolina Wings, Hardee's, Lucky Sports Burgers, McDonald's, Sonic, Starbucks, Subway, Quality Inn, Firestone

113 SC 302, Cayce, **N** G.S./dsl, Marathon, Shell/Burger King, JT's Grill, Waffle House, Inn, Masters Inn, Motel 6, $General, AutoZone, O'Reilly Parts, Save-A-Lot, Walgreens, **S** Circle K, Exxon/dsl, RaceWay, Shoney's, Waffle House, Country Inn&Suites, Days Inn, Red Roof Inn, Sleep Inn, Travelers Inn, NAPA

LEXINGTON

111b a US 1, to W Columbia, **N** Murphy USA, RaceWay, Shell/Circle K/dsl, Chick-fil-A, Dominos, Dunkin, Firehouse Subs, Hardee's, Little Caesar's, Moe's SW Grill, Ruby Tuesday, San Jose, Sonic, Starbucks, Taco Bell, Tokyo Grill, Waffle House, Zaxby's, Clarion, Delta Motel, Quality Inn, $General, $Tree, Hobby Lobby, IGA, Pet Supplies+, to USC, Walgreens, Walmart/gas, **S** Murphy Express, Speedway/dsl, Applebee's, Nick's Gyros, Popeyes, Wendy's, ALDI, BigLots, Lowe's, U-Haul, vet

110 US 378, to W Columbia, Lexington, **N** Blossom Buffet, Cucinella's Pizza, Denny's, Grecian Gardens, Groucho's Deli, Lizard's Thicket, McDonald's, Rush's Rest., Starbucks, Subway, Waffle House, Best Value, Hampton Inn, Hilton Garden, CVS Drug, Food Lion, Toyota, **S** Circle K, Mobil/dsl, Murphy USA, Bojangles, Dunkin, East Bay Deli, Firehouse Subs, Freddy's, La Fogata, Pizza Hut, Executive Inn, Residence Inn, TownePlace Suites, H, URGENT CARE, vet

108b a I-126 to Columbia, Bush River Rd, **N** Citgo/dsl, Capt D's, Chick-fil-A, Cinnabon, Cook Out, Dunkin, Schlotzsky's, The Melting Pot, Wendy's, Zaxby's, Comfort Inn, InTown Suites, Palmetto Inn, $General, Advance Parts, Firestone/auto, Midas, Office Depot, Riverbanks Zoo, Verizon, **S** Marathon, Murphy USA/dsl, Sunoco/dsl, Bamboo House, Pizza Hut, Tokyo Grill, Baymont Inn, Best Western, DoubleTree, Hawthorn Suites, Knights Inn, Sleep Inn, AutoZone, GNC, Walmart

107b a I-20, E to Florence, W to Augusta

106b a St Andrews Rd, **N** Exxon/dsl, QT, ChuckECheese, Dunkin, IHOP, Papa John's, Steve's Burgers, $Tree, Camping World RV Ctr, Infiniti, Nissan, U-Haul, **S** BP/dsl, Shell, Speedway/dsl, Domino's, Maurice's BBQ, McDonald's, Ms. B's, Nick's Grill, Taqueria Jalisco, Tokyo Buffet, Waffle House, WG's Wings, Zaxby's, Red Roof Inn, $General, KJ's IGA, NTB

104 Piney Grove Rd, **N** Spinx/dsl, Hardee's, San Jose Mexican, Starbucks, Waffle House, Rodeway Inn, Costco/gas, Sportsmans Whse, vet, **S** Exxon, QT/dsl, Shell/dsl, Country Inn&Suites, Super 8, Carmax, Land Rover

103 Harbison Blvd, **N** Applebee's, Hooters, Wendy's, Hampton Inn, Chevrolet, funpark, Home Depot, Lowe's, **S** Circle K/dsl, EVC, Speedway/dsl, Tesla Charger, BJ's Rest., Blaze Pizza, Bojangles, BoneFish Grill, Buffalo Wild Wings, Carolina Alehouse, Carrabba's, Chick-fil-A, Chicken Salad Chick, Chipotle Mexican, Crumbl Cookie, Denny's, Fazoli's, Firehouse Subs, Five Guys, Flaming Grill, Honey Baked Ham, Jimmy John's, Kiki's Chicken & Waffles, Longhorn Steaks, Marble Slab, McAlister's Deli, McDonald's, Miyo's, Olive Garden, Outback Steaks, Panera Bread, Poke Bros, Rioz Brazilian, Rush's BBQ, Sonic, Starbucks, Taco Bell, Tokyo Grill, Tropical Smoothie, Tsunami Steaks,

= gas = food = lodging = other = rest stop

INTERSTATE 26 Cont'd

103 Continued
TX Roadhouse, Yamato Japanese, Aloft, Comfort Suites, Fairfield Inn, Hilton Garden, Holiday Inn Express, Home Towne Suites, InTown Suites, $Tree, Academy Sports, AT&T, Belk, Best Buy, Buick/GMC, Dick's, Dillard's, Firestone/auto, Goodyear/auto, JC Penney, Kohl's, Marshalls, Michael's, Midas, NTB, Old Navy, Petco, PetSmart, Publix, Ross, Sam's Club/dsl, Staples, Target, TJ Maxx, Verizon, Walmart

102 SC 60, Ballentine, Irmo, N Cracker Barrel, Extended Stay Deluxe, Hyatt Place, H, S 76, Circle K, Shell, Arby's, Bellacino's Pizza, CAVA, Domino's, Dunkin', Firehouse, KFC, Marco's Pizza, Maurice's BBQ, McDonald's, Moe's SW Grill, Papa John's, Pizza Hut, Smashburger, Smoothie King, Starbucks, Subway, Taco Bell, Wendy's, Zaxby's, Home2 Suites, Residence Inn, AAA, auto repair, CVS Drug, Jiffy Lube, Kroger, park, same as 103

101b a US 76, US 176, to N Columbia, N Murphy Express, Shell/dsl, Bojangles, Jersey Mike's Subs, Silver Fox Grill, $General, Food Lion, Food Lion, Harley-Davidson, Honda, Publix, Walgreens, S Circle K, Shell/7-11/Burger King/dsl, Burger King, Lucky's BurgerShack, Starbucks, Waffle House, $General, Toyota

PEAK

97 US 176, to Ballentine, Peak, N China 1, Subway, Food Lion, S Sunoco/dsl, Burger King

94mm weigh sta wb

91 SC 48, to Chapin, S BP/dsl, Exxon/Taco Bell/dsl, Shell/dsl, Bojangles, Farm Boys BBQ, McDonald's, Zaxby's, to Dreher Island SP, URGENT CARE

85 SC 202, Little Mountain, Pomaria, S to Dreher Island SP

82 SC 773, to Prosperity, Pomaria, N Circle K/Subway/dsl/24hr, Pilot/Wendy's/dsl/scales/24hr, Waffle House

81mm weigh sta eb

NEWBERRY

76 SC 219, to Pomaria, Newberry, N Love's/McDonald's/Chester's/dsl/scales/24hr, S 7-11/dsl, BP, Murphy USA, Shell, Burger King, Dunkin, Hardee's, KFC, Little Caesars, McDonald's, Pizza Hut, Starbucks, Subway, Taco Bell, Waffle House, Wendy's, Hampton Inn(4mi), Holiday Inn Express, Home2 Suites, Quality Inn, $General, AutoZone, CVS, Lowe's, to Newberry Opera House, Walmart

74 SC 34, to Newberry, N BP/dsl, Shell/dsl, Bill&Fran's Café, S Arby's, Capt D's, Sonic, Waffle House, Days Inn, Days Inn, Economy Inn, Food Lion, H, to NinetySix HS

72 SC 121, to Newberry, S Shell/dsl, H, to Newberry Coll

66 SC 32, to Jalapa

63.5mm **full facilities, litter barrels, petwalk, both lanes, vending**

60 SC 66, to Joanna, S BP/dsl, Newberry KOA

54 SC 72, to Clinton, N BP/dsl, S Shell/dsl, Arby's, Bojangles, Fatz Cafe, Starbucks, Zaxby's, Hampton Inn, H, to Presbyterian Coll, W QT

52 SC 56, to Clinton, N ONE9/Subway/dsl/scales/24hr, Blue Ocean Rest., McDonald's, Comfort Suites, Quality Inn, S Shell/dsl, Hardee's, Waffle House, Wendy's, Days Inn, $General, H

UNION

51 I-385, to Greenville(from wb)

45.5mm Enoree River

44 SC 49, to Cross Anchor, Union

41 SC 92, to Enoree, N Valero

38 SC 146, to Woodruff, N HotSpot/Shell/Hardee's/dsl/scales/24hr

35 SC 50, Walnut Grove Rd, to Woodruff, S BP/dsl

33mm S Tyger River

32mm N Tyger River

28 US 221, to Spartanburg, N Circle K/dsl/24hr,

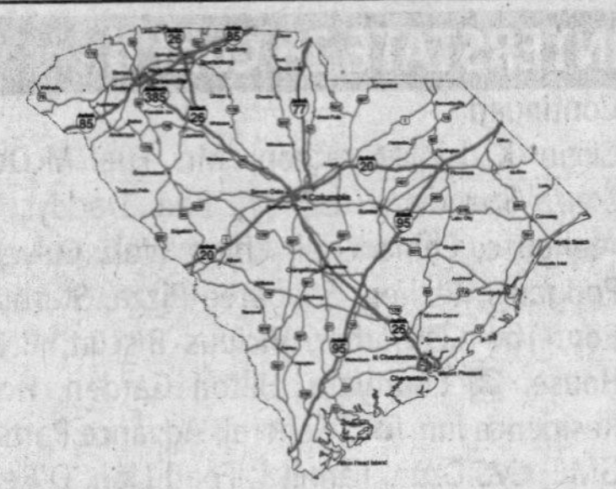

28 Continued
Shell/Subway/dsl, Arby's, Bojangles, Burger King, Italian Pizza, Waffle House, Zaxby's, $General, H, Pine Ridge Camping(3mi), to Walnut Grove Plantation

SPARTANBURG

22 SC 296, Reidville Rd, to Spartanburg, N Exxon/dsl, Marathon/CircleK/dsl, Spinx/dsl, Arby's, Blue Bay Rest., Bruster's, Cook Out, Five Guys, Fuddrucker's(1mi), Little Caesars, McDonald's, Outback Steaks, Shane's BBQ, Starbucks, Substation II, Waffle House, Wasabi Japanese, Wayback Burger, Zaxby's, $General, Advance Parts, to Croft SP, vet, S 7-11/dsl, QT/dsl, Clock Rest., Denny's, Domino's, Dunkin', Hardee's, Hunan K, Papa John's, Rosa's BBQ, Sleep Inn, Super 8, $General, $Tree, Abbott Farms, CVS Drug, Food Lion, Hyundai, Midas, Toyota, vet, VW, Walgreens

21b a US 29, to Spartanburg, N Marathon/Circle K, Spinx/dsl, Tesla Charger, A&W/LJ Silver, Bojangles, Buffalo Wild Wings, Burger King, Chick-fil-A, Chipotle Mexican, ChuckECheese, City Range Steaks, Corona Mexican, DQ, Dunkin, Firehouse Subs, FoodCourt, Golden Corral, Jack-in-the-Box, Jason's Deli, Kanpai Tokyo, KFC, La Taverna Italian, Longhorn Steaks, Marco's Pizza, McAlister's Deli, Moe's SW Grill, NY Hibachi, Olive Garden, Panera Bread, Papa's Mexican, Red Crab Seafood, Red Lobster, Starbucks, Subway, TX Roadhouse, Wendy's, Wingstop, Comfort Suites, Hampton Inn, Hilton Garden, Holiday Inn Express, Residence Inn, ALDI, Barnes&Noble, Belk, Best Buy, Costco/gas, Dillard's, Discount Tire, Firestone/auto, Hamrick's, Home Depot, JC Penney, Lowe's, Meineke, Michael's, Office Depot, Old Navy, PetSmart, Ross, TJ Maxx, USPO, Verizon, Walgreens, Walmart/McDonald's, S BP/dsl, Shell/dsl, Apollo's Pizza, Applebee's, IHOP, McDonald's, Taco Bell, Waffle House, Tru Hotel, $Tree, Academy Sports, Advance Parts, BigLots, Hobby Lobby, H, Ingles Foods/Starbucks/gas, Kohl's, NTB, Sam's Club/gas, Target, URGENT CARE

19b a Lp I-85, Spartanburg, N BP/dsl, Valero, Cracker Barrel, Subway, Residence Inn, Sheraton, S Valero, Brookwood Inn

18b a I-85, N to Charlotte, S to Greenville

17 New Cut Rd, N U-Haul, S BP/dsl, Exxon/dsl, Burger King, McDonald's, Waffle House, Days Inn, Howard Johnson, Red Roof Inn, Rodeway Inn

16 John Dodd Rd, to Wellford, N Exxon/Circle K/Aunt M/dsl, Camping World RV Ctr

15 US 176, to Inman, N BP, Circle K/dsl/scales, Waffle House, S QT/dsl, Optimum RV Ctr

10 SC 292, to Inman, N Shell/Hot Spot/EVC/Subway/dsl/scales/24hr

7.5mm Lake William C. Bowman

5 SC 11, Foothills Scenic Dr, Chesnee, Campobello, N Circle K/Subway/dsl/scales/24hr, S Marathon/dsl, truck repair

3mm **full facilities, info, litter barrels, petwalk, vending, Welcome Ctr eb, wi-fi**

1 SC 14, to Landrum, S Shell/Burger King/dsl, Bojangles, China Cafe, Domino's Pizza, Starbucks, Subway,

INTERSTATE 26 Cont'd

1 Continued
$General, Ingles/café/gas, Verizon, vet

0mm South Carolina/North Carolina state line

INTERSTATE 77

91mm South Carolina/North Carolina state line

90 US 21, Carowinds Blvd, E QT/dsl, Bojangles, Burger King, McDonald's, Zaxby's, Woodspring Suites, fireworks, H, W Circle K/Subway, Circle K/Wendy's/dsl, Exxon/7-11, QT/dsl, Cracker Barrel, Culver's, Famous Dave's, KFC, Moe's SW, Panchito's Mexican, Best Western, Clarion, Comfort Inn/Tesla EVC, Motel 6, Quality Inn, Sleep Inn Suites, Cabela's, Carowinds Camping, Carowinds Funpark

89.5mm **full facilities, info, litter barrels, petwalk/weigh sta nb, vending, Welcome Ctr sb**

88 Gold Hill Rd, to Pineville, E Tru, URGENT CARE, W Exxon/dsl, QT/dsl, Shell/dsl, Dunkin, Hardee's, Marco's Pizza, TWF Burgers, WingBonz Cantina, Chrysler/Dodge/Jeep, Fiat, Ford, Hyundai, KOA, Publix, vet

85 SC 160, Ft Mill, Tega Cay, E Exxon, Brixx Pizza, Carolina Alehouse, Cold Stone, Epic Chophouse, Panera Bread, Smashburger, Starbucks, Taco Molino, Courtyard, H, W BP/dsl, Circle K/dsl, QT/dsl, Akahana Asian, Burger King, Charanda Mexican, Chick-fil-A, Empire Pizza, Fish Market Rest., Five Guys, Fratelli's Italian, Jimmy John's, Killington's Rest., Konnichiwa Japanese, McAlister's Deli, Moe's SW Grill, Papa John's, Pizza Hut, Starbucks, Wendy's, Hampton Inn, Holiday Inn Express, CVS Drug, Firestone/auto, Goodyear/auto, Harris-Teeter, Lowe's, Meineke, vet, Walgreens

84.5mm weigh sta sb

83 SC 49, Sutton Rd, E Circle K, W Love's/Chesters/Subway/dsl/scales/24hr, Bojangles

82.5mm Catawba River

82c US 21, SC 161, Rock Hill, Ft Mill, E 7-11, Exxon, Freddy's, IHOP, Sonny's BBQ, Steak'n Shake, Zaxby's, Comfort Inn, Ramada, Home Depot, Lidl, PetSmart, W Circle K, Mobil/Circle K/dsl, QT/dsl, Shell/dsl, Valero, Chinese Bistro Deli, Dominos, Empire Pizza, Hooters, Krispy Kreme, McDonald's, Outback Steaks, Rock Hill Bagels, Sonic, Starbucks, The Dixie Pig, Courtyard, $General, Food Lion, H, Mavis, Walgreens

82b a E Exxon, 7-11, Comfort Inn, Ramada Inn, W Shell/Circle K/dsl, Arby's, Bojangles, Burger King, Chick-fil-A, China Kitchen, Chipotle, CiCi's Pizza, Cookout, Fuji Japan, Golden Corral, HoneyBaked Ham, HongKong Chinese, Jasmine Grill, Little Caesar's, Luigi& Sons Italian, Mario's Pizza, McDonald's, Penn Sta. Subs, Pizza Hut, Popeyes, Rock Hill Diner, Sakura Japanese, Subway, Taco Bell, Waffle House, Wendy's, Baymont, Baymont Inn, Best Way, Best Western, Country Inn&Suites, Days Inn, EconoLodge, Economy Express Inn, Howard Johnson, Microtel, Quality Inn, Red Roof Inn, Regency, $General, $Tree, Advance Parts, ALDI, AutoZone, BigLots, Cadillac/Chevrolet, city park/EVC, Family$, Firestone/auto, Midas, NAPA, O'Reilly Parts, Office Depot, PepBoys, Publix, Verizon, York Co Museum

79 SC 122, Dave Lyle Blvd, to Rock Hill, E BP/dsl, Murphy USA/dsl, Amber Buffet, Applebee's, Buffalo Wild Wings, Charanda Mexican, Chick-fil-A, Cracker Barrel, El Manhattan Tacos, Five Guys, Hardee's, Jersey Mike's, Longhorn Steaks, O'Charley's, Ruby Tuesday, TX Roadhouse, Comfort Suites, Fairfield Inn, Hampton Inn, Holiday Inn, Home2 Suites, La Quinta, Staybridge Suites, TownePlace Suites, Tru, Wingate Inn, $Tree, AT&T, Belk, Buick/GMC, Discount Tire,

YORK

79 Continued
Food Lion, Harley Davidson, Hobby Lobby, Honda, JC Penney, Kohl's, Lowe's, Meineke, Nissan, NTB, Sam's Club/dsl, Toyota/Scion, Verizon, Walmart/gas, W Circle K/dsl, Baskin Robins/Dunkin, Bob Evans, Chili's, DQ, Firehouse Subs, Jack-in-the-Box, McAlister's Deli, McDonald's, Moe's SW Grill, Olive Garden, Panera Bread, Subway, Taco Bell, Wendy's, Wild Wing Cafe, Extended Stay America, Hilton Garden, Holiday Inn, Best Buy, Books-A-Million, Dick's, Ford, Michael's, Ross, Target/Starbucks, TJ Maxx, URGENT CARE

77 US 21, SC 5, to Rock Hill, E BP/Subway/dsl, ONE9/dsl, QT/scales/dsl, Arby's, to Andrew Jackson SP(12mi), W Tabo Bell, Waffle House, to Winthrop Coll

75 Porter Rd, E Crown

73 SC 901, to Rock Hill, York, E Exxon/dsl, Flying J/Denny's/dsl/scales/LP/24hr, W H

66mm **full facilities, litter barrels, petwalk, both lanes, vending**

65 SC 9, to Chester, Lancaster, E BP/Papa John's/dsl, Citgo/dsl, QT/dsl, Shell/Subway/dsl, Bojangles, China Wok, Sabor Mexican, Waffle House, Days Inn, EconoLodge, Holiday Inn, $General, IGA Foods/gas, W Exxon/dsl, Burger King, Country Omelet, Front Porch Rest., KFC/Taco Bell, McDonald's, Zaxby's, Motel 6, Quality Inn, Super 8, H

62 SC 56, to Fort Lawn, Richburg

55 SC 97, to Chester, Great Falls, E Exxon/dsl, W H, to Chester SP

RIDGEWAY

48 SC 200, to Great Falls, E Shell/Grand Central Rest./scales/dsl/@, W Pilot/Wendy's/DQ/dsl/scales/24hr

46 SC 20, to White Oak

41 SC 41, to Winnsboro, E to Lake Wateree SP

34 SC 34, to Winnsboro, Ridgeway, E Am Pm/dsl, Ridgeway Motel(1mi), Bryan's Auto/tire, U-Haul, W Exxon/dsl, Waffle House, Executive Inn

32 Peach Rd, Ridgeway, Little Cedar Creek Camping(2mi)

27 Blythewood Rd, E BP/Dunkin Donuts, Exxon/Bojangles/dsl/24hr, Carolina Ribs, Chubby's Burgers, Hardee's, KFC/Pizza Hut, McDonald's, Papa John's, Prince Pizza, San Jose Mexican, Scott Benny's, Subway, Waffle House, Wendy's, Zaxby's, Comfort Inn, Days Inn, Holiday Inn Express, Home2 Suites, $General, IGA Foods, repair/tires, USPO, vet, W Lizard's Thicket, Food Lion, Groucho's Deli

COLUMBIA

24 US 21, to Wilson Blvd., E BP/dsl, QT/scales/dsl, Shell/Subway/dsl, auto repair, vet, W 7-11, Exxon/dsl

22 Killian Rd, E Murphy Express/dsl, Shell/Burger King/dsl, Applebee's, Bojangles, Chick-fil-A, Chipotle, Eggs Up, Firehouse Subs, Freddy's, McDonald's, Panda Express, Panera Bread, Popeyes, Salsarita's, Starbucks, Subway, Tropical Smoothie, Zaxby's, Hampton Inn, Acura, ALDI, AutoZone, BMW, CVS Drug, Discount Tire, Firestone, Honda, Kia, Kroger/dsl, Lowe's, Mazda, Subaru, Toyota/Scion, VW, Walgreens, W China Dragon, Monterrey's Mexican, Lexus/Buick/GMC/Cadillac, Verizon, Walmart/McDonald's

19 SC 555, Farrow Rd, E BP/dsl, Exxon, Shell/dsl, Bojangles, Cracker Barrel, Sonic, Subway, Wendy's, Courtyard, Hilton Garden, Residence Inn, H, W Shell/dsl, China Kitchen, Waffle House, SC Archives

18 to SC 277, to I-20 W(from sb), Columbia

17 US 1, Two Notch Rd, E BP, Citgo, Exxon, Shell/Circle K, Arby's, Burger King, TX Roadhouse, Waffle House, Columbia NE Hotel, Holiday Inn Express, InTown Suites, Quality Inn, Family$, to Sesquicentennial SP, U-Haul, USPO, vet, Walgreens, W Mobil, Chili's, Fazoli's, Hooters, IHOP, Lizard's Thicket, Outback Steaks, Waffle House, Best Western+, Comfort Suites, EconoLodge,

= gas = food = lodging = other = rest stop

INTERSTATE 77 Cont'd

COLUMBIA

Exit	Services
17	Continued Fairfield Inn, Hampton Inn, La Quinta, Microtel, Red Roof Inn, Home Depot
16b a	I-20, W to Augusta, E to Florence, Alpine Rd
15b a	SC 12, to Percival Rd, W Shell
13	Decker Blvd(from nb), W El Cheapo, Spinx/dsl
12	Forest Blvd, Thurmond Blvd, E to Ft Jackson, Panda Express, W Circle K/dsl, Shell/dsl/24hr, Chick-fil-A, Cookout, Domino's, Eastern Buffet, Golden Corral, Juicy Crab, McDonald's, Panda Express, Panera Bread, San Jose Rest., Sonic, Subway, Wendy's, Wingstop, Extended Stay America, Super 8, $Tree, AT&T, H, museum, Petco, Sam's Club/gas, U-Haul, Verizon, vet, Walmart
10	SC 760, Jackson Blvd, E to Ft Jackson, Saky Japanese, W QT/dsl, Shell, Applebee's, Bojangles, Broken Egg, Buffalo Wild Wings, Dave's Chicken, Maurices BBQ, Moe's SW, Subway, EconoLodge, Food Lion, Staples, Walgreens, Whole Foods Mkt
9b a	US 76, US 378, to Sumter, Columbia, E BP, Citgo, Gulf, Murphy USA/dsl, Shell, Spinx/dsl, Arby's, Bojangles, Capt D's, Chick-fil-A, Cookout, Domino's, KFC, McDonald's, Pizza Hut, Popeyes, Ruby Tuesday, Rush's Rest., Sawasdee Kitchen, Shoney's, Subway, Taco Bell, Waffle House, Waffle House, Zaxby's, Baymont Inn, Candlewood Suites, Comfort Inn, Country Inn&Suites, Days Inn, Hampton Inn, Holiday Inn Express, Home2 Suites, La Quinta, Microtel, Quality Inn, Sleep Inn, SpringHill Suites, TownePlace Suites, $Tree, Advance Parts, ALDI, AutoZone, CVS Drug, Family$, Firestone/auto, Ford, Lowe's, Mavis, NTB, O'Reilly Parts, URGENT CARE, USPO, Verizon, Walgreens, Walmart, W Circle K, Shell, Firehouse Subs, Hardee's, Jimmy John's, Krispy Kreme, MOD Pizza, Panera Bread, Sonic, Starbucks, Sub Station, Wendy's, Best Value Inn, $General, BigLots, Express Oil & Tire, GNC, Goodyear/auto, H, Target/Starbucks, Walgreens
6b a	Shop Rd, W fairgrounds, to USC Coliseum
5	SC 48, Bluff Rd, W Love's/McDonald's/Subway/dsl/scales/24hr/@, Shell/Burger King/dsl, Bojangles(2mi), $General, Petro/Starbucks/dsl/scales/24hr/@
3mm	Congaree River
2	SC 35, to Cayce, W Columbia, W Courtyard
1	US 21, US 176, US 321(from sb), Cayce, W accesses same as SC I-26, exit 115.
0mm	I-77 begins/ends on I-26, exit 116.

CAYCE

INTERSTATE 85

SHELBY

Exit	Services
106.5mm	South Carolina/North Carolina state line
106	US 29, to Grover, W Exxon/dsl, Hickory Point/gas, Mobil/dsl/fireworks, Pilot/Wendy's/DQ/dsl/scales/24hr
104	SC 99, Tribal Rd, E Love's/McDonald's/Subway/dsl/scales/24hr/@, W fireworks
103mm	**full facilities, info, litter barrels, petwalk, vending, Welcome Ctr sb**
102	SC 198, to Earl, E BP/dsl, Exxon, Hardee's, W Citgo/dsl, Flying J/Denny's/dsl/scales/LP/24hr, McDonald's
100mm	Buffalo Creek
100	SC 5, to Blacksburg, Shelby, W Citgo
98	Frontage Rd(from nb)
97mm	Broad River
96	SC 18, E Circle K/Krystal/dsl
95	SC 18, to Gaffney, E Exxon/Circle K/dsl, PetroMax/dsl, Mr Waffle, H, to Limestone Coll
92	SC 11, to Gaffney, E Circle K/Subway/dsl, Fast Point/dsl, Murphy USA/dsl, Aegean Pizza, Applebee's, Bojangles, Burger King, Chick-fil-A, China Express, Chipotle, CookOut,

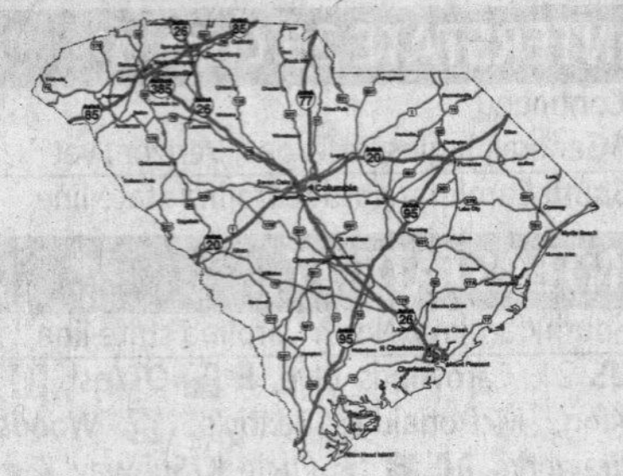

SPARTANBURG

Exit	Services
92	Continued Daddy Joe's BBQ, Domino's, Firehouse Subs, Jersey Mike's, KFC, McDonald's, Osaka Sushi, Papa John's, Pete's, Pizza Hut, Popeyes, Sonic, Starbucks, Taco Bell, US Wings, Waffle House, Wendy's, Wings Etc., Zaxby's, Baymont Inn, Super 8, $General, $Tree, Advance Parts, ALDI, AT&T, Belk, BigLots, Ingles Foods, Lowe's, O'Reilly Parts, to Limestone Coll, USPO, Verizon, Walgreens, Walmart/gas, W EconoLodge, Quality Inn, Chevrolet, Foothills Scenic Hwy, to the Peachoid
90	SC 105, SC 42, to Gaffney, E Pilot/Arby's/dsl/scales/24hr, QT/dsl, Bojangles, Clock Rest., Starbucks, Subway, Waffle House, Red Roof Inn, Sleep Inn, W BP/dsl, Exxon/Burger King, Cracker Barrel, El Michoacan, Food Court, Outback Steaks, Hampton Inn, Holiday Inn, Gaffney Outlets/famous brands, Hamrick's
87	SC 39, E KOA
83	SC 110, E Shell/Hot Spot, fruit stand, W ONE9/dsl/scales/24hr/@, to Cowpens Bfd
82	Frontage Rd(from nb)
80.5mm	Pacolet River
80	SC 57, to Gossett, E Shell/Hot Spot/EVC/dsl
78	US 221, Chesnee, E 76/dsl, Hardee's, Red Roof Inn, W Burger King, QT/dsl, RaceWay/dsl, Arby's, Bojangles, McDonald's, Southern BBQ, Starbucks, Subway, Waffle House, Wendy's, Hampton Inn, Holiday Inn Express, $General, Advance Parts, Harley-Davidson, Ingles Foods/cafe/dsl
77	Lp 85, Spartanburg, services along Lp 85 exits E
75	SC 9, Spartanburg, E Spinx/EVC/dsl, Bojangles, Denny's, Best Western+, $General, U-Haul, W QT/dsl, RaceWay/dsl, Bruster's, Capri's Italian, CookOut, Copper River Grill, Grapevine Rest, La Paz Mexican, McDonald's, Waffle House, Willy Taco, Zaxby's, Comfort Inn, Days Inn, CVS Drug, Ingles/Starbucks/gas, Parr 3 Automotive, USPO
72	US 176, to I-585, E 7-11, Chrysler/Dodge/Jeep, to USCS, Wofford/Converse Coll, W Circle K/dsl, RaceWay/dsl, China Fun, El Limon Mexican, Green Olive Grill, Subway, Waffle House, $General, Ingles Foods/Starbucks/gas
70b a	I-26, E to Columbia, W to Asheville
69	Lp 85, SC 41(from nb), to Fairforest
68	SC 129, to Greer
67mm	N Tyger River
66	US 29, to Lyman, Wellford, E 7-11, Exxon/Subway/dsl, Waffle House
63	SC 290, to Duncan, E Exxon/Circle K/dsl, QT/dsl, Spinx/Dunkin/dsl, Arby's, Bojangles, Chick-Fil-A, Clock Rest., Cracker Barrel, Culver's, El Primo Mexican, Firehouse Subs, Fuddruckers, Fuji Japanese, Jersey Mike's, KFC, Paisanos Italian, Pizza Inn, Starbucks, Taco Bell, Tipsy Taco, Waffle House, Wayback Burgers, Whataburger, Zaxby's, Baymont Inn, Fairfield Inn, Hampton Inn, Home2 Suites, Microtel, W Marathon/dsl, Pilot/Wendy's/dsl/scales/24hr, TA/BP/DQ/rest./dsl/scales/24hr/@, El Molcajete Mexican,

INTERSTATE 85 Cont'd

Exit	Services
63	Continued Hardee's, McDonald's, Rte 290 Grill, Holiday Inn Express, Quality Inn, Red Roof Inn, Woodspring Suites, Blue Beacon, Blue Compass RV Ctr, Speedco
62.5mm	S Tyger River
60	SC 101, to Greer, E Marathon, QT/dsl, Mi Familia Mexican, Subway, Theo's Rest, Wendy's, Junior's Tire, W Spinx/Burger King/dsl, Bojangles, Waffle House, stayAPT Suites, Super 8, BMW Visitor Ctr
58	Brockman-McClimon Rd
57	W Greenville-Spartanburg
56	SC 14, to Greer, E Citgo/dsl, $General, H, W QT/Burger King/dsl, Spinx/dsl, Waffle House, Goodyear Truck Tires, Ledford's Adventure RV Ctr
55mm	Enoree River
54	Pelham Rd, E Exxon/Circle K, Stop-A-Minute/dsl, Burger King, Corona Mexican, SBH BBQ, Starbucks, Subway, Tropical Burger, Waffle House, Best Western, Comfort Suites, W Asian Kitchen, Bertolos Pizza, California Dreaming Rest., Chick-fil-A, Chicken Salad Chick, Chipotle, Chophouse 47, Clean Eatz, Duck Donuts, Dunkin, Eggs Up Grill, Firehouse Subs, Five Guys, Frankie's Pizza, Jimmy John's, Joe's Crabshack, Joy of Tokyo, Lieu's Asian Bistro, Logan's Roadhouse, McDonald's, Moe's SW Grill, On the Border, Panera Bread, PDQ Rest., Poke Bros, Rapid Fired Pizza, Schlotzsky's, Sidewall Pizza, Starbucks, Taco Bell, Taziki's Cafe, Travinia Italian, Tropical Cafe, Courtyard, EconoLodge, Extended Stay America, Fairfield Inn, Hampton Inn, Holiday Inn Express, Home2 Suites, MainStay Suites, Marriott, Residence Inn, Wingate Inn, Advance Parts, Bi-Lo, CVS Drug, EarthFare Foods, GNC, Goodyear/auto, Verizon, Walgreens, Walmart
51	I-385, SC 146, Woodruff Rd, Poke Bros, E Brixx Pizza, Buffalo Wild Wings, Chicken Salad Chick, Chipotle Mexican, Coldstone, Cracker Barrel, First Watch, Fuddrucker's, Fusion Japanese, Genghis Grill, IHOP, La Parrilla, Lieu's Bistro, Longhorn Steaks, Oriental House, Panera Bread, PF Chang's, Red Robin, Volcano Korean BBQ, Wingstop, Drury Inn, Hampton Inn, Hilton Garden, Homewood Suites, Residence Inn, Staybridge Suites, Tru Hilton, Barnes&Noble, Best Buy, Dick's, Frankies Fun Park, Goodyear/auto, Hamrick's Outlet, Lowe's, Marshalls, PetCo, PetSmart, REI, Ross, Verizon, vet, Whole Foods Mkt, W QT/dsl, RaceWay/dsl, Bad Daddy's Burger, Carolina Alehouse, Carrabba's, Cheddars, Chuy's Mexican, Dave&Busters's, Firebirds, Grimaldi's, HuHot Mongolian, McDonald's, MidTown Deli, Panda Express, Ruby Tuesday, Ruth's Chris Steaks, Starbucks, Strossner's Cafe, Subway, TGIFriday's, Tin Lizzy's, Tropical Cafe, Tucanos Brazilian Grill, Twin Peaks Rest., Waffle House, Wild Wing Cafe, Yardhouse Rest., Zoe's Kitchen, Baymont Inn, Candlewood Suites, Comfort Inn, Crowne Plaza, Days Inn, Embassy Suites, Holiday Inn Express, La Quinta, Microtel, My Place, AT&T, Cabela's, Costco/gas, Firestone/auto, Home Depot, Hyundai, Old Navy, Target, Trader Joe's
48b a	US 276, Greenville, E QT/dsl, Red Roof Inn, BMW/Mini, CarMax, to ICAR, W Shell/dsl, Arby's, Bojangles, Burger King, Culver's, Happy China, Hooters, McDonald's, Olive Garden, Starbucks, Subway, Taco Bell, Embassy Suites, $Tree, Acura, Audi/Porsche/VW, Buick/GMC, Chevrolet/Cadillac, Chrysler/Dodge/Jeep, CVS, Food Lion, Ford/Lincoln, GNC, Honda, Infiniti, Jaguar, Kia, Lexus, Mazda, Meineke, Mercedes, Michael's, Nissan, Office Depot, Old Time Pottery, PepBoys, PetSmart, Subaru, Toyota, Volvo
46c	rd 291, Pleasantburg Rd, Mauldin Rd, W Citgo/dsl, Energy Market, QT/dsl, Jack-in-the-Box, Papa John's, Subway,

GREENVILLE

Exit	Services
46c	Continued Greenville Inn, InTown Suites, Super Lodge, Woodspring Suites, Aamco, Advance Parts, ALDI, Home Depot, NTB, same as 46ba
46b a	US 25 bus, Augusta Rd, E Citgo, Mike&Jack/dsl, QT/dsl, Spinx/dsl, Vgo, Burger King, Waffle House, Armstrong Inn, Econo Lodge, Motel 6, Studio 6, Uptown Tires, W QT/dsl, Jack in the Box, Little Caesars, Papa John's, Pizza Hut, Subway, InTown Suites, Traveler's Inn, WoodSpring Suites, $General, Advance Parts, ALDI, Family$, Home Depot, NTB, O'Reilly Parts, same as 46c
44	US 25, White Horse Rd, E Spinx/dsl, W BP/dsl, Citgo/McDonald's, Waffle House, Freightliner, H
44a	SC 20(from sb), to Piedmont
42	I-185, to Greenville, I-185 S(toll), Columbia, W H
40	SC 153, to Easley, E 7-11/dsl, BP/dsl, Waffle House, W 7-11/dsl, QT/dsl, RaceWay/dsl, Spinx/dsl, Antonio's Pizza, Arby's, Big Clock, Burger King, Chick-Fil-A, Cracker Barrel, Dunkin, El Sureno Mexican, Firehouse Subs, KFC, Little Caesar's, Los Amigos, McDonald's, Papa John's, Pizza House, Pizza Hut, Shane's BBQ, Starbucks, Subway, Taco Bell, Tropical, Wendy's, Zaxby's, Best Western+, Comfort Suites, Executive Inn, Hampton Inn(4mi), Holiday Inn Express, Super 8, $General, Advance Parts, ALDI, AutoZone, CVS Drug, Ingles, O'Reilly Parts, Verizon, Walgreens, Walmart
39	SC 143, to Piedmont, E Vgo/dsl, W Shell/dsl
35	SC 86, to Easley, Piedmont, E BP/Subway(1.5mi), Phillips 66, Pilot/McDonald's/dsl/scales/24hr, Burger King, Cancun Mexican, Domino's, Hardee's(1.5mi), Tony' Pizza, $Tree(1.5mi), O'Reilly Parts, repair/tires, USPO, Walgreens, W QT/dsl, Spinx/dsl, Bojangles
34	US 29(from sb), to Williamston
32	SC 8, to Pelzer, Easley, E 7-11/dsl, Shell/dsl, $General, W Love's/Hardees/dsl/24hrs/@
27	SC 81, to Anderson, E BP/dsl, Exxon/dsl, Stop A Minit/dsl, Arby's, McDonald's, Papa's Mexican, Waffle House, Hampton Inn, Holiday Inn Express, H, W Exxon/dsl
23mm	**full facilities, litter barrels, petwalk, sb, vending**
21	US 178, to Anderson, E BP/dsl, QT/dsl, Burger King, Waffle House
19b a	US 76, SC 28, to Anderson, E Exxon/dsl, QT/dsl, Shell/dsl, Stop A Minit/dsl, AJ's Grill, Applebee's, Barbarito's, Bojangles, Carson Steaks, Chick-fil-A, Chili's, Chipotle, CookOut, Denny's, Five Guys, Fuddruckers, Golden Corral, Golden Corral, Grand China, Hardee's, Hardee's, Hibachi Grill, Jack-in-the-Box, Logan's Roadhouse, Longhorn Steaks, O'Charley's, Olive Garden, Panera Bread, Red Lobster, Starbucks, Tucker's Rest., TX Roadhouse, Zaxby's, Best Value Inn, Days Inn, Hilton Garden, Holiday Inn, Rodeway Inn, Super 8, $General, $Tree, Advance Parts, ALDI, AT&T, Best Buy, Chrysler/Dodge/Jeep, Dick's, Ford/Mazda, GNC, Goodyear, Harley-Davidson, Hobby Lobby, Home Depot, Honda, Kohl's, Lowe's, Meineke, Michael's, Nissan, O'Reilly Parts, Office Depot, Old Navy, PetSmart, Publix/deli, Ross, Sam's Club, Staples, Target, TJ Maxx, Toyota, Verizon, vet, Walmart/Subway, W RaceWay/dsl, Shell/McDonald's, Arby's, Cracker Barrel, Hooters, Outback Steaks, Puerto Mexican, Rigsby Grill, Starbucks, Subway, Subway, Waffle House, Wendy's, Wild Wing Cafe, Baymont Inn, Comfort Suites, Country Inn&Suites, Fairfield Inn, Hampton Inn, Holiday Inn Express, Microtel, Residence Inn, to Clemson U(11mi)
18mm	**full facilities, litter barrels, petwalk, nb, vending**
15mm	Lake Hartwell

EASLEY

= gas = food = lodging = other = rest stop

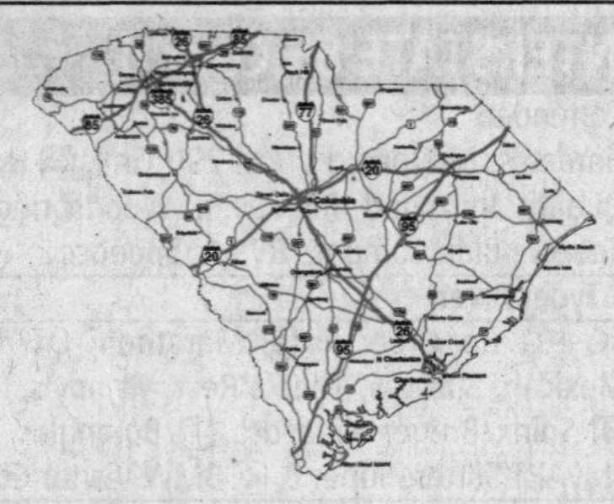

ANDERSON

INTERSTATE 85 Cont'd

Exit #	Services
14	SC 187, to Clemson, Anderson, E Marathon/dsl, Foobar'd Grille, W Mi Casa, Budget Inn, $General, to Clem Research Pk
12mm	Seneca River, Lake Hartwell
11	SC 24, SC 243, to Townville, E Exxon/dsl, Sunoco/dsl, Subway, to Savannah River Scenic Hwy, W Shell/dsl, Neighbors Pub
9mm	weigh sta nb
4	SC 243, to SC 24, Fair Play, E Amoco/dsl, Love's/Arby's/dsl/scales/24hr, Tesla Charger
2	SC 59, to Fair Play, W fireworks
1	SC 11, to Walhalla, W Gazebo Rest., fireworks, to Lake Hartwell SP
0.5mm	**full facilities, info, litter barrels, petwalk, vending, Welcome Ctr nb**
0mm	South Carolina/Georgia state line, Lake Hartwell, Tugaloo River

INTERSTATE 95

DILLON · FLORENCE · OLANTA · MANNING · SANTEE

Exit #	Services
198mm	South Carolina/North Carolina state line
196mm	**full facilities, info, litter barrels, petwalk, vending, Welcome Ctr sb**
195mm	Little Pee Dee River
193	SC 9, SC 57, to N Myrtle Beach, Dillon, N Speedway/Speedy Cafe/dsl/24hr, E Exxon/dsl, Mobil/dsl, Murphy Express/dsl, Sunoco/7-11/dsl, B&C Steak/BBQ, Burger King, CookOut, Firehouse Subs, Huddle House, Little Caesar's, Pizza Hut, Popeyes, Starbucks, Subway, Taco Bell, Tokyo Cafe, Wendy's, Zaxby's, Days Inn, Dillon Express Inn, Quality Inn, Red Roof Inn, Royal Regency Inn, $General, $Tree, Advance Parts, AutoZone, CVS Drug, fireworks, Food Lion, H, O'Reilly Parts, Walgreens, Walmart, W Economy Inn, Bass Lake RV Camp/LP
190	SC 34, to Dillon, E QT/dsl, W Love's/Arby's/dsl/scales/24hr
181	SC 38, Oak Grove, E BP/Subway/dsl/EVC/24hr, Flying J/dsl/LP/scales/24hr, Shell/McDonald's/dsl/24hr, Shuler's BBQ(5mi), Holiday Inn Express, fireworks, W Pilot/DQ/Wendy's/dsl/scales/24hr, Best Western
175mm	Pee Dee River
170	SC 327, E BP, Pilot/Wendy's/dsl/scales/24hr, McDonald's, Subway, Waffle House, Zaxby's, Holiday Inn Express, Harley Davidson, Missile Museum, to Myrtle Beach, W Buc-ee's/Tesla EVC
169	TV Rd, to Florence, E dsl repair, Florence RV Park, W BP, Petro/Shell/Iron Skillet/dsl/scales/24hr/@, Florence Express Inn, Blue Beacon, dsl repair, Peterbilt
164	US 52, to Darlington, Florence, E Exxon/dsl, RaceWay, Shell/dsl, Cracker Barrel, McDonald's, Quincy's, Ruby Tuesday, Waffle House, Wendy's, Baymont Inn, Best Western, Clarion Inn, EconoLodge, Suburban Lodge, Super 8, Chrysler/Dodge/Jeep, H, W Mobil, Pilot/Subway/Taco Bell/dsl, TA/BP/Popeyes/dsl/scales/@, Arby's, Biscuitville, Cook Out, Dickey's BBQ, Dunkin, Hardee's, Krispy Kreme, Shoney's, Starbucks, Young's Pecans, Zaxby's, Comfort Suites, Country Inn&Suites, Days Inn, Hampton Inn, La Quinta, Microtel, Motel 6, Sleep Inn, Travel House Inn, Tru Hilton, to Darlington Raceway, transmissions, vet
160b	I-20 W, to Columbia
160a	Lp 20, to Florence, E Exxon/dsl, Murphy USA/dsl, Tesla EVC, Arby's, Bruster's Ice Cream, Buffalo Wild Wings, Burger King, Chick-fil-A, Chili's, Chipotle, ChuckeCheese, Firehouse Subs, Florence Crab House, Golden Corral, Hibachi Grill, Hwy 55 Cafe, IHOP, Jersey Mike's, Longhorn Steaks,
160a	Continued Margaritas Mexican, Mellow Mushroom, Olive Garden, Outback Steaks, Panera Bread, Red Bowl Asian, Red Lobster, San Jose's, Subway, Taco Bell, TX Roadhouse, Waffle House, Western Sizzlin, Comfort Inn & Suites, Courtyard, Days Inn, Fairfield Inn, Hampton Inn, Hilton Garden, Holiday Inn Express, Home2 Suites, Homewood Suites/Tesla EVC, Quality Inn, Red Roof Inn, Residence Inn, SpringHill Suites, Staybridge Suites, TownePlace Suites, $Tree, ALDI, AT&T, Barnes&Noble, Belk, Best Buy, Big Lots, Dick's, Discount Tire, Hamrick's, Hobby Lobby, Home Depot, JC Penney, Kohl's, Lowes Whse, PetSmart, Sam's Club/dsl, Target, Verizon, Walmart
157	US 76, Timmonsville, Florence, E Amoco/dsl, Exxon/Circle K/dsl, Marathon/dsl, Shell/McDonald's, Peking Chinese, Waffle House, Florence Inn, Travelodge, W Mobil/dsl, Tree Top Inn, Swamp Fox Camping
153	Honda Way, W Exxon/dsl, Honda Plant
150	SC 403, to Sardis, E Mobil/dsl/scales, Budget Inn, W Marathon/dsl
147mm	Lynches River
146	SC 341, to Lynchburg, Olanta
141	SC 53, SC 58, to Shiloh, E DonMar RV Ctr, to Woods Bay SP, W Shell/EVC
139mm	rest area both lanes, **full facilities, litter barrels, petwalk, vending**
135	US 378, to Sumter, Turbeville, E BP/dsl, Mobil/dsl/24hr, W Exxon/Subway/dsl
132	SC 527, to Sardinia, Kingstree
130mm	Black River
122	US 521, to Alcolu, Manning, W Exxon/dsl
119	SC 261, to Paxville, Manning, E Amoco, Murphy USA/dsl, QT/dsl, Shell/dsl, TA/BP/Pizza Hut/Popeyes/dsl/scales/24hr/@, Bojangles, Burger King, Chick-fil-A, CookOut, Jalisco Mexican, McDonald's, Pizza Hut, Shoney's, Sonic, Subway, Taco Bell, Waffle House, Wendy's, Zaxby's, Baymont Inn, Days Inn, Hampton Inn, Quality Inn, SureStay, $General, AutoZone, Chrysler/Dodge/Jeep, CVS Drug, Ford, H, O'Reilly Parts, Verizon, Walmart/gas, W Enmarket/dsl/e85, Marathon, Super 8
115	US 301, to Summerton, Manning, E OYO, W Shell/dsl, Georgio's Rest, Ashburn Inn
108	rd 102, Summerton, E Citgo/dsl, Texaco/DQ/Tesla EVC, TawCaw Camping(6mi), W Love's/McDonald's/Subway/dsl/scales/24hr/@
102	US 15, US 301 N, to N Santee, E Marathon/dsl, KOA, Palmetto Shores Resort, W enmarket/dsl/e85, to Santee NWR
100mm	Lake Marion
99mm	rest area both lanes, **full facilities, info, litter barrels, petwalk, vending**
98	SC 6, to Eutawville, Santee, E BP/Bojangles, Citgo, Exxon, Mobil, Captain's Quarters, Craig's Deli, Huddle House, Pizza Hut, Subway, Taco Bell, Best Western+, Econolodge, Fairfield Inn, Hampton Inn, Red Roof Inn, Rodeway Inn, Super 8, Travelodge, $General, IGA Foods,

SC

INTERSTATE 95 Cont'd

HOLLY HILL

98 Continued
Enmarket/dsl/e85, Exxon, Marathon/dsl, Sunoco, Cracker Barrel, McDonald's, Waffle House, Wendy's, Baymont Inn, Clark Inn/rest., Comfort Inn, Holiday Inn, Lake Marion Inn, Quality Inn, Tru, CarQuest, CVS Drug, Family$, Food Lion, Rivers Country Store, to Santee SP(3mi), USPO

97 US 301 S(from sb, no return), to Orangeburg

93 US 15, to Santee, Holly Hill

90 US 176, to Cameron, Holly Hill, W Exxon/dsl

86b a I-26, W to Columbia, E to Charleston

82 US 178, to Bowman, Harleyville, E Enmarket/Subway, Pilot/Wendy's/DQ/Dunkin'/dsl/scales/24hr, Peachtree Inn, W Shell/dsl, tires/truck repair

77 US 78, to Bamberg, St George, E Citgo, Enmarket/Subway/dsl/e85, Flying J/Denny's/dsl/scales/24hr, Sunoco, Georgio's Rest., Hardee's, KFC, McDonald's, Pizza Hut, Skynyrd's Grill, Waffle House, Best Value Inn, Days Inn/RV Park, EconoLodge, $General, Ace Hardware, Chevrolet/GMC, CVS Drug, Family$, Food Lion/Tesla ECV, USPO, W BP, Shell/Taco Bell/dsl, Budget Inn, Knights Inn, Red Roof

74mm weigh sta nb, parking area commercial vehicles only sb

68 SC 61, Canadys, E BP, Crosco Express, Shell/Subway/dsl, to Colleton SP(3mi)

62 McLeod Rd

57 SC 64, Lodge, Walterboro, E Enmarket/e85, Mobil/dsl, Shell/DQ, Sunoco/dsl, Arby's, Barrel House Grille, Bojangles, Bucks Pizza, Burger King, Capt D's, Cook Out, Dimitrio's Rest., Dunkin', Huddle House, Olde House Café, Popeyes, Starbucks, Subway, Taco Bell, Waffle House, Carolina Lodge, Sleep Inn, Southern Inn, $General, Ace Hardware, Advance Parts, AutoZone, Belk, Family$, Ford, H, O'Reilly Parts, W Murphy USA/dsl, China Buffet, Fat Jack's, IHOP, KFC, Papa Johns, Zaxby's, Super 8, $Tree, AT&T, PetCo, Verizon, Walmart/gas/EVC

BEAUFORT

53 SC 63, to Varnville, Walterboro, Hampton, E BP/McDonald's, El Cheapo, Exxon, Shell/DQ, Ruby Tuesday, Waffle House, Baymont Inn, Best Western, Budgetel, Comfort Inn, EconoLodge, Ramada Inn/Tesla EVC, Rodeway Inn, fireworks, W Enmarket/dsl, Cracker Barrel, Days Inn, Hampton Inn, Holiday Inn Express, Microtel, Motel 6, Quality Inn, New Green Acres Camping

47mm rest area both lanes, **full facilities, litter barrels, petwalk, , , vending**

42 US 21, to Yemassee, Beaufort

40mm Combahee River

38 SC 68, to Hampton, Yemassee, E Enmarket/dsl/e85, Dollar General, Family$, W 76/Subway/TCBY, Love's/Hardee's/dsl/scales/24hr, Shell/dsl

33 US 17 N, to Beaufort, E BP/dsl, Exxon/McDonald's, Mobil/Subway/TCBY, Shell, 17 W Kitchen, Waffle House, Wendy's/Tesla EVC, Best Western, Econolodge, Hampton Inn, Motel 6, Red Roof Inn, Confederate Railroad Museum, KOA, Thousand Oaks RV Camping

RIDGELAND

30.5mm Tullifinny River

29mm Coosawhatchie River

28 SC 462, to Coosawhatchie, Hilton Head, Bluffton, W Exxon/dsl, Gen Store

22 US 17, Ridgeland, W Sunoco

21 SC 336, to Hilton Head, Ridgeland, E Amoco/dsl, Marathon/dsl, McDonald's, Wendy's, Camping World, W BP/DQ/dsl, Enmarket/dsl, Shell, Burger King, Hong Kong Chinese, KFC, Pizza Bella, Subway, Waffle House, Baymont, Carolina Lodge, Days Inn, Quality Inn, $General, Harvey's Foods, H, Walgreens

18 SC 13, to US 17, US 278, to Switzerland, Granville, Ridgeland

HARDEEVILLE

17mm parking area both lanes, commercial vehicles only

8 US 278, to Bluffton, Hardeeville, E Circle K/McDonald's, Enmarket/dsl/scales, Exxon, Dunkin, Taco Bell, Waffle House, Fairfield Inn, Hampton Inn, H, W Enmarket/Subway/dsl, Shell/dsl, Days Inn, Holiday Inn Express

5 US 17, US 321, to Savannah, Hardeeville, E BP/dsl, Parker's/Tesla EVC/dsl, Pilot/Subway/dsl/scales/24hr, QT/dsl/scales/24hrs, Chicken Lickin, Mi Tierrita Mexican, Waffle House, Days Inn, Economy Inn, Sleep Inn, to Savannah NWR, W Butlers/dsl/repair, Shell/dsl, Speedway/dsl, Sunoco/dsl, Burger King, Wendy's, Best Western+, Deluxe Inn, Econolodge, Quality Suites, Red Roof Inn, Super 8, Travelodge, $General, Advance Parts, Family$, NAPA

4.5mm Welcome Ctr nb, **full facilities, info, litter barrels, petwalk, , , vending, wi-fi**

4mm weigh sta both lanes

0mm South Carolina/Georgia state line, Savannah River

INTERSTATE 385 (Greenville)

42 US 276, Stone Ave, to Travelers Rest, I-385 begins/ends on US 276., E vet, W Spinx/dsl/EVC, multiple services on US 276, to Greenville Zoo

40b a SC 291, Pleasantburg Dr, E Sunoco, Jack-in-the-Box, Little Caesar's, S&S Cafeteria, Sonic, Starbucks, Subway, Taco Casa, Wendy's, $Tree, CVS Drug, Furman U, to BJU, Walgreens, W Citgo/dsl, QT/dsl, Asia Pacific Rest, Krispy Kreme, Sleep Inn, Cottman Transmissions, Midas

39 Haywood Rd, E Exxon, Spinx, Outback Steaks, Portofino's, Tony's Pizzeria, Courtyard, Hilton, Hyatt Place, La Quinta, Quality Inn, Woodspring Suites, Firestone/auto, Jiffy Lube, USPO, W Spinx/dsl, Applebee's, Basilico Italian, Burger King, Cheesecake Factory, Chick-fil-A, Chili's, Chipotle, ChuckeCheese, CiCi's Pizza, CityRange Steaks, Clock Rest., Copper River Grill, Firehouse Subs, Five Guys, Fried Green Tomatoes, Harbor Inn Seafood, Jason's Deli, Jimmy John's, Kanpai Tokyo, McAlister's Deli, Moe's SW Grill, Monterrey Mexican, Panera Bread, Papa's&Beer, Starbucks, Steak'n Shake, The Melting Pot, Waffle House, Comfort Inn, Extended Stay America, Hampton Inn, AT&T, Barnes&Noble, Belk, Dillard's, Discount Tire, JC Penney, Jo-Ann, Macy's, TJ Maxx, Verizon, vet

37 Roper Mtn Rd, W QT/dsl, RaceWay/dsl, Bad Daddy's Burgers, Carrabba's, Cheddar's, Chuy's Mexican, Crab Du Jour, Crumbl Cookies, Dave&Busters, Firebirds Grill, McDonald's, MidTown Deli, Panda Express, Ruths Chris Steaks, Starbucks, Strossner's Cafe, Sushi Kingdom, TGI Friday's, Twin Peaks Rest., vet, Waffle House, Wild Wing Cafe, Yardhouse Rest., Baymont Inn, Best Western, Candlewood Suites, Crowne Plaza, Days Inn, Embassy Suites, Extended Stay, Holiday Inn, Microtel, AT&T, Cabela's, Costco/gas, Express Oil Change, Firestone/auto, Home Depot, Hyundai, Old Navy, Target, Trader Joe's

36b a I-85, N to Charlotte, S to Atlanta

35 SC 146, Woodruff Rd, E BP/dsl, Marathon, QT/dsl, Bonefish Grill, Boston Pizzeria, Bruster's, Burger King, Chick-fil-A, China Buffet, CHPSTX Chinese, CookOut, Crab Du Jour, Culver's, Eggs Up Grill, Firehouse Subs, Great Harvest Bread, Green Tomato Buffet, Hardee's, Krispy Kreme, Little Caesar's, McDonald's, Moe's SW Grill, Pita Mediterranean, Pizza Hut, Pizza Inn, Smoky Dreams BBQ, Sonic, Starbucks, Subway, Taco Bell, The Flat, Tropical Grille, Waffle House, Wayback Burgers, Wendy's, Your Pizza Pie, Zaxby's, $Tree, AAA, Ace Hardware, ALDI, BigLots, Discount Tire, Hobby Lobby, Kohl's, Lidl Foods, NTB, O'Reilly Parts, Publix, Sam's Club/gas, Sprouts, Staples, URGENT CARE, Walmart, W Red Robin, Brixx Pizza, Buffalo Wild Wings, Cambria Hotel,

INTERSTATE 385 (Greenville) Cont'd

MAULDIN

35 Continued
Chicken Salad Chick, Chipotle Mexican, Coldstone, Cracker Barrel, First Watch, Fuddrucker's, Fusion Japanese, Genghis Grill, IHOP, La Parrilla Mexican, Lieu's Bistro, Longhorn Steaks, Oriental House, Panera Bread, PF Chang's, Poke Bros, Red Robin, Tipsy Taco, Viva Chicken, Volcano Korean BBQ, Wingstop, Drury Inn, Hampton Inn, Hilton Garden, Homewood Suites, Residence Inn, Staybridge Suites, Tru Hilton, auto repair, Barnes&Noble, Best Buy, Dick's, Frankies Fun Park, Hamrick's Outlet, Lowe's, Marshall's, PetSmart, REI, Ross, Verizon, vet, Whole Foods Mkt, World Mkt

34 Butler Rd, Mauldin, E QT/dsl, Spinx/dsl, Arby's, W Circle K/dsl, Bojangles, Dino's Rest., Moretti's Pizzeria, Sub Sta. 2, Waffle House, Courtyard, $General

33 Bridges Rd, Mauldin

31 I-185 toll, SC 417, to Laurens Rd, E Sunoco , Chik-fil-A, Hardee's, Jersey Mike's, McDonald's, Papa John's, Sheriff Burger, Starbucks, Subway, The Station, auto repair, Food Lion, Walmart/gas, W Spinx/dsl, $General

30 I-185 toll, US 276, Standing Springs Rd, W Spinx/dsl

29 Georgia Rd, to Simpsonville, W Stop-A-Minit/dsl, Waffle House, Woodspring Suites, CVS, Food Lion

27 Fairview Rd, to Simpsonville, E Sav Way, Carolina Rest., CoachHouse Rest., Domino's, Little Caesar's, McDonald's, Milano Pizzeria, Subway, Palmetto Inn, $General, Advance Parts, AutoZone, Big Lots, CVS Drug, H, O'Reilly Parts, W Murphy USA, Spinx, Spinx/EVC/dsl, Anthony's Pizza, Applebee's, Arby's, AZ Steaks, Baskin-Robbins, Bellacino's, Bruster's, Burger King, Chick-fil-A, Chili's, Cracker Barrel, El Tejano Mexican, Epic Buffet, Firehouse Subs, Five Guys, Hibachi House, Honey Baked Ham, Hungry Howie's, IHOP, Jack-in-the-Box, Jersey Mike's, KFC, La Fogata Mexican, McDonald's, Mei Mei House, Moe's SW Grill, O'Charley's, Outback, Panera Bread, Panera Bread, Pizza Hut, Sonic, Starbucks, Subway, Taco Bell, Tequila's Mexican, Waffle House, Wendy's, Zaxby's, Days Inn, Fairfield Inn, Hampton Inn, Holiday Inn Express, Motel 6, Quality Inn, $Tree, ALDI, AT&T, Belk, CVS Drug, Food Lion, GNC, Goodyear/auto, Home Depot, Ingles Foods, Kohl's, Lowe's, Michaels, NTB, Petco, PetSmart, Publix, Ross, Target, TJ Maxx, URGENT CARE, USPO, Verizon, Verizon, Walgreens, Walmart

26 Harrison Bridge Rd, E U-Haul, W same as 27, 7-11/dsl, QT/dsl, Bojangles, Culver's, Comfort Suites

24 Fairview St, E Marathon, Frank's Pizza, Georgia Street Cafe, Hardee's, Waffle House, auto repair, auto repair

23 SC 418, to Fountain Inn, Fork Shoals, E Exxon/pizza/subs/dsl, Bojangles, McDonald's, Starbucks, Zaxby's, $General, $Tree, O'Reilly Parts, USPO, W 7-11, Sunoco/dsl

ENOREE

22 SC 14 W, Old Laurens Rd, to Fountain Inn

19 SC 14 E, to Gray Court, Owings

16 SC 101, to Woodruff, Gray Court

10 rd 23, Barksdale, Ora

9 US 221, to Laurens, Enoree, E 7-11/dsl, Waffle House, Budget Inn, W Walmart Dist Ctr

6mm **full facilities, litter barrels, petwalk, both lanes(both lanes exit left), vending**

5 SC 49, to Laurens, Union

2 SC 308, to Clinton, Ora, W H, to Presbyterian Coll in Clinton

0mm I-26 S to Columbia, I-385 begins/ends on I-26 at 52mm.

INTERSTATE 526 (Charleston)

33mm I-526 begins/ends.

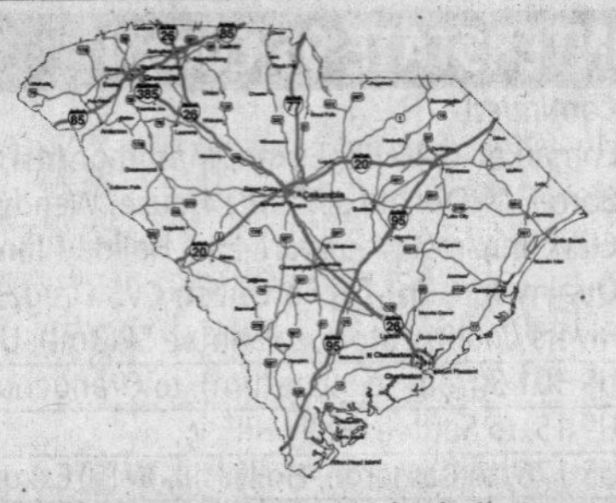

DANIEL ISLAND

32 US 17, N 7-11/Dunkin/dsl, Shell, Sunoco/dsl, Tesla EVC, Bojangles, Burton's Grill, Cane's, Chipotle, CookOut, Crumbl Cookies, Domino's, First Watch, Five Guys, Grimaldi's Brick Oven, IHOP, Jeni's Ice Cream, Jersey Mike's, LongHorn, Marble Slab, PF Chang's, Sonic, Starbucks, Subway, Taco Bell, TGIFriday, Courtyard, Hampton Inn, Home2 Suites, Residence Inn, Advance Parts, AT&T , auto repair, Barnes&Noble, Belk, Chevrolet, CVS Drug, GNC, Lowes Whse, Marshall's, Michaels, Midas, O'Reilly Parts, Old Navy, Petco, REI, TJ Maxx, TrueValue, Verizon, Walgreens, Walmart Supercenter, S Exxon/Cinnabon/dsl, Shell, Shell/Circle K, Arby's, Chick-fil-A, Firehouse Subs, Grace & Grit, McDonald's, Melvin's Ribs& Cue, Moe's SW Grill, Orlando Pizza, Outback Steaks, Wendy's, Best Western, Candlewood Suites, Clarion, Double Tree, Extended Stay America, Hampton Inn, Hilton Garden, Holiday Inn Express, Quality Inn, Quality Inn, Red Roof Inn, Sleep Inn, SpringHill Suites, Staybridge Suites, TownePlace, ALDI, CVS Drug, Dick's, Firestone/auto, Harris Teeter, Jiffy Lube, Publix, Staples, Trader Joe's, USPO, Verizon, vet, VW, Walmart, Whole Foods Mkt

28 Long Point Rd, N Exxon, Shell, Another Broken Egg, Bamboo Garden, Chick-fil-A, McAlister's, Moe's SW Grill, Starbucks, Subway, Waffle House, Wendy's, Charles Pinckney NHS, CVS Drug, Harris Teeter Foods, PetSmart

26mm Wando River

24 Daniel Island, S Exxon, Domino's, Starbucks, Subway, Wasabi, Hampton Inn, Publix

23b a Clements Ferry Rd

21mm Cooper River

20 Virginia Ave(from eb)

19 N Rhett Ave, N Circle K/dsl, Exxon, Pilot/Arby's/dsl/scales/24hr, Bojangles, Waffle House, Family$, Food Lion, URGENT CARE, S Kwikstop

18b a US 52, US 78, Rivers Ave, N Circle K/dsl, auto repair, Family$, H&L Foods, S 76/dsl, Extended Stay

17b a I-26, E to Charleston, W to Columbia

16 Montague Ave, Airport Rd, S Bonefish Grill, Chili's, Jersey Mike's, La Hacienda, Panera Bread, Starbucks, Wendy's, Double Tree, Embassy Suites, Hilton Garden, Homewood Suites, Residence Inn, Sam's Club/gas, Staples, Tanger Outlet/famous brands, Walmart/Subway

15 SC 642, Dorchester Rd, Paramount Dr, N Circle K, $General, auto service, Family$, O'Reilly Parts, S Citgo/dsl, Sunoco, Burger King, Checker's, China Chef, East Bay Deli, Little Caesar's, Subway, Suburban Studios, Advance Parts, CVS Drug, Family$, Food Lion, Harley-Davidson, U-Haul

14 Leeds Ave, S Woodspring Suites, boat marina

13mm Ashley River

11b a SC 61, Ashley River Rd , N Chick-fil-A, McDonald's, O'Charley's, Food Lion, Home Depot, H, Lowes Whse, Marshall's

10 US 17, SC 7, E Circle K, EVC, Sunoco/dsl, Tesla EVC, Bessinger's BBQ, Capt D's, Chick-fil-A, CookOut, Dunkin', Krispy Kreme, La Fontana Italian, McDonald's, Panera Bread,

INTERSTATE 526 (Charleston) Cont'd

10 Continued

Ruby Tuesday, Taco Bell, Best Western, Evergreen Motel, Holiday Inn Express, Home2 Suites, Sleep Inn, Town & Country, Towne Place, West Ashley Inn, AutoZone, Belk, Best Buy, BMW/Mini, Buick/GMC/Cadillac, Chevrolet, Chrysler/Dodge/Jeep, Dick's, Ford/Lincoln, Honda, Honda, Infiniti, Jaguar/Range Rover/Porsche, Maserati, Mercedes,

10 Continued

NAPA, Nissan, Pepboys, PetSmart, Piggly Wiggly, Ross, Smart, Target, Tire Kingdom, Verizon, vet, **W** Circle K, Mobil/dsl, China Fun, Hachiya Japanese, Hardees, Subway, Taco Kitchen, Waffle House, Clarion Pointe, Comfort Suites, Hampton Inn, InTown Suites, Quality Inn, Acura, Advance Parts, Audi, Carmax, Costco/gas, CVS Drug, DriveTime, Family$, Food Lion, Kia, Lexus, Toyota

9 I-526 begins/ends on US 17.

NOTES

SC

= gas = food = lodging = other = rest stop

SD

SOUTH DAKOTA

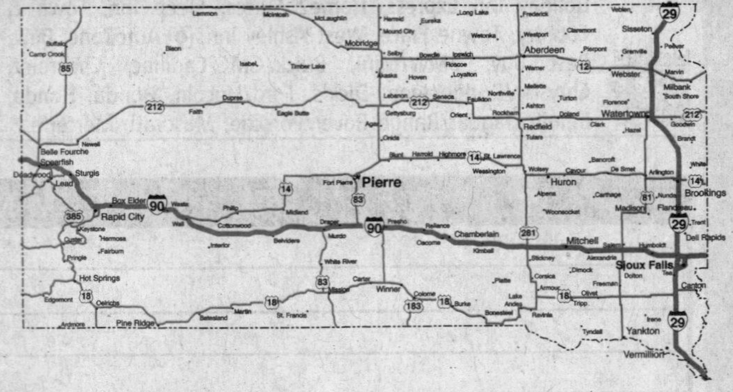

INTERSTATE 29

NEW EFFINGTON

Exit #	Services
253mm	South Dakota/North Dakota state line
251mm	**full facilities, info, litter barrels, petwalk,** RV dump, **Welcome Ctr sb**
246	SD 127, to Rosholt, New Effington, **W** Sica Hollow SP/RV Camping(24mi)
242	110th St
235mm	weigh sta sb
232	SD 10, Sisseton, **E** Dakota Connection/dsl/casino/24hr, **W** ARCO, Cenex, FuelMax/dsl, Marathon/dsl, Sinclair/dsl/e85, DQ, Pizza Hut, Rosalie's Rest., Subway, Taco John's, Holiday Motel, I-29 Motel, Super 8, $General, $General, Camp Dakotah, Family$, Ft Sisseton SP(35mi), H, NAPA, NAPA, Teals Mkt, to Roy Lake SP(25mi)
224	Peever, Sioux Tribal Hqtrs, **E** I-29 Food'n Fill/dsl, **W** Pickerel Lake(16mi)
213	SD 15, to Wilmot, **full facilities, litter barrels, petwalk, both lanes, RV dump, st patrol, E** to Hartford Beach SP(17mi)
207	US 12, Summit, **E** TA Express/Pizza Hut/Subway/dsl/scales/24hr, $General, County Line Camping(1mi), **W** Blue Dog Fish Hatchery(15mi), Waubay NWR(19mi)
201	to Twin Brooks
193	SD 20, to South Shore, Stockholm
185	to Waverly, **W** Dakota Sioux Casino/Cenex/rest.(4mi)
180	US 81 S, to Watertown, **W**, Bramble Park Zoo

WATERTOWN

Exit #	Services
177	US 212, Watertown, **E** Marathon/dsl/24hr, Best Western, fireworks, Kenworth/truck repair, WW Tires, **W** Cenex/dsl, Cenex/dsl(2), Sinclair/dsl, Tesoro/dsl, Applebee's, Arby's, Buffalo Wild Wings, Burger King, China Buffet, Culver's, Domino's, DQ, Firehouse Subs, Godfather's, Guadalajara Mexican, Hardee's, Jimmy John's, Little Caesar's, Marco's Pizza, McDonald's, McDonalds, Papa Murphy's, Perkins, Pizza Hut, Qdoba, Senor Max's Mexican, Starbucks, Taco Bell, Taco John's, Zesto Drive-In, Budget One Motel, Country Inn Suites, Days Inn, Econolodge, Hampton Inn, Quality Inn, $Tree, Advance Parts, AT&T, Chrysler/Dodge/Jeep, Ford/Lincoln, Harley-Davidson, Hobby Lobby, H, Hy-Vee Foods, Menards, NAPA, O'Reilly Parts, Target, Tires+, to Sandy Shore RA(10mi), Verizon, Walgreens, Walmart/Subway
164	SD 22, to Castlewood, Clear Lake, **E** Cenex/dsl(2mi), Best Value Inn(2mi), H(2mi)
161mm	**full facilities, litter barrels, petwalk, both lanes, vending**
157	to Brandt
150	SD 28, SD 15 N, to Toronto, **W** Lake Poinsett RA(15mi)
140	SD 30, to White, Bruce, **W** Oakwood Lakes SP(12mi)

BROOKINGS

Exit #	Services
133	US 14 byp, Brookings, **E** WW Tires, **W** Laura Ingalls Wilder Home(43 mi), museums, to SD St U
132	US 14, Lp 29, Brookings, **E** Cenex/dsl, Applebee's, Whiskey Creek Grill, Country Inn & Suites, Hampton Inn, Holiday Inn Express, My Place Hotel, Super 8, auto repair, Larson RV Park, **W** BP/Taco Express, Arby's, Backyard BBQ, Buffalo Wild Wings, Burger King, Culver's, DQ, Firehouse Subs, Guadalajara Mexican, Hardee's, Jimmy John's, KFC, King's Wok, La Cantina Mexican, McDonald's, Papa John's, Papa Murphy's, Perkins, Qdoba Mexican, Starbucks, Subway, Taco Bell, Brookings Inn, Comfort Suites, Econolodge, Quality Inn, Advance Parts, AT&T, city park, H, Lowe's, O'Reilly Parts, URGENT CARE,

BROOKINGS

Exit #	Services
132	Continued Walmart/Subway
127	SD 324, to Elkton, Sinai
124mm	Big Sioux River
121	to Nunda, Ward, **full facilities, litter barrels, petwalk, both lanes, RV dump, st patrol, vending**
114	SD 32, to Flandreau
109	SD 34, to Madison, Colman, **W** Shell/Crossroads Rest./dsl, Sinclair/Prairie Jct/dsl, Dakota St U, museum, to Lake Herman SP
104	to Trent, Chester
103mm	parking area both lanes
98	SD 115 S, Dell Rapids, **E** Cenex(3mi), Shell(3mi), DQ(3mi), Pizza Ranch(3mi), Bilmar Inn(3mi), Chevrolet, dsl service, H(3mi), vet
94	SD 114, to Baltic, **E** Cenex/dsl, to EROS Data Ctr(10mi), US Geological Survey(10mi)
86	to Renner, Crooks
84b a	I-90, W to Rapid City, E to Albert Lea

SIOUX FALLS

Exit #	Services
83	SD 38 W, 60th St, **E** Flying J/Denny's/dsl/LP/scales/24hr/@, Burger King, Quality Suites, Harley-Davidson/EVC, Indian Motorcycles, Truckwash, **W** BP, fireworks, hwy patrol, Walmart/Subway
82	Benson Rd, **E** Blue Rock Grill, Fairfield Inn, F&F/gas, **W** Subway
81	SD 38 E, Russell St, Sioux Falls, **E** BP, BP/Quiznos, Americinn, Baymont Inn, Best Western+, Motel 6, Ramada Inn, Sheraton, Sioux Falls Inn, Sleep Inn, golf, Schaap's RV Ctr, Schaap's RV Ctr, U-Haul
80	Madison St, **E** Sinclair/dsl, to fairgrounds
79	SD 42, 12th St, **E** BP, Freedom, Burger King, Burger Time, Fry'n Pan, Golden Harvest Chinese, Jacky's Burrito, KFC, McDonald's, Subway, Taco Bell, Taco John's, The Keg Chicken, Wendy's, Ramada, Woodspring Suites, $General, Ace Hardware, BMW/Cadillac/Mercedes, Chevrolet, city park, H, Lewis Drug, Nissan, to Great Plains Zoo/museum, Toyota/Scion, USPO, Walgreens, **W** BP/dsl, Cenex/Chester's/dsl, Hardee's, Tower RV Park
78	26th St, Empire St, **E** BP/dsl/e85, Buffalo Wild Wings, Carino's Italian, Carnaval Brazillian Grill, Chevy's Mexican, ChuckeCheese, Coldstone, Cracker Barrel, Culver's, Domino's, Granite City Rest, Outback Steaks, Puerto Vallarta, Ruby Tuesday, Sickies Burgers, Slim Chickens, Sonic, ClubHouse Suites, Hampton Inn, Holiday Inn Express, StayBridge Suites, ALDI, Home Depot, Michael's, PetSmart, Sam's Club/gas, USPO, World Mkt, **W** DQ, Papa John's, Starbucks, Hyatt Place, TownePlace Suites, Hy-Vee Foods/gas, Lowe's, Verizon
77	41st St, Sioux Falls, **E** BP, SA/dsl, All Day Cafe,

INTERSTATE 29 Cont'd

SIOUX FALLS

77 Continued
Applebee's, Arby's, Burger King, Chick-fil-A, Chili's, Chipotle, Culver's, Fazoli's, Firehouse Subs, Fry'n Pan Rest., Fuddrucker's, HuHot Mongolian, KFC, McDonald's, Olive Garden, Oppa Korean, Pancake House, Panda Express, Papa Murphy's, PepperJax Grill, Perkins, Pizza Hut, Pizza Ranch, Pizzashop, Potbelly, Qdoba Mexican, Red Lobster, ROAM Kitchen, Starbucks, Subway, Szechwan Chinese, Taco Bell, TX Roadhouse, Best Western, Candlewood Suites, Comfort Suites, Courtyard, Fairfield Inn, Microtel, MyPlace Hotel, Quality Inn, Red Rock Inn, Residence Inn, SpringHill Suites, Super 8, Advance Parts, Barnes&Noble, Best Buy, Dick's, Ford/Lincoln, Goodyear/auto, Hy-Vee Foods/dsl, Hyundai, JC Penney, Kohl's, Macy's, Mazda, Meineke, Menards, Old Navy, PetCo, Target, Tires+, TJ Maxx, Verizon, Walgreens, Walmart/Subway/gas, **W** Citgo/dsl, Burger King, Dave&Busters, Freddy's Burgers, Gateway Grill, Godfather's, Guadalajara Mexican, IHOP, Little Caesar's, Perkins, AmericInn, Baymont Inn, Days Inn, La Quinta, B&G Milkyway, USPO

75 I-229 E, to I-90 E

73 Tea, **E** Sinclair/dsl, Marlin's Rest, **W** Casey's/dsl, Red Barn Camping

71 to Harrisburg, Lennox, **E** repair

68 to Lennox, Parker

64 SD 44, Worthing, **W** Buick/Chevrolet

62 US 18 E, to Canton, **E** Cenex/pizza/dsl, Countryside RV park/motel

BERESFORD

59 US 18 W, to Davis, Hurley

56 to Fairview, **E** to Newton Hills SP(12mi)

53 to Viborg

50 to Centerville, Hudson

47 SD 46, to Irene, Beresford, **E** BP/Burger King, Casey's/dsl, Sinclair/dsl, Bertz, Subway, Crossroads Motel, $General, CarQuest, Chevrolet, Family$, Fiesta Foods, Jet Auto Repair, Lewis Drug, **W** Truck Towne/dsl/scales/24hr

42 to Alcester, Wakonda

41mm truck check(from sb)

38 to Volin, **E** to Union Co SP(3mi)

31 SD 48, to Akron, Spink

26 SD 50, to Vermillion, **Welcome Ctr/ both lanes**, **E full facilities, info, litter barrels, petwalk**, **W** Casey's/dsl(6mi), TA Express/dsl/scales, Burger King(6mi), DQ(6mi), McDonald's(6mi), Taco John's(6mi), Best Western(6mi), Holiday Inn Express(6mi), Red Roof Inn(6mi), National Music Museum(6mi), to U of SD(6mi)

JEFFERSON

18 Lp 29, to Burbank, Elk Point, **E** Casey's, Sinclair/dsl, HomeTowne Inn

15 to Elk Point, **E** Kum&Go/dsl, **W** fireworks

13mm weigh sta nb, parking area sb

9 SD 105, Jefferson, **E** Conoco

4 North Shore Dr, McCook, **W** Adams Homestead/nature preserve, KOA(seasonal)

2 SD 105, N Sioux City, **E** Casey's, Goode/casino/dsl/E10/20/30, McDonald's, Subway, Taco John's, $General, auto repair, fireworks, USPO, **W** Casey's, Clark, Days Inn, Hampton Inn, Red Carpet Inn, Super 8, KOA

1 Dakota Dunes Blvd, **E** Holiday Inn Express, **W** Cenex/dsl, Graham's Grill, Country Inn&Suites, Dakota Dunes Golf Resort

0mm South Dakota/Iowa state line, Big Sioux River

INTERSTATE 90

412.5mm South Dakota/Minnesota state line

412mm **full facilities, info, litter barrels, petwalk,**

412mm Continued
RV dump(wb), weigh sta(wb), Welcome Ctr wb/ eb

HARTFORD

410 Valley Springs, **N** Palisades SP(7mi), **S** Beaver Creek Nature Area

406 SD 11, Brandon, Corson, **N** Palisades SP(10mi), **S** BP, BP/dsl, Holiday/McDonald's/dsl, Brandon Steaks, El Tapatio Mexican, Papa Murphy's, Pizza Hut, Pizza Ranch, Subway, Taco John's, Tailgator's Grill, Holiday Inn Express, Quality Inn, Ace Hardware, Lewis Drug, Sturdevant's Parts, Sunshine Foods, to Big Sioux RA(4mi), Verizon

402 EROS Data Ctr, **N** Jellystone RV Park

400 I-229 S

399 SD 115, Cliff Ave, Sioux Falls, **N** Camping World, KOA, **S** BP/Get'n Go/dsl, Holiday/dsl/e85, Love's/Subway/dsl/scales/24hr/@, Sinclair/dsl, Arby's, Burger King, McDonald's/truck parking, Cloud 9 Motel, Days Inn, EconoLodge, Super 8, Graham Tire, H, Kenworth, Peterbilt

398mm Big Sioux River

396b a I-29, N to Brookings, S to Sioux City

395 Marion Rd, Marion, **S** Walmart/Subway/gas

390 SD 38, Hartford, **N** Pizza Ranch(3mi), Goos RV Ctr, **S** Buffalo Ridge Co Store/ghost town

387 rd 17, Hartford, **N** BP/dsl, $General(1.5mi), Hartford Steaks(1.5mi), Pizza Ranch(1.6mi), Subway(1.5mi), AmericInn, Ace Hardware

379 SD 19, Humboldt, **N** Sinclair/dsl, Big J's BBQ, USPO

375mm E Vermillion River

CANOVA

374 to SD 38, Montrose, **S** Battle Creek Res., Lake Vermillion RA

368 to Canisota, Canistota

364 US 81, to Salem, Salem, **N** Cenex(5mi), Home Motel(5mi), Dakota Sunset RV Camping(2.5mi)

363.5mm W Vermillion River

363mm **full facilities, litter barrels, petwalk, both lanes, RV dump, st patrol, vending**

357 to Bridgewater, Canova

353 Spencer, Emery

352mm Wolf Creek

350 SD 25, Emery, Farmer, **N** to DeSmet, Home of Laura Ingalls Wilder

344 SD 262, to Fulton, Alexandria, **S** Sinclair/dsl

337mm parking area both lanes

335 Riverside Rd, **N** KOA(1mi)

334.5mm James River

MITCHELL

332 SD 37 S, to Parkston, Mitchell, **N** Cenex/dsl, Clark, I-90/Holiday/Marlin's Rest./Subway/dsl/scales/24hr, Sinclair/Jimmy John's, Arby's, Cattleman's Club Steaks, Corona Village Mexican, McDonald's, Perkins, Pizza Hut, Pizza Ranch, Starbucks, Twin Dragon Chinese, AmericInn, Corn Palace Inn, Days Inn, Quality Inn, Super 8/truck parking, Thunderbird Motel, Advance Parts, AutoZone, Chrysler/Dodge/Jeep, Dakota Discovery Museum, H, O'Reilly Parts, Rondee's Campground, to Corn Palace, transmissions, Verizon, Walgreens, **S** Blarney's Grill, Culver's, Hardee's, Ruby Tuesday, Shell/Godfather's/Taco Bell/dsl/24hr, Whiskey Creek Grill, Comfort Inn, Hampton Inn, Holiday Inn Express, Kelly Inn, $Tree, AT&T, Cabela's, Menards, Verizon, Walmart/Subway

330 SD 37 N, Mitchell, **N** Cenex/Chester's/dsl, Sinclair/dsl, Tesla EVC, DQ, Budget Inn, Motel 6, Siesta Motel, Travelodge, County Fair Foods, H, Jack's Campers/RV Ctr, Lewis Drug, Mr. Tire, museum, to Corn Palace, weigh sta, **S** Dakota RV Park

325 Betts Rd, **S** Betts Campground

319 Mt Vernon, **N** Sinclair/dsl, Westey's One Stop/dsl

310 US 281, to Stickney, **S** Cenex/Pizza/dsl/24hr,

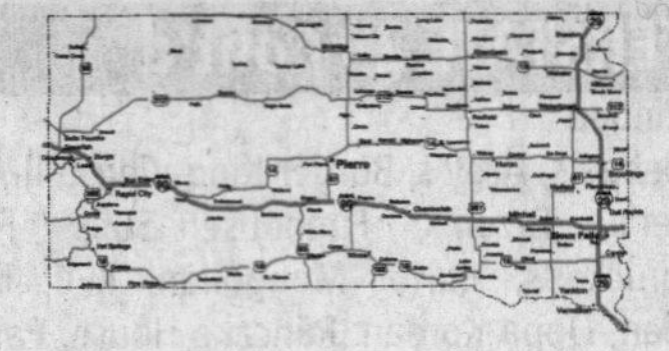

INTERSTATE 90 Cont'd

CHAMBERLAIN

310 Continued to Ft Randall Dam

308 Lp 90, to Plankinton, N Sinclair/dsl, Rodeway Inn, Hills RV Park, USPO

301.5mm full facilities, litter barrels, both lanes, RV dump

296 White Lake, N Hillman's/dsl, Jake's, Pour House Grill, A-Z Motel, USPO, S Siding 36 Motel/RV Park

294mm brake check area

289 SD 45 S, to Platte, S to Snake Cr/Platte Cr RA(25mi)

284 SD 45 N, Kimball, N Clark, Conoco/Ditty's/Diner/dsl, Frosty King, Dakota Winds Motel, Westwood Inn, Parkway Campground, repair/tires, S Love's/dsl/24hr/scales, tractor museum

272 SD 50, Pukwana, S Snake/Platte Creek Rec Areas(25mi)

265 SD 50, Chamberlain, N Cenex/DQ/dsl, AmericInn, Ace Hardware, H, St Joseph Akta Lakota Museum(4mi), S Speedway/dsl, Happy Camper Campground

264mm full facilities, info, litter barrels, both lanes, scenic view

263 Chamberlain, N Casey's, Sinclair/dsl, Charly's Rest.(1mi), McDonald's(1mi), Mi Pueblo Mexican, Subway(1mi), Taco John's, A Bridge View Inn(1mi), Bel Aire Motel(1mi), Best Western(1mi), Super 8, Crow Creek Sioux Tribal Hqtrs, SD Hall of Fame

262mm Missouri River

260 SD 50, Oacoma, N Phillips 66/Arby's/dsl, Shell/dsl, Sinclair/dsl, Tesla EVC, Al's Oasis/Saloon/cafe/mkt, Baymont Inn, Cedar Shore Motel/Camping(3mi), Econolodge, Howard Johnson, Quality Inn, Buick/Chevrolet, Camp Pleasant, Oasis Camping, S USPO

251 SD 47, to Winner, Gregory

248 SD 47, Reliance, N Cenex(1mi), Family$, Sioux Tribal Hqtrs, to Big Bend RA

PRESHO

241 to Lyman

235 SD 273, Kennebec, N Clark/dsl, The 605 Grill, Gerrys, Kings Inn, auto repair, KOA, USPO

226 US 183 S, Presho, N Cenex/dsl, Sinclair/dsl, Hutch's Motel/café, New Frontier RV Park, vet

225 lp 90, Presho, same as 226

221mm full facilities, info, litter barrels, petwalk, wb, RV dump

220 no services

218mm full facilities, info, litter barrels, petwalk, eb, RV dump

214 Vivian

212 US 83 N, SD 53, to Pierre, N Sinclair/dsl, H(34mi)

208 no services

201 Draper

194mm parking area both lanes

MURDO

192 US 83 S, Murdo, N Cenex/dsl, Pilot/Subway/dsl/Lp/scales/24hr, Buffalo Rest., Circle E Drive-In, Covered Wagon Cafe, Prairie Pizza, Rusty Spur Steaks, Star Rest., American Inn, Best Western, Dakota Lodge, Iversen Inn, Range Country Lodge/Tesla EVC, Sioux Motel, Super 8, auto museum, city park, Ford, Murdo Foods, USPO, vet, S Country Inn, to Rosebud

191 Murdo, N same as 192

188mm parking area both lanes

183 Okaton, S ghost town

177 no services

175mm central/mountain timezone

172 to Cedar Butte

170 SD 63 N, to Midland, N 1880's Town, KOA

167mm full facilities, litter barrels, petwalk, wb, RV dump

KADOKA

165mm full facilities, litter barrels, petwalk, eb, RV dump

163 SD 63, Belvidere, S Belvidere Store/dsl, JR's Grill

152 Lp 90, Kadoka, N Yesway/rest./dsl/parking/24hr

150 SD 73 S, Kadoka, N Lakota Lodge/rest., S Conoco/dsl, Sinclair/pizza/dsl, Subway, Sunset Grill, Best Value Inn, Budget Host, El Centro Motel/rest., Ponderosa Motel/RV Park, Wagon Wheel Motel, West Motel, $General, Kadoka Kampground, repair, to Buffalo Nat Grasslands

143 SD 73 N, to Philip, N H(20mi)

138mm scenic overlook wb

131 SD 240, N Minuteman Missle NHS, S Conoco, Badlands Inn(9mi), Cedar Pass Lodge/rest.(9mi), KOA(11mi), Prairie Home NHS, to Badlands NP

129.5mm scenic overlook eb

127 no services

WALL

121 Bigfoot Rd

116 239th St

112 US 14 E, to Philip

110 SD 240, Wall, N Conoco/dsl/EVC, Exxon, Phillips 66/Subway, Tesla EVC, 3 Amigos Cantina, Badlands Grille, DQ, Red Rock Steaks, Ann's Motel, Best Value Inn, Best Western, Days Inn, EconoLodge, Sunshine Inn, Super 8, Travelodge, Welsh Motel, Ace Hardware, Arrow Campground, Badlands Parts, Harley Davidson, National Grasslands Visitor Ctr, Sleepy Hollow RV Park/Camping, Wall Drug/cafe, Wall Foods, S Frontier Cabins Motel, to Badlands NP

109 W 4th Ave, Wall, N access to same as 110

107 Cedar Butte Rd

101 Jensen Rd, to Schell Ranch

NEW UNDERWOOD

100mm full facilities, info, litter barrels, petwalk, both lanes, RV dump, vending

99.5mm Cheyenne River

98 Wasta, Wasta, N 24 Express/dsl, Redwood Motel, USPO

90 173rd Ave, to Owanka

88 171st Ave(from eb, no re-entry)

84 167th Ave

78 161st Ave, New Underwood, S BJs/dsl/motel/rest., Harry's Hideaway Rest,, BJ's Motel, Boondocks Camping

69mm parking area both lanes

67 to Box Elder, N Love's/Hardee's/dog park/dsl/scales/24hr/@, Domino's, Ellsworth AFB, SD Air&Space Museum, USPO

63 (eb only) to Box Elder, Ellsworth AFB, S Sinclair/dsl

61 Elk Vale Rd, N Exxon/dsl, Flying J/Conoco/CountryMkt/dsl/e-85/LP/RV dump/scales/24hr/@, Sickies Burgers, Cambrian Suites, MainStay Suites, My Place, Black Hills Visitor Ctr, Cabela's, Dakota RV Ctr, S Conoco/dsl, Sinclair/dsl/e85, Arby's, Dakotah Steakhouse, Marco's Pizza, McDonald's, Perkins, Subway, Taco Bell, Baymont Inn, Best Western+, Comfort Suites, Courtyard Inn, Fairfield Inn, Home2 Suites, La Quinta, Residence Inn, Sleep Inn, Freightliner, KOA(2mi seasonal)

60 Lp 90, to Mt Rushmore, Rapid City, N Buick/GMC, Chevrolet, Ford/Lincoln, Great Western Tire, Honda,

 = gas = food = lodging = other = rest stop

INTERSTATE 90 Cont'd

RAPID CITY

60 Continued
Kenworth/Volvo, Nissan, Toyota, S Holiday/dsl, Blaze Pizza, Burger King, Cambell Street Cafe, Culver's, Five Guys, Fuji Japanese Steaks, Golden Fortune Chinese, Gyro Hub, Hardee's, HuHot Mongolian, Longhorn Steaks, MacKenzie River, Noodles&Co, Old Chicago, On the Border, Panera Bread, Pizza Ranch, Popeyes, Qdoba Mexican, Sonic, Starbucks, Storming Crab, Tropical Smoothies, Staybridge Suites, $Tree, Aamco, AT&T, dsl repair, Gordman's, H, Menards, Michael's, Nat Coll of Mines/Geology, PetCo, Ross, Sam's Club/dsl, Scheel's Sports, Target/Starbucks, TJ Maxx, Verizon

59 La Crosse St, Rapid City, N Phillips 66, Burger King, Denny's, Los Dos Mexican, Maple Street BBQ, Minerva's Rest., Outback Steaks, Puerto Vallarta Mexican, TX Roadhouse, Best Western, Country Inn&Suites, EconoLodge, Hilton Garden, Holiday Inn Express, Serena Inn, Hobby Lobby, mall/Tesla EVC, st patrol, S Exxon/24hr, Sinclair, Golden Corral, Little Caesar's, MillStone Rest., Mongolian Grill, Pacific Rim Cafe, Perkins, Subway, AmericInn, Clarion, Days Inn, Fair Value Inn, Foothills Inn, Grand Gateway Hotel, Hampton Inn, Microtel, Motel 6, Quality Inn, Rodeway Inn, Tru, URGENT CARE, AT&T, Walgreens, Walmart/McDonald's

58 Haines Ave, Rapid City, N Yesway/dsl, Applebee's, Boba Cafe, Chili's, Hardee's, IHOP, Maple Street BBQ, Olive Garden, Red Lobster, Grand Stay Motel, Super 8, BAM!, Best Buy, JC Penney, Kohl's, Lowe's, PetSmart, Tires+, to Rushmore Mall, S Loaf'n Jug, Maverik/dsl, Papa John's, Pizza Hut, Sweet Treats FroYo, Taco John's, Wendy's, Family$, H, URGENT CARE

57 I-190, US 16, to Rapid City, Mt Rushmore, S Exxon, Ichiban Japanese, Murphy's Grill, Panchero's Mexican, Holiday Inn, Howard Johnson, The Rushmore Hotel, Knecht Home Ctr, Office Depot, Verizon

BLACK HAWK

55 Deadwood Ave, N Dakota RV Ctr, Harley-Davidson/cafe, S Pilot/Subway/dsl/scales/24hr/@, Country Market 2, dsl repair

52 Peaceful Pines Rd, Black Hawk, N JR's BBQ, Lazy JD RV Park, Three Flags Camping(1mi), S BJ's/Godfather's Pizza/dsl, USPO

48 Stagebarn Canyon Rd, S Conoco/Haggar's Mkt/food, PitStop/dsl, Pizza Hut, Summerset, $General, Camping World RV Ctr, O'Reilly Parts

46 Piedmont Rd, Elk Creek Rd, N Elk Creek Steakhouse, Elk Creek RV Park, Teachout's Back 40 Tent Camping (1mi), to Petrified Forest, S Mobil/Papa John's/mart/dsl, Sacora Sta Camping

44 Bethlehem Rd

42mm parking area both lanes, S tent camping

40 Tilford

39mm weigh sta eb

37 Pleasant Valley Rd, N Kickstands Camping, S Bulldog Camping, Rush-No-More Camping

34 S Black Hills Nat Cemetary, No Name City RV Park

STURGIS

32 SD 79, Jct Ave, Sturgis, N Conoco/dsl, Exxon/dsl, Red's Grill, Taco John's, Sturgis Lodge, Ford, Grocery Mart, H, tire repair, to Bear Butte SP, vet, S Mobil/Arby's/Papa John's/dsl, Ford

30 US 14A W, SD 34E, to Deadwood, Sturgis, N Cenex/dsl, Yesway/dsl, McDonald's, Pizza Hut, Sturgis Coffee Co, $General, CarQuest, Day's End Camping, Indian Motorcycles, O'Reilly Parts, Speedy Lube, tires, U-Haul, USPO, S Conoco/dsl, Burger King, DQ, Pizza Ranch, Subway, Baymont Inn, Days Inn, Super 8, BMW Motorcycles,

30 Continued
Chevrolet, Verizon

SPEARFISH

23 SD 34 W, to Belle Fourche, Whitewood, N Northern Hills RV Ctr, Williams & Soutner Tent Camping, S BJs/dsl, Mobil/Sonset Sta/dsl, Hideaway Diner, USPO

17 US 85 S, to Deadwood, S Cenex/dsl, Deadwood NLH(17mi), Elkhorn Ridge RV Resort, KOA(9mi)

14 US 14A, Spearfish Canyon, N Sinclair/dsl, Applebee's, Culver's, Fairfield Inn, Hampton Inn, Holiday Inn/rest., Quality Inn, $Tree, AutoZone, Verizon, Walmart, S Phillips 66/dsl, KFC/LJ Silver, Perkins, Pizza Ranch, Baymont Inn, Super 8, Travelodge, Ford/Lincoln, transmissions

12 Jackson Blvd, Spearfish, S Conoco/dsl, Exxon, Loaf'n Jug, Phillips 66/dsl, Antunez, Arby's, Barbacoa's, Basecamp Kitchen, Burger King, Domino's, Domino's, Dough Trader Pizza, Fujisan Japanese, Jade Palace Chinese, Jimmy John's, Killian's Foods, McDonald's, Millstone Rest., Nonna's Kitchen, Papa Murphy's, Qdoba, Spearfish Steaks, Subway, Taco John's, Uncle Loui's Diner, Best Western, Days Inn, Black Hills St U, CarQuest, Chrysler/Dodge/Jeep, historic fish hatchery, H, Lookout Mtn Trailhead, same as 10, URGENT CARE, Walgreens

10 US 85 N, to Belle Fourche, S Burger King, City Brew, Domino's, Golden Dragon Chinese, Guadalajara, Jimmy John's, McDonald's, Qdoba, Subway, Taco Bell, Days Inn, Buick/Chevrolet, Cadillac/GMC, H, KOA, Safeway/dsl, same as 12, USPO, Walgreens

8 McGuigan Rd, W Spearfish, S Phillips 66/Tesla EVC/dsl, Cowgirl Pizza, KOA(1mi)

2 N McNenny St Fish Hatchery

1mm **full facilities, info, litter barrels, petwalk, RV dump, Welcome Ctr eb**

0mm South Dakota/Wyoming state line

INTERSTATE 229 (Sioux Falls)

10b a I-90 E and W. I-229 begins/ends on I-90, exit 400.

9 Benson Rd, W Casey's, Sinclair/dsl, Jimmy John's, Marlin's Rest., Tarquin Argentinian, Ford Trucks

7.5mm Big Sioux River

7 Rice St, W Casey's, Lam's Vietnamese

6 SD 38, 10th St, E Sinclair, A&W, Applebee's, Arby's, Denny's, Domino's, DQ, Fryn' Pan Rest., Gilbertos Mexican, Jacky's Guatemalan, Jimmy John's, KFC, Pizza Hut, Pizza Ranch, Taco Bell, Tokyo Hibachi, Tomacelli's Italian, Extended Stay, Super 8, AT&T, AutoZone, Discount Tire, Hy-Vee Foods/Starbucks, O'Reilly Parts, Sturdevant's Parts, U-Haul, USPO, Valvoline, vet, W Amoco, BP/dsl, Casey's/dsl, Local, Burger King, BurgerTime, Charbroiled Steaks, Hardee's, Little Caesar's, McDonald's, Pita Pit, Popeyes, Puerto Vallarta, Qdoba Mexican, Slim Chickens, Taco John's, Rushmore Motel, vet

5.5mm Big Sioux River

5 26th St, E Circle K/dsl, Burger King, Cherry Creek Grill, Dareo's Pizza, McDonald's, Saigon Panda, city park, W H

4 Cliff Ave, E city park, W vet

3 SD 115, Lp 229, Minnesota Ave, E city park, W BP/dsl, Sinclair, Arby's, Boss' Pizza, Culver's, DQ, Famous Dave's BBQ, Golden Bowl Chinese, Grill'N Smoke BBQ, Hardee's, Little Caesar's/TCBY, McDonald's, Ramen Fuji, Subway, $Tree, Ace Hardware, Acura, Buick/GMC, Costco/gas, Hy-Vee Foods/dsl, Kia, Staples, tires, USPO, vet

2 Western Ave, E Holiday/dsl, DQ, Flyboy Donuts, Scooters Coffee, Starbucks, W Holiday, Backyard BBQ, Burger King, China Express, Huhot Mongolian, Inca Mexican, Oppa Korean Chicken, Papa Murphy's, PepperJax Grill, Perkins, Potbelly, Qdoba Mexican, Scheel's,

SD

INTERSTATE 229 (Sioux Falls) Cont'd

2	Continued Advance Parts, AutoZone, Best Buy, Goodyear/auto, Hancock Fabrics, H, Tuesday Morning, Verizon
1.5mm	Big Sioux River
1c	Louise Ave, E Holiday/dsl, Arby's, B&G Milkyway Ice Cream, Culver's, kRav'N Grill, Starbucks, Comfort Suites, Hampton Inn, Holiday Inn Express, Homewood Suites, TownePlace Suites, Chrysler/Dodge/Jeep, Fiat, H, Lewis Drug, W BP, Casey's, $Tree, Burger King, Five Guys, Honey Baked Ham, Jersey Mike's, Jimmy John's, Marco's Pizza, McDonald's, Noodles&Co, Panchero's Mexican,
1c	Continued Panera Bread, Popeyes, Qdoba Mexican, Royal Palace, Taco John's, Hilton Garden Inn, Staybridge Suites, Dick's, Honda, Hy-Vee Foods/USPO/dsl, JC Penney, Kohl's, mall, Target
1b a	I-29 N and S. I-229 begins/ends on I-29, exit 75.

NOTES

TENNESSEE

TN

INTERSTATE 24

Exit #	Services
185b a	I-75, N to Knoxville, S to Atlanta. I-24 begins/ends on I-75, exit 2.
184	Moore Rd, S Chef Lin's Buffet, Provino's Italian, $Tree, H, Shell/dsl, URGENT CARE
183	(183a from wb), Belvoir Ave, Germantown Rd
181a	US 41 S, to East Ridge(from eb), S Giardino, Sugar's Ribs
181	Fourth Ave, to TN Temple U, Chattanooga, N Exxon/dsl, Shell/dsl, Texaco/dsl, USA Fuels/dsl, Burger King, Capt D's, Hunan Wok, Krystal, Subway, Waffle House, Chatt Inn, $General, Family$, Food City, Mack/Volvo Trucks, NAPA, O'Reilly Parts, vet
180b a	US 27 S, TN 8, Rossville Blvd, N Best One Tires/service, to UT Chatt, S Mapco/dsl, Mobil/dsl, Family$, to Chickamauga Battlefield
178	US 27 N, Market St, to Lookout Mtn, Chattanooga, N BP/dsl, Citgo, PURE, Good Eats BBQ, District 3 Hotel, Marriott, Staybridge Suites, Chevrolet, Ford/Lincoln, Midas, Nissan, to aquarium, to Chattanooga ChooChoo, U-Haul, S RaceWay/dsl, KFC, Papa John's, Comfort Inn, Motel 6, Red Roof+
175	Browns Ferry Rd, to Lookout Mtn, N BP/Circle K, QT, Spirit/dsl, China Gourmet, La Quinta, Studio 6, CVS Drug, vet, S Mapco/dsl, Hardee's, McDonald's, Comfort Inn, EconoLodge, Howard Johnson, DG Market
174	US 11, US 41, US 64, Lookout Valley, N Days Inn, Racoon Mtn Camping(1mi), st patrol, S BP/dsl, Exxon/Circle K/dsl, Murphy USA/dsl, Cracker Barrel, Jack's Rest., Logan's Roadhouse, Los 3 Amigos, New China, Sonic, Waffle House, Wendy's, Best Western, Clarion, Country Inn&Suites, Fairfield Inn, Hampton Inn, Holiday Inn Express, Knights Inn, Quality Inn, Red Roof Inn, Super 8, $Tree, Ace Hardware, O'Reilly Parts, URGENT CARE, Walmart/Subway
172mm	rest area eb, **full facilities, litter barrels, petwalk, , , vending**
171mm	Tennessee/Georgia state line
169	GA 299, to US 11, N Mapco/dsl, S Citgo, Exxon/dsl/24hr, ONE9/Subway/dsl/scales/24hr, $General
167	I-59 S, to Birmingham
167mm	Central/Eastern time zone, Tennessee/Georgia state line
161	TN 156, to Haletown, New Hope
160mm	Tennessee River/Nickajack Lake
159mm	**full facilities, litter barrels, petwalk, , , vending, Welcome Ctr wb/ eb**
158	US 41, TN 27, Nickajack Dam, Speedway/Speedy's Cafe/24hr, N Love's/McDonald's/Subway/dsl/scales/24hr, S Shellmound Campground(2.5mi)
155	TN 28, Jasper, N Hi-Tech/dsl, Hardee's, Huddle House, Western Sizzlin, Quality Inn, S BP/Subway/dsl, H
152	US 41, US 64, US 72, Kimball, S Pittsburg, N RaceWay/dsl, Shell/dsl, Arby's, China Buffet, Cracker Barrel, Domino's, Dunkin', El Toril, KFC, Krystal, Little Caesar's, McDonald's, Subway, Taco Bell, Waffle House, Wendy's, Best Western, Clarion, Hampton Inn, Holiday Inn Express, $Tree, Buick/Chevrolet/GMC, fireworks, Lowe's, O'Reilly Parts, Walmart, S Lodge Cast Iron, to Russell Cave NM
143	Martin Springs Rd, N Citgo/dsl
135	US 41 N, Monteagle, N Marathon/dsl, Pilot/Dunkin/dsl/scales/24hr, Dixie Lee Diner, High Point Rest., Shan Chinese, Taco Bell, $Tree, USPO, S Red Roof Inn
134	US 64, US 41A, to Sewanee, Monteagle, N BP/McDonald's/dsl, Mountain Goat Mkt, Papa Ron's Pizza, Sonic, Monteagle Inn, Quality Inn, CVS Drug, to S Cumberland SP, S Exxon/Kangaroo, Shell/dsl, Hardee's, Pizza Hut, Smokehouse BBQ, Subway, Waffle House, Mountain Inn, Super 8, The Smokehouse Lodge, $General, Auto/tire repair, Fred's, Piggly Wiggly, to U of The South
133mm	**full facilities, litter barrels, petwalk, , , both lanes, vending**
128mm	Elk River
127	US 64, TN 50, to Winchester, Pelham, N Citgo, Marathon/dsl, S Exxon/dsl, $General, to Tims Ford SP/RV camping
119mm	trucks only parking area both lanes
117	to Tullahoma, N Love's/Hardees/scales/dsl/24hr/@, S Arnold AF Base
116mm	weigh sta both lanes
114	US 41, Manchester, N BP/dsl, Exxon/24 Truckers/scales/dsl, Murphy USA/dsl, Shell/dsl, Chick-fil-A, Great Wall Chinese, Jeffersons Rest., Logan's Roadhouse, O'Charley's, Starbucks, Comfort Suites, Holiday Inn Express, La Quinta, Motel 6, Quality Inn, Scottish Inn, Sleep Inn, Truckers Inn, $Tree, AT&T, Home Depot, KOA, Nissan, tire/truck repair, Toyota, Verizon, Walmart/Subway, S Mobil/Circle K, RaceWay/dsl, Arby's, Baskin-Robbins, Bojangles, Burger King, Capt D's, Dunkin, Hong Kong Buffet, KFC, Krystal, La Rivera, McDonald's/playplace, Papa John's, Subway, Taco Bell, Waffle House, Wendy's, Zaxby's, Days Inn, Microtel, Regency Inn, Royal Inn, Advance Parts, AutoZone, Ford/Lincoln, O'Reilly Parts, Russell Stover, USPO, vet
111	TN 55, Manchester, N Circle K, Co-Op, H, to Rock Island SP, vet, S Marathon/dsl, Hardee's, J&G Pizza/Steaks, Jiffy Burger, Little Caesars, Pizza Hut, Ramsey Grill, Sonic, $General, auto repair, Food Lion, Gateway Auto, Old Stone Fort SP, Save Alot, to Jack Daniels Dist HS, Walgreens
110	TN 53, Manchester, N Exxon, Marathon/dsl, Mobil/Circle K/dsl, Cracker Barrel, Emma's Rest., Las Fajitas Mexican, Oak Rest., Ambassador Inn, Econolodge, Economy Inn, Hampton Inn, H, S Shell/dsl, Los 3 Amigos, Prater's BBQ, Waffle House, repair
110mm	Duck River
105	US 41, N Exxon/dsl, S $General, Dickel HS, tire/repair, to Normandy Dam, Whispering Oaks Camping(1.5mi)
97	TN 64, to Shelbyville, Beechgrove, S Marathon/dsl
89	Buchanan Rd, N Love's/McDonald's/dsl/scales/24hr, Love Thai Sushi, S Shell/dsl, $General, A&L RV Ctr
84	Joe B. Jackson Pkwy, N Exxon, Key Oil , Shell, Burger King, Subway, Waffle House
81	US 231, Murfreesboro, N Exxon, Mapco, Shell, Cracker Barrel, Krystal, Los 3 Potrillos, Mexico Tipico, Parthenon Grille, Waffle House, Wendy's, Best Value Inn, Knights Inn, Quality Inn, Ramada, Regal Inn, Chrysler/Dodge/Jeep, H, Hyundai, S Mapco/dsl, Mobil, Mobil, Pilot/Arby's/scales/dsl/24hr, Bojangles, Burger King, Golden Mongolian Grill, La Siesta Mexican, Little Caesars, McDonald's/playplace, Pizza Hut, Popeyes, Rick's BBQ, Sonic, Starbucks, Subway,

CHATTANOOGA

JASPER

MONTEAGLE

MANCHESTER

MURFREESBORO

INTERSTATE 24 Cont'd

MURFREESBORO

81 Continued
Taco Bell, Waffle House, Zaxby's, Wingate, $General, Advance Parts, AutoZone, Discount Tire, Gateway Auto, Kia, Kroger/dsl, O'Reilly Parts, vet

80 New Salem Hwy, rd 99, **S** RaceTrac, Speedway/Speedy's Cafe/dsl, Domino's, Dunkin, Marco's Pizza, Smoothie King, Sonic, Subway, Costco/gas

78 TN 96, to Franklin, Murfreesboro, **N** Exxon, Marathon/dsl, Murphy USA/dsl, Shell/Jack-in-the-Box, Arby's, Bad Daddys Burger, Baskin-Robbins, Bonefish Grill, Cajun Steamer, Carrabba's, Cheddar's, Chick-fil-A, Chipotle, Chophouse, ChuckECheese, Coconut Bay Cafe, Crab Fever, Cracker Barrel, Egg&I Cafe, Fazoli's, Firehouse Subs, Five Guys, Fresh Bite Cuban, IHOP, Jason's Deli, Jim'n Nick's BBQ, Jimmy John's, KFC, Krispy Kreme, McDonald's, Mi Patria, Miller's Ale House, Moe's SW Grill, Olive Garden, Outback Steaks, Panda Express, Panera Bread, Red Lobster, Red Robin, Sam's Grill, Samurai's Cuisine, Sandwich Factory, Slim Chickens, Starbucks, Steak'n Shake, Waffle House, Wendy's, Whataburger, Zaxby's, Baymont Inn, Best Western, Candlewood Suites, Clarion, Comfort Suites, Days Inn, DoubleTree, EconoLodge, Fairfield Inn, Hampton Inn, Holiday Inn Express, Howard Johnson, InTown Suites, Microtel, Motel 6, Red Roof Inn, Sleep Inn, Super 8, $Tree, ALDI, AT&T, Books-A-Million, Dillard's, Firestone, Hobby Lobby, Home Depot, JC Penney, Jo-Ann Fabrics, Lowe's, NTB, PetSmart, Ross, Sportsman's Whse, Staples, Target, tire/auto repair, TJ Maxx, to Stones River Bfd, Verizon, vet, Walgreens, Walmart, **S** BP, Mobil/Circle K/dsl, RaceTrac, Shell/dsl, Burger King, Capt D's, China Garden, Dos Rancheros, DQ, Hardee's, Jersey Mike's Subs, Little Caesars, McDonald's, O'Charley's, Pizza Hut, Sonic, Starbucks, Subway, Taco Bell, transmission repair, TX Roadhouse, vet, Waffle House, Wasabi Japanese, Wingstop, MainStay Suites, Woodspring Suites, $General, Advance Parts, AutoZone, Express Oil Change, Kohl's, Kroger/dsl, O'Reilly Parts, Old Time Pottery, Sam's Club/gas, Walgreens

FRANKLIN

76 Fortress Blvd, Manson Pike, Medical Center Pkwy, **N** Thornton's/dsl, Bar Louie, BJs Rest., Buffalo Wild Wings, Chicken Salad Chick, Chili's, Culver's, Genghis Grill, Longhorn Steaks, McCalisters Deli, McDonalds, Mimi's Cafe, Newk's Eatery, Starbucks, Subway, Courtyard, Embassy Suites, Hilton Garden/EVC, Holiday Inn/EVC, Residence Inn, Barnes&Noble, Belk, Best Buy, Dick's, H, Michael's, Old Navy, Petco, Tire Discounters, to Stones River Nat. Bfd, World Mkt, **S** Exxon/dsl, Blue Coast Burrito, Sonic, Starbucks, Zaxby's, Starbridge Suites, Chevrolet/Cadillac/GMC/Buick, Honda, Mazda, Toyota/Scion

74b a TN 840, to Lebanon, Franklin

70 TN 102, Lee Victory Pkwy, Almaville Rd, to Smyrna, **N** Speedway/Speedy Cafe/dsl/scales, Bojangles, Burger King, Chagos Mexican, Jets Pizza, Starbucks, Zorba Cafe, Publix, **S** Circle K/dsl, Mapco, Shell/dsl, Arbys, Captain D's, Legends Steaks, McDonald's, Sonic, Taco Bell, Thai Phooket, Deerfield Inn, $General

66 TN 266, Sam Ridley Pkwy, to Smyrna, **N** 7-11, RaceTrac, Shell/dsl, A&W/LJ Silver, Arby's, Asuka Hibachi, Blue Coast Burrito, Buffalo Wild Wings, Burger King, Camino Real, Canes Chicken, Cheddar's, Chick-fil-A, Chicken Salad Chick, Chili's, Chipotle, CiCi's Pizza, DQ, Famous Dave's BBQ, Firehouse Subs, First Watch, Five Guys, Freddy's Steakburgers, Hickory Falls Cafe, IHOP, Jamba Juice, Jersey Mike's Subs, Jim'n Nick's BBQ, La Siesta Mexican, Logan's Roadhouse, Longhorn Steaks, Moes SW Grill, Panda Express, Panera Bread, Penn Sta Subs, Smoothie King, Sonic,

66 Continued
Starbucks, Subway, Toots Chicken, Twisted Tenders, Waffle House, Wendy's, Whataburger, Zaxby's, Courtyard, $General, $Tree, AT&T, BJs Warehouse, CVS Drug, Discount Tire, Firestone/auto, Home Depot/gas, H, Kohl's, Kroger/dsl, Lowe's, Nashville I-24 Camping(3mi), PetSmart, Publix, Ross, Staples, Target, Tire Discounters, URGENT CARE, Verizon, Walgreens, **S** Cracker Barrel, Avid, Candlewood Suites, Comfort Suites, Fairfield Inn, Hampton Inn, Hilton Garden, Holiday Inn Express, Home2 Suites, La Quinta, Sleep Inn, TownePlace Suites, Tru, WoodSpring Suites

64 Waldron Rd, to La Vergne, **N** Exxon/Circle K, Kwik Sak, Pilot/Subway/dsl/scales/24hr, Shell, Arby's, Hardee's, McDonald's, RaceTrac, Waffle House, Econo Lodge, Quality Inn, Ramada Inn, **S** Mapco/dsl, Thorntons/Popeyes/scales/dsl, $General

62 TN 171, Old Hickory Blvd, **N** Exxon/Subway/dsl, Shell, TA/BP/Burger King/Popeyes/dsl/scales/24hr, Thorntons/dsl, Acapulco Burrito, EVC, **S** $General

60 Hickory Hollow Pkwy, **N** Exxon/dsl, Gulf, Mapco, Thorntons/dsl, Burger King, ChuckECheese, Hunt Brothers Pizza, Jimmy John's, Little Caesars, McDonald's, Panda Express, Papa John's, Red Lobster, Slim & Husky's Pizza, Starbucks, Subway, Taco Bell, Waffle House, Wendy's, Zaxby's, Best Western, Comfort Inn&Suites, Hampton Inn/EVC, Holiday Inn Express, Buick/GMC, Chevrolet, Chrysler/Dodge/Jeep, Family$, Firestone/auto, Kroger/gas, mall, URGENT CARE, **S** MAPCO/dsl, Shell/dsl, Casa Fiesta Mexican, Dunkin, IHOP, La Costa Mexican, Olive Garden, Steak'n Shake, Waffle Taco, Antioch Qtrs, Knights Inn, Super 8, Home Depot, Kia, Valvoline Oil Change, vet

59 TN 254, Bell Rd, same as 60

57 Haywood Lane, **N** Kwik Sak/dsl, Hardee's, Pizza Hut, Taco Stand, $General, Family$, Food Lion, O'Reilly Parts, Walgreens, **S** Circle K/dsl, Shell/dsl

56 TN 255, Harding Place, **N** Exxon/7-11/dsl, MAPCO/dsl, Shell/dsl, Chicago Gyros, Dunkin, KFC, McDonald's, Mikado Japanese, Subway, Taco Bell, Waffle House, Wendy's, Executive Inn, Stay Lodge, Woodspring Suites, $Tree, Sam's Club/gas, Toyota, **S** MAPCO/dsl, Philiips 66/dsl, Burger King, Gyro Grill, Hooters, San Jose Fiesta, Travelodge, H

54b a TN 155, Briley Pkwy, **N** Gulf/dsl, **S** Subway, Kroger/dsl/EVC

53 I-440 W, to Memphis

52 US 41, Murfreesboro Rd, **N** Shell, Waffle House, Best Western, Hillside Crossing, Holiday Inn Express, Rodeway Inn, Super 8, Super 8, **S** Mapco/dsl, Speedway/dsl, BP/dsl, NAPA

52b a I-40, E to Knoxville, W to Memphis

51.5mm **I-24 and I-40 run together 2 mi. Exits 212-213.**

50b I-40 W

49 Shelby Ave(from wb only), , **S** Exxon, Comfort Inn, La Quinta, to Nissan Stadium

48 James Robertson Pkwy, **N** Citgo, **S** Exxon, Nashville Kitchen, Comfort Inn, Drift Nashville, La Quinta Inn & Suites, Nissan Stadium, st capitol

47a US 31E

47 N 1st St, Jefferson St, **N** Citgo, **S** Phillip 66/dsl, Clarion, Knights Inn

46mm I-24 and I-65 merge. See I-65, exit 87b a.

44b a I-65, N to Louisville, S to Nashville

43 TN 155, Briley Pkwy, Brick Church Pike

INTERSTATE 24 Cont'd

ASHLAND CITY · FT CAMPBELL · TRENTON

Exit #	Services
40	TN 45, Old Hickory Blvd, N Marathon/dsl, Marathon/Subway/dsl, Shell/dsl, Dunkin, El Rey Azteca, Super 8
35	US 431, to Joelton, Springfield, N H, S BP/Heritage TC/DQ/Subway/dsl, Hightail/dsl, Shell/dsl, Country Junction Rest., Firecracker Pizza, Mazatlan Mexican, McDonald's, Taco Bell, Days Inn, $General, O'Reilly Parts, OK Camping
31	TN 249, New Hope Rd, N Citgo, S Marathon/dsl, Shell/dsl, Jardin Mexican
24	TN 49, to Springfield, Ashland City, N Mapco/dsl, Marathon/Pizza Hut/dsl, Quality Inn, H, S Shell/dsl, SS/Dunkin/Wendy's/dsl, Burger King, Firecrackers Pizza, Hardee's, KFC/Taco Bell, Pedro's Cocina, Sidelines Grill, Sonic, Subway, Hampton Inn, city park, Hill Foods, O'Reilly Parts, USPO, vet
19	TN 256, Maxey Rd, to Adams, N Shell/dsl, S Shell/dsl, $General
11	TN 76, to Adams, Clarksville, N Shell/dsl, S Citgo, Exxon/dsl, Domino's, El Rancho Grande, Freddys Steakburgers, Huddle House, McDonald's, Pancho Villa Grille, Subway, Waffle House, Baymont Inn, Days Inn, Quality Inn, Super 8, $General, H, Publix, vet
9mm	Red River
8	TN 237, Rossview Rd, N Shell, Burger King, Popeyes, Taco Johns, S QT/scales/dsl, Dunbar Cave SP
4	US 79, to Clarksville, Ft Campbell, N Exxon/dsl, Shell/dsl, Cracker Barrel, Best Western+, Hilton Garden, Holiday Inn Express, Sleep Inn, Sam's Club/gas, Spring Creek Camping(2mi), S Marathon/dsl, Murphy USA/dsl, Shell/dsl, Shell/Subway/dsl, Applebee's, Arby's, Baskin-Robbins, Buffalo Wild Wings, Canela Mexican, Capt D's, Cheddar's, Chick-fil-A, Chili's, China King, Chipotle, ChuckeCheese, Cook Out, Crumbl Cookies, Culver's, Fazoli's, Firehouse Subs, Golden Corral, Harbor Cafe, IHOP, Jiffy Lube, KFC, Krispy Kreme, Krystal, Logan's Roadhouse, Longhorn Steaks, McDonald's, Moe's SW Grill, Noodles&Co, O'Charley's, Old Chicago Pizza, Olive Garden, Outback Steaks, Panda Express, Panera Bread, Rafferty's, Red Lobster, Shogun Japanese, Shoney's, Slim Chickens, Smoothie King, Starbucks, Steak'n Shake, Subway, Taco Bell, Tilted Kilt, TX Roadhouse, Waffle House, Wendy's, White Castle, Zaxby's, Baymont Inn, Candlewood Suites, Clarksville Inn, Comfort Suites, Country Inn&Suites, Courtyard, Days Inn, EconoLodge, Fairfield Inn, Gateway Inn, Hampton Inn, Howard Johnson, InTown Suites, La Quinta, Microtel, Quality Inn, Red Roof Inn, Rodeway Inn, Super 8, TownePlace, Travelodge, Woodspring Suites, $Tree, AT&T, Belk, Best Buy, Books-A-Million, Buick/GMC, Dick's, Dillard's, Firestone/auto, Goodyear/auto, Hobby Lobby, Home Depot, H, Hyundai, JC Penney, Kohl's, Kroger/dsl, Lowe's, Mazda, Michaels, Office Depot, Petco, PetSmart, Ross, Subaru, Target, TJ Maxx, to Austin Peay St U, to Land Between the Lakes, Toyota, U-Haul, vet, Walmart/McDonald's
1	TN 48, to Clarksville, Trenton, N Exxon/dsl, Shell/dsl, $General, Clarksville RV Camping, S 7-11, Exxon/dsl, Shell/dsl, Arbys, Bojangles, Burger King, Coldstone, Dunkin, El Bracero Mexican, Little Caesar's, Marco's Pizza, McDonald's, Sonic, Starbucks, Subway, Taco Bell, Zaxby's, $General, AT&T, AutoZone, Walgreens
0.5mm	**full facilities, litter barrels, petwalk, vending, Welcome Ctr eb**
0mm	Tennessee/Kentucky state line

INTERSTATE 26

ELIZABETHTON

Exit #	Services
54.5mm	Tennessee/North Carolina state line
54mm	runaway truck ramp wb
52mm	runaway truck ramp wb, scenic overlook eb (no trucks)
50	Flag Pond Rd
47.5mm	scenic overlook wb (no trucks)
46mm	**Welcome Ctr/ both lanes, N full facilities, litter barrels, petwalk**
44mm	Higgins Creek
43	US 19 W, rd 352, Temple Hill Rd
42mm	S Indian Creek
40	Jackson-Love Hwy, Erwin, Jonesborough, N Shell/dsl, Pancho's & Amigo's, Mtn Inn, H, Nolichucky Gorge Camping(2mi), Red Banks Campground
37	TN 81, rd 107, Erwin, Jonesborough, N Shell, Bojangles, Domino's, Dunkin, McDonald's, Pal's, Taco Bell, Food City/gas, H, USPO, Walgreens, S Super 8, A. Johnson NHS(31mi), River Park Camping(5mi)
36	Main St, Erwin, N BP/dsl, Exxon/dsl/e-85, Clarence's Drive In, Don Manuel Mexican, Hardee's, KFC, Little Caesars, Rocky's Pizza, $General, $Tree, Advance Parts, AutoZone, Food Lion, O'Reilly Parts, tire repair
34	Tinker Rd, N Murphy USA/dsl, Los Jalapenos, Primo's Pizza, Walmart
32	rd 173, Unicoi Rd, to Cherokee NF, N Shell, Whistle Stop Deli, $General, Grandview Ranch Camping(7mi), USPO, S Woodsmoke Campground, Woodsmoke Camping
27	rd 359 N, Okolona Rd, N BP
24	US 321, TN 67, Elizabethton, N Shell/Dunkin Donuts/dsl, $General, Roan Mtn SP, S BP/dsl, Exxon/dsl, Arby's, Burger King, Fox's Pizza, Little Caesar's, LJ Silver, Comfort Inn, Advance Parts, Food City/gas, H, Price Less Foods, to ETSU, Walgreens
23	rd 91, Market St, N DQ, McDonald's, USPO, S museum
22	rd 400, Unaka Ave, Watauga Ave
20b a	US 11 E, US 19 N, to Roan St, N QM/dsl, Shell/dsl, Arby's, Capt. D's, Cootie Brown's Rest., Harbor House Seafood, Hardee's, Little Caesar's, LJ Silver, Mellow Mushroom Pizza, Mona Lisa's Gelato, Moto Japanese, Pizza Hut, Popeyes, Sonic, Waffle House, Baymont, Best Western, Days Inn, Holiday Inn, Staybridge Suites, Super 8, Acura, Advance Parts, AutoZone, BigLots, Honda, Hyundai, O'Reilly Parts, Subaru, UHaul, VW, S Applebees, Babylon Grill, Bojangles, Bonefish Grill, Brusco's Pizza, Crumbl Cookies, Fazoli's, Five Guys, Greg's Pizza, Hibachi Grill, Hooters, Jersey Mike's, KFC, Longhorn Steaks, McAlister's Deli, McDonald's, O'Charley's, Olive Garden, Red Lobster, Shoney's, Smokey Bones BBQ, Starbucks, Subway, TX Roadhouse, Zaxby's, Doubletree, Motel 6, Red Roof Inn, $Tree, Belk, Books-A-Million, Dick's, FreeService Tire/auto, JC Penney, Kroger, mall, Office Depot, Target, TJ Maxx, Verizon, Walgreens
19	TN 381, to St of Franklin Rd, to Bristol, N Murphy USA/dsl, Shell/McDonald's, Golden Corral, Honeybaked Ham, Logan's Roadhouse, Mellow Mushroom, Outback Steaks, Pizza Hut, Subway, Comfort Suites, Walmart, S Amigo Mexican, Barberito's Grille, Buffalo Wild Wings, Carrabba's, Cheddar's, Chick-fil-A, Chili's, ChuckECheese's, East Coast Wings, IHOP, Mad Greek, Ming's Asian, Panera Bread, Wendy's, Courtyard, Fairfield Inn, Hampton Inn, Sleep Inn, AT&T, Barnes&Noble, Best Buy, Hobby Lobby, Home Depot, H, Kohl's, Lowe's, Michael's, Natural Foods Mkt, Old Navy, PetSmart, Ross, Sam's Club/gas, USPO, Verizon, vet
17	Boone St, N BP, Beef'O Brady's, Bob Evans,

TN

INTERSTATE 26 Cont'd

17 Continued
Giovanni's Italian, Hardee's, McDonald's, Pal's Drive-in, $General, Ingles Foods/dsl, **S** Exxon/e-85, Shell/Subway/dsl, Cracker Barrel, Domino's, Poblano's Mexican, Waffle House, Wendy's, Holiday Inn Express, Quality Inn, Woodspring Suites

13 rd 75, Bobby Hicks Hwy, **N** BP, Shell, Burger King, China Luck, DQ, Dunkin, Hot Dog Corner, KFC, La Carreta, McDonald's, Pal's Drive-Thru, Papa John's, Pizza Hut, Si Senor, Subway, Taco Bell, Yong Asian, $Tree, Advance Parts, Food City/gas, NAPA, O'Reilly Parts, USPO, vet, Walgreens, **S** Exxon/dsl

10 Eastern Star Rd, **N** Phil's Dream Pit BBQ

8b a I-81, to Bristol, Knoxville

6 rd 347, Rock Springs Rd, **S** Rite Quik/dsl

5mm Welcome Ctr/rest area, full(handicapped)facilities both lanes, picnic tables, litter barrels, petwalk

4 TN 93, Wilcox Dr, **N** BP/Subway, Mobil/McDonald's/dsl, Burger King, Hardee's, La Carreta Mexican, Pizza Hut, Wendy's, Comfort Suites, Fairfield Inn, Hampton Inn, Holiday Inn Express, Quality Inn, $General, Cave's Drug, Price Less Foods, **S** Exxon, Mobil/Arby's/dsl/e-85, Pizza+

3 Meadowview Pkwy, **N** MeadowView

1 US 11 W, West Stone Dr, **N** Shell, El Patron Mexican, Little Caesar's, Thai Noodle, Super 8, H, U-Haul, Walgreens, **S** Exxon, Murphy USA/dsl, Bojangles, China Star, Sonic, $Tree, Lowe's, Walmart

0mm I-26 begins/ends on US 23.

INTERSTATE 40

451mm Tennessee/North Carolina state line

451 Waterville Rd

447 Hartford Rd, **N** Citgo/dsl, **S** BP/dsl, Bean Tree Cafe, Pigeon River Smokehouse, Foxfire Camping, USPO, whitewater rafting

GATLINBURG

446mm **full facilities, litter barrels, NO TRUCKS, petwalk, vending, Welcome Ctr wb**

443 Foothills Pkwy, to Gatlinburg, Great Smoky Mtns NP

443mm Pigeon River

440 US 321, to Wilton Spgs Rd, Gatlinburg, **N** 76/440 Trkstp/cafe/dsl, **S** Marathon, Arrow Creek Camping(14mi), CrazyHorse Camping(14mi)

439mm Pigeon River

435 US 321, to Gatlinburg, Newport, **N** C&C, Exxon, JSK Express, Marathon/dsl, Weigel/dsl, Arby's, Big Boys Country Kitchen, Burger King, Hardee's, KFC, McDonald's, Pizza Hut, Taco Bell, Motel 6, CVS Drug, H, O'Reilly Parts, Town&Country Drug, URGENT CARE, USPO, Walgreens, **S** Mobil/dsl, Murphy USA/dsl, Bojangle's, Cracker Barrel, Monterrey Mexican, Papa John's, Ruby Tuesday, Subway, Waffle House, Wendy's, Best Western, Family Inn, Hampton Inn, Holiday Inn Express, Quality Inn, $General, $Tree, AT&T, Lowe's, Marshall's, Verizon, Walmart/Subway

432b a US 70, US 411, US 25W, to Newport, **N** Exxon/dsl, Love's/Godfather's/RV/dsl/scales/24hr/@, TimeOut TC/BP/Huddle House/dsl/scales, Cancun Mexican, Econolodge, Relax Inn, Buick/Chevrolet, KOA(2mi), Tana-See RV Park, truck service, U-Haul, Westgate Tire, **S** Mobil/dsl, Shell/dsl, Sunoco/dsl, Family Inn/rest., $General

426mm **full facilities, litter barrels, petwalk, wb, vending,** **S** Milestone Rest., Sherman Oaks Campground, truck repair

425mm French Broad River

DANDRIDGE

424 TN 113, Dandridge, **N** Marathon/dsl, Family$, vet, **S** $General

421 I-81 N, to Bristol

420mm **full facilities, litter barrels, petwalk, eb, vending**

417 TN 92, Dandridge, **N** Marathon/dsl, Pilot/ONE9 Travel Center/dsl/scales/24hr/@, Capt's Galley, Hardee's, McDonald's, Perkins, Ruby Tuesday, Taste of Dandridge, Red Roof Inn, Goodyear, **S** Exxon/Wendy's/dsl, Marathon/dsl, Weigel's/dsl, Arby's, Bojangles, Shoney's, Taco Bell, Waffle House, Hampton Inn, Holiday Inn Express, Jefferson Inn, Quality Inn, Super 8, Advance Parts

415 US 25W, US 70, to Dandridge, **S** Marathon/dsl, Sonic(3mi)

412 Deep Sprgs Rd, to Douglas Dam, **N** Love's/Chester's/Subway/dsl/scales/24hr, Speedway/Speedy's Cafe/dsl, $General

407 TN 66, to Sevierville, Pigeon Forge, Gatlinburg, **N** Shell/Subway/dsl, Chophouse, Cracker Barrel, McDonald's, Taco Bell, Fairfield Inn, Hampton Inn, Holiday Inn Express/EVC, Smokies Motel, Bass Pro Shops, Harley Davidson, RV Camping, Smoky Mtn Visitor's Ctr, **S** multiple services/outlets, Buc-ee's/gas/EVC, Exxon/dsl, Mobil/dsl, Shell/Krystal/dsl, FlapJack's, Wendy's, Best Western, Comfort Suites, Courtyard, Days Inn, Quality Inn, Chrysler/Dodge/Jeep, flea mkt, Russell Stover, RV Camping, USPO

402 Midway Rd

398 Strawberry Plains Pk, Strawberry Plains Pk, **N** BP/dsl, Citgo/dsl, Exxon/dsl, Shell/dsl, Aubrey's Rest., McDonald's, Waffle House, Wendy's, EconoLodge, Hampton Inn, Holiday Inn Express, Motel 6, Red Roof Inn, Rodeway Inn, Super 8, Travelodge, Lazydays RV, TN RV Ctr, **S** Pilot/Subway/dsl/scales/24hr, Weigel's, Arby's, Burger King, Cantina Amigos, Cracker Barrel, KFC, Krystal, Taco Bell, Best Value, Best Western+, Comfort Suites, Fairfield Inn, La Quinta

395mm Holston River

394 US 70, US 11E, US 25W, Asheville Hwy, **N** BP, goodstop/dsl, Shell/dsl, Domino's Pizza, Dunkin, Papa John's, Subway, Wendy's, Gateway Inn, $General, Advance Parts, AutoZone, city park, **S** Kwik Stop, Mapco/dsl, Habaneros Mexican, Pizza Hut, Scott's Place, Waffle House, Days Inn, $General, CVS Drug, Family$, Kroger/gas, NAPA, vet, Walgreens

KNOXVILLE

393 I-640 W, to I-75 N

392 US 11W, Rutledge Pike, **N** Citgo/dsl, $General, truck repair, U-Haul, **S** Shell, Buddy's BBQ, Shoney's, $General, Kroger/gas, Sav-A-Lot Foods, to Knoxville Zoo, transmissions

390 Cherry St, Knoxville, **N** Marathon/dsl, Top Fuel Mart, Weigel's/Subway, Happy Garden Chinese, Knoxville Inn, tires, **S** Exxon, goodstop/dsl, Arby's, Capt. Jack's, Dulcie's Cafe, KFC, Little Caesar's, McDonald's, Wok N Roll, Deluxe Inn, Regency Inn, $Tree, Advance Parts, AutoZone, Family$, O'Reilly Parts, O'Reilly Parts

389 US 441 N, Broadway, 5th Ave, **N** Caseys/dsl, Shell/dsl, Burger King, Domino's, KFC, Krystal, McDonald's, Sonic, Subway, Taco Bell, Wendy's, $General, CVS Drug, Family$, Firestone/auto, Kroger/dsl, Save-A-Lot Foods, USPO, Walgreens/24hr

388 US 441 S(exits left from wb), **S** Crowne Plaza, Hilton, Marriot, downtown, to U of TN

387a I-275 N, to Lexington

387 TN 62, 17th St, **N** Caseys/dsl, Royal Inn, Siegel Select,

INTERSTATE 40 Cont'd

WEST HILLS

387 Continued
$General, $General, Food City/gas, vet, S [H]

386b a US 129, University Ave, to UT

385 I-75 N, I-640 E

384mm I-40 W and I-75 S run together 17 mi.

383 Papermill Rd, N [lodging] Red Roof Inn, S [gas] Exxon/dsl, Pilot/dsl, [food] Barberitos, Buddy's BBQ, Burger King, Five Guys, Krispy Kreme, Sonic, Twin Peaks, Waffle House, [lodging] Courtyard, Hampton Inn, Holiday Inn Express, Travelodge, [other] Food City, same as 380, Walgreens

380 US 11, US 70, West Hills, S [gas] Delta Express, Mapco/dsl, [food] Arby's, Brazeiro's Brazilian Steaks, Brixx Pizza, Burro Flojo Mexican, Cheesecake Factory, Chick-fil-A, Chili's, Cookout, Doc's Grille, Dunkin Donuts, Firehouse Subs, Hardee's, Honeybaked Ham, Hooters, IHOP, Jets Pizza, Jimmy John's, Longhorn Steaks, McAlister's Deli, McDonald's, Mooyah Burger, Mr Gatti's, O'Charley's, Olive Garden, Papa John's, Penn Sta Subs, Petro's Chili, PF Chang's, Pizza Hut, PlumTree Chinese, Qdoba Mexican, Red Lobster, Salsarita's Cantina, Starbucks, Subway, Taco Bell, Tropical Smoothie Cafe, TX Roadhouse, Zaxby's, [lodging] Extended Stay America, Ramada Inn, [other] $Tree, AT&T, Barnes&Noble, Belk, Dillards, Food City, JC Penney, Kohl's, mall, O'Reilly Parts, Office Depot, Old Navy, PetSmart, REI, Ross, Steinmart, Target, TJ Maxx, Trader Joe's, U-Haul, Walgreens, Whole Foods Mkt

379 Bridgewater Rd, N [gas] Exxon/Subway/dsl, Pilot/McDonald's/dsl, [food] Taco Bell, [other] Sam's Club/gas, Walmart/Subway, S [gas] Conoco/dsl, Marathon/dsl, [food] Asia Kitchen, Buddy's BBQ, Burger King, Cheddar's, ChuckeCheese, CiCi's Pizza, Makino Japanese, Misaki Japanese, Shoney's, Sonic, Wendy's, [lodging] InTown Suites, [other] Aamco, Advance Parts, AutoZone, Books-A-Million, Buick/GMC, Chrysler/Dodge/Jeep, Firestone/auto, Ford/Lincoln, Hyundai/Subaru, Mazda, Nissan, NTB, Tire Barn, Transmission World

378 Cedar Bluff Rd, N [gas] Casey's/dsl, Shell, Weigel's/dsl, [food] Arby's, CookOut, Cracker Barrel, Dunkin, KFC, Little Caesar's, McDonald's, Old Mill Bread Company, Panda Express, Papa John's, Starbucks, Subway, Waffle House, Wendy's, [lodging] Country Inn&Suites, Days Inn, Hampton Inn, Holiday Inn, [other] $General, AutoZone, [H], Mazda, S [gas] Exxon, [food] Applebee's, Blaze Pizza, Bojangles, Cancun Mexican, Capt D's, Carolina Ale House, Carrabba's, Chipotle, Chuy's Mexican, Culver's, Famous Dave's BBQ, Firehouse Subs, Hardee's, Jason's Deli, Jimmy John's, Koko Japanese, Krystal, Newk's Cafe, Outback Steaks, Panera Bread, Parkside Grill, Penn Sta. Subs, Pizza Hut, Salsarita's, Starbucks, Which Wich?, Zaxby's, [lodging] Baymont Inn, Best Western+, Comfort Inn, Courtyard, Drury Inn&Suites, Embassy Suites, Hilton Garden, Home2 Suites, MainStay Suites, Microtel, Motel 6, Residence Inn, TownePlace Suites, [other] $Tree, ALDI, AT&T, Best Buy, Cadillac, Chevrolet, CVS Drug, Dick's, Ford/Lincoln, Home Depot, Kia, Kroger/dsl, Lowe's, Maserati, Pepboys, Staples, Verizon, Volvo, Walgreens

376 I-140 E, TN 162 N, to Maryville, N to Oak Ridge Museum

374 TN 131, Lovell Rd, N [gas] Shell/dsl, Speedway/Speedy Cafe/dsl/scales/24hr, TA/Country Pride/dsl/scales/24hr/@, [food] Bojangles, Subway, Waffle House, [lodging] Econolodge, [other] Harley-Davidson, S [gas] Pilot/Wendy's/dsl/24hr, [food] Abuelo's Mexican, Arby's, Baskin-Robbins, Bonefish Grill, Brixx Pizza, Buffalo Wild Wings, Calhoun's Rest., Chick-fil-A, Chipotle, Connor's Rest., Egg&I Cafe, Flemings, Hurricane Grill, IHOP, Jimmy John's, Kabuki Japanese, Krystal, Lenny's Subs, McAlister's Deli, McDonald's, Mimi's Cafe, Moe's SW Grill, Noodles&Co, O'Charley's, Olive Garden, Panera Bread, Pei Wei, Red Robin, Salsarita's Cantina, Smokey Mtn Brewery,

374 Continued
Sonic, Starbucks, Steak'n Shake, Taco Bell, TX Roadhouse, Wasabi Japanese, Zoe's Kitchen, [lodging] Budget Inn, Candlewood Suites, Homewood Suites, SpringHill Suites, [other] $Tree, Advance Parts, AutoZone, Belk, Best Buy, BMW/Mini, CarMax, Costco/gas, EarthFare Foods, GNC, Hobby Lobby, Honda, [H], Land Rover, Lexus, Marshall's, Mercedes, Old Navy, PetSmart, Ross, Target, Toyota/Scion, Walgreens, Walmart/Subway, World Mkt

373 Campbell Sta Rd, N [gas] Marathon/dsl, Shell/dsl, [lodging] Comfort Suites, Country Inn&Suites, Fairfield Inn, Holiday Inn Express, Super 8, [other] Buddy Gregg RV Ctr, S [gas] Exxon/dsl, Pilot/dsl, Weigel's, [food] Bad Daddy's Burger, Cracker Barrel, Dunkin Donuts, Hardee's, La Parrilla, Longhorn Steaks, Mellow Mushroom, Newk's Grill, Panda Express, Potbelly, Seasons Grille, Taco Boy, Wild Wing Cafe, Zaxby's, [lodging] Clarion, Hampton Inn, Staybridge Suites, [other] AT&T, JC Penney, Publix, Verizon, Walgreens

372mm weigh sta both lanes

369 Watt Rd, N [gas] Flying J/Denny's/dsl/LP/scales/RV dump/24hr, Speedco, [other] Blue Beacon, S [gas] Petro/Iron Skillet/dsl/scales/24hr/@, TA/Marathon/Burger King/Pizza Hut/Popeyes/Subway/dsl/24hr/@, [other] Knoxville Coach & RV

368.5mm I-40 E and I-75 N run together 17 mi.

368 I-75 and I-40

KINGSTON

364 US 321, TN 95, Lenoir City, Oak Ridge, N [other] Crosseyed Cricket Camping(2mi), S [gas] Love's/McDonald's/Subway/dsl/24hr, [food] Ruby Tuesday, [lodging] Days Inn, EconoLodge, Hampton Inn, Holiday Inn Express

362 Industrial Park Rd

360 Buttermilk Rd, N [other] Soaring Eagle RV Park

356 TN 58 N, Gallaher Rd, to Oak Ridge, N [gas] Marathon/dsl, Weigels/dsl, [lodging] Motel 6, [other] $General

355 Lawnville Rd, N [gas] goodstop/Subway/dsl

352 TN 58 S, Kingston, N [lodging] Lakeview Inn, S [gas] Exxon/dsl, Mobil/dsl, [food] Buddy's BBQ, Handee Burger, Hardee's, Little Caesar's, McDonald's, Sonic, Subway, Taco Bell, [lodging] Super 8, [other] Cash Saver Foods, Family$, Marina RV Park, to Watts Bar Lake, USPO

351mm Clinch River

350 US 70, Midtown, S [gas] Weigel's/dsl, [food] Bojangles, Burger King, Burger Station, Dunkin, Gondolier Italian, Subway, Zaxby's, [other] AT&T, Caney Creek Camping(3mi), [H], Kroger, Lowe's, O'Reilly Parts, Walgreens

CRAB ORCHARD

347 US 27, Harriman, N [gas] Marathon/dsl, [food] Hardee's, K's Kitchen, KFC, Los Primos Mexican, McDonald's, Pizza Hut, Ruby Tuesday, Taco Bell, Wendy's, [lodging] Days Inn, [other] Big S Fork NRA, to Frozen Head SP, Verizon, S [gas] Shell/Krystal/dsl/24hr, [food] Cracker Barrel, Shoney's, [lodging] Baymont, Comfort Inn, Holiday Inn Express

340 TN 299 N, Airport Rd

339.5mm eastern/central time zone line

338 TN 299 S, Westel Rd, N [gas] Shell/dsl, S Exxon/dsl, [food] Hunt Brothers Pizza, [other] Boat-N-RV Ctr/Park

336mm litter barrel, parking area/weigh sta eb

329 US 70, Crab Orchard, N [gas] Marathon/dsl, Shell/dsl, [other] $General, KOA(4mi), S Cumberland Trails SP, Wilson SP

327mm full [handicapped] facilities, litter barrels, petwalk, [phone], [picnic], [RS] wb, vending

324mm full [handicapped] facilities, litter barrels, petwalk, [phone], [picnic], [RS] eb, vending

322 TN 101, Peavine Rd, Crossville, N [gas] Exxon/Subway/dsl, [food] Hardee's, McDonald's, [lodging] Holiday Inn Express, [other] Deer Run RV Resort, KOA Camping, Roam-Roost RV Campground, to Fairfield Glade Resort, S [gas] Shell/dsl, [food] Cancun Mexican, Los Toritos Mexican, Taco Bell, [lodging] Comfort Suites, Hampton Inn, Super 8, [other] $General, Chestnut Hill Winery,

TN

TN

INTERSTATE 40 Cont'd

CROSSVILLE

322 Continued
Cumberland Mtn SP, H

320 TN 298, Crossville, N Pilot/Wendy's/dsl/scales/24hr, Tesla EVC, Bramble Berry Cafe, Lefty's BBQ, antiques, winery, S Buc-ee's/EVC/dsl, Shell/DQ/dsl, Speedway/dsl, auto repair/tires, Crossville Outlet/famous brands, H, Save-A-Lot Foods

318mm Obed River

317 US 127, Crossville, N Circle K/Dunkin/dsl, Exxon/dsl, Shoney's, Subway, Baymont Inn, Executive Inn, Quality Inn, repair, to Big South Fork RA, to York SP, S 7-11/dsl, Murphy USA/dsl, Arby's, Bojangles, Chick-fil-A, Cracker Barrel, Firehouse Subs, Jersey Mike's, La Costa Mexican, Marco's Pizza, Papa John's, Romo's Mexican, Ruby Tuesday, Vegas Steaks, Waffle House, Zaxby's, Economy Inn, Red Roof Inn, $Tree, Chevrolet/GMC, Chrysler/Dodge/Jeep, Ford, H, Lowe's, Shaddon Tire, Staples, to Cumberland Mtn SP, Walmart

311 Plateau Rd, S Exxon, Lucky Stop/dsl

307mm litter barrels, parking area/weigh sta wb

301 US 70 N, TN 84, Monterey, N Shell, Burger King, DQ, Subway, Taco Bell, Quality Inn

300 US 70, Monterey, N Citgo/dsl, DQ, Hardee's

291mm Falling Water River

COOKEVILLE

290 US 70, Cookeville, S Super Gas, Fiesta Cancun, Baymont

288 TN 111, to Livingston, Cookeville, Sparta, N Hull SP, S Sunoco/dsl, Super Truck&TravelCtr/dsl/24hr, Subway, Fall Creek Inn

287 TN 136, Cookeville, N Exxon/7-11/dsl, Marathon/dsl, Murphy USA/dsl, Arby's, Blue Coast Burrito, Buffalo Wild Wings, Burger King, Capt D's, Cheddars, Chick-fil-A, Chicken Salad Chicks, Chili's, Chipotle, Cookout, Cracker Barrel, Dunkin, Fazoli's, Firehouse Subs, Five Guys, Fuji Japanese, Golden Corral, Hibachi Buffet, IHOP, Jersey Mike's, Krystal, Logan's Roadhouse, Longhorn Steaks, McAlister's, McDonald's, Nick's Rest., O'Charley's, Olive Garden, Outback Steaks, Panda Express, Panera Bread, Papa Murphy's, Pizza Hut, Popeyes, Red Lobster, Romo's Mexican, Smoothie King, Sonic, Starbucks, Steak'n Shake, Subway, Taco Bell, TX Roadhouse, Wendy's, Best Western, Comfort Inn, Comfort Suites, Days Inn, Hampton Inn, Home2 Suites, Red Roof Inn, Super 8, ALDI, BigLots, Firestone/auto, Harley-Davidson, JC Penney, Kroger/gas, Lowe's, Nissan/EVC, OfficeMax, Publix, st patrol, transmissions, Verizon, Walmart, S Marathon/dsl, ONE9dsl, KFC, Waffle House, Country Inn&Suites, Fairfield Inn, Holiday Inn Express, La Quinta, Motel 6, TownePlace Suites, Sam's Club/gas, URGENT CARE

286 TN 135, Burgess Falls Rd, N Exxon/dsl, Shell/dsl, Arby's, Bojangles, Hardee's, Waffle House, auto repair, Chrysler/Dodge/Jeep, Ford/Lincoln, H, Hyundai, Kia, to TTU, Toyota/Scion, USPO, S Exxon/dsl, Shell/dsl, Star Motor Inn, Burgess Falls SP(8mi)

BAXTER

280 TN 56 N, Baxter, N Love's/McDonalds/Subway/dsl/scales/24hr, Shell/dsl, Speedway/dsl/24hr, Huddle House, Papa John's, Taco Bell, Camp Discovery(2mi), NAPA, Twin Lakes RV Park(2mi)

276 Old Baxter Rd

273 TN 56 S, to Smithville, S Shell, Rose Garden Rest., $General, USPO

268 TN 96, Buffalo Valley Rd, N Grandville Marina Camping(11mi), S to Edgar Evins SP/RV camping, Edgar Evins SP/RV camping, USPO

267mm Caney Fork River

267mm full facilities, info, litter barrels, petwalk, both lanes, vending

266mm Caney Fork River

263mm Caney Fork River

258 TN 53, Gordonsville, N Exxon/dsl, Shell/dsl, McDonald's, Subway, Timberloft Café, Waffle House, Quality Inn, to Cordell Hull Dam, S BP/dsl, Pilot/Wendy's/dsl/scales/24hr, Arby's, BB's Bistro, Bellacino's Pizza, KFC/Taco Bell, $General

254 TN 141, to Alexandria

252mm litter barrels, parking area/truck sta both lanes

245 Linwood Rd, N $General

LEBANON

239 US 70, Lebanon, N Shell, Subway, $General, O'Reilly Parts, S QT/dsl, Jalisco Mexican

238 US 231, Lebanon, N Exxon/7-11, Mapco/dsl, Murphy Express/dsl, Arby's, Chick-fil-A, Chipotle, Cici's Pizza, Cook Out, Cracker Barrel, Demo's Steaks, Dunkin, El Molino Mexican, Gondola, Hardee's, KFC, Logan's Roadhouse, Los Compadres, McAlister's , McDonald's, Panda Express, Panera Bread, Pizza Hut, Shoney's, Starbucks, Subway, Taco Bell, Waffle House, Wendy's, Whataburger, Zaxby's, Cedar Valley Inn, Days Inn, EconoLodge, Holiday Inn Express, Quality Inn, Quality Inn, Ramada, $Tree, ALDI, AT&T, Discount Tire, H, Lowe's, to Bledsoe SP(23mi), Verizon, Walgreens, Walmart/Subway, S Pilot/Subway/DQ/dsl/scales/24hr, Shell/dsl, Speedway/dsl/e85, Domino's, O'Charley's, Sonic, Comfort Suites, Knights Inn, La Quinta, Travel Inn, $General, Shady Acres Camping, Timberline Campground, to Cedars of Lebanon SP, USPO

236 S Hartmann Dr, N Mapco/dsl, Shell/dsl, Bojangles, Chili's, Outback Steaks, Subway, Candlewood, Fairfield, Hampton Inn, Buick/Chevrolet/GMC, Home Depot, H, Rose Tire

235 TN 840 W, to Murfreesboro

232 TN 109, to Gallatin, N Mapco/dsl, Shell/McDonald's/dsl/24hr, Speedway/dsl, Thornton's, Bellacino's Pizza, Coach's Grille, Dunkin, Gyro & Philly Steak, Jersey Mike's, Sonic, Subway, Subway, Taco Bell, Waffle House, Wendy's, Whataburger, Zaxby's, Sleep Inn, WoodSpring, Publix, S KOA(3mi)

228mm truck sta, wb only

226mm truck sta

229b a Beckwith Rd

226 TN 171, Mt Juliet Rd, N BP/McDonald's/dsl, BP/McDonald's/dsl, EVC, Exxon/dsl, Murphy Express/dsl, Shell/dsl, Arby's, Big Bad Wolf BBQ, Capt D's, Cheddars, Chipotle, Culver's, Dos Sisters Mexican, Far East Buffet, Five Guys, IHOP, Longhorn Steaks, Panda Express, Comfort Suites, $Tree, ALDI, Firestone/auto, Lowe's, NTB, URGENT CARE, Walmart, S Mapco/Quiznos/dsl, Blue Coast Burrito, Buffalo Wild Wings, Burger Republic, Chick-fil-A, ChuckECheese, Cori's Dog House, Cracker Barrel, Crumbl Cookies, Firehouse Subs, Fulin's Asian, Jason's Deli, Jonathan's, Little Caesars, Logan's Roadhouse, Martin's BBQ, McDonald's, Moe's SW Grill, Nobu Hibachi , O'Charley's, Olive Garden, Oscar's Taco Shop, Panera Bread, Papa John's, PDK Southern , Pizza Hut, Red Lobster, Red Robin, Red Robin, Salsarita's Cantina, Sonic, Starbucks, Steak'n Shake, Taco Bell, Taziki's Cafe, Waffle House, Wendy's, Which Wich?, Zaxby's, Courtyard/EVC, Hampton Inn, Holiday Inn Express, Home2 Suites, Quality Inn, Advance Auto, AT&T, Belk, Best Buy, Books-A-Million, Dick's, Discount Tire, Ford, GNC, Hobby Lobby, Honda, JC Penney, JoAnn Fabrics, Kroger/dsl, Old Navy, PetSmart, Publix, Ross, Staples,

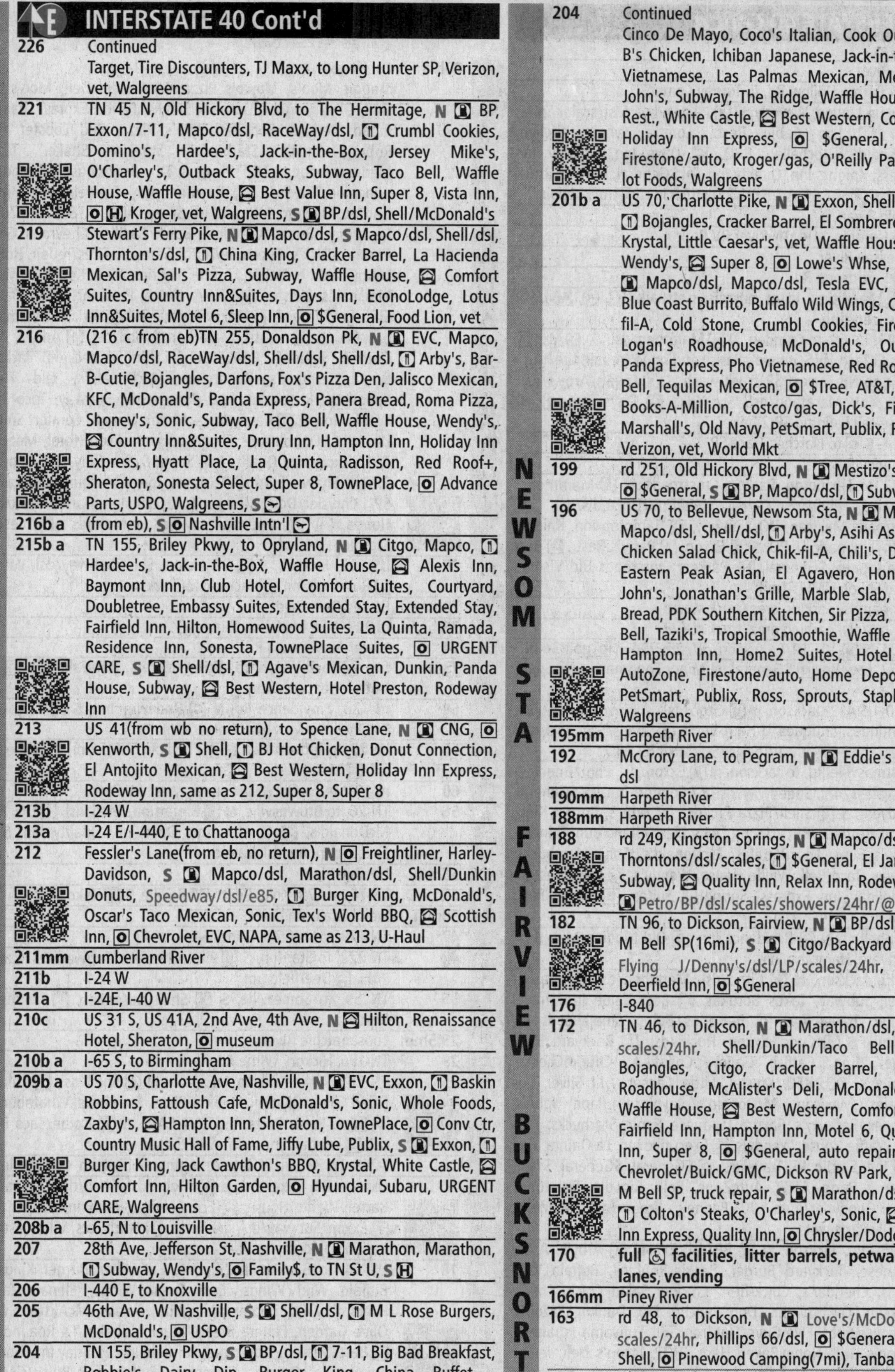

INTERSTATE 40 Cont'd

226 Continued
Target, Tire Discounters, TJ Maxx, to Long Hunter SP, Verizon, vet, Walgreens

221 TN 45 N, Old Hickory Blvd, to The Hermitage, N BP, Exxon/7-11, Mapco/dsl, RaceWay/dsl, Crumbl Cookies, Domino's, Hardee's, Jack-in-the-Box, Jersey Mike's, O'Charley's, Outback Steaks, Subway, Taco Bell, Waffle House, Waffle House, Best Value Inn, Super 8, Vista Inn, Kroger, vet, Walgreens, S BP/dsl, Shell/McDonald's

219 Stewart's Ferry Pike, N Mapco/dsl, S Mapco/dsl, Shell/dsl, Thornton's/dsl, China King, Cracker Barrel, La Hacienda Mexican, Sal's Pizza, Subway, Waffle House, Comfort Suites, Country Inn&Suites, Days Inn, EconoLodge, Lotus Inn&Suites, Motel 6, Sleep Inn, $General, Food Lion, vet

216 (216 c from eb)TN 255, Donaldson Pk, N EVC, Mapco, Mapco/dsl, RaceWay/dsl, Shell/dsl, Shell/dsl, Arby's, Bar-B-Cutie, Bojangles, Darfons, Fox's Pizza Den, Jalisco Mexican, KFC, McDonald's, Panda Express, Panera Bread, Roma Pizza, Shoney's, Sonic, Subway, Taco Bell, Waffle House, Wendy's, Country Inn&Suites, Drury Inn, Hampton Inn, Holiday Inn Express, Hyatt Place, La Quinta, Radisson, Red Roof+, Sheraton, Sonesta Select, Super 8, TownePlace, Advance Parts, USPO, Walgreens, S

216b a (from eb), S Nashville Intn'l

215b a TN 155, Briley Pkwy, to Opryland, N Citgo, Mapco, Hardee's, Jack-in-the-Box, Waffle House, Alexis Inn, Baymont Inn, Club Hotel, Comfort Suites, Courtyard, Doubletree, Embassy Suites, Extended Stay, Extended Stay, Fairfield Inn, Hilton, Homewood Suites, La Quinta, Ramada, Residence Inn, Sonesta, TownePlace Suites, URGENT CARE, S Shell/dsl, Agave's Mexican, Dunkin, Panda House, Subway, Best Western, Hotel Preston, Rodeway Inn

213 US 41(from wb no return), to Spence Lane, N CNG, Kenworth, S Shell, BJ Hot Chicken, Donut Connection, El Antojito Mexican, Best Western, Holiday Inn Express, Rodeway Inn, same as 212, Super 8, Super 8

213b I-24 W

213a I-24 E/I-440, E to Chattanooga

212 Fessler's Lane(from eb, no return), N Freightliner, Harley-Davidson, S Mapco/dsl, Marathon/dsl, Shell/Dunkin Donuts, Speedway/dsl/e85, Burger King, McDonald's, Oscar's Taco Mexican, Sonic, Tex's World BBQ, Scottish Inn, Chevrolet, EVC, NAPA, same as 213, U-Haul

211mm Cumberland River

211b I-24 W

211a I-24E, I-40 W

210c US 31 S, US 41A, 2nd Ave, 4th Ave, N Hilton, Renaissance Hotel, Sheraton, museum

210b a I-65 S, to Birmingham

209b a US 70 S, Charlotte Ave, Nashville, N EVC, Exxon, Baskin Robbins, Fattoush Cafe, McDonald's, Sonic, Whole Foods, Zaxby's, Hampton Inn, Sheraton, TownePlace, Conv Ctr, Country Music Hall of Fame, Jiffy Lube, Publix, S Exxon, Burger King, Jack Cawthon's BBQ, Krystal, White Castle, Comfort Inn, Hilton Garden, Hyundai, Subaru, URGENT CARE, Walgreens

208b a I-65, N to Louisville

207 28th Ave, Jefferson St, Nashville, N Marathon, Marathon, Subway, Wendy's, Family$, to TN St U, S

206 I-440 E, to Knoxville

205 46th Ave, W Nashville, S Shell/dsl, M L Rose Burgers, McDonald's, USPO

204 TN 155, Briley Pkwy, S BP/dsl, 7-11, Big Bad Breakfast, Bobbie's Dairy Dip, Burger King, China Buffet,

NASHVILLE

NEWSOM STA

FAIRVIEW

BUCKSNORT

204 Continued
Cinco De Mayo, Coco's Italian, Cook Out, Domino's, Hattie B's Chicken, Ichiban Japanese, Jack-in-the-Box, Kien Giang Vietnamese, Las Palmas Mexican, Melissa's Pizza, Papa John's, Subway, The Ridge, Waffle House, Wendell Smith's Rest., White Castle, Best Western, Comfort Inn, Days Inn, Holiday Inn Express, $General, $Tree, CVS Drug, Firestone/auto, Kroger/gas, O'Reilly Parts, PepBoys, Sav-a-lot Foods, Walgreens

201b a US 70, Charlotte Pike, N Exxon, Shell/dsl, Thornton's/dsl, Bojangles, Cracker Barrel, El Sombrero, Jim 'N Nick's BBQ, Krystal, Little Caesar's, vet, Waffle House, Wayback Burger, Wendy's, Super 8, Lowe's Whse, Walmart/Subway, S Mapco/dsl, Mapco/dsl, Tesla EVC, Baskin Robbins, Blue Coast Burrito, Buffalo Wild Wings, Chicago Gyros, Chick-fil-A, Cold Stone, Crumbl Cookies, Firehouse Subs, IHOP, Logan's Roadhouse, McDonald's, Outback Steakhouse, Panda Express, Pho Vietnamese, Red Robin, Starbucks, Taco Bell, Tequilas Mexican, $Tree, AT&T, Best Buy, Big Lots, Books-A-Million, Costco/gas, Dick's, Firestone/auto, GNC, Marshall's, Old Navy, PetSmart, Publix, Ross, Target, U-Haul, Verizon, vet, World Mkt

199 rd 251, Old Hickory Blvd, N Mestizo's Mexican, Shell/dsl, $General, S BP, Mapco/dsl, Subway

196 US 70, to Bellevue, Newsom Sta, N Mapco/dsl, S BP, EVC, Mapco/dsl, Shell/dsl, Arby's, Asihi Asian, Baskin Robbins, Chicken Salad Chick, Chik-fil-A, Chili's, DeSano Pizzeria, DQ, Eastern Peak Asian, El Agavero, HoneyFire BBQ, Jimmy John's, Jonathan's Grille, Marble Slab, O'Charley's, Panera Bread, PDK Southern Kitchen, Sir Pizza, Sonic, Subway, Taco Bell, Taziki's, Tropical Smoothie, Waffle House, Wendy's, Hampton Inn, Home2 Suites, Hotel Avery, $Tree, AutoZone, Firestone/auto, Home Depot, Michaels, PetCo, PetSmart, Publix, Ross, Sprouts, Staples, USPO, Verizon, Walgreens

195mm Harpeth River

192 McCrory Lane, to Pegram, N Eddie's Market(1mi), Shell/dsl

190mm Harpeth River

188mm Harpeth River

188 rd 249, Kingston Springs, N Mapco/dsl, Shell/dsl, Sunoco, Thorntons/dsl/scales, $General, El Jardin Mexican, Sonic, Subway, Quality Inn, Relax Inn, Rodeway Inn, USPO, S Petro/BP/dsl/scales/showers/24hr/@, vet

182 TN 96, to Dickson, Fairview, N BP/dsl, Fairview Inn, M Bell SP(16mi), S Citgo/Backyard Burger/Dunkin/dsl, Flying J/Denny's/dsl/LP/scales/24hr, Subway, Deerfield Inn, $General

176 I-840

172 TN 46, to Dickson, N Marathon/dsl, Pilot/Wendy's/dsl/scales/24hr, Shell/Dunkin/Taco Bell/dsl, Arby's, Bojangles, Citgo, Cracker Barrel, Hardee's, Logan's Roadhouse, McAlister's Deli, McDonald's, Ruby Tuesday, Waffle House, Best Western, Comfort Inn, EconoLodge, Fairfield Inn, Hampton Inn, Motel 6, Quality Inn, Rodeway Inn, Super 8, $General, auto repair, Chappell's Foods, Chevrolet/Buick/GMC, Dickson RV Park, Ford, Nissan, to M Bell SP, truck repair, S Marathon/dsl, QT/dsl, Shell/dsl, Colton's Steaks, O'Charley's, Sonic, Days Inn, Holiday Inn Express, Quality Inn, Chrysler/Dodge/Jeep

170 **full facilities, litter barrels, petwalk, both lanes, vending**

166mm Piney River

163 rd 48, to Dickson, N Love's/McDonald's/Subway/dsl/scales/24hr, Phillips 66/dsl, $General, truck repair, S Shell, Pinewood Camping(7mi), Tanbark Camping

152 rd 230, Bucksnort, N Sunoco/dsl, Travel Inn

= gas = food = lodging = other = rest stop

TN

INTERSTATE 40 Cont'd

Exit #	Services
149mm	Duck River
148	rd 50, Barren Hollow Rd, to Turney Center
143	TN 13, to Linden, Waverly, N Pilot/Arby's/dsl/scales/24hr, Shell, Log Cabin Rest., Loretta Lynn's Kitchen, McDonald's, Rochelle's BBQ, Days Inn, Holiday Inn Express, Knights Inn, Quality Inn, $General, KOA/LP, truck repair, S Speedway/dsl, Scottish Inn, truck repair
141mm	Buffalo River
137	Cuba Landing, N TN River RV Park
133mm	Tennessee River
133	rd 191, Birdsong Rd
131mm	**full facilities, litter barrels, petwalk, both lanes, vending**
126	US 641, TN 69, to Camden, N Marathon/dsl, ONE9/dsl, Tacos El Taco, $General, Paris Landing SP, repair, tire/truck repair, to NB Forrest SP, truck wash, S Love's/Arby's/dsl/scales24hr, Marathon/dsl, Shell/dsl, Days Inn, Mouse-tail Landing SP(24mi)
116	rd 114, S to Natchez Trace SP
110mm	Big Sandy River
108	TN 22, to Lexington, Parkers Crossroads, N Marathon / dsl/24hr, Phillips 66/dsl, Shell/McDonald's/dsl, Crossroads Mexican, DQ, Subway, Hampton Inn, Knights Inn, city park, USPO, S Exxon, Patty's Rest., Best Value Inn, $General, Parkers Crossroads Bfd Visitors Ctr, to Shiloh NMP(51mi)
103mm	litter barrels, parking area/truck sta eb
102mm	litter barrels, parking area/truck sta wb
101	rd 104, N 101 TP/Real Food/dsl/tires/24hr, golf(3mi)
93	rd 152, Law Rd, $General, N Minor Foodmart, S Shell/dsl
87	US 70, US 412, Jackson, N Citgo/dsl, Mapco/Deli/dsl/e85, antiques, antiques, U-Haul, vet, S Love's/Hardee's/dsl/scales/24hr, Speedway/dsl/e85, Exit 87 BBQ
85	Christmasville Rd, to Jackson, N Exxon/dsl, Pilot/Denny's/dsl/scales/24hr, Speedway/dsl, Comfort Inn, $General, Goodyear, S Shell/Pizza Pro/dsl, Arby's, Burger King, Clifton Brothers BBQ, Jack's, Jet's Pizza, Jiang Jun Chinese, Lenny's Subs, Los Portales, McDonald's, Sonic, Starbucks, Subway, Taco Bell, Waffle House, Wendy's, Best Western +, Holiday Inn Express, SpringHill Suites, $Tree, Food Giant
83	Campbell st, N Residence Inn, Old Madina Mkt, S Courtyard, Hampton Inn
82b a	US 45, Jackson, N Citgo/dsl, Marathon/dsl, Cracker Barrel, Subway, Takos Borukas, Best Value Inn, Travel Lounge, Travelodge, Batteries+Bulbs, Smallwoods RV Ctr(4mi), S Citgo, Exxon, Hucks/dsl, Backyard BBQ, Burger King, Catfish Galley, Chik-fil-A, ChuckeCheese, Domino's, DQ, KFC, Krystal, Little Caesar's, LJ Silver, Los Portales Mexican, McDonald's/playplace, Papa John's, Popeyes, Rafferty's, Sakura Japanese, Sonic, Starbucks, Taco Bell, Waffle House, Wendy's, Executive Inn, La Quinta, Red Roof Inn, Studio 45, Travelers, $General, $General, $Tree, Advance Parts, AT&T, AutoZone, Belk, BigLots, Firestone/auto, Goodyear/auto, JC Penney, Kroger/dsl, Meineke, O'Reilly Parts, vet
80b a	US 45 Byp, Jackson, N BP/dsl, Exxon, Arby's, Asahi Japanese, Backyard Burger, Baskin-Robbins, Buffalo Wild Wings, Cheddar's, Chick-fil-A, Chicken Salad Chick, Chili's, CookOut, Country Inn, Don Pancho, DQ, Dunkin, Fazoli's, Firehouse Subs, Five Guys, Flat Iron Grill, Fujiyama Japanese, Genghis Grill, HoneyBaked Ham, IHOP, Jason's Deli, Jersey Mike's, Jimmy John's, LJ Silver, Longhorn Steaks,

PARKERS CROSSROADS · JACKSON

Exit #	Services
80b a	Continued Maggie Moo's, Marco's Pizza, McAlisters Deli, Moe's SW Grill, Olive Garden, Outback Steaks, Panda Express, Panera Bread, Perkins, Popeyes, Pyro's Pizza, Red Lobster, Red Robin, Sonic, Starbucks, Steak'n Shake, Taziki Mediterranean, TGIFriday's, TX Roadhouse, Wendy's, Wingstop, Zaxby's, Baymont Inn, Fairfield Inn, Hilton Garden, Howard Johnson, $Tree, ALDI, AT&T, AutoZone, Best Buy, Books-A-Million, Buick/Cadillac/Chevrolet/GMC, CarMax, Dick's, Firestone/auto, Gateway Tires/repair, Hobby Lobby, Home Depot, JoAnn Fabrics, Kia, Kohl's, Lowe's, Marshall's, Nissan, Old Navy, Petco, PetSmart, Ross, Sam's Club/gas, Target, TJ Maxx, Toyota/Scion, Verizon, Walmart/gas/EVC, S 76/dsl, Marathon, Mobil/dsl, Arby's, Asia Garden, Baudo's Rest., Burger King, Checkers, Jackson Donuts, Logan's Roadhouse, McDonald's, Old Town Spaghetti, Pizza Hut, Red Bones Grill, Subway, Taco Bell, Waffle House, Casey Jones Motel, Clarion, Comfort Suites, Days Inn, DoubleTree, EconoLodge, Jackson Hotel, Motel 6, Old Hickory Inn, Quality Inn, Super 8, SureStay, $General, Brooks Shaw's Store/EVC, Casey Jones Museum, Chickasaw SP, Chrysler/Dodge/Jeep, Ford/Lincoln, Harley-Davidson, Honda, Hyundai, to Pinson Mounds SP, Tuesday Morning, U-Haul
79	US 412, Jackson, S BP, Exxon, Shell/Subway/dsl, Valero, Rodeway Inn, Jackson RV Park
78mm	Forked Deer River
76	rd 223, S McKellar-Spines
74	Lower Brownsville Rd
73mm	**full facilities, info, litter barrels, petwalk, both lanes, vending**
68	rd 138, Providence Rd, N Rodeway Inn, S Citgo/dsl, TA/Shell/Subway/dsl/scales/24hr/@
66	US 70, to Brownsville, N Ft Pillow SHP(51mi), S Exxon/dsl, Motel 6
60	rd 19, Mercer Rd, S Country View RV Park
56	TN 76, to Brownsville, N Marathon, Shell/dsl, DQ, KFC, McDonald's, Comfort Inn, Days Inn, Quality Inn, S Exxon/parking/dsl, Valero
55mm	Hatchie River
52	TN 76, rd 179, Koko Rd, to Whiteville, S Koko Mkt
50mm	weigh sta both lanes
47	TN 179, to Stanton, Dancyville
42	TN 222, to Stanton, S Pilot/Chester's/Subway/dsl/scales/24hr, Deerfield Inn
35	TN 59, to Somerville, S Shell/dsl/scales, Longtown Rest.
29.5mm	Loosahatchie River
29	TN 196, Hickory Withe Rd
25	TN 205, Airline Rd, to Arlington, N Shell/dsl, Chicken Salad Chick, Olympic Steak & Pizza, Starbucks, Whataburger, O'Reilly Parts, URGENT CARE, S Exxon/Taco Bell/dsl, Fairfield Inn, SpringHill Suites, vistor ctr
24	I-269, TN 385, rd 204, to Arlington, Millington, Collierville
20	Canada Rd, Lakeland, N Mobil/dsl, Shell/dsl, Cracker Barrel, Waffle House, EconoLodge, Relax Inn, Super 8, S Exxon/Subway/dsl, fireworks, Starbucks, Villa Castrioti Italian, Memphis East Camping
18	US 64, to Bartlett, N EVC, EVC, Shell/Burger King, Buffalo Wild Wings, East Coast Wings, Elena's Tacos, Firebird's Grill, Hooters, Longhorn Steaks, McAlister's Deli, Olive Garden, Panera Bread, Steak'n Shake, TX Roadhouse, Best Western, Courtyard, Fairfield Inn, Holiday Inn, Home2 Suites, La Quinta, SpringHill Suites, Buick/GMC,

JACKSON · DANCYVILLE

INTERSTATE 40 Cont'd

18 Continued
Firestone/auto, Jiffy Lube, Lowe's, Pepboys, Sam's Club/gas, same as 16, Verizon, Walmart, S Circle K/dsl, Marathon, Shell, Backyard Burger, Dunkin, KFC, Papa John's, Pizza Hut, Smoothie King, Subway, Zaxby's, AT&T, Family$, Kroger/dsl, Sprouts Mkt, Walgreens

16b a TN 177, to Germantown, N Circle K, EVC, Shell/Circle K, Arby's, Bahama Breeze, Baskin Robbins, Burger King, Casa Mexicana, Cheesecake Factory, Chick-fil-A, Chik-fil-A, Chili's, Colton's Steaks, Cook Out, Dave & Buster's, Gus's, IHOP, J. Alexander's, Joe's Crabshack, Logan's Roadhouse, McDonald's/playplace, On-the-Border, Red Lobster, Red Sun Buffet, Starbucks, Subway, Taco Bell, Taziki's, Waffle House, Wendy's, Extended Stay America, Hampton Inn, Hyatt Place, $Tree, Barnes&Noble, Best Buy, BigLots, CarMax, Chevrolet, Chrysler/Dodge/Jeep, Dillard's, Ford, Hobby Lobby, Home Depot, Honda, [H], Hyundai, JC Penney, Macy's, Michael's, Nissan, Office Depot, Old Navy, PetSmart, Target, TJ Maxx, Walgreens, S Circle K, EVC, Texaco, Abbay's Rest., Arby's, Burger King, Cheddar's, ChuckeCheese, Corky's BBQ, Genghis Grill, Honeybaked Ham, Howard's Donuts, Jason's Deli, Jim'n Nick's BBQ, Jimmy John's, Little Caesars, Margarita's Mexican, McDonald's, Osaka, Pei Wei Chinese, Pyros Pizza, Shogun Japanese, Smoothie King, Waffle House, Wendy's, Comfort Suites, Country Inn & Suites, Extended Stay, Hilton Garden, Microtel, TownePlace, $Tree, ALDI, AT&T, AutoZone, Costco/gas, Dick's, Family$, IKEA, Kohl's, Kroger/gas, Marshall's, Ross, Toyota/Scion, Verizon

15b a Appling Rd, N Circle K/dsl, Exxon/dsl, vet, [H], S Marathon/dsl, Subway, Family$

14 Whitten Rd, N Mapco, Shell/Burger King, Valero/dsl, Walmart/dsl, Bojangles, Hardee's, McDonald's, Orale Bakery, Sidecar Café, Smoothie King, Starbucks, Taco Bell, $Tree, AutoZone, Firestone/auto, Harley-Davidson, Walmart, S Circle K, Dunkin, Subway, Supreme Hot Wings, Candlewood Suites, Family$, Walgreens

12 Sycamore View Rd, N Murphy Express/dsl, Shell/dsl, Sunoco/dsl, America Deli, Capt D's, Church's TX Chicken, Cracker Barrel, Dixie Queen, IHOP, Krystal, McDonald's, Mi Terra, Sonic, Starbucks, Taco Bell, Waffle House, AmericInn, Baymont Inn, Best Value Inn, GardenTree Hotel, Motel 6, Red Roof Inn, WoodSpring Suites, AutoZone, Family$, Midas, O'Reilly Parts, Walgreens, S Exxon, Mapco, Burger King, Crumpys Wings, Pizza Hut, Popeyes, Subway, Tops BBQ, Wendy's, All Seasons, Comfort Inn, Econolodge, Fair View Inn, FairBridge Inn, Memphis Inn, Quality Inn, Shelby Inn, Wingate, Bass Pro Shops

10.5mm Wolf River

10b a (from wb)I-240 W around Memphis, I-40 E to Nashville

12c (from eb)I-240 W, to Jackson, I-40 E to Nashville

12b Sam Cooper Blvd(from eb)

12a US 64/70/79, Summer Ave, N Mapco/dsl, Marathon/dsl, Hotel Elite, NAPA, U-Haul, S Exxon, McDonald's, Subway, $Tree, Firestone/auto

10 TN 204, Covington Pike, N Mobil, McDonald's, Wendy's, Audi/VW, Buick/GMC, Chevrolet, Chrysler/Dodge/Jeep/Fiat, Honda, Hyundai, Kia, Mazda, Nissan, Pep Boys, Sam's Club, Subaru, SuperLo Food, Superlo Foods

8b a TN 14, Jackson Ave, N Motel 6, Quality Inn, Cooper Tire, S Sunoco/dsl, AutoZone, O'Reilly Parts, tires

6 Warford Rd, N Exxon/dsl

5 Hollywood St, N Marathon, Shell, Valero/dsl, Burger King, Popeyes, Family$, S Memphis Zoo

3 Watkins St, N BP, Highway/dsl, Jubilee/dsl, Marathon, Valero, Family$, tires, U-Haul

MEMPHIS

2a rd 300, to US 51 N, Millington

2 Smith Ave, Chelsea Ave, S Valero

1e I-240 E

1d c b US 51, Danny Thomas Blvd, N Ronald McDonald House, St Jude Research Ctr, S Exxon, KFC

1a 2nd St(from wb), downtown, S Crowne Plaza, Holiday Inn, Sheraton, Conv Ctr

1 Riverside Dr, Front St(from eb), Memphis, S Comfort Inn, Courtyard, Moxy, SpringHill Suites, Conv Ctr, Riverfront, Visitors Ctr

0mm Tennessee/Arkansas state line, Mississippi River

INTERSTATE 55

13mm Tennessee/Arkansas state line, Mississippi River

12c Delaware St, Memphis, W Super 8

12b Riverside Dr, downtown Memphis, E TN Welcome Ctr

12a E Crump Blvd(from nb), E Exxon, Mobil, Capt D's, KFC, Peppers Fish & Chicken, Taco Bell, Family$

11 McLemore Ave, Presidents Island, industrial area

10 S Parkway, E Marathon/dsl

9 Mallory Ave, industrial area

8 Horn Lake Rd(from sb)

7 US 61, 3rd St, E Exxon, Shell, Church's TX Chicken, Interstate BBQ, JJ's Fish & Chicken, Little Caesars Pizza, Lot A Burger, McDonald's, $General, AutoZone, Kroger, Roses, Walgreens, W MapCo, Marathon/dsl, Don Dons Wings, KFC, McDonald's, Subway, Rest Inn, Fuller SP, Indian Museum

6b a I-240

5b US 51 S, Elvis Presley Blvd, to Graceland, W BP/dsl, Dodge's/dsl, Exxon, Marathon, Shell/dsl, Baskin-Robbins, BJ's Wings, Burger King, Checker's, Exline Pizza, KFC, Krispy Kreme, Little Caesar's, McDonald's, Pep Boys, Piccadilly's, Subway, Taco Bell, Days Inn, Guesthouse at Graceland, Holiday Inn Express, Memory Lane Inn, Red Roof Inn, Super 7 Inn, $Tree, Advance Parts, ALDI, CVS, Family$, Graceland RV Park, [H], Marathon, Memphis Visitors Ctr, to Graceland, Walgreens

5a Brooks Rd, E Exxon, Mapco/dsl, Mobil, Burger King, Papa John's, Popeyes, Inn, Motel 6, Travelodge, Freightliner, Peterbilt

2b a TN 175, Shelby Dr, Whitehaven, E Exxon, Marathon/dsl, Qmart/dsl, Colonial Inn, W Exxon/dsl, Shell, Shell/dsl, Crumpy's Wings, Dixie Queen Burgers, McDonald's, Pizza Hut, Popeyes, Starbucks, $General, Family$, Kroger/gas, tire/auto repair, Toyota/Scion, Walgreens

0mm Tennessee/Mississippi state line

INTERSTATE 65

121.5mm Tennessee/Kentucky state line

121mm **full facilities, litter barrels, petwalk, vending, Welcome Ctr sb**

120 Highland Rd

119mm weigh/insp sta both lanes

117 TN 52, Portland, E Exxon/Godfather's/Quiznos/dsl, Shell/dsl, SureStay+, Bledsoe Cr SP(20mi), [H], W Shell/dsl, Budget Host, $General

116mm Red River

113mm Red River

112 TN 25, Cross Plains, E Shell/dsl/fireworks, $General, antiques, Bledsoe Cr SP(20mi), W Mapco/Subway/dsl

108 TN 76, White House, E Murphy USA/dsl, Nervous Charlie's/Shell/dsl, Shell, Speedway/dsl, A&W/KFC, Arby's, AutoZone, Burger King, Captain D's, China Spring, Cracker Barrel, DQ, Dunkin, Hardee's, Los Agaves, Los Jalapenos, McDonald's, Sonic, Subway, Taco Bell, Waffle House, Wendy's, Zaxby's, Comfort Inn, Hampton Inn,

CROSS PLAINS

INTERSTATE 65 Cont'd

MILLERSVILLE

108 Continued
Holiday Inn Express, Motel 6, Quality Inn, $Tree, Ace Hardware, AT&T, city park/playground, Kroger/Starbucks/gas, O'Reilly Parts, USPO, vet, Walgreens, Walmart/Subway, W Love's/Chesters/Godfathers Pizza/dsl/scales/24hr/@, Shell/dsl

104 rd 257, Bethel Rd, W Shell/dsl, Owl's Roost Camping

98 US 31 W, Millersville, E QT/dsl/scales, Shell/dsl, Subway, $General, auto repair, Grand Ol' RV Resort, W Marathon, Lagniappe Bayou Kitchen, Economy Inn, fireworks

97 rd 174, Long Hollow Pike, E BP/dsl, Exxon/7-11, Mapco, Arby's, Chef's Market Cafe, Cracker Barrel, Domino's, KFC, McDonald's, Papa Murphy's, Plaza Mexican, Quiznos, Subway, Taco Bell, Waffle House, Wendy's, Baymont Inn, Candlewood Suites, Courtyard, Days Inn, Hampton Inn, Holiday Inn Express, Quality Inn, Red Roof+, Somotel, TownePlace Suites, Wingate Inn, Kroger/dsl, USPO, Walgreens, W Shell/dsl, Buck's BBQ, DQ, Hardee's, Krystal, Liz's Kitchen, Poncho Villa Grill, Sonic, Starbucks, La Quinta, Motel 6, Advance Parts, Walgreens

96 Rivergate Pky, E Racetrac/dsl, Shell/dsl, Arby's, Bar-B-Cutie, Burger King, Checkers, Chicago Gyros, Chick Fish, Chick-fil-A, Chili's, Chipotle, ChuckeCheese, CiCi's, Cookout, Domino's, Fazoli's, HoneyBaked Ham, Hooters, IHOP, Jersey Mike's, Jets Pizza, Jimmy John's, Krispy Kreme, Las Palmas Mexican, Longhorn Steaks, McDonald's, O'Charley's, Outback Steaks, Panda Express, Panera Bread, Pollo Campero, Popeyes, Red Lobster, Sir Pizza, Sonic, Starbucks, Steak'n Shake, Subway, Sushi Kingdom, Taco Bell, TGI Friday's, Wendy's, Whataburger, Zaxby's, Best Value Inn, Comfort Suites, Country Inn Suites, Executive Inn, Rodeway Inn, WoodSpring Suites, $General, $Tree, $Tree, AT&T, Best Buy, Big Lots, Books-A-Million, Buick/GMC, CarMax, Chevrolet, Chrysler/Dodge/Jeep, Dick's, Dillard's, Discount Tire, Firestone/auto, Harley-Davidson, Hobby Lobby, Home Depot, H(2mi), JC Penney, Kia, Lowe's, mall, Midas, Nissan, O'Reilly Parts, Office Depot, Old Navy, PepBoys, PetSmart, Target, TJ Maxx, U-Haul, URGENT CARE, Verizon, VW, Walgreens, Walmart/Subway/gas, W Marathon, Olive Garden

95 TN 386, Vietnam Veterans Blvd(from nb)

92 rd 45, Old Hickory Blvd, E to Old Hickory Dam

90b TN 155 E, Briley Pkwy, E to Opryland

90a US 31W, US 41, Dickerson Pike, E Citgo/dsl, Exxon/7-11/dsl, Mapco/dsl, Shell, Arby's, Capt D's, Chicago Gyros, Church's TX Chicken, Domino's, Jay's Rest., KFC, Little Caesar's, McDonald's, Nashville Gyros, Taco Bell, Waffle House, Wendy's, Days Inn, EconoLodge, Sleep Inn, Super 8, $General, Advance Parts, AutoZone, O'Reilly Parts, Walgreens, W Murphy USA/dsl, $Tree, H, Lowe's, Walmart

88b a I-24, W to Clarksville, E to Nashville

87b a US 431, Trinity Lane, E Love's/Subway/dsl/scales/24hr, Krystal, Sonic, Cumberland Inn, Delux Inn, Piggly Wiggly, W 7-11, Exxon, Marathon, Shell/dsl, Victory/dsl, Daddys Pizza, Jack's BBQ, McDonald's, Subway, Taco Bell, Best Value Inn, Best Western, Halmark Inn, King's Inn, Red Roof Inn, Regency Inn, $General, auto repair

86 I-24 E, to I-40 E, to Memphis

86mm Cumberland River

85 US 41A, 8th Ave, E Sugaboat's, Kroger/gas, to st capitol, W Exxon, Arby's, Chick-fil-A, Chipotle, Dunkin, Jersey Mike's, McDonald's, Starbucks, Subway, Taco Bell, Wendy's, Wingstop, Fairfield Inn, Holiday Inn Express,

KNOXVILLE

85 Continued
Home2 Suites, Millennium Hotel, SpringHill Suites, Cadillac, Honda, Lexus

84b a I-40, E to Knoxville, W to Memphis

209[I-40] US 70, Charlotte Ave, Church St, E Exxon, McDonald's, Sheraton, Firestone, W Exxon, Shell/dsl, Burger King, Jack Cawthon's BBQ, Krystal, Sonic, Subway, White Castle, Comfort Inn, Hilton Garden, Hyundai, URGENT CARE, Walgreens

82b a I-40, W to Memphis, E to Nashville

81 Wedgewood Ave, W BP, Exxon, Shell/dsl, Burger King, Subway, U-Haul

80 I-440, to Memphis, Knoxville

79 Armory Dr, E Shell, Applebee's, Chipotle, Firehouse Subs, Logan's Roadhouse, Panda Express, Panera Bread, Rafferty's, Subway, Taco Bell, Thai Kitchen, Wendy's, BMW, CarMax, Home Depot, Michael's, PetSmart, Ross, TJ Maxx, Walmart

78b a rd 255, Harding Place, E Mapco/Subway, Pure, Shell, Cracker Barrel, Waffle House, Candlewood Suites, La Quinta, Red Roof+, auto repair, CVS Drug, URGENT CARE

74 TN 254, Old Hickory Blvd, to Brentwood, E Coldstone, Fulin's Asian, Longhorn Steaks, Panera Bread, Waffle House, Best Western, Holiday Inn Express, Hyatt Place, Sheraton, Target/Tesla EVC, W Gulf, Mapco, Shell/dsl, Twice Daily/dsl, Blaze Pizza, Bruegger's Bagels, Chick-fil-A, Chili's, Chipotle Mexican, Chuys, Corky's BBQ, Duck Donuts, Dunkin, First Watch, Five Guys, Jason's Deli, Jimmy John's, Marriott, McAlister's Deli, McDonald's, Moe's SW Grill, Papa John's, Pei Wei, Starbucks, Starbucks, Subway, Taco Bell, Taziki 's Cafe, Uncle Julio's, Wendy's, Comfort Inn, Courtyard, Extended Stay (2), Extended Stay America, Hampton Inn, Hilton, Hilton Garden, Mainstay Suites, Cadillac, CVS Drug, Firestone/auto, Fresh Mkt Foods, Kroger, Land Rover, PetCo, Publix, REI, TJ Maxx, Walgreens

71 TN 253, Concord Rd, to Brentwood

69 rd 441, Moores Lane, Galleria Blvd, E MapCo/dsl, Shell, Amerigo Italian, Baskin-Robbins, Cheddar's, Dicky's BBQ, Dunkin, Fuji Japanese, Mexicali Grill, Outback Steaks, Shogun Japanese, Sonic, Sportsman's Grille, Starbucks, Extended Stay America, Hilton Garden, Holiday Inn, Holiday Inn Express, Hyatt Place, Acura/Lexus, Christian Bros. Auto, CVS Drug, Home Depot, Michael's, PetSmart, Publix, vet, Walgreens, W BP, Shell/dsl, Buca Italian, Burger King, CA Pizza Kitchen, Cheesecake Factory, Chili's, Cracker Barrel, Fairfield Inn, HoneyBaked Ham, Honeysuckle Grill, J Alexander's Rest., Krispy Kreme, McDonald's, Millers Ale House, Olive Garden, Pizza Hut/Taco Bell, Red Lobster, Schlotzsky's, Stoney River Steaks, Twin Peaks, Sleep Inn, $Tree, Barnes&Noble, Belk, Best Buy, Costco/gas, Dillard's, Discount Tire, Firestone/auto, JC Penney, Macy's, mall, NTB, Old Navy, Ross, Target, U-Haul

68b a Cool Springs Blvd, E Jersey Mike's, Noodles&Co, Swankys Tacos, Tupelo Honey Cafe, Courtyard, Embassy Suites, Marriott, Residence Inn, W Exxon, Shell, BoneFish Grill, Burger Up, Canton Buffet, Carrabba's, Chick-fil-A, Chipotle, ChuckeCheese, Chuy's Mexican, Five Guys, Genghis Grill, Greek Cafe, J Christopher's, Jack-in-the-Box, Jason's Deli, Jersey Mike's, Jim 'N Nicks BBQ, Jimmy John's, Jonathan's Grille, Las Palmas, McAlister's Deli, McDonald's, Moe's SW Grill, Newk's Eatery, Old Chicago, Panda Express, Panera Bread, Papa John's, PF Chang's, Pie Five Pizza, Pizza Hut, Pollo Tropical, Saladworks, Sperry's, Starbucks, Subway, TGIFriday's, Wendy's, Which Wich, Wild Wing Cafe,

TN

INTERSTATE 65 Cont'd

68b a	Continued Zoe's Kitchen, ALoft, Country Inn&Suites, Hampton Inn, TownePlace Suites, Acura, AT&T, Dick's, GNC, Harley-Davidson, Jo-Ann Fabrics, Kroger, Lowe's, Marshall's, Mazda, Office Depot, Sam's Club/gas, Staples, TJ Maxx, to Galleria Mall, Verizon, vet, Walgreens
67	McEwen Dr, E Homewood Suites, W Blue Coast Burrito, Brick Top's, Buffalo Wild Wings, Culver's, Firehouse Subs, Granite City, Jamba Juice, Little Caesar's, Marco's Pizza, Pei Wei, Sonic, Subway, Tazikis Mediterranean Cafe, Drury Inn, CarMax, CVS, Kohl's, Petco, Toyota/Scion, Walmart, Whole Food Mkt
65	TN 96, to Murfreesboro, Franklin, E Mapco, Shell/Krystal, Cracker Barrel, Sonic, Steak'n Shake, Baymont Inn, Best Value Inn, Clarion, Comfort Inn, Days Inn, La Quinta, Buick/GMC, Chevrolet, Honda, H, Kia, O'Reilly Parts, Subaru, URGENT CARE, Volvo, Walgreens, W Chick-fil-A, Mapco/dsl, Shell, Shell/dsl, Arby's, Bar-B-Cutie, Cinco De Mayo, Don Pepe's, Einstein Bros Bagels, Franklin Chophouse, Hardee's, Jersey Mike's, Jimmy Johns, KFC, McDonald's, Nashville Pizza, O'Charley's, Pancho's Mexican, Papa John's, Smoothie King, Starbucks, Taco Bell, Waffle House, Wendy's, Whitts BBQ, Zaxby's, Best Western, Candlewood Suites, Quality Inn, $Tree, ALDI, BigLots, Chrysler/Dodge/Jeep, Discount Tire, Fiat, Ford/Lincoln, Hobby Lobby, Home Depot, Kroger/gas, Publix/gas, Sprouts Mkt, Verizon, vet, Walgreens
64mm	Harpeth River
61	TN 248, Peytonsville Rd, to Spring Hill, E Shell, TA/BP/Country Pride/dsl/scales/24hr/@, Nashville RV, W Shell/dsl, Chick-fil-A, Edley's BBQ, McDonald's, Panda Express, Sonic, Hampton Inn, Holiday Inn Express, Residence Inn, Publix
59b a	I-840, Memphis, Knoxville
58mm	W Harpeth River
53	TN 396, Saturn Pkwy, Spring Hill, to TN Scenic Pkwy, Columbia
48mm	truck insp/weigh sta nb
46	US 412, TN 99, to Columbia, Chapel Hill, E Love's/Arbys/dsl/scales/24hr, Marathon/dsl, Sleep Inn, Camper's RV Park, Harley-Davidson, Henry Horton SP, W Exxon, Shell, Stan's/Country Store, Burger King, Cracker Barrel, McDonald's, Waffle House, Candlewood Suites, Comfort Suites, Fairfield Inn, Hampton Inn, Holiday Inn Express, Red Roof Ihn, Super 8, H
40.5mm	Duck River
37	TN 50, to Columbia, Lewisburg, W BP/dsl, to Polk Home
32	rd 373, to Lewisburg, Mooresville, E BP/dsl
27	rd 129, to Lynnville, Cornersville, E Stoney Creek RV Park
25mm	parking area sb
24mm	parking area nb
22	US 31A, to Pulaski, E BP, McDonald's, Subway, EconoLodge, W Pilot/dsl/scales/24hr, Shell/dsl
14	US 64, to Pulaski, E Exxon/dsl, Shell/dsl, Nicks Grill, Motel 6
6	rd 273, Bryson, E Chevron/dsl, Rodeway Inn
5mm	weigh sta nb
4mm	Elk River
3mm	**full facilities, info, litter barrels, petwalk, Welcome Ctr nb**
1	US 31, rd 7, Ardmore, Ardmore, E Chevron/dsl, Exxon/Huddle House/dsl
0mm	Tennessee/Alabama state line

FRANKLIN

CHAPEL HILL

BRYSON

INTERSTATE 75

Exit #	Services
161.5mm	Tennessee/Kentucky state line
161mm	**full facilities, litter barrels, petwalk, vending, Welcome Ctr sb**
160	US 25W, Jellico, E BP/dsl, Sunoco/dsl, W Exxon/dsl, Shell/Arby's/dsl, McDonald's, Subway, Days Inn, fireworks, H, to Indian Mtn SP
156	Rarity Mtn Rd
144	Stinking Creek Rd, E Ride Royal Blue Camping(4mi)
141	TN 63, to Royal Blue, Huntsville, E Shell/dsl, El Rey Azteca, W Pilot/Subway/dsl/scales/24hr, Shell/dsl, TA/Shell/Popeyes/dsl/@, Hardee's, Smokin' Butts BBQ, Comfort Inn, to Big South Fork NRA
134	US 25W, TN 63, Caryville, E Shell, Hibachi Express, Waffle House, Hampton Inn, Holiday Inn Express, Red Roof Inn, Super 8, $General, to Cove Lake SP, to Cumberland Gap NHP, W Exxon/dsl, Scotty's Hamburgers, Shoney's, Tennessee Motel, USPO
129	US 25W S, Lake City, W BP/dsl, Caseys/dsl, Marathon/Sonic/dsl, Shell/dsl, Cracker Barrel, Glenn's Pizza, KFC/Taco Bell, La Fiesta Mexican, McDonald's, Subway, Econolodge, Executive Inn, Rocky Top Inn, $General, Family$, same as 128
128	US 441, to Lake City, E Sunoco, Mtn Lake Marina Camping(4mi), W BP/dsl, Marathon, Weigel's/dsl, Little Caesars, $General, Advance Parts, Family$, same as 129
126mm	Clinch River
122	TN 61, Bethel, Norris, E Mobil/dsl, Wiegel's/dsl, Shoney's, KOA, Museum of Appalachia, Toyota/Scion, W Exxon/Dunkin/Subway/dsl, Git'n Go/dsl, Phillips 66/dsl, Shell/dsl, Speedway, Arby's, Bojangles, Firehouse Subs, Golden Girls Rest., Gondolier Italian, Hardee's, Harrison's Grill, Krystal, McDonald's, Penn Sta Subs, Petro's Chili, Sonic, Taco Bell, Waffle House, Wendy's, Zaxby's, Baymont Inn, Fairfield Inn, Hampton Inn, Holiday Inn Express, Quality Inn, Red Roof Inn, Super 8, $Tree, Ford, Verizon, Walgreens, Walmart/McDonald's
117	rd 170, Racoon Valley Rd, E ONE9/dsl/scales/24hr, $General, W Valley Inn, Racoon Valley RV Park, Volunteer RV Park
112	rd 131, Emory Rd, to Powell, E Casey's/dsl, Shell/Buddy's BBQ/dsl, Arby's, Bruster's, Burger King, Chick-fil-A, Cook Out, Firehouse Subs, Five Guys, Krystal, McDonald's, Petro's Cafe, Ruby Tuesday, Starbucks, Steak'n Shake, Taco Bell, Wendy's, Zaxby's, Comfort Inn, Holiday Inn Express, La Quinta, $Tree, CVS Drug, H, Ingles/Starbucks/gas, O'Reilly Parts, Rigg's Drug, W Shell/dsl, Weigel's/dsl, Aubrey's Rest., Freddy's, Shoney's, Waffle House, Super 8, Kroger/dsl
110	Callahan Dr, E Weigel's/dsl, Asian Cafe, Elidios's Pizza, Baymont Inn, Days Inn, Honda, W Scottish Inn, Chrysler/Dodge/Jeep, Kia, Mack/Volvo
108	Merchants Dr, E BP/dsl, Citgo, Delta/Mapco/dsl, Mobil/dsl, Pilot/dsl, Anafres Grill, Applebee's, Cracker Barrel, El Chico, Hooters, Monterrey Mexican, Pizza Hut, Starbucks, Waffle House, Best Western, Clarion, Comfort Suites, Hampton Inn, Mainstay Suites, Quality Inn, Red Roof Inn, Rodeway Inn, Tru, Ingles, Valvoline, W Exxon/dsl, Goodstop/Domino's/dsl, Austin's Steaks, Burger King, Capt D's, Dunkin, IHOP, Little Caesars, McDonald's, Nixon's Deli, Outback Steaks, Red Lobster, Subway, Taco Bell, Best Value Inn, EconoLodge, Fairfield Inn, Holiday Inn, Motel 6, Super 8, CVS Drug, Walgreens
107	I-640 & I-75

CARYVILLE

= gas = food = lodging = other = rest stop

INTERSTATE 75 Cont'd

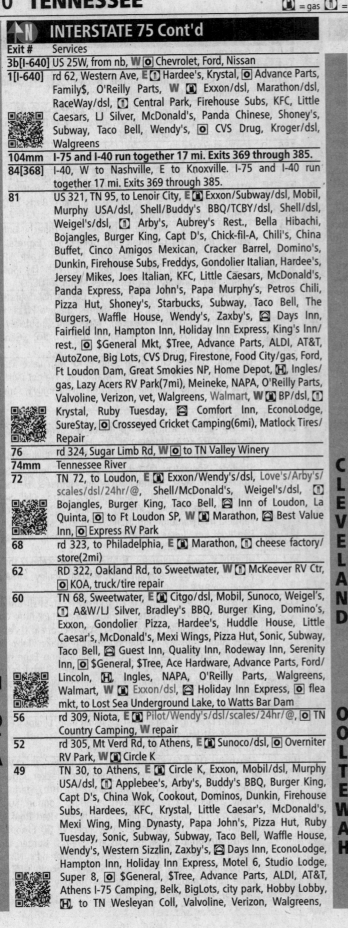

Exit #	Services
3b[I-640]	US 25W, from nb, W Chevrolet, Ford, Nissan
1[I-640]	rd 62, Western Ave, E Hardee's, Krystal, Advance Parts, Family$, O'Reilly Parts, W Exxon/dsl, Marathon/dsl, RaceWay/dsl, Central Park, Firehouse Subs, KFC, Little Caesars, LJ Silver, McDonald's, Panda Chinese, Shoney's, Subway, Taco Bell, Wendy's, CVS Drug, Kroger/dsl, Walgreens
104mm	**I-75 and I-40 run together 17 mi. Exits 369 through 385.**
84[368]	I-40, W to Nashville, E to Knoxville. I-75 and I-40 run together 17 mi. Exits 369 through 385.
81	US 321, TN 95, to Lenoir City, E Exxon/Subway/dsl, Mobil, Murphy USA/dsl, Shell/Buddy's BBQ/TCBY/dsl, Shell/dsl, Weigel's/dsl, Arby's, Aubrey's Rest., Bella Hibachi, Bojangles, Burger King, Capt D's, Chick-fil-A, Chili's, China Buffet, Cinco Amigos Mexican, Cracker Barrel, Domino's, Dunkin, Firehouse Subs, Freddys, Gondolier Italian, Hardee's, Jersey Mikes, Joes Italian, KFC, Little Caesars, McDonald's, Panda Express, Papa John's, Papa Murphy's, Petros Chili, Pizza Hut, Shoney's, Starbucks, Subway, Taco Bell, The Burgers, Waffle House, Wendy's, Zaxby's, Days Inn, Fairfield Inn, Hampton Inn, Holiday Inn Express, King's Inn/rest., $General Mkt, $Tree, Advance Parts, ALDI, AT&T, AutoZone, Big Lots, CVS Drug, Firestone, Food City/gas, Ford, Ft Loudon Dam, Great Smokies NP, Home Depot, H, Ingles/gas, Lazy Acers RV Park(7mi), Meineke, NAPA, O'Reilly Parts, Valvoline, Verizon, vet, Walgreens, Walmart, W BP/dsl, Krystal, Ruby Tuesday, Comfort Inn, EconoLodge, SureStay, Crosseyed Cricket Camping(6mi), Matlock Tires/Repair
76	rd 324, Sugar Limb Rd, W to TN Valley Winery
74mm	Tennessee River
72	TN 72, to Loudon, E Exxon/Wendy's/dsl, Love's/Arby's/scales/dsl/24hr/@, Shell/McDonald's, Weigel's/dsl, Bojangles, Burger King, Taco Bell, Inn of Loudon, La Quinta, to Ft Loudon SP, W Marathon, Best Value Inn, Express RV Park
68	rd 323, to Philadelphia, E Marathon, cheese factory/store(2mi)
62	RD 322, Oakland Rd, to Sweetwater, W McKeever RV Ctr, KOA, truck/tire repair
60	TN 68, Sweetwater, E Citgo/dsl, Mobil, Sunoco, Weigel's, A&W/LJ Silver, Bradley's BBQ, Burger King, Domino's, Exxon, Gondolier Pizza, Hardee's, Huddle House, Little Caesar's, McDonald's, Mexi Wings, Pizza Hut, Sonic, Subway, Taco Bell, Guest Inn, Quality Inn, Rodeway Inn, Serenity Inn, $General, $Tree, Ace Hardware, Advance Parts, Ford/Lincoln, H, Ingles, NAPA, O'Reilly Parts, Walgreens, Walmart, W Exxon/dsl, Holiday Inn Express, flea mkt, to Lost Sea Underground Lake, to Watts Bar Dam
56	rd 309, Niota, E Pilot/Wendy's/dsl/scales/24hr/@, TN Country Camping, W repair
52	rd 305, Mt Verd Rd, to Athens, E Sunoco/dsl, Overniter RV Park, W Circle K
49	TN 30, to Athens, E Circle K, Exxon, Mobil/dsl, Murphy USA/dsl, Applebee's, Arby's, Buddy's BBQ, Burger King, Capt D's, China Wok, Cookout, Dominos, Dunkin, Firehouse Subs, Hardees, KFC, Krystal, Little Caesar's, McDonald's, Mexi Wing, Ming Dynasty, Papa John's, Pizza Hut, Ruby Tuesday, Sonic, Subway, Subway, Taco Bell, Waffle House, Wendy's, Western Sizzlin, Zaxby's, Days Inn, EconoLodge, Hampton Inn, Holiday Inn Express, Motel 6, Studio Lodge, Super 8, $General, $Tree, Advance Parts, ALDI, AT&T, Athens I-75 Camping, Belk, BigLots, city park, Hobby Lobby, H, to TN Wesleyan Coll, Valvoline, Verizon, Walgreens,
49	Continued Walmart/Subway, W Mobil/dsl, Speedway/Speedy's Cafe/dsl, Weigels, Cracker Barrel, Best Value Inn, Comfort Inn, Fairfield Inn
45mm	rest area both lanes, **full facilities, litter barrels, petwalk, vending**
42	rd 39, Riceville Rd, E BP/dsl, Relax Inn, Rice Inn(2mi), $General(2mi)
36	rd 163, to Calhoun, E to Hiwassee/Ocoee River SP
35mm	Hiwassee River
33	rd 308, to Charleston, E Exxon/dsl, Hardee's, W Love's/McDonald's/Subway/dsl/scales/24hr/@
27	Paul Huff Pkwy, E Murphy USA, Shell/dsl, Applebee's, Buddy's BBQ, Buffalo Wild Wings, Capt D's, Cheddars, Chicken Salad Chick, Chili's, CiCi's, Crumbl Cookies, Crumbl Cookies, DQ, Fazoli's, Five Guys, Freddy's Steakburgers, IHOP, Juicy Seafood, Little Caesar's, Longhorn Steaks, Marco's Pizza, McCalisters Deli, McDonald's, O'Charley's, Olive Garden, Outback Steaks, Panda Express, Panera Bread, Popeyes, Six Happiness, Sonic, Starbucks, Steak'n Shake, Subway, Taco Bell, Tropical Smoothie, Wendy's, Zaxby's, Baymont Inn, Holiday Inn Express, $Tree, Advance Parts, ALDI, auto repair/tires, AutoZone, Belk, Buick/Cadillac/GMC, CVS Drug, Discount Tire, Food Lion, Hobby Lobby, Home Depot, Lowe's, Michaels, NTB, PetCo, PetSmart, Publix, Staples, TJ Maxx, URGENT CARE, Verizon, Walgreens, Walmart, W Exxon/dsl, Orbit/dsl, Shell/Subway/EVC, Burger King, Chick-fil-A, Fulin's Asian, Hardee's, Honeybaked Ham, Shane's Ribshack, Taco Bell, Waffle House, Wendy's, Clarion, Classic Suites, Hampton Inn, Quality Inn, Red Roof Inn, Royal Inn, Super 8, TownePlace Suites, AT&T, Books-A-Million, Kohl's, Ross, Target/Starbucks
25	TN 60, Cleveland, E RaceTrac/dsl, Shell/dsl, Sunoco/dsl, Valero/dsl, Arby's, Bojangles, Burger King, Checkers, City Cafe Diner, Cook Out, Cracker Barrel, Dunkin', Hardee's, KFC, Las Margaritas, McDonald's, Old Fort Rest., Papa John's, Pizza Hut, Sonic, Subway, Taco Bell, Waffle House, Wendy's, Zaxby's, Days Inn, Douglas Inn, Fairfield Inn, Heritage Inn, Knights Inn, Motel 6, $General, $Tree, Ace Hardware, BigLots, Cherokee Drug, H, NAPA, to Lee Coll, vet, W Mapco, Best Western+, La Quinta, Mountain View, Mtn View Inn, Wingate/EVC
23mm	truck/weigh sta nb
20	US 64 byp, to Cleveland, E FuelMart, Ford, Honda, Kia, W Exxon/dsl, Pilot/McDonald's/Subway/dsl/scales/24hr, Taco Bell, fireworks, KOA(1mi), Nissan, Toyota
16mm	scenic view sb
13mm	truck/weigh sta, litter barrels sb
11	US 11 N, US 64 E, Ooltewah, E BP/Circle K, EVC, Mapco, Marathon/dsl, Murphy USA/EVC/dsl, Arby's, Bojangles, Burger King, Chick-fil-A, China Rose, Cracker Barrel, El Cortes Mexican, Firehouse Subs, Georgi's Pizzeria, Hardee's, Jersey Mike's, Little Caesar's, Local Goat Rest., McDonald's, Panda Express, Pizza Hut, Salsarita's Mexican, Shane's BBQ, Sonic, Starbucks, Subway, Taco Bell, Wendy's, Zaxby's, Hampton Inn, Holiday Inn Express, Springhill Suites, stayAPT Suites, $General, ALDI, antiques, auto repair, AutoZone, Food City/gas, GNC, Michelin, O'Reilly Parts, Verizon, vet, Walgreens, Walmart/Subway, W BP/Circle K/Dunkin', Exxon/7-11/dsl, Baskin-Robbins, Beef'o Brady's, Dunkin, KFC, Marco's Pizza, Waffle House, Super 8, Publix, Tire Discounters, to Harrison Bay SP
9	TN 317, Apison Pk, Volkswagen Dr, E Shell
7b a	US 11, US 64, Lee Hwy, E Exxon/dsl, W BP, EVC, Mobil,

NIOTA

CLEVELAND

OOLTEWAH

TN

INTERSTATE 75 Cont'd

7b a Continued
Speedway/Speedy's Cafe/dsl, [food] City Cafe, Subway, Taco Bell, Waffle House, Wendy's, [lodging] Inn, Best Inn, Best Value Inn, Best Western, EconoLodge, Motel 6, Woodspring Suites, [other] Denton's Repair, Harley-Davidson, Jaguar/Land Rover/Porsche/Infiniti

5 Shallowford Rd, same as 4a, E [food] Acropolis Grill, Arby's, Chuy's, CiCi's, Forbidden City Chinese, J. Alexanders, Krystal, McAlister's Deli, Mellow Mushroom Pizza, Miller's Alehouse, Newk's Eatery, Olive Garden, Outback Steaks, Panda Express, Pier 88, Red Lobster, Ruth's Chris Steaks, Smokey Bones BBQ, Starbucks, Steak'n Shake, Taco Bell, Zaxby's, [lodging] Embassy Suites, Sonesta, Studio 6, Wingate Inn, [other] Best Buy, Firestone/auto, Fresh Mkt, Hobby Lobby, Home Depot, Lowe's, Michaels, Office Depot, Old Navy, Petco, PetSmart, Publix, REI, Target, U-Haul, Walgreens, World Mkt, W [gas] BP, Citgo/dsl, Exxon/dsl, Shell, Speedway/Speedy's Cafe/dsl, [food] Cracker Barrel, Fazoli's, Firebox Grill, Fuji Steaks, Mariscos Mexican, O'Charley's, Papa John's, Sonic, TX Roadhouse, Waffle House, Wendy's, [lodging] Baymont Inn, Comfort Inn, Days Inn, DoubleTree, Fairfield Inn, Hilton Garden, Home2 Suites, Homewood Suites, La Quinta, MainStay Suites, Microtel, Quality Inn, Red Roof Inn, Residence Inn, Sleep Inn, Staybridge Suites, Super 8, SureStay+, SureStay+, TownePlace Suites, Travelodge, Tru Hilton, [other] CarMax, CVS Drug, Food City, Goodyear/auto, [H], U of TN/Chatt

4a (from nb)Hamilton Place Blvd, same as 5, E [gas] Shell, Tesla EVC, [food] Abuelo's, Bad Daddy's Burgers, Big River Grille, BoneFish Grill, Capt D's, Carrabba's, Cheddar's, Cheesecake Factory, Chick-fil-A, Chili's, DQ, Duck Donuts, Firebirds, Firehouse Subs, Five Guys, Hana Steak, Honeybaked Ham, Jason's Deli, Jimmy John's, Jim'n Nick's BBQ, LongHorn Steaks, McDonald's, Moe's SW Grill, Panera Bread, PF Chang's, Popeyes, Red Robin, Salsarita's Mexican, Smoothie King, Starbucks, Sticky Fingers BBQ, Taziki's Cafe, Volcano Korean BBQ, [lodging] Hampton Inn, InTown Suites, [other] $Tree, ALDI, AT&T, auto repair, Barnes&Noble, Belk, Big Lots, JC Penney, Kohl's, Marshall's, Michael's, Pepboys, Ross, Target, TJ Maxx, Trader Joe's, Verizon, Walmart Supercenter, Whole Foods Mrkt, World Mkt

4 TN 153, Chickamauga Dam Rd, airport

3b a TN 320, Brainerd Rd, E [gas] Circle K/dsl, [food] Baskin-Robbins, W [other] BMW

2 I-24 W, to I-59, to Chattanooga, Lookout Mtn

1.5mm **Welcome Ctr nb, full [handicapped] facilities, [picnic], litter barrels, vending, petwalk, [phone]**

1b a US 41, Ringgold Rd, to Chattanooga, E [gas] Circle K/dsl, Shell/dsl, [food] Buddy's BBQ, Chick-fil-A, Dos Bros Mexican, DQ, Jonathan's Grille, Starbucks, Wendy's, [lodging] Baymont, Best Western+, EconoLodge, Hampton Inn, La Quinta, Motel 6, [other] Bass Pro Shops, Family$, fireworks, W [gas] Citgo/dsl, Exxon/dsl, Mapco/dsl, Valero/dsl, VP Racing Fuels, [food] Apna Kitchen, Arby's, Baskin-Robbins, Burger King, Champy's, Checkers, Cracker Barrel, Don Juan Mexican, Dunkin', Firehouse Subs, Haiku Hibachi, Hardee's, Krystal, McDonald's, Pizza Hut, Popeyes, Portofino's Rest., Sonic, Subway, Taco Bell, Waffle House, [lodging] Budgetel, Fairfield Inn, Holiday Inn Express, Stay Express Inn, Super 8, [other] $General, Advance Parts, antiques, AutoZone, Family$, Food Lion, Honda, [H], O'Reilly Parts, U-Haul, Walgreens

0mm Tennessee/Georgia state line

INTERSTATE 81

75mm Tennessee/Virginia state line, **full [handicapped] facilities, info, litter barrels, petwalk, [phone], [picnic], vending, Welcome Ctr sb**

BLOUNTVILLE

74b a US 11W, to Bristol, Kingsport, E [lodging] Fairfield Inn, Hampton Inn, [other] [H], URGENT CARE, W [gas] Tesla EVC, Valero/dsl, Weigel's, [food] Aubrey's Rest., Bojangle's, Brusco's Pizza, Chick-fil-A, Chicken Salad Chick, Chipotle, Drake's Rest., Dunkin, Five Guys, Jersey Mike's, La Carreta, McDonald's, Moe's SW, Outback Steaks, Pal's Drive-Thru, Panda Express, Starbucks, Waffle House, Zaxby's, [other] Bass Pro Shops, Belk, Best Buy, CarMax, Dick's, GNC, Marshall's, Michael's, Old Navy, Verizon

69 TN 394, to Blountville, E [gas] BP/Subway/dsl, [food] Arby's, The Fox's Cafe, [other] Advance Parts, Bristol Int Speedway, fireworks, Lakeview RV Park(8mi), Shadrack Camping

66 rd 126, to Kingsport, Blountville, W [gas] Shell/dsl, [food] McDonald's

63 rd 357, E [gas] BP/dsl, Shell/Subway/dsl, [food] Cracker Barrel, Wendy's, [lodging] La Quinta, Sleep Inn, [other] Hamricks, Tri-Cities [airport], W [gas] Citgo/dsl, [lodging] Econolodge, [other] KOA, Rocky Top Camping

60mm Holston River

59 rd 36, to Johnson City, Kingsport, E [gas] Marathon/dsl, [lodging] Super 8, W [gas] Exxon/dsl, Marathon, Shell/Dunkin/dsl, Sunoco, [food] Arby's, Fisherman's Dock Rest., Hardee's, HotDog Hut, Jersey Mike's Subs, La Carreta Mexican, Little Caesar's, McDonald's, Moto Japanese, Pal's Drive-Thru, Perkins, Raffaele's Pizza, Sonic, Subway, Taco Bell, The Shack BBQ, Zachary's Steaks, [lodging] Comfort Inn, Motel 6, [other] $General, Advance Parts, auto repair, CVS Drug, Food City/gas, Ingles/deli, Murphy's Automotive, O'Reilly Parts, to Warrior's Path SP, URGENT CARE, USPO, Verizon, vet, Walgreens

57b a I-26

56 Tri-Cities Crossing

50 TN 93, Fall Branch, W [other] $General, auto auction, st patrol

44 Jearoldstown Rd, E [gas] Marathon

41mm **full [handicapped] facilities, litter barrels, petwalk, [phone], [picnic], [RS] sb, vending**

38mm **full [handicapped] facilities, litter barrels, petwalk, [phone], [picnic], [RS] nb, vending**

36 rd 172, to Baileyton, E [gas] Pilot/Subway/dsl/scales/24hr, W Marathon/dsl, Shell/Subway/dsl/24hr, TA/Papa John's/IHOP/dsl/scales/24hr/@, [food] Cuz's Drive Thru, Pizza+, [other] $General, antiques, Around Pond RV Park, Family$, KOA(2mi)

30 TN 70, to Greeneville, E [gas] Marathon/Stuckey's/dsl, W Love's/Arby's/dsl/scales/24hr/@, [other] $General

23 US 11E, to Greeneville, E [gas] Marathon/Wendy's, Mobil/Subway/dsl, [other] $General, Crockett SP, to Andrew Johnson HS, Tri-Am RV Ctr, W [gas] Exxon/DQ/dsl, Phillips 66/dsl/scales, [food] McDonald's, Pizza+, Taco Bell, [lodging] Quality Inn, Super 8, [other] truck repair

21mm weigh sta sb

15 rd 340, Fish Hatchery Rd

12 TN 160, to Morristown, E [gas] Phillips 66/dsl, W Gulf/dsl, [lodging] Days Inn(6mi), Hampton Inn(12mi), Holiday Inn Express(5mi), Super 8(5mi), [other] to Crockett Tavern HS

WHITE PINE

8 US 25E, to Morristown, E [food] Sonic(2mi), W [gas] Weigel's/dsl, [food] Bojangle's, Cracker Barrel, Fastop/Subway/dsl, Hardee's, McDonald's, [lodging] Best Western+, Hampton Inn, Parkway Inn, Super 8, [other] $General, to Cumberland Gap NHP

4 rd 341, White Pine, E [gas] Pilot/McDonald's/dsl/scales/24hr, [food] Subway, W [gas] Pilot/Dunkin/Wendy's/dsl/scales/24hr, Weigel's/dsl, [food] Taco Bell, [lodging] Econolodge, [other] to Panther Cr SP

2.5mm **full [handicapped] facilities, litter barrels, petwalk, [phone], [picnic], [RS] sb, vending**

1b a I-40, E to Asheville, W to Knoxville. I-81 begins/ends on I-40, exit 421.

INTERSTATE 640 (Knoxville)

TN

INTERSTATE 640 (Knoxville)

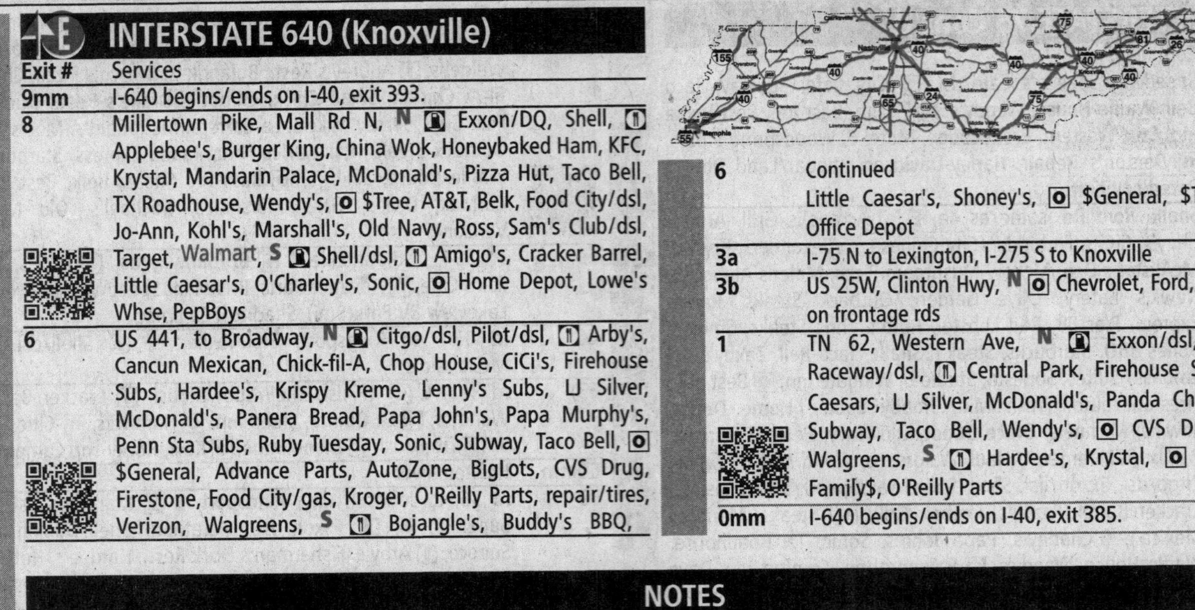

Exit #	Services
9mm	I-640 begins/ends on I-40, exit 393.
8	Millertown Pike, Mall Rd N, **N** [gas] Exxon/DQ, Shell, [food] Applebee's, Burger King, China Wok, Honeybaked Ham, KFC, Krystal, Mandarin Palace, McDonald's, Pizza Hut, Taco Bell, TX Roadhouse, Wendy's, [other] $Tree, AT&T, Belk, Food City/dsl, Jo-Ann, Kohl's, Marshall's, Old Navy, Ross, Sam's Club/dsl, Target, Walmart, **S** [gas] Shell/dsl, [food] Amigo's, Cracker Barrel, Little Caesar's, O'Charley's, Sonic, [other] Home Depot, Lowe's Whse, PepBoys
6	US 441, to Broadway, **N** [gas] Citgo/dsl, Pilot/dsl, [food] Arby's, Cancun Mexican, Chick-fil-A, Chop House, CiCi's, Firehouse Subs, Hardee's, Krispy Kreme, Lenny's Subs, LJ Silver, McDonald's, Panera Bread, Papa John's, Papa Murphy's, Penn Sta Subs, Ruby Tuesday, Sonic, Subway, Taco Bell, [other] $General, Advance Parts, AutoZone, BigLots, CVS Drug, Firestone, Food City/gas, Kroger, O'Reilly Parts, repair/tires, Verizon, Walgreens, **S** [food] Bojangle's, Buddy's BBQ,
6	Continued Little Caesar's, Shoney's, [other] $General, $Tree, Food City, Office Depot
3a	I-75 N to Lexington, I-275 S to Knoxville
3b	US 25W, Clinton Hwy, **N** [other] Chevrolet, Ford, Nissan, services on frontage rds
1	TN 62, Western Ave, **N** [gas] Exxon/dsl, Marathon/dsl, Raceway/dsl, [food] Central Park, Firehouse Subs, KFC, Little Caesars, LJ Silver, McDonald's, Panda Chinese, Shoney's, Subway, Taco Bell, Wendy's, [other] CVS Drug, Kroger/dsl, Walgreens, **S** [food] Hardee's, Krystal, [other] Advance Parts, Family$, O'Reilly Parts
0mm	I-640 begins/ends on I-40, exit 385.

NOTES

TEXAS

INTERSTATE 10

ORANGE

Exit #	Services
880.5mm	Texas/Louisiana state line, Sabine River
880	Sabine River Turnaround
879mm	**full facilities, litter barrels, petwalk, , , vending, Welcome Ctr wb**
878	US 90, Orange, **N** Gulf/dsl, airboat rides, RV Park, **S** Western Store
877	TX 87, 16th St, Orange, **N** Exxon/dsl, Valero/dsl, Pizza Hut, Subway, Tacos La Shula, Hampton Inn, Ace Hardware, Market Basket/deli, **S** Citgo/dsl, Get'n Go/dsl, Shell/dsl, Casa Ole, Chick-fil-A, Church's TX Chicken, DQ, Golden Chick, Little Caesars, Lucky Wok, Mama Martha Seafood, McDonald's, Popeyes, Sonic, Starbucks, Taco Bell, The Hut, $General, CVS Drug, Family$, HEB Foods, Kroger/dsl, Modica Tires, O'Reilly Parts, Superior Tire, Verizon, Walgreens
876	Adams Bayou, frontage rd, Adams Bayou, **N** 2 Amigos Mexican, Ten West Diner, Waffle House, Best Price Motel, Days Inn, Executive Inn, Hampton Inn, SureStay Hotel, Value Inn, Toyota, **S** Valero/Dickey's BBQ/dsl, Holiday Inn Express, same as 877
875	FM 3247, MLK Dr, **N** Exxon/dsl, Civil War Memorial, **S** Chrysler/Dodge/Jeep, H
874	US 90, Womack Rd, to Orange, **S** JB's BBQ, H
873	TX 62, TX 73, to Bridge City, **N** Chevron/dsl, Flying J/Denny's/dsl/LP/scales/24hr, Studio 6, Blue Beacon, Oak Leaf RV Park, truck repair, **S** Phillips 66/dsl, Pilot/Subway/Wendy's/dsl/scales/24hr, Valero/dsl, Bliss Box, Burger King, McDonald's, Sonic, Taco Bell, Waffle House, Waffle House, Whataburger, Best Western, Comfort Inn, La Quinta, truck repair
872	N Mimosa Ln, Jackson Dr, from wb
870	FM 1136
869	FM 1442, to Bridge City, **S** Exxon/dsl
867	frontage rd(from eb)
865	Doty Rd(from wb), frontage rd
864	FM 1132, FM 1135, **N** TX Star RV Park
862	Lakeside St, Timberlane Dr, **N** Conoco
861	FM 105, Vidor, **N** Chevron/dsl, Citgo/dsl, Conoco/dsl, Valero/Circle K/dsl, Bayou Cafe, Casa Ole, Domino's, DQ, Happy Donuts, HealthyWays Cafe, Hushpuppy Seafood, Jack-in-the-Box, Little Caesars, McDonald's, Ming's Buffet, Novrosky's Burgers, Popeyes, Waffle House, Wright's Bar-B-Q, AutoZone, CVS, Mktbasket Foods, Modica Bros Tires, O'Reilly Parts, Verizon, Walgreens, Walmart, **S** Citgo/dsl, Exxon/dsl, Burger King, Dunkin', Jingo Cajun, Pizza Hut, Sonic, Subway, Taco Bell, Whataburger, Woogie's, Best Western+, Holiday Inn Express, auto repair, Family$

ROSE CITY

Exit #	Services
860	Dewitt Rd, frontage rd, W Vidor, **S** Citgo, Exxon, Mobil/dsl, Burger King, Dunkin', Jingo Cajun, Pizza Hut, Sonic, Subway, Taco Bell, Whataburger, Woogie's, Best Western, Holiday Inn Express, Family$, repair
859	Bonner Turnaround(from eb), Asher Turnaround(from wb), **N** Boomtown RV Park, **S** Chevron/Gateway/dsl/24hr
858	Rose City
856	Old Hwy 90 (from eb), Rose City
855b	Magnolia St (from wb)
855a	US 90 bus, to downtown, Port of Beaumont
854	ML King Pkwy, Beaumont, **N** Chevron/dsl, Valero/dsl, Jack-in-the-Box, **S** Jet/dsl, Shamrock/dsl, McDonald's
853b	11th St, Al Basha, **N** Valero/dsl, Cafe Del Rio,

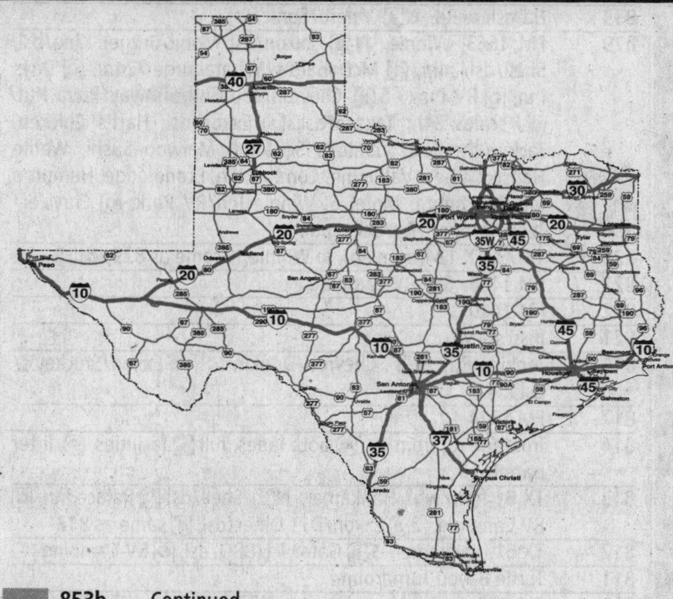

BEAUMONT

Exit #	Services
853b	Continued Red Lobster, Days Inn, EconoLodge, Grand Hotel, Holiday Inn, Merit Inn, Studio 6, Travel Inn, MktBasket, **S** Citgo/dsl, Shamrock, Checker's, Dunkin', Jack-in-the-Box, Luby's, HomeBridge Suites, Midtown Inn, H
853a	US 69 N, to Lufkin
852	Harrison Ave, Calder Ave, Beaumont, **N** Shell/dsl, Casa Ole Mexican, Casa Tapatia Mexican, Chili's, Frankie's Italian, Olive Garden, Saltgrass Steaks, Tony's BBQ, **S** Church's TX Chicken, McDonald's, Popeyes, La Quinta, Scottish Inn, H
851	US 90, College St, **N** Chevron/dsl, Exxon/Subway/dsl, Raceway/dsl, Carrabba's, Chicken Express, Floyd's Cajun Cafe, Golden Corral, Hooters, Lupe Tortilla, Outback Steaks, Tokyo Japanese, Waffle House, Howard Johnson, Quality Inn, Red Roof Inn, Super 8, Advance Parts, AutoZone, Harley-Davidson, Indian Motorcycles, O'Reilly Parts, URGENT CARE, Verizon, Volvo Trucks, **S** Exxon/dsl, Shell/dsl, Cane's, Chick-fil-A, DQ, IHOP, Jason's Deli, Sonic, Starbucks, Taco Bell, Wendy's, Whataburger, Wingstop, Best Value, Courtyard, Elegante Motel, Fairfield Inn, Regency Inn, Woodspring Suites, $Tree, AT&T, BMW, Chrysler/Dodge/Jeep, CVS Drug, Discount Tire, Firestone/auto, HEB Foods, Honda, H, Mercedes, Nissan, NTB, Office Depot, Sam's Club/gas, U-Haul, VW, Walgreens
850	wb only, same as 851
849	US 69 S, Washington Blvd, to Port Arthur, **N**

FANNETT

Exit #	Services
848	Walden Rd, **N** Shell/dsl, Pappadeaux Seafood, Sonic, Subway, Taco Bell, Avid Hotel, Comfort Suites, Days Inn, Holiday Inn/rest., La Quinta, USPO, **S** Chevron/dsl, Petro/Black Bear Diner/dsl/scales/24hr/@, Shell/dsl, Cheddar's, Chicken Shack, Cracker Barrel, Twin Peaks, Waffle House, Candlewood Suites, Executive Inn, Hampton Inn, Hilton Garden, Home2 Suites, Homewood Suites, Residence Inn, Super 8
847	Brooks Rd(from wb), (845 from eb), **S** Gulf Coast RV Resort
845	TX 364, **S** Hidden Lake RV Park
843	Smith Rd, **N** Love's/Godfather's/dsl/scales/24hr/@
838	FM 365, Fannett, **N** Shell/Dunkin'/dsl, Alligator Park/Rest., T&T RV Park, **S** $General

= gas = food = lodging = other = rest stop

INTERSTATE 10 Cont'd

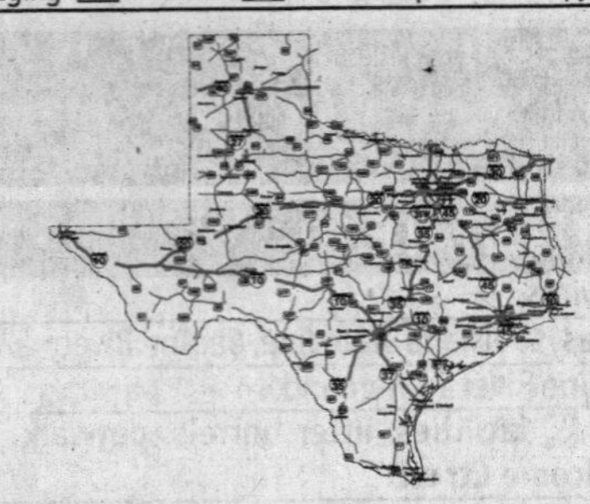

Exit #	Services
837.5mm	no services
833	Hamshire Rd, N Valero/Sonic/dsl
829	FM 1663, Winnie, N Exxon/dsl, Mobil/Burger King/dsl, Shell/dsl/24hr, McDonald's, Whataburger/24hr, Days Inn, RV Park, S Chevron/dsl, Gulf/Subway/Pizza Hut/dsl/scales/24hr, Texaco/dsl, Exxon/dsl, Hart's Chicken, Jack-in-the-Box, Juanita's Seafood, Maiwoo Sushi, Waffle House, Best Value Inn, Comfort Inn, Econolodge, Hampton Inn, La Quinta, Motel 6, Winnie Inn/RV Park, Chrysler/Jeep/Dodge, H, truck repair
828	TX 73, TX 124(from eb), to Winnie, S same as 829, H
827	FM 1406, S RV Camping
822	FM 1410
821	insp sta wb
819	Jenkins Rd, N Chevron/Dunkin'/dsl, S Exxon/Stuckey's/dsl
817	FM 1724
814	frontage rd, from eb, both lanes, full facilities, litter barrels
813	TX 61(from wb), Hankamer, N Shell/dsl, Palace Inn, RV Camping, S Exxon/DJ's Diner/dsl, same as 812
812	TX 61, Hankamer, S Gator Jct/BBQ/dsl, RV Camping
811	Turtle Bayou Turnaround
810	FM 563, to Anahuac, Liberty, N fireworks, S Chevron/dsl, Texaco/Jack-in-the-Box/dsl
807	to Wallisville, N RV Camping
805.5mm	Trinity River
804mm	Lost, Old Rivers
803	FM 565, Cove, Old River-Winfrey, N Shell/Church's TX Chicken/Subway/dsl/scales/24hr, Crawfish Hideaway, Lost River RV Park, S Chevron/Checkers/dsl, Valero/dsl
800	FM 3180, N Exxon/dsl, Burger King, Floyds Seafood, McDonald's, MOD Pizza, Popeyes, Red River Cantina, Starbucks, HEB/deli/gas, vet
799	TX 99, Grand Pkwy
797	(798 from wb) TX 146, 99 toll, Baytown, N Chevron/Subway/dsl/scales, Conoco/dsl/scales, Shell/dsl, DQ, Hacendado Mexican, Iguana Joe's Mexican, McDonald's, Tony's BBQ, Waffle House, Best Value, Motel 6, Super 8, L&R RV Park, Value RV Park, S RaceWay/7-11/dsl, Stripes/Taco Co/dsl, Texaco/dsl, Chick-fil-A, Chipotle, CK's Seafood, Domino's Pizza, Freddy's, Jack-in-the-Box, KFC/Taco Bell, Pho House, Sonic, Wendy's, Whataburger, Wing Boss, Magnuson Hotel, Houston East RV Park, vet, Walmart/Subway
796	frontage rd
795	Sjolander Rd, S Chevron/dsl
793	N Main St, S Valero/Dickey's BBQ/dsl/24hr
792	Garth Rd, N Chevron/dsl, Circle K, Chicken Express, Cracker Barrel, Denny's, Jack-in-the-Box, Red Lobster, Shipley Donuts, Sonic, Starbucks, Subway, Tuscany Italian, Waffle House, Whataburger, Comfort Suites, Days Inn, Extended Stay/EVC, Hampton Inn, Hilton Garden, Holiday Inn Express, Home2 Suites, La Quinta, Motel 6, Regency Inn, SpringHill Suites, Staybridge Suites, Buick/GMC, Chrysler/Jeep/Dodge, Honda, Hyundai, Kia, Nissan, O'Reilly Parts, Toyota, Walgreens, S Exxon/dsl, Shell/dsl, Buffalo Wild Wings, Carino's Italian, Chili's, DQ, Firehouse Subs, Hooters, McDonald's, Olive Garden, Outback Steaks, Panda Express, Panera Bread, Pizza Hut, Pizza Hut/Taco Bell, Popeyes, Salata, Subway, TX Roadhouse, Wendy's, Palace Inn, Quality Inn, Scottish Inn, $General, AT&T, H, Kohl's/EVC, Macy's, Michael's, Tuesday Morning, Verizon
791	John Martin Rd, N Exxon/7-11/Chick-fil-A/dsl,
791	Continued Chevrolet/Buick/GMC, Hyundai, S Buc-ee's/dsl, Cheddar's, Mambo Seafood, Saltgrass Steaks, Best Western+, Woodspring Suites, Cadillac/Chevrolet, Ford
790	Ellis School Rd, N Super 8
789	Thompson Rd, N Love's/McDonald's/dsl/scales/24hr/@ Super 8, S Flying J/Denny's/dsl/scales/24hr/@ TA/Country Pride/dsl/scales/24hr/@ Blue Beacon, Truck Lube
788.5mm	**full facilities, litter barrels, petwalk, [ ], [ ], [ ] eb**
788	sp 330(from eb), to Baytown
787	sp 330, Crosby-Lynchburg Rd, to Highlands, N Exxon/Domino's/dsl, RV Camping(1mi), S Sunoco/dsl, 4 Corners BBQ, to San Jacinto SP
786.5mm	San Jacinto River
786	Monmouth Dr
785	Magnolia Ave, to Channelview, N Shell/dsl/scales, S Exxon/grill/truck parts/dsl, truckwash
784	Cedar Lane, Bayou Dr, N Valero/dsl, Birrieria Mexican, Red Roof Inn, Relax Inn
783	Sheldon Rd, N Chevron/dsl, Shell/dsl, Valero/dsl, Burger King, Church's TX Chicken, Fajitas Taqueria, Jack-in-the-Box, Pizza Hut, Popeyes, Restaurant Flores, Subway, Taco Bell, Tomas Mexican, Whataburger, Wingstop, Comfort Suites, Extended Stay, Holiday Inn, La Quinta, Palace Inn, Palace Inn, Parkway Inn, Sapphire Inn, AutoZone, Family$, fireworks, FoodFair, USPO, S Chevron/dsl, Texaco/dsl, McDonald's, Wendy's, Deluxe Inn, Fairfield Inn, Scottish Inn, auto repair
782	Dell-Dale Ave, N Exxon/dsl, Dell-Dale Motel, Luxury Inn, H, S Channelview RV Ctr
781b	Market St, N Clarion, H, S Starlight Inn
781a	TX 8, Sam Houston Pkwy, S Gulf/dsl
780	(779a from wb)Uvalde Rd, Freeport St, N Chevron/dsl, Texaco/dsl, Capt Tom's Seafood, IHOP, Panda Express, Shipley Donuts, Szechwan Wok, Taco Cabana, Studio 6, $Tree, Aamco, Ace Hardware, H, Office Depot, U-Haul, S Bombshell's Grill, Chick-fil-A, Chipotle, Golden Corral, Subway, Whataburger, AT&T, Firestone/auto, Home Depot, Sam's Club/gas, U-Haul, Verizon, Walmart/McDonald's
779b	N Gulf, Valero/dsl, China Dragon, IHOP, Panda Express, Shipley's Donuts, Sonic, Subway, Taco Cabana, Interstate Motel, $Tree, Aamco, Ace Hardware, Office Depot
778b	Normandy St, N Shell/Jack-in-the-Box, Texaco/dsl, R&K BBQ, La Quinta, S Mobil/7-11/dsl, Church's TX Chicken, Normandy Inn, Palace Inn, Scottish Inn
778a	FM 526, Federal Rd, Pasadena, N Exxon, Spark/dsl, Burger King, Casa Ole Mexican, China Star, Jason's Deli, KFC/Taco Bell, Luby's, Mambo Seafood, Pizza Hut, Popeyes, Subway, Candlewood Suites, Econolodge, S Cevron/dsl, Circle K, James Coney Island, Pappa's Seafood, Pappadeaux Seafood, Pappas BBQ, Peking Bo Chinese, Saltgrass Steaks, Sonic, Swamp Shack Rest., Taqueria Los Reyes, Lamplight Inn, Scottish Inn, Super 8, AutoZone, Discount Tire, O'Reilly Parts, transmission repair

INTERSTATE 10 Cont'd

Exit #	Services
776b	John Ralston Rd, Holland Ave, N [gas] Chevron/dsl, Exxon, Texaco, [food] Denny's, Luby's, Mambo Seafood, Pappasito's Cantina, Tostada Regia, [lodging] Candlewood Suites, Days Inn, Econolodge, Palace Inn, Red Roof Inn, Regency Inn, [other] Family$, NTB, URGENT CARE, S same as 778, [gas] Mobil/dsl, [food] Blue Bayou, Chicharrones Mexican, Chilli's, Saltgrass Steaks, [other] tire repair
776a	Mercury Dr, N [food] Arandas Mexican, Burger King, McDonald's, Tepatillan Mexican, TX Grill, [lodging] Best Western, Hampton Inn, Motel 6, Premier Inn, Quality Inn, TownePlace Suites, [other] Volvo Trucks, S [gas] Circle K, Shell/dsl, Tony's Seafood, [food] Chili's, Cici's Pizza, Donald Donuts, Murphy's Deli, Pizzini's Italian, Tony's Seafood, [lodging] Holiday Inn Express, [other] CVS Drug, URGENT CARE
775b a	I-610
774	Gellhorn(from eb) Blvd, S [other] Anheuser-Busch Brewery
773b	McCarty St, N [gas] Chevron/dsl, Shell, S [food] Don Chile Mexican, [other] tire repair
773a	US 90A, N Wayside Dr, N [gas] Speedy/dsl, [food] Jack-in-the-Box, Whataburger, S [gas] Chevron/dsl, Shell/dsl, Valero, [food] Church's TX Chicken, Subway
772	Kress St, Lathrop St, N [gas] Exxon, Pemex, [food] Popeyes, [other] Family$, O'Reilly Parts, tire repair, S [gas] Chevron, [food] Burger King, Taqueria El Nopalito
771b	Lockwood Dr, N [gas] Chevron/Subway/dsl, [food] McDonald's, Taco Bell, [other] CVS, Family$, Walgreens, S [gas] Fuel Depot, Shell/dsl, [food] JR's Tacos, Pizza Hut, [lodging] Palace Inn
771a	Waco St
770c	US 59 N
770b	Jenson St, Meadow St, Gregg St
770a	US 59 S, to Victoria
769c	McKee St, Hardy St, Nance St, downtown
769a	Smith St(from wb), to downtown
768b a	I-45, N to Dallas, S to Galveston
767b	Taylor St
767a	Studemont Dr, Yale St, Heights Blvd, N [lodging] Courtyard, [other] Stude Park/public pool, S [gas] Shell/dsl, [food] Chick-fil-A, Chili's, KFC/Taco Bell, McDonald's, MOD Pizza, Panda Express, Pizza Hut, Southwell's Burgers, Starbucks, Subway, World of Sourdough, [other] AT&T, PetSmart, Staples, Target
766	(from wb), Heights Blvd, Yale St, N [food] Pizza Hut, Pizza Hut, S [gas] Shell, [food] 1751 Seafood, Chipotle, L&L Hawaiian BBQ, Luna Pizza, Salata, Smashburger, Starbucks, Taco Cabana, [other] Walmart/EVC
765b	N Durham Dr, N Shepherd Dr, N [gas] Shell/dsl, [food] Cane's, Wendy's, [lodging] Howard Johnson, [other] vet, S [gas] Valero/dsl, [food] Saltgrass Steaks
765a	TC Jester Blvd, N [food] Elliot's Table, S [gas] Exxon/dsl, Texaco/dsl, [food] Samurai Noodle, Starbucks, [other] vet
764	Westcott St, Washington Ave, Katy Rd, N [food] Denny's, [lodging] Hampton Inn, S [gas] Chevron, [food] IHOP, McDonald's, [lodging] Scottish Inn
763	I-610
762	Silber Rd, Post Oak Rd, N [food] Chick-fil-A, Dave&Buster's, El Pollo Loco, Jersey Mike's, Jimmy John's, Panda Express, Ranchero Buffet, Red Robin, Whataburger, [other] Chrysler/Dodge/Jeep, EVC, Fiat, Firestone/auto, IKEA, Walmart, S [food] Jack-in-the-Box, [lodging] Crowne Plaza, Holiday Inn Express
761b	Antoine Rd, S [gas] Exxon/dsl, [other] CVS Drug
761a	Wirt Rd, Chimney Rock Rd, N [gas] Shell, [food] Sushi Sakura, [other] vet, S [gas] Exxon/dsl, [food] McDonald's, Shipley Do-Nuts, [other] CVS Drug
760	Bingle Rd, Voss Rd, N [food] Hunan Chef, KP's Kitchen, Patagonia Grill, Starbucks, Subway, [other] AT&T, Home Depot,
760	Continued Shell/dsl, [food] Sweet Tomatoes
759	Campbell Rd(from wb), same as 758b, N [food] Campbell Pizza, Jonathan's The Rub, [other] Ranch Mkt, S [food] Goode Co., Saltgrass Steaks, Starbucks
758b	Blalock Rd, Campbell Rd, N [food] Sonic, Wingstop, [other] [H], Lowe's, S [gas] Chevron/McDonald's/dsl, [food] Corner Bakery Cafe, Goode Co TX BBQ, Pappy's Cafe, Saltgrass Steaks, Starbucks, [other] cleaners, Kroger, Walgreens
758a	Bunker Hill Rd, N [gas] EVC, [food] Cafe Chopstix, Dennys, Five Guys, Freebirds Burritos, Genghis Grill, Jimmy John's, MOD Pizza, Olive Garden, Panda Express, Pappa Geno's, Schlotzsky's, Which Wich?, [other] Best Buy, Costco/gas, GNC, HEB Foods/gas, Jo-Ann, Lowe's, Michael's, PetSmart, S [food] Buffalo Wild Wings, Ciro's Italian, Corner Bakery Cafe, Ember & Greens, Firehouse Subs, Guadalajara Mexican, Hunan Inn, Island Grill, Longhorn Steaks, Lupe Tortilla, Masraff's, Subway, [lodging] Hotel ZaZa, [other] EVC, Kroger, Marshall's, Ross, Verizon
757	Gessner Rd, N [food] McDonald's, Mia's Table, Murphy's Deli, Niko's Greek, Taco Bell, Torchy's Tacos, Wendy's, Whataburger, [lodging] Holiday Inn Express, [other] AT&T, CVS Drug, Hobby Lobby, Home Depot, Honda, Sam's Club/gas, U-Haul, S [food] 59 Diner, Cheesecake Factory, Fuddrucker's, Goode Co. Seafood, Jason's Deli, Pappadeaux Seafood, Pappasito's, Perry's Steaks, Taste of TX, [lodging] Westin Hotel, [other] Firestone/auto, Ford, [H], Macy's, Office Depot, Target
756	TX 8, Sam Houston Tollway
755	Willcrest Rd, N [food] Bahama Buck's, [lodging] Fairfield Inn, Home2 Suites, [other] Discount Tire, Lincoln, NTB, U-Haul, S [gas] Exxon/dsl, [food] Brenner's Steaks, Denny's, IHOP, McDonald's, Pizaro's Pizza, Subway, Taste of TX, [lodging] Candlewood Suites, Extended Stay America, Hampton Inn, Sheraton
754	Kirkwood Rd, N [lodging] Embassy Suites, [other] Audi/Porsche, Lincoln, Toyota/Scion, S [gas] Shell/dsl, [food] Avalon Diner, Carrabba's, Pho 9, Shipley Do-Nuts, Starbucks, Twin Peaks, Whataburger, [other] Chevrolet
753b	Dairy-Ashford Rd, N [other] Infiniti, Lexus, Nissan, S [gas] Exxon/dsl, [food] Becks Prime, Chili's, Hibachi Grill, Pappy's Cafe, Subway, Whataburger, [lodging] Comfort Inn, Courtyard, Hilton Garden, [other] Cadillac, URGENT CARE
753a	Eldridge Pkwy, N [lodging] Hyatt, S [gas] Valero/dsl, [other] Kwik Kar
751	TX 6, to Addicks, N [gas] Shell, [food] Brooks Place, Bros Pizza, Chicken Houz, Christian's Tailgate Grill, Pho Kim, Waffle House, [lodging] Best Western, Homewood Suites, Studio 6, S [food] Ginger Thai, Lomontes Italian, Lupe Tortilla Mexican, North China, Salata, Subway, [lodging] Extended Stay America, Fairfield Inn, Hyatt House, La Quinta, Motel 6, TownePlace Suites, [other] USPO
750	Park Ten Blvd, eb only, N [lodging] Red Roof+, SpringHill Suites, S Embassy Suites, Marriott, [other] Acura, Audi/BMW, Buick/GMC, EVC, Hoover RV Ctr
748	Barker-Cypress Rd, N [gas] Exxon/Subway, Mobil, Shell, [food] El Rancho Mexican, Firehouse Subs, Pho Tan, Popeyes, Starbucks, Taco Bell, Tony's Mexican, [lodging] Courtyard, Hampton Inn, Residence Inn, [other] [H], S [food] Cracker Barrel/EVC, [other] Hyundai, Subaru, VW
747b a	Fry Rd, N [gas] Shell/dsl, [food] Applebee's, Arby's, Buffalo Wild Wings, Burger King, Cane's, Chipotle, Denny's, First Watch, Five Guys, Freddy's Frozen, Green Garden, Jimmy John's, Mambo Seafood, McDonald's, MOD Pizza, Panda Express, Panera Bread, Pizza Hut, Pollo Campero, Smoothie King, Sonic, Starbucks, Subway, Taco Bell, Waffle House, Whataburger, [lodging] Candlewood Suites, [other] AAA, Best Buy, HEB Food/gas, Hobby Lobby, Home Depot, Kohl's, Kroger/dsl, Ross, Sam's Club/gas, URGENT CARE, Verizon, vet, Walgreens, Walmart/McDonald's, S [gas] Shell/dsl, Valero,

TX

= gas = food = lodging = other = rest stop

TX

INTERSTATE 10 Cont'd

747b a Continued
Captain Tom's Seafood, Chick-fil-A, Corner Bakery, El Tiempo, IHOP, Kolache Factory, McDonald's, Ostioneria Michoacan, Potbelly, Shipley Do-Nuts, Smashburger, Star Chinese, Starbucks, Torchy's Tacos, Wendy's, Willie's, Four Points Hotel, WoodSpring Suites, AT&T, H, Katy Drug, Lowe's, NTB, Office Depot, PetSmart, Randall's Mkt, Target, TJ Maxx, U-Haul

746 W Green Blvd, N BJ's Rest., Chang's Chinese, Cheddar's, Chuy's Mexican, Eggcellence Cafe, Firehouse Subs, Longhorn Steaks, Maika'i Hawaiian BBQ, Nagoya Japanese, Olive Garden, Orleans Seafood Kitchen, Russo's Pizza, Springcreek BBQ, TX Borders Grill, TX Roadhouse, Wild Wings Cafe, Days Inn, Holiday Inn Express, Hyatt Place, Palace Inn, S Jimmy Changas TexMex, Taco Bueno, Home2 Suites, Christian Bros Automotive, CVS Drug, Ford, Honda, Honda

745 Mason Rd, N Fadi's, JINYA Ramen, McAlister's Deli, Pho Oh Yeah, Pinchy's TexMex, Salata, CarMax, S Exxon, Shell/dsl, Valero/Circle K/dsl, Atami, Babin's Seafood, Brett's BBQ, Burger King, Cabo Bob's, Cane's, Chick-fil-A, Chili's, CiCi's, Craft Burger, Dimassi's Buffet, DQ, Ephesus Grill, Freebirds Burrito, Harvest Kitchen, Hooters, J&D Caribbean, Jack-in-the-Box, Jason's Deli, Kabob Korner, KFC, LA Crawfish, Landry's Seafood, Luby's, McDonald's, Nere Express, Panda Express, Papa John's, Pastel Pizza, Pizza Hut, Pollo Loco, Popeyes, Project Pollo, Rosa's Pizza, Rudy's BBQ/gas, SaltGrass Steaks, Schlotzsky's, So Gong Korean, Starbucks, Taco Bell, Taco Cabana, Tacos La Bala, Tarator Grill, Tiger Noodle House, Whataburger, Comfort Inn&Suites, Hampton Inn, Motel 6, Palacio Royale, Super 8, $Tree, 99c Store, AutoZone, Chevrolet, Chrysler/Dodge/Jeep, Discount Tire, Fiesta Foods, Firestone/auto, Goodyear/auto, HEB Food/gas, Jiffy Lube, Kia, Toyota/Scion, transmissions, vet, Walgreens

743 TX 99, Grand Pkwy, Peek Rd, N Black Bear Diner, Chipotle, Church's TX Chicken, HaiDiLao, La Madeleine, Red Robin, Whiskey Cake Kitchen, Dicks, Field&Stream, H, JC Penney, PetSmart, S Catfish Station, Cooper's BBQ, First Watch, Freddy's Steakburgers, Harris County BBQ, Ichiban, Jersey Mike's, Subway, Toasted Yolk, Tru, Costco/gas, URGENT CARE

741 (742 from wb)Katy-Fort Bend County Rd, Pin Oak Rd, N Clutch City Burgers, In-N-Out, S Murphy USA/dsl, Texaco/dsl, Alegra Brazilian, Antonia's Rest, ChuckECheese, Denny's, IHOP, Jack-in-the-Box, Jimmy John's, KFC, Kokai Japanese, LJ Silver/Taco Bell, Maxi Arepa, Old Chicago Pizza, Pizza Hut, Starbucks, Subway, Taco Cabana, Taizzi Sushi, Taqueria El Toluca, Twisted Grilled Cheese, Best Western+, Comfort Suites, Country Inn & Suites, Hilton Garden, SpringHill Suites, $Tree, AT&T, Discount Tire, Firestone, Midas, Walmart/McDonald's

740 FM 1463, N Exxon/dsl, S Mobil/7-11, Shell/McDonald's/dsl, Alicia's Mexican, Burger King, Chick-fil-A, Cicis Pizza, Kolache Factory, Los Cucos, Panera Bread, Pearl & Vine, Rainforest Cafe, Red Lobster, Starbucks, Teriyaki Madness, The Chipper, Wendy's, Whataburger, Best Value, Courtyard, Holiday Inn, Homewood Suites, La Quinta, Residence Inn, BassPro Shops, BooksAMillion, HEB/gas, H, Katy Mills Outlet/famous brands, Marshall's, Ross, URGENT CARE

739 Cane Island Pkwy, N Buc-ee's/dsl, S Camping World

737 Pederson Rd, N Buc-ee's/dsl, Love's/Arby's/dsl/scales/repair/24hr/@, S Camping World RV Super Ctr, Holiday World RV Ctr

735 Igloo Rd

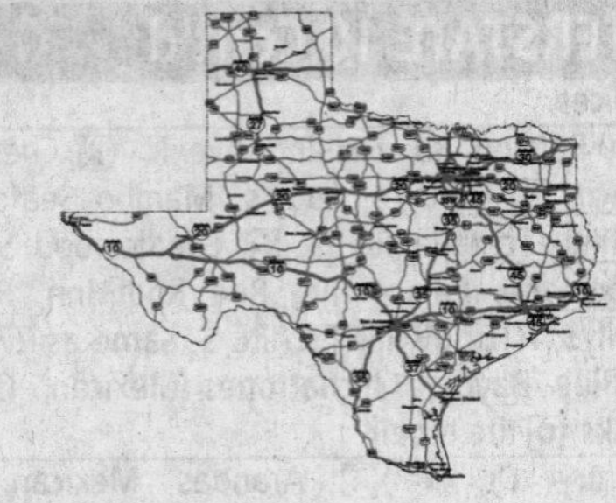

734 Woods Rd

732 FM 359, to Brookshire, N Exxon/rest./dsl, Flying J/Dunkin'/dsl/LP/scales/24hr/@, Shell, Church's TX Chicken, Orlando's Pizza, Subway, Executive Inn, S Burger King, Chevron/dsl, Shell/McDonald's/dsl, Jack-in-the-Box, Popeyes, Taco Bell, Holiday Inn Express, Super 8, truck lube, truckwash

731 FM 1489, to Koomey Rd, N Exxon/dsl, Ernesto's Mexican, Brooke Hotel, Houston W RV Park, S Texaco/Dickey's BBQ/dsl, La Quinta/EVC

729 Peach Ridge Rd, Donigan Rd(730 from wb), S Kathy's/dsl/rest./24hr

726 Chew Rd(from eb), S golf

725 Mlcak Rd(from wb), S Kathy 's Korner/dsl

723 FM 1458, to San Felipe, N Exxon/Subway/dsl/scales/24hr, Peterbilt, to Stephen F Austin SP(3mi), S Riverside Tire, RV Camping

721 (from wb) US 90, N Shell/Chester's/dsl, Chrysler/Dodge/Jeep, Ford

720a Outlet Ctr Dr, N Shell/dsl

720 TX 36, to Sealy, N Shell/dsl, DQ, Hartz Chicken Buffet, McDonald's, Sonic, Tony's Rest., $General, Jones RV Ctr, O'Reilly Parts, Sealy RV Park, Walgreens, S Chevron/Burger King/dsl, Murphy USA/dsl, Shell/dsl, Texaco/dsl, Cazadores Mexican, Chicken Express, Domino's, Ernesto's Cantina, Hinze's BBQ, Jack-in-the-Box, Jin's Asian, Pizza Hut, Starbucks, Subway, Whataburger, American Inn, Countryside Inn, Holiday Inn Express, Super 8, $Tree, T-Mobile, Walmart

718 US 90(from eb), to Sealy, N Valero/Subway/dsl, S Exxon/Prasek's BBQ/dsl

716 Pyka Rd, N Sunoco/dsl/rest./showers/24hr/@

713 Beckendorff Rd, S Road Ranger/rest./showers/24hr

709 FM 2761, Bernardo Rd, N TA/Carl's Jr/Dunkin'/dsl/scales/24hr

704 FM 949, N Pilsner's Cafe, Happy Oaks RV Park(3mi)

699 FM 102, to Eagle Lake, N Happy Oaks RV Park, S Eagle Lake SP(14mi)

698 Alleyton Rd, N Mikeska's BBQ, S Exxon/Taco Bell/BBQ/dsl, Valero/Subway/dsl, Chrysler/Dodge/Jeep, Ford

COLUMBUS

697mm Little Colorado River

696 TX 71, Columbus, N Exxon/Burger King/dsl, Shell/dsl, Donald's Donuts, Formosa Chinese, Jack-in-the-Box, Joe's Italian, Pizza Hut, Schobel's Rest., Whataburger, Columbus Inn, Holiday Inn Express, AT&T, AutoZone, HEB Foods, H, Walmart, S Chevron/dsl, Conoco/Subway/dsl, Phillips 66/dsl, Los Cabos Mexican, McDonald's, Nancy's Steaks, Baymont Inn/EVC, Best Value, LaQuinta, Columbus RV Park

695 TX 71(from wb), to La Grange

693 FM 2434, to Glidden

692mm **full facilities, litter barrels, petwalk, both lanes, RV dump, vending**

689 US 90, to Hattermann Lane, N Whispering Oaks RV Park

682 FM 155, to Wiemar, N Shell/dsl, Valero/dsl, DQ, McDonald's, Subway/Texas Burger, SureStay Hotel,

TX

INTERSTATE 10 Cont'd

SCHULENBURG

Exit	Services
682	Continued $General, H, Tire Pros, S Love's/Chester's/Wendy's/dsl/scales/repair/24hr/@, Buick/Chevrolet/GMC
678mm	E Navidad River
677	US 90
674	US 77, Schulenburg, N Pilot/Taco Bell/PJ Fresh/dsl/scales/24hr, Oak Ridge Smokehouse, Best Value Inn, Executive Inn, Ford, Potter Country Store, S Valero, DQ, Lucy's Grill, Whataburger, Best Western+, Holiday Inn Express, $General, O'Reilly Parts, Schulenberg RV Park
672mm	W Navidad River
668	FM 2238, to Engle
661	TX 95, FM 609, to Flatonia, N Citgo/dsl, Valero/Sonic/truckwash/EVC/dsl, Jessito's Mexican, Joel's BBQ, Robert's Steaks, Flatonia RV Ranch(1mi), S Shell/McDonald's/motel/dsl, DQ, Subway, Best Western+, Carefree Inn, Sunset Inn, $General, NAPA Parts
658mm	picnic areas both lanes, tables, litter barrels
653	US 90, Waelder, N Exxon/dsl, S tire repair
649	TX 97, to Waelder
642	TX 304, to Gonzales
637	FM 794, to Harwood
632	US 90/183, to Gonzales, N Love's/Subway/dsl/scales/24hr, Best Western+, Coachway Inn(2mi), La Quinta, S Buc-ee's/dsl, camping, to Palmetto SP(5mi)
630mm	San Marcos River
628	TX 80, to Luling, N Citgo(2mi), Exxon/dsl, Valero/dsl/24hr, H, Patriot RV Park
625	Darst Field Rd
624.5mm	Smith Creek
621mm	weigh sta both lanes
620	FM 1104
618mm	**petwalk, both lanes, full facitlities**
617	FM 2438, to Kingsbury
614	toll 130 N, to Austin, Waco
612	US 90
611mm	Geronimo Creek
610	TX 123, to San Marcos, N Exxon/Circle K/dsl, Shell/Subway/dsl, Chili's, Giuseppe's, IHOP, Los Cucos Mexican, Starbucks, Comfort Inn, Days Inn, Hampton Inn, Holiday Inn Express, TownePlace Suites, Carters Tires, S Valero/dsl, Taco Cabana, H
609	TX 123, Austin St, N QT/dsl, S Sunoco/7-11/dsl, Chevrolet, Home Depot
607	TX 46, FM 78, to New Braunfels, N Chevron/Jack-in-the-Box/dsl, Motel 6, Ford, S Circle K/dsl, Shell/Circle K/dsl, Bill Miller BBQ, Dixie Grille, Garcia's Mexican, McDonald's, Subway, Whataburger, La Quinta, Super 8, Chrysler/Dodge/Jeep, EVC
605	FM 464, N Twin Palms RV Park
605mm	Guadalupe River
604	FM 725, to Lake McQueeney, N Love's/Arby's/dsl/scales/24hr/@, Twin Palms RV Park
603	US 90 E, US 90A, to Seguin, N Seguin Hilltop RV Park, Seguin RV Ctr, S ExploreUSA RV Ctr, Patriot RV Park, truck repair
601	FM 775, to New Berlin, N Chevron/Subway/dsl/scales/24hr
600	Schwab Rd
599	FM 465, to Marion
599mm	Santa Clara Creek
597	Santa Clara Rd, N auto racetrack/EVC
595	Zuehl Rd
594mm	Cibolo Creek
593	FM 2538, Trainer Hale Rd, N Texaco/dsl,

KIRBY

Exit	Services
593	Continued Kountry RV Park, tires, S Exxon/dsl/24hr
593mm	Woman Hollering Creek
591	FM 1518, to Schertz, N repair, S Valero/Circle K/dsl/e85
589	Pfeil Rd, Graytown Rd
589mm	Salatrillo Creek
587	LP 1604, Randolph AFB, to Universal City, S Shell/McDonald's/dsl, Whataburger
585.5mm	Escondido Creek
585	FM 1516, to Converse, N Best Western+, S Kenworth, Peterbilt/GMC/Freightliner
585mm	Martinez Creek
583	Foster Rd, N Flying J/Denny's/dsl/LP/scales/24hr/@, QT/dsl, Valero/Subway/dsl/24hr, Jack-in-the-Box, McDonald's, Comfort Inn, La Quinta, La Quinta, Blue Beacon, Speedco Lube, Tire Mart, S TA/Chevron/Burger King/Popeyes/dsl/24hr/@, Holiday Inn Express
582.5mm	Rosillo Creek
582	Ackerman Rd, Kirby, N Pilot/Subway/dsl/scales/24hr, tire repair, S Petro/Iron Skillet/dsl/scales/24hr/@, El Rodeo Mexican, Blue Beacon, Petrolube
581	I-410
580	LP 13, WW White Rd, N Chevron/dsl, Valero/dsl, La Playa Seafood, Radicke's Grill, Wendy's, Garden Inn, HomeTowne Studios, Red Roof Inn, tires, S Exxon/7-11, Valero/Circle K, Bayseas Seafood, Bill Miller BBQ, El Rodeo Mexican, Lazaritas Mexican, McDonald's, Pizza Hut, Popeyes, Subway, Budget Inn, Motel 6, Super 8, Family$, Ford/Volvo Trucks, tires/repair
579	Houston St, N Valero/dsl, Starbucks, Quality Inn, Penske, S Chevron, Stripes/Valero/dsl, Days Inn, Knights Inn, Upland Inn
578	Pecan Valley Dr, ML King Dr, N Skinny Black BBQ, S Shell/Subway/dsl
577	US 87 S, to Roland Ave, S Whataburger, Best Western+, Super 8
576	New Braunfels Ave, Gevers St, S Valero/Circle K, McDonald's
575	Pine St, Hackberry St, S Little Red Barn Steaks
574	I-37, US 281
573	Probandt St, N Jack-in-the-Box, Miller's BBQ, Santa Cruz BBQ, S Valero/Circle K, Gyro's Drive Inn, tires/repair, to SA Missions HS
570mm	I-10 and I-35 run together 3 miles. See I-35, exits 156-154a.
569c	Santa Rosa St, downtown, to Our Lady of the Lake U
568	spur 421, Culebra Ave, Bandera Ave, S to St Marys U
567	Lp 345, Fredericksburg Rd(from eb upper level accesses I-35 S, I-10 E, US 87 S, lower level accesses I-35 N)
566b	Fresno Dr, S Exxon/dsl, Galaxy Inn
566a	West Ave, N Exxon/7-11, DQ, Subway, Whataburger, auto repair
565c	(from wb), access to same as 565 a b, S Shell, Jimador Mexican, Starbucks, La Quinta
565b	Vance Jackson Rd, N Murphy USA/dsl, Bill Miller BBQ, IHOP, Comfort Inn, Days Inn, Motel 6, Walmart, S Shell/dsl, Holiday Inn Express
565a	Crossroads Blvd, Balcone's Heights, N Shell/dsl, Howard Johnson, vet, S Exxon, Valero/dsl, Babe's Burgers, Charcoal Grill, Chick-fil-A, Dave&Buster's, Denny's, El Pollo Loco, Grady's BBQ, McDonald's, Peter Piper Pizza, Pizza Hut, Subway, Wendy's, Whataburger, SpringHill Suites, Firestone/auto, Hobby Lobby, Kia, Mazda, Office Depot, Target
564b a	I-410, services off of I-410 W, Fredericksburg Rd
563	Callaghan Rd, N Valero, Jimmy John's, Las Palapas Mexican, Embassy Suites, Marriott, $General,

INTERSTATE 10 Cont'd

563 Continued
auto repair, Ford, Sprouts Mkt, **S** Exxon/7-11, Mamacita's, Country Inn & Suites, La Quinta, Lowe's

561 Wurzbach Rd, **N** Texaco/dsl, 54th St. Rest., Bolo's Grille, County Line BBQ, Firehouse Subs, First Watch, Honeybaked Ham, IHOP, Jason's Deli, Pappasito's Cantina, Popeyes, Sea Island Shrimphouse, Surfing Crab, Wasabi Grill, Extended Stay America, Homewood Suites, Hyatt Place, Motel 6, Sonesta Suites, Westin, AutoZone, BigLots, HEB Food/gas, Office Depot, Porsche, Tuesday Morning, **S** Shell/dsl, 210 Ceviche Seafood, Alamo Café, Asian Star, Chester's Burgers, Denny's, Embers Grill, Jack-in-the-Box, Mamma Margie's Mexican, McDonald's, Pizza Hut, Sumo Japanese, Taco Bell, Taco Tote, Wendy's, Candlewood Suites, Drury Inn, Flex Studios, La Quinta, Motel 6, Sleep Inn, CarMax, H

560b frontage rd(from eb), same as 561

560a Huebner Rd, **N** CA Pizza Kitchen, Chipotle, Fare Wok, Freebirds, La Madeleine, Panda Express, Panera Bread, Potbelly, Salata, SaltGrass Steaks, Snooze Breakfast, Umiya Sushi, Cadillac, Chrysler/Jeep/Dodge, Nissan, Old Navy, Ross, **S** Chevron, Exxon/7-11, Texaco/Jack-in-the-Box/dsl, Bush's Chicken, Cracker Barrel, Jim's Rest., Magnolia Pancake Haus, Miller's BBQ, Holiday Inn Express, TownePlace Suites

559 Lp 335, US 87, Fredericksburg Rd, **N** Best Western, Acura, **S** Krispy Kreme, Shell/Jack-in-the-Box/dsl, Comfort Suites, Days Inn, HomeGate Studios; Rodeway Inn, SpringHill Suites, Studio 6, Infiniti

558 De Zavala Rd, **N** Chevron, Shell/Subway, Bill Miller BBQ, Burger King, Carrabba's, Chick-fil-A, Chili's, Crawfish Cafe, Five Guys, Fox&Hound, KFC/Taco Bell, McDonald's, Outback Steaks, Sonic, Starbucks, Taco Cabana, The Earl of Sandwich, Wendy's, HEB Foods, Home Depot, Marshall's, PetCo, PetSmart, Steinmart, Target, **S** Cici's, HuHot Mongolian, IHOP, LJ Silver, Popeyes, Schlotzsky's, Twin Peaks, Whataburger, Days Inn, SpringHill Suites, Studio 6, Discount Tire, Sam's Club/gas, Verizon, Walmart

557 Spur 53, **N** Exxon/7-11/dsl, Cheddar's, Chicken N Pickle, Chuy's Mexican, Pluckers Wings, Taco Palenque, Best Western, Embassy Suites, Magnuson Hotel, Sleep Inn, Super 8, University Inn, BMW/MINI, Chevrolet, Hyundai, **S** Valero/Subway/dsl, A&W/LJ Silver, Cici's Pizza, Dimassi's Mediterranean, Matamoro's Cantina, Popeyes, Schlotzsky's, Starbucks, Holiday Inn, Costco/gas, Discount Tire, Honda, Land Rover/Jaguar, Sams Club/gas, Univ of TX at San Antonio, Walmart.

556b frontage rd, **N** Embassy Suites

556a to Anderson Lp, **S** to Seaworld, Six Flags

555 La Cantera Pkwy, **N** 54th St Rest., BJ's Rest., Bob's Chophouse, Cane's Chicken, Chick-fil-A, Coldstone, Freddy's Steakburger, IHOP, Lupe Tortilla, Maggiano's Little Italy, McDonald's, Mi Familia, Panera Bread, Popeyes, Potbelly, Red Robin, Sonic, Starbucks, Tiago's, Whataburger, Which Wich?, Courtyard, Hilton Garden, Home2 Suites, Residence Inn, Tru, $Tree, AT&T, Bass Pro Shops, Best Buy, Dick's, GNC, Hobby Lobby, JC Penney, Lowe's, Michaels, Old Navy, PetSmart, Ross, Staples, Target, TJ Maxx, World Mkt, **S** Applebee's, J. Alexander's, Longhorn Steaks, Olive Garden, Red Lobster, Drury Inn, Eilan Hotel, La Quinta, Motel 6, Honda, to La Cantera Pkwy

554 Camp Bullis Rd, **N** Texaco/dsl, Brasão Brazilian, Russell CP, **S** Exxon/dsl, HillView Inn

552 Dominion Dr, Stonewall Pkwy, **N** TX Roadhouse, **S** Acu Bistro, Aldo's Rest., Bourbon St. Kitchen, Dunkin',

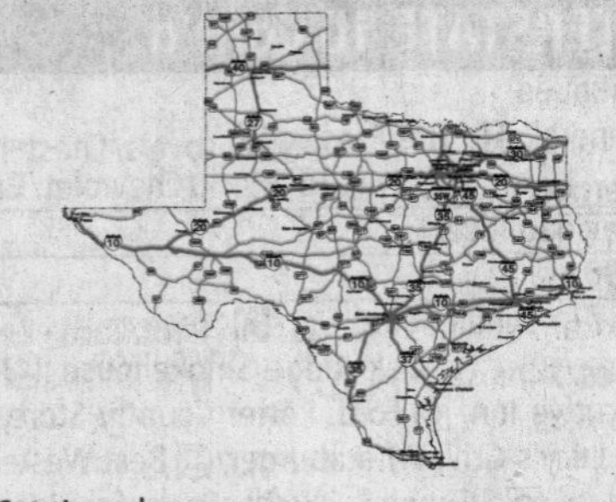

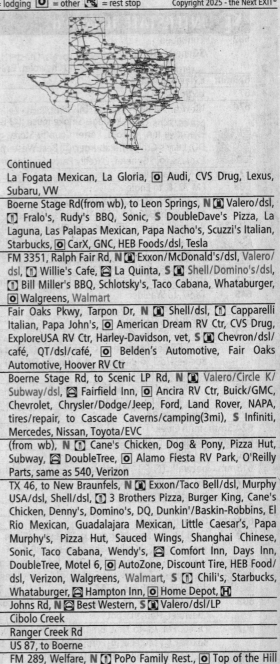

552 Continued
La Fogata Mexican, La Gloria, Audi, CVS Drug, Lexus, Subaru, VW

551 Boerne Stage Rd(from wb), to Leon Springs, **N** Valero/dsl, Fralo's, Rudy's BBQ, Sonic, **S** DoubleDave's Pizza, La Laguna, Las Palapas Mexican, Papa Nacho's, Scuzzi's Italian, Starbucks, CarX, GNC, HEB Foods/dsl, Tesla

550 FM 3351, Ralph Fair Rd, **N** Exxon/McDonald's/dsl, Valero/dsl, Willie's Cafe, La Quinta, **S** Shell/Domino's/dsl, Bill Miller's BBQ, Schlotsky's, Taco Cabana, Whataburger, Walgreens, Walmart

546 Fair Oaks Pkwy, Tarpon Dr, **N** Shell/dsl, Capparelli Italian, Papa John's, American Dream RV Ctr, CVS Drug, ExploreUSA RV Ctr, Harley-Davidson, vet, **S** Chevron/dsl/café, QT/dsl/café, Belden's Automotive, Fair Oaks Automotive, Hoover RV Ctr

543 Boerne Stage Rd, to Scenic LP Rd, **N** Valero/Circle K/Subway/dsl, Fairfield Inn, Ancira RV Ctr, Buick/GMC, Chevrolet, Chrysler/Dodge/Jeep, Ford, Land Rover, NAPA, tires/repair, to Cascade Caverns/camping(3mi), **S** Infiniti, Mercedes, Nissan, Toyota/EVC

542 (from wb), **N** Cane's Chicken, Dog & Pony, Pizza Hut, Subway, DoubleTree, Alamo Fiesta RV Park, O'Reilly Parts, same as 540, Verizon

540 TX 46, to New Braunfels, **N** Exxon/Taco Bell/dsl, Murphy USA/dsl, Shell/dsl, 3 Brothers Pizza, Burger King, Cane's Chicken, Denny's, Domino's, DQ, Dunkin'/Baskin-Robbins, El Rio Mexican, Guadalajara Mexican, Little Caesar's, Papa Murphy's, Pizza Hut, Sauced Wings, Shanghai Chinese, Sonic, Taco Cabana, Wendy's, Comfort Inn, Days Inn, DoubleTree, Motel 6, AutoZone, Discount Tire, HEB Food/dsl, Verizon, Walgreens, Walmart, **S** Chili's, Starbucks, Whataburger, Hampton Inn, Home Depot, H

WELFARE

539 Johns Rd, **N** Best Western, **S** Valero/dsl/LP

538mm Cibolo Creek

538 Ranger Creek Rd

537 US 87, to Boerne

533 FM 289, Welfare, **N** PoPo Family Rest., Top of the Hill RV Park(1mi)

532mm Little Joshua Creek

531mm picnic area wb, tables, litter barrels

530mm Big Joshua Creek

529.5mm picnic area eb, tables, litter barrels

527 FM 1621(from wb), to Waring

526.5mm Holiday Creek

524 TX 27, FM 1621, to Waring, **S** Chevron, Shell/dsl, Los Jarritos

523.5mm Guadalupe River

523 US 87 N, to Comfort, **N** Chevron/Chicken Express/dsl, Love's/McDonald's/Subway/dsl/scales/24hr/@, **S** Exxon/dsl, Mar's Kitchen, Executive Inn, $General, RV Park/LP, tire repair

521.5mm Comfort Creek

520 FM 1341, to Cypress Creek Rd

515mm Cypress Creek

514mm **full facilities, litter barrels, petwalk,**

TX

INTERSTATE 10 Cont'd

KERRVILLE

Exit	Services
514mm	Continued **playground, both lanes, RV dump, vending, wireless internet**
508	TX 16, Kerrville, N Exxon/dsl, Buick/Cadillac/Chevrolet, S Shell/McDonald's/dsl/24hr, Stripes/7-11, Acapulco Mexican, Bella Sera Italian, Cracker Barrel, IHOP, Qdoba, Schlotzsky's, Sonic, Starbucks, Best Western, Days Inn, Hampton Inn, Holiday Inn Express, La Quinta, Motel 6, Quality Inn, Super 8, Yo Ranch Hotel, Home Depot, H, Kerrville RV Ctr, Lowe's
505	FM 783, to Kerrville, S Exxon/dsl
503.5mm	scenic views both lanes, litter barrels
501	FM 1338, N Buckhorn RV Resort, S KOA(2mi)
497mm	scenic views both lanes, picnic tables litter barrels
492	FM 479
490	TX 41
488	TX 27, to Ingram, Mountain Home
484	Midway Rd
477	US 290, to Fredericksburg
476.5mm	service rd eb
472	Old Segovia Rd
465	FM 2169, to Segovia, S Valero/Sonic/dsl
464.5mm	Johnson Fork Creek
462	US 83 S, to Uvalde
461mm	picnic area eb, tables, litter barrels
460	(from wb), to Junction
459mm	picnic area wb, tables, litter barrels
457	FM 2169, to Junction, N Shell/dsl, S Econolodge, RV camping, S. Llano River SP
456.5mm	Llano River
456	US 83/377, Junction, N Alon/dsl, Chevron/dsl, Shell/McDonald's/dsl/24hr, Tesla EVC, Cooper's BBQ, Tia Nena's Mexican, Motel 6, S Conoco/dsl, Exxon/dsl, Phillips 66/dsl, Pilot/Subway/PJ Fresh/dsl/scales/24hr, Cowboy Grill, DQ, Isaack Rest., Junction Burger, La Familia Mexican, Lum's BBQ, Sonic, Americas Inn, Best Western, Holiday Inn Express, Lazy T Motel, Rodeway Inn, Sun Valley Motel, The Hills Motel, $General, Family$, H, Lowe's Mkt, N Llano RV Park, to S Llano River SP
452.5mm	Bear Creek
451	RM 2291, to Cleo Rd
448mm	North Creek
445	RM 1674
444.5mm	Stark Creek
442mm	Copperas Creek
442	RM 1674, to Ft McKavett, N to Ft McKavett SHS
439mm	N Llano River
438	Lp 291(from wb), to Roosevelt
437	Lp 291(from eb, no EZ return), to Roosevelt
429	RM 3130, to Harrell
423mm	parking area both lanes, litter barrels
420	RM 3130, to Baker Rd
412	Allison Rd, RM 3130
404	RM 3130, RM 864, N to Ft McKavett St HS, S Love's/Subway/dsl/scales/24hr/@, H
400	US 277, Sonora, N Road Ranger/Chester's/dsl, Sutton Co Steaks, Motel 6, S Alon/7-11/dsl, Sunoco/dsl, Sunoco/Stripes/dsl, DQ, La Mexicana Rest., Pit Stop BBQ, Pizza Hut, Sonic, Taco Grill, Quality Inn, Super 8, Surestay, Elite RV Park, Family$, H, USPO
399	(from eb)LP 467, Sonora, N vet, S H, RV camping
394mm	**full facilities, litter barrel, petwalk, both lanes, RV dump**
392	RM 1989, Caverns of Sonora Rd
388	RM 1312(from wb)
381	RM 1312(from eb)
372	Taylor Box Rd, N Sunoco/dsl/scales/24hr, Super 8, auto museum, Circle Bar RV Park
368	LP 466, N same as 365 & 363
365	TX 163, Ozona, N Stripes/Godfather's/dsl, Sunoco/dsl, Valero/dsl, DQ, Hitchin Post Steaks, Mi Taco, Pepe's Cafe, Sonic, Subway, Best Value Inn, Economy Inn/RV Park, Hampton Inn, Hillcrest Inn, Holiday Inn Express, Quality Inn/Tesla EVC, Travelodge, $General, Encino RV Park, NAPA, tire repair, to David Crockett Mon, S Sunoco/Stripes, Bryan's Poco Taco, El Chato's, Wagon Wheel BBQ, city park, Southern Living RV Park
363	Lp 466, to Ozona
361	RM 2083, Pandale Rd
357mm	Eureka Draw
351mm	Howard Draw
350	FM 2398, to Howard Draw
349mm	parking area wb, litter barrels
346mm	parking area eb, litter barrels
343	TX 290 W, S Ft. Lancaster Historic Site
337	Live Oak Rd
336.5mm	Live Oak Creek
328	River Rd, Sheffield
327.5mm	Pecos River
325	TX 290, TX 349, to Iraan, Sheffield
320	frontage rd
314	frontage rd
309mm	**full facilities, litter barrels, petwalk, both lanes, wireless internet**
307	US 190, FM 305, to Iraan
298	RM 2886
294	FM 11, Bakersfield, N Exxon, S Chevron/dsl
288	Ligon Rd, N many windmills
285	McKenzie Rd, S winery
279mm	picnic area eb, tables, litter barrels
277	FM 2023
273	US 67/385, to McCamey, picnic area wb, tables, litter barrels
272	University Rd
264	Warnock Rd, N Fort Stockton RV Park
261	US 290 W, US 385 S, S Alon/dsl, Love's/Carl's Jr/dsl/scales/24hr/@, Mingo's Tacos, All Inn, Budget Inn, Deluxe Inn, Executive Inn, RV camping, to Big Bend NP
259b a	(259 from eb)TX 18, FM 1053, Ft Stockton, N Chevron/Burger King/dsl, La Quinta, I-10 RV Park, S Flying J/Subway/dsl/scales/EVC/24hr, H
257	US 285, to Pecos, Ft Stockton, N Stripes/Sunoco/dsl/24hr, Camp Stockton RV Park, golf, S Chevron/dsl, Valero/dsl, Billy's Phillies, Bush's Chicken, McDonald's, Pizza Hut, Sonic, Steak House, Subway, Taco Bell, Atrium Inn, Baymont, Best Western+, Candlewood Suites, Days Inn, Fairfield Inn, Hampton Inn, Quality Inn, Texan Inn, Town & Country, $General, $Tree, Ace Hardware, Advance Parts, AutoZone, Buick/Chevrolet, Comanche Land RV Park, Firestone/auto, Lowe's Foods, O'Reilly Parts, Walmart/EVC/gas, Williams Tires
256	to US 385 S, Ft Stockton, N HillTop RV, S Chevron/dsl, Domino's, Howard's Drive-In, K-Bob's Steaks, Subway, Baymont, Comfort Suites, Holiday Inn Express, Motel 6, Sleep Inn, Super 8, Big Bend NP, Chrysler/Jeep/Dodge, Flying G RV Park, Ford, Honey Badger RV Camping, to Ft Stockton Hist Dist, vet, Walmart/EVC/gas
253	FM 2037, to Belding
248	US 67, FM 1776, to Alpine, S to Big Bend NP
246	Firestone
241	Kennedy Rd
235	Mendel Rd
233mm	**full facilities, litter barrels, petwalk,**

Margin town labels: KERRVILLE, JUNCTION, SONORA, OZONA, SHEFFIELD, FT STOCKTON

INTERSTATE 10 Cont'd

BORACHO STA / ALLAMORE

Exit	Services
233mm	Continued **both lanes**
229	Hovey Rd
222	Hoefs Rd
214	(from wb), FM 2448
212	TX 17, FM 2448, to Pecos, N picnic area, litter barrels, S I-10 Fuel Stop/Saddleback RV Camping, Valero/I-10 Fuel/dsl
209	TX 17, S Ft Davis NHS, Kiko & Tina's RV Camping, to Balmorhea SP, to Davis Mtn SP
206	FM 2903, to Balmorhea, Toyah, S Alon, Matta's Burgers, The Eleven Inn, Ropers RV Park, to Balmorhea SP, USPO
192	FM 3078, to Toyahvale, S to Balmorhea SP
188	Giffin Rd
187	I-20, to Ft Worth, Dallas
186	I-10, E to San Antonio (from wb)
185mm	picnic area both lanes, tables, litter barrels
184	Springhills
181	Cherry Creek Rd, S Chevron/dsl
176	TX 118, FM 2424, to Kent, S Davis Mtn SP, Ft Davis, to McDonald Observatory
173	Hurd's Draw Rd
166	Boracho Sta
159	Plateau, N Exxon/rest./dsl/24hr, tire repair
153	Michigan Flat
146	Wild Horse Rd, Wild Horse Rd
146mm	weigh sta wb
145mm	**full facilities, litter barrels, petwalk,** both lanes, **wireless internet**
140b	Ross Dr, Van Horn, N Love's/Subway/dsl/scales/24hr/@, Valero/dsl, Days Inn/EVC, Desert Inn, Sands Motel/rest., repair, Wild West RV Park, S Mountain View RV Park/dump
140a	US 90, TX 54, Van Horn Dr, N Alon/dsl, Hotel El Capitan, Village Inn, auto/dsl repair, H, NAPA, USPO, S Pilot/Wendy's/dsl/scales/24hr, Valero/dsl, Chelas Mexican Restaurant, Van Horn RV Park/dump
138	Lp 10, to Van Horn, N Chuy's Rest., Van Horn Cattle Company, Budget Inn, EconoLodge, Economy Inn, Knights Inn, Motel 6, Red Roof Inn, Value Inn, $General, city park, Oasis RV Park, Porter Foods, Southern Star RV Park, visitor info, S Chevron/dsl/24hr, Tesla EVC, McDonald's, Hampton Inn, Holiday Inn Express, Quality Inn, Super 8, tires/repair
137mm	weigh sta eb
136mm	scenic overlook wb, picnic tables, litter barrels
135mm	Mountain/Central time zone
133	(from wb)frontage rd
129	to Hot Wells, Allamore
108	to Sierra Blanca(from wb), same as 107
107	FM 1111, Sierra Blanca Ave, N Valero/dsl/24hr, Black Bear Burgers, Small Town Grill, SB Historic Lodge, to Hueco Tanks SP, USPO, S Chevron/dsl, Delfina's Mexican, Americana Inn
105	(106 from wb)Lp 10, Sierra Blanca, same as 107
102.5mm	insp sta eb
99	Lasca Rd, picnic area both lanes, N litter barrels, no restrooms
98mm	picnic tables eb, litter barrels, no restrooms
95	frontage rd(from eb)
87	FM 34, S TX 87/dsl
85	Esperanza Rd
81	FM 2217
78	TX 20 W, to McNary

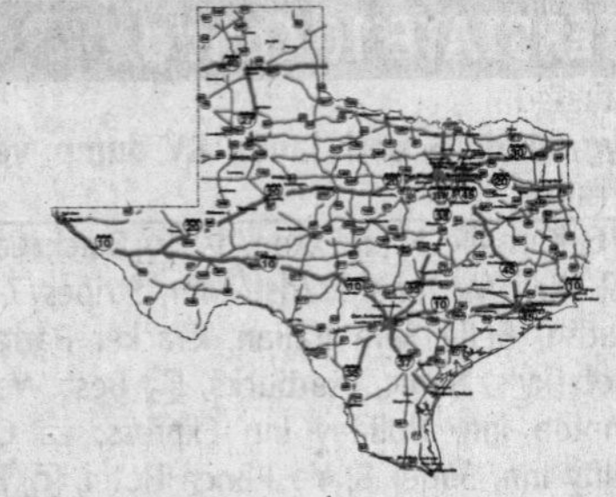

FABENS / EL PASO

Exit	Services
77mm	truck parking area wb
72	spur 148, to Ft Hancock, S Shell/dsl, Cowboy's Land, Ft Hancock Motel, Family$, tire repair, USPO
68	Acala Rd
55	Tornillo
51mm	**full facilities, litter barrels, petwalk,** both lanes
49	FM 793, Fabens, S Speedway/dsl, Church's TX Chicken, Little Caesar's, McDonald's, Subway, Wienerschnitzel, Fabens Inn/Cafe, Family$, San Eli Foods
42	FM 1110, to Clint, N mexitaco El güero, S Xpress/Little Caesars/dsl, Cotton Eyed Joe's, Mamacita's Rest., Adobe Inn, Best Western
37	FM 1281, Horizon Blvd, N Flying J/dsl/scales/24hr/@, Love's/Chester's/Subway/dsl/scales/24hr/@, Carl's Jr, Americana Inn, Freightliner, RV Camping, Speedco Lube, S Petro/Valero/Iron Skillet/Subway/dsl/scales/24hr/@, McDonald's, Deluxe Inn, Blue Beacon
35	Eastlake Blvd.
34	TX 375, Americas Ave, N Circle K/Subway/dsl, Marathon, Motel 6, Woodspring Suites, Mission RV Camping, Peterbilt, U-Haul, S El Paso Museum of Hist
32	FM 659, Zaragosa Rd, N Alon/7-11, Applebee's, Arby's, Baskin-Robbins, BJ's Rest., Butter Smith Kitchen, Cheddar's, Chick-fil-A, Chico's Tacos, Chipotle Mexican, Corner Bakery Cafe, Crave Kitchen, Craze FroYo, Don Carbon, Dunkin', Famous Dave's, Five Guys, Genghis Grill, Great American Steaks, Hook & Reel Seafood, IHOP, Jack-in-the-Box, Jason's Deli, Krispy Kreme, La Malinche Mexican, Logan's Roadhouse, McDonald's, Outback Steaks, Pei Wei, Peter Piper Pizza, Sonic, Starbucks, Taco Bell, Taco Cabana, West TX Steaks, Whataburger, Courtyard/EVC, Hampton Inn, Holiday Inn Express, AT&T, Chevrolet, GNC, Kia, Kohl's, Lowe's, Michaels, Nissan, Office Depot, Ross, Walgreens, World Mkt, S Circle K/dsl, Gallego's Mexican, city park, Mazda, vet, Volvo/Mack
30	Lee Trevino Dr, N Valero, Denny's, Desert Oak BBQ, Quik Wok, Whataburger, La Quinta, Motel 6, Red Roof+, Studio 6, TownePlace Suites, Discount Tire, Firestone/auto, Ford, Home Depot, Kenworth/Ford Trucks, Lexus, Toyota, S Teppanyaki Grill, Chrysler/Dodge/Jeep
29	Lomaland Dr, S Alon/7-11, Ramada, Harley-Davidson
28b	Yarbrough Dr, El Paso, N Murphy USA, Speedway/Coldstone/dsl, Buffalo Wild Wings, Burger King, Corner Bakery, Dunkin', Grandy's, Hayashi Japanese, LJ Silver, McDonald's, Peter Piper Pizza, Sonic, Subway, TX Roadhouse, Wendy's, Whataburger, Wienerschnitzel, Days Inn, $Tree, AT&T, Midas, Ross, Walmart/McDonald's/EVC, S Circle K/dsl, Applebee's, Cabo Joe's, Cuñado's Mexican, El Paso Roadrunner RV Park, Julio's Cafe, La Malinche Mexican, Lin's Buffet, Pizza Hut, Rudy's BBQ/gas, Villa Del Mar, InTown Suites, La Quinta, Quality Inn, H
28a	FM 2316, McRae Blvd, N Speedway, Carl's Jr, ChuckECheese, Jack-in-the-Box, Brake Masters, H, Walgreens, S Circle K/dsl, Gabriel's Mexican, NAPA,

INTERSTATE 10 Cont'd

EL PASO

28a Continued
vet

27 Hunter Dr, Viscount Blvd, N Circle K/dsl, Burger Bros, Chih'ua Rest., El Cometa, Grand China Buffet, T-Coasters, Taco Bell, La Quinta, $General, $Tree, Hobby Lobby, S Chevron/dsl, Gom Ramen, Whataburger, Family$, Food City

26 Hawkins Blvd, El Paso, N Shamrock, Speedway, Cane's Chicken, Chipotle Mexican, Chuy's Mexican, Cici's Pizza, Crave Kitchen, Crazy Crab Seafood, Firehouse Subs, Grimaldi's Pizzeria, Jersey Mike's, Kona Grill, la Madeleine, Landry's Seafood, Luby's, Melting Pot, Menchie's FroYo, Mooyah Burgers, Olive Garden, P.F. Changs, Panda Express, Red Lobster, Ruth's Chris, Starbucks, Starbucks, Tony's Grill, Verde Salad Co, AT&T, Barnes&Noble, Best Buy, Dick's, PetSmart, Sam's Club/gas, Steinmart, TJ Maxx, Verizon, Walgreens, Walmart, S Circle K/dsl, Lotaburger, McDonald's, Super 8, Tony Lama Boots

25 Airway Blvd, N Speedway/dsl, Carino's, Chick-fil-A, Corner Bakery, corralito steaks, Jimmy John's, Piara Pizza, Starbucks, West TX Steaks, Whataburger, Best Western+, Comfort Inn, Courtyard, Fairfield Inn, Hampton Inn, SpringHill Suites, TownePlace Suites, El Paso, vet, VW/Volvo/Mercedes, S Speedway/dsl/24hr, Hilton Garden, Holiday Inn Express, Homewood Suites, Staybridge Suites

24b Geronimo Dr, N El Taco Tote, Taco Cabana, Holiday Inn, Residence Inn, $Tree, Costco/gas, Kohl's, Marshall's, Office Depot, Ross, Target, Walgreens, S Alon/7-11/dsl, Circle K, Denny's, IHOP, Tacos Chinampa, Embassy Suites, Hyatt Place, La Quinta, URGENT CARE

24a Trowbridge Dr, N McDonald's, Whataburger, Ford, Nissan

23b US 62/180, to Paisano Dr, N Jack-in-the-Box, McDonald's, Pizza Hut, Subway, Whataburger, Wingstop, Budget Inn, Soluna Inn, Ford, to Carlsbad, U-Haul, S Mi Pueblo Nuevo

23a Raynolds St, S Americas Hotel, H

22b US 54, Patriot Fwy

22a Copia St, El Paso, N Alon/7-11, Shamrock, Church's TX Chicken, KFC

21 Piedras St, El Paso, N Burger King, McDonald's, Monteleone's Ristorante, $General

20 Dallas St, Cotton St, N Circle K, Rafa's Burritos, Subway

19 TX 20, El Paso, downtown, S The Pizza Joint, DoubleTree Inn, Holiday Inn Express, Hotel Paso Del Norte

18b Franklin Ave, Porfirio Diaz St

18a Schuster Ave, N Sun Bowl, S to UTEP

16 Executive Ctr Blvd, N Circle K, Extend-a-Suites

SUNLAND PARK

13b a US 85, Paisano Dr, to Sunland Park Dr, N Circle K, Buffalo Wild Wings, Carino's Italian, ChuckECheese, Corner Bakery Cafe, Five Guys, IHOP, NY Pizza Diner, Olive Garden, PF Chang's, Red Lobster, Sonic, Whataburger, $Tree, AT&T, Barnes&Noble, Best Buy, Dillard's, Marshall's, Michael's, Office Depot, Old Navy, PetSmart, Ross, Sprouts Mkt, Target, Verizon, vet, S Circle K/dsl, Speedway, Baskin-Robbins, Bob-O's Funpark, Gorditas Tony's, King Crab, La Malinche Mexican, La Palmita, Little Caesar's, McDonald's, Pollo feliz, State Line BBQ, Wingstop, Best Western, Extended Stay America, Holiday Inn, Quality Inn, Sleep Inn, Buick/GMC, Chrysler/Dodge/Jeep, Family$, Vista Mkt

12 Resler Dr(from wb)

11 TX 20, to Mesa St, Sunland Park, N Chevron/dsl, Circle K/dsl, Ali Baba Mediterranean, Chick-fil-A, Chili's, CiCi's, Coldstone, Cracker Barrel, Domino's Pizza, Famous Dave's BBQ, Golden Corral, Jason's Deli, Krispy Kreme,

11 Continued
Leo's Mexican, Los Cabos Seafood, PacoWong's Chinese, Panda Express, Papa John's, Pei Wei, Popeyes, Red Wok, Saltgrass Steaks, Starbucks, Sushi Zen, Taco Bell, Tacotote!, TX Roadhouse, Weck's, Wendy's, Wienerschnitzel, Wing Daddy's, Zino's Greek, Comfort Suites, EconoLodge, Fairfield Inn, La Quinta(2), LaQuinta, Red Roof Inn, SpringHill Suites, $Tree, Albertson's, BigLots, Firestone/auto, GNC, Home Depot, PepBoys, TirePros, USPO, Verizon, Walmart/McDonald's, S Speedway/dsl, Valero/dsl, Ay Caramba Mexican, Burger King, Butter Smith Kitchen, Church's TX Chicken, Jack-in-the-Box, Jun's Ramen, Ke' Flauta, KFC, McDonald's, Pizza Hut, Starbucks, Taco Cabana, Days Inn, Motel 6, Travelodge, AutoZone, CVS, Food King, Hobby Lobby, Martin Tires, Sam's Club/gas, Walgreens

9 Redd Rd, N Circle K, Applebee's, Bahama Buck's, Burger King, China House, Peter Piper Pizza, Starbucks, Albertson's, Ford, Kohl's, Lowe's, O'Reilly Parts, S Circle K, Circle K/dsl, Los Jarrones, Chevrolet, Honda, Mazda, URGENT CARE, VW, Walmart Mkt

8 Artcraft Rd, N Walmart Gas/dsl, Boss Tenders, Cane's, Chick-fil-A, Chipotle, Freddy's Steakburgers, Jersey Mike's, McDonald's, Menchie's, Panda Express, Pieology, Silverlake Ramen, Starbucks, Taco Bell, The Crab Station, AT&T, Cabela's, Ross, TJ Maxx, Tuesday Morning, Verizon, Walmart, S Speedway/dsl, Carl's Jr, Church's TX Chicken, Rudy's BBQ/dsl, Subway, Wingstop, Hampton Inn, Holiday Inn Express, Quality Inn, $Tree, Infinity

6 Lp 375, Transmountain Rd, to Canutillo, N Giant/DQ/dsl, Franklin Mtns SP, to Trans Mountain Rd, S Shell/McDonald's, IHOP, Pizza Hut, Popeyes, Sonic, Starbucks, Tacotote!, Whataburger, Discount Tire, El Paso Shops/Famous Brands, GNC, Martin Tire

5mm truck check sta eb

ANTHONY

2 Westway, Vinton, N TA/Subway/dsl/scales/24hr/@, Extended Stay, American RV Park, Camping World(1mi), truck repair/tires

1 **full facilities, info, litter barrels, petwalk, weigh sta wb, Welcome Ctr eb**, S Great American Steaks, Anthony RV Ctr, funpark

0 FM 1905, Anthony, N Flying J/Denny's/dsl/LP/RV dump/24hr, Love's/Chester's/McDonald's/dsl/scales/24hr/@, Don Carbon, Anthony Inn, S Alon/7-11/dsl, Pilot/Wendy's/dsl/24hr/@, Burger King, Domino's Pizza, KFC/Taco Bell, Best Western, $Tree, Anthony RV Ctr, funpark, Lowes Foods, tires, truckwash, Walgreens

0mm Texas/New Mexico state line

INTERSTATE 20

636mm Texas/Louisiana state line

635.5mm **full facilities, litter barrels, petwalk, Welcome Ctr/ wb**

MARSHALL

635 TX 9, TX 156, to Waskom, N Chevron/Burger King/dsl, Exxon/McDonald's/dsl, DQ, Jim's BBQ, Family$, USPO

633 US 80, FM 9, FM 134, to Waskom, N Shell, Catfish Village Rest., S Miss Ellie's RV Park

628 to US 80, to frontage rd

624 FM 2199, to Scottsville, S Marshall Woods RV Camping (1mi)

620 FM 31, to Elysian Fields, N Timberline RV Park(3mi)

617 US 59, Marshall, N Exxon/dsl, Shell, Applebee's, Burger King, Cafe Italia, Dinne Belle, El Taco, Golden Chick, Golden Corral, IHOP, Injapan Steaks, Jalapeño Tree, Jose Tequila's, KFC, Little Caesars, McDonald's, Pizza Hut, Porky's Smokehouse, Sonic, Subway, Taco Bell, Waffle House, Whataburger, Best Western, Clarion, Comfort Suites/EVC, Days Inn, Fairfield Inn, Hampton Inn, Quality Inn, Texas Inn,

TX

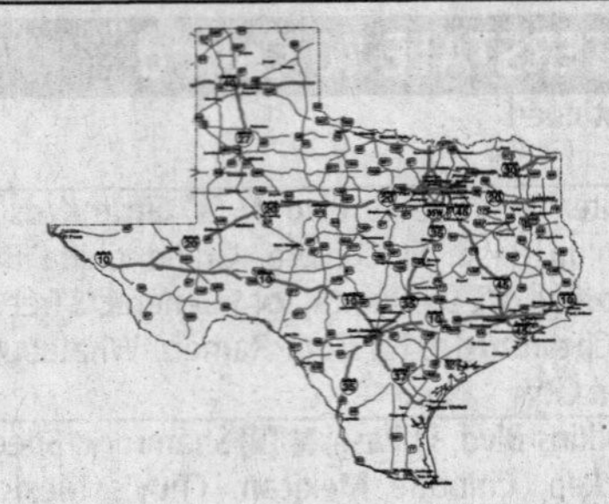

INTERSTATE 20 Cont'd

HALLSVILLE

617 Continued
$General, Chevrolet, Chrysler/Dodge/Jeep, Ford/Lincoln, NAPA, Toyota/Scion, S Chevron/dsl, Conoco/Pony Express/dsl/scales/@, Valero/dsl, Arya Inn, Best Value Inn, Holiday Inn Express, La Quinta, Motel 6, Holiday Springs RV Park(2mi), Laguna Vista RV Camping(2mi)

614 TX 43, to Marshall, S to Martin Creek Lake SP

610 FM 3251

604 FM 450, Hallsville, N Phillips 66/dsl, 450 Hitchin' Post RV Park, to Lake O' the Pines

600mm Mason Creek

599 FM 968, Longview, N Kenworth, S Exxon/Sonic/dsl, Wanda's Burgers/@, Cowboy RV Park(5mi), Goodyear Truck Tire, truck repair, truck/rv wash

596 US 259 N, TX 149, to Lake O' Pines, N Exxon/Grandy's/dsl, Shell/Sonic/TX Smokehouse/dsl, Burger King, Denny's, Whataburger, Holiday Inn Express, Quality Inn, Super 8, H, S Valero/dsl, Cracker Barrel, Best Western+, Hampton Inn, to Martin Lake SP

595b a TX 322, Estes Pkwy, N Exxon/dsl, EZ Mart, Donut Delux, Fat Boyzzz, McDonald's, Waffle House, Best Value Inn, Express Inn, Guest Inn, Knight's Inn, La Quinta, Red Roof Inn/EVC, Family$, S Alon/dsl, Murphy USA/dsl, Domino's, Jucys Taco, KFC/Taco Bell, Baymont Inn, Days Inn, Motel 6, auto repair, Walmart/Subway

KILGORE

593mm Sabine River

591 FM 2087, FM 2011, N Pine Ridge RV Park(1mi), Wise RV Park, S Fernbrook RV Park(2mi), Pinewood RV Park

589b a US 259, TX 31, (exits left from wb), Kilgore, S Exxon/dsl, Gulf/dsl, Chili's, Jalapeno Tree, Mazzio's, McDonald's, McKay's Ranch, Pizza Hut, Taco Bell, Taco Bueno, Wingstop, Best Value Inn, Best Western, Comfort Suites, Executive Inn, Hampton Inn, Holiday Inn Express, Motel 6, Motel 6, AutoZone, Chevrolet, E Texas Oil Museum, Ford, O'Reilly Parts

587 TX 42, Kilgore, N Exxon/dsl, Bodacious BBQ, S TA Express/Exxon/Dunkin'/Wendy's/dsl, Denny's, Sunriser Inn, E TX Oil Museum, Fleet Lube/Tires, Walmart(3mi)

583 TX 135, to Kilgore, Overton, N EZmart/dsl, Shallow Creek RV Resort

582 FM 3053, Liberty City, N Exxon/Subway/dsl, Shell/Whataburger/dsl, Docs Tacos, DQ, Los Enchilado's, Sonic, Gateway Lube, S fireworks

579 Joy-Wright Mtn Rd, N truckwash, S 579 Crawfish

575 Barber Rd, N Love's/dsl/RV hookup/24hr/@, S Stillwater RV Resort

TYLER

574mm picnic area both lanes, handicapped accessible, tables, litter barrels

571b FM 757, Omen Rd, to Starrville

571a US 271, to Gladewater, Tyler, S Cefco/Carl's Jr/Subway/dsl/scales/24hr, Shell/Sonic/TX Smokehouse/dsl/scales/24hr

567 TX 155, Winona, N Valero/dsl/24hr, S DQ(2mi), Country Side Inn, Freightliner, H

565 FM 2015, to Driskill-Lake Rd

562 FM 14, N C Rojo's Taqueria, to Tyler SP, S Pilot/McDonald's/dsl/scales/24hr, Northgate RV Park(4mi)

560 Lavender Rd, N Trails RV Park, S 5 Star RV Park(2 mi)

557 Jim Hogg Rd, N 76/dsl, Happy Trails RV Park(1mi), TX Rose RV Park

556 US 69, to Tyler, N Murphy USA/dsl, QT/dsl, RaceWay/dsl, Burger King, Chicken Express, Chili's, Cinco de Mayo, Domino's, Eastern Buffet, IHOP, Italian Garden, JT2 Burgers, Juanita's Express, Lindale Donuts, McDonald's, Pizza Hut,

CANTON

556 Continued
Posado's Cafe, Schlotzsky's, Sonic, Subway, Taco Bell, Wingstop, Best Western, Comfort Suites, Hampton Inn, Holiday Inn Express, La Quinta, Motel 6, $General, $Tree, Kwik Kar, Lowe's, Verizon, Walmart/Subway, S Chick-fil-A, Cracker Barrel, Panda Express, Starbucks, Apple Tree Inn

554 Harvey Rd

553 TX 49 S(toll), CR 411

552 FM 849, N Exxon/dsl, Collin St Bakery/Tesla EVC, Subway, vet

548 TX 110, to Grand Saline, N Exxon/dsl, S Valero/dsl

546mm cmv insp sta both lanes

544 Willow Branch Rd, N Willow Branch RV Park

540 FM 314, to Van, N Love's/Carl's Jr/dsl/scales/24hr/@, Love's/Arby's/dsl/scales/24hr, DQ, Farmhouse Rest, Sonic, Soulmans BBQ, Subway, Taco Bell, Fairfield Inn, Van Inn

538mm **full facilities, litter barrels, petwalk,** both lanes, **vending**

537 FM 773, FM 16

536 Tank Farm Rd, S Wagon Train RV Park(1mi)

533 Oakland Rd, to Colfax, N Shell/Pilot/A&W/LJ Silver/scales/dsl

530 FM 1255, Canton

528 FM 17, to Grand Saline, N Chrysler/Dodge/Jeep

527 TX 19, N Exxon/dsl, Bunker Rest., Chicken Express, Denny's, Jalapeño Tree, Panda Express, Whataburger, Motel 6, Quality Inn, Super 8, S Circle K/dsl/24hr, Shell/dsl, Valero/dsl, Dairy Palace, Domino's, DQ, Jerry's Pizza, McDonald's, Schlotzsky's, Subway, Taco Bell, Trade Days Donuts, Wing Dingers, Best Western, Days Inn, Ford, Mill Creek Ranch RV Resort, to First Monday SP

526 FM 859, to Edgewood

523 TX 64, Wills Point, N Shell/dsl/24hr, Craft 64 Burgers, Taco Casa, Bluebird RV Park, repair, S Rolling Oaks RV Park

521 Myrtle Springs Rd, S Explore USA RV Ctr, repair

519 Turner-Hayden Rd, S Canton RV Park

516 FM 47, to Wills Point, N to Lake Tawakoni, Fourwinds Steaks, S Texaco/dsl, Robertson's Café/gas, Interstate Motel

512 FM 2965, Hiram-Wills Point Rd

512mm cmv inspection sta both lanes

509 Hiram Rd, S Shell/dsl/cafe/24hr

506 FM 429, FM 2728, College Mound Rd, N Blue Bonnet Ridge RV Park

503 Wilson Rd, S TA/Shell/Country Pride/Pizza Hut/Subway/dsl/LP/24hr/@

501 TX 34, to Terrell, N QT/dsl/scales/24hr, Shell/Subway/dsl, Church's TX Chicken, Gorditas Cafe, Schlotzsky's, Sonic, Starbucks, Two Jalapeno Mexican, Waffle House, Baymont Inn, Motel 6, Quality Inn, Red Roof Inn, Super 8, Home Depot, S Valero/Circle K/dsl, Applebee's, Golden Chick, IHOP, McDonald's, Silver Saloon BBQ, Wendy's, Holiday Inn Express, SureStay, Old Navy, Tanger Outlet/famous brands

INTERSTATE 20 Cont'd

Exit #	Services
499b	Rose Hill Rd, to Terrell
499a	to US 80, W to Dallas, same as 498
498	FM 148, to Terrell, N Buc-ee's/dsl, Exxon/Denny's/Subway/dsl, Shell/dsl, Cane's, Chick-fil-A, Chili's, Chipotle, DQ, Freddy's, Olive Garden, Panda Express, Soulman's BBQ, Starbucks, Taco Bueno, Taco Cabana, TX Roadhouse, Whataburger, Fairfield Inn, La Quinta, Tru Hilton, AT&T, Chrysler/Dodge/Jeep, Discount Tire, Ford, Marshall's, S Terrell RV Park
493	FM 1641, S Exxon/Pizza Inn/Taco Mayo/dsl, Sonic
491	FM 2932, Helms Tr, to Forney, N Shell/Subway/dsl, Domino's, Stinky Ribs BBQ
490	FM 741, to Forney
487	FM 740, to Forney, S Lakeside RV park
483	Lawson Rd, Lasater Rd
482	Belt Line Rd, to Lasater, N Exxon/dsl, Marathon, Denny's, Fuzzy's Tacos, Sonic, TX Smokehouse BBQ, S Shell/Subway/EVC
481	Seagoville Rd, N Shell/rest., Valero/dsl, Motel 6, $General, S Lindy's Rest.
480	I-635, N to Mesquite
479b a	US 175, S Marlow/dsl
477	St Augustine Rd, N Family$, S Shell/dsl, Sonic, Taqueria Ricardo's
476	Dowdy Ferry Rd
474	TX 310 N, Central Expsy
473b a	JJ Lemmon Rd, I-45 N to Dallas, S to Houston
472	Bonnie View Rd, N Flying J/Denny's/dsl/LP/scales/24hr/@, Shell, Jack-in-the-Box, Express Inn, Blue Beacon, Kenworth, Speedco Lube, S TA/Exxon/Burger King/Taco Bell/dsl/scales/24hr/@
470	TX 342, Lancaster Rd, N Chevron/dsl, Exxon/Popeyes/Subway/dsl/scales/24hr, Soulman's BBQ, S Pilot/Wendy's/dsl/scales/24hr, LJ Silver/Taco Bell, McDonald's, Sonic, Whataburger, William's Chicken, Days Inn
468	Houston School Rd, S Exxon/dsl/EVC, QT/dsl, Whataburger
467b a	I-35E, N to Dallas, S to Waco, N Shell
466	S Polk St, N 24-7/dsl, Exxon/dsl, Quick Track, Dan's Seafood, DQ, Sonic, Subway, Family$, S Love's/Carl's Jr/dsl/scales/24hr
465	Wheatland/S Hampton Rds, N Shell/Subway, Cane's Chicken, Chick-fil-A, Chili's, Chipotle, $Tree, ALDI, CVS Drug, GNC, Office Depot, PetSmart, Ross, Target, S Chevron/McDonald's, Mobil/dsl, Murphy USA/dsl, QT/dsl, Arby's, Burger King, Cheddar's, Jack-in-the-Box, Panda Express, Popeyes, Sonic, Spring Creek BBQ, Taco Bell, Wendy's, Super 8, Home Depot, Honda, [H], Hyundai, Kia, Lowe's, Nissan, Sam's Club/gas, Toyota, Walmart
464b a	US 67, Love Fwy
463	Camp Wisdom Rd, N Chevron/7-11, Exxon, Catfish King Rest., Denny's, Hangry Joe's Chicken, Pollo Regio, Taco Bell/LJ Silver, Taco Cabana, Rodeway Inn, Royal Inn, Super 7, TownHouse Suites, $Tree, Chrysler/Dodge/Jeep, S Shamrock, Burger King, Chubby's Rest., Dave's BBQ, Olive Garden, Red Lobster, Sabor Mexican, Subway
462b a	Duncanville Rd(no EZ wb return), S QT, Shell/dsl, Church's TX Chicken, El Patron, Jack-in-the-Box, Little Caesars, Los Lupes Mexican, McDonald's, Popeyes, Smokey D'Z BBQ, Subway, Whataburger, Hampton Inn, Hilton Garden, Motel 6, Firestone/auto, Kroger
461	Cedar Ridge Rd, S RaceTrac/dsl
460	TX 408
458	Mt Creek Pkwy, N Exxon/BBQ/dsl
457	FM 1382, to Grand Prairie, N Shell/7-11/dsl, Valero/Circle K/dsl, Waffle House, S RaceTrac/dsl, Jack-in-the-Box, to Joe Pool Lake
456	Carrier Pkwy, to Corn Valley Rd, N QT, Texaco, Chick-fil-A, Dickey's BBQ, Domino's, Pollo Regio, Popeyes, Simply Asia, Sonic, Taco Cabana, Whataburger, AutoZone, Home Depot, Target, S Exxon, Baskin-Robbins, Boston Mkt, Chapp's Cafe, Cheddar's, Chili's, Chipotle, Denny's, IHOP, Little Caesar's, McDonald's, Panera Bread, Rusty Taco, Spring Creek BBQ, Starbucks, Subway, Holiday Inn Express, Albertsons/gas, CVS Drug, GNC, Tom Thumb Foods/gas, Verizon, Walgreens
455	TX 151, S QT/dsl
454	Great Southwest Pkwy, N Exxon/dsl, Mobil/7-11/dsl, Beto's, Cheesesteak House, ChuckeCheese, DQ, Golden Corral, Hooters, KFC, McDonald's, Taco Bell, Taco Bueno, TX Roadhouse, Waffle House, Wendy's, Wienerschnitzel, Candlewood Suites, Heritage Inn, Quality Inn, Firestone/auto, Harley-Davidson, [H], U-Haul, S Mobil/7-11, QT/dsl, Shell/Subway/dsl, Valero/Circle K/dsl, Applebee's, Arby's, Buffalo Wild Wings, Burger King, Schlotzsky's, Sonic, Home2 Suites, La Quinta, Super 8, $Tree, ALDI, AT&T, Discount Tire, Kroger, Office Depot, PetSmart, RaceTrac/dsl, Sam's Club, to Joe Pool Lake, Walgreens, Walmart/McDonald's
453b a	TX 360
452	Frontage Rd
451	Collins St, New York Ave, N Exxon/dsl, RaceTrac/dsl, Rudy's Store/BBQ/dsl, Cotton Patch Cafe, Egg Bar, Golden Corral, Jack-in-the-Box, Starbucks, Taco Casa, Whataburger, Aloft, Hilton Garden, Chrysler/Dodge/Jeep, Kia/Mazda/VW, URGENT CARE, S QT, Shell, Valero/dsl, Chicken Express, KFC/Taco Bell, McDonald's, Sonic, Subway, Taco Bueno, Hampton Inn, Buick/GMC, Nissan
450	Matlock Rd, Golden Chick, N Abuelo's Mexican, BJ's Rest., Black-eyed Pea, Bone Daddy's, Boomer Jack's Grill, Chuy's Mexican, Coldstone, Dave&Buster's, Dog Haus, Freebirds Burrito, Genghis Grill, Gloria's, Jason's Deli, Kincaide's Burgers, Lazy Dog, McAlister's Deli, Melting Pot, Mercado Juarez, Mimi's Cafe, PF Changs, Piranha Killer Ramen, Pluckers's Wings, Potbelly, Red Robin, Starbucks, Sweet Tomatoes, The Keg Steaks, Torchy's Tacos, Walk-On's, Wendy's, Which Wich, Courtyard, Quality Inn, Residence Inn, AT&T, Costco/gas, [H], Jo-Ann Fabrics, Lowe's, Old Navy, PetSmart, Staples, World Mkt, S Exxon/7-11, RaceWay/dsl, Shell/7-11, China King, Good Time BBQ, Joe's Pizza, Panda Delite Chinese, Pizza Patron, Starbucks, Sunny Thai, Tarboosh Gyro, Fry's Electronics, O'Reilly Parts
449	FM 157, Cooper St, N Shell/dsl, Bon KBBQ, Cane's, Cheesecake Factory, Chili's, Corner Bakery, Five Guys, Honey Baked Ham, IHOP, In-N-Out, McDonald's, On-the-Border, Outback Steaks, Panera Bread, Pei Wei, Razzoo's Cajun Café, Red Lobster, Ricky's Chicken, Rockfish Seafood, Salt Grass Steaks, Souper Salad, Spaghetti Whse, Days Inn, Holiday Inn Express, La Quinta, Motel 6, Studio 6, Super 8, Barnes&Noble, Best Buy, Dick's, Dillard's, Discount Tire, JC Penney, Macy's, mall, Michael's, Target, TJ Maxx, Treetops RV Camping, Verizon, S Applebee's, Arby's, Baskin-Robbins, Boston Mkt, Burger St, Chamas Brazilian, Chick-fil-A, Chipotle, Denny's, Dunkin', El Arroyo, El Fenix Mexican, El Pollo Loco, First Watch, LJ Silver, Macaroni Grill, McDonald's, Mr Hibachi, Ninja Ramen, Ninja Sushi, Olive Garden, Panda Express, Peter Piper Pizza, Pullita Chicken, Red Claws Seafood, Starbucks, Taco Cabana, TGIFriday, Tong's Mongolian, InTown Suites, Microtel, $Tree, AAA, Acura, Chevrolet, Ford, Hobby Lobby, Home Depot, Honda, Hyundai, NTB, Ross, Suzuki, Toyota, Walmart/McDonald's

TX

= gas = food = lodging = other = rest stop

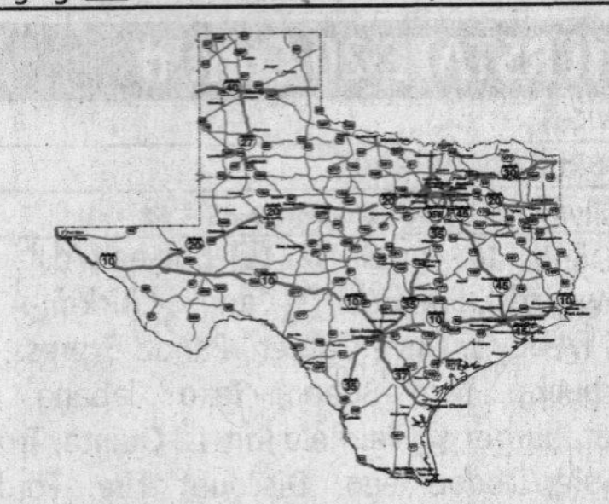

INTERSTATE 20 Cont'd

Exit #	Services
448	Bowen Rd, N QT, RaceTrac/dsl, Chicken Express, Cracker Barrel, Sonic, S Shell
447	Kelly-Elliott Rd, Park Springs Blvd, N 7-11, Valero, S Exxon/Subway, city park
445	Green Oaks Blvd, N Chevron/dsl, Shell/7-11/dsl, Arby's, Boston Mkt, Braum's, Burger St, Cafe Acapulco, Chapp's Cafe, Chick-fil-A, Chipotle, CiCi's, Colter's BBQ, Dunkin', Fuzzy's Tacos, Hooters, Jack-in-the-Box, Jay Jay Rest., Joe's Pizza, Oldwest Cafe, Quizno's, Schlotzsky's, Starbucks, Taco Bell, Taco Cabana, Taco Casa, The Catch, Wendy's, Whataburger, Wingstop, $Tree, Ace Hardware, Albertsons, AT&T, CVS Drug, Firestone, Kroger/dsl, Meineke, Office Depot, Verizon, Walgreens, S Murphy Express/dsl, QT/dsl, Quick Track, Valero/dsl, Cheddar's, Chili's, Corky's Pizza, Golden Buffet, Gyros Xpress, IHOP, Little Caesars, McDonald's, Pancho's Mexican, Panda Express, Sonic, Subway, Taco Bueno, Thai TX, Waffle House, $General, ALDI, AutoZone, BigLots, Discount Tire, O'Reilly Parts, vet, Walmart/Subway
444	US 287 S, to Waxahatchie, from eb, same as 445
443	Bowman Springs Rd(from wb)
442b a	I-820 to Ft Worth, US 287 bus, N Texaco/dsl, Valero, Great Western Inn, Knights Inn, S QT/dsl, Burger King, McDonald's, Popeyes
441	Anglin Dr, Hartman Lane, S Chevron/dsl
440a	Forest Hill Dr, N Starbucks, Woodspring Suites, S Shell/7-11/dsl, Braum's, Capt D's, CiCi's Pizza, Jack-in-the-Box, Luby's, Shipley Do-nuts, Sonic, Subway, Taco Bell, La Quinta, $General, $Tree, AutoZone, CVS Drug, Discount Tire, O'Reilly Parts, Super 1 Foods, Walgreens
440b	Wichita St, N QT/dsl, #1 Chinese, Taco Casa, Wendy's, S Exxon/dsl, Valero, Burger King, Chicken Express, Denny's, Domino's, McDonald's, Pizza Hut, Schlotzsky's, Whataburger, Best Western+, Hampton Inn, La Quinta
439	Campus Dr, N Chrysler/Dodge/Jeep, Ford, S Scottish Inns, Sam's Club/gas
438	Oak Grove Rd, S Valero
437	I-35W, N to Ft Worth, S to Waco
436b	Hemphill St, N Shell/dsl, S Chevrolet
436a	FM 731(from eb), to Crowley Ave, N Conoco/dsl, Valero/dsl, China Express, tires/repair, S BurgerBox, Pizza Hut/Taco Bell, tires
435	McCart St, N 76, Shell/dsl, Antojitos Morazan, Samwon Garden, Sona Taquiera, S Mobil/dsl, QT/dsl, Mexico Real
434b	Trail Lakes Dr, S Shell, Domino's, Sonic, Starbucks, Subway, Wendy's, CVS Drug, Family$
434a	Granbury Rd, S QT/dsl
433	Hulen St, N Shell/dsl, ChuckECheese, Honeybaked Ham, Ninja Sushi, Olive Garden, Original Pancake House, TX Roadhouse, TownePlace Suites, Albertsons, Home Depot, NTB, PetSmart, Sprouts Mkt, TJ Maxx, S Abuelo's Mexican, BJ's Rest., Chili's, Denny's, Five Guys, Freebirds Mexican, In-N-Out, Jack-in-the-Box, Jamba Juice, Kincaide's Burgers, Kyoto Japanese, McDonald's, Mexican Inn, Panera Bread, Potbelly, Red Lobster, Red Robin/EVC, Torchy's Tacos, Hampton Inn, Barnes&Noble, Dillard's, Hobby Lobby, Macy's, Michael's, Office Depot, Old Navy, Ross, T-Mobile
431	(432 from wb), TX 183, Bryant-Irvin Rd, N Chevron, Bonnell's, Chipotle Mexican, Genghis Grill, Keg Steaks, Mimi's Café, On-the-Border, Best Buy, Cavender's Boots, Kohl's, Lowe's, PetSmart, Sam's Club/gas, S Exxon/dsl, BoomerJack's, Chick-fil-A, Chicken Express, Cousin's BBQ, Firehouse Subs, Hawaiian Bros, Home2 Suites, IHOP,
431	Continued Jimmy John's, Lonestar Oysters, Outback Steaks, Pei Wei, Pizza Hut, Razzoo's Cajun, Rio Mambo, SaltGrass Steaks, Schlotzsky's, Sonic, Starbucks, Szechuan, Wingstop, Courtyard, Extended Stay America, Extended Stay America, Fairfield Inn, Hampton Inn, Holiday Inn Express, Homewood Suites, Hyatt Place, La Quinta, AT&T, Costco/gas, Firestone/auto, Ford, Goodyear/auto, H, Infiniti, Kwik Kar, Lexus, Mazda, Petco, Staples, Target, Verizon, Walgreens
430mm	Clear Fork Trinity River
429b	Winscott Rd, N Circle K/dsl, Cracker Barrel, Comfort Suites, SureStay
429a	US 377, to Granbury, N Circle K, Cracker Barrel, Comfort Suites, SureStay Plus, S 7-11/dsl, QT/dsl, RaceTrac/dsl, Shell/dsl, Valero, 3 Parrots Tacos, Arby's, Braum's, Cane's Chicken, Chick-fil-A, Chicken Express, Chipotle, Domino's, DQ, Hoffbrau Steaks, Jimmy John's, Lonestar Grill, McDonald's, Paisano's Pizza, Panda Express, Popeyes, Riscky's BBQ, Sonic, Starbucks, Taco Bueno, Taco Casa, Waffle House, Wendy's, Whataburger, Motel 6, $General, AT&T, AutoZone, CVS Drug, O'Reilly Parts, USPO, Walgreens, Walmart
428	I-820, N around Ft Worth
426	RM 2871, Chapin School Rd
425	Markum Ranch Rd, S Shell/Taco Bell/Dunkin'/dsl/scales/parking/24hr
421	I-30 E(from eb), to Ft Worth
420	FM 1187, Aledo, Farmer, S Cowtown RV Park (1mi), park & ride
419mm	weigh sta eb
418	Ranch House Rd, Willow Park, N Exxon/Taco Casa, Shell/dsl, Pizza Hut, Sonic, Subway, Taco Casa, Whataburger, S Chevron/dsl, Chicken Express, CiBi Italian, Domino's, Fuzzy's Tacos, McDonald's, Railhead BBQ, Starbuck's, Quality Inn, $General, Brookshire Foods/gas, Cowtown RV Park, Texas RV Outlet
417mm	N Cafe 23:5, Drake's BBQ, Hot Chicken, Sunny Street Cafe, SpringHill Suites, H
415	FM 5, Mikus Rd, Annetta, N vet, S Shell/dsl
413	(414 from wb), US 180 W, Lake Shore Dr, N H-E-B/gas, Murphy USA/dsl, RaceTrac/dsl, AutoZone, Big Burger, Chick-fil-A, DQ, Golden Chick, La Playa Mexican, Mama's Pizza, McDonald's, Sonic, Subway, Taco Bell, Waffle House, Buick/Cadillac/Chevrolet/GMC, Ford, HEB Mkt, Hyundai, Nissan, Toyota, Verizon, VW, Walgreens, Walmart/Subway, S Valero/dsl, W Starbuck's
411	Service Rd(from wb), same as 413
410	Bankhead Hwy, S Love's/Godfather's/dsl/repair/24hr/@
409	FM 2552 N, Clear Lake Rd, N Petro/Valero/Popeyes/Iron Skillet/dsl/scales/24hr/@, Antonio's Mexican, Jack-in-the-Box, Little Panda Chinese, R&K on Santa Fe, Heritage Inn, SleepGo Motel, Blue Beacon, H, S Exxon/dsl
408	TX 171, FM 1884, FM 51, Tin Top Rd, Weatherford, N Exxon, Exxon, Mobil, Murphy USA/dsl, RaceTrac, Baker's Ribs, Braum's, Buffalo Wild Wings, Cane's, Chicken Express, CiCi's Pizza, Cotton Patch Cafe, Dickey's BBQ,

ANNETTA

INTERSTATE 20 Cont'd

WEATHERFORD

408 Continued
El Fenix Mexican, Firehouse Subs, IHOP, Jimmy John's, KFC, LJ Silver, Logan's Roadhouse, Marco's Pizza, McAlister's Deli, McDonald's, MT Rest., Oaxaca, Olive Garden, Panda Express, Panera Bread, Rosa's Cafe, Rule the Roost, Schlotzsky's, Slim Chickens, Starbucks, Taco Bell, Taco Bueno, Whataburger, Wingstop, Clarion, La Quinta, Super 8, $Tree, ALDI, AT&T, AutoZone, Belk, Christian Bros Auto, Discount Tire, Firestone/auto, JC Penney, Just Brakes, Michael's, TJ Maxx, Verizon, Walgreens, Walmart/Subway, S Exxon/Subway/dsl, Shell/Steak'n Shake/dsl, Chick-fil-A, Chili's, Chipotle, Cracker Barrel, Hawaii Grill, On-the-Border, Subway, Tokyo Steaks, TX Roadhouse, Waffle House, Whataburger, Best Western+, Fairfield Inn, Hampton Inn, Holiday Inn Express, Motel 6, OYO, Red Roof Inn, Rodeway Inn, Woodland Suites, Best Buy, GNC, Kohl's, Lowe's, NTB, PetSmart, Ross, Target, URGENT CARE

407 Tin Top Rd(from eb), N Home Depot, S KOA, same as 408

406 Old Dennis Rd, N QT/dsl/scales/24hr, Truck'n Travel, Chuck Wagon Rest., Quest Inn, S Pilot/Wendy's/Dunkin'/dsl/scales/24hr, EconoLodge, Quality 1 Motel, Boss Truck Repair, Honda

404 Williams Memorial Dr

402 (403 from wb), TX 312, to Weatherford, N El Pollo Rico, Outlaw BBQ, Greenwood RV Park, Ranger Land RV Park, Tired Traveler RV Park(1.5mi), S Camp Eagle RV Park (1mi)

397 FM 1189, to Brock, N Chevron/dsl, Read's BBQ, Oak Creek RV Park, S Sonic

394 FM 113, to Millsap

393mm Brazos River

391 Gilbert Pit Rd, N Brazos River Cafe, Hillbilly Haven RV Park

386 US 281, to Mineral Wells, Stephenville, N Shell/Subway/dsl, Chicken Express, Coffee Creek Cabins & RV, Gilbert Pecans, S Chevron/Maverick TC/Taco Casa/dsl, Sunoco/Stripes/dsl, DQ

GORDON

380 FM 4, Santo

376 Blue Flat Rd, Panama Rd

373 TX 193, Gordon

370 TX 108 S, FM 919, Gordon, N Texaco/Bar-B/dsl, S Exxon/dsl, Cactus Rose RV Park, Longhorn Inn/Country Store

367 TX 108 N, Mingus, N Smoke Stack Café, Thurber Sta, S NY Hill Rest.

364mm Palo Pinto Creek

363 Tudor Rd, litter barrels, picnic area, tables

362mm Bear Creek, litter barrels, picnic area both lanes, tables

361 TX 16, to Strawn

359mm rest area wb, full(handicapped)facilities, picnic tables, litter barrels, petwalk

358 (from wb), frontage rd

356mm Russell Creek

354 Lp 254, Ranger

353 rest area eb, full(handicapped)facilities, picnic tables, litter barrels, vending

351 (352 from wb), College Blvd

OLDEN

349 FM 2461, Ranger, N Love's/Godfather's/Subway/dsl/scales/24hr, DQ, Rodeway Inn, RL RV Park, tires/repair, truck wash, S Phillips 66/dsl, repair

347 FM 3363(from wb), Olden

345 FM 3363(from eb), Olden, S Starr Stop Cafe

343 TX 112, FM 570, Eastland, Lake Leon, N Alon/7-11/Subway, Murphy USA/dsl, Shell/Taco Casa, Chicken Express, Domino's, DQ, Heff's Burgers, Mae's Meat Mkt, Maverick Grill, McDonald's, Pizza Heaven, Sonic, Subway, Holiday Inn Express, La Quinta, Super 8/RV park,

343 Continued
$General, AT&T, AutoZone, Buick/Cadillac/Chevrolet/GMC, Chrysler/Dodge/Jeep, O'Reilly Parts, TrueValue, U-Haul, Walmart/EVC, S Exxon/dsl, Pulido's Mexican, Budget Host, Quality Inn

CISCO

340 TX 6, Eastland, N Valero/dsl, H, S Texaco/Burger King/dsl

337 spur 490, N Wild Country RV Park

332 US 183, Cisco, N Alon/Allsups/dsl, Chicken Express, Dalia's Cafe, DQ, Guadalajara Taqueria, Pizza Heaven, Sonic, Subway, Cisco Inn, Executive Inn/RV Park, $General, Hilton Mon(1mi), NAPA, S Road Ranger

330 TX 206, Cisco, N Sunoco/Stripes/Tacos/dsl/scales/24hr, Lone Star Inn, H, S Flying J/Denny's/dsl/scales/24hr

329mm picnic area wb, litter barrels, accessible

327mm picnic area eb, litter barrels, accessible

324 Scranton Rd

322 Cooper Creek Rd

320 FM 880 N, FM 2945 N, to Moran

BAIRD

319 FM 880 S, Putnam, N USPO

316 Brushy Creek Rd

313 FM 2228

310 Finley Rd

308 Lp 20, Baird

307 US 283, Clyde, N Love's/Chester's/Subway/dsl/scales/lube/24hr, DQ, Best Value/RV park/dump, S Alon/Allsups/7-11, Conoco/dsl, Robertson's Café, Lone Star RV Park

306 FM 2047, Baird, N Chevrolet/GMC, Hanner RV Ctr, S Sundance RV Park

CLYDE

303 Union Hill Rd

301 FM 604, Cherry Lane, N Exxon/dsl, McDonald's, Sonic, Whataburger, NAPA, S Alon/7-11/dsl, Chicken Express, Subway, Family$, United Mkt, USPO

300 FM 604 N, Clyde, N Chrysler/Dodge/Jeep, S Texaco/dsl, El Mercado, White's RV Park/dump

299 FM 1707, Hays Rd, S Burger King

297 FM 603, Eula Rd

296.5mm **full facilities, litter barrels, petwalk**, both lanes, **wireless internet**

294 Buck Creek Rd, N Buck Creek RV Park/dump, Patriot RV Park, RV repair/parts, S Abilene RV Park

292b Elmdale Rd, S Elmdale RV Ranch

292a Lp 20(exits left from wb)

ABILENE

290 TX 36, Lp 322, S, zoo

288 TX 351, N Alon/7-11/dsl, Murphy USA/dsl, Betty Rose's BBQ, Buffalo Wild Wings, Cane's Chicken, Chick-fil-A, Chili's, Cracker Barrel, DQ, Heff's Burgers, Hooters, Jason's Deli, Oscar's Mexican, Panda Express, Starbucks, Subway, Taco Casa, Wingstop, Comfort Suites, Courtyard, Executive Inn, Holiday Inn Express, Home2 Suites, Motel 6, Quality Inn, Residence Inn, TownePlace Suites, Whitten Inn, $Tree, AT&T, Lowe's, Walmart, S Super 8, H

286c FM 600, Abilene, N Alon/Allsups/7-11/dsl, Denny's, Best Western, Hampton Inn, Holiday Inn, La Quinta, S Alon/7-11, Alon/7-11/dsl, Sleep Inn

286 US 83, Pine St, Abilene, S Alon/Allsups, Frontier Inn, H

285 Old Anson Rd, S Alon/Allsups/dsl, Best Value Inn

283b N US 277, U83, Anson

283a US 277 S, US 83(exits left from wb)

282 FM 3438, Shirley Rd, S Motel 6, KOA

281 Fulwiler Rd, to Dyess AFB, S to Dyess AFB

279 US 84 E, to Abilene, S access to facilities

278 Lp 20, N Conoco/dsl/24hr, S Westgo TC/Phillips 66/Huddle House/dsl/scales/24hr/@, Mack Trucks/Volvo

TX

INTERSTATE 20 Cont'd

TX

Exit #	Services
277	FM 707, Tye, N Flying J/Denny's/dsl/LP/24hr, Peterbilt, truck lube, Tye RV Park, S Alon/7-11/dsl, Southern Tire Mart, USPO
274	Wells Lane
272	Wimberly Rd
	MERKEL
270	FM 1235, Merkel, N Allsup's/DK/24hr/dsl, Alon/dsl/24hr, Windmill RV Camping, S Iron Horse/DK/dsl/24hr
269	FM 126, N Spring Mkt/mart/dsl, Sonic, Subway, Scottish Inn, S Alon/7-11/dsl, DK/dsl, Skeet's BBQ, CarQuest, Family$
267	Lp 20, Merkel, S access to gas, food, lodging
266	Derstine Rd
264	Noodle Dome Rd
263	Lp 20, Trent
262	FM 1085, N Tires+, S Alon/7-11/dsl
261	Lp 20, Trent
259	Sylvester Rd
258	White Flat Rd, oil wells
257mm	**full facilities, litter barrels, petwalk,** both lanes, **vending**
256	Stink Creek Rd
255	Adrian Rd
251	Eskota Rd
249	FM 1856, N Lonestar RV Park
247	TX 70 N, Sweetwater, N Blue Bonnet RV Park
246	Alabama Ave, Sweetwater
245	Arizona Ave(from wb), same as 244
	SWEETWATER
244	TX 70 S, Sweetwater, N Alon/7-11/dsl/24hr, Chevron/Subway/dsl, Murphy USA/dsl, Domino's, DQ, Gills Chicken, Golden Chick, Heff's Burgers, McDonald's, Subway, Wendy's, Whataburger, Best Western+, Marifa Inn, Quality Inn, Studio 6, AutoZone, H, Medicine Place Drug, Verizon, Walmart/EVC, S Shell/dsl, Big Boy's BBQ, Bigg's Pizza, Buck's BBQ, Schlotzsky's, Skeet's Grill, Taco Bell, Econo Lodge, Hampton Inn, Holiday Inn Express/EVC, La Quinta, Ranch House Motel/rest., Ford, Freedom RV Park, Rainbolt RV Park
243	Hillsdale Rd, Robert Lee St, N Family RV Ctr
242	Hopkins Rd, N Love's/Arby's/dsl/scales/repair/24hr/@, Microtel, Bar J RV Park, S TA/Alon/Pizza Hut/Popeyes/dsl/scales/24hr/@, Freedom RV Park, truck lube, truck wash, truck/tire repair
241	Lp 20, Sweetwater, N gas, food, lodging, S RV camping
240	Lp 170, N
239	May Rd
238b a	US 84 W, Blackland Rd
237	Cemetery Rd
	ROSCOE
236	FM 608, Roscoe, N Alon/dsl, Sunoco/Stripes/dsl, Rockin' S Cantina, Carquest
235	to US 84, Roscoe
230	FM 1230, many wind turbines
229mm	picnic area wb, litter barrels, accessible
228mm	picnic area eb, litter barrels, accessible
227	Narrell Rd
226b	Lp 20(from wb), Loraine
226a	FM 644 N, Wimberly Rd
225	FM 644 S, S access to gas, food
224	Lp 20, to Loraine, S gas, food
223	Lucas Rd, S Comfort Zone RV Park
221	Lasky Rd
220	FM 1899
219	Lp 20, Country Club Rd, Colorado City
	COLORADO CITY
217	TX 208 S, N Sunoco/Stripes/dsl/scales/24hr,

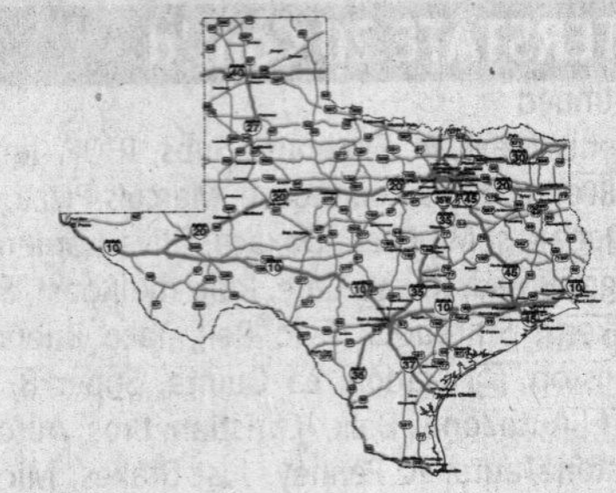

Exit #	Services
217	Continued La Quinta, S Santiago's, Lone Wolf RV Park
216	TX 208 N,, N Chevron/Subway/dsl, DQ, Best Western+, S Sunoco/Stripes/Taco Co/dsl, Golden Chick, Pizza Hut, Sonic, American Inn, Motel 6, Super 8, $General, H
215	FM 3525, Rogers Rd, N Studio 6, S access to gas, H
214.5mm	Colorado River
213	Lp 20, Enderly Rd, Colorado City
212	FM 1229
211mm	Morgan Creek
210	FM 2836, S DK/dsl, camping, picnic area, to Lake Colorado City SP
209	Dorn Rd
207	Lp 20, Westbrook, S Buck's Cafe
206	FM 670, to Westbrook
204mm	**full facilities, litter barrels, petwalk,** wb
200	Conaway Rd
199	Iatan Rd
195	frontage rd(from eb)
194a	E Howard Field Rd
192	FM 821, many oil wells
191mm	**full facilities, litter barrels, petwalk,** eb
190	Snyder Field Rd
189	McGregor Rd
188	FM 820, Coahoma, N Sunoco/Stripes/dsl, DQ, Coahoma Inn, Coahoma RV Park
186	Salem Rd, Sand Springs
184	Moss Lake Rd, Sand Springs, N Alon/dsl, $General, S RV camping, Whip in RV Park
182	Midway Rd
	BIG SPRING
181b	Refinery Rd, N Alon Refinery
181a	FM 700, , N , RV camping, S H
179	US 80, Big Spring, S Alon/7-11, Denny's, Quality Inn, Super 8, $General, Buick/Cadillac/Chevrolet
178	TX 350, Big Spring, N Shell/dsl, Eagle's Den Suites, tire/truck service, S Pilot/McDonald's/dsl/scales/24hr, Sleep Inn
177	US 87, Big Spring, N Exxon/dsl, TA/Subway/Popeyes/dsl/scales/24hr/@, TX Cajun Cafe, Advantage Inn, La Quinta, Plaza Inn, W Texas Inn, S Alon/dsl, Sunoco/Stripes/dsl, Casa Blanca Mexican, DQ, McAlister's Deli, Starbucks, Baymont Inn, Best Western, Comfort Suites, Hampton Inn, Sleep Inn MainStay Suites, TownePlace Suites, Chrysler/Dodge/Jeep
176	TX 176, Andrews, N Arena RV Park
174	Lp 20 E, Big Springs, S Shell/dsl, , Big Spring SP, H, RV camping
172	Cauble Rd
171	Moore Field Rd
169	FM 2599
168mm	picnic area both lanes, litter barrels
165	FM 818
158	Lp 20 W, to Stanton, N RV camping
156	TX 137, Lamesa, N Valero, S Phillips 66/Stripes/Subway/dsl/24hr, Luchi's BBQ, Sonic, Comfort Inn, Stanton Inn,

INTERSTATE 20 Cont'd

LAMESA / MIDLAND

156 Continued
Super 8

154 US 80, Stanton, N RV camping, S access to gas, food, lodging

151 FM 829(from wb)

144 Loop 250, N services in Midland

143mm frontage rd(from eb)

142mm picnic area both lanes, ,litter barrels, hits marker

140 FM 307(from eb)

138 TX 158, FM 715, Greenwood, N Pilot/dsl, Texaco, Valero/dsl, Bush's Chicken, KD's BBQ, Whataburger, S Flying J/Moe's/dsl/scales/24hr, Sunoco/Stripes/Subway/dsl, Sunoco/Stripes/Taco Co/dsl, Avid, Baymont Inn

137 Old Lamesa Rd, N Mainstay Suites

136 TX 349, Midland, N Murphy USA/dsl, Sunoco/Stripes/Taco Co/dsl, Cici's Pizza, Dickey's BBQ, Dominos, Garley's Mexican, IHOP, Jack-in-the-Box, Little Caesar's, McAlister's Deli, McDonald's, Sonic, Starbucks, Best Western+, Candlewood Suites, Comfort Inn, Hampton Inn, Holiday Inn Express, Microtel, Quality Inn, Super 8, TownePlace Suites, West Texas Inn, $Tree, Advance Parts, AutoZone, Chavez Tires, Discount Tire, Family$, Petroleum Museum, Verizon, Walmart/Subway/EVC, S Exxon/Subway/dsl, Pilot/dsl, Stripes/dsl, Burger King, Popeyes

135 Cotton Flat Rd

134 Midkiff Rd, N DK/dsl, Exxon/dsl, Shell, Sunoco/Stripes/dsl, Denny's, DQ, Natalia's Cafe, Best Value Inn, Bradford Inn, Days Inn, Executive Inn, HomeTowne Inn, La Quinta, Super 8, Chevrolet, Chrysler/Dodge/Jeep, Ford/Lincoln, Honda, H, Midland RV Park, Subaru

131 TX 158, Midland, N Super 7 Inn, Midland RV Park, S DK/dsl, Love's/Chester's/Subway/dsl/scales/24hr/@, Tesla EVC, Suburban Inn, Family$

126 FM 1788, N Pilot/McDonald's/dsl/scales/24hr, Shell/dsl, Sunoco/Stripes/dsl, Steak'n Shake, Carquest, Main Street Mkt/dsl, museum, Western Auto

121 Lp 338, Odessa, N Alon/7-11, Alon/DK, Stripes/Taco Co/dsl, Cheddar's, Chili's, Dickey's BBQ, Fazoli's, Five Guys, Fuddruckers, Hooters, IHOP, KFC, Logan's Roadhouse, McDonald's, Olive Garden, Panda Express, Pho House, Pizza Hut, Red Lobster, Rosa's Cafe, Schlotzsky's, Sonic, Starbucks, Starbucks, Subway, Subway, Twin Peaks Rest, Wendy's, Whataburger, Best Inn, Elegante Hotel, Fairfield Inn, Hampton Inn Express, Hilton Garden, Holiday Inn, Holiday Inn Express, HomeTowne Inn, La Quinta, MCM Grande Hotel, Mircotel, Parkway Inn, Ramada, Sleep Inn, TownePlace Suites, Travelodge, $General, $Tree, AT&T, Buick/GMC, Chevrolet, Hobby Lobby, Home Depot, Honda, Hyundai, JC Penney, Lowe's, Mazda, Mkt Street, Nissan, Sam's Club/gas, Target, Toyota, U of TX Permian Basin, USPO, Walmart/Subway, S Flying J/McDonald's/dsl/scales/24hr

120 JBS Pkwy, N Candlewood Suites, Comfort Inn, Days Inn, Hawthorn Suites, Staybridge Suites, Studio 6, Super 8, Mack/Volvo

118 FM 3503, Grandview Ave, N Alon/dsl, Freightliner/Peterbilt

116 US 385, Odessa, N Chevron/dsl, Stripes/Taco Co/dsl, DQ, La Margarita, Panchitos Burritos, Watt's Burger, Delux Inn, SureStay+, Villa West Inn, $General, city park, Family$, H, S Alon/dsl, Valero/dsl, Annie's Cuban, Holiday Inn Express, MainStay Suites, Motel 6

115 FM 1882, N Sunoco/Stripes/Taco Co/dsl, S Love's/McDonald's/Subway/dsl/scales/24hr/@, Blue Beacon

113 TX 302, Odessa

ODESSA / MONAHANS / PECOS

112 FM 1936, Odessa, N Shell/Main Street Mkt/Jimmy John's/dsl

108 Moss Ave, Meteor Crater, Meteor Crater, N Road Ranger/Subway/dsl/scales/24hr, RV camping, S Pilot/PJ Fresh/Dunkin'/dsl/scales/24hr

104 FM 866, Meteor Crater Rd, Goldsmith, N RV park

103.5mm weigh sta both directions

101 FM 1601, to Fenwell, Penwell

93 FM 1053, to Ft Stockton

86 TX 41, N Monahans Sandhills SP, S Pilot/Dunkin'/Subway/dsl/scales/24hr

83 US 80, Monahans, N H, RV camping

80 TX 18, Monahans, N Chevron/dsl, Bar-H Steaks, Bennigans, Domino's, DQ, Great Wall Buffet, McDonald's, Meza's Mexican, Pappy's BBQ, Pizza Hut, Sonic, Candlewood Suites, Hawthorn Suites, Holiday Inn Express, Microtel/EVC, Motel 6, $General, Family$, H, Lowe's Foods, O'Reilly Parts, repair/tires, Verizon, S Sunoco/Stripes/Subway/dsl, Texaco/Huddle House/dsl/24hr, Huddle House, Best Value Inn, Best Western+, Comfort Inn, Comfort Inn, Texan Inn, Buick/Chevrolet/GMC, Chrysler/Dodge/Jeep, RV park, vet

79 Lp 464, Monahans, S Road Ranger/dsl, La Quinta

76 US 80, Monahans, N RV camping, to Million Barrel Museum

73 FM 1219, Wickett, N Alon/Allsup's/dsl, RV camping, S Main St/Shell/Subway/dsl

70 TX 65

69.5mm **full facilities, litter barrels, petwalk, , , both lanes, wi-fi**

66 TX 115, FM 1927, to Pyote, N Alon/dsl, Sook's Rest., RV camping, S Pilot/dsl/scales/24hr

58 frontage rd, many oil wells

52 Lp 20 W, to Barstow

49 FM 516, to Barstow

48mm Pecos River

44 Collie Rd

42 US 285, Pecos, N Alon/Allsup's/dsl, Flying J/Denny's/dsl/scales/EVC/24hr, Sunoco/Stripes/dsl/e85, Valero, Alfredo's Mexican, Burger King, DQ, El Rodeo Mexican, Golden Palace Chinese, KFC, King Shark Seafood, Pizza Hut, Sonic, Holiday Inn Express, Quality Inn, Rodeway Inn, Staybridge Suites, Travelodge, Woodspring Suites, AutoZone, museum, RV camping, tire repair, Walmart, S Love's/McDonald's/Subway/Chester's/dsl/scales/24hr/@, Microtel, repair

40 Country Club Dr, N Dickey's BBQ, Domino's, Comfort Suites, Fairfield Inn, st patrol, S Alon, Alpine Lodge Rest., Best Western+, La Quinta, municipal park, Pecos Park/Zoo, RV camping

39 TX 17, Pecos, N Pilot/Dunkin'/PJ Fresh/dsl/scales/24hr, Home2 Suites, H, S Sunoco/Stripes/Subway/dsl/24hr, Hampton Inn, Red Roof Inn, Buick/Chevrolet/GMC, Eagles Nest RV Camping, tires, Trapark RV Park

37 Lp 20 E

33 FM 869

29 Shaw Rd, S to TX AM Ag Sta

25mm accessible, litter barrels, tables, picnic area both lanes

22 FM 2903, to Toyah, N Valero/dsl, USPO

13 McAlpine Rd

7 Johnson Rd

3 Stocks Rd

0mm I-20 begins/ends on I-10, 187mm.

INTERSTATE 27

123.7mm I-27 begins/ends on I-40, exit 70 in Amarillo.

123b I-40, W to Albuquerque, E to OK City

TX

TX

INTERSTATE 27 Cont'd

W HILLSIDE

Exit #	Services
123a	26th Ave
122c	from sb only
122a	34th Ave, Tyler St, E $General
122b	FM 1541, Washington St, Parker St, Moss Lane, E Valero/Toot'n Totum, Sonic, W Taco Bell, Thai Express
121a	Hawthorne Dr, Austin St, E Amarillo Motel, W Scottie's Transmissions
121b	Georgia St, E Murphy USA/dsl, Buick/GMC, Gander RV Ctr, Honda, Mazda, Subaru, Walmart
120b	45th Ave, E Waffle House, Budget Inn, O'Reilly Parts, W Toot'n Totum, Valero, Abuelo's Mexican, Donut Stop, Gatti's Pizza, Grandma's Cocina, McDonald's, Red River Steaks, Rise N Shine Donuts, Rosa's Cafe, Sonic, Whataburger, $General, Advance Parts, BMW, Chrysler/Dodge/Jeep, Drug Emporium, Family$, NAPA, vet, Walgreens
120a	Republic Ave
119b	Western St, 58th Ave, E Phillips 66/dsl, Sonic, Subway, $General, Fiesta Foods, W Valero/dsl, Arby's, Braum's, Pizza Hut, Potato Factory, Thai Palace, Wendy's, Aamco, U-Haul, USPO
119a(from nb)	W Hillside
117	Bell St, Arden Rd, W Valero/dsl, Benjamin's Donuts, Chicken Express, Popeyes, Sonic, $General
116	Lp 335, Hollywood Rd, E Love's/dsl/scales/24hr, Phillips 66/dsl, McDonald's, Starbucks, Taco Bell, Waffle House, Wendy's, Whataburger, Comfort Suites, Motel 6, W Holiday Inn Express, H(8mi)
115	Sundown Lane
113	McCormick Rd, E Conoco/dsl, Chile Willy's, $General, Ford, W Family Camping Ctr
112	FM 2219, E Stater's RV Ctr
111	Rockwell Rd, W Buick/GMC
110	US 87 S, US 60 W, Canyon
109	Buffalo Stadium Rd, W stadium
108	FM 3331, Hunsley Rd
106	TX 217, to Palo Duro Cyn SP, Canyon, E Palo Duro Canyon SP(10mi), Palo Duro RV Park, W Valero/Allsup's, Best Thai, Dominos, Fat Boy's Diner, Feldman's Diner, McDonald's, Pepito's Mexican, Pizza Hut, Taco Bell, Wendy's, Best Western, Buffalo Inn, Holiday Inn Express, Plains Museum, to W TX A&M
103	FM 1541 N, Cemetery Rd
99	Hungate Rd
98mm	parking area both lanes, litter barrels
96	Dowlen Rd
94	FM 285, to Wayside
92	Haley Rd
90	FM 1075, Happy
88b a	US 87 N, FM 1881, Happy, same as 90
83	FM 2698
82	FM 214
77	US 87, Tulia
75	NW 6th St, Tulia, E Phillips 66, Valero/dsl, tire repair, W same as 74
74	TX 86, Tulia, E El Camino Dining, Pizza Hut, Lasso Motel, H, W Pilot/Valero/Subway/dsl/scales/24hr, Executive Inn
70mm	parking area both lanes, litter barrels
68	FM 928
63	FM 145, Kress, E Jeff's, tire repair, USPO
61	US 87, County Rd
56	FM 788

CANYON

TULIA

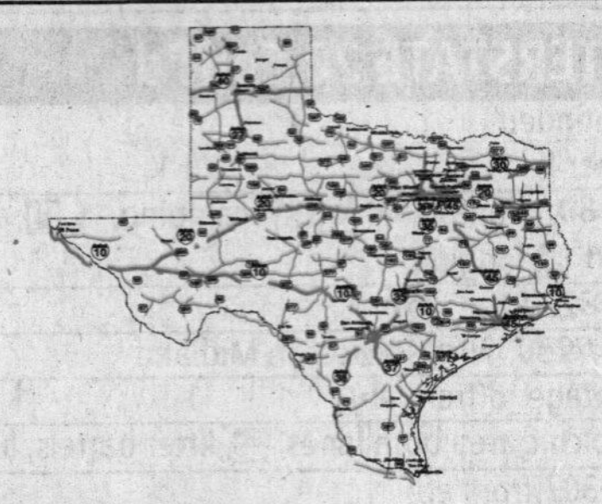

PLAINVIEW

ABERNATHY

FLOYDADA

Exit #	Services
54	FM 3183, to Plainview
53	Lp 27, Plainview, E access to gas, camping, food, H, lodging
51	Quincy St, E Hitchin' Post RV Camping
50	TX 194, Plainview, E CEFCO/dsl, H, to Wayland Bapt U
49	US 70, Plainview, E Allsup's, CEFCO/dsl, Conoco, Phillips 66, Phillips 66/Stripes/dsl, Arby's, Braum's, China Dragon, Church's TX Chicken, Cotton Patch Café, Farmhouse Rest., Fieldhouse Sandwiches, Jumbo Joe's, KFC, Leal's Mexican, Pizza Hut, Budget Inn, Comfort Suites, Quality Inn, $Tree, AutoZone, GNC, NAPA, O'Reilly Parts, United Foods, W Allsup's/dsl, CEFCO/dsl, Murphy USA/dsl, Burger King, Chicken Express, Chili's, Dos Jefes, Empire Buffet, IHOP, McDonald's, Mia's Italian, Sonic, Subway, Taco Bell, Wendy's, Holiday Inn Express, Plainview Inn, Super 8, AT&T, GNC, Verizon, Walmart/McDonald's
48	FM 3466, Plainview(from nb), E Chevrolet/Buick/GMC, Chrysler/Dodge/Jeep
45	Lp 27, to Plainview
43	FM 2337
41	County Rd
38	Main St
37	FM 1914, Cleveland St, W Allsups/dsl, city park, Family$, Lowe's Foods
36	FM 1424 , Hale Center
32	FM 37 W
31	FM 37 E
29mm	**full facilities, litter barrels, petwalk, both lanes, tornado shelter, vending**
27	County Rd
24	FM 54, W RV park/dump
22	Lp 369, Abernathy
21	FM 597, Main St, Abernathy, W Alon/Allsup's, HH Farms/dsl, DQ, Mi Familia, $General, USPO
20	FM 597, Abernathy(from nb)
17	CR 53
15	Lp 461, to New Deal, same as 14
14	FM 1729, E Alon/rest./dsl/scales/24hr
13	Lp 461, to New Deal
12	access rd(from nb)
11	FM 1294, Shallowater
10	Keuka St, E Fed Ex
9	Airport Rd, E aviation museum, W Lubbock RV Park/LP/dump
8	FM 2641, Regis St, E W Love's/Subway/Chester's/dsl/scales/24hr
7	Yucca Lane, E Pharr RV Ctr
6b a	Lp 289, Ave Q, Lubbock, E Pharr RV Ctr
5	B. Holly Ave, Municipal Dr, E Mackenzie SP
4	US 82, US 87, 4th St, to Crosbyton, E funpark, W Flying J/Subway/dsl/LP/scales/24hr, to TTU
3	US 62, TX 114, 19th St, Floydada, E Phillips 66/Stripes, NAPA, W Cast Iron Grill, Mavis, Murphy Express
2	34th St, E Phillips 66/dsl, Pete's Drive Inn, W Valero, Christakis Burgers, Josie's Mexican, Phillips 66, Simple Simon Pizza, Subway, AutoZone, U-Haul

INTERSTATE 27 Cont'd

Exit #	Services
1c	50th St, E (gas) Buddy's, (food) El Charro, (other) Family$, W (gas) Conoco, Valero/dsl, (food) A&W/LJ Silver, Bryan's Steaks, Burger King, China Star, Church's TX Chicken, Domino's, KFC, La Bella Pizza, La Parilla, McDonald's, Taco Bell, Whataburger, Wienerschnitzel, (lodging) Howard Johnson, Microtel, (other) $General, O'Reilly Parts, United Food/gas, USPO, Walgreens
1b	US 84, E (lodging) Best Value Inn, Days Inn, W Best Western+, Country Inn Suites, EconoLodge, Holiday Inn Express, La Quinta, Motel 6, Quality Inn, Red Roof Inn, Super 8, Woodspring Suites, (other) Chevrolet
1a	Lp 289
1	82nd St. I-27 begins/ends on US 87 at 82nd St in S Lubbock, W (gas) Phillips 66/dsl

INTERSTATE 30

TEXARKANA

Exit #	Services
223mm	Texas/Arkansas state line
223b a	US 59, US 71, State Line Ave, Texarkana, N (gas) Exxon/dsl, EZ Mart, Valero, (food) Denny's, IHOP, Naaman's BBQ, Waffle House, (lodging) Baymont Inn, Best Western+, Comfort Suites, Hampton Inn, Holiday Inn, Holiday Inn Express, Ramada, Red Roof Inn, Regency Inn, Super 8, Travelodge, Wyndham Garden, (other) KOA, water park, S (gas) Chevron/dsl, Murphy USA/dsl, RaceWay/dsl, Shell, (food) Burger King, China Inn, El Chico, Fuzzy's Tacos, Hooters, KFC, Little Caesar's, LJ Silver, McDonald's, Papa John's, Pizza Hut, Popeyes, Schlotzsky's, Slim Chickens, Starbucks, Subway, Taco Bell, Wendy's, Whataburger, Wingstop, (lodging) Best Value Inn, EconoLodge, Executive Inn, Magnuson Hotel, Motel 6, Motel 6, (other) $General, $Tree, Albertson's/Sav-On, AT&T, CVS Drug, O'Reilly Parts, VW, Walgreens, Walmart/Subway
223mm	**full (handicapped) facilities, info, litter barrels, petwalk, (phone), (picnic), vending, Welcome Ctr wb**
222	TX 93, FM 1397, Summerhill Rd, N (gas) Shell, Valero/Subway/dsl, (food) Applebee's, McDonald's, The One Buffet, Waffle House, (lodging) Motel 6, (other) AT&T, Goodyear Truck Tire, (H), Hyundai, T-Mobile, S (gas) Exxon/dsl, (food) Julie's Rest., Sonic, (other) Mavis Auto Repair, Nissan, URGENT CARE, Walmart Mkt/gas
220b	FM 559, Richmond Rd, N (gas) Shell, (food) Burger King, Cane's, Chick-fil-A, Chicken Express, Chipotle, CiCi's Pizza, Coldstone Creamery, Cracker Barrel, Domino's, DQ, Fuji Grill, Gusano's Pizza, Jason's Deli, Jimmy John's, Juicy Seafood, Longhorn Steaks, McAlister's Deli, Mooyah Burgers, On-the-Border, Red Lobster, Reggie's Cafe, Smashburger, Sonic, Starbucks, Taco Bell, TaMolly's Mexican, TX Roadhouse, (lodging) Comfort Suites, Courtyard, Residence Inn, TownePlace Suites, (other) $Tree, AT&T, Best Buy, Chevrolet, Discount Tire, Home Depot, Honda, Kohl's, Office Depot, Old Navy, PetSmart, Sam's Club/gas, Super 1 Food/gas, Target, TJ Maxx, Valvoline Oil Change, Verizon, Walmart Mkt/dsl, S (gas) Valero/dsl, (food) Arby's, Chili's, ChuckeCheese, Firehouse Subs, Golden Chick, Golden Corral, Grandy's, Lee's China, McDonald's, Newk's, Olive Garden, Outback Steaks, Pizza Hut, Subway, Taco Bueno, Tacos 4 Life, (lodging) Candlewood Suites, Hampton Inn, Hilton Garden/Conv Ctr, Holiday Inn Express, (other) Albertson's/Sav-On, AT&T, Books-A-Million, Cavender's Boots, CVS Drug, Dillard's, Hobby Lobby, JC Penney, Michael's, Ross, Tuesday Morning, Walgreens
220a	I-369 S, US 59 S, Texarkana
219	Pecan St, University Ave, N (food) Osaka Japanese, Silver Star BBQ, Walk-On's, S (gas) Murphy USA, (food) Subway, (lodging) Country Inn&Suites, Fairfield Inn, (other) Buick/GMC, Cadillac, Chrysler/Dodge/Jeep, Harley-Davidson, Kia, Lowe's, Mazda, Mercedes, vet, Walmart

NASH

Exit #	Services
218	FM 989, Nash, N (gas) Road Runner/dsl, (food) Dixie Diner,

NEW BOSTON — MT PLEASANT — SULPHUR SPRINGS

Exit #	Services
218	Continued 76/TX Best BBQ/Golden Chick/Steak'n Shake/Dunkin'/dsl, Exxon/Burger King/dsl, (food) Sonic, (other) GMC/Peterbilt, to Lake Patman, Toyota, USPO, vet
213	FM 2253, Leary, S (gas) Love's/McDonald's/Subway/dsl/scales/24hr, (food) Mr. D's BBQ, (other) truck wash
212	spur 74, S (gas) Exxon
208	FM 560, Hooks, N (gas) 7 Star/dsl, S Truckstp/dsl/scales/24hr, (food) DQ, Sonic, The Grill, (other) $General, Family$, Hooks Tire
207	rd 594, Red River Army Depot
206	TX 86, S (food) RC's Place
201	TX 8, New Boston, N (gas) Circle K, Exxon/Burger King/dsl, Road Ranger/Wendy's/dsl, (food) Pitt Grill, (lodging) TexInn, (other) Chevrolet, Chrysler/Dodge/Jeep, S (gas) Murphy USA/dsl, Shell/dsl, (food) Burger Joint, Catfish King, Church's TX Chicken, Domino's, DQ, KFC/Taco Bell, McDonald's, Pizza Hut, Randy's BBQ, Sonic, (lodging) Best Value Inn, Bostonian Inn, Holiday Inn Express, (other) $Tree, Brookshire's Foods/gas, Ford, O'Reilly Parts, Verizon, Walmart/Subway
199	US 82, New Boston, N (gas) VP/dsl, S Exxon/Denny's/dsl
198	TX 98, N (gas) VP/dsl
193mm	Anderson Creek
192	FM 990, N (other) Lovin' Life RV Camping, tire repair
186	FM 561
181mm	Sulphur River
178	US 259, to DeKalb, Omaha
174mm	White Oak Creek
170	FM 1993
165	FM 1001, N (food) Lala's Mexican, S (gas) Shell/Cubbies Travel Center/dsl
162b a	US 271, FM 1402, FM 2152, Mt Pleasant, N (gas) Exxon/dsl, (food) Applebee's, JoJack's BBQ, Thai Lanna, (lodging) Holiday Inn Express, Super 8, (other) $General, KOA, S (gas) Shell/dsl, (food) Burger King, McDonald's, Popeyes, Sonic, (lodging) Best Western, (other) Cadillac/Chevrolet, Chrysler/Dodge/Jeep, Ford, (H)
160	US 271, FM 1734, Mt Pleasant, N (gas) Mobil/dsl, (food) Senorita's Mexican, (lodging) La Quinta, (other) Buick/GMC(1mi), Lowe's, Ramblin Fever RV Park(2mi), Toyota, S (gas) Exxon/dsl, Shell/dsl, (food) IHOP, Jalapeño Tree, (lodging) Executive Inn, Hampton Inn, Motel 6, Quality Inn, (other) Sandlin SP
158mm	(other) weigh sta both lanes
156	frontage rd
153	spur 185, to Winfield, Miller's Cove, N (gas) Exxon/Winfield Cafe/dsl/EVC, Phillips 66/dsl, S (food) Tacos El Amigo
150	Ripley Rd
147	spur 423, N (gas) Love's/Chester's/Subway/dsl/scales/24hr/@, (lodging) American Inn, (other) tires/repair, S (gas) Duke's/TA Express/Shell/Taco Casa/BBQ/dsl
146	TX 37, Mt Vernon, N (food) Papa J's, Sonic, (other) $General, auto repair, Brookshire Foods/gas, O'Reilly Parts, S (gas) CEFCO/Huddle House/dsl/24hr, Exxon/dsl, (food) DQ, Los Arcos, McDonald's, (lodging) Super 8, (other) auto/dsl repair, Still Meadow RV Park (2mi), to Lake Bob Sandlin SP
142	County Line Rd(from eb)
141	FM 900, Saltillo Rd
136	FM 269, Weaver Rd
135	US 67 N
131	FM 69
127	US 67, Lp 301, N (lodging) Days Inn, Motel 6, Quality Inn, (other) (H), S (gas) Shell, (lodging) Best Western
126	FM 1870, College St, S (gas) Shell, (lodging) Best Western, (other) same as 127, tire repair
125	Bill Bradford Rd, same as 124
124	TX 11, TX 154, Sulphur Springs, N (gas) Exxon/dsl, (food) Bodacious BBQ, Broadway Buffet, Chicken Express, Don Ialo's Mexican, Fulgham's, IHOP, Juan Pablo's, Metro Diner, Pizza Hut, Schlotzsky's, Slaughter's BBQ, Soulman's BBQ, Subway,

= gas = food = lodging = other = rest stop

TX

INTERSTATE 30 Cont'd

SULPHUR SPRINGS

124 Continued Wendy's, Wingstop, Hampton Inn, Holiday Inn Express, Royal Inn, $General, AutoZone, Brookshire's Foods/gas, CVS Drug, Ford/Lincoln, FSA Outlet/famous brands, H, NAPA, O'Reilly Parts, USPO, VF Outlet/famous brands, Walgreens, S Exxon/dsl, Mobil/dsl, Murphy USA/dsl, Braum's, Burger King, Chick-fil-A, Chili's, Domino's, DQ, Jack-in-the-Box, McDonald's, Panda Express, Pizza Inn, Romas Italian, Sakura Sushi, Sonic, Starbucks, Taco Bell/LJ Silver, Whataburger, AT&T, Cody Drug, Discount Wheel&Tire, Lowe's, Verizon, Walmart/Subway

123 FM 2297, League St, N Shamrock/dsl, Shell

122 TX 19, to Emory, N Shamrock/dsl, Chrysler/Dodge/Jeep, H, to Cooper Lake SP, Travel Time RV Ctr, S CNG, Love's/Carl's Jr/dsl/scales/24hr, Pilot/Arby's/dsl/scales/24hr, Valero/dsl, dsl repair

120 US 67 bus

116 FM 2653, Brashear Rd, S USPO

112 FM 499(from wb)

111mm rest area both lanes, full facilities

110 FM 275, Cumby, N Valero/dsl, S Valero/dsl, Cumby Tire

104 FM 513, FM 2649, Campbell, S to Lake Tawakoni

101 TX 24, TX 50, FM 1737, to Commerce, N Exxon/dsl, to TX A&M-Commerce

GREENVILLE

97 Lamar St, N Budget Inn, S vet

96 Lp 302

95 Division St, S H

94b US 69, US 380, Greenville, N Valero/dsl, Golden Chick, Knights Inn, Royal Inn, H, S Exxon, QT/dsl, Arby's, McDonald's, Racho Viejo, Economy Inn, Guest Inn, Motel 6, Quality Inn, Super 8

94a US 69, US 380, Greenville, S QT/dsl, Valero/Subway/dsl, Chrysler/Dodge/Jeep

93b a US 67, TX 34 N, N Alon, Chevron/Taco Casa/dsl, RaceTrac/dsl, Shell/dsl, Texaco, Applebee's, Braum's, Buffet Palace, Chick-fil-A, Chicken Express, Chipotle, CiCi's, Cotton Patch Cafe, DQ, El Fenix, IHOP, Jack-in-the-Box, Jimmy John's, KFC, Little Caesar's, Panera Bread, Pizza Hut, Schlotzsky's, Sonic, Starbucks, Subway, Sunffers, Taco Bell, Taco Bueno, Tony's Italian, Wendy's, Whataburger, Wingstop, Hampton Inn, ALDI, AT&T, Belk, BigLots, Brookshire's Foods, Discount Tire, Hobby Lobby, H, Kwik Kar, Lowe's, Marshall's, O'Reilly Parts, Petco, PetCo, Ross, Staples, T-Mobil, URGENT CARE, USPO, Verizon, Walgreens, S Exxon/dsl, Murphy USA/dsl, Shell/dsl, Burger King, Chili's, Cracker Barrel, Freddy's Burgers, Molina's Mexican, Panda Express, Papa John's, Popeyes, Red Lobster, Rib Crib BBQ, Shogun' Hibachi, Soulman's BBQ, Subway, TaMolly's Mexican, Wings To Go, Best Western+, Comfort Suites, Holiday Inn Express, $Tree, Buick/GMC, Ford/Lincoln, Home Depot, Hyundai, Nissan, NTB, Walmart

CADDO MILLS

92 Stratton Pkwy, S Chevrolet/Cadillac

90mm Farber Creek

89 FM 1570, N 1770 West I-30 RV Park

89mm E Caddo Creek

87 FM 1903, N Shell/dsl, fireworks, S Pilot/McDonald's/dsl/scales/24hr, Texaco/Huddle House/dsl, Baker's Ribs, tire repair

87mm Elm Creek

85 FM 36, Caddo Mills, N Dallas NE RV Park

85mm W Caddo Creek

83 FM 1565 N, N Exxon/Pizza Inn/dsl

79 FM 2642, N Budget RV Ctr, S Buc-ee's/dsl, vet

77b FM 35, Royse City, N Texaco/dsl/scales/24hr,

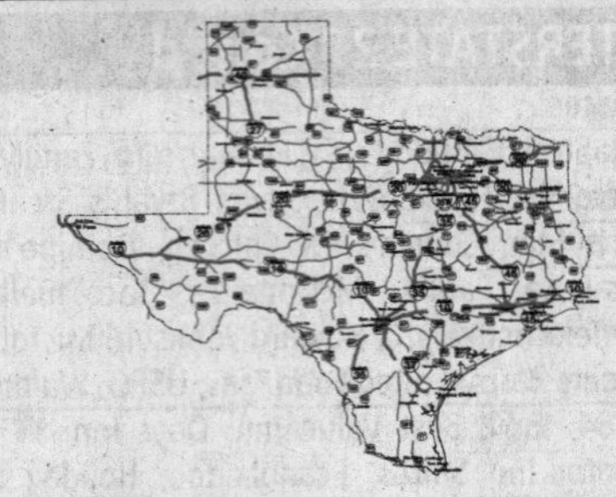

ROYSE CITY

77b Continued Soulman's BBQ, Family$

77a TX 548, Royse City, N Shell/dsl, Jack-in-the-Box, McDonald's, American Inn, AutoZone, tires, S Exxon, Charlie's Burgers, Denny's, Fuzzy's Tacos, Golden Chick, Pizza Hut, Rice Express, Sonic, Taco Bell, Holiday Inn Express

76 Campbell Blvd, Wingstop, N Murphy Express/dsl, Arby's, Burger King, DQ, Palio's Pizza Cafe, Panda Express, Papa John's, Popeyes, Starbucks, Taco Bauno, Whataburger, AT&T, CVS Drug, Kwik Kar, O'Reilly Parts, URGENT CARE, Walmart/Subway

75 Campbell Rd(from wb, same as 76)

74 frontage rd(from eb)

73 FM 551, Fate, N Sonic, S Brookshire's/mkt, Shell/Stag Plaza/dsl

70 FM 549, N Fun Town RV Ctr, McLains RV Ctr, S Love's/Carl's Jr./dsl/scales/24hr, Kia

69 (from wb), frontage rd, N Super 8, S Honda, Hyundai, Nissan, Nissan, Toyota

68 TX 205, to Rock Wall, N Exxon/7-11/dsl, Murphy USA/dsl, QT/dsl, Braum's, Chicken Express, China Taste, DQ, Fireside Chicken, Joe Willy's Grill, Luigi's Italian, Starbucks, Subway, Taco Casa, TX Roadhouse, Whataburger, Best Western+, Rockwall Inn, Woodspring Suites, Buick/GMC, Chevrolet, Chrysler/Dodge/Jeep, Ford, Hobby Lobby, vet, Walmart/Subway, S RaceTrac/dsl, TA/Burger King/Starbucks/dsl/24hr/scales/@, Cane's, Firehouse Subs, Freebird Burritos, In-N-Out, Olive Garden, Rosa's Cafe, Soulman's BBQ, Torchy's Tacos, Belk, Costco/gas, Jo-Ann Fabrics, Toyota/Scion

ROWLETT

67b FM 740, Ridge Rd, N Chevron, Murphy USA/dsl, Buffet City, Culver's, Denny's, Edohana Hibachi, Grandy's, IHOP, LJ Silver, Logan's Roadhouse, McDonald's, Mellow Mushroom Pizza, Popeyes, Schlotzsky's, Steak'n Shake, Taco Bueno, Taco Cabana, Waffle House, Wendy's, Hampton Inn, Firestone/auto, Goodyear/auto, S Exxon, Kroger/dsl, Shell, Applebee's, Bahama Buck's Ice Cream, Blackeyed Pea, Buffalo Wild Wings, Chick-fil-A, Chili's, Chipotle Mexican, ChuckeCheese, CiCi's, Cotton Patch Cafe, Crisp & Green, Dickey's BBQ, El Chico, Five Guys, Jack-in-the-Box, Jason's Deli, Jimmy John's, La Madelein, Mi Cocina, Olive Garden, On-the-Border, Panda Express, Panera Bread, Pizza Hut, Samee's Pizza, Sonic, Soulman's BBQ, Starbucks, Subway, Taco Bell, Which Wich?, La Quinta, $Tree, AT&T, Beall's, Belk, Best Buy, CVS Drug, Dick's, Discount Tire, Home Depot, H, JC Penney, Jo-Ann, Kohl's/EVC, Lowe's, Michael's, NTB, Old Navy, PetCo, PetSmart, Ross, Staples, SteinMart, Target, TJ Maxx, to Lake Tawakoni, Verizon, vet, Walgreens

67a Horizon Rd, Village Dr, N Genghis Grill, Kyoto Japanese, Saltgrass Steaks, Snuffer's Rest, Starbucks, Hampton Inn, Hyatt, S Culpepper Steaks, Oar House, Papa Johns, Hilton, SpringHill Suites/EVC, Tru

66mm Ray Hubbard Reservoir

64 Dalrock Rd, Rowlett, N Shell/dsl, Valero/dsl,

INTERSTATE 30 Cont'd

ROWLETT

64 Continued Alejandro's Grill, Church's TX Chicken, Comfort Suites, Home2 Suites, H

63mm Ray Hubbard Reservoir

62 Bass Pro Dr, N Quality Inn, to Hubbard RA, S Shell/dsl, Texaco, Valero/dsl, CiCi's Pizza, Flying Saucer Grill, Hooters, Primo's Tex-Mex, TLC on the Lake, Whataburger, Holiday Inn Express, Bass Pro Shops, EVC

61b Bush Tpk

61a Zion Rd(from wb), N Exxon/dsl Discovery Inn

60b Bobtown Rd(eb only), N 7-11/dsl, Jack-in-the-Box, La Quinta, S Shell

GARLAND

60a Rose Hill Dr

59 Beltline Rd, Garland, N Mobil/7-11/dsl, QT, Charleys' Cheesesteaks, Chili's, China City, Denny's, IHOP, KFC, Little Caesar's, McDonald's, Papa John's, Popeyes, Starbucks, Subway, Taco Bell, Taco Cabana, Taco Casa, Wendy's, Whataburger, Wingstop, Albertson's, Discount Tire, Tuesday Morning, Walgreens, Walmart S RaceTrac/dsl, Baker's Ribs, Captain D's, DQ, JT Cajun Seafood, Sonic, Waffle House, Best Value Inn, Motel 6, Super 8, AT&T, Kroger

58 Northwest Dr, N Valero/dsl, Valero/dsl, Ziggy Gas, Hyundai, Nissan/EVC, S Exxon/dsl, QT/dsl, Texaco, Jack-in-the-Box, Lowe's

56c b I-635 S-N

56a Galloway Ave, Gus Thomasson Dr(from eb), N Star USA, Texaco, Valero/dsl, Golden Chick, KFC, McDonald's, Sonic, Taco Bell, AutoZone, USPO, Walgreens, S 7-11, Fox Fuels, Murphy Express, Black Bear Diner, Dicky's BBQ, El Fenix, Hooters, Olive Garden, Outback Steaks, Posado's Cafe, Razzoo's Cajun, Red Lobster, Sports City Cafe, Subway, TGIFriday's, Wendy's, Courtyard, Delux Inn, Fairfield Inn, HomeTowne Suites, ALDI, BigLots, Celebration Sta Funpark, Firestone/auto, Gander RV, Kroger/dsl

55 Motley Dr, N Shell/dsl, Astro Inn, Red Roof Inn, to Eastfield Coll, S Exxon/7-11, Quality Inn

BUCKNER

54 Big Town Blvd, N Texaco, Valero/dsl, Chicken Chris, Mesquite Inn, S Explore RV Ctr, Holiday World RV Ctr

53b US 80 E(from eb), to Terrell

53a Lp 12, Buckner, N Circle Grill, Super 8, Chevrolet, Toyota/Scion, S Asian Star Buffet, McDonald's, Panda Express, Taco Cabana, Whataburger, Wingstop, $Tree, Sam's Club/gas, Staples, Walmart

51 (52 a from wb), Highland Rd, Jim Miller Blvd, N Exxon/7-11, Country China, Denny's, McDonald's, Waffle House, Hampton Inn, Holiday Inn Express, La Quinta, Stay Express, S RaceWay/dsl, Shell/dsl, BoomerJack's, Burger King, Capt D's, CiCi's Pizza, Grandy's, KFC, Popeyes, Taco Bell, Wendy's, Motel 6, Super 7 Inn, auto repair, AutoZone, CVS Drug, O'Reilly Parts

E GRAND

50b a Longview, Ferguson Rd, N Texaco, S Brake-O, U-Haul

49b Dolphin Rd, Lawnview Ave, Samuell Ave, N Valero, El Rinconcito Mexican, Downtown Suites

49a Winslow St, N Shell/dsl, Jack-in-the-Box, McDonald's, S Circle K, Shell/dsl, tires

48b TX 78, E Grand, N arboretum, S fairpark

48a Carroll Ave, Central Ave, Peak St, Haskell Ave, N 7-11, Shamrock, Valero, Hamm's Tires, H, S Divino's Pizza, Joe's Rest

47 2nd Ave, S Shell, McDonald's, Cotton Bowl, fairpark

46b I-45, US 75, to Houston

46a Central Expswy, downtown

45 I-35E, N to Denton, to Commerce St, Lamar St, Griffin St, S Gulf/dsl, McDonald's, Ambassador Inn

44b I-35E S, Industrial Blvd

44a I-35E N, Beckley Ave(from eb)

43b a Sylvan Ave(from wb), N 7-11/dsl, Banh Mi, TEN Ramen, Avalon, $Tree, H, USPO

42 Hampton Rd, S Chipotle, Crown Buffet, DQ, Lupita's, Wendy's

41 Westmoreland Ave, N Exxon, Sinclair, S QT, Buffalo Wild Wings, Olive Garden

39 Cockrell Hill Rd, N Shell/dsl, IHOP, KFC/Taco Bell, Pollo Campero, Sonic, Wing Stop, Comfort Suites, Fairfield Inn, Hampton Inn, Staples, S Murphy USA/dsl, Burger King, Chick-fil-A, Chili's, CiCi's, Dickey's BBQ, Golden Corral, Little Caesar's, Lucky Rice, McDonald's, Panda Express, Starbucks, Subway, Taco Cabana, Wendy's, Whataburger, Holiday Inn Express, $Tree, Lowe's, Ross, Walmart/McDonald's

38 Lp 12, N Exxon/7-11, Texaco/dsl, VP/dsl

ARLINGTON STADIUM

36 MacArthur Blvd, S U-Haul

34 Belt Line Rd, N QT/dsl, RaceTrac/dsl, La Quinta, Studio 6, Super 8, Ford, Ripley's Museum, S RaceTrac/dsl, Shell/Subway/dsl, Texaco/dsl, Burger King, Popeyes, Schlotzsky's, Starbucks, Wingstop, city park, vet

32b a George Bush Tpk, toll, N Valero/dsl, NY Pizzeria, S Texaco, Church's TX Chicken, Fresh Catch Seafood, Whataburger, Motel 6

30 TX 360, Six Flags Dr, Arlington Stadium, N Shell, Valero/dsl, Boston's, Cracker Barrel, Saltgrass Steaks, Steak'n Shake, Take a Bao, Wendy's, Budget Suites, Crowne Plaza, Doubletree, Extended Stay America, Extended Stay America, Fairfield Inn, Hawthorn Suites, Hilton, Hilton Garden, Holiday Inn Express, Hyatt Place, Motel 6, R Nite Star Inn, Residence Inn, Sonesta Suites, Studio 6, Tru, S Valero, Al-Amir, Bombshell's, Denny's, Mariano's Mexican, Red Crab, Subway, Baymont Inn, Baymont Inn, Days Inn, Four Points, Homewood Suites, Hyatt Place, La Quinta, Ranger Inn, Red Roof Inn, Sleep Inn, Ford/Lincoln, Six Flags Funpark

29 Ball Park Way, N Mobil/7-11, QT, Valero/dsl, Dicky's BBQ, Rio Mambo, Sonic, Aloft, Hampton Inn, Springhill Suites, Towneplace Suites, Auto Nation/Toyota/Scion, USPO, S On-the-Border, Vila Brazil, Howard Johnson, Sheraton, Six Flags Funpark

28b a FM 157, Collins St, N Exxon/dsl, Biscuit Bar, Chicago Pizza, Chipotle, IHOP, Jersey Mike's, la Madeleine, Starbucks, Subway, Torchy's Tacos, Waffle House, Holiday Inn, BMW, Cadillac, Chrysler/Dodge/Jeep, MINI, Walmart, Whole Foods Mkt, S Airways Burgers, Arby's, Asian Buffet, BoomerJack's, Buffalo Wild Wings, Cane's, Chick-fil-A, Chili's, Gino's East Pizzaria, Golden Chopsticks, Hooters, Jason's Deli, Joe's Crab Shack, Olive Garden, Omi Korean, Panda Express, Panera Bread, Pappadeaux, Popeyes, Shell Shack, Sprouts Pho, Subway, Taco Bell, Taco Bueno, TGIFriday's, TX Land&Cattle, Wendy's, Wingstop, Courtyard, Days Inn, $Tree, GNC, Home Depot, Michael's, Office Depot, PepBoys, PetSmart, Ross, SteinMart, TX Stadium, Walgreens, Walmart/McDonald's

27 Lamar Blvd, Cooper St, N Gulf, Bek's Pizza, Jack-in-the-Box, Subway, Family$, Kroger/dsl, vet, S QT/dsl, Shell/dsl, Burger King, Pappasito's Cantina, Tom's Burgers, Comfort Suites

26 Fielder Rd, S to Six Flags(from eb)

25mm Village Creek

24 Eastchase Pkwy, N Panda Express, La Quinta, CarMax, Lowe's, Sam's Club/gas, URGENT CARE, Walmart/McDonald's, S Exxon/7-11/dsl, RaceTrac/dsl, Shell/7-11/dsl, Arby's, Burger King, Chicken Express, CiCi's Pizza, IHOP, McDonald's, No Frills Grill, Pizza Hut, Popeyes,

TX

= gas = food = lodging = other = rest stop

TX

INTERSTATE 30 Cont'd

FT WORTH

Exit	Services
24	Continued Schlotzsky's, Taco Bell, Wendy's, Whataburger, Wingstop, $Tree, ALDI, AT&T, GNC, Marshall's, Office Depot, Ross, Target
23	Cooks Lane, S Shell/dsl
21c b	I-820
21a	Bridgewood Dr, N Chevron/dsl, Phillips 66, Braum's, Chicken Express, Dan's Seafood, DG, Italy Pizza, Jack-in-the-Box, KFC, Los aibertos, Soinic, Subway, Taco Casa, Wendy's, $General, Albertson's/Starbucks, Discount Tire, Family$, Firestone/auto, Home Depot, U-Haul, Valvoline Oil Change, S Phillips 66/dsl, QT, Texaco, Domino's, Whataburger/24hr, Williams Chicken
19	Brentwood Stair Rd(from eb), N Exxon, Sunoco, S Shamrock, Texaco, Family$
18	Oakland Blvd, N Circle K, Shell/dsl, Lisa's Chicken, Taco Bell, Waffle House, OYO
16c	Beach St, S 7-11, Motel 6, Stay Express Hotel
16b a	Riverside Dr(from wb), S Great Western Inn
15b a	I-35W N to Denton, S to Waco
14b	Jones St, Commerce St, Ft Worth, downtown
14a	TX 199, Henderson St, Ft Worth, downtown
13b	TX 199, Henderson St, N Texaco, Holiday Inn Express, Omni, Sheraton
13a	8th Ave, N Texaco, Holiday Inn Express, S Jack-in-the-Box
12b	Forest Park Blvd, N Pappadeaux Café, Pappasito's, URGENT CARE, S H
12a	University Dr, City Parks, S Ol' South Pancakes, Romano's, Extended Stay, Fairfield Inn, SpringHill Suites
11	Montgomery St, S Shell/dsl, Flying Fish, Railhead BBQ, Taco Bell, Whataburger, TownePlace Suites
10	Hulen St, Ft Worth, S Chick-fil-A, McDonald's, Mi Cocina, Pho Noodle, Potbelly, Slice City Pizza, Starbucks, Central Mkt, WorldMkt
9b	US 377, Camp Bowie Blvd, Horne St, N Uncle Julio's Mexican, S 7-11, Exxon/7-11, Texaco/dsl, Campisi's Italian, Chipotle, Helen's Chicken, Jack-in-the-Box, Jason's Deli, Jersey Mike's, Jimmy John's, Marco's Pizza, McAlister's, McDonald's, Mexican Inn Cafe, Ohana BBQ, Qdoba, Schlotzsky's, Sonic, Starbucks, Toque Mexicano, Wendy's, Zeke's Fish'n Chips, AT&T, Batteries+Bulbs, URGENT CARE, Walgreens
9a	Bryant-Irvin Rd, S same as 9b, Shell
8b	Ridgmar, Ridglea
8a	TX 183, Green Oaks Rd, N Applebee's, Arby's, Asia Bowl, Chick-fil-A, Chipotle, Cowtown BBQ, Del Taco, Don Pablo's, DQ, Firehouse Subs, Grand Buffet, Jack-in-the-Box, Krispy Kreme, McDonald's, Olive Garden, Panda Express, Papa Murphy's, Rule the Roost, Sonic, Subway, Taco Bueno, Woody Creek BBQ, Courtyard, $Tree, Albertson's, ALDI, AT&T, Best Buy, BigLots, Dillard's, JC Penney, Jo-Ann Fabrics, Lowe's, NTB, Office Depot, Old Navy, PetCo, PetSmart, Ross, Sam's Club/gas, Target, U-Haul, Verizon, Walmart/Subway, S Fairfield Inn, Hampton Inn
7b a	Cherry Lane, TX 183, spur 341, to Green Oaks Rd, N Chevron/dsl, Shell/7-11, Texaco/dsl, IHOP, Popeyes, Subway, Wendy's, Comfort Inn, Motel 6, Scottish Inns, Studio 6, same as 8a, U-Haul, S QT/dsl, Parton's Pizza, Country Inn & Suites, Holiday Inn, La Quinta, Quality Inn, Super 8
6	Las Vegas Trail, N Texaco/dsl, Jack-in-the-Box, Love Donuts, Days Inn, Executive Inn, Hyundai, Lincoln, S QT/dsl, Shell/7-11/dsl, Texaco, Best Value Inn, Budget Suites, Relax Inn, AutoZone, Kia, vet
5b c	I-820 N and S
5a	Alemeda St(from eb, no EZ return)
3	RM 2871, Chapel Creek Blvd, S Exxon/Church's TX Chicken/Subway/dsl, Sonic, Starbucks
2	spur 580 E
1b	Linkcrest Dr, S Gulf/dsl
0mm	I-20 W. I-30 begins/ends on I-20, exit 421.

INTERSTATE 35

GAINESVILLE

Exit	Services
504mm	Texas/Oklahoma state line, Red River
504	frontage rd, access to Texas Welcome Ctr
503mm	parking area both lanes
502mm	**full facilities, litter barrels, TX Tourist Bureau/info, Welcome Ctr sb, wireless internet**
501	FM 1202, Prime Outlets Blvd, E Chrysler/Dodge/Jeep, Ford, W Conoco/café/dsl, Applebee's, Cracker Barrel, Hampton Inn, La Quinta, Prime Outlets/famous brands, RV camping, Western Outfitter
500	FM 372, Gainesville, E Exxon
498b a	US 82, to Wichita Falls, Gainesville, Sherman, E QT, Shell/dsl, Valero, Valero/dsl, Chick-fil-A, Luigi's Italian, Panda Express, Whataburger, Budget Host, Super 8, AT&T, H, URGENT CARE, W Exxon/dsl, Burger King, Comfort Suites, Days Inn, Rodeway Inn
497	frontage rd, E Fairfield Inn, W Gulf/Rumpy's
496b	TX 51, FM 51, California St, Gainesville, Taco Bueno, E Chevron, Braum's, Fera's Italian, IHOP, McDonald's, Sonic, Starbucks, Taco Bell, Taco Casa, Wendy's, Holiday Inn Express, Quality Inn, Cavender's Outfitters, Kwik Kar/auto, Lowe's Mkt, W Gulf/Rumpy's/dsl, Chili's, RibCrib, Villa Grande, Gainesville Zoo, N Central TX Coll
496a	to Weaver St
496mm	Elm Fork of the Trinity River
495	frontage rd
494	FM 1306
492mm	litter barrels, picnic area sb, tables
491	Spring Creek Rd
490mm	litter barrels, picnic area nb,
489	FM 1307, to Hockley Creek Rd
487	FM 922, Valley View, W Shell/Subway/Taco Tico/dsl, Valero/dsl, DQ, USPO
486	Fm 1307, W Texaco/dsl, Valero, $General
485	frontage rd(from sb)
483	FM 3002, Lone Oak Rd, E Shell/Church's TX Chicken/Subway/dsl, Roberts Lake SP, RV Guys

BOLIVAR

Exit	Services
482	Chisam Rd
481	View Rd, W McClain's RV Ctr
480	Lois Rd
479	Belz Rd, Sanger, same as 478, E Miguelito's, RV Park
478	FM 455, to Pilot Pt, Bolivar, E DQ, Fuzzy's Tacos, Pizza Hut, Roma's Italian, Sonic, Subway, Taco Bell, Holiday Inn Express, Sanger Inn, USPO, W Chevron/dsl, Conoco/Chicken Express/dsl, Domino's, Jack-in-the-Box, McDonald's, Chevrolet, Kwik Kar Lube, O'Reilly Parts, Ray Roberts Lake and SP
477	Keaton Rd, E Exxon/dsl, Pellegrino's Italian,

TX

INTERSTATE 35 Cont'd

Exit	Services
477	Continued Traildust Steaks
475b	Rector Rd
475a	FM 156, to Krum (from sb)
474	Cowling rd(from nb)
473	FM 3163, Milam Rd
472	Ganzer Rd, W Crandell RV Ctr
471	US 77, FM 1173, Lp 282, to Denton, Krum, E TA/Burger King/Boston Mkt/dsl/scales/24hr/@, W Love's/Godfather's/Subway/Wendy's/dsl/scales/24hr/@, Foster's Western Shop, to Camping World RV Supply
470	Lp 288, same services as 469 from sb
469	US 380, University Dr, to Decatur, McKinney, E Mobil/7-11/dsl, RaceTrac/dsl, Braum's, Cane's, Cheddar's, Chick-fil-A, Chili's, ChinaTown Café, Cowboy Chicken, Cracker Barrel, Dickey's BBQ, El Pollo Loco, Freebird's Burrito, Hanasato Japanese, In-N-Out, McDonald's, Panda Express, Panera Bread, Starbucks, Taco Cabana, Taco Casa, Villa Grande, Whataburger, WhichWich?, Wing Stop, Best Western, Embassy Suites, Fairfield Inn, Albertson's/Sav-On, AT&T, GNC, Kohl's, Kwik Kar, PetCo, Ross, Sam's Club/gas, to TX Woman's U, Verizon, Walmart, Winco Foods, W Exxon/dsl, QT/dsl, Brisket Burger, Denny's, DQ, Shell/dsl, Waffle House, Comfort Inn, Days Inn, Holiday Inn Express, Howard Johnson, La Quinta, Motel 6, WoodSpring Suites, Camping World RV Supply, I-35 RV Ctr
468	FM 1515, Airport Rd, W Oak St, E H
467	I-35W, S to Ft Worth
466.7mm	I-35 divides into E and W sb, converges into I-35 nb. See Texas I-35 W.
466b	N TX Blvd, E NY Sub Hub, Oriental Express, to NTSU
466a	McCormick St, E Ekon, Shell/dsl
465b	US 377, Ft Worth Dr, E RaceTrac/dsl, Valero, McDonald's, Taco Bell, Whataburger, Studio 6, U-Haul, W 7-11/dsl, Frosty Drive N, Sonic, Deluxe Inn
465a	FM 2181, Teasley Ln, E 7-11, Applebee's, Braum's, ChuckeCheese, Domino's, Hooters, KFC, Little Caesar's, Pizza Hut, Subway, Budget Host, Hampton Inn, W Shell/dsl, Valero, Jonuzi's Pizza, La Milpa Mexican, Outback Steaks, Rudy's BBQ/gas, Economy Inn, Super 8
464	US 77, Pennsylvania Dr, Denton, same as 463
463	Lp 288, to McKinney, E Murphy USA, RaceTrac/dsl, Arby's, Buffalo Wild Wings, Buffet King, Buffet King, Burger King, Cane's Chicken, Chick-fil-A, Chipotle, CiCi's Pizza, Dillas Mexican, Great Egg Cafe, Hawaiian Bros, Jason's Deli, Jersey Mike's, Jimmy John's, LJ Silver, Lone Spur Cafe, McAlister's Deli, McDonald's, Olive Garden, On-the-Border, Panda Express, Panera Bread, Patriot Sandwiches, Popeyes, Red Lobster, Sonic, Starbucks, Taco Bell, Taco Bueno, TX Roadhouse, Wendy's, Whataburger, Best Western, Courtyard, Hilton Garden, $General, $Tree, AT&T, Barnes&Noble, Best Buy, BigLots, Burlington Coats, Dillard's, Firestone/auto, Goodyear/auto, Hobby Lobby, Home Depot, JC Penney, Kroger/dsl, Kwik Kar, Lowe's, Macy's, Michael's, NTB, Office Depot, Old Navy, PetCo, PetSmart, Ross, Target, TJ Maxx, Verizon, Walgreens, Walmart, W Buc-ee's/dsl, Chevron/dsl, Chili's, Oldewest Cafe, Papa John's, R G Burgers, Wing Stop, Homewood Suites, EMERGENCY CARE, same as 464, vet
462	State School Rd, Mayhill Rd, E QT, Dickey's BBQ, Subway, Residence Inn, H, URGENT CARE, W Exxon, BJ's Rest., Catahoula's Kitchen, Chuy's Mexican, Shogun Japanese, Sonic, Holiday Inn Express, Buick/GMC, Cadillac, Chevrolet, Chrysler/Dodge/Jeep, Honda, Toyota/Scion
461	Sandy Shores Rd, Post Oak Dr, E Explore USA RV Ctr, Ford, Hyundai, W Christian Bros Auto, Chrysler/Dodge/Jeep, Mazda, Nissan
460	Corinth Pkwy, E Fairfield Inn, McClains RV Ctr, W Harley-Davidson
459	frontage rd, W Destiny RV Resort
458	FM 2181, Swisher Rd, E Circle K, QT/dsl, Arby's, Chipotle, Panda Express, Popeyes, Best Western+, Comfort Inn, Burger King, Discount Tire, O'Reilly Parts, T-Mobile, W Chevron/McDonald's, Exxon/7-11, Murphy USA/dsl, RaceTrac, Chick-fil-A, Chicken Express, Chicken Express, Denny's, Genti's Italian, Jack-in-the-Box, Joey O's, KFC/Taco Bell, Los Cabos, Palio's Pizza, Pizza Hut, Sonic, Starbucks, Subway, Wendy's, Whataburger, Albertson's, ALDI, AT&T, AutoZone, Firestone/auto, GNC, Kwik Kar, Walgreens, Walmart
457b	Denton Rd, Hundley Dr, Lake Dallas
457a	Hundley Dr(from nb), Lake Dallas
456	Highland Village
456mm	Lewisville Lake
454b	Garden Ridge Blvd
454a	FM 407, Justin, E Valero, Old House BBQ, W QT/dsl, Kretzschy's BBQ, McDonald's, Pizza Hut, Rusty Beagle, Kwik Kar
453	Valley Ridge Blvd, E Ford, Travelcamp RV, W Exxon/7-11/dsl, Burger King, Subway, Tacos Sabrositos, Home Depot, Kohl's/EVC, Lowe's
452	FM 1171, to Flower Mound, E Motel 6, H, W Shell, Burger King, Cane's, Chick-fil-A, Chipotle Mexican, CiCi's Pizza, Korner Cafe, McDonald's, Panda Express, Pizza Hut, Regal Buffet, Sonic, Taco Bell, Taco Cabana, The Catch, Whataburger, Wingaholic, $Tree, CVS, DQ, Sam's Club/gas, same as 451, transmissions, U-Haul, URGENT CARE, Walmart/Subway
451	Fox Ave, E Shell/dsl, Braum's, W Citgo/dsl, Cracker Barrel, Starbucks, Baymont Inn, EconoLodge, VW
450	TX 121, Grapevine, E 7-11, Exxon/dsl, Red Roof Inn, Chrysler/Dodge/Jeep, W 7-11, Burger King, Church's TX Chicken, Luci's Bakery, Mariscos 2000, Taco Bell, Taco Hut, Firestone/auto, Nissan, Take 5 Lube, Toyota/Scion
449	Corporate Drive, E Valero/dsl, Hooters, On-the-Border, Razzoo's Cajun, Extended Stay America, Home2 Suites, Motel 6, Suburban Lodge, Cavender's Boots, Chevrolet, W 7-11, Chili's, InTown Suites, Best Western+, La Quinta
448b a	Round Grove Rd, TX 121, Rayburn Fwy, E Exxon, A&W/KFC, Cane's, ChuckeCheese, Jack-in-the-Box, Jason's Deli, LJ Silver/Taco Bell, Olive Garden, Starbucks, Subway, Taco Casa, Homewood Suites, Honda, Target, W Exxon/7-11, RaceTrac/dsl, Applebee's, Arby's, BJ's Grill, Buffalo Wild Wings, Chick-fil-A, Chipotle Mexican, Christina's Mexican, Cotton Patch Rest., Firehouse Subs, Five Guys, Freebirds Burrito, Honeybaked Ham, IHOP, Jason's Deli, Jimmy John's, McDonald's, Panda Express, Panera Bread, Parma Pasta, Popeyes, Potbelly, Red Lobster, Rosati's Pizza, Saltgrass Steaks, Schlotzsky's, Sonic, Spring Creek BBQ, Starbucks, Taco Bueno, Taco Cabana, Twin Peaks, Wendy's, Which Wich?, Wing Snob, Wu Wei, Comfort Suites, Country Inn&Suites, Courtyard, Fairfield Inn, Hampton Inn, Hilton Garden, Holiday Inn Express, Residence Inn, Springhill Suites, TownePlace Suites, AT&T, Barnes&Noble, Best Buy, Costco/gas, Dillard's, Discount Tire, EVC, mall, Michael's, Old Navy, T-Mobile, URGENT CARE, Verizon
447a	TX 121, Rayburn Fwy
446	Frankford Rd, E RaceTrac, Buick/GMC, Kia
445b a	Pres Geo Bush Tpk

KRUM · DENTON · LAKE DALLAS · GRAPEVINE

= gas = food = lodging = other = rest stop

TX

INTERSTATE 35 Cont'd

IRVING

Exit #	Services
444	Whitlock Lane, Sandy Lake Rd, E Shell, Brother's Pizza, Subway, Rodeway Inn, W Scottish Inns, Harley-Davidson
443	Belt Line Rd, Crosby Rd, E Babe's Chicken, Burger Island, Ford, Hyundai
442	Valwood Pkwy, E Chevron/Subway/dsl, Exxon/7-11, Texaco/dsl, DQ, Jack-in-the-Box, McDonald's, Taco Bueno, Guest Inn, LoneStar Inn, Super 8, W transmissions
441	Valley View Lane, E Chipotle, Starbucks, W Chevron, Days Inn, Motel 6
440b	I-635 E
440c	I-635 W, to DFW
439	Royal Lane, E Shell/dsl, Valero/7-11/dsl, McDonald's, Wendy's, W Chevron/7-11, Exxon/dsl, Jack-in-the-Box
438	Walnut Hill Lane, E Burger King, Denny's, Wild Turkey Grill, Best Western+, La Quinta, Quality Inn, W Gulf/dsl, Shell/dsl
437	Manana Rd(from nb), same as 438
436	TX 348, to DFW, Irving, E Chevron, Shell/dsl, Finish Line Grill, IHOP, Starbucks, Waffle House, Baymont Inn, Country Inn Suites, Days Inn, Elegante Hotel, Holiday Inn Express, Motel 6, SpringHill Suites, Studio 6, W Exxon/dsl, Shell/dsl, Cane's, Chili's, Jack-in-the-Box, Jason's Deli, Joe's Crabshack, King Buffet, McDonald's, Ojos Locos Cantina, Olive Garden, Papadeaux Seafood, Pappa's BBQ, Pappas Bros Steaks, Pappasito's Mexican, Red Lobster, Taco Bell, Wendy's, Budget Suites, Century Inn, Fairfield Inn, Holiday Inn Express
435	Harry Hines Blvd(from nb)
434b	Regal Row, E Chevron/dsl, Whataburger, Motel 6
434a	Empire, Central, E Shell/McDonald's, Golden Chick, Kay's Rest, Sonic, Budget Suites, Candlewood Suites, InTown Suites, Wingate Inn, W Exxon/dsl, Burger King, Schlotzsky's, Taco Bell
433b	Mockingbird Lane, E QT, Shell/dsl, Jack-in-the-Box, Budget Suites, Comfort Inn, Crowne Plaza, Hawthorn Suites, Sonesta Suites, Love Field, W Bombshells Rest., Starbucks
433a	(432b from sb)TX 356, Commonwealth Dr
432a	Inwood Rd, E Exxon/7-11, Chevrolet, H, URGENT CARE, W Chevron/Subway/dsl, Whataburger, Comfort Inn, Extended Stay America, Hampton Inn, Homewood Suites
431	Motor St, E Chevron, Denny's, H, W Shell/7-11, Taco Cabana, Embassy Suites, Marriott Suites
430c	Wycliff Ave, E Holiday Inn, Renaissance Hotel, W Hilton Anatole, Hilton Garden
430b	Mkt Ctr Blvd, E World Trade Ctr, W Denny's, Medieval Times Rest., Best Western, Courtyard, Days Inn, DoubleTree, Fairfield Inn, Sheraton Suites
430a	Oak Lawn Ave, W Shell/dsl, Tru
429c	HiLine Ave(from nb)
429b	Continental Ave, Commerce St W, downtown, E Hooters, SpringHill Suites, W Exxon, Burger King, Jack-in-the-Box, McDonald's, Popeyes
429a	to I-45, US 75, to Houston
428e	Commerce St E, Reunion Blvd, Dallas, downtown
428d	I-30 W, to Ft Worth
428a	I-30 E, to I-45 S
428b	Industrial Blvd, E Exxon, W Fuel City/dsl, Texaco
427b	I-30 E
427a	Colorado Blvd
426c	Jefferson Ave
426b	TX 180 W, 8th St, E Shell/dsl, Trinity Suites,

DALLAS

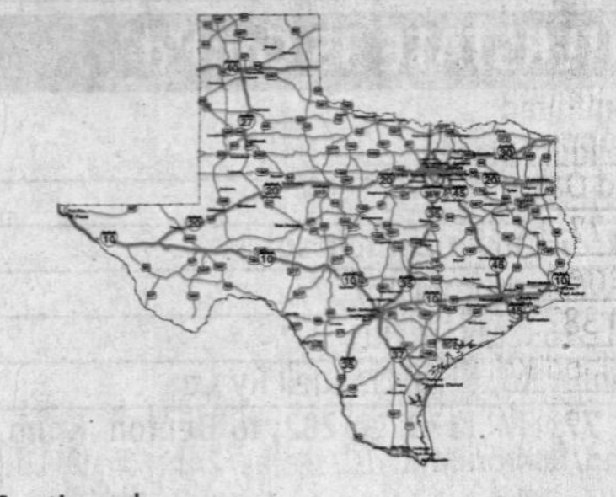

LAURELAND

Exit #	Services
426b	Continued Sabor a la Mexicana
426a	Ewing Ave, E McDonald's, Popeyes, King Tire, W City Inn
425c	Marsalis Ave, E Dallas Zoo, W Chevron, Valero, Jack-in-the-Box
425b	Beckley Ave, 12th St, sb only, W QT, Shell, Wendy's
425a	Zang Blvd, same as 425b
424	Illinois Ave, E Chevron, Exxon, KFC, William's Chicken, AutoZone, CVS, W Exxon/7-11, Burger King, Cane's, Church's TX Chicken, Jack-in-the-Box, Little Caesars, Pancake House, Popeyes, Sonic, Subway, Taco Bell, Wingstop, Oak Tree Inn, Kroger, Ross, Walgreens
423b	Saner Ave
423a	(422b from nb)US 67 S, Kiest Blvd, E OYO, W Shell/repair, Golden Chick, McDonald's
421b	Ann Arbor St, W Exxon/dsl
421a	Lp 12E W, E Chevron/dsl, Henderson Chicken, Motel 6, W QT/dsl, IHOP, Panda Express, Pizza Hut, Taco Bell, Wendy's, Wingstop, $Tree, Walmart/Subway
420	Laureland, E 7-11/dsl, Luxury Inn, Plaza Inn, W Exxon/dsl, Texaco, H&J BBQ, Smokey Joe's BBQ, Linfield Inn, tire repair/lube
419	Camp Wisdom Rd, E Exxon, Jack-in-the-Box, tire repair, W Chevron, Shell, McDonald's, Grand Inn, U-Haul
418c	Danieldale Rd(from sb)
418b	I-635/I-20 E, to Shreveport
418a	I-20 W, to Ft Worth
417	Wheatland Rd(from nb)
416	Wintergreen Rd, W 7-11, Cracker Barrel/EVC, Waffle House, Comfort Suites, Days Inn, Hampton Inn, Holiday Inn Express, Home2 Suites
415	Pleasant Run Rd, E Phillips 66/Church's TX Chicken/dsl, QT, Shell/dsl, Chicken Express, Chili's, CiCi's Pizza, Dan's Seafood, IHOP, In-N-Out, Mariscos Seafood, Pier7, Sonic, Subway, Taco Cabana, Waffle House, Great Western Inn, Hwy Express Inn, Motel 6, Spanish Trails Motel, Family$, Home Depot, H, Tire Kingdom, W Burger King, KFC, LJ Silver, Luby's, McDonald's, On the Border, Outback Steaks, Pizza Patron, Starbucks, Taco Bueno, Tastee Ice, Wendy's, La Quinta, Scottish Inns, AT&T, Chevrolet, Discount Tire, Firestone/auto, Ford, Kroger, Office Depot, Ross, T-Mobile
414	FM 1382, Desoto Rd, Belt Line Rd, E Murphy USA/dsl, Taco Bell, Whataburger, Verizon, Walmart/McDonald's, W QT/dsl, $Tree
413	Parkerville Rd, W Exxon/Subway/dsl, U-Haul
412	Bear Creek Rd, W Shell/Sonic/dsl, Jack-in-the-Box, transmissions
411	FM 664, Ovilla Rd, E Exxon/dsl, Murphy USA/dsl, RaceTrac, Arby's, Burger King, Chick-fil-A, Chicken Express, Denny's, Dickey's BBQ, DQ, KFC, La Quinta, Little Caesars, LJ Silver/Taco Bell, McDonald's, Panda Express, Pizza Hut, Starbucks, Whataburger, Wingstop, Comfort Inn, AT&T, AutoZone, Brookshire's Foods, CVS, USPO, Walgreens, Walmart, W Exxon, Mamacita's Rest., Valero,

INTERSTATE 35 Cont'd

411 Continued Snoops Ice Cream
410 Red Oak Rd, E Shell/Pizza Inn/dsl, Motel 6
408 US 77, TX 342, to Red Oak
406 Sterrett Rd, E fireworks
405 FM 387, E Phillips 66/dsl, QT/dsl
404 Lofland Rd, industrial area
403 US 287, to Ft Worth, E Murphy USA/dsl, RaceTrac/dsl, Shell/dsl, Valero, A&W/LJ Silver, Carino's, Chick-fil-A, Chili's, Chipotle, Domino's, DQ, El Fenix, IHOP, Jack-in-the-Box, KFC, Logan's Roadhouse, McDonald's, MOD Pizza, Olive Garden, Panda Express, Panera Bread, Pizza Hut, Starbuck's, Taco Bueno, Taco Cabana, Waffle House, Wendy's, Wingstop, Wingstreet, Comfort Suites, Fairfield Inn, Hampton Inn, Holiday Inn Express, LaQuinta, Belk, Best Buy, Buick/GMC/Chevrolet, Discount Tire, Firestone, Hobby Lobby, Home Depot, H, JC Penney, Lowe's, Office Depot, PetSmart, Ross, Target, Walmart, W Exxon, Chrysler/Dodge/Jeep, Ford

MAYPEARL

401b US 287 bus, Waxahatchie, E Motel 6, Super 8
401a Brookside Rd, E Dallas Suites, Executive Inn
399b FM 1446
399a FM 66, FM 876, Maypearl, E Texas Inn, W Exxon/dsl, Shell/Sonic/dsl, McDonald's
397 to US 77, to Waxahachie
391 FM 329, Forreston Rd
386 TX 34, Italy, E Love's/Carl's Jr/dsl/EVC/scales/24hr/@, Shell/TX BBQ/dsl, Jack-in-the-Box, McDonald's, Sonic, $General, W Pilot/Exxon/Stuckey's/dsl/scales, Denny's, Golden Chick, Taco Bell
384 Derrs Chapel Rd
381 FM 566, Milford Rd
377 FM 934

HILLSBORO

374 FM 2959, Carl's Corner, W Petro/Exxon/dsl/scales/24hr
373 I-35W
371 I-35 W. I-35 divides into E and W nb, converges sb, See Texas I-35 W.
370 US 77 N, FM 579, Hillsboro, E Buc-ee's/dsl, TA/Shell/Country Pride/Burger King/dsl/scales/24hr/@
368b FM 286(from sb), E LoneStar Café, Taco Bell, Wendy's, Hampton Inn, W Exxon, Valero/dsl, Braum's, El Conquistador Mexican, El Taco Jalisco, Pizza Hut, Up In Smoke BBQ, Best Value Inn, EconoLodge, La Quinta, H
368a TX 22, TX 171, to Whitney, E 7-11, Love's/Chester's/Subway/dsl/scales/24hr/@, DQ, El Charro, Golden Buffet, IHOP, McDonald's, Starbucks, Days Inn, Motel 6, Quality Inn, Rodeway Inn, Super 8, Hillsboro Outlets/Famous Brands, W Chevron/dsl, Murphy USA/dsl, Chicken Express, Jack-in-the-Box, Schlotzsky's, Sonic, Whataburger, Wok Express, Thunderbird Motel/rest., $Tree, AT&T, Chrysler/Dodge/Jeep, Ford, H, Walmart/Subway
367 Old Bynum Rd(from nb), same as 368
364b TX 81 N, to Hillsboro(from nb, exits left)
364a FM 310(from sb)
363 CR 3111

ABBOTT

362mm **full facilities, litter barrels, petwalk, both directions**
359 FM 1304, W Exxon/Tesla EVC/dsl, Gulf/dsl/24hr, truck service
358 FM 1242 E, Abbott, E Still Smokin' BBQ
356 Co Rd 3102
355 County Line Rd, E Waco North RV Park
354 Marable St
353 FM 2114, West, E Chevron/dsl, Shell/Czech Bakery, Bush's Chicken, Sonic, Subway, Ford, Continued Exxon/Slovacek's/dsl, McDonald's, Starbucks, Holiday Inn, Chevrolet, Vintage Automotive

ELM MOTT

351 FM 1858, E tires/repair
349 Wiggins Rd
347 FM 3149, Tours Rd
346 Ross Rd, W Valero/dsl/24hr, antiques, I-35 RV Park/LP, tire repair
345 Old Dallas Rd
345a frontage rd, same as 345
343 FM 308, Elm Mott, E Exxon/DQ, Sunoco/dsl/scales/24hr, Waco RV Resort, W $General
342b US 77 bus, E Road Ranger, W North Crest RV Park
342a FM 2417, Crest Dr, E Texaco, W Valero/Circle K/dsl, Bush's Chicken, DQ, Motel 6, auto repair, Family$
341 Craven Ave, Lacy Lakeview, E Freightliner, W Chevron
340 Myers Lane(from nb)
339 to TX 6 S, FM 3051, Lake Waco, E Murphy USA, QT, Valero/dsl, Casa Ole, Domino's, El Conquistador, IHOP, Jack-in-the-Box, Marco's Pizza, Pizza Hut, Popeyes, Wendy's, Whataburger, Wingstop, Holiday Inn, $General, $Tree, Advance Parts, Discount Tire, Home Depot, to Walmart, W 7-11/dsl, Chevron, Shell, Valero/dsl, Burger King, Cracker Barrel, Heitmiller Steaks, KFC, McDonald's, Starbucks, Taco Bell, Fairfield Inn, Hampton Inn, TownePlace Suites, AT&T, URGENT CARE
338b Behrens Circle(from nb), same as 339, E Little Caesar's, Sonic, W Shell/dsl/LP, Best Western, Days Inn, Delta Inn, EconoLodge, Motel 6, Quality Inn
338a US 84, to TX 31, Waco Dr, E Tesla EVC, Chopstix, Collin St Bakery, Denny's, Pollo Regio, Subway, Woodspring Suites, AutoZone, Family$, HEB Food/gas, O'Reilly Parts, Sam's Club/gas, W Comfort Suites, H
337 US 77 business
335c Lake Brazos Dr, MLK Blvd, E Baylor Stadium, W Buzzard Billy's, Red Roof Inn, H
335mm Brazos River
335b FM 434, University Parks Dr, E Starbucks, Baylor U, TX Ranger Museum, W 7-11/dsl, Twisted Root Burgers, Residence Inn, SpringHill Suites
335a 4th St, 5th St, E Exxon/Subway/dsl, Pizza Hut, La Quinta, Baylor U, W Valero/Circle K/dsl, Cane's, Chick-fil-A, Chipotle, Fazoli's, Freddy's, Hawaiian Bros, In-N-Out, Jersey Mike's, LJ Silver, McAlister's Deli, McDonald's, Panera Bread, Papa John's, Roy's Taqueria, Sonic, Taco Bell, Torcy's Tacos, Wendy's, Whataburger, Aloft, CVS Drug
334b US 77 S, 17th St, 18th St, E CEFCO/dsl, Valero/dsl, Cupp's Drive Inn, Fuego Grill, Hawk's Chicken, Jimmy John's, Schlotzsky's, Vitek's BBQ, Budget Inn, Deluxe Inn, La Quinta, Studio 6, Super 8, W Chevron, George's Rest., Golden Chick, H
333a Lp 396, Valley Mills Dr, E Health Camp, Magnolia Cafe, Rudy's BBQ/gas, Trujillo's Mexican, TX Roadhouse, Comfort Suites, Days Inn, Kia, Mazda, W Exxon/dsl, RaceWay/dsl, Bubba's 33, Bush's Chicken, Catfish King, Chili's, Church's TX Chicken, Jack-in-the-Box, Little Caesar's, Pizza Patron, Starbucks, Subway, TX Teriyaki, Zoe's Kitchen, Home2 Suites, Advance Parts, AutoZone, CVS Drug, Family$, HEB Foods/dsl, RNR Tires, Verizon, Walgreens
331 New Rd, E Conoco/dsl, Candlewood Suites, Motel 6, New Road Inn, Relax Inn, W Flying J/Denny's/dsl/scales/24hr, Burger King, Dave's Chicken, Hooters, IHOP, Quality Inn, Harley Davidson
330 Lp 340, TX 6, Wendy's, W CEFCO/dsl, Buffalo Wild Wings, Bush's Chicken, Chuy's Mexican, Don Carlo's Mexican, Heitmiller Steaks, la Madeleine, Logan's Roadhouse, Newk's Eatery, Old Chicago Pizza,

TX

TX

INTERSTATE 35 Cont'd

LORENA / TEMPLE

330 Continued
Panda Express, Panera Bread, Saltgrass Steaks, Sonic, Starbucks, Subway, Walk-On's, Hampton Inn, Hilton Garden, Holiday Inn Express, Homewood Suites, Hyatt Place, Residence Inn, TownePlace Suites, Tru, $Tree, AT&T, Belk, Best Buy, Cabela's, Cavender's Boots, Fiat/Alpha Romeo, Ford, Honda, H, Hyundai, Kohl's, Marshall's, Nissan, Office Depot, Old Navy, Petco, Ross, Toyota/Scion, URGENT CARE, World Mkt

328 FM 2063, FM 2113, Moody, E Pilot/Subway/Wendy's/dsl/scales/24hr/@, McDonald's, Robinson Inn, Kenworth, W Chevron/dsl, Valero/dsl, Cracker Barrel, DQ, Golden Chick, Ramada Inn, Sleep Inn, Walmart/gas

325 FM 3148, Moonlight Dr, W Valero/dsl, FunTown RV Ctr, RV Station

323 FM 2837(from sb), Lorena, W Brookshire Bros/Conoco/dsl, Bush's Chicken, Pizza House, Sonic

322 Lorena, E Conoco/dsl, Ace Hardware, W Bush's Chicken, Pizza House, $General

321 Callan Ranch Rd

319 Woodlawn Rd

318b a Bruceville, E Bruceville-Eddy RV Park

315 TX 7, FM 107, Eddy, W Family$, to Mother Neff SP

314 Old Blevins Rd

311 Big Elm Rd, E fireworks

308 FM 935, Troy, E Chevron/dsl, Love's/Subway/McDonald's/dsl/scales/24hr/@, Valero/dsl, W $General

306 FM 1237, Pendleton, W Goodyear Truck Tires

305 Berger Rd, W Lucky's RV Park

304 Lp 363, Dodgen Loop, E Buc-ee's/dsl, Burger King, Starbucks, Taco Bell, Belaire Junction RV Park, W CEFCO/Wendy's/dsl, Freightliner

303 spur 290, N 3rd St, Temple, E S-2 Gas, Texas Inn

302 Nugent Ave, E Exxon/dsl, Best Value Inn, EconoLodge, Quality Suites, Rodeway Inn, W Chevron, TX Roadhouse, Best Western, Days Inn, Knights Inn, Motel 6, Studio 6

301 TX 53, FM 2305, Adams Ave, E Cefco/dsl, Valero, Chick-fil-A, KFC, Little Caesar's, McDonald's, Pizza Hut, Subway, Taco Bell, Tapa Tapas, Whataburger, La Quinta, Advance Parts, HEB Foods/dsl, H, O'Reilly Parts, URGENT CARE, W Estella's, TX Roadhouse, Best Western

300 Ave H, 49th –57th Sts, E Clem Mikeskas BBQ, Los Tres Mexican, Rylander's Burgers, W Marvin Fenn Park

299 US 190 E, TX 36, E 7-11, Shell/dsl, Clem Mikeska's BBQ, Cracker Barrel, Jack-in-the-Box, Olive Garden, Smoothie King, Sol de Jalisco, Budget Inn, Residence Inn, Travelodge, AT&T, Chrysler/Dodge/Jeep, H, Natural Grocers, Tires To You, URGENT CARE, Verizon, W BJ's Rest., Chili's, Chipotle Mexican, IHOP, McDonald's, Mee Mee's Thai, Pizza Hut, Taco Cabana, Hampton Inn, Best Buy, Firestone/auto, GNC, Home Depot, Michael's, PetSmart, Target

298 nb only, to frontage rd, E Longhorn Steaks, Residence Inn

297 FM 817, Midway Dr, E Sunoco/dsl, Golden Corral, Holiday Inn, Super 8, Buick/GMC/Cadillac, Nissan, W Circle K/dsl

294b FM 93, 6th Ave, E CEFCO/dsl, McDonald's, Chevrolet, Ford/Lincoln, Toyota, W Subway, River Forest Inn, Harley-Davidson, U of Mary Hardin Baylor

294a Central Ave, E Popeyes, Taco Bell, W CEFCO/dsl, Arby's, Burger King, El Mexicano Grill, Jimmy John's, Pizza Hut, Schlotzsky's, Schlotzsky's, Schoepf's BBQ, Sonic,

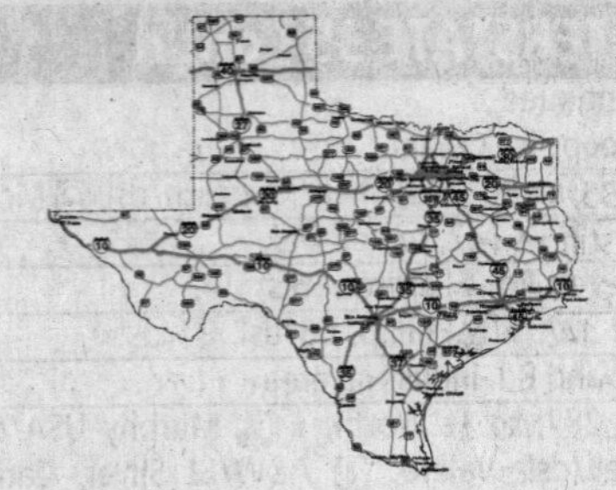

SALADO / GEORGETOWN / LEANDER

294a Continued
Starbucks, Whataburger, Knights Inn, AutoZone, city park, O'Reilly Parts, USPO

293b TX 317, FM 436, Main St

293a US 190 W, to Killeen, Ft Hood

292 Lp 121(same as 293a), E Valero/dsl/24hr, Budget Host, W 7-11/dsl, Exxon/dsl, Oxbow Steaks, La Quinta, Belton RV Park, Sunbelt RV Ctr

290 Shanklin Rd

289 Tahuaya Rd

287 Amity Rd

286 FM 2484, E Days Inn, Holiday Inn Express, Salado RV Park, W to Stillhouse Hollow Lake, Tranquil RV Park(2mi)

285 FM 2268, Salado, E Conoco/dsl, Subway, Holiday Inn Express, Brookshire Foods/gas, W CEFCO/dsl, Gulf, Bush's Chicken, Cowboy BBQ, Robertson's Rest., Sonic

284 Stagecoach Rd, E The Shed, Shady Villa, W Johnny's Steaks

283 FM 2268, FM 2843, to Holland, Salado

282 FM 2115, E Valero/dsl

281mm rest area both lanes, **full facilities, litter barrels, petwalk, RV dump, vending**

280 Grainger Rd, Hackberry Rd, Prairie Dell

279 Hill Rd

277 Rd 305

275 FM 487, to Florence, Jarrell, E Exxon/dsl, $General, W Chevron/dsl, Shell/DQ/dsl, USPO

274 Rd 312, E CEFCO/Dominos/Subway/dsl, Flying J/Burger King/Denny's/dsl/scales, McDonald's

271 Ronald Reagan Blvd, W Shell/Subway/dsl/24hr

268 fm 972, Walburg, E Crestview RV Ctr

266 TX 195, E Shell/Huddle House/dsl/scales/24hr, W Shell/dsl

265 TX 130 Toll S, to Austin

264 Lp 35, Georgetown

262 RM 2338, Lake Georgetown, E Valero/Circle K, Chipotle Mexican, KFC, Louisiana Crab Shack, McDonald's, Papa John's, Pizza Hut, Sonic, $Tree, CVS Drug, Eagle Auto Parts, URGENT CARE, W DQ, Frankie's Pizza, Plaka Greek, Whataburger, Candlewood Suites, Days Inn, Holiday Inn Express, Rodeway Inn

261 TX 29, Georgetown, E Shell/dsl, Applebee's, Burger King, Chili's, Domino's, First Watch, Jack-in-the-Box, Jersey Mike's, Jimmy John's, Olive Garden, P. Terry's Burgers, Schlotzsky's, Taco Bell, Willie's Grill, Best Western+, Comfort Suites, Hampton Inn, ALDI, HEB Foods, Hobby Lobby, Midas, O'Reilly Parts, same as 262, W Murphy USA/dsl, Arby's, Buffalo Wild Wings, Cane's, Carl's Jr, Chick-fil-A, Cotton Patch Cafe, Five Guys, IHOP, Kyoto Japanese, Longhorn Steaks, McAlister's Deli, MOD Pizza, Panda Express, Panera Bread, Popeyes, Starbucks, Taco Cabana, Wendy's, Wingstop, AT&T, Best Buy, Discount Tire, Home Depot, Kohl's, Michael's, Natural Grocers, Office Depot, Old Navy, PetSmart, Ross, Target, TJ Maxx, Walgreens, Walmart

260 RM 2243, Leander, E H, USPO, W Chevron/dsl,

INTERSTATE 35 Cont'd

LEANDER

260 Continued
Exxon/dsl, Texaco, [food] Jack-in-the-Box, [lodging] Motel 6

259 Lp 35, **W** [other] Ron Hoover RV Ctr, to Interspace Caverns

257 Westinghouse Rd, **E** [other] Buick/Chevrolet, Chrysler/Dodge/Jeep, Ford/Lincoln, Mazda, Mercedes, Subaru/Volvo, VW

256 RM 1431, Chandler Rd, **E** [food] BJ Rest., Cane's, Chick-fil-A, Chipotle, Freebirds Burrito, Ike's Love, In-N-Out, Jimmy John's, McDonald's, Mighty Fine Burgers, Mooyah Burger, Panda Express, Papa John's, Pei Wei, PhoNatic, Popeyes, Razzoo's Cajun, Santiago's Tex-Mex, Whataburger, [other] Bass Pro Shops, GNC, HEB/dsl, [H], IKEA, JC Penney, Mazda, PetSmart, Ross, Round Rock Outlet/famous brands, Volvo, Walgreens

ROUND ROCK

254 FM 3406, Round Rock, **E** [gas] Chevron/dsl, [food] Casa Garcias, Gatti's Pizza, Kerby Lane Cafe, La Tapatia, McDonald's, P. Terry's Burgers, Pizza Hut, Tumble22 Chicken, [lodging] Best Western, [other] $General, Firestone/auto, Harley-Davidson, Honda, Kia, Toyota/Scion, vet, **W** [gas] Shell/dsl, [food] Chuy's Mexican, Cracker Barrel, Denny's, DoubleDave's Pizza, Hopdoddy Burgers, IHOP, Jack Allen's Kitchen, Pinthouse Pizza, Rudy's BBQ/gas, Salt Traders Rest., SaltGrass Steaks, [lodging] Courtyard, Hilton Garden, Holiday Inn, Holiday Inn Express, La Quinta, Red Roof Inn, SpringHill Suites, Tru, WoodSpring Suites, [other] CVS Drug, GMC, Nissan

253b US 79, to Taylor, **E** [gas] Chevron/dsl, Valero/dsl, [food] Baskin-Robbins, Casa Garcia's, DQ, KFC, LJ Silver, Pacific Star, Short Stop Dogs, Sirloin Stockade, Taco More, [lodging] Best Western, Wingate Inn, [other] Advance Parts, AutoZone, Just Brakes, **W** [food] GattiTown Pizza, La Margarita, Poke Joe's BBQ, Popeyes, Starbucks, Taco Bell, Thundercloud Subs, Torchy's Tacos, [lodging] Country Inn&Suites, Motel 6, Red Roof Inn, WoodSpring Suites, [other] $Tree, USPO

253a Frontage Rd, same as 253 b

252b a RM 620, **E** [gas] Shell/dsl, [food] Golden Chick, [lodging] Candlewood Suites, Extended Stay America, **W** [gas] Tesla EVC, [food] Corner Cafe Bakery, Freddy's Steakburgers, Jimmy John's, Little Caesar's, McDonald's, Starbucks, [lodging] Comfort Suites, Staybridge Suites, [other] Office Depot, Sprouts Mkt, Tuesday Morning

251 Lp 35, Round Rock, **E** [gas] QT, [food] CiCi's Pizza, Gino's, Joe's Crabshack, Outback Steaks, Papa John's, Pluckers Wings, Roman's Grill, Smokey Mo's BBQ, Whataburger, [lodging] Hampton Inn, Homewood Suites, Residence Inn, [other] Aamco, BigLots, Brake Check, Jiffy Lube, **W** [gas] Shell, [food] Burger King, Jack-in-the-Box, Taco Cabana, [lodging] Marriott, Quality Inn, Sleep Inn, [other] Austin's Automotive, NTB, transmissions, Walgreens

PFLUGERVILLE

250 TX 45, Lp 1, **E** [food] Cajun Crabs & Shrimp, Chick-fil-A, Chili's, Firehouse Subs, Five Guys, Jason's Deli, Joe's Crabshack, Macaroni Grill, McDonald's, Panda Express, Red Lotus Vietnamese, Subway, Taco Palenque, Twin Peaks Rest., Zorba Greek, [lodging] Hampton Inn, Residence Inn, [other] $Tree, AT&T, Best Buy, Discount Tire, Home Depot, Michael's, Target, URGENT CARE, Walmart, **W** [food] Applebee's, Chipotle, Deckhand Oyster, Eddie's Tavern, Egg&I Cafe, Honey Baked Ham, Hooters, Logan's Roadhouse, Longhorn Steaks, Olive Garden, Pho Vietnamese, Red Lobster, Schlotzsky's, Tokyo Steaks, [lodging] Extended Stay America, Holiday Inn Express, La Quinta, TownePlace Suites, [other] Barnes&Noble, Hobby Lobby, Kohl's, Lowe's, Marshall's, Old Navy, PetCo, Sam's Club, World Mkt

248 Grand Ave Pkwy, **E** [gas] 7-11/dsl, Chevron, Shell/dsl, [food] Gatti's Pizza, Gossip Shack, Thundercloud Subs, TX Roadhouse, [lodging] Comfort Suites, [other] URGENT CARE, **W** [gas] Exxon/McDonald's/dsl, [other] Goodyear, J&J Tire Service

247 FM 1825, Pflugerville, **E** [gas] Exxon/7-11/dsl,

247 Continued
Bombshells Rest., Burger King, Cheddar's, Domino's, FD's Grillhouse, Jack-in-the-Box, Subway, Taco Cabana, Wendy's, [lodging] Comfort Suites, [other] Firestone/auto, GNC, HEB Foods/gas, **W** [gas] Exxon/7-11, [food] Inka Chicken, KFC, Miller's BBQ, Sonic, [lodging] Best Western, Country Inn Suites, [other] McSpadden Automotive

246 Howard Lane, **E** [gas] Citgo, Exxon/7-11/dsl, [food] Arby's, Baby Acapulco, Charm Korean, Ka-Prow, McDonald's, Wings'n More, [other] Home Depot, Kohl's, NTB, **W** [gas] Valero/Circle K/dsl, [food] Davi's Tacos, IHOP, Spinners, Whataburger, [lodging] Sleep Inn, [other] CarMax

245 FM 734, Parmer Lane, to Yager Lane (244 from nb), **E** [food] Asadas Grill, Bep Saigon, Carino's, Chick-fil-A, Chili's, Freebirds Burrito, In-N-Out, Jersey Mike's, Jimmy John's, Kublai Khan, MOD Pizza, Niki's Pizza, Panda Express, Schlotzsky's, Souper Salad, Subway, [lodging] Homewood Suites, [other] $Tree, HEB Food/E-85, Hobby Lobby, JC Penney, PetCo, PetSmart, Ross, Sears Grand, Verizon, **W** [gas] Conoco/dsl, Exxon/7-11/dsl, Murphy USA/dsl, [food] Buffalo Wild Wings, Denny's, French Quarter Grille, Golden Corral, Hoho Chinese, Mkt Street Pizza, Panera Bread, Red Robin, [lodging] Courtyard, Fairfield Inn, Hilton Garden, Residence Inn, SpringHill Suites, Staybridge Suites, [other] AT&T, Discount Tire, Lowe's, Walmart/McDonald's

244 Tech Ridge Blvd, Yager Lane, from nb, same as 245

243 Braker Lane, **E** [gas] QT, Valero/dsl, [food] Whataburger, **W** [gas] Citgo, Exxon/dsl, [food] Oakwood BBQ, [lodging] Austin Motel, ValuePlace

LOCKHART

241 Rundberg Lane, **E** [gas] Exxon/7-11, [food] Fujian Chinese, Jack-in-the-Box, [lodging] Orangewood Inn, [other] $General, Chevrolet, U-Haul, **W** [gas] Chevron, Shell, [lodging] Budget Inn, Economy Inn, Motel 6

240a US 183, Lockhart, **E** [food] McDonald's, Taco Bell, [lodging] Extended Stay, Hampton Inn, [other] Walmart, **W** [food] Buffalo Wild Wings, Mario's Seafood, [lodging] Holiday Inn Express, La Quinta, Motel 6, Sonesta, Super 8

239 St John's Ave, **E** [gas] Shell, [food] Burger King, Chili's, Habesha Ethiopian, Pappadeaux, Pappasito's Mexican, Sushi Japon, [lodging] DoubleTree, Drury Inn, Embassy Suites, Radisson, Studio 6, Studio 6, [other] USPO, **W** [gas] Exxon/7-11, Mobil/dsl, Valero/dsl, [food] Denny's, Easy Tiger, IHOP, Lima Criolla, Ojos Locos, Panda Express, Pluckers Wings, VIVO Tex-Mex, Wendy's, [lodging] Best Value Inn, Best Western+, Comfort Inn, Holiday Inn, La Quinta, [other] Ford, Office Depot

238b US 290 E, RM 222, frontage rds connect several exits, same as 238a

238a 51st St, **E** [food] Buffet King, Chi'Lantro, Chipotle, Church's TX Chicken, CiCi's, Jamba Juice, Kebab Shop, La Madeleine, Little Caesars, McDonald's, P. Terry's Burgers, Residence Inn, Starbucks, Subway, Which Wich?, [lodging] DoubleTree Hotel, Drury Inn, EconoLodge, Embassy Suites, [other] $Tree, Advance Parts, AutoZone, Best Buy, Home Depot, Marshall's, Old Navy, PetSmart, Ross, Staples, Target, Walgreens, **W** [gas] Shell, [food] Capt Benny's Seafood, Charoen Express, [lodging] Courtyard, Fairfield Inn, Motel 6, Super 8

237b 51st St, same as 238a

237a Airport Blvd, **W** [food] Freebirds Burritos, In-N-Out, Jack-in-the-Box, Jason's Deli, Pok-e-Jo's BBQ, Wendy's, [other] Firestone, Goodyear, HEB Foods, PetCo

236.7 lower level accesses downtown, upper level is I-35 thru

236b 39th St, **E** [gas] Chevron/dsl, [food] El Pollo Loco, Short Stop Burgers, [other] Fiesta Foods, O'Reilly Parts, U-Haul, **W** [gas] Shell/dsl

236a 26th-32nd Sts, **E** [food] Los Altos Mexican, Subway, [lodging] Days Inn, **W** [food] Aster's Ethiopian, [lodging] Rodeway Inn, [other] [H], to U of TX

235b Manor Rd, same as 236a, **E** [food] Denny's, [lodging] DoubleTree,

INTERSTATE 35 Cont'd

TOWN LAKE

Exit	Services
235b	Continued Rodeway Inn, U of TX
235a	MLK, 15th St, E Denny's, DoubleTree Hotel, W H, st capitol
234.9mm	lower level accesses downtown, upper level is I-35 thru
234c	11th St, 12th St, downtown, E Chevron/dsl, Shell/dsl, Wendy's, Super 8, CVS Drug, W Gulf/dsl, Shell, Hilton, Hilton Garden, La Quinta, Marriott, Omni Motel, Radisson, Sheraton, H, museum, st capitol
234b	8th-3rd St
234a	Cesar Chavez St, Holly St, downtown, E Shell/dsl, W Chevron/dsl, IHOP, Holiday Inn
233mm	Little Colorado River
233	Riverside Dr, Town Lake, E Gulf, Shell/dsl, 1618 Asian, Chipotle, MOD Pizza, Rosita's Mexican, Starbucks, AT&T, Walgreens
232b	Woodland Ave
232a	Oltorf St, E Chevron/dsl, Gulf, Shell/dsl, Chipotle, Donn's BBQ, Whataburger, La Quinta, Motel 6, Parkwest Inn, W Exxon/7-11, Denny's, Starbucks, Best Western
231	Woodward St, E same as 232, Travelodge, Wyndham Garden, W Home Depot, Walmart
230b a	US 290 W, TX 71, Ben White Blvd, St Elmo Rd, E Austin Southpark Hotel, Courtyard, Fairfield Inn, Hampton Inn, Homewood Suites, Marriott, Quality Inn, Red Roof+, Residence Inn, SpringHill Suites, WoodSpring Suites, Acura, W Burger King, La Quinta, Skylite Inn, Sonesta Suites, Audi, CarMax, Chrysler/Dodge/Jeep, Ford, H, Hyundai, Kia, Mazda, Nissan/EVC, Toyota/Scion
229	Stassney Lane, W Buffalo Wild Wings, Chili's, Chipotle, Dimassi's Grill, Jimmy John's, Krispy Kreme, Logan's Roadhouse, Pizza Hut, Trudy's Grill, Twin Peaks Rest., TX Cattle Co Steaks, Holiday Inn Express, Staybridge Suites, TownePlace Suites, Fiesta Foods/gas, Lowe's
228	Wm Cannon Drive, E Exxon, Valero, Applebee's, McDonald's, Subway, Taco Bell, Discount Tire, HEB Foods, W Valero/dsl, China Harbor, Gatti's Pizza, Golden Corral, KFC, Taco Bueno, Taco Cabana, Tucci's Subs, Wendy's, Whataburger, Advance Parts, AT&T, BigLots, Chevrolet, Firestone, Lone Star RV Resort

S CONGRESS

Exit	Services
227	Slaughter Lane, Lp 275, S Congress, E Circle K/dsl, ChuckECheese, Domino's, Don Dario's, IHOP, Home Depot, U-Haul, W Murphy USA/dsl, Valero, Carino's, Chick-fil-A, Chili's, Chipotle Mexican, Crawfish ATX, DQ, Dunkin', Gabriela's Mexican, Gatti Town, Jack-in-the-Box, Jason's Deli, Longhorn Steaks, Luby's, Mama Fu's, Miller BBQ, Panda Express, Pho With Us, Serrano's TexMex, Sonic, Starbucks, Subway, Taco Bell, TX Roadhouse, Wendy's, Whataburger, Wingstop, $Tree, AT&T, Best Buy, Firestone/auto, Hobby Lobby, JC Penney, Marshall's, PetSmart, Ross, Sam's Club/dsl, Target, URGENT CARE, Verizon, Walgreens, Walmart/McDonald's
226	Slaughter Creek Overpass
225	FM 1626, Onion Creek Pkwy, E Exxon, Valero, CraigO's Pizza, Harley-Davidson, W Valero/Circle K
224	frontage rd(from nb)
223	FM 1327, rd 45 toll

BUDA

Exit	Services
221	Lp 4, Buda, E Chevron/McDonald's, Popeyes, Starbucks, Best Value Inn, Best Western+, Candlewood Suites, Comfort Suites, Holiday Inn Express, Ford, Kenworth, W 7-11, Murphy USA/dsl, Shell/dsl, Chick-fil-A, Chili's, Cracker Barrel, Dan's Burgers, Domino's, DoubleDave's Pizza, Freddy's Steakburgers, Hat Creek Burgers, Jack-in-the-Box, Jalisco's Rest., Jersey Mike's,

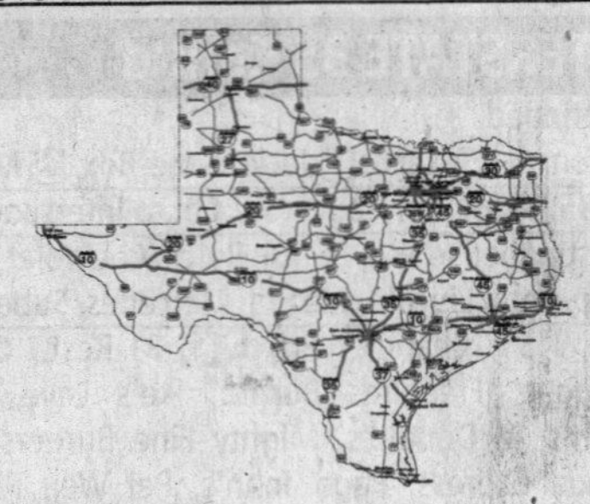

BUDA

Exit	Services
221	Continued KFC/LJ Silver, Little Caesar's, Logan's Roadhouse, Marble Slab, Miller BBQ, Panda Express, Papa John's, Pizza Hut, Sonic, Subway, Taco Bell, Whataburger, Zaxby's, Fairfield Inn, Hampton Inn, Microtel, AutoZone, Cabela's, HEB Food/dsl/E-85, O'Reilly Parts, USPO, Verizon, Walgreens, Walmart
220	FM 2001, Niederwald, E Burger King, Studio 6, Camper Clinic RV Ctr, Marshall's RV Park, W Crestview RV Ctr/Park, Peterbilt
217	Lp 4, Buda, E Exxon/dsl, La Quinta, Mack/Volvo, W QT, Sunoco/Schlotzky's/dsl, Valero/dsl, Burger King, Starbucks, Quality Inn, Christian Bros Auto, Home Depot
215	Bunton Overpass, E Exxon/KFC/LJ Silver, Abby's Crab Shack, Arby's, Dunkin'/Baskin Robbins, Firehouse Subs, Hawaiian Bros, Popeyes, Taco Bell, Taco Cabana, Wendy's, Hampton Inn, AT&T, Discount Tire, Firestone/auto, H, Lowe's, Walgreens, Walmart/dsl, W Applebee's, Casa Garcia's, Chick-fil-A, Chicken Express, Five Guys, IHOP, Ilario's Italian, Jack-in-the-Box, Jersey Mike's, Little Caesar's, Mama Fu's, McDonald's, MOD Pizza, Panda Express, Papa Murphy's, Phở Tháisơn, Starbucks, Subway, Whataburger, Wingstop, Comfort Suites, $Tree, Explore USA RV Ctr, GNC, HEB Foods/dsl/e85, Kohl's, PetCo, Ross, Target, URGENT CARE

KYLE

Exit	Services
213	FM 150, Kyle, E 7-11/dsl, Valero/7-11/dsl, DQ, Sonic, Starbucks, AutoZone, Goodyear, O'Reilly Parts, W Conoco/dsl, Casa Maria Mexican, Advance Parts, CVS Drug, repair
210	Yarrington Rd, E Hyundai, W Buick/Chevrolet/GMC, Ford, Plum Creek RV Park
209	weigh sta (sb only)
208mm	Blanco River
208	Frontage Rd, Blanco River Rd, W Hilton Garden, Buick/Chevrolet/GMC
206	Lp 82, Aquarena Springs Rd, TX Bean & Brew, E Texaco, Valero/dsl, San Marcos RV Park, W Exxon/dsl, Shell, Shell/dsl, Chick-fil-A, Hawaiian Bros, Inn-N-Out, Popeyes, Sonic, Howard Johnson, La Quinta, Motel 6, Motel 6, Quality Inn, San Marcos Inn, Summit Inn, Super 8, to SW TX U

BASTROP

Exit	Services
205	TX 80, TX 142, Bastrop, E 7-11/dsl, 76, Exxon/7-11/dsl, Little Caesar's, Shell/dsl, Valero/dsl, Cane's, China Palace, Fazoli's, Freebirds Burrito, Jason's Deli, Pizza Hut, Subway, Wingstop, Executive Inn, Fairfield Inn/EVC, $General, AutoZone, CVS Drug, Hobby Lobby, Walmart, W Valero, Chuy's, Earth Burger, Five Guys, IHOP, KFC, Kobe Steaks, McCalister's Deli, McDonald's, Mucho Taco, P. Terry's Burgers, Saltgrass Steaks, Taco Cabana, Wendy's, Best Western, Budget Inn, Classic Inn, Days Inn, Red Roof Inn, Rodeway Inn, White Rock Inn, Brake Check, city park, HEB/gas, Office Depot, Walgreens
204mm	San Marcos River
204b	CM Allen Pkwy, W Shell/dsl, Shell/dsl, Casa Maria, DQ, Krispy Kreme, La Fonda Rest., Mazatlan, Plucker's Grill,

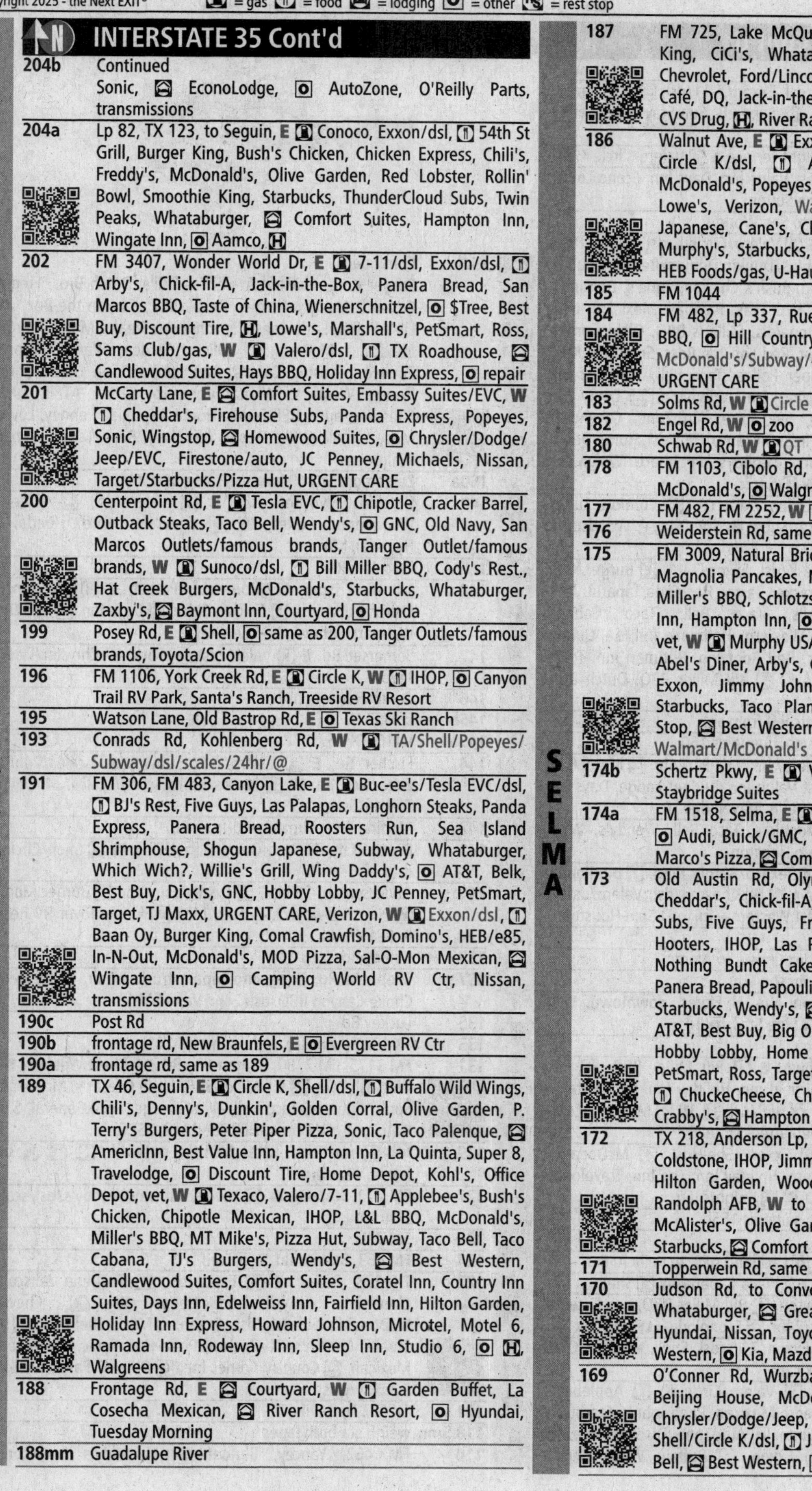

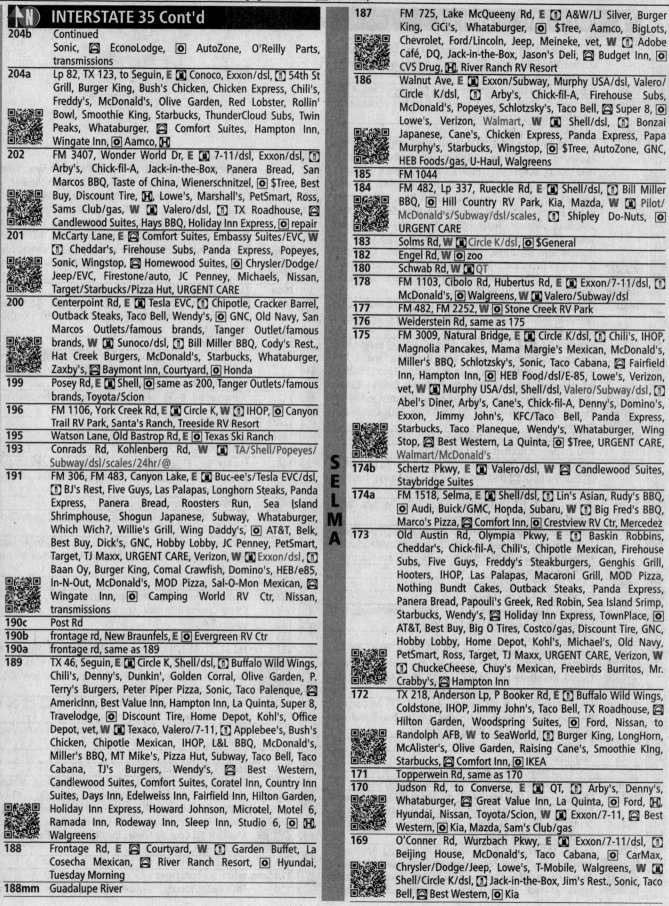

INTERSTATE 35 Cont'd

204b Continued
Sonic, EconoLodge, AutoZone, O'Reilly Parts, transmissions

204a Lp 82, TX 123, to Seguin, E Conoco, Exxon/dsl, 54th St Grill, Burger King, Bush's Chicken, Chicken Express, Chili's, Freddy's, McDonald's, Olive Garden, Red Lobster, Rollin' Bowl, Smoothie King, Starbucks, ThunderCloud Subs, Twin Peaks, Whataburger, Comfort Suites, Hampton Inn, Wingate Inn, Aamco, H

202 FM 3407, Wonder World Dr, E 7-11/dsl, Exxon/dsl, Arby's, Chick-fil-A, Jack-in-the-Box, Panera Bread, San Marcos BBQ, Taste of China, Wienerschnitzel, $Tree, Best Buy, Discount Tire, H, Lowe's, Marshall's, PetSmart, Ross, Sams Club/gas, W Valero/dsl, TX Roadhouse, Candlewood Suites, Hays BBQ, Holiday Inn Express, repair

201 McCarty Lane, E Comfort Suites, Embassy Suites/EVC, W Cheddar's, Firehouse Subs, Panda Express, Popeyes, Sonic, Wingstop, Homewood Suites, Chrysler/Dodge/Jeep/EVC, Firestone/auto, JC Penney, Michaels, Nissan, Target/Starbucks/Pizza Hut, URGENT CARE

200 Centerpoint Rd, E Tesla EVC, Chipotle, Cracker Barrel, Outback Steaks, Taco Bell, Wendy's, GNC, Old Navy, San Marcos Outlets/famous brands, Tanger Outlet/famous brands, W Sunoco/dsl, Bill Miller BBQ, Cody's Rest., Hat Creek Burgers, McDonald's, Starbucks, Whataburger, Zaxby's, Baymont Inn, Courtyard, Honda

199 Posey Rd, E Shell, same as 200, Tanger Outlets/famous brands, Toyota/Scion

196 FM 1106, York Creek Rd, E Circle K, W IHOP, Canyon Trail RV Park, Santa's Ranch, Treeside RV Resort

195 Watson Lane, Old Bastrop Rd, E Texas Ski Ranch

193 Conrads Rd, Kohlenberg Rd, W TA/Shell/Popeyes/Subway/dsl/scales/24hr/@

191 FM 306, FM 483, Canyon Lake, E Buc-ee's/Tesla EVC/dsl, BJ's Rest, Five Guys, Las Palapas, Longhorn Steaks, Panda Express, Panera Bread, Roosters Run, Sea Island Shrimphouse, Shogun Japanese, Subway, Whataburger, Which Wich?, Willie's Grill, Wing Daddy's, AT&T, Belk, Best Buy, Dick's, GNC, Hobby Lobby, JC Penney, PetSmart, Target, TJ Maxx, URGENT CARE, Verizon, W Exxon/dsl, Baan Oy, Burger King, Comal Crawfish, Domino's, HEB/e85, In-N-Out, McDonald's, MOD Pizza, Sal-O-Mon Mexican, Wingate Inn, Camping World RV Ctr, Nissan, transmissions

190c Post Rd

190b frontage rd, New Braunfels, E Evergreen RV Ctr

190a frontage rd, same as 189

189 TX 46, Seguin, E Circle K, Shell/dsl, Buffalo Wild Wings, Chili's, Denny's, Dunkin', Golden Corral, Olive Garden, P. Terry's Burgers, Peter Piper Pizza, Sonic, Taco Palenque, AmericInn, Best Value Inn, Hampton Inn, La Quinta, Super 8, Travelodge, Discount Tire, Home Depot, Kohl's, Office Depot, vet, W Texaco, Valero/7-11, Applebee's, Bush's Chicken, Chipotle Mexican, IHOP, L&L BBQ, McDonald's, Miller's BBQ, MT Mike's, Pizza Hut, Subway, Taco Bell, Taco Cabana, TJ's Burgers, Wendy's, Best Western, Candlewood Suites, Comfort Suites, Coratel Inn, Country Inn Suites, Days Inn, Edelweiss Inn, Fairfield Inn, Hilton Garden, Holiday Inn Express, Howard Johnson, Microtel, Motel 6, Ramada Inn, Rodeway Inn, Sleep Inn, Studio 6, H, Walgreens

188 Frontage Rd, E Courtyard, W Garden Buffet, La Cosecha Mexican, River Ranch Resort, Hyundai, Tuesday Morning

188mm Guadalupe River

CANYON LAKE

SEGUIN

187 FM 725, Lake McQueeny Rd, E A&W/LJ Silver, Burger King, CiCi's, Whataburger, $Tree, Aamco, BigLots, Chevrolet, Ford/Lincoln, Jeep, Meineke, vet, W Adobe Café, DQ, Jack-in-the-Box, Jason's Deli, Budget Inn, CVS Drug, H, River Ranch RV Resort

186 Walnut Ave, E Exxon/Subway, Murphy USA/dsl, Valero/Circle K/dsl, Arby's, Chick-fil-A, Firehouse Subs, McDonald's, Popeyes, Schlotzsky's, Taco Bell, Super 8, Lowe's, Verizon, Walmart, W Shell/dsl, Bonzai Japanese, Cane's, Chicken Express, Panda Express, Papa Murphy's, Starbucks, Wingstop, $Tree, AutoZone, GNC, HEB Foods/gas, U-Haul, Walgreens

185 FM 1044

184 FM 482, Lp 337, Rueckle Rd, E Shell/dsl, Bill Miller BBQ, Hill Country RV Park, Kia, Mazda, W Pilot/McDonald's/Subway/dsl/scales, Shipley Do-Nuts, URGENT CARE

183 Solms Rd, W Circle K/dsl, $General

182 Engel Rd, W zoo

180 Schwab Rd, W QT

178 FM 1103, Cibolo Rd, Hubertus Rd, E Exxon/7-11/dsl, McDonald's, Walgreens, W Valero/Subway/dsl

177 FM 482, FM 2252, W Stone Creek RV Park

176 Weiderstein Rd, same as 175

175 FM 3009, Natural Bridge, E Circle K/dsl, Chili's, IHOP, Magnolia Pancakes, Mama Margie's Mexican, McDonald's, Miller's BBQ, Schlotzsky's, Sonic, Taco Cabana, Fairfield Inn, Hampton Inn, HEB Food/dsl/E-85, Lowe's, Verizon, vet, W Murphy USA/dsl, Shell/dsl, Valero/Subway/dsl, Abel's Diner, Arby's, Cane's, Chick-fil-A, Denny's, Domino's, Exxon, Jimmy John's, KFC/Taco Bell, Panda Express, Starbucks, Taco Planeque, Wendy's, Whataburger, Wing Stop, Best Western, La Quinta, $Tree, URGENT CARE, Walmart/McDonald's

174b Schertz Pkwy, E Valero/dsl, W Candlewood Suites, Staybridge Suites

174a FM 1518, Selma, E Shell/dsl, Lin's Asian, Rudy's BBQ, Audi, Buick/GMC, Honda, Subaru, W Big Fred's BBQ, Marco's Pizza, Comfort Inn, Crestview RV Ctr, Mercedez

173 Old Austin Rd, Olympia Pkwy, E Baskin Robbins, Cheddar's, Chick-fil-A, Chili's, Chipotle Mexican, Firehouse Subs, Five Guys, Freddy's Steakburgers, Genghis Grill, Hooters, IHOP, Las Palapas, Macaroni Grill, MOD Pizza, Nothing Bundt Cakes, Outback Steaks, Panda Express, Panera Bread, Papouli's Greek, Red Robin, Sea Island Srimp, Starbucks, Wendy's, Holiday Inn Express, TownPlace, AT&T, Best Buy, Big O Tires, Costco/gas, Discount Tire, GNC, Hobby Lobby, Home Depot, Kohl's, Michael's, Old Navy, PetSmart, Ross, Target, TJ Maxx, URGENT CARE, Verizon, W ChuckeCheese, Chuy's Mexican, Freebirds Burritos, Mr. Crabby's, Hampton Inn

172 TX 218, Anderson Lp, P Booker Rd, E Buffalo Wild Wings, Coldstone, IHOP, Jimmy John's, Taco Bell, TX Roadhouse, Hilton Garden, Woodspring Suites, Ford, Nissan, to Randolph AFB, W to SeaWorld, Burger King, LongHorn, McAlister's, Olive Garden, Raising Cane's, Smoothie KIng, Starbucks, Comfort Inn, IKEA

171 Topperwein Rd, same as 170

170 Judson Rd, to Converse, E QT, Arby's, Denny's, Whataburger, Great Value Inn, La Quinta, Ford, H, Hyundai, Nissan, Toyota/Scion, W Exxon/7-11, Best Western, Kia, Mazda, Sam's Club/gas

169 O'Conner Rd, Wurzbach Pkwy, E Exxon/7-11/dsl, Beijing House, McDonald's, Taco Cabana, CarMax, Chrysler/Dodge/Jeep, Lowe's, T-Mobile, Walgreens, W Shell/Circle K/dsl, Jack-in-the-Box, Jim's Rest., Sonic, Taco Bell, Best Western, Kia

SELMA

TX

= gas = food = lodging = other = rest stop

TX

INTERSTATE 35 Cont'd

Exit #	Services
168	Weidner Rd, E Citgo/dsl, Exxon/7-11/dsl, Days Inn, La Quinta, W Chevron, Super 8, SureStay+, Harley-Davidson, Volvo Trucks
167b	Thousand Oaks Dr, Starlight Terrace, E Valero/Circle K/dsl
167a	Randolph Blvd, W Best Value Inn, Days Inn, Econo Lodge, Extended Stay, Midtowne Suites
166	I-410 W, Lp 368 S, W to Sea World
165	FM 1976, Walzem Rd, E Valero/Circle K/dsl, Al's Pitas, Applebee's, Baskin Robbins/Dunkin Donuts, Benny's, Buffalo Wild Wings, Burger King, Bush's Chicken, Cane's, Domino's, Dutch Bros, In-n-Out, KFC, Las Palapas Mexican, Little Caesar's, LJ Silver, McDonald's, Miller's BBQ, Olive Garden, Panda Express, Pizza Hut, Red Lobster, Ross, Smoothie King, Starbucks, Subway, Super Pollos, Taco Bell, Taco Cabana, Tokyo Express, Wild Wing Sta., Wingstop, Drury Inn, Holiday Inn, $Tree, 99c Store, AutoZone, Cavender's Boots, CVS Drug, EVC, Firestone/auto, HEB/dsl, Home Depot, Jiffy Lube, Office Depot, PepBoys, PetSmart, Walgreens, Walmart/Subway/dsl, W Sonic
164b	Eisenhauer Rd, E Exxon/7-11, QT, Comfort Suites, Hampton Inn, La Quinta, Super 8, Sure Stay+, Woodspring Suites, $General
164a	Rittiman Rd, E Circle K/dsl, Exxon/7-11, Burger King, Church's TX Chicken, Cracker Barrel, Hacienda Tapatia, Jack-in-the-Box, McDonald's, Taco Bell, Taco Cabana, Whataburger, Best Western, Hallmark Inn, La Quinta, Motel 6, Quality Suites, Red Roof Inn, Rittiman Inn, Travel Inn, W Valero/Circle K, Bill Miller BBQ, Dutch Bros, Popeyes
163	I-410 S(162 from nb, exits left from sb)
161	Binz-Engleman Rd(from nb). Same as 160.
160	Splashtown Dr, E Valero/Circle K/dsl/24hr, Motel 6, W Grady's BBQ, Best Value Inn, Budget Lodge, Days Inn, Quality Inn, Studio 6, Super 8, Travelodge

BROADWAY

Exit #	Services
159b	Walters St, E McDonald's, Taco Bell, Wendy's, W EconoLodge, to Ft Sam Houston
159a	New Braunfels Ave, E Texaco/Burger King, Big Poppas Tacos, auto/dsl repair, W Chevron/dsl, Valero/dsl, Miller BBQ, Sonic, Best Western+, to Ft Sam Houston
158c	N Alamo St, Broadway
158b	I-37 S, US 281 S, to Corpus Christi, to Alamo
158a	US 281 N(from sb), to Johnson City
157b a	Brooklyn Ave, Lexington Ave, N Flores, downtown, E Super 8, W Luby's, Sure Stay, H
156	I-10 W, US 87, to El Paso
155b	Durango Blvd, downtown, E Bill Miller BBQ, Best Western, Courtyard, Fairfield Inn, Holiday Inn, La Quinta, La Quinta, Residence Inn, HEB/dsl, H, W McDonald's, Candlewood Suites, Doubletree, Motel 6
155a	South Alamo St, E Exxon, Shell/dsl, McDonald's, Wendy's, Best Western, Holiday Inn, The Inn, Travelodge, Advance Parts, USPO, W Knights Inn
154b	S Laredo St, Ceballos St, same as 155b
154a	Nogalitos St
153	I-10 E, US 90 W, US 87, Lackland AFB, to Kelly AFB
152b	Malone Ave, Theo Ave, E Taco Cabana, W Shell
152a	Division Ave, E Chevron, Bill Miller BBQ, Las Cazuelas Mexican, Whataburger/24hr, Econolodge, W Sonic
151	Southcross Blvd, E Exxon/7-11/dsl, Shell, W Shell/Circle K/dsl, Mazatlan Mexican
150b	Lp 13, Military Dr, E Valero/Circle K, Applebee's, Arby's, Denny's, Don Pedro Mexican, Papa John's, Starbucks, Taco Cabana, La Quinta, AutoZone, Discount Tire, tire repair, U-Haul, W Exxon, Buffalo Wild Wings,

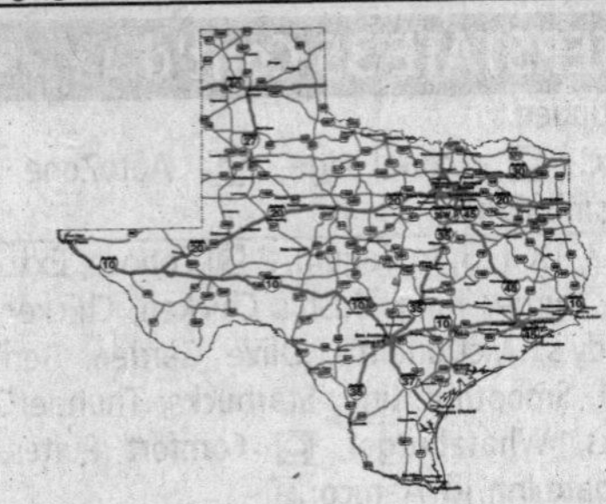

Exit #	Services
150b	Continued Burger King, Chick-fil-A, Chili's, CiCi's, Dutch Bros, Freddy's Custard, Hungry Farmer Rest, IHOP, Jack-in-the-Box, KFC, Lin's Buffet, Little Caesar's, Longhorn Steaks, Mama Margie's Mexican, McDonald's, Olive Garden, Panda Express, Popeyes, Raising Cane's, Red Lobster, Sea Island Shrimp House, Wendy's, Whataburger, $Tree, AT&T, Dick's, Firestone/auto, HEB Foods, Home Depot, JC Penney, Lowe's, Macy's, mall, Office Depot, Old Navy, Ross, Target, Verizon, Walgreens
150a	Zarzamora St(149 fom sb), same as 150b
149	Hutchins Blvd(from sb), E Valero/dsl, Motel 6, WoodSpring Suites, W Chevrolet, Ford, Honda, H, Hyundai, Kia
148b	Palo Alto Rd
148a	TX 16 S, spur 422(from nb), Poteet, E Chevron/dsl, Murphy USA/dsl, Golden Chick, Days Inn, CVS Drug, Walmart/Subway, W $General
147	Somerset Rd, E Valero/dsl, Ford, W Chrysler/Dodge/Jeep
146	Cassin Rd(from nb)
145b	Lp 353 N
145a	I-410, TX 16
144	Fischer Rd, E Valero/7-11/Subway/dsl/scales/24hr, Executive Inn, W Love's/Carl's Jr/dsl/scales/24hr/@, Toyota/Scion
142	Medina River Turnaround(from nb)
141	Benton City Rd, Von Ormy, E USPO, W Shell/Circle K/dsl
140	Anderson Lp, 1604, E Exxon/dsl/24hr, Burger King, W Pilot/Subway/dsl/scales/24hr, Alamo River RV Resort, to Sea World
139	Kinney Rd
137	Shepherd Rd, E auto repair, truck repair, W Exxon/Choke Canyon BBQ/dsl/24hr, Valero/dsl
135	Luckey Rd
133	TX 132 S(from sb), Lytle, same as 131
131	FM 3175, FM 2790, Benton City Rd, E Best Western, W HEB/dsl/24hr, Bill Miller BBQ, Little Caesar's, McDonald's, Sonic, Subway, Taco Bell, Whataburger, $General, $Tree, AutoZone, CVS Drug, HEB Food/dsl, USPO
129mm	**full facilities, litter barrels, petwalk, both lanes, vending**
127	FM 471, Natalia, W Love's/Subway/Wendy's/dsl/scales/24hr/@
125	FM 770
124	FM 463, Bigfoot Rd, E Ford
122	TX 173, Divine, E Exxon/dsl, Taqueria Jalisco, Chevrolet, Chrysler/Dodge/Jeep, W Chevron, McDonald's/Subway/dsl, Exxon, QT/dsl, Shell/dsl, CC Steaks, Church's TX Chicken, Pizza Hut, Sonic, Viva Zapata Mexican, Country Corner Inn, O'Reilly Parts, Walmart Subway/gas
121	TX 132 N, Devine
118.5mm	weigh sta both lanes
114	FM 462, Yancey, Bigfoot, E Addy's Snowcone,

POTEET LYTLE BIGFOOT

INTERSTATE 35 Cont'd

BIGFOOT DILLEY ENCINAL

114 Continued
Valero/dsl, USPO

111 US 57, to Eagle Pass, W Road Ranger/Valero/Subway/Chester's/dsl/scales/24hr

104 Lp 35

101 FM 140, Pearsall, E Chevron/dsl, Cowpokes BBQ, Jalisco's Mexican, Baymont Inn, Hampton Inn, OYO Inn, Pearsall Inn, Royal Inn, HEB Foods/dsl, W Exxon/Subway/Church's TX Chicken/dsl/24hr, Petro/Valero/Iron Skillet/dsl/scales/24hr, Hungry Hunter Grill, Days Inn, Holiday Inn Express, La Quinta, Rio Frio Motel, H

99 FM 1581, to Divot, Pearsall

93mm parking/picnic area both lanes, handicapped accessible, litter barrels

91 FM 1583, Derby

90mm Frio River

86 Lp 35, Dilley

85 FM 117, E Garcia Café, Best Western, Relax Inn, Super 8, W Exxon/dsl, Phillips 66/Church's TX Chicken/dsl/CNG/24hr, DQ, Sona Inn, RV park

84 TX 85, Dilley, E Mobil/Burger King/dsl, $General, auto repair, Chevrolet, Lowe's Mkt/dsl, W Shell/Pollo Grande/dsl/24hr, Valero/Subway/dsl/24hr, Best Value Inn, Executive Inn, NAPA, RV park

82 County Line Rd, to Dilley, Dilley

77 FM 469, Millett

74 Gardendale

69 (68 from nb), Lp 35, Cotulla, E Phillips 66/dsl, Archy's, Family$, Lowe's Mkt, W Flying J/Subway/PJ Fresh/dsl/scales/24hr, Stripes/Taco Co/dsl/scales/24hr, McDonald's, Sonic, Express Inn, Fairfield Inn, Mainstay Suites, Microtel

65 Lp 35, Cotulla

67 FM 468, to Big Wells, E Exxon/Wendy's/dsl/24hr, Valero/deli/dsl/24hr, DQ, El Charro Mexican, Golden Chick, Pizza Hut, Subway, Taco Palenque, Baymont Inn, Candlewood Suites, Comfort Suites, Executive Inn, Hampton Inn, Holiday Inn Express, La Quinta, Scottish Inns, Super 8, Village Inn, W Chevron/dsl/scales/24hr, LaSalle Steakhouse, Hotel Cotulla, Residency Suites, Whitten Inn/RV Park

63 Elm Creek Interchange

59mm full facilities, litter barrels, petwalk, , , both lanes, vending

56 FM 133, Artesia Wells

48 Caiman Creek Interchange

39 TX 44, Encinal, E Love's/Chester Fried/Subway/dsl/scales/24hr, Road Ranger/Church's TX Chicken/dsl/scales/24hr, W Chevron/dsl, Family$

38 TX 44(from nb), Encinal

32 San Roman Interchange

29mm inspection sta nb

27 Callaghan Interchange

24 255 toll, Camino Colombia toll rd, to Monterrey

22 Webb Interchange

18 US 83 N, to Carrizo Springs, E **full facilities, litter barrels, petwalk, , TX Travel Info Ctr(8am-5pm)/, wireless internet**, W RV Camping

14mm parking area sb

12b (13) Uniroyal Interchange, E Pilot/McDonald's/Subway/dsl/scales/24hr, Blue Beacon, Southern Tire Mart, W Flying J/Denny's/dsl/scales/24hr, TA/Burger King/Subway/Taco Bell/dsl/scales/24hr/@

12a Port Loredo

10 Port Laredo Carriers Dr(from nb)

9 Industrial Blvd, to Bob Bullock Lp(from sb only)

MILO

8b Lp 20 W, to Solidarity Bridge

8a Lp 20 W, to to World Trade Bridge, Milo

5 San Isidro Pkwy

4b Las Cruces Dr, E Valero/dsl, El Pescador

4a FM 1472

4 FM 1472, Del Mar Blvd, E Exxon/Burger King/dsl, Applebee's, Carino's Italian, IHOP, Jack-in-the-Box, McDonald's, Whataburger, Extended Stay America, Hampton Inn, Best Buy, BigLots, HEB Foods/gas, Marshall's, Old Navy, Target, W La Noria/dsl, Days Inn

3b Mann Rd, E Buffalo Wild Wings, Krispy Kreme, Lin's Chinese, Residence Inn, Ford/Lincoln, Kia, Lowe's, Mazda, W Chili's, Golden Corral, Kettle Pancake House, Subway, Taco Palenque, TX Roadhouse, Whataburger, Best Value, Best Western, Family Garden Inn, La Hacienda Motel, Motel 6, Red Roof Inn, SpringHill Suites, $Tree, AT&T, Home Depot, Kohl's, Michael's, Office Depot, PetCo, Ross, Walmart/McDonald's

3a San Bernardo Ave, E Chick-fil-A, Chick-fil-A, ChuckeCheese, El Taco Tote, Fuddrucker's, LJ Silver, Logan's Roadhouse, LongHorn, Luby's, Olive Garden, Peter Piper Pizza, Red Lobster, Fairfield Inn, $General, Advance Parts, HEB Foods/gas, Macy's, mall, NAPA, PepBoys, W Valero, Burger King, Danny's Rest., DQ, McDonald's, Pizza Hut, Popeyes, Taco Bell, Taco Kissi, Wendy's, Best Western, Family$, O'Reilly Parts, Sam's Club/gas

2 US 59, Saunders Rd, E Conoco, Jack-in-the-Box, H, W Exxon/Burger King/dsl, Shell/dsl, Church's TX Chicken, Denny's, Subway, Best Western, Courtyard, Hotel Ava, La Quinta, Sky-Palace Inn, Advance Parts, AutoZone, AutoZone

1b Park St, to Sanchez St, W Conoco/dsl, La Reynera, Pizza Hut, Popeyes

1a Victoria St, Scott St, Washington St (from sb), E Texaco, W Chevron, Valero/dsl, McDonald's, Wendy's, Firestone/auto

0mm USA/Mexico Border. I-35 begins/ends in Laredo.

INTERSTATE 35W TX

ARGYLE

85.5mm I-35W begins/ends on I-35, exit 467.

85b W Oak St, E H

85a I-35E S

84 FM 1515, Bonnie Brae St

82 FM 2449, to Ponder

79 Crawford Rd

76 FM 407, to Justin, Argyle, W Exxon/dsl, Papa John's, Corral City RV Park, Mkt at Corral City

76mm picnic area both lanes, tables, litter barrels

74 FM 1171, to Lewisville

72 Dale Earnhardt Way, W TX Motor Speedway

70 TX 114, to Dallas, Bridgeport, E QT/dsl, Shell/dsl, Valero/dsl/e85, Amano Italian, BurgerIM, IHOP, Popeyes, Rosa's Cafe, Sonic, TX Roadhouse, Holiday Inn Express, Home2 Suites, La Quinta, Motel 6, Quality Inn, Northlake RV Park, to DFW, W Buc-ee's/dsl, EVC, Buffalo Wild Wings, Burger King, Cane's, Chick-fil-A, Chipotle, In-N-Out, McDonald's, Newk's Eatery, Olive Garden, Panda Express, Smoothie King, Starbucks, Whataburger, Marriott, Firestone, Jiffy Lube, Tanger Outlets/famous brands, TX Motor Speedway, Verizon

68 Eagle Pkwy, W to Alliance

67 Alliance Blvd, W to Alliance

66 to Westport Pkwy, Keller-Haslet Rd, E Hampton Inn, Hilton Garden, Residence Inn, W 7-11/Wendy's/dsl, Popeyes, Schlotzsky's, Snooty Pig, Starbucks, Subway, Taco Bueno

65 TX 170 E, E Pilot/PJ Fresh/dsl/scales/24hr, IHOP,

TX

INTERSTATE 35W TX Cont'd

PARK GLEN

65 Continued
Cabela's/cafe, W WoodSpring Suites

64 Golden Triangle Blvd, to Keller-Hicks Blvd, E QT/dsl, RaceTrac/dsl/e85, Burger King, Starbucks, Whataburger, Holiday Inn, Chrysler/Dodge/Jeep, H, Kia

63 Heritage Trace, Park Glen, E Exxon, BJ's Rest., Cheddar's, Chick-fil-A, Chipotle, Chuy's, Coldstone, Costa Vida, Firebirds Grill, First Watch, Freebirds Burritos, Jason's Deli, Kincaid's Burgers, McAlister's Deli, McDonald's, Mi Cocina, MOD Kitchen, Panera Bread, Pei Wei, Piada Italian, Pie Five, Razzoo's Cajun, Shell Shack, Smoothie King, Subway, Towne Grill, Which Wich?, Courtyard, Belk, Best Buy, Dick's, GNC, JC Penney, Kroger/dsl, PetSmart, Verizon, W Exxon/dsl, LongHorn Steaks, Outback Steaks, Sonic

62 North Tarrant Pkwy, Cristina's TexMex, E 54th St Grill, Chili's, Firehouse Subs, Five Guys, Fuzzy's Tacos, HaNaBi Hibachi, Olive Garden, Pizza Inn, Pluckers, Thai Fusion, H, W Cane's, Chick-fil-A, ChuckECheese, El Pollo Loco, Hawaiian Bros, Honey Baked Ham, In-N-Out, Jack-in-the-Box, Jimmy John's, La Madeleine, Old Chicago, Panda Express, Potbelly, Qdoba, Red Robin, Starbucks, Uncle Julio's, Wendy's, Whataburger, $Tree, AT&T, Costco/gas, Hobby Lobby, Old Navy, Petco, Ross, Target, TJ Maxx, Tuesday Morning, URGENT CARE, Winco

60 US 287 N, US 81 N, to Decatur

59 Basswood(sb only), E Chevron/Jack-in-the-Box/dsl, Chicken Express, DQ, Sonic, Subway, Taco Bell, Home Depot, NTB, W QT, Einstein Bros.

58 Western Ctr Blvd, E 7-11/dsl, Shell/Church's TX Chicken, 7 Mile Cafe, BoomerJack's, Braum's, Chili's, Denny's, Domino's, Dublin Square Rest., Flips Grill, Genghis Grill, Jimmy John's, Lisa's Chicken, Lone Star BBQ, Moe's Gyro, On-the-Border, Rudy's BBQ, SaltGrass Steaks, Shady Oak Grill, Twin Peaks, Wingstop, Avid, Four Points, Quality Inn, Sonesta Suites, AT&T, W Boston's, Chick-fil-A, Firehouse Subs, Joe's Crabshack, McDonald's, Popeyes, Rosa's Cafe, Smoothie King, Starbucks, Subway, Waffle House, Whataburger, Comfort Inn, Holiday Inn Express, Sleep Inn, Staybridge Suites, Tru, repair, URGENT CARE

57b a I-820 E&W

56b Melody Hills Dr

56a Meacham Blvd, E Shell/7-11, Hilton Garden, La Quinta, Studio 6, W Texaco/dsl, Cracker Barrel, McDonald's, Subway, Days Inn, Holiday Inn, Radisson, Super 8, USPO

55 Pleasantdale Ave(from nb)

54c 33rd St, Long Ave(from nb), W Motel 6

54b a TX 183, NE 28th St, E Lisa's Chicken/dsl, Firestone, W 365 Travel Center, QT/dsl, Burger King, Popeyes, Tres Betos Taqueria, Motel 6

53 North Side Dr, Yucca Dr, E Shell/7-11/dsl, W Mercado Juarez Café, Country Inn&Suites

53mm Trinity River

52e Carver St(from nb)

52d Pharr St(exits left from nb)

52b US 377N, Belknap

52a US 377 N, TX 121, to DFW

51a I-30 E, to Avalene(from nb), downtown Ft Worth, W Sheraton

50c a I-30 W, E to Dallas

50b TX 180 E(from nb)

49b Rosedale St, E 7-11/dsl, Jack-in-the-Box, Mama E's BBQ, W H

49a Allen Ave, E Shell, Valero/dsl, W H

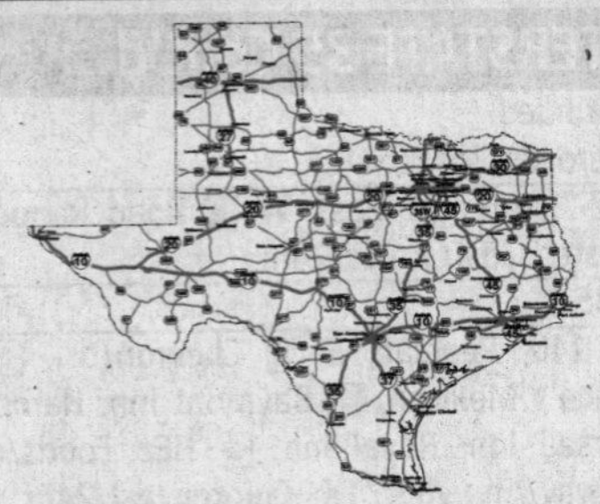

48b Morningside Ave(from sb), same as 48a

48a Berry St, E Chevron/McDonald's, Domino's, Golden Chick, Lisa's Chicken, Papa John's, AutoZone, El Rio Grande Foods, Family$, tire repair, W RaceTrac/dsl, U-Haul, zoo

47 Ripy St, E transmissions, W Astro Inn

46b Seminary Dr, E Bonefire Grill, Jack-in-the-Box, Taco Cabana, Whataburger, Days Inn, Delux Inn, Motel 6, Super 7, NAPA, W Shell, Tesla EVC, Valero, Chalios Mexican, ChuckECheese, Denny's, Hamburguesas Nochistlan, Firestone/auto, Pepboys, Ross, T-Mobile

46a Felix St, E Valero, Chikas Bariscos, Dalworth Inn, W Cesar's Tacos, McDonald's, Family$

45b a I-20, E to Dallas, W to Abilene

44 Altamesa, E Holiday Inn, W Texaco/dsl, Best Value Inn, Red Roof Inn, South Lp Inn, Super 8

43 Sycamore School Rd, W Exxon/7-11/dsl, Jack-in-the-Box, Jimmy John's, Joe's Pizza, Mariscos Mexican, Sonic, Subway, Whataburger, Scottish Inn, $General, Home Depot

42 Everman Pkwy, E Burger King, McDonald's, Panda Express, Popeyes, Starbucks, W QT/dsl/scales, Shell/dsl

41 Risinger Rd, E Chrysler/Dodge/Jeep, W Camping World RV Service/Supplies, McClain's RV Ctr

40 Garden Acres Dr, E Love's/Subway/dsl/scales/24hr, Motel 6, H, W 7-11/dsl, Chicken Express, Taco Bell

39 FM 1187, McAlister Rd, E QT/dsl, Cheddar's, Chipotle, Rudy's BBQ, Starbucks, H, W Shell/dsl, Buffalo Wild Wings, Charley's Subs, Firehouse Subs, Logan's Roadhouse, McAlister's Deli, Mooyah Burger, Olive Garden, Panda Express, Red Lobster, Twisted Tenders, Waffle House, Studio 6, AT&T, Best Buy, Kohl's, Michael's, Old Navy, PetSmart, Ross, Staples, TJ Maxx, URGENT CARE

BURLESON

38 Alsbury Blvd, E Mobil/dsl, Chili's, Cracker Barrel, Hibachi Japanese, IHOP, McDonald's, Mexican Inn Cafe, On-the-Border, Our Place Grill, Outback Steaks, Spring Creek BBQ, Fairfield Inn, Hampton Inn, Holiday Inn Express, La Quinta, Red Roof+, Super 8, Discount Tire, Ford, Lowe's Whse, W Chevron/dsl, Exxon, Applebee's, Arby's, Burger King, Chick-fil-A, Cotton Patch Cafe, Denny's, El Fenix, Sonic, Taco Cabana, Wendy's, Albertson's, Chevrolet, JC Penney, Michael's, PetSmart, Ross, URGENT CARE, vet

37 TX 174, Wilshire Blvd, to Cleburne, from sb

36 FM 3391, TX 174S, Burleson, E 7-11/dsl, Mobil, Hard 8 BBQ, Miranda's Cantina, Rio Mambo TexMex, Sonic, Waffle House, Best Western+, Days Inn, Quality Inn, Harley Davidson, Honda, Hyundai, Nissan, Sam's Club/dsl, tire repair, W Fish City Grill, Fuzzy's Tacos, Ol' South Pancakes, The Rim, $General

35 Briaroaks Rd(from sb), E same as 36, W Mockingbird Hill RV Park(2mi)

32 Bethesda Rd, E Valero, Five Star Inn, RV Ranch Park, W Mockingbird Hill RV Park (2.5mi)

30 FM 917, Mansfield, E Shell/Sonic/dsl, $General, W Exxon/dsl

27 Rd 604, Rd 707, E Camping World,

ALVARADO

INTERSTATE 35W TX Cont'd

27 Continued
Motor Home Specialist, W Holiday World RV Ctr

26b a US 67, Cleburne, E Chevron/dsl, Exxon/dsl, Texaco/dsl, Benny's Italian, Chicken Express, Domino's, DQ, El Rey Alvarado, Lin's Chinese, McDonald's, Papa John's, Pizza Hut, Sonic, Subway, Taco Bell, Taqueria Torres, TX Teriyaki, Waffle House, Whataburger, Comfort Inn, Holiday Inn Express, La Quinta, Motel 6, Super 8, $General, AutoZone, Brookshire Foods, Eagle Auto Parts, Family$, O'Reilly Parts, tire repair, W QT/dsl, Burger King, Jack-in-the-Box, Starbucks, CVS Drug

24 FM 3136, FM 1706, Alvarado, E Shell/dsl/scales/24hr, Señorita Tex Mex, Haven RV Park (2mi)

21 Rd 107, to Greenfield

17 FM 2258

16 TX 81 S, Rd 201, Grandview

15 FM 916, Maypearl, W Mobil/dsl, Shell/Burger King/dsl, Subway, USPO

12 FM 67

8 FM 66, Itasca, W Shell, $General, Ford

7 FM 934, 7H RV Park, E litter barrels, W Exxon/dsl, Golden Chick Cafe

3 FM 2959, E to Hillsboro

0mm I-35W begins/ends on I-35, 371mm.

INTERSTATE 37

142b a I-35 S to Laredo, N to Austin. I-37 begins/ends on I-35 in San Antonio.

141c Brooklyn Ave, Nolan St(from sb), downtown

141b Houston St, E Comfort Suites, Red Roof Inn, Theo's Tires, W Denny's, Crockett Hotel, Days Inn, Fairfield Inn, Hampton Inn, La Quinta, Marriott, Sonesta, SpringHill Suites, Tru, Macy's, to The Alamo

141a Commerce St, E Smoke BBQ, Best Western+, City Inn, Holiday Inn, Staybridge Suites, W Denny's, Ruth's Chris Steaks, Hilton, Hyatt, La Quinta, Marriott, LEGOLAND, Macy's, to San Antonio River Walk

140b Durango Blvd, downtown, E Bill Miller BBQ, to Alamo Dome

140a Carolina St, Florida St, E Shell/dsl

139 I-10 W, US 87, US 90, to Houston

138c Fair Ave, Hackberry St, E DQ, Jack-in-the-Box, La Tapatia Mexian, Popeyes, $General, Brake Check, Home Depot, W Chevron, Exxon/7-11

138b E New Braunfels Ave(from sb), E Arby's, Burger King, Chick-fil-A, Golden Chick, McDonald's, Panda Express, Taco Bell, Taco Cabana, Wendy's, Wingstop, Discount Tire, HEB/dsl, Marshall's, W Exxon, Sonic

138a Southcross Blvd, W New Braunfels Ave, E McDonald's, Taco Cabana, Wendy's, Golden Chick, Panda Express, W Exxon, Burger King, Sonic

137 Hot Wells Blvd, E Chevron/dsl, QT/dsl, W IHOP, Motel 6, Super 8

136 Pecan Valley Dr, E Citgo/dsl, Church's TX Chicken, Domino's, KFC/Taco Bell, Pizza Hut, Pecan Valley Inn, AutoZone, O'Reilly Parts, W H

135 Military Dr, Lp 13, E Shell/dsl, Valero, Jack-in-the-Box, La Parilla, Quality Inn, CVS Drug, Valero, vet, W Valero/Subway/dsl, A&W/LJ Silver, Buffalo Wild Wings, Buffet City, Burger King, Chaba Thai, Chick-fil-A, Chili's, Chipotle, Cracker Barrel, IHOP, Little Caesar's, Longhorn Cafe, Marco's Pizza, Olive Garden, Panda Express, Papa John's, Peter Piper Pizza, Sonic, Starbucks, Subway, Whataburger, Wingstop, Fairfield Inn, Hampton Inn, Holiday Inn Expess, La Quinta, $Tree, Advance Parts, AT&T, AutoZone,

BRAUNIG LAKE

135 Continued
Best Buy, BigLots, Discount Tire, HEB Food/gas, Home Depot, H, Lowe's, Office Depot, PetCo, Sam's Club/dsl, Target, to Brooks AFB, Walgreens, Walmart/McDonald's

133 I-410, US 281 S

132 US 181 S, to Floresville, E Exxon/dsl, La Tapatia, $General

130 Donop Rd, Southton Rd, E Valero/7-11/dsl, Tom's Burgers, Days Inn, Braunig Lake RV Resort, W Shell/dsl, car/truckwash

127 San Antonio River Turnaround(from nb), Braunig Lake

127mm San Antonio River

125 FM 1604, Anderson Lp, E Mobil/dsl/24hr, Burger King, Frank Tacos, W Exxon/dsl, Pilot/Subway/dsl/scales/24hr, QT/dsl, Miller's BBQ, Sonic, Whataburger, Best Western, tires

122 Priest Rd, Mathis Rd, E Valero/dsl, Joe's BBQ, $General

120 Hardy Rd

117 FM 536

113 FM 3006

112mm picnic area both lanes, tables, litter barrels

109 TX 97, to Floresville, E Chevron/dsl, Exxon/dsl, Portrillo's Mexican, Chrysler/Dodge/Jeep

106 Coughran Rd

104 spur 199, Leal Rd, to Pleasanton(no immediate sb return), same as 103

103 US 281 N, Leal Rd, to Pleasanton, E Valero/dsl, Kuntry Inn

CAMPBELLTON

98 TX 541, McCoy

92 US 281A, Campbellton

88 FM 1099, to FM 791, Campbellton

83 FM 99, Whitsett, Peggy, E Shell/cafe/dsl, W C Fuels/dsl, Exxon/dsl, Choke Canyon BBQ

82mm full facilities, litter barrels, sb

78mm full facilities, litter barrels, nb

76 US 281A, FM 2049, Whitsett

75mm truck weigh sta sb

74mm truck weigh sta nb

72 US 281 S, Three Rivers, W Love's/McDonald's/dsl/scales/24hr/@, Emblaze Hotel, to Rio Grande Valley

69 TX 72, Three Rivers, W Valero/Circle K/Subway/dsl/24hr, to Choke Cyn SP

65 FM 1358, Oakville, E Van's BBQ

59 FM 799

56 US 59, George West, E Flying J/McDonald's/dsl/scales/24hr, Stripes/dsl/24hr, W Valero/Stripes/dsl/24hr

51 Hailey Ranch Rd

47 FM 3024, FM 534, Swinney Switch Rd, W Bart's Mkt/gas, Mustang Hollow Camping(4mi)

44mm parking area sb

42mm parking area nb

40 FM 888

36 TX 359, to Skidmore, Mathis, W Exxon/Subway/dsl/scales, Shell/McDonald's/dsl, Valero/dsl(1mi), China Express, Pizza Hut, Smolik's Smokehouse, La Quinta, Lake Corpus Christi SRA

EDROY

34 TX 359 W, E tire repair, Totem Pole RV Park, W Valero/dsl, Butter's BBQ, Church's TX Chicken, DQ, Sonic, $General, O'Reilly Parts, to Lake Corpus Christi SP

31 TX 188, to Sinton, Rockport

22 TX 234, FM 796, to Odem, Edroy, E Camp Stryker RV Park

20b Cooper Rd

19.5mm accessible, litter barrels, picnic area both lanes, tables

17 US 77 N, to Victoria

16 LaBonte Park, W info, litter barrels,

15 Sharpsburg Rd(from sb), Redbird Ln

TX

TX

INTERSTATE 37 Cont'd

ROBSTOWN

Exit #	Services
14	I-69, US 77 S, Redbird Ln, to Kingsville, Robstown, W Shell/dsl, Valero, Valero/Burger King/dsl, Chick-fil-A, Chili's, CiCi's, Denny's, El Tapatio Mexican, Good'n Crisp Chicken, Miller's BBQ, Nolan's Poorboys, Papa John's, Pizza Hut, Popeyes, Rock Star Hibachi, Sonic, Subway, Whataburger, Wienerschnitzel, Best Western, Holiday Inn Express, $General, $Tree, AT&T, AutoZone, CVS Drug, Discount Tire, Firestone/auto, GNC, Hobby Lobby, Home Depot, H, O'Reilly Parts, Petco, Ross, Verizon, Walmart/McDonald's
13b	Sharpsburg Rd(from nb)
13a	FM 1694, Callicoatte Rd, Leopard St
11b	FM 24, Violet Rd, Hart Rd, E Shell/Subway/dsl, Chicken Shack, W Exxon/dsl, Valero/dsl, Domino's, DQ, Fliz Amancer Mexican, KFC/LJ Silver, Little Caesar's, McDonald's, Pizza Hut, Schlotzsky's, Sonic, Subway, Taco Bell, Whataburger, Hampton Inn, Super 8, AutoZone, Family$, HEB Food/gas, NAPA, O'Reilly Parts, Walgreens
11a	McKinzie Rd, E Jack-in-the-Box, Best Western+, La Quinta, W Valero/dsl
10	Carbon Plant Rd
9	FM 2292, Up River Rd, Rand Morgan Rd, W Valero/Circle K/dsl, Whataburger
7	Suntide Rd, Tuloso Rd, Clarkwood Rd, W ExploreUSA RV Ctr, Freightliner
6	Southern Minerals Rd
5	Corn Products Rd, Valero Way, E Kenworth/Mack, W Jalisco II Rest., Howard Johnson, Motel 6, OYO
4b	Lantana St, McBride Lane(from sb), W Inn, Motel 6
4a	TX 358, to Padre Island, W Valero, Best Western, Walmart(4mi)
3b	McBride Lane(from nb), W Gulf Coast Racing
3a	Navigation Blvd, E Valero/dsl, W Exxon/7-11/dsl, Denny's, La Milpas, Miller BBQ, The Bar-BQ Man, Hampton Inn, Holiday Inn Express, La Quinta, Red Roof Inn, Super 8, CarQuest
2	Up River Rd, E refinery, W Mr G's BBQ
1e	Lawrence Dr, Nueces Bay Blvd, W Valero/Stripes/dsl, Church's TX Chicken, $Tree, Aamco, AutoZone, Firestone, HEB Foods, USPO
1d	Port Ave(from sb), W Coastal, Shell, Frank's Spaghetti, Vick's Burgers, EconoLodge, Port of Corpus Christi
1c	US 181, TX 286, Shoreline Blvd, Corpus Christi, W H
1b	Brownlee St(from nb)
1a	Buffalo St(from sb), Sunoco/dsl, Burger King, Joe's Crabshack, Landry's Seafood, Railroad Seafood, Subway, Waterstreet Seafood, Whataburger, Best Western, Holiday Inn, Omni Hotel, Residence Inn, U-Haul, USPO
0mm	I-35 divides into E and W sb, converges into I-35 nb. See Texas I-35 W.

CORPUS CHRISTI

INTERSTATE 40

Exit #	Services
177mm	Texas/Oklahoma state line
176	spur 30(from eb), to Texola
169	FM 1802, Carbon Black Rd
167	FM 2168, Daberry Rd
165mm	check sta wb
164	Lp 40(from wb), to Shamrock, S Motel 6, check sta eb, H, museum
163	US 83, to Wheeler, Shamrock, N Chevron/Taco Bell/dsl, Best Western+, Irish Inn, Ace Hardware, tire repair, S CEFCO/Subway/dsl, Conoco/dsl, Tesla EVC, McDonald's, Blarney Inn, Holiday Inn Express, Route 66 Inn, Shamrock Country Inn, Sleep Inn, Sleep Inn, Western Motel,

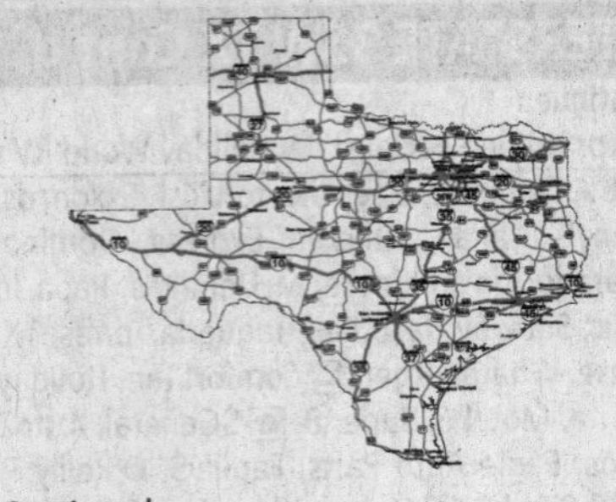

LELA

Exit #	Services
163	Continued Family$, museum
161	Lp 40, Rte 66(from eb), to Shamrock
157	FM 1547, Lela, S TX RV Park
152	FM 453, Pakan Rd
148	FM 1443, Kellerville Rd
146	County Line Rd
143	Lp 40(from wb), to McLean, N to Rte 66
142	TX 273, FM 3143, to McLean, N Conoco/dsl, Red River Steaks, Cactus Inn, auto repair, USPO, W barbed wire museum
141	Rte 66(from eb), McLean, same as 142
135	FM 291, Rte 66, Alanreed, S Longhorn RV Camping, USPO
132	Johnson Ranch Rd, ranch access
131mm	**full facilities, litter barrels, petwalk, wb**
129mm	**full facilities, littler barrels, petwalk, playground, eb**
128	FM 2477, to Lake McClellan, N Lake McClellan RA/RV Dump
124	TX 70 S, to Clarendon, S RV camping/dump(11mi)
121	TX 70 N, to Pampa
114	Lp 40, Groom, N dsl repair, Leaning Tower of TX
113	FM 2300, Groom, N Conoco, S Phillips 66/dsl, Chalet Inn
112	FM 295, Groom, S Alon, Biggest Cross
110	Lp 40, Rte 66
109	FM 294
105	FM 2880, grain silo
98	TX 207 S(from wb), to Claude
96	TX 207 N, to Panhandle, N Love's/Subway/dsl/24hr, S Executive Inn, OYO, Slug Bug Ranch
89	FM 2161, to Rte 66
87	FM 2373
87mm	picnic areas both lanes, litter barrels
85	Amarillo Blvd, Durrett Rd, access to camping
81	FM 1912, N Valero/dsl
80	FM 228, N AOK RV Park
78	US 287 S(from eb), FM 1258, Pullman Rd, same as 77
77	FM 1258, Pullman Rd
76	spur 468, N Flying J/Denny's/dsl/LP/RV dump/scales/24hr, Phillips/dsl, Buffalo Wild Wings, Fairfield Inn, Holiday Inn Express, La Quinta, American Indian Museum, Mack/Volvo Trucks, S Custom RV Ctr, Speedco, TX info
75	Lp 335, Lakeside Rd, N Pilot/Subway/McDonald's/dsl/scales/24hr/@, Valero/Wendy's/dsl, Mitch's BBQ, Hampton Inn, Holiday Inn, Super 8, KOA(2mi), Overnite RV Park, S Petro/dsl/rest./scales/@, Blue Beacon
74	Whitaker Rd, Home2 Suites, N Big Texan Steaks, Big Texan Inn, RV camping, S Love's/Subway/Godfather's/dsl/scales/@, TA/Exxon/FoodCourt/dsl/scales/24hr/@, Blue Beacon, Eagle Truckwash, Peterbilt
73	Eastern St, Bolton Ave, Amarillo, N Toot'n Totum/dsl, Express Inn, Motel 6, Wood Spring Suites, Big Texan RV Ranch, S CEFCO/dsl, Best Western
72b	Grand St, Amarillo, N Valero/dsl, Henk's BBQ, Value Inn, O'Reilly Parts, S Murphy USA/dsl, Phillips 66,

GROOM

AMARILLO

INTERSTATE 40 Cont'd

AMARILLO

Exit	Services
72b	Continued Valero, Braum's, Chicken Express, McDonald's, Sonic, Starbucks, Subway, Taco Villa, Whataburger, Wingstop, Best Value Inn, $Tree, Advance Parts, Amigo's Foods, AutoZone, BigLots, same as 73, URGENT CARE, Walmart
72a	Nelson St, **N** Cracker Barrel, Ashmore Inn, La Kiva Hotel, Rest Inn, Sleep Inn, Super 8, Qtrhorse Museum, **S** Valero/dsl, Domino's, Camelot Suites, transmissions
71	Ross St, Osage St, Amarillo, **N** Chevron/dsl, Valero, Burger King, IHOP, KFC, McDonald's, Schlotsky's, Subway, Wienerschnitzel, Best Western+, Comfort Inn, Days Inn, Fairfield Inn, Microtel, Quality Inn, Discount Tire, **S** Arby's, Denny's, Fiesta Grande Mexican, Sonic, Taco Bell, Wendy's, Baymont Inn, La Quinta, Chevrolet, Ford, Hyundai, Sam's Club/gas, USPO
70	I-27 S, US 60 W, US 87, US 287, to Canyon, Lubbock, to downtown Amarillo
69b	Washington St, Amarillo, **S** TT/dsl, DQ, Subway, CVS Drug
69a	Crockett St, access to same as 68b
68b	Georgia St, **N** Valero/dsl, Dyer's BBQ, Schlotzky's, Sharky's Burrito Co, **S** Valero, Burger King, Chick-fil-A, Chipotle, Church's TX Chicken, Coldstone, Denny's, Firehouse Subs, Jason's Deli, Jersey Mike's, Jimmy's Egg, Pizza Hut, Sonic, Starbucks, TX Roadhouse, Whataburger, Holiday Inn Express, Home Depot, Walgreens
68a	Julian Blvd, Paramount Blvd, **N** Chili's, Rosa's Cafe, same as 67, **S** Valero, Bubba's BBQ, El Patron, Pacific Rim, Popeyes, Red Lobster, Saigon Vietnamese, TX Roadhouse, Atrea Inn, Holiday Inn Express, Motel 6, Super 8, Home Depot
67	Western St, Amarillo, **N** Phillips 66, Aspen Creek Grill, Bahama Buck's, Burger King, Chili's, McAlister's Deli, McDonald's, Sonic, Subway, Taco Bell, Wendy's, **S** Murphy Express/dsl, Rudy's/BBQ/dsl, Valero, Blue Sky Rest., Cedars Mediterranean , Cheddar's, IHOP, Jimmy John's, Olive Garden, Waffle House, Wienerschnitzel, Candlewood Suites, Comfort Suites, Extend-A-Suites, Staybridge Suites, Discount Tire, Firestone/auto, Michael's, O'Reilly Parts, Petco, same 68, URGEN CARE
66	Bell St, Amarillo, **N** Cefco/dsl, Red Roof Inn, Relax Inn, Residence Inn, Harley-Davidson, **S** Donut Stop, Phillips 66
65	Coulter Dr, Amarillo, **N** Arby's, Golden Corral, Subway, Taco Bell, Waffle House, Days Inn, Executive Inn, La Quinta, Cadillac/Chevrolet, Chrysler/Dodge/Jeep, Firestone/auto, H, H, URGENT CARE, **S** Conoco/Chicken Express/dsl, ChinaStar, ChuckeCheese, CiCi's, Hoffbrau Steaks, Outback Steaks, Pizza Hut, Whataburger, 5th Season Inn, Hampton Inn, Sleep Inn, TownePlace Suites, AT&T, Goodyear/auto, Verizon
64	Soncy Rd, to Pal Duro Cyn, Hyatt, **N** Jimmy John's, Kabuki, Lin's Chinese, Logan's Roadhouse, Longhorn Steaks, Plaza Rest., Red Robin, Saltgrass Steaks, Comfort Inn, Country Inn&Suites, Courtyard, Drury Inn, Drury Inn, Extended Stay America, Hilton Garden, Holiday Inn/Tesla EVC, Home2 Suites/Tesla EVC, Homewood Suites, My Place, SpringHill Suites, Tru, Cavender's Boots, Discount Tire, USPO, **S** Valero/dsl/24hr, Applebee's, Crackin' Crab, DQ, Fazoli's, Hooters, Marble Slab Creamery, McAlisters Deli, McDonald's, Smoothie King, Starbucks, $Tree, Barnes&Noble, Best Buy, Dillard's, Ford, Home Depot, JC Penney, Kohl's, Lincoln, Old Navy, PetSmart, Ross, Sam's Club/dsl, Target, Verizon, World Mkt

BUSHLAND

Exit	Services
62b	Lp 40, Amarillo Blvd, **N** Camping World, Gander Outdoors, **S** Rte 66 RV Ranch
62a	Hope Rd, Helium Rd
60	Arnot Rd, **S** Love's/Subway/scales/dsl, Oasis RV Resort/dump
57	RM 2381, Bushland, **N** Falcon Stop/dsl, **S** Phillips 66/dsl, Joe's Pizza, USPO, vet
55mm	parking area wb, litter barrels, **litter barrels, parking area wb**
54	Adkisson Rd
53.5mm	parking area eb, litter barrels
49	FM 809, Wildorado, **S** Crist Fuel/dsl/LP
42	Everett Rd
37	Lp 40 W, to Vega, **N** same as 36
36	US 385, Vega, **N** Shamrock, Valero/Allsup's/dsl/scales/24hr, Lucy's Kitchen, Bonanza Motel, Days Inn, $General, Walnut RV Park, **S** Pilot/PJ Fresh/dsl/scales/24hr, Vega Trk Stop/cafe/dsl
35	to Rte 66, to Vega, **N** Best Value Inn, same as 36, Walnut RV Park(1mi)

ADRIAN

Exit	Services
32mm	picnic area both lanes, litter barrels
28	to Rte 66, Landergin
23	to Adrian, Vega, same as 22
22	TX 214, Adrian, **N** Midpoint Cafe, Fabulous 40s Motel, USPO, **S** Valero/dsl
18	FM 2858, Gruhlkey Rd
15	Ivy Rd
13mm	picnic area both lanes, picnic tables, litter barrels
0	Lp 40, to Glenrio
0mm	Texas/New Mexico state line, Central/Mountain time zone

INTERSTATE 44

SCOTLAND PARK

Exit	Services
15mm	Texas/Oklahoma state line, Red River
14	Lp 267, E 3rd St, **W** historical marker, KOA
13	Glendale St, **W** La Familia Mexican, Subway
12	Burkburnett, **E** Valero/dsl, Best Western, **W** Alon/7-11/dsl, Braum's, Chicken Express, Chief's Corner Cafe, Feedlot Rest., Lite Pan Asian, McDonald's, Taco Bell, Whataburger, Chevrolet, Ford, NAPA
11	FM 3429, Daniels Rd
9mm	picnic area both lanes, litter barrels, petwalk, picnic table
7	East Rd
6	Bacon Switch Rd
5a	FM 3492, Missile Rd, **E** El Mejicano Rest., Marco's Pizza, st patrol, **W** Exxon/dsl
5	Access Rd
4	City Loop St
3c	FM 890, **W** Murphy USA/dsl, Cracker Barrel, Golden Chick, Jack-in-the-Box, KFC/Taco Bell, Northside Grill, Subway, T-Mobile, Walmart/Subway
3b	sp 325, Sheppard AFB
3a	US 287 N, to Amarillo, **W** Shell/dsl, Carl's Jr, Howard Johnson
2	Maurine St, **E** Alon/7-11/dsl, Executive Inn, Motel 6, OYO, Quality Inn, Chevrolet, Mazda/VW, **W** Alon/7-11, Denny's, Whataburger, Candlewood Suites, Comfort Inn, La Quinta, Red Roof Inn, Super 8
1d	US 287 bus, Lp 370, **E** Pioneer 3 Rest., **W** Valero/dsl, Fairfield Inn, OYO
1c	Texas Travel Info Ctr, **E** $Saver, **W** Wichita Bend RV Park
1b	(from nb), Scotland Park
1a	US 277 S, to Abilene, **W** Arby's, EconoLodge
1	Holliday St, **W** Valero/dsl, Arby's, Burger King, Carl's Jr, IHOP, McDonald's, Subway, Delux Inn, EconoLodge, Family$, H, Walgreens
0mm	Witchita Falls. I-44 begins/ends on US 287.

= gas = food = lodging = other = rest stop

TX

INTERSTATE 45

Exit #	Services
286	to I-35 E, to Denton. I-45 begins/ends in Dallas.
285	Bryan St E, US 75 N
284b a	I-30, W to Ft Worth, E to Texarkana, E access to H
283b	Pennsylvania Ave, to MLK Blvd
283a	Lamar St
281	Overton St(from sb), W Chevron
280	Illinois Ave, Linfield St, E Star Motel, W Exxon, Shell/dsl
	HUTCHINS
279b a	Lp 12
277	Simpson Stuart Rd, W to Paul Quinn Coll
276b a	I-20, W to Ft Worth, E to Shreveport
275	TX 310 N(from nb, no re-entry)
274	Dowdy Ferry Rd, Hutchins, E Exxon/Subway/dsl, Shell/McDonald's/dsl, Gold Inn, La Quinta, Motel 6, auto repair, W Top Fuel/dsl, DQ, Jack-in-the-Box, The Grill, Whataburger
273	Wintergreen Rd, W QT/dsl/scales/24hr, Popeyes
272	Fulghum Rd, weigh sta both lanes, E Love's/Carl's Jr/dsl/scales/24hr/@
271	Pleasant Run Rd
270	Belt Line Rd, to Wilmer, E Chevron/Pizza Inn/dsl, tire and brake repair, W Exxon/Sonic/dsl, Shell/Church's TX Chicken/dsl, Denny's, $General, Family$, USPO
269	Mars Rd
	FERRIS
268	Malloy Bridge Rd
267	Frontage Rd
266	FM 660, E Jack-in-the-Box, Taco Bell, W Valero/dsl, DQ, I-45 Donuts, Pizza Hut
265	Lp 45, Ferris, nb only
263a b	Lp 561
262	frontage rd
260	Lp 45, W Shell/Sonic/dsl
259	FM 813, FM 878, Jefferson St
258	Lp 45, Palmer, E Chevron/Subway/dsl/scales/24hr
255	FM 879, Garrett, E Gulf/dsl, W Chevron/dsl
253	Lp 45, W Shell/Subway/dsl
	ENNIS
251b	TX 34, Ennis, E Alon/dsl, QT/dsl, Bubba's BBQ, Chick-fil-A, Cotton Patch Cafe, Hwy 55 Burgers, McDonald's, Panda Express, Schlotzsky's, Comfort Suites, Days Inn, Holiday Inn Express, La Quinta, Motel 6, Ennis RV Camping, Ford, URGENT CARE, W Chevron/dsl, Exxon/dsl/24hr, Mobil, Murphy USA/dsl, Braum's, Burger King, Chili's, Denny's, Domino's, DQ, Grand Buffet, Hilda's Kitchen, IHOP, Jack-in-the-Box, KFC, Little Caesar's, Papa John's, Sonic, Starbucks, Subway, Taco Bell, Taco Cabana, Waffle House, Wall Chinese, Wendy's, Whataburger, Wingstop, Quality Inn, $Tree, AT&T, AutoZone, Beall's, Chevrolet, Chrysler/Dodge/Jeep, H, RV camping, Walmart/McDonald's
251a	Creechville Rd, FM 1181, Ennis, E Buc-ee's/dsl, W H
249	FM 85, Ennis, E Budget Inn, W Exxon/Subway/dsl, Ennis Rest., Blue Beacon, repair
	ALMA
247	US 287 N, to Waxahatchie
246	FM 1183, Alma, E Love's/Subway/dsl/scales/24hr/@, W Exxon/BBQ/dsl
244	FM 1182
243	Frontage Rd
242	Calhoun St, Rice, W Shell/Sonic/dsl, Family$
239	FM 1126, W Conoco/dsl, Rendell RV Ctr
238	FM 1603, E Exxon/rest./dsl/24hr, Casita RV Trailers
237	Frontage Rd
235b	Lp I-45(from sb), to Corsicana
235a	Frontage Rd
232	Roane Rd, E 5th Ave
231	TX 31, Corsicana,, E Mobil/Taco Casa/dsl, Valero/dsl,

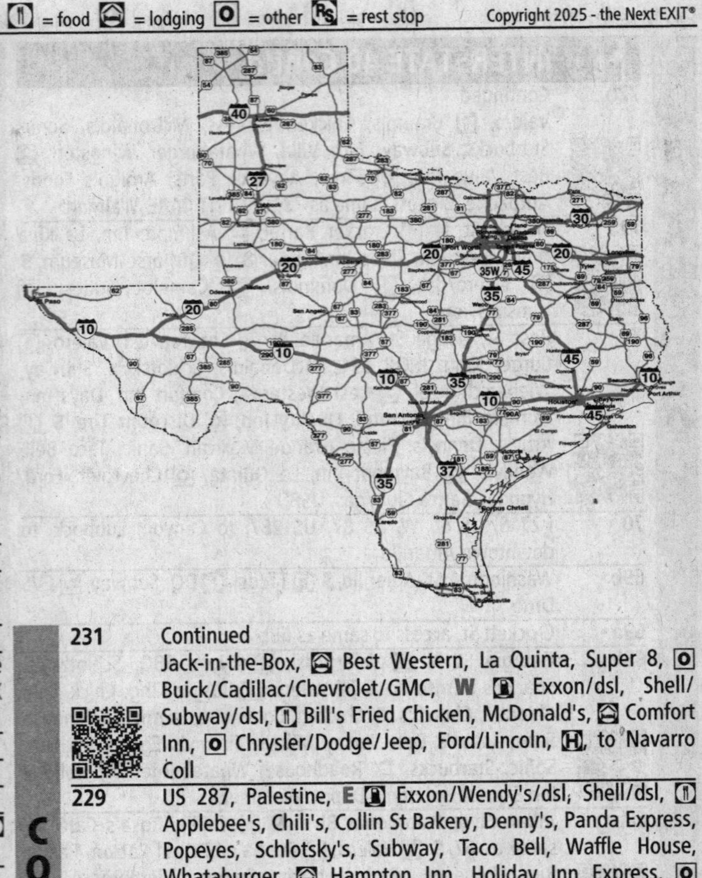

Exit #	Services
	CORSICANA
231	Continued Jack-in-the-Box, Best Western, La Quinta, Super 8, Buick/Cadillac/Chevrolet/GMC, W Exxon/dsl, Shell/Subway/dsl, Bill's Fried Chicken, McDonald's, Comfort Inn, Chrysler/Dodge/Jeep, Ford/Lincoln, H, to Navarro Coll
229	US 287, Palestine, E Exxon/Wendy's/dsl, Shell/dsl, Applebee's, Chili's, Collin St Bakery, Denny's, Panda Express, Popeyes, Schlotsky's, Subway, Taco Bell, Waffle House, Whataburger, Hampton Inn, Holiday Inn Express, Corsicana Outlets, Home Depot, Russell Stover Candies, W QT/Starbucks/dsl, Chick-fil-A, Days Inn, Motel 6, Traveler's Inn
228b	Lp 45(exits left from nb), Corsicana, W services in Corsicana
228a	15th St, Corsicana, W Toyota/Scion
225	FM 739, Angus, E Lucky 7, RV park, to Chambers Reservoir
221	Frontage Rd
220	Frontage Rd
219b	Frontage Rd
219a	TX 14(from sb), to Mexia, Richland, W Shell
218	FM 1394(from nb), Richland, W Shell
217mm	**full facilities, litter barrels, petwalk, both lanes, vending**
213	TX 75 S, FM 246, to Wortham, W Exxon/dsl, Valero/dsl
211	FM 80, to Streetman, Kirvin
	BUFFALO
206	FM 833, W I-45 RV Park(3mi)
198	FM 27, to Wortham, E Shell/Cole's BBQ, TA Express/Whataburger/dsl, La Quinta, H, W Cooper Farms/dsl, Love's/Burger King/dsl/scales/24hr, Budget Inn, I-45 RV Park(4mi)
197	US 84, Fairfield, E Chevron/dsl, Exxon/dsl, Shell/dsl, Bush's Chicken, DQ, Jack-in-the-Box, McDonald's, Sam's Rest., Something Different Rest, Sonic, Subway/TX Burger, Days Inn, Holiday Inn Express, Super 8, Brookshire Foods/gas, Chevrolet, Chrysler/Dodge/Jeep, W Shell/dsl, I-45 Rest., KFC/Taco Bell, Pizza Hut, Ponte's Diner, Te'Jun Grill, Budgetel, Regency Inn, Ace Hardware, Ford
189	TX 179, to Teague, E Exxon/Dinner Bell Rest/dsl, W Valero/Chester's/Sonic/dsl
180	TX 164, to Groesbeck
178	US 79, Buffalo, E Chevron/dsl, Mobil/dsl, Shell/dsl, Pizza Hut, Subway, TX Burger, $General, Brookshire Foods/gas, Family$, W Exxon/Church's TX Chicken/Pizza Inn/dsl/scales, Pilot/PJ Fresh/Taco Bell/dsl/scales/24hr,

TX

INTERSTATE 45 Cont'd

BUFFALO

178 Continued Texaco/dsl, Anthony's Rest., DQ, McDonald's, Rancho Viejo, Sonic, Hampton Inn, Quality Inn, Red Roof Inn, Super 8, Horseshoe RV Park (1mi)

175mm Bliss Creek

166mm weigh sta sb

164 TX 7, Centerville, E Chevron, Shell/Woody's BBQ/dsl, Country Cousins BBQ, Duran's Italian, Subway/TX Burger, Days Inn, W CNG, Exxon/dsl, Shell/Woody's BBQ/dsl, DQ, Roble's Mexican

160mm picnic area sb, tables, litter barrels

159mm Boggy Creek

MADISONVILLE

156 FM 977, to Leona, E dsl repair, W Exxon/dsl

155mm picnic area nb, tables, litter barrels

152 TX OSR, to Normangee, W Shell/Arby's/dsl, Yellow Rose RV Park

146 TX 75

142 US 190, TX 21, Madisonville, E Buc-ee's/Tesla EVC/dsl, Mallett Bros BBQ, Shipley's Donuts, Subway, Best Western, Quality Inn, URGENT CARE, W Exxon, Mobil/Church's TX Chicken/dsl, Shell/Subway, Lakeside Rest, McDonald's, Pizza Hut, Sonic, Taco Bell, TX Burger, Budget Motel, Days Inn, Motel 6, Ford, H, Toyota

136 spur 67, E Home on the Range RV camping/LP(3mi)

132 FM 2989

124mm full facilities, litter barrels, petwalk, both lanes, vending

123 FM 1696

118 TX 75, E Exxon/Hitchin Post/dsl/24hr/@, Texas Prison Museum, truckwash, W Pilot/Wendy's/PJ Fresh/dsl/scales/24hr, Shell/BBQ/dsl, Chicken Express

HUNTSVILLE

116 US 190, TX 30, E Conoco/dsl, Phillips 66/dsl, Valero/dsl, 1836 Steaks, 7 Leguas, Arby's, Bandera Grill, Church's TX Chicken, Lone Star BBQ, Los Pericos, Mama Juanita's, McDonald's, McKenzie's BBQ, Popeyes, Schlotzsky's, Sonic, Days Inn, EconoLodge, Holiday Inn Express/Tesla EVC, La Quinta, Motel 6, AutoZone, Brookshire Foods/gas, Buick/Cadillac/Chevrolet/GMC, Cavander's Boots, Chrysler/Dodge/Jeep, CVS Drug, Family$, Jiffy Lube, O'Reilly Parts, vet, Walgreens, W Chevron/dsl, Exxon/dsl, Murphy USA/dsl, Bahama Buck's, Buffalo Wild Wings, Burger King, Cane's, Chick-fil-A, Chili's, Chipotle, Denny's, Firehouse Subs, Freddy's Steakburgers, Grand Buffet, Hartz Chicken, IHOP, Jack-in-the-Box, Little Caesar's, McAlister's Deli, Olive Garden, Panda Express, Pizza Hut, Rodeo Mexican, Shogun Japanese, Starbucks, Subway, Taco Bell, Whataburger, Wing Stop, Yummy Mongolian, Best Western, Hampton Inn, $Tree, AT&T, Discount Tire, GNC, Hobby Lobby, Home Depot, H, JC Penney, Kroger/dsl, Marshall's, Office Depot, Petco, Ross, Target, USPO, Verizon, Walmart

114 FM 1374, E Exxon/dsl, DQ, La Mision Grill, Red Roof+, Super 8, W Texaco/dsl, Valero/dsl, Country Inn Steaks, Quality Suites, Studio 6, Ford, H

113 TX 19(from sb), Huntsville, W Ford

112 TX 75, E Smiley's, Houston Statue, museum, to Sam Houston St U

109 Park 40, W to Huntsville SP

103 FM 1374/1375(from sb), to New Waverly, E vet, W Chevron/dsl

102 FM 1374/1375, TX 150(from nb), to New Waverly, E Valero/Circle K/dsl(1mi), Dickey's BBQ, Jack's Shack, Subway, Waverly Rest.

101mm weigh sta nb

98 TX 75, Danville Rd, Shepard Hill Rd, E Convenience RV Ctr/repair

97 Calvary Rd, E Valero/Circle K

95 Longstreet Rd, Calvary Rd, Willis, E Holiday World, W Love's/Subway/Wendy's/dsl/scales/24hr/@

MONTGOMERY CO PARK

94 FM 1097, Longstreet Rd, to Willis, E Kwik Stop/dsl, Jack-in-the-Box, Sonic, Taco Bell, Zully's Latin American, $General, AutoZone, W Exxon/Popeyes, Burger King, Chick-fil-A, Cilantros Mexican, Little Caesar's, McDonald's, Panda Express, Papa John's, Pizza Hut, Sakura Japanese, Scholtzsky's, Shipley's Donuts, Starbucks, Whataburger, Red Roof Inn, AT&T, CVS, Kroger/Starbucks/dsl, URGENT CARE, Walgreens

92 FM 830, Seven Coves Dr, W Lake Conroe RV Park(3mi), Omega Farms RV Park(2mi)

90 League Line Rd, E Mobil/McDonald's, Shell/dsl, Mama Juanita's Mexican, Waffle House, Wendy's, Comfort Inn, Days Inn, La Quinta, Scottish Inns, Conroe Outlets/famous brands, W Chevron/Jack-in-the-Box, Cracker Barrel

89 FM 3083, Teas Nursery Rd, Montgomery Co Park, E Exxon/dsl, Applebee's, Buffalo Wild Wings, Popeyes, Red Lobster, Smokey Mo's BBQ, Fairfield Inn, Homewood Suites, AT&T, Kohl's, PetSmart, Ross, TJ Maxx, W Firehouse Subs, Olive Garden, Wengs Wok, TownePlace Suites, WoodSpring Suites, Cavender's Boots, JC Penney, Verizon, Wild Ginger Japanese

CONROE

88 Lp 336, to Cleveland, Navasota, E Valero/Circle K/dsl, Arby's, Burger King, Carl's Jr, Chili's, China Delight, Denny's, Domino's, Dunkin'/Baskin Robbins, La Marisquera Mexican, Marble Slab Creamery, Margarita's Mexican, McDonald's, MOD Pizza, Papa John's, Pizza Hut, Potbelly, Sonic, Subway, Supreme Buffet, TX Roadhouse, Whataburger, Wing Stop, Hampton Inn, Holiday Inn Express, $Tree, Advance Parts, Discount Tire, Discount Tire, GNC, HEB Foods/gas, Hobby Lobby, Kroger/gas, Michael's, Walgreens, W Chevron/24hr, Casa Ole Mexican, Culver's, Hunan Village, Jack-in-the-Box, Jason's Deli, Jersey Mike's, KFC, Starbucks, 99c Store, Big Lots, Lowe's, PetCo, Sam's Club/gas, Tuesday Morning, Walmart

87 TX 105, Conroe, E 7-11, Valero, Burger King, CiCi's, El Bosque, Freebirds Burrito, Golden Corral, McDonald's, Outback Steaks, Popeyes, Saltgrass Steaks, Super 8, $General, CVS Drug, Firestone/auto, NTB, W Exxon, Cane's, Chick-fil-A, Chipotle, Five Guys, Luby's, Panda Express, Panera Bread, Papa Murphy's, Pedro's Mexican, Schlotzsky's, Shogun Japanese, Smoothie King, Starbucks, Subway, The Catch, Toasted Yolk, Vero Italian, Whataburger, Best Buy, Buick/GMC, GNC, Home Depot, H, Hyundai, Office Depot, Target, Verizon

85 FM 2854, Gladstell St, E Shell/dsl, Ford, Honda, Kia, Nissan, U-Haul, W Valero, Motel 6, Palace Inn, Chevrolet, Chrysler/Dodge/Jeep, DeMontrond RV Ctr, H, Mazda, Toyota/Scion

84 TX 75 N, Frazier St, E Chevron/dsl, Corporate Inn, Hotel elev8, W Shell/dsl, Chick-fil-A, China Buffet, IHOP, Incredible Pizza, McAlister's Deli, Pizza Hut, Starbucks, Subway, Taco Cabana, Waffle House, Wasabi Chinese, Baymont Inn, Discount Tire, H, Kroger/dsl, Verizon

MAGNOLIA

83 Crighton Rd, Camp Strake Rd

82 River Plantation Dr

82mm San Jacinto River

81 FM 1488, to Hempstead, Magnolia, E Chevron/dsl, W Valero/Circle K/dsl, CamperLand RV Ctr

80 Needham Rd(from sb)

79 TX 242, Needham, E Shell/McDonald's, Adriatic Grill, BJ's Rest., Black Bear Diner, Buca Italian, Chuy's TexMex, Dave & Buster's, Mama Juanita's Mexican, MOD Pizza, Pappadeaux Seafood, Pappasito's Cantina, Spring Creek BBQ, Wingstop, Best Western+, EVEN Hotel, Hyatt House,

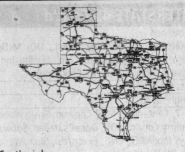

INTERSTATE 45 Cont'd

79 Continued
Costco/dsl, Mercedes, Mini, Sam's Club, VW, **W** Exxon, Murphy USA/dsl, Arby's, Burger King, Chicken Salad Chick, Chipotle, ChuckeCheese, Denny's, Domino's, Dunkin', LJ Silver/Taco Bell, Mia's Table, Outback Steaks, Panera Bread, Popeyes, Red Lobster, Sonic, Starbucks, Starbucks, Taco Cabana, Twin Peaks, Wendy's, Whataburger, Willie's Grill, Candlewood Suites, Days Inn, Fairfield Inn, Homewood Suites, La Quinta, Springhill Suites, TownPlace Suites, BMW/Mini, Firestone/auto, H, Kohl's, Lowe's Whse, Walgreens, Walmart

78 Needham Rd(from sb), Tamina Rd, access to same as 77

77 Woodlands Pkwy, Robinson, Chateau Woods, Marriott, **E** Pallotta's Italian, Valero/Circle K, Chi's Japanese, **W** Cane's Chicken, Kirby's Steaks, Lama Mediterranean, Luby's, Olive Garden, Drury Inn, Embassy, Hyatt Place, Residence Inn, Westin, H, USPO

76 Research Forest Dr, Tamina Rd, **E** Pappas BBQ, Office Depot, **W** Shell/dsl, Benihana, Chili's, Firehouse Subs, Jack-in-the-Box, Jason's Deli, Landry's Seafood, Luby's, Macaroni Grill, Salata, Starbucks, TGIFriday's, Torchy's Tacos, Courtyard, Drury Inn, Residence Inn, JC Penney, Woodlands Mall

73 Rayford Rd, Sawdust Rd, **E** Shell/dsl, Valero, Buffalo Run Grill, Cane's, Crab Daddy Seafood, Golden China, Hartz Chicken, Jack-in-the-Box, McDonald's, Sonic, Starbucks, Zara's Mediterranean, Holiday Inn Express, La Quinta, Aamco, AutoZone, O'Reilly Parts, Walgreens, **W** Shell/dsl, Burger King, Carrabba's, Chick-fil-A, IHOP, KFC, Koji Ramen, Pizza Hut, Wendy's, Whataburger, Wingstop, Extended Stay America, Fukuda Japanese, Hotel Blue, Super 8, Brake Check, Discount Tire, Harley-Davidson, HEB Foods

72a Spring Crossing Dr, **W** Texaco/dsl, Fairfield Inn

72b to Hardy Toll Rd from sb

70b Spring-Stuebner Rd, **E** Hampton Inn, Homewood Suites, Vaughn RV Ctr

70a FM 2920, to Tomball, **E** Exxon/dsl, Rudy's BBQ/dsl, Shell/dsl, Arby's, Chick-fil-A, El Palenque Mexican, Golden Jade Chinese, Hartz Chicken, McDonald's, Subway, Taco Cabana, Wendy's, Whataburger, Zaxby's, Best Western, Comfort Suites, $Tree, Hyundai, Kohl's, Michael's, O'Reilly Parts, Ross, Toyota/Scion, Vaughn's RV Ctr, Verizon, Walmart, **W** 7-11, Palace Inn, AT&T, vet

68 Holzwarth Rd, Cypress Wood Dr, **E** Burger King, Freddy's, Golden Corral, Gringo's TexMex, McAlister's Deli, Pizza Hut/Taco Bell, Sonic, Starbucks, AT&T, Pepboys, **W** Exxon/dsl, Murphy Express/dsl, Bombshells Rest., Brother's Pizza, Cheddar's, Chipotle, Denny's, Dickey's BBQ, DQ, Firehouse Subs, Golden Bowl Chinese, Jack-in-the-Box, Lenny's Subs, Marco's Pizza, Panera Bread, Pizza Hut, Popeyes, Razzoo's Cajun, Schlotsky's, Smashburger, Starbucks, Best Value Inn, Express Inn, Red Roof Inn, Scottish Inn, Best Buy, Chrysler/Dodge/Jeep, Firestone/auto, Ford/Lincoln, Home Depot, Jiffy Lube, Lowe's Whse, Office Depot, PetCo, Staples, Target, Walgreens

66 FM 1960, to Addicks, **E** Chevron/dsl, ChuckECheese, Subway, TX Roadhouse, Waffle House, Motel 6, Acura, BMW, Chevrolet, Honda, Mercedes, PetSmart, Subaru, **W** Exxon, Mobil, Valero/Circle K, Chick-fil-A, Cilantros Mexican, Crafty Crab, Hooters, James Coney Island, McDonald's, Panda Express, Pollo Campero, Red Lobster, Fairfield Inn, Hampton Inn, Hilton Garden, Quality Inn, Red Roof Inn, $Tree, Audi, Chevrolet/Buick/GMC, H, Infiniti, Jaguar/LandRover, Kroger/dsl, NTB, U-Haul

64 Richey Rd, **E** Black Bear Diner, Buffalo Wild Wings,

64 Continued
Chipotle, McDonald's, Olive Garden, Taco Bell, Downtowner Inn, Siegel Suites, Super 8, CarMax, Discount Tire, Sam's Club/dsl, **W** Flying J/Denny's/dsl/scales/24hr, Clio's Mexican, Lupe Tortilla, Mamacita's Mexican, Michoacan Rest, Ojos Locos Cantina, SaltGrass Steaks, Spanish Flowers Mexican, Subway, Toasted Yolk, Wings'n More, SpringHill Suites

63 Airtex Dr, **E** Shell/Golden Chick/dsl, Sunoco/dsl, Valero, Checkers, China Bear, Pappasito's Cantina, Eagles Fly Inn, Woodspring Suites, Cadillac, LoneStar RV Ctr, Nissan, **W** Exxon/dsl, Chicken Express, Cracker Barrel, Jack-in-the-Box, Popeyes, Whataburger, Whataburger, Best Western+, Holiday Inn Express, RestWell Inn

62 Rankin Rd, Kuykendahl, **E** Jack-in-the-Box, Waffle House, Best Classic Inn, Scottish Inn, **W** Chevron/McDonald's, RaceWay/7-11/dsl, Shell, Cajun's Seafood, Shiply Donuts, Sonic, Extended Stay, Extended Stay America, Motel 6, Palace Inn, Kia, Lamborghini, Volvo, VW, Walgreens

61 Greens Rd, **E** Exxon, Brown Sugar's BBQ, IHOP, Jack-in-the-Box, McDonald's, Wendy's, Hilton, Knights Inn, Dillard's, mall, **W** Burger King, Church's TX Chicken, Rocky's Subs, Subway, 99c Store, Burlington Coats

60c Beltway E

60(b a from nb) TX 525, **W** Pappas Seafood, U-Haul

59 FM 525, West Rd, **E** Shell/dsl/repair, A&W/LJ Silver, Burger King, Burger King, Cane's, Chick-fil-A, CiCi's, Denny's, Domino's, El Muelle Seafood, Hanz Diner, Mambo Seafood, McDonald's, Ostioneria Mexican, Holiday Inn Express, AutoZone, Chrysler/Dodge/Jeep, Firestone/auto, T-Mobile, **W** Exxon/dsl, Shell/dsl, Best Western+, Bonfire Wings, Charley's Cheesesteaks, Chili's, Chipotle, Jalisco's Mexican, Panda Express, Papa John's Pizza, Starbucks, Subway, Taco Bell, Taco Cabana, Wendy's, Whataburger, Wing Stop, Best Value Inn, $Tree, AT&T, Best Buy, Discount Tire, Home Depot, Office Depot, PepBoys, PetCo, Ross, Verizon, Walmart

57(b a from nb) TX 249, Gulf Bank Rd, Tomball, **E** Chevron, Gulf/dsl, Texaco/Church's TX Chicken, Subway, **W** Shell, Sonic, Tampico Seafood, Days Inn, Quality Inn, Family$, Giant$

56 Canino Rd, **E** Taj Inn Suites, **W** Texaco, Denny's, Luby's, Deluxe Inn, Gulfwind Motel, Isuzu, Walgreens

55(b a from nb) Little York Rd, Parker Rd, **E** Exxon/dsl, Mobil/dsl, Texaco, Burger King, China One, McDonald's, Pizza Hut, Ranchero King Buffet, Whataburger, Advance Parts, AT&T, Family$, **W** KFC, La Chicken, Popeyes, Wendy's, Walgreens

54 Tidwell Rd, **E** Exxon/dsl, Burger King, Chacho's Mexican, Pho Now, Subway, Thomas BBQ, 99c Store, CVS Drug, **W** Chevron, Shell, Hartz Chicken, McDonald's, Guest Motel, Southwind Motel, Symphony Inn, Town Inn, Family$, U-Haul

53 Airline Dr, **E** Discount Tire, Fiesta Foods/drug, **W** Citgo, Shell/dsl, Little Mexico, Whataburger, Best Value Inn, Luxury Inn, Palace Inn

 = gas = food = lodging = other = rest stop

INTERSTATE 45 Cont'd

HOUSTON

Exit #	Services
52(b a from nb)	Crosstimbers Rd, E Murphy Express/dsl, Baskin-Robbins, Burger King, Charley's Cheesesteaks, Chick-fil-A, China Star, ChuckeCheese, Cici's, Hungry Farmer BBQ, IHOP, Jack-in-the-Box, James Coney Island, KFC, LA Fish House, McDonald's, Ojos Locos Cantina, Panda Express, Pappas BBQ, Pizza Hut, Subway, Taco Bell, Twin Crab, Wingstop, $Tree, AT&T, CVS Drug, GNC, Marshall's, Ross, Verizon, Walmart, W Texan Inn
51	I-610
50(b a from nb)	Patton St, Calvacade St, Link Rd, E Chevron, Exxon, Love's/Wendy's/dsl/scales/24hr, Shell, Best Value Inn, Luxury Inn, W Heights House, AutoZone, Family$, NAPA, USPO
49b	N Main St, Houston Ave, E Chevron, Love's/Wendy's/dsl/scales/24hr, Best Value Inn, Hoilday Inn Express, Luxury Inn, W Exxon/dsl, Domino's, McDonald's, Subway, Whataburger/24hr, Sleep Inn, O'Reilly Parts
48b a	I-10, E to Beaumont, W to San Antonio
47d	Dallas St, Pierce St(from sb), E H
47c	McKinney St(from sb, exits left)
47b	Houston Ave, Memorial Dr, downtown, W DoubleTree
47a	Allen Pkwy(exits left from sb)
46b a	US 59, N to Cleveland, S to Victoria, W Chevron, Texaco, Bonchon Asian, Good Times Grill, LA Fried Chicken, McDonald's, BMW
45b a	South St, Scott St, Houston, E Chevron/Church's TX Chicken/dsl, Shell, Scott Inn, W Burger King, Popeyes, to TSU
44	Cullen Blvd, Houston, E Valero, W to U of Houston
43b	Telephone Rd, Houston
43a	Tellepsen St, W U of Houston
41b	US 90A, Broad St, S Wayside Dr, E McDonald's, Houston Inn, Palace Inn, Walmart/McDonald's, W Chevron/dsl, Exxon, 7Spice Cajun, Burger King, Chick-fil-A, Jack-in-the-Box, Little Caesar's, McDonald's, Taco Cabana
41a	Woodridge Dr, E Shell, Burger King, Cane's, Chick-fil-A, Denny's, McDonald's, Pizza Hut, King$, W Boudreaux Cajun, China Star, ChuckeCheese, CiCi's, Doneraki Mexican, IHOP, KFC/Taco Bell, Panda Express, Pappas BBQ, Starbucks, Subway, Taco Palenque, Taqueria Mexico, Wendy's, Whataburger, Wingstop, Best Buy, HEB Food/gas, Home Depot, Lowe's, Marshall's, Office Depot, Old Navy, Ross, Verizon
40c	I-610 W
40b	I-610 E, to Pasadena
40a	Frontage Rd(from nb)
39	Park Place Blvd, Broadway Blvd, E Valero/dsl, Maria's Kitchen, W Pemex/dsl, Shell/dsl, Kelley's Rest., Papa John's, Subway, Chrysler/Dodge/Jeep
38b	Howard Dr, Bellfort Dr(from sb), E Shell, Jack-in-the-Box, Wendy's, W Shell/dsl, Texaco/dsl, Chilo's Seafood, VStar Seafood Buffet, Camelot Inn, Moonlight Inn, Mustang Inn, Palace Inn
38	TX 3, Monroe Rd, E Shell/dsl, Sunoco/Stripes/dsl, Valero/dsl, DQ, Jack-in-the-Box, Las Hamacas, Las Mamalonas Burgers, Ninfa's Mexican, Starbucks, Wendy's, Palace Inn, AutoZone, Family$, URGENT CARE, W Chevron/dsl, Valero/dsl, Mannie's Seafood, Maria Rita's, Pappa's BBQ, Subway, Tacos Tec, V Star Chinese, Fairfield Inn, Sheraton, tire/auto repair, U-Haul
36	College Ave, Airport Blvd, E Valero, Aranda's Bakery, Burger House 45, Church's TX Chicken, DQ, Jack-in-the-Box, Knights Inn, Shipley Donuts, Subway, T-Mobile, Waffle House, Holiday Inn Express, TownePlace,

ELLINGTON FIELD

LEAGUE CITY

Exit #	Services
36	Continued O'Reilly Parts, W Gulf/dsl, Shell/dsl, Valero/dsl, Denny's, Denny's, Inn, Best Western+, Comfort Suites, Courtyard, Days Inn, GreenTree Hotel, Hampton Inn, Hilton, Holiday Inn, La Quinta, Luxury Inn, Marriott, Motel 6, SpringHill Suites, Discount Tire
35	Edgebrook Dr, E Chevron, RaceWay/7-11/dsl, Shell/dsl, Arranda's Mexican, Burger King, Chilo's Rest., Jack-in-the-Box, KFC, Popeyes, Subway, Taco Bell, Family$, Fiesta Foods, Office Depot, vet, W Citgo/dsl, Mambo Seafood, McDonald's, Pizza Hut, Whataburger, $General, Cavender's Boots, O'Reilly Parts, Verizon
34	S Shaver Rd, E Conoco, McDonald's, Island Suites, Ford, Kia, Nissan, Toyota/Scion, W MurphyUSA/dsl, Arby's, Chick-fil-A, Halal Shawarma, Ojos Locos, Pancho's Mexican, Starbucks, Subway, Waffle House, Wendy's, Baymont Inn, $Tree, 99c Store, AT&T, Discount Tire, Firestone/auto, GNC, Honda, Macy's, Marshall's, NTB, PetSmart, Ross, Staples, Walmart/McDonald's
33	Fuqua St, E Chili's, Las Haciendas, Luby's, Olive Garden, Ostioneria Seafood, Schlotzky's, TGIFriday's, Extended Stay, Studio 6, Lincoln, Volvo, W Bayou City Wings, Bombshells Grill, Boudreaux's, Casa Ole, Cici's Pizza, Famous Crab Cajun, Golden Corral, Gringo's Mexican, House of Pies, IHOP, Joe's Crabshack, McDonald's, Subway, Taco Bell, Taco Cabana, Twon Crab, Whataburger, Buick/GMC, CarMax, Chevrolet, Home Depot, Sam's Club/gas
32	Sam Houston Tollway
31	FM 2553, Scarsdale Blvd, W DQ, Shell/Wendy's, Scottish Inn, Chevrolet
30	FM 1959, Dixie Farm Rd, Ellington Field, E Shell/dsl, Subway, Chrysler/Dodge/Jeep, H, Infiniti, Subaru, W Exxon/dsl, Mobil, McDonald's, Popeyes, Palace Inn, Lonestar RV, VW
29	FM 2351, Clear Lake City Blvd, to Clear Lake RA, Friendswood
27	El Dorado Blvd, E Exxon/dsl, Carl's Jr, Chick-fil-A, Panera Bread, Starbucks, Taco Bell, Firestone/auto, Home Depot, W Gloria's Salvadoran, Maggiano's, Perry's Steakhouse, Red Robin, TX Roadhouse, Whataburger, Yardhouse Grill, Cadillac, Hyundai, Kohl's, Lexus, Sam's Club/gas, Walmart/McDonald's
26	Bay Area Blvd, E BB's Cajun, BJ's Rest., Buffalo Wild Wings, Chick-fil-A, Dimassi's, Escalante's, First Watch, Freebird's Burrito, Genghis Grill, Jason's Deli, la Madeleine, Longhorn Steaks, Lupe Tortilla, Mia's Table, Pei Wei, Potbelly, Red Lobster, Snooze, Taco Cabana, Best Western, Extended Stay, Hampton Inn, Hilton Garden, InTown Suites, La Quinta, Barnes&Noble, Best Buy, H, Lowe's, Michael's, Staples, to Houston Space Ctr, World Mkt, W Valero/dsl, Burger Joint, Cane's, CAVA, Cheesecake Factory, Chick-fil-A, ChuckeCheese, Dave&Buster's, Denny's, Eggcellence Cafe, Five Guys, Grimaldi's Pizzeria, McDonald's, Olive Garden, Outback Steakhouse, Panda Express, PF Chang's, Subway, Swamp Shack Cajun, Holiday Inn Express, Tru, Costco/gas, Dillard's, JC Penney, Macy's, mall, Marshall's, Office Depot, Old Navy, PetSmart, Ross, Target, Verizon
25	FM 528, NASA rd 1, E 7-11/dsl, Chevron/dsl, Exxon, Mobil, Cheddar's, Chili's, Chuy's Mexican, El Tiempo, Las Hacienda Mexican, Luby's, Main Event, Marble Slab, McAlister's Deli, Michiru Asian, Pappa's Seafood, Pappas Delta BBQ, Pappasito's Cantina, Pizza Hut, Plucker's Wings, Rudy's BBQ/dsl, Saltgrass Steaks, Twin Peaks Rest., Waffle House, Motel 6, Springhill Suites, BigLots, Cavendar's Boots, Hobby Lobby, H, H, Mazda, W Floyd's Cajun, Hooters, James Coney Island, Subway, Tuesday Morning
23	FM 518, League City, E Mobil/7-11/dsl, Shell/dsl,

TX

INTERSTATE 45 Cont'd

LEAGUE CITY

23 Continued
Crafty Crab, Domino's, Juanderful Burrito, La Brisa, Popeyes, Sonic, [other] $Tree, Kroger, **W** [gas] Valero, [food] Cracker Barrel, McDonald's, Starbucks, Taco Bell, Waffle House, Wendy's, [lodging] Super 8, [other] Discount Tire, Space Ctr RV Park, U-Haul

22 Calder Dr, Brittany Bay Blvd, **E** [other] [H], Mercedes, Nissan, Toyota/Scion, **W** Acura, Holiday World RV Ctr

20 FM 646, Santa Fe, Bacliff, **E** [gas] MurphyUSA/dsl, [food] Chick-fil-A, Chipotle, Cici's Pizza, Denny's, First Watch, Five Guys, Freebirds Burrito, Jack-in-the-Box, Jimmy Changas, Little Daddy's Cajun, Logan's Roadhouse, Marble Slab, McDonald's, NY Pizzaria, Panda Express, Panera Bread, Schlotzky's, Spring Creek BBQ, Starbucks, Whataburger, Wingstop, [lodging] Candlewood Suites, Hampton Inn, [other] $Tree, AT&T, Best Buy, Firestone/auto, GNC, Hobby Lobby, Home Depot, JC Penney, Lowe's, Michael's, NTB, PetSmart, Ross, Staples, Target, TJ Maxx, URGENT CARE, Walmart/McDonald's, **W** [gas] Chevron/dsl, [food] 888 Chinese Rest., Black Bear Diner, Chili's, Coco Crepes, Freddy's, Fuji Ramen, Jason's Deli, Kabuki, Mod Pizze, Salata, Subway, Taco Cabana, Toasted Yolk, TX Crawfish & Seafood, [other] Cabela's, HEB Foods/gas, Kohl's, PetCo, Verizon, Walgreens

19 FM 517, Dickinson Rd, Hughes Rd, **E** [food] Gator's, Little Mexico, [other] Buick/GMC, CVS Drug, Family$, Kia, **W** [gas] Phillips 66, Shell/dsl, [food] Dickinson Seafood, KFC, McDonald's, Pizza Hut, Rancho's Taqueria, Sonic, Starbucks, Taco Bell, Wendy's, [lodging] Days Inn, Palace Inn, [other] Chrysler/Dodge/Jeep, Ford, Kroger

17 Holland Rd, **W** [gas] Buc-ee's/dsl, [lodging] SpringHill Suites, [other] Tanger Outlets/Famous Brands

HITCHCOCK

16 FM 1764 E(from sb), Texas City, same as 15

15 FM 2004, FM 1764, Hitchcock, **E** [gas] Chevron, [food] Beyond Burger, Gringo's Mexican, Jack-in-the-Box, Olive Garden, Starbucks, [lodging] Best Western, Comfort Inn, Holiday Inn Express, Home2 Suites, La Quinta, Quality Inn, Woodspring Suites, [other] Chevrolet/Toyota/Scion, DeMontrond RV Ctr, [H], Hyundai, mall, **W** [gas] MurphyUSA/dsl, Shell, Valero/dsl, [food] Best Wok, IHOP, Little Caesar's, Sonic, Taco Bell, Waffle House, Wendy's, Whataburger, Wing Street, WingStop, [other] AT&T, Sam's Club/gas, URGENT CARE, Verizon, Walmart/McDonald's

13 Century Blvd, Delany Rd, **W** [food] Barcena's Mexican, [lodging] Best Value Inn, Super 8, [other] Lazy D RV Park, TX RV Park, VF Factory Outlet/famous brands

TEXAS CITY

12 FM 1765, La Marque, **E** [gas] Chevron/dsl, Exxon, [food] Chicken Plus, Domino's, Jack-in-the-Box, Kelley's Rest., Sonic, [lodging] Highway Inn, Motel 6, [other] $General, CVS Drug, Family$, **W** [gas] Valero/dsl, [lodging] Travel Inn, [other] Little Thicket RV Park, UHaul

11 Vauthier Rd

10 **E** [gas] Valero/Circle K, [food] McDonald's, PitStop BBQ, **W** [gas] Shell/dsl, [food] Jack in the Box, [other] Big State RV Park, Hoover RV Ctr, Oasis RV Park

9 Frontage Rd(from sb, no return/turnaround)

8 Frontage Rd(from nb)

7c Frontage Rd

7b TX 146, TX 6(exits left from nb), Texas City

7a TX 146, TX 3

6 Frontage Rd(from sb)

5 Frontage Rd

4 Frontage Rd, Village of Tiki Island, **W** Welcome Ctr, [gas] Valero/dsl, [other] public boat ramp, Tiki Tom's RV Park

4mm West Galveston Bay

1c TX 275, FM 188(from nb), Port Ind Blvd, Teichman Rd, Port of Galveston, **E** [gas] Citgo, Exxon/dsl, Valero/dsl, [food] Yanni's, [lodging] Galveston Inn, Howard Johnson, Motel 6, Sleep Inn,

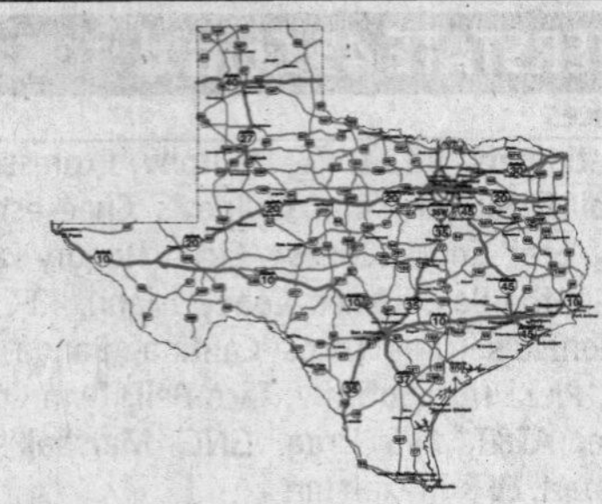

PORT OF GALVESTON

1c Continued
Buick/Chevrolet/GMC, Ford, Honda, Hoover RV Ctr, Toyota/Scion, **W** [food] Number 13 Seafood

1b 71st St(from sb), **E** [gas] same as 1c

1a TX 342, 61st St, to W Beach. I-45 begins/ends on TX 87 in Galveston., **E** [gas] Exxon/7-11, [food] Subway, Wingstop, [lodging] Candlewood Suites, [other] Big Lots, GNC, Home Depot, NTB, PetSmart, Target, **W** [gas] Exxon, Murphy USA/dsl, Shell/Burger King/dsl, Texaco/dsl, Valero/Circle K, [food] Cajun Greek, Darlene's Shrimp, Domino's, Gino's Italian, Golden Corral, Happy Buddah, IHOP, Jack-in-the-Box, Jimmy John's, KFC, Little Caesar's, Marble Slab, Mario's, McDonald's, Panda Express, Papa John's, Popeyes, Schlotsky's, Sonic, Starbucks, Subway, Taco Bell, Taco Cabana, TX Pit Stop BBQ, Waffle House, Whataburger, Yamato Japanese, [lodging] Baymont, Beachcomber Inn, Beachfront Palms, Comfort Inn, Hampton Inn, Hilton, Holland House, La Quinta, La Quinta, Quality Inn, Rodeway Inn, Springhill Suites, Super 8, [other] $Tree, AT&T, AutoZone, CVS Drug, Firestone/auto, Kroger/dsl, KwikCar, Marshall's, O'Reilly Parts, Office Depot, Randall's Food/gas, Ross, to Moody Gardens, Tuesday Morning, URGENT CARE, USPO, Verizon, Walgreens, Walmart

INTERSTATE 410 (San Antonio)

53 I-35, S to Laredo, N to San Antonio

51 FM 2790, Somerset Rd, **S** [food] KFC

49 TX 16 S, spur 422, **N** [gas] Chevron, Texaco/dsl, [food] Church's TX Chicken, Domino's, Little Caesars, Sonic, Subway, Taco Bell, Whataburger, [lodging] Days Inn, [other] [H], to Palo Alto Coll, **S** [gas] Valero/Circle K/dsl, [food] Jack-in-the-Box, [lodging] Best Western+

48 Zarzamora St, **S** [gas] Valero/dsl

47 Turnaround (from eb)

46 Moursund Blvd

44 US 281 S, spur 536, Roosevelt Ave, **N** [gas] Shell/McDonald's/dsl, Valero/dsl, [food] Subway, **S** Jack-in-the-Box, Judy's Mexican, [lodging] Holiday Inn Express

43 Espada Rd(from eb)

42 spur 122, S Presa Rd, **N** [gas] Exxon, [other] to San Antonio Missions Hist Park, **S** [gas] Valero/dsl, [food] BBQ Republic

41 I-37, US 281 N

39 spur 117, WW White Rd

37 Southcross Blvd, Sinclair Rd, Sulphur Sprs Rd, **N** [gas] Shell/dsl, Valero, [other] Family$, [H], **S** [gas] Shell, [other] $General

35 US 87, Rigsby Ave, **E** [gas] Exxon/7-11, Murphy USA/dsl, QT, Valero/dsl, [food] Denny's, El Rodeo Mexican, Jack-in-the-Box, KFC/Taco Bell, McDonald's, Subway, [other] $Tree, AT&T, Walmart/McDonald's, **W** [gas] Chevron/dsl, [food] Bill Miller BBQ, Burger King, Domino's, El Tapico Mexican, Hoffman's Steaks, Laguna Madre, Sonic, Taco Cabana, Whataburger, [lodging] Days Inn, Holiday Inn Express, [other] Aamco, Advance Parts, U-Haul, vet, Walgreens

KIRBY

34 FM 1346, E Houston St, **W** [gas] Valero/dsl, [other] USPO

33 I-10 E, US 90 E, to Houston, I-10 W, US 90 W, to San Antonio

32 Dietrich Rd(from sb), FM 78(from nb), to Kirby

31b Lp 13, WW White Rd

31a FM 78, Kirby

TX

INTERSTATE 410 (San Antonio) Cont'd

Exit #	Services
30	Binz-Engleman, Space Center Dr(from nb)
29mm	**Exits 161 thru 165.**, I-410 and I-35 run together 7 mi
27	I-35, N to Austin, S to San Antonio
26	Lp 368 S, Alamo Heights
25b	FM 2252, Perrin-Beitel Rd, N Chevron/dsl, Valero/dsl, Arby's, KFC/Taco Bell, Schlotsky's, Subway, Tastee-Freez/ Wienerschnitzel, Budget Lodge, Brake Check, Family$, S Jim's Rest., vet
25a	Starcrest Dr, N Valero, Jack-in-the-Box, H
24	Harry Wurzbach Hwy, S BBQ Sta., VW
23	Nacogdoches Rd, N Shell/dsl, Bill Miller BBQ, Earth Burger, Formosa Chinese, Jimmy John's, La Marginal, Mama's Cafe, Pizza Hut, Schlotzsky's, Taco Cabana, Crowne Plaza, S Chevron/7-11, Volvo
22	Broadway St, N Shell/dsl, Cabo Bob's, Chili's, Fuddrucker's, McDonald's, Courtyard, Hilton Garden, Home2 Suites, S Citgo, Valero/dsl, Cane's, Chesters Hamburgers, Frontier Burger, Jim's Rest., Little Caesar's, Magic Time Machine, Taco Palenque, Whataburger, Wild Barley Kitchen, Residence Inn, TownHouse Motel
21	US 281 S, Airport Rd, Jones Maltsberger Rd, N Applebee's, Drury Suites, Hampton Inn, Holiday Inn Express, Marriott, PearTree Inn, S Murphy USA/dsl, Cracker Barrel, Pappadeaux, Plucker's Wings, Saltgrass Steaks, Whataburger, Best Western, Courtyard, Days Inn, Fairfield Inn, Home2 Suites, La Quinta, Springhill Suites, Staybridge Suites, TownePlace Suites, Nissan, TJ Maxx, Walmart/McDonald's/24hr
20	TX 537, N Valero, Arby's, Cheddar's, Chick-fil-A, Jack-in-the-Box, Jason's Deli, LA Crawfish, Project Pollo, Rosario's Mexican, DoubleTree, Barnes&Noble, Best Buy, Brake Check, Cavender's Boots, Chevrolet, Honda, Jo-Ann Fabrics, Lexus, Lincoln, Mazda, Mercedes, PetCo, Ross, S Cheesecake Factory, Chipotle, Dickey's BBQ, Earth Burger, El Pollo Loco, First Watch, Freddy's, Jimmy John's, la Madeleine, Longhorn Steaks, Panda Express, Salata, Shake Shack, Starbucks, Taco Cabana, Twin Peaks, Aloft, AT&T, Chrysler/Dodge/Jeep, CVS Drug, Dillard's, JC Penney, Macy's, mall, Saks 5th, Target, Verizon
19b	FM 1535, FM 2696, Military Hwy, N QT, Guajillos Mexican, Kobe Japanese, S Denny's, Dough Pizzaria, Ilsong Garden
19a	Honeysuckle Lane, Castle Hills
17b	(18 from wb), S Bill Miller BBQ, Burger King, DQ, Las Palapas, Wing Daddy's, HEB Foods/gas, NAPA, vet
17	Vance Jackson Rd, N 7-11, Valero/dsl, Jack-in-the-Box, Kai Sushi, McDonald's, Sonic, Starbucks, Taco Cabana, Whataburger, Embassy Suites, Marriott, Aamco, AT&T, Discount Tire, S Petronic, Shell/Church's TX Chicken, Bill Miller BBQ, Church's TX Chicken, U-Haul
16b a	I-10 E, US 87 S, to San Antonio, I-10 W, to El Paso, US 87 N
15	Lp 345, Fredericksburg Rd, E EVC, Exxon, Dave&Buster's, Denny's, El Pollo Loco, El Rodeo, Jack-in-the-Box, Jim's Rest., La Tequilla, Luby's, McDonald's, Wendy's, Whataburger, SpringHill Suites, Family$, Firestone/auto, Hobby Lobby, SteinMart, Target, W Chevron/7-11/dsl, CVS Drug
14	(c b a from sb) Callaghan Rd, Babcock Ln, E Chevron/dsl, Valero/dsl, Popeyes, Red Lobster, Whataburger, Quality Inn, Hyundai, W Exxon, Shell, Valero, Bill Miller's BBQ, Burger King, Chili's, ChopSticks Chinese, DingHow Chinese, Golden Corral, IHOP, Las Palapas Mexican, Louie Italian, McDonald's, Nicha's Mexican, Pizza Hut, Quizno's, Subway, Wendy's, Cavander's Boots,
14	Continued Home Depot, H, PetSmart, Sam's Club/gas, Walmart/ Subway/24hr
13	(b a from sb) TX 16 N, Bandera Rd, Evers Rd, Leon Valley, E Panda Express, Audi, HEB Foods/dsl, Office Depot, Toyota/Scion, UHaul, W Valero/dsl, Bill Miller BBQ, Henry's Tacos, IHOP, Schlotzsky's, Taco Cabana
12	(from sb), E Days Inn, W Jason's Deli, Ojos Locos, Olive Garden, Sea Island Shrimp House, Starbucks, $Tree, AT&T, Barnes&Noble, Best Buy, Marshall's, Michael's, Old Navy, Petco, Ross
11	Ingram Rd, E Shell/dsl, KFC/Taco Bell, Saltgrass Steaks, TX Roadhouse, Vallarta Mexican, Comfort Suites, Courtyard, Days Inn, Holiday Inn Express, Red Roof Inn, Residence Inn, Aamco, Chrysler/Dodge/Jeep, Mazda, Nissan, W Chick-fil-A, ChuckeCheese, Denny's, Jack-in-the-Box, Whataburger, Best Western, HomeTowne, Dillard's, JC Penney, Macy's, mall
10	FM 3487, Culebra Rd, E Denny's, J Anthony's Seafood, McDonald's, Wendy's, Ramada Ltd, Super 8, Harley-Davidson, to St Mary's U, W Phillips 66, Ford
9	(b a from sb) TX 151, W Murphy USA/dsl, 54th St Grill, Buffalo Wild Wings, Carino's Italian, Cheddar's, Chili's, Chipotle Mexican, Cracker Barrel, Dimassi's , Firehouse Subs, IHOP, McAlister's Deli, MOD Pizza, Panda Express, Schlotsky's, Starbucks, The Shack, Twin Peaks, Whataburger, Homewood Suites, Quality Inn, Springhill Suites, SureStay, $Tree, AT&T, GNC, Home Depot, Lowe's Whse, Office Depot, PetSmart, Ross, Target, to Sea World, URGENT CARE, Verizon, Walmart/McDonald's
7	(8 from sb) Marbach Dr, E Exxon/7-11, Church's TX Chicken, Golden Wok, IHOP, $General, PepBoys, W Chevron/dsl, Shell/dsl, Chick-fil-A, Jack-in-the-Box, Jim's Rest., KFC, LJ Silver's, McDonald's, Peter Piper Pizza, Pizza Hut, Popeyes, Red Lobster, Sonic, Subway, Taco Bell, Taco Cabana, Whataburger/24hr, Econo Lodge, Motel 6, $Tree, Advance Parts, BigLots, BrakeCheck, Firestone/auto, HEB Foods/gas
6	US 90, E Country Inn, to Lackland AFB, W Shell/dsl, Valero/dsl, Best Western, Explore USA RV Ctr
4	Valley Hi Dr, to Del Rio, San Antonio, E Valero/dsl, Burger King, Church's TX Chicken, Little Caesar's, McDonald's, Panda Express, Pizza Hut, Sonic, Subway, $Tree, AutoZone, HEB Food/gas, O'Reilly Parts, W Valero, Jack-in-the-Box, to Lackland AFB, Walgreens
3	(b a from sb) Ray Ellison Dr, Medina Base, E Shell/dsl, W Chevron/dsl, Valero/Subway/dsl, Walmart/Subway
2	FM 2536, Old Pearsall Rd, E Shell/dsl, Valero/dsl, Bill Miller BBQ, Church's TX Chicken, Domino's, Little Caesar's, McDonald's, Mexico Taqueria, Sonic, Subway, Taco Bell, AutoZone, CVS Drug, O'Reilly Parts, W QT, Valero/Circle K/dsl, KFC
1	Frontage Rd, W Toyota/Scion

CASTLE HILLS

LEON VALLEY

MEDINA BASE

INTERSTATE 610 (Houston)

Exit #	Services
38c a	TX 288 N, access to zoo, downtown
37	Scott St, N Citgo, Exxon, Navy Seafood, Papa's BBQ, Family$
36	FM 865, Cullen Blvd, N Crystal Inn, S Exxon/ McDonald's, Shell, Crown Plaza, Cullen Inn, tire repair
35	Calais Rd, Crestmont St, MLK Blvd, N Baked Potato Factory, S Valero, Subway, Timmy Chan
34	S Wayside Dr, Long Dr, N Shell/dsl, Sunoco/Stripes/dsl, Church's TX Chicken, S One Stop, Valero/dsl, Jack-in-the-Box, Leo's Country Kitchen, NAPA
33	Woodridge Dr, Telephone Rd, N Shell/dsl, Boudreaux's Cajun, ChuckeCheese, Cici's Pizza, Doneraki TexMex, IHOP,

INTERSTATE 610 (Houston) Cont'd

SHAMROCK

33 Continued KFC/Taco Bell, McDonald's, Panda Express, Pappas BBQ, Starbucks, Taco Palenque, Wendy's, Wingstop, South Loop Inn, Advance Parts, Best Buy, Brake Check, Harley Davidson, HEB Foods/gas, Lowe's, Marshall's, Old Navy, Ross, Verizon, S Exxon/dsl, Spanky's Pizza

32b a I-45, S to Galveston, N to Houston, to

31 Broadway Blvd, S Phillips 66/dsl, Valero/Circle K/dsl

30c b TX 225, to Pasadena, San Jacinto Mon

29 Port of Houston Main Entrance

28 Clinton Dr, to Galina Park, E Texaco, W Shell/Burger King/scales/dsl

27 Turning Basin Dr, industrial area

26b Market St

26a I-10 E, to Beaumont, I-10 W, to downtown

24(b a from eb) US 90 E, Wallisville Rd, E Chevron/dsl, Gulf/dsl, Love's/Arby's/dsl/scales/24hr, Pilot/McDonald's/dsl/scales, Texaco/dsl, Valero/Hartz Chicken/dsl/scales/24hr, Blue Beacon, W Exxon/dsl

23b N Wayside, N Valero

23a Kirkpatrick Blvd

22 Homestead Rd, Kelley St, N Shell/dsl, Whataburger, Best Value, Super 8, S Chevron/Subway/dsl/scales

21 Lockwood Dr, N Exxon/McDonald's, Shell/dsl, Timmy Chan Chinese, Family$, Fiesta Foods, H, W Texaco/Subway/dsl, MJGs Grill, Hutcheson Hike/Bike Park

20a b US 59, to downtown

19b Hardy Toll Rd

19a Hardy St, Jensen Dr(from eb)

18 Irvington Blvd, Fulton St, N Chevron, S Shell/dsl

17b c I-45, N to Dallas, S to Houston

17a (eb only) Airline Dr, S Shell/dsl, Jack-in-the-Box, Western Inn

16(b a from eb) Yale St, N Main St, Shamrock, N Exxon/dsl, Harley-Davidson, S Burger King, KFC/Taco Bell

15 TX 261, N Shepherd Dr, N Five Guys, Gabby's BBQ, Sonic, Starbucks, Taco Cabana, S Chevron/dsl, Shell, Texaco, Chick-fil-A, Starbucks, Wendy's, Whataburger, Wingstop, Home Depot, PepBoys

14 Ella Blvd, N Exxon, Burger King, Cane's, Dunkin', El Pollo Loco, Halal Guys, KFC, McDonald's, Popeyes, Taco Bell, auto repair, S Murphy USA/dsl, Shell, Chipotle, Hungry Farmer BBQ, Tecate, BrakeCheck, CVS Drug, H, Lowe's Whse, Office Depot

13c TC Jester Blvd, N Shell, Antone's Po' Boys, Denny's, Juanita's Mexican, Courtyard, SpringHill Suites

13b a US 290 (exits left from nb)

12 W 18th St, E Applebee's, Whataburger, W Shell, Burger King, Sheraton

11 I-10, W to San Antonio, E to downtown Houston

10 Woodway Dr, Memorial Dr, W Chevron/Pizza Inn/dsl, Shell/dsl, Goodyear

9b Post Oak Blvd, E Drury Inn, La Quinta, Memorial Park, W McCormick&Schmick's Café, Mendocino Farms,

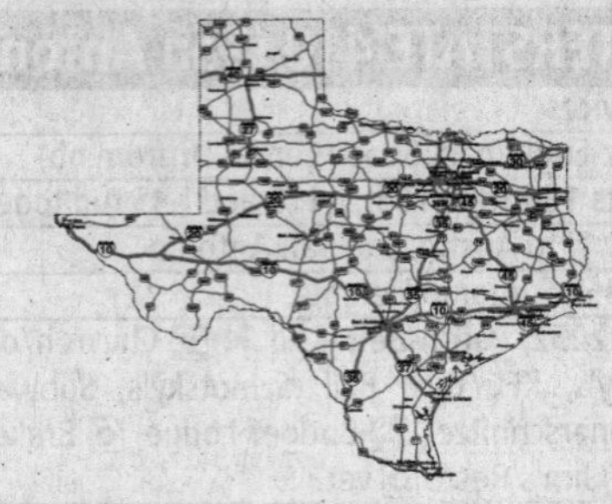

BRASSWOOD

9b Continued Songkran Thai Kitchen, Starbucks, The Rustic

9a San Felipe Rd, Westheimer Rd, FM 1093, E Chevron/dsl, Shell, Antone's PoBoys, Grotto Rest., Jack-in-the-Box, Le Peep Cafe, Sullivan Steaks, Extended Stay America, Hampton Inn, La Quinta, CVS Drug, Target, W Shell, Five Guys, Jamba Juice, Panera Bread, Courtyard, Extended Stay America, Marriott, Sheraton, AT&T, Dillard's, Nieman-Marcus, Whole Foods Mkt

8a US 59, Richmond Ave, E Bayou City Seafood, W Shell, Holiday Inn, Best Buy, Dillards

7 Bissonet St, West Park Dr, Fournace Place, E Beudreax's Kitchen, Sonesta Suites, Home Depot, PetSmart, W Shell/dsl/repair

6 Bellaire Blvd

5b Evergreen St

5a Beechnut St, E Chevron, Boston Mkt, IHOP, Lowe's, McDonald's, Panda Express, Subway, Hobby Lobby, Verizon, W Phillips 66, Shell, Becks Prime, Chick-fil-A, Escalante Mexican Grill, Fadi's Grill, First Watch, James Coney Island, la Madeleine, Los Tios Mexican, Russo's NY Pizza, Saltgrass Steaks, Smoothie King, Starbucks, AT&T, Best Buy, CVS, GNC, JC Penney, Marshall's, Old Navy, Ross, SteinMart, Target

4a S Post Oak Rd, Brasswood, E Starbucks, W Walmart

3 Stella Link Rd, N Domino's, 99c Store, Discount Tire, O'Reilly Parts, S Valero/dsl, Brake Check, vet

2 US 90A, N Exxon/dsl, Mobil, Valero, Burger King, Cane's, Chacho's Cantina, Clucker's Chicken, Denny's/24hr, Dunkin', KFC, Marco's Pizza, McDonald's, Popeyes, Sleepy's Po-Boys, Starbucks, Subway, Wendy's, Astro Best Inn, Holiday Inn Express, CVS Drug, Discount Tire, Family$, Ford, Honda, Mazda, S Chevron/dsl, Arby's, Taco Bell, Whataburger, 7 Diamond Inn, Candlewood Suites, Motel 6, RainTree Inn, Rest Up Inn, Nissan, to Buffalo Speedway

1c Kirby Dr(from eb), N Brewingz Wings, Timmy Chan Chinese, Quality Inn, Sterling Inn, Wingate, Wyndham, S Pappadeaux Seafood, Pappasito's Cantina, Cavender's Boots, Chevrolet, Hyundai, NTB, Toyota/Scion

1b a FM 521, Almeda St, Fannin St, N Chevron/dsl, Shell, Burger King, Scottish Inn, NRG Arena, S Shell/Checkers/dsl, McDonald's, Aamco, Chrysler/Dodge/Jeep, to Six Flags

NOTES

UTAH

INTERSTATE 15

BRIGHAM CITY

Exit #	Services
400.5mm	Utah/Idaho state line
398	Portage
392	UT 13 S, Plymouth, E Green Mart/A&W/dsl
385	UT 30 E, to Riverside, Fielding, E Sinclair/dsl
381	Tremonton, Garland, E H
379	I-84 W, to Boise
376	UT 13, to Tremonton, E Chevron/Arby's/dsl/scales/24hr, Maverik, JC'S Diner
372	UT 240, to UT 13, to rec area, Honeyville
370mm	sb, full facilities, info, litter barrels, vending, petwalk
365	UT 13, Brigham City
363	Forest St, Brigham City, E Love's/Carl's Jr/Subway/dsl/scales/24hr, Holiday Inn Express, Love's RV Stop, W Bear River Refuge
362	US 91, to US 89, Brigham City, Logan, N Galaxie, E 7-11/dsl, Chevron/dsl, Exxon, Floriberto's Mexican, Phillips 66/dsl, Arby's, Burger King, Burgers & Scoops, Cafe Rio, Costa Vida, Dutch Bros, Hunan Chinese, J&D's Rest., Jersey Mike's, KFC/Taco Bell, Little Caesars, McDonald's, Old Grist Mill Bread, Pizza Hut, Sonic, Subway, Taco Time, Wendy's, Wingers, Best Western, Howard Johnson Express, $Tree, AutoZone, Buick/Cadillac/Chevrolet, Chrysler/Dodge/Jeep, Golden Spike RV Park, H, John Watson, Chiropractor(5mi), KOA(4mi), LDS Temple, O'Reilly Parts, Schwab Tires, to Yellowstone NP via US 89, Verizon, Walmart/gas, W Maverick/DQ/dsl/scales/24hr, Days Inn
361mm	nb, full facilities, litter barrels, vending, petwalk

FARR WEST

Exit #	Services
359	Port of Entry both lanes
357	UT 315, to Willard, Perry, E Flying J/Subway/dsl/LP/scales/24hr, KOA(2mi), Willard Peak Camping
351	UT 126, to US 89, to Utah's Fruit Way, Willard Bay, W Smith & Edwards Hardware
349	UT 134, N Ogden, Farr West, E 7-11, Maverik/dsl, Phillips66/Wendy's/dsl, Shell, Arby's, Bella's Mexican, Costa Vida, Del Taco, Domino's, Dutch Bros, Jimmy John's, Jumbo Burger, McDonald's, Subway, Taco Bell, Comfort Inn, Jiffy Lube, W Chevron/dsl, URGENT CARE
346	to Harrisville, W Chevron/Subway/dsl, Maverik/dsl, GriDeli's, Zhang's Chinese, Cal Ranch, O'Reilly Parts, vet

OGDEN

Exit #	Services
344	UT 39, 12th St, Ogden, E 7-11/dsl, Chevron/dsl, Maverik, Old Frontier, Best Western+, to Ogden Canyon RA, W One 9/Subway/Taco Bell/dsl/24hr, Sleep Inn, Sierra RV Ctr
343	UT 104, 21st St, Ogden, E Flying J/Denny's/dsl/LP/24hr, West Haven Travel/dsl, Cactus Red's SW Grill, McDonald's, Comfort Suites, Extended Stay, Holiday Inn Express, Motel 6, truck repair, W Shell/Blimpie/dsl, Super 8, Bideaux RV Ctr, Century RV Park
342	(from nb, no return) UT 53, 24th St, Ogden
341b a	UT 79 W, 31st St, Ogden, E 7-11, Exxon, Cafe Rio, Cane's, Chick-fil-A, Costa Vida, Del Taco, Denny's, Dutch Bros, Goodwood BBQ, In-N-Out, Krispy Kreme, Longhorn Steaks, Lucky Buffet, Napoli's, Olive Garden, Panda Express, Popeyes, Ruby River, Rumbi Grill, Scratch Kitchen, Shake Shack, Starbucks, TX Roadhouse, Warrens, Big O Tires, Cafe Zupas, Chevrolet, Costco/gas, Dillard's, Discount Tire, Ford, H, Hyundai, JC Penney, Jiffy Lube, Lowe's, Michaels, Old Navy, Pep Boys, PetCo, Ross, Staples, Subaru, TJ Maxx,

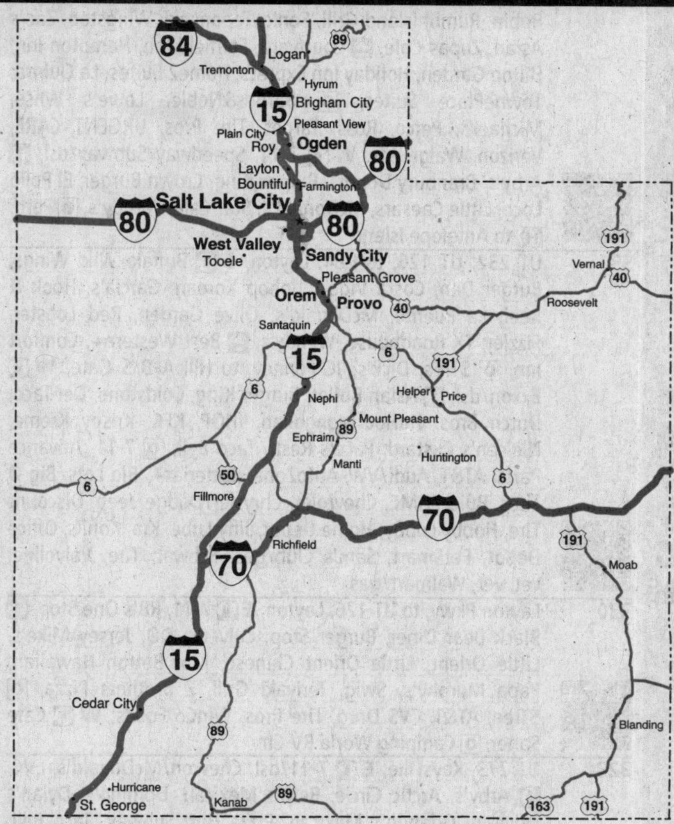

OGDEN

Exit #	Services
341b a	Continued to Weber St U, U-Haul, W
340	I-84 E(from sb), to Cheyenne, Wyo
339	UT 26(from nb), to I-84 E, Riverdale Rd, E Maverik/dsl, Sinclair/dsl, Speedway/dsl, Applebee's, Arby's, Buffalo Wild Wings, Carl's Jr, Chili's, Chipotle, El Pollo Loco, Honeybaked Ham, IHOP, Jamba Juice, Jersey Mike's, McDonald's, MOD Pizza, Starbucks, Subway, The Habit, Wendy's, Wingstop, Zao Asian, Motel 6, $Tree, Best Buy, Buick/GMC, Chrysler/Dodge/Jeep, Good Earth Natural Foods, Harley-Davidson, Hobby Lobby, Home Depot, Honda, Jiffy Lube, Kia, Nissan, PetSmart, Sam's Club/gas, Schwab Tire, Target, Toyota, Verizon, Walmart

CLEARFIELD

Exit #	Services
338	UT 97, Roy, Sunset, E Air Force Museum, W EVC, Exxon/dsl, Maverik/dsl, A&W/KFC, Arby's, Beez Cafe, Burger King, City Buffet Chinese, Greek Olive Rest., Japanese Wasabi, Lolo Hawaiian BBQ, McDonald's, Papa Murphy's, Rancherito's Mexican, Taco Bell, Wendy's, AutoZone, Citte RV Ctr, CVS Drug, Harmon's Mkt, Midas, O'Reilly Parts, Ocean Mart, Sacco's Fresh Mkt, Schwab Tires, Smith's/dsl, Valvoline, vet, Walgreens
335	UT 103, Clearfield, E Jimmy John's, Popeyes, Starbucks, Tru, Hill AFB, W Phillips 66/dsl, Shell/dsl, Sinclair, Beto's Mexican, Carl's Jr, Dutch Bros, KFC, McDonald's, Subway, Taco Bell, Winger's, Ameri-Stay, Charin Inn, Days Inn, $Tree, C&M Tires
334	UT 193, Clearfield, E Chevron/dsl, Maverik, Sinclair, to Hill AFB, W 7-11, Maverik/dsl, AutoZone
332	UT 108, Syracuse, E Applebee's, Cafe Rio, Cane's, Carl's Jr, Chick-fil-A, Chili's, Chipotle, Cracker Barrel, Golden Corral, Jersey Mike's, Jimmy John's, Jimmy John's, Lucky Slice Pizza, MOD Pizza, Moe's SW, Noodles&Co, Outback Steaks,

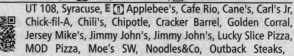

= gas = food = lodging = other = rest stop

UT

INTERSTATE 15 Cont'd

SYRACUSE

332 Continued
Panda Express, Papa Murphy's, Pizza Pie Cafe, Popeyes, Red Robin, Rumbi Island Grill, Sonic, Tepanyaki, Wingstop, Zao's Asian, Zupas Cafe, Courtyard, Fairfield Inn, Hampton Inn, Hilton Garden, Holiday Inn Express, Home2 Suites, La Quinta, TownePlace Suites, Barnes&Noble, Lowe's Whse, Michael's, Petco, Ross, Target, Tire Pros, URGENT CARE, Verizon, Walgreens, W 7-11, Speedway/Subway/dsl, Arby's, Branbury Donuts, Burger King, Crown Burger, El Pollo Loco, Little Caesars, McDonald's, Star Cafe, Wendy's, Ford, H, to Antelope Island

LAYTON

331 UT 232, UT 126, to I-84, Layton, E Buffalo Wild Wings, Burger Den, Costa Vida, Cupbop Korean, Garcia's, Hook & Reel, La Puente, McDonald's, Olive Garden, Red Lobster, Sizzler, TX Roadhouse, Wendy's, Best Western+, Comfort Inn, $Tree, Dick's, JC Penney, to Hill AFB S Gate, W Exxon/dsl, Asian Buffet, Burger King, Coldstone, Del Taco, Dutch Bros, HuHot Mongolian, IHOP, KFC, Krispy Kreme, Nielsen's Custard, Pace's Rest., Taco Bell, 7-11, Advance Parts, AT&T, Audi/VW, AutoZone, Batteries+, Big Lots, Big O Tires, Buick/GMC, Chevrolet, Chrysler/Dodge/Jeep, Discount Tire, Hobby Lobby, Home Depot, Jiffy Lube, Kia, Kohl's, Office Depot, PetSmart, Sam's Club/gas, Schwab Tire, Valvoline, vet, vet, Walmart/gas

330 Layton Pkwy, to UT 126, Layton, E 7-11, RB's One Stop, Black Bear Diner, Burger Stop, Culver's, DQ, Jersey Mike's, Little Orient, Little Orient Chinese, Mo' Bettah Hawaiian, Papa Murphy's, Swig, Teriyaki Grill, Z Brothers Pizza, $Tree, AT&T, CVS Drug, Tire Pros, WinCo Foods, W Cafe Sabor, Camping World RV Ctr

328 UT 273, Kaysville, E 7-11/dsl, Chevron/McDonald's, EVC, Arby's, Arctic Circle, Beto's Mexican, Domino's, Dylan's Drive-In, Orlando's Mexican, Pizza Hut, Subway, Taco Bell, Taco Time, Wendy's, $Tree, Ace Hardware, AutoZone, Big O Tire, Bowman's Mkt, O'Reilly Parts, Schwab Tire, USPO, Valvoline, Walgreens, W Maverik/dsl, Camping World

325mm parking area both lanes

CENTERVILLE

325 UT 225, Lagoon Dr , Farmington, E Chevron, McDonald's, Hampton Inn, funpark, Mercedes, W AT&T, Blaze Pizza, Cafe Rio, Cafe Zupas, Chick-fil-A, Chipotle, Costa Vida, Dutch Bros, Habit Burger, McDonald's, Panda Express, PF Chang's, R&R BBQ, Red Barn Chicken, Starbucks, Tucanos Grill, Waffle Love, Wendy's, Best Buy, Cabela's, Harmon's Mkt, Marshall's, Old Navy, Petco, Ross, World Mkt

324 US 89 N, UT 225, Legacy Pkwy(from sb), E Chevron/dsl, Maverik/dsl, Smith's Foods/dsl, Chopstix Chinese, Javier's Mexican, Little Caesars, Papa John's, Papa Murphy's, Subway, Hampton Inn, Burt Bros, Mercedes, RV Park

322 UT 227(from nb), Lagoon Dr, to Farmington

319 UT 105, Parrish Lane, Centerville, E 7-11/dsl, Chevron/Jimmy John's/dsl, Phillips 66/dsl, Arby's, Branbury Donuts, Carl's Jr, Chick-fil-A, Chili's, Chipotle, Costa Vida, Domino's, Dutch Bros, IHOP, In-N-Out, Jersey Mike's, Little Caesar's, McDonald's, Papa Murphy's, Rancheritos, Starbucks, Subway, Taco Bell, Wendy's, $Tree, Burt Brothers, Dave's Auto Repair, Dick's Mkt, Home Depot, Honda, Jiffy Lube, Kohl's, O'Reilly Parts, PetSmart, Summit Trucks, Target, Walmart

317 US 89 S(exits left from sb), UT 131, 500W, S Bountiful, E Exxon/dsl, Shell, Sinclair, Arella Pizzeria, Culver's, Ramblin Roads, Holiday Inn Express, Chrysler/Dodge/Jeep, Valvoline

316 UT 68, 500 S, W Bountiful, Woods Cross, E Shell, Barbacoa Mexican, Cafe Rio, Carl's Jr, Chipotle, ChuckaRama, Coldstone, Cubby's, Cupbop, Del Taco, Five Guys,

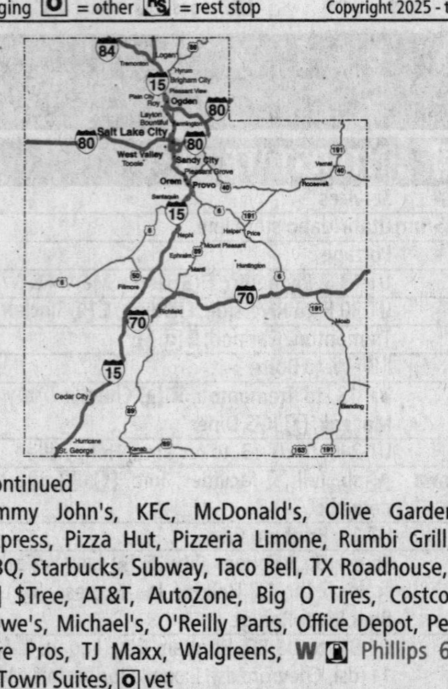

N SALT LAKE

316 Continued
Jimmy John's, KFC, McDonald's, Olive Garden, Panda Express, Pizza Hut, Pizzeria Limone, Rumbi Grill, Smokin' BBQ, Starbucks, Subway, Taco Bell, TX Roadhouse, Wendy's, $Tree, AT&T, AutoZone, Big O Tires, Costco/gas, H, Lowe's, Michael's, O'Reilly Parts, Office Depot, Petco, Ross, Tire Pros, TJ Maxx, Walgreens, W Phillips 66/DQ, InTown Suites, vet

315 26th S, N Salt Lake, E Chevron, Chevron/dsl, Sinclair, Apollo Burger, Arby's, Black Bear Diner, Cafe Rio, Cafe Zupas, Costa Vida, Jersey Mike's, Kneaders Bakery Cafe, McDonald's, MOD Pizza, Nielsen's Frozen Custard, R&R BBQ, Starbucks, Subway, Sweet Burrito, Taco Time, Wendy's, Zao's Asian, Best Western+, Comfort Inn, Buick/GMC, Burt Bros Tires, Chevrolet, Discount Tire, Ford/Lincoln, Honda, Mazda, Nissan, Schwab Tire, Smith's Foods, Southfork Hardware, Toyota, U-Haul, Verizon, Walgreens, W IHOP, Lorena's Mexican, Hampton Inn, Motel 6

314 Center St, Cudahy Lane(from sb), N Salt Lake, E Chevron, JJ Donuts, Nacho House

313 I-215 W(from sb), W to

312 US 89 S, to Beck St, N Salt Lake

311 2300 N

310 900 W(from sb), W Chevron, Don Daniel Mexican, Donut House, El Cabrito, Santo Taco

309 600 N, E H, LDS Temple, W to UT State FairPark

308 I-80 W, to Reno, W

307 400 S (downtown)

CHEYENNE

306 600 S, SLC City Ctr, E Chevron, Fastbreak/dsl, Maverik, Sinclair, Tesla EVC, Alberto's Mexican, McDonald's, R&R BBQ, Starbucks, Street Tacos, Comfort Inn, Crystal Inn, DoubleTree, Grand America, Hampton Inn, Hilton Garden, Little America, Metropolitan Inn, Motel 6, Quality Inn, Sheraton, SpringHill Suites, 7-11, Hyundai, LDS Church Offices, Nissan, to Temple Square, Toyota

305c-a 1300 S, 2100 S UT 201 W, SLC, downtown, E Chevron/dsl, Carl's Jr, ChuckECheese, Egg Break, IHOP, Jimmy John's, McDonald's, Mo Bettahs Hawaiian, Wienerschnitzel, $Tree, Best Buy, Costco/gas, Home Depot, Lowe's, Office Depot, PetSmart, Sams Club/dsl, U-Haul, Verizon, Walmart, W Flying J/Denny's/dsl/LP/24hr, Blue Beacon

304 I-80 E, to Denver, Cheyenne

303 UT 171, 3300 S, S Salt Lake, E 7-11, Maverik, Apollo Burgers, Carl's Jr, Crown Burger, McDonald's, Starbucks, Taco Bell, InTowne Suites, Motel 6, W Maverik, Sinclair, Buick/GMC

301 UT 266, 4500 S, Murray, Kearns, E Chevron, Maverik, McDonald's, Subway, Discount Tire, W Chevron/Burger King/dsl, Shell/dsl, Speedway/dsl, Denny's, Mr. Charlie's Chicken, Wendy's, Fairfield Inn, Hampton Inn, Lowe's Whse

UT

INTERSTATE 15 Cont'd

MIDVALE

Exit #	Services
300	UT 173, 5300 S, Murray, Kearns, E Cafe Zupas, Carl's Jr, Chick-fil-A, Chipotle, Cold Stone, IHOP, Mimi's Cafe, Noodles&Co, Pier 49 Pizza, Starbucks, Zao Asian, Holiday Inn Express, Residence Inn, TownePlace Suites, Barnes&Noble, Costco, H, W Chevron/dsl, Holiday/dsl, Papa Murphy's, Subway, Comfort Inn, Smith's Foods
298	I-215 E and W
297	UT 48, 7200 S, Midvale, E Chevron, Phillips 66/dsl, Arctic Circle, Betos Mexican, Denny's, Korean BBQ, McDonald's, Mi Rico Burrito, Midvale Mining Cafe, Day's Inn, Discovery Inn, InTowne Suites, La Quinta, Motel 6, Park Inn, $General, 7-11, Schwab Tire, Solitude Ski Areas, to Brighton, vet, Walgreens, W Chevron/dsl, Arby's, Cafe Rio, Culver's, Freddy's, Mo Bettahs Hawaiian, Popeyes, R&R BBQ, Subway, Swig, Zaxby's, Staybridge Suites, Tru, Jiffy Lube, WinCo Foods
295	UT 209, 9000 S, Sandy, E Chevron/dsl, Arby's, Beto's Mexican, Korean BBQ, Sizzler, Starbucks, Subway, Alta Ski Areas, Jiffy Lube, NAPA, Real Salt Lake, to Snowbird, W Maverik/dsl, URGENT CARE, BMW Motorcycles, Aamco, Harley-Davidson, H
293	106th S, Sandy, S Jordan, E Exxon, Maverik, Carl's Jr, Carver's Steak & Seafood, Chick-fil-A, Chili's, Chipotle Mexican, Dog Haus, Einstein Bagels, El Pollo Loco, Firehouse Subs, Five Guys, HuHot, HuHot Mongolian, IHOP, Jamba Juice, Jimmy John's, Krispy Kreme, Legends Grill, Los Cucos Mexican, Olive Garden, Pei Wei, Potbelly, Rumbi Island Grill, Slackwater Sandy, Slapfish, Sonic, Starbucks, Subway, Sunday Best, Taco Bell, TX Roadhouse, Wendy's, Best Western+, Courtyard, Extended Stay America, Hampton Inn, Hilton Garden, Holiday Inn Express, Hyatt House, Residence Inn, Barnes&Noble, Chrysler/Dodge/Jeep, Goodyear/auto, Honda, JC Penney, Marshalls, Mazda, Mitsubishi, Old Navy, PetSmart, REI, Subaru, Target, W Tesla EVC, Brickstone's, R&R BBQ, Embassy Suites, Holiday Inn, LaQuinta, Sleep Inn, Super 8, Buick/GMC, Honda, Kia, VW
292	UT 175, 11400 S, E Buffalo Wild Wings, Cane's, Habit Burger, Handel's Ice Cream, Jersey Mike's, McDonald's, Original Pancake House, Pizzeria Limone, Shake Shack, Toscano, Trader Joe's, AT&T, Best Buy, Costco/gas, Duluth Trading Post, Home Depot, Scheel's, W CarMax, Chevrolet, Ford, Mercedes, Nissan, Sam's Club/dsl, Toyota, Walmart
291	UT 71, 12300 S, Draper, Riverton, E Holiday/dsl, Arctic Circle, Astro Burger, Black Bear Diner, Burt Brothers, Cafe Rio, Cafe Zupas, Chick-fil-A, Chuck-A-Rama, Coldstone, Costa Vida, Cubby's, Del Taco, Dutch Bros, Empire Wok, Goodwood BBQ, Great Harvest, Guadalahonky's Mexican, Hash Kitchen, In-N-Out, Jamba Juice, Jimmy John's, La Hacienda, McDonald's, Mountain Mike's Pizza, Noodles&Co, Panda Express, Papa Murphy's, Penny Ann's Cafe, Pizza Hut, Rancheritos, Rumbi Grill, Teriyaki Grill, Waffle Love, Wing Nutz, Fairfield Inn, Quality Inn, Ramada, Springhill Suites, $Tree, aquarium, AT&T, auto repair, AutoZone, Camping World RV Supplies(1mi), Discount Tire, Goodyear/auto, H, Kohl's, Michael's, Mountain Shadows Camping, Office Depot, Petco, Ross, Smith's Foods, TJ Maxx, URGENT CARE, Verizon, Verizon, W 7-11/dsl, Chevron/Holiday, Lolo Hawaiian, Port of Subs, Starbucks, Swig
289	Bangerter Hwy, E Sinclair, Jimmy John's, Kneaders, Little Caesar's, Mo Bettahs Hawaiian, NY Pizza, Subway, Wendy's, TownePlace Suites, Harmon's Mkt, Jiffy Lube, Walgreens, W Maverik/dsl, McDonald's, Hampton Inn, Homewood Suites, IKEA
288	UT 140, Bluffdale, E 7-11/dsl, Chevron/dsl, Maverik/dsl,

BLUFFDALE

Exit #	Services
288	Continued General RV Ctr
284	UT 92, Timpanogas Hwy, to Alpine, Highland, E Blaze Pizza, Braza Grill, Cafe Rio, Chick-fil-A, Chipotle, Five Guys, Jamba Juice, Jersey Mike's, McDonald's, Noodles&Co, Pancake House, Panda Express, Roxberry Juice, Shake It, Slapfish, Sub Zero, Summit Pizza, Taco Bell, Teriyaki Grill, Tsunami Japanese, Village Baker, Wendy's, Wingstop, Zao Asian, Hilton, Hyatt Place, Staybridge Suites, AT&T, Audi/Porsche, Cabela's, Harmon's Mkt, Marshalls, Traverse Mtn Outlets/famous brands, Verizon, W 7-11, Maverik/dsl, Apollo Burger, Arby's, Carl's Jr, Costa Vida, Cubby's Cafe, Curry Pizza, Firehouse Subs, JCW Burgers, JDawgs, Mo Bettahs Hawaiian, Popeyes, Slab Pizza, Smashburger, Starbucks, Zulu Grille, Zupas, Courtyard, Hampton Inn, Holiday Inn Express, Home2 Suites, SpringHill Suites, museum

LEHI

Exit #	Services
283	Triumph Blvd, W Tru, Jaguar, Land Rover
282	2100 N, UT 194, Lehi, E Chevron, Maverik, U-Haul, W Exxon/dsl, K9 Sport Sack
279	UT 73, to Lehi, E Chevron/Holiday, Apollo Burger, Arby's, Buffalo Wild Wings, Cafe Rio, Chili's, ChuckARama, Culver's, Del Taco, Denny's, El Mexiquense, El Pollo Loco, IHOP, Jimmy John's, La Fountain Mexican, Namasthe Cafe, One Man Band Diner, Panda Express, Pizzeria Limone, Popeyes, Red Tacos, Roxberry Juice, Rumbi, Slim Chicken, Starbucks, Swig, TX Hot Chicken, TX Roadhouse, Via 313 Pizza, Zao Asian, Motel 6, AutoZone, Best Buy, Costco/gas, Discount Tire, Home Depot, Lowe's Whse, PetSmart, Ross, Schwab Tire, Valvoline, Verizon, Walgreens, Walmart/Burger King, W 7-11/Wendy's, Chevron/dsl, Arctic Circle, Edna's Mkt, KFC/Pizza Hut, McDonald's, Noble Roman's Pizza, Papa Murphy's, Spudly Donuts, Subway, Tepanyki Japanese, Best Western, Comfort Inn, Day's Inn, $Tree, Big O Tire, Macey's, O'Reilly Parts, USPO

PLEASANT GROVE

Exit #	Services
278	Main St, American Fork, E Chevron, Exxon, Baskin-Robbins, Black Bear Diner, Cafe Zupas, Chick-fil-A, Costa Vida, Cubby's, Cupbop Korean, Five Guys, In-N-Out, MOD Pizza, Nazca Grill, Olive Garden, Pier 49, Root's Place, Sol Agave, Sonic, Super Chix, Waffle Love, Wallabys Smokehouse, $Tree, CAL Stores, Chrysler/Dodge/Jeep, Dick's Sports, Five Below, Hobby Lobby, H, Kia, Kohl's, Michaels, Office Depot, Old Navy, Subaru, Suzuki, Target, TJ Maxx, W Phillips 66/dsl, Extended Stay
276	5th E, Pleasant Grove, E Phillips 66, Speedway, Arby's, Beto's, Carl's Jr, Del Taco, Gandolfo's Deli, Great Harvest, JCW's Burgers, Jim's, KFC, La Costa Mexican, Little Caesars, Los Aribertos, McDonald's, Rocky Mtn Wingshak, Starbucks, Subway, Sushi Bistro, Sushi House, Taco Bell, Wendy's, Holiday Inn Express, AutoZone, Big Lots, Big O Tires, CVS Drug, H, W Buick/GMC, Chevrolet, Ford
275	Pleasant Grove, E Holiday/dsl, Shell, Burger King, Cafe Rio, Chipotle, Costa Vida, Dutch Bros, Jersey Mike's, Mo Bettahs Hawaiian, Panda Express, Papa Murphy's, R&R BBQ, Rancherito's Mexican, Slim Chickens, Smoked Taco, Sodalicious, Starbucks, Summit Pizza, Village Baker, Walgreens, Wingstop, Hyatt House, BMW, Macey's Foods/gas, Tesla
273	Orem, Lindon, E Chevron, Chevron, Maverik/dsl, Beto's Mexican, Costa Vida, Del Taco, Little Caesars, Pizza Pie Cafe, Swig, Discount Tire, Home Depot, Hyundai, Lexus, Schwab Tire, W Harley-Davidson
272	UT 52, to US 189, 8th N, Orem, E Chevron, Maverik/dsl, Arby's, Culver's, Dutch Bros, Gandolfo's Deli, McDonald's, Milagros, Pizza Hut, Sonic, Starbucks, Taco Bell, TacoTime, Fairfield Inn, La Quinta, TownePlace Suites, Family$, Honda, H, Macey's, to Sundance RA, Winco Foods

[gas] = gas [food] = food [lodging] = lodging [other] = other [RS] = rest stop

UT

INTERSTATE 15 Cont'd

Exit #	Services
	OREM
271	Center St, Orem, **E** [gas] 7-11, Chevron, Sinclair, [food] Burger King, Cafe Rio, Cafe Zupas, Chick-fil-A, Corner Bakery, Domino's, Ernie's, Fat Daddy's Pizzeria, Jersey Mike's, Jimmy John's, King Buffet Chinese, Little Caesars, McDonald's, McDonald's, Menchie's, Mo Bettah's Hawaiian, Panda Express, Papa John's, Rancherito's Mexican, Sodalicious, Taco Bell, Wendy's, Zaxby's, [other] [H], Smith's/gas, Target, The Chocolate, USPO, **W** [gas] Maverik/dsl, [food] 5 Star BBQ, DQ, Starbucks
269	UT 265, 12th St S, University Pkwy, bla bla, **E** [gas] Chevron, [food] Applebee's, Arby's, Artic Circle, Blaze Pizza, Chili's, Dave's Chicken, El Pollo Loco, Golden Corral, HoneyBaked Ham, IHOP, In-n-Out, J Dawgs, Krispy Kreme, McDonald's, Mo Bettahs Hawaiian, Noodles & Co., Outback Steaks, Pizza Hut, Sodalicious, Starbucks, Swig, Trader Joe's, Via 313 Pizza, Zao Asian, [lodging] Comfort Inn, Hampton Inn, La Quinta, [other] $Tree, AutoZone, Barnes&Noble, Best Buy, Discount Tire, Hobby Lobby, Honda, Lowe's Whse, Mazda, Michaels, Nissan, O'Reilly Parts, Office Depot, Old Navy, PetCo, PetSmart, Ross, Sprouts, Staples, TJ Maxx, to BYU, Toyota, Valvoline, Verizon, VW, Walmart, **W** [gas] Chevron/dsl, [food] Domino's, Roxberry Juice, Subway, [lodging] Holiday Inn Express
	PROVO
265b a	UT 114, Center St, Provo, **E** [gas] Maverik/dsl, [food] Joe Vera's Mexican, [lodging] Marriott, [other] auto repair, Fresh Mkt, [H], **W** [gas] Chevron, Phillips 66/7-11, Shell/dsl, [food] Great Steak Rest., Subway, [lodging] Colony Inn, [other] Family$, Lakeside RV Camping, to Utah Lake SP
263	US 189 N, University Ave, Provo, **E** [gas] Exxon/dsl, Maverik/dsl, Shell/dsl, [food] A&W/KFC, Arby's, Burger King, Cafe Rio, ChuckaRama, Freddy's, Little Caesars, McDonald's, Papa Murphy's, Rancheritos, Ruby River Steaks, Sizzler, Starbucks, Taco Bell, Village Inn Rest., Wendy's, [lodging] Fairfield Inn, Hampton Inn, Little Suites, Ramada, Residence Inn, Sleep Inn, [other] Discount Tire, Home Depot, JC Penney, Les Schwab, NAPA, Ross, Sam's Club/gas, Staples, Target, to BYU, transmissions
261	UT 75, Springville, **E** [gas] Flying J/Denny's/dsl/scales/24hr, Maverik, [food] McDonald's(1mi), [lodging] Best Western, Holiday Inn Express, [other] KOA, **RestStop**
260	UT 77, Springville, Mapleton, **E** [gas] Phillips 66/7-11/dsl, [food] Arby's, Cafe Rio, Del Taco, IHOP, Jersey Mike's, Jurassic Tacos, McDonald's, Mongolian Grill, Pizza Hut, Sodalicious, Starbucks, Taco Bell, Tropical Smoothie, Wendy's, Zeppe's Italian Ice, [other] Advance Parts, Big O Tire, JiffyLube, Smith's/gas, Walmart, **W** [gas] Exxon, Love's/McDonald's/dsl/scales/24hr, [food] Cracker Barrel, [lodging] Days Inn, Microtel, [other] Quality RV Ctr
	PAYSON
257b a	US 6 E, UT 156, Spanish Fork, **E** [gas] Chevron, Chevron/dsl, Exxon, Maverik, Shell, Texaco, Texaco/dsl/LP, [food] Arby's, Arctic Circle, Beto's Mexican, Burger King, Cafe Rio, Cafe Zupas, Carl's Jr, Chick-fil-A, Chili's, China Wok, Chipotle, Costa Vida, Cubby's Cafe, Culver's, Cupbop, Five Guys, In-N-Out, Italian Place, JDawgs, Jersey Mike's, Jimmy John's, Jurassic Tacos, KFC, Kneaders, Little Caesar's, McDonald's, Mo Bettahs Hawaiian, Mod Pizza, Olive Garden, Panda Express, Papa Murphy's, Pizza Factory, Popeyes, R&R BBQ, Roxberry Juice, Slim Chicken, Sonic, Starbucks, Swig, Taco Bell, Teriyaki Grill, TX Roadhouse, Wendy's, Zao Asian, [lodging] Hampton Inn, Quality Inn, [other] $Tree, Ace Hardware, AT&T, AutoZone, Big O Tire, Cal Store, Costco/gas, Discount Tire, Good Earth Mkt, Hobby Lobby, Jiffy Lube, Lowe's, Macey's Foods, O'Reilly Parts, PetCo, Ross, Target, TJ Maxx, Verizon, Walmart, **W** Chevrolet, Chrysler/Dodge/Jeep
253	UT 164, to Spanish Fork
250	UT 115, Payson, **E** [gas] Chevron/dsl, [food] McDonald's, Subway,

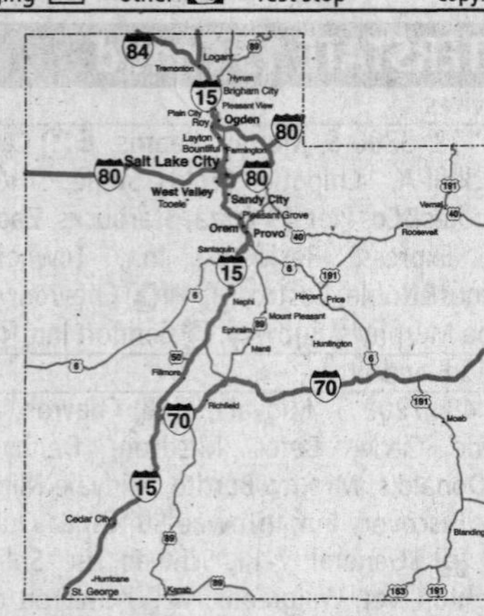

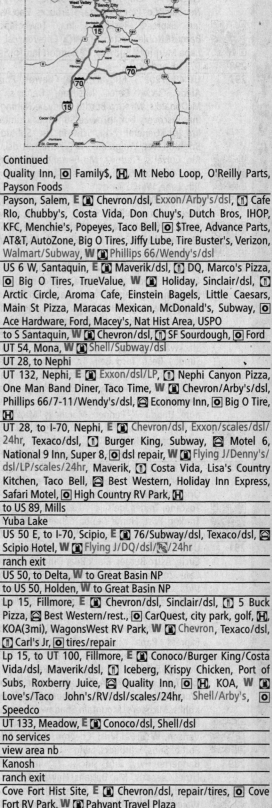

Exit #	Services
250	Continued Quality Inn, [other] Family$, [H], Mt Nebo Loop, O'Reilly Parts, Payson Foods
248	Payson, Salem, **E** [gas] Chevron/dsl, Exxon/Arby's/dsl, [food] Cafe Rio, Chubby's, Costa Vida, Don Chuy's, Dutch Bros, IHOP, KFC, Menchie's, Popeyes, Taco Bell, [other] $Tree, Advance Parts, AT&T, AutoZone, Big O Tires, Jiffy Lube, Tire Buster's, Verizon, Walmart/Subway, **W** [gas] Phillips 66/Wendy's/dsl
244	US 6 W, Santaquin, **E** [gas] Maverik/dsl, [food] DQ, Marco's Pizza, [other] Big O Tires, TrueValue, **W** [gas] Holiday, Sinclair/dsl, [food] Arctic Circle, Aroma Cafe, Einstein Bagels, Little Caesars, Main St Pizza, Maracas Mexican, McDonald's, Subway, [other] Ace Hardware, Ford, Macey's, Nat Hist Area, USPO
	NEPHI
242	to S Santaquin, **W** [gas] Chevron/dsl, [food] SF Sourdough, [other] Ford
233	UT 54, Mona, **W** [gas] Shell/Subway/dsl
228	UT 28, to Nephi
225	UT 132, Nephi, **E** [gas] Exxon/dsl/LP, [food] Nephi Canyon Pizza, One Man Band Diner, Taco Time, **W** [gas] Chevron/Arby's/dsl, Phillips 66/7-11/Wendy's/dsl, [lodging] Economy Inn, [other] Big O Tire, [H]
222	UT 28, to I-70, Nephi, **E** [gas] Chevron/dsl, Exxon/scales/dsl/24hr, Texaco/dsl, [food] Burger King, Subway, [lodging] Motel 6, National 9 Inn, Super 8, [other] dsl repair, **W** [gas] Flying J/Denny's/dsl/LP/scales/24hr, Maverik, [food] Costa Vida, Lisa's Country Kitchen, Taco Bell, [lodging] Best Western, Holiday Inn Express, Safari Motel, [other] High Country RV Park, [H]
207	to US 89, Mills
202	Yuba Lake
188	US 50 E, to I-70, Scipio, **E** [gas] 76/Subway/dsl, Texaco/dsl, [lodging] Scipio Hotel, **W** [gas] Flying J/DQ/dsl/[RS]/24hr
	FILLMORE
184	ranch exit
178	US 50, to Delta, **W** to Great Basin NP
174	to US 50, Holden, **W** to Great Basin NP
167	Lp 15, Fillmore, **E** [gas] Chevron/dsl, Sinclair/dsl, [food] 5 Buck Pizza, [lodging] Best Western/rest., [other] CarQuest, city park, golf, [H], KOA(3mi), WagonsWest RV Park, **W** [gas] Chevron, Texaco/dsl, [food] Carl's Jr, [other] tires/repair
163	Lp 15, to UT 100, Fillmore, **E** [gas] Conoco/Burger King/Costa Vida/dsl, Maverik/dsl, [food] Iceberg, Krispy Chicken, Port of Subs, Roxberry Juice, [lodging] Quality Inn, [other] [H], KOA, **W** [gas] Love's/Taco John's/RV/dsl/scales/24hr, Shell/Arby's, [other] Speedco
158	UT 133, Meadow, **E** [gas] Conoco/dsl, Shell/dsl
153mm	no services
151mm	view area nb
146	Kanosh
138	ranch exit
135	Cove Fort Hist Site, **E** [gas] Chevron/dsl, repair/tires, [other] Cove Fort RV Park, **W** [gas] Pahvant Travel Plaza
132	I-70 E, to Denver
129	Sulphurdale

UT

INTERSTATE 15 Cont'd

Exit #	Services
125	ranch exit
120	Manderfield

BEAVER

Exit #	Services
112	to UT 21, Beaver, Manderfield, E Chevron/dsl, Conoco/dsl, Sinclair/dsl, Craigo's Pizza, Crazy Cow Cafe, Loaded Burgers, McDonald's, Subway, Best Western, Country Inn, De Lano Motel/RV Park, Lotus Hotel, Motel 6, auto/RV/dsl repair, Big O Tires, Family$, H, KOA(1mi), W Flying J/cafe/dsl/scales/24hr, Denny's, Wendy's, Days Inn, to Great Basin NP
109	to UT 21, Beaver, E Shell/Burger King/dsl/RV dump, Spirit/dsl, Comfort Inn, Beaver Camping, W Chevron/DQ/dsl, KanKun Mexican, Timberline Rest., Wingate, to Great Basin NP, truck wash
100	ranch exit
95	UT 20, to US 89, to Panguitch, E Bryce Canyon NP
88mm	**both lanes, full facilities, litter barrels, petwalk, hist site**
82	UT 271, Paragonah
78	UT 141, E Chevron/dsl, Maverik, Pizza Barn, Mtn View Lodge, Family$, NAPA, ski areas, W TA/Shell/LP/dsl/scales/24hr/@
75	UT 143, E Chevron, Maverik, Phillips 66/dsl, DeDe's Cafe, Pizza Barn, Rolling Stone, Mtn View Lodge, Painted Hills RV Resort, Parowan Mkt, to Brian Head/Cedar Breaks Ski Resorts
71	Summit

CEDAR CITY

Exit #	Services
62	UT 130, Cedar City, E Love's/Carl's Jr/Subway/dsl/scales/24hr, Phillips 66/dsl, 5 Buck Pizza, Alfredo's Mexican, Arctic Circle, The Hub Pizza, Cedar Breaks RV Park, H, st patrol, The Tire, W Maverik/dsl, Travelodge, truck stop/@
59	UT 56, Cedar City, E Chevron, Chevron/DQ/dsl, Maverik, Phillips 66/dsl/LP, Shell/dsl, Sinclair/dsl, A&W/KFC, Arby's, Burger King, Denny's, Domino's, Firehouse Subs, Great Harvest Bread Co., Hermie's Drive-In, Hong Kong Buffet, IHOP, Jimmy John's, Little Caesar's, McDonald's/playplace, Papa Murphy's, Rita's, Sizzler, Taco Bell, Teriyaki Grill, Wendy's, Zaxby's, Abbey Inn, Best Value Inn, Best Western, Best Western+, Quality Inn, Buick/Chevrolet, Lin's Mkt, NAPA, The Tire, Tire Company, Tire Pros, to Southern Utah U, USPO, Verizon, W Maverik/dsl, Sunoco/dsl, Chef Alfredo's, Mkt Grill, Subway, Tropical Smoothie, Motel 6, Ramada, Super 8, Carquest
57	Lp 15, to UT 14, Cedar City, E Chevron/repair/24hr, Maverik, Phillips 66/dsl, Culver's, DoughnutsVille, DQ, Dutch Bros, Golden Corral, Jamba Juice, Mo Bettahs Hawaiian, Pizza Hut, Subway, Swig, Comfort Inn, Courtyard, Holiday Inn Express, La Quinta, SpringHill Suites, Wingate, $Tree, AT&T, AutoZone, Big O Tire, Bryce Cyn, CAL Ranch, Duck Crk, H, Navajo Lake, O'Reilly Parts, Ross, Smith's Food/dsl, TJ Maxx, to Cedar Breaks, Verizon, W Chevron/dsl, 5 Buck Pizza, Applebee's, Cafe Rio, Chili's, Chipotle, Costa Vida, Del Taco, Jack-in-the-Box, Lupita's Mexican, Ninja Japanese, Panda Express, Papa John's, Starbucks, Subway, Tropical Smoothie, Hampton Inn, Home Depot, Schwab Tire, Verizon, Walgreens, Walmart
51	Kanarraville, Hamilton Ft
44mm	both lanes, full facilities, litter barrels, petwalk, hist site
42	New Harmony, Kanarraville, E Kolob RV Resort, W Shell/dsl
40	to Kolob Canyon, E scenic drive, to Zion's NP, tourist info/
36	Black Ridge

BROWSE

Exit #	Services
33	Snowfield
31	Pintura
30	Browse
27	UT 17, Toquerville, E Grand Canyon, Lake Powell, to Zion NP
23	Leeds, Silver Reef, E Leeds RV Park, Zion West RV Park, W Silver Mine
22	Leeds, Silver Reef, same as 23

WASHINGTON

Exit #	Services
16	UT 9, to Hurricane, E Texaco/dsl, Holiday Inn Express, Coral Springs Resort, Harley-Davidson, Walmart Dist Ctr
13	Washington Pkwy, E Chevron, Maverik/dsl, 7 Brothers Burgers, Black Bear Diner, Culver's, McDonald's, Papa John's, Best Western+, Settlers Point RV Resort
10	Middleton Dr, Washington, E Phillips 66/dsl, Bishop's Cafe, Burger King, Costa Vida, Crepe Station, Cupbop, Del Taco, Don Pedro's Mexican, Dutch Bros, El Pollo Loco, Freddy's, Hungry Howie's, IHOP, In-N-Out, Jack-in-the-Box, Jimmy John's, Little Caesar's, Mad Pita, McDonald's, Pizza Factory, Pizza Hut, Red Robin, Royal Thai, Rumbi Grill, Sonic, Starbucks, Subway, Taco Bell, TX Roadhouse, Wendy's, Comfort Inn, Quality Inn, $Tree, Albertsons, AT&T, AutoZone, Best Buy, Cal Stores, Costco/gas, Discount Tire, Home Depot, Kohl's, Natural Grocers, O'Reilly Parts, PetCo, Ross, vet, Walmart, W Chevron, Maverik, Spring Hill, auto repair, St George RV Park/camping

ST GEORGE

Exit #	Services
8	St George Blvd, St George, E Chevron, Texaco/dsl, Applebee's, Buffalo Wild Wings, Cafe Zupas, Carl's Jr, Chick-fil-A, Chili's, Chipotle, ChuckaRama, Coldstone, Cubby's, Einstein Bagels, Firehouse Subs, Five Guys, Golden Corral, Habit Burger, Jimmy John's, Olive Garden, Outback Steaks, Panda Express, Pieology Pizzeria, Pizzeria Limone, Red Lobster, Starbucks, Subway, Super Chix, Winger's, Best Inn, Courtyard, Hampton Inn, Ramada Inn, TownePlace Suites, $Tree, AT&T, Dick's, Harmon's Foods, H, Lowe's, Old Navy, PetSmart, Ross, Staples, Sunrise Tire, Target, TJ Maxx, Verizon, Zion Outlets/famous brands, W Maverik/Cinnabon, Shell/dsl, Sinclair/dsl, Texaco/dsl, A&W/KFC, Denny's, El Patron Mexican, Iceberg Drive-In, La Botana, McDonald's, Menchie's, Nielsen's Custard, Ocean Buffet, Papa John's, Pinkbox Doughnuts, Sakura Japanese, Smoked Taco, Swig, Taco Bell, Wendy's, Best Western, Chalet Motel, Coronada Inn, Days Inn, EconoLodge, Economy Inn, Knights Inn, Motel 6, Rodeway Inn, Sands Motel, Super 8, Auto Tech/tires, Big O Tire, NAPA, O'Reilly Parts, to LDS Temple, vet
6	UT 18, Bluff St, St George, E Chevron/dsl, Delta, Texaco/dsl, Cracker Barrel, Culver's, Jack-in-the-Box, Rib Chop House, Comfort Inn, Fairfield Inn, Hilton Garden, Hyatt Place, My Place Hotel, Staybridge Suites, Tru, Buick/GMC, Hyundai, Kia, museum, Subaru, VW, W Chevron, Maverik, Shell, Arby's, Black Bear Diner, Blaze Pizza, Burger King, Chef Alfredo's, Chick-fil-A, Denny's, Jersey Mike's, Jimmy John's, LongHorn Steaks, McDonald's, Mo Bettahs Hawaiian, Rusty Crab Daddy, Swig, TX Hot Chicken, Best Western, Claridge Inn, Clarion Suites, Howard Johnson, Quality Inn, Red Lion Hotel, Red Roof Inn, St George Inn, auto/truck repair, AutoZone, Big O Tire, Cadillac/Chevrolet, Chrysler/Dodge/Jeep, Ford/Lincoln, funpark, Honda, H, Lazydays RV, Mazda, Mercedes, Nissan, Toyota, Verizon
5	Dixie Dr
4	Brigham Rd, Bloomington, E Pilot/Burger King/parking/dsl/scales/24hr, Southern Utah Pizza, La Quinta, W Chevron/Subway/Taco Time/dsl, EVC, Baskin-Robbins, Dickey's BBQ, Hungry Howie's, Pepper's Rest., Tiki Hawaiian, Wendy's, Wingate Inn, Walmart
2	UT 7 E, Southern Pkwy, E, W Chevron/dsl, EVC, Hampton Inn

= gas = food = lodging = other = rest stop

UT

INTERSTATE 15 Cont'd

Exit #	Services
1	port of entry/weigh sta both lanes
0mm	Utah/Arizona state line

INTERSTATE 70

WESTWATER

Exit #	Services
232mm	Utah/Colorado state line
227	Westwater
221	ranch exit
214	to Cisco
204	UT 128, to Cisco
193	Yellowcat Ranch Exit
190mm	Welcome Ctr wb, full facilities, litter barrels, vending, info
187	Thompson, N Exxon/7-11/dsl, Ballard RV Park, Desert Moon Hotel & RV/Tent camping
185mm	parking area eb
182	US 191 S, Crescent Jct, to Moab, N Papa Joe's, S to Arches/Canyonlands NP
181mm	eb, full facilities, litter barrels, scenic view

GREEN RIVER

Exit #	Services
175	ranch exit
164	UT 19, Green River, N Conoco/Champs/Little Caesars/dsl, Pilot/rest/dsl/scales/24hr, Silver Eagle/Blimpie/dsl, Tesla EVC, Tamarisk Rest., Best Value Inn, Comfort Inn, First Choice, Motel 6, River Terrace Inn, Super 8, Travelodge, KOA, Powell River Museum, same as 160
160	UT 19, Green River, N Love's/Arbys/RV Hookup/dsl, Maverik/dsl, Chowhound, La Veracruzana, Ray's Rest., Budget Inn, Holiday Inn Express, River Rock Inn Utah, Sleepy Hollow Motel, Ace Hardware, city park, Green River SP, NAPA/repair, same as 164, Shady Acres RV Park, USPO
157	US 6 W, US 191 N, to Price, Salt Lake
149	UT 24 W, to Hanksville, to Capitol Reef, Lake Powell, S Goblin Valley SP
146	**restrooms wb, view area**
144mm	runaway truck ramp eb
143mm	toilets both lanes, view area both lanes
142mm	runaway truck ramp eb
138mm	brake check area eb, toilet eb
131	Temple Mt Rd
122mm	Ghost Rock View Area both lanes, toilets both lanes
116	to Moore, restrooms wb
115	Devil's Canyon View Area eb, toilets eb

PRICE

Exit #	Services
108	ranch exit
105mm	**Salt Wash View Area both lanes**
99	ranch exit
91	UT 10 N, UT 72, to Emery, Price, S Capitol Reef NP
86mm	both lanes, full facilities, littler barrels, petwalk
73	ranch exit
63	Gooseberry Rd

RICHFIELD

Exit #	Services
56	US 89 N, to Salina, US 50 W, to Delta, NEXT SERVICES 109 MI EB, N Exxon/dsl, Maverik, Phillips 66/Carl's Jr/dsl, Sinclair/dsl, Denny's, El Mexicano Mexican, Mom's Cafe, Subway, EconoLodge, Quality Inn, Super 8, Barretts Foods, Butch Cassidy RV Camp, Family$, NAPA, truck/RV/auto repair, S Love's/Arby's/dsl/scales/24hr, Xpress/parking/dsl
48	UT 24, to US 50, Sigurd, Aurora, S Capitol Reef NP, Fishlake NF
40	Lp 70, Richfield, S Chevron/dsl, Flying J/PJ Fresh/dsl/LP/rest./24hr, Maverik/dsl, Texaco/dsl, Arby's, Papa Murphy's, Ross's Pizza, Subway, Taco Time, Best Western, Holiday Inn Express, OYO, Ramada Inn, Super 8, Big O Tire, Buick/Cadillac/Chevrolet/GMC, Chrysler/Dodge/Jeep, city park, Fresh Mkt, H, IFA Store, NAPA, RV/truck repair, USPO

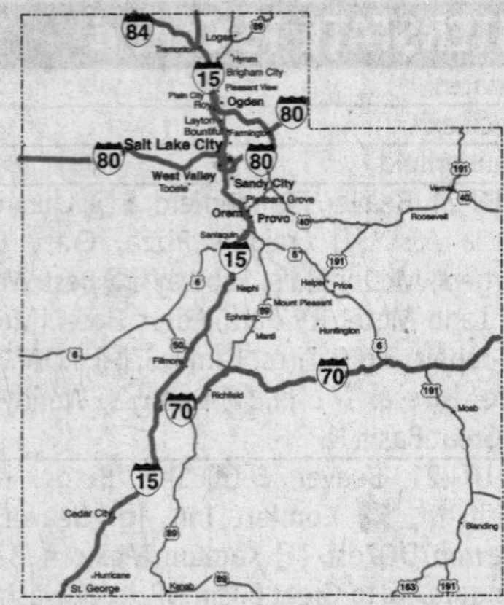

BRYCE CANYON

Exit #	Services
37	Lp 70, Richfield, S Phillips 66/Wendy's/dsl, Silver Eagle/Burger King/dsl, Black Bear Diner, Costa Vida, Domino's, KFC/Taco Bell, Little Caesar's, Lotsa Motsa Pizza, McDonald's, Pizza Hut, Sagebrush Steakhouse, Wingers, Comfort Inn, Fairfield Inn, Hampton Inn, New West Motel, Quality Inn, Royal Inn, Sandi's, $Tree, Ace Hardware, AutoZone, Fish Lake/Capitol Reef Parks, Ford, golf, Home Depot, KOA, O'Reilly Parts, Pearson Tire, to Fish Lake/Capitol Reef Parks, Verizon, Walmart/auto
31	Elsinore, Monroe, S Silver Eagle/Carl's Jr/dsl
25	UT 118, Joseph, Monroe, S Flying U Country Store/dsl/RV park
23	US 89 S, to Panguitch, Bryce Canyon
17	N camping, chain-up area wb, Fremont Indian SP, S Castle Rock Camping
13mm	brake test area eb
7	Clear Creek Canyon Rd
3mm	Western Boundary Fishlake NF
1	N Cove Fort Historic Site
0mm	I-15, N to SLC, S to St George. I-70 begins/ends on I-15, exit 132.

INTERSTATE 80

ECHO

Exit #	Services
197mm	Utah/Wyoming state line, Utah/Wyoming state line
191	Wahsatch
187	ranch exit
185	Castle Rock
182mm	Port of Entry/weigh sta wb
178	(from wb), Emery
170	**full facilities, litter barrels, petwalk, RV dump, vending, Welcome Ctr wb/ eb**
169	Echo
168	I-84 W, to Ogden, I-80 E, to Cheyenne
166	view area both lanes
162	Coalville, 164 Coalville, N Phillips 66/dsl/mart, Best Western, Echo Island RV Park, Holiday Hills RV Camp/LP, S Chevron/dsl, Sinclair/dsl, Polar King, Subway, Burt Bros Tires, NAPA, Neena's Mkt, to Echo Res RA, USPO
155	UT 32 S, Wanship, S Sinclair/dsl, Rockport SP
150	toll gate promontory
146b a	US 40 E, to Heber, Provo, N Sinclair/Subway/Pizza Hut/dsl, Lush's Tennessee BBQ, S Exxon/7-11/dsl, Burt Bros Tires, Home Depot
146mm	view area/chain up wb
145	UT 224, Kimball Jct, to Park City, N Chevrolet, Ford, Park City RV Park, vet, S Chevron/dsl, Arby's, Big Daddy's Pizza, Cafe Rio, Coldstone, Cortona, Del Taco, Domino's, Five Guys, Ghidottis Italian, Glyn Thai, Great Harvest Bread Co, Hearth & Hill, I Love Moo, Jimmy John's, Loco Lizard Cantina, Maxwell's, McDonald's, Panda Express, Protein Foundry, Red Rock Cafe, Sammy's Bistro, Starbucks, Sterling Steaks,

INTERSTATE 80 Cont'd

PARLEY'S SUMMIT

145 Continued
Szechwan Chinese, Taco Bell, Vessel Kitchen, Wendy's, Whole Foods Mkt, Zupas, AC Hotel, Best Western, Holiday Inn Express, Newpark Resort, Best Buy, Enterprise Car Rental, Michaels, Outlet Mall/famous brands, Park City Ski Area, Petco, Smith's Foods/dsl, Staples, TJ Maxx, USPO, Verizon, visitors info, Walmart

144mm eb

141 ranch exit, **N** Phillips 66/Subway/dsl, Burt Bros Tires, **S** Billy Blanco Mexican, O'Shucks Grill, Park City Bread Co., Starbucks, Macey's Mkt

140 Parley's Summit, Parley's Summit, **S** Shell/dsl, The Moose Café

137 Lamb's Canyon

134 UT 65, Emigration Canyon, East Canyon, **N** Little Dell RA

133 utility exit(from eb)

132 ranch exit

131 (from eb) , Quarry

130 I-215 S(from wb)

129 UT 186 W, Foothill Dr, Parley's Way

128 I-215 S(from eb)

127 UT 195, 23rd E St, to Holladay

126 UT 181, 13th E St, to Sugar House, **N** Chevron, A&W/KFC, Cafe Rio, Chick-fil-A, Olive Garden, Red Lobster, Starbucks, Taco Bell, Target, Wendy's, Extended Stay America, Verizon

125 UT 71, 7th E St, **N** Cubby's, Dee's Rest., Jimmy John's, Jinya Ramen, Little Caesar's, Olympian Rest.

124 US 89, S State St, **N** 7-11, Cafe Rio, Cane's Chicken, Chipotle, Del Taco, Jack-in-the-Box, Moochie's Sandwiches, Rusted Sun Pizza, Strarbucks, Subway, Chrysler/Dodge/Jeep, Discount Tire, Mom's Kitchen, WinCo, **S** Drunken Chinese, Comfort Inn

123mm I-15, N to Ogden, S to Provo

122mm I-80 and I-15 merge for approx 4 mi. See I-15, exits 305-307.

121 600 S, to City Ctr

120 I-15 N, to Ogden

118 UT 68, Redwood Rd, to N Temple, **N** Chevron/dsl, Love's/Arby's/dsl/scales/24hr, Apollo Burger, Burger King, Carl's Jr, Denny's, Taco Bell, Wendy's, Comfort Suites, Dream Inn, Holiday Inn Express, Motel 6, Radisson, Sonesta Suites, The Point, 7-11, **S** Maverik/dsl, H

117 I-215, N to Ogden, S to Provo

115b a Bangerter Hwy, **N** Salt Lake

114 Wright Bros Dr(from wb), **N** same as 113

113 5600 W(from eb), **N** Phillips 66/dsl, Perkins, Port of Subs, Subway, Best Western+, Clarion, Comfort Suites, Courtyard, DoubleTree, Fairfield Inn, Hampton Inn, Hilton Garden, Holiday Inn, Homewood Suites, Hyatt Place, La Quinta, Microtel, Quality Inn, Residence Inn, Sheraton, SpringHill Suites, Super 8, Tru Hilton

111 7200 W

104 UT 202, Saltair Dr, to Magna, **N** Great Salt Lake SP

102 UT 201(from eb), to Magna

101mm view area wb

99 UT 36, to Tooele, **N** Starbucks, **S** Chevron/dsl, Flying J/Denny's/dsl/scales/LP/24hr, Sinclair/dsl, TA/Burger King/dsl/scales/24hr/@, Arby's, Del Taco, McDonald's, Comfort Inn/Suites, Oquirrh Motel/RV Park, H, SpeedCo

94mm New Exit

88 to Grantsville

84 UT 138, to Grantsville, Tooele

77 UT 196, to Rowley, Dugway

70 to Delle, **S** Delle/Sinclair/café/dsl

62 to Lakeside, Eagle Range

BONNEVILLE SPEEDWAY

56 to Aragonite

55mm **full facilities, litter barrels, petwalk, both lanes, vending**

49 to Clive

41 Knolls

26mm architectural POI (The Tree)

10mm **full facilities, litter barrels, observation area, petwalk, both lanes, vending**

4 Bonneville Speedway, **N** Sinclair/dsl/café/24hr

3mm Port of Entry, weigh sta both lanes

2 UT 58(no EZ wb return), Wendover, **S** Shell/AM Best/dsl, Sinclair/dsl, Rolberto's Mexican, Subway, Best Western+, Bonneville Inn, EVC, Knights Inn, Motel 6, Quality Inn, Super 8, Western Ridge Motel, Carquest, Family$

0mm Utah/Nevada state line, Mountain/Pacific time zone

INTERSTATE 84

120 I-84 begins/ends on I-80, exit 168 near Echo, Utah.

115 Ut 65 S, to Henefer, Echo, to Henefer, Echo, **S** E Canyon SP, USPO

112 UT 86 E, Henefer

111 Croydon

111mm Devil's Slide Scenic View

108 Taggart, **N** Taggart's Grill

106 ranch exit

103 UT 66, Morgan, **N** Ford, **S** Chevron/dsl, Exxon/dsl, Deb's Spicy Pie, McDonald's, Milk Barn Creamery, River Burger, Smokin' Boxcar BBQ, Subway, Cobblestone Hotel, Ace Hardware, city park, E Canyon SP, Family$, NAPA, Ridley's Mkt, URGENT CARE, USPO

96 Peterson, **N** ski areas, **S** Phillips 66/dsl

94mm **full facilities, litter barrels, petwalk, wb**

92 UT 167(from eb), to Huntsville, ski areas, **N** Sinclair/dsl, city park

91mm **eb, full facilities, litter barrels, petwalk**

87b a US 89, to Ogden, Layton, Ogden, **N** Best Western+, Goodyear/auto, **E** Seven Brothers, Starbucks, **W** EVC

85 S Weber, Uintah

81 to I-15 S, UT 26, Riverdale Rd, **N** Maverik/dsl, Sinclair/dsl, Speedway, Applebee's, Arby's, Buffalo Wild Wings, Carl's Jr, Chili's, Chipotle, El Pollo Loco, Habit Burger, Honeybaked Ham, IHOP, Jamba Juice, Jersey Mike's, McDonald's, MOD Pizza, Starbucks, Subway, Super Chix, Wendy's, $Tree, AT&T, Best Buy, Buick/GMC, Good Earth Foods, Hobby Lobby, Home Depot, Honda, Kia, Lowe's Whse, Nissan, PepBoys, PetSmart, Sam's Club/gas, Schwab Tire, Target, Toyota, Verizon, Walmart, **S** Motel 6, Chrysler/Dodge/Jeep, **E** Wingstop, Zao Asian, Jiffy Lube, **W** Maverik, Golden Spike Park/restrooms, Harley-Davidson

80mm I-84 and I-15 run together. Exits 344-379.

41 I-15 N to Pocatello

40 UT 102, Tremonton, Bothwell, **N** Chevron/dsl/wash/24hr, Maverik/dsl, Sinclair/Burger King/dsl/scales/@, Tesla EVC, McDonald's, Wendy's, Hampton Inn, Western Inn, H(4mi), O'Reilly Parts, **S** to Golden Spike NHS, **E** Exxon, The Grille, True Value

SNOWVILLE

39 to Garland, Bothwell, **N** H

32 ranch exit

26 UT 83 S, to Howell, **S** to Golden Spike NHS

24 to Valley

20 to Blue Creek

17 ranch exit

16 to Hansel Valley(from wb)

12 ranch exit

7 Snowville, **N** Flying J/Pepperoni's/dsl/LP/24hr, Sinclair/A&W/dsl, Mollie's Café, Ranch House Diner, Black Pine Inn, city park, Hitching Post RV Park, USPO

UT

UT

INTERSTATE 84 Cont'd

Exit #	Services
5	UT 30, to Park Valley
0mm	Utah/Idaho state line

INTERSTATE 215 (Salt Lake)

Exit #	Services
29	I-215 begins/ends on I-15.
28	UT 68, Redwood Rd, E Pony Express RV Park, W Flying J/dsl/LP/24hr/@, Maverik/dsl
26	Legacy Pkwy
25	22nd N
23	7th N, E Chevron, Exxon/dsl, Love's/Arbys/dsl/scales/24hr, Maverik, Apollo Burger, Burger King, Carl's Jr, Denny's, McDonald's, Papa Murphy's, Subway, Taco Bell, Wendy's, Motel 6, $General, $Tree, Lucky Mkt, W Inn, Comfort Suites, Holiday Inn Express, Radisson, Sonesta Suites
22b a	I-80, W to Wendover, E to Cheyenne
21	California Ave, E Maverik, Sapp Bros/Sinclair/Burger King/dsl/@, Shell/7-11/dsl, RV/Truckwash, W Chevron/dsl, Horn of Africa, Port of Subs, auto repair
20b a	UT 201, W to Magna, 21st S, W Maverik/dsl, Charley's Sandwiches, Del Taco, Goodyear, Kenworth
18	UT 171, 3500 S, W Valley, E 7-11, Applebee's, Burger King, Cracker Barrel, Greek Souvlaki, IHOP, La Fountain Mexican, Best Western, Comfort Inn, Country Inn Suites, Crystal Inn, Extended Stay, Extended Stay America, Holiday Inn Express, Sleep Inn, Staybridge Suites, Advance Parts, H, PepBoys, W Chevron, Arby's, AT&T, Cafe Rio, Cupbop, Dutch Bros, In-N-Out, Jamba Juice, Jimmy John's, Olive Garden, Panda Express, Pizza Hut, Pizza Hut, Red Robin, Starbucks, Waffle Love, Wendy's, Wienerschnitzel, Winger's, Zupas, Embassy Suites, SpringHill Suites, Big O Tire, Costco/gas, CVS Drug, Hobby Lobby, JC Penney, Old Navy, Petco, Ross, URGENT CARE, Verizon
15	UT 266, 47th S, Sinclair/dsl, E 7-11, Speedway, Speedway, Arctic Circle, Beto's Mexican, Dee's Rest., Del Taco, KFC, Moki's Hawaiian Grill, Pizza Hut, Swig, Wendy's, $Tree, auto repair, Macey's, Walgreens, W Chevron/dsl, Arby's, Arctic Circle, vet
13	UT 68, Redwood Rd, S Great Harvest, E Chevron, Speedway, Apollo Burger, Applebee's, Arby's, Carl's Jr, Domino's, Francesco's Rest., Jamba Juice, King Buffet, LoLo Hawaiian BBQ, McDonald's, Panda Express, Starbucks, Subway, HomeTowne Studios, $Tree, AT&T, Harmon's Mkt, PetSmart, Ross, Verizon, Walmart, W 7-11, 5 Guys, Cafe Rio, Chick-fil-A, Del Taco, Dutch Bros, Marco's Pizza, Old Spaghetti Factory, Papa Murphy's, Penny Ann's Cafe, Pizza Hut, Taco Bell, TX Roadhouse, Wendy's, Zaxby's, AutoZone, Discount Tire, Petco, Smith's/gas, Target, TJ Maxx, USPO, Valvoline
12	I-15, N to SLC, S to Provo
11	same as 10(from eb)
10	UT 280 E, E Phillips 66, AutoZone, Sam's Club/gas,

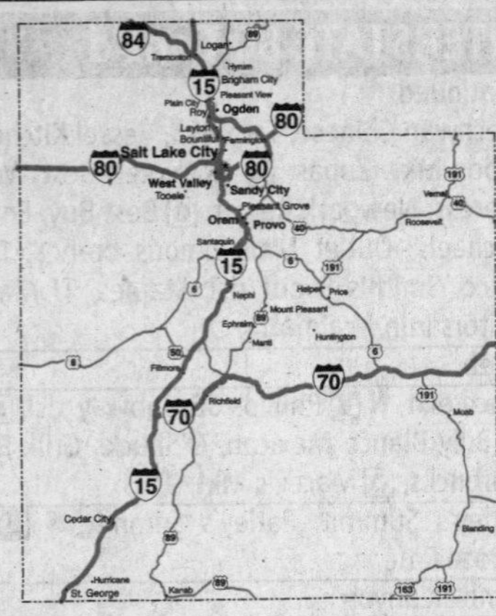

HOLLADAY

Exit #	Services
10	Continued Arby's, Cafe Rio, ChuckARama, Corner Bakery Cafe, East Coast Subs, Macaroni Grill, McDonald's, Olive Garden, Panda Express, Red Lobster, Red Robin, Roxberry Juice, Shake Shack, Subway, Taco Bell, Village Inn, 7-11, Dillard's, Honda, H, Midas, Nordstrom, Pepboys, Ross, Sprouts Mkt, Verizon
9	Union Park Ave, World Mkt, E Maverik, 5 Guys, Arby's, Bucca Italian, Buffalo Wild Wings, Burger King, Cafe Rio, Cafe Zupas, Cane's, Carl's Jr, Chick-fil-A, Chili's, Chipotle, Costa Vida, Cubby's, Dave's Chicken, Denny's, Firehouse Subs, Golden Corral, Handel's Ice Cream, In-N-Out, JDawgs, Jersey Mike's, Jimmy John's, Kneaders, Longhorn Steaks, McDonald's, MOD Pizza, Noodles&Co, Original Pancake, Panda Express, Pizzeria Limone, Sonic, Starbucks, The Habit, Wendy's, Wienerschnitzel, Zao Asian, Holiday Inn Express, Homewood Suites, MainStay Suites, Royal Inn, $Tree, Barnes&Noble, Dick's, Home Depot, Michaels, O'Reilly Parts, Old Navy, Petco, Ross, Smith's Foods, Target, TJ Maxx, Trader Joe's, Verizon, Walmart, W Speedway, Crystal Inn, Studio 6, Wheeler Historic Farm
8	UT 152, 2000 E, E Chevron, KFC, McDonald's, Starbucks, Swig, Taco Bell, Whole Foods Mkt, W Chevron, China Grill, TacoTime, Fairfield Inn, 7-11, Ace Hardware, Discount Tire, Jiffy Lube
6	6200 S, E Tropical Smoothie, Hampton Inn, Hyatt Place, Residence Inn, Alta, Brighton, Snowbird, Solitude/ski areas
5	UT 266, 45th S(from sb), Holladay, W Chevron/7-11
4	39th S, E Chevron/dsl, Sinclair/dsl, Barbacoa Grill, Einstein Bagels, Subway, Macey's, W H
3	33rd S, Wasatch, W Smith's/dsl, Betos Mexican, Cafe Rio, Cafe Zupas, Cupbop, Domino's, Five Guys, KFC/Taco Bell, McDonald's, Menchie's, Pan Wok Chinese, Wendy's, AT&T, PetSmart, REI, Savers, Smith's Mkt, USPO
2	I-80 W
0	I-215 begins/ends on I-80, exit 130.

NOTES

VERMONT

INTERSTATE 89

ST ALBANS

Exit #	Services
130mm	US/Canada Border, Vermont state line, I-89 begins/ends
22(129)	US 7 S, Highgate Springs, E Irving/dsl, DutyFree
129mm	Latitude 45 N, midway between N Pole and Equator
128mm	Rock River
21(123)	US 7, VT 78, Swanton, E Shell/dsl, W Mobil/Subway/dsl, Shell, Sunoco/dsl, Dunkin', McDonald's, Pam's Pizza, Shaggy's Snack Bar, $General, Aubuchon Hardware, Hannaford Foods, NAPA
20(118)	US 7, VT 207, St Albans, E Chevrolet, Toyota, W Mobil/Subway/dsl, Sunoco, Burger King, Dunkin', KFC/Taco Bell, McDonald's, Oriental Kitchen, Pizza Hut, Advance Parts, AT&T, Aubuchon Hardware, Buick/GMC/Cadillac, Ford, Hannaford Foods, H, Jo-Ann Fabrics, Kinney Drug, PriceChopper Foods, TJ Maxx, URGENT CARE, Verizon, Walmart/Subway
19(114)	US 7, VT 36, VT 104, St Albans, W Mobil/dsl, Shell/dsl, Dunkin', Subway, La Quinta, H, st police, vet
111mm	**full facilities, info, litter barrels, petwalk, both lanes, vending, wifi**
18(107)	US 7, VT 104A, Georgia Ctr, E Mobil/dsl, Shell/dsl, GA Farmhouse Rest., $General, GA Auto Parts, repair
17(98)	US 2, US 7, E Mobil, Shell/dsl, camping(4mi), W camping(6mi)
96mm	weigh sta both lanes
16(92)	US 7, US 2, Winooski, E Mobil, Lighthouse Rest., Hampton Inn, Costco/gas, CVS Drug, Osco Drug, Shaw's Foods, W Citgo, Shell/dsl, Athens Diner, Burger King, McDonald's, Subway, Motel 6, Quality Inn
15(91)	VT 15(from nb no return), Winooski, E Days Inn, Handys Extended Stay Suites, to St Michael's Coll, W Mobil/dsl, Shell
90mm	Winooski River
14(89)	US 2, Burlington, E Gulf, Mobil, Shell/dsl, Sunoco/dsl, Valero, Al's Cafe, Applebee's, Chicken Charlie's, Dukes Public House, Dunkin', Hana Japanese, IHOP, Leonardo's Pizza, McDonald's, Moe's SW Grill, Outback Steaks, Pulcinella's, Rotisserie, Starbucks, Subway, Wind Jammer Rest., Zachary's Pizza, Anchorage Inn, Best Western+, Comfort Inn, Delta Hotel, Holiday Inn, Homewood Suites, La Quinta, Aubuchon Hardware, Barnes&Noble, CVS, Hannaford Foods, Healthy Living Mkt, JC Penney, Jo-Ann Fabrics, Kohl's, Midas, PriceChopper, Target, Trader Joe's, USPO, W Mobil/dsl, Shell, DoubleTree, Advance Parts, H, Michael's, PetCo, Staples, to UVT, Verizon
13(87)	I-189, to US 7, Burlington, N Citgo/dsl, Sunoco/dsl, Buffalo Wild Wings, China Express, Chipotle, Five Guys, Starbucks, Subway, $Tree, GNC, Hyundai/Subaru, Kinney Drug, PriceChopper Mkt, Shaw's Foods, TJ Maxx, USPO, Walgreens, S Gulf, Irving, Mobil/dsl, Shell/dsl, Sunoco, Burger King, Chicago Grill, Denny's, Koto Japanese, Lakeview House Rest., McDonald's, Olive Garden, Panera Bread, Pauline's Cafe, Zen Garden, Comfort Suites, Holiday Inn Express, North Star Motel, Travelodge, Acura/Audi, Advance Parts, Buick/Cadillac/GMC, Chevrolet, Chrysler/Dodge, Ford, Hannaford Foods, Jeep, Lowe's, Nissan, O'Reilly Parts, Tire Whse, Toyota, URGENT CARE, Verizon, VW
12(84)	VT 2A, to US 2, to Essex Jct, Williston, E EVC, Mobil, Sunoco/Dunkin'/dsl, 99 Rest., Chili's, Friendly's, Longhorn Steaks, Moe's SW Grill, Panera Bread, Starbucks,

WINOOSKI

BURLINGTON

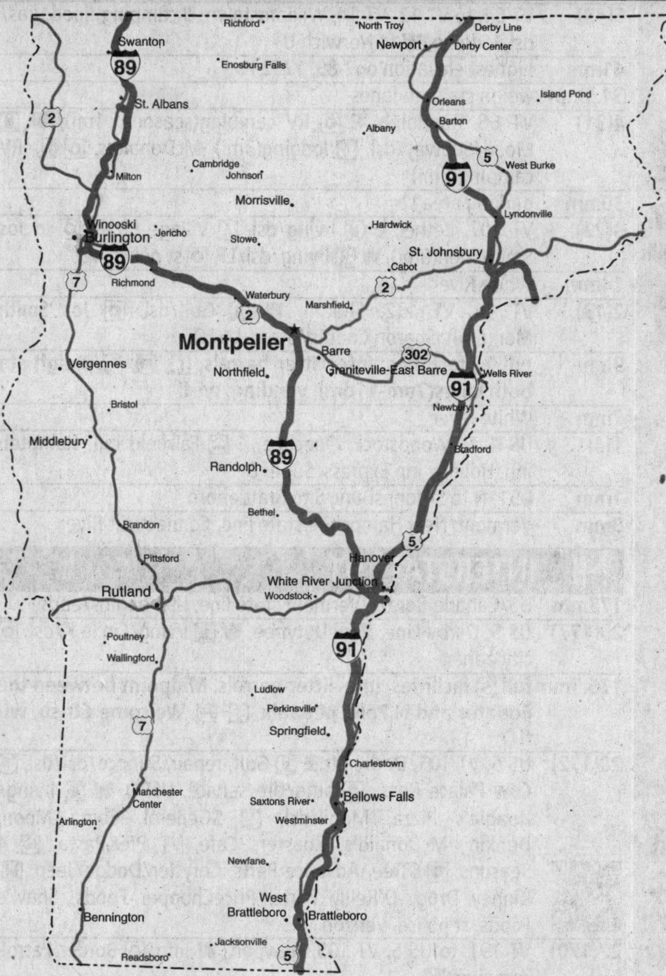

RICHMOND

Exit #	Services
12(84)	Continued TX Roadhouse, VT Taphouse, Fairfield, Best Buy, CVS Drug, Dick's, Hannaford Foods, Home Depot, Marshall's, Natural Provisions Mkt, Old Navy, PetSmart, Shaws Foods/Osco, st police, Staples, Town Fair Tire, Verizon, Walmart, W Courtyard, Sonesta Suites
82mm	**full facilities, litter barrels, petwalk, both lanes(7am-11pm), vending, WiFi**
11(79)	US 2, to VT 117, Richmond, W Mobil/dsl
67mm	parking area/weigh sta sb
66mm	weigh sta nb
10(64)	VT 100, to US 2, Waterbury, E Mobil/dsl, Shell/dsl, Hong Kong Chinese, Thai Smile, Best Western+, Fairfield Inn, Shaws Foods/Osco Drug, TrueValue, W Citgo/dsl, Maxi's Rest., Zachary's Pizza, USPO
9(59)	US 2, to VT 100B, Middlesex, W EVC, Red Hen Baking Co, museum, st police
8(53)	US 2, Montpelier, E Citgo, Cumberland Farms /dsl, Mobil/dsl, Shell/dsl, China Star, Domino's, Dunkin', Julio's, Sarducci's Rest., Capitol Plaza Hotel, Aubuchon Hardware, camping(6mi), O'Reilly Parts, Shaw's Foods, Sunoco/repair, to VT Coll
7(50)	VT 62, to US 302, Barre, E Irving/dsl, Tesla EVC, Applebee's, Comfort Suites, Hilltop Inn, camping(7mi), Honda, H, JC Penney, Shaw's Foods, Subaru, Toyota, Walmart

BARRE

VT

VT

INTERSTATE 89 Cont'd

BETHEL

Exit #	Services
6(47)	VT 63, to VT 14, S Barre, E camping, food, gas, info, lodging
5(43)	VT 64, to VT 12, VT 14, Williamstown, E camping, food, gas/dsl, lodging, W to Norwich U
41mm	highest elevation on I-89, 1752 ft
34.5mm	weigh sta both lanes
4(31)	VT 66, Randolph, E [other] RV camping(seasonal 1mi), W [gas] Mobil/Subway/dsl, [food] lodging(3mi), McDonald's, [other] [H], RV camping(5mi)
30mm	parking area sb
3(22)	VT 107, Bethel, E [gas] Irving/dsl, [food] Village Pizza, [other] to Jos Smith Mon(8mi), W [gas] Irving/dsl/LP, [other] st police, vet
14mm	White River
2(13)	VT 14, VT 132, Sharon, W [gas] Gulf/dsl, [other] Jos Smith Mon(6mi), Sharon Country Store, USPO
9mm	**full [handicap] facilities, info, litter barrels, [phone], [picnic], [RS]/weigh sta both lanes(7am-11pm), vending, wi-fi**
7mm	White River
1(4)	US 4, to Woodstock, Quechee, E [lodging] Fairfield Inn, Hampton Inn, Holiday Inn Express, Super 8
1mm	I-91, N to St Johnsbury, S to Brattleboro
0mm	Vermont/New Hampshire state line, Connecticut River

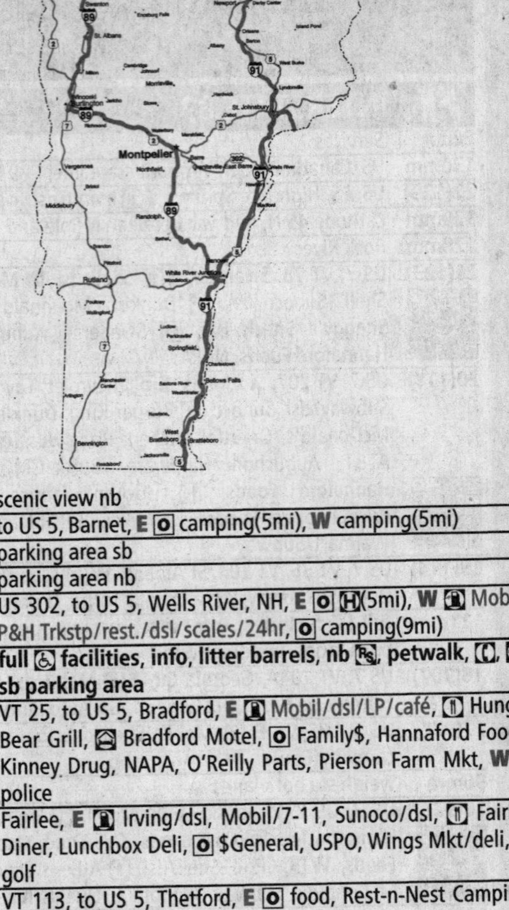

INTERSTATE 91

NEWPORT · ST JOHNSBURY · BARNET · WILDER · ASCUTNEY

Exit #	Services
178mm	US/Canada Border, Vermont state line, I-91 begins/ends.
29(177)	US 5, Derby Line, E [other] Dutyfree, W [gas] Irving/Circle K/dsl, [other] city park
176.5mm	**full [handicap] facilities, info, litter barrels, Midpoint between the Equator and N Pole, petwalk, [phone], [picnic], Welcome Ctr sb, wi-fi**
28(172)	US 5, VT 105, Derby Ctr, E [gas] Gulf, repair, Sunoco/dsl/dsl, [food] Cow Palace Rest., [other] auto/tire service, USPO, W [gas] Irving/Hoagie's Pizza, Mobil/dsl, [food] $General, China Moon, Dunkin', McDonald's, Roasters Cafe, VT Pie&Pasta, [lodging] 4 Seasons, [other] $Tree, Advance Parts, Chrysler/Dodge/Jeep, [H], Kinney Drug, O'Reilly Parts, PriceChopper Foods, Shaw's Foods, st police, Verizon
27(170)	VT 191, to US 5, VT 105, Newport, W info, [other] Border Patrol, camping, [H]
167mm	parking area/weigh sta both directions
26(161)	US 5, VT 58, Orleans, E [gas] Pit Stop, Sunoco/dsl, [food] Subway, [other] Family$, Thibaults Mkt, TrueValue, USPO
156.5mm	Barton River
25(156)	VT 16, Barton, E [gas] Irving/Circle K/dsl, [food] Parson's Corner Rest., [other] C&C Foods, Kinney Drug, O'Reilly Parts, USPO
154mm	parking area nb
150.5mm	highest elevation on I-91, 1856 ft
143mm	scenic overlook nb
141mm	**full [handicap] facilities, info, litter barrels, [phone], [picnic], [RS] sb**
24(140)	VT 122, Wheelock, E food, gas, lodging
23(137)	US 5, to VT 114, Lyndonville, E [gas] Irving/dsl, Mobil/Dunkin', [food] Hoagie's Pizza, Lyndon Buffet, McDonald's, Miss Lyndonville Diner, Pizza Man, [lodging] Colonnade Inn, [other] $General, CarQuest, Kinney Drug, TrueValue, White Mkt Foods, W [lodging] Lyndon Motel
22(132)	to US 5, St Johnsbury, E [gas] Sunoco/dsl, [food] KFC/Taco Bell, Kham's Cuisine, Pizza Hut, [other] Buick/GMC, Chrysler/Dodge/Jeep, [H], Kinney Drug, O'Reilly Parts, PriceChopper Foods, repair, Subaru
21(131)	US 2, to VT 15, St Johnsbury, E services
20(129)	US 5, to US 2, St Johnsbury, E welcome ctr, [gas] Mobil, Sunoco/dsl, Valero/dsl, [food] Anthony's Diner, Domino's, Dunkin', East Garden Chinese, Subway, Winegate Rest., [other] Family$, Kevin's Repair, NAPA, W [lodging] Comfort Inn, [other] st police
19(128)	I-93 S to Littleton NH
122mm	scenic view nb
18(121)	to US 5, Barnet, E [other] camping(5mi), W camping(5mi)
115mm	parking area sb
113mm	parking area nb
17(110)	US 302, to US 5, Wells River, NH, E [other] [H](5mi), W [gas] Mobil/P&H Trkstp/rest./dsl/scales/24hr, [other] camping(9mi)
100mm	**full [handicap] facilities, info, litter barrels, nb [RS], petwalk, [phone], [picnic], sb parking area**
16(98)	VT 25, to US 5, Bradford, E [gas] Mobil/dsl/LP/café, [food] Hungry Bear Grill, [lodging] Bradford Motel, [other] Family$, Hannaford Foods, Kinney Drug, NAPA, O'Reilly Parts, Pierson Farm Mkt, W st police
15(92)	Fairlee, E [gas] Irving/dsl, Mobil/7-11, Sunoco/dsl, [food] Fairlee Diner, Lunchbox Deli, [other] $General, USPO, Wings Mkt/deli, W golf
14(84)	VT 113, to US 5, Thetford, E [other] food, Rest-n-Nest Camping, W camping
13(75)	US 5, VT 10a, Hanover, NH, E [other] [H], to Dartmouth, W [gas] Citgo, [food] Norwich Inn Rest., [other] auto service, USPO
12(72)	US 5, White River Jct, Wilder, E [gas] Cumberland Farms/dsl, Mobil
11(71)	US 5, White River Jct, E [gas] Mobil/dsl, Shell/Subway/dsl, [food] China Moon, Crossroads Country Café, McDonald's, [lodging] Comfort Inn, [other] Chevrolet, Hyundai, Subaru, Toyota, USPO, W [gas] Sunoco/dsl, [food] Dunkin', [lodging] Fairfield Inn, Hampton Inn, Holiday Inn Express, Super 8, White River Inn, [other] [H]
10N(70)	I-89 N, to Montpelier
10S	I-89 S, to NH, [airport]
68mm	Welcome Ctr sb, full facilities, weigh sta nb
9(60)	US 5, VT 12, Hartland, E [other] [H], W [gas] Mobil(1mi), [food] Hartland Diner
8(51)	US 5, VT 12, VT 131, Ascutney, E [gas] Irving/Subway, Sunoco/dsl, [food] Ascutney House Rest., [other] Getaway Camping(2mi), [H], USPO
7(42)	US 5, VT 106, VT 11, Springfield, W [gas] Irving/Circle K/Subway/dsl/scales/24hr, [lodging] Holiday Inn Express, [other] [H](5mi)
39mm	weigh sta both lanes, weigh sta sb
6(34)	US 5, VT 103, to Bellows Falls, Rockingham, E [gas] Shell/dsl, [food] Leslie's Rest., [lodging] Rodeway Inn, W [gas] Sunoco/dsl
5(29)	VT 121, to US 5, to Bellows Falls, Westminster, E food, gas, lodging, [phone]
24mm	parking area both lanes
22mm	weigh sta sb
20mm	weigh sta nb
4(18)	US 5, Putney, E [lodging] Putney Inn/rest., W [gas] Rod's/repair, Sunoco/dsl/24hr, [food] Putney Diner, Putney Food Coop/deli, [other] Putney Gen Store/deli, USPO
3(11)	US 5, VT 9 E, Brattleboro, E [gas] Agway/dsl, Citgo/dsl,

INTERSTATE 91 Cont'd

3(11) Continued
Mobil/dsl, Sunoco, 99 Rest., China Buffet, Dunkin', Fast Eddy Cafe, KFC, McDonald's, Panda North, Ramunto's Brick Oven, Taco Bell, Village Pizza, Wendy's, Black Mtn Inn, Colonial Motel, Comfort Inn, Covered Bridge Inn, Hampton Inn, Holiday Inn Express, Motel 6, Quality Inn, Advance Parts, ALDI, AT&T, Buick/Chevrolet/GMC, Chrysler/Dodge/Jeep, Family$, Ford, GNC, Hannaford Foods, O'Reilly Parts, Staples, Subaru, TrueValue, URGENT CARE, USPO, Verizon

2(9) VT 9 W, to rd 30, Brattleboro, **W** VT Country Deli,

2(9) Continued
to Marlboro Coll

1(7) US 5, Brattleboro, **E** Gulf/dsl, Irving/Circle K/dsl, Mobil/Dunkin Donuts, Shell/Subway/dsl, Domino's, FC Chinese, VT Inn Pizza, EconoLodge, $Tree, H, PriceChopper Mkt, to Ft Dummer SP, vet, Walgreens

6mm **full facilities, info, litter barrels, petwalk, playground, vending, Welcome Ctr nb, wi-fi**

0mm Vermont/Massachusetts state line

INTERSTATE 93

0 see New Hampshire Interstate 93.

NOTES

= gas = food = lodging = other = rest stop

VIRGINIA

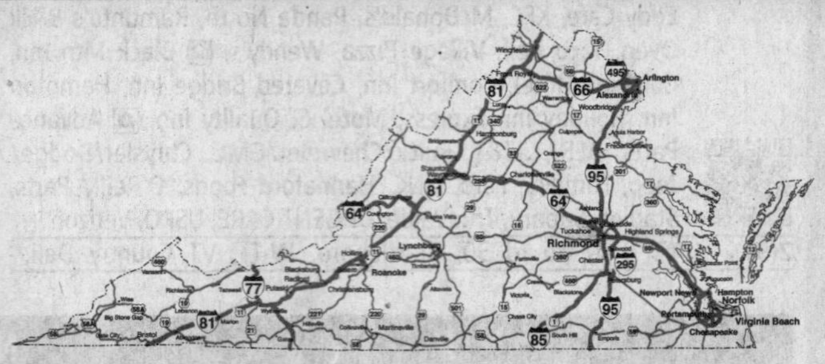

INTERSTATE 64

Exit #	Services
299b a	I-264 E, to Portsmouth. I-64 begins/ends on I-264.
297	US 13, US 460, Military Hwy, N 7-11, Exxon, McDonald's, Papa John's
296b a	US 17, to Portsmouth, N 7-11, Wawa/dsl, BBQ Shack, Brooklyn Pizza, Hardee's, McDonald's, Papa John's, Pizza Hut, Subway, Zino's Cafe, Comfort Inn, $General, $Tree, Food Lion, USPO, vet
294mm	S Br Elizabeth River
292	VA 190, to VA 104(from eb, no EZ return), Dominion Blvd, S Exxon, #1 China, Royal China, Subway, Family$, Food Lion
291b a	I-464 N, VA 104 S, to Elizabeth City, Outer Banks, same services as 292
290b a	VA 168, Battlefield Blvd, to Nag's Head, Manteo, N Arby's, Bubba's 33, La Hacienda Mexican, Popeyes, Starbucks, Woodspring Suites, $General, BigLots, Dick's, Kroger, NAPA, NTB, S 7-11/dsl, Shell, Applebee's, Baskin-Robbins, Carrabba's, Chick-fil-A, ChuckECheese's, CookOut, Denny's, Dunkin Donuts, Five Guys, Golden Corral, Krispy Kreme, Little Caesar's, MOD Pizza, Panda Express, Sonic, Starbucks, TGIFriday's, Tropical Smoothie Café, TX Roadhouse, Waffle House, Wendy's, Wildwing Café, Hampton Inn, InTown Suites, Quality Inn, Studios For Less, $Tree, Discount Tire, Home Depot, H, Kohl's, Lowe's, Nissan/EVC, Sam's Club/gas, USPO, Verizon, Walgreens, Walmart
289b a	Greenbrier Pkwy, N 7-11, Sunoco/dsl, WaWa/dsl, McDonald's, Subway, Taco Bell, Wendy's, Extended Stay America, Hampton Inn, Holiday Inn Express, Marriott, Red Roof Inn, Staybridge Suites, TownePlace Suites, Wingate Inn, Acura, auto repair, Chevrolet, Chrysler/Jeep, Dodge, Ford, GMC, Hyundai, Kia, Lincoln, Mazda, Toyota/Scion, U-Haul, vet, VW, S 7-11, Baker's Crust, Buffalo Wild Wings, CAVA, Chick-fil-A, Chipotle, Coldstone, Cracker Barrel, Fazoli's, Firehouse Subs, Hooters, Jason's Deli, Jimmy John's, Kyoto Japanese, Los Burritos, McDonald's, Moe's SW, Olive Garden, Panera Bread, Pizza Hut, Pop's Diner, Red Robin, Ruby Tuesday, Smokey Bones BBQ, Starbucks, Subway, Zero's Subs, Aloft Hotel, Comfort Suites, Courtyard, Extended Stay, Fairfield Inn, Hilton, InTown Suites, Residence Inn, SpringHill Suites, Tru, AT&T, Barnes&Noble, Best Buy, Dillard's, Food Lion, Harris Teeter, Macy's, mall, Michaels, Old Navy, PetSmart, Ross, Target, TJ Maxx, Verizon, Walgreens
286b a	Indian River Rd, N BP/dsl, Marathon, SkyMart/dsl, Dunkin, Golden China, Hardee's, 7-11, CVS, S Exxon/dsl, CookOut, Ellen's BBQ, Oriental Cuisine, Waffle House, 7-11
285mm	E Branch Elizabeth River
284a	I-264, to Norfolk, to VA Beach(exits left from eb)
284b	Newtown Rd
282	US 13, Northampton Blvd, N Citgo/dsl, Chick-fil-A, Duck Donuts, Krispy Kreme, McDonald's, Mission BBQ, Starbucks, Taco Bell, Waffle House, Wendy's, Comfort Inn, Fairfield Inn, Hilton, Quality Inn, Sleep Inn, to Chesapeake Bay Br Tunnel
281	VA 165, Military Hwy(no EZ eb return), N Shell/dsl, EconoLodge, Aamco, Chysler/Dodge/Jeep, Fiat, H, S 7-11, WaWa, Burger King, Chick-fil-A, Chipotle, CookOut, Firehouse Subs, Hooters, IHOP, Jersey Mike's Subs,
281	Continued Jimmy John's, KF€, Little Caesar's, Panera Bread, Qdoba, Ruby Tuesday, Sonic, Starbucks, Wendy's, Candlewood Suites, Days Inn, Doubletree, Hampton Inn, Holiday Inn, Holiday Inn Express, InTown Suites, La Quinta, Residence Inn, ALDI, BJ's Whse/dsl, FarmFresh Foods, Food Lion, Home Depot, Lowe's, Nissan/EVC, OfficeMax, Pep Boys, PetSmart, Target/CVS, TJ Maxx, Verizon, Walgreens, Walmart/Subway
279	Norview Ave, N WaWa/dsl, China House, Franco's Italian, Wendy's, $General, $Tree, 7-11/dsl, Food Lion, Tire City, to ✈ & botanical garden, S Citgo/dsl, Cal'z Pizza, China Town, KFC, McDonald's, Family$
278	VA 194 S(no EZ return)
277b a	VA 168, to Tidewater Dr, N 7-11, Shell, Bojangles, Cook Out, Fuddrucker's, Hardee's, Philly Steaks&Subs, Ruby Tuesday, Advance Parts, Family$, Food Lion, Walmart/Subway, S Honda, U-Haul
276c	to US 460 W, VA 165, Little Creek Rd, fromwb, N Race Coast/dsl, URGENT CARE, S 7-11, Chipotle, Firehouse Subs, KFC, McDonald's, Moe's SW, Pancake House, Papa John's, Taco Bell, Wendy's, $Tree, AutoZone, Harris Teeter/gas, USPO, Walgreens
276b a	I-564 to Naval Base (exits left from wb)
274	Bay Ave(from wb), S to Naval Air Sta
273	US 60, 4th View St, Oceanview, N 7-11/dsl, Economy Inn, Motel 6, Oceanview Pier
272	W Ocean View Ave, N Willoughby Seafood, S Willoughby Fish House
270mm	Chesapeake Bay Tunnel
269mm	weigh sta eb
268	VA 169 E, to Buckroe Beach, Ft Monroe, N Citgo, McDonald's, S H, to VA Air&Space Ctr
267	US 60, to VA 143, Settlers Ldg Rd, S Marco's Pizza, Starbucks, Subway, Tropical Smoothie, Wendy's, H, to Hampton U
265c	(from eb), to Armistead Ave, N to Langley AFB
265b a	VA 134, VA 167, to La Salle Ave, N RaceTrac/dsl, Burger King, Super 8, Home Depot, S Citgo, KFC/Taco Bell, McDonald's, Advance Parts, Family$
264	I-664, to Newport News, Suffolk
263b a	US 258, VA 134, Mercury Blvd, to James River Br, N 7-11, BP, Exxon/dsl, Miller's/dsl, Shell, Abuelo's Mexican, Applebee's, Bojangles, Burger King, Cane's, Chick-fil-A, Chicken Salad Chick, Chili's, Chipotle Mexican, Cook Out, Denny's, El Azteca, Firehouse Subs, First Watch, Five Guys, Freddy's, Hooters, IHOP, Jason's Deli, McDonald's, Moe's SW Grill, Olive Garden, Panda Express, Panera Bread, Parklane Rest., Pizza Hut, Rally's, Red Lobster, Starbucks, Subway, Taco Bell, Tokyo Japanese, Tropical Smoothie, Waffle House, Wendy's, Best Western, Courtyard, Days Inn, Embassy Suites, Extended Stay America, Holiday Inn Express,

INTERSTATE 64 Cont'd

263b a Continued
Hyatt Place, Red Roof Inn, $Tree, ALDI, AT&T, Barnes&Noble, Chevrolet/Mazda, Food Lion, Ford, JC Penney, Kroger/gas, Michael's, NAPA, Nissan/EVC, PetCo, Ross, Target/Starbucks, tires, U-Haul, USPO, Verizon, Volvo, Walgreens, Walmart, **S** Miller's/dsl, Sunoco/dsl, WaWa/dsl, Anthony's Seafood, Chick-fil-A, CiCi's Pizza, Coldstone, Cracker Barrel, Domino's, Dunkin Donuts, La Parrilla, Little Caesar's, Longhorn Steaks, Pizza Hut, Rita's, Sonic, Taco Bell, Waffle House, Zaxby's, Economy Inn, Hilton Garden, InTown Suites, Relax Inn, SpringHill Suites, $General, 7-11, Aamco, BassPro Shop, BJ's Whse/Subway/gas, CVS Drug, Firestone/auto, Lowe's, Office Depot, PepBoys, Toyota, Walmart Mkt

262 VA 134, Magruder Blvd(from wb, no EZ return), **N** 7-11, Comfort Inn&Suites, Studio 6, Audi, H, Hyundai

261b a Center Pkwy, to Hampton Roads, **N** Hampton Inn(2mi), Sonesta Suites, **S** 7-11, Sunoco, Anna's Italian, ChuckECheese's, Fortune Garden Chinese, Gus's NY Pizza, McDonald's, Pizza Hut/Taco Bell, Plaza Azteca, Subway, $Tree, Ace Hardware, Food Lion

258b a US 17, J Clyde Morris Blvd, **N** 7-11/dsl, BP/dsl, Sunoco/dsl, Domino's, New China, Waffle House, BudgetLodge, Country Inn&Suites, Holiday Inn Express, Host Inn, PointPlaza Hotel, Super 8, Advance Parts, Family$, Food Lion, **S** 7-11, BP, Citgo/dsl, WaWa/dsl, Angelo's Steaks, Burger King, Jimmy John's, KFC/Taco Bell, McDonald's, Papa John's, Starbucks, Subway, Vinny's Pizza, Wendy's, Holiday Inn, Motel 6, H, Jiffy Lube, museum, Subaru, VW

256b a Victory Blvd, Oyster Point Rd, **N** Mobil/dsl, WaWa/dsl, Arby's, Burger King, Cane's, Chick-fil-A, China Ocean, Hardee's, McDonald's, Panda Express, Saisaki Asian, Sonic, Starbucks, Subway, Taco Bell, Three Amigos Mexican, TX Roadhouse, Uno Grill, CandleWood Suites, Courtyard, Extended Stay America, Hampton Inn, Hilton Garden, Homewood Suites, $Tree, Kroger/gas, tires, Walgreens, Walmart/gas, **S** Shell, WaWa/dsl, BJ's Rest., CAVA, Crumbl Cookies, First Watch, Mellow Mushroom, PF Chang's, Plaza Azteca, Starbucks, InTown Suites, Oyster Point, Whole Foods Mkt

255b a VA 143, to Jefferson Ave, **N** Exxon/dsl, Millers/dsl, Chili's, CookOut, Donato's Pizza, Dunkin, Firehouse Subs, Five Guys, Golden Corral, HoneyBaked Ham, Juan's Mexican, Krispy Kreme, Longhorn Steaks, McDonald's, Mission BBQ, Moe's SW Grill, Olive Garden, Panera Bread, Red Lobster, Smokey Bones BBQ, Sonic, Starbucks, Starbucks, Comfort Suites, Acura, ALDI, Buick/Cadillac/GMC, Chrysler/Dodge/Jeep, CVS Drug, FarmFresh Foods/deli, Home Depot, H, Kohl's, Lowe's, NAPA, PetCo, Ross, Sam's Club/gas, TJ Maxx, Trader Joe's, Tuesday Morning, Walgreens, Walmart, **S** Applebee's, Buffalo Wild Wings, Carrabba's, Cheddar's, Chick-fil-A, Chipotle Mexican, Coldstone, Cracker Barrel, KFC, McDonald's, Outback Steaks, Red Robin, Starbucks, Subway, Taco Bell, TGIFriday's, Waffle House, Wendy's, Best Western, Comfort Inn, Courtyard, Extended Stay America, Hampton Inn, Microtel, Residence Inn, 7-11, Barnes&Noble, Best Buy, Costco/dsl, Dick's, Dillard's, Fresh Mkt, JC Penney, Macy's, mall, PetSmart, Target, Verizon, World Mkt

250b a to US Army Trans Museum, **N** 7-11/gas, Exxon/dsl, Hardee's, Subway, B&L Auto Repair, Newport News Campground/Park(1mi), to Yorktown Victory Ctr, **S** Ft Eustis Inn, Holiday Inn Express, Mulberry Inn, 7-11

247 VA 143, to VA 238(no EZ return wb), **N** 7-11/gas, Burger King, auto repair, to Yorktown, U-Haul,

CAMP PEARY TOANO QUINTON

247 Continued
to Jamestown Settlement

243 VA 143, to Williamsburg, exits left from wb, **S** same as 242a

242b a VA 199, to US 60, to Williamsburg, **N** Wyndham Garden, Best Buy, Kohl's, Target, to Yorktown NHS, water funpark, **S** Exxon/dsl, Shell/dsl, Sunoco, Sunoco, WaWa/dsl, KFC, McDonald's, Sportsmans Grille, Starbucks, Subway, Taco Bell, Wendy's, Whaling Co Rest., Courtyard, Double Tree, Holiday Inn, Busch Gardens, to Jamestown NHS, to William&Mary Coll

238 VA 143, to Colonial Williamsburg, Camp Peary, **S** Exxon/7-11, Aberdeen Barn Rest., Another Broken Egg, Chipotle Mexican, Cracker Barrel, Five Guys, Freddy's, Golden Corral, Hooters, House of Pancakes, Jefferson Steaks, Jose Mexican, KFC, McDonald's, Plaza Azteca, Popeyes, Smokehouse Grill, Subway, Taco Bell, America's Inn, Best Western, Comfort Inn, Comfort Suites, Country Inn&Suites, Days Inn, Embassy Suites, Fairfield Inn, Hampton Inn, Hilton Garden, Holiday Inn Express, Holiday Inn/rest., Homewood Suites, La Quinta Inn, Patriots Inn, Residence Inn, Sleep Inn, SpringHill Suites, CVS Drug, Goodyear/auto, H

234 VA 646, to Lightfoot, **N** Williamsburg Campark, **S** Exxon/dsl, Burger King, BurgerFi, IHOP, Sonic, Starbucks, Subway, Taco Bell, Tokyo Express, Great Wolf Lodge, Holiday Inn, Holiday Inn Express, $Tree, BigLots, Ford, Home Depot, H, Lowe's, Ross, Toyota/Scion, Walmart

231b a VA 607, to Norge, Croaker, **N** 7-11/gas, to York River SP, **S** Shell/dsl, China Star, Daddy-O's Pizza, Honey Butter's Kitchen, Pizza Hut, Economy Inn, $General, 7-11, American Heritage RV Park, CVS Drug, Food Lion, Honda, Hyundai, O'Reilly Parts, USPO, vet

227 VA 30, to US 60, to West Point, Toano, **S** Shell/dsl, Sunoco, McDonald's

220 VA 33 E, to West Point, **N** BP/Circle K/dsl, Mobil/7-11/dsl

214 VA 155, to New Kent, Providence Forge, **S** Exxon/DQ/dsl/EVC, Antonio's Pizza, Tops China

213mm **both lanes, full facilities, vending, litter barrels, petwalk**

211 VA 106, to Talleysville, to James River Plantations, **S** Love's/Arby's/dsl/scales/24hr, Pilot/Subway/dsl/scales/24hr, Burger King, auto repair

205 VA 33, VA 249, to US 60, Bottoms Bridge, Quinton, **N** Exxon/dsl, Sunoco, Maria's Italian, Panda Garden, Pizza Hut, Subway, Wendy's, Food Lion, USPO, Verizon, **S** BP/dsl, Mobil/dsl, Bojangle's, Domino's, Dunkin, McDonald's, Taco Bell, Waffle House, $General, Food Lion, Walgreens

204mm Chickahominy River

203mm weigh sta both lanes

200 I-295, N to Washington, S to Rocky Mount, to US 60

197b a VA 156, Airport Dr, to Highland Springs, **N** 7-11, Shell/dsl, Antonio's Pizza, Domino's, Hardee's, Subway, Top's China, $General, 7-11, Advance Parts, CVS Drug, Family$, O'Reilly Parts, **S** BP, Sheetz/dsl, Shell/7-11, WaWa, Arby's, Burger King, El Torito Mexican, Mexico Rest., Pizza Hut, Roberto's Italian, The Patron, Waffle House, Capital Inn, Courtyard, Double Tree, Express Inn, Fairfield Inn, Hampton Inn, Hilton Garden, Holiday Inn Express, Homewood Suites, Microtel, Motel 6, Quality Inn, Rodeway Inn, Sandston Inn, Super 8, to

195 Laburnum Ave, **N** Sunoco, auto repair, Walmart, **S** 7-11, Applebee's, Chick-fil-A, China King, CookOut, Cracker Barrel, Firehouse Subs, Five Guys, Hibachi Grill, Longhorn Steaks, Marco's Pizza, McDonald's, Olive Garden, Panda Express, Panera Bread, Papa John's, Popeyes, Qdoba Mexican, Red Lobster, Starbucks, Subway, Taco Bell, TGIFriday's, Hyatt Place/Tesla EVC, Sheraton, $Tree, AT&T, JC Penney, Lowe's, Michael's, PetSmart, Publix,

VA

INTERSTATE 64 Cont'd

RICHMOND

195 Continued
Target, Verizon

193b a VA 33, Nine Mile Rd, N BP/Subway/dsl, Citgo/dsl, PepBoys, S

192 US 360, to Mechanicsville, N Exxon/dsl, Shell, McDonald's, auto parts, S Shell, Valero

190 I-95 S, to Petersburg, 5th St. I-64/I-95 run together, see VA I-95 exits 76-78., S Hilton, Marriott, coliseum, conv ctr, st capitol

187 I-95 N(exits left from eb), to Washington. I-64 E and I-95 S run together.

186 I-195, to Powhite Pkwy, from wb, Richmond

185b a US 33, Staples Mill Rd, Dickens Rd

183c from wb, US 250 W, Broad St, Glenside Dr N, same as exit 183

183b a US 250, Broad St E, Glenside Dr S., N Mobil/dsl, Sheetz/dsl, McDonald's, Mission BBQ, Olive Garden, Taco Bell, TGIFriday's, Waffle House, Best Western, Econolodge/Rodeway, Embassy Suites, Extended Stay America, Hampton Inn, Home2 Suites, Knights Inn, Residence Inn, Super 8, Woodspring Suites, AutoZone, Honda, vet, Volvo, S Chipotle, Denny's, Jersey Mike's, mezeh, Plaza Azteca, Starbucks, Candlewood Suites, Courtyard, Residence Inn, Westin, ALDI, auto repair, Home Depot, Target, to U of Richmond, vet, Walmart

181b a Parham Rd, N Exxon, Chrysler/Dodge/Jeep, Mercedes, Tropical Smoothie

180 Gaskins Rd, N BP, Exxon, Shell/dsl, Apollo's Pizza, Applebee's, Arby's, Chick-fil-A, Chicken Salad Chicks, Cracker Barrel, Golden Corral, IHOP, Kickback Jack's Rest., Marco's Pizza, McDonald's, Penn Sta Subs, Starbucks, Subway, Taco Bell, Wendy's, 7-11, Extended Stay America, Fairfield Inn, Holiday Inn Express, Mapco, SpringHill Suites, $Tree, 7-11/dsl, AutoZone, Cadillac, Costco/gas, Goodyear/auto, Kroger/gas, Lowe's, Mazda, Michael's, Publix, Sam's Club/gas, Subaru, Tesla, Toyota, S Jiffy Lube

CHESTERFIELD

178b a US 250, Broad St, Short Pump, N 7-11, Wawa/dsl, BurgerWorks, Capital Alehouse, Charley's, Chipotle Mexican, Corner Bakery Cafe, DQ, Dunkin, Firehouse Subs, Five Guys, Hondo's Rest., Joey's Hotdogs, Leonardo's Pizza, Mama Cucina, Moe's SW Grill, Noodles, Panera Bread, Potbelly, Silver Diner, Starbucks, Taziki's, Comfort Suites, Courtyard, Drury Plaza, Extended Stay America, Hampton Inn, Hilton Garden, Homewood Suites, Hyatt Place, Residence Inn, CarMax, CVS Drug, Firestone/auto, Ford, Marshall's, Ross, URGENT CARE, Verizon, S 7-11, Shell, Arby's, BJ's Rest., Bonefish Grill, Burger King, Carrabba's, CAVA, Cheesecake Factory, Chick-fil-A, Chili's, Chipotle Mexican, Chopt, Chuy's Mexican, CookOut, Dave&Buster's, Domino's, Dunkin, First Watch, Genghis Grill, HoneyBaked Ham, Jersey Mike's Subs, Kanpai, KFC, LJSilver, Longhorn Steaks, Maggiano's Italian, McDonald's, Olive Garden, Panda Express, Panera Bread, Plaza Azteca, Qdoba, Sonic, Starbucks, Taco Bell, TGIFriday's, Torchy's Tacos, Tropical Smoothie, Wendy's, Zara Grill, Candlewood Suites, Hilton, Home2 Suites, Hyatt House, Wingate Inn, $Tree, Advance Parts, AT&T, Barnes&Noble, Best Buy, Buick/Chevrolet/GMC, CarQuest, Dick's, Dillard's, Hobby Lobby, Home Depot, Jiffy Lube, Kohl's, Kroger, Lowe's, Macy's, Midas, Nissan/EVC, NTB, Petco, PetSmart, Publix, REI, Staples, Target, Tom Leonard's Mkt, Trader Joe's, Walmart, Whole Foods Mkt, World Mkt

177 I-295, to I-95 N to Washington, to Norfolk, VA Beach, Williamsburg

175 VA 288, Chesterfield

173 VA 623, to Rockville, Manakin, S Shell/dsl,

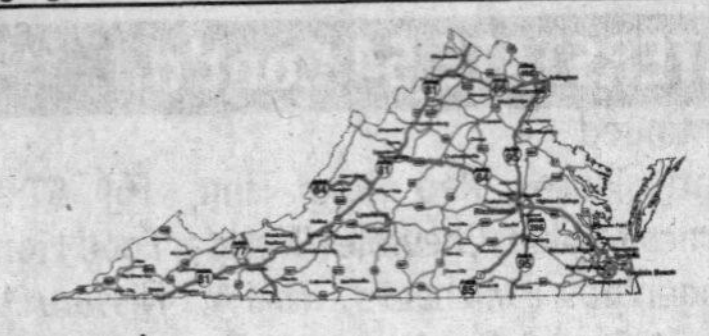

FERNCLIFF

173 Continued
Valero/Subway/dsl, McDonald's, Sunset Grill, Taco Bell, $General, Advance Parts, Food Lion, vet

169mm both lanes, full facilities, litter barrels, petwalk,

167 VA 617, to Goochland, Oilville, N Exxon/dsl, S Exxon/dsl, Mi Jalisco Mexican, USPO

159 US 522, to Goochland, Gum Spring, N Exxon/dsl, S BP/DQ/dsl, Citgo

152 VA 629, Hadensville, S Exxon, $General, auto parts, USPO

148 VA 605, Shannon Hill

143 VA 208, to Louisa, Ferncliff, N Small Country Camping(7mi), S Citgo/dsl, Exxon/dsl

136 US 15, to Gordonsville, Zion Crossroads, N 7-11, Sheetz/dsl, Arby's, Checkers, Dunkin, El Mariachi Mexican, IHOP, Popeyes, Starbucks, Subway, Taco Bell, Wendy's, Best Western+, $Tree, Advance Parts, Lowe's, O'Reilly Parts, Verizon, vet, Walmart, S BP/McDonald's/dsl/24hr, Exxon/Burger King/dsl, Shell/dsl/scales, Crescent Rest.

129 VA 616, Keswick, Boyd Tavern

SCOTTSVILLE

124 US 250, to Shadwell, N BP, Exxon, Mobil/dsl, Shell, Speedway, WaWa/dsl, Applebee's, Bojangle's, Chick-fil-A, Chipotle, Guadalajara Mexican, Jersey Mike's, Jimmy John's, Marco's Pizza, McDonald's, Sbarro Pizza, Starbucks, Taco Bell, TipTop Rest., Tropical Smoothie, Wendy's, Hilton Garden, Audi, Audi/VW, auto repair, BMW, CarMax, Food Lion, Giant Foods, Jiffy Lube, Kia, Mazda, Mercedes, Porsche, Toyota/Scion, URGENT CARE, VW, Walgreens, S Comfort Inn

123mm Rivanna River

121 VA 20, to Charlottesville, Scottsville, N BP/dsl, Moose's by the Creek, S to Piedmont Comm Coll

120 VA 631, 5th St, to Charlottesville, N Exxon/dsl, Shell/dsl, Burger King, BurgerFi, Christian's Pizza, Coldstone, Domino's, Jersey Mike's, Krispy Kreme, Panera Bread, Starbucks, Subway, Taco Bell, Affordable Suites, Holiday Inn, Sleep Inn, $Tree, AT&T, CVS Drug, Dick's, Family$, Food Lion, Marshalls, PetSmart, vet, Wegmans

118b a US 29, to Lynchburg, Charlottesville, N BP, to UVA

114 VA 637, to Ivy

113mm **full facilities, litter barrels, petwalk, wb, vending**

111mm Stockton Creek

108mm N KOA, S Cenex/dsl, Exxon/dsl/scales/24hr, Gasamat/dsl, Maverik/dsl, Domino's, Kim's Rest., McDonald's, Pizza Hut, Verizon, Bramble Motel, Budget Inn, Rodeway Inn, Stage Stop Motel, Super 8, Super Saver Motel, Trails End Motel/rest., Peerless Tires, W Common Cents/dsl

WAYNESBORO

107 US 250, Crozet, N BP/dsl, Citgo, Exxon/dsl, S Misty Mtn Camping

105mm eb, full facilities, litter barrels, vending, petwalk,

104mm scenic area eb, litter barrels, no truck or buses

100mm scenic area eb, hist marker, litter barrels, no truck or buses

99 US 250, to Waynesboro, Afton, N Grey Pine Lodge, Skyline Drive, to Blue Ridge Pkwy, to Shenandoah NP

96 VA 622, to Lyndhurst, Waynesboro, N Shell, Speedway, Quality Inn, Kroger, Walmart/gas, Waynesboro Camping, S Iris Inn & Cabin

95mm South River

94 US 340, to Stuarts Draft, Waynesboro, N 7-11/dsl, Exxon/dsl, Sheetz/dsl, Applebee's, Buffalo Wild Wings, Chipotle,

VA

INTERSTATE 64 Cont'd

FISHERSVILLE

94 Continued
Cracker Barrel, Five Guys, Golden Corral, KFC, Los Panchos Mexican, Outback Steaks, Panera Bread, Pizza Hut, Plaza Azteca, Popeyes, Silk Road Rest., Sonic, Starbucks, The Fishin' Pig, Waffle House, Wendy's, Best Western+, Comfort Inn, Days Inn, Holiday Inn Express, Residence Inn, Super 8, Wingate, Batteries+, Home Depot, H, Lowe's, Martin's Food/gas, Verizon, vet, Walmart, Waynesboro N 340 Camping(9mi), S Mobil/dsl, Chick-fil-A, Dunkin, McAlister's Deli, McDonald's, Taco Bell, Tropical Smoothie, ALDI, AT&T, Books-A-Million, Discount Tire, Kohl's, Michael's, PetSmart, Ross, Target, Valvoline

91 Va 608, to Stuarts Draft, Fishersville, N Citgo/Subway(1mi), Shell/dsl, Hampton Inn, Eaver's Tires, H, S 7-11, Sheetz/dsl, McDonald's, Wendy's, Shenadoah Acres Camping(8mi), Walnut Hills Camping(9mi)

89mm Christians Creek

87 I-81, N to Harrisonburg, S to Roanoke

86mm I-64 and I-81 merge for 20 miles. See I-81, exits 195-220.

55 US 11, to VA 39, N Exxon, Burger King, Jersey Mike's, Mr. G's Donuts, Rockbridge Pizza, Ruby Tuesday, Waffle House, Best Western+, Sleep Inn, Super 8, Wingate Inn, $Tree, AutoZone, Ford, Lowe's, Stonewall Jackson Museum, Verizon, Walmart, S Marathon/7-11/Subway, Mobil/DQ/dsl, Applebee's, Dunkin, Starbucks, Best Western, Comfort Inn, Country Inn&Suites, Holiday Inn Express, Motel 6

50 US 60, rd 623, to Kerrs Creek, Lexington

43 rd 780, to Goshen

35 VA 269, rd 850, Longdale Furnace

33mm truck eb

CLIFTON FORGE

29 VA 269, VA 42 E, S Sunoco/dsl

27 US 60 W, US 220 S, VA 629, Clifton Forge, N NAPA, tires, to Douthat SP, S BP/dsl, Exxon, Bella Pizza, Domino's, auto repair, CVS Drug, Kroger

24 US 60, US 220, Clifton Forge, S Shell/dsl, auto repair, DQ, Hardee's

21 to rd 696, Low Moor, N Love's/McDonald's/Subway/dsl/scales/24hr, S Family Tree Cafe, Penny's Diner, Travelodge, H, USPO

16 US 60 W, US 220 N, to Hot Springs, Covington, Taco Bell, N Exxon/dsl, Shell, Burger King, Cucci's, San Juan Mexican, Subway, Hampton Inn, Magnuson Hotel, Pinehurst Hotel, to ski area, S Domino's, McDonald's, Compare Inn

14 VA 154, to Hot Springs, Covington, N BP, Exxon/Arby's, KFC, LJ Silver, Subway, Wendy's, $General, Advance Parts, AutoZone, CVS Drug, Family$, Food Lion, URGENT CARE, S China House, Trani's Grille, $Tree, Chevrolet, Walmart

10 US 60 E, VA 159 S, Callaghan, S Marathon/dsl/LP

7 rd 661

2.5mm Welcome Ctr eb, full facilities, litter barrels, petwalk, no trucks

1 Jerry's Run Trail, N to Allegheny Trail

0mm Virginia/West Virginia state line

INTERSTATE 66

77mm Constitution Ave, to Lincoln Mem. I-66 begins/ends in Washington, DC.

76mm Potomac River, T Roosevelt Memorial Bridge

75 US 50 W(from eb), to Arlington Blvd, G Wash Pkwy, I-395, US 1, S Iwo Jima Mon

73 US 29, Lee Hwy, Key Bridge, to Rosslyn, N Homewood Suites

FALLS CHURCH

72 to US 29, Lee Hwy, Spout Run Pkwy(from eb, no EZ return), N Shell, Dunkin, Virginia Inn, Safeway/EVC, S Starbucks, Tarbouch Grill, CVS Drug, Giant Foods, Walgreens

71 VA 120, Glebe Rd(no EZ return from wb), N H, S Sunoco, Big Buns Burgers, Booeymonger Grill, Melting Pot, PF Chang's, SER Rest., Comfort Inn, Holiday Inn, The Westin

69 US 29, Sycamore St, Falls Church, N Exxon/7-11, S EconoLodge, vet

68 Westmoreland St(from eb), same as 69

67 to I-495 N(from wb), to Baltimore, Dulles

66b a VA 7, Leesburg Pike, to Tysons Corner, Falls Church, N Exxon, Sunoco, China King, Ledo Pizza, Noodles&Co, Subway, 7-11, Trader Joe's, Verizon, vet, Whole Foods Mkt, S Citgo, Crumbl Cookies, Domino's, Jersey Mike's, Jimmy John's, McDonald's, Starbucks, Tropical Smoothie, CVS Drug, Giant Foods/EVC, Kia, Staples

64b a I-495 S, to Richmond

62 VA 243, Nutley St, to Vienna, S Citgo, Domino's, Starbucks, CVS Drug, EVC, Michael's, Safeway Foods/gas, Walgreens

60 VA 123, to Fairfax, S Exxon, Mobil, Shell, Sunoco, Denny's, El Pollo Rico, Five Guys, Freddy's, Fuddruckers, Hooters, Hooters, Marco's Pizza, McDonald's, Panera Bread, Red Lobster, Starbucks, Best Western, Hampton Inn, Holiday Inn Express, Residence Inn, 7-11, AutoZone, Chevrolet, CVS Drug, Kia, Mazda, Mazda, NAPA, NTB, Petco, Subaru, to George Mason U, Toyota, Toyota/Scion, URGENT CARE, Verizon

57b a US 50, to Dulles Airport, N Brio Tuscan, Cheesecake Factory, Dave&Buster's, Extended Stay America, Marriott, access to same as 55, Barnes&Noble, JC Penney, Macy's, Macy's, mall, Old Navy, S BP, Shell/dsl, Boston Mkt, Buffalo Wild Wings, CAVA, Chipotle, Chuy's, McDonald's, PF Chang's, Subway, Wendy's, Candlewood Suites, Comfort Inn/EVC, Courtyard, SpringHill Suites, 7-11, Ford, Honda, Lowe's, Nissan, NRA Museum, REI, VW/Volvo, Walmart

CENTREVILLE

55 Fairfax Co Pkwy, to US 29, N Exxon, Sunoco/7-11, Applebees, Blue Iguana Café, Burger King, Cantina Italiana, Chick-fil-A, China Taste, Chipotle, Crumbl Cookies, Dunkin, Guapo's, Jason's Deli, Jersey Mike's, Jimmy John's, McDonald's, Noodles&Co, Olive Garden, Red Robin, Sakura Japanese, Starbucks, Taco Bell, Tony's NY Pizza, Wendy's, Hilton Fairfax, Sonesta Suites, ALDI, Best Buy, BJ's Whse/gas, CVS Drug, Fair Oaks Mall, Hobby Lobby, H, Kohl's, Michael's, PetSmart, Target, Verizon, Walmart, Whole Foods Mkt, S Sunoco, Costco/gas, Home Depot, Office Depot

53b a VA 28, to Centreville, S same as 52

52 US 29, to Bull Run Park, Centreville, N Sunoco/dsl, auto repair, Bull Run Park/RV Dump, Dunkin, S Exxon, Sunoco, Sunoco/dsl, Burger King, Carrabba's, Firehouse Subs, IHOP, McDonald's, My Thai, Panda Express, Starbucks, Subway, Wendy's, Extended Stay America, $Tree, Advance Parts, AT&T, Giant Foods, SpringHill Suites, Trader Joe's, USPO, vet, Walgreens

49mm both lanes, full facilities, litter barrels, petwalk

47b a VA 234, to Manassas, N Shell/dsl, Cracker Barrel, Golden Corral, Uno, Wendy's, Courtyard, Hilton Garden, Holiday Inn Express, La Quinta, Wyndham Garden, Duluth Trading Co, Kohl's, Manassas Nat Bfd, Old Navy, S BP, Exxon, Shell/repair, Sunoco, WaWa/dsl/Tesla EVC, Arby's, Bob Evans, Burger King, Cafe Rio, Checker's, Chick-fil-A, Chili's, Chipotle Mexican, ChuckECheese, DQ, Dunkin, Jersey Mike's, KFC, Little Caesars, Logan's Roadhouse, McDonald's, Olive Garden, Panda Express, Pizza Hut, Pollo Campero, Red Lobster, Sonic, Starbucks, Subway, Subway, Taco Bell,

INTERSTATE 66 Cont'd

MANASSAS

47b a	Continued Candlewood Suites, Comfort Suites, Days Inn, Hampton Inn, Holiday Inn, Quality Inn, Red Roof Inn, Residence Inn, Woodspring Suites, $Tree, auto repair, AutoZone, Best Buy, BigLots, Buick/GMC, Burlington Coats, Camping World RV Ctr, Chevrolet, Costco/gas, Dick's, GNC, Home Depot, Honda, Jiffy Lube, Lowe's, Marshalls, Michael's, NTB, PepBoys, PetSmart, Ross, Shopper's Foods, URGENT CARE, Walgreens
44	VA 234 S, Manassas, S to Bristoe Sta Bfd SP
43b a	US 29, to Warrenton, Gainesville, S 7-11, BJ's/gas, Shell/dsl, Sunoco/dsl, WaWa, BJ's Rest, Buffalo Wild Wings, Burger King, CAVA, Chick-fil-A, Chipotle, Coldstone, Domino's, Famous Dave's, Firebirds Grill, Five Guys, Honey Baked Ham, IHOP, Joe's Pizza/Subs, KFC, McDonald's, MOD Pizza, Out of the Blue Seafood, Outback Steaks, Panda Express, Panera Bread, Pizza NY, Potbelly, Qdoba, Rockwood, Smashburger, Starbucks, Subway, Taco Bell, Uncle Julio's, Hampton Inn, SpringHill Suites, Woodspring Suites, Advance Parts, Best Buy, Cabela's, CVS Drug, Giant Food/drug, Hobby Lobby, Jiffy Lube, Lowe's, PetSmart, Piedmont Tire/auto, Target/Starbucks/CVS, Verizon, Walgreens
40	US 15, Haymarket, N Greenville Farms Camping(5mi), H, S Sheetz/dsl, Bruster's, Checkers, Chick-fil-A, Foster's Grille, Giuseppe's Italian, Jersey Mike's, Little Caesar's, McDonald's, Papa John's, Popeyes, Smoothie King, Starbucks, Subway, Young Chow Cafe, Hilton, ALDI, CVS Drug, Home Depot, Kohl's, Valvoline, Verizon, Walmart
31	VA 245, to Old Tavern, N Sunoco/dsl, auto repair, USPO
28	US 17 S, Marshall, N BP/McDonald's/dsl, Liberty/7-11, Anthony's Pizza, Foster's Grille, Old Salem Cafe, Subway, Food Lion, vet
27	VA 55 E, Rd 647, Marshall, N Citgo/dsl, Exxon/dsl/LP, Marshall Diner, The Rosemary, 7-11, vet
23	US 17 N, VA 55, (no re-entry from eb), Delaplane
20mm	Goose Creek
18	VA 688, Markham
13	VA 79, to VA 55, Linden, Front Royal, S 7-11/dsl, Exxon/dsl, Applehouse Rest./BBQ/gifts, to Shenandoah NP
11mm	Manassas Run
7mm	Shenandoah River
6	US 340, US 522, to Winchester, Front Royal, N 7-11, EVC, Mobil/7-11/dsl, Royal/dsl, Tesla/EVC, Applebee's, Chipotle, Cracker Barrel, IHOP, Las Caverns, Ledo Pizza, Los Potrillos, McAlister's Deli, Mikado, Panda Express, Roy Rogers, Starbucks, Taco Bell, TGIFriday's, TownePlace Suites/EVC, $Tree, ALDI, AT&T, auto repair, Buick/GMC, Ford, Lowe's, Michael, Petco, Target, URGENT CARE, Valvoline, Walmart, S 7-11, Exxon/Dunkin, Shell, Hampton Inn, Twin Rivers Camping(2mi)
1b a	I-81, N to Winchester, S to Roanoke
0mm	I-66 begins/ends on I-81, exit 300.

MARSHALL

INTERSTATE 77

BLAND

67mm	Virginia/West Virginia state line, East River Mtn
66	VA 598, to East River Mtn
64	US 52, VA 61, to Rocky Gap
62	VA 606, to South Gap
62mm	Welcome Ctr sb, full facilities, litter barrels, vending, petwalk, info
59mm	nb, full facilities, litter barrels, vending, petwalk
58	US 52, to Bastian, E BP/dsl, W Exxon/Circle K, Love's/Arby's/dsl/scales/24hr
56mm	runaway ramp nb
52	US 52, VA 42, Bland, E Sunoco, Subway, $General,
52	Continued Circle K/dsl, Big Walker Motel
51.5mm	weigh sta both lanes
48mm	Big Walker Mtn
47	VA 717
41	VA 610, Peppers Ferry, Wytheville, E Sleep Inn, Super 8, SureStay+, W Circle K, TA/BP/Popeyes/Subway/dsl/scales/24hr/@, Comfort Suites, Country Inn&Suites, Fairfield Inn, Hampton Inn, Ramada Inn, Tru Hilton, U-Haul
40	I-81 S, to Bristol, US 52 N
39.5mm	I-77 and I-81 merge for 9 mi. See I-81, exits 73-80.
32	I-81 N, to Roanoke
26mm	New River
24	VA 69, to Poplar Camp, E Shell, New River Trail Info Ctr, to Shot Tower HP, W Circle K/dsl
19	VA 620, W
14	US 58, US 221, to Hillsville, Galax, farmers mkt, E Circle K/Subway, Red Roof Inn, H, LakeRidge RV Resort(14mi), W Amoco, BP, Circle K/dsl, Fiddler's, McDonald's, Pizza Inn, TCBY, Wendy's, Comfort Inn, Hampton Inn, Holiday Inn Express, Motel 6, Quality Inn, Super 8, Chevrolet
8	VA 148, VA 775, to Fancy Gap, E Amoco, Lakeview, The Gap Deli, Mountain Top, $General, Chance's Creek RV Ctr, KOA(2mi), to Blue Ridge Pkwy, USPO, Utt's Campground, W BP/dsl, Circle K/dsl, Countryview Inn, Motel 6, Peterbilt
6.5mm	runaway truck ramp sb
4.5mm	runaway truck ramp sb
3mm	runaway truck ramp sb
1	VA 620, E Love's/McDonald's/Subway/dsl/scales/24hr, $General
0.5mm	Welcome Ctr. nb, full facilities, litter barrels, petwalk, info
0mm	Virginia/North Carolina state line

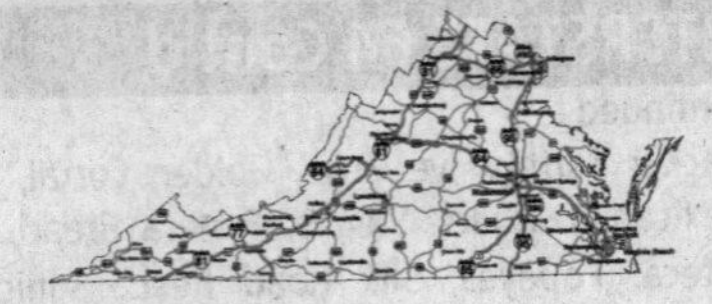

GALAX

INTERSTATE 81

CLEARBROOK

324mm	Virginia/West Virginia state line
323	rd 669, to US 11, Whitehall, E Exxon/Dunkin, Shell/Dunkin, W Flying J/Denny's/dsl/LP/scales/24hr
321	rd 672, Clearbrook, E Sunoco/Olde Stone Truckstop/dsl, Woolen Mill Grill, Freightliner, USPO, vet
320mm	Welcom Ctr sb, full facilities, litter barrels, vending, petwalk
317	US 11, Stephenson, E Chick-fil-A, Chipotle, Glory Days, Guan's Garden, Las Trancas, McDonald's, Red Robin, Subway, Tropical Smoothie, TX Roadhouse, SpringHill, AT&T, Lowe's, PetSmart, T-Mobile, Target/Starbucks/CVS, URGENT CARE, W 7-11/Burger King, Exxon/Dunkin/dsl, Sheetz, Denny's, Pizza Hut/Taco Bell, Days Inn, Holiday Inn Express(3mi), Microtel, Quality Inn, Tru, Candy Hill Camping, H, NTB
315	VA 7, Winchester, E Exxon, Sheetz/dsl, Bojangles, Little Caesars, Skrimp Shack, Sonic, Starbucks, Waffle House, TownePlace Suites, $Tree, Chrysler/Dodge/Jeep, Martin's Foods/gas, tires, Walgreens, W Exxon/Dunkin/Subway, Liberty/dsl, Royal, Shell/dsl, Arby's, Bro Bears, Checkers, Chinatown Kitchen, Domino's, Five Guys, KFC, McDonald's, Wendy's, APM Inn, Hampton Inn, AutoZone, CVS Drug, Family$, Food Maxx, Sharp Shopper Mkt, TrueValue

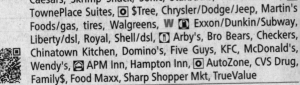

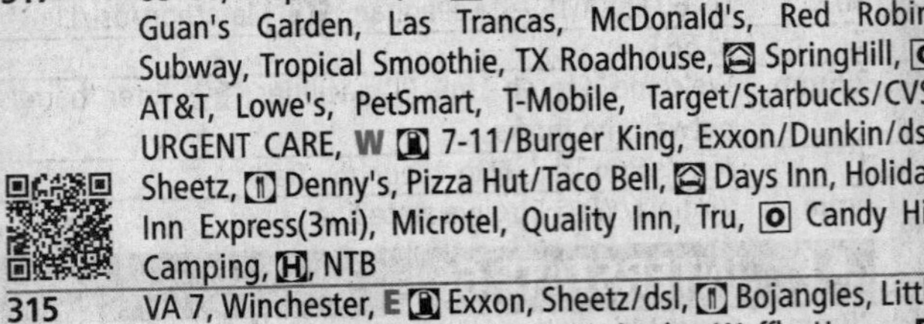

INTERSTATE 81 Cont'd

WINCHESTER

Exit #	Services
314mm	Abrams Creek
313	US 17/50/522, Winchester, E Exxon/Dunkin, Liberty/dsl, Mobil/7-11/dsl, Shell/dsl, Chinatown, Cracker Barrel, Golden Corral, Hibachi Grill, IHOP, Los Tolteco's Mexican, Taste of India, Umberto's Pizza, Candlewood Suites, Fairfield Inn, Holiday Inn, La Quinta, Red Roof Inn, Sleep Inn, Super 8, Travelodge, BigLots, Costco/gas, Nissan, Valvoline, vet, W Sheetz/dsl, Buca Italian, Chick-fil-A, Chili's, China Jade, China Wok, Chipotle Mexican, ChuckECheese, CiCi's, CookOut, Firehouse, Five Guys, Glory Days Grill, Ichiban Japanese, Jersey Mike's, Jimmy John's, Longhorn Steaks, McDonald's, Mission BBQ, Okinawa Steaks, Olive Garden, Panera Bread, Rancho Mexican, Red Lobster, Starbucks, Subway, Taco Bell, TGIFridays, Tropical Smoothie, Waffle House, Wendy's, Hampton Inn, Hilton Garden, Spark Hotel, $Tree, $Tree, Belk, Best Buy, Books-A-Million, Dick's, Hobby Lobby, Home Depot, JC Penney, Kohl's, Lowe's, mall, Martin's Foods, Michaels, NTB, Old Navy, PepBoys, Petco, PetSmart, Ross, Staples, Target/Starbucks/CVS, TJ Maxx, to Shenandoah U, URGENT CARE, Verizon, Verizon, Walgreens, Walmart/gas
310	VA 37, to US 50W, W 76/dsl, Shell/7-11/dsl, Carrabba's, McDonald's, Outback Steaks, Subway, Comfort Inn, Country Inn&Suites, ALDI, Candy Hill Camping(6mi), CarQuest, Honda, H, Mitsubishi, Volvo, VW
307	VA 277, Stephens City, E 7-11, BP/dsl, Shell/dsl, Arby's, Del Rio Mexican, Domino's, Ginger Asian, Gino Pizza, KFC/Taco Bell, McDonald's, Roma Italian, Starbucks, Waffle House, Holiday Inn Express, Qualtiy Inn, $General, $Tree, Advance Parts, AutoZone, Martin's Foods/gas, O'Reilly Parts, vet, W Exxon, Sheetz/dsl/EVC
304mm	weigh sta both lanes
302	rd 627, Middletown, E Exxon/dsl, W 7-11, Liberty/dsl, Italian Touch, McDonald's, Econolodge, $General, to Wayside Theatre
300	I-66 E, to Washington, Shenandoah NP, Skyline Dr
298	US 11, Strausburg, E Exxon/McDonald's/dsl/LP, Shell/7-11/dsl, Anthony's Pizza, Arby's, Burger King, Castiglia Italian, Ciro's Pizza, Golden China, Great Wall, Strasburg Diner/EVC, Fairfield Inn, Ramada Inn, Advance Parts, Family$, Food Lion, O'Reilly Parts, W Battle of Cedar Grove Camping, to Belle Grove Plantation, Walgreens
296	US 48, VA 55, Strausburg
291	rd 651, Toms Brook, W Love's/Arby's/dog park/dsl/scales/24hr, Pilot/Taco Bell/Subway/dsl/scales/24hr, Speedco, truckwash/repair
283	VA 42, Woodstock, E Liberty/7-11, Sheetz, Shell/Dunkin, Arby's, Asian Spice, China Wok, KFC, Las Trancas, McDonald's, Pizza Bella, Pizza Hut, Taco Bell, Wendy's, Comfort Inn, Hampton Inn, Holiday Inn Express, CVS Drug, Family$, Food Lion, H, to Massanutten Military Academy, Walgreens, W Citgo, Exxon/dsl, China Wok, Cracker Barrel, Domino's, Starbucks, Chrysler/Jeep/Dodge, Ford, Lowe's, vet, Walmart/EVC
279	VA 185, rd 675, Edinburg, E Exxon, Exxon/dsl, Shell/dsl, Bean's BBQ, Sal's Italian Bistro, $General, Creekside Camping(2mi), USPO
277	rd 614, Bowmans Crossing
273	VA 292, RD 703, Mt Jackson, E 7-11, Exxon/dsl, Liberty/dsl/scales/24hr, Sheetz/dsl/scales/24hr/Tesla EVC, Burger King, China King, Hardee's, Italian Touch, Motel 6, $General, Family$, Food Lion, USPO
269	rd 730, to US 11, Shenandoah Caverns, E Shell/dsl, W antiques, Shenandoah Valley Camping
269mm	N Fork Shenandoah River
264	US 211, New Market, E Exxon, Exxon/dsl, Exxon/dsl, Liberty/Dunkin/dsl, Shell/dsl, Godfather's Pizza, Italian Job, Jalisco, McDonald's, Quality Inn, $General, Endless Caverns Camping, Skyline Dr, to Shenandoah NP, U-Haul, USPO, W 7-11, Days Inn
262mm	both lanes, full facilities, litter barrels, vending, petwalk
257	US 11, VA 259, to Broadway, E Liberty/7-11/dsl, Endless Caverns Camping, W $General
251	US 11, Harrisonburg, W Exxon/dsl, Pilot/Dunkin/dsl/scales/24hr, BBQ Ranch, Smokin'Q, Economy Inn, tires
247b a	US 33, Harrisonburg, E Exxon/dsl, Liberty/dsl, Royal/dsl, Sheetz/dsl/Tesla EVC, Shell/dsl, Applebee's, Bruster's, Buffalo Wild Wings, Burger King, Chick-fil-A, Chili's, Chipotle, CiCi's Pizza, Cinnamon Bear, Cook Out, Domino's, Dunkin, El Charro Mexican, Five Guys, Hangry Joe's, Honey Baked Ham, IHOP, Jimmy John's, Krispy Kreme, LongHorn Steaks, Marco's Pizza, McDonald's, Mr. J's Bagels, O'Neill's Grill, Olive Garden, Oriental Cafe, Oriental Hibachi, Outback Steaks, Panda Express, Panera Bread, Pizza Hut, Popeyes, Potbelly, Red Lobster, Starbucks, Sushi Village, Taco Bell, Tropical Smoothie, TX Roadhouse, Waffle House, Wendy's, Wood Grill Buffet, Candlewood Suites, Clarion Pointe, Comfort Inn&Suites, Courtyard, DoubleTree, EconoLodge, Fairfield Inn, Hampton Inn, Holiday Inn Express, Howard Johnson, Hyatt Place/EVC, Quality Inn, Residence Inn, Sleep Inn, $Tree, ALDI, AT&T, AutoZone, Barnes&Noble, Belk, Best Buy, Books-A-Million, Chevrolet, Costco/gas, Dick's, Firestone/auto, Hobby Lobby, Home Depot, JC Penney, Jiffy Lube, Kohl's, Kroger, Lowe's, Martin's Foods/gas, Michael's, Mr. Tire, Nissan, Old Navy, PetCo, PetSmart, Ross, Staples, Target, TJ Maxx, to Shenandoah NP, to Skyline Dr, URGENT CARE, Walmart/gas, W Exxon/dsl, Liberty/dsl, Royal/dsl, Sheetz/dsl, Arby's, Chanello's Pizza, Chuy's Mexican, Ciro's Pizza, DQ, El Sol, Flaming Grill, Golden China, Hardee's, Kangham Style, KFC, Kyoto, Little Caesars, McDonald's, Sam's Hotdogs, Subway, Tacos El Primo, Budget Inn, Advance Parts, antique, BigLots, CVS Drug, Family$, Food Lion
245	VA 659, Port Republic Rd, E Circle K/Dunkin, Citgo, Exxon/7-11/dsl, Liberty/dsl, Royal/dsl, Fiesta Mexican, McDonald's, Starbucks, Subway, Tropical Smoothie, Vito's Italian, CVS Drug, Food Lion, H, W Starbucks, to James Madison U
243	US 11, to Harrisonburg, W Exxon/7-11/dsl, Harrisonburg Travel Ctr/diner/dsl/scales, Liberty, Sheetz/dsl, Shell/7-11/dsl, Burger King, China King, Cracker Barrel, Dunkin, Kline's Dairy Bar, McDonald's, Pizza Hut, Sub Sta., Subway, Taco Bell, Best Western+, Country Inn&Suites, Hampton Inn, Microtel/EVC, Motel 6, Ramada Inn, Super 8, Tru, Advance Parts, AutoZone, CarMax, Ford, Honda, Hyundai, Kia, Lincoln, O'Reilly Parts, Penske, Subaru, Toyota, U-Haul, USPO
240	VA 257, rd 682, Mount Crawford, E Shell/7-11/dsl, McDonald's, W Exxon/Burger King/dsl(1mi)
235	VA 256, Weyers Cave, E Shell/dsl, W BP/Subway/dsl, Exxon/dsl, Mi Rancho Mexican, antiques, Freightliner
232mm	**full facilities, litter barrels, petwalk, , , both lanes, vending**
227	rd 612, Verona, E BP/Subway/dsl, W 7-11, Exxon, Shell/dsl, Arby's, Burger King, China City, Ciro's Pizza, Hardee's, McDonald's, Rackem Ribs, Quality Inn, Suburban Studios, $General, antiques, auto repair, Food Lion, vet, Walgreens
225	VA 262, Woodrow Wilson Pkwy, E Motel 6, W Holiday Inn, Red Roof Inn

STRAUSBURG
EDINBURG
HARRISONBURG
MOUNT CRAWFORD

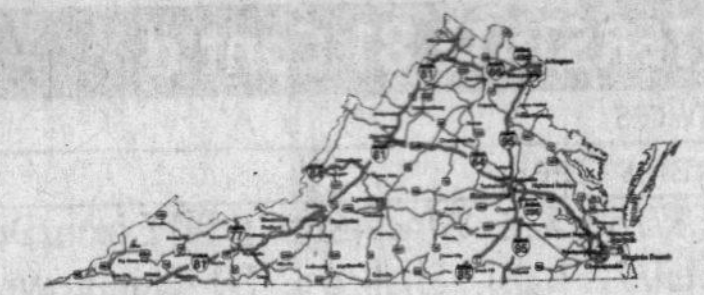

VA

INTERSTATE 81 Cont'd

Exit #	Services
	STAUNTON
222	US 250, Staunton, E Exxon/dsl, Royal/dsl, Cracker Barrel, Hometown Grill, Hometown Grill, Mrs Rowe's Rest., Avid Hotel, Best Western/Tesla EVC, Sleep Inn, Sleep Inn, W BP/dsl, Sheetz/dsl/Tesla EVC, Speedway/dsl, Baskin-Robbins/Dunkin, Bojangles, Burger King, Chick-fil-A, Chili's, Cook Out, Firehouse Subs, Hot Wok, Jersey Mike's, KFC, Massaki Japanese, McDonald's, Pizza Hut, Starbucks, Waffle House, Wendy's, Clarion Pointe, Comfort Inn, EconoLodge, Fairfield Inn, Tru, 7-11, ALDI, American Frontier Culture Museum, auto repair, AutoZone, Lowe's, Martin's Foods/gas, O'Reilly Parts, T-Mobile, Toyota, URGENT CARE, Walmart/Subway
221	I-64 E, to Charlottesville, Skyline Dr
220	VA 262, to US 11, Staunton, W Citgo, Exxon, Applebee's, Brother's Pizza, McDonald's, Red Lobster, Sam's HotDogs, Starbucks, Budget Inn, Hampton Inn, Holiday Inn Express, $Tree, Advance Parts, auto repair, Belk, Charlie Obaugh RV Ctr, Chevrolet, Chrysler/Dodge/Jeep, CVS Drug, Food Lion, Ford/Lincoln, Honda, Kia, Mitsubishi, Nissan, Subaru, TJ Maxx, U-Haul, vet, VW
217	Rd 654, to Mint Spring, Stuarts Draft, E GB/dsl, Days Inn, Walnut Hills Campground/RV Park, W Exxon/Circle K/dsl/24hr, Liberty, Relax Inn, $General
213b a	US 11, US 340, Greenville, E BP/Subway, Love's/McDonald's/tires/dsl/scales/24hr, Pilot/Arby's/dsl/scales/24hr, Edelweiss Rest., Hometown Inn, Walnut Hills Campground & RV Park
	FAIRFIELD
205	Rd 606, Raphine, E BP/dsl, Exxon/Subway/Burger King/dsl, Petro/Papa John's/Popeyes/dsl/scales/24hr/@, Blue Beacon, truck repair, W Pilot/Wendy's/dsl/scales/24hr/truck repair, Comfort Inn/Tesla EVC, auto repair, Peterbilt
200	RD 710, Fairfield, E BP/McDonald's/dsl, Frank's Pizza, Fox Hill B&B, Dottie's Mkt, W Exxon/Subway/dsl, Shell/dsl, auto repair
199mm	sb, full facilities, vending, litter barrels, petwalk
195	US 11, Lee Hwy, E Church Hill, W Exxon/dsl, TA/Shell/IHOP/dsl/scales/24hr/@, Days Inn, Howard Johnson, Quality Inn, Campground at Lee Hi, repair
191	I-64 W(exits left from nb), US 60, to Charleston
188b a	US 60, to Lexington, Buena Vista, E BP, Exxon, Burger King, Hardee's, $General, Family$, Food Lion, to Blue Ridge Pkwy, to Glen Maury Park, W Exxon/dsl, Exxon/McDonald's/dsl, Hardee's, Pizza Hut, Taco Bell, Hampton Inn, Food Lion, H, NAPA, to Washington&Lee U, VMI
180	US 11, Natural Bridge, (180a exits left from sb), E Exxon, Shell, Herring B&B, Relax Inn, Cave Mtn NF, Jellystone Camping, W Shell/dsl, Pink Cadillac Diner, Budget Inn, KOA, st police
	BUCHANAN
175	US 11 N, to Glasgow, Natural Bridge, E Exxon, Inn at Forest Oaks, Natural Bridge Hotel/rest.(2mi), Jellystone Camping(6.5mi), to James River RA
168	VA 614, US 11, Blue Ridge Pkwy, Arcadia, E Shell/dsl, Mtn Cafe, Middle Creek Camping(6mi)
167	US 11(from sb), Buchanan
162	US 11, Buchanan, E Exxon/dsl, to BR Pkwy, W Citgo/Subway
158mm	sb, full facilities, vending, litter barrels, petwalk
156	RD 640, to US 11, E Exxon/Brugh's Mill/dsl/EVC
150	US 11/220, to Fincastle, E Citgo/dsl, Mobil, ONE9/Subway/dsl/24hr/scales, Angelle's Diner, Bella Pizza, Best Wok, Cracker Barrel, Hardee's, McDonald's, Taco Bell, Best Western, Comfort Inn&Suites, Holiday Inn Express, Motel 6,
	CLOVERDALE
150	Continued Quality Inn, $General Mkt, Berglund RV Ctr, truckwash, W BP/dsl, Exxon/dsl, GB, Bojangle's, Pancho's Mexican, Three Lil' Pigs BBQ, Wendy's, Super 8, Kroger/dsl, Verizon, vet
149mm	weigh sta both lanes
146	VA 115, Cloverdale, E BP/dsl, Exxon, Mobil, Shell/dsl, Agave Mexican, Alejandros, Burger King, Dunkin, Harbor Inn Seafood, McDonald's, Subway, Wendy, Country Inn&Suites/Tesla EVC, Days Inn, Fairfield Inn, Hampton Inn, SpringHill Suites, Tru Hilton, Camping World, CVS, Kroger, Mr. Tire, Take 5 Oil Change, tires, to Hollins U, Verizon
143	I-581, US 220, to Roanoke, Blue Ridge Pkwy(exits left from sb), WoodSpring Suites, 7-11, E Kroger/dsl, El Toreo, Subway, Waffle House, Knights Inn, Quality Inn, Super 8, Travelodge, Honda
	SALEM
141	VA 419, Salem, E Liberty/7-11/dsl, Marathon/Burger King, China Fresh, Hardee's, Hibachi Express, Mamma's Pizza, McDonald's, Starbucks, Baymont Inn, Days Inn, Fairfield Inn, Holiday Inn Express, La Quinta, AT&T, Chevrolet, GMC, H, Kia, Kroger/gas, NAPA, W BP/Subway/dsl, Citgo
140	VA 311, Salem, E Mac&Bob's Cafe, W BP/Subway/dsl, Exxon
137	VA 112, VA 619, Salem, E BP, Exxon/dsl, Go-Mart, Marathon, Sheetz/dsl, Alejandro's Mexican, Angelle's Diner, Anthony's Cafe, Applebee's, Arby's, Bojangle's, Burger King, Chick-fil-A, China Wok, Chipotle, Denny's, DQ, Dunkin, El Rodeo Mexican, Firehouse Subs, Hardee's, Jersey Mike's, Jimmy John's, KFC, Mamma Maria Italian, McDonald's, Moe's SW Grill, Sam's Hot Dog, Sonic, Starbucks, Subway, Taco Bell, Waffle House, Wendy's, Comfort Suites, Motel 6, Quality Inn, Super 8, $General, $Tree, Advance Parts, auto repair, AutoZone, BigLots, Food Lion, Goodyear, Kroger/dsl, Mr. Tire, NTB, O'Reilly Parts, Valvoline, Verizon, Walgreens, Walmart, W Avid Hotel, Hampton Inn, Howard Johnson
132	VA 647, to Dixie Caverns, E Mobil/dsl, Which Wich, Dixie Caverns Camping, park
	CHRISTIANSBURG
129mm	nb, full facilities, vending, litter barrels, petwalk
128	US 11, VA 603, Ironto, E Shell, W Exxon/dsl/24hr
118c b a	US 11/460, Christiansburg, E Shell, Cracker Barrel, Days Inn, Fairfield Inn, Holiday Inn Express, Homewood Suites, Quality Inn, Super 8, Tru, Wyndham, RV Park, W Liberty/7-11/dsl, Sheetz/dsl, Shell, Dunkin, Hardee's, LJ Silver, McDonald's, Ruby Tuesday, Starbucks, Wendy's, EconoLodge, $General, Advance Parts, Chevrolet, Chrysler/Dodge/Jeep, Food Lion, Ford, Honda, H, Kia, Mitsubishi, Subaru, to VA Tech, Toyota
114	VA 8, Christiansburg, E to Blue Ridge Pkwy, W Exxon/dsl, Burger King, Pizza Inn, Subway, Budget Inn, $General Mkt, USPO
109	VA 177, VA 600, E H, W Sunoco/dsl, Starbucks, Comfort Inn, La Quinta, Quality Inn, Super 8, Tru, Buick/Cadillac/Chevrolet, Food City/drug, RV repair
107mm	both lanes, full facilities, vending, litter barrels, petwalk
105	VA 232, RD 605, to Radford, W Exxon/dsl, Sportsman RV Campground
101	RD 660, to Claytor Lake SP, E The Mason Jar, Claytor Lake Inn, Wingate, McGuire Family Campgrounds, W Exxon/DQ/dsl, Shell/dsl/scales/@

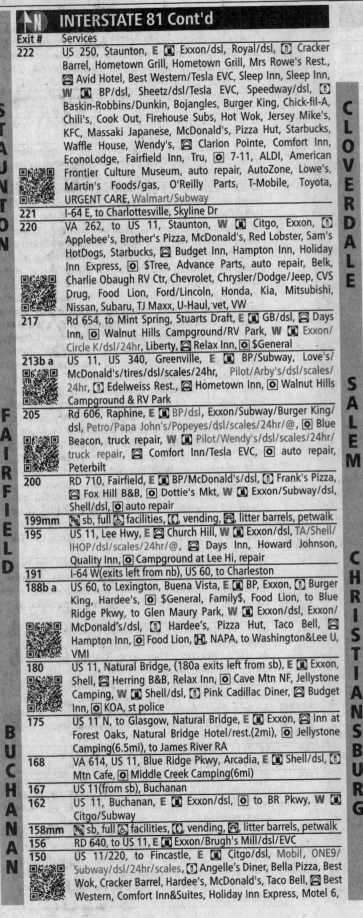

INTERSTATE 81 Cont'd

Exit #	Services
98	VA 100 N, to Dublin, E BP, Marathon/dsl, Bojangles, Cinco De Mayo, Fazoli's, Hampton Inn, Holiday Inn Express, Quality Inn, to Wilderness Rd Museum, W Liberty/dsl, Marathon/dsl, Shell/Papa John's/dsl, Arby's, Burger King, Domino's, El Ranchero Mexican, McDonald's, Taco Bell, Waffle House, Wendy's, Knights Inn, $General, $Tree, Ace Hardware, NAPA, O'Reilly Parts, U-Haul, Walmart/Subway
94b a	VA 99 N, to Pulaski, W BP, Exxon/dsl, Speedway/dsl, Compadre's Mexican, Domino's, Hardee's, Hunt Brother's Pizza, Little Caesar's, McDonald's, Sonic, Taco Bell/KFC, Wendy's, $General, $Tree, Advance Parts, CVS, Family$, Food City, Food City, Food Lion, H, O'Reilly Parts, Suzuki, T-Mobile, tires, tires
92	Rd 658, to Draper, E Citgo, to New River Trail SP, USPO
89b a	US 11 N, VA 100, to Pulaski
86	Rd 618, Service Rd, W truck stop, U-Haul
84	Rd 619, to Grahams Forge, W Exxon/Circle K/dsl/24hr, Love's/Chester's/Subway/dsl/scales/24hr, Cholula Mexican, Fox Mtn Inn
81.5mm	I-81 S and I-77 N run together 9 mi.
81	I-77 S, to Charlotte, Galax, to Blue Ridge Pkwy, Galax
80	US 52 S, VA 121 N, to Ft Chiswell, S Family$, E Exxon/Burger King/dsl, Flying J/Denny's/dsl/scales/24hr/@, Cinco de Mayo Mexican, Wendy's, Hampton Inn, Super 8, Ft Chiswell RV Park, truck repair, W Circle K/dsl, McDonald's, Comfort Inn, Speedco
77	Service Rd, E Circle K/dsl/24hr, Flying J/Denny's/dsl/scales/LP/RV Dump/24hr, Speedway/dsl, Burger King, KOA, W Exxon/dsl, Pilot/Arby's/DQ/dsl/scales/24hr, st police
73	US 11 S, Wytheville, E Exxon/dsl, Go-Mart, Applebee's, Bob Evans, Cracker Barrel, Dawghouse, El Puerto Mexican, Hardee's, Papa John's, Peking Chinese, Shoney's, Sonic, Waffle House, Wendy's, Budget Host, Days Inn, EconoLodge, Holiday Inn Express, La Quinta, Motel 6, Quality Inn, Red Roof Inn, Rodeway Inn, Travelodge, $General, AutoZone, Buick/Chevrolet/GMC, CVS Drug, Food Lion, Ford, Goodyear/auto, Harley-Davidson, H, Nissan, Rural King
72.5mm	I-81 N and I-77 S merge for 9 mi
72	I-77 N, to Bluefield, Circle K/dsl/24hr, TA/Popeyes/Subway/Taco Bell/IHOP/dsl/scales/24hr/@, Mami's Cafe, Best Western, Comfort Suites, Country Inn&Suites, Fairfield Inn, Hampton Inn, Ramada, Sleep Inn, Super 8, Tru Hilton, U-Haul
70	US 21/52, Wytheville, E BP/dsl, Sheetz/dsl, Bojangle's, Capt. D's, China Wok, El Patio Mexican, KFC/Taco Bell, Little Caesar's, McDonald's, Ruby Tuesday, Starbucks, Subway, Tokyo Japanese, Wendy's, $Tree, Food Lion, H, Lowe's, O'Reilly Parts, PetCo, Verizon, Walmart, W Shell, Comfort Inn
67	US 11(from nb, no re-entry), to Wytheville
61mm	nb, full facilities, vending, litter barrels, petwalk, NO TRUCKS
60	VA 90, Rural Retreat, E Shell/dsl, Spirit/dsl, McDonald's, $General, camping, Dutch Pantry Mkt, RV service/repair, to Rural Retreat Lake
54	rd 683, to Groseclose, E Exxon, Sunoco/dsl, El Burrito Loco, SweetWater Rest., Relax Inn
53.5mm	sb, full facilities, vending, litter barrels, petwalk
50	US 11, Atkins, W Circle K/Subway/dsl/24hr, Exxon, Comfort Inn, NAPA Care
47	US 11, to Marion, W Citgo, Gas'N Go, Shell/dsl, Arby's, Burger King, Charley's Philly Steaks, China House, Domino's,
47	Continued KFC/Taco Bell, Little Caesar's, McDonald's, Mi Puerto Mexican, Pizza Hut, Sonic, Starbucks, Wendy's, EconoLodge, Red Roof Inn, Travel Inn, $General, $Tree, Ace Hardware, Advance Parts, AutoZone, Buick/Chevrolet/GMC, CVS Drug, Food City, Food City, Food Lion, H, Ingles, Marion Drug, O'Reilly Parts, to Hungry Mother SP(4mi), Verizon, Walgreens, Walmart
45	VA 16, Marion, E Valero/dsl, Mt Rogers NRA, to Grayson Highlands SP, W Exxon, Sunoco, Hardee's, Collin House B&B, auto parts, NAPA, tires, USPO
44	US 11 , Marion, W $General, tires, vet
39	US 11, rd 645, Seven Mile Ford, W Interstate Camping
35	VA 107, Chilhowie, E Hardee's, Motel 6, U-Haul, W Exxon/dsl, Gas'N Go, Mobil/Main St Mkt, Shell/dsl, Fiesta Jalisco, McDonald's, Riverfront Rest., Subway, Taco Bell, $General, antiques, Food City, Greever's Drugs, NAPA, USPO
32	US 11, to Chilhowie
29	VA 91, to Damascus, Glade Spring, E Marathon/Subway/dsl, Petro/Arby's/Sbarro/dsl/24hr/@, Giardino's Italian, Pizza+, Wendy's, EconoLodge, Knights Inn, $General, Peterbilt, W Exxon, Shell/dsl, Spirit, El Burrito Loco, vet
26	rd 737, Emory, W The Emory House B&B, USPO(1mi)
24	VA 80, Meadowview Rd, E Love's/McDonald's/Subway/dsl/scales/24hr, $General, vet, W USPO
22	rd 704, Enterprise Rd, E Marathon/dsl, H
19	US 11/58, to Abingdon, E Shell/Subway/Dunkin/dsl, Bojangle's, China Wok, DQ, McDonald's, Pizza+, Royal Farms, $Tree, Lowe's, to Mt Rogers NRA, vet, Walmart/dsl, W BP/dsl, Domino's Pizza, Exxon/dsl, Bella's Pizza, Burger King, Cracker Barrel, Puerto Mexican, Alpine Motel, Country Inn Suites, Fairfield Inn, Quality Inn, Red Roof Inn, $General
17	US 58A, VA 75, Abingdon, W Exxon, Arby's, Capt D's, Charley's Philly Steaks, Fiddler's, Fuji Express, Hardee's, Jersey Mike's, Little Caesar's, Los Dorados, McDonald's, Pal's Drive-In, Papa John's, Pizza Hut, Taco Bell, Wendy's, Hampton Inn, Holiday Inn Express, Super 8, Advance Parts, Food City/gas, Kroger/dsl
14	US 19, VA 140, Abingdon, W BP/Dunkin/dsl, Exxon, Shell/dsl, McDonald's, Milano's Italian, Moon Dog Cafe, Subway, Clarion Pointe, Comfort Suites, antiques, Chevrolet, Ford/Lincoln, Riverside Camping(10mi), Verizon
13.5mm	TRUCKERS ONLY nb, full facilities, vending, litter barrels
13	VA 611, to Lee Hwy, W Shell/dsl, vet
10	US 11/19, Lee Hwy, W Exxon, Marathon/dsl, Shell/dsl, Deluxe Inn, Economy Inn, Skyland Inn, auto repair
7	Old Airport Rd, E Shell/dsl, Bojangles, Cheddar's, Cracker Barrel, Sonic, Extended Stay America, Hilton Garden, W Marathon, Valero/dsl, Wendy's, Chick-fil-A, Chili's, Cook-Out, Crumbl, Domino's, DQ, Golden Corral, IHOP, Jersey Mike's Subs, Logan's Roadhouse, Los Arcos, Mellow Mushroom, Olive Garden, Osaka Japanese, Pal's Drive-In, Perkins, Puerto Mexican, Red Lobster, Starbucks, Subway, Taco Bell, Courtyard, Delta, Motel 6, Quality Inn, $General, $Tree, Advance Parts, Advance Parts, AutoZone, Books-A-Million, Discount Tire, Food City/gas, Home Depot, Office Depot, PetSmart, Ross, Sam's Club/gas, Sugar Hollow Camping, Target, TJ Maxx, Verizon, Walmart
5	US 11/19, Lee Hwy, E Shell, Arby's, Hardee's, KFC, LJ Silver, McDonald's, Budget Inn, Red Roof Inn, Harley-Davidson, O'Reilly Parts, Price Less Foods, W Sheetz/Tesla EVC/dsl, Buffalo Wild Wings, TX Roadhouse, Zaxby's, Bristol Inn, ALDI, Buick/GMC, Firestone, Hobby Lobby,

WYTHEVILLE · ATKINS · MARION · EMORY · ABINGDON

INTERSTATE 81 Cont'd

BRISTOL

5 Continued
Kings Tire, Lowe's

3 I-381 S, to Bristol, E Gas'n Go/dsl, Mobil/dsl, Royal Farms/dsl, Shell/dsl, Little Caesar, McAlister's, EconoLodge, $General, Ace Hardware, Food City, tires, vet

1b a US 58/421, Bristol, E Exxon/dsl, Shell, Arby's, Capt D's, DQ, KFC, McDonald's, Pizza Hut, Pizza+, Sakura Japanese, Sonic, Subway, Taco Bell, Wendy's, Budget Inn, $Tree, CVS Drug, H, Hyundai, Kroger/dsl, Toyota, U-Haul, UHaul, URGENT CARE, Verizon, vet, Walgreens, W Shell, Travel Inn

0mm Virginia/Tennessee state line, Welcome Ctr nb, full facilities, info, vending, litter barrels, petwalk, NO TRUCKS

INTERSTATE 85

ALBERTA

69mm I-85 begins/ends on I-95.

69 US 301, I-95 N, Wythe St, Washington St, Petersburg

68 I-95 S, US 460 E, to Norfolk, Crater Rd

65 Squirrel Level Rd, E to Richard Bland Coll, W Marathon, Valero, Family$

63b a US 1, to Petersburg, E Amoco/dsl, Exxon/KFC/dsl, Shell/Burger King/dsl, Hardee's, Taco Bell, Waffle House, Holiday Inn Express, $General, st police, W BP, Mobil, Shell, Brother's Pizza, McDonald's, Pizza Hut, Advance Parts, auto repair, Family$, Food Lion, NAPA, O'Reilly Parts , Walgreens

61 US 460, to Blackstone, E Shell/Subway/dsl, Joe's Rest., W

55mm both lanes, full facilities, litter barrels, vending, petwalk

53 VA 703, Dinwiddie, W BP, Exxon, Exxon/dsl, Dinwiddie Diner, $General, NAPA, to 5 Forks Nat Bfd, USPO

52mm Stony Creek

48 VA 650, DeWitt, W USPO

42 VA 40, McKenney, W BP, Citgo/Quick Mart, Exxon, Dairy Freeze, Little Italy, $General, Family$

40mm Nottoway River

39 VA 712, to Rawlings, W Davis TC/Exxon/Subway/dsl/scales/24hr

34 VA 630, Warfield, W Exxon/dsl, USPO

32mm both lanes, full facilities, litter barrels, vending, petwalk

28 US 1, Alberta, W Exxon, Family$

27 VA 46, to Lawrenceville

24 VA 644, to Meredithville, E USPO

22mm weigh sta both lanes

20mm Meherrin River

15 US 1, to South Hill, E Hines, W Love's/Subway/McDonald's/dsl/scales/24hr, Fiesta Mexico, Kahill's Rest., Holiday Inn Express

12 US 58, VA 47, to South Hill, E Exxon/dsl, Pilot/Shell/dsl, RaceWay, Sunoco/dsl, Applebee's, Arby's, Bojangles, Domino's, Five Guys, Glass House Grill, Luca's Italian, Papa John's, Sonic, Starbucks, Best Western+, Comfort Inn, Fairfield Inn, Hampton Inn, Microtel, $Tree, AT&T, Chrysler/Jeep/Dodge, Honda, Verizon, Walmart/Subway, W BP/dsl, Exxon, Marathon, Burger King, Cracker Barrel, Hardee's, KFC/Taco Bell, McDonald's, New China, Pizza Hut, Subway, Wendy's, Americas Express Inn, Quality Inn, $General, Advance Parts, AutoZone, CVS Drug, Family$, Food Lion, Home Depot, O'Reilly Parts, Roses, TJ Maxx

4 VA 903, to Bracey, Lake Gaston, E Exxon/Simmon's/dsl/scales/24hr/@, Sunoco/7-11/Subway/Papa John's/dsl, Huddle House, Top It Pizza, $General,

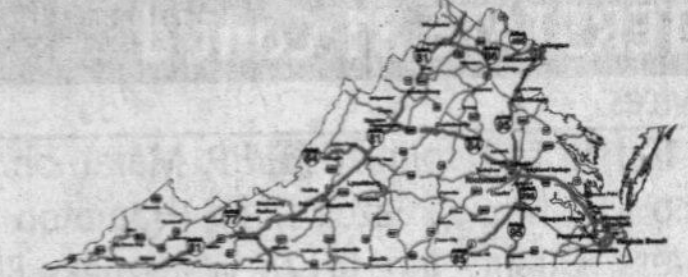

4 Continued
Americamps Camping(5mi), W Shell/Pizza Hut/Quizno's, Lake Gaston Inn

3mm Lake Gaston

1mm Welcome Ctr nb, full facilities, phone, litter barrels, vending, petwalk

0mm Virginia/North Carolina state line

INTERSTATE 95

FT BELVOIR

178mm Virginia/Maryland state line, Potomac River, W Wilson Br

177c b a US 1, to Alexandria, Ft Belvoir, E Applebees, Boston Mkt, Chili's, Chipotle, Famous Dave's BBQ, Five Guys, Krispy Kreme, McDonald's, Outback Steaks, Panda Express, Papa John's, TGIFridays, Budget Host, Days Inn, Fairfield, Hampton Inn, Holiday Inn Express, Red Roof Inn, Relax Inn, SpringHill Suites, $Tree, 7-11, Advance Parts, ALDI, Chevrolet, Chrysler/Dodge/Jeep, Giant Food, Jiffy Lube, Lowe's, NTB, Office Depot, Petco, Target/CVS Drug, Walgreens, Walmart, W Exxon, Liberty/repair, Speedway, District Taco, Ace Hardware, CVS Drug, Safeway

176b a VA 241, Telegraph Rd, E BP, Speedway/dsl, W Aldo's Italian, Dunkin, Jimmy John's, Panera Bread, Pasara Thai, Potbelly, Starbucks, Ted's MT Grill, Courtyard, Embassy Suites, Extended Stay America, Hilton, Holiday Inn, Hyatt, Residence Inn, SpringHill Suites, The Westin, CVS Drug, USPO, Wegmans, Whole Foods

174 Eisenhower Ave Connector, to Alexandria

173 rd 613, Van Dorn St, to Franconia, E Comfort Inn, W Exxon, Dunkin, McDonald's, Red Lobster, Jiffy Lube, Mr. Tire, Starbucks

170a I-495 N, I-495 & I-95 N run together to MD, to Rockville

170b I-395 N, to Washington

169b a rd 644, Springfield, Franconia, E Bertucci's, Silver Diner, Starbucks, Subway, Best Western, Comfort Inn, Courtyard, Extended Stay America, Hilton, Wingate, Barnes&Noble, Best Buy, Dick's, Firestone/auto, Ford, Home Depot, H, JC Penney, Macy's, Marshalls, Michael's, Old Navy, PetSmart, Staples, Target/Tesla EVC, W Liberty, Shell, Sunoco/7-11, Blue Pearl Buffet, Bob Evans, Chick-fil-A, Chipotle Mexican, Cold Stone, Deliah's Grill, Domino's, Dunkin, El Paso Mexican, Hard Times Cafe, Jersey Mike's, KFC, McDonald's, Noodles&Co, Outback Steaks, Paisano's Pizza, Panda Express, Popeyes, Potbelly, Starbucks, Subway, Wingstop, Holiday Inn Express, Homewood Suites, Motel 6, Residence Inn, TownePlace Suites, $Tree, 7-11, 7-11, Advance Parts, ALDI, auto, CVS Drug, Giant Food, Jiffy Lube, Lidl, Midas, Mr Tire, Nissan, Subaru, Trader Joe's, USPO, Verizon, vet, VW, Whole Foods

LORTON

167 VA 617, Backlick Rd(from sb), W InterFuel/dsl

166b a VA 7100, Newington, to Ft Belvoir, E Exxon/7-11, Denny's, Wendy's, Embassy Suites, NAPA, NTB, Toyota, U-Haul, USPO, W Exxon/7-11/dsl, McDonald's, AT&T, Costco

163 VA 642, Lorton, E Shell/repair, Sunoco/dsl, Chipotle, Dunkin, Glory Days Grill, Paisano's Pizza, Panera Bread, Tropical Smoothie, auto repair, W Shell/dsl, Antoneli's Pizza, Burger King, Naty's Tex-Mex, TX Donuts, Holiday Inn Express, H

161 US 1 S(exits left from sb, no reentry nb), to Ft Belvoir, Mt Vernon, Woodlawn Plantation, Gunston Hall

160.5mm Occoquan River

INTERSTATE 95 Cont'd

Exit # Services

160b a VA 123 N, Woodbridge, Occoquan, E Sunoco, Hampton Inn, Quality Inn, ALDI, Food Lion, W BP, Exxon/repair/dsl, Fast Fuels, Shell, Shell/dsl, Domino's, Hibachi Express, KFC, Madigan's Waterfront Rest., McDonald's, Wendy's, 7-11, same as 161

158b a VA 294, Prince William Pkwy, Woodbridge, W 7-11, Exxon, Mobil/dsl, Shell, Bungalow Alehouse, Carrabba's, Chick-fil-A, Chipotle Mexican, ChuckeCheese, Chuy's, Coldstone, Famous Dave's BBQ, Firehouse Subs, First Watch, Five Guys, Fuddruckers, Hooters, IHOP, Jersey Mike's, McDonald's, Mission BBQ, Noodles&Co, On-the-Border, Panda Express, Panera Bread, Qdoba, Red Lobster, Red Robin, Smokey Bones BBQ, Starbucks, Starbucks, Taco Bell, Tropical Smoothie, Wendy's, Country Inn&Suites, Courtyard, Fairfield Inn, Holiday Inn Express, Home2 Suites, Residence Inn, Sleep Inn, SpringHill Suites, TownePlace Suites, $Tree, Advance Parts, ALDI, AutoZone, Best Buy, CarMax, Dick's, GNC, Hobby Lobby, Home Depot, Lowe's, Michael's, PetSmart, Sam's Club/gas, Target, URGENT CARE, Verizon, Walmart/Subway

156 VA 784, Potomac Mills, E Brixx Woodfired Grill, BurgerFi, CAVA, Duck Donuts, Firebirds Grill, Potbelly, Starbucks, Uncle Julio's Grill, Hilton Garden, Homewood Suites, AT&T, Barnes & Noble, H, Old Navy, REI, to Leesylvania SP, Wegman's Mkt, W Shell/7-11, Shell/dsl, Sunoco/dsl, Bahama Breeze, Bob Evans, Buffalo Wild Wings, Burger King, Char Broil Grill, Cheesecake Factory, Chili's, DQ, El Charro, Guapo's, McDonald's, McDonald's, mezeh, Olive Garden, Outback Steaks, Popeyes, Sakura Japanese, Silver Diner, Subway, TX Roadhouse, Wendy's, Best Western, Comfort Suites, Costco/gas, Family$, Firestone/auto, IKEA/EVC, Marshalls, Nordstrom Rack, NTB, Potomac Mills Outlets/Famous Brands, Staples, U-Haul

154mm /weigh sta both lanes

152 VA 234, Dumfries, to Manassas, Red Roof Inn, E BP/dsl, Citgo, Exxon/dsl, Valero/Subway, China One, Dunkin, KFC, KFC, McDonald's, Pizza Hut, Taco Bell, Super 8, ALDI, auto, AutoZone, Food Lion, Jiffy Lube, Walmart, Weems-Botts Museum, W 7-11, Exxon, Sunoco/dsl, Chick-fil-A, Cracker Barrel, El Paso Mexican, Five Guys, IHOP, Jerry's Subs, MontClair Rest., Panera Bread, Popeyes, Starbucks, Subway, Tropical Smoothie, Waffle House, Candlewood, Comfort Inn, Days Inn, Hampton Inn, Holiday Inn, Motel 6, Prince William Camping, Shoppers Foods, Target, URGENT CARE

150 VA 619, Quantico, to Triangle, E 7-11, Sunoco/dsl, Dunkin', McDonald's, Papa John's, Ramada Inn, $General, Harley Davidson, Walgreens, W Prince William Forest Park

148 to Quantico, E Marathon/dsl, McDonald's, Subway, Courtyard, WoodSpring Suites, to Marine Corps Base

143b a to US 1, VA 610, Aquia, E 7-11, Exxon/7-11/dsl, Sunoco, El Gran Charro, KFC, McDonald's, Mick's Rest., Papa John's, Subway, Best Western, Fairfield Inn, Hampton Inn, Home2 Suites, Staybridge Suites, Suburban Studios, Towne Place Suites, Aquia Pines Camping, Nissan, tires, Tires+, W 7-11, Circle K, Exxon/dsl, WaWa/Tesla EVC, 5 Guys Burgers, Applebee's, Baskin-Robbins/Dunkin, Bob Evans, Buffalo Wild Wings, Burger King, Chick-fil-A, Chili's, China Wok, Chipotle, CiCi's, Firehouse Subs, Hardee's, IHOP, Jersey Mike's, Kobe Japanese, Little Caesar's, McDonald's, Mission BBQ, Outback Steaks, Pancho Villa, Panera Bread, Popeyes, Starbucks, sweetFrog, Taco Bell, Umi Japanese, Wendy's, Comfort Inn, Holiday Inn, Quality Inn, Red Roof Inn, Super 8,

POTOMAC MILLS

AQUIA

143b a Continued
$Tree, ALDI, AT&T, AutoZone, Best Buy, Giant Foods, Home Depot, Jiffy Lube, Lowe's, Michael's, NTB, Old Navy, PetCo, PetSmart, Ross, Shopper's Foods, Staples, Target, TJ Maxx, Toyota, URGENT CARE, Verizon, Walmart

140 VA 630, Stafford, E 7-11, Sheetz/dsl, Valero, Chik-fil-A, Starbucks, Wendy's, H, W Chipotle, Five Guys, Jersey Mike's, McDonald's, Starbucks, Publix

137mm Potomac Creek

136 rd 8900, Centreport, E Wawa/dsl

133b a US 17 N, to Warrenton, E Exxon/dsl, Arby's, Motel 6, Red Roof Inn, 7-11, auto/truck repair, CarQuest, W Shell, Shell/Subway/dsl, WaWa/dsl, Burger King, Chipotle, Dunkin', Freddy's, Hardee's, IHOP, Little Caesars, McDonald's, Pancho Villa Mexican, Panera Bread, Popeyes, Subway, Taco Bell, Tropical Smoothie, Waffle House, Wendy's, Best Value Inn, Clarion, Comfort Suites, Country Inn&Suites, Days Inn, Excel Inn & Suites, Holiday Inn, Holiday Inn Express, Quality Inn, Sleep Inn, Super 8, 7-11, Advance Parts, AutoZone, Big Lots, Blue Beacon, Honda, Jiffy Lube, NAPA, PetSmart, Target, tires, U-Haul

132.5mm Rappahannock River

132mm **sb, full facilities, , litter barrels, petwalk, vending**

130b a VA 3, to Fredericksburg, AT&T, E Royal Farms/dsl, Shell/dsl, Wawa, America's Wings, Cook Out, Dunkin', El Rey Mexican, Honeybaked Ham, Mama's Fried Chicken, McDonald's, Mi Rancho Mexican, Mission BBQ, Popeyes, Starbucks, Subway, Wendy's, Best Western, Quality Inn, $General, Batteries+Bulbs, Home Depot, H, PepBoys, Staples, tires, U-Haul, URGENT CARE, W 76, BJ's, Exxon/dsl, Sheetz/dsl, Valero, WaWa/dsl, 5 Guys Burgers, Applebee's, BJ's Rest., BoneFish Grill, Buffalo Wild Wings, Burger King, Cancun Mexican, Carrabba's, CAVA, Checker's, Cheddar's Kitchen, Chick-fil-A, Chili's, Chipotle Mexican, ChuckeCheese, Cold Stone, Cracker Barrel, Domino's, Dunkin, Firebirds, Firehouse Subs, Great American Buffet, IHOP, Krispy Kreme, Logan's Roadhouse, McDonald's, McDonald's, Melting Pot, Noodles&Co, Oishi Japanese, Olive Garden, Outback Steaks, Paisano's, Panda Express, Panera Bread, Park Lane Grill, Peter Chang, Potbelly, Qdoba, Quaker Steak, Raising Cane's, Red Lobster, Sam's Pizza, Starbucks, Starbucks, Subway, Subway, Taco Bell, Tito's Diner, TX Roadhouse, Clarion, Comfort Inn, Econolodge, Extended Stay, Hampton Inn, Hilton Garden, Homewood Suites, Residence Inn, WoodSpring Inn, $Tree, $Tree, $Tree, AAA, ALDI, AT&T, AutoZone, Barnes&Noble, Belk, Best Buy, BJ's Whse, Books A Million, Costco/gas, CVS Drug, Dick's, GNC, Hobby Lobby, JC Penney, Kohl's, Lowe's, Macy's, mall, Meineke, Mercedes-Benz, Michael's, NTB, NTB, Office Depot, Old Navy, PetSmart, Target, TJ Maxx, URGENT CARE, USPO, Valvoline, Verizon, vet, Volvo/EVC, Walmart/gas, Wegman's Foods, Weis Mkts

126 US 1, US 17 S, to Fredericksburg, E Exxon/7-11, Marathon/dsl, Royal Farms, Sunoco/dsl, Wawa, 4 Seasons, Chik-fil-A, Denny's, DQ, Dunkin, Golden Corral, Hardee's, Hooters, McDonald's, Pizza Hut, Poncho Villa Mexican, Subway, Taco Bell, Waffle House, Country Inn&Suites, Econolodge, EconoLodge, Fairfield Inn, Garden Inn, Hampton Inn, Knights Inn, Red Roof Inn, Royal Inn, Stay4 Less, Super Value Inn, TownePlace Suites, Travelodge, $General, $Tree, Advance Parts, ALDI, AutoZone, BMW Cycles, Buick/GMC, Chrysler/Dodge/Jeep, CVS Drug, Family$, Harley Davidson, H, H, Hyundai, Jeep, Jiffy Lube, Kia, Little Tires, Mazda, Nissan, O'Reilly Parts, Subaru, Tires+, VW, W 7-11, Citgo/dsl, Exxon, WaWa/dsl/Tesla EVC, 5 Guys, Arby's, Asian Diner, Bob Evans,

AQUIA

VA

INTERSTATE 95 Cont'd

126 Continued
Buffalo Wild Wings, Burger King, Chick-fil-A, Chili's, China King, Chipotle Mexican, Coldstone Creamery, Cook Out, Cracker Barrel, Dickey's BBQ, Dunkin, Golden China, KFC, Kobe Japanese, Ledo Pizza, Legends Grill, Longhorn Steaks, McDonald's, Mexico Palace, Panera Bread, Papa John's, Red Robin, Salsarita's Cantina, Sonic, Starbucks, Starbucks, Subway, Taco Bell, Tropical Smoothie, Wendy's, Candlewood Suites, Comfort Suites, Holiday Inn Express, Home2 Suites, Sleep Inn, AT&T, AutoZone, Carmax, CVS Drug, Firestone/auto, Goodyear, Kohl's, Lowe's, Marshalls, NTB, PetSmart, Publix, Ross, Target, URGENT CARE, Valvoline, Verizon, Verizon, vet, Walmart/Subway, World Mkt

118 VA 606, to Thornburg, E Sheetz/dsl, Shell/dsl, Tru, to Stonewall Jackson Shrine, W Citgo/dsl, Exxon, Shell/DQ/dsl, Angela's Italian, Domino's, McDonald's, Poco Loco, Subway, Taco Bell, Best Western+, Holiday Inn Express, Quality Inn, $General, Family$, Food Lion, NAPA, to Lake Anna SP, USPO

110 VA 639, to Ladysmith, E BP, Shell/dsl, W Citgo/dsl, Exxon/dsl, Sheetz/dsl, Domino's, Guiseppe's Rest., Lin's Gourmet, McDonald's, Subway, Timbers Rest., $General, Advance Parts, Family$, Food Lion, Verizon

108mm **both lanes, full facilities, litter barrels, petwalk, vending**

104 VA 207, to US 301, Bowling Green, E Exxon/DQ/dsl, Flying J/Golden Corral/dsl/Lp/scales/24hr/@, Gulf/7-11/dsl, Love's/Subway/dsl/scales/24hr, Mr Fuel/dsl, Valero/dsl, Arby's, McDonald's, Taco Bell, Wendy's, Knights Inn, Super 8, Blue Beacon, SpeedCo, to Ft AP Hill, URGENT CARE, W Exxon/dsl, Flying J/dsl/scales/RV dump/24hr, Mi Jalisco Mexican, Waffle House, Comfort Inn, Days Inn/rest., EconoLodge, Quality Inn, NAPA, USPO

98 VA 30, Doswell, E 7-11, Citgo/Doswell motel/dsl/scales/24hr/@, Exxon, Burger King, Country Inn&Suites, Days Inn, La Quinta, King's Dominion Camping, KOA, to King's Dominion Funpark, truckwash/service

ASHLAND

92 VA 54, Ashland, E BP/Circle K, Sunoco, W Amoco/dsl, Exxon/dsl, Shell/dsl, Sunoco/dsl, TA/BP/Fuddruckers/dsl/scales/24hr/@, Wawa/dsl, Anthony's Pizza, Applebees, Brickoven Rest., Capt D's, Chick-fil-A, Chipotle, Cook Out, Cracker Barrel, DQ, El Azteca, Hardee's, Jersey Mike's Subs, KFC/LJ Silver, Little Caesars, Marco's Italian, McDonald's, Panda Express, Panera Bread, Popeyes, Starbucks, Subway, Taco Bell, Waffle House, Wendy's, Ashland Inn, Days Inn, EconoLodge, Hampton Inn, Holiday Inn Express, Knights Inn, Motel 6, Quality Inn, Sleep Inn, Tru, $General, $Tree, Ace Hardware, Advance Parts, AutoZone, Buick/GMC, CarQuest, CVS Drug, Food Lion, O'Reilly Parts, Petco, Verizon, Walgreens, Walmart

89 VA 802, to Lewistown Rd, E Exxon, TA/Shell/Pizza Hut/dsl/scales/24hr/@, Americamps RV Camp, W Bojangles, Perfect Pollo, Subway, Wendy's, Country Inn Suites, Fairfield Inn, WoodSpring Suites, Bass Pro Shops, Harley Davidson, Hobby Lobby, Kosmo Village Camping, McGeorge's RV Ctr

86b a VA 656, Elmont, to Atlee, E Sheetz/dsl, Valero/dsl, Domino's, Mario's Italian, McDonald's, Pizza Hut, CVS Drug, Food Lion, O'Reilly Parts, tire/auto repair, vet, Walmart/gas, W Exxon/dsl, Wawa/dsl, Arby's, BBQ, Buffalo Wild Wings, Chick-fil-A, Chili's, Chipotle Mexican, Coldstone Creamery, IHOP, Jade Chinese, Jersey Mike's Subs, Luca's Pizza, Marco's Pizza, McDonald's, O'Charley's, Panera Bread, Papa John's, Plaza Azteca Mexican, Popeyes,

86b a Continued
Red Robin, Sonic, Starbucks, Starbucks, Taco Bell, Tropical Smoothie, TX Roadhouse, Vinny's Italian Grill, Virginia BBQ, Wendy's, Candlewood Suites, Comfort Suites, Courtyard, Hampton Inn, SpringHill Suites, $Tree, 7-11, AT&T, Barnes&Noble, Best Buy, Dick's, Firestone/auto, GNC, Home Depot, Jiffy Lube, Michael's, NTB, OfficeMax, PetSmart, Publix, Ross, Target, Walgreens

84b a I-295 W, to I-64, to Norfolk

83b a VA 73, Parham Rd, W 7-11, Exxon, Exxon/DQ, Wawa, Burger King, Charlie's Way, Chicken Fiesta, Dunkin, Firehouse Subs, Frida's Cafe, McDonald's, Popeyes, Starbucks, Subway, Waffle House, Wendy's, Best Western+, Cavalier Manor, Days Inn, EconoLodge, Quality Inn, Sleep Inn, Travelodge, $Tree, $Tree, BigLots, Food Lion, Lowe's, O'Reilly Parts, Verizon, Walmart

82 US 301, Chamberlayne Ave, E BP/dsl, Sunoco/dsl, Valero/dsl, Wawa, KFC, Pizza Hut/Taco Bell, Subway, Super 8, $General, $Tree, Food Lion, USPO, W Exxon/7-11, Arby's, Bojangles, La Casita, Wendy's, Jiffy Lube, Walmart/gas

BELVIDERE

81 US 1, Chamberlayne Ave(from nb), same as 82

80 Hermitage Rd, Lakeside Ave(from nb, no return), W Marathon, park, tires

79 I-64 W, to Charlottesville, I-195 S, to U of Richmond

78 Boulevard(no EZ nb return), E BP, Brickhouse Diner, Quality Inn, W Wawa/dsl, stadium

76 Chamberlayne Ave, Belvidere, E, VA Union U

75 I-64 E, VA Beach, to Norfolk

74c US 33, US 250 W, to Broad St, W, Museum of the Confederacy, st capitol

74b Franklin St

74a I-195 N, to Powhite Expswy, downtown

73.5mm James River

73 Maury St, to US 60, US 360, industrial area

69 VA 161, Bells Rd, E Port of Richmond, W Exxon/McDonald's/dsl, Shell/dsl, McDonald's, Starbucks, Best Western, Candlewood Suites, Hampton Inn, Red Roof Inn

67b a VA 895 (toll E), VA 150, to Chippenham Pkwy, Falling Creek, W BP/dsl, RaceWay/dsl, Shell/dsl, Speedway, Burger King, Hardee's, 7-11, flea mkt, Food Lion, U-Haul

64 VA 613, to Willis Rd, E Exxon/7-11/dsl, Marathon/Krispy Chicken, Waffle House, Best Value Inn, Rodeway Inn, W 7-11, BP/Burger King, Shell/dsl, Sunoco, Maury's BBQ, McDonald's, Subway, Country Inn&Suites, La Quinta, Sleep Inn, VIP Inn, flea mkt

62 VA 288 N, to Chesterfield, Powhite Pkwy, W to

CHESTER

61b a VA 10, Chester, E RaceWay/dsl, Don Pepe Mexican, Hardee's, Comfort Inn, Courtyard, Hampton Inn, Holiday Inn Express, Homewood Suites, Quality Inn, W BP/dsl, Exxon/7-11/dsl, Mobil/7-11/dsl, Shell/dsl, Applebee's, Bojangles, Buffalo Wild Wings, Capt D's, Chik-fil-A, Chili's, Chipotle, Cracker Barrel, Dunkin, Hooters, IHOP, La Reina Mexican, McDonald's, O'Charley's, Panda Express, Panera Bread, Patron Mexican, Peking Chinese, Pizza Hut, Popeyes, Raising Cane's, Sonic, Starbucks, Taco Bell, Tropical Smoothie, Wendy's, Zaxby's, Country Inn&Suites, Days Inn, Fairfield Inn, InTowne Suites, SpringHill Suites, Suburban Lodge, Super 8, $Tree, Aamco, AT&T, Big Lots, Chevrolet/EVC, CVS Drug, Discount Tire, Food Lion, GNC, Home Depot, Jiffy Lube, Kohl's, Kroger/gas, Lowe's, NAPA, Office Depot,

CHESTER

INTERSTATE 95 Cont'd

61b a Continued
PetCo, Rite Aid, Target, to Pocahontas SP, Verizon

58 VA 746, to Ruffinmill Rd, E Pilot/Wendy's/dsl/scales/24hr, Honda, Hyundai, Kia, Nissan/EVC, Subaru, Toyota, VW, W 7-11, Shell/Subway/dsl, Wawa/Tesla EVC/dsl, McDonald's, Candlewood Suites, Comfort Inn, Rodeway Inn, Family$

54 VA 144, Temple Ave, Hopewell, to Ft Lee, E Exxon/Burger King, Sheetz/Tesla EVC/dsl, Shell, Sunoco/7-11/dsl, Wawa/dsl, Applebee's, Arby's, Buffalo Wild Wings, Casa Mexican, Chick-fil-A, China Buffet, Chipotle, CiCi's Pizza, Denny's, Firehouse Subs, Five Guys, Golden Corral, IHOP, Longhorn Steaks, McDonald's, Mission BBQ, Olive Garden, Outback Steaks, Panera Bread, Pizza Hut, Red Lobster, Sonic, Starbucks, Subway, Taco Bell, TX Roadhouse, Wendy's, Comfort Suites, Extended Stay, Hampton Inn, Hilton Garden, Holiday Inn, Woodspring Suites, $Tree, AAA, AT&T, Best Buy, BooksAMillion, Dick's, Discount Tire, Home Depot, JC Penney, Macy's, Marshall's, Michael's, NTB, Old Navy, PetSmart, Sam's Club/gas, Staples, Target, URGENT CARE, Verizon, Walmart/Subway, W Circle K/dsl, Dunkin, Hardee's, Jersey Mike's, KFC, Little Caesars, LJ Silver's, Waffle House, Wendy's, AutoZone, Family$, Goodyear, NAPA, O'Reilly Parts, to VSU, U-Haul

53 S Park Blvd, E same as 54

52.5mm Appomattox River

52 Washington St, Wythe St, E Marathon/dsl, Valero/dsl, Tortilleria Mexican, Best Inn, Motel 6, Royal Inn, Travel Inn, Petersburg Nat Bfd, W Liberty, Church's, Krispy Chicken, $General, H

51 I-85 S, to South Hill, US 460 W

50d Wythe St, from nb, same as 52

50b c E 7-11, Flagship Inn

50a US 301, US 460 E, to Crater Rd, County Dr, E Mobil, RaceWay/dsl, Sunoco, Roma Ristorante, American Inn, Budget Inn, California Inn, EconoLodge, H, restrooms

48b a Wagner Rd, W Marathon/dsl, Shell, Wawa, Arby's, Bojangles, Burger King, Capt D's, KFC, Little Caesar's, Pizza Hut, Sam's Crab House, Subway, Taco Bell, Taste of China, Country Inn&Suites, Super 8, $General, $Tree, Advance Parts, H, O'Reilly Parts, PepBoys, USPO, Verizon, Walgreens, Walmart

47 VA 629, to Rives Rd, same as 48 on US 301, W Citgo, Shell/dsl, Arby's, Bojangles, Capt. D's, KFC, Subway, Heritage Motel, Ace Hardware, H, Walmart

46 I-295 N(exits left from sb), to Washington

45 US 301, E Shell/dsl, Rams Cafe, W Exxon/7-11, Star Express/Sunoco/Huddle House, El Arriero Mexican, Mama Rita's, Nanny's Rest., Comfort Inn, Days Inn, Hampton Inn, Holiday Inn Express, Quality Inn, Red Roof Inn, Travelodge, $General

CARSON

41 US 301, VA 35, VA 156, E Exxon/dsl/scales/24hr, Cathy's Grill, Gateway Inn, $General, South 40 Campground

40mm weigh sta both lanes

37 US 301, Carson, W BP/dsl, Shell/dsl

36mm Rest stop nb, full facilities, vending, litter barrel, petwalk

33 VA 602, W Davis/Exxon/Starbucks/dsl/scales/24hr/Tesla EVC, Mobil/Wendys/dsl, Little Italy, Los Compadres Mexican, Popeyes, Fairfield Inn, Hampton Inn, Sleep Inn, dog park

31 VA 40, Stony Creek, to Waverly, W Citgo/dsl, Shell/dsl, Big Pig BBQ, antiques, Family$

24 VA 645

JARRATT

20 VA 631, Jarratt, W Exxon/Blimpie/Pizza Hut/dsl/24hr, Sunoco/dsl, $General, Ford

17 US 301, E Knights Inn, Reste Motel, Emporia KOA

13 VA 614, to Emporia, E Exxon/Chester's/dsl, Shell/dsl

12 US 301(from nb)

11b a US 58, Emporia, to South Hill, E BP, Citgo/Burger King, Shell/dsl, Arby's, Cracker Barrel, Domino's, Dunkin, Hardee's, KFC, Krispy Krunchy, McDonald's, Pizza Hut, Starbucks, Subway, Taco Bell, Val's Pizza, Wendy's, Wong's Garden, Country Inn&Suites, Fairfield Inn, Rodeway Inn, Advance Parts, Buick/Chevrolet/GMC/EVC, CVS Drug, Family$, Food Lion, H, NAPA, O'Reilly Parts, URGENT CARE, Verizon, Walmart, W Exxon, Pilot/5 Guys Burgers/dsl/scales/24hr/@, Race-In/Quiznos/dsl, Shell/Sadler Rest., Bojangles, El Ranchero Mexican, Pino's Pizza, Best Western, Comfort Inn, Days Inn, Hampton Inn, Holiday Inn Express, Quality Inn

8 US 301, E Marathon, Simmons/Exxon/Huddle House/dsl/scales/24hr, Relax Inn, Studios&Suites

4 VA 629, to Skippers, E Love's/McDonald's/dsl/scales/24hr, Pilot/Dunkin/Subway/dsl/scales/24hr, Bojangles, W truck repair

3.5mm Fountain's Creek

0.5mm Welcome Ctr nb, full facilities, vending, litter barrels, petwalk, W Spring Church B&B

0mm Virginia/North Carolina state line

INTERSTATE 264 (Norfolk)

23mm I-264 begins/ends, BP, Shell, convention ctr

22 Birdneck Rd, N Pizza Hut, museum, vet, S Shell/dsl, Dunkin, McDonald's, Subway, DoubleTree, $Tree, Food Lion, O'Reilly Parts, Virginia Beach Conv. Ctr.

21 VA Beach Blvd, First Colonial Rd, N BP, Shell, Burger King, Chick-fil-A, China Wok, Chipotle, Crumbl, DQ, Five Guys, IHOP, Jersey Mike's, Las Palmas, McDonald's, Moe's SW Grill, Otani Japanese, Outback Steaks, Panda Express, Pizza Hut, Schlotzsky's, Shogun Japanese, Sonic, Starbucks, Starbucks, Subway, Taco Bell, Wendy's, Zero's Subs, Advance Parts, CVS, Discount Tire, GNC, Kroger/dsl, PetSmart, SteinMart, Target, Toyota/Scion, Trader Joe's, USPO, Verizon, vet, Walgreens, Walmart, Whole Foods Mkt, S 7-11, Amoco, Wawa/dsl, Firestone/auto, NAPA

20 US 58 E, to VA Beach Blvd(eb only), N Kangaroo/7-11, Wawa/Tesla EVC/dsl, Bojangle's, Capt. George's Seafood, China Moon, Citrus Breakfast & Lunch, Dunkin, Hardee's, Starbucks, Tropical Smoothie, $Tree, 7-11, Buick/GMC, Food Lion, Kia/Lincoln, Lowe's, Meineke, PepBoys, TJ Maxx, Toyota, vet

19 Lynnhaven Pkwy, N 7-11, Wawa, Duck Donuts, Ensenada Mexican, First Watch, Iggle's, Audi, Chevrolet, Ford, Hobby Lobby, Jaguar/Land Rover, Porsche, Subaru, vet, VW, S Chipotle, Five Guys, Jersey Mike's, Jimmy John's, Noodles&Co, Olive Garden, Starbucks, Taco Bell, Dick's, Walmart

18 Rosemont, N EVC, Exxon, Bonefish Grill, Burger King, Denny's, Hardee's, Jade Garden, KFC, LJ Silver, McDonald's, Mi Casita Mexican, Papa John's, Pizza Hut, Starbucks, Taco Bell, Wendy's, Wingstop, Zero's Subs, $Tree, $Tree, Acura, antiques, AT&T, AutoZone, BJ's Whse/gas, CarMax, Chrysler/Dodge/Jeep, Food Lion, Harris Teeter, Home Depot, Honda, Jiffy Lube, Kroger/gas, Nissan, NTB, PetSmart, Sam's Club/gas, Walgreens, S Hyundai/EVC, Mobil/dsl, Wawa/dsl, Jerrrk Time Cuisine, Krazy Mexican, EconoLodge, $General, CVS, tires

17.5mm wb only

17a b Independance Blvd, N Exxon, Tesla Charger, Arby's, Bahama Breeze, Cheesecake Factory, Chik-fil-A, Chipotle,

VA

INTERSTATE 264 (Norfolk) Cont'd

17a b Continued
Crumbl, Honey Baked Ham, IHOP, Jason's Deli, McDonald's, Mission BBQ, Panera Bread, PF Chang's, Ruby Tuesday, Sakura Japanese, Smokey Bones BBQ, Starbucks, Taco Bell, Village Inn, Wendy's, Candlewood Suites, Crowne Plaza, Days Inn, Extended Stay, Fairfield, Hilton Garden, Hyatt Place, Motel 6, Residence Inn, Westin, Barnes&Noble, Best Buy, Kohl's, Michael's, Office Depot, Old Navy, PetSmart, REI, Target, tires, URGENT CARE, Walgreens, Walmart Supercenter, Wegmans, **S** 7-11, Exxon/dsl, Wawa/dsl, Arby's, Azteca Mexican, Buffalo Wild Wings, Domino's, Golden Corral, Hardee's, KFC, Starbucks, Subway, Taco Bell, TX Roadhouse, Zero Subs, InTown Suites, WoodSpring Suites, auto repair, Food Lion, Mazda, O'Reilly Parts, vet

16 Witchduck Rd

15a b Newtown Rd, **N** 7-11, Wawa/dsl/24hr, Capt D's, Domino's, McDonald's, Taco Bell, Wendy's, Extended Stay America, Homewood Suites, AutoZone, CVS Drug, **S** 7-11, Denny's, Plaza Mexican, Courtyard, Hampton Inn, Holiday Inn, La Quinta, Red Roof Inn, SpringHill Suites, Rite Aid

14b a I-64, US 13, to Military Hwy

13 US 13, Military Hwy, **N** Shell, Arby's, Dunkin, McDonald's, Mongolian BBQ, Norfolk Garden Korean, Waffle House, Days Inn, EconoLodge, Motel 6, Ramada Ltd, Costco/gas, CVS, Firestone/auto, Ross

12 Ballentine Blvd, **N** BP/7-11, Domino's, Norfolk SU, tires

11b a US 460, VA 166/168, Brambleton Ave, Campostello Rd, **N** 7-11

10 Tidewater Dr, City Hall Ave, exits left from eb, **N** Popeyes, Courtyard, Marriot, Sheraton

9 St Paul's Blvd, Waterside Dr, **S** to Harbor Park Stadium

8 I-464 S, to Chesapeake

7.5mm tunnel

7b a VA 141, Effingham St, Crawford St, **N** Shell, Naval H, tires, **S** 7-11/24hr, Citgo, $General, Shipyard

6 Des Moines Ave(from eb)

5 US 17, Frederick Blvd, **N** WaWa/dsl, Chick-fil-A, Chipotle, Dunkin, Little Caesar's, Panda Express, Rally's, Starbucks, Subway, Taco Bell, Waffle House, Wendy's, Wong Chinese, Advance Parts, CVS Drug, H, Kroger/gas, TJ Maxx, to Midtown Tunnel, Valvoline, Walgreens, Walmart, **S** BP/dsl, $General, Harley-Davidson

4 VA 337, Portsmouth Blvd

3 Victory Blvd, **N** 7-11, Exxon, WaWa/dsl, Bojangles, Capt D's, CookOut, Domino's, Firehouse Subs, KFC, Krispy Kreme, McDonald's, Pizza Hut, Taco Bell, Wendy's, $Tree, Advance Parts, AutoZone, Jiffy Lube, Lowe's, PepBoys, **S** Freedom/dsl, Royal Farms/dsl, 7-11, Discount Tires

2b a Greenwood Dr

0mm I-264 begins/ends on I-64, exit 299.

INTERSTATE 295 (Richmond)

RICHMOND

53b a I-64, W to Charlottesville, E to Richmond, to US 250, I-295 begins/ends.

51b a Nuckols Rd, **N** Miller's/dsl, Valero, Cheeburger, Chen's Chinese, Home Team Grill, McDonald's, Nonna's Pizzaria, Pizza Hut, Rico's Mexican, Samurai Japanese, Starbucks, Subway, Tropical Smoothie Cafe, CVS Drug, Food Lion, Walgreens, **S** Exxon/Mkt Cafe, USPO

49b a US 33, Richmond, **S** JJ's Grille, Little Angela's, Little Caesar's, Little Szechuan, Nuevo Mexico, $ General, 7-11, CVS

45b a Woodman Rd, **S** 7-11, Little Caesar's, $General, CVS Drug, Meadow Farm Museum

43 I-95, US 1, N to Washington, S to Richmond(exits left from nb), **N** Shell/dsl, Applebee's, Arby's, BBQ, Buffalo Wild Wings, Chick-fil-A, Chili's, Chipotle Mexican, Coldstone, Famous Dave's BBQ, Firehouse Subs, McDonald's, O'Charley's, O'Dragon buffet, Panera Bread, Papa John's, Pizzaro, Plaza Azteca Mexican, Red Robin, Roda Japanese, Shoney's, Starbucks, Subway, TX Roadhouse, Wendy's, Candlewood Suites, Comfort Suites, Courtyard, Hampton Inn, SpringHill Suites, $Tree, AT&T, Barnes&Noble, Best Buy, Burlington, Dick's, Firestone/auto, GNC, Goodyear/auto, Home Depot, JC Penney, Macy's, mall, Martin's Foods, Merchant's Tire, Michael's, PetSmart, Ross, Target, Tire America, Walgreens, **S** 7-11, Shell, WaWa, Aunt Sarah's, Burger King, Frida's Mexican, Hardee's, KFC/Taco Bell, McDonald's, Ming's Dynasty, Starbucks, Subway, Waffle House, Wendy's, Best Value Inn, Cavalier Motel, Days Inn, EconoLodge, Knights Inn, Sleep Inn, $Tree, Food Lion, Lowe's, Walmart

41b a US 301, VA 2, **E** BP/dsl, Valero/dsl, WaWa/dsl, Bojangles, Burger King, China Kitchen, Dunkin Donuts, Marty's Grill, McDonald's, Popeyes, Stevi B's, Subway, Tropical Smoothie Cafe, Wendy's, Zheng Chinese, $General, AT&T, AutoZone, Kroger/gas, URGENT CARE, Verizon, vet, Walgreens, **W** Exxon/dsl, Friendly's, Holiday Inn, Super 8, Travelodge

38b a VA 627, Pole Green Rd, **E** 7-11, Exxon/dsl, Sunoco/dsl, Antonio's Pizza, Bell Cafe, Bruster's, Chen's Rest., Mimmo's Rest., Patron Mexican, Subway, Food Lion, vet, **W** 7-11, Valero, Pasta House, CVS, H

37b a US 360, **E** BP, Shell/dsl, Valero, Applebee's, Arby's, Buffalo Wild Wings, Burger King, Chick-fil-A, Cookout, Cracker Barrel, DQ, Franco's, Gus' Italian, IHOP, Jersey Mike's, KFC, McDonald's, Mexico Rest., Moe's SW Grill, Noodles&Co, Outback Steaks, Panera Bread, Papa John's, Peking Chinese, Pizza Hut, Roma Italian, Ruby Tuesday, Shoney's, Starbucks, Subway, Taco Bell, Waffle House, Wendy's, Hampton Inn, Holiday Inn Express, $Tree, Advance Parts, ALDI, AT&T, Best Buy, BJ's Whse/gas, CVS, Food Lion, GNC, Home Depot, Kohl's, Marshall's, Old Navy, PetSmart, Target, Verizon, Walgreens, Walmart/Burger King, **W** 7-11, Sunoco/dsl, Valero/dsl, $General, to Mechanicsville

CHARLES CITY

34b a VA 615, Creighton Rd, **E** 7-11, Valero

31b a VA 156, **E** Exxon/dsl, to Cold Harbor Bfd, **W** Shell(4mi), Valero, Hardee's(4mi), Courtyard(4mi), EconoLodge(4mi), Holiday Inn Express(4mi), Motel 6(4mi)

28 I-64, to US 60, **W** museum

25 Rd 895 W(toll), to Richmond

22b a VA 5, Charles City, **E** Exxon/dsl, DQ, Shirley Plantation, **W** Valero/Subway/dsl, China Taste, Portabella's Cafe, Food Lion, Richmond Nat Bfd

18mm James River

16 Rivers Bend Blvd

15b a VA 10, Hopewell, **E** BP/dsl, Burger King, H, James River Plantations, **W** EC/Subway/dsl, Exxon/McDonald's/dsl, Sheetz, WaWa/dsl, Cesare's Ristorante, Chen's Rest., Jalapeno's, Rivers Bend Grill, Taco Bell, Wendy's, Wing's Pizza, Hyatt Place, Residence Inn, CVS Drug, Food Lion

13mm Appomattox River

HOPEWELL

INTERSTATE 295 (Richmond) Cont'd

Exit #	Services
9b a	VA 36, Hopewell, E Citgo, Gulf, WaWa/dsl, Bojangles, El Nopal, Hardee's, KFC, Little Caesar's, McDonald's, Rosa's Italian, Best Western, EconoLodge, Fairfield Inn, StayOver Suites, $General, Advance Parts, AutoZone, Family$, O'Reilly Parts, Verizon, vet, Walgreens, W BP/dsl, Exxon, Shell/dsl, Sunoco/dsl, Burger King, Denny's, DQ, Dragon Express, Dunkin Donuts, Kanpai Japanese, McDonald's, Papa John's, Pizza Hut, Ruby Tuesday, Shoney's, Starbucks, Subway, Taco Bell, Top's China, Waffle House, Wendy's, Baymont Inn, Candlewood Suites, Hampton Inn, Quality Inn, $Tree, Chevrolet, Family$, Food Lion, to Petersburg Nat Bfd, U-Haul, US Army Museum
5.5mm	Blackwater Swamp
3b a	US 460, Petersburg, to Norfolk, E Pilot/Wendy's/dsl/scales/24hr, Sheetz/dsl, Shell/Subway/dsl, Hardee's, Prince George BBQ, W BP/dsl, McDonald's
1	I-95, N to Petersburg, S to Emporium, I-295 begins/ends.

FAIRFAX

INTERSTATE 495 (DC)

Exit #	Services
57	I-95 S, I-395 N, I-95 N. I-495 & I-95 N run together.
54b a	VA 620, Braddock Rd, S Shell/dsl, Jersey Mike's, 7-11, to Geo Mason U, USPO
52b a	VA 236, Little River Tpk, Fairfax, E Liberty/dsl, Sunoco/repair, Chicken Loco, KFC/Taco Bell, Kogiya KBBQ, Little Caesar's, McDonald's, Wendy's, $Tree, 7-11, Advance Parts, Petco, Safeway Foods
51	VA 657, Gallows Rd, W Exxon, 7-11, H
50b a	US 50, Arlington Blvd, Fairfax, Arlington, E Marriott, W Shell, Sunoco/dsl, Five Guys, Five Guys, Guapo's Mexican, McDonald's, Panda Express, Panera Bread, Papa John's, Pho Cyclo, Sophia's Cafe, Starbucks, Sweetwater Tavern, UNO Grill, Wendy's, Extended Stay America, Residence Inn, ALDI, CVS Drug, H, Midas, Target, URGENT CARE, vet
49c b a	I-66(exits left from both lanes), to Manassas, Front Royal
47b a	VA 7, Leesburg Pike, Tysons Corner, Falls Church, E Atrium KBBQ, Westin, W BP/dsl, Exxon, Shell, Shell/dsl, BJ's Rest., Capital Grille, CAVA, Crust Pizzaria, Dunkin', Jimmy John's, Lei'd Hawaiian, McDonald's, MOD Pizza, Olive Garden, Panera Bread, Patsy's, Silver Diner, Starbucks, Subway, Super Chicken, Wendy's, Embassy Suites, Hilton Garden, Marriott, Residence Inn, Best Buy, Buick/Chevrolet/GMC, Chrysler/Dodge/Jeep, CVS Drug, Lidl Foods, mall, Marshall's, Old Navy, PetSmart, REI, Subaru/VW, TJ Maxx
46b a	VA 123, Chain Bridge Rd, W Gulf/dsl, Sunoco/dsl, Cheesecake Factory, PF Chang's, The Palm, Courtyard, DoubleTree, Hilton, Macy's
45b a	VA 267 W(toll), to I-66 E, W to Dulles
44	VA 193, Langley
43	G Washington Mem Pkwy(no trucks)
42mm	Virginia/Maryland state line, Potomac River. Exits 41-27 are in Maryland.

BETHESDA

Exit #	Services
41	Clara Barton Pkwy(no trucks), Carderock, Great Falls
40	Cabin John Pkwy(no trucks), Glen Echo(from sb)
39	MD 190, River Rd, Washington, Potomac
38	I-270, to Frederick
36	MD 187, Old Georgetown Rd, S H
35	(from wb), I-270
34	MD 355, Wisconsin Ave, Bethesda
33	MD 185, Connecticut Ave, N LDS Temple, S Carrol/repair, Giant/dsl, Liberty, CVS, Manoli Canoli, Starbucks
31b a	MD 97, Georgia Ave, Silver Spring, N H, S Exxon, Exxon/dsl, Shell, Sunoco/dsl, W Express/dsl, 7 Starr Wings, Crown Fried Chicken, Domino's,

COLESVILLE

Exit #	Services
31b a	Continued La Casa del Mofongo, Meleket Ethiopian, Silvestre Chicken, ALDI, CVS Drug, Snider's Foods, vet
30b a	US 29, Colesville, N BP/dsl, Citgo, Shell, Shell, Chipotle, McDonald's, Papa John's, Pizza Hut, Red Maple Asian, Starbucks, 7-11, Safeway Foods
29b a	MD 193, University Blvd
28b a	MD 650, New Hampshire Ave, N BP, Exxon/dsl, Shell/repair, Cheesesteak Mikes, Chipotle, Domino's, Starbucks, Home2 Suites, Safeway Foods
27	I-95, N to Baltimore, S to Richmond. I-495 & I-95 S run together. See MD I-95, exits 25b a-2b a.

INTERSTATE 664 (Norfolk)

Exit #	Services
15b a	I-64 to Chesapeake, I-264 E to Portsmouth & Norfolk. I-664 begins/ends on I-64, exit 299.
13b a	US 13, US 58, US 460, Military Hwy, E Shell/Frank's/scales/dsl, Bowers Hill Inn
12	VA 663, Dock Landing Rd
11b a	VA 337, Portsmouth Blvd, E 7-11, Citgo, Millers/Dunkin'/dsl, Sunoco, Applebee's, Arby's, Bubba's 33, Buffet City, Chick-fil-A, Chili's, Chipotle, ChuckECheese, DQ, Five Guys, IHOP, Jersey Mike's, McDonald's, Olive Garden, Outback Steaks, Pizza Hut, Pizza Hut, Red Lobster, Red Robin, Starbucks, Taco Bell, Twisted Crab, Wendy's, Zaxby's, Hampton Inn, Holiday Inn Express, Studios & Suites 4 Less, $Tree, AutoZone, Best Buy, Big Lots, BJ's Whse/gas, dog park/playground, Firestone/auto, Food Lion, Ford, Home Depot, Lidl, Merchant's Auto Ctr, Old Navy, PetSmart, Ross, Sam's Club/gas, Target, Tuesday Morning, USPO, Walmart, W 7-11, Burger King, Cracker Barrel, Old Bay Seafood, Subway, Waffle House, Candlewood Suites, Fairfield Inn, Lowe's
10	VA 659, Pughsville Rd, E 7-11, Citgo, Shell, El Puente Mexican, Food Lion, vet, W city park/playground
9b a	US 17, US 164, E 7-11, Speedway/dsl, Wawa, Burger King, Capt D's, Dennis Steaks, DQ, Dunkin', KFC, McDonald's, Papa John's, Philly Wok, Pizza Hut, Rodman's BBQ, Sakura Sushi, Sonic, Taco Bell, Waffle House, Wendy's, Budget Lodge, Extended Stay America, Sleep Inn, Studios & Suites for Less, Super 8, $Tree, Advance Parts, Chevrolet, Honda, Hyundai, NAPA, Nissan, O'Reilly Parts, Subaru, tires, Toyota/Scion, W Buffalo Wild Wings, Ninja Steaks, Starbucks, Subway, Comfort Suites, Hilton Garden, H, to James River Br
8b a	VA 135, College Dr, E 7-11, Murphy USA/dsl, Applebee's, Arby's, Chick-fil-A, Chipotle, Domino's, Duck Donuts, Firehouse Subs, Freddy's, IHOP, Jersey Mike's, Kickback Jack's, McDonald's, Michaels, MOD Pizza, Panda Express, Panera Bread, Ruby Tuesday, Subway, Taco Bell, TX Roadhouse, Village Inn, Wendy's, Which Wich, Zaxby's, Dick's, Discount Tire, Food Lion, Kohl's, Kroger, PetCo, PetSmart, TJ Maxx, Walmart, W Riverstone Chophouse, Courtyard, TownePlace Suites
11.5mm	**insp sta nb**
9mm	James River
8mm	tunnel
7	Terminal Ave
6	25th St, 26th St, E 7-11, McDonald's, $General, W Benny Cantiere's Pizza, Subway, USPO
5	US 60 W, 35th St, Jefferson Ave, E Rennies Gas, #1 Chinese, Burger King, Church's TX Chicken, Family$, Hornsby Tire, W Dunkin', Subway
4	Chesnut Ave, Roanoke Ave
3	Aberdeen Rd, E Sunoco/dsl, Zooms Gas, Family$, tires, W 7-11, Quarles Gas, Hardee's, McDonald's, Wendy's
2	Powhatan Pkwy, E 7-11

VA

INTERSTATE 664 (Norfolk) Cont'd

Exit #	Services
1b a	I-64, W to Richmond, E to Norfolk. I-664 begins/ends on I-64.

NOTES

WASHINGTON

INTERSTATE 5

BLAINE

Exit #	Services
277mm	USA/Canada Border, Washington state line, customs
276	WA 548 S, Blaine, E Chevron/dsl, Exxon/dsl, Shell/dsl, Speedway, Northwoods Motel, NAPA, to Peace Arch SP, W Welcome Ctr, Chevron/dsl/repair, Black Forest Steaks, Border Town Pizza, Chada Thai, Edaleen Dairy, Monte's Rest., Paso Del Norte, Railway Cafe, Rustic Fork Pizza, Starbucks, Anchor Inn, Bay Side Motel, Cottage by the Bay B&B, Motel International, Blaine Marine Park, EVC, USPO
275	WA 543 N(from nb, no return), E Bens Mkt/TA Express/ Carl's Jr/dsl, Marathon/dsl, Sinclair/dsl, Burger King, McDonalds, Subway, Taco Bell, $Tree, CostCutter Foods, truck/tire repair
274	Peace Portal Drive(from nb, no return), Blaine, W Shell/ dsl, Semi-ah-moo Resort
270	Birch Bay, Lynden, W Shell/Domino's/Subway/dsl, Bob's Burgers, Jack-in-the-Box, Sahara Pizza, Subway, Semi-ah-moo Resort, Birch Bay Mkt, vet
269mm	**Welcome Ctr sb, full facilities, info, , litter barrels, petwalk, vending**
267mm	**nb, full facilities, info, , , litter barrels, petwalk, vending**
266	WA 548 N, Grandview Rd, Custer, W Petro, Birch Bay SP
263	Portal Way, E Pacific Pride/dsl, Shell/dsl, El Nopal Mexican, AA RV Park, Cedars RV Park, W Edaleen Creamery
263mm	Nooksack River
262	Main St, Ferndale, E Chevron/dsl, Pilot/Subway/dsl/ scales/24hr, McDonald's, Taco Bell, Super 8, Nor'west RV Camping, tire repair, vet, W Gull/dsl, Shell/ dsl, Coconuts Kenny's Pizza, Domino's, DQ, Jack-in-the-Box, Papa Murphy's, Starbucks, Taco Time, Woods Cofee, $Tree, Grocery Outlet, Haggen's Foods, NAPA, O'Reilly Parts, Schwab Tire, Verizon, Walgreens
260	Slater Rd, Lummi Island, E Arco/dsl, El Monte RV Ctr, W Silver Reef Hotel/Casino, Lummi Indian Res.
258	Bakerview Rd, E Five Guys, IHOP, Jack-in-the-Box, Papa Murphy's, Port of Subs, Starbucks, Subway, Taco Time, Hampton Inn, La Quinta, Costco/dsl, Fred Meyer/dsl, Verizon, W Arco, Chevron/7-11, Yorky's Mkt/76/dsl, Best Western, Holiday Inn Express, Shamrock Motel, , Bellingham RV Park, st patrol
257	Northwest Ave, E Jack-in-the-Box, Starbucks, Hampton Inn, Home2 Suites, La Quinta, SpringHill Suites, TownePlace Suites, Cadillac/GMC/Chevrolet
256b	Bellis Fair Mall Pkwy(from nb), same as 256a, E Chipotle, McDonald's, Red Robin, Sliced Pizza, JC Penney, Kohl's, Target
256a	WA 539 N, Meridian St, E Arco, Shell/dsl, Arby's, Asian 1, Buffalo Wild Wings, Burger King, Chipotle, Denny's, Domino's, DQ, Jimmy John's, Lilia's Mexican, McDonald's, Mi Mexico, Olive Garden, Red Robin, Shari's, Sliced Pizza, Subway, Taco Bell, Taco Time, Thai House Rest., Wendy's, Wonderful Buffet, Baymont Inn, Comfort Inn, Holiday Inn Express, Oxford Suites, Quality Inn, Wingate Inn, $Tree, AT&T, Barnes&Noble, Best Buy, Dick's, Hobby Lobby, Home Depot, JC Penney, Jiffy Lube, Kohl's, Macy's, Marshall's, Michael's, Midas, O'Reilly Parts, O'Reilly Parts, PetCo, PetSmart, Ross, Schwab Tire, Sierra Trading Post, Target,

CUSTER

BELLINGHAM

Exit #	Services
256a	Continued TJ Maxx, Verizon, Walgreens, Walmart/auto, WinCo Foods, W Slo Pitch Grill, Bellis Inn, MorningGlory
255	WA 542 E, Sunset Dr, Bellingham, E Chevron/dsl, Marathon, Shell/dsl, A&W/KFC, Applebee's, COA Mexican, El Gitano Mexican, Hawaii BBQ, Jack-in-the-Box, Panda Express, Panda Palace, RoundTable Pizza, Starbucks, Taco Bell, Jo-Ann Fabrics, Lowe's, Safeway/dsl, to Mt Baker, USPO, Verizon, Walgreens, W H
254	Iowa St, State St, Bellingham, E 76, Mobil/dsl, Audi/ VW, Chrysler/Dodge/Jeep, Honda, Hyundai, Kia, Nissan, Subaru, Toyota, W Chevron/dsl, Shell, DQ, McDonald's/24hrs, Starbucks, Subway, AutoZone, Ford, Midas, NAPA, O'Reilly Parts
253	Lakeway Dr, Bellingham, E Little Caesar's, Menchie's, Papa John's, Papa Murphy's, Port of Subs, Rhodes Cafe, Sol de Mexico, Subway, Woods Coffee, Guesthouse Inn, Sheraton Four Points, 7-11, Discount Tire, Fred Meyer/dsl, URGENT CARE, Whole Foods Mkt
252	Samish Way, Bellingham, E same as 253, W 76, Chevron/ dsl, Sinclair/dsl, Boomers Drive-In, Busara Thai Cuisine, Domino's, El Agave, Five Columns Greek, Kyoto Steaks, McDonald's, Starbucks, Subway, Taco Time, Wendy's, Bay City Motel, Bellingham Lodge, Coachman Inn, Days Inn, Motel 6, $Tree, Ace Hardware, Haggen Foods, REI, vet, Walgreens
250	WA 11 S, Chuckanut Dr, Bellingham, Fairhaven Hist Dist, W Arco, Starbucks, Subway, to Alaska Ferry, to Larrabee SP
246	N Lake Samish, E Lake Padden RA, W Shell/dsl
242	Nulle Rd, S Lake Samish
240	Alger, E Shell/dsl/LP/RV dump, Alger Grille, Cat Nap B&B, Whispering Firs Motel/RV Parking
238mm	**both lanes, full facilities, , , litter barrels, vending, petwalk**
236	Bow Hill Rd, E Skagit Mart/dsl, Skagit Hotel Casino/ rest./dsl/LP
235mm	weigh sta sb
234mm	Samish River
232	Cook Rd, Sedro-Woolley, E Arco, Chevron/dsl, Shell/dsl, Tesla EVC, Bob's Burgers, Jack-in-the-Box, Starbucks, Fairfield Inn, KOA
231	WA 11 N, Chuckanut Dr, E Camping World RV Ctr, Kia, vet, W Larrabee SP, st patrol
230	WA 20, Burlington, E Chevron, Shell/dsl, 4 Season Buffet, Applebee's, ChuckECheese, Coconut Kenny's, Jack-in-the-Box, Mi Mexico, MOD Pizza, Papa Murphy's, Pasqually's Pizza, Pizza Factory, Pizza Hut/Taco Bell, Popeyes, Red Robin, Starbucks, Swan's Korean, Tepic Mexican, Cocusa Motel,

ALGER

WA

INTERSTATE 5 Cont'd

BURLINGTON

230 Continued
Motel 6, $Tree, 7-11, AutoZone, Country Farms, Fred Meyer/dsl, Haggen Foods, H, O'Reilly Parts, Schwab Tire, Target, TJ Maxx, to N Cascades NP, Walgreens, W Pacific Pride/dsl, McDonald's, Holiday Inn Express, Hyundai, to San Juan Ferry

229 George Hopper Rd, E Arco, Speedway Express/dsl, Carl's Jr, Chipotle Mexican, Five Guys, Jamba Juice, Jimmy John's, Just Peachy Fro-Yo, McDonald's, Olive Garden, Panera Bread, Sakura Japanese, Starbucks, Subway, Taco Del Mar, Wingstop, Candlewood Suites, Comfort Suites, Hampton Inn, La Quinta, AT&T, Best Buy, Costco/gas, Dick's, Discount Tire, Home Depot, Kohl's, Michael's, NAPA, Old Navy, Outlet Shops/famous brands, PetSmart, Ross, See's Candies, Verizon, vet, W Chrysler/Jeep/Dodge, Ford/Lincoln, Honda, Mazda, Nissan, Subaru, Toyota/Scion, U-Haul, VW

228mm Skagit River

MT VERNON

227 WA 538 E, College Way, Mt Vernon, E A&W, Big Scoop Rest., Blue Taco, COA Mexican, Darren's Donut, Denny's, Firehouse Subs, Hong Kong Rest., Jack-in-the Box, Jersey Mike's, KFC, Max Dale's Steak Chops, Moreno's Mexican, Papa Murphy's, Pizza Hut, Riverside Cafe, RoundTable Pizza, Starbucks, Subway, Taco Bell, Taco Time, Days Inn, Skagit Valley Inn, West Winds Motel, $Tree, Ace Hardware, auto/tire repair, AutoZone, Circle K, Coastal Farm & Ranch, Grocery Outlet, Hobby Lobby, Motorworks, O'Reilly Parts, Office Depot, PepBoys, PetCo, Safeway/dsl, Verizon, vet, W Pacific Pride/dsl, Shell/dsl, Arby's, Burger King, Burgermaster, DQ, Fortune Chinese, IHOP, Panda Express, Royal Star Buffet, Quality Inn, Tulip Inn, 7-11, Blade RV Ctr, Chevrolet, Jiffy Lube, Lowe's, Skagit Valley RV Park, URGENT CARE, Walmart/Subway

226 WA 536 W, Kincaid St, E H, Lincoln Grocery, W Pacific Pride, Old Towne Grainery Rest., Skagit River Brewing Co, Wendy's, 7-11, Auto Plus, Red Apple Mkt, visitor info

225 Anderson Rd, E 76/dsl, Country Motorhomes, W Chevron, Freightliner, Poulsbo RV Ctr, RV Country Ctr

224 WA 99 S(from nb, no return), S Mt Vernon

221 WA 534 E, Conway, Lake McMurray, E 76/dsl, W Chevron/dsl/LP, Shell/dsl, Conway Deli, USPO

218 Starbird Rd

215 300th NW, W Interstate/dsl

214mm weigh sta nb

212 WA 532 W, Stanwood, Bryant, W Chevron/dsl, Shell/Burger Stop/dsl, Camano Island SP(19mi)

210 236th NE, E River Rock/dsl, Angel Of The Winds Casino/gas

209mm Stillaguamish River

208 WA 530, Silvana, Arlington, E 76, A1/dsl, Arco/dsl, Chevron/dsl, Pilot/PJ Fresh/Arbys/dsl/scales/24hr, Denny's, Subway, Arlington Motel, Chevrolet, to N Cascades Hwy, W Exxon/dsl

207mm **both lanes, full facilities, litter barrels, vending, RV dump, petwalk**

LAKEWOOD

206 WA 531, Lakewood, E 76/dsl, Arco, Shell, Buzz Inn Steaks, Domino's, Galbi Burger, Jack-in-the-Box, Jersey Mike's, Jimmy John's, KFC, Little Caesar's, McDonald's, Moose Creek BBQ, Olympia Pizza, Panda Express, Papa Murphy's, Starbucks, Subway, Taco Time, Tokyo House Japanese, Wendy's, Best Western+, Medallion Inn & Suites, Quality Inn, Smoky Point Inn, $Tree, AT&T, AutoZone, Camping World RV Ctr, Chrysler/Dodge/Jeep, Ford, Harley-Davidson, Honda, Jo-Ann Fabrics, Lowe's, O'Reilly Parts, Safeway/dsl, Schwab Tire, Subaru, Toyota, vet, Walmart/Subway/auto, W Bonefish Grill, Boston's,

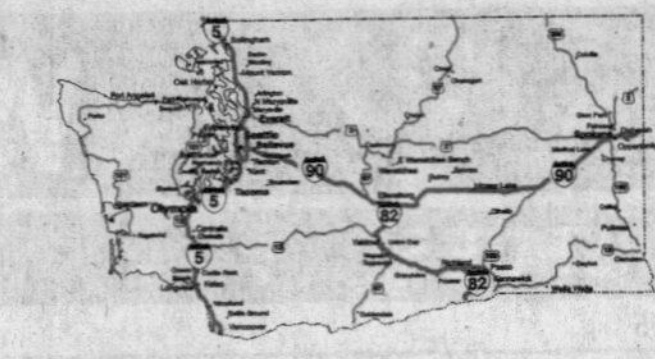

206 Continued
Buffalo Wild Wings, Burger King, Chipotle, Coldstone, Firehouse Subs, Five Guys, Hop N Drops Grill, IHOP, Jamba Juice, MOD Pizza, Outback Steaks, Pizza Hut, Popeyes, Qdoba, Red Robin, Starbucks, Taco Bell, The K BBQ, AT&T, Best Buy, Costco/gas, Dick's, Discount Tire, Firestone/auto, Hobby Lobby, Marshall's, Michael's, Office Depot, Old Navy, PetCo, Target, Verizon

202 116th NE, E Shell/dsl, Arby's, Blazing Onion Burger, Carl's Jr, DQ, Papa John's, Popeyes, Sonic, Starbucks, Subway, Taco Bell, Home2 Suites, $Tree, Kohl's, PetSmart, Ross, URGENT CARE, Verizon, WinCo Foods, W Donna's Trkstp/Gull/dsl/scales/24hr/@, Tulalip Market/dsl, McDonald's, Olive Garden, RAM Rest., Seattle Outlets/famous brands, st patrol, Tulalip Resort/Casino

200 88th St NE, Quil Ceda Way, E 7-11, Shell/dsl/LP, Applebee's, I-5 & 88th, Jersey Mike's, Korean House BBQ, Starbucks, Starbucks, Holiday Inn Express, Haggen's Foods, W Bob's Burgers, Panera Bread, Port of Subs, Cabela's, casino, Home Depot, Walmart/McDonald's

199 WA 528 E, Marysville, Tulalip, E 76, Arco, Shell/dsl, Burger King, Don's Rest./24hr, DQ, Jack-in-the-Box, Jimmy John's, Las Margaritas Mexican, MOD Pizza, Subway, Village Motel/Rest., Albertson's, AT&T, Big Lots, JC Penney, Petco, Staples, Verizon, Walgreens, W 76, Chevron/dsl, McDonald's, Taco Time, Wendy's, Quality Inn, casino, Chevrolet, Robinson RV Ctr, to Tulalip Indian Res

EVERETT

198 Port of Everett(from sb), Steamboat Slough

195mm Snohomish River

195 Port of Everett(from nb), Marine View Dr

194 US 2 E, Everett Ave, W Shell/dsl, H, Schwab Tire

193 WA 529, Pacific Ave(from nb), W Marathon, Hunan Palace, Lew's BBQ, Best Western, Delta Hotel, Travelodge, Lowe's

192 Broadway, to 41st St, W 76/dsl, Arco, Shell, Baskin-Robbins, Erwin's Cheese Steaks, IHOP, Ivar's Seafood, Joa Teriyaki, McDonald's, Quiznos, Red Rock Subs, Starbucks, Subway, city park, H, Jiffy Lube, Safeway/gas, Verizon

189 WA 526 W, WA 527, Everett Mall Way, Everett, E Arco, Shell/dsl, Burger King, Buzz Inn Steaks, Subway, Wendy's, Extended Stay America, Costco/gas, Jiffy Lube, vet, WinCo Foods, W Chevron, Shell/dsl, Applebees, Arbys, Basil Vietnamese, Blazing Crawfish, Bob's Burgers, Buffalo Wild Wings, Jack-in-the-Box, Jimmy John's, Olive Garden, Red Robin, Extended Stay America, Woodspring Suites, Best Buy, Michael's, Old Navy, PetSmart, TJ Maxx, Trader Joe's, Verizon, Walmart

188mm **/weigh sta sb, full facilities, info, litter barrels, RV dump**

186 WA 96, 128th SW, E Marathon, Mobil/dsl, Shell/dsl, O'Donnells Rest., Quality Inn, Lakeside RV Park, park, W Arco, Chevron, Shell, A&W/KFC, Acropolis Pizza, Chinnie's Chinese, Denny's, Dickey's BBQ, DQ, McDonald's, Papa John's, Pizza Hut, Starbucks, Subway, Taco Bell, Taco Time, Teriyaki Plus, Holiday Inn Express, La Quinta, Motel 6, $Tree, Lakeside RV Park, PepBoys, Safeway, vet

183 164th SW, E Arco, Shell/dsl, Domino's, Jack-in-the-Box, Panda Express, Quiznos, Starbucks, Subway, Taco Del Mar, Taco Time, Walgreens, Walmart, W Chevron/dsl,

WA

INTERSTATE 5 Cont'd

LYNNWOOD

183 Continued
Five Guys, Indigo Lynnwood Rest., Mechie's FroYo, MOD Pizza, Stabucks, Subway, Fred Meyer/dsl, vet

182 WA 525, Alderwood Mall Blvd, to Alderwood Mall, I-405 S, W Arco, Baekjeong KBBQ, Bazille, Blazing Onion, Buffalo Wild Wings, Cafe Rio, Caliburger, Cheesecake Factory, Chipotle, Chops Asian, Crumbl, Dave & Buster's, Isarn Thai, Jamba Juice, Keg Steaks, Panda Express, PF Chang's, Red Robin, See's Candies, Shake Shack, Homewood Suites, Residence Inn, Costco/gas, JC Penney, Kohl's, Macy's, Nordstrom, REI, Ross, Target, vet, World Mkt

181 44th Ave W, to WA 524, Lynnwood, E 76/dsl, Arco, Shell, I-5 & Alderwood Rest., Jimmy John's, Little Caesar's, McDonald's, Old Spaghetti Factory, Papa Murphy's, Starbucks, Subway, Teriyaki Garden, Embassy Suites, Extended Stay America, Hampton Inn, Holiday Inn Express, Barnes&Noble, Best Buy, Jaguar, Land Rover, Lowe's, O'Reilly Parts, Old Navy, PetCo, Safeway, Verizon, vet, Whole Foods Mkt, W 76/dsl, Arco, Shell/repair, Applebee's, Arby's, Chipotle Mexican, Denny's, Ezell's Chicken, IHOP, Jack-in-the-Box, KFC, McDonald's, Moonshine BBQ, Olive Garden, Panda Express, Red Lobster, Starbucks, Taco Bell, Taco del Mar, Taco Time, Todo Mexico, Wendy's, WuJu KBBQ, Zeeks Pizza, Best Value Inn, Best Western, Courtyard, Hilton Garden Inn, La Quinta, city park, Fred Meyer/dsl, Goodyear/auto, Schwab Tire, URGENT CARE, USPO, vet

179 220th SW, Mountlake Terrace, Mountlake Terrace, W Shell/dsl, Azteca Mexican, Fork Mediterranean , Port of Subs, Subway, Teriyaki Bowl, H, vet

EDMONDS

178 236th St SW(from nb), Mountlake Terrace, E Baguus Little Asia

177 WA 104, Edmonds, E Chevron/dsl, Domino's, Gabriel's Fire BBQ, Las Brasas, Mazatlan Mexican, McDonald's/playplace, Pagliacci Pizza, Starbucks, Subway, Time Out Greek, Studio 6, Jiffy Lube, O'Reilly Parts, RiteAid, Thriftway Foods, URGENT CARE

176 NE 175th St, Aurora Ave N, to Shoreline, E Peking House, Safeway/dsl

175 WA 523, NE 145th, 5th Ave NE

174 NE 130th, Roosevelt Way

BOTHELL

173 1st Ave NE, Northgate Way, E EVgo EVC, AT&T, Azteca Mexican, BlueFin Grill, CA Pizza Kitchen, Chipotle Mexican, Domino's, Five Guys, Jimmy John's, Pizza Hut, Red Robin, Stanford's Rest., Hampton Inn, Barnes&Noble, Best Buy, Dick's, Discount Tire, JC Penny, Nordstrom, Old Navy, Petco, Target, Verizon, W 76, Chevron, Shell/dsl, McDonald's, Saffron Grill, Starbucks, Courtyard, Hotel Nexus, 7-11

172 N 85th, Aurora Ave

171 WA 522, Lake City Way, Bothell

170 Ravenna Blvd, E Shell/Circle K/dsl, Olympic Pizza, One Bite Cafe, Rain City Burgers, Taco Del Mar, The Wayward Vegan, Whole Foods

169 NE 45th, NE 50th, E Chevron, Shell, Residence Inn, Subway, H, PetCo, U of WA, vet, W to Seattle Pacific U, zoo

168b WA 520, to Bellevue

168a Lakeview Blvd, downtown

167 Mercer St(exits left from nb), Fairview Ave, Seattle Ctr

166 Olive Way, Stewart St, E H, W Hilton Garden, Hyatt, Residence Inn, SpringHill Suites, WA Convention Ctr

165a Seneca St(exits left from nb), James St, E H

165b Union St, E Pike Grocery, H, W Cheesecake Factory, Ruth's Chris Steaks, Crowne Plaza, Fairmont, Hilton, Kimpton Hotel, Renaissance Inn, Sheraton

164b 4th Ave S, to Kingdome, downtown

164a I-90 E, to Spokane, downtown

163 6th Ave, S Spokane St, W Seattle Br, Columbian Way, W Arco/dsl, Gull/dsl, Shell, Albierto's Mexican, Burger King, By's Burger, Denny's, Jack-in-the-Box, KFC, McDonald's, Subway, Subway, Taco Bell, Costco/gas, USPO

162 Corson Ave, Michigan St(exits left from nb), same as 161

161 Swift Ave, Albro Place, W 76/dsl, Shell, Shell/dsl, Mezzanotte Italian, Starbucks, Georgetown Inn

158 Pacific Hwy S, E Marginal Way, W Chevron/dsl, NAPA

157 ML King Way

BURIEN

156 WA 539 N, Interurban Ave(no EZ return to sb), Tukwila, E Pacific Pride/dsl, Billy Baroos Rest., golf, W 76/dsl, Shell/dsl, Jack-in-the-Box, Quiznos, Starbucks, Sunny Teriyaki, Days Inn

154b WA 518, Burien, W Extended Stay America

154a I-405, N to Bellevue

153 S Center Pkwy, from nb, E Chevron/dsl, Applebee's, Azteca Mexican, Bahama Breeze, BJ's Rest., Boiling Point Mongolian, Buffalo Wild Wings, Burger King, CA Pizza Kitchen, Cheesecake Factory, Chipotle Mexican, ClaimJumper, Coldstone, Duke's ChowderHouse, Famous Dave's, Five Guys, Grazie Ristorante, Habit Burger, IHOP, Jersey Mike's, McDonald's, Mizuki Buffet, MOD Pizza, Old Spaghetti Factory, Olive Garden, Outback Steaks, Panda Express, Panera Bread, Peir 88 Seafood, Qdoba Mexican, Red Robin, See's Candies, Shake Shack, Simply Thai, Starbucks, Thai Cuisine, Wingstop, DoubleTree Inn, Holiday Inn Express, Home2 Suites, Hotel Interurban, Tru Hotel, $Tree, $Tree, Acura, AT&T, Barnes&Noble, Best Buy, Firestone/auto, H, JC Penney, Jo-Ann Fabrics, Kohl's, Lowe's, Macy's, Michael's, Nordstrom, Nordstrom Rack, Old Navy, PetCo, PetSmart, REI, Ross, Target, Verizon, World Mkt, W Courtyard, Element Hotel

152 S 188th, Orillia Rd, W 76/dsl, Denny's, Jack-in-the-Box, Marathon, Taco Bell, Aloft, Courtyard, Days Inn, DoubleTree Hotel, Hampton Inn, Hilton Garden, La Quinta, Motel 6, Quality Inn, city park, to

DES MOINES

151 S 200th, Military Rd, E 76/Subway/dsl, Motel 6, W 7-11, Chevron, Shell, Bob's Burgers, IHOP, Best Value Inn, Best Western, Comfort Inn, Fairfield Inn, Hampton Inn, Holiday Inn Express, Residence Inn, Sleep Inn, AutoZone, city park, O'Reilly Parts, U-Haul

149 WA 516, to Kent, Des Moines, E Century Motel, Poulsbo RV Ctr, W Arco, Chevron/dsl, Shell/dsl, Burger Meister, CA Burrito, Church's TX Chicken, Los Cabos Mexican, McDonald's, Menuderia María, Moe Vegan, Pizza Hut, Subway, Garden Suites, Red Lion Inn, $Tree, Lowe's, Meineke, to Saltwater SP, Walgreens

147 S 272nd, E Chevron/dsl, W Arco, Shell/dsl, Dutch Bros, Jack-in-the-Box, Little Caesar's, McDonald's, Papa Murphy's, Starbucks, Subway, Taco Bell, AutoZone, Bartell Drug, Safeway

143 S 320th, Federal Way, W 76/dsl, Applebee's, Azteca Mexican, Baskin-Robbins, Black Angus, Black Bear Diner, Buffalo Wild Wings, Cafe Rio, Chick-fil-A, Chipotle Mexican, Church's TX Chicken, Coldstone, Crawfish Island, Domino's, El Rinconsito, Ezell's Chicken, Grand Peking, Ivar's Seafood, Jersey Mike's, Jimmy John's, Katsu Burger, L&L HBBQ, McDonald's, MOD Pizza, Pac Island Grill, Panda Express, Panera Bread, Papa Murphy's, Red Lobster, Red Robin, Starbucks, Subway, Tokyo Japanese Steaks, Village Inn, Vince's Italian, Vons Chicken, Comfort Inn, Courtyard, Hampton Inn, La Quinta, Staybridge Suites, AT&T, Barnes&Noble, Best Buy, Campeon Mkt, Dick's, Jo-Ann Fabrics, Kohl's, Macy's, Marlene's Natural Mkt, Michael's, O'Reilly Parts, PetCo, PetSmart, Ross, Safeway/dsl, Target,

WA

INTERSTATE 5 Cont'd

PORT OF TACOMA

143 Continued
TJ Maxx, to Dash Point SP, Trader Joe's, Tuesday Morning, Verizon, Walmart/auto

142b a WA 18 E, S 348th, Enchanted Pkwy, E funpark, W Chevron, Shell/dsl, Arby's, Biscuits Cafe, Burger King, Del Taco, Denny's, Jack-in-the-Box, Jamba Juice, Jersey Mike's, Jimmy Mac's Roadhouse, McDonald's, Menchie's, Olive Garden, Panda Express, Popeyes, Puerto Vallarta, RoundTable Pizza, Starbucks, Subway, Super Chix, Taco Bell, Taco Del Mar, Taco Time, Thai Bistro, The Chopped Leaf, The Rock Pizza, Time Out Grill, Wendy's, Day's Inn, Quality Inn, Chevrolet, Costco/gas, Discount Tire, Hobby Lobby, Home Depot, H, Lowe's, O'Reilly Parts, Office Depot, Pepboys, Schwab Tire, T-Mobile, UHaul, Walmart/Subway

140mm rest area both lanes, full facilities, litter barrels, petwalk, RV dump, weigh sta nb

137 WA 99, Fife, Milton, E 76/dsl, Chevron/dsl, Shell, DQ, Starbucks, Warthog BBQ, Motel 6, Acura, Baydo's RV Ctr, Cadillac, RV Country, visitor info, W 76/dsl, 76/dsl, Arby's, Burger King, Church's Chicken, Denny's, Domino's, Fife Thai Rest., Hefy's Burger, Jersey Mike's, Jimmy John's, McDonald's, Pick Quick Burgers, Pizza Hut, Poodle Dog, Sapporo Japanese, Starbucks, Taco Bell, Taco Time, Wendy's, Wienerschnitzel, Emerald Queen Hotel/casino, Niwas Inn, Quality Inn, $Tree, 7-11, Audi/Porsche, Camping World RV Ctr, Infinity, Jiffy Lube, Mercedes, O'Reilly Parts, Schwab Tire, Tacoma RV Ctr, Verizon

136b a Port of Tacoma, E CFN/dsl, BMW, Costco, Honda, Mini, Peterbilt, W 7-11/dsl, 76/dsl, Gull/dsl, Love's/Chester's/Subway/dsl/scales/LP/RV dump/24hr, Jack-in-the-Box, Pick-Quick, Extended Stay America, Guesthouse Inn, Sunshine Motel, Travelodge, Fife RV Ctr, Goodyear, Harley-Davidson, Johnson RV Ctr, Land Rover/Jaguar/Lexus, Lexus, Meineke, Mercedes, NAPA, Porsche, Poulsbo RV Ctr, Volvo

135 Bay St, Puyallup, E 76/Tahoma Express, W La Quinta, Tacoma Dome

134 Portland Ave(from nb), same as 135

133 WA 7, I-705, E Stanley & Seafort's Rest., W El Gaucho Steak, Jack-in-the-box, Comfort Inn, Courtyard, Holiday Inn Express, museum, Tacoma Dome

132 WA 16 W, S 38th, Gig Harbor, to Bremerton, E Safeway/fuel, W BJ's Rest., Buffalo Wild Wings, Cheesecake Factory, Chick-fil-A, Five Guys, Jamba Juice, Jimmy John's, Jollibee, Krispy Kreme, MOD Pizza, Panera Bread, Red Robin, Starbucks, Wendy's, $Tree, Costco/gas, Firestone/auto, Ford/Toyota, Goodyear/auto, JC Penney, JoAnn Fabrics, Macy's, Nordstrom, Old Navy, PetCo, REI, to Pt Defiance Pk/Zoo, Verizon, World Mkt

130 S 56th, Tacoma Mall Blvd, W Shell/dsl, Azteca Mexican, ChuckeCheese, Jack-in-the-Box, Extended Stay America, Best Buy

129 S 72nd, S 84th, E Chevron, Applebee's, Burger King, Cambodian Grill, DQ, Elmer's, Famous Dave's, IHOP, Jack-in-the-Box, Jimmy John's, Olive Garden, Popeyes, Red Lobster, RoundTable Pizza, Shari's, Starbucks, Subway, Motel 6, Thea Tacoma Inn, Bass Pro Shops, WinCo Foods, W La Perla Mexican, Oasis Inn, Home Depot, to Steilacoom Lake

128 S 84th St (from nb)same as 129, E 76, Shell/dsl, Denny's, Subway, Best Western, Hampton Inn, Holiday Inn, Holiday Inn Express, Howard Johnson, Quality Inn & Suites, Rothem Inn, Travelodge, W 7-11/dsl, $Tree, Discount Tire, vet

127 WA 512, S Tacoma Way, Puyallup, Mt Ranier, W 7-11,

CAMP MURRAY

127 Continued
76/7-11, Arco/dsl, Aliberto's Mexican, Black Bear Diner, Captain Crab, DQ, Ivar's Seafood, Mazatlan Mexican, McDonald's, Starbucks, Taco Time, Wendy's, Western Inn, Advance Parts, O'Reilly Parts

125 to McChord AFB, Lakewood, W 76/Circle K/dsl, Chevron, Mobil, Shell/dsl, A&W/KFC, Bruno's, Carr's Rest., Church's TX Chicken, Denny's, Domino's, Jack's BBQ, Jack-in-the-Box, Pizza Hut, Pizza Pizazz, Subway, Wendy's, Holiday Inn Express, Home Motel, TownePlace Suites, Aamco, Ford, H, O'Reilly Parts, tires/repair, U-Haul

124 Gravelly Lake Dr, W 76/Circle K, Arco/repair, El Toro Mexican, Puget Sound Pizza, same as 125

123 Thorne Lane, Tillicum Lane

122 Berkeley St, Camp Murray, W Chevron/repair, Aceituno's Mexican, CA Tacos, Jack-in-the-Box, Kwang's Chinese, McDonald's, Popeyes, Starbucks, Subway, Taco Bell, AutoZone

120 Ft Lewis, E Ft Lewis Military Museum

119 Du Pont Rd, Steilacoom, E to Ft Lewis, W 76, Happy Teriyaki, Starbucks, Subway, Hampton Inn, Home2 Suites

118 Center Dr, W Chevron/dsl, Bruceski's Pizza, Farrelli's Pizza, Jack-in-the-Box, Koko's Wok, McDonald's, McNamara's Eatery, Pizza Hut, Quiznos, Starbucks, Subway, Viva Mexico, Best Western, Fairbridge Inn, Fairfield Inn

117mm weigh sta nb

116 Mounts Rd, Old Nisqually, E golf, W Eagles Pride Grill

115mm Nisqually River

114 Nisqually, E Arco/dsl, Chevron/repair/Lp, Medicine Creek Cafe, Nisqually Grill, Lost Lake RV Camping, Nisqually Auto Repair, Nisqually RV Park, River Bend RV Camping

111 WA 510 E, Marvin Rd, to Yelm, E 76/Circle K, Chevron/dsl, Shell/dsl, Burger King, Chick-fil-A, Chipotle, Coldstone, Domino's, Dutch Bros, Firehouse Subs, Jack-in-the-Box, Jamba Juice, Jersey Mike's, KFC/LJ Silver, L&L HBBQ, Lemon Grass Rest., McDonald's, Panda Express, Panera Bread, Papa Murphy's, Popeyes, Puerto Vallarta, RAM Rest., Red Robin, Starbucks, Subway, Super Buffet, Taco Bell, Taco Del Mar, Taco Time, Vinny's NY Pizza, Best Western+, $Tree, AutoZone, Best Buy, BigLots, casino, Costco/gas, Grocery Outlet, Harley Davidson, Home Depot, Jiffy Lube, O'Reilly Parts, Petco, Safeway/gas, Schwab Tire, Verizon, Walgreens, Walmart/Subway, WLYH RV Park(2mi), W 7-11/dsl, Mayan Mexican, Meconi's Subs, MOD Pizza, Pizza Hut, Starbucks, Super Chix, Cabela's, Tolmie SP, URGENT CARE

109 Martin Way, Sleator-Kenny Rd, E Main Chinese Buffet, Taco Bell, The Rock Pizza, Discount Tire, W 76/dsl, Shell/dsl, Brewery City Pizza, Burger King, Casa Mia, Denny's, Domino's, Jimmy John's, Red Lobster, Shari's, Comfort Inn, La Quinta, Quality Inn, Ramada Inn, Super 8, Point S Tire

108 Sleater-Kinney Rd, E 7-11, Shell/dsl, Applebee's, Arby's, Carl's Jr, Chipotle, Five Guys, McDonald's/playplace, MOD Pizza, Pizza Hut/Taco Bell, Starbucks, T-Mobile, Wendy's, Candlewood Suites, Holiday Inn Express, Firestone/auto, Fred Meyer/dsl, GNC, Jiffy Lube, Kohl's, Marshall's, Michael's, Office Depot, PetSmart, Target, W Arco/dsl, Casa Mia, Dirty Dave's, El Sarape Mexican, Jack-in-the-Box, Jersey Mike's, Panda Express, Starbucks,

INTERSTATE 5 Cont'd

BLACK LAKE

108 Continued
Subway, Hampton Inn, Woodspring Suites, H, Lowe's, Point S Tires, Safeway/gas, same as 109

107 Pacific Ave, E Shell/dsl/E-85, Corona's Mexican, DQ, Shari's, Taco Time, Albertson's, Home Depot, Ross, vet, W Coumbs RV Ctr, H

105 St Capitol, W 76/Subway/dsl, Chevron/dsl

104 US 101 N, W Olympia, to Aberdeen, W 7-11, Arco, Chevron/dsl, Shell/dsl, Jack-in-the-Box, Extended Stay America, Buick/GMC, Chevrolet/Cadillac, Ford, Honda, Hyundai, Jeep, Kia, Lincoln/Mazda, Nissan, Subaru, VW

103 2nd Ave, Deschutes Ave

102 Trosper Rd, Black Lake, E Shell, Brewery City Pizza, Burger King, DQ, Dutch Bros, Happy Teriyaki, Jack-in-the-Box, KFC, La Patrona Mexican, McDonald's, Starbucks, Subway, Taco Bell, Taco Time, Best Western, Motel 6, Tumwater Inn, Jiffy Lube, O'Reilly Parts, Schwab Tire, Tumwater Auto Repair, Verizon, W Chevron, Speedway, Denny's, L&L HBBQ, Little Caesar's, Panda Express, Papa Murphy's, Subway, The Brick Rest., Alderbrook RV Park, AutoZone, Costco/gas, Fred Meyer/dsl, GNC, Home Depot, Safeway, URGENT CARE, Walgreens, Walmart

101 Tumwater Blvd, E Chevron, Shell/dsl, Domino's, Flaming Pig BBQ, Koibito Japanese, Meconi's Pizza, Red Wagon Burgers, Colony Inn, 7-11, Olympia Camping, USPO, USPO

99 WA 121 S, 93rd Ave, Scott Lake, E Pilot/McDonald's/Subway/dsl/scales/24hr, Ace Hardware, American Heritage Camping, Olympia Camping, W Chevron

95 WA 121, Littlerock, E Millersylvania SP, RV camping, W Freightliner

93.5mm **sb, full facilities, info, litter barrels, vending, petwalk**

91mm **nb, full facilities, info, litter barrels, vending, petwalk**

CENTRALIA

88 US 12, Rochester, E Blair's I-5 RV Ctr, I-5 Truckwash, W 76/Taco Bell, Arco, CFN/dsl, Sinclair, Sta 88/Arby's/Burger King/dsl, Burger Claim, DQ, Figaro's Pizza, Jack-in-the-Box, Mariachi Mexican, McDonald's, Quiznos, Starbucks, Fairfield Inn, Great Wolf Lodge, Outback RV Park, Peterbilt

82 Harrison Ave, Factory Outlet Way, Centralia, E Arco, Alibertos Mexican, Burgerville, Casa Ramos Mexican, DQ, Dutch Bros, Hometown Rest., Jimmy John's, Nuby's Steaks, Panda Chinese, Pizza Hut, Quiznos, Wendy's, Centralia Inn, King Oscar Motel, Quality Inn, AutoZone, Jiffy Lube, VF/famous brands, W Chevron/dsl, Mobil/dsl, Texaco, Arby's, Bill&Bea's, Country Cousin Rest., Denny's, Domino's, Firehouse Subs, Jack-in-the-Box, McDonald's, Papa Murphy's, Starbucks, Subway, Taco Bell, AT&T, Centralia Outlets/famous brands, city park, Midway RV Park, O'Reilly Parts, Safeway/dsl, Schwab Tire, Verizon

82mm Skookumchuck River

81 WA 507, Mellen St, E Chevron/dsl, Shell/dsl, Subway, La Quinta, Lakeview Inn, Peppermill Inn, W H

79 Chamber Way, E Mobil/dsl, Jalisco Mexican, Chrysler/Dodge/Jeep/Fiat, GCR Tires/Service, museum, vet, visitor info, W Chevron/dsl/LP/e85, Applebee's, Burger King, Dutch Bros, McDonald's, Sonic, Starbucks, Subway, Taco Bell, Taco Del Mar, Wendy's, $Tree, GNC, Grocery Outlet, Home Depot, Honda, Michael's, O'Reilly Parts, st patrol, Toyota/Scion, Verizon, Walgreens, Walmart/McDonald's

CHEHALIS

77 WA 6 W, Chehalis, E 76/dsl, Cenex/dsl/LP, Dairy Bar, Jeremy's Cafe, Sahara Pizza, Holiday Inn Express, NAPA, Schwab Tire, USPO, W Rainbow Falls SP,

77 Continued
veterans museum

76 13th St, E Arco, Chevron/dsl, Burger Den, Denny's, Jack-in-the-Box, Ocean Prime Rest., Subway, Best Western+, Relax Inn, Awesome I-5 RV Ctr/RV dump, Baydo's RV Ctr, Ford, W RV park/dump

74 Labree Rd

72 Rush Rd, Napavine, E Chevron/dsl/scales, Burger King, Jack's Ribeye Rest., McDonald's, Subway, Country Canopy RV Ctr/repair, W Arco, Love's/Carl's Jr/dsl/scales/24hr/@, Shell/dsl, Arby's, Starbucks, Taco Bell

72mm Newaukum River

71 WA 508 E, Onalaska, Napavine, E 76/dsl

68 US 12 E, Morton, E Arco/dsl, PA/dsl, Papa Bear's Rest., Lewis&Clark SP, Mt Ranier NP, W 76/rest./dsl

63 WA 505, Winlock, W Shell/Chesters/dsl/LP

60 Toledo Vader Rd, Toledo

59 WA 506 W, Vader, E Shell/dsl, Beesley's Cafe, RV Park, W Chevron/Subway/dsl

59mm Cowlitz River

CASTLE ROCK

57 Jackson Hwy, Barnes Dr, E R&R Tires, W Texaco/GeeCee's/café/dsl/scales/24hr/@, repair

55mm **both lanes, full facilities, litter barrels, vending, petwalk**

52 Barnes Dr, Toutle Park Rd, E Paradise Cove RV Park/general store, W Toutle River RV Resort

50mm Toutle River

49 WA 504 E, Castle Rock, E Chevron/dsl/LP, Shell/dsl, Burger King, C&L Burgers, El Compadre Mexican, Papa Pete's Pizza, Subway, Castle Rock Tire/oil change, Mt St Helens Motel, Timberland Inn, Seaquest SP, W McDonald's, visitor info

48 Castle Rock, W city park

46 Pleasant Hill Rd, Headquarters Rd, E Cedars RV Park/dump

44mm weigh sta sb, weigh sta sb

42 Bridge Dr, Lexington, W Chevron/dsl, Lexi's Pizza, Subway, auto repair

40 to WA 4, Kelso-Longview, W Texaco, Econolodge

39 WA 4, Kelso, to Longview, E Arco, Chevron, Denny's, Dutch Bros, Jack-in-the-Box, McDonald's, Shari's, Starbucks, Subway, Taco Time, Motel 6, Red Lion Hotel, Sleep Inn, $Tree, Brook Hollow RV Park, city park, Verizon, W Burger King, DQ, Fiesta Bonita Mexican, Panera Bread, Red Lobster, Taco Bell, Comfort Inn, GuestHouse Inn, JC Penney, museum, Safeway/dsl, Sportsman's Whse, Target

36 WA 432 W, to WA 4, to US 30, Kelso, E RV Country Ctr, W RV Camping, Toyota

KALAMA

32 Kalama River Rd, E Fireside Café, Camp Kalama RV Park/camping/gifts

31mm Kalama River

30 Kalama, E Chevron/dsl, Burger Bar, Columbia Rest., Lucky Dragon Chinese, Playa Azul Mexican, Poker Pete's Pizza, Subway, antiques, Godfrey's Drug, USPO, W Jubitz CFN/dsl, McMenamin's Kalamazoo Inn, RV camping

27 Todd Rd, Port of Kalama, E Rebel/Shell/café/dsl/24hr

22 Dike Access Rd, E Popeye's, Wayback Burgers, Belmont RV Park, W Arco, Taco Bell, Columbia Riverfront RV Park, O'Reilly Parts, Schwab Tire, Verizon, Walmart/Subway

21 WA 503 E, Woodland, E Arco/dsl, Chevron, Pacific Pride/dsl, Shell/LP/dsl, Burgerville, Casa Tapatia, Daddy D's BBQ, DQ, Fat Moose Grill, Grocery Outlet, Little Caesars, Mali Thai, Mat and Mandy's Diner, OakTree Rest., Pizza Factory, Rosie's Rest., Best Western, Lewis River Inn, OYO, Ace Hardware, Hi-School Pharmacy, Woodland Shores RV Park, W Astro, Antony's Pizzaria, Carl's Jr, Dutch Bros,

[gas] = gas [food] = food [lodging] = lodging [other] = other [RS] = rest stop

INTERSTATE 5 Cont'd

BATTLEGROUND · HAZEL DELL

21 Continued
Guadalajara Mexican, Los Pepes Mexican, McDonald's, Papa Murphy's, Starbucks, Subway, [O] $Tree, NAPA, Safeway/dsl, Woodland Tire

20mm N Fork Lewis River

18mm E Fork Lewis River

16 NW La Center Rd, La Center, E [gas] Shell/dsl, [food] Twin Dragons Rest., [O] Paradise Point SP, Tri-Mountain Golf/rest., W [gas] Chevron, [lodging] Ilani Casino/Hotel

15mm weigh sta nb

14 WA 501 S, Pioneer St, Ridgefield, E [gas] 7-11/dsl, Arco, [food] Country Café, Domino's, Papa Pete's Pizza, Subway, Teriyaki Thai, [O] Battleground Lake SP, Big Fir RV Camping, Tri-Mountain RV Park, vet, W [gas] Chevron/dsl, [food] Chipotle, MOD Pizza, Starbucks, Taco Bell

13mm **[RS] sb, full [handicapped] facilities, info, [phone], [picnic], litter barrels, vending, petwalk, RV dump**

11 WA 502, Battleground, [RS] nb, full [handicapped] facilities, info, [phone], [picnic], litter barrels, vending, petwalk, RV dump

9 NE 179th St, W [gas] Chevron/dsl, [O] RV Park

7 I-205 S(from sb), to I-84, WA 14, NE 134th St, E [gas] 7-11, 76, Speedway, [food] Applebee's, Billygan's Roadhouse, Black Rock Coffee, Burger King, Burgerville, Domino's, Jack-in-the-Box, McDonald's, Muchas Gracias, Panda Express, Round Table Pizza, Starbucks, Subway, Taco Bell, [lodging] Holiday Inn Express, Quality Inn, Red Lion, [O] 99 RV Park, [H], Safeway, Safeway/dsl, URGENT CARE, Verizon, Walgreens, W [gas] Shell, [food] Baskin-Robbins, Bruchi's, Creekside BBQ, Freshii, KC Teryaki, Kitchen Table, Los Tacos Locos, Mio Sushi, Papa Murphy's, Planet Thai, [lodging] La Quinta, [O] AT&T, Fred Meyer

5 NE 99th St, E [food] Blind Onion Pizza, Burgerville, Carl's Jr, Del Taco, Domino's, Fat Dave's Rest., K-Town BBQ, Popeyes, Quiznos, UnPHOgettable, [O] AutoZone, Walgreens, Walmart/Subway, Winco Foods/gas, W [gas] Arco/dsl, Chevron/dsl, [food] Amaro's Table Rest., Bortolami's Pizza, Dutch Bros, Joy Teriyaki, McDonald's, Subway, [O] $Tree, Grocery Outlet, Kohl's, Office Depot, PetCo, Target, Verizon

4 NE 78th St, Hazel Dell, E [food] 99 Saloon & Grill, Baja Fresh, Baskin Robbins, Burger King, Canton Chinese, Domino's, Don Pedro Mexican, Dutch Bros, Izzy's Grill, KFC, McDonald's, Megabite Pizza, Panera Bread, Patras Greek, PeachTree Rest., Rib Joint BBQ, Sakura Japanese, Starbucks, Subway, Taco Bell, [lodging] Quality Inn, [O] Aamco, CarQuest, CostLess Parts, Firestone, Fred Meyer, Jiffy Lube, Jo-Ann, O'Reilly Parts, U-Haul, W [gas] Shell/dsl/LP, [food] Buffalo Wild Wings, Chipotle, Five Guys, Jack-in-the-Box, Jamba Juice, Jersey Mike's, Jimmy John's, Killer Burger, Little Caesar's, MOD Pizza, Nekter Juice, Panda Express, Starbucks, Wendy's, Wingstop, [O] Hancock Fabrics, Marshalls, Natural Grocers, PetSmart, Ross, Safeway

3 NE Hwy 99, Main St, Hazel Dell, E [gas] 7-11, [food] El Tapatio Mexican, Muchas Gracias Mexican, Oh My Teriyaki, Valentina Mexican, [O] Valvoline, W transmissions

2 WA 500 E, 39th St, to Orchards, W [gas] Arco, Chevron, [O] Safeway

1d E 4th, Plain Blvd W, to WA 501, Port of Vancouver, E [food] Burgerville, Dominos, Don Taco, McDonald's, Starbucks, Subway, TacoTime, [O] vet, W [food] DQ

1c Mill Plain Blvd, City Ctr, E [O] Clark Coll, W [gas] Chevron, [food] Black Angus, Starbucks, [lodging] Comfort Inn, [O] st patrol

1b 6th St, E [food] Who Song & Larry's Mexican, W Smokin' Oak BBQ, [lodging] EconoLodge, Hilton

1a WA 14 E, to Camus, E [O] [H], W [food] WildFin Grill, [lodging] AC Hotel, Hilton, Hotel Indigo

0mm Washington/Oregon state line, Columbia River

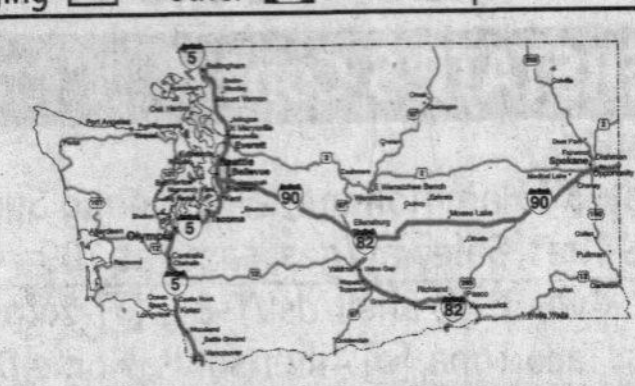

INTERSTATE 82

PLYMOUTH · BENTON CITY · GRANDVIEW

Exit #	Services
11mm	I-82 Oregon begins/ends on I-84, exit 179.
10	Westland Rd
5	Power Line Rd
1.5mm	Umatilla River
1	US 395/730, Umatilla, W [gas] Circle K/Subway/dsl, Shell/Crossroads Trkstp/dsl/rest./24hr, Texaco/dsl, [food] Rae's Dayz Donuts, [lodging] Econolodge, Umatilla Inn&Suites, [O] $General, Harvest Foods, Umatilla Marina/RV Park, USPO, weigh sta
132mm	Washington/Oregon state line, Columbia River
131	WA 14 W, to McNary Dam, Plymouth, W [O] Agate Acres RV Park
130mm	weigh sta wb
122	Coffin Rd
114	Locust Grove Rd
113	US 395 N, to I-182, Kennewick, Pasco, st patrol, N [gas] Circle K/dsl, Royal/dsl, [food] Bob's Burgers, Burger King, Chipotle, Costa Vida, Dutch Bros, Fuego Mexican, McDonald's, Original Pancake House, Osaka Asian, Starbucks, Subway, Taco Bell, [lodging] Baymont Inn, Best Western+, Comfort Suites, Hampton Inn, La Quinta, [O] AT&T, auto/tire repair, Home Depot, [H], PetCo, st patrol, Verizon, vet, Walgreens, Walmart/Subway
109	Badger Rd, W Kennewick, N [gas] Exxon/Circle K/Subway/dsl, Shell/dsl, S [O] Columbia Sun RV Park
104	Dallas Rd, N [gas] 76
102	I-182, US 12 E, to US 395, Richland, Pasco, Spokane
96	WA 224 E, Benton City, N [gas] Conoco/cafe/dsl, [O] Beach RV Park, S [gas] Shell
93	Yakitat Rd
88	Gibbon Rd
82	WA 22, WA 221, Mabton, S [gas] Conoco/dsl, [O] [H], museum, wine tasting
82mm	Yakima River
80	Gap Rd, **full [handicapped] facilities, litter barrels, [phone], [picnic], [RS] both lanes, rv dump,** S [gas] Chevron/dsl, Love's/Carl's Jr/dsl/scales/24hr/@, Pacific Pride/dsl, Shell/dsl/scales, [food] Birrieria Mexican, Burger King, Domino's, Dutch Bros, Golden Horse Chinese, Jack-in-the-Box, KFC/Taco Bell, McDonald's, Palomas Mexican, Starbucks, Subway, [lodging] Best Western+, Holiday Inn Express, Vintners Inn, [O] Ford, Schwab Tire, URGENT CARE, Verizon, vet, Wine Country RV Park
76mm	weigh sta eb
75	County Line Rd, Grandview, S [gas] Marathon/dsl, same as 73, [food] McDonald's, Papa Murphy's, [lodging] Grandview Inn, [O] O'Reilly Parts, Safeway/gas, U-Haul/repair
73	Stover Rd, Wine Country Rd, Grandview, S [gas] Chevron/dsl, [food] 10-4 Café, DQ, Eli&Kathy's Rest., Garcia's Mexican, Little Caesars, [lodging] Apple Valley Motel, [O] Chrysler/Dodge/Jeep, IGA Mercado, RV park/dump, Schwab Tire
69	WA 241, to Sunnyside, N [gas] Arco/dsl, Shell/dsl/scales/24hr, [food] A&W, Burger Den, Burger King, Carl's Jr, China Buffet, Denny's, Dutch Bros, El Charrito Mexican, KFC, McDonald's, Panda Garden, Papa Murphy's, Pizza Hut, Popeyes, Sakura Teriyaki, Subway, Summer Fiesta, Taco Bell, [lodging] Best Western+, FairBridge Inn, [O] $Tree, AT&T, auto repair, AutoZone, Chrysler/Jeep/Dodge, Fiesta Foods, Grocery Outlet, Nissan, O'Reilly Parts, Ross, Walmart/Subway

INTERSTATE 82 Cont'd

TOPPENISH

Exit #	Services
67	Sunnyside, Port of Sunnyside, N Chevron/CFN/dsl, Conoco/dsl/e85, Jack-in-the-Box, BiMart Foods, H, S DariGold Cheese
63	Outlook, Sunnyside
58	WA 223 S, to Granger, S Conoco/dsl, Granger Travel Plaza/Chevron/dsl/scales, $General
54	Division Rd, Yakima Valley Hwy, to Zillah
52	Zillah, Toppenish, N Chevron/Circle K/dsl, Shell/Circle K/dsl, Burger King, El Porton Mexican, McDonald's, Pizza Hut, Subway, Best Western+, vet
50	WA 22 E, to US 97 S, Toppenish, S Legends Buffet/casino, McDonald's, Quality Inn, H, Murals Museum, RV Park, to Yakima Nation Cultural Ctr
44	Wapato, N Donald Store/dsl, HopTown Pizza
40	Thorp Rd, Parker Rd, Yakima Valley Hwy
39mm	Yakima River
38	Union Gap(from wb)
37	US 97(from eb)
36	Valley Mall Blvd, Yakima, S Arco/dsl, Cenex/dsl, Chevron/Gearjammer/dsl/scales/24hr/@, A&W/KFC, Applebee's, Buffalo Wild Wings, Burger King, Carl's Jr, Denny's, DQ, Dutch Bros, Famous Dave's, Five Guys, Fuji Asian, Jack-in-the-Box, Jersey Mike's, Krispy Kreme, McDonald's, Miner's Drive-In, MOD Pizza, Nino's Mexican, Old Town Sta Rest., Outback Steaks, Panda Express, Panera Bread, Starbucks, Starbucks, Subway, Taco Bell, Taco Time, Best Western+, Great Valley Inn, Holiday Inn Express, Super 8, AT&T, Best Buy, Cabela's, Canopy RV Ctr, Chrysler/Dodge/Ram, Circle K, Costco/gas, Dick's, Discount Tire, Frank's Tire, Hobby Lobby, Home Depot, JC Penney, Kohl's, Lowe's, Macy's, Marshall's, Michael's, NAPA, Office Depot, Old Navy, Penske, PetCo, PetSmart, Ross, Schwab Tire, st patrol, TJ Maxx, Toyota/Scion, URGENT CARE, Verizon, WinCo Foods
34	WA 24 E, Nob Hill Blvd, Yakima, N Sportsman SP, U-Haul, S 76/dsl, Arco/dsl, CFN/dsl, Chevron/dsl, Conoco/Circle K, Little Caesars, Circle H RV Park, Fiesta Foods, Freightliner, Kenworth, O'Reilly Parts, Penske, Peterbilt, truck repair
33	Yakima Ave, Yakima, N Chevron/dsl, Maverick, Shell/dsl, Burger King, El Mirador Mexican, Baymont Inn, My Place, Oxford Inn&Suites, Chevrolet, Honda, Walmart/McDonald's, S 7-11, Arco, Bob's Burgers, Domino's, DQ, Pizza Hut, Starbucks, Taco Bell, Fairfield Inn, Hilton Garden, Holiday Inn, LaQuinta Inn, Ledgestone Hotel, Motel 6, Red Lion Hotel, $Tree, BigLots, Ross, Schwab Tire, Target, visitor ctr
31b a	US 12 W, N 1st St, to Naches, S 76/dsl, Arco, Benchmark, Jack-in-the-Box, NY Teryaki, Red Lobster, Tammy's Mexican, Waffle's Cafe, Best Western+, Days Inn, Economy Inn, The Hotel Y, Yakima Inn, auto repair, Harley-Davidson, Yakima RV Park
30	WA 823 N, Rest Haven Rd, to Selah
29	E Selah Rd, N fruits/antiques
26	WA 821 N, to WA 823, Canyon Rd, N 76/Bullseye Burger/dsl
24mm	eb, full facilities, litter barrels, RV dump
23mm	Selah Creek
22mm	wb, full facilities, litter barrels, RV dump
21mm	S Umptanum Ridge, elevation 2265
19mm	Burbank Creek
17mm	N Umptanum Ridge, elevation 2315
15mm	Lmuma Creek
11	Military Area, Military Area
8mm	Manastash Ridge, elevation 2672, view point both lanes
3	WA 821 S, Thrall Rd
0mm	I-90, E to Spokane, W to Seattle. I-82 begins/ends on I-90, exit 110.

YAKIMA

INTERSTATE 90

GREENACRES

Exit #	Services
300mm	Washington/Idaho state line, Spokane River
299	State Line, Port of Entry, N Panda Express, Cabela's, Post Falls RV Camping, Walmart/Subway
297	weigh sta wb
296	Otis Orchards, Liberty Lakes, N 76/dsl, Legend's Grill, Best Western+, Buick/GMC, Kia, Mercedes, Porsche, S Chevron/LP, NomNom/dsl, Barlow's Rest., Brother's Pizzeria, Carl's Jr, Ding How Asian, Domino's, Field House Pizza, Fujiyama, Jimmy John's, McDonald's, Palenque Mexican, Papa Murphy's, Pita Pit, Starbucks, Subway, Taco Bell, Quality Inn, Home Depot, O'Reilly Parts, Peterbilt, RnR RV Ctr, Safeway, TireRama, URGENT CARE, vet, vet, Walgreens, Yoke's Mkt
294	Country Vista Dr, Appleway Ave
293	Barker Rd, Greenacres, N Conoco/dsl, Dutch Bros, Wendy's, Blue Compass RV Ctr, Camping World RV Ctr, Harley-Davidson, S Exxon/Subway/dsl, Mobil/dsl, Starbucks, NW RV Ctr, repair, USPO
291b	Sullivan Rd, Veradale, N Arby's, Hong Kong Buffet, Krispy Kreme, Outback Steaks, Panera Bread, Hampton Inn, My Place, Oxford Suites, Residence Inn, Barnes&Noble, Best Buy, Jo-Ann Fabrics, Verizon, S 76/dsl, Chevron/dsl, Atilano's Mexican, Chipotle, DQ, Dutch Bros, Five Guys, Jack-in the Box, Jersey Mike's, Jimmy John's, KFC, Killer Burger, Little Caesar's, Max Rest., McDonald's, Mongolian BBQ, Noodle Express, Panda Express, Pizza Hut, Pizza Pipeline, RoundTable Pizza, Starbucks, Taco Bell, Wendy's, Zelia's Cafe, Mirabeau Park Hotel, Ramada Inn, $Tree, Ace Hardware, Fred Meyer/dsl, Jiffy Lube, Kohl's, Lowe's, Michael's, NAPA, PetCo, PetSmart, Ross, Schwab Tire, USPO, Walgreens, Walmart/McDonald's
291a	Evergreen Rd, N Azteca Mexican, Black Angus, Boston's Rest, Buffalo Wild Wings, Cafe Rio, Honeybaked Ham, Hops n Drops Grill, IHOP, Red Robin, Twigs Bistro, Dick's, Hobby Lobby, JC Penney, Macy's, Old Navy, Staples, TJ Maxx, S Exxon/dsl, Maverik/dsl
289	WA 27 S, Pines Rd, Opportunity, N Maverik, Sam's/dsl, Black Pearl Rest., Subway, 7-11, S 76/dsl, Chevron, Circle K/dsl, Applebee's, DQ, Jack-in-the-Box, Jimmy John's, Qdoba Mexican, Comfort Inn, H, NW Auto, repair
287	Argonne Rd, Millwood, N Holiday/dsl, Maverik, Atilano's Mexican, Caruso's Sandwiches, Chipotle, Denny's, Domino's, DQ, Jack-in-the-Box, Longhorn BBQ, McDonald's, Panda Express, Papa Murphy's, Pizza Hut, Pizza Pipeline, Starbucks, Subway, Taco Time, Wendy's, Motel 6, SilverSton Inn, Super 8, $Tree, AutoZone, O'Reilly Parts, Safeway, URGENT CARE, Valvoline, Verizon, vet, Walgreens, Yoke's Foods, S 76, Casa de Oro Mexican, Jimmy John's, Pete & Belle's Creamery, Starbucks, Fairfield Inn, Holiday Inn Express, Ace Hardware
286	Broadway Ave, N Chevron/dsl, Flying J/Conoco/rest./dsl/LP/scales/24hr/@, Smacky's Cafe, Zip's Burgers, Rodeway Inn, Goodyear, International Trucks, Kenworth, Schwab Tire, S Amerimart/Chester's, 7-11
285	Sprague Ave, N AK Asian, Beard Papa's, IHOP, Jack-in-the-Box, McDonald's, Panda Express, Phillycious, Tacos Cabron, Wendy's, ParkLane Motel/RV Park, $Tree, Advance Parts, AutoZone, Costco/gas, Home Depot, Lowe's, O'Reilly Parts, tire repair, Volvo Trucks, Walmart, S C-stop, Cottage Cafe, Puebla Mexican, Zip's Drive-In, Acura, CarMax, Chevrolet, Chrysler/Dodge, Ford, Honda, Hyundai,

MILLWOOD

WA

INTERSTATE 90 Cont'd

285 Continued
Nissan, Toyota/Scion, transmissions, vet

283b Freya St, Thor St, N Chevron/dsl, Mobil/dsl, Atilano's Mexican, Subway, S Conoco/dsl, Dominos, Dutch Bros, Fred Meyer/fuel, Valvoline

283a Altamont St

282b 2nd Ave

282a WA 290 E, Trent Ave, Hamilton St, N Conoco/dsl, Ramada, Office Depot

281 US 2, US 395, to Colville, N 7-11, Amerimart, Conoco, Exxon, Arby's, Dick's Hamburgers, Frankie Doodles Rest., Taco Time, La Quinta, Firestone/auto, U-Haul, S Hampton Inn, H, URGENT CARE

280b Lincoln St, N 76/dsl, Chevron, Atilano's Mexican, Carl's Jr, Churchill's Steaks, Domino's, Jack-in-the-Box, McDonald's, Molly's Rest., Old Spaghetti Factory, Taco Bell, Wild Sage Bistro, Zip's Burgers, Baymont, Honda, Lexus, Schwab, Subaru, Toyota/Scion, S H

280a Spokane, downtown, N 76, 76/dsl, Chevron/McDonald's/dsl, Conoco, Frank's Diner, Pizza Hut, Red Dragon Chinese, Rusty's Diner, Starbucks, Subway, Tiki Lodge, Grocery Outlet

279 US 195 S, Pullman, to Colfax

277b a US 2 W (no ez wb return), to Grand Coulee Dam, N Blvd Motel, Hampton Inn, Motel 6, Fairchild AFB

276 Geiger Blvd, N Flying J/Subway/dsl/LP/24hr, Denny's, Best Western+, Sleep Inn, st patrol, USPO, S 76/dsl

272 WA 902, Medical Lake, N Mobil/dsl, Overland Sta/RV Park, S Exxon/Subway/dsl, Petro/Iron Skillet/Subway/dsl/scales/24hr/@, Domino's, McDonald's, Super 8, Freightliner, Ponderosa Falls RV Resort, Speedco, truck repair

270 WA 904, Cheney, Four Lakes, S 76, E WA U

264 WA 902, Salnave Rd, to Cheney, Medical Lake, N RV camping

257 WA 904, Tyler, to Cheney

254 Fishtrap, S Fishtrap RA, Fishtrap RV camping/tents

245 WA 23, Sprague, S Chevron/dsl, Viking Drive-In, Sprague Motel/RV park, Sprague Lake Resort/RV Park

242mm both lanes, full facilities, litter barrels, tourist/weather info, petwalk, RV dump(eb)

231 Tokio, S Templin's Corner/Subway/dsl

226 Schoessler Rd

221 WA 261 S, Ritzville, City Ctr, N Chevron/McDonald's, Circle K/Subway/dsl, Conoco/dsl, Mi Jalisco Mexican, Porky's Grill, Starbucks, Taco Del Mar, Zip's Rest., Best Western, Days Inn/RV park, Empire Motel, Top Hat Motel, H, railroad museum, S Love's/Carl's Jr/dsl/scales/24hr/@

220 to US 395 S, Ritzville, N Bronco/Pacific Pride/dsl, Texaco/dsl, Jake's Cafe, Empire Hotel, Top Hat Motel, Harvest Foods, NAPA, Schwab Tire, st patrol

215 Paha, Packard

206 WA 21, Odessa, to Lind

199mm both lanes, full facilities, litter barrels, vending, RV dump, petwalk

196 Deal Rd, to Schrag

188 U Rd, to Warden, Ruff

184 Q Rd

182 O Rd, to Wheeler

179 WA 17, Moses Lake, N Chevron/dsl, Conoco/Subway/dsl, Ernie's Trkstp/76/café/dsl/24hr, Shell, Sunval/dsl, Texaco/dsl, Arby's, Bob's Cafe, Burger King, Carl's Jr., Chipotle, Denny's, DQ, Dragon Express, McDonald's, Shari's, Starbucks, Subway, Taco Bell, Wendy's, Baymont, Comfort Suites, Fairfield Inn, Holiday Inn Express, Moses Lake Inn, Ramada Inn, Wingate Inn, $Tree, Chevrolet,

179 Continued
Chrysler/Dodge/Jeep, Ford, Honda, H, Lowe's, Peterbilt, Toyota/Scion, Valvoline, vet, S I-90 RV, Mardon RV Park(15mi), Potholes SP(22mi), Willows RV Park(2mi)

177mm Moses Lake

176 WA 171, Moses Lake, N 76/dsl, Cenex/dsl, Chevron/dsl, Conoco/dsl, Shell, Sunval/dsl, El Rodeo Mexican, Michael's Rest., Subway, Taco Del Mar, Best Western+, Interstate Inn, Motel 6, Oasis Motel, Quality Inn, $General, auto repair, Harvest Foods, H, Lake Front RV Park, transmissions, vet, S Half-Sun TP/Chevron/dsl/scales/24hr, Lakeshore Motel

175 Westshore Dr(from wb), to Mae Valley, N Blue Heron SP, S st patrol

174 Mae Valley, N Suncrest Resort/RV, S Chevron/dsl, Love's/Taco John's/dsl/scales, Pier 4 RV Park, st patrol

169 Hiawatha Rd

164 Dodson Rd, N Sunbasin RV park/camp(1mi)

162mm wb, full facilities, litter barrels, petwalk, RV dump

161mm eb, full facilities, litter barrels, petwalk, RV dump

154 Adams Rd

151 WA 281 N, to Quincy, N Shell/dsl, Grand Coulee Dam, Shady Tree RV park

149 WA 281 S, George, S Cenex/Chester's/dsl, Shree's Trkstp/Subway/dsl/scales/24hr, Fatburger, Scalehouse Cafe, Microtel, $General

143 Silica Rd, N The Gorge Ampitheatre/campground, S Sage Creek Tent Camping

139mm N scenic overlook, S Wild Horse Monument

137 WA 26 E, to WA 243, Othello, Richland

137mm Columbia River

136 Huntzinger Rd, Vantage, N Chevron/dsl, Ginkgo Petrified Forest SP, Riverstone Vantage Resort/RV Park, Vantage Gen. Store, S Wanapum SP

126mm Ryegrass, elevation 2535, both lanes, full facilities, litter barrels, petwalk

115 Kittitas, N Shell/dsl/LP, $General, Olmstead Place SP

110 I-82 E, US 97 S, to Yakima

109 Canyon Rd, Ellensburg, N 76, Astro/dsl, Chevron, Circle K, Arby's, Burger King, Carl's Jr, Dutch Bros, Fiesta Mexican, Golden Dragon Chinese, Jimmy John's, Los Cabos Mexican, McDonald's, Oyama Japanese, Roadhouse Grill, Starbucks, Subway, Taco Bell, Taco Del Mar, Teriyaki Wok, Wendy's, Best Western+, Comfort Inn, Holiday Inn Express, Red Lion Inn, SureStay, AutoZone, Chevrolet, EVC, H, NAPA, O'Reilly Parts, Schwab Tire, Super 1 Foods, TrueValue, S Flying J/dsl/scales/LP/24hr, Buzz Inn Steaks, Days Inn/RV park

106 US 97 N, to Wenatchie, N Chevron/dsl, Conoco/dsl, Love's/Subway/dsl/scales/24hr/@, Pilot/PJ Fresh/scales/dsl, DQ, IHOP, Perkins, Econolodge, Hampton Inn, Buick/Cadillac/GMC, Chrysler/Dodge/Jeep, Rodeo City RV Ctr, truck repair, Truck/RV Wash, S KOA, st patrol

101 Thorp Hwy, N Arco/Shree's/dsl, antiques/fruits/vegetables

93 Elk Heights Rd, Taneum Creek

92.5mm Elk Heights, elev 2359

FISHTRAP · MOSES LAKE · GEORGE · ELLENSBURG · WA

INTERSTATE 90 Cont'd

Exit #	Services
89mm	Indian John Hill, elevation 2141, [rest stop] both lanes, full [handicapped] facilities, [phone], [picnic], litter barrels, RV dump, petwalk, vending
85	WA 970, WA 903, to Wenatchie, N [gas] 76/dsl, Shell/dsl, Storey/dsl, [food] Cottage Café, Red Arrow Burgers, [lodging] Aster Inn, Chalet Motel, Cle Elum Traveler's Inn, Quality Inn, [other] Trailer Corral RV Park, Twin Pines Drive-In, vet
84	(from eb, return at 85), Cle Elum, N [gas] Chevron/dsl, Short Stop/Subway/dsl, Warrior's/dsl, [food] Beu's Pizza, DQ, El Caporal Mexican, MaMa Vallones, McDonald's, Starbucks, Sunset Café, Taco Bell, Wendy's, [lodging] Best Western Snowcap, Stewart Lodge, Timber Lodge Inn, [other] $Tree, Cle Elum Hardware, Les Schwab, museum, Safeway/dsl, URGENT CARE, USPO
81mm	Cle Elum River
80	Roslyn, Salmon la Sac, N [lodging] Suncadia Resort/rest.(4mi)
80mm	weigh sta both lanes
78	Golf Course Rd, S [other] Sun Country Golf/RV Park
74	W Nelson Siding Rd
71	Easton, S [gas] Easton Store/dsl/LP, [other] Iron Horse SP, John Wayne Tr, USPO
71mm	Yakima River
70	Sparks Rd, Easton, Lake Easton SP, N [gas] Shell/RV Town/dsl/café, [food] Mtn High Burger, [other] repair, Silver Ridge Camping, S Lake Easton RV Camping, Lake Easton SP
63	Cabin Creek Rd
62	Stampede Pass, elev 3750, to Lake Kachess, N [other] Lake Kachess Camping
54	Hyak, Gold Creek, S ski area
53	Snoqualmie Pass, elev 3022, S [gas] Chevron, [food] Summit Pancake House, [lodging] Summit Lodge, [other] Lee's Summit Mkt, ski areas
52	(from eb), W Summit
47	Tinkham Rd, Denny Creek, Asahel Curtis
45	USFS Rd 9030, N [other] Talapus Lake Hiking
42	Tinkham Rd
38	no services
35mm	S Fork Snoqualmie River
34	468th Ave SE, Edgewick Rd, N [gas] Gull/dsl/deli, Shell/dsl, TA/Country Pride/Popeyes/dsl only/24hr/@, [lodging] Edgewick Inn, [other] Norwest RV Park, S Twin Falls NA
32	436th Ave SE, S [other] Iron Horse SP(3mi), South Fork Gen. Store
31	WA 202 W, North Bend, Snoqualmie, N [gas] Chevron/dsl, Shell/dsl, [food] Arby's, Best Burgers, Burger King, Los Cabos, McDonald's, Rent's Due BBQ, Starbucks, Taco Time, [lodging] North Bend Motel, Sallish Lodge, Sunset Motel, [other] NorthBend Outlets/famous brands, O'Reilly Parts, Safeway/dsl
27	(from eb), North Bend, Snoqualmie
25	WA 18 W, Snoqualmie Pkwy, Tacoma, to Auburn, N [gas] Chevron/dsl/e85, [food] MOD Pizza, [lodging] Snoqualmie Inn, [other] Safeway/fuel
22	Preston, N [gas] Shell/dsl, [food] Rhodes BBQ, Subway, [other] USPO, S Blue Sky RV Park
20	High Point Way
18	E Sunset Way, Issaquah, S [gas] Shell(1mi), [food] Flying Pie Pizza, Las Margaritas, Macky's Chinese, Stan's BBQ, Sunset Alehouse, [other] $Tree
17	E Sammamish Rd, Front St, Issaquah, N [gas] 76, Chevron, [food] Coho Cafe, Coldstone, Fatburger, Ivan's Rest., Jamba Juice, Krispy Kreme, McDonald's, Panda Express, Paseo Issaquah, Qdoba Mexican, Starbucks, Subway, Teriyaki Bistro, Zushi Sushi, [other] AT&T, Best Buy, Fred Meyer, Home Depot, URGENT CARE, Walgreens, S [gas] Arco/dsl, Cenex/dsl, Chevron/dsl, Shell/dsl, [food] Boehms Chocolates, Enzo's Italian, Las Margaritas, Stan's BBQ, Subway, XXX Rootbeer,
17	Continued Big O Tire, USPO
15	WA 900, Issaquah, Renton, N [gas] Arco/dsl, Chevron, [food] IHOP, O'Char Thai, Taco Time, [lodging] Fairfield Inn, Motel 6, [other] Costco/gas, Lake Sammamish SP, Lowe's, Michael's, PCC Natural Mkt, PetSmart, S [gas] Shell/dsl, [food] 12th Ave Cafe, Baskin-Robbins, Burger King, Cafe Rio, Chipotle Mexican, Dickey's BBQ, Five Guys, Frankie's Pizza, Issaquah Cafe, Jack-in-the-Box, Jamba Juice, Jersey Mike's, KFC/Taco Bell, McDonald's, Panera Bread, Papa Murphy's, Potbelly, Starbucks, Subway, Taco Time, Tipsy Cow Burgers, Tuttabella Pizza, WildFin Grill, [lodging] Hilton Garden, Homewood Suites, SpringHill Suites, [other] Chevrolet, Firestone/auto, Ford, Hobby Lobby, O'Reilly Parts, PetCo, QFC Foods, REI, Ross, Safeway, Target, Trader Joe's, Verizon, vet
13	SE Newport Way, W Lake Sammamish
11	SE 150th, 156th, 161st, Bellevue, N [gas] Shell, [food] Crab Season, DQ, Jack-in-the-Box, Lil' Jon Rest., McDonald's, Starbucks, Subway, [lodging] Eastgate Hotel, Embassy Suites, Hyatt House, Quality Inn, [other] LDS Temple, Nissan, Subaru/VW, Toyota/Scion, vet, S [gas] Chevron, Chevron/dsl, Shell/dsl, Texaco, [food] Outback Steaks, Pagliacci Pizza, Starbucks, [lodging] Larkspur Landing Suites, [other] Honda, O'Reilly Parts, Safeway, Trailer Inn RV Park
10	I-405, N to Bellevue, S to Renton, services located off I-405 S, exit 10
9	Bellevue Way
8	E Mercer Way, Mercer Island
7c	80th Ave SE(exits left from wb)
7b a	SE 76th Ave, 77th Ave, Island Crest Way, Mercer Island, S [gas] Chevron/dsl, Shell/dsl, [food] Einstein Bagels, Gourmet Teriyaki, McDonald's, Qdoba, Shawn's Cafe, Starbucks, Starbucks, Vivienne's Bistro, [other] QFC Mkt, True Value Hardware, vet, Walgreens
6	W Mercer Way(from eb), same as 7
5mm	Lake Washington
3b a	Ranier Ave, Seattle, downtown, N [gas] Shell/dsl
2c b	I-5, N to Vancouver, S to Tacoma
2a	4th Ave S, to stadiums. I-90 begins/ends on I-5, exit 164., to King Dome

INTERSTATE 182 (Richland)

Exit #	Services
14.5mm	I-182 begins/ends on US 395 N.
14b a	US 395 N, WA 397 S, OR Ave, N [gas] Flying J/dsl/scales/24hr, King City/76/rest/dsl/@, [food] Burger King, Subway, [lodging] Knights Inn, [other] Arrowhead RV Park, Peterbilt
13	N 4th Ave, Cty Ctr, N [gas] CFN/dsl, [lodging] Starlite Motel, S [gas] 76/dsl, Conoco/dsl, [other] [H], tires, vet
12b	N 20th Ave, N [lodging] Best Western+, Marriott, Red Lion Hotel
12a	US 395 S, Court St, [other] Walgreens, S [gas] 76/dsl, Chevron, Circle K/dsl, Conoco, Exxon/Jack-in-the-Box, Speedway Express, Texaco, [food] A&W/KFC, Andy's Rest., Burger King, Domino's, Dutch Bros, El Mirador Mexican, Little Caesar's, McDonald's, Monarca Kitchen, Papa Murphy's, Pizza Hut, RoundTable Pizza, Starbucks, Subway, Taco Bell, Wendy's, [other] $Tree, Albertson's, AutoZone, Cadillac/Chevrolet, Camping World, Ford, Jiffy Lube, Mazda, Nissan, U-Haul, USPO, Walgreens
9	rd 68, Trac, N [gas] Circle K/dsl, Maverik/dsl, Porter's/dsl, [food] Antonio's Pizza, Applebee's, Arby's, Bruchi's, Burger King, Chipotle, Costa Vida, Domino's, DQ, Dutch Bros, Fiesta Mexican, Hacienda Del Sol, IHOP, Jack-in-the-Box, Jamba Juice, Jersey Mike's, Jimmy John's, Little Caesar's, McDonald's, Panda Express, Pizza Hut, Shakey's Pizza, Starbucks, Subway, Taco Bell, Teriyaki Grill, Wendy's, Wingstop, [lodging] Hampton Inn, Holiday Inn Express, MyPlace, [other] $Tree, AT&T, Discount Tire, Firestone/auto, Franklin County RV Park, Grocery Outlet, Lowe's, O'Reilly Parts, Petco,

EASTON · W SUMMIT · ISSAQUAH · MERCER ISLAND · TRAC

WA

INTERSTATE 182 (Richland) Cont'd

TRAC

Exit	Services
9	Continued Schwab Tire, URGENT CARE, URGENT CARE, USPO, Verizon, Walgreens, **Walmart/Subway**, Yokes Foods, **S** Maverik/dsl
7	Broadmoor Blvd, **N** Sleep Inn, Camping World, Subaru/GMC, vet, **S** Exxon/Circle K/dsl, Broadmoor RV Ctr, KOA
6.5mm	Columbia River
5b a	WA 240 E, Geo Washington Way, to Kennewick, **N** Conoco/dsl, Anthony's Rest., Applebee's, Budd's Broiler, Jack-in-the-Box, Starbucks, Courtyard, Hampton Inn, Holiday Inn, Riverfront Hotel, The Lodge, TownePlace Suites, $Tree, AT&T, Valvoline, Winco Foods
4	WA 240 W, **N** 76/dsl, Coleman Oil, Del Taco, El Agave Mexican, McDonald's, Starbucks, Audi, BMW, Fred Meyer/dsl
3.5mm	Yakima River
3	Keene Rd, Queensgate, **N** Circle K, Maverik/dsl, A&W/KFC, Bob's Burgers, Burger King, Chipotle, Costa Vida, Dickey's BBQ, DQ, Fiesta Mexican, Five Guys, Fujiyama Japanese, Krispy Kreme, LJ Silver, McDonald's, My Fro-Yo, Panda Express, Panera Bread, Starbucks, Sterling's Rest., Stick+Stone Pizza, Subway, Taco Bell, The Habit, AT&T, Home Depot, Marshall's, PetCo, Ross, Schwab Tire, Target, Tire Factory, Verizon, **Walmart/Subway**, **S** Chevron/dsl, MOD Pizza, Taco Time, tires/repair
0mm	I-182 begins/ends on I-82, exit 102.

QUEENSGATE

INTERSTATE 405 (Seattle)

BOTHELL

Exit	Services
30	I-5, N to Canada, S to Seattle, I-405 begins/ends on I-5, exit 182.
26	WA 527, Bothell, Mill Creek, **E** McDonald's, Rama House Thai, Starbucks, Extended Stay America, **W** Shell/dsl, Applebee's, Arby's, Bamboo House, Bangkok Cafe, Baskin-Robbins, Bonefish Grill, Chick-fil-A, Crystal Creek Cafe, Five Guys, Grazie Ristorante, Imperial Wok, Jack-in-the-Box, Jimmy John's, Little Caesar's, MOD Pizza, Outback Steaks, Papa Murphy's, Qdoba Mexican, Starbucks, Subway, Taco Bell, Taco Time, Wendy's, Zeek's Pizza, Comfort Inn, Extended Stay America, Hilton Garden, Holiday Inn Express, 7-11, Bartell Drug, Goodyear/auto, Lake Pleasant RV Park, QFC Foods, URGENT CARE, vet
24	NE 195th St, Beardslee Blvd, **E** Chevron/dsl, Subway, Country Inn&Suites, Holiday Inn&Suites, Residence Inn, Exotic Animal vet, **W** Starbucks
23b	WA 522 W, Bothell
23a	WA 522 E, to WA 202, Woodinville, Monroe
22	NE 160th St, **E** Chevron, Shell/dsl, Top Mkt/deli
20	NE 124th St, **E** Arco, Shell/dsl, Cafe Veloce, Chik-fil-A, Chipotle, Jack-in-the-Box, MOD Pizza, Panda Express, Pizza Hut, Salt&Straw, Santa Fe Mexican, Shari's, Subway, Taco Bell, Baymont Inn, Comfort Inn, Motel 6, AutoZone, Chrysler/Dodge/Jeep, Discount Tire, Fiat, Firestone/auto, Ford, Jiffy Lube, NAPA, Nissan, O'Reilly Parts, Ross, Schwab Tire, Toyota/Scion, Trader Joe's, URGENT CARE, Verizon, VW, Whole Foods Mkt, **W** Arco/dsl, Azteca Mexican, Five Guys, Izumi Japanese, McDonald's, Mediterranean Kitchen, Olive Garden, Papa Murphy's, Romio's Pizza, Starbucks, Subway, Taco Time, Wendy's, Courtyard, Fred Meyer/dsl, QFC Foods, vet
18	WA 908, Kirkland, Redmond, **E** 76, 76/dsl, Mobil, Little Caesar's, McDonald's, Starbucks, Taco Time, Tres Hermanos, $Tree, Chevrolet, Costco, Honda, Kia, Mazda, O'Reilly Parts, PepBoys, Safeway, U-Haul, vet, Walgreens, **W** Shell/dsl, Acropolis Pizza, Starbucks, Subway, The Heathman Hotel, QFC Foods, Tire Pros, USPO
17	NE 70th Pl

FACTORIA

Exit	Services
14b a	WA 520, Seattle, Redmond
13b	NE 8th St, **E** Arco, Chevron/dsl, Shell/dsl, Burger King, Chick-fil-A, Starbucks, Hotel 116, Best Buy, Chevrolet, Ford, Home Depot, Infiniti, Mercedes, Porsche, REI, Trader Joe's, Volvo, Whole Foods Mkt, **W** Starbucks, Courtyard, Hyatt, The Westin, QFC Foods
13a	NE 4th St, **E** Extended Stay America, Hampton Inn, Chrysler/Dodge/Jeep, Lexus, Target, **W** Subway, Hilton, Hotel Bellevue, Marriott, Red Lion/Bellevue Inn, Residence Inn
12	SE 8th St, **W** Residence Inn
11	I-90, E to Spokane, W to Seattle
10	Cold Creek Pkwy, Factoria, **E** 76, Chevron, Applebee's, Burger King, Chipotle, Coldstone, Domino's, El Tapatio Mexican, Great Harvest Bread, Jamba Juice, Jimmy John's, KFC, McDonald's, MOD Pizza, Novilhos Brazilian Steaks, Panda Express, Panera Bread, Red Robin, Starbucks, Starbucks, Subway, Taco Bell, Taco Time, Thai Ginger, Tokyo Japanese, Extended Stay America, AT&T, Honda, Jiffy Lube, Midas, O'Reilly Parts, Old Navy, PetCo, QFC Foods, Target, TJ Maxx, USPO, vet, Walmart
9	112th Ave SE, Newcastle,
7	NE 44th St, **E** McDonald's, Starbucks, Subway, Taco Del Mar, Teriyaki Wok, Lake Washington Inn
6	NE 30th St, **E** Arco, **W** Chevron/dsl, Shell/dsl, 7-11
5	WA 900 E, Park Ave N, Sunset Blvd NE, **W** Five Guys, Jimmy John's, Panda Express, Panera Bread, Potbelly, Red Robin, Torero's Mexican, Wingstop, Hampton Inn, Hyatt House, Residence Inn, AT&T, Lowe's, Marshall's, PetSmart, Ross, Staples, Target, URGENT CARE, Verizon
4	WA 169 S, Wa 900 W, Renton, **E** Mitzu Japanese, Best Western+, **W** Shell, Burger King, Momoya Sushi, Subway, Westernco Donut, Renton Inn, $Tree, 7-11

AUBURN

Exit	Services
2	WA 167, Rainier Ave, Auburn, **E** Hilton Garden, Larkspur Landing, Sonesta Select, tires, **W** Arco/dsl, Chevron, Chevron, Shell/7-11, Speedway Express/dsl, Applebee's, Baskin-Robbins, Chick-fil-A, Chipotle, Domino's, Dutch Bros, IHOP, Jack-in-the-Box, Jimmy John's, Jimmy Mac's Roadhouse, KFC, King Buffet, Little Caesar's, Mazatlan Mexican, McDonald's, Papa Murphy's, Popeyes, Starbucks, Subway, Taco Bell, Taco Time, Wendy's, $Tree, AutoZone Buick/Cadillac/GMC, Chevrolet, Chrysler/Dodge/Jeep, Discount Tire, Ford, Fred Meyer/dsl, Hyundai, Kia, Mazda, Midas, O'Reilly Parts, Safeway/gas, Schwab Tire, Subaru, Toyota/Scion, U-Haul, vet, Walgreens, Walmart
1	WA 181 S, Tukwila, **E** Chevron/dsl, Jack-in-the-Box, Taco Bell, Wendy's, Courtyard, Embassy Suites, Extended Stay America, Hampton Inn, Ramada, Residence Inn, Woodspring Suites, 7-11, **W** Shell, Subway, Taco Del Mar, Comfort Suites, Homewood Suites, fun center
0mm	I-5, N to Seattle, S to Tacoma, WA 518 W. I-405 begins/ends on I-5, exit 154.

NOTES

WEST VIRGINIA

INTERSTATE 64

Exit #	Services
184mm	West Virginia/Virginia state line
183	VA 311, from eb, no reentry, Crows
181	US 60, WV 92(no ez wb return), White Sulphur Springs, N GoMart/dsl, Marathon/Godfather's, Shell, April's Pizzaria, Hardee's, Budget Inn, Greenbrier Resort, autocare, Family$, Family$, Food Lion, ski area, to Midland Trail, USPO, Walgreens
179mm	**full facilities, info, litter barrels, petwalk, Welcome Ctr wb**
175	US 60, WV 92, Caldwell, N BP/Mountaineer Mart/dsl, Exxon, Cook's Country Kitchen, McDonald's, Wendy's, $General, U-Haul, S Greenbrier SF
173mm	Greenbrier River
169	US 219, Lewisburg, Hist Dist, N Shell, Biscuit World, Relax Inn, auto parts, Federated Parts, U-Haul, S Exxon/dsl, Gomart, Shell, Applebee's, Arby's, Bellacino's, Bob Evans, China Palace, Dickey's BBQ, Hardee's, Papa John's, Ruby Tuesday, Shoney's, Subway, Taco Bell, Fairfield Inn, Hampton Inn, Holiday Inn Express/EVC, Home2 Suites, Quality Inn, Super 8, $Tree, AT&T, AutoZone, Buick/Chevrolet, Ford, H, Lowe's, URGENT CARE, Verizon, Walmart/gas
161	WV 12, Alta, S Mobil/dsl, Meeting Place, Greenbrier River Camping(14mi), truck repair
156	US 60, Midland Trail, Sam Black Church, N Exxon/Arby's/dsl, Shell/dsl
150	rd 29, rd 4, Dawson, S Exxon, Dawson Inn, RV camping
147mm	runaway truck ramp wb
143	WV 20, Green Sulphur Springs, N Liberty/dsl
139	WV 20, Sandstone, Hinton, S Citgo/dsl, Blue Stone SP(16mi), Richmonds Store/USPO, to Pipestem Resort Park(25 mi)
138mm	New River
136mm	eb runaway truck ramp
133.1mm	Sandstone Mtn, elev 2765
133	WV 27, Pluto Rd, Bragg, mandatory truck stop eb, S RV camping
129	WV 9, Shady Spring, N to Grandview SP, S Exxon/dsl, Shell/dsl, Little Beaver SP
125b a	WV 307, Airport Rd, Beaver, N Shell/dsl, Biscuit World, Sleep Inn, S GoMart/gas, Marathon/dsl, Sheetz/dsl, Arby's, Dickey's BBQ, DQ, El Mariachi, Hardee's, KFC, Little Caesar's, LJ Silver, McDonald's, Subway, Wendy's, Advance Parts, CVS Drug, Family$, Kroger, USPO, Walgreens
124	US 19, Eisenhower Dr, E Beckley, N GoMart/gas, Capt D's, Microtel, $General, H, last exit before toll rd wb
121	I-77 S, to Bluefield, Chippewa River
120mm	I-64 and I-77 merge for 61 mi. See I-77, exits 42-100.
59	I-77 N(from eb), to I-79
58c	US 60, Washington St, N Exxon, GoMart/dsl, Mobil, Family$, S Tesla EVC, Capt D's, Chop House, Outback Steaks, Starbucks, Tidewater Grill, Wendy's, Courtyard, Embassy Suites, Hampton Inn, Holiday Inn Express, Marriott, civic ctr, Goodyear/auto, H, Macy's, mall
58b	US 119 N(from eb), Charleston, downtown, same as 58c
58a	US 119 S, WV 61, MacCorkle Ave
56	Montrose Dr, N Exxon/dsl, Marathon/dsl, Speedway/dsl/EVC, Hardee's, Los Agaves Mexican, Fairfield Inn/EVC, Holiday Inn, Microtel, $General, Advance Parts,

CALDWELL — ALTA — BEAVER

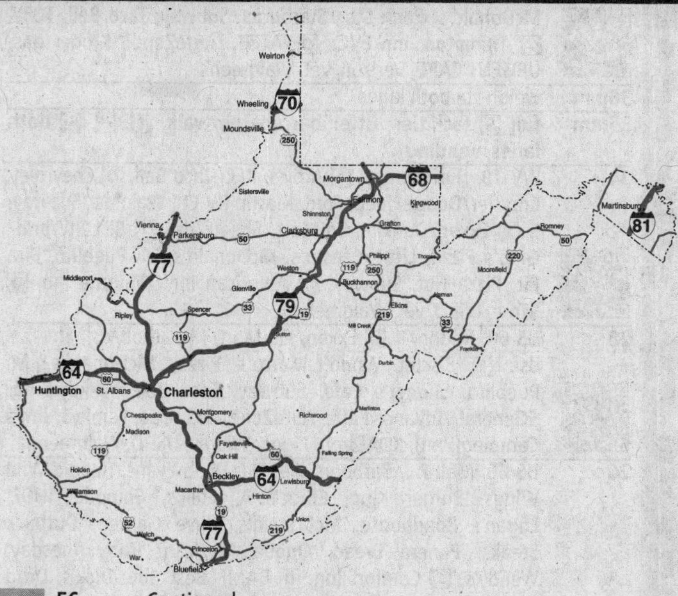

Exit #	Services
56	Continued Chevrolet, Chrysler/Dodge/Jeep, EVC, Hyundai, Kia, NAPA, vet, VW, Walgreens
55	Kanawha Tpk(from wb)
54	US 60, MacCorkle Ave, N Burger King, Casa Garcia, Chick-fil-A, Graziano's Pizza, Krispy Kreme, Subway, $Tree, AT&T, Kroger/dsl, TJ Maxx, S Bob Evans, KFC, LJ Silver, McDonald's, Pizza Hut, Sheetz, Taco Bell, Wendy's, Aamco, Family$, Harley-Davidson, Honda, H, Mazda, URGENT CARE
53	Roxalana Rd, to Dunbar, S GoMart/dsl, BiscuitWorld, Gino's Pizza, Graziano's Pizza, Los Agaves, McDonald's, Subway, Taco Bell, Wendy's, Super 8, Advance Parts, ALDI, CVS Drug, Family$, Kroger/gas, NTB
50	VW 25, Institute, S GoMart/dsl, Ridge View BBQ
47b a	WV 622, Goff Mtn Rd, N Exxon/dsl, Speedway/dsl, BiscuitWorld, Bob Evans, Capt D's, Cookout, Domino's, Dunkin, Little Caesar's, Los Amigos, McDonald's, Papa John's, Pizza Hut, Subway, Taco Bell, Tim Hortons, Wendy's, Rodeway Inn, $General, Advance Parts, Autozone, Family$, Kroger/gas, O'Reilly Parts, Save-a-Lot, URGENT CARE, Walgreens, S Sheetz, Arby's, Asian Buffet, Buffalo Wild Wings, Burger King, Cracker Barrel, Golden Corral, HoneyBaked Ham, La Roca Mexican, Sakura Japanese, TGIFriday's, Holiday Inn Express, Sleep Inn, Wyndham Inn, $Tree, Lowe's, Staples, Walmart
45	WV 25, Nitro, N Pilot/Arby's/dsl/scales/24hr, Chevrolet, S Exxon/dsl, GoMart, Speedway/dsl, BiscuitWorld, Checker's, DQ, Gino's Pizza, Guadalajara Mexican, McDonald's, Subway, Wendy's, $General
44.3mm	Kanawha River
44	US 35, St Albans
40	US 35 N, Winfield, Pt Pleasant, S Sheetz/dsl, Speedway/dsl, DQ, Save A Lot
39	WV 34, Winfield, N Exxon/Arby's, GoMart/dsl, Applebee's, Bob Evans, Panera Bread, Rio Grande Mexican, Taste of Asia, Holiday Inn Express, Red Roof Inn, Sleep Inn, $General, $Tree, Advance Parts, ALDI, BigLots, Home Depot, PetCo, Target, USPO, S GoMart, TA/Country Pride/dsl/scales/24hr, Biscuit World, Burger King, Capt D's, China Chef, Dough Daddy's Pizza, El Rancho Grande,

INSTITUTE — NITRO

WV

= gas = food = lodging = other = rest stop

WV

INTERSTATE 64 Cont'd

WINFIELD

39 Continued
Fat Patty's, Fireside Grille, Five Guys, Gino's Pizza, KFC, McDonald's, Penn Sta., Starbucks, Subway, Taco Bell, TCBY, Hampton Inn/EVC, AT&T, AutoZone, Kroger/gas, URGENT CARE, Verizon, vet, Walgreens

38mm weigh sta both lanes

35mm **full facilities, litter barrels, petwalk, both lanes, vending**

34 WV 19, Hurricane, N Arby's, KFC, Taco Bell, Chevrolet, Chrysler/Dodge/Jeep, Ford, Martin RV Ctr, Walmart/Subway, S Exxon/Dunkin, Go-Mart, Sheetz/dsl, BiscuitWorld/Gino's Pizza, Little Caesar's, McDonald's, Mi Pueblito, Pita Pit, Pizza Hut, Subway, American Inn, Wingate Inn, $Tree, USPO, vet, Walgreens

28 US 60, Milton, S Exxon, Go-Mart, Marathon/dsl, Sheetz/dsl, Biscuit World, Marco's Pizza, McDonald's, Mi Pueblito, Shonet's Cafe, Subway, Taco Bell, Wendy's, $General, Advance Parts, AutoZone, CVS Drug, Family$, Jim's Camping(2mi), KOA(3mi), Piggly Wiggly, USPO, Walgreens

BARBOURSVILLE

20 US 60, Mall Rd, Barboursville, N Bob Evans, Buffalo Wild Wings, Burger King, Chick-fil-A, Chili's, Chipotle, IHOP, Logan's Roadhouse, McDonald's, Olive Garden, Outback Steaks, Panera Bread, Qdoba Mexican, Ruby Tuesday, Wendy's, Comfort Inn, BAM!, Best Buy, Dick's, Drug Emporium, Firestone/auto, Hobby Lobby, JC Penney, Kohl's, Lowe's, Macy's, mall, Michael's, NTB, Old Navy, Walmart/Subway, S Exxon/Dunkin/dsl, Sheetz/dsl, 3 Amigos Mexican, Billy Bob Pizza, Cracker Barrel, Fat Patty's, Sonic, Steak&Shake, Subway, Taco Bell, Tortilla Factory, Waffle House, Best Western, Delta Hotel, Hampton Inn/EVC, Toyota

18 US 60, to WV 2, Barboursville, N Bellacino's, O'Charley's, Starbucks, $Tree, Home Depot, Marshall's, Office Depot, Petco, Target, S Shell/7-11, Biscuit World, Fratelli's Italian, Gino's, Giovanni's Pizza, Papa John's, Food Fair, Kia, Kroger/gas, NAPA, Walgreens

15 US 60, 29th St E, N GoMart/dsl, Speedway/dsl, #1 Kitchen, Arby's, Biscuit World, Jolly Pirate Donuts, Subway, Waffle House, Wendy's, Econolodge, Motel 6, $General, AT&T, H, NAPA, st police, Walmart/McDonald's, S BP, Fazoli's, KFC, Marco's Pizza, McDonald's, Penn Sta. Subs, Taco Bell, Days Inn, Red Roof Inn, Buick/Cadillac/GMC, CVS Drug, Honda, Nissan, Subaru, VW

11 WV 10, Hal Greer Blvd, N Marathon/Subway, Arby's, Baskin-Robbins, Biscuit World, Bob Evans, Frostop Drive-In, McDonald's, Po-Boys Tire, Taco Bell, Wendy's, Comfort Inn, Fairfield Inn, Hampton Inn, Super 8, TownePlace Suites, AutoZone, Chrysler/Dodge/Jeep, H, Walgreens, S Beech Fork SP(8mi), truck tire ctr

10mm **full facilities, litter barrels, petwalk, vending, Welcome Ctr eb**

8 WV 152 S, WV 527 N, N URGENT CARE, vet, S GoMart/dsl, Speedway/dsl

6 US 52 N, W Huntington, Chesapeake, N Sheetz/dsl, Speedway/dsl, #1 Kitchen, Fox's Pizza, Wendys, AutoZone, H, NAPA, Save-A-Lot Foods

KENOVA

1 US 52 S, Kenova, N BP/dsl, Exxon, Burger King, Evaroni's Pizza, Gino's Pizza, Hermanos Nunez Mexican, McDonald's, Rocky Tops Pizza, Stewart's Hotdogs, Taco Bell, Hollywood Motel, $General, Advance Parts, CVS Drug, O'Reilly Parts, Save-A-Lot, USPO

0mm West Virginia/Kentucky state line, Big Sandy River

INTERSTATE 68

32mm West Virginia/Maryland state line

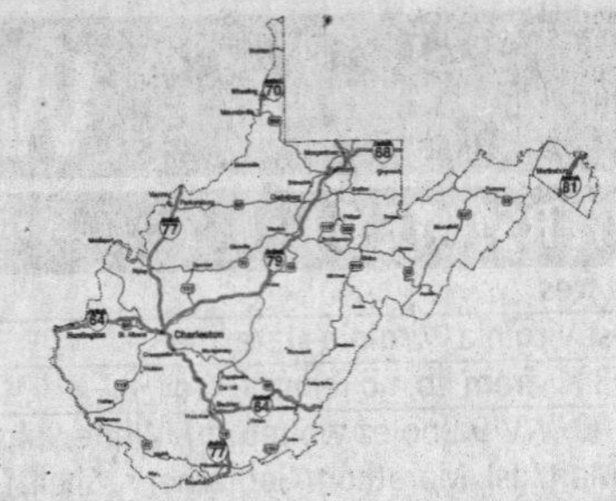

BRUCETON MILLS

31mm **full facilities, litter barrels, petwalk, vending, Welcome Ctr wb**

29 rd 5, Hazelton Rd, N Sunoco/dsl, Microtel(1mi), S Big Bear Camping(3mi), Pine Hill Camping(4mi)

23 WV 26, Bruceton Mills, N BFS/Subway/dsl/24hr, Sunoco/dsl/24hr, Pizza Pro, Maple Leaf Motel, antiques, Bruceton Auto, Family$, USPO

18mm Laurel Run

17mm runaway truck ramp eb

16mm weigh sta wb

15 WV 73, WV 12, Coopers Rock, N Chestnut Ridge SF, Sand Springs Camping(2mi)

12mm runaway truck ramp wb

10 WV 43 N, to rd 857, Fairchance Rd, Cheat Lake, N BFS/Little Caesar's/Subway/dsl, Exxon/dsl, Angelo's Pizza, Dragon Cafe, Ruby & Ketchy's, Walzzy's Hotdogs, $General, vet, S Burger King, Tropics Rest., Lakeview Resort, The Cranberry Hotel

9mm Cheat Lake

MORGANTOWN

7 rd 705, Pierpont Rd, N BFS/Little Caesar's/Subway/TCBY, Exxon/Taco Bell/dsl, Big Red's Hamburgers, Fox's Pizza Den, Fujiyama Steaks, Honeybaked Ham, IHOP, McDonald's, Outback Steaks, Ruby Tuesday, Wendy's, Holiday Inn Express, Super 8, Books-A-Million, Family$, Lowe's, Michael's, Price Cutter, to WVU Stadium, S Sunoco/dsl, Apple Annie's, Super Red Bowl

4 rd 7, to Sabraton, N BFS/Subway/dsl, Sheetz/dsl/EVC, Arby's, Burger King, Dunkin, Hardee's, KFC, LJ Silver, McDonald's, Popeyes, Sabraton Sta. Grill, Shoney's, Sweet Southern Smoke BBQ, Wendy's, SpringHill Suites, Suburban Lodge, $General, $Tree, Advance Parts, ALDI, AutoZone, CVS Drug, Family$, Kroger/gas, USPO, Valvoline Lube, S Amoco/dsl, Marathon/Circle K, China City, Homegrown Pizza

3mm Decker's Creek

1 US 119, Morgantown, N GoMart/Burger King, Quality Inn, tires, USPO, S Sheetz/dsl/Tesla EVC, Denny's, Devino's Pizzeria, Mariachi Loco, $Tree, Walmart/Subway/auto

0mm I-79, N to Pittsburgh, S to Clarksburg. I-68 begins/ends on I-79, exit 148.

INTERSTATE 70

14mm West Virginia/Pennsylvania state line

13.5mm **full facilities, litter barrels, petwalk, vending Welcome Ctr wb**

11 WV 41, Dallas Pike, N TA/Country Pride/dsl/scales/24hr/@, Comfort Inn, S Amoco/DQ/dsl, Exxon, EconoLodge, RV camping

10 rd 65, to Cabela Dr, N Sheetz/dsl, Bob Evans Cheddar's, Chick-fil-A, Chipotle, Coldstone, DiCarlo's Pizza Eat'n Park, El Paso Mexican, Five Guys, Fusion Steaks, Jimmy John's, Logan's Roadhouse, McDonald's, Olive Garden Panera Bread, Primanti Bros, Quaker Steak, Starbucks, Taco Bell, TX Roadhouse, Wendy's, Fairfield Inn, Hampton Inn EVC, Hawthorn Suites, Microtel, AT&T, Best Buy,

INTERSTATE 70 Cont'd

ELM GROVE

10	Continued Books-A-Million, Cabela's, Harley Davidson, JC Penney, Kohl's, Old Navy, PetCo, Russell Stover Candies, Target/Starbucks, TJ Maxx, Verizon, Walmart/Subway, S Sheetz/dsl, Holiday Inn Express, Suburban Lodge, Chevrolet/Buick/GMC, Ford/Lincoln, Honda, Hyundai, Nissan, Toyota
5	US 40, WV 88 S, Tridelphia, N Marathon/dsl, Pizza Hut, Subway, Wendy's, Super 8, Chrysler/Dodge/Jeep, Family$, Riesbeck's Foods, Subaru/VW, URGENT CARE, S Marathon/dsl, Arby's, DQ, McDonald's, Patsy's Pizza, Undo's Rest., Grove Terrace Motel, AT&T, AutoZone, Walgreens
5a	I-470 W, to Columbus
4	WV 88 N(from eb), Elm Grove, same as 5
3.5mm	weigh sta eb
2b	Washington Ave, N $General, S Figaretti's Italian, H
2a	rd 88 N, to Oglebay Park, N Marathon/dsl, Sheetz, Bob Evans, DeFelice Bros Pizza, Little Caesar's, Papa John's, Perkins, Subway, Taco Bell, Tim Hortons, TJs Sports Garden, Hampton Inn, SpringHill Suites, Advance Parts, CVS Drug, Kroger/gas, NTB, URGENT CARE, Verizon
1b	US 250 S, WV 2 S, S Wheeling
1mm	Wheeling Tunnel
1a	US 40 E, WV 2 N, Main St, downtown
0	(from wb)US 40 W, Zane St, Wheeling Island, N Marathon/dsl, Burger King, KFC
0mm	West Virginia/Ohio state line, Ohio River

INTERSTATE 77

MINERAL WELLS

186mm	West Virginia/Ohio state line, Ohio River
185	WV 14, WV 31, Williamstown, W **full facilities, info, litter barrels, WV Welcome Ctr/**, GoMart/dsl, Tonyas County Kitchen, Super 6, $General, Glass Factory Tours
179	WV 2 N, WV 68 S, to Waverly, E Exxon/dsl, Holiday Inn Express, to , W BFS/Tim Hortons/dsl, Burger King, Hardee's(3mi), Motel 6, Sleep Inn
176	US 50, 7th St, Parkersburg, E to North Bend SP, W BP/7-11, GoMart, Domino's, DQ, Little Caesar's, McDonald's, Omelette Shoppe, Taco Bell, Wendy's, Economy Inn, Red Roof Inn, Travelodge, $Tree, Advance Parts, AutoZone, Chrysler/Dodge/Jeep, CVS Drug, Family$, Ford/Lincoln, Hyundai, Kroger/gas, Mazda, Mercedes, NAPA, to Blennerhassett Hist Park, Toyota, vet
174	WV 47, Staunton Ave, E GoMart/dsl, $General
174mm	Little Kanawha River
173	WV 95, Camden Ave, E Marathon/dsl, W BP
170	WV 14, Mineral Wells, E BP/dsl/repair, GoMart/Taco Bell/dsl, McDonald's, Wendy's, Comfort Suites, Hampton Inn, W Cracker Barrel, Napoli's Pizza, Holiday Inn Express, Microtel, Quality Express Inn
169mm	weigh sta both lanes
166mm	**full facilities, litter barrels, petwalk, , , both lanes, RV dump, vending**
161	WV 21, Rockport, W Marathon/dsl
154	WV 1, Medina Rd
146	WV 2 S, Silverton, Ravenswood, E Ruby Lake Camping(4mi), W Exxon/DQ, Marathon/dsl, McDonald's(3mi), Subway(4mi), Wendy's(3mi)
138	US 33, Ripley, E BP/dsl, Marathon/dsl, Murphy USA/dsl, Sheetz/dsl, Arby's, China Buffet, KFC, Las Trancas Mexican, LJ Silver, McDonald's, Taco Bell, Wendy's, Holiday Inn Express, Super 8, $Tree, AutoZone, Kroger/gas, NAPA, Verizon, Walgreens, Walmart/Subway,

FAIRPLAIN

138	Continued Exxon/dsl, Bob Evans, Cozumel Mexican, Roadhouse 2081, Subway, Econolodge, H
132	WV 21, Fairplain, E GoMart/dsl, Speedway/dsl/24hr, Burger King, Samurai Hibachi, $General, Ford, Statts Mills RV Park(6mi), W Love's/Chester's/McDonald's/dsl/scales/24hr/@, Hinzman's Auto Repair
124	WV 34, Kenna, E Exxon, Your Family Rest.
119	WV 21, Goldtown, same as 116
116	WV 21, Haines Branch Rd, Sissonville, E Rippling Waters Camping(2mi)
114	WV 622, Pocatalico Rd, E Exxon/dsl, $General, Save-A-Lot
111	WV 29, Tuppers Creek Rd, W Exxon/Subway/dsl
106	WV 27, Edens Fork Rd, W Marathon/dsl/country store
104	I-79 N, to Clarksburg
102	US 119 N, Westmoreland Rd, E BP/7-11, GoMart, Hardee's, Piggly Wiggly
101	I-64, E to Beckley, W to Huntington
100	Broad St, Capitol St, W Black Sheep Burritos, First Watch, Soho's Italian, Subway, Best Western, Embassy Suites, Marriott, Quality Inn, Sheraton, Cadillac/GMC, Firestone, H, H, USPO, Walgreens
99	WV 114, Capitol St, E , W BP/7-11, Exxon/Noble Roman's, Domino's, McDonald's, Taco Bell, Wendy's, museum, st capitol

BELLE

98	35th St Bridge(from sb), W Shell/7-11/dsl, Husson's Pizza, KFC, McDonald's, Rio De Grill, Starbucks, Steak Escape, Subway, Taco Bell, Wendy's, H, to U of Charleston, Walgreens
97	US 60 W(from nb), Kanawha Blvd
96	US 60 E, Midland Trail, Belle, W Biscuit World, Gino's, Budget Host
96mm	W Va Turnpike begins/ends
95.5mm	Kanawha River
95	WV 61, to MacCorkle Ave, E GoMart/dsl/24hr, Marathon/Subway/dsl, Bob Evans, IHOP, McDonald's, Country Inn&Suites, Days Inn, Econo lodge, Holiday Inn Express, Knights Inn, Quality Inn, Red Roof Inn, Advance Parts, AutoZone, NAPA, O'Reilly Parts, tire repair, W Exxon/dsl, GoMart, Shell/7-11/dsl, Applebee's, Arby's, Burger King, Capt D's, China Buffet, Cook Out, Cracker Barrel, Firehouse Subs, Fujiyama Japanese, Jimmy Johns, Little Caesar's, Pizza Hut, Taco Bell, $Tree, AT&T, Drug Emporium, King Tire, Kroger/gas, Lowe's, Piggly Wiggly, URGENT CARE, Verizon, vet

EAST BANK

89	WV 61, WV 94, to Marmet, E Exxon/Subway/dsl/24hr, GoMart/dsl, Sunoco/dsl, BiscuitWorld, Chum's Hotdogs, Gino's Pizza, Hardee's, LJ Silver, Wendy's, $General, Family$, Ford, Kroger/gas, tire repair, USPO
85	US 60, WV 61, East Bank, E Exxon/Arby's/dsl, Marathon/dsl, Gino's Pizza, McDonald's, Shoney's, $General, Chevrolet
82.5mm	toll booth
79	Cabin Creek Rd, Sharon, W $General, USPO
74	WV 83, Paint Creek Rd
72mm	Morton Service Area nb, , Exxon/dsl, Burger King
69mm	**full facilities, litter barrels, , , sb**
66	WV 15, to Mahan
60	WV 612, Oak Hill, to Mossy, E Exxon/dsl, RV Camping
56.5mm	toll plaza
54	rd 2, rd 23, Pax, E Corner/dsl
48	US 19, N Beckley, E Exxon, Sheetz/dsl/EVC, Arby's, Buffalo Wild Wings, Days Inn, Belk, Chevrolet, Dick's, JC Penney, PetSmart
45mm	Tamarack Service Area both lanes, W Beckley Travel Plaza/Exxon/gifts/dsl

WV

INTERSTATE 77 Cont'd

BECKLEY

Exit #	Services
44	WV 3, Beckley, E Exxon/dsl, Shell, Burger King, Chick-fil-A, DQ, El Bandito, Fujiyama Japanese, Hooters, IHOP, McDonald's, Omelet Shoppe, Outback Steaks, Pizza Hut, Sonic, Taco Bell, Best Western, Courtyard, Howard Johnson, Quality Inn/rest., SMART, Super 8, Travelodge, Advance Parts, CVS Drug, H, Kroger/gas, mini golf, Tires, URGENT CARE, W BP/Subway/dsl, Go-Mart/dsl, Bob Evans, Cracker Barrel, Pasquale Italian, Ruby Tuesday, TX Steaks, Wendy's, Baymont Inn, Clarion Inn, Country Inn&Suites, Hampton Inn, Holiday Inn, Microtel, Tru
42	WV 16, WV 97, to Mabscott, W BP/dsl, Go-Mart, Arby's, Gino's Pizza/Biscuit World, Subway, AutoValue Repair, O'Reilly Parts, USPO, Walmart
40	I-64 E, to Lewisburg
30mm	toll booth
28	WV 48, to Ghent, E Exxon/dsl, Marathon/Subway/dsl, $General, Glade Springs Resort(2mi), to ski area
26.5mm	elevation 3252, Flat Top Mtn
20	US 19, to Camp Creek, W Camp Creek SP/RV camping
18.5mm	Bluestone River, scenic overlook/parking area/weigh sta sb
17mm	**Bluestone Service Area/weigh sta nb, full facilities, picnic area, scenic view, Exxon/dsl**
14	WV 20, Athens Rd, E Pipestem Resort SP(6mi), to Concord U
9mm	WV Turnpike begins/ends
9	US 460, Princeton, **Welcome Ctr/ both lanes, full facilities, litter barrels, petwalk,** E Campestre Mexican, Kimono Japanese, Outback Steaks, $Tree, AT&T, Country Inn&Suites, Fairfield Inn, URGENT CARE, Verizon, Walmart/Subway/gas, W BP/dsl, Exxon, Mobil, Sheetz/dsl, Tesla EVC, Applebee's, Arby's, Bob Evans, Bojangles, Capt D's, Chick-fil-A, Chili's, Cracker Barrel, Dolly's Diner, DQ, Hardee's, McDonald's, Shoney's, Starbucks, Taco Bell, TX Steaks, Wendy's, Days Inn, Hampton Inn, Holiday Inn Express, Microtel, Quality Inn, Sleep Inn, Turnpike Motel, H, Hyundai, Lowe's
7	WV 27, Twelve Mile Rd
5	WV 112(from sb, no re-entry), to Ingleside
3mm	East River
1	US 52 N, to Bluefield, W KFC/LJ Silver, Wendy's, EconoLodge, Quality Inn, H, to Bluefield St Coll
0mm	West Virginia/Virginia state line, East River Mtn

PRINCETON

INTERSTATE 79

Exit #	Services
160mm	West Virginia/Pennsylvania state line
159	**full facilities, info, litter barrels, petwalk, vending, Welcome Ctr sb**
155	US 19, WV 7, E GetGo, Sheetz/dsl, Cheddar's, Chili's, Chipotle, Cracker Barrel, Kome Buffet, Longhorn Steaks, McDonald's, Olive Garden, Pizza Al's, Red Lobster, Starbucks, Fairfield Inn, Motel 6, OYO Hotel, Quality Inn, $Tree, Barnes&Noble, Best Buy, Buick/Chevrolet/GMC, CVS Drug, Dick's, Giant Eagle Foods, H, Nissan, Old Navy, PetCo, Sam's Club/dsl, Target, TJ Maxx, to WVU, Valvoline Express, Walmart/Subway, W BFS/DQ/Tim Horton's/dsl, Burger King, Firehouse Subs, Candlewood Suites, La Quinta, Harley-Davidson, Hobby Lobby, Honda, Sportsmans Whse
153	University Towne Ctr, E Buffalo Wild Wings, Fusion Japanese, Wendy's, Courtyard, Hampton Inn, Kia
152	US 19, to Morgantown, E BFS/dsl, Exxon, Arby's, China Wok, J&D BBQ, McDonald's, Pizza Hut, Subway, Taco Bell, EconoLodge, Advance Parts, BigLots, NAPA, URGENT CARE, W Bob Evans, Burger King, Microtel, JC Penney, Lowe's

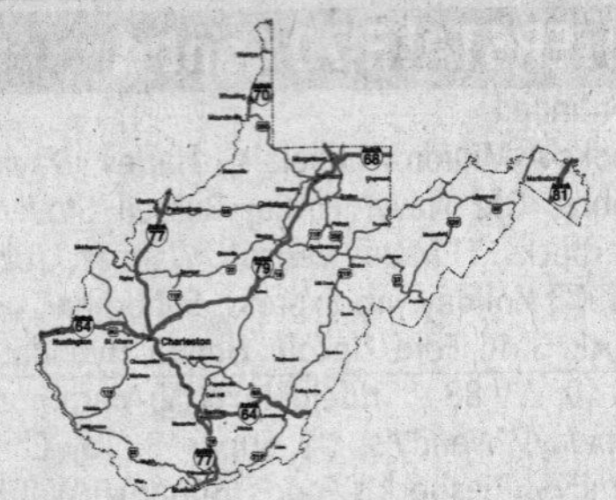

E FAIRMONT

Exit #	Services
150mm	Monongahela River
148	I-68 E, to Cumberland, MD, E Sheetz/dsl/Tesla EVC, Denny's, Devino's Pizza, Mariachi Loco, Quality Inn, $Tree, Walmart/Subway/auto
146	WV 77, to Goshen Rd, W Pilot/PJ Fresh/dsl/scales/24hr
141mm	weigh sta both lanes
139	WV 33, E Fairmont, E Exxon, W Exxon, K&T/dsl/scales, to Prickett's Ft SP(2mi)
137	WV 310, to Fairmont, E Exxon, Exxon/Teryaki Madness/dsl, Clarion, vet, W BP/dsl, Domino's, KFC, McDonald's, Subway, Wendy's, $General, Advance Parts, Family$, Price Cutter
136	rd 273, Fairmont
135	WV 64, Pleasant Valley Rd
133	Kingmont Rd, E Exxon/A&W/dsl, Marathon/Subway/dsl, Cracker Barrel, Hampton Inn, Holiday Inn Express, Super 8, W Amoco/dsl, Sunoco, Copper House Grill, DJ's Diner, Quality Inn
132	US 250, S Fairmont, E BFS/DQ/dsl, Applebee's, Arby's, Bob Evans, Colasessano's Italian, Dutchman's Daughter, Firehouse Subs, Hardee's, McDonald's, Mi Pueblo, Subway, Taco Bell, Days Inn, Fairfield Inn, Microtel, Red Roof Inn, $General, Advance Parts, ALDI, Chrysler/Dodge/Jeep, NAPA, Walmart/Subway/gas, W BP/dsl, GoMart/dsl, Burger King, Steak Escape, AT&T, Camping World, Ford/Lincoln, Toyota/Scion
125	WV 131, Saltwell Rd, to Shinnston, E Kia, W BFS/Burger King/dsl, Exxon/dsl, Dunkin
124	rd 279, Jerry Dove Dr, E BFS/Little Caesar's/DQ, Exxon/Dunkin/dsl, Buffalo Wild Wings, Firehouse Subs, Mi Margherita, Wingate Inn, W Sheetz/dsl, IHOP, Starbucks, Subway, TGIFridays, Wendys, Comfort Suites, Courtyard, Hawthorn Suites, Holiday Inn Express, H
123mm	**full facilities, info, litter barrels, petwalk, both lanes, RV dump, vending**
121	WV 24, Meadowbrook Rd, E GoMart/Biscuit World, Sheetz/dsl, Bob Evans, Hampton Inn, Hyundai/Subaru, vet, W Exxon/dsl, Burger King, Outback Steaks, Super 8, Dick's, Honda, JC Penney, NTB, Old Navy, Target
119	US 50, to Clarksburg, E A&W/LJ Silver, Brickside Grille, Chick-fil-A, Denny's, KFC, Las Trancas, Little Caesar's, Longhorn Steaks, McDonald's, McDonald's(2), Panera Bread, Papa Johns, Pizza Hut, Primanti Bros, Shogun Japanese, Starbucks, Taco Bell, TX Roadhouse, Wendy's, Best Western+, Days Inn, Qdoba, Quality Inn, SpringHill Suites, Townplace Suites, $Tree, Advance Parts, Autozone, BigLots, Hobby Lobby, Home Depot, Kohl's, Kroger/dsl, Lowe's, Monro Tire, Sam's Club/gas, URGENT CARE, USPO, Walgreens
117	WV 58, to Anmoore, E BFS/Tim Hortons/dsl, Applebee's, Arby's, Burger King, Honeybaked Ham, Olive Garden, Ruby Tuesday, Hilton Garden, ALDI, AT&T, El Rey Mexican, Staples, Walmart
115	WV 20, Nutter Fort, to Stonewood, E BP/7-11/dsl, Exxon/dsl, Adventure Grill, $General

WV

INTERSTATE 79 Cont'd

Exit #	Services
110	Lost Creek, E General Store/dsl, USPO
105	WV 7, to Jane Lew, E Jane Lew Trkstp/dsl/rest., Valero/dsl/rest., Days Inn, Mountaineer RV Ctr, W GoMart, $General, Kenworth/Mack/Volvo
99	US 33, US 119, to Weston, E GoMart/dsl, Marathon/DQ/dsl, Sheetz/dsl/Tesla EVC, Burger King, Gino's Pizza, McDonald's, Patron Mexican, Peking Buffet, Subway, Taco Bell, Hampton Inn, Holiday Inn Express, Quality Inn, Super 8, $Tree, Advance Parts, Walmart/gas, W Exxon/Arby's, Go-Mart, Buns Burgers, Domino's, Fox's Pizza, Giovanni's, Hardee's, KFC, LJ Silver, Subway, Wendy's, $General, Chrysler/Dodge/Fiat, CVS Drug, Family$, Ford, NAPA
96	WV 30, to S Weston, E Broken Wheel Camping, to S Jackson Lake SP
91	US 19, to Roanoke, E Stonewall Resort/rest./camping/Tesla EVC(2mi)), to S Jackson Lake SP
85mm	**full facilities, info, litter barrels, petwalk, both lanes, RV dump, vending**
79.5mm	Little Kanawha River
79	WV 5, Burnsville, E Exxon, Motel 79, Burnville Dam RA, Little Kanawha RV Camping, NAPA, W GoMart, Cedar Cr SP
76mm	Saltlick Creek
67	WV 4, to Flatwoods, E BP/Arby's/Dunkin/dsl/Tesla EVC, Go-Mart/Little Caesars/dsl, Shell/dsl, Custard Stand, KFC/Taco Bell, McDonald's, Subway, Days Inn, antiques, Buick/Chevrolet, KOA, to Sutton Lake RA, W Exxon/dsl, Pilot/Moe's SW Grill/Cinnabon/dsl/scales/24hr, China Buffet, El Gallo Mexican, Shoney's, Starbucks, Wendy's, Flatwood Factory Stores, Walmart
62	WV 4, Gassaway, to Sutton, E Elk Motel, $General, NAPA, Sutton Lake RA(3mi), W GoMart, LJ Silver, Pizza Hut, Microtel, AutoZone, CVS Drug, Elk River RV Camping, Family$, Ford, H, Kroger/deli
57	US 19 S, to Beckley
52mm	Elk River
51	WV 4, to Frametown
49mm	**full facilities, litter barrels, petwalk, both lanes, RV dump, vending**
46	WV 11, Servia Rd
40	WV 16, to Big Otter, E GoMart/dsl, W Exxon/dsl, Country Kitchen
34	WV 36, to Wallback, E $General, Wallback Lake
25	WV 29, to Amma, E Exxon/dsl
19	US 119, VW 53, to Clendenin, E BP/7-11/dsl, Frostbite Dairy Bar(3mi), Walgreens(3mi), W NAPA
9	WV 43, to Elkview, E GoMart/dsl, Burger King, Penn Sta Subs, Roni's Pizza, AutoZone, W Exxon/Hunt Bros Pizza/dsl, Speedway/dsl, Hens & Heifers, KFC, La Carreta, McDonald's, Pizza Hut, Subway, Taco Bell, La Quinta, $Tree, Advance Parts, CVS Drug, Kroger/gas
5	WV 114, to Big Chimney, E Exxon, Hardee's, Smith's Foods
1	US 119, Mink Shoals, E Barone Bros Pizza, Harding's Family Rest., Sleep Inn
0mm	I-77, S to Charleston, N to Parkersburg. I-79 begins/ends on I-77, exit 104.

BURNSVILLE

MINK SHOALS

INTERSTATE 81

Exit #	Services
26mm	West Virginia/Maryland state line, Potomac River
25mm	**full facilities, info, litter barrels, petwalk, Welcome Ctr sb**
23	US 11, Marlowe, Falling Waters, E Exxon/dsl, Dunkin, Kings Rest., Red Lantern Chinese, $General, Falling Waters Camping(1mi), Food Lion, W BP/dsl, 7-11, Outdoor Express RV Ctr
20	WV 901, Spring Mills Rd, E Sheetz/dsl, China Spring, Cinco de Mayo, Kitzie's Rest., Little Caesar's, McDonald's, Montese's Pizza, Popeyes, Taco Bell, Motel 6, $Tree, Advance Parts, Walmart/Subway, W BP/dsl, Burger King, Domino's, DQ, Dunkin, Jakki's Grill, Wendys, Quality Inn
16	WV 9, N Queen St, Berkeley Springs, E Citgo/dsl, Exxon/Subway/dsl, Sheetz/Tesla EVC, Arby's, China King, Dunkin, Firebox55, Hoss's Steaks, Just In Time Seafood, KFC, Laddies Grill, LJ Silver, McDonald's, Pizza Hut, Subway, Taco Bell, Waffle House, APM Inn, Comfort Inn, Knights Inn, Super 8, Advance Parts, ALDI, AutoZone, Carquest, CVS Drug, Family$, Martin's Foods, URGENT CARE, USPO, Walgreens, W ROCS/mart/dsl, Shell/Subway/dsl
14	rd 13, Dry Run Rd, E H, W Butler's Farm Mkt(1mi)
13	rd 15, Kings St, Martinsburg, E BP/Subway/dsl, Sheetz/dsl, Angelos Pizza, Applebee's, Buffalo Wild Wings, Burger King, Cracker Barrel, Daily Grind, Fiesta Tapatia, Kobe Japanese, Las Trancas, Outback Steaks, Red Roof Inn, Wendy's, Fairfield Inn, Holiday Inn/rest., Chevrolet/Toyota, H, Office Depot
12	WV 45, Winchester Ave, E Sheetz/dsl, Sunoco/dsl, Arby's, Asian Garden, Blaze Pizza, Bob Evans, Chick-fil-A, Chipotle, Dunkin, Five Guys, Martinsburg Family Diner, McDonald's, Olive Garden, Panda Express, Panera Bread, Papa John's, Starbucks, Taco Bell, Hampton Inn, Home2 Suites, Advance Parts, AutoZone, Hobby Lobby, Lowe's, Martin's Foods/gas/EVC, Nahkeeta Camping(2mi), Walmart, W Jersey Mike's, Ledo Pizza, Logan's Roadhouse, Tropical Smoothie, Hilton Garden, $Tree, ALDI, Best Buy, Books-A-Million, Dick's, GNC, Michael's, PetSmart, Target/Starbucks, TJ Maxx, URGENT CARE
8	rd 32, Tablers Sta Rd, E Rutters/dsl, Sheetz/dsl
5	WV 51, Inwood, to Charles Town, E BP/dsl, Liberty, Sheetz/dsl, Arby's, AutoZone, Burger King, Dominos, DQ, McDonald's, Pizza Hut, Pizza Oven, Subway, Taco Bell, Waffle House, Hampton Inn, Advance Parts, CVS Drug, Family$, NAPA, URGENT CARE, USPO, Walgreens, W Lazy A RV Campground(9mi)
2mm	**full facilities, info, litter barrels, petwalk, vending, Welcome Ctr/weigh sta nb**
0mm	West Virginia/Virginia state line

BERKELEY SPRINGS

WV

NOTES

WISCONSIN

INTERSTATE 39

MERRILL

Exit #	Services
211	US 51, rd K, Merrill, W Cenex, Chip's Burgers, Hardee's, Pine Ridge Rest., Pizza Hut,
208	WI 64, WI 17, Merrill, E KFC, Taco Bell, W KwikTrip/dsl, Mobil/Arby's/dsl, China Inn, Culver's, Los Mezcales, Mama De Luca's Pizza, McDonald's, Subway, Americinn, Cobblestone Inn, EconoLodge, $Tree, Chrysler/Dodge/Jeep, H, O'Reilly Parts, to Council Grounds SP, Verizon, Walmart
206mm	Wisconsin River
205	US 51, rd Q, Merrill, E BP/Hwy 51/rest./dsl/24hr, fireworks
197	rd WW, to Brokaw, W Mobil/dsl
194	US 51, rd U, rd K, Wausau, E F&F/dsl, KwikTrip/dsl, McDonald's, Subway, Taco Bell, W BP/Arby's/dsl, Ford, Kia, Nissan, Subaru, Toyota
193	Bridge St, E CVS Drug, W H
192	WI 29 W, WI 52 E, Wausau, to Chippewa Falls, same as 191 b
191b	Sherman St, E BP, Holiday/dsl, Shell, Applebee's, Buffalo Wild Wings, Great Dane Rest., Jimmy John's, King Buffet, Little Caesar's, McDonald's, Milwaukee Burger Co, Noodles&Co, Panera Bread, Papa Murphy's, Pizza Hut, Qdoba, Starbucks, Subway, Toppers Pizza, Courtyard, Hampton Inn, La Quinta, Motel 6, Plaza Hotel, Super 8, County Mkt/USPO, Trig's Foods, Walgreens, W KwikTrip/dsl, 2510 Deli, Hardee's, Cadillac, Home Depot, Honda, H, Menards
191a	WI 29, Chippewa Falls
190mm	Rib River
190	rd NN, E BP/Burger King, El Tequila Salsa, IHOP, Hilton Garden, W The Store/Subway/dsl, Quality Inn, Granite Mtn Ski Area, Rib Mtn Ski Area, st patrol
188	rd N, E KwikTrip/dsl, Dunkin', Fazoli's, HuHot, McDonald's, Olive Garden, Panda Express, Red Robin, Rococo Pizza, Ropa Pizza, Starbucks, TX Roadhouse, Days Inn, $Tree, ALDI, AT&T, Audi/VW, Barnes&Noble, Best Buy, Chevrolet, Dick's, GNC, Gordman's, Hobby Lobby, Hyundai, JoAnn Fabrics, King's RV Ctr, Kohl's, Michael's, Old Navy, PetCo, PetSmart, Sam's Club/gas/dsl, Tires+, TJ Maxx, Walmart/Subway, W Rib Mtn SP
187mm	I-39 begins/ends. Freeway continues N as US 51.
187	WI 29 E, to Green Bay
186mm	Wisconsin River
185	US 51, Rothschild, Kronenwetter, E BP/dsl, Arby's, Culver's, Denny's, Green Mill Rest., Subway, Wausau Grill, Best Western+, EconoLodge, Grand Lodge, Holiday Inn, Motel 6, Stoney Creek Inn, Harley-Davidson, Pick'n Save Foods
181	Maple Ridge Rd, Kronenwetter, Mosinee, E Peterbilt, vet, Volvo, W Kenworth
179	WI 153, Mosinee, W BP/Subway/dsl, KwikTrip/dsl, Shell/dsl, McDonald's, StageStop Rest., Quality Inn, vet
175	WI 34, Knowlton, to WI Rapids, W Mullins Cheese Factory
171	rd DB, Knowlton, W gas, food, lodging, Rivers Edge Camping
165	US 10 W, to Marshfield(no nb re-entry)
163	Casimir Rd
161	US 51, Stevens Point, W BP, Kwik Trip/dsl, The Store, Burger King, China Wok, Coldstone, Cousins Subs, Culver's, Hardee's, Jimmy John's, KFC, McDonald's, Michele's Rest., Noodles&Co, Perkins, Pizza Hut, Rococo's Pizza, Starbucks,

CHIPPEWA FALLS

KNOWLTON

WI

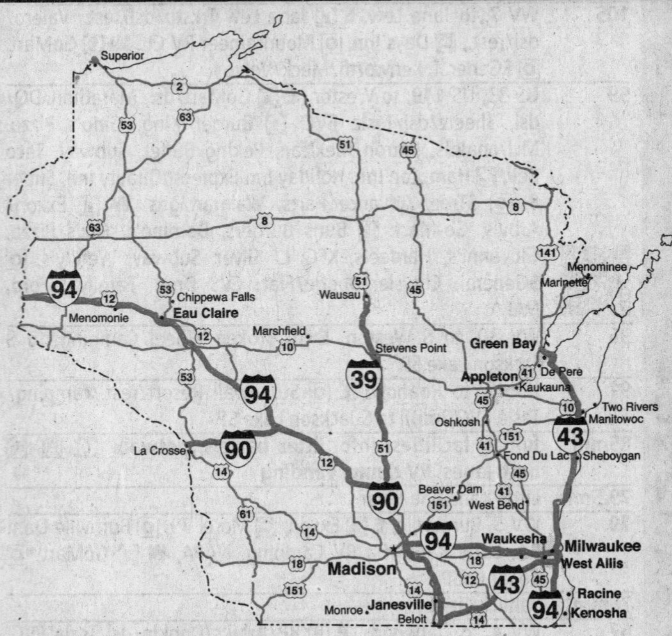

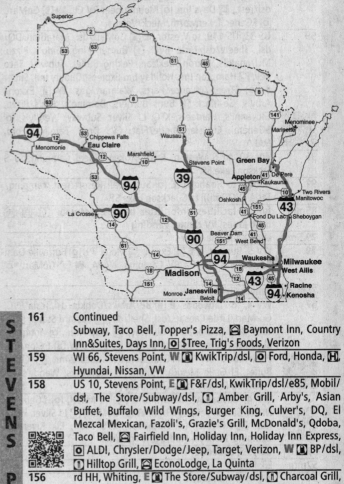

STEVENS POINT

Exit #	Services
161	Continued Subway, Taco Bell, Topper's Pizza, Baymont Inn, Country Inn&Suites, Days Inn, $Tree, Trig's Foods, Verizon
159	WI 66, Stevens Point, W KwikTrip/dsl, Ford, Honda, H, Hyundai, Nissan, VW
158	US 10, Stevens Point, E F&F/dsl, KwikTrip/dsl/e85, Mobil/dsl, The Store/Subway/dsl, Amber Grill, Arby's, Asian Buffet, Buffalo Wild Wings, Burger King, Culver's, DQ, El Mezcal Mexican, Fazoli's, Grazie's Grill, McDonald's, Qdoba, Taco Bell, Fairfield Inn, Holiday Inn, Holiday Inn Express, ALDI, Chrysler/Dodge/Jeep, Target, Verizon, W BP/dsl, Hilltop Grill, EconoLodge, La Quinta
156	rd HH, Whiting, E The Store/Subway/dsl, Charcoal Grill, Chili's, McDonald's, Monk's Grill, Panda Express, Panera Bread, Pizza Ranch, Starbucks, $Tree, AT&T, Best Buy, GNC, JoAnn Fabrics, Kohl's, Lowe's, Michael's, PetCo, Staples, TJ Maxx, Walmart/Subway
153	rd B, Plover, W BP, Kwik Trip/dsl, Mobil/Dunkin'/dsl, Arby's, Bamboo House, Burger King, Culver's, Happy Wok, IHOP, Jimmy John's, KFC, McDonald's, Papa Murphy's, Subway, Taco Bell, Tempura House Asian, AmericInn, Comfort Inn, Hampton Inn, city park, Copp's Foods, dsl repair, Menards, NAPA, Toyota, Verizon, vet
151	WI 54, to Waupaca, E KwikTrip/rest./dsl/scales/24hr, Four Star Family Rest., Shooter's Rest., Best Western, Super 8, tires/repair
143	rd W, Bancroft, to WI Rapids, E Citgo/dsl, Pop A Top Grill, USPO
139	rd D, Almond
136	WI 73, Plainfield, to WI Rapids, E BP/dsl, Budda's Grill, service/repair, W Citgo/Subway/dsl
131	rd V, Hancock, E Citgo, Smiley's Diner, W Oasis Camping
127mm	weigh sta both lanes(exits left)
124	WI 21, Coloma, E Mobil/A&W/dsl, Red Hill Cafe, Subway, Mecan Inn(4mi), Coloma Camping, W BP/Chester's/dsl, Buick/Chevrolet
120mm	rest area sb, **full facilities, litter barrels, petwalk, vending**

ALMOND

PORTAGE

INTERSTATE 39 Cont'd

Exit #	Services
118mm	rest area nb, **full facilities, litter barrels, petwalk, vending**
113	rd E, rd J, Westfield, W BP/Burger King, Cenex, Mobil/dsl, McDonald's, Subway, Pioneer Motel/rest., city park, Family$
106	WI 82 W, WI 23 E, Oxford, E Crossroads Motel, W Citgo/dsl
104	(from nb, no EZ return)rd D, Packwaukee
100	WI 23 W, rd P, Endeavor, E BP/dsl
92	US 51 S, Portage, E KwikTrip/dsl, Asian Express, Culver's, Dino's Rest., Jimmy John's, KFC, La Tolteca Mexican, McDonald's, Papa Murphy's, Pizza Ranch, Subway, Suzy's Steaks, Taco Bell, Best Western, Ridge Motel, Sunset Motel, Super 8, $Tree, ALDI, AutoZone, Chrysler/Dodge/Jeep, Festival Foods, Ford/Lincoln, GNC, H, Walgreens, Walmart
89b a	WI 16, to WI 127, Portage, E BP/dsl, Hitching Post Eatery
88.5mm	Wisconsin River
87	WI 33, Portage, W ski area
86mm	Baraboo River
85	Cascade Mt Rd
84mm	I-39, I-90 & I-94 run together sb/eb

INTERSTATE 41

Exit #	Services
171	I-43 S, to Milwaukee, US 41/141 N, to Marinette
170	US 141 S, Velp Ave, E Mobil, Burger King, Taco Bell, W BP/A&W/dsl, Shell/dsl, Gilligan's Rest., Julie's Rest., McDonald's, River St Grill, Sunny Chinese, Watering Hole Rest., AmericInn, Bumper Parts, CVS Drug, Family$, Harley Davidson
168c b	WI 29, WI 32, Shawano Ave, Dousman St, E KwikTrip, Tesla EVC, Comfort Suites, Buick/Cadillac/GMC, Meijer
168	WI 32, WI 54, Mason St, E Pizza Hut, Home Depot, W Mobil, Shell/Papa John's/dsl, Bon Orient Buffet, Chili's, Fazoli's, Hardee's, Little Caesar's, Los Banditos, McDonald's, Schlotsky's, Festival Foods, GNC, O'Reilly Parts, Petco, Sam's Club, Walmart/Subway
167	CR VK, Lombardi Ave, Hazelwood Ln, E Shell, ChuckeCheese, Margaritas, Red Lobster, Cabela's, Lambeau Field, Pick'n Save
165	WI 172, to I-43
164	CR AAA, Oneida St, Waube Ln, E KwikTrip/dsl, Shell/dsl, Applebee's, Cousins Subs, Culver's, Denny's, Domino's, Five Guys, Grazie's Italian, Olive Garden, Perkins, Starbucks, Subway, Wendy's, Baymont Inn, Comfort Inn, Delta Hotel, EconoLodge, Fairfield Inn, Hampton Inn, Holiday Inn, Motel 6, Super 8, $Tree, Honda, Jo-Ann, W BP/dsl, KwikTrip, Erbert & Gerbert's, Country Inn Suites, Microtel
163b	WI 32 N, Green Bay
163a	CR G, Main Ave, E Shell/dsl, Tobacco Outlet/dsl, Burger King, Dunkin', Jimmy John's, McDonald's, Papa John's, Papa Murphy's, Starbucks, Subway, ALDI, AutoZone, CVS Drug, Festival Foods, Peterbilt, USPO, Walgreens, W BP/A&W/Taco Bell/dsl/scales, UHaul.
161	CR F, Scheuring Rd, De Pete, E KwikTrip/Arby's/dsl, Shell/dsl, Culver's, DQ, Sleep Inn, $Tree, Menard's, Verizon, Walmart/Subway, W Plank Road Rest.
157	CR S, Freedom, W KwikTrip/dsl
154	CR U, Wrightstown
153	weigh sta nb
150	CR J, Kaukauna, E Chrysler/Dodge/Jeep, W BP/dsl, Freightliner
148	WI 55, Seymour, Kaukauna, E KwikTrip/dsl,
148	Continued Shell/Arby's/dsl, Days Inn, W Chevrolet/Buick/GMC
146	CR N, Little Chute, Kimberly, E BP/McDonald's/Subway/dsl, Shell/dsl, Burger King, Culver's, Taco Bell, Tom's Drive In, Country Inn Suites, W Simon's Cheese Store
145	WI 441 S
144	CR E, Ballard Rd, E Shell/dsl, Baskin Robbins, Hardee's, McDonald's, H, W AmericInn, Cambria Suites
142	WI 47, Richmond St, Black Creek, E Mobil, Arby's, Fazoli's, Jimmy John's, Little Caesar's, McDonald's, Starbucks, Taco Bell, Snug In Motel, Kohl's, Walgreens, W KwikTrip/dsl, Meijer/dsl
139	WI15, CR OO, Northland Ave, Greenville, Hortonville, W EVC, KwikTrip/dsl, Acura, BMW, Hyundai, Infiniti, Land Rover/Jaguar/Porsche, Lexus, Mazda, Mercedes, Mini, Nissan, Volvo, VW/Audi
138	WI 96, Wisconsin Ave, Fremont, E KwikTrip/dsl, Arby's, Culver's, Famous Dave's, Golden Corral, Wendy's, Comfort Suites, CarX, Home Depot, PetSmart, Sam's Club, Woodman's, W Mobil, Cheddar's, Chili's, IHOP, Jimmy John's, Noodles&Co, Olive Garden, Osaka Japanese, Papa Murphy's, Qdoba, Red Lobster, Schlotsky's, Solea Mexican Grill, Starbucks, TGI Friday, Walmart/Subway, Holiday Inn, Wingate Inn, $Tree, AT&T, Best Buy, Costco/dsl, Dick's, Discount Tire, JC Penney, Jo-Ann, Macy's, Menard's, Michael's, Petco, Scheel's, Target, Tires+, TJ Maxx, Verizon, Walgreens
137	WI 125, College Ave, E BP/dsl, KwikTrip, Mobil, Applebee's, Burger King, Chick-fil-A, Denny's, HuHot, McDonald's, Panda Express, Panera Bread, Perkins, Popeyes, Starbucks, Subway, Taco Bell, TX Roadhouse, Baymont Inn, Clarion, La Quinta, Motel 6, Quality Inn, Rodeway Inn, Super 8, Big Lots, Chrysler/Dodge/Jeep, Firestone/auto, Ford, Goodyear/auto, Honda, Kia, Office Depot, Subaru, Woodman's Gas, W KwikTrip/dsl, Asian Garden, Buffalo Wild Wings, Chipotle, ChuckECheese, Fairfield Inn, Fazoli's, Five Guys, Machine Shed Rest., Outback Steaks, TGIFriday's, AmericInn, Candlewood Suites, Country Inn Suites, DoubleTree, GrandStay Suites, Hampton Inn, Home2 Suites, Microtel, Residence Inn, Barnes&Noble, Hobby Lobby, Old Navy, USPO, vet
136	CR BB, Prospect Ave, W BP, Mobil/Subway, Van Zealand Autocare
134	US 10 E, WI 441 N
133	CR II, Winchester Rd
132	Main St, Oak Ridge Rd(no return nb or sb), E BP/dsl, Citgo/dsl, Bradke's Rest., Chevrolet/Buick/Cadillac
131	WI 114, CR JJ, Winneconne Ave, Hilbert, Sherwood, E Citgo/dsl, Fox Point, KwikTrip/dsl, Cousins Subs, Ground Round, Hardee's, KFC, Little Caesar's, McDonald's, Papa Murphy's, Pizza Hut, Starbucks, Subway, Best Western, Days Inn, $Tree, Advance Parts, ALDI, CVS Drug, Festival Foods, Firestone/auto, Ford/Lincoln, GNC, Pick'n Save, W A&W, Applebee's, Arby's, Culver's, Jimmy John's, Perkins, Qdoba, Taco Bell, AT&T, Kohl's, Verizon, Walgreens, Walmart/Subway
129	Bell St, Breezewood Ln, W Mobil, Solea Mexican
124	WI 76, Jackson St, E Mobil, W KwikTrip/dsl/CNG, Ole & Lena's, truck repair
120	US 45, US 10 W, New London
119	WI 21, Omro Rd, Oshkosh, E DQ, La Quinta, W KwikTrip/dsl, Shell/McDonald's, Cousins Subs, Culver's, Panera Bread, Papa Murphy's, Rocky Rococo Pizza, Subway, Wendy's, Holiday Inn Express, Chevrolet/Buick/GMC/Cadillac, Dick's, Festival Foods, H, Lowe's, Menard's, Verizon, Walgreens
117	9th Ave, E KwikTrip/dsl, Benvenuto's Italian,

WI

INTERSTATE 41 Cont'd

117 Continued
Buffalo Wild Wings, China King, Cousins Subs, Golden Corral, IHOP, Jimmy John's, Little Caesar's, McDonald's, Olive Garden, Pizza Hut, Potbelly, Qdoba, Red Robin, Starbucks, Taco Bell, Comfort Suites, AT&T, Best Buy, CVS Drug, Duluth Trading, Hobby Lobby, Jo-Ann, Ross, TJ Maxx, Verizon, Walgreens, **W** Burger King, Domino's, Huhot, Perkins, Pizza Ranch, Goodyear/auto, NAPA, Walmart/Subway

116 WI 44, WI 91, S Park Ave, Ripon Rd, **E** BP/dsl, Mobil/dsl, Applebee's, Arby's, Culver's, Durango's, Fazoli's, Firehouse Subs, Friar Tuck's Rest., Hangar Grill, Hardee's, Noodles&Co, Subway, Cobblestone Inn, Fairfield Inn, Hilton Garden, Super 8, $Tree, Advance Parts, air museum, ALDI, CarX, GNC, Petco, Pick'n Save, Target, Tires+, **W** KwikTrip/dsl, Shell/dsl, Johnny Rockets, Hawthorn Suites, Honda, Kia, Nissan, Oshkosh Outlets/famous brands, Subaru, Toyota, vet, VW

113 WI 26, CR N, Rosendale, Waupun, Pickett, **E** Sleepy Hollow Camping(2mi), **W** Planeview/Subway/dsl/scales/24hr, Cobblestone Inn

106 CR N, Van Dyne

101 CR OO, Winnebago St, **E** BP/Rest./dsl/scales, Mack/Volvo, truck wash

99 WI 23, Johnson St, Rosendale, Ripon, **E** 11:11 Burger, Ala Roma Pizza, Applebee's, Buffalo Wild Wings, Burger King, DQ, Faro's Rest., Fazoli's, Hardee's, KFC, McDonald's, Panda Express, Panera Bread, Popeyes, Qdoba, Rocky Rococo Pizza, Schriener's Rest., Starbucks, Days Inn, Hampton Inn, Super 8, AT&T, AutoZone, Best Buy, Jo-Ann, Kohl's, Pick'n Save, Staples, TJ Maxx, **W** KwikTrip/dsl, Shell/Subway/dsl, Arby's, Culver's, Pizza Hut, Pizza Ranch, $Tree, ALDI, CarX, Chevrolet/Buick/GMC/Cadillac, Ford, Harley Davidson, Mazda, Menard's, PetSmart, Target, Verizon, Walmart/Subway

98 CR D, Military Rd, **E** McDonald's, Microtel, F&F/dsl, Schiek's Campers, **W** BP/dsl, Rolling Meadows Rest., Comfort Inn, Holiday Inn Express, Radisson, Chrysler/Dodge/Jeep, st patrol

97 CR VVV, Hickory St, **E** KwikTrip/dsl, Pump&Pantry/dsl, **W** Love's/Subway/dsl/scales/24hr, Country Inn Suites

95 US 152, Madison, Manitowoc, **E** H

92 CR B, Oakfield, Eden, **E** Breezy Hill Camping(2 mi)

87 WI 49, CR KK, Brownsville, Waupun

85 WI 67, Lomira, Campbellsport, **E** Exxon/dsl, **W** BP/Taco Bell/dsl, Shell/Subway/dsl, Bublitz's Rest., McDonald's, AmeriVu Inn, $General, Ford, Piggly Wiggly

82.5mm rest area both lanes, full(handicapped)facilities, picnic tables, litter barrels, petwalk

81 WI 28, Mayville, Kewaskum

76 CR D, **W** fireworks

72 WI 33, CR W, West Bend, Allenton, **W** BP/dsl, Mobil, Alma's Cafe, Subway

68 CR K, **W** Mobil/dsl, MJ Stevens Rest.

66 WI 144, West Bend, Slinger, **W** Freedom RV Ctr, Held's Cheese/sausage, Slinger Speedway

64 WI 60, to Jackson, Slinger, Hartford, **E** Scenic RV Ctr, **W** BP/dsl, KwikTrip/dsl, Burger King, China Town, Cousins Subs, Polanco's Mexican, Chevrolet, Chrysler/Dodge/Jeep, H, O'Reilly Parts, Piggly Wiggly, Schaefer's Service Ctr

60 CR FD, to WI 145, Richfield, **E** Mobil/dsl/e85, Cabela's, **W** BP/McDonald's/dsl/scales/24hr

59 (from nb)US 45 W

57 WI 167, Holy Hill Rd, **E** Mobil/Subway/dsl, **W** BP, Sawmill Rest.

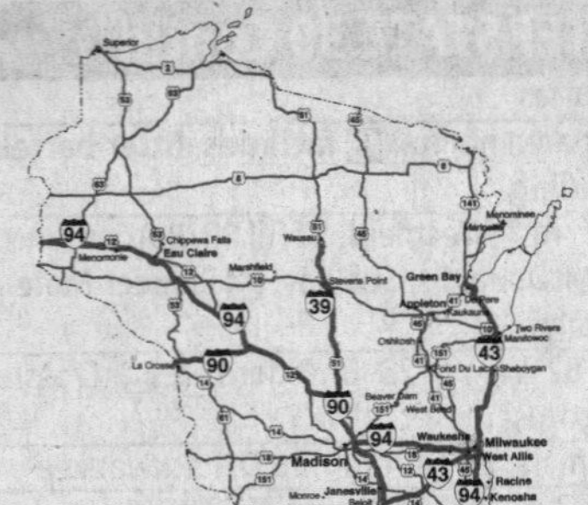

54 WI 167, CR Y, Lannon Rd, Germantown, **E** KwikTrip/dsl, Best Western, Country Inn Suites

52 CR Q, County Line Rd, **E** Briscoe Co Wood Grill, **W** Mobil/dsl, Speedway/dsl, Applebee's, Arby's, Buffalo Wild Wings, Burger King, Cracker Barrel, Jimmy John's, KFC, McDonald's, Panda Express, Pizza Hut/Taco Bell, Qdoba, Starbucks, Wendy's, Holiday Inn Express, Super 8, AT&T, Best Buy, Costco/dsl, Hobby Lobby, Kohl's, Metro Mkt, Target

51b a Pilgrim Rd, **W** KwikTrip, Kraverz Custard, Toppers, AutoZone

50b a WI 74 W, WI 100 E, Menomonee Falls, **E** VW, Buick/GMC, Ford, **W** BP, De Martinis Pizza, Monro

48 WI 145, **E** ALDI, Sam's Club/gas, Woodman's Mkt/gas

47b CR PP, Good Hope Rd, **E** Broken Egg, Cousins Subs, Point Burger Bar, Comfort Suites, Hilton Garden, CarMax, Chevrolet, Mazda, Nissan, Toyota

47 WI 175, Appleton Ave

46 CR E, Silver Spring Dr, **E** Marathon/dsl, Mobil/dsl, Athens Rest., Cousins Subs, KFC, McDonald's, Subway, Taco Bell, Wendy's, Hampton Inn, Quality Inn, Goodyear/auto, Harley Davidson, Petro Mart, **W** Speedway/dsl, Domino's, Hyatt Place

45 CR EE, Hampton Ave, **E** Citgo, **W** BP/dsl

44 WI 190, Capitol Dr, **E** Subway, Walgreens, **W** Arby's, Burger King, Chick-fil-A, Chipotle, Culver's, Jimmy John's, McDonald's, Noodles&Co, Potbelly's, Qdoba, Starbucks, Taco Bell, Advance Parts, GNC, Home Depot, Metro Mkt, O'Reilly Parts, Petco, Ross, Target

43 Burleigh St, **E** Corner Bakery Cafe, Osgood's Rest., Pizza Man, Homewood Suites, Dick's, H, Meijer, Old Navy, TJ Maxx, **W** Wendy's, Cousins Subs, ALDI, Firestone/auto, Lowe's

42b North Ave W, **E** BP, Buffalo Wild Wings, Cheesecake Factory, Dave&Buster's, Denny's, Five Guys, Maggiano's, Panera Bread, PF Chang's, Potbelly, Texas de Brazil, Extended Stay America, Holiday Inn Express, Radisson, Barnes&Noble, Best Buy, Macy's, Nordstrom's, Walgreens, **W** Papa John's, vet

42a WI 100, Mayfair Rd, North Ave E(from nb), **E** Dave&Buster's, Walgreens, **W** Firehouse Subs, Crowne Plaza, Kia, Pick'n Save, USPO

40 Watertown Plank Rd, Swan Blvd, **E** H, **W** Crowne Plaza

39 US 18, Wisconsin Ave, Bluemound Rd, **E** H

1b a I-94

1d WI 53, Greenfield Ave, **E** Jets Pizza, Subway, CVS Drug, Family$, **W** Speedway/dsl, DQ, Fazoli's, Las Fajitas, McDonald's, Starbucks, Wendy's, O'Reilly Parts

1e (from sb)Lincoln Ave, **E** same as 2 E

2a (from sb)National Rd(wb)

2b (from sb)Oklahoma Ave, **E** Citgo, auto repair, H

3 Beloit Rd

4 I-41 S runs with I-43 N/I-894 E, then I-94 E. See I-43 exits 5-9 and I-94 exits 316-347

0mm Wisconsin/Illinois state line

PORT OF GREEN BAY

BELLEVUE

MANITOWOC

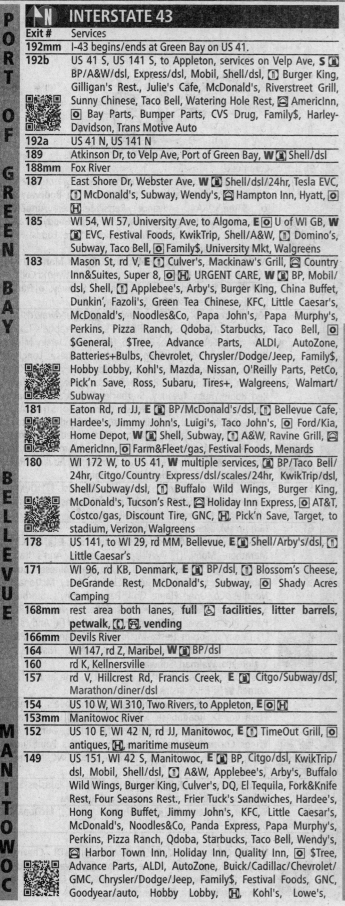

INTERSTATE 43

Exit #	Services
192mm	I-43 begins/ends at Green Bay on US 41.
192b	US 41 S, US 141 S, to Appleton, services on Velp Ave, **S** [gas] BP/A&W/dsl, Express/dsl, Mobil, Shell/dsl, [food] Burger King, Gilligan's Rest., Julie's Cafe, McDonald's, Riverstreet Grill, Sunny Chinese, Taco Bell, Watering Hole Rest, [lodging] AmericInn, [other] Bay Parts, Bumper Parts, CVS Drug, Family$, Harley-Davidson, Trans Motive Auto
192a	US 41 N, US 141 N
189	Atkinson Dr, to Velp Ave, Port of Green Bay, **W** [gas] Shell/dsl
188mm	Fox River
187	East Shore Dr, Webster Ave, **W** [gas] Shell/dsl/24hr, Tesla EVC, [food] McDonald's, Subway, Wendy's, [lodging] Hampton Inn, Hyatt, [other] [H]
185	WI 54, WI 57, University Ave, to Algoma, **E** [other] U of WI GB, **W** [gas] EVC, Festival Foods, KwikTrip, Shell/A&W, [food] Domino's, Subway, Taco Bell, [other] Family$, University Mkt, Walgreens
183	Mason St, rd V, **E** [food] Culver's, Mackinaw's Grill, [lodging] Country Inn&Suites, Super 8, [other] [H], URGENT CARE, **W** [gas] BP, Mobil/dsl, Shell, [food] Applebee's, Arby's, Burger King, China Buffet, Dunkin', Fazoli's, Green Tea Chinese, KFC, Little Caesar's, McDonald's, Noodles&Co, Papa John's, Papa Murphy's, Perkins, Pizza Ranch, Qdoba, Starbucks, Taco Bell, [other] $General, $Tree, Advance Parts, ALDI, AutoZone, Batteries+Bulbs, Chevrolet, Chrysler/Dodge/Jeep, Family$, Hobby Lobby, Kohl's, Mazda, Nissan, O'Reilly Parts, PetCo, Pick'n Save, Ross, Subaru, Tires+, Walgreens, Walmart/Subway
181	Eaton Rd, rd JJ, **E** [gas] BP/McDonald's/dsl, [food] Bellevue Cafe, Hardee's, Jimmy John's, Luigi's, Taco John's, [other] Ford/Kia, Home Depot, **W** [gas] Shell, Subway, [food] A&W, Ravine Grill, [lodging] AmericInn, [other] Farm&Fleet/gas, Festival Foods, Menards
180	WI 172 W, to US 41, **W** multiple services, [gas] BP/Taco Bell/24hr, Citgo/Country Express/dsl/scales/24hr, KwikTrip/dsl, Shell/Subway/dsl, [food] Buffalo Wild Wings, Burger King, McDonald's, Tucson's Rest., [lodging] Holiday Inn Express, [other] AT&T, Costco/gas, Discount Tire, GNC, [H], Pick'n Save, Target, to stadium, Verizon, Walgreens
178	US 141, to WI 29, rd MM, Bellevue, **E** [gas] Shell/Arby's/dsl, [food] Little Caesar's
171	WI 96, rd KB, Denmark, **E** [gas] BP/dsl, [food] Blossom's Cheese, DeGrande Rest, McDonald's, Subway, [other] Shady Acres Camping
168mm	rest area both lanes, **full [handicapped] facilities, litter barrels, petwalk, [phone], [picnic], vending**
166mm	Devils River
164	WI 147, rd Z, Maribel, **W** [gas] BP/dsl
160	rd K, Kellnersville
157	rd V, Hillcrest Rd, Francis Creek, **E** [gas] Citgo/Subway/dsl, Marathon/diner/dsl
154	US 10 W, WI 310, Two Rivers, to Appleton, **E** [other] [H]
153mm	Manitowoc River
152	US 10 E, WI 42 N, rd JJ, Manitowoc, **E** [food] TimeOut Grill, [other] antiques, [H], maritime museum
149	US 151, WI 42 S, Manitowoc, **E** [gas] BP, Citgo/dsl, KwikTrip/dsl, Mobil, Shell/dsl, [food] A&W, Applebee's, Arby's, Buffalo Wild Wings, Burger King, Culver's, DQ, El Tequila, Fork&Knife Rest, Four Seasons Rest., Frier Tuck's Sandwiches, Hardee's, Hong Kong Buffet, Jimmy John's, KFC, Little Caesar's, McDonald's, Noodles&Co, Panda Express, Papa Murphy's, Perkins, Pizza Ranch, Qdoba, Starbucks, Taco Bell, Wendy's, [lodging] Harbor Town Inn, Holiday Inn, Quality Inn, [other] $Tree, Advance Parts, ALDI, AutoZone, Buick/Cadillac/Chevrolet/GMC, Chrysler/Dodge/Jeep, Family$, Festival Foods, GNC, Goodyear/auto, Hobby Lobby, [H], Kohl's, Lowe's,

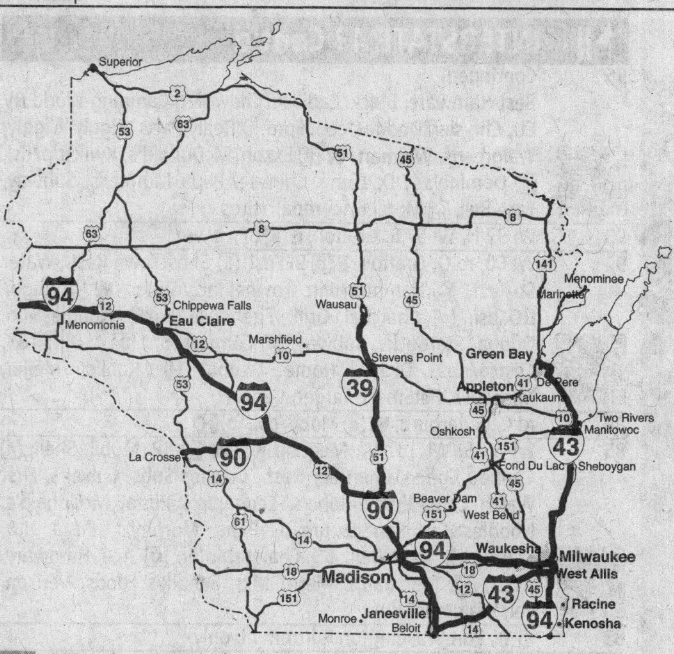

NEWTON

SHEBOYGAN

BELGIUM

Exit #	Services
149	Continued O'Reilly Parts, PetCo, Pick'n Save, USPO, Verizon, vet, Walgreens, **Walmart/Subway**, **W** [gas] Shell/McDonald's, [food] Subway, [lodging] AmericInn, [other] Harley-Davidson, Menards
144	rd C, Newton, **E** [gas] Mobil/dsl
142mm	weigh sta sb
137	rd XX, Cleveland, **E** [gas] **Citgo/Subway/dsl**, [other] Kunes Co RV Ctr
128	WI 42, Howards Grove, **E** [gas] **BP/dsl/24hr**, **KwikTrip/dsl**, [food] Culver's, Hardee's, Harry's Diner, Shuff's Rest., TX Roadhouse, [lodging] Quality Inn, [other] Pomp's Tire, **W** [gas] **Mobil/dsl/scales**, [other] Menards, **Walmart/Subway**
126	WI 23, Sheboygan, **E** [gas] BP, KwikTrip/dsl, Tesla EVC, [food] Applebee's, Cousins Subs, Culver's, McDonald's, New China, Noodles&Co, Panera Bread, Pizza Hut, Pizza Ranch, [lodging] La Quinta, Super 8, [other] ALDI, Batteries+Bulbs, BigLots, Festival Foods, Ford/Kia, Goodyear/auto, Honda, [H], Hyundai/Mazda, Kohl's, NAPA, Subaru, Toyota
123	WI 28, rd A, Sheboygan, **E** [gas] **Citgo/dsl/24hr**, Mobil/McDonald's/dsl, [food] Coldstone, Jimmy John's, Perkins, Qdoba, Rocky Rococo's Pizza, Starbucks, Subway, Wendy's, [lodging] AmericInn, Holiday Inn Express, [other] Harley-Davidson/Cruisers Burgers, **Walmart/Subway**, **W** [food] Arby's, Buffalo Wild Wings, Chili's, Starbucks, [other] $Tree, AT&T, Best Buy, GNC, Home Depot, Jo-Ann Fabrics, PetSmart, Target, TJ Maxx
120	rds OK, V, Sheboygan, **E** [gas] **KwikTrip/dsl, Love's/Hardee's/Subway/dsl/scales/24hr**, [food] Parkside Rest., [lodging] Sleep Inn, [other] camping, Nissan, to Kohler-Andrae SP, VW, **W** Horn's RV Ctr
116	rd AA, Foster Rd, Oostburg, **W** [gas] Sunoco, [food] Judi's Place Rest., Pizza Ranch, Subway, [other] Piggly Wiggly/gas
113	WI 32 N, rd LL, Cedar Grove, **W** [gas] **Citgo/dsl/repair**, Mobil/dsl, Sunoco/Fueling Depot, [food] Country Grove Rest.(1mi), Sunrise Rest., [lodging] Lakeview Motel
107	rd D, Belgium, **E** [lodging] Lake Church Inn/grill, [other] Harrington Beach SP, **W** [gas] **BP/McDonald's/dsl/24hr**, How-Dea Trkstp/Hobo's Korner Kitchen/dsl/scales, Mobil/dsl/24hr, [food] Kyote's Grill, Subway, [lodging] Belgium Inn, [other] repair, USPO
100	WI 32 S, WI 84 W, Port Washington, **E** [gas] BP/dsl, Mobil, [food] Arby's, McDonald's, Pizza Hut, Subway, [lodging] Country Inn&Suites, Holiday Inn(2mi), [other] Allen-Edmonds Shoes, Goodyear/auto, Piggly Wiggly, True Value, vet, **W** [lodging] Hundred Mile House Rest.
97	(from nb, exits left), WI 57, Fredonia
96	WI 33, to Saukville, **E** [food] Culver's(1mi), [other] Advance Parts,

WI

= gas = food = lodging = other = rest stop

INTERSTATE 43 Cont'd

GRAFTON

96 Continued
Best Hardware, Buick/Cadillac/Chevrolet, Camping World RV Ctr, Chrysler/Dodge/Jeep, Ford, O'Reilly Parts, Piggly Wiggly, Walgreens, Walmart, W Exxon/McDonald's, KwikTrip/dsl, Domino's, DQ, Lam's Chinese, Papa Murphy's, Subway, Taco Bell, Motel 6, repair/tires

93 WI 32 N, WI 57 S, Grafton, E BP, vet

92 WI 60, rd Q, Grafton, E BP/dsl, GhostTown Rest., Water St Rest., Hampton Inn, TownePlace Suites, W Citgo/DQ/dsl, Charcoal Grill, Firehouse Subs, Noodles&Co, Qdoba, Starbucks, Subway, Comfort Inn, ALDI, AT&T, Costco/gas, Dick's, Home Depot, H, Kohl's, Meijer, Michael's, PetSmart, Target, Verizon

89 rd C, Cedarburg, W Mobil/dsl, H

85 WI 57 S, WI 167 W, Mequon Rd, W BP, Mobil, Shell, Caribou Coffee, Chancery Rest., Cousins Subs, Culver's, First Watch Cafe, Jimmy John's, Leonardo's Pizza, McDonald's, Noodles&Co, Panera Bread, Papa Murphy's, Pizza Hut, Starbucks, Taco Bell, Chalet Motel, Ace Hardware, AT&T, H, Marshall's, Metro Mkt, Sendik's Foods, Verizon, vet, Walgreens

83 rd W, Port Washington Rd(from nb only)

82b a WI 32 S, WI 100, Brown Deer Rd, E BP, Mobil/dsl, Baskin-Robbins, Benji's Deli, Jose's Blue Sombrero, Maxfield's Pancakes, McDonald's, Noodles&Co, Peking Chef, Qdoba, Starbucks, Subway, Toppers Pizza, Best Buy, CVS Drug, GNC, Land's Inlet, Walgreens

WI

80 Good Hope Rd, E Mobil, Dr Dawg, Jimmy John's, King's Wok, Samurai Japanese, Fairfield Inn, Residence Inn, Pick'n Save, to Cardinal Stritch U

78 Silver Spring Dr, E BP, Mobil, Arby's, Bar Louie, Boston Mkt, Buffalo Wild Wings, CA Pizza Kitchen, Cheesecake Factory, Cousins Subs, Devon Steaks, Fiddleheads Coffee, Five Guys, Kopp's Custard, McDonald's, Panera Bread, Papa Murphy's, Perkins, Potbelly, Qdoba, Taco Bell, La Quinta, Motel 6, AT&T, Barnes&Noble, Batteries+Bulbs, Goodyear/auto, Kohl's, Nissan, Trader Joe's, USPO, Verizon, Walgreens, W H

BROADWAY

77b a (from nb), E Anchorage Rest., Solly's Grille, Holiday Inn

76b a WI 57, WI 190, Green Bay Ave, E Home Depot, W BP/dsl, Burger King

75 Atkinson Ave, Keefe Ave, E Mobil, W BP

74 Locust St

73c North Ave(rom sb), E Wendy's, W McDonald's

73b North Ave(from nb), downtown

73a WI 145 E, 4th St(exits left from sb), Broadway, downtown

72c Wells St, E Doubletree, Hilton, Civic Ctr, H, museum

72b (from sb), I-94 W, to madison

72a (310c from nb, exits left from sb), I-794 E, I-94 W to Madison, to Lakefront, downtown

311 WI 59, National Ave, 6th St, downtown

312a Lapham Blvd, Mitchell St, W BP, Citgo

312b (from nb), Becher St, Lincoln Ave

314a Holt Ave, E SP Mart/dsl, Applebee's, Arby's, China King, Jimmy John's, Little Caesar's, Rosati's Pizza, Starbucks, Subway, Taco Bell, Wendy's, AutoZone, Family$, Home Depot, Pick'n Save Foods, Piggly Wiggly, Target, vet, W H, to Alverno Coll

314b Howard Ave

10b I-94 S to Chicago, E

9b a WI 241, 27th St, E Flying Eagle, Saifron/dsl, Arby's, Benny's Cafe, Dunkin', Famous Dave's, Sonic, Subway, Suburban Motel, AutoZone, Subaru, USPO, Walgreens, W Buffalo Wild Wings, Chipotle Mexican, Denny's, Jimmy John's, McDonald's, New China, Omega Rest.,

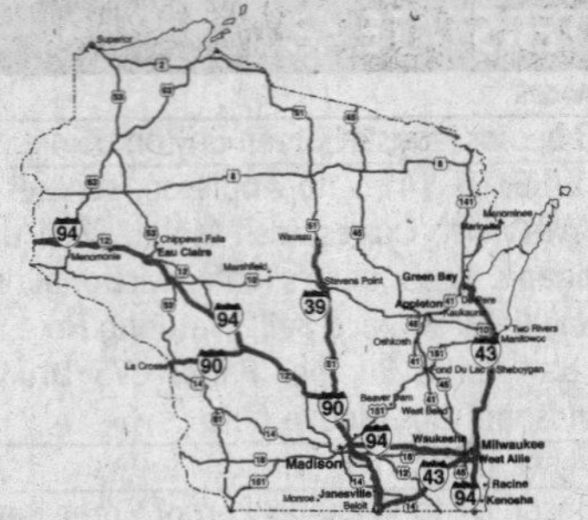

9b a Continued
Panda Express, Papa John's, Rich's Cakes, Starbucks, Taco Bell, Wong's Wok, Zebb's Rest, Quality Inn, Rodeway Inn, $Tree, AAA, Advance Parts/Meineke, AutoZone, Chevrolet, CVS Drug, Firestone/auto, Ford, Goodyear/auto, H, Kohl's, Marshall's, Michael's, Pick'n Save Foods, Ross, Walgreens, Walmart

8a WI 36, Loomis Rd, E BP/dsl, Citgo, Los Mariachi's, ALDI, Walgreens, W Griddler's Cafe, to Alverno Coll

7 60th St, E Speedway/dsl, Culver's, Subway, Harley-Davidson, Meijer/dsl, W Speedway/dsl

5b 76th St(from sb, no EZ return), E Speedway/dsl, Applebee's, Bakers Square, Burger King, Carrabba's Italian, Chick-fil-A, Cousins Subs, El Beso, Habaneros, Jersey Mike's, Jimmy John's, Kopp's Burgers, Kyoto Japanese, Longhorn Steaks, McDonald's, Noodles&Co, Old Country Buffet, Olive Garden, Panda Express, Panera Bread, Qdoba, Red Lobster, Red Robin, Ruby Tuesday, Starbucks, TGIFriday's, Topper's Pizza, Traditional Pancake House, Wendy's, $Tree, AT&T, Barnes&Noble, Best Buy, Firestone/auto, Goodyear/auto, JC Penney, Jo-Ann Fabrics, Macy's, Midas, PetCo, PetSmart, Sendik's Food Mkt, TJ Maxx, Tuesday Morning, Verizon, Walmart, W Arby's, Pizza Hut, Subway, Advance Parts, Family$, Pick'n Save Foods, USPO, Walgreens

5a WI 24 W, Forest Home Ave, E Citgo/dsl, Outback Steaks, Portillo's, Boerner Botanical Gardens, Fresh Thyme Mkt, Kohl's, Marshall's, Ross, Welk's Auto

61 (4 from sb), I-894/US 45 N, I-43/US 45 S

60 US 45 S, WI 100, 108th St(exits left from sb), E BP, Citgo, Marathon, Mobil, A&W, Amore Italian, Ann's Italian, Burger King, Chipotle Mexican, Confucious Chinese, Cousins Subs, Culver's, Dunkin', George Webb Rest., McDonald's, Noodles&Co, Open Flame Grill, Papa Murphy's, Starbucks, Subway, Taco Bell, $Tree, AutoZone, Chevrolet, O'Reilly Parts, Pick'n Save, USPO, vet, Walgreens, W Andy's/dsl, Denny's, Forum Rest., McDonald's, Organ Piper Pizza, Subway, ALDI, Goodyear/auto, NAPA, Nissan, vet, Walgreens, Walmart/Subway

59 WI 100, Layton Ave(from nb, exits left), same as 60, Hales Corner, W BP/Cousins Subs

BIG BEND

57 Moorland Rd, E KwikTrip/dsl, Applebee's, Stonefire Pizza Co, TX Roadhouse, Zaffiro's Pizza, La Quinta, Costco/dsl, W Speedway/dsl, Arby's, Buffalo Wild Wings, Cocina Real, Panera Bread, Papa John's, Point Burger, Holiday Inn Express, Firestone/auto, GNC, Michael's, Target

54 rd Y, Racine Ave, E BP/dsl, KwikTrip, Cousins Subs, Culver's, McDonald's, Piggly Wiggly, Walgreens

50 WI 164, Big Bend, W KwikTrip/dsl/e85, McDonald's, Subway

44mm Fox River

43 WI 83, Mukwonago, E BP/dsl, ALDI, Chevrolet, Chrysler/Dodge/Jeep, Home Depot, H, Walmart, W Citgo, Boneyard Grille, Chen's Kitchen, Domino's, DQ, Starbucks, Taco Bell, Baymont Inn

EAST TROY

INTERSTATE 43 Cont'd

Exit #	Services
38	WI 20, East Troy, W Pilot/Road Ranger/Subway/dsl/24hr, Shell/McDonald's, Ale Sta Rest., Cousins Subs, Dos Amigos, Genoa Pizza, LD's BBQ, Roma's Ristorante, $General, Carquest
36	WI 120, East Troy, E Alpine Valley Resort, W Quality Inn Suites
33	Bowers Rd, E to Alpine Valley Music Theatre
32mm	rest area both lanes, **full facilities, litter barrels, petwalk, , , vending**
29	WI 11, Elkhorn, W fairgrounds
27b a	US 12, to Lake Geneva, E
25	WI 67, Elkhorn, E Love's/Hardee's/dsl/scales/24hr, Mobil/dsl, AmericInn, Buick/Chevrolet/GMC, Chrysler/Dodge/Jeep, vet, W Speedway/dsl/24hr, Burger King, Subway, Hampton Inn(2mi), Kunes Country RV Ctr
21	WI 50, Delavan, E Brodie's Beef, Chili's, China 1, Culver's, Domino's, Jimmy John's, Panera Bread, Papa Murphy's, Starbucks, Subway, Yoshi Japanese, ALDI, AT&T, F&F Tires, Kohl's, Lowe's, PetSmart, Verizon, Walmart, W Mobil/Dunkin'/dsl, KFC, Little Caesar's, McDonald's, Perkins, Wendy's, Comfort Suites, Super 8, $Tree, AutoZone, Cadillac/Chevrolet, Ford/Lincoln, GNC, NAPA, O'Reilly Parts, Piggly Wiggly, Walgreens
17	rd X, Delavan, Darien, W BP/dsl
15	US 14, Darien, E Mobil/dsl, West Wind Diner
6	WI 140, Clinton, E Citgo/Subway/TCBY/dsl, $General, Ford
2	rd X, Hart Rd, E Butterfly Fine Dining
1b a	I-90, E to Chicago, W to Madison, S Mobil/McDonald's, Pilot/Taco Bell/dsl/scales/24hr, Shell, Speedway/dsl, Applebee's, Arby's, Buffalo Wild Wings, Culver's, Doc's Rest., Dunkin', Jimmy John's, Little Caesar's, Little Mexico, Noodles&Co, Qdoba, Road Dawg Rest., Starbucks, Subway, Wendy's, Baymont Inn, Fairfield Inn, Hampton Inn, Holiday Inn Express, Home2 Suites, Quality Inn, Rodeway Inn, Super 8, $Tree, ALDI, AT&T, Buick/GMC, Cadillac/Chevrolet, GNC, Menards, NTB, O'Reilly Parts, Walmart
0	exit 185 in Beloit., I-43 begins/ends on I-90

CLINTON

INTERSTATE 90

Exit #	Services
187mm	Wisconsin/Illinois state line, I-90 & I-39 run together nb.
187mm	**full facilities, info, litter barrels, petwalk, , , vending, Welcome Ctr wb**
185b	I-43 N, to Milwaukee
185a	WI 81, Beloit, S Mobil/McDonald's/dsl, Pilot/Taco Bell/dsl/scales/24hr, Shell, Speedway/dsl, Applebee's, Arby's, Buffalo Wild Wings, Culver's, Doc's Rest., Dunkin', Jimmy John's, Little Caesar's, Little Mexico, Noodles&Co, Papa Murphy's, Qdoba, Road Dawg Rest., Starbucks, Subway, Wendy's, Baymont Inn, Fairfield Inn, Hampton Inn, Holiday Inn Express, Home2 Suites, Quality Inn, Rodeway Inn, Super 8, $Tree, ALDI, AT&T, Buick/GMC, Cadillac/Chevrolet, GNC, Menards, NTB, O'Reilly Parts, Walmart
183	Shopiere Rd, rd S, to Shopiere, S , repair
181mm	weigh sta, wb
177	WI 11 W, Janesville, S KwikTrip/dsl, S WI , to Blackhawk Tec Coll
175b a	WI 11 E, Janesville, to Delavan, N BP/Subway/dsl, Baymont Inn, , vet, S Lannon Stone Motel, city park
171c b	US 14, WI 26, Janesville, N TA/Mobil/Wendy's/dsl/scales/24hr, Coldstone, Cozumel Mexican, Golden Corral, IHOP, Starbucks, Subway, TX Roadhouse, Holiday Inn Express, Microtel, ALDI, Best Buy, GNC, Home Depot, Michael's,

JANESVILLE

Exit #	Services
171c b	Continued NTB, Old Navy, PetCo, Staples, TJ Maxx, S Citgo, Exxon/dsl, KwikTrip/dsl, Applebee's, Arby's, Buffalo Wild Wings, Burger King, Chipotle, ChuckeCheese, Culver's, Dunkin', Famous Dave's, Fazoli's, Fuji Steaks, Hacienda Real, Hardee's, Jersey Mike's, Jimmy John's, KFC, Mac's Pizza, McDonald's, Milio's Sandwiches, Milwaukee Grill, Mo's Taasbag, Noodles&Co, Olive Garden, Panda Express, Panera Bread, Papa Murphy's, Peking Chinese, Pizza Hut, Prime Quarter Steaks, Qdoba Mexican, Red Robin, Road Dawg Eatery, Subway, Taco Bell, Taco John's, Tacos Neno, Toppers Pizza, Quality Inn, Super 8, TownePlace Suites, $Tree, ALDI, AT&T, AutoZone, Big Lots, CarQuest, CVS Drug, Dick's Sports, F&F, Festival Foods, Ford/Lincoln, Harley-Davidson, Hobby Lobby, , Hyundai, JoAnne Fabric, Kohl's, mall, Mazda, Menards, Nissan/Kia/Subaru, O'Reilly Parts, Target, Toyota/Scion, USPO, Verizon, Walgreens
171a	WI 26, N BP/dsl, Cracker Barrel, Hampton Inn, Motel 6, Ramada/rest., Chrysler/Dodge/Jeep, Sam's Club, URGENT CARE, VW, Walgreens, Walmart, S same as 171c b
168mm	**full facilities, litter barrels, petwalk, , , eb, vending**
163.5mm	Rock River
163	WI 59, Edgerton, to Milton, N Mobil/Subway/dsl, Shell/Dunkin Donuts/Taco John's/dsl, Blue Gilly's Rest., Culver's, McDonald's, WI Cheese Store, Quality Inn, KOA, marina
160	US 51S, WI 73, WI 106, Oaklawn Academy, to Deerfield, S BP/dsl/scales/rest./24hr/@, Creek View Camping(2mi),
156	US 51N, to Stoughton, S Coachman's Inn/rest.,
147	rd N, Cottage Grove, to Stoughton, S BP/Arby's/dsl, Road Ranger/Subway/dsl/scales, Roady's, Badgerland Camping (2mi), Lake Kegonsa SP
146mm	weigh sta eb
142b a	(142a exits left from wb)US 12, US 18, Madison, to Cambridge, N BP/dsl, Roadhouse Rest., Best Value Inn, Magnuson Grand Hotel, casino, Harley-Davidson, S Citgo/dsl, Phillips 66/Arby's/dsl, Shell/dsl, Denny's, Days Inn, Sleep Inn, , Menards, UWI
45	I-94 W, to St Paul, I-90 E and I-94 E run together for 93 miles
43	US 12, WI 16, Tomah, N BP/dsl, KwikTrip/dsl/24hr, Burnstadt's Café, DQ, Daybreak Inn, Rest Well Motel, Burnstadt's Mkt, , vet
41	WI 131, Tomah, to Wilton, N KwikTrip/dsl/24hr, Mobil/dsl, Burnstadts Cafe, Daybreak Inn, vet
28	WI 16, Sparta, Ft McCoy, N BP/diner/dsl/scales, Best Western,
25	WI 27, Sparta, to Melvina, N Cenex/Arby's/dsl, KwikTrip/dsl, Mobil/Taco Bell, Shell/dsl, Burger King, Culver's, DQ, KFC, McDonald's, Pizza Hut, Sparta Rest., Subway, Country Inn, Super 8, $General, $Tree, Buick/Chevrolet, Family$, Ford, Hansens IGA, , O'Reilly Parts, Walgreens, Walmart/Subway
22mm	**full facilities, litter barrels, petwalk, , , wb, vending**
20mm	**full facilities, litter barrels, petwalk, , , eb, vending**
15	WI 162, Bangor, to Coon Valley, N gas
12	rd C, W Salem, N Cenex/cafe/dsl/24hr, Coulee Region RV Ctr, NAPA, Neshonoc Camping, S BP/Subway/dsl, AmericInn, Peterbilt
10mm	weigh sta eb
5	WI 16, La Crosse, N Arby's, BA Burrito, Buffalo Wild Wings, Ciatti's Italian, Coldstone, Manny's Mexican, Outback Steaks, Baymont Inn, Hampton Inn, Microtel, $Tree, ALDI, Freightliner, Home Depot, Walmart/Subway,

TOMAH

LA CROSSE

WI

LA CROSSE

INTERSTATE 90 Cont'd

5 Continued
Woodman's Foods/gas/lube, S Kwik Trip/dsl/24hr, Bamboo House, Burracho's Mexican Grill, Carlos O'Kelly's, ChuckeCheese, Culver's, Fazoli's, HuHot Grill, Jimmy John's, McDonald's, Olive Garden, Perkins, Starbucks, TGIFriday's, TX Roadhouse, Holiday Inn Express, Barnes&Noble, Best Buy, Chevrolet, Dick's, F&F, Ford/Lincoln, Hobby Lobby, H, JC Penney, Kohl's, Michael's, Target, Walgreens

4 US 53 N, WI 16, to WI 157, La Crosse, N Harley-Davidson, S Kwik Trip, TO, Applebee's, Burger King, Caribou Coffee, China Inn, Cousins Subs, Famous Dave's BBQ, Grizzly's Rest., Ground Round, Panera Bread, Papa Murphy's, Red Lobster, Rococo's Pizza, Shogun Hibachi, Subway, Taco Bell, Wendy's, Comfort Inn, Festival Food/24hr, GNC, Goodyear/auto, H, La Crosse River St Trail, Office Depot, Old Navy, PetCo, PetSmart, Sam's Club, Tires+, TJ Maxx, Verizon

3 US 53 S, WI 35, to La Crosse, S Clark/dsl, Kwik Trip, Econolodge, Hardee's, KFC, La Crosse Rest., McDonald's, North Country Steaks, Perkins, Pizza Hut, Subway, Best Value Inn, Best Western, Motel 6, Quality Inn, Settle Inn, Super 8, to Great River St Trail, U-Haul, Viterbo Coll, Walgreens

2.5mm Black River

2 rd B, French Island, N , S BP/dsl, Days Inn/rest., Quillin's Mkt

1mm **full facilities, info, litter barrels, petwalk, vending, Welcome Ctr eb**

0mm Wisconsin/Minnesota state line, Mississippi River

WI

INTERSTATE 94

349mm Wisconsin/Illinois state line, weigh sta nb

348.5mm weigh sta wb

347 WI 165, rd Q, Lakeview Pkwy, E **Welcome Ctr nb, full facilities, litter barrels, petwalk,** BP/dsl, Chancery Rest., Culver's, McDonald's, Radisson, Old Navy, Premium Outlets/famous brands

345 rd C, E Holiday Inn Express(1mi)

345mm Des Plaines River

344 WI 50, Lake Geneva, to Kenosha, E Buffalo Wild Wings, Cheddar's, Cousins Subs, Dickey's BBQ, Famous Dave's, Mobil/dsl, Noodles&Co, Olive Garden, Panda Express, Perkins, Pizza Hut, Shell/Dunkin Donuts/dsl, Sparti's Gyros, Starbucks, Subway, Tuscany Bistro, TX Roadhouse, White Castle, Woodman's/gas, Candlewood Suites, Holiday Inn Express, La Quinta, Super 8, AT&T, Best Buy, Chevrolet, Dick's, GNC, H, JC Penney, PetSmart, Target, Verizon, Walgreens, W BP/dsl, Speedway/dsl, Arby's, Birchwood Grill, Cracker Barrel, KFC, McDonald's, Phoenix Rest., Wendy's, Best Western, Comfort Inn, Country Inn&Suites, Hampton Inn, Value Inn, BratStop Cheese Store, CarMax, Honda, Nissan, Subaru, Toyota/Scion

342 WI 158, to Kenosha, E Harley-Davidson, W antiques

340 WI 142, rd S, to Kenosha, E Kenosha TP/BP/Subway/dsl/E85/LP/scales/24hr, H, W Mars Cheese Castle Rest., Oasis Inn, Fun Time RV Ctr, to Bong RA

339 rd E

337 rd KR, to Mt Pleasant, W Apple Holler Rest./orchard

335 WI 11, to Mt Pleasant, Burlington, to Racine

333 WI 20, Waterford, to Racine, E KwikTrip/dsl/24hr, Shell/Cousins Subs/dsl, Burger King, McDonald's, Days Inn, Excel Inn, Holiday Inn Express, H, Toyota/Scion, W Citgo/Wendy's/dsl/24hr, Petro/Mobil/Iron Skillet/dsl/scales/24hr/@, Chicken'n Waffles, Culver's, Route 20 Outhouse Grill, Subway, Quality Inn, Burlington RV Ctr, visitor info

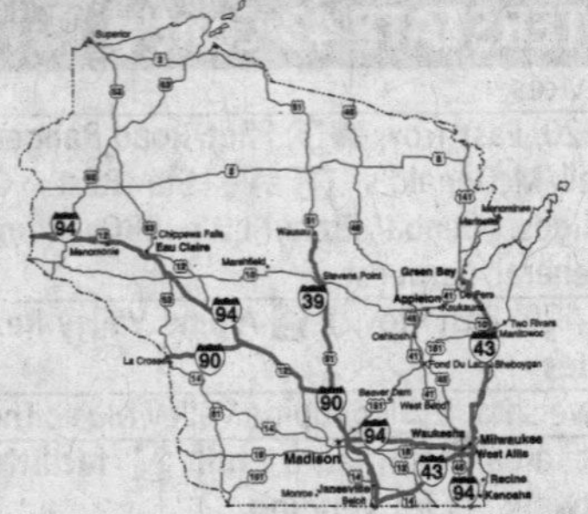

329 rd K, Thompsonville, to Racine, E Pilot/Arby's/Subway/dsl/scales/24hr, A&W, dsl repair

328mm weigh sta eb

327 rd G, W fireworks

326 7 Mile Rd, E BP, Mobil/dsl, Jellystone Park, W Seven Mile Fair

325 WI 241 N(from wb), to 27th St

322 WI 100, to Ryan Rd, E KwikTrip/dsl, McDonald's, Wendy's, dsl repair, W Love's/Denny's/dsl/LP/scales/RV dump/24hr, Mobil, Pilot/Subway/dsl/LP/scales/24hr, Shell/A&W/KFC/dsl, Arby's, Cousins Subs, Dish Bakery, Dunkin Donuts, Perkins, Starbucks, Yen Hwa Chinese, Staybridge Suites, Value Inn, AutoZone, Blue Beacon, Freightliner/repair, H, Pick'n Save, vet, Walgreens

321 Drexel Ave

320 rd BB, Rawson Ave, E BP/7-11/dsl, Mobil, Applebee's, Burger King, La Quinta

319 rd ZZ, College Ave, E Shell/Subway, Speedway/dsl, Branded Steer Rest., McDonald's, Candlewood Suites, Comfort Suites, Country Inn&Suites, Crowne Plaza, Days Inn, EconoLodge, Fairfield Inn, Hampton Inn, Holiday Inn Express, MainStay Suites, Motel 6, Red Roof Inn, Burlington Coats, W Royal

318 WI 119, E

317 I-43, I-894(from wb)

316 I-43 S, I-894 W(I-94 exits left from eb), to Beloit, E Clark/dsl, Martino's Hotdogs

312b a Becher St, Mitchell St, Lapham Blvd, W BP, Citgo

310a 13th St(from eb), E H

310b I-43 N, to Green Bay

310c I-794 E, E Hilton, Lake Michigan Port of Entry, to downtown

309b 26th St, 22nd St, Clybourn St, St Paul Ave, N H, to Marquette U

309a 35th St, N URGENT CARE

308c b US 41

308a VA Ctr, S Miller Park

307b 68th-70th St, Hawley Rd

307a 68th-70th St

306 WI 181, to 84th St, N H, S Olympic Training Facility

305b I-41 N, US 45 N, to Fond du Lac, N H

305a I-894 S, I-41 S, US 45 S, to Chicago, S to

304b a WI 100, N 7-11, Amstar/dsl, BP, Shell/dsl, Cousins Subs, Domino's, Ghengis Khan BBQ, Habanero's Mexican, HoneyBaked Cafe, Jimmy John's, Mo's Irish Grill, Peony Chinese, Qdoba, Rococo's, Starbucks, Subway, Taco Bell, Crowne Plaza, Forty Winks Inn, H, zoo, S Amstar, BP/dsl, Speedway/dsl, Culver's, DQ, Fazoli's, McDonald's, Pallas Rest., Starbucks, Toppers Pizza, Wendy's, Days Inn, ALDI, Midas, O'Reilly Parts, Sam's Club, U-Haul, Walgreens

301b a Moorland Rd, N BP/dsl, Mobil, Bakers Square, Bravo Italiano, Buffalo Wild Wings, Chipotle, CiCi's, Cooper's Hawk, Culver's, Five Guys, Fleming's Rest., Food Court, Fuddrucker's, Hooters, Jamba Juice, Jersey Mike's,

 = gas = food = lodging = other = rest stop

INTERSTATE 94 Cont'd

301b a Continued
Marty's Pizza/subs, McDonald's, Mitchell's Fish Mkt, Noodles&Co, Original Pancake House, Qdoba, Red Robin, Starbucks, Stir Crazy, Subway, TGIFriday's, Courtyard, Sheraton, TownePlace Suites, AT&T, Barnes&Noble, CVS Drug, F&F Tire, Firestone/auto, Fresh Mkt Foods, Goodyear/auto, JC Penney, Jo-Ann Fabrics, mall, Metro Mkt, Michael's, Office Depot, PetCo, PetSmart, SteinMart, TJ Maxx, Verizon, vet, Walgreens, World Mkt, S Champp's Grill, Outback Steaks, Panera Bread, Starbucks, Best Western Midway, Brookfield Suites, Country Inn&Suites, Residence Inn, golf, Pick'n Save Foods, Walgreens, Walmart

297 WI 164 S, US 18, rd JJ, Blue Mound Rd, Barker Rd, N BP, Clark, Applebee's, BoneFish Grill, Boston Mkt, Brookfield Rest., Bullwinkle's Rest., Carrabba's, Chili's, ChuckECheese's, Cousins Subs, Emperors Kitchen, George Webb Rest., Hom Woodfired Grill, Jimmy John's, Jose's Mexican, KFC, Kopp's Custard, Laredo's Mexican, Mama Mia's, McDonald's, Melting Pot, Olive Garden, Perkins, Potbelly, Starbucks, Subway, DoubleTree, Extended Stay America, Hampton Inn, La Quinta, Motel 6, Quality Inn, $Tree, Acura, Advance Parts, ALDI, Best Buy, GNC, Hobby Lobby, H, Lexus/Mazda/VW, Meineke, Metro Mkt, S Clark, PDQ, Arby's, Burger King, Chancery Rest., Cousin's Subs, Culver's, Famous Dave's BBQ, La Fuente Mexican, McDonald's, Meiji Chinese, New China, Oscar's Burgers, Papa Murphy's, Sonic, Starbucks, Subway, Taco Bell, Topper's Pizza, TX Roadhouse, Wendy's, Baymont Inn, Extended Stay America, Super 8, AT&T, Buick/GMC, Cadillac, CarMax, Chevrolet, Farm&Fleet, Firestone/auto, Ford, Home Depot, Honda, Hyundai, Infiniti/Maserati/Mercedes/Porsche, Jaguar/Land Rover/Volvo, Kia, Kohl's, Menards, Midas, Nissan, Sam's Club, st patrol, Subaru, Target, Tires+, Walgreens, Woodman's/gas

PEWAUKEE

295 rd F, to WI 74, Waukesha, N KwikTrip/dsl, Jimmy John's, Marriott, S H, to Carroll U

294 WI 164, rd J S, to Waukesha, N Mobil/Subway/dsl, Machine Shed Rest., Thunder Bay Grille, Holiday Inn, Wildwood Lodge, S Expo Ctr, Peterbilt

293c WI 16 W, from wb, Pewaukee, N GE Plant

293b a rd T, Wausheka, Pewaukee, S KwikTrip/dsl, Mobil, Arby's, Asian Fusion, Canyon City Wood Grill, Cousins Subs, Culver's, Denny's, Dunkin Donuts, Feng's Kitchen, Jimmy John's, McDonald's, Mr. Wok, Papa Murphy's, Qdoba, Rococo's Pizza, Spring City Rest., Subway, Taco Amigo, Topper's Pizza, Weissgerber's Gasthaus Rest., Wendy's, Best Western, $Tree, AutoZone, CVS Drug, Firestone/auto, GNC, Goodharvest Mkt, Jo-Ann Fabrics, Office Depot, Pick'n Save Foods, Verizon, Walgreens

291 rd G, rd TT, N Country Springs Inn

290 rd SS, Pewaukee

DELAFIELD

287 WI 83, Hartland, to Wales, N Applebee's, Five Guys, Hardee's, McDonald's, Noodles&Co, Panera Bread, Perkins, Qdoba, Starbucks, Water St Brewery/rest., Country Pride Inn, Holiday Inn Express, Albrecht's Mkt, Best Buy, GNC, Kohl's, Marshalls, Verizon, Walgreens, S BP, PDQ/dsl/24hr, Burger King, Coldstone, DQ, Jimmy John's, Marty's Pizza, Pacific Asian Bistro, Pizza Hut, Rocky Rococo Pizza, StoneCreek Coffee, Subway, La Quinta, $Tree, Ace Hardware, Home Depot, PetCo, Target, Tires+, vet, Walmart/Subway

285 rd C, Delafield, N BP/dsl, Mobil/deli, Delafield Hotel, to St John's Military Academy, S to Kettle Moraine SF

283 rd P, to Sawyer Rd

282 WI 67, Dousman, to Oconomowoc, N KwikTrip/dsl, Mobil,

282 Continued
Chili's, Cousins Subs, Culver's, Eat Smart Cafe, Feng's Kitchen, Jimmy John's, Pizza Hut, Qdoba, Quiznos, Rococo's Pizza, Rosati's Pizza, Starbucks, Stone Creek Coffee, Subway, Hilton Garden, Olympia Resort, Ace Hardware, ALDI, AT&T, Brennan's Mkt, Ford, GNC, K-Mart, Pick'n Save, vet, Walgreens, S Staybridge Suites, Harley-Davidson, H, Old World WI HS(13mi), to Kettle Morraine SF(8mi)

277 Willow Glen Rd(from eb, no return)

275 rd F, Ixonia, to Sullivan, N Mobil/dsl, Concord Gen Store, S camping

267 WI 26, Johnson Creek, to Watertown, N BP/McDonald's/dsl, Shell/dsl/rest./scales/24hr, Arby's, Hi-Way Harry's Cafe, Comfort Suites, Days Inn, Goodyear/auto, Johnson Creek Outlet Ctr/famous brands, Old Navy, S KwikTrip/dsl, Culver's, Qdoba, Starbucks, Subway, Taco Bell, H, Kohl's, Menards, to Aztalan SP

266mm Rock River

264mm **full facilities, litter barrels, petwalk, wb, vending**

263mm Crawfish River

261mm **full facilities, litter barrels, petwalk, eb, vending**

259 WI 89, Lake Mills, to Waterloo, N Mobil/rest/dsl/24hr, Best Value Inn, truck repair, S BP/dsl/E85, KwikTrip/dsl, Jimmy John's, McDonald's, Pizza Pit, Subway, Pyramid Motel/RV park, Ace Hardware, Buick/Chevrolet, Country Campers, to Aztalan SP, URGENT CARE, vet, Walgreens

250 WI 73, Deerfield, to Marshall

244 rd n, Sun Prairie, Cottage Grove, N BP/dsl, Subway, S BP/dsl, KwikTrip, Arby's

240 I-90 E. I-94 and I-90 merge for 93 miles. See I-90, exits 48-138.

138a I-94, E to Milwaukee, W to La Crosse(exits left from eb), I-90 W and I-94 W run together for 93 miles.

138b WI 30, Madison

135c b US 151, Madison, N BP/dsl, Erin's Pub, Happy Wok, Milio's Sandwiches, Uno Pizzaria, Cambria Suites, Courtyard, Fairfield Inn, GrandStay Suites, Holiday Inn, Staybridge Suites, Buick/GMC, Chrysler/Dodge/Jeep, Ford, Honda, Hyundai, Kia, Mazda, Nissan, Subaru, Toyota/Scion

MADISON

135a US 151, Madison, N Chick-fil-A, S BP, Citgo, Mobil, Shell, Tesla EVC, Applebee's, Arby's, Arod's TexMex, Buffalo Wild Wings, Chili's, Chipotle Mexican, Cracker Barrel, Culver's, Denny's, Dickey's BBQ, DoLittle's Woodfire Grill, Dumpling House, Hardee's, Hooters, IHOP, Jimmy John's, McDonald's, Moka, Noodles&Co, Olive Garden, Outback Steaks, Panera Bread, Perkins, Pizza Hut, Popeyes, Potbelly, Qdoba, Red Lobster, Red Robin, Starbucks, Sumo Steaks, Taco Bell, Takumi Japanese, TGIFriday's, Toppers's Pizza, TX Roadhouse, Wendy's, Best Western, Comfort Inn, Crowne Plaza Hotel/rest., EconoLodge, Hampton Inn, Howard Johnson, Microtel, Motel 6, Premier, Quality Inn, Red Roof Inn, Residence Inn, Rodeway Inn, Super 8, $Tree, ALDI, AT&T, Barnes&Noble, Best Buy, Burlington Coats, city park, Dick's, Firestone/auto, Goodyear/auto, Gordman's, Hobby Lobby, Home Depot, Hy-Vee Foods, JC Penney, JoAnn Fabrics, Kohl's, Marshalls, Michaels, Office Depot, Old Navy, PetSmart, st patrol, Target, Verizon

132 US 51, Madison, De Forest, N Shell/Pinecone Rest/dsl/24hr, Gander RV Ctr, S TA/Subway/Popeyes/dsl/scales/24hr/@, Freightliner/GMC/Volvo/White, Goodyear, Peterbilt, WI RV World

131 WI 19, Waunakee, N Kwik Trip/dsl, Mobil/dsl, Speedway/dsl, A&W, McDonald's, Rodeside Grill, Days Inn,

WI

= gas = food = lodging = other = rest stop

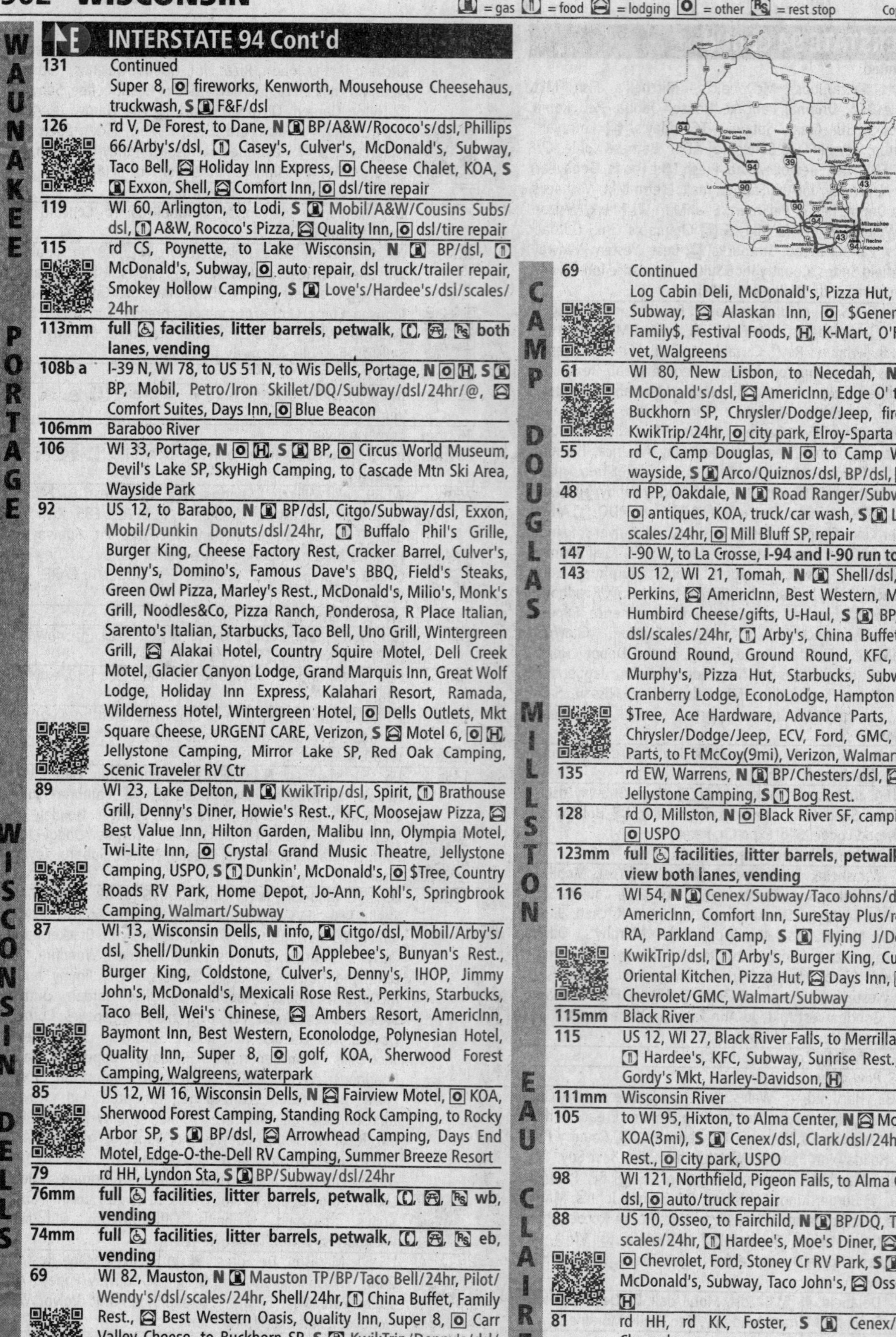

INTERSTATE 94 Cont'd

WAUNAKEE

131 Continued
Super 8, fireworks, Kenworth, Mousehouse Cheesehaus, truckwash, S F&F/dsl

126 rd V, De Forest, to Dane, N BP/A&W/Rococo's/dsl, Phillips 66/Arby's/dsl, Casey's, Culver's, McDonald's, Subway, Taco Bell, Holiday Inn Express, Cheese Chalet, KOA, S Exxon, Shell, Comfort Inn, dsl/tire repair

119 WI 60, Arlington, to Lodi, S Mobil/A&W/Cousins Subs/dsl, A&W, Rococo's Pizza, Quality Inn, dsl/tire repair

115 rd CS, Poynette, to Lake Wisconsin, N BP/dsl, McDonald's, Subway, auto repair, dsl truck/trailer repair, Smokey Hollow Camping, S Love's/Hardee's/dsl/scales/24hr

113mm **full facilities, litter barrels, petwalk, both lanes, vending**

PORTAGE

108b a I-39 N, WI 78, to US 51 N, to Wis Dells, Portage, N H, S BP, Mobil, Petro/Iron Skillet/DQ/Subway/dsl/24hr/@, Comfort Suites, Days Inn, Blue Beacon

106mm Baraboo River

106 WI 33, Portage, N H, S BP, Circus World Museum, Devil's Lake SP, SkyHigh Camping, to Cascade Mtn Ski Area, Wayside Park

92 US 12, to Baraboo, N BP/dsl, Citgo/Subway/dsl, Exxon, Mobil/Dunkin Donuts/dsl/24hr, Buffalo Phil's Grille, Burger King, Cheese Factory Rest, Cracker Barrel, Culver's, Denny's, Domino's, Famous Dave's BBQ, Field's Steaks, Green Owl Pizza, Marley's Rest., McDonald's, Milio's, Monk's Grill, Noodles&Co, Pizza Ranch, Ponderosa, R Place Italian, Sarento's Italian, Starbucks, Taco Bell, Uno Grill, Wintergreen Grill, Alakai Hotel, Country Squire Motel, Dell Creek Motel, Glacier Canyon Lodge, Grand Marquis Inn, Great Wolf Lodge, Holiday Inn Express, Kalahari Resort, Ramada, Wilderness Hotel, Wintergreen Hotel, Dells Outlets, Mkt Square Cheese, URGENT CARE, Verizon, S Motel 6, H, Jellystone Camping, Mirror Lake SP, Red Oak Camping, Scenic Traveler RV Ctr

WISCONSIN DELLS

89 WI 23, Lake Delton, N KwikTrip/dsl, Spirit, Brathouse Grill, Denny's Diner, Howie's Rest., KFC, Moosejaw Pizza, Best Value Inn, Hilton Garden, Malibu Inn, Olympia Motel, Twi-Lite Inn, Crystal Grand Music Theatre, Jellystone Camping, USPO, S Dunkin', McDonald's, $Tree, Country Roads RV Park, Home Depot, Jo-Ann, Kohl's, Springbrook Camping, Walmart/Subway

87 WI 13, Wisconsin Dells, N info, Citgo/dsl, Mobil/Arby's/dsl, Shell/Dunkin Donuts, Applebee's, Bunyan's Rest., Burger King, Coldstone, Culver's, Denny's, IHOP, Jimmy John's, McDonald's, Mexicali Rose Rest., Perkins, Starbucks, Taco Bell, Wei's Chinese, Ambers Resort, AmericInn, Baymont Inn, Best Western, Econolodge, Polynesian Hotel, Quality Inn, Super 8, golf, KOA, Sherwood Forest Camping, Walgreens, waterpark

85 US 12, WI 16, Wisconsin Dells, N Fairview Motel, KOA, Sherwood Forest Camping, Standing Rock Camping, to Rocky Arbor SP, S BP/dsl, Arrowhead Camping, Days End Motel, Edge-O-the-Dell RV Camping, Summer Breeze Resort

79 rd HH, Lyndon Sta, S BP/Subway/dsl/24hr

76mm **full facilities, litter barrels, petwalk, wb, vending**

74mm **full facilities, litter barrels, petwalk, eb, vending**

69 WI 82, Mauston, N Mauston TP/BP/Taco Bell/24hr, Pilot/Wendy's/dsl/scales/24hr, Shell/24hr, China Buffet, Family Rest., Best Western Oasis, Quality Inn, Super 8, Carr Valley Cheese, to Buckhorn SP, S KwikTrip/Denny's/dsl/scales/24hr, Mobil, Speedway, Culver's, Hardee's,

CAMP DOUGLAS

69 Continued
Log Cabin Deli, McDonald's, Pizza Hut, Roman Castle Rest., Subway, Alaskan Inn, $General, Buick/Chevrolet, Family$, Festival Foods, H, K-Mart, O'Reilly Parts, Verizon, vet, Walgreens

61 WI 80, New Lisbon, to Necedah, N BP/dsl, Shell/McDonald's/dsl, AmericInn, Edge O' the Woods Motel, Buckhorn SP, Chrysler/Dodge/Jeep, fireworks, Ford, S KwikTrip/24hr, city park, Elroy-Sparta ST Tr, USPO

55 rd C, Camp Douglas, N to Camp Williams, Volk Field, wayside, S Arco/Quiznos/dsl, BP/dsl, to Mill Bluff SP

48 rd PP, Oakdale, N Road Ranger/Subway/dsl/scales/24hr, antiques, KOA, truck/car wash, S Love's/Hardee's/dsl/scales/24hr, Mill Bluff SP, repair

147 I-90 W, to La Crosse, **I-94 and I-90 run together 93 miles**

143 US 12, WI 21, Tomah, N Shell/dsl, A&W/LJ Silver, Perkins, AmericInn, Best Western, Microtel, Super 8, Humbird Cheese/gifts, U-Haul, S BP, KwikTrip/Denny's/dsl/scales/24hr, Arby's, China Buffet, Culver's, Dunkin', Ground Round, Ground Round, KFC, McDonald's, Papa Murphy's, Pizza Hut, Starbucks, Subway, Taco Bell, Cranberry Lodge, EconoLodge, Hampton Inn, Quality Inn, $Tree, Ace Hardware, Advance Parts, ALDI, Burger King, Chrysler/Dodge/Jeep, ECV, Ford, GMC, H, NAPA, O'Reilly Parts, to Ft McCoy(9mi), Verizon, Walmart/Subway

MILLSTON

135 rd EW, Warrens, N BP/Chesters/dsl, 3 Bears Resort, Jellystone Camping, S Bog Rest.

128 rd O, Millston, N Black River SF, camping, S Cenex/dsl, USPO

123mm **full facilities, litter barrels, petwalk, /scenic view both lanes, vending**

116 WI 54, N Cenex/Subway/Taco Johns/dsl/LP, Perkins, AmericInn, Comfort Inn, SureStay Plus/rest., Black River RA, Parkland Camp, S Flying J/Denny's/dsl/24hr/@, KwikTrip/dsl, Arby's, Burger King, Culver's, McDonald's, Oriental Kitchen, Pizza Hut, Days Inn, $General, Buick/Chevrolet/GMC, Walmart/Subway

115mm Black River

115 US 12, WI 27, Black River Falls, to Merrillan, S Holiday/dsl, Hardee's, KFC, Subway, Sunrise Rest., Ace Hardware, Gordy's Mkt, Harley-Davidson, H

EAU CLAIRE

111mm Wisconsin River

105 to WI 95, Hixton, to Alma Center, N Motel 95/camping, KOA(3mi), S Cenex/dsl, Clark/dsl/24hr, Timber Valley Rest., city park, USPO

98 WI 121, Northfield, Pigeon Falls, to Alma Center, S Cenex/dsl, auto/truck repair

88 US 10, Osseo, to Fairchild, N BP/DQ, TA/Osseo Rest./dsl/scales/24hr, Hardee's, Moe's Diner, 10-7 Inn, Super 8, Chevrolet, Ford, Stoney Cr RV Park, S Speedway/dsl, McDonald's, Subway, Taco John's, Osseo Inn, Family$, H

81 rd HH, rd KK, Foster, S Cenex/dsl/LP, Foster Cheesehaus

70 US 53, Eau Claire, Holiday/dsl, Applebee's,

WI

INTERSTATE 94 Cont'd

EAU CLAIRE

70 Continued
Asia Palace, Buffalo Wild Wings, Caribou Coffee, Chipotle, Coldstone, Culver's, Fazoli's, Fired Up Pizza, Firehouse Subs, Fuji Steaks, Grizzly's Grill, HuHot Chinese, Jade Garden, Jimmy John's, Johnny's Italian Steaks, Mancino's, Manny's Grill, McDonald's, Noodles&Co, Olive Garden, Panera Bread, Papa Murphy's, TGIFriday's, TX Roadhouse, Baymont Inn, Country Inn&Suites, Grandstay, Holiday Inn, $Tree, ALDI, AT&T, Bam!, Best Buy, JC Penney, Jo-Ann Fabrics, Kohl's, Menards, Michael's, PetCo, PetSmart, Ross, Sam's Club, Scheel's Sports, Target, TJ Maxx, Tuesday Morning, Verizon, Walmart/Subway, Younkers, S Gander Outdoors, st police

68 WI 93, to Eleva, N Holiday, KwikTrip/dsl, Burger King, Cousins Subs, DQ, Famous Dave's BBQ, Great Harvest Bread Co, Hardee's, Red Robin, EconoLodge, BigLots, Chrysler/Dodge/Jeep, Festival Foods, Firestone/auto, Goodyear/auto, Gordy's Mkt, Kia, NAPA, Nissan, Subaru, transmissions, vet, S Holiday/dsl, Metropolis Resort, Audi/VW, Ford/Lincoln, Honda, Hyundai

65 WI 37, WI 85, Eau Claire, to Mondovi, N Holiday/dsl, KwikTrip/dsl, Arby's, China Buffet, Godfather's Pizza, Green Mill Rest., Hardee's, Jimmy John's, Mancino's, McDonald's, Pizza Hut, Randy's Rest., Red Lobster, Starbucks, Subway, Taco Bell, Wendy's, Best Value Inn, Best Western, Clarion, Hampton Inn, Motel 6, Plaza Hotel, Quality Inn, Scottish Inn, Super 8, Adams Automotive, Gordy's Mkt, H, Verizon, Walgreens, S tires

64mm no services

59 to US 12, rd EE, to Eau Claire, N Holiday/Burger King/dsl/24hr, Holiday/Subway/dsl/24hr, Dana's Grill, McDonald's, North Crossing Rest., AmericInn, Days Inn, Knights Inn, Freightliner, H, Mack/Volvo Trucks, Peterbilt, S dsl repair

MENOMONIE

52 US 12, WI 29, WI 40, Elk Mound, to Chippewa Falls, S U-Fuel/e85

49mm weigh sta wb

45 rd B, Menomonie, N Cenex/Subway/dsl/scales/24hr, Love's/Hardee's/dsl/scales/24hr, Exit 45 Rest., S KwikTrip/dsl/scales/24hr, Cantinas Grill, Quality Inn, H, Kenworth/dsl repair, truckwash, Walmart Dist Ctr

44mm Red Cedar River

43mm **full facilities, litter barrels, petwalk, both lanes, vending, weather info**

41 WI 25, Menomonie, N Cenex/Dunkin'/E85, Applebee's, Caribou Coffee, China Buffet, Los Cabos Mexican, Menominee Rest., Papa Murphy's, Pizza Hut,

41 Continued
Subway, ALDI, AT&T, Twin Springs Camping, Walmart/Subway, S F&F/dsl, Holiday, Speedway/dsl, Tesla EVC, Arby's, Denny's, Dickey's BBQ, Jimmy John's, Little Caesar's, McDonald's, Perkins, Starbucks, Taco Bell, Taco John's, Wendy's, AmericInn, Best Western+, Hampton Inn, Motel 6, Super 8, $Tree, Advance Parts, Buick/GMC, Chevrolet, Chrysler/Dodge/Jeep, Ford, H, Mkt Place Foods, O'Reilly Parts, to Red Cedar St Tr, Verizon, Walgreens

32 rd Q, to Knapp

HAMMOND

28 WI 128, Wilson, Elmwood, to Glenwood City, N KwikTrip/Denny's/dsl/24hr, S camping, dsl repair, Eau Galle RA

24 rd B, to Baldwin, N BP, Woodville Motel, $General, S camping, Eau Galle RA

19 US 63, Baldwin, to Ellsworth, N Freedom/dsl, KwikTrip/Subway/dsl, A&W, Culver's, DQ, Hardee's, McDonald's, Cobblestone, H, S Baymont, fireworks

16 rd T, Hammond

10 WI 65, Roberts, to New Richmond, Roberts, to New Richmon, N BP/dsl(2mi), Flying J/McDonald's/dsl/scales/24hr, Barnboard Rest.(2mi), S Freightliner

8mm weigh sta eb

HUDSON

4 US 12, rd U, Somerset, N Holiday/dsl, TA/Country Pride/dsl/scales/24hr/@, Regency Inn, to Willow River SP, vet

3 WI 35 S, to River Falls, S U of WI River Falls

2 rd F, Carmichael Rd, Hudson, N BP/repair, Freedom/dsl, Holiday, Applebee's, Caribou Coffee, Culver's, Domino's, Fiesta Loca, Jimmy John's, KFC, Papa Murphy's, Taco John's, Royal Inn, $Tree, Family Fresh Foods, GNC, repair, Target, Verizon, Walgreens, S F&F/dsl, Holiday/dsl, KwikTrip/dsl, Shell, Arby's, Buffalo Wild Wings, Burger King, Caribou Coffee, Chipotle Mexican, Coldstone, Denny's, Five Guys, Green Mill Rest., Jersey Mike's, Kingdom Buffet, Kirin Ichiban, Leeann Chin, Little Caesar's, McDonald's, Noodles&Co, Panda Express, Panera Bread, Perkins, Pita Pit, Pizza Hut, Popeyes, Sapporo Japanese, Smashburger, Starbucks, Subway, Taco Bell, Wendy's, AmericInn, Best Western/Tesla EVC, Comfort Suites, Hampton Inn, Hudson House Hotel, Quality Inn, Super 8, ALDI, AT&T, AutoZone, Chevrolet/GMC, Chrysler/Dodge/Jeep, County Mkt Foods, Ford, Home Depot, H, Menards, NAPA, O'Reilly Parts, TirePros, Tires+, to Kinnickinnic SP, USPO, Verizon, Walmart

1 WI 35 N, Hudson, N Freedom/dsl, Holiday, Carbones Pizzeria, DQ

0mm Wisconsin/Minnesota state line, St Croix River

WI

NOTES

= gas = food = lodging = other = rest stop

WYOMING

INTERSTATE 25

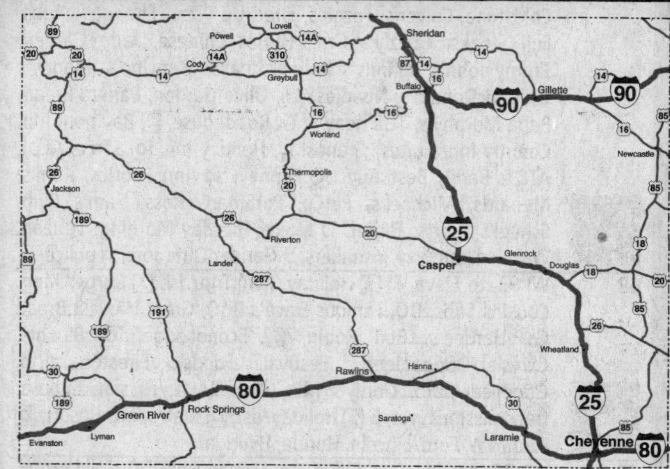

BUFFALO

Exit #	Services
300	I-90, E to Gillette, W to Billings. I-25 begins/ends on I-90, exit 56.
299	US 16, Buffalo, **E** Cenex, Maverik/dsl, Buffalo Inn, Hampton Inn, Holiday Inn Express, SureStay, Deer Park Camping, KOA, tire/auto repair, vet, **W** Cenex/dsl/24hr, Bozeman Tr Steaks, Dash Inn Rest., Domino's, Hardee's, McDonald's, Pizza Hut, Subway, The Breadboard, Alamo Inn, Quality Inn, Rodeway Inn, Super 8, Ace Hardware, Family$, H, Indian RV Camp, O'Reilly Parts, to Yellowstone
298	US 87, Buffalo
291	Trabing Rd
280	Middle Fork Rd
274mm	parking area both lanes
265	Reno Rd
254	Kaycee, **full facilities, litter barrels, petwalk, both lanes, E** Shell/dsl, Country Inn Diner, Invasion Rest., Cassidy Inn Motel, Siesta Motel, Kaycee Gen. Store, museum, NAPA Repair, Powder River RV Park, USPO, **W** Sinclair/dsl/LP/motel, KC RV Park
249	TTT Rd
246	Powder River Rd
235	Tisdale Mtn Rd
227	WY 387 N, Midwest, Edgerton
223	no services
219mm	parking area both lanes
216	Ranch Rd
210	Horse Ranch Creek Rd, Midwest, Edgerton
197	Ormsby Rd
194	Westwinds Rd
191	Wardwell Rd, to Bar Nunn, **W** Loaf'N Jug/dsl, Family$, KOA
189	US 20, US 26 W, to Shoshone, Shoshoni Port of Entry
188b	WY 220, Poplar St, **E** McDonald's, The Fort Eatery, Hampton Inn, Hilton Garden, La Quinta, Motel 6, Quality Inn, Ramkota Hotel, **W** Exxon, Burger King, DQ, Hokkaido Ramen, to Ft Casper HS
188a	Center St, Casper, **E** Conoco/dsl, Shell/dsl, National 9 Inn, Riverside Hotel, **W** Starbucks, Subway, Best Western, Days Inn, USPO
187	McKinley St, Casper, **E** Ranch House Motel
186	US 20, US 26, US 87, Yellowstone St, **E** city park, dsl repair, transmissions/repair, **W** Exxon, auto repair, Chevrolet/Subaru, H, Kia, O'Reilly Parts
185	WY 258, Wyoming Blvd, E Casper, **E** Kum&Go/dsl, Loaf'n Jug/dsl, Chili's, Outback Steaks, Southern BBQ HQ, TX Roadhouse, Baymont Inn, C'mon Inn, Comfort Inn, Super 8, Murdoch's Ranch Store, Smith RV Ctr, vet, **W** Exxon/dsl, Flying J/Conoco/Subway/dsl/LP/scales/24hr, Arby's, Buffalo Wild Wings, Burger King, Denny's, DQ, Firehouse Pizza, Five Guys, Hamburger Stand, Homestretch Grill, Jersey Mike's, Jimmy John's, KFC/LJ Silver, McDonald's, Mongolian Grill, Old Chicago Grill, Olive Garden, Perkins, Pizza Hut, Pizza Ranch, Qdoba, Red Lobster, Sanford's Cafe, Starbucks, Subway, Taco Bell, Taco John's, Wendy's, Candlewood Suites, Courtyard, Holiday Inn Express, Rodeway Inn, AutoZone, Best Buy, Dick's, Home Depot, JC Penney, Natural Grocers, Nissan, PetCo, Ridley's Foods/dsl, Ross, Sam's Club/gas, Schwab TIre, Sportsmans Whse, Staples, Target, Verizon, Verizon, Walgreens, Walmart
182	WY 253, Brooks Rd, Hat Six Rd, **E** Sinclair/dsl, Sonic,

CASPER

E CASPER

GLENROCK

Exit #	Services
182	Continued Sleep Inn, Rivers Edge Camping, to Wilkins SP, **W** FireRock Rest., Keg&Cork Rest., Subway, Wyo Aleworks, Best Western+, Holiday Inn, Mainstay Suites, Buick/Cadillac/GMC, Chrysler/Dodge/Jeep, H, Kohl's, Marshall's, Menards, PetSmart, Toyota, Verizon, VW
171mm	parking area both lanes
165	Glenrock, **E** Classic Pizza, Higgins Hotel, dinosaur museum
160	US 87, US 20, US 26, E Glenrock
156	Bixby Rd
154	Barber Rd
153mm	parking area both lanes
151	Natural Bridge
150	Inez Rd
146	La Prele Rd
140	WY 59, Douglas, **E** Conoco/Subway/dsl, Maverik/dsl, Shell/dsl, Arby's, La Costa Mexican, McDonald's, Taco John's, Douglas Inn, Hampton Inn, Holiday Inn Express, Sleep Inn, Super 8, $General, city park, H, KOA, Lone Tree Village RV Park, Pioneer Museum, WY St Fair
135	US 20, US 26, US 87, Douglas, **E** Loaf'n Jug/dsl, Sinclair/rest./dsl/24hr, Speedway, 4 Seasons Chinese, Dominos, Pizza Hut, Plains Trading Post Rest., Village Inn, 1st Interstate Inn, Budget Inn Express, Plains Motel, The Blue Buffalo, $General, AT&T, Douglas Hardware, Family$, H, O'Reilly Parts, repair, Safeway Foods/dsl, Verizon
129mm	parking area both lanes
126	US 18, US 20 E, Orin, **Orin Jct both lanes, E full facilities, litter barrels, petwalk, RV dump,** Sinclair/Orin Jct Trkstp/dsl/café
125mm	N Platte River
111	Glendo, **E** Sinclair/dsl, Bullfrogs Grill, Glendo Marina Café, Kim's Rest., Old Western Steaks, Glendo Lakeside RV camping, to Glendo SP, USPO
104	to Middle Bear
100	Cassa Rd
94	El Rancho Rd, **W** El Rancho Village RV
92	US 26 E, Dwyer, **full facilities, litter barrel, petwalk, both lanes, RV dump, E** Ft Laramie NHS, to Guernsey SP
87	Johnson Rd
84	Laramie River Rd
84mm	Laramie River
80	US 87, Laramie Power Sta, Wheatland, Laramie Power Sta, **E** Sinclair/A&W/dsl, Tesla EVC, Guadalajara Mexican,

DOUGLAS

DWYER

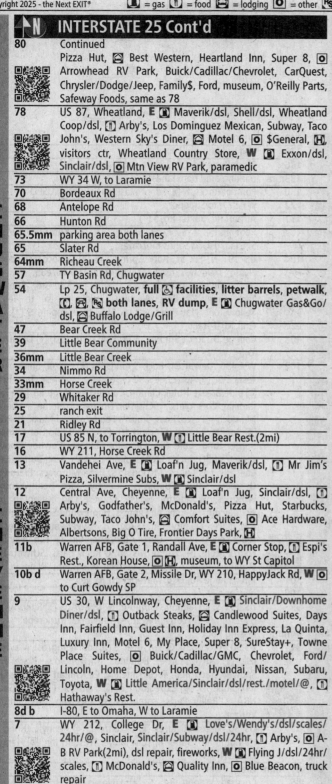

INTERSTATE 25 Cont'd

Exit	Services
80	Continued Pizza Hut, Best Western, Heartland Inn, Super 8, Arrowhead RV Park, Buick/Cadillac/Chevrolet, CarQuest, Chrysler/Dodge/Jeep, Family$, Ford, museum, O'Reilly Parts, Safeway Foods, same as 78
78	US 87, Wheatland, **E** Maverik/dsl, Shell/dsl, Wheatland Coop/dsl, Arby's, Los Dominguez Mexican, Subway, Taco John's, Western Sky's Diner, Motel 6, $General, H, visitors ctr, Wheatland Country Store, **W** Exxon/dsl, Sinclair/dsl, Mtn View RV Park, paramedic
73	WY 34 W, to Laramie
70	Bordeaux Rd
68	Antelope Rd
66	Hunton Rd
65.5mm	parking area both lanes
65	Slater Rd
64mm	Richeau Creek
57	TY Basin Rd, Chugwater
54	Lp 25, Chugwater, **full facilities, litter barrels, petwalk, both lanes, RV dump, E** Chugwater Gas&Go/dsl, Buffalo Lodge/Grill
47	Bear Creek Rd
39	Little Bear Community
36mm	Little Bear Creek
34	Nimmo Rd
33mm	Horse Creek
29	Whitaker Rd
25	ranch exit
21	Ridley Rd
17	US 85 N, to Torrington, **W** Little Bear Rest.(2mi)
16	WY 211, Horse Creek Rd
13	Vandehei Ave, **E** Loaf'n Jug, Maverik/dsl, Mr Jim's Pizza, Silvermine Subs, **W** Sinclair/dsl
12	Central Ave, Cheyenne, **E** Loaf'n Jug, Sinclair/dsl, Arby's, Godfather's, McDonald's, Pizza Hut, Starbucks, Subway, Taco John's, Comfort Suites, Ace Hardware, Albertsons, Big O Tire, Frontier Days Park, H
11b	Warren AFB, Gate 1, Randall Ave, **E** Corner Stop, Espi's Rest., Korean House, H, museum, to WY St Capitol
10b d	Warren AFB, Gate 2, Missile Dr, WY 210, HappyJack Rd, **W** to Curt Gowdy SP
9	US 30, W Lincolnway, Cheyenne, **E** Sinclair/Downhome Diner/dsl, Outback Steaks, Candlewood Suites, Days Inn, Fairfield Inn, Guest Inn, Holiday Inn Express, La Quinta, Luxury Inn, Motel 6, My Place, Super 8, SureStay+, Towne Place Suites, Buick/Cadillac/GMC, Chevrolet, Ford/Lincoln, Home Depot, Honda, Hyundai, Nissan, Subaru, Toyota, **W** Little America/Sinclair/dsl/rest./motel/@, Hathaway's Rest.
8d b	I-80, E to Omaha, W to Laramie
7	WY 212, College Dr, **E** Love's/Wendy's/dsl/scales/24hr/@, Sinclair, Sinclair/Subway/dsl/24hr, Arby's, A-B RV Park(2mi), dsl repair, fireworks, **W** Flying J/dsl/24hr/scales, McDonald's, Quality Inn, Blue Beacon, truck repair
6.5mm	Port of Entry nb
4	High Plains Rd, **both lanes, full facilities, litter barrels, petwalk, rest/info ctr**, WY Welcome Ctr
2	WY 223, Terry Ranch Rd, **E** fireworks, Terry Bison Ranch RV camping
0mm	Wyoming/Colorado state line

INTERSTATE 80

Exit	Services
402mm	Wyoming/Nebraska State line
401	WY 215, Pine Bluffs, **Welcome Ctr/ both lanes, full facilities, info, playground, nature trail, litter barrels, petwalk, N** Exxon/Subway/dsl, Sinclair/A&W/dsl/24hr/@, Currie's Rest., Estella's Mexican, Cobblestone Inn/EVC, NAPA, Pine Bluff RV Park, USPO
391	Egbert
386	WY 213, WY 214, Burns, **N** Antelope Trkstp/Sinclair/dsl/cafe
377	WY 217, Hillsdale, **N** TA/Burger King/Taco Bell/dsl/scales/24hr/@, Tumbleweed Grill, Wyo RV Camping
372mm	Port of Entry wb, truck insp
370	US 30 W, Archer, **N** Sapp Bros/dsl/scales/24hr/@, T-Joe's Steaks, Rodeway Inn, RV park, truck repair
367	Campstool Rd, **N** Pilot/Subway/dsl/scales/24hr, Best Western+, Camping World, KOA(seasonal), Volvo Trucks
364	WY 212, to E Lincolnway, Cheyenne, **N** Kum&Go/dsl, Loaf'n Jug/Subway, Shari's Rest., Rodeo Inn, $Tree, Big O Tire, BigLots, Harley-Davidson, H, Murdoch's Ranch Store, O'Reilly Parts, Sierra Trading Post, Walmart/auto/gas, **S** Peterbilt
362	US 85, I-180, to Central Ave, Cheyenne, Greeley, **N** Hi Mkt/dsl, Arby's, Carls' Jr, Hacienda Mexican, Jimmy John's, Papa John's, Village Inn, CarQuest, Family$, H, museum, st capitol, Verizon, **S** Loaf'n Jug/dsl, Sinclair/dsl, Burger King, Little Caesar's, McDonald's, Pizza Hut, Silver Mine Subs, Sonic, Subway, Taco John's, Comfort Inn, Home2 Suites, Red Lion Hotel, Roundup Motel, SpringHill Suites, Tru, $General, AutoZone, Family$, Hideaway RV Village, Safeway/gas
359c a	I-25, US 87, N to Casper, S to Denver
358	US 30, W Lincolnway, Cheyenne, **N** Little America/Sinclair/dsl/motel/@, Sinclair/dsl/24hr, Outback Steaks, Candlewood Suites, Cheyenne Guess Inn, Days Inn, Fairfield Inn, Holiday Inn Express, La Quinta, Luxury Inn, Motel 6, My Place, Super 8, SureStay+, TownPlace Suites, Buick/GMC/Cadillac, Chevrolet, Ford/Lincoln, Home Depot, Honda, H, Hyundai, Nissan, Subaru, Toyota
357	Wy 222, Roundtop Rd
348	Otto Rd
345	Warren Rd, **N** truck parking
342	Harriman Rd
339	Remount Rd
335	Buford, **S** Buford Trading Post/dsl
333mm	parking area both lanes, Tree in The Rock
329	Vedeauwoo Rd, **N** camping, **S** Ames Monument
323	WY 210, Happy Jack Rd, **elev. 8640, full facilities, Lincoln Monument, litter barrels, petwalk, both lanes, to Curt Gowdy SP**
322mm	chain up area both lanes
316	US 30 W, Grand Ave, Laramie, **N** Loaf'N Jug, Sinclair/dsl, Tumbleweed Express, Applebee's, Arby's, Burger King, Chili's, Chipotle, Dickey's BBQ, Freddy's Burgers, Jersey Mike's, Jimmy John's, McAlister's Deli, McDonald's, Mr Jim's Pizza, Papa Murphy's, Perkins, Sonic, Starbucks, Taco Bell, Taco John's, Wendy's, Wyo Steakhouse, AmericInn, Hampton Inn, Hilton Garden, Holiday Inn, Quality Inn, Buick/Chevrolet/GMC, Ford/Lincoln, GNC, H, Ridley's Mkt, Toyota, U of Wyo, URGENT CARE, Verizon, Walgreens, Walmart/auto
313	US 287, to 3rd St, Laramie, Port of Entry, **N** GasaMat, Maverik, Shell/dsl, Corona Village Mexican, Fernandito's Mexican, Qdoba, Laramie Valley Inn, Motel 8, Travelodge, H, Laramie Plains Museum, NAPA, **S** Budget Inn, Motel 6, USPO, vet
312mm	Laramie River
311	WY 130, WY 230, Snowy Range Rd, Laramie, **S** Conoco/dsl, Exxon/Chester's/Papa John's/dsl, Sinclair/dsl,

CHUGWATER CHEYENNE ARCHER LARAMIE WY

= gas = food = lodging = other = rest stop

INTERSTATE 80 Cont'd

LARAMIE

Exit	Services
311	Continued McDonald's, Subway, Americas Best Value, to Snowy Range Ski Area, repair/tires
310	Curtis St, Laramie, N Love's/Carl's Jr/Subway/dsl/scales24hr/@, Pilot/Wendy's/dsl/scales/24hr, Best Western, Days Inn, EconoLodge, Super 8, H, repair, S Blue Beacon, Petro/Sinclair/dsl/scales/24hr/@, Comfort Inn, Fairfield Inn
307mm	parking area both lanes
297	WY 12, Herrick Lane
290	Quealy Dome Rd, S Exxon
279	Cooper Cove Rd
272mm	Rock Creek
272	WY 13, to Arlington
267	**both lanes, full facilities**
262mm	no services
260	CR 402
259mm	E Fork Medicine Bow River
257mm	Medicine Bow River
255	WY 72, Elk Mtn, to Hanna, N Conoco/dsl, trucking parking area, S Elk Mtn Hotel/rest
238	Peterson Rd
235	WY 130, S US 30/87, N Shell/dsl
229mm	N Platte River
228	**both lanes, litter barrels, petwalk**
221	E Sinclair, N Sinclair/rest/dsl/24hr, to Seminoe SP
219	W Sinclair, N Su Casa Cafe, to Seminoe SP, USPO

RAWLINS

Exit	Services
215	Cedar St, Rawlins, N Conoco/dsl, KFC/Taco Bell, Sinclair/dsl, Burger King, McDonald's, Penny's Diner, Pizza Hut, Starbucks, Subway, Baymont, Comfort Inn, Days Inn, Econolodge, Fairfield Inn, Hampton Inn, Holiday Inn Express, Rawlings Western Lodge, Bomgaars, Buick/Chevrolet/GMC, CarQuest, Chrysler/Dodge/Jeep, City Mkt/dsl, Frontier Prison NHS, museum, O'Reilly Parts, to Yellowstone/Teton NP, U-Haul, Walmart/dsl, S 1st Choice
214	Higley Blvd, Rawlins, N Microtel, KOA, S TA/Conoco/Subway/dsl/scales/24hr/@, Pronghorn Inn
211	WY 789, to US 287 N, Spruce St, Rawlins, N Conoco/dsl, Loaf'n Jug, Sinclair, Sinclair/dsl, Michael's Big Steaks, Best Western, La Bella, Motel 7, Quality Inn, Rodeway Inn, Super 8, Travelodge, Family$, H, Red Desert Rose Camping
209	Johnson Rd, N Flying J/Denny's/dsl/LP/scales/24hr
206	Hadsell Rd(no return)
205.5mm	continental divide, elev 7000
204	Knobs Rd
201	Daley Rd
196	Riner Rd

RED DESERT

Exit	Services
190mm	parking area wb, litter barrels
189mm	parking area eb, picnic tables, litter barrels
187	WY 789, Creston, Baggs Rd
184	Continental Divide Rd
173	Wamsutter, N Love's/Subway/dsl/24hr/@, S Conoco/dsl/repair/café/24hr, ONE9 Travel Ctr, Sunset Inn
170	Rasmussen Rd
165	Red Desert
158	Tipton Rd (continental divide, elev 6930)
156	GL Rd
154	BLM Rd
152	Bar X Rd
150	Table Rock Rd
146	Patrick Draw Rd
144mm	**full facilities, litter barrels, petwalk, both lanes**
143mm	parking area both lanes, litter barrels

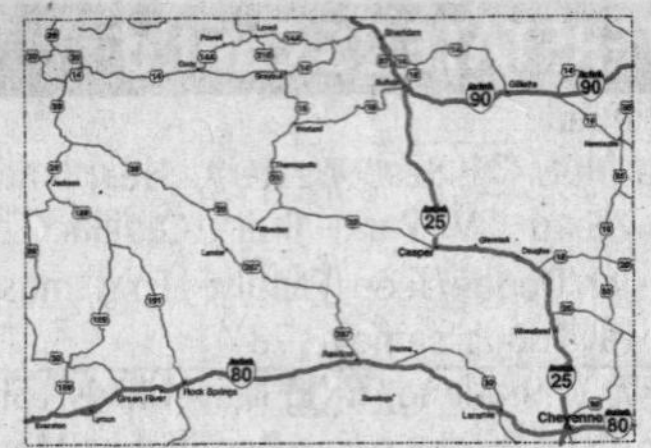

ROCK SPRINGS

Exit	Services
142	Bitter Creek Rd
139	Red Hill Rd
136	Black Butte Rd
133mm	parking area both lanes
130	Point of Rocks, N Conoco/dsl, fireworks, USPO
122	WY 371, to Superior
111	Airport Rd, Baxter Rd, S
107	Pilot Butte Ave, Rock Springs, S Kum&Go/dsl/e85, Sinclair/dsl, Sands Inn/cafe
104	US 191 N, Elk St, Rock Springs, N Conoco/dsl, Exxon, Flying J/Denny's/dsl/LP/24hr, Kum&Go/dsl/e85, Pwi, McDonald's, Renegade Rest., Santa Fe SW Grill, Subway, Taco Time, Best Western, Studio 6, to Teton/Yellowstone Nat Parks via US 191, truck repair, S Chill Grill, U-Haul
103	College Dr, Rock Springs, S Loaf'n Jug/dsl, Domino's, H, W WY Coll
102	WY 430, Dewar Dr, Rock Springs, N Exxon, Sinclair/dsl, Tesla EVC, Applebee's, KFC, Sapporo Japanese, Taco Time, Blue Breeze Hotel, Clarion, Comfort Inn, Motel 6, $Tree, Cadillac/Chevrolet, Chrysler/Dodge, Home Depot, Murdoch's, Petco, Ross, Smith's Foods/gas, TJ Maxx, USPO, S Loaf'N Jug/dsl, Sinclair/dsl, Arby's, Bonsai Chinese, Burger King, Cafe Rio, Chopstix Chinese, Cowboy Donuts, Dickey's BBQ, Jack's Crepes, Jimmy John's, King Buffet, Little Caesar's, Los Cabos, McDonald's, Papa Murphy's, Pizza Hut, Quizno's, Sonic, Starbucks, Subway, Taco Bell, Wendy's, Winger's, Wonderful House Chinese, Hampton Inn, Holiday Inn, Holiday Inn Express, Homewood Suites, Motel 8, My Place, Quality Inn, Super 8, Sweetwater Lodge, Albertsons/Sav-on, AT&T, AutoZone, Big O Tire, Family$, Ford/Lincoln, H, NAPA, Nissan, O'Reilly Parts, Schwab Tire, Staples, Valvoline, Verizon, Verizon, Walgreens, Walmart
101	Interchange Rd, N Maverik/dsl, vet
100	new exit

GREEN RIVER

Exit	Services
99	US 191 S, E Flaming Gorge Rd, N KOA, S Shell/A&W/dsl/24hr/@, Log Inn Rest., fireworks, truck repair
94mm	Kissing Rock
91	US 30, to WY 530, Green River, S Loaf'N Jug/dsl, Maverik/dsl, Arctic Circle, Dominos, McDonald's, Pizza Hut, Subway, Taco Bell, Taco Time, Coachman Inn, Mustang Inn, Super 8, Expedition NHS, Family$, Flaming Gorge NRA, O'Reilly Parts, same as 89, Schwab Tire, Smith's, Verizon
89	US 30, Green River, S Exxon/dsl, Penny's Diner, Hampton Inn, Super 8, Travelodge, Western Inn, Flaming Gorge NRA
87.5mm	Green River
85	Covered Wagon Rd, S Love's/Carl's Jr/Speedco/dsl/scales/24hr/@, Green River RV Park
83	WY 372, La Barge Rd, N Fontenelle Dam
78	(from wb)
77mm	Blacks Fork River
72	Westvaco Rd
71mm	parking area both lanes
68	Little America, N Sinclair/Little America/dsl/24hr/@, Little America Hotel/RV Park, RV camping
66	US 30 W, to Teton, Yellowstone, Fossil Butte NM, Kemmerer

INTERSTATE 80 Cont'd

LYMAN

Exit #	Services
61	Cedar Mtn Rd, to Granger
60mm	parking area both lanes
53	Church Butte Rd
49mm	parking area wb
48	Lp 80, Lyman, Ft Bridger, Hist Ft Bridger
45mm	Blacks Fork River
41	WY 413, Lyman, **full facilities, litter barrels, petwalk,** **both lanes, N** Gas'n Go/cafe/dsl, **S** Taco Time, Gateway Inn, KOA
39	WY 412, WY 414, to Carter, Mountain View
34	Lp 80, to Ft Bridger, **S** Highlander Inn, Flaming Gorge NRA, Ft Bridger NHS, Ft Bridger RV Camp
33.5mm	parking area eb
33	Union Rd
30	Bigelow Rd, **N** TA/Shell/Burger King/Taco Bell/dsl/scales/24hr/@, **S** fireworks
28	French Rd
28mm	parking area both lanes
24	Leroy Rd
23	Bar Hat Rd
21	Coal Rd
18	US 189 N, to Kemmerer, to Nat Parks
15	Guild Rd(from eb)
14mm	parking area both lanes
13	Divide Rd
10	Painter Rd, to Eagle Rock Ski Area
6	US 189, Bear River Dr, Evanston, **Welcome Ctr both lanes, N** Pilot/Subway/dsl/scales/24hr, Shell/dsl, Don Pedro's Mexican, Jalisco Mexican, Jody's Diner, Extended Stay, Prairie Inn, Travelodge, Freeway Tire, Phillips RV Park, Wyo Downs Racetrack, **S** Bear River SP, **full facilities, litter barrels, petwalk, playground, RV dump(seasonal)**
5	WY 89, Evanston, **N** Chevron/Taco Time/dsl, Maverik/dsl, Arby's, Costa Vida, Domino's, DragonWall Chinese, Jimmy John's, McDonald's, Mother Mae's Kitchen, Papa Murphy's, Subway, Wendy's, $Tree, Ace Hardware, AutoZone, Chevrolet, Jiffy Lube, Murdoch's, NAPA, O'Reilly Parts, Verizon, Walmart/Subway, **S** WY St H
3	US 189, Harrison Dr, Evanston, **N** Anderson Service/gas, Chevron/dsl, Flying J/Subway/dsl/scales/24hr, Shell, Tesla EVC, Ichiban Japanese, Legal Tender Rest., Lincoln Highway Grill, Pancho's Mexican, Affordable Inn, Comfort Inn, Days Inn, Hampton Inn, HillCrest Motel, Holiday Inn Express, Quality Inn, Super 8, Chrysler/Dodge/Jeep, USPO, **S** Loaf N Jug, KFC/Taco Bell, Basecamp RV Ctr, Big O Tires, fireworks, H, Smith's
0.5mm	Port of Entry eb, weigh sta wb
0mm	Wyoming/Utah state line

EVANSTON

INTERSTATE 90

BEULAH

Exit #	Services
207mm	Wyoming/South Dakota state line
205	Beulah, **N** Sinclair/dsl/LP, Buffalo Jump Rest., Sand Creek Trading Post/gas/cafe, Beulah Campground, USPO, **S** Ranch A NHP
204.5mm	Sand Creek
199	WY 111, to Aladdin, **Welcome ctr/ (both directions), full facilities, litter barrels, petwalk, N** Devil's Tower NM, Vore Buffalo Jump NHP
191	Moskee Rd
189	US 14 W, Sundance, **full facilities, info, litter barrels, petwalk, playground,** port of entry/weigh sta, **both lanes, RV dump, N** Conoco/Subway/dsl/24hr, Cowgirl Pizza, Serena Inn, Devil's Tower NM, H,
189	Continued Mtn View Camping, museum
187	WY 585, Sundance, , **N** Fresh Start/dsl, Sinclair/dsl, Yesway, Bear Lodge, Best Western, Budget Host Arrowhead, Deer Lodge, auto repair, Decker's Foods, H, museum, NAPA, to Devil's Tower
185	to WY 116, to Sundance, **S** Conoco/dsl, same as 187
178	Coal Divide Rd
177mm	parking area both lanes
172	Inyan Kara Rd
171mm	parking area both lanes, litter barrels
165	Pine Ridge Rd, to Pine Haven, **N** Cedar Ridge RV Park, to Keyhole SP
163mm	parking area both lanes
160	Wind Creek Rd
154	US 14, US 16, **S** Sinclair/dsl, Donna's Diner, Subway, Cozy Motel, Moorcourt Motel, Old Corner B&B, $General, city park, Diehl's Foods/gas, museum, USPO
153	US 16 E, US 14, W Moorcroft, **full facilities, litter barrels, petwalk, both lanes**
152mm	Belle Fourche River
141	Rozet, **S** All Seasons RV Park
138mm	parking area both lanes
132	Wyodak Rd
129	Garner Lake Rd, **S** Maverik, Arbuckle Lodge, auto repair, Crazy Woman Camping, Harley-Davidson, High Plains Camping
128	US 14, US 16, Gillette, **N** Maverik/dsl, MG Oil/dsl, Mona's Cafe, Howard Johnson, Mustang Motel, National 9 Inn, Quality Inn, Crazy Woman Camping, East Side RV Ctr., Port of Entry, **S** Arbuckle Lodge, High Plains Camping
126	WY 59, Gillette, **N** Cenex/dsl, Sinclair/Papa John's/dsl, China King Buffet, Dickey's BBQ, Hardee's, Little Caesar's, McDonald's, Pizza Carrello, Pokey's BBQ, Prime Rib Rest., Alamo Inn, $General, city park, Family$, Smith's, Smith's Foods, Verizon, **S** Exxon, Flying J/dsl/24hr, Loaf'N Jug/dsl, A&W/LJ Silver, Applebee's, Arby's, Armando's Taco, Buffalo Wild Wings, Burger King, DQ, Goodtimes Grill/Taco John's, Great Wall Chinese, Jimmy John's, KFC, Las Margarita's Mexican, Main Bagel, Old Chicago Grill, Papa Murphy's, Perkins, Pizza Hut, Qdoba Mexican, Ruby Tuesday, Smiling Moose Deli, Sonic, Starbucks, Subway, Taco Bell, Wendy's, Wyo Rib Chophouse, Candlewood Suites, Country Inn&Suites, Days Inn, Fairfield Inn, Holiday Inn Express, Home2 Suites, La Quinta, Ramada Plaza, Travelodge, Wingate Inn, $Tree, Advance Parts, Albertson's, AT&T, AutoZone, Big O Tire, city park, Discount Tire, Home Depot, Menards, Midas, O'Reilly Parts, Office Depot, Osco Drug, Petco, Schwab Tire, Tire-O-Rama, Verizon, Walgreens, Walmart/Subway
124	WY 50, Gillette, **N** Kum&Go/dsl, Shell/Burger King/dsl, Sinclair/Papa John's/dsl, Hong Kong Rest., Los Compadres Mexican, Pizza Hut, Sherpa Indian, Subway, Baymont, Best Western/rest., Budget Inn, Comfort Inn, Summit Suites, Super 8, TownePlace Suites, Crazy Woman Camping, Don's Foods, Ford, H, **S** Kum&Go/dsl, McDonald's, Bighorn Tire, Buick/Chevrolet/GMC
116	Force Rd
113	Wild Horse Creek Rd
106	Kingsbury Rd
102	Barber Creek Rd
91	Dead Horse Creek Rd
89mm	Powder River
88	Powder River Rd, **full facilities, litter barrels, petwalk, both lanes**
82	Indian Creek Rd

SUNDANCE

ROZET

GILLETTE

WY

= gas = food = lodging = other = rest stop

INTERSTATE 90 Cont'd

BANNER

Exit #	Services
77	Schoonover Rd
73.5mm	Crazy Woman Creek
73	Crazy Woman Rd
69	Dry Creek Rd
68.5mm	parking area wb
65	Red Hills Rd, Tipperary Rd
60mm	parking area both lanes, litter barrels
58	US 16, to Ucross, Buffalo, S Cenex, Cenex/dsl/24hr, Exxon/dsl, Sinclair/dsl, Bozeman Tr Steaks, Dash Inn Rest., Hardee's, McDonald's, Pizza Hut, Subway, The Breadboard, Alamo Inn, Buffalo Inn, Hampton Inn, Holiday Inn Express, Quality Inn, Rodeway Inn, Super 8, SureStay, Ace Hardware, Bighorn Tire, Deer Park Camping, Family$, H, Indian RV Camp, KOA, O'Reilly Parts, vet
56b	I-25 S, US 87 S, to Buffalo
56a	25 Bus, 90 Bus, to Buffalo
53	Rock Creek Rd
51	Lake DeSmet, N Lake Stop gas/motel/cafe
47	Shell Creek Rd
44	US 87 N, Piney Creek Rd, to Story, Banner, N Ft Phil Kearney
39mm	scenic turnout wb
37	Prairie Dog Creek Rd, to Story
33	Meade Creek Rd, to Big Horn
31mm	parking area eb
25	US 14 E, Sheridan, N Quality Inn, Dalton's RV Ctr, S Exxon/dsl, Farmers Co-op, Holiday/dsl, Maverik/dsl, Arby's, El Rodeo Mexican, Goodtimes, Jimmy John's, Little Caesar's, McDonald's, Mr. Jim's Pizza, Papa Murphy's, Perkins, Qdoba, Starbucks, Subway, Taco Bell, Wendy's,

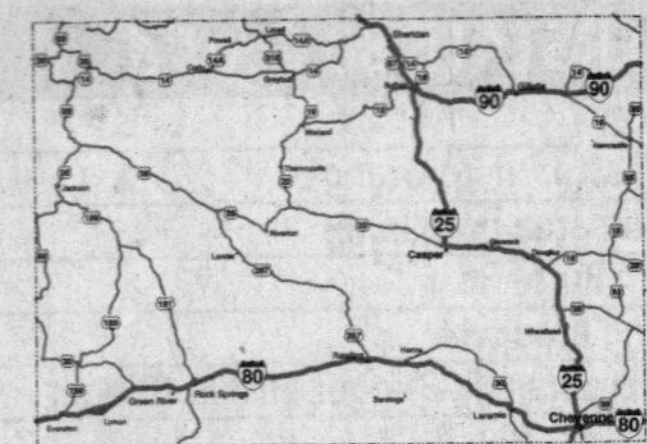

SHERIDAN

Exit #	Services
25	Continued Candlewood Suites, Days Inn, Days Inn, Fairfield Inn, Holiday Lodge, Mill Inn, Ramada, $Tree, Ace Hardware, Albertson's/Osco Drug, AT&T, AutoZone, Firestone/auto, Ford/Lincoln, GNC, Home Depot, NAPA, O'Reilly Parts, Petco, Schwab Tire, Sheridan Coll, Tire-Rama, Toyota, Verizon, vet, vet, Walgreens, Walmart
23	WY 336, 5th St, Sheridan, **both lanes, full facilities, litter barrels, petwalk, RV dump,** N Bucks Travel/dsl, Comfort Inn, S Cenex, Holiday/dsl, Tesla EVC, DQ, La Herradura Mexican, Pad Thai, Powder River Pizza, Silver Spur Cafe, Wyoming's Chop House, Alamo Motel, Baymont, Best Western, Evergreen Studios, Hampton Inn, Sheridan Inn, city park, Family$, Honda, H, Peter D's RV Park, radiators
20	to Main St, Sheridan, N KOA, S Exxon/Common Cents/dsl, Pizza Hut, Krispy Krunchy Chicken, McDonald's, Bramble Motel, Budget Inn, Wyo Inn, U-Haul
16	to Decker, Montana, port of entry
15mm	Tongue River
14	WY 345, Acme Rd
9	US 14 W, Ranchester, S Conoco/dsl, Ranchester Western, Conner Bfd NHS, Foothills Campground, Lazy R Campground, to Yellowstone/Teton NPs, U-Haul, USPO
1	Parkman
0mm	Wyoming/Montana state line

NOTES

Contents

Foreword

Responsible Drinking: A Moderation Management Approach for Problem Drinkers presents an excellent blend of scientific information, common sense, and practical tips on an important topic, moderation as a route to recovery from alcohol problems. Most importantly, *Responsible Drinking* makes a compelling objective argument that moderation is a realistic, achievable, clinically responsible, and preferred goal for many problem drinkers.

Given the convincing evidence in support of moderation, why are moderation programs for problem drinkers rare? Two factors have limited the availability of moderation approaches. The first is a belief that all alcohol problems are progressive and irreversible. A corollary of this belief is that continued drinking by those who develop an alcohol problem will worsen their problem, and that this downward progression will continue until the individual stops drinking or dies. However, a plethora of evidence has accumulated over the years contradicting the progressivity assumption (see reviews in Pattison, Sobell and Sobell 1977; Sobell and Sobell 1993). For example, Schuckit and his colleagues recently tracked the fate of individuals who initially met diagnostic criteria for alcohol abuse but not alcohol dependence. They concluded that "alcohol abuse predicts a less persistent, milder disorder that does not usually progress to dependence" (Schuckit, Smith, Danko, et al. 2001, p. 1084). In other words, mild alcohol problems do not inexorably worsen, even if people continue to drink alcohol. This applies to most individuals referred to in this book as problem drinkers. An important but not unexpected exception to the lack of progressivity is that once an individual's problems become very serious, the likelihood of them worsening increases without treatment (Fillmore and Midanik 1984). Unfortunately, most of this evidence has been ignored by most traditional alcohol programs.

The second factor limiting the availability of moderation approaches has been a concern that such services will be misused (that is, severely dependent individuals will use moderation goals to rationalize continued heavy drinking) or will interfere with abstinence-oriented treatments for those who are unable to moderate their drinking. However, validated reports of moderation services being misused are lacking. Moreover, moderation programs, including Moderation Management, uniformly recommend that moderation is *not* advisable for individuals whose problems are severe.

The availability of moderation approaches encourages people with mild alcohol problems to take action to change their drinking earlier than would otherwise occur. That's because moderation is seen as attainable and realistic. This is in contrast to programs that require lifelong abstinence, a commitment that problem drinkers view as unnecessary and overly intensive. Because there are large numbers of problem drinkers, widespread availability of moderation programs is long overdue.

Responsible Drinking: A Moderation Management Approach for Problem Drinkers demonstrates responsible writing at its best and will help bridge the gap between alcohol research and practice. This book is a welcome addition to the field and will allow those with drinking problems to make more informed, earlier, and better decisions about changing their drinking. Having spent three decades in the alcohol field advocating for allowing problem drinkers to make their own choices and to take responsibility for changing their drinking, we applaud Rotgers, Kern, and Hoeltzel for their courage and willingness to take the issue of responsible drinking to the public.

Mark B. Sobell, Ph.D., ABPP
Linda C. Sobell, Ph.D., ABPP
Professors at the Center for Psychological
Studies and former Senior Scientists at
the Addiction Research Foundation

Preface

Mine is a story about problem drinking with an ending Americans don't often hear: I didn't end up a lifetime alcoholic, dead, institutionalized, or in Alcoholics Anonymous (AA). I'm not an alcoholic, but I certainly did drink too much and too often. My drinking put me at risk for serious health and social problems. I was one of America's estimated thirty-two million problem drinkers, who drink above safe levels but are *not* alcoholics.

However, with the help of a program called Moderation Management (MM), I learned how to cut down, and, as the program says, came to consider "an occasional drink to be a small, but enjoyable part of life." This book contains, as AA might put it, my experience, strength, and hope—and that of other MM members who have found the program useful. It also includes specific techniques and skills to help you moderate your drinking—techniques that have been shown by clinical research to make a difference.

Let's start my story from the beginning. Alcohol was a part of my family life from my earliest memories. I remember my parents "cocktailing" most evenings. Social events always involved drinking. I can recall wondering what was it about this stuff that made the adults different and seemed to change the whole atmosphere.

Like most people, I experimented with alcohol in high school, getting drunk a few times in my junior and senior years with friends. I liked the warm feeling and the way alcohol raised my spirits. In college, again, like 40 percent of students, I drank quite heavily on weekends and during the summer, but this didn't interfere with my schoolwork and didn't appear to be particularly outrageous, though I was sometimes on the heavier end of the norm. I studied English lit undergraduate, and then got a Master's in Business Adminstration.

After getting my MBA, I started work at an advertising agency in New York City at a time when the three-martini lunch was *de rigueur*. Drinking was glamorous and social, and though when I drank, I drank heavily, I considered this simply part of my lifestyle. Martinis were my drink of choice. I got married, and over time, my drinking increased.

By 1980, I recognized that I had a real problem with alcohol. I had started to drink during the day on weekends and was alarmed to realize I had "blacked out" part of an evening. As a result, I quit drinking altogether, on my own, for about two years.

I attended some AA meetings during the first couple of months of this period. Before going to my first meeting, I had a skid-row-drunk image of AA, but I found the people there were just regular, good people with drinking problems. The anti-alcohol fervor of the meetings, and the graphic stories of what could happen down the line to those who continued drinking heavily, helped support my decision to abstain. However, my problems were clearly less severe than those of the regular attendees. Also, since I wasn't having any trouble staying away from alcohol, and began to find the stories repetitive, I never got fully involved in the program, and stopped going.

In 1982, I started drinking again—quite moderately at the beginning. My new regimen included saying no to martinis and seldom using hard liquor. But by the third year after I'd started drinking again, I can remember getting drunk. Over time, the quantity crept back up. I only drank in the evening, and it never got as bad as it was before 1980. I knew where the deep water was and kept well clear. But I certainly felt under par during the day on many occasions.

In 1994, I took an early retirement offer from my job; at this point I was working in marketing in the pharmaceutical industry. I started doing consulting work from home. Without the structure of an office job, my nighttime drinking became even more of a problem.

In late 1995, I saw an article in my local paper about a program called Moderation Management. Actually, I didn't just see it; my wife clipped it for me. From the description, I knew right away that the program was something that I could do—and that I needed to do. But it took me a few months to get around to buying and reading the book, *Moderate Drinking: The Moderation Management Guide.* It took another few months after reading the book and doing the written exercises it contained to start the thirty-day no-drinking period that is necessary to begin the program.

I guess I had been mentally preparing myself, however, because doing the "Thirty" was actually pretty easy. I had slight urges to drink at five o'clock for a few days, and then they were gone. After the Thirty, I had great respect for alcohol. For several months, I treated it with great caution.

But to my surprise, about six weeks after returning to drinking, I got quite drunk on a Saturday night. I had been making my periodic visit to my mother, who was in a nursing home in Massachusetts. Since I live in New Jersey, I stayed the night with a relative near the nursing home for these weekend visits, which, because my mother was declining, were becoming increasingly depressing.

When I considered what had happened, I realized that my visits to her had been a regular occasion for overdrinking in the past. It was the perfect combination of a sad situation and the opportunity to drink because I was far from home on a Saturday night. After that, I knew I had to be extra careful on those weekend trips. Speaking later to MM members, I found that it is quite common for people learning moderation to run into situations that they are not yet equipped to handle, and to need to develop additional coping strategies when these arise. So an incident like that can be another step along the way to learning moderation.

I believe that drinking to relieve a low or "down" frame of mind is behind my tendency to overdrink—aside from the pure habit part of it, which came from overdrinking on a regular basis over time. While I've never been clinically depressed, depression does run in my family.

As a result, my biological makeup may aggravate the aftereffects of overdrinking, which leads to more to counter that, and so on. Keeping busy with purposeful work and with pleasurable activities is important for me, if I am to continue to be a moderate drinker.

I've also found that regular exercise is a great help. I've run five marathons since starting to deal with my drinking problem, including Boston. I've backpacked 800 miles on the Appalachian Trail over the last couple of summers. Just this morning, I ran three miles, and I continue to be a regular distance runner. The MM program has worked wonderfully for me.

Probably due to my age (I'm now sixty-seven) and the number of years I had overused alcohol, I find that temptations seem to pop up periodically, and I do need to maintain vigilance, and keep working at it, as the price of being able to use alcohol. As a former daily drinker, I have found the MM guidelines on nondrinking days (detailed later in this book) to be particularly helpful. On a long vacation to Italy a couple of years ago, I got back to daily drinking, and had to work hard when I returned to stop that. It also helps me to do an annual month of abstinence early in each year.

A couple of months after doing my first Thirty, another person and I started an MM meeting in Morristown, New Jersey. We've been meeting for five years now. Leading a meeting, which involves a great deal of sharing of personal issues, has been a wonderful new experience for me. I have certainly benefited greatly, and have seen all kinds of other people come and share and get better in the program. One of the most striking things about dialogue in MM is the optimistic, forward-thinking attitude that prevails. The feeling of confidence that one can deal with the problems of overdrinking with the right kind of effort is infectious. It buoys everyone up. (However, you don't need to attend a meeting to moderate successfully.)

People who have felt they were living with an unspeakable dirty secret find that their problems are common, manageable, and not at all reprehensible. They learn that they can become responsible drinkers and that they are not powerless.

The basic process of change is outlined in the original 1994 book for the MM program, *Moderate Drinking*. But it seemed to me that people working together and sharing their experiences in MM group sessions and on the Internet had provided a rich treasury of additional ideas on how to carry out this process.

Those experiences are the basis of *Responsible Drinking*, which not only shows you how to moderate, but also uses the insights of many people in the program to provide support and techniques for dealing with the issues that arise on the road to positive change. People who decide to confront their alcohol problems before they have become seriously dependent usually have all the strengths and capabilities they need to handle their problems on their own. However, they may need to learn to mobilize and focus those strengths and capabilities, and can benefit from specific approaches and insight developed through the experience of others. In the introduction, we'll give more details about the best way to use this book.

—Rudy Hoeltzel

Acknowledgments

The words of sixty-one participants in the Moderation Management (MM) program are quoted anonymously in this book. The overwhelmingly favorable response to requests for permission to quote reflects the group's wonderful sense of community and sharing in dealing with a common problem. Quotations are from postings to the MM online discussions, in-person meetings recorded for the book, and, in the last chapter, personal histories written especially for this book. We hope that readers who use this book to pursue moderation on an individual basis without other contact with MM will feel the sense of empathy and support from all these voices.

Maia Szalavitz, a writer who specializes in addiction subjects and who coauthored the book *Recovery Options* with Dr. Joseph Volpicelli, provided invaluable help in revising, editing, and adding to the draft in midcourse, improving considerably the readability and human interest of the text.

William R. Miller, Ph.D., Distinguished Professor of Psychology and Psychiatry, University of New Mexico, provided permission to use the Blood Alcohol Concentration tables in appendix 1. See Markham, M.R., W.R. Miller, and L. Arciniega 1993. Guilford Publications provided permission to use the Psychological Symptom Inventory (PSI-32) in appendix 2, developed by Joseph Volpicelli, M.D., Ph.D., Associate Professor of Psychiatry, University of Pennsylvania. For the Short Alcohol Dependence Data Questionnaire (SADD) in chapter 3, see Raistrick, D., G. Dunbar, K. Davidson 1983.

As well as our literary agent, Henry Shaw of Professional Publishing Services, Inc., we wish to thank the literary agent Denise Marcil for considerable assistance early in the project in organizing many practical aspects.

Introduction

This book aims to offer a wide menu of practical and specific ideas. We recognize, of course, that there are major differences in people's problems and circumstances and how they deal with them. As a result, the suggestions in *Responsible Drinking* provide a great deal of leeway for adaptation to particular situations and to different ways of looking at things. You'll probably find certain ideas more meaningful for you than others, and the sequence in which you take them up may differ from the way this book happens to be organized. You may write out all the exercises for which there are worksheets, or you may prefer to just think some or all of them through. Taking the suggestions made here in the way that makes sense to you, rather than strictly as they are presented, will work best for you. After all, the leading expert on yourself is *you*.

Here is an overview of the key concepts and phases of the change process covered in this book.

A central concept is that moderation is a reasonable and attainable goal for many with less severe drinking problems. The choice of moderation or abstinence for each person should be a considered one, based on looking at the pros and cons of each, and taking full responsibility for one's own actions. Personal choice and empowerment are critical for success, and success in moderation will further build self-efficacy.

Key phases of the process of becoming moderate are as follows:

- **A period of abstinence** of thirty days or more is useful early in the process. This period starts to break old habits, provides a space in which to prepare for practicing moderation, and has other benefits.
- **Guidelines for moderation,** which should be learned and internalized early on, include:

- Not drinking for more than three to four days per week.
- For women, an upper limit of three drinks per occasion, and not more than nine per week.
- For men, an upper limit of four drinks per occasion, and not more than fourteen per week.
- Alcohol should be consumed at a slow pace, keeping the blood alcohol concentration under .055 percent.
- Don't drink and drive.
- A key aspect of becoming a moderator is that alcohol becomes a much smaller, though enjoyable, part of life.

- Getting clearly in mind the **problems that overdrinking has caused you,** and **benefits of moderation,** including **new activities and interests,** will provide motivation and direction.
- There are a variety of **techniques for dealing with urges to drink,** and **techniques for controlling drinking** when you do choose to drink, and you can select ones that fit your individual style.
- **Identify triggers for your overdrinking** and **develop strategies to manage these triggers** more effectively.
- Bring a **high degree of attention to any drinking situation** when starting to practice moderation. It is most helpful to **keep a diary** at this time.
- Use any **slips as valuable learning experiences.** Don't let them decrease your motivation.

The path to moderation may be a long one, as was your path into overdrinking, with ups and downs along the way, so don't be discouraged if success doesn't come early and easily. However, if you are not seeing a trend toward improvement, do consider the alternative of abstinence as a resolution. Reaching a clear understanding that either moderation or abstinence is a secure resolution for your drinking problem is a very positive accomplishment. In either case, continuing vigilance is the price of continuing success.

The book aims to assist you in achieving a responsible relationship with alcohol. What do we mean by "responsible"? *Responsible drinking is drinking that provides pleasure and relaxation without putting oneself or others at increased risk for negative consequences.* Most drinkers can drink responsibly by following the guidelines discussed later in this book.

Caution: *For some drinkers, responsible drinking means no drinking.* We do not mean to tempt anyone back into drinking who has found in abstinence a secure resolution for a previous severe alcohol problem. For anyone who has previously had a very severe alcohol problem, the health and other risks of even moderate drinking are certainly increased, and to an unknown degree. We would also caution anyone who currently has a very severe alcohol problem against attempting moderation, because the chances of success decline with severity of the problem, and the risks of continued drinking are greater. The self-assessment quiz in chapter 3 will help you get a handle on the degree of your current alcohol problem. Chapter 3 also has advice on some other contraindications for continued drinking. Heavier chronic drinkers (those drinking more than five or six drinks per day) should not stop drinking suddenly on their own, which could be fatal, but should seek medical help.

The aim, then, is to help you build a healthy and risk-free relationship with alcohol, whether that means moderation in drinking or abstinence. Whichever way your path leads, we wish you a good journey. Cheers!

Chapter 1

Moderation and the Debate

Lucy, a thirty-three-year-old biotechnology company employee, started drinking regularly at fifteen. Her father, an abusive alcoholic, had left her mother when Lucy was ten. Her first boyfriend "liked to drink as much as I did," she says, as did the man she married. At age thirty, Lucy realized that she had been drinking daily for ten years. "The hangovers were getting harder to shake," she said, and added that she was probably drinking "about a gallon" of beer per night.

Danny, forty-three, works in sales on the Internet. He comes from a working-class Irish Catholic family in the Bronx. A shy, serious adolescent, he didn't start drinking until the then-legal age of eighteen, because "it wasn't worth getting caught." But after he got his girlfriend pregnant and quickly married her in his late twenties, he started drinking heavily. By his early thirties, he was drinking twelve beers daily and was "legally drunk" every day.

Terry, a forty-four-year-old middle manager, started drinking when she was fourteen. From early on, she was aware that she drank more than most of her friends. During her three pregnancies, she didn't drink—but after each birth, she was glad to get back off the wagon. After twenty-one years, her first marriage disintegrated and she got divorced. She remarried soon thereafter. However, merging her family with that of her second husband, coping with her ex-husband's terminal illness, and changing careers led to a period in which her drinking escalated to a bottle of wine per day.

Like Rudy's account in the preface, these sound like they might be the openings of stories of members of Alcoholics Anonymous, but they are not. All three—Danny, Lucy, and Terry—successfully coped with their drinking using Moderation Management (MM) techniques. In this book, you'll find out how—and learn whether the program is right for you.

Get Ready for a Surprise

You're about to learn some surprising things. In fact, you may even find out that everything you thought you knew about alcohol problems is wrong. America has historically had a weird relationship with alcohol, swinging between Puritanism and the pursuit of pleasure. This has led to a strange disconnect between "conventional wisdom" about alcohol problems and what research data actually demonstrate. As a result, the following is likely to be a pleasant and important surprise to those dealing with a drinking problem.

Why Moderation?

In most areas of medicine, doctors start with the least drastic treatments and use more difficult and costly interventions only if these fail. When high blood pressure is initially diagnosed, for example, drugs are not the most common first-line treatment—changes in diet and exercise are. For alcohol problems, the National Institute on Alcohol Abuse and Alcoholism (NIAAA) recommends that physicians assess patients in brief intervention procedures, and then direct patients to one of two goals: abstinence if they seem to be alcohol dependent, or alcoholics, and to moderation if they are not alcohol dependent (NIAAA 2000).

However, NIAAA recommendations notwithstanding, the concept of different goals for different degrees of alcohol problems has been slow to catch on in the U.S., though it is the common approach in Western Europe and Canada. In general, American providers have taken the approach that alcohol is so dangerous that total abstinence is the appropriate treatment for even the most modest problems. A belief that alcohol problems inevitably progress from moderate to severe has also contributed to this perspective. The fact is that most people with alcohol problems are not alcoholics, and can reasonably choose whether to resolve their alcohol problems through moderation or abstinence. Consider the following support for the point that moderation is a reasonable objective. We'll elaborate on all these points later in the chapter:

- There is very clear evidence that large numbers of people with alcohol problems *do* effectively learn to moderate. Indeed, moderation is actually by far the most common resolution for people with less severe problems and for people who do not undergo professional treatment.

- Further supporting the reasonableness of moderation is the evidence that professional moderation-focused treatment, usually *behavioral self-control training* (BSCT), is quite effective.

- The success of *brief intervention* also supports the use of moderation for less dependent individuals. In brief intervention, people with less severe drinking problems learn to drink more moderately with fairly minimal guidance, after a health-care professional has intervened to focus attention on the issue and get them started.

Let's look at the solid evidence for each of these.

Most People with Alcohol Problems Are Not Alcoholics

Due to questions about the adequacy of the nation's systems for dealing with alcohol problems, the NIAAA called upon the prestigious Institute of Medicine (IOM) of the National Academy of Sciences to study and report on this area.

In its 1990 report, IOM found that for every one alcoholic, there are approximately three *problem drinkers* who are at risk for serious health problems as a result of their drinking, but who do not meet the criteria for the clinical diagnosis of alcoholism, which is called *alcohol dependence*. This discovery was reaffirmed by the NIAAA in 2000 when the agency stated, "estimates suggest that alcohol dependence is found in only one in four persons seen in primary care settings [i.e., regular doctor's offices] who drink above recommended limits of alcohol use" (p. 429). This means that there are about 32 million nondependent problem drinkers in the U.S. (16 percent of the adult population)—but just 5 percent of the population are alcoholics. (The term *alcoholic* has been used in many different ways and does not have an exact meaning, but we'll use it here to mean a person with more severe alcohol problems who could be clinically diagnosed as alcohol dependent.)

In plain language, these problem drinkers have some problems related to their control over their drinking, and they may drink often and excessively, and may even take dangerous risks like drinking and driving. But they have not developed the nearly total and consistent loss of control over drinking, and the series of repeated negative consequences related to it, that marks alcoholism. A classic problem drinker is the college student who sometimes engages in binge drinking or the housewife whose nightly glass of wine turns into a nightly half bottle or bottle. These problem drinkers can usually stop or moderate when they wish to.

The IOM report pointed out, however, that most treatment programs in the U.S. are designed for the minority of drinkers with the most severe problems. In fact, 93 percent of treatment facilities base their programs on the principles of Alcoholics Anonymous (AA), requiring an admission of total powerlessness over alcohol and a commitment to attempt lifelong abstinence (Roman and Blum 1997). For the 75 percent of drinkers with less severe problems who still maintain some control over their drinking, this approach often doesn't make much sense.

The IOM suggested, as a result of its findings, that treatment be expanded to offer options for treatment of problem drinkers, not just alcoholics. It called for more programs aimed at people on the less acute end of the problem spectrum, such as brief interventions, "to reduce or eliminate the individual's alcohol consumption in a timely and efficient manner, with the goal of preventing the consequences of that consumption" (IOM 1990, p. 213). Unfortunately, appropriate alternatives for nondependent drinkers are not yet being offered in the U.S. in any widespread way.

Moderation Works for Many

Moderation is the most common resolution for people with less severe problems and for untreated people. The noted researchers Linda and Mark Sobell of the Addictions Research Foundation of Toronto were asked in 1995 what were the most important things that had been learned in the past twenty-five years of research on controlled drinking. They singled out these two conclusions: "Recoveries of individuals who have been severely dependent on alcohol predominantly involve abstinence," and "Recoveries of individuals who have not been severely dependent on alcohol predominantly involve reduced drinking" (p. 1149).

The next year, a U.S. study provided major additional evidence to support the Sobells' point. This study, called the National Longitudinal Alcohol Epidemiological Study (NLAES), was conducted by the U.S. Bureau of the Census for the NIAAA to determine what happened to people who had once been alcohol dependent (Dawson 1996). NLAES is an unusually high-quality study, as the sample was quite large and representative of the total U.S. population, and all interviews were done in person. The study reports current (past year) alcohol use and problems of 4,585 adults who had been alcohol dependent at some previous time—from one to twenty years before the interview.

The table below shows in the first column the outcomes for all people in the study, in the second column the outcomes for people who had never been treated for their problem, and in the third column the outcomes for people who had been professionally treated. In general, studies have shown a strong association between problem severity and undergoing treatment; that was again seen in this study. Compared to untreated people, those who had been treated averaged over 65 percent higher on number of drinking-related problems and over 55 percent higher on amount of alcohol consumed while alcohol dependent. Therefore, people in the second column also had less severe initial problems on average, and people in the third column had more severe alcohol problems.

As can be seen in the third column, the most frequent outcome for the treated and more severely dependent people was abstinence, with 38.8 percent achieving that goal, which was in almost all cases the aim of the treatment. But in the second column the most frequent outcome for the untreated individuals, with the less severe problems, was reduction of drinking so as to be no longer diagnosed as alcohol dependent or abusing. (An abuse diagnosis reflects lesser severity than dependence, but where drinking is causing some life problems for the individual.) Specifically, 57.8 percent, or well over half of these individuals, had moderated their drinking to the degree that they were no longer dependent or abusing.

The first column shows that overall, just about half, or 49.9 percent, of all the individuals in this study resolved their drinking problem via reduced drinking. For all these formerly dependent people, reduction in drinking was more than twice as common an outcome as abstinence. This is a very strong, clear, real-world demonstration of the practicability of reduced drinking objectives.

Current Status of Formerly Alcohol-Dependent Persons—NLAES

Current (Past-year) Status Percentages by Column:	**Total Sample**	**Never Treated**	**Ever Treated**
Alcohol Dependence or Abuse	27.8%*	25.8%*	33.2%*
Drinking Without Dependence or Abuse	49.9%	57.8%	28.0%
Abstinent	22.3%	16.4%	38.8%
Subtotal Improved (Drinking Without Dependence or Abuse, or Abstinent)	72.2%	74.2%	66.8%
Total Persons in Study	100.0%*	100.0%*	100.0%*

Percentages Across:			
Subtotal Improved	100.0%**	75.2%**	24.8%**
Total Persons in Study	100.0%**	72.9%**	27.1%**

* Percentage by column
** Percentage across

It might be noted that the treated group also had more people who continued to be alcohol dependent or abusing (33.2 percent) than the untreated group (25.8 percent). This does not reflect ineffectiveness of treatment, but rather that positive resolutions of any kind are less common in people with more severe problems. That's another good reason to deal with alcohol problems at earlier, less severe stages!

Moderation and Self-Control

One of the largest and most positive bodies of outcome data in the alcohol treatment literature is for behavioral self-control training (BSCT). BSCT seeks to strengthen individuals in using their own resources and abilities to control their own behavior in positive directions, by emphasizing individual autonomy, responsibility, choice, and competence. These same principles and many of the techniques form the backbone of the program outlined in this book. Positive outcomes have been found in extensive studies conducted since the early seventies by Miller in New Mexico, Marlatt in Washington State, Sanchez-Craig and the Sobells at the Addiction Research Foundation in Toronto, Heather in Australia and the U.K., and Duckert in Norway (Heather 2000). This provides an international body of supportive data.

An example of such treatment is a study whose results were announced in September, 2001, at the University of Buffalo, where 144 women who had drinking problems less severe than dependence were given treatment directed at drinking reduction and minimizing alcohol-related harm, rather than abstinence. At follow-up eighteen months after the outpatient treatment sessions, there were not only highly significant decreases in drinking, but also decreases in drinking consequences, increases in general self-esteem, assertiveness, and psychological functioning, and greater confidence in controlling drinking.

A review of all comparative studies of behavioral self-control training (moderation-focused) vs. traditional abstinence-oriented treatment, found BSCT to be at least equally effective and perhaps more effective than abstinence treatment (Walters 2000).

Brief Intervention

The technique for addressing alcohol problems with the largest and most positive body of research support of all is called *brief intervention*. Brief intervention studies have most often been done with people with less severe alcohol problems, and most often with moderation as a goal or option. *Brief* means short periods of face-to-face contact between health-care professionals and patients, sometimes as short as five minutes of consultation after assessment procedures. *Intervention* means that the people in the studies are not seeking treatment for alcohol problems. Rather, they are identified through screening questions about medical history in which alcohol consumption questions were included amongst questions about other health issues. Following the brief in-person sessions, individuals are left to pursue moderation on their own with fairly minimal guidance, such as short leaflets on moderation techniques. The kind of commonsense guidance typically offered in such leaflets (including NIAAA's "How to Cut Down on Your Drinking") is integral to the program offered in this book. In some studies, there are brief follow-up sessions or phone check-backs, but often not.

The largest brief intervention study was carried out by the World Health Organization (WHO) and published in 1996. The WHO study involved 1,490 heavy but nondependent drinkers at ten different sites around the world. Most persons in the study received just five to twenty minutes of counseling after assessment. Nine months after the brief intervention, drinkers had reduced their alcohol consumption on average by about one third, with impressive consistency across cultures and sites.

A key U.S. brief intervention study was carried out in Wisconsin and reported in the *Journal of the American Medical Association* (Fleming 1997). A year after the brief intervention, alcohol consumption by the participants declined 40 percent and the percent who drank excessively the week before the initial and year-later interviews declined from 47.5 percent to 17.8 percent.

A painstakingly thorough review of *all* available research studies on efficacy of different treatments for alcohol problems was reported in 1995 by Dr. William Miller and his associates. This review found brief intervention to be the approach with far and away the strongest evidence of effectiveness of all 30 types of treatment for which there was data!

Brief Intervention and Self-Change

For people who want to change their own alcohol habits without professional treatment, the significance of these findings on brief intervention is threefold.

First, they add to the very large body of evidence that people with alcohol problems short of dependence (and even some who are dependent) can and do achieve moderation.

Second, there are strong similarities between the change process in brief intervention and the self-initiated change you may be considering. Brief intervention essentially uses a doctor's appointment to bring the alcohol problem forcefully to the attention of the patient and to get him or her focused on improving it. Beyond that, however, brief intervention offers little support. Patients are typically told that their drinking habits are their own responsibility and choice. Often, a specific goal of reduction or elimination of drinking is worked out between the professional and the patient. Some brief advice on means to change may be provided verbally and some written material on how to do it may be provided. And that's about it.

Brief intervention works on the basis that the patient has the capabilities and strengths to change successfully, once started on the path. The program detailed in this book, which helps to marshal the strengths and capabilities of each person, has a strong similarity to brief intervention, but actually provides more guidance, support, and specific advice.

Third, while the brief intervention studies show that impressive changes can be made by people who were not seeking change at the time of intervention, the outlook for motivated self-changers is even better. James Prochaska and his colleagues studied thousands of ex-smokers who had quit on their own to determine how they had done it and what they could teach others who wanted to kick the habit (Prochaska

1994). They found a series of stages through which people progress when making a major change in behavior. The critical early steps include recognizing that one has a habit in need of change and bringing oneself to the point of seeking ways to make that change. Few people involved in brief intervention studies were at the point of deliberately seeking a way to change their alcohol habits. However, those who are reading this book most likely are actively seeking means to change, and are thus several critical steps ahead of those studied in brief intervention research.

Overall, then, we've seen that moderation is a reasonable and attainable objective for many people with alcohol problems. Even people who are alcohol dependent most often resolve their problems through moderation, although this book is not aimed at those who are dependent, due to their greater risk from continued drinking. Moderation-directed BSCT has a strong record of successful results. And brief intervention studies demonstrate the ability of nondependent problem drinkers to resolve their problems through moderation with only a small amount of guidance.

The Dominance of Twelve-Step Programs

So why don't most people know about this research, and about the hundreds of other studies that support moderation as a way of coping with drinking problems?

The answer comes down to politics—and the popularity of the self-help group Alcoholics Anonymous (AA). When America prohibited alcohol in 1919, it was because people had increasingly come to believe that alcohol was a dangerous poison—not just dangerous for heavy drinkers, but for everyone. It was believed that there was no chance of controlling it. If anyone—even the most upright citizen—drank enough booze for long enough, he or she would get hooked. Alcohol was viewed in much the same way we now view cocaine.

This led to the outright ban on alcohol sales, and all the crime and corruption everyone associates with Prohibition. But how could America repeal Prohibition if the demon rum still contained the devil? The answer was a new look at alcohol, and at those who had problems with it. The end-of-Prohibition and post-Prohibition view became that most people can handle alcohol, but a small minority—alcoholics—cannot. The problem no longer resided in the substance, but in those few who developed serious problems with it.

This view was given a huge boost by Alcoholics Anonymous, the first group to report widespread success helping alcoholics. Founded in 1935 by Bill Wilson and Dr. Bob Smith, it claimed that only alcoholics could understand the problems of other alcoholics—and that the only way to solve these problems was for one alcoholic to help another. Though AA promotes what is largely a moral cure—involving confession, repentance, atonement, and giving one's will over to a higher power—many in AA believe that alcoholism is a disease.

Since psychiatry and the rest of medicine had largely given up on alcoholics during Prohibition, AA filled a void, and its ideas began seeping into detoxification programs and other facilities devoted to treating alcoholism. Soon treatment centers, mainly run by people who had recovered through AA, sprang up. The proprietors of these centers came to believe that they had an unbeatable system for treating alcoholism. Not coming from a medical or scientific background, they didn't feel the need to prove their efficacy with outcome studies or other research. They believed that the success stories of those who recovered were proof enough. Those who relapsed, or who didn't think they needed abstinence, were just "in denial." Their problems were not considered to be the program's or the rehab center's fault. Overgeneralizations like these, based on an unsystematic view of the experience of the heaviest-drinking alcoholics, began to spread beyond treatment centers and into public opinion about alcohol problems.

AA began to develop a view of the problem based on the special circumstances of AA meetings. Members never saw anyone who went from heavy drinking to moderation at their meetings. Such people were highly unlikely, after all, to show up at an AA meeting, or to discuss their experience with those who would be likely to disbelieve or denigrate it. Similarly, AA members rarely met drinkers who had gotten sober on their own, because such people would be unlikely to identify themselves as former alcoholics or go to AA.

While AA had warned against people becoming "Professional AA's" and getting paid for their work in promoting the program, nonetheless there emerged a whole class of paraprofessionals whose experience of counseling was largely limited to what they had learned in AA and in rehab based on AA. They began to promote the idea that any loss of control over drinking was a sign of incipient alcoholism—and that any denial of an alcohol problem was a sign that one existed.

In the late 1980s and early 1990s, these rehabs and counselors came to dominate the discussion of alcohol and other drug problems. Twelve-step programs for all sorts of problems became popular—so much so that in 1990, 13 percent of the American population reported having attended at least one meeting either as a participant or a guest of a friend.

Insurance would pay for thirty days of inpatient care for alcoholics. Suddenly, anyone with such coverage who had a drinking problem at any level was really "in denial" of just how bad it was and needed thirty days of confrontation to become convinced. Many of these programs, based strongly on AA, were truly well-intentioned, and they helped thousands to recover. Unfortunately, others used the rhetoric to treat people who didn't need such intense care—and to convince them that their alcohol problem required a lifetime of abstinence and lengthy aftercare therapy.

Though AA was based on a foundation of voluntary acceptance of its steps and a philosophy of "attraction not promotion," coercive measures like confrontational therapy and "interventions" became increasingly popular. AA's main book ("the big book") suggests a trial of controlled drinking if a person is not convinced that he or she is an alcoholic (Wilson 1976, p. 31–32). Now, however, those who suggest such a trial are seen as "enablers" who are keeping alcoholics drinking, rather than helping them recover. And so, any treatment that does not demand abstinence from people with drinking problems on day one is demonized.

Today, despite the continually growing scientific evidence that moderation is not only feasible, but preferred by most nonalcoholic problem drinkers and the most likely resolution for drinking problems, American treatment centers still believe it is too controversial to offer. In 2000, the Smithers Center—a rehab noted for treating such famous patients as Truman Capote and Darryl Strawberry—started offering patients a choice of treatment goals, since a number of severe alcoholics are reluctant to commit to abstinence initially, but generally opt for abstinence as they progress through treatment. The medical director was thereupon fired summarily after an outcry from twelve-step devotees.

Tellingly, in other countries, which never made alcohol sales illegal and where AA never took hold, moderation treatments for problem drinking and even for alcoholics are common and not at all disputed. For Americans to benefit from moderation therapies in this country, however, it is likely that we will have to help ourselves.

The Power of Belief

Here's what one person, looking into MM as a way to change a distressing drinking problem, said in an online discussion. He was troubled by a feeling common to those with drinking problems: a loss of power over alcohol. AA takes that feeling to be an unchangeable fact, but this person was seeking a way to regain that power.

> *I am powerless over alcohol. I tell myself that I will not drink, and then I do. I decide that I will not drink during the week, only weekends, but I fall short. Once I start drinking, I cannot stop. I get annoyed when alcohol runs out or I don't have any when I want it.*
>
> *My life is unmanageable due to alcohol because my career suffers. I cannot give 100 percent to anything, work or personally related. I say and do embarrassing things that I feel embarrassed about afterward. I suffer from all-day hangovers.*

A person who had achieved moderation through MM replied:

> *You could call it powerless; it feels like powerless. When I really believed it was fun to get drunk, or that I "needed" to drink to get through my life, then, of course I drank. But the truth is, I set myself up for it. Right now, I am very much involved in changing and refixing the strength of my belief.*
>
> *I think most of us know the power of belief. I think we all have different little particulars about our drinking history or why we do it. We all shared the same beliefs about it. We believed we needed to drink to get through certain situations. We believed if we drank we would be happy. By a certain point in our lives we realized more and more that drinking to get through situations could create more and different and bad situations. But somehow, that didn't necessarily stop us from using it to get away from the bad situations in front of us at the moment. Additionally, we realize that we only feel happy when we're drinking. Maybe it is a function of age, but after a while, I wasn't really happy for too long even while I was drinking. And I certainly wasn't happy after.*
>
> *So I, like you, set myself up for feeling worse about myself by now saying I was going to do something about my drinking and then drinking anyway and just feeling like a big fat loser. But take heart. This is just part of the process of healing!! It's not easy to change our beliefs and the habits that have evolved over many years. First we need that inkling. An inkling that all is not as it should be. That inkling needs to be walked around, stared at, thought about, and it grows, slowly, little by little. And works its way into "I want to change" and transforms itself into "I can change" and moves on to "change." For most of us, "I want to change" doesn't magically result in change. We have to work the steps, the baby steps everyone talks about.*

This dialogue reflects how hopeless and out of control people can feel when they start to confront a drinking problem. Chances are you've tried sporadically to bring the drinking problem under control, without really giving it your full attention, and failed. But now you're giving the issue a new priority in your life. You're taking time to focus your attention and efforts in this area. Be aware that, "to change your beliefs and habits that have evolved over many years," you've started on a journey that is made up of many small steps. As you take each step forward, your belief and confidence in your own ability to succeed will grow. So far, you have seen that large numbers of people do resolve drinking problems, and that for many, moderation is a viable alternative to abstinence. In the next chapter, we'll come to understand better how alcohol affects us in different ways. Then, in the following chapter, we'll deal with your choice of goals.

Summing Up

- Drinking and problems associated with it may make your life seem hopeless right now, but for most people the odds of resolving their drinking problems are quite good—once they begin to pay serious attention to the issue.
- At least 75 percent of people who drink above healthful levels are not alcoholics—but help for such people is not widely available in the U.S.
- Alcoholics Anonymous and treatment programs modeled on it have so dominated the approach to alcohol problems in America that other effective approaches have been overlooked.
- The Moderation Management program is based on solid scientific evidence for techniques that work in dealing with alcohol problems.
- A large percentage of people with alcohol problems resolve them through learning to moderate their drinking.
- A trial of moderation is a reasonable first step for those who think their drinking may be getting out of control.
- Most people with alcohol problems resolve them without professional treatment, and there is overwhelming evidence that self-managed efforts can be effective for nonalcoholic problem drinkers.
- Critical initial steps in dealing with problem behaviors include recognition of a need for change and starting to actively seek means to change. If you are reading this book, then you have probably already taken several of the most important steps along the path to positive change.

Chapter 2

Alcohol's Effects

Because you're reading this book, it's clear that you've been giving some thought to the effects of alcohol. Still we believe you'll learn something new from this chapter.

First we'll hear more from Lucy, whom you met in chapter 1. Lucy's earliest memories of how alcohol affected her framed her later experience of it. She recalls:

> *My very first experience with alcohol came in a loving environment. After dinner at my grandparents' house on holidays, they would allow us to have one small shot of chocolate mint liqueur. I loved the way it tasted and I loved the way it made me feel all warm inside. It just perfectly matched all the love I felt at Grandmom's house. It was very good and I would ask for more, but one was all they would ever allow.*

Another person, Lisa, from New Mexico, aged fifty-two, describes the effects drinking had on her:

> *I would wake up at 2:00 A.M. and start to experience panic attacks. I would wrestle with myself into the morning hours, deciding that, today, I would cut down or would not drink. By 3:00 P.M., the resolve I had felt at 4:00 A.M. had faded. I felt trapped, like I was on a hamster wheel and couldn't step off to do anything differently. I was also frustrated that I didn't feel in control, but instead was being controlled by this habit.*

The first quotation touches on how experience can shape your expectations of the way alcohol will affect you. The second touches on the paradox of continued overuse of alcohol despite continuing negative consequences. The human response to alcohol is complex indeed, and this chapter will explore both the physical and psychological aspects of alcohol use.

Overall, you'll see that overuse of alcohol has a wide range of negative effects, and that the positive experiences of alcohol are really limited to moderate use. In order to understand why less is more and how our expectations of alcohol use are shaped, you first need to understand the physiological effects of alcohol.

General Physical Effects

Alcohol is classified as a sedative or depressant substance because its most prominent effects are to impair mental and physical functioning and cause sedation. (*Depressant* in this sense refers to its ability to impair functioning rather than to change mood). The following table shows the increasing interference with mental and physical functions as the amount of alcohol in the body increases. The level of alcohol in the body is measured by blood alcohol concentration (BAC), which is directly related to how much you drink, along with several other factors that will be discussed later. You probably recall learning about BAC while studying for your road test—it is the measure used by police to determine whether or not a driver is impaired. The legal BAC limit for driving in many states is 0.08 percent, in some states 0.10 percent, and all states will likely soon phase over to that lower limit due to new federal regulations.

Common Alcohol Effects for People Without Tolerance

BAC	Common Effects
0.02%	Light and moderate drinkers begin to feel some effect.
0.04%	Most people begin to feel relaxed.
0.06%	Judgment is somewhat impaired; people are less able to make rational decisions about their capabilities (such as driving).
0.08%	Definite impairment of muscle coordination and driving skills is evident; increased risk of nausea and slurred speech.
0.10%	Clear deterioration of reaction time.
0.15%	Balance and movement are impaired; risk of blackouts, passing out, and accidents increase dramatically.
0.30%	Most people lose consciousness. Central nervous system is substantially depressed; risk of death.

Despite this strong profile of progressively depressing effects on the body, the first effect most people notice is the drug's paradoxical initial stimulant action. Low doses of alcohol increase measures of arousal (like heart rate), while additional drinking and simply the passage of time after one drink will reduce energy and awareness (Marlatt 1999).

Alcohol also has effects on at least one of the *reward centers* of the brain (Cowen 1999). The evolutionary function of these areas is to motivate animals—or in this case, people—to do things that promote the survival of their genes. These can be loosely characterized by what biologists call the four Fs: feeding, fighting, fleeing, and fucking. Doing any of these successfully feels good. One thing alcohol and other drugs do is stimulate the release of chemicals (in the best-understood case, the body's own opioids and dopamine) in brain areas that normally release them during a triumph in one of these activities so basic to survival. The good feeling from an actual triumph probably comes from multiple, as-yet-unknown pathways and is fuller and richer than that from alcohol. But in learning to drink, we're learning to experience the effects of alcohol as similar to the experience of a real triumph. Nature meant to reward us for positive activity, but alcohol and drugs can give some of the same rewards more easily. That can of course lead to overuse.

Research has also found that nature has a kind of counterbalancing system to help keep emotions from staying in extreme states (Solomon 1980). That is, a rapid and strong movement toward a positive or negative emotional state is soon met by a countering movement in the opposite direction. This *opponent process* effect may have both physical and psychological roots. Examples of negative states that people undergo to induce a positive after-feeling are skydiving, bungee jumping, roller coaster rides, and very hot saunas. Examples of strong positive mood states that induce negative after-feelings are those involved with heavy drinking and use of other euphoriant drugs.

A striking feature of this decline in mood is that it is often somewhat more extreme and longer lasting than the initial high. That is, the countering mood movement has a momentum of its own, and often seems to overdo it a bit. However, you can keep from triggering this kind of effect with alcohol, or at least keep it at a low level, by keeping consumption moderate. After moderate drinking, there should be little noticeable crash—which is another good reason to favor it.

The Power of Belief

Our expectations or expectancies about alcohol—our beliefs about what drinking will do to us—are also essential factors in determining how we will perceive and respond to this drug. You may have heard of the *placebo effect* in medicine, where an inert substance can sometimes bring about cures or changes. It is so powerful that new drugs must be tested in comparison to placebo before they are approved in order to ensure that the substance itself has actions above and beyond this effect. The impact of expectancies on drinkers is similarly dramatic.

Some now-classic experiments illustrate the importance of expectancies to drinking experiences (Marlatt 1999). In these experiments, social drinkers were given tonic-flavored drinks. Half were told that the drinks contained alcohol, and the other half were told that they were drinking soft drinks. But half of each group were misled— they were told that their drinks contained alcohol, when in fact, they did not, or vice versa.

The behavior of participants depended almost entirely on what the subjects were told the drinks contained—*not* their actual alcohol content. As Dr. Marlatt reported, "Those who expected to receive alcohol showed disinhibited responsiveness, regardless of the alcohol content of the beverage" (p. 234). These types of experiments have demonstrated that expectancies condition many types of social behavior related to drinking, including openness about disclosing personal information and aggression. In one experiment of this type, young male subjects were exposed to sexually violent tapes, and the degree to which they had erections reflected whether they were told their drinks contained alcohol, rather than whether the drinks actually contained alcohol (Briddell 1978). However, it is always actual alcohol content that depresses measures of functioning, including motor performance and reaction times. Those effects do not depend on expectancies.

Since expectancies can be so powerful in conditioning our responses to alcohol, it's important to think about what exactly they are, and where they come from. Expectancies are automatic associations between things. These are learned associations, not inborn ones. With drinking, most of us have learned to automatically associate it with a variety of pleasurable experiences. Many of these automatic associations are learned from others (most strikingly in college fraternities and sororities where the situation seems to teach that overdrinking is *the* way to have fun), and some are related to our own personal experiences. So people who automatically associate drinking with pleasure have seen others appear to derive pleasure from it, and have also experienced pleasure from it themselves.

But if alcohol can produce both positive and negative experiences, why do people expect mainly positive experiences from alcohol, as surveys repeatedly show (Leigh 1999)? The reason has to do with biases in the way our brains process information. Things that happen repeatedly and in quick succession in time are more likely to be interpreted as related to each other than those that happen less often and a long time apart. With alcohol, the positive effects do happen quickly, and, with some help from our expectations, fairly reliably. The negative effects happen later and not as consistently—and, worse, our memories of them may be hazy.

For example, hangovers don't happen every time we drink—and they happen a day later. So the association between drinking and hangovers isn't as emotionally strong as that between drinking and pleasure. Hangovers also may be taken by regular heavy drinkers to be a normal part of life. And some of the worst consequences of drinking, such as liver failure or auto fatalities, are never experienced by most drinkers. As a result, the positive associations between alcohol and pleasure are much more likely to be strengthened than those that link alcohol to pain. Fortunately, since this is a learned connection, it can also be unlearned.

Another expectancy many people have about alcohol is that more is better. The feeling of enjoyment from the first drink or two may make us reach for more in an attempt to sustain or increase these good feelings. Normal people who do not overdrink get a signal from their bodies that they have had enough after a drink or two, when the alcohol starts to interfere with functioning in a way that they perceive as unpleasant. They say to themselves, "I am starting to feel as though I'm losing control—I'd better stop." People who overdrink, however, may disregard or never get that signal. Steps discussed later will help you become more sensitive to these normal body feelings of "enough is enough," and can also give you mental tools to help control your consumption.

BAC, Gender, and Weight Differences

One way to understand and control the effects of alcohol is to know about and use information regarding your BAC. Your BAC is directly related to how much you drink: the more alcohol you consume, the higher your BAC.

But the BAC that results from a given amount of alcohol also varies by weight, the time-span in which the alcohol is consumed, and gender (Markham 1993). It's easy to see why most of these factors matter. The more you weigh, the more fluid you will have in your body, so any given dose of alcohol will be more diluted and less impairing. The more time since you consumed alcohol, the more time your body will have had to metabolize it and get it out of your system.

Gender is a bit more complicated. For a number of reasons, women tend to achieve higher BACs from a given amount of alcohol than men do. Women, of course, weigh less on average. Women also have a higher proportion of fat in their bodies in relation to water, so they have relatively less water to dilute the alcohol. In addition, women have less of the gastric enzyme that metabolizes and deactivates alcohol.

A 120-pound woman would have a 0.027 percent BAC an hour after drinking one drink, a 0.071 percent BAC after two drinks in one hour, and would be just at the 0.055 percent BAC after two drinks in two hours. But if a 180-pound man consumes two drinks in two hours, his BAC will be only 0.016 percent. The differences by sex and weight, as you can see, can be quite dramatic. A complete set of BAC tables is furnished in appendix 1 so that you can see what your own BAC is likely to be at different drinking levels.

The drinking guidelines and limits of the MM program suggest keeping BAC under 0.055 percent, or below the level where significant judgment and performance impairment occur.

Tolerance to Alcohol

Another factor that can affect your response to alcohol is tolerance. Tolerance results from the body's attempt to stay in balance despite regular alcohol consumption. When you develop tolerance, you feel less of the initial stimulating effect from a drink. Many take this as a positive sign that they can now hold their liquor better and stay more in control. But in fact, tolerance reduces your ability to feel pleasure from small amounts of alcohol and it also seems to increase the depressing effects of higher doses.

Also, as tolerance develops, the "had enough" signal that your body sends to tell you to stop drinking (which nonproblem drinkers recognize and respond to) is diminished or lost. People with tolerance are likely to drink more as a result. And so tolerance exposes your body to higher levels of alcohol and, as a result, a greater probability of negative health consequences.

Do Genes Matter?

To some extent, your reaction to alcohol is also determined by your genes (NIAAA 1995; NIAAA 2000). If one or more of your first-degree relatives (parents or siblings) have had significant alcohol problems, your chance of developing such problems is increased.

It is not clear, however, how and to what extent genetic influences work (Peele and DeGrandpre 1995). Some people with alcohol problems seem to be predisposed to feel greater pleasure from alcohol—and less pleasure from other life experience. Others with drinking problems have a somewhat opposite reaction—they have innate or inborn tolerance and are less affected by alcohol. People with innate tolerance probably have increased risk of developing alcohol problems because they lack the "had enough" signal. In addition, some alcohol problems may be linked to genes that make people more likely to take risks, and others to genes that make them less likely to do well socially or more likely to be depressed or have other mental illnesses. Obviously, it is a very complex area.

Nonetheless, it is clear that no one is predestined to have alcohol problems. Most children of alcoholics do not become alcoholics. It is also clear that genetic factors must interact with the environment (for example, upbringing and culture) and other factors to produce alcohol problems.

For instance, genetics make most East Asians tend to flush (develop a burning redness in their faces) and feel uncomfortable when drinking. They have a defect in the enzyme system that metabolizes alcohol—and consequently, their experience is a much milder version of what happens when someone takes Antabuse (a drug that blocks the enzyme system entirely). As a result, Asians with these genes tend to drink much less than Americans and Europeans. However, Native Americans have the same genetically-determined physical reaction to alcohol, and those living on reservations have some of the highest rates of alcohol use and alcohol problems in the world.

So if alcohol problems run in your family, it is possible that you may have inherited a response to alcohol that will make controlling its use more difficult for you—but genetics does not wholly determine what will happen. The choices you make about when, where, how much, and with whom you drink also have a large influence. Nonetheless, if you come from a family with a history of alcohol problems, and seem to be running into a stone wall in attempts to curb drinking, be alert to potential genetic influences. If you have a very atypical response to alcohol (can hold your drinks much better than anyone you know, for example, or get much more euphoric than your friends), it may be genetic, and this may make learning to moderate more difficult or even impossible.

Harmful Health Consequences

Long-term heavy drinking causes liver disease in over 2 million Americans and is the most common cause of liver failure (NIH 1999). Heavy drinking also increases the risk of cardiovascular problems, including high blood pressure, heart disease, and certain kinds of stroke. In addition, high levels of alcohol consumption increase the risk of cancer, especially of the throat and mouth, and probably also of the colon and rectum. The risk of pancreatitis—an extremely painful inflammation of the pancreas, which produces insulin—is also dramatically elevated. Fetal alcohol syndrome—which can result from overdrinking by pregnant women—is the number one cause of mental retardation in children.

The most common alcohol-related health risk, however, is in the area of accidents and injuries. Because most of these are not reported, or are not associated with alcohol when reported, the total number of injuries from alcohol use is not known. But the impact of alcohol on traffic fatalities is well documented, and more than 16,000 people are killed annually in the U.S. in alcohol-related motor vehicle crashes (U.S. Dept. of Transportation 2000). Alcohol is involved in 39 percent of fatal motor vehicle crashes. Research also finds that alcohol is involved in about 50 percent of homicides, 15 percent of robberies, 26 percent of assaults, and 37 percent of rapes and sexual assaults—far more than any other drug (NIAAA 2000). And a study of fatal, nonintentional injuries that did not involve motor vehicles found that 31 percent involved blood alcohol levels of 0.10 percent or above (Smith, 1999).

A recent survey of alcohol-related verbal and physical violence in the general population found that drinking was involved in 38.1 percent of serious arguments, 56.5 percent of threats, and 67.9 percent of incidents of physical aggression. This survey also found that physical violence was associated with intoxication rather than simply with drinking moderately (Wells 2000).

People with alcohol problems are much more likely to smoke, to smoke heavily, and to have great difficulty stopping smoking. Alcohol and smoking may be synergistic in promoting dependency, and are clearly synergistic in causing health problems, notably certain cancers and cardiovascular problems. In fact, it has been established that more alcohol abusers die of smoking-related diseases than die directly from the effects of alcohol (Hurt 1996).

The Liver

Because the liver plays a key role in metabolizing alcohol, it is amongst the organs most likely to suffer damage (NIAAA 1998). This damage occurs in three stages. The first two of these can often be reversed, but the last stage is usually fatal.

The first phase is called *fatty liver*. Here, liver cells have switched to using alcohol as fuel instead of breaking down fat, which is one of their key jobs as part of digestion. Unprocessed fat accumulates inside liver cells, which stresses them, and if drinking is not reduced, this stress begins to kill them.

The second stage is known as *alcoholic hepatitis*. In this condition, liver cells start dying from the changed fat metabolism and from the direct toxic effect of alcohol. The body's immune defenses then cause inflammation (the "-itis"). In someone with hepatitis, the liver is enlarged, may be sore, and is tense and tender to the touch. The person feels generally unwell, with nausea, vomiting, and perhaps even a yellowish tinge to the skin and eyeballs and bloody-looking urine and grey bowel movements. At this stage, if a person quits or severely limits drinking, the liver may return to normal or close enough to cause few problems.

But if the drinker keeps drinking, the liver will continue to decline. In the final stage, which is called *cirrhosis*, many liver cells have died and been replaced by fibrous scar tissue. The liver has now become small, lumpy, and hard, and there are a number of associated symptoms. These include a worsening and intensifying of all the symptoms of hepatitis, with frequent nausea, vomiting, diarrhea, and digestive problems (often everything eaten or drunk gives a feeling of being poisoned or weighed down). Again, if alcohol use is stopped, many people can live with decreased liver function. But this stage is terminal if alcohol use continues or if the cirrhosis has been allowed to progress to the point of no return. Liver transplants can help some people—but they are hard to obtain and anyone who has not maintained consistent sobriety for a period of time (usually a year or so) is ineligible.

In order to determine the health of your liver, liver function tests or liver enzyme tests can be performed. These indicate the amount of enzymes that are flowing out of liver cells into the bloodstream due to cell damage. If a physician indicates that your liver enzymes are elevated, listen carefully to the advice given. If there is any mention of cirrhosis or borderline cirrhosis, it is best never to drink again, because your liver is at the very least highly sensitive to alcohol, and may have suffered permanent damage. Getting these tests done can also be a way of determining for yourself if your drinking has harmed your body—and if it has, that can help strengthen your resolve to change. If not, as you become a moderate drinker, just think about the nasty symptoms you won't have to worry about developing!

Alcohol and Sleep

Alcohol normally helps people fall asleep, but it can decrease the time spent in the most restful stage of sleep: REM sleep, where most dreams occur and which is believed to be important for storing and later recalling memories (NIAAA July 1998b). Drinking may also cause early morning awakening—not at 7:00 A.M., but at 2:00 to 4:00 A.M. (as in Lisa's story, above), when depressing thoughts often come to mind and it becomes impossible to get back to sleep.

As a result, it's a short-term solution to insomnia, at best, which can have negative long-term results if repeated. In the long run, those who drink heavily often find that alcohol doesn't even help them fall asleep—and that awakening at the hour of the wolf is even more common and unpleasant. In fact, problems related to poor sleep account for a good part of the most unpleasant feelings that follow a night of heavy drinking.

How Does Alcohol Compare to Other Substances?

Comparing alcohol to other psychoactive substances gives an interesting additional perspective on its nature and physical effects. Two experts on addiction, Dr. Jack Henningfield of the National Institute on Drug Abuse, and Dr. Neal Benowitz of the University of California at San Francisco, ranked six legal and illegal substances on five problem areas (Hilts 1994). The substances were nicotine, heroin, cocaine, alcohol, caffeine, and marijuana.

Interestingly, two of the legal substances—alcohol and nicotine—were amongst the most dangerous on several dimensions. Nicotine ranks highest on difficulty of quitting and likelihood that users will develop dependence, with alcohol rated only fourth on that dimension. While heroin ranks highest on tolerance (the need for increasing amounts over time) and cocaine ranks highest on reinforcement (wanting to use over and over, in preference to all other activities and drugs), alcohol ranks highest on two important dimensions: intoxication and withdrawal.

Withdrawal won't be a problem for most people seeking to moderate because the vast majority won't have developed this high a level of dependence on the drug. However, it's important to point out that alcohol withdrawal—unlike that from heroin or cocaine—can kill. If you have developed dependence to the point where you get "the shakes" when you go without a drink, it is important to seek medical attention if you wish to quit or seriously cut back.

Intoxication, on the other hand, is an important consideration for most moderate drinkers. Heroin, cocaine, and marijuana can certainly have profound mind-altering capabilities—and most people believe that they are illegal in part as a result of the intensity of this intoxication. What a surprise, then, to learn that alcohol can derange thinking the most of any of these drugs! If you were going to get into a car with an intoxicated driver, you'd be safer (though not as safe as with a sober driver, of course) with someone on cocaine or marijuana than with a heavy drinker—and if you had to cope with an intoxicated person, a heroin user or potsmoker would be more likely to be cooperative and follow instructions than a drunk.

As Dr. George Vaillant, a Harvard professor and one of the country's leading alcohol researchers, put it: "No other drug of addiction impairs one's aversion to punishment the way alcohol does . . . When drinking, people are much more likely to engage in all kinds of dangerous, life-threatening behavior—wife beating, child abuse, unprotected sex with strangers, smoking, drunk driving. You can be five foot two and willing to take on anyone in the bar" (Lambert 2000).

The Health Benefits of Moderation

However, unlike any other recreational drug known, alcohol, if used moderately can actually protect your health. At first, researchers couldn't believe that the link seen in a number of studies between moderate drinking and lowered risk of heart disease and the most common type of stroke was real. They thought it must be connected to other positive health behaviors exhibited by moderate drinkers, like exercising more and having better diets than heavy drinkers. But a major study, which separated the effect of alcohol consumption from other diet and lifestyle factors, has now demonstrated that an effect on coronary heart events is real and is related to moderate drinking itself (Stampfer 2000). These benefits appear to be due to modest positive effects on cholesterol levels and on two factors involved in blood clotting (Baer 2002).

In what is known as the "French paradox," the death rate from coronary heart disease is lower in France than, say, in the U.K., despite comparable diets and higher alcohol consumption in France. This may be due to the French preference for wine rather than other alcoholic beverages. And, studies in non-French populations have indicated that, at moderate intake levels, wine may provide more cardiovascular benefits than other alcohol drinks (Gronbeck 2000). More recently, a factor has been found in certain red wine varietals such as cabernet sauvignon that blocks a peptide involved in atherosclerosis—so it may be red wine rather than wine in general that has an extra benefit (Corder 2001).

Several well-conducted studies that have followed older people over time have now indicated a protective effect of moderate alcohol consumption against dementia and Alzheimer's disease (Galants 2000; Peele, 2000; Ruitenberg 2002). This may be due to preservation of brain vascular integrity or to positive effects on one of the major brain neurotransmitters. Moderate alcohol consumption has also been associated with decreased incidence of osteoporosis (Turner 2000). These effects have not yet been as strongly supported as those on cardiovascular health, but the possible dementia/Alzheimer's benefit could be very important because of the current lack of preventive means for these conditions.

Note that all of these health benefits are reversed with drinking above moderate levels, however.

Environment Matters

The effects of alcohol are also related to the overall atmosphere of a country where someone is drinking at a given time. The U.S. has tended historically to run to extremes in alcohol use. Levels were high in colonial times and prior to the Civil War (Nephew 2000). They were very low before and during the early part of Prohibition (1920–1933), then rose up through World War II, and afterward dropped a bit. Drinking levels reached their highest peak in the early eighties (when rates of other drug use were also at all-time highs) and have declined 21 percent since. The table below shows the low in 1954 and the peak in 1981.

U.S. Per Capita Total Alcohol Consumption

Population 14 and Older	
1860	2.53 (gallons of ethanol)
1946	2.30
1954	1.96
1981	2.76
1998	2.19

In addition to a change in total quantity, there has been a shift in recent years toward the lower-alcohol beverages like beer and wine, with distilled spirits falling from 37 percent of total consumption in 1981 to 29 percent in 1998.

The environment in America is thus becoming increasingly favorable to more moderate use of alcohol. According to the *Tenth Special Report to the U.S. Congress on Alcohol and Health:* "One of the factors consistently identified in the epidemiologic literature is that the overall level of consumption in a society, that is, its relative 'wetness' or 'dryness,' is related to the rate of alcohol problems" (NIAAA 2000, p. 38). Against the background of lower total alcohol consumption and use of the lighter alcoholic beverages, there are also anti–drunk driving media campaigns and tougher criminal sanctions. Social approval of heavy drinking is low now, whereas in the past, in many businesses, the three-martini lunch or complaining about hangovers on Monday were accepted social rituals, and being able to "hold your liquor" was an important part of masculinity.

As a result of the shift away from heavy consumption, you are more likely to find today an ideal climate of approval and support for your efforts to moderate than at most other times.

Summing Up

- Alcohol initially has a stimulating effect, but at higher doses it has an overall depressing effect on the nervous system and the body, and there are unavoidable impairments that occur at increasing blood alcohol concentrations (BACs).
- Through the "opponent process" effect, a strong positive mood change caused by alcohol is often followed by a later negative swing in mood.
- Our expectations greatly affect our experiences of drinking. Many studies show that expectancies and not the alcohol itself cause much of the positive mood change and social disinhibition that we associate with drinking.
- We tend to automatically associate drinking with its positive early effects rather than its later negative effects, because we form automatic associations based on consequences that happen quickly and predictably. So we need to keep reminding ourselves and reinforcing in our minds the negative side of overdrinking.

- The Moderation Management program recommends that BAC be kept under .055 percent, to avoid impaired judgment. This book provides a set of BAC tables by gender, weight, and alcohol intake.
- Genetics play a role in alcohol problems, and may make it more difficult for some individuals to overcome an established drinking problem. However, no one is destined to have alcohol problems due to genetics alone, and other, controllable, factors seem to be of greater importance.
- Heavier consumption of alcohol can cause a host of health and other problems, especially related to violence of all kinds.
- Truly moderate use of alcohol may actually confer some health benefits.

Chapter 3

Choosing Your Goal

Now's the time to choose your own goal. We'll start by looking at some successful moderators. The stories of Lucy, Danny, and Terry, whom we met at the beginning of chapter 1, all have positive outcomes.

Lucy, the thirty-three-year-old biotechnology company employee, says of her alcohol problem:

> *MM reaffirmed what I believed. I was not sick and I had the power. All I had to do was find it, strengthen it, and use it.*

Lucy has been abstaining for six months and plans to drink very moderately again at some time in the future.

Danny, the salesman, says of his discovery of the moderation approach:

> *I felt like I could exhale and actually talk about my behavior as opposed to simply "don't drink" and "go to meetings."*

Danny has cut his drinking dramatically, and it no longer causes him problems at work or with his family.

Terry, the forty-four-year-old middle manager, says of her discovery of moderation and taking part in the MM online discussions:

> *I went on the e-mail list and was totally flabbergasted to learn that there were problem drinkers out there who did not have to hit bottom, and even some who had, but were able to turn their drinking around and were actually drinking socially again.*

Terry has been a moderate drinker for over a year, with just one heavy drinking incident. She abstains entirely four to five days a week, and drinks within healthy limits on days she does drink.

Each of these people achieved their positive outcome through their own efforts, with a little guidance from the MM program in focusing those efforts. This included some hard thinking about whether abstinence or moderation would be the right goal for them, including assessment of the level of their current drinking problem as one indicator of which goal would be best, thinking through the pros and cons of both moderation and abstinence, and looking at what moderation really entails and the steps necessary to get there. Those are the subjects that you'll tackle in this chapter.

Moderation or Abstinence?

A first step is to get an objective measure of the level of your drinking problem. Your score from the following questionnaire will provide a rough guide as to the likelihood of achieving a moderation objective, if you choose that objective. The questions here were developed by Raistrick, Dunbar, and Davidson (1983).

The Short Alcohol Dependence Data Questionnaire

The following questions cover a wide range of topics having to do with drinking. Please read each question carefully, but do not think too much about its exact meaning. Think about your *most recent* drinking habits and answer each question by placing an "X" in the box under the most appropriate heading:

	Never	Sometimes	Often	Nearly Always
1. Do you find difficulty in getting the thought of drinking out of your mind?	☐	☐	☐	☐
2. Is getting drunk more important than your next meal?	☐	☐	☐	☐
3. Do you plan your day around when and where you can drink?	☐	☐	☐	☐
4. Do you drink in the morning, afternoon, and evening?	☐	☐	☐	☐
5. Do you drink for the effect of alcohol without caring what the drink is?	☐	☐	☐	☐
6. Do you drink as much as you want irrespective of what you are doing the next day?	☐	☐	☐	☐
7. Given that many problems might be caused by alcohol, do you still drink too much?	☐	☐	☐	☐
8. Do you know that you won't be able to stop drinking once you start?	☐	☐	☐	☐
9. Do you try to control your drinking by giving it up completely for days or weeks at a time?	☐	☐	☐	☐

10. The morning after a heavy drinking session do you need your first drink to get yourself going?	☐	☐	☐	☐
11. The morning after a heavy drinking session do you wake up with a definite shakiness of your hands?	☐	☐	☐	☐
12. After a heavy drinking session do you wake up and retch or vomit?	☐	☐	☐	☐
13. The morning after a heavy drinking session do you go out of your way to avoid people?	☐	☐	☐	☐
14. After a heavy drinking session do you see frightening things that later you realize were imaginary?	☐	☐	☐	☐
15. Do you go drinking and the next day find that you have forgotten what happened the night before?	☐	☐	☐	☐

Is Moderation Right for You?

To figure out your score, give yourself zero points for each "never" answer; one point for "sometimes"; two points for "often"; and three points for "nearly always." Out of a possible total of 45, the guidelines for interpretation are as follows: 1-9 is considered low dependence; 10-19 points medium dependence; and 20 (or greater) high dependence (Raistrick 1983). If you scored 15 points or less, and you do not suffer withdrawal symptoms when you stop drinking, a self-management goal of moderation may be appropriate for you, and a support group like MM may be helpful.

If you scored higher than 15 (but below 20) you should consider seeing a professional therapist before trying a moderation-based program, as you may need more intensive help than a support group alone can offer. A comprehensive assessment of your drinking history will identify other factors that should be taken into account when selecting the best recovery goal for you. If you scored 20 or above, you might want to consider an abstinence goal. The subject of support for an abstinence goal is discussed in chapter 12.

If you are uncertain after taking this questionnaire whether moderation is right for you, there are two options: 1. Give this program a try, but be vigilant for problems in moderating, such as frequently going over the limits; or 2. Seriously consider abstinence as your goal.

> ***Caution:*** People should not attempt moderation if they have signs of physical dependence, including withdrawal symptoms, drinking to avoid withdrawal symptoms, or if they have liver damage or other medical or psychological contraindications. People with very high chronic blood alcohol levels should not cease drinking abruptly, which could be fatal, and should seek medical treatment.

Please note that the risks of attempting moderation are especially high if you exhibit signs of physical dependence on alcohol. These signs include high tolerance (whether it's innate or you develop the need to consume much larger amounts of alcohol to feel the same effect as before) and the withdrawal symptoms noted above.

In addition, moderation is not the best goal for you if you suffer any significant physical medical condition which would be made worse by alcohol; if you take a prescription medication with which use of alcohol is discouraged; or if you have any psychological condition where alcohol should not be used. Women should not drink at all during pregnancy.

In a number of cases where people have tried unsuccessfully to resolve alcohol problems on their own, the overuse of alcohol seems to coexist with another psychological condition such as major depression or an anxiety condition, or with a physical condition such as chronic pain. Although in the main, women are more likely than men to successfully moderate, women with the most serious drinking problems are more likely than men to suffer additional psychological difficulties, particularly depression. When people suffer both an alcohol problem and another psychological problem, the two disorders are often intertwined, and the other psychological condition often stands in the way of resolving the alcohol problem. The best approach is that both problems be treated concurrently by a professional who specializes in these complex disorders. The same is true if there is a problem with other drugs in addition to alcohol.

In appendix 2, you'll find a Psychological Symptom Inventory self-assessment, which you can use to help determine if you have another psychological problem that might benefit from professional attention. If you do have such a condition and have been using alcohol to self-medicate, you may be amazed to find how good you feel when you stop drinking and get the proper treatment for your disorder. Many people fear seeking help for such troubles because they imagine that it will make them feel worse—but in the vast majority of cases, appropriate treatment improves both mood and productivity, rather than diminishing them. Once your problem has been treated, you can reconsider the issue of alcohol moderation if it seems appropriate.

Pros and Cons

Once you have determined the level of your drinking problem, and considered whether or not there are other conditions for which you need help, you'll also want to consider the pros and cons of abstinence versus moderation more generally. Most readers of this book may already assume that moderation is a superior goal. But this is a critical decision, and it is important to thoroughly examine your thinking about your goal.

First, let's take a look at some of the pros and cons of moderation.

Some Pros and Cons of Moderation

Pros	**Cons**
• Still enjoy positive aspects of alcohol use	• Requires a significant effort to achieve and maintain

• A balanced, pragmatic approach	• Risk of relapse to overuse
• Learning valuable habit-change skills that can apply elsewhere	• Takes freedom and spontaneity out of drinking

You may find it helpful to make your own personal list. Take a look at the example below, then create your own list.

Joe's List of Pros and Cons of Moderation

Pros	**Cons**
• *Still drink on social occasions*	• *Might be tempted to drink and drive*
• *Shows self-control*	• *Might take too much effort and worry*
• *I enjoy fine wine*	• *Wife wants me to quit*

Here's some space if you'd like to list your own moderation pros and cons:

My Moderation Pros and Cons

Pros	**Cons**
______________________	______________________
______________________	______________________
______________________	______________________
______________________	______________________
______________________	______________________
______________________	______________________
______________________	______________________

Your list should give you a clearer sense of some of the advantages of achieving moderation, as well as a better understanding of some of the costs of learning how to moderate and the risks of engaging in moderate drinking. The more consideration you give this decision, with your eyes open, the better and firmer your decision is likely to be.

Of course, many people ask: Why even think about continuing to use alcohol at all, if you are having problems with it and its use can pose serious risk, while not using poses little or no risk at all? You need to consider this question thoroughly in making your decision about which goal to pursue. Are the benefits of drinking worth the risks to you? Driving, sex, eating fatty foods, and playing sports carry risks as well—but most people don't think giving them up entirely is the best way to handle those risks. Whether this is true of alcohol for you is something *only you can decide.*

Next, consider the pros and cons of *abstinence*. You are probably reading this book with a primary interest in achieving moderation, but it's important to consider abstinence as well. People with drinking problems sometimes overestimate the costs of abstinence and underestimate its benefits due to fears about what life without alcohol may be like. This program recommends a thirty-day initial period of abstinence. The abstinence period will help you break the habit of overdrinking, and will also give you some experience of abstinence.

Some Pros and Cons of Abstinence

Pros

- The safest choice
- Simpler to achieve and maintain
- Saves all the monetary cost of drinking

Cons

- A less common social practice
- If you do drink, you haven't learned how to control it
- Can't enjoy positive aspects of alcohol use

Again, you might make up a list of pros and cons that seem important to you personally, like this sample:

Jack's List of Pros and Cons of Abstinence

Pros

- *Simpler, no more decisions to make*
- *Healthiest choice*
- *No more risks of drinking*
- *Everyone will support this goal*

Cons

- *Hate to think I've lost control*
- *Conspicuous at a party*
- *No more enjoying fine wine*
- *Others might think I'm a recovering alcoholic.*

Here's some space if you'd like to make your own list of abstinence pros and cons:

My Abstinence Pros and Cons

Pros	**Cons**
______________________	______________________
______________________	______________________
______________________	______________________
______________________	______________________
______________________	______________________
______________________	______________________
______________________	______________________

Now that you've thought through the advantages and disadvantages of abstinence in your own terms, it's likely that you have a better understanding of all the reasons that many people do choose not to drink. And remember, abstinence is your friend, offering you a safe place to hang out for a while if you encounter problems in your efforts to moderate.

As discussed earlier, many people with alcohol problems ultimately opt for abstinence. A common reason is that they find that maintaining moderation involves more effort and diligence than they want to expend in this area of their lives. The safety and simplicity of abstinence are strong points indeed. When people in treatment for more serious alcohol problems are given a choice of an abstinence or moderation goal, those with the most serious problems most often choose abstinence, and the number that choose abstinence continually rises as they continue in the program. This seems to reflect both greater recognition of the problems that alcohol has caused, and a greater appreciation of the effort needed to maintain moderation.

One note: Any decision you make needn't be considered permanent. If you can't figure out which approach seems better in your situation, you can experiment. If you are honest about your progress and carefully monitor it, it will become clear relatively quickly whether abstinence or moderation is best for you.

The Moderate Drinker

In making your choice of moderation as a goal, it's also important to consider what moderation really consists of. Moderation Management founder Audrey Kishline wrote the following description of a moderate drinker (Kishline 1994). Some parts of the description include the frame of mind in which a moderate drinker approaches alcohol, and some are specific practices and skills that will be discussed in the following pages.

The moderate drinker:

- Considers an occasional drink to be a small, though enjoyable, part of life
- Has hobbies, interests, and other ways to relax and enjoy life that do not involve alcohol
- Usually has friends who are moderate drinkers or nondrinkers
- Generally has something to eat before, during, or soon after drinking
- Usually does not drink for longer than an hour or two on any particular occasion
- Usually does not exceed the 0.055 percent BAC (blood alcohol concentration) drinking limit
- Usually does not drink faster than one drink per half-hour
- Feels comfortable with his or her use of alcohol (never drinks secretly and does not spend a lot of time thinking about drinking or planning to drink)

The first statement about making alcohol a small, though enjoyable, part of life is the core idea of what moderation is about. When you can really say that alcohol is a small part of your life, you're a moderator. The other statements are about practices that support that core idea. The abstinence period or early part of your work in this program is a time to begin to get these attitudes and practices strongly in mind, and to form a picture of yourself as a moderator.

To get a further feel for what moderation looks like in practice, here's how Julie, fifty-one, who has long been a very moderate drinker, describes how the concept works in her life:

Here's what moderation looks like for me.

Snapshots: There I am, most times, having a fine time with no alcohol. There I am, out with friends, having two glasses of wine during the evening, and sipping reallllly slowly. There I am, in my apartment, with no liquor in the house, or maybe a bottle of wine, which I'm saving for a special occasion.

What does it sound like? I think to myself: Well, I don't want to drink tonight, because I have a long day tomorrow. Or: I think I'll have wine with dinner tonight. I'll start with club soda and have a glass of wine with dinner.

What does it feel like? Needing only seven hours of sleep instead of nine. Waking up clear, with good energy right away. Looking for an underlying feeling if I have an urge to drink. Am I depressed? Sad? Bored? Angry? Tired? Hungry? Thirsty?

Describing myself to myself: I am a person who doesn't drink much. I have a drink or two sometimes, to make good moments even better. A drinking occasion is usually a celebratory one. I am careful about what I put in my body.

Julie fills in another part of the picture of successful moderating, with the notion of using alcohol to enhance good feelings rather than to counter negative feelings. She knows how to have rewarding experiences without alcohol, and appreciates the natural good feelings she has through avoiding overuse of alcohol. When she does use alcohol, she is careful and conscious about what she is doing. And she has a strong self-identity as an aware and moderate person.

Drinking Limits

An essential part of moderation is having definite limits to drinking. There is a lot of evidence that setting specific limits—rather than just having a general intention to drink less—is a key part of successful moderation. People who achieve moderation on their own without following a program usually set specific limits for themselves (Tucker 1999). And the many successful professionally-directed "brief intervention" studies almost always include working out specific drinking limits.

The limits suggested here are a starting point; the ones you ultimately set should make sense to you and can be adjusted based on your own personal experience. Those listed below are based on what successful moderators who have previously had drinking problems actually do in real life, not on some theory. Researchers at the Addiction Research Foundation of Toronto (one of the world's premiere alcohol research centers) followed people who had been through moderation programs, and determined the drinking levels of those who were successful moderate drinkers, *i.e.*, those whose drinking caused them no problems (Sanchez-Craig 1995).

Drinking Limits

Recommended Limits for Men
Not more than fourteen drinks per week, and not more than four per occasion.

Recommended Limits for Women
Not more than nine drinks per week, and not more than three per occasion.

For Both Men and Women
No moderate drinker should drink on more than three to four days per week.

A "drink" for this purpose is a twelve-ounce bottle of regular beer (5 percent alcohol), 5 ounces of table wine (12 percent alcohol), or 1.5 ounces of eighty-proof liquor (40 percent alcohol), which contain equal amounts of alcohol.

It happens that these limits, if the drinks are consumed at a slow pace, keep the Blood Alcohol Concentration (BAC) below 0.055 percent, which is the recommended upper limit for a moderate drinker. And happily, below that level you are likely to experience all of the pleasant effects of alcohol. Above that level, however, judgment tends to become impaired and significant depressant effects come into play. A person who weighs substantially more may be able to consume more and keep the BAC under that limit, and a much lighter person may want to consume less (see BAC tables). Also, older people tend to metabolize alcohol more slowly, so if you fall into this category, you may want to trim the limits a bit.

The U.S. Department of Agriculture—in its health and nutrition guidelines—recommends that men drink no more than fourteen drinks per week, and women no more than seven, which is close to the limits given here. In addition, a large longitudinal study in the U.S. published in 2000 suggests that for women weekly consumption up to the limit recommended here is consistent with good health, especially from a cardiovascular standpoint (Stampfer 2000).

But remember, while the limits given above make sense, they are not cast in stone. Other higher and lower limits are recommended by different sources in the U.S. and around the world. And as you progress in the MM program, you will learn more and more about what works best for you.

Resources of the Moderation Management Organization

Attending MM meetings if they are available locally and joining in discussions on the Internet can greatly enhance your process. The most convenient access to MM is at its Web site at www.moderation.org. There, you will find a range of additional information about the program, tips concerning things that people working on moderation have found helpful, bibliographies for further reading, and more.

The Web site also tells you how to access the various MM online forums, which can provide ongoing support for your change process. The most heavily used are the national listserv discussion groups. These operate in "bulletin board" fashion, sending posted messages to all subscribers. They bring you instant access to others working the program at all stages, and are extremely lively and free-flowing. There is nothing quite like hearing from others who are facing and dealing with the same issues as yourself. The Web site also provides information on MM face-to-face meetings. Most of these are in major cities at present, but the number is growing and access is spreading. Face-to-face meetings offer a unique depth and immediacy of interchange.

Overview of the Program

Once you have decided to pursue moderation as a goal or to simply try it and see whether it is right for you, the real work begins. First, it's necessary to develop the *commitment* to make a proper start; the tools and support you'll need are discussed in the next chapter. Then, in most cases, people formally begin the program with a thirty-day period of abstinence. This helps break the hold of alcohol, allows a period free of alcohol to prepare you for moderate drinking, and gives you a feel for daily life without alcohol. Chapter 5 contains an overview of the "Thirty."

Control skills that can apply to most drinking situations are discussed in chapter 6. Another basic step is to find out which special situations are likely to lead you to overdrink, and how to cope. You'll need these coping skills, covered in chapters 7 and 8, whether your goal is moderation or abstinence.

Chapter 9 discusses activities that can displace drinking and give you more satisfaction than alcohol can. Chapter 10 deals with the critical period of starting to drink moderately, when moderate drinking skills are put into practice and learned. Chapter 11 discusses coping with any slips or relapses that occur, and how to maintain moderation in the long run. For those who find that moderation is not an appropriate goal, other avenues for help are discussed in chapter 12.

So, if you've decided moderation might be for you, let's get started!

Summing Up

- Your score on the self-test indicates whether moderation is likely to be a reasonable goal for you.
- Be alert to any physical or psychological reasons why continuing to drink may not be a good idea. You can use the psychological test in appendix 2 to get a fix on whether there may be other psychological problems that need attention.
- Think through the pros and cons of both moderation and abstinence for yourself before you choose your goal.
- Get clear on what a moderate drinker is. MM defines a moderate drinker as a person who "considers an occasional drink to be a small, though enjoyable part of life." When you can truly say that alcohol's role in your life has become a minor one, you will have achieved the essence of moderation.
- Recommended drinking limits for men are not more than fourteen drinks per week and not more than four per occasion. For women, the limits are nine drinks per week and three per occasion. And one should not drink on more than three or four days per week.
- If your choice of goal is moderation, this program will guide you through a series of steps that progressively build your ability to moderate successfully.

Chapter 4

Building the Commitment

A useful prelude to the action phase of habit change is building a strong sense of commitment to the process. Mary, for instance, got to the point of feeling "it's really important." Before starting her Thirty, she told some friends about her process so that she'd have social support, and to reinforce her commitment.

> *I've told a couple of friends here about my concern about my drinking, and about the Thirty. That's helped to make me more committed. It's really important that I take this step. It'll be good to have company.*

This chapter will help you build the sense of commitment that's so necessary for successful change in your drinking habits. There are several crucial tasks:

- First, you need to take responsibility for your actions—including those done under the influence.
- Next, it's helpful to review and see how you can utilize the various assets you already have for carrying out your change.
- The third task is to closely examine and recognize all the problems that drinking is causing in your life.
- Finally, it's important to focus on the positive effects you expect to experience from achieving moderation.

These steps will help solidify your resolve, helping you to reach the level of commitment needed for success. They should give you momentum to move forward, help keep you on track, and give you strength to deal with any rough patches.

Some people find it helpful to work through these steps before starting their period of thirty days' abstinence. Others are "sick and tired of feeling sick and tired" and just want to get away from alcohol for a while without further preparation. *It's up to you.* You can do the steps outlined here during your period of abstinence, or you can do them in advance—whichever feels appropriate in your situation.

Taking Responsibility

One of the first steps in making a successful change in your behavior is taking full responsibility for your actions. Taking responsibility means that you must clearly acknowledge that drinking is not something that "just happens to you," but something that you do. Although you may have been encouraged to believe that you are "powerless" once you take a drink, and that alcohol itself can take control of you, you cannot change your drinking behavior unless you believe you control it. That old nursery tale about the little engine that could holds some serious truth here. Though some people do find that the urge to continue drinking once they start is so strong that resisting it takes more energy than they have, this is not true for most problem drinkers.

Max addressed the responsibility issue in this way:

> *It's personal responsibility. I'm not going to obey alcohol, let it run my life. And, therefore, I've got to take that responsibility. I don't want to use one of my reasons—you know, it was very easy to say "I'm drinking because I'm still depressed about my divorce," or "I'm frustrated because I don't have a lot of money." But you stop drinking and you say, you're just making excuses.*

Taking responsibility means recognizing that *you are making choices* in every aspect of your drinking. You are choosing to go into a situation where alcohol will be served, you are choosing a high or low alcohol content drink, you are choosing to order another, you are choosing whether to eat or not. Of course, high levels of alcohol can impair judgment. But there are many choices to be made before you get into that situation.

Your Assets for Change

Everyone has strengths and weaknesses, assets and liabilities. To change your drinking, you need to find sources of support to bolster your weak spots when you feel challenged. You may be surprised to find that you already possess all or most of the assets you need to overcome your drinking problem.

- First, consider the various controls and disciplines you bring to bear on your life now. These may include getting to work on time, meeting work deadlines and carrying out job responsibilities, making and getting to appointments, making shopping lists and shopping within a budget, providing and maintaining clothing for the family, operating and maintaining a car, filing tax returns, and on and on. Modern life is complex and demanding. You wouldn't be functioning in it without a very wide range of capabilities and disciplines.
- Also, there's one discipline you already have that will likely surprise you. That is your control over your drinking. If you score anywhere in the middle or lower ranges on the self-assessment in chapter 3, you're not an out-of-control drinker. Think about it. You don't drink until you pass out. You don't wake up in Vegas and wonder how you got there. At times you may drink quite

moderately. In addition, you have some definite limits on your drinking, which you enforce. These limits may be set much too high and too loosely now, and you need to strengthen and adjust them. But you do actually have some working controls on drinking already. If you didn't, you probably wouldn't have avoided sliding into severe dependence.

- Next, *think about bad habits you have already overcome.* You may have had to deal with getting up on time on school or work days despite a serious desire to sleep in, remembering to do certain things on time, keeping paperwork organized, learning and remembering names or other information, exercising or avoiding too many snacks, and dieting. If you have quit smoking, you have actually overcome the substance that is the hardest of all to beat.

So just what is a habit, and why are they so hard to change? A habit is a behavior you have learned to do automatically, often by repeating it consistently over months or years. To form or change a habit, the process that most people naturally follow is to give the area extra focus for a while, to make activity in that area subject to conscious control, until the habit is changed in the right direction. Then you can go back to acting essentially automatically in that area with the changed habit.

In changing drinking habits, you'll be following a pattern of change you have used naturally before with success, only now you'll do it in an even more conscious and purposeful way.

Consider something as simple as brushing your teeth. Many people have returned home from an unpleasant trip to the dentist and sworn that they will take more care next time to avoid problems. Those who make successful changes in their behavior usually create a specific routine and time for brushing and flossing their teeth, and they repeat it daily, despite tiredness and other excuses. They can tell the new habit is securely in place when, on the rare occasions that they skip tooth care, they feel uncomfortable. This feeling is actually similar to the alcohol craving that habitual drinkers get when they skip a usual drink—it can happen whenever an entrenched behavior routine is disrupted.

To create new habits, you simply need to persist in the changed behavior long enough that it becomes automatic.

Of course, drinking behavior is harder to change than tooth care routines, because unlike flossing, drinking feels good. Addictive behaviors are supported by the pleasure of the behavior, plus the pain often involved in not doing the behavior, on top of the automatic, routine aspect of the behavior. Although changing behaviors that have an addictive aspect is more difficult, the process of change is exactly the same. It just takes consistent, sustained effort.

Tools for Success

Research finds that young people, women, those who have been drinking heavily for shorter periods of time, and those who have less severe problems with alcohol all have better odds for achieving moderation (Larimer 1998). If any of these factors are in your favor, great—you can use them to increase your confidence about success in drinking moderately. If not, note that the researchers are far from discovering all the factors that make for success, and many who do not meet the above profile at all do well.

In fact, your **mental outlook** may be the most important factor of all. In one landmark study of problem drinkers in Great Britain, there was no correspondence between pretreatment dependence levels and successful outcomes of abstinence or moderation (Orford 1986). The key influences on outcomes were instead the problem drinkers' starting beliefs about appropriate treatment goals, the beliefs of the treatment personnel, and whether or not the clients and counselors agreed on the goals. Those who did best were those who believed they could attain their goal and were supported by their counselors in their attempts, no matter which goal was sought.

The NIAAA states that through research, several "factors contributing to successful recovery during treatment have been identified" (NIAAA 2000). These include "increased self-efficacy, fewer coexisting psychiatric problems, a supportive social network, experiences with the negative consequences of drinking, and readiness to change." Patients in treatment programs have more severe problems than most people who would work toward a moderation goal on a mainly self-guided basis with this book, but these same factors very likely apply.

Self-efficacy is belief in your own ability to succeed at what you set out to do. The tools and techniques of MM are designed to reinforce your self-efficacy. Unfortunately, many people with alcohol problems have low opinions of themselves. These may become tinged with self-hatred, which leads to drinking to feel better, which can lead to more negative feelings, etc. In order to increase self-efficacy, you need to learn to ignore any inner voices of self-hatred. If such thoughts or feelings arise, turn your thoughts instead toward what you are doing now to take action to address the problem. The more progress you make, the more self-confident and self-respecting you will feel, and the less ammunition your self-loathing side will have to torment you. For more information on this issue, see the section called "Self-Criticism, Guilt, and Self-Acceptance" in chapter 8.

Regarding **psychiatric problems,** once again we stress that you should seek help for any significant ones that plague you. If you don't take this step, your chances of successfully addressing your drinking problem are much lower.

Social support is a crucial asset for anyone wishing to make major life changes. Think about the people in your life, including family, friends, and coworkers. Your relationships will play a key role in your change process. In some cases, they may actively assist you. In others, you may need to be aware that they could have a negative influence unless you work to defuse that.

Some people find it helpful to announce plans to change drinking habits to close friends or relatives, for instance. Most people who do that get a very good response—their loved ones are usually quite supportive. Of course, some will ask, "Why don't you quit entirely?" So you'll need to be prepared with an answer, and the material in this book can be a source for that.

"Going public" can be really helpful if done when you are determined to change. Don't tell people if you aren't yet comfortable with your goals or timetable for action. You may invite unwanted scrutiny of your drinking habits before you are ready to handle it. When you are ready, however, knowing that others are supportive and may be disappointed if you don't live up to expectations can be highly motivating, and can increase your commitment if it should waver.

Jackie got some very positive feedback through telling others:

I came out right away. I just figured they all had seen me drink too much, you know. They didn't say: "Oh, that's awful." They would say: "Oh, what a good thing to do, how wonderful."

Another described her "coming out" this way, emphasizing how it made her commitment to complete the Thirty stronger:

It's important to me to make it through this Thirty. I told some friends. Close friends who know my stories are happy for me. Other friends are a bit perplexed, but still supportive. (They're perplexed because they don't know the truth about things I've done while drunk.)

Max also found it easy to talk to close friends about it, and got positive responses:

I'm a person who has a few very close friends. Of course, they always recognized the situation. When I told them what I was doing, what was going on, and that I was taking care of my situation, then they were happy about it. And they were supportive. It was not difficult to tell them what was going on.

Others can have an important passive role in your changes. That is, you may want to change in order to feel better about how you stand with your circle of friends or in society more generally. In the book *Coming Clean*, which contains stories of people who beat various addictions on their own, one drug user said that his main motivation for quitting was to avoid needle scars on his arms, which would mark him as an intravenous drug addict (Granfeld 1999). He wasn't aiming to show any particular person that he wasn't an addict, but wanted to be seen by society in general as a respectable person. This type of thinking about our standing with others around us, including our self-image, can be a powerful asset for change.

Moderation Management can also be a source of social support, whether you attend meetings or get involved online. These contacts can provide the special encouragement of others who understand your problems and the effort you are making. Others in MM will be warmly supportive of your progress. If you are not ready to tell people close to you about your moderation efforts, talking to other people who are following the MM program can provide a replacement for that. And even if you do have other support, contact with people in MM can provide an important bolster.

Another important factor listed by NIAAA as important to success is experience of **negative consequences.** It is more than likely that some negative experience with drinking has impelled you to seek to change your behavior. The exercise in the next section of this chapter involves unearthing and reviewing all the problems that alcohol is causing you. By emphasizing these negative consequences, you increase your motivation to take action.

The last factor mentioned in the NIAAA list is **readiness to change.** The fact that you are reading this book means that you are starting to take action against your problem, which indicates that you are ready to make some important changes in your life. Building on that, the exercises of this chapter will help reinforce your desire and readiness for such changes.

Your Reasons for Change

If you are drinking so much that you have come to consider alcohol a problem, it's likely that drinking is causing difficulties in many areas of your life. Now is the time to get a square look at all these problems. This can be an excellent motivator, even though it might be a bit painful. It will also help you later if you hit any rough spots and need to remind yourself why you decided to make this change.

Though the role of "denial" as a part of alcohol problems has been greatly exaggerated and seen incorrectly as being unique to addictions (it's actually common in all medical conditions, including fatal ones), it certainly is possible to delude yourself about the extent of your problem. The less you do so, the easier it will be for you to cope with your problem.

It will help you to remember your findings—and make them more real for you—if you write things down. Making a mental list can work, but most people find that it is more effective in writing. See below for a sample form you can use.

There are a number of different areas you'll want to examine. A very concrete area is any *legal issues*, such as drunk driving—regardless of whether you were arrested or not—and any other legal issues. *Financial issues* are also very concrete. Try to estimate your total yearly spending on alcohol and any lost income or extra expenses related to overdrinking. *Physical health* would include any illness or disability related to alcohol, as well as physical hangover symptoms, poor sleep, etc. You may also have gained weight from the excess calories of alcohol, or be out of physical shape due to lack of exercise. *Work issues* include absence or lateness due to drinking, and complaints from supervisors, coworkers, or customers which you think might be caused by your drinking. *Inner feelings* would include feeling depressed or having low self-esteem due to drinking, or feeling out of control. *Relationships* includes complaints and problems between you and your family, significant other, or friends. *Nonwork activities* are things like hobbies, physical exercise, and other outside interests you may have neglected due to drinking.

Here's an example:

Marcy's Problems of Current Drinking

Legal Issues	*Risked a drunk driving arrest last week.*
Financial Issues	*$5,000+ on alcohol last year.*
Physical Health	*Many hangovers, days of feeling bad. Out of shape.*
Work Issues	*Hanging on, but missed promotion, forgot follow-up with two big customers.*
Inner Feelings	*Often feel like I'm letting myself and my family down.*
Relationships	*Some big arguments with wife about drinking.* *Don't do outdoor things with the kids anymore.*
Nonwork Activities	*Stopped playing tennis, seldom go to church with wife.*

And here's a place for your own list:

My Problems of Current Drinking

Legal Issues

____

____

Financial Issues

____

____

Physical Health

____

____

Work Issues

____

____

Inner Feelings

____

____

Relationships

____

____

Nonwork Activities

____

____

If you've done a thorough job of digging up all the problems alcohol is causing you, you'll probably be surprised at the length of your list. Most of the time, we tend to avert our gaze from all these difficulties. There are natural reasons for that. We have gotten used to living with a lot of these problems. And most of us don't want to dwell on things that make us feel bad, which is healthy when those things can't be changed or when we aren't ready to change them.

Another reason we may have avoided looking at these problems is that most of us have used alcohol so much that we have come to feel that drinking is the only thing that will, quickly and reliably, allow us to feel good and get away from it all for a while. It's not a crazy thing to shield our use of alcohol from too much scrutiny, including self-scrutiny, if it's really the only way we can feel good.

But, of course, it isn't the only way. And too much of a good thing often backfires, because our brains have feedback mechanisms to keep our pleasure chemicals under tight control. Tolerance prevents alcohol from working as well and as often as we'd like. To feel really good, our systems need a variety of pleasurable experiences and activities, not just one substance over and over. You'll be getting back in touch with feeling good without alcohol during the abstinence period.

But for now, it's time to take a hard look at the whole list of negative experiences, feelings, and consequences your drinking has caused. Be sure to consider the problems alcohol was leading you toward, as well as the problems you actually had. Maybe you haven't had a drunk driving arrest or accident, but you're risking that if you drive after drinking, for example. Think about how alcohol has cast a shadow over your life. Think about how alcohol has deformed and twisted the person you really are and intend to be. This tangle of problems is a part of ourselves we want to shed and leave behind. So take a look at it, shudder a moment, and then start looking ahead to better things.

Positives from Moderation

There are two ways to look at the benefits of moderation. You can focus on immediate, concrete benefits, or you can look more abstractly, highlighting your life goals and priorities and how moderating your drinking will bring you closer to them. You can do either or both—different people have different perspectives. With either approach, an objective is to identify what you care about most, and how your drinking is getting in the way of it. As a result, you will gain some strong emotional leverage in your efforts to stop overdrinking. Whenever you feel inclined to excess, you can remind yourself why this is harmful rather than helpful in terms of what you most want out of life.

The thing or things that are most important to you will be very much your own. Noted alcohol researchers Miller and Rollnick tell the story of a man who had a whole range of problems related to his drinking (Miller 1991). He had liver damage, he was breaking up with his partner, and he had just lost his job. The researchers figured that recognizing these problems and their relationship to his drinking might spur him to quit. However, it turned out that he was actually relieved to be leaving his partner, and he had hated his job. He planned to start a new business with his severance payment, and was very excited about that. And he didn't really understand the severity of his liver problem. However, "his prime concern was his dog. Indeed, he eventually decided to quit drinking because when he did drink he neglected his pet, and this was the source of a great deal of personal sorrow" (p. 239–40).

Benefits of Moderation

The simplest approach in this area, then, is to think up and list the reasons why you want to drink less, in terms of the specific *benefits of moderation* you expect. You may want to have better relations with family and friends, have better health, sleep better, do better on the job, or get back to regular exercise and sports participation. You may want to read more, go back to school, or be nicer to your pet. Some men find that overdrinking impairs their sexual performance; for women, the fact that cutting down will improve their appearance and help them lose weight may be motivating. Again, what matters most is what matters to you.

Here's what one person wrote down for benefits of moderation:

Emily's Benefits of Moderation

1. *Health. I would never want to have my liver damaged by drinking.*
2. *I'd like to set a better example for my kids, who see me getting my "refills" in the kitchen.*
3. *I want to feel I am in control of this and not that the wine is in control of me.*
4. *I don't want to choose a restaurant based on whether they serve alcohol.*
5. *I want to explore doing other things in the evenings such as a class, activity, or whatever.*
6. *I'd like to sleep through the night more soundly because I am not getting up to get a drink of water or pee from the diuretic effects.*
7. *I want to take action* now *and not wait till I have a worse situation. I think it will be much easier for me to tackle this now than if I wait.*
8. *I want to find pleasure in other things.*

That's a fine list, simply written and clear, and it covers a wide range of external and internal life factors.

Creative writing ability is especially important to another person, and so it features on his list:

Danny's Benefits of Moderation

Doing it for yourself is the best reason, and in my opinion, no other is needed.

Here are just a few benefits:

1. *Better health*
2. *Improved appearance*
3. *More energy*
4. *Self-esteem & confidence*
5. *Self-discipline*
6. *Save money*
7. *Ability to think clearly*
8. *Enhanced creativity*
9. *Your writing will be improved greatly when you stop abusing alcohol. Even though there is a rich history of heavy-drinking writers, there is nothing romantic about drinking your brain away! Even Kerouac admitted that everything he wrote while drinking was shit!!!*

Here's a place where you can list yours:

My Benefits of Moderation

____

____

____

____

____

____

____

____

____

____

____

Life Goals and Priorities

Alternatively, you can look at positives of moderation somewhat more abstractly in terms of your *life goals and priorities*. You may have thought about these in the past, but lost track of them in the busyness of life and with the influence of heavy drinking. Also, priorities can naturally change over time as we pass through different stages of life. On the other hand, many people are quite unaccustomed to thinking in abstract terms about life goals. If so, this will take some shifting of mental gears. But it may be a helpful tool for looking at your current situation and imagining your future.

Life goals and priorities can come in many forms, and be stated in many different ways, but here is a list of some possibilities:

- Health
- Financial security
- Family, marriage, children
- Career or vocation
- Education
- Personal freedom
- Inner peace and focus
- Contribution to community/society
- Friendships

- Avocation or other interests
- Balance and moderation

Here's an example of what one person did in this area:

Carrie's Life Goals and Priorities

I thought about ways to reclaim my lost passion for teaching, and to balance my less fulfilling work hours with something creative and meaningful. I thought about my need for love versus my craving for independence. Finally, I thought about the necessity of moderating the excesses in my life, of getting control of some really bad habits that were keeping me from . . . what? Obviously, it was time to write down my priorities. I found a list I had written twelve years ago when I was going through another life change. Not surprisingly, the priorities had not changed so much as they had slipped out of focus. The newly polished, abbreviated version is:

1. *Love*
2. *Self-worth*
3. *Passion and balance*
4. *Personal freedom with self-control*
5. *Mental & emotional growth*

I can't wait to get on with it.

If you'd like to list benefits of moderation in terms of life goals and priorities, here's a space for that:

My Life Goals and Priorities

Once you have your list or lists of positives of moderation set down, you can think through what your heavy drinking habit looks like alongside them. You can see that the overdrinking actually runs counter to every one of them!

Whether you've chosen to focus here simply on the tangible benefits of moderation, or the possibly more abstract life goals and priorities, it's certainly an interesting exercise to step back and take a look at where you want to go next in your life. There are really some attractive benefits out there you can reach by getting the alcohol problem under control, aren't there?

At this point you may very well feel some concern about giving up your current pattern of use of alcohol, despite working through these exercises. In that case, take a moment and identify your worst fear about changing your current overuse of alcohol. Look at that fear squarely, and you will probably be able to see that it is not a rational fear. For most people, the key fear is of loss of a source of pleasure or escape. But as you'll see, there are better ways to achieve both of those goals—and alcohol in moderation can actually offer more pleasure at much less cost.

Keep your list of benefits or core goals/priorities in mind now as you move ahead. It will help give you an overall sense of direction. And when you reach chapter 9, where new nondrinking activities are discussed, it will be a handy reference.

Early Benefits of Moderation

At this point, it's helpful to look ahead to some of the first benefits of moderation that you will experience. Better morning feelings are one of the first things you'll be likely to notice:

> *I'm still just giddy over the idea of waking up on a Saturday morning without feeling sluggish. Geeez, I woke up at 5:30 this morning with a smile on my face. That's way early for me on a Saturday. I'm also on vacation this week. Another feat too, as my former alcohol-abusing self would have surely tied one on the first Friday night of a vacation.*

Another put it this way:

> *For years, my entire life I reckon, I'd hit the snooze bar enough times so that I was running around throwing on clothes getting ready for work. "If I hit it one more time, I can put on my makeup at work." Now, for the past few months, I wake up an hour earlier than I need to (gasp!). I drink my decaf, I read my posts, I even . . . make my lunch! And I love this time of day! It's quiet, there's no kids yelling in the street. Maybe for years I just dreaded "waking up". . . .*

There can be real satisfaction in just performing ordinary responsibilities well, as Lucy says, instead of feeling overwhelmed by them:

> *I used to think that I work so hard, damn it, I need a break, some time to myself, and I would take that time to drink and smoke 'til I smelled like a brewery on fire, staggering around getting stuff done 'til I decided enough for one day, I'll go to bed now. And pass out and wake up in the morning trying very hard to remember what exactly it was that I did last night. And usually it was nothing serious. Mostly it would be conversations and/or commitments forgotten. Oh, sorry, must've been drunk. Well, all that is gone now. I've taken on a lot more of the household tasks. I haven't felt overwhelmed by them—more proud, I think, a real feeling of accomplishment.*

Better mental focus and self-possession can pervade your whole experience, replacing feelings of emptiness:

> *Learning to be aware and observant of everything going on around me and being in the present moment was another outcome from moderating that has brought me a lot of inner peace. Given the circumstances of my life right now, I* really *know how important learning to enjoy the precious present is. When I was drinking on a daily basis, the drinking dulled my senses. I wasn't really* aware *with all my being. I have continued to enjoy the wonderful benefit of moderating and I'm not racing the clock of restlessness or boredom anymore!*

Freeing the mind from aftereffects of alcohol can lead to key accomplishments and moments of experience we would not otherwise have. As another person reported:

> *Tonight turned out to be a truly wonderful night. My older son and I had a nice, long conversation about his college options for next year. We needed to do that, but it seems like often we are all just jumping in ten different directions. Tonight he was in a delightful mood, and willing to talk with me!! With a seventeen-year-old, it's rather rare. And you know, the wine* will *always be there, but he will not be. (Boo hoo.)*
>
> *Anyway, if I had given in to the wine, I would have missed a special moment with him and never have known it. It's not a huge deal, but sometimes I think it's the total of all the little things that makes the biggest differences in life.*

Costs of Learning Moderation

Achieving moderation is not all benefits, however. There are some costs, which you should acknowledge up front in order not to be startled or discouraged by them. First, it will take a significant effort over at least three months or longer to establish your new habit of moderating. It may even take a period of several years to get your drinking under completely satisfactory control and your life moving in a new direction. The effort will require some change in your pattern of activities and require some serious mental attention. Working on moderating may not be the most important thing you'll be doing in this period, but it will need a fairly high priority in your life if you are to succeed. Some find that the focus needed to maintain moderation isn't worth the costs, and decide to shift to an abstinence goal.

Another cost is that you may have some mental discomfort during the abstinence period, perhaps a feeling of irritability early on, and possibly difficulty falling asleep at the beginning. For most people, these soon give way to positive experiences, however.

If you have heavy-drinking friends as frequent companions, you may have to avoid their company for a while. Many people find that they can see such friends again after they have established a new drinking pattern, but some find that these friends are likely to prompt a return to old habits if seen regularly. Others find that spending time with heavy drinkers simply isn't pleasurable when you yourself aren't getting drunk. And so you may find that your circle of friends shifts when you moderate.

Also, you may be concerned about standing out from the crowd in drinking situations during the abstinence period. We'll talk more about that later, but you'll actually be surprised at how seldom people even notice that the drinks you are sipping are nonalcoholic.

The cost that prompts the most fear is that of losing the enjoyment and relaxation of drinking. It's certainly true that periods of definite change and growth can be unsettling, especially a change in something as fundamental as where we get some of our sharpest feelings of enjoyment and relaxation. You'll feel some anxiety and sense of loss of your old drinking self and the good old drinking times. Fortunately, however, most people discover in the abstinence period that they are not so dependent on alcohol for good feelings. And you will find that you can enjoy alcohol without overdoing it. When you drink moderately in the future, you'll be having good times that are much less colored by alcohol, more keenly appreciated at the time, and better remembered.

Making the Commitment

After going over the problems of current drinking, your potential benefits of moderation, and the costs of moderating, you will probably arrive at a real sense of commitment to moderation. If you feel remorse in adding up the problems list, let yourself feel the remorse. It can help move you forward—just don't let it daunt you or discourage you from trying. Instead, try to picture the new you ahead as vividly as you can, and get a bit keyed up about getting on to that new life. Visualization will help you internalize what you have found, and to reach a real, strongly felt *desire* for change.

Barry described the value of the desire for change this way:

> *It's a visceral desire. I quit smoking for eighteen months in the early 1970s. I quit then out of sheer willpower, not desire. Then I started again. In 1991 I developed the visceral desire to become a nonsmoker and I did it without any problems. Instead of willing yourself to do it, it is so much easier if you develop a gut desire to be a nonsmoker or—in our case—a moderate drinker. Once that level of desire is achieved, it's a piece of cake. You have to really—deep down inside—want it to work.*

And how the desire can head off feelings of deprivation:

> *Going on sheer willpower is unstable. It requires you to do something you don't want to do just because your higher intellect says you should. Any time you decide to reward yourself and tell that higher intellect to get lost, you're back in the old habit.*
>
> *But when you develop that deep-down-in-your-gut belief that you're better off in a new state, then you are no longer depriving yourself. You're actually rewarding yourself by pursuing the new state.*

Nevertheless, if you don't yet feel a burning desire for moderation, just keep moving ahead. As it turns out, the experience of abstinence and the experience of practicing moderation will often give you vivid firsthand experiences of benefits, which then increase your commitment level. Also, the process of working out your particular path to moderation can gradually give you a deep sense of ownership in the changes going on. Tammy said:

There is an element of self-determination in MM that is critical to its success. It is the "visceral desire" we have all talked about so much. Instead of an outside program that we must "work" to succeed, MM is an inside compulsion that we must learn to recognize, develop, and honor on our own. How we decide to manage our drinking is a matter of individual choice. MM just offers guidelines.

When someone else or an outside authority tells me that I must do something a certain way, my immediate reaction is negative. My heels dig in so hard the dust cloud obscures any benefits that might be there. However, with a program like MM, I am the one telling myself what to do and how to do it.

Finding the Time

If you are worried about not having enough time to go online, or to meetings, or to think about your drinking, consider how much time you are spending hungover or too drunk to concentrate. When you start your Thirty and when you learn to moderate, all that time becomes free.

Another trick is to just set aside certain periods of the day or week, when you can be uninterrupted, to focus on your drinking and drinking-related things. This could be when the husband has left for work and the kids are off for school or having naps. If you travel to work, you can spend part of the commute reflecting on the subject without the radio on or without reading the newspaper on the train or bus. Or you might use the period late in the evening before going to bed.

Another way to spend time focused on the subject is to read other books about it. You'll find a number listed in the Recommended Reading list in appendix 3 at the end of this book.

Whatever means you find to stay focused on the subject of moderating, it is really critical to spend enough time with your thoughts focused on the process to make it work. Like an exercise program, it won't work unless repeated regularly and frequently. But once you start, you'll feel the benefits almost immediately, and these will help keep you going.

Summing Up

- You already have a number of strengths and capabilities for positive change that can now be focused on resolving your drinking problem.
- A number of factors have been identified that favor success in resolving alcohol problems, and this program will reinforce those factors.
- Social support, which can include many different kinds of contact with others, ranks as a key success factor.
- A necessary step is to take full responsibility for all your own actions with respect to drinking.
- The next step is to bring out into full daylight all the problems that overdrinking has caused you.
- The third step is to define in your own terms the benefits you expect from achieving control.

- You need to come to a strong "visceral" desire for change.
- You'll also need to commit the necessary time and attention to the process.
- The sense of commitment will build as you begin to experience the benefits of moderation.

Chapter 5

Taking a Break from Drinking

This chapter discusses the benefits of a period of abstinence (we call it the Thirty) and gives you an idea of what the experience has been like for others. You can also learn how others felt about starting this part of the program—and how they did it. If you are not ready to try a month of abstinence yet, there are other very productive things you can do at this point, like tapering down or trying just a day or two without drinking. Skills that you'll get to practice during the Thirty are covered here, such as specific techniques for drink refusal, and coping with urges to drink. And you'll begin to draw up your own personal set of "rules" concerning drinking. As noted previously, anyone drinking more than five or six drinks a day should seek medical treatment rather than stopping drinking abruptly.

Sam, a thirty-eight-year-old sales representative from Kansas, describes his experience in the thirty-day abstinence period:

> *A few days into my Thirty, the feeling that I was completely out of control with alcohol started to fade away. The real me started to come back together.*
>
> *I began to look ahead and see the possibility of a better life. When I was trapped in the drinking, I was just surviving from day to day and couldn't—or didn't dare—look ahead. Now I'm more positive about the future, actually upbeat, feeling energy I thought I'd lost for good, and back in charge of my life.*

Why Do the Thirty?

Researchers have found that becoming abstinent for a period is one of the key techniques used by people who successfully moderate their drinking on their own (Tucker 1999). There are a number of reasons for this:

- For one, if you have a feeling that your use of alcohol is slipping out of control, you may have become a bit demoralized about your ability to cut back.

But with abstinence, the tide promptly turns in your favor. People often take a real sense of pride and accomplishment from the abstinence period. For example, Bernie wrote:

> *Finished up my Thirty last Tuesday, and it felt great. It's just the kind of reminder you need to show you that it really is* you *in control and that* you *can be in control. Now I know better—that my bad habit is just bad behavior, not a disease, and only I can change it. I am ready for the challenge.*

- Abstinence also gives you a period unclouded by alcohol in which you can work out your strategies for moderate drinking. And it gives you a space in which to get your strategies well in mind, to rehearse ahead of time how you will apply them in your life, and to develop a sense of commitment to them. Lisa wrote when she reached the end of her Thirty:

> *I can't believe I'm on day thirty today! This time really has gone fast! I realize now that I would have never gained the perspective I have without taking this thirty-day break from drinking. I feel stronger, more committed, more focused, and very confident that I can moderate successfully. I have a much clearer understanding of my triggers now.*

- In addition, while doing the Thirty, most people rediscover how good life can be without alcohol and how unnecessary and counterproductive drinking can be in many circumstances. They find that situations in which they thought they "needed a drink" can actually be handled better sober. And all of this can help give alcohol a much smaller role in your life. Says Elise:

> *When I did my Thirty, my birthday fell during that period. My husband gave me a surprise party. I didn't drink anything, and it was the best birthday I ever had. I learned how much fun you can have when you don't get drunk.*

- During the Thirty, you also practice saying no to alcohol. This is important, because there's a lot of saying no to alcohol in moderate drinking. Many days you won't drink at all, and when you do drink, you'll have to say no when you reach your limit.

- In this period, you may also get a chance to see how you and other people really behave while drinking heavily. It is hard to get a clear picture of that while drinking heavily, because alcohol impairs judgment and perception. But when you remain stone cold sober, you can see how heavy drinkers actually behave. It won't be pretty. A few mental snapshots like that taken during your abstinence period can be valuable possessions. (For the most part, however, you'll of course want to avoid situations where others are drinking heavily during the Thirty.)

- Finally, abstaining for a month dramatically reduces your tolerance for alcohol. If you have been drinking daily, tolerance has probably reduced your sensitivity to the effects of drinking. After thirty days abstinence, the ability to sense the effects of modest amounts of alcohol returns.

What the Thirty Feels Like

As you embark on the abstinence period, focus your mind on your goals in moderating your drinking and why they are important to you. Then help yourself stick to your plan by reminding yourself of the real sense of accomplishment and empowerment that will come with success.

Of course, individual experiences vary widely. Some people have smooth sailing all the way, and soon get to feeling noticeably better than when they were drinking. Some find themselves eating a lot of candy or drinking really large quantities of nonalcoholic beverages at this time—as a short-term substitute for booze. Others feel nervous and irritable at the start, have trouble sleeping for a few nights, and are bothered by thoughts of drinking. However, most people do get to a feeling of greater well-being within their abstinence period, and they often rediscover a pre–heavy-drinking self they'd lost touch with over the years. In the MM online discussions, one person told another who was feeling edgy and jittery at the beginning:

> *I assure you that it is only the first few days—or maybe it is a different time for everyone. You have to trust that it will get easier. You may think that the edginess and those unpleasant emotions are your* life *and you may also think that you can't handle your life* without *the booze. But have you ever thought some of those edgy, negative feelings are not life but the effects of alcohol on your body? And, yes, drinking will get rid of the symptoms it causes itself, but wouldn't it be better to wait it out and just get the toxins out and overcome the withdrawal? Know that each step in the right direction is a good thing, even if it doesn't feel good along the way.*

Another (a Texan) modestly reported a few improvements:

> *Now on day thirteen. If I felt any better I would be able to throw lightning bolts out of my fingertips. This is the longest period of no booze I have put in in five years. I shave daily. I now tie my shoes when I go out. I can put my pants on in the morning, standing up. My alligator syndrome (you know: all mouth and no ears) is under control. When I look at my wife, I can see the tombstones fading from her eyes, and her hand will touch me out of the blue with a reserved but intense affection. The dog wags his tail when he sees me. I am starting to like daylight.*

In the middle of her Thirty, Lisa described finding some gifts that had been lost in her life:

> *I am finding myself more content with the "ordinary." I started thinking about some of the changes in me since I started the Thirty. If I were writing a book, some of these would make great chapter titles. For example, "Drinking and the Lost Pastime of Reading." I've really enjoyed reading for a while when I get into bed at night before I go to sleep. Gee, I think, this is what ordinary people do, and isn't it wonderful? Drinking wine and reading didn't really go together very well. Then there would be the chapter entitled "Drinking and the Lost Gift of Spontaneity." I am finding myself much more spontaneous in the last couple of weeks. It's fun to decide to run out and do something different on the spur of the moment. I hadn't realized how dull the daily rut had become! Now there would be the chapter "Drinking and the Lost Art of Child Play." This requires spontaneity also, but there is another dimension to this one. It's great to have*

the "child" in me come out to play!!! I guess the "child" didn't feel like playing with an adult who had been drinking, so she just stayed hidden! Then there would be "Drinking and the Lost Ability to Fall Asleep." I am sleeping much better now, and after the first week, I stopped having a difficult time falling asleep.

Of course, some people fall off the wagon during their Thirty. You should be flexible with yourself if this happens. Thirty or more consecutive days is the objective. But if you drink, don't fall into the trap of chastising yourself for it, and then creating additional urges to drink, and falling back into the old cycle. It's not just how many consecutive days, but what you do with them in learning and becoming more healthy that matters. As one person said:

I've seen a lot of people go for Thirty, make a few days, then stumble and beat themselves up to no end because they view themselves as having "failed" (which they haven't—every time you try, you learn something, like why *did I not make it,* what *caused me to trip up?).*

It is crucial not to take one failure as evidence that you can never succeed. Just dust yourself off, figure out why you drank on that occasion, and focus your thinking again on getting ready for the next abstinence period. Instead of feeling bad about failing, feel pride that you did abstain for a time and that you are making progress. That first try is valuable experience for the next try, and each time of abstinence is time well spent.

In fact, you can often learn much more from mistakes and difficulties than you do when things go smoothly. If things go too well, you might even get a false sense of security about a single way of approaching things. So, if you have problems getting through the abstinence period, just keep going. Remember that progress can sometimes be a bit painful.

Skills for the Thirty and Beyond

The Thirty, of course, gives you a concentrated period of learning and practicing a range of abstinence skills. These skills are necessary to get through the Thirty, and they also have considerable use later on, on all the occasions and days where as a moderator you choose not to drink.

How to Say No

One of the first and most important skills is the ability to refuse drinks when you don't want them—whether you are trying to do a Thirty, or taper down. In the past, you may have said yes automatically, so it will be a bit of a turnaround to say no.

It's helpful to distinguish situations where a simple "no" statement is all that's needed from situations where a brief explanation formula fits better. A simple "no" statement can range from just "no thanks" to a host, or "not right now" to a waiter, to asking for a non-alcoholic drink. Choosing something that looks the same as an alcoholic drink—like tonic and lime, ginger ale, or nonalcoholic beer—can work well when others are drinking. In these situations, you needn't feel compelled to offer any explanation at all.

However, at other times, more may be required because some people will question your new behavior. A brief explanation formula, say in the company of people you ordinarily drink with, could be something like "No thanks, I'm not drinking now," "I'm on a diet," "I'm the designated driver," "I've got an early one tomorrow morning," or "I'm cutting back on drinking." Or, you can have a little fun with the "ulcer" gambit one person thought up:

> *The times I have felt pressured and obligated to drink, I whip out the ol' ulcer scenario. The relief in their faces when they realize they must accede to a physical problem that has nothing to do with booze is immense.*

If someone presses, be prepared to be firm, and don't feel you have to give a detailed and explicit explanation. Say something like "Look, not right now. Okay?" or "I'll tell you when I want a drink."

While it's not uncommon to fear that you will be very conspicuous in not drinking, you will usually be pleasantly surprised at how seldom people notice—and the situations where you have to provide an explanation are fortunately much rarer than you might imagine. In fact, it's usually only the minority of drinkers who really try to pressure others to keep up with them. If you find that you know many such people, you may have to spend less time with them, at least at first, in order to work on moderation.

Coping with Urges

When it's not someone else who wants you to drink, but your own desire that is pushing you, you need a different approach. You may or may not have significant urges to drink during the abstinence period. But it's more than likely that at some time in the future you will feel urges to drink in circumstances where you have decided not to—so this is an important skill area.

First, it's important to recognize that urges or cravings are normal, learned behaviors that unfortunately will never go away completely. They are actually learned somewhat the way you learned to ride a bicycle—through lots of practice. Think about it: how many times have you bent your elbow with a drink in your hand in your lifetime? How many times have you done so in similar settings—for example your favorite chair in front of the TV, at your favorite bar with friends, at parties? Just as you never completely forget how to ride a bicycle, you never completely lose the memories you've generated through all that practice. That's the bad news.

The good news is that no one ever died, went crazy, or had any other bad things happen to them just because they had an urge or craving! Urges that aren't acted upon are harmless. And they are relatively easy to overcome (though hard to eliminate entirely). You simply have to be aware of what they are, that they will subside—like an ocean wave, peaking then disappearing over time—and that the key is to have a plan for what to do while you wait out the cresting and disappearance of the wave.

Some important urge-management skills include avoidance, confrontation, distraction, and combinations of those techniques, which are described below.

Avoidance

Avoidance techniques lessen the chances of urges coming up in the first place, so they are particularly useful. They include the following:

1. Make booze harder to get. You can remove alcohol from the house for the time being, or keep only minimal amounts for guests in a special place removed from the regular place you usually keep alcohol. This helps make you think before you drink.

2. Stay away for the time being from places where you typically drink, like favorite bars and restaurants or sporting events. If your regular way home takes you past them, or past liquor stores, go home a different way.

3. Avoid heavy-drinking friends. Staying away from people you like can be a little tough. But right now it's just for a month.

4. Stay busy. Especially if you're a regular at-home drinker, try to avoid passive activities that regularly go with your drinking, like watching TV. Try to make plans for your down time, or get out of the house to nondrinking situations.

5. Minimize stress. You should also try to avoid other situations that you know will trigger reactive drinking on your part, if possible. In the next chapter, you'll go on a hunt for those types of situations, but there may be some that come to mind right away—like arguing with a spouse, visiting a difficult relative, or seeing certain acquaintances.

6. Take care of yourself. If you are tired, thirsty, hungry, or lonely, you may start to feel a drinking urge in the making. At such times, tend to your need for rest, sustenance, or human contact, and the inkling will not bloom into a full urge.

Confronting Your Urges

Confrontation is willpower, skillfully applied. Confrontation techniques include:

Outwait the urge: Urges are paper tigers. An urge seems really powerful because it tells you that it's making you miserable right now, and that it will keep on making you just as miserable until you give in. But actually, the urge isn't that strong, and won't last that long.

Urge surf: Using the wave analogy above, you can go urge surfing, which means consciously recognizing the urge as a wave that will rise and fall, and then riding it out. Rather than worrying about the urge and obsessing about whether or not it will get too strong to resist, just step back, check out the craving, examine it, and understand it for what it is. It is a thought/feeling that is the result of years of learning, not some irresistible force that must be heeded. Looking at the urge objectively and studying it will help detach you from it.

Substitute positive messages: Urges often come in the form of self-talk that gives you permission to drink. Like: "I'll just sip on one; that's not really drinking," or "I'll be drinking again in a few weeks anyway—why not now?" When this kind of idea comes up, spot it for what it is and substitute a more rational thought for it. Such as: "Not drinking at this time is key to my plan," or "Each time I refuse a drink, I get stronger." Also, you can talk directly back to the urge. Say, "Get out of here—I'm not drinking tonight," or whatever. This will help mobilize your resolve on the issue.

Consider your long-term goals: Bring to mind your list of reasons for moving to moderation that you put together earlier. Having a drink just at this moment may not then seem so important. And think about how you will feel tomorrow if you give in, and how you will feel if you don't give in. You gain some real power when you refuse to give in. As Terry said:

> *The urge passes. That is a guarantee. No matter how strong, how tempting, how deviously convincing, the urge to take a drink to relieve the stress will pass. But that sense of pride, of strength, of self-worth will not pass. It will stay with you and make you even stronger.*

Distracting Yourself

Distractions are activities you can call on quickly to take your mind off the urge and point it in a healthier direction. Here are a quick three dozen:

1. Take a walk.
2. Take a drive.
3. Do exercises at home or go to the gym.
4. Go jogging.
5. Listen to favorite music.
6. Telephone a friend.
7. Clean out the garage.
8. Cook something interesting.
9. Go to the library or bookstore.
10. Work in the yard.
11. Clean and polish the car.
12. Take a shower or bath.
13. Read the newspaper, a magazine, or a book.
14. Drink something nonalcoholic.
15. Get a video.
16. Write a letter or e-mail.
17. Plan your next vacation.
18. Make up a grocery store or hardware store shopping list.
19. Go shopping or window-shopping.
20. Plan on redecorating a room.
21. Clean out the refrigerator.
22. Have sex.
23. Go to a driving range.
24. Pay the bills.

25. Make up a household budget or plan future finances.
26. Check stock market action and look for investments.
27. Talk to your children.
28. Get a haircut or manicure.
29. Get a massage.
30. Work on a sewing project.
31. Start a journal.
32. Look into your genealogy on the Internet.
34. Visit a friend.
35. Get the snapshot collection in order.
36. Make popcorn.
37. Start a woodwork project.

Do you have ideas for other distractions that might work for you? If so list them here:

____

____

____

____

____

____

Here's an example of how Maxine used distractions and confrontation to cope with an urge:

> *I feel so very proud of myself this morning. Had a little urge to drink wine last night, however, I did not give in to the urge. Realized it was a habit. I worked like a fool yesterday, enjoyed it mind you. Finished painting two bedrooms, and after it was all done, I thought gee, I need a reward. My reward in the past has been a drink. Realized this and turned the TV on instead. Made supper, and while making supper thought about MM, and how not to dwell on drinking thinking, that it is really no big deal, really minimized it, and kept telling myself if you want to become a moderate drinker you have to take steps and learn new skills. The urge disappeared. Instead I made my hubby and myself two raw juice cocktails, with fresh carrots, apples, celery and parsley. When hubby came home, he said,"Oh, Mocktails." It was delicious, had supper, did a little bit of work after supper. Watched the news, and by 8:15 we went to bed to read. Life felt soooooo good, and a sense of accomplishment settled in my heart. Slept like a baby.*

Another person, who lives in New York City, was having a terrible time with an urge to drink in the middle of the day. He got in touch with a friend, who suggested going to the park and feeding the pigeons. This might seem like a simplistic answer to a major emotional problem. But the fact is that ordinary activities—which we have often taken to be of little interest compared to drinking—can be surprisingly absorbing and fulfilling. And many activities like that are right at hand. While in the grip of overdrinking, we may not be able to appreciate them. Once we get our heads clear, we can. Mike advises:

> *If you're feeling the urge to drink, go do something, anything, as long as it's not something you normally do while drinking. Go for a walk. Drink some iced tea. Write a letter to a friend. Better yet, call a friend and enjoy the fact that you'll be clearheaded enough to remember it tomorrow.*

One reason it's important not to give into urges is that they are not just isolated events. If you feel an urge and give into it by using alcohol, you may satisfy the urge at the moment. But the giving in at this time increases the odds that your automatic response to the next urge will be to give in again. On the other hand, every time you stand up to an urge, you build strength for controlling it in the future. In upcoming chapters, you'll learn ways to determine the triggers that are most likely to cause urges for you—and additional techniques for coping with them.

Why Just Thirty?

The main reason for an abstinence period of thirty days is that this amount of time will eliminate most or all alcohol tolerance for people who are not physically dependent on alcohol. A period of four weeks also gives you plenty of time to accomplish the steps that will help prepare you for successful moderation. However, some people sense that longer periods are needed to get them to where they need to be to start moderate drinking. Your inner sense on that is absolutely brilliant. Trust it. As one person put it:

> *It feels really good to have done this, and now I'm going to go to sixty days. I continue to be bothered by urges to drink. I think to be the kind of moderate drinker I want to be, I shouldn't have urges, or be looking forward to drinking. I want to be able to drink occasionally, at dinners or whatever, but not be consumed by it. So I'm going to continue to abstain until it doesn't matter anymore to me. Does that make sense to anyone? When I get to the point where I don't care, then I'll allow myself to indulge.*
>
> Another answered:
>
> *Congrats on your Thirty. I think it is a great idea to continue. I know several of the successful moderators are those that have spent more than thirty days abstinent. Good luck to you.*

What If You're Not Ready for a Thirty?

If you don't feel ready for a month's abstinence, then you're not ready. No one on earth is a better judge of your own needs than you are. You can do mini-abstinence periods of a few days here and a few days there, if you want. Preparing to do short periods can be much less daunting. One described her experience this way:

> *It was really scary when I realized I had become an every-night drinker (usually four to five glasses of wine each night). I haven't mastered a Thirty yet, but since I started MM, I have certainly reduced my drinking. There are usually people doing weekly abstinence . . . not drinking three, four, or five consecutive days out of the week. This is the way I started, and it works wonders. I had a short period of falling back into my old wicked ways, but knowing that I had improved myself once before, I knew I could do it again. . . .*

If you can do a month's abstinence or longer, that is good. But if you can only do, say, three days at the beginning, that is also better than overdrinking every day. Many people find they get the experience and confidence from mini-periods to do a longer period. And some people start on a "mini", find it's going well, and just continue on.

Tapering Down

Others find that it's easier for them to just taper down rather than start with an abstinence period. This is one approach people naturally use on their own and research shows that it can work (Tucker 1999; Miller 1991). The abstinence period does have the benefits listed above, and it does compress the process, but it is not the only way.

To taper down, for a regular or daily drinker, means cutting back on both the number of days on which you drink and the quantities per day. If you're not a regular or daily drinker, it simply means gradually cutting back on the amount you drink per occasion. For people who are drinking five or six drinks per day or less, the rate at which you cut back is a matter of what seems realistic and achievable to you.

However, for people who are drinking more than five or six drinks per day, there is a caution about stopping too suddenly, as there is a significant risk of possibly life-threatening seizures. In such cases, you might want to seek medical assistance for cutting back. If you decide to cut down on your own from more than five or six drinks per day, then cutting down slowly is the safest way to do it. In such cases, we'd recommend that you reduce your drinking by no more than 50 percent each day until you reach zero.

For any tapering-down effort, it will help to set some specific number goals for days and quantities per day as you go along, rather than just having a general aim to reduce drinking. Research has shown that number goals work better than general intentions. And it will help to keep a written diary to track progress. Some find it encouraging to note their typical number of drinks per week before starting moderation efforts, and then note their reduction from that number each week as they progress in tapering down. Don't be too rigid about this, particularly at the beginning, or you could get discouraged. Your aim is for a definite downtrend in drinking, not necessarily hitting certain numbers exactly. As you notch down your number goals and your drinking, you'll probably take a lot of satisfaction from the process. And if you're not doing a Thirty, you'll still find that all the other techniques and exercises in this program can work for you.

In tapering down, then, you can aim to drink less on drinking occasions, and also use short periods of abstinence. With short periods of abstinence, there is less chance of failure.

Mary, a writer, age forty-two, describes the benefits she found in this route:

Just my two days of abstinence a week gives me practice, and interrupts the "habit" of drinking wine every night. And I drink less when I do drink. I still have a way to go, but now it's been many weeks since I woke up feeling remorseful. I'm more purposeful elsewhere in my life too. I don't think it's drinking less that caused it: rather, both things came out of some common source. Whatever, it's self-generating. I used to think I couldn't do anything right (despite what looked like "achievements" to other people, what a fraud I felt like). Now I really live in each day (some are tough, but that's cool because it's real) and look forward with hope, not dread.

Another successful moderator gave this advice about planning ahead when tapering down:

Plan ahead for your moderate days. Get your goal limit set in mind and make plans to back it up. Such as only having on hand a smaller amount, sipping if you're normally a fast drinker, starting later than your "habit" time, something to signify "caboose" (mine was eating), etc. And be realistic and honest about where you're setting your limit too! If you're saying two but thinking four—don't be surprised (or beat yourself up) when you stop at four. If your "normal old way" is six, this is another step at reducing. Each success fosters the confidence, experience, and knowledge of "what works" as you go along. As does each "what doesn't" as the journey unfolds.

Your Drinking Diary

For those who are not ready to start a month of abstinence, or who are tapering down, keeping a drinking diary is highly recommended. In the diary, note on each day if you drink, how much you drink, what you drink, the occasion (where and with whom), and how you were feeling. If you've started to take up activities that displace drinking, which we'll discuss more later, you could make notes on progress there as well. Some use the diary as a planning tool as well, for example, marking in advance days planned to be abstinent with an "A," and moderating days with an "M."

Keeping this diary will help you focus on what you are actually doing and where you want to go with your drinking. On any occasions when you over-drink, figure out what made that occasion different from other occasions. It often happens that the effect of paying increased attention to drinking through a diary will in itself reduce the level of drinking. A diary can also be a very important tool when you start practicing moderation. Use of the diary at that time is discussed more thoroughly in chapter 10.

Here's an example of a diary, with two drinking occasions over the MM limits and one within, and the restart of a positive nondrinking activity:

Patrick's Diary

Date	# of Drinks	What Drink	Time Spent Drinking	The Occasion	Feelings at Time and/or Positive Activity Progress
5/5	5	beers	3 hrs	watching football at Hi Note bar	excited thru a close game, not counting my drinks
5/6	0				
5/7	2	wine	1½ hrs	dinner out with Sue	quiet & comfortable
5/8	0				
5/9	0				rejoined the health club
5/10	6	tequila	4 hrs	office group TGIF	carried away doing shots
5/11	0				

Here's a blank form that you can make copies of for ongoing use:

My Diary

Date	# of Drinks	What Drink	Time Spent Drinking	The Occasion	Feelings at Time and/or Positive Activity Progress

Drinking Rules

During the Thirty—or early in the program if you're not ready for a Thirty—is a good time to work out an initial set of drinking rules. A main purpose of these rules is to keep you away from situations in which you are most likely to violate your limits.

Though most rules should be made to fit individual situations, there is one that we strongly believe should be part of anyone's regimen and that is *never to drink and drive* (and likewise, don't drink in any other situations where doing so would endanger yourself or others). In the case of driving, the possible damage is just too great to risk. Even if you *know* you are under the legal limit, *any* alcohol can impair you—and with driving, every millisecond of reaction time counts.

The nature of the rules you make for yourself is completely up to you—they should reflect your life, your experience, and your knowledge about your own weak spots. The list should be short and simple enough to keep clearly in mind. It is good to make up this list during the abstinence period and mentally rehearse using both your rules and your limits. Later on, you may reshuffle the list of rules to stop focusing on the ones you now follow habitually and add new rules, dealing with other problem situations that may have come to light.

An initial list, focusing on the particular problem areas of an individual might look like this:

- *No drinking in bars.*
- *Cut out the nightcap routine.*
- *No drinking when feeling low.*

One person working out his rules wrote:

Frank's Initial Drinking Rules

Never drink when you're angry. Every time I drank in the past when I was angry, I lost all control. I have done a lot of anger work and know today to stay away from the booze when I am annoyed at someone. Also when I am too tired or have had a stressful day, my body wants more rest and sleep than alcohol. And I've learned not to drink while grieving. I lost my father in March, and in coming back I was drinking twice a week, and it did not help matters. I have given myself permission to feel my loss and pain. I am applying this, and to me that is progress.

Here's a place to set down your first ideas about your drinking rules:

My Initial Drinking Rules

These, your very own guidelines, are now your roadmap to moderation, so you've just taken a big step. This is a vital part of your program, and you'll probably develop and change this set of personal guidelines as you move along.

Rehearse Your New Thinking and Behaviors

Once you have your limits and rules set, think ahead to how you will use them in the weeks when you begin to moderate. Consider typical situations you will encounter, and picture just what you will say and do about drinking in those situations. Keep coming back to this exercise as often as you can during the Thirty. If you have a big event coming up after your Thirty, like a wedding, graduation, or family gathering, make specific plans for that event. This thinking ahead is a critical part of internalizing your limits and rules, developing commitment to them, and starting to make them second nature.

Telling yourself what you will do in advance is what psychologists call an *action intention statement*. When you have fixed the response to a given type of situation in your mind in this way, it becomes more likely that you will respond that way in the actual situation. The rehearsal helps set up a new automatic action of the desired type.

At the end of the next chapter, after the discussion of control techniques for drinking situations, there's space provided to make notes on a plan for an upcoming event.

Finally, during the abstinence period or as you start the program, you should begin to visualize yourself as the new person you wish to become, with moderate drinking as a new habit. Think about the definition of the moderate drinker given in chapter 3, and picture yourself being and acting in that mode.

Summing Up

- A thirty-day abstinence period early in the program puts you back in control and provides a period removed from alcohol in which to plan and prepare for using alcohol in moderation.
- The Thirty has a number of other benefits, including the experience that you can handle the ups and downs of life and many kinds of situations better without alcohol than with it. The abstinence period will also reduce your tolerance for alcohol and give your body a better sense of feedback on how much is "enough."
- You'll practice a number of abstinence skills during the Thirty, including refusing drinks, which you'll probably find easier than you expect.
- There are a number of ways of dealing with drinking urges, but the most important is to realize that the urge will pass.
- If your first try at a Thirty doesn't work, don't consider yourself a failure. Count your good days, and get ready for another try.
- If you feel you are not ready to start a Thirty, just go ahead and do the written exercises in this chapter, and start a drinking diary.
- You can then find yourself ready later to try a Thirty, or try mini-periods of abstinence and work up to a Thirty, or you can try tapering down.
- Many find repeats of the Thirty are helpful later.
- Work out an initial set of drinking rules that fit your particular situation, aiming to avoid or better manage activities or situations that most put you at risk of overdrinking.
- During the Thirty, picture yourself in the days ahead as a moderator, and mentally rehearse applying your limits and rules to upcoming events and in your daily activities.

Chapter 6

General Drinking Control Skills

Now it's time to learn some skills that will help you become a successful moderator, just as they have helped many others. Let's take a look at Lucy's case for a start. Drinking fast had become a habit for her, and the habit asserted itself, especially when her attention was focused on something else:

> *I used to drink beer in "chug mode" while cleaning. Probably a six-pack in two hours. If you drink like that over and over again, it just becomes a habit, a reflex, and no matter what you drink, it goes down like that. So it takes concentrated attention to s-l-o-w i-t d-o-w-n. Learn to s-a-v-o-r each s-i-p. Appreciate the flavor. Or drink water or juice.*

The general drinking control skills covered in this chapter should be useful in almost any drinking situation, from the most to the least challenging. They have been gleaned from research on how people become successful moderate drinkers, as well as from the experiences of people like Lucy. From learning how to read your body's "stop" signals, to measuring, counting drinks, and eating while drinking, they offer practical methods for staying in control. Since everyone is different, some techniques that are critical for one person may not be critical for another. You'll need to experiment to find which work best for you. In chapters 7 and 8, you'll learn to identify and cope with the special situations that are triggers for overdrinking for you.

Understanding What Is "Enough"

Probably the most important single factor that determines moderation is true commitment to the insight that you get all of the real positives of drinking from a small number of drinks. As Tammy described it:

> *The positives almost always happen for me during the first two, or maximum three, glasses. After that, the negatives kick in. I use that fact to help me moderate by reminding myself before the second drink that it is the last "good one."*

You don't need to come to this commitment immediately. But keep it in mind as a conviction that you would like to arrive at through your own experience. The exact number of "good ones" will vary by individual, of course—in ways related to sex, weight, and other factors—but it will almost invariably be a small number, probably one, two, or three.

Here is an experiment you might try to help you experience this for yourself. Some evening when you are not in an abstinence period, drink one drink, and observe all your feelings and sensations. Write down the taste and all the subjective feelings you have. Then have a second, an hour later. Again, observe all your experiences closely and write them down, but keep them separate and don't compare them to the first. Then, an hour later, have a third drink, and again write down your observations in detail about how it tasted and everything about how you feel. A woman might stop this experiment at three, and a man at four drinks, if those are your limits per occasion.

The next day, sit down and review your notes. See how your experiences differ over time, if at all. You will probably find that after a drink or two, the additional drinks do not add much if anything to your positive experience. And if enjoyment is what you are after, this will give you a good idea of what the drinks themselves contribute to your enjoyment over time.

You might then try this experiment (minus the note-taking) at a party. If your second drink during a party produces very different feelings from the second drink when you are alone, it is clear that the party atmosphere is contributing as much to your feelings as the drinks. If that is the case, why do you need the extra drinks? Wouldn't a nonalcoholic drink do as well?

Another thing you might try when you start to moderate is to carefully check the effect of just one drink. Here's how Morgan describes the benefit of having a single drink:

> *Previously, I never considered a single drink pleasurable and worth seeking out in its own right. Drinks came in sets of two or more, never in singlets. Why bother? There's no buzz from just one drink. Consumed grudgingly, it frequently left an aftertaste of resentment.*
>
> *The other day I had orchestra rehearsals into the evening, after a really horrid drive to the rehearsal site, fighting major construction delays. I had a two-hour dinner break and headed to my usual pub. I ordered a pint of beer and an Asian-style grilled chicken salad. About a third of the pint went down very fast—and then I said to myself, "sip" at it for god's sake, you can always have another if you really want it. So the salad came, and I ate that and sipped my beer and finished them both at the same time without trying. The relaxation from alcohol came on slowly, subtly, not at all the powerful rush I used to get.*

Relief, yes—from the over-the-top stress I'd put myself through that day. But not the answer to all life's problems, not any more. When I left the pub, I felt full but not stuffed, and pleasantly relaxed from the beer. I felt so grateful that I had refused myself a second pint. I had had just a little soft twilight spot in my day, which faded pleasantly after dinner and was already fading out as we sat down to the next Mozart session.

Thinking Ahead

As mentioned earlier, picturing yourself in the specific situations in which you will be drinking is a key exercise you should undertake during your Thirty or any later abstinence periods. That is, you should bring to mind as graphically as possible a future drinking situation, and mentally rehearse the specific actions you will take in the situation. As you start the exercise, get your commitment to moderation, your limits, and the control tools you'll use in the situation in mind. Then, track through what you will do and say in the situation as it unfolds. Picture yourself entering the situation, being offered or offering yourself a drink, just how you will handle that drink, and how you will handle successive offers of drinks as the event unfolds. This rehearsing ahead during the abstinence period is a key way of starting to own the tools and habits of moderation. At the end of this chapter, after we've gone through the various control skills for drinking situations, there's a suggestion that you write down notes about what you would do in various drinking situations.

It's important to practice mentally because after the Thirty, when you start moderate drinking, you'll need to have a plan when going into any potential drinking situation. First, of course, you need to decide whether it is a situation in which you can safely drink, or one in which you should avoid drinking, or a situation to avoid entirely.

If you are going to drink, decide in advance on a specific limit on drinks for that occasion. And keep in mind your commitment to moderation and the key drinking control skills you will use. It has recently been shown that even in nondependent social drinkers, there is often a slight *priming* effect from initial doses of alcohol (Kirk 2000). This priming effect is an increase in liking for alcohol, and seems greatest in those who experience the greatest subjective positive mood effects from it. So make your decision about your limit for the occasion *before* you start drinking, and stick with it.

Control Tools for Drinking Situations

The list of tools that can be helpful is so long that no one could keep them all in mind. And you don't need to. The first three—measuring, counting and eating—are basic and should be used at all times if possible. In addition to those, just pick out a couple of other tools that seem to deal with your key problems and keep them in mind for a time. You might even make one or another of these tools a part of your set of drinking rules. After using those has become a habit, you may find it helpful to target a couple of others.

Measuring

As mentioned earlier, the standard drinks for the BAC tables are twelve ounces of regular beer, five ounces of table wine, and 1.5 ounces of eighty-proof hard liquor. Obviously you need to measure to know how many drinks you're having. Since beer comes in twelve ounce bottles and cans, it is easy to measure. With wine, you can take a home wine glass and measure out exactly five ounces to see what that looks like. Restaurant wine glasses vary in size, but you can generally see whether the serving is in that range or not. Hard liquor is the trickiest, since a little goes a long way. Again, check your home shot glass or other measuring device to get a clear mental image of what the 1.5-ounce standard looks like.

Mixed drinks (sangria, punches, martinis, etc.) make measuring and keeping track a lot harder, and are best to avoid. If the mixed drink is hard liquor with a mixer or over ice, try to make it yourself or observe the maker. If the beverage contains a higher-than-standard amount of alcohol, such as "ice" beer, dessert wine, or ninety-proof liquor, just be advised and leave a little in your glass or whatever.

Counting

This may seem a bit silly, since it's easy enough to keep track of, at least, single-digit numbers. But sometimes in the past you probably haven't kept a count at all. Now you want to establish a firm habit of keeping count and keeping to your limits. And a somewhat exaggerated focus on counting will actually help keep you mindful of your moderation goals overall at the beginning of moderating drinking.

One earlier book on moderation actually advised carrying around a card on which the person noted each drink at the time. Another idea is to carry a coin for each drink you're planning in one pocket and transferring one of these coins to the other pocket with each drink. You can also announce to others what your limit for the occasion will be, if you are comfortable doing so. One woman marked drinks on her forearm with a ballpoint pen, during a long night around town! Of course, you don't need to take these kinds of public actions unless they appeal to you. But do focus at the beginning on keeping a clear mental count of each drink on each occasion, and make counting a habit.

Eating

Having something to eat before or with alcoholic drinks delays the rate at which alcohol gets into the bloodstream and has its effects, and so makes it considerably easier to handle. On a completely empty stomach, alcohol can take us by surprise and get us off-balance almost before we know what's going on. One successful moderator, Mike, features eating in his set of ongoing rules:

1. *Always drink on a full stomach. It makes a world of difference.*
2. *Always drink water or soda in between alcoholic beverages. I am a fast eater and drinker so this helps me slow down.*
3. *Keep the booze out of the house. If there's some lying around, I'll drink it.*
4. *No drinking on consecutive days. When I find I've been breaking this rule, I find that it's time to refocus on moderation.*

The First Few Minutes Count

Somehow, what you do in the first few minutes of a drinking episode can be critical for the way the whole episode goes. It's a matter of your frame of mind going in, and the physical actions you take are important too. If, at a social event, you rush to the bar and have a quick one to get in the swing of things, you may be in for trouble. People have a tendency to start as they mean to go on and to tell themselves things like, "I've already blown it, so I may as well go for it," if they find themselves doing things that violate their rules.

However, if you take time to settle into the situation, get comfortable with it, and then after a while start out with a nonalcoholic drink or start sipping a drink very slowly, you'll probably be okay for the rest of the time. You've told yourself by those actions that you are going to be moderate. Those first actions somehow get us on the track of being moderate or not for the rest of the episode, whether it's out in company or home alone.

Thirst Management

This may sound obvious, but don't go into a drinking situation thirsty. Quench your thirst with water, juice, or a soft drink before the drinking situation, or start out with a nonalcoholic drink when you arrive. Sometimes an overpowering lust for alcohol turns out to be a simple thirst for water. One beer drinker we know loads up on several glasses of water beforehand. (If you do that, of course, be sure you know where the restroom is!)

Delaying

To delay, just postpone the time when you allow yourself to have your first drink. This may mean getting to an event late, or delaying the start of drinking on any occasion. Or, you can leave an event early, especially if the event is getting a little too alcohol-saturated for you to feel comfortable drinking moderately, or if you're feeling resolve slip away. Says Paul:

> *You might try the old "arrive late and leave early" trick. If I arrive after everyone is reasonably plied, I find the sight of other people's drunkenness motivating and fascinating enough to entertain myself for quite a while. Practice your moderation for a while, and you will still have the capacity to leave under your own recognizance. It doesn't sound as fun at first, but it pays great dividends the following day—not only for your confidence but physically as well.*

You may also have the best bits of gossip! In addition, leaving early can actually be a plus for your public image, as Amy put it:

> *My number one rule even during partying days was: always be one of the first to split! That way, it looks good in public, like you have something way more interesting to attend.*

Jenny found these techniques helpful to her image as a business person:

> *My department are* big *drinkers and partyers . . . there's always something going on. Because of that, I started doing exactly what you've suggested here. I get there a couple of hours into the party, drink two or three drinks, and leave.*

Usually, by the time I get home, it's late and I end up going straight to bed. No one has seen me totally ripped! I use my kids as the excuse to leave. Works great!

Diluting

There is a wide range of possibilities here that can help make moderation easier. Studies of people who moderate without assistance find that they often move to a less-preferred beverage—which in itself can often help you to slow down (Sobell 1992; Tucker 1999). The move is generally to a lighter beverage, such as from hard liquor to wine or from wine to beer. It happens that alcohol is absorbed more quickly by the body the higher its concentration, so a drink with a lower percentage of alcohol will get into your system more slowly.

Said Gretchen:

I find that when I drink the less potent drinks like beer, I get full first. Drinking a martini too fast—now that's an entirely different story. Too much alcohol too fast spells disaster. Gone is any sense of sense, and I don't even know what it is I'm trying to achieve, except stupidity.

In addition, for many people, different drinks have quite different images. In one survey, people associated straight liquor with heavy drinking, and wine more with contentment and sociability (Leigh 1999). If different drinks carry different meanings for you, go for the ones you associate most with moderate use.

There are also many ways to dilute a given beverage. Instead of liquor on the rocks, try a highball. Wine can become a spritzer. There is 3.2-percent-alcohol beer. And there is the never-empty glass trick that Barry finds helpful:

You get a mixed drink, such as gin and tonic. When the glass is half empty, refill it with just a little more ice and tonic. Then when it is half empty again, repeat the drill ad infinitum. You're there with an alcoholic drink the whole night but end up drinking just one standard drink. Or if you want two standard drinks, decide at what point, i.e. after how many refills with tonic, you are going to drink the whole glass. Then repeat the drill. I like doing it this way. No one has ever noticed—or at least commented on it. And the fact that the gin is successively diluted is almost imperceptible. This is probably because the concentration of gin goes down at about the same speed as its effect on me goes up.

Alternating

Many find alternating nonalcoholic drinks with alcoholic drinks particularly helpful. Some tips from Lisa:

Get some nonalcoholic beer or other "not-tail" drink (club soda, lime, a splash of bitters; cranberry juice and club soda; diet Snapple; nonalcoholic bloody mary; nonalcoholic beer and V8 juice, etc.), and alternate drinking nonalcoholic drinks with alcoholic drinks.

Start out with a nonalcoholic and put off drinking the alcohol for longer. Many people find that just having something in their hand to hold while talking with others helps, even if it's an nonalcoholic drink.

Elise describes alternating at two occasions:

Friday night, a cookout at a friend's house with an out-of-town friend present. Two drinks the whole night. I alternated with water and drank slowly. On Saturday I attended a wedding—three glasses of wine spread out over about five hours. I also drank a lot of sparkly water and the fact that it was an outside reception and it was quite hot helped my motivation for water.

And a formerly heavy beer drinker, Tom, described a moderate drinking weekend this way:

As for my little plan, this past weekend . . . lots of work around the house and in the yard . . . late Saturday afternoon after five months and seven days of abstinence, I bought a six-pack of light beer and a twelve-pack of nonalcoholic beer . . . Sat out by the pool admiring all my hard work . . . drank two nonalcoholic beers for every one regular beer . . . and still have three regular ones in the fridge . . . it really works for me.

Sipping

Another useful technique is learning to sip rather than gulp. Slowing down the intake by consciously taking smaller sips and spacing them out can be a big help, especially for people who are inclined to guzzle. Kimberly explains how the group dynamics at a social event can lead to faster drinking if one isn't paying attention to pacing:

Allowing more time per drink really helps. You know, it seems that, at cocktail parties and weddings, at big family functions, you tend to drink faster. And it's amazing when you slow down how you notice, even when you go out to dinner, that you're probably only halfway through that glass of wine and everybody else is finished—they're ordering a second drink.

Gretchen's motto is SKIS, or is it KISS?

So borrowing the KISS advice: "Keep It Simple, Stupid," we might say, "Simply Keep It Slow." Unfortunately instead of a kiss we get skis, but we do stay sober. I suppose if one insisted on a kiss, it would be "Keep It Slow, Stupid." I just hate calling myself stupid.

For training purposes, some people have even made a game out of seeing how many sips, and how long an interval of time, they can get out of one drink.

Put the Glass Down

Another drinking control skill involves putting your glass down during drinking occasions. To do this, try not to keep the glass in your hand, either at the table or while standing up, except when you are actually drinking from it. Often even while standing up at a social event, you can find a place to perch your glass. This helps with the sipping business and with making you conscious of your consumption. Of course, this won't work if you are self-conscious about not having a glass in your hand—but it can be helpful in situations where that is not a concern.

Timing

If sipping or putting a drink down doesn't work for you, you can also get about the same effect by noting the timing of your drinking. The simplest way is to plan in advance the number of drinks you will have and the interval between the start of each drink, such as an hour or forty-five minutes. Then just watch the clock for the time you can start each drink. This technique may make you slightly more self-conscious—but again, different things work for different people and some have found that timing works best for them.

Self-Talk

Another crucial tool—which perhaps underlies all the others—is having a little internal dialogue with yourself before each drink. This makes the act of having a drink more subject to conscious control and helps you keep your goal of moderation firmly in mind. Says Rick:

> *All of our "have a plan" and "count measured drinks" rules are just ways to help us stop after having one or two drinks. I don't have "the" answer, but I have found something that works for me. Before* each *and* every *drink I run through a little test in my head that goes something like "Do I want this drink? Will it really taste good? Will it interfere with anything I have planned for the next few hours?" If I can answer "yes," "yes," and "no," I have it, and I make sure that it is one* standard *drink. This takes some of the "carefree abandonment" out of the drinking experience, but perhaps that's a* good *thing.*

Bring Your Own Alternatives

Some have found that bringing their own nonalcoholic beverages to social events works for them. It can be helpful either in abstinence periods or if you just want to be sure you have your preferred nonalcoholic beverage to alternate with hard drinks. Says Fred:

> *I generally take along my own assortment of alternative drinking matter. Some nonalcoholic beer, some Perrier water, cranberry juice, whatever I feel like* I *will want to have. If I have to rely on the host(ess)'s selection I find I feel uncomfortable and wish I were having what everyone else is having. But if I have my own stash I do not feel deprived. Also I find it important to bring a variety of things so I don't get bored. I have never had anyone be offended by my bringing my own.*

Focus on the Fun

Especially when you start to learn new moderation habits, you need to pay close attention to what you're doing when you are drinking. But try not to center on the alcohol as the main or only source of enjoyment in a drinking situation. Focus on what else is going on that is pleasurable, and try to give alcohol a back seat. For example, you could focus your attention on the people you like, the conversation, the music, or whatever other activities are going on. If you are successfully moderating, you'll be more open to what others are saying, better at making conversation, and more able to appreciate and take part in socializing. If you're drinking alone, try to be content to relax and enjoy the play of your thoughts, without looking for a big kick from the alcohol. You can spotlight the pleasure of the taste and the subtle relaxation that comes from a first drink—but keep it in context and try to see it as just one aspect of an enjoyable experience.

Think about Tomorrow

No, don't get the Fleetwood Mac song stuck in your head—but it can be helpful while you are in a drinking situation to literally consider what you have to do the next day. Many of us have a tendency to focus on the short term, rather than the long term—and that can lead to overdrinking. Instead, consider your obligations and goals when the thought of "having just one more" pops into your head, or just as a way of keeping your focus on moderation. This works especially well if you have something important to do, or will be attending an early morning event like an early tennis game or business breakfast meeting. Says Rob:

> *I would borrow tomorrow's feelings today. I'd say, you know when I wake up tomorrow I'm going to be very happy with myself, both physically and mentally, because I'm not going to have a hangover and I'm going to feel good about myself. And I'd start these nice feelings the night before while I'm there, saying, hey, I'm already patting myself on the back and the cocktail party's only halfway over.*

Heed the "Stop" Signal

After an abstinence period of thirty days, your body's natural signal that tells you when you have "had enough" should be in better working order. When you plan to have more than one drink, you should pay particular attention to the physiological sensations that arise from additional drinks as well as any internal voice reminding you that more might make you lose control. The signals are different for everyone, but with awareness, most of us can recognize the form they take in our own mind and body. The thing is, when the buzzer sounds, you have to pay attention to it. As Paul said:

> *In the past, I have experienced a natural feeling like "I don't want any more." But the difference was that stupid me would just drink through it! How insane is that? Not only did I not really want to drink, but I forced myself into ruining the following day.*

As you can see from Paul's experience, the sensitivity to alcohol is partly physical and partly psychological. The abstinence period, and then having three or four no-drinking days in the week, should give you back the physical sensitivity. The psychological part of sensitivity comes in good part from your particular mind-set at the moment. If you've ever had a drink during an important business luncheon or when you had pressing things to do after lunch, for instance, you may have noted that you could feel almost the very first sip, and that it didn't feel particularly good. When we really want to keep our minds clear and fully functioning, we don't welcome the mental blurring from even small amounts of alcohol.

But if we're looking for relief and escape from pressures, we just go with the flow of what alcohol does to us and see that as a sign of the release to come. If it's part of a wanted change in our feelings, somehow the unpleasant aspects of losing control that come with intoxication are less noticeable than when we're trying to keep on top of things. And so if what you really want to do is just let loose without concern about the consequences, then you may not get or acknowledge any signal of "enough" from your body. Thus, keeping a moderation mind-set is critical for being able to hear and heed the "stop" signal that may come after a couple of drinks.

Managing Overdrinking Urges

For many of us, there comes a time after we have had a drink or two where a voice in our head says "why not go for it?" and tries to convince us to abandon our plans for moderation. This voice often comes in response to the "stop" signal, as a counter to it.

A big cause of getting to this "what the hell" point, where having another drink seems more important than moderation, is simply your BAC getting above that magic .055 percent. At that point your judgment and self-control start to become impaired, and things can easily get out of hand. In fact, this is sometimes called "the point of no return." So the best answer is just to work hard to keep your BAC below that .055 percent danger point.

Another major cause of overdrinking urges is drinking in circumstances that involve your overdrinking triggers. Though you may have made plans to avoid doing this, these triggers can sometimes sneak up on you, or you may not be aware of them until they occur during your first tries at moderation. So, how should you cope?

Basically, overdrinking urges generally come from a state of somewhat fuzzy judgment where you fall into the trap of thinking more is better. Says Morgan:

> *This does not mean that you/we are "powerless" over alcohol, but rather that we have taken enough of the drug to interfere with our higher thought centers, the place where we are able to defer immediate gratification in favor of long-term benefit. For me, that point occurs halfway through the third strong drink.*

Rationally, we know by now that more really isn't better. But rationality is about to go by the wayside. The aim is to try to bring rationality back into control, and quickly. So, whenever you realize you are about to overdrink, recognize the situation for what it is and declare an emergency to yourself. If you can, just stop whatever you are doing, put down your drink if you have one, and try to focus on what is happening.

Some of the same techniques we discussed earlier, in the section on how to deal with drinking urges during the abstinence period, work here as well—especially learning to recognize and outlast the urge.

Often the urge to overdrink will come via a voice that tells you the rules can slip a little bit on this occasion. This relates to what AA calls "drinking thinking," a nice term. Leading psychologists such as Albert Ellis and David Burns have made recognition of these wayward inner voices a central part of their self-help programs for behavior change. You may be telling yourself things like "I'm holding the drinks really well tonight," "There's nothing big on tomorrow anyway," "I've been working hard and deserve a good time."

The trick is to get to know your typical self-talk that gives you excuses for overdrinking, recognize it clearly when it comes up, and counter it. A good way to do this is to talk back directly. You can say things to that voice like: "You still there? Get lost!" Or substitute a more rational thought: "No sir, three's my limit," "I made a promise to myself," etc. Making these mental statements can bolster your resolve, and you can repeat them to yourself like a mantra for extra effect. Try not to say them out loud in public unless you are prepared to explain them, however!

Next, bring to mind the consequences of overdrinking. Not the consequences for your long-term goals, or what you plan for the rest of the year, but for right now and tomorrow. Immediate consequences have more power when your will is wavering. Try to picture that you'll be getting loose and sloppy, saying things you don't mean, or finding yourself unable to keep up with the conversation. And think of the last bad hangover you had and what it will feel like tomorrow to wake up like that. Says Morgan:

> *I have educated myself that if I continue to drink beyond this point, I'm very likely to end up hungover in the morning, unable to wake on time or to work well when I do finally get up. I'm able to deal with this because it's a general physical limitation that my body enforces, rather than a rule that my intellect tries to enforce.*

These are some specific suggestions, but the general idea is to get the rational part of your mind back into play, working against the urge to overdrink. These are tough situations, which are much better to avoid in the first place. Use whatever helps in your case.

Unexpected Situations

Drinking situations can come up unexpectedly, like a boss or good friend suddenly wanting to have a drink with you. These situations can be dangerous because you haven't had a chance to get into your moderation mind-set or to plan in advance. Instead of just going along with the drinking occasion, the thing to do now is to stop first and make a few conscious decisions.

Your first decision is whether to take part in the occasion at all. It's recommended earlier that you make and update a simple set of drinking rules, which often pick out a few types of situations in which you do not want to drink. You might, say, have a rule against drinking in bars at this point. But what if your boss wants to talk about something important, or there is some other special benefit to taking up the invitation? Well, you have to adapt the rules to real-life situations, but if you bend the rules, at least you can do so with extra care. Or, it might be an unexpected emotion-laden situation, like a sudden breakup, job loss, or death. You may just instinctively feel in some of these situations that it's not safe to drink.

Then there is the question of your running count of drinks over the past days. A written diary of drinks by day makes this especially easy to bring to mind. If you have just had three consecutive days of drinking, for instance, there's a red flag on the field.

Next, if it's an okay situation for drinking, decide on a specific drink limit for the occasion. Especially as you go into practicing moderate drinking, have your limit set at the beginning of any drinking occasion. And keep in mind that you can go for nonalcoholic drinks if that seems best.

So, when unexpected situations come up, focus your mind on your choices and make some decisions quickly.

Make Up Your Own

Odd control techniques you make up for yourself seem to work especially well. They fit your particular situation, and they are yours and you own them. Says Gail:

> *Here's what I've done that has worked for me, since two drinks sometimes seems too few. I bought small wine glasses and only fill them half full (about two ounces). I get to go back to the bottle, which seems to be important to me. I "intentionally" (at first but on habit now) leave my glass sitting somewhere and when I'm away from it I say to myself "Oh . . . I'll get it in a minute." Lots of times I find it the next morning, still full. I brush my teeth, clean my face, and give myself a foot-soaking (pedicure) while reading or writing something (with a little buzz). By the time the buzz wears off, I'm de-stressed already.*
>
> *Also, I drink water (before, during, and after). That, to me, is logical in that the water replenishes me, is on my list of to-do's anyway, and makes me feel full (in about ten minutes). It also dilutes the wine and my tolerance is less.*
>
> *Oh . . . and this is funny (to me). In the book* How to Think Like Leonardo da Vinci (Seven Steps to Genius Every Day), *there is a list of things Leonardo did that are signs of genius . . . one of them is to* drink water with wine. *First of all, you gotta love the title of the book.* Then, *to find that Leonardo loved wine and believed it was best (for one's health) to follow the glass of wine with a glass of water.*

An experienced moderator, Lisa, summed it up:

> *Some techniques to cope include: Starting out with a nonalcoholic drink or glass of water; alternating alcoholic beverages with nonalcoholic beverages; sipping two glasses of water for every alcoholic beverage you drink; eating before going to the event; having something to eat along with the alcoholic beverage; finding "mocktails" that you enjoy; visualizing how good you will feel in the morning waking up refreshed after not overindulging; thinking about how much you don't want to wake up in the middle of the night with a dry mouth you can't open or close; carrying your list in your purse of all the reasons you want to reduce your drinking in the first place; focusing on the social aspects of the evening instead of drinking (dance, converse, ask people lots of questions and learn lots of new things).*
>
> *The more you practice these new habits, the more natural they begin to feel.*

What's Your Plan?

As discussed, there can be a lot of benefit in mentally picturing yourself going through future drinking situations, using your moderation skills. So, you might pick out some major upcoming event that you'll be attending after the Thirty that will involve drinking, or just pick a typical situation you will be in that could involve drinking, and make up a list of some of the techniques you will use as you go through the situation. Here's an example:

Denise's Plan for a Drinking Situation

The Situation: *Becky & Jack's wedding reception*

The Techniques I'll Use: *Start with a soda and lime, then have a glass of wine, and then another soda and lime. Get a plateful of appetizers shortly after arriving. Introduce self to Jack's family and spend some time talking with them. Don't let them pour wine at the table. Drink the champagne toast, but if they get into pouring more wine for a whole series of toasts, turn my champagne glass upside down and do the toasts with water.*

And here's some space for you:

My Plan for a Drinking Situation

The Situation: ______________________________

The Techniques I'll Use: ______________________________

____

____

____

____

____

____

____

____

Summing Up

- Recognize that the positive effects of alcohol are generally achieved with only truly moderate amounts.
- General drinking control techniques include:
  - Measure quantities
  - Count drinks
  - Eat something while drinking
  - Take care with what you do in the first few minutes
  - Drink other liquids for thirst

- Delay the start a bit
- Dilute your drinks
- Alternate with nonalcoholic drinks
- Sip to slow the intake
- Put the glass down
- Time your drinks
- Think before each drink
- BYO nonalcoholic beverage
- Get your fun from the occasion more than from the booze
- Think about tomorrow
- Heed the "stop" signal

- Overdrinking urges are best avoided by keeping the pacing and amounts within the guidelines, so that BAC does not get too high. If you do get to that point, declare an emergency to yourself, and try to break the chain of events.

Chapter 7

Pinpointing Your Drinking Triggers

Almost everyone can think of a situation where the thought immediately comes to mind: "It's time for a drink." Overdrinking situations may involve coping with negative emotions, simply drinking for pleasure, drinking from habit in certain circumstances, or a mixture of these. Examples of coping situations might be after a frustrating day at work, a breakup, a death in the family, the loss of a job, or a visit with the in-laws. All of us have stressful experiences, and people with alcohol problems tend to respond to them by overdrinking.

Says Rick:

> *My main trigger is coming home. I'm so used to pouring a nice drink when I get home that I look forward to it at about 3 or 4 o'clock when I'm still at work.*

Whatever our individual triggers for drinking are, we've come to automatically think of drinking in those situations, and to act on that thought, without considering alternatives. Exercises in this chapter will help you pinpoint the circumstances that lead to your heavy drinking. These circumstances can involve both the things going on around you and your internal thoughts and feelings. With these circumstances clearly identified, you can then decide on a better kind of response for the future. The response could involve not drinking, coping with the situation in another way, avoiding that type of situation, and others. Then, when one of your trigger situations comes up in the future, you can be alert to avoid your old automatic response, and instead respond in a more rational and beneficial way.

In the following exercise, you can think about your life and experiences from a number of different dimensions, to help pinpoint your individual triggers for heavy drinking. Each section invites you to think about a different aspect of experience, to help tease out all the many particulars. Then you can put together at the end a composite picture of your key triggers for heavy drinking.

In each of these sections, think about your situations of heavy drinking in the last few months, and especially the circumstances that have been involved in your heaviest drinking, or most often involved.

Timing

Here, list the time(s) of day, days of week, particular seasons. Examples could be: Every evening after work, Fridays on the way home after work, or end-of-year holiday season, etc.

____

____

____

____

____

____

Locations

List places, such as at home, at a bar, club, sports arena, etc.

____

____

____

____

____

____

Activities

List the particular things you've been doing at the time, such as reading, cooking, eating in or out, watching TV, playing cards, etc.

____

____

____

____

People Involved

List types of people or particular people present, such as coworkers or spouse, and whether these are male, female, or both, etc. If you drink alone, include that here as well.

Work-Related Circumstances

List things directly or indirectly related to work, such as after meeting monthly deadlines, when things are slow and boring at work, after criticism by boss, etc.

Finance-Related Circumstances

List things involving your and your family's finances, such as when paying the bills, when short of funds, when there is extra money, after an argument with spouse about money, after financial losses, etc.

Your Physical State

List here things involving your own physical state and physical feelings. Examples would be when feeling tired, to help sleep, when feeling pain, when thirsty, etc.

Relations with Others

Focus here not so much on particular people, but on aspects of your interchanges and relationships with others. Examples would be when feeling misunderstood by another, when unduly criticized, to be one of the gang, when nervous before meeting someone, when angry at someone, to help express feelings, etc.

Relationship with Spouse or Significant Other

Here list any aspects of this primary relationship that are involved with your heavy drinking. These might include when relaxing and having fun, when having sex, when the other doesn't understand, when the other doesn't pay attention, before, during, or after arguing, etc.

Parents or In-Laws

List things related to people in the senior generation in your life, positive or negative. These could include before, during, or after a visit by in-laws, celebrating their anniversaries or birthdays, when concerned about their health or financial situations, feeling guilty about not seeing and caring for them enough, etc.

Children

Aspects of your relationship with your children might include when they are acting out, when proud of their achievements, after arguments with spouse about handling children, when they are seriously ill, when they seem to be a nuisance, when grown children don't keep in touch enough, etc.

Feelings

List here emotions that precede your heavy drinking, rather than those that arise during or after it. The full gamut of human emotions are possible triggers for different people. On the positive side, these might include joy, elation, or feelings of success, relaxation, and comfort. On the negative side, these might include when feeling anxious, depressed, worn out, bored, restless, etc.

____

____

____

____

____

____

Major Life Events

These tend to stand out in one's mind, so you might think back a couple of years on this dimension, if it seems pertinent. Examples here are deaths of anyone close to you; your own marriage, separation, or divorce; change or loss of job; moving residence; significant health changes; job advancement or downgrade; retirement; significant new recreational or outside interests; major religious experiences, legal difficulties, etc.

____

____

____

____

____

____

Pattern of Drinking

The first section of this exercise on times of drinking bears on this, but the following are some common overall patterns of drinking that often typify the drinking of different individuals. Just note the one or ones that seem to fit.

- ☐ ____ Regular daily drinking
- ☐ ____ Regular weekend or holiday but not daily drinking
- ☐ ____ Occasional drinking with no particular time pattern, but often to excess
- ☐ ____ For fun and recreation
- ☐ ____ To relieve stress and bad feelings

Summarize and Characterize Your Triggers

Once you have finished going through the above sections, go back and study them to see the pattern in the factors that stimulate your problem drinking. You can use the list below to identify, for instance, which are the five most important problem areas for you. Then rank them from 1 to 5, with 1 being the most important.

- ☐ ____ Timing
- ☐ ____ Locations
- ☐ ____ Activities
- ☐ ____ People Involved
- ☐ ____ Work-Related Circumstances
- ☐ ____ Financial-Related Circumstances
- ☐ ____ Your Physical State
- ☐ ____ Relations with Others
- ☐ ____ Relationship with Spouse or Significant Other
- ☐ ____ Parents or In-Laws
- ☐ ____ Children
- ☐ ____ Feelings
- ☐ ____ Major Life Events

In addition to these broad categories, look for other patterns in things that go together and typify your key problem drinking situations. Do most of them involve social occasions, or being alone, or being with the immediate family? Are you usually under stress, or tired, or in a celebratory mood? The description of your most troublesome drinking situations will probably be a combination of factors that are special to you and your life. You can now make a short written summary description of the key circumstances that trigger your problem drinking.

Such a list for Andy might read:

Andy's Triggers

After work, when I'm feeling a bit tired and looking forward to relaxing with buddies at the bar

After arguing with wife about the kids or family finances

At sports events on the weekends

Anytime I'm feeling really angry

For Barbara, it might be:

Barb's Triggers

In social situations, to feel more easy and to get up for having a good time

When the kids are at school and I'm home alone, feeling nervous and down

After visiting the in-laws

During the Christmas and New Year's period

The number of items on the list can vary a great deal from one person to another. The problem circumstances may be simple single-factor situations, or the situations may combine several factors.

Here you can note your own particular list of triggers for heavy drinking:

My Triggers

____

____

____

____

____

____

It may have taken a fair amount of work to profile your trigger situations. But now you've isolated the problem to certain areas of your life, and you can focus your efforts on finding better ways of handling those particular areas.

Now, on the positive side, make a short written summary of the key situations in which you generally drink moderately. These situations often involve social controls, such as being with another person or people, or involve performance aspects, such as work or other activities that require your best attention. You can look back over the previous sections that go through different aspects of living, to help bring to mind the aspects of occasions when you drink moderately. For one person, that might be:

Ethan's Moderate Drinking Situations

Business lunches with customers

Scottish dance evenings

Bowling team nights

Here's a space for your list:

My Moderate Drinking Situations

____

____

____

____

____

____

____

____

____

____

____

Whether these occasions of drinking moderately have been times when you've been under special constraints, or times when you've just naturally managed your drinking better, they show that you do have the capability to be moderate. And, calling to mind these situations can show you the behaviors and feelings that go with your responsible drinking, which you may be able to apply to your other drinking situations. Here's an example:

Ethan's Things to Do to Drink Moderately in Those Situations

Situation	**What I Do to Moderate**
Lunch with customers	*If customer has a drink, I usually have one, but keep it to just one. The whole afternoon's ahead, and I don't need that let-down feeling.*
Scottish dance nights	*One or two drinks spaced over the whole evening. I'm more interested in the dancing than drinking, and want to get the steps right. And others usually aren't drinking much.*
Bowling team	*No more than a couple of beers—no hard stuff, and I drink it slowly. Don't want to let the teammates down—and they post the scores on the dept. bulletin board.*

Here's a space for your own notes:

What I Do to Drink Moderately in Those Situations

Situation	What I Do to Moderate
______________	______________________________
	______________________________
______________	______________________________
	______________________________
______________	______________________________
	______________________________

So, it seems you already have some kinds of situations where it is safer for you to drink. And you already have some tools in your toolkit that work well for you.

Update Your Rules List

Now that you have identified your triggers, the next step is to learn to either *avoid* or *cope* with them. After you determine which strategy to use for which triggers, you can update your rules list to reflect this new information.

Since avoidance is the simplest thing to do, at first you will want to just avoid as many situations as you can that are likely to provoke overdrinking. Later—or when there is no other choice but to go through a particular emotion or experience—you may use other strategies.

To see which trigger situations you can deal with by avoidance right now, look over your list and see which kinds of situations you can currently keep out of your life. Some examples are optional activities like going to sports events with heavy-drinking friends, drinking in bars, drinking at lunch on shopping days, maybe visiting difficult relatives, etc. If you come up with some triggers that need to be avoided, just add those to your short list of rules at this point.

For those drinking triggers that are unavoidable—or which are simply very important for you to keep in your life—the next chapter discusses some ways to cope without using alcohol excessively. In unavoidable situations where you have negative emotional or physical feelings, the best strategy is just not to drink, as the next chapter will discuss.

If you'd like to update your rules list at this point, here's a space for that:

My Drinking Rules

Summing Up

- The written exercise will highlight where and when your drinking problems most often occur.
- Coming up with some summary statements about your most common types of trigger situations for overdrinking will help fix those insights in your mind.
- Listing the situations where you tend to drink moderately will show the kind of occasions where it is safest for you to drink, and help uncover the techniques you already use to moderate.
- You can then update your rules list with initial ideas about how to deal with these trigger situations. This may include types of situations that are best to simply avoid, at least for the near future. And there may be unavoidable situations where you'd just decide not to drink at this point.
- Any situations where you typically drink moderately may give you ideas about how to handle your problem situations, and can be included in your list as positive rules about when you will choose to drink.

Chapter 8

Managing Your Drinking Triggers

Now that you have identified the areas that are most likely to trigger problem drinking for you, you can develop skills to either avoid or cope with these situations. Amy reports on the satisfactions of handling triggers well, and how she blows off a little steam when she feels the need:

> *The great thing about identifying triggers is to learn not to drink "through" them. You feel ten times more powerful when you come through the other side! Once you know what sets you off, you can see it coming a mile away, and think of alternatives. Blasting radical music is always good. I like to dance in my home office (with the door shut) and play air guitar. Use a hairbrush as a microphone, stuff like that.*

Where practical, avoiding problem situations is the simplest and safest way to deal with them. If your triggers include, say, drinking with certain people or in bars, you might just avoid those people and the bars, at least until your moderation habits are well established.

On the other hand, there may be trigger situations for you that involve positive feelings—situations that you really don't want to avoid. These could include celebratory situations like holiday times, or parties or special events. Those kinds of situations may be handled best by taking part in them without drinking. In fact, repeatedly being in situations that have triggered your overdrinking in the past, and not drinking at all, is one very good way to break those habits. If you do choose to drink in these kinds of situations, do so with extra forethought and care.

Trigger situations that bring up negative feelings may sometimes be unavoidable, and simply a part of life. Upcoming sections of this chapter deal with negative emotions in general and with several major types of negative feelings. A particular danger with negative feelings is that one may drink just to get numb. In the case of getting numb, more alcohol does indeed work better, so there is a real downside to that use of alcohol.

Negative feelings may point to particular problem areas in your life. Perhaps you have been overdrinking to avoid dealing with difficulties in your marriage or at work. Perhaps you have been using alcohol heavily because there is a change you know you need to make, but you can't seem to move forward. Or perhaps you are inherently depressed or anxious. In such cases, coping with triggers means taking action against these unsolved problems in your life. Importantly, clearing your mind from the effects of overdrinking will give you new ability and resolve to address those problems.

In the case of drinking that is mainly habitual, or drinking simply for pleasure, it is especially important to find nondrinking activities to displace your overdrinking habit, which will provide better, more meaningful satisfactions. That is the subject of chapter 9.

The rest of this chapter explores some of the areas where people have most often had problems, and how they have coped with them.

Social Situations

Some people drink primarily to feel more comfortable around friends; others find it eases their discomfort with strangers. In the first case, the drinking can go with a lot of shared warmth and good times, and these situations can be hard to let go of. You can test whether these situations still work for you by drinking nonalcoholic drinks while you're doing your Thirty. Your success or failure on this test and your feelings during it may indicate whether later on you can drink moderately with these friends. Some situations and people lend themselves easily to moderation, while others just don't. As Gretchen described it:

> *Sometimes that group dynamics thing really gets everybody hyped up and devil may care. It really is hard to stay moderate when everyone around you is laughing and appearing to have fun and getting drunk. Try staying sober with them one night and see how witty they really are. Sometimes one night is all it takes . . . and you think, yuck, do I look like that?"*

It's important to set your priorities and consider what friendships are for. As Jim said:

> *Perhaps the fact that you find it easier to control your drinking in certain settings is telling you that these are the circumstances you should be looking toward to fulfill your social needs. Maybe the social situations that cause you to overindulge are scenarios where you are telling yourself that this is not your niche anyway, for a whole host of reasons, not just the alcohol. It could be intuition.*

While some people are most tempted to overindulge when they are with heavy-drinking friends, for others the temptation is strongest when meeting new people. It is quite common to use alcohol to loosen up a bit and get in a social mood, especially when you're not completely comfortable. But it's awfully easy to overdo that.

Maggie and Sandy had the following interchange regarding socializing and drinking.

Said Maggie:

Maybe I need to learn some other ways to unwind, let go, be social. I'm always really careful when I'm with other people, and getting high just lets me do whatever and not care—and that's a relief. But I want to be able to be more of myself around people without needing to get drunk to do it (because then at some point I'm definitely not myself anyway). Any thoughts?

Sandy replied:

I think that was one of the feelings that got me started on this path. I wanted to relax enough to be funny and spontaneous. And at first, to be honest, it did help. But that slope was slippery, and one day I realized that I had been careening out of control for some time. Eventually I began having my two drinks before I even got to the social event, apparently thinking that in this way I could arrive, and already be there, so to speak.

In general, I think the increased tolerance led to a desire to "pound" at a certain point, in an effort to grab for that relaxed feeling, which took more and more alcohol to get. Trying to grab at it was like trying to grab at a speck of dirt in a glass of water. And I would find myself just drunk. Not pleasantly relaxed and warmly social, but drunk.

So I'm taking these steps back. And for instance, tonight I found that I was able to warm up and join in the joking without a glass of wine or two, etc. I did warm up to the table, even though several there were strangers. I felt more connected. I think that practice makes perfect. And the more I go out and be social without the assistance of alcohol, the more likely I am to have pleasant social experiences and to be present and connected to those around me, which is attractive.

Here, Sandy highlights the fact that there's often a little uneasiness at the outset of a social meeting that one just needs to get through. And that being clearheaded can distinctly improve the quality of contact in social occasions and the pleasure you take from them.

Quite a few people are uneasy in social situations, especially at the outset, and at the extreme, social phobia actually has the status of a psychiatric diagnosis. If you find socializing simply too terrifying to contemplate when sober, you may want to seek help to determine whether you have this condition—which can be successfully treated by either medication, cognitive therapy, or a combination of the two. Fortunately, for most of us, it's not that severe. It helps to realize that others around us are probably feeling uneasy too. As one person described being in a social situation and not relying on alcohol:

With the loosening-up part, actually, it didn't happen in the first ten minutes, but I just listened and stayed with the flow. It's funny, but you notice that you are not the only one who is maybe a little shy and uncomfortable and it makes it easier to think of something to say to get things going.

Terry replied:

This jumped out at me. I think that next time I'm in a social situation where people are drinking, this is going to be what I key in on. Instead of reaching out for a drink (and hitting the disconnect button) I'm going to try to reach out to someone who may be just as uncomfortable as I am feeling. It's sort of like public speaking. People who think that they are the only ones who feel uncomfortable with it sometimes don't realize that no one is really all that comfortable with it—at first. Maybe I've been blundering along, feeling that everyone else has some connection and sense of ease, and that I'm the only one feeling awkward, when in fact, everyone is feeling a little awkward. By disconnecting with alcohol, I never get a chance to find out. And I seem to miss out on some good conversations, and the opportunity to get to know others, and this in turn perpetuates that feeling of disconnectedness.

Bottom line? The good news is that moderation or not using alcohol can very definitely improve social experiences. It just takes a little willingness to go through the initial discomfort—but it can be wonderful when you realize that this passes even without the help of alcohol.

Drinking Alone

Another situation that can prompt overdrinking is being alone. George Bernard Shaw once said that marriage is a popular institution because it combines maximum temptation with maximum opportunity. Both temptation and opportunity for overdrinking are increased when alone, because normal social controls are all off. When we're with others, we have in mind how we appear to them, and we are often occupied with the social interaction. As Amy describes it:

I'm waaaay less likely to drink, period, in a social situation. Maybe because I learned long ago the bummers associated with drinking and driving. But even with guests at my home, I'm always extremely moderate. Perhaps I learned the bummers associated with overdrinking in front of anyone.

But when we're alone, that all goes by the board. As Christen put it:

Just the wonderful "aloneness" of it all, with a lovely drink and no one judging me! *To whittle one's self away to blessed aloneness and then add the excess of alcohol, oh boy, no need to describe the aftermath.*

To counter this, Christen focuses on maintaining her self-possession while her partner is away:

Sometimes if he takes off and I'm solo, lo and behold, I want to enjoy me *and not dive into the drink. And those are the times I focus on more than my burning desire to do what I want to do. No bad thing to feel the desire in a strong way. Just shows that you can feel deep yearnings and not act upon them, which is where the miracle begins.*

Another helpful tool to fight the tendency to overdrink alone is to change some of the physical settings associated with the habit. Amy details one such technique that worked for her:

One method that has helped is to figure out the wheres and whys of your at-home drinking, and to rustle up those habits a bit. For instance, I used to sit in my home office with the wine bottle on the piano behind me, so I started putting the wine in the fridge. People have had success with drinking in a totally different room, out of a different glass (anything beats a dark blue coffee mug), or even sitting in a different chair.

Figuring out the "whys" is also crucial. The setting may facilitate overdrinking, but the basic trigger that releases it may be an emotional state. If you are more prone to overdrinking when alone, it may be serving a different function for you than your drinking in social situations. Does boredom/loneliness play a role in your drinking when alone? One way to find out is to do a self-assessment of your moods when you are alone. Look at the difference between times you are alone and don't drink at all, and times when you do drink or drink to excess. Once you have a handle on what it is about drinking while alone that seems to lead to more drinking, you can brainstorm alternative activities to do that are incompatible with drinking a lot.

Even if you can't discover a specific trigger, finding alternative positive activities to keep your time pleasurably occupied can be a very strong counter to any desire to overdrink that may arise—and they also have their own benefits. Karen describes what works for her:

> *I think I have the social stuff under control. I don't seem to have a problem abstaining or moderating then, but I still struggle with drinking when at home alone. My husband and I have worked together to come up with alternative activities. These include, but are not limited to: starting an herb garden, volunteering at the local dog shelter, playing chess, and creating meals that do not need to be cooked.*

Habitual Daily Drinking

If your alcohol problem takes the form of daily drinking, there are some specific techniques for coping with that. Three key ways of dealing with a daily drinking habit are:

- Be especially alert to the problem and ready to counter it during the habitual hours of drinking
- Keep firmly in mind your commitment at that time, especially the part of the commitment related to recognition of negative consequences, and especially the near-term negatives
- Use alternative activities to displace the habit

Says Lisa:

> *What I have done, and it's been very successful—I actually conjure up the feelings or symptoms I used to get when I was drinking daily. I used to always order wine when we went out to lunch (even at eleven thirty!!!). After I would have the wine I would go home and want to continue from there. The day was shot. I always felt groggy and sluggish during the day and lost any motivation to do a thing, plus I was embarrassed to go anywhere afterward except home because I didn't want people to smell wine on my breath! So, now I just remember how it felt and I really didn't like any of those feelings and don't want to duplicate them again.*
>
> *Staying to my limits at nighttime is a bit trickier but I pretty much do the same thing when I'm having something to drink. I put the vacuum stopper in the bottle after I pour my second glass of wine. No ifs, ands, or buts anymore. I also think about how I hated to wake up in the middle of the night with my*

mouth so dry I could hardly move it. When I conjure up all those memories and physical symptoms, it really helps to keep me where I want to be.

So Lisa keeps the picture of really near-term negative consequences to help control drinking both at noon (spoiling the afternoon) and in the evening (waking up in the middle of the night feeling awful). She also uses the act of putting the stopper back in the wine bottle as a clear, physical signal of her commitment to stop after two drinks.

Daily drinking is also often associated with some sort of passive off-hours activity like watching television or reading. It can help to find alternatives to that associated activity for a time to break the connection. In Scott's case, the problem was drinking and reading.

> *I drank when I read, and I read a lot. I'd read four or five hours a night. So when I joined MM the first thing I did was decide that I had to do something else in the evening, at least for part of the night. So for a period of time I scheduled some sort of an activity other than just sitting and reading, just to break the habit and the connection of get home, take off my shoes, sit down, have a drink, open a book. And I did that. Now I'm back to reading a lot. I drink liquid, but not booze. I drink seltzer.*

Scott's "something else" was often some out-of-the-house activity, so this took an effort, but the effort really paid off.

For many people who work nine to five, alcohol has a special allure at the "witching hour" at the end of the workday. For such drinkers, it's important to keep alcohol out of that postwork time of transition to your "own time." Here's a nice regimen that Julie uses, which also helps enrich her evening hours:

> *Once I realized my after-work glass(es) of wine was my signal to myself that it was relaxation time, I hit on a new ritual:*
>
> > *Take a hot shower, wash off all makeup, let the day go.*
> >
> > *Plan evening while in the shower.*
> >
> > *Change into comfy house-clothes.*
>
> *By then, I've processed the day, consciously decided what I want to do with my evening, and made the transition from work and stress to "my time."*

After the press of a busy day's work, it's easy to find yourself at home in the evening with nothing planned to do. Julie's evening regimen gives her a little space to decide on a satisfying way to spend that time. Her ritual also provides a nonalcoholic way to destress from the day's activities.

Another thing that comes up frequently is the habit of drinking while cooking supper. An alternative nonalcoholic beverage is one thing that works well for some. Making the cooking more interesting and challenging is another trick. Says Polly:

> *I started out by replacing the wine with a glass of V-8 (you could also spice it up to make a Virgin Mary). Now, I don't even think about needing/wanting anything while I'm cooking. Just find a nonalcoholic replacement for your drink of choice while doing any other activities. Tonic with a dash of bitters and twist of lime is a favorite of mine. (The bitters is alcohol, but we're talking about a splash!!) I also drink Crystal Lite, iced*

cappuccino, sparkling water, a diet Coke. Many things from which to choose! The point is to break the habit: cooking = wine, etc.

Some people who have been daily drinkers find that when moderating they need to avoid putting drinking days back-to-back. For some, three days in a row are too much, and for some, even two days in a row. If you alternate drinking and nondrinking days, it's easier to avoid slipping back into old patterns.

Coping with Negative Emotions

You may have used alcohol to exert control over your entire flow of feelings, believing it could insulate and protect you from your responses to events in the world. You won't realize until you learn to moderate that acceptance of your own experiences, thoughts, and feelings is an important part of actually having control over your life. It is much better to learn to let your feeling responses happen in a natural way, experience them, and let them pass. Otherwise, you become less aware of your own reactions and needs and therefore less able to make appropriate changes to improve your life and your moods. Facing some of the more deep-seated negative feelings squarely can be tough at first, however, as Lucy found:

These last ten months I have been feeling feelings that I had put off or buried for some ten years. It hurt the first time but I just drowned them out. The second time it hurt just as much, but I felt them this time. Experienced it, flowed with it, and then released it, finally. It was strange, but in a good way.

Of course, heavy drinking to escape negative emotions simply postpones and confuses these feelings—and worse, compounds them with drinking-related problems. And moderate drinking won't eliminate negative feelings or numb you the way getting drunk can. So, in order to moderate successfully, you will need new ways to cope. One benefit of the Thirty is the experience of starting to face and deal with negative emotions with a clear mind. As Lisa put it:

I don't think any of us enjoy feeling negative emotions (stress, depression, grief, and boredom are the ones that get to me). I did learn, however, that I could experience negative feelings without drinking and live through it! Then the more I experienced them without drinking, the easier it became to deal with them. I actually made lists of coping mechanisms and activities for my different emotional states and still refer to them from time to time. These feelings were more uncomfortable in the earlier days of moderation, but now feel manageable and less intimidating or overwhelming. I call it the three Ps that help me—patience, practice, and persistence. You can add a fourth "P"—preparation. If you know you will experience a negative emotion and live through it without alcohol, it isn't as terrible when it occurs!

Per the above passage, these negative events and feelings are better managed with a clear mind. And over time, with experience, one tends to get better and better at dealing with the inevitable down times of life.

To a person with a series of problems, Terry's advice was to prioritize and focus on one area at a time so as not to get overwhelmed. She asked:

Can you deal with one issue at a time, and just let the others hang for a bit? Is there one thing you can do today that will improve that one issue you've decided to focus on? I know that when I started moderation, I decided to put everything else on the back burner, and look at it all again later. For me, moderation was enough of a project without throwing everything into the mix.

Sometimes the issues that are bothering us are things we just can't do anything about, at least at present. Life will never be perfect, and there are some things we have to learn to live with. It is good to be able to spot those kinds of wrinkles in the fabric of our lives, and to wear them with good grace.

Here is Maggie's account of her newfound ability to deal with a negative development without resorting to overdrinking:

I'm feeling good about myself today. My habits are taking a definite turn for the better. My boyfriend broke up with me and so my friends took me out for drinks to make me feel better. But pretty quickly, I realized that the drinks weren't making me feel better. If anything, they were making me feel worse, and . . . I actually lost my urge to drink. This was a new development, a first! I've talked myself out of it before, yes, but a natural feeling of "Well, I just don't feel like drinking a lot tonight"? Halfway through my second beer, over dinner, I simply stopped drinking. Just like a normal moderate drinker. Well, I know I can't expect that every time, but that was a great experience. A couple of months ago a parting like that would have made me dive into the booze.

Times when you feel strong negative feelings can be good times to avoid alcohol altogether, or at least be very careful. As Mara put it:

I know that one drink doesn't make me a drunk. Drinking when I feel like getting drunk probably does. In my opinion, when I feel like getting drunk is exactly the time when I should be teetotaling it. So for me, having a drink with friends is not foreplay, it is an extremely enjoyable experience in itself. Getting drunk isn't orgasmic—it destroys that experience.

As mentioned earlier, when people drink to overcome negative feelings, the objective is often to just blot out all sensation and get numb. But this is one case where alcohol really will do just what we expect, and so there is an increased chance of overdoing it. On the other hand, if we are in a very low mood state and expect to get to a high state with alcohol, that may be asking more than alcohol can do on that occasion, and we may pump in too much trying to get there. In either case, if we overdrink in a low mood state, the natural counterswing back to a low mood state afterward will be particularly painful and prolonged. Probably for all these reasons, research shows that drinking to cope with negative feelings is more likely to be associated with alcohol abuse than is drinking to enhance positive feelings (Peele 2000).

So, if alcohol is being used to solve certain negative issues in your life, it is important to find other, better answers to those issues. It may be that the issues are things you would rather suppress, things like fears and hostilities and hurts and shortcomings—things you think of as your bad side. But if you get to know those issues, those inner needs, a little better, they may not seem so bad after all. They are parts of you that deserve your kindly attention and care. It may turn out that something as simple as going to the gym will help make you feel strong and well when you need that, or a little loud music will help you blow off steam, or joining some kind of club or activity will bring you friends and connections to help make you less lonely.

Stress Reduction

Negative feelings frequently involve stress or feeling overburdened. The following simple, portable relaxation exercise can be quite helpful in reducing stress. The exercise is focused on your breathing and involves five steps:

1. Breathe in very slowly through your nose, and as your breath goes in, say veeerrrryyy sssllllooowwwwllly to yourself "Innnnnnnn," trying to make the end of the "in" correspond with complete filling of your lungs.
2. Hold your breath for a few counts (one Mississippi, two Mississippi).
3. Exhale through your mouth, also veeeerrrrryyyyy slooowwwlllyyy, and say to yourself slowly "Ouuuuttttt," trying to make the end of the "out" correspond with the complete emptying of your lungs.
4. Repeat steps 1 through 3 at least five times.
5. Check out how you feel. Most people find this sort of exercise puts them in a state of comfortable relaxation.

There are of course numerous other stress relief techniques—and many good books devoted to handling it. Try to find something that suits your lifestyle and makes you feel relaxed—whether that's yoga, making chocolate chip cookies, or bungee jumping.

The following sections take up some of the major negative emotions, and you will also find a list of helpful books in the Recommended Reading section at the back of this book.

Anger

Anger is one of the most common negative feeling states, and often happens in combination with other negative emotions. One technique for handling anger is simply to become quickly aware of it when you become angry, and see if you can't steady yourself and cool down a bit, rather than letting the anger grow. Amy says:

> *It took me years, but I realized that seething with anger was really self-defeating. The angrier I was, the angrier I became. The only solution, and this is easier said than done, is to let it go. The way I managed to do this was to think about how unhealthy it is to be pissed off all the time. I thought about my heart and blood pressure. I came to the realization that it isn't worth it to get angry.*

In other words, a little internal, rational appeal to her own self-interest often helps her become cooler.

Many people believe that the way to deal with anger is to express it, let it all out and "blow off steam." But that can actually make matters worse. As Alan said:

> *I spent so much time during the day in control, hiding what I thought, that I'd become trapped in my own prison of sorts. And when I drank, I* raged. *I once, in my drunken state, tore an abandoned house apart with my bare hands. A friend once asked me about the house thing, "Did it lessen your rage?" In a horrified realization, I replied, "No, it made it stronger." Like wood added to a fire.*

Then I realized something about myself. All I was ever allowing myself to feel was anger. So much easier to be angry than to be scared. Can't be sad, so I'll be angry instead. I saw emotions as a weakness and fed my rage as a way to avoid the others. There was no end to my rage, because I hid everything behind it, feeding that fire, as it were.

An extremely valuable tool is realizing, as Alan did, that anger often has to do with being scared at some level. If you can discover what the fear behind your rage is, you can often channel your energy into more productive pursuits and this itself will make you less likely to overdrink. Says Ozzie:

The feeling of anger is almost always a feeling that has lying beneath it the feeling of being threatened—that is, fear. A simple example: When someone cuts you off on the freeway, what emotion do you experience? Anger, right? (I myself am infuriated.) Yes, but why? It's not just because "they ought to respect the rules of the road," etc. No, you feel threatened because you were *threatened.*

This relationship between anger and feeling threatened is much more subtle when you shift to talking about threats that are not physical. For example, why are you enraged when someone spreads a vicious lie about you? Because your reputation, which is quite close to your core self, has been threatened. Once you identify the threat, you can decide whether it is truly a threat or not, and if it is, how should you react—fight or flight—and how that would manifest itself.

In other words, switch the issue from the emotional to the rational level, and things will work out much better.

For Amy, the threats that led to her anger and urges to overdrink often seemed to be threats to aspects of her self-esteem:

I realized that most of my vulnerable feelings have to do with "un-" words: unloved, unneeded, and unimportant. Most of my anger can usually be traced to feeling plain old unimportant. I know it's extremely difficult to say to your spouse, "You know, it really made me feel unimportant *when your sister didn't invite me to her wedding," when you really want to throw things and just yell bloody murder. But you get a much better reaction when you express the vulnerable feelings. (Bummer! It's so much more "fun" to act like a kid.)*

Often, too, we get angry because something negative has been done to us and we haven't responded or handled it the best we could. If a tree falls on our car, we don't get angry at the tree. But if someone gets the better of us, we get hopping mad partly because we feel that *we* didn't handle the situation better. In this kind of area, and situations like the one cited above, assertiveness training can be very helpful. This kind of assertiveness is not about being loud or pushy, but about quietly and effectively asserting your rights, while respecting those of others. If this sounds like your ticket, some excellent books on the subject are listed in the Recommended Reading section.

And, depending on your taste, there's even some music out there that can help you when you feel the need to express your anger harmlessly. Said Alan:

The one that always works for me when I am angry is music. When I'm angry I throw on Rage Against the Machine, Misery Loves Company, bands like that. I turn up the sound, I shut out the world, and I just let myself listen to angry music, feel angry, and then I'm done, I feel kind of purged.

Depression

Depression involves sadness, lack of energy and motivation, emptiness, low self-esteem, boredom, and inability to take pleasure in things that used to make you happy. It is often tinged with anxiety and may be accompanied by feelings of worthlessness and hopelessness. When such feelings last without respite for more than two weeks or become incapacitating (or if you have recurring or intrusive suicidal thoughts), depression is considered a mental illness and you should seek professional help to cope with it. You wouldn't be ashamed about seeking help for a problem with your kidney or heart—and wouldn't feel weak if you had to take medication or participate in physical therapy to treat such conditions—so you shouldn't suffer needlessly when the problem is with a different organ, your brain.

For people with drinking problems, depression can be either a cause or a result of heavy alcohol use—or both. Depression is significantly related to overuse of alcohol, in a vicious cycle. Feeling down leads to overuse of alcohol in an attempt to feel better, but then the hangover involves more feeling down, leading to more alcohol, and so on. If you are seriously depressed, you simply shouldn't drink. As one report on the research in the area concluded, "The combination of depression and alcohol use disorders is particularly lethal, conferring a higher risk of suicide than any other clinical or demographic predictor" (Mueller 1999, p. 51).

A key point is that with people who are depressed or have that tendency, the negative aftereffects of alcohol seem to be amplified. As Sandy said:

> *I can tell you from experience, that alcohol* really really *makes depression worse. And I think it is not just during the hangover stage—I think it lingers in the sad mind for days after.*

It is not uncommon for people to suffer along for many years with symptoms of depression, perhaps aggravated by overdrinking, without getting professional treatment. It can seem that life is just like that, and the condition often robs you of initiative to reach out for help as well. And worse, the vicious cycle of the two can make it more difficult to break out of either one. Trevor describes his starting to break the cycle of depression and overdrinking by stopping drinking for a time:

> *Last April, I was so depressed I couldn't imagine doing one day of abstinence, let alone three, four, or god forbid thirty. I began to realize that my drinking was just making the depression worse, so how bad could going abstinent for a little while be? I tried it and, no, it wasn't easy, but it was better than I had been doing. With a little success here and there I began to feel good enough about myself to take on a Thirty.*

The good news is that most people with depression can get real help from professional treatment. This may involve the use of antidepressant drugs, and it often takes some experimentation to find the best drug and dose for an individual. The most effective treatment often involves a combination of medication and counseling.

For people suffering depression, it's important not to "play doctor" and stop taking medication because you feel you are cured or because you start to feel that medication is a "crutch," or an "addiction." Addiction is compulsive use of a substance despite negative consequences—and use of medication to treat depression doesn't fit this definition at all! As one put it:

> *I tried going off Paxil because life was so good for me. I was doing all the natural things to help myself—walking, running, doing volunteer work, eating*

well, doing yoga, and meditating/chanting. Within six weeks I felt incredibly low. I considered drinking but I was so depressed I wasn't interested in anything. I felt so bad, I no longer cared if I was "drug free" or not. Now, back on the Paxil, life is more "normal" for me.

Treatment may not be short or inexpensive, but it is getting better. The pace of research in this area is extraordinary and new drugs are always being developed. If one drug or therapy doesn't work for you, try another. Almost everyone can get some level of relief with modern treatment.

Apart from real clinical depression, of course, many of us have days when we are just feeling down for the time being. Going ahead with activities instead of giving in to the feeling can be helpful in this case. Said Trevor:

After goading myself into a bike ride, I at least had that positive thing to reflect on for the rest of the day. Did it totally change my negative attitude? No. Did it miraculously turn my day into a Disney film of singing birds and cute little animals dancing around me? Of course not, but it was sure better than the alternative, which would have been giving into the doldrums and might well have led to a drinking evening.

Julie described a similar experience:

I was in danger of being enveloped by depression yesterday. I decided I couldn't feel any worse if I just went ahead and did everything I would have happily done if I were feeling fine—so I did. Went to the gym—one hour's exercise actually helped; did business paperwork; dealt w/ all the cleaning and laundry; got food in the house; bought peonies; did a bit of housecleaning; ate healthy foods; finished reading a book; listened to Carolyn Myss tapes. I no longer feel like crying and throwing things. Think I'll go to the park and see what my squirrels are up to. Happy Sunday.

Another condition sharing some of the same symptoms as depression is bipolar disorder or manic-depression. This involves extreme mood swings up and down. It is highly associated with alcohol overuse, as people with bipolar disorder often seek to self-medicate. When alcohol use is stopped, the swings may become even more extreme, so this is definitely a condition calling for professional assistance. In the manic phase, uncontrolled behavior can be quite dangerous, including binge drinking, wild spending, and taking all kinds of physical risks. Again, it's important to stick to the medication regime you develop with your doctor. Many people with this disorder try to talk themselves out of taking their meds because they like the manic highs and forget the terrible lows that follow.

Anxiety

Like depression, anxiety can be a disease in need of medical treatment, or it can be a milder and less problematic state that many people experience off and on. As with depression, alcohol can relieve anxiety temporarily. But, too, you become more sensitive to the negative aftereffects of even slight overuse. When alcohol is overused, the fear and worry can rebound with greater intensity and lead into the spiral of more drinking. Both anxiety and panic states are highly associated with overdrinking.

Again, professional treatment can help, so if anxiety has been a significant factor in your life over time, it is worth trying professional treatment. Sally said:

I'm on medication now for anxiety disorder. It's a real disease and it's no fun to deal with. It's a serious disease and if you don't know what you are dealing with it can cripple and destroy your life. Because of the medication, I am leading a normal life now. I work as an administrative assistant in a substance abuse counseling center. It's an extremely social and busy job. A year ago I couldn't have handled it. I had trouble even going to the store back then.

Treatment of anxiety may involve counseling and any of a number of medications. Both anxiety and depression may stem from stress and trauma, including that experienced as a child. Post-traumatic stress disorder is a recognized syndrome that can follow traumatic experiences and that often involves anxiety, depression, and flashbacks or nightmares related to the experience. This, too, frequently requires professional treatment in order to mitigate or eliminate symptoms.

Another anxiety disorder is panic disorder, in which people have intense experiences of overwhelming anxiety and frequently feel as though they will die of a heart attack. These have led many people to overdrink as a form of medication. Christen describes the relationship between her drinking and this problem:

My first panic crushed me at age twenty-six. Today panic attacks pop up once in a while under heavy stress. Had a bad time with them for three weeks in March but I noticed that when I quit having two coffees and a smoke for breakfast, they eased up rapidly. Another point of interest is that when I stopped drinking for thirteen months, I didn't have a single attack.

I've had three dips on my path to moderation; on two occasions I felt "those sensations" rising up again on the morning after drinking. The temptation to "medicate" the fear with more booze was overwhelming and automatic, almost as if at the snap of a finger I'd forgotten all I'd learned that proved otherwise. Had to fight like hell to remind myself that there was a better way and to run toward it. On the other occasion the panic slammed me first and, horrified, I cried "to hell with moderation, make me numb, dear bottle." Again, I had to snap out of this illusion before the treadmill sped up out of control.

It's very hard to break away and stay away from the instant relief of alcohol when it comes to panic, but I've seen such a significant change in the nature of my panics since I quit/cut down on my intake.

So Christen has found a strong relationship between drinking and her panic attacks, and is using that knowledge to great benefit.

There are a variety of cognitive behavioral approaches that often work as well as medication for anxiety and panic. One of the main treatments for panic disorder is having the person realize that the symptoms are actually natural processes over which the person has some control. That is, certain actions tend to bring on the symptoms. Accepting that to some degree one will always have such feelings, and that they're a part of life, is helpful as well.

In addition, there's also plain old worry, which can be a habit of mind for many of us. If we see past experience in a negative light, this can condition our thoughts about the future. It's human and resourceful to look ahead. But looking ahead and worrying can lead to overly negative expectations. And so often our expectations come true through how we interpret and react to events in daily life. As a result, it's important to recognize the way we frame the world, and try to change it to allow us a more positive perspective.

Here's Trevor, reflecting on the fact that a day that he expected to be filled with problems turned out to be a very good one:

> *Way too much of my energy goes into worrying about the unrealized outcomes of wrong assumptions. All too often I am either analyzing yesterday or fretting about tomorrow, letting life slip by while hardly noticing. Alcohol is fuel to that flame. It denies the moment. We have all heard (or given) the joking answer to the question, "Why do you drink? Well, I drink sometimes because I am sad, and other times because I am happy, and always when I am angry, and sometimes because I am bored." Basically, I could add that I drink because of my assumption that it is the only way to get from yesterday to tomorrow unscathed by now.*
>
> *This day was one during which I was defenseless, living in the moment, as assumption after assumption fell away. The lesson? I want to stop wallowing in yesterday and assuming the worst for tomorrow. I want to get on with purely enjoying—or at least truly experiencing—my now.*

In short, Trevor plans to focus his thoughts more on positive actual experiences, as a way of dealing with his tendency to worry about things to an unhealthy degree.

Self-Criticism, Guilt, and Self-Acceptance

It's a normal and positive thing to correct our actions based on feedback from experience. If we forget to buy things at the supermarket, we tell ourselves to make a shopping list. If we have a close call driving because we didn't use the turn signal, we remind ourselves to use it next time, and so forth. Normally there's little emotion in this type of self-correction—it's simply a rational behavior. But when we're stuck in a bad habit, that internal voice gets louder and the tone gets nastier. We wind up saying a lot of bad things to ourselves, repeatedly, and that can be a major source of guilt and negative feelings. Said Lisa:

> *What useless emotions guilt and worry are—they are only good to the point that they prod you to plan what you can for the future (vs. worry) or learn what you can from the past and move on (vs. guilt).*

If guilt is caused by a habit of doing something that really runs against your values and beliefs, the only effective solution may be to change the habit that is the source of your guilt feelings. As Lisa continues:

> *This may not be what you want to hear, but the only way I've found to get rid of the guilt was to change the habit or behavior that was causing the guilt. Once I felt good about what I was doing, ta da! No more guilt! As long as I continued behaviors that I knew internally were opposed to my personal core value system, I continued to have guilt.*

The problem is, a heavy burden of guilt gives us a negative image of ourselves. And that negative image may stand in the way of positive change, making us view ourselves as weak and incapable. After all, if we are continuing to do things we feel bad about, we can't be very good people, can we? In order to move on, it's crucial to break free of that burden of guilt and its resultant self-hatred. As Annette explains:

Oddly, it wasn't until I quit guilting myself that I began to do something about how I was treating my body, how I was wasting my life. It was as if the guilt made *me keep doing it. When I began to forgive myself, things shifted.*

Guilt—like anxiety and depression—can also create a vicious cycle. Negative self-feelings lead to overdrinking, which leads to more negative self-feelings, etc. Annette continues:

When I'd drink too much and wake up berating myself, I reminded myself that that would only make things worse, make me feel like a bad person, and bad people do bad things, which is of course, a really good excuse to drink again. So instead I was kind and loving and understanding, as I knew a parent should be to a child. Or, if you prefer, to a much loved friend.

To help break the cycle, it sometimes helps just to identify the source of the guilt, and to tell yourself rationally that you are now doing something about it. Recognize and take pride in each step of your movement away from problems with alcohol. Squarely facing the problem for what it is, is a big step that many people delay for years or never get to. You can take positive feelings from each small action you take against the problem—and each lesson you learn when things don't go as well as you'd hoped. Many people take real pride in their control over alcohol in the thirty-day abstinence period, for instance.

Another helpful tip for coping with urges that result from guilt and self-hatred is to list and consider your positive attributes. This is what Sandy does:

Make five Positive Statements about yourself. Here are mine. . . .

1. *I am thrifty.*
2. *I am creative.*
3. *I am caring.*
4. *I am a deep thinker/intuitive.*
5. *I am an independent rebel in that I'm convinced to do only that which makes sense to me.*

And Rebecca:

I am not ashamed to admit that my life has touched many. Yes, I have had my battles with the bottle; it touched my children and my husband and anyone choosing to be around me . . . but I continued to enhance the lives of others. The hours I drank paled in comparison to the hours I lived and worked. I am a wonderful mother who has sacrificed her career and goals to stay at home. I am a wonderful wife whose hubby has never gone to work hungry or in dirty clothes without a fresh made dinner with goodies. I am an accomplished medical professional, aiding dozens of people through the pain and fear of leaving this world. At times my face was the last they saw as they clung to my hand (and I know it takes a special kind of person to work in the hospice field). I have a magic for healing animals of all kinds and have fostered everything from monkeys, to ferrets, to my own pups. You need to look beyond all the pain and sorrow and pity to the God-given talents you and everyone else possesses. I have learned that although at times alcohol seemed to rule my life, it was only a small facet and I always had the power to refocus its role.

One of the slogans used by AA members is, "If you want self-esteem, do estimable actions." And it's really a healthy exercise to bring the good things we have done to the front of our minds, as Rebecca illustrates. Listing all your positive points is likely to be an unaccustomed exercise, and you may be surprised by the results. As you get your alcohol problem under control, you will also get more self-respect from that basic change.

As also discussed in the next chapter, you will get a greater sense of self-worth from almost any kind of positive service to others. Activities that involve service to others seem to provide an extra emotional uplift. You get back what you give. Said Jake:

> *Many books and people that I respect advise that we can get out of our depression and boredom if we give to others. If we start doing little things that make others feel good, we get a sincere pleasure from seeing them happy. Give to the community at large. See your little step (picking up roadside garbage or giving blood) as a contribution and a loving statement to your environment.*

As well, sometimes there's an obsessive-compulsive streak in the temperament that feeds guilt, and that needs to be recognized. As Terry put it:

> *In the end, it doesn't matter which came first, the chicken or the egg, because I know that I need to tackle both my drinking and my obsessive/perfectionist behavior. I guess I was hoping that I could moderate one, and the other would just naturally follow, but that is my way of looking for an easy answer. I do know that each aspect of my personality exacerbates the other—the drinking is fed by obsessiveness and the obsessiveness is worsened by overdrinking.*

Beyond just a tendency to be perfectionist, there is also a diagnosed psychological disorder called obsessive-compulsive disorder (OCD). OCD is an anxiety disorder characterized by unremitting worry that forestalls action, continuing mental fixations, constantly rechecking and recounting things, and repeating behaviors that look like rituals. This is another condition that can be treated effectively by therapy and by medication. So if your obsessions seem beyond your control, or if you feel overwhelming shame or guilt about them, do seek help. It can be hard to get the courage to do so, but effective treatment is an extraordinary relief for people with this condition.

Relationships with Others

In working on your drinking problem, the best case is, of course, to have the wholehearted support of your significant other. But you may have to carry on without support, with attempts to oversee or steer your process in ways that make you uncomfortable, or even with covert or open opposition to your changes.

First, keep in mind that change itself is hard on both parties. And that the initial adjustment period will likely be harder for both of you, than will life after you have accommodated to your new habits. Said Annette:

> *I know that if I am successful with moderation, or even decide on abstinence, he is well aware that it will impact his life, regardless of the fact that I do not expect, nor do I ask, for him to do what I am doing. He just hates change of any kind.*

Other family members may well be used to criticizing your drinking. They may not be able to change that pattern quickly, despite your progress. Gretchen said:

> *Sometimes the people closest to us are the hardest to reach. And sometimes they don't know how to help. I come from a family of critics. They thought simple criticism was the only way to help . . . hey, you're gonna get faaaaat eating those chips, etc.*

Your partner may have been very concerned about your drinking for years—but that doesn't mean that he or she will automatically understand what you are trying to do now. Because American culture is so dominated by the AA perspective, many people believe that moderation is impossible for anyone with any level of alcohol problem. Some open communication helps. As Sarah put it:

> *He gives me a much needed pat on the back when I moderate for a brief time, and now during my Thirty, but there is that now unspoken but very definite "you keep messing up now it's time to quit" (abstinence forever) that's constantly in the air. Maybe it's good, maybe it'll keep me on track, but it also puts me under pressure.*

Bonnie advised Sarah to try some open two-way communication with her husband. The issues can be as complex as the marriage relationship itself, and this will never be easy, but an effort by both partners to talk and listen can be productive. And frequently it's the one with the drinking problem who needs to break the ice about the subject:

> *At some point, when you feel the time is right, it might be helpful to discuss this with him. That this is "yours" (your journey of self-awareness, strength, and positive change), that you are doing it for you and will continue to do it with or without his support. But that if he wants to be helpful and supportive, you would appreciate it. Mention that some of what he says/does, his seeming attitude, not only feels negative, but is causing you to feel pressured. Give him examples of this, etc. Also, be ready to listen—he may have (with reason) some of his own discomfort at times too (even if he does believe in you wholeheartedly!). He can work through this of course, as you work through your stuff—but communication and support are a two-way street.*
>
> *My own husband was nothing but supportive from the start as far as belief goes—even before I found MM. But I noticed right away once I started moderating after my abstinence, that he seemed to cringe whenever he walked in and saw a glass in my hand. He knew that things were different, but still* felt *the tension of all the old ways and automatically would do an eggshell stepping dance, bracing for an argument. Quite uncomfortable to say the least!! I felt pressure too.*
>
> *But once I started to talk to him about it, I found that many times my perception of when he would ask me something (that I took as him being disapproving or trying to control me somehow) was totally off the wall!! And at others, his mind was totally on other things than my drinking. And the discomfort he felt when it* was *about that, he admitted to and was able to own and process through himself over time. A tremendous relief for both of us and weight off my shoulders. Very supportive—which was how he'd wanted to be and thought he'd been all along!*

I'm a firm believer in true communication, again though, when the time is right (meaning without blame or accusations). It's working for us and has eased my journey a lot since I'm no longer busy working around him. I stick with this being mine and leave him to his own end of things and he quite happily does the same.

Rebecca touched on many of the same themes when she advised a person whose spouse seemed to be avoiding talking about the whole area:

Don't make too much of your hubby's attitude; maybe he is not saying much because he is not sure what to say or how to say it. Just because we change, does not mean everything and everyone around us can make the transition as quickly or easily or readily, and they should not be expected to. I can understand his seeming wait-and-see attitude, and I can hear your need for him to play a role as cheerleader. It can't hurt for you to initiate the conversation and open things up for discussion. He may not realize your needs or your goals or your obstacles. It can't hurt to put yourself out there and give him the okay to respond without upsetting what he may view as your "fragile" condition.

Sometimes what is intended as helpful monitoring by a spouse feels like interference. We can be quite reactive when we feel someone is trying to control our inner processes. Bonnie gave this advice for dealing with these situations:

Sometime before *you begin your moderation time (or at least a day where you're not planning to have anything), bring up how "you know he's just trying to help" (and you do appreciate it), by "reminding" you of your goals/limits at certain times, but how that's triggering for you a feeling of being controlled. (And that you know that's not what he's trying to do, but that's how you feel at that moment.) And let him know that if he really wants to help, then "allowing" you to keep track for yourself and yes, even "allowing" you to make your own mistakes if it happens, will be the best help/support that he can give. You are seeing to this and need the space to work on it for yourself.*

Keep it from a place of you simply sharing your own assessment of where you're at, what works for you. (Doesn't hurt to blow your own horn a bit about your success and progress so far either!) Keep ownership of what you're doing.

If that open communication doesn't work, you have to be ready to row your own boat in working on your drinking problem. Said Danny:

It was only after I completely discounted her feelings about me and booze, that I was I *able to begin, let me repeat that, begin, to understand what my drinking was about. My drinking was about my feelings. If I had had the sense to keep her feelings out of my decisions about what was right or wrong for me, my drinking habits probably would not have escalated to the level that they did, and our present relationship would be much healthier.*

It's important to consider the possibility that perhaps the basic relationship has gone bad, and is itself a main trigger for the overdrinking. Getting a handle on your drinking, and not using alcohol to avoid confronting the truth, will be essential to sorting this out, and seeing whether the relationship can be saved or needs to be broken. As Talia put it:

It took me twenty-one years to figure out that all marriages aren't like this . . . that there are some absolutely wonderful marriages. When I broke from his mean grip, that's how I found out how really strong I am. Sometimes things don't change until you start cleaning house and throwing out all the poisonous feelings that are keeping you from being the great human being you were meant to be. I know . . . I did it. After being single for five years, I found my soul mate. He also happens to be my best friend. We pull each other up . . . that is one of the cool things about a good marriage and it should be built on a strong foundation. To me it just sounds like you're at a dead end . . . maybe it's time to start digging a new path for yourself.

Managing Your Triggers

Now that you've seen how a variety of drinking trigger situations can be handled, you may have some specific thoughts about managing yours. Here's an example of the kind of brief notes that could be helpful:

Jane's Trigger Management Plans

The Trigger	How I'll Deal With It
Hubby's off on a business trip, staying in fancy hotels and living off the expense account.	*Go with Marge to see that Jane Austen movie that Dick wasn't interested in seeing. Volunteer to lead the book discussion group that week.*
Going out with the office group after working long hours for the quarterly closing.	*Skip the drinkathon the office group usually has. Buy myself one of those expensive photography books I've been thinking about. Go out for dinner with Chris and Jane Schmidt. Chris doesn't drink at all, but he's one of the funniest storytellers I know, and I usually remember a few good ones when we get together too.*

And here's a place where you could note down the specifics of how you might handle some of your more important trigger situations in the future. We'd suggest going back over the categories in this chapter as you make your list:

My Trigger Management Plans

The Trigger	How I'll Deal With It
______________________	______________________
______________________	______________________
______________________	______________________
______________________	______________________
______________________	______________________
______________________	______________________
______________________	______________________

Summing Up

- Many people find stressful or emotional situations to be their "triggers" for overdrinking. But a fair number of people also report that they simply drink out of habit or to enjoy themselves.
- In social situations many find that, contrary to expectations, their experiences are enhanced by not drinking or drinking moderately, rather than drinking heavily.
- Anger is one of the most common negative emotions that trigger overdrinking, and a feeling of being threatened often is at its root.
- Depression, anxiety, and other psychological situations call for medical attention when they are at significant levels.
- Low self-esteem is often involved as a cause and as a consequence of overdrinking, and there are a number of effective self-management tools to cope with this.
- More often than not, there will be some conflict with your significant other over both the overdrinking problem and your work to overcome it. So recognize that such conflict is common, and be as patient and communicative as circumstances permit.

Chapter 9

Finding More Rewarding Activities

Moderation involves more than changing your drinking behavior. It's also about taking the time to explore some new pursuits.

Sandy speaks of the value of finding rewards in "that new life" from activities she really cares about, that make her feel "more alive":

> *I have tasted that freedom. That new life. How it feels to feel good about myself. How much better it feels to take yoga at lunchtime with one friend, a drawing class another night with another friend. Doesn't it feel* so *good to know that I can have companionship outside a bar, that all it takes is a little planning? Doesn't it feel* good *to know I make continual progress on my life—not a day of progress, followed by a night of drinking/reward, followed by two days of being lost in the dark, making no progress, forgetting about what I had set out to accomplish? It does feel good.*
>
> *I think that what we aim for with our "fix" is . . . legitimate(?) . . . admirable(?). Wanting to escape from the mundane, wanting to feel more alive. But what happens with abuse is the opposite—we become much more dead.*
>
> *I'm also thinking that drunkenness and hangovers, and whatever other penalties one gets from drinking, are a kind of drama that fools you into thinking you are so much more alive, that your life is just so much more exciting than those mundane lives everyone else lives. You are so much closer to life and death (poisoning yourself, driving drunk). It really is hard sometimes to get over the lack of thrill that just paying the bills, doing the dishes, getting a good night's sleep provide. I think it is important to find some really* above average *activities that really (I hate this expression, but) turn you on.*

The Importance of Other Activities

Nondrinking activities and interests are an extremely important part of successful moderation. First, there's the matter of simply filling the time you used to spend drinking. Earlier, we discussed a number of activities you can draw upon quickly to displace use of alcohol. But it's also important to find activities and goals that can give you better experiences and more long-term rewards than alcohol can. The more you can discover and develop these, the more you will be drawn away from overdrinking. People often drink heavily to drown out a sense of emptiness or purposelessness—so the fuller and more meaningful your life is, the less desire there will be to fill the gaps with alcohol.

Of course, if you have been hitting the booze heavily for years, you may have put many plans and dreams on hold. When you are overusing alcohol, other things seem of much less interest than the instant gratification of drinking. And you're also less able to pursue activities with mental and physical demands. But when alcohol gets put in its place, a whole world of new possibilities opens.

Developing rewarding alternatives to drinking is also an important counterbalance to the effort you put into restraining yourself from overusing alcohol. Psychologists have studied this phenomenon of *restraint,* which they define as the effort that people make in working to restrict a highly rewarding behavior (like eating, drinking, sex, drug use, etc.). *Restrainers* are people who put a great deal of effort into keeping within their personal guidelines. They tend to be rigid in the rules they set for themselves. ("I'll *never* eat chocolate cake again.") Such people do well so long as they keep within their guidelines. But if they violate them, they tend to violate them in spades, and then become very self-punishing. It may take restrainers years to start trying again after the kinds of relapses that this provokes.

A healthier approach is to not be overly rigid about your guidelines and not overly self-critical if they are violated (though obviously you need a certain amount of firmness to get new habits into place). Finding positive satisfaction in new activities can offset the negative effort of restraint. If you are enjoying your life, after all, you'll feel much less desire to escape from it.

In essence, you need to find new things that give you pleasure and satisfaction. Relapse prevention expert Alan Marlatt has said the idea is to increase the ratio of things you *want* to do, compared to the things you feel you *should* do (Marlatt 1985).

Envisioning and moving into more positive life experiences once you get free of alcohol problems involves covering some unaccustomed ground, and can be a little uncomfortable at times. Despite all its problems, the old cycle of overdrinking is familiar and in some ways comfortable. As you shed alcohol problems and move on to better things, there are bound to be occasional twinges of feeling that this is too good to be true, this isn't really you, this can't last, etc. The following quote from Nelson Mandela's inaugural speech can be applied to such concerns:

> *Our deepest fear is not that we are inadequate. Our deepest fear is that we are powerful beyond measure. It is our light, not our darkness, that most frightens us. We ask ourselves: Who am I to be brilliant, gorgeous, talented, fabulous?*
>
> *Actually, who are you not to be? You are a child of God. Your playing small does not serve the world. There's nothing enlightened about shrinking so that other people won't feel insecure around you. You were born to make manifest the glory of God that is within you. It's not just in some of us; it's in everyone. And as we let our own light shine, we unconsciously give other people*

permission to do the same. As we're liberated from our own fear, our presence liberates others.

Nondrinking activities—old ones that have lapsed, or new ones we discover—are what life is really about. Some of them bring out our finest capabilities. As we engage in them, our true life comes back into being and progresses, and the allure of alcohol fades.

It's really a matter of balance. Balance can be an abstract idea, but Kimberly brought it down to earth with the simple statement:

To establish balance in your life—that to me would be a certain amount of exercise, a certain amount of intellectual activities. I'm doing more of those things. I mean, you just become interested in so many more things.

In other words, you need to find some fulfilling engagement of both the physical and intellectual aspects of your being. If you have a job, some of this may come from work, and some from outside activities. Research on recovering addicts has found that one of the best correlates of long-term success is having a satisfying job. If alcohol problems have been standing in the way of your doing well in your current job or finding a better one, you now have a better chance of making progress in your career.

Counter Your Triggers

If you are having some difficulty deciding what types of hobbies or alternative activities to pursue, a good first choice can be activities that directly counter your drinking triggers in some way. If drinking has been your main recreation, then come up with other recreational activities. If you've been using alcohol to relieve stress and other negative emotions, search for other ways of stress relief that work for you. Says Gerry:

One helpful thing is to try to determine what it is that makes you drink. Then you can come up with alternative activities. If you drink because of stress, you can exercise, meditate, read something uplifting, etc. If you drink because you are alone and lonely or bored, you can get out of the house and meet a friend for lunch (in a place that doesn't serve alcohol). You can visit the elderly or shut-ins, do volunteer work, etc., which gets you outside of yourself and in a place where others become the focus. And believe me, volunteering really lifts your spirits and takes your mind off drinking.

Finding Other Activities That Appeal

Of course, if finding meaningful goals and satisfying activities were easy, many of us would never have taken up overdrinking in the first place. As Gary put it:

I think I'm in real need of some new hobbies, but since drinking has been my only one for so long, I really have no idea where to start. Maybe some kind of sport. The only problem is that would only take up a few hours per week, which couldn't possibly make up for the half-dozen or more hours I spend in the pub.

It may take some effort to discover activities you really like. So Terry replied:

You'll be amazed at how many things you want to do, once you allow yourself the time out of the pubs. It takes a while, though, because at first it doesn't feel like anything is as much "fun," when really it's just that nothing is as "comfortable"—or routine. If you stay with it, though, you'll have new routines, ones that you love even more!

Multiple Benefits of Exercise

We've all been told to exercise more—and yet most of us find it hard to get going. But once you get over the initial inertia, and when you are doing an activity you like, it can be helpful in numerous ways. First, many types of exercise may stimulate some of the same endorphin reward systems as alcohol. You don't have to run to get this—bicycling, swimming, aerobics, in-line skating, even weight lifting—anything that keeps you going in a sustained, rhythmic fashion can produce it. Exercise can give a tangible feeling of increased health and well-being, relieve stress, and aid sleep. And the feeling of physical improvement can reinforce the increased mental sense of control and competence. Says Annette:

To put something in the place of alcohol, probably a walk, yoga, t'ai chi, exercise bike, bike ride. I tend to do better with something physical. If I just sit down and read I would probably get distracted and still think about that nice glass of Chardonnay. Ummmm . . . wouldn't it be the perfect complement to this novel?

Elise makes exercise a priority:

I actually turned down a happy hour invitation tonight because I was afraid it would be hard to deal with. But it is also my aerobics night and I am trying to make exercise a new habit and priority, and know that if I had a couple of drinks after work I wouldn't come home and work out. I need to start planning other activities to do with friends that don't include drinking or eating junk food while drinking.

Remember to ease into any exercise regimen in a gradual way. Exercise may not feel good at first if you haven't done it for a long time, so be patient with yourself. Once you get started, you can move on to more rigorous workouts if you like. These can include biking, jogging, swimming, cross-country skiing, aerobics, kick boxing, and others too numerous to list. Shop around and see what's out there.

Get Out of the House

Many of us have found that it's important to spend less time at home inside and get out into the world. This can be aimed at breaking the early-evening drinking habit, as Lisa found:

My biggest trigger was the same—time of day—aka the witching hour! What helped me the most in the beginning was to do things outside the house during that time. My husband and I went to the movies, to plays, walking, to the gym, to the library, hiking . . . anything we could think of. We actually found a new world opening up to us as we became more spontaneous about going out in the evening. I used to feel like my butt was glued to the couch.

Getting out of the house can also give you a whole different mental focus. Adds Sandy:

I am just thinking back to what was different that made me overcome the drinking at home to deal with emptiness and sorrow. I had joined a gym for the first time in my life. It got me out of the house, gave me a goal, gave me an outlet for stress, was just something different to get my mind—as well as my body—out of the rut.

I can't say I go all that often now, but mostly I like to do things outside so I can have sun, fresh air, and my dog's company. So, I guess I'm suggesting you just do something different *and* out *of the house.*

Nondrinking Activities

This might sound obvious, but it's best if your new activities do not take you into situations where others are drinking. Said Annette:

As to what you can do to replace the alcohol, it depends a lot upon what you enjoy. This can be problematic for longtime habitual "numb-ers." Many of us don't know *what we enjoy, if it doesn't involve drinking! You just have to try different things. It's important, however, at least in the beginning, to make certain that the things you try aren't associated with drinking. For example, if you enjoy dancing, or think you might, don't go to a nightclub right off the bat. Take a class in tango or ballroom, or take a belly dancing class or tantric dance (this is especially wonderful for women who have trouble fully expressing themselves). Some of you are talking about yoga. I've been doing yoga on and off since the sixties, and I can't say enough good things about it.*

Some ways of making new social connections that are not based on alcohol include joining religious organizations, political organizations, health clubs, special-interest clubs, and sports teams. Once you start looking, you may be surprised at the range of opportunities. Advises Lisa:

Are there any old hobbies you would like to start doing again? Or new hobbies you always wanted to try? I started taking an oil-painting class. I also took a meditation class. Other things we did included plays, concerts, socializing with friends (all of our friends are either moderate drinkers or nondrinkers), evening walks, finding new places to watch the sunset, off-road exploring, visiting the library, going to town events. Also, we enrolled in courses at the college—film and literature. Working out at the gym and swimming for exercise. Massages, facials for rewards. Bookstores. Surf the Internet on subjects of interest. Read!! I finally started catching up on all the books I had bought but never felt like reading when I was drinking.

Service to Others

Community service activities can involve especially meaningful contact with others, and can really help with the feeling of uselessness and purposelessness that sometimes pushes us to drink. Terry asks:

How about volunteering a few hours a week to a cause you believe in? Big Brothers, Big Sisters, or going to the convalescent hospital to read aloud. Most cities have volunteer programs with all sorts of ideas, from working with the public works department to plant trees, to working with the recreation department or the police with their programs. In Monterey they have volunteers help keep sea lions off the pier!

On the same theme, Talia says:

Here's one that a friend of mine did in Florida. She volunteered at the hospital in the newborns' nursery. There she just held them and rocked and talked to them, when the mothers couldn't. I don't know if other hospitals do this . . . but at least for a while you're not thinking about drinking, and you're helping another human being. Can't lose on that one.

Finding Time

Of course, if you drink to relieve the stress related to being overextended and overscheduled, the last thing you may want to do is add new activities or commitments. Here, cutting back may be in order so that you can do things that are not for anyone else—not your partner, not your kids, but just for you. This may be hard for some people—particularly women—who have come to believe that everyone else's needs must come first. But if you don't take care of yourself properly, you won't be at your best when trying to help others, especially if you become resentful and feel that you "need" that extra drink as a reward.

Sandy found that she just had to let up on her housewife performance standards for a bit while she was bringing new interests into her life. She had to live with the feeling of "letting things go" a bit, in order to achieve better long-term balance in her life:

I've been slightly cruel to myself about the housework, but today, as I practiced the piano for the first time in four days, I remembered that I sort of made a deal with myself. And it was kind of a fair deal. When I decided to bring new interests into my life, I realized that it would be difficult to make them a habit. I got so sick of wanting to do something and then not following through. I thought, by God, if I change anything about myself, I should change that. The follow-through ability. So I made this deal: If I would go to the gym or would practice the piano, or would draw, or practice Spanish, then I did not have to do housework. *I figured it was like this: The housework would* always *be there to remind me to do it, but how long would my desire to learn Spanish last?*

Also, I have all my mother's and her generation's ideas about what really is clean. Talk about perfectionism. And then there is all that guilt that can so easily attach itself to housework. What a great way to see how you just don't measure up. So what I have to strive for is balance.

Being Good to Yourself

Often, people who overdrink are seen as self-indulgent. But, at least in some cases, it seems that people with drinking problems are people who do not know how to "take care" of their feelings in other ways. Everyone needs to have times when they feel rewarded by life, when they can feel good and feel relaxed for a bit. We need to find small, harmless indulgences that we call on readily and regularly, so that we don't end up needing a big, harmful one. These little indulgences can have large benefits in helping us maintain a healthy, balanced frame of mind. Says Rebecca:

> *The best thing I have found is to do something each and every day that makes me happy. I take a bubble bath, I purchase something I really want, I go for a long walk, anything that makes my soul feel alive. Also, I keep lots of nonalcoholic stuff around to drink. Last night instead of cocktails I had root beer floats with my children.*

Overdrinking has given us opportunities to periodically blow off steam, and we can miss that. So it can be good to seek out some really fun—and even outlandish—things to do as a replacement.

Liz talked to Sandy, who was having trouble with urges, about having a ready list of just such really fun things to do:

> *Is there anything that you absolutely* love *to do? Something that is slightly (or very) extravagant that you could do in place of drinking to get your ya-yas out? I've found that doing stuff that I adore and planning on making it a non-drinking activity (or a moderate activity) is a great replacement.*
>
> *Some stuff that works for me:*
>
> *Seeing a hockey game*
>
> *Going to Atlantic City*
>
> *Visiting the track*
>
> *Taking a trip to pinball/air hockey arcade*
>
> *Taking classes (improv is my passion)*
>
> *Going to a movie I'm dying to see*
>
> *Going to a live show of anything I like*
>
> *Make a list of your own and next time you are feeling like you gotta depressurize, pull it out and treat yourself!*

Your Special Needs and Spirituality

Keep in mind that these alternatives to drinking, while often directed at the world outside, are really there to serve the inner you. Try to be sensitive to your own internal needs, unique to you, as you carry on. Says Terry:

> *I was just staring into a murky pool, wondering if I'd ever get a clear look at the bottom, or if I should just say to hell with it and jump in. I think I still believed that the "outside world" would provide me with the information I needed to finally get a handle on the drinking. I wanted to find the answers "out there" so I could finally have some inner peace. My feeling was that my inner self was a reflection of what was going on outside of me, and that I would not have inner peace until I resolved the external issues: drinking, some family and work conflicts, not enough hours in the day, a need to be more organized.*
>
> *I have slowly come full circle, to the point where I realize that it is just the opposite: All of the external issues cannot be resolved until I get to inner peace.*

> *The external world is the reflection! So my pursuit is no longer about counting drinks/days/hours/goals/conflicts—it's become about making the time for meditation, reading, journal writing, and exercise. If I focus on the inner me, my external world will take care of itself.*
>
> *It's a nice change of pace, and feels so natural. I should add that had I not searched for answers "outside," I wouldn't have found MM, would not have been able to complete a Thirty (and regain some of my confidence to move forward), would not have come around to where I am now.*

Overdrinking blunts spiritual life, and when drinking comes under control, spiritual feelings often begin to return. Said Max:

> *At least a couple of Fridays I've gone to Temple, which is something that I had not done in many years. Though I may not necessarily believe all the words that I'm hearing, it gives me a sense of peace.*

And here's how one person applies the Buddhist concept of freeing oneself from "attachment" to moderation in drinking:

> *I think that the Eastern philosophers didn't mean that you shouldn't* enjoy *physical, emotional, or even spiritual feelings, but that you shouldn't get attached to them. Meaning that you should be aware and present for every moment of that passion and emotion. But when the event is over, you shouldn't be preoccupied with trying to hold on to that good feeling or to recreate it. Each moment is separate, and we should experience it fully for what it is without clinging to it.*
>
> *It's like the pleasure we often get from our first drink. We enjoy the taste and the sensation so much that we try to recreate that experience by having a second or third or sixth. And they are never like the first. Yet we cling to the hope and ambition that we can recreate that feeling by recreating the situation that first caused it. But because everything is always changing every moment, we can't ever recreate that experience. Of course, the converse is that we should experience pain fully as it's happening without trying to push it away. Then, of course, let go of it when it's over. It's simple, but it's certainly not easy.*

The Conversion Experience

A conversion experience is one where a person's self-image or self-definition is significantly changed—for some during a flash of insight, for others more slowly over time. The classic example is AA founder Bill W.'s experience during detoxification, when he asked for a sign of God's presence and felt a burst of joy that helped free him from the desire to drink. Such experiences, whether of the blinding turnaround variety or of the slower "educational" variety, can be extremely helpful in moving beyond alcohol problems.

One woman who had started to have a serious drinking problem came to her first MM meeting. She had also just discovered that she had a real talent for pottery-making. She was alive with the excitement of that, and was never seen at another MM meeting. She later told us that she didn't need another MM meeting, because she had transformed herself from Mrs. X the drinker to Mrs. Y the artist—and Mrs. Y didn't have much time for drinking.

Another, Morgan, had achieved a large reduction in drinking with a lot of effort, but had still not achieved stable moderation. She finally found that through developing a practice of meditation, the desire for alcohol seemed to drop away without effort.

> *I now do intense Zen meditation, for thirty minutes in the morning and fifteen or twenty minutes in the evening. Most days I sit alone; some days I go to a Buddhist sitting group. After about a month I noticed that my alcohol consumption was way down. After two months, I had a glass of wine, and I felt* nothing *beyond a pleasant sensation of slight body/mind relaxation. Incredulous, I checked with a second glass. More bodily relaxation, and a slightly confused mind began to arise. But still no euphoria, none at all. So I closed up the bottle. Not because I felt I should, or had promised myself, or was over my limit, or for any other "outside" reason. I shut up the bottle because* I really wanted to, *for the first time in my life.*
>
> *A wall of denial has collapsed. There had been a difference between what I was getting out of drinking and what so-called "normals" get out of it. But now, in place of the powerful high from alcohol, there is a higher emotional baseline all the time—more confidence and mental clarity; more joy in the little beauties of daily life; less fear that the world will come to an end if everything does not go "exactly my way, right this very minute." Even some spontaneous and genuine smiles. Right now I simply don't care enough about alcohol anymore to fight with it, and in any case there's no fight necessary.*

A conversion experience, then, involves a new activity, which becomes an important enough part of your life that it changes your self-definition and experience of life. Becoming deeply involved in religion and spirituality can do that. A significant job change or beginning to study for a new career (and therefore defining oneself as a future worker in that field) can do it. Even changing from a couch potato to a fit-and-trim athlete can work. Don't worry if the sudden turnaround doesn't happen for you—this is the less common version of this type of change. Over time, you can work to see yourself in new ways that will help you develop an identity and a new, fuller life as a moderate drinker.

Making Your Plan

Well, something as big as a conversion experience may not come your way, but this area of alternative activities can be quite important even with seemingly less consequential activities. Going jogging a few days a week, or joining a book discussion group or a bowling team may seem a bit trivial compared to your drinking problem. But, as discussed, they can function directly as replacements for and counters to key aspects of your drinking problem. Once you get into them, you may find them surprisingly rich and rewarding, and they may lead to other good experiences.

So you might make some notes here of ideas for activities you'll renew or start up. These can just be some initial thoughts at this point. But if so, do come back to it and make some firm plans, because this can be a very significant and rewarding part of your path to a better life with moderation. A suggestion would be to start out by "brainstorming" a bit, i.e., let your imagination run on, and just put down anything that comes to mind. Some things that look like oddballs at first might prove to be things you've sort of had in the back of your mind, and could prove to have more promise than they seem to at first glance. And the list could include some simple and easy things that you can get going on right now, and some more ambitious or far-out things that need some more thought and preparation. To keep moving on this, you might note for the activities you've selected what the next steps will be to get started. Here's an example:

Ray's Activities to Start or Renew

Activity	**Next Step to Get Started**
Regular workouts	*Check membership prices at the Y and the two health clubs, and sign up at one of them. Get new cross-training shoes.*
Habitat volunteer work	*Call Alex to find out what times they work weekends and get on the list for a regular shift.*
Astronomy club	*Check dates for next meetings and put on calendar. Finish reading that book on quasars.*

And here's some space for you:

Activities to Start or Renew

Activity	**Next Step to Get Started**
____________	____________
____________	____________
____________	____________
____________	____________
____________	____________
____________	____________

Getting these activities thought out and planned is a very worthwhile step, because they can become a key part of the architecture of your more rewarding life ahead. So thinking about these activities and then pursuing them are big action steps toward that more rewarding life.

Summing Up

- Positive alternatives to drinking are essential, because putting effort only on restraint can be self-defeating.
- New activities can be targeted to counter specific triggers. If your overdrinking is at home, for example, take up new out-of-the-house activities.
- Exercise has multiple benefits.
- Service to others provides very positive experiences.
- Being good to yourself and taking time for your own needs is not an indulgence, but a necessity.
- Regaining spiritual pursuits is a benefit for many.
- Overcoming alcohol problems may involve changes in basic self-identity, whereby you come to identify yourself more with nondrinking activities that are central to your life.

Chapter 10

Practicing Moderation

Becoming a moderate drinker requires practice—just like becoming a heavy drinker did. When you start moderating, you may find it takes a great deal of energy at first. And—as Mike says below—this might "feel weird" as you start out. Don't worry though, it won't always be this hard. The idea is have your drinking become a highly conscious activity for a time, to help you keep things on track while you establish your new habits. You'll need to practice the patterns of moderation in drinking very mindfully for a time, until they become second nature. Then, as Mike says, "you have captured lightning in a bottle."

Mike found that moderation was a habit that felt a little odd at first:

> *When I was a kid, I went to a baseball camp one summer. They were teaching a different way of playing the infield than most people taught at the time. Many of us complained that it "felt weird" to do it the way we were being taught. The response? Keep working at it, and pretty soon, it will feel weird not to do it the right way. Sounds clichéd, but I went from riding the bench to making the all-star team in my league by trying that new method that felt weird at first. So I've always been very receptive to the notion that if you've been doing it the wrong way for years, doing it the right way will feel strange at first. But if you can turn doing it the right way into a habit, you have captured lightning in a bottle. As with many things, if it's true in baseball, it's true in life.*

In this chapter, you'll learn more about how to practice and learn the habits of moderation in drinking. Up to this point, you've been developing and learning a mental framework to guide you in moderation. But the most important learning comes from doing. Says Rick:

> *In the spirit of "practice makes perfect," I believe you have to "drink in moderation" to learn to moderate. For example, I believe that drinking two drinks and* then stopping *does much more to help teach moderation than*

periods of abstinence do. In practice, drinking at most two drinks, then stopping, is a great way to learn moderation.

If you've been doing an abstinence period of thirty days or longer, and thinking through the exercises in the preceding chapters, it's a good idea to review your progress and plans before you start moderate drinking. Says Sarah:

Last time I did the Thirty I couldn't wait until it was over so I could drink again, and no wonder I fell into old habits quickly. This time I have a plan in place, and will stick with it or I'll immediately start my third Thirty!

Here is an example of careful planning for the start of practicing moderation, by Lisa, who was exceptionally cautious about drinking in this period:

I made a decision that I found worked very well. I decided to take the next thirty days after my Thirty one at a time. I actually ended up extending the first Thirty to forty-six days. I had decided not to bring any wine home to drink by myself (since that was my daily habit that needed to be changed). I only bought a bottle when we had company and split it three ways. I actually only drank six glasses in the month following the first Thirty. And then I made plans for the next thirty days.

Update Your Rules and Guidelines

In chapter 5 we suggested sketching out some initial "rules" or key points to guide yourself in moderating, and subsequent chapters have led you through some exercises to help refine those. As you begin to try to practice moderation, you can take another look at these now, and see if any adjustments are in order.

First, look at what you have thought out about your key triggers for overdrinking. What are they, and what are your plans for dealing with your key triggers at this point? Are there certain drinking situations you are just going to avoid, or other situations where you will be present but abstain? Do you have any plans for situations where you will drink but need to be particularly on guard?

Other aspects of your rules or guidelines for drinking are your weekly quantity limits and any days-of-the-week guidelines. Some people start low on the quantity limits for safety's sake, and adjust them upward if they feel comfortable. On the other hand, a number of people start with the limits suggested in chapter 5, find them too high for themselves, and wind up with lower limits. And some people find days-of-the-week guidelines helpful, such as not drinking on a particular number of consecutive days or not drinking on weekdays. Says Bonnie:

I struggled for several weeks before realizing that "Less is more"!!

So in my opinion, it's best to start s-l-o-w-l-y instead of jumping right in with several times a week and trying to maintain three drinks per occasion. Better maybe to drink once a week (or even other week) and only one or two drinks, and definitely with food. Old habits die hard, as they say, and if you're trying to break a daily or several days per week habit, then going back to the usual frequencies is going to make it more difficult to build new habits. That's also when I figured out that for me, three is a lot!

Chapter 9 discussed activities you might want to increase or start to give you a more balanced lifestyle. Undertaking some action in this area is fairly important.

Your current lifestyle has been the setting for overdrinking. If you expect to just change the drinking and keep everything else the same, that may not work out so well. And you would also be missing the opportunity, while making major improvement in one area of life, not to use the momentum to make other positive life changes. Says Laura:

I think doing it all at once is exactly the point, because what you do is substitute healthy, positive lifestyle activities for unhealthy ones. If you just go along and try not to drink, but don't change other aspects of your life as well, it becomes the white-knuckle "dry drunk" thing.

Some people find it handy to formulate their drinking rules or guidelines into very brief statements that they can easily keep in mind and refer to. These can be quite simple, such as:

No hard liquor

Drink only with meals or with snacks right before meals

Gym at least twice a week

Here's how Alan explained his guidelines:

Here are a few things that I had to actually work at:

1. *I used to go out of my way to make sure I had drinking partners, surrounding myself with people who helped me on a daily basis to justify my own drinking. In moderation, I've had to go just as much out of my way to establish nondrinking buddies . . . folks who I connect with and spend that social time with and have a connection with that's based on more than just drinking. Linux system users groups, nonprofit/charity work, etc. It really is interesting how something as simple as a change of "cast" in the theater that is your life can really affect the overall performance. The difference between having a co-star of Bobcat Goldthwait or Patrick Stewart, I guess. I also find that my social interactions are deeper and more meaningful when we have more in common than "Man, that tequila kicked my ass last night."*
2. *I save the money that I would have spent on booze and weekly give myself a sort of treat. Typically a book, in my case, although I am sure other people do other things. But I made it a fairly nice little production of going out and getting a "good boy" present. After all, Pavlov's dog can't salivate if he's not given food when the bell rings. Positive reinforcement was really important, considering the way I react to negative. So I went out of my way to congratulate myself, rather than beat the crap out of myself for my mistakes. In the end, I like the positive better than always feeling like I had screwed up.*
3. *I have a "shut down" room that's quiet, and relaxing. I can turn off the phone and ignore the world. Sometimes a little "me" time is a good thing, considering I spend more time working than most people know. I'm not a workaholic or anything . . . it just seems to always happen that I work for three days straight. Anyway, I try to make sure that when I feel myself sorta freaking out, I can close the door, shut off the phone, lay on the floor, and pet my cat for a few hours.*

4. *I quit stocking large amounts of booze in my house. There was no point in having that much around, except for me to overdrink. If I want a beer? I go buy a six-pack, nothing more, no cases, no matter how much I might think, "Well, this will save me another trip next week if I want a few." I'd rather make the trip next week, inconvenient or not, than overdrink tonight and feel like shit in the morning. If I want to have a rum and Coke in the privacy of my own home? I buy a pint, not a fifth. A fifth is just pushing the temptation a little too far, in my mind, to have it sitting around available.*

So Alan's set of guidelines involves 1) lifestyle changes of avoiding former drinking companions and finding new friends, with charitable service work one avenue to those new connections, 2) a "reward" system, which we'll discuss later, 3) a plan for countering the trigger of overstress from work, and 4) a simple rule of no extra alcohol in the house.

Sue's rules were somewhat different:

I want to share what really helped me, and I hope others can benefit:

1. *I don't drink any alcohol with lots of excess sugar, especially white wine. I notice even after margaritas, I start feeling that uncomfortable out-of-control feeling after about two glasses. So I stay away from those types of drinks entirely. I don't even tempt myself, not even a sip of the evil white wine. Red wine or vodka with club soda works best for me.*

2. *I drink LOTS of water.*

3. *I recognize a trigger when it happens, such as feeling all amped or nervous before going out. I take some time to do a few yoga moves, calm down, and remember what's important.*

4. *I write in my journal.*

So this set of guidelines includes some rules about types of drinks, alternating with water, dealing with emotional triggers, and keeping a diary.

Here's a place to set down your drinking rules, if you've updated them since the list you made at the end of chapter 7. You may want to include your quantity and occasion limits here, or at least mentally check on where you are on those factors.

My Drinking Rules

____

____

____

____

____

Your Diary

It is recommended that you keep a diary of your drinking, making daily entries as you start moderate drinking. The Addiction Research Foundation in Ontario, one of the most highly regarded in the English-speaking world, reports that alcohol treatment clients "consistently rate this strategy as one of the most important in their progress" (Sanchez-Craig 1993). There are many other studies of the use of diaries by people who are working on changing habits, especially in the weight-loss area, which clearly show the benefits of such monitoring.

One reason that keeping a diary is effective is that the diary focuses a little more of your time each day on the subject, and thus helps make drinking more conscious. Said Maureen:

> *I* hated *the idea of keeping a record, but for some reason, it seemed manageable. I've been doing it with cigarettes and it is making a world of difference. I never could even think that I would have no more than four a day. And that's what I've successfully done for the last two weeks. It's just a matter of not grabbing one when I want it without giving it a thought. I am conscious of each and every one. Lord knows how it is working, but I'm not questioning it.*

Keeping a written record is likely to be more accurate than just recollection. Said Becky:

> *After my Thirty, I tried to use forms for tracking drinks each day. It helped because one time I thought I was within the allowed amounts, when I charted it out, I had gone over my limits because of the time frame. It was really an awakening as to how much thought I had to put into the times and amounts when I did drink. That is why abstinence is almost easier, a no-brainer.*

Keeping a diary helps you look back to see your progress and to plan ahead to stay within the limits. Adds Sandy:

> *COUNT. Count how many you drink—best to write it somewhere because you won't remember. So even if it doesn't slow you down while you are doing it, when you look back at it you will probably want to make those numbers smaller.*

You will often find that you get real satisfaction from putting down good numbers and keeping to a good running total. The thought of having to record a bad number can even help you keep to the limits at times of temptation.

As to its format and content, the diary can be as simple as just writing numbers of drinks or no-drinks down on a regular calendar. Or, you can add information, such as the length in time of the drinking occasion, the place, people you were with, even your mood, what it was that you drank, etc. You can also note any action toward your goals in lifestyle changes such as activities you want to increase or start. Additionally, if you like to write, you may find it interesting and useful to keep a journal of thoughts during this period.

Here's the prepared diary form (discussed in chapter 5) that you can use, if you'd like:

My Diary

Date	# of Drinks	What Drink	Time Spent Drinking	The Occasion	Feelings At Time and/or Positive Activity Progress

For all that, some people just don't like the idea of keeping a diary. People really do vary in that respect. But there's no single path to moderation, and you can still successfully moderate without keeping a diary

How Does It Feel to Start?

So how do you start—and should you make a big deal of your first drink after an abstinence period? As always, it's best to do what makes you most comfortable. We've found that it's a good idea to have your first drink in a "safe" situation—that is, not one where you have been prone to overdrink in the past. Plan it carefully, and structure your environment and activities to support moderation. For instance, you can measure carefully, eat while you are drinking, and try to be with someone you care about who is supportive of your efforts. Then, as you feel able, gradually work your way toward "harder" situations, again with plans carefully worked out beforehand.

Let's follow Laura as she starts her moderate drinking:

> *After forty-eight days of abstinence, I had two glasses of wine on a Friday night two weeks ago, as a test, to sort of check out the feeling in preparation for the inevitable days of summer moderation to come. Then I went abstinent through the rest of that weekend and the following week to Saturday night, when I had the rest of the bottle from the week before, about two and a half glasses.*
>
> *Again, I successfully abstained all week, until Friday night, when I left the house at 9:30 to drive out and pick up my husband at the airport. When I arrived, I discovered that his plane was delayed an hour and a half. So into the bar I went, ordered a glass of wine, drank it, then left and sat by the gate for*

half an hour. I then went back and had another, and waited for him to arrive. Totally in control.

Saturday, my niece graduated from college, so we went to lunch with my sister and her husband who were in from out of town, where I had two glasses of wine. Later that afternoon, we got ready to go to the graduation, then we all had one more drink. That's three in five hours I think. And afterward, a glass of champagne, then two glasses of wine with a very nice dinner out. Now that sounds like a hell of a lot of wine, but it was over a ten-hour period, and I was very much in control of myself the entire time. At 10:30 that night when we got home from the restaurant, everyone went outside to sit by the fire, but I went to bed. I didn't want to have a hangover, and I was tired, so I just went to bed.

On Sunday, we all went out to brunch, and I had two glasses of champagne. Went home, laid in the pool, had another glass of wine, out to dinner, two more, and another after dinner back at home. Too much.

Now, today when I woke up, it's still the Memorial Day weekend, and I was very glad not to have a hangover, and feeling a little bad because I drank a little more than I should have in a shorter span of time Sunday. But I was looking forward to another day of relaxation before the work week began. And I thought, I'd really like to have a glass of wine by the pool, so my husband went to the grocery store to buy stuff to barbecue and get me a bottle of wine. But still I was feeling a little uncomfortable with this idea because there's no real reason to have a drink, because all the company is gone, and that would make four days in a row, not good I know. Although it is a holiday, right?

Anyway, while he was gone I decided to catch up on my e-mails. So I'm drinking red raspberry Sprites today, and feeling great about that decision. Whew!!

So for those wondering, my moderation plan includes no drinking on days before work (Sunday through Thursday), or days just at home with my husband. I only plan to drink socially on Friday or Saturday, and then I will *learn to pace myself. I have proved to myself that I can, so I will continue to strive for that.*

I was beating myself up a little bit for Sunday, because I drank enough where I was pretty buzzed, and I can't let myself get over that edge, but I will use that as a learning experience. I know what the trigger was that day, and have already talked with my husband about it.

Next weekend I'm going for a girls' weekend to my best friend's cabin in the mountains. She lost her brother last December. And she's a drinking buddy of mine. But I'm going to pace and moderate, and stay in control, and not be hung over on Sunday. There is nothing between then and my niece's wedding that should involve drinking, so I'm planning on abstinence until then.

So, what happened during that "girl's weekend"?

I spent this weekend with the friends who do the "monster drink thing." When I arrived at the cabin, they were already on their way to a big buzz. And I'm very *proud to say that I did it!! Moderated, I mean.*

Moderating techniques that I used were:

1. *Arrive late*

2. *Alternate sodas/mineral waters with wine*

3. Drink slowly, and wait awhile between drinks

My friends made a few comments, in a teasing way, but I continued to pace my way along while they eventually got smashed. One passed out in the chair as we sat in the sun having a great time. Yuck. None remembered much of the great dinner we had, and all were amazed at how I was able to remember every detail of the evening as we rehashed it all the next day. I loved it!! Ha—What an awesome feeling.

Sunday the discussion did come up again with one of my best friends about reducing drinking, and I recommended she read up on Moderation Management. So sometimes drinking buddies can be very supportive!!

I did drink more than moderate limits dictate on Sunday, but it was over a long day and night. And, I had a couple of glasses of wine Friday night, and on Sunday, so I'm going to go for abstinence until my niece's wedding.

For those who feel themselves slipping back into old patterns, I know from experience that can happen all too easily. That's why I'm going to go another three weeks abstaining.

So what's going on here—is Laura working the program or is she setting herself up to slide back into heavier drinking? She certainly does have quite a few experiences of successful moderation, but she also exceeds her limits several times. To look at the particulars, one thing to note is the initial forty-eight-day period of abstinence, versus the thirty days given as a reference in this program. That is an instance of someone thinking about her own particular needs and feelings and adapting the program guidelines to what feels right for her. So that's a positive. Then, there's a very mindful and cautious approach to the start of drinking, in starting with a two-drink occasion, then waiting several days, and then having another moderate-drinking occasion, then waiting a few more days.

Another important thing Laura is doing is returning to nondrinking as a safety base when things don't feel right or the limits are exceeded. Other safety mechanisms you could use include a strong fixation on your drinking limits and rules, which might include any of the techniques discussed in chapters 6, 7, and 8, enlisting the help of a spouse or friend to monitor your drinking, and so on.

There's also a fine example here of some pieces of "drinking thinking" coming up at the poolside ("*it's still the weekend . . . looking forward to another day of relaxation*"), identifying it, and countering ("*no real reason to have a drink . . . all the company is gone, and that would make four days in a row, not good I know*")

Additional positives are the careful planning ahead for how to handle the weekend at the cabin with heavy-drinking friends, and the overall high level of attention to drinking behavior as evidenced by her ability to play back events of these days in such detail. The ability to recognize and congratulate herself for progress ("*Totally in control,*" "*I'm very proud . . .* ") is very important reinforcement for the change process. Conversely, she did not castigate herself for exceeding limits. Instead, she took a realistic look at what was going on and took practical remedial action. So the balance of feeling here—and the reality—is of very positive progress.

Finally, Laura's story brings up the special risk of social situations where drinking is going on over many hours. That was the case in the two instances where Laura went over her limits. Prolonged drinking situations place an extra burden on your controls and need special treatment. That might be placing a time limit on your own drinking at the event, special attention to counting, arriving late and/or leaving early, or others.

Check Out Your Response to Drinking

The start of your moderation period can be a good time to make careful observations about your response to successive drinks. As discussed earlier, your actual response when you observe it closely may be quite different from your impression of what drinking does for you. Laura did this as well:

> *Last night, Friday, I found myself home alone for the first time in eons! My sons were out at a friend's house for the night, and my husband has gone to Florida for the week. I decided to treat myself to some wine. So last night, being all alone, I carefully monitored my feelings as I drank. I measured out a six-ounce glass of chardonnay, and drank it over a half-hour period. I discovered that I wasn't as buzzed as I like, so I had another. Then I felt fuzzy! And it was definitely enough!! The happy buzz lasted about half an hour. Then I was totally tired, so I went to bed at nine.*

Laura recognized her body's "stop" signal, obeyed it (even though she did set out to seek a certain level of 'buzz'), and stayed within her limits.

Watch Out for Special Situations

When you first start to moderate, you need to be particularly careful about situations that present special temptations. Maureen was invited to a party with imaginative staging, but decided it looked like trouble:

> *Hey, there was this very wild party I was invited to tonight where more than a hundred people were going, dressed as punkers or some type of angry something. There was to be a car in the backyard to bash in. Sounded like a wonderful day in the park to me. How often can a person take out rage like that? But everyone would be wasted and I'm tired, so I didn't go.*

Vacations and holiday times also present special temptations, partly because they give us a chance to relax and loosen up a bit from the restrictions of the daily grind. It's not uncommon to go a bit overboard at such times. Since these occasions are an exception to our regular routines, it may be easy enough to get back on track afterward. But it's worth taking a look at the thinking under "It's New Year's, right?" or "Vacations were made for fun!" There's a thread here of equating times of greatest pleasure with drinking or overdrinking. It can be helpful to look at any such thinking directly, and counter it. Here's a report from Christen of practicing moderation during a big vacation trip, experiencing things more keenly than before, and going only slightly over the normal limit on one night.

> *Such a difference to behold the world with clear eyes. So rewarding to lay sober footsteps on tourist trails compared to our initial visit four years ago.*
>
> *On my birthday in Coimbra, found a nontouristy Fado cave and got swept away by the atmosphere-wine-port. But it was wonderful, not like we were chugging drinks—we'd stuffed in a jumbo meal beforehand and just slowly sipped the night away. Once in a while we'd look at each other as if to say, "Can you believe it, this is what dreams are made of." Of course, if we were getting "el blotto," no amount of atmosphere would have meant much if it ultimately led to a throbbing headache or retching dawn.*
>
> *It was only a "dream come true" because I didn't cross over to the excess*

of my past. I was able to feel, see, and experience so much that would normally have been briskly dismissed in my quest to guzzle and do what "came naturally." Even though I've strived to claim moderation as a lifestyle and have lived thus for only slightly more than one year, it still blows me away.

It is worth doing some extra planning ahead for vacations, because of the special temptations, and that can be rewarding. Says Terry:

Last weekend was a four-day vacation for me. Spent the four days reading, sunbathing, watching movies, exercising, and moderating. It was not difficult, either, and I think that is the first time I've had that experience with a vacation.

I've been putting some extra effort into this, and also some extra abstinent days, knowing that the summer is a trigger—as is vacation. The results? Not one day was sullied by a hangover. Woke up bright and early every day of the four feeling energetic and ready to go. Not one moment of guilt (okay, one moment of guilt, but it was over eating a whole bag of chips).

And did I have one big blowout to celebrate my success? My last night of vacation? To make the transition back to work a little easier? Did I even want to? Nope! Now I'm back at my desk feeling as good as can be expected considering the vacation is over. MM, I love ya!

Indeed, vacations and holidays can be an opportunity to imbed the experience of having some vivid good times without alcohol—or with moderation.

Pay Close Attention

Extra mindfulness when a drinking situation comes up is particularly critical at the beginning of moderation. Fredrika caught herself automatically going for another beer:

Funny thing was, after he left, I went without thinking to the fridge and grabbed another and opened it. I took a sip, realized what I was doing (i.e. that I was headed toward a third, fourth, or fifth beer perhaps), and put it back for another night. I did not feel deprived. I felt strong. Today I was able to spend a day off with one of my kids doing stuff that I never would have done with a hangover.

Those automatic drinking actions are more than likely to come up at the start of moderating, and we need to spot them and head them off. As well as automatic drinking actions, there is the beckoning of the old "more is better" thinking. Here's another beer story, from a similar situation experienced by Sandy. That first beer felt awfully good, but she stopped and felt that having another in that particular situation could be a problem:

Last night I offered the guy—a friend of a friend—who tuned my piano a beer. Our mutual friend was also here, having wine left over from the book club. I was thinking, "that beer sounds delicious." Then I had the thought. "I can have one. I am not doing abstinence, I'm trying moderation." So I had one. Soon after, they left to go to a bar. They didn't ask me—I was relieved. I seemed to have gotten a pretty big buzz from the one beer. (I had dinner, so I'm not sure why.) And it felt really good. It was like I had forgotten how good it felt. I seriously debated having another one—I figured two more and I would still be succeeding at moderation. But then I figured that I'd better not. If I felt that way after one, I knew my judgment would be gone after two. And I was glad I didn't go with them. Because if someone had encouraged me while I was seriously "debating" the pros and cons . . . I really felt a compulsion to continue on with the buzz.

I just waited it out. I thought about my life and my goals. I had been doing paperwork for the previous two hours (probably a lot of the reason it felt so good and the escape to its fuzzy warm jolliness would have been nice), and was able to see in the baskets of papers how out of control my life has been and was also able to see how little by little I would gain control back. So I just continued with my bills and receipts. And I soon realized that the buzz and the compulsion to have more had passed. I was back to myself. I was so happy to know that I could just go to bed, not be hungover and filled with grief and regret and not have to start the whole ugly vicious cycle over again.

I think I need to be careful when I make the decision to just have a drink. Like do I ever even want to have one in my house . . . well, I guess I do, but I don't want to put myself in a situation where temptation is too strong. What a learning process it is. But I am very happy with my little big step last night. And I feel great today.

This is a really fine example of not just taking the drinking limits as they are, but judging one's frame of mind carefully in a particular situation. Sandy took what was going on to a highly conscious level. She outwaited an urge. She reflected on and learned from experience early in the moderating process. And she recognized and congratulated herself for her positive achievement.

Consider Extra Rewards for Yourself

Heavy drinkers tend to get their rewards from alcohol, and may not be good at treating themselves well in other ways. In fact, many of us have spent a lot of time tearing ourselves down with guilt about the drinking. So giving yourself rewards for good behavior with alcohol can be a useful reinforcement to your new habits. You can simply give rewards to yourself on a regular basis, or you can plan ahead on the basis of, "If I do so and so, then I'll get such and such." The rewards can be small regular ones, like the example earlier in this chapter of buying books about once a week, or they can be big, milestone ones. Here's an example of how Talia used rewards to stave off a drinking urge. The style is fanciful, but it's a true story, in its way. . . .

Okay, so here's the story of talking myself out of stopping at the liquor store on the way home. I decided to take a trip to the big city with hubby today. He had to get a colonoscopy, and I went along to cover his ass. After it was over I had to drive.

So we were toolin' happily down the highway and my evil twin yells from the back seat: "stop at the liquor store."

I pretended not to hear her.

So she starts chanting: "Lic ker store! lic ker store! lic ker store!"

So I reach back and I tried to slap her from the front seat. You know, just like our parents did when we were kids? Ya see that dang hand just a swingin' and a slappin', trying to swat at least one of us kids? And we're all just a laughin', and, and. . . . Then you toss your little brother up in the way of "the hand" and he gets "the slap." Aah, the good ol' days. Oops, got off the track. Evil twin settles down and starts pouting.

"I want to have a drink tonight."

"I deserve to have a drink tonight."

"I'm not going to drink more than two drinks anyway."

"I mean it's been four days since we had one."

"I'll be really quiet and sweet, you won't even know I'm drinking."

"I promise I won't dance, or make long distance calls this time!"

"Okay?"

"Okay?"

"Can you even hear me??"

So good twin yells: "No!"

Evil twin: "No? You mean 'no' you can't hear me, or 'no' you won't stop at the dang liquor store?"

Good twin: "I'll tell ya what . . . remember that video game we looked at last week?"

Evil twin: "Yes."

Good twin: "It's yours in exchange for a bottle.

Evil twin: "Hmm . . . throw a homemade pizza in there and it's a do'er."

Whew! The things I do to keep my MM magic dust from drying up! Chalkin' another night up for not drinking. The good twin wins again!

Summing Up

- When you start drinking moderately, give the whole area a high degree of attention for a time.
- Update the rules/guidelines you've been developing, and get them well in mind.
- Start a drinking diary and keep it for at least a couple of months.
- Monitor your progress carefully and learn from experience as you go along.
- Be extra alert in special situations, and try to spot the problem situations in advance.
- Give yourself rewards for good behavior.

Chapter 11

Coping With Slips and Relapses

What are slips and relapses? A slip could be defined as an incident of drinking beyond your new limits, and a relapse as going back to a regular pattern of drinking beyond your new limits. These are common enough events that we should discuss them here. We'll also offer advice about maintaining moderation over the long term.

Says Rick:

I tell beginning skiers that if you don't fall, you're not learning anything.

What Rick is referring to is that there are few people who can start a new activity or skill and make no mistakes during their learning process. As a result, occasions of overdrinking are not unusual when people first try to moderate. Some people go into their first moderation period with a great deal of caution and keep right to their limits and rules for a time. Then, as they begin to relax and feel more confident, a slip or relapse may occur as they let down their guard, or as unusual occasions come up for which an appropriate response had not been thought out. Slips and relapses are certainly not required, and there are some people who sail into complete moderation without a hitch. But since slips and relapses are common experiences, it's important for everyone to be prepared.

Dealing with Slips

Here is a framework for dealing with slips that can turn them into positive learning experiences:

1. Don't get discouraged—instead, see the progress you are making. The way you interpret the slip is critical. If you see it as proof that you just don't have

what it takes to handle moderation, the slip will take you in a harmful direction. The trick is to manage the slip in a way that gives you a positive outcome.

2. Figure out what went wrong. Then you will have learned something useful from the slip, and that will strengthen you in your journey toward moderation.

3. Figure out how you will handle that kind of situation the next time.

4. Mentally rehearse the new behavior. The slip in itself increases the likelihood that you will do the same thing again. Mentally practicing a better response increases the chances that your first thought in a similar situation will be toward the better behavior you are aiming for.

When a slip occurs, you may know right away what caused it and how to deal with it or you may not—either way, you will probably need to do some evaluation. Here's a checklist:

- ☐ Did you have a plan and a limit in your mind going into the situation?

- ☐ Is there one of the general drinking control tools, like measuring or drink counting, that you need to pay more attention to?

- ☐ Have you been keeping a drinking diary? Was your pattern a bit off (like too many drinking days in a row) going into the situation?

- ☐ What were you doing at the time? What were you feeling? Whom were you with? What prevented you from paying enough attention to how you were drinking? Does this slip identify another trigger situation you need to watch out for? If so, you may need to come up with another strategy to deal with it. (Such as: "When I pay the bills, I need to make sure there's enough time set aside, and recognize that it will take patience," or "Next time I don't feel up for a big party like that, I will just stay a short time or skip it," or "Watch out when Sammy comes to visit.") Research with recovering alcoholics has found that half of their relapses occur due to negative emotions, either internal negative states or interpersonal conflict situations (Larimer 1999). And another 20 percent of relapses occur due to social pressures, direct or indirect. The same may be true with people learning moderation, so those are likely places to look for causes of your slips.

- ☐ Commitment to moderation is central. You can help renew this by looking back at your list of problems overdrinking has caused, and your list of benefits of moderation or life goals/objectives. And are you really convinced that the better experiences come from moderate than from immoderate drinking? Think carefully about your moderate vs. immoderate experiences, both the immediate and the overall longer-term effects. That conviction that moderation is best is really critical, and if you don't feel it for sure, keep working on that theme.

If you'd like to make notes on your review and planning after any slip that might occur, here's an example and a simple form for you to fill in:

The Problem and the Solution for Walt

What happened

Drank two beers and three scotches on Saturday night. Started with the beer late Saturday afternoon while watching TV.

What went wrong

Drinking alone has been a problem. Had no plans for the evening and no plans for Sunday. I was feeling there was nothing interesting to do and whatever I drank just didn't matter.

What I'll do differently next time

If I'm feeling lonesome and have nothing to do in the evening, I'll get out of the apartment, even if it's just to go to a movie, shopping, or to eat out. Have some kind of plan for the weekend. Come up with some kind of regular club or group activity for the weekends I can plug into if I don't have other plans. Make it a rule never to start drinking in the afternoon when alone.

And here's one for you to use:

The Problem and the Solution

What happened

____

____

What went wrong

____

____

What I'll do differently next time

____

____

____

____

That's not a fun exercise to have to do. But as you can see, squarely facing up to a mishap can be quite productive. An exercise like this turns your focus away from guilt and sorrow and toward positive thinking about the future.

Some slips seem to come from out of the blue, with no obvious causes. These may be preceded by what Alan Marlatt's group calls SIDs (seemingly irrelevant decisions), like bringing a bottle of liquor home in case guests show up (Marlatt 1985).

Such slips may be due more to little negative experiences or unresolved stresses building up over time, until they add up to enough negative feeling to cause an overdrinking episode. These can be hard to sleuth out, but the basic problem is an imbalance of positive and negative experiences and feelings in your life. One solution is to increase the positive experiences, or activities that you want to do and find rewarding, as discussed in chapter 9. Also, you may need to learn ways to better manage the negative experiences that you can't avoid.

It's particularly important not to get discouraged by slips, but to see them as part of a positive process. Says Terry:

> *I think it is like taking a trip. Say your dream is to climb Mt. Everest. You study, you evaluate your own capabilities, you prepare and you pack. And then you begin the ascent. Can you only say that you are climbing Mt. Everest when you arrive at the summit? No. As soon as you start the journey, you are climbing Mt. Everest. Even if you need to take a break. Even if you get altitude sickness and need to return to base camp for a while. I think that as long as you are committed in your goal, and have the unshakeable belief that you will achieve that goal, and are actively involved in a plan (however flexible that plan may need to be), you are climbing Mt. Everest.*
>
> *I believe that the same is true in defining a successful moderator. If you have studied, evaluated (honestly) your own capabilities, have made a plan, and are now actively engaged in pursuing the goal, you are a successful moderator. The key for me is "active engagement." To me this means that you have some way to monitor and measure your own progress. It means that you allow for setbacks, and do not consider them defeats. It means that your plan is flexible enough to allow for alternate routes. It means that your plan and goals are also subject to honest evaluation, and that you are not so rigid in your definition of "success" that you cannot question your plan, and adapt to a new one, if needed. Maybe your initial goal was unrealistic. Maybe it was too vague. As long as you have a plan, and are honestly and diligently working at it, you are a success.*

Alan adds these thoughts about seeing and valuing your own progress:

> *So what if you slip, and you stumble along the way? Remember that you aren't falling backward and getting dumped on your ass . . . you're falling forward, into warm hugs and support, because you are changing, growing, and getting better every day. Four months not drunk? Ask around your office/workplace sometime . . . you'd be surprised to learn that you are now in the minority of people that don't get drunk every/other weekend, and they are "normal." Hang onto that, not the negativity and guilt. It helps make the rest of the road easier as you continue to progress.*

Dealing with Relapses

A return to old drinking habits may of course go beyond a single episode, and become a relapse for a period to the old pattern of overdrinking. It's best in such cases to stop drinking completely, say by doing another Thirty, while you take a hard look at where you are. If you haven't been able to sustain any significant periods of moderation and it's pretty much a complete failure, then moderation may just not be the thing for you. In that case, your trial of moderation will have led you to a very valuable finding, that moderation is not a practical goal for you at this time. The next chapter on routes to abstinence will help you think through that direction.

If, on the other hand, you can see that you were making some progress against your problem before the relapse, then another try at moderation is worthwhile. In that case, it's best to use this abstinence period to do some real thinking about that next try, rather than just going through another time without alcohol. And keep a positive outlook. Says Bonnie, advising another on coming back after a relapse:

> *First off for the abstinence. Why not abstain for the next few days and see what you think then? But also at the same time, rethink your moderation plan. Meaning, where is it that it's not working? Frequency? Limits not being adhered to? And maybe some "whys" about that from your own perspective.*
>
> *Are there more triggers surfacing—so they'd seem "new"—that need to be examined and included in the equation? Do you need to do some planning for those like you did for the ones you found during your Thirty? Or some old ones that you need to "put the halt" on drinking through again? (Like to not drink until whatever it is is worked out and you feel differently—like not "in anger," etc). Even if it means waiting until sometimes the next day?*
>
> *You are wise to take stock and nip things in the bud if you feel yourself relapsing. Re-evaluate what works and hold onto that, and "tweak" your plan accordingly. For instance, do you need to make sure to eat? Make sure of what mind-set you're in before you begin? Start later in the day? Actually, consciously set your limits before you begin? Keep or buy lesser amounts for a while? Where is your plan going out the window, or where is it "too difficult" the way it's been going?*
>
> *At one point for myself I had to make sure I didn't have three "on" days in a row—it became too difficult that third day to stick to limits. Now it's not an issue, but I'm less likely to have three in a row anyway.*
>
> *Are you charting your drinks? For quite some time I kept a log on the kitchen calendar—different color dots for abstinence days, and one, two, three, or "over." It did make a difference having (and knowing I would!) a visual record. It can also help to be able to go back and see your progress when things aren't going as right as you'd like.*
>
> *Commit yourself to however many abstinent days that you want and think you'll need to regain your strength, get your wits about you, and make some changes with your plan. Then whenever you decide to have a moderation day, make sure you plan for it. These are new habits we're trying to establish, and old ones die hard. It takes practice, patience, and sometimes, trial and error.*
>
> *See your goals and look ahead—not back—forward motion is what's important. If you must look back, see all the successes you've had so far!!! Know that you can change, and believe in yourself. Progress is not perfection. You can look forward to the "trips" being fewer and further between and the new habits taking form as you go along. It does get easier! Just focus on what you want and as much as possible see yourself already there, then feel it when you're on the right path. It takes a minute to absorb the "truth of insight" that's right there and store it for that changed mind-set. Use what works!*

Especially in the case of a relapse as opposed to a slip, the thing lacking may well be your basic level of commitment to moderation. You may need to go back and seriously redo the steps of looking at the harm alcohol has done to your life, and the benefits you expect from moderation, to help build that commitment.

Another key piece often missing in relapses is the critical belief that the better experiences with alcohol come from using moderate amounts. You have to review your own experiences with alcohol clearly and honestly to see if you can get to that belief.

On the positive side, you have a tool in your kit now that you may not have had at the beginning of this project. That is your actual experiences of successful moderation, showing what you can do and what the world beyond alcohol problems looks like. It may not be easy, and your process may have to go on for several years to be complete, but just keep working at it. Says Ron:

> *The short abstinences have become a part of my routine. As boring and obvious as it sounds, repeating a behavior over and over again will make it a habit. It's a little over a year now that I have returned . . . and I have made progress during that time. Guess I have got a bit of "visceral desire" in me!*
>
> *My pattern has been to work on this (for me a daily drinking habit), ignore it for a time, and then return to it again. Each return has found me a bit further along in my resolve to make the change that I want for myself.*
>
> *When I think of my habits from my initial entry into MM-ism in 1996 compared to now, I am truly amazed. If you are just beginning this journey, please know that it can sometimes take longer than you would wish it to, but the changes can be made. Don't give up on yourself, look for support in all the right places, and be ready to forgive yourself. What may seem to be a major slip or lack of progress may just be a fallow time before your next success.*

Professional Help

If you just aren't enjoying life, be sure that there isn't a physical or psychological problem like depression or certain medical conditions that has gone untreated. This type of suffering can often lead to relapse—and it's just not pleasant—so keep actively seeking solutions until you find one.

And if you're having real trouble progressing toward moderation, you might want to consider professional help for moderating. There is a growing group of therapists who work with people seeking to moderate their drinking—information about some of them can be found on the internet at:

www.moderation.org

www.behaviortherapy.com

www.doctordeluca.com (for clinicians in the greater NYC area)

www.addictionalternatives.com (Los Angeles and Santa Ana, CA)

The support of a professional who can help you track your drinking, reinforce trigger avoidance and relapse prevention skills, and encourage you to do your best may be just what you need. If the Web sites here do not list a therapist in your locality, your best bet is to look for a psychologist practicing cognitive behavioral therapy or trained in harm reduction approaches.

Professional treatment might include use of naltrexone (trade name ReVia) as well as counseling. Naltrexone is currently officially approved for alcohol-related use only in abstinence-focused programs. There, its effect has often been to reduce rather than eliminate drinking (a common effect in abstinence programs in general). When heavy drinkers take naltrexone in abstinence-focused treatment, they find that it reduces their craving for alcohol. But interestingly, it seems to reduce the craving for a second drink more than it does the craving for a first. People who never had "just one" have found that doing so is much easier with naltrexone—suggesting that it may be useful for those seeking moderation.

If naltrexone is approved for help in moderating, it will require close medical supervision because of the potential for side effects in early use, and because, as the label now states: "ReVia has not been shown to provide any therapeutic benefit except as part of an appropriate plan of management for the addictions." And, a key question to be answered is whether people who achieve moderation via a drug will do as well in the long term as those who have learned to control their drinking without drug assistance. A research study which measured efficacy for fourteen weeks after treatment found that there was no significant lasting benefit fourteen weeks after stopping use of the drug (Anton 2001). So there are many issues to be resolved, but this is an interesting area to keep an eye on.

Maintaining Moderation

Preventing relapse is certainly preferable to having to cope with it. While some people learn moderation, find a more fulfilling pattern of activities, and seldom or never have problems with alcohol thereafter, it is not uncommon to find old ways emerging at times or new problems emerging. Moderation involves constantly making choices, and to stay on track we have to keep making the right ones. Says Mike:

> *What I can tell you for sure is that living in the world of moderation, which is inherently a shade of gray, requires more intellectual acumen than living in the world of abstinence, which merely requires one to say "no" for the rest of one's life.*

Even if the going seems to be smooth, it pays to stay on the alert for problems, just as you would do if trying to maintain abstinence. Says Rick:

> *I too have felt the "I've kicked the habit" feeling. It is wonderful. And in fact I drink tons less than I used to. I've fessed up to the few overindulgences I've had over the past year, but by and large I'm doing great. But my one big problem is feeling that "I've kicked the habit." Like it is in the past. Constant vigilance. Constant vigilance. As soon as I feel that "I've kicked the habit," I then feel that I don't have to pay attention/be careful anymore, and I screw up big time.*

Backsliding can happen gradually, so that we don't notice. This happened to Fredrika:

> *I felt I had learned how to control it. However, I imperceptibly slipped back into my old ways bit by bit. You know, saying "what the hell" to that glass of wine right after work while I am getting the dinner ready. Not that frozen Pogo Dogs actually require that a bottle of Chardonnay accompany them. And then a few days later having two or three glasses. . . .*

Things can look fine on the surface, but not so good on closer inspection. Says Christine:

> *Well, then "the Porsche of my heart" was lifted toward the heavens and I was invited to walk 'neath her belly to inspect the situation, I was horrified. Cancer*

of the exhaust system, what a sight, rust holes everywhere. Boing, here comes my revelation. My car looks good for an '89 Celica, not one ding, no visible rust, but underneath my exhaust system was ready to litter the pavement.

And so comes a reaffirmation to constantly monitor my moderation. Yes, oh yes, I like to think that I'm sailing along and doing fine because sometimes I can have a bit more than moderation and not feel any consequences—however—after today I'm jolted back into a fresh reality. I can think I'm doing okay by getting away with a little excess here and there, but will it add up to a whack of rust one day? I must constantly consider my living "vehicle" as something to be protected, inspected, and meeting certain requirements lest I grow sleepy and figure that I can decide what "moderation" really means and mush my way toward another downfall.

Checkups and Diary-Keeping

One way of monitoring yourself is to keep a drinking diary going over the long term, maybe in the simplest form of entering number of drinks or no-drinks on a calendar. Another is periodically to check back mentally over the previous week or so as to your drinking quantities and pattern.

Also, you can check back to the latest version of your own rules and guidelines for drinking, to see how your current practice measures up. One of the important practices is to have some days in the week on which you do not drink. The suggested guideline is, as mentioned earlier, to not drink on more than three or four days per week. Says Rob:

So I think for me it's important that there are days I don't drink anything at all, you know. If I drink anything, even if it's just a couple, I know the more I put in my system on a consistent basis it makes me want more. I know that for sure—it's like nicotine. Some people think even if they drink one or two it's not so bad because it's a small amount, but I think for myself if it's in there every day, over a period of time I want more.

Also, consider the goals you had for nondrinking activities. These may, of course, change and evolve over time, but some positive progress in pursuing nondrinking activities is critical. You need to have other reliable means to pleasure, and ways of dealing with negative states, than using alcohol. You need to get to a place where when you feel, for instance, uncomfortably tense, you have an urge to go jogging, rather than an urge to have a drink.

Refining Your Guidelines

If you have had a slip—or just seem to be encountering difficulty controlling your drinking—you may well need to change your drinking guidelines and practices. Says Terry:

My overall drinking is down to about a third of what it was, on a weekly basis. I'm pretty good at holding the number of drinks down, just still find it tempting to want to end every day with a relaxing chilled glass of wine! I also found summertime to be a trigger for me. It was news to me that the longer daylight hours and beautiful long evenings would be such a draw to drink. So to get a little firmer grip on that, I'm picking my days for moderation in June carefully, to coincide with special weekends and/or events, and the other days will be abstinent. Started a twelve-day stretch yesterday, so I feel great! Went to the gym on my lunch break to work out. Going to the store to stock up on sparkling water after work. And home to enjoy the long evening on the deck, with my sparkly water and lemon.

Maintaining Commitment

We can't stress enough that one of the most important parts of moderation is the true, deeply felt desire to be moderate. We had that feeling when we went through the steps of change to learn moderation. But we may lose some of that sense of commitment over time as we go on to other things. One thing that can help, interestingly, is additional periods of abstinence. Says Mike:

Moderation isn't something you accomplish and forget about. In the press of day-to-day life, it's easy to let the focus on it slide, and it is good to bring it back periodically to the forefront and refocus and rededicate oneself to moderation and one's moderation plan. For the newer folks here, one way that more veteran moderators employ to do this is a shorter version of the Thirty. You will often see references to three, five, seven, ten, or other periods. I find I am at that point now. So as of today, I'm up for seven.

And Bonnie as well felt a need to reinforce her commitment:

It's time for me to put some more distance between myself and alcohol. I've been wanting to do another Thirty since May or so. I have felt and continue to feel my mind-set slipping over the past few weeks (as well as amounts/frequencies gradually increasing) and it's time to reinforce my visceral desire and grab a better hold of ultimate goals again. For quite some time drinking was not on the list as a way to get "high"—that list is made up of natural things (sunsets, a walk around the yard and garden, etc.) but I'm noticing it ever so subtly sneaking its way back and I'm tired of having to watch for it and kick it off. So I'm starting a Thirty today. I know I'm in good company.

Also, if your sense of commitment seems to be slipping, you can go back and review some of the exercises we suggested that you do during the Thirty, especially your list of problems related to your former drinking pattern. Reminding yourself of the problems you had before can be quite salutary. In addition, look at where you are now compared to where you were before learning moderation. Seeing and feeling your success a bit can be quite motivating as well. Says Terry:

One year ago this month I found MM. Was searching for help online and stumbled serendipitously upon MM. For about a month I lurked, thought about my drinking, started the exercises, and thought about my drinking some more. Tried skipping a couple of days . . . but it was agony, and I wasn't sure how or if I could ever go thirty days abstinent. Two days seemed to be the most I was capable of.

Sept. 5, 1999 was my one year wedding anniversary. My husband and I celebrated with a lovely dinner out, and we drank two bottles of wine. I'm sure I had more than one whole bottle to myself, but that was my norm. What was different about the evening was my awareness of my consumption, and not in my normal chronically neurotic "Oh shit I've got a problem" sense, but

"Hmmm, I'm about to do something about this."

One year later, I've finished two Thirties since that evening. I've cut my consumption by a huge *amount. I have had only one occasion since that evening where I've been drunk. And last night we went back to the same restaurant. I had two drinks over the course of three hours, with a lovely dinner. And today I am starting a two-week abstinence—just as sort of a celebration and a mini-salute to MM.*

I felt like I was celebrating two anniversaries, really, my wedding and MM. Hubby gave me a beautiful diamond bracelet, but MM gave me something a whole lot more valuable. I like myself so much better this year. I have so much more confidence, not just in moderation, but I think in all aspects of my life. Amazing how overdrinking just bled into everything—relationships, hobbies, fitness, reading, eating, health—all dominoes that I was constantly struggling to keep from tipping over. Life takes a whole lot less effort. Happy MM anniversary to me!

Keeping in Touch

Attending MM meetings, whether online or in person, can also be really helpful after a slip or if you are just in need of rededication. Remember how supportive that sharing was to your initial progress. Says Sue:

It's like, if you can come to MM and vent and tell secrets and things you keep bottled up inside, that alone can help you get the strength to moderate. But reading others' posts has been truly inspiring. I see that I'm not alone, but in the company of amazing people who struggle with moderation like I do. It's just kind of cool. It does become a part of everyday life, even if you don't read all the e-mail every day or post all the time.

The face-to-face meetings can also be a convenient way to spend some time focused on the moderation issue. Says Scott:

The other thing was to attend the MM meetings, which at least once a week caused me to focus on the fact that I really don't want to drift back into those habits. And I remember a book many years ago called Delinquency and Drift. *The notion of drifting into bad habits has been a powerful notion for me. I think that explains a lot of misbehavior. I didn't want to drift back, so attending this meeting focuses me at least once a week on that fact.*

Going on to Other Issues and Possibilities in Your Life

The alcohol issue may have poisoned your life in many ways. Once free of that problem, you may see positive changes spreading throughout other areas of your life. Says Trudy:

I don't think I realized when I was drinking that I was walking around for twenty-five years with a headache all the time. I discovered what it was like not to have a headache because I wasn't hungover every morning.

And one of the things I rejected was the idea of a higher power as being necessary to changing my life, but I found myself back in church and very active in church when I was thinking again and putting my life together in different ways.

My husband and I renewed our vows. Our relationship is just worlds better than it was. And it was surprisingly good despite my drinking. So there's a lot of good things you don't even know you're missing when you're drinking all the time.

Freeing ourselves of the alcohol problem allows us to come to terms with other significant problems and issues. And the change skills and confidence that come from success can be applied to other challenges. Says Jack:

I think the thinking part is primary. I mean you think much more clearly, and as a result of that I've been able to develop a new nonprofit organization, which I would never have been able to do if I wasn't moderating. And also I've become involved in some art that I also would never have been able to do. Before moderating I was sort of getting through, and I didn't have any leftover energy to be creative or, you know, to do anything different and new.

Summing Up

- If slips occur:
  - Don't get discouraged, but focus on the progress you have made.
  - Figure out what went wrong and how to deal with it next time.
  - Rehearse the new behavior mentally.
- If major slips occur, you may need to repeat earlier steps of the program, including additional abstinence periods.
- Keep at it, because your overdrinking habit took a while to develop and may take a while to resolve.
- If you are really having trouble making progress, consider professional help for moderating.
- Continued tracking of drinking is very helpful—even the simplest recording of quantities on a calendar.
- Use periodic checkups to monitor progress, refine guidelines, and renew commitment.

Chapter 12

If Moderation Doesn't Work: Routes to Abstinence

Cary has come to realize that, despite some good efforts, he just can't seem to stop drinking once he starts. He has decided on abstinence as the final resolution of his drinking problem:

> *The crossover effect comes too low for me. My rational mind weakens and my animal brain strengthens at only two or three drinks. Two a night are not enough. I drank to get ripped. Stopping at two is worse than coitus interruptus. Two is enough to rouse, inflame, and enrage my beast. Two is enough to loosen my grip on its collar. Then in a matter of maybe hours, perhaps months, twelve each weekend will not be enough, and twenty or more each weekend day will not slake its thirst!*

Patty's work in the MM program has also led her to a decision for abstinence, but with a shorter time horizon:

> *For the moment I have chosen to abstain, but nothing is written in stone. At some point I may decide to give moderation a try. Or, I may not. I am not so foolish as to say I will never drink again. Never is a looooong, loooong time. We are all here for the same reason: To examine our relationship with alcohol and determine how (or if) we want to proceed in that relationship. Whether we choose moderation or a long-term abstinence, the work is the same, the feelings that rise to the surface are the same. Therefore, we are all pretty much in the same boat and can cheer each other on as we attempt to reach whatever shore it is we're swimming toward.*

By now you have probably gotten a good idea of whether moderation is achievable for you. If you've been able to moderate successfully, GREAT—keep up the good work! If not, you may want to begin to think about the possibility that abstinence may be the best way for you to achieve the healthiest lifestyle with respect to alcohol. So, how do you go about making the decision to pursue abstinence?

Important Things to Remember in Considering Abstinence

As you reevaluate your relationship to alcohol, there are a number of things you might want to keep in mind.

First of all, it's important that you *not* be discouraged because you found moderation wasn't for you. It's no shame to be an abstainer—at least a third of the U.S. adult population, by recent estimates, don't drink at all! If alcohol has been creating significant problems in your life, it's a responsible, healthy course to rethink whether you want to drink at all. After all, if you want to reduce risks associated with drinking to zero, abstinence is the best way to do so!

Second, it's important to remember that the decision to abstain does not have to be a lifetime commitment. It may be easier to commit yourself to simply doing a repeated thirty days of abstinence, reevaluating after each thirty-day period how you feel and whether the potential benefits of again attempting moderation outweigh the potential costs and risks. You can even adopt the AA approach—abstinence "one day at a time." What's important is not "how long," but how healthy you become as a result of a commitment to abstinence.

Third, people change and their circumstances change. Recently the National Institute on Alcohol Abuse and Alcoholism (NIAAA), in their Tenth Report to Congress (2000), pointed out that even among people who are alcohol dependent, many find that they resolve their dependence and return to nonharmful drinking after a period of abstinence. The key to deciding what's right for you is to use the knowledge you have accumulated about your drinking triggers and high-risk situations to guide you in making healthy decisions about alcohol. If, after a period of abstinence, you are no longer reacting to previous triggers or high-risk situations the same way you used to, then it may be possible to resume your efforts at moderation. We know that people often "mature out" of drinking problems—and you might, too. The only way to know is to continually reevaluate your health goals, the reasons you want to resume drinking moderately, and the risks associated with that choice.

In this chapter you'll see what some people in the MM program have said about their decision to shift from moderation to abstinence. In a surprising number of cases, people choose abstinence not because they couldn't moderate, but because moderation just seemed to involve too much effort, or uncertainty, or concern. Said Maggie:

> *The last month hasn't been easy. There were some close calls. But it's been worth all the work. I was thinking, now it will be so great to enjoy a drink in a moderate mode. But then I got worried. I saw I'd feel tense all the time worrying about getting back in the scrapes I'd been in before. I've never told anyone about some of those. And the limits and counting and all that stuff aren't my thing. I think I'm on the wagon for good. In fact, I know I'm on the wagon for good.*

The abstinence period at the start of the MM program provides a wonderful opportunity to get reacquainted with the experiences of life without alcohol, as well as a time to learn about drink refusal and dealing with urges. For some, the positives experienced from abstinence during that time simply come to outweigh any benefits of renewed drinking. And when and if you start to moderate after the abstinence period, don't just take it for granted that you will be drinking from that point on. See how your initial experiences of moderation measure up to abstinence. Said Peter:

After a while, I was able to start a Thirty, and it went all right. To my surprise, I actually went forty days without extra effort. In fact, I was comfortable and sort of rolling along with it, feeling so good after the crazy times of getting way too drunk. My mind was sharp again, my body felt like I could live in it, and life just seemed better all over. So, at a point where I was relaxed and taking stock of things, I had a drink to see what it would be like. It wasn't like much of anything. And I thought, if I have a few more, then I'll get pumped up some, but is it worth it? Do I want to get back to feeling miserable? No, drinking just doesn't seem attractive right now. Maybe some time later, it will be nice to have a glass or two in the right setting. But right now, I'm enjoying having myself together again.

Also, for some people, the attempt to moderate after the initial abstinence period, or after repeated abstinence periods, just doesn't work out well. This program gives a person considerable support toward achieving moderation, so that moderation is being attempted under more or less optimum circumstances. But if a person cannot achieve moderation—or a sense of definite progress toward moderation—that person has made an extremely valuable discovery. The program has been a success for that person, because its central goal is to assist people in making informed choices for themselves. Says Lucy:

I found MM a year ago and immediately jumped into a Thirty with no prior preparation (which can make for piss-poor performance) and I only made it two weeks. So in September I did a successful Thirty. I then tried moderation, but not successfully. It was not long at all till I was right back where I started. So I decided to do another Thirty in November. It went well. I tried moderation with a little success, but again was back into my old patterns in short order. So I did another Thirty in January. Again, moderation would start off okay, but then again, same pattern.

So I thought I'd do a Thirty in March, but we were going on vacation and I wanted to drink on vacation in Florida with my husband's family who are all drinkers. The very first day of vacation I didn't eat much and I drank a lot and drank whiskey, which I never drink and something really bad happened that I barely remember at all. I have no idea how I let myself get in a situation so bad that it could almost destroy my marriage. So in an effort to restore and retain our relationship I swore I would never ever drink again. And so I have not. He is just too important to me. Although, I do believe after some long period of time I would be able to have one glass of wine with dinner once a month or so, but maybe I'm just kidding myself. Anyway, I have found that abstinence is much easier and maybe it is the final answer. . . .

The decision that one has tried enough and that it isn't working is a highly personal and subjective one. You weigh in the risks of your past pattern and current pattern of drinking, and evidence of progress. Then, you just have to set a go/no-go decision point that makes sense for yourself. Said Sandy:

I think the first thing you would do is to look at your life. Do you have legal, financial, family, etc. problems that are directly related to your drinking? Have you tried to stop before? Do you really/honestly see improvement after joining MM? What price do you pay by continuing to drink? I don't think you need a brain scan, just some honest introspection. This is a program all about self-responsibility.

Why not set your own time limit or some other personal measure of success or failure and determine whether you should be here or not? Like, "If I don't see at least a 50 percent improvement in the amount I drink"? For me, I feel good about it because I see improvement, but in the long run I'm going to have to reevaluate if I'm still going over "limits," like how much is too much and too often?

So You've Decided Abstinence Is for You: What Now?

If you have decided on abstinence, how should you go about achieving that goal? There are many routes to abstinence, ranging from purely self-directed efforts, to support groups, to professional counseling, inpatient treatment, and combinations of these. All of these can be effective for different people, as demonstrated in Anne Fletcher's book *Sober for Good* (see the Recommended Reading List at the back of the book). Because support groups are widely available and have the advantages of providing social support and helping keep you focused on the subject, we'll discuss those first. If this proves to be insufficient, more intensive treatment options are in the following sections.

While we don't think most really seriously dependent, chronic drinkers would be reading this book, especially given the warnings in chapter 3, we'll repeat here some special advice for persons who have high chronic blood alcohol levels: *Stopping abruptly can be very dangerous and even fatal for serious chronic alcoholics.* It is recommended that such persons go to medical treatment facilities for medical detoxification, rather than quitting cold turkey on their own.

Alcoholics Anonymous (AA)

More than 90 percent of treatment programs in the U.S. focus on encouraging their patients to affiliate with AA, the leading self-help group. That doesn't mean that AA is necessarily "better" than other abstinence support groups. It simply reflects the fact that AA is much more widely available than the others—and that people who recover via AA often choose to work in the field. AA is widely available and generally familiar, at least in its broad outlines, to most people.

Before you decide on attending a face-to-face AA group, you might want to pick up a copy of *Alcoholics Anonymous,* also known in AA as "The Big Book." This book outlines the basic program and tenets of AA in a way that may differ somewhat from what you may hear at AA meetings. As an independent decision-maker, it may pay dividends for you to read about AA and develop some understanding of the organization and its principles before you decide if it is for you. And if you don't like the first AA meeting you go to, try out others. Since there are so many different people in

AA and so many different kinds of meetings, you may find that some suit you while others don't.

An outstanding feature of the better AA groups is their spirit of fervent commitment to the program, and AA is exceptional in the amount of support it can offer. An example is that many areas have a meeting going on every day of the week, so that people in need can get to a meeting literally on any day of the year.

Said Maggie:

> *Time to say goodbye to my friend in MM. I've now found an AA meeting that feels comfortable, and it's just the answer for me. The AA meetings around here each have different characters, so I've had to try different ones to find one right for me. My time in MM was a turning point in my life. MM was the first place I could open up on my drinking problem without being lectured at, and gave me a chance to sort out what I needed to do about it.*

There are more than 50,000 local AA chapters in the U.S., and you will find a contact number for local groups in any phone book.

SMART Recovery

SMART stands for Self-Management And Recovery Training. This program deals with addictive behavior related to substance abuse (psychoactive substances of all kinds, including alcohol, nicotine, caffeine, food, illicit and prescribed drugs) and activities (gambling, sexual behavior, eating, spending, relationships, etc.). With respect to substance abuse, the program aims for abstinence, although it points out that many of its techniques are helpful to people who aim for moderation. Since alcohol abuse is by far the most common substance abuse, the group meetings are likely to include many people with drinking problems.

Weekly meetings are in a self-help group format, led by trained chairpersons who may be professionals or lay people who have recovered from an addictive behavior. The program teaches people how to develop and maintain motivation to abstain, cope with urges, think rationally, and lead a balanced lifestyle. Cognitive behavioral therapy, especially the rational emotive behavior therapy principles developed by Albert Ellis, make important contributions to the program. SMART contrasts itself to AA in rejecting self-labeling as "alcoholic" and "powerless," and is secular rather than religion-based.

Meetings are free, although a voluntary contribution is requested, and it is assumed that individuals who succeed in the program will graduate from it in time. Several hundred meetings are ongoing in the U.S. There is also an online national discussion group.

SMART Recovery Self-Help Network
7537 Mentor Avenue, Suite #306
Mentor, OH 44060
Phone: (440) 951-5357
email: SRMAIL1@aol.com
Web site: http://www.smartrecovery.org/

Secular Organization for Sobriety (SOS)

SOS takes a self-empowerment approach to recovery from alcoholism and drug addiction through abstinence. It therefore gives the SOS acronym the second meaning of "Save Our Selves." SOS maintains that sobriety is a separate issue from religion or spirituality. SOS credits the individual for achieving and maintaining his or her own sobriety, without reliance on any "higher power." SOS respects recovery in any form, regardless of the path by which it is achieved. It is not opposed to or in competition with any other recovery program. SOS respects diversity, welcomes healthy skepticism, and encourages rational thinking as well as the expression of feelings.

The following passage from SOS's "Your Sobriety Toolkit" (on their Web site) gives the flavor of this program: "Watch for tools . . . If you feel it may work for you, try it. You are fighting for your life, nothing less. You are the owner of your life. You are responsible for the caretaking of your life and you have decided to find better ways to live. Other people have gone before you and put together their own 'tool kits.' Ask them to share."

The program was founded by its current executive director, Jim Christopher, in the mid-1980s. Today there are a number of local meeting groups in the U.S. and in several foreign countries. SOS also has an online forum and a newsletter, as well as other publications. Local meetings are led by nonprofessionals.

Secular Organization for Sobriety (SOS)
4773 Hollywood Blvd.
Hollywood, CA 90027
Phone: (323) 666-4295
email: SOS@cfiwest.org
Web sites: http://www.cfiwest.org/sos/ (main Web site)
http://www.sossobriety.org/ (international-oriented)

If a local meeting does not turn up on the main Web site, it is worth calling the phone number above for further information.

LifeRing Secular Recovery

LifeRing started as a breakaway organization that includes some people and local groups formerly associated with SOS. The break may have had more to do with organizational issues than with its philosophy, which seems extremely close to that of SOS. For instance, LifeRing offers the "Three-S" Philosophy of Sobriety, Secularity, and Self-Help, wherein "sobriety" always means abstinence. Since LifeRing and SOS are very close in their approach to abstinence, it's worth checking out the Web sites of both for informative material, and for a meeting near you if you're interested in a face-to-face meeting group.

Its Web site, http://www.unhooked.com, offers a variety of information about the program, a list of local meetings, and a listing of scheduled online chat events.

Women for Sobriety (WFS)

Women for Sobriety is an abstinence-focused support group specifically for women. It was founded by Jean Kirkpatrick as a feminist alternative to AA.

Kirkpatrick realized that AA's emphasis on becoming more humble and doing more service for others might not be helpful for women who already suffer low self-esteem and spend most of their time catering to other people's needs. Kirkpatrick felt that many women need a program that is "empowering" rather than focused on "powerlessness."

The easiest way to get information about WFS is to visit their website:

http://www.womenforsobriety.org.

Moderation Management

One of the major objectives of MM is to help people determine whether the objective of moderation or of abstinence is best for them. MM therefore applauds people who make the decision to pursue abstinence, and counts the program a success in assisting in making that critical decision. Its ongoing support, on the other hand, is more for people who are working on moderation. Although many people leave the MM program if their decision is for abstinence, there are a few who remain in the program because of its openness of approach, and because so many of its tools and techniques apply so well to abstinence.

Abstinence-Based Treatment: Professional Care

There are a number of types of treatment for alcohol problems available in the U.S.—although unfortunately, their actual methods don't vary much. Most are based on what is called the "Minnesota Model," which was pioneered by Hazelden and other programs in Minnesota and which involves formally introducing patients to twelve-step principles and the AA program.

The least intensive treatment is simply outpatient counseling, where you meet one-on-one with a professional counselor and discuss your problems and your progress. Many states require such counselors to be licensed as specialists in substance abuse problems—but this doesn't mean that they will be knowledgeable about anything other than twelve-step programs. If you want someone with greater training, you may wish to see a licensed psychologist or social worker, who will have at least a Master's degree—and some have Ph.D.s. Look for a psychologist or social worker who practices *cognitive behavioral therapy*, a modality that is very useful for coping with alcohol problems, or a psychologist trained in harm reduction approaches. Traditional psychotherapy—Freudian, psychodynamic, insight-oriented, "eclectic"—has not been shown to help people with substance problems.

If you still can't get a handle on your drinking problem through counseling and self-help, you may want to try intensive outpatient therapy. This ranges from programs that are two to four hours every day or evening on most weekdays to those that run a full eight-hour day, every day or most days. During this time, you will be provided with information about relapse prevention, coping with urges, and the effects of alcohol on your body. There will also be group sessions, individual sessions, and usually classes on how to incorporate AA into your life. Family or couples therapy is often included as part of the program.

Some programs include anti-craving medications like naltrexone, which can help reduce your desire to drink—and can also help prevent a slip where you have one drink from becoming a big binge. This medication can be prescribed by any physician, and it has been found to cut the chances of major relapse by 50 percent if taken regularly. If you think it might be a useful adjunct to your treatment but have not been offered it, you may want to ask your doctor about it.

Most people's insurance no longer covers twenty-eight-day inpatient treatment—which is simply the same program described above as intensive outpatient, but with the people in treatment living at the center and often attending additional AA meetings together. If you have a really good policy, you might get seven to ten days covered—but probably not unless you have physical dependence and need to spend the first few days hospitalized to deal with withdrawal symptoms.

If you feel that your current living situation is part of the problem, and that getting away for a month or longer might allow you to make a new start, you might want to consider a "halfway house" or "Oxford House." Halfway houses have formal treatment, usually including groups and relapse prevention lectures, but more in the range of two to four hours a day, rather than longer. Work is an important part of the program—people are expected to pay a (usually low) rent and also to keep their rooms and the general living areas clean. Oxford Houses have less of an organized program: they are simply houses or apartment buildings where people in recovery live and support each other in going to meetings and staying sober.

If you wish to avoid AA-focused treatment but do want a more intensive program, see if there is a university near you conducting studies on alcohol problems. Some will be studying medications; others new types of talk therapies. Many provide top-notch treatment in the course of their research—and even if you end up in a study of a new anti-craving medication in the group that doesn't receive the active medication, you will be offered free psychosocial treatment either during the study or afterward. There are also lists on the Internet of the few providers who offer different types of care—you can access one via the SMART recovery site listed above.

The Recommended Reading List describes three books that give further information on alternative approaches to resolving alcohol problems: *Alternatives to Abstinence*, *Recovery Options*, and *Sober for Good*.

Please note: If you are relapsing repeatedly or just don't feel good over the long term when you are abstinent, we urge you to get a thorough psychiatric evaluation. A large percent of people with alcohol problems have an additional problem like depression, various anxiety disorders, post-traumatic stress syndrome, bipolar disorder, or others—and this can prevent recovery if it is not properly treated.

Above all, just keep up the effort against your alcohol problem. Don't be discouraged if you don't achieve complete abstinence on your first try. A recent review of major treatment outcome studies found that after one course of professional treatment aimed at abstinence, on average about one out of four abstained from alcohol throughout the first year.

However, the others on average showed major reductions in drinking, and about one in ten became truly moderate in drinking. Furthermore, the study found that among those who did not achieve complete sobriety, the chances of benefiting from further professional treatment were probably still favorable (Miller 2001). So keep at it.

Finally, keep in mind that your decisions are yours alone. People do best when they feel they have deliberately chosen their goals. If you have tried moderation and found that it is too much effort for too little reward, or that moderation just isn't achievable for you at this time, then you have made an informed choice about what will work best for you. We wish you well—no matter what your goal.

Summing Up

- A decision to pursue abstinence is not a failure, but a very positive step in progress toward overcoming a drinking problem.
- AA is the most widely available program, and offers a high intensity of support.
- SMART Recovery, Secular Organization for Sobriety (SOS), and LifeRing are secular alternative self-help group programs for abstinence.
- Women for Sobriety is a feminist-oriented alternative to AA.
- Professional treatment options—like counseling, intensive outpatient treatment, anti-craving medications, and inpatient treatment—may be helpful if your problem is particularly persistent.
- Never give up—research shows that the more you try, the more likely you are to succeed.

Chapter 13

Life Stories

In the previous chapters, we've looked at the elements of resolving alcohol problems in some detail, and have heard comments from sixty-one different people on specific parts of the process as we went along. Most of those are quoted, with permission, from messages posted in the ongoing course of MM online discussions, or in a couple of MM in-person group meetings specially recorded for this book.

Now it's time to take a look at how the overall process of getting into and out of problems with alcohol unfolds in real lives. We've asked several people in the MM program to write out their stories, and seven of those stories follow. The names are pseudonyms.

Some of these people have overcome far greater obstacles in life than most of us are likely to encounter, such as the highly traumatic childhoods of Alan, Tony, and Gretchen. But we'll also see that alcohol can cause deep distress in outwardly smooth and successful lives, such as those of Terry, Mike, and Lisa.

Several speak of alcohol problems as not just existing in certain parts of their lives, but as reaching into and poisoning every aspect of their being. Part of Terry's description of that is: "I felt flawed as a person, as though I was contaminated." Alan says: "The booze was a sort of spiritual/intellectual death." And several have had close brushes with physical death, due to overdrinking.

Several speak of realizing for some time that they had a significant problem with alcohol, but feeling unable to do anything effective about it. Part of Lisa's description of that is:

"I felt trapped, like I was on a hamster wheel and couldn't step off to do anything differently." Yet all retained a belief in their ultimate ability to control their own actions, and so to maintain responsibility for them. As Tony says: "I refused to admit I was powerless!"

Often being in a rather defeated frame of mind, these people had to reach into some well of inner strength to undertake a real search for a means to resolve their problems. Several speak of finding that path in MM as a truly galvanizing event.

There is a good deal of variability in what parts of the MM process these people single out as being particularly meaningful for them. All have put a lot of work into the process, and all have had reversals along the way. For instance, Mike's DUI arrest a year after starting in MM might have been extremely demoralizing, but he just learned from it and got back to work.

Some common themes? All have guidelines they have formulated for themselves and can articulate well. All have been abstinent for at least thirty days at a time, and often have repeated abstinent periods and used longer periods. A strong and often-repeated theme is having a continuing higher level of awareness concerning one's drinking, and, indeed, concerning other related choices about how one spends one's time. Part of that is commonly record-keeping of drinking quantities and occasions.

There's a good deal of discussion here of moving toward non-alcohol-related positives in life. It's a reinforcing pattern, of course, of liberation from overdrinking allowing one to take up better things, and the experience of better things then supporting the movement away from habits related to overdrinking. Gretchen's wonderful ending commentary covers both major career-related experiences teaching young children, and a range of smaller but significant leisure time activities that enrich her life. The sense of better life experiences can be strong, as Terry reports: "I feel a sense of lightness—of contentedness—and of wholeness that I did not feel. . . ."

Of course, life is not always good, but controlling drinking restores strength in dealing with the negatives. Part of Tony's report on this: "My life is so much easier to handle, especially in stressful times. . . ."

Some of the most powerful things that people do for themselves are things they invent that are not strictly in the MM program as described in this book. Examples are Lucy's decision to remain abstinent for a good many months before she attempts very occasional drinking, and Lisa's practice of writing down a daily list of positives in her life.

Everybody here views moderation as a work in progress—not a fixed destination. Mike says: "Remember that moderation is a process, not an event." Therefore, they see their current moderation as conditional on continuing successful efforts. Most intersperse periods of moderation with periods of abstinence beyond the MM suggested guidelines, and several speak of the possibility of stopping drinking completely at some time in the future.

These people, because they've taken a very active part in MM online discussions, have all successfully enlisted social support for their moderation efforts. And several speak of responsibilities for and concern about others, despite the focus here on their own resolutions. Yet several also speak of realizing that, in the end, the most powerful motivation for moderation is doing something for themselves. Self-preservation and self-worth are the most fundamental motivators.

You, dear reader, are doing something that many never do or do too late. That is, to stop in your tracks on the slow road into oblivion through overdrinking, and finally take a stand and begin a real effort to come back. Excerpting Alan: "Thank yourself for being strong enough to take the hard road. . .You took a long hard look at a very dark and scary road and had the strength . . . We have people dealing with the most amazing things. . . date rape, divorce, terminal illness . . . The easy way would be to go back to the bottle. . . . But they don't do it. . . . They want change so badly, even if the world smacks them down, they dust themselves off, stand back up and say, 'Okay, maybe this time.'"

As you can see, these people are awfully good at speaking for themselves, telling us their experiences and what they have learned. So let's hear from them directly:

Terry

I am a forty-four-year-old woman, working in middle management. I started drinking at around age fourteen with a group of friends and my sixteen-year-old sister. We drank beers and smoked joints. At around sixteen, I gave up marijuana, but remained loyal to alcohol. I always considered myself a social drinker, even though I was always aware that I drank more than most of my friends, and later on, more than my husband.

I quit entirely during each of my three pregnancies, but was happy to return to my cocktail hour after each birth. I think that my drinking was still within moderate range, although at the upper limit, through most of these years.

I was able to work, raise my kids, and get my degree, all with little or no interference from alcohol. About two or three times a year I would get drunk, and sometimes embarrass myself and/or my kids, but I still saw this as within reason.

About five years ago I entered a very stressful time in my life. My marriage of twenty-one years was breaking up, and my response was to quit drinking almost entirely. I felt that I needed a clear head to deal with all of the emotional issues—my own and my children's. But once the crisis phase was passed, I returned to drinking, socially, as before, but the amounts and frequency began to creep up on me.

My marriage ended. Shortly thereafter I met my current husband and we merged families. Although I was riding high on the new romance, I was still dealing with some heavy issues from the end of the first marriage—my ex-husband became terminally ill, I was dealing with stepchildren, and I had a major career change preceded by a brief period of unemployment. Through it all, I was coping, but alcohol was my tool. Every night I would come home and relax with wine. Sometimes two or three glasses, but more and more often the whole bottle. I started every day with a mild hangover, but never enough to keep me from work or other responsibilities.

In 1998, we bought a new house and did a major remodel. I started a new job. I was drinking every single night, almost always a whole bottle of wine or more. I began to see that my drinking was no longer "social" and wanted to cut down, but couldn't. Every day I would vow to skip a day of drinking, but by happy hour, my resolve was down the drain, and I'd decide to "start tomorrow."

I began to despair of ever gaining control, and felt that deep down inside I was headed for the proverbial "bottom" and AA. My pride kept me from seeking counseling or even discussing the problem with friends or family. I dreaded the thought of how much lower I would have to sink before things would fall apart completely. I would guess that I had five or fewer days without alcohol from September 1998 to September 1999. One day, feeling totally sickened by my situation, and feeling both physically and mentally fatigued from trying to hold it all together, I got up the courage to go online and search for help.

That was the day Moderation Management entered my life. I went on the e-mail list, and was totally flabbergasted to learn that there were actually problem drinkers out there who did not have to hit bottom, and even some who had, yet were able to turn their drinking around, and were actually drinking socially once again. I ordered the book and lurked on the list for a little over a month, still struggling with attempts to give up drinking for longer than a day.

In October of 1999 I came out of hiding on the list, and after a couple of weeks of getting comfortable with talking about my drinking problem, tried for and successfully completed thirty days of abstinence, with my day thirty being Thanksgiving 1999. Since that time, I have completed one additional thirty-day abstinence, and numerous shorter periods, for needed reinforcement. I have successfully moderated on all but one occasion, and that was a major learning experience for me, and a catalyst to take my moderation plans more seriously. I keep diligent calendars to record all drinks; I plan four to five abstinent days every week.

I don't drink on every single available Friday or Saturday. I am able to limit myself to two drinks on almost every occasion. My tolerance is quite a bit lower, and this limit is not something I struggle to maintain—it seems to be my own natural limit, something that had been obscured by years of overdrinking and knowing no limits. I learned what a five-ounce glass of wine looked like (I had been using fourteen-ounce water goblets!). I no longer have a drink to "warm up" before we go out, and I don't continue drinking after we get home.

I still have to work at moderation; I notice a tendency to want to fudge on the four to five days a week of abstinence. This has been the most persistent aspect of my problem. But I also see continued progress, even a year after beginning this program. I am very comfortable with my drinking right now, and feel like I am in control. I can choose to drink or not to drink, and it is no big deal. What was once the center of my every day, every holiday, every occasion, and something I thought about constantly, is now in far better and healthier perspective. If I think of my life as a circle, with me in the middle, my drinking used to be a thin shield that surrounded me. Then the next layer out was family, then friends, then activities, job, etc. Now when I think of myself, it is still me in the center, but right next to me up close is family—with nothing between us—and drinking is in the outermost ring.

How did I give myself permission to drink so much? It's like a kid who is playing in the street: "Who said you could play in the street?" And the kid looks up at you, and you can see it in her face—she was having such a good time, she didn't even realize that she *was* playing in the street!!

In my case, it was that slow slide into the gray area that allowed me to continue to think that it was okay. I didn't click overnight from "light drinker" to "moderate drinker" or from "moderate" to "flat-out drunk." So I could easily excuse one or two indiscretions. And then three or four, especially when spread out over a long and gradual slippery slope. It was not so much a case of giving permission, as of not paying attention.

Now I have a heightened awareness, and I will never allow my drinking to be something out on the periphery of my consciousness again. I want it to be always right in front of me. I know that at times I have thought that I yearned for the day when I no longer have to think about moderation—it would just come naturally. Now I am at a place where I know that part of being an aware person means that I *always* think about being moderate, and I don't want it any other way.

I plan to continue recording drinks on a calendar, writing daily in a journal, including my thoughts on drinking (but more and more about other things), and participating with the online discussion. In addition to these, I have used meditation and visualization as powerful tools to help me with my lifestyle change.

I don't think I drank to hide from emotions. I, too, just like the feeling of being pleasantly buzzed. What I needed to get in touch with again was the feeling of relaxing *without* being pleasantly buzzed. It was, at first, well, not too pleasant. I felt like something was missing. (Fun? Relaxation? My ritual? Probably all of those. . . .) So I had to ask myself if I was going to need to go through the rest of my life always with a buzz, but more and more stepping over that line to *drunk*, and feeling guilt the next morning. It was all in the name of fun and relaxation, but in fact it was a poor substitute for the real thing. No, better to seek out a new habit.

Now I find that I actually *love* going home and having nothing to drink. It is very mellow, very relaxing, very fun. And, rather than my ritualistic behavior, I find myself doing lots of other things—and some of them are even healthy, like walks on the beach, romantic dinners with my husband, movies, stitchery, etc. I still like the buzz, I just like the no-buzz, too. That's what is new. And now I have the choice. Before I really didn't. It makes me feel good. The work I had to do to break the habit has paid off in so many subtle ways, but none more strongly felt than the freedom of choice and the freedom from guilt and worry.

I wish I could say that life was always wonderful without alcohol, but it still has ups and downs. I still have days that I would like to blot out! But all in all, my self-esteem is better than it has ever been in my adult life. I feel like I am returning myself to a more natural, more spiritual sense of self. I am kinder to myself. I am more tolerant of my shortcomings, and more accepting of who I am. I no longer feel the need to judge myself a loser.

I think this is indeed the gold nugget that MM has to offer. Whenever we engage in behaviors that are hurtful to ourselves (and often, by extension, to our families, friends, and communities), we carry around that little ache. For me it was a constant shadow lurking just outside of my awareness. (Once it entered fully into my awareness, I decided to do something [MM] about it!) It cast just the slightest pall over everything, keeping me from having moments of pure joy. I felt flawed as a person, as though I was contaminated. I was very harsh in my self-judgments.

Even if I had a day of not drinking, which was, believe me, rare, I could still condemn myself for what I had done the day before, the week before, or knew that I was about to do again the next day. It's very hard to feel good about yourself when you *know*—even if you have yourself convinced that nobody else does—what a weak person you are. Or not weak, but overindulgent. Or not overindulgent, just blatantly uninhibited. Whatever.

It didn't matter what labels I put on myself, or what justifications I could offer, and sometimes even believe! I did not feel strong and I did not feel proud. My self-acceptance/self-worth/self-esteem, my *sense of self*, was tainted, and I felt less than whole.

I am still a somewhat shy person by nature, but I find myself feeling much more confident about who I am and all aspects of my being. I'm okay being a bit of a clown—I no longer associate that silly side of me with being tipsy. I like to sing, even though I can't carry a tune. I like to dance, even though I have two left feet. And I feel a sense of lightness—of contentedness—and of wholeness that I did not feel when I was drinking immoderately.

So, finding the ability to moderate my drinking has also allowed me moderation, and balance, in other aspects of my life. Moderation Management was/is a turning point in my life, and is a program that I will be eternally grateful for.

Alan

I'm Alan, I'm twenty-eight years old, and I work in advanced computer applications.

In my home, with an abusive father beating my mother senseless, a two-year-old me defiantly stood between my mother and father, daring to risk my father's wrath to say, "Don't hit mommy anymore!" (That is my mother's recollection, honestly, and not mine.) She says it was the moment she realized, as she stared at me, that soon it wouldn't be just her that was being beaten, and while the good Catholic in her had to try to stay in an abusive marriage "till death do you part," her religion was not worth her son's life. So we left shortly afterwards.

Years later, the ages from nine to sixteen were spent in an almost daily struggle for sanity and my own sense of self in the institutions I had been placed in. On one side I had a host of psychiatrists trying to pick my brain apart to make me "the perfect little kid," and on the other I had the staff members, some of whom had long ago succumbed to that thing Fyodor Dostoyevsky referred to when he said there was something about the helplessness of children that brought out the evil in men. I learned a lot about waging war, choosing battles, and tactics in that environment.

I learned that you could never let your guard down. I learned that no one anywhere could be relied on, trusted, or you found yourself having lost the war because someone left a dagger in your back. The fact that I walked out of there with my sanity in one piece is a testament to the stubborn kid I used to be, spitting in my father's eye.

But then I was suddenly loose in a world I wasn't fully prepared for. People out here don't have "enemies." They don't fight wars. And most of them seemed pretty bewildered by me and my constant looking over my shoulder. Friends would be baffled at the ends I would go to in retribution against someone who I felt had wronged me or those I cared for. Shortly after that, the first man I ever fell in love with took it upon himself to declare himself my "enemy." He hurt me worse than my father or any of those staff members ever could have. I trusted—and I got the knife in between the shoulder blades. The battle lasted one year. It was ugly. No, it was way beyond ugly.

It was after that I had my little nervous breakdown that most abuse victims seem to suffer around ages twenty-three to twenty-eight. I can tell you classically that the reason for this breakdown, in most of us, has to do with the fact that all the defense mechanisms that served us so well for so many years become almost suicidally deadly when we are no longer in the abusive environments. Those very same things that kept us safe and warm are the same things that later keep us from getting the things we need so desperately to stay alive: love, compassion, understanding. I wasn't any different. People around me reached out, trying to help, and I lashed out violently, slashing with broken glass and razor blades, to keep them away. I *wanted* them to help me, but I was trapped and couldn't get out. That's where the booze in my personal history enters in.

Standing on a street corner, sixteen years old. Alone. Cold. Tired. Hungry. Been sleeping in parking garages for weeks now. My knees are starting to show signs of being pretty messed up from the cold winter weather and sleeping in the back seats of parked cars, crunching my six-foot-two form into them. A guy pulls up. I'm terrified. But this is why I came here. He offers. I accept. When we get to his place, I find that after six rum and Cokes, I really don't care what's going on. That continues for some time, kinda hazy. Take the money and get an efficiency apartment in sleazeville. Take the next batch of money and get my GED. Start working at a bookstore during the day, Hardee's drive-thru at night, and drinking a whole lot to forget. Wishing the taste of rum would wipe away my memories as easily as it did my fears.

Standing in the corner of a bar. Just like every Friday and Saturday night. Standing there on the outside. Watching the Pretty People. They're laughing, having fun. Doing that stuff that somehow I wasn't destined to do. Sipping my drink, I finally get the nerve to say hi to one of them. He fixes me with a rather disdainful glare and says, "Why are you talking to me, you fat fucking cow?" I spend the rest of the night trying to quench, with the deeply soothing rum, the fires of my anger, my loneliness, my fear that I will forever be that shadow in the corner, unknown.

Later that night, I tap him on the shoulder. Fear gone. Nervousness gone. Shyness gone. I feel *alive*. And I deck that sorry son of a bitch so hard he flips over a table and shatters a mirror.

I am escorted out. But my victory smells of rum, tastes of gin. My friend Scott asks me why I can't just stop? And my quiet knowing that somehow, somewhere, I signed a deal with the devil and now it was time to pay my dues. The pact had protected, saved, soothed, and healed me all it was going to, and now the piper was at my door, wanting payment for the rats he dealt with. And I had nothing to give him. Except myself.

I told Scott to fuck off. And I never talked to him again. Locked myself in a dorm room and gave the piper his due. Spiraling down . . . down . . . down. The end of the road. Just me. An empty bottle of Southern Comfort, and an Exacto knife. Something needs to end.

I'm glad I chose to end the right thing. The ending is rather anticlimactic compared to the beginning and middle. The result is a fat blond guy with too many computers, plus degrees in Theatre and Psychology, who somehow ended up being an applications developer and UNIX Systems Administrator who spends too many nights alone with a bowl of popcorn, his cat, and a movie. In short . . . I succeeded in spite of myself and everyone else. If ever there was a man who should believe in guardian angels, it's me.

I've always been one of those drinkers who can drink a *lot* and no one would ever know. I don't get spinnies, I don't pass out, until I've consumed *so* much that people have a hard time believing me when I tell them how much I used to drink on a nightly basis in a short period of time, trying to get to oblivion. So for me, I could and can probably drink four stiff rum and Cokes and be none the worse for wear. I don't. But I could. And for me, part of the magic of succeeding at moderation was the fact that I gave myself the choice. I can, right now, without any guilt whatsoever, go buy a fifth of rum and drink it right now in the next hour. All gone. By not stressing over what a bad person I am for wanting to get drunk, by not hanging onto the details of how much I should beat myself up because I got drunk. . . . I don't drink.

See, AA had me thinking I was a pretty miserable sot because I couldn't *not* have a drinking night once every nine months. And then one day I took a hard look at all those "normal" drinkers in my life and realized I drank less than they did, but spent a good hour a day in a meeting beating myself up for it! After a while, it just became a pattern for me. I order Coke by default because I drank Coke for years. In order to override that setting, I have to stop and think "I want a drink," which is then usually followed by a brief weighing of things like "how early do I have to get up," "do I have stuff I have to do tonight," and after the checklist is run down, if I still want the drink, I drink it.

So I've not been a traditional MMer, I don't think. I never used that chart we have on the Web site. I never stopped to figure out BAC. I just have a drink if I want one, but since I've not been drinking hard for years, I just don't tend to drink by default. That isn't to say I don't get drunk. I've had at least one good rip-roaring drunk since I joined MM. It was full of fun, laughter, friends, one really really really cute man who kissed me like I've rarely been kissed, and a bunch of really burly furry guys singing at the top or their lungs "BLAME CANADA!" while doing the bunny hop or some other strange dance. I don't regret it at all! And you won't hear one moment of wasted guilt on it either. Because I don't do it every week, every month, or even every three or four months. And that's a lot better than most of the "normals" around me. So why stress about it?

It took me almost five years of mostly abstinence via AA (I'd go nine months abstinent, drink one night, do nine months abstinent, drink one night . . . cycle repeat) before I even considered moderation as an alternative. I can say without a doubt that for all of AA's faults, if I had not spent five years maintaining a mostly abstinent life, I would never have succeeded at moderation. I needed time away from the pied piper. Prolonged time. Thirty days would never have cut it for me. On day thirty-one, I would have been drinking my two fifths again. I spent years getting to that point; it shouldn't really be surprising that it took years to unlearn the behaviors.

Even after five years, I came to this program scared to death I was on my way back to where I used to be for just considering trying moderation. So here's what I do: major abstinence periods. Rules like not keeping liquor in the house. I experimented briefly with keeping a stocked bar for guests, but in the end, still found that because I am someone who is constantly drinking *something* (water, coke, etc.), the temptation wasn't to get drunk, it was simply to drink . . . so best to not keep it around. I force myself to be outside in a social environment if I want to drink. (My drinking was always alone, behind locked doors for the most part.) These have been the keys to changing my ways after all that time abstinent. Just what worked for me.

You know one of the most helpful things that I ever did? I stopped thinking "I am going to limit myself to two drinks" and started thinking "I'm going to allow myself a drink or two." Turn the negative to positive, and you tend to want to succeed more, in my experience. People rarely feel like they want to succeed at "punishment."

One of the things, lest I sound too heavy on AA, that they helped me identify over my time spent with them, was *what* it was I sought from alcohol. As phony baloney as some of their "spirtual" crap was, for me, they were right on the money when they asked me to remember the first time I'd ever gotten drunk. Young kid, home alone, who drank a bunch of the rum sitting in the cupboard, and then immediately refilled the bottle with water, knowing my mom didn't drink and would throw the bottle away some weeks later thinking it was "bad." For years, that pattern followed me. Drinking alone out of boredom/depression/anger/apathy, trying to achieve something, and then instant fear and paranoia and attempting to cover all my tracks so no one would be the wiser. I got pretty good at it too.

Some time back, a girl I knew told me I was looking in my bottles of booze for a shut-off switch for my head. I said I agreed with her assessment. At some point, I reached the impasse. That line in the sand. The one that reads "Abandon hope all ye who enter here." I had a choice to make. I could keep drinking, keep being drunk, keep trying to die—and eventually find that final switch that would turn my head off for the last time. Or I could fix it. Make it better. I don't think most people choose to fix it. I am one of the lucky ones. Alcoholism, hard drinking, whatever you want to call it, it consumes lives, families . . . everything.

And it's a pretty rampant destroyer in our world today. Stop and think about the uncle everyone laughs about, the wino in the street begging for his spare change to go get a bottle, the frat boys who never stop partying. It just shifts from their frat house to "out with the boys." But also, part of what I am trying to say is that it had nothing to do with luck. It took real strength to stand at the abyss, and then walk away. Fight my way back to a normal life.

I don't think very many people stop and realize what booze is actively doing in their lives. I don't think most people stop and actively try to change it. In that regard, I agree with AA and their idea that "you have to want to change," because if I hadn't hit that line in the sand . . . I don't think I would have stopped. If even three different variables in my life had resulted in me looking at the sky rather than the ground, I would have gone flying off that very dark and scary cliff without a care in the world.

Most of you here didn't/don't drink as much as I did. But inside, no matter how much we drank, I think we all agree that the booze was a sort of spiritual/intellectual death. A surrender. An escape. A way to cope with what we feared we could not cope with, whatever that may have been. We had the strength to give that up and choose life. To fight for life. To struggle for life. Even if it hurts. The stuff that led us to the bottle was still there—that's part of the reason drinkers keep drinking. The problems don't go away, you just forget about them for a while. But we chose to deal with them. Struggle with them. Fight with them.

I don't think most people make that decision. I really don't. And part of me thinks that the reason AA succeeds with those it does is because of its total embrace of the passivity and weakness in regards to drinking. To someone like me, that's anathema . . . you don't embrace weakness. You don't joyfully stand up and tell the world, "Hi, I'm so and so and I'm a total loser!" at every chance you get and that somehow makes it better. Eventually you either quietly die from the weakness or you make yourself stronger and actively *change* what's wrong. You don't turn it over to God. God gave you those hands, that heart, and that head to *use*, not to cry to him "fix what's wrong with my world please, I'm too lazy to do it."

Thank yourself for being strong enough to take the hard road. You may not have succeeded yet, or found all the answers, or fixed it so there is world peace. . . . but you took a long hard look at a very dark and scary road and had the strength to fight your way down it. I mean, we have people dealing with the most amazing things, date rape, divorce, terminal illness, etc. And they still fight. *They don't lie down and die.* The easy way would be to go back to the bottle. To embrace its deadening effects. But they don't do it. They fight. They want change so badly, even if they fail, even if the world smacks them down, they dust themselves off, stand back up, and say "Okay, maybe this time."

That's amazing. We are all warriors. Each and every one of us. And we will win the battle. Because we chose to fight it, not hide from it, not ignore it, and most certainly, not to just lie down and die when the enemy came knocking.

Today I give myself credit for the strength I have. Because I've spent so long beating myself up for being weak and becoming a hard drinker in the first place, I almost missed the sheer and amazing strength I had that night, staring at an Exacto knife and my wrists, to choose life, for all its difficulties and the hard road it would be. To pick back up my sword and shield, dust them off, and return to battle. The strength I have to spend each day living my life, not hiding from it in a bottle of rum. I don't think most people do that. So we are the strong. And deserve to be proud of ourselves for that fact.

Lucy

I'm Lucy, I'm thirty-three, and I work in a biotechnology company. This is just one person's story. This is my story of alcohol in my life. Take from it what you will and leave the rest.

My father was an alcoholic and abusive to my mother. But he left us when I was only ten years old. My very first experience with alcohol came in a loving environment. I must have been about seven or eight. After dinner at my grandparents' house on holidays, they would allow us to have one small shot of chocolate mint liqueur. I loved the way it tasted and I loved the way it made me all warm inside. It just perfectly matched all the love we felt at Grandmom's house. It was very good and I would ask for more, but one was all they would ever allow.

I remember being sick when I was twelve and my mom telling me to drink a shot of blackberry brandy. I didn't like it straight, so I would make hot chocolate and add it to that. That was very good. Again, I loved that warm feeling inside—it was comforting, like a hug from the inside out.

When I was thirteen, my mom took us to a friend's wedding. My mother let me try the punch. It was very, very good. She said I had had enough. When she wasn't looking I got some more. This was the first time I actually got drunk. I remember on the way home I was all giddy and silly and happy. Mom warned, wait until tomorrow. True to her word, I must have felt pretty yucky for awhile the next day. I don't remember exactly how I felt, but I remember saying I'd never drink again.

When I was fourteen, my grandfather died and within three months both my dog and my rabbit died too. One night I got up, and crying hysterically, I drank a whole bottle of wine. It was a dry, bitter wine and I didn't like it, but I drank it anyway, probably in an effort to re-find that happy, warm feeling from the wedding and to stop feeling so bad about my losses.

By fifteen, I was drinking beer with my friends. My mom would even get it for me. I don't really know what she was thinking. I imagine she hoped I would stay home and out of trouble rather than go out with God knows who doing God knows what. When she wouldn't get beer for me I would drink whatever was in the house and then replace it with water.

At sixteen, I got a boyfriend who liked to drink as much as I did. Together we spent the next six years drinking and partying. Every once in awhile I would get so drunk as to totally lose control of myself and do something really stupid and embarrassing—so embarrassing that I'm still embarrassed today. I've done things that to this day I can not figure out why I would have ever done such a thing.

From ages eighteen to twenty I went away to a junior college for computer science. Every weekend I would go home and drink and hang with this boyfriend. When returning to the dorm, I would bring a case of beer. That would usually last me until Friday when I headed home again. I didn't get drunk every night, but I did drink every single night.

I got out of college and started working for a local computer company. We used to have board meetings every Friday after work; that is, we'd go talk about work at the local bar.

Ironically, shortly after I turned twenty-one, I stopped drinking and went to AA. I didn't go for me. My boyfriend had gotten drunk and stolen a four-wheeler. Part of his probation was to go to AA. I just went with him. I didn't get anything out of it. We quit drinking for maybe four months. I remember that maybe the third time we went out drinking again, there was this guy from AA out drinking too. Then it was back to the way it was before.

When I was twenty-two, my mother became very ill with cancer and died. My drinking increased. She never liked that boyfriend of mine and on her deathbed told me to get rid of him and find a nice guy. Within six weeks I did dump him.

So I had been drinking alone for about six weeks when I met my now husband. He liked to drink as often as I did. We spent almost every night at the bar, until our favorite bar burned down. Then we just started drinking at home. When the money got tight, we just started drinking cheaper beer.

And the years rolled by. Although the stupid, embarrassing events were fewer and fewer and came farther and farther apart and were not nearly as bad, I believe my drinking was slowly creeping up so that while I was not getting quite as drunk as often, I was actually drinking more than ever.

Then one day when I was thirty I realized that I had been drinking every night for almost ten years. The hangovers were getting harder to shake. I started to think maybe I was drinking too much, too often. I started asking my husband what he thought. He said he didn't really think it was a problem, but that if I thought it was, maybe it was.

I would wake up in the wee hours of the morning and start thinking I'm not going to drink tomorrow. But then the day would wear on and by the time I got home from work I had forgotten that and would just start drinking again. I was drinking a gallon of water during the day and probably as much beer at night.

Then I don't know what happened, but my husband began to say that he thought I was drinking too much, but he kept on drinking. The thing is, somehow I had progressed to drinking in the mornings. I could drink two to his one. So finally it was time to figure out what to do.

I knew there was no way that I could or would make the time to go to those meetings where you admit you are powerless and diseased. Call it denial if you want, but I am neither. I knew it was me making choices and with some exercise I could have the power to make better choices. I knew the power was within me. Thank God for the Internet. I began searching for alternatives to AA and I found MM. MM reaffirmed what I knew I believed; that I was not sick and I had the power, all I had to do was find it, strengthen it, and use it.

At thirty-two I embarked on my first Thirty. I only made it two weeks. The list was encouraging and supportive. My second attempt was successful. What was special extra special about the second attempt was that it was in September, the month my mother had died. It was historically a very tough time of year for me, and this was the first time in ten years that I faced it completely sober.

This is when I began to learn about feeling the feelings instead of drowning them out. Let the feelings flow over you and through you and around you and then they'll pass on. It was very therapeutic, but I don't think that I could have done it without the support of my newfound friends in MM.

But then moderation was difficult, very difficult. So I did another Thirty in November. That was cool, my first Thanksgiving sober was much easier and dinner was not late for a change. Moderation in December was again difficult but the Thirty in January was a breeze. Unfortunately I let loose again in February and I drifted from the list and I just drank into March.

March 17, 2000. The most embarrassing, stupid, awful thing I have ever done—getting drunk and saying some really awful things to some important people—nearly destroyed my marriage. The only thing I had to blame it on was how drunk I was. I hadn't been that drunk in a long, long time. Since that was the only thing to blame it on and I never ever wanted something like that to ever have the remotest possibility of ever happening again, I vowed to never drink again.

Fortunately we have recovered and grown from that horrible experience.

I am learning a lot from being sober for this long. It's been a really, really long time since I was sober for this long. I'm learning a lot about myself and how to deal with what life throws at me. The thing is that my husband keeps drinking. And I miss the taste of good wine with a fine dinner or even a cold beer with a hot pizza. I don't miss the hangovers, yuck mouth, irritable bowel syndrome, guilty feelings, loss of control, all that comes with too much, too often.

I think I have learned enough and gathered enough strength or power to moderate in the strictest fashion. I have a plan. My moderation plan is one drink a month. Some may see that as too strict, but for me, I see it as just right. I figure there's one holiday or event a month that is traditionally celebrated with a drink. I don't want to be an outcast. I like and miss the taste. I shall not lose control again.

I look at it like I look at my dieting. I like the taste of nacho-flavored tortilla chips, but they are full of fat. I figure I have three choices: 1) I can deny myself the pleasure for the rest of my life and on some level be miserable, 2) I can say to hell with it and eat a bag a day for the rest of my life and on some level be miserable as the weight goes on, or 3) I can eat one serving of fourteen chips once or twice a month to satisfy that craving without going overboard and putting on the pounds. And I know I can do that with food because I do.

Now that the habit portion of drinking is broken and with this much time under my belt I feel that the psychological part is almost completely broken too (I say "almost" because I do still get urges to let loose), I will be able to drink occasionally like a normal person. I'll be back to the time when it was one special drink on a special occasion that tastes really good and makes you feel warm inside—but one is enough to savor until the next special occasion.

My sister just celebrated five years in AA. It works great for her. I wouldn't be able to stand the restrictiveness of the whole thing. She won't even taste a spaghetti sauce that has a touch of wine in it, because its got alcohol in it. As my own little way of moderating during this extended abstinence I've begun collecting and using recipes that have alcohol in them. Beer boiled shrimp, champagne scallops, kahlua pumpkin pie, chicken braised in lambrusco, steak diane with brandy, and on and on. There's more variety in my liquor cabinet now than ever before. I don't drink alcohol anymore, I eat it! As far as I'm concerned, this just proves the strength of my power to control myself. And like it or not, that's my story and I'm sticking to it!

Mike

I'm Mike, I'm thirty-five, and I've been a lawyer since I was twenty-five. My childhood history is entirely unexceptional. I had a good home life and nothing really bad happened while I was growing up. As I got into junior high and high school, I was generally not a social butterfly, but I did have a circle of friends that I hung out with. Largely because most of my friends didn't drink, I had very few experiences with alcohol before I left high school. I got drunk three times my senior year—at a cousin's wedding, the night of our last football game, and the night before graduation.

When I went to college, I started drinking more often, but still not on a really regular basis. I probably drank three to four nights a month on average my freshman and sophomore years. When I did drink, it was usually at a party. Since everywhere was within walking distance, it was never a big deal to drink a little too much. Plus, at that age, I had astonishing powers of recovery. I started to drink more my junior year. A couple of things led to that. One was that a relationship that had started shortly after I got to college ended. The other was that a number of my friends had turned twenty-one, so it was a lot easier to obtain alcohol. I was hit hard by the end of that relationship, and I like to joke that I spent the next six months drunk dealing with it. That's an exaggeration, but there's no doubt that I was drinking a lot more. Even then, it wasn't so much the number of days in the week that I drank as the amount I drank on the days I did drink. That pattern continued through law school and into my professional career, and it continues to this day. I can quite easily go several days without drinking or having just one or two drinks. But if I don't make sure to pay attention to what I'm doing, I can have nights where I go past my limits and have way too many drinks.

The main problem drinking has caused in my life is that it contributed to problems I had with my wife. The problems existed apart from the drinking, but my behavior on a couple of occasions when I exceeded the limits didn't help. Both involved my getting falling-down drunk in front of people she worked with. With one or two exceptions, those were the only times I'd ever met those people, so I didn't make a real good impression. As I said, there were a lot of other problems, but my drinking didn't help.

In fact, I found MM after an episode where I'd had too much to drink and said some very mean things to her. I knew that I wanted to work on getting those "over the top" nights under control. I'd also noticed that I was starting to drink more every day just to help myself ignore the problems in our marriage. Just after I'd started my Thirty, though, things went from the "problem" stage to the "crisis" stage when we separated about three weeks into my Thirty.

I am very proud of the fact that I finished the Thirty rather than simply retreating into alcohol as I had ten years earlier in college. There were times during those days when working my way toward moderation was the only positive that I had in my life. So let me encourage you not to let the feeling of having too much else going on in your life keep you from working toward moderation. After all, if many people drink to relieve stress, it makes some sense to work on moderation instead at those times.

I found MM by looking on the Internet for groups offering assistance with drinking issues that didn't simply preach abstinence. Also, from what I had seen of AA-style approaches, I knew that I could not deal with having to repeat the mantra of "I am powerless" when I knew it just wasn't true. At the same time, I knew that things were not right and I was really looking for a direction to follow, and not someone who would try to force a solution down my throat.

I chose to pursue moderation rather than abstinence because I knew I could be abstinent if I wanted to. About five years previously, I had gone through a six-month period where I wasn't drinking because of a medical issue. So I knew that I could give it up, but I also knew that I liked having alcohol in my life if I could keep it in the proper place. That led me to try following a moderation program. I figured that, at the least, I would be drinking less, and if it didn't work, I could always conclude that I was better off not drinking at all. I find that when I'm not drinking, I sometimes start to focus on the fact that I'm not drinking, whereas with moderation, I simply have to keep track of how much I've had and know when to stop.

I found that doing the Thirty was a wonderful chance to take a hard look at myself—not just my actual drinking behavior, but what I was doing and what I could be doing differently to make myself happier. I found that my drinking issues were bound up with a general personality trait of mine, which is simply drifting along, and letting things happen, rather than consciously taking control of them and trying to influence them.

And when I took a hard look at my drinking patterns, I realized it was because I had never developed the good habits to ensure that I stopped at one or two drinks. I had never tried to work on pacing myself. As a result, I had developed some bad drinking habits. And as an attorney, waking up hung over and running late were the top two on my stress list, even if I'd gotten drunk the night before to escape whatever work-related stress I was suffering from. If you step away and take an honest look at it, drinking can often make the stress worse rather than better.

I have learned that it is absolutely imperative to be aware of what I am doing with regard to my drinking, to formulate a plan and stick to it. It's not a big production or anything, maybe just a couple of minutes on my way to a party to set a limit and figure out what to do to stick to that limit. Some techniques that work for me are (1) making sure that I'm eating something when I have a drink in my hand and (2) always alternating an alcoholic drink with a nonalcoholic drink. I also try to follow a rule that I don't drink at all at at least one out of every three social events I attend. Since I'm a fairly withdrawn person, I have a tendency to use alcohol to loosen up and feel more comfortable, especially at business events where I don't know many people.

To break my established drinking pattern, I found nothing more effective than going out for a walk with my dog at times I'd otherwise have been drinking, particularly after coming home from work. As an attorney I work twelve to fourteen-hour days just about every day. I drank every day before getting into MM. Now I look forward to walking my dog down to the mailbox and then heading out to see the world . . . at least that's how Alfie (my dog) sees it. I see it as walking around a parking lot, but it seems so much more exciting through his eyes. I know there's a lesson for me somewhere. . . .

I find that when I let myself drink without paying conscious attention to what I'm doing, I can overdo it—especially when I get all self-congratulatory about being a "successful" moderator. As with many other areas of life, few things can undermine your focus on moderation like overconfidence. I stopped drinking for four months a while back because of a little run-in I had with the police. About a year into MM, and feeling very proud of myself for being so successful a moderator, I went to a party and totally ignored everything I'd learned. I compounded it by trying to drive home, and was pulled over and cited for DUI. I even got handcuffed.

I decided that day that I needed to rethink what I was doing. Here's the last paragraph of what I posted to the list at that time: "I feel embarrassed, humiliated, angry, but mostly I feel stupid. I've decided that at least for the time being I'm going to stop drinking entirely. As I sit here now, I can't see a single good thing that alcohol is doing for me."

And I didn't drink again for four months. During the time I wasn't drinking, I spent a lot of time trying to figure out what the best approach was for me. There are so many folks out there who constantly preach that only an abstinence-based approach will work that I was doubting myself and my decision.

When I started drinking again, it was half a glass of wine when I went to visit my brother and see my baby nephew for the first time. We had a family get-together and my brother had opened up some of his best wine for the occasion. I had been thinking that I was ready to try drinking again, and that turned out to be an appropriate time to do it. And I found that when I took that first sip of that wine, the world didn't come to an end. I didn't grab the bottle and run outside and drink the whole thing. I had my half a glass of wine, enjoyed it thoroughly, and had a great time with my family.

The other thing I find that I need to do is to periodically check in with myself to see how I'm doing, and whether I need to tweak my plan at all. Moderation is not an event. It's a process. It's not something you achieve once, file away, and move on ever upward. It was easy for me to reach a point of moderation for a month or two. It has been much harder for me to avoid losing focus and slipping back into unhealthy ways of dealing with stress. By saying that it is a process, I don't mean to suggest the old AA theory that you're only one drink away from falling down in the gutter. I am simply saying that, just as problem drinking is often a learned habit that can be unlearned, the good habits you replace them with can also be unlearned.

The idea of periodically reviewing where you stand with your drinking does not mean you are stuck in an endless cycle. It's simply something that has worked to help me identify times when I was slipping a little bit. Sometimes I decide no change is needed. As mentioned, I once decided that I needed to stop drinking entirely, and did so for over four months. The point is that I now do a review of where I stand with drinking every forty-five days, where eighteen months ago I was doing it weekly.

The last thing that I found to be helpful is to find people to talk to about things. The MM listserv has been wonderful for me. It is very helpful to know that you're not alone and have people to share your troubles with.

I guess the main way that MM has affected my feelings and experiences is that I'm more "there" when I do things. For one thing, I go out and do things more often, and when I'm out, I can actually participate and respond to what's going on without it being dulled through an alcoholic haze. I can focus more on the places I'm at and the people I'm with. I just enjoy things more.

The main impact that this has had at work is that I don't make a fool of myself at social events the way I used to, and I have a lot fewer mornings where I wake up and wonder how I'm ever going to make it through the day.

With regards to my marriage, another big issue has been eliminated. I'm not overdrinking and doing stupid things that cause more problems. I'm not making a fool out of myself at her work functions or picking a fight with her because I've had too much to drink.

Maybe a better way to describe it is to say that it takes two people to make a marriage work, and when one of them is overdrinking several nights a week, that person is really not fully participating in the relationship. Overdrinking can very quickly help to create a distance in the relationship that helps lead to all sorts of marriage problems. I can't say that participating in MM has directly made my marriage better, but it definitely has taken one of the major problems and made it a much smaller issue.

The most obvious impact that it has had on me is that it made it possible for me to deal with all of the problems I've gone through without winding up at the bottom of the bottle. In the past, that is how I've dealt with the end of relationships, and I was worried that it could happen again. Instead, I made MM part of a program of personal rediscovery that in many ways has been a lot of fun. By controlling my drinking, I have been able to continue with that process and grow as a person, rather than use alcohol to numb myself to the difficult emotions I was confronting.

Remember that at the beginning, if you only make it without drinking for a week, or five days, or three, you've still done better than you would have done without trying at all. The point is to spare your body for a while from the effects of alcohol and at the same time take a hard look at your drinking habits. That way you can learn about yourself and use the insights you gain as you move forward. Remember that moderation is a process, not an event.

Lisa

My relationship with alcohol began about thirty-two years ago. I did the normal experimenting that kids will do in high school. I'm both amazed and thankful that I lived through some of the stupid stunts I pulled.

I married very young, as soon as I graduated from high school. We were horribly mismatched. We had a couple of children and remained together for eight years. Drinking became part of our lives—our social circle of young friends would also drink a lot.

I became extremely depressed during the marriage, to the point that I didn't care whether I lived or died. The only thing that really kept me from feeling suicidal was my love for my children. It was an extremely abusive relationship. My husband had a dark side that I hadn't seen before jumping into this marriage. He became very abusive over time, both emotionally and physically—and the episodes grew more intensive and frequent as time passed. They were especially common when we had been drinking.

My episodes of drinking heavily also became more intensive and frequent, to the point of regular blackouts. It became a catch-22. I was depressed, yet I drank to escape my reality. I felt guilt after every episode but felt too weak emotionally to make changes.

I also suffered from the "beaten wife syndrome." One of the most common characteristics of an abused person is lack of self-esteem. Between the abuse and my heavy drinking, my self-esteem or self-worth was nonexistent.

But, then, something happened when I decided to go to work. I started to gain a smidgen of self-esteem because I was my own person at work. That little bit of confidence led me to the decision to quit drinking. And the dynamics of our marriage changed completely once I quit. My husband lost his ability to dominate me, I didn't fit in with our social circle, and I began to regain my independence. We divorced within less than a year.

And I remained abstinent for eighteen years! I never sought any support when I stopped drinking, and quitting was very easy. My life was so much happier and I began to find fulfillment. At that time, the concept of alcoholism being a disease, and very possibly hereditary, was a common belief. My mother had a long history of drinking, as did her father. I assumed I had alcoholic tendencies and it was best I didn't drink.

Then, I met a wonderful man and remarried, went back to school to get my degree and eventually my MBA. As the eighteen years passed, my children grew up and I had a very successful career. I was really content, both in my personal and professional life. The idea began to occur, to both my husband and me, that an occasional glass of wine or cordial might be something we would enjoy for relaxation in the evenings. I also questioned the idea of whether I was really an alcoholic, or had just abused alcohol when I was in extremely unhappy circumstances.

So, about six years ago, we decided to try having an occasional drink in the evenings. My husband enjoyed cordials, but found he didn't care for the taste of wine. I, however, really enjoyed wine. Unlike the old days, when I drank mostly hard liquor (but also beer and wine), I limited my intake to wine only since that was what I particularly enjoyed.

My intake was moderate for the first couple of months. But it gradually increased to daily drinking after I came home from work. One glass soon turned to two, then three, then four . . . etc. In the meantime, my husband, who had never drank before, was satisfied with one small cordial in the evening. Although I really enjoyed my work, I also found myself exhausted and stressed at the end of the day, so this became my excuse for multiple glasses of wine in the evening. My drinking, however, was much different than in my younger days. I didn't get drunk, didn't experience blackouts—but my tolerance to the wine was steadily increasing.

After a couple of years of following this pattern, we retired. We had planned this for several years. We built a home and moved to another state for our retirement. My husband had been growing concerned with my drinking, primarily how it might be affecting my long-term health. We both talked about the fact that it would be easier to cut back when I wasn't so stressed from work.

But that didn't happen. I found myself facing depression as I couldn't figure out what I wanted to do with my life at such a young age (from a retirement standpoint, anyway!). The daily drinking continued, only now I found myself starting earlier in the day. We'd go out to lunch and I would have wine with lunch at noon and continue when we returned home. I started feeling more and more frustrated with myself, but kept the feelings inside. My husband would occasionally express concern that he was afraid of what this could be doing to my body. I was also experiencing chronic stomach problems and insomnia.

I would wake up at two in the morning and start to experience panic attacks. I would wrestle mentally with myself into the morning hours, deciding that today I would cut down, or would not drink. By three in the afternoon, the resolve I felt at four in the morning had faded. I felt trapped, like I was on a hamster wheel and couldn't step off to do anything differently. I was also frustrated that I didn't feel in control, but that I was being controlled by this habit. Through all of these feelings, however, I still did not feel that I was an alcoholic.

One night I started to search the Internet to see if I could find information about reducing one's drinking. This is when I stumbled onto the site, Moderation Management, and found out about the book, *Moderate Drinking*. I told my husband about it the next day, and checked the book out from the library. As I read the book, I found that it really made sense to me.

But the idea of abstaining for thirty days from drinking was frightening, to say the least. I joined the list, but did not participate for the first few months. Being on the list did give me the support and courage to try baby steps and start with a day or two of abstinence. After several months, I finally worked up the courage to try a Thirty.

I decided to journal my thoughts and feelings during my Thirty and posted these daily to the list as my "reflections." I started reading them to my husband, who became eager each day to hear what I had posted. This was a rather frightening proposition in itself! By sharing my innermost thoughts and discoveries with my husband, they really came out in the open where I could no longer hide from them. Many of these discoveries were things that I had not really allowed myself to think about while I was caught up in the habit of daily drinking.

I found myself feeling much better emotionally and physically during the Thirty. The real turning point for me occurred when I worked through one of the steps of listing my priorities in life. I examined my core values as my priorities. I discovered that daily drinking was in direct conflict with every one of my core values! This was a major eye-opener. I immediately reframed the way I viewed drinking and the role I wanted it to play in my future.

My husband and I began to discover new activities together, enrolled in classes, and started finding a lot more romance in our daily lives again! The experience from this Thirty (which I extended for sixteen more days) was so profound that I was extremely cautious about starting to moderate. I planned my next two months very carefully and only had something on special occasions. I did another Thirty about three months after my first. This reinforced what I had learned, and it helped to shrink the importance of drinking in my life. I repeated another Thirty about three months later!

I started to find that I liked doing these quarterly thirty days of abstinence because they reduced the role that drinking played in my life to a very small part, which is where I wanted it to stay.

As tends to happen in life, however, we were thrown a major curve while I was in the middle of a Thirty. We found out that my husband was suffering from a form of chronic cancer, a blood disorder. Although my first reaction was one of "if anything happens to my husband, I'll lose all motivation to moderate," I didn't break my Thirty. The stress of his illness, and our subsequent dealings with treatments, has created a stress like I've never experienced.

I have found myself breaking my own guidelines for moderation more than I wanted to in the last six months. However, I still find that doing a Thirty every few months helps to keep me on track, even though I might step off sometimes. One great result of working on this over the last couple of years is that I find that I can only step off track for a month (or two at the most) before my moderation "conscience" takes over and reminds me it's time to take a break and do a Thirty to regain my perspective.

Having dealt with my husband's illness for a year now, I have also come to realize a couple of other important points. I didn't embark on this moderation journey for him, but for me. So, even though I feel like I could lose my motivation to moderate if something were to happen to him, I realize that all I have learned on this journey has been for me—and that isn't going away. I might *feel* like I wouldn't be motivated to moderate, but the truth is I *am* motivated!!! It has changed my world! I also realized that it was not *coincidence* that I learned to moderate when I did—it was necessary, so that I could be fully present for my husband. Life has a funny way of working out sometimes, but it always does!

Last week I was thinking about the different emotional states that are triggers for me to drink. I decided that in the future I am really going to pay attention to both my mental/emotional state and my physical state. If I'm not feeling well either emotionally or physically, I'm not going to drink. I want to drink when I am happy and add to the pleasurable feeling! So I started thinking of alternative things to do that could help me get out of funks. This listing is a work in process, as I keep adding to it when I think of something else. Yesterday I was feeling bored at about ten o'clock after I had gone for my morning swim. My husband suggested we go for a walk (which is one of the things on my list) and it was great. Then I checked my list and did several other things on my list, and before I knew it the day was half over and the boredom had disappeared!

I've also been keeping the daily journal of things I'm grateful for. Some days are easier than others, but every day I make myself write at least three things. This is a good exercise for me. I want to stay focused on all of the good in my life . . . it's too easy to see the negative. Some days I am struggling to come up with anything.

When I started taking a shower this morning I wasn't feeling very good physically (not from drinking!), and I noticed how wonderful the shower felt. Then I started thinking about a whole bunch more things that made me happy or that I was grateful for. So I finished my shower and wrote in the journal for today and must have written about ten things! According to the philosophy behind doing this, the more we focus on what we are thankful for, the more we find to be thankful for.

I think the perspective of "balance" is critical. This really applies to many things—if I exercise too much (which does happen often) I actually end up more exhausted than if I exercise within balance. If I eat too much at a meal, I'm terribly uncomfortable. A problem for me is that I didn't really experience hangovers often. I was a daily drinker and could easily drink a bottle of wine a day without hangover effects. When I drank more than that, then I could feel yucky the next day! And I know a bottle a day isn't a balanced amount of alcohol! That's why I need to set my own guidelines for my moderation plan. I also need to set them before I start drinking—waiting until after my second glass of wine to make the decision doesn't work very well because my resolve weakens. It's a pretty structured approach, but it's been working for me.

So resolve and commitment are critical, too. It is our resolve/commitment that will cause us to start making a significant change in our life, will help keep us focused on that change, and will help bring us back when we stray off the path of change.

Tony

My name is Tony. I'm thirty-nine, and manage information systems for an engineering firm. My mother was a major rageaholic trained in the "I'm okay, you're okay, let it all hang out" encounter group therapy aura of the sixties. If you bottled it up, it would fester, so the solution was to scream out every irritation you felt. There was nonstop yelling. Of the three of us kids, I got it the worst. I resembled her and reminded her the most of herself, and that angered her.

She didn't drink, in fact was down on drinking. I don't remember one compliment on anything I ever did. In first grade they said my IQ tested over 140 and they wanted to skip me two grades in school. That's the only fight I recall between my parents before my dad left. He advocated skipping me the two grades (which I wanted as well) and she was against it on the grounds I'd get a swollen head. I'd bring her home a painting and she'd sneer and point out the flaws. I'd show her a piece of writing and she'd say, "Don't name the character Mr. Sipcowicz, that's slanderous to Poles, call him Smith." She found fault in everything I did.

Around the time I turned ten, it was cool to rebel. We were the original grunge gang with ripped-up coats and holes in our jeans. My mother was always kicking me out of the house. I usually ran to my best friend Chris', but a lot of the times I had to sleep in the hills or in unlocked cars, trying to wake up before the owner came to go to work in the morning. So, during this grunge phase of the early seventies drugs and alcohol came into the picture. We took our first LSD trip at age ten around the time we smoked our first weed. There were some minor amounts of beer around. It was mostly weed, acid, and "beans" (benzedrine). It was all a huge lark, a lot of fun.

When I was fifteen I was permanently kicked out of my mother's house and went to live with my girlfriend Sarah. Sarah drank beer with her girlfriends, but I don't recall ever having it in the house. I just didn't get the attraction. I quit smoking weed at age sixteen because it made me paranoid. I did my last LSD at age seventeen. I have always been very good at quitting things, which makes it odd that booze turned out to have such sway over me.

My first real time getting drunk was when I'd just turned twenty-one. I drank gin by myself at the kitchen table and felt this euphoria and I just wrote and wrote until I passed out. Around the same time I got back friends with Chris who was now a heavy-duty punk rocker. I was acting as much of a punk rocker as I dared, since I worked full-time at the largest software firm of the time. Every weekend it'd be a nonstop party downtown, popping Quaaludes and slam dancing until you were lying under the table in shards of broken glass, all "Isn't this *great*?" Even then I was the square one, always the driver, always the one who peeled Chris away and helped him up the stairs to his apartment.

A few months after all this started, Sarah calmly announced one day she wanted to split up. I moved in with a coworker from the software company, Dave. Cocaine started looming large. I was probably only into it for about six months. I will never forget the day I quit cocaine at age twenty-two. Me, Dave, and Chris had been up all night doing an eight-ball of coke and drinking screwdrivers. I lay down to sleep, but my heart was pounding out of my chest. Suddenly I leaned over and just vomited profusely. Then I started pulling a rope of snot out of my nose. It was like an umbilical cord with blood entwined in it; it felt like I was pulling my brains out. So I said "That's it, we've got to quit this shit."

Somehow I saved enough money for a plane ticket to Africa. I wound up spending six months there traveling overland alone, and it was the most empowering time of my life. I went through Zaire, Uganda, Rwanda, and Zambia. I finally had to leave; I left Nairobi with eight dollars in my pocket.

It was a letdown to return—nothing had changed, all anyone wanted to do was buy a BMW, snort cocaine, listen to Dead records, and be trendy. None of the great lifestyles I'd envisioned for myself while sitting by the side of a dirt road in Africa materialized. I think this is when I started drinking destructively, at age twenty-four. I was still high on the self-esteem I'd gained, so I was going full-on ahead barreling through life just steam-rolling over anyone in my path. This is when I started drinking daily, mostly beer or cheap rosé wine. I would go weeks on nothing but booze, partying till three in the morning, making it home to pass out and get up at five to go to work.

I got pulled over a few times for drunk driving but never actually got arrested. I'd drink a beer on my lunch hour, and I always stopped after work to get beer, and would drive with one between my legs. It still seemed cool because nothing bad (that I noticed) was ever happening, and everyone else was doing it. I never blacked out or fell down or did anything stupid. In retrospect I know you can take a lot more in your twenties.

When I met my first wife, I noticed on our first date she was doing cocaine in the nightclub bathroom. I told her my stance on coke, and she swore up and down she "used to do a lot of it, and was just getting out of it." By that time I was hopelessly in love, and more importantly I was loved. I moved in with her, and we were flying high. We were the perfect trendy yuppie couple. Her father was a record company exec so we got free backstage passes to everything. I mostly overlooked her cocaine use because it didn't seem to be having a negative effect—except on certain occasions. I also learned to love red wine at her family's Italian get-togethers, and I drank every night. Maybe not enough to get drunk every night, but I drank.

So I was getting drunk about once a week. Something would start off an argument and soon I'd be raging with anger. I'd scream abusive things at five o'clock in the morning. I always felt embarrassed to see our neighbors, knowing they'd heard all this yelling. This is where, when I looked back later, I was repeating the example my mother had set with her rageaholism.

After five years, I walked out. There followed a huge drinking spree. I was fired a week after moving into a rental, for having an affair with a coworker. For the first time ever, I could not find a job. I was hanging with ex-girlfriend Sarah and another woman. That's where I developed the drinking in the morning thing. I got a DUI in 1992 when I crashed into a stalled car and broke my nose. My brother (who saw fit to invite my mother) came to pick me up at the jail, and I got the huge lecture. Talk about "hitting bottom." Now I had to go to work with a cast on my nose and have plastic surgery.

Around the time of the plastic surgery, I started dating a coworker. For the first time in my life I felt truly loved. I felt accepted the way I was. Donna would never utter one critical word. Yet I just kept drinking destructively. Why? *I saw no reason not to.* Booze was starting to also have a heavier effect on me, probably due to the simple fact of getting older. Donna would go to bed at ten o'clock on the dot no matter what day of the week it was, and I'd stay up later drinking, way later drinking lots if it was the weekend.

There were no more DUIs because I adhered strictly to the one-drink legal limit if out with friends, but I had Donna to drive all other places, so I saw nothing standing in the way of gulping a few mugs of wine before going on an outing with her. Still, she said nothing. Around 1996 my two brothers had a mini-intervention with me after a scene I caused at one of their houses. I decided that so-called "moderation" was the watchword for me. I started buying cases of Calistoga and from Sunday to Thursday nights I was moderate. Problem was, I continued to be out of control on the weekends. That was the scene that was set in 1997 when the shit hit the fan.

Best friend Chris let me know that my brother had arranged an intervention which also included my mother and father and coworker/boss, and it was only through Chris telling them interventions are only for teens or people otherwise dependent on someone and they do *not* work, that the idea died a happy death. He told them, "Usually the person winds up rebelling and hating you." Well, that's what happened. I still don't talk to my brothers, and I rebelled by drinking even more. I was fired for "poor attendance" and didn't argue. Then I got a good long-term temp job and a couple days later I "happened" to be wandering in the bookstore in the self-help or addiction section. I grabbed *Moderate Drinking*. It was May 1999.

I was ready. I think I just had to gross myself out to come to that point. I've always been one to tell myself what to do—it doesn't work if it's someone else telling me what to do. I will never forget the part where she talks about going thirty days without drinking. "When you first read this, most of you will feel some sort of anxiety about this idea." I laughed to myself and said yeah, I do feel some anxiety, but it didn't stop me for half a second from plunging right into the program.

The first thirty days was hard work and extremely empowering. Another of the first things that grabbed me in the book was the concept that you are not powerless over alcohol. I'd always felt that in my bones, but I never even formulated it into an idea with words in my head. I just knew I'd never been able to even make it to Step One of AA because I refused to admit I was powerless! I thought I was the only person on the planet who saw the basic flaw in this line of thinking. To read it in the MM book was a revelation.

The first thirty days I planned out every moment of my days in fifteen-minute intervals. Yes, it was weird at first, but only because it was a *habit* of more than twelve years of daily drinking. As the book says, if you've spent a decade putting your left shoe on first, it'll seem weird putting your right shoe on first . . . until the new habit is ingrained in you. I followed the program rigorously with a few slips here and there. The main thing I can say is that every day that I stick with MM it gets easier and easier. That was a huge revelation. Every abstinence day, abstinence week, and currently abstinence month are more spontaneous and require less planning or thought.

Donna's relationship with her adult daughter is my #1 button. Whenever the daughter comes up with more financial demands I get irritated, and of course I'm not informed about anything remotely to do with her. I learned a huge lesson in making life more serene in general. "The definition of insanity is doing the same thing over and over, and expecting different results." I realized I kept "going there" with my anger about the daughter and the answer was always the same: "She's my daughter and I'm gonna do what I want and it's none of your business!!" I had to unlearn my mother's teaching that every single irritant needs to be vented at the top of your lungs. I learned that it's ten times easier to let things go when you're sober. When in drinking mode, which is what I call anything more than moderate drinking, I seem to be ten times more liable to "go there" about issues that I don't have control over, and it always escalates into a huge screamfest. Sober (or moderate) I am much more likely to walk away or even laugh at it.

In the past, I could never envision going on a day trip with Donna without first having a couple of mugs of wine. Since MM, the mug is out the window. I used to keep the bottle on the piano behind me in my office—now the bottle, when there is one, stays in the fridge! I haven't bought one of those huge bottles of wine I used to exist on in the one and a half years I've been in MM. The wine is better quality so I suppose I'm not saving much financially but I am also learning more about appreciating wine and how to be a "wine snob." Before it would be like "Well, that's one step up from Thunderbird." Now I look at labels and make notes because after all, isn't that why we choose to continue drinking moderately? The good things about drinking we didn't feel it was necessary to give up? About a year ago I actually sent back a glass of wine in a restaurant!

I still have slips where I go over the limit, as zillions of dieters do (I like the food analogy! It's very similar) but they're fewer and farther between. You don't become a perfect moderator overnight. As even AA (I do believe in a lot of what that program espouses) says, "Progress, not perfection." I even say, "MM works if you work it." Since we know we are powerful over alcohol and it's not someone else or an outside force moving our hand to the bottle and uncorking it, that makes it all the easier for me to say, "Nah, I don't really feel like drinking at all tonight." The stress level in my life is at an all-time high right now but I've gone weeks abstinent or extremely moderate.

And conversely, my life is so much easier to handle, especially in stressful times, if I abstain or moderate. In drinking mode everything seems like a crisis. I would get anxiety attacks, freak out to my friends about what a nightmare my life was, and have a destructive fight with Donna. Then of course show up to work (if I was lucky) all trashed and feeling like shit, do a crappy job, get in trouble. MM may not have saved my marriage; if we divorce it was obviously unsalvageable, but it has saved me. I feel so much better physically and mentally, and thus prepared to tackle new things. I was one of those people who needed to "mature out of" destructive drinking.

We become moderate drinkers for ourselves. That is the best way any change is effected for good, if you do it for yourself. At least, if you're a rebel like me and don't like being told what to do.

Gretchen

I'm Gretchen. I'm forty-two, and I work as an instructor at a nature preserve.

Writing this wasn't as easy as I thought it would be, for talking about my past is bringing back to life a part of me that has long been buried—a part of me that I'd prefer not to revive. But if it is useful to someone else to read about it, then I guess it's worth it.

My "happy kid" days ended when I was about six and a half. My mother and I had been living with my grandparents up until that time. I thought it was a normal progression to go from outgoing and fun-loving to sad and frightened. It wasn't until years later when I looked back and wondered how I had become a sad, depressed person that I narrowed it down to pre- and post-trial. That was when my mother remarried and I fell in love with my new stepfather. The price I paid for the love of this stepfather was my innocence.

When my mother realized he was a pedophile, she had him arrested. Unfortunately I was the one put on trial. As in so many sexual assault situations, the victim became the accused. I was required to sit in a witness stand in a courtroom full of men, prosecutors, defense lawyers, and a curious public. I was required to describe the kind of underwear I wore and what we called our private parts. I still cringe with shame when recounting this. I was told later that there were two trials. One was declared a mistrial and the pedophile was acquitted after the second. That year pretty much marked the end of my joyful days. I knew way too much. I never put it together until later in counseling that I had been carrying the guilt and shame and feelings of worthlessness, a burden far too huge for a child to carry all of those years.

After my mother's disastrous second marriage, we moved back in with my grandparents and no one ever said one word to me about the whole series of events. I was sent to catechism classes and prepared for my First Holy Communion and wondered whether I had to confess my "sins" committed with stepfather.

My first taste of alcohol was from my grandfather's beer as he sat at the kitchen table after work. On a hot day, it was cool and bitter yet something I liked to taste. Family gatherings at my grandmother's house were always loud drunken parties, except for my grandparents. She didn't drink and my grandfather drank one or two beers a day. For some reason all of my aunts—there were five—drank heavily or if they didn't, their boyfriends or husbands did. It seemed as though there was always some catastrophe: a fight, or argument during the party, or a car crash after the party. This was how I saw family social interaction.

I discovered the soothing qualities of getting drunk when I was about twelve or thirteen. I tried to get drunk on something I found in my grandmother's kitchen pantry but couldn't swallow it. My friend and I had heard you could get drunk on aspirin and Coca-Cola but all it did was make us sick and very wired. My uncle showed me how to smoke marijuana. I remember on Christmas Eve coming back from smoking it and falling backwards into the pile of gifts under the Christmas tree. No one seemed to notice—probably because they were all getting drunk. Drinking was liberation to me. It was the only time I could talk. But then it turned on me too.

By the time I was fifteen, I was pregnant and married to an older man—he was seventeen. At age eighteen, I was the mother of three. (I still considered myself a Catholic and so was committed to marriage for life.) The foundation of this marriage was built on alcohol and drugs. I would try anything then—marijuana, red devils, bennies—but my favorite was plain old alcohol. This "marriage" lasted until I was twenty-one.

My plunge into the real world was life on welfare, in a very scary housing project where people got jumped taking their trash out to the bins. I celebrated my newfound freedom by getting drunk almost every night with my roommate and sometimes driving around with my kids asleep in the back of my beat up '57 Chevy station wagon. Unlike me, my roommate was very outgoing and made friends easily. She considered me her sister and my kids her nieces and nephew. We helped each other in some ways but harmed in other ways. She too had demons and sometimes when she got drunk she'd go off the deep end and try to kill herself. One day she finally succeeded. She was my best friend.

I am thankful that my kids have no memory of much of this. Of course, I shudder now to think of how many times I put their lives at risk. One of the gods must have felt sorry for me in my ignorance and pain and let us live through this horrible time.

What transformed me? A hit-and-run car crash that could have sent me to jail, at the age of twenty-two, for three years. We hit and ran because we were all drunk and didn't want to get in trouble for drunk driving! Luckily, no one was injured, although my car was totaled. I was given three years of probation. This for me was hitting bottom as they say in AA. I went to night school and finished high school. My children survived having me as their mother, and we all trundled along going to school and living a single-parent-family lifestyle. My youngest daughter and I graduated from the same college the same year.

Eventually I met and married a fine, responsible man who—though he liked to drink—didn't do so out of control. We built a life together, and started our own business, which we had for several years. When we closed that business, I went to work as an educator at a nature preserve where I still work sharing my passion for the natural world with schoolchildren. This has worked as a wonderful symbiotic relationship, for in a way I can recapture the years I missed with my children—I am mature enough now to enjoy their unique preciousness—while I give them a wonderful gift as well. And for some reason I have become an animal rescuer of sorts, bringing home strays and the unwanted creatures that cross my path. I guess I have always identified with their innocent helplessness. At the moment, we are home to six rabbits, seven cats, and five turtles of various species.

I have never sunk back to the drinking levels of those earlier years but there has always been the deep knowledge or perhaps just fear that I could again—that alcohol could take over my life if I didn't keep my awareness up. Knowing this about myself, yet unable to relate to what I saw and heard in the few AA meetings I had explored, I was very interested when I read an article in the paper about Moderation Management. Finally, a different view than the black-and-white dogma of AA was being voiced.

I found the MM group online and began lurking and eventually participating. I was and continue to be fascinated by the stories shared in this forum. The amazing thing is that we all share a common bond even though we come from very diverse backgrounds. All of us want to put alcohol in its proper place in our lives and don't want it to be a controlling element. We want to be able to have a glass of wine with dinner now and then, drink a champagne toast at our kid's wedding—just a normal, healthy relationship with alcohol.

Following the MM guidelines I have found that I can get through and actually enjoy social settings with little or no alcohol being consumed. It has been a small transformation in some ways. I don't think of myself as having a drinking problem and I can't recall the last time I've abused alcohol.

I do have a few rules that I can follow that really seem to help. I don't start drinking past a certain hour, so if I am out at a class or movie or whatever, when I get home I am done for the day. I never drink on an empty stomach. I pace myself. Sip. I keep track. Drink water. Listen to your body. Are you tired? Hungry? Thirsty? Take care of those things first. Be nice to yourself. (I know this sounds corny but this is important to those of us who grew up not feeling very nice about ourselves.)

I think it is about setting up a reward system for yourself (especially at first). When I have things to look forward to that I have set out for myself, the chores and tasks of life don't seem so enormous. For me, replacing the "happy hour" times (those made fake happy with alcohol) with other activities that involve people is key. For me it was finding a few things that filled the evenings (because that's when I drink). I have recently rediscovered my love of dance and am taking some jazzercise classes (kind of dancy). Now I am looking for a line dance . . . it's movement, it's music, it's people, it's fun, and it's an alcohol-free environment. I joined a city college jazz choir (translation: they'll take anybody!) a few years ago and that night is a guaranteed abstain. I would be too embarrassed to be hollering—I mean singing—with beer breath to my classmates. When I get home, it's too late to start drinking. Okay, that's one day of abstinence.

And so on. . . .

Think substitution, not restriction. Somehow make it a game. Charts are good. Points are good, whatever. Measuring is good. Positive thinking: I choose to have this or that tonight. I choose to avoid the heavy drinkers tonight. I choose to wake up tomorrow hangover free. (Actually that is one of my main motivators . . . I just hate hate hate that feeling of a hangover and really want to have the other feeling of waking up relatively clearheaded and knowing that if things don't feel so hot it's just because things don't feel so hot and not because of some self-induced poisoning.)

Which reminds me: another way to look at it is similar to medicine. Almost all of it can be toxic or even lethal if taken in excess. If you want, think of alcohol as a very potent medicine. Just as you take aspirin to relieve a headache, you don't take the whole bottle. Keep alcohol at the medicinal level. That's why I like Sapphire gin, because it has so many botanicals in it. You only need a small amount for the "cure."

Make drinking a very elegant ritual. Pour it just right into a just-right piece of stemware or glass. Sip and savor. Have dinner cooking or ready to eat so that after your selected number of drinks, you must treat yourself to the meal. If you like wine, have one with your pre-dinner snack (remember we're supposed to eat while drinking—no empty stomach) and the second with dinner. Then take a walk. Or, read some really horrible medical articles about the effects of alcohol on the brain and liver. Sometimes that helps me, though other times it just sends me into denial.

Don't beat yourself up. Make a tally sometime and see how many times you say something good about yourself in a day. It can be very eye-opening. If you're like me, it is a joke and everything is a problem that I've created. Instead of it's just the tire is flat, I'm an idiot for driving over a nail. It is everywhere . . . can you see it? Once you see it, you can change it. It's amazing—it's like magic. Just shift your viewpoint two inches that way. . . .

These are just some of the tricks I use. I am sure you have ones up your sleeve that you might try. You know yourself better than anyone else. Any ideas? What do you like?

I am grateful that I found MM. And if for some reason, someday in the future I decide that no alcohol shall ever pass my lips again, then that will be okay too. I know that MM will be helpful to me in making and keeping that decision as well.

Appendix 1

Blood Alcohol Concentration (BAC) Tables

To use these tables to estimate your blood alcohol concentration, first find the correct chart for your sex and weight. Then look down the Number of Drinks column and across the Number of Hours row to find your BAC. The tables cover ranges of drinks from one to twelve, consumed over one to eight hours. Weight ranges covered for females are 100 to 220 pounds, and for males 120 to 280 pounds.

A BAC of .055 percent is a sensible limit or maximum for moderate drinking. In these tables, the shaded areas indicate BACs that are over the moderate limit of .055 percent.

A Standard Drink, on which these tables are based, contains .6 ounces of pure alcohol, and equals:

One 12-oz beer, 5 percent alcohol

or

One 5-oz glass wine, 12 percent alcohol

or

One 1½ oz shot 80 proof liquor, 40 percent alcohol

The BAC percentages shown in these tables can help you *estimate* your blood alcohol level, based on the number of drinks you have over a given length of time. Though useful information, the figures provided are only estimates, because blood alcohol levels are influenced by several other factors that are difficult to account for in a chart. Your age, how much food you've eaten, your metabolism, physical condition, percentage of body fat, and a woman's phase in her hormonal cycle, can all affect your BAC.

As people get older, their percentage of body fat usually increases, which means the percentage of body weight in water available to dilute the alcohol decreases. On average, a fifty-five-year-old will reach BACs that are 20 percent *higher* than those shown on the charts.

In the interest of providing full information, these tables show all of the BACs that would be reached based on one to twelve drinks over one to eight hours. The moderate drinking limit is .055 percent. Most people become extremely intoxicated at .200 percent and become unconscious at .300 percent. BACs from .450 percent to .500 percent are usually fatal.

100-pound Female

Number of Drinks	*Number of Hours* 1	2	3	4	5	6	7	8
1	.036	.020	.004	0	0	0	0	0
2	.088	.072	.056	.040	.024	.008	0	0
3	.140	.124	.108	.092	.076	.060	.044	.028
4	.192	.176	.160	.144	.128	.112	.096	.080
5	.244	.228	.212	.196	.180	.164	.148	.132
6	.295	.279	.263	.247	.231	.215	.199	.183
7	.347	.331	.315	.299	.283	.267	.251	.235
8	.399	.383	.367	.351	.335	.319	.303	.287
9	.451	.435	.419	.403	.387	.371	.355	.339
10	.503	.487	471	.455	.439	.423	.407	.391
11	.555	.539	.523	.507	.491	.475	.459	.443
12	.607	.591	.575	.559	.543	.527	.511	.495

110-pound Female

Number of Drinks	*Number of Hours* 1	2	3	4	5	6	7	8
1	.031	.015	0	0	0	0	0	0
2	.078	.062	.046	.030	.014	0	0	0
3	.126	.110	.094	.078	.062	.046	.030	.014
4	.173	.157	.141	.125	.109	.093	.077	.061
5	.220	.204	.188	.172	.156	.140	.124	.108
6	.267	.251	.235	.219	.203	.187	.171	.155
7	.314	.298	.282	.266	.250	.234	.218	.202
8	.361	.345	.329	.313	.297	.281	.265	.249
9	.409	.393	.377	.361	.345	.329	.313	.297
10	.456	.440	.424	.408	.392	.376	.360	.344
11	.503	.487	.471	.455	.439	.423	.407	.391
12	.550	.534	.518	.502	.486	.470	.454	.438

120-pound Female

Number of Drinks	Number of Hours 1	2	3	4	5	6	7	8
1	.027	.011	0	0	0	0	0	0
2	.071	.055	.039	.023	.007	0	0	0
3	.114	.098	.082	.066	.050	.034	.018	.002
4	.157	.141	.125	.109	.093	.077	.061	.045
5	.200	.184	.168	.152	.136	.120	.104	.088
6	.244	.228	.212	.196	.180	.164	.148	.132
7	.287	.271	.255	.239	.223	.207	.191	.175
8	.330	.314	.298	.282	.266	.250	.234	.218
9	.373	.357	.341	.325	.309	.293	.277	.261
10	.417	.401	.385	.369	.353	.337	.321	.305
11	.460	.444	.428	.412	.396	.380	.364	.348
12	.503	.487	.471	.455	.439	.423	.407	.391

130-pound Female

Number of Drinks	Number of Hours 1	2	3	4	5	6	7	8
1	.024	.008	0	0	0	0	0	0
2	.064	.048	.032	.016	0	0	0	0
3	.104	.088	.072	.056	.040	.024	.008	0
4	.144	.128	.112	.096	.080	.064	.048	.032
5	.184	.168	.152	.136	.120	.104	.088	.072
6	.224	.208	.192	.176	.160	.144	.128	.112
7	.263	.247	.231	.215	.199	.183	.167	.151
8	.303	.287	.271	.255	.239	.223	.207	.191
9	.343	.327	.311	.295	.279	.263	.247	.231
10	.383	.367	.351	.335	.319	.303	.287	.271
11	.423	.407	.391	.375	.359	.343	.327	.311
12	.463	.447	.431	.415	.399	.383	.367	.351

140-pound Female

Number of Drinks	Number of Hours 1	2	3	4	5	6	7	8
1	.021	.005	0	0	0	0	0	0
2	.058	.042	.026	.010	0	0	0	0
3	.095	.079	.063	.047	.031	.015	0	0
4	.132	.116	.100	.084	.068	.052	.036	.020
5	.169	.153	.137	.121	.105	.089	.073	.057
6	.206	.190	.174	.158	.142	.126	.110	.094

7	.244	.228	.212	.196	.180	.164	.148	.132
8	.281	.265	.249	.233	.217	.201	.185	.169
9	.318	.302	.286	.270	.254	.238	.222	.206
10	.355	.339	.323	.307	.291	.275	.259	.243
11	.392	.376	.360	.344	.328	.312	.296	.280
12	.429	.413	.397	.381	.365	.349	.333	.317

150-pound Female

Number of Drinks	*Number of Hours* 1	2	3	4	5	6	7	8
1	.019	.003	0	0	0	0	0	0
2	.053	.037	.021	.005	0	0	0	0
3	.088	.072	.056	.040	.024	.008	0	0
4	.122	.106	.090	.074	.058	.042	.026	.010
5	.157	.141	.125	.109	.093	.077	.061	.045
6	.192	.176	.160	.144	.128	.112	.096	.080
7	.226	.210	.194	.178	.162	.146	.130	.114
8	.261	.245	.229	.213	.197	.181	.165	.149
9	.295	.279	.263	.247	.231	.215	.199	.183
10	.330	.314	.298	.282	.266	.250	.234	.218
11	.365	.349	.333	.317	.301	.285	.269	.253
12	.399	.383	.367	.351	.335	.319	.303	.287

160-pound Female

Number of Drinks	*Number of Hours* 1	2	3	4	5	6	7	8
1	.016	0	0	0	0	0	0	0
2	.049	.033	.017	.001	0	0	0	0
3	.081	.065	.049	.033	.017	.001	0	0
4	.114	.098	.082	.066	.050	.034	.018	.002
5	.146	.130	.114	.098	.082	.066	.050	.034
6	.179	.163	.147	.131	.115	.099	.083	.067
7	.211	.195	.179	.163	.147	.131	.115	.099
8	.244	.228	.212	.196	.180	.164	.148	.132
9	.276	.260	.244	.228	.212	.196	.180	.164
10	.308	.292	.276	.260	.244	.228	.212	.196
11	.341	.325	.309	.293	.277	.261	.245	.229
12	.373	.357	.341	.325	.309	.293	.277	.261

170-pound Female

Number of Drinks	*Number of Hours* 1	2	3	4	5	6	7	8
1	.015	0	0	0	0	0	0	0
2	.045	.029	.013	0	0	0	0	0
3	.076	.060	.044	.028	.012	0	0	0
4	.106	.090	.074	.058	.042	.026	.010	0
5	.137	.121	.105	.089	.073	.057	.041	.025
6	.167	.151	.135	.119	.103	.087	.071	.055
7	.198	.182	.166	.150	.134	.118	.102	.086
8	.228	.212	.196	.180	.164	.148	.132	.116
9	.259	.243	.227	.211	.195	.179	.163	.147
10	.289	.273	.257	.241	.225	.209	.193	.177
11	.320	.304	.288	.272	.256	.240	.224	.208
12	.350	.334	.318	.302	.286	.270	.254	.238

180-pound Female

Number of Drinks	*Number of Hours* 1	2	3	4	5	6	7	8
1	.013	0	0	0	0	0	0	0
2	.042	.026	.010	0	0	0	0	0
3	.071	.055	.039	.023	.007	0	0	0
4	.099	.083	.067	.051	.035	.019	.003	0
5	.128	.112	.096	.080	.064	.048	.032	.016
6	.157	.141	.125	.109	.093	.077	.061	.045
7	.186	.170	.154	.138	.122	.106	.090	.074
8	.215	.199	.183	.167	.151	.135	.119	.103
9	.244	.228	.212	.196	.180	.164	.148	.132
10	.272	.256	.240	.224	.208	.192	.176	.160
11	.301	.285	.269	.253	.237	.221	.205	.189
12	.330	.314	.298	.282	.266	.250	.234	.218

190-pound Female

Number of Drinks	*Number of Hours* 1	2	3	4	5	6	7	8
1	.011	0	0	0	0	0	0	0
2	.039	.023	.007	0	0	0	0	0
3	.066	.050	.034	.018	.002	0	0	0
4	.093	.077	.061	.045	.029	.013	0	0
5	.121	.105	.089	.073	.057	.041	.025	.009
6	.148	.132	.116	.100	.084	.068	.052	.036
7	.175	.159	.143	.127	.111	.095	.079	.063

8	.203	.187	.171	.155	.139	.123	.107	.091
9	.230	.214	.198	.182	.166	.150	.134	.118
10	.257	.241	.225	.209	.193	.177	.161	.145
11	.284	.268	.252	.236	.220	.204	.188	.172
12	.312	.296	.280	.264	.248	.232	.216	.200

200-pound Female

Number of Drinks	*Number of Hours* 1	2	3	4	5	6	7	8
1	.010	0	0	0	0	0	0	0
2	.036	.020	.004	0	0	0	0	0
3	.062	.046	.030	.014	0	0	0	0
4	.088	.072	.056	.040	.024	.008	0	0
5	.114	.098	.082	.066	.050	.034	.018	.002
6	.140	.124	.108	.092	.076	.060	.044	.028
7	.166	.150	.134	.118	.102	.086	.070	.054
8	.192	.176	.160	.144	.128	.112	.096	.080
9	.218	.202	.186	.170	.154	.138	.122	.106
10	.244	.228	.212	.196	.180	.164	.148	.132
11	.269	.253	.237	.221	.205	.189	.173	.157
12	.295	.279	.263	.247	.231	.215	.199	.183

210-pound Female

Number of Drinks	*Number of Hours* 1	2	3	4	5	6	7	8
1	.009	0	0	0	0	0	0	0
2	.033	.017	.001	0	0	0	0	0
3	.058	.042	.026	.010	0	0	0	0
4	.083	.067	.051	.035	.019	.003	0	0
5	.108	.092	.076	.060	.044	.028	.012	0
6	.132	.116	.100	.084	.068	.052	.036	.020
7	.157	.141	.125	.109	.093	.077	.061	.045
8	.182	.166	.150	.134	.118	.102	.086	.070
9	.206	.190	.174	.158	.142	.126	.110	.094
10	.231	.215	.199	.183	.167	.151	.135	.119
11	.256	.240	.224	.208	.192	.176	.160	.144
12	.281	.265	.249	.233	.217	.201	.185	.169

220-pound Female

Number of Drinks	*Number of Hours* 1	2	3	4	5	6	7	8
1	.008	0	0	0	0	0	0	0
2	.031	.015	0	0	0	0	0	0
3	.055	.039	.023	.007	0	0	0	0
4	.078	.062	.046	.030	.014	0	0	0
5	.102	.086	.070	.054	.038	.022	.006	0
6	.126	.110	.094	.078	.062	.046	.030	.014
7	.149	.133	.117	.101	.085	.069	.053	.037
8	.173	.157	.141	.125	.109	.093	.077	.061
9	.196	.180	.164	.148	.132	.116	.100	.084
10	.220	.204	.188	.172	.156	.140	.124	.108
11	.244	.228	.212	.196	.180	.164	.148	.132
12	.267	.251	.235	.219	.203	.187	.171	.155

120-pound Male

Number of Drinks	*Number of Hours* 1	2	3	4	5	6	7	8
1	.020	.004	0	0	0	0	0	0
2	.056	.040	.024	.008	0	0	0	0
3	.092	.076	.060	.044	.028	.012	0	0
4	.128	.112	.096	.080	.064	.048	.032	.016
5	.164	.148	.132	.116	.100	.084	.068	.052
6	.200	.184	.168	.152	.136	.120	.104	.088
7	.236	.220	.204	.188	.172	.156	.140	.124
8	.272	.256	.240	.224	.208	.192	.176	.160
9	.308	.292	.276	.260	.244	.228	.212	.196
10	.344	.328	.312	.296	.280	.264	.248	.232
11	.380	.364	.348	.332	.316	.300	.284	.268
12	.417	.401	.385	.369	.353	.337	.321	.305

130-pound Male

Number of Drinks	*Number of Hours* 1	2	3	4	5	6	7	8
1	.017	.001	0	0	0	0	0	0
2	.051	.035	.019	.003	0	0	0	0
3	.084	.068	.052	.036	.020	.004	0	0
4	.117	.101	.085	.069	.053	.037	.021	.005
5	.150	.134	.118	.102	.086	.070	.054	.038
6	.184	.168	.152	.136	.120	.104	.088	.072
7	.217	.201	.185	.169	.153	.137	.121	.105

8	.250	.234	.218	.202	.186	.170	.154	.138
9	.283	.267	.251	.235	.219	.203	.187	.171
10	.317	.301	.285	.269	.253	.237	.221	.205
11	.350	.334	.318	.302	.286	.270	.254	.238
12	.383	.367	.351	.335	.319	.303	.287	.271

140-pound Male

Number of Drinks	*Number of Hours* 1	2	3	4	5	6	7	8
1	.015	0	0	0	0	0	0	0
2	.046	.030	.014	0	0	0	0	0
3	.077	.061	.045	.029	.013	0	0	0
4	.108	.092	.076	.060	.044	.028	.012	0
5	.138	.122	.106	.090	.074	.058	.042	.026
6	.169	.153	.137	.121	.105	.089	.073	.057
7	.200	.184	.168	.152	.136	.120	.104	.088
8	.231	.215	.199	.183	.167	.151	.135	.119
9	.262	.246	.230	.214	.198	.182	.166	.150
10	.293	.277	.261	.245	.229	.213	.197	.181
11	.324	.308	.292	.276	.260	.244	.228	.212
12	.355	.339	.323	.307	.291	.275	.259	.243

150-pound Male

Number of Drinks	*Number of Hours* 1	2	3	4	5	6	7	8
1	.013	0	0	0	0	0	0	0
2	.042	.026	.010	0	0	0	0	0
3	.071	.055	.039	.023	.007	0	0	0
4	.099	.083	.067	.051	.035	.019	.003	0
5	.128	.112	.096	.080	.064	.048	.032	.016
6	.157	.141	.125	.109	.093	.077	.061	.045
7	.186	.170	.154	.138	.122	.106	.090	.074
8	.215	.199	.183	.167	.151	.135	.119	.103
9	.244	.228	.212	.196	.180	.164	.148	.132
10	.272	.256	.240	.224	.208	.192	.176	.160
11	.301	.285	.269	.253	.237	.221	.205	.189
12	.330	.314	.298	.282	.266	.250	.234	.218

160-pound Male

Number of Drinks	*Number of Hours* 1	2	3	4	5	6	7	8
1	.011	0	0	0	0	0	0	0
2	.038	.022	.006	0	0	0	0	0
3	.065	.049	.033	.017	.001	0	0	0
4	.092	.076	.060	.044	.028	.012	0	0
5	.119	.103	.087	.071	.055	.039	.023	.007
6	.146	.130	.114	.098	.082	.066	.050	.034
7	.173	.157	.141	.125	.109	.093	.077	.061
8	.200	.184	.168	.152	.136	.120	.104	.088
9	.227	.211	.195	.179	.163	.147	.131	.118
10	.254	.268	.222	.206	.190	.174	.158	.142
11	.281	.265	.249	.233	.217	.201	.185	.169
12	.308	.292	.276	.260	.244	.228	.212	.196

170-pound Male

Number of Drinks	*Number of Hours* 1	2	3	4	5	6	7	8
1	.009	0	0	0	0	0	0	0
2	.035	.019	.003	0	0	0	0	0
3	.060	.044	.028	.012	0	0	0	0
4	.086	.070	.054	.038	.022	.006	0	0
5	.111	.095	.079	.063	.047	.031	.015	0
6	.137	.121	.105	.089	.073	.057	.041	.025
7	.162	.146	.130	.114	.098	.082	.066	.050
8	.188	.172	.156	.140	.124	.108	.092	.076
9	.213	.197	.181	.165	.149	.133	.117	.101
10	.238	.222	.206	.190	.174	.158	.142	.126
11	.264	.248	.232	.216	.200	.184	.168	.152
12	.289	.273	.257	.241	.225	.209	.193	.177

180-pound Male

Number of Drinks	*Number of Hours* 1	2	3	4	5	6	7	8
1	.008	0	0	0	0	0	0	0
2	.032	.016	0	0	0	0	0	0
3	.056	.040	.024	.008	0	0	0	0
4	.080	.064	.048	.032	.016	0	0	0
5	.104	.088	.072	.056	.040	.024	.008	0
6	.128	.112	.096	.080	.064	.048	.032	.016
7	.152	.136	.120	.104	.088	.072	.056	.040

8	.176	.160	.144	.128	.112	.096	.080	.064
9	.200	.184	.168	.152	.136	.120	.104	.088
10	.224	.208	.192	.176	.160	.144	.128	.112
11	.248	.232	.216	.200	.184	.168	.152	.136
12	.272	.256	.240	.224	.208	.192	.176	.160

190-pound Male

Number of Drinks	*Number of Hours* 1	2	3	4	5	6	7	8
1	.007	0	0	0	0	0	0	0
2	.030	.014	0	0	0	0	0	0
3	.052	.036	.020	.004	0	0	0	0
4	.075	.059	.043	.027	.011	0	0	0
5	.098	.082	.066	.050	.034	.018	.002	0
6	.121	.105	.089	.073	.057	.041	.025	.009
7	.143	.127	.111	.095	.079	.063	.047	.031
8	.166	.150	.134	.118	.102	.086	.070	.054
9	.189	.173	.157	.141	.125	.109	.093	.077
10	.212	.196	.180	.164	.148	.132	.116	.100
11	.234	.218	.202	.186	.170	.154	.128	.122
12	.257	.241	.225	.209	.193	.177	.161	.145

200-pound Male

Number of Drinks	*Number of Hours* 1	2	3	4	5	6	7	8
1	.006	0	0	0	0	0	0	0
2	.027	.011	0	0	0	0	0	0
3	.049	.033	.017	.001	0	0	0	0
4	.071	.055	.039	.023	.007	0	0	0
5	.092	.076	.060	.044	.028	.012	0	0
6	.114	.098	.082	.066	.050	.034	.018	.002
7	.135	.119	.103	.087	.071	.055	.039	.023
8	.157	.141	.125	.109	.093	.077	.061	.045
9	.179	.163	.147	.131	.115	.099	.083	.067
10	.200	.184	.168	.152	.136	.120	.104	.088
11	.222	.206	.190	.174	.158	.142	.126	.110
12	.244	.228	.212	.196	.180	.164	.148	.132

210-pound Male

Number of Drinks	*Number of Hours* 1	2	3	4	5	6	7	8
1	.005	0	0	0	0	0	0	0
2	.025	.009	0	0	0	0	0	0
3	.046	.030	.014	0	0	0	0	0
4	.066	.050	.034	.018	.002	0	0	0
5	.087	.071	.055	.039	.023	.007	0	0
6	.108	.092	.076	.060	.044	.028	.012	0
7	.128	.112	.096	.080	.064	.048	.032	.016
8	.149	.133	.117	.101	.085	.069	.053	.037
9	.169	.153	.137	.121	.105	.089	.073	.057
10	.190	.174	.158	.142	.126	.110	.094	.078
11	.211	.195	.179	.163	.147	.131	.115	.099
12	.231	.215	.199	.183	.167	.151	.135	.119

220-pound Male

Number of Drinks	*Number of Hours* 1	2	3	4	5	6	7	8
1	.004	0	0	0	0	0	0	0
2	.023	.007	0	0	0	0	0	0
3	.043	.027	.011	0	0	0	0	0
4	.063	.047	.031	.015	0	0	0	0
5	.082	.066	.050	.034	.018	.002	0	0
6	.102	.086	.070	.054	.038	.022	.006	0
7	.122	.106	.090	.074	.058	.042	.026	.010
8	.141	.125	.109	.093	.077	.061	.045	.029
9	.161	.145	.129	.113	.097	.081	.065	.049
10	.181	.165	.149	.133	.117	.101	.085	.069
11	.200	.184	.168	.152	.136	.120	.104	.088
12	.220	.204	.188	.172	.156	.140	.124	.108

230-pound Male

Number of Drinks	*Number of Hours* 1	2	3	4	5	6	7	8
1	.003	0	0	0	0	0	0	0
2	.022	.006	0	0	0	0	0	0
3	.040	.024	.008	0	0	0	0	0
4	.059	.043	.027	.011	0	0	0	0
5	.078	.062	.046	.030	.014	0	0	0
6	.097	.081	.065	.049	.033	.017	.001	0
7	.116	.100	.084	.068	.052	.036	.020	.004

8	.134	.118	.102	.086	.070	.054	.038	.022
9	.153	.137	.121	.105	.089	.073	.057	.041
10	.172	.156	.140	.124	.108	.092	.076	.060
11	.191	.175	.159	.143	.127	.111	.095	.079
12	.210	.194	.178	.162	.146	.130	.114	.098

240-pound Male

Number of Drinks	*Number of Hours* 1	2	3	4	5	6	7	8
1	.002	0	0	0	0	0	0	0
2	.020	.004	0	0	0	0	0	0
3	.038	.022	.006	0	0	0	0	0
4	.056	.040	.024	.008	0	0	0	0
5	.074	.058	.042	.026	.010	0	0	0
6	.092	.076	.060	.044	.028	.012	0	0
7	.110	.094	.078	.062	.046	.030	.014	0
8	.128	.112	.096	.080	.064	.048	.032	.016
9	.146	.130	.114	.098	.082	.066	.050	.034
10	.164	.148	.132	.116	.100	.084	.068	.052
11	.182	.166	.150	.134	.118	.102	.086	.070
12	.200	.184	.168	.152	.136	.120	.104	.088

250-pound Male

Number of Drinks	*Number of Hours* 1	2	3	4	5	6	7	8
1	.001	0	0	0	0	0	0	0
2	.019	.003	0	0	0	0	0	0
3	.036	.020	.004	0	0	0	0	0
4	.053	.037	.021	.005	0	0	0	0
5	.071	.055	.039	.023	.007	0	0	0
6	.088	.072	.056	.040	.024	.008	0	0
7	.105	.089	.073	.057	.041	.025	.009	0
8	.122	.106	.090	.074	.058	.042	.026	.010
9	.140	.124	.108	.092	.076	.060	.044	.028
10	.157	.141	.125	.109	.093	.077	.061	.045
11	.174	.158	.142	.126	.110	.094	.078	.062
12	.192	.176	.160	.144	.128	.112	.096	.080

260-pound Male

Number of Drinks	*Number of Hours* 1	2	3	4	5	6	7	8
1	.001	0	0	0	0	0	0	0
2	.017	.001	0	0	0	0	0	0
3	.034	.018	.002	0	0	0	0	0
4	.051	.035	.019	.003	0	0	0	0
5	.067	.051	.035	.019	.003	0	0	0
6	.084	.068	.052	.036	.020	.004	0	0
7	.100	.084	.068	.052	.036	.020	.004	0
8	.117	.101	.085	.069	.053	.037	.021	.005
9	.134	.118	.102	.086	.070	.054	.038	.022
10	.150	.134	.118	.102	.086	.070	.054	.038
11	.167	.151	.135	.119	.103	.087	.071	.055
12	.184	.168	.152	.136	.120	.104	.088	.072

270-pound Male

Number of Drinks	*Number of Hours* 1	2	3	4	5	6	7	8
1	0	0	0	0	0	0	0	0
2	.016	0	0	0	0	0	0	0
3	.032	.016	0	0	0	0	0	0
4	.048	.032	.016	0	0	0	0	0
5	.064	.048	.032	.016	0	0	0	0
6	.080	.064	.048	.032	.016	0	0	0
7	.096	.080	.064	.048	.032	.016	0	0
8	.112	.096	.080	.064	.048	.032	.016	0
9	.128	.112	.096	.080	.064	.048	.032	.016
10	.144	.128	.112	.096	.080	.064	.048	.032
11	.160	.144	.128	.112	.096	.080	.064	.048
12	.176	.160	.144	.128	.112	.096	.080	.064

280-pound Male

Number of Drinks	*Number of Hours* 1	2	3	4	5	6	7	8
1	0	0	0	0	0	0	0	0
2	.015	0	0	0	0	0	0	0
3	.030	.014	0	0	0	0	0	0
4	.046	.030	.014	0	0	0	0	0
5	.061	.045	.029	.013	0	0	0	0
6	.077	.061	.045	.029	.013	0	0	0
7	.092	.076	.060	.044	.028	.012	0	0
8	.108	.092	.076	.060	.044	.028	.012	0
9	.123	.107	.091	.075	.059	.043	.027	.011
10	.138	.122	.106	.090	.074	.058	.042	.026
11	.154	.138	.122	.106	.090	.074	.058	.042
12	.169	.153	.137	.121	.105	.089	.073	.057

Appendix 2

Psychological Symptom Inventory (PSI-32)

Following is a list of problems and complaints that people sometimes have. Please read each one carefully, and circle the number that best describes how much you were bothered by that problem during the past week. PLEASE CHOOSE ONLY ONE. For the past week, how much were you bothered by:

	Not at all	**A little bit**	**Moderately**	**Quite a bit**	**Extremely**
1. Nervousness or shakiness inside	0	1	2	3	4
2. Unwanted thoughts, words, or ideas that won't leave your mind	0	1	2	3	4
3. Loss of sexual interest or pleasure	0	1	2	3	4
4. Trouble remembering things	0	1	2	3	4
5. Worrying about sloppiness or carelessness	0	1	2	3	4
6. Feeling easily annoyed or irritated	0	1	2	3	4
7. Feeling low in energy or slowing down	0	1	2	3	4
8. Thoughts of ending your life	0	1	2	3	4
9. Crying easily	0	1	2	3	4
10. Feeling shy or uneasy with the opposite sex	0	1	2	3	4

11. Feelings of being trapped or caught	0	1	2	3	4
12. Suddenly feeling scared for no reason	0	1	2	3	4
13. Blaming yourself for things	0	1	2	3	4
14. Feeling blocked in getting things done	0	1	2	3	4
15. Feeling lonely	0	1	2	3	4
16. Feeling blue	0	1	2	3	4
17. Worrying too much about things	0	1	2	3	4
18. Feeling no interest in things	0	1	2	3	4
19. Feeling fearful	0	1	2	3	4
20. Having your feelings easily hurt	0	1	2	3	4
21. Feeling that others do not understand you or are unsympathetic	0	1	2	3	4
22. Feeling that people are unfriendly or are unsympathetic	0	1	2	3	4
23. Having to do things very slowly to ensure correctness	0	1	2	3	4
24. Feeling inferior to others	0	1	2	3	4
25. Having trouble falling asleep	0	1	2	3	4
26. Having to check and double-check what you do	0	1	2	3	4
27. Difficulty making decisions	0	1	2	3	4
28. Having to avoid certain things, places, and activities because they frighten you	0	1	2	3	4
29. Having your mind go blank	0	1	2	3	4
30. Feeling hopeless about the future	0	1	2	3	4
31. Having trouble concentrating	0	1	2	3	4
32. Feeling tense or keyed up	0	1	2	3	4

To score, add up the numbers related to the answers you gave. If you score over 30, you should see a professional for further evaluation.

Appendix 3

Recommended Reading

Controlling Use of Alcohol

Alternatives to Abstinence: A New Look at Alcoholism and the Choices in Treatment by Heather Ogilvy (Hatherleigh 2001) shows how decades of well-established research contradict popular beliefs about the nature of alcoholism as an irreversible disease, and how expanded treatment options can lead to greater overall recovery rates. Twelve treatment alternatives to traditional twelve-step programs are described, and there is a comprehensive listing of public and private organizations and individual therapists specializing in a range of types of treatment.

Behavioral Self-Control Program for Windows by Reid K. Hester, Ph.D. is an interactive software program that helps the problem drinker moderate in eight sessions. Based on the most current data available, it provides individualized feedback based on answers to many questions. Session topics include: assessing of your chances for success, keeping track of your progress using self-monitoring cards (included), learning to deal with social pressures to drink, setting up a system of rewards to keep you motivated, discovering events that trigger drinking, learning techniques to keep you from relapsing into old patterns, and even a graduation! (Two 3.5 inch diskettes and manual included). To order call (505) 345-6100. Also available as a download from rhester@behaviortherapy.com.

Drinker's Check-Up by Reid K. Hester, Ph.D. is an interactive software program that provides a comprehensive assessment of the user's drinking and drug use, feedback that provides motivation for change as indicated, and assistance in making decisions about changing drinking. The assessment stage covers quantity/frequency of drinking with estimated peak blood alcohol concentrations, alcohol dependence, frequency of other drug use, perceived benefits from, styles of, and consequences of drinking, motivation for change, family history of alcoholism, and number and severity of alcohol-related problems. Ordering information same as for software above.

Moderate Drinking: The Moderation Management Guide for People Who Want to Reduce Their Drinking by Audrey Kishline (Three Rivers Press 1996) is a lay person's introduction to moderation and to the program of Moderation Management (MM). It contains Ms. Kishline's personal story of how she came to start MM, as well as the basics of the MM program. These basics can also be found on the MM website at http://www.moderation.org.

Recovery Options: The Complete Guide, by Joseph Volpicelli, M.D., and Maia Szalavitz (Wiley 2000) is for readers who are interested in a comprehensive, readable handbook on addictions, what they are, how they come about, and what paths are available to overcome them. This book is invaluable. Covers a variety of treatment and self-help options, including moderation approaches.

7 Weeks To Safe Social Drinking: How to Effectively Moderate Your Alcohol Intake by D.J. Cornett, M.A. (iUniverse 2001) is a version of the text used in the fee-based Drink/Link Moderation Counseling program, and provides a list of exercises to carry out over seven weeks to achieve moderation. Diagrams clarify the sequences of events involved in various aspects of problem drinking, and countering strategies are outlined. Offers many practical tips and ideas for moderating drinking.

Sober for Good: New Solutions for Drinking Problems—Advice from Those Who Have Succeeded by Anne M. Fletcher (Houghton Mifflin 2001), explores the variety of routes to resolution of drinking problems in 222 people, nine out of ten of whom are abstinent. The other 10 percent are moderate, occasional, or near-abstinent drinkers. More than half of all these people did not follow traditional (AA or professional twelve-step-oriented) paths. The book illuminates various techniques these former problem drinkers discovered and used effectively in their recoveries, and reports on the spectrum of alternative programs available to problem drinkers.

The Miracle Method: A Radically New Approach to Problem Drinking by Scott D. Miller, Ph.D. and Insoo Kim Berg, M.S.S.W. (Norton 1995) presents a useful method for self-change in which two steps—imagining oneself changed and then implementing the behaviors one imagines—play a central role. Highly motivational, the book takes no position with regard to whether abstinence or moderation is the better goal, and the authors believe (as do the authors of this book) that people have within themselves the power to change, if only that power can be focused and used in the service of healthy changes.

The Truth About Addiction and Recovery by Stanton Peele, Ph.D. and Archie Brodsky (Fireside 1991) is another self-help book that many people have found useful in guiding the process of overcoming problem drinking using a moderation goal. As with other books we have recommended, Peele and Brodsky focus on empowering the individual to make his/her own decisions, and are not prescriptive with respect to whether or not abstinence or moderation is the best goal for any person. A book with a cause, it is often a real eye-opener for people who have had extensive contact with the traditional, twelve-step-based, abstinence-only treatment system here in the U.S.

Scientific Background on Alcohol Issues

Problem Drinking by Nick Heather, Ph.D. and Ian Robertson, Ph.D. (Oxford University Press 1997) is a masterful summary of research and research-based approaches to the solution of drinking problems. Gives a history of views of and approaches to alcohol problems, and thoroughly refutes the disease theory of alcoholism. Provides an overview of social-learning theories as applied to alcohol, including classical conditioning, instrumental learning, modeling, self-management/self-regulation, and higher cognitive processes, and discusses their implications for alcohol treatment and policies.

General Self-Change

Changing for Good by James O. Prochaska, Ph.D., John C. Norcross, Ph.D., and Carlo C. DiClemente, Ph.D. (Avon 1994) is an excellent introduction to the Transtheoretical Model of behavior change that also provides guidance as to how to both assess your own readiness to change and begin the process of moving yourself through the stages. It is a general book on how to change unwanted behaviors, with a brief section relating its ideas to alcohol problems. It can be useful in helping people change almost any bad habit.

Take Control Now! by Marc F. Kern, Ph.D. (Life Management Publishing 1994) tells how to overcome unhealthy habits that steal our happiness, productivity, health, and self-esteem. As well as touching on several of the major negative habits. From understanding the role that bad habits play, to learning to value the results of change more than the feelings produced by the old habits, the book provides a depth of guidance at each stage, and helpful worksheets.

Negative Emotions

Anger

The Angry Book by Theodore I. Rubin, M.D. (Simon & Schuster 1998) shows that anger is one of our most powerful emotions, and that suppressed or twisted anger can lead to various emotional problems. Presents clear, concise advice on how to arrest and reverse the perversion of anger, and how to manage its normal, natural free flow, leading to greater mental health and emotional wholeness.

The Dance of Anger: A Woman's Guide to Changing the Pattern of Intimate Relationships by Harriet Lerner, Ph.D. (Harper 1997) demonstrates how anger may be used to maintain an unsatisfactory status quo in a relationship, and how to use anger to change the relationship for the better. Women tend to silence their anger, deny it, or vent it in unhealthy ways. Teaches women to identify their sources of anger and to use anger as a vehicle for creating positive change.

Anxiety

The Anxiety & Phobia Workbook by Edmund J. Bourne, Ph.D. (New Harbinger 2001) is the book that therapists most often recommend to clients struggling with anxiety disorders. It provides detailed treatment outlines for each of the seven major anxiety disorders (including panic) discusses medications available, and also provides information on herbs and supplements that have recently become popular.

Depression

Feeling Good (Avon 1980) and *The Feeling Good Handbook* (Plume 1999) by David D. Burns, M.D. are two excellent self-help manuals for people who want to overcome feelings of anxiety and depression, as well as improve other behaviors such as minimizing procrastination and enhancing communication with spouses, partners, and family members. Based on the theory of cognitive therapy, these books are among the most widely read and effective self-help books on changing negative feelings.

The Depression Workbook: A Guide for Living with Depression by Mary Ellen Copeland, M.S. (New Harbinger 1992) is based on the responses of 120 survey participants who share their insights, experiences, and strategies for living with extreme mood swings. Interactive exercises teach essential coping skills, such as building a strong support system, bolstering self-esteem, fighting negative thoughts, finding appropriate professional help, and using relaxation and exercise.

Guilt and Self-Criticism

Self-Esteem by Matthew McKay, Ph.D. and Patrick Fanning (New Harbinger 2000) is the most comprehensive book on the subject, and the only one that uses proven cognitive techniques. It's a book about talking back to the self-critical voice inside you, healing the old wounds of hurt and self-rejection, and changing the perceptions and feelings you have about yourself.

Marital Issues

Relationship Rescue: A Seven-Step Strategy for Reconnecting with Your Partner by Phillip C. McGraw, Ph.D. (Hyperion 2000) starts out by exploding ten popular myths about relationships. Then it talks about "bad spirits" people use, often unconsciously, to damage relationships. It provides exercises to diagnose yourself and your relationship, and a step-by-step process for reconnecting with your partner and reclaiming your dignity and self-respect. A companion workbook is also available with the same title.

Lack of Assertiveness

Don't Say Yes When You Mean to Say No: Making Life Right When It Feels All Wrong by Herbert Fensterheim and Jean Baer (Dell 1978) is one of the earliest such manuals. It guides readers in targeting their own assertiveness difficulties and setting goals. It enables the reader to visualize and actualize assertiveness techniques through exercises designed to develop new behavior patterns. Shows the reader how to develop self-control, change self-sabotaging habits, and apply assertiveness to different life areas, including the job and marriage.

Asserting Yourself: A Practical Guide to Positive Change by S.A. Bower and G.H. Bower (Perseus 1991) provides a number of assertiveness exercises and many specific means to deal with what it calls "detours" that stand in your way. It provides model scripts for standard situations as helpful starting points for the individual, and deals with related subjects including looking and feeling assertive and developing supportive friendships.

References

Anton, R.F., et al. 2001. Posttreatment results of combining naltrexone with cognitive-behavior therapy for the treatment of alcoholism. *Journal of Clinical Psychopharmacology* 21:72-77.

Baer, J. D., et al. 2002. Moderate alcohol consumption lowers risk factors for cardiovascular disease in postmenopausal women fed a controlled diet. *American Journal of Clinical Nutrition* 75:593-599.

Briddell, D. W., et al. 1978. Effects of alcohol and cognitive set on sexual arousal to deviant stimuli. *Journal of Abnormal Psychology* 87:418-430.

Corder, R., et al. 2001. Endothelin-1 synthesis reduced by red wine. *Nature* 414:863-864.

Cowen, M. S., and A. J. Lawrence. 1999. The role of opioid-dopamine interactions in the induction and maintenance of ethanol consumption. *Progress in Neuro-Psychopharmacology & Biological Psychiatry* 23:1171-1212.

Davidson, R., et al. 1986. The validity of the short alcohol dependence data (SADD) questionnaire: A short self-report questionnaire for the assessment of alcohol dependence. *British Journal of Addiction* 81:217-222.

Dawson, D. A. 1996. Correlates of past-year status among treated and untreated persons with former alcohol dependence: United States, 1992. *Alcoholism: Clinical and Experimental Research* 20(4):771-779.

Fleming, M. F., et al. 1997. Brief physician advice for problem drinkers: A randomized controlled trial in community-based primary care practices. *Journal of the American Medical Association* 277:1039-1045.

Galants, D. J., et al. 2000. A longitudinal study of drinking and cognitive performance in elderly Japanese American men: The Honolulu-Asia aging study. *American Journal of Public Health* 99(8):1254-1259.

Granfeld, R., et al. 1999. *Coming Clean: Overcoming Addiction Without Treatment.* New York: New York University Press.

Gronbeck, M., et al. 2000. Type of alcohol consumed and mortality from all causes, coronary heart disease, and cancer. *Annals of Internal Medicine* 133(6):411-419.

Heather, N., et al. 2000. A randomized controlled trial of moderation-oriented cue exposure. *Journal of Studies on Alcohol* 61:561-570.

Hilts. P.J. 1994. Is nicotine addictive? *The New York Times,* August 2, p. C3.

Hurt, R. D., et al. 1996. Mortality following inpatient addiction treatment: Role of tobacco use in a community-based cohort. *Journal of the American Medical Association* 275:1097-1103.

Institute of Medicine (IOM). 1990. *Broadening the base of treatment for alcohol problems: Report of a study by a committee of the Institute of Medicine, Division of Mental Health and Behavioral Medicine.* Washington, D.C.: National Academy Press.

Kirk, J. M. and DeWit, H. 2000. Individual differences in the priming effect of ethanol in social drinkers. *Journal of Studies on Alcohol* 61(1):64-71.

Kishline, A. 1994. *Moderate Drinking: The Moderation Management Guide.* Three Rivers Press: New York.

Lambert, C. 2000. Deep cravings. *Harvard Magazine,* March-April, p. 60-68.

Larimer, M. E., et al. 1999. Relapse prevention: An overview of Marlatt's cognitive-behavioral model. *Alcohol Research & Health* 23(2):151-160.

Larimer, M. E., et al. 1998. Harm reduction for alcohol problems: Expanding access to and acceptability of prevention and treatment services. In *Harm Reduction: Pragmatic Strategies for Managing High-Risk Behaviors,* edited by G. A. Marlatt. New York: The Guilford Press.

Leigh, B.C. (1999). Thinking, feeling and drinking: alcohol expectancies and alcohol use. In S. Peele & M. Grant, eds., *Alcohol and Pleasure: A Health Perspective.* (pp. 215-231). Philadelphia: Taylor & Francis.

Markham, M. R., et al. 1993. BACCus 2.01: Computer Software for Quantifying Alcohol Consumption. *Behavior Research Methods, Instruments, and Computers* 25:420-421.

Marlatt, G. A. 1999. Alcohol, the magic elixir? In S. Peele and M. Grant, eds., *Alcohol and Pleasure: A Health Perspective,* (pp. 233–248). Philadelphia: Taylor & Francis.

Marlatt, G. A. and J. R. Gordon. 1985. *Relapse Prevention: Maintenance Strategies in the Treatment of Addictive Behaviors.* New York: Guilford Press.

Miller, W. R., et al. 2001. How effective is alcoholism treatment in the United States? *Journal of Studies on Alcohol* 62:211-220.

Miller, W. R., et al. 1995. What works? A methodological analysis of the alcohol treatment outcome literature. In *Handbook of Alcoholism Treatment Approaches, 2nd ed.,* edited by R. K. Hester and W. R. Miller. Boston: Allyn and Bacon.

Miller, W. R., and S. Rollnick. 1991. *Motivational Interviewing: Preparing People to Change Addictive Behavior.* New York: Guilford Press.

Miller, W. R., and A. C. Page. 1991. Warm turkey: Other routes to abstinence. *Journal of Substance Abuse Treatment* 8:227-232.

Mueller, T. I. 1999. Depression and alcohol use disorders: Is the road twice as long or twice as steep? *Harvard Review of Psychiatry* 7(1):51-53.

Nephew, T. M., et al. 2000. *Surveillance Report: Apparent Per Capita Alcohol Consumption: National, State and Regional Trends.* Rockville, Md.: National Institute on Alcohol Abuse and Alcoholism (NIAAA), Division of Biometry and Epidemiology.

National Institute on Alcohol Abuse and Alcoholism (NIAAA). 2000. *Tenth Special Report to the U.S. Congress on Alcohol and Health: Highlights from Current Research, From the Secretary of Health and Human Services, Public Health Service, National Institute of Health, National Institute on Alcohol Abuse and Alcoholism.* Rockville, Md.: NIAAA.

National Institute on Alcohol Abuse and Alcoholism (NIAAA). 1998a. Alcohol and the liver. *Alcohol Alert,* October, No. 42. Rockville, Md.: NIAAA.

National Institute on Alcohol Abuse and Alcoholism (NIAAA). 1998b. Alcohol and sleep. *Alcohol Alert,* July, No. 41. Rockville, Md.: NIAAA.

National Institute on Alcohol Abuse and Alcoholism (NIAAA). 1995. The genetics of alcoholism. *Alcohol Alert,* July, No. 18. Rockville, Md.: NIAAA.

National Institute on Alcohol Abuse and Alcoholism (NIAAA). 1996. "How to Cut Down on Your Drinking." NIAAA Publication No. 96-1770. Rockville, Md.: NIAAA.

National Institutes of Health (NIH). 1999. "Alcohol: What You Don't Know Can Harm You." NIH Publication No. 99-4323. Bethesdam Md.: NIH.

Orford, J., and A. Keddie. 1986. Abstinence or controlled drinking in clinical practice: A test of the dependence and persuasion hypothesis. *British Journal of Addiction* 81:495-504.

Pattison, E. M., M. B. Sobell, and L. C. Sobell. 1977. *Emerging Concepts of Alcohol Dependence.* New York: Springer.

Peele, S. and A. Brodsky. 2000. Exploring psychological benefits associated with moderate alcohol use: A necessary corrective to assessments of drinking outcomes? *Drug and Alcohol Dependence* 60:221-247.

Peele, S. and R. DeGrandpre. 1995. My genes made me do it. *Psychology Today,* July, p. 52-53; 62-68.

Prochaska, J. O., et al. 1994. *Changing for Good: A Revolutionary Six-Stage Program for Overcoming Bad Habits and Moving Your Life Positively Forward.* New York: Avon Books.

Raistrick, D., et al. 1983. Development of a questionnaire to measure alcohol dependence. *British Journal of Addiction* 78(1):89-95.

Roman, P. M. and T. C. Blum. 1997. *National Treatment Center Study Summary Report.* Athens, Ga.: University of Georgia.

Ruitenberg, A., et al. 2002. Alcohol consumption and risk of dementia: The Rotterdam Study. *Lancet* 359:281-286.

Sanchez-Craig, M., et al. 1995. Empirically based guidelines for moderate drinking: 1-year results from three studies with problem drinkers. *American Journal of Public Health* 85:823-828.

Sanchez-Craig, M. 1993. *DrinkWise: How To Quit Drinking Or Cut Down, 2nd ed.* Toronto: Addiction Research Foundation.

Schuckit, M. A., T. L. Smith, G. P. Danko, K. K. Bucholz, and T. Reich. 2001. Five-year clinical course associated with DSM-IV alcohol abuse or dependence in a large group of men and women. *American Journal of Psychiatry 158*:1084-1090.

Smith, G., et al. 1999. Fatal non-traffic injuries involving alcohol: A meta-analysis. *Annals of Emergency Medicine* 33:699-702.

Sobell, L. C., et al. 1992. Recovery from alcohol problems without treatment. In *Self-Control and Addictive Behaviors,* edited by N. Heather, W. R. Miller, and J. Greeley. New York: Maxwell Macmillan.

Sobell, M. B. and L. C. Sobell. 1995. Controlled drinking after twenty-five years: How important was the great debate? *Addiction* 90(9):1149-1153.

Sobell, M. B. and L. C. Sobell. 1993. *Problem Drinkers: Guided Self-Change Treatment.* New York: Guilford Press.

Solomon, R. L. 1980. The opponent-process theory of acquired motivation: The cost of pleasure and the benefits of pain. *American Psychologist* 35(8):691-712.

Stampfer, M. J., et al. 2000. Primary prevention of coronary heart disease in women through diet and lifestyle. *The New England Journal of Medicine* 343:16-22.

Tucker, J. A. and M. P. King. 1999. Resolving alcohol and drug problems: Influences on addictive behavior change and help-seeking processes. In *Changing Addictive Behavior: Bridging Clinical and Public Health Strategies,* edited by J. A. Tucker, et al. New York: The Guilford Press.

Turner, R. T. 2000. Skeletal response to alcohol. *Alcoholism: Clinical and Experimental Research* 24(11):1691-1701.

U.S. Department of Transportation. 2001. *Traffic Safety Facts 2000: Alcohol*. Washington, D.C.: National Center for Statistics and Analysis. DOT HS 809 323.

University of Buffalo. 2001. Research Institute on Addictions Public Communications Office Release: "Treatment Program Effective in Helping Women Decrease Alcohol Use." September 26.

Walters, G. D. 2000. Behavioral self-control training for problem drinkers: A meta-analysis of randomized control studies. *Behavior Therapy* 31:135-149.

Wells, S., et al. 2000. Alcohol-related aggression in the general population. *Journal of Studies on Alcohol* 61(4):626-632.

Wilson, W. 1976. *Alcoholics Anonymous: The Story of How Many Thousands of Men and Women Have Recovered from Alcoholism. 3rd ed.* New York: Alcoholics Anonymous World Services, Inc.

World Health Organization (WHO) Brief Intervention Study Group. 1996. A cross-national trial of brief intervention with heavy drinkers. *American Journal of Public Health* 86:948-955.

Frederick Rotgers, Psy.D., is Chairman of the Board of Directors for Moderation Management Network Inc., and has been in the forefront of using Moderation Management techniques as a component of comprehensive alcohol treatment since the mid-1990s. Dr. Rotgers is the former Director of the Program for Addictions Consultation and Treatment, at the Center of Alcohol Studies at Rutgers University in Piscataway, New Jersey. He also served as the Assistant Chief Psychologist at the Smithers Alcoholism Treatment and Training Center at St Luke's/Roosevelt Hospital Center in New York City. A private practice psychologist, researcher, and teacher, Dr. Rotgers is currently an Associate Professor of Psychology with the Philadelphia College of Osteopathic Medicine. He lives in Metuchen, New Jersey.

Marc F. Kern, Ph.D., is the Founder and Director of Addiction Alternatives in Los Angeles, California, and a member of the Board of Directors for Moderation Management Network, Inc. A founding board member of both Rational Recovery and SMART Recovery, Dr. Kern is a licensed clinical psychologist, Certified Addictions Specialist, Certified Rational Addictions Therapist, and is Certified by the American Psychological Association in the treatment of alcohol and other psychoactive substance use disorders. He has been featured on 20/20 and Larry King Live on the topic of moderate drinking. With over 25 years of clinical experience helping people to overcome a variety of self-defeating habits, Dr. Kern has overcome his own problems with addictions, and now enjoys alcohol in moderation. To learn more about him, visit his Web site at . Dr. Kern lives in Los Angeles, California.

Rudy Hoeltzel resolved a drinking problem in the Moderation Management program and has led a local Moderation Management self-help group meeting for six years. A member of the Board of Directors for Moderation Management Network Inc., Rudy's experience is recounted in the book's preface. He lives in Morristown, New Jersey.

Some Other New Harbinger Titles

A Cancer Patient's Guide to Overcoming Depression and Anxiety, Item 5044 $19.95
The Diabetes Lifestyle Book, Item 5167 $16.95
Solid to the Core, Item 4305 $14.95
Staying Focused in the Age of Distraction, Item 433X $16.95
Living Beyond Your Pain, Item 4097 $19.95
Fibromyalgia & Chronic Fatigue Syndrome, Item 4593 $14.95
Your Miraculous Back, Item 4526 $18.95
TriEnergetics, Item 4453 $15.95
Emotional Fitness for Couples, Item 4399 $14.95
The MS Workbook, Item 3902 $19.95
Depression & Your Thyroid, Item 4062 $15.95
The Eating Wisely for Hormonal Balance Journal, Item 3945 $15.95
Healing Adult Acne, Item 4151 $15.95
The Memory Doctor, Item 3708 $11.95
The Emotional Wellness Way to Cardiac Health, Item 3740 $16.95
The Cyclothymia Workbook, Item 383X $18.95
The Matrix Repatterning Program for Pain Relief, Item 3910 $18.95
Transforming Stress, Item 397X $10.95
Eating Mindfully, Item 3503 $13.95
Living with RSDS, Item 3554 $16.95
The Ten Hidden Barriers to Weight Loss, Item 3244 $11.95
The Sjogren's Syndrome Survival Guide, Item 3562 $15.95
Stop Feeling Tired, Item 3139 $14.95
Responsible Drinking, Item 2949 $19.95
The Mitral Valve Prolapse/Dysautonomia Survival Guide, Item 3031 $14.95
The Vulvodynia Survival Guide, Item 2914 $16.95
The Multifidus Back Pain Solution, Item 2787 $12.95
Move Your Body, Tone Your Mood, Item 2752 $17.95
The Woman's Book of Sleep, Item 2493 $14.95
The Trigger Point Therapy Workbook, second edition, Item 3759 $19.95
Fibromyalgia and Chronic Myofascial Pain Syndrome, 2nd edition, Item 2388 $19.95
Rosacea, Item 2248 $14.95
Coping with Chronic Fatigue Syndrome, Item 0199 $13.95

Call **toll free, 1-800-748-6273,** or log on to our online bookstore at **www.newharbinger.com** to order. Have your Visa or Mastercard number ready. Or send a check for the titles you want to New Harbinger Publications, Inc., 5674 Shattuck Ave., Oakland, CA 94609. Include $4.50 for the first book and 75¢ for each additional book, to cover shipping and handling. (California residents please include appropriate sales tax.) Allow two to five weeks for delivery.

Prices subject to change without notice.